William Anthony Smith

The Transforming WORD

ONE-VOLUME COMMENTARY ON THE BIBLE

The Transforming WORD

Mark W. Hamilton
General Editor

Kenneth L. Cukrowski
Nancy W. Shankle
James Thompson
John T. Willis
Associate Editors

Abilene, Texas

THE TRANSFORMING WORD
One-volume Commentary on the Bible

Abilene Christian University Press

1648 Campus Court
Abilene, Texas 79601
www.abilenechristianuniversitypress.com
www.transformingwordcommentary.com
1-877-816-4455 toll free

Copyright © 2009 Abilene Christian University Press
ISBN 978-0-89112-521-1
LCCN 2007942406

Dustjacket · Nicole Weaver, Zeal Design Studio
Book design · William Rankin
Typesetting · William Rankin & Sandra Armstrong
Maps & graphics · William Rankin with Lawson Soward

Unless otherwise noted, all scripture quotes are either the authors' own translation or from the NIV®. Copyright © 1973, 1978, 1984 by International Bible Society. Used by permission of Zondervan Publishing House. All rights reserved.

All rights reserved. Except as provided in the Copyright Act of 1976, no part of this book may be reproduced, stored in a retrieval system, or transcribed, in any form or by any means, electronic, mechanical, photocopying, recording or otherwise, without prior written permission from ACU Press. Printed in the United States of America.

09 10 11 12 13 14 15 16 / 10 9 8 7 6 5 4 3 2 1

To faithful students of the Bible

past, present, & future

Contents

Contributors iii
Preface v

CONTEXTS
The Pentateuch 1
The Wisdom & Lyric Literature 9
The Gospels & Acts 17
The Biblical Canons 25
Israel in the Ancient Near East 33
Greco-Roman New Testament Backgrounds 41
The Archaeology of Israel 55
Old Testament Prophecy 65
Old Testament Theology 69
New Testament Theology 77
The Bible & Literature 85
Religion & Science 93
The Bible & Music 99

THE OLD TESTAMENT
Genesis 107
Exodus 143
Leviticus 167
Numbers 185
Deuteronomy 203
Joshua 237
Judges 249
Ruth 267
1 Samuel 271
2 Samuel 291
1 Kings 309
2 Kings 329
1 Chronicles 353
2 Chronicles 373
Ezra 395
Nehemiah 407
Esther 417
Job 423
Psalms 445
Proverbs 505
Ecclesiastes 523
Song of Songs 529
Isaiah 533
Jeremiah 577
Lamentations 617

Ezekiel 621
Daniel 653
Hosea 665
Joel 675
Amos 679
Obadiah 685
Jonah 689
Micah 693
Nahum 699
Habakkuk 703
Zephaniah 707
Haggai 711
Zechariah 713
Malachi 719

THE NEW TESTAMENT
Matthew 723
Mark 761
Luke 789
John 825
Acts of the Apostles 855
Romans 893
1 Corinthians 917
2 Corinthians 937
Galatians 949
Ephesians 957
Philippians 965
Colossians 973
1 Thessalonians 979
2 Thessalonians 985
1 Timothy 989
2 Timothy 997
Titus 1003
Philemon 1007
Hebrews 1013
James 1027
1 Peter 1032
2 Peter 1041
1 John 1047
2 John 1055
3 John 1057
Jude 1059
Revelation 1063
Topical Index 1087

Contributors

Rodney Ashlock   PhD, Baylor University; Assistant Professor of Old Testament, Abilene Christian University; Abilene, Texas.

Allen Black   PhD, Emory University; Professor of New Testament, Harding University Graduate School of Religion; Memphis, Tennessee.

Mark Black   PhD, Emory University; Professor of New Testament, Hazelip School of Theology, Lipscomb University; Nashville, Tennessee.

Philip G. Camp   PhD, Union Theological Seminary & Presbyterian School of Christian Education; Assistant Professor of Old Testament, Hazelip School of Theology, Lipscomb University; Nashville, Tennessee.

Larry Chouinard   PhD, Fuller Theological Seminary; Adjunct Professor, Gonzaga University; Spokane, Washington.

Kenneth L. Cukrowski   PhD, Yale University; Associate Professor of New Testament, Abilene Christian University; Abilene, Texas.

Everett Ferguson   PhD, Harvard University; Professor Emeritus of Church History; Abilene Christian University; Abilene, Texas.

Brandon L. Fredenburg   PhD, University of Denver & Iliff School of Theology; Associate Professor of Biblical Studies, Lubbock Christian University; Lubbock, Texas.

Sara Fudge   PhD, Hebrew Union College, Jewish Institute of Religion; Associate Professor of Hebrew & History, Cincinnati Christian University; Cincinnati, Ohio.

Jennifer S. Green   PhD, Princeton Theological Seminary; Adjunct Professor of Old Testament, Columbia Theological Seminary; Atlanta, Georgia.

Mark W. Hamilton   PhD, Harvard University; Associate Professor of Old Testament, Abilene Christian University; Abilene, Texas.

Preston Harper   PhD, Texas Christian University; Professor Emeritus of English, Abilene Christian University; Abilene, Texas.

R. Christopher Heard   PhD, Southern Methodist University; Associate Professor of Religion, Pepperdine University; Malibu, California.

Christopher R. Hutson   PhD, Yale University; Associate Professor of New Testament, Hood Theological Seminary; Salisbury, North Carolina.

Ira J. Jolivet, Jr.   PhD, Baylor University; Associate Professor of Religion, Pepperdine University; Malibu, California.

Paul J. Kissling   PhD, University of Sheffield; Professor of Old Testament & Biblical Languages, TCMI Institute; Heiligenkreuz, Austria.

Nathaniel D. Lollar   Graduate Student, Abilene Christian University; Abilene, Texas.

Jesse C. Long, Jr.   PhD, Drew University; Professor of Old Testament, Syro-Palestinian Archaeology & Preaching and Dean of the College of Biblical Studies & Behavioral Sciences, Lubbock Christian University; Lubbock, Texas.

Rick R. Marrs   PhD, The Johns Hopkins University; Dean of Seaver College A Professor of Old Testament, Pepperdine University; Malibu, California.

Mark A. Matson   PhD, Duke University; Vice President for Academic Affairs & Dean, Associate Professor of Bible, Milligan College; Milligan College, Tennessee.

Phillip E. McMillion   PhD, Vanderbilt University; Professor of Old Testament, Harding University Graduate School of Religion; Memphis, Tennessee.

Allan J. McNicol   PhD, Vanderbilt University; A. B. Cox Professor of New Testament, Austin Graduate School of Theology; Austin, Texas.

Michael S. Moore   PhD, Drew University; Faculty Associate in Hebrew Bible, Arizona State University & Fuller Theological Seminary; Phoenix, Arizona.

Curt Niccum   PhD, University of Notre Dame; Professor of New Testament, Abilene Christian University; Abilene, Texas.

CONTRIBUTORS

Thomas H. Olbricht PhD, University of Iowa; STB, Harvard University; Distinguished Professor Emeritus of Religion, Pepperdine University; Malibu, California.

Richard E. Oster, Jr. PhD, Princeton Theological Seminary; Professor of New Testament, Harding University Graduate School of Religion; Memphis, Tennessee.

Heather Dana Davis Parker MAR, Emmanuel School of Religion; PhD candidate, Johns Hopkins University; Baltimore, Maryland.

Glenn Pemberton PhD, University of Denver & Iliff School of Theology; Associate Professor of Old Testament, Abilene Christian University; Abilene, Texas.

Jeffrey Peterson PhD, Yale University; Jack C. & Ruth Wright Professor of New Testament, Austin Graduate School of Theology; Austin, Texas.

Paul Pollard PhD, Baylor University; Professor of New Testament, Harding University; Searcy, Arkansas.

Christopher A. Rollston PhD, Johns Hopkins University; Toyozo W. Nakarai Professor of Old Testament & Semitic Studies, Emmanuel School of Religion; Johnson City, Tennessee.

Keith N. Schoville PhD, University of Wisconsin; Professor Emeritus of Hebrew & Semitic Studies, University of Wisconsin-Madison; Madison, Wisconsin.

Tim Sensing PhD, University of North Carolina at Greensboro; Associate Professor of Ministry & Homiletics, Abilene Christian University; Abilene, Texas.

Nancy W. Shankle PhD, Texas A&M University; Professor of English, Abilene Christian University; Abilene, Texas.

David I. Shaw MA, Abilene Christian University; Minister, Hawley Church of Christ; Hawley, Texas.

Kelly Shearon Graduate Student, Abilene Christian University; Abilene, Texas.

R. Mark Shipp PhD, Princeton Theological Seminary; Pat E. Harrell Professor of Old Testament, Austin Graduate School of Theology; Austin, Texas.

David Skelton Graduate Student, Abilene Christian University; Abilene, Texas.

Mark Sneed PhD, Drew University; Associate Professor of Hebrew & Old Testament, Lubbock Christian University; Lubbock, Texas.

Charles B. Stephenson ThD, New Orleans Baptist Theological Seminary; Professor of New Testament, Lubbock Christian University; Lubbock, Texas.

Gregory M. Stevenson PhD, Emory University; Professor of Religion & Greek, Rochester College; Rochester Hills, Michigan.

Gregory Straughn PhD, University of North Texas; Assistant Professor of Music, Abilene Christian University; Abilene, Texas.

James W. Thompson PhD, Vanderbilt University; Onstead Chair for Biblical Studies, Abilene Christian University; Abilene, Texas.

Jennifer Thweatt-Bates MA, Abilene Christian University; PhD candidate, Princeton Theological Seminary; Princeton, New Jersey.

Jonathan Wade PhD, University of Texas at Dallas; Fellow, North Carolina Center for the Advancement of Teaching; Cullowhee, North Carolina.

James Walters PhD, Boston University; Associate Professor of New Testament & Christian Origins, Boston University; Boston, Massachusetts.

Paul L. Watson PhD, Yale University; Adjunct Professor of Bible & Ministry, Graduate School of Theology, Amridge University; Montgomery, Alabama.

Stephen Weathers PhD, Florida State University; Associate Professor of English, Abilene Christian University; Abilene, Texas.

Christian W. Willerton PhD, University of North Carolina at Chapel Hill; Professor of English, Abilene Christian University; Abilene, Texas.

John T. Willis PhD, Vanderbilt University; Burton & Sissy Coffman Distinguished Chair of Biblical Studies, Abilene Christian University; Abilene, Texas.

Wendell Willis PhD, Southern Methodist University; Professor of New Testament, Abilene Christian University; Abilene, Texas.

Richard Wright PhD, Brown University; Assistant Professor of Bible, Oklahoma Christian University; Oklahoma City, Oklahoma.

Preface

The book you are holding primarily concerns another book, the Bible. The editors and authors of this book, in their fervent belief that the Bible reveals to human beings the path to God and thus to meaningful human existence, offer this commentary on the church's central texts. In doing so, we stand in a long tradition of interpreters of Scripture going back to ancient times, as readers sought to understand the stories, prophecies, songs, prayers, and letters making up the great anthology that is the Bible. More than that, they—and we—seek to hear afresh transforming words that will quicken the life of the church as it shares in God's redeeming work in the world.

The authors and editors of this book share a common history. They are all members of churches that emerged in the nineteenth century in North America following the direction of such great leaders as Barton Stone, Walter Scott, Alexander Campbell, and others. Their "present Reformation," as they named it, began as an effort to purify the Christianity they had inherited of its divisions and corruptions. By returning to the Bible as the only rule in faith and practice, they believed that they could restore primitive Christianity and thus help welcome God's in-breaking kingdom.

For these men and women of faith, the Bible offered a picture of a healed world in which God's will was done on earth as it was in heaven. Thus teaching the Bible was an act of redemption, not merely a technical exercise. As Thomas Campbell put it in 1809,

> [A]ll that are enabled, thro' grace, to make such a profession, and to manifest the reality of it in their tempers and conduct, should consider each other as the precious saints of God, should love each other as brethren, children of the same family and father, temples of the same spirit, members of the same body, subjects of the same grace, objects of the same divine love, bought with the same price, and joint heirs of the same inheritance. Whom God hath thus joined together, no man should dare to put asunder.

This commentary thus has a past. It is one of reform and division and now hopeful reconnections. We trust that it will also have a future as a source of healing for all who read the Bible as what Alexander Campbell called "the living oracles of God." We thus offer this volume as a gift to all God's people in the Stone-Campbell tradition and far beyond. And we pray that it will be a source of enlightenment for all who use it.

THE METHODS OF THIS WORK

Contemporary biblical scholarship offers a wide range of methods and conclusions on some points of the ancient texts, while producing broadly agreed upon understandings on others. In this commentary, the editors have imposed no method upon authors, nor have we censored their interpretative conclusions, which range across the broad mainstream of current biblical interpretation. Everyone whose work appears here has received advanced training in biblical studies, which includes command of the original languages and a deep awareness of the literary shape and flow of the Bible, the relevant archaeological and textual evidence from the ancient Near East or Greco-Roman worlds, and the history of biblical interpretation, ancient, medieval, and modern. Authors drew upon such bodies of knowledge for their comments, but their works have differing emphases. In every case, however, the reader should expect to gain an understanding of the organization and arguments of each biblical book, the main historical issues bearing on its interpretation, and the theological meaning of each book and part thereof. A single volume cannot hope to include every relevant issue or fact, but we have written with the reader in mind so as to help him or her encounter the biblical text with greater understanding and commitment.

PREFACE

Alongside their work as scholars, each author of this volume lives as an active Christian. Many of them teach in Christian seminaries or universities. Thus their interest in the Bible is not merely theoretical but connects to an active faith working to bear the good news of God's redeeming work in Christ to the world.

Each author uses the best available editions of the original Hebrew, Aramaic, or Greek texts of the Bible, but comments refer to several English translations – and frequently to the translations of the authors themselves.

THE LAYOUT OF THIS WORK

This volume includes a commentary on each biblical book as well as additional articles on the background of the Old and New Testaments. The commentaries include a chapter outline, a discussion of the contexts of the biblical book, a detailed commentary, a brief essay on the book's theological implications, a list of texts for further study, and a list of works cited. The reader may dip in wherever he or she likes or read straight through. The supplementary essays at the beginning of this book are designed for continuous reading.

Each chapter may also includes maps, graphics, and sidebars. Rather than collecting this material in one place, we have sought to locate it where readers will need it most. An index of these special supplementary materials appears at the end of this volume. Most of these materials are the responsibility of the editors and may not reflect the precise point of view of the authors of the commentary in which they appear.

ABBREVIATIONS & ATTESTATION

In the interest of readability, this work avoids most abbreviations – even those common in biblical scholarship. However, a few abbreviations do appear, including:

ASV	American Standard Version
AV	Authorized Version
NAB	New American Bible
NASB	New American Standard Bible
NEB	New English Bible
NIV	New International Version
NJPS	Tanakh: The New Jewish Publication Society Translation
NKJV	New King James Version
NRSV	New Revised Standard Version
REB	Revised English Bible
RSV	Revised Standard Version
BCE	Before the Common Era (formerly called BC)
CE	Common Era (formerly called AD)

In addition, the names of biblical books are abbreviated in parentheses accordingly:

GEN	Genesis
EXOD	Exodus
LEV	Leviticus
NUM	Numbers
DEUT	Deuteronomy
JOSH	Joshua
JUDG	Judges
RUTH	Ruth
1 SAM	1 Samuel
2 SAM	2 Samuel
1 KGS	1 Kings
2 KGS	2 Kings
1 CHRON	1 Chronicles
2 CHRON	2 Chronicles
EZRA	Ezra
NEH	Nehemiah
ESTH	Esther
JOB	Job
PS/PSS	Psalms
PROV	Proverbs
ECCL	Ecclesiastes
SONG	Song of Solomon
ISA	Isaiah
JER	Jeremiah
LAM	Lamentations
EZEK	Ezekiel
DAN	Daniel
HOS	Hosea
JOEL	Joel
AMOS	Amos
OBAD	Obadiah
JONAH	Jonah
MIC	Micah
NAH	Nahum
HAB	Habakkuk
ZEPH	Zephaniah
HAG	Haggai
ZECH	Zechariah
MAL	Malachi

PREFACE

MATT	Matthew
MARK	Mark
LUKE	Luke
JOHN	John
ACTS	Acts
ROM	Romans
1 COR	1 Corinthians
2 COR	2 Corinthians
GAL	Galatians
EPH	Ephesians
PHIL	Philippians
COL	Colossians
1 THESS	1 Thessalonians
2 THESS	2 Thessalonians
1 TIM	1 Timothy
2 TIM	2 Timothy
TITUS	Titus
PHLM	Philemon
HEB	Hebrews
JAS	James
1 PET	1 Peter
2 PET	2 Peter
1 JOHN	1 John
2 JOHN	2 John
3 JOHN	3 John
JUDE	Jude
REV	Revelation

THE LANGUAGES OF THE BIBLE

Although this volume assumes no knowledge of the Bible's original languages on the part of readers, words in those languages occasionally appear here when the biblical author's use of wordplay – a very prominent feature in both the Old and New Testaments – would otherwise be lost. Readers interested in a more detailed look at the original languages may consult the texts listed in the chapter's bibliographical entries.

A brief note about the languages of the Bible and our representation of them may be in order. Most of the Bible was written in Hebrew over about a millennium. During this time, Hebrew developed (as every language does), so that the Hebrew of, say, old poems like Judges 5 or Exodus 15 differs significantly from that of a later book, such as Chronicles. The Bible contains several dialects of Hebrew and three basic stages of the language (Early, Classical, and Late). Ancient Hebrew is otherwise attested in inscriptions, letters, seals and seal impressions.

A few parts of the Old Testament survive in Aramaic (Ezra 4:8–7:26; Jer 10:11; and Dan 2:4b-7:28). Like Hebrew, Aramaic is a language in the Northwest Semitic family, a group that also included Phoenician, Moabite, Ammonite, Edomite, and other languages. Hebrew and Aramaic were not mutually intelligible (though Phoenician and Hebrew probably were), but many ancient Jews probably spoke both.

This volume transliterates Hebrew and Aramaic words following an informal system. Scholars may easily recognize the original behind the transliteration, so we have made no effort at reproducing a fully scientific system. Spirantized consonants (consonants spoken with a continuous expulsion of breath) are not represented except with ב and פ (*v* and *f* respectively), following modern Israeli conventions. The correspondences are as follows:

א	'	ב	*b* (*v* after vowels)	ג	*g*	ד	*d*
ה	*h*	ו	*w*	ז	*z*	ח	*ch* (as in "choir")
ט	*t*	י	*y* or *i*	כ	*k*	ל	*l*
מ	*m*	נ	*n*	ס	*s*	ע	'
פ	*p* (*f* after vowels)	צ	*ts*	ק	*q*	ר	*r*
ש	*s* or *sh*	ת	*t*				

Originally the writing systems for these languages, which are identical, did not include signs for vowels. Scribes added vowel signs below and above the consonants long after the biblical period. The vowels for these languages differ from those in English, and include short and long *a* (like the second *a* in *garage*), short and long *i* (like the *i* in *machine*), *o* (as in *long*), short and long *e* (as in *bet* and *beta* respectively), and short and long *u* (as in *umbrella* and *parachute* respectively). A schwa sound (like the first *a* in *garage* or *barrage* as Americans pronounce those words) also exists, represented here by *e*. When the consonants represented by ch, ts, or sh are doubled in Hebrew, we have indicated the letter only once (thus *matsevot*, not *matstsevot*) in order to avoid confusion.

PREFACE

While the Old Testament is written in two Semitic languages, the New Testament is written primarily (with the exception of a few Latin and Aramaic words) in one Indo-European language: Greek. During the first century CE, Greek language and culture dominated the eastern Mediterranean world. The upper classes even in Rome spoke and wrote in Greek. The Greek of the New Testament closely resembles that used by non-Christians at the same time. The authors use the language with varying degrees of sophistication, from the marketplace level of Mark to the educated language of Paul to the highly sophisticated text of Hebrews.

Again, as with Hebrew, this commentary uses Greek words only when necessary for explaining the argument of the biblical author. Readers should consult the bibliography for further references. Here we follow a transliteration system closely resembling that of the *SBL Handbook of Style* (Hendrickson, 1999).

α	a	β	b	γ	g	δ	d
ε	e	ζ	z	η	e	θ	th
ι	i	κ	k	λ	l	μ	m
ν	n	ξ	x	ο	o	π	p
ρ	r	σ	s	τ	t	υ	u
φ	f	χ	ch (as in "choir")	ψ	ps	ω	o

ACKNOWLEDGEMENTS

The production of a book as large as this requires many hands and eyes. The editors wish to thank the following colleagues, in addition to their fellow contributors to this book: from ACU Press, to Thom Lemmons and Karen Cukrowski, who worked with us at the beginning stages of this work, and especially Leonard Allen who materially aided its completion; from friends who read earlier drafts of parts of the book, to Kris Southward, Dan Brannan, David Shaw, Gerardo Lara, Eddie Sharp, Jack Reese, Dwayne VanRheenen, and members of the Highland Church of Christ, University Church of Christ, and the Hillcrest Church of Christ; to Hannah Nielsen, Sandra Armstrong, and Crystal Perry for their valuable proofreading, typesetting, and corrections; to Bill Rankin and Sherry Rankin, whose skills as typesetter and proofreader only begin the list of their accomplishments; to Harry Conner, Kelly Shearon, and David Skelton, Mark Hamilton's assistants, who worked diligently on turning editorial marks into typescript; and most of all to our families, who saw us through to the end. Without all their help, this volume would not exist at all.

AN INVITATION

Finally, we wish to invite our readers to join us in the study of the words of Scripture. As the Apostle Paul put it when connecting the Old Testament to the Christian message, *whatever was previously written was written for our instruction, so that through endurance and encouragement from the Scriptures we might have hope* (Rom 15:4). We pray that this book may contribute in some measure to the life of hope that its readers seek. Such a result will justify our labors.

The Editors

INTRODUCTION TO
The Pentateuch

Mark W. Hamilton

CHAPTER CONTENTS

Textual Issues   1
The Structure of the Pentateuch   2
Literary Traditions before the Pentateuch   2
The Pentateuch as Literature   3
Authorship & Date   5
Theological Implications   7
For Further Study   8
Works Cited   8

The Pentateuch, traditionally also called the Five Books of Moses, or Torah, opens the Old Testament with the foundation story of the people of Israel and its fundamental practices. These five large books have been the cornerstone of Jewish religious reflection from ancient times until today. The 613 laws of the Torah and the story of Israel's origins, redemption, wandering, and preparation to enter the promised land form a carefully interwoven whole. As the eighteenth-century theologian Jonathan Edwards put it, "History and law are everywhere so grafted one into another ... that there is all appearance of their originally growing together ..." (Edwards 441).

Most modern scholars would express reservations with Edwards's statement, because the Pentateuch appears to preserve several streams of tradition that did not necessarily originate at the same time and place. Yet he is right to argue that law and story belong together as an organic whole. The law guides the people rescued from slavery, in Egypt or elsewhere, from the patterns of life in which some humans command while others merely obey. The story feeds the collective memory and moral imagination of a people that repeats it at their major festivals and on other occasions.

For Christians, reading the Pentateuch presents more than merely a literary or historical challenge. It also presents a theological one. While Matthew's Jesus (Matt 7:12) and Paul (Rom 13:8–10; 15:4) argue that followers of Christ must read Torah in moral and spiritual terms, and while the New Testament contains numerous quotations of and allusions to stories in the Pentateuch (for example, 1 Cor 10:7–10; 2 Cor 3:1–18; Gal 3; 2 Pet 2:4–10; Rev 2:14), Christians have never raised these texts to quite the same level Jews have, since Jesus is to Christianity as Torah is to traditional Judaism. Still, early Christians saw Genesis-Deuteronomy as far more than a series of edifying stories. The Pentateuch offered them a framework for life under God.

TEXTUAL ISSUES

The Pentateuch existed in several forms in antiquity: the Samaritan Pentateuch, the Greek Septuagint (LXX), translated from a Hebrew original, and the immediate ancestor of the traditional Jewish Masoretic Text (MT). All five books are represented in the Dead Sea Scrolls. Fragments of twenty manuscripts of Genesis, seventeen of Exodus, seventeen or eighteen of Leviticus, seven of Numbers, and twenty-eight (possibly thirty) of Deuteronomy have survived in the caves near Qumran. Commentaries and retellings of the stories of the Pentateuch also exist, as do the rules of the Qumran community, which quote extensively from the laws of Leviticus and Deuteronomy.

> **The Samaritan Pentateuch**
> *The Samaritans regard only the Pentateuch as Scripture, though they use other books, including a version of Joshua. Their edition of the five books makes minor alterations to the Hebrew text, most obviously in identifying the "place where Yahweh will choose to set his name" as Mount Gerizim, the location of their ancient temple. The sect apparently broke with other Jews in the second century BCE.*

The stories of the Pentateuch also figured in Jewish art and literature. The third century CE synagogue from Dura-Europos in Mesopotamia, for example, contained a fresco with many scenes from Genesis, Exodus, and the historical books of the Old Testament (see Schreckenberg and Schubert 162–88). (Similar artistic motifs show up in the earli-

INTRODUCTION TO THE PENTATEUCH

est Christian catacombs a couple of centuries later.) As early as the third century BCE, Jewish texts such as *Jubilees* and the earliest parts of *1 Enoch* retold the stories of Genesis, filling in gaps, explaining the actions of characters, and applying the stories to the moral needs of their own readers. In the second century BCE, a Greek-speaking Jew named Ezekiel wrote a play in Greek poetry based on the book of Exodus, thus making the ancient story available to a broader audience.

Like Hellenized Jews, early Christians knew the five books primarily in Greek. Church fathers of the second and third century quote Genesis, Exodus, and Deuteronomy extensively (and Leviticus and Numbers less often) to argue with heretics, train young Christians, and otherwise do the work of the church. The earliest sustained Christian commentaries on them come from the third century in the form of homilies by Origen (died 254 CE). As the opening of the Christian's two-part canon, the Pentateuch offered a set of moral examples and spiritual insights usable to the new faith.

THE STRUCTURE OF THE PENTATEUCH

To understand the theological import of the Pentateuch for its ancient and modern readers, it is important to pay attention to its structure. It consists of several narrative and legal blocks of material and can be outlined as follows:

Genesis 1–11 · *The story of humankind*

Genesis 12–50 · *The story of Abraham's family*

Exodus 1–15 · *The exodus from Egypt*

Exodus 16–Numbers 36 · *Israel in the wilderness and at Sinai*
    Exodus 16–19 · *The first wilderness treks*
    Exodus 20 · *The Ten Commandments*
    Exodus 21–23 · *The Covenant Code*
    Exodus 24–31 · *Instructions for Building the Tabernacle, Part 1*
    Exodus 32–34 · *The Golden Calf Episode and the Second Revelation of Torah*
    Exodus 35–40 · *Instructions for Building the Tabernacle, Part 2*
    Leviticus 1–16 · *The Laws of Sacrifice and Cleanness*
    Leviticus 17–27 · *The Holiness Code*
    Numbers 1–10 · *Rules for the Camp of Israel*
    Numbers 11–25 · *Stories of Conflict*
    Numbers 26–36 · *Laws and Stories on Worship and Inheritance*

Deuteronomy 1:1–34:4 · *Instructions on the Plains of Moab*
    Deuteronomy 1–11 · *Homilies on Israel's Past and Future*
    Deuteronomy 12–26 · *Laws*
    Deuteronomy 27–31 · *Concluding Homiletical Material*
    Deuteronomy 32–33 · *Hymns*
    Deuteronomy 34:1–4 · *Conclusion*

Deuteronomy 34:5–12 · *The Death of Moses*

This structure interweaves narratives of many types with laws, songs, and genealogies. The stories, especially in Genesis 1–36 and Numbers, relate to each other fairly loosely, often lacking clear chronological sequencing and occasionally repeating the same themes or similar events (for example, Gen 12, 15, 17). At the same time, the Pentateuch includes a number of internal cross-references that show an effort to form the pieces into an integrated work, such as the foreshadowing of the exodus in Genesis 15:13–14 or the reflections on it in Deuteronomy 1–3. That is, the Pentateuch as a whole does not seem to be merely a hodgepodge of ancient stories but rather an intentionally (although loosely) structured work.

Although ancient people thought of books differently than we do and did not necessarily expect to read them straight through with every loose end tied up (see van der Toorn), the Pentateuch transcends the chronicles, law codes, and ritual texts from the ancient Near East that serve as its model, rising above them to a new level of sophistication. The division into five books, incidentally, reflects the word limits of scrolls (no readable, manipulable scroll could have contained all the Pentateuch). However, Exodus 1 and Deuteronomy 1 clearly start new sections of material. Leviticus 1 flows smoothly from Exodus 40.

LITERARY TRADITIONS BEFORE THE PENTATEUCH

Within this overarching structure, the Pentateuch uses many kinds of literary material. Ancient Near Eastern societies produced several genres that served, in part, as literary models for the Pentateuch. Some, such as king lists and prayers, are attested

INTRODUCTION TO THE PENTATEUCH

before 2000 BCE, while others probably existed in oral form long before being written down.

Such literary types found in the Bible and in Mesopotamian, Canaanite, or Egyptian texts include: King lists (Gen 36:31–39; "Sumerian King List"); stories of dreams (Gen 28:10–17; 40–41; "Aqhat"); stories of wise experts at a royal court (Gen 38–50; "Ahiqar"); creation narratives (Gen 1–2; *Enuma Elish*; "The Song of the Hoe"; "The Memphite Theology"); law codes (Exod 20–23; Lev 17–27; "Code of Hammurabi"; "Middle Assyrian Laws"); rules for sacrifice (Lev 1–10; "The Marseilles Tariff"; rituals texts from Ugarit); judicial rulings (Exod 18; thousands of receipts and contracts from ancient archives); death scenes (Gen 48–50; Deut 34; "Aqhat"); hymns (Deut 32–33; "Hymn to Shamash"); speeches (Deut 1–3; *Epic of Gilgamesh*, column 3); travel stories (Exod 2:11–22; "Sinuhe"); and war songs (Exod 15:1–18; Num 21:27–30; numerous semi-poetic royal inscriptions). To read translations of some of these ancient works, see the large collection in Hallo and Younger or the excerpts in Matthews and Benjamin.

> **The Pentateuch & Ancient Near Eastern Law Codes**
> *Beginning in the late third millennium BCE, Mesopotamian kings began to inscribe collections of laws on stone monuments. These lists were not codes, strictly speaking, in that they did not attempt comprehensiveness, nor did judges rigidly follow them. The most famous of these is the Code of Hammurabi, named for the seventeenth-century king of Babylon by that name. His code has numerous similarities with Exodus 21–23, indicating the existence of a region-wide legal culture in antiquity.*

In most cases, the parallels between the Pentateuch and texts from outside Israel are loose, with three exceptions. First, an inscription on plaster from Deir Alla in what is now the Kingdom of Jordan tells the story of a seer named Balaam son of Beor; the language is not Hebrew, and the site is not Israelite. Second, the story of the birth of Sargon of Agade, a third-millennium ruler of Mesopotamia, describes him being drawn from a basket floating down the Euphrates, in a manner similar to the infant Moses. The story in this version comes from the first millennium BCE. Third, the flood story in Tablet XI of the *Epic of Gilgamesh* portrays Utanapishtim, the equivalent of Noah, sending forth a dove and then a raven from his boat. On leaving it, he offers sacrifices to the gods. There are several possible explanations for these similarities, but it seems most likely that Israelites were seeking to read well-known stories through the lenses of their own theology. In addition, Deuteronomy uses some of the elements of ancient treaties (oaths of loyalty, sanctions for loyalty and disloyalty), though it significantly alters them.

In assessing the fact that the Pentateuch uses widespread literary techniques and occasionally even entire stories, it is important to recognize two things. First, what the Bible omits is almost as interesting as what it includes. For example, although one of the most popular scholarly genres in Mesopotamia was the omen list, in which diviners or astrologers collected examples of their own work for the guidance of their successors, the Bible consciously omits such material, even though its authors had some knowledge of the practices involved (see Ezek 21:21). Since Yahweh controlled the flow of information about the future, such practices were illicit.

> **The Pentateuch & Contemporary Literature**
> *Unlike many ancient texts, the Pentateuch contains no story describing the origins of God (theogony), activities in heaven, or conflicts with other supernatural beings. That is, it radically curtails the mythological element so prominent in non-Israelite religions.*

Second, any text must engage readers with ways of communication to which they are accustomed, even if it uses them in new ways. The Pentateuch does so masterfully and from the point of view of its major theological ideas.

THE PENTATEUCH AS LITERATURE

In reconfiguring ancient genres for new purposes, the Pentateuch places them in the service of an overarching story of Yahweh's interactions with the human race through the people of Israel. Although many of the stories in Genesis especially seem to fit the sort of oral culture of Israel's life as farmers and shepherds – in short, to be what we would call in any other context folklore – their apparent artlessness and detachment from one another mask the extraordinary care with which they were collected and organized.

Here it is important to consider several elements of the Pentateuch as literature. First, most of the narratives in Genesis-Numbers consist of brief

INTRODUCTION TO THE PENTATEUCH

episodes, usually told with a minimum of detail and leaving open to the reader's imagination all sorts of elements. Consider, for example, the story of the binding of Isaac in Genesis 22. The author does not tell us why God decided after so many trials to test Abraham again, nor why Abraham accepted the test unquestioningly. We hear nothing of the internal state of any of the characters. The story does not tell us how old Isaac was, his level of awareness, or his subsequent reaction to near death. Although the common ancient Near Eastern custom of child sacrifice lies in the background of the story, Genesis itself neither endorses nor explicitly condemns the practice. Isaac's binding serves as a model for no subsequent act, either positively or negatively. The point of the story comes at its end when the narrator speaks of Yahweh as the provider who now knows Abraham in some new way and can thus share with him a level of intimacy that gives new meaning to the older promise of chapter 12 and its fulfillment in Exodus.

> **Torah or Law?**
> *The Hebrew word* torah *literally means "instruction." Ancient Israelites and, later, Jews conceived of torah as far more than merely a list of rules which one either followed or broke at the risk of punishment. Torah was a way of life, a window into God's vision for the human race, and a manifestation of the divine wisdom that informs all creation.*

Second, the reticent, under-specified technique of storytelling evident in Genesis 22 and many other parts of the Pentateuch forces the reader to ask how a given episode connects to all those around it. Why, to continue this example, should the God who promised an heir to Abraham and Sarah three times (Gen 12, 15, 17) attempt to kill him? What does such an event say about the divine promise, the election of Israel, the nature of faith, and other major aspects of Israel's religious views? Only by juxtaposing one story upon another can the total picture become clear.

Third, this style of storytelling owes a great deal to the oral world behind the written text. Oral stories tend to consist of short episodes. Oral storytellers remember the basic structure of the story and tell it with catch phrases and stock expressions that skilled bards easily remember. The same themes appear repeatedly, as for example when Adam and Eve lose their chance at immortality (Gen 3), just as Gilgamesh does (see Blenkinsopp 93–96).

Genesis, Exodus, and parts of Numbers certainly have an oral stamp. But at the same time, they are written texts, and as such they preserve a higher level of order than one might expect from a purely oral tradition. These books result from the careful blending of oral tradition and a careful, artistic work of written composition.

Fourth, the structure of the oral tradition provides the skeleton for the Pentateuch's storyline, but not every episode in it. This becomes apparent from Exodus 15:1–18, an ancient text that all modern scholars agree uses the oldest Hebrew in the Bible. The hymn must date to sometime before 1100 BCE. It follows a basically three-part structure: Yahweh rescued Israel from Egypt, brought them to the holy mountain (Sinai/Horeb or the promised land), and made the nations afraid of them. Exodus-Numbers expands upon this basic storyline, while Genesis explains how Israel got to Egypt in the first place. Deuteronomy knows the storyline (see Deut 1–3) but embeds it in a series of theological and legal reflections.

Fifth, the Pentateuch does not consist simply of stories. It also contains other types of literature. The stories provide the framework, but the other genres, especially law, provide a large part of its substance. The laws may take the form of either apodictic ("thou shalt not") or casuistic ("if ... then") statements and in some cases may become fairly elaborate to reflect the complexities that arise from their implementation (see, for example, Exod 21:28–32).

The 613 laws of Torah fall into seven major, and partly overlapping collections, or codes:

The Ten Commandments (Exod 20; Deut 5),

The Covenant Code (Exod 21–23),

The Ritual Decalogue (Exod 34),

The Levitical Code (Lev 1–16),

The Holiness Code (Lev 17–27),

The Deuteronomic Code (Deut 12–26), and

The Curses Code (Deut 27:15–26).

Although the individual laws often resemble those of other ancient Near Eastern collections, the overall biblical collections take on a larger life. As Deuteronomy 30 makes clear, the laws function as guides for those in covenant with God. Israelites keep the law with joy, not grudgingly, because they remember their liberation from slavery.

INTRODUCTION TO THE PENTATEUCH

Moreover, the laws of the Pentateuch challenge the power structures to seek the rights of all members of the society, not just the powerful. Thus Deuteronomy radically limits royal power (17:14–20), and rules on tithing, landlessness for the priesthood (Num 35), and the periodic redistribution of property during the Jubilee (Lev 25) insure a relative equality of goods and status. As Levinson (118) puts it, "law does not merely enshrine or reflect the existing social order but provides a vantage point independent of it." Lawmaking presupposes an attempt to find a particular kind of order and meaning in life. Law makes arguments as to what is moral or immoral, just or unjust. To some extent, the laws help determine which stories get told (Freedman), just as the stories Israel remembered shaped their understanding of their laws.

AUTHORSHIP & DATE

In reading the Pentateuch, it becomes obvious that several different points of view shape the text. To take a small example, Torah forbids the erection of unhewn stones [Hebrew *matsevot*] as funerary or cultic objects (Lev 26:1; Deut 16:22), although Moses (Exod 24:4) and Jacob (Gen 28:18, 22) both do so. Or, again, Abraham and Sarah eat non-kosher meals (Gen 18:7–8), Joseph practices a form of divination (Gen 44:5; but see Lev 19:31; Deut 18:19–14), the number of festivals varies by text (three in Exod 23:14–15; six plus the Sabbath in Lev 23 and Num 28–29), and the number of the cities of refuge may or may not depend on the extent of Israelite territory (Num 35; but Deut 19).

Such minor differences in perspective indicate that the Pentateuch contains material of varying sorts. It records a dialogue, not a monologue. Yet readers have been more troubled by what seem to be logical problems or outright discrepancies. Thus, although ancient traditions ascribed all of the Pentateuch to Moses, its most important human character, as early as the fifth century CE, the Babylonian Talmud (*Baba Bathra* 15a) wondered how Moses could record his own death, concluding that "Joshua wrote the book which bears his name and [the last] eight verses of the Pentateuch," although it also reports the guess of one Rabbi Simeon that from Deuteronomy 34:5 on, "God dictated and Moses wrote with tears," that is, that he predicted his own death.

In the Middle Ages, the commentator Ibn Ezra listed five historical problems: the end of Deuteronomy; the statement "Moses wrote" (Deut 31:22) referring to Moses in the third person; "then the Canaanites dwelled in the land" (Gen 12:6) as though from the point of the author they no longer did so; Genesis 22:14, which he apparently understood to refer to a future appearance of God in Jerusalem, long after Moses' time; and the reference to the iron bed of Og as a museum piece "until this day," again implying some time lag between the time of Moses and the time of writing.

> **Traditional Jewish Commentary**
> *Several medieval Jewish commentators left valuable works on the Pentateuch. The greatest of them, the French rabbi Rashi (Rabbi Solomon ben Isaac; 1040–1105) combined careful language study and attention to the literal reading of the text with traditional Jewish homiletical interpretations, all in a clear, straightforward style. Ibn Ezra (1092–1167) also offered a careful literal reading of the text. Both of their works are frequently reprinted in Jewish texts.*

In the late sixteenth and early seventeenth century, Christian scholars began to notice the same phenomena, as well as others. Among many other examples, they recognized that the mountain on which Moses received the law was in some instances Sinai and in others Horeb; he brought forth water at Massah/Meribah, which could be at Rephidim (Exod 17:8) or Kadesh (Num 20:1), and so on. Sometimes God was called Elohim, sometimes Yahweh, and, rarely, Yahweh Elohim. Genesis 1 lays out a clear week-long pattern of creation through divine decree, while Genesis 2 speaks of "the day that Yahweh Elohim made the earth and the heavens" and connects the growth of plants to human activity. Abraham twice tries to pass his wife off as his sister, while Isaac does so once, all with the same results. Exodus 6:2–3 notes that God revealed a new name to Moses, the divine name Yahweh, which the ancestors did not know. However, Genesis uses the name 131 times, sometimes in the mouths of the patriarchs. (Some scholars try to explain away this data by noting that one can know a name without knowing its "power," but such a magical view of names has little basis in the Bible and fails to explain the actual occurrences in Genesis.) Numbers 12 calls Moses "the humblest man in the world," an odd statement if Moses wrote the Pentateuch himself! And so it goes.

INTRODUCTION TO THE PENTATEUCH

Most significantly, early modern scholars noticed that some patterns of word uses tended to cluster and to coincide with changes of style and approach in various texts. They thus began to ask how to explain this evidence. Over the past two centuries, scholars have thought of the origins of the Pentateuch in several ways. No hypothesis is entirely satisfactory, but each deserves some attention.

THE DOCUMENTARY HYPOTHESIS

The most common explanation has been to think of four major sources, combined together by an editor. In the early nineteenth century, scholars identified these sources as the Older Elohist (or E; using Elohim as the divine name), the Younger Elohist (using Elohim until Moses' call to be a prophet), the Yahwist (or J; using Yahweh – Jahweh in German, the language of these scholars), and the Deuteronomist (or D, consisting mostly of the book of Deuteronomy or some version of it). Later scholars changed the name of the Younger Elohist to the Priestly Source (P).

For much of the nineteenth century, scholars debated the sequence, extent, date, and purposes of the sources. The most influential presentation came from Julius Wellhausen (1844–1918). His 1878 book, *Prolegomena to the History of Ancient Israel*, accepted the sequence of sources JEDP, which he dated to about 850 BCE, 750 BCE, 620 BCE, and 550 BCE respectively. More significantly, Wellhausen believed that, if one could date the sources correctly, they could serve to reveal the development of Israelite religion. For him, the faith of Israel began as a beautiful nature religion, which the law fossilized and caused to deteriorate. The thoroughness of his arguments made his book the definitive work for nearly a century.

Despite the brilliance of his work, several problems have surfaced with Wellhausen's overall scheme. First, his belief that the material in Leviticus presupposes Deuteronomy is not altogether persuasive. In some cases, the influence appears to go in the other direction (for example, see Weinfeld). Second, Wellhausen's view that the law was a degenerate form of religion simply reflects the biases of his German setting, in which several forms of anti-Semitism were prevalent. Third, the dating of his sources is debatable, with some recent scholars dating the Yahwist last (Van Seters) or arguing that it is not a single source at all (the studies in Dozeman and Schmid). And, finally, it is not clear that the various layers of material in the Pentateuch should properly be described as sources that existed independently of each other until an editor combined them. None of this challenges the basic assumption of prior scholars that the Pentateuch consisted of material coming from many times and places, but it does mean that contemporary scholars are working hard to resolve old problems formerly thought solved. The combination of completely independent documents does not explain the literary evidence sufficiently well.

THE DEFENSE OF MOSAIC AUTHORSHIP

In response to the previous view, a minority of scholars, Jews and Christians, have defended some form of the idea that Moses wrote the Pentateuch or at least was responsible for its basic shape. These scholars have pointed out that some proponents of the documentary hypothesis assume that Israel's religion was purely human and espouse low views of the Bible's inspiration (see Archer 113–18). They also note that some features of the Pentateuch, such as the name of Moses himself ("Mose" is an Egyptian name common during the second millennium BCE), are very old, that the "atmosphere of Exodus through Numbers is unmistakably that of the desert" (Archer 122–23), and that, in short, many of the customs in the Pentateuch have parallels in second, not first millennium texts. They show that Wellhausen and his predecessors ignored archaeology and the rapidly increasing knowledge of ancient Near Eastern languages (Harrison 509; however, Wellhausen was one of the most accomplished scholars of Arabic in modern times).

Some arguments for Mosaic authorship rest on theological assumptions. For example, Archer (and Edwards, much earlier) claims that the historicity of the Pentateuchal characters and stories is essential to their value. He also cites an example like Matthew 19:1–9, which portrays both Jesus and the Pharisees assuming Mosaic authorship of Deuteronomy 24 ("Moses says"; Archer 30).

Those who approach the problem in this way raise important points, especially with regard to the need to pay careful attention to the archaeological and literary evidence that bears on the interpretation of the Bible. They are surely correct that Wellhausen and some of his immediate followers were overly skeptical. However, serious problems remain with their own arguments. First, arguing from the New Testament prooftexts seems to be a logical fallacy, a case of begging the question. Second, and even more seriously, Archer and others misrepresent what the New Testament actually says. For example, the Pharisees in Matthew 19 do not ask Jesus who wrote the Pentateuch but rather how a person should live based on Scripture. For them and for Jesus, the author of the Bible was God, and arguments for or against Moses' authorship were irrelevant.

Third, archaeology rarely bears directly on a given story in the Bible or elsewhere. Archaeology can tell us about customs, but many of them remained in practice for millennia, and often later generations remembered earlier, obsolete practices (see Ruth 4:7; 1 Sam 9:9). Fourth, we do know that many ancient texts arose through the combination of discrete sources, and many were revised multiple times in the course of their transmission. The *Epic of Gilgamesh* is a good example. Fifth, it is not at all clear that the documentary hypothesis necessarily undermines a high view of the inspiration of the Bible. A theory of inspiration should arise from the evidence of the text, not the other way around. Sixth, volumes like Archer's read more like a lawyer's brief than a careful analysis of the literary shape and flow of the text of the Pentateuch. There is no substitute for close reading. And, seventh, it is not quite true that arguing against Mosaic authorship means breaking with the long history of Christian reading of the text, since earlier generations focused primarily on the theological import of the text, that is, on its claim on the life of the church.

OTHER ALTERNATIVES

In contemporary scholarship, many of the old battles for the Bible have become passé as new concerns and more creative solutions have arisen. For example, already in the early twentieth century, numerous scholars began to argue for a process by which many small elements came together in the oral tradition to form series of stories that could be put into writing (see Gunkel vii-lxix; however, we should distance ourselves from his label "legend" for these stories). They speak of schools of thought rather than "authors," since authorship in antiquity did not mean what it does to us today. They also show that finding close connections among individual stories, such as one would expect of a single author, sometimes poses insurmountable problems (Rendtorff 177–206).

> **Ancient Authorship**
> *In ancient times there were no copyrights, and authors freely copied each other's texts or added their own material to that of others.*

This research has also shown that theology – reflection on Yahweh's interactions with Israel – drove the composition of these stories (von Rad 1–78). Or put another way, "the final editors of the Pentateuch wanted to respect long-standing traditions, and they did not alter them" (Ska 230). That is, they sought to conserve the Mosaic legacy, not to bend it to their own purposes. Yet preservation also meant connecting the old word to a new situation (see Isa 40:1–10). Rather than being a word to one time that later times merely passed on and tried to imitate in some way, the Pentateuch embeds a living tradition that continued to draw on the experiences of Israel before Yahweh. Such a view of Torah is more dynamic and more likely both to pay attention to the literary evidence of the Pentateuch itself and to respect the reality of a developing revelation within the Bible as a whole.

SUMMARY

However one thinks of the immensely complex problem of the authorship of the Pentateuch, it is clear that the answer does have implications for an understanding of Christian theology. Not many people would find Wellhausen's reconstruction of Israelite history persuasive in all (or even many) of its details, and not many seem to find the defense of unitary authorship mounted in the late nineteenth and early twentieth centuries to be a careful enough handling of the evidence. The crucial turn comes when all of us try to understand the Pentateuch as a whole greater than the sum of its parts and as a fitting witness to God's work in Israel and its heir, the church.

THEOLOGICAL IMPLICATIONS

To make this final turn, we must ask what theological claims the Pentateuch as a whole does make. First, it claims that one deity, Yahweh, the God of Israel, exercises universal sovereignty. This deity created the world, sustains and blesses all its creatures, places them in order for the mutual benefit of themselves and humankind, and repairs the defects in the human condition. Second, Yahweh has elected Israel, liberated them from slavery, and called them to a life of creative freedom in their own land. This election serves to testify to all human beings of Yahweh's greatness and mercy. Third, Israel need not wonder how it should live. It has received torah (literally, "instruction"), which orients it toward a life in which the community lives together in peace and justice. Fourth, Israel should care for the "strangers" among them. Justice does not extend merely to them. And, fifth, the fitting response of the redeemed people is worship that centers upon the one God, shows proper concern for human beings (especially those who are vulnerable), and reinforces the basic identity Israel has as a nation of priests.

For Christian readers of the Pentateuch, these basic theological claims still inform how we live. Far from being a dead letter, the stories, songs, homilies, and laws of the first five books of the Bible still speak.

FOR FURTHER STUDY

Albert Kirk Grayson, *Assyrian and Babylonian Chronicles* (Winona Lake, Ind.: Eisenbrauns, 2000).

Göran Larsson, *Bound for Freedom: The Book of Exodus in Jewish and Christian Traditions* (Peabody, Mass.: Hendrickson, 1999).

WORKS CITED

Gary Anderson, *The Genesis of Perfection: Adam and Eve in Jewish and Christian Imagination* (Louisville: Westminster John Knox, 2001).

Gleason Archer, *A Survey of Old Testament Introduction* (third ed.; Chicago: Moody, 1994).

Joseph Blenkinsopp, *The Pentateuch: An Introduction to the First Five Books of Moses* (New York: Doubleday, 1992).

Thomas B. Dozeman and Konrad Schmid, eds., *A Farewell to the Yahwist? The Composition of the Pentateuch in Recent European Interpretation* (Atlanta: Society of Biblical Literature, 2006).

Jonathan Edwards, *Notes on Scripture* (ed. Stephen J. Stein; New Haven: Yale University Press, 1998).

David Noel Freedman, *The Nine Commandments* (New York: Doubleday, 2000).

Hermann Gunkel, *Genesis* (original edition 1901; trans. Mark Biddle; Macon, Ga.: 1994).

William W. Hallo and K. Lawson Younger, eds., *The Context of Scripture* (3 vols.; Leiden: Brill 1997–2002).

R. K. Harrison, *Introduction to the Old Testament* (Grand Rapids: Eerdmans, 1969).

Abraham Ibn Ezra, *The Commentary of Abraham ibn Ezra on the Pentateuch*, vol. 5: *Deuteronomy* (trans. Jay Shachter; Hoboken, N.J.: Ktav, 2003).

Gary Knoppers and Bernard Levinson, eds., *The Pentateuch as Torah: New Models for Understanding Its Promulgation and Acceptance* (Winona Lake, Ind.: Eisenbrauns, 2007).

Bernard M. Levinson, "Deuteronomy's Conception of Law as an 'Ideal Type': A Missing Chapter in the History of Constitutional Law." *Maarav* 12 (2005): 83–119.

Victor H. Matthews and Don C. Benjamin, *Old Testament Parallels: Laws and Stories from the Ancient Near East* (third ed.; New York: Paulist, 2006).

Gerhard von Rad, *The Problem of the Hexateuch and Other Essays* (New York: McGraw-Hill, 1966).

Rolf Rendtorff, *The Problem of the Process of Transmission in the Pentateuch* (Sheffield: Sheffield Academic Press, 1990).

Heinz Schreckenberg and Kurt Schubert, *Jewish Historiography and Iconography in Early and Medieval Christianity* (Minneapolis, Minn.: Fortress, 1992).

Jean-Louis Ska, *Introduction to Reading the Pentateuch* (Winona Lake, Ind.: Eisenbrauns, 2006).

Karel van der Toorn, *Scribal Culture and the Making of the Hebrew Bible* (Cambridge: Harvard University Press, 2007).

John Van Seters, *The Life of Moses: The Yahwist as Historian in Exodus and Numbers* (Louisville: Westminster John Knox, 1994).

Moshe Weinfeld, *The Place of the Law in the Religion of Ancient Israel* (Leiden: Brill, 2004).

Julius Wellhausen, *Prolegomena to the History of Ancient Israel* (original edition 1878; New York: Meridian, 1957).

INTRODUCTION TO
The Wisdom & Lyric Literature
Michael S. Moore

CHAPTER CONTENTS

The Book of Job   10
The Book of Proverbs   11
The Book of Ecclesiastes   11
The Lyric Literature   12
For Further Study   14
Works Cited   14

Students of the Bible are becoming increasingly aware of two developments in contemporary study of the Old Testament Wisdom literature: the numerous parallels between Israelite wisdom and that of the ancient Near East, and the impact of the plural nature of our world on the interpretive process itself.

First, the inscriptional evidence from Egypt and Mesopotamia continues to inform contemporary study about the phenomenon of "wisdom" in the ancient Near East. No serious interpreter can ignore this evidence (Lichtheim; Lambert), and while it may be possible to overinterpret it, it is impossible to overstate its importance. Wisdom has "as many non-biblical contacts as biblical" (McKenzie 27). Thus the ancient Near Eastern Wisdom literature is an indispensable resource for understanding Old Testament wisdom.

Egyptian wisdom breaks down into two types: "didactic" and "pessimistic" (Lichtheim). The first focuses on the education of scribes and diplomats for bureaucratic service, while the second tends to address deeper philosophical questions. Students of Proverbs are familiar with didactic wisdom because Proverbs 22:17–24:22 practically translates into Hebrew the thirty sayings of *The Instruction of Amenemopet*, a didactic text from the New Kingdom (about 1500–1000 BCE). Students of Job and Ecclesiastes, however, are more familiar with pessimistic texts and would feel more at home in Egyptian texts like *The Dispute Over Suicide*, *The Tale of the Eloquent Peasant*, and *The Song of the Harper*.

In Babylon, sages and scribes tended to work within categories encompassing religious, scientific, historical, and/or wisdom points of view (Wiseman). Whereas they thought of religious literature as the product of divine revelation (often incorporating the very words of Ea and Marduk, the revered "lords of wisdom"), *nemequ* (the Babylonian word for "wisdom") comes from human intelligence and common sense, although in the first millennium BCE scholars began to think of it as sacred lore (van der Toorn). With Job, the closest structural parallel is a text conventionally named after its first line, *ludlul bel nemeqi* ("I Will Praise the Lord of Wisdom," the so-called "Babylonian Job"; Lambert 32–62). The so-called "Babylonian Theodicy" preserves a number of striking structural parallels to Ecclesiastes (Lambert 70–91).

In Syria-Palestine, the text known as "The Sayings of Ahiqar" preserves a very old wisdom tradition. A fifth century BCE Aramaic copy calls Ahiqar a "wise and skillful scribe," and line 3 of the texts describes him as "the [ke]eper of Sennacherib's seal," referring to the Assyrian ruler (705–689 BCE).

Second, recent decades have witnessed a veritable explosion of interpretive approaches to Old Testament wisdom. Many of the newer approaches downplay the problems of historical development, emphasizing instead the meaning of the final form of the text. Historically minded critics still profitably interpret Old Testament wisdom through classical methods of philological criticism, form criticism, inner-biblical criticism, comparative literary-historical

> **Mesopotamian Wisdom Literature**
> *Some of the world's oldest, deepest, and most reflective wisdom literature comes from Mesopotamian scribes. They wrote justifications of the goodness of the gods (theodicies), disputations, dialogues, instructions, proverbs, parables, fables, folktales, short essays, and love songs.*

> **The Ahiqar Tradition**
> *The Ahiqar tradition survived into the apocryphal book of* Tobit, *and even Christian writers like Clement of Alexandria (died 215 CE) quote from it, as did even later scribes writing in Syriac, Arabic, Ethiopic, Armenian, Turkish, and Slavonic.*

INTRODUCTION TO THE WISDOM LITERATURE

criticism, and "sapiential spiritual" criticism (Ceresko, O'Connor). Some also speak of wisdom as an aspect of the entire Old Testament (Sheppard; Morgan).

Biblical theologians engage Old Testament wisdom in a number of interesting ways. Some theologians ask whether Wisdom (with capital "W") might have been an ancient goddess (see Schroer) or merely an extension of Yahweh's wisdom (Prov 8:1; Ringgren). Another polarity pits Lady Wisdom against Lady Folly (Prov 1–9), sometimes as a literary foil (Clifford), sometimes as a competing demigod (Lang). Scholars interested in the history of the biblical traditions wonder whether Wisdom literature originated in the life of clans, in the royal court, or in schools. Others see in wisdom a theological bridge between the Old and New Testaments (Terrien 350–89).

Regardless of approach, most interpreters agree that wisdom contributes several important elements to Old Testament theology: first, it argues that the purpose of humanity is to pursue *shalom*, not live in fear of constant contamination from foreigners and other "defilements." Second, biblical wisdom holds that the authority for pursuing *shalom* comes from common experience, not cultic or political hierarchy. Third, biblical wisdom teaches that the responsibility for making religious and moral decisions lies in human hands, not divine hands alone. Fourth, biblical wisdom teaches that human beings are created to live orderly lives in an orderly cosmos, not a disorderly cosmos in constant need of disruption. Last, biblical wisdom celebrates humanness as the crown of God's creation; humanity is not simply fallen and reprobate, but whole and good.

As Hebrew wisdom went through the changes generated by the invasion of Hellenism (fourth through the first centuries BCE), several notable adaptations occurred. Roman Catholic/ecumenical Bibles document these changes via two books now missing from Protestant Bibles: the *Wisdom of Jesus ben Sirach* (or *Ecclesiasticus*) and the *Wisdom of Solomon*. Although Protestant Bibles relegate these books to the "Apocrypha" (literally, "hidden things"), each preserves valuable details about the process through which Hebrew wisdom eventually becomes thoroughly Hellenized (Hengel).

Sirach, for example, probably represents the work of a single scribe, Jesus ben Sirach, who writes to Hellenized Jews living in the second century BCE. Comprised of moralistic proverbs, psalms of praise and lament, theological and philosophical reflections, homiletic exhortations, illustrative histories, autobiographical essays, and rambling diatribes, *Sirach* is the longest of the "apocryphal" books. Some of its noteworthy ideas focus on "wisdom" as synonymous to *torah* (*Sirach* 1:26; 24:23; 39:1–5), the tongue as a "fiery evil" (28:12–26; compare Jas 3:1–12), and the "house of instruction" as a place for disseminating wisdom (51:23).

The *Wisdom of Solomon*, probably written in the first century BCE (and listed by some early Christians as part of the New Testament; see the Muratorian Canon), drinks more deeply from the Hellenistic well, as even a quick glance at its primary themes makes clear: the exclusion of doubt as antithetical to faith (*Wisdom* 1:2; compare Mal 3:10 on "putting Yahweh to the test"); the limitation of wisdom only to "righteous" Israel (*Wisdom* 1:4; in contrast to the broader boundaries in *Sirach*); and the independence of the "immortal soul" from the "mortal body" (*Wisdom* 3:1–9; 9:13–15).

As contemporary study of Second Temple wisdom literature continues, interpreters of the Dead Sea Scrolls and related literature (especially *1 Enoch*) are beginning to fill in gaps in our knowledge. Fragmentary wisdom texts from Cave 4 of Qumran, for example (especially *4QWisdom* and *4QMystery*), help illuminate the idiosyncratic literary, historical, and ideological processes by which the Greek New Testament adopts and adapts its Old Testament heritage (Hengel; Kloppenborg; Kirk; Hempel).

> **Second Temple Period**
> *The era between the restoration of Judah by the Persians (after 539 BCE) and the destruction of the temple by the Romans (70 CE). Earlier scholars sometimes referred to the same era as the Intertestamental Period.*

THE BOOK OF JOB

Like wisdom itself, the book of Job remains subject to several interpretations. Theodore of Mopsuestia (fourth century CE) read it as a Greek tragedy, while John Milton transformed it into an epic poem some thirteen centuries later. Theologically speaking, scholarly focus on human suffering (Dell) continues to stand in tension with approaches focusing on the problem of Yahweh's "honor" (Gammie; Muenchow). Third world interpreters are uncovering insights in the book largely undetectable to first world interpreters (Gutierrez), and recent inscriptional discoveries are forcing interpreters to reassess whether Job's fear of the Almighty [Hebrew *shadday*] might be deeply rooted in Canaanite demonology (see *shaddin* in Job 19:29; Moore, "Job's Texts").

Most of the book's "problems," however, spring from approaches designed to reduce all of the book to hypotheses about historical "sources" and "stages of composition." For example, Karl Budde and Bernhard Duhm presume the prose narrative (Job 1–2 and 42:7–17) to be part of a preexisting folktale into which a later editor spliced the poetic dialogues (Job 3–31). Though several of their contemporaries rejected this approach, the Budde-Duhm "school" dominated twentieth-century scholarship. Today it is under strong attack from those interested in literary (Good), canonical (Habel; Seitz), metaphorical (Perdue), deconstructionist (Clines), comparative (Pope, *Job*), comedic (Whedbee), and polyphonic (Newsom) dimensions of the book.

THE BOOK OF PROVERBS

At first glance, the book of Proverbs looks like a disconnected anthology of short "comparisons" [Hebrew *meshalim*, "proverbs"] set within a literary framework. In reality, however, this Hebrew teacher-training manual is laid out in seven well-defined sections: chapters 1–9, a series of short essays admonishing "my son" to embrace the call of Lady Wisdom (1:20–33; 8:1–21; 9:1–6) and avoid the lure of teenage gangs (1:10–19), sexual immorality (5:1–7:27), and Lady Folly in all her disguises (9:13–18); 10:1–22:16, a series of mostly contrasting proverbs pleading the case for moral integrity in all areas of life; 22:17–24:34, thirty sayings fashioned after the Egyptian *Instructions of Amenemopet*; chapters 25–29, several proverbs preserved by the "men of Hezekiah" about political and moral leadership (25:2–7; 28:2, 15–16; 29:2, 4, 12, 14, 26); 30:1–9, "The Words of Agur," featuring quotations from several parts of the Bible; 31:1–9, the "Exhortation to King Lemuel," featuring instructions to a king from his queen mother about sobriety, charity, sexual decorum, and the dispensing of justice; and finally, 31:10–31, a justly famous 22-line acrostic poem about "the virtuous woman," apparently designed to recapitulate in metaphorical language the figure of Lady Wisdom introduced in section one.

According to Proverbs, human beings cannot function without "discipline." Thus a "wise person" possesses both knowledge and the discipline to control his or her moral behavior (Prov 5:12, 23; 6:23). Fools, by definition, hate discipline (1:7; 12:1; 13:1), and for this reason they often fall into moral and financial ruin (13:18; 24:32). Of all God's creatures, children need "discipline" the most (3:11; 13:24; 19:18; 22:15; 23:13) because without it they easily fall victim to the curse of negative self-esteem (15:32).

THE BOOK OF ECCLESIASTES

Many consider Ecclesiastes to be the most pessimistic of all the Old Testament wisdom books, and it fits well what we know about ancient Near Eastern pessimistic literature. Some of the closest structural parallels occur with the so-called "Babylonian Theodicy" (Lambert 70–91), but perhaps the closest thematic parallels occur in a text not usually associated with wisdom at all, the *Epic of Gilgamesh* (George 1:32–33). While it is true that *Gilgamesh* is an "epic," the Akkadian *Catalogue of Texts and Authors* lists it alongside several other narrative texts as part of the wisdom scribal curriculum. This raises several pertinent questions about the striking parallels between Ecclesiastes and *Gilgamesh*, of which there are many examples. Just a few suffice to illustrate how similar the books are:

ON IMMORTALITY

Gilgamesh Epic III.iv.5–9

> *Gilgamesh to the beast-man Enkidu:*
>
> Who, my friend, can scale he[aven]?
> Only the gods [live] forever under the sun.
> As for humankind, their days are numbered.
> Whatever they achieve is but the wind
>   [*compare the Hebrew keyword* hevel,
> "vapor," *throughout Ecclesiastes*]

Ecclesiastes 3:21

> Who knows whether the spirit of sons of
>   men go upward
> And the spirit of a beast goes downward to
>   the netherworld [*literally* "earth"]?

INTRODUCTION TO THE WISDOM LITERATURE

Gilgamesh Epic IX.iii.3–8

> *Gilgamesh*: "[I have come] on behalf of Utnapištim [*the Mesopotamian Noah*], my father, who joined the assembly [of the gods, in search of life].
> [I wish to ask him] about death and life."
>
> *Scorpion-man*: The scorpion-man opened his mouth to speak,
> Saying to Gilgamesh,
> "Never was there, Gilgamesh, [a mortal who achieved that]."

Ecclesiastes 3:11

> God has put eternity into the human mind,
> Yet so that he cannot find out what God has done....

ON THE LIMITATIONS OF BEING HUMAN

Gilgamesh Epic X.iii.7–14

> As for you, Gilgamesh, let your stomach be full!
> Celebrate every day and every night!
> Dance and play every day, every night!
> Always wear new, clean clothes!
> Take a shower! Wash your hair!
> Give your children the attention they need!
> Take care of your wife's needs!
> For this is the task of [humankind]!

Ecclesiastes 9:7–9

> Go, eat your food with enjoyment.
> Drink your wine with a merry heart....
> Let your clothes be sparkling clean (*literally, "white"*).
> Anoint your head with oil.
> Enjoy life with the wife whom you love....

Ecclesiastes 3:12

> I know that there is nothing better for them than to be happy and
> enjoy themselves as long as they live.... It is God's gift that
> every person should eat and drink and take pleasure in their work.

As this comparison makes clear, Ecclesiastes is much more than merely the confessions of a cynic. Like all "pessimistic" literature, the goal of Ecclesiastes is not to "prove" wisdom's efficacy, but to provoke discussion about how to deal with intellectual disappointment. That so many interpreters struggle to understand this book seems an indication that Ecclesiastes has succeeded in accomplishing this goal.

THE LYRIC LITERATURE

For many interpreters, modern study of Hebrew poetry begins with Robert Lowth's contention long ago that semantic parallelism, whether synonymous, antithetical, or synthetic, is its most basic, significant, and fundamental characteristic (Lowth). In general, contemporary interpreters still accept this thesis, albeit with numerous updates, revisions, and qualifications. Some realign Lowth's thesis according to the insights generated by more sophisticated linguistic analysis (Jakobson). Others expand it beyond purely semantic analysis to include phonological, morphological, and syntactic categories as well (Geller; Berlin; Pardee).

THE PSALMS

Modern social and historical study of the Psalms begins with Hermann Gunkel's attempt to catalogue the various social settings within which each psalm originates and functions. Prior to Gunkel, most interpreters tend to view the psalms as abstract compositions created in private settings by poets unaware of their actual function. Gunkel rejects this highly privatized approach as romantic and naive. Noting the existence of praise and lament literature elsewhere in the ancient Near East, and noting that the Psalter categorizes itself in terms of "prayer" [Hebrew *tefillah*; see Ps 72:20] and "praise" [*tehillah*; see Ps 22:4], he creatively proposes the following subcategories: psalms of lament, hymns, thanksgiving songs, psalms of trust, royal psalms, Zion songs, wisdom psalms, torah psalms, psalms of historical recital, and liturgies.

Later analyses (many from Gunkel's own students) streamlined these categories somewhat, but none of them dislodge Gunkel's original thesis. In fact, the Qumran evidence solidly confirms it. Many copies of the Psalms have been found at Qumran, and, taken together, these fragments demonstrate that the shape of the book varied a good deal. Therefore the Qumran Psalm fragments validate Gunkel's original decision to focus on the history and function of individual psalms versus a hypothetically finished Psalter (Sanders; Flint).

INTRODUCTION TO THE WISDOM LITERATURE

Contemporary theological analyses attempt to translate the results of this socio-historical research into practical categories such as psalms of "orientation," "disorientation," and "reorientation" (Brueggemann). Whereas some interpreters of the Psalter's canonical shape claim to find an "editorial center" in Book 4 (Wilson), pastoral interpreters emphasize the spiritual power of the entire Psalter as the prayerbook of the church (Peterson). Recent research reimagines the Psalter as a literary depository of metaphorical images designed to nourish Israel's aesthetic as well as spiritual needs (Creach; Brown).

Many of the psalms come packaged with superscriptions designed to connect them to specific historical events (Miller). Only Psalm 137, however, remains even approximately dateable. For a fuller description of the structure and meaning of the Psalms, see the commentary elsewhere in this volume.

> **The Structure of Psalms**
> *The literary structure of the Psalter breaks down into five "books" (Pss 1–41, 42–72, 73–89, 90–106, and 107–150), a design which is probably intended to parallel the five books of Torah. Whereas God speaks to Israel in Torah, Israel answers God back in the Psalms.*

SONG OF SONGS

The Song of Songs [Hebrew *shir hash-shirim*] is a remarkable anthology of erotic love poems inserted right into the Bible, apparently to help creatures made in the image of God learn how to experience one of God's greatest gifts: heterosexual love. Like all poetry, the Song can be appreciated for itself on its own terms; it does not need an interpretive key to be understood. Because this is *biblical* poetry, however, the Song's presence in the canon often bothers some readers persuaded of the body's "inherent evil," in spite of the conviction of Genesis 1:27 and many other texts that we are made in the image of God in all our faculties. Thus two interpretive approaches have arisen to explain the Song's character and purpose.

First, given the presence and influence of amazingly similar love poetry in Egypt and Mesopotamia, interpreters aware of the Song's literary and historical context tend to interpret it as straightforward erotic poetry. Just as Sumerian love poetry portrays males as "shepherds/brothers" and females as "brides/sisters" (Kramer), so the Song uses the same language, now cleansed of all cultic connotations (see Pope, *Song*). And just as Egyptian love poetry focuses on themes of mutual admiration, sexual yearning, explicit description, lovesickness, and praise of the beloved (White 150–53), so the Song of Songs highlights these same themes. In short, ancient Near Eastern erotic poetry (like all erotic poetry) tends to focus on the senses (touch, sight, sound, smell, taste) instead of the intellect, and the Song of Songs is no exception to this literary rule (Fox).

To include such erotic love poetry within the Bible, therefore, is to make a bold theological statement about the vision of the biblical Creator. According to the Song, heterosexual love is both a power *strong as death* (Song of Songs 8:6) and a delicate creation easily abused (note the cautionary refrain, *Do not arouse or awaken love until it so desires* in 2:7; 3:5; and 8:4). Given the debates over celibacy in the Roman Catholic church and homosexuality in the mainline Protestant church, the Song invites readers to consider what a biblical vision of sexuality is designed to accomplish.

Second, given the predilection of Scripture to portray God's love via this same metaphor of heterosexual love (Hos 2:2–23; Eph 5:21–33), it is not surprising that so many pastorally minded interpreters approach the Song from perspectives emphasizing the "fuller sense" of Scripture (the *sensus plenior*). Ancient and medieval interpreters often resorted to allegory. Not all allegorical interpretations are equal, of course. Some allegorize the Song because they bristle at and refuse to accept its overt theology of sexuality. Others allegorize it because it helps them see the connection between human love vis-à-vis divine love. Thus the Aramaic targum interprets the Song as an allegory of God's deep love for Israel, the chosen people God patiently shepherds from exodus to exile to eventual restoration (Gollancz). Similarly, Origen allegorizes the Song to help his flock learn how to celebrate Christ's unfathomable love for his beautiful bride, the church (Lawson). Thus even a celibate monk like Bernard of Clairvaux can mine it for no fewer than eighty-six

> **Targum**
> *An ancient expanded translation of the biblical text into Aramaic is called a targum. Several different targums were written from just before the time of Jesus until late in the first millennium CE.*

sermons on the subject of God's love – and this from the first two chapters alone (Murphy).

FOR FURTHER STUDY

Claudia Camp, *Wisdom and the Feminine in the Book of Proverbs* (Sheffield: Almond Press, 1985).

Stephanie Dalley, ed., *Myths from Mesopotamia: Creation, the Flood, Gilgamesh, and Others* (Oxford/New York: Oxford University Press, 1998).

Stuart Weeks, *Early Israelite Wisdom* (Oxford: Clarendon, 1994).

Roger N. Whybray, *Wealth and Poverty in the Book of Proverbs* (Sheffield: JSOT, 1990).

WORKS CITED

Gabriele Boccaccini, *Beyond the Essene Hypothesis: The Parting of the Ways between Qumran and Enochic Judaism* (Grand Rapids: Eerdmans, 1998).

Adele Berlin, *The Dynamics of Biblical Parallelism* (Bloomington, Ind.: University of Indiana Press, 1985).

William P. Brown, *Seeing the Psalms: A Theology of Metaphor* (Louisville: Westminster John Knox, 2002).

Walter Brueggemann, *The Message of the Psalms: A Theological Commentary* (Minneapolis, Minn.: Augsburg, 1984).

Anthony R. Ceresko, *Introduction to Old Testament Wisdom: A Spirituality for Liberation* (Maryknoll: Orbis, 1999).

Richard J. Clifford, *The Wisdom Literature* (Nashville: Abingdon, 1998).

David J. A. Clines, "Deconstructing the Book of Job," in *The Bible as Rhetoric* (ed. M. Warner; New York: Routledge, 1990), 65–80.

Jerome Creach, *Yahweh as Refuge and the Editing of the Hebrew Psalter* (Sheffield: Academic Press, 1996).

Katharine Dell, *Shaking a Fist at God: Struggling with the Mystery of Undeserved Suffering* (San Francisco: Harper Collins, 1995).

Peter Flint, *The Dead Sea Psalms Scrolls and the Book of Psalms* (Leiden: Brill, 1997).

Michael V. Fox *The Song of Songs and the Ancient Egyptian Love Songs*. Madison, Wis.: University of Wisconsin Press, 1985.

John Gammie, "Behemoth and Leviathan: On the Didactic and Theological Significance of Job 40:15–41:26," in *Israelite Wisdom: Theological and Literary Essays in Honor of Samuel Terrien* (ed. John Gammie et al.; Missoula, Mont.: Scholars Press, 1978), 217–31.

Steven Geller, *Parallelism in Early Biblical Poetry* (Missoula, Mont.: Scholars Press, 1979).

Andrew F. George, *The Babylonian Gilgamesh Epic: Introduction, Critical Edition and Cuneiform Texts* (Oxford: Oxford University Press, 2003).

H. Gollancz, "The Targum to the Song of Songs," in *The Targum to the Five Megilloth* (New York: Hermon, 1973), 171–252.

Edwin Good, *In Turns of Tempest: A Reading of Job, with a Translation* (Stanford: Stanford University Press, 1990).

Hermann Gunkel, *Introduction to Psalms* (trans. James Nogalski; Macon, Ga.: Mercer University Press, 1998).

Gustavo Gutierrez, *On Job: God-Talk and the Suffering of the Innocent* (Maryknoll: Orbis, 1987).

Norman C. Habel, *The Book of Job* (Philadelphia: Westminster, 1985).

Charlotte Hempel, Armin Lange, and Hermann Lichtenberger, eds., *The Wisdom Texts from Qumran and the Development of Sapiential Thought in the Ancient Near East, the Hebrew Bible, Ancient Judaism, and the New Testament* (Sterling, Va.: Peeters, 2001).

Martin Hengel, *Judaism and Hellenism* (Philadelphia: Fortress, 1974).

Roman Jakobson, "Grammatical Parallelism and its Russian Facet," *Language* 42 (1966): 399–429.

Alan Kirk, *The Composition of the Sayings Source: Genre, Synchrony & Wisdom Redaction in Q* (Leiden: Brill, 1998).

John S. Kloppenborg, *The Formation of Q: Trajectories in Ancient Wisdom Collections* (Philadelphia: Fortress, 1987).

Samuel N. Kramer, *The Sacred Marriage Rite* (Bloomington, Ind.: University of Indiana, 1969).

W. G. Lambert, *Babylonian Wisdom Literature* (Oxford: Clarendon, 1960).

R. Lawson, *Origen: The Song of Songs: Commentary and Homilies* (Westminster, Md.: Newman, 1957).

Miriam Lichtheim, *Late Egyptian Wisdom in International Context* (Göttingen: Vandenhoeck und Ruprecht, 1983).

James M. Lindenberger, "Ahiqar," *The Old Testament Pseudepigrapha* 2 (1985): 479–507.

Tremper Longman, *The Book of Ecclesiastes* (Grand Rapids: Eerdmans, 1998).

Robert Lowth, *De Sacra Poesi Hebraeorum* (1787; Hildesheim, N.Y.: G. Olms, 1969).

James L. Mays, *The Lord Reigns: A Theological Handbook to the Psalms* (Philadelphia: Westminster, 1994).

John L. McKenzie, *A Theology of the Old Testament* (Garden City, N.Y.: Doubleday, 1974).

Patrick D. Miller, *Interpreting the Psalms* (Philadelphia: Fortress, 1986).

Michael S. Moore, "Resurrection and Immortality: Two Motifs Navigating Confluent Theological Streams in the Old Testament (Dan 12.1–4)," *Theologische Zeitschrift* 39 (1983): 17–34.

———, "Job's Texts of Terror," *Catholic Biblical Quarterly* 55 (1993): 662–75.

Donn F. Morgan, *Wisdom in the Old Testament Traditions* (Atlanta: John Knox, 1981).

Charles Muenchow, "Dust and Dirt in Job 42:6," *Journal of Biblical Literature* 108 (1989): 597–611.

Roland E. Murphy, "Patristic and Medieval Exegesis – Help or Hindrance?" *Catholic Biblical Quarterly* 43 (1981): 505–16.

Carol A. Newsom, *The Book of Job: A Contest of Moral Imaginations* (New York: Oxford, 2003).

Kathleen M. O'Connor, *The Wisdom Literature* (Wilmington: Michael Glazier, 1988).

Dennis Pardee, *Ugaritic and Hebrew Poetic Parallelism* (Leiden: Brill, 1988).

Leo G. Perdue, *Wisdom and Creation: The Theology of Wisdom Literature* (Nashville: Abingdon, 1994).

Eugene A. Peterson, *Answering God: The Psalms as Tools for Prayer* (New York: Harper & Row, 1989).

Marvin Pope, *The Book of Job* (Garden City, N.Y.: Doubleday, 1965).

———, *The Song of Songs* (Garden City, N.Y.: Doubleday, 1977).

Gerhard von Rad, *Wisdom in Israel* (London: SCM, 1972).

Helmer Ringgren, *Word and Wisdom* (Lund: Hakan Ohlssons Boktryckeri, 1947).

James A. Sanders, *The Psalms Scroll of Qumran Cave 11* (Oxford: Oxford University Press, 1965).

Sylvia Schroer, *Wisdom Has Built Her House: Studies on the Figure of Sophia in the Bible* (Collegeville, Minn.: Liturgical Press, 2000).

Christopher R. Seitz, "Job: Full-Structure, Movement, and Interpretation." *Interpretation* 43 (1989): 5–17.

Gerald T. Sheppard, *Wisdom as a Hermeneutical Construct* (Berlin: de Gruyter, 1980).

Nili Shupak, *Where Can Wisdom Be Found? The Sage's Language in the Bible and in Ancient Egyptian Literature* (Göttingen: Vandenhoeck und Ruprecht, 1993).

Samuel Terrien, *The Elusive Presence: The Heart of Biblical Theology* (San Francisco: Harper & Row, 1978).

Karel van der Toorn, "Why Wisdom Became a Secret: On Wisdom as a Written Genre," Paper presented to the Annual Meeting of the Society of Biblical Literature, San Antonio, Tex., November 22, 2004.

Claus Westermann, *Praise and Lament in the Psalms* (Atlanta: John Knox, 1981).

J. B. White, *A Study of the Language of Love in the Song of Songs and Ancient Egyptian Poetry*. (Missoula Mont.: Scholars Press, 1978).

J. William Whedbee, *The Bible and the Comic Vision* (Minneapolis, Minn.: Fortress, 2002).

Gerald R. Wilson, *The Editing of the Hebrew Psalter* (Atlanta: Scholars Press, 1985).

Donald J. Wiseman, "Babylonia," *New Bible Dictionary* (1996): 112–17.

INTRODUCTION TO
The Gospels & Acts
Larry Chouinard

CHAPTER CONTENTS

- Matthew   17
- Mark   18
- Luke & Acts   19
- John   21
- For Further Study   23
- Works Cited   24

The four gospels and Acts are our primary sources for understanding the life of Jesus and the expansion of the early Christian community. These works communicate their message by means of story, and thus readers must consider how stories communicate and what kind of information they provide. In the past, studies in these books have been focused on "what really happened" or have attempted to reconstruct the process by which these documents may have emerged. However, these attempts are rarely satisfying, since elaborate attempts to uncover the processes and reconstruct the sources that each evangelist may have used often appear too speculative, and since the authors seem to have incorporated whatever oral or written sources they may have used creatively into the coherent flow of their stories.

Contemporary readers should listen carefully to the individual stories as a whole before contrasting them with the other accounts. The gospels offer four verbal portraits of Jesus, each having a particular focus and message (Guelich). Each work tells of Jesus' life and teachings from a particular point of view, informed both by the primary events and the theological concerns and needs of the expanding church. The following introductions look at the historical factors giving rise to these documents, the literary features used by each author to illumine the flow and meaning of his story, and the major theological themes peculiar to each account.

MATTHEW

For the first two centuries of the Christian era, Matthew's gospel prevailed as the most popular of the gospel accounts. Not only was it the most frequently quoted New Testament book among second-century Christians, virtually all textual witnesses and canonical lists place Matthew first.

The anonymity of the canonical gospels necessitates dependence on external evidence to establish authorship. The external testimony from the second century is virtually unanimous that Matthew the tax collector authored the book. While the heading "according to Matthew" probably did not appear in the original manuscript, the heading did appear when copies began to circulate among Christian communities (see Hengel 78–106). Early patristic evidence for Matthean authorship comes from Papias, the Bishop of Hierapolis (60–130 CE), whose comments survive in Eusebius's *Ecclesiastical History* (3.39.14–16). All subsequent patristic testimony depended on Papias.

> **Patristics**
> The study of the "church fathers" who wrote and lived during the first through the sixth centuries CE.

There is nothing inherent in the gospel itself that convincingly argues against Matthean authorship. Given the obscurity of the Apostle Matthew, the burden of proof rests with those who think the early church got it wrong. However one solves the problem, no significant exegetical or theological concern hangs on the issue.

> **Papias on Matthew**
> According to Eusebius, Papias wrote that "Matthew collected [or "composed" or "arranged"] the oracles [or "sayings"] in the Hebrew [or "Aramaic"] language and each interpreted them as best he could." The meanings of some of the quotation's words are debatable, but the basic idea is clear enough.

Efforts to recover the setting that best explains the form and content of Matthew's gospel have not satisfied everyone. There are two basic proposals for the book's date. Most scholars argue that Matthew was written after Mark, around 80 to 100 CE. However, the arguments for such a dating depend on Mark coming first and on theories about the split between the church and the early rabbinic movement at the end of the first century. Others have made a strong case for a pre-70 dating for Matthew's gospel. The gospel does not suppose that its readers have severed all contact with the synagogue. Furthermore, not enough is known about pre-70 Pharisaism. Fortunately understanding Matthew's gospel does not depend on precisely reconstructing the community from which the work emerged.

While the setting and date of the book remain uncertain, its purpose deserves serious consideration. However, it is precarious to assume only one purpose. The writer obviously knows the law of Moses and the Old Testament stories. The gospel assumes that the readers believe the Jewish Scriptures. The story creates a sense of the culmination of God's plan in Jesus and in an alternative community initially composed of twelve disciples. The story shows Jesus shaping the worldview of the disciples as they experience the kingdom of God (compare 6:10 and the five "teaching blocks" of chapters 5–7, 10, 13, 18, and 24–25). Jesus' alternative vision challenges the religious establishment (and indirectly the Roman Empire) with a nonviolent, suffering Messiah and a community of those on the social margins. Ultimately, Jesus expects all his disciples to take seriously their call to embrace his story as their own. The way of discipleship is forever linked to the way of the cross.

As the commentary in this volume will show, Matthew narrates a story in which the various episodes are interrelated by causal and thematic developments. The unifying factor giving coherence to the overall sequence of events is the explicit and implicit presence of Jesus, the central character in virtually every episode. Within Matthew's story, events of similar nature are often clustered or repeated for their cumulative impact as various themes are reinforced and developed.

MARK

In contrast to the popularity of Matthew in the early church, Mark was perhaps the most neglected of the canonical gospels. Early assessments viewed Mark as an inferior abbreviator of Matthew. While incidental comments could be found among the church fathers about Mark, the first commentary on Mark did not appear until early in the seventh century.

However, early in the nineteenth century perceptions of Mark changed as scholarship began to explore the literary relationships of the Synoptic Gospels; a consensus emerged that Mark was the first gospel written and was therefore the primary source for reconstructing the life of the historical Jesus. As noted by Ralph Martin (37), it was with the "life of Jesus movement" that Mark "came into its own, after centuries of neglect." Mark's brevity, alleged literary inferiority, and so-called "primitive theology," alongside the supposition that Gospel composition proceeded from the "more primitive" to the "more advanced," convinced many that Mark must replace Matthew as the earliest of the canonical gospels (see Farmer 1).

> **Synoptic Gospels**
> *Matthew, Mark, and Luke show a close literary relationship with one another and thus are called "synoptic" (from the Greek "seen together").*

Far from being a mere editor who pasted together random Jesus stories, Mark was a creative literary genius who crafted an engaging story with theological sophistication. Although Mark may lack the artistry of Matthew and the command of Greek prose of Luke, Mark tells his story in an engaging way, challenging the reader to rethink conventional values and to see reality through a radically different lens.

> **Biographies of Jesus**
> *In the nineteenth century, European scholars wrote many so-called lives of Jesus, highly critical biographies that sought to go behind the canonical gospels. Their contemporary successors include the "Jesus Seminar," among others.*

Mark, like Matthew, contains no explicit reference to the author. Also, like Matthew, the earliest and most important source attributing the work to Mark comes from Papias, whom Eusebius quotes: "Mark having become the interpreter of Peter wrote down accurately whatever he remembered of the things said and done by the Lord, but not however in order" (*Ecclesiastical History* 3.39.15).

While some find the statement by Papias to lack credibility, it is difficult to account for his identifying such an obscure person as Mark as the author unless he had authentic information. (However, since Mark was a common Roman name, we do not know whether Papias had in mind the John Mark of Acts 12:25; 13:4, 13.)

While the patristic tradition states that Mark wrote in close association with Peter, we do not know if the book follows or precedes Peter's death in the mid-60s. It does appear from Papias that Mark wrote as Peter recounted events.

Since Mark has been linked to Peter, and since tradition locates Peter in Rome at the end of his life, most scholars point to Rome as the place of Mark's writing. Obviously such conclusions depend on the reliability of patristic tradition. The gospel hints, however, that the original readers were Gentile rather than Jewish Christians (see Bauckham): Mark's explanation of Jewish customs (7:3–4), his defining of Aramaic phrases (5:41), his presupposition of a setting where women have a right to divorce their husbands (10:11–12), and his explanation that the widow's two copper coins were worth "a fraction of a penny" (*lepton*, a coin not used in Syria and Galilee), all point to the original recipients as non-Jewish. So unlike the distinctive Jewish flavor of Matthew, Mark has a distinctive Gentile flavor.

Although only about 7 percent of Mark's gospel has no parallels in either Matthew or Luke, Mark nevertheless weaves a remarkably dramatic portrayal of Jesus. Mark describes his work as "the gospel [Greek *euangelion*] about Jesus Christ, Son of God" (1:1). In Greco-Roman documents the term *euangelion* announced a military victory or a momentous event in the life of the emperor. Mark's gospel, by contrast, proclaims the "good news" about Jesus' victory and a subsequent exaltation that completely overshadows the claims of the Roman emperor. In Christian circles prior to Mark, the term referred to the oral proclamation of the salvation in Jesus. As far as we know, Mark was the first to use the term "gospel" to refer to the "content rather than the form of the book" (France 4–5). For Mark, the entire story of Jesus constitutes the "good news," not just his death and resurrection (compare 1 Cor 15:1–4).

While all four gospels highlight the importance of the cross as the defining moment of Jesus' mission, Mark stands out in his emphasis on Jesus' passion (Hooker 22). There is a reason that Mark has been described as "a passion narrative with an extended introduction," since almost half of the book focuses on the last week of Jesus' life. Early in the story, two themes capture the Markan portrayal of Jesus: Jesus is uniquely and supremely authoritative, and yet he remains unassuming in his service.

As observed by Best (45), it is "probable that he [Mark] wrote down a story which he was already accustomed to telling in the Christian community." Mark, the consummate storyteller, stands on the "boundary between oral and written literature" (Best 47). His gospel is meant to be heard, since the vast majority in the ancient world was illiterate, and the modern practice of reading texts silently was unusual for ancient readers.

> **The Messianic Secret**
> *In spite of the fact that his majestic presence stirred the crowds and brought instant recognition by the demons, Jesus sought to silence all discussion about his miracles (1:44; 5:43; 7:36; 9:9; compare 5:19) and refused the disclosure of his identity by the demons (1:25, 34; 3:11). Only in the cross does his identity become clear. His instructions to his disciples to keep his identity to himself was not a rhetorical trick but a witness to his most basic nature as the one who gave up all for the sake of humanity.*

Mark's breathless narration is illustrated in chapter 1, as virtually every episode begins with "and" [Greek *kai*, used to introduce 88 episodes in Mark], and everything seems to happen "immediately" or "at once" [Greek *euthus*; verses 10, 12, 18, 20, 21, 23, 30, 42, 43]. The lightning pace continues throughout Mark with the same adverb used over 40 times. These stylistic features, along with his frequent use of the historical present (150 times) to depict past action [Greek *legei*, "he says"] adds to Mark's liveliness, particularly suited to oral narration. The effect is to draw the reader/hearer into the action of the story and heighten a sense of urgency.

To the casual reader, Mark may appear to be a random collection of episodes. But episodes in oral narratives are "not grouped according to cause and effect, that is, in linear plot development, neither are they necessarily arranged in chronological order" (Dewey 38). By repeating words or placing similar situations side by side, Mark uses literary techniques that provide aids to memory in an oral culture.

LUKE & ACTS

The relationship of Luke and Acts may escape the modern reader because of their separation by John in the canon. Nevertheless, there is a scholarly consensus that the two volumes came from the same author. In addition to the similarities of prologues (Luke 1:1–4 and Acts 1:1–2), the two share common

INTRODUCTION TO THE GOSPELS & ACTS

theological themes: the culmination of God's redemptive plan in Jesus; the Spirit's work in the ministry of Jesus and of the disciples; the concern for "the least, last, and lost" (Witherington 70); the universality of the gospel's appeal; and the signs of the kingdom in the lives of both Jesus and the church.

> **Luke-Acts or Luke & Acts?**
> *The author of Luke and Acts originally intended the books to go together. Therefore, modern scholars often speak of a single work, Luke-Acts. However, by the end of the second century, the books were circulating independently, probably because Luke had become part of a four-gospel assembly, along with Matthew, Mark, and John.*

Only Luke has Jesus' petition on behalf of his executioners (23:34), while in Acts, Stephen, the first Christian martyr, utters a similar sentiment (7:60). Luke intentionally highlighted similarities between Jesus and the disciples. Jesus' empowerment by the Spirit as he begins his public ministry (Luke 3:21–4:30) is paralleled by the disciples' reception of the Spirit and empowerment for service (Acts 1–2). The last days of Jesus in Luke (19:28–24:53) have many parallels to Paul's arrest, trials, and eventual arrival in Rome (Acts 20:13–28:31). It also seems apparent that Luke's closure highlighting the ascension (24:49–53) links to the opening chapter in Acts (1:1–11). Just as Luke has Simeon praising the infant Jesus as "a light for revelation to the Gentiles" (Luke 2:32), Acts narrates Gentile inclusion in God's redemptive plan. As noted by Bock (1; compare Marshall 16–17), "Luke's Gospel often lays the foundation for many of the issues whose answers come in Acts." Taken together, Luke-Acts constitutes 25 percent of the New Testament.

The nature of Luke's literary production has stimulated a "storm center" of controversy (van Unnik), especially concerning Luke's competence as an historian. Although not an eyewitness to most of the incidents he records, Luke shows a historian's sensitivity to the sources at his disposal (Luke 1:1–4). He anchors his story in real events involving the major players dominating Palestinian and the broader Greco-Roman world of the first century. More than any other evangelist, Luke is most influenced by the conventions of Hellenistic historiography and biography. It follows that Luke's writings must be assessed in terms of ancient historiographical conventions rather than the protocols expected of the modern historian.

Luke was not a careless historian, but he does rearrange events and summarize lengthy speeches in order to highlight their theological significance. Since he writes to believers, not skeptics, he is more concerned to interpret events than to prove their veracity. However, foundational to the Christian claim is that the story retold by the evangelist has its roots in real time-place events.

In neither the third gospel nor Acts does the author reveal his identity. However, the tradition in the early church is virtually unanimous that the author was Luke. As noted by Fitzmyer (*Luke* 41), "If the Gospel and Acts did not already pass under [Luke's] name there is no obvious reason why tradition should have associated them with him [Luke]." Hence, the heading found in the earliest manuscripts (such as ms. *P* 75, dated to the end of the second century, "according to Luke" [Greek *kata Loukan*]), probably provides the best testimony we have.

Luke appears in the New Testament three times (Col 4:14; 2 Tim 4:11; Phlm 24). The so-called "we" sections in Acts (16:10–17; 20:5–15; 21:1–18; 27:1–28:16) probably limit the authorship of Acts to one of Paul's traveling companions. While Luke does appear as the most likely candidate, it is strange that he ignores an abundance of material about Paul and his letters (see 2 Cor 11:24–35; Gal 1:17–22). While the exact ethnic background of Luke has been disputed, he was probably a Gentile who had strong connections to Judaism before becoming a Christian.

As for the date of the book, the fact that Acts ends without any reference to events detailing the outcome of Paul's trial in Rome may suggest a writing date preceding Paul's trial. On the other hand, it may be argued that Luke's purpose for closing his second volume the way he did was to end the story by portraying Paul in the heart of the empire announcing the good news of an alternative kingdom right under the nose of the emperor (28:30–31).

Also, Luke's relationship to Mark requires explanation. If Luke used Mark, and if Mark wrote in the mid-60s, then Luke must come later, perhaps in the 80s. Indeed, Luke's reference to the "many" who have written before him (Luke 1:1) may include Mark, but exactly how long Mark circulated before Luke had access to it is anybody's guess.

Another fixed point often used to establish a date for Luke-Acts is the destruction of Jerusalem in 70 CE. If Luke's two volumes were composed

INTRODUCTION TO THE GOSPELS & ACTS

after 70, it would seem odd that the books make no concrete reference to Jerusalem's destruction. While certainty may not be possible, it is not unreasonable to date the composition of Luke-Acts sometime between the late 60s and the mid-70s.

As with date and authorship, any proposal concerning the purpose of Luke-Acts must take seriously the gospel's opening prologue (Luke 1:1–4), which introduces both Luke and Acts. Luke writes to Theophilus to provide assurance concerning the things he had been taught (1:4). Luke tries to demonstrate that the Christian community to which he now belongs is the fulfillment of God's redemptive plan in Jesus. As noted by Tannehill (69), the phrase "plan of God" gives Luke-Acts a "unitary story" (Luke 7:30; Acts 2:23; 4:28; 5:38–39; 13:36; 20:27). Theophilus and others like him, who live on the boundary of Jewish and Hellenistic cultures, must understand that in spite of the rejection by the synagogue, God's plan has always intended for both Jew and Gentile to find their spiritual identity united in Christ.

> **Theophilus**
> *Theophilus probably was a Gentile believer, perhaps once associated with the synagogue, like other God-fearing Gentiles Paul had encountered (Acts 13:43; 14:1; 17:4, 12, 17; 18:6; 19:8–10).*

Luke, therefore, defends the Christian movement by grounding his story in Israel's past and demonstrating through Jewish Scripture that Jesus and the new community fulfill God's promises. In spite of overwhelming odds and the fierceness of Christianity's opponents, God seems to turn every adversity into an opportunity for witness. From every social stratum people come to faith and thus challenge the Roman Empire with an alternative reality.

JOHN

To move from the Synoptic Gospels to John seems at first to enter a different world. About 92 percent of John's material is unique to that gospel. Even where the four overlap, John's distinctive style, order of events, and literary imagery differ radically from that of the other three gospels. John invites his readers to enter a symbolic world where dimensions of Jesus' identity and mission develop differently than they do in the Synoptics.

Although a few allusions to John come from second- and third-century Christian writers, its popularity within Gnostic circles probably brought the gospel to the forefront of discussion in the early church. Because of Gnostic interest in the work, some suspected its orthodoxy. It was Irenæus in the second century who came to the defense of John as a reliable witness to orthodox theology. Irenæus claims to have been taught by Polycarp, who in turn was instructed by John himself, one of the original disciples. Accordingly, Irenæus affirms the integrity of the fourth gospel because it comes from John's own eyewitness testimony. While not all were persuaded, by the end of the fourth century a strong consensus endorsed John's place in the canon.

> **Gnosticism**
> *Historical Gnosticism involved a cluster of religious movements emphasizing "secret knowledge" (the name comes from the Greek gnosis, "knowledge") that allowed the "enlightened" to escape the corruption of the physical world. Some Gnostics claimed Christianity, while other Christians regarded them as heretics who misunderstood the nature of Christ and redemption.*

John's revered status continued until the 18th century, which brought a diminishing assessment concerning the value of the book for recovering reliable information about Jesus. Modern scholars saw John as a late, heavily Hellenized theological reflection on Jesus' ministry and teachings. Such views influenced scholarly thinking until the middle of the twentieth century.

Scholars argue for literary dependency among the Synoptic Gospels where they agree, almost word for word, in retelling an episode they share in common. John is different. Unlike the Synoptics, which focus on Jesus' Galilean ministry, John's story narrates Jesus' movement back and forth between

> **John's Historical Value**
> *Recent trends have seen a renewed interest in John as a valuable source for understanding the historical Jesus. The fourth gospel, like the Synoptic Gospels, tries to report Jesus' story accurately and with theological richness. Furthermore, since the discovery of the Dead Sea Scrolls, it has become clear that John's dualistic language and the categories of his christological thought have parallels in the Jewish writings of the first century. As Matson (78) puts it, "Indeed, it could well be said that John actually represents the most Jewish of all the Gospels, as opposed to being Hellenistic in its framework."*

Galilee and Judea (2:13; 5:1; 7:1–10), largely within the framework of three Passovers (2:13; 6:4; 13:1; compare Mark 14:1). John's account of the cleansing of the temple early in his story (2:13–20) seems to conflict with the synoptic portrayal of the cleansing as a climatic prophetic act that precipitated events leading to Jesus' arrest and eventual execution (Mark 11–13). Many scholars have struggled to harmonize John's account of the time and events surrounding Jesus' crucifixion (John 18–19) with the synoptic portrayal (see Blomberg).

Numerous stories in the synoptic tradition are absent from John's narrative (for example, baptism of Jesus, temptation, transfiguration, confession in Cæsarea, the Lord's Supper, and the prayer in Gethsemane). On the other hand, John has his own distinctive collection of episodes not found in the Synoptics (for example, the wedding at Cana, the Nicodemus encounter, the Samaritan woman, raising of Lazarus, foot washing, and unique resurrection appearances). Even in those episodes where John and the Synoptics overlap, John writes with his own unique style and theological concerns.

When addressing the identity and mission of Jesus, John writes with theological flair. Jesus' discourses in John, unlike those in the Synoptics, focus not on the kingdom but upon himself (5:1–47; 6:25–59; 9:1–10:42; 13:1–38). In John, Jesus makes some of the most extraordinary affirmations about himself and his relationship to God (for example, calling himself the "bread of life," the "light of the world," the "good shepherd," "the way the truth and the life," and also saying "I and the Father are one" and "before Abraham was I am"). Though John reports no exorcisms, his Jesus has come to do battle with the cosmic forces of evil (6:70; 8:44; 13:2, 27) and will not succumb to the powers of darkness (1:5; 3:19; 8:12; 12:35, 46). The parables of the Synoptics are replaced by seven signs (2:11; 4:54; 9:16; 10:41; 11:47; 12:18, 37; 20:30), which also demand "eyes to see" and "ears to hear" in order to properly interpret.

Finally, John's exalted Christology seems to take the reader into revelatory realms to which the other gospels only hint (see Carson 57). John identifies Jesus as the incarnate "word" (1:1–14) who has come to manifest, as no one else has, the character and will of God (1:18; 8:19; 14:9). While the Synoptics primarily refer to Jesus as God's son to stress his role as an obedient son, in John, Jesus' intimacy with the Father is based upon identity and nature (see 5:24, 30; 10:36; 11:42; 12:44–45; 17:8; 20:21). John emphasizes more than anyone else that one's relationship with God depends upon faith in Jesus as God's divine Son. While John may have access to the same wellspring of tradition (both written and oral) that informed the Synoptic Gospels, John certainly shows an independence of thought in theologically shaping his story of Jesus.

> **Christology**
> Systematic theological reflection on the nature, life, work, and significance of Jesus the Christ. Much of Christian history and theology concerns the place of Jesus in the eternal plan of redemption that God is carrying out in the world.

Like the Synoptic Gospels, John contains no explicit reference to the identity of the author. Scholars debate whether enough evidence exists to identify the author, with some insisting that available evidence implicitly points to John, the son of Zebedee, as the most likely candidate (see Burge 37–54; Carson 68–81). The mysterious figure referred to as "the beloved disciple" (13:23; 19:26–27; 20:1–9; 21:7, 20–24; compare 18:15; 19:35) may have been John. If so, then John 21:24 constitutes our earliest testimony concerning Johannine authorship: "This is the disciple who testifies to these things and who wrote them down. We know that his testimony is true." Obviously, even if John is the "disciple" to whom the gospel refers, the reference assumes an editorial hand in the final collection of John's eyewitness material. On the other hand, not everyone is persuaded that John refers to himself as "the disciple whom Jesus loved." The integrity and authority of the fourth gospel do not depend upon establishing John the apostle as the author.

However, the earliest patristic testimony does unanimously point to John as the author of the fourth gospel. But, again, it is primarily the testimony of Irenæus, bishop of Lyons in the second century, who is our primary source for identifying John the apostle as the author of the document that bears his name. While the specifics of Irenæus's claims have been disputed (Barrett 83–106), his testimony carried the day, and by the end of the second century Johannine authorship was widely accepted. Although no conclusive evidence exists to dispute John as the author of the fourth gospel, the value of the gospel does not depend upon a definitive answer to the question.

As for the date of the gospel's composition, nothing in the text enables one to speak with certainty. The silence of John with respect to Jerusalem's destruction (but see 2:19–22) may point to a date before 70, but the absence of any reference to the Sadducees may indicate a date after 70. Some scholars point to a date late in the first century to accommodate John's advanced Christology. However, there appears to be no reason to assume a gradual evolutionary development of Christology in the early church (see the early writings of Paul, such as Rom 1:3–6; Phil 2:5–11). Furthermore, efforts to situate John in a late first century setting are at best hypothetical and fail to take seriously the widespread circulation of gospel materials (Bauckham). So while a date of 70–90 CE may make the most sense, it is by no means certain.

Unlike the other gospels, John explicitly states why he wrote his gospel: *Jesus did many other miraculous signs in the presence of his disciples which are not recorded in this book. But these are written that you may believe that Jesus is the Christ, the Son of God, and that believing you may have life in his name* (20:30–31). While John's affirmation appears straightforward, the term translated "that you may believe" reflects a textual problem that complicates a precise understanding of John's intention. Some manuscripts read the verb as a form meaning "that you might believe," while others contain a present subjunctive meaning meaning "that you might go on believing" (Metzger 256). The first possibility focuses on evangelism and the second on encouraging Christians. Conceivably, as Beasley-Murray (lxxxix) has plausibly suggested, "the Fourth Gospel was written with both evangelistic and didactic aims in view." While John writes to strengthen the Christian community in the face of opposing and compromising views, his gospel also becomes the basis of an apologetic appeal to those outside the faith. What is necessary is to properly read and interpret the *signs*, of which John says there were too many to record in a single volume (20:31).

While John's literary artistry has been widely recognized, no comprehensive structural scheme seems to do justice to the literary complexities of the fourth gospel. Rather than a clear linear sequencing of events, John's gospel is "christocentric" (Johnson 478), with virtually every episode hovering around Jesus and vibrating between the tensions of faith and unbelief. John's story dramatizes the affirmation of the prologue (1:1–18) that "the light shines in the darkness, but the darkness has not understood [or "overcome"] it" (1:5), and "he came to that which was his own, but his own did not receive him" (1:11). Especially in the first part of John's story (1:19–12:50), the narrative flow reflects repetitive accounts, highlighting the tensions between faith and unbelief. As noted by Culpepper (89), "Plot development in John, then, is a matter of how Jesus' identity comes to be recognized and how it fails to be recognized. Not only is Jesus' identity progressively revealed by the repetitive signs and discourses...but each episode has essentially the same plot as the story as a whole." Also, each episode seems to dramatize the message of the prologue: "He was in the world, and though the world was made through him, the world did not recognize him" (1:10).

After narrating a series of episodes highlighting the revelation of Jesus through "signs" and discourses (1:19–12:50), in the next section (13:1–17:26), Jesus discloses his glory and salvific intent "to those who believed in his name" (that is, the disciples, 1:12). Though they cannot follow Jesus in his departure, they are promised the resources for survival (Holy Spirit), given insight into what they can expect (persecution and suffering), and encouraged to exhibit a community of love and solidarity.

When the darkness approaches (18:1–11), events move quickly through the trials (18:12–40) and the eventual execution of Jesus (19:1–42). However, the darkness was not able to "overcome" the light (1:5), as Jesus' glory is revealed through his resurrection and subsequent restoration of his disciples (20:1–21:25). The *Word*, who was acknowledged as God in the beginning of the story (1:1), is now recognized and confessed at the end as *my Lord and my God* (20:28).

FOR FURTHER STUDY

Larry Chouinard, *Matthew: The College Press NIV Commentary*, (Joplin, Mo.: College Press, 1997).

Jack D. Kingsbury, *Matthew as Story* (second ed.; Philadelphia: Fortress, 1988).

INTRODUCTION TO THE GOSPELS & ACTS

D. Rhoads, J. Dewey, and D. Michie, *Mark as Story* (second ed.; Minneapolis, Minn.: Fortress, 1999).

WORKS CITED

Richard Bauckham, *The Gospels for All Christians: Rethinking the Gospel Audience* (Grand Rapids: Eerdmans, 1998).

C. K. Barrett, *The Gospel According to St. John* (London: SPCK, 1972).

George Beasley-Murray, *John* (Waco, Tex.: Word, 1987).

Ernest Best, "Mark's Narrative Technique," *Journal for the Study of the New Testament* 37 (1989): 43–58.

Craig L. Blomberg, *The Historical Reliability of John's Gospel: Issues and Commentary* (Downers Grove, Ill.: InterVarsity, 2001).

Darrell L. Bock, *Luke 1:1–9:50* (Grand Rapids: Baker, 1994).

Gary M. Burge, *Interpreting the Gospel of John* (Grand Rapids: Baker, 1992).

D. A. Carson, *The Gospel According to John* (Grand Rapids: Eerdmans, 1991).

R. Alan Culpepper, *Anatomy of the Fourth Gospel: A Study in Literary Design* (Philadelphia: Fortress, 1983).

Joanna Dewey, "Oral Methods of Structuring Narrative in Mark," *Interpretation* 43 (1989): 32–44.

Eusebius, *Ecclesiastical History* (trans. Paul Maier; Grand Rapids: Kregel, 1999).

W. R. Farmer, *The Synoptic Problem*, (Dillsboro, N.C.: Western North Carolina, 1976).

Joseph A. Fitzmyer, *The Acts of the Apostles* (New York: Doubleday, 1998).

———, *The Gospel According to Luke I-IX* (New York: Doubleday, 1981).

R. T. France, *The Gospel of Mark* (Grand Rapids: Eerdmans, 2002).

Joel B. Green, *The Gospel of Luke* (Grand Rapids: Eerdmans, 1997).

Robert Guelich, "The Gospels: Portraits of Jesus and His Ministry," *Journal of the Evangelical Theological Society* 24 (1981): 117–25.

Martin Hengel, *The Four Gospels and the One Gospel of Jesus Christ* (Harrisburg, Pa.: Trinity Press International, 2000).

Morna D. Hooker, *The Gospel According to Saint Mark* (Peabody, Mass.: Henrickson, 1991).

Luke Johnson, *The Writings of the New Testament*, (Philadelphia: Fortress, 1986).

I. H. Marshall, *The Acts of the Apostles* (Sheffield: JSOT, 1992).

Ralph Martin, *Mark: Evangelist and Theologian* (Grand Rapids: Zondervan, 1972).

Mark A. Matson, "Current Approaches to the Priority of John," *Stone-Campbell Journal* 7 (Spring 2004): 73–100.

Bruce M. Metzger, *A Textual Commentary on the Greek New Testament* (New York: United Bible Society, 1971).

Robert C. Tannehill, "Israel in Luke-Acts: A Tragic Story," *Journal of Biblical Literature* 104 (March 1985): 69–85.

W. C. van Unnik, "Luke-Acts, a Storm Center in Contemporary Scholarship," in *Studies in Luke-Acts* (ed. L. E. Keck and J. L. Martyn; Philadelphia: Fortress, 1980), 15–32.

Ben Witherington, *The Acts of the Apostles: A Socio-Rhetorical Commentary* (Grand Rapids: Eerdmans, 1998).

HISTORICAL CONTEXTS
The Biblical Canons
Everett Ferguson

CHAPTER CONTENTS

- The Canon of the New Testament 25
- The Canon of the Old Testament 29
- Theological Reflections 32
- For Further Study 32
- Works Cited 32

The Greek word *kanon* (derived from the Semitic *qaneh*, "reed") was used of a rod and a measuring line, then metaphorically of a standard or model, and so a rule or norm. The first person certainly to use the word for a list of authoritative books was Athanasius in the fourth century.

> **Athanasius of Alexandria**
> A church father from Egypt and the Bishop of Alexandria, Athanasius (about 293–373 CE) is best known for his writings against the Arian heresy.

The presuppositions for a canon of Scripture are revelation and inspiration, and a corollary is authority. These theological points are not the primary task of this article, which is concerned with the history of the canons of the Old and New Testaments, but the history does require some theological reflections.

> **The Canon**
> The subject of canon has to do with books, not their precise wording (textual criticism) nor their titles (often added in the course of transmission).

Focusing on the last meaning of canon as "list" and defining canon as necessarily involving a definitively closed collection, some assert that a New Testament canon did not exist until the fourth century. If, however, one takes the concept for which the word "canon" stood, namely a collection of authoritative writings, then a Christian "canon" existed much earlier. Different definitions of canon often lead to different judgments about the history of the canon.

Historical study normally seeks a beginning point and moves forward chronologically. Yet sometimes it is helpful to begin at the end of a development and move backward. Although this procedure carries the danger of reading later results back into an earlier period, the end product often shows what was implicit earlier, and it may be useful in identifying significant trends, attitudes, and statements.

THE CANON OF THE NEW TESTAMENT

The general acceptance of our closed New Testament canon came even later than the fourth century. In the Syriac church, Tatian's *Diatessaron* (a harmony of the four gospels) was replaced by the four "separated" gospels in the fifth century, and only in the early sixth century did all Christians include 2 Peter, 2 and 3 John, Jude, and Revelation. The Ethiopian church still has a broader canon that includes various books on church order.

> **Syriac**
> The term "Syriac" refers both to an eastern dialect of Aramaic and an early branch of eastern Christianity.

The earliest list corresponding to the now accepted twenty-seven book New Testament comes from Athanasius, bishop of Alexandria (*Festal Letter* 39.5-6 for the year 367). His order is the four Gospels, Acts, the seven General Epistles, fourteen Epistles of Paul (Hebrews follows 1-2 Thessalonians and precedes 1-2 Timothy), and Revelation. The list is exclusive: "In these alone is proclaimed the doctrine of godliness. Let no one add to these, neither let him take away from these." The grouping of Gospels, Acts, Epistles, and Revelation gave a four-part New Testament.

Athanasius did not end discussion of the canon in the Greek church. Gregory of Nazianzus (*Songs* 12.31) omits Revelation from his New Testament list, as does the compiler (about 380 CE) of the *Apostolic Canons* 85 (adding 1-2 Clement and the *Apostolic Constitutions*). Even in Alexandria, Didymus the Blind's quotations show him to have been less precise about the limits of the New Testament canon than was Athanasius.

THE BIBLICAL CANONS

In the fourth century, scribes began to produce the great codices, bringing together all the biblical books in one volume. Codex Sinaiticus includes the *Epistle of Barnabas* and the *Shepherd*, and Codex Alexandrinus includes *1 Clement*, *2 Clement*, and the *Psalms of Solomon*. The Greek manuscripts place Acts and the General Epistles together and usually before the letters of Paul (Sinaiticus is an exception in placing them after Paul). The order of the General Epistles usually agrees with the listing in Galatians 2:9 (James, Peter, and John), followed by Jude.

> **Codex**
> *A book made of leaves bound together, as opposed to a scroll, the codex format began in the early Roman Empire. It has remained the normal method of binding a book until this day. Christians preferred the codex technology as well.*

Shortly after Athanasius's time, the Latin churches ratified the same twenty-seven book New Testament but put the General Epistles after Paul: see councils in Hippo in 393 and Carthage in 397 (canon 24), Jerome (*Letter* 53.9), Rufinus (*Commentary on the Apostles Creed* 37-38, which in addition to the "canonical" books designates the *Shepherd* and the *Didache* as "ecclesiastical" books suitable for reading but not for establishing doctrine), and Augustine (*On Christian Teaching* 2.8-9.12-14).

Despite continuing uncertainties on the fringe of the canon, whether to include the shorter General Epistles or exclude some of the works now called "Apostolic Fathers," Athanasius was not an innovator. Rather, his list was a consensus derived from an earlier stage of usage in the churches. He represents the common ascription in the Greek churches of Hebrews to Paul, the removal of lingering doubts about the shorter General Epistles recorded by Eusebius, bishop of Caesarea (about 313-339 CE), and a reversal of the latter's judgment on Revelation (*Church History* 3.25; 2.23.24-25).

Eusebius, following the literary criticism of his day, listed books in three categories: the "acknowledged books" [Greek *homologoumena*] – four Gospels, Acts, letters of Paul, 1 John, 1 Peter, and Revelation (rejected by "some"); the disputed books [Greek *antilegomena*], but recognized by "most" – James, Jude, 2 Peter, and 2-3 John; and the spurious books [Greek *nothoi*], not deriving from their supposed authors (but orthodox) *Acts of Paul, Shepherd, Revelation of Peter, Barnabas*, and *Didache*. Eusebius preferred to put Revelation in the last category, as written by a different John from the gospel and epistles. He also noted heretical books put forward in the name of apostles – gospels attributed to Peter, Thomas, or Matthias and Acts of Andrew, John, or other apostles. Eusebius recognized that his "disputed" books were read publicly in most churches. He was aware that some in the church at Rome denied that Paul wrote Hebrews. Eusebius's term for what Athanasius called "canonical" writings was "covenantal," belonging to the covenant.

Eusebius, in turn, was greatly influenced by Origen, and his classification of books closely corresponds to Origen's comments. Eusebius compiled Origen's explicit statements on the canon: four undisputed Gospels, letters of Paul, Hebrews, 1 Peter (2 Peter disputed), 1 John (2-3 John questioned), and Revelation (*Church History* 6.25-3-14). Origen made extensive use of Acts, and in passages not quoted by Eusebius he used James and Jude with recognition that some did not accept them. One passage in Origen, preserved only in the Latin translation of Rufinus, gives the twenty-seven book canon, although without enumeration and a full listing: four Gospels; General Epistles of Peter (2), James, Jude, and John; Revelation; Acts; and fourteen Letters of Paul (*Homilies on Joshua* 7.1). Suspicion that the passage is not Origen's results from its absence in Eusebius's quotations, its lack of reservation about some of the General Epistles that Origen expressed elsewhere, and its survival only in a Latin translation. However, much of the passage reflects other texts among Origen's writings, and in later life he may not have felt the reservations some had about the shorter New Testament writings. Eusebius's views on the canon, therefore, reflect an outlook that Origen expressed a century earlier.

> **Origen**
> *Origen (185–254 CE) was a theologian and biblical scholar and died in Cæsarea.*

By the end of the second century, the basic contents of the New Testament canon had taken shape. Ecclesiastical writers of the late second and early third century – Tertullian, Hippolytus, Clement of Alexandria, Irenæus – do not offer lists of the New Testament books, but their extensive quotations and manner of argumentation show which books they considered authoritative. Among them for the first time appears the titles "Old Covenant (Testament)" and "New Covenant (Testament)" for these books. There was clearly a collection of authoritative books, if not yet an authoritative collection of books.

Tertullian often uses the language of two testaments, or "dispensations," contrasted as law and gospel, but he more expansively describes their content as "the Law and Prophets united in one volume with the writings of Evangelists and Apostles" (*Prescription Against Heretics* 36). That work mounted an argument against the heretics over who possessed the Christian Scriptures ("from them we have our being") and the right to interpret them, the whole premise of which would be an identifiable group of writings (explicitly in *Prescription Against Heretics* 38). These Scriptures supply the "records of the faith," and the revelation contained in them is implied to be complete (*Prescription Against Heretics* 9, 14). Tertullian shows a "canonical" sense in arguing that the "New Testament" is short in comparison with the regulations of the Law (*Against Marcion* 4.1.3), in his reasoning on the authorship of the Gospels (*Against Marcion* 4.2 and 5), in stating that Acts is Scripture (*Prescription Against Heretics* 22-23), and in declaring that Paul "in writing to one church did in fact write to all" (*Against Marcion* 5.17). He cites all the writings of the New Testament except 2 Peter, James, 2 and 3 John. He rebukes Marcion for not accepting the Acts and the Pastoral Epistles. Initially favorable to the *Shepherd*, he came to reject it, as he claimed all the churches did.

> **Tertullian**
> *Quintus Septimus Florens Tertullianus (155–230 CE) was a Romanized African and church leader from Carthage. He is sometimes called "The Father of the Latin Church."*

Clement of Alexandria made use of the widest range of literature of any early Christian author. For him, two parts of Scripture are the prophetic and apostolic, also designated the Old and New Covenants. The teaching of the Lord comes "by the Prophets, the Gospel, and the blessed Apostles" (*Miscellanies* 7.16). Clement mentions all the New Testament books except Philemon and 3 John. He testifies to the Pauline authorship of the Pastoral Epistles, and he regularly attributes Hebrews to "the divine apostle" (Paul). His *Hypotyposeis* comments on the General Epistles (he assigns 1 John to "the elder"), *Barnabas*, and the *Revelation of Peter*. He treats Hermas as inspired, cites *Barnabas* ("one of the seventy") and *1 Clement* as apostles (perhaps in the sense of belonging to apostolic times), and quotes the *Didache* as Scripture. Clement's terminology shows he was thinking primarily of "inspired" and "authoritative" writings without trying to reduce them to a canonical list.

> **Clement of Alexandria**
> *Born Titus Flavius Clemens, Clement (150–215 CE) combined Christian doctrine with Greek traditions of philosophy. He is best known for his trilogy: Exhortation to the Greeks, Instructor, and Miscellanies.*

Irenæus offers various formulations of what was authoritative. Some are twofold, as "the entire Scriptures, the Prophets and Gospels" or "the Law and the Gospel." He frequently mentions the threefold "Prophets, Lord, and Apostles" in varying sequence, or even a fourfold classification of writings, the "Law and the Prophets" set alongside the "Evangelists and Apostles" (*Against Heresies* 1.3.6; see 2.35.4). Irenæus is the first author whose surviving work argues from Scripture as a whole, Old and New Testament.

> **Irenæus**
> *A noted opponent of heresies and bishop of Lugdunum in Gaul (now Lyons, France), Irenæus died in 202 CE.*

Irenæus was the first to assert a four-gospel canon and argue that there must be four and only four gospels (*Against Heresies* 3.11.8). He opposed heretics who appealed to only one gospel (Ebionites and Marcion) or had other gospels than the four (Gnostics). Furthermore, Irenæus proceeds to argue from our other New Testament books as fully authoritative. Acts contains "the truths of Scripture" (*Against Heresies* 3.12.9), and the epistles of Paul are grouped with Luke as Scriptures (*Against Heresies* 3.12.12). Irenæus cites every New Testament book except Philemon and 3 John with uncertain allusions to 2 Peter and Jude. He also quotes from the *Shepherd* as Scripture (*Against Heresies* 4.20.2) and makes use of *1 Clement* without clarifying what status he gave to it (*Against Heresies* 3.3.3).

The apparent lack of a listing of New Testament books from about 200 or earlier may be supplied by the Muratorian Canon. Some scholars have recently challenged this canon's traditional date and provenance of the late second century in the West (Italy) with arguments for a fourth century date in the East (Palestine/Syria), but the debate seems to be swinging back in favor of the earlier date. The document does not simply list books in the fashion of the fourth century sources, but it includes explanatory information on each book in the fashion of the early prologues to the New Testament books. (The prologues date from the second to the fourth centuries.)

The Muratorian Canon, a fragment, begins with the end of a sentence presumably about the Gospel of Mark. It then describes Luke, John, the "Acts of All the Apostles," thirteen letters of Paul, Jude, two letters of John, Revelation, *Apocalypse of Peter*, and *Wisdom of Solomon*. Missing are Hebrews, James, one letter of John (unless the letter mentioned in the discussion of the Gospel of John is 1 John and the two Letters of John listed later are 2 and 3 John), 1 Peter, and 2 Peter. Since the discussion of the Gospel of John also mentions a letter, it is possible that 1 Peter was included in the now lost discussion of Mark.

All the evidence suggests, then, that about 200 CE a basic, or core, "canon" functioned in the mainstream of the church. It included four Gospels, Acts, thirteen (or fourteen) letters of Paul, and varying General Epistles (with 1 Peter and 1 John best attested). Eastern churches included Hebrews among the letters of Paul, but had doubts about Revelation, while in the West the situation was reversed. Some books not later included found acceptance, especially the *Shepherd* and the *Didache* and less often *Barnabas* and *1 Clement*. The developments in the next two centuries cleared up these ambiguities.

> **Early Christian Texts**
> Christian leaders in the late first and early second centuries produced a set of documents such as letters (1 Clement, seven letters by Ignatius), vision (Shepherd), and instruction for church practices (Didache).

For the most part, in the second century Christian leaders sought to articulate right doctrine in contrast to heretical and schismatic movements, but some evidence points to the beginning of what may be called a "canon consciousness" in the sense of identifying or recognizing authoritative writings.

The central contents of the later New Testament canon (the Gospels and Epistles) result from collections that go back to the early second, if not the late first, century. Prior to Irenæus's staunch affirmation of a four-gospel canon, Tatian (about 170) had woven the four canonical gospels into a single harmony, using John as the chronological framework. Rather than expressing a lack of regard for the four gospels, his enterprise derived from respect for them and the desire to show that they told one story; he acted on the analogy of the Jewish practice of rewriting the Bible, precisely to emphasize its authority. Tatian's teacher, Justin Martyr, had combined passages from the Synoptic Gospels for study and teaching purposes and testified to the reading of the "Memoirs (Gospels) of the Apostles" in church assemblies in the mid-second century on a level with the Prophets (1 *Apology* 67).

Manuscript evidence (P45; P75; and P4, 64, and 67 from the same codex) and the uniform titles for the gospels (Gospel According to Matthew, Mark, etc.) point to their combination at least

> **Papyrus**
> Some ancient manuscripts were written on papyrus. Such manuscripts of the New Testament are classified by number and the letter "P": hence P46 refers to "Papyrus 46."

by the mid-second century and probably earlier. No manuscript evidence exists for a "fifth gospel" alongside the four. Marcion, writing in the 130s or 140s CE, knew Luke but not Acts, which suggests that these books already circulated separately, and the only likely explanation for this separation would have been Luke's placement in a collection of Gospels.

The usage of several of Paul's letters by Clement of Rome, Ignatius of Antioch, and Polycarp of Smyrna by the beginning of the second century indicates that they knew these letters in a collection. The varying order in which the letters were arranged suggests more than one independent collection, but the process had likely begun with associates of Paul or (on the pattern of secular writers in antiquity) with Paul himself. Collections of the Gospels and Paul's letters did not equal canonization but were a preliminary step for it.

There are other early indications that the writings that became our New Testament had authority from an early period. Gnostic teachers from the early and mid-second century started from Scripture in constructing their religious systems and often provide some of the earliest evidence for the authority of New Testament books. The production of apocrypha in the second century according to the genres of the later canonical books shows the pattern of literature that had impressed itself on the Christian consciousness. The widespread circulation of certain books attested in the papyri and their quotation by Christian writers suggests more than simply use.

THE BIBLICAL CANONS

The most famous early heretic, Marcion made a collection of New Testament books: the Gospel (Luke) and Apostle (ten letters of Paul, without the Pastorals) in an edited version. Although some suggest that Marcion was the first to have a New Testament (to replace the Jewish Scriptures), the reaction of the church against him indicates that his true innovation lay in giving precision and abridgement to the usage of the church. His editing of Paul's letters implies, as Tertullian later argued, that there was already a collection of Paul's letters in a probably relatively definite text form. Marcion's canon did not cause the church to create a canon but did perhaps cause it to reflect on the nature of the Scriptures it was already using.

> **The New Testament's Authority**
> The New Testament books themselves make a declaration of authority – for instance, by Paul himself (1 Cor 14:37; 2 Thess 2:15; 3:14) and about Paul (2 Pet 3:15). They also anticipate a wider circulation of the writings (Col 4:16). The four gospels appear to have been written as conscious efforts to produce Scripture and continue the Old Testament record of God's dealings with his people (now culminating in Jesus Christ). Such were the premises behind the later recognition that certain books were at the foundation of the Christian church and its life.

THE CANON OF THE OLD TESTAMENT

Early Christians based themselves on the Jewish Scriptures. When the Hebrew canon received its definitive form is likewise a matter of debate. That canon contains three parts: *Torah*, or "Law," *Nebiim*, or "Prophets," and *Kethubim*, or "Writings." The Law consists of the five books of Moses; the Prophets include the Former Prophets (Joshua, Judges, Samuel, and Kings – each counted as one book) and the Latter Prophets (Isaiah, Jeremiah, Ezekiel, and the twelve minor prophets as one book); the Writings are the remainder (Psalms, Job, Proverbs, Ruth, Song of Songs, Ecclesiastes, Lamentations, Esther, Daniel, Ezra-Nehemiah, and Chronicles). This totals twenty-four books, but the contents are the same as the current 39-book Protestant Old Testament canon.

> **Tanakh**
> An acronym for the Jewish Bible using the initial consonants of the names of the divisions of the Jewish canon (T-N-K).

The earliest Rabbinic attestation of this canon comes from the Babylonian Talmud, *Baba Bathra*, 14b-15a – an early tradition (second or third century CE) incorporated later in the Talmud. The passage assumes the Law and then gives the books of the Prophets in the following order: Joshua, Judges, Samuel, Kings, Jeremiah, Ezekiel, Isaiah, and the twelve, and finally the Writings as Ruth, Psalms, Job, Proverbs, Ecclesiastes, Song of Songs, Lamentations, Daniel, Esther, Ezra-Nehemiah, and Chronicles. On the authorship of the books, the passage gives the bookends as Moses and Ezra. One of Jerome's listings of the Scriptures enumerates the twenty-four books of the Hebrew canon but in an unusual order, closer to the Christian arrangement of the books (*Letter* 53.8, c. 394). The earliest attestation of the number 24 for the books in the Jewish canon (without naming them) is *4 Ezra* 14:45 (which equates to *2 Esdras*, about 100 CE).

Jerome's other listing of the Old Testament books, giving the Hebrew as well as Latin names and following the Hebrew grouping in three parts, presents the total as twenty-two, to correspond to the number of letters in the Hebrew alphabet (*Helmeted Prologue* to Samuel and Kings, about 394 CE). This enumeration counts Ruth with Judges and Lamentations with Jeremiah, but Jerome observes that some (Jews) put those short books with the Writings and so have twenty-four books. The number twenty-two was the most popular figure among Christian authors who spoke about the Jewish canon.

> **Jerome**
> A scholar and prolific author, Jerome (around 347–420 CE) is best known for his Latin translation of the Bible, known as the Vulgate.

The earliest certain reference to twenty-two Jewish sacred books is by Josephus at the end of the first century (*Against Apion* 1.37-43). (A possible earlier correlation of the twenty-two books with the letters of the alphabet is in *Jubilees* 2:23 from the second century BCE.) Josephus's claim that the Jews have "only twenty-two" books implies a closed collection of long standing. It comprised the five books

> **Josephus**
> A first-century Jewish priest and historian, Josephus was best known for his account of the Roman destruction of Jerusalem in 70 CE.

of Moses, thirteen books of Prophets, and four books of "hymns and precepts for the conduct of human life" (these "remaining books" did not yet have a common title but were not an open-ended category). The threefold grouping is consistent with earlier sources; the arrangement within the groups may precede Josephus, for the rabbinic classification is only attested later. Josephus did not name the books but said that the Prophets wrote the events from the death of Moses to Artaxerxes, king of Persia. From references in his other writings, it seems likely that Josephus included here Job, Joshua, Judges (possibly Ruth was here or with the Psalms), Samuel, Kings, Isaiah, Jeremiah (with Lamentations), Ezekiel, the twelve, Daniel, Chronicles, Ezra-Nehemiah, and Esther. That would leave Psalms, Proverbs, Ecclesiastes, and Song of Songs for the last category. Without using the word "canon" (a Christian word), Josephus does give the formula that nothing was added to, removed, or altered in the transmission (no doubt an exaggeration, but a strong affirmation of authoritative Scriptures). Josephus presumably represents the canon of the Pharisees and indicates it was more or less complete decades before his time, even if other Jewish groups did not accept it.

> **History & Prophecy**
> *Josephus notes that historians had recorded the history of the Jews from Artaxerxes to his own time, but such records were not "deemed worthy of the same trust with the earlier records because of the failure of the succession of the prophets." The theme of prophecy's demise also appears in rabbinic texts.*

In the period after 70 CE, the rabbinic academy at Jamnia discussed the status of the books of Ecclesiastes and Song of Songs. Previous generations of scholars believed that this was the time of the final closing of the Hebrew canon. However, the rabbis inherited a more or less agreed on set of writings. They continued in the second and third centuries to debate the merits of certain books, but these discussions asked "why do we have these books?" rather than "should we accept them?"

Some statements in the New Testament reflect on the Hebrew Bible. Luke 24:44 refers to the "Law, the Prophets, and the Psalms." "Psalms" may be the title of the third section of the Bible. Matthew 23:35 (which parallels Luke 11:49-51), "the blood of righteous Abel to the blood of Zechariah son of Barachiah," may refer to the first and last murdered prophets in the Hebrew canon, which began with Genesis and ended with Chronicles. A problem with this interpretation is that "son of Berechiah" refers to the prophet Zechariah (1:1), whereas the murdered Zechariah of 2 Chronicles 24:19-22 is identified as "son of Jehoida." Perhaps the latter was actually a grandson of Jehoida, or perhaps the Jewish homiletic device of conflating persons of the same name explains the designation (the *Targum on Lamentations* 2:20 makes the same identification). More significant evidence for the authoritative status of the Old Testament for early Christian writers comes from the numerous quotations, allusions, and arguments based on it (John 10:35; 1 Cor 15:3, 5). For the New Testament, the Old Testament had canonical significance (2 Tim 3:16 indicates a whole entity).

Other notices of authoritative writings show a three- or fourfold division, the imprecision due to the lack of a clearly defined title for the books beyond the Law and the Prophets. Philo groups biblical books much as do Josephus and Luke: "The Laws, and the Oracles given by inspiration through the Prophets, and the Hymns [Philo's standard term for the Psalms], and the other books whereby knowledge and piety are increased and completed" (*Contemplative Life* 25). Philo's main interpretive work concerned the five books of Moses, but he makes use of most of the other canonical books and not the Apocrypha.

> **Philo of Alexandria**
> *A Jewish scholar and philosopher living in Egypt, Philo (about 20 BCE–50 CE) was heavily influenced by Greek tradition.*

The *Halakhic Letter* from Qumran (from the first century BCE) contains a similar description: "the Book of Moses, the Prophets, and David and the history of the generations." David would stand for the Psalms. The Dead Sea Scrolls offer abundant evidence of authoritative Scriptures but have frustrated researchers' efforts to find firm indications of their limits. Qumran authors introduce quotations as Scripture only from books now in the canon.

Much like the later rabbis, the "Prologue" (132 BCE) to *Sirach*, by the author's grandson, gives formulations of what his grandfather had devoted himself to studying and teaching: "The Law and the Prophets and the others that have followed in their steps"; "the Law and the Prophets and the other Books of the fathers ["ancestral books"—what was ancient was authoritative]; and "the Law itself, the Prophecies, and the rest of the Books." The use of the definite article for "the books" implies that the third part was an identifiable group, even if its exact boundaries remained unclear. The grandfather himself had spoken of "study of the law...wisdom...and prophecies" (*Sirach* 39:1; compare Jer 18:18), and in his historical treatment of great men of Israel's past he names Joshua, the judges, Samuel, David, Solomon, other kings and prophets, Isaiah, Jeremiah, Ezekiel, the twelve prophets, Zerubbabel, and Nehemiah (*Sirach* 46:1-49:13), a sequence suggesting that the Former and Latter Prophets had already taken shape as a closed group.

> **Sirach**
> "The Wisdom of Ben Sira," also called *Ecclesiasticus*, this text was written in Hebrew about 180–175 BCE by Jeshua ben Sira and translated into Greek by his grandson in Alexandria.

Some consider the collection of authoritative writings to be the work of the Hasmonean dynasty in the second century BCE. *Second Maccabees* 2:14-15 says that Judas Maccabee "collected all the books that had been lost on account of the war." The collection of books at the temple signified special authority. Some conjecture that the non-Mosaic books were divided at this time into two groups of Prophets and other Writings (although the third category received this name only later). The passage indicates a parallel between Judas Maccabee's activity and that of Nehemiah after the Exile (*2 Maccabees* 2:13). That statement would correspond to the categories of Former Prophets, Latter Prophets, and Psalms, and the letters about votive offerings could refer to the contents of Ezra. If we believe this passage, the collection of Scriptures would have begun in the time of Nehemiah. Jewish tradition about Ezra's place in collecting and preserving the sacred writings might confirm this possibility (see *4 Ezra* above).

> **The Hasmonean Kingdom**
> The Hasmonean Kingdom was an autonomous Jewish government in Israel from the second to the first centuries BCE.

Christians used the term "Prophets" to refer to the whole Old Testament, treating Moses and David as prophets. The phrase "Law and the Prophets" (*2 Maccabees* 15:9; or "Moses and the Prophets" in 1QS 1, 1-3; 8, 15-16) came into use early for the Hebrew Scriptures (for example, John 1:45; Acts 24:14; Rom. 3:21; compare *4 Maccabees* 18:10-19 to include Daniel, Psalms, and Proverbs) and continued to be a standard designation by the rabbis and by Christians for the whole of Jewish Scripture long after the third division was undoubtedly recognized. Therefore, we must be careful about concluding from this phrase that no third group of writings was acknowledged. There are indications in the Old Testament text that "law and prophets" designated authoritative writings in general (not separate categories), and that they became canonical at essentially the same time (see Deut 34:10-12 and Mal 4:4-6 for the conclusions of the collections of law and prophets). Indeed, the authors or final editors of Old Testament books make claims of canonical closure (for example, Deut 4:2; 12:32; Jer 26:2; Prov 30:5-6).

> **The Dead Sea Scrolls**
> The Dead Sea Scrolls are classified by the number of the cave in which they were found and the number of scrolls in the cave. Thus, "4QS 21" refers to the twenty-first scroll fragment from Cave 4 at Qumran.

Early Christian authors who set forth the books of the Old Testament followed the Jewish reckoning; these authors include: Melito of Sardis (about 180 CE), but with the omission of Esther and in the order law, history, poetry and wisdom, and prophets (cited by Eusebius *Church History* 4.26.13-14); and Origen, giving the number of books as twenty-two and giving the Hebrew names (*Church History* 6.25.1-2).

Later, Athanasius gave an Old Testament list of twenty-two books but arrived at that number by counting Ruth separately and omitting Esther, and by including *Baruch*, Lamentations, and the *Epistle of Jeremiah* with Jeremiah. He acknowledged an intermediate category: after his Old Testament and New Testament lists he refers to noncanonical books that one may read profitably: *Wisdom of Solomon*, *Sirach*, Esther, *Judith*, *Tobit*, *Didache*, and *Shepherd*. Apocryphal writings are those by heretics. Jerome used "Apocrpha" differently. After listing the books in the Jewish canon in the *Helmeted Prologue*, he adds that what was not in the list was to be placed among the apocryphal writings: *Wisdom of Solomon*, *Sirach*, *Judith*, *Tobit*, the *Shepherd*, *1 Maccabees*, and *2 Maccabees* (so also in his preface to the books of Solomon he says that the church reads these books but does not admit them to the canon). In the Middle Ages,

> **Hugh of St. Victor**
> Hugh was an 11th century religious philosopher from what is now Germany.

THE BIBLICAL CANONS

Hugh of St. Victor wrote that the *Wisdom of Solomon*, *Sirach*, *Judith*, *Tobit*, and the books of the *Maccabees* are to be read but not included in the canon (*Didacalicon* 4.2). This intermediate category of noncanonical continued to be acknowledged in the Middle Ages.

Manuscripts of the Greek translation of the Old Testament, made and preserved by Christians, included varying numbers of other books besides those officially recognized by Jews as biblical. (All such works originated among Jews, however.) These Greek Bibles divided the longer Hebrew books (such as Kings and Chronicles) into two, separated the twelve Minor Prophets, and rearranged the entire collection. This order followed literary categories of law, history, poetry, and prophecy, perhaps derived from an alternative Jewish grouping. Whereas the Hebrew order emphasized the law, exhortations and applications of the law, and then the human response to it, the Greek order emphasized past history, present human life, and climaxed with the prophets, looking to the future.

> **Augustine's Canon**
>
> *Augustine of Hippo (died 430 CE) gave a listing of forty-four books in the Old Testament, adding to the usual thirty-nine the books of Tobit, Judith, 1–2 Maccabees, Wisdom, and Sirach, not grouped separately but as in the Greek and Latin translations interspersed among the historical or poetic works* (On Christian Teaching 2.8.13). *His practice increasingly prevailed, and the larger canon was officially recognized at the Council of Trent (1546). The Orthodox Church recognizes a still larger canon than the Roman Catholic Church. These intermediate books are called by Roman Catholics "Deuterocanonical" and by Protestants "Apocrypha."*

THEOLOGICAL REFLECTIONS

The canon belongs in the context of the church. Hence, the role of the church in recognizing a canon of Scripture should not be misunderstood. Acknowledging a canon of Scripture was not an act of authority by the church over Scripture but an act of submission. In recognizing a canon, the church testified to what was the authoritative word and source of its teachings, practices, and life. A canon acknowledges and limits authoritative books; it does not bestow authority. The recognition of authority came first. The church recognized a canon; it did not create a canon.

The Christian writers who speak about their authoritative books regularly state that these were the books that the church received. They did not say, "we decide," but "we received" these books. Sometimes they comment on signs or "criteria" of canonicity. But these comments always come "after the fact," that is, why these books are accepted as authoritative. They served as tests only in the cases of books rejected by the church, not for determining to accept given books.

With both the Old and New Testaments, a few books sat on the edge, some less widely accepted but ultimately included and some with a certain degree of usage and approval but ultimately not included. A person who wonders about the judgments involved should read the alternatives – the Jewish and Christian apocrypha, pseudepigrapha – and other contemporary literature. The result is not likely to be any extensive or effective clamor for widening or contracting the present canon.

FOR FURTHER STUDY

J.-M. Auwers and H. J. de Jonge, eds., *The Biblical Canons* (Leuven: University Press, 2003).

Roger Beckwith, *The Old Testament Canon of the New Testament Church* (Grand Rapids: Eerdmans, 1985).

F. F. Bruce, *The Canon of Scripture* (Downers Grove, Ill.: InterVarsity, 1988).

Stephen B. Chapman, *The Law and the Prophets: A Study in Old Testament Canon Formation* (Tübingen: Mohr Siebeck, 2000).

Everett Ferguson, *Early Christians Speak*, vol. 2 (Abilene: ACU Press, 2002).

A. van der Kooij and K. van der Toorn, eds., *Canonization and Decanonization* (Leiden: Brill, 1998).

Lee Martin McDonald and James A. Sanders, eds., *The Canon Debate* (Peabody, Mass.: Hendrickson, 2002).

Bruce M. Metzger, *The Canon of the New Testament: Its Origin, Development, and Significance* (Oxford: Clarendon, 1988).

WORKS CITED

The ancient texts cited above can be found in the following collections:

Ancient Christian Writers: The Works of the Fathers in Translation (Mahwah, N.J.: Paulist).

The Ante-Nicene Fathers (reprint ed.; Peabody, Mass.: Hendrickson).

Nicene and Post-Nicene Fathers (reprint ed.; Peabody, Mass.: Hendrickson).

James H. Charlesworth, ed., *The Old Testament Pseudepigraph* (Garden City, N.Y.: Doubleday).

I. Epstein, ed., *The Babylonian Talmud* (London: Soncino).

HISTORICAL CONTEXTS

Israel in the Ancient Near East

Mark W. Hamilton

CHAPTER CONTENTS

Writing & Literature   35
Politics & Warfare   36
Agriculture, Trade, & Manufacturing   36
Architecture   37
Art & Music   37
Science & Mathematics   38
Religion   38
Conclusion   39
For Further Study   39
Works Cited   39

When Israel emerged during the early Iron Age (around 1200–586 BCE), it inherited the cultural achievements of centuries. Major technological and social developments, such as writing, agriculture, government, trade, small-scale manufacturing of textiles and metal goods, and urban life emerged millennia before, and Israel made no important innovations in these areas. Although it occasionally sought to eliminate foreign influence in religion, even here Israel adapted much from outside its borders, filtering it through the theological tradition of emerging ethical monotheism. Much of the Old Testament can be better understood by taking account of the cultural influences of Israel's neighbors. The comparative method of historical study involves examining both similarities and differences among the cultures compared and tracing both direct influences and shared behaviors or technological solutions rooted in either the physical or social environment (or both).

The period from which the Old Testament comes (around 1200–200 BCE) saw numerous political and social changes. Political history centered around the fortunes of the states that dominated the two great river systems of the Near East, the Nile in north Africa and the Tigris and Euphrates in Mesopotamia. Along the Nile, a large state developed by 3100 BCE, and even when Egypt fell into small, competing kingdoms, its rulers sought to reclaim the unity of the past. In Mesopotamia, urban centers, or city-states, arose even earlier, but few kingdoms were able to subjugate the entire area before 1000 BCE. Throughout the first millennium BCE, these great cultures influenced Israel, sometimes using its land as a battleground and eventually ruling it outright.

Israel's first contact was with Egypt, from which at least some Israelites fled in the exodus. Egyptians had long dominated Palestine, often through local dynasties. In the mid-1300s BCE, for example, these petty rulers, from such places as Jerusalem and Shechem, wrote letters to the pharaoh requesting his help policing rebels. Some 350 letters, called the Armana Letters after the place of their discovery, Tell el-Amarna in southern Egypt, reveal the turbulent state of life in the Palestinian city-states just before the advent of Israel. They address the pharaoh as "the sun" (reflecting Egyptian royal religion with its emphasis on the sun-god) and communicate military, economic, and social problems with the Egyptian court (James). Some of the ancestors of the Israelites must have been among the Semitic-speaking peoples who lived as slaves in Egypt itself.

The first extrabiblical mention of Israel itself comes from the Stele of Merneptah, the son of Ramses II, possibly the pharaoh of the exodus, who in around 1209 BCE boasted of destroying a tribal, non-urban people in northern Palestine called "Israel" (Hallo and Simpson 277–78). Over the succeeding centuries, Egypt continued to exert influence over Israelite politics. Solomon married a daughter of Pharaoh (1 Kgs 3:1). Sheshonq probably invaded Israel soon after Solomon's death. Egyptian courts harbored Israelite refugees and dissidents (1 Kgs 12:2–3; Jer 41:17–43:13). But the internal weakness of Egypt during this period,

> **"Near East" & "Middle East"**
> The terms "Near East" and "Middle East" describe approximately the same geographic region, southwest Asia and northeast Africa. Scholars of antiquity usually refer to the area as the "Near East."

when Libyans (945–715 BCE) and Kushites (760–656 BCE) ruled parts of the country (Kitchen), meant that influence over Israel was primarily economic and cultural, not political. When Necho, a native Egyptian ruler bent on reclaiming past glories, executed Josiah of Judah after the latter had tried to halt Egyptian assistance of the dying Assyrian empire, this was the last gasp of Egyptian pretensions to regional rule until the Greek-speaking Ptolemies ruled the region three centuries later.

Not so with the great Mesopotamian empires, Assyria and Babylonia. The Assyrian emperor Shalmaneser III fought a coalition of Syro-Palestinian kingdoms led by Ahab of Israel at Qarqar in 853 BCE. Though he probably lost the battle, Shalmaneser later did subjugate much of Syria (see Hos 10:14). After his long reign, Assyria did not menace Israel or Judah until the reign of Tiglath-pileser III (745–727 BCE). This great general, ranking with Napoleon or Alexander, annexed the northern half of Israel and exacted tribute from Judah (Isa 7). His successors Shalmaneser V (727–722 BCE) and Sargon II (722–705 BCE) destroyed Samaria and annexed all of Israel, deporting over 200,000 Israelites (the so-called Ten Lost Tribes) and settling others in the land. Throughout the seventh century, Judah remained a vassal of Assyria. Assyrian artistic conventions appear on seals and paintings (on pottery) from Judah. Samaria was rebuilt by Assyrian planners on a grid pattern, with monumental architecture similar to that in their homeland (borrowed ultimately from Syria). The new settlers in northern Israel bore Mesopotamian names (as seen in legal documents from Samaria, written in Akkadian: Hallo and Younger 3.122), though they adopted the worship of Yahweh (2 Kgs 17:24–34; Hallo and Younger 1.99, a story by and about some of the foreigners settled in Israel by the Assyrians).

The collapse of Assyria in 612–609 BCE did not mean independence for Judah, however. Rather, the country became a reluctant vassal of Babylon, which now ruled the Near East. After quashing a series of rebellions, Nebuchadrezzar (less correctly spelled Nebuchadnezzar) II sacked Jerusalem and deported much of Judah's population in 586 BCE. Babylon ruled the entire region, much of which lay devastated, until its last king, Nabonidus, was defeated by Cyrus the Great of Persia in 539 BCE.

A new era came with the absorption of Babylon into the vast Persian empire, which stretched from India to Greece and embraced scores of nationalities and languages. Cyrus the Great and his successors placed Palestine in the great satrapy "Beyond the River" (Euphrates), which embraced all of modern Syria, Lebanon, Jordan, Israel, and Palestine. Samaria and Yehud (Judah) were sub-provinces, ruled by hereditary Israelite princes (Briant 487–90). The architecture, coinage, and art of the region, though it had local features, borrowed much from the styles of the greater empire. Palestine was militarily important as a border region and economically significant as a grower of wine and olive oil and as a transit point in the Arabian spice trade with the Mediterranean world. A comment on the dynamics of the empire appears in Ecclesiastes 5:8–9: *one official is eyed by a higher one, and over them both are others higher still*. An Israelite mercenary colony existed during this period on Elephantine Island, in the Nile near the modern border with Sudan. The archive of a contemporary Jewish banking family, the Murashus, survives from Nippur, near Babylon, showing that Jews did survive and even flourish under Persian rule.

> **Jews or Israelites?**
> *During the Persian period, we begin to speak of "Jews" rather than "Israelites," for what was originally the name of people in a region (Judah) became the label for an entire ethnic group.*

In the Old Testament, allusions to foreign powers, their politics and military, and even cultural practices are commonplace. Isaiah 1–39 reflects the time of Assyrian expansion in the eight century, Jeremiah and Zephaniah the Babylonians' supplanting of Assyria in the late seventh century, and Chronicles Persian practices (for example, when mentioning, anachronistically, Persian coins, *darics*, in 1 Chron 29:7). Isaiah 10 quotes Assyrian propaganda. There are many, more subtle influences from outside Israel on the Bible, for Scripture arose in the midst of a diverse, international culture.

These influences and parallels are of several types: writing and literature; politics and warfare; agriculture, trade, and manufacturing; architecture; art and music; science and mathematics; and religion. These categories overlap in practice, but they offer useful ways of classifying the evidence, which can derive either from written texts or from archaeological artifacts.

WRITING & LITERATURE

Writing originated in Mesopotamia around 3200 BCE, probably as a notation system for business records. It spread to Egypt, India, and intervening regions soon afterward. At first pictographic, writing quickly evolved into an elaborate system of syllabic script. Mesopotamian cuneiform (wedge-shaped) scripts consisting of over 500 characters were written on clay tablets, seals, wax tablets, and stone until the first century CE. The first language employing cuneiform was Sumerian, but most texts in the script are in Akkadian, a language distantly related to Hebrew. Cuneiform was also used for writing Hittite, a language in Anatolia. Perhaps 1,000,000 cuneiform texts exist, spanning three millennia.

Egyptian writing, hieroglyphics, drew on Mesopotamian pictographs but soon went its own way. Again, the symbols represented syllables or whole words. Texts were on stone, wood, or papyrus (a reed growing in the marshes along the Nile from the pulp of which sheets of paperlike material could be manufactured).

> **Ancient Documents**
> *The evolution of writing allowed the preservation of many types of documents. Most cuneiform and hieroglyphic texts are business and legal documents, such as contracts, dockets, accounting records, receipts (for examples, see Hallo and Younger vol. 3). These offer interesting insights into the economic and social lives of these ancient societies.*

Around 1900 BCE, in Egypt or north of it, speakers of Canaanite invented the alphabet. This radical simplification of the writing system, in which each symbol represented a consonant (representations of vowels came 2500 years later for Semitic languages), made writing accessible to far more people than before. Each letter sign was originally a picture of something starting with that letter (*aleph* was a cow, *beth* was a house, etc.), though the representational features quickly disappeared as the letter shapes developed. All Hebrew texts are alphabetic.

Ancient Near Eastern literature includes love poems, city laments, dialogues and proverbs, historiography, myths, epics, hymns and prayers, descriptions of rituals, incantations, omens, and even humor (Bottéro; Michalowski; Redford). Although only fragments of what must have existed in antiquity survive, enough remains to prove that ancient Near Easterners enjoyed a robust intellectual and artistic life.

Some of these texts are quoted directly in the Old Testament, particularly by wisdom-oriented texts. For example, Proverbs 22:17–23:11 borrows freely from the Egyptian *Instruction of Amenemope* (Hallo and Younger 1.47), Jeremiah 9:22 shares a proverb also found in the contemporaneous wisdom text, *Ahiqar*, and Ecclesiastes knows the *Epic of Gilgamesh* (Eccl 4:12, 9:7–9; Seow 64–65). The style of opening wisdom texts (Prov 1:1–7; Eccl 1:1–2) is borrowed from Egyptian models.

Administrative documents also appear in the Bible, as when Ezra quotes Persian decrees (circular letters), or Isaiah 10 quotes Assyrian royal propaganda. Some psalms can plausibly be understood as drawing directly on foreign models (Pss 29 and 104). Psalm 20 is also known in an Aramaic version from Egypt (praising Egyptian gods), though it remains unclear who borrowed from whom.

Direct quotations are uncommon, however. Instead, biblical texts draw on ancient Near Eastern genre rules and literary devices. Mesopotamian, Egyptian, Anatolian, and Syrian texts provide illuminating parallels to the biblical material. Thus, Song of Songs is similar to both Egyptian and Mesopotamian love poetry, involving both humans and deities. The Sumerian female lover's address, "Oh my one fair of locks! Sweet one, tree well grown!" could easily fit in Song of Songs (Jacobsen 91). All these poems use brother-sister imagery to describe close intimacy, and all present both male and female as equal actors in the drama of love.

Another genre is the city lament, seen in Lamentations 1–4, and in the centuries-older Sumerian "Lament for Ur" (Jacobsen 447–74) and the end of the "Curse of Agade" (Jacobsen 359–74, especially lines 192–209). In all these texts, disaster befalls a city because the deity has abandoned it after some human failing.

Wisdom-oriented texts include proverb collections (often in the form of instructions of a father to a child or a teacher to a student) and dialogues. Proverbs and Ecclesiastes fit the first category and the poetic core of Job the second.

Historiographic and quasi-historiographic texts from the region also exerted influence on Israelite writing, though less directly. Egyptian travel stories about Palestine exist from the early and late second millennium (*Sinuhe* and *Wenamun* in Hallo and Younger 1:38, 41), but other than royal inscriptions recounting battles, history writing was not an endeavor of Egyptian scribes. Mesopotamians, on the other hand, documented the reigns of individual rulers, particularly their wars and building projects, and compiled chronicles of many reigns (texts translated in Grayson). Some of these chronicles synchronize the kings of two different kingdoms, paralleling the much more elaborate structure of 1–2 Kings.

Perhaps the most complex relationships exist with specifically religious texts (myths, hymns, omens, prophecies, and prayers). Egyptians composed hymns, cosmologies (stories on the origins of the world), prayers, and myths, which expressed deep commitment to deities and belief in a divinely ordained order [Egyptian *ma'at*]. Thus a hymn to Re-Harakhty (Hallo and Younger 1:29) asks the deity, "Visit not my many offenses upon me, I am one ignorant of himself," a sentiment not unlike that of many Israelite psalms.

In Mesopotamia, meanwhile, hymns and prayers can express deep theological reflection. Thus a prayer to Babylonian deities (Hallo and Younger 1.114) opens: "O warrior Marduk, whose anger is the deluge, whose relenting is that of a merciful father," while another prayer for a righteous sufferer (called in Akkadian *Ludlul bel nemeqi*; Hallo and Younger 1.153) says, "I will praise the lord of wisdom, solicitous god, furious in the night, growing in the day: Marduk … whose anger is like a raging tempest, but whose breeze is sweet as the breath of morn." The complexity of the divine-human relationship finds elegant expression in these texts, even if they remain polytheistic and uncertain of divine reliability.

> **Borrowed Images for God**
> *Biblical religion did not emerge in a vacuum, but in a world of often pious people, some of whose ideas and expressions proved salvageable for Israelite monotheism. The Bible borrows some images of God from the larger environment, including God as warrior, king, creator, father, mother, or farmer, among others. However, the God of the Bible is the only God, without sexuality or self-conflict, and thus some images of the deity prevalent in the ancient Near East were not deemed suitable for Yahweh. Comparing biblical literature to that of surrounding cultures demonstrates the significant differences between the two.*

POLITICS & WARFARE

All ancient Near Eastern states after the third millennium were hereditary monarchies in which the king sat atop a social pyramid of which he was thought of as the paterfamilias. Beneath him were landed nobles who held the major governmental and military offices and often raised troops at their own expense. The king must maintain justice in the land and insure its prosperity and social stability (see, for example, Psalm 101; Hallo and Younger 2.23, 2.29, 2.30). Politics thus consisted of the nobility's jockeying for position at court and the king seeking to play them off against each other. Political action by the populace was virtually unknown.

Warfare, similarly, was carried out by the king as the head of his army, or, if the king were old or infirm, by his generals. An army in the first millennium consisted of several types of infantry (spearmen, archers, slingers), a chariot unit used on flat terrain as shock troops, and later cavalry equipped with lances or bows. Auxiliary troops such as cooks, drovers, foragers, and smiths accompanied the troops. The Assyrian armies also included engineering corps, intelligence and signal units, and propaganda units. In the absence of artillery, only later invented by the Romans, fighting took place at close range by armies numbering at most in the tens of thousands. Campaigns might last one or more years, with supplies coming from the invaded land (though the Assyrians' in-kind taxes were often paid in arrowheads and other weapons).

Biblical stories rarely describe military tactics. First Samuel 11:11, 1 Kings 22:29–36, and 2 Chronicles 35:22–23 are exceptions.

AGRICULTURE, TRADE & MANUFACTURING

The economies of the ancient Near East rested on the production of grain (especially barley and wheat), as well as such plants as dates, figs, grapes, olives (along the Mediterranean coast), and such animals as cows, sheep, and goats as their basis. Most people worked the land, and the surpluses produced allowed others to engage in other activities, including the production of goods for local use or trade. Pottery, textiles (especially of wool and linen, but later also of cotton and hemp), tools of bone, wood, or metal, and leather goods were typically produced locally and circulated in comparatively small areas.

Other products, such as wood, copper, iron, tin, gold, silver, glass, semiprecious stones (notably lapis lazuli), and some textiles were traded over wide areas, as were wine and oil. Lapis lazuli could move from Iran to Egypt, wine from Israel and Phoenicia to points inland, and metals from Anatolia to the rest of the region. Trade in metals, wines, oils, and such woods as the famous cedars of Lebanon often took place over sea routes. Spices and perfumes from Arabia and Ethiopia, luxury goods available only to the rich, entered the trade routes through either Palestine or southern Mesopotamia. Other finished products, such as bronze mirrors, fine pottery, jewelry, or rugs could travel long distances as trade goods.

Though mass production was essentially unknown, large establishments for the production of wine and oil did exist (King and Stager 95–101). Their owners accessed many acres of vineyards.

It is important to note that ancient economies were not primarily driven by market forces. Royal decrees and longstanding local customs often set prices. Most people engaged in subsistence agriculture and home-based trade only (Yoffee). Much, though far from all, of the long-distance trade was motivated by military and political activities such as the collection and redistribution of booty and the forming of diplomatic alliances through gift-giving. The invention of coinage in the sixth century BCE may have expedited a more market-based economy, but only in the very long run.

Ancient Israel functioned in this regional economy as an exporter of wine and other agricultural products and as a transit point in the spice and wood trades. It undoubtedly imported precious metals (1 Kgs 9:26–28) and exotic plants (King and Stager 280–82).

ARCHITECTURE

Many building styles existed in the ancient Near East. The colossal granite pyramids of third-millennium Egypt and the mud-brick ziggurats of Mesopotamia are best-known today, but were uncommon buildings in antiquity. Most people lived in simple mud-brick houses clustered in family compounds, whether in villages or fortified cities (which could reach a population of 100,000 or more).

Beginning in the third millennium, cities were encircled by massive walls, often made of a mud-brick core covered with a stone façade, or of stone or brick casemates. Especially after the mid-second millennium, a glacis (slope) and moat surrounded many city walls, protecting them from battering rams and tunneling. Towers and fortified gate houses (up to 20 × 20 meters) were also common (Mazar).

Within the city an elite precinct, often on an acropolis in Syria and Palestine, included temples, a palace, and garrison buildings. These structures were situated to catch the prevailing breezes and provide additional safety for their dwellers. The surrounding houses were of different sizes linked by narrow, winding streets usually without a distinct market section (though exceptions exist). The Assyrians invented the grid (or Hippodamian style) of city planning, on which they rebuilt even Israelite cities such as Megiddo and Samaria.

Most people lived in irregularly shaped houses roughly 100 square meters (about 1000 square feet) in size, with stone foundations and plastered mud-brick or stone walls. Flat roofs allowed outside sleeping during warm weather and provided work space. Stone or wooden pillars in larger rooms supported roofs of wood beams covered with mud and plaster. Typical houses in Palestine had four rooms for the family (often upstairs above a stable for the family's cattle, sheep, and goats). At times, houses in cities were arranged in *insulæ*, or blocks in which all houses adjoined and were surrounded by streets (Holladay). Larger houses for wealthy landowners or merchants also existed. They differ from ordinary houses in size and in the quality of goods inside them (such as precious metals, imported pottery, or art objects). Since most ancient people were farmers or artisans, separate structures for work were rare in antiquity, except in cities where shops and warehouses did exist.

ART & MUSIC

The first art works predate Israel by many millennia. During the Middle (2000–1600 BCE) and Late (1600–1200 BCE) Bronze Ages, conventions of representation of nature and the human body originated that would influence Israelite art, as well.

Like sculpture, fresco painting, pottery decoration, and other art forms, music played an important role in ancient life. Reliefs, seals, and other sculptural forms from Egypt, Syria-Palestine, and Mesopotamia show pictures of lyres, drums, flutes, pipes, shakers, trumpets, harps, bells, horns (from animals), and other instruments. Actual bells, plectra, flutes, cymbals, rattles, scrapers, clappers, and pipes also survive from the land of Israel (Braun). Superscriptions to the Psalms give titles of tunes (now lost), and also indicate the existence of orchestras and choirs in the temple.

> **Ancient Musical Notation**
> *Unfortunately, no undisputed musical notation predating the Roman Empire exists, so reconstructing ancient music requires guesswork, although instruments resembling ancient pictures of them have been constructed and their approximate range and timbre can be conjectured. They used a heptatonic (octave) scale like the Western one (von Soden 244). Perhaps this ancient music sounded somewhat like contemporary east Asian or African music. It was used for worship, parties, funerals, and to accompany storytelling, among other occasions.*

SCIENCE & MATHEMATICS

Science in the river valley civilizations chiefly consisted in the development of technology. Theoretical work, at least in writing, remained rudimentary and was not part of the school curriculum. The great exceptions are mathematics and astronomy, which in both Egypt and Mesopotamia were quite advanced. The Babylonians, by careful observations of stellar movements (by the naked eye), could calculate eclipses and predict planetary movements. They understood the Pythagorean theorem and elements of geometry, though they left no tracts in mathematical theory (the invention of the Greeks, who borrowed much from Mesopotamia). Drawing no distinction between astrology and astronomy, they employed their skills in the casting of horoscopes, for states in the second millennium and for individuals beginning after 400 BCE. Their accomplishments remained state of the art until the fifteenth century CE (Aaboe). Both Mesopotamians and Egyptians pioneered other fields of scholarship, such as the study of language (with multilingual glossaries), biology, medicine, and pharmacology, all of which influenced Israel only tangentially (von Soden 145–65).

RELIGION

Ancient Near Eastern religions, with the possible exceptions of a few esoteric circles in Egypt (notably during the reign of Akhenaten) and Mesopotamia, were uniformly polytheistic. The vast numbers of gods were associated with virtually every natural phenomenon, pushing ancient religions toward pantheism, the belief that deity inhabited everything (Hallo and Simpson 169). Unlike the modern West, ancient societies did not think of religion as a separate sphere of life: the actions of the gods interpenetrated all human experience. Yet this should not be exaggerated: deities did not intermingle with humans; they could be approached through worship in temples, not directly. Thus it was possible for humans to exist and develop culture (see Assmann 18).

Dozens or hundreds of deities could be worshiped in a given area, though most cities had temples to only a few of them. The Sumerians claimed 3,600 deities, and other societies were not far behind. Most deities were associated with natural phenomena, with sky gods dominating in the second and first millennia especially. The social structure of the pantheon mirrored that of human society, with a divine king and court, and then below them lower-ranked gods. Moreover, humans ordinarily worshiped deities whose place in the hierarchy corresponded to their own (kings worshiped the high gods, peasants served minor deities).

> **Ancient Piety**
> *Although rituals in the temples on major festivals often involved primarily the priests and could be highly stereotyped, individual humans could and did form deep personal lives of piety focused on a deity. An example of this is Adad-guppi, the mother of the last Babylonian king Nabonidus, whose attachment to the moon-god Suen (or Sin) was commemorated in inscriptions her son made after she died at age 103. She spent her life renovating Suen's temples and persuading others to worship him.*

The rituals and beliefs of Near Eastern priests are well documented in letters, myths, and lists of sacrifices. Ritual actions include sacrifices of animals and plants (especially grains and spices), parades of worshipers on pilgrimage, singing, and the parades of statues of deities at major festivals. These ceremonies structured time, space, and human life so as to conform society to the imagined order appointed by the gods for the universe.

All cultures of the region worshiped by means of sacrifice, music and dance, and prayers. Sacrifice centered around the presentation of valuable objects, notably animals, to the deity in order to mend the offerer's relationship with the deity and thus to heal the cosmos itself. While Israelite prophets and others critiqued the idea that sacrifice worked apart from the behavior of the worshiper, this view was not universal in the ancient world. Music and dance were key elements in worship, as well. Prayer likewise could be spontaneous and simple but was more often transmitted within a community of worshipers. Such prayer, often of great literary sophistication, as in the book of Psalms or the Babylonian prayer to Marduk (Hallo and Younger 1.114) or the Egyptian prayer for healing to the god Re-Harakhty (Hallo and Younger 1.29), expressed the worshiper's deep longing for communion with deity and the solution of earthly problems stemming from such communion. They could also be theologically sophisticated, as in the prayer to Marduk: "O warrior Marduk, whose anger is the deluge, whose relenting is that of a merciful father...." Here we touch human feeling at its deepest and most compelling level.

Alongside these practices were methods of divination, by means of which humans discerned the will of the gods. Reading of the entrails of sacrificed animals was the most common method of divination in Mesopotamia, and collections of thousands of omens existed, allowing the priest examining the liver, kidneys, or intestines of the animal to map out future events in their shapes.

> **Ancient Divination**
> *Ancient people believed that the gods revealed themselves in animal entrails, as well as in the movement of the stars, the flight of birds, the circulation of wine or oil in a cup, and other means. The surviving omen texts show great sophistication among diviners.*

Ancient Israel emerged in such a religious world. Yet Israel carefully accepted some practices and excluded others (such as divination or fortune-telling) on the basis of the perceived nature of the one God. Since God could not be manipulated, divination gave way to prophecy. Since sexuality is inappropriate as an attribute of deity, God was neither male nor female. Since God is the guarantor of all human life, human sacrifice is wrong. However, some images of God, such as God as warrior, protector, sun, or king, could be acceptable with qualifications. Artistic evidence from ancient Israel, as well as the sermons of the prophets against idolatry, indicate clearly that many Israelites were polytheists, seeking help from such deities as the Egyptian cow-headed god Bes or the Canaanite deities Baal and Asherah (Keel and Uehlinger 401). These conclusions did not triumph immediately, but over time it became clear to Israelites that its God was qualitatively different than neighboring deities. This growing understanding of revelation, not any technological, political, or military advancement, is the lasting legacy of ancient Israel.

CONCLUSION

To summarize, Israel became a nation in a world already old. On many levels, Israel borrowed from its neighbors, particularly in the areas of technology and the arts. Its primary arena of innovation was religion, where the worship of the one God became the most important element and distinction of the society, and the Bible its most important legacy to the world. Understanding the Bible, however, requires attention to the larger world from which Israel sprang.

FOR FURTHER STUDY

The Epic of Gilgamesh (trans. and ed. Benjamin Foster; New York: W. W. Norton, 2001).

Glenn Markoe, *Phoenicians* (Los Angeles: University of California Press, 2000).

WORKS CITED

Asger Aaboe, "Babylonian Mathematics, Astrology, and Astronomy," *Cambridge Ancient History* 3.2 (1991): 276–92.

Rainer Albertz, *A History of Israelite Religion in the Old Testament Period* (2 vols.; Louisville: Westminster/John Knox, 1994).

Jan Assmann, *The Search for God in Ancient Egypt* (Ithaca: Cornell University Press, 2001).

Jean Bottéro, "Akkadian Literature: An Overview." *Civilizations of the Ancient Near East* 4 (1995): 2293–2303.

Joachim Braun, *Music in Ancient Israel/Palestine: Archaeological, Written, and Comparative Sources* (Grand Rapids: Eerdmans, 2002).

Pierre Briant, *From Cyrus to Alexander: A History of the Persian Empire* (Winona Lake, Ind.: Eisenbrauns, 2002).

A. Kirk Grayson, *Assyrian and Babylonian Chronicles* (1975; reprint ed.; Winona Lake, Ind.: Eisenbrauns, 2000).

William Hallo and William Kelly Simpson, *The Ancient Near East: A History* (second ed.; New York: Harcourt Brace Jovanovich, 1998).

William Hallo and K. Lawson Younger, eds., *The Context of Scripture* (3 vols.; Leiden: Brill, 1997–2002).

John S. Holladay, "House: Syro-Palestinian Houses," *Oxford Encyclopedia of the Ancient Near East* 3 (1997): 94–114.

Thorkild Jacobsen, *The Harps That Once...: Sumerian Poetry in Translation* (New Haven: Yale University Press, 1987).

Alan James, "Egypt and Her Vassals: The Geopolitical Dimension," in *Amarna Diplomacy: The Beginnings of International Relations* (ed. Raymond Cohen and Raymond Westbrook; Baltimore: Johns Hopkins University Press, 2000), 112–24.

Othmar Keel and Christoph Uehlinger, *Gods, Goddesses, and Images of God in Ancient Israel* (Minneapolis, Minn.: Fortress, 1998).

Philip J. King and Lawrence Stager, *Life in Biblical Israel* (Library of Ancient Israel; Louisville: Westminster/John Knox, 2001).

Kenneth Kitchen, *The Third Intermediate Period in Egypt (1100–650 BC)* (Warminster: Aris and Phillips, 1973).

Amihai Mazar, "The Fortification of Cities in the Ancient Near East." *Civilizations of the Ancient Near East* 3 (1995): 1523–37.

Piotr Michalowski, "Sumerian Literature: An Overview." *Civilizations of the Ancient Near East* 4 (1995): 2279–91.

Patrick Miller, *The Religion of Ancient Israel* (Louisville: Westminster/John Knox, 2000).

William Moran, *The Amarna Letters* (Baltimore: Johns Hopkins University Press, 1992).

Dennis Pardee, *Ritual and Cult at Ugarit* (Atlanta: Society of Biblical Literature, 2002).

Donald Redford, "Ancient Egyptian Literature: An Overview." *Civilizations of the Ancient Near East* 4 (1995): 2223–41.

Erica Reiner, "First-Millennium Babylonian Literature." *Cambridge Ancient History* 3/2 (1991): 293–321.

J. David Schloen, *The House of the Father as Fact and Symbol: Patrimonialism in Ugarit and the Ancient Near East* (Studies in the Archaeology and History of the Levant 2; Winona Lake, Ind.: Eisenbrauns, 2001).

C. L. Seow, *Ecclesiastes* (New York: Doubleday, 1997).

Wolfram von Soden, *The Ancient Orient: An Introduction to the Study of the Ancient Near East* (Grand Rapids: Eerdmans, 1985).

Norman Yoffee, "The Economy of Western Asia," *Civilizations of the Ancient Near East* 4 (1995): 1387–99.

HISTORICAL CONTEXTS

Greco-Roman New Testament Backgrounds

Richard Wright

CHAPTER CONTENTS

City versus Country 41

Religion in the Roman Empire 48

Conclusion 53

For Further Study 53

Works Cited 53

MAPS, TABLES, & FEATURES

Mysteries 52

The world in which the church came into existence was a worldwide web of interconnections linking individuals to a number of different groups. These groups combined to populate the cities of the larger Roman Empire. Until the coming of Alexander the Great, cities had been independent, self-governing entities. Alexander infused these cities of the east with a common Greek culture and with common civic structures. One could move from city to city and feel a sense of familiarity. With the coming of Rome, these cities became part of a united empire. Rome took advantage of the common culture and structures to pull the cities together. Religion was the mechanism that connected individuals to cities and cities to the empire.

> **Cities in Early Christianity**
> *Jesus' ministry took place in and around the cities surrounding the Sea of Galilee and terminated with his death, burial, and resurrection in the city of Jerusalem. The church's movement described in the book of Acts radiates out into the cities — to the Jews first and then to the Gentiles. The epistles provide insights into the lives of churches located in cities.*

The Christianity witnessed to in the New Testament arose in this urban web (Meeks 9–50). So we will look at Greek and Roman life in the first century from the perspective of those who lived in cities of the eastern part of the Roman Empire.

CITY VERSUS COUNTRY

City dwellers distinguished themselves from those who lived in the surrounding countryside. The economy of the Roman Empire was driven by agriculture, but it was not those who worked the land who became wealthy but rather those who owned the land; and these people, for the most part, lived in cities.

Slaves often worked the land. Independent, small landowners did exist but found it increasingly difficult to hold on to their land. More and more of the land was coming into the hands of fewer and fewer wealthy individuals. Those who did own land were constantly trying to acquire more land and to exploit the resources from the properties they owned. This could be accomplished through robbery, physical threats, and attempts to drive out weaker owners through economic oppression. The slightest misfortune, such as drought or personal loss, could force a small landowner to borrow to sustain his family's existence. Loans were offered at usurious rates. The slide from debtor into tenancy or even slavery was a short one. Most absentee landlords owned land only around the cities in which they lived. But the wealthiest families in the provincial cities and the aristocratic orders in Rome owned land all over the empire.

> **Wealth in the First Century**
> *In the first century CE, Pliny the Elder wrote that half of Roman Africa (today's Tunisia, Algeria, and Morocco) was owned by only six families.*

CITIES & THEIR PHYSICAL LAYOUT

The sizes of cities in the empire varied greatly. Rome, the capital of the empire, and Alexandria had populations of close to a million people. Carthage and Antioch had populations of around 250,000 each. Perhaps six or eight cities had populations greater than 75,000. But the majority of cities were around 20,000 people.

Cities in the east followed a similar physical layout. Walls enclosed shops, houses, and public facilities that were laid out in a grid. The buildings of the city were filled with color: frescoes, friezes, statues, and even inscriptions were all painted. At the center of the grid was the agora, which served as marketplace but also the general gathering place for civic activities. The agora was lined by stoa – columned walkways that provided shade and opportunities for conversations and lectures. Temples, theaters, odea, gymnasia, and hippodromes surrounded the agora.

> **Greco-Roman Public Buildings**
> *Temples served as locations not only for religious rituals but also for civic functions and meetings. Theaters put on classical plays as well as new tragedies and comedies. The* odea *were venues for lectures, poetry, orations, music, and songs. Gymnasia were places for both physical exercise and educational enterprises. Periodically, competitions were held in drama, music, and athletics. In Roman times, circuses or hippodromes were constructed for the purpose of chariot races. Arenas showcased gladiators battling both man and beast. Everywhere one looked there was sculpture and art – often depicting scenes from religious life.*

Living quarters for most were small. Single-family houses could only be purchased by the wealthy. Greek houses separated the living quarters of women from men. Romans liked to focus their houses around a central atrium. Most people lived in apartment-style complexes. These could be from two to five or six stories tall. The structures were prone to fire or collapse. Often these complexes were set up so that a business could operate in one room of a ground floor house. Larger businesses might take up the entire floor.

Because living spaces for most people were crowded and uncomfortable, people lived in the public sphere. There was little privacy.

> **Urban Organization & Trade**
> *Often the city was laid out into specialized areas by function or ethnic group. For example, all the tentmakers or lampmakers might live in a single quarter. In some cities, Alexandria for example, a section of the city was identifiable as Jewish.*

CITIES & SOCIAL STRUCTURE

Just as the cities were laid out physically in structured ways, so also was the social fabric. In the first century CE, especially in the east, Roman citizenship still indicated status, though decreasingly so. Citizenship was rarely conferred on non-Italians in that period, and so its possession was coveted. The death penalty could result from a false claim to citizenship. Citizens could not be punished without a trial and could appeal a legal case to the emperor.

Another major distinction was between slave and free. Slaves could be prisoners of war, captives of pirates, debtors, or they could be slaves by birth. Aristotle described slaves as "living property"; others spoke of slaves as "speaking tools." They had no legal rights; they could not, for example, marry. Their children belonged to the owner of the slave mother. Slaves were part of the household of their owner.

On the next tier up from the slaves were the free – both those born free and those who were freed slaves. The vast majority of these city dwellers lived in poverty. The slaves of wealthy households often lived more comfortably than these poor. These were primarily tradesmen or merchants. A few could accumulate considerable wealth but not on the order of the wealthier landowners, and they could not enter the aristocratic orders (Garnsey and Saller 107–125).

> **Slaves**
> *The economic situation and responsibilities of slaves varied widely. Slaves who worked in the country or in the mines suffered more than anyone else in the ancient world. Life in these contexts could be deadly. Slaves in urban areas whose owners were not themselves well off could live difficult lives. But slaves of prosperous owners could hold positions of authority and, with their owners' permission, accumulate some property. Upon manumission, these freedpersons could begin a comfortable existence. Freedmen themselves did not have access to public offices, but some offices and opportunities were open to their children.*

The highest order someone in a provincial city could attain was that of decurian. Augustus set the property qualification for decurians at 25,000 denarii. These were mostly landowners with property around their own cities. The city of Rome itself, however, might draw from the provincial ranks to repopulate its aristocratic orders.

> **Denarius**
> *The denarius was the basic silver coin of the Roman Empire, equal to about a day's wages for a common laborer.*

Rome provided two aristocratic orders: senators and equestrians (MacMullen 88–120). Equestrians needed property worth at least 100,000 denarii. The political distinction between this order and that of senator was not always economic or social. Equestrians served as military tribunes, prefects, and procurators. Augustus did not limit the number of equestrian families.

> **"Equestrian"**
> The name "equestrian" originally referred to men who could afford to outfit their own horse.

Augustus set the minimum property qualification for senators at 250,000 denarii. The number of senators was limited to 600. These were the elite families. They served as praetors, quaestors, and consuls – the principle offices of Rome. Senators wore a broad purple stripe on their robes. This order filled the chief civic and military offices of the empire. The career of a senator might take the following path. After serving in a minor office in Rome, the young man would then enter military service as one of the six tribunes of a legion. Next followed the office of quaestor and a seat in the senate. The office of quaestor was a financial role and could be filled in one of the provinces. Some might occupy the judicial office of praetor. Those who had served as praetors could then become governors in the provinces, judges, or commanders of legions. For the ambitious, the role of consul would mark the culmination of a distinguished career with the possibility of a governorship of a major province.

> **Greco-Roman Aristocracy**
> Movement between the Roman aristocratic orders was frequent. The son of a senator frequently did not become a senator in his father's place. In fact, 75 percent of senators needed to be replaced with each generation (Garnsey and Saller 123).

Because wealth was lodged predominantly in land, it was difficult to move from being a tradesman to being a landowner. In fact, all goods, agrarian and social, remained in limited supply. People thought that one person's success could only come at the expense of someone else. It was a static system. One inherited everything: land, trade, and even customers. One did not break out of one's class.

Military service was the best way to improve one's social and economic standing. Aristocrats filled higher ranking offices and only for short terms. Centurions, on the other hand, were career military men. Upon retirement, those not already citizens received that status along with some land in one of the imperial provinces.

CITIES CONNECTED TO THE EMPIRE

When Rome moved into the Greek east, it could take advantage of an environment that Alexander the Great and his successors had already united in a common culture and civic structure. Rome used these features to its advantage by working with the provincial aristocratic families to bring the cities into its empire. In governing the east, the emperor could then focus on two goals: collecting taxes that were used to pay for administering the empire, and keeping the peace.

> **The Importance of Provinces**
> Rome depended on crops and money from the provinces to feed its population. The size of the city and the bureaucratic structure for the empire required more resources than Italy could produce on its own.

Rome governed the provinces in different ways. Provinces that required no standing army were administered by the senate through a former consul. Africa, Greece, and Asia are examples of areas under this kind of governance. The emperor himself administered Egypt through a legate. Because of its economic importance as the chief source of grain to the empire, he could not risk entrusting it to a senator.

> **Taxation in Rome**
> In the Roman Empire, only non-citizens paid direct taxes, and so they were disproportionately paid by the provinces. The governor of the province collected these taxes. The main object of these taxes was agricultural produce. In addition, conquered lands had to pay rent, land leases, and real estate taxes. Everyone paid indirect taxes such as customs duties, sales taxes, and rental fees for use of public facilities.

Provinces that required a military presence were administered by the emperor who appointed a governor (a legate), prefect, or procurator. All administrators received a fixed salary to discourage officials from extorting funds from their region.

The Roman Empire provided an environment that facilitated travel. Trade extended into the Far East as far as India and China. People moved from one location to another by both land and sea. Romans constructed roads to improve troop movement and communications from city to city. Greeks and Romans traveled by sea only when necessary. Improved security for travelers came

> **Travel in the First Century**
> One could sail from Ostia or Puteoli on the east coast of Italy to Alexandria. One could take the Appian Way down to Brundisium and sail from there to Corinth and on to other destinations. From Corinth, one could sail to Ephesus and then take roads inland to Asia Minor. From Brundisium, it was also possible to sail across the Adriatic to Dyrrachium and take the Egnatian Way across Macedonia.

with a military presence in areas of unrest. Inns existed but could be dangerous. Whenever possible, travelers stayed with friends or with friends of friends. Travel on both land and sea was affected by weather. Sea travel and certain roads generally shut down during the winter months. Four main routes connected Rome to the eastern part of the empire.

CITIES & SOCIAL INTERACTION

The primary motivator in Greco-Roman society was not money, but honor—that is, a combination of one's own evaluation of self-worth and the acknowledgment of that self-evaluation by others in society. Honor could be ascribed or acquired. One was ascribed honor because of who he was, not because of anything he had done. Birth into an aristocratic family was an example of ascribed honor. One acquired honor by performing favors for one's city, province, friends, or clients (Malina 25–48).

One took every opportunity to put on public display the honors one accumulated. By wearing the right clothes, accumulating many clients and friends, erecting statues and buildings bearing one's image, and dedicating inscriptions that bore one's name, it was possible to display one's honor. A prominent role in rituals also demonstrated one's place in society. The number and rank of offices one held also indicated honor.

> **Meals**
> Meals were an important part of social interaction either as part of a sacrifice or on other occasions. Where a person sat (or reclined) at the table indicated his or her relative position among those who were eating. The same was the case for the quality and quantity of food, and the order in which one was served.

Civic and religious offices were filled from the aristocratic orders. But rather than being salaried posts, these offices operated under a liturgical system. A liturgy was a service an official provided to the city at his own expense: for example, the rebuilding of a temple, the restoring of a road, or the staging of a celebration. In return for these acts of service, the benefactor received honor.

Interactions between individuals operated as part of this competition for honor. Relationships between men of unequal rank worked according to a patron and client system. Favors done by the patron were to be returned by favors in proportion to the ability of the client but especially in terms of honors attributed to the patron. Clients assisted patrons in public and personal affairs. Manumitted slaves became the clients of their former masters.

> **Symmetrical Relationships**
> Symmetrical relationships (relationships between persons of equal social status) operated according to the obligations of friendship. Reciprocation brought honor to both friends; to return a favor with lesser value was dishonorable. A technical vocabulary developed to describe the relationship between friends. Friends were sometimes said to have the same mind or to hold all things in common.

There were opportunities for the exchange of honor even among the nonaristocratic social orders. Many merchants and tradesman organized themselves into guilds, or *collegia*. These societies did not function primarily to improve the economic well-being of the members but rather provided opportunities for the members to exchange honor and friendship. In many instances, these guilds provided, through the collection of dues, for the funeral expenses of their members.

Even in a system that was designed to parade status and honor before the public eye, trying to exceed one's social position was viewed negatively. A person who tried to move beyond his or her inherited position was viewed as trying to usurp someone else's possessions.

CITY & HOUSEHOLD

If agriculture and land drove the economy, the household was the mechanism through which property moved from generation to generation. This was particularly the case in the Greek east, but it was also the case to a lesser extent in the Roman west.

The primary bond between husband and wife was an economic one. Marriages insured the best economic result for the two families, creating a relationship by which a family's possessions could be maintained and passed on to the next generation. This did not mean that there were not feelings of endearment between husband and wife. Such feelings appear repeatedly in letters and inscriptions.

Roman men married in their late twenties or early thirties. Women married in their teens. Men from aristocratic families tended to marry women on the younger end of the scale. In Rome marriage appears to have been less stable than in the Greek east.

Childbirth was dangerous to both mother and child. The average life expectancy at birth for a Roman was 20–30 years. What reduced this average life expectancy to such a low number was the infant mortality rate: twenty-five percent of children did not survive the first year, and fifty percent did not make it to age ten. Those who did survive, however, could expect to live another 35–40 years. By the time of Augustus, each woman needed to bear five or six children just to keep the population from declining. Augustus was so concerned that he introduced legislation to encourage husbands and wives to produce children.

Being born, however, did not automatically make the child part of the family. In both Greece and Rome, the father had to accept and receive the child formally.

The practice of exposing children has been misunderstood by many modern interpreters. Families usually exposed only children they did not believe they could afford to raise. When exposing a child, parents expected someone to rescue it, if only to sell it into slavery. Girls tended to be exposed more than boys.

In Greek cities, the civic organization consisted of individual households connected through kinship groups. Households were collected into clans. The clan centered around an eponymous ancestor who was worshiped at a common cult center. The *phratry* (also a collection of households based on kinship) controlled access to civic rights. It determined citizenship and with it, important economic and political privileges. The deme and tribe were larger kinship groups.

EDUCATION & THE CITY

The role of education was to train the children of citizens to be the next generation of citizens. As a result, education was typically available for only a few slaves, usually those belonging to aristocratic families or the emperor's household, where they occupied positions that required the ability to read or write (Gamble 1–41).

Wealthy families would entrust their children to a nurse until age seven. At this age, children learned to read, write, and perhaps do some arithmetic. Some children received additional education, usually until the ages of 11 or 12. Studies at this stage tended to include grammar, rhetoric, dialectic, geometry, arithmetic, astronomy, and music. Physical education was a component of education at all levels. Additional educational opportunities could take different forms, such as law or medicine, or rhetoric and philosophy.

The study of rhetoric was the most common form of higher education. Because public life required the ability to speak on any number of occasions (in court, at assemblies, or at ceremonies), this was a very practical skill to acquire. Topics included the arrangement of ideas, memorization, diction,

> **Women in the Greco-Roman World**
> *Women, throughout most of the Mediterranean world, remained under the authority of a male, first their fathers, then their husbands. For most Romans, the wife remained under the authority of her father. Thus the woman was the primary heir of her father and became an independent property owner on his death. To some extent, this gave Roman women more independence from their husbands (Meeks 23–5). In both Greek and Roman settings, the woman brought a dowry into the marriage. If the couple should divorce, the dowry stayed with the woman.*

> **Education**
> *Schooling was not widely available in the Roman Empire. Many wealthy families taught their children to read and write. Those who sent their children to school typically paid for the teacher on their own, so only prosperous families tended to educate their children. The most recent estimates regarding literacy in the Roman Empire put the figure at 10 percent on average and never more than 15 to 20 percent.*

> **Philosophy**
> *Philosophers often drew the comparison between the work of the physician for the body and the work of the philosopher for the soul. In treating these moral illnesses, they often went to great lengths to describe accurately the way the world worked. In the ancient world, those who were concerned about living moral lives turned to philosophers, not to priests and religion (Nussbaum 13–47).*

style, and delivery. Classes might take place in gymnasia or even in the streets.

While the study of rhetoric equipped the student to participate in the civic structures, the study of philosophy challenged those structures and challenged the student to reorient himself or herself to the environment. The three schools with the strongest influence during the period of the birth of Christianity were the Cynics, Stoics, and Epicureans. Philosophies in the ancient world were less "logical," "rational" systems of thought than, according to their own descriptions, attempts to heal what was wrong with the human soul.

Cynics argued that human traditions and social customs in most cases opposed what is natural. Therefore, the Cynics showed disregard for social convention. They were sharply critical of misplaced values and of foolishness. They rejected pleasure and sought to take care of the body only to the extent necessary for survival. They thought of wealth as problematic because it allows the satisfaction of desires and therefore produces enslavement to immorality.

> **Cynics**
>
> *The word "cynic" comes from the Greek word for "dog" (kune). Our English word connotes someone who is disdainful of others and of their behaviors or organizational structures. The Greek word does not necessarily carry such an association.*

The origins of Cynicism go back to Antisthenes, a student of Socrates. Diogenes of Sinope who lived in the fourth century BCE and his student Crates were its most famous practitioners. Diogenes argued that true happiness is found in a simple life. To see how one should live, one need only observe the animals. Animals do not worry about shelter or food. They eat what they find and live where they find shelter. Likewise, a person's goal should be to become self-sufficient. Thus Diogenes gave away his possessions and begged for his food. He once observed a child drinking water with his hands and so Diogenes threw away his cup. He felt the child had surpassed him in simplicity. To make his philosophical points, Diogenes reportedly engaged in behavior designed to shock the public. He allegedly urinated and had sex in public because these are natural acts.

In the spirit of Diogenes, some Cynics made their points with abusive language and shocking actions. Cynics earned a reputation for using frank or bold speech. They were not interested in flattering people or sugarcoating the truth. These Cynics stressed radical individualism and the moral superiority of the Cynic over the rest of humanity. Other Cynics practiced a milder form of the philosophy. They saw the same problems with society as their harsher philosophical siblings but believed in using gentler methods to bring about change.

Wandering Cynics were a common sight in cities in the Roman world. They kept a distinctive appearance. They wore a woolen, threadbare cloak, carried a walking stick and a beggar's bag, and wore a long beard and hair.

Probably the most influential of the Hellenistic philosophies was Stoicism. Stoics argued that the world needs individuals who can subject culture and their own perceptions to rigorous, thoughtful examination. The untrained mind does not see the world as it truly is. Culture and habit distort its vision. One must learn to make good judgments about available information. Each person, regardless of his or her place in the social order, has the rational capacity to perform these evaluations of self and culture. Rather than rejecting culture, a person needs to become a skilled critic. Intellectual activity becomes the basis of social and political order. This order, however, is larger than the individual city. Since every person has the capacity to function in a fully human manner, the Stoic is truly a citizen of the world.

Stoicism was founded by Zeno, who came to Athens from Cyprus and lived in the late fourth and early third centuries BCE. Zeno was a student of Crates the Cynic, and so Stoicism shares some Cynic ideas. Because Zeno was a foreigner, he could not purchase property in Athens. He began his teaching under the "Painted Porch." The name of the school derived from the location of its teaching (the Greek word for porch is *stoa*).

> **Stoics**
>
> *Like the Cynics, Stoics argued that nature provides the clue to understanding how humans should act. But whereas the Cynic did not really distinguish humans from any other animal, Stoics observed something fundamentally distinctive about humans – they are rational. Humans, therefore, owe it to themselves to live in a fully rational manner.*

The study of physics showed the Stoic the nature of the world, the nature of deity, and the relationship between the two. For the Stoics, there is one god, and his nature is both matter and reason (*logos*, which they described as a kind of fiery breath). They did not find this idea incompatible with polytheism because the myths about multiple gods, when rightly interpreted by means of allegory, point to the one god.

Not only is god composed of matter and *logos*, but in creating the world, he infused in it and its creatures those two components, as well.

> **Gods in Pantheism**
> *Stoicism describes a pantheistic world: god is in everything. God is, in a sense, the father of humans. He is interested in their well-being. God shows his concern through providence and makes his will known through oracles.*

One of the implications of this understanding of deity for Stoics is that one can discern the nature of god from the creation. Another implication from the Stoic description of the world is that, because it is fully rational, all things must be in order and, therefore, determined. Stoics strongly believed that life is a series of fated causes. They did not find fatalism incompatible with an idea of individual liberty. The truly wise person learns to conform to his or her destiny.

In their ethics, Stoics tried to work out a very precise account of virtue and vice. If humans are essentially rational, then virtue is anything that contributes to living in a fully rational manner. Vice is anything that detracts from rational life. The early Stoics described the human challenge as cutting out the passions that inhibit sound perceptions and judgment. Later Stoics decided that one cannot completely get rid of passions but should moderate them.

Humans are not just rational, they are also physical. Stoics decided that anything that affects the physical aspect is a matter of indifference. On the other hand, both health and sickness affect one's physical nature, and since health is clearly better than sickness, then among things that are indifferent, there are preferred things and things that are not preferred.

Only the virtuous person can act virtuously. Unfortunately this cannot be determined from outside appearances. A nonvirtuous person can perform the same action but his or her motivations are not correct and therefore that act, for that person, is merely acceptable, not virtuous.

If the Cynic scoffs at society, and the Stoic rationally evaluates the civic structures, then the Epicurean avoids society altogether. Epicureanism came into existence at about the same time as Stoicism. The Epicureans gathered in a garden, the exact location of which is not known. Their leader Epicurus, in contrast to Cynics and Stoics, argued that the goal of life is pleasure. Epicurus looked to nature like the Cynics and Stoics, but he concluded that the prime instinct for the animal

> **Epicurus & Pleasure**
> *Epicurus talked about three classes of pleasures: those that are both natural and necessary; those that are natural but not necessary; and those that are not natural and not necessary. He asserted that pain, if it is intense, is of limited duration; otherwise it can be easily endured.*

is for pleasure. He defined pleasure as simply the cessation of pain. So for him the goal of human life is to attain a state of calmness and serenity, an absence of concerns or anxiousness. The gods, according to Epicureans, model this kind of life. The gods are not concerned with humans: they neither answer prayers nor interfere with human activities. The gods bring neither material blessings nor curses. They are a source of pleasure for humans because they model the serene life that the philosopher attempts to attain.

Epicurean physics dealt with things invisible to the senses. The universe consists of void and an infinite number of atoms that are indivisible. They entangle to form shapes, whether worlds, people, or animals. There is an infinite number of worlds continually being created and destroyed. The gods live in between the separate worlds.

Many of the fears that trouble humans come from misinterpretations of celestial phenomena. Humans attribute unpleasant celestial phenomena to divine action. Epicurean physics offers natural explanations for these events and preserves the peacefulness of the gods.

One of the greatest causes of anxiety for humans, argued the Epicureans, is the fear of death. They assuaged this fear by claiming that there is

> **Epicurus' Four-Fold Way**
> *Epicurus offered a fourfold way: the fear of gods and the world is empty; the fear of death is absurd; pleasure that is understood correctly is available for all; and evil is either of short duration or easily endured.*

nothing after death, so there is nothing to fear. The soul does not survive the death of the body. Finally, public life is to be avoided as a distraction. Civic striving for honor cannot contribute to a pleasurable existence and so is to be given up in exchange for the Epicurean community of friends. Friendship provides the context for a truly pleasurable life.

RELIGION IN THE ROMAN EMPIRE

One can speak of religion in antiquity as a technology if by technology one means processes that, when repeated, return the same results. This was effectively how religion functioned for both Greeks and Romans. Honor is a deity's function, and in return for performing that function, the deity receives honor from people. The god, in response, repays the honor received. To describe the working of the gods in terms of honor also illustrates the way in which religion itself fitted into the larger society that operated on the exchange of honor (Mikalson, *Honor*, 185–190).

Individual gods have special areas of expertise and activity, but, taken together, they give fertility and health to humans and their crops and animals. They offer protection against hazards such as disease, sea travel, and war.

Religion and city were inseparably joined. Places that conducted civic business also had a sacred identity. Sacred boundaries marked the marketplaces, which served as hubs around which sacred shrines were constructed. In Athens, the agora, in addition to being a commercial and civic center and a place for parades and festivities, was the center of the civic concern with religious matters. A major portion of it was marked off by boundary stones. It contained basins holding water for ritual purification. Religious sanctions and regulations governed its use. The forum in Rome had similar religious features.

Temples were the most prominent landmarks in the city, thickly clustered in public spaces, but also distributed throughout the city. Sanctuaries and religious shrines ordered both the city's territory as a whole and its urban center. The precincts of temples offered a place to sit and rest and enjoy a formal garden. In Rome, temples contained botanical gardens, zoological parks, and aviaries. Poets studied and assembled for recitations and competitions. Public lectures took place in temples. Resident experts helped explain various aspects of a particular temple. Temples in both the Greek and Latin areas of the empire held libraries. Beggars and the homeless found refuge in temples.

Houses contained altars for domestic gods. As groups moved from one city or region to another, they took their religions with them. These cults would probably begin meeting in a room of someone's house. As the group began to grow, they would modify the house so that more of the space became dedicated to the cult. Eventually the group might take over the entire building. In this way even domestic architecture was infused with religion (White 31–47).

To live in a city was to participate in the festivals and rich religious life of the calendars of that city. Each city had its own calendar respecting the gods that protected it. Within a city, households, clans, phratries, demes, tribes, and associations all had separate religious calendars. Religious festivals were distributed through the year on fixed dates of a calendar. In setting the dates of religious festivals, these calendars determined when business could and could not be conducted. The sequence of rites in the calendar sustained a stable, enduring order, across generations and

> **Hosting Meals**
> For most people whose houses had no dining room, the only place they could host their friends was in the dining complex of temples.

> **Greco-Roman Polytheism**
> Greco-Roman polytheism was extremely complex. For example, Athena Polias, Athena Skira, and Athena Hygieia were for all practical purposes independent deities to the Athenians. They had separate myths, sanctuaries, cult officials, festivals, and rites; and they provided different services. In a particular place, a particular deity could fulfill a particular need. As the place (even within the same city) or need changed, so did the deity (Mikalson, *Honor*, 10).

> **Greco-Roman Priesthood**
> Rather than being closed groups with special initiations, priesthoods were offices that men held as a normal part of their career path. Most men in Greece and Rome offered sacrifices either as the heads of households, as civic officials, or in the role of official priest for a cult.

seasons, and within households. Daily life in an ancient city, therefore, was calculated according to religious markers.

Greek and Roman religions largely did without priests. Although there were priesthoods in both religious systems, there was no priestly caste as a closed group with fixed traditions, education, initiation, and hierarchy. By way of example, sacrifices could be performed by just about anyone; the tradition of rites and myths was easily learned through imitation and participation.

RELIGION, COMMUNITY & SACRIFICE

The places and the actions of groups in the eastern empire were essentially the same: the agora, sanctuaries, and gymnasia were the meeting grounds for these groups; sacrifices, meals with meat, and communal drinking were the major events of their gatherings. These rituals included a series of communal practices, the repetition of which brought the group together. Sacrifices and meals were the chief means of group cohesion in ancient Greek and Roman cities.

The characteristic form of religious expression was sacrifice. This ritual lay at the heart of life in the Greco-Roman world. Those offering sacrifices to deities included magistrates of the city, members of a club/association, and private individuals. Families offered sacrifices at weddings, birthdays, and funerals. A military campaign, engagement with an enemy, the conclusion of a treaty, works commissioned on a temporary basis, the opening of an assembly, or the assumption of office by magistrates each began with a sacrifice that involved a meal.

Sacrifice was a straightforward process: the slaughter and consumption of a domestic animal for a god. The sacrifice was a festive occasion for the community. Participants washed, dressed in clean garments, and wore a garland woven from twigs on the head. A procession escorted the animal to the altar. A girl at the front of the procession carried a sacrificial basket, which concealed the knife under barley grains. Worshipers also brought along water and often an incense burner. One or more musicians accompanied the procession. Once the procession arrived at the sacred spot, someone drew a circle to inscribe the altar, the animal, and the participants. Water was poured from the jug over the hands of each participant in turn. The animal was sprinkled with water causing it to jerk its head; this was interpreted as the animal giving its assent to the sacrifice. After recitations by the official, the participants hurled their barley onto the altar and the sacrificial animal. The official then took the knife, concealing it from the victim, and cut a few hairs from its forehead and threw them on the fire. The slaughter followed. The offerer collected the blood in a basin and poured it over the altar and its sides. As the blade struck the victim, the women cried out in shrill tones. The worshiper then skinned and butchered the animal, consecrating the inedible remains and laying the bones on the pyre prepared on the altar. Afterwards, the inner organs, especially the heart and liver [Greek *splanchna*], were roasted on the fire on the altar. The innermost circle of participants shared these choice pieces of meat. The worshipers burned food offerings, cakes, and broth in small quantities. The official poured wine over the fire so that it flamed up. Once the assembled party ate the *splanchna* and the fire had died down, the preparation of the actual meat meal began. Meat that was not eaten was taken to markets for sale to the public (Burkert 56–57).

SACRIFICE & SOCIAL ORDER

This constant ritual negotiated and reinforced social roles. In large sacrifices that involved a procession, the procession itself broadcast these relationships. The procession began a delineation of community that continued through to the conclusion of the sacrifice with a meal. The participants separated themselves from the larger community, took their places in the procession according to rank, and moved toward the altar. There the circle drawn around the participants, animal, and altar separated them from the rest of the city. The participants assumed distinct roles in the communal action based on their place in that sacrificial community. The hierarchy of the group was both constituted and exhibited in the order of procession and in the assignment of activities for the sacrifice.

Processions accompanied only larger sacrifices. But in every sacrifice with a meal, the distribution of the animal's flesh established and reinforced the hierarchy of the community. This act made social groups and the distinctions between them recognizable to all concerned. The gods received their portion first (the bones wrapped in fat). Then the most prestigious men roasted and ate the choice *splanchna*. The rest of the meat was boiled and distributed in fixed order: priests, officials, honored guests, and finally remaining participants.

In uniting men and women in community such sacrificial meals separated participants from foreigners, the defiled, and all those not entitled by descent or invitation to participate. One belonged to the religious community of one's own city or ethnic group; in another city, even in pan-Hellenic sanctuaries, one could only participate as a foreigner. Foreigners were kept away from the altars and were unable to make sacrifices without the official mediation of a citizen, who would answer for him before the gods and the local community (Mikalson, *Athenian*, 85–86).

> **Sacrifice & Society**
>
> *A good example of the complicated social dimensions of sacrifice occurred at the oracle at Delphi. The oracle's religious personnel consisted of Delphians. Non-Delphians could participate only with the help of citizens who acted on their behalf and offered a preliminary sacrifice. Even the order of consultation reflects the way the cult defined relationships between groups. Greeks came before barbarians; among Greeks, the Delphians came before all other Greeks; after the Delphians and before the other Greeks came the ethnic groups and cities who were members of the Delphic league.*

SACRIFICE & GENDER

One of the major movements of sacrifice is to separate men from childbearing women. In both Greece and Rome, women at a sacrifice were treated like foreigners. Women could not function as full members of the community. Just as women required a representative in court for any legal proceeding, they entered the larger circle of sacrificial participants only by an intermediary.

A simple example of the place of women in sacrifice comes from one of the associations. The principals in the sacrifice were adult males. Their sons shared in the sacrificial feast on all occasions, but their portions of meat were half or less that of the portions given to their elders. When the sacrifice consisted of an ox, the women of the club who were adult females of citizen status received similar portions to those of the men, while their daughters and female slaves were given portions on the same basis as their sons; when the sacrifice did not consist of an ox, the women received no meat at all.

This separation of men from women also served to create inheritance rights between fathers and sons. Because continuity between males was important in ancient societies, inheritance could not be left to the uncertainty of biology – birth cannot provide sure evidence of paternity. Membership in family and kinship groups did not come by virtue of birth alone. Rather, sacrifice was the mechanism used to establish these relationships (Jay 41–43).

Cities in the Greek east illustrate the use of sacrifice to establish kinship. For example, Athens defined the membership of its citizen body in terms of descent. Each family and household was tied to its ancestral land and tombs. These provided evidence of ownership and formed the location for the family's worship. Before a male could run for office, he had to demonstrate that he had an ancestral cult with its inheritance of land. These family citizens owned all the land and houses in Attica, and only they could inherit property from Athenians, participate in tribal feasts, or serve in a public festival. Only persons within a family could offer sacrifices to its gods. Thus ancestor cults were not simply "worship" of the dead; they were ways of organizing relations among the living.

Again, the household was the foundational kinship unit. The household had its own distinct religious identity. In Athens, for example, provided that a child survived birth, and that the father decided not to expose it, it was still necessary to incorporate the baby into the family. After the birth of a child, following a sacrifice to purify the household from the pollution of the child's birth, the father recognized the child as legitimately his. When a family member died, the hearth was extinguished. Later it was rekindled, and a sacrifice at the hearth followed.

> **The Hearth**
>
> *The hearth was the domestic sacrificial site. The head of the house sacrificed at the hearth, poured drink offerings into the flames, and threw in offerings before every meal. It was at the hearth that brides, children, and slaves became members of the household.*

Although social groups in Rome were not defined on the basis of kinship to the extent that they were in Greece, descent was traced through the father in Rome as it was in Athens. Tribes, *curiae*, centuries, and clans were the basic divisions for grouping the people. Each clan (*gens*) had its own cults. The *curiae* also held sacrifices and banquets for their members. From Josephus we find that even during the reign of Vespasian, the people of Rome could gather by tribe, clan, and neighborhood for sacrifices and banquets.

In addition to kinship groups, Romans associated by street; these were the neighborhood gatherings that took place at the street corners, the *compitalia*. Shrines were dedicated to the *lares*, or household deities. Sacrifices, banquets, and games were celebrated annually at the winter solstice. Every Roman family worshiped its own *lares*, but households gathered together periodically at the crossroads to feast in honor of the *lares*.

> **Phratries**
> Phratries, *or extended families, also determined their membership by sacrifice. Once a year in Athens the* phratries *celebrated a three-day festival. On the third day three sacrifices took place: at the first, fathers presented male infants born that year; at the second, fathers swore that initiates were their legitimate sons; at the third, a husband and his family "pledged" his bride as the daughter of a legitimate family. For each rite, the sacrifice validated the act. Any member of the* phratry *who doubted the legitimacy of the initiate could stop the sacrifice. Completing the sacrifice established kinship. Similar sacrifices took place elsewhere in Greece.*

PERSONAL PIETY

The discussion of religion to this point has focused primarily on its role in weaving together groups. But the participants in these rituals were individuals with a number of personal motivations. These motivations largely revolved around a person's four primary relationships toward unrelated individuals or groups, another member of the family, the city-state, and the gods (Mikalson, *Honor*, 166). People believed that all acts of piety and impiety caught the attention of the gods. This idea should not be confused with the Judeo-Christian idea of God holding people responsible for their moral actions, for in Greek and Roman religion, what the gods were interested in was receiving their proper due – honor.

Popular piety focused on divination, oaths, the rights of foreigners, hospitality, and burial rites. Divination sought to discover proper actions for the future. It was a way to validate the introduction of new cults, the engagement of war, or marriages. Dreams were also an important avenue for interpretation of divine will.

Oaths were a key to individual piety. They provided the most temptation to act impiously. An oath involved the gods with matters that they were not usually interested in. Deities became witnesses to certain actions or inactions (Mikalson, *Athenian*, 31–38).

In addition to these religious opportunities, people looked to religion to solve personal issues. The cult of Asclepius, for example, spread throughout the Roman Empire. People turned to this god for healing. A temple complex for Asclepius included a temple proper, a place to wash for purification, and sleeping quarters where people could await healing. The god could heal either directly or by giving instructions to the priests, who interpreted them for the recipient.

> **Honoring the Dead**
> *Giving honor to one's parents in death was equal to giving honor in life. Ancient people usually attributed death to fate or lower* daimons *rather than to the work of the gods. Traditional burial rites must be performed. Mourners participated in banquets for several days after the burial. Later, annual presentations of offerings and libations occurred.*

NON-LOCAL RELIGIONS

To this point we have been looking at religions specific to a particular place and a particular group. Under the Roman Empire, another form of religious practice increased in popularity: the so-called mystery religions.

These religions, some of which date back at least to the fourth century BCE, began to take on more prominence in the imperial period. Several characteristics set these cults apart from the religious phenomena described so far. First, they were secret societies. Whereas civic and family cults took place in public, mysteries took place behind closed doors, at times of night when most people slept.

Second, the mysteries were voluntary cults. Members often paid some kind of initiation fee. Most other religious practices were determined by one's birth and kinship. Mysteries did not replace the family and city cults, but did supplement them.

> **Mysteries**
>
> The oldest and most famous of the mysteries were those based at Eleusis – just fourteen miles outside of Athens. The myth for the mysteries is found in the Homeric Hymn to Demeter. Demeter, the goddess of grain, loses her daughter Kore (or Persephone) to Hades, the god of the underworld, who abducts her; Demeter wanders the earth searching for her daughter; while she searches, the crops die because of her sorrow. During her wanderings, she arrives in the guise of an old woman at Eleusis, where the king welcomes her into the his house as the nurse for his son. Demeter reveals herself to the Eleusinians and in return for their hospitality, teaches them the rites that would assure them a happy immortality. Zeus intervenes on behalf of Demeter with Hades, and Kore is allowed to return to her mother for two-thirds of the year while remaining with Hades for the other third. The myth clearly reflects the agricultural growing season.

Third, mystery cults offered secret knowledge, which most practitioners thought to offer salvation. This knowledge was described in terms of things seen, things recited, and things performed. Special objects were shown to initiates and members. In many cases the content of the mystery derived from myths involving agrarian deities and may have originated in commemoration of the agricultural cycle. What little we do know about some of these mysteries we learn from Christians who converted from them.

Fourth, to gain access to this knowledge, one had to proceed through one or more initiations into levels of the religion. And finally, the initiate was sworn to secrecy. The members were forbidden from sharing their knowledge with the uninitiated.

There were apparently three stages or degrees of initiation into the Eleusinian mysteries: the Lesser Mysteries, the Greater Mysteries, and the *epopteia*. The Lesser Mysteries were celebrated in February-March and involved fasting, sacrifices, sprinkling or washing, the singing of hymns, and the carrying of a sacred vessel. The Greater Mysteries occurred in September. At this time, worshipers brought the sacred things from Eleusis to Athens. A proclamation was given inviting those who wished to be initiated. Candidates went to the sea with a small pig to be washed along with themselves. They then sacrificed the pig to Demeter. A great procession was then made to Eleusis. Priestesses led the procession carrying the sacred things in baskets on their heads. They arrived in Eleusis at night by torchlight, and spent the rest of the night singing and dancing. The worshiper spent the next day fasting for the initiation proper that evening. During the initiation, some of the sacred things were revealed. Those who were there to take the final stage (*epopteia*) remained another day for the revelation of more of the sacred things. Libations and rites for the dead were also celebrated. The initiates finally returned to Athens. One could not progress to the *epopteia* in the same year he or she was initiated into the Greater Mysteries.

The rites surrounding the god Dionysus (the Romans called him Bacchus) are difficult to evaluate. One must distinguish among different types of religious devotion to this god. Associations devoted to Dionysus functioned like any other religious association, offering community, meals, and burial rites for its members. But some associated mysteries with the god, as well as engaging in communal, sexual, and ecstatic activity. Not much is actually known about the specific rites of the mystery cult. A villa just outside Pompeii contains a room with wall paintings that depict scenes believed to show aspects of the initiation. Literary evidence suggests that the initiate received instructions, went through a period of fasting and sexual abstinence, and then took a bath and swore an oath of secrecy.

> **The Followers of Bacchus**
>
> Euripides' play *The Bacchæ* describes the attempt by a Greek king to keep out the Dionysian followers. The Roman historian Livy also describes Roman attempts to keep the mysteries out of Italy.

The cult and mysteries associated with the Egyptian goddess Isis and her consort Osiris (replaced by Sarapis in the Greek world) were widespread. These mysteries combined aspects of Egyptian and Hellenistic cultures. The basic myth for the deities recounts how Typhon tricks Osiris to get into a chest. Typhon then locks the chest and throws it into the Nile. Isis looks for Osiris everywhere. She eventually finds him and brings him back to Egypt. Typhon, however, finds Osiris and cuts him into fourteen pieces that he then scatters. Isis gathers the pieces together again and gives Osiris a proper burial. Having been properly buried, Osiris becomes lord of the underworld. Cult and mysteries were related for Isis. As with the Dionysian rites, there were different levels of participation. One could attend public ceremonies and participate in processions. One could become initiated into the mysteries of Isis. One could become a priest in the service of Isis. A full description of one person's path through the religious rites for Isis is given by Apuleius in Book 11 of his *Metamorphoses*.

> **Mithras**
>
> *Still another important set of mysteries are associated with Mithras. The origins of the cult go back to Persia, but in the Roman Empire it had been thoroughly Hellenized. The mysteries of Mithras identified seven stages of initiation, each identified with one of the seven planets known at the time. Each stage had its own set of rites. The places of association were in rooms constructed to look like caves, since Mithras himself supposedly lived in a cave.*

IMPERIAL CULT · WEAVING TOGETHER AN EMPIRE

The imperial cult had its roots in the Hellenistic cults of kings. These cults expressed gratitude and loyalty to individuals who had acted in a powerful way for a city or a region. When Rome came on the scene, cults in honor of the goddess Roma, the Hearth of the Romans, or the People of the Romans, became established. Greeks accounted for these external powers by fitting them into the cultic system with which they were already experienced. The Greeks often "worshiped" kings and other extraordinary human beings.

The imperial cults fit into this context. In the case of the emperor, however, the comparisons with the gods are drawn even closer. The imperial cults became part of the competition between citizens for status and honor. Members of the aristocracies of the cities desired to hold offices in these cults. This competition could even grow such that cities competed against one another. Even though the aristocracy competed for the priesthoods of these cults, the celebrations and festivals involved the whole city or, in some cases, an entire province (Price 101–132).

> **Emperor Worship**
>
> *In Rome, emperors were worshiped only after death. In the east, however, the cults focused on the living emperor and even depended on his acceptance of these honors and his participation. He could take advantage of these competitions to fold cities and provinces peacefully into the empire. The imperial cult constructed a united empire from what had previously been independent regions and cities.*

CONCLUSION

Urban life in the eastern part of the Roman Empire was a complex web of interconnections between individuals and, more importantly, groups. Households formed the building blocks for larger groups within the city. In a world viewed as having limited goods, individuals competed with one another for honor. Religion was a crucial mechanism for connecting individuals within households, households to larger groups within the cities, and, through the emperor cult, those cities into the Roman Empire. It is into this competition for honor among gods and humans that Christianity was born.

FOR FURTHER STUDY

Everett Ferguson, *Backgrounds of Early Christianity* (third ed. Grand Rapids: Eerdmans, 2003).

Ronald F. Hock, *The Social Context of Paul's Ministry: Tentmaking and Apostleship* (Philadelphia: Fortress, 1980).

Helmut Koester, *Introduction to the New Testament*, vol. 1: *History, Culture, and Religion of the Hellenistic Age* (New York: Fortress, 1982).

Hans-Josef Klauck, *The Religious Context of Early Christianity: A Guide to Graeco-Roman Religions* (Edinburgh: T & T Clark, 1999).

WORKS CITED

Walter Burkert, *Greek Religion* (Cambridge: Harvard University Press, 1985).

Harry Y. Gamble, *Books and Readers in the Early Church: A History of Early Christian Texts* (New Haven: Yale University Press, 1995).

Peter Garnsey and Richard P. Saller, *The Roman Empire: Economy, Society and Culture* (London: Duckworth, 1987).

Nancy Jay, *Throughout Your Generations Forever: Sacrifice, Religion, and Paternity* (Chicago: University of Chicago Press, 1992).

Ramsay MacMullen, *Roman Social Relations, 50 BC to AD 284* (New Haven: Yale University Press, 1974).

Bruce J. Malina, *The New Testament World: Insights from Cultural Anthropology* (Atlanta: John Knox, 1981).

Wayne A. Meeks, *The First Urban Christians: The Social World of the Apostle Paul* (New Haven: Yale University Press, 1983).

Jon D. Mikalson, *Athenian Popular Religion* (Chapel Hill: University of North Carolina Press, 1983).

———, *Honor Thy Gods: Popular Religion in Greek Tragedy* (Chapel Hill: University of North Carolina Press, 1991).

Martha C. Nussbaum, *The Therapy of Desire: Theory and Practice in Hellenistic Ethics* (Princeton: Princeton University Press, 1994).

S. R. F. Price, *Rituals and Power: The Roman Imperial Cult in Asia Minor* (Cambridge: Cambridge University Press, 1984).

L. Michael White, *Building God's House in the Roman World: Architectural Adaptation among Pagans, Jews, and Christians* (Baltimore, Md.: American Schools of Oriental Research/John Hopkins University Press, 1990).

HISTORICAL CONTEXTS
The Archaeology of Israel
Jesse C. Long, Jr.

CHAPTER CONTENTS

Archaeology & the Bible 55

The Emergence of Israel 58

Conclusion 63

For Further Study 63

Works Cited 63

MAPS, TABLES, & FEATURES

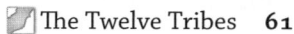 The Twelve Tribes 61

An unexpected and contentious chapter has been added to the scientific study of the Bible.

The Old Testament accounts of the exodus of Jews from Egypt and the settlement of ancient Israel have been challenged by evidence emerging from large-scale archaeological excavations, chiefly conducted in the territory conquered or occupied in 1967 by Israel.

Archaeologists now generally agree that their discoveries ... have produced a new consensus about the formation of ancient Israel that contradicts significant parts of the biblical version (Strauss).

So begins a newspaper article that calls into question the historicity of the biblical text. Since its publication, the challenge to the accuracy of the Bible has only intensified, most recently in questions raised about the veracity of the biblical accounts of the reigns of David and Solomon (see Niebuhr; Dever, *What Did the Biblical Writers Know*).

How should the Christian who believes that the Bible is trustworthy, in matters of history as well as matters of faith, assess these challenges? How can the very archaeologists who are uncovering the record of Israel raise such questions, when the popular view is that archaeology "proves" the Bible to be historically reliable? What does archaeology actually say about the history of Israel? We need to offer a balanced view of the role of archaeology in biblical studies, and here we wish to give direction on one example of a contemporary issue in the archaeology of Israel, the emergence of Israel in Palestine, all in a context that maintains a high view of Scripture.

ARCHAEOLOGY & THE BIBLE

A brief overview of the rise and decline of "Biblical Archaeology" will help frame a discussion of the role of archaeology in biblical studies. The early exploration of Palestine (before 1900) could, for the most part, be more accurately described as treasure hunting. Each new discovery raised popular interest, especially when there was even a hint of correlation with the Bible. In the face of nineteenth-century liberal attacks on the historicity of the Bible, relics of the ancient Near East were offering the promise of proving the Bible true.

In time, archaeology in Palestine began to develop as a scientific discipline, with a better understanding of tell formation and stratigraphic excavation. In the first half of the twentieth century, William F. Albright played a leading role in the transformation of the discipline and at the same time created the American phenomenon of "Biblical Archaeology." Albright came to believe that archaeology, with its objective evidence, supports the historicity of the Bible. While he confined his scholarly concern for the Bible to questions of history, his student, G. Ernest Wright, addressed the theological implications of Albright's view of archaeology and the Bible. A theologian and an archaeologist, Wright saw in archaeology the possibility of demonstrating the Hebrew Bible's theological claim that God was acting in history. His excavations in Palestine (Shechem in 1956–68; Gezer in 1964), however, only disillusioned the champion of

> **Tell**
> A "tell" is a mound formed by the remains of cities, one layer upon another. Archaeologists seek to identify the layers, or strata, of each site. Some sites consist of a dozen or more strata spanning thousands of years.

THE ARCHAEOLOGY OF ISRAEL

the Biblical Theology movement (a twentieth century American reaction to nineteenth century liberalism). In the dirt, Wright discovered that the archaeological data are often ambiguous. When assessing a destruction layer, for example, an excavator cannot identify the people who caused it. Israel's material remains are subject to a variety of interpretations.

The 1970s and 1980s saw the further development of the archaeology of Palestine into a more scientific discipline with the conscious call to discard the label "Biblical Archaeology." At the forefront of these developments, William G. Dever aggressively worked to remake the archaeology of Palestine, calling for a more professional, secular discipline, where science, not the Bible, sets the agenda. Dever led the charge to transport the "New Archaeology" begun in the American Southwest into Palestine. This new approach sought to apply the techniques of the physical sciences and anthropological theory to the archaeological record. Dever lobbied for the designation "Syro-Palestinian Archaeology," which in time became the moniker most often used for the discipline.

The move to make the archaeology of Palestine a more scientific discipline, distinct from biblical studies, was methodologically sound – especially when one factors in the excesses of Biblical Archaeology and misguided attempts to "prove" the Bible. At Bethel, for example, James Kelso described remains that he said went back to the time of Abraham. Subsequent analysis qualified his interpretation. A "temple" from the time of Abraham, as a case in point, turned out to be an early phase of the northwest gate complex of the city. Dever ("Archaeological Methods," 464–65) lamented the "vicious circle in which the archaeological evidence is viewed naively with Biblical blinders on and then, not surprisingly, becomes confirmation of a particular Biblical view."

In the late 1980s and 1990s, "postprocessual" archaeology, which emphasized context in interpretation and the complexity of human behavior, emerged as a reaction to the overemphasis on science in the New Archaeology (see Long, "Theory in Archaeology"). In this context, there has also been increased discussion on how Syro-Palestinian archaeology can and should dialogue with biblical studies (for example, Rast), although there is little chance of returning to the days of Albright.

The rise and decline of Biblical Archaeology provide an important framework for understanding current discussions in Syro-Palestinian archaeology. When the changing perception of the role of archaeology in biblical studies accompanies a corresponding decline in belief in the historicity of the Bible, even in whether the Bible contains reliable history or not, it is easy to explain the newspaper account with which this essay began. But even more importantly, the history of archaeology as a discipline bears witness to what is perhaps the most important archaeological discovery of the twentieth century, the ambiguity in the archaeological record itself. Realizing this can help one chart a balanced course through the confusion surrounding discussions of archaeology and the Bible. With this said, the following ideas should provide direction for using archaeological discoveries to enhance reading the Bible.

ARCHAEOLOGICAL RESEARCH & RESULTS IN PALESTINE

As has already been stressed, and as Wright discovered at Shechem and Gezer, there is ambiguity in the archaeological record (see Merling 37–42; Davies, "Theory and Method," 27). Archaeology is not an exact science. The data are empirical, but they still have to be interpreted, from the debris layers, pottery shards, and stratigraphy of a mound to the broader issues of settlement patterns, culture change, and synthesis of an ever increasing database. The nature of the evidence leaves much room for interpretation and therefore for allowing one's own assumptions and attitudes about the Bible (whether liberal or conservative) to influence conclusions. So the issue is not only the historicity of the Bible but also the subjective nature of the interpretation of archaeological finds.

THE BIBLE MUST BE UNDERSTOOD ON ITS OWN TERMS

It is not uncommon for archaeologists and even Bible scholars to make assumptions about the biblical text (conservative or liberal) that the archaeological data do not support. Like archaeology, the Bible must also be interpreted. David Merling (40) succinctly states the issue:

> The real dilemma, when archaeology and a Bible story do not seem to support each other, is that the archaeological evidence found, as

interpreted, does not mesh with the biblical account, as *interpreted* [italics added].

When interpreting the Bible, one must consider the "three impulses" of Scripture, its historical, literary, and theological aspects (see Long, "Art," 327). History is an important element but not the main focus of the Bible. For example, the Monolith Inscription of Shalmaneser III of Assyria records Ahab's participation in the battle of Qarqar in 853 BCE, but the Bible does not mention the event, despite its political significance (occurring sometime between chapters 21 and 22 in 1 Kings). Even though Kings gives more attention to Ahab (and the Omride dynasty) than to any other king after Solomon, the author's purpose is not history. It is theology – offering a glimpse of Ahab's character before Yahweh. Challenges to the historicity of the Ahab narrative often overlook the literary and theological motives in Scripture (Long, *1 & 2 Kings*, 241–47). Many claims of biblical inaccuracies come from misreading the Bible. Historical issues must be filtered through the literary and theological dimensions of the text.

ARCHAEOLOGY DOES NOT PROVE THE BIBLE

Because of the ambiguity inherent in the archaeological record, "proving the Bible" is not a legitimate approach to the dialogue between archaeology and the Bible. This point is reinforced by the incomplete nature of the archaeological record (as a result, for example, of erosion, destruction by subsequent settlement, and so on) and the more general nature of archaeological finds (with the exception of inscriptions, which are rare) as opposed to the specific nature of the biblical record of people and events in Israel's history.

> **Archaeology & Biblical Events**
> *Archaeological discoveries seldom relate directly to events in the Bible. Most significantly, archaeology cannot validate the claim of Scripture that Yahweh was working in Israel's history.*

ARCHAEOLOGY DOES NOT DISPROVE THE BIBLE

If it is true that archaeology does not prove the Bible, the corollary is also true: archaeology does not disprove the Bible (Merling 32–33). There is something illogical in the way many scholars address archaeology and the Bible. Adamant that archaeology cannot be used to prove the Bible, almost in the same breath these scholars will try show how archaeology demonstrates the Bible to be unhistorical, not reliable in matters of history – positions that are obviously inconsistent. If the subjective nature of the archaeological data means that one cannot prove the Bible, the conclusion that archaeology disproves the Bible is logically flawed.

ARCHAEOLOGY HAS AN IMPORTANT ROLE TO PLAY IN APOLOGETICS

The archaeology of Palestine is still an important arena for defending the Bible, although not in the traditional sense of proving the Bible true. The battle for the Bible in the twenty-first century is, in many respects, taking place in the dirt, as, more and more, archaeologists are marshalling evidence that "demonstrates" that the Bible is not historical. At the same time, however, one can amass an equally impressive amount of evidence that indicates the Bible's reliability. In the arena of ideas, let the debate be joined, calling attention to the subjective nature of the evidence, the assumptions and biases that too often are covered over, and the fact that conservative interpretations of the evidence are often just as valid – all performed in a spirit of humility, opening one's own assumptions and interpretations up for critique.

> **Negative Evidence in Archaeology**
> *In this context, archaeologists and biblical scholars must remember that negative evidence is no evidence at all. Too often, the lack of evidence in the material record is championed as proof that the events in the Bible did not happen as recorded (for example, the lack of significant Late Bronze Age occupation at Ai [et-Tell]; compare Josh 7:1–26). Typically, other explanations for the incongruities are not explored (Merling 33–39).*

ARCHAEOLOGY ILLUMINATES THE BIBLE

By far the most useful aspect of the archaeology of the Bible, at least as far as the church is concerned, is illumination. The archaeology of Palestine and the ancient Near East (including monuments and texts) sheds light on the world of the Bible. As the only primary data other than Scripture, archaeology provides context for interpretation that enables reading the Bible more on its own terms. By supplying background information, archaeology may also help bridge the gap between what a text meant and what it means, by explaining ancient culture and customs.

THE ARCHAEOLOGY OF ISRAEL

At times, illumination from archaeology and the ancient Near East enables seeing new meanings in Scripture. For example, the claim in Exodus that Pharaoh's heart was hardened makes more sense in light of what we now know about New Kingdom religion in Egypt. In particular, the weighing of the heart ritual in the *Book of the Dead* (a document of incantations designed to enable one's journey through the underworld to eternal life, popular in the New Kingdom, the period of Moses and the Exodus), where the heart is weighed on the scales of justice by the god Anubis against the feather of Maat (truth), may lie behind statements about Pharaoh's heart in Exodus. Nine times, the text says that Pharaoh hardened his own heart (Exod 7:13, 14, 22; 8:15, 19, 32; 9:7, 34, 35). Nine times, God hardened his heart (4:21; 7:3; 9:12; 10:1, 20, 27; 11:10; 14:4, 8). Of the three Hebrew words used for "harden" in these passages, the word *kaved* ("heavy/to be heavy") is used six times, and in one key passage. When Yahweh says to Moses, "Pharaoh's heart is hardened [*kaved*]; he refuses to let the people go" (7:14), the author of Exodus, through the literary technique of allusion, is intimating that "the one who [actually] keeps the balance" (a label for Anubis in the *Book of the Dead*) is, in effect, judging Pharaoh's heart as "heavy" or unworthy (Currid 83–103).

Archaeological discoveries may also modify naive, Sunday school readings of Scripture, or at least place them in a different light. For example, the story of David and Goliath takes on a different light when one realizes that the sling in the ancient Near East was a weapon of war and that its long range gave David an advantage over Goliath. When Agatha Christie, who excavated with her archaeologist husband, Max Mallowan, in Iraq, first saw the local bird-scarer at Nimrud defending the crops with his sling, she

> suddenly realized for the first time that it was Goliath against whom the dice were loaded. David was in a superior position from the start – the man with a long-distance weapon against the man who had none. Not so much the little fellow against the big one, as brains versus brawn (quoted in Hoerth 240).

When one also notices that David is described as a "man of valor, a warrior" in the preceding chapter (1 Sam 16:18), the narrative takes on a different focus. While David's faith response is still intact, the story is much less about the "little boy" overcoming incredible odds. In any case, the world of the Bible, mediated through archaeology, provides a cultural/historical context for reading Scripture.

THE EMERGENCE OF ISRAEL

The discovery of around three hundred small settlements in the central hill country west of the Jordan, through both excavation and survey, has brought to the forefront once more the question of the emergence of Israel in Canaan. These small agriculturally based compounds (including the excavated sites of Raddana, Giloh, 'Izbet Sartah, and Shiloh, among others; see Dever, *Who Were the Israelites*, 75–100) appear in the central hills by about 1200 BCE (King and Stager 9–19 on Judg 17–18; Stager, "Family"). Though securely dated to the beginning of the Iron I period (1200–1000 BCE), the new sites raise questions about Israel's appearance. Are these villages Israelite? If they are Israelite, do they represent

Basic Chronology of Ancient Israel & Its Neighbors:

1550–1200 BCE	Late Bronze Age
1200–1000 BCE	Iron Age I
1000–589 BCE	Iron Age II
589–334 BCE	Persian Period
334–31 BCE	Hellenistic Period

recent or long-term presence in the region, and what do they say about the nature of the settlement process? In early discussions, the date and manner of the settlement were central issues.

With respect to date, the biblical text can be read to indicate either an early or late date for the exodus and conquest. An early fifteenth-century date is suggested by the reference in 1 Kings 6:1 to the exodus at the construction of the Solomonic temple: "In the four hundred and eightieth year after the Israelites came out of the land of Egypt, in the fourth year of Solomon's reign over Israel... he began to build the house of the Lord" (compare Judg 11:26). If Solomon began his reign in 970, the fourth year of Solomon would be 966/67, and the exodus would have occurred in 1446/47 BCE. It follows, then, that the conquest/settlement would have taken place around 1400 BCE.

On the other hand, Exodus 1:11b suggests a late date for the exodus: "They built supply cities, Pithom and Rameses, for Pharaoh." Since "Rameses" was a popular name for the New Kingdom pharaohs of the Nineteenth and Twentieth Dynasties (Kitchen 255), a date for the exodus in the thirteenth century BCE would best fit this text. The first reference outside the Bible to Israel places them in Canaan by the last quarter of the thirteenth century (Merneptah Stele, about 1210 BCE), so Rameses II (1279–1213) would be a good candidate for the Pharaoh of a late exodus. The four hundred and eighty years of 1 Kings 6:1 may be explained as representing not actual years, but generations. If this chronological reference refers to twelve generations, represented by the symbolic figure "forty," the exodus would have occurred sometime in the first half of the thirteenth century (20 to 25 years for an actual generation; 12 × 25 = 300; 966/67 + 300 = 1266/67 BCE). If the 480 in 1 Kings 6:1 stands for literal years, "Rameses" in Exodus 1:11b probably represents an anachronistic reference to a city whose name changed over time. Since the time of Albright and the discovery of numerous destructions in Palestine at the end of the Late Bronze Age, the late date has dominated discussions of the settlement.

In terms of the settlement process, there have been three schools of thought. First, Albright (beginning in the 1920s) saw in Late Bronze II–Iron I destruction levels evidence for a conquest right out of the book of Joshua. When questions surfaced, however, about the variance in dates for the destructions and whether one could with any confidence identify the culprit, the conquest model was brought into question. Problems with the conquest model arose with difficulties in the interpretation of key sites. For example, Kathleen Kenyon excavated Jericho and determined that the city fortifications were destroyed in about 1500 BCE, well before a Late Bronze Age conquest by Joshua, whether one assumes an early (fifteenth century) or late date (thirteenth century) for the exodus and conquest. Similarly, there are few Late Bronze remains at Ai or Gibeon to correspond with the stories in Joshua (Josh 8–9) of their conquest.

Second, drawing more on the book of Judges, Albrecht Alt and Martin Noth (1920s and 1930s) saw the settlement as a peaceful infiltration and settling down of pastoral nomads – including a group of Yahwists, perhaps from Egypt (the mixed multitude of Exod 12:38), a model that reflected a growing awareness of the dynamic relationship between the desert and the sown in ancient civilizations. Third, applying social science and especially Marxist theory to the biblical and archaeological record, George Mendenhall (1960s, further developed by Norman Gottwald, 1970s) proposed a peasants' revolt model to explain the emergence of Israel. In this view, early Israelites were Canaanites who, revolting against the controlling city-state system, moved to the highlands of central Palestine.

While each model has its flaws, aspects of the three approaches may be reflected in biblical tradition (Hess 492–503). In any case, more recent approaches have emphasized the indigenous nature of Israelite settlement. Often dismissing an exodus altogether, and relying primarily on the archaeological data, some scholars believe that Israel is seen to emerge out of Canaanite culture. A conservative reaction attempts to maintain a more balanced dialogue between the text and the extant material record.

An Israeli archaeologist who has actively participated in the survey and excavation of Iron I sites in the central hill country, and representing the "indigenous" approach, Israel Finkelstein (for example "The Great Transformation") has proposed a more sophisticated sedentarization model. Based on survey data that appear to show cycles of settlement and abandonment from as early as the late fourth millennium BCE, he argues that the sites in the hill country represent a natural process of the sedentarization of a pastoral-nomadic, Canaanite population, who in time become the Israelites. With Neil A. Silberman, Finkelstein (118) writes:

> **Sedentarization**
> *The process by which nomads settle down to farm and raise livestock is known as sedentarization.*

> The process that we describe here is, in fact, the opposite of what we have in the Bible: the emergence of early Israel was an outcome of the collapse of the Canaanite culture, not its cause. And most of the Israelites did not come from outside Canaan – they emerged from within it. There was no mass Exodus from Egypt. There was no violent conquest of Canaan…. The early Israelites were – irony of ironies – themselves originally Canaanites!

William G. Dever (*Who Were the Israelites*, 153–89) disagrees with Finkelstein's hypothesis, even though he also envisions an indigenous process for the emergence of Israel. Arguing that there were not enough nomads to explain the explosion of settlements in the hill country in Iron I, Dever believes these settlements represent a "withdrawal" from Canaanite society of those who were on the social periphery. With an updated "peasants' revolt" approach, Dever sees the 'Apiru of the Amarna tablets (a fourteenth century collection of letters from Palestinian city-states to the Egyptian court at Amarna; see *Ancient Near Eastern Texts*, 483–90) as representing an analogous cultural phenomenon. In the Amarna tablets, the city-state kings of Canaan often request reinforcements against the 'Apiru, who appear to be disenfranchised brigands. Dever argues that the Iron I hill country settlements may reflect the settlement of similar 'Apiru who, with other "urban dropouts," refugees, and local pastoral nomads, become "proto-Israelites." Reasoning that "the historical memory of the Bible is accurate by and large," he suggests that this "motley crew" is reflected in the story of the Gibeonites (Judg 9) and in Shechem's role (Josh 24) in the emerging Israelite confederation. Both Finkelstein and Dever concur in the belief that the Bible contains two contradictory accounts of the settlement of Canaan, with the book of Judges containing a more accurate memory of an indigenous development as opposed to the conquest narrative of Joshua.

An important aspect of the origins of the Iron I settlers (whether they are from outside Palestine or not) has been the question of ethnicity. Are there distinctive features of the hill country material remains which can be interpreted as Israelite? Four-room houses, collar-rim jars, agricultural terraces, silos, and plastered cisterns have been singled out as indicators of Israelite occupation. However, these items also existed in earlier periods and in regions not associated with Israel. In addition, the Iron I ceramic assemblage has clear connections with earlier, Late Bronze Age, Canaanite forms. The material culture in the hill country is not in itself unique. Nevertheless, the sum total of the above mentioned features in the Iron I hill country settlements (allowing that not all reflect the same ethnic identity) appears to represent early Israel. The almost complete absence of pig bones in hill country sites, when compared with significant percentages of pigs among the animal remains in the coastal areas of Philistine and Canaanite occupation (with pigs also evidenced before and after the Iron Age in the hill country), reinforces this conclusion. When one also considers the reference to Israel in the Merenptah Stele (about 1210 BCE), where Israel seems to be located in the central hills, the convergence of the data in concert with the biblical text which locates early Israel in the hills of Canaan indicates that the 300 small Iron I settlements in central Palestine are Israelite (see Dever, *Who Were the Israelites*, 113–25, 201–8). But does the fact that the Iron I highland remains are not unique to Israel imply indigenous origins, as suggested by Finkelstein and Dever, a theory that undermines the biblical claim of an exodus from Egypt and conquest of Palestine?

Marshaling a persuasive array of evidence locating the exodus and conquest in the thirteenth century BCE (for example, in parallels between the form of the Mosaic covenant and late-second-millennium Hittite treaties), Kitchen (159–312) defends the biblical story of Israel's origins in exodus and conquest. He argues that the rapid population growth in the new highland settlements of Iron I Palestine is better explained by the settlement of outsiders coming in (that is, the Israelites coming out of Egypt), than the settling down and/or revolt of Canaanites already in the land (226–27, 239).

In another recent conservative treatment, Provan and his colleagues (138–92) also see the archaeological record as being consistent with the biblical story of Israelite origins as slaves in Egypt. Their analysis also highlights the connection between the Bible and archaeological evidence. Their survey of problem sites suggests that the biblical account should not be dismissed. For example, at Jericho the crucial issue is the dating of the destruction of City IV, which

> **Amarna Letters**
> *A group of 380 clay tablets from Tell el-Amarna (ancient Akhetaten) in Egypt is known as the Amarna Letters. These letters to the Pharaoh Akhenaten come from rulers in Palestine, Syria, and beyond. At this time the Canaanties were subjects of Egypt.*

> **Ceramic Assemblage**
> *A collection of all types of pottery vessels available at a give time and place is known as a "ceramic assemblage." A well-stocked house might contain dozens of pots of many sizes and shapes.*

Kenyon set at the end of the Middle Bronze Age, about 1500 BCE. Bryant Wood cites imports from Cyprus, local ceramic forms, Egyptian scarabs, and Late Bronze Age burials as indicating a destruction in about 1400 BCE, which would correspond with the early date for the exodus suggested by 1 Kings 6:1. While Wood's views have not generally been accepted, Provan and his coauthors (174–76) caution that we should not discount them out of hand. Erosion could also explain the lack of evidence for a Late Bronze Age destruction at Jericho (early or late date). If Ai has been correctly identified with the site of et-Tell, the lack of significant Late Bronze Age material there is a problem, although Merling (34–39) outlines a range of possible explanations for the apparent problem. At Gibeon, Late Bronze Age tombs were identified, and much of the site remains unexcavated (Pritchard, *Gibeon*, 156–58).

Just as important are the archaeological discoveries that appear to correspond with the biblical story. The site of Hazor displays evidence of massive destruction in the thirteenth century, including the burning of a large palace that is consistent with the biblical description of Hazor as "the head of all those kingdoms" (Josh 11:10; Ben-Tor and Rubiato). An earlier Late Bronze Age destruction could correspond with an early date for the exodus.

At Laish/Dan, following a thirteenth century destruction layer, a change in material culture occurred in the twelfth century BCE. The new stratum is characterized by silos and collar-rim storage jars typical of the Iron I highland sites, which the excavator believes corresponds with the destruction of Laish by the Danites as recorded in Judges 1:34; 19:40–48 (Biran 125–46).

Other evidence seems to fit the biblical picture. Excavations at Shiloh show evidence of an Iron I central settlement with satellite communities consistent with the biblical story. Its destruction in about 1050 BCE corresponds chronologically with the battle of Ebenezer in 1 Samuel 4 (compare Jer 7:12; Finkelstein, "Shiloh Yields Some"). Excavations at Shechem have uncovered a massive temple that is probably referred to in Judges 9:4, 46 (the temple of Baal-berith/El-berith). A massive standing stone from the courtyard of the temple may be the stone of witness referred to in Joshua 24:26–27 (Stager, "Shechem Temple"). Adam Zertal believes he has uncovered Joshua's altar on Mount Ebal (Josh 8:30–35), although there have been objections to his interpretation. A small Iron I highland enclosure in the hills of Manasseh produced a bronze statue of a bull (5 × 7 inches) that may reflect the idolatrous practices mentioned in the book of Judges (for example, Judg 6:25; Mazar).

The Twelve Tribes

For Provan and his coauthors (138–92), however, an accurate history of Israel must also carefully weigh the witness of the biblical tradition. Current approaches to the emergence of Israel too often misread the biblical sources. Even the conquest model distorts the claims of Scripture. When describing Joshua's northern campaign, the narrator in Joshua 11:13 indicates that of the cities on mounds (that is the fortified cities), Israel burned only Hazor. In the narrative of the conquest, the only other cities that were "burned" were Jericho (Josh 6:24) and Ai (8:28; Laish/Dan was also burned according to Judges 18:27). Related to this is the biblical tradition that Yahweh gave Israel the cities of Canaan, which they did not build (Josh 24:13; Deut 6:10–12). Reconstructions of the settlement that look for massive destruction layers in the archaeological record are flawed, as are those that discount the biblical tradition because of the absence of widespread destruction.

Scholars who see the books of Joshua and Judges as representing two contradictory traditions of the settlement (Joshua as military conquest, Judges as the sedentarization of nomads) miss the literary and theological dimensions of the story. They make a "genre mistake," by viewing the narratives primarily as a source of historical information. On one level, this happens when the documents are severed from their ancient moorings. Lawson Younger (197–266; see also Provan and colleagues 148–49, 168) has demonstrated that Joshua 9–12 is a typical Near Eastern conquest account, in which figurative language, even exaggeration for effect, was a characteristic element. For example, the summary statement in Joshua 10:40 that "Joshua defeated the whole land ... he left no one remaining, but utterly destroyed all that breathed" is inconsistent with the subsequent picture of all of the Canaanites who remained in the land (Judg 1:27–36), unless this statement is in some sense intentional exaggeration, consistent with ancient conquest accounts (Provan and coauthors 149).

From a literary perspective, Joshua and Judges read together exhibit tension between what God does for Israel and what God asks them to accomplish. God gives them the land as a possession, fights their battles, and directs them to take the land. This is the difference between "subjugating" and "occupying" the land (Provan and colleagues 156, 167–68). The military campaigns of Joshua enable the subjugation of Canaan, but occupation is a process that happens over time and is never completed. The theological message is that Yahweh has kept his promise to Abraham (Gen 13:14–17), even though Israel does not follow through on their responsibility to occupy the land in faith. So, the author/theologian's answer to Gideon's question, "If the Lord is with us, why then has all this happened to us?" (Judg 6:13) is that it is not Yahweh's fault (compare Josh 21:43–45; 23:14). Israel's inadequate faith response explains their circumstances. To miss the literary-theological thrust of the composition is to misread the story.

A literary and theological reading of Joshua-Judges is at odds with the view that Israelite culture and religions evolved from Canaanite culture. The plot of the biblical story is that Yahweh reveals himself to the descendants of Abraham, separates them as a people, covenants with them on Sinai, and leads them victoriously into the land of Canaan, directing the people to dispossess the inhabitants of the land. In the course of the story in Joshua and Judges, however, the people fail to destroy the nations, and Yahweh allows them to remain as a snare among them (Josh 23:12–13; Judg 2:1–5). This theme looms large in the book of Judges as Israel spirals away from God. By the end of the story, the Israelites have broken covenant and, morally and ethically, have become Canaanites. For example, when the Levite on his way home with his concubine in Judges 19 tells his servant that they will not stay in Jebus because there are foreigners there, they go instead to Israelite Gibeah, whose citizens, like those of Sodom, rape and murder his concubine. The storyteller in an indirect, creative way is saying that descendants of Abraham have become Canaanites (see Deut 28:64–68; Long, *1–2 Kings*, 449–53, 538).

The discovery of the highland Iron I sites may be interpreted as reflecting the biblical version of events and not the indigenous theory. Remarkably consistent with the biblical record, small agricultural settlements emerged in the highlands of Canaan sometime around 1200 BCE. The Merneptah Stele supports their identity as Israelites. The appearance of these villages may represent a process of settling down as Israel moves from a semi-nomadic lifestyle to settled life. If 1 Kings 6:1 indicates a fifteenth-century date for the Exodus, this process may have taken a much longer period of time (see Provan and others 188–89). That the hill country material remains reflect Late Bronze Age, Canaanite cultural traditions does not imply Canaanite origins. As Hess

(499, 502) points out, even if the hill country dwellers came from outside Canaan, since they were ethnically related to the West Semitic culture of the region, one would not expect a distinctive assemblage of archeological remains. And, the absence of pig bones in the highland faunal assemblages not only indicates Israelite ethnicity, it dramatically reflects the food restrictions of the Mosaic covenant (Lev 11:1–47; Deut 14:3–20), the covenant being the cornerstone of the biblical account of how Israel becomes a nation set apart from her Canaanite neighbors.

> **Faunal Assemblage**
> *A collection of bones and other animal parts found together in archaeological sites and representing a particular time and place is known as a "faunal assemblage."*

CONCLUSION

Contemporary challenges to the reliability of the Bible often cite the archaeology of Israel as proof that the Bible is historically unreliable, even with the ambiguity in the archaeological record. A cursory survey of the archaeological evidence for the emergence of Israel in dialogue with the biblical text suggests that those challenges are far from convincing. Provan and others (192) express it well: "All in all, we believe that such archaeological evidence as is known to us in no way invalidates the biblical testimony (provided that both text and artifact are properly read) and that at least some promising 'convergences' exist." The same can be said for other issues in the archaeology of Israel. Avraham Faust has recently argued, for example, that the decline in highland settlements at the end of Iron I (about 1000 BCE) corresponds with the events described in 1 and 2 Samuel, where external pressures from the Philistines led to Israelite state formation and the concentration of population in larger, more urban centers. While difficult issues (both archaeological and textual) and problems in reconstructing events remain, there is no reason, based on the archaeology of Palestine, to doubt the biblical story of Israel in Scripture.

FOR FURTHER STUDY

Thomas W. Davies, *Sifting Sands: The Rise and Fall of Biblical Archaeology* (Oxford: Oxford University Press, 2004).

Lee I. Levine, *Jerusalem* (Philadelphia: Jewish Publication Society, 2002).

Robert D. Miller II, *Chieftains of the Highland Clans* (Grand Rapids: Eerdmans, 2005).

WORKS CITED

Amnon Ben-Tor and Maria Teresa Rubiato, "Excavating Hazor, Part Two: Did the Israelites Destroy the Canaanite City?" *Biblical Archaeology Review* 25/3 (1999): 22–39.

Avraham Biran, *Biblical Dan* (Jerusalem: Israel Exploration Society, 1994).

John D. Currid, *Ancient Egypt and the Old Testament* (Grand Rapids: Baker, 1997).

Thomas W. Davies,, "Theory and Method in Biblical Archaeology" in *The Future of Biblical Archaeology: Reassessing Methodologies and Assumptions* (ed. James K. Hoffmeier and Alan Millard; Grand Rapids: Eerdmans, 2004), 20–28.

William G. Dever, "Archaeological Methods and Results: A Review of Two Recent Publications." *Orientalia* 40 (1971): 459–71.

———, *What Did the Biblical Writers Know and When Did They Know It? What Archaeology Can Tell Us about the Reality of Ancient Israel* (Grand Rapids: Eerdmans, 2001).

———, *Who Were the Early Israelites and Where Did They Come From?* (Grand Rapids: Eerdmans, 2003).

Avraham Faust, "Abandonment, Urbanization, Resettlement and the Formation of the Israelite State." *Near Eastern Archaeology* 66/4 (2003): 147–61.

Israel Finkelstein, "Shiloh Yields Some, But Not All, of Its Secrets." *Biblical Archaeology Review* 12/1 (1986): 22–41.

———, "The Great Transformation: The 'Conquest' of the Highlands Frontiers and the Rise of the Territorial States," in *The Archaeology of Society in the Holy Land* (ed. by Thomas E. Levy; New York: Facts on File, 1995), 349–65.

Israel Finkelstein, and Neil A. Silberman, *The Bible Unearthed: Archaeology's New Vision of Ancient Israel and the Origin of Its Sacred Texts* (New York: The Free Press, 2001).

Richard S. Hess, "Early Israel in Canaan: A Survey of Recent Evidence and Interpretations," in *Israel's Past in Present Research: Essays on Ancient Israelite Historiography* (ed. V. Philips Long: Winona Lake, Ind.: Eisenbrauns, 1999), 492–503.

Alfred J. Hoerth, *Archaeology and the Old Testament* (Grand Rapids: Baker, 1998).

Philip J. King and Lawrence E. Stager, *Life in Biblical Israel* (Louisville: Westminster John Knox, 2001).

Kenneth A. Kitchen, *On the Reliability of the Old Testament* (Grand Rapids: Eerdmans, 2003).

Jesse C. Long Jr., *1 & 2 Kings* (Joplin, Mo.: College Press, 2002).

———, "Theory in Archaeology: Culture Change at the End of the Early Bronze Age," in *Near Eastern Archaeology: A Reader* (ed. Suzanne Richard; Winona Lake, Ind.: Eisenbrauns, 2003), 308–429.

V. Philips Long, "The Art of Biblical History," in *Foundations of Contemporary Interpretation* (ed. Moisés Silva; Grand Rapids: Zondervan, 1996), 281–429.

Amahai Mazar, "Bronze Bull Found in Israelite 'High Place' from the Time of the Judges." *Biblical Archaeology Review* 9/5 (1983): 34–40.

David Merling, "The Relationship between Archaeology and the Bible: Expectations and Reality," in *The Future of Biblical Archaeology: Reassessing Methodologies and Assumptions* (ed. James K. Hoffmeier and Alan Millard; Grand Rapids: Eerdmans, 2004), 29–42.

Gustav Niebuhr, "The Bible, as History, Flunks New Archaeological Tests; Hotly Debated Studies Cast Doubt on Many Familiar Stories." *New York Times* Late Edition–Final (July 29, 2000): Section B, 9.

James B. Pritchard, *Gibeon, Where the Sun Stood Still: The Discovery of the Biblical City* (Princeton: Princeton University Press, 1962).

———, ed. *Ancient Near Eastern Texts Relating to the Old Testament* (3d ed. Princeton: Princeton University Press, 1969).

Iain Provan, V. Philips Long, and Tremper Longman, *A Biblical History of Israel* (Louisville: Westminster John Knox, 2003).

Walter E. Rast, "Bible and Archaeology," in *Near Eastern Archaeology: A Reader* (ed. Suzanne Richard; Winona Lake, Ind.: Eisenbrauns, 2003), 48–53.

Lawrence E. Stager, "The Archaeology of Family in Ancient Israel." *Bulletin of the American Schools of Oriental Research* 260 (1985): 1–35.

———, "The Shechem Temple: Where Abimelech Massacred a Thousand." *Biblical Archaeology Review* 29/4 (2003): 26–35, 66, 68–69.

Stephen Strauss, "Archaeologists Question Biblical Accounts." *Montgomery Advertiser and Alabama Journal* (March 12, 1988): Section B, 5, 8.

Bryant G. Wood, "Did the Israelites Conquer Jericho? A New Look at the Archaeological Evidence." *Biblical Archaeology Review* 16/2 (1990): 44–58.

K. Lawson Younger Jr., *Ancient Conquest Accounts: A Study in Ancient Near Eastern and Biblical History Writing* (Sheffield: JSOT, 1990).

Adam Zertal, "Has Joshua's Altar Been Found on Mt. Ebal?" *Biblical Archaeology Review* 11/1 (1985): 26–43.

THE GOSPEL ACCORDING TO
Old Testament Prophecy
John T. Willis

CHAPTER CONTENTS

- Functions of Israelite Prophets   66
- Materials in Prophetic Books   67
- Development & Arrangement of Prophetic Books   67
- False Prophets   68
- Religious Teachings of the Prophets   68
- For Further Study   68

A prophet is Yahweh's spokesperson to a designated audience, as three lines of study show. First, the Old Testament states that a prophet *speaks for* God. When Moses tries to avoid accepting Yahweh's charge at the burning bush to return to Egypt to lead Israel out of bondage, Yahweh replies: *[Aaron] will speak for you to the people; he shall serve as a mouth for you, and you shall serve as God for him* (Exod 4:16). Later, in Egypt, when Moses tries to avoid speaking to Pharaoh, Yahweh responds: *I have made you like God to Pharaoh, and your brother Aaron shall be your prophet* (Exod 7:1). Since Aaron *speaks for* and is a *mouth* for Moses, he is Moses' *prophet*. Likewise, Amaziah, priest of Bethel, prohibits Amos from declaring Yahweh's word in Israel, saying: *Do not prophesy against Israel, and do not preach against the house of Isaac* (Amos 7:16). To "prophesy" is to "preach," or to "speak for" God. When Yahweh tells Jeremiah: *I appointed you a prophet to the nations*, Jeremiah responds: *Ah, Lord God! Truly I do not know how to speak* (Jer 1:5–6; compare 15:19; 1 Cor 14:3).

Second, the Old Testament uses terms for prophet derived from four realms of ancient Israelite life, all of which indicate that a prophet is Yahweh's spokesperson to a designated audience. Four terms (council, servant, man, and messenger) come from the royal court. To begin, a prophet belongs to Yahweh's *council*, analogous to royal cabinets. Ancient Near Eastern kings gathered a few trusted people, the king's *council*, before them early each day to assign them tasks, often carrying a message from the king to some person or group. Yahweh condemns false prophets with these words in Jeremiah 23:21–22b:

I did not send the [false] prophets, yet they ran; I did not speak to them, yet they prophesied. But if they had stood in my council, then they would have proclaimed my words to my people.

As a member of Yahweh the King's council, a prophet speaks Yahweh's words to the audience Yahweh designates. Moreover, a prophet is a *servant* who does the King's (Yahweh's) bidding. *My (His) servants the prophets* is a common Old Testament expression (Amos 3:7; Jer 7:25; 26:5). Also, a prophet is the King's special "man" (or woman) commissioned to declare a certain message to some audience.

The Old Testament frequently calls a prophet a *man of God* (1 Sam 9:6–10; 1 Kgs 17:18, 24; 2 Kgs 4:9, 16, 21, 25, 40; 5:13–15). Then again, a prophet is the King's "messenger." Second Chronicles 36:15–16 says: *The Lord ... sent persistently to them by his messengers ... ; but they kept mocking the messengers of God, despising his words, and scoffing at his prophets....*

One term comes from means of protecting walled cities. Ancient peoples posted sentinels on walls to watch for signs of danger on the horizon and to warn the proper authorities or the people within by shouting out or blowing a trumpet. Second Samuel 18:19–32 reports that when Ahimaaz approached the walled city of Mahanaim, *the sentinel ... looked up, [and] he saw a man running alone. The sentinel shouted and told the king ...* (verses 24–25; compare Isa 21:6, 8, 11–12). Drawing from this familiar sight, Yahweh charges Ezekiel to be a *sentinel [watchman] for the house of Israel* and thus *warn* his hearers of impending punishment (Ezek 3:16–21; 33:1–9).

One term comes from divination. Micah 3:6c–7b says: *The sun shall go down upon the prophets, and the day shall be black over them; the seers shall be disgraced, and the diviners put to shame.* "Prophets," "seers," and "diviners" stand in synonymous parallelism here. Apparently, composers of the Old Testament borrowed

> **Divination**
> Any of a set of practices (such as reading the entrails of sacrificed animals) by which ancient persons sought to discover the future or determine the will of the gods is known as divination.

OLD TESTAMENT PROPHECY

the term "seer" from divination, which was popular in the ancient world, including Israel (Deut 18:10, 14; 1 Sam 9:9; 28:8; Isa 29:10; Jer 29:8; Ezek 21:21–29; Mic 3:11). A prophet is like a diviner in that he/she communicates with the unseen world to receive information helpful to those he or she addresses (see 1 Sam 9:6; Isa 37:1–7).

One term derives from the ancient method of refining metals. Ore dug from the ground was impure. Assayers heated it in a furnace, which melted the alloys at different temperatures, leaving the metal much purer than when mined. Jeremiah 6:27–30 compares a prophet's task with refining metals. His or her message removes corruption from the heart as Yahweh's purifying process (compare Isa 1:21–26).

Third, a careful oracle-by-oracle study of relevant Old Testament prophetic texts verifies that their presenters understood a prophet to be a *speaker* or *mouthpiece* for God to some audience. As Yahweh's spokesperson to a designated audience, the prophet often refers to past events and teachings (Isa 1:9–10; Hos 11:1–4; Amos 3:1–2; 4:6–11; Mic 6:3–5), present situations (Isa 8:16–20; Jer 5:1–6; Hos 5:1–7; Amos 5:4–17), and future activities of Yahweh (Isa 28:16–22; 40:1–11; Amos 6:11–14; Hos 11:5–11). In all cases, the prophet aims to change or guide the hearts and lives of audiences. Most prophetic predictions announce events to occur in the near future. The few proclamations of distant forthcoming events reassure the hearers that Yahweh controls nations and individuals throughout human history. There is no unequivocal specific prediction of the coming of Jesus Christ and/or the church in the Old Testament. New Testament speakers reinterpreted and reapplied Old Testament texts to Christ and/or the church.

> **Non-Israelite Ancient Near-Eastern Prophets**
>
> *Prophets were common in ancient Near-Eastern societies. The Old Testament refers to Balaam the Mesopotamian prophet (Num 22–24; 31:8, 15–16; Deut 23:4–5; Josh 13:22; 24:9–10; Neh 13:2; Mic 6:5; compare 2 Pet 2:15–16; Jude 11; Rev 2:14) and the prophets of Baal (1 Kgs 18:17–40; 19:1–14; 2 Kgs 10:19). Extrabiblical texts from Tell Deir 'Alla east of the Jordan in the region inhabited by the ancient Ammonites (eighth century BCE), Mari in northern Mesopotamia (eighteenth century BCE), and Assyria in northern Mesopotamia (eighth-seventh centuries BCE) extensively corroborate the existence of prophets throughout the ancient Near East. These prophets worked in ways similar to those reported of Israelite prophets in the Bible.*

FUNCTIONS OF ISRAELITE PROPHETS

Israelite prophetism arose with Samuel. Scattered texts refer to Abraham (Gen 20:7), Miriam (Exod 15:20), Aaron (Exod 7:1), Moses (Deut 18:15–22), Eldad, Medad and seventy elders (Num 11:16–30), Deborah (Judg 4:4), and an anonymous man in the days of Gideon (Judg 6:7–10) as *prophets*. However, these individuals were not "prophets" in the sense of those succeeding Samuel. For example, Genesis 20:7 calls Abraham a *prophet* because he prayed for Abimelech king of Gerar, since one function of a prophet is to intercede for others (for example, Jer 7:16; 11:14; 14:11; Amos 7:2, 5). Exodus 7:1 calls Aaron a "prophet" of Moses, because he speaks for Moses to Pharaoh or to the people of Israel.

Prophets arose as a divine check on kings. Yahweh was the true king of Israel, with the earthly king as Yahweh's representative. Prophets also anointed kings. Yahweh charges Samuel to anoint Saul (1 Sam 9:15–16; 10:1) and David (1 Sam 16:1–13) as *prince* (not king) over Yahweh's (not the earthly king's) people; David commissions Nathan (in conjunction with Zadok the priest and Benaiah) to anoint Solomon king in his place (1 Kgs 1:32–39). Yahweh instructs Elijah (1 Kgs 19:16), whose mantle empowered Elisha (2 Kgs 2:1–15), who in turn tells a young prophet in his prophetic group to anoint Jehu king over the northern kingdom of Israel (2 Kgs 9:1–6).

Moreover, prophets denounced kings who sinned against Yahweh. Thus Samuel reproves Saul for not waiting until he arrived to offer the sacrifice at Gilgal (1 Sam 10:8; 13:8–15) and for not utterly destroying the Amalekites (1 Sam 15). Nathan condemns David for committing adultery with Bathsheba and having Uriah murdered (2 Sam 12:1–15). Elijah rebukes Ahab for having Naboth murdered and seizing his vineyard (1 Kgs 21).

On the other hand, prophets encouraged kings to be faithful to Yahweh. For example, Azariah urges Asa to be courageous; thus Asa destroys foreign idols in Judah and restores the worship of Yahweh (2 Chron 15). Isaiah assures Hezekiah that Yahweh will deliver Jerusalem from the Assyrians who had been deployed by Sennacherib to capture the city (Isa 37:21–35).

Prophets even announced Yahweh's rejection of kings when they turned against Yahweh. Samuel informs Saul that Yahweh has rejected him from being king because of his disobedience (1 Sam 13:13–14; 15:22–23, 28–29).

OLD TESTAMENT PROPHECY

In sum, prophets addressed God's chosen people, charging them to be faithful to or return to Yahweh, who had acted on their behalf in various ways in the past by giving instructions as to how they should live in the law at Sinai and by continuing to work for the good of the people. The prophets did not establish a new religion but used Israel's traditions to call their hearers to God. They often referred to Yahweh's bringing Israel out of Egypt at the exodus, leading them through the wilderness forty years, and giving them the land of Canaan (Isa 43:14–21; Jer 2:4–7; Hos 2:14–15; 12:9; 13:4–5; Amos 2:9–11). They appealed to specific laws, including the Ten Commandments, to support their message (Jer 7:8–11; 17:19–27; Hos 4:1–3).

Prophets could pray for nations or individuals. Biblical writers cite the prophet Samuel as a model of a praying person (1 Sam 7:8–9; 12:19, 23; Ps 99:6). Jeroboam I begs a prophet to pray for him that Yahweh restore his withered hand (1 Kgs 13:6). Amos prays that Yahweh would not destroy north Israel (Amos 7:2, 5). Jeremiah prays for his enemies (Jer 18:20). King Zedekiah asks Jeremiah to pray for the Judeans as Babylon threatens Jerusalem (Jer 37:3), and Johanan and his associates implore Jeremiah to pray for them (Jer 42:2, 20).

> **Prophets & Foreigners**
>
> Prophets proclaimed Yahweh's words to foreign nations (Isa 13–23; Jer 46–51; Ezek 25–32; Amos 1–2; Obadiah; Nahum). Sometimes they announced forthcoming doom to a nation, such as Assyria (Isa 14:24–27; 17:12–14) or Babylon (Isa 13:1–14:23; 46–48; Jer 50–51); and sometimes they declared hope to a nation, such as Egypt (Isa 19:18–25) or Phoenicia (Isa 23:17–18).

MATERIALS IN PROPHETIC BOOKS

Prophetic books contain various types of material: narratives (Isa 36–39; Jer 40–44), descriptions of symbolic (sign) acts, usually with an explanation of the meaning (Isa 20; Jer 13:1–11; 27–28; Ezek 4–5; 37:15–28), reports of prophetic calls (Isa 6; Jer 1; Ezek 1–3), visions (Amos 7–9; Jer 1:11–19; Ezek 1; 8), oracles of doom (announcing punishment on a nation or an individual, often with reasons) (Isa 2:6–22; Amos 3:9–15), including woe oracles (Isa 5:8–30; 28–33; Amos 5:18–20; 6:1–7), covenant lawsuits (Isa 1:2–20; Mic 6:1–8), laments (Jer 8:18–9:1; Amos 5:1–2; Mic 1:8–16), songs (Isa 5:1–7), allegories (Ezek 17:1–21), acrostics (Nah 1:2–8), and oracles of hope announcing deliverance of a nation or individual from distress or oppression (Isa 40–55; Jer 29–33; Ezek 33–48; Amos 9:10–15; Mic 2:12–13; 4–5; 7:7–20). Usually, hope oracles depict a complete reversal of the present negative situation.

DEVELOPMENT & ARRANGEMENT OF PROPHETIC BOOKS

Old Testament prophetic books are the final product of a long process of development, as generations of prophetic groups reapplied, revised, rearranged, and reinterpreted earlier materials and added oracles, explanations, modifications, and grammatical links of their own. The book of Jeremiah mentions at least three stages in its growth: a collection of prophetic oracles from 627 to 605 BCE (Jer 36); the insertion of prophetic materials from 605 to 587 BCE (Jer 1:1–3); and the insertion of prophetic materials from 587 to 550 BCE (Jer 52:31–34). Prophetic authors did not simply add later materials to earlier collections – for example, several passages in Jeremiah 1–35 date after the event related in Jeremiah 36 (605 BCE); Jeremiah 21, 32, and 34:8–22 (588 BCE), or chapters 24 and 29 (597 BCE). Rather, they interwove earlier and later materials, creating a new work.

> **Performance & the Prophets**
>
> The structure of prophetic books seems designed in part to help people remember their content for performance or recitation. To take one typical case, the book of Amos falls into three structural sections after the superscription (1:1):
>
> Eight similarly structured doom oracles against the nations (1:2–2:16).
>
> Three sections, each beginning with Hear this word (3:–5:17), followed by two sections beginning with Woe (5:18–6:14).
>
> Five visions announcing that Yahweh will soon punish the sinful people (7:1–3 and 7:4–6; 7:7–9 and 8:1–3; and 9:1–10). A related section follows each of the last three visions: a dispute between Amos and Amaziah (7:10–17), an oracle against injustice (8:4–14), and a hope oracle (9:10–15).

Composers of prophetic books arranged their materials coherently for effective use in oral proclamation or performance at festivals of faith communities and other occasions, using repetition, or juxtaposing doom and hope oracles, for example.

OLD TESTAMENT PROPHECY

FALSE PROPHETS

The Old Testament often denounces Israelite prophets (for example, 1 Kgs 22:1–28; Isa 28:1–8; 29:9–10; Jer 23:9–40; 27–28; Ezek 13; Mic 3:5–12). Audiences who heard messages by prophets had no obvious way to know whether God sent these spokespersons. When Jeremiah announces the Jews will be in Babylonian captivity seventy years, but Hananiah declares they will be there only two years, Jeremiah says to Hananiah: *The prophets who preceded you and me from ancient times prophesied war, famine, and pestilence against many countries and great kingdoms. As for the prophet who prophesies peace, when the word of that prophet comes true, then it will be known that the Lord has truly sent the prophet*. Jeremiah's two criteria for determining a true prophet are: the typical messenger proclaims impending punishment; and if a spokesperson announces hope and it comes to pass (see Deut 18:15–22), that person is a true prophet. However, these general principles do not always apply. For example, Jeremiah announces a bright future for God's people in Jeremiah 29–33, yet his declarations that the northern kingdom of Israel would return to Yahweh (Jer 31:15–20) never happen.

RELIGIOUS TEACHINGS OF THE PROPHETS

Various prophets spoke at different times to many audiences, but certain religious themes permeate the prophetic books. First, Yahweh is creator and sustainer of everything (Isa 42:5; 45:12; Amos 4:13). God is more powerful than all nations, who are like *a drop [hanging] from a bucket, dust on the scales, grasshoppers*, and *less than nothing* in his sight (Isa 40:15, 17, 22). As *king of the nations, the true God, the living God*, and *the everlasting King* (Jer 10:7, 10), Yahweh exerts power over all earthly kings, so that Cyrus of Persia is his *shepherd* and *anointed one* [Hebrew *meshiach*, "messiah"] (Isa 44:28–45:1), and Nebuchadrezzar II of Babylon is his *servant* (Jer 25:9).

Second, Yahweh entered into an intimate relationship with Israel at the exodus (Jer 2:1–8; Hos 2:14–15; 11:1; 12:9; 13:5; Amos 3:1–2), like that of a husband and wife (Hos 2:2–15), parent and child (Hos 11:1–9), gardener and vineyard (Isa 5:1–7), shepherd and flock (Isa 40:11), doctor and patient (Jer 30:12–17), and potter and clay (Jer 18:1–11). Yahweh instructed Israel how to be religiously faithful and how to treat other human beings (Jer 7:8–11; Ezek 18:5–10; Hos 4:1–3).

Third, Yahweh will soon punish a foreign nation (Isa 13:1–14:23) or the chosen people (Isa 1:2–20; Hos 8; Amos 3:9–15; 6:11–14) because of their sins (Isa 1:4, 16–17; 13:19; 14:4, 11–14; Hos 8:1, 3, 7; Amos 5:10–12). Sin is a heart problem (Jer 3:10; 4:3–4; 9:25–26; 17:9–10). The primary sin of the heart is pride or self-centeredness or ingratitude (Isa 2:6–22; 10:5–19; 13:19; 16:6; 23:9; Obad 3–4). The prophets denounce those who forsake Yahweh to serve other gods (Isa 44:9–20; Jer 10:1–16; Ezek 8; 20:1–31; Hos 2:2–13) and those who oppress and manipulate their fellows (Isa 58; Jer 9:2–9; Amos 8:4–6; Mic 2:1–11).

Fourth and finally, Yahweh's ultimate purpose in punishing sinners is not to destroy but to refine and redeem. As a doctor inflicts pain on a sick patient in order to heal, so Yahweh punishes those who are unfaithful in order to bring them to repentance and save them. Isaiah 30:26 speaks of *the day when the Lord binds up the injuries of Israel, and heals the wounds inflicted by his blow* (compare Jer 30:12–17). So the prophets announce hope for the penitent *remnant* of God's people (Isa 10:20–23; Jer 31:7–9; Mic 2:12–13; 4:6–8). Yahweh will overthrow the people's captors (Isa 44:24–45:7; Jer 51), gather the remnant of Israel from captivity and return them to Zion (that is, Jerusalem; Isa 52:7–12; 54:4–17), reunite Israel and Judah as in the days of David and Solomon (Jer 30:1–3; 31:10–14; Ezek 37:15–28), place a *new David* over them (Jer 23:5–8; 30:9; 33:14–16; Ezek 37:24), namely, Zerubbabel (Zech 3; 6:9–14), remarry the divorced wife Israel (Jer 3:6–11; 31:31–34; Hos 2:2, 14–16) because she will love her divine husband from the heart rather than with mere external religion (Deut 6:6–9; Jer 31:31–34; 32:36–41; Ezek 36:22–32), and restore her spiritual health (Jer 30:12–17). The prophets thus provide readers even today with a bold vision of God's redeeming work in a broken world. As such, they deserve our close attention.

FOR FURTHER STUDY

Ronald E. Clements, *Old Testament Prophecy: From Oracles to Canon* (Louisville: Westminster John Knox, 1996).

Donald E. Gowan, *Theology of the Prophetic Book: The Death & Resurrection of Israel* (Louisville: Westminster John Knox, 1998).

David L. Petersen, "Introduction to Prophetic Literature," *The New Interpreter's Bible*, vol. 6 (Nashville: Abingdon, 2001), 1–23.

A. Rofé, *Introduction to Prophetic Literature* (Sheffield: Sheffield Academic Press, 1997).

Odil Hannes Steck, *The Prophetic Books and their Theological Witness* (trans. James D. Nogalski; St. Louis: Chalice, 2000).

THEOLOGICAL BACKGROUNDS
Old Testament Theology

Thomas H. Olbricht

CHAPTER CONTENTS

- Creation 69
- The Promise to the Ancestors 70
- The Exodus 70
- The Wilderness 71
- The Conquest 73
- Inheritance of the Land 74
- A Shepherd for His People 74
- A History of Old Testament Theology 75
- Old Testament Theology in the Modern World 75
- Conclusion 76

MAPS, TABLES, & FEATURES

- The Mosaic Covenant 72
- Lord of Hosts 74

Old Testament theology focuses upon God's saving actions on behalf of all creation. The theological thread running through the Old Testament is that God loves the creation, especially humankind. Humans, however, continually aspire to be gods in their own right and to defy the Lord God. God brings disasters upon the human lot, but he also sets apart Abraham and calls him to be the father of a special nation that in turn will become a servant to the nations: *In you all of the families of the earth shall be blessed* (Gen 12:3). The various statements of basic religious orientations (credos) in the Old Testament (Deut 26:1–11; Pss 105; 106; Neh 9) reiterate the milestones in God's struggles with humans. The chief theological topics of the Old Testament center upon a loving God working in creation, through the patriarchs and matriarchs, the exodus, the wilderness, the covenant, the law, the conquest, the land, and the promise to David. These topics are interlaced throughout and provide a skeleton upon which to flesh out a theology of the Old Testament.

CREATION

The fundamental reflections on creation in the Old Testament appear in Genesis 1–11, with only a few observations on the creation of the universe and biological life. Most of the comments are on the accomplishments and failures of humankind. God is affirmed as the beneficent maker and sustainer.

After creating on each day, God saw that the work was good (Gen 1:4, 10, 12, 14 25, 31). It was good because it was beneficial to the creatures God made (1:29–31). The Genesis presentation makes a theological statement, not a biological one. Humans appear last on the scene after God readied the rest of creation for their arrival.

Humans are made in the image of God: *They shall have dominion* over all the other creatures God made (1:26). God created by speaking a word: *Let there be light* (1:3). Humans, likewise, create by words. Adam named every living creature, and the name he assigned gave each its identity (2:19–20).

> **Humans as Caretakers**
> *Humans occupy the same position in their sphere as God does in the universe; they are caretakers (2:15). They are to be godlike in their dominion, that is, exhibiting loving care.*

God created male and female. Sin disrupted their companionship with God. By defying God and eating from the tree of the knowledge of good and evil, humans became gods, deciding what is right and wrong.

All those who stood before the tree suffered. The new human domain became infested with evil. Individuals went from bad to worse. Cain killed his brother Abel. As people multiplied, *every inclination of their hearts* was evil (6:5). God grieved that he had made humankind and determined to wipe them off the face of the earth by water. But one man, Noah, found favor in God's sight (6:8). After the flood, God made a promise (or covenant) to Noah and all living creatures never again to decimate all flesh. Regardless, humans continued to live for themselves rather than God, saying, *Come, let us build ourselves a city, and a tower with its top in the heavens, and let us make a name for ourselves* (11:4). As a result, they suffered in that their language was confused, and they were scattered across the face of the earth (11:7–8). As Psalm 104 makes clear, God not only created the world, but he sustains it.

THE PROMISE TO THE ANCESTORS

One important part of the Old Testament's theology involves the role of God in blessing humankind. God created everything good, but humans went from bad to worse. In order to maintain some semblance of goodness on earth, God will act through Abraham and his descendants (Gen 12:1–3). Through this relationship, the theme of God's blessing of humanity becomes prominent.

The promise to Abraham contained four blessings (12:1–3): Abraham will be blessed; his descendants will comprise a great nation; those Abraham blesses will be blessed and those he curses will be cursed; and through him all the families of earth will be blessed. By the end of Genesis, God has fulfilled these blessings. Abraham becomes rich (Gen 13:2). In turn, his nephew Lot, who is to father the nations of Moab and Ammon, becomes wealthy (13:5). The Philistines even request that Isaac enter into a covenant with them so that they, too, will benefit from God's blessings (26:26–31).

Jacob, fearful for his life, flees to Laban, his mother Rebekah's brother in Haran, and marries Rachel and Leah, Laban's daughters. When Jacob prepares to return home, Laban announces that he has discovered by divination that God has wonderfully blessed him because of Jacob's presence (30:25–30).

Jacob's favoritism to Joseph causes his brothers to hate him and sell him as a slave. Yet in Egypt, Joseph becomes a servant to Potiphar (39:1), whose house is abundantly blessed because a descendant of Abraham is present (39:2–6). Because of Potiphar's wife, Joseph is thrown in prison. Even those in the prison are blessed because of him. After he interprets the Pharaoh's dream, Joseph wins his freedom and power over the conservation of food. At the height of the famine, Joseph's brothers come to Egypt to purchase grain, and *soon all the nations came to Joseph in Egypt to buy grain* (41:57). The promise to Abraham and his descendents is realized numerous times in Genesis. Isaiah declared that Israel, God's servant, was a light to the nations (Isa 49:1–8).

THE EXODUS

During the exodus, God reveals the divine name Yahweh, launches Israel as a community of faith, and makes believers of the nations. Thus, the ever-present nature of God is integral to Old Testament theology.

Moses on a mountain in Midian sees a bush afire but not consumed. God speaks out of the bush and announces to Moses the impending deliverance of Israel from Egypt. Moses asks God's name, only to hear the enigmatic response, *I am who I am*, a pun in Hebrew on the name "Yahweh."

> **God's Name**
> Exodus 6:2–3 tells us that God appeared to Abraham, Isaac, and Jacob as God Almighty [El Shaddai] but did not make the name Yahweh known to them. This revelation must await the decisive saving act of the exodus.

The initial sign that God has called Moses and Aaron is the turning of a staff into a snake, a healthy hand into a leprous one, and Nile water into blood. When these are demonstrated, *The people believed and … they bowed down and worshiped* (Exod 4:31). What happens at the sea, however, establishes that Yahweh is with the people. After Pharaoh expels the Israelites, the Lord hardens his heart once again. Moses tells them to stand firm and not be afraid, for the Lord will fight for them. Moses lifts his staff, the sea opens, and the people go across on dry land. *Israel saw the great work that the Lord did against the Egyptians. So the people feared the Lord and believed in the Lord and in his servant Moses* (Exod 14:31). The Passover celebration repeatedly reenacts the original exodus events (Exod 13:14). Wherever the Passover is observed, the believing community continues.

The power and uniqueness of God are also major elements of Old Testament theology. By the plagues and the opening of the sea, God also makes believers of the nations: *For by now I could have*

> **References to the Exodus**
> *Psalms 105:23–43, 106:9*, and *136:10–11* celebrate the exodus as a time of great deliverance. Hosea declares that, because of Israel's sins, God will send them back to Egypt: *Now he will remember their iniquity, and punish their sins; they shall return to Egypt* (Hos 8:13). Jeremiah declares that, though the people must face divine punishment, God will act again as before in Egypt and lead the people to their own land (Jer 16:14–15; 23:7–8).

stretched out my hand and struck you and your people with pestilence, and you would have been cut off from the earth. But this is why I have let you live: to show you my power, and to make my name resound through all the earth (Exod 9:15–16). In Exodus 15:14, the inhabitants of Philistia, Edom, Moab, and Canaan tremble at what they hear. Jethro, Moses' father-in-law and a priest of Midian, declares that Yahweh is greater than all gods. Rahab, a prostitute in Jericho, hearing about Yahweh's deeds, joins the people of God (Josh 6:25), declaring, *The Lord your God is indeed God in heaven above and on earth below* (Exod 2:9–11).

THE WILDERNESS

The wilderness is a time between Egypt and the land promised. It is a training ground for preparing God's people for occupancy of the land. In the wilderness, God is preparing, protecting, providing, punishing, and parenting Israel. Here, the theme of God's providence, as well as his role in disciplining those he loves, takes a prominent place in the theology of the Old Testament.

PREPARING

God does not lead Israel directly to Canaan by the way of the land of the Philistines, where there are Egyptian garrisons, but diverts them toward the Reed Sea so they will not have to face war immediately (Exod 13:17–18).

God protects Israel in the wilderness. Moses reminds them how *the Lord your God carried you, just as one carries a child, all the way that you traveled until you reached this place* (Deut 1:31). The Lord goes before Israel in fire by night and a cloud by day (Deut 1:33).

God provides the people with manna and quail (Exod 16:4–21), as well as with water from the rock (Exod 17:6). As later reflections on the event note, *these forty years the Lord your God has been with you; you have lacked nothing* (Deut 2:7), and *the clothes on your back did not wear out and your feet did not swell these forty years* (Deut 8:4).

While accomplishing all these feats, God also punishes the older Israelites because they refuse to obey him. God announces to them, *of all your number ... from twenty years old and upward ... not one of you shall come into the land* (Num 14:29–30).

During the forty years in the wilderness, God parents and disciplines the people so that they will keep all his commandments. Israel learns to become utterly dependent on God for food, drink, clothing, and shelter (Deut 8:1–3). God lets them hunger, then feeds them with manna, *In order to make you understand that one does not live by bread alone, but by every word that comes from the mouth of the Lord* (Deut 8:3; see Matt 4:4). If all these other gifts are good, then obviously God's commandments are also good, for they come from the same source.

The human inclination is to attribute whatever one has to hard work, and the Old Testament acknowledges: *Then do not exalt yourself, forgetting the Lord your God ... for it is he who gives you power to get wealth ...* (Deut 8:18). When the redeemed people no longer feel dependent on God, disaster overtakes them (Deut 8:20).

The theme of the Name of God also functions as an integral part of Old Testament theology. The wilderness is a time in which God acts for the sake of his own name. While Moses is on the mountain, the people, with Aaron's help, create a replica of a calf in gold and declare it to be the god who brought them up out of Egypt. Angry, God determines to wipe out Israel and make a great nation from the offspring of Moses (Exod 32:10). Moses begs God to reconsider, lest the Egyptians will say that Yahweh brought the people out to kill them (Exod 32:11–12). In order to fulfill earlier promises to Abraham, Isaac, and Jacob (Exod 32:13), Yahweh relents (Exod 32:14; see Num 14:1–30).

It goes far better for God's people than they deserve because they wear God's name. God wants all the peoples of the world to come to Israel and learn God's ways (Exod 9:16; Isa 2:2–4). Thus Jeremiah intercedes for Israel in the midst of a great drought: *Although our iniquities testify against us, act, O Lord, for your name's sake; our apostasies indeed are many, and we have sinned against you* (Jer 14:7, 20–22). But sometimes God's people depart so far from God's will that it is not in God's best interest to vindicate them. They have brought reproach upon God's great name and so must suffer the consequences (Jer 15:1–2).

Ezekiel particularly notes that God forgave Israel many times because of the name they wore, even when

> **God Changes His Mind**
> *It may seem strange that Moses' arguments could change God's mind. God repents after Moses points out how humans will perceive God's intended action. This should not be surprising, since God has always gone to great lengths to listen to humans.*

they failed to cast away their detestable idols in Egypt (Ezek 20:7–8), rebelled in the wilderness (20:10–13), and disobeyed God's statutes and ordinances (20:16–21). In each case, God declared, *Then I thought I would pour out my wrath upon them and spend my anger against them in the wilderness. But I withheld my hand, and acted for the sake of my name, so that it should not be profaned in the sight of the nations* (Ezek 20:21–22).

PROMISE THROUGH THE COVENANTS

The theme of God's willingness to bind himself through promises, or covenants, to his creation also plays a major role in the theology of the Old Testament. The covenants with Noah, Abraham, and David are in the mode of a personal covenant.

> **Covenants**
> *Covenants traditionally involve two parties, one of which is dominant. In every case in the Bible, it is God who decides to offer the covenant.*

God, out of supreme goodness, makes a covenant with Noah, his descendants, and all the creatures of the earth: *never again shall all flesh be cut off by the waters of a flood* (Gen 9:11). The sign of the covenant, that is, the assurance that God had signed off on it, was the *bow in the clouds* (Gen 9:13). God alone is the guarantor. Regardless of what humans or other earth creatures do or do not do, the covenant will continue inviolate.

When making the promise to Abraham (Gen 15:1–11), God requests that he cut a heifer, goat, ram and a turtledove in half, and form a passage through the middle. As the sun goes down, a smoking fire pot and flaming torch pass between the pieces (Gen 15:7), and *On that day the Lord made a covenant with Abram* (Gen 15:18). God alone ratifies the covenant and sets out no stipulations for Abraham. The sign of the Abrahamic covenant is circumcision (Gen 17:11). This promise is likewise made to Isaac (Gen 26:3–5) and Jacob (Gen 28:13–15).

The Davidic covenant contained two parts: that God would *establish the throne of his kingdom forever*; and that if the Davidic heir committed iniquity, God would *punish him with a rod such as mortals use, with blows inflicted by human beings* (2 Sam 7:12–16). The Davidic covenant did not cancel out the Mosaic but built upon it.

God gives Israel a covenant through Moses. Humans, by flaunting the laws, can indeed be excluded from the blessings of the Mosaic covenant, but they cannot destroy or put the covenant out of commission. God promises not to break the covenant, despite what people do (Judg 2:1). The sign for the Mosaic covenant is the Sabbath (Exod 31:12, 17).

The same basic perspective or theology underlies both the Mosaic and the Davidic covenants. The ruler extends covenant out of the goodness of his heart, as does Yahweh. The covenant will continue in force at the pleasure of the ruler. He may, however, end the covenant owing to constant violations by the vassal state. The Mosaic covenant remains in force because of Yahweh, and it is an eternal covenant (Deut 12:28).

God gives Israel the covenant, not because of Israel's intrinsic merits or numbers, but out of unsolicited love (Deut 7:7–9). Israel is not righteous and does not "earn" the covenant, although it is superior to the nations it dispossesses (Deut 9:4–5).

The prophets, beginning with Hosea, offer the marriage metaphor as a means of depicting the relationship of God with the people. Gomer is unfaithful to Hosea, just as Israel, God's bride, prostitutes herself to other lovers by worshiping the Baals (Hos 2:4–13). Jeremiah depicts Judah as an adulterous bride who becomes unfaithful (Jer 2:2–3). Ezekiel declares that, though Yahweh loves the bride Israel dearly and provides all her needs, she actively seeks lovers. Nevertheless, God will forgive and redeem the bride and enter into an everlasting marriage covenant (Ezek 16:60–63).

> **The Mosaic Covenant**
> *The Mosaic covenant somewhat resembles an ancient suzerainty treaty. A powerful emperor, or suzerain, befriended a small vassal state on his border by offering a treaty. These treaties typically had six features, as did also the Mosaic covenant:*
>
> Preamble – the ruler's name is given (Deut 5:6).
>
> The suzerain describes the manner in which he had befriended the small vassal state (Deut 5:6).
>
> The stipulations are laid out (Deut 5:7–26:19).
>
> Prescriptions for preserving (Deut 31:25–26) and reading the covenant are established (Deut 31:9–11).
>
> The witnesses are named. In Hittite treaties, the witnesses were numerous gods and natural phenomena. In the Old Testament, of course, no deities were cited, though natural phenomena were (Deut 32:1, Mic 6:1).
>
> The curses (Deut 27:15–26) and blessings are enumerated (Deut 28:1–8).

Jeremiah envisions a new covenant. The existing law will now be in the hearts of God's people, not on tables of stone (Jer 31:31–33). Moreover, God will *forgive their iniquity and remember their sin no more* (Jer 31:34).

THE LAWS

The law of God plays a central role in the Old Testament's theology, as well. God's laws for Israel are covenant stipulations given out of love: *The precepts of the Lord are right, rejoicing the heart* (Ps 19:8). The Ten Commandments establish the boundaries beyond which one does not step. The first four commandments stipulate relations with God, the last six relationships with others.

The main body of laws in Exodus (25–40) sets out the features of the tabernacle. God graciously provides the ground rules for dwelling among the people: *And have them make me a sanctuary, so that I may dwell among them* (Exod 25:8–9).

The key to the main body of laws in Leviticus is holiness: *You shall be holy, for I the Lord your God am holy* (Lev 19:20). God declares specific guidelines for holiness, and when violations occur, he provides forgiveness by sacrifice. God's decrees in Numbers guarantee the safety of the tent of meeting by placing it in the center of the armies (Num 2:17). The presence of the Levites insures the well-being of the people. *Moreover, I have given the Levites as a gift ... to make atonement for the Israelites, in order that there may be no plague among the Israelites for coming too close to the sanctuary* (Num 8:19). Deuteronomy shows God's love for Israel in that, if they keep the law, they will occupy the land, realize much increase in crops and animals, and live to an old age (Deut 6:1–2, 8:1).

When God brings charges against Israel, the prosecution proceeds in the form of a covenant lawsuit. Hosea declares the Lord's indictment against Israel: they are guilty of swearing, lying, murder, stealing, and adultery (Hos 4:2). Micah also depicts a covenant lawsuit: *Hear what the Lord says, 'Rise, plead your case before the mountains, the controversy of the Lord, and you enduring foundations of the earth; for the Lord has a controversy with his people, and he will contend with Israel'* (Mic 6:1–23).

Since God gave the law, God can transcend the law. For example, in the time of Hezekiah, several Israelites from the north come to Jerusalem, and despite not arriving in time to undertake the cleansing ceremony, they eat of the Passover in violation of the law (2 Chron 30:18). Hezekiah prays for God to pardon them, and *The Lord heard Hezekiah, and healed the people* (2 Chron 30:20). God does not simply waive law as though it were inconsequential, but neither are God's hands tied by the law.

THE CONQUEST

The story of the conquest of the promised land reinforces aspects of Old Testament theology, such as the importance of obedience to God, God's role as a keeper of promises, and God's compassion on all peoples, not only on the Israelites. God promises the people of Israel a land. To obtain it, God also battles on their behalf. According to Psalm 136, *Yahweh struck down great kings, and killed famous kings, Sihon, king of the Amorites, and Og, king of Bashan, and gave their land as a heritage, a heritage to his servant Israel.* Israel's God was Yahweh Sabaoth, the "Lord of hosts" – the general of the heavenly armies.

The battle rules differ depending on whether the enemy is within the boundaries of the promised land or in outside countries. As to those who dwell in the land, everything that breathes must be destroyed *so that they may not teach you to do all the abhorrent things that they do for their gods, and you thus sin against the Lord your God* (Deut 20:18). Some of the *abhorrent things* were child and human sacrifice, male and female cult prostitution, and sorcery (Deut 18:9–14; 23:17–18). God is long-suffering toward the occupants, delaying the destruction of the Canaanites by the Israelites, as indicated in Genesis 15:16: *And [the Israelites] shall come back [to Canaan] in the fourth generation; for the iniquity of the Amorites is not yet complete.*

> **Rules of Warfare**
> *Deuteronomy 20 sets forth the rules for warfare. Israel is not to be afraid, since the Lord your God is with you (20:1). The priest first addresses the troops, reminding them that it is the Lord who gives victory. Afterward, the officials determine who will fight and who will be exempted. Victory comes owing to the heavenly armies, not because of the number of human fighters (Deut 20:5–8).*

Joshua and Judges demonstrate the application of the rules. Jericho is taken because the commander of the army of the Lord is present behind the scene (Josh 5:14). Several Israelites die because the devoted things are not destroyed (Josh 7:1–5). Israel also suffers because the Gibeonites claim to be from another region and thereby trick the Israelites

> **Lord of Hosts**
>
> *God is often identified as Yahweh Sabaoth (Hebrew for "Lord of hosts"), a name especially important early on at the sanctuary at Shiloh. The term was a military one, used to identify a king and his army, as is clear from David's battle with the Philistine strong man, Goliath:* But David said to the Philistine, You come to me with sword and spear and javelin; but I come to you in the name of the Lord of hosts, the God of the armies of Israel, whom you have defied *(1 Sam 17:45). Similarly, the story of Elisha and his servant Gehazi depicts vividly the heavenly hosts behind the scenes. One morning, Gehazi discovers that the horses and chariots of the Arameans surround the city. He hurries back to Elisha in alarm. Elisha responds,* Don't be afraid, for there are more with us than there are with them *(2 Kgs 6:16), whereupon Gehazi suddenly sees* the horses and chariots of fire all around Elisha *(2 Kgs 6:17).*

into disobeying God's injunction to destroy the inhabitants of Canaan.

The theme of God's role as ruler of Israel is also prominent. Gideon assembles many warriors, but God selects only three hundred. Because of Gideon's victory, the people request that he rule over them, but Gideon declares, *I will not rule over you, and my son will not rule over you; the Lord will rule over you* (Judg 8:23).

INHERITANCE OF THE LAND

The inheritance of the promised land reinforces the theme of God's providence for his own namesake and God's role as a gracious provider of unmerited gifts. Israel does not deserve the land, nor does it acquire the land on its own. It is a divine gift (Josh 1:2), as are the improvements upon it. It is *a land with fine, large cities that you did not build, houses filled with all sorts of goods that you did not fill, hewn cisterns that you did not hew, vineyards and olive groves that you did not plant* (Deut 6:10–11).

Out of love, God *gave their land as a heritage ... to his servant Israel* (Ps 136:21–22). God, however, retained ownership: *for the world is mine and all that is in it is mine* (Ps 50:12; also 50:8–11). Or again, *The land shall not be sold in perpetuity, for the land is mine; with me you are but aliens and tenants* (Lev 25:23–24). Israel may occupy the land as long as it is faithful to God, but Israel is a tenant. Naboth refuses to sell or trade his vineyard to King Ahab of Israel because to do so would be to violate the law about selling God's land (1 Kgs 21:1–6).

God desires that the land sustain the poor, the widows, and the orphans: *When you reap your harvest in your field, you shall not go back to get it; it shall be left for the alien, the orphan, and the widow, so that the Lord your God may bless you in all your undertakings* (Deut 24:19–20). The same was true for olives and grapes (Deut 24:20–22). God's ownership of the land is also implied in his ability and right to protect and create as well as destroy it: *For I am about to create new heavens and a new earth* (Isa 65:17–18; 66:22–23).

A SHEPHERD FOR GOD'S PEOPLE

Another important theological theme is kingship and the roles played by the kings, particularly the promise to David of a dynasty. David becomes king of Israel and makes many important contributions to the religious life of the people. The psalmist declares that God prepared David: *He chose his servant David, and took him from the sheepfolds; from tending the nursing ewes he brought him to be the shepherd of his people Jacob, of Israel, his inheritance. With upright heart he tended them, and guided them with skillful hand* (Ps 78:70–72). As his capital, David selects Jerusalem, which he takes from the Jebusites. The citadel was Zion, and the walled area became known as the city of David.

David brings the ark of the covenant to Jerusalem and places it in the tabernacle (2 Sam 6:17). He sets up a schedule whereby the priests take turns in serving at the tabernacle and appoints praise leaders (1 Chron 16:7–13). According to Nehemiah, David and Solomon were lawgivers: *They performed the service of their God and the service of purification, as did the singers and gatekeepers, according to the command of David and his son Solomon* (Neh 12:45).

After his monarchy stabilizes, David anticipates building a temple to house the ark. The Lord appears to Nathan with the message that David's son will build the house (2 Sam 7:13; 1 Kgs 5:3). The Lord declares that he will build David a house, meaning a dynasty (2 Sam 7:11).

The covenant of God with David consists of two parts: descendants of David will rule forever, and wayward descendants will be punished. As 1 Samuel 7:13–15 puts it: *I will establish the throne of his kingdom forever. I will be a father to him, and he shall be a son to me. When he commits iniquity, I will punish him with a rod such as mortals use, with blows inflicted by human beings. But I will not take my steadfast love from him* (see also Ps 89:30–33).

The prophets remind God's people that the promise to David is the ground of hope for a stable future. Micah declares, *But you, O Bethlehem of Ephrathah, who are one of the little clans of Judah, from you shall come forth for me one who is to rule in Israel* (Mic 5:2–3).

The dynasty of David extended to Zerubbabal – almost five hundred years (Hag 2:21–22), longer than dynasties of Egypt or China. Yahweh promises an unending dynasty, but it was over by 500 BCE. Did God forget this promise? The promise was completed in Jesus, David's seed, who died and arose, never to die again (Acts 2:33–36; Ps 89:29; Matt 1:1; 12:23).

A HISTORY OF OLD TESTAMENT THEOLOGY

Anyone who writes a summary of the Bible's key claims like the one in this essay does so as a practitioner of biblical theology. The following pages summarize some basic approaches to the discipline and offer extensive resources for further reading.

One of the earliest examples of such an enterprise occurs in the covenant theology of Johannes Cocceius (1603–1669), who argued against his contemporaries that Scripture did not neatly follow the topics of traditional dogmatic theology (God, Christ, the Holy Spirit, church, etc.) but rather emphasized covenants. Anticipating twentieth century developments, he also emphasized that Scripture highlights God's saving action in history. He contended that "there are three dispensations – that of the Promise during the time of the patriarchs, that of the Law given from Sinai, and that of the Gospel ..."

Old Testament theology began as a separate discipline in the late eighteenth century. Georg Lorenz Bauer's *Theologie des alten Testaments* (1796) was the first major work. The Old Testament theology of Gustav Friedrich Oehler (1873–1874, 2 vols.) was the first to be translated into English. After a long decline, interest in biblical theology revived in the 1930s.

OLD TESTAMENT THEOLOGY IN THE MODERN WORLD

Scholars have reached no agreement on precisely how to write a theology of the Old Testament. A few of the basic approaches are described below.

DOGMATICS

These authors assemble texts from various parts of the Old Testament to flesh out Christian theological topics. For example, the chapters in Baab's work are: God, Man, Sin, Salvation, Kingdom of God, Death and the Hereafter, and Evil. The difficulty with the dogmatic approach is that it uproots texts from their historical setting and fails to highlight the significant themes located in the Old Testament itself. Examples of works taking this approach include: Otto J. Baab's *The Theology of the Old Testament* (Abingdon, 1949); Millar Burrows's *An Outline of Biblical Theology* (Westminster, 1946); Ludwig Koehler's *Old Testament Theology* (Westminster, 1957); John L. McKenzie's *A Theology of the Old Testament* (Doubleday, 1974); and Samuel Terrien's *The Elusive Presence: The Heart of Biblical Theology* (Harper & Row, 1978).

CHRISTOLOGICAL

Certain Old Testament theologians have argued that ultimately the theology of the Old Testament must be interpreted from a christological perspective. Christ is the interpretative key through prophetic fulfillment, or Old Testament typology. The danger of the christological approach is that Old Testament theology is not given serious consideration in its own right, and the historical contexts are ignored. Examples of this approach appear in: Edmond Jacob's *Theology of the Old Testament* (Harper, 1958); G. A. F. Knight's *A Christian Theology of the Old Testament* (John Knox, 1959); and Walter Vischer's *The Witness of the Old Testament to Christ* (SCM, 1949).

COVENANTAL

The major Old Testament theologian taking this view in the twentieth century was Walther Eichrodt. Eichrodt attempted to construct Old Testament theology around the concept of covenant, especially the Mosaic covenant. He fleshed out topics by tracing their chronological unfolding. In volume 2, he dropped the word "covenant" from the chapter headings. Payne and Kaiser emulated the dispensational approach of Cocceius, with Payne taking up the covenants in order, and Kaiser the successive promises. Sample works include: Walther Eichrodt's *Theology of the Old Testament* (2 vols.; Westminster, 1961, 1967); Walter C. Kaiser's *Toward an Old Testament Theology* (Zondervan, 1978); and J. Barton Payne's *The Theology of the Older Testament* (Zondervan, 1962).

CREDO

More recently, some Old Testament scholars have focused on the themes found in Old Testament credos, or statements of basic beliefs, such as Deuteronomy 26:1–11, Psalms 105, 106, and Nehemiah 9. The most influential and impressive work in this direction was by Gerhard von Rad. Modern authors vary considerably as to what items of the credos are central. The credo approach focuses upon the topics emphasized in the Old Testament itself. These can be commented upon historically, thus resulting in serious engagement with the themes in their own settings. Some works taking this approach are: James Barr's *The Concept of Biblical Theology: An Old Testament Perspective* (Fortress, 1999); Christoph Barth's *God With Us: A Theological Introduction to the Old Testament* (Eerdmans, 1991); Walter Brueggemann's *Old Testament Theology: Essays on Structure, Theme and Text* (Fortress, 1992), and his *Theology of the Old Testament: Testimony, Dispute, Advocacy*, (Fortress, 1997); Brevard Childs's *Biblical Theology in Crisis* (Westminster, 1970), *Old Testament Theology in a Canonical Context* (Fortress, 1985), and *Biblical Theology of the Old and New Testaments: Theological Reflections on the Christian Bible* (Fortress, 1993); Ronald E. Clements's *Old Testament: A Fresh Approach* (John Knox, 1980); Hartmut Gese's *Essays on Biblical Theology* (Augsburg, 1981); Gerhard Hasel's *Old Testament Theology: Basic Issues* (Eerdmans, 1991); Thomas H. Olbricht's *He Loves Forever* (College Press, 2000, revised); Gerhard von Rad's *Old Testament Theology* (2 vols.; Harper, 1962, 1965); Claus Westermann, *Elements of Old Testament Theology* (John Knox, 1982); Hans Walter Wolff's *The Vitality of Old Testament Tradition*, with Walter Brueggemann (John Knox, 1975); G. Ernest Wright's *God Who Acts* (Allenson, 1952), and his *The Old Testament and Theology* (Harper, 1969); and Walter Zimmerli's *Old Testament Theology in Outline* (John Knox, 1978)

OLD TESTAMENT THEOLOGY IN THE STONE-CAMPBELL MOVEMENT

One might think that Old Testament theology had no role in the Stone-Campbell movement, because the Campbells, Stone, and Scott argued that only the New Testament was authoritative for Christians, and because they were wary of theology. Despite Alexander Campbell's designating the Old Testament as "Israel's book," his longest published exposition on the Bible was his *Familiar Lectures on the Pentateuch* (1867). More importantly, the two most significant theologians in the movement during the nineteenth century, Walter Scott (*The Gospel Restored*, 1836 and *Messiahship or Great Demonstration*, 1859) and Robert Milligan (*The Scheme of Redemption*, 1869), utilized much material from the Old Testament. Furthermore, all the key early leaders were opposed to dogmatic theology, particularly that based upon a metaphysical system, but not to theology located in the Scriptures.

Both Scott and Milligan emulated the covenantal theology inaugurated by Cocceius and highlighted the human propensity to sin and the anticipation of a savior in the Old Testament. Scott devoted the first 128 pages of *The Gospel Restored* to the first three chapters of Genesis. In the next section (129–191), he laid out a Christology utilizing Old Testament as well as New Testament components. In his book *The Messiahship*, Scott set aside the first 119 pages for tracing the anticipation and need for a messiah through the Old Testament. In *The Scheme of Redemption*, Milligan devoted the first 209 pages to the Old Testament and focused upon God and humans, as well as sin and punishment, in the early part of Genesis. In the second book of the work, he amplified "Scheme of Redemption in Process and Development" through scrutinizing the rest of the Pentateuch.

Both of these authors located in the theology of the Old Testament initial human innocence, disobedience, punishment, and the prospect of redemption specifically in the Torah (or the Pentateuch). God created the universe with human needs in mind. He foresaw sin and hence punishment and mortality. The gospel, that is, what God did in Christ, is the remedy and must be embraced by sinners.

As this brief summary shows, the Old Testament continues to provide the church with a basic understanding of the ways of God with human beings. The works cited here can help us understand this important part of the biblical canon in a better and more constructive way.

CONCLUSION

Emphasizing God's salvation, Old Testament theology stresses God's love of the entire creation, but particularly humankind. Despite human rebellion, God continues to bless as well as discipline and correct humanity. Although the topics of the Old Testmament are many and varied, the theme of God's work dominates the text and provides a framework for a theology of the Old Testament.

THEOLOGICAL BACKGROUNDS

New Testament Theology

Thomas H. Olbricht

CHAPTER CONTENTS

- Summary of Jesus' Life & Teachings   77
- The History of New Testament Theology   82
- The Heart of the New Testament   82
- Conclusion   84

New Testament theology as a discipline grew out of the focus of the Reformation on the theology of the Bible. Those who work in this field of study concentrate on the theology found in the various New Testament documents. However we work out the technicalities of New Testament theology, we should recognize that the documents of the New Testament were written and then collected because of the unique way in which God's love is demonstrated through Jesus' deeds and words. The focus of the New Testament is not upon a body of doctrine, a set of laws and rules, or a series of propositions, but upon a man – Jesus the Galilean.

It is not enough, however, simply to locate Jesus as the focus of the message. Down through the centuries, the views about Jesus have been legion, as Albert Schweitzer documented in *The Quest for the Historical Jesus*. The important topics pertaining to Jesus may be discovered in the basic declarations as to the centers of the faith in sermons or songs (for example, Matt 23:23; 1 Cor 15:1–9; 1 Tim 3:16). The fuller outlines appear in the sermons of Acts (2:17–36; 4:8–12; 7:1–35; 10:34–43; 13:16–41; and 17:16–31). The most complete declaration is Peter's sermon to Cornelius and his household. Many years ago, C. H. Dodd pointed out that an outline of Peter's Acts 10 sermon fits neatly over the structure of the Gospel of Mark.

SUMMARY OF JESUS' LIFE & TEACHINGS

By drawing upon Peter's sermon, it is possible to identify the following declarations regarding Jesus. He: was the Son of God come in the flesh; was heralded by John the Baptist; was anointed by the Holy Spirit; engaged in doing good; preached good news; gave his life as a ransom for many; was raised for our justification; had witnesses sent out to announce his amazing resurrection (so that his ministry continued under the auspices of the Holy Spirit, which called the church into being); showed no partiality; and is coming back in judgment in order to claim his own.

JESUS THE SON OF GOD CAME IN THE FLESH

The New Testament writers present diverse images of Jesus. Mark emphasizes that Jesus pledged the demons and those he healed to silence and shunned the limelight. Both Jesus' life and death were the way of the cross. Jesus was the servant, the Messiah, who *came not be served but to serve, and to give his life a ransom for many* (Mark 10:45). Jesus' self-designation was "Son of Man." Sometimes, this label may highlight Jesus' humanness, as in Psalm 8:4: *What is man that you are mindful of him, and the son of man that you care for him*? But Jesus can also pinpoint himself as the one who receives an everlasting kingdom (Mark 14:61–62; compare Dan 7:13). Mark depicts Jesus as possessing the prerogatives of God. He tells the paralytic who is let down through the roof, *Son, your sins are forgiven* (Mark 3:5). Mark therefore commences his gospel: *The beginning of the good news of Jesus Christ, the Son of God* (1:1).

Matthew, in his gospel, highlights Jesus as son of David prior to designating him son of Abraham (Matt 1:1). Jesus was born of Mary, conceived of the Holy Spirit (Matt 1:20–25). He was a king of the Davidic line who reigned over a kingdom (Matt 3:8–1) and proclaimed its rules (Matt 5–7). In the Old Testament, prophets anointed the Davidic king, and thus the title referring to anointing, Hebrew *mashiach* ["messiah"; Greek *Christos*] appears more frequently in Matthew than in any other gospel (seventeen times as compared with four in Mark). The heart of Jesus' message in Matthew is: *Repent, for the kingdom of heaven has come near* (Matt 4:17). Jesus is the center of the New Testament writings, not only for his word and work, but also because of who he is.

NEW TESTAMENT THEOLOGY

John declares at the beginning of his gospel that Jesus is God: *In the beginning was the Word, and the Word was with God, and the Word was God* (John 1:1). The gospel also identifies Jesus as God's *only* Son. (John 3:16). He is God enfleshed (John 1:14). He is the savior of the world (John 1:29; 11:51–53). He has prepared a place beyond death for those who believe in him (John 14:1–3).

JESUS WAS HERALDED BY JOHN THE BAPTIST

All four gospels, as well as Acts 10:37, mention that John the Baptist preceded Jesus. The disciples of John provided certain leaders and members for the growing Christian churches (John 1:35–42; Acts 18:25; 19:3). The story of John, therefore, played a role in the proclamation concerning Jesus. John the Baptist testified that Jesus was the true light coming into the world (John 1:6–9) and the *Lamb of God who takes away the sins of the world* (John 1:29). He declared that he was *The voice of one crying out in the wilderness: Prepare the way of the Lord, make his paths straight* (Mark 1:3). John insisted that he must decrease, while Jesus must increase (John 3:30), and that he was not worthy to carry Jesus' sandals (Matt 3:11). John first declared Jesus Son and savior.

> **Preparing the Way**
> John preceded Jesus and cleared the route, just as ancient servants leveled roadways and removed stones and brush prior to the journey of a king.

John and Jesus preached the same message (Matt 3:2, 4:17), the call for repentance in view of the dawning kingdom of heaven. Those who become disciples must bear fruit worthy of repentance (Matt 3:8). John declared that he baptized with water to secure the forgiveness of sins (Mark 1:4), yet Jesus would baptize with the Holy Spirit (Mark 1:8). John declared that people with two cloaks and extra food should share them with others (Luke 3:10), and Jesus taught the same (Matt 5:40–42). John charged the tax collectors to collect no more taxes than prescribed (Luke 3:13), and when the tax collector Zacchaeus met Jesus (Luke 19:8), he announced his decision to stop fraudulently collecting taxes. John told soldiers not to extort money and to be satisfied with their wages (Luke 3:14), while Jesus condemned the love of money (Matt 6:24). In all these ways, John prepared the way for the teachings of Jesus.

When questioned, John replied that he was neither the messiah nor Elijah the prophet (John 1:20–21). Jesus announced that John was greater than all those born of women (Matt 11:11) and was the Elijah to come (11:14). John only identified himself as a servant preparing the way for Jesus. Jesus attributed to him an even higher status, that of fulfilling the role of Elijah in arriving before the terrible day of the Lord.

JESUS WAS ANOINTED BY THE HOLY SPIRIT

One of the key claims in Peter's sermon is that God anointed Jesus with the Holy Spirit: *God anointed Jesus of Nazareth with the Holy Spirit and with power* (Acts 10:38); all four gospels agree (Matt 3:16–17; Mark 1:10; Luke 3:22; John 1:32). Matthew 3:16 reports, following upon Jesus' baptism by John: *suddenly the heavens were opened to him and he saw the Spirit of God descending like a dove and alighting on him*. Luke 4:18–19 quotes Isaiah 61:1–2 to affirm the anointing by the Spirit. Jesus is the anointed one (the Messiah, the Christ) because he was anointed by the Spirit of God.

The Holy Spirit anointed Jesus in order to empower his ministry. Jesus was conceived by the Holy Spirit (Luke 1:35). But as the writer of Hebrews declares, *Therefore he had to become like his brothers and sisters in every respect....* (2:17). He emptied himself (Phil 2:6). Jesus commenced his ministry under the empowerment of the Holy Spirit. As Jesus faced momentous tasks, God affirmed him as Son, first, at the commencement of his ministry (Matt 3:17), and again as his death grew imminent (Matt 17:5).

> **The Model of Jesus**
> Jesus launched his ministry after being baptized, anointed by the Spirit, affirmed as Son, and tempted by Satan (Luke 4:1–13). The disciples of Jesus commence their ministry in the same manner. They are baptized in water and of the Spirit (John 3:5; 1 Cor 12:13). They are affirmed as sons of God (John 1:12–13). They are tempted, but overcome (1 Cor 10:13).

JESUS WENT ABOUT DOING GOOD

Jesus was acclaimed for his work as well as for his words. Peter declared that Jesus *went about doing good and healing all who were oppressed by the devil, for God was with him* (Acts 10:38). In Mark, the works of Jesus predominate over his words. Jesus heals the sick (1:30–34), restores limbs, sight, and hearing (3:3–5; 8:22–25; 7:31–35), casts out demons (1:23–27), feeds the multitudes (6:40–44), stills the storm (4:37–41), and raises the dead (5:40–43).

Why did Jesus do these mighty works? Did he wish to be known as a wonder-worker? Was it to establish his claim to messiahship? No; in each case, he demonstrated God's care. He was the Son of a God of compassion (see Ps 103:8–14). Upon marveling that Jesus raised the son of the widow of Nain, the onlookers declare, *God has come to help his people* (Luke 7:16). Mark explicitly pronounces the compassion of Jesus as he has pity on the leper (1:41), views the multitudes as sheep without a shepherd (6:34), feeds the hungry in the wilderness (8:2), and casts the evil spirit out of the young man who has seizures (9:22).

In the Gospel of John, the works of Jesus are signs pointing to his messiahship: *But these are written so that you may come to believe that Jesus is the Messiah, the Son of God* (John 20:31). Many signs are mentioned in John: Jesus announces to Nathanael that he saw him under the fig tree (John 1:48); the water is changed to wine (2:11); Jesus tells the woman at the well that she has had five husbands (4:18); the official's son is healed (4:54). He also heals at the pool (5:1–15), he feeds the 5,000 (6:1–13), walks on water (6:16–21), heals the blind man (9:1–34), raises Lazarus (11:38–44), and supervises a catch of 153 fish (21:1–14). The most significant signs showing that Jesus was sent from God and is returning to God are his death, resurrection, and post-resurrection appearances. The signs give rise to faith.

> **Sign Stories in John**
> *Each sign story in John follows a pattern. First, an unusual puzzle occurs: for example, the water changed into wine (2:10). Second, a true believer who is present serves as a catalyst, in this case Mary the mother of Jesus (2:5). And third, an openness to the work of God is required (2:2), which thereupon results in faith in Jesus as Son of God (2:11; 13:1).*

JESUS PREACHED GOOD NEWS

The teachings of Jesus are many. He himself pinpoints the center: *Woe to you, scribes and Pharisees, hypocrites! For you tithe mint, dill, and cummin, and have neglected the weightier matters of the law: justice and mercy and faith. It is these you ought to have practiced without neglecting the others* (Matt 23:23). Or, again, *You shall love the Lord your God with all your heart, and with all your soul, and with all your mind. This is the greatest and first commandment. And a second is like it: You shall love your neighbor as yourself* (Matt 22:37–39). Taking these challenges seriously requires a major life change. Hence, Jesus calls, *Repent, for the kingdom of heaven has come near* (Matt 5:17).

A major collection of Jesus' teachings appears in the Sermon on the Mount (Matt 5–7). In the Beatitudes, Jesus heralds the virtues of humility, physical non-aggression, passionate seeking of God, mercy, purity in heart, and peace seeking. In the rest of the sermon, he requires a right heart in order to bring about correct action. Love is to be genuine, and it extends to enemies as well as friends. Human beings should trust God to provide the needs of life. Judgment is God's prerogative. Jesus elsewhere stresses forgiveness (Matt 18:21–22). Luke contains a lengthy section of Jesus' affirmation that God gives possessions in order that they may be shared with the less fortunate (Luke 12–19). The gospels also quote Jesus extensively regarding the church (Matt 16:13–20; 18:15–20), the Holy Spirit (John 14–16), and his own death and resurrection (Matt 16:21–26; 26:26–29).

JESUS GAVE HIS LIFE AS A RANSOM FOR MANY

The death and resurrection are central to the proclamation about Jesus. God carries out these actions in order to provide the pad from which to launch much of the theology of the New Testament. The Gospel of Mark makes it clear that one cannot fathom the work of Jesus without coming face-to-face with him upon the cross (Mark 14:39). Paul places the cross and resurrection at the center of his ministry: *Jesus Christ our Lord … was handed over to death for our trespasses and was raised for our justification* (Rom 4:24–25; compare 1 Cor 2:2). The death and resurrection are the focal point for the entry into Christ by baptism (Rom 6:1–4) and for being sustained in the faith through the Lord's Supper (Matt 26:26–29; 1 Cor 11:23–26). John clearly declares the import of Jesus' death by saying, *Here is the Lamb of God who takes away the sin of the world* (John 1:29). The cross and resurrection are the focal points of Jesus' mission (John 12:32–36). Jesus removed sin once for all by the sacrifice of himself (Heb 9:26).

NEW TESTAMENT THEOLOGY

JESUS WAS RAISED FOR OUR JUSTIFICATION

The cross and the resurrection are two sides of the same coin. The significance of the one is secured by the actuality of the other. Jesus is one of a kind because God raised him never to die again. According to the gospels, he anticipates his own resurrection (Mark 8:31). Because of his resurrection, he continues his earthly ministry by working through the disciples. In the Gospel of John, Jesus is lifted up not only on the cross (12:32–33) but in his return to the Father (20:17). Those who believe in the death and resurrection of Jesus will be forgiven and justified because he was *handed over to death for our trespasses and raised for our justification* (Rom 4:25).

The resurrection of Christ commends a lifestyle for those who believe. As Romans 6:4 puts it, *Therefore we have been buried with him by baptism into death, so that, just as Christ was raised from the dead by the glory of the Father, so we too might walk in newness of life.* Or again, *So if you have been raised with Christ, seek the things that are above, where Christ is, seated at the right hand of God. Set your minds on things that are above, not on things that are on earth* (Col 3:1–4). Believers have been transferred *into the kingdom of his beloved Son, in whom we have redemption, the forgiveness of sins* (Col 1:13–14). Believers rise from the grave just as their Lord did, with a spiritual body (1 Cor 15:44).

> **"Take up your cross ..."**
> *The cross clearly defines the life of the disciple*: If any want to become my followers, let them deny themselves and take up their cross and follow me (*Mark 8:34*). *They are to wash feet, as did Jesus (John 13:1–17) so as to remove grime. Because of the cross, believers have newness of life (Rom 6:3–4; Gal 2:19–20), their flesh is crucified (Gal 5:24–25), they are united with Christ and each other (1 Cor 1:12–13), they recognize that their brothers and sisters are those for whom Christ died (Rom 14:13–15; 1 Cor 8:9–11), their ministry is empowered (2 Cor 13:1–4), and they interact with spouses, children, masters, and workers in a cruciform manner (Eph 4:31–6:2). Believers should go to Christ outside the camp where he died, and they should bear the abuse he bore (Heb 13:13).*

WITNESSES WENT FORTH TO ANNOUNCE JESUS' RESURRECTION

According to Peter, God prepared special witnesses (Acts 10:40–43). The witnesses are those who see the risen Lord. They included the Twelve (Acts 1:22; 3:14–15; 4:33; 5:30–32) as well as many others (Acts 13:30–31), including women (Luke 23:55–24:5). Paul likewise knows of multiple witnesses to the resurrection (1 Cor 15:6). Jesus' ministry of forgiveness and resurrection-inspired hope continue after his ascension.

> **Jesus' Origins**
> *In John, the witness or testimony focuses upon Jesus as sent from God (1:15; 3:31–32; 5:37). He is also the one who will return to God (13:1; 3; 14:3). The witnesses include John the Baptist (5:32, 33), works provided by God (5:36), and especially God (5:37) and the Scriptures (5:39).*

JESUS' MINISTRY CONTINUED UNDER THE AUSPICES OF THE HOLY SPIRIT

Jesus ushers in a new age by baptizing in the Spirit (Luke 3:16–17; see Ezek 36:26–27). The Spirit does not come upon the disciples during the ministry of Jesus (John 7:39). The disciples receive the Spirit in a private bestowing before his ascension (John 20:21–22) and in a public display on the feast of Pentecost, afterward (Acts 2:1–4). The Spirit is promised to all who believe and are baptized (Acts 2:38–39). In Luke-Acts, the Holy Spirit opens up the ministries, first of John the Baptist (Luke 1:15), and of Jesus (Luke 3:22; 4:18), then of the apostles (Acts 2:1–4), the ministry to the Samaritans (Acts 8:15–17), and finally to the Gentiles (Acts 10:44–48). Special phenomena may accompany these ministry openings, for example, speaking in such a manner that all hear in their own language (Acts 2:6; 10:46; 19:6). All believers, however, are baptized with water and with the Spirit (John 3:5; 1 Cor 12:13).

In John, Jesus asks God to send the Holy Spirit [Greek *parakletos*, "counselor, helper"] to accompany the disciples when he departs (John 14:16, 16:7). The Holy Spirit will enable them to do the works of Jesus (John 14:12) and will teach and remind them of what Jesus said (John 14:26). The Spirit will also convict the world of sin, righteousness, and judgment (John 14:8). The Spirit not only descended upon the Twelve but also upon all those who believe (1 John 2:27; Acts 1:15, 2:1–3).

For Paul, the Spirit accompanies Jesus in ushering in the new age (Gal 3:2–5). In fact, Paul can declare the Lord and the Spirit one: *for this comes from the Lord, the Spirit* (2 Cor 3:18). The Spirit pours love into the heart of the believer (Rom 5:5), leads

NEW TESTAMENT THEOLOGY

the children of God (Rom 8:14), and produces the fruits of the Spirit – love, joy, peace, patience, kindness, generosity, faithfulness, gentleness, and self control (Gal 5:22–23). The Holy Spirit may be resisted (1 Thess 5:19). All believers have gifts [Greek *charismata*] of the Spirit (1 Cor 7:7; 1 Pet 4:10–11). These gifts [*charismata*] are not all spectacular but include giving and serving (Rom 12:3–6). The greatest gift [Greek *charisma*] is love (1 Cor 13:13). Flashy gifts for self-aggrandizement that disrupt the gathering of believers are not from God (1 Cor 14:32, 39). The gifts provided for the believer are not so much for his or her own benefit but for the welfare of the body, the church (1 Cor 12:4–7).

JESUS CALLED THE CHURCH INTO BEING

In Paul's view, the church is that body brought about by the suffering of the body of its Lord on the cross (1 Cor 11:29; Phil 2:1–11). At the end of Matthew, Jesus charged church leaders to continue his earthly ministry. He will continue to empower from the right hand of God: *And remember I am with you always, to the end of the age* (Matt 28:20). The Synoptic Gospels identified the church as the kingdom of God (in Matthew the kingdom of heaven). It begins small, but like mustard seed, grows into a significant entity (Matt 13:31–32).

> **The Kingdom**
> *The church is a manifestation of the visible kingdom of God on earth (Matt 16:18–19), but it does not exhaust the full meaning of the kingdom. The kingdom of God is God's everlasting kingly sway that existed from time immemorial (Matt 12:38; Luke 17:21) and will continue even after the church is absorbed into the kingdom at the end time (Matt 8:11; 1 Cor 6:10).*

The Gospel of John also believes that the Holy Spirit empowers the church (14:25–26). It is a sheepfold with Christ as the shepherd (John 10:11–18). The church is also depicted as the branches of a vine. Christ is the vine. God is the vinedresser. Believers (the church) are the branches nourished by the vine, and they in turn produce fruit (John 15:1–8). In 1 John also, the church is a fellowship of the forgiven who in turn forgive: *But if we walk in the light as he himself is in the light, we have fellowship with one another, and the blood of Jesus his Son cleanses from all sin* (1:9).

Moreover, according to Ephesians, God has subjected all things to Christ, the head over the church, which is his body (1:22). Christ loves and sustains the church in order to purify it for its final destiny (Eph 5:25–27).

Entry into the church is through baptism into Christ: *For in one Spirit we were all baptized into one body* (1 Cor 12:13). The one baptism (Eph 4:5) is of water and of the Spirit (John 3:5; 1 Cor 12:13–13). Baptism depicts the death, burial, and resurrection of Jesus Christ (Rom 6:3–4). Similarly, in partaking of the Lord's Supper, believers remember the death, burial, and resurrection of Jesus Christ and are sustained and maintained until he comes (1 Cor 11:23–26).

JESUS SHOWED NO PARTIALITY

Peter declares, *I truly understand that God shows no partiality, but in every nation anyone who fears him and does what is right is acceptable to him* (Acts 10:34–35). Jesus charges the disciples to disciple all nations (Matt 28:19). Yet Christ's work involves more than the establishment of a new relationship with God. It also opens up a new relationship between one human and another.

> **Babel**
> *Genesis 11 tells of estrangement resulting from multiple languages. When the believers gathered in Jerusalem, that language barrier collapsed* because each one heard the disciples speaking in the native language of each *(Acts 2:6), a reversal of the Babel curse that the Old Testament anticipated (Isa 2:2–4; 19:24–25; Zeph 3:9).*

Paul particularly emphasizes the breaking down of human barriers: *There is no longer Jew or Greek, there is no longer slave or free, there is no longer male and female; for all of you are one in Christ Jesus* (Gal 3:27–28). He charges the ethnically and socially diverse Roman believers to *welcome one another, therefore, just as Christ has welcomed you, for the glory of God* (Rom 15:7). Jesus, by his death, broke down the walls that separate humans from each other, *for he is our peace; in his flesh he has made both groups into one and has broken down the dividing wall, that is, the hostility between us* (Eph 2:14).

JESUS IS COMING BACK IN JUDGMENT & TO CLAIM HIS OWN

In his sermon, Peter declares that Jesus is *the one ordained by God as judge of the living and the dead* (Acts

10:42) in the end time. Jesus proclaimed the end of human history and the coming judgment (Matt 24:30–31), noting however, that *about that day and hour no one knows, neither the angels of heaven, nor the Son, but only the Father* (Matt 24:36). Paul believes that the resurrected Jesus will return and take his own to God (1 Thess 4:14). Before that happens, however, Paul believes that a larger remnant of the Jews will come to faith in Christ (Rom 11:1). They will accept him, jealous of the increasing numbers of Gentiles who believe (Rom 11:11). After the full number of Gentiles has accepted Jesus as Lord, all the true remnant of Israel will be saved (Rom 11:24–26). Before that time, defection and immorality will develop among the believers (1 Tim 4:1–5). The return of Christ may be delayed, but it is certain (2 Pet 3:3–10).

The book of Revelation is especially focused upon the passing away of the heaven and earth and on the New Jerusalem coming down from heaven (Rev 21:1–2). The separation between heaven and earth in the old age has collapsed in the new, for God now reigns in the New Jerusalem (Rev 21:3–5). Before the descent of the heavenly city, however, the churches will undergo tribulation and apostasy (Rev 2–3). Not only will the churches face attack, but all those who reject Christ as Lord will also experience trouble.

Christ himself, because of his death, is able to open the seals that bring future scourges upon the earth (Rev 5:1–5). The seven seals disclose disaster and destruction (Rev 6:1–8:1), as do the seven trumpets (Rev 8:2–11:19) and the seven bowls (Rev 15:7–16:20). After these terrible afflictions, the beast and the false prophet are defeated and thrown into the lake of fire (Rev 19:17–21). The devil is sealed in the pit for a thousand years, then released, defeated, and likewise thrown into the lake of fire (Rev 20:1–10). During the binding of Satan, Christ will reign for a thousand years, along with those who have overcome evil and have been beheaded for Jesus. Apparently this reign will take place where the heavenly thrones are located (Rev 20:4–6) and not on earth, though earth-dwellers will be affected by this reign. After that, the New Jerusalem will come down out of heaven, and God and the Lamb will reign forever (21:1–22:5).

A HISTORY OF NEW TESTAMENT THEOLOGY

Anyone who writes a summary of the Bible's key claims like the one in this essay does so as a practitioner of biblical theology. The following pages summarize some basic approaches to the discipline of New Testament theology and offer extensive resources for further reading.

An influential formulation of New Testament theology was that of J. P. Gabler in his 1787 address, "On the Proper Distinction between Biblical and Dogmatic Theology," in which he proposed a method for distinguishing biblical theology from the church's dogmatic theology that developed after the Bible. For Gabler, biblical theology focused upon concepts of the divine in the individual books of the Bible, and he distinguished between the Old and New Testaments as well as among the individual authors. He first noted the differences in the documents and then systematized the larger views while still preserving the specific views of the individual books. The New Testament theologian then identifies the unchanging forms of Christian teaching, and systematic theologians proceed to construct dogmatic theology based upon these insights. This basic approach has shaped the field ever since.

It was not until the work of later scholars such as F. C. Baur, Johannes Weiss, Albert Schweitzer, Wilhelm Bousset, Wilhelm Wrede, Rudolf Bultmann, and Ernst Käseman, that the historical ramifications of New Testament theology were more precisely formulated. But Gabler clearly set the agenda for all of us – see Henrikus Boers's "New Testament Theology," in *Dictionary of Biblical Interpretation* (Abingdon, 1999).

In the Stone-Campbell restoration movement, the study of the New Testament has focused upon the doctrine of the church rather than the proclamation of Jesus – see Everett Ferguson's *The Church of Christ* (Eerdmans, 1996).

THE HEART OF THE NEW TESTAMENT

Several major New Testament theologies have been written since the 1930s. A few scholars have despaired of locating a central thrust in the theology of the New Testament. But most of them, while recognizing differences, have attempted to pursue a thread or threads running throughout the whole. It is commonly recognized that, whereas God is the focal point of the Old Testament, God as revealed through Jesus Christ is the focus of the New Testament. Studies of

New Testament theology depict Jesus' role in various ways.

> **New Testament Theological Models**
> Broadly speaking, there are five different approaches to explaining the theology of the New Testament: dogmatics, a focus on key Christian doctrines; ecclesiology, a focus on the life of the church; Heilsgeschichte, concentration of the mighty saving deeds of God; anthropology, an emphasis on the nature of humankind; and Christology, a centering of theology on the person and work of Jesus Christ.

These approaches each have strengths and weaknesses, a fact that testifies to the complexity of New Testament theology. Perhaps we can never have a completely satisfactory solution to the problem because the New Testament witnesses to the ongoing work of a universal God among all creation, including an ever-changing human race.

DOGMATICS

Donald Guthrie, in *New Testament Theology* (InterVarsity, 1981), declared that a center is not apparent in the New Testament and that therefore the best procedure is to take up the traditional topics of dogmatic theology such as faith, the Scriptures, God, the Holy Spirit, the church, salvation, and eschatology. Based upon that approach, the systematic theologian can build upon the conclusions of New Testament theologians. Guthrie, however, fails to give appropriate consideration to the divergent ways in which theology permeates the various New Testament books.

ECCLESIOLOGY

C. H. Dodd influenced a generation of British New Testament scholars with the claim that realized eschatology, the view that the end time began with the life or resurrection of Jesus, prevailed in early Christianity. He asserted that the church is at the center of the New Testament, because the goal [Greek *eschaton*] of Jesus' mission was the church. Two of his works were especially influential: *Apostolic Preaching* (Hodder 1936, 1963) and *The Authority of the Bible* (Nisbet, 1952). Based upon Dodd's work, Alan Richardson produced *An Introduction to the Theology of the New Testament* (Harper, 1959), in which he focused upon the core New Testament claims about the church. The problem with Richardson's thesis is that the church is the body that came about because of the body of Christ on the cross, and so Christ's work is logically more central than the church itself.

HEILSGESCHICHTE

The German word *Heilsgeschichte* means "holy history," or, in biblical language, the "mighty acts of God." A theological movement in Germany identified as *Heilsgeschichte*, or salvation history, centered around J. C. K. Hofmann (1810–1877). This movement had some influence upon later New Testament theologians, namely: Ethelbert Stauffer's *New Testament Theology* (SCM, 1963); Oscar Cullmann's *Christ and Time* (third edition, SCM, 1967), and his *Salvation in History* (Harper, 1967); Werner G. Kümmel's *The Theology of The New Testament* (Abingdon, 1973); George Eldon Ladd's *A Theology of the New Testament* (Eerdmans, 1974, 1993); and Leonard Goppelt's *Theology of the New Testament* (2 vols., Eerdmans, 1981, 1982)

In this manner of thinking, Jesus Christ is the center and culmination of God's mighty acts in history. The salvation history perspective has merit as long as the mighty acts are not held to be superior to and isolated from the biblical affirmations interpreting them.

ANTHROPOLOGY

Drawing on contemporary scientific approaches to reality, Rudolf Bultmann took the position that all causes in this world are of this world. Therefore, the theology of the New Testament focuses upon the human appropriation of the Christ figure (for Bultmann, a non-deity) who points the way to authentic human existence. His approach has therefore been designated anthropological – that is, human focused (Rudolf Bultmann, *Theology of the New Testament*, 2 vols., Scribners 1951, 1955). Though Käsemann and Conzelmann questioned Bultmann's indebtedness to the philosophy of Heidegger, they retained his basic presuppositions. See Ernst Käsemann's *Essays on New Testament Themes* (SCM, 1960), and Hans Conzelmann's *An Outline of the Theology of the New Testament* (Harper, 1969). Bultmann's assumptions are, however, not those of the New Testament, which presupposes a supernatural preexistent Christ.

NEW TESTAMENT THEOLOGY

CHRISTOLOGY

Several New Testament theologians have assumed that the heart of the theology in the New Testament books focuses upon Jesus of Nazareth. They vary considerably, however, in the manner in which they depict Jesus. The theology of the New Testament focuses upon Jesus Christ, but as fleshed out from the theological explorations in early Christian preaching. New Testament theologies with this perspective include: Vincent Taylor's *The Formation of the Gospel Tradition* (Macmillan, 1957), *The Names of Jesus* (Macmillan, 1953), *The Atonement in New Testament Teaching* (Epworth, 1958), and his *Jesus and His Sacrifice* (Macmillan, 1937); Eduard Schweizer's *Jesus* (John Knox, 1971), and *New Testament Theology* (1993); Joachim Jeremias's *New Testament Theology: The Proclamation of Jesus* (Scribners, 1971); Stephen Neill's *Jesus Through Many Eyes: Introduction to the Theology of the New Testament* (Fortress, 1976); Gerhard Hasel's *New Testament Theology: Basic Issues in the Current Debate* (Eerdmans, 1978); Leon Morris's *New Testament Theology* (Zondervan, 1986); Robert Morgan's *The Nature of New Testament Theology* (SCM, 1973); John Reumann's *Witness of the Word: A Biblical Theology of the Gospel* (Fortress, 1986), and *The Promise and Practice of Biblical Theology* (Fortress, 1991); Peter Balla's *Challenges to New Testament Theology* (Hendrickson, 1998); Georg Strecker's *Theology of the New Testament* (Westminster John Knox, 2000); and I. Howard Marshall's *New Testament Theology: Many Witnesses, One Gospel* (InterVarsity, 2004).

CONCLUSION

The depictions of what Jesus said and did are the skeleton upon which the theology of the New Testament is fleshed out. The presence of the risen Lord shapes the church's actions in worship, service, and moral decision-making. While the New Testament does not try to think systematically through all the ways in which Christians should imitate Christ, the gospels, epistles, historical work, and apocalypse that make up the New Testament canon give enough guidance for the church to flourish in a world awaiting the return of God.

CONTEMPORARY CONTEXTS

The Bible & Literature

Jonathan Wade & Nancy W. Shankle

CHAPTER CONTENTS

The Bible in Literature 85

Christian Approaches to Reading 87

Literature's Power to Influence 88

Understanding the Christian Worldview 90

For Further Study 91

Works Cited 91

MAPS, TABLES, & FEATURES

Sin Depicted in Literaure 86

Fantasy & the Young Adult 88

The Bible is still the best-selling and most reprinted book in the world. Numerous writers in varying fields, in various forms, and in multiple languages have used the Bible as inspiration for their own creative works. It is quoted in titles, in text, and in song. In English, the cadence and rhythm of the King James Version of the Bible still influences the way we speak and write.

THE BIBLE IN LITERATURE

Many stories adapt the biblical text or retell it in a different way. Others attempt to illuminate biblical principles by allegory. There are also allusions to the Bible in numerous texts. Examples include "the mark of Cain," "the Ten Commandments," "love your neighbor," and "the gifts of the magi."

There are also quite a few extra-biblical texts with biblical themes. Some examples from the Middle Ages include the stories of King Arthur and his knights and Dante's *Divine Comedy*. The "Matter of Arthur," as it has been called, has been told in numerous ways. In almost every case, the stories share the idea of Arthur as a bringer of goodness, civilization, and perhaps salvation, who is ultimately betrayed by his wayward bride and faithless friends. This tale clearly echoes the Christian story of a savior betrayed by a faithless humanity. Of course, in many of the stories, the connection is less clear because Arthur is portrayed less sympathetically while Lancelot and Guinevere are made more sympathetic.

In his *Divine Comedy*, Dante, the great medieval Italian poet, writes about a journey from Earth through hell, purgatory, and heaven. Dante appears to have been attempting to adapt the Greek and Roman myths of journeys to the underworld to a Christian conception of the nature of reality. This journey illustrates much about the medieval conception of the afterlife, about the nature of God's relationship with humankind, and about the political situation in Italy in Dante's time. It is worth noting that the *Divine Comedy* tries to explain and explore an idea that the biblical text did not adequately explain. So in these poems, Dante attempts to explore the possibilities at which the Bible only hints.

> **The Bible & Literature**
> *The Bible has had a great effect in shaping the character and form of Western literature. It has served as a template, an encouragement, an inspiration, and a source to be contested for many authors and traditions. Biblical phrases still linger in the popular mind and in the literary record. Biblical cadences still echo in our poems and our songs. Whatever one's belief stance, the Bible is an important piece of the knowledge of humankind. Even discounting its great literary importance, for those who believe, the Bible is a gift from a God who seeks to embrace humanity with all its weaknesses, it is a message from beyond that can connect humankind to that which is truly real and truly beautiful.*

Later works like John Milton's *Paradise Lost* continue in the same vein. In *Paradise Lost*, Milton describes the war in heaven between the forces of Lucifer and the forces of God. He describes the event where Lucifer and his minions are cast into hell, and he depicts the fall of humanity as yet another skirmish in the war that Satan wages against the works of God. In telling this story in poetic form, Milton, whether he meant to or not, depicts a Satan who is more vivid, comprehensible, and perhaps more sympathetic than the sketchy depictions of him in some biblical texts. At the very least, Milton makes it more possible to understand how Satan might have justified his rebellion against God to himself. *Paradise Lost* remains one of the central and valuable texts in English.

Another text worth considering is John Bunyan's *A Pilgrim's Progress*. In this short work, Bunyan tells the story of Christian as he tries to make his way from the City of Destruction to the Celestial City. On his way, he encounters obstacles like the Slough of Despond and Vanity Fair. Eventually, by the grace of God (and with a good bit of work on his own) he accomplishes his goal. This book is a superb example of religious allegory. From a modern perspective it is, perhaps, a bit morally heavy-handed and not particularly subtle, but it is a beautiful and touching work, nonetheless.

A good bit of short poetry also exists on biblical themes. Some poets, like Alfred Lord Tennyson in his *In Memoriam*, use poetry as a way to question and praise God. The prelude to *In Memoriam* is a plaintive prayer from a person saddened by the sudden and untimely death of a loved one:

> Strong Son of God, immortal love,
> Whom we, that have not seen Thy face,
> By faith, and faith alone, embrace,
> Believing where we cannot prove.
>
> Thou wilt not leave us in the dust;
> Thou madest man, he knows not why,
> He thinks he was not made to die:
> And Thou hast made him: Thou art just.
>
> Thou seemest human and divine,
> The highest, holiest manhood, Thou.
> Our wills are ours, we know not how;
> Our wills are ours, to make them Thine.
>
> Our little systems have their day;
> They have their day and cease to be;
> They are but broken lights of Thee,
> And Thou, O Lord, art more than they.
>
> We have but faith: we cannot know;
> For knowledge is of things we see;
> And yet we trust it comes from Thee,
> A beam in darkness: let it grow.
>
> Let knowledge grow from more to more,
> But more of reverence in us dwell;
> That mind and soul, according well,
> May make one music as before.
>
> But vaster. We are fools and slight;
> We mock Thee when we do not fear;
> But help Thy foolish ones to bear –
> Help Thy vain worlds to bear Thy light.

In this poem, Tennyson echoes the odd mixture of faith and doubt that is produced even in those with the strongest belief in times of trouble. He sounds very much like the prophet Habakkuk in Habakkuk 1:1–4:

> *The oracle that Habakkuk the prophet received. How long, O Lord, must I call for help, but you do not listen? Or cry out to you, Violence! but you do not save? Why do you make me look at injustice? Why do you tolerate wrong? Destruction and violence are before me; there is strife, and conflict abounds. Therefore the law is paralyzed, and justice never prevails. The wicked hem in the righteous, so that justice is perverted.*

In reading the Psalms, one is often struck by the way that the writers explore the goodness of God while still acknowledging or even questioning the power of wickedness in the world. The Victorian

---

Sin Depicted in Literature

Literature as a whole does not depict fools, hypocrites, or the cruel in a positive light. It is therefore no surprise that the literature of western civilization, steeped as it is in Christian history and tradition, has no qualms about pointing out the sins of those who claim to be righteous. In the English language, one can look as far back as Chaucer's Canterbury Tales *and find numerous examples of hypocrisy. Chaucer illustrates the fleshly sins of the Pardoner, the Summoner, and the Friar who are all employed in some way by the church. In continental literature, we have works like Voltaire's* Candide *in which the reader meets many churchmen but finds them all to be horrible people. In Jane Austen's* Pride and Prejudice, *the character Mr. Collins depicts the churchman as a boring social climber. In Leo Tolstoy's* Anna Karenina, *Karenin, the title character's husband, is "religious" but unbelieving and cold. In Dostoevsky's* The Brothers Karamazov, *Rakitin, the student of religion, is a calculating and godless person.*

poet, Gerard Manley Hopkins, often praised for his innovative poetic form, explores both God's greatness and humanity's suffering in his poetry. In poems like "The Windhover," Hopkins explores the beauty of nature as it reflects the goodness of God. In another group of poems, called his "terrible sonnets," Hopkins explores the worst experiences of humanity. For example, in his "Carrion Comfort," the speaker of the poem is struggling with depression but eventually realize – by defying his dark thoughts – that God is seeking him.

Lately, many of the adaptations have served as a criticism of the Bible. For example, Oscar Wilde's *Salome* is a play that attempts to get at the aesthetic beauty behind the story of John the Baptist's beheading. The play attempts to fill in the gaps in the biblical story by expanding the characters of Salome and John the Baptist. Wilde's explicit text still condemns Salome, but implicitly he also condemns John as a man too proud to love. Another more recent example might be *Job: A Comedy of Justice* written by Robert A. Heinlein. In this book, a modern retelling of Job, Satan becomes one of the heroes and God figures as the one who torments Job.

There are, however, some positive depictions of Christians and Christianity in literature. Chaucer gives us the Parson, an honest and caring man. Victor Hugo gives us the Bishop of Digne who rescues the hero of his *Les Misérables* from a life of sin and dissipation. Even Voltaire, who opposed Christianity for several reasons, shows us in the character of the kind Anabaptist in *Candide* that some people do actually live the Christian ethic. Finally, also in his *The Brothers Karamazov*, Dostoevsky gives us positive examples of both otherworldly Christianity (in the person of the elder Zossima) and concrete day-to-day Christianity (in the person of Alyosha).

In recent times, there has been a shift toward allocating all explicitly Christian fiction to publishers who cater specifically to Christian audiences. In fact, Christian fiction has become as much a separate genre as science fiction or young adult fiction. However, there are two possible problems with sequestering most Christian works in a specifically Christian genre. The first is that authors and readers have to choose between secular and religious works. Although this approach has given us such best-selling fiction as the *Left Behind* series, the audience for such works are usually self-selected Christians. This leads us to the second problem: whenever a group sequesters itself from the world, it automatically excludes the majority of people who do not at least partially agree with its precepts. The current Christian fiction market is predominantly white, middle-class, evangelical, and Protestant. This leaves out people from other Christian traditions, ethnicities, classes, as well as those who do not believe. This market, then, mainly centers upon encouraging and reinforcing a worldview rather than spreading it. Christians should support great Christian writers like Calvin Miller or Stephen Lawhead whether their books are published by Christian presses or not, but they should also seek out good writing from Christians who are publishing in the mainstream presses. There are many contemporary writers who explore the reality of life from a Christian perspective and are being published by mainstream publishers. Some worth noting are Walker Percy, Frederick Buechner, Annie Dillard, and Anne Lamott.

Before the Christian book market became a separate entity, mainstream works often dealt with Christian themes. One example of explicitly Christian themes that are buried in a work intended for all people is C. S. Lewis's *The Chronicles of Narnia*. In this seven-book series, intended for grade-school children, Lewis crafts a beautiful world that is parallel to our own. In doing so, he creates stories that stand on their own but still point to central Christian beliefs. This series is beautiful and encouraging for people of all ages.

J. R. R. Tolkien, a friend of Lewis, in his *Lord of the Rings* trilogy, creates a world that is less specifically related to Christianity but which clearly shows the struggle between good and evil. One could argue that Tolkien's legacy has shaped the entire genre of fantasy, so that, even today one can still find books like J. K. Rowling's *Harry Potter* series that, while not specifically Christian, do support the idea that the forces of good and the forces of evil are constantly battling each other.

CHRISTIAN APPROACHES TO READING

When Christians approach any text, we should carefully attempt to discern the immediate aesthetic effect, the author's intent, and the possible implications of the text. We should be able to examine texts logically and appreciate them for their quality, their

THE BIBLE & LITERATURE

Fantasy & the Young Adult

Some Christians are concerned with the "occult" references in popular series like the Harry Potter series by J. K. Rowling. Others have even condemned C. S. Lewis for portraying witchcraft or Tolkien for writing about wizards and sorcerers. Often the condemnation of such writing is based, not on a well formulated critique, but instead upon a general dislike for fantastic literature or, perhaps, for fiction in general. It is important for Christian leaders to realize that Jesus explicitly condoned fiction in his use of parables, and he, to some extent, seems to have condoned fantasy in his description of the woman married to many brothers and in the story of the rich man and Lazarus. Even if one decides that fiction is permissible but that fantasy is not, one still has to face the facts that the literature is very popular, and that censoring works without thought or persuasive argument usually compels young people to want to read them. In the case of popular series, parents can choose three paths. They can ignore the issue, which avoids responsibility. They can attempt to completely separate their children from all outside influences. Or they can logically and prayerfully encounter the texts and discuss them with their children. The third way seems preferable.

If one examines the Harry Potter series logically, it is very difficult to find much to condemn. The "sorcery" in Harry Potter is obviously fanciful and quite different from the depictions of witchcraft in historical accounts and even the rhetoric of modern self-proclaimed witches. In most cases, the spells and magical creatures are loosely influenced by earlier works of fantasy but are primarily products of the author's imagination. They are light, enjoyable books that center on adolescent issues of growing up and the battle of good versus evil. Parents should be more concerned with works that are explicitly occult oriented. Many books classified as Teen Horror books portray occult activities in a positive manner, but are not nearly as popular as the Harry Potter series. If a parent cannot steer his or her children to less troublesome books, he or she should read the book and use it as a starting point for discussion.

One fantasy series that might be treated as an opportunity for discussion is Phillip Pullman's His Dark Materials trilogy. These three books are exceedingly well-written and interesting. They are also part of Pullman's effort to deconstruct and criticize the Christian worldview. They subtly undermine the Christian tradition while weaving a captivating story. Even in this case, however, parents and youth workers would be best advised to logically analyze Pullman's arguments against Christianity and to discuss them critically with any child who decides to read (or who is assigned) this series. In this way, a work that is aesthetically beautiful can be appreciated as a work of art and as a persuasive argument. Once Pullman's argument is unmasked, it is easily countered, and in the encounter between his arguments and the reader's counterarguments comes an opportunity for growth in both mind and spirit.

It is not the genre (fantasy, science fiction, or even horror) that makes a work anti-Christian. It is the intent and the effect. Careful reading and honest and prayerful critique are important weapons in the arsenal of good.

stance, and their truthfulness. We can consider the effects of a text on ourselves and on others. We can also look at the historical, social, artistic, and even religious context of the work.

It may be that we encounter a text with which we already agree, but we will also, almost certainly, encounter texts with which we do not agree. In the latter case, we should not allow our dogmatism to override the opportunity to understand the perspective of another human being. Censorship should be the last resort. The Bible gives us an example of the value of candid reporting. If God had censored the Bible, we would not have the stories of Abraham's attempted deceit, of Jacob's successful deceit, of David's indiscretion with Bathsheba, or of Peter's denial. All of these stories, though negative in one sense, illuminate the power and love of God.

LITERATURE'S POWER TO INFLUENCE

The children's rhyme, "Sticks and stones may break my bones, but names will never hurt me," belies the power of language to shape our ideas, build our moral consciousness, or tear down our fragile beliefs. Most people can easily recall a book they read as a child or young adult that shaped their development in powerful ways. For many famous writers, it was more than simply one book; it was the amazing world of books. For example, Eudora Welty, in her autobiography *One Writer's Beginnings*, wrote about her trips to the library as a child. Mrs. Calloway, the librarian, had strict rules; she allowed only two books to be checked out at a time and patrons could not return the books on the same day they were checked out. As a result, young Eudora pedaled her bicycle back and forth to the library reading her books two by two. She had an eclectic, impressionable, and insatiable appetite for reading. As an adult, she reported that she had lived a sheltered life in Jackson, Mississippi, but it was nonetheless a "daring life" because "all serious daring comes from within" (104). Welty began an intense, sustained life of the mind with her countless bicycle trips to the library as a child. In the same way, people today continue to prosper from a rich habit of reading.

Gene Edward Veith Jr. argues that "the habit of reading is absolutely critical today, particularly for Christians" (xiv). In a time of increasing influence of pop culture, habits of reading reinforce important skills of thinking – analyzing, evaluating, exploring, questioning. Moreover, Christians are heirs to a rich tradition of literature that examines our faith and nurtures our beliefs (read, for example, Milton's *Paradise Lost* or Flannery O'Connor's short stories).

Throughout the Bible, the Word figured prominently. John reminds us: *In the beginning was the Word, and the Word was with God, and the Word was God* (John 1:1). God spoke our world into existence and gave us a revelation in written word. We remember the biblical narratives told to us as children long after we are grown, for *the word of God is living and active* (Heb 4:12).

Still more evidence of the power of language is the frequency with which some books are banned. Book banning has a long history, and Christians have often led the call for censorship of reading. Famously censored are some of the great works of literature: Shakespeare's *Othello*, Mark Twain's *Huckleberry Finn*, Harriet Beecher Stowe's *Uncle Tom's Cabin* for their racial themes; James Joyce's *Ulysses* and Walt Whitman's *Leaves of Grass* for sexuality; or even Grimm's *Fairy Tales* for violence. Christians usually have good motives – to protect others from dangerous ideas – yet banning books deprives everyone of the opportunity to examine ideas and form independent opinions on their content. Ironically, the Bible itself is frequently banned.

There is no doubt that literature can be a positive, sustaining influence for Christian readers, yet some books can lead to what Veith describes as "vicarious sin"; that is, through reading, people vicariously experience the events being depicted in the work. In this way, a Christian can be led to sin – through titillating sexual fantasies, violent disregard for humanity, or other immoral subjects. The goal of good literature is to entertain and to instruct. The problem with bad literature is that bad books are simply bad – they have predictable plots, undeveloped characters, and they pander to prurient interests. There is a market for bad books; smut sells. However, even books judged as good literature may prove to be harmful if the content leads to vicarious sin.

How then, should a Christian judge a work of literature with questionable content? First of all, simply depicting a sordid element of life does not automatically lead to vicarious sin. There are many biblical stories that depict sin – from the sexual sin of David and Bathsheba to the violence of the passion of Christ. Reading these stories should inspire us to live better lives, not to sin vicariously or, more dangerously, to duplicate the portrayed sins in our own lives. In the same way, many literary stories reinforce biblical themes because they do show the dangers of sin. We can vicariously experience the temptation, the guilt of having committed sin, and perhaps even the release that comes from confession and redemption.

> **Personal Reactions to Literature**
> We should also recognize that our past experiences influence our responses to literature individually. One woman I know who experienced a sexual assault as a young woman cannot read any passage depicting sexual violence without the painful memories returning in a flood of emotion. Anyone who has watched a loved one die knows the emotion behind Dylan Thomas's lament "Do not go gentle into that good night" or the measured acceptance of Alfred Tennyson's "'Tis better to have loved and lost than never to have loved at all." However, young people who have not yet lived through the depths of grief rarely find similar comfort from Tennyson or Thomas.

Regular reading sharpens our abilities to read critically; thus, an inexperienced reader may not understand the aesthetic technique or purpose that generates a powerful response to a work from a more experienced reader. Too often, Christian critics will attack a work for its use of profanity, sexuality, or violence, without considering the real message of the book. In its goal to instruct, literature must often challenge us, asking us to question our unstated assumptions about life. For example, Frederick Douglass was born a slave, taught himself to read and write, and escaped from slavery.

Once freed, he wrote a narrative of his life as a corrective to the commonplace arguments of many pro-slavery men and women who declared the black slaves to be little more than animals – incapable of normal emotional ties to family, unable to live independently, and in need of constant discipline. Douglass chronicles the beatings, the humiliations, the sexual abuse of female slaves by their owners, and the tearing apart of slave families. His story has been criticized for its violence, and the book is violent. It is a difficult book to read. However, Douglass's truth-telling was influential in bringing people of his day to acknowledge truths about slavery and thus to bring public opinion toward the side of the abolitionists. Christian readers of the book today learn that many Christians in Douglass's time supported slavery, either through willful blindness to the inhumanity of slavery or through twisting Scripture to support the institution of slavery. We must learn always to be on guard against the dangers of popular opinion, even (or especially) in a democratic society.

UNDERSTANDING THE CHRISTIAN WORLDVIEW

Our worldview is most easily explained as the lens through which we view the world. However, it is far more complex than a simple lens. Our worldview contains our core values and beliefs, especially beliefs about what happens in the world and why. These core values and beliefs explain the world to us and thus shape our image of the world. They drive our behavior and actions in the world and our interactions with others. Our worldview gives us our purpose in life. It guides us as we set priorities.

Throughout time, believers in God have had conflict with other people whose explanations of God contrasted sharply with our own. Arthur F. Holmes describes the development of a monotheistic worldview among the Israelites. When Abraham left Chaldea for the promised land, the journey was an "act of faith in a God who called him to a markedly different view and way of life" (7). Similarly, the Israelites' flight from Egypt was more than an economic or political act; the migration sought to preserve their monotheistic view. In the Greco-Roman world of the New Testament, Holmes notes that Paul confronted mystics who "tried to find salvation by escape from physical and earthly involvements" (8). This error led to "the dualism of flesh and spirit" which "confused the meaning of good and evil" and affected "attitudes toward marriage, toward work, and toward social relationships in general" (8). Our beliefs about the world will influence our actions today as surely as in past centuries.

A worldview is rarely static. It is the product of many influences – our life experience, our culture, our family, and our ethnicity, our national politics. Worldview is the result of many influences, especially culture. Brian J. Walsh and Richard Middleton assert that cultural life is "not only *rooted* in the dominant world view; it also *orients* life in terms of that world view" (33).

> **Christians & Cultural Influence**
> *Christians should acknowledge the ways their lives are affected by their culture's beliefs regarding children, education, politics, marriage, economics, art, and more. Furthermore, our worldview may change over time as we mature through life experiences, reflect on national events or technological change, and practice a spiritual lifestyle.*

Differences in how one worldview compares with another can be subtle until one looks carefully at underlying beliefs. For example, conservative Christians and conservative Muslims share many assumptions about modesty, alcohol consumption, and dating, even though our beliefs about sacred texts differ radically. Thus, I could count on the family of one of my son's friends, members of the Ba'hai faith, to share our family rules about restrictions on movies our son was allowed to watch because of their conservative values. Our local zoo has an exhibit explaining the work being done to protect the environment and save endangered species. I, too, support most environmental issues. However, the language of the exhibit demonstrates that while the zoo and I have a shared response to the environment, our motives are completely different. The zoo exhibit argues that all species are equal and thus no one has a right to exploit one species for the benefit of another. In contrast, I see the underlying cause for my environmentalist attitudes due to biblical teachings that God created our world for us to be stewards. As in the parable of the vineyard, one day I will be held accountable for how I treated the creation. Thus we share similar responses to the problems of the environment, but from vastly different assumptions about the purpose of my work.

How does our worldview influence our reading? Our worldview drives our understanding of a text. In one of my college classes on multicultural literature, I start with a short story by a Native American author, Leslie Marmon Silko, called "Yellow Woman." In the story, a contemporary woman, married with a baby and extended family, leaves her home (voluntarily or under duress?) to spend three days with a stranger on the mountain in an adulterous relationship. At the end of the story, she returns to her family. For most of my students with a strong Christian worldview and little experience with non-Christian literature, the story makes no sense. They perceive little motive for Yellow Woman's behavior, nor do they comprehend the resolution at the end of the story. In class, we read about Native American legends, however, and discuss how the main character is reenacting the legend of Yellow Woman. In doing so, she reconnects to her past heritage and returns to her family with a renewed commitment to family tradition. The story shows my students the significance of our worldview in interpreting events, and that our assumptions of the world may vary considerably from other worldviews.

The first step in reading is to adopt Alan Jacobs' "hermeneutics of love" through "charitable reading." Jacobs posits that Christ's great commandment to love God and love your neighbor as yourself influences every human interaction, including reading. If we are to love our neighbor as God commands, then we must be willing to hear what our neighbor has to say and to understand who our neighbor is. Jacobs says, "the hermeneutics of love requires that books and authors, however alien to the beliefs and practices of the Christian life, be understood and treated as neighbors" (13). Further, Jacobs warns us that we should be humble when approaching a text because we are not gifted in the same way as the author nor had the same experiences as the author: thus, we must understand "the role that humility – or, to be more specific, an honest recognition of another's gifts – can play in reading. Surely such honesty and humility are necessary in a reader who would love God and her neighbor through the act of reading" (75). When we read literature in this way, we may be able to grow in our understanding of the gospel itself.

> **Literature & Its Influence**
>
> *How does our reading influence our worldview? Everything we read adds a layer to it. At times, our reading so transforms our ideas that it causes us to exchange one idea or layer of our worldview for another. We should never accept the idea that what we read is unimportant. However, limiting our reading to texts that we know in advance support our worldview will limit our development of a critical apparatus necessary to read with understanding. In other words, we must learn to be effective judges of what we read because reading is an essential element in developing our worldview.*

FOR FURTHER STUDY

Paul Cavill and Heather Ward, eds., *The Christian Tradition in English Literature* (Grand Rapids: Zondervan, 2007).

Hannibal Hamlin, *Psalm Culture and Early Modern English Literature* (Cambridge: Cambridge University Press, 2004).

WORKS CITED

Arthur F. Holmes, *Contours of a World View* (Grand Rapids: Eerdmans, 1983).

Alan Jacobs, *A Theology of Reading: The Hermeneutics of Love* (Boulder, Colo.: Westview, 2001).

Leslie Marmon Silko, *"Yellow Woman."* (ed. Melody Graulich; New Brunswick, N.J.: Rutgers University Press, 1993).

Gene Edward Veith Jr., *Reading between the Lines: A Christian Guide to Literature* (Wheaton, Ill.: Crossway, 1990).

Brian J. Walsh and J. Richard Middleton, *The Transforming Vision: Shaping a Christian Worldview* (Downers Grove, Ill.: InterVarsity, 1984).

CONTEMPORARY CONTEXTS
Religion & Science

Jennifer Thweatt-Bates

CHAPTER CONTENTS

The Good Times...& The Bad   93

Dialogue · A Therapeutic Enterprise   94

For Further Study   97

Works Cited   97

MAPS, TABLES, & FEATURES

Faith versus Science   94

I used to imagine religion and science as siblings, squabbling incessantly because they share the same rational living space. By this I meant to say that science and religion are two closely related – and therefore occasionally competing – ways of investigating and knowing the world. We accept squabbling siblings as a natural and inevitable reality, and so the image of science and religion as an arguing brother and sister does not bother us. Rather, it comes as a relief that no one is to blame for it – it is just the way things are. Ideological bloodshed is the norm.

But siblings grow up, and as they do, they learn how to get along without the incessant arguing that drives parents crazy. They learn how to communicate constructively, cooperate, and even appreciate their differences. Now we should explore the ways we can go beyond the relational model of conflict and enter a more constructive dialogue between religion and science.

The question is, then, how do we do this?

THE GOOD TIMES...& THE BAD

To understand any relationship, a sense of history is required. The history of the relationship between religion and science is much too long and complex to summarize here, but we can get a sense of the relationship's troubled history by briefly examining one of the more famous conflicts between religion and science: Galileo Galilei and the medieval Catholic church in the 17th century.

The censorship of Galileo Galilei and the suppression of the Copernican heliocentric (sun-centered) model of the universe is inarguably an example of the extreme form that the conflict between science and religion may take. The medieval church had adopted a geocentric (earth-centered) model of the universe, doing so with a consciousness of the importance of Earth as the place at which God saves creation (Southgate 27). This marriage of doctrine and science lasted until the first hint of trouble in 1543, when Nicolaus Copernicus' *De Revolutionibus* was published, challenging the geocentrism espoused by the church.

In the 1600s, when Galileo championed Copernicus's heliocentric cosmology, he did so believing that Christian faith and Copernicanism were compatible. Galileo's method of reconciling this new cosmology, this new picture of the universe, was multifaceted, but one of the most important elements in Galileo's position is the way he understood the Bible.

Galileo clearly subordinated accepted interpretations of Scripture to demonstrated truths of science. Galileo believed that Scripture had layers of meaning, or could signify truth in different ways. For instance, he argued that when Scripture refers to God's bodily parts, we know better than to think that God has a body. If the conflict in this case was the result of misinterpreting Scripture by taking the bare words too literally, then the key to resolution was a better understanding of Scripture. Galileo believed strongly that not only should old interpretations of biblical passages give way before scientific truth, but also that, in the end, the Copernican heliocentric universe was closer to the Bible than the old geocentric idea.

This way of understanding the Bible was not new or unique to Galileo. The idea that Scripture

> **Galileo on Science & Faith**
> In "The Letter to the Grand Duchess Christina," Galileo makes the case that "Scripture was given to show how to go to heaven, rather than how the heavens go" (Southgate 30). In asserting this, Galileo sought to separate the realm of science and the realm of faith.

> **Faith Versus Science**
>
> From our point of view, it may seem obvious that there is no advantage in a geocentric model of the universe in terms of biblical interpretation or Christian theology. But to the 17th-century mind, the shift in perspective required by Copernicanism would be something like the shift required of us today if we were to discover that there is indeed life on other planets. The heliocentric cosmological model espoused by Copernicus and Galileo seemed to question the accepted place of humanity in the universe.
>
> The adoption of the geocentric cosmology had not simply been an issue of the physical location and movement of heavenly bodies. It had been deliberately incorporated into Christian doctrine as proof that the relationship of God to humankind on Earth was the center of reality. Prying apart this belief from the geocentric model of the universe was not impossible, but it required the ability to see that the two could indeed come apart.
>
> The problem, then, is not that the Copernican model of the universe was in direct opposition to the Christian faith, or to Scripture, but rather in opposition to a previous scientific position that had been endorsed by the church as a foundation for their belief about the importance of the salvation of humankind as the story of the universe.

has layers of meaning, not all of them literal, has a long history reaching back to the earliest Christians. So, given that both the church and Galileo agreed on this principle of interpretation, an easy resolution to the conflict would seem to have been within reach. Yet no such resolution was found. This suggests that the conflict involved much more than the question of how to read the Bible in light of these new scientific findings. What was at stake was not just how to read the Bible but the theology driving the biblical interpretation.

DIALOGUE · A THERAPEUTIC ENTERPRISE

The story of Galileo offers us a clear picture of just how bad things can get. How might things have been different? How can we learn from this stellar example of how *not* to relate religion and science? It may be helpful at this point to take a step back and evaluate our options. Ian Barbour has offered the following list of the possible relationships between religion and science: conflict, independence, dialogue, and integration (Barbour 77–103).

CONFLICT

Conflict is unfortunately the most familiar type of relationship in many ways. The story of Galileo shows how extreme that conflict can become. Some – among them both scientists and Christian believers – clearly believe that an antagonistic relationship is the only possible one. This view is often the result of a particular way of reading the Bible but is equally often the result of a shallow and one-dimensional view of science, as well. For the sake of simplicity, let's label these views "biblicism" and "scientism." Both views claim that science and religion make opposing statements about the world and that one must choose between them.

Scientism is a label for the belief that science is the only reliable kind of knowledge we can have about the world, and that the kinds of realities science investigates (matter and energy) are the only really real things in the world. The preference for scientific knowledge comes from the sense that the scientific method produces objective, reproducible, universal results. Religion, on the other hand, is unprovable, untestable, and no one can agree on anything; science, therefore, seems clearly superior. However, the assumption that the only real things are material and observable by science goes beyond science itself into the realm of philosophy and metaphysics, or more simply, it is a claim of faith. It is, in fact, not too different from the kind of faith claims made by religion. Thus, conflict between science and religion is really conflict between *scientism* and religion – two competing faiths making opposing claims about the nature of reality.

All too often, scientism is accepted as the necessary scientific worldview, explicitly by (some) scientists and then by default by Christians. It then becomes the Christian task to refute science. This brings us to biblicism. Just as the scientific materialist uses science to make broad philosophical claims, the biblical literalist uses the Bible to make claims about scientific matters. One might say that one group tries to make science a religion, and the other tries to make religion science; both clearly misunderstand what science is and what it tells us about the world.

INDEPENDENCE

One way to resolve this conflict is to conceive of science and religion as two completely *independent* areas of thought – something along the lines of Galileo's proposal that Scripture is supposed to "show how to go to heaven, rather than how the heavens go." Clearly, religion and science differ a great deal in their goals, methods, and content; perhaps, the argument goes, they differ so much that no interaction is necessary or possible between religious beliefs and scientific knowledge.

The ease with which this solution suggests itself, however, should make us suspicious. Is it really the case that we can solve problems in religion and science by simply not dealing with them? If so, why is our religious history marked with this cycle of cozying up to, breaking up with, then making up with, science?

Independence, in the end, is a deceptively easy answer to the problem of conflict. Separation is impossible because of the very nature of human beings and the nature of human rationality or intelligence. Scientific materialism implies a very narrow view of rationality and therefore devalues religion because it falls outside this narrow definition. Independence does not challenge this view of rationality; instead, religion is spared conflict with science only by withdrawing into its own irrational corner. But rationality, we are discovering, is a much broader capacity than we may have thought. There is a sense in which all human activity is rooted in a basic kind of rationality, a "pre-analytic reasonableness," that influences all goal-directed action (van Huyssteen 22).

The phrase "pre-analytic reasonableness" suggests that rationality, though it can take analytic and logical forms, is not necessarily constituted by the kind of rigorous analysis one finds in science. Science is an expression of this more basic rationality, but it is no more rational than any other kind of human enterprise. It is a process of forming beliefs about the world and the nature of reality, which differs somewhat from other belief-forming processes in its specific methods and goals, but not in its basic rationality.

Science, like everything else, is done by people, and people always have preconceived ideas and theories about the world that affect how they conduct experiments and interpret data. Consider, for example, James Watson's comment from his first-person account of the discovery of the double helical structure of DNA: "science seldom proceeds in the straightforward logical manner imagined by outsiders. Instead, its steps forward (and sometimes backward) are often very human events in which personalities and cultural traditions play major roles" (Watson 13).

Just as science is no more rational than any other enterprise, religion is no less so. Religion, too, is a process of forming beliefs about the world, the nature of reality, and so on. When viewed in this way, the chasm of difference between science and religion narrows. This is not to say that science and religion are the same, but that they share a common resource in basic human rationality. This is why religion cannot ignore science – and, in fact, does not. Think about the internet rumors of finding Noah's ark on a mountain somewhere, or that scientists have found Joshua's "missing day" in their calculations. Why do these claims circulate? As human beings, we want to understand, and science is a powerful explanatory tool. In these instances, however misguided, the human impulse to understand and explain becomes evident.

INTEGRATION

This leads us to the possibility of *integration*. Integration of science and religion may sound far-fetched, the stuff of science fiction novels rather than a serious proposal for Christians in the real world. Certainly, some attempts to integrate religion and science have resulted in outcomes approaching the bizarre. Yet there have been serious attempts to integrate religious belief with scientific knowledge in a systematic way. For example, one common argument for the existence of God, the argument from design, was revitalized by Isaac Newton's idea of the universe as a giant law-abiding machine. Following Newton, Robert Boyle (known to chemistry students as the discoverer of Boyle's Law of Gases) famously likened the universe to a clock. This image was picked up later by William Paley, who proposed that the evident design of the universe implied a

> **Reason & Creativity**
>
> *As Watson describes the events that led to the discovery of the double helix, it is clear that not only did "personalities and cultural traditions" play a role, but also that Watson and Crick's preconceived notions about the structure of DNA led them into several dead ends before they stumbled upon the right answer.*

Designer, just as the design of a watch implies a watchmaker. The physical details of nature, they believed, revealed a God who was purposeful, inventive, and benevolent. This kind of "natural theology" assumes that God is evident in the natural world and can be discovered through science.

Integration can also take the form of a "theology of nature," beginning with religious convictions and harmonizing religious beliefs with scientific knowledge. This differs from "natural theology" in an important way. In the above example, science leads one to religion, not the other way around. Thus, in a way, science dictates what is reasonable to believe religiously. In a theology of nature, on the contrary, religious beliefs take center stage, and theology works to state these beliefs in ways that are consistent with science.

Finally, integration can also take the form of a synthesis of religious and scientific knowledge in a framework that encompasses both. One contemporary example of this kind of integration is process theology, which uses the process philosophy of Alfred North Whitehead as a means to bring together Christian beliefs and scientific knowledge. (Process theology assumes that God, humans, and other beings make choices that affect each other, and thus that God cannot fully control all events in the universe.) In these attempts at integration, both science and religion are subordinated to a controlling system of metaphysics. This may be an unattractive option to many Christians, because in the end, it requires faith in a system unrelated to Christian belief in order to achieve harmony with science. It may be that this strategy loses more than it gains.

At its most modest level, the project of integrating science and religion is simply a matter of wanting to embrace coherence. Yet, a word must be said here about the danger of overcommitment. Overcommitment invites subsequent conflict; permitting doctrine to piggyback on scientific knowledge is an unstable arrangement because of the nature of all human knowledge, including science.

> **The Dangers of Integration**
> *The conflict with Galileo could not have happened if the church had not previously wed itself to the scientific theory Galileo challenged. When faith finds science congenial, it is not wrong to acknowledge their fit, or what some have called "consonance," but it is unwise to take the further step of making religion dependent on that consonance.*

DIALOGUE

For this reason, it is the concept of *dialogue* that I find to be the most helpful of Barbour's options. Dialogue permits exchange in a way that acknowledges the integrity of science and religion as distinct sources of knowledge while insisting that they cannot remain strictly independent. This type of relationship strikes a balance between the necessary autonomy of individual disciplines and the holistic nature of the human search for understanding. In dialogue, science and religion are equal partners investigating areas of common interest: the natural world, human nature, and the question of how God acts in the world.

> **Challenges & Opportunities**
> *Taking science seriously does not mean that we must accept the overblown claims of scientism; in fact, one of the contributions religion can make to the dialogue is to challenge the uncritical acceptance of this philosophy. In our own turn, we also need to hear science's challenge of uncritical faith.*

But it is a little misleading to suggest that a single dialogue exists. In reality, there are dialogues between particular sciences and particular religions and theologies on particular topics. Conversations about human nature, for example, may engage biology, psychology, and anthropology, while conversations about nature may partner with physics and chemistry. The conclusions reached in these specific conversations may differ from each other, or there may be no conclusions reached at all. But this should be no surprise to theologians and Christians in general, who, after all, ought perhaps to be more sensitive to the limitations of human rationality than anyone else. Human reason is fallible, so all conclusions must be open to continued examination.

Finally, unpredictability in the dialogue between religion and science is a fact to be accepted, if the conversation is really to be genuine. As an English teacher in China, I was frequently frustrated with the ubiquitous scripted conversations in English textbooks. They were fine for classroom practice, but they in no way prepared students for the reality of live conversations in English with real foreigners. The truth is, not everyone answers "Fine, and how are you?" to the question, "How are you?" We cannot afford to ignore that dialogue brings with it the possibility of disagreement, if it is in fact an honest conversation. Yet there is a positive side to this as well: dissonance often opens the door for renewed investigation and creativity. It is only when conflict is assumed to be a permanent and inevitable condition that it becomes detrimental to dialogue, because the motivation to find resolution disappears.

Perhaps we do well to end with a prayer by Ingrid Schafer:

Prayer

*Let us give thanks for chaos and logos and
explicate, implicate, and superimplicate orders;
for black holes, bright galaxies, and nonlocal connections;
for crystals and continents;
for the emergence of mind and memes from matter;
for Lucy's skull and Mary Leakey's
footprints in volcanic ash; for Thales' water,
Heraclitus' fire, and Pythagorean music of the spheres
that choreographs
the elementary particle dance of Heisenberg's
fundamental symmetries;
for Aristotle's taxonomy and Bacon's idols;
for the Indian zero, algebra, and algorithms; for the
oscillations of the Yin and the Yang; for
acupuncture, Su Sung's astronomical clock, and
Huang Tao P'i's textile technology; for Arabic
alchemists on the Old Silk Road and Ibn Sina's
Canon of Medicine;
for Euclid and Newton and Einstein's space-time;
for Leonardo's bio-art and Rembrandt's
meditative merging of darkness and light;
for Kepler's snowflake and Kekule's dream;
for Mendel's monastery peas and the genetic
Tetragrammaton on the spiral staircase of life;
for fractals, ferns, and fall foliage; for
caterpillars and cocoons; for the infant's first
cry; for Pachelbel's Canon; for stained glass
windows, Leeuwenhoek's microscope, and the Galileo
probe; for Sheldrake's morphogenetic fields
of archetypal information exchange and Teilhard's
noogenetic vision of the emergent higher consciousness;
for the World Wide Web to help us become aware
of ourselves as co-creators of cosmic interconnectedness;
and most of all, let us give thanks for the twin passions
which make us fully human – the meaning-making
yearning to transcend the boundaries of time and space
by learning and by loving.*

FOR FURTHER STUDY

M. Eugene Boring, *Disciples and the Bible: A History of Disciples Biblical Interpretation in North America* (St. Louis: Chalice, 1997).

Edward J. Larson, "The Scopes Trial in History and Legend," in *When Science and Christianity Meet* (ed. David C. Lindberg and Ronald L. Numbers; Chicago: The University of Chicago Press, 2003), 245–64.

WORKS CITED

Ian Barbour, *Religion and Science: Historical and Contemporary Issues* (San Francisco: HarperCollins, 1997).

Christopher Southgate, ed., *God, Humanity and the Cosmos: A Textbook in Science and Religion* (Harrisburg, Pa: Trinity Press International, 1999).

J. Wentzel van Huyssteen, "Postfoundationalism in Theology and Science: Beyond Conflict and Consonance." *Rethinking Theology and Science: Six Models for the Current Dialogue* (ed. Niels Henrik Gregersen and J. Wentzel van Huyssteen; Grand Rapids: Eerdmans, 1998), 13–49.

James Watson, *The Double Helix: A Personal Account of the Discovery of the Structure of DNA* (New York: W. W. Norton, 1980).

CONTEMPORARY CONTEXTS
The Bible & Music

Gregory Straughn

CHAPTER CONTENTS

The Grammar of Music · Functions, Sounds, & Forms   99

Music in the Bible   100

Music from the Bible   101

Conclusion   105

For Further Study   105

Works Cited   106

Music has always played an important role in worship. The account of David calming Saul's evil spirit (1 Sam 16:14–23) is a particularly vivid testament to the power of music to change one's frame of mind. Yet, it is precisely this power that often places music in an awkward position when one examines its service in the church. Since the church was the primary sponsor of the creation of Western music, its development parallels the history of the church for almost 1500 years; and it was from the Bible, particularly the Psalms, that composers sought inspiration for setting this music. Before surveying this development, it is important to have a framework from which to examine music's power.

THE GRAMMAR OF MUSIC · FUNCTIONS, SOUNDS & FORMS

Music is a synthesis of many elements: melody, rhythm, tempo, and words all unite to create an art form greater than any of its individual parts. Music is also a twofold creative act: the composer conceives it, and musicians perform it. This double creation reflects God's own creative character, and as such, music can take any number of styles, forms, or sounds, reflecting the diversity of God's creation. Underneath this myriad appearance, music can act on its hearers in three broad dimensions: ecstatic, symbolic, and rhetorical. The ecstatic dimension of music entails an unconscious response (such as foot tapping or swaying) that is directly tied to the sound of the music. This is the kind of instinctual response that would have soothed Saul's spirit. The symbolic dimension of music signals ideas or theology that lie beyond the surface sounds. For example, the very act of congregational singing reflects the "harmonious arrangement [of]... the entire cosmos" (Wilson-Dickson 12). Finally, the ancient study of rhetoric was tied to the art of persuasion. Music's rhetorical ability lies in its synthesis of ecstatic and symbolic elements. Music can articulate for the hearer abstract ideas such as grief, longing, and awe in ways both subtle and profound, and it is this kind of emotional persuasion that defines much of the worship music of the last 150 years.

It is difficult to give an accurate description of what ancient music sounded like, since no written musical notation and very little description survives. Our knowledge of this music comes from later historical developments that can be retrofitted to match the physical artifacts we have available. Ancient music was primarily monophonic (with one musical line), though multiple singers or instrumentalists might perform this single line. Polyphony (with different melodies and rhythms sung simultaneously) did not develop until around 1000 CE. A form of polyphony that would define church music after 1500 is homophony, the movement of all the voices to the same rhythm. This is the basic plan for almost all of the traditional hymns sung in churches today.

The actual sound of ancient songs would have been radically different from that with which we are familiar. Even Jewish cantillation sung at synagogues today only partially represents the ancient sound. In a situation that parallels most Protestant churches, contemporary Jewish worship music is rooted in the sounds and styles of the mid- to late-nineteenth century. Ancient music would have made use of a variety of modes, arrangements of pattern of pitches to many different scales. The Greeks adapted and expanded this system in the half-millennium before Christ and imbued each mode with a kind of ethos said to effect one's mood. A system of eight modes was firmly in place during the first 1,600 years of the Christian church. After 1600, two modes were privileged over the rest. These became our major and minor scales. It has only been recently (in the last half century) that Christian church music has explored the possibilities of reusing the other modes in new compositions.

The transition from monophony to polyphony is often seen as Western civilization's most important contribution to musical development. While it is true that this transition increased music's level of complexity, that alone is not sufficient reason to negate solo singing in contemporary practice. Indeed, to use solo song would be to reclaim an ancient tradition.

MUSIC IN THE BIBLE

OLD TESTAMENT

In the thousand years that encompass the writing of the Old Testament, the sound, elements, and style of music did not change appreciably. What did change was its function, especially in the service of worship. The very few references to sung music in the Old Testament place it most frequently in the context of ritual, especially as songs of thanksgiving (Num 21:17–18). The songs of Moses (Exod 15:1–18), Miriam (Exod 15:21), and Deborah (Judg 5) are some of the earliest Hebrew examples of fully developed songs.

The Psalms formed what has been called the "womb of church music" (Westermeyer 23). They are the hymnal of the Old Testament, and their varied expression set the model for all church music to follow. The poetic structure of the psalms in parallel parts (couplets, or stichs) lead naturally to a balanced musical structure. The rhyming of ideas (though not of words) between the first and second half of the verse leads to an artistically pleasing presentation of the psalm, and this idea defined some of the earliest forms of psalmody. The Talmud gives explicit instructions for psalm singing in the temple and instructs for specific psalms to be sung on subsequent days of the week. This structure remains in place today in a variety of both Jewish and Christian forms.

None of the musical melodies for the psalms survive from biblical times; however, written accounts tell us that one of the most important features of the music was its intimate tie to the language. The synagogue practice of cantillation (the name for the heightened inflection of speech when declaiming in Hebrew) provides such an emphasis by allowing vertical (pitch-wise) and horizontal (length-wise) stretching of the notes (Sendrey and Norton 72–81).

Another key factor in musical emphasis was the addition of instruments to accompany the singing of the psalms. Instruments that would have been used in the temple services include a *kinnor* (a lyre), the *nevel* (like a kinnor, but lower), and the *halil* (a reed instrument like the two-reeded pipe). Outdoor wind instruments would have announced temple services and include the *shofar* (ram's horn) and the *magrepha* (a primitive type of organ). Percussion instruments such as cymbals, bells, and the *tof* (a small drum or castanet) would have also been used in temple worship (Sendrey and Norton 113–31).

> **Instrumental Music in Jewish Tradition**
> While synagogue practices did not require the use of instruments, they were prominent in temple worship and usually duplicated the cantillated line or added a decoration to it.

NEW TESTAMENT

Compared with the Old Testament, our knowledge of music in the New Testament is even less. Certainly, we can draw comparisons with earlier Jewish practices, especially in regards to the ordering and styles of the worship services, but very little is specifically mentioned in terms of style, practice, or sound. Throughout the Epistles, Paul exhorts the church to sing to the Lord. He then specifies "psalms, hymns, and spiritual songs" (Eph 5:19 and Col 3:16), a distinction that has opened up many interpretations over the last 2,000 years. It is clear that "psalms" refer to any of the canon of Old Testament Psalms. The modern definition of "hymn" later denoted a text in rhymed verses, but this structure did not exist in the first century. Writing in the late fourth century, Augustine defined hymns as "songs containing the praise of God" (McKinnon 158). Hymns might also refer to other sung portions of the Bible (the Christian canticles) excluding the psalms. The term "spiritual song" probably refers to spontaneous songs of praise given under the direction of the Holy Spirit (Wilson-Dickson 25). With this last form, Paul calls for a continuous renewal of Christian song rather than limiting it to preexisting forms. It should be noted, however, that scholars also view the three terms as interchangeable and as having connotative rather than denotative meanings. Retaining these ancient texts in modern times strengthens our connection to past Christian practices, as we see in the ancient hymns "Hail! Gladdening Light" and "Shepherd of Tender Youth."

Our understanding of music in the earliest Christian worship comes from sources one or two centuries later. Singing was common at meals in homes and at assemblies on the first day of the week, as the Roman governor Pliny noted in about 110 CE. Beyond that, very little is specified until the fourth century, by which time liturgical and musical practices had changed dramatically.

One of the most important distinctions the early church tried to make was a separation from pagan cults. To do this, the early church fathers vehemently opposed instrumental music and dancing. In the early third century, Clement of Alexandria exclaimed that "the irregular movements of auloi, psalteries, choruses, dances, Egyptian clappers and other such playthings become altogether indecent and uncouth ... [and lead to] a theater of drunkenness" (McKinnon 32). In the late fourth century, however, the view had changed: "We must not shun music because of the superstition of the heathen," Augustine writes, later adding, "citharas and other instruments ... might be of aid in comprehending spiritual things" (McKinnon 4–5).

MUSIC FROM THE BIBLE

CHRISTIAN ANTIQUITY & THE EARLY MIDDLE AGES

Worship in Christian antiquity grew from the psalms and canticles to included nonscriptural hymns, call-and-response acclamations, and two important three-part songs: the *Kyrie* ("Lord have mercy") and *Sanctus* ("Holy, Holy, Holy"). The last two would form the kernel of the most important form of Christian worship to develop in the early Middle Ages: the mass.

Central to the mass is the celebration of the Lord's Supper. Two large-scale cycles dictate the readings and music used to add propriety to the celebration: the Proper of the Saints (fixed days that commemorated the lives of famous church leaders) and the Proper of the Time (movable dates based on Easter and Christmas that celebrated the life of Christ). Virtually all of the texts for a given mass were sung, and while the mass used certain readings every day (the Ordinary), other readings (called Proper) were appropriate to a specific day in one of the cycles. These Proper texts were gathered from the Psalms or from newly created poetry that referenced a saint or an event.

> **Early Christian Music**
> For the first 1,000 years of the Christian era, music was performed with all voices singing one line. The most common way of performing chant was direct, or all voices singing together from start to finish. This style characterizes the Ordinary chants of the mass. To add variety to this uniformity of style, Proper chants were performed either antiphonally (with one choir alternating with another choir) or responsorially (with the choir alternating with a soloist). The question and answer structure of many of the psalms lends itself to this kind of sung performance.

The sung parts of the mass that appeared every day included: the *Kyrie* ("Lord have mercy"), the *Gloria* ("Glory to God in the highest"), the *Credo* ("the Nicene Creed"), the *Sanctus* ("Holy, Holy, Holy"), and the *Agnus Dei* ("Lamb of God"). In the Middle Ages, a limited number of tunes would have been used to set these texts, though later in history, composers vastly expanded the musical settings. Since musical notation did not exist in the early Middle Ages, the frequent repetition of these chants throughout the year helped stabilize and codify a standard body of chants used by churches in specific geographic regions.

HIGH MIDDLE AGES

The need for worship music precipitated two important musical developments that marked the transition to the high, or later, Middle Ages. The first was a notational system that could accommodate the growing repertoire of Gregorian chant. Though the earliest examples come from the late eighth and ninth centuries, notation did not firmly establish itself until the tenth century. The best hypothesis for the development of notation recognizes the growing need for a mnemonic system that would represent the shape of a given chant melody.

Aside from facilitating the move from an oral and fluid repertoire to one that was both fixed and more diverse, notation also permitted one of the most important textural developments in the history of music: composition for multiple voices, or polyphony. Around the end of the eleventh century, the chants for especially solemn days (like Christmas and Easter) were enhanced with a second part written a few notes higher but in strict parallel motion. This sound, characteristically medieval, was thicker and more sonorous than a single melodic line, and it did not take long (within 150 years) for most of the liturgical feast days to incorporate polyphony into their chanted services.

The development of notation allowed for both a greater number of chants and the polyphonic elaboration of any given of chant. At the same time, the text used for chants underwent a significant amount of change. Tradition ascribes the entire corpus of Gregorian chant to Pope Gregory I (540–604), who himself received the melodies from the Holy Spirit in the form of a dove. However, the historical evidence shows that the collection and codification took place almost a century later, in the early eighth century, during the papacy of Gregory II (715–731). While there can be no doubt that both popes were influential in organizing liturgical practices, there was still a great deal of variety among the major cities in Christendom. What was sung in Paris was not necessarily (or usually) heard in Milan, Rome, or Madrid.

The Carolingian Renaissance, as the period of Charlemagne's rule is sometimes called, witnessed the addition of increasingly poetic texts to the main collection of chants. One of the most important genres of this new poetic music was the Sequence. The music for Sequences grew out of the final syllable of the Alleluia chants, where a long string of notes was sung to the "-ia." Taking a simple structure of paired verses (AA BB CC, etc.), new words were placed over the existing melody, and the end rhymes of each verse help give it structure. The result was a well-liked chant style that was replicated thousands of times by the mid-sixteenth century, although by then both new words and music had been composed.

The early thirteenth century in Paris saw the creation of the next major musical genre. A combination of the symbolic dimension of texts with the liturgical elaboration of polyphony, the motet would remain a popular compositional medium for 650 years. The motet used a preexisting chant as its basis (usually the lowest sounding part), while newly written voices (music and text in various rhythms) were added above it. In this way, the original chant was privileged as authoritative, and any chant could accept this kind of elaboration, so long as none of its notes were changed.

By 1400, motets were no longer based on preexisting chants. Instead, they were newly composed throughout. In this respect, motets were one of the first polyphonic genres in Western music to be the inspiration of a single composer writing for a specific occasion. This modern idea – a single composer writing music for a specific event – is actually a late medieval concept, one that gained currency as a function of music in the context of worship.

THE RENAISSANCE

As might be expected, the humanistic perspectives of the Renaissance radically altered the shape of music in the fifteenth and sixteenth centuries. Though the forms of music were still the same

> **Charlemagne & Music**
> *The single most important person in the establishment and implementation of an "authoritative" chant body was the great Frankish King Charlemagne (742–814). His desire was to unify the newly established Holy Roman Empire with a "pure" chant that was true to its Roman source. In doing so, it would create consistency and uniformity from city to city throughout his empire (Westermeyer 102–10). To some extent he succeeded, though true worldwide codification would not come until the end of the nineteenth century as we see in the hymns "Of the Father's Love Begotten," "All Glory, Laud, and Honor," and "Jesus the Very Thought of Thee."*

> **Medieval Chant**
> *The very nature of the Sequence's rhymed poetry encouraged the growth of a symbolic dimension to chant texts. References to Mary, particularly as she was personified by flowers and other natural phenomena, numerological symbolism, and objects connected to Christ's life (such as the wood of the cross, nails, or sandals), were all frequent topics in later medieval chants.*

(chants, motets, and polyphonic masses), there was an increased secularization of these forms, and the church slowly began to lose its position as arbiter of musical innovation.

Central to all Renaissance composition was the polyphonic mass. More masses were composed during the two centuries of the Renaissance than any other time before or since. The primacy of the mass, with its unchanging text, gave composers an opportunity to explore more complex musical settings. Voices were expanded, both in range and in number; compositional devices such as canon (imitation of one voice by another), backwards canons, and upside-down canons regularly found their way into Renaissance masses (Douglas 58–64; Wilson-Dickson 72–77). A small-scale example of this kind of imitation is the seven-fold "Amen" from "The Lord Bless You and Keep You."

All of this complexity tended to obscure the worshipers' ability to hear and understand the words of the mass. What had once been the primary objective of church music – the clear delivery of text in a large space to be heard by many people – had now been usurped by musical concerns. This was true in another important aspect of Renaissance sacred music, the source on which masses and motets was based.

> **Motets**
> Early motets drew their melodic inspiration from preexisting chants. In the Renaissance, however, secular music, such as dance tunes or bawdy songs, became an increasingly frequent model for motets and masses. Thus a composer might write a six-part mass for a particular feast and base his melody on a drinking song.

THE REFORMATION

Many of the issues leading to the Reformation had direct connections to the use of music in worship: music had become more important than textual exegesis by the local priest; the complexity of the musical texture, plus its rigid adherence to archaic Latin, left most of the congregation unable to understand what was being sung; and congregational participation the service (specifically in the celebration of the Lord's Supper) was almost completely marginalized.

Redressing these concerns, Reformation musical practices sought to increase the importance of the sermon by lessening the overall amount of music heard in a service. Simultaneously, music was opened up to congregational participation, with its presentation in the vernacular and in simpler settings appropriate to congregational singing.

A much more severe reaction against Roman Catholic practices emerged with the Calvinist tradition. For at least a short time, both Calvin and his Zurich predecessor Ulrich Zwingli banned music completely from their services. Both would eventually restore music, though in a much more narrowly defined role. Calvin disbanded the choir and removed the organ in favor of *a cappella* congregational singing only. To promote good congregational singing, Calvin adopted a setting of the psalm texts in a metrical pattern – a series of short and long notes in which all the parts moved in the same rhythm (for example, "Praise God from Whom All Blessings Flow" and "God Himself is with Us"). The result was a collection of musical tunes that could be used to a number of different psalm texts, and this collection was printed as the *Geneva Psalter* in 1562. Calvin's historic distrust of music lead him to confine congregational singing to the 150 Psalms, noting that "Only God's Word is worthy to be used in God's praise" (Hustad 362).

While Calvin's ban on hymns was eventually loosened to include nonbiblical texts, the most lasting musical effect of his efforts was the adoption of metrical Psalm singing. In the newly formed Anglican church, leaders saw the benefits of this kind of congregational singing and quickly crafted a metrical translation of the Psalms in English. The

> **Martin Luther & Music**
> *Martin Luther, himself a musician, called for specific changes in musical practice in many of his early Reformation documents (Westermeyer 142–49). In the Deutsche messe (German mass) of 1526, he translated the Roman mass into German and provided folksong settings of the music appropriate for congregational singing. Luther's work with composer Johann Walter produced one of the first hymnbooks intended for wide distribution, the* Church Chorale Book *(1524), a collection of four- and five-part settings of simple tunes to popular devotional texts. Some of these include "A Mighty Fortress," "O Sacred Head," and "Now Thank We All Our God". Like Gregorian chants from the Middle Ages, Luther's chorales formed the basis of many more complex musical genres in succeeding centuries by composers such as Bach, Mozart, and Brahms.*

translator, Thomas Sternhold, was aided by the composer John Hopkins, who lent their last names to the Psalter – an edition that remained in use for over 250 years after its initial publication in 1562.

The Catholic church reacted to the Protestant Reformation with its own so-called Counter-Reformation, a move to correct all excesses of music and to restore a more balanced and blended form to fit its revised view of worship. Composers were urged to use only certain Latin texts and to free their settings from elaborate imitation and other musical devices that obscured the intelligibility of these texts. Over the next 200 years, the Catholic church reinvented the styles of music deemed appropriate for its worship, though the "Golden Age of Polyphony" (the designation given to those Counter-Reformation composers who sought the perfect balance of text and music) never lost its popularity.

REVIVALIST TRADITIONS

Metrical psalm singing was the most common form of music in Protestant churches throughout the late sixteenth, seventeenth, and early eighteenth centuries. The revivalist tradition, whose devotionalist stance stressed a personal relationship with God, relied upon the ease, interchangeability, and familiarity of these tunes and texts to form its worship music. Indeed, what distinguishes Isaac Watts's texts from those of Calvin's era is the frequency with which Watts uses the first person: for example, "Come, We that Love the Lord" and "When I Survey the Wondrous Cross."

The camp meetings and revivals that characterized the spread of Christianity throughout America in the nineteenth century frequently employed simple, highly emotional, and repetitious hymns that were improvisatory or folk-like in nature (such as "Come to Jesus" and "Give Me That Old Time Religion"). Like the Wesleyan hymns, these songs tended to stress personal involvement with salvation and a constant petition for grace. The majority of "invitation songs" comes from this time period and reflects these two primary concerns. In the 1840s, when the evangelistic thrust of these campaigns began to center on children, the Sunday school movement was born. This yielded a number of important trends that defined church music for the remainder of the century: simple songs with catchy melodies and a mandatory refrain (coined a "gospel song" by Philip Phillips); singing schools designed to teach these songs; and a system of shaped notes used to facilitate music reading at sight.

All of these elements were present in the important campaigns lead by Dwight L. Moody and his lead musician Ira D. Sankey. Together, they traveled throughout America and England in a barnstorming evangelism characterized by large crowds, frequent singing, and large-scale invitations. A similar plan was adopted by Billy Sunday and Homer Rodeheaver in the early twentieth century and was continued by Billy Graham and Cliff Barrows in the 1950s and 1960s (Eskew and McElrath 196–205). While each generation contributed its own theological, poetic, and musical tastes to the sound of their gospel songs, a great deal of homogeneity exists between the music and lyrics from the 1860s through the 1960s. Compare, for example, "Softly and Tenderly" (Will Thompson, 1880) and "He Touched Me" (Bill Gaither, 1963), which share a similar melodic contour, including the opening phrase and an "echo" effect in the chorus, as well as an intensely personal character in their texts.

Radio, and later television, in the mid-twentieth century created a constant demand for new music that could accompany evangelistic programming. Several groups created a self-perpetuating cycle of songbooks and professional gospel quartets that would promote this new music. Among the most successful was the Stamps-Baxter Music and Printing Company, whose more than 200 paperback hymnals contain over 10,000 songs. Squarely in the tradition

---

Isaac Watts & the Wesleys

Watts's contemporaries, John and Charles Wesley, have often been credited with freeing church music from the bonds of metrical psalmody. Their musical sources broke from the common meters used for over a century to include folksongs, opera melodies, and their own original melodies (such as "Come, Thou Almighty King," "Christ the Lord Has Risen Today," and many others). The freedom and popularity found in these new tunes led to the quick adaptation of Wesleyan hymns in the various revivals happening in England and America, and the songbooks associated with the Great Awakening of the late eighteenth century contained mostly Watts's and Wesleyan hymns. Combined, these three hymn writers covered almost every aspect of the Christian devotional life, and in this way they can be seen as the foundations of the modern gospel song (Bailey 48–62, 82–88).

of the late nineteenth century gospel songs, Stamps-Baxter songs employ highly descriptive language to express an especially sentimental view of the Christian life, as in, for example "Paradise Valley" or "No Tears in Heaven."

LITURGICAL REVIVALIST TRADITIONS

Two major trends in worship renewal track throughout the twentieth century, and both have significantly impacted Christian music: liturgical renewal and multicultural worship. The former grew out of the Oxford Movement in England at the turn of the century. In an attempt to revive ancient liturgical traditions, scholars and theologians translated early Christian prayers and hymns into modern English for use with congregations. The result produced two important collections of music: *Hymns Ancient and Modern* (1862) and the *English Hymnal* (1906). Along with ancient music and texts such as "O Come, O Come, Emmanuel," compilers included traditional English folksongs melodies (for example, "Be Thou My Vision") as a way to connect the liturgical community with the local communities these hymnals served (Westermeyer 273–80).

> **Liturgical Revival**
>
> The trend toward liturgical revival continued in the late twentieth century with movements based in Taizé, France and Iona, England. The simplicity of their music (a good example is "Jesus, Remember Me") and brevity of their texts (usually a pair of phrases to make one sentence) makes them easily repeated, and as such, they capitalize on the ecstatic and rhetorical aspects of music's grammar.

The trend toward including non-Western elements in Anglo-European and American worship began in the late nineteenth century with the inclusion of Negro spirituals in printed hymnals. A reflection of slaves' interpretations of camp meeting songs, spirituals were rooted in biblical images of liberation (see "Go Down, Moses" and "My Lord, What a Morning"). After the abolition of slavery, black gospel music developed in a similar course to its white counterpart. Tunes were memorable, and texts, while often expressing heightened emotions, frequently engaged feelings of distress and the need for divine help (such as in "Stand By Me" or "Take My Hand, Precious Lord," Wilson-Dickson 191–95).

The charismatic immediacy of black gospel music is a vital part of, and is well represented in, the Western hymnic tradition. In the last quarter century, African hymns, along with songs from east Asia, South America, and Latin America, have increasingly found a presence in North American hymnals. A testament to the spread of Christianity throughout the world, these songs often incorporate one or more verses in the original language along with English translations such as "*Somos uno en Cristo*" ("We Are One in Christ") or "*Ososo*" ("Come Now)."

CONCLUSION

The history of music in the service of Christian worship brings together many disparate and complex elements. Indeed, the history of music is itself bound inextricably with the history of the church for almost 1,500 years. Throughout this mutual development, and over the past half millennium as well, church music has struggled to maintain the careful balance between biblical truth and aesthetic worth. In the era of Watts and Wesley, poetry examined a single aspect of this truth with an infinite variety of images (for example, the idea of majesty in "God Moves in a Mysterious Way"). In the nineteenth century, a single image illustrated a number of different biblical principles (such as the love of Christ, his sacrifice, and his will as manifest in his name in "Oh, How I Love Jesus"). In the late twentieth century, poetic amplification frequently gave way to scriptural paraphrase, leaving the singer (or the context of other songs) to provide thoughtful commentary (for example, "As the Deer" [Ps 42:1–2] or "We Shall Assemble" [Ps 24:3–6]). Whatever form its metaphorical or allegorical dimension might take, the best hymns amplify some aspect of the biblical narrative and combine it with ecstatic, symbolic, or rhetorical musical elements. The result is a form of worship that withstands countless repetitions, each of which will embed itself into the heart and mind of the singer.

FOR FURTHER STUDY

Frank Burch Brown, *Good Taste, Bad Taste, and Christian Taste* (Oxford: Oxford University Press, 2000).

Donald P. Hustad, *Jubilate! Church Music in the Evangelic Tradition* (Carol Stream, Ill.: Hope, 1981).

THE BIBLE & MUSIC

———, *Jubilate II: Church Music in Worship and Renewal* (Carol Stream, Ill.: Hope, 1993).

James McKinnon, *Music in Early Christian Literature* (Cambridge: Cambridge University Press, 1987).

David W. Music, *Hymnology: A Collection of Source Readings* (Lanham, Md.: Scarecrow, 1996).

WORKS CITED

Albert Edward Bailey, *The Gospel in Hymns* (New York: Scribner's, 1950).

Winfred Douglas, *Church Music in History and Practice* (New York: Scribner's, 1962).

Harry Eskew and Hugh T. McElrath, *Sing with Understanding* (Nashville: Church Street, 1995).

Donald P. Hustad, "Music of the Reformation," in *The Complete Library of Christian Worship*, vol. 4: *Music and the Arts in Christian Worship* (ed. Robert E. Webber; Nashville: StarSong, 1994), 221–27.

James McKinnon, *Music in Early Christian Literature* (Cambridge: Cambridge University Press, 1987).

Alfred Sendrey and Mildred Norton, *David's Harp* (New York: New American Library, 1964).

Paul Westermeyer, *Te Deum: The Church and Music* (Minneapolis, Minn.: Fortress, 1998).

Andrew Wilson-Dickson, *The Story of Christian Music* (Minneapolis, Minn.: Fortress, 1996).

Genesis

R. Christopher Heard

CHAPTER CONTENTS

Contexts **107**

Commentary **108**
- An Account of Creation · 1:1–2:4a **108**
- The Garden of Eden · 2:4b–3:24 **110**
- The Story of Cain · 4:1–16 **112**
- Antediluvian Genealogies · 4:17–5:32 **112**
- Humanity's Degradation · 6:1–8 **113**
- The Flood · 6:9–9:17 **113**
- Noah After the Flood · 9:18–28 **115**
- The Table of Nations · 10:1–32 **115**
- The Tower of Babel · 11:1–9 **115**
- From Shem to Abram · 11:10–32 **116**
- Abraham & His Children · 12:1–25:18 **116**
- Isaac & His Children · 25:19–36:43 **126**
- Jacob & His Children · 37:1–50:26 **132**

Theological Reflections **138**

For Further Study **140**

Works Cited **140**

MAPS, TABLES, & FEATURES

- An Ancient Near-Eastern Model of the Cosmos **109**
- Genesis 1 & Modern Science **110**
- Ancient Near-Eastern Flood Stories **114**
- The Nations of Genesis 10 **116**
- Abram's Migration to Canaan **117**
- Sacrificing Isaac **124**
- Jacob's Travels to Paddan-Aram **128**
- Jacob's Travels to Esau **130**
- Joseph & Egyptian History **135**
- The Twelve Tribes **137**

Genesis opens with stories about God's interactions with all humanity, then focuses on Israel's earliest ancestors – Abraham, Isaac, and Jacob. Although often mined for children's stories, Genesis challenges all readers, unashamedly presenting Israel's beloved ancestors as fully human, flawed, and sinful, yet deeply engaged in God's activity.

CONTEXTS

Scholars call Genesis 1–11 the "primeval narratives," indicating that these stories treat humanity's most distant past. A panoramic account of creation (chapter 1) introduces the book, followed by a second account focused more tightly on human beings in the Garden of Eden (chapters 2–3). The story of Cain and Abel (chapter 4) leads into a pair of genealogies (chapters 4 and 5). The longest sustained primeval narrative concerns the great flood, with its antecedents and its aftermath (chapters 6–9). Genesis 10, "the table of nations," relates various ancient peoples to Noah's sons. Finally, the tower of Babel story brings readers into the more familiar world of diverse languages and nations. Terah's genealogy bridges the book's two major sections.

Focusing on Abraham's family and immediate descendants, chapters 12–50 constitute the "ancestral narratives." The Abraham stories, including his migration from Mesopotamia, his journeys in and outside Canaan, and his relationships with his wives and children, occupy most of chapters 12–25. Chapter 25 introduces Jacob's story, while chapter 26 briefly features Isaac. Chapters 27–36 focus on Jacob's conflicts with Esau and the growth of Jacob's family. With an interlude about Judah in chapter 38, chapters 37–50 tell Joseph's story. Some scholars see this last section as a separate unit, calling it the "Joseph narrative."

A series of *generations* [Hebrew *toledoth*] notices divides the book into ten or eleven sections of unequal length. The NIV translates *toledoth* as *account* in the phrase *This is the account of...* (normally followed by a person's name).

Genesis does not stand alone. The narrator assumes readers' familiarity with many of the characters and places named in the book. Moreover, Genesis begins

> **Toledoth**
> *The* toledoth *notices mention heaven and earth (Gen 2:4), Adam (Gen 5:1), Noah (Gen 6:9), Noah's sons (Gen 10:1), Shem (Gen 11:10), Terah (Gen 11:27), Ishmael (Gen 25:12), Isaac (Gen 25:19), Esau (Gen 36:1, 9), and Jacob (Gen 37:2). Some* toledoth *sections include only genealogies; others feature long narratives.*

a story that continues into Exodus, and indeed through the end of 2 Kings.

Like any narrative, Genesis has its own characters, settings, and plot twists. Poetic fragments appear when these serve to advance the plot. Thus the primary skill readers need to make sense of Genesis is attentiveness to the storyline. However, Genesis also includes several specialized genres, each with distinct characteristics.

Blessings and curses usually appear as poetry. A blessing or curse pronounced by God (as in Gen 3:14–15) announces that something good or bad will happen. People, too, can bless or curse (as Isaac blessing Jacob, Gen 27:27–29), but human blessings and curses constitute wishes or prayers that God will bring about certain things.

Genealogies serve important functions in Genesis. Most simply, they link episodes from different time frames into chronological sequence. Genealogies also express ancient understandings of interrelationships between Israel and other peoples. Other biblical genealogies verify eligibility for kingship or priesthood, but Genesis's genealogies do not serve this function.

Brief itineraries – lists of places Israel's ancestors traveled – appear sporadically (for example, Gen 13:1–4). Itineraries link geographically diverse stories into meaningful sequences.

Most individual episodes within Genesis may be labeled "stories." Some specialists in literary genres distinguish among "stories," "tales," "sagas," "legends," and such, but these fine distinctions help little in understanding Genesis. However, two special types of stories deserve attention.

"Etiologies" explain the origin of a custom, practice, or name. Genesis contains few pure etiologies but includes numerous etiological comments. For example, the story of Jacob's wrestling match (Gen 32:22–32) is not chiefly about diet (Gen 32:32), but the narrator does add an explanatory note on that topic. Many etiological comments in Genesis explain personal and place names.

Some etiologies, called "cult stories," describe how certain places became worship or cultic sites. Genesis repeatedly describes Israel's ancestors building altars or receiving divine revelations at certain places. Perhaps the most famous such story in Genesis derives from the theophany, or visible appearance of God, at Luz, which then becomes Bethel, "house of God" (Gen 28).

COMMENTARY
AN ACCOUNT OF CREATION · 1:1–2:4A

1:1–2 The NIV follows the traditional English rendering *in the beginning God created*, implying that God created the *formless and void* earth, then ordered and shaped it. This rendering fits Western philosophical notions of creation "out of nothing" (*ex nihilo*). However, creation of a chaotic earth would jar an ancient Near Eastern reader, who would understand creation as the taming and ordering of chaos (Isa 45:18). The translation *When God began to create* (JPS, NRSV) better fits ancient perspectives. God acts on a *formless and void* earth, an undifferentiated mass of waters (*the deep*). *Formless and void* together mean "uninhabitable" (compare Isa 34:11). The terminology suggests an original chaos from which God orders the universe.

> **The Spirit of God**
> In the NIV, Spirit of God *implies a Christian understanding of the "Holy Spirit" unknown to Genesis's author and earliest readers. In the Old Testament, "God's spirit" roughly equates to "God's power," and is not an independent divine personality. Hebrew* ruach *(NIV "Spirit") includes the senses "wind" and "breath," both almost always representing the Hebrew usage better than the translation "spirit." In Genesis 1:2, God's* ruach *is the same sort of "wind" God uses to disperse the floodwaters in Genesis 8:1 (Orlinsky).*

1:3–5 God's first few acts of creation differentiate opposites, beginning with darkness and light. The existence of sourceless light and the rotation of evening and morning without sun and moon to mark time's passage form a literary, not a scientific, pattern. Throughout Genesis 1, God creates by commanding. Here, God commands light to exist, and the previously nonexistent light obediently appears. The account thus depicts God as a cosmic king, commanding obedient subjects.

1:6–8 The NIV's *expanse* implies a large empty space, but the Hebrew term *raqia'* implies a physical object. "Dome," or even *firmament* (KJV), better expresses the image. The *water under the expanse* will become the sea; ancient readers would have understood the *water above it* as the source of precipitation (see Gen 7:11).

1:9–13 *Dry ground* likewise emerges through differentiation, as the *waters* obediently gather

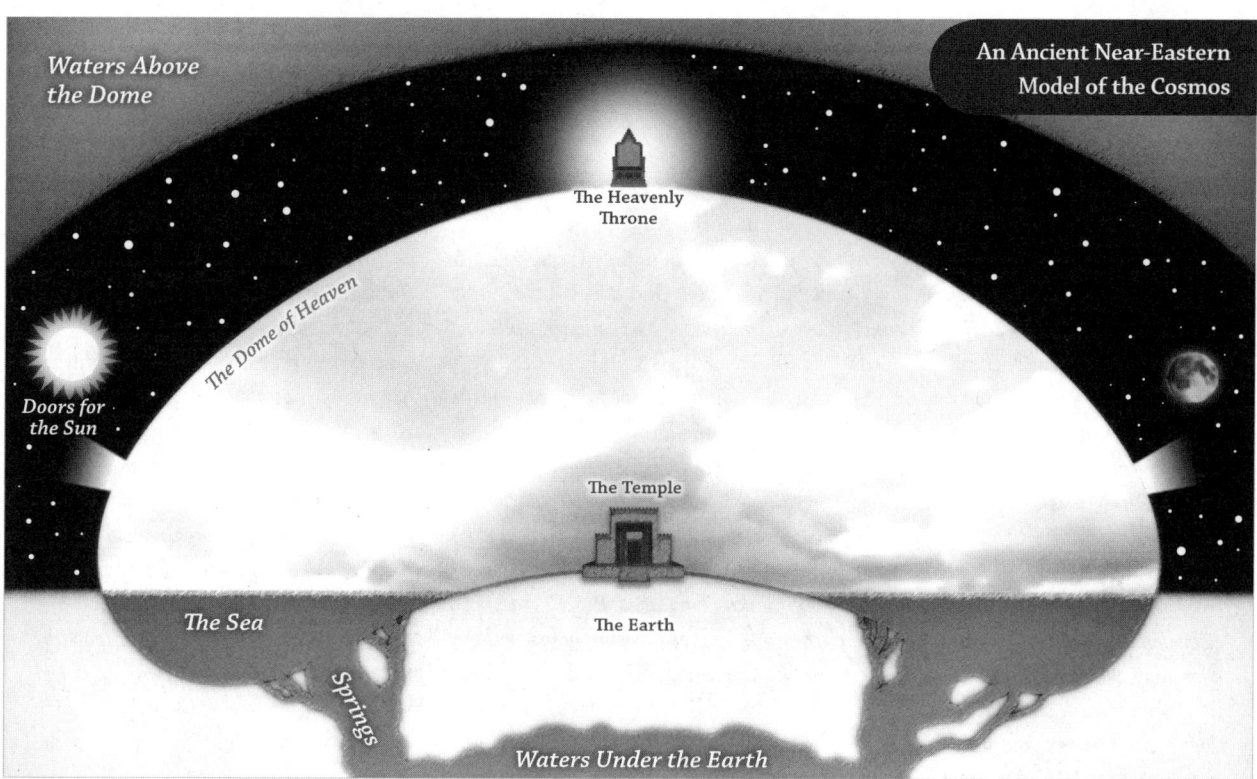

An Ancient Near-Eastern Model of the Cosmos

together, exposing dry ground. Notably, rather than creating vegetation directly, God commands the dry ground to produce vegetation.

1:14–19 On the first three days, God forms various habitats; on the fourth through sixth days, God fills them with appropriate inhabitants. Thus, *the lights in the expanse of the sky*, created on the fourth day, inhabit (in a sense) the light. God charges the lights to *govern the day and the night*, not "ruling" (as if they were gods) but "regulating" time's flow.

1:20–25 *Sky* and *sea* next receive inhabitants, followed by land. Again, God commands and creation obeys. The narrator means the same thing by saying that *the land produce[d] living creatures* (obeying God's command, verse 24) and that *God made* those creatures.

1:26–30 Although grammatically plural in Hebrew, the term for *God* often takes singular verbs and pronouns in the Hebrew Bible, testifying to biblical writers' belief in the singularity of God. Here, however, plural pronouns and verbs appear. God's use of the plural suggests a king addressing a royal – here, divine – council. Several biblical passages (for example 1 Kgs 22:19–23; Job 1:6–12; Ps 82) depict God as a king attended by a council of *sons of [the] god[s]* or simply *gods*. Genesis 1 stresses the function of the *image of God* in humans more than its nature. Humans represent God on earth, *rul[ing] over* other creatures. In this idyllic scene, *everything that has the breath of life in it* eats only *every green plant*, not another creature's flesh.

1:31–2:3 God recognizes each day's work as *good*. The sixth day ends with God's evaluation of *all that he had made* as *very good*, the added emphasis drawing the overall presentation toward its close. God then blesses and sanctifies the seventh day by resting. God's rest implies victory, not fatigue, and shows God to be the unchallenged divine king of heaven and earth (Batto 78).

2:4A This sentence marks part of Genesis as *the account of the heavens and the earth when they were created*. The Hebrew verb *bara'* – used in Genesis only to describe God's creative activity – here and in 1:1 links the two verses as bookends. Here alone, the formula *this is the account of* concludes rather than introduces the section it governs.

The Mesopotamian, Egyptian, and Hebrew cosmologies, or descriptions of the physical world, were all very similar, each depicting a three-tiered world. Humans and animals live in the middle tier, bounded above by sky (understood as a solid object holding back water, except when opened to allow precipitation) and

Genesis 1 & Modern Science

Surface differences between Genesis 1 and modern science generate much controversy. Christians hold many opinions on the biblical and scientific descriptions of terrestrial origins. Only a few important points can be addressed here.

Literalistic readings of Genesis 1 preclude scientifically assessed geologic time. Some Christians think the Bible, read literally, must be correct, and modern science must be wrong. However, the Hebrew Bible contains three distinct models of creation. In Genesis 1, God creates by commanding an obedient cosmos, in Genesis 2 by crafting human beings and animals from soil, and in Psalm 74:12–17 and elsewhere, by (or only after) defeating the monster Leviathan or Rahab. One cannot take all three models literally, because they do not blend harmoniously. A literal reading trims down biblical creation faith.

Readers should not overlook God's use of intermediate creative agents. In Genesis 1, God does not directly create plants, sea life, and land animals, but commands the obedient land and sea to produce these things (verses 11, 20, 24). This is how God created the giant creatures of the sea (verse 21) and God made the wild animals (verse 25). A literal reading does not rule out scientific theories, if the latter explain how land and sea obeyed God.

Some Christians try to reconcile the Genesis chronology with geological time. The "day-age theory" casts the "days" of creation as long ages. Proponents note that one cannot measure hours without the sun, nonexistent before the fourth "day." Moreover, "day" is as flexible in Hebrew as in English, denoting twenty-four-hour periods, eras, or indeterminate time periods.

The "gap" or "ruin-restoration" theory posits a "time gap" between Genesis 1:1 and 1:2. Since Isaiah 45:18 claims God did not create the world to be empty, while Genesis 1:2 describes it as formless and empty, proponents think the earth became formless and empty between two creative episodes. Advocates differ about the mechanism but agree that this gap of unnarrated time allows the earth to age in accordance with the geological record.

Some consider such theories unnecessary. These approach Genesis 1 as a theological discourse crediting Israel's God – and no other – with drawing an orderly world from chaos. Such readers may accept many aspects of modern science, if God receives credit for starting and superintending the processes science describes.

---

below by ground and sea. Still lower lies the underworld, including underground oceans (*springs of the great deep*, Gen 7:11) and Sheol (where the dead stay).

The Mesopotamian story *Enuma Elish* (Hallo and Younger 1:390–402) begins, like Genesis 1, with watery chaos. In *Enuma Elish*, however, the chaos is itself two gods, Tiamat and Apsu, "their waters commingling as a single body." From this union, Tiamat bears new gods. The elder and younger gods clash, until a third-generation god, Marduk, attacks Tiamat and her allies. After killing Tiamat, Marduk creates the three-tiered world, using half of her body to create the sky and half to create the earth. Marduk mixes the blood of another elder god, Kingu, with dirt to create human beings as agricultural serfs to reduce the gods' workload.

While the Genesis and *Enuma Elish* cosmologies have some similarities, the stories' theologies differ widely. Genesis 1 omits any story of the birth of the gods because Israel only knows one God. Modern readers of Genesis 1, surprised by the presence of the primordial watery chaos at the beginning of creation, may ask, "Where did the chaos come from?" Ancient Near Eastern readers would find the idea of chaos routine, but would ask, "Where did God come from?" The lack of conflict in the creation story would surprise them. In Genesis 1, God need not fight the chaos to create the world. God simply commands, and the chaos obeys. By introducing God as a king who commands primordial chaos, Genesis 1 departs sharply from its Mesopotamian counterpart (but see Job 26:7–14; Ps 74:12–17; 89:9–12).

Egyptian religion likewise produced multiple creation stories. The Memphite Theology (third millennium BCE; Hallo and Younger 1:21–23) and Genesis 1 both feature a god creating through speech who rests after creating. However, the Memphite Theology emphasizes Ptah's creation of the nine chief gods. Genesis 1 has no such story.

THE GARDEN OF EDEN · 2:4B–3:24

2:4B–7 The sequence of events marks the chapter as an independent account of humanity's creation, not "day six" in more detail. Here, God creates *the man* when *no shrub of the field had yet appeared on the earth and no plant of the field had yet sprung up*; in Genesis 1, plants precede humans. Genesis 2:5 specifies that vegetation had not yet appeared, precisely because *there was no man to work the ground*. By creating *the man*, God supplies one of the earth's basic needs: a caretaker. The text emphasizes the connection between the man [Hebrew *'adam*] and the earth [Hebrew *'adamah*].

2:8–9 Attempting to reconcile the Genesis 2 sequence with Genesis 1, the NIV implies that *the Lord God had planted a garden in the east, in Eden*, before creating the man. In the Hebrew syntax, however, the planting follows human creation. The extraordinary properties of *the tree of life* and *the tree of knowledge of good and evil* are described later. All other trees are *pleasing to the eye and good for food*, supplying basic human needs just as the man supplies their need for caretaking.

> **The Rivers of Eden**
>
> *The Tigris and Euphrates rivers define Mesopotamia. No river separates to form these two; they originate separately in Armenia, converging as they flow into the Persian Gulf. The narrator locates the otherwise unknown* Pishon *in* Havilah, *somewhere between Canaan and Egypt (Gen 25:18; 1 Sam 15:7). A spring outside Jerusalem bears the name* Gihon *in 1 Kings, but here the* Gihon *flows in the land of Cush,* usually Ethiopia. *No known headwater separates into rivers running through Mesopotamia, northern Sinai, and Africa. This conundrum spurs some attempts to relocate* Havilah *and* Cush *nearer the Persian Gulf, but such attempts imply that Genesis 2 uses place names differently from the rest of the Bible. The author hardly intends to help readers locate Eden geographically.*

2:10–14 The description of the *four headwaters* cannot be located on a map.

2:15–17 Without the man's help, verse 5 implies, the garden would wither. Reciprocally, every *tree in the garden* nourishes the man. Of all these, only one tree's fruit is off-limits. God's proclamation that the man *will surely die* upon eating fruit from *the tree of the knowledge of good and evil* institutes a penalty for violating the prohibition rather than describing some inherent property of the fruit.

2:18–24 The NIV attempts to reconcile Genesis 1 and 2 by casting verse 19 as a flashback, but the Hebrew syntax places the animals' creation *after* God's decision to *make a helper* for the man. *Suitable* is usually a geographical or architectural term denoting a counterpart or mirror image. This specification belies any attempt to read inferiority or superiority into *helper*.

The narrator does not clarify why God brings the animals to the man for naming. *No suitable helper was found*, but as God surely realizes, no animal will correspond to the man. This task is not trial and error. Perhaps the narration builds readers' anticipation, or perhaps God intends to build the man's anticipation, or both. The man's isolation ends when God *took part of the man's side* (NIV margin; *rib* is too specific) and *made a woman*. The *one flesh* saying underscores the isolated man's prior incompleteness.

2:25 Biblical writers normally consider shameless nudity to be foolish or immature. The narrator passes no explicit judgment but probably does not consider this state worthy of emulation.

3:1–5 Identification of *the serpent* as Satan (or Satan's agent), common among Christians, contradicts the text's explicit location of the serpent among *the wild animals the Lord God had made*. Genesis knows of no malevolent quasi-deity opposed to God. The narrator does not reveal the serpent's motive.

3:6–7 The desire for *gaining wisdom* (other trees are also *good for food and pleasing to the eye*, 2:9) persuades the woman and *her husband, who was with her*, to eat. The serpent's claim finds partial confirmation, as the humans' *eyes* are *opened* to their nudity.

3:8–15 The serpent's punishment resembles an etiology for enmity between humans and snakes. Christians often read verse 15 with reference to Christ defeating Satan, but the text does not support this interpretation. The verse does not depict humans defeating serpents. In temporal sequence, human crushing of snakes' heads *causes* (it does not *answer*) snakebites; the crushing precedes the striking.

3:16 Despite the NIV and most English translations, God increases the woman's "toil and pregnancies," not *pains in childbearing* (Hebrew uses different terms for pregnancy and parturition). The pronouncement concerns the multiplication of pregnancies in an agrarian lifestyle rather than physical pain at childbirth. Both woman and man will experience *pain*[*ful toil*]: both must struggle to extract food from an uncooperative earth (verses 17–19), and this toil does not abate during pregnancy (Meyers, *Discovering Eve*, 95–121).

3:17–19 God curses *the ground*, but the man feels the brunt of the curse. The man's eventual *return to the ground* does not enact God's original death threat. God had told the man that death would occur *when you eat of it* (2:17), allowing little room for delay. Continued life, however bleak, represents a stay of execution. God foregoes the stated penalty, applying less severe sanctions instead.

3:20–24 By expelling the couple, God seeks to prevent them from acquiring immortality. God's statement, *the man has now become like one of us, knowing good and evil*, confirms the serpent's claims. The humans have taken on the ability, previously reserved for divinity, to make value judgments. God's concern that the humans might *take also from the tree of life and eat, and live forever* implies both that they had not yet done so and that they were mortal all along. The angelic guard prevents any subsequent bid for immortality. After all this, the humans' vocation remains *to work the ground*. God's original purpose for humans remains intact, though they must pursue that purpose under catastrophically modified conditions.

THE STORY OF CAIN · 4:1–16

4:1–5 The humans cannot achieve individual immortality; humanity's survival depends on reproduction.

Cain and Abel (in that order, verses 3–4) each bring *an offering to the Lord*. God's unequal reception of Cain's and Abel's offerings leads many readers to wonder why. The phrases *some of the fruits of the soil* and *fat portions from some of the firstborn of his flock* do not clearly mark Cain's offering as inferior to Abel's. Similarly, the narrator nowhere implies that Cain brings his offering grudgingly or with any attitudinal defect. The narrator actually implies that the offerings were Cain's idea: he brings his offering first, without any divine prompting. The narrator simply does not explain God's disregard for Cain's offering. Cain's anger and depression suggest that he, at least, cannot perceive any reason for God's discrimination.

4:6–7 The Lord challenges Cain to *do what is right* and thereby *master* the *sin … crouching at [his] door*. This challenge may refer to Cain's offering, implying some defect in it. Alternately, the challenge may refer to Cain's response to his perceived mistreatment. The imagery of sin as a predatory animal favors the latter reading. Sin does not yet have Cain, and Cain might yet master it. The Lord does not charge Cain with prior sin (defective sacrifice) but warns him against imminent sin. Cain, sadly, does not rise to the challenge.

4:9–11 Cain's question, *Am I my brother's keeper?* does not so much deny brotherly responsibility ("Why should I care?") as reject the question itself ("Does my brother need a babysitter?").

4:12–16 Agriculture, difficult for Adam (3:17–19), now becomes impossible for Cain. He must now fear that someone will kill him to exact blood vengeance for Abel, or that he, a defenseless stranger, will be brutalized by those among whom he wanders. God addresses Cain's fears by granting a protective mark, but the narrator neither describes its appearance nor specifies how it will ward off antagonists. Cain, however, accepts the mark's usefulness and migrates eastward (the Hebrew word *Nôd* resembles *nod*, "wanderer," used in verses 12, 14).

ANTEDILUVIAN GENEALOGIES · 4:17–5:32

4:17 Cain's story ends with social cohesion: marriage, fatherhood, and city-building. These activities may represent a divine reprieve of Cain's rootlessness or Cain's acts of resistance to divinely imposed isolation (perhaps anticipating the story of Babel).

> **Antediluvian & Postdiluvian**
> Antediluvian = before the flood
> Postdiluvian = after the flood

4:23–24 The Lamech anecdote acknowledges the increasing human violence that culminates in the flood story (Gen 6–9). God promised Cain sevenfold retribution to deter violence. Lamech seizes that promise, multiplies it eleven times, reduces the "trigger" from death to injury, and twists its purpose from divine protection into human revenge.

4:26 *To call on the name of the Lord* is to worship.

5:1–2 Recapitulating Genesis 1:26–27, these verses contain the second *toledoth* formula (see Gen 2:4a). The

> **Cain's Offering**
> Cain's plant products could be thought accursed by extension from God's curse on the ground (see 3:17–19; Herion 57–62). Cain and his tilled plants are more closely associated with the cursed ground than Abel and his livestock (*though these too graze on uncultivated plants*), perhaps accounting for God's differing responses (Spina 323–28). The Torah prescribes grain offerings, but in the Pentateuch's chronology those offerings come only after God lifts the ground's curse (Gen 8:21–22).

repetition and structure pick up on the creation story in chapter 1 more than intervening stories do, almost as if chapters 2–4 have been a long parenthesis.

5:24 The strange report of Enoch's departure from earthly life fascinates many readers. In contrast to the customary notice *and then he died*, the narrator reports that Enoch *was no more, because God took him away*. The narrator offers no further details, and Enoch plays no further role in the Old Testament, although Jewish writers later write stories about him (see *1 Enoch*; Jude 4–15).

5:29 Lamech does not specify what *comfort* he envisions, nor does the narrator clarify how Noah fulfills this expectation (but see Gen 9:20).

HUMANITY'S DEGRADATION · 6:1–8

6:1–2 *The sons of God* belong to the divine council (see Gen 1:26–30). Interpreters later equated *the sons of God* with angels (see "fallen angels" in 2 Peter and Jude).

> **Divine Council**
> The assembly of beings who surround God and serve as a court are known as the "divine council" (see Job 1–2; Isa 6).

Some readers uncomfortable with the story's "mythological" overtones recast these characters as aristocrats consorting with commoners, or Sethites marrying Cainites, but these explanations have no real support. *Sons of God* so clearly denotes members of the divine council elsewhere in the Hebrew Bible that the same sense must prevail here. This episode inverts Genesis 3. There humans seek to become more godlike; here, divine beings (included by God in *us*, Gen 3:22) condescend to become more humanlike. Both initiatives transgress the divine/human boundary that God wants to maintain.

6:3 God's decision to limit human *days* to *a hundred and twenty years* seems to result from divine-human intermarriages, but that link remains implicit. God will impose this limit by withdrawing the divine *ruach*. The NIV translates *ruach* as *Spirit*, probably reminding Christian readers of concepts of the Holy Spirit alien to the original audience. God's *ruach* – wind, breath, or spirit – gives humans life (Gen 2:7). When that breath departs, humans die (see Eccl 12:6–7).

A hundred and twenty years may be a new limit to the average human lifespan. Curiously, most people listed in Shem's genealogy (Gen 11:10–26) live considerably longer than that, though human lifespans in Genesis do generally trend downward. Jacob dies at 147 (Gen 47:28) and Joseph at 110 (Gen 50:26). However, the limit might apply to the entire species rather than individuals, indicating the time left before the flood.

6:4 Readers sometimes consider the *Nephilim* (which means "fallen") the offspring of *the sons of God* and *the daughters of men*. The narrator clearly assigns the Nephilim to this time period *and also afterward* but does not label them divine-human hybrids. The narrator simply calls them *men*, albeit *heroes of old*. (Strangely, they seem to survive the flood; see Num 13:33.)

6:5–7 The narrator assigns human wickedness not to outside causes (for example, temptation) but to an evil inclination within the human mind (the *heart* functions in Hebrew idiom as the mind does in English). Human depravity bothers God. To be *grieved* fundamentally means "to change one's mind." When used of God, the verb indicates a reversal of some divine decision, whether blessing (for example, Jer 18:10), election (for example, 1 Sam 15:11), or (as often) punishment (Exod 32:14; Jer 18:8; Joel 2:13; John 4:2). Here God decides to undo the creation of humanity.

THE FLOOD · 6:9–9:17

Attentive readers sense a double telling of the flood story, a literary "split screen." Although this commentary focuses on Genesis's canonical form, the explanation that two slightly different stories have been merged here best explains some of the text's puzzling features.

6:9–22 The first introduction shows characteristics of the so-called "priestly material": the "account" formula, the name "God" (not "the Lord"), and an interest in divine covenants. God seeks not only to wipe away evil generally, but more specifically to redress humans' inhumanity toward one another.

God's description of the ark suggests a long, three-story barge. *Cypress wood* is a guess. Hebrew *gofer* may name a specific tree species, or may simply mean "lumber."

Verse 18 contains Genesis's first reference to a *covenant*, or binding agreement, between God and another party. Here, God promises to spare Noah and his family from the flood and charges Noah to preserve male-female animal pairs as well as food for both animals and humans.

7:1–5 This second introduction portrays the Lord distinguishing between clean and unclean animals, commanding Noah to take seven individuals, or perhaps seven *pairs* (NIV margin), of each type of clean animal and bird, but only one pair of each type of unclean animal. (Other parts of the text studiously avoid attributing knowledge of "clean" and "unclean" to persons living before the exodus.)

7:6–23 Priestly material dominates Noah's actual entry into the ark and the flooding as such. The narrator mentions pairs (not sevens, nor seven pairs) of both clean and unclean animals in verses 8 and 15. The narrator reuses phrases from both of Genesis's creation stories. References to *every creature ... according to its kind* echo Genesis 1, while references to creatures *that have the breath of life in them* recall Genesis 2. Verse 11 depends on Genesis 1's portrait of the universe. By "unplugging" the *springs of the great deep* and opening *the floodgates of the heavens*, God reverses the division between the waters above the sky and the waters below, returning the earth, in a sense, to its original chaotic state. However, the survival of the ark's passengers indicates God's intention to repopulate the earth.

7:24–8:14 The flood's chronology resists easy explanation. According to Genesis 7:11, the flood begins on the 17th day of the second month of Noah's 600th year. The *waters flooded the earth for a hundred and fifty days* (7:24), until the seventeenth day of the seventh month (8:4), when the waters start receding. The ark then runs aground on Mount Ararat; the waters still stand *more than twenty feet* above the mountains (7:20), but the ark itself is *45 feet high*. The waters recede for *the hundred and fifty days* following the ark's landing (8:3; both context and mathematics place the recession after the landing on Ararat). Halfway through that period, *on the first day of the tenth month, the tops of the mountains became visible* (8:5). The flood thus lasts three hundred days.

On the other hand, it rains for forty days (7:12, 17). After forty (more?) days, *Noah opened the window* (8:6). He sends out a raven, then a dove; waiting a week, he sends the dove out again, then again the next week (8:7–12). The dove's olive branch (8:11) tells Noah *the water had receded from the earth*. The dove's failure to return from its third flight shows that the earth is ready for repopulation. The "enclosed ark" portion of the flood thus lasts forty or eighty days, and the "open window" portion fourteen or twenty-one days (depending on whether Noah waits a week between sending out the raven and the dove, as he does between each of the dove's flights), yielding a flood of 54, 61, 94, or 101 days. Apparently Genesis has no interest in reconciling every detail in the flood story.

8:15–19 The exit from the ark represents a kind of second creation of humanity and animals. As in Genesis 1:22, God tells living creatures to *multiply on the earth and be fruitful and increase in number upon it*.

8:20–22 Immediately after disembarking, Noah sacrifices to God. The scene presupposes the distinction between *clean animals and clean birds* and their unclean counterparts, picking up on Genesis 7:1–4. God's decision *never again [to] curse the ground because of man* apparently results from God's pleasure with *the pleasing aroma* of Noah's sacrifice. However, God's assessment of humanity in general has not changed. Even after the flood, God still perceives that *every inclination* of the human *heart is evil from childhood*. "Human nature" after the flood is no different than before (see 6:5). Even so, God vows never again to use "uncreation" to cleanse

---

Ancient Near-Eastern Flood Stories

Flood stories were well-known in ancient Near-Eastern writing about early humanity. The famous Atrahasis *and* Gilgamesh *epics record flood stories very similar to the one in* Genesis. *The pervasiveness of ancient Near-Eastern flood stories suggests the author(s) of Genesis felt obligated to describe and explain this primeval flood. However, greater significance lies in the differences between the biblical and other versions than in their similarities. In the older Mesopotamian stories, the gods' motives are petty: humans make too much noise. In* Genesis *(and perhaps in* Gilgamesh*), the flood answers human corruption. Most strikingly, Genesis attributes all divine activity in the flood to one god. In the Mesopotamian versions, one god warns the flood survivor, working against other gods bent on destruction. In Genesis the same God who destroys humanity also preserves humanity.*

the earth of human evil. In verse 22, God poetically promises to maintain the regular cycles of life *as long as the earth endures*.

9:1–4 This new world will not, however, mirror Genesis 1 precisely. The humans' menu now includes animal flesh (with the *lifeblood* drained). Human violence toward animals, in search of food, will inspire *fear and dread* in other creatures. God may have added meat to the human diet to divert human violence to a more constructive purpose.

9:5–7 God's stance on interpersonal human violence appears ambivalent; God limits human violence, but not entirely. God does not want wanton killing and insists on *an accounting* from any murderer (including animals that kill people). The motive clause – *for in the image of God has God made man* – seems to mean that God sanctions blood vengeance because the practice makes *the image of God* concrete in humans by implementing the *accounting* God demands for human *lifeblood*. God also attempts to limit human violence by asking humanity to *be fruitful and increase in number*; unchecked interpersonal violence opposes that goal.

9:8–17 God's commitment to increasing the terrestrial population extends beyond humanity to *every living creature*. In Hebrew, the same word names a *rainbow* and an archer's bow, enabling this sign to evoke images of God, a divine warrior shooting arrows of lightning, peacefully retiring the weapon. The rainbow reminds God (not humans) of this covenant.

NOAH AFTER THE FLOOD · 9:18–28

9:20–21 Noah's *vineyard* and *wine* may grant Lamech's wish that Noah would provide humans with *comfort* from their *labor and pain[ful toil]* (Gen 5:29), since wine *gladdens the human heart* (Ps 104:15) and helps the afflicted *remember their misery no more* (Prov 31:7). However, irony pervades any such fulfillment. In a poignant, or pathetic, inversion of the Eden story, Noah consumes a fruit product that robs him of his ability to discern between good and evil. Noah *lay uncovered inside his tent*, too *drunk* to know better. Eating opened Adam's and Eve's eyes to their nudity; drinking closes Noah's eyes to his.

9:22–23 Some readers imagine a sexual encounter between Ham and one of his parents; "to uncover someone's nakedness" sometimes indicates sexual intercourse. Leviticus 18:7 uses *uncover the nakedness of your father* and *uncover the nakedness of your mother* synonymously, referring to sexual intercourse with one's mother. However, Ham does not "uncover his father's nakedness." Rather, Noah "uncovered himself." The narrator's terminology casts Ham as a witness, not a participant.

9:24–25 By telling his brothers, Ham shames Noah. Strangely, Noah curses Ham's son Canaan rather than Ham himself. This redirection of the curse probably reflects Israel's ongoing hostile relations with Canaanite populations. In context, it mirrors the offense; Ham shames his father, so his father curses Ham's son.

THE TABLE OF NATIONS · 10:1–32

10:1–32 The "table of nations" presents major population groups in the Middle East and beyond as descendants of *Noah's sons*. It expresses the author's understanding of interrelationships between various peoples of the readers' world.

THE TOWER OF BABEL · 11:1–9

11:1–2 In the logic of Genesis, this story is a flashback to a time when people had *one language and a common speech*, preceding the postdiluvian multiplication of nations, *each with its own language* (chapter 10). But the episode also provides an alternative, catastrophic account of the origins of nations, as opposed to the more gradual account in chapter 10.

11:3–4 The builders want to avoid being *scattered over the face of the earth*. Their underlying attitude is more likely fear of separation and isolation than arrogance, pride, or aspirations to divinity. The *name* they wish to make for themselves is not fame – according to the story, no other humans exist who might hear of the builders' reputation – but a physical, visible monument, a sort of lighthouse to keep individuals from getting lost.

11:5–6 Readers who think the Lord feels threatened by the humans' potential discovery that *nothing they plan to do will be impossible for them* must note what the humans have actually planned. All they have yet planned is to remain together. However, this human plan runs counter to God's plan for human beings to *be fruitful and increase in number and fill the earth* (9:1).

GENESIS

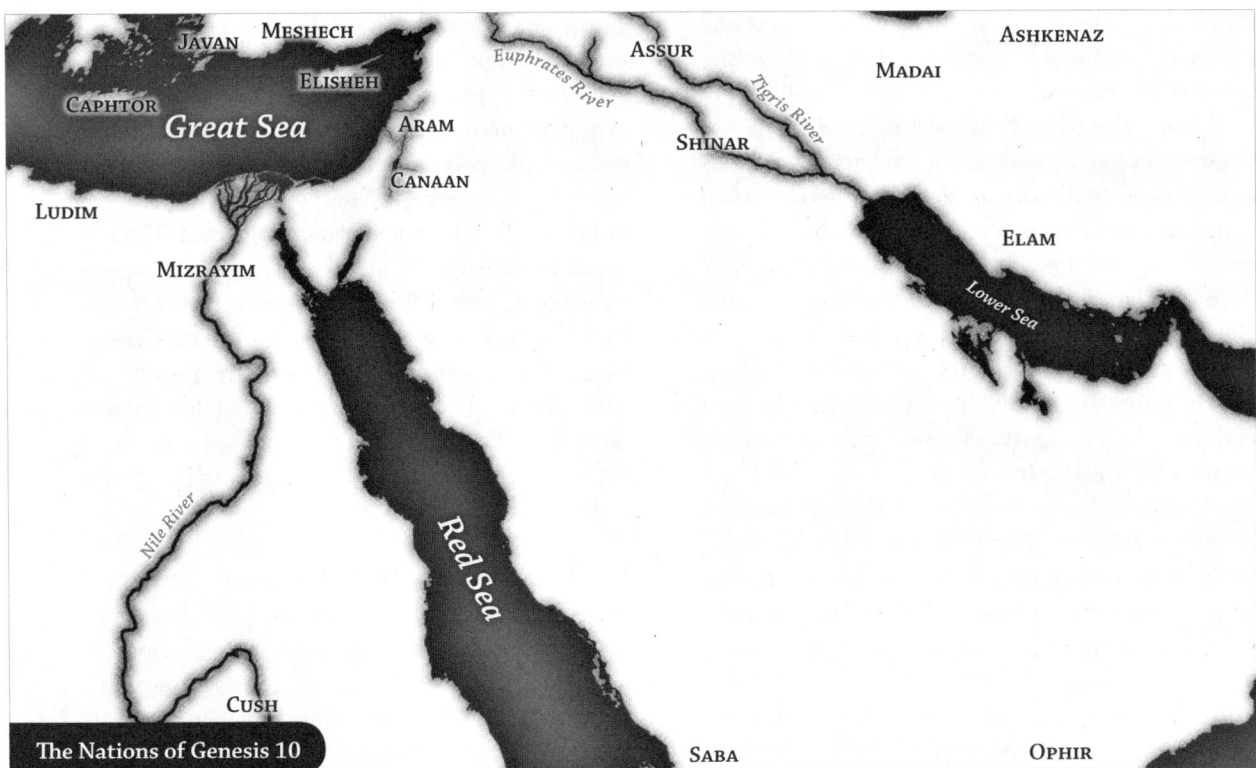

The Nations of Genesis 10

11:7–9 Thus, when *the Lord confused the language of the whole world* and thereby *scattered* people *over the face of the whole earth*, God overturns human resistance to divine plans. Linguistic diversity helps spread humans around the world and is not punishment for sin.

FROM SHEM TO ABRAM · 11:10–32

11:10–26 Shem's genealogy links Noah to Abram. The entries connect Abram's ancestry to the larger human population, with many unspecified branches on this family tree. Simultaneously, the genealogy focuses readers' attention on the one line that leads down to Abram.

11:31 This section presents migration *to Canaan* as Terah's initiative, although later passages (for example, Gen 15:7) will credit God with bringing Abram out of Ur. Abram, Sarai, and Lot set out for Canaan, along with Terah, but settle in Haran for a time instead of completing their journey.

ABRAHAM & HIS CHILDREN · 12:1–25:18

Abram's Call · 12:1–9

12:1–3 God plans to increase Abram's progeny, prosperity, and fame. *You will be a blessing* and *all peoples on earth will be blessed through you* can be understood in two ways. The latter clause could be translated "all peoples on earth will bless themselves by you." This claim might mean that people would someday use Abram's name in expressions of blessing formulae, such as, *May God make you like Abram* (Gen 48:20; Ruth 4:11–12). Alternately, God may want Abram and his descendants to act in ways that benefit ("bless") others. Neither sense excludes the other; the narrator may want readers to perceive both.

12:4–5 As Lot's uncle, Abram may have taken responsibility for Lot's welfare after Haran's death (11:28). Given Sarai's barrenness, he might even consider Lot the channel through which he will become a great nation. Abram is already relatively wealthy when he leaves Haran, though he may or may not yet be an experienced pastoralist (the narrator mentions possessions and people but not livestock).

12:6–9 God does not explicitly send Abram to Canaan, but he now confirms *this land* as the one promised to his offspring. God's appearances and Abram's worship suggest these brief notices derive from stories about holy places.

Abram in Egypt · 12:10–20

12:10–13 Genesis features three "wife-sister stories" in which a patriarch–twice Abra(ha)m and once Isaac–passes his wife off as his sister in a land bordering

Canaan. Here, Abram claims to be afraid of the Egyptians, though some readers may doubt his claim about his motives, given his deception of Pharaoh.

12:14–20 Abram's fear, if genuine, is unwarranted. Pharaoh's indignant speech shows that he would not have taken Sarai as a wife had he known her to be married.

Abram & Lot Separate · 13:1–18

13:1–7 Lot now apparently has the resources to survive, perhaps even flourish, as head of his own household. The impact of *the Canaanites and Perizzites* on the herders' conflict is unclear. Perhaps the narrator mentions them only to emphasize competition for resources.

13:8–9 Abram suggests separation to end the herders' quarreling. Some readers consider Abram generous, since he gives Lot the first choice of land. Others consider Abram foolhardy, threatening to give away half the promised land. Still others think Abram's offer misleading, if he believes God will eventually return to his descendants any land he now grants to Lot. The NIV's *left* and *right* (verse 9) in an east-oriented geography actually mean north and south, respectively. Abram proposes to mark two zones, northern and southern, meeting between Bethel and Ai. Each man will pasture his flocks in one of those zones.

13:10–13 Lot's option for the east actually introduces a possibility Abram had not proposed. Lot leaves Abram both north and south. Many interpreters blame Lot for selfishness, overlooking two factors. First, Lot leaves behind plenty of fertile grazing land. Second, given the presence of cities in the Jordan plain, Lot surely realizes he must share that land; indeed, as a newcomer, he will be disadvantaged. Genesis 14:3 may locate Sodom near the southern end of the Dead Sea.

13:14–18 God's words may carry a gentle rebuke to Abram, who has offered to split the land north/south with Lot. God also reassures Abram that Lot's departure does not spell the end of Abram's household.

Four Kings against Five · 14:1–24

14:1–7 All attempts to identify *Amraphel*, *Arioch*, *Kedorlaomer*, and *Tidal* with known historical figures have failed (Emerton, "False Clues" and "Riddle").

14:13–16 Oddly, the narrator describes Abram as *the Hebrew*, as if readers needed more specification than just his name. Abram's Amorite allies accompany his raid (verse 24), perhaps motivated also by kinship with *the Amorites who were living in Hazazon Tamar* (verse 7). Once rescued, Lot plays no role in the aftermath. The narrator's focus shifts to Abram's interactions with two local leaders.

14:17–24 Abram's encounter with *Melchizedek*, king of Salem (later Jerusalem), intrudes into his encounter with the *king of Sodom* (who either survives the battle or rapidly ascends the throne upon his predecessor's death), and the two conversations complicate one another. After Melchizedek

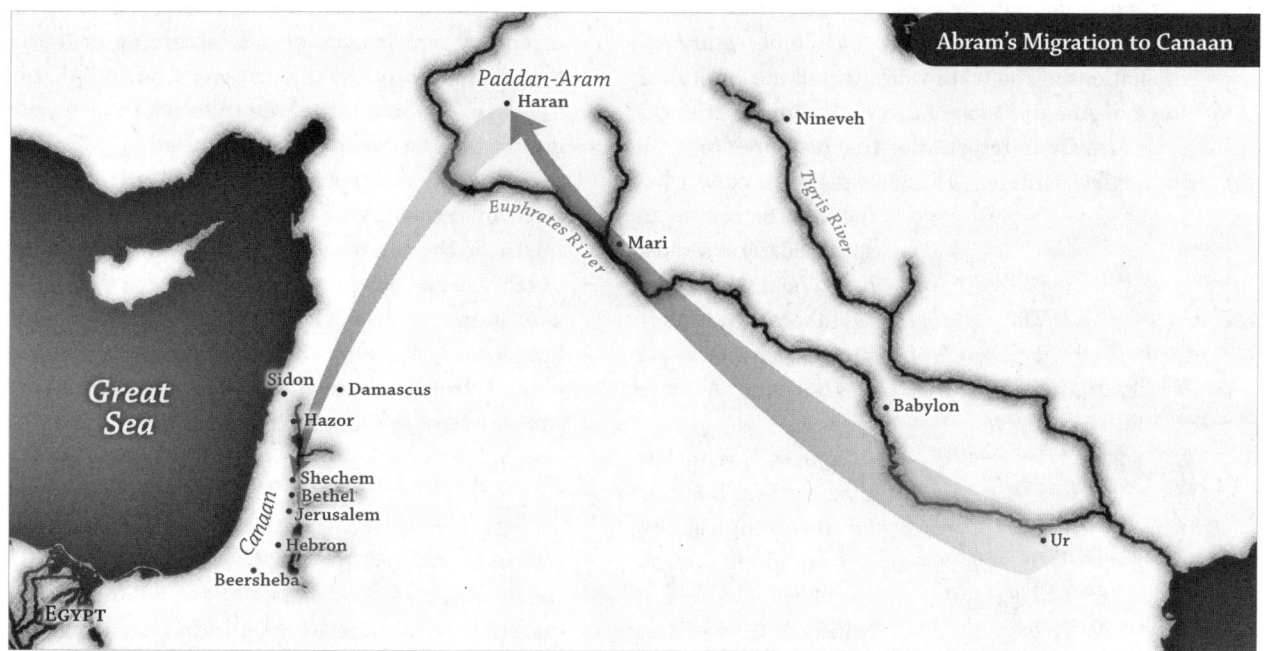

Abram's Migration to Canaan

blesses both Abram and God Most High, the source of Abram's victory, *a tenth of everything* changes hands. The narrator merely says, *he gave him a tenth of everything*, leaving the giver's and receiver's identities unclear. The NIV suggests that Abram tithes to Melchizedek. If so, the tithe presumably comes from the spoils of war (verse 16), but Abram explicitly disavows any claim to the spoils (verse 24). For Abram to tithe those spoils would contradict his disavowal. Perhaps, then, Melchizedek gives a tithe to Abram. However, Abram's attitude in verses 23–24 contradicts receiving a tithe as much as giving one. Readers can resolve the latter difficulty by supposing that Abram objects only to receiving wealth from Sodom's king, not from Melchizedek, though the narrator does not explain why this should be so.

Melchizedek serves *God Most High*, whose name in Hebrew, *El Elyon*, points to El, the Canaanite high god. Melchizedek labels El Elyon *Creator of heaven and earth*. Abram accepts these names completely, but equates El Elyon with Yahweh. This irenic, even inclusive attitude toward El characterizes the ancestral narratives. El emerges unscathed from biblical polemic against the Canaanite gods. Abram implies that he and Melchizedek worship the same deity.

The Covenant of the Pieces · 15:1–21

15:1–3 Still childless, Abram responds unenthusiastically to God's promise of protection and reward. Abram's speech in verse 2 is difficult in Hebrew. The NIV smoothes out the sense, inserting into verse 2 words borrowed from verse 3. Such unnecessary manipulations of the text's wording dull the emotional force of Abram's reply. At first, Abram experiences such surprise and frustration that he cannot form an intelligible sentence. He must pause to collect his thoughts before he can speak clearly. *A servant in my household* (literally "a son of my house") implies that Eliezer was born into Abram's service.

15:4–5 God insists that Abram's heir will be his biological son, not an adopted nephew (Lot) or servant (Eliezer). God invites Abram to *look up at the heavens and count the stars*, but thinks he cannot. Readers familiar with Genesis 22:17 may picture a nighttime scene: God showing Abram innumerable stars as a sign of the number of Abram's descendants. However, if all the activity in chapter 15 happens on one day, God's reference to the stars happens before sundown (see verse 17). God invites Abram to count the stars in the daytime sky. God thus seeks to convince Abram that his unseen descendants are nevertheless reliably "out there" in the future, just as the stars, invisible in daylight, are still "out there" in the heavens. Readers may, alternatively, imagine a long time gap between verses 6 and 7, though the narrator wants to link the two scenes (verses 1–6 and 7–21) thematically.

15:6–8 New Testament quotations make verse 8 particularly famous. In context, the narrator does not generalize about Abram's character but focuses on only one issue: Abram finally believes that God intends for him to father children. Immediately thereafter, however, Abram presses God for a sign to confirm the promise of land.

15:9–11 God performs a covenant-making ceremony to give Abram that sign. Abram must understand the ritual, as God merely lists the needed animals and Abram already knows what to do with them. The ritual may have been more common than the few passages describing it would imply.

15:17 Jeremiah 34:17–20 clarifies the ceremony's symbolism. Passing between the pieces of slaughtered animals during a covenant-making ceremony means symbolically accepting death as the penalty for covenant violations. God tells Abram, in effect, "I would rather die than fail to give your descendants the land I have promised."

15:18 The *river of Egypt*, or the "Wadi of Egypt," a seasonal river along the Mediterranean seacoast north of the Sinai peninsula, forms the ancient northeastern boundary of Egypt (2 Kgs 24:7) and the southwestern boundary of David's and Solomon's kingdoms (1 Kgs 8:65; 2 Chron 7:8). The *Euphrates* extends from Syria down to the Persian Gulf; God's promise here references the northwestern end.

Hagar & Ishmael · 16:1–16

16:1–2 A few ancient Near Eastern marriage contracts required the wife, if barren, to provide her husband with a concubine to bear children; a few ancient Near Eastern law codes address similar issues

---

Eliezer

Some interpreters identify Eliezer as Abram's chief servant (24:2), *though the text does not confirm this speculation. Some scholars cite ancient adoption contracts to suggest Abram had adopted Eliezer* (Speiser 112; Gordon 2–3), *but the relevant adoption contracts concern freeborn persons, not slaves* (Thompson, Historicity, 203–30).

(for example, the "Code of Hammurabi" 144–47). Some interpreters take these texts as evidence for a widespread and long-lived sense of obligation along these lines (Gordon 3; Hamilton, *Genesis 18–50*, 444–45), citing not only Sarai's actions but also those of Rachel and Leah (Gen 29–30). However, the contracts place limitations on a husband's widely accepted option to take additional wives (Thompson, *Historicity*, 252–69). Similarly, the law codes focus narrowly on certain social and religious classes. Moreover, careful examination reveals that the scenarios in the ancestral narratives differ sharply from those in the contracts and laws.

> **Sarai & Hagar**
> *Readers often criticize Abram for acting impatiently, hurrying up God's promise of offspring. Neither the narrator nor any character, however, says anything like that. Sarai expresses no interest in any divine covenant, nor does she seem to care whether Abram has descendants. She acts for her own sake, to counteract the social stigma besetting a barren wife. The* NIV*'s* perhaps I *can build a family through her* obscures Sarai's self-interest; she literally says, "perhaps I can be built up through her."

16:3 The figure *ten years* provides a touchstone for chronological reconstructions of Abram's life. Hagar's quick conception confirms Sarai's claim, *The Lord has kept me from having children* (verse 2).

16:4–5 Despite the NIV's rendering, the narrator does not say Hagar *began to despise her mistress*. The Hebrew text reads, "her mistress was lessened in her eyes." The second "her" could refer either to Hagar or to Sarai. The NIV and most other English translations rewrite the sentence. The narrator may mean that Hagar thinks less of Sarai, or that Sarai thinks less of herself, once Hagar's pregnancy becomes known. Sarai asserts the former (verse 5), but she could be projecting her own loss of self-esteem onto Hagar. Even if Sarai is correct, Hagar may simply have regarded Sarai with less deference and respect than previously (not with outright contempt). Hagar's new status as a childbearing wife (verse 3; she is not a concubine) would lessen the gap between her social standing and Sarai's. At worst, Hagar may have claimed equality with Sarai as Abram's wife. The "Code of Hammurabi" 146 (Hallo and Younger 2:345) and the "Laws of Ur-Nammu" 25 (Hallo and Younger 2:410) envision similar situations.

The wrong I am suffering is literally "my violence," referring either to "violence" done to Sarai (according to the NIV) or by Sarai (see verse 6). The former rendering suggests that Sarai blames Abram for her loss of household status, while the latter suggests that she blames him for whatever action Sarai might take against Hagar. Sarai even invokes God as judge, although she patently tries to blame someone else for the success of her own plan.

Abram's disinterest in Hagar's welfare may surprise readers, especially those who think he might consider Hagar's pregnancy a step toward fulfillment of God's promises of progeny. Surely Abram realizes harsh treatment could cause Hagar to miscarry, yet he does not restrain Sarah. Readers may imagine several possibilities: Abram thinks God will protect the child to fulfill the promise; he thinks God will provide another child if this one dies; he does not consider the child real while unborn; he wants to preserve peace with Sarai at all costs; or he simply does not care about Hagar or her baby. The narrator does not tell what Abram thinks.

16:6B–10 Some readers are startled by God's appearance to a non-Hebrew woman, but this reflects such readers' biases more than the narrator's (or God's). Other non-Hebrews (*Abimelech*, Gen 20:3–7; *Pharaoh*, Gen 41) receive such revelations (albeit in dreams), as does another expectant mother (*Rebekah*, Gen 25:21–23). *The angel of the Lord* appears to be the Lord himself (verse 13) in some visible form. Hagar must have received the message ambivalently. Only *the angel of the Lord*, among all characters in this chapter, addresses Hagar by her name, but the angel immediately pairs her subservient status with her name when he does so. The angel's instruction precisely inverts verse 6 (*mistreated* and *submit* are forms of the same word in Hebrew). Words of blessing accompany the instruction to return to an abusive situation: Hagar's descendants will be too numerous to count, as will Abram's (Gen 22:17).

16:11–12 Perhaps the assurance that her son will grow to adulthood gives Hagar the resolve needed to return to Abram's household. The etymology for

> **Ishmael the "Wild Donkey"**
> *Calling Ishmael* a wild donkey of a man *is not necessarily an insult. Elsewhere, wild donkeys symbolize independence (Hos 8:9), freedom (Job 39:5), and resourcefulness (Job 24:5). Usually, no valuation is involved; only Jeremiah 2:24 refers to wild donkeys negatively.*

Ishmael's name ("God hears") explains that *the Lord has heard of* [*Hagar's*] *misery*. In biblical idiom, saying God "hears" someone means God answers a prayer for help.

The NIV's *his hand will be against everyone and everyone's hand against him* represents one of two opposite but syntactically legitimate translations. *Against* renders the Hebrew preposition *b–*, normally translated "in." The preposition *b–* can have an adversative ("against") or cooperative ("in") sense, depending on the accompanying verb. For example, "to stretch out a hand *b–*" means "to assassinate" (Esth 2:21), while "to strengthen your hand *b–* him" means "take him by the hand" (Gen 21:18). The angel's phrase, however, contains no verb at all, reading merely "his hand *b–* everyone and everyone's hand *b–* him." Without a verb to govern "hand," the sense of *b–* remains ambiguous. Guided by stereotypes of Ishmael's descendants as Bedouin raiders, or by assumptions about Israelite attitudes toward Ishmaelites, many translators render the statement as predicting that Ishmael will live a life of "hand-to-hand" combat with others. Alternately, the message may be that Ishmael will live "hand in hand" with others, unlike Hagar's life "under Sarai's hand" (*submit to her* is literally "humble yourself under her hand," verse 9).

Likewise, the NIV's *he will live in hostility toward all his brothers* renders the Hebrew clause incorrectly. The Hebrew word rendered *in hostility* can be used adversarially, but the sense of hostility stems from the context or surrounding verbs, not from the word itself. The verb "to live" always refers to staying in a particular place. In Hebrew, then, the angel says Ishmael will reside near his relatives.

Hagar probably receives the angel's message favorably. God has heard and answered her prayers. Unlike her, Ishmael will be free, independent, and cooperative but not subservient; moreover, he will live near his relatives (see 25:12–18).

16:13–14 Hagar actually names God *the God who sees me* [Hebrew *El Roi*] and the spring *Beer Lahai Roi*, or "Well of the Living One Who Sees Me." These two names, as well as Ishmael's, commemorate God's care for Hagar.

16:15–16 The narrator credits Abram with naming Ishmael, without reporting any conversation between Hagar and Abram about her experiences. Abram may intend to commemorate God's attention to Abram's own childlessness rather than to Hagar's affliction.

The Covenant of Circumcision · 17:1–27

17:1–2 By Genesis's chronology, thirteen years pass between Ishmael's birth and God's institution of the covenant described here. This covenant places more obligations on Abram than did the covenant of the pieces (chapter 15): Abram must *walk before* [*God*] *and be blameless* and accept circumcision.

17:3–8 God intends the new name "Abraham" to underscore the promise of many descendants. "Abram" probably derives from "father [*'ab*] is exalted [*ram*]," "father" naming God, not Abram. The narrator connects the longer "Abraham" to *father of many nations*, but "father [*'ab*] of many [*hamon*]" should be "Abhamon" instead. If "Abraham" derives from a "father of …" phrase, biblical Hebrew offers no word that fills in the blank. Divided differently, "Abraham" could abbreviate "chief [*abir*] of many [*hamon*]," but ancient Semitic sentence names normally commemorate deities, not the humans bearing the names. Perhaps *father of many nations* does not explain the name etymologically; the syllable *ham* in "Abraham" and *hamon* ("many") may constitute the connection.

17:9–14 Circumcision, elsewhere in the world a puberty or prenuptial rite (as in Egypt), here attaches to a boy's eighth day of life so as immediately to incorporate newborn males into the covenant community. Lack of circumcision entails dismissal from that community.

17:15–16 Both "Sarai" and "Sarah" derive from Hebrew *sarah*, "noblewoman." Before this, God had only announced Abraham's paternity, not Sarah's maternity.

17:17–18 Abraham's laughter reflects his incredulity. Biology renders God's promise "impossible," in Abraham's view. Moreover, Ishmael renders God's promise unnecessary.

17:19–22 The Hebrew text includes neither the NIV's *Yes* (verse 19) nor NRSV's *No*. God blesses both sons with many descendants but restricts the covenant to Isaac.

17:23–27 Abraham circumcises Ishmael (the narrator emphasizes this point by stating it three times) in strict obedience to God's command to circumcise every male in his household. This act, however, endows Ishmael with the sign of a covenant from which God has explicitly excluded him. Perhaps Abraham wishes to include Ishmael in the covenant community despite God's announcement of his exclusion in verses 19 and 21.

Another Annunciation of Isaac · 18:1–15

18:1–8 Abraham apparently does not yet know the visitors' identities when he offers them hospitality. At first the visitors seem fully human while they are eating, resting, and washing their feet.

18:11–15 Sarah's surprise suggests that Abraham had not told her of the first announcement of Isaac's birth (historically, chapters 17 and 18 come from parallel traditions). Sarah's incredulous laughter parallels Abraham's earlier laughter (17:17); both doubt the announcement for the same reason.

The Destruction of the Cities of the Plain · 18:16–19:38

18:16–19 God seems to think out loud so Abraham can hear. God implies that Abraham's destiny to become a great nation and a channel of blessing qualifies him to receive the forthcoming information. Neither quality stems from Abraham himself; both derive from divine promises. God's reminder that *all the nations of the earth shall be blessed in* Abraham may prompt Abraham's subsequent intercession. For the first time in Genesis, God specifies an overarching goal in choosing Abraham: *that he may charge his children and his household after him to keep the way of the Lord by doing righteousness and justice.*

18:20–21 *Whether they have done altogether* is better translated "whether they have dealt destruction," focusing the issue on Sodom's violence.

18:22–33 That God might treat *the righteous and the wicked alike* disturbs Abraham, who therefore presses God, *the Judge of all the earth*, on the propriety of *sweep[ing] away the righteous with the wicked.*

Righteous and *wicked* could also be translated "innocent" and "guilty," especially in judicial contexts. Abraham labels God *Judge of all the earth*, implying a judicial outlook. "Innocent" raises problems; readers may doubt that Sodom truly lacks ten innocents (for example, small children). Readers more easily believe Sodom lacks ten "righteous" or meritorious individuals, but the emphasis on justice and judging (verses 19, 25) commends the judicial interpretation.

> **The "Ten Righteous"**
> Abraham's decision to stop the dialogue at ten people, rather than pressing the number lower, remains a conundrum. Some interpreters think Abraham has reached the limits of charity (Skinner 306; see von Rad, 214). Others suppose Abraham calculates Lot's family to include ten persons (Youngblood 176). Still others construe ten persons as the smallest possible group; nine or fewer persons are treated as individuals (Loader 30–31; Westermann, Genesis 12–36, 232).

19:1–3 In ancient walled cities, citizens conducted civic business in the gate complex. By *sitting in the gateway*, Lot casts himself as a citizen participating in community life. Lot's hospitality rivals Abraham's. His insistence that the men lodge with him may reflect his suspicion that they might be harmed in the square or simply the pastoralist's commitment to hospitality.

19:4–5 Sodom's men announce a desire to *know* the strangers; Lot's answer confirms the NIV's interpretation of "know" as a euphemism for "have sex with." However, Sodom's men do not seek sexual pleasure. Instead, they seek to humiliate the visitors by raping them, a stereotypical way for locals to assert dominance over strangers (see *Phibis* in Lichtheim, 226–27; also 102 note 92). Moreover, Sodom's men themselves admit they intend harm (verse 9).

19:6–8 Lot apparently undermines his bravery by offering his virgin daughters to the mob. Most interpreters take Lot's offer seriously, inferring that Lot considers his daughters expendable to protect visiting males' honor. Interpreters debate the narrator's and early audiences' evaluations of Lot's offer, but an ancient Israelite author or audience would hardly have approved.

Possibly, Lot's offer is not straightforward. The narrator places *all the men from every part of the city of Sodom – both young and old* at his house (verse 4). This presumably includes his *sons-in-law, who were pledged to marry his daughters* (or had already married two older daughters). Lot may try to turn the mob against itself, thinking that his sons-in-law (and perhaps their close friends) will object to having their fiancées (or sisters-in-law) raped, shattering the crowd's solidarity and defusing the situation.

Alternately, Lot may speak sarcastically, saying one thing while meaning the opposite. Lot sandwiches his offer between two statements advocating a "do no harm" ethic. A straightforward offer to allow the mob to rape his virgin daughters would contradict those statements. If Lot speaks sarcastically, the speech makes good sense. A sarcastic offer implies that he has no intention of allowing anyone to rape anybody, as long as he can help it.

19:9–14 The mob hears Lot's words as condemnation, not concession. Lot tries to convince his sons-in-law to leave and cannot be faulted for their refusal to believe his surprising claims.

19:15–22 Interpreters sometimes criticize Lot's slowness, attributing it to materialism or other faults. Lot may feel reluctant to abandon his beloved home and neighbors. Perhaps he hopes to revisit his sons-in-law. Maybe he is exhausted from the harrowing night before. Perceiving the strangers' commitment to his survival (verses 12–13, 15; see verse 22), Lot may actually see himself as a human shield protecting his neighbors. Readers who doubt this possibility should evaluate it in light of Lot's effective preservation of Zoar (verses 18–22).

19:30–32 The older daughter's pessimism about marriage prospects may have a regional or worldwide scope. The Hebrew word *erets* means both "land, region" and "earth, world." *Erets* appears twice in verse 31, and the NIV renders each instance differently. *There is no man around here* renders "there is no man in the *erets*," and *as is the custom all over the earth* renders "according to the way of the whole *erets*."

> **Lot's Daughters**
> *Readers all know there are men elsewhere "in the world," but the daughters may not know this. Living in isolation, they may think themselves and their father the sole survivors of a worldwide catastrophe – a latter-day version of Noah's family – now responsible for repopulating the scorched earth. The NIV obscures this possibility by having the older daughter wish to* preserve our family line; *the Hebrew text reads "bring offspring to life." The daughters may think they alone can preserve the human species.*

19:33–38 In contrast with Isaac's miraculous birth (chapter 21), this episode mocks the origins of Moab and Ammon, longtime antagonists of Israel and Judah.

Abraham, Sarah & Abimelech · 20:1–18

20:1–2 This episode parallels those in Genesis 12:10–20 and 26:6–11, with some unique features. Many scholars believe these episodes now stand in an artificial chronological framework.

20:3–7 Abimelech's response to God's charge suggests that Abimelech would not have taken Sarah had he known her to be married. God calls Abraham *a prophet* only here, though Abraham acts as an intercessor, not a messenger (that is, in a secondary rather than primary prophetic role).

20:8–13 Abimelech accuses Abraham of scheming to *bring guilt upon [Abimelech] and [his] kingdom*. The canonical sequence makes Abraham's "fear" ambiguous. Abraham has previously discovered in Egypt (chapter 12) that he can survive without misrepresenting Sarah as his sister, and that the Egyptians considered the deception immoral, but also that he can accrue wealth when a local ruler (temporarily) marries Sarah. Readers might wonder whether a man who will lie about his marital status would not also lie about his motives for lying. They might also wonder whether Sarah really is Terah's daughter; the narrator neither confirms nor denies this, here or in any genealogy.

Abraham may fear the locals but may also manipulate the situation to gain wealth. A scam seems ridiculous to readers who consider Abraham a hero of faith, but he claims in verse 13 that he and Sarah undertake similar deceptions *everywhere* they travel. Surely Abraham has learned by now that his fears are unwarranted. Those fears certainly misconstrue the case in Gerar. If Abraham really thinks *there is surely no fear of God in this place*, he errs considerably. Abimelech and his officials demonstrate more fear of God than does Abraham himself. Of course, even a legitimate fear of strangers would hardly justify Abraham's actions.

20:14–16 Intentionally or not, Abraham benefits from his lie. The silver, intended to *cover the offense* against Sarah, is neither hush money (the incident is already known to Abraham's company and Abimelech's household and officials) nor reparations, but a protestation of Abimelech's innocence. By accepting it, Abraham acquits Abimelech of any wrongdoing.

20:17–18 The narrator had not previously mentioned the misfortunes of Abimelech's household. *Have children* refers to giving birth, not becoming pregnant; pregnant women's inability to deliver would be more quickly noticed than other women's inability to conceive. In the canonical chronology, Sarah must not yet have conceived Isaac or must have been too early into the term for her pregnancy to show. Otherwise, Abimelech would undoubtedly have detected the trick without divine intervention – or Sarah might have faced execution for consorting with other men while in the king's harem.

Isaac's Birth & Ishmael's Expulsion · 21:1–21

21:6–7 Sarah may respond joyfully to Isaac's birth, as NIV's *God has brought me laughter, and everyone who hears about this will laugh with me* suggests. Or she may respond cynically or defensively: "God has made me a joke, and everyone who hears about this will laugh at me."

> **Ishmael and Isaac**
> The NIV's *mocking* oversteps the narrator's description of Ishmael's activity; nowhere else does the NIV translate the Hebrew verb tsachaq – *the verb at the core of "Isaac" [yitschaq] – as "mocking."* The translators apparently want to explain or justify Sarah's hostile reaction. However, the Hebrew text merely asserts that Ishmael is "playing," "joking," "entertaining himself," or perhaps "clowning around." Indeed, the verb describes Ishmael's actions less than it puns on Isaac's name. Sarah sees Ishmael "Isaac-ing," reminding her of Ishmael's status as Abraham's firstborn. Her insistence on Ishmael's expulsion hangs on inheritance issues, not Ishmael's behavior. Sarah cannot stand to have Ishmael and Isaac share Abraham's estate.

21:8–10 Isaac's weaning may come as late as his third birthday.

21:11–13 God endorses Sarah's demand, reminding Abraham that *it is through Isaac that [his] offspring will be reckoned.* Yet God also shows compassion for Ishmael and for Hagar.

21:14 Readers may wonder why Abraham provides such meager provisions for Hagar and Ishmael. He may have given Hagar only what she could carry, but if so, he surely had better alternatives (for example, sending a well-provisioned donkey along). Perhaps he hopes to keep Hagar and Ishmael nearby, though expelled from the household. Maybe he cannot do more on such short notice, though his wealth makes this unlikely.

21:15–18 Several source critics think the phrases *she put the boy under one of the bushes* and *crying as he lies there* depict Ishmael as an infant or toddler, not a teenager as required by the canonical chronology, but the story makes good sense as it stands. *Put* (verse 15) is often a technical term for preparing a body (of any age) for burial, and *crying* does not actually appear in the Hebrew text. The end of verse 17 literally reads, "God has heard the boy's voice where he is." "God heard someone's voice" means that God responded favorably to that person's prayer, especially a plea for help. Even adults frequently utter such pleas.

21:19–21 True to the divine word, God blesses Ishmael, giving him the skills and relationships needed to thrive in the wilderness. Hagar's initiative in getting *a wife for him from Egypt* parallels and anticipates Abraham's initiative in getting a wife for Isaac from Abraham's extended family.

The Treaty at Beersheba · 21:22–34

21:22–24 The lack of an introduction implies that this is the same *Abimelech* with whom Abraham dealt in chapter 20. In light of earlier experiences, Abimelech's concern that Abraham or his descendants might harm Abimelech or his descendents through false dealings seems reasonable. Returning to the theme of 12:2–3, Abimelech presses Abraham to fulfill his role as a conduit of blessing to all nations.

21:25–32 By accepting *seven ewe lambs*, Abimelech accepts Abraham's testimony to having dug the well.

21:33–34 Abraham's *tamarisk tree* seems to mark a worship site, as *there he called upon the name of the Lord* (see Abram's earlier altar among Mamre's oaks, Gen 13:18). Abraham here (as in chapter 14) applies a Canaanite divine name, *the Eternal God* (*'el 'olam* – "El" being the Canaanite high god), to *the Lord*.

> **Beersheba**
> Beersheba – *"Well [be'er] of the Oath"* – puns on both the number of ewe lambs [sheba', "seven"] and the oath [shaba', "to swear"].

The Binding of Isaac · 22:1–19

22:2 God characterizes Isaac as Abraham's *only son*, ignoring Ishmael. The NIV's *your son, your only son, Isaac, whom you love* rearranges the Hebrew text's order: "your son, your only son, whom you love, Isaac." Each of the first three descriptors could apply equally well to Ishmael and Isaac: both are Abraham's sons, each is his mother's only son, and Abraham can love two sons (Gen 17:18 and 21:11 reflect Abraham's affection for Ishmael). The string of identifiers emphasizes the identity of Isaac as the child of promise.

God's command – "sacrifice Isaac" – shocks modern readers, but Abraham seems neither shocked nor appalled (contrast his displeasure in Gen 21:11). He may be too stunned to respond, numbed by shock. Abraham may have learned to trust God's promises, supposing that God's purposes will be served no matter what happens (Isaac's very birth proves that God can do the impossible). Maybe Abraham does not really love Isaac after all and thinks the sacrifice may allow him to reclaim Ishmael as his heir; perverse as this possibility may sound, the narrator drops hints (Gen 17:17; 21:11) that Abraham loves Ishmael and may prefer him to Isaac. Or perhaps, Abraham simply does not consider it strange for a god to make unreasonable demands. The text does not tell us which interpretation is correct.

22:3–5 Abraham's prompt action in verse 3 mirrors his prompt action in 21:14. Abraham's assurance to the servants, *we will come back to you*, may imply that he already believes Isaac will somehow survive. Alternately, he may simply be masking his plans from his companions.

22:6–8 Abraham reverses normal sacrificial logistics by placing the wood *on his son Isaac*'s back or shoulders. *God himself will provide* masks a double entendre. The Hebrew text literally reads "God sees [or 'will see'] for himself," implying both that God will "see to" (*provide*) the lamb and that God already "sees" (visually) the lamb. *My son* addresses Isaac but also stands in apposition to *the lamb*, equating Isaac with the sacrifice.

22:9 Isaac apparently does not struggle against his father. Isaac could be anywhere from nine or ten (old enough to carry firewood) to thirty or more years old by the narrative chronology (the next marker comes in Genesis 23:1; born when Sarah is ninety years old, Isaac would be thirty-seven at her funeral).

22:10–19 Abraham passes the test by not withholding Isaac from God. Most interpreters think God commends Abraham for his obedience even to the unthinkable extent of sacrificing his *only son*. That willingness apparently motivates God's reiteration of the promises of blessing and descendants. This view construes Abraham's actions as demonstrating remarkable trust and obedience to a command that seems counter to God's earlier promises. On this interpretation, Abraham's not withholding Isaac consists in being willing to kill Isaac regardless of the consequences for Abraham's lineage.

God reiterates that *all nations on earth will be blessed* through Abraham's descendants, but adds that Abraham's descendants will *take possession of the cities of their enemies*. These notices stand in tension. At least some of *the nations on earth* will be displaced, not blessed, by Abraham's descendants (see the book of Joshua).

Sarah's Death & Burial · 23:1–20

23:6 As part of their deal-making rhetoric, the Hittites may overstate their actual esteem for Abraham.

23:7–16 The dialogue feels like a ritualized verbal dance, not a genuine negotiation. Ephron speaks politely but controls the transaction. If Jeremiah 32:8–9 is any indication (even adjusting for price fluctuations), Ephron overprices the field.

23:17–20 This repetitious paragraph emphasizes Abraham's title to the field. Immediately, Abraham can bury Sarah there; the cave provides the family's sole landholding in the promised land, even at the end of the entire Pentateuch.

Isaac & Rebekah · 24:1–67

24:1–9 Readers – but not the narrator – often identify Abraham's *chief servant* with the Eliezer of Genesis 15:2. The hand under the thigh may associate the oath with the covenant of circumcision (Wenham 141), invoke God's life-giving power (Skinner 341), or signify something else entirely. Old Testament writers use the title *God of heaven* only twenty-two times, usually in Aramaic passages and almost always in postexilic passages with clear Persian influences, although the title is much older in nonbiblical texts.

Sacrificing Isaac

Some propose a different interpretation of Abraham's willingness to sacrifice Isaac, which deserves consideration. Since Abraham has little difficulty sacrificing family members in earlier scenes (Gen 12:10–20; 13; 16; 20; 21:1–21), signs suggest that Abraham would probably readily sacrifice a family member. Abraham has previously resisted God's announcement of Isaac's birth (Gen 17), God's plan to destroy Sodom and Gomorrah (Gen 18), and Sarah's insistence on Ishmael's expulsion (Gen 21). Might God hope that Abraham would by now have accepted Isaac as his covenant heir, so that Abraham would intercede on Isaac's behalf, as he did for Sodom and Ishmael? When Isaac's birth was announced, Abraham asked God to favor Ishmael. Might Abraham think that God is now granting that request? If so, Abraham passes the test not by being willing to sacrifice Isaac, but by being willing to abort the sacrifice when told to do so. On this interpretation, Abraham's "not withholding" Isaac consists in preserving Isaac's life as commanded, making Isaac available for God to use as covenant-bearer from Abraham to subsequent generations.

Abraham does not say why Isaac should not marry a Canaanite, though he cites God's land promise to justify his insistence that Isaac remain in Canaan. Indeed, only here does Abraham explicitly invoke God's promises to explain his own actions (mentioning God's "call," but not promises, in Genesis 20:13).

24:12–21 The narrator implies that the servant prays (literally "speaks") out loud. The servant later claims to have prayed silently (verse 45), but readers may suspect rhetorical embellishment there.

24:22–27 Unexpectedly, the servant presents his gifts before Rebekah identifies herself, reflecting confidence in Rebekah's suitability as a wife or prior identification of Rebekah as Abraham's relative.

24:28 Old Testament writers use the phrase *mother's household* only four times (also Ruth 1:8; Song 3:4; 8:2), apparently to emphasize the internal workings of a household (Meyers, "Mother's House," 49–51). Some interpreters think *mother's household* indicates that Rebekah's father, Bethuel, has already died (contrast the servant's use of *father's household* in verse 23, but see verse 50).

24:29–32 Laban may react greedily to *the nose ring, and the bracelets* or enthusiastically to Rebekah's tale itself. His rush to greet Abraham's servant parallels Abraham's rush to greet his visitors (chapter 18), though here the visitor comes from a relative's household, thus deserving outstanding hospitality.

24:33–49 The servant's version of events differs slightly from the narrator's. According to the narrator, Abraham has sent his servant to *my country and my own relatives* (or simply "my native land," as the two terms may be two ways of saying the same thing), a very broad mission. The servant collapses his mission's scope from Abraham's *country* and *relatives* down to his *father's family* and *clan*. The servant claims to have prayed silently at the well, although the narrator mentions no silence. Finally, the servant inverts the order of his gift-giving and Rebekah's self-identification.

24:50–51 The servant's embellishments of his story help him convince Rebekah's family that *this is from the Lord*. Bethuel plays no explicit role in extending hospitality to Abraham's servant (verses 29–33) or in negotiating Rebekah's departure (verse 55), and Abraham's servant gives him no gift (verse 53). Bethuel's absence from these key moments leads some scholars to suspect his name here is a scribal error that crept into the text later and that he has already died.

24:52–61 Rebekah's family blesses her with words echoing Genesis 22:17. They mention numerous descendants and victory over enemy cities, but, chillingly, they omit any reference to blessings for the nations.

24:62–67 Interpreters cannot agree on what Isaac is doing in the field, proposing at least twelve different understandings of the obscure verb used (Vall 513–16); the NIV's *meditate* derives from the Vulgate. Rebekah's connection with Sarah's tent links with the matriarchal line, perhaps foreshadowing her barrenness. Isaac seems to be living in Sarah's tent apart from Abraham's company (as children do in many cultures). Thus Abraham receives no further mention in the episode.

> **Vulgate**
> This Latin translation of the Bible was prepared by Jerome (who lived 345–420). For centuries, this version of the Bible was the Bible in Western Europe.

Epilogue to Abraham's Life · 25:1–11

25:1–6 The Hebrew Bible associates Abraham's descendants through *Keturah* with the Sinai peninsula and Arabia. Biblical writers associate *Midian*'s descendants with the Ishmaelites, sometimes even conflating the two groups (for example, Gen 37:28; Judg 8:22–24).

Ishmael's Descendants · 25:12–18

25:13–15 Few of Ishmael's descendants appear elsewhere in biblical tradition. *Nebaioth*'s sister will later marry Esau (Gen 28:9; 36:3). Nebaioth and *Kedar* appear together as stereotypical herders (Isa 60:7). *Jetur* and *Naphish* recur in 1 Chronicles 5:18–22 as "Hagrites," credited with large flocks. *Kedar*'s descendants reappear more frequently than any other Ishmaelite clan; Psalm 120:5–6 and Isaiah 21:16–17 cite them as accomplished warriors. Other passages portray the Kedarites, like other Ishmaelites, as shepherds and merchants (Jer 49:28–29; Ezek 27:21).

25:18 The NIV's *they lived in hostility toward all their brothers* depicts Ishmaelites as raiders, contradicting the usual view of Ishmaelites as herders and traders. Literally, the clause reads, "he fell near all his brothers." An exact parallel appears only in Genesis 50:1, where *Joseph fell down near* [NIV *threw himself upon*] *his father and wept over him and kissed him*. Surely Joseph does not attack or live in hostility toward his dying father. Presuppositions about Ishmaelites – based more on nineteenth-century stereotypes of Bedouins than on biblical data – lead modern translators to mistranslate this verse. *He fell near all his brothers* precisely parallels *he will dwell near all his brothers* in Genesis 25:19. Here "fall" means "settle" (see Judg 7:12 and compare Josh 13:6 and other passages where the causal form of the same verb means "to allocate land"). The narrator says that Ishmael and his descendants settle near each other, not that they fight each other.

ISAAC & HIS CHILDREN · 25:19–35:29

The Birth of Jacob & Esau · 25:19–26

25:22 In Hebrew, Rebekah babbles incoherently, literally saying "If thus, why this I?" The NIV's *Why is this happening to me?* attempts to make sense of her nonsense by radically altering the syntax. Other translations offer *If it is to be this way, why do I live?* (NRSV) or *If so, why do I exist?* (JPS), supplying words that do not appear in the text. Instead, interpreters should take Hebrew *ken* ("thus") as a form of "to be stable, secure" [*kun*], yielding: "If things are okay [in my womb], why am I like this?" (Janzen 95). Alternatively this verse could contain a sudden break in speech resulting from a speaker's inability or unwillingness to finish. In this reading, Rebekah asks, "If so, why do I ...?"

25:23 The Lord does not answer Rebekah's question directly, but by predicting that her sons will become two *nations* (Israel and Edom), the oracle assures Rebekah that they will come to term. *The older will serve the younger* could equally well be translated "the younger will serve the older." An odd, nonstandard word order allows either *older* or *younger* to function as either the subject or the object of *serve*. The norms of Hebrew syntax render "the younger will serve the older" more plausible, but this translation runs counter to Israelite ethnic pride and to Genesis's theme of younger sons displacing older sons. Nevertheless, Jacob will repeatedly label himself Esau's servant in Genesis 32–33, but nowhere in Genesis does Esau serve Jacob. Translating the final clause "the younger the older will serve" preserves the ambiguity.

25:24–26 No obvious linguistic connection exists between "Esau" and Hebrew terms for ruddiness or hairiness. The narrator relies on readers' awareness that Esau is also called Edom (verse 30) and that Edomite territory was also called Seir; "Edom" sounds like *'adom*, "red," and "Seir" sounds like *se'or*, "hair." Similarly, "Jacob" [*ya'aqob*] sounds like *'aqeb*, "heel." In Genesis 27:36, Esau uses the verb form, *'aqab*, to mean "to cheat."

Jacob Acquires Esau's Birthright · 25:27–34

25:27–28 *A quiet man* is better rendered "a man of integrity" or "a wholesome man," contrasting Jacob's stability with Esau's less predictable lifestyle.

25:29–34 Commentators sometimes accuse Esau of exaggerating his hunger, but his description precisely mirrors the narrator's. In Israelite law, the *birthright* entitles the holder to inherit a double share; perhaps early readers assumed it so functioned in Isaac's family. Readers critical of Esau should consider his alternatives. Esau is not flippant; surely it is better for Esau to accept a reduced inheritance than to risk death through greed.

The idea that *so Esau despised his birthright* functions as a summary evaluation more in English translations than in the Hebrew text. The NIV's *so* (translated "thus" in several other English versions) renders the simple Hebrew conjunction "and." The NIV translates this word "and" three times and "so" once over two sentences: *He ate* and *drank, and then got up* and *left. So Esau despised his birthright.* In Hebrew, the same word also appears before the first verb: "and he ate and he drank and he got up and he left and Esau *bazah* his birthright." "Esau *bazah* his birthright" could stand as one action in a sequence rather than a summary of all the actions. The translation "and Esau did not think about the birthright again" (Gunkel 292) might better capture Hebrew syntax. The narrator's final words may indicate merely that Esau does not dwell on the matter.

> **"Esau despised his birthright ..."** The NIV's *so Esau despised his birthright could mislead readers.* English speakers use "to despise" synonymously with "to hate," although dictionaries supply a second sense, "to treat as worthless." The latter sense resembles the sense of the Hebrew verb, *bazah*. To *bazah* something is to ignore or devalue (not necessarily to hate) it. If so, *Esau despised his birthright* summarizes the narrator's judgment on Esau – Esau underestimates the birthright's value.

Isaac & Abimelech · 26:1–35

26:1–6 This seems to be the same *Abimelech* as in chapter 20.

26:7–11 The episode closely parallels Genesis 12:1–10 and Genesis 20. Here, Abimelech discovers the ruse by observing Isaac's interaction with

Rebekah. (The story ignores Jacob and Esau, making it fit awkwardly in its literary context.) Unlike Sarah in the parallel stories, Rebekah remains in Isaac's household, so Isaac receives no compensation once his deception is discovered.

26:12–16 Abimelech's insistence that Isaac *move away* seems to renege on his treaty with Abraham (chapter 21). His implicit fear of Isaac reminds readers that, while blessing all nations remains part of God's intent for Isaac's descendants (verse 4), possessing enemy cities now accompanies the forecast (Gen 22:17; 24:60).

26:17–18 The Philistines apparently close the wells between Abraham's death and Isaac's sojourn among them. The closures represent conservation, not necessarily aggression.

26:32–33 This etiology for *Beersheba* connects the name's origin to Isaac rather than Abraham (contrast 21:31).

Esau's First Two Marriages · 26:34–35

26:34–35 The narrator does not explain Isaac's and Rebekah's disapproval of Judith and Basemath. Esau later seems surprised to learn that his parents dislike his wives (Gen 28:8).

Jacob's Theft of Esau's Blessing · 27:1–28:5

27:1–4 Isaac's sense of impending death is premature; he survives for at least another twenty years.

27:5–17 Readers may suspect that Rebekah anticipates what blessing Isaac will give and that she acts in accordance with the prenatal oracle she received. If so, her felt need to deceive Isaac in order to protect God's plan seems odd. Jacob earns little sympathy; he expresses no moral reservations about deceiving his father, only a pragmatic fear of detection.

27:27–29 Isaac's blessing resembles God's promise to Abraham and the prenatal oracle Rebekah received. Isaac grants his son lordship over his *brothers* (perhaps in the broader sense of "kinfolk," since Isaac has only two sons). Isaac's intended blessing perfectly suits one reading of the prenatal oracle ("the younger will serve the older"; see the comment on 25:23, while Isaac's actual blessing perfectly suits the other reading "the older will serve the younger"). The oracle's ambiguity, far from unintentional, thus acquires thematic significance. The question of fraternal service now seems closed, but later events will reopen it.

27:30–38 Isaac cannot take back his blessing, but it is not a magic spell with a life of its own. Rather, Isaac's invocation of the Lord's name commits to God his wishes for his son's future. Such a prayer cannot simply be undone. Esau does not dispute this, but he does bemoan his loss of birthright [Hebrew *bekorah*] and blessing [Hebrew *berakah*]. Even so, Esau lobbies Isaac to pronounce multiple blessings. Esau's persistence and grief demonstrate the importance of the blessing as a key moment in the relationship between father and firstborn at the turning of generations.

27:38–40 The NIV turns Isaac's pronouncement into curse, but the Hebrew text does not require this. The NIV's *away from* (verse 39) translates the Hebrew word *min* to mean "from," although it is translated *of* in verse 28. Yet a better translation would render the word to mean "some of the dew of heaven and some of the earth's richness." Isaac would not think heaven's dew and earth's richness can benefit only one son.

> **Esau's "Service"**
> *Since Isaac cannot reverse Jacob's blessing, Esau will have to serve Jacob. However, Isaac gives Esau an escape clause. Esau will serve only as long as he is willing to remain servile. In Genesis, Esau never serves Jacob; rather, Jacob will later call himself Esau's "servant" and will call Esau his "lord" (for example, Gen 32:18).*

That Esau *will live by the sword* need not forecast raiding and warfare. Swords often serve as weapons, of course, but the Hebrew term refers to many bladed implements, including those used for circumcision (Josh 5:2, 3) or chiseling (Exod 20:25). Here, Esau's *sword* might function as a hunting tool for slaughtering, skinning, and dressing game animals shot with bow and arrows (verse 3). A skilled hunter, Esau already lives *by the sword* (and other hunting weapons). Isaac's blessing wishes Esau continued success in his chosen lifestyle rather than predicting a new one.

27:41 Esau's *grudge against Jacob because of the blessing his father had given him* contrasts with Esau's devaluation of the birthright. Esau's murderous plot may merely reflect great anger, or Esau may think killing Jacob will throw off Jacob's yoke (see verse 40). Esau's delay until *the days of mourning for my father* demonstrates Esau's regard for Isaac: he does not want to bereave his living father.

27:42–45 By *both of you*, Rebekah may mean both sons, anticipating blood vengeance against Esau. If so, readers may wonder who would avenge Jacob, as the

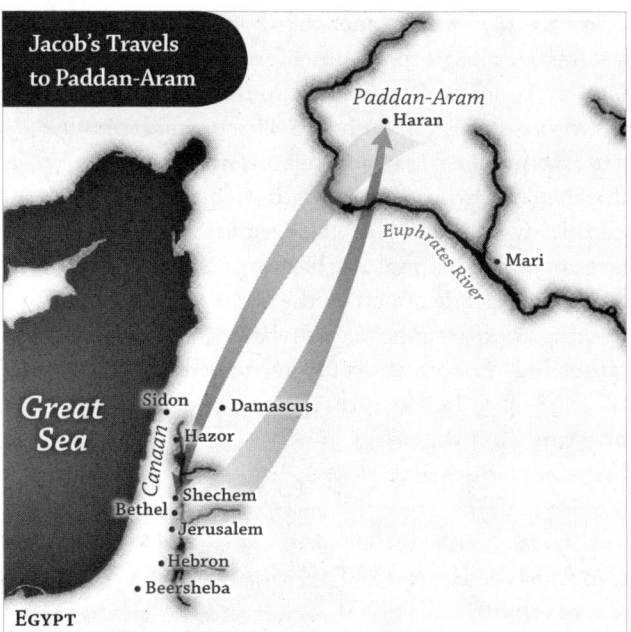

28:12–15 In his dream, Jacob sees a *stairway* or earthen ramp, not a ladder. God's promises to Jacob echo those given to Abraham.

28:16–19 Jacob now recognizes *this place* as *the house of God* [Hebrew *beth 'elohim*], and he names the place *Bethel*, "house of El." El is the Canaanite high god; *el* is also a common Hebrew noun meaning "god." Raising a *pillar* or standing stone to honor a deity was a common practice in Canaanite worship. Ironically, Jacob worships in typically Canaanite fashion while traveling to find a non-Canaanite wife. The NIV normally translates *pillar* as "sacred stone," especially in passages prohibiting such stones or commanding their destruction (for example, Exod 23:24; Lev 26:1; Deut 7:5). Jacob's well-intentioned act demonstrates the similarity of the patriarchs' religion to Canaanite practices and its distinctiveness from later Israelite religion.

Jacob's Marriages · 29:1–30

29:1–12 Jacob's greeting, *my brothers*, politely appeals to social camaraderie but does not assert that these shepherds are blood relatives. The shepherds probably fail to remove the stone from the well because of their social obligations, not because they cannot move it. When Jacob moves the stone, he is not "granted a superhuman power in his service of love" (Westermann, *Genesis 12–36*, 465); rather, he breaks the local social convention to demonstrate his interest in the wellbeing (see verse 6) of Laban, his flocks, and his daughter.

29:14–20 The notice about Leah's *weak eyes* – the NIV's margin *delicate* (others suggest "tender") may be better, as the term describes an observable characteristic of Leah's eyes – seems a mild compliment, highlighting the much stronger compliment paid to Rachel's beauty. In effect, Jacob offers seven years of work as a bride price (money or goods paid by a suitor to a woman's family) for Rachel. He has nothing else to offer.

29:21–26 Though it seems strange to modern readers, the narrator thinks a woman could clothe herself in such a way that a sexual partner might not learn her identity (see Gen 38:15–18). Perhaps the narrator intends this scene along these lines. Alternately, perhaps Jacob's drunkenness (*feast* normally implies drinking wine) and the night's darkness clouded his perceptions. When confronted, Laban appeals to local custom. Jacob has broken local custom before (verse 10) but cannot circumvent this one.

boys lack close male relatives except their infirm father. Moreover, Rebekah has shown no interest in Esau's welfare; rather, she has conspired against him, so her sudden solicitude seems odd. Perhaps Rebekah's *both* refers to Isaac and Jacob, imagining that Esau will kill Jacob immediately upon Isaac's death.

27:46–28:5 Isaac seems ignorant both of Esau's plot and Rebekah's role in Jacob's deceit. Thus Rebekah does not appeal to the brothers' mutual hatred to convince Isaac to distance Jacob from Esau. Instead, Rebekah appeals to the parents' shared dislike for Esau's Hittite wives. Before dismissing Jacob, Isaac blesses him with *the blessing given to Abraham*, including *possession of the land* of Canaan. This blessing seems odd, given Isaac's preference for Esau, and may suggest that Isaac thinks *the blessing given to Abraham* must pass down to a son who marries within Terah's lineage.

Esau's Third Marriage · 28:6–9

28:6–9 Esau's attempt to rectify his marital missteps precisely mirrors Jacob's plans, except that Esau marries a paternal, rather than a maternal, cousin.

Jacob's Dream at Bethel · 28:10–22

28:11 At first, Jacob does not know he has reached a sacred place (verse 16). The idea that Jacob used *one of the stones* as a pillow departs from the Hebrew text. The Hebrew phrase used means "away from his head," not *under his head*. Jacob places the stone behind his head for protection (Westermann, *Genesis 12–36*, 454).

29:27–30 Jacob actually marries Rachel immediately after his honeymoon week with Leah. He completes the additional *seven years of work* after the wedding.

Jacob's Children · 29:31–30:24

29:31–35 God counterbalances Jacob's favoritism by empowering Leah to bear children. Leah names her sons after God's favor.

> **The Names of Leah's Sons**
> In effect, Reuben's, Simeon's, and Judah's names constitute miniature hymns of praise. Reuben's means "behold a son," and Judah's "praised, an object of praise," while Simeon comes from the verb "to hear," perhaps referring to God's hearing a prayer. Levi's sadder name (perhaps "joined") expresses Leah's desire for Jacob's affection.

30:1–8 Rachel's authority to name Bilhah's children shows that this arrangement worked out better, from Rachel's perspective, than that between Sarah and Hagar. Rachel gives Bilhah's children adversarial names, focused on "besting" her sister with Bilhah's two children.

30:9–13 Leah gives both of Zilpah's children names commemorating God's kindness to her. Despite Jacob's disinterest and Rachel's hostility, Leah remains positive and grateful to God.

30:14–16 Rachel believes that the mandrakes will somehow stimulate fertility. Their shape, which resembles that of a human body, may have suggested to ancient peoples their usefulness in fertility rituals. Leah's sharp retort exposes her ongoing emotional pain.

30:17–21 Ironically, Leah becomes pregnant after giving Rachel her mandrakes; Rachel does not. Leah gives her two youngest sons names reflecting her troubled marriage. Interestingly, Leah does not explain Dinah's name. "Dinah" is the feminine equivalent of "Dan," perhaps meaning "vindicated." This name would fit Rachel's hostility better than Leah's gratefulness. Thus the narrator may omit the name's explanation for thematic reasons or because Dinah does not give her name to an Israelite tribe.

30:22–24 When Rachel finally bears a son, she seems dissatisfied. She does declare that God has *taken away* [Hebrew *'asaph*, "gathered up"] her disgrace, but she immediately wishes for the Lord to *add* [Hebrew *yoseph*] *another son* to this one.

Jacob's Prosperity · 30:25–43

30:25–26 Even after Jacob's term of service for Rachel, Jacob and Laban agree that Laban maintains authority over Leah, Rachel, and their children.

30:27–31 *Divination*, or various techniques for learning the future, allows people to question a god. Usually, the diviner manipulated and examined some object (see Ezek 21:18–22) to determine the answer.

> **Teraphim**
> The Torah prohibits Israelite use of divination, except for casting lots (Lev 19:26, 31; Deut 18:9–14). Laban's divination probably uses small idols called teraphim (see Gen 31:19).

30:32–36 The visual distinction between the sheep makes accounting and verification simple. When Laban *placed them in the care of his sons*, he does not steal Jacob's wages. Rather, he separates the herds to prevent Jacob from increasing his flocks at Laban's expense through selective breeding.

30:37–43 Jacob's breeding technique seems almost magic, apparently requiring readers to suppose that visual stimuli at conception affect young animals' coloration. Several commentators (such as Skinner 393; Westermann, *Genesis 12–36*, 453) think the narrator believed this, but none have advanced solid ancient Near Eastern evidence for any such belief (though it appears in rabbinic and medieval texts; Noegel 8–9). One might avoid a magical interpretation by believing Jacob's tale in Genesis 31:8–12, but the narrator's version of events differs strikingly from Jacob's. Readers might think Jacob knows enough about genetics to selectively breed multi-colored animals from monochromatic stock; the rods would be a ruse for Laban's benefit (Hamilton, *Genesis 18–50*, 284). This farfetched interpretation avoids magic but remains unconvincing. The outcome, not the mechanism, drives the story.

Jacob Flees from Laban · 31:1–55

31:4–13 Jacob's story goes beyond the narrator's. The narrator never describes any wage changes. Even if "ten times" is a stereotypical round number, readers must conclude that Jacob's version is either exaggerated or outright false, or that the narrator chose not to mention these wage changes previously. Similarly, Jacob ascribes the birth of multicolored livestock to God alone, but the narrator lengthily describes Jacob's schemes. Some interpreters conflate the narrator's account with Jacob's, suggesting that the rod technique was divinely inspired (see verses 10–13), thus creating a third story that neither the narrator nor Jacob tells.

31:14–16 Leah and Rachel imply that by selling them to Jacob, Laban effectively dismisses them from his household. The NIV's *he has used up what was paid for us* paraphrases what literally states: "he ate and is still eating our silver." The NIV interprets "our silver" as a bride price, but Jacob paid the bride price with labor, not silver. Rachel and Leah focus instead on their inheritance, concluding that Laban has already spent it. Of course, Laban does not literally eat silver, but he may have spent his reserves owing to losses during the last six years of Jacob's stay. Readers sometimes think Laban particularly wealthy, but the text makes no such claim.

31:17–21 *Deceived*, literally "stole the heart of," makes Jacob's covert departure a striking parallel to Rachel's theft of Laban's *household gods*.

31:22–24 God's warning for Laban to say nothing to Jacob, *either good or bad*, means that God does not want Laban either to encourage or discourage Jacob's return to Canaan. Laban speaks with Jacob at length, all the while casting himself as obedient to God's command, so he cannot have understood the command to mean total noncommunication.

31:31–32 The household gods (probably clay figurines) are small enough to be hidden in a camel's baggage, but their function is less clear than their size. Rachel does not want Laban to have them.

Some interpreters think possession of the gods determined inheritance (Jay 65–66), but Rachel would be far away when Laban died, and other claimants (for example, her brothers, Gen 31:1) could challenge her claim as theft (Greenberg 244–45). Other scholars assign to Rachel mere spite (Fuchs 77), estimation of the gods as "good luck charms" (Fokkelman 163–64; Gunkel 334), or sentimental attachment to the gods (Greenberg 246–48). Early Jewish interpreters thought Rachel knew the gods as Laban's divination tools (see Gen 30:27). If so, perhaps she steals them to prevent him from divining her family's route, just as Jacob "stole Laban's heart" by leaving secretly to conceal their itinerary (see *Pirqe de-Rabbi Eliezer* 36 and Heard 163).

31:36–42 Jacob claims that his work continually benefited Laban, omitting any mention of Laban's dwindling flocks. The title *the Fear of Isaac* appears only here and, with slight variation, in verse 53.

31:44–55 The covenant is both a nonaggression pact and a reminder of family responsibility. *Jegar Sahadutha* (Aramaic) and *Galeed* (Hebrew) both mean "witness heap." *Mizpah* ("watchtower") puns on Laban's desire for God to *keep watch* over both parties to enforce the covenant. *The God of Abraham*, *the God of Nahor*, *the God of their father*, and *the Fear of his father Isaac* seem to be four titles for the same God, *the Lord* (verse 49).

Jacob's Reunion with Esau · 32:1–33:17

32:1–2 Jacob has previously encountered *the angels of God* at Bethel in Canaan; here he meets them in Transjordan. *Mahanaim* means "two camps." Jacob's exclamation, *This is the camp of God!* implies that the "two camps" are God's camp and Jacob's. Later, however, Jacob will describe himself as "two camps" (NIV's *two groups*, verse 10).

32:3–5 Somehow, Jacob knows that Esau has moved to *Seir, the country of Edom*, during Jacob's stay in Paddan-Aram. Jacob uses deferential language, calling himself Esau's *servant* and Esau his *master*, thus notably inverting the usual reading of the prenatal oracle about the boys' descendants (Gen 25:23).

32:6–21 The NIV's *I had only my staff when I crossed this Jordan, but now I have become two groups* sounds like Jacob crediting God with making him rich, but this common translation may miss the point. Wealthy shepherds and householders, not poor refugees, carry staffs (Frolov 48–50); the translators

Jacob's Travels to Esau

change a connotation of wealth into one of poverty by inserting *only* (absent from the Hebrew text). Moreover, only after dividing it (Gen 32:7) would Jacob have called his household *two groups*. All this suggests that Jacob *crossed this Jordan* while returning from Paddan-Aram. Jacob actually seems to complain, "I just today crossed the Jordan as a wealthy householder and herder, but will now probably lose half of everything" (Frolov 50–51).

32:22–24 Jacob's movements confound interpreters. Most readers think one crosses the Jabbok river at *the ford of the Jabbok*, and they take *the stream* to be the Jabbok. If so, either Jacob crosses the Jabbok twice, or verse 23 unnecessarily repeats verse 22. The NIV's *after he had sent them across the stream* adds the words "after he had" to the Hebrew text in order to imply only one crossing. "Cross" is intransitive in verse 22, indicating that Jacob himself crossed, but transitive in verse 23, suggesting that he did not cross. Thus the text depicts two crossings, the second of which leaves Jacob alone (verse 24).

Two crossings make the camps end where they started, unless crossing *the ford of the Jabbok* and crossing *the stream* are entirely different, not opposite, geographical moves. Perhaps *the ford of the Jabbok* is not a place to cross the Jabbok, but a place to cross the Jordan where it meets the Jabbok. Jacob must have crossed the Jordan earlier (verse 11). Here, he moves eastward across the Jordan where it meets the Jabbok. He sends his family north or south (depending on the ford's precise location) across the Jabbok itself, leaving him alone as the text demands, but not putting his family back where they started (Frolov 52–54). Jacob either shields his family from Esau (if he is south of the Jabbok) or shields himself from Esau with them (if north of the Jabbok).

32:25–32 *You have struggled with God and with men and have overcome* does not necessarily identify Jacob's opponent as God, because it mentions God and *men* (plural). Since Jacob wrestles only one opponent here, the struggle cannot be this wrestling match alone. The explanation of his name change views Jacob's life more broadly.

The narrator's etymology for *Israel* makes it seem like a description of Jacob, but the name uses a common form of ancient names, which were actually sentences with a god as the subject. Technically, "Israel" translates not as "he struggles with God" but "God struggles" or "God rules."

33:8–11 Esau needs none of Jacob's gifts, but Jacob needs Esau to accept them so Jacob will know all is forgiven. The NIV's *please accept the present* masks a crucial word choice; *the present* is literally "my blessing." Jacob seeks to return to Esau the blessing he took by deceit in chapter 27. Understanding Jacob's need, Esau accepts the gift.

33:12–17 Jacob implies in verse 14 that he will join Esau in Seir; instead, he turns aside to settle at Succoth. Even after Esau's warm reception, Jacob seems to revert to old deceitful ways. However, Esau and Jacob may engage in a verbal banter that both know is not straightforward. Perhaps Esau knows Jacob will not really come to Seir, and Jacob realizes that Esau will not compel him to do anything (Westermann, *Genesis 12–36*, 527).

Jacob's Family at Shechem · 33:18–34:31

33:18–20 The value of Jacob's *hundred pieces of silver* relative to Abraham's four hundred shekels cannot be determined accurately, because *piece* names a unit of unknown weight and value. *El Elohe Israel* means "El is the God of Israel."

34:1–4 Many readers assume that Shechem raped Dinah, but the NIV's *violated her* is appropriately circumspect. Shechem *violated* Dinah by having sex with her outside of a socially approved marriage, but the narrator does not specify whether Dinah consents or not. In fact, the pattern of Hebrew terminology related to shameful sex suggests that Shechem does not rape Dinah but has consensual premarital sex with her, a socially humiliating, but not violent, act (see Bechtel for details).

34:25–29 *Simeon and Levi*, Dinah's full brothers, do the actual killing, while all of *Jacob's sons* loot the city. Readers now learn that Dinah has been in *Shechem's house* throughout the episode. In dark irony, Jacob's sons seize the city's *women and children*, undoubtedly taking the women as concubines or slaves.

Jacob's Wrestling Partner

Jacob himself thinks the attacker is God, but the narrator does not confirm this. The ambiguity leads scholars to identify Jacob's opponent as God, an angel, Esau, Esau's guardian angel, a "river demon," or perhaps even a personification of Jacob's internal fear or guilt (Knight 451). The man's insistence on leaving before daybreak implies something paranormal, but the Bible does normally restrict God's activity to nighttime.

34:30–31 Jacob seems more concerned about good relations with his neighbors than with family honor; his sons reverse those priorities.

Jacob Returns to Bethel · 35:1–29

35:2–5 Anticipating worship at Bethel, Jacob prescribes purification rites for *his household and … all who were with him*. The *foreign gods* may include Laban's household gods and figurines plundered from Shechem. The *earrings* may have come from the idols themselves rather than Jacob's family (Hurowitz).

35:8 *Deborah, Rebekah's nurse*, was mentioned obliquely in Genesis 24:59. It is not clear why the narrator chose to report her death and burial, except perhaps as an explanation of the name *Allon Bacuth* ("Oak of Weeping"). Rebekah herself presumably dies while Jacob is away; the narrator relates no mother and child reunion.

35:16–20 *Ben-Oni* means "son of my trouble" or "son of my suffering." Rachel seeks to commemorate the difficult birth. Perhaps Jacob prefers *Benjamin*, "son of my right hand" or "son of the south," precisely because *Ben-Oni* would remind him too painfully of Rachel's death.

35:21–26 Reuben seeks more than sexual gratification with Bilhah. By sleeping with his father's concubine, he asserts a claim to headship of the household (like Absalom in 2 Sam 16:21–22), perhaps already realizing that Jacob prefers Joseph (see chapter 37).

Esau's Descendants · 36:1–43

36:2–5 This list of Esau's wives differs from that in Genesis 26:34–35; 28:6–9. Some readers try to harmonize the lists by suggesting that Esau had six wives, but this seems unlikely (Driver 313). If Esau had six wives, it seems strange for Esau's genealogy to mention only three wives, especially if Esau married two pairs of sisters (two of Elon's daughters and two of Ishmael's daughters). A possible explanation is that Genesis incorporates two different traditions about Esau's marriages; these traditions agreed that Esau married two Canaanite women and one of Ishmael's daughters, but disagreed about their names and families.

36:6–8 The narrator here transmits an alternate tradition about Esau's separation from Jacob and migration to Seir. This account closely resembles Abram's and Lot's separation (chapter 13); according to this report, Esau migrates to Seir seeking resources for his animals. Esau appears here as a herder, not a hunter as in chapters 25 and 28; Esau leaves Canaan while Jacob is living there (not in Paddan-Aram); and the entire theme of Jacob's deceit and Esau's anger disappears.

36:9–19 *Teman* later appears as an Edomite place name, associated with wisdom (Jer 49:7) and, curiously, with the Lord (Hab 3:3). *Kenaz*'s apparent descendants, the Kennizites, include the spy Caleb (Num 32:12) and the "judge" Othniel (Judg 3:9); however, Kennizites appear in Genesis 15:9 as a group already known to Abraham, so this connection may be incorrect. A kingdom hostile to Israel bears the name *Amalek* in the post-exodus period; the nation may be this Amalek's descendants.

36:31–39 The kings listed reign in the region later called Edom but are not ethnically Edomite (descended from Esau). The transfer of power between these kings is nondynastic, and the kings rule from various royal cities. The phrase *before any Israelite king reigned* suggests the author lived during or after the Israelite monarchy.

JACOB & HIS CHILDREN · 37:1–50:26

Joseph & His Brothers · 37:1–36

37:1–4 Readers might think Jacob favors Joseph because of Rachel, but the narrator attributes Jacob's favoritism to his own age at Joseph's birth (anywhere from fifty-five to one hundred years old by the narrative chronology). The narrator does not detail the content or accuracy of Joseph's *bad report about* his brothers.

The NIV's *richly ornamented robe* renders the Hebrew better than the traditional *coat of many colors* (a reading based on the Septuagint); the NRSV's *long robe with sleeves* is even better. Either way, Joseph's tunic would be inappropriate for everyday manual labor, perhaps exempting him from ordinary chores besides signifying Jacob's favoritism.

> **The Septuagint (LXX)**
> *The Septuagint is the ancient Greek translation of the Old Testament begun, probably in Alexandria, during the third century BCE.*

37:12–17 Jacob seems unwise to send Joseph to check up on his brothers. Perhaps he remains unaware of his other sons' anger (though this seems rather unlikely), or maybe he simply cannot imagine they would defy him by harming his favorite son.

37:18–30 The brothers' attempt to counteract Joseph's dreams by killing him suggests that, despite their earlier scoffing, they cannot completely discount the dreams. The reasons for Reuben's desire *to rescue him from them and take him back to his father* go unstated. Perhaps he cares too much for Jacob to cause him grief, or he feels a sense of responsibility as the firstborn.

Judah apparently finds it less offensive to sell one's *own flesh and blood* into slavery than to murder a brother outright. The alternation between Ishmaelites and Midianites confuses matters (and appears also in Judg 8:22–24). The book of the covenant values a slave at thirty shekels (Exod 21:32); the caravaners get a bargain.

37:31–35 The brothers' use of the robe to deceive Jacob echoes Jacob's use of Esau's clothes to deceive Isaac.

Judah & Tamar · 38:1–30

38:1–5 *Kezib* sounds like the Hebrew verb "to tell a lie"; deception will figure prominently in this episode.

38:6–10 Er's precise offense is irrelevant; his only role is to die, setting into motion the chain of levirate marriage. Deuteronomy 25:5–6 details an Israelite understanding of this custom, intended to provide descendants for as many men as possible. Onan objects to his biological children being counted as Er's.

> **Levirate Marriage**
> *Levirate marriage is a custom by which the childless widow of a man marries his closest male relative and has a child by him, who is nevertheless credited to the dead previous husband. This custom also lies behind Ruth 4:1–10.*

38:12–19 The narrator does not explain Tamar's reasoning, but everything seems to go exactly according to her plan. The *veil* conceals Tamar's identity, rather than identifying her as a prostitute. A veiled prostitute would actually be unusual in the ancient Near East (Huddlestun). Her other clothing, or more likely her position and demeanor by the roadside, leads Judah to think she is a prostitute. Judah's *seal and its cord, and the staff* he carries, mark his identity and authority as a well-to-do householder.

38:20–23 The NIV's *shrine prostitute* implies that Hirah (or Judah) changes vocabulary to make the transaction seem more respectable. However, translating Hebrew *qedeshah* (plural *qedeshot*) as *shrine prostitute* rests on meager evidence. No biblical passage explicitly connects these persons with sexual activity. Hosea 4:14 mentions illicit sex and *qedeshot* in the same context, but even there, *qedeshot* are explicitly linked to sacrificial rituals, not sex. Syrian and Mesopotamian texts use cognate terms for female ritual functionaries, but they do not assign these women sexual roles. Other than a possible annual "sacred marriage" ritual in parts of Mesopotamia, sexual activity seems absent from ancient Syro-Palestinian and Mesopotamian worship. The notion of "sacred prostitution" in ancient Near Eastern religion stems more from Herodotus than from ancient Near Eastern texts (Westenholtz). Consequently, Judah and Hirah apparently try to change the entire terms of the transaction. By asking for a *qedeshah* or "holy woman" while leading a kid goat, Hirah implies a desire to sacrifice, not to pay a prostitute ("sacred" or otherwise).

38:24–26 Tamar's guilt is obvious from her pregnancy; the messengers do not necessarily know about her earlier scheme. Tamar's presentation of Judah's belongings implicates him in her pregnancy and vindicates her.

Joseph in Potiphar's House · 39:1–23

39:1 *Captain of the guard* identifies Potiphar's military authority, perhaps over bodyguards or executioners. The NIV's *official* could also be translated "eunuch," leading to speculation about Potipahar's wife's motives for her later actions. Hebrew *saris* can denote a eunuch or, more frequently in the Hebrew Bible, a government official (castrated or not). The linguistic data cannot close the matter altogether but seem to lean against identifying Potiphar as a eunuch (Péter-Contesse). However, the narrator may exploit the ambiguity to heighten the double entendre in verse 6.

39:2–6A The narrator emphasizes *the blessing of the Lord* to Potiphar's benefit. Here a descendant of Abraham blesses people of other nations. The NIV's *he did not concern himself with anything* translates the Hebrew accurately, but obscures a subtle double entendre. Literally, the Hebrew text reads, "he did not know anything"; "know" often functions as a euphemism for sexual intercourse. By choosing this particular term and describing Potiphar as a *saris*, the narrator hints at a possible cause for the actions Potiphar's wife later takes.

39:6B–10   Joseph's refusal stems less from abstract morality than from loyalty to Potiphar. For Joseph, to violate Potiphar's trust would constitute sin against God. The note about Joseph's appearance may lead readers to think Potiphar's wife mainly seeks sexual gratification. Alternately, Joseph's newfound household authority may have somewhat displaced her; her sexual advances may represent an attempt to gain leverage over him or to get him dismissed so she can regain some or all of the power her husband has transferred to Joseph (Donaldson 90–92).

39:11–18   If Potiphar's wife seeks sexual pleasure, her accusation stems from anger at having been spurned too many times. If, however, she seeks Joseph's dismissal from the household management, this ruse serves her purposes admirably.

39:19–23   The narrator does not say with whom Potiphar is angry. Readers may think Potiphar is angry with Joseph, because he immediately imprisons Joseph. However, even a highly prized household slave hardly seems qualified for *the place where the king's prisoners were confined*. Curiously, Joseph's prison is overseen by *the captain of the guard* (Gen 40:3–4), Potiphar's title. The narrator does not distinguish *the captain of the guard* in chapter 40 from the one in chapter 39, suggesting that Potiphar may personally oversee the royal prison (note also *house of the captain of the guard* in 40:3 and *his master's house* in 40:7). Notably, the *prison warden* treats Joseph exactly as Potiphar had, by giving Joseph responsibility for *all that was done* in the prison. If the *prison warden* reports to the *captain of the guard*, Potiphar may have been the channel by which *the Lord ... granted [Joseph] favor in the eyes of the prison warden*. All this suggests that Potiphar's anger might be directed toward his wife, who has manipulated events such that Potiphar has to imprison Joseph. Yet Potiphar retains enough control over the situation, and enough regard for Joseph, to commit him to a prison under his own authority and to have him made chief trusty there.

Joseph in Prison · 40:1–23

40:6–8   Joseph's answer to the cupbearer and baker seems presumptuous. He credits God alone with the ability to interpret dreams but then immediately solicits an account of the dreams. Presumably, God reveals the interpretations to Joseph, though the narrator does not confirm that.

40:9–15   In Hebrew idiom, to *lift up [someone's] head* is to show that person favor. *Dungeon* translates the same word rendered "cistern" in chapter 37, thematically linking Joseph's current circumstances to his entry into Egypt.

40:16–19   *Lift off your head* (literally "lift up your head from upon you") darkly echoes the previous interpretation.

40:20–23   Joseph's accuracy establishes him as a divinely gifted dream interpreter for the next episode.

Pharaoh's Dreams · 41:1–57

41:1–8   Joseph's assertion that *interpretations belong to God* (40:8) prepares readers for the magicians' and sages' failure. The text contrasts the God of Israel with the gods of Egypt (see also Dan 2:10–11; 5:8).

41:9–15   The cupbearer's *shortcomings* (literally "my sin") may refer to his offense against Pharaoh or his failure to mention Joseph to Pharaoh, or both.

41:14–32   Joseph tempers his own reputation as an interpreter by insisting again that only God can explain dreams. Nevertheless, Joseph delivers those interpretations to Pharaoh. Joseph understands Pharaoh's dreams to be divine revelation to Pharaoh.

41:33–40   Joseph's dream interpretation, and perhaps also his policy suggestion, convince Pharaoh that *the spirit of God* resides in Joseph. Thus the *wise and discerning man* needed to oversee taxation and storage turns out to be Joseph himself. Joseph's new status in Pharaoh's court mirrors his status within Potiphar's household and in prison: he becomes second-in-command.

41:41–45   Pharaoh's *signet ring* gives Joseph authority to make and enforce proclamations. *On* is Heliopolis, just north of modern Cairo. Joseph's new name, *Zaphenath-Paneah*, serves to "Egyptianize" him.

41:50–52   *Manasseh* resembles the Hebrew verb "to forget." Ironically, Joseph has not in fact forgotten his troubles and his father's household, else he would not name his son after them. The meaning of the word *Ephraim* is hard to explain. Ephraim and Manasseh later replace Joseph in the standard list of the "twelve tribes of Israel" (see Gen 48:1–7; see Deut 33, where Ephraim and Manasseh appear as subsets of Joseph).

> **Joseph & Egyptian History**
>
> In the seventeenth and early sixteenth centuries BCE, a West Semitic people called "Hyksos" (a corruption of the Egyptian phrase for "foreign rulers") in classical Greek sources dominated Egypt. Because the Hyksos were Semites like the Hebrews, some interpreters think the Hyksos period provides an appropriate setting for Joseph's rise to power. Alternately, since Greek sources sometimes call the Hyksos "shepherd kings," readers might relate the Egyptians' disdain for shepherds (Gen 46:34) to a post-Hyksos setting.
>
> Joseph, however, ill fits known Egyptian history. The Egyptian names in Genesis 37–50 (Potiphar, Asenath, Zaphenath-Paneah) follow patterns characteristic of the mid-first millennium BCE, a thousand years later than Joseph's lifetime. On other details, the Joseph story reflects Egyptian concepts long predating Joseph, such as the concept of Pharaoh owning Egypt, with the people as his slaves and the priests as his hired employees (Redford 424–26). Though a literary and theological masterpiece, the Joseph story is difficult to situate historically.

Joseph's Reunion with His Brothers · 42:1–45:28

42:6–9A The narrator almost overuses the word "recognize," echoing the brothers' call for Jacob to "recognize" Joseph's coat (37:32–33). Joseph's harsh treatment of his brothers may stem from vengeful hostility, but subsequent developments suggest that he has already begun to use his position to engineer a reunion with his father and Benjamin.

42:9B–24 By accusing his brothers of spying, Joseph draws out their family self-identification, which in turn gives him the opportunity to demand Benjamin's presence. Joseph's shift from sending one brother back to sending all but one (the choice of Simeon seems arbitrary) enhances the sense that he already plans reconciliation. The brothers' sense of guilt is palpable.

42:25–28 When the brothers ask, *What is this that God has done to us?* they undoubtedly think God is now punishing them for mistreating Joseph years ago.

43:15–25 Joseph's steward agrees with the brothers' assumption that God had placed their silver in their sacks, but interprets this as a blessing, not a punishment.

43:26–34 Joseph's brothers will later receive a false explanation (divination) for Joseph's incredible knowledge about them (Gen 44:5).

45:4–15 Joseph not only forgives his brothers for selling him into slavery but even claims they were doing God's work unawares. In retrospect, Joseph can see the good that has come from his troubles.

Jacob's Reunion with Joseph · 46:1–47:12

46:1–4 Abraham and Isaac worshiped at Beersheba; God now visits Jacob there also. God reassures Jacob that his migration to Egypt does not nullify God's promises regarding descendants and land. Those promises will continue to bear fruit. Egypt will incubate the fledgling people of Israel.

46:28–47:12 The claim that *all shepherds are detestable to the Egyptians* seems odd; if so, expulsion from Egypt would be expected, rather than settlement in *the best part of the land* and charge over Pharaoh's own livestock. No Egyptian source confirms such a bias. Perhaps Joseph wants his brothers to be honest despite any fear they might have about Pharaoh's attitude toward their profession (Hamilton, *Genesis 18–50*, 604).

Joseph's Famine Relief Policies · 47:13–27

47:13–22 Joseph, enslaved in his youth, now enslaves Egypt. Meanwhile, his Hebrew kin occupy fertile land and receive a food allowance, apparently without payment. The narrator claims, in effect, that a Hebrew created the Egyptian slave culture – a darkly ironic foreshadowing of Exodus 1.

47:23–27 By leaving eighty percent of the land's yield with the people, Joseph softens the blow of the Egyptians' newfound slavery to Pharaoh.

Jacob's Burial Wish · 47:28–31

47:28–31 The NIV's marginal note *Israel bowed down* (or better, "leaned over") *at the head of his bed* is correct, not the NIV's in-text translation, *Israel worshiped as he leaned on the top of his staff*. The narrator wants to emphasize the elderly Israel's fragility and approaching death.

Jacob Blesses Ephraim & Manasseh · 48:1–22

48:5–7 Jacob adopts Joseph's sons Ephraim and Manasseh as his own. The story explains how these boys become ancestors of two Israelite tribes named for them.

48:8–11 The sudden switch to the name *Israel*, along with Israel's need to have Ephraim and Manasseh identified, suggests that two sources have contributed to this section. However, Israel's poor eyesight may sufficiently explain why he cannot recognize the boys.

48:12–20 Since the boys can sit on *Israel's knees*, they must be fairly young. However, the narrative chronology requires them to be older than seventeen.

Israel envisions God as *my shepherd*, a metaphor familiar to Bible readers and appropriate to Jacob's occupation, but appearing in Genesis only here and in Jacob's deathbed blessing (Gen 49:24). Israel also calls God *the Angel who has delivered me from all harm*. Jacob's speech may reflect the way the narrator sometimes refers to the Lord as "the angel of the Lord" (Gen 16:7–14; Gen 22:11–19; see Exod 3:1–4).

48:21–22 No other text mentions any battle for land between Jacob and Amorites. The only clash narrated in Genesis between Jacob's family and any Canaanites is the attack on Shechem (chapter 34). However, the narrator calls Shechem's population Hivites (not Amorites), and Jacob's family did not occupy Shechem, but moved southward. More importantly, Jacob repudiates that attack in 34:30 (and perhaps 49:5–7), so he would hardly take credit for it here.

> **Amorites**
> *Group of Semitic-speaking peoples living in Palestine and Syria from at least the second millennium BCE on.*

Jacob Blesses His Sons · 49:1–33

49:1–2 Jacob's long, poetic deathbed speech forecasts *what will happen to you in days to come*. *You* must include the tribes descended from Jacob's sons. Several pronouncements make sense only when applied to the later tribes. The various descriptions of the tribal features use a series of word plays to make their point.

49:5–7 The impulsive violence criticized might be the assault on Shechem (see Gen 34:30), or something from a later tribal context (Gevirtz). Simeon and Levi lacked distinct territory within Israel. The Judahites apparently absorbed Simeonite territory (see Josh 19:1, 9). The Levites received no tribal territory, only individual cities throughout the land (see, for example, Num 18:21–24).

49:8–12 Jacob paints Judah in royal imagery, anticipating the Davidic dynasty. The lion imagery may echo chapter 37, where Judah and his brothers altered Joseph's coat to imply that Joseph had been "torn to pieces." Here, most interpreters take *my son* in *the prey, my son* as direct address, but it may also restate "prey" [Hebrew *tereph*], alluding to Judah's leadership in selling Joseph (Carmichael 438–39).

The NIV's text implies that *until he comes to whom it belongs* refers to David: Jacob says Judah's descendants will enjoy preeminence until they finally achieve kingship (Westermann, *Genesis 37–50*, 230). The NIV's margin suggests two other possibilities. *Until Shiloh comes* or "until he comes to Shiloh" mentions the shrine at Shiloh in Ephraim (Josh 18:1); its connection, if any, to Judah is unclear. The NIV's third option, *until he comes to whom tribute belongs* ("until tribute is brought to him") best parallels *and the obedience of the nations is his*; read thus, the line refers to neighboring kingdoms' tribute and fealty to David (see 2 Sam 8 and elsewhere; Wenham 478).

Donkeys and mules become stereotypical mounts for Israelite leaders (Judg 10:4; 12:14; 1 Kgs 1:44; Zech 9:9). Verses 11b–12 may simply praise the envisioned king's appearance or may anticipate agricultural prosperity during his reign. The image of garments stained with *the blood of grapes*, as if from treading in a winepress, elsewhere describes the divine warrior (Isa 63:1–6).

49:13 Jacob assigns seacoast territory to Zebulun; the allotments described in Joshua do not agree. There, Manasseh and Asher separate Zebulun from the Mediterranean, and Naphtali and Issachar separate Zebulun from the Sea of Galilee. Jacob's description of Zebulun better fits Asher, whose territory stretched along the Mediterranean seacoast from the Kishon River northward toward Sidon.

49:14–15 If *Issachar* reminds readers of the Hebrew word for a worker's wages, the imagery of a beast of burden may play off Issachar's name.

49:16–17 *Dan* sounds like the Hebrew word for "to judge." Otherwise, Dan has no special association with jurisprudence. The metaphor of a *serpent by the roadside* may refer to the Danites' craftiness and treachery in seizing new territory when they could not hold their original allotment (Josh 19:47–48; Judg 18, especially verses 27–29).

49:18 Jacob's plea for *deliverance* sits approximately in the center of the poem, interrupting the train of thought. Wenham (481–82), however,

GENESIS

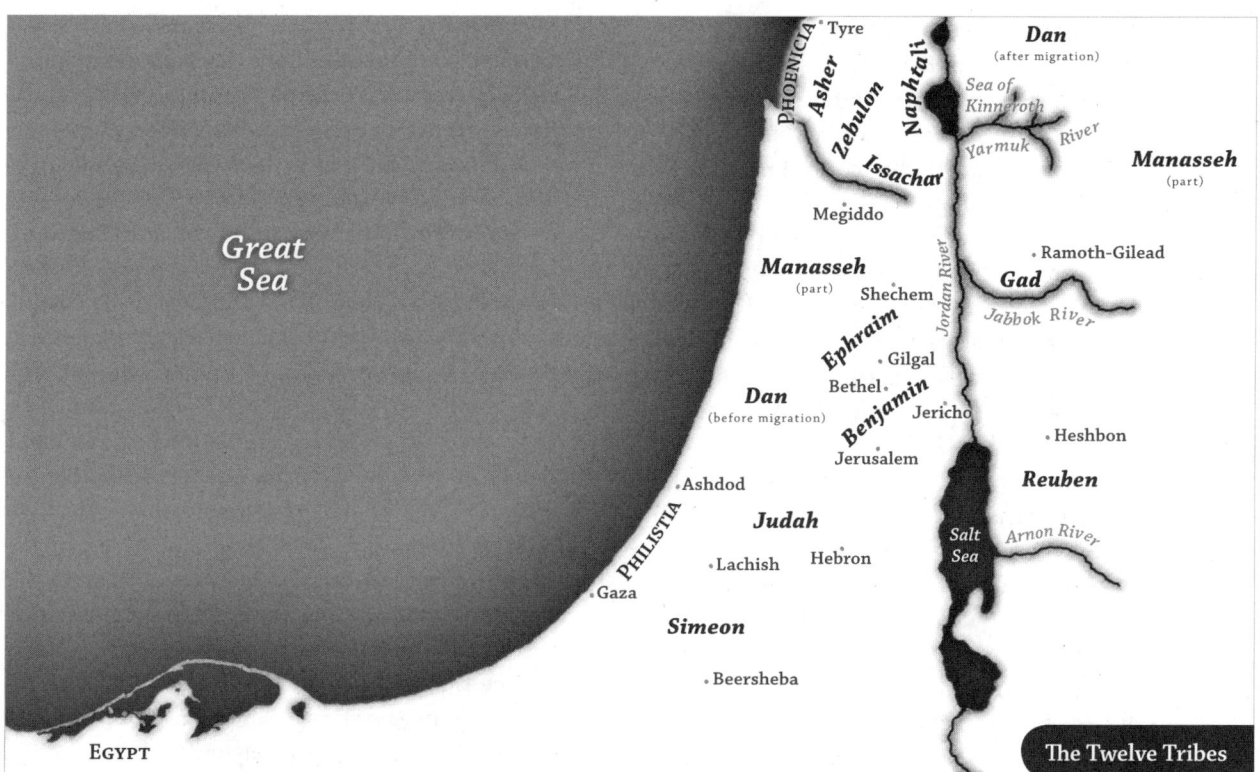

The Twelve Tribes

includes verse 18 in the pronouncement about Dan, suggesting that it anticipates that tribe's difficulties described in Judges 17–18.

49:19 No other text depicts Gadites as raiders, although a few mention invasions of Gad's territory (2 Kgs 10:32–33; Jer 49:1).

49:22–26 Jacob reserves his longest blessing for Joseph, ironic given Joseph's displacement by Manasseh and Ephraim. Perhaps Ephraim and Manasseh implicitly stand together here as "tribes of Joseph" (see Num 36:5; Ps 78:67; Ezek 37:19). *Fruitful* echoes the etiology of Ephraim's name (41:52). No biblical stories describe Joseph fighting defensively, as verses 23–24 imply.

The rare title *Mighty One of Jacob* stresses God's protectiveness, as does *Rock*. Jacob also sees God as a caretaking *Shepherd*. *Almighty* translates Hebrew *Shaddai* poorly; the fuller *El Shaddai* probably means "God of the heights." The *blessings of the heavens above* and the *blessings of the deep that lies below* relate to plant fertility, the *blessings of the breast and womb* to human and animal fertility.

In Genesis, Joseph literally stands as *the prince among his brothers*. In Israelite history, the Ephraimites would prove preeminent among the northern tribes.

49:27 Benjaminites play violent roles in Judges 19–20, possibly inspiring the image of *a ravenous wolf*. Since the blessing on Judah presupposes readers' familiarity with David, the reference to Benjamin may also presuppose readers' knowledge of Saul.

49:29–33 Jacob insists on being buried in *the cave in the field of Machpelah*. Jacob's speech emphasizes Abraham's title to the land. This plot, the family grave, is all Abraham's family owns in Canaan as Genesis ends. Yet even this much property inspires hope: the family may sojourn in Egypt, but God has begun to fulfill the promise of land. Jacob's determination to be buried with his ancestors underscores his conviction that God will give Canaan to his descendants.

Jacob's & Joseph's Deaths · 50:10–26

50:1–9 Given Joseph's warm relationship with Pharaoh, it seems likely that *their children and their flocks and herds were left in Goshen* for their welfare rather than as hostages (see Exod 10:8–11).

50:22–26 Jacob's family, the growing people of Israel, ends Genesis in Egypt, far from *the land [God] promised on oath to Abraham, Isaac, and Jacob*. Joseph, however, knows they will not remain there; his dying wish points forward to Israel's great experience of liberation narrated in Exodus.

GENESIS

THEOLOGICAL REFLECTIONS

In the ancient Near East, Genesis's picture of creation would have been both familiar and revolutionary. The earth's divine creation would have been thought a truism, and the basic storyline of Genesis 1–11 – creation, followed by divine disappointment with humans resulting in a great flood – was common knowledge. Genesis's portrayal of early human experience and the physical world resembled those of Israel's neighbors in some ways. However, Genesis' portrayal of God sharply contrasts with its ancient Near Eastern background.

Most remarkably, Genesis features only one God. This God directs a council of similar beings to whom God occasionally speaks (Gen 1:26; 3:22; 11:7), beings called *gods* or *sons of gods* (Gen 6:1–4), not *angels* (for which biblical Hebrew has other vocabulary). Yet these "gods" act independently, and against God's intention, only once in Genesis. Otherwise, they are God's almost indiscernible entourage. The serpent is not one of those beings.

It follows that God has no divine competitors. Conflict among gods drives other ancient Near Eastern creation and flood epics. In *Enuma Elish*, Marduk slays Tiamat, mother of the gods, then creates the world from her dead body. In *Atrahasis* and parallel flood stories, one god thwarts the other gods' plans by preserving a few humans. No such conflict appears in Genesis 1–11 (except, perhaps, Gen 6:1–4). All creation obeys God's creative commands. Similarly, the God who saves Noah sends the flood itself; there can be no squabbling among gods because only one God wields the power of creation and re-creation. In short, Genesis offers a bold monotheistic claim in a polytheistic context.

Similarly, the ancestral narratives know no rivals to the Lord. These narratives lack any hint of the patriarchs – or, for that matter, any other character – worshiping any other deity. Abimelech (Philistine), Melchizedek (Canaanite, presumably Jebusite), Abraham's extended family (Mesopotamian), and Egyptian officials all the way up to Pharaoh speak as if they know and revere Abraham's God.

Genesis's narrator actually takes an inclusive approach to worshipers of the Canaanite god El, identifying the Lord and El as one God, or at least taking over for the Lord's use divine epithets including El's name: El Elyon ("God Most High," Gen 14:18–20, 22), El Olam ("the Eternal God," Gen 21:33), and especially El Shaddai (NIV "God Almighty," better "God of the Heights," Gen 17:1; 28:3; 35:11; 43:14; 48:3; 49:25). Notably, the name "Israel" incorporates the name "El." Evidently, the narrator accepts patriarchal era worship of the Lord as El (as Exodus 6:2–4 explicitly claims), even to the point of planting sacred trees (Gen 21:33) and erecting sacred stones (Gen 28:18; 35:14), practices that the Torah forbids for Israelites.

Genesis's author(s) may extend this "inclusive monotheism" outside the book into their contemporary setting. Genesis probably reached its canonical form during the postexilic period, when Persia controlled Judea. Evidence for this "inclusive" approach comes especially from Abraham's anachronistic use of the divine title "God of heaven," a characteristically Persian-era epithet apparently used by the Persians themselves. Texts from the Jewish community at Elephantine in Egypt also equate the "God of Heaven" – presumably recognized and revered by the Persian king – with Yahu (a shorter spelling of *Yahweh*, "the Lord"; Bolin).

While the primeval narratives cannot be reduced to just one theme, a "crime and (mitigated) punishment" motif binds the stories together. Often, these offenses violate or threaten the boundary between divinity and humanity. Genesis 1 raises the theological problem: God created human beings "in the image of God," but humans are not gods. Repeatedly, human beings who resemble and even represent God on earth reach for more godlikeness, exerting efforts that transgress God's intention for "the image of God" in humanity.

Moreover, the ancestral narratives emphasize God's intentions for Israel's ancestors, beginning with Abraham. God's summons to Abraham comes with a threefold announcement: God declares that Abraham's descendants will become a great nation, will possess Canaan, and will somehow bless all peoples.

> **Origin Stories**
> *Mesopotamian and Egyptian parallels to Genesis's stories invariably feature multiple gods. Mesopotamian creation stories include theogonies, stories about the birth of the gods. Even in the Egyptian "Memphite theology," the creator god Ptah begins by creating other gods. Yet Genesis's God needs no theogony. God does not even need, as some Egyptian gods do, to will the divine self into existence. For Genesis's narrator, God's existence is a simple fact needing no explanation.*

The matriarchs' barrenness complicates expectation of descendants. Even so, the family's size stands as Genesis's most obvious fulfillment of divine intention. From small beginnings, the family grows in three generations to include seventy people (excluding servants or nonrelatives in the household) when Jacob migrates to Egypt.

In contrast, almost no progress is evident within Genesis toward Abraham's descendants possessing Canaan. As the book closes, the family can claim only the field of Machpelah, a tiny corner of the land. Nevertheless, for the narrator, this foothold is enough to sustain expectations that Jacob's family will possess the land. As their lives (and Genesis) end, Jacob and Joseph speak boldly of a return to Canaan, and their interest in this burial plot underscores their confidence.

Blessing the nations seems even more difficult for the patriarchs than holding land in Canaan. Abraham's dealings with Pharaoh and Abimelech result in plagues on Abraham's hosts; Abimelech fears the same after encountering Isaac. Laban initially prospers from Jacob's work, but his flocks later dwindle under Jacob's care. Certainly the Shechemites find Jacob's family anything but a blessing. Even Joseph, capable of blessing others as administrator of Pharaoh's famine relief effort, uses that position to enslave the Egyptian populace.

Yet it is not as if God's promises fail. God's major intentions for Abraham and his descendants depend heavily on human cooperation. The patriarchs' bad behavior does sometimes resist God's plan, yet their inability or unwillingness to live out God's intentions does not change or invalidate those intentions. Blessing the nations should be seen as an unmet challenge or unheeded call rather than an unfulfilled promise.

In the meantime, "election" refers to God's arbitrary decision to interact with particular people or groups to the exclusion of other people or groups. Abraham, Isaac, Jacob, and the Israelites are "elect." All other nations, even those descended from Abraham through Ishmael and Esau, are not.

To call election "arbitrary" means only that God could have chosen differently. Nothing in Abraham's character forces God to choose him, and the same goes for Isaac and Jacob.

However, the narrator's admission that the patriarchs, like their descendants, are fallible humans, shows clearly that their election is entirely unmerited. The patriarchs do not deserve to be singled out for special relationships with God. Nevertheless, they are, by the unmerited divine favor that Christians call "grace."

However, election, though unmerited, includes expectation. According to Genesis 18:18–19, God wants Abraham's family to increase the righteousness, justice, and blessing within the entire community of nations (even if Abraham's immediate descendants do not always accomplish this goal).

Moreover, God does not simply abandon the non-elect. In Genesis, God shows remarkable care for those excluded from the covenant community. God chooses Isaac over Ishmael but does not curse Ishmael. Instead, God blesses Ishmael, making him the father of nations. Esau too, though non-elect, prospers. The explicit theological claim that God cares even for the non-elect carries an implicit ethical challenge for the elect to care as much as God does. After all, the elect were chosen to increase righteousness, justice, and blessing for all.

Also, the portrait of God as a covenant-maker unites the primeval and ancestral narratives. In Genesis, God's covenants are usually unilateral. That is, God voluntarily enters into covenants committing God to pursue or avoid certain courses of action, without asking much in return. The primeval and ancestral narratives share this emphasis, each highlighting one specific covenant.

Immediately after the flood, God establishes a covenant with Noah, all terrestrial creatures, and the earth itself. God pledges never again to destroy all earthly life by flood. God asks nothing in return for this promise. Indeed, God knows the flood had no fundamental effect on the human tendency toward evil. The "evil inclination" plagues humanity after the flood, just as before. Despite this continuity in human evil, not because of any change, God decisively rules out any repeat of the flood.

Abraham, too, becomes party to a covenant with God, which then passes down to each successive generation among the elect. This covenant, too, is almost completely one-sided. God promises Abraham, Isaac, and Jacob many descendants and a prosperous land. In return, God requires circumcision, a physical sign of the covenant and virtually the only covenant requirement in Genesis 17.

As king and creator of heaven and earth, God could dictate covenant terms, placing all covenant responsibility on the other party. In Genesis, however, God unexpectedly shoulders covenant burdens, committing to the benefit of humanity and of Abraham's descendants without regard for a return on the divine investment.

FOR FURTHER STUDY

Walter Brueggemann, *Genesis* (Atlanta: John Knox, 1982).

Danna Nolan Fewell and David M. Gunn, *Gender, Power, and Promise: The Subject of the Bible's First Story* (Nashville: Abingdon, 1993).

W. Lee Humphreys, *The Character of God in the Book of Genesis: A Narrative Appraisal* (Louisville: Westminster John Knox, 2001).

Richard H. Lowery, "Genesis," in *Chalice Introduction to the Old Testament* (ed. Marti J. Steussy; St. Louis: Chalice, 2003), 29–45.

P. Kyle McCarter and Ronald S. Hendel, "The Patriarchal Age: Abraham, Isaac, and Jacob," in *Ancient Israel: From Abraham to the Roman Destruction of the Temple* (ed. Hershel Shanks; Washington: Biblical Archaeology Society, 1999), 1–31.

Bill Moyers, *Genesis: A Living Conversation* (New York: Doubleday, 1996).

R. Norman Whybray, *Introduction to the Pentateuch* (Grand Rapids: Eerdmans, 1995).

WORKS CITED

Peter R. Ackroyd, *The Chronicler in His Age* (Sheffield: JSOT, 1991).

Lloyd M. Barré, "The Riddle of the Flood Chronology," *Journal for the Study of the Old Testament* 41 (1988): 3–20.

Bernard F. Batto, *Slaying the Dragon: Mythmaking in the Biblical Tradition* (Louisville: Westminster John Knox, 1992).

Lyn M. Bechtel, "What If Dinah Is Not Raped? (Genesis 34)," *Journal for the Study of the Old Testament* 62 (1994): 19–36.

Thomas M. Bolin, "The Temple of יהו at Elephantine and Persian Religious Policy." in *The Triumph of Elohim: From Yahwisms to Judaisms* (ed. Diana Vikander Edelman; Grand Rapids: Eerdmans, 1995), 127–42.

Calum Carmichael, "Some Sayings in Genesis 49," *Journal of Biblical Literature* 88 (1969): 435–44.

Nina Collins, "281 BCE: The Year of the Translation of the Pentateuch into Greek under Ptolemy II." in *Septuagint, Scrolls, and Cognate Writings: Papers Presented to the International Symposium on the Septuagint and Its Relations to the Dead Sea Scrolls and Other Writings* (ed. George J. Brooke and Barnabas Lindars; Atlanta: Scholars Press, 1990), 403–503.

Philip R. Davies, *In Search of 'Ancient Israel'* (second ed.; Sheffield: Sheffield Academic Press, 1995).

Laura E. Donaldson, "Cyborgs, Ciphers, and Sexuality: Re-Theorizing Literary and Biblical Character," *Semeia* 63 (1993): 81–96.

S. R. Driver, *Genesis* (London: Methuen, 1915).

J. A. Emerton, "The Riddle of Genesis 14," *Vetus Testamentum* 21 (1971); 403–39.

———, "Some False Clues in the Study of Genesis 14," *Vetus Testamentum* 21 (1971): 24–27.

Jan Fokkelman, *Narrative Art in Genesis: Specimens of Stylistic and Structural Analysis* (Assen: Van Gorcum, 1975).

Serge Frolov, "The Other Side of the Jabbok: Genesis 32 as a Fiasco of Patriarchy," *Journal for the Study of the Old Testament* 91 (2000): 41–59.

Esther Fuchs, "'For I Have the Way of Women': Deception, Gender, and Ideology in Biblical Narrative," *Semeia* 42 (1988): 68–82.

Giovanni Garbini, "Hebrew Literature in the Persian Period." in *Second Temple Studies, 2: Temple Community in the Persian Period* (ed. Tamara C. Eskenazi and Kent H. Richards; Sheffield: JSOT, 1994), 180–8.

Stanley Gevirtz, "Simeon and Levi in 'The Blessing of Jacob' (Gen 49:5–7)," *Hebrew Union College Annual* 52 (1981): 93–128.

Cyrus H. Gordon, "Biblical Customs and the Nuzu Tablets," *Biblical Archaeologist* 3 (1940): 1–12.

Moshe Greenberg, "Another Look at Rachel's Theft of the Teraphim," *Journal of Biblical Literature* 81 (1962): 239–48.

Hermann Gunkel, *Genesis* (trans. Mark E. Biddle; Macon, Ga.: Mercer University Press, 1997).

Moses Hadas, *Aristeas to Philocrates* (New York: Harper, 1951).

William W. Hallo and K. Lawson Younger Jr., *The Context of Scripture*, vol. 1: *Canonical Compositions from the Biblical World* (Leiden: Brill, 1997).

———, *The Context of Scripture*, vol. 2: *Monumental Inscriptions from the Biblical World* (Leiden: Brill, 2000).

Victor P. Hamilton, *The Book of Genesis, Chapters 1–17* (Grand Rapids: Eerdmans, 1990).

———, *The Book of Genesis, Chapters 18–50* (Grand Rapids: Eerdmans, 1994).

Menahem Haran, "Behind the Scenes of History: Determining the Date of the Priestly Source," *Journal of Biblical Literature* 100 (1981): 321–33.

R. Christopher Heard, *Dynamics of Diselection: Ambiguity in Genesis 12–36 and Ethnic Boundaries in Postexilic Judah* (Atlanta: Society of Biblical Literature, 2001).

Gary A. Herion, "Why God Rejected Cain's Offering: The Obvious Answer," in *Fortunate the Eyes that See: Essays in Honor of David Noel Freedman in Celebration of His Seventieth Birthday* (ed. Astrid B. Beck et al.; Grand Rapids: Eerdmans, 1995), 52–65.

John R. Huddlestun, "Unveiling the Versions: The Tactics of Tamar in Genesis 38:15," *Journal of Hebrew Scriptures* 3 (2001) [online].

Victor Hurowitz, "Who Lost an Earring? Genesis 35:4 Reconsidered," *Catholic Biblical Quarterly* 62 (2000): 28–32.

J. Gerald Janzen, *Abraham and All the Families of the Earth: A Commentary on the Book of Genesis 12–50* (Grand Rapids: Eerdmans, 1993).

Sara Japhet, *I & II Chronicles* (Louisville: Westminster John Knox, 1993).

Nancy Jay, "Sacrifice, Descent and the Patriarchs," *Vetus Testamentum* 38 (1988): 52–70.

Sidney Jellicoe, *The Septuagint and Modern Study* (Oxford: Oxford University Press, 1968).

Henry F. Knight, "Meeting Jacob at the Jabbok: Wrestling with a Text – a Midrash on Genesis 32:22–32," *Journal of Ecumenical Studies* 29 (1992): 451–60.

J. A. L. Lee, *A Lexical Study of the Septuagint Version of the Pentateuch* (Chico, Calif.: Scholars Press, 1983).

Niels Peter Lemche, "The Old Testament – A Hellenistic Book?" *Scandinavian Journal of the Old Testament* 7 (1993): 163–93.

Miriam Lichtheim, *Late Egyptian Wisdom Literature in the International Context: A Study of Demotic Inscriptions* (Göttingen: Vandenhoeck and Ruprecht, 1983).

J. A. Loader, *A Tale of Two Cities: Sodom and Gomorrah in the Old Testament, Early Jewish, and Early Christian Traditions* (ed. T. Baarda and A. S. van der Woude; Kampen: Kok, 1990).

Carol Meyers, *Discovering Eve: Ancient Israelite Women in Context* (New York: Oxford University Press, 1988).

———, "'To Her Mother's House': Considering a Counterpart to the Israelite *Bêt 'āb*," in *The Bible and the Politics of Exegesis* (ed. David Jobling, Peggy L. Day, and Gerald T. Sheppard; Cleveland: Pilgrim, 1991), 39–51.

Jacob Milgrom, *Leviticus 1–16: A New Translation with Introduction and Commentary* (New York: Doubleday, 1991).

E. Theodore Mullen, *Ethnic Myths and Pentateuchal Foundations: A New Approach to the Formation of the Pentateuch* (Atlanta: Scholars Press, 1997).

Scott B. Noegel, "Sex, Sticks, and the Trickster in Gen 30:31–43," *Journal of the Ancient Near Eastern Society* 25 (1997): 7–17.

Martin Noth, *A History of Pentateuchal Traditions* (Englewood Cliffs: Prentice-Hall, 1972).

Harry M. Orlinsky, "The Plain Meaning of *Ruah* in Gen 1.2," *Jewish Quarterly Review* 48 (1957): 174–82.

René Péter-Contesse, "Was Potiphar a Eunuch? (Genesis 37.36; 39.1)," *Bible Translator* 47 (1996): 142–46.

James D. Purvis, *The Samaritan Pentateuch and the Origins of the Samaritan Sect* (Cambridge: Harvard University Press, 1968).

Gerhard von Rad, *Genesis* (Philadelphia: Westminster, 1972).

Donald B. Redford, *Egypt, Canaan, and Israel in Ancient Times* (Princeton: Princeton University Press, 1992).

Rolf Rentdorff, *The Problem of the Process of Transmission in the Pentateuch* (Sheffield: JSOT, 1990).

John Skinner, *A Critical and Exegetical Commentary on the Book of Genesis* (Edinburgh: T & T Clark, 1930).

E. A. Speiser, *Genesis: Introduction, Translation, and Notes* (Garden City, N.Y.: Doubleday, 1964).

Frank Anthony Spina, "The Ground for Cain's Rejection (Gen 4): *adamah* in the Context of Gen 1–11," *Zeitschrift für die Alttestamentliche Wissenschaft* 104 (1992): 319–32.

Thomas L. Thompson, *The Historicity of the Patriarchal Narratives: The Quest for the Historical Abraham* (Berlin: de Gruyter, 1974).

———, *The Mythic Past: Biblical Archaeology and the Myth of Israel* (New York: Basic, 1999).

Emmanuel Tov, *Textual Criticism of the Hebrew Bible* (Minneapolis, Minn.: Fortress, Van Gorcum, 1992).

Gregory Vall, "What Was Isaac Doing in the Field?" *Vetus Testamentum* 44 (1994): 513–23.

John Van Seters, *Prologue to History: The Yahwist as Historian in Genesis* (Louisville: Westminster John Knox, 1992).

Bruce K. Waltke, "The Samaritan Pentateuch and the Text of the OT," in *New Perspectives on the Old Testament* (ed. J. Barton Payne; Waco, Tx.: Word, 1970), 212–39.

Julius Wellhausen, *Prolegomena to the History of Israel* (Edinburgh: Black, 1885).

Gordon J. Wenham, *Genesis 16–50* (Dallas: Word, 1994).

Joan Goodnick Westenholtz, "Tamar, *Qedešah*, *Qadištu*, and Sacred Prostitution in Mesopotamia," *Harvard Theological Review* 82 (1989): 245–65.

Claus Westermann, *Genesis 12–36* (Minneapolis, Minn.: Augsburg, 1985).

——— , *Genesis 37–50* (Minneapolis, Minn.: Augsburg, 1986).

Ronald F. Youngblood, ed., *The Genesis Debate*: *Persistent Questions about Creation and the Flood* (Nashville: Nelson, 1986).

Exodus

Rodney Ashlock

CHAPTER CONTENTS

- Contexts 143
- Commentary 144
    - The Birth & Call of Moses · 1:1–4:31 144
    - The Exodus from Egypt · 5:1–12:42 151
    - Crossing the Red Sea · 12:43–15:21 155
    - The Journey to Sinai · 15:22–18:27 157
    - God's Appearance at Sinai · 19:1–20:18 158
    - The Book of the Covenant · 20:19–23:32 161
    - The Inauguration of the Covenant · 24:1–18 162
    - Instructions Pertaining to the Tabernacle · 25:1–31:18 162
    - The Breaking & Renewal of the Covenant · 32:1–34:35 163
    - The Making, Erection, & Consecration of the Tabernacle · 35:1–40:38 164
- Theological Reflections 166
- For Further Study 166
- Works Cited 166

MAPS, TABLES, & FEATURES

- The Land of Midian 145
- The Prophetic Call 148
- Hardening Pharaoh's Heart 150
- A Possible Route of Wilderness Wandering 156
- Law in the Ancient Near East 159
- Forms of Marriage 160
- Law Codes in the Pentateuch 161
- *Cherem* Warfare 162
- The Tabernacle 163

The name Exodus is derived from the Greek word which means "road or way out" and refers to the Israelites' departure from Egypt after the tenth plague. Its Hebrew title is Shemoth, which refers to the second word of the Hebrew text of Exodus and means "names." This reference to "names" at the beginning of the book of Exodus forges a link with the book of Genesis as it continues Israel's story from its inception that goes back to the call of Abraham from Ur of the Chaldeans to Joseph's, and then Jacob's, descent into Egypt where the book of Genesis ends. Exodus depicts this fledgling people as they begin to grow into a nation.

Exodus instructs us on the importance of covenant and faithfulness. This book reminds the people of God to cry out in times of distress and to have faith that He will respond and deliver. It is a faithful reminder that God is on the side of the oppressed and does not operate according to human conditions. It is finally a story of the continuing presence of God. This presence, to be sure, is both frightening and awesome, life threatening as well as life giving.

CONTEXTS

In many ways, the best-known section of the book of Exodus is the covenant established on Mount Sinai. A covenant is a binding agreement between two parties that results, in this case, in an exclusive relationship between God and Israel. God desires to be in a relationship with Israel, and that relationship takes the form of a covenant. The laws that follow are an expression of the loyalty that Yahweh demands of the covenant partner, because God demonstrated loyalty as Israel's partner by hearing their cry of oppression and bearing them out on eagle's wings from the house of slavery (Exod 19:6). A covenant relationship demands loyalty [Hebrew *chesed*] and trust [*emeth*] – two characteristics God demonstrates consistently to Israel, but which Israel often has a difficult time demonstrating back to God. One significant theological point is that God establishes a covenant with the children of Israel prior to issuing the law. Israel does not keep the law in order to enter into a covenant relationship with God. Rather Israel is already in a covenant relationship with God; therefore, they keep the law.

However, in addition to the theme of covenant, the book of Exodus focuses on a number of other thematic structures as it tells its story – structures that can unlock important aspects of the relationship between God and his people.

Creation · Often overlooked, Fretheim (12–14) has effectively reminded us of the prominent role the theme of creation plays in the book of Exodus. Just as Genesis 1–2 depicts God creating the world, so much of Exodus is concerned with the creation of a nation. The book of Exodus shows the children of Jacob fulfilling the divine mandate to be fruitful and multiply (Gen 1:28) as they flourish in Egypt (1:7). The creation of the tabernacle follows the same scheme as found in Genesis 1 when God finishes the work of creating the universe in six days and then blesses and consecrates the seventh day and then rests. So the Israelites under Moses' direction create a sacred space, and then Moses blesses the people while they rest from their journeys (Exod 39:43). In many ways, the reader should recognize the making of the tabernacle as a way of reordering creation (Blenkinsopp 275–292).

Journey/Encampment · The motif of journey pervades the book of Exodus. The story begins in Egypt but will end with the ancient Israelites encamped at the foot of Mount Sinai. In essence, the experience of the children of Israel alternates between pilgrimage and encampment. At times, Israel will journey through the harsh climate and terrain of the Sinai Peninsula, while at other times they will pitch their tents and settle in for a long stay. While on their way to the mountain to encounter God, they begin to grumble or complain about their conditions and plight (see Exod 15:22–17:7 especially). The Israelites will not resume their journeys until Numbers 10:10, but in between the time they arrive at the foot of Mount Sinai (Exod 19:1) until they depart from it lies the formative period of the Sinai covenant and thus the birth of Israel's life as a nation.

Presence/Guidance · While the book of Exodus begins with God noticeably absent, by the end of the book God's presence saturates the camp of the Israelites (Exod 40:34–38). On the way from Egypt to Sinai, God's presence is vividly marked by the pillar of cloud and fire as the children of Israel march through the wilderness (Exod 13:20–21), the division of the Red Sea (Exod 14:10–31), the provision of water and food in the hostile desert (Exod 15:22–17:7), and in thunder and lightning, fire and smoke, and a dense cloud atop Mount Sinai (Exod 19:16–19). God's abiding presence is marked by the construction of the ark of the covenant and its placement in the holy of holies (Exod 35:1–40:33). Finally, Exodus 40:34–38 dramatically depicts the descent of the glory [Hebrew *kavod*] of Yahweh into the holy of holies. The divine presence is so strong that not even Moses, who often talks to God face-to-face (Exod 33:11; Numb 12:8), ventures into the tabernacle.

Law/Holiness · One of the more interesting features of the book of Exodus is the juxtaposition of the narrative and the legal materials. Scholars have wrestled with the literary and theological relationship of the narrative and legal material with no consensus on the reason the legal materials appear where they do. The best way to understand this arrangement is to see the legal material arising out of the story of ancient Israel and their relationship to God.

> **Law & Relationship**
> The legal materials in Exodus are not designed to be burdensome. Rather, laws are extensions of the relationship Yahweh desires with the covenant people. God's actual act of deliverance or intent to deliver always precedes the law and serves as the rationale behind the law given to Israel. The law, as it appears in Exodus 19–24, aims to help the Israelites know what it means to be a holy people.

The Gospel · As Christian readers, we do not often associate the good news of God with the Old Testament. Furthermore, we tend to individualize and spiritualize the gospel, thus relegating the good news of God to the hereafter and rendering it useless and benign to the material circumstances of people. Exodus demonstrates how God's good news reaches into the real lives of people in the here and now. By seeing God's deliverance affecting the physical and material lives of the people, we recognize that God seeks the well-being, or *shalom*, of all individuals and nations. As Christians, we share God's concern for the oppressed, not just in spiritual categories, but also in the tangible aspects of life.

COMMENTARY

THE BIRTH & CALL OF MOSES · 1:1–4:31

Exodus 1–4 charts the ebb and flow of Israel's relationship with God. Exodus 1:1–7 situates the Hebrews in Egypt and describes the flourishing nature of their existence in the land. Exodus 1:8–22 marks a major shift in the relationship of the Hebrews with Egypt, as a *new king* arises who does not know Joseph and the salvation God wrought through him. He initiates a policy of oppression and genocide. Exodus 2:1–10 details the birth and salvation of Moses through the compassion of Pharaoh's daughter and the cunning of his sister. From the beginning, Yahweh is training Moses to be the leader of the Hebrew people, as Moses will be raised in the court of Pharaoh but nurtured in the bosom of his Hebrew mother. Exodus 2:11–22 signals another transition, this time in the life of Moses, as he must depart Egypt after killing an Egyptian who was beating a Hebrew. He flees to Midian where he rescues (as he will also do for the Israelites) the daughters of Reuel (Jethro), priest of Midian, and marries Zipporah. Here the second stage of his training begins as he learns to shepherd the flocks of his father-in-law in the wilderness around Mount Sinai. God finally enters the picture in 2:23–25 to respond to the cries of the oppressed people of Israel. Exodus 3:1–4:23 depicts the process of Yahweh's self revelation, in which God charges Moses with the task of delivering the Hebrews from their oppressor. Moses proves to be a reluctant savior, but God's will prevails in the end. This first section ends with Moses returning to Egypt (4:24–31) after a narrow escape from the hand of Yahweh, who sought to kill him. Aaron and Moses unite and meet with the Israelite elders, who learn that God has not forgotten them and plans to deliver them. The people respond to this good news with worship (4:31).

1:1–7 The book of Exodus begins with a brief genealogy (*these are the names*) of the sons of Jacob, linking Exodus with Genesis. Exodus 1:1–7 demonstrates that Genesis's God of creation is still busy creating and fulfilling promises and purposes in creation. Seventy persons are mentioned in Exodus, similar to the number listed in Genesis 46:8–27. Whereas Genesis lists the twelve sons in the order of their birth, Exodus arranges them according to their mother. The six sons of Leah begin the genealogy, followed by Benjamin, the only son of Rachel not in Egypt already, then the sons of Bilhah, Rachel's maid servant, and last of all, Gad and Asher, the two sons of Zilpah, Leah's maid servant. Joseph appears last in the list because he is already in Egypt, the result of his having been sold as a slave (Gen 37:12–36). This opening paragraph serves three primary functions: first, the list of names provides a link to the book of Genesis and reminds the reader of how the children of Israel came to be in Egypt in the first place; second, the language of Exodus 1:7 serves to draw the

reader back to Genesis 1:28, where God commanded the first man and woman *to be fruitful and multiply and fill the earth*; and third, it concludes the story of Joseph and his brothers and the generation that was faithful to commands of God. However, their faithfulness to Yahweh does not please the new king of Egypt, who sees them as a threat.

1:8–22 These verses introduce a major theme of the book – oppression. Many modern readers come from affluent backgrounds with very little experience of oppression, much less slavery. It may be difficult, therefore, for readers today to grasp the feeling of despair and brutality that would have permeated the lives of the slaves. Our rather comfortable lifestyles make us strangers to the world of this fledgling people derisively called Hebrews, or *Hapiru*, who suffer under taskmasters who cruelly and ferociously demand of them every ounce of their sweat and blood as they make bricks for

> **Hebrews & Hapiru**
> *A collection of letters from Palestine to Pharaoh Akhenaten (about 1350 BCE) speaks of marauders called "Habiru" or "Apiru," a term that may relate to the ethnic label "Hebrew." However, the label "Habiru" probably does not designate an ethnic group, but rather a loose collection of social outcasts, or a socioeconomic group that later pharaohs could easily exploit. Some of their descendants may have been the Israelites. Interestingly, in the Bible, "Hebrew" is usually the label that non-Israelites use of Israelites. It thus remained an ethnic slur for many centuries.*

the store cities. Rather, one of the central messages of the book of Exodus is the reminder that the gospel, the good news that God desires to proclaim to all people in all times, has every bit as much to do with the here and now as it does the hereafter. Exodus is not a trite book of easy spiritual truths. We must suppress our tendency to dismiss the social and even political teachings of this book.

The new king of Egypt who does not know Joseph may well be a reference to the restoration of a native Egyptian dynasty and the overthrow of a group of Asiatics, known as the *Hyksos*, who had ruled Egypt from roughly 1750 BCE to 1500 BCE. This new king, being an Egyptian, would quite naturally champion a policy that would seek to eradicate any memory of this non-Egyptian dynasty. Included in this eradication process would be any memory of Joseph and the life-giving work of God through him. In contrast to the life-preserving policies of Joseph and his wise counsel, the king embarks on a maniacal policy that, in his attempt to eradicate the Hebrews, will bring death to his own people.

> **Hyksos**
> *The Hyksos were a group of Asiatic tribes expelled from Egypt by Ahmose. Other scholars date the Hebrews' slavery somewhat later.*

The increasing numbers of the Hebrews pose a serious threat to the security of the Egyptians (1:10). Egyptian policy ratified by the Pharaoh involved two steps: first, the Egyptians made the Hebrews' life *bitter* through the oppression of hard labor (1:11–14). This labor concentrated on two Egyptian "store cities," Pithom and Raamses, which were built to store supplies and weapons as part of the defense system established by the Egyptians to protect themselves from invasions from southwest Asia (Hoffmaier 119–21). When this plan fails to slow down the explosive growth of the Israelites, the Pharaoh instructs the midwives to throw every male child into the Nile River, while they are allowed to spare the lives of the female children (1:15–21). The midwives, who are depicted as wise women because they *feared God* (see Proverbs 1:7; 9:10), refuse to obey the Pharaoh's command and spare the male children. Being *wise*, the midwives Shiphrah and Puah discern a certain divine ordering of things. The two women outwit the Pharaoh based on their wisdom. The story is deeply ironic, as the lowly midwives outmaneuver and defy the most powerful figure in Egypt. The irony continues as the midwives are named while the Pharaoh remains nameless. Another point of irony is that, by commanding the slaughter of Hebrew male infants, the Pharaoh is essentially cutting off his future work supply. The decree makes no sense. By their actions and response to the Pharaoh, the wisdom of the women holds life as sacred (Fretheim 32). Having been duped by the midwives, the Pharaoh then commands the Egyptians to throw the male children into the Nile. Ironically, the Nile, which provides life for the Egyptians, threatens death for the Hebrew male offspring. The next paragraph in the story tells how three women work together once again to thwart the schemes of the most powerful man in the land.

> **The "Wise Woman"**
> *The character of the wise woman in the Bible reappears in the stories of Abimelech (Judg 9) and David (1 Kgs 14). In both cases, a wise woman proves superior to the king, who should be the wisest of all.*

> **Water Symbolism**
> *The use of the Nile to cause death anticipates future scenes in Exodus, such as the first plague and the drowning of the Egyptian army as they attempt to cross the sea.*

The text first mentions God in Exodus 1:17. The scant references to God in the first two chapters of Exodus may surprise the reader. This silence of God here resembles that in the story of Joseph, where God never speaks directly to Joseph, and in the book of Esther, which never directly mentions God at all. In both cases, the action of the stories takes place in a foreign land. Exodus 1 also highlights human activity and character. The courage and wisdom of the women are mentioned, with God taking part only indirectly. Perhaps a lesson to be learned in Exodus 1 is the working together of human activity and divine power. (There is direct speech by God to Jacob in Gen 46:1 and following, but it is interesting to note that God never directly addresses Joseph, whose story also primarily occurs outside the land.)

2:1–10 Under these conditions, Moses is born. The mother and father remain unnamed at this point, but both parents are descended from Levi (see 6:16–20). Seeing that he is a handsome baby boy and fearing for his life, Moses' mother makes an *ark* for him out of a papyrus basket, coats it with bitumen and pitch, and places him in the Nile. The boy's sister – presumably Miriam, though she remains unnamed until 15:20 – watches over him from a distance. Once again, the plan of the Pharaoh is thwarted, this time by his own daughter, who adopts the baby and brings him into the Pharaoh's house. The boy's sister offers the mother of the child as a wet nurse until he is weaned. Pharaoh's daughter agrees to this suggestion and gives the little boy an Egyptian name, Moses, which means "son of," but which the text connects by means of a pun to the Hebrew word "to draw out." Even though the child will be raised in the house of the Pharaoh, Moses' Hebrew mother will have the first opportunity to influence and nurture the little boy. Walter Brueggemann has rightly noted that this story is not primarily a birth narrative but a rescue story. The emphasis does not fall on the birth of Moses but on the rescue of Moses by none other than Pharaoh's daughter herself. The birth of Moses also invites comparison with the birth of Jesus. In each instance, an evil tyrant threatens the male children.

Once again, an early story in Exodus emphasizes the role of human beings in the salvation of God's people. God is not the subject of any sentence in the birth and rescue story of Moses. Soon God will appear in power and demonstrate divine supremacy over Pharaoh and the gods of Egypt, but for now five women have served as the hands and feet of God.

2:11–22 The narrative moves quickly as Moses next appears as an adult. Readers can only speculate about the childhood of Moses. Exodus 2:11–22 relates three episodes in the life of Moses that lead to his departure from Egypt and his new life as a shepherd in the wilderness of Sinai. This brief paragraph features the two primary settings of the book of Exodus, Egypt and Sinai. Moses encounters three different groups of people: Egyptians, Hebrews, and Midianites. Moses demonstrates his ability to dispense justice as he attempts to settle disputes in two different cases. Moses also serves as a savior as he rescues both a Hebrew man from his Egyptian oppressor and the daughters of Reuel (also called Jethro) at the well, and additionally he learns the life of a pastoralist as he serves as a shepherd for his father-in-law.

Moses is raised in the house of Pharaoh but apparently never forgets his roots as a Hebrew. One day he comes across an Egyptian striking a Hebrew, and his compassion is stirred. This story foreshadows the notion of Moses as a deliverer but rules out the idea that Moses, by his own violence or initiative, will free Israel.

Moses' flight into the wilderness leads him to Midian. Whereas Egypt stood for power and was a vast and ancient empire, Midian represented the pastoral life, though it did have urban centers (Mendenhall). While a power-hungry Pharaoh ruled Egypt, Moses will encounter a priest in Midian. He comes to a well where the flocks of wandering shepherds are watered. While Moses is at the well, a group of shepherds attack the daughters of a local priest in an effort to prevent them from watering their father's flocks. Moses comes to their defense, drives away their attackers, and waters their flock for them. Impressed, their father extends hospitality to him and gives Moses his daughter Zipporah as a wife. She bears him a son, and Moses names him Gershom, a pun on the word for "sojourner" [Hebrew *ger*].

> **Moses' Name**
> *The name Moses [Egyptian Mose] indicates that the Pharaoh's daughter has every intention of raising him in the royal court (compare the name Moses with the endings of several Egyptian pharaohs, such as Thutmose).*

> **The Ark**
> *A strong tie to Genesis is made through the use of the word ark [Hebrew tevah], which also appears in Genesis 6 and 7. In Genesis 6:14, the word signifies the boat Noah makes to ensure that he and his family do not drown in the flood. In both stories of an ark, God delivers the hero through water.*

> **Wells in Ancient Times**
> *In the ancient Near East, among pastoral societies, wells served as gathering places where the women of the village would water their flocks. Thus in Genesis 26:12–22, Isaac's shepherds quarrel with the servants of Abimelech, the king of the Philistines, over the ownership and use of wells. In Genesis 24:10–23 and 29:1–12, however, the well is the setting for romance as both Isaac, in the person of his father's servant, and Jacob first meet Rebekah and Rachel, who later become their wives. In Exodus these twin themes of conflict and romance converge.*

2:23-24 At this point in the story, God officially enters the scene. While Moses is in Midian, Israel is still in Egypt experiencing the oppression of their masters, the Egyptians. In their affliction, they cry out to God, who *hears* their cry, *remembers* the covenant with the great ancestors Abraham, Isaac, and Jacob, *looks* upon their distress, and *takes notice* of them. These four verbs are vital in our understanding of the nature of God. God, who up to this point has been a passive bystander, now becomes an interested participant in the story of Israel. The names of Abraham, Isaac, and Jacob recall Genesis and the promise made to these ancestors of faith. Here, the children of Israel initiate the encounter, and God responds, whereas in most biblical examples, God initiates and the people respond. Here God remembers a promise made long ago and prepares to deliver the children of Israel. The success of God's plan, however, will hinge on a reluctant shepherd in Midian.

3:1-4:18 This narrative emphasizes the dual roles of divine initiative and human agency. God takes the initiative in "bringing up" the Israelites from Egypt, while the human agent, in this case Moses, is charged with the task of "bringing them out" of Egypt. God calls Moses, but Moses resists the call, giving in only after intense pressure. In essence, the calling of Moses is an excellent example of how God works with, through, and sometimes in spite of human beings. Nevertheless, humans have an indispensable role to play in the working out of God's plan.

Moses is tending the flock of his father-in-law, Jethro, when he comes across a bush that is on fire but is not being consumed. Furthermore, the Hebrew term for bush is *seneh*, which sounds similar to Sinai, the place where Moses is tending the sheep of his father-in-law and the future site of the covenant-making ceremony between God and Israel. Moses witnesses a theophany, or appearance of God on earth. The association of fire with the appearance of God is quite common (see Gen 15:17; Exod 19:18; 2 Kgs 2:11; Isa 6:1-8), but for Moses, this occurrence is unnatural and is a sight that he must *turn aside* to see.

He finds that the ground is holy, but only because of God's presence. It is the presence of God that makes a place and a people holy. What follows is Moses' initial encounter with the divine and a call that accompanies the commissioning of most prophets (1 Sam 3:1-10; Isa 6:1-8; Jer 1:5-7; Ezek 3:1-3).

The conversation between God and Moses reveals God's need for human agents. God is moved by Israel's cries and initiates the encounter with Moses yet is dependent upon Moses to serve as an instrument. Salvation is twofold: God will deliver or save Israel from oppression and bondage in Egypt, and he will bring them to the promised land. God's salvation recalls the promise made to Abraham (Gen 12:1-3) in the covenant ceremony (Gen 15:7-21). In

---

The Prophetic Call

Most prophetic calls contain the following standard elements:

Theophany or a divine appearance by God (3:1-3) · In this case the voice of God appears to Moses in the form of a fiery bush. (Note the association of fire and God later on Mount Sinai.)

Introductory word (3:4-6) · God tells Moses to take off his shoes, for the ground on which he is standing is holy. God also identifies himself as the God of Abraham, Isaac, and Jacob. But upon closer inspection, God also ties his identity into the heritage of Moses—a heritage he might have learned while being nursed by his mother in the court of Pharaoh and one which he has already defended (2:11-12). Thus, God links himself with Moses and links Moses with the Hebrews. As a result, the people of God are the people of Moses.

Divine commission (3:7-10) · God informs Moses that he is well aware of the suffering of the Israelites, just like Moses is, and that he intends to rescue them, just as Moses rescued both the Hebrew who was being beaten (2:11-12) and the daughters of Reuel (2:16-19). God intends to bring the Israelites to a land flowing with milk and honey (3:8). God tells Moses to appear before Pharaoh and demand that the Egyptian king let the people go. This request will be met with rejection (see Isaiah 6).

Objection (3:11, 13; 4:1, 10, 13) · Moses will respond to God's commissioning with a series of five specific objections.

Reassurance (3:12, 14-22; 4:11-12, 14-17) · God responds to each of Moses' objections with a divine word meant to encourage Moses. He will even send his brother Aaron, a concession to the original plan, to speak for Moses.

Sign (4:2-9) · God offers a variety of signs to Moses, involving the divine promise of presence (see Fretheim 51).

addition, the conversation between Yahweh and Moses reveals a flexibility in the divine plan. God wants to send Moses alone; however, when Moses proves reluctant, God adapts the plan to include Aaron. Thus a sovereign God works through us and is willing to change plans to meet us where we are in our spiritual journey.

As with most prophetic calls, Moses is less than thrilled at the prospect of being a deliverer or prophet (see Judg 6:15; Jer 1:6). His resistance to the divine call is a strong one and manifests itself in five objections. First, he claims that he is unworthy of the task through the statement, *Who am I?* God responds by promising to be with Moses (3:11–12). On the surface, God's response does not seem like much of a sign for Moses. However, the promise of divine presence is crucial as Moses begins to muster the courage to meet Pharaoh with the message God has given to him. In many ways, the divine promise of presence (*I am* or *will be with you*) echoes throughout Scripture (see Matt 1:23; 28:20).

Second, Moses claims he will not command Pharaoh's attention because he does not know God's name. God counters by telling Moses to say that *I am* has sent him, giving Moses a form of the Hebrew verb "to be" [*hayah*, which shares the same letter as God's name "Yahweh"]. These four letters will become the sacred name that is too holy to be pronounced or uttered. This name also indicates the power associated with God. It is a causative power that brought both the world and a chosen people into existence. It is the same God who called the great ancestors of the past (Abraham, Isaac, and Jacob) and made a promise to give them land. It is this God, Yahweh, who now sends Moses to Pharaoh and who will speak through him with the demand to release Israel. In 3:20, Yahweh's power will be demonstrated in striking [Hebrew *nakah*] the Pharaoh (the same word used to describe the action of Moses when he strikes the Egyptian in 2:12) and performing wonders in his sight. After performing these wonders, this same God will cause the Egyptians to release the Israelites and allow the Hebrew women to *plunder* their Egyptian masters (3:22).

> **Tetragrammaton**
> The Old Testament spells God's name YHWH, which was probably pronounced Yahweh. Later Jews avoided pronouncing the name out of reverence, substituting "Lord" [Hebrew *adonay*] or "the name" [*hashem*]. Following this lead, the Septuagint renders YHWH as *ho kyrios*, "the Lord," which English translations also follow. "Jehovah" is an early modern misreading of the name, mixing the consonants of YHWH and the vowels of *adonay*.

> **"So you will plunder the Egyptians ..."**
> The plundering of the Egyptians serves as a form of reparation for years of servitude.

Moses' third act of resistance is to argue that the people will not believe him when he arrives in Egypt (4:1). Yahweh offers two proofs of the validity of the call to Moses: changing Moses' staff to a snake and back again, and afflicting Moses with a skin disease (probably not Hansen's disease, the modern form of leprosy). As it turns out, those signs only partially demonstrate Yahweh's presence, since the Egyptian magicians can duplicate the first one. However, they serve to foreshadow the awesome demonstrations of God's power in the ten plagues.

Fourth, still stubbornly refusing to go, Moses claims that he would not make a good messenger for God because he does not speak well or that his tongue is *heavy*. Later readers speculate that Moses may have had a speech impairment, but Exodus does not say this explicitly. Once again, God reassures Moses that he will be with him and speak for him (4:10–11). Finally, Moses sheds all pretense and asks God simply to find someone else (4:13). Yahweh, who is beginning to lose patience with Moses, offers Moses' brother Aaron as a companion. Moses is to put the words of the Lord in the mouth of Aaron, and the latter will speak before the Pharaoh. Moses has no choice but to obey and return to Egypt. He reports to his father-in-law what has transpired and prepares to leave Midian.

At this point, an analysis of the character of Moses proves useful. Exodus 2–4 has given us a fairly good picture of Moses and the type of leader he will be. First, he is beautiful, or literally, "good" [Hebrew *ki tov*]. The phrase *ki tov* is the same one that is used to describe each of the days of creation in Genesis 1 and seems to express the concept that each day turned out exactly the way God intended. Exodus 3:2 seems to indicate that Moses is exactly what God intends for his leader. Second, Moses is from the tribe of Levi, which makes him a member of the "priestly tribe." This association with the tribe of Levi will impact his role as lawgiver for the Israelites. Though never called a priest, certainly Moses assumes the role when he inaugurates the covenant in Exodus 24 and oversees the consecration of Aaron and his sons when they become priests in Leviticus 8 and 9. Third, Moses is nursed by his mother, and we may assume from his concern for his Hebrew kinfolk (2:11) that he is fully aware of his nationality and heritage as one of the children of Israel. Fourth, Moses has a passion for justice (Fretheim 43–46). Twice in the narrative Moses comes across scenes of injustice, and each time he acts on behalf of the oppressed, whether it be one of his Hebrew brothers or the daughters of the priest of Midian. Fifth, Moses is a shepherd, a feature or characteristic associated with a monarch (2 Sam 24:17). Shepherds lead the flock to water and provide for their basic needs. These are tasks Moses will assume during Israel's forty years in the wilderness. Finally, Moses will serve as a prophet for the Israelites. His call is similar to that of other prophets, most notably Jeremiah (Jer 1:6). His death scene eulogizes him as a prophet the likes of whom Israel would never see again, because God spoke to him face to face (Deut 34:10). Thus, Moses will assume the roles of lawgiver/priest, prophet, military leader, and judge – the quintessential leader. Perhaps Moses is the ideal ruler for Israel as one who upholds the law, delivers God's people from their enemies, and acts as a shepherd, leading them to the still waters. In essence, Moses bears the traits and character of a king but does not actually possess the title, and therefore he avoids the traps of the monarch regarding the multiplication of wives and military forces (compare for example, Judg 8:22–27, where Gideon refuses the title of king but ensnares the people by making some sort of image). Moses is a leader par excellence, and, despite his weaknesses and limitations, he serves as both a role model for all leaders and as a foreshadowing of Christ's leadership (see John 1; 2 Cor 3–4; Heb 2–4).

> **God's Leaders Oppose Injustice**
> In Exodus, the Egyptians are the oppressor (1:11), the Israelites cry out (2:23), and God hears their cry (2:24) and raises up Moses to deliver (3:10). Later, leaders in the book of Judges will play a similar role (Judg 2:12–19). When Israel is oppressed by enemies and cries out to God, God will hear their cry and send a deliverer, or judge.

4:19-31 Moses returns from his encounter with Yahweh to ask permission from Jethro to go to Egypt, ostensibly to check on his people. Jethro grants Moses permission, and Moses begins his journey back to Egypt. Once again, Yahweh breaks into the narrative to speak to Moses. Here God promises to perform signs and wonders before Pharaoh, but Yahweh will also *harden his heart* so that Pharaoh will temporarily refuse to let Israel

> **Hardening Pharaoh's Heart**
> The hardening of Pharaoh's heart has proven to be one of the more difficult theological problems in the Bible. Even the apostle Paul in Romans 9 seems to have struggled with the theological implications of this passage. Questions abound. Does Pharaoh harden his own heart, or does Yahweh? If the latter, then does Pharaoh really have a choice? Thus the issue of human free will and divine sovereignty comes to the forefront of the discussion.
>
> Three words are used to describe the hardening of Pharaoh's heart: kavod, qashah, and chazaq. Yahweh says that he will harden [Hebrew qashah] Pharaoh's heart. The verb qashah connotes a stubborn disposition, a refusal to listen (Wilson). At some points, Pharaoh hardens his own heart, while at other points, Yahweh hardens Pharaoh's heart. Evidently, the character of Pharaoh determined the situation. In antiquity, kings in the ancient Near East often regarded themselves as deities (see Isa 14). In ancient Egypt, Pharaohs became Horus at their coronation and Osiris at their deaths. Moreover, Exodus emphasizes Pharaoh's tyrannical nature in chapters 1–2. Human beings were often considered the slaves of the gods, primarily tasked with serving them and avoiding being an annoyance. The hardening of Pharaoh's heart was a recognition of Pharaoh's own arrogance and a statement of the inscrutable will of God. No one, not even a pharaoh who considers himself a divine being, is beyond the power and will of God.
>
> God will use this occasion to display power before the world. The purpose of this hardening is so that God might multiply the signs and wonders in the land of Egypt, *that is, to demonstrate God's universal power and providential care for Israel as an oppressed people.*

go. Yahweh also refers to Israel as his *firstborn son* (see Hos 11:1), foreshadowing the final sign and wonder, the tenth plague, when Yahweh will strike the firstborn of Pharaoh and the Egyptians.

One of the more bizarre episodes in Exodus, and in fact in all of the Bible, appears in 4:24–26. Moses, on his return to Egypt, meets the Lord, who is prepared to kill him (compare Numbers 22, where the angel of the Lord prepares to kill Balaam son of Beor on the road). Reacting quickly, Zipporah circumcises their son and touches the foreskin to either Moses' or Gershom's *feet* (the text is unclear). The Lord spares Moses; but Zipporah is unhappy with her husband, whom she calls a *bridegroom of blood*. The meaning of this episode is difficult to discern. Why would God, who has worked so hard to convince Moses to take on the task of delivering the Israelites, now threaten to kill him? Several interpreters have made associations with the rite of circumcision. The story seems to be a fragment of a larger whole, now lost. As it stands, the story allows Moses to integrate his own family into the people of Israel, who practice circumcision.

After this strange scene, Yahweh tells Aaron to go out and meet his brother, who is on his way to Egypt. The two brothers greet each other, and Moses recounts all the great things Yahweh has done in his presence. Moses and Aaron make their way to Egypt, where they gather the elders together. Aaron assumes his role as spokesperson and tells the leaders of Israel all that Moses had related to him. Upon hearing about the mighty acts of God, the people respond with worship.

THE EXODUS FROM EGYPT · 5:1–12:42

The second major section of Exodus begins with a question, *Who is Yahweh?* (5:2), and ends with an exclamation point as the Hebrews leave Egypt. In between, this section describes a battle of wills between Yahweh and the Pharaoh. Only one can win. This battle is fought with the plagues, or *signs*, given to the king and the nation of Egypt to demonstrate Yahweh's incomparable nature and the distinction between the Israelites and the Egyptians. No one can withstand Yahweh, the God of the Hebrews: not the Egyptians, not the Pharaoh, not the forces of nature, nor the Egyptian gods themselves. Of course, the plagues climax in the slaying of the firstborn by the destroying angel of Yahweh (12:29–30). The Passover feast commemorates this final plague and makes the distinction between the Hebrews and Egyptians concrete.

5:1–23   This section begins with Moses and Aaron making their initial appearance before Pharaoh and uttering the demand, *Let my people go!* Pharaoh responds, *Who is Yahweh that I should let this people go? I do not know Yahweh and I will not let the people go* (5:1–2). This question triggers the contest between Yahweh, Pharaoh, and all the gods of Egypt. The question also advances the story of Exodus, for the book as a whole tries to describe who Yahweh is. Exodus 6:12 closes off this opening episode with the announcement, *I am Yahweh*. The plagues narrative will answer Pharaoh's question and demonstrate beyond a shadow of a doubt who Yahweh is – a powerful deity. Later stories will show that Yahweh is also benevolent. In response to Moses' demand for Pharaoh to allow the Israelites go and worship their God, the king of Egypt tyrannically adds to their labor (5:6–9). The accusation of laziness paints Pharaoh as a brutal, insensitive ruler. It comes as no surprise that the Hebrew slaves are unable to make their quota of bricks. The Pharaoh becomes angry at the Hebrew supervisors and again accuses the slaves of refusing to work hard. Having endured the verbal abuse of the Pharaoh, the foremen go to Moses and complain to him, a foreshadowing of the behavior of the Hebrews throughout the wilderness wanderings. Moses, in turn, complains to God, who reiterates the promise to defeat the Egyptians (5:19–6:1).

6:1–12   In this section, Yahweh rehearses the drama that is about to unfold between Moses and Pharaoh. The appeal to the ancestors (6:8) connects the impending triumph to the ancient stories of promise of redemption. Yahweh will redeem Israel and bring them out of Egypt to the land of promise. Moses tells the people this good news, but the people are too discouraged to hear it because of the cruel oppression the Egyptians have brought upon them. Moses then complains to Yahweh in a manner that suggests, "I told you so." He says, in essence, "I am not a good speaker, you should not have sent me" (6:12).

6:13–30   With what appears to be an attempt to heighten the suspense by delaying the confrontation between Moses and the Pharaoh, the narrative is interrupted by a genealogy. The genealogy not only

EXODUS

reaffirms the connectedness and wholeness of Israel even in bondage, it also highlights the tribe of Levi and the priestly line of Aaron. From this point, the family line of Aaron, as the first high priest, now takes center stage as 6:23 lists the sons of Aaron. The four sons of Aaron are Nadab, Abihu, Eleazar, and Ithamar. Nadab and Abihu will meet their fate in Leviticus 10:1–3 because they offer *unauthorized fire* before the Lord. As the oldest surviving son, Eleazar will become the second high priest. Eleazar's son Phinehas (6:25) will become the third high priest. Also noteworthy is the reference to Korah in 6:21 and 24, who will be the source of future tensions with Moses and Aaron over leadership as a power struggle develops between two clans of Levi (Num 16–17).

7:1–13 Yahweh once again instructs Moses as to how he should encounter Pharaoh. He will serve as God to Pharaoh, and Aaron will function as Moses' prophet. This means that Moses will stand in the place of God and give the words to Aaron, who will then speak those words to the Pharaoh. The challenge between Yahweh and Pharaoh will also become a challenge between the Pharaoh and Moses as Moses takes on an increasingly greater leadership role. It is interesting that Aaron is given the role of prophet, for in the actual interchanges between Moses and the Pharaoh, Moses always speaks.

The first sign that Moses performs before the Pharaoh involves the staff turning into a snake and recalls the earlier scene with Moses and God at Mount Sinai (4:3–5). At this point the magicians of the Pharaoh can perform the same sign that Moses and Aaron do. Their staffs also turn into snakes. As a sign that Yahweh's power is greater than the magicians', Aaron's staff devours the magicians' staffs. However, Pharaoh's heart was hardened (7:13). The introduction of the magicians again allows the story to build tensions – will Yahweh win or not?

7:14–11:10 The next section of Exodus focuses on the contest of will between the Pharaoh and Yahweh. The first nine plagues are described in succession. There also appears to be some pattern surrounding these plagues. The first three plagues center around the contest between Yahweh and the magicians. After the third plague, the magicians fail, which leads them to confess in 8:19, *This is the finger of God!* The next set of three plagues revolves around the distinction that Yahweh makes between the Israelites and the Egyptians. During the three plagues involving insects, cattle disease, and human disease, the Egyptians experience the full brunt of the plague, while the Israelites are spared the damaging effects. The final triad of plagues (hail, locusts, and darkness) highlights the incomparability of Yahweh. Yahweh claims to be the originator of these plagues *so you may know that there is no one like me in all the world* (9:16). Another indicator that there may be a triadic pattern to the first nine plagues is the introductory formulas of each plague. In the first, fourth, and seventh plagues, YHWH tells Moses to meet Pharaoh early in the morning. In the second, fifth, and eighth plagues, God simply tells Moses to go to Pharaoh. In the third, sixth, and ninth plagues, Moses does not meet the Pharaoh at all. Thus, each of the triads follows a particular literary pattern:

First Plague: Water to Blood · 7:14–24

The first plague pits Yahweh against Pharaoh beside the waters of the Nile. The Nile River is the source of life in Egypt and a fitting place for this challenge. Immediately, we learn that Pharaoh's heart is heavy, or dull [Hebrew *kavod lev*]. *Kavod* is the same word used by Moses to describe his tongue when referring to the fact that he could not speak well. The word, when applied to organs of the body, means that they do not function properly. When used to describe the heart of Pharaoh, the term *kavod* serves as another way of depicting the hardness of Pharaoh's heart. By stating that the Pharaoh's heart is heavy, God informs Moses that his heart does not function properly – that is, he is not open to the workings and wonders of God. The purpose of the plague is so that the Pharaoh will *know that I am the Lord* (in response to the question articulated by the Pharaoh in 5:2).

> **The Order of the Plagues**
> Psalms 78:44–51 and 105:28–36 list the plagues in different orders and interpret their theological significance differently as well, though all these text agree on the basic nature and purpose of the plagues.

> **A Pharaoh's Heart**
> *In Egyptian mythology, the dead Pharaoh meets the gods of the underworld for judgment. If Pharaoh's heart weighs more than a feather, he faces a doomed afterlife. The plague thus plays upon the Egyptian understandings of the royal heart.*

By the end of the plague sequence, there will be no doubt who this God is.

Moses meets the Pharaoh by the banks of the Nile early in the morning, and the water is turned into blood. The water, the source of life in Egypt, now has become undrinkable and incapable of sustaining life. In fact, all of the fish in the Nile die. At this point, the magicians step in to duplicate the plague, and the heart of the Pharaoh becomes "hard" [Hebrew *chazaq*]. This is the third term used to describe the hardening of Pharaoh's heart and again refers to a stubborn disposition. The magicians cannot, however, remove the plague. In order for the blood to be removed from the river and channels that flow from the Nile, the Pharaoh has to ask Moses to remove it, and he does.

Second Plague: Frogs · 7:25–8:11

Seven days after the blood vanishes out of the Nile River and its channels, the Lord strikes Egypt with a second plague. Like the first plague, the setting is the Nile River. This time, *frogs* appear from the Nile and infest the entire land. Once again, the magicians are capable of duplicating the plague but prove ineffective in reversing it.

Third Plague: Gnats · 8:12–15

No time lapse is given for the end of the second and the beginning of the third plague. In a very succinct manner, God instructs Moses to tell Aaron to strike the dust of the earth, and *gnats* appear, which then swarm over the earth. The magicians attempt to replicate this plague but are not able to do the same. Instead, they turn to the Pharaoh and confess, *Surely this is the finger of God*! But Pharaoh has "stiffened" his heart [Hebrew *chazaq*].

Fourth Plague: Flies or Insects · 8:16–28

The second triad of plagues begins with Yahweh commanding Moses to meet Pharaoh early in the morning as he comes out to the water (presumably the Nile). This time, the threat is another type of insect (traditionally translated as *flies*). In addition, this second triad of plagues introduces the theme of God distinguishing between the Israelites and the Egyptians. Once the plague strikes, the insects harm the Egyptians but not the Hebrews in the land of Goshen. Pharaoh tells Moses that he can go and sacrifice to God, but he must do so within the land of Egypt. Moses replies that what they sacrifice may be detestable to the Egyptians, who may stone the Hebrews. That is, Israelite sacrifice may violate Egyptian taboos. Therefore, they must be allowed to go into the wilderness a three-day journey to sacrifice. Pharaoh agrees they can go as long as it is not too far away (since a three-day journey would not likely lead to a return trip), but he asks Moses to *plead* on his behalf to remove the swarm of *flies*. Moses agrees to do so after he leaves the Pharaoh's presence. But again, once Yahweh removes the plague, Pharaoh *hardened* [Hebrew *kaved*] his heart.

Fifth Plague: Livestock Disease · 9:1–7

After the Pharaoh has hardened his heart again, God decides to strike the livestock of the Egyptians with a disease. Again, a distinction is made between the Hebrews in the land of Goshen and the Egyptians in the rest of the land of Egypt. Pharaoh hears about the plague but hardens [*kaved*] his heart.

Sixth Plague: Human Disease · 9:8–12

The final plague of the second triad has Moses and Aaron again throwing handfuls of soot in the air. As the soot becomes fine dust over all the land of Egypt, boils, or inflammations of the skin, appear on all the Egyptians. The hurling of dirt in the air is a ritual act symbolizing the pervasiveness of the plague. The magicians reenter the story as a grim sort of comic relief as they too are struck with the boils. This time Yahweh hardens [*chazaq*] the heart of Pharaoh, and he refuses to listen.

Seventh Plague: Hail · 9:13–35

The third triad of plagues begins, as did the first two, with Moses encountering the Pharaoh early in the morning. This time, God expands the rationale for the plagues by reminding Pharaoh and his subjects of God's power to destroy. But instead of eliminating the Egyptians, Yahweh wants to build a reputation throughout all of Egypt and beyond, to the whole world.

Exodus 9:16 explains Yahweh's dealings with the Egyptians thus far: *Nevertheless, for this reason I have left you standing* (or *spared you*) *so that I might show you my power and in order that my name* (that is, *reputation*) *might resound throughout the world*. On the heels of this pronouncement, Yahweh threatens to bring hail on the Egyptians and their property.

God will ultimately stop the storm not because of Pharaoh's plea, but in order to demonstrate that that the earth belongs to God, not to Pharaoh or the Egyptian gods. One of the major theological points of the plague narrative is that all of the earth belongs to God alone (see Isaiah 40–55 for a similar point). Yahweh demonstrates a sovereignty over Egypt and the Egyptian gods by destroying their source of livelihood. Yet, instead of acknowledging the sovereignty of God, once again Pharaoh hardens [*kaved*] his heart and refuses to let the Israelites go.

Eighth Plague: Locusts · 10:1–20

Prior to the plague of locusts, Yahweh again "hardens" [*kaved*] the heart of Pharaoh in order to display signs and wonders among the Egyptians and reduce them to mockery so that Moses and the Israelites will know that Yahweh is God. The plague of locusts will consume and destroy whatever crops have survived the plague of hail. It will, in effect, cripple the economy of Egypt. The back-to-back plagues of hail and locusts bring to mind the story of Joseph, who saved Egypt from a famine by storing grain during the seven years of plenty. Now the tables have been turned. Before the plague begins, the Pharaoh's courtiers beg him to let the Hebrews go and worship their God. Pharaoh agrees but tries to limit the worship to adults. As before, Pharaoh recognizes that the desire to worship Yahweh is really a diplomatic ploy, a way of leaving Egypt altogether. Pharaoh begs for forgiveness, Moses pleads with God on his behalf, and the plague stops. But Yahweh hardens [*chazaq*] the heart of Pharaoh.

> **Locust Plagues**
>
> *In the Middle East, grasshopper populations in deserts or near desert areas may increase so much that the insects metamorphose into winged creatures. The enormous swarms of locust invade settled land, eating plants and laying their eggs underground. The damage to a country can be incalculable.*

Ninth Plague: Darkness · 10:21–29

The final plague of the third triad strikes at the very heart of Egyptian existence. In a land where the sun shines every day and where the sun-god is worshiped, Yahweh challenges the very core of Egyptian life. Darkness symbolizes divine wrath (Amos 5:21) and the forces of chaos (Gen 1:2), two powers from which Pharaoh should protect his people. Pharaoh, of course, is powerless to do anything about the darkness; he tells Moses that he and the people may go and worship their God, but they must leave their flocks and herds behind. Moses argues that they need the animals to offer sacrifices and worship their God. By describing the repeated negotiations over who can leave to worship in the wilderness, Exodus builds dramatic tension, for soon all will leave. Yahweh hardens [*chazaq*] the Pharaoh's heart once again, and the king refuses to let the people go.

Tenth Plague: Death of the Firstborn · 11:1–10

The tenth and final plague provides the climax in the contest between God and Pharaoh. With each plague, Pharaoh has refused to let the people go into the wilderness to worship their God. Now, after the tenth plague, all that will change. Again, the reasons for the plagues are reiterated: to make a distinction between Egypt and Israel (11:7); to cause the court of Egypt to bow before Yahweh and allow the Israelites to go (11:8); to multiply Yahweh's wonders in the land of Egypt (11:9); and to harden the heart of Pharaoh so that Yahweh may completely defeat him (11:10). But before the plague actually takes place, Yahweh instructs Moses to prepare the people for their departure from Egypt. Israel will receive reparations from the Egyptians, who will do whatever it takes to rid themselves of their former slaves. Their departure will be reminiscent of Abraham's departure from Egypt in Genesis 12:16–13:2.

Following the Lord out of Egypt · 12:1–42

12:1–28 After the pronouncement of the tenth plague, the narrative pauses to provide instruction regarding the Passover feast. This feast will become the primary celebration of Israel's freedom from bondage and a marker of the beginning of the year. The Passover meal provides an opportunity for the Israelites to retell their story of freedom (see also Deut 6:4–8; 26:5–10). Also included in the Passover celebration is the Feast of Unleavened Bread (Exod 12 and 13), a seven-day celebration that begins on the fourteenth day of the first month and goes through the twenty-first day. During this time, no leaven was to appear in the houses of the Hebrews as they remember God's wondrous act of deliverance.

At the end of the instructions for the Passover meal and Feast of Unleavened Bread, the people bow low and worship (12:28), something they have not done since Moses first reported to elders of the people in 4:31. These two acts of worship thus bracket the conflict between Yahweh and Pharaoh. Between these times, the people have complained because the initial confrontation between Moses and Pharaoh led to increased labor for them. Yahweh's response was to send the plagues. Now on the eve of the final plague, the people once again engage in worship. The next time we see the people engaged in the worship of Yahweh will be on the other side of the Red Sea.

12:29–34 The narrative picks back up in 12:29 with the tenth plague. The destroying angel passes through Egypt, killing the firstborn of every inhabitant of Egypt, animal and human, from the king to the lowest peasants, while maintaining the distinction between the Egyptians and Hebrews.

12:35–42 Exodus 12:37 mentions that approximately 600,000 Hebrew men leave on foot and that the people had spent 430 years in Egypt. The number of Israelites who depart from Egypt and later wander in the wilderness has caused problems for many scholars, because there is no archeological evidence for the movement of such a huge group. Some have suggested that the number is better understood as a reference to clans. So, rather than 600,000 males leaving Egypt, the word *'eleph* may actually refer to 600 clans, a number much smaller. The number of years spent in Egypt corresponds with the amount of time Yahweh had told Abraham the people would be in Egypt in Genesis 15. Here again is a reminder that the exodus is tied directly to the promise made by Yahweh to the patriarchs. The God of Israel is a God who keeps promises.

CROSSING THE RED SEA · 12:43–15:21

God's mighty act of deliverance of the crossing of the Red Sea constitutes the foundational act of Israel's faith. It is referred to more than any other event in the Old Testament. Pharaoh's heart is hardened one final time so that he pursues the Israelites to his army's demise. The crossing of the Red Sea marks the introduction of one of the primary images of the Old Testament to describe God: the image of the divine warrior. The song in honor of Yahweh's activity on Israel's behalf leads to a resounding chorus of celebration and the proclamation that Yahweh is a warrior. This image of God will remain in the forefront throughout Israel's experience of wandering, conquest, and life in the land.

12:43–13:16 This section takes special care to provide a theological rationale for the devotion of the firstborn to Yahweh. Because God took the firstborn of the Egyptians and spared the Israelites' firstborn, they are to devote every firstborn male to Yahweh. Later, the tribe of Levi will be devoted to Yahweh in place of every family's firstborn (Num 3:45–48; but see Num 18:14–16). This section also mentions another feast that corresponds to the Passover, the Feast of Unleavened Bread. The Passover appears to be the start of the Feast of Unleavened Bread, which lasts for seven days. The Feast of Unleavened Bread marks the celebration of the spring harvest, which coincides with the freedom of the Israelites from their bondage from Egypt.

13:17–22 The Israelites begin their journey in the wilderness. They do not take the most direct route to Canaan, northeast along the Mediterranean coast, for two reasons. First, the coastal road from Egypt to Canaan is littered with Egyptian strongholds and fortified Philistine cities. Second, Yahweh desires to bring Israel to Sinai to establish his covenant with

---

> **The Passover**
>
> *The menu for this feast includes roast lamb, unleavened bread, and bitter herbs. The roast lamb signifies the lamb that is slain, whose blood is smeared on the doorposts and mantel as a sign that the house is Israelite. The unleavened bread signifies the haste in which the already prepared Israelites leave Egypt. The bitter herbs reflect the bitter experience of the oppression the Israelites had undergone in their time as slaves in Egypt. For the Christian community, familiarity with this Jewish festival goes back to the days of Jesus Christ, who used this opportunity to break bread with the disciples to institute the Lord's Supper. The Passover meal, which signified the sparing of Israel's firstborn, links thematically to the Lord's Supper and the sparing of Christians.*

> **Red Sea or Reed Sea?**
>
> *The Bible portrays Israel crossing a body of water called the* Yam Suph, *more properly translated the "Reed Sea." This was probably a lake in the swampy area north of the Gulf of Suez, near the present day Suez Canal.*

EXODUS

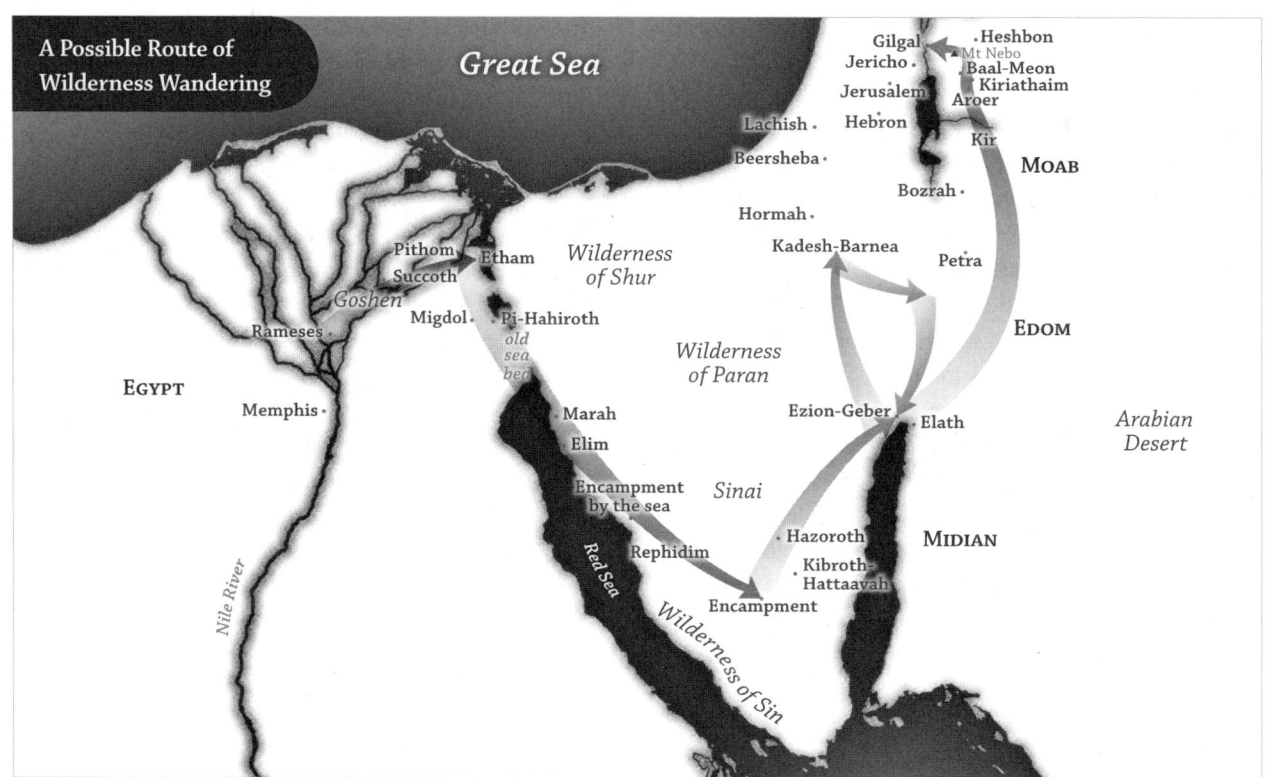

them. Thus, the Israelites turn southward toward the Red Sea to begin their journey. The pillars of cloud and fire represent the divine presence.

14:1–15:21 By turning around and marching his people toward the Red Sea, Yahweh has created the illusion that the Israelites are marching aimlessly through the desert. God will harden Pharaoh's heart one final time in order to gain glory with one final confrontation with the king of Egypt. This final wonder will be Yahweh's greatest sign, and all the Egyptians will know Yahweh's divine identity (see Isa 40:25–26). As before, Gentiles will testify to the might of Israel's God.

This miracle is reminiscent of God's control and authority of the waters of chaos in Genesis 1. Yahweh causes a strong east desert wind to blow, parting the waters and providing an avenue of escape for the Israelites. Whereas 14:22 pictures the wind driving back the waters, 15:8 portrays them being congealed. The Israelites witness the dramatic washing up of the Egyptian soldiers and chariots on the shore and recognize God's power and grace in delivering them from their enemy.

In response to God's gracious act of salvation, Israel breaks out in praise. Exodus 15:1–18 contains the full song of celebration of this event, while 15:21 gives its first line. Perhaps we are to consider Miriam's song as an antiphonal response to Moses'. Both the song of Moses and the song of Miriam reflect Israel's dependence on God for salvation. The song of Moses depicts Yahweh as a Mighty Warrior, an image that will remain dominant as the children of Israel march through the wilderness. Thus in Numbers, the census emphasizes the number of Israelites available for war. Israel marches as an army through the land, with Yahweh leading the Israelites to battle. *Your holy dwelling* in the context of Exodus refers to Mount Sinai, though it could also refer to the promised land. The reference to God's abode (often as a mountain) is common in both Israelite and Canaanite literature. The song is characteristic of other praise songs (Judg 5; Hab 3) found in the Old Testament, especially the book of Psalms. Yahweh's wondrous and mighty acts are met with worship.

> **The Song of the Sea**
> *The Song of the Sea (Exod 15:1–18) is in archaic Hebrew. It consists of three parts: a hymnic opening (1–3), the narrative (4–12), including a dramatic address to God (11–12), and finally a note about the aftermath of victory (13–18).*

THE JOURNEY TO SINAI · 15:22–18:27

The wilderness wanderings described in Exodus do not show Israel in its best light, yet the initial stories do not seem as negative as those recounted in the book of Numbers. Moreover, complaint can be a legitimate expression of faith (see the Psalms of complaint or the book of Lamentations). Like most communities of faith, the Israelites vacillate between faith and despair. Faith leads to praise; despair leads to grumbling.

15:22–27 After the tremendous experience of deliverance at the Red Sea, the Israelites resume their journey through the wilderness. They depart from the Red Sea and go into the wilderness of Shur. Israel first complains about thirst, leading to the miracle of the sweetening of the water and the naming of the place Marah (the Hebrew word for "bitter"). At this point, a warning interrupts the narrative. Israel must realize that the Lord has put them to the test. The test involves obedience and trust. If Israel proves to be an obedient people, then Yahweh will spare them from all the diseases (namely, the plagues) that befell the Egyptians. Here we see the characteristic conditionality of the covenant relationship Yahweh is seeking to enter into with Israel. God will deliver them from their oppressors, provide for them in the wilderness, and lead them into the promised land. In turn, Israel must trust God and be obedient. In Egypt, the children of Israel were exploited and oppressed, but they did receive minimal care and protection from their masters. In the wilderness, they come face to face with the challenge of sheer and utter dependence on God, who will give them everything they need. Trust, however, does not come easily. Yahweh must also prove to be a trustworthy provider. In fact, the character of God will be a major theme in Exodus. The plagues proved God's power, but the events in the wilderness will prove God's benevolence.

After Marah, the Israelites come to the large desert oasis of Elim, which had twelve springs of water and seventy palm trees. The exact location of these sites remains unknown.

16:1–36 The Israelites resume their journey from Elim and soon arrive in the wilderness of Sin. The problem the Israelites encounter in this region is a lack of food. Here the children of Israel complain that they were better off back in Egypt, where they at least had food to eat on a regular basis (compare Num 11:4–6). Their experience in the wilderness does not afford them the luxury of knowing where their next meal will come from. Yahweh responds to the complaint of Israel once again with provision. He provides quail on occasion for meat and manna (literally, "what is it?") on a daily basis, except on the Sabbath day. The Israelites are instructed to gather the manna every day and only enough for the day, except that they gather double before the Sabbath. The manna becomes their primary source of food throughout their journeys in the wilderness.

17:1–7 The Israelites next march out of the wilderness of Sin and encamp at Rephidim. Once again the scarcity of water plagues the people, and they ask to return to Egypt, where they at least experienced a secure water supply. In this instance, Yahweh instructs Moses to strike a rock so water would gush out and provide relief for the people. Moses does so, and the people find relief from their great thirst. This scene anticipates Numbers 20:11, when God will command Moses to speak to a rock, but Moses will strike it and forfeit his opportunity to lead the Israelites into the land. This place was called "Massah" and "Meribah" because it was a place of testing and quarreling before the Lord.

> **Water from the Rock**
> *Exodus 17 and Numbers 20 give two different locations with the same names and two very similar stories explaining their names. Ancient interpreters, like Paul (1 Cor 10:4) and his contemporary Pseudo-Philo (Biblical Antiquities 10:7, 11:25), assumed that the rock moved. Paul expands the story's symbolism even further by equating the rock with Christ.*

17:8–16 While at Rephidim, the Israelites are attacked by the Amalekites. The Amalekites were a nomadic people who continue to be a source of trouble for Israel into the time of Saul (see 1 Samuel 15 and Saul's failure to carry out the total destruction of the Amalekites and their king, Agag) and even into Israel's experience of exile in the days of Esther and Mordecai (Mordecai is descended from the tribe of Benjamin and the line of Kish, the father of Saul, and he destroys Haman, who descends from Agag). Here the text introduces Joshua as the commander of the army. After the battle, Yahweh vows the extinction of the Amalekites (see Deut 25:19).

18:1–27 Chapter 18 details the visit of Jethro, Moses' father-in-law, and the reunion of Moses with his wife Zipporah and sons Gershom and

EXODUS

Eliezer. Exodus 18:3–4 essentially repeats 2:22. The repetition of these verses forms an *inclusio*, "bookends" to emphasize what is between them: God's acts of help in a strange land. An interesting encounter ensues as Moses relates the events in Egypt that God performed for the Hebrews. When Jethro hears these words, he responds with what might be termed a confession of faith. This confession by a non-Israelite foreshadows similar confessions made by other foreigners, such as Rahab the Canaanite (Josh 2:8), the widow of Zarephath of Sidon (1 Kgs 17:24), and Naaman the Syrian (2 Kgs 5:15). One of the purposes of the plagues was to make the name of Yahweh known throughout the world: hence the confession of Jethro and other non-Israelite notables.

> **The Names of Moses' Sons**
> *"Eliezer" means "God is a helper," and "Gershom" is reminiscent of the Hebrew word for "stranger" [ger].*

While staying with Moses and the Israelites, Jethro notices the tremendous pressure Moses is under as he serves as a judge for all the people (18:15–16). Jethro advises his son-in-law to delegate the minor cases to subordinate judges, freeing Moses to hear the major cases and serve as a final appeal. The story explains later Israelite practices and gives a rationale for division of political power. Numbers 11:16–18 gives a different story also explaining the same arrangements.

GOD'S APPEARANCE AT SINAI · 19:1–20:18

Exodus 19–24 describes the covenant established between Yahweh and Israel. Included in this section is the arrival of the Israelites at Mount Sinai. Exodus 3:12 has made the return to Sinai the proof of God's presence, and now that proof has become a reality. Next, God makes a dramatic appearance on the mountain, creating so much fear among the people that they designate Moses as their intermediary with Yahweh. Moses will assume this role and later save the people (Exod 32:1–14). God will begin the legal section of the book with the Ten Commandments, the fundamental laws that will designate Israel as God's chosen people through their demonstration of their love for God and their neighbor. Following the Ten Commandments lies a section known as the book of the covenant (20:22–23:33), a series of case laws that Yahweh provides in order to help the Israelites live together as a holy people. The section ends with a covenant meal between Yahweh, Moses, and a group of Israelite leaders and the inauguration of the covenant as Moses sprinkles blood on the people (24:1–18).

> **The Prophet as Intermediary**
> *In the Bible, prophets function as intermediaries between Yahweh and Israel, speaking to each for the other. See for example, Numbers 14:10–19; Amos 7–8.*

19:1–25 Readers have anticipated the arrival at Sinai since Exodus 3:12, when God first appeared to Moses in the burning bush. Now the entire assembly of Israel, not only Moses, will witness the appearance of Yahweh as the God of Israel descends upon the mountain. The story of God's absence has ended. The covenant begins with God's famous recital of the past act of deliverance from Egyptian bondage. The imagery of *eagle's wings* also occurs in Isaiah 40:31 and is an obvious metaphor for freedom.

Verse 5 sets the covenant in a universal context (*all the earth is mine*) and focuses on Israel's new role as a *nation of priests* – that is, as intermediaries between Yahweh and the rest of humankind. Most importantly, the text puts the law in the context of God's gracious saving acts.

God's appearance on the mountain is another example of a theophany. Earlier, Exodus 3:12 depicted the appearance of God in the form a burning bush; now the manifestation of God takes the more dramatic form of thunder and lightning, a dense cloud, smoke, and the blast of a loud horn. Theophanies are typically terrifying (see Nah 1:1–10). Although the people do encounter God, they go through their representative, Moses. He will prove to be a capable intermediary (Exod 32). However, God's presence on the mountain is not only terrifying, it is also sanctifying. The holiness of God permeates the mountain, making it untouchable. Any Israelite who accidentally touches the mountain will die at the hand of God. For Israel, the threat of such an outbreak from God is real, as will be made more than

> **Biblical Holiness**
> *Holiness in the Bible does not merely concern human ethics. It is a property of God and sometimes of matter (especially of sacred objects like the temple and its furniture). Humans encounter the holy through exterior and interior preparations, such as washing and penitence.*

evident in the cases of Nadab and Abihu, the sons of Aaron, who offer *strange* fire and are consumed by fire (Lev 10:1–5), and Uzzah, who reaches out to steady the ark of the covenant when it appears to be about to topple off the cart carrying it to Jerusalem under the supervision of David (2 Sam 6). Their infractions are violations of ritual taboos.

The Decalogue (20:1–17) serves as an example of "absolute," or "apodictic," law ("thou shalt" or "thou shalt not"). Other biblical law codes consist of "casuistic" law ("if...then"). The first four commandments emphasize the vertical relationship between Yahweh and Israel. The final six stress the importance of horizontal relationships between human beings. Though stated in the negative, these Ten Commandments form the basis for the covenant relationship between Yahweh and the people of Israel and make possible the type of peace, or well-being, that God envisions for Israel. It is important to bear in mind that Yahweh is not requiring the children of Israel to keep the law in order to become a part of the covenant community. Rather, the people are already a part of the covenant community (see Gen 15:9–21). God initiates the relationship, and God's people respond with glad and faithful obedience.

> **The Ten Commandments**
> *Different traditions break up the commandments differently. Most understand verses 3–6 to contain two commands and verse 17 one. Other readings merge verses 3–6 and divide verse 17 into two. All agree on the final number ten, which probably serves as a memory device corresponding to the number of fingers on two hands.*

20:1–2 The Ten Commandments begin with a story that serves as their rationale. Ancient Eastern law codes (for example, Hammurabi's) usually began with a justification for the code. Since God has acted on behalf of the Israelites and delivered them from their oppressors, he therefore has the right and duty to institute a law code (Deut 7:6–8).

20:3 The wording of the first command is curious in that it does not unequivocally deny the existence of other gods; rather, it simply states that other gods are not to come before Yahweh. In essence, this commandment lays claim to Israel's exclusive loyalty (see Deut 30:19; Josh 24:14–27). Israel will constantly be tempted to worship other gods (see Exod 32:1–6; Num 25:1–9; Judg 2:10–15), an action the prophets will characterize as unfaithfulness or adultery (see Hos 2). Furthermore, this command anticipates the "greatest command" found in Deuteronomy 6:4–5, which emphasizes the oneness of God. Although Exodus does not offer a theoretical monotheism, it does call for a practical one.

20:4–6 The second command illustrates a major distinction between the Israelites and their neighbors: the Israelites are forbidden to make images representing God. The command also assumes the three-tiered universe of heaven above, earth beneath, and water below (see Gen 1 and 6). Yahweh is the God of all these regions, in contrast to polytheistic religions, which pictured many gods populating the universe. Since God is everywhere, humans can never adequately represent or understand the divine nature. Verses 5 and 6 anticipate the great description of God's wrath and compassion in Exodus 34:6–7.

20:7 The third commandment forbids the misuse of the name of the Lord. The name "Yahweh" is regarded by Jews to this day as so sacred that readers of the Hebrew Bible do not pronounce it aloud lest they be found in violation of this command. Instead they read another word, *adonai*, Hebrew for "lord or master," in its place. The common English translation of the name as "Lord" goes back to

> **Law in the Ancient Near East**
> *Biblical law drew on precedents in the legal systems of the ancient Near East. Some ancient kings published law codes resembling in certain details the laws of the Bible. For example, Hammurabi of Babylon compiled over 280 laws on various social, economic, and even religious issues. The laws follow a "casuistic" ("if...then") format, much like the laws in Exodus 21–23, in contrast to the "apodictic" ("thou shalt"/"thou shalt not") form of the Ten Commandments. Many ancient contracts and legal decisions about contract law have survived from Mesopotamia, if not from Israel itself. These all indicate a widespread emphasis on fair play, due process of law, and even divine guarantee of justice, all concepts fundamental to biblical jurisprudence. Biblical law differs from other systems, not so much in its details, but in its theological grounding in the mighty, redemptive deeds of Yahweh, who rescued Israel from Egypt.*

ancient Greek-speaking Jews, who rendered the name as *kyrios* ("lord"). However, in Exodus, the command does not forbid the pronunciation of God's name but rather its misuse in oath-taking by swearing an oath and then failing to keep it.

20:8-11 The fourth commandment, *remember the Sabbath day to make it holy*, again echoes Genesis 1 as it recalls the creative process of God, who worked for six days then rested on the seventh. Deuteronomy 5:15 offers a different but complementary rationale for the Sabbath. Rest is necessary for the wholeness that God desires for all of creation; thus this command extends not only to the head of the house, but to the servants, livestock, and even the land, which is to rest every seventh year (Lev 25). The Sabbath thus helps structure the economy and society in a more just way. Work, or vocation, certainly has its place in God's conception of the human life (Gen 2:15), but it must not be obsessive or demeaning to another.

20:12 The fifth command is also the first to be accompanied *with a promise* (Eph 6:2); it also marks a transition in the orientation of the commandments and looks forward to the book of Joshua, when Israel will take possession of the land of promise. Yahweh envisions for the people perpetual existence in the land, but that security depends upon obedience (failure to keep the commandments of Yahweh will result in expulsion from the land; see Deut 28:58-68). By honoring their parents, the Israelites will ensure the *shalom*, or well-being, of every member of their community, even those individuals who are older and therefore vulnerable. The care of the aged marks the just community. Compare Isaiah 65:17-25, which depicts an ideal world where individuals who reach a hundred years of age are considered mere youths. Perhaps included in this command is the admonition of wisdom literature to listen to and respect the teaching of parents (Prov 1:8) who, presumably, have sought the best for their children. In turn, it is the children's responsibility to care for the welfare of their parents.

20:13 The Hebrew word often translated "kill" in the sixth commandment [*ratsach*] normally applies specifically to the act of murder, not to killing in general. The murders of Abel by Cain (Gen 4:8) and Uriah the Hittite by David (2 Sam 11:1-27) are two prominent stories of the violation of this command. To take another person's life violates the sanctity that God, as its creator, places on life. Furthermore, humans are created in God's own image (Gen 1:26), which intensifies the sanctity of life.

20:14 The violation of the marriage covenant prohibited in the seventh commandment recalls the narrative of Genesis 2, when God brings the woman to the man and they become one flesh. Malachi 3:12 proclaims that Yahweh hates divorce. Adultery violates the very nature of this relationship. This commandment also protects the basic fabric of family life. The placing of the sixth and seventh commandments back-to-back inevitably brings to mind King David, who, unlike Joseph (Gen 39), commits adultery with his "neighbor's" wife and then plots and sanctioned his murder. The violence done to Uriah the Hittite does not go unnoticed or unpunished, as the *sword never departed the house of David* (2 Sam 12:10). Life in community demands that marriage be taken seriously and its sanctity be rigorously upheld.

20:15 The eighth command, forbidding the theft of another's possessions, implies that theft does violence to the victim's sense of well being. Ancient Israel considered a person's possessions an extension of the self (Fretheim 325). Thus, stealing from anyone harms that person.

Forms of Marriage

The Old Testament permits several marital structures, including monogamy (the most common option), polygamy, and levirate marriage (a form of polygamy in which the nearest male relative of a deceased, childless male marries the widow and rears a child in honor of the deceased; see Gen 38 and Ruth 3-4). Polygamy, or more properly polygyny, the marriage of one man with multiple women, was generally the practice among wealthy, powerful persons, not among the vast majority, who were peasants. At the same time, fidelity within marriage of whatever structure was an absolute requirement (Lev 18:8-20; Deut 22:22; Prov 12:4, 18:22 etc.). At the same time, Judaism and Christianity, beginning in late antiquity, have strongly disapproved of nonmonogamous marriages, citing the creation ideal of Genesis 2 and appealing to the dignity of women and the need for male spiritual discipline (see Hamilton).

EXODUS

> **Law Codes in the Pentateuch**
>
> *The Pentateuch contains seven distinct law codes: the Decalogue (Exod 20:1–17; Deut 5:6–21), the Covenant Code (Exod 20:19–23:33), the Ritual Decalogue (Exod 34:11–26), the Priestly Code (Lev 1–16, 27; Num 1–10), the Holiness Code (Lev 17–26), the Deuteromic Code (Deut 12–26), and the Curses Code (Deut 27:14–25).*
>
> *The laws relate to agricultural life at various levels, as well as to family life. Although arranged somewhat randomly, the laws do follow several basic legal principles, including: a distinction between intentional and accidental harm (thus the rules on goring oxen in 21:28–32); a principle of punishment fitting the crime (thus the* lex talionis *of 21:23); a distinction between harm to humans and harm to property; and a sense that offenders must be accountable regardless of their social class (even if the punishments for crimes against slaves are less severe than those for crimes against free persons). The laws emphasize due process.*
>
> *Some laws deserve special notice. Thus the "eye for an eye" (*lex talionis*) in 21:23–24 is designed to limit vengeance, not to encourage it. The Sabbath laws of 23:10–13 repeat the rules of the Ten Commandments, even though the rules do make life on farms more difficult in some ways. The three festivals of 23:14–19 include Passover in the early spring, Pentecost in the spring-summer transition, and Tabernacles in the early fall. Leviticus 23 and Numbers 28–29 greatly expand this calendar and tie it to the sacrificial system. The reference to boiling a kid in verse 19 has long puzzled readers, but it may relate to the strong impulse to preserve animal life seen also in Deuteronomy 22:6–7.*

20:16 The ninth commandment pertains to legal testimony. The idea of justice is prominent in the Old Testament, and honesty in the courtroom is a precondition to maintaining justice. The prophets, of course, speak harshly against giving false testimony and state that one of the primary reasons for the punishment of Israel and Judah is the false testimony that takes place there (Amos 5:15).

20:17-18 The purpose of the tenth and final commandment is to encourage contentment with one's possessions. A well-known narrative involving violation of this commandment as well as the commandments regarding murder, stealing, and bearing false testimony is that of King Ahab and Naboth's vineyard (1 Kgs 21). This commandment may be the summation of the previous four. In other words, when humans covet, they tend to commit other crimes, as well (such as murder, adultery, theft, and false witness).

In essence, the first four commandments sum up the "greatest command," cited in Deuteronomy 6:4: *Hear O Israel, the Lord our God is one and you shall love the Lord your God with all your heart and with all your soul and with all your strength.* The final six commandments sum up the "second greatest commandment," found in Leviticus 19:18b: *You shall love your neighbor as yourself.* Neither harsh nor demanding, the commandments serve as a guide or set of instructions, even *a test* (Jer 9:7), to keep the Israelites from going astray. Later Jewish interpreters would see the law as a "hedge" whose primary purpose was to protect the people from disobedience and form a distinction between themselves and the Gentiles, who did not possess the Torah. The commandments, which shape many stories in the Bible (Freedman), are necessary for life in a community that extends both vertically and horizontally.

THE BOOK OF THE COVENANT · 20:19–23:33

Exodus 20:19–23:33 also contains legal material, but the nature of the laws changes from the absolute form found in the Decalogue to case (or casuistic) law. This type of legal material is characterized by the "if...then" formula. The laws in this section bear striking resemblance to law codes found in other ancient Near Eastern countries of this time, most notably, the law Code of Hammurabi. Exodus 24:8 refers to this section of the law as "the book of the covenant." It is unclear if the term refers to laws contained only in Exodus 20:19–23:32 or if it also includes all the other legal material in Exodus. Most interpreters of Exodus believe that the title "book of the covenant" refers to the material found in Exodus 20:19–23:32 and that these laws, along with the Decalogue, constitute the foundation for all other laws found in the Torah. This section describes legislation bearing on matters ranging from slavery to witchcraft to goring oxen. Key points in this legal material focus on a discussion of the nature of God, human rights or social justice, loyalty on the part of Israel, and covenant and promise.

20:19-23:33 This closing section of the book of the covenant offers the book's first detailed description of how Yahweh will go before the Israelites to

Cherem Warfare

The depiction of Yahweh as a warrior who commands the complete annihilation of all the inhabitants of Canaan conjures up disturbing images for modern minds.

Many people today struggle with the idea that a loving God could participate in the slaughter of innocent women and children. For many, this issue is the most perplexing in all of Old Testament studies. Two considerations deserve attention: first, this is a one-time command given for a very special reason; and second, Israel does not completely carry out the command (see Judg 1).

With regard to the first consideration, Yahweh desires to cleanse the land so that the covenant people can live there and in turn (ironically) be a light (or source of salvation) to the nations (Isa 49:6). In order to accomplish this task, all temptations to worship other gods must be removed (see commandments one and two). In Genesis 15:16, God says the Amorites will remain in the land of Canaan until their wickedness is complete. Thus the Pentateuch accepts the logic of the Canaanites' demise.

With regard to the second consideration, a quick reading of Joshua might lead a reader to believe that Israel, in essence, carries out the command of Yahweh and utterly defeats all of their enemies (see especially Josh 12). A closer look, however, reveals that the Israelites do not carry out this command (see, for instance, Josh 9 and the story of the Gibeonites). The book of Judges also acknowledges that the Israelites fail to carry out this command, and that is why they constantly worship the Baals and the Asherahs (Judg 2:1–11; 3:7; 6:28).

The fact that Israel fails fully to carry out this command does not diminish the theological difficulty that God ordered its undertaking, but it does relieve some of the tensions that many modern readers feel.

---

defeat their enemies and give them land. The seven nations listed here – the Amorites, Hittites, Perizzites, Canaanites, Hivites, and the Jebusites – are by and large unknown, except for the Jebusites, who inhabit Jerusalem (see Judg 19:10–12) until the time of David (2 Sam 5:6–8). Two important principles come to the forefront: Yahweh is a warrior, and *cherem* warfare is being declared on the nations in Canaan; and the land is a gift from Yahweh. *Cherem* warfare refers to the command of Yahweh to annihilate every citizen and eradicate all cultural and religious aspects of Canaanite life (Deut 7:1–6). The other difficult lesson Israel will have to learn is that God is magnanimously giving them the land. Deuteronomy 8:12–18 will address this all-too-human tendency to forget the wonderful acts of God.

THE INAUGURATION OF THE COVENANT · 24:1–18

In Exodus 24:1, Yahweh calls Moses, with Aaron, Nadab, and Abihu, and seventy of the elders, to worship. Moses alone, however, will draw near to God. Ancient treaties often end with some ritual of ratification, and these actions serve the same purpose. Verse 10 pictures God walking on a blue floor, a poetic way of describing the sky. *Sapphire* would be better translated "lapis lazuli," a semiprecious blue stone imported from Central Asia and very popular in ancient Near Eastern jewelry-making. The shared meal of verse 11 forms the basis of the idea of the messianic banquet and anticipates certain parables of Jesus.

INSTRUCTIONS PERTAINING TO THE TABERNACLE · 25:1–31:18

During this forty-day encounter with Yahweh, Moses will receive instructions pertaining to the cultic centerpiece of ancient Israel – the "tabernacle" [Hebrew *mishkan*], or "tent of meeting" [Hebrew *'ohel mo'ed*] – where God will dwell. The furniture and utensils that will be used as a part of the religious service of the people include the table of the bread of presence, the lampstand or *menorah*, the altar of incense inside the tabernacle, and the altar of burnt offering and basin outside the tabernacle. Inside the innermost part of the tabernacle, or holy of holies, lies the ark of the covenant, with the mercy seat serving as the throne of God. Included in these instructions are directions for Aaron and his sons, who will function as the priestly family officiating over the services surrounding the tabernacle. This section makes for tedious reading for modern readers, but the painstaking detail demonstrates the care with which Israel is to approach its God. This section anticipates many of the instructions regarding sacrifices and purity rites contained in Leviticus. The Israelites are to take care to follow the instructions carefully and to do *as the Lord commands* because the Lord's holiness will dwell in the midst of the people. And, as Nadab and Abihu later find out (Lev 10:1–5), Yahweh's holiness can be very dangerous.

25:1–9 This section itemizes the materials used for building the tabernacle. Many of the materials are unknown to us today. The tabernacle itself consists of two parts – the holy place and the holy of holies. The priests will carry out their daily administrative tasks in the holy place, such as baking and arranging the bread of presence on the table and lighting the lampstand and burning incense on the altar of incense. Only one piece of furniture occupies the holy of holies, and only one person can enter it and that only on one specific day (the Day of Atonement, according to Lev 16). In a very real way, the holy of holies functions as the epicenter of holiness in the camp of the Israelites as God dwells among the people from the ark of the covenant. As in Leviticus, this text expresses the idea of graded holiness: some places are more holy than others, and therefore some actions are more appropriate in one place than another.

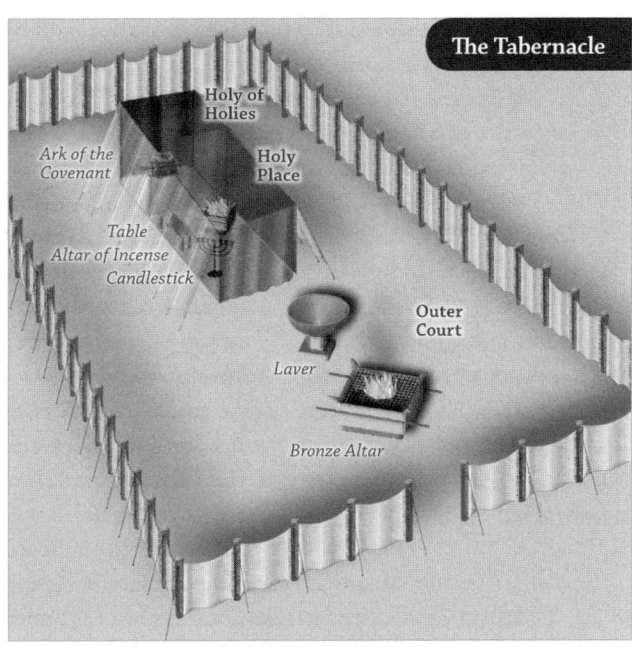

The Tabernacle

25:10–22 The ark of the covenant symbolizes the throne of Yahweh. When the Israelites embark on a journey, the priests carry it before the people (Num 10:33–36). In battle, the ark goes with the army as the Israelites face their enemies (see especially 1 Sam 4, where the Israelites lose to the Philistines, who capture the ark).

25:23–30 The table of the bread of presence symbolizes the presence of God with the people and God's gracious provisions for them while in the wilderness.

25:31–40 The lampstand perhaps recalls the first day of creation. God creates light on the first day, and the pillar of fire symbolizes the presence and sustaining power of God while the Israelites are in the wilderness. It may also symbolize God's dominion over the forces of chaos, represented by darkness. In later Judaism, the *menorah* becomes the most popular Jewish symbol, a reminder of the temple destroyed by the Romans.

27:1–8 Situated just outside the tabernacle proper, this is the altar where the sacrifices of the people are made. The worshiper would bring his or her sacrifice to the priest, who would then officiate over the sacrifice to be made. The types of sacrifices and the instructions for making them appear in Leviticus 1–7 (compare Amos 5:22).

28:1–43 The priestly wardrobe includes the breastpiece, *ephod*, a robe, a tunic, a turban or headgear, and a sash. Of particular interest are the *Urim* and *Thummim*. Not much is actually known about these items, but they were apparently stones placed in the breastpiece and used to discern the will of the Lord pertaining to a particular matter. By means of this type of "lot casting," kings and priests could obtain "yes" or "no" answers from the Lord. Examples of the use of the *Urim* and *Thummim* may be found in the narratives of Saul (1 Sam 14:36–37) and David (1 Sam 23:9).

29:1–46 In this section, Moses received the instructions for what will actually take place in Leviticus 8–9. The priests represent a higher level of holiness than do the general population. Within the tribe of Levi, different clans have different functions and responsibilities within the tabernacle, and from these clans, Aaron's family was selected by Yahweh to become the line of priests and officiate over the sanctuary. Numbers 18:1–7 clarifies this distinction between the priests and Levites, although not all biblical texts observe this distinction. Aaron and his sons, then, have a special and prominent place in the religious structure of ancient Israel (see also Num 16:1–17:11). As such, special procedures are put in place to ensure their sanctity. Before entering the holy place themselves, the priests must be sanctified in order to perform their daily tasks. Thus the priest both represents the people as a whole and substitutes for them.

30:1–10 In front of the curtain that divided the holy place and the holy of holies stands the altar of incense, which burns daily. The curtain that divides the holy place from the holy of holies later hangs also in the temple and is torn in two at the death of Jesus Christ (according to Matt 27:51).

31:1–11 Two individuals, Bezalel and Oholiab, are set apart and gifted by God to oversee the construction of the tabernacle. Bezalel is said to have the Spirit of God in "skill," or "wisdom" [Hebrew *hokmah*], to work with gold, silver and perform other special crafts.

> **Wisdom**
> In the Bible, the word translated *"wisdom"* [Hebrew *chokmah*] *may mean technical skill* (as here), *discernment as to the meaning of life and good choices in it, or an abstract set of ideas governing all reality* (which we would call *natural laws*).

31:12–18 This final section addresses the issue of work limits on the Sabbath. Although the priests "work" on the Sabbath by carrying out sacrifices, the builders of the tabernacle do not. This is a reminder that no job is so important that we should ignore the basic rhythm of life found in the creation itself. That rhythm involves rest. If Yahweh rested on the seventh day after creating the world, then God's people should also rest, even while working on something as significant as the tabernacle. In addition, the Israelites must keep the Sabbath as a way of maintaining the distinction God has given them by consecrating them as a holy people. The section ends with a note about the tablets of stone and a statement that the commands were written by the very finger of God (31:18).

THE BREAKING & RENEWAL OF THE COVENANT · 32:1–34:35

After Moses receives the tablets of stone, but while he is still on the mountain, the narrative shifts its focus to the Israelites at the foot of the mountain. The story interrupts the paired description of the tabernacle, allowing the narrator to contrast Yahweh's gracious forgiveness with the stubbornness and ignorance of the people. The organization of these chapters helps answer the central question of Exodus: "Who is Yahweh?" In an exchange parallel to that in Numbers 14:11–25, Exodus 32:9–14 reaffirms the covenant in spite of Israel. Moses persuades God to change his mind (compare Gen 18:22–33; Amos 7). Yahweh validates Moses as the leader of the people by allowing Moses to see a part of "the divine body." The theme of being unable to see God was part of Israelite popular religion, but we have no stories of anyone actually dying from seeing God.

32:1–35 The story of the golden calf addresses the question of how one depicts God. Calves and bulls were typical images in Canaanite and other Near Eastern religions. First Kings 12:25–33 portrays golden calves as suitable (in the minds of northern Israelites) images of God. The cry *those are your gods, O Israel* (Exod 32:14; 1 Kgs 12:28) was apparently a refrain from the worship services of northern Israel. Moses, who was timid when God first spoke to him on Mount Sinai, is now bold enough to challenge Yahweh in the form of intercession. The most important feature of the discussion between Yahweh and Moses is that Moses fulfills his prophetic role as intercessor on behalf of the people (see Amos 7:1–6 for a similar scene, when Amos intercedes on behalf of the people of God).

Moses' plea for Israel rejects God's proposal to shift the promise to Abraham to Moses himself. He persuades Yahweh to change his mind based on two arguments: that destroying the Israelites will undo all Yahweh's work in Egypt and will cause the Egyptians to question the integrity of God and the mission of deliverance (compare 15:14–15); and that God should *remember* the covenant with Abraham, Isaac, and Jacob. Just as God remembered that covenant by hearing the cries of Israelites in their oppression (2:23–25) and responding with compassion, so now God must *remember* that covenant even in anger.

The story addresses the question of the role of the priests. Though obviously guilty, Aaron does not receive punishment because he is the high priest, and his services will be necessary later in the story. The Levites, by punishing the idolaters, rescue the reputation and status of their tribe. Apparently the Levites are not simply priests but also warriors, a role that the third high priest, Phinehas, will assume in Numbers 25.

33:1–34:35 In chapter 33, Moses must negotiate with Yahweh. Yahweh has promised to go before the people into battle and give them the land of Canaan. Now, the continuing presence of the divine warrior among the Israelites is in jeopardy, though Yahweh does remain with Israel.

The narrative digresses by telling the reader how Yahweh communicates with Moses at the tent of meeting. The "tent of meeting" is an alternate name for the tabernacle. Central to this tradition is the fact that when Moses talks to Yahweh his face shines, and the people are afraid to look upon him (see also 2 Cor 3:12–18), requiring that Moses cover his face. Apparently, the tent was placed outside the camp (in seeming contrast with other traditions), and Moses communicated with God there before returning to the people.

> **"His face was radiant …"**
> The Hebrew word for "was radiant" [qaran] is similar to that for "horn" [qeren], leading to the medieval interpretation that Moses grew horns on Mount Sinai. Accordingly, Michelangelo's great statue of Moses depicts short horns atop Moses' head. Though incorrect, the interpretation has survived for centuries.

Exodus 34:6–7 expresses Israel's basic confession about the nature of God (repeated in Num 14:18; Jonah 4:2 and many Psalms). Yahweh is depicted as a God slow to anger and abounding in steadfast love [Hebrew *chesed*]. The traits of compassion, graciousness, and patience are necessary if God and Israel are to remain in their covenant relationship. After making this core statement about the divine nature, Yahweh next renews the covenant with Israel, despite their idolatry.

Whereas chapter 32 describes illicit worship, the commandments in 34:15–26 focus primarily on aspects of legitimate worship.

THE MAKING, ERECTION & CONSECRATION OF THE TABERNACLE · 35:1–40:38

The final section of the book of Exodus recounts the combined efforts of the people and Moses as they contribute to the making of the tabernacle. Following the disobedience described in the matter of the golden calf, this final section depicts Israel as a faithful people who contribute from their own possessions, combine their energies, and complete the task of building the tabernacle. A key phrase in this section is, *as the Lord commands*. It occurs ten times in Exodus 39 alone and highlights the obedience of the people in regard to building the sanctuary. The book ends with the glory [Hebrew *kavod*] of Yahweh descending upon the tabernacle and a note regarding the resumption of their journeys that will take place in the book of Numbers.

35:1–39:43 Chapters 35–39 in Exodus describe the actual making of the tabernacle. The narrative begins with a tremendous outpouring of generosity by the people (35:20–29). Bezalel and Oholiab begin the work of making the tabernacle and overseeing the people (36:8–39:42). In this section, the description of the making of the tabernacle corresponds to the instructions for each section being made. The infidelity of the golden calf episode gives way to generosity of faith as the people bring the very items that were formerly used to construct an idol to form the tabernacle and its furniture.

In 39:32, the Israelites complete all the work that they had been commanded to do. In language similar to Genesis 2:1–3, the Israelites have finished their work like God had finished the work of creating the earth. In many ways, the building of the tabernacle is similar to the creation of the world, in that both are sacred places. Furthermore, just as God blessed the earth after finishing the work, so Moses blesses the people after they have completed their task (39:42). Blessing and obedience typify this section of Exodus. The way has been prepared for God to enter the tabernacle and reside with the people.

40:1–33 The final chapter of Exodus turns its attention to the erection of the tabernacle. Under discussion since chapter 25, the tabernacle is now finished and only needs to be put up. Aaron and his sons will officiate over the offerings and serve as mediators between Yahweh and the people. The tabernacle is put up in the first month of the year – a year after the exodus itself in the timeline of the book. The tabernacle is now ready for business and only awaits the inauguration of the priesthood, which will take place in Leviticus 8–9.

40:34–38 This final scene both concludes the book of Exodus and serves as a link to Leviticus, even anticipating the resumption of the journeys of the Israelites in the book of Numbers. Now that the tabernacle has been erected, all that it lacks is the presence of Yahweh. A book that begins with Yahweh's absence ends with an overwhelming presence of the divine. The cloud not only symbolizes the presence of Yahweh with the people but also signals to the Israelites when they should leave the place they are camped and begin the next stage of their journey (Num 10:11–12). Israel's stay at the foot of Mount Sinai has only just begun. They will remain encamped at Sinai until Numbers 10, when Moses blows the trumpet and the cloud ascends from the tent of meeting, leading the people of God on to the next stage of their journey.

THEOLOGICAL REFLECTIONS

Exodus confronts the faithful reader on a number of levels with several theological themes contained in both narrative and legal material. First, when Israel cries to God under the tyranny of the Pharaoh's whip, we learn that God hears, remembers, sees, and is concerned about their plight (2:23–25). God is a God who acts and who responds especially to the plight of the poor and oppressed. As God's people, we would do well to respond to the cries of the poor and marginalized in the same manner. Furthermore, we want to make doubly sure we are not the oppressors (see also James 5:1–6).

Second, the call of Moses in the burning bush (chapters 3–4) reminds us that though God is a powerful and holy God, the Lord works through individuals to deliver the poor and oppressed. We are indeed partners with God in this world to promote justice and righteousness.

Third, the account of the plagues against Pharaoh and the Egyptians demonstrate God's power over all of creation and over any other god we might imagine (7:8–12:30). Israel's wilderness experience (13–19) calls us to see God as one who provides. Do we rely on ourselves and our own ingenuity? Or do we really trust God to provide for us as he did the Israelites in the wilderness? At both the foot of Mount Sinai (19:16–19) and the tabernacle (40:34–38), Israel encounters a holy and terrifying God who demands that Israel be holy and faithful as both God and people enter into a covenant relationship (24:1–11).

Finally, this same holy and terrifying God is also "compassionate and gracious, slow to anger and abounding in love and faithfulness" (34:6–7). It is before this God that we the faithful come in search of his grace and mercy.

FOR FURTHER STUDY

Nahum Sarna, *Exploring Exodus* (New York: Schocken, 1986).
Michael Walzer, *Exodus and Revolution* (New York: Basic Books, 1985).

WORKS CITED

Joseph Blenkinsopp, "The *Kerygma* of P," *Catholic Biblical Quarterly* 38 (1976): 275–92.
Walter Brueggemann, *The Book of Exodus* (Nashville: Abingdon, 1995).
Thomas Cahill, *The Gifts of the Jews: How a Tribe of Desert Nomads Changed the Way Everyone Thinks and Feels* (New York: Nan A. Talese/Anchor, 1998).
David Noel Freedman, *The Nine Commandments: Uncovering a Hidden Pattern of Crime and Punishment in the Hebrew Bible* (New York: Doubleday, 2000).
Terence Fretheim, *Exodus* (Louisville: John Knox, 1991).
Victor Hamilton, "Marriage OT and ANE," *Anchor Bible Dictionary* 4 (1992): 559–69.
James K. Hoffmaier, *Israel in Egypt: The Evidence for the Authenticity of the Exodus Tradition* (Oxford: Oxford University Press, 1996).
George Mendenhall, "Midian," *Anchor Bible Dictionary* 4 (1992): 815–18.
George Pixley, *On Exodus: A Liberation Perspective* (Maryknoll, N.Y.: Orbis, 1987).
Pseudo-Philo, "Biblical Antiquities." Pages 297–377 in vol. 2 of *The Old Testament Pseudepigrapha* (ed. James Charlesworth; Garden City, N.Y.: Doubleday, 1985).
Robert R. Wilson, "The Hardening of Pharaoh's Heart," *Catholic Biblical Quarterly* 41 (1979): 18–36.

Leviticus

Glenn D. Pemberton

CHAPTER CONTENTS

Contexts **167**
Commentary **168**
   Sacrifice · 1:1–7:36 **168**
   Institution of the Priesthood · 8:1–10:20 **172**
   Human Uncleanness · 11:1–15:33 **174**
   The Day of Atonement · 16:1–34 **177**
   The Holiness Code · 17:1–26:46 **178**
   Redemption of Vows · 27:1–34 **183**
Theological Reflections **184**
For Further Study **184**
Works Cited **184**

MAPS, TABLES, & FEATURES

Laying on of Hands **168**
The Purpose & Object of the Atonement **170**
Sacrifice **172**
Priesthood **174**
Food Laws **175**
The Day of Atonement **178**

In the book of Exodus, God rescues Israel from Egypt (Exod 1–15), brings them to Sinai (16–18), and proposes a covenant relationship (19:1–6). Israel eagerly accepts (19:8), and both parties ratify the covenant (24:1–18). At its heart, this covenant is about the Lord's desire for an intimate relationship with the new bride, Israel. Consequently, after the covenant is established, the Lord asks the Israelites to "make a sanctuary for me, and I will dwell among them" (25:8).

While Moses is on the mountain receiving instructions for God's tent (25–31), however, the people break the new covenant. At their request, Aaron makes a golden calf and declares, *These are your gods, O Israel, who brought you up out of Egypt* (32:4). Their single-minded allegiance to the Lord does not survive the honeymoon, the months at Sinai.

The crisis is severe. The Lord threatens to destroy these people and start over again with Moses (32:9–10). Moses intervenes and convinces Yahweh not to kill them (32:11–14), but the crisis is not fully resolved. Yahweh next orders the Israelites to leave for the promised land but refuses to go with them *because you are a stiff-necked people and I might destroy you on the way* (33:3). The plans for the tabernacle and the Lord's hopes for this relationship are in jeopardy. The Lord is not going with them so as not to destroy them! Moses intervenes and convinces the Lord to go with the people (33:12–17). Construction on the tabernacle proceeds (35–40), and at the end of the book of Exodus, the glory of the Lord moves into the tent (40:34–38).

The crisis, however, is still not resolved. At Sinai the Lord had stated, *if I were to go with you even for a moment, I might destroy you* (33:5). Yet now the Lord goes with them, without resolution of the problems that threaten their life together. How can a holy God live with the unholy people he loves and not destroy them? That is the question Leviticus seeks to answer.

CONTEXTS

The English title Leviticus suggests that the author of this book addresses the Levites (the tribal family of priests). Leviticus, however, consistently reports the Lord's address to *the people of Israel* (1:2; 7:22; 11:1–2; 15:1–2); only a few texts exclusively address the priests (6:1–7:21; 8:1–10:7; 10:8–15; 16:2–28; 21:1–22:16). Further, only one short passage mentions the Levites as a distinct group (25:32–34). Thus, Leviticus's instructions for maintaining relationship with the Lord are not simply the responsibility of priests but of all the people.

Although Leviticus primarily consists of speeches from the Lord through Moses at Sinai, the book does not specify an author or date of composition. One should not confuse the literary setting and content of a book with its date and authorship. Thus, while a few interpreters still regard Moses as the author, most recognize a later date of composition, probably in postexilic Judah, but using earlier source materials or traditions. There is, however, no consensus on the number, identification, or extent of influence of these earlier sources. For example, some ascribe the entire book to "P" (a priestly source concerned with ritual and law), while others limit the direct influence of P to chapters 8–10; some identify an "H" source (concerned with holiness or ethics) in chapters 17–26, while others deny any such independent document or source. No end to the debate is in sight (Milgrom, *Leviticus 1–16*, 3–35; Hartley xxxv–xliii, 246–260).

COMMENTARY

SACRIFICE · 1:1–7:36

The writer sets instructions for sacrifice within the story of Israel at Sinai. Now that the tabernacle is complete (Exod 40), the Lord speaks to Moses *from the tent of meeting* (1:1). Leviticus 1–7 identifies five types of offerings (burnt, grain, fellowship, sin, and guilt) and the ritual responsibilities of the people and priests. Instruction to the people dominates and surrounds instruction to the priests: to the people (1:2–6:7), to the priests (6:8–7:21), and to the people (7:22–36). The people, not the priests alone, are responsible for proper sacrifice.

The primary purposes for the sacrifices are clear; each plays a role in promoting or maintaining relationship with God. A complete understanding of each sacrifice, however, eludes consensus for two reasons. First, sacrificial texts in Leviticus (and elsewhere) prescribe the rituals of sacrifice with little theological explanation. The writer assumes that the reader already knows the purpose of each sacrifice. Thus the modern interpreter must reconstruct the theology of these sacrifices from scattered clues in the texts. Second, many interpreters observe changes in the rituals and purposes of these sacrifices through history. While acknowledging these problems, this commentary tentatively reconstructs the rituals and purposes of each sacrifice based primarily on the present text of Leviticus.

Instructions to the People of Israel · 1:1–6:7

Theology and regularity dictate the order of 1:2–6:7. The first three sacrifices (burnt, grain, and fellowship) are most frequent and produce *an aroma pleasing to the Lord* (1:9). The last two sacrifices (sin and guilt) are less frequent and focus on atonement and forgiveness.

1:1–17 The distinguishing feature of the burnt offering is the complete incineration of the animal on the altar (1:6–9, 11–13, 15–17). Only the animal's hide and the crop of the bird are not burned (1:16; 7:8). While only the best and most costly are acceptable (1:3, 10, 14; compare 2 Sam 24:24; Mal 1:7, 13), the different monetary value of the animals and birds enables all persons, including the poor, to present a burnt offering (Lev 12:6–8; Luke 2:24).

The worshiper is no passive bystander in the sacrifice. He lays his hand (see below) on the head of the bull (1:4; implied for sheep and goats), slaughters the animal, skins it, cuts it into pieces (1:5–6, 11–12), and washes the legs and inner parts to prevent dirt and excrement from defiling the altar (1:9, 13). Then the priest manipulates the blood (1:5, 11; Exod 27:3), arranges the pieces, and burns the sacrifice on the altar (1:8–9, 12–13). Only in the case of a dove or pigeon does the priest kill the animal (1:15).

The smoke of the burnt offering is *an aroma pleasing to the Lord* (1:9, 13, 17). In addition to gaining the Lord's attentive favor (see Levine 5–6), here the only stated purpose for a burnt offering is *to make atonement* (1:4). This appears to be for sin in general, rather than for specific known sins (but see the sin and guilt

---

Laying on of Hands

In Leviticus 1–7, the worshiper must lay his hand on the burnt offering (1:4), the fellowship offering (3:2, 8, 13), the sin offering (4:4, 15), and the guilt offering (7:7). This ritual has three basic meanings presented elsewhere in the Old Testament: designation of a representative or substitute (Num 8:14–18); transference of authority to a person (Deut 34:9) or guilt to an animal (Lev 16:21); and an act of solemn identification (Lev 24:14).

Substitution or transferral of guilt is a possible meaning for hand placement in Leviticus 1–7, but this is unlikely because it is not required for all atonement sacrifices, such as birds (1:14–17) and grain (5:11–13), and it is also mandated for sacrifices that have nothing to do with sin or guilt, such as the fellowship offering (3:2) and ordination offering (8:22–36). Thus, in Leviticus 1–7, solemn identification seems the best understanding of the ritual. Through laying on of hands, the worshiper declares ownership, dedicates the animal, and stakes a claim to the benefits of the sacrifice (1:4). Since the donor gives birds and grain directly to the priest, an act of formal identification is unnecessary.

offerings). Elsewhere, Leviticus associates the burnt offering with the fulfillment of a vow or a freewill offering (22:17–19). Psalm 66:13–19 illustrates the exuberant joy associated with this sacrifice. Outside Leviticus, the burnt offering accompanies appeals to the Lord (1 Sam 13:12; 2 Sam 24:21–25) and dominates the regular offerings on the Sabbath and holy days (Num 28–29). A burnt offering is, therefore, an act of complete surrender to the Lord that seeks divine favor from a sense of joy, need, or sinfulness.

2:1–16 A grain offering consists of *fine flour* (wheat) that is raw (2:1) or cooked (2:4, 5, 7, 14). Each recipe includes oil and sometimes incense (2:1, 15) but prohibits yeast and honey (2:11). This exclusion is likely due to the ancient association of leaven and honey with decay, deterioration, and death (Milgrom, *Leviticus 1–16*, 188–90; compare 1 Cor 5:8). *The salt of the covenant* must season every grain offering (2:13). As a preservative, salt symbolizes the enduring nature of the covenant (Num 18:19; 2 Chron 13:5).

After preparation of a grain offering, the worshiper brings it to the priest (2:1–2), who presents it at the altar (2:8) and burns a handful as a *memorial portion* that represents all of the offering (2:2, 9, 16). The priest then retains possession of the remainder of the offering (2:3, 10) and eats it (6:16–18; 7:10).

The grain offering may function as an independent sacrifice, in, for example, the offering of firstfruits (2:14; Deut 26:9–10). However, it most often accompanies other types of offerings and supports their purposes, as in the case of the whole burnt offering (Num 15:1–10, 24; 1 Chron 21:23) and the fellowship offering (Lev 7:12–13; Num 6:17). Leviticus 2 gives little clear indication of the purposes for an independent grain offering other than provision of food for the priests, an *aroma pleasing to the Lord* (2:2, 9, 12), and the concept of a *memorial portion* which may prompt the worshiper to remember God's provision and/or ask God to remember the worshiper.

3:1–17 A fellowship offering is voluntary and may be a male or female without defect from the cattle (3:1), the sheep (3:6), or the goats (3:12). The worshiper must present the offering before the Lord (3:1, 7, 12) *at the entrance of the Tent of Meeting* (3:2; see also 1:3), *lay his hand on the head* of the animal (3:8), slaughter it (3:13), and remove the internal organs with their fat (3:3–4,9–10,14–15). The priest then sprinkles the blood against the sides of the altar (3:2, 8, 13) and burns the internal organs and fat (3:5, 11, 16). Like the burnt offering and grain offering, the fellowship offering gains the Lord's favor; its smoke is *an aroma pleasing to the Lord* (3:5; see 3:16).

Interpreters traditionally associate the term for the "fellowship offering" [Hebrew *shelamim*] with "peace" [Hebrew *shalom*], a concept of wholeness, prosperity, and salvation in the Old Testament. Thus a *peace offering* (KJV) celebrates these blessings. Another clue to the purpose of this sacrifice is the disposal of blood and fat at the altar (these belong to God, as indicated in 3:16; 17:10–12; see also Gen 9:16), but not the meat, which humans consume. Indeed, a primary purpose of the fellowship offering is to provide the meat for a meal shared with family and friends in the presence of God (7:11–18; Deut 27:7; 1 Sam 9:12–13). Thus, joy and celebration dominate fellowship offerings (see 2 Chron 5:12–13; Neh 12:35, 41), teaching that a relationship with God includes celebration of the joys of life with God.

4:1–5:13 An appropriate sin offering depends on a person's social and economic position. Greater standing requires a more costly sacrifice. The anointed priest and whole community must bring bulls (4:3,14); a leader must bring a male goat (4:23); a community member must bring a female goat or lamb (4:28,32); a person too poor to bring a lamb must bring two doves or pigeons (5:7); a person too poor to bring these birds must bring a tenth of an *ephah* (1–2 liters) of fine flour (5:11). In the same way, greater ritual and social standing require a more intrusive use of the blood in the tabernacle. The priest brings the blood from his sin offering and that from the community into the tent of meeting, sprinkles it in front of the sanctuary curtain, and puts some of it on the altar of incense (4:5–7, 16–18). The blood from the sin offering from a leader or community member does not enter the tent. Rather, the priest puts some of this blood on the altar in the courtyard (4:25, 30, 34; 5:9). This graduated system of sin offerings and blood manipulation suggests that the greater the standing of the person, the greater the defilement of his or her sin upon the tabernacle.

Ignorance is not bliss. Only when one becomes aware of an unintentional offense (4:13, 23, 28; see 5:2–4) does the person present a sin offering (4:4, 14) and confess the wrong (5:5; see 16:21; 26:40). Deliberate sin can only be removed by the high priest on the Day of Atonement (chapter 16), and the removal does not benefit the sinner. The worshiper lays his hand on the head of large

LEVITICUS

> **Gender in Leviticus**
>
> With rare exception, the ritual laws in Leviticus do not explicitly address women. Their menstrual period and the associated bleeding made it difficult for them to attend to the ceremonies of the community. Leviticus does assess women's economic value more highly than do most ancient texts (27:1–8), however – an attempt to protect their marital rights (see Milgrom, *Leviticus 17–22*, 1412–14).

animals and slaughters them (4:4, 15, 24, 29, 33), but the priest slaughters birds (5:8–10). After ritual manipulation of the blood, the priest pours the remainder at the base of the altar (4:7, 18, 25, 30, 34; 5:9) and burns the internal organs with their fat (4:8–10, 19–20, 26, 31, 35). He then disposes of the remaining portions of his sacrifice and that of the community by burning them outside the camp (4:11–12, 21). Portions remaining from other sin offerings become the property of the priest (see 6:24–30).

5:14–6:7 The only acceptable animal for a guilt offering is a *ram from the flock* that is *without defect and of the proper value* (5:15, 18; 6:6). The unique phrase *of proper value* suggests that in some circumstances a person may bring silver of equivalent value rather than the ram itself. Unlike in preceding instructions, the writer delays description of the ritual procedure for this sacrifice until 7:1–10. The focus here is on the occasions that require a guilt offering and the prerequisites for the offering.

The guilt offering atones for unintentional sins against the Lord's holy things (5:14) or the Lord's commands (5:17, suspected but not known), and intentional sins against a neighbor about which a person swears falsely (6:2–5). Each of these is a serious offense, or *violation* (5:15), against the sacred, whether against holy things (5:15; for example, by eating holy things, 22:14) or by use of God's name in a false oath (6:5). In this way, the guilt offering differs from the sin offering, which focuses on unspecified types of sin.

Before bringing a guilt offering, a person must first recognize his or her guilt. The term "guilt" occurs with two distinct meanings in Leviticus. One is objective guilt. When people sin, they are guilty whether or not they realize their sin or feel guilty (4:13–14; 5:2). However, the term may also denote subjective guilt or remorse (see Milgrom, *Leviticus 1–16*, 339–45). People who have deceived a neighbor and then lied under oath are guilty (6:1–3). However, it is only after they *realize* their *guilt and would restore* what they have taken that they bring a guilt offering (6:4 NRSV). The same is true for a sin offering. A person must first recognize his or her sin and then realize his or her guilt (5:4–5 NRSV;

> **The Purpose & Object of Atonement**
>
> While atonement is the primary focus of the sin and guilt offerings (for example, 4:20; 5:6; 6:7), the precise meaning and object of the Hebrew term *kipper* ("to atone") are elusive. Usage in the Hebrew Bible suggests four interrelated ideas.
>
> First, atonement is an action that may calm or restrain anger caused by some offense. When Jacob sends gifts to Esau, he hopes that *I will pacify (kipper) him with these gifts I am sending on ahead; later, when I see him, perhaps he will receive me* (Gen 32:20). Jacob's action seeks reconciliation with his brother through an atonement gift (compare Prov 16:14; Num 16:44–48; 25:11–13).
>
> Second, atonement is an act of cleansing or removal (10:17, see Deut 21:8–9; Isa 6:7; 27:9). Traditionally, scholars have assumed that the object of cleansing is the person. In recent years, however, Milgrom has persuasively argued that the object of *kipper* is not the person but the tabernacle and objects within it. In the ancient Near East, sin or impurity was thought of as aerial pollution that threatened to contaminate the sanctuary (Milgrom, *Leviticus 1–16*, 77; see Lev 15:31; 20:3; Num 5:2; 19:13, 20). Atonement blood is a ritual detergent (Lev 8:15) that the priest applies to sacred objects (4:7), not persons. Thus, the object of cleansing is the polluted temple, not the person. Milgrom's arguments are persuasive that one important object of atonement is the sanctuary. However, people are also objects of cleansing. For example, Leviticus 16:30 states: *On this day atonement will be made for you, to cleanse you.*
>
> Third, as an action that seeks reconciliation and cleansing, atonement brings forgiveness to the sinner. Indeed, the most common usage of *kipper* in Leviticus is in the refrain *the priest will make atonement for them, and they will be forgiven* (for example, 4:20). Although atonement is not synonymous with forgiveness, the two ideas are inseparable. There is no forgiveness without cleansing, and cleansing brings forgiveness.
>
> Fourth, as an extension of the previous ideas, atonement may consecrate people or things to holy status, especially the altar (Exod 29:36–37; Lev 8:15) and the priests (Exod 29:33). Since an act of atonement cleanses defilement and obtains forgiveness, a further act of atonement produces a sanctified or holy object.

the NIV misses this nuance in both texts). Next, the sinner must make restitution plus twenty percent to the priest for the damaged or destroyed holy things (5:16) or to the person whose property was damaged or destroyed (6:5). Such action mitigates stiffer penalties for theft if the person refuses to admit wrong and make restitution (see Exod 22:7–17).

A clear concern in these prerequisites is the heart of the worshiper. Before bringing a guilt offering, a person must feel remorse and make restitution; that is, he or she must be penitent. Atonement sacrifice is not a mere external ritual but the expression of a broken and contrite heart (as in Ps 51:17).

Leviticus is explicit about the effectiveness of atonement sacrifice: *they will be forgiven* (for example, 4:20, 26, 31). The problem for many Christian interpreters is not the clarity of Leviticus, but such texts as Hebrews 10:4 and Romans 3:25. Lifting these passages from their contexts, some interpreters suggest that God did not really forgive previous sins, but "rolled them forward" to Christ. This flatly contradicts Leviticus. Neither Romans nor Hebrews denies effective atonement or forgiveness in Leviticus (see Heb 9:13); but each claims that this system was not powerful enough to work a final solution (Heb 10:1–3): that is, to take sin away once and for all (Heb 10:10–12). This claim follows Leviticus, for which the sanctuary requires continual cleansing because of the power of sin and impurity. For Christians, Christ resolved this weakness with a more potent sacrifice that took away sin and its power to defile (Heb 9:13–14).

Atonement Sacrifice & Grace
Atonement sacrifice in Leviticus works on the principle of grace. The initiative for atonement sacrifice comes from God, not Moses or the people. The potency of the blood to cleanse is due to God's declaration: For the life of the creature is in the blood (17:11a). *Further, God provides the blood for atonement*: and I have given it to you to make atonement for yourselves on the altar (17:11b). *Israel does not provide its own atonement sacrifices. God owns the lifeblood (Gen 9:3–5), and God gives it for atonement. God only asks Israel to respond appropriately to the offer of grace.*

Instructions to the Priests · 6:8–7:36

For the first time in Leviticus, the Lord tells Moses to speak directly to *Aaron and his sons* rather than to all Israel (6:8). Sacrificial procedure remains the topic, but the emphasis shifts from the rituals before and during a sacrifice to the proper disposal of the remains. Except for the fellowship offering, the Lord assigns the responsibility and rights regarding the unburned portions to the priests, thus the direct address to them.

6:8–13 The priests are responsible for the complete incineration of the burnt offering on the altar and the disposal of the remains. To this end, they leave the offering on the altar overnight and keep the fire burning (6:9, 12–13). The next day, the priest puts on his linen clothes and undergarments (see Exod 28:42–43; 20:26) and removes the ashes from the altar to a temporary place beside the altar (6:10). Then, after changing clothes again, he carries these ashes to a ceremonially clean place outside the camp (6:11).

6:14–23 After the priest offers *the memorial portion* of a grain offering (6:14–15; 2:2,8–9) the remainder of the sacrifice belongs to the priests (6:17–18; 7:10; 2:3,10). It is *most holy* (6:17) and, according to the NIV, *whatever touches it will become holy* (6:18). Levine's translation is preferable: "anyone who is to touch these must be in a holy state" (Levine 37; see Hag 2:11–13: touching holy food does not impart holiness). Consequently, the priests must dispose of the grain offering by eating it in a *holy place*, that is, *in the courtyard of the Tent of Meeting* (6:16).

The exception to this procedure is a grain offering from the priests. The ordination offering or priest's daily offering of grain (6:20; see 8:26–28 and the discussion in Hartley 97–98) or any other grain offering from a priest (6:23) belongs only to the Lord and *is to be burned completely* (6:22). A priest may not benefit (that is, eat) from his own grain offering.

6:24–30 Like the grain offering, the unburned meat of a sin offering is *most holy* (6:25, 29), and *anyone who is to touch its flesh must be in a holy state* (6:27; Levine 40; see above). This meat belongs to the priest who offered it; he and the male members of his family must eat it in the courtyard (6:26, 29). Further, because of the *most holy* status of the meat, the priest must follow special instructions regarding the utensils he uses to cook the meat (6:28) and any garment spattered with blood from the offering (6:27).

The exception to this method of disposal is *any sin offering whose blood is brought into the Tent of Meeting* (6:30), that is, the sin offering of a priest (4:4–5) or the entire congregation, including the priests (4:13, 16). In these instances, the priest may not eat the meat but must incinerate it on the altar (6:30). As with the grain offering, a priest may not profit (eat) from any sin offering made on his behalf.

7:1-10 A guilt offering is also *most holy* (7:1). The priest dashes its blood on all sides of the altar and burns the internal organs with their fat on the altar (7:2-5; the ritual is described here, but not in 5:14-6:7). Like the sin offering, the remaining meat belongs to the priest who offered it (7:7); he and the male members of his family must eat it in the courtyard (7:6; compare 6:16).

The writer offers a brief summary of priestly rights (7:7-10) before turning to the fellowship offering (7:11-34). Sin and guilt offerings belong to the priest who offers them (7:7). He also retains possession of the hide of a burnt offering (7:8) and any cooked grain offering (7:9). The officiating priest shares other grain offerings (those that are uncooked) with *all the sons of Aaron* (7:10).

7:11-21 The regulations for the fellowship offering continue the theme of proper disposal of sacrificial meat. Thus, although these regulations address the worshiper (7:11), not the priest, the writer includes them in this section (6:8-7:36).

A fellowship offering is voluntary and may be of three distinct types: a thanksgiving offering (for example, Ps 56:12-13), a votive offering (at the beginning or completion of a vow; for example, 2 Sam 15:7-8), or a freewill offering (an expression of joy, in, for example, Ps 54:6-7). A thank offering requires the presentation of various cooked grains with and without yeast (7:12-14). The worshiper contributes these *to the Lord*; that is, they become the property of the officiating priest (7:14). Votive offerings and freewill offerings do not require these grain sacrifices.

7:22-36 The worshiper presents the breast of the fellowship offering to the Lord by *waving*, or better, *raising* it (NRSV 7:30); this and the thigh then belong to the priests (7:32-34). The remainder of the meat reverts to the worshiper. Anyone ceremonially clean may eat it (7:19). One must eat a thanksgiving sacrifice on the day it is offered, with no leftovers allowed (7:15). A votive or freewill offering, however, permits a two-day feast (7:16-17). The rationale for such time limits is not clear (see Wenham 124). Nonetheless, it is not difficult to imagine the joy that accompanied a fellowship offering in ancient Israel (compare Deut 27:7).

Because this is the one sacrifice that reverts to the person bringing it, who will take meat presented to God outside the sanctuary, dire warnings accompany its disposal. If anyone consumes the meat after the stipulated time, this person will be held responsible (see 19:5-8), and the sacrifice *will not be credited to the one who offered it* (7:18). Further, an unclean person who eats the meat *must be cut off from his people* (7:20-21). The writer extends these warnings to broader dietary issues in 7:22-27. The people must not eat the fat of any sacrificial animal found dead (7:23-25; compare 17:15) or consume blood from any animal or bird (7:26-27).

INSTITUTION OF THE PRIESTHOOD · 8:1-10:20

God calls all Israelites to be priests to the world (Exod 19:5-6). Nonetheless, the Israelites themselves need a special priesthood to facilitate their relationship to God: to offer sacrifice (Lev 1-7), to teach (10:10-11), to inquire of the Lord (8:8; Exod 28:30), and to determine the clean and unclean (10:10; 11-15). God's instructions for the tabernacle in Exodus included

---

Sacrifice

Sacrifice is God's gift to Israel, a provision for an ongoing relationship. Through sacrifice, God provides the way and the means to maintain the holiness of the tabernacle and the people and thus God's presence among them. God's people respond to this grace with appropriate atonement offerings (the sin and guilt offerings), with acts of complete surrender to the Lord (the burnt offering), and with celebration in the presence of the Lord (the fellowship offering). Sacrifice concerns people who come to God with hearts broken by sin or hearts bursting with joy. The prophets support this view of sacrifice and lash out at its corruption into mere external rituals (Hos 8:11-13; Isa 1:11-17; Mic 6:6-8; Amos 5:21-24).

Vestiges of Israelite sacrifice may be seen throughout the practices of the church: the communion (1 Cor 15:23-26, consumption of the sin and guilt offerings and sharing the fellowship offering), common meals (Acts 2:42, the fellowship offering), giving (Phil 4:18, the pleasing aroma of a burnt offering), the sacrifice of praise (Heb 13:15), and the presentation of your bodies as living sacrifices (Rom 12:1, the burnt offering). The principles of sacrifice from Leviticus live on in the life of the church. Sacrifice does not involve giving up something as much as taking on something.

the ordination of such priests (Exod 28–29, 39); now Moses carries out these instructions. In fact, a major point of emphasis in Leviticus 8–10 is the obedience of Moses and Aaron to the Lord's commands (for example, 8:4, 5, 9, 13; 9:6, 7, 10, 21; 10:7, 13, 15) and the tragedy of disobedience (10:1).

8:1–36 On the first day of ordination, Moses gathers Aaron and his sons, the appropriate ordination sacrifices, and the *entire assembly* (represented by the elders – see 9:1; Wenham 98) at the entrance of the tent of meeting (8:1–4). Throughout this day, Moses takes on the role of a priest. He washes Aaron and his sons and then dresses Aaron in ornate clothes that denote the honor and dignity of the high priest (8:5–9; Exod 28, 39). Included in this clothing are the *Urim and Thummim* (8:8), two small objects distinctively marked in some way so that a priest could determine the Lord's answer to a specific question by casting these *lots* (Exod 28:30; Num 27:21; 1 Sam 28:6).

Moses anoints the tabernacle, its contents, and Aaron with oil to consecrate them (8:10–12; Exod 30:22–33). He then dresses Aaron's sons in their priestly garments (8:13) and turns to offer the sacrifices (8:14–29). The procedure for each type of offering generally follows the directives of chapters 1–7 (for variances, see Hartley 109–15, 194). Moses puts some of the blood from the ordination offering on the right ear, right thumb, and right big toe of Aaron and his sons (8:23–24). These parts stand for the whole body; the right side indicates what is most favored or important (Gen 48:17). Thus this action consecrates the priests wholly to the Lord.

The first day of ordination concludes with two instructions for the priests. First, they must cook and eat the remaining meat of the ordination offering (8:31). Leftover meat and grain should be burned (8:32). Second, they must not leave the entrance of the tent for seven days, until the end of their period of ordination (8:33–35). Ordination demands time and avoidance of anything that might defile them during this week.

9:1–24 Whereas Moses officiates on the first day, on the eighth day he instructs Aaron to begin his priestly ministry by offering the sacrifices (9:2–4). Aaron first offers his own sin and burnt offerings (9:8–14); then he offers sacrifices on behalf of the people (9:15–21). The order is significant, for only after Aaron offers his own sacrifices can he officiate for the people.

The goal of priestly ordination is the presence of God among the people (see Exod 25:8): *so that the glory of the Lord may appear to you* (9:6, 4; symbolized in the cloud, Exod 24:15–18; 40:34–35). After the sacrifices, Aaron blesses the people (9:22; compare Num 6:23–27) and then, for the first time, enters the tent of meeting with Moses. As high priest, Aaron now has full access to the sanctuary. They come out, again bless the people, and *the glory of the Lord appeared to all the people* (9:23). Fire comes out from the presence of the Lord and incinerates the meat and fat already burning on the altar (9:16–17). In response, the people shout for joy and reverently bow (9:24). Unfortunately, not all the priests respond with such reverence.

> **Tent of Meeting**
> *The Pentateuch calls the portable tent shrine in the wilderness several names*: the "Tent of Meeting" [Hebrew ohel moed], the "Dwelling" [mishkan], *and the "Sanctuary" [migdash]. More or less interchangeable, the names emphasize different aspects of the structure's roles in Israelite life.*

10:1–20 Later on the eighth day, Nadab and Abihu each take a censer (a portable ladle for carrying coals), put fire in them, and *offered unauthorized fire before the Lord* (10:1). Immediately, fire again comes out from Yahweh's presence (9:24) and kills them (10:2). What was so wrong with their action that it brought this response from Yahweh? Despite numerous explanations, the nature of their sin may best be explained by careful attention to chapter 10 and the entire book of Leviticus.

First, the writer describes their fire as *unauthorized* [Hebrew *zarah*]. The fire is the problem, not the incense. The Hebrew term *zarah* means "strange," "foreign," or "unlawful." How the fire could be *unauthorized* is explained by 16:12–13. When Aaron enters the sanctuary on the Day of Atonement, he must take fire for offering incense from the altar in the courtyard. It seems reasonable that fire from any other source is *unauthorized*, and, as common (rather than holy) fire, it would pollute God's sanctuary.

Second, their action is *contrary to [God's] command* (10:1) or, more literally, *such as he had not commanded them* (NRSV). Nadab and Abihu break the pattern of obedience to the Lord's commands set forth in chapters 8 and 9. The Lord explicitly instructs Moses, Aaron, and Aaron's sons on the proper procedures for ordination (8:1, 4, 5). Nadab and Abihu forego these instructions in favor of their desires.

Third, immediately after their death, the Lord warns Aaron and his remaining sons not *to drink wine or other fermented drink whenever you go into the Tent of Meeting, or you will die* (10:8). The placement of this warning here, embedded in the context of the death of Nadab and Abihu, may suggest that drinking is a part of mourning rituals or that Nadab and Abihu had been drinking. God warns Aaron and his sons that, if they act in a similar way, they may expect the same fate.

Fourth, Leviticus 16:1–2 explains that Nadab and Abihu *died when they approached the Lord* and then warns Aaron *not to come whenever he chooses into the Most Holy Place*, or else he too will die. Apparently, Nadab and Abihu had decided to enter the most holy place, an action reserved only for the high priest one day a year. Thus, their action may also be an attempt to usurp the role of the high priest.

Nadab and Abihu do not make an unintentional mistake. Rather, perhaps inebriated, they take fire that endangered the purity of the sanctuary and go to enter the most holy place. At the very least, their action threatens to drive away the presence of God; priests must pay great attention to holiness and obedience (10:3).

Moses summons men to carry away the bodies of Nadab and Abihu (10:4–5) and then warns Aaron and his sons not to enact mourning rituals of unkempt hair or tearing clothes (10:6–7; compare 21:1–4, 10–12). Further, for the only time in Leviticus, the Lord speaks solely to Aaron when he warns him that he and his sons must not drink wine when they enter the tent (10:8–9). Their task as priests is to *distinguish between the holy and the profane, between the unclean and the clean* and to teach God's laws to the Israelites. Their task requires clarity of mind while on duty.

After these events, but still during the eighth day, a conflict erupts between Moses and Aaron. Moses reminds Aaron and his sons to eat the grain offering and fellowship offering (10:12–15). When Moses asks whether they have eaten the sin offering as required, he discovers that Eleazar and Ithamar have already burned it (10:16–17; 6:24–30).

Aaron's defense is unclear: *Would the Lord have been pleased if I had eaten the sin offering today?* (10:19). Aaron may have felt that his sons' deaths contaminated the sin offering, and thus it was improper to eat it (see Milgrom, *Leviticus 1–16*, 635–40). Or it may be that these tragic events made it inappropriate, in his opinion, to eat the sin offering. In a remarkable turn, Moses accepts his excuse (10:20); the explicit commands of the law are overridden by the circumstances of the day. The story appears here to insure that no reader would understand the Nadab and Abihu story to imply that God demands unthinking obedience to technical rules rather than religion of the heart.

HUMAN UNCLEANNESS · 11:1–15:33

Thus far in Leviticus, God has provided sacrifice (1–7) and a priesthood (8–10) to facilitate his relationship with Israel. This theme continues in chapters 11–15 with the gift of purity laws to *keep the Israelites separate from things that make them unclean, so they will not die in their uncleanness for defiling my dwelling place* (15:31). God's desire is to live with the people, not kill them. Consequently, Israel must strictly control the uncleanness that threatens to pollute God's tabernacle (10:10).

11:1–47 A clear introduction (11:1) and conclusion (11:46–47) frame the instructions about clean and unclean animals. The three domains of life from Genesis 1 provide internal organization for the first

---

Priesthood

A priest promotes and facilitates relationship with God. Thus Israel is a priestly nation to the world (Exod 19:5–6) while Aaron and his sons are priests to Israel. In the same way, all Christians are priests to the world (1 Pet 2:9–10) while Jesus is the high priest over the church (Heb 7:26; 9:11; 10:21).

The call to priesthood is a wonderful privilege and a grave responsibility. The closer a person lives to God, the more responsible he or she must be to reflect God's holiness (Lev 10:3). New Testament writers adopt this idea. Christians are a "royal priesthood" and, thus, must abstain from sinful desires (1 Pet 2:9, 11–12).

God's judgment of Nadab and Abihu underscores the special accountability of priests. God will not tolerate flagrant and presumptuous disobedience. Yet, this is not the whole story of Leviticus 10.

Aaron and his remaining sons also disobey the Lord. In fact, their sin is much more clearly a violation of explicit law than was the sin of Nadab and Abihu. Why do they not die? While judging disobedience, God also takes account of attitudes and circumstances. In any other circumstance, the flagrant actions of Aaron and his sons are inexcusable, but God sees the heart, not merely external actions.

Food Laws

The food laws stem from God's desire to live with Israel (15:31). But why? Interpreters have proposed various rationales for these laws, the most popular in recent years being a hygienic explanation. Some claim that the distinction between clean and unclean is based on which animals are more likely to carry disease. Yet there are several problems with this view. First, there is no hint in the text that ancient Israel understood these laws in such a way. Second, the omission of dangerous plant life and water is inexplicable. Third, if health is the rationale, why would Jesus declare all foods clean (Mark 7:19), especially when cooking and other hygienic practices had not yet advanced far from those of ancient Israel?

A more likely rationale for the food laws is that they symbolize Israel's place in the world (see Douglas 42–58). Clean animals conform to a pure type of its class (land, water, or air) from a pastoralist's viewpoint. Animals that are ambiguous types are unclean: for example, a lobster (which lives in water but walks as if on land), or a land animal that does not chew the cud and have a cleft hoof. This classification of types appears to symbolize Israel's identity. Like clean food, God has set apart the nation of Israel from the Gentiles and their unclean food. Israel's table laws, therefore, were a constant reminder of its calling to be holy to Yahweh (20:24–26).

This interpretation of the food laws finds support in Acts 10. Here, Peter receives a vision that instructs him to kill and eat unclean food and not to call anything profane that God has made clean (Acts 10:9–16). Although the vision says nothing about the distinction between Jew and Gentile, when Peter later interprets the meaning of the vision, he claims that *God has shown me that I should not call any man impure or unclean* (Acts 10:28). For Peter, the repealing of the foods laws meant that there was no longer a distinction between Jew and Gentile.

---

half of the chapter: land (verses 1–8), water (verses 9–12), and sky (verses 13–23). The second half concerns defilement caused by the carcass of a clean or unclean creature (verses 24–45).

Edible or clean land animals include *any animal that has a split hoof completely divided and that chews the cud* (11:3). Animals with only one of these characteristics are unclean and must not be eaten (11:4–8, 26). Here, *chews the cud* denotes animals that chew their food thoroughly (for example, neither a camel nor a rabbit is a true ruminant, or cud-chewer, yet they are lawful to eat). Further, animals with paws, such as dogs (11:27), and a variety of animals that *move* (*swarm* in the NRSV) *about on the ground* (11:29–30, 41–42) are also unclean.

Edible water creatures must have both *fins and scales* (11:9–12). Sky creatures include two categories: birds (verses 13–19) and insects (verses 20–22). Rather than characterizing detestable birds, the writer provides a list. Although the identity of some birds is unclear, the common feature of forbidden birds appears to be that each one consumes meat with blood (compare Gen 9:4–5). Of insects, those that fly and walk are *detestable* (11:20) but not those that fly and hop (11:21–23).

Contact with the carcass of any unclean creature makes a person unclean (11:24–28), but only for one day (11:25, 28, 31, 40). Concern for this type of defilement leads to two further instructions: what is to be done when the carcass of an unclean animal falls on or into something (11:32–38), and the status of a person who touches or eats the carcass of a clean animal that was not slaughtered as a sacrifice (11:39–40).

12:1–8 Concern now shifts from external threats to cleanness (chapter 11) to internal threats: childbirth (chapter 12), disease (chapters 13–14), and bodily discharges (chapter 15). A woman's monthly period renders her unclean for seven days (15:19). In the same way, the blood of childbirth also makes her unclean (12:2). For ancient Israel, blood had the greatest power to atone, but also the greatest power to defile (see Milgrom, *Leviticus 1–16*, 766–68). Strangely, the duration of uncleanness is less for the birth of a boy (7 days unclean plus 33 days before purification, 12:1–4) than for a girl (14 days plus 66 days, 12:5). This difference is undoubtedly rooted in Israel's patriarchal social structure (27:2–7; see Hartley 167–68). Because of their menstrual cycle, women spent much of their lives ritually impure, a state symbolized even in infants.

Before her purification, a woman must not *touch anything sacred or go to the sanctuary* (12:4) so as not to contaminate it (15:31). She may approach the tabernacle only when her days of purification are over, and then only with an appropriate burnt offering and sin offering (12:6–8; see Luke 2:22–24). The sin offering does not presume that the woman has sinned; rather, the sin offering cleanses the impurity of the blood. As Levine (74) puts it, "Ancient man seldom distinguished between 'sin' and 'impurity.'"

13:1–46 A second internal threat to cleanness is *tsaraath*, traditionally translated *leprosy* (KJV, NASB), but more accurately referring to a wide range of skin ailments. Diagnosis of *tsaraath* is the focus of chapter 13; chapter 14 gives instruction for the ceremonial cleansing of skin diseases. Throughout these processes of purification, the priest makes the crucial diagnosis and performs the key rituals.

In chapter 13, priests take on the role of public health officials. The text prescribes a diagnostic procedure for identifying a skin ailment in six suspicious circumstances and limiting its spread through quarantine: *a swelling or a rash or a bright spot* (13:2–17), *a boil* (13:18–23), *a burn* (13:24–28), *a sore* (13:29–38), *white spots on the skin* (13:38–39), and *baldness* (13:40–44). Any person who suspects that he or she may have an infectious skin disease must go to a priest for an inspection (13:2, 9, 18). The priest will examine the person and pronounce him or her clean (13:12–13, 38) or unclean (13:3, 10–11, 20, 25, 30, 43–44) or, if uncertain, place the person in isolation (13:4, 21, 26, 31). After one week, the priest will again examine the person and pronounce him or her clean (6, 23, 28) or unclean (22, 27), or in some cases require a second period of quarantine followed by a third examination (13:5, 32–34). In the case of a reoccurrence, the patient must reappear before the priest for further examination (13:7–8, 15–17, 35–37). Once declared unclean, a person must move outside the camp, wear torn clothes, have unkempt hair and cover *the lower part of his face* when warning people nearby of his or her unclean status (13:45–46).

13:47–59 A second type of *tsaraath* is *destructive mildew* (translated *leprosy* in the KJV) of any wool, linen, or leather product (13:47–49, 51, 57). A priest must examine any suspicious item and isolate it for seven days (13:51). If after seven days the *mildew* has spread, the entire article is unclean and *must be burned* (13:51–52). If there is no noticeable spread, the priest will order the item washed and isolated for another week (13:53–54). Then, if the spot has faded, the priest will tear out the suspicious area, order the item washed again, then pronounce it clean (13:56–58). If the spot has not faded, the item is unclean and must be destroyed (13:55).

14:1–32 A person who believes *he has been healed of his infectious skin disease* must summon a priest for an examination (14:3). If the priest determines that the person is healed, based on the standards of chapter 13, he performs a purification ritual outside the camp.

> **Ritual Purification**
> *Purification of a person with a skin ailment is not medicinal in our modern sense but reintroduces a person back into the community.*

The priest kills one bird and drains its blood into a pot (14:5). He then takes the second bird (and other items), dips it into the blood, sprinkles the person seven times with the blood, and releases the bird into the open fields (14:6–7).

After the purification ceremony outside the camp, the person washes his or her clothes, shaves, and bathes. Although now clean, he or she must still stay outside his tent for seven more days (14:8). On the seventh day, he or she again washes his or her clothes, shaves, and bathes (14:9). Finally, on the eighth day the person brings offerings to complete his or her purification and reintroduction into the community (14:10). The procedure involving the sacrifices generally follows the instructions of chapters 1–7, with the notable exception of putting some of the blood and oil on the right ear lobe, the right thumb, and the right big toe (14:14–17, 25–28). This ritual, similar to that in the ordination of the priests, cleanses the whole person (compare 8:23–24). Also, like other rituals, this one requires a week.

> **Offerings of the Poor**
> *Special provisions are made for those too poor to bring the regular offerings (14:21–22).*

14:33–57 A third type of *tsaraath* is *mildew* in a house (14:34). When a person suspects *tsaraath* in his house, he must summon a priest. The priest will order the house emptied before his arrival *so that nothing in the house will be pronounced unclean* (14:36). He will then inspect the house and, if it is suspect, close it for seven days (14:37). Upon his return, if the suspicious area has grown, he will order all the contaminated stones replaced, and all the inside walls scraped and replastered (14:39–42). After an unspecified time the priest will return to inspect the house again. If the mildew reappears, the house is unclean and must be destroyed. Otherwise, *he shall pronounce the house clean* (14:48) and perform the same purification ritual for the house as for a person healed of a skin disease (14:49–53; see 14:4–7).

Ancient Israelites thought of growths on the human skin or on buildings as being essentially alike, whatever our modern system of categorization.

15:1–33 This chapter considers how four types of sexual discharges may pollute others and how to remedy such contracted uncleanness (15:3): an abnormal sexual discharge of a male (15:2–15), an emission of semen (15:16–18), a woman's period (15:19–24), and an abnormal sexual discharge of a female (15:25–30). Again, Israel does not think of these issues as morally problematic but as matters of ritual impurity.

A person may contract uncleanness from a man with an unnatural discharge by touching anything on which he lies, sits (15:4–6), or rides (15:9–10), or by touching him (15:7). The man may also communicate his uncleanness by spitting on someone (15:8) or touching someone without first washing his hands (15:11). A person who contracts uncleanness in any of these ways must wash his clothes and bathe (15:5–8, 10–11).

An emission of semen renders the man and anything that comes in contact with the semen unclean (15:16). In an emission during intercourse, both the man and the woman become unclean (15:18). In both instances, a person must bathe and wash any clothes that have become unclean.

A woman's menstruation renders her unclean for seven days (15:20). Her uncleanness may be contracted by touching anything on which she lies or sits (15:21–23). In such cases, the contaminated person must wash his or her clothes and bathe, but remains unclean only until the evening (15:22). However, if a man has intercourse with a woman during her period, he will be unclean for seven days and may contaminate others (15:24).

> **Reflection on the Purity Laws**
> The purity laws highlight inescapable aspects of human life: food, sexuality, reproduction, and disease. These have nothing to do with sin but are intimately connected to our status as created beings and therefore represent what most distinguishes us from God (John 4:24). Thus, while food laws may symbolize boundaries and remind Israel of its special chosen status, the purity laws as a whole remind Israelites of their humanity. Set deep within the culture of ancient Israel, purity laws guard against pride and irreverence, since life in the presence of God demands a recognition of and respect for the difference between us and God.

A woman who has an abnormal discharge of blood is unclean for as long as the discharge lasts; she may spread her uncleanness just as during her monthly period (15:25–26). Those who contract this uncleanness must wash their clothes and bathe with water, but they remain unclean only until evening (15:27).

Purification rituals for a male or female with an abnormal discharge are similar (15:13–15, 28–30). After the discharge has stopped, a man must wash his clothes and bathe. He is then clean, although he must wait seven days before coming to the tabernacle (15:13). Presumably, a woman also washed her clothes and bathed, but she is not ceremonially clean for seven days (15:13, 28). The reason for this difference is not clear. On the eighth day, both the man and the woman must bring a sin offering and burnt offering of doves or pigeons for atonement (15:14–15, 29–30). Again, such emission of bodily fluids comes under neither moral nor medical categories of thinking.

THE DAY OF ATONEMENT · 16:1–34

God's glory is enthroned on the ark in the innermost room of the tabernacle (holy of holies), Yahweh's throne room (16:2; 1 Sam 4:4; Isa 37:15). For God to live with Israel, this room must remain ritually clean. Now, God provides a way for the high priest to cleanse the throne room and send away Israel's sin.

Prior to entering the most holy place, Aaron (or any high priest) gathers the appropriate sacrificial animals for himself (16:3) and the people (two goats and a ram, 16:5). He casts lots for the two goats (see below) and bathes and changes into *sacred garments*: a linen tunic, undergarments, sash, and turban (16:4). This simple linen dress contrasts sharply with Aaron's ornate vestments (Exod 28; Lev 8) and suggests the humility with which he must enter God's presence. Similarly, the community must demonstrate humility by practicing self-denial (fasting, as in Ps 35:13) and not working on this day (16:29, 31).

Aaron first sacrifices a sin offering for himself and his family (16:6). Then as he enters the most holy place, he burns incense, creating a smoke cloud that shields him from seeing God's glory on the throne (16:12–13). Aaron sprinkles some of the bull's blood *on the front of the atonement cover* and *before the atonement cover* (16:14, 16). He then repeats this procedure with the goat for the people's sin offering (16:15) before manipulating the blood of both sacrifices on the incense altar or outside altar (16:18–19; Exod 30:7–10; see Hartley

> **The Day of Atonement**
>
> The Day of Atonement is the most important annual event in Israel. The people's sin and uncleanness pollute God's tent, especially God's throne room. This impurity threatens their relationship. God cannot live with impure people in an unclean, defiled sanctuary (15:31; 16:16). But once again, God provides a way to maintain relationship, the Day of Atonement. On this day, the stain of impurity is cleansed from the most holy place, the entire tabernacle, the priests, and the people (16:33). Further, not only is the stain removed, but the source of the stain is taken away from the camp (16:21–22).
>
> The book of Hebrews explains the work of Jesus in terms of the Day of Atonement. As high priest, Jesus offered himself as a sacrifice (Heb 7:26–28) and entered the true throne room of God with his own blood (Heb 9:11–13). The potency of his blood enabled him to do this once for all time, rather than every year (Heb 9:25–27; 10:11–14). Furthermore, his action removes sin (Heb 9:14, 28; compare 2 Cor 5:21; 1 Pet 2:24). As a result, we have confidence to enter the presence of God in full relationship (Heb 10:19–22).

240–41). These actions cleanse the entire tabernacle, especially the most holy place (16:16).

One of the most fascinating events on the Day of Atonement regards the second goat. Earlier in the day, Aaron casts lots for the two goats: *one lot for the Lord and the other for the scapegoat* [Hebrew *azazel*, 16:8]. While the second goat certainly functions as a scapegoat, the meaning of the word *azazel* is uncertain. Most modern interpreters recognize it as the name of a wilderness demon (so the NRSV's *Azazel*; see Hartley 237–38). Aaron does not kill the second goat for Azazel. Instead, he lays both hands on its head, confesses all the sins of Israel, and thereby puts *them on the goat's head* (16:20–21). This goat, led into the wilderness and released, carries away all their sins (16:21–22; for later Jewish tradition, see Levine 106). Thus, whereas the sacrificed goat cleanses the sanctuary, the living goat removes the cause of defilement from the camp and returns it to its proper abode – in the wilderness with Azazel.

THE HOLINESS CODE · 17:1–26:46

A series of speeches follows the Day of Atonement: to the priests and all Israel (17:1–20:27), to the priests alone (21:1–22:16), and again to the priests and all Israel (22:17–22:45). The theme of these speeches is clear: God calls Israel to be holy. Three times the Lord states, *Be holy because I, the Lord your God, am holy* (19:2; 20:7, 26). The Hebrew root *qadash* for both the noun ("holy") and verb ("be holy") occurs eighty-five times in these ten chapters. In fact, the theme of holiness is so prevalent that most interpreters refer to Leviticus 17–26 as the Holiness Code.

The Holiness Code offers a guide for holy living as an imitation of God. As God calls Israel to be holy, Israel need not wonder what it means to be so. Rather, from sexual conduct to worship, God explains what is and is not holy. Israel's holiness is God-given, not self-achieved: *I am the Lord, who makes you holy* (22:32). The Holiness Code, then, instructs Israel how to live up to her high calling to be like the Lord, not how Israel may achieve her own righteousness.

17:1–16 Leviticus 17 sets forth a general principle based on the equation of blood with life (17:11; Gen 9:4; Deut 12:23). As life, blood belongs to Yahweh, the creator of life, who gives it to Israel only for purposes of atonement (17:11). Consequently, Israel must never grasp what God alone owns; it must handle blood properly and never consume it (17:10, 12, 14). Chapter 17 applies this principle to three cases (17:1–9, 13–14, 15–16).

First, any slaughter of a sacrificial animal must take place at *the entrance to the Tent of Meeting* (17:4, 8–9), where it may be presented as a fellowship offering (17:5) (for discussion of whether this regards only sacrifice or any slaughter, see Hartley 269–71, Levine 112–13; compare Deut 12:13–27). The explicit reason for this command is to stop the practice of sacrificing to *goat idols*, perhaps imagined satyrs, in the open fields (17:5, 7). Improper disposal of the blood may be a second concern (17:6). Priests regulate the disposal of blood at the tabernacle. Elsewhere there are no such controls.

Second, an Israelite or resident alien may hunt and kill a nonsacrificial animal or bird without bringing it to the tabernacle (17:13–14; see Deut 12). It would be impractical to wrestle wild game to the tent entrance before killing it. Nonetheless, the hunter must be careful to drain blood properly.

In these first two cases, the penalty for violation is to be *cut off*, or expelled, from the community (17:4, 9, 14); once Yahweh promises *to cut him off from his people* (17:10). In instances where the Lord imposes "cutting off," the penalty may denote premature death, loss of descendants, or no life after death (see Milgrom, *Leviticus 1–16*, 457–60).

Third, anyone who eats a creature *found dead* becomes unclean and must bathe and wash his or her clothes (17:15–16; see 5:2; Deut 14:21). This uncleanness is likely due to the uncertainty of whether the blood properly drained from the animal (compare 11:39–40).

18:1–30 Leviticus 18 describes the limits of holiness in sexual relationships, primarily delineating who is a proper marriage/sexual partner; the injunction not to *have sexual relations* denotes not only sexual intercourse, but marriage itself (18:18). In ancient Israel, marriage took place within the clan (Gen 24; Num 36). This chapter explains that one's nearest relatives are not eligible marriage candidates, much less appropriate sexual partners (18:6): mother or wife of your father (18:7–8), full-, half-, or stepsister (18:9, 11; compare Gen 20:12), granddaughter (18:10), aunt (18:12–14), daughter-in-law (18:15), sister-in-law (18:16; see Deut 25:5–10), a woman and her daughter or granddaughter (18:17), or a woman and her sister (18:18; compare Gen 29). An obvious omission from this list is one's own daughter. Since a daughter is a closer blood relative than any other person listed, however, sexual relations with her are assumed unthinkable.

> **God's Standards of Holiness**
> The underlying premise of the Holiness Code is that Yahweh is Israel's God (18:2, 4, 29). Consequently, God, not other peoples or gods, sets Israel's moral standards (18:3). In the same way, culture cannot set the standards for God's people today (1 Pet 1:14–16; 2:9–12).
>
> The Lord's holiness code for marriage and sex naturally extends into the New Testament (Rom 1:26–28; 1 Cor 5:1; 6:9) and is the basis of many contemporary state laws. Concerns for family stability, the welfare of women, and the concept of "one flesh" underlie this code and should not be lightly dismissed.

The list of prohibited partners is not limited to blood relations, but extends to relationships created by marriage (for example, an uncle's wife). The more literal translation of the NRSV indicates the rationale. Such a relative is *your father's flesh* (18:12), *your mother's flesh* (18:13), and *your flesh* (18:17). Here, Leviticus 18 takes seriously the claim in Genesis 2 that in marriage the couple becomes *one flesh* (Gen 2:24). Hence, marriage creates "blood" relations among family members. A man may not marry his stepsister because the marriage of their parents has by extension made them near-blood relatives.

In addition to marriage stipulations, Leviticus 18 prohibits some other types of sexual behavior: sex during a woman's menstruation (18:19), adultery (18:20; compare Exod 20:14; Deut 5:18), homosexual behavior (18:22), and bestiality (18:23; Exod 22:19; Deut 27:21).

Leviticus justifies these rules by appealing to history: the former inhabitants of the land polluted their land with these sexual practices, and the land vomited them out (18:24–25, 27). The same will happen to Israel if it does these things (18:26, 28). Thus, any person who violates these standards *must be cut off from their people* (18:29) for the well-being of the whole.

19:1–37 Leviticus 19 likewise stresses Israel's relationship to Yahweh as the foundation for holy behavior. Eight times the chapter repeats, *I am the Lord your God* (19:2, 3, 4, 10, 25, 31, 34, 36) and another eight times the shortened formula, *I am the Lord* (19:12, 14, 16, 18, 28, 30, 32, 37). God calls Israel to *be holy because I, the Lord your God, am holy* (19:2). Israel's holiness is an imitation of the God to whom it belongs.

Holiness includes acceptable worship practices, especially regarding sacrifice (19:5–8) and social conduct, namely, respect for others' property (19:11a), honesty (19:11b–12), fairness (19:11c, 13, 35–36), justice (19:15), and upholding the reputation and well-being of others (19:16). The foundation of these principles is love: *love your neighbor as yourself* (19:17–18).

In addition to these general principles, chapter 19 identifies persons for whom holy people show particular concern: the poor (19:9–10, 13b), the alien (19:10, 33–34), the disabled (19:14), and the elderly (19:3, 32). Each of these groups is marginal in society and thus vulnerable. An imitation of God's holiness demands that special consideration be made for those whom society disregards. In a striking and often overlooked text, Yahweh demands that Israel love the alien, not just fellow Israelites (19:34).

> **Aliens**
> The Hebrew term *ger*, usually rendered "stranger" or "foreigner," designates the non-Israelites who live a long time among the Israelites and thus enjoy many of the privileges and responsibilities of the community, including the economic protection that comes from the law of Sabbath.

Questions typically arise regarding two texts in chapter 19. First, the prohibition of mixed breeding, sowing, and clothing is perplexing (19:19). Three lines of explanation are typical: these mixtures violate the separation of species (Gen 1) and thus symbolize disorder; mixture of wool and linen is a feature of the tabernacle (curtains [Exod 26:1, 31] and priestly garments [Exod 28:6, 15; 39:29]), and thus the prohibition protects the divine sphere (see Milgrom, *Leviticus 17–22*, 1657–65); the prohibited mixtures may be symbolic for intermarriage with non-Israelites. The ethical context of chapter 19 seems to support this last option, as does the use of this text in the Dead Sea Scrolls (Milgrom, *Leviticus 17–22*, 1659 and 2 Cor 6:14).

Second, God prohibits cutting *the hair at the sides of your head* and *the edges of your beard* and tattooing (19:27–28). These customs are a part of pagan mourning rituals (21:1–5; Deut 14:1; Jer 16:16). Thus, the real issue appears to be the close association of these rites with the worship of other gods, especially Baal (for example, 1 Kgs 18:28).

20:1–27 It is inevitable that some people will break the standards of holiness in Leviticus 18–19. What then? According to Leviticus 20, holiness includes a godlike response to those who act in unholy ways (20:7, 22–26). First, the community must stone any Israelite or resident alien who practices child sacrifice (20:2; 18:21). Since God will set his *face against that man* and *cut him off from his people* (20:3), ignoring such a sin implies complicity (20:5).

Second, the penalty for turning to a medium or spiritist is to be cut off by the Lord from the people (20:6; compare 19:31). The community must put to death any medium or spiritist (20:27).

Third, anyone who *curses his father or mother* must be put to death (20:9; Exod 21:17). To curse one's parents is not a matter of flippantly using "curse words" against them. A curse in ancient Israel was a speech act that could bring about a tragic event (see 2 Sam 16:5–13; Job 3:1–10). A curse against one's parents flagrantly violates the command to respect them (19:3).

Fourth, the writer stipulates penalties for a range of sexual sins in order of severity (20:10–21; compare 18:6–23). Violations of sexual holiness that bring a death penalty include adultery (20:10), as well as sexual relations with *one's father's wife* (20:11) or with a daughter-in-law (20:12). In addition, homosexuality, bestiality, and marriage to a woman as well as to her mother merit the death penalty (20:13–16). In all of these cases, the man and his sexual partner(s) must be put to death.

Other sexual violations carry a lesser penalty. Those who marry a sister or have sexual relations with a woman during her menstruation *must be cut off from their people* (20:17–18; compare 15:24). In instances of sexual relations between a brother and sister (but not married), a nephew and aunt, or a man who marries his sister-in-law, both the man and the woman will *be held responsible*, and *they will die childless* (20:19–21).

> **Punishments in Leviticus**
>
> *Although the punishments in Leviticus 20 seem harsh, Wenham suggests this harshness is moderated by other factors. First, these penalties are maximums; mitigating circumstances brought lesser penalties. Second, in some cases Israel accepted compensation in lieu of the death penalty (see Exod 21:30; Num 35:31). Third, the requirement of at least two witnesses in a capital case limits these penalties to the most flagrant violations (Num 35:30). Israel rarely put to death those whose crimes merited the death penalty. When the community did carry out such punishment, it was not to be vengeful but to purge evil from the land and deter others from such crimes (Deut 19:19–20; Wenham 282–85).*

21:1–22:33 Chapters 21 and 22 address the priests (yet Moses also speaks to the whole nation in 21:24). Two topics emerge: the standard of holiness for an officiating priest (21:1–24) and the disposition of sacrificial food (22:1–16). This section concludes with instructions to the priests and all Israel regarding acceptable offerings (22:17–32).

Because they serve in close proximity to the holy, the Lord calls the priests (21:1–9) and high priest (21:10–15) to a higher standard of purity. Contact with a dead body renders a person unclean (Num 19:11–13). Consequently, a regular priest may not *make himself ceremonially unclean* by attending to the burial of anyone except a close relative (21:1–4), nor may he enact the mourning rituals of shaving his head, clipping his beard, or cutting himself (21:5). He must remain holy (21:6). Further, because of his position, a priest ought not marry *women defiled by prostitution or divorced* (21:7), presumably, a safeguard for his reputation.

Stricter standards apply to the high priest. He must not even *enter a place where there is a dead body* (21:11) or observe the most common mourning rituals of unkempt hair and torn clothes (21:10), even for his father or mother (21:11). The phrase *nor leave the sanctuary of his God* does not mean that the high priest could never leave the tabernacle. Rather, he could not leave the tabernacle to attend to a funeral because the incurred defilement would threaten the tabernacle on his return (21:12). Further, his marriage restrictions are greater; he may only marry *a virgin from his own people* (21:13–14), presumably to ensure a legitimate heir for the high priest (21:15).

For ancient Israel, physical wholeness symbolizes holiness. Thus, a priest with a physical defect may not officiate in the tabernacle lest he desecrate it (21:16–23). The intention is not punitive; the priest may still eat from the offerings (21:22). It is simply that within the world view of ancient Israel, physical "abnormalities" represent an opposition to the wholeness of life God intends for creation.

Instruction for the disposition of the priest's share of the offerings begins with a principle: *treat with respect the sacred offerings* (22:1). Any descendant of Aaron may eat from the sacred offerings, with two qualifications. First, a priest who is ceremonially unclean must not *come near the sacred offerings* (to officiate) or eat from them until he is cleansed (22:3–8). A priest who presents an offering in an unclean state *must be cut off from [God's] presence* (22:3; meaning at least dismissal from the priesthood). One who eats an offering in an unclean state may die for his contempt (22:9).

Second, the priest's family does not involve guests or hired hands (22:10). A slave, however, is part of the household (22:11). A daughter will eat of his food until marriage (22:12). Only if she returns to her father's house, divorced or widowed without children, may she eat of her father's priestly food (22:13). A person who eats from a sacred offering by mistake must make restitution plus twenty percent (22:14; compare 5:14–16). A priest, however, must not desecrate offerings by consciously allowing others to eat of them (22:15–16).

Leviticus 1–7 consistently warned the Israelites to bring only animals *without defect* for sacrifice. Now, the writer defines "without defect" (22:17–22). Most striking here is the close parallel between what renders an animal unacceptable and what renders a priest unacceptable (21:16–23; see Levine 141). In essence, an obligatory offering, including a fellowship offering pledged in a vow, must be without any defect (22:24–25). Only a freewill offering may be less than perfect (22:23).

23:1–44 Leviticus 23 is a calendar text that provides the information a common Israelite, not a priest, needed to know in order to observe the Lord's appointed feasts (compare Exod 23:12–19; Num 28–29; Deut 16:1–17). In addition to the weekly Sabbath (23:3), the feasts consist of three festivals, or seasons. First, the one-day Passover (fourteenth day of the first month; based on a lunar calendar, roughly March through April) is immediately followed by the weeklong Feast of Unleavened Bread (23:4–8). Second, Israel marks the beginning of the barley harvest with an offering of firstfruits, followed seven weeks later (50 days) by the Feast of Weeks to celebrate the completion of the harvest (23:9–23; "Pentecost" in Acts 2:1). Third, the seventh month (roughly September through October), which marks the end of the agricultural year, is most holy. Trumpet blasts announce the arrival of the month (a Feast of Trumpets, 23:23–25; Ps 81:1–5). The Day of Atonement follows on the tenth of the month, and the weeklong Feast of Tabernacles begins on the fifteenth (23:26–44).

As a whole, this text presupposes that the readers already understand the purposes of these special occasions. Thus, there are terse explanations for only the Day of Atonement (to make atonement; 23:28) and the Feast of Tabernacles (to commemorate the wilderness years; 23:43). Instead, the writer explains what to do on these days. Two themes emerge: rest and worship. On each of the special days and the first and last day of each festival week, the people are to *do no regular work* but *have a day of rest* (23:3, 7–8, 21, 24–25, 28–32, 35–36). *Sacred assemblies* that include sacrifice and worship (23:27) correspond to these days of rest.

> **The Purpose of Festivals**
> While New Testament writers make optional the observance of special days (Rom 14:5–6; Gal 4:10–11), the principles underlying Israel's calendar endure. Rest is important physically, ecologically, and spiritually. Unceasing work is largely the result of self-reliance. The Sabbath rest asserts that Israel trusts God enough to be still for a day (Exod 16:14–30). Sacred assemblies pursue the same aim: to affirm and proclaim reliance upon God.

> **Holidays of the Jewish Year**
> Ancient Israel used several different calendars, but the most important one included twelve months beginning in our March. Each festival was keyed to a particular month. In the list below, the second name is the month's older name:
>
> **Nisan** (Aviv) – Passover; **Iyyar** (Ziv); **Sivan** – Pentecost/Weeks; **Tammuz**; **Av**; **Elul**; **Tishri** (Ethanim) – Trumpets, Atonement, Tabernacles; **Chislev** – Hanukkah; **Tebeth**; **Shebat**; **Adar** – Purim

24:1–9 Inside the holy place stands an altar of incense, a lampstand, and a golden table (Exod 25:23–40; 30:1–10). Each evening "Aaron" (that is, the high priest) must fill the lamps and light them so that they burn throughout the night (24:1–4). Each Sabbath, he is to set out twelve fresh loaves of bread on the table along with incense (24:5–7). According to Exodus 30:7–8, when Aaron tends the lamp each morning and evening, he is to offer this incense to God *in lieu* of the bread. The priests eat large loaves (*two-tenths of an* ephah *for each loaf*, at least four quarts of flour) as part of their regular share of offerings (but see 1 Sam 21:1–6).

24:10–23 The connection between this story and what precedes and follows is difficult to discern. Like the story of Nadab and Abihu in chapter 10, this story illustrates what can happen when Israel does not listen to Yahweh's commands, and the proper ways to correct such an error. The story illustrates how the people are to resolve ambiguities in the Torah.

Two men fight and one blasphemes *the name of the Lord with a curse* (24:11). Exodus clearly forbids such an action (20:7; 22:8) but does not prescribe a penalty. Further complicating this case is the identity of the man who curses; he is the *son of an Israelite mother and an Egyptian father*, not fully Israelite (24:10). Uncertain what to do in such a case, the people put the man in custody *until the will of the Lord should be made clear to them* (24:12). The Lord's ruling is plain; blasphemy is a capital offense regardless of whether the person is *alien or native born* (24:16).

Resolution of this particular case leads to a brief exposition of two principles of Israelite law (24:17–22). First, resident aliens, non-Israelites who choose to live in Israel, are subject to the same laws as Israelites (24:22). Second is the principle of *talion*: *whatever he has done must be done to him*: *fracture for fracture, eye for eye, tooth for tooth* (24:19–20). Although this seems harsh, the same principle underlies modern law: punishment should match the crime. In practice, this most often limits rather than sets the extent of punishment.

25:1–55 The modern concept of a "sabbatical" derives from the Lord's demand that every seven years Israel observe a Sabbath year (25:2); Israel may not sow or reap the land but only eat whatever grows in the field of itself (25:5–7). The natural objection to a Sabbath year is, *what will we eat in the seventh year if we do not plant or harvest our crops* (25:20)? In response, the Lord promises that the sixth year will produce enough to provide for the intervening years (25:21–22; compare Exod 16:14–30). Although the ecological benefits of crop rotation may support the Sabbath year, the primary issue is trust: will Israel be self-reliant or trust in the Lord?

Once every fifty years, on the Day of Atonement, Israel is to proclaim a Year of Jubilee (25:10). Two features define the Jubilee: release of property and release of persons. Both concepts are rooted in a common theological principle. The land and the people of Israel belong to the Lord (25:23, 42). Israel is God's tenant, not the landowner; it is God's servant, not a servant to another.

The first defining feature of the Jubilee is the return of property. In an agricultural society, a family's well-being depended on keeping their land (see 1 Kgs 21:3). Consequently, Leviticus 25 stipulates that any land "purchase" is only a "lease" based on the number of harvests until the Jubilee, not a permanent sale (25:14–17). Further, in instances in which the lease is due to financial difficulties, a close relative or the owner must be given the right to buy out the lease at any point (25:25–27). In all cases, at the Year of Jubilee, the land returns to the original owner (25:28).

The law is different for houses in an urban area (that is, a walled city). Here, the owner maintains the right of redemption (repurchase) for only one year. After this, the house belongs permanently to the buyer and will not be returned at the Jubilee (25:29–30). Houses in rural areas (or in an unwalled city), however, are classified as an open field and are subject to those rules for redemption (25:31).

The property of the Levites is an exception to all these regulations. Since the Levites do not receive land, but cities (Josh 21), their houses are always redeemable and always revert to them in the Jubilee (25:33). Further, the pastureland surrounding a Levitical town may not be sold or leased under any circumstances (25:34).

Lex Talionis

Ancient Israel considered the circumstances surrounding a crime, and only in instances of premeditated action did they apply the full extent of this law (for example, Num 35:16–28). In other instances, a person could pay compensation for damages (see Exod 21:12–36). Incidentally, in the New Testament, Jesus does not reject this principle as a principle of societal justice but as an illegitimate defense for personal vendettas (Matt 5:38–40).

The second defining feature of the Year of Jubilee is the release of persons (25:35–54). Here, the writer envisions several scenarios: first, if an Israelite is *unable to support himself*, the community should help him (25:35). Under no circumstance should people take advantage of his circumstances to enrich themselves. Interest on loans is forbidden, as is profit from food sales (25:36–37). This injunction is due to the person's impoverished situation, a far different circumstance from most modern economic loans.

> **Loans in Ancient Times**
> *In a world without banks and the financial instruments that make modern capitalism possible, loans were taken out only for desperate people whose crops had failed or unwise persons living beyond their means. To take interest on such loans, which came from neighbors, was to sever the bonds of community. Thus the Bible forbids the practice.*

Second, if an Israelite's poverty becomes so extreme that he sells himself, he is to work as a hired worker, not a slave, until the Year of Jubilee. Then, he and his family will be free and may return to their land (also released in the Jubilee; 25:40–41). Permanent slaves may come only from other nations or resident aliens living in Israel (25:44–46).

Third, in the event that an impoverished Israelite sells himself to a resident alien in the land, the community is to take pains to redeem him. The alien is subject to the laws of Israel; he must allow for redemption, must not treat the Israelite as a slave (but as a hired worker), and must release him in the Year of Jubilee (25:48–54).

26:1–46 As is typical for ancient Near Eastern legal texts, Leviticus concludes with a short statement of blessings for obedience (26:3–13) and a much longer description of consequences for disobedience (26:14–45; compare Deut 28). In response to faithfulness, the Lord promises four blessings, in ascending order of importance: prolific agricultural produce (26:4–5, 10); security from wild animals and invasion (26:6–8); the fertility of the nation (26:9); and Yahweh's presence among the people (26:11). This final promise is central to the book. God's desire is to walk among the people and to be their God, a distinct echo of the relationship lost in Eden (26:12; Gen 3:8).

The Lord threatens five escalating punishments, the reverse of the blessings. If Israel is unfaithful it will experience disease and insecurity before enemies (26:14–17); drought and crop failure (26:18–20); harm by wild animals (26:21–22; 2 Kgs 17:25–26); defeat by enemies during invasion and siege (26:23–26); and destruction of the sanctuaries and cities, resulting in exile (26:27–39). The repeated phrase *seven times over* is proverbial for complete or full punishment (see 26:18). The connection of environmental disaster and sin is common in ancient Near Eastern texts, including Deuteronomy and the prophets.

Yahweh's punishing actions are remedial, not vindictive. After each punishment, the hope is that the people will turn back. Further discipline comes only if the people do not accept correction (26:18, 21, 23, 27). The goal is not to destroy them, but to persuade them to *confess their sins* (26:40) and turn back to God. When *their uncircumcised hearts are humbled* (26:41) and they pay the consequences of their sin in the exile (26:41), Yahweh promises to remember the covenant with the people and the land (26:42–43; compare 25:1–7). In all this, even when the direst punishment of exile is enacted, the Lord does not reject the people or break the covenant (26:44–45).

REDEMPTION OF VOWS · 27:1–34

Leviticus seems to conclude with chapter 26 but continues with chapter 27. Despite its appendix-like appearance, the purpose of the chapter is clear: financing the tabernacle. The laws of Leviticus for God's dwelling in the tabernacle are useless unless financing for operations is secured. Here, funding comes from special vows or dedications (27:1–29) and tithes (27:30–33).

Four types of dedications are possible: of persons (27:2–8), animals (27:9–13), houses (27:14–15), and land (27:16–25). The dedication of a person to the Lord may be an expression of devotion and/or thanksgiving (for example, Hannah dedicates Samuel; 1 Sam 1–2). The expectation is that after dedication, the person making the vow will contribute the monetary value of the person dedicated. Values are computed on the basis of economic productivity (for example, more for a male between 20 and 60 years of age than any other group). As in 5:7–13, the cost is reduced for a person who cannot afford the full valuation (29:8).

A person may dedicate a sacrificial or non-sacrificial animal (27:9–13). A sacrificial animal becomes holy and may not be redeemed or exchanged. A person may, however, redeem other animals at the valuation of the priest plus twenty percent. In this way, the priests would acquire work animals or monies to support the tabernacle.

A person who dedicates a house or field to the Lord must redeem it. As Levine explains, the conditional statement "if ... he redeems it" really states the expectation "when he redeems it" (Levine 192–98). Thus the text explains how to arrive at the cost for redemption or repurchase: for a house, the priest's appraisal plus twenty percent (27:14–15; see 25:29–30); for a field, the crop value until the Jubilee plus twenty percent (27:16–19, 22–24; see 25:14–28). In the exceptional case of a person who dedicates a field belonging to his clan but does not redeem it, the field becomes the property of the priests at the Jubilee (27:20–21). The same applies if the person dedicates the field and then sells it to someone else; it immediately becomes the priests' property (27:20). A person may also dedicate a field under his lease. But in the event that this field is not redeemed, it reverts to the original owner, not to the priests (27:24).

The writer clarifies possible ambiguities in the laws of dedication and redemption in 27:25–29. First, the standard measure for all valuations is the sanctuary shekel (27:25). Second, no one may dedicate a firstborn animal because it *already belongs to the Lord* (27:26; compare Exod 13:2). Third, anything a person *devotes* (*cherem*, a different term than the preceding) to the Lord may not be redeemed. The idea of *cherem* frequently occurs in instances of holy war and the complete destruction of the opponent (for example, Deut 7:1–6). This text speaks, then, of an extreme form of dedication that is not redeemable.

Finally, ten percent of all produce, both agricultural and livestock, belongs to the Lord (27:30, 32–33). A person may redeem his tithe (animal or agricultural), but only by payment of an additional twenty percent (27:31).

The dedication of a person, animal, house, or field, as well as the donation of the tithe, is an expression of a person's devotion to the Lord. For the priests, these acts of devotion support their needs and those of the tabernacle (see 2 Kgs 12:4–5). It is striking that the book of Leviticus, with its dominant concern for God's presence among Israel, concludes on such a pragmatic note. Israel must financially support the tabernacle through its gifts.

The crisis of Sinai is now resolved, for Yahweh has provided a way for the people to live before God through sacrifice, priesthood, purity, holiness, and a financially supported tabernacle. To be sure, both God and the people remain at risk. The people may still defile God's holiness; God may still destroy the people. Yet both are willing to take the risk.

THEOLOGICAL REFLECTIONS

For many Christians, Leviticus carries the unenviable reputation of an obsolete and irrelevant law book. Its counsel for living in the presence of a holy God may sound bewildering to modern ears. Nonetheless, the principles established here are eternal, even if their expression concerns ancient Israel specifically. Two dominant themes merit a brief discussion here.

Leviticus demonstrates that life with God has always been by grace. People cannot resolve the problem of sin, but God can and does. God provides a method (sacrifice, Lev 1–7), empowers it (17:11a), and provides the sacrifice for atonement (17:11b, see above). Israel does not own the life of the animal, which has nothing capable of making atonement. Atonement is by grace through reliance upon God (see Eph 2:8–9). Similarly, God's grace provides a priesthood, the containment of impurity, a Day of Atonement, and instruction in holiness.

God's grace, however, is not a license to sin. Grace summons people to holiness, a second major theme in Leviticus: *Be holy because I, the Lord your God, am holy* (19:2). In Leviticus, holiness includes worship (Lev 1–10) but also reaches into every aspect of life, including sexual ethics (chapter 18), social justice (19:15–16), honest behavior (19:11–13, 35–36), and love for others (19:17–18). This is not works-based righteousness; God calls his people to holiness as a response to grace, not to earn grace.

FOR FURTHER STUDY

Jacob Milgrom, *Leviticus 23–27* (New York: Doubleday, 2000).
Allen P. Ross, *Holiness to the Lord* (Grand Rapids: Baker: 2002).

WORKS CITED

Mary Douglas, *Purity and Danger* (New York: Routledge, 1966).
John E. Hartley, *Leviticus* (Dallas: Word, 1992).
Baruch A. Levine, *Leviticus* (Philadelphia: Jewish Publication Society, 1989).
Jacob Milgrom, *Leviticus 1–16* (New York: Doubleday, 1991).
———, *Leviticus 17–22* (New York: Doubleday, 2000).
Gordon J. Wenham, *The Book of Leviticus* (Grand Rapids: Eerdmans, 1979).

Numbers

Michael S. Moore

CHAPTER CONTENTS

- Contexts 185
- Commentary 186
  - In the Shadow of Sinai · 1:1–10:10 186
  - Community in Conflict · 11:11–20:13 190
  - Preparing for the Promised Land · 20:14–36:13 194
- Theological Reflections 199
- For Further Study 201
- Works Cited 201

MAPS, TABLES, & FEATURES

- Monotheism in Egypt 186
- Pledging Human Beings 188
- Interspersed Thematic Summaries 190

Many reckon Moses to be the "author" of Numbers, but the book itself never makes such a claim. Observant students have long noted that the Pentateuch always speaks of Moses in the third person, includes an account of Moses' death (Deut 34:5) alongside several other anachronisms such as a list of Edomite kings from a period following Moses' death (Gen 36:31–39), and designates Moses as *more humble than any other man on the face of the earth* (Num 12:3). This last passage is particularly difficult to reconcile with Mosaic authorship.

> **Books in the Hebrew Bible**
> *In lieu of titles, biblical books distinguish themselves by their first keyword. Thus the book called Numbers in English Bibles is traditionally called* Bemidbar *("in the desert") in the Hebrew Bible because its first line reads, "the Lord spoke to Moses in the desert." The Septuagint entitles the book* Arithmoi *(The Latin Vulgate's* Numeri*), or "Numbers," because of its obvious preoccupation with lists, instructions, and inventories.*

Nevertheless several passages refer to Moses as writing down the substance of various divine commands (Exod 17:14; 34:27; 38:21; Deut 10:2; 31:19), and Jews embellished these references into a full-blown tradition during the Second Temple period. In the New Testament, Moses' name appears some 84 times, seven referring explicitly to him as a writer (Mark 10:5; 12:19, 26; Luke 20:28; John 1:45; 5:46; Rom 10:5). Thus the evidence from both Testaments indicates that Moses occasionally wrote down specific divine words; the Gospel accounts championed a tradition of Mosaic "authorship"; and these facts make it difficult to reject Mosaic authorship *and* accept a high christology of Scripture.

> **The Second Temple Period**
> *The period from 539 BCE to 70 CE is known as the Second Temple period. This period is also called the intertestamental period.*

Moderates searching for middle ground often suggest that Moses is the author of the Pentateuch's earliest draft but not its final form. The advantage of this position is that it holds firmly to a tradition of Mosaic authorship while simultaneously refusing to ignore the Pentateuch's glaring anachronisms. More to the confessional point, such a view approaches Scripture as the product of a Spirit who graciously watches over the *entire* writing process, from beginning to end.

CONTEXTS

Although extrabiblical evidence for Moses remains elusive, the evidence for Israel's existence is early and certain. The name "Israel" appears in a list of conquered peoples on a twelfth century BCE monument from Egypt, the so-called "Merneptah Stele" (Pritchard 376–78). Because of this evidence, the events behind Exodus-Numbers significantly overlap the events occurring in Egypt's Nineteenth Dynasty (1293–1187 BCE), especially the reigns of Seti I, his son Rameses II, and his grandson Merneptah. A minority view tries to push this date back another 200 years or so (based on innovative interpretations of the pottery evidence), but this view is too speculative for most scholars (contrary to Bimson).

NUMBERS

One of the most important accomplishments of the Nineteenth Dynasty is its successful reestablishment of Egyptian polytheism after the maverick reign of Amenhotep IV (1350–1334 BCE). A pharaoh of the Eighteenth Dynasty, Amenhotep IV comes to power at a time when Egypt's traditional priesthoods controlled practically everything in Egyptian life. Renouncing traditional polytheism, he introduces in its place a monotheistic religious system centered around the worship of the Aten (sun-disc; Zevit 44–48). At first he champions this cult as an alternative to the stifling legalism of Egypt's traditional priesthoods, but eventually he compels its observance.

One indication of his determination is his decision to change his royal name to Akhenaten ("One who is effective on behalf of the Aten") and move Egypt's capital to a brand new city, Akhetaten ("The place of the horizon of the Aten"). Like David centuries later, the pharaoh's strategy is to unite a fragmented country by moving its capital to a "neutral" location. Just as David's Jerusalem strategy moves power away from the traditional capitals of Shiloh (north) and Hebron (south), so Akhenaten's strategy challenges the northern priesthood of Re (Heliopolis) and the southern priesthood of Amun (Thebes).

Numbers continues this theological trajectory. As Israel moves from one polytheistic culture (Egypt) to another (Canaan), Yahweh leads Israel through a number of cosmic confrontations in the wilderness: the desert itself, a bronze seraph (Num 21:1–9; 2 Kgs 18:4), Balaam's "gods" (Num 22:22), and the Baal of Peor (Num 25:3; 1 Kgs 18:20–40). None of these encounters is any less significant than the confrontations with Egypt's gods. On the contrary, these teaching moments effectively grow Israel into Yahweh's image. Compared to the mudpits of Egypt (450 years), the wilderness proves to be a much more effective classroom (only 40 years).

Numbers preoccupies itself with lists and rosters and other kinds of priestly inventories, most notably with two major census lists (chapters 1 and 26). The first is taken at Sinai and includes a muster of Israel's qualified warriors. The second shows Moses and Eleazar (Aaron's son) starting all over again with a new list. Each chronicles the flaws and feats of a separate generation. The Sinai generation begins its journey with promise and potential. The post-Sinai generation picks up the mantle of its parents. Whereas the first shrinks back from following Yahweh, the second reaps the benefits of trusting Yahweh. The first dies in the wilderness (except Joshua and Caleb). The second goes on to inherit the promised land. Numbers accentuates these differences by the way it positions these census lists (Olson 175).

Another way to view the book's structure is to follow the lead of its summary chapter (33) and to telescope the book's major events into one long master list. This approach condenses forty years of wandering into a travelogue comprised of forty separate "stages" (literally, the "pulling-up" of tent pegs), each clustering around one of Israel's major encampments:

COMMENTARY

IN THE SHADOW OF SINAI · 1:1–10:10

Israel yearns for balance. Having just received the law on Sinai, the question now is, "What's next?" Will Israel trust in the law and wean itself from Egypt? Or will the nation reject the law, slink back to Egypt, and settle for a life of institutionalized

---

Monotheism in Egypt

Whether his motivation was political or religious (or both), Akhenaten's monotheism did not survive. His son and successor, Tutankhamun, reinstated the old priesthoods and removed all evidence of sun-disc worship from Egypt's official literature. Historians call this the "Amarna period" because most of our knowledge about it comes from royal letters accidentally discovered at Tell El-Amarna, the site of ancient Akhetaten (about 180 miles south of Cairo).

Presuming the events in Exodus-Numbers to be influenced by this history, the Amarna evidence helps explain why Mosaic monotheism in Exodus so aggressively challenged the traditional gods of Egypt, and why Moses' pharaoh (probably Rameses II) opposed Moses. As the biblical text reports, Pharaoh's heart "hardens" at the very thought of letting Israel leave Egypt. The historical question, though, is not whether Yahweh delights in hardening Pharaoh's heart, but whether Pharaoh's behavior betrays Egyptian sensitivity to any kind of religious innovation. Is it merely coincidental that the monotheist Moses comes along at this precise moment in Egyptian history, or that Exodus credits his expulsion to Yahweh's defeat of Egypt's traditional deities (Exod 7:14–12:32)?

slavery? Yahweh relentlessly puts this choice before them. Each conflict tests whether they will move forward or retreat. Each squabble tests whether they will emulate the ethics of their covenant partner or the survivalist ethics of "the rabble" (Num 11:4).

Numbers 1–10 addresses several key concerns. How is Israel going to deal with internal problems like leadership, identity, and stewardship? How will they address external problems such as enemies, limited resources, and foreign gods in a way firm enough to maintain order, yet flexible enough to allow change? Most importantly, how will Israel stay loyal to its covenant partner, God, in the process?

1:1–54 Census lists serve several functions. Clay tablets from Ebla, for example (Syria, twenty-fourth century BCE), lay out census lists for distributing food and supplies. Census lists from Alalakh and Ugarit (Syria, fourteenth century BCE) list military recruits. Such lists show not only the frequency of famine and war, but also the need of careful preparation for surviving these disasters.

Israel's census lists emphasize that Yahweh's military relates to the practice of holy war. So important is this strategy, in fact, that Yahweh exempts one whole tribe (Levi) from military service in order to give Israel a better chance at survival. Yahweh singles out the Levites to care for the tabernacle and guard it against possible defilement. Anyone who violates its sacred boundaries takes his life in his hands. Anyone who challenges the authority of its priests must suffer the consequences. From the narrator's perspective, boundaries are necessary and punishments appropriate. Just as it is impossible to imagine Israel migrating across the desert without a game plan, so is it impossible to imagine this game plan without the Holy One at its center (Cross 231; Rothenberg).

> **Holy War**
> *Under rare circumstances, ancient cultures thought of war as the result of divine command with the aim of the total destruction of an enemy. No Israelite "holy war" occurred after the time of David.*

> **The War Scroll**
> *The War Scroll from the Dead Sea Scrolls (1QM) is another text written to prepare Israel for holy war. This much later text uses the same terminology as Numbers to describe the "banners" and "signs" that distinguish battalions and build esprit de corps (Num 2:2; 1QM 6.1, 4, 5; 3.13). Like the War Scroll, Numbers reads more like a ballet than a battle strategy, a fact that becomes painfully clear as soon as the opportunity arises to put it into practice (Num 14:45; Josh 7:4).*

2:1–34 Discipline and order are critical to defense planning, so everybody in the camp must have a job and know something about how his or her job interfaces with everyone else's. Numbers is about premodern survival, not postmodern autonomy. The tabernacle itself may be modeled after the Egyptian war camp (Homan 22–36).

3:1–4 Numbers says a great deal about leadership–its goals, challenges, and parameters. Most importantly, the book stresses that the *sons of Aaron* always oversee the Levites in Israel's priestly economy. In fact, the Levites are a divine gift to them (Num 3:9). Kohathite leaders report directly to Eleazar, son of Aaron (3:32). Gershonite and Merarite leaders report directly to Ithamar, son of Aaron (4:28, 33). Israelites are to give all collected monies to Aaron and his sons (3:48), who also pronounce the priestly blessing (6:23) and sound the trumpet alarms (10:8). Only the descendants of Aaron may touch the holy things inside the tabernacle; the Levites merely carry them after they have been bundled up (4:15).

Thus, even though two of Aaron's sons violate the law (Lev 10:2), the failure of some Aaronids in no way challenges the authority of the entire family. Aaron still has two more sons (Eleazar and Ithamar), and one of the main purposes of part 1 (Num 1:1–10:10) is to place tabernacle leadership firmly in their hands.

3:5–39; 4:1–49; 8:1–26 Rules for the Levites are scattered throughout these chapters. Because the Levites do most of the actual work, however, they have their own census list. Each of Levi's sons (Gershon, Kohath, and Merari) bears responsibility for a very important task. The Levites set up the tabernacle at the middle of the camp, the very center of Israelite life, the place where Yahweh *meets* Israel. All divine communication occurs at the *'ohel mo'ed* (tent of "meeting"), a word that, in

> **Tent Shrines**
> *Many parallels to such tent shrines existed in ancient Arabia, Syria, and surrounding cultures (Kitchen 14–23), as well as the Edomite tent sanctuary discovered at Timna (Rothenberg 122–30).*

the cognate literature, denotes the meeting-hall of the divine assembly (Cross 321).

On the north side of the tabernacle, the sons of Merari take care of the large bars and poles forming the framework of the tabernacle. On the south side, the sons of Kohath take care of the packed interior furniture: the ark, the lampstand, the altars, and the rest of Israel's cultic paraphernalia. On the west side, the sons of Gershon take care of the tabernacle's coverings, exterior as well as interior. Finally Moses and Aaron oversee worship on the east side, where messages from Yahweh are received and administrative decisions are made. For a description of the building itself, See Exodus 25–31 and 35–40.

Because leadership is so important, Numbers devotes a great deal of space to it, explaining repeatedly the exact responsibilities assumed by each Levitical clan (Num 4:1–39; 8:5–26). Even though the congregation participates in consecrating the Levites (all Israel lays their hands on them), Aaron and his sons remain firmly in control.

3:40–51 Behind this hierarchy lies a mysterious theological rationale to which Scripture often refers, but never fully explains (Exod 13:2, 12–15; 22:28; 34:1–20; Num 3:11–13; 8:16–18; 18:15). This is the rite of the firstborn. Anthropologically speaking, patrilineal societies celebrate the arrival of firstborn sons because such births guarantee the survival of the family inheritance (thus the special request of Zelophehad's daughters at the death of their father; Num 27:1–12). Aware of this value system, ancient Near Eastern priests sometimes gauge the depth of a family's religious devotion by whether or not it will allow its most precious commodity to be sacrificed to this or that god. King Mesha of Moab, for example, publicly sacrificed his firstborn son to Chemosh, his nation's main deity (2 Kgs 3:27). Mercifully this practice never finds a home in Israel (Jer 7:31), even though isolated instances occur here and there (for example, 2 Sam 21). The redemption of the firstborn preserves a faint trace of this heritage.

5:1–31 Maintaining order is impossible without law, and some laws are more helpful than others (1 Cor 6:12). In addition to the laws at Sinai, this section of Numbers adds laws on how to address various kinds of physical, economic, and social problems. In terms of form, Numbers often intersperses law with narrative (Douglas 83–88), and while some argue for a structuring of the book that privileges the laws over the narrative, most scholars find this literarily impoverishing. In terms of content, no one knows why the narrative singles out these particular problems for discussion (leprosy, restitution, adultery), but these are typical kinds of problems that all societies face. Each ritual illustrates the necessity of priestly involvement, one of the book's most prevalent themes.

Numbers 5:1–5 addresses physical problems. The usual Hebrew term for "leprosy" refers to several kinds of skin disease (Kinnier-Wilson 354–65), but it can also refer to various kinds of defects on cloth, leather, and even the walls of buildings. With Jesus we might summarily reject any simplistic connection between "illness" and "sin" (John 9:1–3), but Israel nevertheless needed some kind of premodern strategy for dealing with physical illness. Further, since priests are the only group even remotely qualified to address these issues (there were no physicians in our sense in the wilderness), priestly involvement met a need.

Numbers 5:5–10 addresses economic problems. Political utopians may imagine forgiveness and reconciliation as universal and normative, but *restitution* is the backbone of most socioeconomic systems (Van de Mieroop 59–94). In Leviticus, this word [Hebrew *'asham*] denotes a specific kind of sacrifice for sin, whether "intentional" or "unintentional" (on the

---

Patrilineal & Matrilineal

Societies may emphasize family relationships and even the inheritance of property either through the father's line (patrilineal descent) or the mother's line (matrilineal descent).

Pledging Human Beings

From business contracts among the Hurrians, a group in Syria during the second millennium BCE, we know that debtors could pledge family members to creditors in exchange for food and supplies and other commodities (Taggar-Cohen 74–94), and this suggests that the Israelite "law of the firstborn" finds parallels in the precepts of ancient Near Eastern law. Translated into Israelite language, this means that Israel's "creditor" (Yahweh) is the party responsible for taking the Levites in "pledge," that is, in lieu of Israel's firstborn sons. While this remains only a possible understanding of the law, Numbers nevertheless assumes a basic understanding of the history behind the Levites' privileged position.

latter, see Lev 5:14–6:7). The only valid question is how such sacrifices help to bring about *restitution*. Payment in full plus one-fifth seems to be the most common equation (Num 5:7; Lev 5:16).

Numbers 5:11–31 addresses social problems. In this ritual Numbers updates and adapts an older non-Israelite ritual (van der Toorn 40). Adultery is a perennial social problem, and this is one of Israel's oldest attempts to deal with it. Much has been written about this strange ritual. Some speculate its purpose to be to check the problem of female "defilement," allegedly because this problem has the potential to defile the land (Frymer-Kensky 11–26). Others see it as something designed to restrict a husband's power, carefully repositioning it under the authority of the priesthood (Haberman 12–42). In any case, this is a primitive attempt to deal with a very delicate social problem. Historically, this is an important text because, compared to other ancient Near Eastern texts, the ordeal described here actually improves a woman's chances for justice (van der Toorn 40–42).

6:1–21 This ritual connects to the preceding one because it too requires priestly involvement. Whereas the descendants of Aaron and the Levites have their own specialized ministries, Nazirites may come from any tribe. They "consecrate" themselves to Yahweh (the name "Nazirite" comes from the Hebrew verb *nazar*, "to consecrate"). Where the previous ritual focuses on bizarre cultic ingredients ("water of bitterness," "one-tenth ephah of barley flour"), the main idea here seems to focus on financial investment. That is, Nazirites become such only after investing a large sum of money: one male lamb, one ewe lamb, one ram, one basket of unleavened bread, several cakes of choice flour mixed with oil, several unleavened wafers spread with oil, one grain offering, and several drink offerings. And this pertains only to the consecration ritual. Should the Nazirite need a *cleansing* ritual too, the price goes up even higher: two turtledoves (or pigeons), plus one male lamb. Many have speculated about the contents of this vow, with its emphasis on avoiding grapes, corpses, and haircuts, but why these particular items are prohibited remains a mystery.

> **Vows**
> *The Old Testament knows of several types of vows that Israelites may make. Vows that lead to evil or are made by non-competent persons (such as minors) are not binding.*

7:1–88 Another major component of Israelite ritual involves the dedication of two key tabernacle items: the altar (Num 7:1–88) and the lampstand (8:1–4). In addition, Israel has to consecrate the Levites for service (8:5–26), begin the preparations for Passover (9:1–14), and hammer out the silver trumpets (10:1–10). The cost for all this is high; everyone most contribute. Thus on the day of the altar's "anointing" and "dedication" Israel responds to the challenge. Though written in artificial prose, this passage documents the first successful offering in support of the Levites.

9:1–14 With Passover, however, Israel faces a cultic contradiction. Put simply, "How are unclean and absentee Israelites to celebrate Passover?" In other words, where, exactly, is the balance between cultic purity and corporate unity? Instead of wrestling with this question by himself, Moses takes it directly to Yahweh, and Yahweh immediately responds: holistic community takes priority over absolute cultic purity. Thus, resident aliens can legally celebrate Passover with the rest of Israel because Yahweh desires to establish an inclusive community, not an exclusive priesthood. To underline this theology, Moses publishes a contrastive law punishing any "pure" Israelite's unexcused absence from Passover.

In other words, the purpose of priestly regulation is to serve the creation, not become an end in itself. As Jesus puts it, *The sabbath is made for man, not man for the sabbath* (Mark 2:27). Non-Hebrews are to be welcomed at Passover because the Creator wants to avoid creating a two-class system. Yahweh wants "one statute for all" (see also Num 14:13–16).

9:15–23 Hovering over the tabernacle, the spirit of Yahweh manifests itself in a cloud by day and a pillar of fire by night. Whenever the cloud moves, Israel moves. Whenever the cloud stops, Israel stops.

10:1–10 Israel uses trumpet blasts to indicate levels of

> **Clouds in Biblical Symbolism**
> *Cloud imagery is deeply rooted in ancient Near Eastern religious language. Baal, for example, is called the "rider on the clouds" in Canaanite mythical texts from Ugarit (Syria, fourteenth century BCE). Psalm 18 preserves the essence of this cloud imagery in an old hymn now thoroughly connected to the God of Israel (verses 9–15). In the Bible, clouds can refer to God's garment (Job 38:9), God's veil (Lam 3:44), and the dust of God's feet (Nah 1:3). The advantage of such imagery is its ability both to reveal and to conceal the mysterious nature of God (Otto 23–63).*

NUMBERS

> **Interspersed Thematic Summaries**
> Interspersed throughout these lists and laws stand several short summaries, each providing in its own way a glimpse into the narrator's style and worldview. These include Israel's obedience to the exemption of the Levites (Num 1:54), Israel's submission to the encampment pattern (2:34), Moses' delivery of the firstborn money to Aaron (3:49–51), Moses' warning to the Kohathites (4:20), Israel's obedience to the leprosy law (5:4), the priestly blessing (6:22–27), the description of the revelation process (7:89), Moses' construction of the lampstand according to the pattern (8:4), and Israel's reliance on the pillar of fire/cloud (9:15–23). Taken altogether, these insertions emphasize Israel's obedience, Yahweh's presence and holiness, Aaronid priestly authority, and the variety of ways Yahweh chooses to communicate the divine word.

danger. When both trumpets *sound*, this is the signal for the assembly to gather. When only one trumpet *sounds*, only the leaders are to gather. When one trumpet "sounds an alarm" the east camps (Aaron, Moses, and company) should begin moving out. A second alarm signals the south camp, and so on, until all the tribes muster out. Only the family of Aaron may blow the silver trumpets.

COMMUNITY IN CONFLICT · 10:11–20:13

When the cloud starts moving, Israel dutifully breaks camp and starts walking. Everything seems to be going well until Sinai disappears over the horizon and Israel finds itself alone for the first time in four hundred years. Then the rabble starts *murmuring* (Coats 1–29), and the *congregation* starts finding fault with Moses.

Their first complaint focuses on food, because Israel remembers the variety of food they formerly enjoyed in Egypt and that everything in Egypt used to be *at no cost* (Num 11:5). As slaves, they learned to rely on Egypt for everything. Now Yahweh wants them to rely upon him.

10:11–36 In Numbers, Israel is trying to do something few nations have ever successfully done. Because the book is so overtly theological, one cannot interpret these events through sociohistorical analysis alone. Viewed theologically, Numbers 11:11–20:13 functions as a cautionary tale (see 1 Cor 10:1–13). By emphasizing the anonymity of death, the absence of proper burial, and the matter-of-fact way Yahweh abandons these rebels in the desert, the book warns future generations about the consequences of disobedience (compare Heb 3:7–19; Leveen 245–72).

11:1–15 Up to this point, Israel has lived out its faith vicariously through its leaders: Moses, Aaron, and Miriam. Moses successfully delivers Israel from Egyptian slavery. Aaron faithfully mediates the holy presence. Miriam dramatically leads worship as a prophetess of Yahweh (Exod 15:20). Israel trusts Yahweh because of what these leaders have accomplished. Now, only a few days out from Sinai, Yahweh tests this faith, and Israel fails the test.

Israel's problem, of course, has nothing to do with food. In fact, the keyword here is not *food*, but *crave*. In some forms this verb can mean "to wish for" or "to desire," but here in its reflexive form it means a continual "wishing/desiring." Israel's stubborn "desire," in other words, is spinning out of control. Demanding meat instead of manna, Israel receives meat in such abundance, it makes them gag and choke. Amazingly it takes only one day in the wilderness for Israel's true identity to emerge, and this leads later generations to name this place *Kibroth Hattaavah* (Hebrew for "Graves of Addiction," Num 11:35).

All this profoundly affects Moses. Frustrated and angry, he pours out his anger before Yahweh in a torrent of questions. Like Jeremiah, he laments the "impossibility" of his ministry, the hiddenness of his deity, the poignant loneliness of his role (see Jer 15:10). Only one of his questions relates to the immediate problem (*Where am I going to find meat for this people?*), but before he can ask the "where" question, he first has to get through the "why" questions: *Why do you treat your servant so badly?*, and *Why do I have to carry this burden?"* This last question seems particularly poignant because this same word can mean either "burden" or "oracle," depending on context (see Jer 23:33). In short, Moses comes to the point where he begins to wonder how long he can carry the burden of an infantile people (literally a "sucking child"; Brueggemann 11–27).

11:16–30 The following story offers Yahweh's response to Moses' cry for help. This is not the first time Moses has had to deal with a leadership crisis. In Exodus 18, before the giving of the law, his father-in-law criticizes his management skills and encourages him to delegate responsibility to others. Both of these passages set up a simple system for leadership delegation and emphasize that leadership should be delegated to recognized leaders. Both demonstrate the necessity of delegation.

Yet the differences in these two events outweigh the similarities for several reasons: first, Moses responds to a suggestion from someone else in Exodus (Jethro), while in Numbers Moses himself takes the initiative; second, Exodus distinguishes between major and minor judicial cases (Exod 18:22), while Numbers rejects all such distinctions, even when Israel tries to segregate those *prophesying at the tent of meeting* from those *prophesying in the camp*; third, Exodus presents the new leadership system without criticism, while in Numbers both Joshua and Miriam raise objections; fourth, Exodus shows God playing an indirect role, while in Numbers God personally directs the process, taking some of the spirit given to Moses and redistributing it to seventy others; and last, Exodus focuses on the creation of a functioning judicial system, while Numbers envisions a deeper purpose. In Numbers, Yahweh gives to Israel a gift it neither deserves nor expects, and Moses is so delighted by the outcome that he wishes that all of Yahweh's people might experience it.

Historical analysis might focus on whether leadership after the giving of the law is somehow different from leadership before the law. Intertextual analysis exposes a correlation between degrees of pressure and degrees of response. In other words, Moses appears to be under greater pressure in Numbers, and this may be why the Spirit chooses to descend at this precise moment.

12:1–16 While the first challenge comes from the rabble, the second comes from Moses' own siblings, Miriam and Aaron (see Jer 11:18–12:6). The alleged reason for this challenge is with Moses' marriage to an Ethiopian woman, but this problem fades from view as the passage unwinds. This text actually focuses on the problem of prophetic authority. Up to this point, Numbers has said little about prophecy because the book focuses mostly on matters of priestly law and priestly authority. This changes in chapter 11 as the Spirit descends, and seventy lay elders suddenly prophesy. The book emphasizes that priestly ritual alone cannot sustain people in the wilderness. Moreover, wilderness wanderers need more than structure to survive and grow. Israel also needs the power of the Spirit, and since the prophetic word is the primary conduit for the Spirit, something eventually has to be said about the purpose, function, and authority of prophecy. Just as Moses responds to Joshua's critique of Eldad and Medad (Num 11:28), so Yahweh responds to Miriam's critique of Moses the prophet (Noth 92–93; Levine, *Numbers 1–20*, 328–33).

In chapter 11 Yahweh addresses Moses' *burden* by redistributing the Spirit at the tent of meeting. Here in chapter 12 he calls Aaron and Miriam to this same tent of meeting and explains to them the nature of prophecy. Aaronid ritual provides priestly structure. Mosaic prophecy fills up that structure with spiritual substance. Thus Moses' obituary reads, *Never was there a prophet like Moses* (Deut 34:10).

By publicly challenging Moses, Miriam publicly challenges Israel's greatest prophet.

> **Moses, the Greatest Prophet**
> *With most prophets, God speaks in dreams and riddles. Not so with Moses. With this prophet God speaks plainly and clearly. Moses is the greatest prophet (compare Deut 18:14–22), and the word he speaks is the very word of God (Brueggemann 11–27).*

Yahweh strikes her with a skin disease and exiles her outside the camp because Israel needs to realize the seriousness of this sin. Just as God disciplines Aaron for his part in the Meribah affair (Num 20:22–29), so he disciplines Miriam for challenging Moses' prophetic authority. Soon Moses will be disciplined too (Num 20:12), but focusing on punishment instead of prophecy misses the whole point of the passage. In its historical context, these texts do not emphasize Yahweh's judgment, nor do they criticize Israelite androcentrism/misogyny (but see Graetz 184–92). The point here is that priests and prophets must work together to survive wilderness.

13:1–14:10A Having survived two crises, Israel now lurches its way toward a third. Twelve men slip into Canaan to spy out the land, and when they report back to Moses, ten of them try to talk him into forsaking the invasion. They argue that the Canaanites are just too strong, and their cities are too well fortified (ironically, the Amarna letters give credence to this; Moran 232–37). Yes, the land is flowing with "milk and honey," they grudgingly admit, but the descendants of the Anakim still live in the land (a word translated "giants" in the Septuagint's Deut 1:28), and they make them feel like *grasshoppers* by comparison.

Joshua and Caleb reject this fatalism. Yes, they argue, the land is populated by strong peoples, but *their protection is gone* (14:10). A better translation would be "their shadow has turned from them." Joshua and Caleb reject the fatalism of their colleagues because underneath it lies the false premise that God wants Israel to inherit the land on their own power, without divine help.

When the congregation gets wind of this debate, they panic. Whereas earlier the congregation simply *mourns* and Miriam simply *speaks* against Moses, here the congregation *raises its voice* and *weeps aloud* (14:1–2). Some of the *rabble* even threaten to *bury them with stones* (14:10).

> **The "Shadow" of the Canaanites**
> *The rare word for "shadow" in 14:10 [Hebrew tsel] denotes the "shadows" of protector-deities elsewhere, so this idiom probably means more than merely, "we've got them where we want them." Rather, it implies that Israel's divine Warrior has gone before Israel to clear their cosmic way. The awful "dread" of Yahweh paralyzes the cosmic defenses of their enemies (Josh 2:9; compare Judg 5:20–21).*

14:10B–45 Again, as in chapter 11, Yahweh appears in order to resolve the problem. Proposing to destroy the entire camp, he invites Moses to become a new Abraham, the father of a new Israel. Whether a test proposal or a real one, this response resonates powerfully with Moses' earlier laments (Num 11:11–14). Apparently the narrator intends via this resonance to highlight several facets of Yahweh's relationship to Moses. Both Yahweh and Moses suffer from the *burden* of spiritual leadership (Fretheim 121). Yahweh responds to Moses' burden by redistributing his Spirit to seventy colleagues. Moses responds to it by pleading Israel's case before an angry deity. This is a classic case of prophetic intercession, one of several in the Hebrew Bible (Exod 32:11–14; 1 Sam 5:1–7:1; 2 Sam 21:1–14; 24:1–25; 1 Kgs 16:29–18:45). As Israel's intercessor, Moses argues three propositions before God, and though this dialogue seems artificial, the arguments he raises nevertheless succeed in establishing Moses' prophetic authority and turning away Yahweh's divine wrath.

First, if Yahweh is to remain Israel's Protector, his "shadow" must continue standing over the tabernacle. For Moses, this truth seems self-evident and non-negotiable. Even Egypt knows that unlike the Canaanite deities (whose "shadows" are nowhere to be found), Yahweh's "shadow" has real cosmic power. Moses therefore wonders why Yahweh would think of abandoning this important role. Second, should Yahweh annihilate his people "as one man," such an atrocity would call into question the commitments made to these people at Sinai. Yahweh's international reputation is at stake (see also Exod 15:14–15; 32:12). Third, Yahweh's problem seems clear to Moses. Somehow he must find a way to forgive human sin without compromising divine holiness. However difficult the task, Yahweh needs to find that delicate balance between unconditional holiness and covenant love.

Hearing these three arguments, God decides to change his mind. Instead of annihilating Israel, he decides to let the Sinai generation perish while the post-Sinai generation matures (Sakenfeld 317–30). This behavior does not imply that Yahweh is capricious or that Yahweh truly does not know the future (but see Boyd 3–16). It simply means that, as human sovereigns can do what they like, so can the divine sovereign (Willis 156–75). Yahweh will keep the promises to the ancestors while still punishing the sins of the present generations. Unfortunately, Israel misses the impact of this truth and decides to invade Canaan anyway, without the divine Warrior's help. Moses warns against such *presumption* (14:44), but Israel decides (again) not to listen to Moses.

15:1–41 In order to limit the number and severity of future rebellions, this chapter follows up the previous one with several layers of priestly instruction, addressing what kinds of sacrifices to offer, how to handle borderline cases, and how to use visual aids to reinforce priestly warnings. Underneath these statutes lies the presumption that Israel at least partially understands the difference between intentional and unintentional sin. The latter is forgivable. The former is not. Unintentional sin can be expiated via animal sacrifice because such gifts provide financial deterrents against following this or that charismatic rebel. In addition to Israel's other sacrifices (Lev 1–7), Moses now adds grain and dough offerings. The more sacrifices one has to offer, the more costly taking the rebellious path becomes.

But what about those borderline cases in which the law needs to be explained (15:34; see Fishbane 98–100)? In cases like these, Numbers suggests a combination of logical analogy and legal precedent. The judges solve the problem of what to do with a man gathering firewood on the Sabbath, for example, by giving intertextual attention to another, similar case. In Leviticus 24:10–23 a man who is half-Egyptian and half-Hebrew breaks one of the Ten Commandments (blaspheming), but it is not yet clear whether the law applies to all peoples or just to Hebrews. Therefore, by analogy, since blasphemy receives a death sentence, so does defiling the Sabbath. Punishment must be the same because both are examples of intentional sin. Both involve a clear violation of revealed law (Exod 20:7, 8).

> **Dry & Liquid Measures**
>
> The actual size of Israelite measures changed over time; however, below is a list of approximate equivalencies:
>
> **kab** = 2.1 quarts = 2 liters
>
> **seah** = 12.6 quarts = 12 liters
>
> **ephah** or **bath** = 38 quarts = 36 liters
>
> **kor** or **homer** = 380 quarts = 360 liters
>
> For a thorough discussion of Israelite measures, see Powell.

To help Israel remember this legal principle, Moses provides a simple visual aid. All educators know the value of visual aids. Israel uses colored fringes on garments, leather phylacteries, kosher food, and scraps of Scripture on doorposts. Visual aids bring clarity and intentionality to the learning process because they condition the mind (Crenshaw 85–113). These particular visual aids help Israel see who Yahweh is and realize that the law is the only way to honor God's holiness.

16:1–50 In this chapter, the virus of rebellion invades Israel's leadership structure. The leader of this rebellion is Korah, son of Izhar, son of Kohath, son of Levi. According to chapter 4, Korah's job is like that of every other Kohathite, to carry the ark of the covenant and other holy objects from camp to camp (Num 4:1–15). Among all the Levitical clans, the Kohathites are the servants who work most closely with the "holy things"; so closely, in fact, that the law warns them not even to look at them, lest they be tempted to touch them (Num 4:20). Korah now wants to move up the priestly ladder and do what the Aaronids do.

> **The Psalms of Korah**
>
> First Chronicles 6:22–24, 33–3 lists the family of Korah as temple singers. The superscriptions of Psalms 42, 44–49, 84–85, and 87–88 attribute these texts to this family.

Instead of going to Moses privately and making his case (like the daughters of Zelophehad), however, Korah gathers an army of 250 men and organizes his own "congregation" (Cross 195–215). Curiously, Korah's name does not even appear in the review of these events in Deuteronomy 11:6, for example, and this omission suggests to some that Dathan and Abiram (the Reubenites) might be playing a more intentional role here than the Numbers account would allow (Goodnick 177–81). Perhaps the Reubenites act out of anger at Moses for replacing them (Jacob's firstborn) with another firstborn (Levi). We can only speculate.

Yahweh's response, however, leaves no doubt about what is going on here. This is not a text about "murmuring" or "complaining." This is a text about full-fledged rebellion, and this means that no punishment involving leprosy, or long-term generational death, or *gouging out the eyes* (as the Reubenites fear in 16:14) will be enough to deter it from recurring over and over again. Thus the ground opens up and swallows Korah's congregation alive into Sheol, animals and all. These horrid events are not a response to "murmuring" against Moses. These rebels die because of their *contempt* for Yahweh (16:30).

> **Sheol**
>
> Sheol is the Hebrew word for the underworld. In the Old Testament, all humans go to Sheol at death. Israel at this period did not believe in a system of postmortem rewards and punishments.

17:1–13 Reviewing these chapters, it is clear to see that Israel's rebellious behavior centers on its allergic reaction to priestly authority, particularly Aaronid authority. Thus Yahweh decides to validate the authority of the Aaronid priesthood via an unforgettable visual aid. Each tribe writes the name of an ancestral leader on a staff and deposits it in the tent of meeting overnight. Aaron's name goes onto Levi's staff. The next morning Aaron's staff bursts with life while the other eleven remain lifeless and inert. Just as Moses' staff turns into a snake, so Aaron's staff turns into a budding almond tree. The blooming symbolizes Yahweh's decision to make Israel's life dependent upon Aaron's life. All the other staffs remain lifeless because "lifelessness" (death) is the fate of any Israelite who dares challenge Yahweh's decision.

18:1–32 This chapter now follows up by summarizing in detail the authority of the Aaronids versus the authority of the Levites. Aaronid priests are to focus on the *area behind the curtain*. For their work they are to be paid in kind, not in land, receiving all the sacrifices generated by the grain, sin, and guilt offerings. All the consecrated oil, wine, and produce belong to them. All the firstfruits and devoted offerings are theirs. All the firstborn creatures, human and animal, are to be theirs. All the fat of the firstborn cows, sheep, and goats belong to Yahweh (that is, the priests incinerate them on the altar), while the meat is to be given to the Aaronid priests. All firstborn human beings and unclean animals are to be theirs as well, though the narrator is quick to add that each human being is redeemable for five shekels of silver (see Num 3:40–51).

The Levites' support, however, comes from the tithes generated by Israel's freewill offerings. Out of these offerings the Levites are to *tithe a tithe*, thus demonstrating by example the genius of the Israelite economy. In addition to this, the Levites receive forty-eight cities for their homes, flocks, and herds (Num 35:1–8).

19:1–22 Since death is the worst kind of defilement, it needs its own special ritual. The bizarre ritual of the red heifer meets this need. Later the priests will offer a supplement to this ritual in order to cleanse Israel of all contact with the Midianites (Num 31:21–24; Wright 213–23). The general presumption behind this ritual is, "Defilement is lethally contagious" (Douglas 24). Like all ancient peoples, Israel abhorred the world of the dead. This passage therefore itemizes a few objects no Israelite should ever try to touch, including: a human corpse; the tent in which this corpse is found; anything else in the defiled tent (for example, any liquid sitting in an unsealed jar); a human bone (even if found in an open field); and graves. Anyone contacting these objects must undergo a complicated purification process involving specially prepared *purification water*. Like the *bitter water* in chapter 5, this ritual also uses a special kind of water, the *water of purification*, prepared beforehand by mixing water with the ashes of a ritually burned red heifer.

The question, of course, is how any priest can participate in the production of this concoction without himself becoming impure (Harris 198–200). Apparently priestly status prevents the priest's defilement in this case.

20:1–13 This is another chapter about death, beginning with Miriam's death and ending with Aaron's death. In between, the narrator addresses one of the great mysteries of the Bible: "Why does God forbid Moses from entering the promised land?" The answer to this question comes in the narrator's reflection on the spies narrative (Num 13–14). Put simply, if Joshua and Caleb are to be the only survivors of the Sinai generation (Num 14:22), then everyone else will have to die in the wilderness, including Moses. Aaron dies at Mount Hor (Num 20:28), Miriam dies at Kadesh (20:1), and Moses dies on Mount Nebo (Deut 34:5).

Numbers 20:12 correlates Moses' disobedience with Israel's *trust*. Prophets must follow a higher standard. Absolute obedience to the word of God is the cardinal value of prophetic Yahwism. For example, in the story of the Judahite man of God, Yahweh commands his prophet to fast, and when he disobeys this command via an innocent meal, Yahweh strikes him dead (1 Kgs 13:24; Moore, *Faith under Pressure*, 237–42). Here in Numbers another prophet disobeys, striking a rock instead of speaking to it. Certainly this is not murmuring or full-blown rebellion. Nevertheless, prophetic disobedience is never innocent.

PREPARING FOR THE PROMISED LAND · 20:14–36:13

With their parents dying and Sinai fading from memory, the post-Sinai generation faces a difficult question. How can a weary, ragtag group of refugees *inherit* (14:24) the promised land when Israel no longer exists (at least not in its earlier form at Sinai), and the Anakim, Amalekites, Hittites, Jebusites, Amorites, and Canaanites already populate the area? This question takes on new urgency with the publication of the second census in chapter 26. The new census list bears witness to the sad truth that the Sinai generation has rejected Yahweh's vision.

The final section of Numbers begins with the post-Sinai generation waiting on Edom's doorstep for another Exodus miracle. From Edom's perspective, allowing them to cross Edomite territory presents too many dangers. Such refugee groups have a long history of agitation and troublemaking in this part of the world dating back centuries before Moses (Moran 326–34; Snell 58–62). Edom therefore rejects Israel's request for transit.

From Israel's perspective, however, Edom stands as one more "uncrossable" boundary in their journey toward Canaan. In Exodus, the uncrossable boundary is the Red Sea (Exod 14:10–25), in Joshua the Jordan River (Josh 3:1–17), and in Numbers the boundaries of Edom and Moab. Final challenges in Numbers become more international than tribal, more political than priestly, more cosmic than mundane. Now Israel must face the terrifying power of the unseen world (seraphim-snakes, Balaam's gods, the Baal of Peor).

20:14–21:9 Edom's rebuff leads to two more incidents in quick succession: Aaron's death and the attack of the seraphim-snakes. No connection seems immediately obvious between these incidents, yet each resonates loudly with the other. Aaron does not simply die on Mount Hor, at least not in the way Miriam dies in the wilderness of Zin (Num 20:1). Instead, Moses strips Aaron of his priestly garments (20:26) and leaves him to die alone on a strange mountain in a strange land. With such brusque prose the narrative duly reports Aaron's punishment for his role in the Meribah incident (20:24). Yet there is something else going on here. Numbers preserves not one, but two stories of leadership transition: the Aaron-Eleazar transition, and the Moses-Joshua transition (27:23). In the latter, Moses does not strip anyone of anything. He rather supports Joshua by publicly acknowledging his authority before the whole congregation (27:22–23). In the former, Israel's high priest perishes outside of the promised land. In the latter, Israel's prophet passes the mantle to the next generation.

Reading these stories together thus makes it easier to understand why the next story appears where it does. Just as Moses strips Aaron, so Yahweh strips Israel, launching against his people a squadron of poisonous seraphim-snakes. Most English Bibles translate this phrase "fiery serpents" or the like, but seraphim are usually cosmic creatures in the Bible (note the seraphim covering the deity in Isa 6:2, as well as the flying seraph in Isa 14:29). When Hezekiah removes one of these bronze seraphim from the temple centuries later (2 Kgs 18:4), this action raises a simple question for the text in Numbers. Why doesn't Yahweh do the same thing in the wilderness? Why not simply remove these seraphim-snakes? Why instead make Israel stare at a bronze image of a seraph-snake?

The answer has to do with the ancient principle of reciprocity. Just as Hittite priestesses burn wax "tongues" to stop gossip, and Philistine diviners use gold cancers to stop plagues (1 Sam 6:5), so Moses makes a bronze snake to cure snakebite (Moore, *Balaam Traditions*, 60–64). This story, in other words, has more to do with the anthropological principle of reciprocity than Yahweh's power over Canaanite snakebite gods (as suggested by Gray 27–34) or Moses' prowess as an exorcist (Joines 245–56). Moses constructs an image of the affliction in order to bring healing to the afflicted. Moses removing the source of the affliction would restrict Israel's opportunity to learn something important about the biblical God, namely that healing is contingent and salvation is conditional.

21:10–25; 31:1–12 Edom's rebuff is not the last challenge Israel will have to face. Others occur mostly in Transjordan, in the general vicinity of Moab; these include the encounters with Sihon, Og, Balaam, Baal Peor, and Midian. Easily dispatching the first two of these challenges, Israel defeats the militias of Sihon and Og. Later writers describe it as Yahweh *hardening the spirit* of Sihon and *giving* Og into Israel's hand (Deut 2:30–33). The last of these challenges, Midian, is more complex because of Israel's ambivalent relationship to Midian. This material comes packaged in a mixture of prose narrative and legal material, as is often the case in Numbers, in order to highlight the middle two conflicts (Balaam and Baal Peor).

Prior to the Moabite material, the narrator inserts a transitional section comprised of several old poems and war songs (Num 21:10–35). Numbers 21:27–29 may be part of a Canaanite war song, now turned on its head to celebrate Israelite victories. Each of these songs has its own history, but strung together they create an important transitional bridge between the encounters in Edom and those in Moab. The text as it stands shows how Israel transforms itself from a group of squabbling tribes into a united confederation. Apart from this bridge, it is impossible to imagine why Balak would suddenly feel *great dread* at the beginning of chapter 22. As

> **The Bronze Snake**
> *Whatever the theological significance of this incident in Numbers, historians can make a strong case for its antiquity because of the many bronze snakes found at sites like Mevorakh and Hazor, not to mention the magnificent bronze snake from a 13th century BCE "tabernacle" at Timna (Rothenberg 129–30).*

Israel changes, so does the tone of the book. Gone now is the constant bickering, the stifling fatalism, and the colorless fear.

King Balak hires a magical specialist to *curse* Israel, a common first volley in ancient Near Eastern warfare (Moore, *Balaam Traditions*, 29). War captains hire magico-religious specialists like Balaam because they want to trick their opponents' deities into abandoning their clients. The usual procedure is to invite an enemies' gods to a specially prepared cultic dinner. Those deities who "take the bait" also take their "shadows" with them, leaving their human clients naked and exposed (see Num 14:9; Moore, *Balaam Traditions*, 29). Balaam tries to do this with Yahweh. He wants to trick Yahweh into abandoning Israel, and when things go awry, this makes for some great satire. The purpose of this satire is not simply to poke fun at Balaam but to satirize every charlatan who thinks he can trick God (Hackett 219–22; Jemielity 21–49). No matter how hard he tries, Balaam will never figure out how to trick Yahweh.

What makes this incident even more interesting is the fact that this portrait of Balaam is not the only one presently known. Here in Numbers, Balaam enacts a fairly complex role-set comprised of divinatory, prophetic, and exorcistic elements, all cleverly packaged into one hilarious comic story (Rofé 51). In other places, however, Balaam enacts simple roles as diviner (Josh 13:22), curser (Josh 24:9), answerer (Mic 6:5), madman (2 Pet 2:15), and seer. Thus, like the multiple self-portraits of Van Gogh, Balaam's portrait changes over time as various writers from various traditions accentuate differing aspects of his character.

> **Balaam Son of Beor**
> *A text on plaster from the Transjordan town of Deir Alla also mentions Balaam. The text predates 700 BCE and is written in a non-Israelite dialect. It refers to Balaam son of Beor as a seer who speaks to the gods and receives from them a vision of future disaster (see Moore, Balaam Traditions, 110–16).*

The Balaam cycle (Num 22–24), however, serves several literary functions. First, like the plagues narrative in Exodus, this text preserves Numbers' final showdown between Yahweh and the gods, a contest Yahweh wins when Balaam finally stops looking for omens (Num 24:1; compare 21:6). Second, the Balaam cycle proclaims to friend and foe alike that no power in heaven or earth can hurt Israel, whether human (Num 21:10–35) or superhuman (Num 22–24). Isaiah proclaims this same message to the Babylonian exiles (Isa 44:1–8), and Paul preaches a similar message to the Roman church (Rom 8:38–39).

Third, Israel is to be led someday by a charismatic messiah (24:17–24). Numbers 24:17 may well be Numbers' most popular verse. The covenanters at Qumran, for example, quoted it to buttress their vision of the Teacher of Righteousness as the fulfillment of Israel's messianic hopes (*Damascus Document* 7:18; Collins 7–26). The Nazarenes saw Jesus as the *bright and morning star* (Rev 22:16; Moore, "Jesus Christ," 82–91). Rabbi Akiba saw Simon bar Kokhba ("son of the Star," who died in 135 CE) as the fulfillment of the messianic hope (Yadin 22–34). Centuries later, the controversial leaders Shabbetai Tzevi and Jacob Frank led failed messianic movements in the seventeenth and eighteenth centuries (Salkin 25–30).

As the Dead Sea is the lowest point on earth, so Baal Peor is the lowest point in Numbers. Where the Moab-Israel conflict ends in stalemate, the Midian-Israel conflict ends in apostasy. Yahweh sends a plague so virulent, it makes Moses issue strict instructions on the purification of Israel from Midianite *defilement* (Num 31:13–24; Josh 22:17). The Baal Peor cult itself remains swathed in mystery. Some believe it to be an orgiastic cult built around "Lord of Fire" gods from Anatolia (Mendenhall 109). Others doubt it has anything to do with sex at all, much less Anatolian religion (Levine, *Numbers 21–36*, 294–7). Whatever its secrets, Numbers sees Israel's "yoking" to Baal Peor as something incredibly horrid, an opinion expressed in several other biblical passages. The psalmist, for example, notes how the participants of the Peor cult *eat sacrifices for the dead* (Ps 106:28). Hosea remembers the Peor incident as a time when Israel *consecrates itself* [Hebrew *nāzar*] to something *vain* and *detestable* (Hos 9:10). Joshua simply speaks of *the Peor iniquity* (Josh 22:17).

As the man responsible for stopping this plague, Phineas forever secures for himself a revered place in priestly history. Granted, the solution he offers is grisly and violent, yet the text emphasizes his status as an *Aaronid* priest (that is, not a Levite or a Reubenite; Levine, *Numbers 21–36*, 297–300). When Phineas *intercedes* (Ps 106:30) with an enraged Yahweh to save Israel's life, the telling of this story constantly reminds Israel of its fundamental debt to the Aaronid priesthood. Whether or not human sacrifice is required to stop the plague is a question complicated by the fact that this is not the only time in Scripture when someone "impales" a cultic violator (25:4; see 2 Sam 21:6, 9). By "piercing" these violators, Phineas satisfies the essence of the divine command. In short, Aaronid *zeal* (25:11) is the focus of this story, not human sacrifice.

Because Midian is responsible for tricking Israel, Yahweh's decision to *treat* them *as enemies* is both just and fair (Num 25:17). When Israel goes on to *take vengeance* against Midian (31:2), the appearance of a much harsher verb highlights Israel's ambivalence toward Midian and things Midianite. On the one hand, Moses' wife (Zipporah) is the daughter of a Midianite priest, a man Moses deeply respects. On the other hand, Midian tries to trick Israel through the hiring of Balaam (22:7) and the yoking of Israel's male population to Baal (25:1–4), and when Israel tries to soften their punishment, Moses reacts negatively (see 1 Sam 15:1–35 for a parallel with Samuel). None of this behavior is explainable apart from a clear understanding of Hebrew holiness theology (Gammie 9–44) and Hebrew prophetic theology (Moore, *Faith under Pressure*, 237–48).

27:1–11; 30:1–16; 36:1–13 At first glance the final chapters of Numbers seem to follow no discernible outline or literary pattern. Traditions about leadership awkwardly bump into statutes about stewardship. Paragraphs about female vow-taking suddenly transition into strategies about war booty. That these chapters are not simply tacked-on appendices, however, becomes clear when the narrative itself draws parallels between the attitude of Gad, Reuben, and Manasseh (Num 32:8–9) and the fatalism of the ten cowardly spies (Num 13–14). The refusal of the Gad-Reuben-Manasseh alliance to cross the Jordan links the flaws of the Sinai generation with the flaws of the post-Sinai generation (Olson 175).

Strikingly, however, this section, like the book of Proverbs (Prov 1, 8–9; 31:10–31), begins and ends with material about women, the daughters of Zelophehad. Literary critics call this kind of parallelism *inclusio*. Should women be excluded from inheriting land just because they are women? If not, then what provisions should be made to protect their inheritance rights?

> **Inclusio**
> Inclusio *occurs when a narrator uses a common theme to frame otherwise miscellaneous material. By thus framing the material, narrators can subtly prioritize the issues on their agenda. In this example, the* inclusio *implies that of all the issues on this narrator's agenda, female inheritance rights must be very important.*

As with previous hard cases (for example, Num 9:1–14; 15:32–36), Moses takes this one directly to Yahweh, and the answer he receives is clear and immediate. Daughters can indeed inherit land in the absence of sons (Num 27:1–11). This ruling shows Yahweh's compassion and Moses' flexibility. Yet left unchecked, this ruling on the condition might easily lead to the unraveling of Manasseh's tribal integrity and its basic rule of male descent. Thus several of Zelophehad's relatives convince Moses to delimit it, and Numbers ends with Zelophehad's daughters inheriting property only provided that they marry men from within their own tribe, the tribe of Manasseh (36:1–13). The statutes regulating female vow-taking make the same assumptions respecting the boundaries between male-dominated households (30:1–16). Vows are essential to everyday commerce, but the transactions they validate remain subject to patriarchal approval in ancient Israel's world.

This section therefore surfaces and highlights the following themes: equitable justice for all Israelites (including those who find themselves landless through no fault of their own); legislative flexibility in the face of unexplored legal territory (the decision awarding land to the daughters of Zelophehad); endogamous marriage (to protect Manasseh's tribal integrity); and a system of checks and balances to protect daily business transactions. Numbers highlights these themes because Israel will have to face these issues when it enters the land (Kunin

> **Endogamous Marriage**
> *Marriage between partners within a clan or tribal unit is known as endogamous marriage, as opposed to exogamous marriage, which involves mating outside such units.*

53–61). That so many of them focus on women is not lost on the rabbis, who continue this discussion in the third order of the Mishnah, the second-century CE collection of Jewish law that constitutes the core of the Talmud (*Nashim*, "Women"; Steinsaltz 280–81).

27:12–23; 34:16–35:8 Yahweh prohibits Moses from entering the land for two reasons. First, Moses actively participated in the rebellion at Meribah, and second, he failed to *honor [God] as holy before their eyes* (Num 27:14). The first reason feels more familiar, perhaps, because Yahweh overtly punishes Moses for what he calls Moses' "faithlessness" (20:12). The narrator later labels this action "rebellion" (27:14), but this contrasts sharply with the telling of the incident in Deuteronomy (3:26).

The second reason is doubtless less familiar to readers because it highlights a basic flaw in Moses' theology, and most (post)moderns have little appreciation for Hebrew holiness theology. In other words, Moses fails not simply to trust Yahweh at Meribah; he fails also to exalt Yahweh's holiness (Num 20:12). Leadership is many things, but from a priestly perspective it centers upon consecrating the name of God, the Holy One of Israel, as the *Holy One in your midst*. This responsibility anchors priestly holiness theology. Thus when Moses asks, *Shall we bring forth water for you?* he crosses the line between the sacred and the profane. By failing *to show [God's] holiness before their eyes*, Moses fails to do the job for which he was originally commissioned, to *serve* God (Exod 3:12).

But another question arises here. Why does the mantle of leadership pass to Joshua instead of, say, to Eleazar (Aaron's son), since the priests already control the community's worship? Perhaps the answer to this question lies not in what the narrative says, but in what it does not say. The conspicuous absence of Aaronid priests in the incident where *the rabble* threaten Joshua and Caleb (Num 13–14), and from the incident in which Moses delegates miraculous spiritual power to seventy lay elders (Num 11:16–30), implies that Numbers believes in a distribution of power among several forces, especially priests and prophets.

Prophetic leadership remains a check against the tendency among all priesthoods to create oligarchical aristocracies (like, for example, Eighteenth Dynasty Egypt). This holds true even though Numbers never even suggests that Joshua is a *prophet like Moses* (Deut 18:15). The Miriam incident makes it clear that God speaks *face to face* to only one prophet (Num 12:8), and the book of Joshua insists that the source of Joshua's authority is faithful interpretation of the law, not miraculous charismatic experience (Josh 1:7–8; Schniedewind 1–37).

28:1–29:40 The offerings in Numbers 28:1–8 echo the offerings in Exodus 29:38–46, though there are a few differences. First, Numbers prescribes this offering at *the appointed time* [Hebrew *mo'ed*] while Exodus has it offered daily [*tamid*]. Second, Numbers calls it a *fire-offering*, while Exodus calls it a *whole burnt-offering*. Third, Numbers augments the daily offering with two more offerings, the Sabbath offering and the monthly offering. The rest of these offerings follow closely the list in Leviticus 23: offering for Passover, the Festival of Weeks, the Festival of Trumpets, the Day of Atonement, and the Festival of Booths. Scripture preserves three different descriptions of Israel's feasts. Deuteronomy 16 stresses the pilgrimages to the feasts, Numbers 28–29 the offerings at the feasts, and Leviticus 23 the feasts themselves. Whether any of these texts depend directly on each other is less likely than the possibility of some kind of common reliance on the traditions underlying Leviticus 23 (Levine, *Numbers 21–36*, 394). This must remain speculative, though, because reconstructing the literary development behind priestly texts is notoriously difficult.

31:1–32:42; 33:50–34:15 Israel's war against Midian destroys many of their most intransigent enemies: the "five kings of Midian" (Evi, Rekem, Zur, Hur, and Reba); Balaam ben Beor, the magician who tries to entice Yahweh into abandoning Israel; and the women responsible for tricking Israel into worshiping Baal Peor. This last task, however, involves a lengthy period of internal struggle as some of Israel's warriors try to bring these women home as slaves. This option, however, violates the fundamental principle of holy war, which by definition requires *complete devotion* [Hebrew *cherem*] of all plunder to Yahweh (von Rad 1:17). Since those who ignore it usually pay dearly (Josh 7; 1 Sam 15), Moses insists that Israel obey the divine imperative in the case of the Midianite women. The only compromise he makes is to spare the virgin Midianite women, presumably because of their innocence at Peor. Intrigued by this compromise, many rabbis question how exactly one might

> **Rabbinic Interpretation**
> *Because the Bible often leaves questions unanswered, ancient interpreters, whether Jewish or Christian, often invented stories that, in homiletical fashion, "explained" the biblical text's gaps. These ancient readers assumed that even the gaps or silences of the Bible allowed God to speak to people of faith (see Kugel).*

identify these virgins. One rabbi suggests that the way to find out is to parade each Midianite woman before the high priest, and if his "forehead plate" turns pale green, this indicates her nonvirginal status (*b. Yevamoth* 60b; compare Exod 28:36). Numbers, of course, does not answer this question.

After a lengthy list of distribution equations and other priestly details, the narrative notes that Reuben, Gad, and Manasseh decide to settle in Gilead, not Canaan. Wary of Reuben (see Num 13–14, 16), Moses nevertheless agrees, but only on the condition that these three tribes first help their brothers secure their own tribal inheritances. Contemporary archaeologists tend to be skeptical about these traditions because there is a lack of corroborative archaeological evidence for "kingdoms" in Transjordan at this period, and the present state of the evidence suggests that the only destructions from this period are farther north (Dever 547–49). Arguments like these will never be definitive, however, until arguments from silence are no longer untenable, and the "present state" of archaeological knowledge no longer makes allowances for new discoveries.

35:1–34 Asylum is an old solution to an old dilemma (Snell 31–62). Unlike modern Western cultures, where crime victims can appeal to legislatures and courts, ancient tribal cultures allow "avengers of blood" to execute justice and reestablish societal equilibrium. One does not have to see the *Godfather* films to realize that such a system might easily spin out of control. As a check against vendetta, the law therefore provides *cities of refuge* to regulate and control this primitive form of tribal justice. Several biblical passages give attention to the functions of these cities (Exod 21:13; Deut 4:41–43; 19:1–13; Josh 20). Some, like Numbers, lump them in with the forty-two Levitical cities (making a total of 48 cities). Others focus on the crimes for which a refugee might seek asylum, carefully distinguishing between intentional (murder) and unintentional homicide (manslaughter). Others give the names and locations of these cities: Bezer, Ramoth, and Golan in Transjordan; Kadesh, Shechem, and Hebron in the hill country.

Continuing questions about these cities later led the Talmud to argue that if a refugee is a scholar, he can he take his school with him into his city of refuge. If a pupil, he can have a teacher brought to him (*b. Makkoth* 10a). To discourage avengers from harassing these cities, the Talmud also bans practicing certain trades within them, such as textile, rope, and weapons manufacturing (*b. Makkoth* 10a; see also *t. Makkoth* 3:9). To make escape easier, the rabbis insist that road signs be put up at intersections indicating the way to the nearest refuge city (*b. Makkoth* 10b; *t. Makkoth* 3:5).

> **The Talmud**
> The Talmuds, or collections of legal material, of Babylonia and Palestine were collected in Late Antiquity. These massive collections of moral reflection and religious insight are divided into "tractates" centering on recognizable topics. They are cited by which Talmud and tractate in which they appear. Thus, b. Makkoth refers to tractate Makkoth in the Babylonian Talmud.

THEOLOGICAL REFLECTIONS

The theology of Numbers contains several important features. First, Numbers documents the persistent conflict between Yahweh and the gods of the nations. Famous for humiliating Egypt's gods (Exod 7:14–10:29), Yahweh takes his war to the wilderness in Numbers, successfully projecting his "dread" over Transjordan (Num 22:3) and his "fear" over Canaan (Josh 2:9–11). When Joshua and Caleb testify to the Canaanites' cosmic nakedness (Num 14:9), this contrasts sharply with the reality of Yahweh's "shadow" over the tabernacle (symbolized by the cloud). Yahweh therefore defeats the schemes of Balaam and scoffs at the crude temptations of his flat-footed pseudo-deities. He surgically removes the Peor cancer using a scalpel made from plague and pestilence. He launches a squadron of seraphim-snakes even as he challenges their victims to trust in him as their divine Healer.

> **Israel's Faithlessness & God's Faithfulness**
> That Numbers would so intentionally focus on Yahweh's cosmic power is not unusual given the culture of the ancient Near East. What is unusual, however, is Numbers's emphasis on the Sinai generation's unwillingness to follow this divine Warrior and Yahweh's determination to keep fighting for them anyway. Unlike any of the gods of the nations, Israel's God makes and sustains covenant. Though finding this burden (Num 11:11) difficult to carry, God never lays it down. Not even Israel's faithlessness can dissuade God from the mission of salvation.

Second, Israel's fatalism is understandable, if tragically naive. After all, who really prefers cold bland manna to hot, fresh vegetables? Had food not been the trigger, doubtless the Sinai generation would have found something else about which to complain. The *rabble* would have found some other pretext for attacking Moses. Fatalism, however, as Numbers takes great pains to point out, is just a synonym for faithlessness. In Numbers, Israel struggles to trust Yahweh in the midst of challenges and difficulties and baffling uncertainties. When things look hopeless, as they often do in the wilderness, Israel has to decide whether to prefer fatalism to faith. Whether the challenge before them is cosmic (Baal Peor), political (Korah, Dathan, Abiram), missional (the spies), financial (Midianite plunder), domestic (ritual of the accused adulterers), or painfully familial (Miriam's attack), Israel must decide which way it wants to live. Only when the post-Sinai generation starts trusting in Yahweh does the tone of the book change.

Third, Israelite leadership breaks down into three categories in Numbers: priestly (Aaronids, Levites), prophetic (Moses, Joshua) and lay (seventy elders, Nazirite vow). Each serves a vital function in Israel's life. Priestly leadership, of course, grabs the lion's share of the narrative as the narrator lays out the structure of the camp and the duties of tribe and clan. Aaronid leadership stands at the top of the priestly hierarchy, while the Levites serve by hauling, carrying, and depositing the holy things in the tabernacle. Prophetic leadership complements this work, especially with regard to preaching and prophetic intercession. Lay leadership manifests itself in the distribution of the Spirit to seventy Israelite elders, the appointment of tribal leaders (34:16–29), and the Nazirite ritual.

Fourth, the wilderness is Yahweh's classroom, a place where conflicts appear not as insurmountable defeats, but as teaching moments. After every major crisis the narrator inserts a bundle of laws based on fundamental principles designed to help Israel avoid similar conflicts in the future. Preeminent among these are the principle of the priority of spiritual mission over priestly method (Num 11:26–29), the principle of financial deterrent (15:1–21), the principles of analogy and precedent (15:22–31), the principle of reciprocity (21:1–9), the principle of legal flexibility (27:1–11), the principle of total devotion (31:13–24), the principle of covenant faithfulness (32:1–32), the principle of asylum (35:9–34), and the principle of tribal integrity (36:1–12). To illustrate these principles, the narrator reports the use of a number of visual aids, including Aaron's budding staff, the fringed garments, the cloud over the tabernacle, and the bronze seraph-snake.

Fifth, the Bible depicts holiness through at least three lenses: as ritual cleanness in the priestly literature, as the cleanness of social justice in the prophets, and as the cleanness of individual morality in the wisdom literature (Gammie 195–98). Numbers preserves laws and rituals rooted most prominently in the first of these categories, including especially the ritual of the accused adulterers, that of the red heifer, and the Nazirite vow. Like all rituals, these function within a well-defined system based on the axiom that "defilement is lethally contagious" (Douglas 24). Yet underneath this system lies the much deeper conviction that Yahweh of Hosts is absolutely, mysteriously, and indescribably holy. The seraphim ceaselessly chant this truth (*holy*, *holy*, *holy*, Isa 6:3), and Moses recognizes its power in the burning bush incident (Exod 3:51). The ritual of the red heifer presumes it as well as it seeks, like all priestly ritual, to clean up that which is defiled and transport it back to the realm of the holy.

This emphasis on ritual and sacrifice comes out of the primitive belief that defilement is as real as holiness is ideal. When someone violates a holy boundary, be it spatial or temporal, priestly ritual is the only effective way to reconnect this violator to the Holy One. Accordingly, priestly theology is the only way for believers to understand that they must steer clear of defilement and experience God's holy presence.

Sixth, prophetic theology is muted, but not absent in Numbers because Moses is the prophet par excellence, and prophetic intercession furnishes an important check against the excesses of priestly hierarchy and oligarchy. When Israel's tendency is to turn inward, the Spirit pushes them outward. When the Aaronids start to become too exclusive, Moses reminds them of Yahweh's desire to be globally inclusive, for example, in the statute permitting aliens and defiled worshipers to celebrate Passover with the rest of the congregation (Num 9:1–14). Thus one of Numbers' most important messages is that all wilderness wanderers need to learn how to live healthy spiritual lives, carefully balanced between priestly structure and spiritual substance.

FOR FURTHER STUDY

Joseph T. Leinhard, ed., *Exodus, Leviticus, Numbers, Deuteronomy* (Downers Grove, Ill.: InterVarsity, 2001).

Dennis T. Olson, *Numbers* (Louisville: Westminster John Knox, 1996).

WORKS CITED

J. J. Bimson, *Redating the Exodus and Conquest* (Sheffield: JSOT, 1981).

Gregory Boyd, *A God of the Possible* (Grand Rapids: Baker, 2000).

Walter Brueggemann, *The Prophetic Imagination*. (Philadephia: Fortress, 1978).

George W. Coats, *Rebellion in the Wilderness: The Murmuring Motif in the Wilderness Traditions of the Old Testament* (Nashville: Abingdon, 1968).

John J. Collins, *The Scepter and the Star: The Messiahs of the Dead Sea Scrolls and Other Ancient Literature* (New York: Doubleday, 1995).

James Crenshaw, *Education in Ancient Israel: Across the Deadening Silence* (New York: Doubleday, 1998).

Frank Moore Cross, *Canaanite Myth and Hebrew Epic* (Cambridge, Harvard University Press, 1973).

Simon Dein, "What Really Happens When Prophecy Fails: The Case of Lubavitch," *Sociology of Religion* 62 (2001): 383–402.

William G. Dever, "Israel, History of: Archaeology and the Israelite 'Conquest,'" *Anchor Bible Dictionary* 3 (1992):545–58.

Mary Douglas, *In the Wilderness: The Doctrine of Defilement in the Book of Numbers* (Sheffield: Academic, 1993).

Michael Fishbane, *Biblical Interpretation in Ancient Israel* (Oxford: Clarendon, 1985).

Terence E. Fretheim, *The Suffering of God: An Old Testament Perspective* (Philadelphia: Fortress, 1984).

Tikva Frymer-Kensky, "The Strange Case of the Suspected Sotah," *Vetus Testamentum* 34 (1984): 11–26.

John Gammie, *Holiness in Israel* (Philadelphia: Fortress, 1989).

Benjamin Goodnick, "Korah and his Aspirations," *Jewish Bible Quarterly* 28 (2000): 177–81.

Naomi Graetz, "Miriam: Guilty or Not Guilty?" *Judaism* 40 (1991): 184–92.

John Gray, "The Canaanite God Horon," *Journal of Near Eastern Studies* 8 (1949): 27–34.

Bonna Devora Haberman, "The Suspected Adulteress: A Study of Textual Embodiment," *Prooftexts* 20 (2000): 12–42.

Joanne A. Hackett, "Some Observations on the Balaam Tradition at Deir 'Allā.," *Biblical Archaeologist* 49 (1986): 216–22.

Rachel T. Harris, "The Ritual of the Red Heifer," *Jewish Bible Quarterly* 26 (1998) 198–200.

Michael W. Homan, "The Divine Warrior in His Tent," *Bible Review* 16 (2000): 22–36.

Thomas Jemielity, *Satire and the Hebrew Prophets* (Louisville: Westminster/John Knox, 1992).

Karen Randolph Joines, "The Bronze Serpent in the Israelite Cult," *Journal of Biblical Literature* 57 (1965): 245–56.

J. V. Kinnier-Wilson, "Medicine in the Land and Times of the Old Testament" in *Studies in the Period of David and Solomon* (ed. T. Ishida; Winona Lake, Ind.: Eisenbrauns, 1982): 337–65.

Kenneth A. Kitchen, "The Desert Tabernacle," *Bible Review* 16 (2000): 14–23.

James Kugel, *The Bible as it Was* (Cambridge: Harvard University Press, 1997).

Seth Daniel Kunin, *The Logic of Incest: A Structuralist Analysis of Hebrew Mythology* (Sheffield: Academic Press, 1995).

Adriane B. Leveen, "Falling in the Wilderness: Death Reports in the Book of Numbers," *Prooftexts* 22 (2002): 245–272.

Baruch Levine, *Numbers* (2 vols.; New York: Doubleday, 1993, 2000).

George E. Mendenhall, *The Tenth Generation* (Baltimore: Johns Hopkins, 1973).

Michael S. Moore, "Jesus Christ: 'Superstar'," *Novum Testamentum* 24 (1982): 82–91.

———, *The Balaam Traditions: Their Character and Development* (Atlanta: Scholars Press, 1990).

———, *Faith under Pressure: A Study of Biblical Leaders in Conflict* (Siloam Springs, Ark.: Leafwood, 2003).

William Moran, ed. *The Amarna Letters* (Baltimore: Johns Hopkins, 1992).

Martin Noth, *Numbers* (Philadelphia: Westminster, 1968).

Dennis T. Olson, *The Death of the Old and the Birth of the New: The Framework of the Book of Numbers and the Pentateuch* (Chico, Calif.: Scholars Press, 1985).

Rudolf Otto, *The Idea of the Holy* (New York: Oxford, 1946).

Marvin Powell, "Weights and Measures," *Anchor Bible Dictionary* 6 (1992): 903–5.

James Pritchard, *Ancient Near Eastern Texts* (Princeton: Princeton University Press, 1969).

Gerhard von Rad, *Old Testament Theology* (New York: Harper and Row, 1962).

Alexander Rofé, *Spr Bl'm* [Hebrew *The Book of Balaam*] (Jerusalem: Simor, 1979).

B. Rothenberg, *Timna* (London: Thames and Hudson, 1972).

Katherine D. Sakenfeld, "The Problem of Divine Forgiveness in Numbers 14," *Catholic Biblical Quarterly* 37 (1975): 317–30.

Jeffrey Salkin, "The Frankists and the Reformers: A Hidden Link," *Journal of Reform Judaism* 35 (1988): 25–30.

William Schniedewind, *The Word of God in Transition: From Prophet to Exegete in the Second Temple Period* (Sheffield: Academic Press, 1995).

Daniel Snell, *Flight and Freedom in the Ancient Near East* (Leiden: Brill, 2001).

Adin Steinsaltz, *The Essential Talmud* (London: Weidenfeld and Nicholson, 1976).

Ada Taggar-Cohen, "Law and Family in the Book of Numbers: The Levites and the Tidennutu Documents from Nuzi," *Vetus Testamentum* 48 (1998) 74–94.

Karel van der Toorn, "Ordeal." *Anchor Bible Dictionary* 5 (1992): 40–42.

Marc Van de Mieroop, "A History of Near Eastern Debt?" in *Debt and Economic Renewal in the Ancient Near East* (eds. M. Hudson and M. van de Mieroop; Bethesda, Md.: CDL, 2002): 59–94.

John T. Willis, "The Repentance of God in the Books of Samuel, Jeremiah, and Jonah." *Horizons in Biblical Theology* 16 (1994): 156–75.

David P. Wright, "Purification from Corpse Contamination in Numbers XXXI 19–24," *Vetus Testamentum* 35 (1985): 213–23.

Yigael Yadin, *Bar Kokhba* (London: Weidenfeld and Nicholson, 1971).

Ziony Zevit, *The Religions of Ancient Israel* (New York: Continuum, 2001).

Deuteronomy

Mark W. Hamilton

CHAPTER CONTENTS

Contexts 203
Commentary 204
    Introductory Sermon · 1:1–4:40 204
    Sermon About Life in the Promised Land · 4:41–11:32 209
    Laws for Relating to God · 12:1–16:17 216
    Laws on Proper Leadership · 16:18–21:9 219
    Laws on Interpersonal Relationships · 21:10–25:19 224
    Ceremony of Renewing the Covenant · 26:1–29:9 228
    Final Sermon Appealing for Loyalty · 29:10–30:20 230
    Moses' Final Exhortations · 31:1–30 232
    The Song of Moses · 32:1–52 232
    Moses' Blessing of Israel · 33:1–29 233
    The Death of Moses · 34:1–12 235
Theological Reflections 235
For Further Study 235
Works Cited 235

MAPS, TABLES, & FEATURES

The Twelve Curses 229

Deuteronomy, the "second law," as the Greek translators of the book called it, brings the Pentateuch to a conclusion and marks a transition in the biblical story as Israel moves from the wilderness to the promised land. The book is the linchpin of the Old Testament, addressing the theological challenges of the ongoing life of the people of God. Joshua through 2 Kings, Jeremiah, and other parts of the Old Testament draw heavily on Deuteronomy's theology, and its basic commitments survive in Christianity. Tellingly, Jesus and Satan quote the book to each other in the story of the temptation in the wilderness (Matt 4:1–11; Mark 1:12–13; Luke 4:1–13).

As a piece of literature, Deuteronomy presents itself as a sermon by Moses on the plains of Moab (in the western part of the modern Kingdom of Jordan). Deuteronomy 1:1–4:40 and 7:12–11:25 are straightforwardly sermonic, full of exhortations and storytelling. But within the sermonic framework come long lists of laws that sometimes reiterate and sometimes modify those of Exodus and Leviticus. Chapters 32–34 step outside the sermon, forming a conclusion for the Pentateuch as a whole and a transition into the Deuteronomistic History (Joshua through 2 Kings minus Ruth).

CONTEXTS

As a theological treatise, Deuteronomy works on several levels. It connects the life of Israel to its founding events, the story of the exodus, which in turn becomes the touchstone for ethics, worship, politics, and all other dimensions of life. It concentrates on the nature of the one God. Monotheism, the belief in only one God who is the gracious sovereign of all, allows Deuteronomy to argue that God is not arbitrary, tyrannical, or unreliable, and that therefore God's human subjects should not be, either. It addresses major theological themes such as election, the land, the nature of community, power and responsibility, economic life, family life, intergenerational spiritual formation, reverence for God and creation, and the cultivation of memory as the lifeblood of the community. Deuteronomy thus touches on all the crucial biblical themes applicable to life here and now.

Modern readers of the book have noted its theological sophistication but have wondered precisely when it was written. Curiously for a book written by Moses, it had no obvious influence on Israelite life before the seventh century BCE. The earliest mention of the book comes from 2 Kings 22, the story of the discovery of the "Book of the Law" by the servants of King Josiah, in about 627 BCE. (The phrase "book of the law" or "book of the law of Moses" also appears in Deut 17:19–20; 28:58; 29:19; 31:11–12; Josh 1:8; 8:34; 23:6; and 2 Kgs 14:6. In the last verse, it introduces a quotation from Deut 24.) Josiah's reform program included the centralization

> **Covenant**
>
> A major theme in Deuteronomy is the covenant, a two-sided agreement obligating both God and Israel to certain behaviors. God imposes the covenant, and Israel accepts it, but it is not a set of arbitrary rules. Rather, it flows out of the redeeming love of the divine sovereign, who rescues a people and calls them to a healthy life. In the deep background behind the idea of covenant lies the ancient Near Eastern treaty between two powers. However, Deuteronomy is not a treaty. It merely assumes the spiritual equivalent of a treaty and calls Israel to carry out its obligations under the treaty.

of the cult in Jerusalem, and he appeals to the prospect of divine curses, both themes in Deuteronomy. Although his activities do not coincide precisely with the program of the book, the best guess still is that his priests found Deuteronomy or some part of it.

Most modern scholars explain this disappearance of Deuteronomy from Israelite history by arguing that it was written in its current form (or some shorter version) only a few decades before the time of Josiah. Certainly, the language of the book for the most part is Hebrew of the late monarchic period, not the period of Moses. On the other hand, it has become increasingly common to recognize that lying behind the final written form are long periods of oral transmission, so that some basic outlooks of the book may go back to the time of Moses himself.

In short, the attribution to Moses is simply a literary device. Certainly, ancient people had no problem with writing speeches that reported, not the exact words of the speaker, but the general tenor of his arguments. And for Christians reading Deuteronomy, it is acceptable to argue that God working through a community of faithful people remembering the religious and ethical commitments of Moses, which were rooted in the saving story of the exodus, could use the magnificent theological treatise that is Deuteronomy at any period in Israel's history, employing any literary convention available to ancient authors.

COMMENTARY

INTRODUCTORY SERMON · 1:1–4:40

This "sermon," as the conclusion in 4:40 makes clear, seeks to persuade Israel to avoid idolatry and keep the laws of the deliverer God (the label "sermon" should not be pressed too far; as Brettler argues, these chapters are a literary creation designed to resemble actual sermons). Far from being a set of mindless rules, the law is a gift that God gives to a rescued people so that they may live free from the tyranny that strangled them in Egypt. This call to an obedient life follows from the nature of God as the sole deity in the universe ("there is no one else" [4:39]) and from the liberation of the exodus. The sermon recites the story of deliverance in order to build God's reputation and the credibility of the moral and spiritual agenda of the book.

Thus the sermon covers the promises to the ancestors (1:8 echoes Gen 12–50), the choice of leaders (1:9–18 echoes Exod 18), the sending of spies (1:19–46 echoes Num 13–14), the wandering in the desert (2:1–23 echoes Exod 26-Num 36), the defeat of Sihon and Og (2:24–3:11 echoes Num 21:21–35; Pss 135:11; 136:18–19), the division of the land (3:12–20 echoes Num 32), and Moses' exclusion from the promised land (3:21–29). Historical recitation buttresses the theological argument of chapter 4.

> **How Deuteronomy Makes Arguments**
>
> At first glance, one might assume that a book full of divine laws would simply assert them without explanation or opening for dissent. Deuteronomy, like all other parts of the Bible, declines to take this approach, however. It makes arguments. It follows rules of persuasion, drawing on knowledge the audience already has to call it to avoid some behaviors or beliefs and accept others (see Willard). It justifies its demands by appealing to the nature of God, to God's gracious acts of deliverance, to precedents in history (both positive and negative), and to reason. Deuteronomy makes a case for what it calls "life," faithful obedience to a gracious God.

1:1–8 This section on the march through the wilderness sets the time and location of the book's opening speech. Verses 1–5 open the book with a list of exotic places in the region south of the Dead Sea. Verse 1 – *These are the words* – is the first of four rubrics introducing major sections of the book; the others are 4:44–45; 29:1 (Hebrew 28:69); and 33:1. The NIV's *east of the Jordan*, though correct, is misleading and apologetic in nature; the Hebrew reads "on the other side of the Jordan," implying that both author and original readers live in the land of Israel. The *Arabah* is the extension of the Great Rift Valley south of the Dead

Sea, while the other place names are part of an itinerary leading backward to Mount Horeb (Nelson 16–17). Verse 5's *this law* refers at least to the speeches of chapters 1–4 and probably to the entire book. Deuteronomy thinks of law broadly to include story and oral performance of both story and rules for life.

Verse 7 lists the areas of the promised land, while verse 8 moves from geography to theology and summarizes the book's opening section. Genesis 17:8 promised Abraham and his descendants the land and the presence of God, and Deuteronomy reaffirms that promise. The text offers a justification for Israel's seizure of land already inhabited: owing to Yahweh's promise, the land belonged, in fact, to Israel.

1:9-18 *At that time* begins a digression (Weinfeld, *Deuteronomy*, 137) following the story in Numbers 11, not that in Exodus 18. The story emphasizes the wisdom of Moses and the people (who do not play significant roles in the texts earlier in the Pentateuch) in agreeing to set up a judicial system (without explicit divine instructions but with divine approval). Verses 10–11 express both a blessing (verse 11) that echoes Genesis 15 and implicitly a prayer of thanksgiving for Yahweh's trustworthiness (verse 10). The organization of the judiciary respects tribal boundaries but also creates new structures within them. The rankings of the judges and their constituencies follow a widespread practice attested in military and political hierarchies in Egypt and the Hittite Empires (Weinfeld, *Deuteronomy*, 140–41), with one exception.

That exception is the lack of a king in this part of Deuteronomy (but see 17:14–20). Just as the law on the judiciary in Deuteronomy 17:8–13 does not name the crown as a court of appeals, so also chapter 1 omits the king. On the other hand, Moses functions much as a king would have in other cultures. For the audience of the book itself (not the literary audience inside the book), the role of Moses has no parallel in their own lives. No human king, in Deuteronomy's view, can play the role of judge, despite the fact that Israelite kings did judge cases on occasion (for example, 1 Kgs 3:16–28; Ps 101; Isa 11:4).

The judges should work impartially. Unlike other legal systems that distinguish parties in a case by class, national origin, or some other accident of birth, Deuteronomy insists that judges "regard no faces" (verse 17; NIV's *Do not show partiality*). Resident aliens have equal rights with native Israelites. The failure of judges to behave in this way can lead to societal disintegration (Isa 1:23).

1:19-46 The historical recitation resumes with the story of the spies (Num 13–14). Unlike the Numbers story, which attributes the idea for spies to Yahweh, Deuteronomy emphasizes that it was the plan of Moses and the people, though again with divine approval. The chapter explains why the original exodus generation did not enter the promised land, and yet why Yahweh's faithfulness stood the test.

Israel makes several theological claims that deny the truth of the exodus faith: Yahweh *hates us* (verse 27; compare Exod 32:12) and favors the Amorites (who would allegedly kill the Israelites), and the indigenous peoples are invincible (verse 28). The *Anakites* are remembered as giants (Deut 2:10, 11, 21; 9:2; Josh 15:13; 21:11).

In contrast to their revolt, Moses offers several defenses of Yahweh's benevolence: God is a successful warrior, an appeal to the most ancient portrayals of Israel's God (verse 30; Exod 15; Judg 5; Hab 3); and God resembles a parent (verse 31). God's blessings will fall on the next generation, as well as on Caleb and Joshua. The latter is famous as the successor of Moses and the bearer of Israel's faith (see Josh 23–24, speeches in the Deuteronomistic style).

> **The Amorites**
> In Mesopotamian literature, the ethnic label "Amorite" referred to any number of groups from west of the Tigris-Euphrates valley, especially in the center of modern Syria. A kingdom of Amurru existed in the Orontes Valley (near later Antioch of Syria) just before the Israelite period, and the stories about Og and Bashan may indicate that some of these people migrated to the Transjordan. In the Pentateuch, the Amorites are one of the nations in the area Israel was to conquer.

The episode ends with an aborted war. Yahweh may permit some decisions without direct instructions (like law courts) but not others (like warfare).

2:1-23 This section collapses thirty-eight years of nomadic life into a few verses. These years served to kill off the warriors who had rebelled (not their wives or children; verse 16). The various instructions about the Edomites, Moabites, and Ammonites (verses 3–9, 16–19) contrast with those for other peoples (verses 10–12, 20–23). Abrahamic peoples receive Yahweh's protection from Israel, while others must be conquered. These verses contain bits of lore about groups in Transjordan.

DEUTERONOMY

In the midst of political line-drawing, verses 4–7 offer instructions and a reminder of blessings. The instructions demand peaceful actions toward the Edomites (*your brothers the descendants of Esau*; verse 4). In contrast to the hostility for Edom in Obadiah or Psalm 60, Deuteronomy expects friendly relations with that country. The blessings emphasize Yahweh's protection of the second generation of exodus people (*you* [verse 8] in chapters 1–4 usually refers to the audience inside the book, that is, the second generation of post-exodus Israelites). *Elath* and *Ezion Geber* lie on the Gulf of Aqaba and were sometimes Israelite, sometimes Edomite.

> **Seir**
> Seir is the wooded slope leading from the plateau southeast of the Dead Sea down to the Wadi Arabah (the valley due south of the Dead Sea), and part of the Kingdom of Edom. Often Seir is a synonym for Edom as a whole.

The references to the Moabites and Ammonites recognize the political integrity of those states, thus confining Israel within smaller boundaries than Numbers 32. Moreover, the text says that Yahweh had located them and destroyed their enemies (verses 19, 21–22). Like many other Old Testament texts (Amos 1–2, 9:7), Deuteronomy regards Yahweh as the ultimate political organizer of the world.

This interest in Israel's neighbors includes available bits of lore about the populations of Palestine and Transjordan before 1000 BCE. The *Rephaites*, or "Rephaim," are usually thought of as peoples of the Middle or Late Bronze Age (Gen 14:5; 15:20), long preceding Israel, and as giants (Deut 3:11, 13; Josh 12:4; 13:12). Deuteronomy thinks of them as an umbrella term for several groups (*Emites* and *Zamzummites*, and possibly *Horites*). Texts from the north Syrian town of Ugarit (destroyed just after 1200 BCE) describe the *Rapi'uma* (equals the Rephaim) as a race of dead heroic kings (like the biblical Og). Thus the word could mean different things to different peoples, but all agreed that it labeled mighty warriors of the past. It would be plausible for later Israelites, who lived at first in poor villages, to attribute the ruins of mighty cities all around them to past giants. But Deuteronomy places this ancient tradition in a theological context: Yahweh has acted to rearrange the world in a way that supports the covenant people.

The *Caphtorites* (from Crete) must be part of the Philistines, themselves part of a large migration of peoples from the Aegean to both western Asia and the western Mediterranean basin about 1200 BCE. Interestingly, Deuteronomy does not say that Yahweh moved the Caphtorites (but see Amos 9:7).

These references reflect an accurate historical memory. The last two centuries of the second millennium BCE saw radical rearrangements of centuries-old political realities throughout the region around Israel. Remarkably, these traditions survived in Israel for centuries and must have been well-known and uncontroversial. Thus Deuteronomy can use them for its overall theological purpose: to emphasize Yahweh's benevolent mastery over time, space, and peoples.

2:24–3:11 This section retells the old story of the conquest of two Transjordanian rulers, Sihon (2:24–37) and Og (3:1–11). Israelites must have recited their names and stories in worship (see Pss 135:11; 136:20; compare Josh 12:2–5; Judg 11:12–18; 1 Kgs 4:19), and Numbers 21:27–30 quotes stanzas of an Amorite war song praising Sihon. The two figures stood for all conquered kings.

> **Heshbon**
> Tell Hesban lies about 12 miles southwest of modern Amman, Jordan. Song of Songs 7:4 mentions a famous pool there, probably the same as a large reservoir from the Iron Age. Remains of Sihon's city have not yet come to light.

The subsection on Sihon describes a diplomatic overture, in which Moses offers the Amorite kingdom payment for safe passage. Since God has promised this land to Israel, Sihon responds to the peaceful proposal with an attack. He loses the battle. Verse 30 is reminiscent of the story of Pharaoh in Exodus. In that case, Pharaoh is a brutal tyrant whom God has decided to destroy. Sihon's character is less clear, and the text does not defend God's actions except in terms of the intention to give this land to Israel. Deuteronomy assumes that parts of Transjordan belonged to the Israelites, despite the counter-claims of neighboring nations such as Moab. Verse 34's *completely destroyed* translates the Hebrew for "put to the ban," a technical term for a practice of holy war in which an army destroyed the conquered nation (see the Achan story in Josh 7). Israel's neighbors also practiced such a policy of massacre. The ninth-century inscription of Mesha of Moab (see also 2 Kgs 3) mentions his "putting to the ban" of Israelites in territories adjacent to his own. This practice died out in Israel after the reign of David and pertained only to the original inhabitants of Canaan. Deuteronomy 20 offers different rules of warfare for other settings.

The story of Og repeats the divine promise of deliverance (3:2) without an offer of parley from Moses. Verse 5 gives a good description of an ancient fortified city, which sat atop a mound and was encircled by stone casemate walls. The city gates were small fortresses within themselves, with massive wooden gates bolstered by timber *bars*. The looting of animals in both these stories differs from the rule for warfare in Deuteronomy 20 and the rules that the Achan story (Josh 7) assumes. Verses 8–11 function as a sort of footnote collecting bits of antiquarian data about Transjordan, including alternative names for various sites and the massive size of Og's bed. Ancient beds resembled our chaise lounges, and Og's was wooden with iron inlay, since in the late second millennium iron was still scarce and would have served as jewelry or decoration on luxury goods (Tigay 35). It measured about 13.5 x 6 feet, an enormous piece of furniture worth preserving as a trophy of war. The note *it is still in Rabbah of the Ammonites* must come from an author somewhat later than Moses, since Ammon emerged as a kingdom only several centuries after him.

3:12–22 The three subsections of this unit (verses 12–17, 18–20, 21–22) relate to the duties of the Transjordanian tribes. Verses 12–17 summarize the events of Numbers 32, giving the boundaries of those tribes and the origins of a few place names. Verse 14's *to this day* again implies a date much later than the time of Moses. *Makir* appears in Judges 5:14 among the list of tribes, though in the Pentateuch the name applies to a clan of Manasseh. Verses 18–20 report an instruction to the tribes settling east of the Jordan River. They too must join the conquering army. The demands of home and hearth must give way to the needs of the entire community and God's call for settlement in the promised land.

The idea of *rest* (verse 20) appears often in the Pentateuch (Exod 10:14; 20:11; 23:12; Deut 5:14; 12:10; 25:19). In Deuteronomy, Yahweh's gift of rest equals the settlement of the land in peace and prosperity. The rest extends to all classes and conditions, in contrast to the state of oppression in Egypt. In later texts, it extends to Israel wherever it lives as long as the people remain obedient (Christensen 62). Finally, verses 20–21 take the command to conquer into the future. The demands of the holy war against the Canaanites extend into the future, to the time of *Joshua*, who receives the charge to conquer the promised land (compare Josh 1). However, the leader of the fight remains Yahweh, the divine warrior.

3:23–29 This section explains the fact that Moses did not enter the promised land. His death in Transjordan created a problem that the Israelite tradition felt obligated to solve. Whereas Numbers 20:12 attributes this turn of events to Moses' failure to honor God when bringing water from a rock, Deuteronomy 1:37 and 3:26 place the blame on the Israelites themselves. Moses could not persuade them to follow God, and thus he must pay the price. Verse 24 presents a prayer that sets forth several major theological claims of Deuteronomy: God is great; God acts (*your strong hand* is a metaphor for God's entire "body," that is, God's vigorous redemptive work); God surpasses all potential rivals (without denying the existence of other deities, Deuteronomy compares their power unfavorably to Yahweh's); and any Israelite may pray to God. Typically in the Bible, the prayer itself consists of words of praise (verse 24) and a petition (verse 25).

> **The Divine Warrior**
> *The image of Yahweh as a warrior carries on very old understandings of deity common through the ancient Near East. In the Bible, God leads in warfare in order to bring justice to the world and to liberate the oppressed (see for example, Exod 15; Judg 5; Hab 3; Zech 9–10).*

Verses 26–29 validate the selection of Joshua and mark God's final verdict on Moses' career. *Pisgah* is the main peak of Mount Nebo, modern Jebel Nebo, which lies about 4 miles southwest of Heshbon (modern Hesban), just across the Jordan River from the land of Israel. On a clear day, viewers atop its 802-meter-high peak can see much of the surrounding area (Weinfeld, *Deuteronomy*, 192). The valley near Beth Peor is probably the Wadi Ayn Musa. It was the location of a famous act of idolatry (Num 25:1–9; Hos 9:10).

4:1–40 The opening "sermon" of the book concludes with an extended exhortation to faithfulness. Von Rad (48) argued that originally the book must have skipped from 3:29 to 31:1, with the intervening chapters interrupting Moses' ascent to

DEUTERONOMY

Pisgah. Perhaps so, but as it stands, chapter 4 links the opening sermon with the first legal material in chapter 5 (Nelson 61) and overlaps with chapter 30. It makes sense where it stands.

Chapter 4 consists of several parts: verses 1–8 introduce the "sermon"; verses 9–14 look to past acts of salvation as a model for all time; verses 15–24, the center of the unit, call on Israel to avoid idolatry; verses 25–31 exhort them to seek God and teach their descendants to do the same; and verses 32–40 engage in theological reflection on Israel's entire experience. The idea of *life* opens and closes the entire unit (verses 1, 40).

Verse 1 opens with a call to listen. The verb *hear*, often in a command form (imperative or imperfect), appears in Deuteronomy 81 times in the simple active form (*Qal*; 1:16, 17, 34, 43, 45; 2:25; 3:26; 4:1, 6, 12, 28, 30, 33, 36; 5:1, 23, 24, 25, 26, 27, 28; 6:3, 4; 7:12; 8:20; 9:1, 2, 19, 23; 10:10; 11:13, 27, 28; 13:4, 5, 9, 12, 13, 19; 15:5; 17:4, 12, 13; 18:14, 15, 16, 19, 20; 20:3; 21:18, 20, 21; 23:6; 26:7, 14, 17; 27:9, 10; 28:1, 2, 13, 15, 45, 49; 29:3, 18; 30:2, 8, 10, 17, 20; 31:12, 13; 32:1, 7; 34:9), once in the simple passive (*Niphal*; 4:32), and four times in the causative (*Hiphil*; 4:10, 36; 30:12, 13). Ordinarily in these texts, to listen is also to assent to, or comply with, the proposals of the speaker. Thus for Israel, to *hear* also means to obey, and for God to hear means to bless. The oral nature of Deuteronomy comes through in these calls to listen.

The text persuades Israel to listen with a series of devices: a warning (verse 2), a reminder of past experiences (verse 3), an appeal to desired reputations (verse 6), and an appeal to fundamental theological assumptions about God (verses 7–8). The warning in verse 2 resembles those from ancient Egypt (von Rad 48), and the form lasted at least as late as Revelation 21:18–19. While using older styles of communication, the text also employs several expressions typical of Deuteronomy and books it influenced, including the synonyms "statutes and judgments" [NIV *decrees and laws*], "keep and do" [NIV *observe carefully*], *the land you are entering*, and so on. These stereotyped expressions, which occur repeatedly in the book, create an air of solid conviction for readers.

Verses 6–8 state Israel's ideal self-understanding. Their wisdom derives from the divinely inspired laws, not from their innate abilities. The idea that the nations will honor Israel and its God is a very old one, dating back to the ancient Song of the Sea (Exod 15:14–16), and it warrants attention in many biblical texts on the condition of these nations. Ultimately, the interest in the foreign nations underlies the promise of international peace of Isaiah 54–55 and other texts.

The nations especially notice Israel's close relationship with God. When Israel lives the high ethical life that the Torah envisions, God will dwell among them, and the reputation of such closeness will spread to neighboring kingdoms. In contrast to polytheistic systems, in which humans rarely felt close to the gods they worshiped, Israel experienced a life of prayer that, in theory, embraced all members of the society.

> **God & His Sanctuary**
> *Since Deuteronomy argues for a single sanctuary, not the multiple holy places that sometimes existed in ancient Israel, its readers were forced to ask what closeness to God entailed. Some ancient Israelites must have felt that closing the sanctuaries outside Jerusalem distanced them from God. At one point, the Assyrian ambassador, the Rabshakeh, exploits their discontent (2 Kgs 18:22).*

Verses 9–14 look both to the past and to the future. Chapter 6 expands the instructions to teach children. The very existence of the nation depends on such education, since to ignore the Sinai covenant is to commit communal suicide. Verse 10 retells the events of Exodus 19–20, while verse 14 emphasizes that the law at Sinai (especially Exod 20–23) applied to life in the promised land. As will become clear later, this is so despite Deuteronomy's minor revisions and reinterpretations of the Covenant Code (Exod 21–23).

Verses 15–24 forbid idolatry (worship of other gods) and iconism (representation of Yahweh in sculpture or other art form). Israel's refusal to make statues of Yahweh must have struck most outsiders as very strange. Ancient Near Eastern rituals for bringing a statue to life, in which priests offered incantations inviting the god to dwell in the new work of art, existed. (The second-century BCE Jewish tale *Bel and the Dragon* ridicules this practice.) Although Israelite statuettes of goddesses and the god Baal exist, no indisputable portrayal of Yahweh has come to light.

Verse 17, like Genesis 1, classifies animals by habitat (*air…ground…water*). This must have been the typical Israelite folk-scientific way of thinking about living things. Deuteronomy underscores the fact that the creation cannot adequately symbolize the creator. Verse 19 adds to this a criticism of the worship of the heavenly bodies. Mesopotamians and Egyptians, by contrast, often identified the chief gods with major astronomical phenomena. Thus an elegant Akkadian hymn, the "Prayer to Gods of the Night," an incantation performed after dark, says, "Shamash, Sin, Adad, and Ishtar are gone off to the lap of heaven. They will give no judgment.... May the princely ones of the gods of the night ... place the truth" (translated by Benjamin Foster in Hallo and Younger 1:417). Shamash was the sun god, Sin the moon god, and Ishtar the morning star (Venus), while the "gods of the night" were the constellations. Israelites should not worship them, though God did allow the nations to do so. By describing God's deliverance from the *iron-smelting furnace*, an image for hard labor in Egypt (1 Kgs 8:51; Jer 11:4), the text clinches an argument for Israel's distinctiveness: they have a different history and thus should behave differently.

Verses 21–24 repeat older material but to make a new point. Israel should avoid idolatry because disrespect of God can cost even their greatest leader his place in the promised land. The text argues from lesser to greater: "if X is so, how much more Y."

Verses 25–31 address the possibility of exile from the promised land. By the time of the completion of Deuteronomy, the exile was a reality, and this section of the text would have encouraged the book's audience to seek restoration (compare 1 Kgs 8:46–51; Jer 11:1–5).

Verse 25 reminds the readers that living in the land does not guarantee the nation's survival there: there are no squatters' rights in Yahweh's land. Rather, the test will be whether Israel engages in idolatry. Verse 26 anticipates the covenant curses of chapter 28, in which the forces of nature bear witnesses on God's behalf, since only they can have a long enough perspective to put Israel's behavior in a proper context. Carrying out the curses of the covenant equates to the expulsion of Israel from its own land. Yet Deuteronomy does not envision the nation's extinction but, instead, the survival of a remnant that God will *scatter among the nations*. Thus even the threat of punishment here contains an implicit note of hope.

As verse 28 recognizes, the difficulty with deportation as a punishment for idolatry is that Israel in a Gentile, polytheistic environment will be more likely to worship other gods. Thus the text ridicules the foreign gods for their inability to sense and thus to act. The theme of the gods' impotence appears in many biblical texts (for example, Isa 40:18–20; Jer 11:2–5; *Bel and the Dragon*).

By contrast, Yahweh can hear prayers from anywhere on earth and can save those who repent (verses 28–31). Verse 31 concludes this speech on repentance with a reminder of God's basic nature (*merciful*; the same adjective, Hebrew *rachum*, occurs in Yahweh's self-description in Exod 34:8) and longstanding relationship with the ancestors. The language of repentance originated in the communal worship of Israel, especially after the fall of Samaria (see Weinfeld, *Deuteronomy*, 220–21).

Verses 32–40 conclude the opening section of Deuteronomy with a grand oration on Israel's history. Moses argues for loyalty to Yahweh on several grounds: no nation has experienced with its gods what Israel has with Yahweh (verse 32, 35); Yahweh communicates better than other gods (verses 33, 36); the might of Yahweh appears most clearly in the deliverance from Egypt (verse 34, 37); and Yahweh has "loved" the ancestors as well as the present generation of Israelites (verse 37). The appeal to *former days*, here the beginnings of the world, draws on a common ancient Near Eastern idea according to which the first humans had the most direct access to wisdom (see Job 15:7–8; 38:4, 21). In other words, Israel should employ all resources of discernment in analyzing their own situation. When they do, they will find themselves renewing their commitment to the ancient faith and will experience life richly (verse 40).

> **Israel's Ancestors**
>
> Deuteronomy repeatedly mentions Abraham, Isaac, and Jacob. The status of Israel as an elect people began with the patriarchs and matriarchs, for whose sake God continues to act. At the same time, Deuteronomy argues that "the realization of the promise to the Patriarchs was conditioned a priori by the fulfillment of the obligatory covenant of the Israelites at Sinai" (Weinfeld 58). The Old Testament usually regards election as both conditional for any generation and unconditional for the nation of Israel over time.

SERMON ABOUT LIFE IN THE PROMISED LAND · 4:41–11:32

4:41-43 These verses fit loosely in the context. They concern the implementation of the law of asylum of chapter 19. The notice of Moses' actions

DEUTERONOMY

at this point marks a transition from speechmaking to action. It also reminds the reader that the Transjordan once belonged to Israel.

4:44–49 This opening section follows the model set forth in 1:1, in which an introduction to the following speech precedes a list of locations and then a brief recitation of events leading to the speech.

5:1–33 The opening section of Moses' second speech consists of the Ten Commandments (verses 1–21) and a description of Moses' mission as a mediator and revealer for Israel (verses 22–33). These two subsections closely relate in that the law derives its authority from God, who speaks through Moses as the prophet par excellence.

One of the most familiar of all biblical texts, the Ten Commandments nevertheless deserves reexamination. First, although the list does not summarize the whole body of Israelite law, since many topics do not easily fit under any of the ten rules, it does offer a basic set of duties deserving the attention of everyone. Second, verse 1 views the giving of these laws as a public event (hence *summoned*). The entire community has an obligation to learn and carry out the law. Third, the laws concern relationships with God and with fellow humans. Like many prophetic texts, the Ten Commandments assume that worship and ethics intimately relate to each other. Fourth, classical Jewish and Christian interpretations use two different ways of counting the commands, while still reaching the number 10 (Weinfeld, *Deuteronomy*, 243–44). One system counts the call to worship only Yahweh and the prohibition of idolatry as a single command, with the rules against coveting a spouse and coveting material goods being separate commands (so Augustine and most subsequent Catholics and Lutherans). Another system does the opposite (so the church fathers and most Protestants and Jews). This commentary follows the second counting. Fifth, the commands use the second person singular verb "as if they were directed personally to each and every member of the community" (Weinfeld, *Deuteronomy*, 249). Sixth, the commands apply to every time and place, hence their lack of qualification or explanation (except with the fourth commandment).

The preface to the Ten Commandments (verse 6a) offers a theological rationale for the following rules. Like other ancient law codes (see the prologue to the "Code of Hammurabi"), this one begins with a rationale for the document: *I am Yahweh your God, who rescued you from Egypt*. God earns the right to give the Torah by rescuing the nation from bondage. Moreover, the law testifies to the grace of God by allowing Israel to escape the sort of tyranny that they experienced in Egypt. Contrary to popular Protestant theology, the law was a vehicle for grace.

The first two commandments are remarkable in their ancient context because they call for a counterintuitive understanding of God and of worship. Unlike all other ancient religions, and unlike the actual practice of ancient Israel, the Bible calls for the worship of God alone. Verses 9–10 contrast the limits of God's punishments for idolatry (up to four *generations*) with the lack of limits of blessing for the faithful (literally, "for thousands"; the NIV's *thousand generations* is a paraphrase). Since ancient Israelite families lived in multigenerational houses and compounds, the punishment would fall at a single time on an entire family. Later texts (Jer 31:29–30; Ezek 18:1–4) shift the responsibility for the sin to the individual sinner, but the Deuteronomistic History still thought that at least some sins could be heinous enough to deserve punishment over an extended period (see 2 Kgs 23:26). Connecting to ideas of worship, the third commandment (literally, "you will not lift up the name of Yahweh your God for a falsehood") forbids using the divine name as an oath for unworthy purposes (compare Lev 19:12) or perhaps even for magic (von Rad 57).

The fourth command extends the basic principles of worship further. An Israelite innovation, the weekly Sabbath has no good precedent in the ancient Near East. The law invites Israel to make the day *holy* by stepping out of the demands of the

---

> **Why Ten Commandments?**
> The most obvious reason for a list of ten commandments is its correspondence to the number of fingers on one's hands. The list served an educational purpose as it oriented all Israelites, not just priests expert in Torah, to the desires of Israel's redeeming God.

> **Monotheism or Monolatry?**
> Deuteronomy does not explicitly deny the existence of other gods. It simply forbids Israelites worshiping them. The book does not advocate a theoretical monotheism (belief that only one God exists) but monolatry (the practice of worshiping only one God).

agricultural economy and resting. Unlike the later commandments, the law of the Sabbath offers several rationales for itself: *God has commanded you*, a right God earned at the exodus (verse 12); *you were slaves*, that is, the liberated community should not copy its oppressors (verse 15); "God rescued you," meaning that Yahweh planned a community in which humans would not measure each other by their economic utility but by their faithfulness to their nature as liberated persons. Later Jews took the restriction on labor seriously enough that some refused even to defend themselves on the Sabbath (see *Jubilees* 50:13; 1 Maccabees 2:38–41).

The command to honor *your father and your mother* (verse 16) addresses adults, not children. Both parents deserve equal respect (Tigay 70). Three rationales undergird the law: Yahweh commanded it; keeping it will prolong life; and this life will be "good for you." The text assumes that a society in which elders receive honor and support will be more stable and prosperous.

The final commands need little explanation, except for the final injunctions against covetousness. The laws may refer to a fixed mental state (Tigay 72; Weinfeld, *Deuteronomy*, 318) or to grasping activities (von Rad 59; Rofé 79–96). Either way to *covet* [Hebrew *tachmod*] or *set your desire* [Hebrew *tit'awweh*] implies more than a passing thought, and as such something difficult to enforce. Thus the law seeks more than outward conformity but inward transformation.

The commentary on the Ten Commandments in verses 22–33 emphasizes the awesome physical effects surrounding their revelation (verse 22), the Israelites' fear and joy at receiving them (verses 23–26), their commitment to obey (verse 27), and God's pleasure at their acceptance of the covenant (verses 28–31). Verses 32–33 close the reminiscence of past events with a new warning to keep all the Torah.

Deuteronomy understands the encounter at Sinai as an offer of covenant and willing acceptance thereof. Yahweh does not coerce Israel. As verse 29 makes clear, Yahweh sought to bless Israel, and the commandments offered opportunities for that to occur. As Weinfeld (*Deuteronomy*, 325) has pointed out, the idea of putting *fear*, or perhaps better, reverence or awe, in human *hearts* was widespread in the ancient Near East and has specific echoes in Jeremiah 32:39–40.

6:1–3 These verses introduce the entire section ending in 7:11. Deuteronomy uses the terms *commands* [Hebrew *mitswot*], *decrees* [Hebrew *chuqqim*], and "judicial decisions" [Hebrew *mishpatim*; better than the NIV's *laws*] interchangeably throughout the book to impress on the reader the comprehensiveness of the Torah. Again, the divine law guarantees social tranquility and religious purity (compare 5:16; 30:11–20).

> **The Land**
> *Deuteronomy emphasizes the blessing of living in the land of promise. The word "land" [Hebrew* erets] *occurs in the book 194 times, usually in reference to the land of Israel. The emotional and spiritual connection to location is crucial to Israelite religion, though difficult for many modern persons to understand.*

6:4–25 This homily encouraging obedience to God makes several moves: a call to faithfulness (verses 4–9), a warning against negligence (verses 10–15), a warning against testing God (verses 16–19), and instructions for passing on the faith (verses 20–25). This emotive section seeks to inspire self-examination and a commitment to responsible action in the reader.

Verses 4–9 begin with a call to the audience to *hear* [Hebrew *shemaʻ*]. The creedal statement in verse 4 takes its name from this verb. The Shema has become the most concise statement of the central confession of Judaism. (See Kugel 503–5; *Sibylline Oracles* 3; *Judith* 8:18–20; *Testament of Zebulon* 5:1; Matt 22:35–40; *Didache* 3:1–2). The repetition of the divine name seems awkward, but it probably comes from the language of worship, where it may have functioned as a call to praise or as a communal confession. The clause might be translated "Yahweh our God is one Yahweh," or "Yahweh our God is Yahweh alone," or "Yahweh our God, Yahweh is one" (Weinfeld, *Deuteronomy*, 337–38). However one translates the confession, it indicates the unity and uniqueness of Israel's God. They hear especially the *words* of the Ten Commandments, which for Deuteronomy constitute the core of the covenant (see Vogt 157).

Israel should respond to Yahweh's singularity with *love* [Hebrew *'ahav*; verse 5]. This term originally appeared in treaties to describe the loyalty of a vassal to an overlord. In Deuteronomy, however, it includes emotional commitment (see 7:9; 10:12; 11:1, 13, 22; 13:4; 19:9; 30:6, 16, 20) brought to life in obedience (Weinfeld, *Deuteronomy*, 351–52). Since *you* is plural throughout verses 5–9, the commands address every individual Israelite. They should be *on your hearts*, not mere outward forms (see Jer 31:33). Jews from the Second Temple period to the present interpreted the *symbols on your hands and ... foreheads* (verse 8) as frontlets or phylacteries, though some understood the command symbolically (for references, see Weinfeld, *Deuteronomy*, 341–42). Deuteronomy's "commemorative culture," as Braulik (183–98) calls it, takes visible form on each person's body.

Verses 10–15 remind Israel that it did not earn its prosperity. Verse 11 refers to labor-intensive forms of agriculture, viticulture and olive growing. These large-scale industries produced wine and oil for domestic consumption and export (King and Stager 95–101). Olive oil served for cooking, fuel for lamps, and as a kind of soap. Plastered "cisterns" (not NIV's *wells*) stored rainwater, a necessity in a dry climate. Since Yahweh gave Israel these things, the book says, they should avoid idolatry.

> **A "Jealous" God**
>
> Deuteronomy calls Yahweh a "jealous" [Hebrew qanna'] God in 4:24, 5:9, and 6:15. A better translation might be "impassioned." The term does not imply divine fickleness but rather divine commitment. It occurs in connection with prohibitions of idolatry and reflects the idea that Yahweh has married Israel and treated it with great love.

Verses 16–19 extend the warning by reminding Israel of murmuring in the wilderness (see Exod 17:1–7; Num 20:1–13) and of God's continuing mercy (*go well ... good land*).

Verses 20–25 return to the theme of verse 7, the teaching of children. Parents have a responsibility to pass on the core story of the people. The recited story probably originated in the community's worship (see Pss 78; 105; 106), and it consists of six fixed points: Israel began as slaves; Yahweh rescued them; miracles attended their rescue; they received a *land*; Yahweh had promised this land to the ancestors; and so Israel must obey the Torah (compare Josh 23–24). These crucial events in Israel's self-understanding portrayed a picture of a nation dependent on divine grace. The conclusion, *that will be our righteousness* (verse 25), might better be translated "that will be our merit" (Weinfeld, *Deuteronomy*, 349; Tigay 83; but Craigie 175), with *righteousness* [Hebrew *tsedaqah*] referring to one's "correct attitude toward claims [of God] upon him" (von Rad 65). To follow the covenant is to be righteous. And children learn from their parents how to do so.

7:1–26 This chapter constructs a dialogue between Yahweh and Israel discussing the proper approach to the aboriginal inhabitants of Canaan. The dialogue opens with a divine command to eradicate the Canaanites (verses 1–5), continues with a justification of such work (verses 6–15) and a response to anticipated objections (verses 16–24), and concludes with a call to destroy idols (verses 25–26).

The criticism of the seven nations of the land distinguishes them from all other ethnic groups. Israel carries out a holy war only against them. In fact, the text reveals contradictory expectations. Verse 2 commands Israel to *destroy them totally*. The Hebrew word *charam* means "to kill in the context of a sacred war," a practice that existed in the ancient Near East and survives in some Muslim conceptions of *jihad* as well as in earlier Christian notions of crusade. However, verse 3 forbids intermarriage, a command that would be unnecessary unless some Canaanites survived the conquest, as they did (see 1 Kgs 9:20–21).

The focus of Yahweh's initial command regarding the Canaanites comes in verses 3–5, which prohibit idolatry. Deuteronomy recognizes that intermarriage can lead to religious corruption. Thus it demands the demolition of religious objects. Many archaeological sites in the land of Israel have revealed circles of small standing *stones* [Hebrew *matstsevot*]. These objects delineated a sacred space that might also contain an *altar*. The "asherahs" were wooden objects (not necessarily *poles*) commemorating the goddess by that name (see also 1 Kgs 15:13; 2 Kgs 23:7). Eighth-century inscriptions from sites in Judah at Kuntillet Ajrud and Khirbet el-Qom mention "Yahweh and his Asherah," referring either to the goddess or the objects in her honor, and thus confirming Israel's continued interest in polytheism. Curiously, the patriarchs and Moses erected *matstsevot* (Gen 28:18, 22; 31:13; 35:14; Exod 24:4), but Deuteronomy condemns the practice.

Verses 6–15 offer a series of theological rationales for the conquest and thereby work out Israel's proper self-understanding. Israel's relationship to God resembles a love affair based not on the success of the nation but on the passion of the deity. Israel is a "royal treasure" (see Nelson 96; Exod 19:5; Deut 14:2; 26:18; 1 Chron 29:3; Eccl 2:8). Israel's election does not rest on what it brings to the partnership – God did not marry Israel for its dowry – but on its smallness and more so on Yahweh's decisive rescue of the slaves in Egypt. Again, the exodus story underwrites Deuteronomy's instructions.

Since God keeps promises and punishes betrayals, Israel should keep the Torah.

Keeping the promise takes concrete shape in fertility of body and soil (verses 13–14). The triad *grain, new wine,* and *oil* includes the most important elements of ancient agriculture, the primary sources of carbohydrates and fats. The animals in verse 13 yielded most of the protein in the Israelite diet, as well as fuel (dung), fertilizer, and fiber. Verse 14 sums up the promised prosperity with slight hyperbole. Although the Bible contains numerous stories of infertility among faithful Israelites (for example, Sarah or Hannah), Deuteronomy values the desire for children and family as a concern of both humans and God.

Verse 15 may refer either to the plagues on Egypt (see Exod 15:26; Weinfeld, *Deuteronomy*, 374) or to skin diseases or a dysentery endemic there (Tigay 88). The medieval Jewish commentator Ibn Ezra (38) distinguishes between ordinary and unnatural diseases, reading the verse to cover both. The verse does not connect to Jewish food or hygienic laws, but to idolatry.

Verses 16–24 return to the tone of command with which the chapter opened. In what sounds like a prebattle speech (Nelson 103), the text whips up Israel's courage. Acknowledging the nation's natural timidity, verses 18–19 call them not to fear but to recall the exodus story, particularly its supernatural aspects. Verses 22–23 explain the gradualness of the Israelite settlement, thus anticipating the stories of Joshua and Judges. Rather than resulting from divine weakness or even Israelite sinfulness, the gradual expansion into the land resulted from a providential awareness of the risks of uninhabited cities, full of wild animals and choked with undergrowth. The text may show an awareness of the state of the land after the Assyrian and Babylonian invasions, but the presence of abandoned tells throughout Near Eastern history probably provides a sufficient background.

The quasi-war sermon concludes in verses 25–26 with a renewed call to destroy the Canaanite (or any other) idols. The *images* were wood covered with gold or silver foil. Since the material was sacred to foreign deities, Israelites could not retain any of it. Verse 26 uses technical terms *abhor* and *detest* for proper treatment of such radically unholy objects (see Weinfeld, *Deuteronomy*, 377).

8:1–20 The chapter follows a chiastic (A B B'A') pattern with slight interruptions at verses 5 and 17 (Tigay 92): a call to keep God's commands (verse 1), recollection of the provision of manna (verses 2–4), two calls to remember God amid prosperity (verses 6–10, 11–14), recollection of the provision of manna (verses 15–16), and a final call to keep God's commands (verses 17–20). The pronoun "you" in this chapter is in the singular (except verse 1's "you shall *be careful to keep*") indicating that each Israelite bears responsibility for observing Torah.

As before, this chapter does not add new information, nor does it give specific instructions about behavior. Rather, it exhorts the hearers to do what they already know. At the same

> **Individual & Communal**
> *Deuteronomy frequently alternates singular and plural second person pronouns (both are rendered "you" in English). No English translation can fully capture this alternation, nor has any scholar convincingly explained every case of it. Taking the book as a whole, it seems that Deuteronomy tries to insure that readers know that its vision of the faithful life embraces the whole nation as well as each individual within it.*

time, it does this by creating pictures of the blessings they have experienced, both in the wilderness (verses 2–6) and in the fertile promised land (verse 8), and by contrasting such a picture with the pain Israel incurred by rejecting God's promise. The dense texture of contrasting images of weal and woe builds the case for accepting Torah.

Several verses demand attention. Verse 2's *to humble and to test you* argues that God sought to "learn" the nation's true intentions. The Old Testament does not assume a rigid view of divine omniscience that precludes human choice (see Gen 18:20–21; 22:12). Therefore, Yahweh must discover whether Israel accepts the covenant out of love, not out of fear or laziness. Verse 3's claim that humans do *not live on bread alone* (see Matt 4:4; Luke 4:4; compare John 4:34) interprets the manna story, not as God's test of Israel's will, but as a provision of divine gifts (see Pss 78:23–25; 105:40; 1 Cor 10:3). The *word* that feeds the nation also gives it life (see 30:15; von Rad 72). Verses 7–9 extend the description of divine blessings to the main crops and mineral resources of the promised land.

Verses 10–18 turn the rhetoric to its point: do not allow prosperity to lead to complacency. For Deuteronomy, the covenant with Israel is unconditional in that God offered it to the nation for the sake of the ancestors, and thus the covenant is irrevocable. But any given generation can reject its terms, leading to the covenant penalties in chapter 28. Hence this chapter's warning against taking matters for granted. Verses 17–18 underscore the point that the blessings of God do not come to a deserving people, nor do they operate automatically. Rather, they remain the blessings of God. That is, they point to a relationship beyond themselves.

Verses 19–20 make this connection explicit by warning against idolatry. Verse 19 describes the phenomenon of idolatry, which includes abandonment of Israel's self-understanding (*forget*), reorientation to other deities (*follow … worship*; or literally: "go after" … "serve"), and use of the body itself (*bow down*). Just as Israel's true faith involves the entire person in community, so too does idolatry. Verse 20 concludes the appeal to faithfulness by reminding Israel that it received its land owing to the wickedness of the previous inhabitants, not to Israel's own intrinsic worth. The unstated point is that God may give the land to others if Israel forgets who it is (see Neh 9:32–36).

9:1–10:22 This sermonic section, like chapters 1–3, retells stories of Israel's rebellion in the wilderness. As von Rad (77) has pointed out, the events of 9:7–29 precede those of the opening of the book. However, the practice of placing last things first (*hysteron proteron*) is not unusual in ancient or even modern literature, and thus the chapter intensifies a point already made earlier: Israel's past should not determine its future in every respect. Chapter 9 contrasts Israel's stubbornness with God's graciousness around several topics: the granting of the land, the nature of worship, and the giving of the law. Several aspects of Israel's self-understanding come into view here.

First is the temptation toward pride (verses 4–6). Although verses 1–3 refute Israel's assumption that the *Anakites* were superior beings by promising their defeat, the text hastens to discourage arrogance. By noting that Israel settled in the land because of the wickedness of the earlier inhabitants, Deuteronomy offers a defense of the replacement of the Canaanites without allowing for Israelite triumphalism. Verse 5 offers a second reason: God fulfilled the promise to the ancestors for their descendants, not because of the descendants' intrinsic worth.

Second is the negative understanding of several aspects of the early history of the nation (verses 7–29). The episode of the golden calf (verses 7–21; Exod 32:1–33:6; see Begg) and the revolts at *Taberah* (verse 22; Num 11:1–3), *Massah* (verse 22; Exod 17:1–7), *Kibroth Hattaavah* (verse 22; Num 11:31–35), and *Kadesh Barnea* (verses 23–24; Num 14–15) all serve as examples of the nation's temptation toward rebellion. Deuteronomy does not seem interested in the sequence of these events, or at least does not follow the order of Exodus and Numbers. Nor does Deuteronomy report redeeming aspects of the stories, such as the restoration of the people in Exodus 34. Rather, the rhetoric aims at warning the reader against similar behaviors. History thus serves a homiletical purpose.

Third is the focus on Moses' role as intercessor. The text portrays him engaging in the spiritual disciplines of fasting and praying (verses 9, 18, 25) for the superhuman length of forty days (compare 1 Kgs 19:8; Matt 4:2; Luke 4:1–2) and then forty days further. As in Exodus 32–33, he petitions God to forgive Israel. The prayer in verses 26–29 returns to the scene with the golden calf, making three arguments for forgiving Israel: Yahweh *redeemed* them from *Egypt* (verse 26); this deliverance fulfilled an earlier promise to their ancestors (verse 27), and killing them would prompt other nations to criticize their God (verse 28). Craigie (196) notes that when Moses addresses the people, he emphasizes their history of disobedience, while he speaks to God of a history of deliverance. One might add that Deuteronomy allows its audience to overhear that contrast in order to accentuate the choice Israel must make (see chapter 30).

> **The Anakites**
> *According to Israelite tradition, some of the earlier population of Canaan were giants (see Num 13:22, 28, 33; Deut 2:10, 11, 21; Josh 15:14). Their gigantic stature came to symbolize the great odds Israel, or rather God, overcame in settling the promised land.*

> **Fasting**
> *In both Judaism and Christianity, fasting has long been a spiritual discipline that, by emptying the body, allows the mind to focus on God. The biblical calendar provides for only one communal fast, the Day of Atonement, although individuals might fast at will, and the community might do so on special occasions to mark their repentance or their search for divine guidance.*

This section of the homily continues into chapter 10. Verses 1–10 conclude the story of Moses' intervention on Israel's behalf, and verses 12–22 call on the readers of the book to follow Moses' Torah.

Verses 1–10 merge two stories, the second carving of the Ten Commandments (Exod 34:4–5, 29–32) and their placement in the ark (Exod 40:20), in order to mark the closure of the original danger to Israel coming from their rebellion. Unlike Exodus 34:4, in which Moses carved the tablets, in Deuteronomy 10:4 Yahweh does so. Classical Jewish interpreters tried to solve these discrepancies by supposing that two arks existed (Tigay 105), though others doubted such a harmonization (ibn Ezra 46–47). A better explanation would be that Deuteronomy adapts Exodus to fits its own rhetorical plan, which contrasts God's saving acts with Israel's tendency toward rebellion. Arguably, Deuteronomy was reading a different version of the story than that of the current form of Exodus (but see Begg).

Verses 8–9 summarize the stories about appointing the tribe of Levi to be priests, a much fuller form of which exists in Leviticus 1–10. The recitation of Israel's history in this section closes with another order to march alongside the people's ever-forgiving God (compare 1:6; 2:31; 3:2).

> **The Poverty of the Levites**
> *Deuteronomy often mentions the Levites, the part of the priestly tribe that did not officiate at the altar in Jerusalem (though they may have done so at other altars). The book understands that these persons lack their own farms and thus must depend on the nation for sustenance (see 10:2; 12:12, 18–19; 14:27–29; 16:11, 14; 18:1, 6–7). Caring for them equates to caring for orphans and widows.*

Chapter 10 continues with another exhortation to serve God (verses 12–22). Again, the text uses multiple ways to underscore the desired conversion of thought and deed. It repeats key verbs such as *fear* [Hebrew *yare'*; verses 12, 20; compare Deut 4:10; 5:26; 6:2, 13, 24; 8:6; 10:20; 13:5; 14:23; 17:19; 28:58; 31:12, 13; Josh 4:24; 1 Sam 12:14, 24; 1 Kgs 8:40, 43; 2 Kgs 17:32–41; Weinfeld, *Deuteronomic School*, 83, 332], *walk* [Hebrew *halak*; see Deut 5:30; 8:6; 11:22; 19:9; 26:17; 28:9; 30:16; Judg 2:22; 1 Kgs 2:3; 3:14; 11:33, 38], *love* [Hebrew *'ahav*; see Deut 6:5; 11:1, 13, 22; 13:4; 19:9; 30:6, 16, 20; Josh 22:5; 23:11; 1 Kgs 3:3], and *observe* [Hebrew *shamar*; verse 13; compare Deut 4:2, 6, 40; 5:1; 6:2, 3, 17, 25; 7:9, 11, 12; 8:1, 6, 11; 11:1, 8, 22, 32; 12:1, 28; 13:1, 5, 19; 15:5; 16:1, 12; 17:10, 19; 19:9; 23:24; 24:8; 26:16, 17, 18; 27:1; 28:1, 9, 13, 15, 45, 58; 29:8; 30:10, 16; 31:12; 32:46; 33:9]. The repetition of the key vocabulary creates a rhetorical effect: it encourages the audience to pay attention to its own obligations under Torah.

Some of the terms in this section are less conventional, however. The verb *serve* [Hebrew *'avad*; verses 12, 20; Deut 6:13; 11:13] appears often throughout the Bible and in Deuteronomy normally refers to the worship of "other gods" (for example, 7:4; 12:2; 13:7, 14; 17:3; 28:14, 36, 47, 64; 29:17, 25), though here it refers to worship of Yahweh alone. Verse 16 commands Israel to *circumcise your hearts*, a metaphor for transformation of attitude and action.

> **"Circumcise your hearts ..."**
> *While circumcision was a widespread surgery throughout the ancient Near East and northern Africa, it took on special significance in Israel as the physical reminder of males' inclusion in the covenant people (see Gen 17:1–27). Circumcision also became a symbol of a rightly attuned heart (Lev 26:41; Deut 10:16; 30:6; Jer 4:4; 9:25–26), lips used well (Exod 6:12, 30), and ears that attend to divine instruction (Jer 6:10). As Hall (1026) has put it, "A circumcised heart is a mind of the right kind, one able to participate in a covenant with God."*

In addition to the repeated call for obedience, verses 14–22 offer a series of arguments for following God, using widely accepted claims about the deity. These claims come from the communal worship of the people: "Yahweh owns the heavens, even *the highest heavens*, *the earth and everything in it*" (verse 14; see, for example, Pss 24:1–2; 50:12; 104:1–35); "Yahweh loved the ancestors" (verse 15; and frequently in the book); "Yahweh is *God of gods and Lord of lords*" (verse 17; see Pss 82; 136:2–3), and "Yahweh defends the vulnerable" (verse 18). These widely accepted claims, which all Israelites would have heard at festivals and any other time of worship, ground Deuteronomy's call for obedience in the most basic language and self-understandings of the people. Thus the laws that follow in chapters 12–26 proceed from the nation's ongoing experience with God.

Like Paul in his letters (see the commentary on Romans in this volume), Deuteronomy moves from the indicative (the reality that God's actions create) to the imperative (the actions that God's people should undertake). Thus verse 18 notes Yahweh's vigilant care for the needy, and verse 19 instructs Israel to make that care a reality in their own lives (compare Job 31). Verse 20 enjoins Israel to swear in Yahweh's name, thus avoiding idolatry and binding their commitments to those of their divine sovereign (but compare the correction of abuses in Matt 5:33–37).

11:1–32 It is not clear where this section begins or ends. Verses 1–9 connect with 10:1–12 (see Christensen 201–3; Nelson 135) and continue the earlier exhortation. At the other end, Tigay (117–18) puts verses 31–32 with the following major unit. Christensen (218–19) makes the break before 11:26, and Craigie (213) and von Rad (85–86) at 12:1. Since chapter 11 as a whole both concludes the homiletic part of Deuteronomy and introduces the following legal code, it makes sense to see the entire chapter as a transition between two distinct literary genres, which the book nevertheless combines into one integrated work.

Verses 1–9 combine exhortation with a recital of Yahweh's mighty deeds. Verse 2, like chapter 6, provides for the instruction of future generations. The NIV's *discipline* translates Hebrew *musar*, a technical term for "education" in wisdom literature (for example, Prov 1:2, 3, 7, 8; 3:11; 4:1, 13; 5:12, 23; 6:23; 7:22; 8:10, 33; 10:17; 12:1; 13:1, 18, 24; 15:5, 10, 32, 33; 16:22; 19:20, 27; 22:15; 23:12, 13, 23; 24:32). Thus, for Deuteronomy, the core of Israelite education should be recitation of God's acts and the spiritual and ethical behaviors that mirror them (again, the indicative and the imperative). Verses 3–7 sound much like a hymn (Weinfeld, *Deuteronomy*, 442); Psalms 78, 105, and 136 might provide models for what Deuteronomy has rendered into prose.

Verses 10–17 offer an extended reverie on life in the promised land. In contrast to Egypt, whose agriculture depends on the annual flooding of the Nile, the land of Israel depends on rainfall. Rainfall averages today a little over 1 inch per year in the Negev up to about 36 inches per year in the northern Galilee. The land may have been wetter in antiquity. Rabbinic interpreters noted the advantages and disadvantages of such a climate pattern, deciding that Israel's dependence on God for rain strengthened its faith (Tigay 112).

Verses 18–21 return to the theme of educating the community, and especially children. See the close parallel in 6:6–9. Even architecture was to serve an educational purpose in Deuteronomy's ideal Israel.

The homiletical introduction to the book closes with two summary calls to obey God (verses 22–25 and 26–30). Verse 24 promises an extended national territory, larger than Israel ever possessed. These verses form an *inclusio* with 26:16–27:26 (Weinfeld, *Deuteronomy*, 451), framing the intervening laws as the Torah that Israel agrees to keep in order to continue in relationship with their redeeming God. It is unclear why Deuteronomy repeats itself in this way, since either summary would provide a fitting transition between the homiletical and legal sections of the book. As so often in the book, repetition emphasizes a point that the audience might otherwise lose. In any case, verses 26–28 do connect chapter 11 with the ceremony of covenant acceptance in chapters 26–27 (Weinfeld 451–54). Thus concludes the exhortation part of the book as it transitions to the patterns of life that characterize its vision of the faithful people.

> **Mezuzot**
> Deuteronomy 11:20 uses the Hebrew word for a doorpost, mezuzah. Israel was to inscribe some teachings of Torah on their doorposts, much as contemporary Muslims write verses of the Quran on the outside of their buildings. Later, the word mezuzah came to mean a small object affixed to the outside of the doorpost. Observant Jews place such boxes for Torah passages at entrances to their houses and communal buildings to this day, again using architecture to teach.

LAWS FOR RELATING TO GOD · 12:1–16:17

The legal section of Deuteronomy opens with instructions for relating to God. However, since Israelite faith consistently connects human-to-human behavior with human-to-God relationships, the text does not focus on liturgical concerns but on their implications for everyday life.

12:1–32 The opening laws seek to centralize the sanctuary (verses 1–14) and clarify rules for non-sacrificial slaughter (verses 15–28). A warning against idolatry (verses 29–32) closes the section. As with other law codes (Exod 20:24–26 for the Covenant Code and Lev 17:1–9 for the Holiness Code), Deuteronomy's opens with rules for the altar (Nelson 146). Although the book does not specify the location of the single sanctuary, it must have in mind Jerusalem. (However, the Samaritan Pentateuch insists on Mount Gerizim as the proper location; see also John 4:20). The Samaritan temple was situated there during the Persian and Hellenistic periods until John Hyrkanos destroyed it around 100 BCE. Samaritans still celebrate major festivals on its site.

The rule of centralization has several parts: destruction of Canaanite sanctuaries (though Israelites long used them; see for example Hos 4:13–14) and the closing of Israelite temples. Referring to these sanctuaries as Canaanite reflects polemics more than a straightforward historical claim (Rofé 101), much as when we call something "un-American" even though many Americans practice it. Verse 3 lists the normal paraphernalia of such open-air shrines: *altars*, *sacred stones* [Hebrew *matstsevot*; rectangular unfinished stones placed in an upright position, often in a semicircle], and *Asherah poles*. See the discussion of chapter 7 above. The reforms of Josiah respond to this law (see 2 Kgs 23), and the law itself reflects the tenor of those times.

Verses 11–14 describe the expected attitudes and behaviors of reforming worshipers. Israel should *rejoice* as a community that includes all its members, no matter their status. As Braulik (85) puts it, Israelite worship "cannot be limited either to a celebration of God's historical deeds through sacrifice or to the creation of a holy people." It is both, and as such it prompts Israel to find joy in their contemporary experiences, as well. Nor does the text worry about the technicalities of ritual (Nelson 146).

Verses 15–28 answer a question that any ancient person would have asked: since we ordinarily kill an animal and offer part of it to a deity, how can we eat meat if we are not at the central sanctuary? Even the word for "a sacrifice" [Hebrew *zevach*; Ugaritic *dhabchu*] also denotes a communal meal. Deuteronomy responds by allowing "secular slaughter," that is, non-sacrificial offering of meat. Ancient Israel categorized animals in three ways: animals that could never be eaten or sacrificed (pigs, predators); those that could be both sacrificed and eaten (cows, sheep, goats); and those that could be eaten but not sacrificed (browsing mammals, herbivorous birds, or most fish). Verse 15's *as if it were gazelle or deer* (see verse 22) allows for the slaughter of animals that could be sacrificed as if they were part of the third category. This law thus extends mercy to persons craving meat, and it also allows for even *unclean* people, who would have avoided a sacrificial meal, to eat. Verse 16 forbids eating blood (see Lev 3:1; 7:26–27; 17:11–14), but commands pouring out the blood on the ground, as in sacrifice (see Lev 4:7, 18, 25, 30, 34). Thus even "secular slaughter" shows respect for the animal's life and prevents barbarism among the eaters.

Verses 29–32 close the law of slaughter as it began, by warning against idolatry. The location seems odd, since the text has discussed legitimate slaughter, but often law codes sequence rules by subject, and thus sacrifice connects to idolatry.

13:1–18 Chapter 13 raises the perennial problem of discerning which alleged spokesperson for God speaks the truth (see also Jer 7:4; 23:9–23; Matt 7:21–23; 24:23–24; Gal 1:8). The problem arises because the speakers of truth often face persecution from those who doubt their word; discerning the truth is difficult (see Moberly 252). Deuteronomy's test draws on the core story of Israel: even if the prophet performs *sign or wonder*, but he or she argues for idolatry, then the message is false. Lest the miracle seem persuasive, verse 3 argues that it must be a test from Yahweh. As 8:2 makes clear, Yahweh sometimes tests Israel's faithfulness (see Tigay 130); in chapter 13, the test comes via those who contest Deuteronomy's theology. Despite the drama of a miracle, the ongoing story of Israel's relationship with God should trump counter-stories (hence the reminder in verses 5 and 10 that Yahweh *brought you out of Egypt*).

Verses 6–11 name potential false prophets and explain that the need to keep the community pure takes priority over family loyalties. Verses 12–18 expand the scope of potential false prophets to any town in Israel.

The Name of Yahweh

Deuteronomy frequently speaks of the name of God, often in the clauses "to put his name there" (12:11; 14:23; 16:2, 6, 11; 26:2) or "to put his name" (12:5; 14:24, 25). Most scholars understand this phrase to express the idea that Yahweh cannot dwell in a temple humans make and thus does so only in a partial or symbolic way. Another possibility is that the name theologically emphasizes God's abiding presence in the land (Richter 215–16). Either way, Deuteronomy underscores God's deep relationship to Israel.

DEUTERONOMY

Verses 15–17 describe a ritual destruction of the idolatrous town's property. The clause *destroy it completely* [Hebrew *hacharem 'otah*] uses the technical language of the holy war (for example, Num 21:2, 3; Deut 2:34; 3:6; 7:2; 20:17; Josh 2:10; 6:18, 21; 8:26; 10:1, 28, 35, 37, 39, 40). As far as we know, Israelites never carried out this law (see Christensen 281).

14:1–21 Chapter 14 opens with two laws: one against self-mutilation as a mourning practice (verses 1–2) and another listing licit and illicit food (verses 3–21). They appear together because both concern Israel's need to be *holy*. The first law does not forbid all tattooing or scarifying, only that associated with mourning. Verse 2 offers a warrant for the law, *you are a holy people*, which must mean that scarification, because non-Israelite religions practiced it (see Craigie 230), compromised Israel's separation from them.

The law of *kashrut* (the Hebrew noun for pure food; *kasher* or *kosher* is the adjective) allows Israel to eat herbivorous mammals and birds, as well as fish that have both fins and scales. Contrary to popular belief, the rules have little to do with hygiene. Rather, they reflect a view of creation as orderly and peaceful. Animals that symbolize disorder or conflict do not reach Israel's table. Like Genesis 1, the food law classifies animals by habitat (land, water, air) and means of locomotion. Israelites may eat animals that fit the categories neatly (Nelson 178; Tigay 137–38). While the precise identity of some of the bird species remains uncertain, the basic classification is clear. More importantly, Deuteronomy 14 resembles Leviticus 11 but differs from it, as well. The differences indicate that Israelites actively debated the meaning and implementation of these laws (Mayes 178).

Verse 21 closes off the main part of the law with a warrant: *you are a people holy to the Lord your God*. Israel's diet marks it as a separate people. While outsiders may find such rules arbitrary or meaningless, keeping them reminds the people to seek nobility of heart and action.

14:22–16:17 This section includes five subsections on miscellaneous laws about: tithes (14:22–29), protecting the poor (15:1–11), freeing slaves (15:12–18), redeeming the firstborn (15:19–23), and celebrating holidays (16:1–17).

The law of tithes (14:22–29) opens with the ancient practice of committing a portion of the crops to a communal meal. The tithes do not leave the control of the giver. Since chapter 12 has called for a central sanctuary, which might be *too distant* for practical transportation of bulky food, the celebrant may sell his food and use the *silver* to purchase proper food in Jerusalem. The family meal there should be an occasion for rejoicing (verse 26) and for providing for the needs of the poor Levites (verse 27). It is difficult to see how a family could consume one-tenth of its annual food during a holiday (Tigay 143); perhaps the law does not require such literal arithmetic.

Verses 28–29 modify the basic rule by providing for a triennial tithe, apparently in lieu of the ordinary one. The tithe took place in the third and sixth years of a seven-year cycle (Craigie 234; Christensen 304) and supported the poor. Again, the purpose was to insure community solidarity and material prosperity.

The law in 15:1–11 has the same goals. In a precapitalist system in which persons borrowed money to meet immediate needs rather than to invest in business, the poor could fall into debt. The solution was to remit all debts every *seven years*. Verse 3 allows debt collection from a *foreigner*, but such cases must have been rare. Verse 6, far from being a boast of Israel's domination (see 7:7–8; 9:4–6), reassures fearful lenders of God's protection of their interests, as well. Verses 7–11 recognize the risk of the basic law of debt remission: prosperous people might not help others in distress. Thus the law overtops the profit motive with loyalty to Yahweh, who brings prosperity.

The law in 15:12–18 expands on the law in Exodus 21:2–6. As part of Deuteronomy's attempt to build communal solidarity, the law enjoins the master to give the manumitted person livestock as the foundation of his own herd.

The law of the *firstborn male* animal (15:19–23) consists of several elements: the removal of the animal from the family's revenue stream, the use of

> **"A young goat in its mother's milk ..."**
>
> *The addendum to the dietary law at the end of Deuteronomy 14:21 has mystified interpreters. In the mid-twentieth century, commentators sought to explain eating such a dish as a pagan practice, but the evidence for that interpretation has proven weak. Classical Jewish interpreters used the verse to forbid eating milk and meat together, since no one could tell whether the milk came from the dead animal's mother. In its original context, the rule must be an attempt to encourage respect for life (compare Deut 22:6–7).*

it in a meal at the temple (unredeemed, unlike the tithe in 14:24–26), and exclusion of defective animals from sacrifice, though not from a communal meal. The law amplifies that in Exodus 22:29–30. Verse 22 allows the family to eat a defective animal, though not to sacrifice it to Yahweh. In this case, honoring God could take place without a sacrifice, since the joy of the people was paramount.

The law of the firstborn connects loosely to rules about festivals (16:1–17). The older list in Exodus 23:14–17 and 34:22–24 included three holidays, while the later lists in Leviticus 23 and Numbers 28–29 expand the total. Deuteronomy follows the shorter list but makes at least two changes, one major and one minor. First, the Passover no longer functions as a *sacrifice* except in Jerusalem. Exodus 12 neither affirms nor denies its sacrificial status, but the prohibition *you must not sacrifice* in Deuteronomy 16:5 implies that some Israelites must have interpreted the slaughter of the paschal lamb as a sacrifice. Exodus 34:25 speaks of the "sacrifice of the festival of Passover." Since Deuteronomy allows only one place of sacrifice, the law here seems to require travel by everyone to Jerusalem for at least the first day of the festival, after which they might return home (Tigay 155–56; but see Christensen 335). Yet given the impracticality of such travel for many persons, it seems more likely that Deuteronomy allows for two options: a sacrificial meal in Jerusalem or a "secular" meal elsewhere.

Second, in keeping with its basic outlook, Deuteronomy highlights the joy of the festivals of Pentecost (verse 11) and Tabernacles (verse 14). Perhaps, as Nelson argues (207), the omission of joy in reference to Passover reflects its role as a memorial of sad times. On the whole, however, worship reflected and augmented Israel's delight in God and their own redemption.

LAWS ON PROPER LEADERSHIP · 16:18–21:9

16:18–17:13 This section addresses several topics, all of which relate to the proper functioning of courts. The section's chiastic arrangement emphasizes the character of judges (16:18–20), the true worship of the lawgiver (16:21–17:1), the punishment for idolatry (17:2–7), and the structure of the courts (17:8–13). Although the laws may have originated separately and still appear loosely connected, their arrangement is not random. Organizing any court system demands that one pay attention to issues of personnel and procedure, as well as of scope or purpose. Hence the various elements of this section.

The Pentateuch includes several stories describing the origins of Israel's judicial system (Exod 18:13–27; Num 11:16–17). Deuteronomy does not specify processes for selecting judges except to entrust the act of selection to the people rather than to the king or the priests.

Deuteronomy 16:18–20 makes the selection of judges the responsibility of the entire community and insists that judges avoid bribery, arbitrariness, and partiality. See also Leviticus 19:15. Verse 19 argues against bribery by citing a sort of proverb, since the negative results of bribery are common knowledge and need no special divine sanction. The law may downgrade the role of the elders, though local elders still play a major role in Deuteronomy 21:19, 22:15, 25:7 (see Nelson 217).

Deuteronomy 16:21–17:1 prohibits three types of religious practices, all associated with the worship of the Canaanite gods Baal and Asherah. Although some great Israelites erected *sacred stones* [Hebrew *matstsevot*; Gen 28:16–22; Exod 24:4; Josh 24:26], the practice eventually was outlawed because of idolatrous connections (Tigay 162). This section connects to the following one on the punishment of idolaters, and so it fits this context, if loosely. Tigay (454) argues that the law emphasizes the importance of enforcing the first commandment as "the primary condition for national welfare."

> **Baal & Asherah**
> *In Canaanite mythology, El was the king of the gods, but in at least some stories Baal (whose name means "lord") conquers the forces of chaos and takes the heavenly throne. Baal was the god of storm and rain, and thus of fertility (see Hos 2). Asherah, often wife of El but perhaps in some cases of Baal, was a queen of the gods. Different ancient stories portray these deities in different ways, and so generalizing about beliefs remains difficult. Older scholarly emphases on fertility cults, ritualized sex, sacred marriage and so on have proven to lack substantial support in the ancient evidence.*

Deuteronomy 17:2–7 understands idolatry as both *evil* and "forsaking the covenant." *Which I have not commanded* corrects contemporary belief that God could be approached by means of the heavenly bodies. Deuteronomy, like Genesis 1, sees these entities as God's creation, not deities in their own right. *Gates* were large, multistoried buildings in the city walls that served for defense but also provided space for commerce and court proceedings (see Prov 31:23), as here. The law forbids summary execution as well as tolerance of idolatry. Due process of law must occur even under dire circumstances. Verse 4 insists on a proper investigation. Verse 5 emphasizes that the idolater may be either male or female, perhaps to recognize that male and female religious practices could differ (see 1 Kgs 15:13; Jer 44). Verse 6 is confusing: how many witnesses are needed? Traditional Jewish interpreters understand the verse to say that all available witnesses should be heard (see Tigay 163). Nelson (220) understands the accuser to be the third witness. The verse establishes a minimum (two) and, again, forbids witch hunts and other abuses of judicial process, even when idolatry is the charge.

Deuteronomy 17:8–13 provides for a referral (not an appeals) process. Whenever the case proves too difficult to decide (for whatever reason), the parties must travel to Jerusalem (*the place the Lord your God will choose*) for the priests to clarify the laws. Verses 10–11 imply that, although the local leaders understand a crime to have occurred, they were uncertain as to its precise nature or penalty. The court consisted of both priestly and lay judges. *The judge who is in office*, a layperson, could offer legal expertise to decide whether a particular case demanded capital punishment or not (Nelson 221), since a homicide did and assault did not. The text does not specify how these judges were chosen, their terms of service, or their qualifications. Nor does it provide a mechanism for helping local judges decide which cases to refer to Jerusalem. That is, the text sketches an ideal legal system without working out its details.

17:14–20 Although Israel adopted monarchy as an institution for monopolizing violence and taxation (1 Sam 8–12; compare Pss 2; 18; 20; 21; 45; 72; 89; 101; 110; 132; and 144), and some Israelites thought of monarchy in much the way neighboring cultures did (Levinson), most strands of the biblical tradition sought to prevent the abuse of royal power. Deuteronomy does so in this law by forbidding the selection of foreign-born rulers, restraining military spending, limiting the size of royal harems (and thus of diplomatic relations, since kings took multiple wives not primarily for sexual reasons but to forge alliances with other kings who gave their daughters), preventing the king from accumulating too much wealth (which he could only have done through oppressive taxation), and most importantly, assigning the *priests, who are Levites* the task of reminding the king of his obligations under Torah.

As so often occurs, this law begins by recalling the core Israelite story of the entry into the land, which Yahweh *is giving you*. Law flows out of divine promise and election. Unlike 1 Samuel 8–9, this text expresses no discomfort with the selection of a king: *like all the nations around us* need not imply God's disapproval of monarchy. Yet monarchy does pose problems, as it tends to draw all the nation's resources to itself. Unlike modern governments, which spend tax money on projects for their citizens, ancient monarchs typically spent their funds on the building of palaces and fortifications, and the pay of the army.

Hence the realistic proposals of 17:16–17. The law intends to ensure the wide distribution of resources. Just as the prophets forbid the nobility from taking goods from the poor (Amos 5–6), so Deuteronomy tries to limit the monarchy. Verse 16's *make the people return to Egypt* apparently forbids the slave trade (on which see also Amos 1:9), but it does so by anchoring the prohibition in God's promise never to return Israel to Egyptian slavery (probably from Exod 14:13; see Reimer 229). The king should follow Yahweh, not his own desires.

> **Royal Generosity**
> *Ancient kings often boasted of their generosity toward their subjects. A good example comes from southern Turkey, a town now called Karatepe, whose eighth-century BCE king, Azatiwada, boasted that his subjects "had everything good, and satiation, and welfare. And I filled the granaries.... And I established peace with every king. And indeed every king treated me as a father because of my righteousness" (Çambel 51). Still, if we could audit the accounts of ancient monarchs, we would find that such expenditures took up a small part of their budgets.*

The law of the king provides for its own enactment by normalizing priestly instruction of the king. Although the ceremony of writing *a copy of this law* (presumably these verses, not the entire book of Deuteronomy) applied to the king's coronation, it set the tone for his entire reign. The priests should shape the king's internal motivations so that he reveres God and practices humility before his subjects (compare 2 Sam 16:5–12; Ps 101). A promise, echoing the dynastic promise of 2 Samuel 7, concludes the law. Thus the law begins and ends with references to God's saving acts, both past and future.

18:1–8 By balancing the powers of judges, kings, priests, and prophets, Deuteronomy seeks to construct a society in which power does not corrupt but instead guides Israel toward obedience to God. The rules of the priesthood here focus only on their pay.

Unlike other texts (Num 4, 18; Ezek 44:10–16), Deuteronomy does not distinguish between priests and other Levites (compare Deut 10:8–9), or perhaps the book wants to contrast Levitical priests with non-Levitical (and therefore for Deuteronomy, illegitimate) ones (Nelson 232). The book does seek to integrate the entire tribe (perhaps including those who officiated at illicit sanctuaries, as in Ezek 44:10–16) into the worship life of Israel. This law forbids the priests' accumulation of wealth. The cuts of meat in verse 3 differ from those in the parallel text of Leviticus 7:32–34, but the basic idea of providing for the priests remains the same. Verse 4 also provides that some unspecified percentage of the firstfruits of all agricultural produce should go to support the priests (see Num 18:12–13; Deut 15:19–23; 26:1–11). Again, the law does not spell out a procedure for collecting, distributing, or accounting for these goods. In Deuteronomy's ideal society, the people will follow the law.

18:9–22 This section consists of two laws on licit and illicit spokespersons (9–13 and 14–22). Deuteronomy 18:9–13 forbids various types of divination or methods of discerning (and perhaps manipulating) the divine will. By marking them as foreign (verse 10), even though Israelites often practiced them, the text says that no Israelite can keep membership in the community while doing such things. The practices include burning children (see Lev 18:21; 20:2–5; Deut 12:31; compare 2 Kgs 3), reading entrails (NIV *practices divination*; compare Num 22:7), soothsaying, and divining omens. The distinctions among these practices are unclear (Tigay 173) and may have been unimportant to the original readers. Ancient people developed elaborate techniques of reading organs of sacrificial animals, the movements of stars and planets, the patterns of animal behavior, and other phenomena in the belief that the gods wrote the future into the natural world. Israelite texts prohibit these practices. Some cultures, notably the ancient Greeks, feared such soothsayers and took steps to protect themselves from them (Hagedorn 156–69), though Deuteronomy takes the drastic step of forbidding their arts altogether.

Verses 14–22 expect the coming of a prophet like Moses. Like the king, he would be a member of the Israelite community (*from among your own brothers*; verses 15, 18), not a foreigner insensitive to Israel's redemptive history. Verse 16 explains his role as the mediator between God and the people by referring them to the story of encountering God at Mount Sinai (see also 5:5). While Exodus does not say that the people sought to distance themselves from God, Deuteronomy understands the role of the prophet as a buffer between God and Israel, owing in part to human awe – or fear – before God. Far from being a criticism of the people, 18:16 recognizes that ordinary persons cannot easily deal with God without specially designated intermediaries, namely, prophets. The problem of the role of prophets also lies behind the stories in Numbers 11–12.

> **A Prophet Like Moses**
> *In late antiquity, some Jews expected the coming of a great, Moses-like prophet, who might or might not be the Messiah. For example, the "Community Rule" from Qumran speaks of the coming of the prophetic one, along with two messianic figures. Still other Jews rejected this possibility, arguing that the Law was a once-for-all revelation. In the New Testament, John 1:19–25 and Acts 3:17–24 identify Jesus as this new Moses. Deuteronomy itself is more ambiguous, and the singular prophet may refer to any succeeding prophet, just as "king" in 17:14–20 refers to any succeeding ruler.*

At the same time, the people bear responsibility for discerning the truthfulness of the prophet's words. Repeating the discussion of chapter 13, 18:20 makes the primary test of a prophet's words their faithfulness to the worship of the one God and the secondary test their historical validity. Israel may ignore a prophet whose words remain unfulfilled but must punish the promoter of idolatry.

19:1–13 The series of judicial rules continues with a provision for cities of asylum. In a social setting in which families practiced blood feud to avenge homicide and in which the central government did not or could not check such behavior, such asylums limited violence and preserved harmony. The law of asylum contains several provisions: the arrangement of the land into three parts (verses 1–3), the qualifications of those seeking asylum (verses 4–7), a provision for expanding the system to meet new conditions (verses 8–10), and a limit on asylum (verses 11–13). Section 1 parallels section 3 and sections 2 and 4 go together. This ABAB organizational pattern probably indicates the growth of the law in several stages (much as one would expect in any law code responding to real-life circumstances).

The earlier law of asylum in Exodus 21:12–14 spoke of a "place I will designate for you, to which one may flee," without specifying its location. First Kings 1:50–53 and 2:28–34 know of a practice of seeking asylum at an altar of Yahweh. A fugitive might remain in the temple for a time until the anger of the suffering family cooled. However, since Deuteronomy allows for only one legitimate altar, and since flight to Jerusalem would not always have been practical, the book allows for *three cities* (again unspecified) and even the possibility of three more (verse 9). Unlike the law in Numbers 35:6–8, Deuteronomy 19 does not assign the cities of refuge to the Levites. The differences between these two texts show that the problem of asylum, not surprisingly, remained a live issue in the Israelite judicial system.

To be qualified for asylum, one must have committed homicide involuntarily. Verse 5 gives an example from everyday life. Conceivably, in such a case, the family of the dead person might simply forgive the killer, recognizing the terrible nature of the accident. The scenario at hand, however, assumes that no one else witnessed the event, and thus that the family of the deceased must take the word of the killer. If they will not, he may seek asylum in a designated place. The family would then appoint an *avenger of blood* [Hebrew *goel haddam*; verse 6], a family member tasked with killing the manslayer. Presumably, a race to the asylum would ensue. We do not know the unwritten rules for this race, though the society may have worked them out in an elaborate way that the text presupposes. Interestingly, Deuteronomy offers no way of assessing his claims of innocence. The community must accept his word.

The expansion of the law in verses 8–10 does not explain the circumstances under which God *enlarges your territory*. Verse 7 uses language characteristic of Deuteronomy to speak of God's longstanding commitment to Israel's success, and thus verse 8 may envision either the final conquest of Palestine (lasting until the time of David) or even imperialistic expansion of some sort (Nelson 241).

Verses 11–13 expand the law still more by disqualifying murderers. Any legal system must take account of the possibility of the abuse of process, and thus Deuteronomy recognizes the intentions of criminals as a factor in any case. Entrapment constitutes grounds for refusing asylum. The onus of charging a villager with such a crime falls on the community's *elders*, presumably the heads of local clans, who would have knowledge of the murderer's motives and actions. To "burn off [Hebrew *bi'arta*] the blood of the innocent" (NIV's *guilt* does not correspond to any Hebrew word in the text) means to insure that the community does not bear guilt for tolerating the murder of one of its members. The text does not imagine that blood haunts a community but rather that a town that allows murderers to escape cannot function properly in the Israelite commonwealth.

19:14 In a chapter of diverse rules for judicial procedure, this verse connects loosely to the previous section. The moving of a *boundary stone*, which must have remained in place for generations, marked a theft of property (*inheritance*) from an entire family. As the story of Naboth's vineyard illustrates (1 Kgs 21:1–19; compare Num 27:1–11; 36:1–12), farms belonged to family units, and individuals could usually sell them only to family members (see Ruth 4:1–10; Jer 32:6–12). The law prohibits both deceptive movement of boundaries and the sale of land in times of economic distress. The law thus maintains the social harmony of the village.

19:15–21 These verses describe the role of witnesses in the judicial system. First, proof cannot rest on the word of one witness (verse 15). In a world without forensic science, such a rule creates a strong predisposition toward acquittal of an accused person. The law demands *two or three witnesses* without explaining how a court can decide which number applies in a given circumstance. Perhaps the third witness was the victim of the crime (Nelson 242), but this is unclear. An exception to this rule may apply to the charge of advocating idolatry (see 13:7–12; Rofé 118).

Second, when a witness bears prejudicial testimony, he or she must swear *in the presence of* God. This phrase ordinarily implies that the person in question would go to a temple. In the context of Deuteronomy, however, such a requirement of location makes no sense (Tigay 184). Thus, "before Yahweh" must refer to the fact that the witness swears by God's name or that the judges somehow represent God. Verse 19 thus echoes the command against "taking Yahweh's name in vain," that is, swearing falsely while invoking God's protection.

Third, the false witness, once exposed, will meet the potential fate of the accused. Verse 20 offers both a motivation for punishing abuse of process (to warn against others doing the same) and a limit to the punishment (*life for life*, etc.).

> **Lex Talionis**
>
> *Contrary to popular opinion, the Bible does not intend the punishment "eye for eye, tooth for tooth," to encourage violence, but rather to limit it. Israelite judges were to avoid drastic punishments for crimes. This limitation of punishment marks the starting point of western law's gradual prohibition of torture and other forms of legalized cruelty.*

20:1–20 Chapter 20 sets forth rules on warfare. Anticipating by many centuries modern efforts at limiting the horrors of war for civilians (a movement in which Christians took the lead), chapter 20 attends to rules for conscription and to the economic consequences of warfare. For much of Israelite history, such rules would have been moot, since the nation rarely engaged in offensive warfare. The chapter divides into three parts: rules for mustering the army (verses 1–9), distinctions among enemies (verses 10–18), and rules for sieges (verses 19–20).

Verses 1–4 open the chapter by encouraging bravery in warfare. Verse 1 does not state conditions for warfare or specify whether it is defensive or offensive in nature. In Israelite history, most conflicts after the reign of David involved defense against invading outside powers. In antiquity, warfare usually involved prayer to the combatants' gods, and usually the king consulted diviners to discern the will of heaven (see 1 Kgs 22 for an Israelite example). Verse 2, however, modifies the ancient norm. As usual, a *priest* will be present with the army, but here *the priest* (of unspecified identity, perhaps the high priest) will give the war speech, encouraging the troops. Such speeches did exist in Israelite worship (Ps 20), but one would expect the king to lead the army. Here, as in 17:14–20, Deuteronomy downplays the monarch's role. It does so in order to highlight Yahweh's (verse 4). Although most ancient persons thought of the human king as the representative of his deity and the deity as the protector of the king, Deuteronomy loosens that connection in order to protect the nation's faith from the abuses of human leaders.

Verses 5–9 extend this protection of the people from the state by exempting anyone engaged in new agricultural improvements, newlyweds, and the fearful from conscription. Behind these deferrals stand some basic assumptions about life, namely, that economic prosperity helps the whole people, that an unconsummated marriage is a tragedy, and that fear is natural and does not merit permanent stigma. Such a war rule shows Deuteronomy's bias toward peace.

Verses 10–18 temper this peaceful spirit by dealing with the economics of warfare and by distinguishing between faraway nations and those close-by. For Deuteronomy, Israel was to destroy the earlier inhabitants of Palestine (verses 16–17). The book justifies this ethnic cleansing on the grounds of the threat of idolatry (*detestable things* is a euphemism for images of deities and the rituals attending them). The practice of "holy war" [Hebrew *cherem*] existed throughout the ancient Near East. Thus King Mesha of Moab in his royal monument, the so-called Moabite Stone or Mesha Stele, says that he "devoted" [Moabite *charam*, the same word as in Hebrew] a whole region's Israelite population to his god Ashtar-Chemosh (line 16–17). Israel's practice followed standards of the region. Moreover, the texts of Joshua and Judges make it clear that Israel did not in fact eradicate the *Canaanites* but intermarried with them and subjected some of them to conscript labor (see 1 Kgs 9:20–21). (*Canaanite* is the generic label for all the groups in the land before the Israelites. The Bible also reports their local names. The *Hittites*, for example, bore no relation to the group of the same name living in Anatolia, and are more properly called the "Hethites.") Thus Deuteronomy and other texts envision an ideal situation (from their point of view), in which foreign influence does not threaten their life in the land.

> **Holy War**
>
> *Most contemporary Christian readers are rightly disturbed by the Old Testament's texts on holy war. However, any rules for such a war apply only to the special circumstances of the conquest of the land of Israel during the late second millennium BCE, not to subsequent wars. Deuteronomy takes pains to distinguish between a holy war and an ordinary one. Thus the book marks the beginning of a long Jewish and Christian reflection on the nature of warfare and a concerted effort to reduce or eliminate it.*

In contrast to the holy war, verses 10–15 envision a war with nations beyond the borders of Palestine. Unlike contemporary Assyrians, who relished bringing the horrors of war to their defeated enemies, this law allows enslavement and plundering of a conquered population. Other texts will impose more severe limits on such behaviors.

21:1–9 This law tells what to do when a village finds a murdered corpse, the identity of whose killer is unknown. In a world without forensic tests or detectives, the most important task was to honor the dead and vindicate the living. The law assumes that a village has some responsibility for the actions of its members; therefore, the village must acquit itself of wrongdoing. The procedure of exoneration here involves the *elders*, who represent the village, and the *priests*, who speak for God. Verse 5 states Deuteronomy's view of the priesthood's responsibility for teaching and enforcing laws and customs. Verses 6–8 describe a ritual of *atonement* [Hebrew *kapper*, "atone for"]. It is not a sacrifice, since no altar is involved, no blood is spilled, and no one eats the animal. The atonement comes about because of the elders' prayer to God, not because of the magic of the ritual (Tigay 193). The ritual apparently imitates the murder (Tigay 474), but it does not transfer guilt to the heifer, since the elders wash after its death, not before. This seemingly primitive ritual thus offers a very sophisticated way of exonerating a community from guilt while still acknowledging the terrible nature of murder.

LAWS ON INTERPERSONAL RELATIONSHIPS · 21:10–25:19

As with many law codes, these chapters do not follow an obvious linear order. Rather, they arrange laws by association or topics (see Rofé 55–77), covering various, but not all, aspects of life in the land of Israel.

21:10–14 This law allows the marrying of Gentile female prisoners of war not from the seven nations of Canaan. It does not forbid battlefield rape outright, but it does assume that marriage would be normal (Nelson 259). Rather than dehumanizing such a person, the law restricts abuse of her in two ways. First, the male must allow her to mourn separation from her family, thus recognizing the value of family ties even outside Israel. Second, he may not sell her into slavery. Later rabbis interpreted the law as a discouragement of intermarriage and a concession to male weakness (Tigay 194).

21:15–17 This law connects topically to the previous one. In a polygamous society, husbands could exercise abusive power over their wives and children, even after death, in the disposition of an estate. This law limits the husband's rights. The firstborn child will inherit the *double share* of the estate, regardless of his mother's relationship to his father. Compare Genesis 29:30.

21:18–21 Again, this law links through association to the previous one: both speak of sons. This law envisions the case of an adult child who disrespects both parents in a sustained way. The procedure protects the rights of everyone by moving the dispute from the household to the community, by requiring both parents to testify against the son (again limiting the father's power), and by requiring specific charges (the roles of "glutton" [NIV *profligate*] *and a drunkard* offer possible examples of disobedience, but they do not exhaust the option and apply only to adolescents and adults). The law aims to protect the community from such a person. Like the previous two, this law explores implications of the command to honor father and mother.

21:22–23 Again connecting to an aspect of the previous law, this one prohibits prolonged exposure of the corpse of an executed person (compare Josh 8:29; 10:26–27). The text gives two reasons: the hanged person is an affront to God, and no one should *desecrate the land*. Neither reason is entirely clear. The Hebrew word for *God* [*'elohim*] can also mean a "spirit," and so the verse may wish to insure the removal of the dead person's ghost (Tigay 198; Nelson 255). More likely, the verse means that God does not wish to leave death exposed so openly before humans, who may grow too accustomed to it. In this case, the second reason would be an explanation of the first. Death brings about ritual impurity, and a corpse eaten by birds would scatter such impurity. Humans cannot be cavalier about that.

22:1–12 This section contains laws centered around two intertwining ideas: found animals needing care and mixing of two unmixable things. Again, the laws link together by association ("speaking of x, here is y"). Verses 1–3 forbid someone to take ownership of unclaimed property, without specifying a timeline. The *brother* must mean a fellow Israelite (see 1:16; 2:4, 8; 3:18, 20; 10:9; 15:3, 7, 9, 11; 17:15, 20; 18:2, 7, 15, 18; 19:18, 19; 20:8; 23:8, 20, 21; 24:7, 14; 25:6, 7, 9, 11; 28:54; 32:50; 33:16, 24).

Verse 8 seems out of place, but it tries to protect life from accidental death. Israelite houses had flat roofs that dwellers used as living and work space. A child could fall off and die.

The laws against mixing objects try to prevent unusual behaviors. Not yoking together animals of different capabilities makes obvious sense. Prohibiting the mixing of crops (see Lev 19:19) may have a practical basis, or it may follow by analogy the prohibition of interbreeding animals (Tigay 202). Verse 9 literally says "lest you make the whole thing unholy" [Hebrew *tiqdash*]. The NIV's options *defiled* and *forfeited to the sanctuary* (NIV note) over-interpret the text, which says merely that the resultant crop cannot enter the normal food supply (Nelson 269; but Craigie 290). The law against mixed fabrics may reflect their usage by the priests. Again, Deuteronomy offers no rationale for these laws, indicating that they must have been widely known.

> **The Law in Deuteronomy**
> Deuteronomy 22:6–8 seeks to enhance the value of life. Its justification, *so that it may go well with you and you may have a long life*, connects it with the fifth commandment (see 5:16; Exod 20:12; Eph 6:2–3). To preserve the lineage even of a bird helps create a world in which the vulnerable receive respect.

22:13–30 This text sets forth a series of possible infractions of marriage rules punishable by death (compare Lev 18:1–20). Verses 13–21 envision a marriage-day ritual of collecting the blood of a virgin as the unspoken condition allowing the challenge to the bride's virginity to occur. The law seems hard to understand, since a husband could divorce his wife for any cause (24:1–4). Therefore, it does not protect the husband, but the accused wife and her family, from false charges (Nelson 269–70). Verses 20–22 extend the law to cases of bridal premarital promiscuity.

The subsequent verses address several scenarios involving extramarital sex. The rules assume that the male bears a greater responsibility and that isolation creates a presumption of innocence for the woman. Verse 26 gives a legal rationale for the surrounding provision: the case involves force (Nelson 272; see Craigie 295). The text thinks of the legal system as an integral whole.

Verses 28–29 describe sex between a male and an unbetrothed woman. The NIV's *rapes* renders the Hebrew *tafas*, "to seize," which implies some level of force, if not necessarily rape. The enormous penalty of fifty shekels (verse 29) paid as a bride price should deter such actions. However, the law, as it stands, protects the family more than the young woman in question. Forbidding later divorce may protect the woman to some extent, but the law hardly seems enlightened to modern readers.

Verse 30 rounds off this section by forbidding outright marrying a *father's wife*, presumably not the marrying person's mother but one of her co-wives (see Gen 49:4; 2 Sam 16:21–22; 1 Cor 5:1–5). Rather than using the "if…then" (casuistic) legal form, the law uses the all-inclusive "thou shalt not" (apodictic) format (see von Rad 143).

23:1–8 This law states entry requirements for those worshiping Yahweh in a community setting. Three negative and one positive law make up the section. First, eunuchs cannot enter the assembly, perhaps because of their inability to contribute to its survival. Isaiah 56:4–5 countermands this law (compare Acts 8:26–40). Second, verse 2 excludes the *mamzer*, a Hebrew word of uncertain meaning. The reading *one of illegitimate birth* (NIV note) is possible but seems unlikely, since the society has a need to include its members, not exclude them. The NIV's *forbidden marriage* is not in the text. The phrase *tenth generation* implies a permanent exclusion. Third, verses 3–6 try to isolate the community from the *Moabites* and *Ammonites*. The rule appeals to the story of Numbers 22–24 as a basis. As in many places of Deuteronomy, law and story intersect to create a behavior norm for Israel. This law does not decree war with those nations, only isolation.

> **The Death Penalty**
> Like other ancient law codes such as the Code of Hammurabi, many Israelite laws provide for the death penalty. Yet there is some evidence that Israel did not always carry out such a punishment owing to its obviously socially destructive quality. Later Jewish law made the death penalty virtually impossible. Exodus 21:28–32 offers an interesting example of the death penalty not being as inevitable as it first seems. That law discusses a case of negligent homicide, first prescribing the capital punishment and then allowing for a money payment. Such flexibility explains why David could escape death for the affair with Bathsheba, for example.

By contrast, verse 7 includes the grandchildren of *Edomites* and even *Egyptians* in the community, reflecting the realities of intermarriage in the monarchic period. The surprising rationale for including Egyptians – "for you were a resident alien [Hebrew *ger*] in his land" – thinks of the exodus story from an enlightened angle. Since Israel lived as guest workers in Egypt, where they experienced oppression, guests in Israel should experience justice (see 5:15).

> **Edom & Israel**
> *These two nations experienced a complex relationship over the centuries. Genesis tells stories of the brothers who were the nations' ancestors. Obadiah condemns Edom for betraying Judah during the siege of Jerusalem. During the Persian period, Edomites moved westward from their ancestral homeland (which fell to the Nabateans, an Arab tribe) into Palestine proper. They became the Idumaeans. In the second century BCE, they converted to Judaism. The most famous Idumaean/Edomite was Herod the Great.*

23:9–14 This section provides for ritual purification outside the camp for males experiencing accidental ejaculation of semen. It also commands the building of latrines outside the camp. Both cases seek to preserve the camp's ritual "holiness" and thus keep it ready for the presence of God. The bodily actions here are not sinful in any sense, and indeed they are normal, but they do render the person unclean to some extent.

23:15–16 This astonishing law forbids repatriating runaway slaves. As in many other cases in Deuteronomy, property rights do not trump human rights.

23:17–18 Israelites should not engage in illicit religion. The NIV's *temple prostitute* mistranslates the Hebrew *qedeshah* (which is feminine) and *qadesh* (which is masculine), two nouns designating some kind of cultic official. The evidence for cult prostitution in the ancient Near East is shaky (Nelson 280; but see, wrongly, Craigie 301–2). The text prohibits any non-Levite from participating in the sacrificial worship.

23:19–20 This text allows collection of interest on non-emergency loans from foreigners. Although Jewish lending practices later became a common theme in anti-Semitic propaganda, this text operates in a pre-capitalist society in which lending took place on an emergency basis among family members. Loans for interest in ancient Israel must have been rare.

23:21–23 Vowing figured prominently in ancient religions. The Hebrew noun *neder* ["vow"] appears 40 times in the Old Testament (see Deut 12:6, 11, 17, 26) and the verb *nadar* ["to vow"] another 30 (see Deut 12:11, 17). A fuller discussion of the issue appears in Numbers 30. As in Ecclesiastes 5:1–7, Deuteronomy holds the one making a vow to his or her words. Since vows are voluntary, keeping them shows a serious commitment to Yahweh.

23:24–25 Residents of a society based on subsistence agriculture may eat of their neighbors' food in an emergency. This law protects landowners from their neighbors. It also explains why Jesus' disciples were not stealing when they picked grain on the Sabbath (Mark 2:23).

24:1–4 Biblical law allows the husband to divorce the wife for *something indecent*, an unspecified cause. Later Jewish *halakhah* generally interpreted this flaw as adultery (hence Matt 19:8–9), though some authorities allowed the husband more leeway. Moreover, Jewish law allowed a wife or her family to petition a rabbinical court to command the husband to divorce his wife, thus partially equalizing their rights. In Deuteronomy, the penalty for adultery is theoretically death, making it probable that *something indecent* (or better, "problematic") is a broader category than adultery. The law also forbids remarriage between divorced partners, since such a casual treatment of marriage offends Yahweh.

> **Divorce Decrees**
> *Numerous marriage and divorce contracts, as well as business receipts for transactions within families, exist from the ancient Near East. From Babylonia, we even have a receipt for the return of wedding gifts: "Shatuwa came and, according to what belonged to him, he reclaimed six talents of copper and two bronze daggers" (Hallo and Younger 3:251). Some things never change!*

24:5 See the comments on chapter 20 above. Marital duties trump the military needs of the nation in Deuteronomy's ideal world. The new husband should *bring happiness* (literally, "cause to rejoice") not only in sex (Tigay 223), but in all aspects of the marriage. On the connection between home life and millstones (the following law), see Jeremiah 25:10 and Job 31:10.

24:6 Women ground the family's grain between a large stone and a smaller one (*the upper one*). To appropriate such kitchenware could cause hardship.

24:7 Kidnapping merits capital punishment.

24:8–9 The law offers a popular view on a topic that Leviticus 13–14 discusses in technical detail. As so often, Deuteronomy connects a prescription to a story, in this case that of Numbers 12 (but see von Rad 151). However, Deuteronomy thinks of that story from a particular angle, Miriam's refusal to listen to instructions of an authority, namely, Moses.

24:10–13 Small lenders within the village may not humiliate borrowers. Amos 2:8 presumes this law or one like it. Two motivations exist for the law: the borrower will "bless" (NIV's *thank* is too weak) the lender, and Yahweh will count the deed as "merit," that is, a deed showing proper solidarity with a fellow Israelite.

> **Law & Justice**
>
> *A seventh-century BCE letter from Mesad Hashavyahu on the Mediterranean coast requests that an official make someone return a garment that someone named Hoshayahu took from a poor farm laborer named Hatsar-Asam. Hatsar-Asam begs for his clothing as a matter of right but finally appeals to the official's sense of mercy. Deuteronomy thus legislates for a real situation in the ancient world.*

24:14–15 Farmers hiring day-laborers should pay a regular wage. Since the poor lived from day to day (hence Jesus' prayer "Give us this day our daily bread"), those with more means must pay daily. The text portrays Yahweh as the protector of the vulnerable. Property rights cannot take precedence over human rights.

24:16 This law works out the implications of 5:9. Only Yahweh can punish descendants of sinners. Deuteronomy also anticipates later texts that assign responsibility to individual sinners (Jer 31:29–30; Ezek 18:1–4).

24:17–18 This law provides a specific example of that in verses 10–13. Since many persons would have owned only one change of clothing, taking garments in pledge could exact great hardship.

24:19–22 The vulnerable triad in Israel (*alien, fatherless, widow*) receive the community's care in part by harvesting what others have missed. This provision allows them the dignity of work and inclusion in the village's ways of life. Verse 22 gives the same rationale as the Sabbath command in 5:15, not surprisingly since both the Sabbath and the law of gleaning make room for social justice in the land. Ruth 2–3 presumes the application of this law or one like it.

25:1–3 Although Israelite law allowed flogging in cases involving non-capital offenses not subject to monetary payments, limits existed on punishment. Cruel and unusual punishment humiliated [Hebrew *qalah*; see 27:16; 1 Sam 18:13; Isa 3:5; 16:14; Prov 12:9] the criminal and thus loosened the bonds uniting society (compare 21:22–23).

25:4 Even animals have rights to food and rest in ancient Israel (see 5:14; Exod 20:10). The law may reinforce the principle of respect in the previous regulation (Nelson 297).

25:5–10 The law has a main section (verses 5–6) and an appendix (verses 7–10). The main law concerns levirate marriage, in which a childless widow capable of childbearing marries her husband's nearest male relative. The appendix provides an escape clause.

25:11–12 The law has no obvious parallel in the Pentateuch in that it involves mutilation for a crime that did not result in bodily damage. The severity of the punishment could correspond to the unfairness of such an attack or the way in which it disrupts family ties (in verse 11, the NIV carelessly omits the phrase "a man and his brother" following *fighting*) or because of the shame coming to a male so bested (see Christensen 611 for other options).

25:13–16 The law against cheating in business rests on two warrants: honesty will allow the nation to live long in the land (see 5:16), and God *detests* dishonesty. See the parallel in Leviticus 19:35–36. Transparency in business protects buyers and sellers and indeed the economic system as a whole, since trade depends heavily on trust.

> **Just Scales**
>
> *Ancient merchants used hand balances to weigh the silver or gold a buyer must pay for a product, since coins came into use only after 600 BCE and one could pay in chunks of precious metal long afterwards. A merchant who used phony weights and measures posed a threat to the well-being of any customer.*

25:17–19 This warning recalls the story in Exodus 17:8–15 (compare 1 Sam 15; Esth 3:1). Although at first it seems out of place, the rule follows the structure of laws in this part of Deuteronomy (Christensen 620–21) and actually echoes 23:4–7 (Nelson 302). The two units form bookends placing the intervening laws in the context of Israel's commitment to live differently than their sometimes treacherous neighbors. Thus, for example, Israel should avoid cheating in business (verses 13–16), lest they be like the Amalekites.

DEUTERONOMY

CEREMONY OF RENEWING THE COVENANT · 26:1–29:9

26:1–19 The law consists of three parts: the basic law (verses 1–11), an appendix (verses 12–15), and an exhortation to keep the law (verses 16–19). The ritual concerns fertility but moves the participant beyond that to an interest in God's saving nature (see Tigay 238). It takes place at the central sanctuary (see chapter 12) every three years. The farmer must present a small part of his crop to Yahweh.

The basic ritual consists of two parts: a presentation of a *basket* of grain to the *priest in office* (better: "in charge") and a recitation of the saving deeds of God. Ibn Ezra (121) explains the phrase *at that time* (literally, "in those days") to mean "as long as a high priest is in office," precluding the ceremony while the temple was in ruins. This may be correct, but the reference may simply reflect the priests' rotation in service at the temple (see 18:6–8).

The recitation itself (verses 5–10) recognizes that Israel began as one nation among many and reached its present status through God's grace. By restating the basic story of Israel's redemption and by inviting each generation to embrace this story, Deuteronomy draws a close connection between what God has done and what Israel should do. Specifically, Israel is to show concern for the poor and those serving as priests, is not to confuse worship with mourning, and is to embrace the commands of God with joy.

The speech makes several claims: the ancestor was a "perishing" (or possibly *wandering*, though this is more difficult) *Aramean*; he became a mighty *nation* in *Egypt*; the Egyptians oppressed Israelites; but Yahweh rescued them from slavery, brought them to the promised land, and gave it (and by implication its produce) to them. The words imply that present agricultural success repeats God's longstanding practice of blessing Israel.

> **The Arameans**
> This group appears in Mesopotamian records about 1100 BCE and formed several kingdoms in what is today Syria shortly thereafter (see Millard). Genesis 11:31–32, 24:10–61, and 27:41–31:55 connect Abraham's family to Aramean territory.

The origins and use of this "credo" remain uncertain. Von Rad (158) noted that the recital contains elements similar to Deuteronomy as well as phrases that seem very old. One example is the label *Aramean*: it is difficult to imagine Israel using such a label for the first time during periods of conflict with Aram (see Tigay 240). On the other hand, the description of the exodus event sounds like much of Exodus and Deuteronomy and so must be a bit younger.

Whatever the origins of the credo or confession, it functions in the book and in proposed ritual of firstfruits to remind the nation of its past. The ancestor (presumably Jacob) experienced growth amid adversity, and now his descendants can experience prosperity without adversity if they submit to Yahweh.

This same theme appears in the appendix to the law (verses 12–15), which adds a second ritual declaration (verses 13–15). The offerer must swear to having lived generously and faithfully. Israelites might not eat the *firstfruits* while *in mourning* (verse 14) in order to differentiate between times of loss and times of gain. In the background may lie the practice of offering food to the dead (see von Rad 160), but more likely the oath reinforces the need to isolate the offering of firstfruits from the impurity that comes from contact with the dead (see Tigay 243–44). The entire ritual of chapter 26 highlighted the joy that God brought to the nation.

> **The Alien, the Widow & the Orphan**
> *Deuteronomy repeatedly highlights this triad of vulnerable persons, singling them out for the faithful people's attention. To ignore their plight would compromise the very reason for the nation's being as a witness to God's generosity toward humankind.*

The exhortation to keep this law (verses 16–19) repeats common Deuteronomic phrases. Verse 18 supplements the expected language with a declaration of divine love. God embraces Israel when it accepts the covenant. The promise to elevate Israel *above all the nations* (compare chapter 28) does not reflect a parochial patriotism, but rather a sense of Israel's mission of bearing witness to Yahweh's glory in the world (compare Isa 49:22–26; Jer 30:16–17; 31:10).

27:1–26 This chapter consists of three parts: an injunction to keep the Torah (verses 1–8), the introduction to a brief law code (verses 9–14), and the so-called Curses Code (verses 15–26). Unlike most of the preceding material, this section claims both Moses and the nation's elders as lawgivers.

The practice of writing on plaster occurred elsewhere in Israel's environs. For example, in the late 1960s, Dutch archaeologists found at a site in Jordan, called Deir Alla, remains of a plaster text concerning the prophet Balaam son of Beor (compare Num 22–24). The text does not come from an Israelite site, nor does it reflect Israelite theology, though it does depict Balaam as a seer of visions. Writing texts on plaster in this way substituted for inscriptions in stone. Joshua 8:30–35 may offer the earliest commentary on this text, though there the writing occurs on an altar, not on steles (see Rofé 214–15). The stone altar at Mount Ebal is not in a temple compound, and so is different from Solomon's. Deuteronomy here records a situation that it would forbid for Israelites during the time of the monarchy.

> **The Mount Ebal Worship Complex**
> *In the 1980s, Adam Zertal and his team discovered a platform covering about 700 square feet and standing about 10 feet above bedrock. They interpreted it as an altar or offering platform. Although other archaeologists remain skeptical, the best explanation seems to be that the site, dating about 1200–1100 BCE, was a cultic site (see Zevit 196–201), perhaps related to that in Deuteronomy 27.*

Verses 9–14 continue the ritual of accepting the law. Verses 9–10 portray the Levites, who taught the Torah, as partners in Moses' call for obedience. Verses 11–14 focus on Moses himself as he arranges the tribes for a ceremony of blessing and cursing. The text does not specify where the tribes should stand. At their closest, the mountains lie within 1700 feet of each other. The ritual does not assume that one set of tribes receives curses and another blessing. Rather, the division symbolizes the choice Israel must make between blessing and cursing. The clustering of specific tribes may correspond to their geographical arrangement or to their genealogical relationships (Tigay 252–53).

The twelve curses in verses 15–26 (eleven for specific sins and verse 26 as a summary statement) address sins unknown to the community and thus not subject to public punishment (Ibn Ezra 127; Tigay 253). By assuming these basic responsibilities, Israel prepares itself for the larger task of keeping all of Torah. Most of the rules have parallels elsewhere in the Pentateuch.

28:1–14 Following this assumption of obligations by Israel, the text offers a series of blessings and curses that Israel must consider as it takes on the yoke of Torah. Verses 1–14 offer one alternative, and verses 15–68 the other.

Verses 1–14 contain several subsections: an introductory blessing (verses 1–2), six beatitudes (verses 3–6), further blessings (verses 7–10), a threefold blessing of fertility (verse 11), and promises amplifying the blessing (verses 12–14). The opening and closing subsections are very similar.

The opening condition *if* does not make the blessing dependent on human whim, since God has already promised the land and accompanying benefits. But Israel does have the option of rejecting the covenant. Because of their brevity and repetitiveness, the sixfold benedictions in verses 3–6 sound like something a priest would say in the worship of the temple. The NIV obscures the rhythm of the original, which begins most clauses with the Hebrew passive participle *baruk* ["blessed"]. The blessings encompass all locations in the land and focus

> **Kneading Trough**
> *A large shallow bowl for mixing bread dough. The image symbolizes provision of adequate food for Israel (see Christensen 672).*

> **The Twelve Curses**
> *Deuteronomy lists a series of curses for "private" sins. With their parallel injunctions from elsewhere in the Pentateuch, they include:*
>
> **27:15** *No idolatry (Exod 20:4–6; Deut 5:8–10)*
>
> **27:16** *Honor parents (Exod 20:12; Deut 5:16)*
>
> **27:17** *Do not remove boundary markers (Deut 19:14; Prov 23:10)*
>
> **27:18** *Do not trick the blind (Lev 19:14)*
>
> **27:19** *Do not oppress the vulnerable (Deut 24:17 and many other texts)*
>
> **27:20** *Do not sleep with one's father's wife (apparently a co-wife, not the mother of the cursed person; Lev 18:8; 20:11)*
>
> **27:21** *Avoid bestiality (verse 21; Exod 22:18)*
>
> **27:22** *Avoid incest even with a half-sister (Lev 18:9, 17)*
>
> **27:23** *Avoid sex with one's mother-in-law (verse 23; Lev 18:17)*
>
> **27:24** *Avoid murder (Exod 20:13; Deut 5:17)*
>
> **27:25** *Avoid bribery in a capital case (see Exod 23:7–8; Deut 16:22)*
>
> *The final curse in verse 26 binds the people together in pursuit of justice and social order. Once again, many of these injunctions protect the disempowered.*

on fertility of body and farm, underscoring God's care for Israel's day-to-day life.

Verses 8 and 10 interact with an old theme in Israel's theology: the nations' attitudes toward the saving acts of Yahweh (see for example, Exod 15:14–16; Jer 30:16). The blessing of Israel does not occur in secret. Verses 12–13 also make sense in this context. Far from being a case of Israel's pride, they express the hope of a small and vulnerable nation that it will flourish among its more powerful neighbors. Contrast 28:37, which describes the divine punishment that comes when the nations scorn Israel.

28:15–68 The curses of verses 15–68 draw on similar lists in ancient Near Eastern loyalty oaths (see Weinfeld, *Deuteronomic School*, 116–29). They cover most aspects of human suffering, from famine to disease to death, and need little explanation in detail. However, a few theological themes occur repeatedly. First, these disasters result from disobedience to God. Second, they lead to disgrace of Israel before the nations. Third, they undo the age-old story of redemption. Thus Israel receives the diseases of Egypt (verse 27; the precise diagnoses of these diseases remain unclear) and return there as slaves (verse 68; compare 17:16). And fourth, they are avoidable and reversible. As the next three chapters make clear, the people of God need never face such punishment.

29:1–9 This paragraph marks a transition to the final exhortations of the book. As verse 3 indicates, now Israel can understand the full implications of their history with Yahweh. The NIV's *to this day* might better be translated "until this day," indicating that attending to the preceding words would lead the reader to adequate understanding of the proper way to relate to God (Tigay 275). The text offers three arguments for accepting the Torah: God delivered Israel from Egypt, provided for them in the wilderness, and dispossessed their enemies.

FINAL SERMON APPEALING FOR LOYALTY · 29:10–30:20

This last homiletical section begins either at 29:1 or 29:10 (see Rofé 193). Either way, it brings to a climax the themes of chapters 1–4. It also links to chapter 28, and in fact chapter 29 interrupts the connection between 28 and 30. The text falls into seven sections (29:10–15, 16–21, 22–28, 29; 30:1–10, 11–14, and 15–20). Each section is carefully balanced by word count and content (see Christensen 713–48). The section works at several levels, both to reinforce Israel's assumptions about God, themselves, the land, and the covenant, and to call them to live according to those truths (see Lenchak 233–42).

29:10–15 The covenant embraces all members of the community, even *aliens* working at menial tasks. Acceptance of the covenant makes Israel God's people and thus confirms the promises to the patriarchs. The term *oath* [Hebrew *'alah*; verses 12, 14], or better "sanctions" (Tigay 278), refers to the blessings and curses of chapter 28. Verse 15 reminds the reader that Deuteronomy does not address a single generation, but all generations, because the covenant is not limited to a single time or place.

29:16–21 The first corollary of keeping the covenant is avoiding idolatry. Verse 16 marks gods other than Yahweh as foreign and thus suspect because of their association with oppression. Verse 17 offers a handy catalogue of possible substances for image-making, and it describes them as *detestable* or, better, "disgusting" [Hebrew *shiqquts*; see also 2 Kgs 23:13, 24; Isa 66:3; Jer 4:1; 7:30; 13:27; 16:18; Ezek 5:11; 7:20; 11:18, 21; 20:7, 8, 30; 37:23], a Hebrew word related to that for vermin [*sheqets*].

Verse 18 returns to the theme of the covenant's comprehensiveness: no one should entertain reservations about entering into a pact with God. The NIV's *bitter poison* smoothes out the Hebrew's more graphic "poison and wormwood." To remain a pagan even after receiving God's gracious gift of national rescue and meaningful moral and spiritual instruction is to live as a noxious weed.

Verses 19–21 extend the warning even further, this time to mental reservations in swearing to keep the covenant. Since God is the universal judge who sees all, no one can avoid the consequences of his or her thoughts. In verse 19, the NIV's *the watered land and the dry* overinterprets an ambiguous Hebrew phrase, "the moist with the dry," perhaps an idiom meaning "everything" (Tigay 280; Christensen 721), or a way of distinguishing between the guilty and the innocent (see options in Nelson 336). Verses 20–21 indicate that the guilt of one person cannot extend to the whole community. Though the text does not state the rationale for such a claim, it assumes that God can judge hearts and bring about justice on individuals as well as groups.

29:22–28 The next paragraph describes the results of national, rather than individual, apostasy. Whereas foreigners and later generations of Israelites could praise a given era for its faithfulness (see 4:6), they could also fault it for its rebellion. The author has in mind the Babylonian exile, which he connects to the well-known story of the destruction of Sodom and Gomorrah. Idolatry leads to destruction. Arguably, the text may also be drawing on political ideas of his time (see Pakkala 101).

29:29 Verse 29 is widely misunderstood. It is a proverbial maxim that refers in general to the gap between human and divine knowledge. Yet in the context of Deuteronomy 29, it must bear on the subject of idolatry somehow. One way to understand it is that of the medieval rabbi Ibn Ezra (144): "if someone practices idolatry in secret, it is for God our God – meaning, his judgment will be at the hand of God … but if it be public, then we, and our descendants are obliged to do what is written in the Torah." Another possibility is the contrast between God's knowledge of the future and Israel's sufficient knowledge of the present need to keep the Torah. Still another is that the author is emphasizing the possibility of keeping Torah here and now (see 30:11–16; Nelson 344).

30:1–10 Returning to the covenant curses of chapter 28, this section opens the door to repentance. Emphasizing the mercy of God, the author still allows for divine punishment. Suffering for sin should be therapeutic.

Verse 4 allows for banishment to *distant* lands, probably an allusion to the Babylonian exile or at least to the policy of both Assyrian and Babylonian empires of transferring populations across their realms (see also 1 Kgs 8:46–51). Yet verses 5–6 provide for repentance.

The exhortation persuades its audience mainly through emotion. By repeating phrases such as "Yahweh *your God*" (verses 1, 2, 3, 4, 6, 7, 9, and 10) and "*return*" [Hebrew *shuv*; verses 2, 3, 8, and 9], the text reminds the audience of its ties to their redeemer and thus to the story of redemption (see Lenchak 199). Yet God does not seek mere repentance, but rather new behavior (Christensen 739–40). This change comes about through the renewal of mind and body (verse 6; the metaphor of circumcising the heart reminds readers that the initiation rite of physical circumcision, though valuable, symbolizes a change of inward state).

The emotion climaxes in verse 9 with the extraordinary image of God taking *delight in*, or better "rejoicing over," Israel. The same expression appears in prophetic texts referring to return from exile (Isa 62:5; 65:19; Jer 32:41; and Zeph 3:17), indicating that the image of a celebrating God resonated with a frightened people.

30:11–14 The Torah does not demand impossible actions of Israel. The metaphors of nearness and distance work at several levels. First, like verse 4, they remind readers of the universal scope of God's rule. Second, they speak of the understandability and accessibility of divine revelation. And third, as Ibn Ezra noticed already (146), they speak of the immediacy of Torah. It is physically present and thus can translate into actions.

By mentioning inaccessible places such as *heaven* and the lands *beyond the sea*, the text alludes to heroic ideals of the ancient Near East. Keeping Torah requires no Gilgamesh or Odysseus (see Craigie 365; Christensen 743; Tigay 286). Anyone can do it, and anyone who does it will receive life and blessing. Since chapter 1 has reminded Israel that it does not contain many heroes, 30:11–14 is poignant in its call to ordinary Israelites to follow the God who redeems them.

30:15–20 Israel may choose between two ways. Keeping Torah leads to a successful life; violating Torah leads to a failed life. The choice lies with the hearer of Torah.

Interestingly, verse 17 returns to the possibility of destruction. Lest the reader believe that verses 1–10 take the edge off God's expectation of an obedient life, verse 17 reminds Israel that the promise for any given generation depends on its obedience.

The witnesses of verse 19 (*heaven and earth*), though often deities in ancient Near Eastern texts, figure here only metaphorically. Since they have experienced everything, they can testify

> **The Two Ways**
> *Later Jewish and Christian interpreters thought about two ways, a distinct choice between moral and immoral lifestyles. Thus Jesus spoke of the wide and narrow ways (Matt 7:13–14) and the* Didache *(1:1) and Letter of Barnabas (18:1–2) described the way of life and the way of death. Deuteronomy does not explicitly set forth the same idea but comes very close to doing so, and thus it is the earliest text in a long tradition of moral and spiritual reflection on the contrast between sets of life choices (see Kugel 527–33).*

to Israel's behavior. The three generations of verses 19–20 (*children*, *you*, and the *ancestors*) link together the nation throughout time in obedience or disobedience.

MOSES' FINAL EXHORTATIONS · 31:1–30

The final exhortation reconnects Deuteronomy to the biography of Moses. Commentators have long noted that the sequence of events in the chapter seems scrambled (Tigay 505). One may explain this by arguing, as Christensen (753) has shown, that the chapter is arranged in a chiasm, the center of which is the divine self-revelation in verses 14–15. The story does not seek chronological order but rather an artful nesting of themes, pivoting around God's self-revelation. The theophany in the center of the story highlights the choice between faithfulness and rebellion that Israel must make.

Thus the chapter includes the following topics: Moses' departure (verses 1–6, 24–30), the appointment of Joshua (verses 7–8, 23), the writing of sacred texts (verses 9–12, 19–22), description of future generations (verses 13, 16–18), and the theophany of Yahweh (verses 14–15).

31:1–6 Deuteronomy recognizes that Moses lives on in Israel through the Torah, but the nation must live without his direct leadership. It survives by remembering the saving events of the wilderness. The order of verses 5 and 6 is significant. God acts to save, and therefore Israel must be *courageous*. Humans must cooperate with God in the work of redemption, but God takes the lead.

31:7–8 Deuteronomy's ideal of leadership includes bravery, remembrance of the promises to the ancestors, and a commitment to lead the people into the land. The book does not envision Joshua as a national administrator. In such a role, Moses has no real successor. Joshua 23–24 returns to this theme, and both chapters owe a great deal to Deuteronomy.

31:9–13 The narrative shifts from sermon to ritual. Moses, like the king in 17:18, writes *this law*. Presumably, the phrase refers to the book of Deuteronomy or at least some large portion of it. Rather than transmitting the book to the people as a whole, Moses entrusts it to the *priests* and *elders*, who must teach it to the people.

Verses 10–13 envision a septennial ritual at the Feast of Tabernacles. The festival should remind Israel of its past and call it to a faithful future. For a parallel, see Nehemiah 8–9.

31:14–15 The divine appearance functions on at least two levels. First, it explains to the readers of the book centuries after Moses why Israel drifted into idolatry and noted that their actions did not surprise Yahweh. Second, it exhorts the readers not to repeat the behavior of their ancestors.

> **The Feast of Tabernacles**
> In Hebrew called Sukkoth ["booths" or "shelters"], this festival on the 14th of Tishri (September-October) commemorated Israel's travels in the wilderness. Associated with the autumn harvests, the festival has figured prominently in Judaism for more than 3,000 years.

31:16–18 Verses 17–18 connect back to chapter 28 and to 29:22–28. To *hide* God's *face* is an idiom signifying God's abandonment of the people. The righteous king will not protect wicked people from others.

31:19–22 Verse 19's *this song* refers to chapter 32. Like Psalm 78, this hymn criticizes Israel's rebellious spirit, but in the context of communal worship, it calls hearers to better choices. The NIV's *have them sing it* translates the Hebrew phrase that literally means, "put it in their mouth," an idiom meaning "have them memorize it" (Tigay 295). Verse 21 explains the purpose of such recitations in the cult: a given generation may remember the sins of its ancestors and avoid repeating them.

31:23 The verse ignores the warnings of the previous lines, indicating that doom is not inevitable. It results from human choices.

31:24–30 The ritual ends when Moses places the written Torah near the ark, symbolizing the close connection between the words of Deuteronomy and the preeminent symbol of God's presence among the people. The indictment of verses 27–29 serves not as an obituary for the people, but as a challenge to serve God. Compare the rhetorical maneuverings of Joshua 24:16–22. Israelite speakers could stimulate their hearers' faithfulness by accusing them of faithlessness.

THE SONG OF MOSES · 32:1–52

As with chapter 33, Deuteronomy here quotes an old poem, which it frames as a set of instructions from Moses to all Israelites for all time. There are different ways to understand the organization of this psalm. For example, Tigay (299) finds four parts: an introduction (verses 1–3), a history of Israel's and

God's relationship (verses 4–18), a description of God's decisions (verses 19–42), and a coda (verse 43). Christensen (787) finds five parts (verses 1–6, 7–14, 15–29, 30–36, and 36–43). Nelson (362–66) also finds five parts, but divides them differently (1–6, 7–18, 19–25, 26–38, and 39–43). Craigie (376–90) finds nine parts (verses 1–3, 4–9, 10–14, 15–18, 19–22, 23–27, 28–33, 34–38, and 39–43). This variety of opinion illustrates, if nothing else, the careful artistry of the poem. Each section flows into the next. For the sake of convenience, this commentary follows Nelson's outline. Verses 44–47 turn the song into moral instruction, and verses 48–52 mark a transition to the final episode of the Moses story.

32:1–6 Verses 1–3 open the poem with a hope for the efficacy of the oral poet's words (compare Ps 45:1). The imagery of moisture on vegetation stands behind later reflections on the power of God's word (see Isa 40:7–8). Verses 4–6 introduce the problem of the poem, Israel's ingratitude to Yahweh. By calling both Yahweh (verses 4, 15, 18, 30, 31) and foreign gods (31) a *rock*, the poem draws on ancient Canaanite names for the deity (Christensen 795), but in a wholly Yahwistic vein.

32:7–18 The next section opens with a call to remembrance (compare Pss 78:4–6; 105:5). In the context of Deuteronomy, verse 7 ties back to chapter 6's instructions for family education. Verse 8 begins the story of Israel with Yahweh's choice of them at the creation. The Dead Sea Scrolls and Septuagint read: "when the Most High divided the nations, as he spread out the children of Adam, he established the portions of the nations according to the number of the angels of God." This reading, because it is harder to fit within a strictly monotheistic framework, must be more original than the Masoretic Text's reading (see the NIV note). God takes a special interest in Israel, in contrast to lesser deities who rule the nations.

Verses 12 and 15–17 insult these gods and criticize Israel (though not Gentiles) for worshiping them. The translation *demons* in verse 17 renders the Hebrew *shedim*, a word borrowed from Akkadian and referring to household spirits. The word does not imply that these beings were evil, but that worshiping them was inappropriate for Israelites.

32:19–25 Like the prophets, this section envisions foreign invasion as the due penalty of idolatry. The descriptions of disaster graphically represent the results of warfare. The *deadly plague* of verse 24 probably refers to smallpox (Christensen 807). For parallels to these forms of suffering, see Jeremiah 15; Lamentations 2. On God as the bringer of plague, see Habakkuk 3:5.

32:26–38 The drama of devastation takes a turn for the better when Yahweh considers the public relations implications of destroying Israel. The concern with the nations' viewpoint on Yahweh and Israel appears elsewhere in the Pentateuch (for example, Exod 15:14–16; 32:12–13; Num 14:13–16). This concern for God's reputation derives from God's love for Israel and eagerness to show mercy to them. Hence God can have compassion (verse 36), demonstrated in part through the removal of false gods, who cannot save in the first place.

32:39–43 The song concludes with God's self-description. Yahweh as the divine warrior, boasts not in an ability to destroy, but in one to save Israel. Verse 43 returns to the theme of the Gentiles' observation of Israel's God at work.

32:44–52 This prose section consists of two subsections, marking a transition to the end of the book. Verses 44–47 close off the poem by inviting its hearers and later singers to teach it to their children (compare chapter 6; Ps 78:1–8). Israel is to be a culture of memory and spiritual reflection. Verses 48–52 move the narrative forward to the scene of Moses' death, Mount Nebo. Together, the paragraphs remind the reader that Moses' words do not concern only his generation but all subsequent ones. Verse 51 explains why Moses did not enter the land. At one level, the text remembers the historical fact that Moses worked only in Transjordan. At a deeper level, it makes a theological point: failure to recognize God's holiness "in the midst of the people" seriously breaches Moses' relationship with God. Whatever Moses' private doubts might be (and Exodus attributes doubt to him), publicly minimizing God's centrality to the work of grace, as Moses did in Numbers 20, keeps him out of the land. As elsewhere in the Bible, the Pentateuch avoids making a human leader an unblemished hero.

MOSES' BLESSING OF ISRAEL · 33:1–29

Like Genesis (with chapter 49), Deuteronomy almost concludes with a blessing of the tribes. Deuteronomy 33 consists of a series of blessings on each tribe (verses 6–25), framed by more general blessings (verses 2–5, 26–29). Verse 1 introduces the song as a *blessing*, thus tying it to a major theme in the Pentateuch (for example, Gen 12; 15; 17) and in Deuteronomy itself (Deut 12:15; 16:17; 23:6; 30:1; 33:1, 23). As elsewhere in the Bible (for example, Exod 15; 1 Sam 2), a poem appears in the middle of a story to remind the reader that this is a well-known story. Apparently, singers recited such poems at major festivals, and such songs may have been well known.

33:1–5 The song opens by describing Yahweh's arrival from a distance. *Seir*, the hilly flanks of Edomite territory and southward from the land of Israel, also appears as Yahweh's place of origin in old poetry (Judg 5:4). Other poetry (Hab 3:3) locates God in Teman and Paran (as here), near the modern border between Jordan and Saudi Arabia. But all these texts agree in finding God outside the land of Israel and to its southeast, probably reflecting the origins of worship of Yahweh in that area (also known as Midian).

The Hebrew of these verses is more obscure than the NIV indicates, and verse 3 in particular is hard to translate, since "his holy ones" and "your hands" seem hard to connect. Verse 4 makes sense in the NIV, and it indicates the centrality of the law of Moses to Israelite life as God's gift to the nation. Verse 5's *He was king* has an uncertain antecedent. The nearest noun is *Moses*, but since he nowhere else wears the title *king*, the more likely bearer of the title here is Yahweh. It is also possible to translate the verse as "let there be a king in Jeshurun," which could be the people's worshipful cry acknowledging their submission to God (Craigie 394). Such acclamations of divine kingship do appear in Psalms 96–99. *Jeshurun* is a poetic name for Israel (much as one calls New York City "the Big Apple").

33:6–25 Nelson (387) divides the blessings into three categories: undirected wishes, prayers addressed to God, and "descriptions of tribal lifestyle and situation." Arguably, the prolonged attention to Joseph indicates that the poem originated in northern Israel, but this is uncertain. The sense that Reuben barely survives (verse 6), the absence of Simeon from the list, and the location of Dan in the northeast (verse 22; on the tribe's move, see Judg 18) all point to a date of composition no earlier than about 1050 BCE and possibly significantly later. On the other hand, the Hebrew of the text cannot be too late, and the poem must date from before the Babylonian exile.

The blessing of Levi (verses 8–11) emphasizes the tribe's role in discerning the will of God, their loyalty at the revolt at Massah and Meribah (merging the stories of Exod 17 and Num 20 with that of Exod 32:26–29; see Nelson 389), and their service as teachers of the nation and as sacrificers. Verse 11's surprising request *smite the loins* (not heads or other body parts) calls for a poetic justice against those who threaten the tribe in a way that puts family loyalty after faithfulness to God.

> **Urim & Thummim**
> *Devices that allowed the priests to answer yes-no questions so as to discover the will of God. This form of divination was permissible in ancient Israel, though it died out by the end of the First Temple period (before 586 BCE). Postexilic Jews often prayed for the restoration of the Urim and Thummim as a sign of divine favor (see Neh 7:65).*

The blessing of Joseph (thus Ephraim and Manasseh, the largest tribes in the northern kingdom) emphasizes material prosperity. The phrase *moon can yield* (verse 14) may refer either to the alleged influence of the heavenly bodies on human life (see Ps 121:6) or to the monthly natural cycles. Quasi-mythological language appears in the pair *ancient mountains* and *everlasting hills* (verse 15), with Israel recognizing its late arrival in a long-cultivated land. Verse 17 uses common princely language (Num 23:22; 24:8; Ps 2:8; Isa 52:10). Nelson (391) guesses that the two horns are Ephraim and Manasseh, but this seems unnecessarily literal-minded. Verse 19 probably refers to Mount Tabor as a place of sacrifice, demonstrating that the poem predates the book of Deuteronomy undoubtedly by a long enough time that it could gather so much authority that the Deuteronomists felt unable to modify it to fit their own theology.

33:26–29 The psalm closes by celebrating Yahweh's, and thus Israel's, incomparability. The image of God as the *one who rides on the heavens ... and on the clouds* (verse 26) draws on ancient Canaanite portrayals of Baal as the "rider on the clouds." Not the foreign deity – but Israel's God – is the true ruler of the universe. Yet this God does not merely rule in power but offers protection to Israel. God's "eternal arms," like the "eternal hills" of verse 15, furnish the nation with stability and orient them to their true identity. God's protection takes tangible form in abundant food, always precarious in premodern societies, and in protection from enemies, a constant need in a small society like ancient Israel. The final verse emphasizes the unity of the nation as more than a band of tribes but as a religious community serving an incomparable God.

THE DEATH OF MOSES · 34:1–12

Medieval Jewish commentators attributed this chapter to Joshua (Ibn Ezra 181), since Moses could not have described his own death. Modern scholars have cited this story as evidence for a complex literary history for the book. As it stands, chapter 34 ends not only Deuteronomy but the entire Pentateuch, by marking the transition from the nation's founder to his successors. Joshua 1 continues the story.

The chapter consists of four parts: Moses' departure (1–4); his death and burial (5–8); the succession of Joshua (9; compare Josh 1:1–9); a summary comment on Moses' career (10–12). The chapter summarizes the key theological ideas of the Pentateuch: God has kept the promises to the ancestors (verse 4), a fulfillment toward which all the Pentateuch leads; and God communicates through prophetic figures, especially Moses, whose legacy remains whenever Israel reads the texts of the Torah.

Verse 6 notes that Moses' grave is unknown, perhaps in order to dissuade would-be pilgrims to it, who might even make offerings to his spirit (Tigay 338). Unlike the patriarchs, he did not receive burial in the promised land.

The concluding paragraph comments not only on Moses but on all subsequent spokespersons for God. Moses' role had no parallel because of his miracle-working. These actions serve also to legitimize his words and thus the words of the book of Deuteronomy.

THEOLOGICAL REFLECTIONS

Deuteronomy both draws together older legal and narrative traditions and interprets them in light of core theological ideas so as to make them usable for a new day. At one level, the key ideas of the book are clear: Israel, the redeemed people, should serve the one God, Yahweh, and in doing so will enjoy a life of joy and plenty in its own land and thus will witness to other nations of the goodness of the redeemer God. While the book sorts through the actual practices of ancient Israelite religion to identify those that reflect the larger vision of the one God and to reject those that do not, it does so by connecting its sometimes innovative thinking to the deepest beliefs of the people.

At another level, however, it is difficult to reduce Deuteronomy to a set of discrete ideas. Rather, the book offers a total picture of the redeemed people. Thus, for example, law serves to better individuals, families, and the nation because, as Fretheim puts it (186), "God is concerned about the best possible life for all of God's creatures." The law does not serve its own ends but gives shape to Israel's vocation as a people finishing God's creation (Fretheim 189).

For Christians, Deuteronomy points to the desire of the God who redeems to be also the God who sanctifies a people. While the Torah does not apply to us in the same way it does to Jews, we recognize in its search for ordered freedom the pursuit we also undertake, for in it we recognize the God who also redeems us.

FOR FURTHER STUDY

Roger E. van Harn, ed., *The Ten Commandments for Jews, Christians, and Others* (Grand Rapids: Eerdmans, 2007).

Joseph T. Leinhard, ed., *Exodus, Leviticus, Numbers, Deuteronomy* (Downers Grove, Ill.: InterVarsity, 2001).

WORKS CITED

C. T. Begg, "The Destruction of the Calf (Exod 32,20/Deut 9,21)," in *Das Deuteronomium: Entstehung, Gestalt und Botschaft* (ed. Norbert Lohfink; Leuven: University Press, 1985), 208–51.

Georg Braulik, *The Theology of Deuteronomy* (trans. Ulrika Lindblad; North Richland Hills, Tex.: BIBAL, 1994).

Marc Brettler, "A 'Literary' Sermon in Deuteronomy 4," in *"A Wise and Discerning Mind": Essays in Honor of Burke O. Long* (ed. Saul Olyan and Robert Culley; Providence, R.I.: 2000), 33–50.

Halet Çambel, *Corpus of Hieroglyphic Luwian Inscriptions*, vol. 2: *Karatepe-Aslantaş* (Berlin: de Gruyter, 1999).

Duane Christensen, *Deuteronomy* (2 vols.; Nashville: Nelson, 2001–2002).

Peter Craigie, *The Book of Deuteronomy* (Grand Rapids: Eerdmans, 1976).

DEUTERONOMY

Abraham ibn Ezra, *The Commentary of Abraham ibn Ezra on the Pentateuch*, vol. 5: *Deuteronomy* (trans. Jay Shachter; Hoboken: Ktav, 2003).

Terence Fretheim, "Law in the Service of Life: A Dynamic Understanding of Law in Deuteronomy," in *A God So Near: Essays on Old Testament Theology in Honor of Patrick D. Miller* (ed. Brent Strawn and Nancy Bowen; Winona Lake, Ind.: Eisenbrauns, 2003), 183–200.

Anselm Hagedorn, *Between Moses and Plato: Individual and Society in Deuteronomy and Ancient Greek Law* (Göttingen: Vandenhoeck & Ruprecht, 2004).

Robert G. Hall, "Circumcision," *Anchor Bible Dictionary* 1 (1992): 1025–31.

William Hallo and K. Lawson Younger, eds., *The Context of Scripture* (3 vols.; Leiden: Brill, 2003).

Philip J. King and Lawrence Stager, *Life in Biblical Israel* (Louisville: Westminster John Knox, 2001).

James Kugel, *The Bible as It Was* (Cambridge: Harvard University Press, 1997).

Timothy Lenchak, *"Choose Life!" A Rhetorical-Critical Investigation of Deuteronomy 28,69–30,20* (Rome: Pontifical Biblical Institute, 1993).

Bernard Levinson, "The Reconceptualization of Kingship in Deuteronomy and the Deuteronomistic History's Transformation of Torah," *Vetus Testamentum* 51 (2001): 511–34.

Norbert Lohfink, *Theology of the Pentateuch: Themes of the Priestly Narrative and Deuteronomy* (trans. Linda Maloney; Minneapolis, Minn.: Fortress, 1994).

A. D. H. Mayes, "Deuteronomy 14 and the Deuteronomic World View," in *Studies in Deuteronomy* (ed. F. García Martínez et al.; Leiden: Brill, 1994), 165–81.

A. R. Millard, "Arameans," *Anchor Bible Dictionary* 1 (1992): 345–50.

Patrick Miller, "The Wilderness Journey in Deuteronomy: Style, Structure, and Theology in Deuteronomy 1–3," in *Israelite Religion and Biblical Theology: Collected Essays* (Sheffield: Sheffield Academic Press, 2000), 572–92.

R. W. L. Moberly, *Prophecy and Discernment* (Cambridge: Cambridge University Press, 2006).

Richard J. Nelson, *Deuteronomy* (Louisville: Westminster John Knox, 2002).

Juha Pakkala, *Intolerant Monolatry in the Deuteronomistic History* (Göttingen: Vandenhoeck & Ruprecht, 1999).

Gerhard von Rad, *Deuteronomy* (Philadelphia: Westminster, 1966).

David Reimer, "Concerning Return to Egypt: Deuteronomy XVII 16 and XXVIII 68 Reconsidered," in *Studies in the Pentateuch* (ed. J. A. Emerton; Leiden: Brill, 1990).

Sandra Richter, *The Deuteronomistic History and the Name Theology* (Berlin: de Gruyter 2002).

Alexander Rofé, *Deuteronomy: Issues and Interpretation* (London: T & T Clark, 2002).

Stephen Sherwood, *Leviticus, Numbers, Deuteronomy* (Collegeville, Minn.: Liturgical, 2002).

Jeffrey Tigay, *Deuteronomy* (Philadelphia: Jewish Publication Society, 1996).

Peter T. Vogt, *Deuteronomic Theology and the Significance of Torah: A Reappraisal* (Winona Lake, Ind.: Eisenbrauns, 2006).

Moshe Weinfeld, *Deuteronomy and the Deuteronomic School* (1972; reprint ed.; Winona Lake, Ind.: Eisenbrauns, 1992).

———, *Deuteronomy 1–11* (New York: Doubleday, 1991).

Charles Arthur Willard, "Argument," in *Encyclopedia of Rhetoric and Composition* (ed. Theresa Enos; New York: Garland, 1996), 16–26.

Ziony Zevit, *The Religions of Ancient Israel: A Synthesis of Parallactic Approaches* (London: Continuum, 2001).

Joshua

Phillip E. McMillion

CHAPTER CONTENTS

Contexts   237
Commentary   237
- Possession of the Land of Canaan · 1:1–12:24   237
- Allocating the Land to the Tribes · 13:1–21:45   242
- Farewell Speeches & Conclusion · 22:1–24:33   246

Theological Reflections   248
For Further Study   248
Works Cited   248

MAPS, TABLES, & FEATURES

Jericho   240
Ai   241
"O Sun stand still…"   242

The book of Joshua continues the story begun in the Pentateuch. Part of God's promise to the patriarchs is the giving of the land of Canaan. Deuteronomy 9:5 repeats this promise, but its primary fulfillment occurs in Joshua. This promise of the land becomes one of the major themes in Joshua. A second theme is that the great victories over the Canaanites come only with God's help. A third theme is the importance of faithfulness and obedience by God's people.

CONTEXTS

The book is primarily prose narrative, although poetry, boundary lists, city lists, and speeches also appear. The style of the book is straightforward, and there are few serious textual problems. In Jewish Bibles, Joshua begins the section called the Former Prophets, which includes Joshua, Judges, Samuel, and Kings. In Christian Bibles these are the Historical Books.

The book relates the events following the death of Moses. Joshua takes the people across the Jordan where they begin to take possession of Canaan. Joshua divides the land among the various tribes and encourages them to be faithful to God. The purpose of the book is not simply to relate historical facts in a modern sense. Rather, the writer uses history to teach Israel what the Lord had done for them and to admonish them to be obedient in the new land.

There is no strong tradition of authorship in Joshua. Joshua 24:25–26 report an instruction to Joshua to write down the newly contracted covenant, but this command does not extend to the entire book. Joshua 24:31 indicates that the book was written a number of years after the death of Joshua, but just how long is uncertain. Some place the writing of the book soon after the events, in the time of the judges or early monarchy. Most scholars date it considerably later and view it as one part of the survey of Israel's history stretching from Deuteronomy through Joshua, Judges, Samuel, and Kings (Noth 12). This larger work, the Deuteronomistic History, comes from a later writer who uses Israel's past to teach lessons about faithfulness and obedience.

COMMENTARY

POSSESSION OF THE LAND OF CANAAN · 1:1–12:24

1:1–18   A new period in Israel's history has begun. Moses, the great leader, is dead. Joshua will guide Israel into their new home. Joshua continues the work of Moses, though, as Deuteronomy 34:10 indicates, without his stature.

As verse 2 first notes, and the rest of the book emphasizes, the *land* is a gift from the Lord. It is not won by military might but through the power of God. God's promise to give the land is about to be fulfilled. To emphasize that the land is a gift, verse 4 situates Israel's borders at the widest possible bounds of Israelite influence. No Israelite state actually governed all that territory, but the book describes its boundaries in order to encourage the readers to trust in God.

The charge, *be strong and courageous*, is repeated in verses 7, 9, and 18. Since God is with him, Joshua should be strong. Along with Joshua's new authority comes the obligation to be a faithful leader. Part of the leader's role is to reflect on Torah (compare Ps 119:15–16, which emphasizes the joy of doing so). This term

JOSHUA

for *meditate* (verse 8) is rare in Hebrew but appears in almost the same form in Psalm 1:2.

> **"Meditate on God's law ..."**
> It is significant that both the opening of the Former Prophets (Josh 1:8) and the opening of the Writings (Ps 1:2), two major segments of the Hebrew Bible, exhort their readers to meditate on God's law day and night. As with the wise person of Psalm 1, if Joshua is faithful, God will be with him.

With his leadership role confirmed (verses 10–11), Joshua begins to make preparations to carry out his commission. This great work is possible only with the Lord's help. He first takes up the task of settlement by granting land east of the Jordan River to two and a half tribes (see Num 32). These tribes must help the others secure their territory west of the Jordan since the same God is giving territory to both groups.

The chapter's conclusion in verses 17–18 reinforces Joshua's role as the new leader. His word is like the word of God. He owns a copy of the law. He will lead them across the Jordan as Moses led them across the Red Sea.

2:1–24 Even though God has promised to give the land, Joshua makes careful preparations for the settlement. The spies select a house where strangers will attract little attention. Their plan fails when the king's informers report these events immediately. Meanwhile, Rahab hides the men and prepares a story to deceive the king's men. The text does not criticize the lie she tells, but celebrates the fact that God can use unexpected people to further the divine purpose.

The speech of Rahab in verses 8–11 both explains why she helped the Israelite spies and allows the narrator to state a theological rationale for the defeat of the Canaanites. The speech echoes several passages from Deuteronomy (Deut 11:25, 3:1–3, 4:39). Rahab expresses her faith that Yahweh is at work in these events. She has heard what the Lord has done for Israel. Even Rahab can find deliverance if she has faith in God (compare Matt 1:5, Heb 11:31). The lesson for Israel is that they should show a similar faith.

However, Rahab is no starry-eyed idealist. In verses 12–13, Rahab asks for a promise of rescue for both herself and her family when Israel takes the city. She shows the Israelites kindness, and asks for kindness in return.

In verse 14, the Hebrew terms translated *kindly* and *faithfully* are the Hebrew words *chesed* and *'emet*, both of which have already appeared in verse 12. Exodus 34:6 and other texts use these same terms to depict God's very nature (compare Pss 25:10, 86:15, and 117:2). The God who gives Israel the land also extends loyalty and mercy to those who cooperate in the divine work, even when they are Canaanites.

Verses 17–24 chart a transition in the story as Rahab conspires with the Israelites against Jericho, marking her house with the scarlet cord, and as the spies return to their people and report the morale of the city. Again, the narrator stresses God's provision of the land to Israel and Israel's protection of the innocent in imitation of God's own work.

3:1–4:24 The story progresses in chapters 3–4 as Joshua leads Israel to the camp beside the Jordan. The people wait three days until they see the *ark* carried toward the Jordan. The ark, as the symbol of God's presence, provides a link to chapter 2 and emphasizes that the Lord will lead them into the land. The

> **The Ark of the Covenant**
> The ark of the covenant represented the presence of the Lord. The top was decorated with two cherubim facing each other. Their wings arched up to form a platform that was the throne for the invisible God (Exod 37:1–9).

presence of the Lord is awesome and dangerous (compare 2 Sam 6:7), so the people keep a safe distance. As part of the unfolding pre-invasion ritual, the people purify themselves as if they are going into battle (1 Sam 21:5). The term used in 3:5 for *amazing things* [Hebrew *nifla'ot*] also appears in Exodus 3:20 and Judges 6:13 of God's work of deliverance from Egypt. The Lord will do amazing things on behalf of Israel.

Verse 6 portrays Joshua instructing the priests to move. Such repetition sounds awkward to modern ears, but is typical of Old Testament narratives.

In verses 7–8 God begins to carry out the promise to be with Joshua. Joshua, like Moses earlier, converses with Yahweh.

Verses 9–13 explore the roles of both God and Israel. God's presence leads to the giving of the land. This list of the groups within the land appears frequently in the Pentateuch and normally contains six to eight groups (see, for example, Deut 20:17). As *Lord of all the earth*, God may give the land to Israel. As for Israel, the reason for this selection of twelve men (one per tribe) does not become clear until 4:2. To underscore the miraculous nature of the divine-human relationship, verse 13 previews what will happen when the priests step into the water.

In verses 14–17, the reference to *flood stage* makes it clear that this is no normal crossing. Various explanations such as an earthquake or a mudslide have been suggested to explain this event. The Bible gives no explanation except that it is the Lord's work. The term *dry ground* appears twice in verse 17 and links the story with the crossing of the sea in Exodus 14. There is also a connection with God's work in Genesis 1 where God created the world by making dry ground.

Joshua 4:1–3 repeat the instructions from 3:12 with slight variations. The men are to carry twelve stones from the river as a memorial for the twelve tribes (see Exod 24:4). The text locates the stones at the spot *where the priests stood*, emphasizing the priests' role and the religious nature of the entry into the land. Joshua insists that God is at work in this process. Thus according to verses 4–7, the stones serve as a reminder of God's action. The historical books show a consistent concern for the instruction of future generations. Israelite history-writing does not simply chronicle events, but teaches the meaning behind the events. The stones give parents an opportunity to retell their children how God worked in these events (see Deut 6:20–25).

In verses 8–9, Israel obeys the Lord's command. The Hebrew text of verse 9 indicates that Joshua set up twelve stones in the midst of the river. These stones were apparently separate from those taken out of the river (see Nelson 69). However, the NIV translation, recognizing the awkwardness of the Hebrew phrasing, assumes that there is only one set of stones that are taken from the river and set up on the bank. This marker, like the ark of the covenant, highlights the theological importance of this event. The writer reflects on these events from a later vantage point.

Verses 10–14 report the fulfillment of promises. *The men of Reuben, Gad, and the half tribe of Manasseh* keep the promise they made to Moses (Num 32:32). God keeps the promises made to Joshua in 1:5 and 3:7. Just as Moses led Israel across the sea, so now Joshua leads them across the Jordan.

In verses 15–18, after everything is completed, the Lord tells Joshua to instruct the priests to *come up out of the Jordan*. The instructions are repeated as Joshua gives the command, and then repeated again as the priests carry out the command. The repetition is characteristic of biblical narratives, and it again emphasizes the solemnity of the occasion.

Verses 19–24 report the creation of a holy site at Gilgal. This site is anticipated in Joshua 4:3 but finally named in verses 19–20. The memorial stones serve as a reminder to future generations of what the Lord has done. The question "What are these stones?" is reminiscent of the question in Deuteronomy 6:20, "What are these statutes?" In both cases, the question concerns the meaning of the stones or the statutes. In each passage the meaning is related to what God has done. In Joshua 4, it is a reminder of how God helped the people cross the Jordan as they had crossed the Red Sea. One purpose was to be a testimony to the nations, and second to remind Israel to obey the Lord. In the Old Testament fear of the Lord is often linked with obedience (Deut 6:2; Josh 24:14).

> **Gilgal**
>
> The name of several locations in the Bible. The Hebrew word *gilgal* probably comes from the verb *galal*, "to roll," thus allowing the wordplay in Joshua 5:9, I have rolled [*galloti*] the reproach.... *Gilgal was an important religious site through early Israelite history*.

5:1–6:27 This section first mentions kings representing all who oppose Israel. Verse 1's "their hearts melted" echoes Joshua 2:11. When the spies went to Jericho, the people had heard of God's work at the sea. Now, they have heard of God's work at the Jordan. In both cases, God gives success if the people trust the Lord. This lesson continued to be important for later generations of Israelites as it is today. The remainder of this chapter narrates three important events that mark a new phase in the life of Israel. Along the way, it intertwines theological reflections on Israel's past and future.

First, God commands circumcision since it was neglected in the wilderness (verses 2–9). The text expands on the first action with several theological reflections, such as explaining the death of the adult men as the fulfillment of God's decree (Num 14:20–35) and repeating the common phrase *a land flowing with milk and honey* (which appears only here in Joshua). In this section, the Israelites renew their practice of circumcision as one aspect of their obedience to God. This is part of their preparation for moving into the new land.

Second, the people prepare to occupy the land by observing the Passover there (verses 10–12). A clear transition occurs when *the manna stopped*, and they begin to eat the produce of the land. The renewal of circumcision and the observance of Passover emphasize the need for obedience as the people move into the land. Faithful obedience is important throughout Israel's history.

Third, a divine messenger appears *with a drawn sword* (verses 13–15). Joshua asks, *Are you for us or our enemies?* The man replies, *Neither, but as commander of the army of the Lord I have come.* The answer may suggest that the Lord does not take sides. Israel must choose the Lord's side. When Joshua asks for a message, the only command given is to recognize and submit to the Lord's control. These words echo the command to Moses in Exodus 3:5. As Moses humbled himself before he led the people out of the old land, so Joshua humbles himself before he leads the people into the new land.

> **The Army of the Lord**
> In a number of passages, God fights on behalf of Israel (Josh 10:14; Judg 5:20–23; 2 Sam 5:24; Hab 3). Joshua 5:14 speaks of, literally, the "commander of the Host of the Lord." Similar language is used in other passages to refer to God as the "Lord of Hosts."

Chapter 6 turns to the siege of Jericho itself. In the ancient world, one method of attacking fortified cities was to cut off all supplies and lay siege. According to 6:2–5, the fall of Jericho is a foregone conclusion since God works on behalf of Israel. Joshua receives careful instructions on how to conduct the campaign. The description sounds more like a worship procession than a battle plan. This emphasizes the fact that the defeat of Jericho is God's work, not the work of a human army. Using the technique of repetition seen so often in these chapters, verses 6–14 picture Joshua passing on the instructions from the Lord to the priests who lead this worship procession. No battle cry is needed since this is not a human battle.

On the last day of the ceremony, the priests lead the procession around the city seven times (verses 15–21). The people shout a battle cry, or perhaps a cry of worship and praise for what the Lord has done. The term *devoted* [Hebrew *cherem*] means totally given over to the Lord through destruction (see verses 18, 21). The concept is similar to a whole burnt offering which is totally given to the Lord when it is consumed on the altar (Lev 27:28–29; 1 Sam 15). However, the *cherem* is not an offering per se. In this case, the devoted city is not used for human gain. It is totally given to God, and is banned from any human use. Rahab and her family are spared because she helps the spies when they come to Jericho. Any spoil goes to the Lord. Anything kept by the people will bring disaster. Interpreters have offered many explanations for the collapse of the walls, from earthquakes to sound vibrations. Scripture does not attempt to explain how this happened except that the Lord did it.

The story concludes by tying up loose ends. In verses 22–23, Joshua instructs the spies to bring Rahab to safety as they had promised. Since Rahab is not Israelite, she may live nearby but outside the camp in order to preserve the purity of the camp that is holy to the Lord. Verses 24–26 emphasize that the instructions of the Lord concerning the destruction are carried out to the letter. As a final blow, the city is cursed and is not to be rebuilt (but see 1 Kgs 16:34). Finally, verse 27 reminds the reader that God has made Joshua Moses' successor. The first victory in the land serves as a model of how faithfulness to the Lord is crucial for the people in their new land. It also speaks to later generations when they look to their own history for lessons to guide them after the exile.

7:1–26 This chapter links to chapter 6 through the mention of the devoted things. Here, however, *Achan's* inattention to them causes a problem that

> **Jericho**
> Jericho has been the site of much scholarly investigation, and it has been the subject of much debate. Three major archaeological investigations have explored Jericho. From 1907–1911 a German team led by E. Sellin and C Watzinger dug there. From 1929–1936, John Garstang led a second work. Kathleen Kenyon led a third work from 1952 to 1958. The first group excavated before the importance of pottery was fully understood and may have discarded important pottery evidence. Garstang believed he had found the destruction layer from the time of Joshua, but Kenyon dated that destruction long before Joshua. Kenyon found only scant evidence of occupation that could be related to the time of Joshua. More recently, Bryant Wood has contested Kenyon's findings, although he has not gained widespread scholarly support. The site is badly eroded and the three expeditions as well as a modern road have disturbed much of the evidence. At present it is difficult to draw any firm conclusions based on the archaeology of Jericho (Holland 224).

> **Ai**
>
> The site of Ai is usually identified with et-Tell, about one mile southeast of Beitin, although other sites in the area have been suggested. Excavating at et-Tell 1933–1935, Judith Marquet-Krause found remains dating from before 2400 BCE. There was a long gap in the occupation of the site, and a later occupation sometime after 1200 BCE. Joseph A. Callaway led a second expedition at et-Tell from 1964 into the 1970s. Callaway found the same gap in occupation that the earlier expedition had found. The later city was much smaller than the earlier one. The problem is that during the period usually suggested for the Israelite settlement, Ai appears to have been unoccupied. Callaway suggested that the conquest of Ai may have been later than traditionally thought and that the city may have been smaller than previously believed. Other possible sites in the area have been explored, but none have won wide support (Cooley 33).

Joshua and the Israelites only discover as the narrative unfolds. Joshua and the army of Israel will feel the weight of God's wrath when they attack Ai (a name that means "ruin").

The initial report (verses 3–5) suggests an easy victory requiring only a small force. The narrative does not explain how the defeat took place. The point is not to emphasize the military tactics, since failure to depend on God is the real cause of defeat.

Verses 6–18 describe a series of rituals by which Joshua discovers the cause of defeat. (The process resembles that for the selection of Saul as king [1 Sam 10:20–22].) Joshua asks why God brought them this far only to allow them to be defeated. He also reminds God of what the nations will think when they hear this (compare Exod 32:12; Num 14:13–16). As part of the conversation with Joshua, Yahweh reveals the cause of Israel's defeat, the theft of the *devoted things* (verses 11–12).

As the ritual of selection unfolds, Joshua discovers the guilty party. He seeks a confession of wrongdoing from Achan (verses 19–21). In a ritual execution (stoning), the nation eliminates Achan and everything connected to him. It may be that Achan's family has participated in the deception, or it may be that anyone who has come in contact with the forbidden goods must be removed. The site is named the "Valley of Trouble" [Hebrew *'emeq 'akor*]. The repeated use of the Hebrew letters *ayin* and *kaf* create a wordplay on the name Achan [Hebrew *'akan*]. In any case, the story reinforces the importance of faithfulness, since any disobedience can bring disaster. However, the story also underscores God's mercy, since only Achan's family is punished, and not all Israel (Auld 53).

8:1–35 The story continues with the charge, *do not be discouraged*, the same words God spoke to Joshua in 1:9. Now that the sin of Achan has been removed, God encourages Joshua to renew the attack on Ai. This time, the rules will change, for Israel may take the goods and livestock. The Israelite army is to use a ruse to draw away the defenders of the city (verses 3–8).

The phrase *thirty thousand* (verse 3) presents a problem, since such a large force could not well move undetected. Gray (71) has argued that the reading must be a scribal error for "three thousand" (Gray 71). Another option is to translate the Hebrew term "thousand" as "unit" or "platoon," hence thirty units of soldiers (Mendenhall 52). Joshua explains the plan of attack and sends out a raiding party. His is one of the classic tactics of military planning, but the victory still comes from Yahweh.

It would take some time to move around the city without being seen, so Joshua waits until the next morning to begin his second stage of the attack (verses 9–17). Joshua positions the remainder of his force. It is unclear whether the *five thousand men* is the group already set in ambush, since the relationship between verses 3 and 12 remains unclear. Critical scholars argue that the text interweaves two versions of the same story (Nelson 110–11). Others suggest that the story intentionally reflects the confusion of the king of Ai. Certainly verses 14–15 do present his confused viewpoint: he knows less than the readers of the narrative. Joshua and his men initiate the plan, and it works perfectly.

Verses 18–29 report the attack. The sign for it resembles that used by Moses at the crossing of the sea (Exod 14:16). At Joshua's signal, the men carry out the attack. The Canaanites are caught between the Israelite forces and destroyed. In accordance with the custom of the ban, the Israelite army kills all the city's inhabitants. Since the name Ai means "ruin," its location memorialized this story in Israel.

Verses 30–35 reflect the instructions of Moses in Deuteronomy 27. Mount Ebal lies 20 miles north of

Bethel and Ai, and it was one of the early centers of Israelite worship (see Josh 24). After the initial success at Jericho and Ai, all the people come together and renew their commitment to the Lord.

> **Taking the Land**
> *The end of Joshua 8 clearly reflects the instructions of Deuteronomy 27. The altar of uncut stones, the people standing on the two mountains, the reading of the law, all are elements from that chapter. As such, they show the Deuteronomistic History's interest in showing Israel as an obedient people in the initial phases of their life in the land.*

9:1–27 Israel's conquest of Jericho and Ai puts all the population on alert. Verse 1's list of peoples is typical and represents all the inhabitants of the land. They will unite against the Israelites, although the war is not described here. A similar coalition with different members appears in chapter 10.

Verses 3–6 introduce Gibeon, an important site in central Israel. Its inhabitants decide to use trickery rather than power to survive. Their plan involves considerable preparation to make it appear as if they have been traveling for many weeks. They carefully choose provisions, utensils, and clothes that support the deception. They seek to assure Israel that they will be no threat since they are from far away.

As the story unfolds (verses 7–15), the Israelites become suspicious until the Gibeonites show their old supplies as proof. The deception works, for Israel contracts a *treaty* [Hebrew *berit*, usually translated "covenant"] with the Gibeonites. The deception works because Israel fails to seek guidance from Yahweh. However, it is too late to go back on their word. The people are upset that their leaders have been deceived. They agree that the Gibeonites will be *woodcutters and water carriers*. At some level, the story explains how a group of Canaanites came to be in relationship to Israel (see verse 27).

In verses 22–23, Joshua confronts the Gibeonites asking why they deceived Israel. When Joshua relays the judgment, he adds woodcutters and water carriers *for the house of my God*.

The story ends with the Gibeonites explaining that they had heard that the Lord would give Israel the land and *wipe out all its inhabitants*. They had heard of the exodus just as the inhabitants of Jericho had. In keeping with the ancient theme of the Gentiles bearing witness to the saving work of Israel's God (see Exod 15:13–16), the Gibeonites testify to Israel's core story. Meekly, they agree to submit to the decision of Joshua. As the summary statement in verses 26–27 reports, Joshua spared them but makes them manual laborers *at the place the Lord would choose* (a phrase reflecting the language of Deuteronomy for Jerusalem; see Deut 12:5).

10:1–43 When *Adoni-Zedek hears* what happened to Ai, Jericho, and Gibeon, he defends his own power. He forms a coalition with four other kings in southern Palestine and attacks Gibeon, seeking its inhabitants to abandon their alliance with Israel and to make an example of them (verses 1–5). In response, the *Gibeonites* ask Joshua to honor their alliance by coming to their aid (verses 6–11). Joshua brings his army on a forced march of 15 miles to launch a surprise attack on the Canaanite kings. The text highlights the fact that Yahweh speaks to Joshua reassuring him that he will be victorious. The providential hailstorm leads to their victory (verses 10–11).

Verses 12–14 cite a poetic passage celebrating God's work for Israel. As in Exodus 14–15 and Judges 4–5, Joshua 10 first reports a victory in prose narrative and then quotes a song about the same event. Here, the victory over the five kings is told in verses 6–11 and then celebrated in the poetry of verses 12 and 13. According to verse 13, this story, or perhaps the poetry about it, comes from the now lost *Book*

> **"O sun, stand still …"**
> *The words* O sun, stand still *begin one of the most fascinating passages in the book. The traditional understanding is that this refers to a massive cosmic miracle where the sun stops, or the earth stops rotating on its axis and begins again. Others suggest that it involves a natural phenomenon such as an eclipse or the diffusion of the sun's light through the clouds of the storm. A third possibility is that this is symbolic language to show that the Lord has acted in a mighty way on behalf of Israel.*
>
> *Judges 5:20 states that* From the Heavens the stars fought *on behalf of Israel. Habakkuk 3:11 says,* The sun and moon stood still *in awe of God's victory. Isaiah 55:12 pictures all nature celebrating God's work for Israel. In each of these passages, elements of nature are personified as praising God. Similarly, Joshua 10 may also use poetic language to highlight the Lord's work.*

of Jashar. That book contained poetry celebrating Yahweh's victories (2 Sam 1:18). In verse 13, the clause *the sun stopped* may explain the poetry, or it may be a continuation of the quotation that goes through the end of verse 13. *There has never been a day like it before or since* refers to the fact that the Lord listened to Joshua and gave Israel the victory.

Verse 15 marks a transition between the preceding campaign and its aftermath in verses 16–42. Some scholars have suggested that this conclusion fits better in verse 43 where is occurs again. Verse 15 does not appear in the Septuagint and so is probably a late addition.

Verses 16–28 report the death of the five Amorite kings, who hide in a cave while the Israelites pursue the Canaanites. Since caves are often used for burial, their location there becomes a metaphor for their ultimate fate. The text chronicles in detail the death of the kings. Joshua commands the Israelite officers to *put your feet on the necks of these kings*. This humbles the kings, but perhaps even more importantly, it strengthens the Israelite leaders by allowing them to dominate their enemies with God's help. The text also specially mentions the destruction of Makkedah, a site in the hill country east of Jerusalem near Azekah, the exact location still unknown.

Verses 29–39 extend the theme of conquest of southern Palestinian cities by summarizing Joshua's campaigns there. Verses 40–42 offer an important summary statement that emphasizes God's role in leading Israel. Israel succeeds because they obey God's commands. Again, the narrator does not simply report the past, but instead teaches a lesson for later audiences as well.

11:1–23 The account now turns from southern to northern Palestine, where *Jabin* organizes a coalition. The author paints a graphic picture of this force that from Israel's perspective is *as numerous as the sand of the seashore*.

In verses 6–9, Yahweh assures Joshua that the Canaanites will lose. Moreover, Israelite should capture the Canaanites chariot units and *hamstring their horses and burn their chariots*. They should do so for two reasons. First, Israel has no experience in using such high-powered weapons and high-spirited horses. Second, these are the weapons of the pagans, and the weapons Israel has been warned against (Deut 17:16).

As the story continues in verses 10–15, *Joshua turned back and captured Hazor* since it was the leading city of the coalition. Once it was defeated, the others would fall. Joshua destroyed Hazor and burned the city. Amnon Ben-Tor, the archaeologist of Hazor, reports that a tremendous fire destroyed the city in the late 1200s BCE, roughly the time of Joshua (Ben-Tor 253–56). Archaeology cannot prove that Israel destroyed the city, but this destruction fits the biblical description. Verse 15 pictures Joshua as the faithful servant who carries on the work of Moses.

Hazor
A major site about 9 miles north of the Sea of Galilee, during the Late Bronze Age (about 1600–1200 BCE), Hazor was the leading city in Canaan, hence Joshua 11:10's reference to it as the head of all these kingdoms. *Judges 4–5 recount a later war between Israel and Hazor, curiously also involving a king named Jabin.*

Verses 16–20 summarize the work of Israel throughout northern Palestine. Since the war continued for a long time, these summary statements encompass a longer period than usually assumed, perhaps even many decades. The fact that the text comes from long after the time of Joshua also becomes clear in verses 21–23. The reference to *Judah* and *Israel* suggests that the writer knows of the division of the land after the death of Solomon. However, the text seeks to illustrate the faithfulness of Joshua and his generation in order to make the argument that the possession of the land comes through obedience.

12:1–24 Chapter 12 summarizes the two major divisions of Israel's conquest, east of the Jordan (verses 1–6) and west of it (verses 7–24). Several place names and personal names deserve explanation. The *Arnon* is the great valley that forms the southern border of the Ammonites. *Sihon* and *Og* are two kings whom Israel defeated (Num 21). The summary in verses 7–24 describes the territory west of the Jordan including a typical list of the six major groups of inhabitants of the land (compare Deut 20:17; Josh 9:1). Chapter 12 thus closes the first section of the book, describing the initial conquest of the land by Joshua.

ALLOCATING THE LAND TO THE TRIBES · 13:1–21:45

13:1–7 The next chapters (13–21) describe the allocation of the now conquered land to the twelve tribes. After the swift conquest, much remains to be done. God will drive out the inhabitants before Israel. Chapter 13 lists kings throughout the region and collects several different regional traditions of Israelite settlement.

In verse 6, *the other half of Manasseh, the Reubenites and the Gadites* are the tribes who receive land east of the Jordan. The boundaries extend from the Arnon in the south to Mount Hermon in the north. Verse 13 indicates that not all the conquest was quick and easy (see Josh 15:63; 16:10; 17:12–13). Verse 14 explains why the tribe of Levi did not receive land. They lived from the offerings that were presented, so they did not need land to grow their food.

The remainder of the chapter details the lands given to the tribes east of the Jordan. Such lists are important in the ancient world. No people could survive without territory. These boundary lists show that Israel has a legitimate claim on this land. They also demonstrate that God is concerned with the survival of Israel and provides a place for them.

14:1–15 Chapter 14 introduces the distribution of the land to the tribes west of the Jordan. The chapter falls into two sections: a summary of the entire distribution west of the Jordan (verses 1–5) and the special allocation to Caleb (verses 6–15).

Verse 2 emphasizes that this is done *as the Lord had commanded through Moses*. The Levites do not receive land but cities. This would make for only eleven tracts of land for the tribes. The number twelve comes from dividing the territory of Joseph between the tribes of Ephraim and Manasseh. Verse 5 concludes this opening subsection by reiterating that all has been done *as the Lord had commanded*. Most important is the fact that the land comes through the word of the Lord.

Verses 6–15 describe the allocation of land to Caleb, who receives the first portion for Judah. Retelling the story of Numbers 13–14 (compare Deut 1:35–36), the text celebrates Caleb's unusual fidelity as one of two survivors of the exodus. Joshua gives Caleb the city of Hebron, 20 miles southwest of Jerusalem. The narrative explains that the city of *Hebron used to be called Kiriath Arba* because its leading citizen was Arba the greatest of the Anakites. The story is thus an etiology explaining why the descendants of Caleb live in Hebron, and how the city once had another name.

> **Etiologies**
> Stories that explain the origins of a custom, name, or structure are known as etiologies. Examples in Joshua include the explanation of the twelve stones in Joshua 4, the name of Gilgal in 5:8–9, and Achor in chapter 7.

Then the land had rest from war repeats a phrase from Joshua 11:23 to emphasize that the major battles have concluded and the division of the land can proceed. Thus the verse introduces the long lists in chapters 15–21, which define the boundaries of the various tribes and their clans.

15:1–63 The boundaries for *Judah* appear first since Judah becomes the political and religious heart of the kingdom and the home of David. The boundary lines are traced with a variety of terms which make the narrative much more vibrant in Hebrew. The border goes out, crosses over, goes up, surrounds, goes down, and turns. This is of special interest to later readers who live within the borders described.

> **Extents of the Lands**
> Joshua 15 weaves together a set of boundaries and a list of towns. The boundary list may come from the united monarchy and the town list from the time of Josiah, or perhaps earlier (see Nelson 186).

The chapter includes several sidebars explaining the dispositions of particular regions. For example, verses 13–19 recount the allotment of Caleb. Verses 20–26 list the towns within the territory of Judah. Although these general locations are known, not all of the cities can be identified today. Verse 63 notes that *Judah could not dislodge the Jebusites*, informing the readers that there were exceptions to the total conquest of the land and explaining why Jerusalem fell only during the reign of David (2 Sam 5:5–10).

16:1–10 The text takes up the Joseph tribes next because they formed the core of the northern kingdom of Israel. The southern border of Joseph begins east of *Jericho* at the northern end of the Dead Sea and goes north into the hill country. There it turns southwest and moves past *Lower Beth-Horon, Gezer*, and to the Mediterranean. This separates Joseph from Benjamin and Judah. The specific boundaries of Ephraim appear in verses 5–9. Many of the place names are unknown, although the general boundaries are clear enough. The conclusion of the boundary section for Ephraim offers a sober reminder of the limits of Israel's control: verse 10's *they did not dislodge the Canaanites* is a reminder that not all people were conquered immediately. Joshua 10:33 states that the king of Gezer is completely defeated, but here Gezer remains in the hands of the Canaanites. The city did not pass to Israelite control until the reign of Solomon (1 Kgs 9:16–17).

17:1–18 Part of the *tribe of Manasseh* has already received the territory of *Gilead and Bashan* east of the Jordan. Manasseh's territory west of the Jordan is the focus of the remainder of the chapter. According to Numbers 26:29–32, Manasseh's son was Makir, and Makir's son was Gilead. Gilead had six sons who head the clans listed in 17:2.

Verses 3–6 link to the story in Numbers 27 and 36, according to which Zelophehad had no sons but five daughters. They remind Eleazar and Joshua that Moses had consulted the Lord on their behalf. They were given an inheritance along with the male descendents, and Joshua upholds this decision so that they receive land in the territory of Manasseh. In Joshua, the story may explain a custom among the tribe of Manasseh (see verse 6).

Verses 7–10 give the borders of Manasseh in general terms with the territory of Asher as its northern border and the southern border running from the city of *Micmethath* past *En Tappuah* and along the northern side of the *Kanah Ravine*. Verses 11–13 explain that Manasseh also had a right to territory within the boundaries of other tribes, Issachar and Asher, but was unable to govern it. Rather, they put the inhabitants to forced labor.

The text then transitions to a report of the Joseph tribes complaining to Joshua about their insufficient territory. Joshua suggests they clear the hill country and use it. They answer that this is still not enough and the cities are difficult to conquer because their troops use iron chariots, the era's state-of-the-art weapons. Joshua's word that they can conquer the cities if they wish is also a lesson intended for later audiences.

> **Chariots**
> *These light horse-drawn vehicles with spoked wheels able to carry one to three passengers came into use a little after 2000 BCE and proved effective weapons until the Greek phalanxes of Alexander the Great made them useless. Chariots charging into the untrained infantry of the Israelite militia would have enjoyed an enormous advantage under normal circumstances.*

18:1–28 Chapters 18 and 19 comprise a unit as indicated by references to *Shiloh* and the *Tent of Meeting* in 18:1 and 19:51. These chapters recount the allotment of the territory to the remaining tribes. Before this, the camp at Gilgal is the focus (Joshua 4:19–20, 5:2–12). Now, Shiloh moves to the center of the narrative, and the tent of meeting (another name for the tabernacle) is mentioned for the first time in Joshua. The tent represents the presence of God and emphasizes God's guidance (see Exod 33:7–11).

In verses 3–7, Joshua gives directions to the remaining tribes to survey the land and bring back a report. Joshua casts lots *in the presence of the Lord*. God is in control. These verses introduce a long section extending through 19:51. The repetition in verses 8–11 emphasizes the importance of these events. The assigning of territory begins with the phrase *the lot came up*. This introduction is repeated for each of the tribes through the end of chapter 19. In each case, the verb in Hebrew means either "came up" or "came out" referring to the lot that was cast.

The first tribe in this new list of allotments is Benjamin (verses 12–20). It comes first because of its proximity to Judah. Benjamin's northern border is the same as the southern border of Ephriam and Manasseh (Josh 16:1–5). Benjamin's short western border runs from *Beth Horon* to *Kiriath Jearim*. The southern boundary is similar to that given for Judah in 15:5–10, but the text here lists sites in reverse direction from west to east. The mention of *Geliloth* is unclear since in Joshua 15:7 it is Gilgal. The Hebrew word *gelilot* means "districts" or "territories," so the reference could be to the districts in this area. Alternatively, it could be a scribal error for Gilgal. The Aramaic paraphrase in the Targum has "Gilgal." The border on the eastern side is the Jordan River.

Chapter 18 concludes two lists of Benjamin's cities (verses 21–25). The first twelve lie in the eastern part of the tribal territory, and the second fourteen in the western part. Interestingly, Joshua 15:61 includes *Beth Arabah* among Judah's cities. Some suggest that it was a shared city, or that this list in chapter 18 reflects a later revision.

19:1–51 Chapter 19 summarizes the boundaries for the remaining tribes of Simeon (verses 2–9), Zebulun (verses 10–16), Issachar (verses 17–23), Asher (verses 24–31), Naphtali (verses 32–39), and Dan (verses 40–48). Joshua himself receives a town within the territory of Ephraim. Each tribal list ends with the phrase "by their clans" [Hebrew *lamishpachot*]. Apparently, each clan of the tribe centered around a single town.

The rest of the chapter locates the various tribes, often surfacing problems for contemporary historians. Verses 1 and 9 repeat that the territory of Simeon lies *within the territory of Judah*. Simeon is given scattered cities within Judah (Gen 49:5–7). Simeon later disappears as a tribe, probably absorbed into Judah.

The borders of Zebulun (verses 10–16) are difficult to identify since some locations such as *Japhia* and *Hannathon* are unknown today. The territory is the central hill country north of Ephraim and Manasseh. Issachar's (verses 17–23) boundaries are also problematic since several of the places are known only from boundary lists. *Beth Shemesh* in verse 22 is not the one in 1 Samuel 6 since that Beth Shemesh is southwest of Jerusalem and borders Philistine territory. Issachar's territory is north of Manasseh bounded by the Jordan on the east.

Verses 24–31 locate Asher north of Manasseh bounded by the Mediterranean on the west and Zebulun on the east (compare Gen 49:13). Verses 32–39 locate Naphtali north of Zebulun and between Asher and the Jordan. This is prime territory by the Sea of Galilee.

The allocation of Dan (verses 40–48) deserves attention. The mention of *Aijalon*, *Timnah*, *Ekron*, and *Gath* identify the original Danite territory along the Mediterranean coast in the land of the Philistines. Dan is unable to take possession of this, however, and abandons it for territory in the north. They conquer the city of Laish and rename it Dan (Judg 18).

This list of land grants closes with that to Joshua (verses 49–50) and a summary statement (verse 51) closing all of chapters 14–19. Fittingly, the land distribution begins with Caleb (Josh 14:6–15) and ends with Joshua. The dramatic summary of verse 51 notes that everything occurred with divine sanction and under divine direction.

20:1–21:45 Chapters 20 and 21 complete the details concerning the settlement of the land. The *cities of refuge* are identified in chapter 20 (compare Exod 21:12–14; Deut 19:1–14) and the Levitical cities in chapter 21. Moses set aside three cities east of the Jordan and gave instructions for the cities west of the Jordan (Deut 4:41–43).

The rest of chapter twenty spells out rules for the cities of refuge. First, the cities give shelter to one fleeing the avenger until there can be a trial. If the person is found innocent, he may return home after the death of the high priest (verses 4–6). The law owes a great deal to Deuteronomy 19. Second, three cities west of the Jordan are named as cities of refuge. Their locations north, central, and south on both sides of the Jordan give refugees convenient routes to safety. And, third, the law extends to *any alien living among them*.

Chapter 21 lists the clans of the tribes of Levi. As the story opens, *the Levites approached* the leaders of Israel asking for territory as the Lord promised. They receive cities within the territory of the other tribes (see also Gen 49:5–7). Whereas Deuteronomy 18:1–8 had allowed the tribe no inheritance, Joshua 21 apparently interprets the prohibition to mean that Levi could not have continuous territory like the other tribes. Thus they receive towns scattered throughout the entire land. They receive these towns owing to their faithfulness at the rebellion in Exodus 33:27–29, and because they are responsible for teaching the people (Lev 10:10). The teaching role will be easier if they live among the people.

Verses 4–42 list the allotments of the tribe. The Levites live in 48 cities and lands according to the descendents of the sons of Levi: Kohath, Gershon, and Merari. Several of the towns such as Gezer, Taanach, and Rehob, are listed in Judges 1 as not yet captured by Israel. Thus, in the context of Joshua, the list states a goal to be achieved over a long period of time, or an ideal achieved if the priests faithfully follow the Lord.

Verses 43–45 constitute a summary emphasizing the completeness of God's work. The Lord is faithful to do all that he promised.

FAREWELL SPEECHES & CONCLUSION · 22:1–24:33

22:1–34 The last three chapters are a series of farewell speeches. The first marks the departure of the tribes of Reuben, Gad, and half of Manasseh. They had promised to help the remaining tribes conquer the land west of the Jordan (see Num 32), and have kept their word. Joshua commends them and releases them to return to their territory. He also charges them to *be very careful to keep the commandment and the law* (verse 5). Using a stock expression of Deuteronomy, this verse combines the Hebrew verbs for "keep" [*shamar*] and "do" [*'asah*] in an idiom meaning "be careful to keep" (as in Deut 5:1, 5:32, 6:3, 6:25, 11:32).

Cities of Refuge

In a culture with inadequate police and judicial structures, the cities of refuge served an important purpose. In the case of accidental homicide, there would be a place of safety for the guilty party. This is necessary because of the practice of blood vengeance, in which a kinsman avenges a death (see Num 35:9–29).

According to verses 6–9, *Joshua blessed them* showing that the Lord approved their departure. All this was done *in accordance with the command of the Lord*. In keeping with the theme of national unity in faith, the narrative reports that the departing tribes build an altar west of the Jordan (verses 10–19). When the other tribes hear of this, they immediately assemble for war. The nine and a half tribes assume this altar is for false worship. They plan to stop this rebellion against God. They are also afraid that this unfaithfulness will bring God's wrath on them.

However, the story ends peacefully (verses 20–29), when *Reuben, Gad, and Manasseh* answer that this altar is not for false worship. It is a memorial to remind later generations of their link with the tribes in Canaan. The peaceful resolution of the conflict leads the Transjordanian tribes to name the memorial altar *A Witness Between Us that the Lord is God* (verses 30–34).

> **Sacrifice**
> This story assumes that the altar law of Deuteronomy 12 was the norm for Joshua's time. That law forbids sacrifice anywhere but Yahweh's designated place, eventually to be Jerusalem. At the same time, the story also acknowledges that some Israelites sacrificed at other locations, and it takes pains to stop that practice.

23:1–16 The conquest took longer than the quick victories at Jericho and Ai suggest. Joshua reminds them that *their victories are not by their own power*. There is still work to be done to possess the land.

Verses 6–13 use the language of Deuteronomy extensively including such expressions as *Be careful to obey* (see the comment on 22:5) and *without turning aside to the right hand or the left*, which means to remain faithful. The text warns the people not to follow the gods of the land, a temptation Israelites felt throughout their history. Rather, Joshua urges them *to love the Lord your God*. Like Deuteronomy 30, Joshua 22 presents two choices: in love and gratitude follow the God who acts on behalf of the people, or *turn away* to impotent idols and fail to receive God's blessing in the land.

The speech concludes (verses 14–16) with Joshua's final words presenting the two choices in clear distinction. They have seen how God has been faithful in keeping every promise. God's warnings are just as reliable as the promises. If they turn away from the Lord, they will not survive long in the land.

24:1–33 A number of scholars have suggested that this chapter has parallels to the typical form of treaties from the ancient Near East. (Mendenhall and Herion, "Covenant," 1179–1202). The chapter describes a ceremony of covenant renewal. This concluding unit of Joshua has five sections: an introduction (verse 1), Joshua's speech (verses 2–18), a dialogue between Joshua and the people (verses 19–24), a summary of the covenant renewal ceremony (verses 25–27), and a final notice of the death and his colleagues (verses 28–33).

> **Famous Last Words**
> *Several texts in the Old Testament contain the speeches of dying leaders. These testaments often predict future events as well as orient descendants to their duties. Examples include Genesis 49, 2 Samuel 23:1–7, and, in some respects, the book of Deuteronomy. Later Jews wrote many such testaments, the best-known being the* Testament of the Twelve Patriarchs.

The speech proper (verses 2–18) recounts God's acts of redemption and calls on Israel to respond by being obedient. As in much of the Bible, *fear of the Lord* (verse 14) is not terror of punishment, but a sense of awe and respect. The nations around Israel believe in many gods, and some of the Israelites are tempted to follow them as well. There were also foreigners present who had joined Israel (Exod 12:38). They are all challenged to *choose for yourselves this day whom you will serve* (verse 15). In light of all God has done for them, they are to choose to be faithful. Joshua leads by example with the rousing words *as for me and my household, we will serve the Lord* (verse 15).

The fitting response to such a stirring speech comes in verses 16–18 when the people affirm that they will serve the Lord. They review what God has done for them and promise to remain faithful.

Surprisingly, however, Joshua responds by questioning their ability to keep the covenant (verses 19–24). Joshua cautions them that it is a serious thing to accept this commitment because Yahweh *is a jealous God* (verse 19), meaning that God accepts no rivals. The people again affirm their commitment and witness against themselves. Joshua tells them they must *throw away the foreign gods*, a frank acknowledgment that the people have worshiped multiple deities in their history. The people reaffirm *we will serve the Lord*. The Hebrew terms for "we will serve the Lord" are the same words used by Joshua in verse 14, and repeated by the people in verses 18, 21, and 24.

Verses 25–27 use common elements in ancient treaties, a provision to keep a copy in a safe place. This was usually in some royal archive, but that is not possible here. The other important element in a treaty was the calling of witnesses. These were usually the gods and goddesses of the parties involved. Here, Joshua sets up a stone as a witness.

Verses 28–33 leave the speech event at Shechem and report the death of Joshua and his generation, tying up the loose ends of the book. The work of Joshua is completed. He led the people and charged them to remain faithful. He dies at the age of 110 and is buried in the land of his inheritance. Owing to his leadership, *Israel served the Lord* during his lifetime (verse 31). This is a fitting legacy to the memory of Joshua.

> **Finishing the Story**
> *Joshua ends by recalling the story of Joseph and the burial of his embalmed body in the land (see Gen 50). The book tries to tie up loose ends left from the Pentateuch.*

The book of Joshua begins with the death of Moses, and the charge to Joshua to be strong and faithful as the new leader. Now, at the end of the book, Joshua dies and is buried. He has fulfilled his role as leader, and has remained faithful to all that God has asked him to do.

THEOLOGICAL REFLECTIONS

The book of Joshua makes several crucial theological points. First, it shows that God fulfills the promises made in the Pentateuch, especially the promise to bless Israel with its own land. God is trustworthy and reliable. Although modern readers might find the details of boundaries and clans tedious, ancient readers would have seen in them the detailed fulfillment of promise and a constant reminder to respond to God's work by remaining faithful and obedient. The covenant is another way of describing this relationship between God and Israel. God has made a covenant with Israel. The Lord is faithful, and Israel is called to remain faithful.

Second, the book illustrates the key role of leaders. Joshua is a leader like Moses, and the people remain faithful during his life and the lives of the elders who follow him. By contrast, the later books of Judges, Samuel, and Kings will show the negative effects of unfaithful leaders.

Joshua thus moves Israel's story forward from the uncertainty of the period of the wilderness to the possibilities of a redeemed life awaiting them in the land. As part of the larger Deuteronomistic History, which ends in the tragedy of Babylonian exile, Joshua helps an exilic audience reflect on what might have been, and could be again. It thus speaks of hope in a redeeming God.

FOR FURTHER STUDY

Antony F. Campbell, S.J., *Joshua to Chronicles* (Louisville: Westminster John Knox, 2004).

Mary E. Mills, *Joshua to Kings: History, Story, Theology* (London: T. & T. Clark, 2006).

Carolyn Pressler, *Joshua, Judges, and Ruth* (Louisville: Westminster John Knox, 2002).

WORKS CITED

A. Graeme Auld, *Joshua, Judges, and Ruth* (Louisville: Westminster John Knox, 1984).

Amnon Ben-Tor, "Tel Hazor, 1993," *Israel Exploration Journal* 43 (1993): 253–56.

Robert E. Cooley, "Ai.," in vol. 1 of *The Oxford Encyclopedia of Archaeology in the Near East* (ed. Eric M. Meyers; Oxford: Oxford University Press, 1997): 32–33.

John Gray, *Joshua, Judges, Ruth* (Grand Rapids: Eerdmans, 1986).

Thomas A. Holland, "Jericho.," in vol. 3 of *The Oxford Encyclopedia of Archaeology in the Near East* (ed. Eric M. Meyers; Oxford: Oxford University Press, 1997): 220–24.

George E. Mendenhall, *Ancient Israel's Faith and History* (ed. Gary A Herion; Louisville: Westminster John Knox, 2001).

George E. Mendenhall and Gary Herion, "Covenant," *Anchor Bible Dictionary* 1 (1992): 1179–1202.

Richard Nelson, *Joshua* (Louisville: Westminster John Knox, 1997).

Martin Noth, *The Deuteronomistic History* (Sheffield: Sheffield Academic Press, 1981).

Judges

Phillip McMillion

CHAPTER CONTENTS

Contexts **249**

Commentary **250**

    Introduction · 1:1–3:6 **250**

    Accounts of the Judges · 3:7–16:31 **251**

    Israelite Society in Decline & Chaos · 17:1–21:25 **262**

Theological Reflections **265**

For Further Study **266**

Works Cited **266**

MAPS, TABLES, & FEATURES

The Twelve Tribes **250**

The book of Judges is a collection of accounts of various heroes who led Israel in the time before kingship. The first two chapters set the stage for this material and give the theme that binds together individual stories. Judges 2:11–19 contains the outline for much of the remainder of the book: Israel does evil in the sight of God, and so God gives them over to the power of their enemies who oppress them. Then the people cry out to God, who sends them a judge to deliver them. After a time, the people again turn away from the Lord, and the cycle begins all over again. One purpose is to show that the Lord gives Israel many opportunities to be faithful, and they continually turn away from God.

CONTEXTS

In chapters 17–21, a second theme appears with the phrase "In those days there was no king in Israel" (17:6; 18:1; 19:1; 21:25). The first and last occurrences add the phrase, "every man did what was right in his own eyes." This suggests a second theme, which is the chaos that occurred in society without a strong leader like a king. A second purpose for Judges, then, would be to illustrate the need for the monarchy in Israel.

The book of Judges is primarily a prose narrative. In addition to the stories about the judges, it also includes lists of cities in chapter 1, a long poem in chapter 5, and a parable in 9:8–15.

The book is set in the period following the initial conquest of the land and before the establishment of the monarchy. During this time, God uses various heroes to deliver Israel from those oppressing them. Israel alternates between periods of faithfulness and rebellion against the Lord. The last few chapters show the breakdown of society and point to the need for a strong central government. The period of the judges is often dated about 1250–1050 BCE (Block 26–27). The book gives a chronology based on the years of oppression and the years the various judges ruled. Some scholars, however, think that there may be some overlapping, with some judges ruling in different parts of the country at the same time.

> **Who Were the Judges?**
> The English term "judge" does not quite describe the role of the leaders in the book of Judges. Some of them did carry out legal or administrative roles, but most were military leaders or deliverers.

The opening chapter of Judges presents a picture of a number of cities in Canaan that still must be taken by Israel. This suggests a more complicated picture of the conquest than a cursory reading of Joshua would suggest. A careful reading of Joshua, however, indicates that not all areas are initially conquered (Josh 15:63; 16:10; 17:12). Scholars now debate the length of time involved and the very nature of the conquest itself. Another important issue is the role of the judges in the period before the monarchy. Some of the judges are military heroes, while others are local rulers. The book of Judges also depicts a transition period between the conquest and the establishment of the monarchy. The reference to the *captivity of the land* in Judges 18:30 suggests that the book was not completed until long after the events described. The book does not name its author, and one suggestion is that Judges is part of a much larger history of Israel stretching from Joshua through Kings. This history is intended to reinforce the principles of blessings and obedience found in the book of Deuteronomy,

COMMENTARY

INTRODUCTION · 1:1–3:6

1:1–7 The reference to the *death of Joshua* links this chapter with the end of the book of Joshua. As seen in Joshua 16:63 and 17:12, Israel did not take all territories at once. The fact that Judah goes up first places Judah in a prominent role in the narrative. This corresponds to the important place of Judah in the books of Samuel and Kings, as well as in later Israelite history. Simeon's role as Judah's helper may foreshadow the later assimilation of Simeon into the tribe of Judah. Cutting off the thumbs and great toes of *Adoni-Bezek* shows that he is humiliated, just as he had humiliated others.

1:8–10 *Judah fought against Jerusalem and took it*, establishing that tribe's claim on the city. They burn the city and move on to conquer Hebron south of Jerusalem.

1:11–15 This passage repeats Joshua 15:15–19 almost exactly. This fact illustrates that Judges 1 is not giving a chronological survey of contemporary events. It is a summary of events, some long past. This chapter is organized geographically and shows a conquest that covers a long time frame. This story about Caleb links this material with the past. The reference to *Othniel* also points to the future, where he will appear again in Judges 3:7–11 as the first judge. The fact that *Acsah* makes a request that is granted also shows that women were not completely ignored in this period. Other important women, such as Deborah and Jael, appear later in Judges.

1:16–21 This section explains why Kenites and Simeonites live in the territory of Judah. Judah is unable to drive out the Canaanites from the plains because the *iron chariots* are too strong for them. The Benjaminites are also unable to capture Jerusalem. This is surprising, since verse 8 says that Judah took Jerusalem. This chapter is likely not in chronological order, and so this could refer to an earlier time. Some have also suggested that Judah took Jerusalem, burned it, and then abandoned it. It was reoccupied by the Jebusites, who kept it until David's time. The fact that both Judah and Benjamin are connected with Jerusalem reflects the location of the city on the border between the territory of Judah and Benjamin.

1:22–26 The house of Joseph is treated as a unit, but the following verses treat Ephraim and Manasseh separately. In the Hebrew text of Joshua 16:2, Luz and Bethel are two different locations, but here they are two names for the same place. The Septuagint in Joshua 16:2 combines the two sites, as does this text in Judges. Joseph conquers Bethel with help from an insider.

1:27–36 Chapter 1 concludes with a series of notices about the various tribes and their failure to conquer the territory assigned to them. In each case, the fortified cities pose problems. Many outposts of resistance remain, and the Israelite possession of the land is much slower than often pictured. Judges 2 explains that this slow process is because of Israel's unfaithfulness. Some of the Canaanites are put to forced labor, but they are not driven out of the land (see 1 Kgs 9:20–24). This opening chapter reflects a combination of successes and failures and provides an appropriate introduction to the judges, who are a fascinating mixture of success and failure, obedience and disobedience.

2:1–5 The angel of the Lord explains why Israel cannot drive out the Canaanites. The angel reminds them of what God has done by delivering them from

The Twelve Tribes

Egypt. They have not responded by being obedient, and so the Lord will not drive out their enemies.

2:6–9 This section repeats the material on the death of Joshua from Joshua 24:28–30 and shows the contrast between the faithful response of Joshua's generation and the lack of faith of the later generations. So the book of Joshua emphasizes the success of their conquest, while Judges 1 shows the failure of a later generation. The emphasis falls not so much on historical developments as on the change from faithfulness to unfaithfulness. Scholars have sometimes emphasized the different historical pictures in Joshua and Judges, but the real concern is for the differences in the faith of Israel (Schneider 28–30). The term *served* [Hebrew *'avad*] the Lord appears in verse 7, in contrast with the same verb in verses 11, 13, 19, and 3:6 with reference to Israel's service to other gods.

2:10–15 These verses recount in detail how Israel forgot what the Lord had done for them and how they began to follow other gods. Because they forgot the Lord, they were defeated and oppressed by their enemies. Their failures were not simply military or political setbacks but were the direct result of their failure to be faithful to God and to show their gratitude for what the Lord had done for them. Verse 10 should serve as a warning of the tragic results of a failure to pass on the basic elements of faith to every new generation.

2:16–19 This passage is important because it outlines the cycle of unfaithfulness, oppression, and deliverance that figures throughout chapters 3–16. Again and again, Israel turns away from the Lord, and yet God is gracious and sends a deliverer each time.

2:20–23 Because of Israel's repeated unfaithfulness, God is angry and determines to test them to see if they will remain faithful or not. God will not drive out their enemies but will use the Canaanites to test Israel.

3:1–6 This section concludes the introduction of the book. Israel does not drive out the other nations as God had instructed. The list of nations remaining is a formula found in a number of other passages (Deut 7:1; Josh 3:10). The nations remain as a test for Israel, and the remainder of Judges shows that Israel does not fare well in that test. As the text indicates, they intermarry with the idol worshipers, and they take up the worship of idols. The writer here is reflecting back on these events from a time long after the results of this failure are well known. This text also says that the nations are left so that Israel may learn war. This is a lesson they learn all too well. By the end of the book of Judges, they are fighting and killing each other.

ACCOUNTS OF THE JUDGES · 3:7–16:31

3:7–11 This passage opens with the typical statement of Israel's disobedience: *did evil in the eyes of the Lord*. This clause also appears in Judges 3:12, 4:1, 6:1, 10:6, and 13:1. This formula introduces each of the major judges who deliver Israel. Israel does evil, they are oppressed, they cry to the Lord, and the Lord sends a deliverer. In 3:8, it is *Cushan-Rishathaim* who oppresses Israel for eight years. He is the *king of Aram Naharaim*, or northwest Mesopotamia. The RSV translates this as "Mesopotamia." In either case, this is a rather general description of a large area, and it is difficult to be certain just what kingdom is intended. The Lord raises up Othniel, who is linked to Caleb, one of the faithful spies from the book of Joshua. Verse 10 emphasizes that God chooses Othniel when the *Spirit of the Lord came upon him*. He goes to war and defeats Cushan-Rishathaim, although no details of the battle are given. The story concludes with the formula that *the land had rest for forty years*. This first account of one of Israel's judges gives only the barest outline with almost no details of how this deliverance took place. Perhaps the writer of Judges knew few details about this earliest judge, or perhaps the story serves simply as an introduction to the stories of God's salvation and so is used here because it highlights all the important elements of the outline in Judges 2:16–19 (Younger 101).

> **Aram**
> The Arameans emerged in what is now Syria and northern Iraq sometime before 1000 BCE. The various tribes may have come from Arabia or Anatolia, or they may have been local populations changing their social structures. Shortly before 1000 BCE, they founded kingdoms, mostly notably Damascus, that encountered Israel.

3:12–30 Israel again does evil in the Lord's eyes, and God allows Eglon of Moab to oppress them for eighteen years. Eglon is joined by the Ammonites and Amalekites. The *City of Palms* is likely a reference to Jericho, as in Deuteronomy 34:3 (Soggin 49). Jericho was the first city taken by Israel in Joshua 6, and now it falls to Eglon. The sin of Israel has caused a reversal of the possession of the land promised by the Lord.

Following the theological pattern of Judges, God sends a deliverer named Ehud, a man of Benjamin, who is left-handed. The Hebrew term used here for left-handed means literally "bound in the right hand." Some have suggested that Ehud was crippled in the right hand, but this seems unnecessary (Block 161). Halpern argues that he bound his right hand in order to develop his skills with his left hand. This was done to trick those who might expect an attack from the right hand. Halpern believes that Ehud was a trained warrior who served as a secret agent for God (41). Whether Ehud was naturally left-handed, or trained to use his left hand, it will be important later in the story that he uses his left hand.

Ehud is selected to deliver the tribute to King Eglon. The conquering king demands tribute, and someone must deliver it. What is unexpected here is the reference to a double-edged sword. Such a weapon would not be needed for delivering tribute. The additional detail that the sword is strapped to his right thigh under his clothes adds an element of intrigue. It is on the right so it can easily be reached with the left hand.

Ehud carries out his duties and presents the tribute to the king. The narrator adds an unexpected detail, that Eglon *was a very fat man*, which points to another important part of the story that follows in verse 22. It is also interesting that the name "Eglon" is similar to the Hebrew word for calf, *'egel*. The writer may be hinting that Eglon is like a fatted calf waiting to be slaughtered (Younger 116).

Verses 18–19 do not name those who carry the tribute but dismiss them before the major action begins. Ehud turns back at the *idols* and returns to Eglon. The meaning of the Hebrew term translated *idols* [*pesilim*] is not clear, but its use here and in verse 26 suggests some type of boundary marker. They may have marked the border of Eglon's territory, and in the narrative they mark the danger zone for Ehud.

As Ehud returns, he proclaims a *secret message* for the king. No king can resist a secret message, and Eglon is immediately intrigued. The king calls out, *Quiet*. It is ironic that the only word that Eglon utters in the story is the call for quiet. Soon he will be silenced for good. His attendants depart, leaving him alone with Ehud. Now Ehud can deliver his secret message. This is also a play on a double meaning of the Hebrew word for "message." It can mean a word or a message, but it can also mean a thing. Eglon expects a message, but Ehud has a secret thing. He delivers the sword hidden under his garment on his right thigh.

Eglon is sitting in an upper chamber, perhaps an elevated throne room located off the main assembly hall. Ehud approaches and repeats the announcement that he has a message for the king. The only difference is that now he calls it a message *from God*. As the king rises in anticipation of the message, Ehud reaches under his robe and pulls out the short sword. Before the obese king can react to defend himself, Ehud plunges the blade into the king's belly so that even the handle disappears into the ample folds of the king's midsection.

In verse 22, the phrase *came out his back* in the NIV is difficult. This phrase in Hebrew occurs at the very end of the verse, and not in the middle where the NIV has placed it. It could mean the sword comes out the back, as the NIV understands it, or more likely that the king's entrails come out or that his bowels empty (so RSV, KJV; McCann 45). This would also explain why the servants assume he is relieving himself in verse 24, if they smell the odor from outside the chamber.

Ehud locks the king in the chamber and makes his escape. Halpern (54–58) argues that Ehud could not have locked the door from the outside as he escaped. He must have locked the door from the inside and then escaped through a secret passage, probably through the hole in the floor for the king's private toilet. Some ancient locks could be bolted from the outside without a key, but they required a key to open them from the outside (King and Stager 32–33). This fits verse 25, where the servants must use a key to open the locked room. If this is correct, then Halpern's theory of an elaborate escape through the toilet is unnecessary.

When the servants return (verses 24–25), they find the door locked. They assume the king is relieving himself. Their long wait may be another element of irony. How long does one wait for a king? Finally, they get a key and open the door to find the king dead on the floor.

While the servants delay (verses 26–27), Ehud has time to escape beyond the boundaries of the danger zone. He sounds the [*shofar*], the ram's horn trumpet, to summon the Israelites to his aid.

In verses 28–30, Ehud proclaims that the Lord has given Israel a great victory. Throughout the book of Judges, God receives credit for their deliverance. The Israelites take possession of the fords of the river to cut off the escape route for the retreating Moabites. Demoralized by the death of their king, and trapped in hostile territory, the Moabites are completely routed. The Ehud story ends with the observation that the land had rest for eighty years.

> **Humor in the Story of Ehud**
> *Humor is difficult to translate from one culture to another. The story of Ehud, however, appears to be filled with irony and humor at the expense of Israel's enemies. Ehud tricks the king grown fat on Israel's tribute, who cannot defend himself in his own palace. The palace guards stand idle outside while Ehud escapes. At the end, the mighty fighting men of Moab die as they try to slink away across the Jordan. All this is the kind of story that could be told around the campfires in Israel while they have a good laugh at the expense of their enemies.*

3:31 The Hebrew here does not include the name Ehud and simply begins, *after him was Shamgar*. The NIV is surely correct in assuming that this "him" refers to Ehud. All we know of Shamgar comes from this single verse. He defeats 600 Philistines, but where and how? The Philistines were known as great warriors. Was Shamgar another mighty man like Samson? Why did he use an oxgoad? All this and more the modern reader would like to know, but the text simply says he saved Israel. He is the first of the minor judges to appear in the book.

4:1–5:31 Judges preserves two accounts of Deborah and Barak's victory over the Canaanites. Chapter 4 gives the narrative account, and chapter 5 tells the story in poetic form. Chapter 4 opens with the formula that Israel *again did evil in the eyes of the Lord*. Shamgar is not mentioned, and the events of this section take place after Ehud has died. Because of Israel's evil, the Lord allows *Jabin*, king of Canaan, to oppress them. He rules from *Hazor*, an important city in northern Israel. The term king of Canaan is interesting, since at this time Canaan was actually a collection of small city-states ruled by individual kings. The Hebrew text here could be understood as "a king of Canaan" or "the king of Canaan." In the context, the NIV reading of *a king of Canaan* is the better reading. Jabin is the leader of a coalition of city-states. In this story, it is Sisera, his general, who is the main antagonist against Israel. Sisera has 900 chariots of iron. This is significant because the chariot was the main shock weapon of ancient warfare, comparable to a modern tank. It was fast and powerful. The chariot was especially difficult for infantry to defeat on open ground where the chariot had room to maneuver. Israel is oppressed for twenty years, and they again cry out to the Lord.

According to verses 4–7, Deborah is leading Israel and must be well known as a judge and a prophetess, since she has an established place for deciding legal cases. As a prophetess, she speaks for the Lord and delivers a message to Barak that he should deliver Israel. Through Deborah, God commands him to take his army to *Mount Tabor*, in northern Israel, and prepare to defeat Sisera.

According to verses 8–10, Barak hesitates and declares that he will go only if Deborah goes with him. Deborah agrees to go, but she adds the enigmatic words that the honor of defeating Sisera will go to a woman. Naturally, the reader would assume that this refers to Deborah, but the story has a surprise in store.

Verse 11 appears unrelated to the previous story, but it prepares for what is to come. The narrative introduces *Heber the Kenite*, an ally of Jabin's (see verse 17). The introduction of Heber here foreshadows important developments later.

> **The Kenites**
> *Taking their name from Cain, this group of nomads lived in close proximity to Israel as their allies (see Judg 1:16; 1 Sam 15:6; 27:10; 30:29; 1 Chron 2:55). They lived mostly in southern Judah, but apparently could migrate north to feed their flocks.*

In verses 12–13, when Sisera learns that Barak and Israel have gone to Mount Tabor, he calls out all 900 chariots and goes to meet them. In verses 14–16, Deborah assures Barak that the Lord is with him, and he must attack. As the Israelite forces advance, Sisera is routed. How does Israel defeat such superior forces? The first answer is that the Lord was with them. In addition, the terrain helped, since Israel is attacking down the hill from the top of Mount Tabor, and chariots would be slowed by driving up hill. Others find a clue in the poem of chapter 5, where verses 4–5 suggest a thunderstorm. If a sudden storm dropped enough water to soften the ground, the chariots would become ineffective. By whatever means the Lord used, the Canaanites lose.

Why would Sisera leave a fast chariot to flee on foot? If the chariot was slowed by the mud after a storm, that would explain this problem. He goes to the tent of Jael, the wife of Heber the Kenite, and asks for safety (verses 14–20). There were peaceful relations between the Kenites and the Canaanites. Jael invites him in and offers him hospitality according to the code honoring guests. When he asks for water, she goes beyond that and gives him milk. She covers him, and he asks her to stand guard while he rests.

In an unexpected twist (verses 21–23), Jael forsakes the expected hospitality and kills Sisera. She uses the tools at hand, a hammer and a tent peg. These are hardly the typical weapons of war but rather the tools of necessity. No doubt, Jael had used these tools many times in erecting tents. Now they serve a darker purpose. The text adds a final ironic phrase in verse 21: *and he died*. As Barak rushes by in pursuit of Sisera, Jael calmly announces that she will show him the man he seeks. There lies Sisera, with the tent peg still in his head. These stories seem shocking, and yet verse 23 affirms that God is at work defeating the enemies of Israel.

Chapter 5 presents an extended poetic account of the defeat of Sisera already narrated in chapter 4. There are other examples in Scripture of the same event given in narrative and poetic form (for example, Exod 14–15). Judges 4 relates the basic story of the defeat of the Canaanite oppressors under Deborah and Barak. The poetic account in Judges 5 celebrates this victory and also highlights God's use of the forces of nature to achieve success.

This poem has been the subject of much scholarly work in recent years (see Younger 147; Block 211–18). Some have suggested that this is one of the oldest sections of the Bible (McCann 55). Scholars have suggested several different ways to organize and outline the poem. One way to think of the poem is in five large sections (Younger 148). The major divisions and verses are: praise to God and need for help (verses 2–8), praise to God for volunteers (verses 9–13), a list of tribes who participated and those who did not (verses 14–18), a report of the battle (verses 19–23), and a contrast between two women, Jael and Sisera's mother (verses 24–31).

The opening verse introduces Deborah and Barak as the leaders who celebrate their victory with this song. Verses 2–8 celebrate the leaders who prepare for battle and those who follow them willingly. The foreign rulers are to take note of this. Verses 4 and 5 use language similar to Deuteronomy 33:2–3 and Psalm 68:8–9, both parts of war poems. Those passages praise God for the covenant made in the wilderness. In Judges 5:4–5, it is God's faithfulness in the covenant that is foremost in mind. That is the basis for any deliverance. The mention of Shamgar and Jael in verse 6 suggests that problems existed for a long time in Israel. Normal travel and village life is disrupted until Deborah arises to defend Israel.

> **War Poems**
>
> *The Bible contains several war poems (for example, Exod 15:1–21; Pss 20, 21, 68; Hab 3). In all of them, Yahweh is the chief hero and foreign nations the major enemy.*

The second section of the poem (verses 9–13) also calls for praise of the Lord. *You who ride on donkeys* may be a reference to royalty or simply to travelers, in parallel with *you who walk along the road*. The poem calls Deborah and Barak to awaken and take charge. All who remain in Israel are to join them for battle.

The central section of the poem (verses 14–18) is perhaps the most crucial. This is a list of the tribes that participated and those who did not. *Ephraim*, *Benjamin*, *Makir* (in most texts a part of Manasseh), *Zebulun*, *Issachar*, and *Naphtali* (verse 18) are all commended for coming to help. Reuben, Gilead, Dan, and Asher are rebuked for failing to do their duty. This passage shows that early Israel was not always united. Why some tribes did not participate is not clear. Passages such as Judges 6:35 and 7:23 indicate that not all of the tribes participated in other battles, either. One point made clear at the end of the book of Judges is that this was a time when there is no central government, and the tribes often went their own way.

The reference to kings of Canaan (verses 19–23) may indicate that the Canaanite army is a coalition of forces from several groups with several tribal kings. Plunder is the reward for the army, but they receive none. Some take the reference to the stars as indicating some special event, such as an eclipse or a comet. Others see it as simply poetic language indicating God's intervention (Block 236). When the flood of the seasonal stream *Kishon* is taken together with the reference to clouds and water in verse 4, the picture is more complete. A sudden thunderstorm drops rain, the brook overflows, and the Canaanite chariots are rendered useless. *Meroz* is probably a town that could have given aid to Israel and failed to do so (compare Succoth and Peniel in Judg 8:6–9).

Verses 24–27 praise Jael for killing Sisera, the enemy general. A literal reading of verse 27 could indicate that Sisera is standing when he is struck and only fell afterward. This would contradict 4:21, where he is lying asleep when he is struck. This controversy is unnecessary, however, since 5:27 is giving a poetic account of the events (McCann 57).

Verses 28–30 present the last woman in this account, Sisera's mother. She waits in vain for the return of her son. She assumes that he and the victorious Canaanite army are gathering their plunder. The poet and the audience know better. Sisera's days of plundering God's people are ended.

The poem concludes with two wishes (verse 31). May all God's enemies perish as Sisera has, and may all those faithful arise with the strength of the morning sun.

6:1–40 Chapter 6 begins the Gideon cycle, one of the longer sections in the book of Judges. The story opens with the familiar notice that Israel sinned before the Lord and that the Lord allowed them to be oppressed by *Midian* and their allies. Midian takes all the produce of the land so that Israel finally cries out to the Lord.

> **Midian**
>
> *A region southeast of the Dead Sea, Midian was populated by city-dwellers and nomads before 1000 BCE. According to the Bible, some Midianites worshiped Yahweh, even before Israel did.*

Before the Lord sends a deliverer, he sends a prophet to remind them of what God has done. The Lord brought them out of Egypt, and they should have responded in faithfulness. Israel failed to show their gratitude. The words of the prophet emphasize a common theme throughout the Deuteronomistic History, that the Lord had acted first on behalf of Israel. Israel should respond in obedience to the Lord.

In spite of Israel's failure, the Lord continues to respond to their cries for help (verses 11–18). God is faithful, even when they are not. The *angel of the Lord* comes to Gideon. The exact location of Ophrah is not known. Wheat was not usually threshed in a wine press, but this was done in order to keep it from the Midianites. The angel's greeting contains two important elements. The Lord is with Gideon, and Gideon is a mighty warrior. Both statements appear questionable at first glance. First, Gideon wonders how God could be with them in light of all that is happening to them. Second, Gideon does not act like a mighty warrior as he hides from Midian and even questions how God could use him. Gideon has heard how the Lord delivered them from Egypt, but asks where the Lord is now in this new crisis. In verse 14, the Lord, not the angel, reassures Gideon. Gideon's protest in verse 15 is similar to that of Moses in Exodus 3:11–13. The Lord promises to be with Gideon and to bring success. Gideon wants to present an offering, but he is worried that the messenger might disappear before he returns (see 1 Kgs 18:12). The Lord promises to wait.

It would take some time to prepare an offering and make bread (verses 19–24). When Gideon returns, the angel instructs him how to present the offering. When the angel touches it with his staff, the offering is consumed, and the angel disappears. Gideon is now certain that this was a divine messenger, and he is sure he will die since no one can see the Lord and live (Exod 33:20). God reassures him that he will not die, and Gideon builds an altar and names it "The Lord is Peace."

In verses 25–27, the Lord gives specific instructions to Gideon. He is to take a particular bull from his father's animals, demolish the altar to Baal and the sacred pole of Asherah, and then build an altar to the Lord and offer the bull on it. Gideon takes ten men with him. He does as the Lord commanded, but he goes at night, because he is afraid of the men of the city.

According to verses 28–32, the following morning, the men of the city discover what has occurred. Even though Gideon acts in secret, it does not take long for word of his actions to spread. It is clear that Gideon has good reason to fear the reaction of the men, who call for his death. Interestingly, in verse 30, the men say Gideon must die because he has pulled down the altar of Baal and cut down the Asherah. No mention is made of the altar to the Lord or the sacrifice there. This reflects a common polytheistic worldview. According to that perspective, it is permissible to worship many gods, but it is very narrow-minded to worship only one. Gideon's father defends his son and says that if Baal is really a god, he should defend himself. This exchange is thus similar to Elijah's challenge to the prophets of Baal in 1 Kings 18. In Gideon's case, the men have no answer, since to press their point would be to admit that Baal cannot defend himself.

In verses 33–35, just as the spirit of the Lord came upon Othniel and Samson, so Gideon does not act on his own, but he acts directed by the spirit of the Lord. Only some of the tribes from the central hill country are involved in this initial call to arms.

> **The Spirit of the Lord**
> In the Old Testament, the phrase "spirit of Yahweh" appears occasionally, often as a synonym of God or as an expression of God's power to enable prophets to discern the future. The understanding of the "spirit" as a person of the Trinity comes only in the New Testament and in early Christian texts reflecting theologically on the New Testament.

In perhaps the best-known section of the Gideon stories (verses 36–40), Gideon asks the Lord for a sign that the Lord will indeed deliver Israel by his hand. Gideon uses a *fleece* to confirm the sign. First he asks that the fleece be wet with dew, while the ground around it is dry. God grants this sign, just as Gideon asks. Gideon then asks the Lord not to be angry if he asks yet again. Gideon knows he is pressing on dangerous ground, but he asks for another sign. Second, he asks that all the ground around be wet and the fleece be dry. This also is granted, and Gideon asks no more. Gideon's fear, mentioned in 6:27, the signs of the fleece, God's selection of the three hundred, and the dream in 7:13–14 present an unusual number of dramatic events in this story before Gideon finally takes action. Gideon appears very hesitant to take action in the first half of the story. His attitude changes dramatically in 7:15, where Gideon finally takes decisive action.

7:1–25 Commanders usually want more men to assure victory in battle. The Lord often acts in unexpected ways, and here he tells Gideon that he has too many men. Lest Israel be tempted to think that they won the victory by their own strength, Gideon must send home all the fearful, cutting his army by two thirds. The reference to *Gilead* is surprising, since that is across the Jordan some distance from their camps. Some think this indicates that those departing should go far out of their way to avoid detection by the enemy. More likely it is a scribal error for Mount Gilboa, which is directly beside the *spring of Harod*.

Gideon's army of ten thousand is still too large (verses 4–6). The Lord sends him down to the water, where more soldiers will be sent home. Gideon watches the men drink, and separates those who lap the water with their tongues like a dog from those who kneel down to drink. Much has been made of this test, which may have identified the most alert soldiers. On the other hand, Josephus says that the three hundred were the most fearful, and that God could win the battle even with the worst soldiers. The test is also difficult to understand, since in verse 5 there appear to be two groups: those who lap like a dog, and those who kneel down to drink. In verse 6, however, there is the added note that three hundred lapped *with their hands to their mouths*. This is not the way a dog laps. One suggestion is that verse 5 refers only to one group, "Those who lap like a dog, that is, they kneel down to drink." That group is then distinct from those who lap with their hands to their mouth in verse 6 (Block 276). The point is that God selects the three hundred based on extraordinary criteria in order to win the victory. After the Lord reassures Gideon, most of the troops depart but leave their extra provisions with the three hundred that remain.

In verses 9–14, God offers to give Gideon another sign if he is still afraid. Gideon might have reason to be afraid, since his army had been reduced from thirty-two thousand to three hundred. He goes into the enemy camp and overhears one soldier telling another his dream. Gideon's reputation is known to the Midianites, since they understand the dream as representing Gideon's victory.

Verses 15–18 mark the turning point in the story. Now, Gideon springs into action, and he believes that the Lord will give Israel the victory. He organizes his men into three companies, gives them their supplies, and instructs them to follow his lead. Their supplies include empty jars, trumpets, and torches, all atypical weapons. Yet they will be effective with the Lord's help. Their battle cry is to be *For the Lord and for Gideon*.

Verses 19–21 describe the climactic moment. If the night were divided into three watches, the second watch would begin at midnight. When the camp is settled for the night, Gideon and his men approach the camp. The stillness of the night is shattered as Gideon and his men break the jars, blow the trumpets, and shout their battle cry. The mention of *a sword* is ironic, since the enemy soldiers turned their own swords on each other in the confusion. One need not assume that Gideon and his men break pitchers, blow trumpets, shout, and wave torches all at the same time. The text is describing a series of events that happens quickly and dramatically.

> **Psychological Warfare**
> The story of Gideon's victory is a classical case of psychological warfare, the use of unconventional means to demoralize and defeat an enemy. Other examples in the Bible appear in 2 Samuel 10:4; 16:15–17:23; 2 Kings 14:9–10; 18:17–36. Methods of deception, propaganda, espionage, and intimidation were widespread in the ancient world because they minimized bloodshed in wartime.

In verses 22–25, in the chaos of the enemy camp, the Midianites begin to slaughter their own comrades. As they flee for their lives, no doubt the Israelites use their swords to attack the remnants of the enemy army. Reinforcements are called out from the neighboring tribes to prevent the enemy escape. Two of the enemy commanders are captured and killed, and their names, *Oreb* and *Zeeb*, are commemorated at the places where they die. Soldiers bring their heads to Gideon as gruesome trophies.

8:1–35 The *Ephraimites* are called to help in the pursuit after the initial attack, and they are angry that they have not been included from the beginning. Intertribal battles could break out, as seen in Judges 19–21, so Gideon has to be diplomatic. Gideon answers by downplaying his own contribution and complimenting the Ephraimites for their capture of the leaders. This soothes their hostility and avoids more trouble.

Gideon pursues the remaining Midianite forces across the Jordan (verses 4–9). Coming to *Succoth*, he asks for supplies for his weary troops. The men of *Succoth* refuse to help him. Perhaps, they are worried about reprisals from the Midianites if they defeat Gideon and return to take vengeance. Gideon assures them that once he has the Midianite leaders, *Zebah* and *Zalmunna*, he will return to repay Succoth for their lack of aid. Next, Gideon asks for aid from *Peniel*, but they, too, refuse to help.

The exact location of *Karkor* remains uncertain, but it lies somewhere east of the Dead Sea. Gideon attacks them by surprise and routs them once again, this time capturing Zebah and Zalmunna.

On his return trip (verses 13–17), Gideon captures a young man of Succoth, who writes down the names of the elders of the city. Gideon then punishes the elders for their failure to help him on his journey. He also demolishes the tower of Peniel, as promised.

Verses 18–21 reveal an additional motivation for Gideon's pursuit. Gideon questions Zebah and Zalmunna about a group of men they killed at Mount Tabor. This battle is not previously mentioned. The leaders reply that they were men like Gideon. Gideon then replies that they were, in fact, his brothers. It is not stated, but perhaps they were captured by Zebah and Zalmunna and then executed after the battle. Gideon's desire for revenge has fueled his desire to catch these enemy leaders. Now he will execute them as they did his brothers. He first offers the right of execution to his son, *Jether*. This was likely a rite of passage, in which Jether would take the lead in avenging this injustice against his family. He refuses, however, and verse 20 says *he was only a boy and was afraid*. The Hebrew term used here for *boy* does not mean a child, but rather a young man who is still under the authority of others. This may have been Jether's first battle. He does accompany the soldiers, and he has his own sword, but he is not a hardened veteran. He has no taste for cold-blooded execution. The two leaders then call on Gideon to kill them himself. He steps forward without hesitation and dispatches them without mercy. The picture of Gideon here is quite different from the hesitant and fearful figure in chapter 6. Gideon is now a forceful leader who takes control and acts decisively.

> **The Code of the Warrior**
> In the ancient Near East, warriors followed codes of conduct emphasizing bravery, loyalty to friends and relatives, and self-restraint. They would not bother to kill an unworthy opponent. The Mesopotamian Epic of Gilgamesh gives the fullest treatment of such a warrior's life, but the stories of some of the judges and of David give other examples.

One of the high points comes when Israel offers Gideon the kingship (verses 22–23). He has delivered Israel and may establish his own family dynasty. Gideon refuses and reminds them, *the Lord will rule over you*. This commentary does not agree with those who see Gideon as a cynical and self-serving individual presented in an entirely negative light (Block 300). Gideon is far from perfect, but in this response, he voices an important truth. If more leaders in Israel had taken this attitude, Israel's history could have been far different.

Gideon does not grasp for power but recognizes that the Lord is the true ruler.

Gideon does ask for a share of the gold taken (verses 24–27), and the people give it to him gladly, along with additional spoil. Gideon makes the gold into an ephod. Normally, an ephod is part of the priestly garments, as is Judges 17:5, 18:14–20. Here, however, it likely represents not only a garment but also a figure that is worshiped. This figure becomes a snare for Gideon and for all Israel.

Like many in Israel's history, Gideon is a mixture of good and bad. He recognizes that God is the true ruler, and yet he allows idolatry to creep into Israel's worship. He delivers Israel, but he multiplies wives and gold for himself. After his death, Israel returns to worship Baal. The people do not remember the Lord who has rescued them.

9:1–57 After the disappointing ending of the Gideon story, chapter 9 begins a new section, but one clearly linked to the Gideon stories since Abimelech is the son of *Jerub-Baal*, apparently another name for Gideon (8:35). Jerub-Baal must have exercised some power, since after his death, Abimelech is interested in who will be in control next. He returns to his clan in Shechem in order to solicit their support for his bid for power. He appeals to family ties and also to the fact that it is better to deal with one ruler that with seventy. He is trying to convince the people that it is better for their interests if he is in power, but he is most concerned with his own interests.

The people of Shechem accept his arguments (verses 3–6) and give Abimelech seventy shekels of silver from the treasury of the temple of Baal. He uses this money to hire a private army and begins to consolidate his power. His first act is to eliminate all his rivals. He goes to *Ophrah* and kills all the other sons of Jerub-Baal. *Jotham*, the youngest son, escapes, and goes into hiding. All the people of the region come together to crown Abimelech as the new ruler.

In verses 7–15, when the people come to crown Abimelech, Jotham stands high on Mount Gerizim and shouts to them. He tells a riddle about the *trees* seeking a king to rule over them. The trees first ask the *olive tree*, then the *fig tree*, then the *vine*, and finally the *thornbush*. All the useful trees decline to rule, while the useless one consents to do so. The point is that only the poorest candidate accepts the job.

The people of Shechem have murdered all the best candidates and have accepted the worst candidate, Abimelech (verses 16–21). Jotham reminds them of all that Gideon did for them, kindness that they have failed to repay to his family. He warns the people that the wrath that came out from Abimelech on his brothers may spill over and consume the people, as well.

Just as Abimelech comes to power through violence, so his short reign will be filled with violence (verses 22–25). The NIV's translation *evil spirit* is unfortunate because it suggests that God sends a spirit of moral evil. The Hebrew word translated "evil" can also simply mean "trouble" or "calamity," and so here "a spirit of calamity" would be better. God sends trouble in order to avenge the wrong that Abimelech has done.

In verses 26–29, the leader of the opposition is *Gaal*. At a festival, he boasts that he would defeat Abimelech if he were in control. There is no shortage of people hungry for power in Israel. In verses 30–33, Zebul the governor sends a warning to Abimelech with the cryptic instructions, *do whatever your hand finds to do*. Zebul supports Abimelech and urges him to kill Gaal. Abimelech marches on Shechem for a surprise attack to reclaim his city (verses 34–41). Gaal is startled, but he organizes a defense and fights against Abimelech. Many of Gaal's followers are wounded, and he is driven out of Shechem. Gaal is not mentioned after verse 41, so it appears that he dies or goes into hiding.

In verses 42–49, Abimelech presses the attack against the remaining inhabitants of Shechem. The survivors retreat into the stronghold of the temple of *El-Berith*. The name means the "God of the Covenant," but it is unclear whether the deity of the temple is a version of Yahweh or a version of the Canaanite god El. Now, Abimelech shows the spirit of revenge at its worst. He piles up wood and burns the stronghold with one thousand people inside.

The location of Thebez is unknown, but it must be nearby. Abimelech plans a similar fate for the people there (verses 50–56). As he approaches the stronghold to set it afire, however, a woman throws down a millstone that strikes Abimelech on the head and mortally wounds him. He asks his armor-bearer to kill him so he may avoid the shame of being killed by a woman. Block (333) suggests that the woman

> **Fables**
> Fables are stories about animals, or in this case, plants, who have humanlike characteristics. Often they make a serious moral or religious point, as here.

must have had extraordinary strength or had help to cast down a heavy millstone. However, small hand millstones about the size of a loaf of bread were common and certainly could have done the job here (Herr and Boyd). The conclusion of the chapter (verse 57) reminds the readers that God brought this fate upon Abimelech because of all he had done to his own family. God also punished the people of Shechem for their wickedness in helping him.

10:1–5 Judges next mentions two more minor judges briefly. Nothing is known about them beyond what this text says. Tola saves Israel, but how he does this is not given. He lives in the central hill country of Ephraim and governs for twenty-three years. After him comes Jair, who leads Israel for twenty-two years. He is from Gilead and has thirty sons who ruled three cities.

> **Minor Judges**
>
> *The editor of Judges used more extensive sources for some judges than for others. In some cases, he must have known only names and lengths of reigns. Since the book does not purport to follow strict chronological order, it is impossible to reconstruct the historical relationships of these various leaders.*

10:6–12:7 In 10:6–18, the cycle of disobedience continues as Israel again turns away from the Lord. The apostasy is growing worse, since they worship not only Baal and Asherah but also the gods of the surrounding nations of Aram, Sidon, Moab, Ammon, and the Philistines. God gives them into the hands of the *Philistines* (on the southwest) and *Ammonites* (on the northeast) for eighteen years. The region of Gilead on the east side of the Jordan suffers most from this oppression, but it spills over into Judah and central Israel, as well. Following Judges' theological pattern of interpreting Israel's history, the text reports that Israel cries for help and receives a warning. Since they have forsaken God, they should cry out to their new gods. Israel responds by accepting whatever punishment God sends and ridding themselves of foreign gods. The Lord listens to their plea.

In verses 17–18, Israel must act when the Ammonites prepare for battle. Israel assembles at Mizpah near Gilead, but no leader is ready to launch the attack.

Judges 11:1–3 introduces Jephthah and gives the background for the story that is to follow. His mother is a prostitute, and his half-brothers drive him out to prevent him from sharing an inheritance. He is a mighty warrior, and other warriors gather around him.

In 11:4–11, when the Ammonites oppress Israel, the elders ignore Jephthah's questionable background and turn to him for help. Jephthah reminds them of their previous hatred toward him, but they assure him that they need his help. The elders agree to Jephthah's terms that they accept him as leader. This they will do if he will only deliver them. In verses 12–13, Jephthah sends a message to the king of the Ammonites to determine the reason for their attack. The Ammonites claim that Israel has taken their land unfairly, and they now demand it back.

Jephthah sends a lengthy reply and summarizes the history of Israel's passage from Egypt to Canaan (11:24–27; compare Neh 9:7–37; Pss 78; 105). Israel tried to avoid conflict, but the king of Ammon forced them into battle. Then Israel's God gave them victory, so Ammon has no right to complain. If Ammon presses the battle, the Lord will decide who is victorious. The three hundred years is probably a round number for the years already mentioned in the period of the judges, but in fact some of the judges may have worked concurrently in different areas.

The spirit of the Lord comes upon Jephthah (verses 28–32). Over and over, the writer of Judges emphasizes that the Judges do not act only by their own power. They are successful because the Lord is with them. Before the battle, Jephthah makes his fateful vow. If he is victorious, he will sacrifice whatever comes to meet him. What does Jephthah have in mind when he makes this vow? Does he expect to make a human sacrifice? Some have argued that he is so corrupt and power hungry that he is ready to make any sacrifice to gain power. That is not consistent with his sorrow expressed in verse 35. There Jephthah sounds truly sorry that his daughter has come out to greet him. This does not sound like he intended a human sacrifice, and certainly not one from his own family. Israelites kept animals in the gates of the courtyard, and he could have intended an animal sacrifice. Jephthah is victorious, and returns in triumph.

In verses 33–35, Jephthah's joy turns to sorrow when he sees his daughter coming out to greet him. She is his only child and surely not the intended sacrifice.

She assures her father that she accepts her fate (verses 36–40). She asks only to be given two months to mourn the fact that she will not marry or have a family. Some have suggested that she lived out her life as a perpetual virgin. The term for sacrifice here is the usual term for a whole burnt offering, so Jephthah almost certainly killed her as a sacrifice. On the other hand, the text never says that God accepted this sacrifice. This was Jephthah's idea that he carried out on his own. The period of the Judges was a harsh and cruel time, and this is one more example of that fact. Jephthah makes a terrible vow, and then feels compelled by the pressures of his society and the importance of honor and shame to carry out that vow no matter how painful it is to him.

> **Human Sacrifice**
>
> *In the ancient Near East, human sacrifice was comparatively rare, but it did occur. The biblical stories of the binding of Isaac (Gen 22) and the offering of Mesha's son (2 Kgs 3), as well as the Greek story of Iphigeneia, provide clear parallels to the story of Jephthah and his daughter.*

In 12:1–7, Jephthah's judgeship comes to a violent end. He is confronted by the *Ephraimites*, much as Gideon had been. The Ephraimites complain that he excluded them from the battle and subsequent plunder. Instead of using diplomacy as Gideon had done, Jephthah calls his troops and attacks the complaining Ephraimites. The test at the fords of the Jordan reflects a different pronunciation in the dialects of the two tribes. Jephthah's judgeship lasts only six years, and there is no mention that it brought rest to Israel. Jephthah is a mixture of both good and bad, as is seen in many of the judges.

12:8–15 We know little of *Ibzan* except that he judged Israel for seven years. The marriage of his *thirty sons* and *thirty daughters* to those outside his clan probably served to cement alliances with neighboring groups. After him comes *Elon*, who judged for ten years. The text offers no details except his length of rule. Abdon judged for eight years and had *forty sons* and *thirty grandsons*, for a total of seventy male descendents. Their *seventy donkeys* symbolized the family's wealth and near-royal status. The minor judges show some periods of relative calm and peace in the midst of this tumultuous period.

13:1–16:31 In 16:1, the Samson story begins with the same notice seen earlier, that Israel again did evil in God's eyes. It is not clear if the forty years precedes Samson's birth or includes the twenty years of his judgeship and even perhaps the years of turmoil beyond.

Verses 2–7 constitute the only narrative in the book of Judges that includes an announcement before the birth of the judge. It is similar to the narrative in 1 Samuel 1 and perhaps points ahead to that story. No reason is given for the selection of this couple, and the only detail revealed is that *Manoah*'s wife is childless. The angel appears first to the unnamed woman. Her husband is named, but nothing more is known of him. The woman should abstain from wine and from anything unclean. The child is not to cut his hair or beard and is to remain a Nazirite (Num 6:1–21). The text says *he will begin the deliverance*, but it implies that he will not complete what he starts. From the opening of the story of Samson, there are hints that his judgeship is less than ideal. When the woman reports all this to her husband, she calls the messenger a *man of God*.

In verses 8–14, Manoah wishes to hear this for himself and prays for the messenger to return. The angel does return and repeats the same message that he had given to the woman.

In verses 15–23, Manoah tries to honor the messenger with an offering. The angel declines and suggests an offering to the Lord, instead. The fact that Manoah does not know that this is an angel suggests that the angel looks like a man rather than the traditional picture from later artwork. Once they do realize that he is an angel, Manoah is afraid. His wife reassures him that they will not die.

In verses 24–25, the woman gives birth, and the child is named Samson. *The spirit of the Lord began to stir him* is the climax to the story. The point is not really the birth but the fact that the Lord will use this child for Israel's deliverance. Throughout the Bible, God uses imperfect people to good ends. Samson is far from ideal; nevertheless, God can use him.

The first episode in Samson's adult life (14:1–9) does not present him in a very favorable light. He is ready to marry, but he selects a woman from among the Philistines, the enemies of Israel. His parents suggest he look among the

> **The Philistines**
>
> *The Philistines migrated from the Aegean region to the coast of Syria and Palestine sometime after 1300 BCE. Related groups moved westward to Sardinia, southern France, and Spain. The group that reached Palestine founded five major cities (Ashkelon, Ashdod, Ekron, Gaza, and Gath) and warred with Israel for generations.*

Israelites, but he insists that this is the right woman for him. A better translation of 14:3 would be, "she is right in my eyes." This echoes almost exactly Judges 17:6 and 21:25, where every man does "what is right in his eyes" (Younger 301). Samson's concern for his own interest symbolizes the selfish concern that will bring ruin to the entire nation. In verse 4, the narrator gives the theological motivation. God is at work in this choice to bring about a confrontation with the Philistines. Often God works behind the scenes, even when the participants do not realize it. There is no more discussion, but Samson's parents accompany him to arrange the marriage. On the trip, Samson turns aside and kills a lion with his bare hands, but his parents do not see it. This event prefigures an important event in the following episode. Some time later, Samson passes by and finds a honeycomb in the carcass of the lion. He eats and gives some to his parents, but they do not know where he found the honey.

At the wedding feast (verses 10–20), Samson poses a riddle for his companions and makes a sizable wager that they cannot guess the answer. This scene suggests a different side of Samson. In the ancient world, riddles were a sign of intelligence and skill. Reporting Samson's skill at riddles adds another dimension to his character. He is not simply a strong back with no brains. He is pictured as both strong and smart. His riddle is based on a secret that only he could know. Out of the *strong* (the lion) came something *sweet* (honey). Out of the *eater* (the lion) came something to *eat* (honey). Since his friends do not know the story of his killing the lion, they cannot guess his riddle. In desperation, the companions force Samson's bride to help them, so they will not be ruined. She cries and pleads with Samson for the entire seven days of the feast and finally persuades him to tell her the answer. She immediately relays it to the companions, who then answer Samson. He knows immediately that they could only have acquired the information from her. This begins the confrontation between Israel and the Philistines foreshadowed in Judges 14:4, and when Samson kills thirty Philistines for their garments, the conflict only intensifies. After Samson departs, his bride marries his best man. This sets the stage for further problems in the following chapter.

In 15:1–8, the narrative continues from the previous chapter. After some time, Samson has second thoughts and decides to visit his bride again. He is unaware that she has married another, but the audience knows this from the end of chapter 14. Samson's action clearly foreshadows trouble ahead. The girl's father prevents Samson from seeing his former fiancée and informs him that she is now married. Samson is enraged, exactly as anticipated, and vows to take vengeance on the Philistines. It is striking that here and in 16:28, Samson speaks of revenge on the Philistines and not of delivering Israel. His motives are personal rather than on behalf of his people. He ties torches to foxes and burns the grain of the Philistines. How Samson does this is not explained, but it fits well into the story of this warrior who kills thirty men for their clothes, kills a thousand men with a jawbone, and pulls down a temple on a throng of his enemies.

When the Philistines discover that Samson has done this, they burn his bride and her father, as they had threatened to do in Judges 14:15. Perhaps this emphasis on fire underlines the destructive nature of this conflict between Samson and the Philistines. Much is destroyed, but no one really benefits from all the destruction. The cycle of violence continues as Samson kills still more Philistines and then withdraws to a cave in the *rock of Etam*.

In verses 9–17, the cycle of violence continues as the Philistines come to find Samson and *to do to him as he did to us*. The men of Israel are afraid that this conflict will engulf them all. Some three thousand of them go to Samson to ask him to consider the danger he is bringing upon them. His reply reinforces the mentality of revenge, as he says he *merely did to them what they did to me*. The Israelites want to save themselves by cooperating with the Philistines, so they agree to hand Samson over. There

> **Samson Reinterpreted**
> *In the centuries before and after the time of Jesus, Jewish readers of the Bible tried to fill in the gaps of its stories and to find application for their own situation. Thus the writer of Hebrews 11:32 listed Samson with miscellaneous heroes who delivered Israel. Sometime in the first century CE, Pseudo-Philo wrote a work called* Biblical Antiquities *in order to retell the Bible's story. He gave Samson's mother a name and otherwise speculated on his moral decision-making. He also emphasized the danger of mixing with Gentiles. Thus Samson, like other biblical figures at many times and places, became the role model he never was in life.*

is a touch of irony in the fact that they send three thousand men to capture this lone warrior. Even in the face of three thousand, Samson can extract a promise that they will not kill him if he surrenders to them. They agree, and Samson is bound and led to the Philistine camp. The three thousand Israelites disappear from the narrative with no hint of what happens to them. The issue now is the continuing confrontation between Samson and the Philistines. The Philistines see Samson from a distance, and they come ready to humiliate their archenemy. The spirit of the Lord comes on Samson, and he bursts the ropes on his arms. He picks up a fresh jawbone nearby and strikes down a thousand Philistines. So, the place is called "Jawbone Hill."

In verses 18–20, Samson cries to God that after this great victory, he is about to die from thirst. God opens up a spring, and Samson revives. *Samson led Israel for 20 years* sounds like it belongs at the end of the Samson story, and it is repeated at the end of chapter 16.

The story in 16:1–3 once again shows Samson humiliating and outsmarting the Philistines. He goes to a prostitute in Gaza, one of the Philistine cities. Samson is too well known to escape notice, and his presence is reported. The people lie in wait, assuming he will stay all night, and they will surprise him in the morning when he is too tired to fight. Samson surprises them, however, and comes out at midnight. The gates of the city are barred, but Samson rips open the gates, pulls up the gateposts, and carries them off toward Hebron.

In verses 4–22, Samson's downfall begins with his interest in another woman. It is ironic that thousands of warriors cannot defeat him, but one woman does. The parallels between this story and the wedding in chapter 14 are striking. The Philistines hear of Samson's interest, and they go to the woman to elicit her help in defeating Samson. She pries the secret from him, just as the first woman did. The Philistines offer a huge reward if Delilah can give them the secret of Samson's strength. Samson treats this all as a great game, and he tells her one big story after another about how his strength can be tamed. Of course, they are all false, and Samson enjoys the game. At last, she pleads until he can bear it no longer. He tells her the truth about his Nazirite vow and his hair. She realizes that this is the truth and rushes to tell the Philistines.

She puts Samson to sleep on her lap and calls in a man to cut his hair. She warns Samson as before, *the Philistines are upon you*. He expects to leap up as before, but now *the Lord had left him*. Samson's great strength comes not from his own power, but from the Lord. The Philistines gouge out his eyes and put him to work in prison. The last line hints that this is not the end of Samson. The statement *his hair began to grow again* foreshadows that Samson will have one more go at the Philistines.

The Philistines hold a great feast at the temple of Dagon to celebrate their victory over Samson (verses 23–31). Dagon is mentioned in 1 Samuel 5:2, where the ark is captured and placed in the temple of Dagon. The name Dagon derives

> **Dagon**
> *The Canaanite god of grain, Dagon was claimed by the Philistines, who adopted the religion and manners of the locals of Palestine. Eventually, they assimilated fully with the original population.*

from the Hebrew word for grain, but little is known about how Dagon was worshiped. At the height of the celebration, his captors bring Samson before the crowd. The temple is so crowded that there are even three thousand on the roof to watch the show. It is ironic that the Philistines gather to celebrate Samson's downfall, and the scene is suddenly reversed when he wins his greatest victory by pulling down their temple on their heads. Samson does not win this victory with his own strength alone, but he prays to the Lord for strength. The answer comes in Samson's actions. The text indicates that God does grant this one last request. Samson pushes down the pillars and dies with the Philistines in the rubble. His family shows their respect by giving him a proper burial. The conclusion does not say the land had peace, but that Samson judged Israel for twenty years. The lack of peace becomes more apparent in the turmoil of the final chapters of Judges.

ISRAELITE SOCIETY IN DECLINE & CHAOS · 17:1–21:25

17:1–18:31 There are no more judges in the book. The final episodes in chapters 17–18 and 19–21 show two examples of the disintegration of Israelite society as it becomes more and more chaotic. Chapter 17 introduces a man named Micah who has stolen 1,100 shekels of silver from his mother. She curses the silver, and he returns it to her. She then consecrates the silver to the Lord, but uses a small part of it for an idol. Perhaps she and her son hope that this will remove the curse, and then they can use the remainder for themselves. Micah installs one of his sons as a priest, although he is not a Levite. The key idea for this entire section is *in those days Israel had no king, and every man did as he saw fit*. There was no central authority, and these stories illustrate what happens in such times.

In 17:7–13, an unnamed Levite from Judah is traveling, looking for a way to make a living. That is the real meaning of verse 8. When he passes by Micah's house, Micah offers him a job at his family shrine. The Levite accepts, and everything appears to be in order. The curse on the silver is removed, Micah has his priest, and the Levite has a job. Micah is sure that the Lord will bless him. It is striking that there is no word from the Lord in these chapters. God gives no assurance that he will bless this situation as Micah hopes. Micah has done what is right in his own eyes, but not in God's eyes.

Chapter 18 opens with a repetition of the phrase *in those days Israel had no king*. The second half of the phrase, that everyone did as he saw fit, is not repeated but is surely implied, as is demonstrated in the actions of this chapter. Like the Levite, the Danites are seeking land. They have lost their territory and must send out spies to find a new place. As they pass by Micah's house, they hear the Levite at the shrine. They recognize him either from previous acquaintance or by his southern speech. The Danites ask him to inquire about the success of their mission. He replies immediately that their mission has God's approval. Since the text does not say that he asked God or gave God's reply, the reader may assume that he says what the Danites want to hear.

> **Tel Dan**
> *An ancient site northeast of the Sea of Galilee near Mount Hermon, Tel Dan was inhabited long before the Israelite period. Pottery from 1200–1000 BCE (Iron Age I) sometimes resembles earlier types but often closely resembles that of the hill country of Ephraim, indicating the presence of the Israelites whom Judges 18 describes.*

In verses 7–10, the Danites travel to *Laish* and find a prosperous city that will be an easy target for their attack. They report back to their leaders and encourage swift action against Laish. The spies echo the words of the Levite that God will give them victory.

In verses 11–26, as the Danites prepare for their attack on Laish, the spies tell them of the shrine at the house of Micah. The phrase *you know what to do* reveals their intention to take this for themselves. Twice, verse 16 states that the six hundred armed men stood at the gate while the spies took the idols from the shrine. The six hundred men would prevent any serious opposition, since they could take it by force if they chose to do so. They also tell the priest that he should go with them and be the priest for a whole clan rather than just one family. *The priest was glad* reinforces the idea that he is in this for his own gain. There is more prestige and more money to be made working for a whole clan. Micah questions the men, but the threat of six hundred soldiers is too much to confront. Their threats silence him, and they go their way.

In verses 27–31, the Danites capture Laish and destroy it. They rebuild the city, calling it Dan, and placing the idols they have stolen in the new city. The priest is finally named and is a descendent of Moses. Judges 2:7 states that the people were faithful all the days of Joshua and his generation. Now, this next generation is no longer faithful, and Jonathan is an example of that unfaithfulness. This line of priests and sanctuary continue until the time of the "captivity," almost certainly referring to the captivity of the northern kingdom by the Assyrians at the end of the 700s BCE. This shrine at Dan begins with stolen silver, and the entire episode is filled with selfish and self-promoting motives. There is no concern for what God wants but only for what each group can seize for itself through greed and violence.

19:1–21:25 Chapters 19–21 make up the final section of the book of Judges. In some ways, this is the most problematic material in the whole book. There is a rape and murder, a dismemberment of a body, and finally civil war among the tribes. One would be hard pressed to find a story that appears more out of place in Scripture than this one. The real challenge for the reader lies not simply in what the passage says but in why it is here. That question must be considered as the story is analyzed.

The clause *in those days Israel had no king* opens 19:1–10. This opening phrase reminds the audience that this was a chaotic time because of the lack of a central government. An unnamed Levite has a concubine from Bethlehem who has left him and returned to her home. After four months, he goes to bring her back. The girl's father insists that they stay and eat and drink and rest. This introduces the theme of hospitality that is important in the remainder of the story. After several attempted departures, on the fifth day, the father tries to make them stay again, but the Levite is anxious to leave. Even though it is late in the day, they depart and travel toward Jebus, that is, Jerusalem.

> **Hospitality**
> In ancient Israel, hospitality was a highly valued set of practices. It included the sharing of food and resources, kind language, and even protection from enemies. Abraham and Sarah, Jethro, Boaz, Samuel, David, and many others demonstrate this approach to strangers. In contrast, the story of Sodom and Gomorrah and this one in Judges demonstrate the radical denial of hospitality and the consequences of such actions.

In verses 11–21, *the day was almost gone* so the servant suggests that they spend the night in Jebus. The Levite rejects this suggestion because Jebus is not an Israelite city. It is still in the hands of the Jebusites. How ironic that the Levite avoids the pagan city in favor of Gibeah, and his stay there results in tragedy at the hands of the Benjaminites. The Levite and his group enter Gibeah and proceed to the city square. Since there were few inns in those days, it was customary for local citizen to offer hospitality to travelers. When no host volunteers, the travelers prepare to spend the night in the square. At evening, an old man from Ephraim returns from his work in the fields. The text makes clear that he lives in Gibeah, but he is not one of the Benjaminites. He offers the travelers a place to stay and takes them home with him.

In verses 22–26, their peaceful evening is interrupted by a crowd of men from the city pounding on the door and demanding that the Levite be given to them so they may have sex with him. Whether this is to satisfy their own lusts or to shame and humiliate the Levite is not clear. The old man goes out to talk with them and to ask them not to do this shameful thing. He even offers his own virgin daughter and the concubine, but the men of the city reject this offer. This passage is similar to the one in Genesis 19, where the men of Sodom ask Lot to bring out his guests for the same purpose. The writer of Judges 19 may be suggesting that the Benjaminites have sunk so low that they are no better than the citizens of Sodom. The attitude of the old man is shocking to modern audiences but must be understood in the context of ancient customs of hospitality. Once a guest has come under his protection, the host is responsible for the safety of the guest. Nowhere does the text suggest that the Lord approves this custom, but it is the practice of the time. The men will not listen, so *the man took his concubine* and put her outside. She is raped and abused all night and finally collapses on the doorstep.

The next morning (verses 27–30), the man comes out and simply says, *Get up, let's go*. There can be little defense for his callous and cruel attitude, and that may well be the point of the narrative. No one does what is right here, since all are doing what is right in their own eyes. The Levite puts the concubine on his donkey and takes her home. He cuts up the body and sends out the pieces to every corner of Israel. Some have suggested that she was still alive, so his action is even more heartless. This is unlikely, and the Septuagint translation says plainly that she is dead.

> **Dismembering the Concubine**
> Dismembering the woman's body reflects one version of an ancient custom. Often, a covenant was sealed with a sacrifice, even a curse, suggesting that those who accept the covenant are bound to keep it or suffer the same fate as the sacrificed animal. This symbolic action may have been intended to remind all Israel of their commitment. They are bound to right this horrible injustice and to purge this evil from their midst. Everyone who hears of this is appalled and is ready to act. A parallel event occurs in 1 Samuel 11:7–8, though there Saul dismembers an ox to call out the national militia.

Chapter 20 opens with an assembly of all Israel, even beyond the Jordan, at Mizpah, in response to this shocking development (verses 1–11). They ask for an explanation of this terrible event. The Levite summarizes the story, but it varies from that given in chapter 19. In his account, the men of the city plan to kill him, but in Judges 19:22 they say they want to have sex with him. He also omits the fact that he put his concubine outside. After his story, he asks for the judgment of the people. They are outraged and begin to plan an attack to avenge this crime.

In verses 12–17, Israel first sends messengers to Benjamin asking for the surrender of those responsible. The tribe of Benjamin ignores this request and begins to prepare for battle. They muster twenty-six thousand troops, along with a special force of seven hundred left-handed men who are especially skillful with the sling. Baruch Halpern (41) argues that the term used here for left-handed means that they were trained to be ambidextrous. This is the same term used of Ehud in chapter 3. The four hundred thousand troops of Israel would appear to give them overwhelming superiority.

Verse 18 sounds much like the opening of the book of Judges in 1:1–2. Judah is to lead the battle. The first attack is a disaster, and Israel loses twenty-two thousand men. On their second attack, despite Yahweh's command to go forward, they face another rout and the loss of eighteen thousand fighting men. The text gives no specific reason as to why the first two attacks fail, but there are subtle differences in the preparations for each attack. In verse 18, there is no doubt about going to battle; the question is only, *Who of us shall go up first?* After the first defeat, they encourage each other and weep before the Lord. After the second defeat, they go up to Bethel to fast and make sacrifices. Then they ask the Lord whether they should go up again or not. Perhaps this indicates a more sincere dependence on the Lord. Finally, the Lord assures them that they will be victorious.

According to verses 29–36, Israel uses an ambush to defeat Benjamin. They prepare to attack Gibeah as before and draw away the Benjaminite army. As Israel pretends to withdraw in defeat, Benjamin rushes in to press their attack. At that point, Israel attacks and springs the trap on Benjamin. The Benjaminites are utterly defeated and their army is almost completely destroyed.

Verses 37–45 recount the tactic of the ambush in more detail. This is not simple repetition but expands the first narrative with additional information about the flight of Benjamin and the pursuit and complete victory by Israel.

Verses 46–48 complete the picture of the defeat of Benjamin. Out of their initial army of twenty-six thousand, only six hundred remain, and they are driven into months of hiding. The army of Israel then marches through Benjaminite territory, destroying everything in their path.

Chapter 21 explains the aftermath of the civil war. According to verses 1–3, only a few hundred survivors remain from Benjamin, and there are no wives so that their tribe may continue. The Israelites have sworn not to give their daughters to anyone of Benjamin. Now, however, they realize that this vow will condemn Benjamin to extinction. This is one of the most shocking chapters in the entire book, since it shows Israel committing further atrocities in order to try to resolve the problems created in chapter 20.

In verses 4–14, Israel assembles to make an offering to the Lord, and they suspect anyone who fails to attend of not supporting their decisions. At the meeting, the question is raised concerning how wives can be provided so that Benjamin will not disappear from the tribes of Israel. It is discovered that the town of Jabesh-Gilead has not attended the meeting. Then a way of combining revenge on Jabesh-Gilead and providing wives for Benjamin is suggested. The Israelites will kill all the men and women who are not virgins, leaving alive only the virgins of Jabesh-Gilead. These are offered to the men of Benjamin. Still, there are not enough women.

The people are still concerned that Benjamin may die out, and so they come up with a second plan to provide them with wives (verses 15–23). The Benjaminites are told to go to Shiloh at the time of the annual festival. When the girls come out to dance, the Benjaminites may seize them and take them away for wives. Then everyone will have a degree of deniability. No one shows concern about the women or their feelings in all this. The men only want to help Benjamin and to be able to deny their own guilt in breaking their vow. Unfortunately, this sounds all too familiar, as they void the spirit of their vow while keeping it in a technical sense.

In verses 24–25, everyone returns home now that this crisis has been resolved. The final line makes clear, however, that Israel is doing what is right in their own eyes. The implication is that it is far from right in God's eyes.

THEOLOGICAL REFLECTIONS

In some ways, Judges appears to be a secular book with little to say about God. It is filled with bloodshed, struggles for power, atrocities, and civil war. In many respects, the book sounds all too familiar to the modern reader. The book does make some important points, however, about the need for remaining faithful to God. After the death of the great leader Joshua, a new generation has to make its own decisions about whether or not to be faithful to God. Over and over, the people turn away from the Lord, and they suffer terrible consequences. This should be an important lesson for every generation. In this transition period, God raises up leaders who are often far from perfect, but God can use them, nevertheless. Even today, God can use imperfect people, if they will accept his guidance. The book ends with a warning about the dangers that may arise when people do what is right in their own eyes. The contemporary world is filled with tragedies that can occur when people do what is right in their own eyes with no regard for anyone else. The book also looks forward to leaders who will provide the right kind of leadership and do what is right in God's eyes. Unfortunately for Israel, they had far too few leaders who were concerned with leading according to God's laws. This finally leads to their downfall. Perhaps today one should take a lesson from that and be more concerned with the types of leaders selected in all aspects of life. The book of Judges is filled with stories from the distant past, but the people and situations look very similar to those in the modern world and thus offer abiding lessons.

FOR FURTHER STUDY

Antony F. Campbell, S.J., *Joshua to Chronicles* (Louisville: Westminster John Knox, 2004).

V. Philips Long, *The Art of Biblical History* (Grand Rapids: Zondervan, 1994).

A. D. H. Mayes, *Judges* (Sheffield: Sheffield Academic Press, 1985).

Richard D. Nelson, *The Historical Books* (Nashville: Abingdon, 1998).

Carolyn Pressler, *Joshua, Judges, and Ruth* (Louisville: Westminster John Knox, 2002).

WORKS CITED

Daniel I. Block, *Judges, Ruth* (Nashville: Broadman & Holman, 1999).

Baruch Halpern, *The First Historians* (San Francisco: Harper & Row, 1988).

D. Herr and M. P. Boyd, "A Watermelon Named Abimelech," *Biblical Archaeology Review* 28 (January-February 2002): 34–37, 62.

Philip J. King and Lawrence E. Stager, *Life in Biblical Israel* (Louisville: Westminster John Knox, 2001).

J. Clinton McCann, *Judges* (Louisville: Westminster John Knox, 2002).

Tammi J. Schneider, *Judges* (Collegeville, Minn.: Liturgical, 2000).

J. Alberto Soggin, *Judges* (trans. John Bowden. Philadelphia: Westminster, 1981).

K. Lawson Younger Jr., *Judges/Ruth* (Grand Rapids: Zondervan, 2002).

Ruth

Mark W. Hamilton & Kelly Shearon

CHAPTER CONTENTS

Contexts 267
Commentary 267
    To Moab & Back · 1:1–22 267
    Ruth in the Fields of Boaz · 2:1–23 268
    Ruth in the Arms of Boaz · 3:1–18 268
    Ruth Becomes an Israelite · 4:1–22 269
Theological Reflections 269
For Further Study 269
Works Cited 270

The book of Ruth paints a charming picture of a vulnerable woman whose loyalty to her Israelite mother-in-law and her God gains her acceptance into the village life of Bethlehem.

CONTEXTS

Though set in Israel's premonarchic period, the book was written later, perhaps as late as the early postexilic era. It reflects, however, the life of small farmers in Israel at many periods. More importantly, it explores the question of what it means to be Israelite, implying that mere genetic origin does not suffice. The true Israelite lives out a set of commitments to family and God.

The Septuagint (the Greek translation of the Old Testament) situates Ruth between Judges and 1 Samuel, the position it holds in most English translations. Such a location makes sense of the setting of the story. However, the Hebrew Bible locates the book after Proverbs, making Ruth a parade example of the "virtuous woman" [Hebrew *eshet chayil*, "woman of strength"].

COMMENTARY

TO MOAB & BACK · 1:1–22

1:1–5 The opening verses set the scene chronologically (*when the judges ruled*), geographically (*Judah* and *Moab*), and economically (*famine*). The opening verse gives the story a non-specific, once-upon-a-time quality. The verses then set up the problem of the book with great literary skill, first by giving the sons of *Naomi* ("pleasant") odd names (*Mahlon* relates to the Hebrew word for "sickness," and *Kilion* to "finished off"), and then by noting that all the males die without issue. Such a state necessitates Naomi's return to Israel and thus sets the story in motion.

1:6–15 Naomi's return home begins with the notice (verse 6) that God has ended the famine in Judah. The text introduces Yahweh as a deliverer and so initiates a discussion that continues across the book as to what one can expect from God.

For the moment, however, the story moves into the discussion among Naomi and her daughters-in-law. The blessing in verses 8–9 makes several moves: Naomi invites them to return to their families of origin, with the unexpected phrase (since fathers ruled daughters until marriage) *mother's home*, which emphasizes the story's location in the world of women; she invokes the name of Israel's God on Gentile women because of their fidelity [Hebrew *chesed*]; and she wishes for them other (presumably Moabite) husbands. Far from being a parochial text, Ruth hopes that even ordinary Gentiles can enjoy the pleasures of a normal life.

When the women beg her not to leave, Naomi makes several arguments for her planned journey. She acknowledges their sexual needs (Sasson 26; see Song of Songs) and appeals to her own inability to conceive new husbands for them.

While many readers censure Orpah's return home, the text does not. Ruth's behavior shows greater risk-taking, but Orpah obeys her mother-in-law and thus deserves respect. Biblical stories usually work by bringing supporting characters onstage and then dismissing them, so there is no reason to denigrate Orpah's actions.

1:16–22 The scene in Moab closes with Ruth's plea to return to Israel with Naomi. She bravely commits herself not only to Naomi, but also to Naomi's God, whom she invokes as a witness to her oath. Verse 17 implies that she expects never to return to

Moab. In moving, Ruth imitates earlier individuals who left their homeland to follow Yahweh, notably Abraham and Sarah.

Verses 19–21 describe a less than happy homecoming. The author reveals Naomi's interior state through the change of her name from Naomi ("pleasant") to *Mara* ("bitter, bitterness") and through her pointed criticism of God (verse 21). Naomi thus becomes a mourner, much as one sees in the psalms of lament (for example, Ps 137; Lam 1–4). The ironic use of the title *the Almighty* calls God's power into question. Like the author of Job, the writer of Ruth does not offer a defense for God's inactivity.

RUTH IN THE FIELDS OF BOAZ · 2:1–23

2:1–16 Boaz may have been either an acquaintance (Sasson 39) or a relative (Nielsen 53) of *Elimelech*'s, depending on how one interprets the Hebrew text. Boaz's introduction here foreshadows the possibility of his marriage to Ruth and his redemption of Naomi. As a poor person, Ruth may glean in the fields of more prosperous landowners (see Lev 19:9; 23:22; Deut 24:19). Verse 3's phrase *she found herself* affirms that Ruth did not choose her fate (see the same phrase in Eccl 2:14–15; compare Gen 24:12).

The conversation between Ruth and Boaz (verses 8–13) deepens the story's portrayal of their characters. Boaz, apparently older, appears as a man sensitive to the needs of others and aware of the attractions of the opposite sex. Ruth comes across as a naïve but grateful *young woman*. She insists on her foreign origins (verse 10), while he, expressing the author's views, details her qualifications for acceptance into the community in Bethlehem (verse 11). She is widowed, hence vulnerable, but she also cares for her mother-in-law (thus keeping the fifth commandment). She takes risk, forsaking her family and land to *live with a people you did not know before* (literally "three days ago").

Boaz's blessing (compare 4:11–12, 14–15) recognizes Ruth's pledge to follow Yahweh as the passport into the community. Ruth accepts this new position in verse 13, referring to herself as *your servant*. Boaz then asks Yahweh to protect Ruth, utilizing a popular Israelite metaphor for the providence of God, *wings* [Hebrew *kanaph*]. Ironically, it is Boaz who must ultimately provide protection for Ruth, as she asks him to spread his *kanaph* over her on the threshing floor (3:9; see Nielsen 60).

2:17–23 Ruth returns with an *ephah* of barley, about ³/₅ of a bushel. Customarily, a male harvester consumed one to two pounds per day, and thus Ruth brought home several weeks' worth of food (Sasson 57). Like the "virtuous woman" of Proverbs 31, she works hard. The narrative contrasts Boaz's abundant provision of food with Ruth's ongoing problem of being a childless, foreign (see *Moabitess* in verse 21) widow (Nielsen 62). The charming conclusion of this story makes it clear that, while the characters in this story experience love as an accident, for the reader, the story's happy ending seems increasingly inevitable. Naomi reveals Boaz to be a *kinsmen redeemer* [Hebrew *goel*; see Job 19:25]. The narrative presents the possibility of ultimate provision (remarriage) for the needs of Ruth *the Moabitess* (verse 21) and also subsequently, for Naomi. Naomi urges Ruth to continue gleaning in the field of Boaz, which she does for about two months.

> **The "Kinsmen Redeemer" & Levirate Marriage**
> *Levirate marriages were a common practice in the Near East, including Israel. A childless widow might marry her deceased husband's brother in order to produce a child who, in theory, carried on the name and reputation of the dead man. The woman and her offspring thus remained in the family of marriage. Subsequent children would count for the new husband. See Genesis 38 for an especially complex case of such a practice.*

RUTH IN THE ARMS OF BOAZ · 3:1–18

This scene of seduction consists of three parts: Naomi's plan (verses 1–5), the encounter with Boaz (verses 6–15), and Ruth's report (verses 16–18). Here two highly self-aware adults choose to marry on grounds of both expediency and attraction.

3:1–5 Naomi's plan counts on Boaz's participation in a post-harvest religious ceremony. Naomi instructs Ruth to *wash and perfume yourself and put on your best clothes*, activities strikingly similar to bridal preparations (see Ps 45:8, 13–14; Esth 2:12). Naomi advises Ruth to *uncover his feet*. This suggestion can be interpreted in several ways, including the possibility that *feet* is a euphemism for either Boaz's or Ruth's genitals (Sasson

> **The Wings of God**
> *Ancient Near Eastern art sometimes portrayed deities with wings. The Bible also uses this metaphor (Pss 17:8; 36:7; 57:1; 61:4; 63:7; 91:4) for the God of Israel.*

70–71). The author deliberately obscures what happened on the threshing floor that night.

3:6–15 Ruth's request in verse 9 discreetly invites Boaz to fulfill his blessing on her in 2:12 by marrying her. (Ezek 16:8 offers a parallel for the spreading of one's cloak over a naked woman to symbolize marriage) Boaz responds favorably to Ruth's request because she has chosen a husband based on his ability to provide security and redemption, rather than on mere virility. He reveals his identity as a *kinsman-redeemer*, previously recognized by only Naomi. We learn there is another man of nearer kinship to Elimelech, but Boaz promises to negotiate with him, swearing *as surely as the Lord lives* as a witness to his intentions (as in 1 Sam 20:3, 21). Ruth *lay at his feet until morning*, apparently asleep. Boaz, in yet another display of generosity, fills her shawl with *six measures of barley*, roughly 30 pounds of grain.

3:16–18 Ruth reports back to Naomi, who expects a satisfactory outcome to her plan.

RUTH BECOMES AN ISRAELITE · 4:1–22

The conclusion of the book consists of three sections: a scene of business and legal activities (verses 1–12), a wedding and birth (verses 13–17), and an appendix connecting the entire story to David (verses 18–22).

4:1–12 The scene now shifts to the *town gate*, a small fortification with a space for meetings (though Bethlehem was an unwalled village in the Iron Age) and the site of the local court (see for example Gen 19:1; 2 Sam 15:2–4; Prov 31:23). The gathering of the *ten elders of the town*, presumably the heads of the local families, to bear witness to the proceedings has parallels elsewhere (Gen 23:10; Job 29:7; Prov 24:7).

The court scene opens with a land sale and ends with a marriage. Since land remained in a family, especially through the male heirs (but see Num 27:1–11; 36:1–12; Job 42:15), the extended family felt a need to settle its ownership (compare Jer 32:6–15).

> **Removing Sandals**
>
> *Verse 7 constitutes an aside to the reader, explaining a custom that had died out by the time of the book's composition. The removal of sandals symbolized the transfer of property or marital rights from the heir of first resort to one further down the line.*

Boaz uses the occasion to persuade the nearest relative to Elimelech to forego his rights, arguing that the addition of Ruth's potential children to the man's family would dilute the value of inheritances on his death (verse 6). He and Boaz work out a business deal by which Boaz gains both the property and Ruth.

This scene closes with a blessing integrating Ruth into the community. The people connect her story to that of the great, fertile ancestresses, then seek for her a high status, and then pray for fertility for her. Interestingly, the people tell the tawdry story of *Tamar* to emphasize instead her crucial place in the tribal story.

4:13–17 The blessing foreshadows the fertility of the couple's marriage. Yet the ultimate reversal of fortunes is Naomi's, because Yahweh has answered her complaint in 1:20–21 with a redeemer and descendents. The village calls the child Naomi's, possibly because his birth not only preserves but redeems her lineage. *They named him Obed*, which means "to serve." Verses 15–16 beautifully describe the duties of adults to their parents, giving concreteness to the fifth commandment.

4:18–22 The book closes with the genealogy of Perez, leading through Ruth to David and indicating that Israel at its best opened the door to righteous Gentiles (compare Isa 56).

THEOLOGICAL REFLECTIONS

Ruth focuses on the small-scale lives of destitute women and the village that welcomes them in order to highlight the large-scale ethical and religious values of Israel. The soaring visions of the law and prophets become tangible in the behavior of ordinary men and women seeking stability, fertility, and meaning in life. While it does not speak to the intricacies of biblical theology in its portrayal of God or Israel, Ruth reminds readers that religion works meaningfully in the everyday, and as such the book deserves the affection it continues to receive.

FOR FURTHER STUDY

André LaCocque, *Ruth* (Minneapolis, Minn.: Fortress, 2004).
Katharine Doob Sakenfeld, *Ruth* (Louisville: Westminster John Knox, 1999).

WORKS CITED

Kirsten Nielsen, *Ruth: A Commentary* (Louisville: Westminster John Knox, 1997).

Jack M. Sasson, *Ruth: A New Translation with a Philological Commentary and a Formalist-Folklorist Interpretation* (2d ed.; Sheffield: Sheffield University Press, 1989).

1 Samuel

Sara Fudge

CHAPTER CONTENTS

Contexts   271

Commentary   272
    Samuel's Leadership · 1:1–8:22   272
    Saul's Kingship · 9:1–15:35   277
    David's Rise to Kingship · 1 Sam 16:1–2 Sam 4:12   281

Theological Reflections   288

For Further Study   289

Works Cited   289

MAPS, TABLES, & FEATURES

The Deuteronomist   272
Children & the Israelite Family   273
The Philistines   275
Baal & Ashtoreth   276
Monarchy & Hardships   277
The High Place   278
The Theology of the Exodus   279
The Teraphim   284
Early Ecstatic Prophets   284
Philistia   286

First and Second Samuel are alive with accounts of prophets and kings, servants and heroes, generals and princes. They are filled with palace intrigue, human drama, with incidents of murder, rape, love, revenge, and war, as well as the fear, faithfulness, hope, and heartbreak that tug at the reader's heart. They tell a remarkable history as an unassuming youth becomes a powerful king. Scripture is not sparing in reporting the events of its heroes. These books tell both the bitter and the sweet in the lives of men and women who work to serve Yahweh but become distracted with their passions and aspirations. More important than these elements of intrigue, however, is the account of the establishment of the kingdom of Israel – the account not only of those who engage in this process, but also of the God who orchestrates it.

CONTEXTS

The books of Samuel primarily record the transition of the nation of Israel from the period of the Judges to the founding of the monarchy. Israel moves from a theocratic state, a nation ruled by God under non-hereditary judges, to a nation ruled by dynasties of kings. Deuteronomy anticipates this political shift: the establishment of kingship (Deut 17:14; 1 Sam 8), the pitfalls of kingship (Deut 17:16, 17; 1 Sam 8) and the disobedience to God's commands (Deut 17:18, 19; 1 Sam 13:13, 14). Three focal characters are key in this transition: Samuel, Saul, and David.

The key story is the founding of the dynasty of David (2 Sam 7:4–16), which lasts four hundred years and provides the lineage of David through which the Messiah will come and an "everlasting covenant" will be established (2 Sam 23:5; Rom 1:2–4).

Several themes interwoven throughout 1 and 2 Samuel are evident in the songs that open and close these books (Hannah's, 1 Sam 2; David's, 2 Sam 22, 23). Hannah and David sing of the blessings they experience in the Lord. Both witness how the righteous receive the Lord's blessing while the wicked perish. They see the Lord humble the exalted and arrogant, while giving victory and blessing to the insignificant and humble. Hannah and David receive the Lord's strength as he delivers them from the enemy; the Lord is our "rock" and "horn" (strength), sing Hannah and David (1 Sam 2:1, 2; 2 Sam 22:3). God not only brings salvation, but does so against the odds by using the small, weak, and few to accomplish mighty works. Another prominent theme is the contrast between the heart of the repentant and the heart of one with little or no concern for his or her own sinfulness and repentance (Samuel and Eli, David and Saul, Abigail and Nabal).

Biblical scholars have shown particular interest in the literary analysis of 1 and 2 Samuel. Critics have noted alleged discrepancies throughout the books of Samuel. For instance, some feel that there is a contradictory response from God to the establishment of a monarchy over Israel, in that 1 Samuel 8 gives a warning to Israel regarding a king, but God anoints a king

1 SAM

1 SAMUEL

> **The Deuteronomist**
>
> Noth proposed that the books from Deuteronomy through Kings (except Ruth) are one unified literary work compiled from several oral and written sources. He contends that this work was revised and edited during the exilic period (about 586–539 BCE) by a single editor he refers to as the Deuteronomist (Dtr).
>
> Samuel makes sense in the context of this larger block of material and how it reflects the theology found in Deuteronomy. The layering of the ideas found in Samuel reflects the multiple authorship of this book and explains the apparent discrepancies found there. The Deuteronomist did his work during the exilic period of Israel's history (about 560 BCE) in an attempt to unify the Jewish history and explain the situation in which Israel now finds itself, driven from the covenant land promised to it in the days of Abraham. This theory proposes that the Deuteronomist composed speeches for the main characters and inserted them throughout the text to unify the history (Josh 1:23; 1 Sam 12; 1 Kgs 8) with Deuteronomy itself being a speech of Moses. For further study see Dillard and Longman; McCarter's 1 Samuel; McKenzie; and Polzin.

for Israel in 1 Samuel 9:16. Another question posed by the text regards Saul's first introduction to David. Does Saul first meet David when he hires him to play the harp and sooth Saul's tormented spirit, or when David challenges Goliath (1 Sam 16:14–23; 17:31–58)?

Other issues that concern literary critics are the duplications and sometimes variations of certain incidents recorded in Samuel. We find two different accounts of Saul's selection as king (1 Sam 10:17–24; 11:15) as well as two accounts of his rejection by God (1 Sam 13:14; 15:23). And who killed Goliath, David or Elhanan (1 Sam 17:51; 2 Sam 21:19)? These inconsistencies have caused scholars to search for explanations for the text and its author(s). These and other issues will be addressed in the commentary section of this study.

Many scholars have suggested solutions to the difficulties found in Samuel, but the one most widely accepted was proposed by Martin Noth, a noted scholar in Old Testament studies. He argued for the existence of a Deuteronomistic History, a single work including Joshua through 2 Kings (minus Ruth). Though it is impossible with the information available today to know exactly how the early writings of the Bible were composed and collected, Noth's theory analyzes Scripture by searching for common denominators that give clues to its origin and composition. It is altogether possible, however, that these books may have been produced essentially in their present form at an earlier time than proposed by Noth.

The events recorded in the books of Samuel take place approximately between 1118–970 BCE. This period spans the birth of Samuel to the end of David's reign. Israel has been living in the land of Canaan since the exodus from Egypt and has not been oppressed or challenged during this time by any of the mighty world powers. The great Egyptian New Kingdom, from which the Israelites fled, no longer poses a threat. Assyrian interference in Israel will not occur until the expansions of Shalmaneser III in about 853 BCE, and Babylon is in a weak period of its own and will not come to the forefront in strength until the Chaldaean Dynasty of the Neo-Babylonian Period, 625–539 BCE.

Israel is thus in an ideal situation to expand despite the continuous raids from immediate neighbors (Amalekites, 1 Sam 15:8–33; Philistines, 1 Sam 21:10–14, 27–29; Ammonites, 1 Sam 11:12, 2 Sam 10:1–4). We should note, though, that "biblical historiography, in contradiction to modern history writing since the Enlightenment, locates the causes of human events in the passions and purpose of Yahweh, the God of Israel" (Arnold 24).

COMMENTARY

SAMUEL'S LEADERSHIP · 1:1–8:22

The period of the judges draws to a close as Israel seeks a different style of leadership. A new era of Israel's history is about to begin. Israel will look to Samuel to implement this change.

Birth & Dedication of Samuel · 1:1–28

First Samuel opens with the birth story of Samuel. This birth motif is similar to several others found in Scripture and characterized by emotional frustration and spiritual intervention (Isaac, Gen 17:17; Moses, Exod 2:1–10; Samson, Judg 13; John the Baptist, Luke 1:5–25). Samuel's father is a *man from Ramathaim, a Zuphite from the hill country of Ephraim, whose name was Elkanah* (1:1). Elkanah has two wives: one who bears him children, Peninnah, and one who is barren, Hannah. As a sign of his affection and favor toward Hannah, Elkanah gives Hannah a *double portion of meat* (1:5). The Hebrew dual form here may be emphasizing the greater quantity given to Hannah, though its exact meaning is ambiguous. Possibly due to jealousy for her husband's attention or common pride, Peninnah mocks Hannah for her infertility, which intensifies Hannah's desperation for children. Elkanah asks Hannah several questions regarding her sadness, but his most impassioned question is, *Don't I mean more to you than ten sons?* (1:8).

> **"A double portion..."**
> Hebrew nouns may be singular or plural, as in English, or dual (referring to two items) as here.

Bearing children was the honor of a woman in the ancient world, and *children's children are a crown to the aged* (Gen 24:60; Prov 17:6). Here we see the tensions typical of some polygamous families. A kind and compassionate husband was a blessing, but he could not replace a child. Hannah deeply mourned her barrenness.

Elkanah would make yearly trips to the sanctuary of Shiloh to bring offerings to the Lord (compare Exod 23:14–17). These were times of celebration and thankfulness before the Lord. Because of Hannah's sorrow, she is unable to celebrate with the others, so she takes this opportunity to pray and petition the Lord for a child. She makes a vow to the Lord. Vows were a contract with the Lord, usually encased in a conditional "if ... then" formula: "If you, O Lord, will do this for me, then I will do this for you." Hannah vows that if the Lord will *give her a son, then I will give him to the Lord for all the days of his life, and no razor will ever be used on his head* (1:11). Hannah vows to give her son to the service of the tabernacle in Shiloh, which raises the issue of Levitical lineage. His genealogy is traced to Levi in 1 Chronicles 6:25–28. Samuel's service to the temple would be brought to a more intense level by what appears to be the Nazirite vow. Hannah vows not to cut his hair, which is one of three requirements of the Nazirite vow, along with abstaining from wine and avoiding dead bodies for a designated period of time. A variation in the Dead Sea Scrolls reads, "and I will give him as a Nazirite for life" (4 QSam), adding credence to Samuel's being a Nazirite (Douglas 808).

> **Nazirites**
> Numbers 6 prescribes rules for those taking the Nazirite vow. These characters apparently served as intermediaries between God and Israel (see Amos 2:11–12), with their lives of abstinence symbolizing the radical commitment to God that all of Israel had assumed. (Samson's mother carried out the Nazirite rules (Judg 13:13–14), and he refrained from cutting his hair.)

Eli, the high priest, is sitting by the door watching Hannah pray. He misunderstands her silent prayer as the result of drunkenness, which is not uncommon during the days of celebration as worshipers overuse wine. This, of course, is not Hannah's state. Apparently, Eli does not have the insight of the Spirit, which will be seen in the yet-to-be born Samuel, to know what will come of Hannah's prayer, but after learning of her circumstances, he expresses a "hopeful blessing" that her petition will be granted (Cartledge 34). This lack of spiritual discernment in Eli's life becomes more serious as the story unfolds.

The Lord hears Hannah's prayer and blesses her with a son, Samuel. After weaning the boy, usually a two- to three-year period, Hannah brings him to

---

Children & the Israelite Family

Children were an integral part of the family structure in the ancient world. Not only were they essential in maintaining the family farm or business, but their duty as caregivers to their parents in their older years was crucial. The elderly had no pension plan to sustain them in later life.

Children were heirs to the family inheritance and carried on the name of the family. If a woman did not bear children for her husband, then other measures could be taken in order to bring children into the family. Adoption, even of an adult, was an option. Abraham considered Eliezer as one to inherit his estate (Gen 15:2, 4). Another solution to the problem was to marry another wife (Abraham, Gen 16:1, 2; Jacob, Gen 30:1–3). This was a very common practice in biblical times and even survives in the Arab world today. Texts from the ancient city of Nuzi attest to these practices.

Scripture does not record the history of Elkanah's two marriages, but it may be that he married Peninnah because Hannah was childless. For further study see de Vaux 41–52 and Thompson, 196–297.

the house of the Lord with a *three-year-old bull* (the Masoretic Text reads "three bulls"; the Septuagint reads a "three-year-old bull"), *an ephah of flour and a skin of wine* (1:24). Leviticus 12:6 specifies that a gift of a year-old lamb and a young pigeon or dove be brought following the days of purification for a son or daughter. Either translation reveals that Hannah and Elkanah brought a generous gift to Yahweh.

Hannah's Prayer · 2:1–11

Hannah's prayer beautifully expresses the themes found in the books of Samuel. God answers her prayer and removes her shame. She sings praises to God for his holiness and strength: *there is no one holy like the Lord* and *there is no Rock like our God* (2:2). This truth carries throughout these pages. Another prominent theme mentioned here is how God exalts the humble and godly, *He raises the poor from the dust and lifts the needy from the ash heap; he seats them with princes and has them inherit a throne of honor* (2:8). Saul and David both come to the throne from humble means. In contrast, the haughty and evil will be broken, *the bows of the mighty are shattered* (2:4), referring to Israel's victory over her enemies and God's care of the poor. Hannah prophesies a coming king who will achieve this victory (2:10). She sings of *his anointed*, "Messiah" (2:10), foreshadowing the future house of David and the Son of God (1 Sam 2:35; 2 Sam 7). The books of Samuel are encased between Hannah's song and a song of David found in 2 Samuel 22 and 23 that reiterates and expounds upon these themes.

Samuel & Eli's Household · 2:12 – 3:21

2:12–26 Unlike the pious Samuel, *Eli's sons were wicked men* or literally, "sons of Belial." *Belial* means "wickedness" or "worthlessness." Their conduct reflected a heart that *did not know the Lord* (2:12). The Hebrew word "to know" carries a sense of intimacy. The actions of Hophni and Phinehas are unworthy of their priestly office. They desecrate the offerings brought to the temple by taking more than their share. The fat of an offering was to be burned to the Lord; the priest was not to eat any fat or blood of an offering (Lev 3:17), yet the family of Eli were *fattening* themselves *on the choicest parts of every offering made by my people Israel* (2:29). In addition, they engaged in sex acts with female worshipers, perhaps a Canaanite practice. Prior to this discussion of Eli's sons, in the middle and at the end of this discussion, the text notes Samuel's role as a priest (2:11, 18), and his winsome behavior (2:26). What a stark contrast between the priests by birth—legitimate Levites—and the boy Samuel.

3:1–21 Samuel receives his first word from the Lord as a boy while sleeping in the sanctuary *where the ark of God was* (3:3). The ark may be mentioned here as a reference to time, for the ark will not reside in an Israelite sanctuary much of Samuel's life.

> **Temple or Tabernacle?**
> 1 Samuel speaks of Yahweh's temple (3:3), *using the common Hebrew noun* heykhal *["temple" or "palace"], hence a masonry structure. The* NIV's *note* tabernacle *has no basis in 1 Samuel and is a harmonization with the Pentateuch.*

More importantly, the story functions as a prophetic call narrative like those of Moses (Exod 3), Isaiah (Isa 6), and Jeremiah (Jer 1). In these stories, the called prophet expresses confusion and reluctance but accepts God's charge. On God's third call, Eli realizes that the Lord is calling to the boy and instructs Samuel to listen to the divine word. Samuel announces the same message Eli had received from an unnamed prophet earlier (2:27). Samuel is *afraid*, but he tells Eli that the guilt of his house *will never be atoned for by sacrifice or offering* (3:14). Later, Samuel will tell Saul, *To obey is better than sacrifice, and to heed is better than the fat of rams* (1 Sam 15:22). God's favor shifts from Eli to Samuel as Eli continues to allow bad decisions.

Eli is portrayed as a kind man. He listens to Hannah and sends her away with a blessing. He takes Samuel into his care, and he even shows his concern for the reverence of the Lord when he confronts his sons for their sin. But Eli lacks both an intimacy with God and moral courage. He confronts his sons but does not purge their evil from the temple, though he was warned repeatedly to do so (2:22–25). As a priest, he should be able to receive the Lord's word, but several times God's message comes from other places. He misinterprets Hannah's cry to the Lord, and it takes three calls to Samuel before Eli understands that it is the Lord calling (3:4–14). Finally, he allows the army to take the ark of the covenant to the battlefield. He knows this is improper, for *he feared for the ark of God* (4:13) but once again did nothing to prevent it. Because of these offenses, Eli's family loses its priestly status (2:31).

There are both immediate and long-term consequences to Eli's actions. Eli will see the death of both of his sons on the same day and then die himself (2:34). Phinehas's wife gives birth to a son on the day of

Phinehas's death, so the family line carries on. The name "Ichabod" means "where is the glory," a commentary on the events of this chapter. Years later, Saul kills the priests at Nob, fugitives from Shiloh, who assist David, with only Abiathar, a descendant of Phinehas, escaping (1 Sam 22:20). Later, Solomon dismisses Abiathar from his service, *fulfilling the word the Lord had spoken at Shiloh about the house of Eli* (1 Kgs 2:27). Scripture closes this episode reiterating the words that *the Lord was with Samuel as he grew up ... and revealed himself to Samuel through his word* (1 Sam 3:19–21), not through Eli and his house. The significance in these verses is the transfer of power and authority from Eli's house to Samuel, illustrating a theme prevalent throughout these books: God favors and rewards faithful people but brings curses to those who disrespect holy things. The story shifts to an incident regarding the ark of the Lord and one last fatal error of Eli's family.

Capture of the Ark of the Lord · 4:1–7:1

4:1–11 Ancient people attributed success or failure in war to the favor or disfavor of the gods. These cultures created and cared for statues of their gods in their cities in order to curry the gods' favor. The presence of the statue represented the presence of the god. Invading nations would, at times, capture the statues of the gods and transport them to their cities as a sign of conquest of the nation and their gods. It is not surprising, then, that after Israel's defeat by the Philistines, they would seek God's favor by bringing the only image-like relic they had, the ark of God, to the battlefield. Their thinking was flawed, for God did not dwell in anything made by the hands of man, and will not be manipulated by the strategic location of the ark. God reinforces this point when Israel falls again to the Philistines, and their sacred ark of the covenant falls to their enemies.

4:12–22 The capture of the ark accompanies disturbing events for Israel. Not only does Israel lose 30,000 men in the battle, but they also lose their religious leaders. The unnamed prophet's prediction comes true. Hophni and Phinehas die on this same day, as well as the old priest Eli, who led Israel for 40 years. The text sadly notes that *the glory has departed from Israel* (4:21).

5:1–12 The story next follows the ark from one Philistine town to another and watches the chaos it brings to each. It is first taken from Ebenezer, where Israel was defeated, to the Philistine town of Ashdod, where it is placed before their god Dagon (1 Sam 5), whose statue twice falls before the ark of the Lord, the second time with head and hands *cut off*, not broken. This gives the image of one slain in battle, an intentional incident, not an accident. The Hebrew word for "hand" sometimes means "power." *The Lord's hand was heavy upon the people of Ashdod* (5:6), whereas Dagon's hands are cut off.

6:1–7:1 The Lord also afflicts the Philistines with *tumors* of an unspecified nature. Literally, the Hebrew word means "hill." This may allude to raised bumps on the skin. The Septuagint uses the dual form of the word meaning two bumps, which the Greek translates as "buttocks." The Masoretic Text may imply that the Philistines suffered from dysentery leading to hemorrhoids. Cartledge observes, "Not only does Dagon lose his head and his hands, but his people lose their dignity" (84).

This plague brings to mind the exodus when God inflicted the Egyptians with many plagues (6:6). Significantly, Philistines remember the devastating

---

The Philistines

The Philistines posed a constant threat to Israel until the reign of King David. They came from the land of Caphtor (probably Crete) and other Aegean islands. Part of a larger group called the Sea Peoples, they migrated to the east (1 Chron 1:12; Jer 47:4; Amos 9:7). By about 1100 BCE, they settled in five cities commonly known as the Philistine Pentapolis (Gaza, Ashkelon, Ashdod, Ekron, and Gath). The zenith of their culture dates from 1150 to 1000 BCE.

Their material remains reflect a blending of foreign and neighboring cultures. Many of their gods were borrowed from the Semitic and Canaanite pantheons (Dagon, the god of grain, and Baal respectively). Mycenaean, Egyptian, and Canaanite art influenced their pottery. Very little of their language has survived, and it is assumed they spoke a dialect of the Canaanite language, at least later in their history. They were well known for their expertise in metalworking, which gave them an advantage in weaponry over the Israelites and explains Israel's fear of them (1 Sam 13:19–21). Following the period of David's reign, in the tenth century, they began to lose their influence and were gradually absorbed into the surrounding Canaanite culture (Dothan 333; see Hoerth, Mattingly, and Yamauchi 231–50).

Baal & Ashtoreth

Israel constantly struggled with the desire to worship a God they could not see or touch. Israelite history saw a struggle to understand God as one and as unrepresentable by human art. All their needs and praises were directed to one deity, whereas other nations had many gods who specialized in different areas of nature and expertise. When Israel needed rain, it was tempting to call upon the Canaanite god of rain, Baal. Israel often merged its notion of God with Canaanite images of deity (see Hos 1–2).

Baal was a major deity in the Canaanite pantheon. His name means "lord." Stories of Baal in creation texts exist from the ancient city of Ugarit, located on the Mediterranean coast of Syria (about 1250 BCE). He is believed to have been worshiped from as early as 2000 BCE. He was the god of storms and rain and later of vegetation and the fertility of the land. Mythologies tell of his victorious battle against Yam, the sea god, and Mot, the god of death. Many times he is depicted with a club or a symbol for lightning in his hand.

Ashtoreth was a goddess of fertility, love, and war. She is equated with the Phoenician goddess Astarte and the Mesopotamian goddess Ishtar. Her symbols include the lion, the dove, and the planet Venus. After killing Saul, the Philistines placed his armor in a temple of Ashtoreth (1 Sam 31:10). People have found many clay plaques depicting a naked female, likely the image of Ashtoreth-Astarte, throughout the region (Jordan 36).

---

power of God at the exodus (compare Exod 15:14), while Israel forgets the saving power of God at the exodus.

After seven destructive months, the Philistines wisely decide to return the ark to its rightful owners. True to ancient tradition, it must be returned with ritual and offerings to appease the God they offended. Approaching any god carelessly can only bring more harm to the people. The Philistines construct a new cart and find two cows that have recently given birth and have never been used as beasts of burden. These animals transport the ark in the direction of the Hebrews, then become a sacrifice to the Hebrew God. Next, the Philistines place offerings of golden tumors and rats beside the ark, corresponding to the number of leaders of the Philistines and their settlements (6:4). This is the first mention of rats. They may have spread the devastating plague or possibly destroyed the fields to add further damage to the Philistine nation. God had won a total victory over the Philistines, their gods, their people, and their land. The cart with its treasures travels toward the Israelite town Beth-Shemesh.

The Israelites should have shown more reverence and caution in their handling of the ark to avoid the calamity they are about to encounter. They remove the ark from the cart and use the wood of the cart to build a fire upon which to offer the cows as an offering to the Lord. Whether it was due to ignorance or disrespect, many Israelites foolishly *looked into the ark of the Lord* (6:19) and died. This places a fear of the Lord in them: *who can stand in the presence of the Lord, this holy God*? (6:20). The Pentateuch sets forth guidelines for the care of sacred objects – how to carry them (Exod 25:14), ways to approach them, and who was to handle them (Lev 16:2, 13) – but Israel here seems unaware of these rules. The ark had been kept in the holy of holies hidden from the people, and only on occasion did the high priest approach the ark.

Like the Philistines, the people of Beth-Shemesh find another home for the ark at Kiriath Jearim for the next twenty years (7:2). They conscientiously consecrate a Levite, Eleazar, son of Abinadab, to tend to the ark (for further reading see Campbell).

The ark disaster reveals the decay that had beset Israel at this time. Through this national tragedy, the prophecy against the Elide dynasty was fulfilled, and Israel must look to a new leader.

Samuel as Judge · 7:2–8:22

7:2–17 The narrative returns to Samuel and sets the stage for the coming monarchy. Samuel now fills the role in Israel as prophet, priest, and judge. As a prophet, he brings Israel to repentance as they rid themselves of the *foreign gods and the Ashtoreths* (7:3). As priest, he leads them in fasting, praying, sacrificing, and confessing their sin. As judge, he leads them to victory against the Philistines, bringing peace to the land. He establishes a circuit of three towns in the hill country to settle disputes among the people (7:16). This may seem like an uneventful chapter, but it is important to see the successful role of Samuel as a leader to the people of Israel and the peaceful state of Israel following her repentance.

8:1–22 There seems to be a forty-year period of silence between chapters 7 and 8 (Smith 117). Chapter 8 records Israel's transition from temporary war leaders to kingship. Israel asks Samuel for a king.

Why now? One possibility is that Samuel, the one who has led Israel with integrity, is now old (8:5), and his years of serving Israel are about to come to an end. A second reason is the lack of integrity found in Samuel's sons (8:3). (Hereditary rule needs checks and balances, which neither the family of Eli nor Samuel supplied.) Finally, Israel wants to be like the other nations governed by human kings (8:5). Samuel understands their request as a personal rejection of his leadership. God consoles him by telling him that *it is not you they have rejected, but they have rejected me as their king* (1 Sam 8:7), while paradoxically accepting the charge.

Verses 11–18 describes a worst-case scenario for kingship. Kingship will bring certain hardships on the people, but it could be successful. Deuteronomy 17:14–20 envisions the coming of a monarchy and states certain guidelines. The king must be chosen by God from among the nation of Israel. He must not amass quantities of horses, silver, or gold. Neither should he accumulate many wives who may lead him astray. He should write a copy of the law for himself and read it daily, so he may learn to fear the Lord. In all of this he is not to consider himself better than his brothers. If he fulfills these requirements, "then he and his descendants will reign a long time over his kingdom in Israel" (Deut 17:20). Sadly, this formula for a godly leader will be lost on future kings. First Samuel 8 and Deuteronomy 17 bear some relationship as stages in Israel's theological reflection on political life.

The question of these chapters is not whether Israel has a temporary war leader or a king, but rather, will Israel and its leaders trust the Lord? The question at hand concerns more than governmental structure.

This section of Scripture contrasts the lives of two individuals, Eli and Samuel. One is a humble boy who gains respect among the people and learns to know the Lord, while the other, established in the priestly office, is dishonored by his family, lacks leadership abilities, and exhibits no repentance. Hannah's song echoes here as it will in the following pages that the Lord *will guard the feet of his saints* (2:9) and *those who oppose the Lord will be shattered* (2:10). The Lord delights in humble trust and desires that his people know him intimately.

SAUL'S KINGSHIP · 9:1–15:35

Samuel has the task of appointing a king over Israel. The Lord will lead him to one *without equal*, but the road to kingship will not be without obstacles.

Saul's Rise to Kingship · 9:1–11:15

9:1–27 Israel's first king will come from the small tribe of Benjamin located in the central territory of Israel, the same district as Samuel's circuit. His name is Saul, son of Kish. Kish is *a man of standing* (9:1). This phrase may refer to his military strength, valor, or noble character. His son is *without equal among the Israelites* (9:2). The NASB translates the verse, *and there was not a more handsome person than he among the sons of Israel*, but the verse refers less to his appearance than to his character and ability: that is, "there was not a man from the sons of Israel better than he." It is curious that God chose a man like Saul, who falters soon after taking office, to be the first king of Israel. His size is one qualification for office (Hamilton 119–28). Looks may be interpreted as divine favor in the Old Testament (Gen 12:11, 14; 39:6; 1 Sam 16:12);

Monarchy & Hardships

Chapter 8 of 1 Samuel predicts that a number of hardships will fall on the people should they choose to have a king. These predictions are borne out and recorded in the books of Samuel, Kings, and Chronicles:

Prophecy	Fulfillment	Prophecy	Fulfillment
8:11–13 He will take your children to serve him	1 Sam 18:24; 2 Sam 15:1; 1 Kgs 1:5	8:16–17 Your menservants and maidservants and the best of your cattle he will take…. He will take a tenth of your flocks, and you yourselves will become his slaves	1 Kgs 4:22–28; 5:13; 12:4
8:14–15 He will take the best of your fields…a tenth of your grain…and give it to his officials	1 Kgs 21	8:18 You will cry out for relief from the king…and the Lord will not answer you in that day	1 Kgs 12:13–17; 2 Chron 16:10

> **The High Place**
>
> The word for "high place" comes from the Hebrew term bamah, *which sometimes refers to a "mountain ridge" or "height," an elevated site. Polytheistic traditions in the ancient world built holy places on these elevated sites, physically placing them as close to the heavenly gods as possible. Thus the word* bamah *denotes a worship site, including its altars, sacred stones, Asherah poles, and other paraphernalia. Deuteronomy 12:1–7 warns Israel about the high places. Prophets condemned these high places as abominations and called for their removal throughout the land (2 Kgs 17:9; Jer 7:3; 19:5; Ezek 6:3, 13). How is Samuel worshiping in the "high places" with no apparent condemnation? The books of Joshua and Judges, which lead up to this passage, do not mention the high places as locations of sin, and at the time of Samuel, these areas still do not appear to carry the stigma they have later in Israel's history during the kings and prophets.*

however, 16:7 notes that it is not the outward appearance that the Lord sees, but rather the heart.

After three days of futile search for the animals, Saul and his servant inquire of the seer Samuel, who is said to be in the area (9:8). The term "seer" was an older term used in the days of Samuel for one who sees visions. The narrator, writing somewhat later, equates the role with that of a prophet, who reveals the word of God. Samuel recognizes Saul as the future king of Israel by anointing him (9:15, 16). He invites Saul to the high place where he has prepared a sacrifice and meal, and he gives Saul unexpected news. Not only have his donkeys been found, but now Israel will be turning their eyes on Saul as king. Naturally, Saul is confused by this statement, since all he was looking for were some donkeys. Furthermore, he was from an insignificant tribe (Benjamin) and an insignificant clan. Like Gideon (Judg 9:22) and Solomon (1 Kgs 3:7–8), Saul protests his unworthiness for the throne. This is precisely the way Yahweh operates: *He raises the poor from the dust ... and has them inherit a throne of honor* (Hannah in 2:8).

10:1–8 The next morning, Samuel *took a flask of oil and poured it on Saul's head and kissed him saying, Has not the Lord anointed you leader over his inheritance?* (10:1). At this time, only Saul and Samuel are privy to this anointing and designation. The appointment of Saul as king does not become public at this time.

God communicates several messages to Saul on his way home. First, Samuel's words can be trusted. Samuel told Saul that his donkeys had been found; the first people he meets confirm this message. Second, all his needs will be met; God provides bread and wine for him on his way. Finally, God will fill him with his own spirit and thereby not only be with him but in him (10:6). Others who receive the spirit include Othniel (Judg 3:9, 10), Gideon (Judg 6:34), Samson (Judg 14:6, 19), and David (1 Sam 16:13). Samuel himself will assist Saul during his rule. He will be there to guide him in future decisions (10:8). Everything he needs to be a godly ruler will be provided by the Lord.

10:9–27 Some scholars question whether Saul receives the spirit when he leaves Samuel (10:9) or when he joins the band of prophets (10:10). These appear to be two different events. In verse 10, God immediately begins to work on the heart of Saul, changing him from a man of timidity and confusion to a man fit for royalty. His experience with Samuel, a man of God, begins to change Saul. The Hebrew word for "change" means "to be turned upside down" or "turned into something else." This does not suggest that he will no longer be Saul; rather, his heart will no longer be concerned for his father's farm, but for a kingdom. The heart can refer to the "character, disposition, or concern" of man. The heart is significant as Saul will fail to guard his heart, while David is characterized as *a man after [God's] own heart* (13:14). The next step in his transformation will come with the help of God, who empowers him with the indwelling of his own spirit (10:10). God's very presence will be with Saul.

Samuel gives Saul final instructions before sending him away (10:8). Some scholars believe these instructions are fulfilled in chapter 13 when Saul waits seven days for Samuel. This interpretation is awkward, however, since chapter 13 occurs possibly two years later (Smith 20). A smoother flow of events would be to interpret *whatever your hand finds to do* as referring to the battle with Nahash (chapter 11). This is followed by a gathering of the people at Gilgal, an ancient religious site, and a reaffirmation of kingship (11:14). The text does not mention the seven days, but we can assume they apply here. Chapter 13 would then be a separate and later event.

On returning home, Saul meets his uncle. Ancient Israelite families emphasized the importance of older males. Yet, although Saul has had the experience of his life, he answers coyly, *looking for the donkeys* (10:14). He mentions to his uncle that he has spoken with Samuel but says nothing of the extraordinary events that have just transpired. Why does Saul keep these things to himself? First Samuel portrays Saul as an unassuming man who poses no threat (see 8:11–13) to his subjects. This is the man who will become Israel's king since they *rejected* (10:19) their God who *delivered [them] from the power of Egypt* (10:18). Thus, kingship can continue the covenantal promises revealed at the exodus, rather than threatening the core of Israel's faith.

Samuel uses the lottery process, seen elsewhere in Scripture, to publicly appoint Israel's first king (Judg 7:14–19; 1 Chron 24:5–19). It was a means by which God's people could discern the will of the Lord. The use of the Urim and Thummim is not specifically mentioned, but it is possible that they were used here. Samuel did not require them to discern God's will, for God had previously revealed this to him.

> **Lot-Casting**
> *Although the Bible forbids divination, methods for discerning the will of God by manipulating objects or observing natural phenomena, it does allow the use of Urim and Thummim. These were evidently objects that allowed yes or no answers to questions posed by the priests using them.*

Saul is found hiding during this selection process, though (or perhaps because) he knows its outcome. The people's acclamation *Long live the king* (10:24) expresses their pleasure and support for their new king. As most new leaders experience, there are *some troublemakers*, called *sons of Belial* (10:27), who do not support Saul (see note at 2:12). There may be several reasons for their lack of support. As Saul himself notes (9:21), he has done nothing to this point to prove his capabilities as king.

These troublemakers further insult the new king by not bringing him gifts that would express their support (10:27). Saul's wisdom may have prompted him not to respond to this act of defiance at this time, but it seems to be in keeping with his personality seen thus far, which is timid, indirect, and lacking confidence (though his first act as king is not one of timidity).

11:1–15 Shortly after Saul's public inauguration, a crisis breaks out in the town of Jabesh Gilead. Nahash, the Ammonite ruler, besieges this town and demands its surrender, threatening to gouge out the right eye of everyone living there. The Dead Sea Scroll 4QSam includes a paragraph not found in the Masoretic Text or the Septuagint that explains the incentive for the conflict. Apparently, a group of seven thousand people rebelled earlier against Nahash and fled to the town of Jabesh. It was customary under such conditions to punish the rebels by gouging out an eye. Gruesome acts of mutilation were not uncommon forms of punishment in the ancient world. Saul rallies the Israelites and secures a victory over Nahash, though his own gruesome threat exposes Israel's hesitancy to follow him into battle. This was an important victory for Saul, for it helped to legitimize his reign and *confirmed Saul as king* (11:15). Saul shows promise as the first king of Israel who can fulfill the military aspirations of the people (see chapter 8). He is led by the Spirit of God, has the support of the people (though some are hesitant), and begins to exhibit some maturity and wisdom in his leadership.

Samuel's Warnings of Kingship · 12:1–25

The aging Samuel addresses the people of Israel after granting their request for a king. He reminds them what *an evil thing* (12:17) they have requested, and that he himself did not take advantage of his position or act improperly in any way to prompt this decision while he led Israel. Using legal jargon, Samuel challenges Israel, *Stand here because I am going to confront you* (12:7). In a speech reminiscent of Joshua 24, Samuel reminds them of their history, the faithlessness of

> **The Theology of the Exodus**
> *The exodus was a major focal point for the Israelites. It symbolized God's saving grace for the people. Reminders of the event could serve as a rallying point for penitent Jews to return to the Lord (Josh 24:17; Judg 6:8; Mic 6:4; Acts 7:20; 13:17). As a major event in their history, it is used in dating as a point of reference: in the four hundred eightieth year after the Israelites had come out of Egypt ... (1 Kgs 6:1). Jews still celebrate yearly at Passover, which commemorates the events that took place just before Israel left Egypt. God's angel of death "passed over" the doorways of those who by faith placed the blood of the lamb on their door frames. Participants eat the unleavened bread and the roasted lamb at this celebration, just as the Hebrews ate it in their haste to leave Egypt.*

their ancestors, and how they themselves showed a lack of faith when confronting King Nahash. But it is possible for a king to rule successfully over Israel if he and the people will *fear the Lord and serve and obey him and not rebel against his commands, and if both [the people] and the king who reigns over [them] follow the Lord [their] God* (12:14). The formula for success is to "fear," "serve," "obey," and "follow" the Lord. It was not the kingship that God opposed, but their lack of faith and disobedience.

Samuel's words are verified by the untimely advent of thunder and rain at the time of the wheat harvest (12:17). The thunder is God's calling card, saying, "I am here." Samuel still has connections to the power of God and prays for his frightened people.

Saul's Decline as King · 13:1–15:35

13:1–22 The opening verses of chapter 13 give the age of Saul and the years ruled, but the text appears to be corrupted here, creating some confusion regarding the exact numbers. This explains why the NIV gives Saul's age as thirty and his years ruled at forty-two, whereas, the NASB makes Saul forty years old, reigning thirty-two years. We simply do not know.

Saul and his son Jonathan gather their forces at Michmash and Gibeah in response to a Philistine threat. Jonathan attacks one of the Philistine outposts, prompting them to move against Saul's army. Israel then reassembles at Gilgal, the same location where Saul received his kingdom and, ironically, the same location where he learns that he will lose his kingdom.

Samuel had given Saul very specific instructions to wait seven days at Gilgal for him to come and offer *burnt offerings and fellowship offerings* (13:9). These are offered before battle to seek God's favor and express thanks (in advance) for deliverance. As Saul waits for Samuel, he sees the Philistines *as numerous as the sand on the seashore* (13:5), and the Israelites in fear hide themselves *in caves and thickets, among the rocks, and in pits and cisterns* (13:6). Seven days pass with no sign of Samuel, so Saul makes the foolish decision to offer the sacrifices himself, a priestly task. Samuel arrives as Saul finishes making the offering, suggesting that Saul may not have waited the full time appointed for Samuel's arrival. When confronted with the offense, Saul rationalizes his every action.

Why would God take the kingdom away for what seems to be a minor procedural infraction? Samuel accuses Saul of not keeping the commands of God (13:13, 14). It is a problem of the heart. He may have been the best man for the job when Samuel anointed him, but this is no longer true. Saul failed to guard his heart. *The Lord has sought out a man after his own heart and appointed him leader of his people* (13:14). Saul's foolishness led to disobedience. The result was loss of the kingdom.

Though Samuel leaves Saul with a warning that his kingdom will not endure, that time is not now. The Lord will deliver Israel this time from the Philistines, but the hero will not be Saul. It will be his son Jonathan. Jonathan, the crown prince, becomes a key figure in the next two chapters as his courage, competence, and faith in the Lord are displayed. As the story continues, Samuel and many of Saul's men abandon Saul (13:15).

The setting for the Philistine encounter is given as the Philistines send out raiding parties into the area. It is not mentioned what weapons, if any, were used against Nahash in chapter 11, but it is noted here that on *the day of the battle not a soldier with Saul and Jonathan had a sword or spear in his hand; only Saul and his son Jonathan had them* (13:22). The Philistines had a monopoly on blacksmiths and were careful not to supply their enemy neighbors the Israelites with iron weapons. Israel probably used makeshift weapons or farm tools. This heightened Israel's fear of the gathering Philistines.

> **Weaponry & Warfare**
> *Large armies in the early first millennium included chariot units, spearmen, bowmen, and slingers. All were highly skilled. An amateur army like Saul's probably lacked chariots. True cavalry was a later invention, since saddles and stirrups did not yet exist (Chapman 338).*

13:23–14:52 Jonathan does not share this fear. Overcoming treacherous terrain and overwhelming odds, Jonathan and his shield bearer win a small victory over a Philistine outpost. This report portrays Jonathan as a man of audacity, physical strength, and incredible faith (14:6). Jonathan recognizes that God does not need the advantage of numbers to overcome the enemy. Compare Jonathan's trust in God to his father's hesitancy to move against the Philistines. Jonathan's initiative once again sets the next battle in motion.

With Samuel gone, Saul seeks God's direction through the priest Ahijah, using the ephod containing the Urim and Thummim along with the ark of God (14:18). This is a risky and foolish move (see chapter 4). Saul will receive no word from God.

Saul continues to make rash and unwise decisions. He creates a precarious situation for his army and his son by making an oath to the Lord (14:24). Oaths were ways of gaining a deity's favor and offering a form of sacrifice to show one's sincerity and dedication to the issue at hand. Saul's oath places a restriction on his army that reduces their ability to complete the task before them and creates a situation for temptation and error (Lev 7:26, 27; 1 Sam 14:31–35).

When Saul inquires of the Lord for approval to continue attacks against the Philistines, the Lord is silent, which usually indicates unchecked sin somewhere (Josh 7). Saul assumes that God's silence is due to someone who has broken his oath, not due to his own sin that Samuel has told him will take his kingdom from him (1 Sam 13:14). Lots determine the offender; it falls to Jonathan, who admits to eating honey in the field, unaware of his father's oath. Saul is ready to carry out his pledge to destroy this one who has broken his oath, when his troops come to Jonathan's defense. The troops remind Saul that it was Jonathan's tenacity that was a major component in Israel's victory. Saul concedes.

What does this story reveal about Saul? Saul's jealousy toward Jonathan is not typical of a father, but it foreshadows his fear of another superior general, David. Verse 39 may indicate that Saul intends to be impartial to the sinner, or that he knows who the sinner is. When Jonathan is chosen, Saul shows no remorse (14:44). Scripture does not say that Saul wants to kill Jonathan at this time, but his intentions are suspicious given his readiness to destroy his son for an unintentional infraction against an irrational oath. Even if Saul did not engineer this plot against Jonathan, he does manage to diminish Jonathan's heroic deed and the honor due him that day. Saul's unguarded heart continues to deteriorate.

A summary of events follows this story that testifies to Saul's success as a military leader. He delivers Israel from its enemies and focuses on building his military. He seeks *mighty or brave* (14:52) men who will enhance his army, though he will continue to lose favor before the Lord as he is distracted by his own personal pursuits.

15:1–35 Samuel has one more directive for Saul: *attack the Amalekites and totally destroy everything that belongs to them* (15:3). He is to place them under a *ban*, and none are to be spared. Saul, consistent with his past, follows only part of Samuel's instructions. Instead of placing the Amalekites under the ban, Saul spares the best, *everything that was good* (15:9), from king to animal, and justifies himself when confronted by Samuel. Samuel reminds Saul that God picked a humble man years ago from a small tribe to lead his people. Now this same man is setting up a *monument in his own honor* (15:12), in the manner of the tyrant warned about in chapter 8.

Saul rationalizes his decision to spare the best by saying that they were to be used for sacrifices to the Lord. Samuel's response is written in poetic form, which accentuates the message: *to obey is better than sacrifice* (15:22). Samuel is not negating the value of sacrifices, but validating obedience (see Hos 6:6). Rebellion and arrogance resemble pagan divination and idolatry (15:23), causing God's rejection of Saul's kingship. This is the last time Samuel appears before Saul's court, though he mourns for Saul and the kingship of Israel (15:11), as the *Lord was grieved that he made Saul king over Israel* (15:35). Although modern readers are inevitably uncomfortable with this story, the text itself regards proper kingship as following God without question.

DAVID'S RISE TO KINGSHIP · 1 SAM 16–2 SAM 4

The narrative shifts its focus to David. Saul has established the office of kingship and protected Israel from her oppressive neighbors, but he is no longer the best of Israel. God has found in the shepherd boy David the essence of a king, a physically attractive orator, warrior, and musician (16:18; compare Pss 45, 101, 144).

> **The Ban**
> In its early history, Israel practiced the ban [Hebrew cherem], or the complete destruction of certain cities. This practice also occurred in Moab. No record of its happening exists after the time of David.

> **The Amalekites**
> The Amalekites are descendants of Esau (Gen 36:12) living in the Negev south of Israel. Their tension with Israel goes back to the exodus. As Israel left Egypt, the Amalekites attacked those who lagged behind (Exod 17:8–16; Deut 25:17–19). They were cursed that day for this action: You shall blot out the memory of Amalek from under heaven. Do not forget (Deut 25:19). They continued to be a source of danger to Israel in the following years. Now that Israel is politically established, the time had come to call in this debt and fulfill prophecy. Saul is given the task of eliminating this nation who made women childless (1 Sam 15:33).

David in the Court of Saul · 16:1–20:42

16:1–23 Samuel is directed to Bethlehem to anoint a new king, but this one-time friend and confidante of Saul fears Saul when called by God to this task. This is evidence of Saul's decline. To protect himself and keep this anointing from public awareness, Samuel's stated purpose for coming to Bethlehem is to offer a sacrifice to the Lord. Before the Deuteronomic reforms of the seventh century (see Deut 12, 16), family sacrifices were apparently part of Israelite family religion. He invites Jesse and his sons. As with the selection of Saul, the rejection of David's older brothers indicates Yahweh's interest in the human heart. A godly heart is one quality this kingly office needs and demands (Deut 17:20) and now will be found in the youngest son of Jesse, the one not worthy to be presented before Samuel until Jesse is specifically asked if he has another son. God chooses the least likely one.

Samuel privately anoints David before his family, and like Saul, David is filled with the spirit of the Lord. The process to move the royal kingship from Saul to David has begun, but this will be a long process. Many years and many trials will pass before David will sit securely on the throne of Israel.

When God rejected Saul, *the spirit of the Lord had departed from Saul, and an evil spirit from the Lord tormented him* (16:14). This evil spirit may be an actual demonic spirit filling the void left by the absence of the spirit of the Lord, but more likely it was a spirit of "misery or unhappiness," referring to his mood. This may be a better interpretation when understanding Israel's conviction that "evil, like everything else, was thought to come from God" (Cartledge 205). In monotheistic belief there is one God, one source for blessings and curses. We can consider psychological conditions that may have troubled Saul, such as paranoia, schizophrenia, or bipolar disease, but one must not reduce Saul's condition to mere psychology and miss the theological illness intended by the narrator. Saul's unrepentant posture is the source of his ruin and torment (Brueggemann 124).

Ironically, the one recommended and invited to the court to soothe Saul's tormented soul is none other than the one who will replace him as king. David is a reputable young man and talented harpist. He pleases Saul, who requests that David remain in his service at the palace, though this may not have happened until after Goliath is slain. For many scholars, the fact that Saul does not know David in the Goliath story indicates the existence of different sources behind the text of 1 Samuel.

17:1–58 Israel finds itself again on the battlefield with the Philistines. This time the challenge comes in a different form. Rather than the two armies facing off in a pitched battle where hundreds or thousands are killed, the Philistines propose a duel to the death between a champion from each camp. The people of the defeated warrior would then become *subjects and serve* (17:9) the nation of the victor.

A common battle tactic used in the ancient world was intimidation, scare tactics expressed through battle cries, fierce looking attire, a reputation of body mutilations, slander against the enemy and its gods, or a brute of a challenger. The Philistine challenger, Goliath, is over nine feet tall (the Greek text puts him at four, rather than six cubits, still a large man) and equipped with the finest armament (17:4–7). The appearance of Goliath and his boastful challenge *dismayed and terrified* Saul and his army (17:11). Note that Saul's faith is limited to his army, not his God. Significantly, we find no mention of a prophet or priest to bring the word of the Lord to Saul concerning this challenger.

David, along with his family, is reintroduced to the reader. He is doing part-time service for the king while tending sheep (17:15). At this time, Saul does not have an established standing army on the state's payroll. Consequently, families needed to send supplies to their young men on the battlefield. David first witnesses the obnoxious giant when he brings provisions for his brothers and their commander.

David does not respond with fear, as do the others, but with indignation at the insults leveled against his God. He calls Goliath *this uncircumcised Philistine* (17:26), one who is not of the covenant of the Lord. Despite his giant size, Goliath lacks the body of an Israelite. Such a one should not *taunt the armies of the living God* (17:36).

David offers his service to the king: *your servant*

> **The Sling**
> The sling is not only a shepherd's tool; it is used as a common weapon in the ancient world. Hardly a child's toy, the sling was the weapon of choice for a unit of any ancient army (Judg 20:16). Assyrian art from the royal palaces depicts soldiers using the sling. It was an inexpensive weapon, but one that required a high level of skill to use accurately. Thus we misunderstand the story if we see David as hopelessly outclassed by the giant.

will go and fight him (17:32). The irony and power of this story lies in this very point. Despite his skill in defeating wild animals (17:34–37), David seems too small for the job. Saul offers David his gear, which is much too awkward for David's use, so he leaves it behind and gathers the shepherding tools to which he is accustomed – his staff, a sling, and few small stones (17:40).

When Goliath sees who Israel sends to challenge him, he is amazed and offended: *Am I a dog that you come at me with sticks?* (17:43). He follows with intimidation and the fear tactics: *I'll give your flesh to the birds of the air and beasts of the field* (17:44). David will not to be intimidated, not by his brothers, not by the king, and certainly not by this uncircumcised pagan giant. David returns his own form of intimidation. Rather than taunting the giant, he appeals to God as the real protector of Israel. Following this defeat, the Philistines flee rather than serve the Israelites according to the agreement of the duel. Israel pursues them to their city gates of Ekron and Gath, leaving a path of slain men.

David took the Philistine's head and brought it to Jerusalem and put the Philistine's weapons in his own tent (17:54). Jerusalem is occupied by the Jebusites at this time, and David is said a few verses later to have the head in his hand when he comes to Saul (17:57). David may have brought the skull to Jerusalem later, after he captured this city. Thus the text is slightly anachronistic. Yet this episode and the story of David's presentation at court in 17:57–58 introduce a theme that will play out for the rest of the book: David's fighting skills surpass Saul's, yet David always modestly submits to his overlord.

18:1–30 No one is more impressed with David's heroism than Saul's son Jonathan. He *became one in spirit with David and he loved him as himself* (18:1). Some have suggested a homosexual relationship between David and Jonathan, but the text does not support such an interpretation. The text literally reads, "the soul of Jonathan was bound up (or "knit together") with the soul of David." David's friendship will outlive Jonathan, for even after his death, David will provide for Jonathan's family who survive him (2 Sam 9). Again 1 Samuel emphasizes David's innocence of the death of Saul, even though he was its primary beneficiary (Halpern, *David's Secret Demons*).

David becomes a full-time employee of the court, but his favor with Saul is short-lived. It was customary in ancient times to have a joyous celebration for the homecoming of the troops from a victorious battle. As the women sing praises, they credit David with greater success than Saul, saying: *Saul has slain his thousands, and David his tens of thousands* (18:7; see Hamilton 187–96). Rather than joining in congratulating David or recognizing the victory as the Lord's, *from that time on Saul kept a jealous eye on David* (18:9). Saul can see that the Lord is with David and no longer with Saul. David's harp no longer soothes Saul's tormented soul. In fact, it agitates him the more, so that he unsuccessfully attempts to kill David (18:11). Saul will later connive other schemes to eliminate David. Meanwhile, an uneasy peace must have been established, for David remains in the royal court.

After an unspecified amount of time passed since David defeated Goliath, Saul decides to fulfill his promise to give his daughter to the champion of that duel (17:25). When he offers his daughter to David in return for his faithful service in battle, it is with hopes that the Philistines will kill him (18:17). David willingly serves the king but humbly refuses Saul's daughter, feeling he is not worthy of a royal wife; he has no bride price to bring the father of the bride. When Saul's second daughter desires David, Saul approaches David again. This time, Saul figures the way to move David is not by persuasive words but a courageous challenge. He tells David that the *price* for his daughter is *a hundred Philistine foreskins to take revenge on his enemies* (18:25). Saul requests foreskins as a derogatory ethnic statement against this pagan people. There is also a sense of warped humor, as the Philistines are humiliated by the mark of the Hebrew. Again, Saul hopes that David will lose his life in the process, but the Lord is with David. He kills not one hundred Philistines but two hundred and brings the foreskins to his future father-in-law. Michal becomes David's wife and *was in love* with him (18:20). We do not know if David returned her love. Saul's own children have cast their allegiance with David, and Saul feels all the more threatened. Saul regards David from here on as his enemy (18:29).

The Bride Price
A marriage usually included a bride price, a gift from the groom to the father of the bride, and a dowry, a gift from the father of the bride to his daughter. David did not have a gift worthy of a king's daughter.

19:1–24 Saul's emotional state continues to deteriorate as his actions become more irrational

> **The Teraphim**
>
> What are David and Michal doing with an idol in their home? These idols are common household items found in many Israelite homes. Here, as well as in the story of Rachel stealing the teraphim *from her father's home, there is a pejorative element associated with these idols. Rachel's idol is small enough to fit in a saddlebag and there seems to be no concern for its purity as she sits on it, particularly in her own impure state (Gen 31:34–35). Michal's idol may have been life size and used as a dummy ("At least they are useful for something" [Brueggemann 143]), again, a less than respected treatment of the* teraphim. *These idols likely served a legal function associated with family leadership and property rights as well as instruments of divination. Later reformers prohibited such objects (2 Kgs 23:24), which they associated with techniques of divination.*

and inconsistent. As Saul moves to eliminate David, his children move to aid David in escaping from the royal court. Saul tells his attendants and his son, Jonathan, *to kill David* (19:1), but before Saul can send his men into David's home, Michal lowers David through the window to make his escape. She stalls her father's men by placing *teraphim*, one or more figures used in worship, in David's bed with goat's hair on the head (19:13). When the men come to capture David, she lies by telling them he is ill. By the time the king receives the report and gives the order to take him anyway, David is well on his way to safety. Saul confronts his daughter for aiding his enemy. To protect herself and possibly stay in the good graces of her irrational father, Michal lies and tells her father that David threatened her if she would not help him escape.

David seeks refuge at Ramah with the old prophet who first anointed him, Samuel. Together they go to a particular location in Ramah called Naioth. When Saul receives word of this, he immediately sends men to capture David. In fact, Saul sends three contingents of men after David because each contingent is distracted from its orders; when they see the prophets prophesying with Samuel, *the Spirit of God came upon Saul's men and they also prophesied* (19:20). The gift of "prophecy" here refers to uncontrollable, ecstatic experience, not the sort of thing one sees in Isaiah or Amos. (Compare also the story in 2 Kgs 1:9–15.) Finally, Saul goes but finds himself in the same state as his men, prophesying among the prophets and stripped of his robes. God spares Saul at the same time he reminds him of earlier days when he prophesied and praised his Lord. Saul could have recognized God's hand at work, repented of his ways, and cast his support behind David. Instead, he chooses to keep his hard heart and continue his murderous pursuit. Brueggemann (145) notes, "The pitifully embarrassing scene is that of this once great man, still tall but no longer great, exhausted by demanding religious exercise (v 24), clearly not in control, shamed, now rendered powerless in a posture of submissiveness. This episode is an act of dramatic delegitimation of Saul."

20:1–42 What follows is a detailed account of an encounter between God's newly anointed and the current royal heir to the throne. Unlike Saul, Jonathan realizes he will not be king, David will. The

> **Early Ecstatic Prophets**
>
> *Prophets from many nations of the ancient world exhibited behavior that included dancing, playing music, chanting, visions, and divining. Some are recorded to have expressed more ecstatic actions such as stripping, self-flagellation, and self-mutilation (1 Kgs 18:28). The ecstatic behavior is a means of transporting people into an altered or euphoric state of mind. This is not uncommon today as people will be overcome by the "power of the spirit" that may lead them to fall into a trance, jerk uncontrollably, or laugh hysterically. There has been a distinction made between Israel's early prophets, who seemed to exhibit at times ecstatic behavior as the "Spirit of Lord came upon" them, and the later writing prophets who received their message by more "rational" means, a "word from the Lord." Wood (104) questions this distinction between the early and late prophets: "all the prophets were equally sane people who received their messages by revelation from God," whether by "Spirit" or "by word." The story of Elijah and the prophets of Baal is an example of a comparison between the more ecstatic prophets of Baal, who* slashed themselves, *and Elijah, who merely prayed to the Lord (1 Kgs 18:27–39).*

text emphasizes David's innocence of the death of Jonathan by portraying Jonathan as his unflinching supporter. Jonathan seeks and receives David's pledge that he and his family will be protected.

Due to escalating tensions, David cannot not risk dining with the king, as was his custom. Courtiers in ancient times dined with the king to await his instruction (see Prov 23:1–3). Saul waits until David's second absence, assuming that the first absence from dinner is due to being *ceremonially unclean* (a condition that may be caused by contact with a dead body or perhaps by a nocturnal emission; see Deut 23:10; Lev 15:2–26). When Jonathan explains David's absence, Saul rightly discerns the partnership between his son and his enemy and feels betrayed. He reminds his son of David's threat to the dynasty (20:31). Jonathan understands this and, having made peace with David, defends David's innocence, infuriating his father all the more. Saul hurls his spear at Jonathan *to kill him* (20:33), as he has done more than once to David.

Jonathan signals to David the danger at the palace, and David now faces life as a fugitive. He will be on the run for six years (Smith 19). Jonathan returns to his father, to whom he will remain loyal to the day of his death.

David a Fugitive in Israel · 21:1–27:12

21:1–15 David has become a fugitive of the court. The king's allies are now David's enemies, and David's friends are now enemies of the state. He obtains assistance from Ahimelech the priest at a town just north of Jerusalem, Nob (21:6). From there, he seeks protection among Saul's enemies, the Philistines. He may have hoped that the Philistines would not recognize him without the Israelite army with him or that they may accept him as a refugee from Saul's court. David miscalculates. The Philistines do recognize him and remember the songs about him, *Saul has slain his thousands, and David his tens of thousands* (21:11; see 18:7). To save his own life, David feigns insanity, thereby convincing the Philistines that he is not a threat, but an unwanted madman. Ironically, his behavior resembles that of Saul in 19:23–24. David continues on to the *cave of Adullam* (22:1) about sixteen miles southwest of Jerusalem, and is joined by about four hundred malcontents, along with his family and the prophet Gad. His alliance with the king of Moab foreshadows his later friendship with the Philistines.

22:1–23 Back at the court, Saul's dread and suspicion consumes him as he accuses his entire court, including his son, of conspiring against him. Doeg, a servant who overheard David with the priest at Nob, comes forward with information. Saul summons the priest Ahimelech for interrogation. He denies knowing that David had become an enemy of Saul. Nonetheless, Saul orders the execution of the priest, his family, and everyone in the priestly town of Nob, including the women and children. *That day he killed eighty-five men who wore the linen ephod*. The ephod is a vest-like garment worn by the priests as they serve the Lord; it sets them apart from the common folk (22:18). Abiathar, the son of Ahimelech, escapes to report the events to David. This horrible tragedy shows Saul's obsession with David's demise and his contempt for God. The story explains the loyalty of the Nob priests to David and the later prominence of Abiathar.

23:1–29 David had enjoyed enthusiastic support from the people of Israel when he served under Saul, but without the court behind him, he loses the support of the masses, though his band of fugitives grows. As David moves about the area west of the Dead Sea, staying out of the reach of Saul, he encounters some hostile people and groups: Keilah (whom David rescued from the Philistines) and the Ziphites. These may be isolated cases of hostility, or they may represent the general mood of the land toward David. In any case, the stories illustrate Saul's lack of control over most of the land of Israel. Jonathan recognizes that David *will be king over Israel* (23:17) but erroneously and sadly believes he will himself *be second* (23:17) to David. Again the narrator prepares the reader for Jonathan's death and seeks to establish David's innocence.

24:1–22 David's loyalty and faith are put to the test when he is given an easy opportunity to take Saul's life. Saul leaves the protection of his men to *relieve himself* (24:3) in the privacy of a cave where, unknown to him, David and his men are hiding. God has delivered the king into David's hands, so his men believe. Saul may be seeking David's life, but David still regards him as his king, his father-in-law, and most importantly, the anointed of God. David will wait on the hand of the Lord. He decides to show his loyalty to the king by proving to him that he could have taken his life (at a most humiliating moment) but chose instead to spare him. He *crept up unnoticed* *and cut off a corner of Saul's robe* (24:4). When Saul leaves the cave, David calls to him, addressing him as father, and shows Saul the corner of his robe. He *prostrated himself* (24:8) before Saul and in a beautiful speech declares himself innocent and no threat to the king. David's words soothe Saul's spirit, as did his harp. Saul recognizes his own sin and the righteousness of David. He acknowledges that the kingdom will one day be David's and pleads for the life of his descendants, who will be at David's mercy when he becomes king. David reassures Saul of his loyalty to Saul's family (24:20–21), but he does not return to the palace. The story depicts him as a righteous man waiting on the Lord, rather than seeking after his own ambition. Again, the story seeks to exonerate David of charges of treason.

25:1–44 The story leaves Saul for the moment and relates an incident that occurs while David is a fugitive. David had hoped to benefit from a service his men offer to a wealthy farmer, Nabal. David had graciously stationed his men where they could protect Nabal's flocks from wild animals and thieves, a hospitable gesture worthy of gratitude. With the respect and humility of a servant, David requests provisions for his men in return for the protection he had provided Nabal. Ancient peoples were dependent on the hospitality of one another, but while Nabal accepts David's protection, he reciprocates nothing. David can endure the irrational behavior of the Lord's anointed, but this foolish man (the name "Nabal" literally means "fool") is not to receive this same courtesy. Nabal's wife is quite the opposite of her foolish husband, described as an *intelligent and beautiful woman* (25:3), as opposed to her husband, who is described as *surly and mean in his dealings* (25:3). When the servants report to Abigail the approach of David and his armed men, she quickly gathers a large quantity of food to give to David, along with a thoughtful and wise apology for her husband's behavior. David accepts her gift and kind words, which stays his hand from an ugly retaliation. A few days later, Nabal dies of heart failure; justice is served by the hand of the Lord, not the hand of David (so shall the case be with Saul). From this near disaster, David learns the "importance of self-control and reliance upon Yahweh" (McCarter, *I Samuel*, 401).

Abigail becomes David's wife. At this time, David has two wives, Abigail and Ahinoam of Jezreel. According to verse 44, Saul had given Michal to possibly an official in Saul's court. David lost his marital connection to the court of Saul when Michal was taken from him. Now he forms a new marital alliance with the people of Hebron in Judah, his future center of control, through Abigail, widow of a prominent Calebite, a leading family clan in Hebron (25:3; McCarter, *I Samuel*, 402).

26:1–25 This passage returns to the conflict between David and Saul. This story parallels the account of David sparing the life of Saul in chapter 24. Some scholars believe this to be a retelling of the previous story, but the details are too distinct to draw this conclusion. The repetition of similar stories emphasizes David's moral stature in contrast to Saul's. David finds himself a second time in a position where Saul is vulnerable and exposed. His men again encourage him to take this opportunity to end Saul's life, but David chooses to maintain his stance of integrity and respect for God's anointed, which once again humbles Saul. This time, Saul invites David to return with him, but David refuses, not trusting Saul. David will wait.

David does not feel safe moving about in Israelite territory. The Ziphites and others have served as informants against him. Earlier, when David first became a fugitive, he sought refuge at the gates of the Philistines (21:10–15), Israel's mortal enemy. He quickly learned that though he is a fugitive from Saul, the Philistines still remember him as a formidable adversary. Now that several years have passed and he has proven truly to be an exile, the Philistines stand to benefit from his experience.

David and his supporters are permitted to move into Ziklag, a town near Gath in Philistine territory. He wins the favor of Achish, king of Gath, by raiding neighboring towns and bringing in the spoils of war, which he likely shares with the king. Achish assumes these were Israelite towns. Actually, they were Philistine enemies of Israel south of Ziklag whom David completely annihilated, leaving no survivors to report differently (27:11).

Saul's Final Battle & Death · 1 Sam 28:1–2 Sam 1:27

28:1–25 While David and his men are living in Ziklag, the final events of Saul's life take place. The Philistines have gathered their men to do battle against Israel. Achish is under the impression that David's loyalty lies securely with him, not with Israel. He believes this so confidently that he appoints David his personal *bodyguard for life* (28:2; literally "a keeper for my head." The memory of Goliath's head must have been fading!). The narrator makes two points that are important to the following story. One, Samuel has died; he is no longer accessible to Saul. Two, Saul had *expelled the mediums and spiritists from the land* (28:3) according to the law (Deut 18:10–12).

Saul inquires of the Lord before going against the Philistines, *but the Lord did not answer him by dreams or Urim or prophets* (28:6). In desperation, Saul finds an expelled medium to call up Samuel from the dead, but before she begins her work, to her amazement, Samuel appears. Only she can see his form, for Saul asks, *What do you see*? She describes Samuel as *an old man wearing a robe* (28:13), which confirms the appearance of Samuel (possibly the robe that Saul tore when the kingdom was torn from him, 1 Sam 15:27). Saul does not receive the comfort from Samuel he had hoped to receive. Instead, Samuel rebukes him and reminds him of his sin that tore his kingdom from him; furthermore, *tomorrow you and your sons will be with me* (28:19). Samuel's harsh and condemning words contrast with his mournful demeanor seen earlier when God first strips Saul of his kingdom (16:1). The narrator evokes a sense of pity for a now pathetic king frantically seeking a word from the Lord. Tragically, Saul is no longer aligned with God's prophet; instead, he finds nourishment and strength through a kind, yet illegal and abhorrent necromancer, a new association further denoting his regression.

Why does God allow Saul to find his answers through an illegitimate medium? Does he in fact find his answers through a medium? It is likely that Samuel's appearing was not the result of the woman's magic, since Scripture does not record any action on her part to call up Samuel (though this silence may be due to a reluctance to describe outlawed religious practices). Her surprise at Samuel's appearance may allude to the fact that she has nothing to do with bringing up this spirit.

29:1–11 Meanwhile, as Saul is preparing to face the Philistines (and having his rendezvous in Endor), David and his men, who appear to be allied with them, are *marching at the rear with Achish* (29:2), king of the Philistines, into battle against Israel. Achish's trust in David is not shared among the other Philistine leaders, who protest David and his men marching behind them. How easy would it be for these Israelites to turn on the Philistines and annihilate them from the rear! David is ordered to return to Ziklag with apologies from Achish.

30:1–31 Before David reaches home, the Amalekites (the people Saul failed to annihilate; 1 Sam 15) raid Ziklag, capture the families of David and his men, and burn their city (30:3). The men are so distraught that they *were talking of stoning* David. *David found strength in the Lord his God* (30:6) and inquires of him through the priest Abiathar if he should pursue the Amalekites. Because of the divine promise in verse 8, David finds strength and direction in the Lord through his priest. In contrast, Saul is strengthened by the medium at Endor.

David successfully *recovered everything the Amalekites had taken, including his two wives* (30:18,

---

Abode of the Dead

The ancient world had a dreary view of the netherworld where the souls of the dead went. Sheol was the underworld located below the grave in a subterranean realm. It was characterized by darkness, dust, silence, and where "neither working nor planning nor knowledge nor wisdom" exist (Job 17:13; 17:16; Ps 94:17; Eccl 9:10). The NIV translates the word sheol as "grave," denoting the place where all go at the end of life, whether good or evil. The New Testament likewise refers to the abode of the dead, but by that time an idea of the separation of the wicked and righteous has developed (Luke 16:19–31).

19). He distributes the plunder among his men, even those who did not aid in the rescue, as well as among other neighboring cities that had also been raided by the Amalekites. Thus David exhibits an intolerance for greed among his men, and furthermore, shows himself to be upright and shrewd. Smith lists four benefits of David's generosity: to reimburse these people for losses to these and other raiding desert tribes; to thank those who did encourage him during his wilderness wanderings; to remove any reservations about his loyalty to Israel despite his sixteen-month stay in Philistine territory; and to be positioned for kingship by his native tribe following Saul's death (334).

31:1–13 Saul now faces his final battle against the Philistines. He incurs a wound that will end his life, but not immediately. Fearing torture and abuse by the Philistines if they find him alive and wounded, Saul asks his armor bearer to run him through with his sword and end his life. The young man *was terrified and would not do it* (31:4), so Saul falls on his own sword. (A variation of Saul's death is recorded in 2 Samuel 1. The differences are discussed there.) Samuel's prediction is fulfilled. Saul and his sons, including Jonathan, lie slain on Mt. Gilboa (1 Sam 28:19). Saul is not spared the disgrace and mutilation he feared. His and his sons' bodies are decapitated. Their heads are placed in the temple of Dagon (1 Chron 10:10) and their bodies stripped and attached to the wall of the newly captured city, Beth-shan (a highly elevated and visible city), to intimidate and discourage future rebellion and encourage compliance with the conquering peoples.

> **Dagon**
> *Although 1 Samuel 31:9 has the heads being placed in various temples in Philistia, 1 Chronicles clarifies this verse by emphasizing the key Philistine god Dagon. Dagon was the god of grain and therefore physical prosperity and was originally a Canaanite (or even earlier people's) deity.*

Saul is not completely without honor. The *valiant men* (31:12) of the neighboring city of Jabesh Gilead, whom Saul had rescued years earlier, come at night to steal the royal bodies from the city wall and give them a proper burial (1 Sam 11; 2 Sam 21:12). The men of Jabesh Gilead burn the decomposed and defiled bodies of the royal family and bury the bones under a tamarisk tree at Jabesh (2 Sam 21:13, 14). This was not a common practice among Israelites but may have been done given the state of the decomposing bodies or "perhaps as a means of purifying them from the offensive handling of the unclean Philistines" (Cartledge 343).

First Samuel ends on a minimally positive note with the men of Jabesh, unlike the closing recorded in 1 Chronicles 10:13, 14: *Saul died because he was unfaithful to the Lord; he did not keep the word of the Lord and even consulted a medium for guidance, and did not inquire of the Lord. So the Lord put him to death and turned the kingdom over to David son of Jesse.*

Thus Hannah's song introduces a key theme in the book, and her song serves as an appropriate epitaph for Saul. *It is not by strength that one prevails; those who oppose the Lord will be shattered. He will thunder against them from heaven* (1 Sam 2:9, 10).

THEOLOGICAL REFLECTIONS

The books of Samuel are alive with stories of men and women entangled in the web of life's experiences and the God who is sovereign over all. These stories reflect human triumphs and failings in life and a God who is merciful yet just and immovable in his holiness. He forgives David as he repents of his sin against Bathsheba, yet the unrepentant priesthood under the Elide dynasty and the defiling of the holy ark of God do not go unanswered. A holy and righteous God seeks obedience and righteousness from Israel. *To obey is better than sacrifice* (1 Sam 15:22). God raises those of humble means and humble hearts to immeasurable heights.

These books are part of a greater work, the Hebrew canon, which reflects the nature of God and God's relationship with Israel. First and Second Samuel fit securely into the larger theological picture of the Old Testament. The anticipation of kingship in Deuteronomy 17:14–20 is realized in the establishment of David's dynasty. This theological picture continues in the books of Kings, where David's reign of justice and righteousness sets the standard for future rulers who either *did what was right in the eyes of the Lord, as [their] father David* (1 Kgs 15:11) or *did evil in the eyes of the Lord [by not following] the Lord completely as [their] father David had done* (1 Kgs 11:6). God's promise to bless and bring security to those who walk in obedience but ruin to those who fail to obey divine commands appears in Deuteronomy and comes to fruition in Samuel and Kings as well as in the prophetic writings. First and Second Samuel look to the New Testament as it establishes the house through which salvation will ultimately come, not only to the remnant of Israel returned to the promised land, but to all nations through this covenantal house and heir, Jesus Christ.

FOR FURTHER STUDY

Simcha Brooks, *Saul and the Monarchy: A New Look* (Burlington, Vt.: Ashgate, 2005).

Walter Brueggemann, *Ichabod Toward Home: The Journey of God's Glory* (Grand Rapids: Eerdmans, 2005).

WORKS CITED

A. A. Anderson, *2 Samuel* (Dallas: Word, 1989).

Bill Arnold, *1 & 2 Samuel: The NIV Application Commentary* (Grand Rapids: Zondervan, 2003).

John Bright, *A History of Israel* (Philadelphia: Westminster, 2000).

Walter Brueggemann, *First and Second Samuel* (Louisville: John Knox, 1990).

Anthony F. Campbell, *The Ark Narrative* (Chico, Calif.: Society of Biblical Literature, 1975).

———, *2 Samuel*. (Grand Rapids: Eerdmans, 2005).

Tony Cartledge, *Smyth & Helwys Bible Commentary: 1 & 2 Samuel* (Macon, Ga.: Smyth & Helwys Publishing Co., 2001).

Rupert Chapman, "Weapons and Warfare," *The Oxford Encyclopedia of Archaeology in the Near East* 5 (1997): 334–39.

Raymond B. Dillard and Tremper Longman III, *An Introduction to the Old Testament* (Grand Rapids: Zondervan, 1994).

Trude Dothan, "Philistines," *Anchor Bible Dictionary* 5 (1992): 328–33.

J. D. Douglas, "Nazirite," *New Bible Dictionary* (1999): 808–9.

S. R. Driver, *Notes on the Hebrew Text of the Books of Samuel* (Oxford: Clarendon, 1913).

Jenni Ernst and Claus Westermann, *Theological Lexicon of the Old Testament* (Peabody, Mass.: Hendrickson, 1997).

Baruch Halpern, *The Constitution of the Monarchy in Israel* (Chico, Calif.: Scholars Press, 1981).

———, *David's Secret Demons: Messiah, Murderer, Traitor, King* (Grand Rapids: Eerdmans, 2001).

Mark Hamilton, *The Body Royal: The Social Poetics of Kingship in Ancient Israel* (Leiden: Brill, 2005).

Alfred J. Hoerth, Gerald L. Mattingly, Edwin M. Yamauchi, *Peoples of the Old Testament World* (Grand Rapids: Baker, 1998).

Michael Jordan, *Encyclopedia of Gods* (New York: Facts on File Inc., 1993).

Philip J. King and Lawrence E. Stager, *Life in Biblical Israel* (Louisville: Westminster John Knox, 2001).

Theodore J. Lewis, "Dead, Abode of the," *Anchor Bible Dictionary* 2 (1992): 102–3.

Mario Liverani, "The Deeds of Ancient Mesopotamian Kings," in *Civilizations of the Ancient Near East* (ed. Jack M. Sasson; New York: Hendrickson, 2000), 2353–66.

Kyle P. McCarter, *I Samuel* (New York: Doubleday, 1980).

———, *II Samuel* (New York: Doubleday, 1980).

Steven L. McKenzie, "Deuteronomistic History," *Anchor Bible Dictionary* 2 (1992): 160–68.

Martin Noth, *The Deuteronomistic History* (Sheffield: JSOT, 1981).

Robert Polzin, *Samuel and the Deuteronomist* (San Francisco: Harper & Row, 1989).

Ronny Reich and Eli Shukron, "Light at the End of the Tunnel," *Biblical Archaeology Review* 25 (January-February 1999): 22–33, 72.

Allen Ross, *Holiness to the Lord: A Guide to the Exposition of the Book of Leviticus* (Grand Rapids: Baker, 2002).

James E. Smith, *The College Press NIV Commentary 1 & 2 Samuel* (Joplin, Mo.: College Press, 2000).

Thomas Thompson, *The Historicity of the Patriarchal Narratives* (1974; repr. Harrisburg, Pa.: Trinity International, 2002).

Roland de Vaux, *Ancient Israel* (Grand Rapids: Eerdmans, 1997)

Leon J. Wood, *The Prophets of Israel* (Grand Rapids: Baker, 2001).

2 Samuel

Sara Fudge

CHAPTER CONTENTS

Contexts   291

Commentary   291
- David's Rise to Kingship · 1 Sam 16:1–2 Sam 4:12   291
- David's Reign Established Over Israel · 5:1–10:19   294
- Trouble in the House of David · 11:1–21:22   297
- Psalms of David · 22:1–23:7   305
- David's Men & Their Numbering · 23:8–24:25   306

Theological Reflections   307

For Further Study   308

Works Cited   308

MAPS, TABLES, & FEATURES

- A King's Harem   293
- Ancient Jerusalem   294
- The Water Tunnel   295
- Violated Women   299
- Geshur   300
- Wise Women   304
- Royal Inscriptions   307

The books of Samuel were originally one scroll. Due to its great length, it was separated into two smaller sections in the Septuagint for easier use (Dillard and Longman 136). Therefore, 2 Samuel flows smoothly from 1 Samuel as it reports the rise and rule of David.

CONTEXTS

The books of Samuel primarily record the transition of the nation of Israel from the period of the Judges to the founding of the monarchy. Israel moves from being a nation ruled by God under nonhereditary judges to a nation ruled by dynasties of kings. The key story is the founding of the dynasty of David (2 Sam 7:4–16), which lasts four hundred years and provides the lineage of David's through which the Messiah will come and an "everlasting covenant" will be established (2 Sam 23:5; Rom 1:2–4).

Several themes interwoven throughout 1 and 2 Samuel are evident in the songs that open and close these books (Hannah's, 1 Sam 2; David's, 2 Sam 22, 23). Hannah and David sing of the blessings they experience in the Lord. Both witness how the righteous receive the Lord's blessing while the wicked perish. They receive the Lord's strength as he delivers them from the enemy, not only bringing salvation, but doing so against the odds by using the small, weak, and few to accomplish mighty works.

The events recorded in the books of Samuel take place approximately between 1118–970 BCE. This period spans the birth of Samuel to the end of David's reign. Israel has been living in the land of Canaan since the exodus from Egypt and has not been oppressed or challenged during this time by any of the mighty world powers. Israel is thus in an ideal situation to expand despite the continuous raids from immediate neighbors (Amalekites, 1 Sam 15:8–33; Philistines, 1 Sam 21:10–14, 27–29; Ammonites, 1 Sam 11:12, 2 Sam 10:1–4). We should note, though, that "biblical historiography, in contradiction to modern history writing since the Enlightenment, locates the causes of human events in the passions and purpose of Yahweh, the God of Israel" (Arnold 24).

For a more detailed discussion of the historical and literary contexts of 2 Samuel, see the discussion of 1 Samuel's contexts on page 271.

COMMENTARY

DAVID'S RISE TO KINGSHIP · 1 SAM 16:1–2 SAM 4:12
The opening section of 2 Samuel continues the story of David's rise to power. One by one, remaining opponents fall by the wayside as he moves from rule of Judah to rule of all Israel and beyond.

1:1–27 The tragic end of Saul and his sons is reported to David by a young man who claims to have escaped the battle. After he gives his report, David has the young man killed (1:15). Why kill the messenger? First, this young man claims to have assisted Saul in bringing about his death, perhaps thinking to please David since Saul had sought David's life. Contrary to this thinking, David has a different perspective. He says, *Why were you not afraid to lift your hand to destroy the Lord's anointed?* (1:14). David could have but did not raise his hand against God's anointed and neither should this self-serving young man. Only God can kill the king.

Second, this man was an Amalekite (1:8, 13), part of the people Saul was commanded to destroy but did not. Unfortunately for the young man, David had just returned from his own battle against this very people (1 Sam 30:1, 2). The irony of the story should be obvious.

This account of Saul's death differs from the account in 1 Samuel 31 (see above). Many scholars bridge this discrepancy by understanding that the young Amalekite embellishes his story to gain favor and privilege in David's eyes. This is uncertain, however. One of the few war poems in the Bible (compare Judg 5; Pss 20; 21; 68), this funeral hymn mourns a failed warrior. David appears here as a loyal subject innocent of his master's death.

David respectfully mourns the death of Saul and Jonathan and makes it a national lament as he *ordered that the men of Judah be taught this lament of the bow (it was written in the book of Jashar)* (1:18). "Lament of the Bow" may be the title of this dirge (Cartledge 354). The lament credits Saul for the economic strength he brought Israel (1:24). It then moves to the first person as David grieves for Jonathan *my brother* (1:26), one of the most genuine and heartfelt friendships recorded in history.

> **The Book of Jashar**
> *This book appears to have been a collection of songs and poems that commemorated remarkable deeds and events in Israel's history, especially battles. There is one other reference to this book in Joshua 10:13, where* the sun stood still and the moon stopped, till [Israel] avenged itself on its enemies, as it is written in the book of Jashar. *The book no longer survives; we know of its existence only through these two references.*

2:1–32 David's new capital, Hebron (2:1), sits less than twenty miles south of Jerusalem. Here David reigns for the next seven years. *Up* refers to elevation, not a northern direction. The men of Judah come here to anoint David and make him *king over the house of Judah* (2:4). From here, David begins to put his house in order by recognizing the men of Jabesh Gilead who buried the body of Saul (2:4–7). The dynasty of Saul still has a hold in the north through Saul's military leader, Abner, and a surviving son, Ishbosheth.

What follows in chapter 2 is a clash between the generals of Saul and David, Abner and Joab respectively. Abner "was clearly the power behind the throne in Israel" following Saul's death and possibly served as interim leader before Ishbosheth's two year reign (Cartledge 373). Abner, Joab, and their men meet around the pool of Gibeon as twelve chosen men from each side challenge one another (2:13). Some archaeologists believe they have found this pool/cistern. It is 37 feet in diameter and is located on the northern side of the city. The Hebrew word describing this exchange (2:14) literally means to "entertain" or "contest." This event may have begun as an entertaining show of strength, but the contest ends in a stalemate as each man kills his opponent and fighting breaks out. Such competitions of strength and military skill bespeak a situation of rival war parties and political instability.

Scripture focuses on the pursuit of Abner by one of Joab's brothers, Asahel. Asahel is a less skilled soldier than Abner but a swift and determined adversary. Abner, an experienced soldier and official, knows that if he kills Asahel, the revenge of Joab and the political tension caused between the two camps could be devastating. He tells Asahel to *turn aside* (2:21), but the latter is relentless. Asahel, who is literally at Abner's heels, is killed when the butt end of Abner's spear runs through his stomach and out his back. Abner may have stopped suddenly, hoping only to knock the breath out of Asahel with the blunt end of his spear, but Asahel's momentum is such that he runs himself through as he comes abruptly upon Abner. Joab aborts the pursuit late that evening when Abner calls out, *Don't you realize that this will end in bitterness? How long before you order your men to stop pursuing their brothers?* (2:26). The tone of the question serves to cast Abner as a man of rough integrity, unlike the fierce Joab. Curiously however, Joab is David's assistant. Joab will get his revenge later for his brother's death (3:27). This encounter is representative of the hostility between the house of Saul and the house of David. David continued to grow stronger *while the house of Saul grew weaker and weaker* (3:1).

3:1–29 *Abner had been strengthening his own position in the house of Saul* (3:6), but tensions within the palace walls are exposed when Ishbosheth accuses Abner of sexual relations with one of the royal concubines, Rizpeh (see chapter 21). This angers and insults Abner, who replies: *Am I a dog's head*? (3:8). Abner's reference to the dog may reflect common wisdom: "Sexual promiscuity of dogs is proverbial" (Smith 359).

Following this accusation, Abner swears to *transfer the kingdom from the house of Saul and establish David's throne over Israel* (3:10), further evidence of his power in the royal court. He acknowledges that the Lord promised *on oath* to give the kingdom to David (3:9, 10, 18). It seems to have been well known, at least in the court, that David would succeed Saul. Abner approaches David with a proposal (3:12). David agrees but demands the return of Michal (3:13). David may have wanted Michal back because of his deep love for her, or he may have believed that his marriage to Saul's daughter would aid in uniting the northern tribes to his house. Either way, she seems to be a pawn in the political maneuvers of powerful men. With complete support from the men of Benjamin, the elders of Israel, and Michal, Abner aligns Israel with David politically and militarily. David welcomes Abner, and they share a feast together. Three times Scripture mentions that they departed in peace, making it clear that David had no part in the events that are about to take place (3:21–23).

When Joab returns from a raid and learns of the arrangement between David and Abner, he becomes indignant with David (3:24). Acting without the approval or knowledge of David, Joab forms a posse to bring Abner back to Hebron to avenge his brother Asahel's death and thus eliminate any threat of losing his position to Abner as commander-in-chief of David's army. Abner trusts that he will be safe with David's men. Joab takes Abner *aside* (using the same verb used by Abner when asking Asahel to "turn aside"), *into the gateway, as though to speak with him privately,* then *stabbed him in the stomach* (3:27). Joab chooses the same deadly wound that Abner inflicted on Asahel. According to Hebrew law, if a person is intentionally killed, the next of kin of the one murdered has the right as the "avenger of blood" to seek vengeance for his relative's murder (Num 35:19–21). The law did not exactly apply here, for Abner did not intentionally seek out Asahel to kill him and had actually tried to avoid the encounter. Joab steps outside the law and disregards the king's peace negotiations and the good of the nation to seek his own revenge. Ironically, Hebron is a city of refuge, a safe-haven for those accused of murder (Josh 20). This incident could have threatened the new merger of Judah and Israel, but David prudently disassociates himself completely from this act. He publicly recognizes it as a wrongful deed, acknowledges Abner as a *prince and a great man* (3:38), and properly mourns his death, thus averting what could have been a disastrous situation (3:36–37).

David does not take action at this time against this murderous act of Joab, but he does curse Joab's house and place the bloodguilt for Abner's death on Joab's head (3:29). These are typical curses one would find among ancient texts against one's enemy. He recognizes (as will Ishbosheth) the control held by the commander-in-chief of the armies: *these sons of Zeruiah [Joab] are too strong for me* (3:39). David does not feel he has the strength to discipline Joab, who has the power of the military behind him.

A King's Harem

Polygamy was an accepted practice in the ancient Near Eastern society as seen in Hannah's home with her husband having two wives (1 Sam 1–2). In this situation it served a practical purpose of bringing children into a barren home. A large harem was a sign of wealth and power, as well as a sign of male virility. "Harem" here means simply a collection of wives, not necessarily a separate set of buildings as existed in later royal courts.

Foreign alliances were often formed by a marriage agreement. A foreign princess could become a part of the king's harem, creating a family tie between the two nations. A king's harem was part of the royal inheritance and was passed on to the new heir to the throne. To sleep with or even request a king's concubine was a show of power and aggression to the throne. This helps to explain Absalom's first act as king to defile David's harem (2 Sam 16:21, 22; also Adonijah and Abishag, 1 Kgs 2:13–25).

If Abner had indeed slept with a concubine of Saul's harem, that would support the theory that Abner had become an interim ruler during those first few years following Saul's death. God warned future kings against taking many wives that may lead a man's heart astray (Deut 17:17; see also 1 Kgs 11:1–3).

This practice raises the question of incest: cursed is the man who sleeps with his father's wife, for he dishonors his father's bed (Deut 27:20). This law certainly includes rulers but may not extend to secondary wives or concubines (Ezek 22:10; de Vaux 115–117).

4:1–12 Abner had been able to keep David contained to the south, but Ishbosheth proves too weak to maintain this hold and unable even to sustain his position in the north. Two Benjaminites, leaders of a marauding band, kill Ishosheth as he sleeps, hoping to gain David's favor. David's response is the same as when the Amalekite claimed to have killed Saul. He has these two men killed for their deed against *an innocent man in his own house and on his own bed* (4:11), a royal man. He has their bodies hung in public view with their hands and feet cut off to further disgrace these criminals. David makes a public statement once again that he is innocent of these crimes against Saul's house.

The text adds a note about another possible heir to the throne, a son of Jonathan who has survived, Mephibosheth. He is described by his physical handicap, crippled in both feet. Being handicapped makes him less acceptable for the throne and, therefore, not a threat to David's position. Being a son of Jonathan endears him to David.

DAVID'S REIGN ESTABLISHED OVER ISRAEL · 5:1–10:19

The elders of Israel, those who had backed Abner and Ishbosheth, publicly transfer their allegiance to David and anoint him. With Abner dead and Ishbosheth's power hold in the north broken, David is in a position to rule over all Israel and Judah. He will set up a new location for his rule, confirm his military capabilities, and honor the Lord before the people as their God. David rules seven and a half years from Hebron over Judah and thirty-three years over Judah and Israel from Jerusalem. He lives to the age of seventy (5:4, 5).

5:1–6:23 Jerusalem becomes the new capital city for the united Judah and Israel. At this time it is under the control of the Jebusites, a Canaanite people. Its advantage lies in its central location between Israel and Judah, with defenses including its elevation, walls, citadel, and water shaft. It is surrounded by the Kidron Valley to the east and the Hinnom Valley to the west, which meet on the south side of the city. Joab cunningly secures the city by a sneak attack through the water shaft leading from the Gihon spring in the Kidron Valley, under the fortified wall, into the city (5:8).

> **Jerusalem & Its Names**
> *Egyptian texts mention Jerusalem by the eighteenth century BCE. Jerusalem is first referred to as Salem when Melchizedek, its king, meets Abraham (Gen 14:18). The Jebusites, a Canaanite people, managed to maintain their control over the city until the time of David (Judg 19:10). When David captures the city, he refers to it as the fortress of Zion, which may be the fortified section of the city (2 Sam 5:7). Zion is later used in a poetic context as it refers to the city of God (Ps 2:6). Jerusalem is also referred to as the City of David (2 Sam 5:7). This designation usually refers to the oldest section of Jerusalem occupied by David, located on the southeastern slope of the mount between the Central and Kidron valleys.*

Another sign of success for David comes when he is recognized as king in Jerusalem by foreign rulers such as Hiram, the king of Tyre, who offers his famous cedar wood, along with men skilled in wood and stone, to assist in constructing a palace for David (5:11). Cedar was the building material of choice for ancient temples and palaces, and Phoenicia provided the best cedar. It also provided the best artisans. Israelite art from the Iron Age II (1000–586 BCE) often followed Phoenician conventions.

Continued success to establish David in Jerusalem comes when David is victorious over the Philistines as the Lord is present *marching in the tops of the balsam trees* (5:24). Israel carries off the Philistine idols as a statement on the dominance of Israel's God, Yahweh (5:21). Thus, David's kingship is confirmed with his

> **The Water Tunnel**
>
> The Canaanites, and later the Israelites, had skilled engineers that designed a variety of water systems for their towns. They included large water shafts tapping into the water table, large cisterns or reservoirs collecting water, and sophisticated underground water tunnels.
>
> Jerusalem was a prime location for a city due to a spring located at the base of the Kidron Valley that produced a generous amount of water. Its name, Gihon, comes from the Hebrew word meaning "gusher." During the Middle Bronze Age (about 2000–1550 BCE), a channel was cut near the surface, funneling this spring into a pool at least four hundred meters away at the south end of the city. Great towers were constructed at the source of the spring to protect the waters from enemy attack. Another access to the water was a tunnel leading from inside the Jebusite wall to a pool fed by the spring. This tunnel was accessed from a shaft lined with steps leading to the tunnel. With the threat of an Assyrian assault, King Hezekiah (727?–698 BCE) later constructed another tunnel. This tunnel began at the spring and ran under the city parallel to the Kidron Valley, ending in the Pool of Siloam at the south end of the city, possibly replacing the pool fed by the channel. The Pool of Siloam was located safely within the walls of the city. Tourists today can walk through Hezekiah's tunnel. (Reich and Shukron; King and Stager 210–15).

new capital city, recognition among the nations, and victory over his enemy.

Another important step in establishing David's kingship is to honor the Lord and bring the sacred ark of the covenant to the royal city of David. For twenty years, the ark remained in Kiriath Jearim (about eight miles west of Jerusalem) after its capture and return from the Philistines (1 Sam 7:2). Many had died in connection to its previous move, creating an atmosphere of fear (1 Sam 4–6). David begins preparations to bring the ark to Jerusalem.

David makes the return of the ark a joyous national celebration as he orders thirty military units to transport the ark. This is approximately 150–420 men, if one translates the Hebrew word *eleph* to mean "military unit" rather than the number "thousand" (Cartledge 433). The ark is magnificently described as the *ark of God, which is called by the Name, the name of the Lord Almighty, who is enthroned between the cherubim that are on the ark* (6:2). The sacredness of the ark is emphasized because it helps to explain God's reaction when the ark is defiled.

Israel follows the example of the Philistines by making a new cart to carry the ark. When the oxen pulling the cart stumble, Uzzah reaches out to steady the ark, bringing the wrath of God and death upon himself (6:6, 7). David becomes angry and fearful. Uzzah's was a protective reflex, not a premeditated crime. Assuming the applicability of the law of Moses to this occasion, the issue is not the punishment served on Uzzah, but rather, the holiness of God. God had warned Israel, *they must not touch the holy things or they will die* (Num 4:15). His holiness was compromised when they neglected to transport the ark properly, thus disregarding its sacredness. Uzzah had violated a ritual instruction and so paid a terrible price.

For three months following this tragic event, the ark remains in the house of Obed-Edom, who reaps blessings from the Lord during its stay (6:11). David makes a second attempt to move the ark.

With much celebration, the ark comes safely into Jerusalem. David's excitement is visibly evident as he is *leaping and dancing before the Lord* (6:16). He offers burnt and fellowship sacrifices to the Lord and shares cakes of dates and raisins (a special gift) with the people. In the eyes of Michal, David's wife, this blatant show of enthusiasm is not appropriate public behavior befitting a king, for she reprimands him when he returns home to bless his family. This unacceptable behavior may be the setting aside of his royal garb for the ephod, a short garment that perhaps proved immodest. This is a critical moment for the house of Saul. Three times Michal is referred to as *the daughter of Saul*, not the wife of David, connecting her to the house of Saul rather than the house of David. David, in the past, defended Saul and his house, but now he makes a sharp distinction between Saul and himself. He reminds Michal that Yahweh *chose me rather than your father or anyone from his house* (6:21). It is possible to argue that this was not an arrogant statement but quite the opposite. He says, *I will become even more undignified than this, and I will be humiliated in my own eyes* (6:22). His "humility" is emphasized twice in this verse. Scholars have interpreted this passage in several ways: David engaged in worship practices that Michal believed illegitimate; Michal is arrogant and jealous, while David is not; David is arrogant, while Michal is the victim of his crass behavior. As is typical, the text does not tell us which reading is correct.

The passage ends with: *Michal, daughter of Saul, had no children to the day of her death* (6:23). It does not state whether this was due to the Lord closing her womb or David refusing to have relations with her. There is no blood union between the house of Saul and the house of David. David begins a new dynasty completely separate from and unrelated to the previous rule.

God's Blessing on the House of David · 7:1–8:18

The events of this chapter may have taken place closer to the end of David's career, when there was rest in the land. They may have been placed here to connect them to the movement of the ark in the preceding chapter.

7:1–17 David has established his capital city and his reputation in the land, but he cannot justify his beautiful palace while the Lord lives in a tent. The ark of the covenant was placed in a tent in Jerusalem, rather than the tabernacle located in Gibeon (2 Sam 6:17; 1 Chron 16:39, 21:29). David turns his attention to constructing a temple. Temple building in the ancient world served to legitimate a king's rule as one sanctioned by the gods. David takes council with the prophet Nathan regarding this project. Nathan responds, *go ahead and do it, for the Lord is with you* (7:3). This appears to be good council, but later that night, the Lord gives Nathan a different message for David.

Second Samuel and 1 Chronicles give different explanations for David's disqualification from building the temple. In 1 Chronicles, Nathan informs David that he will not build a temple to the Lord for *you have shed much blood on the earth* (1 Chron 22:8). Instead, David's son Solomon, a man of peace, will be the one to build the temple. For 2 Samuel, the Lord simply does not desire a structure of cedar. God would not be manipulated by the ark (1 Sam 4–6) nor be contained in a house made with hands (7:5–7). The Chronicler's explanation is odd, since temple building and warfare often went hand-in-hand in the ancient Near East.

However, the Lord promises to establish a house for David. The word "house" is used repeatedly in this chapter in a wordplay to denote both something literal and something metaphorical. It refers to a physical dwelling and a family, a present existence and a future hope: *Your house and your kingdom will endure forever before me, your throne will be established forever* (7:16; Arnold 475). God has blessed David's house by taking him from shepherding sheep to ruling over his people. He will continue to bless his house through future generations to secure his dynasty and legacy. Moreover, this chapter is foundational to understanding Old Testament theology. It establishes God's covenant with the dynasty of David in Jerusalem. Many Old Testament passages are grounded in this promise (for example, 1 Kgs 9:4–9; Ps 89:29–37; Isa 9:7; Jer 33:17). The New Testament looks back to this passage as it looks forward to David's *kingdom enduring forever* in Christ (for example, Matt 1:1; Acts 13:22, 23; Heb 1:5).

7:18–29 David *went in and sat before the Lord* (7:18). He humbly recognizes the things the Lord has done for him and Israel, not only in the present, but in *the future of the house of your servant* (7:19). He asks, *Is this your usual way of dealing with man, O Sovereign Lord?* (7:19). The Hebrew does not pose a question here. Literally it reads, "and this is the law for a human being, O Lord, Yahweh." This is the only place where this phrase occurs in Scripture. A possible translation of "law" (*torah*) here would be "custom" or "manner," giving the word the idea of contrasting the manner of man with the manner of God. Humans would not take someone of such low social status as David, a shepherd boy, and honor him in such a magnificent way as God has. David boldly accepts this honor from the Lord. The verb for *be pleased* (7:29) is in the imperative form, revealing David's confidence and boldness before the Lord.

8:1–18 One means by which God blesses the house of David is through victory over the enemy. David's conflicts come from the neighboring nations living in present-day Palestine, Jordan, and Syria: Philistines, Moabites, and Arameans respectively. This text sounds like an ancient inscription celebrating a king's victories. The systematic execution of the Moabites where he *measured them off with a length of cord* (8:2) is curious, since David has Moabite blood in him (Ruth 4). Also, he sought safety for his parents with them while he was a fugitive (1 Sam 22:3). David the conqueror comes to the fore.

David expands the borders greatly, and thus the wealth in the kingdom, through tribute from these conquests: *The Lord gave David victory wherever he went* (8:14). This favor came by the Lord's grace and David doing what was *just and right for all his people* (8:15). This theme is seen as later rulers will be characterized by doing *what is right in the eyes of the Lord* as David did (2 Kgs 18:3; 22:2; 2 Chron 29:2; 34:2) as opposed to *walking in the ways of Jeroboam*, noted for his evil, leading the people away from God (1 Kgs 15:34; 16:7, 19; 22:52; 2 Kgs 13:2; 13:11; 14:24; 15:9, 18, 24, 28). This theme continues in the message of the prophets, who seek *One who in judging seeks justice and speeds the cause of righteousness* (Isa 16:5; compare Isa 9:7; Jer 9:24; Hos 2:19; Amos 5:24).

David's high court officials are listed, including military leaders, archivists, and religious leaders (see also 2 Sam 20:23–26; 1 Kgs 4:1–6; 1 Chron 18:14–17). His sons serve as royal advisors, or "priests." The word "priest" may imply "that they stood in some special relation to the king. It seems not improbable that they were 'domestic priests' appointed specially to perform religious offices for the king" (Driver 285). Chronicles, uncomfortable with the Samuel text, calls David's sons *the chief officials at the king's side* (1 Chron 18:17).

David's Kindness · 9:1–10:19

It is rare that a new regime would show kindness to the family of a displaced ruler. But, as David was fleeing Saul's court, he made a promise to Jonathan, Saul's son, that he would not cut off "kindness" from Jonathan's family (1 Sam 20:15). Now David searches for a descendant of Saul to whom he can fulfill this promised kindness (9:1).

A surviving son of Jonathan is brought to David—Mephibosheth, who was crippled as a child (2 Sam 4:4) and exiled from his father's lands. When he appears before David he bows as his *servant* and refers to himself as a *dead dog*, a common word picture found in Samuel for self-abasement (Goliath in 1 Sam 17:43; David in 1 Sam 24:14; Abner in 2 Sam 3:8) Mephibosheth receives honor as David invites him to eat at his table for the rest of his days. His family estate is returned to him and assistance is provided through Ziba, a servant of Saul. David honors an unlikely individual, a handicapped man from a deposed family. Twice the text mentions Mephibosheth's crippled feet, a fact which exemplifies David's exceptional grace.

We see another example of David's kindness when he shows compassion to the Ammonites whom he believes to be a new ally developed from earlier days of war. The Ammonites, descendants of Nahash, mourn the death of their king (compare 1 Sam 11). David sends a delegation *to express sympathy* (10:2). However, the Ammonites accuse them of being spies. Their beards, a sign of their masculinity, were half shaved and their robes torn exposing their nakedness. They are sent away in a most undignified state (10:5).

This begins a series of conflicts between Israel and the Ammonites, which is the setting for the following chapter. During this Ammonite conflict, the mood will change dramatically for the house of David.

TROUBLE IN THE HOUSE OF DAVID · 11:1–21:22

Thus far, David has been depicted as a man of integrity and mercy (righteousness and justice). Scripture does not spare its heroes the humiliating truth of personal and spiritual failings. David makes poor choices in his personal life that overshadow the storybook success he has had to this point.

David & Bathsheba · 11:1–12:31

There is a season for battle, in the summer when the cold is past and the rains ease to allow freedom of movement for the troops and abundance of food for the soldiers and animals, a time when kings go out to battle. David sends Joab and his troops against the Ammonites, while he stays behind in Jerusalem. The reader is not informed of the reasoning, but it is evident that David is distracted from the affairs of the kingdom.

One evening David got up from his bed and walked around on the roof of the palace (11:2). He notices a beautiful woman bathing on her rooftop. She may have been engaging in a ritual cleansing following her menstrual period, indicating she was not pregnant at this time (Lev 15). She is Bathsheba, the daughter of Eliam (possibly one of David's mighty men, 2 Sam 23:34), and the wife of Uriah the Hittite, one of David's mighty men. Many have attempted to judge Bathsheba's role in this act; was she a willing participant, or did she consider or even fear the imperial position of her suitor and comply? We cannot know the answer to this, only that she did submit and become pregnant. A parenthetical note follows that *she had purified herself from her uncleanness* (11:4). This notice may refer back to her bath on her roof or a cleansing following sexual intercourse. It would be ironic that she would be conscientious of this minor form of purification following a sinful act worthy of death (see Ross 307).

The text next sets up a contrast between the "righteous and just," King David and a Gentile foreigner, Uriah the Hittite (Uriah's nationality is mentioned eight times in Samuel). God's anointed becomes the malefactor, while the foreigner (a stranger deserving the king's protection) exhibits loyalty and integrity.

Plan A is to bring Bathsheba's husband home from the war under the guise of seeking intelligence concerning *how the war was going* (11:7). Once home, David expects Uriah to sleep with his wife so that the child would appear to be his. To David's disappointment, Uriah's conscience will not allow him such pleasure (11:11). We see the contrast in the honorable Uriah and David at home enjoying the pleasures of his palace with this man's wife.

David moves to Plan B, a more drastic plan. He devises a scheme whereby Uriah will be placed in the *fiercest* battle. Nearby soldiers will withdraw so he will be killed (11:15). The plan is written in a letter and – in a brutal irony – carried to Joab by Uriah himself. Joab understands David's instructions. He must employ poor battle tactics and place his men in unnecessary danger, within the range of archers on the city wall, to carry out this order. He reports back a coded message that describes the battle situation and justifies the losses incurred by Israel. Most importantly, he reports the death of Uriah. David responds, and again the true message underlies the façade of words: *Don't let this upset you*; *the sword devours one as well as another ... Say this to encourage Joab* (11:25), which means, "Thank you for killing Uriah; many die in battle; no regrets."

Until verse 27, the narrator makes no comment on these events, but the sentence *But the thing David had done displeased the Lord* sets in motion a series of disasters for the hitherto successful king.

The Lord sends the prophet Nathan to David to confront him (12:1). Nathan's parable draws David (and the reader) into a sense of outrage and concern. David says the rich man *deserves to die* (12:5) though his sin was not a capital crime. Nathan points to David and says, *You are the man* (12:7). One scholar describes this scene as perhaps "the most dramatic sentence in the Old Testament" (Smith 428). The Lord had given David the houses of Saul, Judah, and Israel. *If all this had been too little, I would have given you even more* (12:8). David did not need to take from the house of Uriah. David had made a personal assault against the Lord, as the statement *you despised me* indicates (12:10). As the true king of Israel, Yahweh must punish the human king for injustice (compare Ps 101).

Unlike Saul, David repents, recognizing his sin against the Lord. Nathan's reply is extraordinary: *The Lord has taken away your sin* (12:13). Without sacrifice, without purification, without any kind of action, God graciously forgives David as he repents. Though forgiven, David will realize the consequence of the sin. Notice the effect of his sin against the "house" with which the Lord blessed him: because he murdered one of his trusted men, *the sword will never depart from your house* (12:10); because of David's adultery, *out of your own house I am going to bring calamity upon you ... another will lie with your wives* (12:11). However, the story does not end in hopelessness. Inserted into the story at this point is the birth of Solomon. The house of David will continue.

Meanwhile, Joab battles the Ammonites. The text emphasizes David's personal distractions at home when Joab sends messengers to David to advise him of his responsibility to the nation's foreign conflicts. He is about to inflict the final blow and conclude the Ammonite campaigns when he judges it best to give the victory to David rather than claim it for himself, but David must come to the battlefield for this honor. David makes his appearance in Rabbah, overpowering the capital city of the Ammonites, claiming its royal crown and an abundance of spoils from its surrounding sister towns.

Why add this story to the Bathsheba incident? Though David has stumbled in his righteousness, the Lord continues to be with this repentant king. However, Nathan's words of warning are about to be realized. The real heartache will come from within David's house, from his own offspring.

Absalom & Sheba's Rebellion · 13:1–20:26

Following David's transgression, the temper of the kingdom changes. David's house is riddled with conflict and anguish. The reader's attention turns to the princes of the kingdom, Amnon, David's firstborn son, and Absalom, his third son. David's second son Kileab, son of Abigail, mentioned only in 2 Samuel 3:3, may have died at an early age.

13:1–38 Amnon sets his eyes on his beautiful half-sister Tamar, a full sister of Absalom. Scripture says he *fell in love with Tamar* (13:1) with a desire so intense he *became frustrated to the point of illness* (13:2). Amnon devises a scheme to be alone with Tamar and then rapes (literally, "humiliates") her. Tamar pleads with Amnon not to do such a thing; she will be disgraced, and he will be as a *wicked fool* (13:13). She then says something we would not expect; she suggests marriage. He refuses to listen. After he finishes "humbling" her, his feelings of "love" turn to hate (13:15). Further disgrace comes to her when he sends her away (13:17). This is the same Hebrew word used for "divorce." She is now stripped of her innocence, dignity, and value as a woman. As a sign of her reproach, she tears the ornamented robe of her virginity, puts ashes on her head, and weeps.

Tamar's brother, Absalom, learns of his sister's tragedy. (A similar incident occurs in Genesis 34 with Dinah and Shechem.) His immediate response appears composed: *Be quiet now, my sister; he is your brother. Don't take this thing to heart* (13:20), yet in fact he is furious and bides his time before taking action (13:21–22). Meanwhile, Tamar finds refuge in the home of Absalom now that she is no longer eligible to live among the virgin princesses in the palace. Absalom, and not her father as one should expect, becomes her protector. Her standing among the women has moved to an "unwanted divorcee" (Cartledge 540).

After two years, Absalom invites the family to a celebration. David declines the invitation and questions the presence of Amnon's name on the guest list, possibly due to suspicions from previous events. Eventually, David is persuaded to send Amnon along with his brothers. Fathers control the actions of sons, even adult sons, yet David has not acted on behalf of Tamar. After filling Amnon with wine, Absalom's servants kill him (13:28). Absalom flees to Geshur, north of Israel, homeland of Absalom's maternal grandfather. *David mourned for his son every day* (13:37), not only Amnon, but Absalom as well.

14:1–33 Absalom remains in Geshur for three years. He receives no word from his father, though David's *heart longed for Absalom* (14:1). Joab determines that David needs to resolve this issue with his son. It may be that David's grief is distracting him from governmental affairs, or Joab may be concerned for the personal well-being of the king. He uses a similar tactic Nathan used to convict David of his sin against Uriah. Joab recruits *a wise woman* (14:2) to present a fictitious version of David's predicament. (Tekoa, south of Jerusalem, was later Amos's hometown.) See the discussion of chapter 20 below. She delivers her story well, evoking the sympathy and protection of David for her son. Once she has achieved this, she confronts David with his own family situation. David catches the parallel as it relates to himself, but his response is different than it was with Nathan. He does not seek the Lord's word in this time of confusion, as he had in the past. Nor does he repent of any injustice on his part. He agrees to call Absalom back to Jerusalem, but he does not meet with him for two years and then only when pressed. There is no genuine reconciliation between father and son. This behavior of David indicates a lack of decisiveness.

Joab personally brings Absalom back to Jerusalem. The text gives a physical description of Absalom (14:25). As with Saul and David, physical appearance will contribute to Absalom's political success. His *heavy* hair is noted, as this will be important to the story later (14:26).

Things seem to be going well for Absalom in Jerusalem, but two years pass without seeing his father. Two times he calls for Joab to send a message to the king to settle the affair, since Absalom is forbidden to approach the king himself, but Joab does not answer Absalom's call. Absalom gets Joab's attention by setting his fields on fire. He demands a judicial decision (14:32). David grants an audience with Absalom, who bows in reverence to his father. David kisses Absalom as a sign of forgiveness, though restoration and mutual respect are still lacking in this relationship. David, of course, faces a political dilemma: he dare not punish Absalom since

---

Violated Women

Why would a girl about to be raped offer to marry her rapist? In Israelite culture it was a great humiliation and shame for a women to be defiled and lose her virginity prior to marriage. She would be unfit and unwanted by any proper man.

According to Mosaic law, if a man violates an unbetrothed virgin he must offer marriage and pay an "enhanced" brideprice to her father (Exod 22:16, 17; de Vaux 30). Her other option is to remain celibate in the home of her father, or next of kin, the rest of her days. All things being equal, a woman without husband or children was held in lesser esteem than one with a family.

The law states,

If a man happens to meet a virgin who is not pledged to be married and rapes her and they are discovered, he shall pay the girl's father fifty shekels of silver. He must marry the girl, for he has violated her. He can never divorce her as long as he lives (Deut 22:28–29).

Another odd feature behind Tamar's proposal is the fact that she and Amnon have the same father. It is forbidden by law for siblings of one or both parents to marry (Lev 18:9). Tamar was either unaware of this law (which may have been ignored at the time) or perhaps hoped her words would save her from the immediate situation.

Tamar deserved a defense, and he dare not acquit him, since he had killed his brother. David avoids making a decision, thus insuring continued instability.

The previous years have not been kind to Absalom's reputation. He is a murderer and a returned exile who has fallen from the grace of the king. For any hope of the throne, he must win the favor of the people and overcome the bad publicity that follows him. He begins by creating an image for himself as he travels with a chariot and horses along with an entourage of fifty men to run along the chariot, assuming a countenance of distinction as royal prince. The men may have served as bodyguards for him. Next, he will promote himself as one concerned for justice and the needs of the people.

15:1–12 It was a common practice for the royal court to receive cases from individuals who for some reason felt they had not received justice through the courts or whose cases were unusual (for example, the "wise woman" in 2 Sam 14). Absalom begins to station himself along the road *leading to the city gate* (15:2) in order to intercept those coming to the king with their case. Justice in the ancient world came from the intervention of powerful individuals. With a friendly greeting and a listening ear, Absalom endears himself to those petitioners as a fellow Israelite who desires to bring justice to the people. He tells them their *claims are valid and proper* (15:3), aligning himself with them. He says he would be their advocate if he were *appointed judge* (15:4), thereby revealing (or creating an appearance of) weakness in the current justice system and indicating his candidacy for higher office. Add a touch of his hand and a kiss (it did not hurt being a man of extreme good looks!), and *Absalom stole the hearts of the men of Israel* (15:6).

After four years, Absalom rallies enough support that he feels ready to move against David. Under the pretense of fulfilling a vow he made while living in exile in Geshur, Absalom travels to Hebron (15:7). David appears to have no problem with this trip, which is somewhat surprising, considering Absalom duped the king earlier when he requested a gathering of his brothers. It is also curious that David appears oblivious to Absalom's scheming at the city gate. He sends Absalom off with a word of *peace* (15:9), his last word to him. All the congenial language is there, but Absalom's intentions are anything but congenial. Absalom has *secret messengers throughout all the tribes of Israel* ready to declare him king at the *sound of the trumpets* (15:10). Hebron was a likely city in which to stage a coup. It was Absalom's hometown, where he could more easily gather support, placing David in a precarious position between Absalom's forces in the south and weak supporters to the north among the Israelites. It was apparently a rallying location for the tribe of Judah, since it was David's first capital.

15:13–37 Word reaches David that Absalom is approaching Jerusalem with an overwhelming army that may have either outnumbered David's force or were arriving too quickly for David to muster his troops, causing him to flee across the Kidron Valley.

Did David lose his edge, or does the fact that the enemy he now faces is his son affect his judgment? With David are the six hundred men who have been with him since he left Saul's court, along with the loyal Kerethites and Pelethites, his special force, suggesting that Absalom's approach was so sudden and unexpected that David and Joab could not strategize in time to safeguard the city. The text notes that he leaves behind ten concubines (15:16). This will be significant later as it fulfills an aspect of Nathan's prophecy.

> **Kerethites & Pelethites**
> *This group, apparently made up of foreigners and probably groups from the Aegean and nearby regions and thus relatives of the Philistines, formed a personal army for David, separate from the Israelite militia, that he could mobilize during wartime.*

The following verses emphasize the despair in this turn of events; *the whole countryside wept aloud* (15:23) as David and his company pass by. *All the people with him covered their heads too and were weeping* (15:30). Even David weeps as he flees with his head covered and his feet bared, signs of deep mourning. The king is not on his royal donkey; there are no horses or chariots to carry this royal entourage away.

As David flees, he encounters several individuals. Some remain with David as military and advisory personnel; some he sends back to Jerusalem to serve his purposes there; others taunt him. These characters include Ittai, a Gittite, a Philistine from Gath, who had just joined with David's company the previous day. David suggests that the new recruit return home. Why become a wanderer with an exiled king? Ittai insists on being faithful to David to the death. Later, he is seen commanding a contingency of troops along with Joab and Abishai (2 Sam 18:2). In addition, he encounters Zadok, chief priest of Yahweh. Zadok and the Levites followed David with the ark of the covenant of God. David gives instructions to Zadok and his son Ahimaaz along with Abiathar and his son Jonathan to return to Jerusalem with the ark as informants to relay information to David about Absalom's intentions. David is not abandoning his kingdom. He is setting strategies into motion that will reinstate him in Jerusalem. Ahithophel has been a counselor to David. David does not encounter Ahithophel as he flees; rather, he hears that Ahithophel has betrayed him and is now serving Absalom. David prays that Yahweh will confound his counsel to Absalom (15:31). In addition, David meets Hushai, a friend, confidant, and counselor to David. Possibly unable to handle the rigors of flight, Hushai is instructed to return to Jerusalem and pretend to transfer his loyalties from David to his son. He is then to misdirect Absalom with his counsel and send intelligence from within the court back to David through Zadok's messengers (15:32–37).

16:1–23 On the road, David also encounters Ziba, steward of the estate of Saul's grandson Mephibosheth (Jonathan's crippled son). Ziba offers food to the king and his company and promises his loyalty. He accuses his master, Mephibosheth, of taking advantage of this coup to reclaim his grandfather's kingdom. To reward Ziba for his loyalty and punish Mephibosheth for his treacherous act, David gives *all that belonged to Mephibosheth* (16:4) to Ziba. Later, David is informed that Ziba's report is inaccurate (19:26). More ominously, David's army meets Shimei, a relative of Saul. He pelts David and his men with stones, dirt, and insults as they pass by (Exod 22:28). Abishai, Joab's brother, enthusiastically offers to behead *this dead dog* (16:9). David stays his hand. If David's own son seeks his life, how much more this Saulide. The story emphasizes David's restraint, in contrast to the portrait of a tyrant in 1 Samuel 8 (compare 1 Sam 11:12–13).

The text depicts David as a humbled man out of harmony with the Lord, yet he still has many supporters and military savvy. Absalom and his followers enter an undefended Jerusalem, but unknown to him, David has strategically placed a few of his own men in Jerusalem, even in the inner circle of Absalom's cabinet.

Absalom consults with Ahithophel, the traitor from David's court, regarding the establishment of his sovereignty in Jerusalem and throughout Israel. Ahithophel's advice *was like that of one who inquires of God* (16:23) – that is, a prophet or diviner. His advice that Absalom make a public display of his virility and his ascendancy over the kingdom, *lie with your father's concubines* (16:21), reflects the fact that "possession of the harem was a title to the throne" (de Vaux 115–16). Absalom pitches a tent on the roof and takes David's concubines inside, where he "humiliates" (that is, rapes) them *in the sight of all Israel* (16:22; 2 Sam 15:16). With this action, Absalom becomes ten times the offender his brother Amnon had been and does in "broad daylight" what David had done "in secret." Ironically, this is the same roof where David desired Uriah's wife. Nathan's prophecy is fulfilled (2 Sam 12:11–12).

17:1–29 Absalom may take David's city, his women, and many of his supporters, but he will never be secure in his position as king as long as David is alive. Ahithophel's next advice is to take advantage of the *weary and weak* (17:2) state of David and his men who have just fled the city. He advises Absalom to take 12,000 men and overwhelm David (17:2). He suggests that Absalom kill only the king and bring the people home unharmed. The Hebrew uses the cohortative verb, suggesting that Ahithophel wants to lead the attack, putting himself in the position of commander-in-chief of Absalom's forces. This sounds like a good plan, but there is another in the court whom Absalom trusts, Hushai, David's friend and informant. Absalom summons Hushai and presents Ahithophel's plan. Hushai diplomatically undermines Ahithophel (17:7). As promised, he is about to *turn Ahithophel's counsel into foolishness* (15:31).

Hushai's strategy is given in detail. He stresses what Absalom already knows and fears: *your father is a fighter and that those with him are brave* (17:10). If Absalom follows Ahithophel's plan, David's superior forces will overwhelm him. Hushai uses his "rhetoric and his charismatic ability to appeal to the war council's emotions rather than to logic" (Cartledge 585). He suggests that Absalom gather as many men as possible from one end of Israel to other (*Dan to Beersheba*, 17:11), overwhelm David with numbers, and kill everyone. Absalom should be in front of his army leading this attack. This would appeal to his egotism and make him personally vulnerable to David's army. In reality, this plan would eliminate the element of surprise that would be catastrophic to David. It would give Hushai time to warn David, and David time to plan his strategy. But the advice appeals to Absalom's vanity and exposes his unfitness for kingship.

This intelligence is sent to David through Zadok and Abiathar with a warning that it be delivered immediately or *the king and all the people with him will be swallowed up* (17:16). The story has some suspense, as the dispatchers are spotted by Absalom's people, pursued, and lost. David receives the word and immediately moves his people across the Jordan and prepares for battle at Mahanaim, Ish-Bosheth's old capital in the Transjordan. He receives provisions from some unlikely sources, Ammonites and relatives of Saul.

Before the battle begins, Ahithophel learns that his advice is not heeded. He may realize that Hushai's plan will fail, making him a traitor when David returns. He goes home while there is still time to do so; *he put his house in order and then hanged himself* (17:23). He is buried in his father's tomb, which is a more honorable burial than the burial he would have received as a traitor.

18:1–18 With the time that Hushai buys for David, the exiled king musters his troops. They are divided into three companies under the commands of Joab, Abishai, and Ittai. As Anderson (224) notes, this way of organizaing the army was common practice in Israel. David's passion is seen as he emphatically states that he himself *will surely march out with you* (18:2). This expresses a different attitude than seen in chapter 11. His men insist that he stay a safe distance from the battle, different advice than given to Absalom by Hushai, but appropriate for a general. David is more valuable than *ten thousand* of his men (18:3). He agrees to stay behind but gives the command to be *gentle* (18:5) with Absalom. This is specifically directed to the three commanders, but it is pronounced in the hearing of all the people. Despite the son's transgression, the father's love is steadfast. Compare this to Saul's response to his son's loyalty to David (1 Sam 20:30–33).

David chooses the battlefield, the forest of Ephraim located just west of Mahanaim, an unusual place for a battle. Scholars surmise that "David had selected this terrain, where the experience and courage of each individual soldier counted more than sheer numbers" (Smith 272). The location is uncertain, since Ephraim is north of Jerusalem and west of the Jordan, but Mahanaim is east of the Jordan. The forest setting makes it difficult for armies to maneuver, diminishing any strength in numbers Absalom may have enjoyed. Absalom's beautiful hair, likely a mark of his vanity, becomes entangled in the branches. He is one that is *claimed* (literally, "consumed or eaten") by the forest (18:8). Unfortunately for him, there is no royal treatment for this royal dissident.

> **The Death of Absalom**
> Absalom leaves no descendants; the three sons born to him must have died at an early age. A pile of stones is all that is left of him. The narrator, writing sometime afterwards, knows the location of the tomb; others must have also known.

18:19–33 The commanders are next faced with the awkward task of telling the king that the son who was to be protected is dead. David is known to kill messengers who carry what they believe is good news to the king (2 Sam 1:14, 15; 4:9–12). Ahimaaz, son of Zadok, volunteers to run the communication to David. He had been key in the transmission of intelligence from Jerusalem to David. Joab recognizes the danger in delivering this message and refuses Ahimaaz's request. He prefers to risk a nameless and expendable Cushite, a foreigner from eastern Africa in David's service. Ahimaaz counts the cost and says, *Come what may, I want to run* (18:23). Both carry the message. Ahimaaz must have run the words through his head a million times before he arrives ahead of the Cushite. He delivers a positive message, *All is well, Praise be to the Lord your God! He has delivered up the men who lifted their hands against my lord the king* (18:28). David has one concern: *Is the young man Absalom safe?* (18:29). Ahimaaz is either too frightened or careful not to answer this question, though he knows quite well the welfare of Absalom. The Cushite can bring the king this element of the report and does so. The messengers are spared, but *the king was shaken* (18:33). The depth of his despair is expressed in the Hebrew with a repetitive, *Absalom, my son* (18:33). David mourns so profoundly that the soldiers' return to the city is not met with a victor's welcome. There is no celebration for their bravery; rather, they *stole* (NASB return *by stealth*) into the city as men *who are ashamed when they flee from battle* (19:3).

19:1–43 Joab, who has been in control of this operation, rebukes David without formal courtesies: *Today you have humiliated all your men* (19:5). David's mourning, so appropriate on another occasion (for example 2 Sam 3:31–39), here shows more regard for the one seeking his life than for those who have protected it. Joab emphatically orders the king to get up from his mourning and *encourage your men* (19:7), or the whole military will defect *by nightfall* (19:7). Cartledge (606) suggests that Joab "would personally lead the troops in a mass desertion" if David did not act immediately. David does as Joab directs, though Joab's act of defiance does not go unnoticed (echoes of 2 Sam 3:39, *these sons of Zeruiah are too strong for me*).

David prepares to return to his capital city. The northern and southern tribes renew their allegiance to David and support his return to Jerusalem. David makes a cabinet change. He replaces Joab, his commander-in-chief, with Amasa, the army leader of Absalom. Joab has been unmanageable since he killed Abner. Amasa seems an unlikely candidate for the office, but he is a skilled and capable commander and a strategic player in David's return to the throne. The text raises, however, the question of loyalty to subordinates.

The list of characters David met as he was fleeing Jerusalem (see chapters 15–16) parallels the individuals he meets on his return. These encounters reflect the mood of David. First he meets Shimei, the one who cursed him and his men as they fled. Realizing his error in supporting Absalom, Shimei begs for mercy. He even fills his gallery with a thousand Benjamites to emphasize his newfound devotion. David rejects the advice of Abishai, his commander who earlier had offered to behead Shimei (19:22), preferring to engage in celebration, not bloodshed. We see here David's political savvy return as he proves himself not to be a tyrant. Shimei's fate will be in the hands of David's son Solomon, who will execute judgment for his contempt (1 Kgs 2:8, 9; 36–46).

Next he meets Ziba once again, but no words are exchanged. This meeting leads David quickly to Mephibosheth, grandson of Saul, and son of Jonathan. His haggard appearance is designed to express the sincerity of his devotion to David. David questions his loyalty due to Ziba's earlier report. Mephibosheth explains that his steward, Ziba, had betrayed him as he was preparing to flee with David. Unable or unwilling to decide the merits of the case, David redistributes the estate equally between Mephibosheth and Ziba. Mephibosheth surrenders his share to Ziba in order to live at court.

Similarly, David meets the nobleman Barzillai. He had provided David and his people with supplies as they fled Jerusalem (17:27). There may have been a history between David and this generous elderly gentleman, for David invites him to live in Jerusalem under his care. Barzillai declines the kind proposal but offers, in his place, a man named Kimham, possibly his son (1 Kgs 2:7).

Through these encounters, we see the king of earlier days, a king of compassion, strength, justice and righteousness. The list of personal encounters, mirroring the earlier list, illustrates the restoration of David to his earlier position.

20:1–26 Yet peace is short-lived. Second Samuel presents next an event that may have occurred at any point in David's reign but appears here as an example of the theme of rebellion. An Israelite by the name of Sheba takes advantage of this discord to promote himself and persuades Israel to break their allegiance with David and Judah to follow him. Judah continues to follow David to Jerusalem, where David will gather a force under the command of his new general, Amasa, to pursue Sheba. Before sending out this force, David separates his violated secondary wives (better translation than "concubines") from the other women and provides for them but has no further relations with them. They live the rest of their lives as if they are widows (20:3).

Amasa meets up with the troops at Gibeon, located about six miles north of Jerusalem, likely with the militia of Judah. Surprisingly, Joab approaches Amasa with a friendly greeting, the same deceptive greeting he gave Abner before stabbing him to death (3:27). Joab's dagger drops from its sheath into his left hand where the unsuspecting Amasa would not expect it (since warriors were trained to fight right handed), and as he takes hold of his beard to kiss him, he *plunged it into his belly* (20:10) with a wide enough slit to disembowel

Amasa. This cruel murder (20:12) may be recompense for Amasa's part in Absalom's rebellion as well as retaliation for Joab's loss of position as commander of the army. Joab refuses to relinquish his position to this man, and with flagrant disregard for David's orders, he maintains his hold on the military. The troops have followed Joab for years; they march past the body of Amasa to follow Joab now as they always have.

Sheba seeks protection behind the walls of the fortified city Abel Beth Maacah, a city in Israel noted for its wisdom, peace, and faithfulness. It was said of this *mother* (20:19) city, *Get your answer at Abel and that settled it* (20:18). Joab is in the process of attacking Abel when a *wise woman* (20:16) from the city questions his attack. After hearing Joab's report, the woman takes the army's issue to the people with her wise advice and promptly delivers the head of Sheba to Joab. Joab and his men withdraw from Abel and return to Jerusalem, thus ending the short-lived Sheba revolt. Joab's murder of Amasa receives no reprisal from David at this time; Joab maintains his position. David rules in Jerusalem over Judah and Israel, though conflict batters his government.

This section is summed up with a list of David's royal cabinet. Interestingly, Joab is listed first as being *over Israel's entire army* (20:23). This list of officers forms a neat conclusion to 2 Samuel 9–20, as the previous section ended with a list of David's officers (2 Samuel 8). These officials held office in part on a hereditary basis, but always at the sufferance of the king.

Justice for the Gibeonites & Feats of David's Men · 21:1–22

A series of appendices follow that conclude the book of Samuel and do not necessarily proceed in chronological order. They interrupt the flow of the narrative in order to describe certain abiding features of Davd's reign and offer material for later reflection.

21:1–14 The first narrative, the Gibeonite resolution, probably occurs closer to the beginning of David's reign. Famine ravages the land for three years, signaling the Lord's displeasure. David inquires of the Lord about this affliction, only to find that it is the result of a sin incurred by Saul when he shed the blood of the Gibeonites (in a case of ethnic cleansing) who were under his protection by treaty (Josh 9:3, 15–27). The Bible does not record this event, but David's resolution of the problem is given. After consultation with the Gibeonites, David hands over seven descendants of Saul (sparing Mephibosheth, son of Jonathan) for execution *during the first days of the harvest* (21:9). This is a case of blood for blood. Conceivably, the descendants of Saul were involved in Saul's treachery and deserving of death, since at least one Israelite tradition forbade children being *put to death for their fathers* (Deut 24:16). But the text does not say this, nor does the character Rizpah find it to be the case. God ends the famine. This restitution may have fallen under David's rule due to the sudden death of Saul before justice could be served. This incident shows the importance given to protecting a people under one's guardianship, whether it is a nation or an individual, such as a widow. God is a God of justice, and protection of the indigent is not to be neglected.

21:15–22 The next appendix recounts four Philistine encounters. Each one involves a descendant (or perhaps follower) of a man named Rapha of Gath (one of the five major Philistine cities) and one of David's warriors. These may be the Rephaim depicted as exceptionally large and daunting men who

Wise Women

There are two references to "wise women" in the books of Samuel. The first reference is the wise woman Joab brings from Tekoa, home of the prophet Amos, to speak with David concerning Absalom's exile (2 Sam 14:2). The second reference is the wise woman of Abel who calls to Joab, questioning his attack on her city (2 Sam 20:16). Prophetesses may also be considered along with the wise women as those who were sought after for advice and for the word of the Lord. Deborah, who judged Israel, was referred to as a prophetess (Judg 4:4) to whom many came for guidance. Huldah the prophetess was approached by King Josiah seeking advice after finding the book of the law (2 Kgs 22:14). Anna the prophetess was one of the first to see Jesus as an infant (Luke 2:36).

These wise women, similar to "wise men," were renowned for their mastery of speech and rhetoric and for their skill of persuasion. In Hebrew, "wisdom" carries the idea of one who is "clever, cunning, or wise." These two wise women in Samuel were able to use their artful speech to resolve conflict and avert disaster. They serve as "bookends" on either end of the Absalom crisis. Scholars note that the source of her power comes from her ability to sway an audience (Arnold 607).

lived among the Canaanites. The chronology is vague, but it is likely that these battles took place earlier in David's reign. Abishai, one of David's chief commanders, saves David's life when Ishbi-Benob, a powerfully outfitted Philistine, seeks to kill David; Sibbecai the Hushathite, one of David's mighty men, kills a descendant of Rapha named Saph (compare 1 Chron 11:29); Elhanan, according to this passage, kills Goliath. The parallel passage in 1 Chronicles 20:5 states that it is the *brother of Goliath* that Elhanan kills. "Bethlehemite" in the Samuel passage may have been miscopied by the scribe and instead should read "brother of" (Driver 354–55). Or, Chronicles may have sought to reconcile an inconsistency in the Samuel text (see Anderson 255); David's nephew, Jonathan son of Shimeah, kills yet another descendant of Rapha who has six fingers on each hand and six toes on each foot.

These four episodes emphasize the valor and capability of David's men against the formidable forces of the Philistines. These hero stories also emphasize the basic splendor of David's reign and God's favor toward him.

PSALMS OF DAVID · 22:1–23:7

Two psalms appear near the end of 1 and 2 Samuel. The first and longer of the two is dated to the height of David's reign. It is a psalm of praise to the Lord for his deliverance from David's enemies and can also be found in Psalm 18 with slight variations. The second psalm is the *last words of David* (23:1). It acknowledges that the Lord has established his house and *made with me [David] an everlasting covenant* (23:5). Chapter 22 combines elements of the thanksgiving song with those of the hymn of praise (Campbell, *2 Samuel*, 97).

Though the superscription of the first psalm assigns the poem to early in David's reign, it is placed at the end of the story of David's life because it makes a theological statement about the dynasty of David. David's house is established and sustained by the power of Yahweh. Smith writes, "the compilers intended for the history of David to be read theologically, i.e., in the light of this psalm. It is not David, the great and powerful king, upon whom readers should focus, but David's great and powerful God" (509).

22:1–7 The opening lines exalt Yahweh as David's deliverer. The Lord is everything a soldier needs: a rock (a protective shield), fortress, deliverer, shield, horn (calls one to battle or to retreat), stronghold, refuge, and savior. Being all these things, God is worthy of praise.

22:8–16 The psalm moves to a fierce description of the Lord as a warrior fighting against David's enemies from the heavens, causing the earth and the heavens to tremble, as illustrated by a mighty dark storm. As Cartledge (654) puts it:

> The plethora of images used to describe God's heavenly arrival demonstrates the poet's inability to capture Yahweh's awesome appearance in human words. He stretches the imagination to the breaking point yet fails to arrive at a single image that does justice to the thought of Yahweh's personal and perceivable descent through the sky. Multiple metaphors will have to do.

22:17–25 The psalm notes that Yahweh *rescued me because he delighted in me* (22:20). David "delighted" the Lord by: righteousness, cleanness of hands, keeping the ways of the Lord, refraining from doing evil, keeping his laws before him, being blameless, and abstaining from sin. The psalmist is not boasting of a sinless life but recognizes the fulfillment of the Lord's promises to bless those who love the Lord and keep God's demands before them. Blessings come through righteousness and obedience to the Lord.

22:26–30 The Lord's response to the faithful and the wicked are compared. If one is *blameless* and *pure*, the Lord will respond appropriately. If one is *crooked* (literally, "tortuous" or "twisted"), again an appropriate response is given. This reflects God's words to Moses, *I will have mercy on whom I will have mercy and I will have compassion on whom I will have compassion* (Exod 33:19, compare Rom 9:15). The *humbled* (God's people) are delivered, but the *haughty* (those who oppose God and God's people) are humbled (22:28).

22:31–46 Praise the Lord for *his way is perfect* (22:31). David's strength and success come directly from the Lord – not by any feat or ability of his own (22:31–46).

22:47–51 The psalm ends with praises to the Lord. *He gives his king great victories; he shows unfailing kindness to his anointed, to David and his descendants forever* (22:51). This reflects back to Nathan's oracle in 2 Samuel 7 where David's house is established as everlasting. The reference to David in the third person shows that David did not actually author the psalm; it is traditional material used by the composer of 2 Samuel.

23:1–7 The second psalm was written toward the end of David's reign (23:1). It sings of the blessings

2 SAMUEL

that come as one rules in righteousness and fear of God, while justice prevails over the wicked. It furthermore reiterates that God has made an *everlasting covenant* with the house of David (23:5). The text of the psalm has not been preserved in the manuscripts, but its essential meaning is clear enough.

These two psalms at the end of 2 Samuel create a poetic bookend with Hannah's psalm at the beginning of 1 Samuel. The poems frame the books theologically, focusing the reader's attention on the sovereignty of the Lord and the salvation he provides for those who look to him.

DAVID'S MEN & THEIR NUMBERING · 23:8–24:25

David had a personal bodyguard and an inner circle of warriors who were known for their heroic deeds (2 Sam 21:15–22). These fell into distinct groups: the three and the thirty. These groups seem to overlap, and other heroes were in neither group. Presumably, the author knew more stories about them because verse 19 appeals to the audience's knowledge of them.

The story of 23:13–17 illustrates both the valor and loyalty of David's men and his own skill at leading them. Their heroic story tells how David longs for water located at the gate of Bethlehem, David's hometown, where, surprisingly, the Philistine garrison was camped. (This event must date to very early in David's reign.) These three men risk their lives to acquire the water and bring it to David. David responds, *Far be it from me, O Lord, to do this! Is it not the blood of men who went at the risk of their lives?* (23:17). The language used is that of a pledge and sacrificial offering. David does not feel worthy of such a sacrifice; only the Lord deserves this magnitude of a gift, so David pours it on the ground to God. This act would bring honor to the three warriors for their loyalty and bravery as well as recognize the value of his men's lives.

The references to Abishai indicate some confusion as to his exact status (was he part of the three or not?). The description of Beraiah, commander of the Kerethites and Pelethites, the royal bodyguard, is clearer. His exploits include striking down *two of Moab's best men*, killing a lion in a pit on a snowy day, and slaughtering a *huge Egyptian* armed with a spear while he carried a mere club (23:20, 21). Following David's death, Solomon commissions him to execute Joab (whom he will succeed, 1 Kgs 2:34, 35) and eliminate Adonijah (another rebellious son of David, 1 Kgs 2:25) and Shimei (the one who cursed David as he fled Jerusalem, 1 Kgs 2:46).

The second, slightly less illustrious group of warriors was "the thirty." The list concludes with a total count of thirty-seven in all, perhaps indicating that the group's membership changed over time. There is some variation to this list in 1 Chronicles 11. The numbers do not add up, but this discrepancy may be explained by the adding of new men through loss of life and retirement. Joab is listed among the court officials in 2 Samuel 20:23. In any case, the list functions in 2 Samuel to enumerate David's accomplishments in defending the nation and welding together its leaders under a central monarchy.

24:1–25 The final appendix to the book of Samuel recounts an episode in which David takes a census of the nation. This appears innocent, but Joab and the other commanders are concerned: *Why does my lord the king want to do such a thing?* (24:3). David *overruled Joab and the army commanders* (24:4) and sends the men throughout the land, from its northern to southern borders. This action brings the wrath of God and the prophet Gad to David with three options for punishment for his actions: three years of famine, three months of fleeing from his enemies, or three days of plague in the land. David chooses the three days of plague, preferring to be at the mercy of the Lord rather than at the the mercy of men. Several thousand Israelites die.

The story opens with Yahweh's anger burning against Israel. It does not state the cause for this anger. Throughout Samuel, the Lord is provoked by injustice and a lack of faith and obedience revealing a dependency on oneself rather than on God (2 Sam 21; 1 Sam 13, 15). David may have conducted a census of his fighting men, an evaluation of the physical strength of his nation, possibly to mount an attack not sanctioned by God. The warnings against royal abuse of power in

> **The Census**
> *Censuses were taken in Israel periodically to number* those twenty years old or more who are able to serve in the army of Israel (*Exod* 30:14; *Num* 1:3; 26:2). *It registered the people for service, whether in the army or in service to the temple. A tax or "ransom" was collected from the people at this time for an atonement for life (Exod 30:12) and given to the temple. Such a practice was used* for the service of the Tent of Meeting *and to do repairs on the temple (Exod 30:16; 2 Kgs 12:4, 5).*

> **Royal Inscriptions**
>
> Many ancient royal inscriptions have been discovered throughout the Near East. They typically contain inflated rhetoric as rulers record their successes, particularly in battle. It is common for them to begin with the favor they received from the gods and move to their magnificent accomplishments. They end with curses on their enemies and praises to the gods for destroying their foes.
>
> The purpose for such propaganda can be understood in many ways. A king hopes for immortality and a better afterlife through the favor of the gods. The preservation of his name and accomplishments through these records, even if they are not recorded exactly as they occurred, will accomplish this. To quote one scholar, "they were written for self-justification, or to obtain or increase sociopolitical control, or to mobilize, or to impress, or even to frighten" (Liverani 2354). The documents are likely read before the people to justify the cost and casualties of war and render better conditions for the people. The gods have sanctioned the war and therefore support it. The spoils of war have covered the costs incurred and the human casualties have brought peace.
>
> David's psalms contain much of this same outline and purpose. The Lord is with David as he rules in righteousness and fear of the Lord, and God has secured (23:5) the land while the evil men are all to be cast aside like thorns (23:6). Such a text serves to inspire the confidence of Israel and instill fear in the enemy. Immortality comes for David in the establishment of his house and an everlasting covenant with the Lord (23:5; see Liverani 2353–366).

1 Samuel 8 may also offer a possible explanation of David's action.

According to 2 Samuel 24:1, the *Lord incited* David against Israel, encouraging him to *take a census*. According to 1 Chronicles 21:1, *Satan ... incited* David to *take a census*. Which is correct? Evidently, Chronicles seeks to distance God from this event. Actually, David acts on his own initiative and free will. He becomes *conscience-stricken* and confesses that *I have sinned greatly in what I have done ... I have done a very foolish thing* (24:10). A closer look reveals that both the divine and demonic are served by this incident. Evil is accomplished prior to the census in an undefined sin and then an unsanctioned census resulting in the deaths of seventy thousand people. The divine is accomplished through the purging of sin, repentance, and restoration to a faith in the Lord. Israel, being a monotheistic culture, may have understood all supernatural activity as coming from one source, God.

David sees the angel *who was striking down the people* (24:17) at the threshing floor of Araunah the Jebusite, in Jerusalem, the site of the future temple of Solomon. Gad instructs David to build an altar to the Lord at this site to stop the plague. Araunah, out of his generosity and respect for the king, offers to donate the sacrifices and wood needed for the offerings to the Lord. David's response exemplifies the proper attitude toward one's offerings to the Lord: *No, I insist on paying you for it. I will not sacrifice to the Lord my God burnt offerings that cost me nothing* (24:24). The story, then, explains why the temple was built where it was.

What makes David stand above Saul and future rulers is that he repents and brings his kingdom back in accord with the Lord, which is exactly what the punishment is designed to do. We should not focus on the plague and punishment in this passage; rather, we should emphasize God's merciful response to David's wholehearted repentance and return to the Lord, which solidified his house for eternity. This is what makes David such a remarkable character and superior to all of his successors. Everyone stumbles, but only the extraordinary get up and humble themselves to a restored relationship with their creator.

THEOLOGICAL REFLECTIONS

The books of Samuel are alive with stories of men and women entangled in the web of life's experiences and the God who is *sovereign* over all. These stories reflect human triumphs and failings in life and a God who is merciful yet just and immovable in his holiness. He forgives David as he repents of his sin against Bathsheba, yet the unrepentant priesthood under the Elide dynasty and the defiling of the holy ark of God do not go unanswered. A holy and righteous God seeks obedience and righteousness from Israel. *To obey is better than sacrifice* (1 Sam 15:22). God raises those of humble means and humble hearts to immeasurable heights.

These books are part of a greater work, the Hebrew canon, which reflects the nature of God and God's relationship with Israel. First and Second

Samuel fit securely into the larger theological picture of the Old Testament. The anticipation of kingship in Deuteronomy 17:14–20 is realized in the establishment of David's dynasty. This theological picture continues in the books of Kings, where David's reign of justice and righteousness sets the standard for future rulers who either *did what was right in the eyes of the Lord, as [their] father David* (1 Kgs 15:11) or *did evil in the eyes of the Lord [by not following] the Lord completely as [their] father David had done* (1 Kgs 11:6). God's promise to bless and bring security to those who walk in obedience but ruin to those who fail to obey divine commands appears in Deuteronomy and comes to fruition in Samuel and Kings as well as in the prophetic writings. First and Second Samuel look to the New Testament as it establishes the house through which salvation will ultimately come, not only to the remnant of Israel returned to the promised land, but to all nations through this covenantal house and heir, Jesus Christ.

FOR FURTHER STUDY

Walter Brueggemann, *David's Truth in Israel's Imagination and Memory* (Minneapolis, Minn.: Fortress, 2002).

William Schniedewind, *Society and the Promise to David* (New York: Oxford University Press, 1999).

WORKS CITED

A. A. Anderson, *2 Samuel* (Dallas: Word, 1989).

Bill Arnold, *1 & 2 Samuel: The NIV Application Commentary* (Grand Rapids: Zondervan, 2003).

John Bright, *A History of Israel* (Philadelphia: Westminster, 2000).

Walter Brueggemann, *First and Second Samuel* (Louisville: John Knox, 1990).

Anthony F. Campbell, *The Ark Narrative* (Chico, Calif.: Society of Biblical Literature, 1975).

———, *2 Samuel* (Grand Rapids: Eerdmans, 2005).

Tony Cartledge, *Smyth & Helwys Bible Commentary: 1 & 2 Samuel* (Macon, Ga.: Smyth & Helwys Publishing Co., 2001).

Rupert Chapman, "Weapons and Warfare," *The Oxford Encyclopedia of Archaeology in the Near East* 5 (1997): 334–39.

Raymond B. Dillard and Tremper Longman III, *An Introduction to the Old Testament* (Grand Rapids: Zondervan, 1994).

Trude Dothan, "Philistines," *Anchor Bible Dictionary* 5 (1992): 328–33.

J. D. Douglas, "Nazirite," *New Bible Dictionary* (1999): 808–9.

S. R. Driver, *Notes on the Hebrew Text of the Books of Samuel* (Oxford: Clarendon, 1913).

Jenni Ernst and Claus Westermann, *Theological Lexicon of the Old Testament* (Peabody, Mass: Hendrickson, 1997).

Baruch Halpern, *The Constitution of the Monarchy in Israel* (Chico, Calif.: Scholars Press, 1981).

———, *David's Secret Demons: Messiah, Murderer, Traitor, King* (Grand Rapids: Eerdmans, 2001).

Mark Hamilton, *The Body Royal: The Social Poetics of Kingship in Ancient Israel* (Leiden: Brill, 2005).

Alfred J. Hoerth, Gerald L. Mattingly, Edwin M. Yamauchi, *Peoples of the Old Testament World* (Grand Rapids: Baker, 1998).

Michael Jordan, *Encyclopedia of Gods* (New York: Facts on File Inc., 1993).

Philip J. King and Lawrence E. Stager, *Life in Biblical Israel* (Louisville: Westminster John Knox, 2001).

Theodore J. Lewis, "Dead, Abode of the," *Anchor Bible Dictionary* 2 (1992): 102–3.

Mario Liverani, "The Deeds of Ancient Mesopotamian Kings," in *Civilizations of the Ancient Near East* (ed. Jack M. Sasson; New York: Hendrickson, 2000), 2353–66.

Kyle P. McCarter, *I Samuel* (New York: Doubleday, 1980).

———, *II Samuel* (New York: Doubleday, 1980).

Steven L. McKenzie, "Deuteronomistic History," *Anchor Bible Dictionary* 2 (1992): 160–68.

Martin Noth, *The Deuteronomistic History* (Sheffield: JSOT, 1981).

Robert Polzin, *Samuel and the Deuteronomist* (San Francisco: Harper & Row, 1989).

Ronny Reich and Eli Shukron, "Light at the End of the Tunnel," *Biblical Archaeology Review* 25 (January-February 1999): 22–33, 72.

Allen Ross, *Holiness to the Lord: A Guide to the Exposition of the Book of Leviticus* (Grand Rapids: Baker, 2002).

James E. Smith, *The College Press NIV Commentary 1 & 2 Samuel* (Joplin, Mo.: College Press, 2000).

Thomas Thompson, *The Historicity of the Patriarchal Narratives* (1974; repr. Harrisburg, Pa.: Trinity Press International, 2002).

Roland de Vaux, *Ancient Israel* (Grand Rapids: Eerdmans, 1997).

Leon J. Wood, *The Prophets of Israel* (Grand Rapids: Baker, 2001).

1 Kings

Christopher A. Rollston & Heather Dana Davis Parker

CHAPTER CONTENTS

Contexts 309

Commentary 310
- David's Death & the Reign of Solomon · 1 Kgs 1:1–11:43 310
- Division of the Monarchy & Narratives about Israel & Judah to 722 BCE · 1 Kgs 12:1–2 Kgs 17:41 319

Theological Reflections 327

For Further Study 327

Works Cited 327

MAPS, TABLES, & FEATURES

Gezer 312
Shalmaneser & Ahab 326

First and Second Kings, originally one continuous work, were derived from numerous sources, including the "Chronicles of Solomon" (1 Kgs 11:41), "the Chronicles of the Kings of Judah" (1 Kgs 14:9; 15:7), and the "Chronicles of the Kings of Israel" (1 Kgs 14:19; 15:31). These "chronicles," or "annals," were apparently the royal records commissioned by the king and his administration (compare Esth 6:1 for a reference to Persian royal records). Various additional sources may have been used as well, including the narratives of the "Elijah-Cycle," the "Elisha-Cycle," and "Temple Records." None of these sources survives outside of 1 and 2 Kings, however. In any case, the important point is that the books of Kings draw on various sources, and some of these are actually named within the books of Kings (Cogan 89–95).

CONTEXTS

Through the centuries, traditions within Judaism (for example, the Talmud) and Christianity have often affirmed that Jeremiah authored the books of Kings. However, the books of Kings are anonymous, and their author (or perhaps authors) is referred to by scholars as the "Deuteronomist," with this term being chosen because the books of Kings and Deuteronomy use similar language and reflect similar theological perspectives. The "Deuteronomist" is often credited with authoring Joshua, Judges, and the books of Samuel as well. For this reason, Joshua, Judges, Samuel, and Kings are traditionally referred to as the "Deuteronomistic History."

There has been much debate regarding the dating of the final version of the books of Kings. Currently, most scholars believe that the next-to-last version of the "Deuteronomistic History" was produced during the reign of King Josiah (640–609 BCE) and the final version during the Babylonian Exile, that is, during the sixth century BCE. Phrases such as "unto this day," "then," and "at that time" (2 Kgs 8:22; 14:7; 16:5–6; 17:41; 18:16; 20:12; 24:10) actually suggest a time of composition long after the occurrence of the actual events.

Although the final composition may date to the sixth century, the history detailed within the books of Kings spans the tenth century to the sixth century BCE. The text provides precise information about the various Israelite and Judean kings, and the duration of their reigns. Moreover "synchronisms," the coordination of events in the two kingdoms, also run through the book. Here we use conventional dates for the reigns of the kings of Israel and Judah, even though some dates are debatable because some rulers shared the throne with their eventual successors (Thiele; Bright).

Though Kings contains a substantial amount of historical information, it was not intended to be solely a recitation of data. That is, the author(s) did not merely record a string of events, but commented on them, in light of a particular theology. For example, although Omri was a powerful king of the northern kingdom of Israel, he receives little attention in the books of Kings. Moreover, although Jehu of Israel became a vassal of the great Assyrian king Shalmaneser III (something described in detail in an Assyrian text), 2 Kings does not refer to this event. Josiah's reign is discussed in detail, but his religious reforms are the focus, not his international political activities (though it was the latter that brought about

1 KINGS

his death). The point is that Kings is not "history"; it is "religious history," or "historical theology."

Significantly, the "theology" most clearly reflected in the books of Kings is that found within the book of Deuteronomy. The "Deuteronomistic theology" is complex, and we will discus it in detail at the end of our commentary. The major components of the theology of the Deuteronomist include: righteous people (and good kings) could anticipate the blessings of God, and wicked people (and kings) could anticipate the curses of the covenant; good Yahwists (worshipers of Yahweh) sacrificed solely in Jerusalem, not on the "high places"; and any king that worshiped a deity other than (or in addition to) Yahweh was condemned.

> **High Places**
> *Outdoor holy sites, often located on hilltops and always condemned in the Old Testament.*

One of the most striking features of the books of Kings is that these books demonstrate that ancient Israel and Judah did not exist in a cultural vacuum. References to Assyria, Babylon, and Egypt suggest that intercultural contact was common. Moreover, Syria and Lebanon also frequently appear within the narratives. Finally, there are also references to the Moabites, Ammonites, Edomites, and Philistines within the Deuteronomistic History, as well.

Within the books of Kings, there are often also stock numerals. For example, the number three often occurs within the narratives of Kings (1 Kgs 12:5; 17:1; 17:21; 18:34; 2 Kgs 13:18). The number seven is often employed, as well (for example, 1 Kgs 8:65; 2 Kgs 4:35; 5:10; 8:1). Of course, the number forty also occurs numerous times in Kings (for example, 1 Kgs 2:11; 11:42; 19:8; 2 Kgs 12:1), and fifty-two occurs several times (2 Kgs 2:24; 10:14), as does 70, as well (2 Kgs 10:1). Because these numbers often occur as stock numerals in much of ancient Near Eastern literature, readers of the Bible should not press these biblical numbers very hard, for they are often not to be understood in a strictly literal sense.

COMMENTARY

DAVID'S DEATH & THE REIGN OF SOLOMON · 1:1–11:43

1:1–4 This chapter concludes the Deuteronomist's narrative of David's life and a description of the ensuing rivalry regarding succession. Initially, however, there is a reference to the need for finding a beautiful virgin woman that might assist in maintaining David's body temperature. The Hebrew *sokeneth* (used of Abishag, the virgin woman selected) implies that she not only functioned as a "nurse" but also served some sort of administrative function as well.

1:5–10 Adonijah (meaning "Yahweh is Lord") was born to David and Haggith (2 Sam 3:3) during David's royal residency in Hebron, before Jerusalem became the capital. Adonijah's older full-siblings were the now-deceased Absalom (2 Sam 18:14–15) and Chileab (2 Sam 3:3; compare 1 Chron 3:1), arguably also now dead. Therefore, as the heir apparent (based on the principle of primogeniture), the handsome Adonijah begins preparations for the assumption of the Israelite monarchy, including the creation of an entourage of chariots, horsemen, and runners. Significantly, David never rebukes Adonijah for these actions, although the text affirms that David had actually promised that Solomon, his son with Bathsheba (2 Sam 12:24–25), would succeed David as king.

> **Primogeniture**
> *The practice by which the oldest son inherits the bulk of the estate and related social responsibilities.*

Within the court, there is division regarding the succession. Adonijah is supported by David's military commander, Joab (2 Sam 8:16), as well as by the priest Abiathar, whose father Ahimelech had harbored David at Nob (1 Sam 22:20). However, Nathan the prophet, Zadok the priest, as well as Benaiah (2 Sam 8:18), Shimei son of Ela (compare 1 Kgs 4:18), Rei, and David's warriors do not support Adonijah. As part of the coronation preparations, Adonijah sacrifices at En-Rogel (see also 2 Sam 17:17), inviting all of his brothers, the king's sons, and all the royal officials, except for Nathan, Benaiah, David's warriors, and Solomon. Although Adonijah's actions are calculated to preempt Solomon's forthcoming coronation, they are also nevertheless public, in contrast to Absalom's earlier conspiracy to usurp the throne (2 Sam 15:1–12).

1:11–31 Because of Bathsheba's status as the primary wife of David, she has the privilege of immediate access to the king. Nathan prompts her to visit the king and remind him of his oath (in the name of Yahweh) to orchestrate Solomon's coronation and also to report that Adonijah is in the process of executing his own coronation. Nathan promises to enter the king's presence and affirm the accuracy of Bathsheba's synopsis of Adonijah's activities. Bathsheba does as

Nathan has instructed, enters the king's room (with Abishag also present), and petitions David to remember his oath regarding Solomon's kingship. She also alludes to the fact that if Adonijah does become king, she herself and Solomon will become outcasts. At this juncture, Nathan enters the king's room and confirms Bathsheba's account. Nathan specifically states that he himself was not invited to Adonijah's coronation festivities. After listening to Nathan, David summons Bathsheba and reiterates his vow that Solomon will be his successor. Bathsheba responds with the standard court greeting, "May my lord King David live forever" (verses 34, 39; 2 Sam 15:10; 2 Kgs 11:12). There may have been a strong relationship between Solomon and Nathan for some time (2 Sam 12:25); hence, one of Nathan's motivations in coaching Bathsheba was probably fidelity to Solomon; however, Nathan's desire to retain his status within the kingdom was doubtless another motivation.

1:32–37 After his meeting with Bathsheba and Nathan, David commands the coronation of Solomon, with the priest Zadok and the prophet Nathan anointing him with olive oil, as was the custom (compare 1 Sam 10:1; 15:1, 17; 16:13; 2 Sam 2:4, 7; 5:3; 1 Kgs 19:15–21; 2 Kgs 8:7–15; 9:1–13; 11:12; 23:30). It is significant that the coronation was to occur at the Gihon spring, within the hearing of those in the process of crowning Adonijah at En-Rogel. Those present were to blow the ram's horn (*shofar*) and shout: "May King Solomon live!"– a customary affirmation (see verse 31). Then all were to proceed to the palace, where Solomon would sit upon David's throne. Benaiah confirms his support of the wisdom of this course of action with an oath. This process of coronation seems to be reflected in Psalms 2, 45, and 110.

1:38–53 This narrative details the enactment of David's instructions, under the direction of the priest Zadok and the prophet Nathan, with the full support of Benaiah and David's foreign mercenaries. The ceremony included Solomon's riding upon David's mule, an act often associated with kingship (see Zech 9:9; Matt 21:1–11). Adonijah's supportive attendees (including Joab and Abiathar) hear the celebrative din from the Gihon spring and become alarmed, because they learn that David has endorsed the inauguration of Solomon and that Solomon is already seated on the throne. With this sudden demise of his claim to the throne, Adonijah seeks "sanctuary" (see Exod 21:14), grasping the horns of the altar (Ps 18:2; Amos 3:14; see Keel 146). Solomon honored his brother's act of subjection by letting him live, but with the caveat that any disloyalty would be met with revenge (see 1 Kgs 2:13–25).

2:1–12 Within this section, the Deuteronomist affirms that David encourages Solomon to be faithful to Yahweh (see Deut 17:14–20), keeping his commandments as written in the "law of Moses" (see Deut 4:40; Ezra 3:2; 7:6; Neh 10:29; 2 Chron 23:18). He also reiterates the fact that Yahweh has indeed promised loyalty to the Davidic dynasty, with the caveat that the Davidic king must be faithful to Yahweh (2 Sam 7; Ps 89; 1 Kgs 9:4–9). In addition, David here instructs Solomon to kill Joab and Shimei. Joab, a kinsman of David, had earlier killed Abner (Saul and Ishbaal's commander) because of a blood feud (1 Sam 17:55; 2 Sam 2:8–10; 3:22–30; compare 2 Sam 2:17–28), even though David had made peace with Abner (2 Sam 3:6–21). Joab (1 Chron 2:16) had also killed Absalom's commander Amasa (2 Sam 17:25; 20:4–10), a military figure who had displaced him as David's commander during the period after Absalom's rebellion (2 Sam 19:11–15). Joab killed professional rivals. In any case, David also instructed Solomon to kill Shimei son of Gera, a decendant of Saul, who had cursed David during his flight from Absalom (2 Sam 16:5–13), even though Shimei had subsequently "repented" (2 Sam 19:16–23). Finally, David also requests that Solomon show kindness to the sons of Barzillai (2 Sam 17:27–29; 19:31–40). Note that "instructions" to successors and heirs are often attested in biblical (Gen 47:29–50:14; Deut 33–34; Josh 23–24; *1 Maccabees* 2:49–70) and ancient Near Eastern (Lichtheim 1:135–139) literature. This narrative concludes with references to David's death (about 961 BCE), to the durations of his reigns in Hebron (2 Sam 5:4–5) and Jerusalem (a total of forty years;

> **Cherethites & Pelethites**
> *Probably Cretan and Philistine soldiers in David's service.*

> **The Royal Purge**
> *Solomon's elimination of all potential rivals ties up many literary loose ends from 2 Samuel, and thus the narrator reports his acts of "justice." On the other hand, most readers have difficulty avoiding the comparison to twentieth-century coups d'etat and their purges. Solomon's first act does not bode well for him to live up to his name, a pun on the word for "peace" (shalom).*

1 KINGS

for the implications of this number, see our introduction above), and to the establishment of Solomon's kingdom. The text also notes that David was buried in the city of Jerusalem, presumably in a chamber-tomb (Borowski 83–85).

> **Cave Burials**
> *During the period of the monarchy, prosperous Israelites often buried their dead in hollowed-out caves of one or more rooms. Each chamber might contain several benches carved into the wall, and each bench could receive one or more bodies.*

2:13–46 According to the Deuteronomist, Adonijah asked Bathsheba to facilitate his marriage to Abishag the Shunamite. Bathsheba goes to Solomon, transmitting the request of Adonijah. However, Solomon is enraged, as he considers this to be indicative of Adonijah's continued desire to become king. Solomon's conclusions are based on the fact that within the ancient Near East, "concubines" (better, secondary wives) of the previous monarch (or patriarch) often became the property of the new monarch (Gen 35:22; 49:4; 2 Sam 16:20–23; 1 Chron 5:1–2; but see Deut 22:30; Lev 18:8). Solomon takes an oath affirming that Adonijah must die, and Benaiah carries out this instruction (1 Kgs 1:50–53).

Because Abiathar and Joab had supported Adonijah's earlier attempt to succeed David as king (1 Kgs 1:7), Solomon assumes that they might be in collusion with Adonijah in this second "attempt." For this reason, he orders that Abiathar return to Anathoth, thus concluding his tenure as priest, and fulfilling the prophetic utterance from the time of Eli (1 Sam 2:27–36; see 1 Kgs 4:4). Subsequently, although Joab enters the tent of Yahweh for sanctuary (fearing retaliation), Solomon orders that Benaiah kill him there. Benaiah carries out this order, as well; Joab is subsequently buried in the family tomb in Bethlehem (2 Sam 2:32). At this juncture, Solomon makes Benaiah the commander of the army and replaces Abiathar (as the senior priest) with the priest Zadok (2 Sam 8:17; 15:24). Significantly, from this point on, the priesthood will often trace its lineage back to Zadok (Ezek 40:46), a descendant of Aaron (Ezra 7:2). To ensure the security of his kingship, Solomon also requires Shimei to remain always in Jerusalem. However, Shimei subsequently goes to the Philistine city of Gath (and its King Achish), seemingly in pursuit of some fugitive slaves, and for this, Solomon orders him killed. Again, Benaiah fulfills the request. Since David and Achish of Gath had enjoyed a congenial relationship (1 Sam 21:10–11), Shimei's journey seems imprudent. The text concludes with the following words: "And the kingdom was established by the hand of Solomon," a summary statement concluding chapters 1–2 and affirming that many potential rivals were eliminated so as to ensure the security of the fledging monarchy.

3:1–15 Earlier Egyptian kings were often reluctant to give their daughters in marriage to foreign monarchs (see El Amarna Letter 4, in Moran 8–10); however, this text affirms that Solomon married a daughter of the Pharaoh, and the Deuteronomist later states that this Pharaoh gave Gezer, a city near the Philistine-Israelite border, to his daughter as a dowry (1 Kgs 7:8; 9:15–16; 11:1). This marital alliance may have been possible because of Egypt's relative weakness during the Twenty-First Dynasty.

Solomon chooses to inaugurate his reign with sacrifices at the "great high place" in Gibeon (1 Chron 16:39; 21:29; 2 Chron 1:3–6), a site near Jerusalem, rather than at Jerusalem itself. Levitical priests may have been responsible for the actual sacrifices, but royal figures often functioned as priests (2 Sam 6:17–18; 1 Kgs 8:63), including some of David's sons (2 Sam 8:18), something that the Chronicler later found difficult to explain and so modified (1 Chron 18:17). (For a negative view of kings administering sacrifices, see also 1 Kgs 12:32; 13:1–2; 2 Kgs 15:5; 16:12–13.)

Dreams were often believed to reveal the future (Gen 20:3–7; 26:24; 28:12–16; 1 Sam 3:1–15; 28:6). Thus the Deuteronomist affirms that Yahweh appeared to Solomon at Gibeon in a dream in order to endorse his

Gezer

legitimacy, affirm his status as the heir to the Davidic covenant (see 2 Sam 7), and offer the new king whatever he wants. Solomon admits his youthfulness and then petitions Yahweh for a "listening heart" (understanding and humility), so as to judge the numerous people well and to have moral direction. In the ancient Near East, a primary responsibility of a monarch was to promote and to ensure justice within his realm, often acting as the final arbiter (2 Kgs 6:26–31; 8:1–6; Preamble to the Code of Hammurabi in Roth 71–142; Weinfeld; Gunkel 155–56; for an example of abuse of this power, see 1 Kgs 21:1–29).

Yahweh approvingly promises to grant Solomon's request and add riches and honor, and, conditional on loyalty to the covenant, a long life as well. Riches, honor, and wealth were signs of divine favor to ancient people (1 Kgs 10:1–13). At this juncture, the text notes that Solomon awakes from the dream, returns to Jerusalem, and offers sacrifices there before the ark of the covenant (see 1 Kgs 8:62–64; 9:25–28). Throughout this story, Solomon is depicted as the ideal king, a docile servant of God.

> **Kingship & Divinity**
> *Elsewhere in the ancient Near East, kingship was considered to be a divine gift. For example, this motif is present in biblical texts (1 Sam 9:15–17; 16:1–13) and in Israelite inscriptions, as well (for example, The Tel Dan Inscription in Biran and Naveh).*

3:16–28 Two prostitutes seek justice at the feet of the king. Within this narrative, the king determines accurately the true mother of the living child. The narrative concludes by noting that the entire country learned of the king's sage judgment and marveled at the wisdom God had given him. Of course, the ultimate purpose of this story is to demonstrate that Solomon possesses the wisdom that he had so astutely requested (verses 9–12). Interestingly, the text makes no moral judgment on the women, highlighting instead the puzzling nature of their problem.

4:1–6 The names of the members of Solomon's chief officials appear here. Among the official titles are priest, scribe, herald, commander of the army, prefect, palace overseer, and head of forced labor (1 Kgs 5:14; 12:18). The precise functions of these officials have been discussed at length (Fox 81–203) and presumably varied as new needs arose. It is significant that among these officials are two sons of Nathan, one of Solomon's strongest supporters during the period of his contention for the throne (1 Kgs 1:11–31). Some of these official titles are also present in the narratives about David's court (2 Sam 8:16–18; 20:23–26; 1 Chron 18:15–17). Abiathar's presence in the list reflects his status as priest before his subsequent banishment (1 Kgs 2:26–27).

4:7–19 Solomon divides the kingdom up into twelve administrative districts, rather than attempting to work through the old tribal boundaries (as in Josh 13–22; Judg 1). Each district is responsible for providing for the king's household for one month each year, a sizeable financial burden, given the quantity of provisions listed as consumed per day by the court (1 Kgs 4:22–23). Also, the Deuteronomist affirms that Solomon had also imposed the corvée (tax) on segments of the northern tribes (1 Kgs 11:28). Also of importance is the fact that at least two of the officials in this list married daughters of Solomon, a prudent mechanism for ensuring the fidelity of his officials. Finally, it should be noted that some of the territory referred to is in Transjordan, thus suggesting the breadth of Solomon's territory (Fritz 48–52).

> **Judah & Taxation**
> *Based on the list in 1 Kings 4:22–23, it is arguable that Judah (with just one official) was not taxed as heavily as was the heartland of Israel. Archaeological excavations indicate a small population for Judah during the tenth century, another possible explanation.*

4:20–28 The Deuteronomist states that Israel and Judah were as "numerous as the sands of the sea," an affirmation suggesting the fulfillment of the promises (Gen 12:1–3; 13:14–17; 15:18–19; 22:17; 32:12; Deut 1:7–8). He also states that Solomon controlled at some level much of the Levant, receiving tribute from numerous vassal states. Further reference is made to the immense food provisions necessary for the throne and those associated with the royal administration and to the horses and horsemen of the Israelite kingdom. Finally, there is reference to the fact that there was peace [Hebrew *shalom*] in Israel and Judah during Solomon's reign (in an idyllic world with vines and fig trees) and a statement affirming that this peace reached from Dan in the north to Beersheba in the

> **The Levant**
> *The region between the eastern Mediterranean and the Arabian Desert, including the modern states of Israel, Jordan, Lebanon, and Syria, is known as the Levant.*

south, traditional phraseology describing Israel's ideal borders. The statement reflects Solomon's fulfillment of a major obligation of ancient Near Eastern kings, maintaining the security of the nation. The assertions in this story may reflect historical reality, but some may be hyperbolical, reflecting grandiose rhetoric lauding a royal figure of a "golden age" in Israelite history.

4:29–34 This chapter also contains grandiose descriptions of Solomon's wealth and wisdom, with his wisdom purported to surpass that of Egyptian and various neighboring sages. Just as the Assyrian emperor, Assurbanipal, was lauded within Mesopotamian literature for learning to write, so also Solomon is lauded for composing proverbs and songs, dwarfing even the famous wisdom of Ethan and Heman (see Pss 88–89). Significantly, Solomon's proverbs and songs focus on flora and fauna, subjects that are not a predominant focus of the book of Proverbs. Nevertheless, these verses are often cited in connection with an endorsement of the Solomonic authorship (or sponsorship of) at least part of Proverbs. Solomon is the sage par excellence, but this tradition may be based on Solomon's patronage of wise traditions, not on actual authorship (Crenshaw 35–54).

5:1–18 A Phoenician king named Hiram from the city of Tyre (Cogan 226) had been instrumental in the building of the Davidic palace in Jerusalem, supplying David his "friend" (better, "ally," a standard treaty term) with materials and artisans (2 Sam 5:11), for which Phoenicia was famous (as in the term "cedars of Lebanon"). Although David had also considered building a temple for Yahweh during his reign (2 Sam 7; 1 Kgs 7:51; 1 Chron 22:2–7; Ps 89), the task of securing his throne and defending his country had made this impractical. Moreover, there is a strong tradition in Chronicles suggesting that David was not considered the best person for this project because of the bloodshed that marked his reign (1 Chron 22:8).

In any case, Hiram now sends a delegation in order to renew diplomatic relations with David's successor. This sort of diplomatic action was common during periods of royal succession (2 Sam 10:1–5), but it certainly shows that the Israelite king was an important potential ally. The text notes that Solomon responds by sending Hiram's ambassadors back to Tyre with a cordial letter, requesting Hiram's assistance (shipments of cedars and cypress) for the temple in Jerusalem. Solomon also affirms that he would be pleased to send some of his workmen to assist in the cutting of the Phoenician timber and to pay the wages of the Phoenician coworkers. Hiram is said to have rejoiced at hearing Solomon's reply and to have stated, "Blessed be Yahweh today, who has given David a wise son." Hiram then replies to Solomon with a message affirming that he would be happy to supply the cedars and cypress and that he would send these materials via the Mediterranean Sea to a designated port (Joppa in 2 Chron 2:15). He notes that Solomon could orchestrate the transportation of the timber from the Israelite port to the city of Jerusalem. Also within this letter, he requests that Solomon, in return, provide agricultural commodities for Tyre, namely wheat and olive oil (commodities often raised in abundance in the fertile territory of Israel). The text also affirms that Hiram and Solomon made a treaty (literally "cut a covenant"). Note that the presence of ambassadors and international communication via formal letters was standard practice in ancient Near Eastern diplomacy (Moran; Pardee).

> **Trade in Cedars**
> *Large forests of cedars existed in the Lebanon mountains in antiquity. Since the trees can grow up to 90 feet high, and their aromatic, attractive wood resists insects and rot, it was a prized product all over the Near East and a valued building material, especially for palaces and temples.*

The workers that Solomon contributed to the project were predominantly forced laborers (see 1 Kgs 9:15–22). Forced labor was often viewed as royal oppression (Exod 1:8–14; Judg 1:28; 1 Sam 8:11–17). The practice is attested throughout much of the ancient Near East (Weinfeld 75–151). Note that Adoniram (1 Kgs 4:6) is referred to as the superintendent of Solomon's forced labor (and later Rehoboam's), a significant reference in light of the fact that he is also a figure (sometimes referred to as Adoram and Hadoram) associated with David's administration (2 Sam 20:24; 1 Kgs 12:18; 2 Chron 10:18). In this connection, it also should be mentioned that Solomon's extensive use of conscripted laborers became a source of tension during his reign and contributed to the disintegration of the so-called united monarchy (1 Kgs 11:28; 12:1–20). Also of significance is the fact that reference is made to those quarrying the stone and dressing it, work that was done in conjunction with artisans from Phoenician

Byblos (*Gebal*, north of Tyre), a city famous for its majestic monumental architecture (Mazar).

Kings in the ancient Near East often engaged in public works, especially the erection of large-scale monumental architecture. Therefore, Solomon's commissioning of the building of the temple, the palace, and massive fortification projects at Jerusalem, Gezer, Hazor, and Megiddo (1 Kgs 9:15–19) is characteristic of the work of a powerful king. Some massive fortifications (at Gezer and Hazor) have been excavated and are traditionally dated to the Solomonic era (Mazar 375–402).

The features and dimensions of the Solomonic temple are discussed in some detail (often using very rare Hebrew vocabulary). Based on the architectural information provided here, the Solomonic temple was rectangular, and about 90' x 30' and about 45' high. There were two major "rooms," the main room about 60' long, and the inner sanctuary ("holy of holies") about 30' long, wide, and high (thus a perfect cube). The temple was built with stone finished at the quarry, with the assembly occurring in Jerusalem. The roof of the house consisted of cedar beams and planks. In addition, the interior walls of the temple were lined with cedar, and the floor was covered with cedar. Wooden carvings overlaid in gold adorned the temple, as well. Of course, the ark of the covenant was placed in the inner sanctuary. The Chronicler affirms that the Solomonic temple was built on the site of Ornan's threshing floor, where David built an altar to Yahweh (1 Chron 22:1). It should be mentioned in this connection that the Solomonic temple is similar in architectural structure to Late Bronze Age (1550–1200 BCE) Canaanite temples (for example at Ugarit, Hazor; see Mazar 248–57; Akkermans and Schwartz 335–41; Keel 111–76), and also to non-Israelite Iron Age temples (for example, the temple at Ayn Dara in Syria). Finally, it should be reiterated that Yahweh's presence in the temple and his dynastic promise are conditional, based on religious obedience (verses 11–13).

6:23–38 The furnishings and decorations of the temple are described in some detail. The text repeatedly mentions cherubim, that is, mythological creatures having features associated with both humankind and beasts (see 2 Sam 22:11; Ps 18:10; Ezek 1:10), well attested in the ancient Near East. Palm trees and open (blooming) flowers sometimes reflect notions of royalty, peace, and even fertility (Exod 28:36; Ps 92:12–15; Song 7:7–13; Keel 166–71). The chapter concludes with reference to the fact that the temple was completed in seven years, during the Canaanite month of *Bul*.

7:1–12 Solomon's palace complex required thirteen years to complete. In addition to Solomon's private residence, various other components of the palace complex are mentioned, including "the house of the forest of the Lebanon," "the hall of pillars," and "the hall of the throne," the last also apparently referred to as "the hall of justice." It is important to note that there is a special residence for Pharaoh's daughter, an indication of the fact that she was of higher status than the rest of Solomon's royal wives (1 Kgs 3:1).

7:13–51 Hiram is the name of the Phoenician king, and it is also the name of the Phoenician artisan responsible for making some of the most elaborate features of the palace complex (and this personal name is attested in Phoenician sources; see Benz). The Deuteronomist states that the artisan (Hiram) was a descendant of an Israelite woman and a Tyrian father.

Two pillars of bronze were erected in the vestibule (and so were highly visible) but do not appear to have had any structural function. Significantly, the pillars were given names "Jachin" and "Boaz," which mean respectively "may he (God) establish" and "with strength" (with the former name attested in Old South Arabic as the name of a gate).

The molten sea is an interesting structure. Its capacity was some two thousand baths, that is, some twelve thousand gallons. It may have functioned as a priestly wash basin of sorts (2 Chron 4:6), but the nature of the structure (with its rim some ten feet from the

> **Dating the Exodus**
> *There is an important date-formula (the fourth year of Solomon and the 480th year after the Israelite exodus from Egypt) in this text. Because Solomon began to reign about 960 BCE, this text seems at first to suggest that the Israelite exodus from Egypt occurred during the mid-fifteenth century BCE. However, based on the archaeological evidence (and some biblical evidence), most biblical scholars date the exodus to the mid-thirteenth century BCE (Mazar 328–355; Sarna and Shanks 33–54). The month of Ziv is the name of the second Canaanite month. Several Canaanite month names are used within the Hebrew Bible (for example, Abib, Bul, Ethanim), although it is more common for the writers of the Hebrew Bible to use Babylonian month names.*

pavement) would have presented some logistical problems for such a use. In any case, just as the two pillars had symbolic significance, so also the molten sea may have had special significance, perhaps symbolizing some sort of life-giving water, or as a symbol of the watery forces of chaos overcome in the creation of the world (Coogan). The rich iconography that was part of this sea (lions, oxen, and cherubs on the borders and twelve cattle underneath) reflects traditional ancient Near Eastern artistic motifs (Keel).

> **Watery Chaos**
>
> *In creation stories from northern Syria, Baal defeated the god Yamm/Nahar (Sea/River) in order to create the world. The Bible knows of such an idea (Ps 24:2), but downplays it, or rather demythologizes it. Still, the molten sea could symbolize the created world governed by Yahweh.*

Regarding the ten "stands" (verse 27), it should be mentioned that some cult stands (with similar artwork) have been found in Israel, including the Iron II levels of Taanach (Mazar 380). In addition, the Deuteronomist also states that Hiram made various cultic implements, such as pots, basins, and shovels (the ones of precious metal probably reserved for special rites). Similar cultic utensils have been found at religious sites in Israel (for example, Tel Dan; see Mazar 492–95). Finally, the reference to David's involvement in the creation of the cult (verse 51) may, in part, reflect later traditions that are also described in Chronicles.

8:1-21 The dedication of a temple was a major event in the ancient Near East; therefore the pomp and circumstance is predictable and apropos. It is significant that the temple was completed in *Bul*, the eighth month (1 Kgs 6:38), but the dedication did not occur until the *month of Ethanim* (note the fact that this is also a Canaanite month name), some eleven months after the completion. The Masoretic Text states that the dedication occurred at the *festival* (perhaps Tabernacles). In any case, the priests help transfer the ark of the covenant from the portable tabernacle to the permanent temple. It is placed in the most holy place using poles (see 2 Sam 6:6–7; 1 Chron 15:13–15), and God's presence is symbolized by the *cloud* in the temple, analogous to the cloud in the tabernacle (Exod 40:34–35). The Deuteronomist notes that there was nothing in the ark except the two stone tablets of Moses. Note that the Pentateuch refers to Aaron's rod and the jar of manna as being "before the covenant" (Exod 16:33–34; Num 17:10).

Within this narrative, Solomon also addresses the entire assembly, blesses Yahweh the God of Israel, and affirms Yahweh's selection of, and fidelity to, David. Solomon also affirms that although David had desired to build the temple, Yahweh had given his son this responsibility and privilege (1 Kgs 5:3), an accomplishment that this text celebrates.

8:22-66 Solomon here utters a prayer that celebrates Yahweh's faithfulness in keeping the covenant, especially with the Davidic line. He affirms that Yahweh is incomparable (verse 23). A most interesting component of this prayer is Solomon's affirmation that Yahweh cannot be "contained" in all the heavens and so certainly not within an earthly temple. Nevertheless, Solomon declares, God is present in some fashion in the Israelite temple (the reference in verse 29 to Yahweh's *name* dwelling there is a euphemism). Furthermore, Solomon petitions Yahweh for the forgiveness of the people's future sins and for their restoration (after military defeats, droughts, famines, etc.), based on the penitence of the people. Some consider verses 41–53 to be a postexilic addition to Solomon's prayer. The presence of monotheism in verse 60 and of "universal salvation" motifs (verses 41–43) analogous to those of Isaiah 44–55 strengthen this position. Finally, it should be noted that "blessings" (verse 56) were often considered priestly duties (Num 6:24–26), as were sacrifices (verses 62–64; see 1 Kgs 3:4). At the conclusion of the seven day festival, Solomon sends the people (some of whom had come from distant borders, Lebo-hamath in the north to the Wadi of Egypt in the south; see 2 Kgs 14:25) to their homes, and they go away blessing the Davidic king.

9:1-9 After Solomon's completion of the temple, Yahweh appears to him again, but this time at Jerusalem, not Gibeon. This serves to affirm Yahweh's complete acceptance of Jerusalem as the official cult site. In addition, there are reaffirmations of the dynastic promises made to David and his descendants (1 Kgs 2:1–12). Note that the promises are conditional, with the Davidic line required to be loyal always to Yahweh. Infidelity, the text affirms, will result in destruction of the dynasty, the temple, and the city.

9:10-14 This section constitutes an interlude in the narrative. The essence of the narrative is that Solomon gives Hiram ten cities as a gesture of royal benevolence to the supportive Phoenician king (and in response to Hiram's gift of 120 talents of gold). However, when Hiram sees the cities, he is displeased and refers to them as "Cabul," that is, "like nothing." Royal gift giving was a prominent feature of international diplomacy in the ancient Near East, and such is reflected in the Amarna Letters and in this narrative, as well (Moran).

9:15–25 Reference is made to the Millo of Jerusalem and the fortification walls of Jerusalem, as well as the walls of Hazor, Megiddo, and Gezer (see 1 Kgs 6:1–22). The word "Millo" derives from a Hebrew word meaning "to fill," and so it probably refers to some sort of earthen rampart or terracing made by "filling in" with dirt. Fortification walls often associated with the reign of Solomon (or with Omri and Ahab of ninth-century Israel) have been excavated in Israel (Mazar 380–87; 469; see 1 Kgs 10:26–29 for the store cities and chariot cities mentioned in 1 Kgs 9:19). The Masoretic Text also refers to a pharaoh (often identified with Pharaoh Siamun) who gives the city of Gezer to his daughter as a dowry. No Egyptian sources have yet been found that refer to this event (Fritz 110). Note that the narrative repeats (verse 24) that Solomon built a house for Pharaoh's daughter (1 Kgs 3:1), an indication of her high status in his harem.

Regarding borders, there are references in the Masoretic Text (verses 18–19) to Solomon's rule over portions of Lebanon and Tadmor (that is, Palmyra, an oasis in the desert of Syria). There are no archaeological or ancient Near Eastern historical data suggesting that Solomon ruled over parts of Lebanon or Aram; therefore, these references are often considered idealized statements. Moreover, a better Hebrew reading would be "Tamar," a city in Judah, not Tadmor (verse 18), in Syria.

> **Forced Labor**
> *Regarding building projects and workers, the Masoretic Text affirms that the Canaanites of the land who had not been annihilated had become slaves to the Israelites (and were conscripted for Solomon's building projects). The Israelites, however, were his soldiers and officials, not conscripted slaves.* However, clearly Solomon had conscripted at least some Israelites for his building projects, for 1 Kings 11:28 refers to Solomon's appointment of Jeroboam I "over the forced labor of the tribe of Joseph."

9:25–28 Of course, the narrative notes Solomon's cultic activities, with Solomon himself again said to offer sacrifices (as in 1 Kgs 3:4). In addition to his cultic activities, Solomon is reputed to have built a fleet of ships harbored at Ezion Geber in the region of modern Elat (biblical Eloth), on the coast of the Red Sea in the land of Edom (the Edomites, from the time of David, were sometimes subjects of Israel; see 2 Sam 8:12–14; 1 Kgs 11:14–22; 22:47; 2 Kgs 3:8–9; 8:20–22; 14:7, 22; 16:6). It is significant that Israelite kings normally did not establish navies (because the Philistines normally occupied the coastal areas, not the Israelites). However, the Phoenicians were famous for their nautical abilities, and the biblical text affirms that Solomon was assisted by them. Finally, an inscription from Tel Qasile (near the Mediterranean coast) refers to the "gold of Ophir" (see Naveh, "Writings," 16–17), a striking parallel to the reference here (compare 1 Kgs 10:11–12, 22; 22:47–49; 2 Kgs 14:22; 16:6; Job 22:24; 28:16; Ps 45:9; Isa 13:12).

10:1–13 This text serves to demonstrate Solomon's fame and wisdom and thus constitutes another example of the fulfillment of Yahweh's promises to him (see 1 Kgs 3:1–15). Indeed, this narrative may affirm that Yahweh's promises were fulfilled to the superlative degree, with the result that distant monarchs sought Solomon (compare Ps 72). *Sheba* is normally considered to be Saba (of the Sabean people), a region in Southwest Arabia (modern Yemen), and so this "Queen of Sheba" had traveled a great distance to see the splendor of Solomon's royal court and to hear words of wisdom from his lips (resulting from her queries). Note the presence of the personal name "Sheba" in genealogical texts in Genesis (25:3; compare Gen 10:7), even as a brother of Ophir (Gen 10:28–29).

In keeping with ancient Near Eastern customs of royal gift giving, she brings numerous gifts for the Israelite king. Among the presents are *spices*, something that probably reflects Sheba's role in the incense trade. The narrative portrays the queen not only praising Solomon's legendary wisdom, but even blessing Yahweh, Solomon's God. Thus even foreigners acknowledge the uniqueness of Israel's God. Solomon, also following traditional ancient Near Eastern protocol, gives many gifts to the queen as well, in return for her gifts and her visit to his kingdom.

> **The Incense Trade**
> *Many plant products could serve as incense or perfumes in ancient Israel. Some grew throughout the Near East, while some (frankincense, myrrh) came from southwestern Arabia or northeastern Africa, and others (cinnamon) from India or further east.*

Indeed, the text even states that Solomon gave her "every desire that she requested" (verse 13), a text that has given rise to many legends (for example, Ethiopic, Yemenite, Jewish, and Muslim traditions; see Qur'an, Surah 27) suggesting the presence of a romantic relationship between Solomon and the Queen of Sheba. Finally, it should be noted that verses 11 and 12 are intrusive, and continue with contents that are present in 1 Kings 9:26–28 (see verse 22).

10:14–29 This text contains a further description of Solomon's purported opulence as well as the trappings of power and prestige associated with his court. The text notes that among Solomon's trade partners were the Phoenicians (verse 22) and Arabian kings (verse 15). Furthermore, the presence of prestige items such as golden and silver shields is characteristic of the ostentatious nature of many ancient Near Eastern courts. Naturally, thrones with reliefs of lions are part of the same sort of desire for majestic royal presentation (see Keel). Import items are often associated with wealth and fame – hence, Solomon's fleet of Tarshish ships (a term that refers to the style of the ships and essentially means that they were capable of crossing large open waters such as the Mediterranean; see 1 Kgs 9:26–28) is coupled with reference to the importation of precious metals and exotic fauna (verse 22). The chapter concludes with reference to Solomon's military prowess (chariots and horses), the ubiquitousness of Phoenician cedars, and Solomon's status as a middleman for Neo-Hittite and Aramean kingdoms to his north (see also Deut 17:16; 1 Kgs 9:15–25).

> **Ivory**
> Carved ivory was an important product of Syrian and Phoenician artisans (Winter 1–18); therefore, the reference to carved ivory (verse 18) is unsurprising (see Amos 6:4 and Mazar 503–5 for carved ivories at Iron Age II Samaria).

11:1–13 The religion of the nations of Edom, Moab, and Ammon was a "national god religion" (see the conclusion of 2 Kings). For ancient Israel, the national God was Yahweh. This narrative notes that Solomon was a king with a large harem, consisting of 700 wives of royal birth (often the result of international alliances and relations, for which Solomon was famous; 1 Kgs 3:1) and 300 concubines (for the significance of the numbers three and seven, see note in contexts). The foreign wives are reported to have caused Solomon to compromise his own Yahwistic faith (see Exod 34:16; Deut 7:1–6; 23:2–8; Ezra 9:2; Neh 9:12), probably precipitated initially by his willingness to accommodate their religious practices (note that foreign women are often considered culpable in Old Testament narratives – for example, Potiphar's wife, women of Baal-Peor, Jezebel). The end result is that Yahweh punishes Solomon, stating that his kingdom will be divided (but not until after his own death; see 1 Kgs 12:1–24).

11:14–25 The material here is intended to demonstrate Solomon's religious infidelity and its consequences. Namely, Yahweh *raised up* Hadad the Edomite (see 1 Kgs 9:26–28). Of course, this text notes that Hadad had fled to Egypt during David's reign, and a strong marital alliance had been formed between him and the Pharaoh. In addition, God raised up an Aramean adversary, namely, Rezon son of Eliada, a usurper that ascended the throne in place of the Aramean king Hadadezer of Zobah (2 Sam 10:15–19).

11:26–43 Solomon had struggled to gain and establish the throne (1 Kgs 1–2), and now the Deuteronomist affirms that, with his death, the division of the kingdom will come. Moreover, the leader of the revolt was to be Jeroboam the son of Nebat, a northern Israelite whom Solomon had placed in a position of importance (1 Kgs 5:1–18). It is a prophetic figure named Ahijah of Shiloh who announces to Jeroboam (with the symbolic act of tearing a garment into twelve pieces; see 1 Sam 15:27–28; 1 Kgs 20:35–43; 2 Kgs 9:1–13) that he will soon reign over ten of the Israelite tribes, with one tribe (LXX "two tribes," that is, with Benjamin understood not yet to have been assimilated to Judah; compare 1 Kgs 12:21) remaining for the Davidic kings and thus insuring the continuation of the Davidic dynasty (see 2 Sam 7:1–17; "lamp" in 1 Kgs 15:4; 2 Kgs 8:19; 19:34; 20:6; 22:2; 25:25, 27–30). Ahijah informs Jeroboam that Solomon's abandonment of Yahweh has precipitated Yahweh's decision to divide the kingdom. Note that Ahijah promises Jeroboam a dynasty as well, provided that he and his descendants remain faithful to Yahweh (1 Kgs 12:1–24). This text then implies that Solomon learns that Jeroboam will soon reign over a large portion of the kingdom and so attempts to kill him. Nevertheless, Jeroboam flees to Egypt and to the court of Shishaq (Sheshonq, founder of the Twenty-Second Dynasty) of Egypt, remaining there until Solomon's death (1 Kgs 14:25–28). This section of the text concludes with a reference to the annals of Solomon's reign and to his great wisdom, stereotyped statements about the duration of his reign, references to his death (sometime between 930 and 922 BCE) and to his successor.

DIVISION OF THE MONARCHY & NARRATIVES ABOUT ISRAEL & JUDAH TO 722 BCE · 1 KGS 12:1–2 KGS 17:41

12:1–24 Solomon's son Rehoboam is the heir apparent (reigns 922–915 BCE). Significantly, he travels to the historic northern cult site of Shechem (see Josh 24) to be crowned king by *Israel*, an act intended to consolidate his power within both Judah and Israel. Jeroboam I (son of Nebat; referred to as Jeroboam I, as there is a subsequent king of Israel with this name as well, 2 Kgs 14:23–29) learns of Solomon's death and of the coronation of Rehoboam, so he returns from Egyptian exile to meet with the new king, and to determine the prudence of Israel's accepting Rehoboam's kingship in the north (see 1 Kgs 11:26–40). The text notes that Jeroboam is willing for the northern tribes to be subjects of the kingdom of Rehoboam, but he desires some assurances that Rehoboam will not engage in the oppressive policies (1 Kgs 5:1–18) that characterized Solomon's reign. Rehoboam requests three days to consider. His older counselors advise him to "lighten the load," but his younger counselors (lacking the wisdom that ostensibly comes with age) encourage him to increase the number of oppressive policies, suggesting that he say, "my father disciplined you with whips, but I will discipline you with scorpions," and even the euphemistic phrase "my little finger is thicker than my father's loins" (verses 10–11). Rehoboam foolishly accepts the advice of the young counselors, and the kingdom divides, thus fulfilling Yahweh's words to Solomon (1 Kgs 11:11–13) and the prophetic oracle of Ahijah (1 Kgs 11:29–39). David had succeeded in unifying north and south, and Solomon had maintained and strengthened it, but Rehoboam cannot.

Jeroboam and the northern delegation depart, affirming that they have no "share with David, no portion with the son of Jesse" (verse 16; compare the similar terminology in 2 Sam 20:1). Subsequently, Rehoboam sends a *corvée* officer named Adoram (perhaps a descendant of the Adoram of David's reign; 2 Sam 20:24; see also 1 Kgs 4:6 for a similar name) to the north, but "all Israel" (that is, the people of the north) "stone him to death." Ultimately, Jeroboam I is crowned king in Israel. At this juncture, Rehoboam returns to the capital city of Jerusalem and assembles a massive number of Judean troops, with the explicit purpose of forcing Israel to remain part of his kingdom. However, a divine oracle comes to Shemaiah, affirming that Judah should not go into battle against Israel, because they are "kindred." From this point on, there were two kingdoms in "Israel": the northern kingdom of Israel (often called Ephraim) and the southern kingdom of Judah.

12:25–33 Jeroboam I (reigns 922–901 BCE) engaged in building projects at Shechem and Penuel, historic sites in the northern tribal territory. From the perspective of the Deuteronomist, however, Jeroboam's most important act is the erection of cult sites at Dan and Bethel, including the making of golden calves. Religion in the region often associated bovine imagery with deities, especially Baal and El (see Exod 32; Smith, *Early History*, 83–85). In addition, Jeroboam institutes a new festival on the fifteenth day of the eighth month. Finally, he establishes a northern Israelite priesthood of some sort. The Deuteronomist considers all of these actions to be idolatrous, though many Israelites obviously disagree.

13:1–34 Jeroboam I stands at the altar of Bethel to offer incense (1 Kgs 3:4). However, a prophet from Judah, who had been commanded to travel to Bethel, pronounces a curse upon the altar, resulting in its immediate destruction; he also indicates that a future Judean king, namely Josiah (reigned 640–609 BCE), will one day burn the bones of this altar's priests upon it (2 Kgs 23:15–18), thus desecrating it. The editor of the book, writing in Josiah's time, emphasizes God's foreknowledge of the course of Israel's history.

> **Corvée**
> *A day's unpaid labor owed by a vassal to his lord, or forced labor exacted in place of taxes.*

> **Bethel**
> *Bethel was a site associated with Jacob and his dream of the ladder going to heaven (Gen 28:19; compare Gen 32 on Penuel). Dan was a historic religious site, with roots back to the grandson of Moses (Judg 18:30). The point is that Jeroboam's decisions to engage in building and cultic activities at Bethel, Penuel, and Dan can be framed as his attempt to reconnect with sites associated with patriarchal and Mosaic religion. Also, it is important to note that Jeroboam gives his son a Yahwistic name (Abijah, meaning, "Yahweh is my father"). Together, these facts suggest that Jeroboam worshiped Yahweh, but not in a way that met the approval of the Deuteronomist.*

Jeroboam's command to seize the Judean prophet results in the withering of Jeroboam's hand. Jeroboam implores the prophet to entreat Yahweh for the hand's restoration, and the request is granted.

Jeroboam attempts to convince the prophet to dine with him, but the Judean prophet refuses, indicating that he has divine instructions not to do so (and not even to travel the same road home). Nevertheless, an old prophet from Bethel deceives the Judean prophet and convinces him to sup with him, then later pronounces God's judgment upon the Judean prophet for violating the divine instructions. The result is that a lion kills the Judean prophet after he departs for home (compare 1 Kgs 20:36; 2 Kgs 17:25–26). The old prophet later learns the location of the Judean prophet's body, provides it with a proper burial, and then requests that, when he dies, his sons bury him near the Judean prophet. The odd story, so troubling to modern readers, underscores the risks of prophecy and the importance of the individual prophet's sense of and obedience to the divine will.

This narrative concludes by affirming that even after this event, Jeroboam I continues to worship at high places and to employ his own priests. The Deuteronomist then states that this "sin of Jeroboam" would lead to the termination of Jeroboam's line (also see 1 Kgs 15:29–30).

14:1–20 Jeroboam I's son Abijah becomes gravely ill, and Jeroboam asks his wife to go from Tirzah (in disguise) to Shiloh to ask the prophet Ahijah about his recovery (for inquiring of a prophet or deity at the time of sickness, see 2 Kgs 1; 5:1–19; 8:7–15; 20:1–11). He instructs that she take loaves, cakes, and honey to serve as some form of compensation. Although Ahijah is elderly and nearly blind, Yahweh had told him of the coming of Jeroboam's wife. Ahijah informs her that Jeroboam's religious faithlessness will result in the termination of Jeroboam's "male" line (literally, "those who urinate on the wall"; 1 Kgs 16:1–4, 11–12; 21:19–29; 22:37; 2 Kgs 9:7–10:17). This will begin in the near future, starting with the death of his sick son. Moreover, Ahijah states that all of Jeroboam's relatives will die violent deaths, with animals consuming their flesh (see Pritchard 538 for a similar statement), will not receive proper burial (with the exception of his son Abijah, in whom Yahweh found something pleasing), and that the northern kingdom will fall (see 1 Kgs 15:25–16:7; 2 Kgs 17). This story also refers to the *Asherah poles*, a component of Jeroboam's state religion that the Deuteronomist considers offensive (Smith, *Early History*, 108–47). Finally, the chapter concludes in the traditional manner, with reference to the "Book of the Annals of the Kings of Israel," to the duration of Jeroboam's reign, and to the name of his successor.

14:21–29 These verses summarize Rehoboam's reign. The text notes that he becomes king at the age of 41 and reigns for 17 years in Jerusalem. Striking is the fact that Jeroboam's mother is an Ammonite (probably an Ammonite princess). The Deuteronomist affirms that Judah "did what was evil," using "high places, pillars, and asherim on every high hill and under every green tree." Moreover, there is even reference to the presence of male temple prostitutes in Judah during this period (see 2 Kgs 23:7; Deut 23:17–18). Temple prostitutes apparently existed in ancient Near Eastern religion.

One of the most important historical events during the reign of Rehoboam was Shishaq's campaign into Judah (Cogan 387–88). The biblical text (here) mentions his plundering of Jerusalem (including the temple and palace), and one might conclude that this was a punitive campaign intended to demonstrate support for Jeroboam I (1 Kgs 11:40).

> **The Campaign into Judah**
> *Shishaq's own record of this campaign has been preserved on the Bubastite Portal (at the Egyptian Temple of Amun at Karnak in Thebes) and reveals that he campaigned heavily in the Judean Negev. Significantly, though, sites in the northern kingdom (Megiddo, Taanach) are also listed as conquered, and, in addition, a fragment of a stele has been found at Megiddo that contains the cartouche (hieroglyphic name and symbol) of Shishaq (Mazar 395–98).*

This chapter concludes with the standard reference to the presence of records of Rehoboam's reign in the "Book of the Annals of the Kings of Judah," to his burial in Jerusalem (*city of David*), to his mother's name (*Naamah the Ammonite*), and to his successor. Note that there is war between Rehoboam and Jeroboam I continually (compare 1 Kgs 12:24).

15:1–8 This text notes that in the eighteenth year of Jeroboam I of Israel, Abijam (Abijah), son of Rehoboam, begins to reign in Judah (reigns 915–913 BCE). Abijam's mother is Maacah, daughter of Absalom (2 Chron 11:20; 13:2). According to the Deuteronomist, Abijam is not faithful to Yahweh;

however, because of Yahweh's faithfulness, David still had a *lamp* in Jerusalem (see 1 Kgs 11:36). The wars between north (Israel) and south (Judah) continue all the days of Abijam's life. This section concludes with the traditional summary (source and successor).

15:9–24 The Deuteronomist begins by providing the standard synchronism, in this case noting that Asa (son or brother of Abijam and son or grandson of Maacah) begins to reign in Judah (reigned 913–873 BCE) during the twentieth year of Jeroboam I of Israel. Significantly, Asa receives praise for his religious reforms, even though he continues to allow worship on the high places. Some have argued that the queen mother held some sort of official position, and here the text notes that Asa removes Maacah from this role [Hebrew *gevirah*]; (see 2 Kgs 8:26; 10:13; 11:1–16; 24:12; Ackerman, "The Queen Mother," 385–401). During Asa's reign (in Judah), there is continual warfare between Judah and Israel, culminating during the reign of Baasha of Israel. To strengthen his military position, Asa of Judah forms an alliance (using precious metals from the temple as a "gift"; see also 1 Kgs 6:1–7:51; 2 Kgs 12:18; 16:8; 18:15; 24:13; 25:13–17) with Ben-Hadad I of Damascus (reigns about 885–870 BCE), who had formerly had an alliance with Baasha of Israel. This alliance succeeds in forcing Baasha (Israel) to withdraw from Ramah (near Jerusalem, the capital of Judah). Some have suggested that the destruction of Dan (and Hazor Stratum IX) might be associated with a campaign of Ben Hadad I, both being strategic cities on the border between Israel and Aram (undertaken after his alliance with Asa against Baasha; see Mazar 494; Halpern 72). The narrative concludes with the formulaic reference to records of Asa's reign, to his death, and to his successor.

> **Hadad**
>
> *Hadad was the Syrian storm god (similar to Canaanite Baal), and Aramean kings would often be referred to as* Ben-Hadad, *that is, "son of Hadad," as a means of affirming fidelity to this deity. The Aramean king of this narrative is often referred to as Ben-Hadad I, as he is the first Aramean king known by the name Ben-Hadad (also 1 Kgs 20:1–22; 2 Kgs 13:1–9).*

15:25–16:7 Nadab (reigns 901–900 BCE), son of Jeroboam I, begins to reign in Israel in Asa's second year. He is reported to have been *evil*. Moreover, the text notes that a coup led by Baasha results in Nadab's assassination during the third year of Asa (of Judah), and then provides the standard formula about sources. The fact that Nadab is assassinated during a battle against Philistine Gibbethon probably demonstrates that he was attempting to expand his borders, seize plunder, or gain tribute.

Immediately after usurping the throne of Israel, Baasha (reigns 900–877 BCE) succeeds in annihilating all members of the dynasty of Jeroboam I, thus fulfilling the word of the prophet Ahijah the Shilonite (probably not, of course, the same Ahijah as the father of Baasha; 1 Kgs 14:7–16). The text affirms that Baasha's capital was at Tirzah (1 Kgs 14:17), that he reigned for twenty-four years, and that he was *evil*. During Baasha's reign, a prophet named Jehu son of Hanani (2 Chron 16:7–10) delivers an oracle condemning Baasha for his sins and promising that his dynasty will not endure, but his heirs will all die violent deaths (verse 4, compare verse 11; 1 Kgs 14:1–20). Baasha's reign is then summarized, with the traditional reference to sources, to death and burial, and to his successor.

16:8–14 Elah (reigns 877–876 BCE) son of Baasha begins to reign in Israel during the twenty-sixth year of King Asa (Judah). However, Zimri (an official in the Israelite army) assassinates him. Zimri begins by killing the royal line of Baasha, thus fulfilling the prophecy of Jehu (verse 11; compare 1 Kgs 14:1–20). The narrative concludes by referring to the sources for Elah's reign.

16:15–28 Zimri (reigns 876) begins to reign in Israel during the twenty-seventh year of Asa (Judah). During the army of Israel's continued siege of the Philistine city of Gibbethon, it becomes known that Zimri has assassinated Elah. The army, displeased with this turn of events, declares their *commander* Omri to be king. Omri's first act is to lay siege to the capital city of Tirzah. Knowing that he cannot repel the army, Zimri sets the palace ablaze and dies in the conflagration. The narrative concludes with a reference to Zimri's *walking in the ways of Jeroboam*, to his conspiracy, and to the sources used for the description of his reign.

Chaos continues to reign in Israel, with some supporting Tibni's kingship (876 BCE) and some supporting Omri. However, Omri crushes the supporters of Tibni (and Tibni himself is killed), although this process may have taken as many as three years (compare 16:15, 21–23). The synchronism of the text affirms that Omri (reigns 876–869 BCE) begins to reign (as the sole ruler) in the thirty-first year of Asa (Judah). Although he begins his reign in Tirzah, he makes Samaria the new capital of the northern kingdom of Israel (Tappy 1:145–212). Significantly, Omri is affirmed to have done more evil than *any of those before him*, but the remaining textual notations are brief and formulaic (sources, successor).

> **Omri**
> Omri must have been a very powerful monarch, as Assyrian inscriptions refer to the kingdom of Israel as the "House of Omri" until the time of the fall of Israel in 722 BCE (see Pritchard 284–85). Moreover, he is also mentioned in the Mesha Inscription as a powerful king of Israel that ruled over the Moabites (Pritchard 320; Rollston, "Mesha"; compare 2 Kgs 1:1; 3:4–27; 13:20; 24:2). Furthermore, the text's statement that Omri rested with his fathers suggests that he received proper burial in the capital city of Samaria.

16:29-34 Omri's son Ahab (reigns 869–850 BCE) begins to reign in Israel during the thirty-eighth year of Asa (of Judah), and he is said to have reigned for twenty-two years and to have been "more evil than all who were before him." Among the acts of Ahab that the Deuteronomist considers most offensive is Ahab's marriage to the Phoenician princess Jezebel (whose name means "here is the royal one"), daughter of the Sidonian king Ethbaal (Rollston, "Ethbaal"). Ahab is credited with supporting the worship of Baal and Asherah (Smith, *Early History*, 65–147), precipitated by the foreign wives who bring foreign cults into Israel (see 1 Kgs 11:1–8 for similar statements about Solomon). Finally, the text provides a historical footnote, affirming that Hiel of Bethel rebuilt the city of Jericho, at the cost of his youngest son (Josh 6:26), who may very well have been ritually sacrificed and buried as a "foundation" deposit.

17:1-7 Elijah of Tishbe is introduced into the narrative here. This inaugurates a series of stories that revolve around the prophets Elijah and Elisha. These stories are sometimes referred to as the "Elijah and Elisha Cycle." They are probably used as source materials by the Deuteronomist.

Importantly, Elijah seems to have been considered a paradigmatic prophet, analogous to the lawgiver and prophet Moses (Exod 18:9–22; 33:17–23; Num 19:11–15; Deut 18:9–22; 2 Kgs 2). In any case, within this narrative, Elijah proclaims that there will be a drought in the land for three years (for the number "three," see note in 1 Kings introduction). Then, Yahweh instructs Elijah to cross the Jordan River so as to be outside Ahab's jurisdiction. The narrator also affirms that during Elijah's time in Transjordan, the ravens fed him bread and meat in the morning and evening, as he lived in a seasonal riverbed. Because there is normally no rain during the dry season, ravines dry up. The fact that the *Ravine Cherith* dries up, therefore, is quite typical.

17:8-24 Elijah travels to the town of Zarephath, in the territory of Sidon (in Phoenicia). There he meets a poor widow (as he had been told he would), also suffering from the drought (see Luke 4:26).

Striking is the fact that Phoenician territory suffers from the drought, for within Phoenicia the god Baal was believed to be the "storm god," the god that controlled the rain (see Green). However, this text affirms that Yahweh is omnipotent, even in the land of Phoenicia. Also important is the fact that Elijah is sent (by Yahweh) from the land of Israel to the land of Phoenicia, the very region from which Jezebel hailed, again a demonstration of Yahweh's power in the region of Phoenicia (and perhaps a demonstration of Ethbaal's weakness).

> **Options for Women**
> Widows were often vulnerable and downtrodden members of society in ancient times (Exod 22:22–24; Deut 24:19–21; Ruth 2; Luke 7:12–15). Although there are some exceptions, women's roles often revolved around the family. Vocational options for a widow were few, and those that did exist garnered only the most modest compensation. Widows without (grown) male children could be in dire straits (King and Stager 53).

Elijah requests a drink from the widow, and as she is bringing it to him, he also asks her for some food. She responds, however, by stating that she has only a handful of meal and a little oil and that she is about to cook a final meal for herself and her son. Elijah tells her to prepare the meal, but to feed him first and then to make more for herself and her son. Then Elijah vows that the widow and her son will have enough grain and oil to suffice until the drought has ended. The text concludes by affirming that all occurs just as Elijah (through Yahweh) predicts (see 2 Kgs 4:1–7).

At some point, the widow's son nearly dies. The widow assumes that this is some sort of divine judgment for some (unnamed) sin, and she rails against Elijah. However, Elijah revives the boy. One of the most interesting components of this narrative is the fact that Elijah *stretched himself out on the boy three times* (for the number "three," see above) and prays to Yahweh for the child's life. The end result is that the child is restored to life and that the Phoenician widow feels compelled to affirm that Elijah is indeed a man of God and that the word of Yahweh is truth (2 Kgs 4:8–37). That is, the text now affirms that, not only does Yahweh's power reach beyond Israel, but even that non-Israelites are capable of realizing this.

18:1–19 During the third year of the drought, Yahweh reveals to Elijah that he is to meet with Ahab. However, in the meantime, Ahab sets out to find pasturage, along with his servant Obadiah (a faithful Yahwist who has hidden prophets of Yahweh from Jezebel, but not to be confused with the prophet of the book of Obadiah). Elijah and Obadiah meet, and Elijah tells him to summon Ahab. Although Obadiah is reluctant at first, fearing that Elijah will be transported by Yahweh's spirit to another place (see 2 Kgs 2:16; Acts 8:39; *Bel and the Dragon* 36) before Ahab can return, he concedes, and Elijah and Ahab meet. Ahab ridicules Elijah, but Elijah replies with a stern condemnation of his own, accusing Ahab of abandoning Yahweh. Then, Elijah throws down the gauntlet, calling Ahab and the court prophets of Baal and Asherah to a contest.

18:20–40 Mount Carmel was historically associated with the storm god Baal; hence Elijah's desire to duel on Mount Carmel indicates his confidence in Yahweh's power and dominance in all realms. Nevertheless, Elijah also affirms (perhaps with hyperbole) that he is the sole prophet of Yahweh in the land at that time, with all others having abandoned Yahweh or having been killed (1 Kgs 19:10). Ultimately, it is agreed that two bulls will be prepared for sacrifice, with the deities being responsible for the *fire*. Elijah permits the prophets of Baal to prepare their bull first; however, Baal fails to consume the sacrifice with fire. The prophets of Baal engage in a ritual dance during their attempts to "summon" Baal (see 2 Sam 6:14; Pss 149:3; 150:4). For this reason, Elijah taunts (compare Jer 10:1–16; Isa 44:9–20) the worshipers of Baal, suggesting that Baal may be "meditating," "on a journey," or "asleep" (perhaps a trip to the "underworld," as is affirmed in Ugaritic literature; compare Smith, *Early History*, 67–69) or that he may have "wandered away" (perhaps a euphemism for defecating and urinating). The worshipers of Baal even resort to cutting themselves (Lev 19:28; Deut 14:1; Hos 7:14; Coogan 109) as part of their attempt to gain Baal's attention. Nevertheless, nothing happens.

Elijah reconstructs the altar, using twelve stones (Josh 4:3–9, 20–24), and prepares the sacrifice. Finally, he requests that four jars be filled with water and dumped onto the altar, repeating this (again) three times. Then Elijah calls upon the name of Yahweh, and Yahweh answers by consuming the sacrifice, the water, and even the stones with fire. Within the narrative, this event functions as an empirical demonstration of the power of Yahweh and the impotence of Baal. Immediately after this, Elijah commands that the prophets of Baal be seized and killed (as some laws describe; Deut 13:1–5).

18:41–46 The culminating event that exposes Baal's powerlessness is that, after this demonstration of Yahweh's power, the rain comes. Yahweh, not Baal, the narrator affirms, is lord of nature. Although Samaria was the primary national capital, Jezreel was also a capital city (2 Kgs 8:29). For this reason, Ahab returns to Jezreel, and Elijah runs alongside the chariot of Ahab. Elijah's telling Ahab to eat and drink before the journey may be an indication that Ahab can begin to celebrate the conclusion of the drought.

19:1–18 Although Elijah has been victorious on Mount Carmel, Jezebel's vow to take Elijah's life terrifies him (see 1 Kgs 18:20–39). He flees from the northern Israelite city of Jezreel to Judean Beersheba (in the deep south), and from there he travels even further south. During this period of discouragement, he pleads to God for death (compare Job 3; Jer 20:14–18). Instead, an angelic visitor encourages Elijah to eat and drink; however, he drifts off into sleep. A second time, Yahweh's angel comes to him and tells him to eat. Then Elijah rises and travels for forty days (for the number "forty," see introduction), arriving at Mount Horeb (Sinai; compare Exod 19–34; Deut 5–30), thus essentially reversing the journey of the Israelites from Horeb to the promised land.

After Elijah again affirms that he is the sole remaining prophet of Yahweh (compare 1 Kgs 18:1–22), Yahweh instructs him to go out and stand on the mountain and wait for Yahweh's presence. Theophanies (appearances of God) are often attested within the biblical narrative, and the accompanying components often

> **Theophany**
>
> *An appearance by God, especially to a prophet or other spokesperson for the divine, is known as theophany. Elijah's theophany deliberately downplays the majestic features that Moses' prior vision of God at the same location leads one to expect.*

include thunder and lightning, fire, quaking, wind, etc. (compare Exod 19:16; Deut 5:22–24; Judg 5:4–5; Isa 6:1–4; Ezek 1:4). Striking within this text, however, is the fact that Yahweh is present in the silence. During this theophany, Yahweh instructs Elijah that his prophetic ministry is to continue, and he commands him to anoint Jehu as king of Israel and Hazael as king of Aram (compare 1 Kgs 1:39). These directives, of course, necessitate Elijah's departing from the south and returning to the north, and reveal the fact that Yahweh is still the God of Israel and even holds sway over Aram, as well. Significantly, there is reference (verse 17) to some sort of an alliance between Hazael and Jehu, a fact that is evidenced also by the Tel Dan Inscription (Biran and Naveh 2–18; compare 2 Kgs 8:7–10:36; 12:17–13:7).

> **Tel Dan Inscription**
> *Three fragments of this inscription were discovered in 1993–94. Though broken, the inscription testifies to an Aramean victory over Israel: "Hadad went before me.... king of Israel and [ ]yahu son of [ ] I [over thr]ew the House of David...."*

19:19–21 Although the text does not specifically state that Elijah anoints Elisha (compare 1 Kgs 1:39), the text does affirm that Elijah travels from Mount Horeb and meets Elisha as he is plowing fields. Moreover, Elijah's casting of his mantle onto Elisha is indicative of his desire for Elisha to serve as a prophetic voice in Israel. Elisha requests permission to give a parting kiss to his parents and then returns to prepare a final meal for various people (for example, coworkers with whom he was plowing the field). Elijah responds with the enigmatic phrase: "go and return, for what have I done to you." In any case, the fact that Elisha slaughters his oxen and burns their yokes reveals that he is renouncing his agricultural past in favor of the prophetic life. Finally, with the words *he became his attendant*, the text affirms Elisha's fidelity to Elijah, as well as Elisha's secondary status in the relationship (compare Num 27:12–23 and Deut 31:7–23, for the relationship between Joshua and Moses).

20:1–22 The Ben-Hadad of this text is often referred to as Ben-Hadad II (reigned in Aram about 870–842 BCE; compare 1 Kgs 15:9–24). Within this narrative, he (along with an alliance of Aramean city-state rulers) besieges the northern Israelite capital of Samaria, demanding plunder in exchange for his withdrawal. Ahab of Israel, although a very powerful king, is willing to meet these demands. However, Ahab refuses to grant Ben-Hadad's subsequent demands for permission to search the royal residence and the residences of high officials, so as to seize more. Ben-Hadad is so angry at Ahab's refusal that he vows (verse 10) to destroy Samaria. Rather than succumbing to Ben-Hadad's anger, Ahab responds with a proverb, stating that warriors should not boast until they have vanquished a foe (and thus are able to take off their armor after a victory). Significantly, a prophet of Yahweh approaches Ahab with a word: attack the Arameans. Ahab accepts the prophetic word and wins a great Israelite victory. Nevertheless, the prophet affirms that Ben-Hadad will return in the spring for battle again (compare 2 Sam 11:1; 2 Kgs 13:20). Although one might deduce from the "Elijah and Elisha Cycle" that Ahab was not a Yahwist, it is important to note that this narrative (not necessarily part of that cycle per se) affirms that Ahab did not always reject all Yahwistic prophets (compare 22:5–28).

20:23–43 Within the ancient Near East and Mediterranean, gods were often associated with mountains. Thus some of the Aramean officials assert that Yahweh's power is confined to the mountains; therefore, they propose to do battle with Israel on the plain, near the city of Aphek (which appears to have been on the Israel-Aram border and in Aramean hands, although its precise location has been debated).

> **Gods & Mountains**
> *Many cultures associated deities with mountains. For example, the Ugaritic pantheon was associated with Mount Zaphon, and the gods of Greece were associated with Mount Olympus. Yahweh was associated with mountains as well (Sinai, Horeb, and Zion). Furthermore, the term El Shaddai likely means "God of the Mountains" (not "God Almighty").*

Israel marshals a modest force (*like small flocks of goats*) in the face of superior Aramean forces. A prophet of Yahweh verifies that Yahweh will deliver the Arameans into Israel's hands, especially because of the Arameans' presumptive assertion that Yahweh's power is confined to the mountains. The Arameans engage in various strategic actions (for example, replacing the city-state kings with Ben-Hadad's own loyal commanders) to ensure success in battle. Nevertheless, Israel succeeds, and the wall of the city of Aphek is even reported to have fallen on the Arameans that fled to the security of this city. Ultimately, Ben-Hadad II surrenders after some negotiation, dressed in such a way so as to signify submission. Ahab is lenient with Ben-Hadad, welcomes him into the chariot as a peer, and permits him to return home. However, certain members of the "company of the prophets" (compare 1 Sam 19:20–24; 2 Kgs 2:1–18; 4:1–7; 5:22; 6:1–7; for lions doing Yahweh's bidding, see 1 Kgs 13:24; 2 Kgs 17:25–26) rebuke him severely (using symbolic acts; see 1 Kgs 11:26–40) for sparing Ben Hadad. Note that a prophet pretends to be a soldier wounded in the battle (hence his request to have another prophet strike him) and uses the ruse of wounds and bandages to gain the king's attention (see 2 Sam 12:1–12 for another example of a king's being duped into pronouncing his own punishment). The reason for this rebuke is that Yahweh *had determined* that Ben-Hadad *should die* (verse 42; see Deut 20; Josh 6:17; 1 Sam 15:3). The narrative concludes by noting that Ahab will lose his life because of his decision and that he returns to Samaria a sullen man.

21:1–29 Naboth owns an impressive vineyard in the northern Israelite city of Jezreel, near one of Ahab's palaces (his main palace is in Samaria). This land is Naboth's ancestral inheritance and, as such, is inalienable. That is, based on ancient Israelite legal traditions, this land cannot be sold (see Lev 25:8–17, 23–25; 27:16–25). Nevertheless, Ahab wishes to possess this land and offers to compensate Naboth for it. For the pious Naboth, however, this is not an option, because it would be a violation of ancient Israelite custom. Jezebel notices that her husband is sullen, and after learning the reason for his morose behavior, she takes matters into her own hands. She forges letters in Ahab's name and uses his seal to authenticate them (for seals, see Avigad and Sass). The fact that she acts in the king's name, rather than her own, seems to suggest that her own power was limited. The purpose of these letters is to create a public festival where Naboth can be accused of cursing (Masoretic Text has "bless," an obvious euphemism; compare Job 2:9 and 1 Sam 3:13, for the same basic phenomenon) God and country (Exod 22:28; Lev 24:14–16). Ironically, the occasion chosen for accusing Naboth of grievous sins is a fast, usually a time to atone for sins. Based on Israelite legal custom, it was necessary that a charge resulting in punishment by death be brought by two or more witnesses (compare Num 35:30; Deut 17:6–7, 19:15; there were severe penalties for giving false testimony according to Exod 20:16; Deut 5:20, 19:16–21); hence, multiple "witnesses" make the accusation. For the Deuteronomist, it is reprehensible that the Phoenician Jezebel repudiates Israelite law, but it is especially tragic that the Israelite Ahab does, as well. After all, it is the duty of the king to maintain the law (2 Sam 11:1–12:25; 1 Kgs 3:9–12). In any case, regarding the land itself, either Naboth had no surviving family to lay claim to it, or perhaps it was common practice for the property of accused criminals (especially those who had wronged the state) to go to the king. Regardless of the operative component, Ahab is able to take possession of the vineyard.

Elijah the prophet comes to Jezreel to rebuke Ahab for this heinous act and pronounces that Ahab will die in the very place where Naboth was murdered and that he and his line, like those of previous guilty Israelite kings (14:1–20), will die shameful and violent deaths, that is, being eaten by dogs or birds (1 Kgs 22:37). The text affirms that there was no king before Ahab who had acted more wickedly, comparing him to the *Amorites* (a term often used as a synonym for the term Canaanites see 2 Kgs 21:11), who had been driven from the land by Israel and were abhorred as idol worshipers. It is noteworthy, however, that it is not idol worship, but rather an act of social injustice, that is the final straw, precipitating the pronouncement of punishment against Ahab. Upon hearing Elijah's words, Ahab mourns and "humbles himself," rending his garments, dressing in sackcloth, and fasting (standard acts to express mourning, distress, and despair; compare Gen 37:34; 2 Sam 13:31; 2 Kgs 2:12; 5:7; 6:30; 11:14; 18:37; 19:1; 22:11; Job 1:20). This causes Yahweh to proclaim that the disaster that is to befall Ahab's house will occur not during Ahab's lifetime but rather during the lifetime of his son (see 2 Sam 12:13–14; 2 Kgs 9:25–26; 22:11–20).

22:1–40 There is peace between Israel and Aram (1 Kgs 20:31–34) at times, but Aram retains control of Ramoth-gilead (perhaps part of some treaty negotiation). The king of Israel proposes to Jehoshaphat, the king of Judah, that they form a coalition against the king of Aram and retake Ramoth-gilead (a seat of provincial government under Solomon; 1 Kgs 4:13; 2 Kgs 8:28–9:15). Jehoshaphat agrees, and the alliance is formed (compare 2 Kgs 8:18, 26).

While the kings gather at one of Samaria's main threshing floors (arguably a public meeting place; see Gen 50:10; 2 Sam 24:18), Jehoshaphat states that he desires some sort of prophetic confirmation. Four hundred Yahwistic prophets (compare 20:13–43) are summoned, and they prophesy that "Yahweh will give [Ramoth-gilead] into the hand of the king" (verse 6). Nevertheless, Jehoshaphat is suspicious and requests

> **Shalmaneser & Ahab**
>
> *According to his Monolith Inscription, Shalmaneser III met a coalition that consisted of (among others) Irhuleni of Hamat, Hadad-Ezer of Damascus, and Ahab of Israel. This Assyrian text notes that Ahab contributed 10,000 foot soldiers and 2,000 chariots; these are sizeable numbers and reflect the fact that Ahab was a powerful monarch (text in Pritchard 279). The powerful Assyrian King Shalmaneser III made several military campaigns into Syria-Palestine (Cogan 498). During these campaigns he often encountered serious resistance from the local kings. One of the most important of these resulted in the battle of Qarqar (853). The Deuteronomist does not mention the battle of Qarqar or even this important coalition between Aram and Israel. In any case, at some point Ahab's relationship with certain Aramean states (perhaps Damascus) deteriorated, so the Deuteronomist notes that Judah and Israel form an alliance against Aram.*

more prophetic confirmation. The Yahwistic prophet Micaiah ben Imlah is, therefore, summoned. However, Ahab states that he hates Micaiah and anticipates a negative oracle (for which the pious Jehoshaphat rebukes him). During this intervening time, Zedekiah ben Kenaanah makes some iron horns and prophesies in dramatic fashion that the king of Israel will *gore* (as if with horns) the Arameans (compare 1 Kgs 20:23–43). Micaiah then appears and affirms that he will prophesy whatever Yahweh tells him. Initially, he prophesies victory, but it is a ruse, and after some royal prodding, he prophesies the death of the king of Israel.

> **Divine Approval**
>
> *Often within the ancient Near East, kings desired some sort of sign demonstrating that the patron deity (or deities) supported them during a military campaign or a time of national distress (compare 1 Sam 28:3–19 with Saul's seeking out the witch of Endor; 2 Kgs 3:11–19; 19:1–7; 22:11–20). Extispicy, the ritual reading of an organ or organs of a slaughtered animal (see Oates 178–80), was a traditional rite employed for this purpose. Prophetic oracles and omens were also sought at times (compare Ezek 21:21–23; Cogan and Tadmor 45, n. 11; 49, n.3).*

Of course, Micaiah feels compelled to account for the "false prophecy" of Zedekiah; hence, he states that there was a meeting of Yahweh's divine council (Job 1, 2; Smith, *Origins*, 41–53; Rollston, "The Rise of Monotheism," 102–10), and Yahweh himself proposed that some member of the celestial court *entice* Ahab so that he might fall. One of the members of the celestial council then proposed that he himself be a *lying spirit* in the mouth of all the king's prophets. Naturally, Zedekiah considers this to be a frontal assault on him, and he slaps Micaiah, still claiming to be the true prophet of Yahweh. At this juncture, Micaiah is ushered out as a prisoner (with the governor and the king's son serving as the guards), but as he is being taken away, he declares that if the king returns in peace, he has spoken falsely.

During the course of the battle, the Arameans focus on killing the king of Israel, perhaps knowing that he has initiated the formation of the coalition. Nevertheless, Ahab is disguised (while Jehoshaphat of Judah still wears royal robes). Jehoshaphat is pursued for a time, but he cries out (presumably identifying himself), and the Arameans cease pursuit of him. In spite of the ruse, a random arrow strikes Ahab, and he dies at some point as he watches the battle. With Ahab's death in battle and the scattering of Israel's troops (verse 36), the words of Micaiah are fulfilled (verse 17). Moreover, the dogs lick up Ahab's blood, thus fulfilling the words of Elijah (1 Kgs 21:19, but with no mention of prostitutes washing; compare 1 Kgs 14:1–20), although this occurs in Samaria, not Jezreel. The narrative concludes not only with the standard formulas (sources, successor), but also with reference to Ahab's "house of ivory" (see Tappy 2:443–503; Amos 3:15; 6:4). Although Ahab dies a violent death, he receives a proper burial in the capital. One final note must be made regarding this narrative: it is striking that Ahab's name is not mentioned within the narrative proper (at least not until the end). The Deuteronomist may not have been comfortable with the fact that Jehoshaphat formed an alliance with the notorious Ahab, so he refers to him throughout the majority of the narrative as the "king of Israel."

22:41–53 Although the narrative has already summarized an event in the life of Jehoshaphat (as part of its discussion of Ahab's reign), it now focuses on the reign of Jehoshaphat himself (reigns 873–849 BCE), inaugurating the synopsis in the formulaic manner (for example, age, mother's name). The text evaluates his religion approvingly, but notes that the high places were not removed. The text then refers to a war that is recorded in the royal archives. There may be an implication here that Jehoshaphat ruled Edom (verse 47; compare 1 Kgs 9:26–28). Moreover, the text makes a striking reference to Jehoshaphat's building "ships of

Tarshish," but the fleet is reportedly wrecked at Ezion-geber (1 Kgs 9:26–28), much further south than the traditional borders of Judah. Subsequently, Ahaziah, son of Ahab, suggests a joint shipping venture, but Jehoshaphat rejects the offer. The text then concludes with the standard formulas (death, burial, successor).

The narrative now discusses the reign of Ahaziah (850–849 BCE) of Israel in detail, provides the synchronism (with Judean king Jehoshaphat), and notes that Ahaziah reigns only two years in Israel. He is described as *doing evil* in the way of his father and mother (1 Kgs 16:29–22:40) and as walking in the way of Jeroboam I, even worshiping Baal.

THEOLOGICAL REFLECTIONS

The Old Testament is an ancient Hebrew and Aramaic library of documents, with a long and complicated textual history. The books of the Old Testament are not "history" in the modern sense of the term. Rather, these books are ancient religious literature anchored in history. In addition, for ancient Israel and Judah, there was often no clear separation (or delineation) of the sacred and the secular, such as is often made in modern cultures. Modern interpreters often err in biblical interpretation because of the sincere but misguided desire to read the biblical text through a modern interpretive lens. Nonetheless, the books of 1 and 2 Kings do explore religious and theological ideas that deserve our attention.

First, the Old Testament affirms that there was a "covenant" between Yahweh and Israel. This relationship required Israel's complete religious and moral fidelity to Yahweh, with faithfulness bringing a multitude of blessings and faithlessness bringing divine retribution. Second, these books affirm that Yahweh controls all historical events, whether within Israel proper or without. Regardless of the precise context, the books of Kings affirm the magnitude of Yahweh's power. Third, the setting up of cultic sites at Dan and Bethel by Jeroboam I, the first king of the northern kingdom of Israel after its separation from Judah, violated the commandments found in Deuteronomy 12. All of the following kings of Israel were deemed wicked because of the use of cultic sites outside of Jerusalem. Fourth, several of the northern Israelite kings received explicit criticism not only for the worship of Yahweh at a site other than Jerusalem, but also for the worship of other deities and/or for cultic practices associated with the deities of other nations. Those kings who received commendation were those who abolished the high places and made extensive reforms. Fifth, prophets (as well as priests) appear as Yahweh's representatives, even in politics. Prophets, in essence, attempted to call people (high and low) back to the covenant. Within the books of Kings, numerous prophetic voices speak. Sixth, the religions of the southern neighboring states of Moab, Ammon, and Edom were "national god religions" (that is, each nation believed it had a "patron deity"; compare Deut 32:8–9; 1 Kgs 20:23; 2 Kgs 17:8, 29–41; 18:33; 19:10–13; Smith, *Early History*). Yahweh was Israel's God (see, for example, Deut 32:8–9), and it was to Yahweh that Israel was to be faithful, as Yahweh had made a binding covenant relationship with the nation. Finally, the Deuteronomistic History was written in such a way as to presuppose exile (Deut 4:27; Josh 23:13, 16; 1 Sam 12:25; 1 Kgs 8:34, 46; 9:6–9). However, divine forgiveness and mercy stood over against punishment (Deut 4:25–31; 1 Kgs 8:46–53). The author intentionally ended Kings with Jehoiachin's release from prison (2 Kgs 25:27–30), reminiscent of the *lamp* that is promised to remain for David in Jerusalem (2 Sam 7:1–17; 1 Kgs 11:34; 15:4; 2 Kgs 8:19; 19:34; 20:6; 22:2; 25:25, 27–30). For a full discussion of these various elements in 1 and 2 Kings, see the Theological Reflections sections in 2 Kings on page 348.

FOR FURTHER READING

Frank M. Cross, *Canaanite Myth and Hebrew Epic* (Cambridge: Harvard University Press, 1971).

John H. Hayes, *An Introduction to Old Testament Study* (Nashville: Abingdon, 1979).

WORKS CITED

Susan Ackerman, "The Queen Mother and the Cult in Ancient Israel," *Journal of Biblical Literature* 112 (1993): 385–401.

———, *Under Every Green Tree: Popular Religion in Sixth-Century Judah* (Atlanta: Scholars Press, 1992).

Peter M. M. G. Akkermans and Glenn M. Schwartz, *The Archaeology of Syria: From Complex Hunter-Gatherers to Early Urban Societies (ca. 16,000–300 BC)* (Cambridge: Cambridge University Press, 2003).

N. Avigad and Benjamin Sass, *Corpus of West Semitic Stamp Seals* (Jerusalem: Israel Exploration Society, 1997).

Frank L. Benz, *Personal Names in the Phoenician and Punic Inscriptions* (Rome: Biblical Institute, 1972).

Avraham Biran and Joseph Naveh, "The Tel Dan Inscription: A New Fragment," *Israel Exploration Journal* 45 (1995): 2–18.

Joseph Blenkinsopp, *A History of Prophecy in Israel* (Louisville: Westminster John Knox, 1996).

Oded Borowski, *Daily Life in Biblical Times* (Atlanta: Society of Biblical Literature, 2003).

Joachim Braun, *Music in Ancient Israel/Palestine* (Grand Rapids: Eerdmans, 2002).

John Bright, *A History of Israel* (3rd ed.; Philadelphia: Westminster, 1981).

Mordechai Cogan, *1 Kings: A New Translation with Introduction and Commentary* (New York: Doubleday, 2000).

Mordechai Cogan and Hayim Tadmor, *2 Kings: A New Translation with Introduction and Commentary* (New York: Doubleday, 1988).

Dan P. Cole, *Archaeology and Religion* (Washington, D.C.: Biblical Archaeology Society, 1991).

Michael Coogan, *Stories from Ancient Canaan* (Louisville: Westminster, 1978).

James L. Crenshaw, *Old Testament Wisdom: An Introduction* (Louisville: Westminster John Knox, 1998).

Frank M. Cross, "Epigraphic Notes on the Amman Citadel Inscriptions," *Bulletin of the American Schools of Oriental Research* 193 (1969): 13–19.

Israel Eph'al and Joseph Naveh, "Hazael's Booty Inscriptions," *Israel Exploration Journal* 39 (1989): 192–200.

Nili Sacher Fox, *In the Service of the King: Officialdom in Ancient Israel and Judah* (Cincinnati: Hebrew Union College Press, 2000).

Volkmar Fritz, *1 and 2 Kings* (trans. Anselm Hagedorn; Minneapolis, Minn.: Fortress, 2003).

Seymour Gitin, Trude Dothan, and Joseph Naveh, "A Royal Dedicatory Inscription from Ekron," *Israel Exploration Journal* 47 (1997): 1–16.

Alberto R. W. Green, *The Storm-God in the Ancient Near East* (Winona Lake, Ind.: Eisenbrauns, 2003).

Jonas Greenfield, "Ramman/Rimmon," *Israel Exploration Journal* 26 (1976): 195–98.

Hermann Gunkel, *The Folktale in the Old Testament* (trans. Michael D. Rutter; Sheffield: Almond, 1987).

Baruch Halpern, *David's Secret Demons* (Grand Rapids: Eerdmans, 2001).

Othmar Keel, *The Symbolism of the Biblical World: Ancient Near Eastern Iconography and the Psalms* (Winona Lake, Ind.: Eisenbrauns, 1997).

Philip King and Lawrence Stager, *Life in Biblical Israel* (Louisville: Westminster John Knox, 2001).

Miriam Lichtheim, *Ancient Egyptian Literature* (Berkeley, Calif.: University of California Press, 1973).

James M. Lindenberger, *Ancient Aramaic and Hebrew Letters* (2nd ed.; Atlanta: Society of Biblical Literature, 2003).

Amihai Mazar, *Archaeology of the Land of the Bible: 10,000–586 BCE.* (New York: Doubleday, 1992).

William Moran, *Amarna Letters* (Baltimore: Johns Hopkins University Press, 1992).

Joseph Naveh, *Early History of the Alphabet* (2nd ed.; Jerusalem: Magnes, 1987).

———, "Writing and Scripts in Seventh-Century BCE Philistia: The New Evidence from Tell Jemmeh," *Israel Exploration Journal* 35 (1985): 8–21.

Joan Oates, *Babylon* (New York: Thames & Hudson, 1986).

Dennis Pardee, *Handbook of Ancient Hebrew Letters* (Chico, Calif.: Scholars Press, 1982).

Wayne Pitard, *Ancient Damascus* (Winona Lake, Ind.: Eisenbrauns, 1987).

James Pritchard, ed., *Ancient Near Eastern Texts* (Princeton: Princeton University Press, 1969).

Christopher A. Rollston, "Ethbaal," in *Eerdmans Dictionary of the Bible* (Grand Rapids: Eerdmans, 2000), 431.

———, "Mesha," in *Eerdmans Dictionary of the Bible* (Grand Rapids: Eerdmans, 2000), 887–88.

———, "The Rise of Monotheism in Ancient Israel: Biblical and Epigraphic Evidence," *Stone-Campbell Journal* 6 (2003): 95–115.

Martha T. Roth, *Law Collections from Mesopotamia and Asia Minor* (Atlanta: Scholars Press, 1995).

Nahum M. Sarna and Hershel Shanks, "Israel in Egypt: The Egyptian Sojourn and the Exodus," in *Ancient Israel* (rev. ed.; ed. Hershel Shanks; Washington, D.C.: Biblical Archaeology Society, 1999), 33–54.

Mark S. Smith, *The Early History of God: Yahweh and the Other Deities in Ancient Israel* (2nd ed.; Grand Rapids: Eerdmans, 2002).

———, *The Origins of Biblical Monotheism* (New York: Oxford, 2001).

Ronald Tappy, *The Archaeology of Israelite Samaria* (2 vols.; Winona Lake, Ind.: Eisenbrauns, 1992 and 2001).

Edwin R. Thiele, *The Mysterious Numbers of the Hebrew Kings* (Grand Rapids: Zondervan, 1983).

Karel van der Toorn, ed., *Dictionary of Deities and Demons in the Bible* (rev. ed.; Grand Rapids: Eerdmans, 1999).

Andrew G. Vaughn, *Theology, History, and Archaeology in the Chronicler's Account of Hezekiah* (Atlanta: Scholars Press, 1999).

Moshe Weinfeld, *Social Justice in Ancient Israel* (2nd ed.; Jerusalem: Magnes, 2000).

Irene Winter, "Phoenician and North Syrian Ivory Carving in Historical Context: Questions of Style and Distribution," *Iraq* 38 (1976): 1–18.

2 Kings

Christopher A. Rollston & Heather Dana Davis Parker

CHAPTER CONTENTS

Contexts   329

Commentary   329

    Division of the Monarchy & Narratives about Israel & Judah to 722 BCE · 1 Kgs 12:1–2 Kgs 17:41   329

    Narratives about Judah to Its Destruction (587 BCE) & the Assassination of Gedaliah · 2 Kgs 18:1–25:30   342

Theological Reflections   348

For Further Study   351

Works Cited   351

First and Second Kings, originally one continuous work, were derived from numerous sources, including the "Chronicles of Solomon" (1 Kgs 11:41), "the Chronicles of the Kings of Judah" (1 Kgs 14:9; 15:7), and the "Chronicles of the Kings of Israel" (1 Kgs 14:19; 15:31). These "chronicles," or "annals," were apparently the royal records commissioned by the king and his administration (compare Esth 6:1 for a reference to Persian royal records).

CONTEXTS

The author (or perhaps authors) of 1 and 2 Kings, though not explicitly identified, is referred to by scholars as the "Deuteronomist." This term was chosen because the books of Kings and Deuteronomy use similar language and reflect similar theological perspectives. In addition, the "Deuteronomist" is often credited with authoring Joshua, Judges, and the books of Samuel as well. For this reason, Joshua, Judges, Samuel, and Kings are traditionally referred to as the "Deuteronomistic History."

Currently, most scholars believe that the next-to-last version of the "Deuteronomistic History" was produced during the reign of King Josiah (640–609 BCE) and the final version during the Babylonian Exile, that is, during the sixth century BCE. Phrases such as "unto this day," "then," and "at that time" (2 Kgs 8:22; 14:7; 16:5–6; 17:41; 18:16; 20:12; 24:10) actually suggest a time of composition long after the occurrence of the actual events.

Though Kings contains a substantial amount of historical information, it was not intended to be solely a recitation of data. The author(s) did not merely record a string of events, but commented on them, in light of a particular theology. For this reason, Kings cannot be identified as "history"; it is "religious history," or "historical theology."

For a more detailed discussion of the historical and literary contexts of 2 Kings, see the discussion of 1 Kings' contexts on page 309.

COMMENTARY

DIVISION OF THE MONARCHY & NARRATIVES ABOUT ISRAEL & JUDAH TO 722 BCE · 1 KGS 12:1–2 KGS 17:41

1:1–18   Since 1 and 2 Kings originally formed one book, 2 Kings 1:1 constitutes a final statement about the conclusion of Ahab's reign (and opens the reign of his son and successor, Ahaziah): Moab rebelled against Israel after the death of Ahab (see 1 Kgs 16:15–28; 2 Kgs 3:4–27). This same basic material is contained in the Mesha Inscription, but the Mesha Inscription states that this rebellion occurred during the reign of Omri's son Ahab (Rollston, "Mesha").

Ahaziah of Israel falls through the lattice of the palace in Samaria, and he fears that his injuries may be mortal. Rather than inquiring of Yahweh (and thus accepting Yahweh's victory at Carmel), he sends messengers to a Philistine deity said to be *Baal-Zebub* (1 Kgs 14:1–20).

> **Baal-Zebub**
> *The name "Baal-Zebub" would be a very strange name for a deity, for this would mean "lord of flies." However, Baal-Zebul ("Baal the prince") would be an acceptable name for an ancient deity, and indeed it is attested at Ugarit. Moreover, the New Testament actually preserves this name with the term Beelzebul (Matt 10:25; 12:24; Mark 3:22; Luke 11:15). It is also certain that, at times, names of villainous people were turned into insults. For example, detractors of the cruel Antiochus IV Epiphanes ("Antiochus the Divine") sometimes referred to him as Antiochus Epimenes ("Antiochus the Insane").*

Elijah intercepts Ahaziah's messengers, rebukes them for Ahaziah's attempt to inquire of *Baal-Zebub*, and predicts the impending death of Ahaziah. Of course, the messengers return rapidly and inform Ahaziah that a "hairy man with a leather belt" had given them this message (compare Matt 3:4). Based on this description (of the distinctive dress), Ahaziah knows that it must have been Elijah that gave them this message. Ahaziah sends out troops to find Elijah, but they are consumed by fire, a demonstration of God's power and protection of Elijah. Because of instructions from the "angel of Yahweh" (and also because of the deference of the third commander), Elijah receives the commander and goes with him to speak to the king. Elijah's prediction of the king's death comes true, and Jehoram (Ahaziah's brother) succeeds him as king, during the second year of King Jehoram son of Jehoshaphat of Judah. At this juncture, the narrative concludes with the standard statements about sources.

2:1–18 Yahweh is about to take Elijah into heaven in a whirlwind of fire (compare 1 Kgs 19:11–12; 2 Kgs 6:17; 13:14). Elijah and Elisha set out from the site of Gilgal (see Josh 4:7–19) toward the city of Bethel. Elisha vows that he will travel with Elijah, not leaving him as Elijah had instructed. Although it is possible that the "prophetic company" of the biblical texts are "prophetic disciples," or "learners," under a master prophet, this narrative suggests that such groups were capable of discerning future events in a prophetic fashion. In any case, Elijah and Elisha meet a company of prophets who ask Elisha if he is aware of Elijah's impending departure (compare 1 Kgs 20:35–43). Elisha indicates that he is. Elijah and Elisha travel on from Bethel to Jericho, where they encounter another company of prophets (suggesting that there may have been numerous such prophetic bands throughout Israel), and they, too, mention that Elijah is soon to be taken away. Ultimately, Elijah, Elisha, and the company of the prophets from Jericho arrive at the Jordan River. Significantly, the waters part before Elijah (using his rolled mantle as a "staff"), much as the waters of the Yam Suph (Sea of Reeds) had parted before Moses (Exod 14:21–22) and the Jordan River had parted before Joshua (Josh 4:7–17). After crossing, Elijah tells Elisha that he will be happy to "do something" for him, so Elisha requests a *double portion* of Elijah's spirit (analogous to the firstborn receiving a double share of the inheritance; see Deut 21:17; compare Num 11:17, 25). Elisha is told that if he watches Elijah's ascension, his request will be granted. Of course, he does witness it (and cries out *my father, my father*, a traditional term for a teacher) and then picks up Elijah's mantle (a symbol of the transfer of spiritual power). He rends his garments as a sign of mourning (see 1 Kgs 21:27). Then, he parts the waters of the Jordan himself (demonstrating that he is Elijah's true successor, something that the company of the prophets perceives as well; verses 19–22; 1 Kgs 17:1–7; 19:16). At times, prophetic figures would simply be transported to another place (1 Kgs 18:12; *Bel and the Dragon* 33–36; Acts 8:39–40), hence the prophets' desire to search for Elijah.

> **Elijah & Enoch**
> Elijah and Enoch (Gen 5:24) are the two people that the Bible affirms never died. Later Jewish and Christian traditions affirmed that Elijah might return, especially as a precursor to the Messiah's coming (Mal 4:5; 1 Maccabees 2:58; Matt 16:13–14; 17:3–4, 10–13; Mark 8:27–28; 9:4–5, 11–13; Luke 1:17; 9:18–19, 30–33; see also the traditional Jewish Passover Seder, in which a place at the table is traditionally set for Elijah).

2:19–25 Both narratives within this section testify to the power of Elijah and reveal the esteem (and even fear) in which his contemporaries held him. Salt was used for various purposes, but purification of a well was not one of them, which demonstrates the miraculous nature of this narrative. Salt was often associated with curses and destruction (Judg 9:45; "Sefire Treaty" A.36 in Fitzmyer), but it obviously had preservative qualities, as well. This text serves to demonstrate the similarities between Moses and Elisha (Exod 15:23–25; compare verses 13–14). Moreover, Elisha's pronouncement of "no more death or miscarriage" constitutes a reversal of traditional curse terminology. Within the next narrative, Elisha travels to Bethel. Along the way, he curses some children because they insult his

> **Bethel**
> Literally, Bethel means "house of God." A city north of Jerusalem that was the site of a famous sanctuary. Genesis 28 gives a version of the story of its founding as a holy site. Its location at a major crossroads probably enhances its importance.

baldness (see Lev 19:27; 21:5). Two female bears maul forty-two of them (for forty-two as a number associated with religious problems and punishment, see 2 Kgs 10:14; Rev 11:2; 13:5). This chapter concludes with a travelogue, noting that Elisha journeyed from Mount Carmel, and then to the capital city of Samaria to continue serving as a Yahwistic prophetic voice, as had Elijah.

3:1–3 The narrative begins with the customary synchronism, noting that Jehoram son of Ahab began to reign (849–843/2 BCE) during the eighteenth year of Jehoshaphat of Judah and reigned for twelve years. Kings evaluates him in the customary way for his response to the cult of Baal and Israel's high places. He receives credit for attempting to removing his father's Baal pillar (1 Kgs 16:32–33) but criticism for not removing the high places.

> **Synchronisms**
> *Like a few Babylonian chronicles of its time, 1–2 Kings tries to coordinate two historical tracks simultaneously. The biblical books switch back and forth between Israel and Judah. This strategy is difficult to carry out, a fact that partly explains why 1–2 Chronicles abandoned the practice.*

3:4–27 Mesha of Moab, who had been under the rule of Omri, rebels at some point after Omri's death (2 Kgs 1:1; Rollston, "Mesha"). Of course, vassal kings were routinely forced to pay some sort of tribute, and this narrative states that Mesha (as a sheep breeder) paid a large tribute in sheep and wool. However, when he ceases to pay the tribute, Jehoram decides to make a punitive campaign against him, with Jehoshaphat of Judah and the (presumably vassal) king of Edom (see 1 Kgs 9:26–28) assisting him. They choose to travel through Judah around the southern tip of the Dead Sea, into Edom (a place name that derives from a word for "red") and then into Moab (hoping to flank the Moabites, no doubt). The campaign, though, is on the verge of collapse because of a shortage of water, so Jehoshaphat proposes that they inquire of Yahweh (through a prophet; see 1 Kgs 22:1–40). Elisha is in the region (and *he used to pour water on the hands of Elijah*, that is, was Elijah's understudy), and when questioned, he affirms that Yahweh is supportive of the campaign, that the wadi will fill with water (even though no rain will occur in the immediate vicinity), and that a victory will occur against the Moabites. Of course, Elisha's initial retort contains a caustic element: "What have I to do with you, go to your father's prophets or to your mother's" (1 Kgs 18:19; 22:6, 10–12), but Jehoram's reply reveals that he believes that Yahweh has summoned them against Moab. Elisha concedes, but affirms that he does so simply because of Jehoshaphat's piety (1 Kgs 22:8). Striking, though, is the fact that Elisha requests a musician before he begins to convey his message (compare 1 Sam 10:5–6; see Braun 115, 175, 219).

The next morning the wadi (ravine) is full and there are pools of water in the region (wadis are often dry, except during periods of rain). The Moabites, knowing that a confederation of kings opposes them, assume that there must have been a fracture of the coalition, resulting in a battle between the partners, for as the sun shines on the water laden with the reddish soil of the region, the wadi and pools appear red (as if filled with blood). Thus, the Moabites rush the allied camp but are confronted by a large force that drives them back. The coalition makes a concerted effort to destroy Moabite cities, wells, trees, to fill tillable fields with stones (although wreaking such havoc was a breach of Israelite law according to Deut 20:19–20). After the king of Moab determines that he cannot break through the lines of the besieging

> **The Mesha Stele**
> *Also known as the Moabite Stone, this monument was found in the nineteenth century by Bedouin traders who sold it to French scholars. The monument, written about 835 BCE, records Mesha's revolt against Ahab ("Israel has gone to ruin, yea, to ruin forever") and his subsequent building activities ("I have built gates ... the royal palace ... reservoirs").*

> **Human Sacrifice**
> *Human sacrifice was practiced at times in the Near East. It is often argued that human sacrifice was never acceptable in Israel. However, certain biblical texts reveal a more complicated picture, namely, that some good Yahwists offered human sacrifices (see Gen 22; Judg 11:30–31, 39; Mic 6:7), although redemption was also possible (Exod 13:2, 11–26; 34:19–20; Num 3:11–15, 41, 45; 8:17; 18:15; 2 Kgs 23:10). Later this practice was repudiated, and those that practiced were impugned in the strongest terms (Lev 18:21; 20:2–5; Deut 18:10; 2 Kgs 16:3; 17:17; 21:6; 23:10; Jer 7:31; 19:5; 32:35; see Cogan and Tadmor 47, n. 27).*

force of *Kir Hareseth*, he sacrifices his firstborn son on the city wall. After this event, the text notes that "there was a great anger against Israel," with the result that Israel withdrew from the siege. Strikingly, the text does not affirm that this was Yahweh's anger "against Israel." Indeed, it seems that this text (reflecting an ancient view) actually suggests that the Moabite king's act of sacrifice (to the Moabite god Chemosh) resulted in Chemosh directing punitive anger against Israel, ending in their withdrawal (for national gods, see below).

4:1–7 The miracle stories present throughout this chapter demonstrate further that the miraculous power of Elijah had been perpetuated in the person of Elisha (compare the similar miracle in 1 Kgs 17:8–16). This story revolves around the tragic death of a member of the *company of the prophets* (compare 1 Kgs 20:35–43) and the dire financial state of his widow and children. A creditor has arrived to seize the widow's two children as debt slaves. Within ancient Israel, it was legal for a family that was deep in arrears to sell a member of the family into debt slavery (Exod 21:7; Deut 15:12–18; Lev 25:39–46; Jer 34:8–16) as a means of payment. The widow appeals to Elisha, and with his help (and the neighbors' pots), she is able to repay her debts and supports the family for a time.

4:8–37 A wealthy Shunammite woman deduces that Elisha is a *holy man of God* (note that the word "holy" is not normally used of prophets but rather of priests or Nazarites; Exod 19:6; Num 6:5, 8; 16:5) and suggests to her husband that they prepare a room for him on the second floor of their home. Naturally, Elisha feels indebted to this family, so he requests that his servant Gehazi determine the sort of favor that Elisha might do for them, such as speaking a word to the king or commander of the army (revealing the power and access that Elisha possessed). After talking with the woman, Gehazi informs Elisha that she and her husband have no pressing request (all her needs are met by her family or surrounding community). When Elisha presses Gehazi, he mentions that the woman has no child (note the motif of barrenness throughout the biblical corpus: Gen 18:9–15; 30:1–24; Judg 13:2–24; 1 Sam 1:1–28), and her husband is old (and thus she will one day be a widow who has no son to care for her in her old age). For this reason, Elisha speaks with the woman and tells her that she will bear a son within one year.

The second episode reinforces a sense of Elisha's (and Yahweh's) power and benevolence. The husband's questioning of the woman's going to the prophet, as he states that it is neither *the New Moon or the Sabbath*, highlights the traditional days to worship or consult a religious figure. Perhaps he was not yet aware that the child was dead, or perhaps he doubted that the prophet could do anything. The wife, by contrast, trusts Elisha's power enough to travel to Mount Carmel. Gehazi functions in the story as a helper of Elisha and an illustration of the prophet's power, since no surrogate can heal the boy. Only Elisha can. Sneezing here is a sign of returned breath. For the significance of the number seven, see the introduction to 1 Kings. Significantly, this narrative revolves primarily around the woman and the child, and it is the woman who seems to have the stronger relationship with Elisha. In this connection, note that the text begins with the statement that there was a "wealthy Shunammite woman" (2 Kgs 4:8), rather than referring to her husband as wealthy (see 2 Kgs 8:1–6).

4:38–44 Two final miracle stories are contained in this chapter. The first revolves around Elisha's servant's making a pot of stew using poisonous vines and gourds. After one of the company of prophets (1 Kgs 20:35–43), who is eating some of the stew, declares, "there is death in the pot!" Elisha throws some flour in the pot and all eat without harm. The second story revolves around a gift of first fruits (see Lev 2:14; 23:9–20) to Elisha (revealing that not only priests, but also prophets might receive donations from the people). Within the narrative, twenty loaves of barley are given, but it is noted that this is not sufficient to feed a hundred people. Nevertheless, at the behest of Elisha, the bread is distributed, all eat, and there is still some left over (compare Exod 16:1–17:7; Num 11; Matt 14:13–21, 15:32–38; Mark 6:30–44, 8:1–10; Luke 9:10–17). Again, the prophet cares for the needy.

Roofs in Ancient Architecture
Homes in ancient Israel often had flat roofs used for various purposes. Here, the widow proposes to wall off a segment of their roof for Elisha (compare Judg 3:20). For home architecture, see King and Stager 34–35.

5:1–27 Naaman is the commander of the army of the (unnamed) king of Aram (Damascus), and he has been very successful in battle (because Yahweh has given him victory, according to the text). However, this great commander is afflicted with *leprosy*.

> **Leprosy**
> *Within the Hebrew Bible, leprosy is a term used for various skin diseases, not necessarily Hansen's Disease, the form of leprosy best known today. Moreover, Naaman's leprosy was probably not Hansen's Disease, in light of the fact that he was not excluded from interaction with non-lepers (compare Lev 13:46; Num 12:14–16; 2 Kgs 7:3; 15:5).*

A captured Israelite servant girl mentions the powerful prophet in Samaria who can cure Naaman. Therefore, based on this statement, Naaman receives a "letter of recommendation" from the Aramean king and travels to Israel, bearing many gifts (compare 1 Kgs 14:1–20). Nevertheless, the king of Israel (unnamed – perhaps Jehoram; compare 2 Kgs 3:1–3) is concerned (his tearing his clothes being a sign of this; see 1 Kgs 21:27), because he feels the request cannot be met. In addition, he feels that the request may be intentional diplomatic entrapment by the king of Aram. Elisha learns of these events and requests that the king of Israel send Naaman to him. Striking is the fact that Elisha does not receive this important Aramean himself, but rather sends a messenger out to instruct Naaman to dip seven times (for the significance of the number "seven," see the introduction to 1 Kings) in the Jordan. Initially, Naaman is irate (reasoning that the muddy waters of the Jordan River are nothing compared to the great rivers of Aram), but his servants convince him to dip himself in it. Perhaps the author intends to poke fun at the Arameans here. This results in his healing and also in his affirmation of the fact that Yahweh is the only *God in all the world* (verse 15).

Naaman attempts to compensate Elisha generously, but Elisha refuses. Naaman's request for Israelite soil on which to worship reflects a belief that the land of Israel itself is holy (Josh 22:19; 2 Kgs 16:10–12). In addition to this, Naaman makes another striking request: that he not be faulted for standing and kneeling next to the king in the temple of Rimmon (normally Rimmon, "thunder," is an epithet for the storm god Hadad; see Greenfield 195–98), when the king is *leaning on my arm* (a term used to describe Naaman's vocational responsibilities as a chief advisor to the king; compare 2 Kgs 7:2). Elisha tells him to "go in peace," indicating approval of both of these requests.

The appendix to this story faults Gehazi for greed and again emphasizes Elisha's power. On leprosy as a curse, see Numbers 12:10–11; 2 Kings 15:4–5.

6:1–7 Some component of the *company of the prophets* (1 Kgs 20:35–43) states that the "place where we are residing is too small for us." The use here of the Hebrew word translated "reside" could imply that some permanent residential structure had become too small. However, it is also possible to understand this verb to imply that some non-residential meeting place had become too small. That is, this text may or may not imply some sort of communal living arrangements for the prophets. In any case, Elisha concurs that it is acceptable to build a larger facility, and the group cuts timber near the Jordan River (where trees could readily grow because of the moisture in the soil). However, a borrowed ax head falls into the water. Elisha cuts a stick, tosses it into the water, and the ax head floats to the top, where it is retrieved. Again, this story constitutes another demonstration of Elisha's miraculous power.

6:8–6:23 This narrative details some espionage by the king of Israel (unnamed – perhaps Jehoram; see 2 Kgs 3:1–3) against Aram (perhaps during the reign of Ben-Hadad II; compare 1 Kgs 20). In essence, Elisha conveys information about Aramean troop movements, with the result that Israel avoids meeting their army. The king of Aram senses that someone is conveying strategic information and discusses this with his officers. His advisors tell him that Elisha is revealing (apparently clairvoyantly) the information to the king of Israel, with the dubious hyperbole that Elisha knows "even the words that you speak in your bedchamber." The king sends a large contingent of troops to Dothan to seize Elisha. After learning that this contingent has come for him, Elisha tells his attendant that the Aramean troops are surrounded by *horses and chariots of fire* (compare 2 Kgs 2:11–12) in the service of Yahweh (for Yahweh as a warrior, forces against Israel's enemies, see Exod 15:3; Josh 5:13–15; Judg 5:20, and also note that the term "Yahweh Sebaoth" literally means "Yahweh of armies"). When the Arameans approach Elisha's location, he prays that Yahweh might blind them. Elisha then leads them (under false pretenses!) to Samaria (the capital of Israel), and, when there, Elisha petitions Yahweh to open their eyes. Addressing Elisha as *father* (showing deference to the great prophet), the king asks if he should kill the captives. Rather than permitting the king to kill these Arameans, Elisha responds by stating that they should receive sustenance and be allowed to depart (perhaps so that the released captives might laud Israel and its god; see Cogan and Tadmor 75, n. 2, for this practice in the ancient Near East), because they were not captured with *your sword or bow* (see 1 Kgs 20 for the treatment of those captured in battle and under the "ban"). The narrative concludes by stating that, for a time, the Arameans no longer raided the land of Israel.

6:24–7:20 Although there is some respite for Israel for a time, the king of Aram (perhaps Ben-Hadad II) besieges the city of Samaria. Sieges of cities often result in starvation and disease (2 Kgs 18:27; 25:2). During this siege, food becomes so scarce that even a donkey's head (with the donkey being an unclean animal, Deut 14:3–8) and dove's dung (for fuel; see Ezek 14:3–8) are garnering substantial sums. Cannibalism is also practiced. For example, one woman comes to the king seeking "justice" (see 1 Kgs 3:9–12, 16–28) against another woman; however, her "case" is horrific, as her complaint is that the other woman has reneged on her promise to kill her son so that the two of them can consume him (see Lam 2:20; 4:10; Ezek 5:10 on cannibalism; see also Fritz 269; Cogan and Tadmor 79, n. 25, for the dire situation during Assurbanipal's siege of Babylon in 650 BCE). Upon hearing this complaint, the king rends his garments in despair (exposing his sackcloth; see 1 Kgs 21:27) and vows that the Yahwistic prophet Elisha must be beheaded (as the king believes this siege is of Yahweh; compare Deut 28:53–57 for a siege's resulting in cannibalism as a curse from Yahweh; however, this text names no specific sin as precipitating the siege).

Elisha, though, is aware of the king's intent and tells the elders with him to bar the door (apparently the elders, like the company of the prophets [see 1 Kgs 20:35–43], could go to Elisha for counsel), as the "son of a murderer" (perhaps a term for an executioner, but maybe just an insult; compare 1 Sam 20:30) wishes to take off his head. The king, preceded by his messenger, comes to the house and accuses Yahweh of bringing this calamity upon Israel. Elisha responds, however, by stating that within one day, the siege will be lifted and there will be an abundance of food (this is to function as a sign for the king, whose faith in Yahweh, by his own admission, is wavering). After hearing Elisha's words, the captain ("on whose hand the king leaned"; as in 2 Kgs 5:18) disbelieves. Elisha, therefore, says that the captain will see the fulfillment of the prophecy but will not live to eat the food.

The narrative now turns to the conversations and actions of four lepers. They are residing outside the city wall (see 2 Kgs 5:1 on lepers) and determine to travel to the Aramean camp, with the hope that the Aramean soldiers will feed them. They find the camp abandoned, because God caused the Arameans to "hear the sound of a great army" coming, so they assumed that powerful Anatolian or Egyptian rulers (the term in Hebrew is *mtsrym*, which could be *Mitsrayim* [Egypt] or *Mutsrim*, an area in northern Syria) were coming to attack them. After gathering food and plunder, the lepers decide to tell the king and his officials. Naturally, the king believes that it could be a ruse, but he permits a small contingent of soldiers to reconnoiter. Upon determining that the Arameans had indeed fled, the people of Samaria gather plunder, thus fulfilling Elisha's words about the abundance of food (for similar low prices after a siege, see the text in Pritchard 299). The captain who had doubted that deliverance would come is trampled at the gate, fulfilling Elisha's words about him (compare Deut 18:19).

Alliances
Small nations often paid larger nations to help them in times of war. See 2 Samuel 10:6 and Isaiah 7:20. Kilamuwa, king of the nation of Samal at about this time, paid Assyria for just such an intervention.

8:1–6 Elisha instructs the Shunammite woman, whose son he had raised from the dead (2 Kgs 4:8–37), to leave the land of Israel because of the coming famine (compare Gen 12:10; 26:1; Ruth 1:1), which is to be of seven years' duration (as in Gen 41; see also Pritchard 31–32 for a seven-year famine in Egypt). She flees to the land of the

Philistines along the Mediterranean coast (with important cities such as Gaza, Ashkelon, Ashdod, Ekron, Gath, and Timnah) and then decides to return to her ancestral estate in Israel. However, someone (perhaps a neighbor, caretaker, or royal official) has laid claim to her land, so she decides to appeal to the king for justice (see 1 Kgs 3:9–12, 16–28; Weinfeld 45–56). At this time, the king of Israel (unnamed – perhaps Jehoram, compare 2 Kgs 3:1–3) requests that Gehazi (perhaps still leprous?) recount the great deeds of Elisha. As Gehazi is relating the miracle of Elisha's raising a child from the dead, the woman appears before the king to articulate her claim. Of course, Gehazi recognizes the woman, and she tells her story to the king. Immediately, therefore, the king appoints an official to restore her land plus revenue derived from the field during her absence. Significantly, the woman is a strong character here (as in 2 Kgs 4:8–37), and it is she (not her husband) who appeals to the king for her land (perhaps, however, her husband is now dead; see 2 Kgs 4:14).

8:7–15 Elijah had been commanded to anoint Hazael as king of Aram (1 Kgs 19:15–16; compare 1 Kgs 1:39), but he was not able to fulfill this command. This narrative, however, affirms that Hazael will indeed be king as the result of an assassination. Elisha travels to Damascus (in Aram). The king of Aram (probably Ben-Hadad II; see 1 Kgs 20) is very ill, and because of his respect for Elisha's reputation, he asks Hazael (one of his high officials) to inquire about a potential recovery (compare 1 Kgs 14:1–20). This story also reaffirms that Yahweh's power cannot be confined to the borders of Israel. The term *your son* is not to be taken literally.

Elisha instructs Hazael to lie to Ben-Hadad, saying, *you will certainly recover*, though Ben-Hadad actually will die. The prophet Elisha, though, begins to weep (after one of them stares intently at the other, although it is not possible to discern who is doing the staring) and then states that Hazael will become king and then pillage and kill in Israel, engaging in a most cruel form of warfare (compare 1 Kgs 9:15–17; 2 Kgs 10:32–33; 12:17–13:7). Hazael rebuffs these statements at first (using the term *dog* of himself, a traditional ancient Near Eastern term signifying inferior status; see the Amarna Letters in Moran 132–33 and Lindenberger 2:125, 127–29 for a reference in one of the Lachish Letters), but subsequently returns to Ben-Hadad's palace and suffocates him. Assyrian inscriptions refer to Hazael as a "son of nobody," that is, a usurper (in Pritchard 280). The story emphasizes Yahweh's control of politics.

8:16–29 The text begins with a synchronism, affirming that Jehoram (or Joram) of Judah (reigned 849–843 BCE) begins to reign during the fifth year of Jehoram (or Joram) of Israel. The reason for the indictment *he walked in the way of the kings of Israel* is that he had married the daughter of Ahab (compare 1 Kgs 22:4) and Jezebel, the princess Athaliah (see 1 Kgs 15:13; 2 Kgs 11:1–16). However, the text also affirms that Yahweh did not destroy Judah because of the promise to "give a lamp" (1 Kgs 11:36) to David and his descendants. Edom revolts (for it was a vassal) at this time and establishes a monarchy (see 1 Kgs 9:26–28), and, although Jehoram of Judah attempts to regain control, his army loses. The prominent city of Libnah, which had been Judean at times, also revolts (Josh 21:13; 2 Kgs 19:8; 23:31; 24:18). The traditional formulaic statements summarize Jehoram's reign.

Ahaziah (843/2 BCE) son of Jehoram succeeds his father as king of Judah, and the synchronism places his reign in the twelfth year of Jehoram (Joram) of Israel (but see 2 Kgs 9:29). As is customary, his age at ascension is given, along with the duration of his reign (one year). He, too, walked in the ways of his grandfather Ahab (1 Kgs 16:29–22:40). At one point, Ahaziah accompanies Jehoram of Israel to wage war against Hazael of Aram at the border town of Ramoth-gilead (note the shortened form *Ramoth* of verse 29; also 1 Kgs 22:1–36). However, Jehoram is wounded in the battle. During a period of recovery in Jezreel (see 1 Kgs 18:45), Ahaziah of Judah travels to visit him.

9:1–13 Jehoram (Joram) of Israel is reigning, but Elisha tells a member of the company of the prophets (see 1 Kgs 20:35–43) to prepare to travel (carrying olive oil for anointing, as in 1 Kgs 1:39) to Ramoth-gilead (1 Kgs 22:1–36; 2 Kgs 8:28) to anoint Jehu, a commander in the army, as the new king of Israel (and then to depart immediately, as those loyal to Jehoram would understand this as participation in a coup). The young prophet is able to find Jehu in the company of other commanders, and he anoints him, stating that he should annihilate *every last male* of the house of Ahab, as had happened to the dynasties of Baasha and Jeroboam (including the Phoenician princess Jezebel, in fulfillment of Elijah's prediction; see 1 Kgs 14:1–20; 16:1–4, 11; 21:19–29; 22:37). After Jehu returns to the group of commanders, they ask him what the *madman* (on the term, see Jer 29:26; Hos 9:7; compare 1 Kgs 11:26–40) said, but Jehu deflects the query by characterizing the actions of such prophets as strange. They press him, though, and he then confides in them that the prophet has anointed him as king of Israel (reigned 843/2–815 BCE). Immediately, the commanders affirm his kingship and their loyalty to him (see 1 Kgs 1:31).

9:14–29 After the anointing, Jehu travels to Jezreel. Note his request that no one convey news of the anointing in Jezreel, lest Jehoram have advanced warning of the impending coup détat. Both Jehoram of Israel and Ahaziah of Judah are in the city of Jezreel (the latter having gone there to see about the former's recovery; see 2 Kgs 8:29). The sentinels see a company of soldiers approaching, and two horsemen investigate. However, when both men fall in behind Jehu (after Jehu implies that they are serving a bloody regime), Jehoram and Ahaziah go out to meet him. Immediately they deduce that he has not come for peaceful purposes (and he accuses them of following the religious practices of Jezebel; see Exod 34:16; Lev 17:7; Deut 31:16; 1 Kgs 16:31–33; 18:1–19:18; Hos 1:2), so they attempt to flee. Jehu, in an act of poetic justice, casts the unburied body of Jehoram onto Naboth's land (see 1 Kgs 21), but Ahaziah manages to flee, first to the city of Megiddo (still in the territory of the northern kingdom; but see 2 Chron 22:9). Upon his death, Ahaziah's body is transported to the city of Jerusalem for burial in the royal tomb complex. Jehu kills Ahaziah in addition to Jehoram, although there had been no prophetic instruction to do so. (Compare 2 Kgs 8:25 with verse 29, concerning the religious irregularities of Jehoram's and Ahaziah's reigns.)

9:30–37 After eliminating Jehoram and Ahaziah, Jehu rides into the city of Jezreel. Jezebel, having heard of the recent events, paints her eyes and adorns her head (perhaps with the hope of seducing the new king, but more likely in preparation for death and burial). Ultimately sensing that Jehu comes solely with violent intent, she calls out to him, referring to him as Zimri, perhaps now a watchword for a disloyal royal assassin (compare 1 Kgs 16:8–14). Jehu calls out to the eunuchs attending her (to ensure sexual purity, eunuchs often attended royal women – 2 Kgs 23:11; Fritz 287), and in response to his request, they throw her down to her death. This action fulfills the gruesome words of prophecy of Elijah and Elisha (verses 8–29; 1 Kgs 14:1–20; 21:19–29; 22:37; 2 Kgs 10:1–17). Interestingly, Jehu states that, because Jezebel is a king's daughter, her remains should be buried.

10:1–17 The narrative asserts that Ahab had *seventy sons* in Samaria (*seventy* is a round number, not necessarily to be taken literally; see Judg 9:5; 12:14). Jehu is intent on ruling as the sole king of Israel. Therefore, he tells the nobles of Samaria (and Jezreel) to select a king who will replace Jehoram (from among Jehoram's sons) so that he might engage the new king's troops in battle (and thus win a complete victory). However, the leaders send Jehu a letter stating that they will be loyal to him. Jehu sends them a second letter requesting that they take the *heads* (the Hebrew makes a pun on two meanings of the word: high official or the body part) of their master's sons and bring them to Jezreel. When the nobles fulfill this request, Jehu affirms that the people of Samaria have no legal liability in this matter (verse 9). Moreover, he states that this is all in fulfillment of Elijah's prophecy (1 Kgs 19:15–18; 21:17–24; compare 1 Kgs 14:1–20; 22:37; 2 Kgs 9:7–10:17). Note that the purge of Omrides (the descendants of Omri, the father of Ahab) extends not only to family but also to close friends who were political and religious leaders. Indeed, Jehu even kills 42 (compare 2 Kgs 2:24) relatives of Ahaziah of Judah as well (for the queen mother, see 1 Kgs 15:13). Note that subsequent prophetic critique of Jehu demonstrates that his extensive purge exceeded the prophetic directives

---

The Tel Dan Inscription

The Tel Dan Inscription was arguably commissioned by Hazael of Aram (see Biran and Naveh 2–18 and Eph'al and Naveh 192–200). Within this inscription, Hazael arguably claims to have killed Jehoram of Israel and Ahaziah of Judah (though the text is partially broken). Based on this evidence, it is possible that Jehu of Israel and Hazael of Aram had formed an alliance, the purpose of which was to put Jehu on the throne of Israel (1 Kgs 19:17). Naturally, this would have been attractive to Hazael, who was frequently at war with both Jehoram and Ahaziah.

he had received (Hos 1:4–5). In any case, in this purge, he has the support of Jehonadab, a powerful Rechabite, whose lineage is well known for its asceticism and repudiation of everything related to the cults of Canaan (see Jer 35).

10:18–31 After sending notification throughout the kingdom to announce the event, Jehu gathers all of the worshipers of Baal under the pretext of a great sacrifice to Baal. Upon entering the temple of Baal, they begin to offer sacrifices. After the sacrificial worship concludes, Jehu summons 80 armed men to kill all of the worshipers. In addition, they burn the pillar (2 Kgs 3:2) of Baal (and the entire area becomes a latrine and public dump). Jehonadab is, of course, at Jehu's side. The text concludes with a promise from Yahweh to Jehu's descendants, and then with a succeeding statement affirming that he did not follow the law of Yahweh.

> **Cultic Sites**
> *Jehu wiped out Baal worship, but also continued in the sins of Jeroboam I (with cult sites at Dan and Bethel, rather than just at Jerusalem). The Bible thus tacitly admits that Jeroboam's cult sites were Yahwistic. The Deuteronomist rejected them, because he rejected all worship centers other than Jerusalem, whether or not Yahweh was worshiped there.*

10:32–36 Although there was an alliance between Hazael and Jehu at one point, there must have been a fracturing of the relationship, as Hazael seized portions of Israel in fulfillment of Elisha's prophecy (1 Kgs 19:15–17; 2 Kgs 8:7–15; 12:17–13:7). The text concludes in the standard formulaic fashion, referring to sources, burial, and successor, as well as to duration of reign. There is also a tantalizing reference to "all his power" (verse 34). Significantly, a famous monumental Assyrian inscription referred to as "The Black Obelisk of Shalmaneser III" credits the subjugation of the northern kingdom of Israel to Shalmaneser and actually depicts Jehu prostrating himself at the feet of this Assyrian king. The biblical text does not even refer to this event, a striking omission (Pritchard 280–81). The Black Obelisk also refers to Jehu as the son of Omri. Technically, this is an historical error; however, it may just reflect the fact that, for centuries, the Assyrians considered the Omride Dynasty to be the royal family of Israel.

11:1–21 After the death of Ahaziah of Judah, Athaliah (the wife of the late King Jehoram and the mother of Ahaziah; 1 Kgs 15:13; 2 Kgs 8:26) decides to seize the throne and kill all family members who might contest her queenship. She reigns 842–837 BCE. However, Jehosheba (the daughter of King Jehoram, probably by a different wife) takes Jehoash (or Joash) son of Ahaziah and hides him for some six years from Athaliah. When Jehoash is seven years old, the priest Jehoiada (whose wife was Jehosheba, according to 2 Chron 22:11) orchestrates a heavily guarded coronation ceremony and proclaims Jehoash king (reigned about 837–800 BCE; see 1 Kgs 1:31, 39). Note that the text mentions putting *the crown on him* and giving him *the covenant* (the Hebrew word translated *covenant* could be a reference to the book of the law or to some sort of royal adornment; see 2 Sam 1:10). For the ceremony, spears and shields that had belonged to King David's administration are used (perhaps because there was a shortage of weaponry but perhaps as a public display of the new king's connection to the founding monarch of the dynasty; 2 Sam 8:7; 1 Kgs 11:12). Athaliah hears the commotion, sees the king standing by a pillar (1 Kgs 7:15–22; 2 Kgs 23:3), realizes the nature of the activities, tears her clothes (1 Kgs 21:27), and shouts *treason*. Then, Athaliah is brought out and taken to the king's house and killed.

Jehoiada the priest makes a covenant among Yahweh, the king, and the people (see 1 Kgs 2:1–12). This covenant renewal ceremony may have been considered necessary as some sort of reaffirmation of Yahweh's covenant with the people and the dynasty (something precipitated because of the unorthodox religion that is assumed to have marked Athaliah's reign, even though her name is Yahwistic, meaning "Yahweh has declared his eminence"). The *people of the land* is often understood to be a term for ordinary people, but because they often appear at coronations, especially after assassinations or an interregnum, the term could also refer to some sort of elite class (2 Kgs 14:21; 21:24; 23:30). In any case, they tear down the temple of Baal and destroy various components of

> **Carites**
> *It is significant that the* Carites, *a non-Israelite group (likely of Aegean origin, perhaps to be identified with the Cherethites that seem to have functioned as hired mercenaries, as in 2 Sam 20:23) appear among those serving as guards at the coronation of Joash.*

the cult. In addition, they kill Mattan, a priest of Baal (2 Kgs 8:18, 26–27), and, as a security measure to prevent retaliation, Jehoiada posts guards at the temple of Yahweh. Note that the Chronicler eliminates all reference to these foreigners (2 Chron 23). Under this heavy guard, the king takes the throne, and all the people rejoice at the conclusion of Athaliah's reign. The text does not summarize her reign in the traditional formulaic manner, an indication that it was not viewed as legitimate.

12:1–16 The reign of Jehoash is reported to have been *forty years* (a round number often found in the Old Testament), and his mother's name and city of origin are mentioned. He is credited with doing that which was right, because of the influence of the priest Jehoiada, though he failed to remove the *high places*.

Jehoash instructs the priests to collect required monies (Exod 30:11–16; Lev 27:1–8) from those coming to worship and then commissions needed repairs for the temple (2 Kgs 22:4–7). However, no repairs are made, even as late as the twenty-third year of Jehoash's reign (though money has been collected). Therefore, Jehoash instructs the priests not to collect any more money. The priests agree, but still no repairs are made. Jehoash, therefore, makes alternate arrangements to raise funds. Namely, he places a chest, with a hole in its lid, by the entrance to the temple (near the altar of incense), so that people can make donations. Significantly, when the chest needs to be emptied, the king's scribe and the high priest collect and count the money together (so as to ensure that the money is indeed spent as intended). The same sort of practice is attested to in Mesopotamia (Cogan and Tadmor 138, n. 11). The funds go directly to those executing the repairs (carpenters, masons, stonecutters, etc.), and these artisans carry out the work without being required to give a precise accounting of expenditures. Curiously, no money is allocated for the reacquisition of some of the cultic utensils (perhaps lost during a previous reign), and none of the money can be melted down and made into cultic utensils. The narrative concludes with a statement that the priests continued to receive money from various offerings brought to the temple. Significantly, the narrative portrays Jehoash positively, while some suspicion falls upon the priests. In contrast, however, Chronicles praises the priests that are lauded for piety, while Jehoash becomes an apostate of sorts (2 Chron 24).

12:17–21 Hazael of Aram (1 Kgs 19:15–17; 2 Kgs 8:7–15; 10:32–33; 13:3–7) makes a successful raid against the Philistine city of Gath, and Jehoash deduces that he will soon raid Judah. Therefore, Jehoash sends numerous precious royal commodities to Hazael, with the result that Hazael lifts his siege of Jerusalem (1 Kgs 15:18). The narrative then concludes with formulaic references to sources and successor; however, because Jehoash is assassinated, various details appear about the place of the assassination and the names of the assassins.

13:1–9 The synchronism states that in the twenty-third year of King Jehoash (or Joash) of Judah, Jehoahaz son of Jehu (reigned 815–802 BCE) began to reign in Israel (Samaria). The text notes duration of his reign and his imitation of the sins of Jeroboam I. For this reason, Yahweh gives him into the hands of Hazael of Aram (1 Kgs 19:15–17; 2 Kgs 8:7–15; 10:32–33; 12:17–21) and then into the hands of Hazael's son Ben-Hadad. However, after Jehoahaz entreats Yahweh, Yahweh raises up an unidentified savior for Israel (Judg 2:11–23), permitting the Israelites to return to their homes. Nevertheless, the people continue to engage in the "sins of Jeroboam" (for a description of these sins and for the Asherah pole, see above), and the military strength of Israel is depleted. The narrative contains the traditional formulaic summary of the reign of Jehoahaz, with reference to burial and successor.

> **Ben-Hadad III**
> Ben-Hadad III, *referred to in the "Zakkur Inscription," is also to be identified with the "Mari" of the inscriptions of the Assyrian ruler Adad-Nirari III; see Pritchard 281–82 and 1 Kings 15:9–24.*

13:10–13 The narrative begins with the traditional synchronism, citing the reign of Jehoash (or Joash) of Israel (802–786 BCE), son of Jehoahaz, as beginning in the thirty-seventh year of Joash of Judah. There is reference to his perpetuating the *sins of Jeroboam*. The narrative concludes with references to his battles with Amaziah of Judah (2 Kgs 14:1–14) and to sources, burial, and successor (Jeroboam II; 2 Kgs 14:15, 23–29).

13:14–21 With Elisha's death imminent, Jehoash (Joash) of Israel visits him, weeping and referring to him as *my father* (showing reverence and respect) and mentioning the *chariots and* *horsemen of Israel* (see 2 Kgs 2:12). Elisha instructs the king to shoot a victory arrow eastward out of the window. Jehoash complies. Then Elisha tells him to strike the remaining arrows against the ground. Jehoash does so, but only three times (for the number "three," see the introduction to 1 Kings). Elisha is disturbed, because the number of strikes is to determine the number of victories Jehoash will win against Aram (1 Kgs 20:35–43). After the death of Elisha, during the burial of an Israelite man, a group of raiding Moabites approaches them (1 Kgs 16:15–28) in the spring of the year (1 Kgs 20:22). Because the Israelites wish to avoid detection, those attending the funeral take the body and throw it into the grave of Elisha. However, after touching the bones of Elisha, the man comes to life, thus demonstrating Elisha's miraculous power, even after death.

13:22–25 The text notes that Hazael oppressed Israel throughout his reign, but Yahweh was gracious to Israel and would neither destroy it nor banish the people. The basis for this mercy is the promises to the patriarchs (Gen 15:1–21; 26:23–25; 28:10–22; 2 Sam 7:1–17). Finally, the text concludes by stating that Jehoash of Israel was successful in battles against Aram three times, just as had been predicted (verse 19).

> **Kings of Aram & Damascus**
> *The Bible and scattered texts from Assyria or Aram itself give the names of several kings of Damascus. These include Hadad-ezer (tenth century), Ben-Hadad I (ninth century), Tab-Rimmon, or Ben-Hadad II (ninth century), Hazael (843–797 BCE), Ben-Hadad III (or II) (797–?), Hadianu (mid-eighth century), and Rezin (730s). The kingdom fell to the Assyrians in the last third of the eight century BCE.*

14:1–22 The narrative begins with the traditional synchronism, with the rise of Amaziah (son of Jehoash) of Judah (reigned 800–783 BCE) to the throne corresponding with the second year of Jehoash (Joash) of Israel. Information about Amaziah's age at the time of his ascension to the throne, the duration of his reign, and his mother's name is also provided. He is critiqued for not removing the high places, although the text notes that he generally *did what was right in the eyes of Yahweh* (essentially doing as his father Joash had done; 2 Kgs 12). Because his father had been assassinated (2 Kgs 12:20–21), Amaziah first secures the throne and then kills his father's conspirators. The children of the conspirators, however, are not killed, in keeping with certain legal directives (Deut 24:16). In addition, he kills *ten thousand Edomites* (a round and aggrandizing but not necessarily literal number; see 1 Kgs 9:26–28) in the region of the Dead Sea. He names the area Joktheel.

After his successful campaign against the Edomites, Amaziah sends a provocative message to Jehoash (Joash) of Israel, attempting to provoke him to war. King Jehoash, however, rebuffs Amaziah, citing a proverb that implies that Amaziah of Judah (the *thistle*) hardly has the capacity to interact in any fashion with the northern kingdom of Israel (a stately *cedar*). Nevertheless, Amaziah refuses to desist (perhaps assuming that the northern kingdom has grown weak during its constant warfare with the Arameans; see 2 Kgs 13:3–8, 22–25). Thus Judah and Israel engage in battle. Judah is soundly defeated, resulting in the capture of Amaziah, the breaching of the wall of Jerusalem from the Ephraim Gate to the Corner Gate, the plundering of the temple and palace in Jerusalem, and the taking of Judean hostages. The narrative then concludes with the formulaic summary of Jehoash of Israel's reign, with references to sources, burial, and successor (Jeroboam II; 2 Kgs 13:12–13). In addition, there is also a formulaic summary of the reign of Amaziah of Judah, with a notation that Amaziah continued to reign for some fifteen years after the death of Jehoash of Israel. References are given to sources, to a conspiracy against Amaziah that spread from Jerusalem to Lachish (a fortified royal city near Jerusalem; 2 Kgs 18:14; 19:8; 24:8; 25:22–26; Mazar 384–89), to his burial in Jerusalem, and to his successor. Note that there is also reference to the restoration of the seaport city of Elat, something that was made possible by Judah's subjugation of Edom (see verse 7; 1 Kgs 9:26–28).

14:23–29 This narrative begins with the traditional synchronism for Jeroboam II (reigned 786–746 BCE; see 1 Kgs 12:20–24), son of Jehoash (Joash) of Israel. He is reported to have reigned some forty-one years (longer than any other king of Israel) and to have walked in the ways of Jeroboam I. He is credited with restoring Israelite territory (after a period of weakness, verse 26) from

Lebohamat in the north to the *Sea of the Arabah* (the Dead Sea; compare the purported extent of Israel's territory during the reign of Solomon, 1 Kgs 8:65). The fact that Jeroboam II is said to have ruled as far south as the Dead Sea suggests that he ruled much of the territory of Judah. Significantly, although Assyria had been powerful throughout much of the ninth century (1 Kgs 22; 1–20; 2 Kgs 10:32–36), during the first half of the eighth century Assyria was weak, creating a power vacuum and thus an opportunity for the south Syrian states (such as Israel) to vie for power.

The text notes that this fulfilled the words of the prophet Jonah the son of Amittai, but there is no reference to this particular prophecy either in that book or in this text. The narrator feels compelled to account for the expansion of Israel's borders and wealth (for a critique of Israel's social injustice in the face of opulence, see Amos 3:15–4:1; 6:4, 14) during the reign of a "wicked king." Yahweh had not said that he would completely blot out Israel, and also the narrator asserts that Yahweh saw the distress of Israel (and so decided to show mercy in spite of sin). The text concludes in the traditional manner, with reference to sources, burial, and successor. Note that there is reference to Jeroboam's "recovering" the important Aramean cities of Damascus and Hamath, as well. However, the Hebrew text appears to be corrupt at this point, and so the precise reading of this verse (and its reference to Hamath and Damascus) is in dispute.

> **The Megiddo Seal**
> *Archaeologists have found a seal at Megiddo that bears the following inscription: "Belonging to Shema, Servant of Jeroboam" (Avigad and Sass 49–50). Although some have attempted to argue that this seal belonged to a servant of Jeroboam I, the script demonstrates that it must be associated with Jeroboam II.*

15:1–38 Azariah (or Uzziah; compare verses 13, 32; Isa 1:1; 6:1) of Judah (reigned 783–742 BCE) is reported to have begun to reign during the twenty-seventh year of Jeroboam II. The customary references to his age, mother's name, and duration of reign are given. Notably, he is said to have had leprosy and not to have lived in the royal palace (2 Kgs 5:1). Chronicles considers his leprosy to have resulted from his attempt to offer sacrifices (2 Chron 26:16–23; but see 1 Kgs 3:4; on leprosy as a curse, see 2 Kgs 5:27). The text notes that Azariah's son, Jotham, functioned in certain royal capacities, probably as regent (verses 32–38), and then summarizes Azariah's reign in the traditional manner (sources, burial, successor). Jotham's reign (742–735 BCE) is described briefly (verses 32–38), with reference to his age at ascension, the duration of his reign, and his mother's name. Significantly, he is reported to have done that which was *right in the eyes of Yahweh, just as his father Uzziah had done*. However, he is impugned for not removing the high places. It is important to note that he is credited with some public works (verse 35) in the area of the temple. Moreover, the narrative notes that Rezin of Syria (reigned about 740–732 BCE) and Pekah of Israel (736–732 BCE) made military campaigns into the Judean territory of Jotham. His reign is summarized in the traditional manner, with reference to sources, burial, and successor (his son Ahaz).

A primary focus of this chapter is the rise and demise of various kings in the northern kingdom of Israel. The text recounts the reign of Zechariah (reigned 746–745 BCE) the son of Jeroboam II, his evil acts, and his assassination by Shallum. The Deuteronomist affirms that with Zechariah's death, the dynasty of Jehu concluded, just as had been prophesied (2 Kgs 10:30). Shallum is reported to have reigned for one month, and then he was assassinated by Menahem, a cruel ruler who sacked the city of Tiphsah and ripped open the wombs of pregnant women (2 Kgs 8:12; compare Hos 13:16; Amos 1:13). Menahem is reported to have reigned for ten years (745–737 BCE). Significantly, Tiglath-Pileser III (745–727 BCE) of Assyria (sometimes referred to as *Pul*) made a raid on Israel (about 738 BCE) during Menahem's reign, mandating the payment of heavy tribute, something also recorded in the Assyrian inscriptions of Tiglath-Pileser III (in Pritchard 283). Menahem died and was succeeded by his son. Pekahiah (737–736 BCE) son of Menahem reigned two years, did *evil*, and then was killed in a conspiracy by his general, Pekah. The Deuteronomist notes that, during Pekah's reign (736–732 BCE), Tiglath-Pileser III made another campaign into the region. This precipitated a palace coup détat orchestrated by Hoshea (732–724 BCE). Significantly, Tiglath-Pileser III claims to have placed Hoshea (compare 2 Kgs 17:1) on the throne of Israel after Pekah's assassination (Pritchard 284) and deported a portion of the population (verse 29). This chapter reflects the social and political chaos present during the final years of the northern kingdom, with repeated bloody revolutions being the norm.

16:1–20 Ahaz of Judah (reigned 735–715 BCE) came to the throne during the seventeenth year of Pekah of Israel. He is reported to have *walked in the ways of the kings of Israel*. The Deuteronomist refers to the various cultic practices performed by Ahaz, including the sacrifice of his son as a burnt offering (compare 2 Kgs 3:27) and the sacrificing of offerings on the high places, on hills, and under every green tree. It is possible that the severe critique of Ahaz was, in part, a reflection of the Deuteronomist's disappointment at his alliance with Assyria (Isa 7).

Certain aspects of the Syro-Ephraimite War (735–734 BCE) are narrated here in some detail (see Isa 7:1–8:10). In essence, the setting for this war is as follows: Rezin of Syria and Pekah of Israel (2 Kgs 15:25–37) are concerned about the growing might of Assyria under Tiglath-pileser III (745–727 BCE) and have formed a coalition to resist him. However, Ahaz of Judah refuses to become part of this futile coalition (hence, Rezin and Pekah's desire to replace Ahaz with a puppet king, namely the son of Tabeel; Isa 7:6), and actually sends messengers to Tiglath-pileser III, affirming that he is willing to be his vassal (this would necessitate Tiglath-pileser's protection of Ahaz). Of course, Ahaz's decision to appeal to Assyria for help is an indication of Judah's relative weakness, as is also the fact that the Edomites are able to rebel against Judah (as in 1 Kgs 9:26–28). To seal the relationship, Ahaz sends precious items from the temple treasury (as an initial payment) to Tiglath-pileser III (compare 1 Kgs 15:18). Of course, Tiglath-pileser is willing to accept Judah as a vassal (giving Assyria a strong foothold in the region). Consequently, he travels to Damascus, sacks it (in 732 BCE), kills Rezin, and deports the residents of Damascus to Kir (Pitard 187–88; Cogan and Tadmor 191; see 2 Kgs 17).

> **The Iran Stele**
> Tiglath-pileser III mentions in his inscription, called the "Iran Stele," that he took tribute from "Rezin the Damascene, Menachem the Samarian," including precious metals, elephant hides, ivory, and beautiful clothing.

To symbolize his fidelity and gratitude, Ahaz goes to Damascus and meets with Tiglath-pileser III. Following this meeting, Ahaz commissions the Judean priest Uriah (Isa 8:2) to replicate the (arguably Assyrian style) altar that he had seen in Damascus. Ahaz goes up on the altar (compare Exod 20:26), offers sacrifices (1 Kgs 3:4), and commands Uriah to offer sacrifices upon this altar as well. The frames of the stand, laver, sea, and bronze oxen (1 Kgs 7:23–37) are removed "because of" (that is, "given to") the king of Assyria. The bronze altar is retained (but moved), with Ahaz affirming that he will use this altar to inquire of God. For the *royal entryway* of the king, see the Amman Citadel Inscription (Cross, "Amman Citadel," 13–19). The precise meaning of the "covered portal for use on the Sabbath" is unclear. This narrative concludes in the traditional manner, referring to sources, burial, and successor.

17:1–6 The narrative begins with the standard synchronism and formulaic statements, formally introducing Hoshea (732–724 BCE) as the new king of Israel (compare 2 Kgs 15:30). He is reported to have done evil, yet *not like* the previous kings of Israel. During his reign, Shalmaneser V (726–722 BCE) of Assyria comes to Israel, because Hoshea had withheld tribute from Assyria and had attempted to form a coalition with *King So* of Egypt (there is no known Egyptian ruler bearing this exact name; for discussion see Cogan and Tadmor 196, n. 4) as well as with various neighboring states. Consequently, Shalmaneser V imprisons Hoshea. After a siege of some three years, Samaria is captured (722–721 BCE), and a substantial portion of the northern kingdom's population is deported to northern Syria (Halah), Mesopotamia, and Persia. Note that Deuteronomy contains a prophecy of the destruction of the northern kingdom (Deut 29:10–29).

> **The Destruction of Israel**
> The destruction and deportation of Israel are associated with Shalmaneser V and also with Sargon II (721–705 BCE, a fragment of whose victory monument was found in excavations at Samaria), Shalmaneser V's successor to the Assyrian throne (Cogan and Tadmor 199–201 and illustration 11a).

17:7–23 This text recites the theological rationale for the destruction of Israel. Numerous sins play a role, including references to high places and asherim, worship of Baal and the host of heaven, to child sacrifice, divination, and augury, and to the golden calves (see Exod 32; Deut 4:19; 6:4–15; 7:1–6; 12:2–4; 17:2–5; 18:9–14; 2 Kgs 3:27; Hos 13:2). The text also affirms that the Israelites refused to listen to the oracles of the prophets (for example, Amos and Hosea). Judah is also impugned for "walking in the customs that Israel had introduced" (compare 2 Kgs 21:1–18). There is also reference to the original division of the kingdom, with Jeroboam reigning in the north (see 1 Kgs 14:15, with a prophecy to Jeroboam that the north would fall).

17:24–41 In addition to deporting residents of the northern kingdom, the Assyrians bring people from various vanquished territories and move them into the cities of Samaria (here, *Samaria* refers to the whole country, not just the city; Cogan and Tadmor 209–10, n. 24). The text emphasizes the fact that those deported from various regions to Israel "did not worship Yahweh; therefore, Yahweh sent lions among them" (verse 25; compare 1 Kgs 13:24; 20:36), arguably an indication that in Yahweh's territory, all must worship Yahweh, regardless of ethnicity. According to the Deuteronomist, Yahweh's punitive measure precipitates a request that a deported Israelite priest be returned to the land of Israel to teach the non-Israelite settlers how to worship Yahweh, the God of the land. Nevertheless, the text remarks that the deportees continued to worship the various deities (see van der Toorn; for national gods, see theological implications below) associated with the regions from which they had come, alongside Yahweh, appointing their own priests as well (Exod 30:30; Ezek 40:46). Sargon II reported that he vanquished Samaria and the cities of Israel and exacted tribute from them after their destruction (Pritchard 284).

NARRATIVES ABOUT JUDAH TO ITS DESTRUCTION (587 BCE) & THE ASSASSINATION OF GEDALIAH · 18:1–25:30

18:1–12 Hezekiah (reigned 715–687 BCE) becomes king of Judah in the third year of Hoshea of Israel. The text lists his age at ascension to the throne, the duration of his reign, and the name of his mother. He is credited with "doing that which was right in the sight of Yahweh," with "no king like him before or after him" (2 Kgs 23:25). This is, of course, Deuteronomistic language for the removal and destruction of diverse cultic sites and objects, especially the high places and the Asherah poles. In essence, the text affirms that Hezekiah made a concerted effort to mandate the standardization of worship at a single worship center, the Jerusalem temple (for cultic practices, see theological implications below). There is also a reference to his removing the bronze serpent

> **Hezekiah's Reforms**
> *There is archaeological evidence for the reforms of Hezekiah, including an altar that was dismantled at Beersheba during his reign (Mazar 495–98).*

from the Mosaic period (Num 21:4–9), referred to as Nehushtan (a Hebrew term, based on a root that can mean both "bronze" or "snake").

Hezekiah rebels against the king of Assyria, refusing to pay tribute, hence, rejecting the vassal treaty his father had accepted (2 Kgs 16:7–18). There is archaeological evidence for this period that reveals the sophisticated administrative apparatus of Hezekiah (Vaughn). This suggests that Hezekiah had substantial power; therefore, the report that he raided Philistine territories (for the purpose of plunder or territory) is entirely plausible. Finally, this section concludes with a statement about the fall of the northern kingdom of Israel to the Assyrians and the deportation of many Israelites (2 Kgs 17).

18:13–26 During the fourteenth year of Hezekiah (701 BCE), Sennacherib of Assyria (704–681 BCE) attacks the cities of Judah (2 Kgs 19; Isa 36). Hezekiah sends emissaries from Jerusalem to the fortress city of Lachish (2 Kgs 14:19) and sues for peace, apparently asking forgiveness for a failure to pay tribute. He pays a massive amount of tribute, which includes gold stripped from the doors of the temple (1 Kgs 15:18). However, the Assyrians are not satisfied and send officials from Lachish to Jerusalem, meeting at the "conduit of the upper pool," apparently where meetings sometimes occurred (Isa 7:3). These Assyrian officials speak to high officials in the Judean kingdom (for the roles of these officials, see Fox 89, 115, 118, 201). The Assyrian officials presume that Hezekiah has been attempting to form an alliance with Egypt (verse 21; perhaps Pharaoh Shebitku; see Cogan and Tadmor 221), and the Rabshakeh (a title essentially meaning "Chief Cupbearer") affirms that this would be fruitless (as Egypt was like a "broken reed," and those who attempted to lean on it would be injured, not helped). He tells the Judeans that he will give them 2,000 horses if they can find soldiers to mount them (he believes the Judeans have few soldiers left). He even affirms that Yahweh will not "save" the people because, after all Hezekiah has been destroying all of the high places and altars devoted to Yahweh; and it is Yahweh that has summoned the Assyrians to vanquish Judah. It is striking that the Assyrians are privy to Hezekiah's religious reforms and believe them to have been destructive. Their intelligence service has accurate information about Judah's domestic affairs. It is also notable that the Assyrians state that they have come at the behest of Yahweh. Although the latter may seem problematic, Habakkuk himself will later state that Yahweh summoned a foreign nation (namely, Babylon) to punish Judah by vanquishing them (Hab 1:6).

18:26–37 The Judean officials entreat the Assyrians to speak in Aramaic (the *lingua franca* of much of the ancient Near East; Naveh, *Early History*, 78–89) rather than Hebrew, because they do not want the ordinary people of Jerusalem to hear what the Assyrians are saying (this is the earliest historic reference to the use of Aramaic in Judah; during the Second Temple period, Aramaic would supplant Hebrew as the primary language). However, the Rabshakeh refuses and begins to speak directly to the common people (Cogan and Tadmor 242), affirming that they should not listen to Hezekiah, because he is "deceiving" them, and because it is they, the common people, who must suffer (2 Kgs 6:24–7:2). He encourages them to surrender to him, as this will be easier for them than siege or battle, and he notes that no god of any other nation has been able to resist the power of Assyria (verses 34–35; 2 Kgs 17:6, 24; for national gods, see below). The Judean officials report all of these events to the king, appearing with torn clothes as a sign of distress (1 Kgs 21:27). This text gives a window onto the political savvy of the Assyrians as they used popular discontent in Judah against Hezekiah's regime.

19:1–7 The entire court of King Hezekiah is concerned (1 Kgs 21:27) about the Assyrian threat, as is the king himself. Because it was customary to seek out divine guidance during a time of crisis (1 Kgs 22:1–40), high Judean officials go to the prophet Isaiah (compare Isa 37), conveying King Hezekiah's great concern and his ire at the arrogant words of the Rabshakeh. Isaiah responds by instructing these officials to convey to Hezekiah the fact that he should not be afraid, as Sennacherib is about to return to his own land (after he hears a "rumor," likely about problems brewing back in Assyria) and would be slain there.

19:8–13 The Rabshakeh leaves Jerusalem and travels to Libnah (2 Kgs 8:22), for Sennacherib has already destroyed Lachish (2 Kgs 14:19; 18:14). Sennacherib hears that Tirhakah of Cush might be setting out to fight against him (summoned, Sennacherib believes, at the behest of Hezekiah), and he sends a letter to Hezekiah affirming that Jerusalem's fall is inevitable, as no nation's deity (2 Kgs 18:33–35) is capable of stopping him.

> **Cush**
> *Typically Ethiopia or Nubia, in this case Cush is a reference to the Twenty-fifth Cushite Dynasty of Egypt. Tirhakah was probably a general at the time of Sennacherib's siege rather than a king, as he did not begin to reign until about 690 or 688 BCE.*

19:14–34 After receiving the letter, Hezekiah goes to the temple ("house of Yahweh") and prays to Yahweh, enthroned above the cherubim (1 Kgs 6:23–28), for deliverance. Isaiah then conveys a response to Hezekiah, affirming that his prayer has been heard. This precipitates a beautiful poetic section (verses 21–28) criticizing Assyria for its arrogance, noting that Assyria's previous successes (including drinking the waters of Egypt, something that might be more readily associated with Esarhaddon; Pritchard 292) were ordained by Yahweh, and also affirming that Assyria itself will be brought low (much like a prisoner of war, led back to a captive area, with a hook in the nose or a bit in the mouth). Moreover, Isaiah prophesies that for two years the Judean people will eat the after-growth of grain, but in the third year, they will plant and reap abundant crops. That is, Isaiah affirms that a remnant will survive. Jerusalem will not be further besieged. Yahweh himself will protect it out of loyalty to David (1 Kgs 11:32).

19:35–37 Then, on "that very night," the angel of Yahweh strikes down 185,000 Assyrian soldiers, and Sennacherib himself returns to Nineveh and is subsequently assassinated by his sons while worshiping in the temple of Nisroch (a god that has not been identified with certainty). Sennacherib's son Esarhaddon (680–669 BCE) succeeds him. Note that

Josephus states that a "plague" caused the deaths of the Assyrian soldiers (Josephus, *Antiquities of the Jews*, 10:1; Cogan and Tadmor 239, n. 35, 250–51).

There is an abundance of archaeological and textual data from Assyria and Israel that converges with the contents of 2 Kings 18–19 (compare Mazar, 405, 420–22, 432–34, 483–85). First, Sennacherib commissioned a detailed Assyrian (in the Akkadian language) account of his campaigns in Syria-Palestine, including those against Hezekiah of Judah. He states that he destroyed some 46 cities of Judah, that he destroyed the Judean fortress of Lachish, and that he had Hezekiah trapped in the city of Jerusalem "like a bird in a cage." Second, Sennacherib's palace in Assyria has been excavated and magnificent reliefs (carved depictions) of his siege of Lachish were found, complete with depiction of the walls of Lachish, Judean dead, and Sennacherib's siege works and warriors. Third, the city of Lachish has been excavated, and decisive evidence has been found for the Assyrian destruction of Lachish at the end of the eighth century (701 BCE). Fourth, because Hezekiah knew that the Assyrians might make a punitive campaign against Judah (2 Kgs 18:14), and because he knew that the city of Jerusalem's major water source was vulnerable (as it was outside the city wall), he commissioned the fortification of the walls of Jerusalem and the building of a tunnel to bring water into the city (2 Kgs 20:20). The fortified city wall has been excavated. Fifth, Sennacherib's Assyrian records testify to the fact that pro-Assyrian King Padi of Ekron was removed from the throne by Hezekiah in Jerusalem. Subsequently, however, the Assyrians restored him to the throne of Ekron. An inscription found at Tel Miqne (ancient Ekron) mentions King Padi (Gitin, Dothan, and Naveh 1–16). Sixth, King Assurbanipal of Assyria (reigned 668–627 BCE) reports that his grandfather Sennacherib was assassinated, an event also mentioned in various other Mesopotamian sources (in Pritchard 289–90, 309). The cumulative biblical (2 Kgs 19; Isa 37), archaeological, and inscription evidence combine to provide a nuanced description of Sennacherib's siege, with the extrabiblical material essentially confirming the biblical material.

20:1–11 Hezekiah becomes sick (with a boil being one of the symptoms). The prophet Isaiah comes to him (compare 1 Kgs 14:1–20), tells him that this sickness will result in his death, and then leaves (Isa 38). However, Hezekiah utters a petitionary prayer, affirming his strong piety (2 Kgs 18:3–7). Before Isaiah can leave the royal court, Yahweh instructs him to return and tell Hezekiah that his prayer has been heard and that he will be granted fifteen additional years of life and will be delivered from the king of Assyria, for David's sake and for Yahweh's sake (1 Kgs 11:32). In addition, Isaiah requests that a poultice made of figs be placed on Hezekiah's boil to aid in the recovery. Hezekiah solicits a sign as proof that he will be healed. Consequently, his "sundial" retreats ten intervals (see Josh 10:12–13, for a similar miracle).

20:12–19 Merodach-baladan (see Isa 39), king of Babylon (reigned 722–710 BCE and 703–702 BCE), sends gift-bearing representatives (1 Kgs 10) to Hezekiah (perhaps because he is interested in forming an alliance with him against Assyria, hence part of Isaiah's resistance to this visit). Hezekiah shows the emissaries all of the royal treasures in Jerusalem. Isaiah rebukes Hezekiah for this and then prophesies that all these treasures will be taken as plunder to Babylon, as will some of Hezekiah's own descendants (2 Kgs 21:10–15; 22:16–20; 23:26–27; 24:1–25:30). Hezekiah's response is interesting; he considers this prophecy of doom to be tolerable, as it will not occur during his reign. Note that this chapter is chronologically out of place, as there is a reference to the future deliverance "from the hand of the king of Assyria" (compare 1 Kgs 19), and Merodach-baladan's reign was before, not after, Sennacherib's siege of 701 BCE.

20:20–21 The narrative concludes in the traditional way, with references to sources, death, and successor. In addition, there is reference to Hezekiah's constructing the pool and the water channel (see 2 Kgs 19).

21:1–18 This section summarizes Hezekiah's son Manasseh's reign (687–642 BCE), beginning in the traditional manner with reference

---

The Siloam Tunnel

In 1880, an inscription came to light in the Siloam Tunnel, dug by Hezekiah beneath Jerusalem (see 2 Chron 32:30). The inscription does not mention the king. But it does describe the process of digging: "while [they were wielding] their pickaxes, each toward his co-worker, and while there were yet three cubits for the breach, a voice was heard, each calling to his co-worker..." (Hallo and Younger 2:145–46).

to age, duration of reign, and mother's name. However, after these summary statements, the Deuteronomist begins to discuss the manifold sins of Manasseh (for a further discussion of these "sins," see theological implications below; 2 Kgs 17:19). These include the rebuilding of the high places destroyed by Hezekiah (2 Kgs 18:4). An important strand of the Deuteronomistic literature is the emphasis on "one place of worship" (namely Jerusalem); hence, Hezekiah was perceived as implementing Yahweh's will for a single worship center, and Manasseh was understood as undermining it in dramatic ways (1 Kgs 9:3–9). Manasseh makes a sacred pole to Asherah and worships Baal, as well as the host of heaven. Significantly, some of this worship occurs within Yahweh's temple in Jerusalem (not just at distant sites throughout the region). Manasseh sacrifices his son, practices soothsaying and augury, and even consults mediums and wizards (2 Kgs 3:27; 17:7–23).

Ultimately, the narrative states that Manasseh did even more evil than the Canaanites (sometimes referred to as *Amorites*; see 1 Kgs 21:26). Because of these many sins, Yahweh affirms that he will "bring evil" (NIV *disaster*) upon Judah and its capital city of Jerusalem (2 Kgs 20:12–19; 22:16–20; 23:26–27; 24:1–25:30). This destruction will be comparable to the destruction of Samaria (2 Kgs 17), using the same "measuring line and plummet" (architectural tools). In addition to using these tools, he will *wipe Jerusalem as one wipes a dish*, that is, will purge Jerusalem of all its impure contents (that is, its citizenry). Yahweh's prophets (verse 10) convey this message about Manasseh, much as prophets (such as Elijah and Elisha; 1 Kgs 17- 2 Kgs 13) often condemned the northern kings for religious error. In any case, Manasseh's reign is summarized by stating that he *shed much innocent blood* (see also the *Ascension of Isaiah* of the Old Testament Pseudepigrapha), and by the formulaic references to sources, burial (in some *garden of Uzza*), and successor. Manasseh's reign is recorded as fifty-five years, the longest of any king of Judah. Note that he is mentioned in Assyrian records as a vassal of Assyrian kings Esarhaddon and Assurbanipal (Pritchard 290, 291, 294).

The Prayer of Manasseh
Significantly, Chronicles states that Manasseh uttered a penitential prayer (2 Chron 33:10–17; see also the Prayer of Manasseh *in the Old Testament Apocrypha). This led to God forgiving him. 2 Kings takes a harsher view of his reign.*

22:19–26 Amon's age at ascension appears (reigned 642–640 BCE), along with the duration of his reign and his mother's name (strikingly, her family hails from the northern Israelite city of Jotbah; perhaps they had immigrated south after the destruction of the northern kingdom, as had so many from that region). He did that which was *evil in the sight* of Yahweh, in the same way that his father Manasseh had done (verses 1–18). He is killed in his house during a palace coup détat. The *people of the land* (see 2 Kgs 11:14) kill the assassins and then put his son Josiah on the throne. The text concludes in the traditional formulaic way.

22:1–20 Josiah is eight years of age when he begins to reign, and he reigns thirty-one years (640–609 BCE). The text names his mother, as is the custom for Judean kings. Striking is the fact that Josiah is commended without restraint throughout the narrative, as someone who did that which was "right in the eyes of Yahweh, walking in the ways of his father David" (compare 1 Kgs 11:32).

Josiah's reforms begin in the eighteenth year of his reign, when he sends high court officials to the high priest Hilkiah. These officials instruct Hilkiah to count the money that has been collected and give it to the artisans who might repair the temple. No accounting for expenditures is required of the artisans (compare 2 Kgs 12:1–16 for a similar narrative about repairs made to the Jerusalem temple during the reign of Jehoash).

During the restoration process, Hilkiah reports to the scribe Shaphan that he has found *the Book of the Law* in the temple. Arguably, this narrative suggests that during the reigns of Josiah's wicked predecessors (2 Kgs 21), *the Book of the Law* had fallen into disuse and been temporarily "lost." However, modern scholarship has sometimes suggested that the book may actually have been produced during Josiah's reign to bolster the support for Josiah's sweeping reforms (Deut 12; 16:2; 17:2, 18–20; 18:10; 23:18 and compare the reforms in 2 Kgs 23:4–27). More likely, the core traditions of the book were somewhat older. In any case, Shaphan informs the king of the find and then reads it aloud to him. After hearing the contents of the book (clearly a relatively small one as it was read during one sitting), the king tears his clothes (see 1 Kgs

21:27) and then commands that the high officials (see also the names of the high officials in Jer 26:24; 29:3; 36:10–12; 2 Kgs 25:22; Fox 53–248) go and inquire of Yahweh (1 Kgs 22:1–40), fearing that Yahweh's wrath is about to be poured upon Judah due to the people's breaching of the covenant.

A royal delegation then takes the book to a prophetess named Huldah, the wife of Shallum (for prophetesses in the Old Testament, see Exod 15:20; Judg 4:4; Isa 8:3; for prophecy in the ancient Near East, see Blenkinsopp 41–64), who resides in the Second Quarter of Jerusalem. Huldah declares that disaster is at hand because of the religious unorthodoxy of the people (see 2 Kgs 20:12–19; 21:10–15; 23:26–27; 24:1–25:30). However, she also states that Josiah, because of his penitence, will be spared from this disaster and will "go to his grave in peace" (2 Kgs 28–30). This final prediction proves not to be true. Huldah's words are then brought back to the king.

> **Jerusalem**
> *In Hezekiah's time the city of Jerusalem, previously consisting of a small Jebusite city (12 acres) and the Temple Mount, expanded onto the western hill of the city, where Huldah must have lived.*

23:1–27 King Josiah decrees that all should gather near the Jerusalem temple, and he reads *the Book of the Law* (2 Kgs 22) during an event best described as a covenant renewal ceremony (Josh 22–24). He stands near *the pillar*, a place sometimes associated with important political and religious events (2 Kgs 11:14). After reading the text, he commands the temple officials to remove all vessels made for Baal, Asherah, and the host of heaven (2 Kgs 21:2–9) from the temple of Yahweh. These vessels are burned in the Kidron Valley, and their ashes are carried to Bethel (compare 1 Kgs 12:25–33). In addition, Josiah deposes the foreign priests (sometimes rendered "idolatrous priests"), and has the Asherah images removed from the temple, as well. He breaks down the houses of the male temple prostitutes (compare 1 Kgs 14:24), where women did weaving for Asherah. He defiles the Topheth, something connected with child sacrifice and well-attested from the archaeological excavations at Carthage (see 2 Kgs 3:27; King and Stager 359–61). According to Mesopotamian religious texts, the chariot of the Mesopotamian (sun) god, Shamash, was drawn through the sky by horses; therefore, the reference here in Kings to horses *dedicated to the sun* [Hebrew *shemesh*] may very well reflect religious syncretism (see Mazar 380 and Cole 16 for references to horses with sun disks found in Israel). Eunuchs were often part of the religious and political establishment (2 Kgs 9:32), and these horses were near the room designated for Nathan-melech's use. In addition, Josiah removes the altars on the roof of Ahaz's upper chamber (2 Kgs 16:1–20) and the altars that Manasseh had in the courts of the temple (2 Kgs 21:4). Cult sites of Astarte, Chemosh, and Milcom are destroyed (1 Kgs 11:5–7) and even covered with human bones to desecrate them (presumably the bones of those who had worshiped these deities).

Significantly, while attempting to eradicate unorthodox religion in all of Judah (from the northern border of Geba to the southern extreme of Beersheba; see Mazar 498 on the evidence for Josianic reforms at Arad), Josiah also manages to burn down the sacred pole and altar at Bethel located in the region of the old (now devastated) northern kingdom. At Bethel, he removes bones from tombs and burns them on the altar, thus fulfilling the word of God (1 Kgs 13, where the old prophet is reported to have come from Bethel, not Samaria). He also enacts reforms in all the towns of Samaria (2 Kgs 17:24–41) and slaughters all of the priests of their high places and burns the priests' bones on their altars.

As part of his sweeping reforms, Josiah proclaims the observance of the Passover, something neglected during the reigns of all of the previous kings of Judah (a hyperbolic statement, to be sure). It is also stated that Josiah put away mediums, wizards, teraphim (household gods; Gen 31:19–55), idols, and various other abominations (that is, cult paraphernalia associated with gods other than Yahweh). Moreover, the Deuteronomist notes that there were no kings like Josiah, neither before nor after him (see 2 Kgs 18:5 for a similar statement about Hezekiah).

However, the text avers that even the far-reaching reforms of Josiah could not satisfy the indignation of Yahweh, resulting from the extreme sins of Manasseh (2 Kgs 20:12–19; 21:1–16; 22:16–20; 23:26–27; 24:1–25:30). The die had been cast.

23:28–30 The Deuteronomist's narrative concludes with the standard references to sources, death, burial, and successor. However, because

Josiah died in battle (and not in peace as Huldah had predicted; 2 Kgs 22:18–20), some additional details are provided. Josiah goes up to meet in battle the forces of the king of Assyria (recently defeated by the Babylonians and now attempting to establish a stump government in Harran, in northern Syria), but Pharaoh Neco II (reigned 610–594 BCE) intercepts him at the pass near Megiddo (a site of many battles in antiquity) and slays him (as Neco II was an ally of Assur-ubalit II, the Assyrian king; Cogan and Tadmor 291–302). Josiah's body is transported to Jerusalem. Then the *people of the land* (compare 2 Kgs 11:14) crown Josiah's son Jehoahaz and anoint him king (see 1 Kgs 1:39).

23:31–37 The narrative introduces Jehoahaz (reigned 609 BCE) in the traditional formulaic manner (age at ascension, duration of reign, mother's name. Note that his mother was from Libnah; see 1 Kgs 8:22). Jehoahaz was arguably a throne name, as his given name was Shallum (Jer 22:11). He does "evil in the sight of Yahweh." It is, however, difficult to envision Jehoahaz's having had much opportunity to enact the sort of religious reforms acceptable to the Deuteronomist (see verses 1–30) during such a brief reign (three months). In any case, Pharaoh Neco II (now overlord of Judah) confines Jehoahaz to Riblah in the Aramean region of Hamath (2 Kgs 25:6, 20–21), not wanting him to reign in Jerusalem; he also imposes on Judah a heavy tribute. Because Judah has become a vassal of Egypt, Neco II puts Eliakim (Josiah's son) on the throne and gives him the throne name Jehoiakim. Jehoahaz is subsequently taken to Egypt as an exile and dies there. Jehoiakim's reign (609–598 BCE) is introduced in the traditional formulaic manner, with references to his age, the duration of his reign, and his mother's name. The narrative states that Johoiakim "did that which was evil in the eyes of Yahweh."

24:1–7 The narrative begins by noting that, during the reign of Jehoiakim, Nebuchadnezzar (reigned 605/4–562 BCE) came to Judah, and Jehoiakim became a vassal of Babylon, rather than of Egypt (compare 2 Kgs 23:28–35). This is an accurate historical note, as the Neo-Babylonians defeated the Egyptians in the Battle of Carchemish (605 BCE; Jer 46:2), and this defeat temporarily forced Egypt back toward its borders. Nevertheless, just a few years later in 601 BCE, Egypt recovered some of its power and regained control over the Near East for a time. It was at this point that Jehoiakim decided that it was an opportune time to rebel. The narrative of Kings also notes that, during this period, bands of Chaldeans (Neo-Babylonians), Arameans, Moabites (1 Kgs 16:15–28), and Ammonites made raids against Judah, as the day of Yahweh's punishment was drawing nigh. The narrative concludes in the traditional formulaic manner, referring to sources, death, and successor. Moreover, there is a note that, with the surge of Babylonian power, Egypt was not able to make campaigns into Syria-Palestine. Significantly in this connection, an Aramaic letter from this period contains a plea from a Syrian king requesting assistance from the Egyptian throne against the invading Babylonians (Cogan and Tadmor 308, n. 3).

> **The Sins of Manasseh**
> *Second Kings refers to the sins of Manasseh as galvanizing Yahweh's decision to bring judgment on Judah (compare 2 Kgs 21:1–26).*

24:8–20 Jehoiachin (note the two alternate spellings of his name, namely, Jeconiah in 1 Chron 3:16 and Coniah in Jer 22:24) comes to the throne during this turbulent time at the age of eighteen, and reigns for a mere three months (598/7 BCE). His mother's name and his grandfather's name are noted in the text. He does "evil in the sight of Yahweh," although it is difficult to envision his having had much opportunity to enact religious reforms, especially during a political crisis. In any case, when Nebuchadnezzar besieges the city of Jerusalem (see Cogan and Tadmor 311–13, on the *Babylonian Chronicle*'s reference to this), Jehoiachin surrenders (in about 597 BCE; see Jer 52:28), and he is taken captive to Babylon along with various members of the royal family, including the queen mother (see 1 Kgs 15:13), the daughter of Elnathan (26:22; Jer 36:12, 25; 37:5; see Lachish Letter 3 for a reference to an Elnathan; 2 Kgs 14:19, for references to Lachish) and court, as well as many soldiers and artisans (thus making rebuilding in Judah more difficult; 2 Kgs

> **Lachish Letters**
> *Many inscribed ostraca (large pieces of broken pottery reused for written documents) have been found containing letters and lists of names. The letters were sent to the governor of the city of Lachish and describe graphically life just before the fall of Judah to the Babylonians in 586 BCE.*

25:27–30). The numbers of those deported are listed (compare the numbers in verses 14 and 16 with those in Jer 52:28–30). Additionally, the treasures of the Jerusalem temple are plundered (as in 1 Kgs 15:18; Dan 5:1–4), even as prophesied (2 Kgs 20:12–19; 21:10–15; 22:16–20; 23:26–27; 24:1–25:30). Jehoiachin's uncle (a son of Josiah; see 1 Chron 3:15), with the given name Mattaniah, gains the throne and takes the throne name Zedekiah.

Zedekiah's reign (597–587 BCE) is introduced in the traditional manner, with references to his age at ascension, the duration of his reign, and the name of his mother (see Jer 52 for a parallel account). Note that he is the full brother of Jehoahaz (2 Kgs 23:31–35). He and the people of Judah do "evil in the sight of Yahweh" to such an extent that Yahweh expels them from his presence. The text also states that he rebelled against the king of Babylon. His decision to do this was arguably galvanized by the resurgence of Egyptian power during the reigns of Egypt's Psammetichus II (reigned 594–589 BCE) and Apries [Hophra] (reigned 589–570 BCE) and by the presence of strife within the Babylonian court (Cogan and Tadmor 322; compare Jer 27:3).

25:1–21 During the ninth year of Zedekiah's reign (587/6 BCE), Nebuchadnezzar besieges Jerusalem as part of a punitive campaign (compare 2 Kgs 6:24:7:2; note the extensive parallel material in the book of Jeremiah, especially Jer 39–41 and 52 and also see the Lachish Letters translated in Lindenberger; also 2 Kgs 14:19). Ultimately, the Babylonians breach the wall, and as a result, Zedekiah and some of his soldiers flee from the city. However, the soldiers abandon Zedekiah, and he is captured and taken to Riblah (see 2 Kgs 23:33). There the Babylonians gouge out his eyes, so that the last thing he sees is the death of his sons (for similar incidents of blinding, see 1 Sam 11:2; Pritchard 533). Subsequently, a high Babylonian official travels to Jerusalem and supervises the destruction of the city, with the result that even the temple is destroyed. The book of Lamentations mourns this destruction. The implements and utensils of the temple are taken to Babylon (compare 1 Kgs 15:18; Dan 5:1–4). Some of the remaining elites are exiled, while some are taken to Riblah and executed; the remaining population of Judah now is primarily composed of the poorest people (2 Kgs 17). The narrative concludes with a statement that "Judah went into exile, out of its land," a sober assessment of all these tragic events (see also 2 Kgs 20:12–19; 21:10–15; 22:16–20; 23:26–27).

25:22–26 Nebuchadnezzar appoints Gedaliah, son of Ahikam, grandson of Shaphan (2 Kgs 22:3, 12), as governor. Some of the remaining Judean soldiers travel to Mizpah (the apparent seat of government after Jerusalem's destruction) and speak with Gedaliah, who affirms that Judah will survive if it shows fidelity to Babylon. However, Ishmael (of the Davidic line; see 1 Kgs 11:36), one of the captains, along with ten men, assassinates Gedaliah and his court. Then, fearing Babylonian retaliation, they flee to Egypt. Jeremiah was taken to Egypt at this time, apparently under duress (Jer 43).

> **Gedaliah's Seal**
>
> A seal impression (bulla) referring to "Gedaliah, the Royal Steward" has been found at Lachish (Cogan and Tadmor 325, note 25; compare 2 Kgs 14:19 for references to Lachish).

25:27–30 The book of Kings concludes with an affirmation that in the thirty-seventh year of the exile of Jehoiachin of Judah, the Babylonian King Evil-Merodach (reigned 562–560 BCE; his name means "Man of Marduk" and is better spelled Amel-Marduk) released Jehoiachin from prison and permitted him to enjoy the amenities of the Babylonian palace (compare 2 Kgs 24:14–16; Jer 52:31–34), something Babylonian records also mention (Pritchard 308). Jehoiachin was arguably still considered the legitimate Judean king even after his exile, as certain biblical superscriptions (Ezek 1:2) still cite the years of his reign. Moreover, the fact that Kings concludes with a reference to the freedom of the exiled Davidic king is certainly a hopeful note, intended to encourage (see 1 Kgs 11:36).

THEOLOGICAL REFLECTIONS

The Old Testament is an ancient Hebrew and Aramaic library of documents, with a long and complicated textual history. The books of the Old Testament are not "history" in the modern sense of the term. Rather, these books are ancient religious literature anchored in history. In addition, for ancient Israel and Judah, there was often no clear separation (or delineation) of the sacred and the secular, such as is often made in modern cultures. Modern interpreters often err in biblical interpretation because of the sincere but misguided desire to read the biblical text through a modern interpretive lens. Nonetheless, the books of 1 and 2 Kings do explore religious and theological ideas that deserve our attention.

First, the Old Testament affirms that there was a "covenant" between Yahweh and Israel. This relationship required Israel's complete religious and moral fidelity to Yahweh, with faithfulness bringing a multitude of blessings, but with faithlessness bringing divine retribution. That is, a good life, dwelling in the land given by Yahweh, would come to those who would obey Yahweh's commandments; however, curses and punishments were promised to those who would disobey (Deut 6:10–25; 10:12–11:32; 12:28–32; 28; 30:11–20; Josh 23:15–16; Judg 2:11–23; 1 Sam 12:14–15; 2 Sam 7:22–24; 1 Kgs 8:22–53; 2 Kgs 17:7–23). This theology is most evident within the books of Kings in the author's reflections on each king's reign and in his comments on crucial historical events. Sin, the Deuteronomist would affirm, consistently has consequences, as does piety. For the Deuteronomist, there is a rigid connection between deed and consequence.

Second, Yahweh controlled all historical events, whether within Israel proper or without. Foreigners often blessed Yahweh and acknowledged his power (1 Kgs 10:9; 11:14, 23; 17–18; 19:15–17; 20; 2 Kgs 5:17–19; 6:8–23; 8:7–15; 24:2–3; for a problem, see 2 Kgs 3:27). The function of prophetic oracles and their fulfillment was to demonstrate such power (1 Kgs 14:1–20; 15:27–29; 21:19–29; 22:37; 2 Kgs 9:7–10:17; but also see 2 Kgs 22:20; 23:29–30). Sometimes Yahweh seemed to use power in a volatile manner (1 Kgs 22:13–28; 2 Kgs 2:23–25; compare 2 Sam 6:6–11). Regardless of the precise context, the books of Kings affirm the magnitude of Yahweh's power.

Third, Jeroboam I, the first king of the northern kingdom of Israel after its separation from Judah, set up cultic sites at Dan and Bethel, complete with bovine images for the worship of Yahweh. He arguably did so to encourage the northern Israelites to remain within the borders of the northern kingdom to worship, because he feared that when the Israelites went to Judah to worship, the kingdom might revert to the house of David (1 Kgs 12:25–33). However, for the Deuteronomist, the worship of Yahweh at a cult site in a location outside Jerusalem violated the commandments found in Deuteronomy 12. That is, although, there is no indication that Jeroboam built these sites in order to worship any deity other than Yahweh, the sites were still deemed offensive. Significantly, it was on the basis of these cultic sites that Jeroboam I and all of the subsequent kings of Israel were evaluated. All of the following kings of Israel were deemed wicked because of the use of cult sites outside of Jerusalem: Nadab (1 Kgs 15:26), Baasha (15:34), Elah (16:13), Zimri (16:19; despite a reign of only seven days), Omri (16:25–26), Jehoram (2 Kgs 3:2–3; even though he removed the Baal pillar of Ahab), Jehu (2 Kgs 10:18–31; even though he destroyed the Baal cult), Jehoash (13:11, 14–19; despite loyalty to Elisha), Jeroboam II (14:24), Zechariah (15:9), Menahem (15:18), Pekahiah (15:24), Pekah (15:28), and Hoshea (17:2, 7–23). The Deuteronomist condemned those who promoted sacrificial worship at sites other than the Jerusalem temple. Of course, kings of Judah were also criticized (but more mildly) for allowing (presumably Yahwistic) worship to continue at the high places within Judah's boundaries: Asa (15:11–15), Jehoshaphat (22:43), Jehoash (2 Kgs 12:2–16), Amaziah (14:3–4), Azariah (15:3–4), and Jotham (15:34–35). Arguably, these Judean kings were critiqued more mildly because they also promoted the worship of Yahweh at the Jerusalem temple. Nevertheless, for kings of both Israel and Judah, the Deuteronomist had the same requirement: sacrificial worship at the Jerusalem temple.

In light of this, it is interesting to note that Israelites had been offering sacrifices at various "high places" for centuries with no critique, even long after they had taken possession of much of the land of Canaan (1 Sam 7:7–17; 9:11–26). Moreover, although the ark of the covenant was in Jerusalem for much of David's reign (2 Sam 6), the Israelites continued to sacrifice at sites in various Israelite cities, with Solomon's sacrifices at the high place of Gibeon being a notable case (1 Kgs 3:3–9; but compare 1 Kgs 11). Also, Naaman the Syrian (Aramean) was given a blessing when he requested permission to build an altar to Yahweh in his home country (2 Kgs 5:17–19), which invites the question: if someone from another nation might worship Yahweh at an altar that was not in Jerusalem, why could not those from the nation of Israel, especially in light of the fact that it was Yahweh who had created the separate nation? Accounting for this equivocal material is, however, not an insurmountable problem, for during the early First Temple period, sacrificial worship of Yahweh often occurred at disparate sites, but during the late First Temple period, there was a concerted effort to restrict sacrificial worship of Yahweh to the Jerusalem temple.

Fourth, several of the northern Israelite kings received explicit criticism not only for the worship of Yahweh at a site other than Jerusalem, but also for the worship of other deities and/or for cultic practices associated with the deities of other nations: Jeroboam I (1 Kgs 14:15), Ahab (16:30; along with Jezebel and the Israelites, 16:31–33; 18:4, 13, 17–19:2, 10, 14, 18; 21:20–26), Ahaziah of Israel (22:52–53; 2 Kgs 1:2–17), and Jehoahaz (2 Kgs 13:2; and the Israelites, 13:6). A summary of these offenses appears in 2 Kings 17:1–23 to account for the fall of the northern kingdom of Israel. The text also warns Judah not to follow in Israel's footsteps (2 Kgs 17:19). Of course, Judean kings committed similar offenses: Rehoboam (14:22–24; compare Deut 23:17–18), Abijam (15:3), Jehoram of Judah (2 Kgs 8:18, son-in-law of Ahab, sinned in the ways of kings of Israel), Ahaziah of Judah (8:27, grandson of Ahab, sinned in ways of Ahab), Athaliah of Judah (11:1–21, no specific reference to cultic sins are cited, but she slaughters her family ruthlessly; 8:18, daughter of Ahab), Ahaz (16:2–4; Deut 18:10), Manasseh (21:1–17), and Amon (21:20–22).

Those kings who received commendation were those who abolished the high places and made extensive reforms: Hezekiah (2 Kgs 18:3–6) and Josiah (22:11–23:27). Josiah removed not only the southern high places but those within the north, as well (2 Kgs 23:4, 15–20). Significantly, no northern kings receive such praise.

From the perspective of the Deuteronomist, the fate of Judah had been decided with certainty because of the sins of the wicked Manasseh (2 Kgs 24:3). Even the reign of the pious Josiah could not prevent the inevitable fall of Judah. For Jehoahaz (2 Kgs 23:32), Jehoiakim (23:37), Jehoiachin (24:9), and Zedekiah (24:19; compare also Gedaliah in 2 Kgs 25:22–26) the die had already been cast and punishment would come. It is significant that there were problems for which the Deuteronomist could not account. For example, Hezekiah's religious reforms do not prevent attack from Assyria (2 Kgs 18–19), nor do Josiah's reforms prevent his death or attack from Babylon (2 Kgs 22:11–25:21). Again, though, the position of the Deuteronomist seems to be that Manasseh's sins were too great to be overcome, even in light of the most sweeping reforms that Judah ever experienced.

Fifth, prophets (as well as priests) appear as Yahweh's representatives, even in politics. They anoint kings, especially when a change of a dynasty occurred (1 Kgs 1:39). They prophesy the fall of kings and their dynasties, even assisting in the replacement of one king with another (1 Kgs 11:26–40; 14:1–20; 19:15–17). A condemnatory prophecy is usually the result of a king's disloyalty to Yahweh or the commitment of a cultic offense (1 Kgs 14:1–20). Kings consulted prophets in instances of sickness or national distress (1 Kgs 14:1–20; 22:1–28). At times, kings respected the prophets and heeded their words (1 Kgs 21:17–29; 2 Kgs 6:21–23; 8:1–6; 13:14; 20; 22:14–23:27); however, at other times, oracles caused prophets to fall out of favor with the court or even endangered their lives (1 Kgs 13:4; 19:1–3; 22:8–28; 2 Kgs 6:31–33). Prophets, in essence, attempted to call people (high and low) back to the covenant. Within the books of Kings, numerous prophetic voices speak.

Sixth, the religions of the southern neighboring states of Moab, Ammon, and Edom were "national god religions." That is, each nation believed it had a "patron deity" (compare Deut 32:8–9; 1 Kgs 20:23; 2 Kgs 17:8, 29–41; 18:33; 19:10–13; Smith, *Early History*). Based on biblical and inscriptional evidence, we know that Ammon affirmed that its national god was "Milkom" (sometimes confused with Molek; 1 Kgs 11:5, 7; 2 Kgs 23:13). Moab claimed as its national god Chemosh (1 Kgs 11:7; 2 Kgs 3:27; 23:13). Edom affirmed that its national god was Qaus. Yahweh was

> **The Falls of Israel & Judah**
> *The fall of the kingdoms of Israel and Judah was horrific. Without being tied to their own land, the people of Israel and Judah ran the risk of being swallowed up by the foreign populace in the lands of their exile. If Yahweh was truly in control, how could the kingdoms have fallen? Such an atrocity had to be accounted for. The answer was in the breach of the covenant; only a sin of that magnitude could have brought on such great punishment. Indeed, the author took great pains to show how almost every king broke the commandments of Yahweh.*

Israel's God (see, for example, Deut 32:8–9), and it was to Yahweh that Israel was to be faithful, as Yahweh had made a binding covenant relationship with the nation. Yahweh was to be worshiped by Israel (Deut 5:7; 6:4, 13–14). To be sure, some Israelites affirmed that Yahweh had a consort: Asherah. For example, stunning epigraphic evidence has demonstrated that some Israelites worshiped Asherah as Yahweh's consort (Smith, *Early History*; Rollston, "Rise of Monotheism"). Nevertheless, orthodox Israelite religion always had Yahweh as its central God.

In conclusion, the Deuteronomistic History was written in such as way as to presuppose exile (Deut 4:27; Josh 23:13, 16; 1 Sam 12:25; 1 Kgs 8:34, 46; 9:6–9). However, divine forgiveness and mercy stood over against punishment (Deut 4:25–31; 1 Kgs 8:46–53). The author intentionally ended Kings with Jehoiachin's release from prison (2 Kgs 25:27–30), reminiscent of the *lamp* that is promised to remain for David in Jerusalem (2 Sam 7:1–17; 1 Kgs 11:34; 15:4; 2 Kgs 8:19; 19:34; 20:6; 22:2; 25:25, 27–30).

FOR FURTHER STUDY

Frank M. Cross, *Canaanite Myth and Hebrew Epic* (Cambridge: Harvard University Press, 1971).

John H. Hayes, *An Introduction to Old Testament Study* (Nashville: Abingdon, 1979).

WORKS CITED

Susan Ackerman, "The Queen Mother and the Cult in Ancient Israel," *Journal of Biblical Literature* 112 (1993): 385–401.

———, *Under Every Green Tree: Popular Religion in Sixth-Century Judah.* (Atlanta: Scholars Press, 1992).

Peter M. M. G. Akkermans and Glenn M. Schwartz, *The Archaeology of Syria: From Complex Hunter-Gatherers to Early Urban Societies (ca. 16,000–300 BC)* (Cambridge: Cambridge University Press, 2003).

N. Avigad, and Benjamin Sass, *Corpus of West Semitic Stamp Seals* (Jerusalem: Israel Exploration Society, 1997).

Frank L. Benz, *Personal Names in the Phoenician and Punic Inscriptions* (Rome: Biblical Institute, 1972).

Avraham Biran and Joseph Naveh, "The Tel Dan Inscription: A New Fragment," *Israel Exploration Journal* 45 (1995): 2–18.

Joseph Blenkinsopp, *A History of Prophecy in Israel* (Louisville: Westminster John Knox, 1996).

Oded Borowski, *Daily Life in Biblical Times* (Atlanta: Society of Biblical Literature, 2003).

Joachim Braun, *Music in Ancient Israel/Palestine* (Grand Rapids: Eerdmans, 2002).

John Bright, *A History of Israel* (3rd ed.; Philadelphia: Westminster, 1981).

Mordechai Cogan, *1 Kings: A New Translation with Introduction and Commentary* (New York: Doubleday, 2000).

Mordechai Cogan and Hayim Tadmor, *2 Kings: A New Translation with Introduction and Commentary* (New York: Doubleday, 1988).

Dan P. Cole, *Archaeology and Religion* (Washington, D.C.: Biblical Archaeology Society, 1991).

Michael Coogan, *Stories from Ancient Canaan* (Louisville: Westminster, 1978).

James L. Crenshaw, *Old Testament Wisdom: An Introduction* (Louisville: Westminster John Knox, 1998).

Frank M. Cross, "Epigraphic Notes on the Amman Citadel Inscriptions," *Bulletin of the American Schools of Oriental Research* 193 (1969): 13–19.

Israel Eph'al and Joseph Naveh, "Hazael's Booty Inscriptions," *Israel Exploration Journal* 39 (1989): 192–200.

Nili Sacher Fox, *In the Service of the King: Officialdom in Ancient Israel and Judah* (Cincinnati: Hebrew Union College Press, 2000).

Volkmar Fritz, *1 and 2 Kings* (trans. Anselm Hagedorn; Minneapolis, Minn.: Fortress, 2003).

Joseph Fitzmyer, *The Aramaic Inscriptions of Sefire* (Rome: Pontifical Biblical Institute, 1995).

Seymour Gitin, Trude Dothan, and Joseph Naveh, "A Royal Dedicatory Inscription from Ekron," *Israel Exploration Journal* 47 (1997): 1–16.

Alberto R. W. Green, *The Storm-God in the Ancient Near East* (Winona Lake, Ind.: Eisenbrauns, 2003).

Jonas Greenfield, "Ramman/Rimmon," *Israel Exploration Journal* 26 (1976): 195–98.

Hermann Gunkel, *The Folktale in the Old Testament* (trans. Michael D. Rutter; Sheffield: Almond, 1987).

Baruch Halpern, *David's Secret Demons* (Grand Rapids: Eerdmans, 2001).

Josephus, *Jewish Antiquities* (ed. and trans. H. St. John Thackeray and Ralph Marcus; 8 vols.; Cambridge: Harvard University Press, 1930–1963).

Othmar Keel, *The Symbolism of the Biblical World: Ancient Near Eastern Iconography and the Psalms* (Winona Lake, Ind.: Eisenbrauns, 1997).

Philip King and Lawrence Stager, *Life in Biblical Israel* (Louisville: Westminster John Knox, 2001).

Miriam Lichtheim, *Ancient Egyptian Literature* (Berkeley, Calif.: University of California Press, 1973).

James M. Lindenberger, *Ancient Aramaic and Hebrew Letters* (2nd ed.; Atlanta: Society of Biblical Literature, 2003).

Amihai Mazar, *Archaeology of the Land of the Bible: 10,000–586 BCE.* (New York: Doubleday, 1992).

William Moran, *Amarna Letters* (Baltimore: Johns Hopkins University Press, 1992).

Joseph Naveh, *Early History of the Alphabet* (2nd ed.; Jerusalem: Magnes, 1987).

———, "Writing and Scripts in Seventh-Century BCE Philistia: The New Evidence from Tell Jemmeh," *Israel Exploration Journal* 35 (1985): 8–21.

Joan Oates, *Babylon* (New York: Thames and Hudson, 1986).

Dennis Pardee, *Handbook of Ancient Hebrew Letters* (Chico, Calif.:Scholars Press, 1982).

Wayne Pitard, *Ancient Damascus* (Winona Lake, Ind.: Eisenbrauns, 1987).

James Pritchard, ed., *Ancient Near Eastern Texts* (Princeton: Princeton University Press, 1969).

Christopher A. Rollston, "Ethbaal," in *Eerdmans Dictionary of the Bible* (Grand Rapids: Eerdmans, 2000), 431.

———, "Mesha," in *Eerdmans Dictionary of the Bible* (Grand Rapids: Eerdmans, 2000), 887–88.

———, "The Rise of Monotheism in Ancient Israel: Biblical and Epigraphic Evidence," *Stone-Campbell Journal* 6 (2003): 95–115.

Martha T. Roth, *Law Collections from Mesopotamia and Asia Minor* (Atlanta: Scholars Press, 1995).

Nahum M. Sarna and Hershel Shanks, "Israel in Egypt: The Egyptian Sojourn and the Exodus," in *Ancient Israel* (rev. ed.; ed. Hershel Shanks; Washington, D.C.: Biblical Archaeology Society, 1999), 33–54.

Mark S. Smith, *The Early History of God: Yahweh and the Other Deities in Ancient Israel* (2nd ed.; Grand Rapids: Eerdmans, 2002).

———, *The Origins of Biblical Monotheism* (New York: Oxford, 2001).

Ronald Tappy, *The Archaeology of Israelite Samaria* (2 vols.; Winona Lake, Ind.: Eisenbrauns, 1992 and 2001).

Edwin R. Thiele, *The Mysterious Numbers of the Hebrew Kings* (Grand Rapids: Zondervan, 1983).

Karel van der Toorn, ed., *Dictionary of Deities and Demons in the Bible* (rev. ed.; Grand Rapids: Eerdmans, 1999).

Andrew G. Vaughn, *Theology, History, and Archaeology in the Chronicler's Account of Hezekiah* (Atlanta: Scholars Press, 1999).

Moshe Weinfeld, *Social Justice in Ancient Israel* (2nd ed.; Jerusalem: Magnes, 2000).

Irene Winter, "Phoenician and North Syrian Ivory Carving in Historical Context: Questions of Style and Distribution," *Iraq* 38 (1976): 1–18.

1 Chronicles

R. Mark Shipp

CHAPTER CONTENTS

Contexts 353

Commentary 356
- Genealogies from Adam to the Restored Community of Judah · 1:1–9:44 356
- The Story of the Kings of Judah · 10:1–29:30 360

Theological Reflections 370

For Further Study 371

Works Cited 371

MAPS, TABLES, & FEATURES

Building the Temple 368
Poetry as Prophecy 369

First and Second Chronicles, though two volumes in our English Bibles, originally formed a single work, and thus the stories of the kings of Judah are continued in 2 Chronicles. The title in Hebrew, *divre hayyamim*, "the words of the days," differs markedly from the title in the ancient Greek translation (the Septuagint), *paraleipomenon*, "things left out." The Greek title suggests that Chronicles provides supplementary information to the books of Samuel and Kings. The Hebrew and English titles suggest that the nature of the work is that of an annal, a "day book" or chronicle of the kings of Judah.

CONTEXTS

Chronicles has suffered neglect in the history of scholarship, at least until the last 200 years. This neglect probably derived from the book's assumed role as a supplement to Samuel and Kings. More recent scholars have increasingly attended to the theological and literary dimensions of the book and have questioned its historical reliability. Since about 1800, debate over Chronicles has gone through three basic stages, with concerns about the books' historical value (most of the nineteenth century), its authorship and its relation to the books of Samuel and Kings on the one hand and Ezra-Nehemiah on the other (until roughly the 1980s), and currently its nature as a work of literary and theological artistry in its own right. Since these three debates still largely define the study of Chronicles down to the present, they provide useful categories for the balance of these introductory comments: Chronicles and history, the extent and authorship of the Chronicler's work, and Chronicles and literature.

The Chronicler claims that his work draws on several literary sources, some of which appear distinct from the sources mentioned in Samuel and Kings. These include the visions of Gad the seer (1 Chron 29:29), the visions of Iddo the seer (2 Chron 9:29), the book of the kings of Israel and Judah (2 Chron 16:11), and many others. The Chronicler's major source, of course, is the canonical books of Samuel and Kings, which provide roughly half of the content of Chronicles.

However, many scholars have doubted the historical reliability of Chronicles, especially since the work of Wilhelm de Wette in 1806–1807. Attitudes toward the reliability or even existence of sources other than Samuel and Kings have ranged from acceptance of them as historically reliable (Rainey and Myers), to their being invented, based upon the preexistent literature of Samuel-Kings and sources mentioned there (Willi and Hoglund), to a more cautious case-by-case analysis of each source (Kalimi). In the absence of corroborating evidence of such sources outside of Chronicles, one should avoid a dogmatic attitude about the Chronicler and his sources.

Related to the issue of sources and historical reliability is that of the question of the Chronicler as a historian. For example, did he write history,

> **The Placement of Chronicles**
> Chronicles closes the Hebrew Bible, while it follows Samuel and Kings in the Septuagint and English versions. This arrangement in the Hebrew is probably due to the lateness of the composition of the book (the postexilic period) as well as its similarity to Ezra-Nehemiah, also found in the "Writings," the last section of the Hebrew Scriptures.

if he simply collated data from a single source or a variety of sources? Does it make sense to speak of him as a historian, if he mainly interpreted the earlier Deuteronomic history of the kings in Samuel and Kings, as Willi maintains? Or was he primarily a theologian, as Ackroyd has suggested, using the medium of narrative to make theological and sermonic points, but not self-consciously a historian?

These questions do not allow easy answers, but perhaps some general guidelines relative to the Chronicler as historian and the historical reliability of Chronicles are in order. First, there are too many historical details in the places where Chronicles does not draw on Samuel-Kings to simply discount them as fabrications. For example, the genealogies of chapters 1–9 frequently do not reveal the Chronicler's main theological ideas, and thus there is no clear reason why he would invent such information (Rainey). On the other hand, even where we do see the Chronicler's theology shaping a major expansion of his sources (for example, the story of Josiah's reform in 2 Chron 34:3–7), these are not necessarily freewheeling interpretations of Samuel-Kings on the Chronicler's part.

Second, it is clear that, while the Chronicler is an interpreter of Samuel-Kings (Willi and North) and a theological writer (Ackroyd), he is primarily a historian (Braun, *1 Chronicles* and Kalimi, *Reshaping*). Whether his sources and his interpretation of those sources is reliable history is another question.

Third, the Chronicler is clearly writing a history of Judah, especially covering the period of Davidic monarchy, for the postexilic community of Jews in the Persian province of Yehud (the area surrounding Jerusalem). The Chronicler has selected and interpreted sources and traditions which make his points. The sections of the work not paralleled in Samuel-Kings reflect his theology no more than the shared material. All of his sources, historical acumen, and creativity serve to make the point of God's faithfulness to the Davidic covenant, priesthood, and temple, and "all Israel" in the past and its continuing relevance to the present. Like all historians of any period, the Chronicler selects and interprets sources.

No less difficult than the issue of the Chronicler as historian is the question of whether the book also includes Ezra and Nehemiah. Jewish tradition as early as the Talmud suggested that the author of Chronicles was Ezra, although it did not necessarily equate Chronicles and Ezra as a single work. L. Zunz first suggested that Chronicles, Ezra, and Nehemiah comprise a single historical work (1832). This thesis was assumed by Martin Noth in 1943 and has, until recent years, been scholarly orthodoxy (see Noth 29: "There is no need to [demonstrate] the work's literary unity"). Since Noth, most scholars have assumed that the Chronicler's history consists of Chronicles, Ezra, and Nehemiah and that these books share common terminology, style, and theological emphases (especially the postexilic concern for priesthood, temple, and *torah*).

While this theory has always had its detractors, beginning with David Freedman's article in 1961 and Sara Japhet's 1968 work, the general consensus on the scope of the Chronicler's work began to break down. Freedman noticed that the theological concerns of the Chronicler are not necessarily those of the author of Ezra-Nehemiah. In particular, concern for Davidic kingship and the covenant with David is paramount in Chronicles and virtually nonexistent in Ezra-Nehemiah. Freedman, however, suggested that there were several editions of Chronicles, finally resulting in our canonical books of Chronicles, Ezra, and Nehemiah.

Cross (15–16) proposed a variation of Freedman's theory of multiple editings. To Cross, there is a literary relationship between Chronicles and Ezra-Nehemiah, as the deuterocanonical work *1 Esdras* suggests. The original work of the Chronicler (according to Cross, "Chron 1") would have consisted of the books of 1–2 Chronicles, minus the genealogies of 1 Chronicles 1–9. The second stage of development (Chron 2) included most of Ezra, and the final stage included the genealogies and Nehemiah. This, he felt, explained why *1 Esdras* contains 2 Chronicles 34–35 and most of Ezra, why 2 Chronicles ends and Ezra begins with almost the same wording, and why they share some themes and terminology in common.

Williamson and Japhet, on the other hand, see few points of contact between Chronicles and Ezra-Nehemiah. Williamson suggested that the

> **1 Esdras**
> *This book in the Apocrypha (or deuterocanonical books) covers the history of Judah from Josiah's reform to Ezra. It revises 1–2 Chronicles, Ezra, and Nehemiah, also adding unparalleled material. Composed sometime between 165 BCE and 50 CE, the book nevertheless reflects older traditions and reveals some of the history of the interpretation of the Chronicler's earlier work.*

book of Chronicles is a unit in itself and the work of the Chronicler consisted of the books of 1 and 2 Chronicles in substantially the form we possess them. He would therefore date the work sometime after the end of the Davidic genealogy in chapter 3, which brings the Davidic line to about 400 BCE. Japhet agrees, but would date the book even later, at the end of the Persian or even the beginning of the Greek period (about 330 BCE). Freedman, on the other hand, suggests editorial additions in the book and therefore sees no reason why it could not have been composed shortly after the return from exile.

The extent and date of the Chronicler's history continues to be debated, although the best arguments seem to show that Chronicles is a unitary work separate from Ezra-Nehemiah. However, some connection does exist between Chronicles and Ezra-Nehemiah, perhaps as the result of an editor's work (see Cross; Tuell). At least, the books have similar themes.

No agreement on the date of Chronicles has come about, although few would now date the work as late as the Greek period (after 332 BCE). Currently, suggestions run from the Greek period (around 300 BCE; Knoppers, *1 Chronicles 1–9*), to a few decades earlier (Ackroyd), to about 400 BCE (Williamson), to early in the postexilic period (Freedman; Throntveit). If one follows Cross's multiple editions, then perhaps the composition spanned the early Second Temple period down to sometime after 400 BCE.

It is impossible to date the book more precisely within the Persian period. The mention of the Persian coin the *daric*, minted during the reign of Darius I, suggests a date after 515 BCE. Likewise, apparent quotations from Zechariah in 2 Chronicles 16:9 (Zech 4:10) and 30:6–9 (Zech 1:2–4) may suggest a date somewhat after 515 BCE and Zechariah's ministry. Likewise, the continuation of the Davidic line in the genealogies of 1 Chronicles 3 to roughly 400 BCE (sometime between 416 and 336, according to McKenzie), suggests a date for composition of 400 or later. On the other hand, Knoppers has recently suggested that the apparent quotations of Zechariah are not quotations at all, leaving only the mention of *darics* and the continuation of the Davidic line to suggest a date of 400 or later. That *darics* would require 100 years or better to be disseminated throughout the Persian Empire and accepted as the medium of exchange, as Knoppers implies, does not follow. In an empire as organized as Persia, little time need have passed from the introduction of the *daric* in 515 to its general use and acceptance throughout the empire.

Attempting to date a document by literary theme is notoriously difficult. Nevertheless, the most predominant themes of the Chronicler's history are those of Davidic kingship, the covenant with David, and his relationship to the temple and its cult. This preoccupation with David and the Davidic covenant is totally lacking in the books that unquestionably date from the middle or the end of the Persian period, such as Ezra-Nehemiah and Malachi. On the other hand, concern for the restoration of Davidic kingship figures prominently in such early postexilic writings as Haggai and Zechariah 1–8. Thus perhaps Chronicles dates to an era when messianic expectation ran high, such as in the early Second Temple period (but before the work of Ezra and Nehemiah in about 450 BCE). The continuation of the Davidic genealogy in 1 Chronicles 3, therefore, would probably be an addition to update the genealogy to the editor's own time. Some ancient manuscripts suggest such a possibility. After Zerubbabel and Shenazzar are mentioned in 1 Chronicles 3:18–20, the text departs from a more or less freeform genealogy and becomes rigid and formulaic, mentioning all of an individual's descendants in the same way (for example, "the sons of X: X, X, X, three").

> **Biblical Genealogies**
>
> *In traditional societies, genealogies help family groups establish their internal and external relationships. In the Bible, the genealogies function in a similar way, but they also serve as metaphors for the basic organization of society or even as arguments for the superiority of one group over another or as a reminder of God's providential care (for example, Exod 6:14–25).*

Chronicles and Literature: The last 20 years have seen a great deal of attention given to Chronicles as a piece of literature. But what kind of literature is Chronicles? Various responses to this question have been posed, ranging from historiography, to Bible study, to midrash (homiletical commentary). I will briefly look at a few of these options and conclude with my own observations.

First, as mentioned above, early readers of Chronicles thought of it as a parallel historical account supplementing Samuel-Kings. While not many would still characterize Chronicles as "Things Omitted," as the Septuagint did, some scholars view the book as predominantly historiographic. That is, it predominantly narrates and interprets history. Williamson suggests that the Chronicler was a master at "retelling the sacred story." Two recent commentators, De Vries and Hooker, suggest "history" as the genre that author self-consciously uses: "No less than Samuel-Kings, Chronicles deserves the genre-name history" (De Vries 16).

Second, other scholars have been more reluctant to apply the term "history" to Chronicles. Due to the large amount of Chronicles which has as its main source other biblical texts, including Samuel-Kings, Psalms, etc., these scholars suggest that Chronicles is primarily an exegesis of Samuel-Kings and other biblical texts. The Chronicler's own additions would therefore be his own interpretations and extrapolations, not reliable history based on ancient sources. Perhaps the most significant proponent of this view is Thomas Willi, but this approach has been espoused recently by such scholars as Tuell, who calls Chronicles a "Bible study," and Mitchell, who refers to Chronicles as "proto-midrash."

Is, then, Chronicles an attempt to rewrite history or a literary product resulting from the exegesis of Samuel-Kings? Williamson (23) puts it well:

> [W]e should beware of attempts simplistically to reduce to a single category the nature of the Chronicler's composition or his use of sources.... But overall the Chronicler shows himself as the master, not the servant, of his sources. His is the last example of Israel's genius for retelling her sacred history in a way which applies its lessons creatively to the demands of a developing community.

As some scholars have recently suggested, Chronicles may be considered the genre of the "rewritten Bible," a reworking and interpretation of older biblical texts, but at the same time a new history carefully selecting biblical and extrabiblical sources for maximum impact on the community of faith in the postexilic Persian province of Yehud.

COMMENTARY

GENEALOGIES FROM ADAM TO THE RESTORED COMMUNITY OF JUDAH · 1:1–9:44

Chronicles is the only book of the Old Testament that begins with an extensive genealogy. Most of the genealogical data contained within this section – and even the precise wording – occur elsewhere in the Old Testament, although there may be some material dependent upon other sources now lost to us.

1:1–54 The names recorded in 1 Chronicles 1:1–4 come from Genesis 5, although the more expanded text of that latter passage is missing from 1 Chronicles. The sons of Noah (Shem, Ham, and Japheth) appear in the flood account of Genesis 6–9 and as the progenitors of the nations in Genesis 10. Verses 4–23 occur almost word for word in Genesis 10, the so-called Table of Nations. Verses 24–27 summarizes the lineal genealogy in Genesis 11:10–26, the line of Shem down to Abraham. Thus, this opening chapter summarizes the primeval history of Genesis 5–11 in genealogical form.

> **Lineal & Branched Genealogies**
> *Genealogies in the Old Testament may be either lineal (one name per generation) or branched (more than one name per generation). The two styles serve different purposes.*

Verses 28–54 comprise the genealogy of tribes related to Israel, tracing their lineage back to Abraham: Ishmael (verses 28–31), Keturah, Abraham's concubine (especially Midian; verses 32–33), and finally the genealogies of the sons of Isaac, Jacob, and Esau (1:34–8:40). Of the sons of Isaac, Esau's genealogy comes first as part of the genealogy of the "nations" that precede Israel's clans in chapters 2–9. The entire genealogy of Esau is an abbreviated form of Genesis 36.

2:1–55 Chapters 2–8 comprise the genealogy of Jacob/Israel, the twelve sons who were the progenitors of the twelve tribes of Israel. It is noteworthy that the list includes all twelve, even though some had ceased to function early on as viable tribes (notably, Simeon, absorbed by Judah – see Judges 1 – and Reuben, whose land was lost no later than the ninth century, according to the Moabite text, the "Mesha Stele," which does not know of a tribe of Reuben to their north). Indeed, all of the northern tribes had been carried off to Assyrian captivity centuries before Chronicles was written. We know from 1 Kings 17 that there were remnants of the northern Israelites who married foreigners settled in Israel by the Assyrians, combining their religion and culture with the eastern Elamites and Medes. Furthermore, the Chronicler speaks of a few north Israelites who returned to the land with the Judeans after the edict of Cyrus in 539 BCE. The Chronicler is concerned with the restoration of "all Israel," representatives of all twelve tribes, not just the southern portion of it.

For the most part, these chapters reflect close familiarity with both the Pentateuch and Joshua–2 Kings, which the Chronicler has undoubtedly used as sources. The list of the twelve tribes in 2:1–2 is identical in order to that of Gen 25:23–26, except that Chronicles lists *Dan* prior to *Joseph*, rather than with *Naphtali* as sons of the concubine Bilhah. The balance of chapter 2 comes primarily from Genesis 38 and 46, as well as Numbers and Joshua. An interesting feature of this chapter is the listing of the Calebites, Jerahmeelites, and Kenites in the genealogy of Judah. The Pentateuch lists them separately from the Israelites, but Joshua includes them in Israel's genealogy.

3:1–24 This section lists David's descendants, from his own children down to roughly the year 400 BCE, including all of the kings of Judah during the divided monarchy. The list continues after the last king of Judah (Zedekiah), with the descendants of the penultimate king, *Jeconiah* (Jehoiachin), including *Shenazzar* (possibly Sheshbazzar, governor of Judah after the exile; see Ezra 1:8), and Zerubbabel (see Ezra 3, 5; Hag 2:23; Zech 4:6). Following Jeconiah, the list of Davidides is dependent upon extrabiblical sources. This is important data for us, as it helps us to understand that the continuation of the Davidic line was important until well into the Persian period. It is also an indication of the Chronicler's concern for Davidic messianism and God's continued faithfulness to the promises to David.

4:1–23 This section returns to the genealogy of Judah and largely repeats information already in chapter 2. This genealogy contains some unusual features, including names of children of Judah who do not otherwise appear in chapter 2 or in the Pentateuch. Judah heads the genealogical lists of the twelve tribes for two reasons: it is the tribe of David and Davidic kingship in Israel, and also because Judeans comprised the greatest part of those returning from Babylonian exile.

5:1–26 Chapter 5 consists of the genealogy of Reuben, Gad, and half of Manasseh, the three Transjordanian tribes that elected to remain to the east of the Jordan after the period of conquest (see Num 32; Josh 22). The Chronicler shows a concern with priority among the tribes, as Reuben was the firstborn and logically should have been listed first. Pride of place goes to Judah in the Chronicler's history, of course, as David's tribe and comprising the majority of the remnant of Israel in his own day. In 5:1, the Chronicler explains that Reuben, otherwise possessing the primogeniture, had "profaned his father's couch" (see Gen 49:4), and so the primogeniture went to the sons of Joseph, specifically Ephraim (Gen 49:22). The Chronicler has further explanations to make, as neither Ephraim nor Reuben retained their primacy in postexilic Judah and, indeed, from at least the time of Assyrian captivity in 721 BCE. The Chronicler's explanation is that, though Ephraim became the most prominent northern tribe, and though Reuben was the firstborn, Judah arose in time as the *strongest of his brothers* and most significantly, *a ruler came from him* (Gen 49:8–10).

> **Primogeniture**
> *The right of the firstborn (usually male) child to inherit more than the other children. In Israel, firstborn males ordinarily received twice the share of other children. In some settings, ultimogeniture, or inheritance by the last child, may have prevailed, as in the patriarchal stories of Isaac, Jacob, and even Joseph, or as in the story of David, who becomes king though the youngest boy of his family.*

Verses 3–10 contain a short list of prominent Reubenite families. The list is abbreviated, containing at most eight generations. The Chronicler has apparently taken the initial list of Reuben's sons from Numbers 26:5, but beginning with 1 Chronicles 5:4 he gives his own special list of eight generations of Reubenites, leading to exile under Tiglath-pileser III of Assyria in 721 BCE. This list is interesting because King Mesha of Moab indicates on the so-called "Mesha Stele" (late 800s BCE) that the men of Gad had lived to his north "for always," betraying no knowledge that Reubenites had ever lived there.

The lion's share of attention in this chapter is given to the war which the Transjordanian tribes fought with the Hagrites, an Arab group living to the east, not otherwise known before the ninth-eighth century BCE (see Eph'al 67, 71, 100, 215). Here, the most significant memory that the Chronicler shares in the genealogical section pertaining to these tribes is the war with the Hagrites. It is possible that a tribe by this name lived near the Reubenites in the time of Saul; also, it is possible that the Chronicler preserves a memory of battles fought with other nomadic groups who lived in the area which during the postexilic era was occupied by Hagrites.

The Gadites (verses 11–16) also have only a truncated genealogy. They are listed as living in the land of Bashan, north of Reuben. Here, the author makes no attempt to provide a lineal genealogy. We do possess some indication of where the Chronicler got at least some of the information he had relative to Transjordanian genealogies: "All of them were enrolled by genealogy in the days of Jotham king of Judah and in the days of Jeroboam king of Israel" (verse 17). What genealogical information he possesses may simply end around this time, on the eve of the Assyrian conquest.

As with Reuben, so the Gadite section largely deals with the Hagrite war (verses 18–22). Two concerns of the Chronicler are evident here: immediate retribution and seeking Yahweh (here, "crying out" and trusting in the Lord). As a result of the Transjordanian tribes' trust in God, many *fell slain, because the battle was God's* (5:22).

The *half-tribe of Manasseh*, in the Transjordan, merits only four verses (verses 23–26). There is but a single verse which gives prominent family names of "fathers' houses." The Chronicler deals with them summarily: "But they acted unfaithfully ... and played the harlot." The final verse dealing with the Transjordanian tribes (verse 26) summarizes their faithlessness and divine retribution that resulted.

5:27–41 (Hebrew 6:1–16) is possibly a list of prominent or high priests from the line of Levi down to the exile of Judah. This list has generated a great deal of discussion, as the names do not always coincide with known high priests of Judah (for example, Jehoiada the high priest under Joash's reign is not mentioned; see Japhet, *I & II Chronicles*, 150–151). Some have suggested that the list is actually a genealogy of a line of Levitical priests during the Persian period, whom the Chronicler wishes to accord legitimacy in the Aaronic line (Japhet, *I & II Chronicles*, 151).

6:1–81 Chapter 6 (in Hebrew; 6:16 in English) is a continuation of the Levitical genealogy begun in the previous chapter. This list begins with the children of Levi, Kohath, Gershom, and Merari, a segmented genealogy. Of these, Kohath receives the most attention as the ancestor of Moses and Aaron. Verses 31–48 detail one of the Chronicler's main concerns: the organization of the temple singers. This group is given legitimacy in all three of the Levitical family lines. Verses 49–81 predominately deal with the the Aaronic/Kohathite priestly family and its allotments of territory, Levitical cities and cities of refuge. Verses 71–80 deal with the territorial allotment for the Gershomites and Merarites. This account is largely dependent upon Joshua 21.

7:1–40 Chapter 7 returns to the other tribes, not earlier recorded. It is the Chronicler's concern to show all Israel as the scope of God's concern and restoration in the postexilic period. To that end, genealogies are given for most of the tribes, with one or two missing and a few with rather brief entries. Issachar is one such (7:1–5). The sons of Issachar (7:1) are listed in Numbers 26:23–25 (also Gen 46:13). Otherwise, this brief listing of Issachar's genealogy comprises only three generations and is not otherwise known to us.

Verses 6–12 contain the first Benjaminite genealogy. While the Chronicler is primarily concerned with Judah (Davidic kingship) and Levi (temple priesthood), Benjamin was also a major player in the postexilic community of Yehud. The first Benjaminite genealogy consists of a segmented genealogy of only three families. There is also a fourth family line mentioned in verse 12, not otherwise clearly connected with what precedes (although see verse 15 for the possible dislocation of verse 12).

In verse 13, Naphtali receives the shortest genealogical entry with the exception of Dan, which has no entry at all. It is at least arguable that those tribes that make appearances in the Chronicler's postexilic community, such as Ephraim and Manasseh, receive greater attention in the genealogies. The author may include others, such as Naphtali, only for the sake of completeness.

Presumably the Manasseh mentioned in 7:14–19 is the Cisjordanian (western Israelite) "half-tribe"

> **Pul or Tiglath-pileser**
> In 1 Chronicles 5:26 Pul and Tiglath-pileser are two names for the same Assyrian king (reigned 745–727 BCE). The name Pul or Pulu comes primarily from Babylonian texts about this monarch, one of the greatest generals of the ancient world. Chronicles seems to recognize that the two names designate the same person (Japhet, *I & II Chronicles*, 142).

of Manasseh, the Transjordanian half having been previously mentioned. This list closely follows the genealogy of Manasseh in Numbers 26:29–34. Of his descendants, Machir and Gilead have pride of place. Zelophehad and his daughters also receive attention, owing to the prominence of their story in Numbers 27 and 36 as the family whose daughters could inherit property in Israel.

Verses 20–29 mention Ephraim. A version of 7:20 occurs in Numbers 26:35–36, although the names are spelled differently there. In a story otherwise unknown to us, the men of Gath kill Ephraim's children. He and his wife have another child, named Beriah, through whom the ensuing genealogy is reckoned (7:21–29).

Verses 30–40 is the genealogy of Asher. Verses 30–31a appears in a more complete form in Numbers 26:44–46. Note that occasionally the text of Chronicles as we have it appears to result from copyists' mistakes on minor points. For example, the text gives *Ishvah* and *Ishvi* as the names of two of Asher's children, while Numbers records the name of the child as *Ishvi*, the father of the *Ishvites*. The Chronicler may have taken these as two separate genealogical entries.

8:1–40 Chapter 8 is a far more exhaustive genealogy of Benjamin, in two sections: first, verses 1–28, presumably a lineal genealogy of Benjamin until the postexilic community in Jerusalem, gives only occasional anecdotal or historical information. The second, verses 29–40, specifically deals with the genealogy of Saul. This information is important, as chapter 10, the beginning of the historical narrative proper, will chronicle God's rejection of Saul and his death on the field of battle.

9:1–44 Chapter 9 is the record of captives who returned from captivity to Babylon. Several interests and concerns of the Chronicler figure prominently here. First, "all Israel was enrolled by genealogies." The Chronicler is self-consciously a keeper and interpreter of ancient records. His records, on the other hand, are not complete, and he tips his hat to other sources: "They are written in the book of the kings of Israel."

Second, the exile of Judah is mentioned tersely: they were taken there *because of their unfaithfulness* (verse 1). Whether for the Transjordanian tribes (chapter 5), or Judah and "all Israel" in the postexilic age (chapter 9), exile is the inevitable result of faithlessness. The Chronicler is not mainly concerned, however, with faithlessness, but rather with restoration. Verses 2–9 deal with the restoration to the land of certain elements of all Israel, prominent among them Judahites and Benjaminites, but also including some Ephraimites and Manassites (compare the attention given to these tribes in chapter 7). Priests, Levites, gatekeepers, and singers fill out most of the remainder of the chapter. These families carry out specific duties in the postexilic worship in the temple. It is apparently not critical for the Chronicler to establish the credentials of these Levitical functionaries all the way back to Levi; simply a few generations back to the period before the exile appears to suffice to show the Levitical continuity between the pre- and postexilic communities (most of the lineal genealogies are three to six generations; see verse 11). While the texts of the preexilic period do not give details of the organization of the temple functionaries, the divisions of the priests and Levites (differentiated in the post-, but not the preexilic periods) are of paramount importance to the Chronicler. Thus he records brief genealogies of some of the prominent families of the priests and Levites (verses 10–16), but gives details of the responsibilities of the gatekeepers and singers (verses 17–34). Most commentators suggest that such detailed organization was unknown prior to the exile and that these functions came to full flower in the temple-centered community of the Persian province of Yehud (Knoppers, *1 Chronicles 1–9*, 512–14). Regardless, it is extremely important to the Chronicler to ground postexilic practice in preexilic bloodlines, in order to establish continuity and legitimacy.

The final section of chapter nine, verses 35–44, is a virtual repetition of the Saulide/Benjaminite genealogy in 8:29–40, with the exception of some variation in spelling and the deletion of the last two verses of chapter 8. Perhaps such a record of Saul's prolific descendants did not sit well with the

---

The People of God

The Chronicler's concern for the legitimacy of the postexilic community is such that he must begin with genealogical data in order to establish the returnees' claim to be the people of God, to retell their story in a new context, and to call the people to faithfulness in that new context.

1 CHRONICLES

Chronicler's understanding of the demise of Saul's dynasty due to his faithlessness. In any event, this genealogy has been duplicated here for the transparent reason of leading the reader into the account of Saul's rejection and death.

THE STORY OF THE KINGS OF JUDAH · 10:1–29:30

The next section of Chronicles should be considered a unit, comprised of the subunits of the reigns of David and Solomon. There is no clear distinction between their reigns: as Braun has pointed out, in Chronicles David and Solomon are the two model kings, whose reigns set the standard for those who follow (Braun, *1 Chronicles*, 219). Indeed, they are portrayed as exemplary in every way, with the sole exception of David's peccadillo in numbering the people in 1 Chronicles 21 (see below). Solomon plays a major part also in 1 Chronicles 22–29, first as heir of David's temple plans (1 Chron 22:6), then as regent over Israel (1 Chron 23:1), and finally as executor of David's "blueprint" [Hebrew *tavnit*] for the temple and king (1 Chron 28–29). The reigns of these two kings may therefore be construed as an idealized unit, as exemplary kings and as originators of the temple and its organization, personnel, and worship.

10:1–14 Chapter 10 comes almost entirely from its source, 1 Samuel 31, with the exception of portions of verses 10, 12, and 13–14. This chapter sets the tone for the remainder of the book: it will specifically address righteous and legitimate kingship, with the king's role as temple and worship patron an important component. The Chronicler begins with the contrast between faithless king Saul and faithful king David. To accomplish this comparison, the Chronicler need do nothing more than quote his source and provide his own interpretation of Saul's death at the end.

The rejection of Saul and his eventual demise require all of 1 Samuel 9–31 to explain. Chronicles, on the other hand, reduces the life of Saul to the single story of his death because of unfaithfulness to God. The author attributes that death to three factors: Saul did not keep the (here unspecified) commandments of God, he "sought" [Hebrew *darash*] a medium, and he did not "seek" [*darash*] Yahweh (verses 13–14).

Chronicles' source does not describe Saul's ending in a complimentary way. First, the Philistines overrun the Israelite army (verse 1), a sure sign to both the Deuteronomist and the Chronicler of Saul's and Israel's faithlessness and God's absence. Second, Saul commits suicide by falling on his sword (verse 4). Third, Saul and his heirs are subjected to the ultimate indignity by having their bodies exposed (verses 8–12; compare with 1 Sam 31:10–12, where Saul's body and the bodies of his sons are fastened to the wall of Beth Shean, something the Chronicler may have felt uncomfortable including). Finally, his head is set up in the temple of the Philistine god Dagon (compare with 1 Sam 31:10, where his armor, and not his head, is placed in the temple of Ashtaroth).

The Chronicler thus introduces the reader to three of his most important themes, which are reiterated throughout the work: legitimate Davidic kingship, immediate retribution for sinfulness, and blessing for seeking the Lord.

> **Dagon**
>
> *1 Chronicles 10:10 may reflect an exegetical move on the Chronicler's part*, as Dagon was the main god of Philistia (see 1 Sam 5) and also because 1 Samuel 31 does not detail the disposition of the king's head. As in many other places, Chronicles tries to explain matters in Samuel through Kings that seem unclear.

11:1–12:40 Chapter 11 is largely a compilation of passages from 2 Samuel 5 and 23. Chapter 12 contains material about David's army from "all Israel," not otherwise attested. These two chapters demonstrate that thousands of armed warriors from all over Israel, north and south, came to David when he was at Ziklag (12:1) and at Hebron (11:1, 10, 12:23). The author takes 11:1–3 from 2 Samuel 5:1–3, although the Chronicler has ended the account of Israel's anointing of David by making it a fulfillment of a prophecy of Samuel (1 Sam 16), in line with his interest in prophets and prophetic fulfillment. Verses 4–9 have as their source 1 Samuel 5:6–10, but with two omissions: the Jebusites' taunting of David and the notice of Joab as the one to respond to David's promise of leadership to the one who would first go up against them. The deletion of the first may be due to the Chronicler's concern to level no criticism against David; the inclusion of the second to show the reason for Joab's prominent place in David's cabinet. Verses 10–47 have as their primary source 1 Samuel 23:8–39, the account of David's 30 mighty men, which the Chronicler transfers to the beginning of David's reign.

The author has written 11:11–41a with virtually no modifications of his source, 2 Samuel 23:8–39, apart from mainly text-critical issues relating to spelling of names and verb forms. The main differences are the abbreviation of the account of Eleazer and Shammah, two of the three mighty men whose exploits against the Philistines appear in 2 Samuel 23:9–12. The Chronicler collapses these two accounts into one and gives credit to Eleazer. Second Samuel 23:10 is simply missing, because of the repetition of the word "were gathered" at the end of verse 9 and the beginning of verse 11. The result is that one ends up in Chronicles with only two, and not three, chief mighty men. The Septuagint fixes this problem, as do some of the ancient versions, by reading about Abishai in verse 20 "he was famous among the three." Other smaller variations abound. For example, 1 Chronicles 11:23 says that an Egyptian warrior measured five cubits tall (almost as tall as Goliath; 1 Sam 17:4) and also had a spear *like a weaver's rod* (1 Sam 17:7). In the 2 Samuel account, the Egyptian man is simply a "man of appearance," perhaps good-looking. Also, several of the names in 2 Samuel 23:34 are missing from 1 Chronicles 11:36 and vice versa, but this may be attributable to confusion in word breaks and consonants by the Chronicler or by later scribes. Besides these, the biggest variation occurs in 1 Chronicles 11:41b–47, which has no parallels in 2 Samuel or anywhere else. While the list in 2 Samuel includes 37 names (see 2 Sam 23:39), the Chronicler's account now contains almost 50 names!

Chapter 12 lists armed men from all of the tribes of Israel which supported David while he was at Ziklag (verses 1–22) and at Hebron (verses 23–37). It is first important for the Chronicler to establish that

> **David's Mighty Men**
>
> *The most significant difference between these two accounts of David's mighty men has to do with the Chronicler's purpose in reporting the account where he does. In Samuel, the lists of David's mighty men seek to chronicle and eulogize David's strength and charisma. In Chronicles, the purpose is to show that these famous warriors came to him before he was proclaimed king over all Israel, while he was still at Hebron, with full intent to see him crowned. It is important that these mighty men came from the entire nation, showing that all tribes united to make David king.*

David inspired loyalty from the northern tribes and even from Saul's kinsmen, the Benjaminites. While he was still a Philistine mercenary, Benjaminites, Gadites, Judeans, and Manassites came to him (David is exonerated in the Philistine battle against Israel, because the Philistines thought he would be faithful to Saul [verse 19]). It is interesting that Manassites and Gadites, also highlighted in the genealogies of chapters 1–9, are here depicted as among David's earliest supporters. In chapter 9, Manassites and Ephraimites are among the remnant living in Jerusalem after the exile, while the Gadites and Manassites were exemplary in chapter 5 for calling on Yahweh in their battle against the Hagrites. To the Chronicler Israel is always "all Israel," north and south, and the mention of northern tribes by name serves to promote unity with the remnants of the northerners living in postexilic Judah (see Japhet, *I & II Chronicles*, 208).

While the numbers of those defecting to David seem overstated, one should probably read this account as idealized and eschatological, pointing forward to a time when all Israel would bow before the Davidic king in a "great army, like an army of God" (verse 22). All Israel unites to make David king (verse 38), eating and drinking in joyful celebration.

13:1–16:43 This section focuses on the escorting of the ark to Jerusalem and the organization of the Levitical singers and gatekeepers. These chapters have as their source 2 Samuel 5:11–6:19, although the initial narrative, the first attempt to bring the ark up from *Kiriath Jearim*, precedes the account of *Hiram* of Tyre and the Philistine wars instead of following them as in 2 Samuel. Furthermore, chapters 13–14 come mainly verbatim from 2 Samuel, while chapters 15–16 are mostly expansions upon that biblical material.

Chapter 13 primarily draws on 2 Samuel 6:1–11, although 1 Chronicles 13:1–5 expands and interprets its source. First, as every ideal king should do, David consults with all the leaders of Israel (verse 1). Second, he suggests to these leaders that all those "who are left" or "who remain" in all the "lands of Israel"—a strange expression for David's time, but understandable in light of the remnants of the people following exile—to be gathered together, along with priests and Levites, to bring the ark of the covenant to Jerusalem. Third, the reason given for this is because they did not *inquire of it* [RSV "we

1 CHRONICLES

neglected it"; Hebrew *darash*, "seek"] in the days of Saul. Again, one is reminded of the way the narrative section of Chronicles begins: Saul is rejected because he did not seek Yahweh. David's first act in Chronicles, after being made king by all Israel, was to begin to do so by means of bringing the ark of the covenant into the center of religious and political life. Indeed, one wonders if "seeking the Lord" to the Chronicler is not a way of saying "inquire of the Lord at the ark of the covenant," or "seek God's presence in worship."

The last verse of chapter 13 without a parallel in 2 Samuel is verse 5. Once again, David assembled *all the Israelites*, coming from the nation's ideal boundaries from the valley between the Lebanon and Anti-Lebanon mountains (*Lebo Hamath*) to the border of Egypt and Canaan (the *Shihor* of Egypt).

Verses 6–14 closely follow 2 Samuel 6. All of Israel comes to *Kiriath Jearim* (Baale-Yehudah in 2 Sam 6:2 and identified with the former city in Chronicles) to bring up the ark. A certain Uzzah drives the ark of the covenant on an ox cart, but when the ox stumbles, he put forth his hand to steady the ark and is smitten by God for his presumptuous act. David is then afraid to bring the ark into Jerusalem, so it is left with the household of Obed-Edom ("the servant of Edom"), whereupon God blesses that household. This is where the narrative from 1 Samuel 6 stops and the Chronicler inserts material from 1 Samuel 5 following it, to subsequently pick up and expand the ark account in chapter 15.

Chapter 14 returns to the text of 2 Samuel 5 as its main source, with an interpretive addition in verse 17. The Chronicler has interrupted the narrative of 2 Samuel 6:1–11, the first, aborted attempt to bring up the ark and its temporary installment in the house of Obed-Edom, with a return to 2 Samuel 5, last used in 1 Chronicles 11:1–10.

> **Praise for David**
> 1 Chronicles 14 praises David for his successes in international diplomacy, the size of his household, and his military success against the Philistines. In verses 11–12, the Chronicler is not overly concerned about David's palace-building venture prior to establishing the ark in Jerusalem, because of David's confidence in Yahweh's support. This knowledge comes as a result of Hiram's aid in building his palace. Also, David needs a palace, for that is going to be the place where the tent for the ark will be pitched (1 Chron 15:1).

There may be two reasons for the reordering of these accounts. First, even more than the author of Samuel, the Chronicler wants to make the bringing of the ark of the covenant into Jerusalem the first act of David's reign. No one can charge him with neglect of the ark such "as in the days of Saul"! Therefore, rather than the account of Philistine wars, international treaties, and David's prolific fathering preceding the ark narrative, as in 2 Samuel, all of these accounts from 2 Samuel 5 come first in order to underscore David's piety.

Second, this shifting of stories leaves the question of where these accounts should be put, as they are also complimentary of David's might, political acumen, and piety. The perfect opportunity presents itself in the ark narrative, as there is a three-month gap in David's activities while the ark rests at Obed-Edom's house. While not everything in 2 Samuel 5:11–25 can have taken place in three months (two battles, the building of a palace, and eleven children!), these accounts do draw attention away from the fiasco of the original attempt to move the ark and onto David's power and fame.

In verses 3–7, David is even more prolific in fathering than even 2 Samuel acknowledges, as Chronicles records thirteen children born in Jerusalem, as opposed to the eleven in 2 Samuel 5:13–16. For the most part, these names are similar or identical to those in 2 Samuel, with the exception of the addition of *Elpelet* (perhaps a dittography for *Eliphelet* in 14:7; the Septuagint lists them both identically) and *Nogah* (next to *Nepheg*, perhaps a scribal slip). The only other significant difference is in the name Eliada ("my god knows"; 2 Sam 5:16) as opposed to the equivalent *Beeliada* ("Baal [or the Lord] knows"; 1 Chron 14:7). The latter name is consistent with the Chronicler's preference for preserving original forms of names, even those mentioning Baal, among the royal household (see the Chronicler's Ishbaal for 2 Samuel's Ishbosheth).

The balance of chapter 14 reports two battles against the Philistines. In both verses 8–17 and its source (2 Samuel 5:17–25), the purpose is to extol David's military prowess and piety. It is apparent that the Chronicler has included these accounts because both of them begin with David *inquiring* (RSV) of God before going into battle. The term for "inquire" or "ask" [Hebrew *sha'al*] is common in Chronicles and virtually synonymous with to verb *darash*, "to seek." These accounts echo the Chronicler's concern to show David's exemplary piety and explain God's rejection of Saul (see 10:13–14), because Saul did not "seek" Yahweh as David did.

The Chronicler has ended both accounts of these Philistine battles differently than his source did. At the end of the first battle, Samuel reports that the Philistines were defeated at *Baal Perazim*, leaving their gods there, whereupon David and his men "carried them away." In 2 Chronicles 14:12, after the defeat of the Philistines David "commanded and they were burned with fire," leaving no ambiguity as to the disposition of the idols. In the second battle account, God fights the battle for Israel (much in the manner of battle accounts in Joshua and elsewhere) and David "smote the camp of the Philistines from Gibeon [2 Sam 5:25: Geba] to Gezer." The Chronicler adds the unparalleled material in verse 17 to his source as a summary of David's greatness portrayed in chapter 14.

Chapter 15 returns to the ark narrative, but with only verses 25–29 parallel to 2 Samuel (2 Sam 6:12b–19a). The balance of chapter 15 is the Chronicler's own additions, primarily dealing with the organization of the Levitical singers and gatekeepers. It is critical for the Chronicler to establish the legitimacy and antiquity of Second Temple Levitical and priestly organization, but his depiction of Levitical offices and musical instruments, according to many scholars, may owe more to his own time than to that of David.

> **Second Temple Worship**
> *It is important to the Chronicler that he ground temple cult rituals and Levitical courses in the ancient practices of worship of David and Solomon, even though 2 Samuel does not mention the Levitical gatekeepers and singers, whose roles appear to be largely Second Temple developments.*

Chapter 15 has four main sections: verses 1–3, introduction to bringing the ark from the house of Obed-Edom (a partial reiteration of 2 Sam 5:11 and 6:17); verses 4–15, the consecration of the Levitical priests to carry the ark; verses 16–24 (the appointment of musicians and gatekeepers); and 5:25–6:3, the transporting of the ark with celebration into Jerusalem and its installation there (parallel to 2 Sam 6:12b–19a). In the first section, the Chronicler has David building a house first (14:1; here *buildings*), then pitches a tent for the ark of the covenant once "houses" have been suitably prepared (compare 2 Sam 6:17). The "tent" pitched is reminiscent of the *mishkan* or tabernacle which housed the ark in the wilderness and at Shiloh. The Chronicler, however, is quite positive that the *mishkan* was at this time at Gibeon, while the tent David pitched for the ark was something else (see 1 Chron 16:39 and the commentary on that passage below). The reason given in Chronicles for the earlier fiasco was that the Levites did not carry the ark as they should have (15:2; a fact not reported in Samuel). David assembled all Israel to Jerusalem to bring up the ark (verse 3, a version of 2 Sam 6:2b).

In the next section, certain Levites are consecrated to carry the ark. These are from the three main Levitical families – the Merarites, the Kohathites, and the Gershomites – as well as three other Levitical families: the sons of Elizaphan, Hebron, and Uzziel. First Chronicles 6:2 indicates that Hebron and Uzziel were children of Kohath, the priestly family of Levites. Elizaphan is otherwise unattested in the Chronicler's genealogies of chapters 1–9, but may be mentioned in Numbers 3:30 as the son of Uzziel and the grandson of Kohath. Elizaphan appears one other time in Chronicles, in connection with Hezekiah's reform (2 Chron 29:13), along with these other prominent Levitical families (Gershom, Merari, Kohath, Uzziel, Shemaiah, Heman, and Jeduthun). It is apparent that certain families of the Levites had become prominent no later than the early postexilic age and the Chronicler correspondingly focuses attention on these family lines.

In verses 11–15, the high priests Zadok and Abiathar, along with the chiefs of the Levitical families mentioned above, learn from David that the reason God *broke out* against them in the first attempt to bring the ark to Jerusalem was because the Levites did not "seek it according to custom" (RSV: *care for it in the way that is ordained*). The text does not mention Uzzah and his violation of the holy object by touching it; the Chronicler focuses on what should have happened based on current practice and his reading of scripture. The *prescribed way* referred to may be the Chronicler's reading of ark passages in the Pentateuch, such as Exodus 25:14–15, 37:5, and 39:35, which mention the ark and its poles for carrying. In terms of who should carry it, the Pentateuch simply specifies "priests" (Deut 31:9), and Joshua 3–4 details the priests transporting the ark of the covenant over the Jordan River into Canaan.

Verses 16–24 describe the organization of the Levitical musicians and gatekeepers, two divisions of Levitical offices not heretofore mentioned in the Old Testament. The families of musicians mentioned here are those of *Heman*, *Asaph*, and *Ethan*, while a *Jeduthun* figures as a prominent musician in 16:41 and *Kenaniah* as a "leader" or "director" of the Levitical musicians in 15:22. Several other names are mentioned who are of the "second order" (15:20–21). Heman, Asaph, Ethan, and Jeduthun achieved prominence in the tradition outside of Chronicles. First Kings 4:31 mentions *Heman the Ezrahite* as being extremely wise (and the superscription of Ps 88 attributes that poem to him). Ethan (also the Ezrahite) is likewise a wise man in 1 Kings 4:31, and the superscription of Psalm 89 attributes the work to him. Jeduthun, besides several occurrences in Chronicles, appears possibly as "choirmaster" in Psalms 38, 61, and 76, all psalms attributed to David. Asaph has preeminence over these others in chapter 16 ("Asaph and his brothers") and is credited with Psalms 50 and 73–83.

The instruments that are mentioned in 15:16, 28 and 16:5–6 and 42 are the *nevel* (large harp or lyre), the *kinnor* (small harp or lyre), the *metsaltayim* (cymbals), the *chatsotserot* (silver trumpets), and the *shofar* (ram's horn trumpet). All of these instruments are attested in the late second and first millennia BCE, although the *chatsotserah* or trumpet rarely occurs in Iron Age archaeological contexts (for more on music, see Braun, *Music*).

Chapter 16 makes explicit what 2 Samuel 6:12–19 leaves implicit. The Chronicler composes a psalm for David, weaving together pieces of several biblical psalms as well as other material. With only minor variations, verses 8–22 repeat Psalm 105:1–15, verses 23–33 equal Psalm 96:1–13, and verses 34–36 are equivalent to Psalm 106:1, 47–48. (For more detail on each psalm, see the Psalms commentary in this volume.) Like some other late biblical authors (for example, see Neh 9), the Chronicler could treat earlier hymns as raw materials for new compositions. This process of revising older material into something new with its own integrity continued into the late Second Temple period, as we see in the *Hodayot* from the Dead Sea Scrolls. Indeed, hymn writers still use such techniques of composition.

As Knoppers (*1 Chronicles 10–29*, 645) has noted, the Chronicler does not make a sloppy patchwork with this psalm, but rather uses it to emphasize major theological points, such as "remembrance, thanksgiving, singing, and praise." He clearly uses this text to portray an ideal worship setting for his own time, in which it would be important for dwellers in Yehud to remember Yahweh's care for them in the past and to celebrate it in the present.

17:1–27 Chapter 17 concludes the section on David's piety in bringing the ark into Jerusalem. This chapter, based almost entirely upon 2 Samuel 7, caps his religious achievements in *seeking Yahweh* begun in chapter 11. David desired a permanent home for the ark of the covenant, a *house* for it to reside in. Initially, Nathan the prophet was supportive of this, but later, in a dream, he received a word from God that David was not to be the temple builder. Rather, God would himself build David a *house* (or dynasty), while David's son would be allowed eventually to build God a *house* (temple) for the ark of the covenant. In this "eternal covenant with David," God binds himself to Davidic kingship and to the temple and its cult, the two major pillars of the Davidic covenant and not incidentally for the Chronicler, the two major pillars of the Chronicler's theology. In the final section of the chapter David responds to God's grace and election by a faithful prayer of gratitude.

It is impossible to overestimate the importance of this chapter to both the Deuteronomist and to the

---

Chronicles & Psalms
The superscriptions of the Psalms, though much later than the psalms themselves, contain ancient tradition about the circles from which these sacred poems arose. Chronicles similarly describes the families or guilds of musicians who created and performed the music of the temple and royal court.

Elaborate Worship
Although the Chronicler updates his history and often gives it "modern" dress, it would be a mistake to suppose that all complex cultic practices and priestly organization must be late as well. Highly organized worship and complex music existed well before the Israelites came on the scene, as we know from the elaborate second millennium Canaanite texts from Ras Shamra or Ugarit.

Chronicler. In the first case, the Deuteronomist uses the covenant with David as the bar to which kings should aspire, and few, perhaps none (with the possible exception of Josiah) live up to the standards of royal behavior (see the warning in 2 Sam 7:14, lacking from the equivalent passage in Chronicles). In spite of it all, of course, the Deuteronomistic Historian is not negative about Davidic kingship as an institution. Indeed, he understands and supports its eternal validity, in spite of the scoundrels who often occupied the throne.

The Chronicler's task, on the other hand, is to celebrate the ideals of Davidic kingship and to ground those ideals in the great exemplars of the past, David and Solomon. He does this in two ways: by placing this narrative at the close of the accounts of "all Israel" helping David bring the ark of the covenant into Jerusalem at the beginning of his reign, and by slightly altering terminology to update the language and to remove any question about David's or Solomon's faithfulness. One can see the latter particularly in his omission of 2 Samuel 7:14b, a text that implies that David's descendants would, in fact sin.

> **The Kingly Ideal**
>
> *As mentioned above, the task of the Chronicler is to lay out the ideals of Davidic and Solomonic kingship as a plan for future kings, not to point out the mistakes of the past.*

18:1–20:8 Chapters 18–20 deal with David's successes in battle against the *Philistines*, *Arameans*, *Ammonites*, *Moabites*, and *Edomites*, in short, virtually all of Israel's antagonistic neighbors (even the Amalekites are thrown in for good measure in 1 Chron 18:11, as well as the Edomites, not mentioned in the equivalent passage in 2 Sam 8:12). Chapter 18 deals with successful wars against Philistia (verse 1), *Moab* (verse 2), *Zobah* (a small kingdom northeast of Israel; verses 3–4), and Damascus (verses 5–8). We also hear of a congratulatory gift from Tou (2 Sam 8:9 reads Toi) of Hamath (verses 9–11), a war against Edom (verses 12–13), and a roster of David's cabinet (verses 14–17). Chapter 19 deals with the Ammonite war (see 2 Sam 10), while chapter 20 deals with the final chapter in the Ammonite conflict (equals 2 Sam 11:1 and 12:30–31, pointedly leaving out the entire affair with Bathsheba and the murder of Uriah in 2 Sam 11–12) in verses 1–3 and with battles with Philistine giants [Hebrew *refayim*] in verses 4–8.

The Chronicler's accounts, while drawing on parallel texts in 2 Samuel, further accentuate David's piety and heroism. They also, incidentally, correct some readings in 2 Samuel (Edom for Aram in the Valley of Salt, for example).

Chronicles makes very clear the extent of David's conquests. In 18:1, David captures *Gath* and its villages from Philistia (compare 2 Sam 8:1, which mentions a town called *Metheg Ammah*, "the bridle of the mother [city?]"). Against *Moab*, 2 Samuel records that David made the defeated Moabites lie down and measured three cord lengths; two cord lengths of Moabites he put to death, while the third he spared. This account is simply missing from Chronicles. In the war with *Aram*, the kingdom centered on Damascus (verses 5–8), David took a great deal of bronze as booty. With this bronze, the Chronicler says, Solomon made the bronze sea, the pillars of the temple, and the temple vessels (verse 8), again a detail absent from 2 Samuel. Verse 12 corrects Samuel's Aramean war (it is Edomite; in Hebrew the letters *daleth* and *resh* are very similar, making confusion between Aram and Edom easy). David consecrates the plunder captured by Joab and Abishai from *all these nations* to Yahweh, an act of military piety (18:11). Verse 13 is a summary statement, retained from his source, underscoring David's success and piety: Yahweh *gave David victory wherever he went*.

The roster of David's cabinet in verses 14–17 parallels 2 Samuel 8:15–18, with a few small text-critical, and perhaps one intentional, variant. Perhaps there is no better way to highlight the greatness and piety of David's rule than the summation of it in 18:14. A better passage for the Chronicler to show David's paradigmatic, righteous rule could hardly be found; also prominent is the Chronicler's emphasis upon "all Israel." The single possible intentional variant is in 18:17. Its source, 2 Samuel 8:18, says that David's sons were priests [Hebrew *kohanim*; see the NIV footnote – the NIV text is an incorrect apologetic translation]. Chronicles may balk at this description of non-Levitical priests, changing the role of David's sons to "leaders at the hand of the king." The Septuagint also balked at the original reading, saying that "the first sons of David were successors to the king."

Chapter 19, the beginning of the Ammonite war, is synoptic with 2 Samuel 10. After David attempts to console *Hanun* of Ammon due to the death of his father *Nahash*, Hanun humiliates the envoys by shaving their beards and cutting their garments in half, assuming that they were spies (verses 1–4). When the Ammonites became aware that David was outraged, they hired Arameans from *Aram Naharaim* (RSV: *Mesopotamia*; compare 2 Sam 10:6: "Aram of the House of Rehob") and Arameans from *Maacah* and *Zobah* to help them in battle against David. Chronicles includes the hiring fee: 1,000 talents of silver. With the Ammonites and their allies arrayed for battle in *Medeba* (actually Moabite territory!), David sent *Joab* and *Abishai* his brother to engage them in battle. The Chronicler's tendency to accentuate David's good qualities spills over onto Joab, whom the author never depicts in a negative light, unlike the picture in 2 Samuel and 2 Kings. In chapter 19, Joab encourages his brother to take half the armed force and encounter the Ammonites while he engaged the Arameans. His final admonition is one of trust in the Lord to do what was right (verse 13), and they should take courage "on behalf of our people and on behalf of the cities of our God." The result, of course, was the routing of the Ammonites and Arameans. When the Arameans had regrouped, David himself arrayed for battle against them (19:17; compare with 2 Sam 10:17, where the Arameans array themselves for battle). Upon the Arameans final defeat, David took 7,000 chariots from the Arameans (compare 700 in 2 Sam 10:18).

First Chronicles 20 is perhaps the most revealing relative to the Chronicler's selection and organization of narratives from his primary source, Samuel and Kings. First Chronicles 20:1 equals 2 Samuel 11:1, but then 20:2–3 equals 2 Sam 12:30–31. The Chronicler omits David's sin with Bathsheba (when he should be with the armies of the Lord in battle, when "kings go forth to war"), his conspiracy to murder Uriah, in which Joab was complicit, Nathan the prophet's parable and denunciation of David, and the birth and subsequent death of the child of David and Bathsheba's union. It is quite clear that the Chronicler was familiar with these accounts of David's failings; they are simply not interesting to him and his messianic agenda in the postexilic age. In 1 Chronicles 20, Joab goes out to battle in verse 1 while David remained in Jerusalem (for no good reason in Chronicles). Joab smote the Ammonites and destroyed the capital city *Rabbah* (verse 1). David appears in Rabbah in verse 2 to put the crown of their king on his head and in verse 3 sets his new subjects to forced labor. Thus a low point in Israel's history in Samuel becomes a great victory over a recalcitrant foe in Chronicles!

The balance of chapter 20 (equals 2 Sam 21:18–22) concerns David's battle with a variety of Philistine warriors, the remnants of the *refayim*. The first was in *Gezer* (in 2 Sam 21:19, Gob), where *Sibbecai the Hushathite* smote *Sippai* (2 Sam 21:18, Saph) of the remnants of the *refayim*. The second occurred in an undisclosed location (likewise Gob in 2 Samuel). *Elhanan* the son of Ya'ur (compare with "the son of *Yare 'Oregim*" in 2 Sam 21:19; the term means "the forests of the weavers," probably an equivalent of the *weaver's rod* at the end of the verse). In Chronicles, Elhanan fought *Lahmi the brother of Goliath*. In 2 Samuel, Elhanan is a *Beth Lachmi*, or Bethlehemite, who fought Goliath of Gath. The question of the identity of Elhanan and the giant he killed could be text critical ("the brother of" could have fallen out of the text in 2 Samuel), or it could be a harmonizing change with 1 Sam 17 (where David, not Elhanan, killed Goliath) on the part of the Chronicler. The third Philistine, a remnant of the *refayim* in verse 6, had 24 digits and was slain by *Jonathan, the son of Shimei*, David's brother. All of these were from Gath of the Philistines, and all met defeat "by the hand of David and by the hand of his servants" (though David himself does not figure in these accounts, unless the mention of Goliath is intended to recall David's exploits in 1 Samuel 17).

21:1–22:1 One of the somewhat startling features of Chronicles is the single account brought over from 2 Samuel which casts David in a less than positive light (2 Sam 24). The Chronicler has a problem: it is very important for David to be shown as the originator of the temple cult, its organization, and the planning of the temple itself, but the origin of the temple site and the altar of burnt offering

---

Talent

A talent is a weight of metal varying between 44 and 88 pounds (20–40 kilograms), usually about 75 pounds. The sums taken as plunder in 1 Chronicles 19 would presumably represent several years of the conquered states' tax revenues.

appear in a narrative about David's sin in numbering the people. The Chronicler deals with this from the very first verse. Whereas 2 Samuel 24:1 says that God, being angry with David, incited him to number the people, 1 Chronicles 21:1 has Satan inciting David to this sin.

> **Satan in Chronicles**
>
> *While for the Chronicler the introduction of Satan to the story of the census does not excuse David, it at least makes this sin understandable and leads smoothly to the recounting of David's repentance and the selection of the site for the temple. As in Job 1–2 and Zechariah 2, Satan does not figure as a character beyond the control of God, and thus we should not read later Christian theology into this text.*

Minor differences between the two accounts abound, with a few significant ones. To name a few: Joab objects to David's plan in Samuel, but in Chronicles his objection is more serious: David will be bringing guilt upon Israel by such a move. Second, the entire itinerary of Joab's travels while numbering disappears from Chronicles, probably due to its lack of significance for the author's agenda. The census figures in Samuel (800,000 men of Israel, 500,000 men of Judah) differ from the version of Chronicles (1.1 million warriors in Israel, and 470,000 in Judah). In 1 Chronicles 21:12, the three options given to David by Gad the seer have been leveled out to three sets of three: three years of famine, three months of being pursued by their enemies, and three days of plague (note that 2 Sam 24:13 allots seven years for the famine).

It is really the end of the account where the Chronicler makes his greatest adaptation of the story. To begin, the destroying *angel* is standing between earth and heaven with a *drawn sword* in Chronicles, while in 2 Samuel the angel does not play so active and personified a role. First Chronicles 21:16 has no parallel in 2 Samuel, underscoring the severity of the situation (angel with drawn sword) and the repentance of the elders. There are minor differences between Ornan's (2 Sam: Araunah) offer to give his threshing floor to David and the Chronicler's account. Another significant difference occurs between 2 Samuel 24:24 and 1 Chronicles 21:25. In Samuel, the threshing floor cost David 50 shekels, while in Chronicles it is 600! With 21:26b, the most significant addition occurs. After David sacrificed on the altar he erected on the threshing floor, the Lord "restrained the plague from Israel" (2 Sam 24), while in Chronicles, fire fell from heaven, reminiscent of Elijah's contest with the prophets of Baal in 2 Kings 18. Finally, 1 Chronicles 21:27–22:1 make clear the reason for the Chronicler's addition of this account which casts a negative light on David: it is because it is the origin story of the location for the temple and the altar.

22:2–19 Chapters 22–29 contain little material that precisely parallels 2 Samuel. Chapter 22 has had the necessary introduction in chapter 21 – the account of David's sin in numbering the people, followed by the sacrifices at the threshing floor of Ornan and its subsequent purchase by David for the temple and the altar of sacrifices. Chapter 22 is his selection of, and exhortation to, Solomon to be the temple builder and his gathering of raw materials for the temple construction. Chapters 22–27 detail the organization of the Levitical courses or divisions, priests, gatekeepers, singers, guards, and others. Chapters 28–29 contain David's final admonitions to Solomon regarding the temple.

First Chronicles 22:1 ends the account of the previous chapter: once fire has fallen from heaven and consumed David's sacrifice for his sin, David selects the future spot for the temple. Verses 2–4 have a fairly close parallel in 2 Samuel 5, where David creates a forced levy to hew stone and cut down cedar for his building projects. Verses 5–19 contain David's instructions to Solomon, who is *young and inexperienced* (literally, "tender"; verse 5). It is very important for the Chronicler to connect the building of the temple to David's own plan and "blueprint" [Hebrew *tavnit*; see chapter 28]. Perhaps this is because, in the Chronicler's understanding, God made the eternal covenant, involving the twin pillars of kingship and temple (see 2 Sam 7; 1 Chron 17), with David, not Solomon.

Chapter 22 gives two reasons why David planned, but Solomon built, the temple. First, David must gather materials because Solomon was as yet too young (verse 5). Second, only Chronicles gives a reasoned explanation for David's failure to build the temple: it is because he was a man of warfare, who had shed much blood (verse 8). It is David's initiative, following the divine oracle, also to appoint Solomon as the temple builder (verse 11) and his successor (23:1).

Verses 11–19 clearly demonstrate the Chronicler's theology of retribution and his agenda for Israel, especially Israel's king, to *seek* Yahweh. The section both begins and ends with David's admonition to Solomon to seek Yahweh so that he might prosper as king. The task is made easier for Solomon, in that David already has a large labor force (verse 15; compare 1 Kgs 5:13–18; 9:15–23), as well as a huge amount of gold, silver, bronze, iron, wood, and stone which David had amassed. Finally, David commands all the leaders of Israel to lend aid to Solomon in the construction of the temple (verse 17). The Chronicler gives a final defense of David's failure to build the temple: it is because David was busy with warfare so that Solomon might be the "man of peace" (Solomon's name in Hebrew, *Shlomo*, comes from the root *shalam*, "to have peace") with the leisure to engage in the peaceful pursuit of building the temple (verses 9, 18).

23:1–27:34 Part of the Chronicler's agenda for the restoration of "all Israel" is to connect practices current in the Second Temple cult and temple organization with their origins in the era of David. While many priests in preexilic Israel were Levitical priests, not all Levites were priests and indeed there was apparently no special class of temple functionary known as Levites. In the course of time, particularly in the postexilic age, Levites who did not function as priests (that is, did not make sacrifices) filled a variety of administrative and cultic functions in the temple and its environs (for example, music performing and directing, gatekeeping, storehouse and treasury guarding, and other functions auxiliary to the temple priesthood). These functions are so central and fixed in the Second Temple period that the Chronicler takes them for granted and accentuates their place in Israel's early history (see Japhet, *I & II Chronicles*, 26). This is not to say that the Chronicler is playing fast and loose with Israel's historical records; it is to say that Chronicles has an eschatological agenda that is concerned with the future restoration of all Israel, including the temple and cultic organization. Once again, this is history "as it should have been," with idealized organizations projected back to David's time and given his authority.

Chapter 23:2, according to McKenzie, gives us the order of the material appearing in chapter 27 in reverse: David assembled all the chiefs/commanders, the priests, and the Levites. Chapter 23 mentions Levitical functions, then that of the priests (distinguished from Levites, as sons of Aaron) appear in chapter 24, a return to Levitical functions as musicians (referred to as prophecy) takes up chapter 25, the gatekeepers feature in 26:1–11, and other guarding/watching functions in 26:12–32. Chapter 27 concludes the list section with David's military, civic, and political organization.

The Levites are organized by David by function and genealogy. Of 38,000 Levites (a greater number than any other count of cultic personnel in Scripture!), 24,000 serve as temple auxiliaries, whose function was apparently to aid the priests. Of the balance, 6,000 worked as "officers and judges," a bit of novelty relative to Levitical function, 4,000 as gatekeepers, and 4,000 as singers. It is interesting that correspondingly little is said about the vast majority of Levites who served in the temple as auxiliaries; the Chronicler reserves his greatest attention for the singers and gatekeepers. The age requirement for a Levitical male is somewhat unclear: in verse 3, only 30-year-olds may qualify (compare Num 4:3), while verses 24 and 27 make the qualifying age 20. Many commentators have seen in this discrepancy the sign of editorial activity, reflecting Levitical requirements at different times. The second division is by genealogy of the three sons of Levi, Gershom, Kohath, and Merari (verses 7–23).

Building the Temple

Chapters 22–29 use a chiastic (A B B'A') structure. Chapter 22 describes David's amassing of building materials and his opening admonition to Solomon. In chapters 23–26 David makes Solomon king and then organizes the divisions of the Levites and priests for the temple work, while he appoints chiefs over civic and military affairs in chapter 27. Chapter 28 again refers to the covenant oracle at the end of chapter 22, in which Solomon is chosen as temple builder and David admonishes him to seek Yahweh. In chapter 29 David amasses yet more treasures for the temple from his own stores and from freewill offerings, as at the beginning of chapter 22. The whole section concludes with David making Solomon his son king "the second time" with the full support of Israel and a summary statement about David's reign.

> **Poetry as Prophecy**
>
> *In the Second Temple period, Jews often thought of prophets as singers and singers in the temple as prophets. In the most famous case of this association, the Dead Sea Scrolls text 11QPsa (col. XVII) describes the career of David:*
>
> David ... wrote 3600 psalms and songs to sing before the altar over the burnt-offering, the daily regular burnt-offering, for all the days of the year 364; and for the sabbath offerings 52 songs; and for the offering of the new moons and for all the days of the assemblies and for the day of atonement 30 songs. And all the psalms which he spoke were 446, and songs to make music over the afflicted, 4. And the total was 4050. All of these he spoke through prophecy which was given to him from before the Most High.

Chapter 24 describes the divisions of the priests, the sons of Aaron. All the priestly line is legitimated through the two sons of Aaron, Ithamar and Eleazar, his other two sons, Nadab and Abihu, having died "before the Lord" (so Numbers; Chronicles reads, *before their father*, perhaps an intentional change). Verses 1–19 describe a 24-family rotation of duties, not mentioned earlier in the Old Testament, but apparently in place in the postexilic age. Furthermore, assignments seem to reflect social necessity as much as pedigree: since the sons of Eleazar greatly outnumbered Ithamar's, they received twice as many slots in the rotation. Verses 20–31 show a similar organization on the part of the other Levites and their selection as the priests: they are also chosen by lot.

Chapters 25–26 describe the organization of the singers and gatekeepers. Once again, as in chapter 6, the singers are organized under the names of Heman, Asaph, and Jeduthun. Chapter 6 described these groups as part of the family of Kohath, the priestly family; perhaps this is why they appear after the sons of Aaron. According to 25:1, they were to "prophesy" with musical instruments – their priestly and prophetic functions merge in this passage (verse 5 also calls Heman *the king's seer*). Their organization, like that of the Aaronic priesthood, was in 24 courses, taken by lots (verses 8–31).

Chapter 26 describes the gatekeepers and other Levitical functionaries of the family of Korah, also reckoned as Kohathites in chapter 6. Verses 1–11 describe the family divisions of gatekeepers, while verses 12–19 describe the appointment and selection by lot of the various families to the gates on each quadrant. Verses 20–32 describe the "security" or guarding function of certain Levitical families over treasuries (verses 20–28) and as officers and judges (verses 29–32).

Chapter 27 ends the section of David's organization with the political divisions and organization of his army, administrators, and counselors. This chapter may be divided into four sections: army commanders for each of the tribes of Israel (verses 1–15); political leaders over the tribes of Israel (verses 16–24); officials over the royal estates (verses 25–31); and counselors and officials of the king (verses 32–34).

Verses 2–15 describe twelve military commanders over divisions of 24,000 from each of the tribes. There are a few unusual aspects to this list. First, the names of the commanders are similar or identical to most of the first twelve on the list of David's thirty mighty men, found in 2 Samuel 23 and 1 Chronicles 11, though some are spelled and ordered somewhat differently. Second, there are striking anachronisms, such as the use of Asahel as a commander of 24,000 at the end of David's life, although he died early on in David's reign. Third is the schematic nature of this list. Note that all the divisions have the same large, round number – 24,000 – regardless of region. The final military figure would, therefore, be in the neighborhood of 3 million, a fantastical number if taken literally. It is more likely that the 24,000 represents an ideal figure (multiple of the twelve tribes by 1,000), symbolic of the Chronicler's vision of a future, restored community.

Verses 16–22 list tribal *sarim* ("chiefs, princes, or rulers"), possibly tribal governors. Besides being unattested elsewhere, this list is striking for other reasons. Gad and Asher strangely do not make the list of leaders, while Manasseh gets two. Levi makes the list of governors, although they did not have tribal territory per se, and Aaron also receives separate mention. Also, Judah is governed by one of David's brothers, otherwise unknown, named *Elihu* (possibly Eliab?). The list may be helpful to get a glimpse of the otherwise murky political organization of the tribes. Verses 23–24 seem to be an addition by a later scribe, as they give an apology for David's numbering of the people and obliquely blame it on Joab, while exonerating David because he did not enumerate those below 20 years of age. Most scholars attribute this section to a later scribe, who understood the lists of the preceding chapters to be the same as that connected with David's sin in 1 Chronicles 21 and 2 Samuel 24.

Verses 25–31 are also otherwise unparalleled in 2 Samuel or anywhere else. They provide a list of David's stewards over royal holdings (storehouses, agriculture, vineyards, wine cellars, orchards, and animals).

> **Royal Property**
> In the ancient world, as also more recently, kings held some property in their own names, some as family estates, and some in their role as king. Rules governing the inheritance of these types of property varied.

28:1–29:30 First Chronicles ends with David's admonitions to Solomon and the people (28:1–10); his giving to Solomon the blueprint for the temple and its vessels (28:11–19); a final word of admonition to Solomon (28:20–21); request for (and receipt of) freewill offerings from the people (29:1–9); a prayer of thanksgiving and request for God to bless the gift (29:10–19); sacrifices of thanksgiving (20–22); Solomon's installation as king for the second time (29:22b–25); and the summary of David's reign (29:26–30).

Chapter 28 carries on the narrative interrupted by the lists of chapters 23–27. Verses 1–8 largely repeat the covenant to David in chapters 17 and 22: God's choice of Judah, his father's house, himself, and finally Solomon to be temple builder. Notable is the public nature of this final discourse with Solomon and the people: "all Israel" once again assembles to hear his final words. Second, David states that he went to great lengths to "make preparation" for building the temple and in fact provides Solomon with the blueprint for it (note the most minute details of David's management of the temple plan in verses 11–19). David's final speech to Solomon includes some of the Chronicler's key theological topics: the need for the king to seek the Lord (verses 8–9), the focus upon the temple and its cult (verse 10), and retribution theology (verses 7–9).

Verses 20–21 recount David's final exhortation to Solomon, encouraging him to follow through with the construction in light of the fact that God was with him and would help him complete it. Along with the architectural blueprint, David also gave Solomon the organization of the priests, Levites, and officers, attributing the religious and cultic organization of Israel to David's own initiative.

Chapter 29 parallels the temple dedication prayer of Solomon in 2 Chronicles 6. First, the temple is meticulously built, and then Solomon offers prayers and sacrifices. Here, the temple plan is given, offerings are taken from the people, and prayers and sacrifices follow. In verses 1–9, he reiterates to the people that in light of Solomon's youth and inexperience, he would need a good deal of support and freewill offerings (compare 22:5). David leads by example: he provided a massive amount of gold, silver, bronze, iron, wood, and stone for the temple and then gave even more from his own wealth for its building. Verses 6–9 demonstrate the success of David's fundraising: the people give thousands of talents of gold, silver, bronze, and iron, along with precious stones. Incidentally, the people gave gold in *darics*, coinage not minted before the time of Darius the Persian, about 515 BCE, the earliest possible date for the writing of the book.

Verses 10–19 comprise David's prayer of thanksgiving to God for the freewill offerings and request for God's blessing upon it and upon Solomon the temple builder, though David recognizes that all these gifts simply return items belonging to God, the great gift giver (verse 16). The chapter ends with all Israel sacrificing, feasting, and making Solomon the king *a second time* (verse 22; see 23:1). Zadok's installation as priest along with Solomon exemplifies the Second Temple conviction that "two anointed ones" coexist in Judah's hierarchy: the political messiah, the son of David, and the high priest of the line of Aaron. Verses 26–30 more or less follow 1 Kings 2:10–11, although expanding the earlier source's praise of David, his reign, and his accomplishments.

THEOLOGICAL REFLECTIONS

Chronicles has often seemed to readers to lack historical importance and theological insight. While the historical reliability of Chronicles continues to be a matter of debate, the issue of the Chronicler's theological acumen is coming increasingly into focus (see Graham, McKenzie, and Knoppers). While much can be said about the Chronicler's theological commitments in what he has taken from his sources, four primary themes appear to be his own creative contributions.

The Chronicler is certainly interested in the temple and its practices, and also their Davidic and Solomonic origins, resulting in a broad focus on king and temple. Additionally, the Chronicler is interested in a retribution theology of "you reap what you sow." This theology is tempered in Chronicles, however, by the examples of good kings like David who did some very evil things and of bad kings like Manasseh who were nonetheless rewarded with long, stable reigns.

Another focus for the Chronicler is the grace made available to all of Israel. In the postexilic age, the author exhorts the entire community to seek [Hebrew *darash*] and repent [*shuv*], as the forefathers did, so that God might once again restore all Israel.

A final characteristic of Chronicles which was not adequately appreciated or understood by earlier commentators is the Chronicler's emphasis upon cultic joy: singing, praising, rejoicing, dancing, and so forth. The Chronicler's view of temple worship, priestly organization and practice, and the cult are all responses to God's unfathomable grace and occasions for rejoicing.

For a fuller discussion of the theological implications of 1 Chronicles, see the theological reflections on 2 Chronicles on page 391.

FOR FURTHER STUDY

William R. Millar, *Priesthood in Ancient Israel* (St. Louis: Chalice, 2001).

James C. VanderKam, *From Joshua to Caiaphas: High Priests After the Exile* (Minneapolis, Minn.: Fortress, 2004).

WORKS CITED

Peter R. Ackroyd, "The Chronicler as Exegete," *Journal for the Study of the Old Testament* 2 (1977): 2–32.

Joachim Braun, *Music in Ancient Israel/Palestine* (Grand Rapids: Eerdmans, 2002).

Roddy Braun, *1 Chronicles* (Waco, Tex.: Word, 1986).

Frank M. Cross, "A Reconstruction of the Judean Restoration," *Journal of Biblical Literature* 94 (1975): 4–18.

Simon De Vries, *1 and 2 Chronicles* (Grand Rapids, Eerdmans, 1989).

Israel Eph'al, *The Ancient Arabs: Nomads on the Borders of the Fertile Crescent 9th-5th Centuries B. C.* (Jerusalem: Magnes, 1982).

David N. Freedman, "The Chronicler's Purpose," *Catholic Biblical Quarterly* 23 (1961): 436–442.

M. Patrick Graham, *The Utilization of 1 and 2 Chronicles in the Reconstruction of Israelite History in the Nineteenth Century* (Atlanta: Scholars Press, 1990).

M. Patrick Graham, Kenneth Hoglund, and Steven L. McKenzie, eds., *The Chronicler as Historian* (Sheffield: Sheffield Academic Press, 1997).

M. Patrick Graham and Steven McKenzie, eds., *The Chronicler as Author: Studies in Text and Texture* (Sheffield: Sheffield Academic Press, 1999).

M. Patrick Graham, Steven McKenzie, and Gary Knoppers, eds., *The Chronicler as Theologian: Essays in Honor of Ralph W. Klein* (Sheffield: Sheffield Academic Press, 2003).

Kenneth Hoglund, "The Chronicler as Historian: A Comparativist Perspective." in *The Chronicler as Historian* (ed. M. Patrick Graham, Kenneth G. Hoglund, and Steven L. McKenzie; Sheffield: Sheffield Academic Press, 1997): 19–29.

Paul Hooker, *First and Second Chronicles* (Louisville: Westminster John Knox, 2001).

Sara Japhet, *I & II Chronicles: A Commentary* (Louisville: Westminster John Knox, 1993).

———, "The Supposed Common Authorship of Chronicles and Ezra-Nehemiah Investigated Anew," *Vetus Testamentum* 18 (1968): 330–71.

Isaac Kalimi, "Was the Chronicler a Historian?" in *The Chronicler as Historian* (ed. M. Patrick Graham, Kenneth G. Hoglund, and Steven L. McKenzie; Sheffield: Sheffield Academic Press, 1997): 73–89.

———, *The Reshaping of Ancient Israelite History in Chronicles* (Winona Lake, Ind.: Eisenbrauns, 2005).

Gary Knoppers, *1 Chronicles 1–9* (New York: Doubleday, 2003).

———, *1 Chronicles 10–29* (New York: Doubleday, 2004).

Daniel D. Luckenbill, *Ancient Records of Assyria and Babylonia, Part 2* (London: Histories and Mysteries of Man, 1989).

Steven McKenzie, *1–2 Chronicles* (Nashville: Abingdon, 2004).

Christine Mitchell, "The Dialogism of Chronicles." in *The Chronicler as Author: Studies in Text and Texture* (ed. M. Patrick Graham and Steven L. McKenzie; Sheffield: Sheffield Academic Press, 1999): 311–326.

Jacob Myers, *1 Chronicles* (Garden City, N.Y.: Doubleday, 1965).

R. North, "Theology of the Chronicler," *Journal of Biblical Literature* 82 (1963): 369–81.

Martin Noth, *The Chronicler's History* (Sheffield: Sheffield Academic Press, 1987).

Anson F. Rainey, "The Chronicler and His Sources – Historical and Geographical." in *The Chronicler as Historian* (ed. M. Patrick Graham, Kenneth G. Hoglund, and Steven L. McKenzie; Sheffield: Sheffield Academic Press, 1997): 30–72.

R. Mark Shipp, "Remember His Covenant Forever: The Chronicler's Use of the Psalms," *Restoration Quarterly* 35 (1993): 29–39.

Mark Throntveit, "Linguistic Analysis and the Question of Authorship in Chronicles, Ezra, and Nehemiah," *Vetus Testamentum* 32 (1982): 201–16.

Steven Tuell, *First and Second Chronicles* (Louisville: John Knox, 2001).

Thomas Willi, *Die Chronik als Auslegung: Untersuchungen zur literarischen Gestaltung der historischen Überlieferung Israels* [*Chronicles as Exposition: Investigations in the Literary Formation of the Historical Tradition of Israel*] (Göttingen: Vandenhoeck & Ruprecht, 1972).

H. G. M. Williamson, *1 and 2 Chronicles* (Grand Rapids: Eerdmans, 1982).

2 Chronicles

R. Mark Shipp

CHAPTER CONTENTS

Contexts 373

Commentary 373
    The Story of the Kings of Judah · 1:1–36:14 373
    The Fall & Rise of Judah · 36:15–23 391

Theological Reflections 391

For Further Study 393

Works Cited 393

First and Second Chronicles originally formed a single book. Thus the stories of the kings of Judah begin in 1 Chronicles and are continued here.

CONTEXTS

Second Chronicles continues the story of the kingdom of Judah, pointing to the history of the northern kingdom only as an illustration of Israel's rejection of the true faith, as Chronicles sees it.

The Chronicler claims that his work draws on several literary sources, some of which appear distinct from the sources mentioned in Samuel and Kings. These include the visions of Gad the seer (1 Chron 29:29), the visions of Iddo the seer (2 Chron 9:29), the book of the kings of Israel and Judah (2 Chron 16:11), and many others. The Chronicler's major source, of course, is the canonical books of Samuel and Kings, which provide roughly half of the content of Chronicles.

No agreement on the date of Chronicles has come about, although few would now date the work as late as the Greek period (after 332 BCE). Currently, suggestions run from the Greek period (around 300 BCE; Knoppers), to a few decades earlier (Ackroyd), to about 400 BCE (Williamson), to early in the postexilic period (Freedman; Throntveit). If one follows Cross's multiple editions, then perhaps the composition spanned the early Second Temple period down to sometime after 400 BCE.

For a more detailed discussion of the historical and literary contexts of 2 Chronicles, see the discussion of 1 Chronicles' contexts on page 353.

COMMENTARY

THE STORY OF THE KINGS OF JUDAH · 1:1–36:14

Second Chronicles 1–9 closely parallels 1 Kings 3–10, with some notable additions and, more significantly, deletions. The omissions include the throne succession intrigues of 1 Kings 1–2, as well as Solomon's dealings with the remainder of the family of Saul (notably, Shimei) and claimants to his throne from his own family (Adonijah) and other detractors. The Chronicler also omits stories of Solomon's many foreign wives and idolatry (1 Kings 11). What remains is an account that glorifies Solomon as the king par excellence of Israel's golden age, without even a minor flaw comparable to David's in 1 Chronicles 21. Along with some rearrangement of material and a few additions, such as the psalmic material in Solomon's temple dedication prayer, the picture presented of Solomon is one of thoroughgoing piety and faithfulness.

> **Solomon**
> *The Chronicler's narrative about Solomon almost entirely concerns the plans, execution, and dedication of the temple and demonstrates his remarkable wisdom, which the Chronicler equates with piety.*

The Chronicler's depiction of Solomon does not begin with the throne succession as in 1 Kings 1–2, but earlier, in a peaceful transition (1 Chron 23, 29). The Chronicler begins Solomon's solo reign with his dream at Gibeon where he requests wisdom. The wisdom God grants him is most manifested in his carrying out the temple construction and dedication, encompassing 2 Chronicles 1:18–7:22 and, indeed, most of chapter 8 also (see below).

Another of the Chronicler's concerns important in these chapters is that of immediate retribution. The Chronicler begins Solomon's reign with his "seeking Yahweh" in worship at the "great high place" in Gibeon. God rewards him with wealth and power. The beginning (1:14–18) and end (chapters 8–9) of this narrative form an inclusio with each element emphasizing retribution.

1:1–17 As in 1 Kings 3, Solomon's ritual dream comes early in his reign, with the exception that here it is the inauguration of it, since he need not "secure" the kingdom as he does in 1 Kings 1–2. Verses 1–13 follow the account in 1 Kings 3, but in abbreviated form. Also, whereas the Kings account does not deem it essential to explain why Solomon worships at the "great high place" (though such places were one of the Deuteronomist's pet peeves), the Chronicler explains that this is entirely appropriate, as the tabernacle of Yahweh was there, as well as the great altar of sacrifice. Verse 4 explains that David had previously taken the ark from *Kiriath Jearim* to Jerusalem, but the tabernacle was in Gibeon (verse 3; here called the *Tent of Meeting*, but identified with the tabernacle in 1 Chronicles 16). We are now left with the curious conundrum that, in order to sacrifice properly, Solomon has to go to Gibeon to the tabernacle and the altar. Most commentators see this an exegetical and apologetic move on the Chronicler's part – why else would pious king Solomon go to Gibeon to sacrifice, unless the tabernacle were there? Furthermore, the Bible says nothing of the fate of the tabernacle or its disposition after the ark narrative in 1 Samuel 4–7. It is a logical conclusion to the Chronicler that it was in Gibeon, where Solomon sacrificed.

Solomon's request for wisdom in his vision of the night is abbreviated from 1 Kings 3 but serves a different purpose than the story does in 1 Kings. The Kings account introduces the wisdom of Solomon and how he manifests it in manifold ways: in judgment (chapter 3), bureaucracy and government (chapter 4), in aesthetics and learning (chapter 4), in architecture (chapters 5–7), in piety (chapter 8), in commerce (chapter 9), and in diplomacy (chapter 10). In Chronicles, he seeks Yahweh in the cult (1:2–6), requests wisdom (1:7–13), and then receives that wisdom, along with power and wealth (1:14–17, parallel to 1 Kgs 10:23–29) in order to build the temple (1:18).

2:1–18 Chapters 2–5 mostly follow 1 Kings 5–7, although in an abbreviated form at several points. First, rather than allow Huram, king of Tyre (1 Kgs 5: *Hiram*), the initiative in corresponding with Solomon, Solomon begins by gathering a large number of forced laborers (see 1 Kgs 5:15). He then informs Huram of his intentions to build the temple and his need for an architect (2:6) and several types of wood found in the Lebanon (verses 7–8). He offers Huram's workers set wages (20,000 *baths* [about 480,000 liters] of wine and oil, and 20,000 *kors* [about 7.2 million liters] of wheat). Note that in the Kings account Solomon allows Hiram to name the wages. Verses 3–5 demonstrate Solomon's great piety and humility in an addition not attested in Kings: Solomon's intent is to build a temple for incense, shewbread, burnt offerings, and for all of the seasonal and weekly observances. Furthermore, the house must be magnificent, as God is greater than all other gods. Huram accepts Solomon's plan (see 1 Kgs 5:7–12).

He offers a skilled artisan for the metal and stone work (here, *Huram-abi*; Hiram in 1 Kings). Huram-abi figures much more prominently in the Chronicles narrative than in that of Kings. Here, he is a son of a Danite (rather than a Naphtalite) woman and a man of Tyre and so is at least partially Israelite and qualified to help with the temple. Huram acquiesces to Solomon's wages and offers his own plan to haul the trees to Jerusalem (verses 14–15). Finally, the Chronicler makes it very clear that the forced labor does not to include any native Israelite, but rather foreigners (verses 16–17, exactly mirroring the number of foreigners set aside for forced labor in 2:1). In so interpreting the forced labor accounts of 1 Kings 5 and 9, the Chronicler removes one of the major reasons for the split of the kingdom following Solomon's death, that of forced labor of the northern tribes and unfair taxation.

3:1–5:1 The next section comes essentially from 1 Kings 6–7, but once again in abbreviated form. The Chronicler leaves out two significant sections of narrative from Kings. First, 1 Kings 7:1–14 reports Solomon's building of his own palace (which took thirteen years to build, as opposed to the seven for the temple). It may be that the relative time it took to build each complex caused the Chronicler to leave this

> **The Temple's Furnishings**
> *The furniture of the temple fascinated ancient Israelites. Thus Ezekiel 1 and 10 refer to the wheels within wheels, drawing inspiration from the offering stands from the temple (seen also in contemporary art from Cyprus and elsewhere). The menorah or multi-branched candlestick has been a symbol for Jews in art and texts until this day. The furniture of the sanctuary, because it served to draw Israel close to God, remained an important symbol for the people's religious life.*

account out, or perhaps the building of palaces was simply not interesting to him. Second, 1 Kings 7:27–37 has been largely reworked. Kings describes the building of ten stands on wheels, while Chronicles replaces them with ten lampstands and ten tables of shewbread.

There are other, minor differences. The first, and most obvious, involves the dimensions of the temple complex. In 1 Kings 6:2, the height of the temple was 30 cubits (about 45 feet), in proportion to its other dimensions, while in Chronicles it is an amazing 120 cubits (180 feet). Also, the height of the pillars varies: in Kings, they are a modest 18 cubits tall, while in Chronicles they are 30 cubits. It is possible that these dimensions reflect the Chronicler's concern that the temple be magnificent and lofty (see 6:1). It is also possible that the numbers in Chronicles reflect an error in the transmission of the text. Another addition the Chronicler makes is that of the huge bronze altar (4:1), not described in 1 Kings but alluded to in the temple dedication (1 Kgs 8:64). The initial verses of these chapters vary also between the two accounts. Kings connects the temple building to the exodus and wilderness wanderings traditions (480 years from exodus to the temple; 12 × 40), providing a theological framework for understanding the temple and connecting it to Israel's earlier traditions. Chronicles relates the temple not to the exodus but to Abraham's near sacrifice of Isaac (Genesis 22) on Mount Moriah, identified as the site of the temple, and with David's purchase of the threshing floor from *Ornan the Jebusite* (1 Chron 22:1–22:1).

5:2–14 Chapter 5:2–14 is partially based upon 1 Kings 8:1–11, but with the Chronicler's own substantial addition. Verses 2–11a come almost verbatim from 1 Kings 5, describing massive sacrifices and the bringing up of the ark of the covenant by the Levites and depositing it under the wings of the cherubim (winged lion/sphinxes, representative of divine sovereignty) in the holy of holies. The Chronicler's cultic emphasis is thus satisfied by the Kings account. With verse 11b, the Chronicler departs from his Kings source. Verses 11b–13 describe the divisions of Levites and their sanctification, especially of the Levitical singers, and connect this account with David's installation of the ark in Jerusalem in 1 Chronicles 15–16. The singers, under *Heman*, *Asaph*, and *Jeduthun*, play cymbals, harps, and lyres alongside 120 trumpeters. The song that the singers and players perform uses the psalmic refrain, sprinkled throughout Chronicles, "for he is good, for his loyalty is everlasting," no doubt a common refrain in postexilic temple worship (see Psalm 136). Only upon the intonation of this music does the cloud of God's glory, known from the earlier exodus and Sinai traditions (see Exodus 19 and 40) fill the temple.

6:1–7:22 2 Chronicles 6 is among the closest of all the accounts in Chronicles to the text of Samuel and Kings. There are only two significant variations between 1 Kings 8:12–52 and 2 Chronicles 6:1–42: first, the description of the platform upon which Solomon stands in 6:13 does not appear in Kings and second, the Chronicler ends (verses 41–42) not with an appeal to Mosaic and exodus traditions as in Kings, but with a quotation again from a psalm, Psalm 132:8–10. Otherwise, the differences between the two accounts are mostly minor text-critical variants.

> **The Theology of History**
> *First Kings 8 is one of the most significant passages for understanding the historian's theology in Joshua through 2 Kings, detailing his understanding of retribution, the gift of the land, centralized worship in Jerusalem, and the loss of land due to idolatry. Second Chronicles 6 utilizes this passage for slightly different reasons. Here, Solomon's temple dedication prayer serves to underscore his piety and wisdom.*

8:1–9:31 Chapter 9 once again underscores the Chronicler's understanding of immediate retribution and mirrors the beginning of the narrative about Solomon in 2 Chronicles 1. There, Solomon's piety in worship and request for wisdom led immediately to his acquisition of wealth and power. In chapter 9, almost completely identical with 1 Kings 9–10, Solomon's wisdom, might, and wealth provide the focus following his exemplary act of piety and faithfulness, the creation of the temple and its dedication in chapters 2–8. For more on these stories, see the commentary on 1 Kings 9–10.

10:1–12:15 The last major division of the book occupies chapters 10–36. Unlike 1–2 Kings, which may be subdivided into two eras, the period of the divided monarchy and that of Judah alone following the exile of the northern kingdom until the exile of Judah to Babylon, Chronicles barely mentions the exile of Israel. This section forms a narrative whole, alternating sections that do and do not parallel 1–2 Kings. Its intent is at least twofold: to focus attention on the kings of Judah, while only mentioning the kingdom of Israel as it intersects with Judah's history; and to emphasize the role of prophets with most of Judah's kings, particularly as relates to his doctrine of retribution.

Second Chronicles 10:1–11:4 more or less reproduces 1 Kings 12:1–24, with the exception that 2 Kings 12:20 disappears from the account in Chronicles. This passage deals with the gathering of northern dignitaries to request of *Rehoboam* better treatment than they experienced under Solomon. After consulting with the older counselors, Rehoboam forsook their gentle counsel for that of the young men, who advised still greater burdens on the northern tribes. This immediately precipitated the breakup of the kingdom, with only the tribe of Judah left to the house of David. When Rehoboam prepared for civil war, *Shemaiah* the prophet admonished him not to pursue this course of action. Thus begins the close connection in 2 Chronicles between the word of the prophet and the actions of the kings of Judah.

First Kings 12:20 is notable for its absence in the Chronicles text. In Kings, this passage specifies that Jeroboam was crowned king over the north, while only Judah remained to David. It is the Chronicler's agenda to magnify the kingdoms of David and Solomon, while giving scant attention or reference to the north. He accomplishes this simply by leaving verse 20 out. The synoptic section of chapter 10 now ends, "So Israel has been in rebellion against the house of David to this day" (RSV; verse 19). While the text in Kings focuses the attention of the reader upon Solomon's and Rehoboam's faithlessness, that in Chronicles emphasizes the rebellion of the north. Chronicles does not criticize Rehoboam himself until 12:1, the fifth year of his reign, when he "forsook Yahweh's law." Even the near civil war with the north is not criticized, but understood to be an act of faithfulness in response to the prophetic word.

The Chronicler introduces a problem into the narrative, however, by leaving out the entire episode of 1 Kings 11, Solomon's idolatry and forced labor. In Chronicles, the people of the north have no reason to protest, much less to rebel.

The balance of chapter 11 is an addition by the Chronicler, intended to demonstrate Rehoboam's faithfulness during his first five years of reign. First, Rehoboam built or strengthened several cities in Judah and Benjamin (surprising, since Benjamin was not firmly in the hands of the southern kingdom until the reign of Asa). Second, priests and Levites from the north, whom Jeroboam had rejected in favor of his own priesthood, were welcomed into Judah. These priests "set their hearts to seek the Lord God of Israel" (11:16) and were a blessing to Rehoboam and Judah "for three years" (verse 17). Third, Rehoboam's wisdom is demonstrated by his various marriages (including the daughter of Absalom, verse 20) and his political appointments in Judah and Benjamin (verses 22–23). Verse 23 specifies that Rehoboam "dealt wisely."

The summary statement in 12:1 does not describe the nature of Rehoboam's offense, only that he and *all Israel* had been unfaithful. Verses 2 and 9–11 parallel 1 Kings 14:25–28, the account of the invasion of Judah by *Shishak* of Egypt, much expanded in Chronicles. Chronicles attributes this invasion to their forsaking Yahweh in the fifth year of Rehoboam. The text describes the invasion itself: 12,000 chariots and 60,000 horsemen, including *Libyans*, *Sukkites*, and *Cushites*, came against Judah. Shemaiah, the prophet who had warned them not to engage in warfare with Jeroboam in chapter 11, once again admonishes them: it is due to their forsaking God that this invasion happened (verse 5). Because of the humbling of the king and rulers, God relented and did not allow them to be destroyed, only to know the "service of the kingdoms" (verses 6–8). Verses 9–11 reproduce the account of Shishak's invasion from 1 Kings 14 (the taking of the gold from the temple). The Chronicler gives a clear interpretation of why Judah and Jerusalem escaped further devastation at the hands of Egypt: it is because they humbled themselves (see verse 12, which has no parallel in 1 Kgs).

Verses 13–16 more or less reproduce 1 Kings 14:21–22 and 29–31, with some expansions. This is the Deuteronomist's summary and evaluation of a king's reign, here combined at the end of the account of Rehoboam. There is one major omission and one major addition in these accounts. The Chronicler has omitted 1 Kings 14:23–24, which tells of how Israel committed gross idolatry and prostitution

> **Retribution**
> *Chapter 12 provides a useful template for understanding the Chronicler's doctrine of retribution and his method of interpreting the reigns of many of the kings of Judah.*

during the reign of Rehoboam. The one addition to his source connects the entire account of Rehoboam to the prophets Shemaiah and *Iddo*, not mentioned in the parallel passage in 1 Kings 14:29–31.

13:1–14:1 The entire reign of Abijah, with the exception of 13:1–2, lack a parallel in 1 Kings. The first two verses parallel 1 Kings 15:1–2, with the exception that Abijah's mother's name is not Maacah daughter of Abishalom, but *Micaiah* (see NIV note) the *daughter of Uriel*. The Kings account (15:1–8) mentions only that Abijah did evil and that there was war between him and Jeroboam. The Deuteronomist takes the opportunity to reiterate God's eternal covenant with David, even though sorry kings such as Abijam/h did not deserve it. God was patient with them for David's sake alone. The Chronicles account takes as its point of departure a single phrase from Kings (1 Kgs 15:6: "Now there was war between Rehoboam and Jeroboam," a curious comment, considering that Rehoboam was dead and Abijam/h was reigning, so several ancient and modern versions replace "Rehoboam" with "Abijah"). The balance of 2 Chronicles 13 deals with an account of this warfare, not otherwise attested in Kings. Jeroboam came out to fight Abijah and Judah with 800,000 warriors, a huge army, twice the size of that which Judah fielded. Apparently, there was no tradition of prophetic ministry at this time relative to Abijah, because Abijah himself acted the part of prophet by speaking the word of Yahweh to Jeroboam and admonishing him to discontinue the battle (compare 2 Chron 35:21). Abijah's speech (13:4–12) is filled with the Chronicler's theological commitments: proper kingship was given to David and his sons eternally (a *covenant of salt*, verse 5). The division in the kingdom happened because Jeroboam rebelled against Solomon and *worthless scoundrels* [Hebrew *'anashim reqim bene beliya'al*, "empty men," "sons of worthlessness"] took advantage of a young and inexperienced Rehoboam. Verses 8–12 turn attention toward the true worship in Jerusalem (with proper Aaronic priests and Levites, proper sacrifices done at the specified times and in the specified way), as opposed to the false worship of Jeroboam's golden calves and false priesthood. Finally, Abijah plays his ultimate trump card: God fights at the head of the army of Judah, with his consecrated priests blowing trumpets (see verse 12).

An account of the battle ensues (verses 13–19). Judah is victorious, in spite of being outnumbered and Jeroboam's clever ambush, because Judah sought divine help, and the priests blew the trumpets. Jeroboam was routed and he "did not recover his power in the days of Abijah" (verse 20). The final evaluation of Jeroboam by the Chronicler is telling: because of his faithlessness and rebellion, "Yahweh smote him and he died" (verse 20).

As with most other accounts of faithful acts by kings, God recompensed Abijah with "might" and a very large family and many children (verse 21). Once again, as with Rehoboam, Chronicles connects Abijah with prophetic writings [*Iddo* the seer], a notice missing in Kings.

14:2–16:14 As with the account of Abijah, much of Asa's reign lacks a parallel in 1 Kings. Chapter 14:1–3 is a rewriting of 1 Kings 15:8–14, the summary of Asa's reign. The Chronicler has epitomized the summary in 1 Kings by condensing the information about the queen mother and her idolatry in the 1 Kings account and by specifying his recompense for a good reign: "the land had rest for 10 years" (verse 1). Whereas the Deuteronomist's benchmark for great kingship – removal of the high places – is not achieved by Asa in Kings (see 1 Kgs 15:14), 2 Chronicles 14:5 unequivocally states that Asa took away the high places and the incense altars. It is also incumbent upon every good king of Judah to "seek Yahweh," and Asa follows suit (verse 4).

Second Chronicles 14:4–15:15 lacks parallels with Kings. The first section, verses 4–8, once again shows how those who seek Yahweh in the beginning of their reign receive blessings. Because Judah under Asa sought God, the land had peace, cities were built and fortified, the army was enlarged and equipped, and Judah prospered.

Second Chronicles 14:9–15:15 gives us valuable information about an otherwise unattested battle

> **Perspectives on the Kings**
> *Perhaps no narrative more clearly gives us insight into the Chronicler's, as opposed to the Deuteronomist's, reporting and evaluation of the kings of Judah than 2 Chronicles 13. The Deuteronomist finds little to praise in virtually any king. Solomon, Jehoshaphat, Hezekiah, and even David fail to one degree or another to meet his standards. The Chronicler, on the other hand, is much more positive about the kings of Judah. Abijah is credited with faithfulness and might. The Deuteronomist, contrariwise, gives Abijam short shrift and evaluates him as an idolater.*

between Asa and *Zerah the Cushite*. Asa deals with the dangerous military situation (according to the text, Zerah came against him with 1,000,000 soldiers) in the manner of Abijah: he cried [Hebrew *qara'*] to Yahweh and confessed that all Judah also relied [Hebrew *sha'an*, "leaned"] on God. As with the Israelites before Jericho, God smote the Ethiopians and then the Judeans plundered their cites and livestock (perhaps the text envisions them raiding Egyptian territory, since the Cushite Dynasty ruled Egypt at that time).

Chapter 15:1–15 lays out the Chronicler's theology from the mouth of *Azariah* the prophet, followed by Asa and Judah's resolve to seek divine help. As with Zerah, the Bible does not otherwise mention *Azariah the son of Oded*. His speech to Asa, as he returned from the slaughter of the Cushites, employs several themes dear to the Chronicler: *if you seek him, he will be found by you* (verse 2); when Israel turns Yahweh, they receive "teaching priests" and the Torah (verses 3–4); and then come his final words to Asa, *your work will be rewarded* (verse 7; the theme of immediate retribution).

Following Azariah's speech, Asa and the people of Judah resolved to put away idols, repair the altar, and seek Yahweh with their whole heart. Judah and Benjamin, along with numerous inhabitants of Ephraim, Manasseh, and Simeon (all Israel) sacrificed and made a covenant with God promising that anyone not religiously loyal would face the death penalty. As so often in Chronicles, such sacrificing and vows precede singing and rejoicing and the notice that Israel met the God they sought (verse 15).

Second Chronicles 15:16–19 once again returns to its source, here 1 Kings 15:13–15, where Asa removed his mother from being queen and destroyed her idols. Here the Chronicler's use of sources and his own additions are in tension: in 14:3, the Chronicler said that Asa removed the high places. In 15:17, he returns to his major source, 1 Kings, which says these high places survived.

Not all is ideal with the reign of Asa. The Chronicler has inherited the tradition from his Kings source that late in life, the king was diseased in his feet. Chapter 16 spells out the reason for this. King *Baasha* of Israel began fortifying Ramah, on the border with Judah, in order to keep Israelites from going south, clearly a threat to Asa. Rather than rely on God to help him, Asa persuaded *Ben-Hadad* of *Aram* to break his covenant with Baasha and make an alliance with him instead. Ben-Hadad complied and promptly invaded the northern kingdom. Now with foes to his north and south, Baasha was forced to cease fortifying *Ramah*, whereupon Asa seized the city and carried away its stones and timber and with them built border forts of his own, at *Geba* and *Mizpah*.

In the next section (verses 7–10), which lacks a parallel in 1 Kings, *Hanani the seer* warns Asa that he had relied on a military alliance rather than on God, so from that point on God would afflict him with wars. Rather than repent, we are told Asa put Hanani in prison and also persecuted many of the people at the same time. Though Asa's foot disease is not directly attributed to the alliance with Ben-Hadad, the latter results in warfare and the former is attributed to his failure to be loyal to Yahweh, beginning with his foray into foreign military alliances.

> **Medicine & God**
>
> *As Sara Japhet* (I & II Chronicles, 736) *points out, neither this text nor any other in the Bible condemns a patient for seeking human medical help. Whatever Asa's disease (gout?), his search for assistance was appropriate, but according to the Chronicler his refusal to combine that with worship of Yahweh was not.*

17:1–20:37 As with the account of Asa, the story of Jehoshaphat's reign has been expanded greatly from that of Kings. Aside from a very brief equivalent introduction (2 Chron 17:1a parallels 1 Kgs 15:24b) and conclusion (2 Chron 20:31–37 parallels 1 Kgs 22:41–49), the only significant parallel is that between 2 Chronicles 18:3–34 and 1 Kings 22:1–35, the longest synoptic account in Chronicles dealing with the northern kingdom. As with Rehoboam and Asa, the author evaluates Jehoshaphat's early reign as faithful, and rewarded accordingly, but his later reign as deviating from faithfulness.

The Chronicler evaluates Jehoshaphat's reign as faithful, in that he *walked in the earlier ways of his father [Asa]* (the Septuagint and some Hebrew manuscripts omit *David* in verse 3, hence some doubt about the NIV's rendering). As with Rehoboam and Asa, the Chronicler divides the reigns of many Judean kings into two distinct periods: an early, faithful period and a later, unfaithful one. The early periods are characterized by military strength, prosperity, peace, and building and commercial enterprises. The later periods of unfaithfulness are characterized by warfare, or disease, or commercial disaster. Jehoshaphat fits in well with two of his three forbears, only Abijah averting disaster by seeking Yahweh. Thus, 17:1–19 illustrates Jehoshaphat's single-minded "seeking" of God and thus his opportunity to rebuild cities (verses 12–13), gain military strength (verses 1–2, 10, 13–19), and acquire riches and honor (verses 5, 11). Like other righteous kings, such as Asa, he sought Yahweh through the Levitical cult and instruction of Torah (verses 7–9) and through the destruction of idols, *asherim*, and high places (verses 3 and 6).

Second Chronicles 18:1–2 summarizes his great faithfulness and the blessing that accrued to him because of it: *great wealth and honor*. Nevertheless, after the initiatory years of his reign, he made a marriage alliance with Ahab of Israel and as a result became involved in military ventures with the northern kingdom. Indeed, verse 2 says that Ahab "incited" Jehoshaphat [NIV *urged*; Hebrew *wayesitehu*] to go to war with him against the Arameans by throwing him a huge party, assuming the same role as Satan in 1 Kings 21:1, who seduced [Hebrew *wayaset*, the same root form] righteous David to number the people. The story thus begins a negative evaluation of Jehoshaphat's reign (19:2–3, an evaluation and account missing in Kings).

The balance of chapter 18 follows its source (1 Kgs 22) almost verbatim as it relates the story of Ahab and Jehoshaphat's military alliance, Micaiah the son of Imlah's prophecy of Ahab's death, and that death on the field of battle against the Arameans. Even though the account deals more with Ahab of Israel than with Jehoshaphat of Judah, the Chronicler retains the story because it shows Ahab and his prophets and alliances in a bad light, illustrates the Chronicler's own principle of retribution, and shows the true prophets as proclaimers of God's word and rebukers of kings (Micaiah, Jehu the son of Hanani, 19:1–3). Whereas the Kings account does not overtly criticize Jehoshaphat for his marriage alliance with Ahab and misbegotten war with Aram, the way the Chronicler begins and ends the narrative reveals his application of the account: Jehoshaphat has allowed himself to enter into marriage and military ventures with the apostate northern kingdom. In seeking God's will, the kings consult false prophets but ignore, at first, the true prophet. Because of this failure to seek Yahweh properly, the battle is lost, Ahab is killed, and Jehoshaphat is severely rebuked upon his return. Perhaps the reason Jehoshaphat does not fall in battle as well is because he was "incited," like David, and thus the greater guilt lay with the inciter, and because according to Jehu the prophet, "some good is found in you, for you destroyed the *asherahs* ... and have set your heart to seek God" (19:3, RSV).

The balance of Jehoshaphat's essentially good reign is mostly marked by sound judgment and faithfulness,

> **God & Deception**
> *The story of the attempt to deceive Ahab (2 Chron 18:18–22) has long troubled readers. But the Bible often portrays God dealing with tyrannical rulers in the ways they understand. The most famous case is that of Pharaoh in Exodus 1–14. Here, as in Exodus, an arrogant monarch receives divine judgment so as to bring about greater peace and justice in the world. Moreover, Ahab's realization that Micaiah is "lying" indicates the political nature of their conversation; words do not mean what they seem on the surface to mean.*

with one exception at the end of this section. As with the "teaching Levites" who instruct Israel in the Torah, so Jehoshaphat appoints judges in 19:4–11 to deal with difficult cases throughout Judah "in the respect of Yahweh and in faithfulness" (verse 9), adjudicating cases with piety and by careful attention to Torah. As with all matters pertaining to worship and Israel's corporate life, Jehoshaphat also appoints Levites to assist these judges.

Second Chronicles 20:1–30, which has no parallel in Kings, recounts Jehoshaphat's battle with the *Edomites*, *Ammonites*, and *Meunites* (according to the Septuagint; the Hebrew text reads "Ammonites" again; the Meunites were from Ma`an, east of Petra; see McKenzie 295; Japhet, *I & II Chronicles*, 785–86). It is remotely possible that the account of the battle against Moab by the Israelites, Judeans, and Edomites in 2 Kings 3 parallels this story in Chronicles; if so, the Edomites and Moabites have become the aggressors in Chronicles rather than partners and the invaded nation. Furthermore, 2 Kings does not specify the kings involved, though perhaps implying the involvement of Jehoshaphat of Judah and Jehoram of Israel. It is perhaps best to suggest an alternate source for the battle in Chronicles, reflecting a different account than the battle with Moab in 2 Kings 3.

2 CHRONICLES

The purpose of this account is to demonstrate Jehoshaphat's piety and proper stance in seeking God (verse 3), when he heard of the great multitude opposing him. Both the king and his nation turn to God (verse 5). Jehoshaphat prays, rehearsing the Israelites' travel itinerary during the wilderness wanderings and that Israel had done no harm to Edom, Moab, and Ammon. While "all Judah" stood expectantly, *Jahaziel*, a Levite, prophesied their salvation, for the battle belonged not to them, but to God. Thus the Chronicler connects the era of the monarchy with Israel's earliest holy war traditions, according to which the Lord was a mighty warrior who fought battles for the nation. The listeners responded to this prophetic pronouncement with worship and singing (verses 18–19). (Verse 21 seems to quote Ps 136 or a similar song.) Jehoshaphat gave instructions to his army to essentially confront the invading forces with worship and song (verses 20–21), whereupon Yahweh *set ambushes* (verse 22) for the enemy armies, who then slaughtered each other (verses 22–23). As Israel did in plundering the Egyptians, Jehoshaphat and his army simply had to pick up the plunder from the field of battle. After returning to Jerusalem amid worship and song, Jehoshaphat lived in peace, for his fame spread to all the nations (verses 27–30).

The closing narrative of Jehoshaphat's reign once again returns to the Kings source. By quoting the Kings source relative to his failure to remove the high places (verse 33), once again the Chronicler introduces a note of tension in his work, for he had previously stated that Jehoshaphat had removed all of them. Secondly, the Chronicler puts a harsher interpretation on Jehoshaphat's commercial maritime ventures with Ahaziah of Israel (compare with his military venture with Ahab). Because he set out on such ventures with the apostate northerner Ahaziah, Yahweh destroyed the ships they had made at *Ezion Geber* on the Red Sea, prophesied by the prophet Eliezer (verse 37).

> **Ezion Geber**
> *Ezion Geber lay on the Gulf of Aqaba near modern Eilat. The location is disputed, with the island of Jezirat Far'on being a good candidate with its artificial harbor and fortifications.*

21:1–20 The Chronicler unequivocally condemns the next two kings, Jehoram and Ahaziah, partially due to their family ties: Jehoram was married to Ahab's daughter (21:6) and Ahaziah to Omri's granddaughter. The Chronicler's account of Jehoram's reign does not begin with details of his reign, but rather with an account of his father Jehoshaphat's many sons and the wealth he lavished on them, emphasizing Jehoshaphat's rather than Jehoram's power and wealth. Verse 3 does indicate that due to the custom of primogeniture (succession by the firstborn son), Jehoram was designated king, a curious and unnecessary note to include, unless it is meant to suggest why someone otherwise unfit to be king should be so designated.

Verses 4–7 emphasize this unfitness to rule. As soon as Jehoram ascended the throne, he slew all his brothers, as well as princes of the royal house of Israel (an interesting addition with parallel in 2 Kings). Why he would slay princes of Israel, with whom he is allied by marriage (verse 6), the Chronicler does not explain. Consequences, of course, immediately follow. In verses 8–10, the Edomites, vassals of Judah since the days of David and Solomon, revolted. Both 2 Kings 8:20–22 and 2 Chronicles 21:8–10 include a short account of this Edomite revolt and Jehoram's attempt to quell it. Apparently, in going to Edom to fight, his army became surrounded by the Edomites. Both texts mention that Jehoram smote the Edomites who had surrounded him, an allusion to his personal valor. Only Kings records that his army had fled, giving a reason why Edom remained in revolt against Judah *to this day*. Verse 10 also records the revolt of Libnah against Judean rule. In Chronicles, both revolts – Libnah and Edom – illustrate the loss of land and military defeat that accompany Jehoram's apostasy (verse 10).

Chapter 21 illustrates well the Chronicler's understanding of retribution and prophetic denunciation. Besides Jehoram's earlier murder of his brothers and marriage to Ahab's daughter, verse 11 says that he *built high places in the mountains* and caused Judah to commit "harlotry." As a direct consequence of these actions, Elijah wrote Jehoram a letter, not otherwise attested in Kings, to the effect that Yahweh was about to bring plagues upon Jehoram and his dynasty, after the manner of the plagues upon Pharaoh and the Egyptians (compare Exod 9:4).

Elijah makes the point in the letter that Jehoram had not conducted himself like the previous great kings (David, Asa, and Jehoshaphat; one wonders why Solomon does not make the list, as he otherwise appears flawless in Chronicles), so God was about to punish his kingdom, family, possessions, and he himself would die of a bowel disease. Due to his faithlessness foreigners invade (Philistines and "Ethiopian Arabs," verse 16), who literally carry away Jehoram's family and possessions, leaving him with a single son. Finally, Jehoram himself dies of a disease of the bowels, strangely reminiscent of Herod's passing in Acts 12:22–23, because of his unfaithfulness. The chapter ends with the postscript that he was not mourned (verse 19), no one regretted his passing, and he was not buried with the kings his fathers (verse 20).

22:1–9 Jehoram's single remaining son, whom chapter 21 refers to as Jehoahaz but chapter 22 knows as Ahaziah, then came to the throne, succeeding Jehoram. Like Jehoram before him, Ahaziah "walked in the ways of Ahab," not surprising considering he was related to the Omride dynasty in Israel through his mother Athaliah, daughter (NRSV: "granddaughter") of Omri. Indeed, Ahaziah's evil (verse 3) is compounded by the fact that the family of Ahab were his counselors (a detail absent from Kings).

Ahaziah's reign was truncated due to God's judgment on him for his wickedness (verse 7, an interpretation of his untimely death, lacking in Kings). Verses 5–8 roughly correspond to 2 Kings 8:28–29 and 9:14–16, 27, but interpreted through the lens of the Chronicler's overarching retribution theology. Ahaziah foolishly allied himself with Jehoram of Israel, engaging the Arameans in battle at Ramoth Gilead. Jehoram of Israel was wounded and subsequently went to Jezreel to recover from his wounds. When Ahaziah went to visit him, Jehoram was killed by the zealous Jehu, who began his coup d'etat in Jezreel. From this point on, the accounts in Chronicles and Kings differ. Jehoram's death is not even mentioned in Chronicles, not surprising considering the Chronicler is writing about Judah's past and is only concerned with the northern kingdom tangentially at best. Ahaziah flees to Samaria, where he hides, but Jehu's followers find him, bring him to Jehu, and put him to death. Inasmuch, however, as he is a descendant of Jehoshaphat, *who sought the Lord with all his heart* (verse 9), he receives a proper burial.

22:10–24:27 The account of Athaliah and the hiding of Joash tracks almost completely with 2 Kings 11, which is clearly its source. There are very few significant variants between these accounts and those, which demonstrates the Chronicler's interest in the political and religious organization of Judah. Rulers not mentioned in Kings came over to Jehoiada in their attempt to throw off the reign of Athaliah (23:1). Priests, Levites, and gatekeepers join the plot to restore the kingdom to Joash (23:2, 4–6, 18). The themes of cultic joy, praise, and purity are also evident in this section (23:13, 18–19). Whereas the overthrow of Athaliah in Kings was largely accomplished by government officials (2 Kgs 11:15–17), in Chronicles it is a thoroughgoing cultic reform, enacted by all the divisions of the priestly and Levitical classes.

> **Queen Athaliah**
> *Chronicles says little about the reign of Queen Athaliah, except that she murdered the royal scions in order to seize power. The account about her is really a prelude to the reign of Joash, whom Jehoiada the priest and his wife Jehosheba had hidden. Probably this silence is owing to the Chronicler's near silence about the northern kingdom.*

Chapter 24 has far fewer parallels to Kings than chapter 23. Since much of 2 Kings 12 deals with Joash's reconstruction project on the temple, the Chronicler's particular concerns are addressed and amplified within the context of that work. In the beginning of his reign, as with other good kings, Joash is blessed with many sons and daughters as recompense for his acts of faithfulness (verse 3).

Verses 4–14 loosely track with 2 Kings 12:5–17. Whereas Kings focuses on the procedure for gathering and utilizing the money to pay the workers on the temple restoration, Chronicles emphasizes obedience to the Torah and the wholehearted involvement of king, priests, and Levites. The reason for the freewill offering in Chronicles is because the Levites had not gone throughout Judah collecting tribute for the temple "according to the law of Moses." In order to comply properly with the requirement of the temple tax (although, interestingly, the Pentateuch does not use the word "tax"), the king had a box made to receive the temple tax and even chided Jehoiada for failing to provide the tax for the maintenance of the temple (compare with 2 Kgs 12:16; apparently, each person should pay according to his or her ability, and the priests also accepted freewill offerings, a detail lacking in

Chronicles). In any case, the people rejoice over the opportunity to pay the tax (verse 10) and thus to support the workers. So much money is taken in that the surplus paid for "utensils for service...dishes for incense...and vessels of gold and silver" (24:14; compare 2 Kgs 2:12:13).

As is so often the case in Chronicles, a king who starts well finishes poorly. Kings ignores Joash's apostasy but does mention his defeat at the hands of Hazael, his tribute taken from the gold and silver items in the temple, and his assassination. Second Chronicles 24:15–27 attributes the downfall of Joash to his apostasy, after the death of the good high priest Jehoiada (verses 15–16). After listening to his princes rather than the good counsel provided by such men as Jehoiada, he began to serve idols (verse 18). As with almost every other king of Judah, prophets are sent to warn and rebuke Joash, but to no avail. Jehoiada's son, Zechariah, goes to warn Joash, but is murdered. Recompense for the idolatry and murder comes swiftly. Connected with these acts of faithlessness, Hazael of Aram invades Judah and "destroys all the princes" (the very group who had drawn Joash's heart toward idols). Rather than tribute from the temple as in Kings, Hazael destroys cities and takes their spoil with "very few men," in retribution for Joash's apostasy. Furthermore, he was first wounded in battle against Hazael, then assassinated by his servants, whom the Chronicler identifies as a Moabite and an Ammonite (verse 26), because of the murder of Zechariah (verse 25). Joash's story closes with his burial outside the tombs of the kings, the ultimate and final act of retribution for apostasy.

25:1–28 The account of Amaziah's reign in Chronicles mostly parallels 2 Kings 14, with the exception of a lengthy nonparallel section (verses 5–16). He followed the ways of his father Joash and began well, but committed apostasy later in his reign. His first act of faithfulness (verses 2–4) was to put to death those who had conspired against his father, but he did not put their children to death, "according to what is written in the *Torah*, in the book of Moses" (verse 4).

According to Chronicles' unique material, verses 6–10, Amaziah mustered 300,000 soldiers, aged 20 and upwards, and also hired 100,000 troops from northern Israel for 100 talents of silver. An anonymous man of God came and admonished Amaziah not to take these mercenaries into battle, because of Yahweh's repudiation of the north (verse 7). A clearer statement of the Chronicler's attitude toward the northern kingdom of Israel could hardly be given! The prophet exhorted him to be faithful to Yahweh, who is able to help in battle (verse 8). So Amaziah released his hired mercenaries from the north, writing off the 100 talents, whereupon the northerners left in anger.

In a curious, but brief, synoptic passage, Amaziah takes his army to the *Valley of Salt* in Edom (Kings; Chronicles says *Seir*). The Edomites were defeated and 10,000 were captured and then cast off of a cliff (this latter unique to Chronicles, but see Japhet, *I & II Chronicles*, 859, 865).

The unparalleled verses 13–16 deal with the disgruntled troops of Ephraim, who raided the cities of Judah and took plunder, and Amaziah's apostasy on his return from Edom. The raid of the northern troops almost constitutes retribution in prospect of Amaziah's idolatry, mentioned in the following verses. On his return, Amaziah brought idols from Edom, which the text says he worshiped. Once again, an anonymous prophet came to Amaziah, asking him why he had "sought" [Hebrew *darash*] the gods of other peoples. After being threatened by Amaziah, the prophet foretells his death. Once again, in this brief section the Chronicler's concerns come to the forefront: blessings for faithfulness (the defeat of Edom), but loss and destruction for faithlessness (his impending defeat by the north and death); the necessity for the king to "seek" Yahweh; and the prophetic warning and admonition.

Verses 17–28 come virtually word for word from 2 Kings 14:8–20, the account of Amaziah's ill-conceived battle against Jehoash of Israel, his defeat at Jehoash's hands, and the tribute levied against Judah. Kings has two verses that the Chronicler omits (2 Kgs 14:15–16). The Chronistic account also has two brief additions (verses 20b and 27a) that place the blame for Amaziah's defeat by Jehoash of

> **"Yahweh is not with you..."**
> Second Chronicles 25:7 makes an evaluation that is common, whether in negative or positive form, in Chronicles. As Sara Japhet (I & II Chronicles, 863) points out, the claim that God is either with or not with Israel is not an "existential declaration," but a statement of God's willingness to help Israel or not. Those who refuse to follow God will lack divine help in doing evil, while those who obey will find God a great help.

Israel on his idolatry (verse 20) and his departure from following Yahweh (verse 27). This latter reference is the reason given for Amaziah's death at the hands of assassins in Lachish, another detail missing in Kings.

26:1–23 Chapter 26 consists of three sections (verses 1–5, 6–20, 21–23), with the first and last section drawn from 2 Kings and the middle section reflecting independent information. The first section (verses 1–4) deals with Uzziah's (2 Kgs 14–15: Azariah) ascent to the throne and some of his building activities (compare 2 Kgs 14:21–22, 15:2–3). As before in Chronicles, good kings often have some of their notable activities included in the summary statement at the beginning of their reign. Here, the Chronicler takes from his Kings source the notice that Uzziah built Eilat and restored it to Judah (2 Kgs 14:22). This notice precedes the summary statement of his age upon taking the throne and his mother's name, another feature of his source.

Verses 6–20 deal with Uzziah's superlative blessing due to his "seeking the Lord," and also with the retribution upon him for his religious violations. As with Rehoboam, Joash, and many others, his reign began faithfully and he enjoyed blessings as a result, but ended tragically as a leper because of his sin.

> **Righteous Kings & Sinful Kings**
> Arguably, 2 Chronicles 26:5 states the Chronicler's purpose in rehearsing the story of the kings for the postexilic Judean community: Uzziah and all the rest prospered as long as they sought divine guidance. It is interesting that Uzziah began to seek the Lord in the days of Zechariah, presumably the son of Jehoiada, a prophet last encountered in 24:20 when he confronted Joash with his sin. Kings need prophets, and kings need to repent.

Verses 6–15 detail in what ways he prospered: success in warfare against the Philistines, Arabs, and Meunites (verses 6–7); expansion of the territory of the kingdom (verses 2, 6, 8), a sure sign of God's blessing; diplomatic success with the Ammonites and the Egyptians (verse 8); success in building activities (verses 2, 9–10); expansion of agriculture and animal husbandry, in short, his economic interests (verse 10); expansion and organization of the military (verses 11–14); and advancement of military technology (verse 15). His success, strength, and fame came when Yahweh "marvelously helped" him (verse 15).

Verses 16–20 give the less savory ending to a powerful and prosperous reign. Uzziah became a leper under quarantine (2 Kgs 15:5, 2 Chron 26:21). No reason is given for the affliction of leprosy in Kings; in Chronicles it is because Uzziah took upon himself the sole prerogative of the priests and attempted to burn incense in the temple. Azariah the priest, here functioning in a prophetic or admonitory role, attempted to intervene and Uzziah became angry. Both Chronicles and Kings assign the leprosy that ensued to God's "touching" Uzziah [NIV *afflicted*; Hebrew *naga'*, a word used in the plague narratives of Exodus]. To the Chronicler, he is smitten because he had become proud in his strength, then rebellious in entering the temple to offer sacrifice. The Chronicler, here and elsewhere in the period of the divided kingdom, follows a method: he explains the defeats in a Judean king's reign, not otherwise given or expanded upon in Kings; and then he demonstrates the necessity of constancy in seeking the Lord, as so many of these kings began well and ended poorly.

The last section (verses 21–23) is the traditional ending summary statement of a king's reign. It slightly modifies its source (2 Kgs 15:5–7). Two of the Chronicler's additions are interesting. The first (verse 26b) demonstrates the close association of virtually every Judean king with one or more prophets. In this case, no less a figure than Isaiah son of Amoz wrote of Uzziah. The second demonstrates again the bad end to which rebellion leads: as with Joash before him, Uzziah is not even buried with his royal ancestors, because he is a leper.

27:1–9 As in Kings, Jotham's reign receives little attention in Chronicles. This may partially be due to the fact that he was regent during his father's long illness. As with Uzziah, one of the first things said about Jotham in Kings is that he *did what was right* and accomplished building projects with the upper gate of the temple and (in Chronicles only) in the Ophel (whose name implies that it was a structure erected on fill) in Jerusalem. Besides these projects, in another plus from Kings, he built many cities, towers, and fortresses. He was successful in building and in warfare because he did what was right and "he did not go into the temple of Yahweh," as his father had done.

In the largest addition to his Kings source, the Chronicler records a battle Jotham fought against the Ammonites, which he won, and exacted the tribute of 100 talents of silver and thousands of bushels of grain. He could defeat the Ammonites, as well as be successful in his building enterprises, because "he established his ways before Yahweh his God" (verse 6).

28:1–27 Chapter 28 has few parallels with 2 Kings except in the introduction (verses 1–4; see 2 Kgs 16:1–4) and conclusion (verses 26–27; see 2 Kgs 16:19–20). Following his Kings source, the Chronicler's evaluation of Ahaz is negative (verses 1–2, similar to the initial summaries of Ahaziah and Jehoram). Not only did he make images to the *Baals* (verse 2) and burn incense and sacrifice to Canaanite deities (verses 3–4), but he did what was unthinkable for his predecessors: he burned his sons (2 Kgs 16:3: his son) as sacrifices to them.

Here the parallel accounts diverge and Chronicles begins a lengthy independent section (verses 5–15). In the Kings account, it is not immediately obvious that the Syro-Ephraimite coalition of Pekah of Israel and Rezin of Damascus fought against Judah as retribution for Ahaz's sins, although one could perhaps infer this from the juxtaposition of the accounts of Ahaz's sin and the invasion of the northerners (Chronicles omits Rezin; but see 2 Kgs 16:5). As a result of Ahaz's sin, large numbers of Judeans went into exile to Damascus (verse 5), 120,000 men of Judah were killed, and even members of the royal household were slain (verses 6–7). Note the marked difference with the Kings account and Isaiah 7:1. In 2 Kings 16:5 and Isaiah 7:1, the coalition is so weak they are incapable of taking Jerusalem, although Eilat on the Red Sea did revert to Aram (according to the Septuagint and the Masoretic text of the Hebrew; NRSV "Edom"). We may gather from this passage insight into the Chronicler's method: it is theological, exegetical, and historical. The details in this text (death of Judean royalty, exile, etc.) are difficult to explain without recourse to some ancient source. At the same time, the juxtaposition of this invasion with the idolatry of Ahaz may allow the Chronicler to conclude that this trouncing of Judah (note that Chronicles mentions neither Jerusalem nor a coalition) is because of God's judgment on Ahaz and his people. Verse 6 interprets this war in unequivocal terms: *because* [or "when"] *they had forsaken the Lord the God of their fathers*.

> **God's Punishment of Idolatry**
> *What the Kings account may imply, the Chronicler makes explicit: the reason the northern coalition comes against Ahaz is because Yahweh sent them in response to Ahaz's idolatry (28:5).*

The continuation of this war with Aram and Israel has no parallel in Kings. It is the account of the exile of 200,000 Judeans to Israel. As with every preceding king of Judah, in reversal of the expected pattern, a prophet indeed comes, but this time with a message against the invading Israelites. Oded, an otherwise unknown prophet (note that 2 Chron 15:1 mentions another Oded, the father of an earlier prophet, but the name is otherwise unattested), tells them that Yahweh had used them to punish Judah (verse 9), but that they had overdone the punishment and were now about to add to their guilt by subjugating and enslaving the Judeans (verses 9–11). Certain wise rulers of Israel, hearing these words, returned the Judeans and dealt kindly with them (verses 12–15). Even in the Chronicler's stringent retributive system, compassion triumphs over judgment.

Verses 16–25 alternate material from Kings with independent material, with the majority being the latter. Ahaz does appeal to the "kings of Assyria" (the Hebrew is plural) for help (verse 16; 2 Kgs 16:17 indicates a single king of Assyria, Tiglath-Pileser III [spelled "Pilneser" by the Chronicler]). The reason for the appeal is unclear, because the war with Aram and Israel had already concluded in verse 15, unless verse 16 is simply retrospective. In any event, verses 18–19 depict invading Edomites and Philistines wreaking havoc in Judah and it is only then that "Tiglath-Pilneser, the king of Assyria" came, leaving the impression that Assyrian presence was invoked due to the invasion of these groups rather than the Syro-Ephraimite coalition. The coming of the king of Assyria, however, did not help Ahaz, but rather oppressed him (verse 20). The Chronicler's retributive system and his theme of "seeking Yahweh" applies here in full measure. Because Ahaz had forsaken Yahweh and pursued other deities and kings for help (namely, Tiglath-Pilneser and the gods of Damascus [verse 23]), the help he thought to get compounded his transgression. Even though he stripped the temple and palace of gold, he found no solution to his political problem (verse 21). The final evaluation of the Chronicler is thoroughly negative. In the time of his great distress, rather than seek Yahweh, he sought idols and military alliances (verses 22–25).

Verses 26–27 return to the Kings source for the closing summary of Ahaz's reign, with one interesting addition: "They buried him in the city in Jerusalem, but they did not bring him to the tombs of the kings of Israel," once again proving that bad kings come to a bad end and a bad burial.

> **Burial**
>
> *In the ancient world, proper burial was extremely important. To be buried outside the ancestral tomb or not to be buried at all was a dreaded fate. For a later era in Israel, burial inside a city also seemed inappropriate, but early Israelites apparently made an exception for the monarchs.*

29:1–32:33 Hezekiah's reign is one of the longest accounts of kings in Chronicles, after the reigns of David and Solomon. Little of the material in Chronicles appears in Kings. Even those sections of it that do come from there, such as the account of his reform, Sennacherib's invasion, and his illness, are reported and interpreted differently than in Kings. Hezekiah provides the Chronicler with an ample supply of examples of the benefits of righteous rule, what it means to seek Yahweh, and the benefits of pure and correct worship and cultic organization. Even those accounts that the Chronicler could interpret negatively, such as Sennacherib's invasion and Hezekiah's severe illness, appear in a positive light, given Hezekiah's response to those situations.

Chapters 29–32 fall into seven sections: 29:1–2 draws on 2 Kings 18:2–3, the initial summary of Hezekiah's reign; 29:3–36 recounts Hezekiah's reform, which mainly consists in Chronicles of the purification of the temple and its sacrificial system; 30:1–31:1 takes a further stage in the reform, the invitation of "all Israel" to the Passover and the response of the people in destroying all of the idols in the land (30:14, 31:1); 31:2–21, the reinstitution of the temple contribution (as in the account of Joash), and a concluding statement about Hezekiah's faithfulness; 32:1–22, an abbreviated version of 2 Kings 18:13–19:37, the story of the invasion of Sennacherib of Assyria and God's deliverance of Judah; 32:23–31, several accounts of Hezekiah's greatness and faithfulness; and 32:32–33, a concluding summary of his reign, parallel to 2 Kings 20:20–21.

Chapter 29 casts Hezekiah's reign into a similar mold as that of King Josiah. It is a thoroughly cultic reformation, extending throughout the nation, north and south. In the Kings account, there is but a single verse attesting to religious reform (2 Kgs 18:4), relating to the removal of the high places – an act endearing him to the Deuteronomistic author of Kings – and destruction of images. To the Chronicler, reform began in the temple and its worship and spread out from there.

Hezekiah's purification of the temple seems to be in response to Ahaz's idolatry and the misuse of temple implements (28:24–25). As with all other good kings and religious reforms in Chronicles, priests and Levites are included at the outset. Hezekiah's speech (verses 6–11), exhorting the priests and Levites, include some of the Chronicler's major concerns: rather than seeking Yahweh, their ancestors had abandoned God and temple (verse 6) by failing to burn incense and make offerings in the prescribed way (verse 7); therefore, many Judeans had died in battle, or had been taken into captivity (a possible reference to the Aramean war in chapter 28, direct retribution for faithlessness, verses 8–9); and a final exhortation for the priests to be faithful in carrying out their duties, especially relative to cleansing the temple and carrying out the prescribed sacrifices (verses 10–11). In verses 12–19, the Levites respond to the king's command – which is really the "words of Yahweh" (verse 15). All three of the main families of the Levites figure here, Kohath, Merari, and Gershon (also spelled "Gershom" in Chronicles; these variant spellings also occur in the Pentateuch), as well as the families of the Levitical gatekeepers, singers, and other functionaries (Elizaphan, Asaph, Heman, and Jeduthun). After sanctifying themselves, they purified the temple and its vessels and removed the "uncleanness" that appeared in it (verses 15–19).

The following section deals with the offering of sacrifices to atone for the sin of Israel (verses 20–30) and voluntary sacrifices brought by the people (verses 31–36). The first sacrifices offered are for a *sin offering…to atone for all Israel* (verse 24). At Hezekiah's instigation, the priests slaughtered the sacrifices and sprinkled their blood on the altar (verses 20–23), consecrating all the people (verse 31).

As with other dedications (see in particular the investiture of the ark in Jerusalem by David, 1 Chron 15–16), this one was accompanied by cultic music and praise (verses 25–30).

The concluding account relating to the temple purification and sacrifices (verses 31–36) is the invitation for all *the assembly* to bring voluntary sacrifices. This they do with great relish: they bring over 4,000 animals, so many that the Levitical helpers must help the priests complete the sacrifices, because the priests had not sanctified themselves in sufficient numbers as the Levites had. The emphasis upon joyful worship, music, and proper sacrifices everywhere become evident in this chapter and form part and parcel of the Chronicler's purpose.

> **The Author of Chronicles**
> *Perhaps two conclusions may be drawn relative to 2 Chronicles 29: first, the Chronicler is himself closely associated with the Levitical functionaries in postexilic Judea and so fills in the gaps in information about them in the Deuteronomic history; and, second, the emphasis upon voluntary giving in Chronicles is quite striking and may also relate to the Chronicler's agenda for his community.*

The Chronicler includes the story in 30:1–31:1 as a continuation of his purification of the temple and the people. In chapter 30, Hezekiah extends an invitation to the former northern kingdom (*Ephraim and Manasseh*; verse 1) to come celebrate the Passover. While this passage lacks a parallel in Kings, the details of the text suggest that the Chronicler may have had another source for this account. Whereas the Kings account focuses upon international intrigue (Sennacherib's invasion and Merodach-Baladan's visit, which the Deuteronomistic historian criticizes), the Chronicles account of Hezekiah depicts him similarly to Josiah. These are the only two kings to be compared favorably with David. As such, they are both purifiers (as David was an initiator) of the temple, and they preside over proper worship. Also, the reigns of Hezekiah and Josiah follow the scheme which the Chronicler has used throughout the narratives of the divided kingdom: many kings begin their reigns well, but then end badly and suffer retribution. In the case of Hezekiah, invasion and illness become tests of his faithfulness, which he passes.

The issue in chapter 30 is not that Passover had been suspended, but that the priests were not sanctified to conduct the slaughtering of the Passover lambs in sufficient number (29:34), presumably the result of the corrupt reign and false worship of the period of Ahaz. This condition results in the delay of the Passover until the second month. The second issue is that the northern Israelites are invited to attend, once again underscoring the Chronicler's "all Israel" emphasis (verses 5–6). However, most of the northerners mock the invitation, with the exception of "a few men from Asher, Manasseh, and Zebulun" (verse 11). An interesting side issue in this passage is the assumption that the reader knows the entire account of the destruction and exile of the north under Shalmaneser V of Assyria, found in 2 Kings 17. As the Chronicler is not particularly interested in the fate of the unfaithful north, this is the first reference we have to their demise (verses 6–9). So Judah, with representatives of the remnant of the north, kept the Passover according to the law of Moses (verse 16). As in chapter 29, Levites take the lead in sacrificing, even though this was not their responsibility, because of the masses of northern Israelites who were not sanctified to make the Passover sacrifice (verses 17–20).

> **Keeping Passover**
> *The Chronicler does not believe in mechanical retribution or "legalistic" following of rules. Here, all Israel keeps the Passover in great numbers, even on the wrong day and conducted by Levites rather than priests. The northerners are not even sanctified. The community keeps Passover in the best way possible under the circumstances, and even extended it for seven additional days, because of the great joy all Israel experienced (verse 21), the likes of which had not occurred since the time of Solomon (verses 23–27). It is the people themselves who destroy the high places and idols in Chronicles in response to Hezekiah's Passover (compare 2 Kgs 18:4).*

Second Chronicles 31:2–21 begins with Hezekiah's organization of the priests and Levites into their respective divisions (verses 2–3). In order for them to fulfill properly their responsibilities, the tithe or "portion of the priests and Levites," needed to be brought in from the people (compare with Joash's temple tax). Verses 4–11 describe the great abundance that the people of Judah (and Israelite refugees; verse 6) brought in, "heaps upon heaps." They give so much that the temple storerooms, which surrounded the outside walls of the main sanctuary, had to be used to hold the surplus (verses 10–11). The final section of this chapter returns to the organization of the Levites in charge of the tithe (verses 12–15), as well as the overall enrollment of the Levites (verse 16) and priests of the "sons of Aaron" (verses 17–19).

The chapter ends with a statement about Hezekiah's faithfulness (verses 20–21). Note the Chronicler's agenda: Hezekiah "began" in the house of God and devoted himself to its worship and organization, kept the Torah, and sought the Lord. As a result, he prospered.

In 32:1–22, the story returns to its source in 2 Kings. In 22 verses the Chronicler covers what the author of Kings takes almost two complete chapters to narrate (2 Kgs 18:13–19:37). Whereas 2 Kings portrays Hezekiah in a negative light for failing to keep covenant with the Assyrian monarch, leading to the invasion of Judah (2 Kgs 18:14), Chronicles brightens the picture. Other than the reason for the invasion, the narrative unfolds in much the same way as in Kings: Sennacherib invades Judah and sends his representative, the *Rabshakeh*, to Jerusalem to demand their capitulation (2 Chron 32:9–17 equals 2 Kgs 18:19–37); Isaiah and Hezekiah pray to Yahweh, who delivers them by an *angel*, who slays the Assyrian army, whereupon Sennacherib returns to his own land only to die, years later, at the hands of his own sons (a condensed version of 2 Kgs 19).

Chronicles portrays Hezekiah as a faithful king, comparable to David. Note how it begins: "After these things and this act of faithfulness..." (32:1). Hezekiah's response to Sennacherib is another act of faithfulness on his part. He is prudent and prepares for the invasion by stopping up the water supplies (verses 3–4), building up the city wall (verse 5), and storing weaponry (verse 5). He is pious in that, when the *Rabshakeh* comes, he partners with the prophet Isaiah and prays. Verses 7–8 also report an encouraging speech of Hezekiah to the people, lacking in the Kings account, in words reminiscent of David's battle with Goliath (1 Sam 17). Because of Hezekiah's faithfulness (verse 1), and his new act of faithfulness and prudence during the crisis with Sennacherib, God saved Judah and "gave them rest on every side" (verse 22).

As with other great kings of Judah, Hezekiah's righteous reign brings personal riches for the king (verse 27), economic prosperity for the nation (verse 28), great architectural projects (verses 27–29), and success in diplomatic relations (verses 23, 31). Two short accounts are embedded in this section, much abbreviated from the Kings narrative. The first is that of Hezekiah's illness (verses 24–26), parallel to the account in 2 Kings 20:1–11. Neither 2 Kings nor 2 Chronicles gives any reason for Hezekiah's illness; he is simply told he will not recover and so he prays and is given a sign pointing to his healing. Once again the Chronicler makes allusion to his Kings source without giving the details of it. In Chronicles, however, once Hezekiah is healed he becomes proud and does not return thanks as he ought, so the Lord sent great wrath upon them. This pride, and the wrath it engenders, is the only negative statement made about him in Chronicles, but the historical details are lost. It may be an allusion to Sennacherib's invasion, or else to the prophecy about wrath coming in Hezekiah's descendants' days relating to his welcome of Merodach-Baladan of Babylon (see 2 Kgs 20:17–19; Isa 39). Regardless of the nature of the penalty for his pride, Hezekiah responds with true repentance, averting the disaster during his days (verse 26).

The second abbreviated account relates to the Babylonian envoy under Merodach-Baladan who visits Hezekiah. In 2 Kings 20:12–19 and Isaiah 39, this is an unfaithful act, leading ultimately to Judah's exile to Babylon many years later. In 2 Chronicles 32:31, Merodach-Baladan comes to inquire [Hebrew *darash*, "seek"] of the "sign" which had been done, either the miraculous delivery from the Assyrians, or more likely the sign [Hebrew *mophet*] mentioned in verse 24 (a probable allusion to the turning back of the shadow on the sun dial in 2 Kings 20:9–11). In Kings, the visit of the rebellious king of Babylon, Merodach-Baladan, and Hezekiah's implication in his conspiracy is the probable occasion for Isaiah's judgment oracle. In Chronicles, after Hezekiah became proud following his illness, Yahweh sent Merodach-Baladan to test him, to *know what was in his heart* (verse 31).

> **Merodach-Baladan**
> *The ruler of Babylonia, known in his own land as Marduk-apla-iddina, began his career as an Assyrian vassal but made several bids for independence. His contact with Judah probably came as part of a plan to gather allies for an empire-wide revolt. He later died as an exile in Elam, modern southern Iran.*

Hezekiah's narrative in Chronicles concludes by returning to its source, here 2 Kings 20:20–21. A couple of small details differ from the parallel account in Kings. First, Chronicles emphasizes Hezekiah's faithfulness [Hebrew *chesed*], rather than his might. Second, the notice of his burial is superlative, befitting a king in David's mold: he is buried close to the tombs of David's sons and all Judah honored him.

33:1–20 Manasseh's account alternates between sections parallel and not parallel to 2 Kings. The first part of the account of Manasseh's reign (verses 1–9) is almost identical with 2 Kings 21:1–9. One small divergence may be significant: the Chronicler does not mention Manasseh's mother, an odd omission considering the Chronicler's method of including most of the initial summary information about a Judean king from the Kings account, including the mother of the king. After the summary statement, the opening section reports that Manasseh engaged in idolatry to Canaanite deities (verses 2–3); worshiped the "hosts of heaven," a particularly, but not exclusively, Assyrian religious practice (verses 3, 5; see Amos 5:26–27); burned his sons as sacrifices in the *Valley of Ben Hinnom*, an addition by the Chronicler (verse 6); practiced sorcery and soothsaying (verse 6); and mixed Israelite and Canaanite worship practices (verses 4, 7). In short, in both Kings and Chronicles he is the antithesis of his father Hezekiah (verse 3).

The section independent of 2 Kings (verses 10–17) reflects the Chronicler's retributive agenda, except in reverse. Here is the paradigmatic evil, idolatrous king, so evil that the Kings account says that destruction and exile were inevitable due to him (2 Kgs 21:11–16). Out of character for his stories, the Chronicler begins Manasseh's reign with unfaithfulness and idolatry, followed by Manasseh's repentance and national reform (absent from 2 Kings), leading to his exceedingly long reign of 55 years.

In Chronicles a prophet warns, rebukes, and exhorts virtually every king. Hezekiah and Manasseh are polar opposites, and the prophetic word also differs in these two cases. Isaiah does not warn Hezekiah, but prays with him (2 Chron 32:20). No prophet is named in the case of Manasseh, but 33:10 and 18 record the unsuccessful activity of prophets (33:10).

In retribution for his idolatry, the Chronicler records the account of Manasseh being taken in chains to Assyria. This account has been verified by one of Esarhaddon of Assyria's inscriptions (Prism S; see Luckenbill 265), which lists Manasseh as a vassal taken to Assyria to engage in heavy labor until he should learn to be quicker to obey. This imprisonment and the repentance and reform that follow are absent from Kings. Verse 14–17 detail the result of Manasseh's later faithfulness: like other good kings, he engages in building projects (verse 14) and cultic reform (verses 15–17). He even rebuilds the high places (see 2 Kgs 21:3), but does not tear them down, apparently forgivable to the Chronicler, since only Yahweh was subsequently worshiped at them. He also expands the military (verse 14). The concluding summary of Manasseh's reign, mostly drawn from 2 Kings, also reports his sin, his prayer, and repentance, not included in the Kings account (verse 19).

> **The Prayer of Manasseh**
> *The Eastern Orthodox Bible includes the apocryphal* Prayer of Manasseh. *Written in Greek, it is an attempt by a much later writer to tell the reader the content of Manasseh's prayer of repentance.*

33:21–25 This brief account loosely parallels 2 Kings 19:21–26. As with Manasseh, the text records no royal mother. Though he did evil, as his father had done in worshiping idols (verses 22–23), Amon is compared unfavorably with Manasseh, who repented. Amon, on the contrary, *did not humble himself* and multiplied guilt (verse 23). In retribution to his idolatry, his servants slew him in his house (verse 24), whereupon the *people of the land* executed the conspirators and placed Josiah his son on the throne (verse 25). Amon's reign therefore concludes with no summary of his reign or burial notice.

34:1–36:1 The account of Josiah's reign alternates sections with parallels in 2 Kings with those without. Chapter 34 largely follows 2 Kings 22, with one fairly extensive addition and one condensation: verses 3–7 condense the story of Josiah's destruction of idols and high places throughout all Israel (2 Kgs 23:4–20); and verses 12–14 add a note about Levites helping with the purification of the temple. Chapter 35 consists almost entirely of expansions of two accounts in Kings: Josiah's Passover celebration, mentioned briefly in 2 Kings 23:21–23 (verses 2–17, with only verses 1 and 18–19 loosely based upon its source in Kings), and his encounter and death at the hands of Pharaoh Necho of Egypt (verses 20–25; with verse 20 loosely drawing on 2 Kgs 23:28). The account of Josiah's reign ends with the summary statement in 2 Chronicles 35:26–27 (roughly equals 2 Kgs 23:28).

Chapter 34 recounts Josiah's reform of the temple worship and the discovery of the book of the law. Contrary to the much longer Kings account of Josiah's iconoclasm, the account of Josiah's reign in Chronicles begins with him "seeking Yahweh" (34:3). The reform that this seeking produced initially consists of the "purification" of Judah and Jerusalem from idolatrous high places and idols (verse 3). Verses 4–7 spell out this program of purification in more detail, preserving the spirit if not the terminology and sequence of similar activities in 2 Kings 23. More importantly, this program of purification of the land from idols leads to the purification of the temple and is not its result, as in 2 Kings 23.

> **Iconoclasm**
> From a Greek word meaning the "smashing of images," the practice of iconoclasm occurred with some frequency in Israel, according to 1–2 Kings. The oldest religion of Israel was aniconic, at least as far as portrayals of Yahweh were concerned. No such pictures exist from antiquity. However, Israelites did make images of other deities, hence the prohibition of such activities in the Ten Commandments and the smashing of images by Josiah and other reform-minded kings.

Verse 8 makes this point all the more clearly. Here, Josiah sends Shaphan (not identified in Chronicles, but a scribe in Kings and the father of leaders in Jeremiah and Ezekiel) and other leaders to "strengthen" (NIV: *repair*) the temple, much as Joash had done. This act in Chronicles is simply an extension of his earlier campaign against idolatry (verses 3–7). Verse 8 connects the preceding purification with the one that follows. The land has just been purified (verses 3–7); the temple is next (verses 9–14). In order to pay for this restoration, a collection is taken, again as with Joash. This collection is not just from the people, as in 2 Kings 22:4, but from the "remnant of Israel, and all Judah, and Benjamin, and the inhabitants of Jerusalem" (verse 9). In short, the text reflects the demographic makeup of Israel in the Chronicler's day probably in order to teach the Jews about cheerful giving from their own sacred history.

As with Joash's work, Josiah's collection is given to the skilled workers in order to pay for repairing the temple (verse 10). Verses 12–14 specify who was responsible for carrying out the temple restoration. In this passage that the Chronicler does not draw from 2 Kings, those in charge of the work are Levites, including singers and gatekeepers. As with every temple or cult restoration in Chronicles, joyful singing accompanies the work (verse 12).

It is in the context of a reformation and purification of the land and temple well under way that Hilkiah the priest finds the book of the law of Moses in the temple. Verse 14 segues between the Chronicler's addition in verses 12–14 and the section drawn from 2 Kings that follows, in words almost identical to verse 15. Verses 15–28 come virtually word for word from 2 Kings 22:8–20, with only slight variations.

> **Finding the Book of the Law**
> There are several good reasons why the Chronicler has incorporated the story of the finding of the book of the law from his Kings source. First, it occurs within the context of temple and ritual purification. Second, Josiah resolves to "seek Yahweh" concerning the words found in the book (verse 21). Third, the court consults the prophetess Huldah (verse 22). It is hard to imagine a passage more reflective of many of the Chronicler's main themes than this one.

Shaphan read the book of the law to the king, who upon hearing tore his garments (verse 20) and sought a prophetic word. When Josiah's men came to Huldah, she indeed had a message from Yahweh, one that threatened destruction upon Judah, Jerusalem, and the temple (verses 22–25). Yet, because of Josiah's humble and penitent response, the destruction would not occur in his days (verses 26–28). Thus in the Chronicler's use of his main source, Samuel-Kings, he introduces a note of ambiguity. Whereas in the Kings account the reason for Huldah's prophecy of destruction was evident – idolatry, high places, and sacrificing contrary to the *torah* existed in the land, and Manasseh was so evil even good king Josiah could not reverse the coming judgment – in Chronicles the reason for the destruction is not obvious. Josiah has just cleansed the land and the temple, has resolved to keep the law of God (verses 30–31), and all the people resolved to keep it as well (verse 31). Afterwards, the people again remove (presumably any remaining) idols and high places from the land (verse 33).

Second Chronicles 35:1–19 continues the story. These verses have few parallels with 2 Kings except in verses 1 and 18–19 (see 2 Kgs 23:21–23). The Chronicler vastly expands his source's story of Josiah's marvelous Passover celebration. In several ways, Josiah is a copy of Hezekiah (and David) in Chronicles: Hezekiah also began his reign with the purification of the temple and worship (chapter 29), followed by a magnificent Passover for "all Israel" (chapter 30). Both kings are excellent and faithful monarchs, in the manner of David, following tremendously evil kings (Ahaz and Manasseh). Both respond positively to the prophetic word (Isaiah and Huldah). Both set their hearts to "seek Yahweh" (see 2 Chron 31:21; 34:3). Both make a covenant with the people of Judah and Yahweh, to avert God's wrath following the reigns of evil kings (see 29:10; 34:25, 31).

The Passover that follows Josiah's cleansing of the land and temple also looks much the same as Hezekiah's. First, the priests and Levites receive for their organization and the slaughtering of the Passover animals (following the directions of David and Solomon, verse 4; compare the detailed organization of the priests and Levites in 1 Chronicles 23–27). Again as with Hezekiah, contributions are made to the temple (in Hezekiah's case, after the Passover, chapter 31). As in every other cultic text in Chronicles, Levitical helpers are prominent, including singers and gatekeepers (verses 10, 14–15). All takes place according to the book of Moses (verse 12) and the instructions of David and Solomon (verse 4). Josiah celebrates an "all Israel" Passover in the style of Hezekiah, the likes of which had never before happened (verses 18–19; equals 2 Kgs 23:22–23, with the Chronicler's added information that all Israel was present, north and south).

Chapter 35 continues with the story of Josiah's death in battle against Necho of Egypt (35:20–36:1). Most of this section is an expansion of 2 Kings 23:28–30, with verses 20, 26–27 taken loosely from it. Second Kings records this final episode in Josiah's life in the concluding summary statement of Josiah's reign (23:28, not quoted by the Chronicler until verse 26). In Kings, Josiah goes out to "meet" Necho of Egypt, who was on his way to aid the king of Assyria encamped at Carchemish on the Euphrates River. When Necho saw him, he killed him. What Kings leaves implicit – that there is a fierce battle between Necho and Josiah – Chronicles makes explicit in verses 21–25. In the heat of battle, archers shot Josiah, who, sorely wounded, was taken in a chariot to Jerusalem, whereupon he died (compare with *1 Esdras* 1:25–33). Apparently, the Chronicler does not understand every disaster as retributive. This death in battle ended an extraordinarily faithful life; hence Josiah received the best of burials (verses 24–25), all Judah mourned him (verse 24), and no less a prophet than Jeremiah wrote his funeral dirge (verse 25). The final summary of his reign includes the Chronicler's addition "the rest of the deeds of Josiah and his faithfulness [Hebrew "his acts of *chesed*"] are written in the Torah of the Lord," high praise for a faithful king.

36:2–14 The final chapter of 2 Chronicles gives brief records and evaluations of the final four kings of Judah. The account of Jehoahaz is very brief (verses 1–4, almost identical to 2 Kgs 23:30–34). After reigning only three months, Jehoahaz was removed by Necho of Egypt who placed the former king's brother Eliakim on the throne, and changed this new king's name to Jehoiakim. The most significant divergence from the text of Kings is the notice in 2 Kings 23:32 that "he did evil in the eyes of Yahweh," missing from the text of Chronicles. Likewise missing from Chronicles is the note that Jehoahaz died in Egypt (2 Kgs 23:34; compare with 2 Chron 36:4).

Similarly, the reign of Jehoiakim in Chronicles consists almost entirely of the summary of his reign in Kings (2 Chron 36:5–6, 8 follows 2 Kgs 23:36–37, 24:1, 5). The Chronicler has left out entirely the account in 2 Kings 24:1b–4, about Jehoiakim's rebellion against the king of Babylon, the invasion of Judah by various neighboring countries, and the reason for such destruction (the sin of Manasseh). Lacking in Chronicles is the first act of Jehoiakim's reign, to give Necho of Egypt money he took in taxation from the land. Missing from Kings, on the other hand, is the notice that Nebuchadnezzar took vessels from the temple and brought them to Babylon, an interesting convergence with Jeremiah 27. Likewise, the Chronicler records that Jehoiakim was taken in chains to Babylon, while Kings only indicates that he "lay down with his fathers and his son Jehoiachin reigned in his place" (2 Kings 24:6). It is interesting that no notice is given of his burial, perhaps prompting the Chronicler to write of his exile. The final evaluation of Jehoiakim's reign includes a phrase also not found in Kings which may sum up his reign: "his abominations and what was found against him" (2 Chron 36:8).

Jehoiachin's reign receives only two verses in Chronicles (36:9–10). These verses closely follow, more or less, 2 Kings 24:8–9 and 17. The Chronicler has omitted, however, the entire narrative of Nebuchadnezzar's taking of Jerusalem, exiling Jehoiachin and most of the populace of Jerusalem, and stripping the temple storehouses, found in 2 Kings 24:10–16. The Chronicler has attributed these events not to Jehoiachin's, but to Jehoiakim's reign (see above). As a result, the only thing the Chronicler can add is "At the turn of the year, king Nebuchadnezzar sent and brought him to Babylon with the precious vessels of the house of the Lord" (verse 10). Since the Chronicler reports that only "some" of the vessels were taken in Jehoiakim's reign (verse 7), some still remain for the king of Babylon to take. The narrative ends with Nebuchadnezzar replacing Jehoiachin with his brother (2 Kings 24:17: "his uncle") Zedekiah, whose name, 2 Kings tells us, Nebuchadnezzar had changed from Mattaniah.

THE FALL & RISE OF JUDAH · 36:15–23

The closing section of 2 Chronicles reports both the fall of Jerusalem and the restoration by Cyrus the Great. The intervening half century does not interest the Chronicler, just as it did not interest his source in Kings (but see Jer 40–44). The reign of Zedekiah appears in 36:11–21, but it follows its source in 2 Kings only loosely in verses 11–12. This account summarizes the Chronicler's message throughout the book. Zedekiah, the priests, and the people of Judah acted unfaithfully in worshiping idols and polluting the temple and did not repent [Hebrew *shuv*] of their sins (verses 13–14). Though they were repeatedly warned by prophets (verses 12, 15–16), they did not listen. Therefore, as a direct result and in retribution for their unfaithfulness, God had sent the Chaldeans against them, killing and exiling the people and despoiling the temple (verses 17–20). All of this also fulfilled the prophetic word of Jeremiah, until the land had enjoyed its sabbatical years, which had not been kept (verse 21).

The book ends (36:22–23) with words identical to Ezra 1:1–2, the only case in the Bible in which one book ends with the beginning of another book. This is a synopsis of Cyrus of Persia's edict, to release the captive Judeans to go home and rebuild their temple. In verse 23, the Chronicler adds to his source with an appeal by Cyrus to "all Israel" to return home.

THEOLOGICAL REFLECTIONS

Chronicles has often seemed to readers to lack historical importance and theological insight. While the historical reliability of Chronicles continues to be a matter of debate, the issue of the Chronicler's theological acumen is coming increasingly into focus (see Graham, McKenzie, and Knoppers). While much can be said about the Chronicler's theological commitments in what he has taken from his sources, I will focus on some of the themes which appear to be his own creative contributions.

KING & TEMPLE

Many 19th- and 20th-century commentators were convinced that the theology of Chronicles was basically the theology of temple and cult. For them, it was a product of a postexilic Jewish community which focused on Torah and ritual and not upon messianism. This view is true in part: temple and cult do loom large. Equally important, however, was the close connection perceived between Chronicles and Ezra-Nehemiah – the ideology of the latter seemed to be normative for the former (since royal theology is not an issue in Ezra-Nehemiah, it must, therefore, not be an issue in Chronicles either). As I have stated above, however, the ideology of king and temple loom large in Chronicles. Indeed, the theology of temple and cult may be subsumed under royal theology in Chronicles, as it is primarily with the period of the united and divided monarchies that the book deals, and it is under the patronage of David and Solomon that the temple and cult originate.

The Chronicler's emphasis upon the temple and its cult is quite clear. Almost half of 1 Chronicles deals in some way with the temple and the organization of the priesthood and Levites (1 Chron 15–17, 21–29), and much of 2 Chronicles does as well (for example, 2 Chron 2–7, 8:12–16, 11:13–17, 13:8–12, 19:8–11, 23:1–11, 16–21). As has often been suggested, the temple, its priesthood, its organization, and its cult were matters of intense concern in postexilic Judah (see Ezra, Nehemiah, and Malachi). It was important to justify worship and the priestly organization, but also important to ground that organization in Davidic and Solomonic origins.

The emphasis upon kingship is less clear. After a lengthy series of genealogies (one of which is the Davidic line, see chapter 3), the narrative of Chronicles begins with the demise of a king (Saul), continues with some of the exploits and deeds of David and Solomon, particularly as they relate to temple and cult, and ends with stories about and evaluations of the kings of Judah. Indeed, even more fundamentally than its emphasis upon the temple, Chronicles is a book about kings and kingship. It begins and ends with kingship and points the way in the postexilic community for the continuation and restoration of Davidic messianism.

> **Messianism**
> *Messianism, or the expectation of a royal, God-led deliverer, became increasingly important for Jews during the Second Temple period. Although Jews understood the messiah in different ways, they agreed in tying him to the story of God's redemption in the life of David. Chronicles is an early example of this hope for a ruler like David.*

How is this so? Besides the lion's share of space devoted to kings and their evaluations relative to the extent to which they sought Yahweh, Chronicles contains several clues to the author's commitment to the Davidic covenant (for the eternal covenant with David, see 2 Sam 7). First, quotations or allusions to Psalms or Psalmic refrains emphasize the eternality of God's covenant, especially God's *chesed* or covenant loyalty related to the covenant with David (1 Chron 16, 2 Chron 13). Two illustrations will suffice. First, in a passage with no parallel in Kings, King Abijah of Judah informs Jeroboam of Israel that "the Lord God of Israel had given the kingdom to David [to be] over Israel forever, to him and to his sons, [as a] covenant of salt" (2 Chron 13:5). In the second example, 2 Chron 21:7, more or less equivalent to 2 Kings 8:19, the Chronicler evaluates the reign of King Jehoram of Judah. In spite of Jehoram's terrible reign, Yahweh "was not willing to destroy the house of David for the sake of the covenant which he had made with David, and because he had promised to give to him and to his sons a lamp always" (author's translation). These few examples serve to illustrate the Chronicler's commitment to the Davidic covenant and its continuing relevance and continuity in the postexilic community.

RETRIBUTION THEOLOGY

If Deuteronomic theology may be characterized as retributive ("what you sow is what you reap"), the theology of Chronicles may be said to be retributive with a vengeance. In a broad sense, good kings are rewarded with lengthy reigns, bad kings with short ones. Retribution also is at work in individual actions on a smaller scale in Chronicles. For example, see 2 Chronicles 21:10 or, better still, 2 Chronicles 20:35–37.

A strict retribution theology poses a problem to the Chronicler, however. Some good kings did tremendously evil things, yet had lengthy reigns and positive evaluation. David is the parade example of this phenomenon. Manasseh, on the other hand, appears in 2 Kings as lacking in any redeeming value, yet had a reign of 55 years, longer than any other king of Israel or Judah. The Chronicler, therefore, reports a repentance and minor revival under Manasseh, justifying the long reign. No such repentance occurs in 2 Kings, which blames Judah's exile ultimately on Manasseh.

Examples can be multiplied. Good King Amaziah's reign was cut short because of his idolatry (2 Chron 25:27). Also, Asa is diseased in his feet, because of his failure to seek Yahweh (2 Chron 16:12; see below on "seeking Yahweh").

Related to the Chronicler's retribution theology is his emphasis upon prophets and prophetic preaching. Each of the kings of Judah receives warnings and exhortations by at least one prophet, usually named. The prophets warn the kings of Judah to seek Yahweh, follow the proper procedures for temple worship, and remove idolatry and false worship from the land. These prophetic warnings give a richer context to what might otherwise be seen as mechanical retribution. Especially as demonstrated in these prophetic rebukes, retribution theology falls under God's sovereignty and faithfulness to covenants.

> **Seeking Yahweh**
> *Another major emphasis is the Chronicler's theme of "seeking Yahweh" [Hebrew darash; 41 occurrences in Chronicles]. Hence, 1 Chronicles 10 condemns Saul partially for not doing so. "Good" kings of Judah, on the other hand, inevitably seek Yahweh. The point cannot be missed for the postexilic community of Judah: if we, too, will seek our God as David, Hezekiah, Josiah, and others in the past did, then God will bless us and restore king, temple, cult, sovereignty, and land.*

Perhaps for this reason, the distribution of justice in the book of Chronicles at times appears uneven.

ALL ISRAEL

R. Braun has suggested that one of the Chronicler's major concerns is the restoration of "all Israel." This concern shows up in manifold ways throughout the book, beginning at least in 1 Chronicles 9 with the list of returning Judeans and Levites, but also with families of the remnants of Ephraim and Manasseh and other northerners. Furthermore, David is proclaimed king over Israel by all the tribes in a manner far more inclusive and unequivocal than 2 Samuel suggests. The reforms of Hezekiah and especially Josiah are more thoroughgoing than in Kings (that is, Josiah's reform reaches to the far north of Israel, rather than only to Bethel in the version in 2 Kings). The whole of Israel – land, political and cultic entities, and representatives of north and south – comprise the sphere of God's grace and judgment in the past. In the postexilic age, the author exhorts the entire community to seek [Hebrew *darash*] and repent [*shuv*], as the forefathers did, so that God might once again restore all Israel.

CULTIC JOY & PRAISE

One of the surprising themes characteristic of Chronicles which was not adequately appreciated or understood by earlier commentators is the Chronicler's emphasis upon cultic joy: singing, praising, rejoicing, dancing, and so forth. McKenzie (55) has recently drawn attention to this aspect of the Chronicler's theology as adjunct to the "major theological tenets" of kingship, temple, all Israel, and retribution. Opposed to the caricature of postexilic religion in nineteenth and twentieth century commentators as dry, legalistic, and inflexible, the Chronicler's view of temple worship, priestly organization and practice, and the cult are all responses to God's unfathomable grace and occasions for rejoicing.

FOR FURTHER STUDY

William R. Millar, *Priesthood in Ancient Israel* (St. Louis: Chalice, 2001).

James C. VanderKam, *From Joshua to Caiaphas: High Priests after the Exile* (Minneapolis, Minn.: Fortress, 2004).

WORKS CITED

Peter R. Ackroyd, "The Chronicler as Exegete," *Journal for the Study of the Old Testament* 2 (1977): 2–32.

Joachim Braun, *Music in Ancient Israel/Palestine* (Grand Rapids: Eerdmans, 2002).

Roddy Braun, *1 Chronicles* (Waco, Tex.: Word, 1986).

Frank M. Cross, "A Reconstruction of the Judean Restoration," *Journal of Biblical Literature* 94 (1975): 4–18.

Simon De Vries, *1 and 2 Chronicles* (Grand Rapids, Eerdmans, 1989).

Israel Eph'al, *The Ancient Arabs: Nomads on the Borders of the Fertile Crescent 9th-5th Centuries B.C.* (Jerusalem: Magnes, 1982).

David N. Freedman, "The Chronicler's Purpose," *Catholic Biblical Quarterly* 23 (1961): 436–442.

M. Patrick Graham, *The Utilization of 1 and 2 Chronicles in the Reconstruction of Israelite History in the Nineteenth Century* (Atlanta: Scholars Press, 1990).

M. Patrick Graham, Kenneth Hoglund, and Steven L. McKenzie, eds., *The Chronicler as Historian* (Sheffield: Sheffield Academic Press, 1997).

M. Patrick Graham and Steven McKenzie, eds., *The Chronicler as Author: Studies in Text and Texture* (Sheffield: Sheffield Academic Press, 1999).

M. Patrick Graham, Steven McKenzie, and Gary Knoppers, eds., *The Chronicler as Theologian: Essays in Honor of Ralph W. Klein* (Sheffield: Sheffield Academic Press, 2003).

Kenneth Hoglund, "The Chronicler as Historian: A Comparativist Perspective," in *The Chronicler as Historian* (ed. M. Patrick Graham, Kenneth G. Hoglund, and Steven L. McKenzie; Sheffield: Sheffield Academic Press, 1997): 19–29.

Paul Hooker, *First and Second Chronicles* (Louisville: Westminster John Knox, 2001).

Sara Japhet, *I & II Chronicles: A Commentary* (Louisville: Westminster John Knox, 1993).

———, "The Supposed Common Authorship of Chronicles and Ezra-Nehemiah Investigated Anew," *Vetus Testamentum* 18 (1968): 330–71.

Isaac Kalimi, "Was the Chronicler a Historian?" in *The Chronicler as Historian* (ed. M. Patrick Graham, Kenneth G. Hoglund, and Steven L. McKenzie; Sheffield: Sheffield Academic Press, 1997): 73–89.

———, *The Reshaping of Ancient Israelite History in Chronicles* (Winona Lake, Ind.: Eisenbrauns, 2005).

Gary Knoppers, *I Chronicles 1–9* (New York: Doubleday, 2003).

Daniel D. Luckenbill, *Ancient Records of Assyria and Babylonia, Part 2* (London: Histories and Mysteries of Man, 1989).

Steven McKenzie, *1–2 Chronicles* (Nashville: Abingdon, 2004).

Christine Mitchell, "The Dialogism of Chronicles," in *The Chronicler as Author: Studies in Text and Texture* (ed. M. Patrick Graham and Steven L. McKenzie; Sheffield: Sheffield Academic Press, 1999): 311–326.

Jacob Myers, *1 Chronicles* (Garden City, N.Y.: Doubleday, 1965).

R. North, "Theology of the Chronicler," *Journal of Biblical Literature* 82 (1963): 369–81.

Martin Noth, *The Chronicler's History* (Sheffield: Sheffield Academic Press, 1987).

Anson F. Rainey, "The Chronicler and His Sources – Historical and Geographical," in *The Chronicler as Historian* (ed. M. Patrick Graham, Kenneth G. Hoglund, and Steven L. McKenzie; Sheffield: Sheffield Academic Press, 1997): 30–72.

R. Mark Shipp, "Remember His Covenant Forever: The Chronicler's Use of the Psalms." *Restoration Quarterly* 35 (1993): 29–39.

Mark Throntveit, "Linguistic Analysis and the Question of Authorship in Chronicles, Ezra, and Nehemiah," *Vetus Testamentum* 32 (1982): 201–16.

Steven Tuell, *First and Second Chronicles* (Louisville: John Knox, 2001).

Thomas Willi, *Die Chronik als Auslegung: Untersuchungen zur literarischen Gestaltung der historischen Überlieferung Israels* [*Chronicles as Exposition: Investigations in the Literary Formation of the Historical Tradition of Israel*] (Göttingen: Vandenhoeck & Ruprecht, 1972).

H. G. M. Williamson, *1 and 2 Chronicles* (Grand Rapids: Eerdmans, 1982).

Ezra

Paul Kissling

CHAPTER CONTENTS

Contexts 395

Commentary 396

    Return from Exile & the Rebuilding of the Temple · 1:1–6:22 396

    Ezra's Return & Reforms · 7:1–10:44 401

Theological Reflections 404

For Further Study 405

Works Cited 406

MAPS, TABLES, & FEATURES

The Persian Empire 396

Along with Nehemiah, Ezra forms the only history that the Old Testament supplies of the crucial period after the return of some Jews from exile to the land of Palestine. Considered one book from earliest times, the two books were not divided until the time of Origen. The older consensus of modern scholarship was that Chronicles and Ezra-Nehemiah were written by the same author. More recently, experts have argued for separate authorship (Japhet, Williamson), although this has been contested by Blenkinsopp.

> **Origen**
> Origen, who lived around 185–254 CE, was an early Christian writer and church father.

CONTEXTS

The traditional view dates Ezra's trip to Jerusalem at 458 BCE (the seventh year of Persian king Artaxerxes I; Ezra 7:8) while Nehemiah arrived in 445 BCE. Others have proposed the seventh year of Artaxerxes II (398 BCE) for Ezra, which would place him after Nehemiah. The later dating can only be sustained by deleting, modifyng, or ignoring Nehemiah 8:9; 12:26, 36, which mention the two as working together. One problem with the traditional chronology is that it requires that Ezra does not hold the public Torah-reading ceremony (Neh 8) until thirteen years after his initial arrival in Jerusalem, which seems implausible. But Ezra may have been back in Persia during the interim. Other objections to the earlier date of Ezra include the fact that the full population of Jerusalem in Ezra 10:1 precedes the underpopulation in Nehemiah 7:4; 11:1–2; the reform of marriage in Nehemiah 13 would not be necessary if Ezra had really succeeded in establishing the Torah as Scripture for the community; Ezra 9:9 alludes to a "wall" before Nehemiah has rebuilt it; and correlating the events of Ezra-Nehemiah with the sequence of high priests is difficult.

But each of these objections has a plausible explanation. The underpopulation in the time of Nehemiah may have come about from unmentioned events in the interim period. The marriage reforms of Nehemiah similarly may be due to a relapse by the community, something the reforms seem to assume. The "wall" in Ezra 9:9 is metaphorical since it encompasses "Judah and Jerusalem." The chamber of Jehohanan, son of Eliashib, to which Ezra retired is not necessarily that of the high priest. Alternatively, the later editor of the final form of the book may have lived in the time when Jehohanan was high priest and described the chamber anachronistically. In short, there is no compelling reason to correct the text or disregard its testimony that Ezra's first trip to Jerusalem preceded Nehemiah's by thirteen years and that they worked together in 445 BCE during Nehemiah's first governorship.

While Ezra-Nehemiah focuses on real events that occurred and real people who existed, the author had no intent to write history in the modern sense. At times, the author telescopes events which are separated in time but are thematically related. Like all historians, the author uses the principle of selectivity in writing about the past; but his/her criteria for selecting what is and is not important are not the criteria of modern historians. The account is not always strictly chronological; examples are Ezra 4,

EZRA

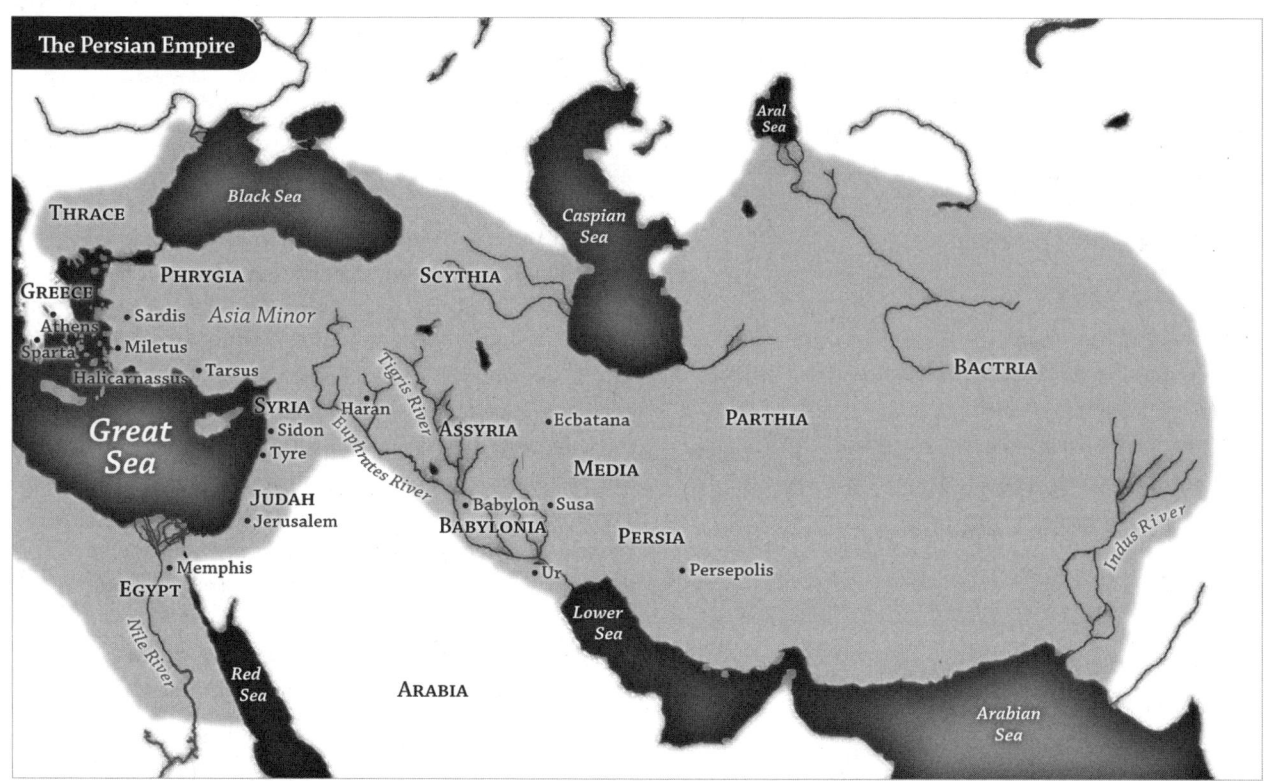

where opposition is the theme irrespective of chronological sequence, and Ezra 6:14, which speaks of a single decree of Cyrus (550–530 BCE), Darius (522–486 BCE) and Artaxerxes I (465–424 BCE), passing over Cambyses (530–522 BCE) and Xerxes (486–465 BCE) entirely.

COMMENTARY

RETURN FROM EXILE & REBUILDING OF THE TEMPLE · 1:1–6:22

> **Life in Babylonia**
> Many of the exiles from Judah settled down in Babylonia, and many remained there after the "return." Jeremiah 29 contains a letter to the Israelites there, urging them to settle down. Banking records from the firm of the Jewish family of Murashu, who were active in central Babylonia during the Persian period, have survived. The famous rabbi Hillel of the time of Jesus came from Babylonia. Jewish life remained intact there until the mid-twentieth century.

1:1–4 King Cyrus of Persia is ultimately under the Lord's hand (see Isa 4:4:28–45:4). God stirs his spirit to issue an edict authorizing the return of the Israelites and their financial support; Cyrus acknowledges that the Lord had given him all the kingdoms of the earth and commanded him to rebuild the temple in Jerusalem. Unlike Pharaoh, whose heart was hardened against the Lord, Cyrus is his willing tool and servant.

1:5–11 Notice the only tribes mentioned are Judah and Benjamin, the two tribes of the southern kingdom exiled by Babylon. Israelites from the north, dispersed by the Assyrians, are not included. Yahweh "stirred up the spirit" of both Cyrus and those who actually went back. The phrase *all their neighbors assisted* (1:6) echoes the reparations paid by the Egyptians at the exodus (Exod 12:36).

Sheshbazzar, the Babylonian name of the governor of Yehud, is mentioned only here and in Ezra 5:14–17. Attempts to identify him with Zerubbabel, while possible, seem unlikely. Piecing together information

> **Judah / Yehud**
> In the Persian period and beyond, the area around Jerusalem was called Yehud, a shortened form of the name of Judah [Hebrew Yehudah].

from the Bible and seals and jar handles of the period yields the following list of Persian-appointed governors of Judah: Sheshbazzar (538–? BCE); Zerubbabel (520–510 BCE); Elnathan (510–490? BCE); Yehoezer (490–470? BCE); Ahzai (470–? BCE); Nehemiah (445–433 BCE).

2:1–67 Significantly, the list of returnees begins with common people, in keeping with the book's emphasis on the community more than its leaders. This is followed by the priests (verses 36–39), the Levites (verse 40), the singers (verse 41), the gatekeepers (verse 42), the temple servants (verses 43–54), and Solomon's servant's descendants (verses 55–58). The basic organization of the temple staff follows the pattern of 1 Chronicles 23–26. Either the names of ancestors (verses 3–20) or the places of residence (verses 21–35) introduce the groups of returnees. Those listed by residence may have been less prominent socially and had no land in their own names (like "the poor of the land" in 2 Kgs 25:12). The towns mentioned are mostly from Benjamin, not Judah. The end of the list has those who came up but were unable to prove their ancestries, both people (verses 59–60) and priests (verse 61). Archaeological evidence suggests the population of the district numbered only 2 to 3 thousand persons.

According to 2:40, evidently not many Levites were willing to return, as Ezra later discovered (8:15; see also Ezek 44:10–14). According to 2:61–63, the lack of priests was rendered even more serious by the fact that many could not locate their genealogical records and so had to be provisionally excluded lest they desecrate the cult. This meant the temporary loss of livelihood. The family of Hakkoz was initially excluded, but later reinstated (Ezra 8:33; Neh 3:4, 21; 1 Chron 24:10). The Hebrew word translated "governor" in 2:63 is unusual and the person referred to unidentified. Sheshbazzar or Zerubbabel is most likely. The Urim and Thummim (see Exod 28:30; Num 27:12–23) were used by the high priest to request divine guidance on irresolvable issues. Jeshua does not take up the high priesthood until about 520 BCE. The clan of Hakkoz was likely reinstated to the priesthood then.

2:68–70 The house (that is, temple) of Yahweh is not yet built, but the returnees came to the site. Evidently the phrase *house of the Lord* means the location of the former temple. The *house of God* may refer to the second temple (see Hag 1–2 and Zech 1).

Like Israel in the wilderness, the returnees give freewill offerings in keeping with Ezra-Nehemiah's understanding of the return as a new exodus. The NIV's *drachmas* is to be preferred. *Darics* (NRSV) were not minted until the time of Darius.

3:1–7 The year in which these events occurred is omitted, although the context would imply the first or second year of Cyrus (538/7 BCE). The seventh month is the sacred month of three festivals – Rosh Hashanah, Yom Kippur, and Sukkoth, or New Year's Day, the Day of Atonement, and Tabernacles respectively (Lev 23:23–36; Num 29:1–38). Israelites were by this time settled in their towns so that they could begin to remember the wilderness (in Sinai and in exile) by dwelling in booths (verse 4).

> **Ancient Coinage**
> *Coins were invented in Lydia (the western part of modern Turkey) around 600 BCE. Earlier, people used gold or silver chunks for commerce. In the Persian period, although the central government and many cities within it minted coins, the standard coin for the entire region was the Athenian tetradrachma. The amount of money in Ezra 2:69 must have constituted a large percentage of the movable wealth of the Jerusalem area.*

Jeshua and his fellow priests lead in founding the altar, the first step in rebuilding the temple community. Zerubbabel here takes the place of Sheshbazzar who laid the foundation of the temple (Ezra 5:16). Explanations for this switch in names include: Zerubbabel is an alternative name for Sheshbazzar; Zerubbabel worked under Sheshbazzar's authority in 538/7 and eventually became governor under Darius; the text has suddenly jumped forward to the time of Zerubbabel in 520 BCE by telescoping history. An altar may have functioned on the temple site throughout the exile (Jer 41:5); if so, it was not regarded by Ezra-Nehemiah as adequate, and thus a new one was needed. The altar was in conformity with the Torah, which was constitutive for the returnees.

The fear of *the peoples of the lands* drove the returnees to obey God exactly and thus receive divine protection, but also prevented them from continuing on immediately to build the temple after completing the altar. These *peoples of the lands* had settled (or remained) in Judah while the nation was in exile and resisted the return and rebuilding, since they had taken over the poor villages that survived the Babylonian invasions.

Careful obedience to the Torah in 3:4–6 shows a radical change on the part of the returnees. The exile had served its purpose, resulting in a far more faithful and obedient, though smaller, nation.

The initial attempt to build the temple began with the amassing of building materials much as David had done (1 Chron 22:2–4). Repetition of details from Solomon's temple (payment with food, drink and oil, Sidonians and Tyrians, shipment by sea to Joppa) indicates a conscious attempt to copy the older building. Tyre in this period was a major port, and all the Phoenician cities would have provided both the capital and the artistic models for the new temple.

3:8–13 Attention turns to the actual building of the new temple in 520 BCE, some seventeen years after the initial return. The foundation laying is celebrated ceremoniously, but those who had seen the first temple as small children wept, evidently disappointed by the comparison (Hag 2:3). The majority, however, joyously celebrated the opportunity to begin again.

Lacking a king and under the thumb of Persian authority, priests lead in the supervision of the temple builders, but their celebration is in accord with the directions of David (according to 1 Chronicles), the great king of the past who accumulated resources for the first temple which his son Solomon built.

4:1–24 This chapter is arranged thematically around "opposition to the rebuilding" rather than chronologically: verses 1–5 refer to opposition during the reign of Cyrus (538–529 BCE), skipping entirely over the time of Cambyses (529–522 BCE) into the reign of Darius (522–486 BCE); verse 6 jumps ahead to an otherwise unknown event during the reign of Ahasuerus (Xerxes 486–465) in his accession year (486–485 BCE); verses 7–23 leap forward to the reign of Artaxerxes (465–424 BCE); while verse 24 brings the reader back to the second year of Darius (about 520 BCE) from which the events of chapter 5 ensue. While historically the opposition to the rebuilding has changed, for Ezra-Nehemiah it is ideologically one continuous chain of opposition that began in Cyrus's time and continued until Artaxerxes.

Scholars debate the identity of the opposition. According to Ezra-Nehemiah, the opposition in the time of Jeshua and Zerubbabel comes from those who had descended from Assyrian deportees to Israel, who worship Yahweh as the god of the land of Israel as well as other gods and want to join the temple building project, bringing their syncretistic practices with them. When they are rebuffed by Jeshua and Zerubbabel, they threaten the returnees with violence and use bribery and political manipulation to stop the building. The author then gives other examples of such opposition later on in candid recognition that the returnees have always (and presumably will always) face serious obstacles and injustices under the thumb of great world empires.

> **Syncretism**
> The merging of religious practices from several different traditions. Although Israelite religion inevitably had certain similarities to those of other nations, the prophets and others strove to eliminate practices and beliefs from the outside that undermined the core of Israelite faith in Yahweh.

4:1–3 As in 1:5, the returnees are here termed *Judah and Benjamin* to indicate the restoration of the southern Davidic kingdom. Their opponents are here termed *enemies*, indicating the author's rejection of their cause. The adversaries of Judah refer to Yahweh as *your* (that is, the returnees') *God*, not as their own. They claim to descend from the mixing of populations by mass deportation under the Assyrian king Esarhaddon (681–669 BCE). Their worship of *God* (not called Yahweh here) reflects the common regionwide understanding of a high god (see Jonah 1:9, which applies this more generic terminology to Yahweh). The leaders of the returnees refuse the offer of help since it comes from those who do not recognize the exclusive claims and history of the relationship between Yahweh and Israel. They refer to the edict of Cyrus that authorized them (and no one else) to rebuild. God is referred to here by the returnees as *Yahweh, the God of Israel*, as the narrator referred to him in 4:1, thus showing the convergence in point of view between the author and the returnees.

4:4–5 The opposition is here referred to as "the people of the land," a much discussed label. Here it

> **The People of the Land**
> The Hebrew phrase am ha'arets ("people of the land") occurs about 73 times in the Old Testament. In the preexilic period, it designated the free landholders of a given part of Israel and Judah, people who could influence the powerful at least occasionally (2 Kgs 21:25; 23:30). In the postexilic period, hence in Ezra-Nehemiah, the term designates those who live in the land but did not get there in the return from Babylonia.

refers to those who did not return from exile, but who already lived in Judah and the surrounding territories, including Samaria. They evidently intimidate the returnees into putting off the rebuilding from the edict of Cyrus (538 BCE) until the time of Darius I (522–486 BCE).

Ahasuerus (more commonly called Xerxes) reigned from 486–465 BCE. The narrator suddenly jumps forward thirty-five years to illustrate how this opposition that began in Cyrus's time continued throughout the period. With the change of king would often come attempts by the new king's subjects to gain advantage in any dispute. Here they accuse the returnees of some unspecified trespass. This is the only specific reference in Ezra-Nehemiah to the long gap between the rebuilding of the temple (520–516 BCE) and the time of Ezra (458 BCE).

Ezra 4:7 mentions a second letter in the time of Artaxerxes I (465–424 BCE). The letter is not supplied, either because the author did not have it or because it was not necessary for his purposes.

> **Ancient Letters**
> Many letters survive from the ancient Near East, including many in Aramaic from the time of Ezra-Nehemiah. From the Jewish military colony Elephantine Island, near the modern Aswan High Dam, come more than two dozen such letters (*on papyrus*), *covering topics both mundane and important. In one, the garrison is told to celebrate Passover:* "be pure and take heed. Do not work … until the 21st day of Nisan at sunset."

In 4:8–23, another letter besides the one mentioned in 4:7 from later in the reign of Artaxerxes is supplied, this time in Aramaic. The author of Ezra-Nehemiah evidently copies the entire document containing the letter and Artaxerxes' response. There is thus a double introduction to the letter in verses 8 and 9–11a respectively. The opponents of the returnees assert that the completion of the walls and complete rebuilding of Jerusalem will result in the Israelites' refusal to pay tribute, dishonoring of the king and outright rebellion against Persia, resulting in Persian loss of control of the key province bordering on mighty Egypt. They use the alleged history of Jerusalem's rebellions against empires as evidence of their real motives in rebuilding. Artaxerxes did find a history of rebellion in Judah, and so he halts the rebuilding until he "made a decree." That decree happened in the time of Ezra.

The Persian kings (4:9–10) claimed to be the successors of the kings of the nations they conquered, Assyria and Babylonia in particular. The descriptions of the peoples currently inhabiting Israel and of Assurbanipal ("Osnappar") are designed to curry the king's favor.

The argument (4:16) that the entire province "Beyond the River" will be lost if Jerusalem is fortified seems an exaggeration designed to gain the king's favor. The allusion in 4:20 to mighty kings who ruled over the Persian province "Beyond the River" is to David and Solomon, whose realms stretched to the western side of the Euphrates in Syria (2 Sam 8:3; 1 Kgs 4:24).

In 4:24, after having jumped ahead in history to cite further instances of opposition to the rebuilding of the nation, the author returns to the time of Zerubbabel and Jeshua (about 520 BCE) and takes up the narrative thread through resumptive repetition (see also 4:5). Redaction critics often assume that the author had inserted verses 6–23 rather haphazardly, but this assumes modern conventions about history writing that are inappropriate for the ancient world. The opposition begun in the time of Cyrus stops the building until the reign of Darius.

5:1–6:22 This section records how the work on the temple was resumed in the second year of Darius, was completed despite attempts to stop it in the sixth year (516 BCE), was dedicated during the twelfth month and saw its first Passover celebrated during the first month of the Jewish year. While their opponents had temporarily stopped the building for nearly 20 years, the returnees were able to resume the work and see its completion. The prophets Haggai and Zechariah supported the work.

> **Jews or Israelites?**
> *Originally the term "Jew"* [*Hebrew* Yehudi *or feminine* Yehudith] *referred to someone living in Judah. However, during the Persian and Hellenistic periods (538–31 BCE), the term became a religious and ethnic label. For the time of Ezra-Nehemiah, it is still a bit anachronisitic to refer to Judaism, though this usage was beginning to be appropriate.*

5:1–2 In order to refocus the returnees on their primary task, Haggai and Zechariah gave oracles ordering them to resume building, which had been stopped throughout the remainder of the reign of

Cyrus and the entire reign of Cambyses. The prophets are said to have "helped" the builders, a word used of sustaining those in need of food or aiding those in distress. The prophecies of Haggai and Zechariah called upon the nation to reestablish their priorities, with questions like: *Why do you dwell in houses with expensive wood paneling while my house lies in ruin?* (Hag 1:4). Yahweh promises to provide the resources needed for the rebuilding by *shaking the nations* (Hag 2:7), and to offer reassurance that the temple would be rebuilt and the land repopulated (Zech 1:16–17; 2:4; 4:8–10; 6:15). The hope for restoration of a Davidic king in Haggai and Zechariah (Hag 2:20–24; Zech 3:8–9; 4:6–10, 14; 9:9, 10; compare Jer 23:5–6) is apparently suppressed by the author of Ezra-Nehemiah. While this could be interpreted as mere political expediency (the Persians would not have taken kindly to the suggestion of a restoration of a Davidic monarchy), more likely the author is making a theological point. The present community, based as it is around the rebuilt temple, is a fulfillment of God's promises. There is no need to focus in exclusively or even primarily on what future work Yahweh may do while the present has enough troubles of its own. Ezra-Nehemiah calls upon Israel to see the work of God in the restoration of the nation and focus on rebuilding the nation.

5:3–5 Again potential opposition arises to the rebuilding, but this time the building is not stopped. According to a cuneiform document dated 502 BCE, Tattenai was the governor of Beyond the River only and subordinate to Ushtannu, who was governor of Babylon and Beyond the River. (Later the provinces were split into two satrapies.) Unlike the opposition in Ezra 4:1–5, here the Persian satrap does not take such an overtly hostile stance but writes to Darius, inquiring as to the legitimacy of the project. This was especially crucial for a satrap in the early years of Darius when his authority as the new king was being contested by a rebellion in Babylon. Persian satraps were known as "the king's eye"; the author makes clear that the "eye of God" overrides any human threat.

5:6–17 The letter of inquiry to Darius is included in Aramaic. Tattenai hopes to impress Darius with his efficiency, diligence, and attention to detail. He also shows the proper respect as a subordinate (verse 17). The letter records the account given by the elders to Tattenai of Persian authorization of the rebuilding along with an explanation of why it was originally allowed to be destroyed by Nebuchadnezzar. The originally authorized Sheshbazzar is mentioned rather than Zerubbabel, the current leader of the effort, lest the change in leadership cause confusion and raise eyebrows. (Another possibility is that Zerubbabel is another name for Sheshbazzar.) The continuous building (verse 16) from the time of Cyrus is misleading, since it was clearly stopped through threats of violence and bribery. Is this Tattenai's massaging of the facts, or is it the elders'? Tattenai wrongly assumes that the edict of Cyrus would still be in the archives in Babylon.

6:1–12 Darius does have a search made in Babylon for the original decree of Cyrus, although oddly it is found in Ecbatana (a city in Iran, apparently with its own archive). The height and width of the temple are idealized, and no length is given. The cost of this impressive project is to be born by the province Beyond the River, even the costs of sacrifices. The Persian government sought to build loyalty and obtain the protection of all the deities within its borders, and so we need not attribute any appreciation of Israel's God to them. Darius directs that Persian officials support the project in every way, issuing a stern warning for disobeying his orders. This remarkable decree is further evidence of God's providential hand guiding the returnees.

The first year of Cyrus (6:3) is the first year of his reign over Babylon, which he conquered in 539. He began reigning in 550. If we supply the length of the temple from Solomon's (60 cubits, or about 90 feet) the envisioned temple is a cube of 90 feet with a volume of six times that of Solomon's, which seems implausible. Compare also the imaginary temple in Ezekiel 40–41. Instead, the author is depicting "the perfect holy space," more reminiscent ideologically of the holy of holies (which was a cube though much smaller) than the actual dimensions of the second

---

Cuneiform

Cuneiform was the writing system used in Mesopotamia. Consisting of about 800 signs, each made of a series of wedge-shaped incisions by a stylus (on clay or stone), the system evolved from pictographs beginning about 3200 BCE. Many copies of older texts date to the Persian period, though most people did not speak the languages that used cuneiform (Akkadian and Sumerian). Aramaic was the dominant language of the Persian Empire.

temple. Darius wants the temple rebuilt in part because *the God of heaven* (compare Jonah 1:9) will be petitioned on account of him and his heirs.

6:13-18 The temple proper was finally completed in 515 BCE on the 23rd (compare 1 *Esdras* 7:5; Masoretic Text has 3rd) of Adar, the last month in the Babylonian calendar. Assuming an eight day festival like that at the dedication of the first temple, New Year's day followed immediately after. The joyous celebration ensued in the organization of the Levites and priests for its continued functioning.

The lavish offerings of 6:17 are appropriate to the significance of the event. The twelve male goats offered for the twelve tribes of Israel indicate that, for the returnees, they were the new Israel in its totality, the loss of the ten tribes to the Assyrian dispersion notwithstanding.

6:19-22 The narrative reverts to Hebrew and records the celebration of the first Passover and Unleavened Bread in the new temple. But unlike the original family Passover (Exod 12), here the newly purified priests and Levites slaughter the Passover lambs, thus linking the feast more closely to the temple. Only those who had returned from exile and those who had separated themselves from the nations surrounding them are allowed to participate.

> **Hebrew & Aramaic**
> Like Daniel, Ezra is written in two languages, Hebrew and Aramaic (4:8–6:18 in the latter). Such a merger of languages became common in much later Jewish texts but may also indicate the book's use of several sources.

The reference to the king of Assyria in 6:22 is perplexing. Either there is a textual problem, or the author is making the point that the Persians regarded themselves as the legitimate successors of the Babylonians who in turn regarded themselves as the legitimate successors of the Assyrians. Blenkinsopp (133) suggests that the author had in mind the story of 2 Chronicles 30:6, Hezekiah's Passover. Regardless, Yahweh's control of history is emphasized as an encouragement to the returnees, who felt themselves at the mercy of the arbitrary decisions of imperial despots.

EZRA'S RETURN & REFORMS · 7:1-10:44

The narrative now leaps forward from 515 BCE to the seventh year of Artaxerxes I (458 BCE), to the story of Ezra's return to Jerusalem, his teaching of Torah and his leading the community to conform its life to it. The intervening fifty-seven years go unmentioned, apparently because the author saw no literary or theological significance in them.

7:1-10 Ezra here appears as a priest and a scribe, both roles related to his most famous legacy as the first expositor of Torah.

Ezra's elongated genealogy goes back all the way to Aaron, the original high priest of Israel and Moses' older brother. He cannot literally have been the son of Seraiah, the high priest executed by the Babylonians when Jerusalem fell (2 Kgs 25:18–21). Since sixteen names are not enough to cover the eight centuries back to Aaron, this genealogy, like most in the Bible, is not intended to be complete and serves a social function, that is to portray Ezra's priestly work as a continuation of the original priesthood ordained at Sinai. While Ezra is never called the high priest, his priestly work was a continuance of that ordained by God.

Ezra is described as a "scribe," which may have meant something like secretary for Jewish affairs at the Persian court. But for the author, his scribal ability was in the study of, obedience to and teaching of the written Torah. God's providential hand was upon Ezra, and so he is authorized to lead a delegation back to Jerusalem to assist the returnees in implementing strict observance of Torah.

> **Scribes**
> In the ancient Near East, writing was a comparatively rare skill and thus a profession. The term "scribe" could refer to a local letter-writer for hire or a highly skilled, powerful intellectual official. Ezra was almost certainly the latter.

In 458 BCE, Ezra planned his journey (notice *for* in verse 10) to coincide with the celebration of the Passover. For the author and for Ezra, this return was a sort of new exodus. Ezra studied God's word in order to obey it, and from the power inherent in that word and through his example he was able to be an effective teacher in Israel. Ezra's example reminds us that it takes diligence (*he set his heart*) in both intellectual preparation and consistent practice to really have the power to influence others to change.

7:11-26 A letter in Aramaic from Artaxerxes is here introduced to establish explicit Persian authorization for the trip to Yehud (Judah) and reform of the community on the basis of Torah. Gifts from both the Persian court and those still in exile are also to be delivered. The form of the letter follows that in Ezra 4:17–22 and the conventions of letter writing from the period. Ezra is authorized to lead in making Torah the basis of communal life.

In 7:11, Artaxerxes describes Ezra in his roles as priest, scribe, and Torah scholar.

The title *king of kings* (7:12), although found occasionally in the Babylonian period, was typical of the Achaemenid (Persian) kings. The title recognizes that their empire had absorbed many previously independent states. The inquiries Ezra was to make (7:14) are perplexing. Perhaps he was to examine to what extent the community was living in conformity with Torah and to determine the boundaries of the community. Since one of his major reforms was addressing the problem of mixed marriages (a community boundary issue), he may also have been authorized to establish concrete criteria to determine who was to be included in the community.

The gifts given to the returnees (7:15) by their Persian captors recalls the "despoiling of the Egyptians" at the original exodus and highlights the new exodus theology of Ezra-Nehemiah.

As was often the case in the Persian Empire, the Jerusalem temple was exempt from taxes (7:24), a sign of the Persian king's respect for the temple community. To some extent, the temple thus falls under royal patronage, and Ezra's mission serves the central government.

The letter of 7:25–26 now addresses Ezra directly. Artaxerxes directs that Ezra appoint those who would teach and enforce obedience to Torah through strict punishments for offenders, including death. Perhaps the delegating of authority is an echo of Moses' similar assignment in Exodus 18.

7:27–28 Ezra here interjects his own first-person commentary (which continues through 9:15) on the events described in the letter just quoted. Ezra does not take credit for the decisions of the king, even though he asked for them; he instead credits Yahweh, who put the glorification of the temple into his heart. Ezra claims that his courage to ask so daringly came from his realization that Yahweh's hand was upon him. The fact that the royal endowment of local cults for reasons of political expediency was a feature of the early Achaemenid imperial policy does not find expression here. According to the book, Yahweh is in control of history, no matter what motivation Artaxerxes may have had.

8:1–20 Ezra now lists the returnee leaders (about 5,000 including women and children) willing to go up to Jerusalem with him, a sign of God's grace in preserving the nation even through the punishment of Diaspora and exile. The list of returnees begins with descendants of the two surviving branches of the Aaronite priesthood and a descendant from David, Hattush, the fourth generation after Zerubbabel (1 Chron 3:21–22). The latter makes the case for a date in the reign of Artaxerxes I (458 BCE) rather than Artaxerxes II (398 BCE) much more likely.

The list continues with the laity, whose status is elevated in the book. All twelve of the clans mentioned for the first return (Ezra 2:3–15) are mentioned again (8:3–14), Ezra evidently seeking recruits from those who had relatives in Jerusalem. The number twelve is crucial to this narrative (8:24, 35) in its portrayal of the returnees as a new Israel involved in a new exodus.

The text probably mentions the Levites as a reminder of their role in moving the camp from Sinai to the promised land in Numbers 10, again an example of the new exodus theology of Ezra-Nehemiah. Ezra sent eleven men to an otherwise unknown place called Casiphia, where a large number of Levites and temple servants had settled. It seems plausible (though unprovable) that some sort of worship center or Jewish temple had been built there by the exiles, else why 220 extra temple servants? The leader of this community was guided by God to send a "man of discretion" to lead the 38 Levites and 220 temple servants who were sent to return with Ezra's company. All belonged to the Levitical clan Merari, which had special responsibilities for carrying the tabernacle and furnishing in the wilderness (Num 4:29–33), another echo of the new exodus theology of Ezra-Nehemiah.

Ezra did not seek an armed escort from the king since he had spoken, perhaps too hastily, about God's power to protect them and did not want to

> **The Elephantine Papyri**
> *From a Jewish colony in southern Egypt, these texts demonstrate that Jewish people did sometimes build temples in the Diaspora when return to Jerusalem seemed unrealistic.*

undermine that witness. But God had not yet promised to work in that way, and so Ezra led the returnees in a fast and petitionary prayer for safety as a testimony to the king.

> **The "Safe Way"**
> The safe journey of English translations (NRSV, NIV) misses the allusion to the "straight way" prophesied in Isaiah 40:3. Ezra's journey is seen as fulfillment of prophecy. The fast which Ezra called in preparation for the dangerous journey involved abstention from food and perhaps also sexual relations (compare 1 Cor 7:5).

The amount of treasure in 8:26–27 seems to some scholars implausibly high. If we understand the Persian weights and measures accurately, they would represent the annual income of 100,000 to 500,000 men (Clines). The amount of precious metals would have amounted to thirty tons. But Artaxerxes's court would have wanted to give gifts worthy of the God of heaven. The Murashu banking family archives from Babylonia make it clear that many Diaspora Jews were quite wealthy, as eighty Jewish names occur among their clients. They also contributed to the gifts.

In 8:28–29, Ezra reminds the twelve priests that both they and the offerings were set apart, or holy, from the ordinary for service to God.

8:31–36 The risky step of taking such a large number of people with such a large amount of money across the Fertile Crescent to Jerusalem was rewarded by God's protecting hand. The gifts were faithfully turned over to the temple personnel and carefully accounted for. The returnees offered lavish sacrifices as part of the new Israel (notice how the number twelve shows up in the sacrifices). The three days' rest at the end of the journey may recall the three-day rest of Israel before crossing the Jordan under Joshua (Josh 3:2) as part of the new Israel/new exodus theology of Ezra-Nehemiah.

9:1–10:44 Ezra is told that the entire people, including their priestly and Levitical leadership, was embracing foreign religious practices through marriage with foreign women. Had they converted to Judaism within the marriage and adopted the faith of their Israelite husbands, this would presumably not have been an issue. According to some biblical texts, intermarriage had been a great danger to Israel as they entered the promised land and had been a primary cause of the fall of the nation into polytheism with its resultant judgment in exile. Having seen the nation miraculously preserved through exile, a remnant return and rebuild the temple, the danger of another slide into the same problems disturbs Ezra and others like him. Ezra reacts as though in mourning for the dead since in his view he is facing the death of the nation. Those who witness Ezra's mourning are moved to repentance. They approach Ezra and ask him to lead them in a national commitment to rid themselves of mixed marriages. He makes them commit to their intentions before calling a national assembly, where an orderly process of dealing with the problems is designed. Over a period of two months, the problem is systematically investigated and dealt with, and 113 men are listed who commit themselves to divorce their wives.

Concerned about the plight of the women cast off and the ethnocentrism if not racism of this text, many modern interpreters can barely disguise their contempt for this section of Ezra. This is hardly fair. Ezra neither raises the problem nor imposes a solution. He leads the community to look at things from the perspective of God's Torah and Israel's experience of receiving God's judgment for violating it. He does not force his will on anyone but persuades by his own expressions of concern for the faithlessness of Israel and the judgment that Israel's recent history had proven it brings.

> **Intermarriage in Israel**
> Israel must maintain a careful tension which allows it to remain open to proselytes without losing its own religious identity. The Torah is the living constitution by which Israel conducts its common life. It warns of the danger that intermarriage posed for Israel (Deut 7:3, 4). Ezra understands that the same danger is present for the returnees.

9:1–4 Four months had passed between the arrival in the fifth month (8:31) and these events in the ninth month (10:9). We do not know what Ezra did during this time. Many interpreters believe that the reading of the Torah in Nehemiah 8 occurred during this period and that Nehemiah's name was added to the event for ideological reasons or by later scribes. The entire narrative was then placed in the middle of Nehemiah for thematic purposes. But there is nothing inherently implausible in gaps in the account, a common enough phenomenon in this theologically oriented narrative history (compare a similar gap from the initial return in 538 BCE and the recommitment to the rebuilding of the temple in 520 that goes unmentioned). The text makes sense as it is. Ezra's silence for five months here and thirteen years later only shows that Ezra-Nehemiah is not an attempt to record everything that happened. The author chooses what to record based on the theological and practical teaching he or she is trying to convey. The people and their leaders have not been separated from the same abominations Israel faced when they first left Egypt to enter the promised land.

Ezra's reaction is grief in mourning at the impending death of Israel, recently redeemed from exile. He is joined by those who fear God enough to tremble at the idea of God's people rebelling against his word.

9:5-15 Ezra's wonderful prayer does not ask for anything, merely confessing the nation's sin, including himself as a leader in that sin, though not individually responsible. He recognizes that he has no foundation upon which to presume upon the Lord's mercy. After all of God's patience and grace in leaving a remnant, the nation is on the brink of falling back into the very sins for which the exile had chastened them! The Torah had warned Israel, says Ezra, quoting a series of passages from Deuteronomy and Leviticus. Ezra expresses the rational fear that, if Israel intermarried and syncretized again, Yahweh would completely destroy the nation.

The wall in *Judah and Jerusalem* is metaphorical, and there is no indication that Ezra came after the building of the wall in Nehemiah's time.

10:1-4 The people are affected by Ezra's concern, joining his mourning for the nation. Led by Shecaniah, one of those guilty of the intermarriage (10:26), the people acknowledge their guilt and suggest the divorce of wives by those committed to God's Torah. Shecaniah claims that if this is done, there is still hope for Israel and prods Ezra into taking responsibility for leading this reform.

10:5-8 Ezra asks those in the crowd for a solemn commitment to follow the course recommended by Shecaniah, spending an additional night in prayer and fasting. The leaders of the returnees call for a public assembly to devise a strategy to deal with the intermarriages. Those failing to come to the assembly risk loss of property and excommunication from the community.

10:9-15 The assembly takes place in December, the month of the heaviest winter rains in Jerusalem, the weather seeming to match the gravity of the situation. Ezra calls upon the men to divorce their idolatrous wives, and they agree (with only four exceptions), but ask for time to deal with the issue in an orderly way. It is not clear what the elder and judges will decide, presumably either what actually qualifies as a forbidden marriage or how to handle the associated issues such as dowries, sudden "conversions," and financial support for children. Those who opposed Ezra may have wanted stricter enforcement of the Torah.

10:16-44 Ezra chooses heads of families to examine the matter. They begin meeting ten days later, their work taking two months. The 113 or so offenders seem surprisingly few given the earlier discussions. Perhaps many of the women chose to convert rather than be divorced, or their husbands may have chosen to leave the community. The list of those who were found guilty and who pledged to divorce their wives begins with the priests, including descendants of the high priest Jeshua from Zerubbabel's time. The guilt offering indicates an unintentional sin (Num 5:8; Lev 5:14-19). There was no specific prohibition in the Torah of intermarrying with the particular nations in existence at that time. They had violated the principle and the point of the Torah, but not its actual words, but they could not be excused on that account.

Ironically, literalist interpreters put the nation in danger of slipping back into syncretism. The Torah did not literally make the women they were marrying off limits. But the principle behind the regulations prohibiting exogamous marriage for Israel in Canaan was being violated. The less literalistic interpreters were more faithful to the intention of the Torah (Clines).

THEOLOGICAL REFLECTIONS

The most distinctive theological idea of Ezra and Nehemiah is that the God who controls history has acted to create a new or at least a restored Israel out of the old exiled Israel. Israel is to be a kingdom of priests and will follow the written Torah rather than the oral pronouncements of prophets and others.

What matters for Ezra-Nehemiah is the community in which every member functions like a priest with a direct and personal relationship with God. Ezra and Nehemiah are fully aware that God's ultimate restorative work on behalf of Israel will have to wait for the distant future. There is a "not yet" element implicit in its ideology. But the focus is on the "now" and "already" of the kingdom. This kingdom has no human king. Hope for the restoration of the line of David is muted in Ezra-Nehemiah, although not entirely gone. The book advises its readers to accept the Persian authorities and see God's hand at work through them. What God will do in the future is up to God. What Israel must do now is focus on becoming the holy nation and kingdom of priests that the old Israel committed itself to becoming but miserably failed at achieving (Exod 19:1–6). Day-to-day living in conformity with the scripturally revealed will of God is the priority for the nation.

The nation is already restored (Ezra 1:1–4; 3:11; 7:27; Neh 12:27) but also in need of restoration (Ezra 3:12; Neh 13). The "already" of the restoration is seen in the depiction of the return as a new exodus/conquest. Ezra departs in the first month (Ezra 7:1–10), the month of the original exodus (Exod 12:2; Num 33:3). The "straight way" prayed for in Ezra 8:21 is a deliberate echo of the new exodus typology in Isaiah 40:3. The departure from the river Ahava in Ezra 8:31 involves Israel celebrating Passover as the end of the sojourn in the house of bondage in Babylon.

> **God's Control of History**
>
> A significant theological theme of Ezra-Nehemiah is God's control of history. Ezra 6:14b notes that the rebuilding of the temple was ultimately commanded by God, not the Persian kings. They may have believed that they were in control, but in actuality they were carrying out God's will. There were several decrees by Persian kings throughout the time period reflected in Ezra-Nehemiah (538 BCE – Cyrus's decree; 520 BCE – Darius's decree; Artaxerxes' decrees in 458 for Ezra and 445 for Nehemiah). But the author of the book refers to the divine decree. All of these kings played a part in fulfilling the one will of God, the restoration of the exiled people. God is still in control of history, no matter what leaders of great empires may think.

The threat that intermarriage poses for the returnees is reminiscent of a similar threat in the time of Joshua (Ezra 9:1–5). The number twelve recurs (Ezra 2:2; 6:17; 8:3–14, 24, 25), alluding to the twelve tribes of Israel even though only two tribes (Judah and Benjamin) return. For the author, the returnees from Babylon are a new Israel. The old Israel leaves Egypt for Sinai where they are offered the privilege of becoming a kingdom of priests and are given detailed instructions for the building of the tabernacle, the predecessor to the temple. In Ezra-Nehemiah, the entire city becomes a temple. The (to us) tedious lists of names that recur throughout the book show that the laity are of the utmost importance, not the priests. The people exercise leadership and initiate change (Ezra 9:1; 10:1–9; Neh 8:1, 2), not the specially called leaders. There is little emphasis on the Davidic promise because this community is priestly in nature, not royal. The returnees from Babylonian exile have the opportunity and the responsibility to become a new Israel.

A final theological theme of Ezra-Nehemiah is the importance of the written, rather than the oral, revelation of God. Ezra leads the returnees in committing themselves to strict obedience to the Torah of Moses. For the first time, Israel as a whole, rather than a small minority, becomes a people of the book, a Scripture-based and Scripture-formed people. This implies a time when spontaneous prophecy has either ceased or is regarded with such suspicion that it no longer is trusted as a means of ongoing guidance for the people of God. Israel will follow the written word of God, and that will trump any oral pronouncements of prophets. Israel will forever be a people of the book while it waits for God's sending of the Messiah.

FOR FURTHER STUDY

Pierre Briant, *From Cyrus to Alexander: A History of the Persian Empire* (trans. Peter T. Daniel; Winona Lake, Ind.: Eisenbrauns, 2002).

Gordon F. Davies, *Ezra & Nehemiah* (Collegeville, Minn.: Liturgical Press, 1999).

Kenneth K. Kitchen, *On the Reliability of the Old Testament* (Grand Rapids: Eerdmans, 2003).

Iain Provan, V. Philips Long, and Tremper Longman III, *A Biblical History of Israel* (Louisville: Westminster John Knox, 2003).

WORKS CITED

Joseph Blenkinsopp, *Ezra-Nehemiah* (Philadelphia: Westminster, 1988).

David J. A. Clines, *Ezra, Nehemiah, Esther* (Grand Rapids: Eerdmans, 1984).

Michael W. Duggan, *The Covenant Renewal in Ezra-Nehemiah (Neh 7:72b–10:40): An Exegetical, Literary and Theological Study* (Atlanta: Society of Biblical Literature, 2001).

Tamara Cohn Eskenazi, *In an Age of Prose: A Literary Approach to Ezra-Nehemiah* (Atlanta: Scholar's Press, 1988).

Sara Japhet, *I & II Chronicles* (Louisville: Westminster John Knox, 1993).

Mark A. Throntveit, *Ezra-Nehemiah* (Louisville: John Knox, 1992).

H. G. M. Williamson *Ezra, Nehemiah* (Waco, Tex.: Word, 1985).

Nehemiah

Paul Kissling

CHAPTER CONTENTS

Contexts 407

Commentary 407

 Nehemiah's First Return to Rebuild Jerusalem · 1:1–13:3 407

 Nehemiah's Second Return · 13:4–31 413

Theological Reflections 414

For Further Study 415

Works Cited 415

MAPS, TABLES, & FEATURES

Known Postexilic High Priests 413

Along with Ezra, Nehemiah forms the only history that the Old Testament supplies of the crucial period after the return of some Jews from exile to the land of Palestine. Considered one book from earliest times, the two books were not divided until the time of Origen. The older consensus of modern scholarship was that Chronicles and Ezra-Nehemiah were written by the same author. More recently, experts have argued for separate authorship (Japhet, Williamson), although this has been contested by Blenkinsopp.

> **Origen**
> Origen, who lived around 185–254 CE, was an early Christian writer and church father.

CONTEXTS

The traditional view dates Nehemiah's arrival in Jerusalem to 445 BCE with Ezra arriving earlier in 458 BCE. Others have proposed the seventh year of Artaxerxes II (398 BCE) for Ezra, which would place him after Nehemiah. One problem with the traditional chronology is that it requires that Ezra does not hold the public Torah-reading ceremony (Neh 8) until thirteen years after his initial arrival in Jerusalem, which seems implausible. Other objections to the earlier date of Ezra include the fact that the full population of Jerusalem in Ezra 10:1 precedes the underpopulation in Nehemiah 7:4; 11:1–2; the reform of marriage in Nehemiah 13 would not be necessary if Ezra had really succeeded in establishing the Torah as Scripture for the community; Ezra 9:9 alludes to a "wall" before Nehemiah has rebuilt it; and correlating the events of Ezra-Nehemiah with the sequence of high priests is difficult, though each of these objections has plausible explanations.

While Ezra-Nehemiah focuses on real events that occurred and real people who existed, the author had no intent to write history in the modern sense. At times, the author telescopes events which are separated in time but are thematically related. Like all historians, the author uses the principle of selectivity in writing about the past; but his/her criteria for selecting what is and is not important are not the criteria of modern historians.

For a more detailed discussion of the historical and literary contexts of Nehemiah, see the discussion of Ezra's contexts on page 395.

COMMENTARY

NEHEMIAH'S FIRST RETURN TO REBUILD JERUSALEM · 1:1–13:3

The book of Nehemiah contains mainly the first-person account of Nehemiah himself. The author introduces his words (1:1), and then the character Nehemiah tells his story. He actually goes to Jerusalem to work on reforming and rebuilding the community twice: here in 445 BCE and later (chapter 13) in 433 BCE. His most noteworthy accomplishment is the rebuilding of the walls of Jerusalem in a remarkable fifty-two days. But he is also involved in the halting of usury against impoverished Jews, the repopulating of the city, and along with Ezra, the establishment of the Torah as the community's standard of conduct. The celebration of the completion of the wall in Nehemiah 12 forms the high point of Ezra-Nehemiah.

1:1–11 Upon hearing of the distressing situation in Judah with the returned community, Nehemiah goes into extended mourning and asks God to grant him success in his plea to Artaxerxes for support in returning and rebuilding Jerusalem. In the twentieth year of King Artaxerxes I (445 BCE), Nehemiah, his Jewish cupbearer, received a report concerning the returnees in Judah. The province's inhabitants were in a state of shame and the wall of Jerusalem was broken down and its gates burned, leaving it defenseless. The authorities in Samaria had been successful in stopping the building of the walls (Ezra 4:8–23). The force mentioned in Ezra 4:23 may allude to their destruction. Nehemiah's reaction is to go into an extended period of mourning and prayer.

> **The Royal Cupbearer**
> *Far from being a minor servant, a royal cupbearer (or wine steward) was a very high-ranking official. In becoming governor of Yehud, Nehemiah took a demotion in order to serve his people.*

His prayer is primarily one of contrition. As a leader, he includes himself in his confession of Israel's sin. He refers back to the Torah of Moses to remind the Lord that he has promised (Deut 30:1–5) to bring a repentant Israel back even from the "end of the heavens" (verse 9; see also 1 Kgs 8:46–53). He asks for success in his approach to "this man" Artaxerxes, for permission and financial backing to return and rebuild the walls of Jerusalem.

2:1–8 Nehemiah waits four months for the right opportunity to address Artaxerxes, showing remarkable tact when doing so. When asked about his sad demeanor, he refers to the place where his fathers' graves are, rather than to the rebellious capital Jerusalem, whose wall-building project the king had halted. He thus appeals to a common interest of ancient kings, the preservation of ancestral tombs. He asks first to return to Judah (not Jerusalem) before asking for the resources for the building project. Nehemiah combines his prayer with a wise pragmatism. He requests and receives authorization and financial backing to rebuild the walls, the military fortress standing on the temple mount, and for his own personal residence (perhaps as governor). While Nehemiah used tact, he attributes the favorable decision to the gracious hand of God (verse 8).

2:9–10 When Nehemiah and company arrive in Jerusalem, his future opponents, Sanballat, the governor of Samaria (though Nehemiah does not give him his title) and Tobiah, the governor of Ammon, are incensed. But given the royal letters and the army backing Nehemiah, they are in no position to resist. Their power and wealth are undermined by a newly appointed governor of Judah.

2:11–20 Before enlisting the support of the returnees for the wall-building project, Nehemiah wisely and secretly surveys the project, counting its cost. He sees the difficulties of rebuilding on the collapsed slope to the east of the Temple Mount and so makes it the eastern edge of the city to be walled in.

> **Jerusalem's Walls**
> *The current walls of Jerusalem date to the sixteenth century CE, to the reign of Suleiman the Magnificent. But their foundations come from the time of Herod and earlier. Part of the foundations may date as early as Nehemiah, but this is uncertain.*

Having surveyed the situation, Nehemiah then recounts to the returnees the disgrace that the lack of a functioning capital with protective walls brings and the providential opportunity God had provided through Artaxerxes to remedy the situation. Nehemiah's rhetorical skills move his audience to an immediate, enthusiastic commitment. The success of Nehemiah in gaining support from the returnees results in a ratcheting up of opposition. Geshem now joins Sanballat and Tobiah, and displeasure turns to ridicule and suggestions of sedition against the king of Persia. Nehemiah recognizes how much he depends upon God for his success and does not even answer the mocking. This political confusion comes in part from the loose organization of the Persian Empire.

3:1–32 Here Nehemiah cites a list of those who repaired the wall. The sheer variety of builders working side by side is striking. The laity matter, but priests also work with them. Whenever possible, Nehemiah makes the builder responsible for that section of the wall nearest his or her home, motivating them to make that portion of the wall as secure as possible. Rulers and ruled (note the exception in verse 5), priests and laity, men and women, the affluent and the poor, merchants and the purchasing public all contribute to the project. In rebuilding the walls, Nehemiah is obviously also restoring the essential unity of the community.

4:1–23 With success again comes opposition. Here Sanballat and Tobiah take their mockery to the people themselves. They discourage the workers from believing that they will actually be able to complete the project with lasting quality given the present difficulties. As elsewhere, Nehemiah's response to opposition is to pray, this time asking God's most severe judgment upon their opponents.

The wall, having been connected, is now elevated to at least half its height. The opposition does not stop the work because of the mindset of the people. They have a heart to do and not just discuss or plan. However, having attempted and failed to stop the rebuilding through threat, ridicule, and discouragement, the opposition begins to scheme. The opposition now comes from every direction: Sanballat from Samaria to the north, Tobiah from Ammon to the east, Arabs to the south, and now the Ashdodites from the west. Military action is suggested, which is yet another increase in the severity of the pressure.

> **Building the Wall**
> In 4:9–21, the text seamlessly moves from God's work to humans' responsibility. Faced with increasing opposition, they both pray and set up guards. Nehemiah and the builders use multiple techniques: reconnaissance in uncovering the plot, strategizing, rallying the troops with encouraging speeches, enlightened self-interest by placing families as guards near their homes, and so on. Eventually the workers carry weapons with them, some standing guard while others work. A signal system is devised to support weak places in the wall. The workers end up living inside of the city to protect themselves and the work they are doing. In all this, God's protection is never questioned.

5:1–19 While this event is recorded out of chronological sequence, the point of putting it here is to emphasize that Nehemiah's work is not merely building the wall. The wall would be meaningless if the community that it protects were fundamentally at odds with God's standards of behavior. In a time of famine, some of the community are taking advantage of their fellow Jews by forcing them to pledge their land as collateral for food and to pay taxes (compare Deut 23:19–20). Some are even forced to sell their children into slavery (and even prostitution), having already lost their lands. The rich are taking advantage of the situation through usury and forcing their kinsmen into perpetual poverty. Throntveit suggests that this event occurs during the time of Nehemiah's second term as governor (432 BCE), when he is dealing with other abuses that had arisen in his absence. It is also possible that the famine referred to here may be the one perhaps implied by Malachi.

In 5:6–13, Nehemiah publicly confronts the abuse, accusing the nobles and officials of selling their Jewish brothers into slavery after only recently being released from a form of debt slavery in exile. Their behavior will only bring ridicule from the very nations they claim their God rules over. He contrasts their behavior with his own, of lending without interest, and calls upon them to restore their property and return the interest they have already collected. Nehemiah takes special care to confirm that the priests in particular keep their promises to make restoration. The rich may have been using a stringent application of the Torah's rules concerning the Year of Jubilee as justification for taking advantage of the poor during a famine (see Lev 25:8–54). Nehemiah knows that building walls without a community ethic that shows concern for one's neighbors will accomplish little. While Nehemiah's leadership style is different from Ezra's, drawing attention to himself and publicly enforcing his norms on the community, he still accomplishes important matters in the rebuilding of the nation.

Nehemiah 5:14–19 quotes the Nehemiah Memoir here again. He claims retrospectively to have never taken advantage of the returnees, not even taking the food allowance or salary due him as governor even though his expenses were significant, feeding more than 150 people daily. He is quoted as praying for God to remember his generosity. Modern readers may be embarrassed by the seeming self-aggrandizement of such passages. Even the original audience would compare him unfavorably with Ezra. But Nehemiah speaks the truth, and the memoir that the author quotes may have contained such self-justification for good reasons.

> **The Nehemiah Memoir**
> The book of Nehemiah, written by someone other than the man of that name, nevertheless quotes extensively from a first-person account that Nehemiah himself may have written as a way of justifying his work. This so-called memoir survives in Nehemiah 1:1–2:20; 4:1–7:5; 12:31–43; and 13:4–31.

6:1–19 We are now back to the time of the rebuilding of the wall that chapter 5 interrupted. With progress on the wall becoming obvious (only the gates remained to be set), Nehemiah's enemies try to lure him away from the project to meet with them outside the city. When Nehemiah rebuffs this trap five times, they send an open letter with an accusation that the returnees are planning a rebellion against the Persian authorities once they have their capital city protected with a wall. This accusation had previously been used to stop the work (Ezra 4:7–23). They also claim that Nehemiah has hired prophets to proclaim him king. They threaten to send this false information to the Persian emperor if Nehemiah will not meet with them. Nehemiah denies the charges and prays for God to make his hands even stronger so that the work will be completed even more quickly. Nehemiah is portrayed here as a leader who will not be stopped by false accusations and political manipulation but turns to God in prayer and continues his focus on the task at hand. His autobiographical memoir is designed to protect him from false accusations. He balances dependence on the Lord with wise and savvy actions. In 6:1, the enemies arise yet again for the sixth time, now including the principals Sanballat, Tobiah, and Geshem, as well as the *rest of [their] enemies*.

In verses 10–14, Nehemiah gives another example of the opposition he faced, again without clear chronological indications. He visits a prophet (verse 12), Shemaiah, who is *shut up*. Perhaps this means that he has sought asylum in the temple by pledging himself to lifelong service as a temple servant (Clines). By prophesying that Nehemiah should seek asylum from his enemies in the temple, Shemaiah is attempting to trick Nehemiah into being accused of cowardice (by running away from trouble into the temple) and impiety (by entering the temple as a nonpriest). Having been accused of hiring false prophets, here Nehemiah discovers that his enemies have done the very thing they have accused him of doing. In the postexilic community where the written Torah is being accepted as normative, this text warns of the alluring dangers of false prophesy.

Noadiah may have been Shemaiah's wife. The *rest of the prophets* shows that this episode is only a representative one. Nehemiah deals with false prophets just as Jeremiah had before the exile.

The remarkably speedy completion of the wall (verses 15–16) deflates the returnees' enemies. There is no explaining it other than as the strong hand of God being on Nehemiah and the community. They have done it with God and not by themselves.

While the absolute chronology of the events recorded in verses 17–19 is not clear, its placement here is another example of the continual (and continuing) problem that Tobiah represents for Nehemiah and the returnees. Nehemiah explains that there may well be documents presented that seem to paint a very different picture from the one he has painted. The correspondence between Tobiah and the nobles of Judah is another way Tobiah attempts to undermine Nehemiah's work. He has connections with the community's elite in both economic (*oaths* verse 18) and relational ways (*marriages*, compare Ezra 2:5), giving him insider information on Nehemiah's activities. Tobiah's allies among the Jewish nobility also tries to influence Nehemiah's view of him by speaking of his good deeds to Nehemiah.

7:1–73A With the walls now built, Nehemiah's next challenge is the protection of the city and the preparation for its development. At this stage, the capital was seriously underpopulated so that the temple could not function in reality as the center of the returnees' communal life. Nehemiah first acts to ensure the safety and security of the city. The gates are not to be opened during the heat of the day while most people in that climate would have a sort of siesta (see Williamson for this translation of verse 3). Further, guards are posted, overseen by trusted men. Nehemiah once again deals with the reality of the situation, all the while trusting in God's providential protection. The conclusion of this narrative comes only in chapter 11, the narrative being "interrupted" by the account of the covenant renewal in 7:73b–10:39.

On the census in 7:5–73, see Ezra 2:1–67. Here the census helps determine who could legitimately move into the holy city because of their Jewish religious background. Nehemiah does not want to introduce pagan worshipers or syncretists into Jerusalem. The policy of government directed resettlement of underpopulated regions was not unusual in the ancient world, though those moved may normally have been less eager than the book of Nehemiah implies.

Most experts believe that the record of an event from the Ezra Memoir, used by the author as one of his sources, is inserted here. It fits the emphasis of this section of Nehemiah on rebuilding the people as well as the walls. Ezra helps the people establish the Torah as the norm for communal life. It is publicly read, explained, and discussed. The Feast of Tabernacles is observed in accordance with the Torah, while Ezra continues to read and teach it. Finally, a national assembly engages in public confession of violation of the Torah and, with Ezra, prays confessionally and recounts the sad history of the people's disobedience to Yahweh. A written document is produced expressing the commitment of the returnees to be faithful to the Torah. Many interpreters believe that Ezra's Torah, the Pentateuch in more or less its final form, is here accepted as holy Scripture by the nation as a whole.

> **The Ezra Memoir**
> *Along with the first-person account of Nehemiah, the author of Ezra-Nehemiah also used a first-person source related to the work of Ezra. This material appears in both Ezra and Nehemiah.*

7:73B–8:12 The seventh month would seem to be September/October of 445 BCE (Artaxerxes' twentieth year; compare Neh 6:15). This month included celebrations of the Feast of Trumpets, the Day of Atonement, and Tabernacles or Booths (beginning on the 15th; see Lev 23). What Ezra did between the seventh and twentieth years of Artaxerxes is unknown; perhaps he returned to Persia. The people as a whole receive the prominent place in this narrative. They gather without being directed to do so (8:1); they tell Ezra to bring out the Torah to read it; their leaders interpret the Torah, which Ezra reads to them; their ears are attentive to it and they express mourning at their failure to follow it. Ezra and other leaders, including Nehemiah, remind the people of the joy they should experience on a day like this. While they had been unfaithful, Yahweh is not and will receive them back gladly.

> **Reading the Torah**
> *The Torah is so important that the people are said to have listened to it being read and explained for half the day. Men, women, and children old enough to understand all participated. The Scriptures were and are for all. Moreover, the careful preparations for the reading of the Torah imply a communal decision to commit publicly to it. The note in verse 8 means that the Levites read the text distinctly and carefully and offered some sort of explanation, either linguistic (since some persons may not have understood Hebrew well) or theological.*

8:13–18 The leaders discover from the Torah that they are to remember God's preservation of Israel in the wilderness by annually living in booths for a week. They hear the Torah as Scripture and obey. This ordinance had not been obeyed by the nation since the time of Joshua upon entering the land. As Joshua, like Moses before him, challenged the people to obey Yahweh, here the new Israel, recently returned from exile, does so as well.

9:1–5 Two days after the conclusion of the feast, the people gather for a public service of repentance that includes the public signs of mourning, formal separation from relationships with people who do not share their covenant commitments, and public confession of the nation's sins. Again the Torah is read and confession of sin and worship of God follow naturally. Ezra takes no part in this ceremony, another demonstration of the book's emphasis on the people rather than their leaders. The nation is becoming a kingdom of priests.

9:6–37 Evidently Ezra, who has been silent up to now, leads in a national prayer of confession. He begins by confessing who God is: the creator (verse 6), the elector of Abram and promiser of the land (verse 7–8), the redeemer from Egypt (verses 9–11), the preserver in the wilderness (verses 12, 15), and the giver of the laws including the Sabbath (verses 13–14). Ezra then turns to confession of Israel's long history of rebellion and Yahweh's merciful faithfulness despite it. This rebellion began at Sinai and in the wilderness (verses 16–25) and continued all the while Israel had the blessings of the promised land (verses 26–30a). The exile was just judgment (verse 30b), and the return was another demonstration of grace (verse 31). Ezra then asks for help in their current difficult circumstances (verse 32). He quickly acknowledges that the nation is not deserving (verses 33–37), but this beautiful prayer ends with an implied trusting of God's continuing grace to unworthy people. Duggan (298) rightly terms this prayer "the theological centerpiece of covenant renewal and the spiritual apex of the Ezra-Nehemiah story." Following Eskenazi, he notes the following about the prayer and the related context: first, the prayer encapsulates the penitential prayers of Ezra (9:6–15) and Nehemiah (1:5–11) and "thereby suggests that the devotion of these protagonists now pervades the community"; second, by moving from creation to the present, the prayer gives a large enough historical context for understanding the recent events in Judah better; third, in light of the opposition to rebuilding, the prayer provides assurance that the land is an irrevocable gift; fourth, the use of words built on the Hebrew root *amen* ("faith [fulness]") links faithful Abraham (9:8a; Gen 15:6) to the people's commitment to faithfulness (10:1); fifth, the lack of mention of exile redefines the people in terms of their present allegiance to the law, not as the survivors of exile; sixth, the law is portrayed as the most intimate and personal communication of God (9:13–14); seventh, the present Persian overlords are "peoples of the lands" (9:30c) who treat Israel as "slaves" (9:36–37) from whom they must separate (Ezra 4:4); eighth, the cycles of peace, rebellion, outcry, and redemption characterize the present as well as the past (Judges, Kings) and speak of hope that Yahweh will listen; ninth, the contrast between ancestral rejection of the law and present commitment to it gives hope for a new beginning; and finally, just as God previously sent prophets to warn the people when they slipped, so Nehemiah is sent as a prophet to warn them (13:4–31).

9:38–10:39 This passage contains a description of a sealed document in which Israel commits itself to follow the Torah. The signatories to the covenant document are listed first (10:1–27), including Nehemiah, but not including Ezra for some reason. Ordinary people are important in this book as the kingdom of priests is reestablished. From the absence of Ezra's name and the content of the document, some scholars infer that this document comes from another time, perhaps after the reforms in Nehemiah's second term as governor in 433 BCE. But the lack of Ezra's name here may be deliberate. Ezra consistently puts the people forward and not himself. The document seems to flow naturally from the public commitments in chapters 8 and 9 and from Ezra's prayer in 9:6–37, although admittedly the introduction is a little rough by modern standards (compare 9:38).

11:1–2 This takes up the narrative, interrupted at 7:5, of the repopulating of Jerusalem now that its walls have been rebuilt and it is safe to live there. The strategy is to use lots to determine the one out of ten families who would move into the city. Some move voluntarily and receive the community's blessing.

11:3–24 This passage seems to list those who settle in Jerusalem, although the information included is confusing. The residents of Jerusalem from the tribes of Judah and Benjamin are mentioned first (verses 4–9), followed by the priests (verses 10–14), Levites (verses 15–18), and gatekeepers (verse 19). Verse 20 reminds us that the rest of Israel, including priests and Levites, live in the other towns of Judah. Verses 21–24 list those in leadership in Jerusalem, particularly supervisors of the temple servants, Levites, and singers, and the Persian king's agent over Jerusalem. Unknown and historically insignificant people are mentioned, a part of the elevation of the laity in this emerging kingdom of priests. Ordinary people matter so much that they get their names in the Bible even though we know nothing else about them.

11:25–36 The author here inserts a list of villages where those who did not move into Jerusalem lived. But the list is not of those who lived nearby. The towns listed are outside of the borders of the Persian province of Yehud (Judah), but for the author are still part of the restored community. They are to be included in the new Israel even if the Persians do not yet recognize that fact. Verse 36 makes clear that Levites lived in Benjamin, not just Judah, to collect tithes and teach people the Torah.

12:1–26 Here the author gives lists of priests and Levites for the returnees to flesh out his picture of the entire community. The lists do not fit into the narrative smoothly. Included are a list of priests and Levites from the time of Zerubbabel in 520 BCE (verses 1–9), an incomplete list of high priests down to the time of Alexander the Great (332 BCE) if Josephus is correct (verses 10–11), and a list of priests and Levites from the time of Joiakim, a contemporary of Ezra in 458 BCE (verses 12–21, 24–26). Verses 22–23 cite the author's sources for his information. The list of high priests

> **Community Rededication**
> *The entire community, including its priests, Levites, and nobles, commits itself to obedience to the Torah. In particular, they promise to end intermarriage with pagans (verse 30), to obey Sabbath laws (verse 31), and to give offerings of money and produce for the temple (verses 32–38), including firstfruits and tithes. They promise not to neglect the temple (verse 39).*

> **Known Postexilic High Priests**
> *The priests below are listed with their known dates and the time of their flourishing. In some cases, external documents add validity to these dates. (All dates below are BCE)*
>
> | Date | Priest |
> |---|---|
> | 520 | Jeshua · time of Zerubbabel. |
> | 458 | Joiakim · time of Ezra. |
> | 445 | Eliashib · time of Nehemiah's first mission. |
> | 433? | Joiada · time of Nehemiah's second mission. |
> | 433 | Jonathan · time of Nehemiah's second mission. |
> | 410 | Johanan · mentioned in the Elephantine Papyri 30:18 |
> | 332 or 404 | Jaddua · Josephus claims Jaddua met Alexander the Great. |

is probably incomplete (notice the gaps in the chart above). Those mentioned in the Bible and at Elephantine, with the exception of Jaddua, were high priests during the focal events recounted in Ezra-Nehemiah.

Darius the Persian (12:22) is presumably Darius III Codomannus (336–331 BCE), if Josephus is correct that Jaddua was a contemporary of Alexander the Great. The alternative is Darius II Nothus (423–404 BCE).

12:27–43 Here we return to the Nehemiah Memoir to hear Nehemiah's first-person account of the dedication of the wall. Extra Levites who live outside of Jerusalem are brought in to staff the huge celebration. Rites of purification are performed for the priests and Levites, the people, the gates and the wall in a fashion reminiscent of the Day of Atonement. Nehemiah then divides the assembled people into two large groups who proceed in opposite directions to walk on top of the walls until they meet again on the other side of the city at the temple. They give thanks, accompanied by musical instruments as they walk, afterwards holding a joyous celebration at the temple. The account of the ceremony is reserved until this point in the book to emphasize the great accomplishment that the completion of the wall symbolizes. With the wall built, the people committing themselves to obey the Torah, the poverty of the people being addressed, and the city repopulated, it is time to celebrate. The entire community is becoming a holy nation and a kingdom of priests. Many individual leaders other than Ezra and Nehemiah are mentioned. The people matter in a kingdom of priests.

12:44–13:3 On the very day of the celebration, the work of reforming the community continues. The people of God are ever in the process of reforming and never actually arrive until God intervenes. Here the organizational structure for the receiving and distributing of tithes and offerings, for ritual purification, and for the singers' and gatekeepers' work is set up. A newly faithful Israel would bring large amounts of offerings that would require adequate administrative structures. Once again, there is public reading and instruction from the Torah and concrete acts of obedience to it in separating from the community those of Moabite and Ammonite religious descent. We see a community that acts to conform its behavior to the Scriptures. The exile had done its disciplinary work in purging Israel of its desire to serve pagan gods.

NEHEMIAH'S SECOND RETURN · 13:4–31

Nehemiah returns to Artaxerxes soon after the walls are rebuilt and the reforms implemented. Some thirteen years later (433 BCE), he is sent back to Jerusalem where he discovers that some of the earlier reforms are now unraveling. In particular, Tobiah, the Ammonite opponent of Nehemiah, is now living in an apartment in the temple, the sacrifices are being neglected, the Sabbath is being routinely disregarded, and intermarriage with pagan women is creeping back into the community. Nehemiah acts to correct all of these abuses and asks God to remember him for his efforts (verses 14, 22, 29). As an ending for the entire book of Ezra-Nehemiah, it serves as a warning of how easy it is for the nation to slip back into its self-destructive patterns of behavior. Ezra and Nehemiah had already dealt with each of these issues previously.

13:4–14 While Nehemiah is back in Persia, a room that was supposed to store offerings brought to the temple was cleared to enable Tobiah, Nehemiah's archenemy and an Ammonite, to live in the temple. When Nehemiah returns, he throws Tobiah's possessions out of the temple and has the room cleansed. He then addresses the failure of the leadership to enforce the Torah's tithing requirements. Levites who had lost their livelihood in Jerusalem in the interim and returned to their towns to make a living are brought back. New leadership is installed to ensure that the problem does not arise again. Nehemiah shows his characteristic energy in chastising the current leadership and in ensuring that the problem does not recur. But what happens when Nehemiah is gone?

13:15–22 While Nehemiah had been back in Persia, Israel had become lax regarding obedience to Sabbath laws. Jews and non-Jews alike were actively buying and selling on the Sabbath. Nehemiah warns the elites of the seriousness of Sabbath violation and sets some of his own servants over the gates to ensure that the Sabbath trading stops. At first the merchants attempt to wait Nehemiah out, but when he warns them of more severe consequences should they continue, they leave and no longer come to trade on the Sabbath.

> **Sabbath for Christians**
> While we as Christians are not under the Sabbath law, the Sabbath principle is a gift to overworked Christians who are tempted to neglect to take the time to worship and fellowship. Israel would not maintain a healthy relationship with God without worship and other communal experiences that allowed them and their servants and animals to refresh and renew themselves. Neither can we.

13:23–31 The problem of intermarriage had been dealt with by both Ezra and Nehemiah. Now the problem arises again in 433 BCE. In this case, the marriages were with women from the old Philistine community of Ashdod and the Transjordanian kingdoms of Moab and Ammon. Even the high priest's son had married the daughter of one of Nehemiah's greatest enemies, Sanballat. These were not marriages in which the non-Jewish woman converted to faith(fulness) in Yahweh alone. Nehemiah takes extreme measures, cursing them, physically beating some and even pulling out their hair. He then extracts solemn oaths from them to stop the practice. Nehemiah warns them of the lesson of history. Even Solomon could not enter into such covenants without being led into sin. While the author merely records Nehemiah's words without giving approval of his actions, the more important point is the seriousness of the issue. Israel's unfaithfulness to Yahweh began with such sins as intermarriage with pagans and accompanying syncretism. Having been severely chastised through dispersion and exile, and having repented of those sins, they are now in danger of falling back into them. This explains the severity of Nehemiah's reaction without justifying the means he uses to make his point. In the larger context, this narrative shows that Israel has not yet put those sins in the past. They are a very present danger for them.

> **The Reformation of Israel**
> If Israel will not learn the sad lessons of their own history of disobedience, they are destined to be cast off forever (Lam 5:19–22). The reforming of Israel, like the reforming of the church, is an ongoing task to which its leadership must devote itself.

THEOLOGICAL REFLECTIONS

The most distinctive theological idea of Ezra and Nehemiah is that the God who controls history has acted to create a new or at least a restored Israel out of the old exiled Israel. Israel is to be a kingdom of priests and will follow the written Torah rather than the oral pronouncements of prophets and others. What matters for Ezra-Nehemiah is the community in which every member functions like a priest with a direct and personal relationship with God. Ezra and Nehemiah are fully aware that God's ultimate restorative work on behalf of Israel will have to wait for the distant future. There is a "not yet" element implicit in its ideology. But the focus is on the "now" and "already" of the kingdom. This kingdom has no human king. Hope

> **God's Control of History**
> A significant theological theme of Ezra-Nehemiah is God's control of history. Ezra 6:14b notes that the rebuilding of the temple was ultimately commanded by God, not the Persian kings. They may have believed that they were in control, but in actuality they were carrying out God's will. There were several decrees by Persian kings throughout the time period reflected in Ezra-Nehemiah (538 BCE – Cyrus's decree; 520 BCE – Darius's decree; Artaxerxes' decrees in 458 for Ezra and 445 for Nehemiah). But the author of the book refers to the one divine decree. All of these kings played a part in fulfilling the one will of God, the restoration of the exiled people. God is still in control of history, no matter what leaders of great empires may think.

for the restoration of the line of David is muted in Ezra-Nehemiah, although not entirely gone. The book advises its readers to accept the Persian authorities and see God's hand at work through them. What God will do in the future is up to God. What Israel must do now is focus on becoming the holy nation and kingdom of priests that the old Israel committed itself to becoming but miserably failed at achieving (Exod 19:1–6). Day-to-day living in conformity with the scripturally revealed will of God is the priority for the nation.

The nation is already restored (Ezra 1:1–4; 3:11; 7:27; Neh 12:27) but also in need of restoration (Ezra 3:12; Neh 13). The "already" of the restoration is seen in the depiction of the return as a new exodus/conquest. Ezra departs in the first month (Ezra 7:1–10), the month of the original exodus (Exod 12:2; Num 33:3). The "straight way" prayed for in Ezra 8:21 is a deliberate echo of the new exodus typology in Isaiah 40:3. The departure from the river Ahava in Ezra 8:31 involves Israel celebrating Passover as the end of the sojourn in the house of bondage in Babylon. The threat that intermarriage poses for the returnees is reminiscent of a similar threat in the time of Joshua (Ezra 9:1–5). The number twelve recurs (Ezra 2:2; 6:17; 8:3–14, 24, 25), alluding to the twelve tribes of Israel even though only two tribes (Judah and Benjamin) return. For the author, the returnees from Babylon are a new Israel. The old Israel leaves Egypt for Sinai where they are offered the privilege of becoming a kingdom of priests and are given detailed instructions for the building of the tabernacle, the predecessor to the temple. In Ezra-Nehemiah, the entire city becomes a temple. The (to us) tedious lists of names that recur throughout the book show that the laity are of the utmost importance, not the priests. The people exercise leadership and initiate change (Ezra 9:1; 10:1–9; Neh 8:1, 2), not the specially called leaders. There is little emphasis on the Davidic promise because this community is priestly in nature, not royal. The returnees from Babylonian exile have the opportunity and the responsibility to become a new Israel.

A final theological theme of Ezra-Nehemiah is the importance of the written, rather than the oral, revelation of God. Ezra leads the returnees in committing themselves to strict obedience to the Torah of Moses. For the first time, Israel as a whole, rather than a small minority, becomes a people of the book, a Scripture-based and Scripture-formed people. This implies a time when spontaneous prophecy has either ceased or is regarded with such suspicion that it no longer is trusted as a means of ongoing guidance for the people of God. Israel will follow the written word of God, and that will trump any oral pronouncements of prophets. Israel will forever be a people of the book while it waits for God's sending of the Messiah.

FOR FURTHER STUDY

Pierre Briant, *From Cyrus to Alexander: A History of the Persian Empire* (trans. Peter T. Daniel; Winona Lake, Ind.: Eisenbrauns, 2002).

Gordon F. Davies, *Ezra & Nehemiah* (Collegeville, Minn.: Liturgical Press, 1999).

Kenneth K. Kitchen, *On the Reliability of the Old Testament* (Grand Rapids: Eerdmans, 2003).

Iain Provan, V. Philips Long, and Tremper Longman III, *A Biblical History of Israel* (Louisville: Westminster John Knox, 2003).

WORKS CITED

Joseph Blenkinsopp, *Ezra-Nehemiah* (Philadelphia: Westminster, 1988).

David J. A. Clines, *Ezra, Nehemiah, Esther* (Grand Rapids: Eerdmans, 1984).

Michael W. Duggan, *The Covenant Renewal in Ezra-Nehemiah (Neh 7:72b–10:40): An Exegetical, Literary and Theological Study* (Atlanta: Society of Biblical Literature, 2001).

Tamara Cohn Eskenazi, *In an Age of Prose: A Literary Approach to Ezra-Nehemiah* (Atlanta: Scholar's Press, 1988).

Sara Japhet, *I & II Chronicles* (Louisville: Westminster John Knox, 1993).

Josephus, *Jewish Antiquities* (ed. and trans. H. St. John Thackeray and Ralph Marcus; 8 vols.; Cambridge: Harvard University Press, 1930–1963).

Mark A. Throntveit, *Ezra-Nehemiah* (Louisville: John Knox, 1992).

H. G. M. Williamson *Ezra, Nehemiah* (Waco, Tex.: Word, 1985).

Esther

Mark W. Hamilton & David Skelton

CHAPTER CONTENTS

Contexts 417
Commentary 417
    Jews in Danger in a Gentile World · 1:1–5:14 417
    Jews Rescued by Their Own · 6:1–10:3 419
Theological Reflections 421
For Further Study 421
Works Cited 421

The book of Esther is many things: a romantic comedy, a satire on Persian rule, a celebration of the festival of Purim, and a meditation on the challenges of Jewish life in a Gentile world. Its prominent place in Jewish worship makes it an important witness to the combination of realism and joy that characterizes religious life.

CONTEXTS

Esther survives in three ancient versions. English translations follow the shorter version of the Masoretic Text. The Septuagint includes several additions: a long introduction, a decree after 3:13, a prayer for deliverance after 4:17, the story of Esther's meeting with Ahasuerus between 5:1 and 5:2, a second decree after 8:12, and a new conclusion after 10:3. The additions fill in gaps and make the text more religious. The reviser apparently felt that the original text, because it did not mention God or religious acts by the heroes, needed augmentation. A third version, called the "Alpha text," derives from a Hebrew text that most scholars believe to be older than the Masoretic Text. The Alpha text lacks the conspiracy of the two eunuchs (2:21–23),

> **Additions to Esther**
>
> *English translations of the Apocrypha often print the additional material in the Septuagint Esther as a separate book, called "Additions to Esther." However, this material never circulated independently in ancient times.*

the practice of irrevocable laws among the Persians (1:19; 8:8), and, like the Septuagint, it mentions God. Most scholars also believe that the Hebrew version from which it was translated did not contain chapters 9–10 (but see Jobes), and that these chapters, along with the additions, were added later to harmonize it with the Septuagint.

The book reflects a basic awareness of Persian politics, including the existence of a postal service and the division of the empire into large satrapies. Although the names Mordecai and Esther were common Mesopotamian names (Marduka and Ishtar), no corroborating evidence for the existence of any of the characters exists (except for Ahasuerus, probably the Xerxes of Greek texts). With brilliant humor, Esther satirizes life in the Persian Empire, highlighting the folly and lust of a king who can rule the world but not himself. Whether one reads this book as historical fiction, as most scholars do, or as a realistic account, the emphasis on wisdom and piety as needed survival skills in a hostile world remains an important lesson for readers today.

COMMENTARY

JEWS IN DANGER IN A GENTILE WORLD · 1:1–5:14
The first half of Esther sets up the problem of the book, namely, the incompetence and selfishness of the rulers of the Persian Empire. Their abuse of power threatens their Jewish subjects. Yet a surprising solution appears in the person of an orphaned Jewish girl, Esther. Ironically, the corruption that comes from absolute power permits justice's victory.

1:1–2:20 The two opening scenes (1:1–22; 2:1–20) explain how Esther becomes queen, not merely another member of the royal harem. Chapter 1 mocks most of the conventions of kingship. For example, the number 127 is exaggerated, since the Persian Empire included about 25 satrapies, each containing dozens of regions and self-governing cities. The phrase *third year* (verse 3) parodies the opening of many ancient inscriptions, in which a king dates his most notable accomplishments to his "first year." Ahasuerus's most notable accomplishment is a six-month-long drinking party. The accurate description of a lavish palace (verses 5–7) provides the author of Esther a setting for self-indulgence and misrule (compare Prov 31:4–7). The list of seven high officials (verses 10, 14) also reflects Persian governmental structure, but the list itself highlights the corruption of a political apparatus that uses its best minds to create foolish schemes. The best example of such a foolish scheme appears in the decree to the empire that forbids women to imitate *Vashti* in refusing to allow their husbands to humiliate them: subjects would not have considered doing so had not the decree itself raised the possibility!

Perhaps the most devastating criticism of Persia appears in the book's use of the Hebrew word *dat*, often translated "law" or "command." In 1:8, the partygoers drink "according to the king's *dat* without restraint" (NIV *command*). In 1:13, the experts in *dat and justice* concoct the decree against women. According to 1:19, the *dat* of the Medes and Persians was not subject to amendment, a legal practice that made for chaos, as it did in this book (and one that no Persian text or Greek text about the Persians corroborates). According to 4:11, the king's *dat* allows him to kill anyone approaching him without permission. Finally, Haman's most serious charge against the Jews is that "their laws [Hebrew *dat*; NIV *customs*] differ from all people, and they are not keeping the king's laws [Hebrew *dat*; NIV *laws*]" (3:8). For the reader, not keeping the king's laws should commend the Jews, not condemn them.

In chapter 2, the hero and heroine of the story enter. The government-sponsored beauty pageant shows that "even the king's sex life requires commissioners" (Levenson 54), so absurd is Persian rule. *Mordecai*'s genealogy connects to that of Saul in 1 Samuel 9:1, importantly since *Haman* is an *Agagite*, a mortal enemy of the Jews (see 1 Sam 15). Verse 7 shows Mordecai as one who cares for the vulnerable, since care of the orphan is a prominent command in the Torah (for example, Deut 10:18). The probation period for Esther (verses 12–15) is reminiscent of that for the boys in Daniel 1, though Esther has no occasion to demonstrate her fidelity to Judaism. She seems a pliant, though beautiful, young woman. The shrewd courage she later shows does not yet seem evident.

2:21–23 These verses foreshadow the episode in chapter 6 in which Haman's humiliation foreshadows his ultimate defeat. The rescued king owes a debt to Mordecai.

3:1–15 This chapter consists of three episodes: the promotion of Haman (verses 1–6), the plot to massacre the Jews (verses 7–11), and the issuance of the genocidal decree (verses 12–15). The story paints a picture of intrigue at court.

Verses 1–6 introduce the villain of the story. Haman was an *Agagite*, an ethnic label that may have been related to the episode in 1 Samuel 15, in which King Agag of the Amalekites threatened Israel (see Exod 17:8–15; Num 24:7; Deut 25:17, 19; 2 Sam 1). As a possible relative of King Saul's (see 2:5; Levenson 56–57), Mordecai refuses to honor a hereditary foe. The scene takes place in the *king's gate*, a monumental building (about 11,000 square feet) in the palace compound (Briant 260). Here courtiers would have displayed their importance. Verse 4 acknowledges the danger from Gentiles by alluding to Genesis 39:10 (*day after day*) and by identifying Mordecai as a *Jew*. Haman's wrath in part reflects the Amalekite-Israelite history of strife.

Verses 7–11 illustrate the cruelty of Haman and the malfeasance of Ahasuerus. Only genocide will satisfy the former, while the latter permits the destruction of his subjects. Verse 7 plays on the word *pur* ("lot") since the festival of Purim ("lots") commemorates the events of the book of Esther. The narrator steps outside the text into the festival that his readers know. See the comments on chapter 10 below. Selecting a day for the massacre long in advance seems odd, but it makes sense in a world of slow communications (by modern

> **Haman & Mordecai**
> *As the Festival of Purim developed through the centuries, comic dramas pitting Haman against Mordecai also developed. The story of their conflict also became a model for the ultimate triumph of the Jewish people against all persecutors. The elaborate rituals of Purim that exist today draw on Esther and rabbinic commentaries on the book, as well as on later encounters with anti-Semitism. See Horowitz.*

standards) in which everyone believed in auspicious and inauspicious days.

Verses 12–15 describe the publication of the decree. In a multilingual empire, the bureaucracy published decrees in many languages.

4:1–17 Chapter 4 depicts Esther as a woman isolated in the harem. She does not know of the royal decree or why Mordecai mourns. Her statement that *thirty days have passed since I was called to go to the king* (verse 11) illustrates his complete control over her marriage. Greek authors state that the Persian king took a different companion from the harem each night, all according to his own pleasure (see Briant 282–86). Such an idea may reflect the Greeks' fascination with Persian hedonism more than actual practice, but the book of Esther agrees that the queen's marriage was under her husband's domination.

In verses 15–16, Esther joins her people in mourning, since *fasting* was a mourning ritual. However, while their practices reflect their helplessness (verse 1), and Mordecai's exclusion from the seat of power (verse 2), Esther's fast leads to her decisive intervention on behalf of Jews.

Verses 13–14, the most famous of the book, more than hint at divine providence in the story. Although they do not explicitly mention God, they do assume that human actions can take on larger signification. As Levenson (81) points out, the question *who knows?* comes from penitential prayers hoping for divine deliverance (2 Sam 12:22; Joel 2:14; Jonah 3:9).

5:1–14 In verses 1–8, Esther shrewdly appeals to Ahasuerus's desires for banqueting and accompanying beautiful women to move toward the salvation of her people. She teases him in verse 8 by declining to make a substantial request.

Verses 9–14 move to another scene anticipating the final resolution. Here, Haman's mood alternates between joy and wrath. His utter self-absorption becomes clear. Verses 11–13 show him bragging about his *vast wealth*, sexual prowess (*many sons*), and special connections to the court. Ironically, his wealth will go to Mordecai, his sons will be executed, and his feast with the monarchs will prove his undoing. The text thus gives an anatomy of the powerful fool whose very successes lead to his undoing. The advice of his *wife* and *friends* (verse 14) is chilling: such an unnecessarily high *gallows* serves to display the horrible death of the executed person. Fittingly, Haman himself will die there.

JEWS RESCUED BY THEIR OWN · 6:1–10:3

6:1–13 The honoring of Mordecai is the turning point of the book. Chapter 6 reveals the author's genius for humor. This chapter, especially verse 13, also offers the strongest evidence for the book's interest in providence.

The story opens when the king, to cure his insomnia, requests *the book of the chronicles, the record of his reign, to be brought in and read to him*. This serves to recall the reader's attention to Mordecai's foiling of a conspiracy (2:23). It is surprising that the king has forgotten Mordecai's deed and whether or not a reward was bestowed on him (verse 3), but this absent-mindedness is another example of Ahasuerus's incompetence, and it also allows the story now to turn to the reversal of fortune for all the Jews.

> **"Record of his reign …"**
> This phrase literally means, "words of the days," a common phrase in 1–2 Kings for two now lost works recording key events of the kings. Unfortunately, no such court documents survive from anywhere in the ancient Near East, although they must have existed. The many surviving royal inscriptions from that region probably used such annals.

The king desires to reward Mordecai for his actions. The practice of keeping a list of those who had done noble deeds worthy of repayment, called the "King's Benefactors," is well known in Persia; such persons could receive compensation when officials verified that their name was on the list (Briant 303). The fact that Mordecai did not ask for a reward accentuates his humility, in contrast to Haman's arrogance in desiring a blessing he did not earn (Levenson 95–96).

Ironically, Haman offers advice on how to reward Mordecai. The greatest irony in the book occurs when Haman must herald Mordecai's greatness through the streets of Susa (verses 8–11). This is especially poignant when one realizes that Haman came to court to discuss killing Mordecai with the king (verse 4) but leaves blessing him. Even more so than his pride, his hatred for Mordecai and all Jews leads to his humiliation (Fox 82–83). Afterwards, Mordecai humbly returns to his place at the king's gate (compare 3:2), and Haman returns home in shame (verse 12).

When Haman reveals the day's events to his wife and friends, they make a foreboding declaration: *Since Mordecai, before whom your downfall has started, is of Jewish origin, you cannot stand against him – you will surely come to ruin!* (verse 13). In Hebrew, the verb for "to fall" [Hebrew *nafal*] occurs three times in this sentence in reference to Haman. It is odd that Haman's wife and friends did not reveal this information to him earlier, for now it is too late to save him.

6:14–7:10 The advice of Haman's wife and friends lingers as he is whisked away to the second banquet with Esther and the king (5:7). Haman's silence contrasts with his boisterousness after the previous banquet (5:9, 12). Nevertheless, 7:1 (compare 3:15; 5:5, 8) still mentions him in conjunction with the king at the start of the banquet. Esther must still consider him a threat.

The dialogue that transpires between Esther and Ahasuerus reveals her political brilliance. She begins her request much as in 5:8 but adds the phrase "in your eyes" (NIV *with you* downplays this connection) to denote intimacy (Fox 83). Likewise, she parrots Xerxes's offer. Her petition is for herself, and her request is for her people (7:3). She includes herself first in this verse as well as the next (*I and my people*; verse 5) out of realization that Ahasuerus is more likely to respond to danger to his wife rather than for her people. Also, Esther parallels herself and her people to demonstrate that their destruction is analogous to her own. Additionally, her failure to mention the Jews and to blame Ahasuerus for their predicament, and her incitement of the king against an unknown perpetrator before naming Haman, all indicate her political savvy. She has outwitted Haman at his own game (Bechtel 67). Furthermore, her ambiguous comment about being sold into slavery versus being *sold for destruction* probably refers to Haman's duping of Ahasuerus in 3:9, since the Hebrew word for "destruction" sounds similar to the word for "enslavement" (Bechtel 64).

The next series of events happens rapidly. Haman is no longer the *enemy of the Jews*, but an *enemy and an adversary* of Persia, as well (verse 6; see Levenson 103). The king storms out, and Haman now stands alone (verse 7). As predicted by his wife and friends in 6:13, Haman falls before Esther (verse 8). Upon returning, the king accuses Haman of attempting to ravish Esther, either out of foolishness or a desire to dissociate himself from Haman's genocidal plot (Crawford 919; Fox 86–87). As in Psalm 7:16–17, the snare that Haman set for Mordecai springs upon him instead (verse 9). Nevertheless, though Ahasuerus has defended his throne, the danger toward the Jews remains.

8:1–17 As in 2:1, the subsiding of the king's anger leads him to appoint Mordecai to fill Haman's role, just as Esther took Vashti's. Now Esther reveals her ethnic identity to her husband, contrary to Mordecai's orders in 2:10, 20. Ahasuerus gives Mordecai his signet ring, signifying Mordecai's appointment to Haman's position (verse 2; compare 9:4; 10:3). Fulfilling the prediction of Haman's wife and friends in 6:13, Mordecai also receives Haman's estates (verse 3; Levenson 107).

Chapter 8 reverses chapter 3 (Berlin 72; Levenson 107). Many of the actions of Esther and Mordecai parallel but counteract those of Ahasuerus and Haman. However, since royal edicts cannot *be revoked* (verse 8; compare 1:19), the reversal must be indirect. Thus, the Jews may defend themselves from attackers. Like Haman's decree, the new counter-decree is carried throughout the empire by the Persian courier service as well as issued in Susa (see 3:13–14), but unlike 3:12–13, the Jews now have special status, as signified by the double mention of them along with the rest of the people and provinces in verse 9 (Fox 230). The new decree is *issued as law* so that no one can contest it (compare Ezra 5:4–6:12).

Unlike in 6:8–11, this time Mordecai gets to keep his clothes and his newfound status (see 9:4; 10:3; Dan 5:29). Mordecai, the Jew, now ranks alongside the king and queen (Fox 94). These garments are also in stark contrast to the *sackcloth and ashes* he donned after Haman's decree (4:1; Levenson 116). Likewise, instead of *mourning* and *fasting* (4:3) the Jews are *feasting and celebrating, and many people of other nationalities became Jews* (better "identified themselves with the Jews"; see Berlin 80, Levenson 117) *because fear of the Jews had seized them* (verses 16–17). Finally, instead of being bewildered (3:15), the city of Susa rejoices (3:15).

9:1–32 This chapter continues the reversal that began in chapter 8 and explains the origins of the Jewish Festival of Purim (Levenson 107). As in the days of the exodus and conquest, the Jews win (*they* *did what they pleased*, verse 5; compare Neh 9:24; Dan 11:26); thus the people cower before them (verse 2; see Exod 15:14–16; Josh 2:8–11; Ps 105:38). Likewise, the assistance of the government officials further demonstrates Persian support of the Jews (verse 3); thus verse 12 pictures Ahasuerus cheering the Jewish victory (Berlin 86). The rise of Jewish prestige and power is personified through Mordecai (verses 3–4), who becomes the dominant figure of the rest of the book.

> **Origins of Purim**
> Although the origins of Purim are obscure, and it may originally have been a non-Jewish feast, by the second century BCE, 2 Maccabees 15:36 refers to the 14th of Adar as the "Day of Mordecai," and Purim was well established by the third century CE, when a whole tractate of the Mishnah, the first comprehensive code of Jewish law, covered rules for its observance.

With the execution of their enemies, especially the sons of Haman (verses 5–10), the Jews do what Saul could not: they annihilate the Amalekites and *did not lay hands on their plunder* (also verse 15; compare 1 Sam 15). Thus, Mordecai has reversed the sin of his ancestor (Bechtel 78; Levenson 122). The list of Haman's ten sons recalls the list of the eunuchs and advisors (1:10, 14) and may imply that they were the leaders of the enemy force (Crawford 932). The Jews outside of Susa were also victorious and *did not lay their hands on the plunder* (verse 16) but only fought on the 13th of Adar, which explains the celebration of Purim on the 14th for *rural Jews* (verse 19).

Mordecai's letter to all the Jews declares Purim to be an official festival (verses 20–22), making explicit that they should *feast and give presents of food to one another and gifts to the poor* (verse 22). These are actual Purim practices and parallel earlier motifs of feasting and giving (see 2:9; Crawford 935). Verses 23–26 are a summary of the events in Esther recorded by Mordecai as part of his letter to all the Jews (verse 20; Levenson 125). It vindicates the king of wrongdoing, thus revealing Mordecai's political savvy (Fox 120; Levenson 127–28). The Hebrew text attributes the letter to both Esther and Mordecai to give added validation for Purim, since the Pentateuch does not mention the holiday (Levenson 127).

> **Celebrating Purim**
> Today, Jews celebrate Purim on the 15th of Adar in Jerusalem but on the 14th everywhere else (late February-early March). Its main components are the reading of Esther, giving food to friends and money to the poor, and a special festival meal.

10:1–3 This chapter may be an addition because it does not appear in the Alpha text, yet it does form an inclusio with 8:1–2 and further accentuates the glorification of Mordecai begun in 8:15 (Crawford 941). The taxation is a parallel to the Joseph story (Gen 47:13–26). The book ends declaring the greatness of Mordecai among the Persians in a manner that recalls the ending of the stories of the kings of Israel and Judah (verse 2). As Carey Moore (lii) says, "Between Mordecai and Esther, the greater hero in the Hebrew is Mordecai."

THEOLOGICAL REFLECTIONS

Although some Christian scholars have condemned Esther for its lack of spirituality or excess of nationalism (see the survey in Horowitz 24–45), such a reading badly misunderstands the book. The author of Esther recognizes the danger Jews faced in a Gentile world because of their differences from polytheists. He or she also recognized that deliverance could occur because the God who repeatedly had saved Israel still lived. Far from being an unholy or secular work, Esther witnesses to the ways in which religious persons under difficult circumstances can cooperate in God's redemptive work. The book's unforgettable portrayal of greed and incompetence among leaders reminds us that power can corrupt. Yet the equally unforgettable scene of a brave young woman confronting a brutal tyrant reminds us that power sometimes settles in the right hands. For that reminder, and for many others, the book deserves our attention and respect.

FOR FURTHER STUDY

Carol M. Bechtel, *Esther* (Louisville: Westminster John Knox, 2002).

Tod Linafelt and Timothy K. Beal, *Ruth and Esther* (Collegeville, Minn.: Liturgical Press, 1999).

WORKS CITED

Carol M. Bechtel, *Esther* (Louisville: Westminster John Knox, 2002).

ESTHER

Adele Berlin, *Esther* (Philadelphia: Jewish Publication Society, 2001).

Pierre Briant, *From Cyrus to Alexander: A History of the Persian Empire* (trans. Peter Daniels; Winona Lake, Ind.: Eisenbrauns, 2002).

Sidnie White Crawford, "The Book of Esther," in *The New Interpreter's Bible Commentary of the Old Testament* (ed. Leander E. Keck, et al; Nashville: Abingdon Press, 1999), 3:855–941.

Michael V. Fox, *Character and Ideology in the Book of Esther* (2d ed.; Grand Rapids: Eerdmans, 2001).

Elliott Horowitz, *Reckless Rites: Purim and the Legacy of Jewish Violence* (Princeton: Princeton University Press, 2006).

Karen H. Jobes, *The Alpha-Text of Esther: Its Character and Relationship to the Masoretic Text* (Atlanta: Scholars Press, 1995).

Jon D. Levenson, *Esther* (Louisville: Westminster John Knox, 1997).

Carey A. Moore, *Esther* (New York: Doubleday, 1971).

Job

Mark Sneed

CHAPTER CONTENTS

- Contexts 423
- Commentary 425
  - Prologue · 1:1–2:10 425
  - Dialogue · 2:11–42:6 427
  - Epilogue · 42:7–17 442
- Theological Reflections 442
- For Further Study 443
- Works Cited 443

MAPS, TABLES, & FEATURES

- Theodicy 423
- The Heavenly Council 425
- Poetic Descriptions of Creation 427
- Sheol 428
- The Doctrine of Retribution 428
- Cosmology 435

Most Christians have used the phrase *the patience of Job* which comes from James 5:11. However, such a description does not do justice to the complexity of the man or his problems. The book divides into two general parts: prose in the prologue (1:1–2:13) and epilogue (42:7–17) and poetry in between (3:1–42:6). Readers often forget the poetic dialogue, and hundreds of years of interpretation have focused instead on the pious Job of the frame narrative, who perseveres and passes the test God allows the *satan* to administer. Modern biblical scholars have tried to compensate by focusing on the poetical dialogue, where Job has a debate with his four friends (Eliphaz, Bildad, Zophar, and Elihu) and God about his suffering condition. In the dialogue, we hear a less pious Job who, instead of quietly accepting God's treatment of him as in the prologue, impiously protests his innocence before God (27:2–6; 31:1–40), verging at times on the blasphemous (chapter 10) and even asking for a semi-divine lawyer who could intervene between him and God (9:33; 16:19; 19:25). Because of the tone of the middle sections, scholars tend to focus on the "radical" Job, perhaps casting him in their own image, while lay readers, intuitively recognizing the near blasphemous character of the dialogic Job, prefer to fix their attention on the frame narrative to understand the book as a whole. Both premodern and lay readers have been correct in recognizing the dominance that the frame narrative has for interpreting the book as a whole.

CONTEXTS

The book as a whole focuses on two primary questions: why is there unjust suffering (the dialogue),

---

Theodicy

"Theodicy" comes from the Greek words for "God" [theos] and "to justify" [dikaioo]; Thus, theodicy is an attempt to justify God in connection with the problem of evil. The problem of evil is the difficulty faced by those who believe in a loving and gracious God who is all-powerful and yet allows moral evil and natural suffering to exist in the world. A deity who is all-powerful and can remove evil and suffering and yet does not calls for an explanation. This problem is especially difficult for religions that are strongly monotheistic, with no other deities to blame for evil and suffering.

The Old Testament is filled with theodicies. The Deuteronomistic History (Joshua–2 Kgs) has been described as an extensive theodicy that explains why the Lord allowed the Assyrians and Babylonians to come into the land of Canaan and defeat and capture the north Israelites and Judeans, taking many into exile. The theodicy is that the Lord has not forgotten earlier promises or covenants and is not powerless. Rather, the blame falls on the people of Israel, who did not abide by the covenant. Thus, defeat and exile is explained as punishment that the Lord has inflicted on the Jews via the hands of the Assyrians and Babylonians.

The doctrine of retribution is also a similar theodicy that attributes individual (versus national) suffering to the lifestyle of the sufferer (see Green).

and should we serve God with no thought of reward/retribution? (The second raises the question of indifferent righteousness. In other words, do we serve God without reward in mind [see 1:9]?) The answer to the latter question actually becomes the solution to the former. In other words, the question of theodicy, or the problem of evil, is never really answered in Job. Instead, the focus shifts to the question of the appropriate form of human piety. Thus, scholars that label the book a theodicy are misunderstanding its main intent. In fact, the book could be described as an anti-theodicy (see Tilley 109).

The problem of theodicy is universal and perennial and found in both Israelite and ancient Near Eastern wisdom traditions. A favorite theodicy strategy of the Israelites was the doctrine of retribution, in which evil persons suffer. The book of Proverbs assumes this concept to explain suffering and bad fortune. The problem comes when bad things happen to good people. This serves to challenge the doctrine, and this is what we see in the book of Job. The Assyrian (722 BCE) and Babylonian (587 BCE) devastations and exiles exacerbated this tension between doctrine and reality. The bad fortunes of the Jews in postexilic times continued to cause people to question this teaching.

The inability of either Job or his three (four) friends to resolve the problem of theodicy (the friends are condemned in the end [42:7], and Job repents of his blasphemous questioning [40:4–5; 42:1–6]) points to the author's conclusion that such debates lead nowhere. Rather, the frame narrative and the divine speeches (chapters 38–41), which represent the voice of the author and are the book's climax, attempt to demonstrate that God's ways are ultimately mysterious and inaccessible to human reason and that the focus should be on the question of human piety in the context of such limitations. The reader should endure like Job, even when circumstances become unbearable. The point of Job is to show the growth of Job's faith, from questioner and almost blasphemer, to one who humbly submits to God's unknowable purposes (see Rodd 82–90).

It is impossible to date Job precisely. Although the book depicts a pre-Mosaic setting (Job is a patriarch like Abraham), it was probably written much later. However, the use of the article "the" with "satan" indicates that the book was written prior to Chronicles (compare 1 Chron 21:1; see Crenshaw 863), a book from the Persian period (6th–3rd centuries BCE). Also, the focus on the question of individual piety in Job was typical for the postexilic period, where nationalistic expressions of Jewish identity were seriously limited (compare Dan 1–6). And as already pointed out, the difficult times of postexilic Judah provide a social and historical rationale for the questioning of the doctrine of retribution such as we see in Job and Ecclesiastes. So, to conclude, the late Persian period looks like the best candidate for dating the book.

Job is technically anonymous, as are most of Old Testament books. The author was certainly a member of the upper class, since at that time literacy was exclusively for the small minority of society. Approximately 2 percent of ancient agrarian societies were part of the governing class, and 5 percent would be part of the retainer class (lower rung of an ancient upper class) (Lenski 219–84), the class to which our author would have belonged. Furthermore, debating about the problem of unjust suffering/indifferent righteousness suits more the activity of an upper class intellectual than a poor peasant (see Clines, *Ideology*, 125–28). His artistic skill as a poet and writer is unquestioned, as has been recognized throughout history. The best guess is that the author was a governmental scribe (probably not priestly), who may have served in the role of a teacher.

It needs noting that there are several ancient Near Eastern parallels to Job. The most illuminating is the *Babylonian Theodicy* (1100 BCE). It concerns a sufferer who goes to a sage for comfort and counsel; a dialogue ensues. At the beginning, the sufferer praises the sage for his great wisdom but complains about his misfortune (5–11). The sage answers with the doctrine of retribution: *He who waits on his god has a protecting angel*; *The humble man who fears his goddess accumulates wealth* (21–22). The sufferer then supplies instances in the animal and human world where retribution falters (45–55). The sage then answers similarly to the divine speeches of Job: ... *the plan of the gods is remote* (58). Later he says similarly, *The divine mind, like the centre of the heavens, is remote*; *Knowledge of it is difficult*; *the masses do not know it* (256–57). But finally, the sage gives in and admits that the gods made mortals inherently evil, and they persecute their own (276–86). The sufferer then thanks the sage and offers a prayer to his god: *May the god who has thrown me off give help*! (295).

COMMENTARY

PROLOGUE · 1:1–2:13

The book opens by introducing us to the character of Job, a man from the East, who excels all his contemporaries in righteousness (like Noah in Gen 6:9). He is identified as non-Israelite, and this may be both because a patriarchal setting is assumed (Job is a patriarch who regularly sacrifices for his children [verse 6]) and because the Eastern sages were renowned for their wisdom (like the *magi* of Matt 2:1–12).

1:1–5 The best guess is that *Uz* is a desert region east of Palestine, perhaps in Edom or northern Transjordan (Weinstein; see Gen 36:28; 1 Chron 2:42; Jer 25:20; Lam 4:21). *Fearing God* is a typical way that Wisdom literature expresses the ideal form of piety (see 1:1; Eccl 7:18; 8:12–13; 12:13). The call to *fear God* is the motto for the book of Proverbs and forms an *inclusio* in that work (1:7; 31:30).

The point of verse 1 is not that Job is absolutely sinless, but that, among his peers, he is exceptionally pious. In addition to his piety, according to verse 2, he has the perfect number of sons (7), and the three daughters brings this number up to another significant Hebrew number (10).

In verse 3, note the similarity in numbering for the cattle (7,000 + 3,000 = 10,000; 500 + 500 = 1,000). All of this suggests that Job is as wealthy as he is righteous. Wealth in patriarchal days was measured in cattle and slaves, since money did not exist yet. The family's great wealth is indicated in the regular feasts held (verse 4). The sisters do not own their own homes because their husbands (assuming they are married), as males, were the usual landowners. The introduction of Job concludes by noting that he "goes beyond the call of duty" to insure that his children's sins are continually atoned for. This serves to confirm his great piety.

1:6–12 This section transfers readers to heaven and the instigation of the testing of Job. The term *angels* literally means "sons of God," the members of the divine council of heavenly beings that served God. The name *Satan* should be rendered "the satan," or "the accuser." This is not necessarily the same person as the devil, or Satan, in the New Testament. The accuser's function among the divine council appears to be as a divine spy who investigates what mortals do on the earth and reports this to the council. Verse 8 states for a second time the virtues of Job, with God's verdict confirming the author's (see verse 1). God assumes the role of a proud parent who is pleased with his exemplary son, Job.

In verse 9, the accuser abruptly questions the sincerity of God's exemplary servant by insinuating that Job has an ulterior motive for being so pious. This is the question of indifferent righteousness (see above). In verse 11, the word *curse* in Hebrew [*barak*] is actually identical to the word *blessed* in the previous verse. Since the Jewish scribes were probably reluctant to connect directly the actual word for "curse" and "God" himself, they used its antonym. This is actually reflected in our modern colloquialism: "I blessed him out!" As verse 12 makes clear, though technically the accuser is the one who directly tests Job, God is ultimately responsible in his permitting of the contest.

1:13–22 This section transfers us back to the earth, and the actual testing of Job begins. Verse 14 links the *donkeys* with the *oxen* because they carried the plowing implements to the field (Clines 31). Verse 15's *Sabeans* were people that lived in the area of modern Yemen in southwest Arabia; the queen of Sheba was from this region (see Boraas). For dramatic effect, the lone surviving servant brings the message of the attack to Job personally.

The Heavenly Council

Though strongly monotheistic, the Jews have often believed that God had a heavenly council, or court, that met from time to time to make decisions. The prologue of the book of Job assumes such a court. The satan, *or "accuser," is simply one such divine being. Angels seem to be part of this group. The first person plural used in Genesis 1–3 –* let us make man... *(1:26); like one of us (3:22) – is a reflection of such a counsel. The phrase* sons of God *in Genesis 6 also reflects this conception. The title* Lord of hosts *(1 Sam 17:45) is connected with this concept. The host is God's army that he uses to defeat his and Israel's enemies (see 1 Kgs 22:19; Isa 6:1–5). The Septuagint version of Jeremiah has a tendency to eliminate this phrase because of its possible polytheistic implications (see Rofé 35–36).*

Obviously, one servant had to survive for the news to reach Job in this way.

Instead of human-brought catastrophe, natural disaster from God strikes Job's household. Thus, verse 16 attributes the fire directly to God (*fire of God*) and not the *satan*. That is, the book of Job does not seek a dualistic solution to the problems it poses. God cannot avoid responsibility. In verse 17, the clause *while he was yet speaking* dramatically compresses the action of the scene so that the reader feels the affect of a bombardment of catastrophes.

In verse 17, the *Chaldeans* are the Babylonians. Since they did not campaign in the region west of the Arabian Desert before the sixth century BCE, the mention of them here gives a date before which the book cannot have been written, at least in the form we have it. The reference to *camels* appropriately depicts the caravanning character of Job as one from Edom or a desert region. Verse 19 refers to a *mighty wind*, a phenomenon often accompanying God's appearances to human beings (for example, Elijah in 1 Kgs 19:11 and Job in Job 38:1). Again, we see God directly involved in the catastrophe (see verse 12). The characters respond to this news with mourning rites. Tearing one's robe and shaving the head were signs of great despair (verse 20; Gen 37:34; 2 Sam 13:31; Jer 16:6). Job's body language at first is actually more emotional than his subsequent worship and praise.

Verses 21–22 conclude this section with two proverbs and a blessing.

Naked I will depart should be translated, more literally, "I will return there." This does not mean that Job will return to his mother's womb; the statement is a poetic way of expressing a return to a state of preexistence. Instead of cursing God, Job *blesses* God this time, and so Job passes the test, and God wins the contest. Verse 22 makes this final resolution clear.

2:1–6 We are transferred up to heaven again for another round of the contest. Verses 1–3 are almost identical to 1:6–8, except for the addition in verse 3b. The repetition creates a sense of balance in the story and prepares the reader for another encounter between the *satan* and God. With the phrase in verse 3, *without any reason*, God reminds the *satan* – and all the readers – of the correctness of the original assessment of Job, a fact that makes the contest essentially pointless. God engages in it only to prove a point. This phrase is only one word in Hebrew and is from the same Hebrew word as *for nothing* in 1:9.

Verse 4's phrase *skin for skin* seems to draw on a proverb describing equal exchange in bartering. No merchant would go beyond this point and suffer loss (Seow 729). In other words, the *satan* is saying that Job's loyalty has its limits. He is willing to give up his possessions but not his physical well-being, much less his life. This scene ends with an escalation of the test; Job may experience physical pain but not death, since death would terminate the contest.

2:7–13 This section transfers readers back to the earth for the second round of testing that provides the context for the dialogue that begins in chapter 3. It is appropriate that Job is stricken with a skin disease, ironically echoing the proverb of verse 4. Verse 7 highlights the extent of his illness: *from the soles of his feet to the top of his head*. The phrase emphasizes that there was no surface on the skin of his body that was not in torment; there was no respite for Job, spatially or temporally: he was continually in pain everywhere! Thus Job sits among the *ashes*; perhaps this is a garbage dump (a midden), which would certainly symbolize his feelings of worthlessness at the time. Ashes are associated with mourning (2 Sam 13:19; Isa 58:5; Jer 6:26), as connected with the first round of the contest. In such a dump, *broken pottery*, or potsherds, would be in abundance. They are one of the few items preserved in ancient sites that archaeologists have uncovered. They are often used by people to write messages on, since papyrus was very expensive.

In a famous scene in verse 9, Job's wife wonders why he still holds on to his *integrity*. This word was used in 2:3 [Hebrew *tummah*] and will appear again in 27:5 and 31:6. This is a key word for understanding Job's position. Though his three *friends* try to get Job to confess sin, Job will never deny his integrity. He even states that he will never deny his integrity, even if he were to appear directly before God (27:5). The wife provides the easy out for Job, but he refuses to give in.

> **Job & Worship**
>
> The book of Job frequently explores the purposes, techniques, and even possibilities of worship. Thus it begins with Job worshiping after his children's feasts, and here he praises God even in times of distress. In the poetic dialogue in chapters 3–25, however, he struggles with whether to praise God and turns lament into a sharp questioning of the ways of the divine.

In verse 10a, Job's rhetorical question implies a strong monotheistic belief that God is responsible for both weal and woe (compare Eccl 7:14; Isa 45:7). The section concludes by emphasizing that Job does not curse God; but the contest has only begun.

2:11–13 These verses set the stage for the dialogue and properly end the prologue. Eliphaz's designation as a *Temanite* (of Edom) recognizes Teman's renown as a place of wisdom (Jer 49:7). *Shuite* names a descendant of Shuah, one of Abraham's sons (Gen 25:2); they were perhaps Arabs and may have lived in Edom (Beck 341). *Naamah* lies somewhere in northwest Saudi Arabia (see Anonymous).

In verse 11, the word *comfort* and the display of concern are interesting because the friends soon become less than comforting when the dialogue begins, and they accuse Job of sin. In fact, in 16:1 Job facetiously refers to his *friends* as *comforters*. We find in the end that Job's other friends, mentioned in the epilogue, are the only ones who can truly comfort him (42:11).

Verse 13 again reveals the importance of numbers for the Israelites (see 1:2–3). The friends sit with Job for a perfect number of days and nights before the dialogue begins. The author appears to be characterizing the friends of Job as just as pious as he is. We thus expect them to behave in a certain way and are confused when they do not.

DIALOGUE · 3:1–42:6

The main section of the book consists of three cycles of dialogues among Job and his friends (3:1–14:22; 15:1–21:24; 22:1–25:6). After their conversation breaks down, Job begins a soliloquy (26:1–31:40), and speeches by Eliphaz (32:1–37:24) and Yahweh (38:1–41:34) follow.

As the poetic conversation in these chapters unfolds, the author explores from many angles the limits of human speech about God, morality, and faith.

3:1–26 Job curses both his birthdate (verses 1–3a, 4–5, 8–10) and the night of his conception (verses 6–7). Verse 1 uses the usual Hebrew word for *curse* [qalal], since Job's oath does not refer to God. However, this verse strongly contrasts with 2:10, where Job refuses to curse God for the latest development. In verses 6–7, the time switches to the night of Job's conception. *Joy* may refer to his parents' wedding night (Clines 85–86).

In verse 8, *those who curse days* are magicians or sorcerers who could declare a certain day unlucky (Clines 86).

Leviathan is poetic allusion to a sea-monster that represented chaos and evil. Magicians roused it up for a destructive purpose (Clines 86–87). According to verse 9, that destructive purpose (verse. 8) is to swallow the sun and thus form an eclipse so that the day (or night) of Job's conception might never happen (Clines 86–87).

In verses 11–19, Job escalates his lament with a series of rhetorical questions concerning his birth to make the point that he wishes he had never come into existence. The imagery in verse 12 depends on the fact that women in ancient times were not supine when delivering but usually squatting (Matthews and Benjamin 70), and thus the first thing the newborn would *see*, as the midwife lifted it out, would be its mother's *knees*.

The Israelites sometimes described the Underworld as a place of sleep (for example, 1 Kgs 2:10 *David rested with his fathers …*). Thus verse 14 refers to death as the great equalizer that never discriminates between the powerful and weak (verse 19;

Poetic Descriptions of Creation

The Old Testament often refers to the Lord's creation with picturesque and poetical language that draws on ancient Near Eastern ideas. The "Enuma Elish" is the name of the Babylonian "Genesis" (see Heidel 3–12), and it depicts a great god, Marduk, who battles and defeats a multi-headed dragoness, Tiamat, who represents the sea water and also chaos and evil. Marduk savagely crushes her head with a club. From her body is made the sky and earth. Tiamat is replaced in the Old Testament with the names Leviathan ("twisted one") and Rahab ("furious one").

Baal also similarly battles the sea god Lothan in Canaanite lore. Instead of Marduk or Baal, the Lord is portrayed as a mighty warrior who crushes the head of a dragoness or sea monster (Pss 74:13–14; 89:10; Isa 51:9; Job 26:12–13). This is a graphic way of describing God's placement of order on the chaos inherent in the early creation (Gen 1:2). It also demonstrates the Lord's superiority to any other pagan deities. This conflict between the Lord and a sea monster is sometimes used to refer to the Lord delivering the Israelites from the Egyptians by parting the waters (Isa 51:9–10).

> **Sheol**
>
> Literally "the pit," Sheol was a metaphor used for the abode of the dead among the Israelites (for example, Prov 9:18). It probably denotes the shaft tombs that the Israelites used to bury their dead. These were family tombs that contained several chambers with three "bench tombs" each. A body was laid on a bench. When the benches became full, the bones were removed and placed in a separate area to make room for the recently deceased.
>
> The phrase used of deceased kings, so-and-so slept with his fathers, literally brings to mind bodies lying next to one another in these chambers. Sheol is depicted as a dark and gloomy place (for example, Eccl 9:5–6), similar to the way the Mesopotamians viewed their afterlife. No one could praise God in Sheol, so the psalmist tries to motivate the Lord do deliver him from death (6:5). Sheol was certainly not the heaven and hell described in the New Testament.

see Eccl 5:15). Job, in his current condition, seems to long for this kind of Underworld that treats everyone the same – that is, justly – unlike God. The exploration of death continues with the phrase *lying in ruins*. The irony of the ruins of once great Egyptian rulers after their deaths is expressed in the Egyptian "A Song of the Harper" (in Pritchard 467).

In verse 16, Job wishes he had been a stillborn fetus. *Hidden* reflects the unnaturalness of having to bury a child (Clines 95). Archaeologists have uncovered numerous infants buried in jars under homes in ancient Middle Bronze Age Canaan; infant mortality was probably high (Mazar 214).

In verse 18, Job probably relates more to the slave than the king (verse 14) (for a discussion of the theme of kingship in Job, see Hamilton 33) and yearns for delivery from his oppression via death.

In verses 20–26, Job wonders why God seems to preserve his miserable life when he prefers death. His speech makes numerous links to previous themes. Thus verse 21's phrase *hidden treasures* contrasts with the treasures of the dead in verse 15. In verse 23, the phrase *whose way is hidden* refers to Job's destiny, which he feels powerless to affect (Clines 101). With a different Hebrew term, Job describes himself as *hedged in* negatively, rather than in the protective way God had formerly provided implied by the *satan* (1:10).

4:1–5:27 In this longer speech, Eliphaz chastises Job for so easily becoming upset in his calamity, when in earlier years he had helped those in dire straits. The speech falls into six sections (4:1–6, 7–11, 12–21, 5:1–7, 8–16, and 17–27). Eliphaz politely but firmly makes a series of arguments against Job's lament.

In verse 4, he picks up the theme of the birthing knees from 3:12. Verse 6's adjective *blameless* echoes the stereotypical description of Job by God as blameless (1:8; 2:3), while the word *ways* echoes Job's *way* hidden by God (3:23). Thus Eliphaz reaffirms a positive assessment of Job's earlier life, which contrasts with his present attitude.

> **The Doctrine of Retribution**
>
> One of the oldest and most basic assumptions of the wisdom tradition that could be challenged from time to time is what German scholarship calls the action-consequence connection. Older wisdom within the ancient Near East assumed that one's actions or lifestyle brought about certain consequences. This is the oldest form of what we call today the cause/effect principle, except that it applies to human behavior. The idea is that the world has been created to be orderly and that the gods (or Yahweh, for Israel) have established patterns of human behavior that can either bring benefit or damage. Israelites and their neighbors believed this cause and effect system existed within the very fabric of the cosmos. As such, it worked itself out automatically without the aid of any deity – an almost deistic notion.
>
> The role of the sage was to observe the world and human behavior and detect those patterns and teach them by casting such rules in the form of proverbs that could be easily taught and memorized. The pragmatic focus on success makes this earlier wisdom appear self-serving and "secular," with little attention paid to the gods. However, in Israel the automatic notion of the action-consequence connection gradually came to be intricately and directly connected with Yahweh: Yahweh himself intervened and brought the negative or positive consequences in the form of punishment and reward; this meant that the older wisdom/folly dichotomy started to give way to a contrast between righteousness and wickedness (Blenkinsopp 41–46). The shift in thought is known as the doctrine of retribution by scholars today.

In verses 7–11, Eliphaz argues that the truly innocent have nothing to fear; only the wicked will be punished. He supports this claim in verses 10–11 with two true proverbs placed together to demonstrate the principle that even the mighty succumb to weaknesses. In this context, the lions represent the wicked.

Verses 12–21 offer a new argument. Eliphaz, a wise man, receives a revelatory dream, something usually associated with prophets. It emphasizes the general wickedness of mortals before the creator, implying that Job has no grounds for questioning God.

Verse 17 is the key verse for this section; it obviously expects a negative answer. However, the question that will play out in the book is precisely why the answer is negative. The phrase *righteous before God* is used in a moral sense. No mortals are sinless before God. This contrasts with the way Job uses this word in 9:2. Verses 19–21 extend the argument by noting the ephemeral nature of mortals in contrast with God's eternality.

In Job 5:1–7, Eliphaz connects Job's vexation with folly, leading to an argument for the doctrine of retribution, which teaches that fools eventually receive their just punishment from God. In verse 1, Eliphaz sarcastically asks Job to whom he will appeal to hear him regarding his condition. Eliphaz ironically foreshadows Job's desire to encounter a divine mediator, or lawyer, who could defend his case against God (16:19; 19:25). The phrase *holy ones* refers to angels in God's divine council. It connects with the reference to angels in 4:18. In the proverb in verse 2, Eliphaz implies that Job's resentment is foolish, which leads him to depict the fate of fools, according to the doctrine of retribution.

Verse 5 uses humor: the fool is so devastated that the hungry leave him nothing, not even harvest land difficult to reap because of thorns. Verses 6–7 offer another proverb built on wordplays involving *earth* [Hebrew *'adamah*; verse 6b] and *man* [Hebrew *'adam*; verse 7a]. It states that trouble is not inherent to mother earth but rather to humanity. Eliphaz returns to the argument for the perversity of humanity that he used earlier in 4:17.

Verses 8–16 push the argument further. The only one to whom Job can appeal, according to Eliphaz, is God. Eliphaz then describes in hymn-like fashion God's greatness and mercy, especially toward the poor. Verse 16 personifies the concept of *injustice*; its *mouth* would devour the poor.

Verses 17–27 close Eliphaz's first speech. He presents the idea that God is disciplining Job, or what is known as the soul-making (God sends suffering to develop us spiritually) theodicy. This is technically a new argument for Eliphaz. It does seem to imply that Job has done wrong, but the punishment is assumed to have the effect of rehabilitation. Eliphaz then argues that one whom the Lord disciplines will receive deliverance and well-being from him. He uses several literary devices to make his argument. Verse 17 is in the form of a beatitude. Verse 19 uses the literary device of ascending numeration: to a number assumed to be sufficient one adds another, to remove any doubt (Clines 150). The message is that one whom God chastens can count on God for deliverance. Job should be patient, says Eliphaz. Verse 23 speaks metaphorically of a *covenant with the stones* to say that the natural world will even be at peace with those whom God blesses. Stones will not be a problem for the farmer's soil. The *wild animals* will not even be a threat.

Verse 25 is a saying coldly insensitive to Job's loss of children. In verse 27, the word *we* refers to the three friends. Eliphaz appears to be the leader and representative of the group. They are boastful and confident that they are right and Job is wrong.

6:1–7:21 In a lengthy response, Job counters Eliphaz's claim that Job has been a whiner in his suffering; he points out how he has reason to question God and complain. Job's response uses several metaphors and arguments to make his point. In verse 2, he employs the metaphor of weighing his grief on scales (compare 31:6). Archaeologists have uncovered many of the weights used for these scales. In verse 3, his statement *my words have been impetuous* does not admit wrong but does explain why he complains. In verses 5–6, his rhetorical questions make the point that animals are not upset unless they are given what is inappropriate. Job is saying that God has dealt out to him what is wrong (Clines 171–72). The point of the second set is that inedible and repulsive food is hard to swallow; Job is saying that he finds God's cuisine hard to swallow (Clines 172).

> **Job's Integrity**
> *Job is arguing that he is not merely whining over nothing; he is justified in defending his integrity.*

In 6:8–13, Job wishes God would just kill him and be done with it; at least he would have his integrity. In verse 10, the word *consolation* signals Job's notion that, should God grant his request of premature death, at least he could take pride in his having maintained his integrity and lived by God's commands (*words of the Holy One*; Clines 174). The phrase *my joy in … pain* signals a temporal switch to Job's current situation from the context of his wish for God to slay him quickly.

In verses 14–23, Job condemns his friends for not being true friends. He compares them to unreliable dry streambeds, or *wadis* (verses 15–20), that offer no refreshment to caravans seeking water. Verse 14 considers the possibility that he might *forsake the fear of the Almighty*, but without admitting to doing so argues that true friends would not give up on him even if he had. Fear of God is the wisdom tradition's typical way of describing piety or religious commitment (see 1:1). In verse 19, *Tema* and *Sheba* are in northern and southwestern Arabia, respectively (Seow 733).

Job continues his plea in verses 24–27, where he challenges his friends honestly to correct him instead of so quickly condemning him. At first he claims that they are not innocent. Thus verse 27 speaks of the undesirable character of those who criticize an innocent sufferer such as himself: they *cast lots for the fatherless*. The image appears to be someone casting lots, the ancient version of today's "drawing straws," to purchase orphans as slaves.

He next challenges them to produce evidence of his sin (verses 28–30). In verse 29, the Hebrew word for *integrity* [*tsedeq*] is literally "righteousness." It is synonymous with the word used earlier for integrity (2:3, 9; compare 25:5; 31:6). Verse 30 climaxes his appeal by saying that he is not lying, and his mouth is personified as having better sense than to try and deceive the friends.

In 7:1–6, Job finds himself longing for the end of the day or night like a laborer or slave. Yet when Job comes to the end of his *day*, he receives misery and long, restless nights. Verse 6 portrays Job lamenting how quickly he is heading for death, though earlier he had wished that God would strike him down and end his life prematurely (6:9). Early death will make his public vindication impossible. The verse uses a pun, for in Hebrew the word for *hope* can also mean "thread"; the image is of the thread quickly running out on the shuttle (Seow 734).

Verses 7–10 expand the meditation on mortality. The previous reference to life's brevity causes Job to reflect on his inevitable journey to the abode of the dead, the place of no return. He does not have the benefit of New Testament teaching on an afterlife. He holds the typical Israelite view of a gloomy, mysterious afterlife, where people sleep forever. The Hebrew word for *grave* is *Sheol*.

Verses 11–21 explore Job's anxieties further, as he insists on his right to vent his frustrations. He is tired of God continuously watching over him and afflicting him. Verse 12 opens with the powerful image of sea monsters, the same kind of poetic figure as in 3:8. Job is questioning why God is treating him like his archenemy, the sea monster, or the forces of disorder (verses 12–18). He wishes that God would leave him alone or simply forgive him for whatever sin that he has committed unwittingly (verses 19–21). In verse 14, Job complains that God frightens him with nightmares. Dreams were understood by ancients to be sent by deities.

8:1–22 Bildad says that the destruction of Job's children

> **Job & Psalm 8**
> *Job 7:17–19 apparently offers a parody of the famous Psalm 8:4–9, where the psalmist praises God for considering and being concerned about lowly humans stationed beneath the angels. Here Job inverts that idea. He wants God to stop noticing and being concerned about him.*

was due to some sin on their part. He tells Job to simply submit to God, who will restore him. He seems to be unaware that Job had gone so far as to offer sacrifices for his children, just in case they had sinned (1:5). Like Eliphaz, he assumes the doctrine of retribution, for which he claims to find support from history and the ideas of the community (verse 8). He also argues that the wicked, though at first prosperous, will eventually succumb to demise. Verses 11–19 couch this claim in plant metaphors.

Several elements deserve comment. In verse 11, the rhetorical questions point out the inability of the wicked to prosper without God's sustenance. Verse 17 describes the wicked as weeds that try to find a place to root, while verse 18 personifies the ground as a being that cannot remember the previously existent *wicked* plant that was pulled out. In verses 20–22, Bildad finishes by reminding Job that God does not punish the innocent nor take sides with the wicked. The phrase *blameless man* in verse 20 uses the same word in Hebrew as that for God's praise for Job in 1:8. Of course, Job continually argues that he is blameless. Verse 22 refers to the *tents of the wicked*, which means simply their dwellings; it does not suggest that they were nomads (compare 11:14).

9:1–10:22 Job presents a hymnic description of God's cosmic powers to demonstrate that no mortal can have a fair debate with the divine. Verse 2 seems to cite Eliphaz in 4:17, making it seem that Job agrees with him (1–3). However, Job is using the word *just* in a different sense than Eliphaz does, a legal sense, thus implying that no one can have a fair chance at legally challenging God (Seow 736). Eliphaz uses the word in a moral sense. Verse 3 heightens the tension by using the word *dispute*, which shows we are dealing with a legal setting. Job pictures himself before God as judge at a trial.

Verses 4–10 foreshadow the divine speeches to Job, in which God's awesome power is displayed in the creation of the earth and its inhabitants (chapters 38–41). Verse 9's names for the constellations are guesses based on the Septuagint. The exact identifications remain uncertain.

In verse 11, the claim, *I cannot see him* points to God's ability to be invisible, another overpowering characteristic that humbles Job.

In verses 13–24, Job argues that he would have no chance in a legal setting with God; even if innocent, he would fail in using the right words, and God would overwhelm him with his power. Job then expresses his innocence but hates his life. He also refers to the extreme conflict in his life by returning again to the image of the sea monster, this time called *Rahab*, a synonym for Leviathan. The name is not the same word as the proper name Rahab of the book of Joshua (see 26:12; Ps 89:10; Isa 30:7; 51:9–10). In verse 20, Job complains that even if he were blameless, his mouth would get him into trouble in this portrayed legal setting (Clines 235). Verse 22's note, *he destroys ... the wicked*, clashes a bit with verse 24, which seems to suggest that God favors the wicked. However, the point emphasized here is that the innocent are punished by God in the same way as the wicked.

In verses 25–35, Job seems to be alluding to his rapidly approaching death, when time will run out for his vindication (see 7:6). Job yearns for a divine umpire, or lawyer, who might intervene between him and God. He also alludes to several artifacts of contemporary material culture, such as *papyrus*, a plant whose fibers yielded writing material and even boats (Clines 240), and *washing soda*, or lye.

Legal Imagery in Job
In 9:33, Job challenges God by wishing to hire an attorney to defend his case before him. Perhaps Job has in mind some angel to intervene. This figure may be the same as the redeemer in 16:19–21 and 19:25. Some scholars see Elihu, Job's fourth friend, taking this role (chapters 32–37).

10:1–17 Job sarcastically accuses God of judging him by showing partiality. Job asks God to reconsider destroying his own creation. Job comes close to blasphemy when he challenges God to produce the evidence of his supposed great sin.

Verses 9–12 offer a beautiful poetic description of God's creation of Job's fetal body in his mother's womb. Verse 10 makes reference to the semen that starts the birth process and, like milk, becomes *coagulated* in the womb for developing the embryo (Clines 248). Of course, the Israelites did not have a scientific and detailed knowledge of fetal development and had to resort to analogies to explain the process.

In verse 17, Job may be blasphemously implying that God has produced false witnesses in this imaginary legal setting so as to indict him.

In verses 18–22, Job again wishes he had never been born, just as in chapter 3. He then reminds God that, since his life will be so brief, he is not worth God's attention. Verse 20's plaintive question, *Are not my days almost over*? returns us to to the theme of 6:9, where Job wants his life to end quickly, and to 7:6, where Job laments the fact that his life will end soon, before he can be vindicated.

11:1–20 Zophar sarcastically condemns Job for being a babbler, full of hot air. He cautions him against claiming to be innocent. In verse 4, the Hebrew word for *pure* is related to the words for innocence Job has used in defending his integrity (see 6:29; 7:20) and that God used to characterize him (1:8; 2:3). The point of verse 6 is not to discredit God for memory loss but to emphasize that God has been very gracious to Job, not even accounting to him all his sins, and that Job should thus be grateful.

In verses 7–12, Zophar begins a speech that foreshadows the divine speeches at the end of the book.

He describes the great and mysterious wisdom of God. He explains that God's judgment is accurate. His humorous proverb in verse 12, *a wild donkey's colt can be born a man*, is functionally equivalent to our expression, "When hell freezes over," stating the impossibility of the situation.

Verses 13–20 bring home Zophar's lesson. He recommends Job turning repentantly to God. If he does, Zophar says, life will turn bright again for him. Zophar calls on Job to practice typical forms of religion: the stretching of the hands toward heaven was the typical prayer posture of the Jews (see 1 Tim 2:8). A pious response should bring Job *hope* (verses 18, 20). Zophar may be alluding to Job's use of this word in 7:6, where he laments that he will die before being vindicated. Here Zophar argues that Job would have hope if he repents. In verse 20, hope has the negative connotation of the wicked person's wish to die quickly instead of enduring his or her fate.

12:1–13:22 Job challenges Bildad's earlier claims to represent ancient wisdom (8:8–10). He boldly states that his wisdom is not inferior to theirs. In verse 4, *he answered me* refers to Job's former life before the tragedy (Clines 290), while *righteous* is the same word used in 6:29 synonymously with the word *blameless* (itself used by God to describe his exemplary servant in the prologue; see 1:8; 2:3).

In verses 7–12, Job rhetorically challenges Bildad to ask the animals and plants whether God has dealt unfairly with him; he is not making it all up. He also uses a series of other images. For example, in verse 11, *the ear tests words ... tongue tastes food* suggests the discriminating capacity of human reasoning (compare 34:3).

In verses 13–25, Job argues that God alone has wisdom, implying that his friends lack this. He describes how God seems deliberately to baffle and humiliate even the wise men and leaders of the people. He uses a series of military images to make this point. Thus in verse 18, *loincloth* refers to the fact that armies often marched captives along the way naked to their destinations. Here God reverses this fate and undoes what the mighty king has done. Similarly, verse 23 sounds like an allusion to the Assyrian and Babylonian invasions, and verse 24 sounds similar to the fate of Nebuchadnezzar in Daniel 4.

In 13:1–12, Job points out that he is not inferior in wisdom to his friends. But his real wish is to encounter God, not debate with them. He then attacks his friends for being worthless and showing favoritism toward God and predicts that God will rebuke them.

> **"Plastering with lies ..."**
> Job uses the language of the courts (*verse 3*) and the graphic image of plastering with lies, metaphorically describing the friends as false healers, since oil was "plastered" on patients (Clines 306).

In verses 13–28, Job wants to take God to court; he is taking a great risk but will defend his integrity before God, anyway. Job challenges God to present the evidence of his sin. Verse 15 illustrates his bravery in making such a request. While saying, *Behold, he will slay me; I have no hope*, Job insists on proclaiming his innocence, perhaps after his own death (see 19:23–29). His lack of confidence in God comes through in verse 26's *write down bitter things against me*, which depicts God as "a judge recording sentence" (Rowley 102). In verse 27, *marks on the soles of my feet* literally reads "roots of my feet" and may refer to tracks made in the soil by walking; the meaning is that God watches over Job like a prisoner, noting every detail (Clines 322–23).

14:1–22 In his response, Job argues that since mortals are transient and perverse, God should leave them and, thus, him alone. The center of his argument comes in verses 7–17, where he notes that there is more hope for vegetation that seems to die but then resurrects than for humans, whose fate is to go to the abode of the dead (see 7:6; 11:18, 20). Job then dreams of being resurrected after his death like these plants, and then he could be vindicated.

In verses 13–17, Job dreams of coming back from the grave to be vindicated, but this is only a dream (Clines 330–32); he knows that mortals only die, never to rise. Like the other Old Testament writers (except for the book of Daniel), Job does not believe in a resurrection or heavenly afterlife; this idea would not become

> **The Dead**
> The character Job assumes that the dead have no knowledge of contemporary events (compare Eccl 9:5), yet they can feel. Thus the first cycle of the dialogue ends with the conclusion that humans can imagine a solution to their problems, but it is only an illusion, not a real possibility.

popular until the Second Temple period. He also dreams, again impossibly, that God will stop analyzing him under a microscope and thus ignore any sins he may have committed (verses 16–17). Job would then be able to defend his case for his innocence and integrity.

Verses 18–22 reveal that his thoughts are only a dream, as Job describes how things are worn away in nature. God wears away humans so that they die.

15:1–35 The second cycle begins with a speech from Eliphaz, who reprimands Job for being filled with hot air and threatening traditional values. He appeals to traditional goals emphasizing piety, literally "fear," a shortened form of "fearing God," the wisdom tradition's favorite expression for piety (see 1:1). In verses 7–16, Eliphaz condemns Job for thinking too highly of his own wisdom; these verses foreshadow the divine speeches. Humans cannot be pure before God. He refers to the wisdom of the ages being on his side (see 8:8–10; 12:1–2). Verse 14 returns to an earlier argument (4:17; Job responds in 9:2) that all mortals are morally impure before God; they have no right to question God about anything.

In verses 17–35, Eliphaz describes how the wicked, though at first prosperous, will eventually get their just deserts. He again appeals to the wisdom of the ages to confirm this idea. Specifically, verse 19 refers to ancient land rights given to the Temanites; it suggests that the Temanites retained a pristine, pure wisdom superior to more recent nations (Clines 355; similarly Obad 8). He also refers to various social practices that seem to confirm his view, such as warfare (verse 24), the obesity of prosperous persons (verse 27), and a series of plant metaphors (verses 29–33; compare 8:16–19). In short, he argues that Job misunderstands the nature of reality and thus his own situation and the role of God.

16:1–17:16 Job responds to these charges by condemning his friends for long-windedness. Job directs his speech toward God and condemns him for attacking him. Yet Job still defends his innocence. Verse 4 dismisses the friends' response as mockery (see 2 Kgs 19:21; Ps 22:7; 44:14), drawing on a theme about the enemies in psalms of lament. Verse 9 (*gnashes his teeth*) also uses an idiom that usually refers to rage or anger (Pss 35:16; 37:12; Lam 2:16). Here God assumes the role of a predator that attacks and eats its prey; gnashing the teeth refers to the hungry predator licking its chops as it prepares to devour its victim.

In verse 13, *kidneys* are the organs that Israelites assumed to be the seat of the emotions. Thus God strikes Job emotionally. *Gall* represents bitterness or negative emotion (Clines 385).

Verse 19 echoes 9:33, where Job wishes there might be a divine lawyer or witness who could stand between himself and God. Here he appeals to anyone in heaven to serve as witness against God if Job is not vindicated and succumbs to death. Unfortunately, there is no such person (see Clines 389–90).

The argument continues in verse 20, as Job subtly condemns his friends for not being friends (compare 6:14–20; 13:4–9; 16:1), even while he seeks a true friend. As 16:22–17:2 makes plain, he fears that he may die before he can be vindicated.

In search of this protector, he turns in 17:3–5 to prayer to the very God he fears. He seeks *the pledge* (verse 3) from God, thus challenging God metaphorically to be a co-signer or guarantee for him, that is, his deliverer, against his so-called friends. Thus the identities of the adversary and protector shift. Job is hoping that God will punish his friends for their disloyalty; this prefigures the friends' eventual condemnation by God (42:7).

In verses 6–16, Job again complains about God's injustice toward him. He has become a laughingstock among the people.

In this speech, Job returns to themes or images that appear in earlier chapters. Thus verse 8 returns to God's stereotypical description of Job in the prologue (1:8; 2:3). In spite of God's injustices toward Job, he is saying that he will hold on and not give up.

> **Job's Fortitude**
> *In his speech in chapter 17, Job makes a statement of faith that he will not give up in spite of the injustices in the world. He laments that he has no hope, only an inevitable journey to the abode of the dead.*

Verse 12 cites Zophar in 11:17, who counseled Job to repent so that his *night* would become *day*. On the word *hope* in verse 15, see 7:6; 11:18, 20; 14:7, 19. And verse 16's phrase *gates of death* returns to the image of Sheol, now describing it as a walled city.

18:1–21 In his response, Bildad begins by condemning Job for not respecting the friends. Bildad's question in verse 4 is saying that Job's criticism of God's moral order of the cosmos would mean turning the world upside down to rectify it (Clines 412). He also argues in verses 5–21 that, whatever apparent imperfections in the world, the wicked will suffer many calamities; he is upholding the doctrine of retribution. He uses several metaphors to describe the fall of the wicked. These include hunting metaphors in verses 8–9 (on the wicked caught in a *net*, see Ps 9:15; 31:4; 35:7–8; Prov 1:17; on traps, see Ps 91:3; 124:7; Prov 7:23; Amos 3:5).

The text ends with a meditation on death, which Job personifies as a leader of demons that will eventually destroy the wicked. The Canaanites believed in a god of the underworld, Mot (Death). His *son* might refer to his vizier, or aide (Clines 417). The phrase *king of terrors* (verse 14) personifies death again.

19:1–29 In his response, Job condemns his friends for cruelty. He then shifts the attack to God, claiming unfair treatment. He constructs his retort in part with words and ideas from earlier parts of the book. Thus in verse 6, *net* echoes Bildad's use of its synonym in 18:8. Here, instead of a net catching the wicked, God has trapped Job. This image also echoes the good hedge the *satan* claims God has placed around Job (1:10; but see Job's negative evaluation of the hedge in 3:23). Also, the word *hope* in verse 10 takes one back to 11:18, 20; 14:7, 19; 17:15. He also introduces new metaphors such as verse 12's *siege ramp*, a military implement of the ancient Near East made of dirt and debris built up on the sloping rampart surrounding the walls so that the attacking army could more easily get at the base of these walls.

In verses 13–22, Job bemoans the fact that, because of his affliction, all his family and friends have deserted him. He appeals to his friends to have some mercy on him and not be like God. Again, we see a range of images. Thus verse 17 says his *breath is offensive*, or better, his relatives find his "life" repulsive (Clines 448). Verse 20's *skin of my teeth* is an idiomatic saying that refers to virtually nothing left of Job (there is no skin on the teeth; he is starving; see Clines 452).

In verses 23–29, Job wants to record his protest of innocence in a permanent form. He ponders that after his death, his *champion* will vindicate him. But he prefers that God should encounter him before his own death. Verse 23, an ironic glance at the reader rather than Job's immediate audience, wants his protest of innocence chiseled into rock, that is, as an inscription so that it will last beyond his death (Rowley 137). Job believes that his *champion* will eventually demonstrate his innocence (Clines 461), even if after his own death (verse 26). Verse 27 expresses a hope to *see God* after death, or better still, in this life. He concludes his defense by warning his friends to show mercy on him.

> **"I know that my redeemer lives ..."**
> *Although Job 19:25 serves as the inspiration for the words of one the most popular Christian hymns, its interpretation does not entirely reflect its meaning in Job. The word* redeemer *[Hebrew* goel*] means kinsmen-redeemer, the same word used for Boaz (Ruth 4:4–6). This person was responsible for taking care of his own kin, as when they might be enslaved for debt. Job is referring to some being in the heavens, probably the lawyer, umpire, or mediator that he has already mentioned (9:33; 16:19).*

20:1–29 Zophar condemns Job for insulting the friends. He then argues that, though the wicked may seem to prosper temporarily, retribution is only delayed.

In verse 8, he returns to a theme of 4:12–16, revelation through a *vision in the night*, either a dream or perhaps a prophetic vision (the Bible does not sharply distinguish between the two). Prophets often received their oracles from God in visions during the night (see 1 Kgs 3:5, where God asks Solomon in a vision what he wants most). The sages, unlike Eliphaz and now Zophar, were often skeptical of such visions of the night (Eccl 5:7). The point is that the wicked will disappear like a night vision that is gone by daybreak.

In verses 12–19, Zophar describes wickedness as if it were a sweet substance the wicked consume, but it turns to bitterness and poison. They will never enjoy the fruit of their labor, especially their unjust activities. Verse 19 describes the oppressive actions of the powerful wicked, who, due to the poor's indebtedness, foreclose on their property (compare Mic 2:2).

In verses 20–29, Zophar describes the wicked as having stuffed bellies because of their greed. God will stuff them some more with his anger as a divine warrior. In verse 25, the *liver* is literally the gallbladder (Clines 496). The point is that this is a mortal injury (see 16:13).

21:1–34 In his response, Job emphasizes that the friends are not listening to him. He argues that the wicked in fact prosper instead of fail; like Midas, everything they touch seems to turn to gold. He also insists that his argument is of deep significance. According to verse 4, he is not merely arguing with friends. He is questioning the entire moral order held up by God (see Newsom 491). In verse 5, he asks his friends to be prepared for what he is about to say; he is not speaking of his physical appearance but rather of their lack of awareness of reality (Newsom 491). The advice, *clap your hand over your mouth*, means being silent due to shock (Seow 749; compare 29:9; Prov 30:32).

In verse 13, *go down to the grave in peace* means that the wicked do not die a violent or premature death (see Eccl 7:17c). A king who does not die a violent death is also described by the author of Samuel or Kings as *sleeping with the ancestors*. Also, to die and possibly not be buried (eaten by wild animals) was considered a particularly horrible fate (as in Goliath's threat to David in 1 Sam 17:44; 46). The deceased's *soul* was somehow still associated with the body and could not *sleep* unless buried properly.

Verse 16 is a strange verse from Job and sounds like Eliphaz in 22:18. Perhaps this is again Job's way of protesting his innocence, or perhaps he is mocking Zophar (Newsom 492).

In verses 17–26, Job counters the argument that the punishment is delayed for their children. He argues that God's judgment seems capricious. Verse 19 considers the idea of delayed retribution, a typical one used by the author of Samuel through Kings (for example, Manasseh's wicked ways explains the early death of Josiah [2 Kgs 23:26–30]). The notion is used to mitigate the problems inherent in the doctrine of retribution. The wicked father might escape the full effect of punishment, but his children will then suffer. He continues to claim that the wicked have it better than the righteous in verse 24, where *rich with marrow* symbolizes a well-fed, healthy animal available for the eater to enjoy.

In verses 27–34, Job anticipates the objection that there is little evidence for the wicked prospering. He notes that, even in death, *watch is kept over his tomb* (verse 32), which means that guards prevent anyone bothering the body (Newsom 494; see Eccl 8:10). When verse 33 says that the *soil in the valley is sweet*, it refers to the horror of a burial procession of the wicked that many attend. The *clods of the valley* taste sweet to the wicked (Good 420) because the proper burial is *sweet* for the wicked, who deserve no such procedure.

22:1–30 Chapter 22 begins the third cycle of the dialogue. Here Eliphaz argues that God is completely impartial and not swayed by any piety on Job's part (Rowley 153–54). Eliphaz then shifts, without evidence to back his charges, to condemning Job for instances of social injustice. Verses 6–9 graphically describe a rich person oppressing the poor, a particularly shameful sin to be leveled against a Jew. Note that Job eloquently

> **Responsibility**
> *Job 21:19 takes up the problem of group versus individual responsibility. Unlike the Ten Commandments, which allow for punishment to the third and fourth generation, and Jeremiah 31:29–30, which allows for individual responsibility, Job does not decide one way or another but notes the pain that any form of retribution leaves behind for the survivors.*

Cosmology
"Cosmology" refers to a people's view of the physical universe. The Israelites, like other ancient peoples, did not hold to a modern, scientific understanding of the universe. The Israelites probably believed the earth was flat, as did other ancient peoples. They also believed that water surrounded the earth. Celestial water (Gen 1:6–7) covered the top of the dome-like structure they referred to as the firmament. These waters were what made the sky look blue. The firmament divided these heavenly waters from the earth beneath; it essentially separated the heavens from the earth. But beneath the earth were waters that came up through springs (Gen 7:11; 8:2). In the flood, these waters served to help flood the earth. The Hebrews believed mountains along the horizon held up the great dome (Job 26:11; 37:18). Rain and snow came through gates in the firmament connected to chambers that held them (Gen 7:11). The sun, moon, and stars were believed to be fixed in the firmament, making their circuits along it (Gen 1:14–19; Ps 19:4, 6). The sun was believed to travel from east to west and then under the earth until the new dawn, when the cycle continued. See page 109 for a representative image.

refutes this (29:12–17; 31:13–23). Eliphaz carefully describes such oppression.

Thus verse 6 describes a lender who *demanded security*. When extending a loan to a debtor, often creditors demanded some type of security to insure payment of it. Sometimes, all the debtors had were the clothes on their backs. This practice is condemned in Scripture (Exod 22:25–27; Deut 24:6, 17). Eliphaz is accusing Job of being a greedy, ruthless oppressor of the vulnerable.

Verse 9 refers to *widows…fatherless*, the most vulnerable social categories in ancient Israel (see Exod 22:22–23; Pss 10:14; 68:5). *Widows* means a once-married woman without children to support her. *The fatherless* means children with no aunts/uncles or grandparents to take care of them. No highly regulated governmental procedures were available to take care of such persons. A person had to depend on kin, who, if nonexistent or poor themselves, were unable to assist. Certain Pentateuchal laws attempt to alleviate the situation to some extent (for example, Lev 19:9–10; Deut 24:19).

Verses 12–20 draw on the previous language about darkness to accuse Job of thinking that God's perception of what happens on the earth is obscured by dark clouds. Job hears again that the way of the wicked is disastrous. Eliphaz notes God's inaccessibility (see verse 14: *vaulted heavens*, an image similar to the *firmament* of Gen 1, though with different terminology). He also turns Job's words against him in verse 18 (see 21:16), perhaps mocking Job.

In verses 21–30, Eliphaz recommends that Job repent and turn to God and then be restored. He is told to forget his materialism and put God first, so that good things will happen to him. In verse 23, *tent* refers to one's habitation or home and is not meant to be taken literally. In verse 24, *nuggets…gold of Ophir* imply Job's guilt as a materialist. Returning gold to a faraway place like Ophir, known for its exotic luxury goods and located perhaps in either in Saudi Arabia or Ethiopia, would be an excessive act but worth it for Job (see Newsom 502). Yet Eliphaz counsels him to fulfill his vows (verse 27), since using his wealth for religious ends would make God restore him (Newsom 503). Eliphaz sums up his argument in verse 29 by saying that, if Job repents, then he will be able to even intervene on others' behalf, the ultimate mark of well-being (Newsom 503).

23:1–24:17, 25 There is evidence that chapter 24 has suffered dislocation in the process of being copied through the centuries. It appears that part of Zophar's last speech has been placed within Job's response (verses 18–24; according to Rowley 158–59, 167). This section is very unlike Job and seems to support the doctrine of retribution.

In 23:1–7, Job bemoans the fact that he cannot find God. If he could, he dreams of finally being acquitted. He extends this point in verses 8–17 by noting that God knows his purity but will not admit it. He begins to mock his friends (verse 10; compare 22:24) and claims that God has made him wish he could hide in darkness (see 22:11, 13). In 24:1–8, he accuses God of injustice for allowing the wicked to oppress the poor, whose plight is despicable. He then explores the nature of oppression, giving such examples as the removal of *boundary stones*, a serious offense in ancient Israel (Deut 19:14), especially since land was the main source of wealth among the people. His reference to *orphans'* and *widows'* plights echoes Eliphaz's accusations against Job (22:9). In verses 9–12, he cites further instances of the wicked's oppression of the vulnerable. An especially offensive case is when an *infant [is] seized*. A debtor might have to sell his own children as slaves to pay off the debt (see Neh 5:4–5).

In 24:13–17, Job depicts the wicked as dwellers of the darkness (compare 23:17; 22:11, 13). This description helps us understand Job's mental anguish, for he believes that wickedness wins in the world, though it should not.

Verses 18–20 are a dislocated part of Zophar's speech. It exudes the doctrine of retribution. Mother Nature is described as opposing the wicked. Verse 20 graphically describes their fate: in the phrase the *womb forgets them*, the womb represents fertility, and in the reference to *the worm*, the recognition is that maggots eat a corpse.

Verses 21–24 are another dislocated fragment of Zophar's speech. Zophar argues that God's retribution on the wicked is only delayed, as he argued earlier in 20:4–11. Job counters in 21:19–21. The reference to *widow* in verse 21 may echo Eliphaz's accusation of Job's oppression of the poor (22:9). Verse 25 ends Job's response to Eliphaz.

25:1–6 AND 26:5–14 This section has also suffered dislocation; 26:1–4 appears to be part of Job's response to Bildad (Rowley 170–71). In 25:1–6,

Bildad describes the vast difference in power and piety between God and humans. This is in response to Job's argument that the wicked prosper and God does nothing. He does not realize that he has contradicted the argument that Job is accountable for his behavior. In verse 6, the phrase *son of man* is an idiomatic way of referring to human beings (see, for example, Eccl 3:10).

Job 26:5–14 continues Bildad's response to Job, which has suffered dislocation (following Rowley 169, 172). They do not fit Job's preceding words (verses 1–4) and better fit Bildad's (25:2–6). Bildad, in hymnic fashion, describes the awesome power of God, before whom mortals cower. This foreshadows the divine speeches in their description of God's creative powers (chapters 38–41). The speech lists several demonstrations of God's power, including death (verse 6), the creation of the cosmos (verse 7–10), the violence of earthquake and flood (verses 11–12), and the return to peace after such events (verse 13).

In verse 6, *death ... destruction* denote the abode of the dead, ultimately mysterious to humans but fully comprehended by God. In verse 7, the note *He spreads out the northern skies over empty space* fits the depiction in Genesis 1:6–8 of a firmament, the sky, which separates the heavens from the earth. The reference to the north is poetic for the residence of a deity. Heaven has been suspended upon nothing, an observation that is not a scientific description of gravity but a poetic description of the tripartite Israelite conception of the cosmos: heavens, earth, and chaotic waters beneath (see Newsom 518).

The rest of the speech describes the act of creation. Verse 8 offers a poetic description of clouds serving as water skin containers for rain (see Newsom 518; see Ps 33:7; Prov 30:4). Verse 10 makes a poetic description of the Israelite view that water surrounded the earth, marking the farthest horizon. The vault of heaven then sat upon this horizon (see Rowley 173). Next, verse 11 speaks of the *pillars of the heavens*, which Israelites believed to be the mountains of the horizon supporting the firmament that held up the heavens. Then verse 12's reference to the death of *Rahab* (not the prostitute in Josh 2) names a poetic sea monster who represents chaos and evil. God controls such forces. Verse 13's *gliding serpent* is the same as *Rahab* in verse 12.

26:1–4 This is part of Job's answer to Bildad that has been dislocated (so Rowley 170). Job sarcastically lauds Bildad's comforting words.

27:1–6 This section resumes Job's answer to Bildad (see Rowley 174). Job once again defends himself against charges of blasphemy or other sins. As in other speeches, Job returns to themes set forth earlier in the book. Thus verse 5 uses the word *integrity* [Hebrew *tummah*], a slightly different form of the word that God used to impress the *satan* with Job's virtue in 1:8 and 2:3. It literally means *blamelessness*.

27:7–23 This is the rest of Zophar's third speech (according to Rowley 175; but see Habel 383, who begins Zophar's speech at verse 13). This section begins with a curse and portrays the woeful plight of the wicked. The wicked's retribution by God is often delayed, yet in wishing, *May my enemies be like the wicked*, Zophar is so sure of the wicked's eventual punishment that he can think of nothing worse for his enemies (Rowley 176). In verse 16, the word *silver* echoes the *gold* of 22:24 (Eliphaz) and 23:10 (Job) and anticipates the mountain of jewels of chapter 28, especially the gold of Ophir in 28:16. In verse 23, *hisses* could be translated "whistles derisively" (Good 424).

28:1–28 Most scholars see this chapter as an addition to the dialogue that anticipates the divine speeches (chapters 38–41) in some ways. Though it is in the mouth of Job, it is better to view it as a supplement by the author in his own voice to extol the value of wisdom (as the author defines it), whose value Job's speeches have seriously questioned. The poem also emphasizes traditional piety at the end but does not connect it with the doctrine of retribution.

> **Ancient Creation Stories**
>
> In the ancient world, stories of creation tended to portray the creator as engaging either in combat against a force of chaos or in sexual activities. The Bible completely avoids the second option, and creation narratives in Genesis 1–2, Proverbs 8, and elsewhere avoid the first, as well. Job uses the combat imagery for creation here, perhaps because it is portraying the theology of Gentiles (Job and his friends).

> **Finding Wisdom**
>
> Job 28 sets up an analogy between the relationship between human miners and animals and the accessibility and value of true wisdom.

Several elements of the text deserve clarification. In verses 1–6, human miners are seeking fine gems and precious metals hidden within a mountain. Verse 6's *nuggets of gold* echoes Eliphaz's speech in 22:24. Verses 7–8 note that animals cannot see or appreciate the value of such hidden treasure. Yet, as verses 9–19 make clear, human miners can get it and use it. Wisdom, however, eludes humans even though it is more valuable than gems.

According to verses 12–14, mortals cannot easily find wisdom (see Eccl 7:23–24). Thus, the point of the contrast comes to light: as the animal world cannot search and find the underground treasures that miners exploit, so humans do not have direct access to God's wisdom, the most valuable of commodities.

The text continues in verses 15–19 by describing wisdom as more valuable than any jewels or precious metals, connecting with the search for jewels in verses 1–6, 9–11. Similarly, verses 20–22 return to the theme of animals, as in verses 7–8. For verse 22's mention of *death* and *destruction*, see the commentary on 26:6. The text mentions these realities in order to point to the "most distant and inaccessible place" (Seow 756).

The meditation on wisdom closes (verses 23–28) by noting that only God knows where it abides. At its creation, God *looked at wisdom and appraised it* (verse 27), an idea similar to the personification of Wisdom as God's master architect at the creation (Prov 8:22–31, especially 30). Here it appears that God creates the world first, then compares his handiwork to Wisdom and sees its great value. The final verse mentions the *fear of the Lord*, a favorite expression for piety in the Wisdom literature (see 1:1).

29:1–31:40 Job wishes for the former days when God blessed him. He describes those golden days when he was esteemed by his village and known for his acts of social justice. Again, a series of images serve Job's response to his friends' charges. In verses 12–13, Job refers to *the fatherless ... widow* in order to counter Eliphaz's accusation that Job had oppressed the poor and vulnerable (see 22:6–9). In verse 19, the reference to *dew ... all night on my branches* reflects the scarcity and preciousness of dew in an arid region; Job's life had known abundance and prosperity. In verse 20, *the bow* is a symbol of strength (see Gen 49:24; see 30:11). In verses 21–25, Job describes how the people used to esteem him and seek his advice.

Chapter 30 contrasts his present life with the former one. Here, Job depicts the irony of outcasts he once comforted who now despise him in his condition (Rowley 190). He now uses images of disgust or discomfort to illustrate his condition. Thus in verse 4, *salt herbs* are saltwort, which has sour leaves and is poor nutritionally (Habel 415). In verses 9–15, Job continues to describe the outcasts whom society despises, who ironically despise Job in his current condition. Verse 11 reverses 29:20, while verse 12 returns to the theme of besieging armies seen in 19:12. In verses 16–23, Job laments his miserable situation. God is like a brawler who throws Job into the mud. Verses 24–31 continue the lament, bemoaning the fact that though Job had been good to the poor in his former days, now he finds himself in terrible straits. His lament ends with a series of metaphors for social isolation. Thus verse 28 says that, ironically, the man who once strutted before the *assembly* (29:7–11) must now cry out for help. Similarly, verse 29 names animals that "inhabited desolate places" (Seow 759).

Chapter 31 seeks resolution of the tension between what was (chapter 29) and what now is (chapter 30). In an oath of innocence, Job says he has been very strict with himself ethically. Why would he turn from God now?

In verse 1, the clause *made a covenant with my eyes*, demonstrates his extreme piety by metaphorically making a pledge with his eyes (his covenant partner) not to lust after women. The point is simply that Job has been vigilant in not falling into wicked lust. Note that Job mentions sexual offenses in verses 7 and 9. Sexual sins were especially condemned by the Jews (see Rosner 36–37, 143).

In verses 5–8, Job proclaims a self-imposed curse that would become effective had he not been ethically and religiously faithful. This section begins Job's famous protest of innocence. This is a legal context, and so Job is preparing to meet God in court. Thus he uses the legal metaphor of *honest scales* (verse 6) to entice God to

> **Dishonest Scales**
> *Biblical texts frequently condemn the use of* dishonest scales *by cheating merchants (for example, Prov 11:1; 20:23; Hos 12:7). Job 31:6 uses a business activity metaphorically to depict God's judgment of Job. Job is saying that if God would only look impartially and clearly at his case, he knows God would find him innocent.*

hear his case. Verse 7 describes his innocence in reference to desires, a theme connecting with verse 1.

The following sections continue the theme of personal integrity, focusing on several aspects of the life of a powerful person such as Job. First, in verses 9–12, Job proclaims a curse on himself if he has committed adultery (on verse 12, compare 26:6; 28:22). Second, in verses 13–15, Job proclaims a self-imposed curse if he has mistreated his slaves. Verse 13 counters Eliphaz's accusation (22:6–9) that he has committed social injustice. Verse 14 implies a punishment but does not state it explicitly. Third, in verses 16–23, Job proclaims a self-imposed curse if he has violated the rights of the poor and vulnerable. Using the common pair *widow ... fatherless*, Job counters Eliphaz's accusation that he had oppressed the most vulnerable poor (22:9). Fourth, in verses 24–28, Job proclaims a self-imposed curse if he has been guilty of materialism or if he has worshiped heavenly bodies that represented deities. The reference to *gold* in verse 24 counters Eliphaz's implication that he has been materialistic (22:24). Verse 27 refers to "throwing kisses to the moon ..." (Rowley 203). Fifth, in verses 29–34, Job proclaims a self-imposed curse if he has mistreated even his enemies or concealed his sins. Job closes this description of his central moral values by expressing a desire to encounter God in court (verses 35–37). By *someone to hear me*, most likely Job is referring to God.

In a final self-imposed curse (verses 38–40), Job sums up his commitments by referring to his tenant-farmers, whom he has sought not to mistreat.

32:1–37:24 Many scholars believe the speeches of Elihu were added to the book later, after its completion. They point out that the speeches seem to interrupt the train of thought and that the epilogue and prologue completely ignore Elihu. Job never responds to him. However, we will consider the speeches as genuine and an integral part of the book. Elihu thinks he can do better at arguing with Job than the three friends (32:3), but he too really does no better. Yet some of what he says prepares the reader for the divine speeches.

Chapter 32 opens with Elihu denying that the three friends were competent enough with their arguments. Unlike the other friends, he seems to be a descendant of Abraham, since Buz was a nephew of Abraham (Gen 22:20–21) and the brother of Uz, the ancestor of Job's tribe (1:1). In verses 6–10, he argues that wisdom does not come necessarily with age; he now promises to demonstrate that youth can be more competent. In verse 13, he notes that the friends admit that Job is too clever for them; only God can refute him. Elihu argues, to the contrary, that all they need is him (Rowley 209).

In verses 15–22, Elihu sarcastically asks whether he should give up like the others have. He will have his say; he cannot hold back the words any longer. However, the text portrays him ironically, as in verse 18's *full of words*, since it is he who is *full of hot wind*.

In 33:1–7, Elihu ends his verbose self-introduction. Job is not to fear him; he is merely mortal, too. He repeats Job's protest of innocence in verses 8–11 but then turns in verses 12–28 to state plainly that Job is wrong and should not challenge God to answer him. He then explains how God answers humans (in dreams at night to warn the individual, and through disease). Verse 14 (*now one way, now another*) uses a literary device known as ascending numeration to signify more than enough ways (see 5:19; Clines 150). Verse 18 returns to the theme of Sheol (*the pit*), literally, the abode of the dead. Verses 19–22 close this section by stating the classic theodicy of soul-making, or suffering, as disciplinary. Eliphaz has already made this argument (5:17–18), so Elihu is not so original, despite his claim in 32:14–22.

In chapter 34, Elihu states that Job has claimed innocence, yet he is guilty. Defending God's justice, he insists that God is sovereign and has no need to be partial (Rowley 218). In verses 16–20, he also argues that it makes no sense that the God who is just would be unjust. Moreover, in verses 21–30, he further defends God's justice by pointing to the ultimate punishment of the wicked, who commit social injustice. In verse 28, he cites a major theme of Israelite ethical reflection,

> **Angels & Mediators**
> *Elihu's reference to* an angel or a heavenly mediator *like the* champion *(see 16:19; 19:25), who will vouch for a human in the divine council, returns to the theme of humankind's need for protection from God, the protector. Elihu draws on the theme in his reference to a* mediator, *or one who interprets God to humans and vice versa. This may be like the* champion *to which Job has already referred (see 16:19; 19:25). The phrase* one out of a thousand *may mean that there are plenty of angels available for this task (Newsom 570; Rowley 214).*

which believes that God hears the *cry of the poor*. Earlier, Job had accused God of ignoring social injustice (24:1–12). In verses 31–37, Elihu intensifies his critique when he sarcastically insinuates that Job wants restoration without repentance. In verse 37's clause, *scornfully he claps his hands*, the meaning of the verb is uncertain, but the intent is clear: to jeer at the friends (Holladay 259).

In chapter 35, Elihu loosely cites Job. Job's piety, whether good or bad, means nothing to God. Verse 2 loosely quotes 13:18; verse 3, 9:29–31; and verse 7, 22:2–3. Again, Elihu is not as unique in his argumentation as he claims (32:14–22). In verses 9–16, Elihu argues that the oppressed who cry out to God are only concerned about themselves and not learning anything (Rowley 225). Verse 10 sounds like the prophets in claiming that *no one says, Where is God my Maker…?* These people cry out only because of oppression; they do not truly seek God (Rowley 225). Similarly, the phrase "because of the arrogance of the wicked" probably refers to these oppressed who are not learning their lesson (see Rowley 225).

In chapter 36, Elihu says he will defend God. He argues (verses 5–12) that God disciplines the righteous so they might be instructed. If they repent, they will be blessed. By saying in verse 10, *he makes them listen to correction*, Elihu returns to an argument Eliphaz has already made (5:17–18) for soul-making, or disciplinary theodicy. Elihu himself made this argument first in 33:19–22. In verse 16, *jaws of distress* may be an allusion to Sheol or death personified, an adversary who swallows his victims (see Ps 141:7). God is, says Elihu, enticing Job to avoid disaster by the infliction of suffering (Habel 508). The phrase *to a spacious place free from restriction* depicts God as offering a place of feasting instead of death (Habel 509).

Elihu continues his speech by trying to turn Job's obsession with divine justice into an opportunity to learn from his suffering and avoid evil. Verse 17 notes that Job is obsessed with the issue of demanding that God appear in court with him (Habel 508). Elihu warns him in verse 18 not to think that he can *bribe* his way out of being consumed by Sheol, the adversary (Habel 509). This phrase contains the same Hebrew word [kofer] as in 33:24, where a mediator hopes to ransom Job out of his predicament. Of course, the fact that Job has lost all his wealth makes Elihu's warning extremely ironic. Verse 20's *long for the night* warns Job not to be seduced by the "dark forces of the night world" (Habel 509). Also, the NIV's *to drag people away from their homes* could better be rendered (with Habel 495), "When peoples disappear from their places."

> **Job & Darkness**
> In chapter 36, Elihu warns Job to repent and not attempt dealing with the forces of darkness or chaos that he had earlier summoned up to curse his birthday (3:8).

In 36:24–33, Elihu praises God's cosmological powers, which provide everything. This theme foreshadows the divine speeches. In verse 29, *pavilion* literally means "hut" (Holladay 255) or covering of clouds (see Ps 18:11).

Chapter 37 concludes Elihu's intervention in the debate. In hymnic language, the text praises God's maintenance of the cosmos. God brings forth meteorological elements (such as *clouds* in verse 13) to both punish and bless mortals. This claim, again, foreshadows the divine speeches. In verses 14–24, Elihu challenges Job with a series of questions about God's creation of the world that emphasize Job's limited perspective. Among the natural phenomena Elihu mentions are the *south wind* (verse 17), which connects with the *north* in verse 22. The sirocco, or east wind, blows off the desert with great intensity in the spring and fall (Rowley 239).

In verse 18, the image *hard as a mirror of cast bronze* alludes to the Israelite belief that the sky, or firmament, was shaped like a beaten out metal dome that covered the earth. Mirrors in those days were made of beaten metal brought to a fine polish. In verse 20, Elihu states that to confront God would be to flirt with disaster. Death may be personified here as the one who swallows (Seow 762). The reference to the *north* (verse 22) connects with *south* in verse 17. The north is the typical direction that symbolizes a deity (Isa 14:13; Ezek 1:4). If God were to appear, it would be like the sun, bright and glorious, which humans could not bear (see Newsom 591).

38:1–41:34 God prepares Job for a series of rhetorical questions that counter the claim that he is unjust. Job cannot answer the questions, because only God can. The point is to humble Job and widen his perspective. Thus the text offers a large number of images emphasizing God's might and basic justice.

Chapter 38 opens with a *storm*, because God's appearances to humans (theophanies) usually are accompanied by bizarre or frightening phenomena like fire, smoke, earthquake, loud thunder or voice, and lightning (see Exod 3:1–6; 19:18–19; 1 Kgs 19:11–13). The point of these phenomena is to represent God's might and glory and to humble humans witnessing such events. Verse 2 asks, how dare Job question the God of the universe. Among questions about the creation of the earth, God speaks of the time when *morning stars sang together* (verse 7), a portrayal of the praise of members of the divine council (Seow 768; see 25:5; Judg 5:20).

Verses 8–11 speak about the creation of the seas, with the clause *shut up the sea behind doors* being a reference to seashores that form a border between the water and dry land. Genesis 1 portrays God as a deity of order, who separates water from dry land in their chaotic state (1:1–2, 9–10). The word for *shut up* is literally "hedge in" as in 3:23, where Job uses it negatively to depict God hedging him in. Robert Alter (85–110) shows how the divine speeches constantly allude to the former dialogue to contrast God's omnipotent perspective versus the narrow views of Job and his friends.

In 38:12–15, God asks Job about the maintenance of the earth's rotation, bringing day and night. God proclaims that the light exposes the wicked, and so they are made vulnerable. Verse 13 speaks poetically of the dark of night being shaken like a sheet by the morning so that the wicked are exposed for what they are in the light (Rowley 243).

Verses 13–15 answer Job's accusation that God favors the wicked (see 9:22–24). "Contrary to Job's claim, however, the 'design' of Yahweh includes exposing the wicked each dawn (verse 15) without necessarily destroying them" (Habel 540). Thus, the *wicked are denied their light*, since their "light" is the darkness (Rowley 243); dawn takes this away.

In verses 16–21, God sarcastically asks Job about the most inaccessible places: the depths of the sea, the abode of the dead, and the sources of light and darkness. Verse 17 portrays the underworld as a city with gates.

Verses 22–30 and 34–38 extend the line of questioning to the operations of meteorological phenomena, about which Job is obviously ignorant. In a related line of thought, verses 31–33 turn to the constellations as the text moves from sea to sky. The identification of the various constellations is uncertain, and translations may vary. Nor is it clear that the ancients "saw" the same patterns in the sky that we do. The point is that, since Job did not create or maintain the constellations, he has no right to question God. Also, verse 37 (*the water jars of the heavens*) refers to clouds, now metaphorically depicted as water-skins (see also *Ecclesiasticus* 43:8). It takes great wisdom to allot the appropriate amount of water to the appropriate places (Newsom 605).

Verses 39–41 begin a larger section (through 39:30) that treats the animal world, especially the undomesticated part of it. God begins to ask Job about the activities of wild animals, for which humans have little concern. The point seems to be that Job's perspective is too limited; he has only human-centered concerns, but God's perspective is much broader and includes unwanted animals that live in desolate wasteland.

Chapter 39 opens with God asking a series of questions about the birthing customs of wild animals (except the war horse, which is domesticated). Particularly interesting is Job's reflections on the ostrich, which the author may not have seen up close, though ostrich feathers were a trade commodity in the ancient Near East. Unlike most birds, it cannot fly, and *God did not endow her with wisdom* (verse 17). And yet God is proud of this animal. A human might have endowed it with great wisdom if he or she were creator, but this passage reveals that God's concerns are not those of mortals and that humans are presumptuous to question God's sense of judgment; the world is not centered on human desires.

> "She laughs at horse and rider ..."
> The observation in 39:18, *she laughs at horse and rider*, means that, although humans consider ostriches misfits among birds, God has made them beautiful and honorable – and fast – in their own way, regardless of human standards of value.

On God's invitation, Job responds to the first divine speech in 40:3–5. Or, rather, he demurs before God and admits that he cannot respond. In verse 5, *once ... twice* is an example of ascending numeration, which implies that Job has spoken more than enough (see 5:19; 33:14; see Clines 150).

In 40:6–9, God again prepares Job to answer a series of rhetorical questions whose effect is to humble Job. On *storm*, see the comment on 38:1.

In verses 10–14, God challenges Job to punish the wicked on the earth himself. Verse 12, in particular, alludes to Job's accusation that God only favors the wicked (9:22–24). Job should punish them himself before he accuses God of wrong.

In verses 15–18, God demands that Job consider his creature Behemoth, which he describes in great detail. Literally "animal" or "beast," the *behemoth* here has mythic or poetic characteristics, and it is not as important to decide precisely what animal the author has in mind behind the symbol (whether hippopotamus, water buffalo [Newsom 618], or crocodile) as to realize that this is a description of a cosmic beast representing chaos that the Lord has control of and Job does not! Even if a real animal is being portrayed, the picture given is highly exaggerated, and the creature is meant to represent power and chaos that humans cannot control and God can. (Verse 17 means that the great muscular thighs of the beast are well constructed by God.)

Verses 19–24 state that God is proud of this creature, which everyone must approach cautiously. It cannot be caught by human hands.

Chapter 41 presents God's next favorite creature: the Leviathan. God questions whether Job or any mortal can catch and tame it. Anyone who tries will be very sorry. The *leviathan* is either a poetical cosmic beast or an exaggerated crocodile. Verses 12–34 describe this awesome beast in detail. It fears nothing and moves about majestically and violently. The reference to *smoke … his breath sets coals ablaze* (verses 20–21) is poetical language either describing the spraying of water out of a crocodile's mouth or the description of a fire-breathing dragon (cosmic beast) similar to medieval lore. Such a creature frightens even *the mighty* (verse 25; literally "gods," a label that shows the cosmic character of this creature). In verse 30, *potsherds* offers a poetic description of a crocodile-like creature whose underside contains sharp and jagged overlaid scales that function like armor. Verse 32's note that *the deep had white hair* refers to the great white churning of the sea caused by the beast; it represents chaos (Habel 573).

> **Threshing Sledges**
> *A threshing sledge was a tool farmers used to separate grain from the husk. It was made of planks of wood studded with sharp stones and dragged across kernels of barley or wheat.*

42:1–6 This section is Job's second response to the divine speech, and it closes the poetic section of the book. Job acknowledges his error in questioning God and speaking rashly. He is happy to have had a direct encounter with God and repents. Verse 5 indicates that the fact that God had personally appeared before Job seems to have been the most comforting thing for Job, even though God never actually answers his many questions.

EPILOGUE · 42:7–17

The epilogue proper begins with verse 7. Yahweh condemns the three friends for their rigid explanations of Job's suffering in terms of the doctrine of retribution. They are told to go and make offerings and have Job pray for them. In verse 8, the number *seven* is the number of completion and order for the Jews.

Yahweh's announcement *You have not spoken of me what is right* indicates that the three friends were wrong to insist rigidly on the doctrine of retribution as an explanation of Job's suffering. Job, however, was wrong, too, in that his frustration is evidence that he still assumed the doctrine in that he connected his suffering with God punishing him.

As the story reaches its conclusion, God restores to Job twofold his former wealth and family. Job begins life anew with new children, who do not replace the old ones but make room for a meaningful life for him. Quite out of character for biblical stories, we learn the names of his daughters but not his sons. He gives these girls unusual names. *Jemimah* means "dove"; *Keziah* means "cinnamon" or the similar spice, "cassia"; *Keren-happuch* means "horn of eyeshadow" or "mascara palette" (Seow 773). Horns were used as containers for cosmetics. It was unusual for women to inherit unless no sons were born (see Num 27:8), but Job's story must end in an unusual way.

THEOLOGICAL REFLECTIONS

Job raises the question of indifferent righteousness, which should be of great significance for Christians today. It raises the question of why we serve God. Do we do it because of who God is and in gratitude for what Jesus Christ did for our sins? Or do we primarily do it because we anxiously await the reward of heaven? What if there were not a heaven? Would we still serve God and Christ? No doubt the New Testament speaks of reward and punishment, but there seems to be a higher standard presented, as well. Paul sometimes resorts to divine sanction (fear of punishment) to persuade his audience, but he prefers to remind his readers with rational arguments versus scare tactics (Hays 39–41). He argues that living immorally does not reflect the change that has been wrought in them through Jesus Christ. It does not reflect their change in allegiance to Christ rather than to sin (see Hays 36–39). Perhaps we too should listen to Job and go beyond turning Christianity into a type of legalism, where we only obey for future reward. A more mature relationship with God is motivated more by love than fear or ulterior motives.

Another benefit of the book is its demonstration that protest is appropriate for Christians, within limits. The author has provided a model of piety (see Boström 57–72) for his readers to show them how to live their lives in the midst of such disturbing data. The encapsulation of the dialogue by the frame narrative again serves to create a balanced effect. The pious Job, who never questions God in the frame narrative, serves to soften the more aggressive protest piety of the dialogue. The Hebrew Bible contains both types of piety, especially in the Psalms. The sandwiching effect of the book serves to show that protest piety is acceptable at times, but ultimately the quietist piety of the frame narrative is dominant and that protest piety has its limits. Doubt and protest can be expressed in Jewish society only within the context of faith. So as modern readers, though we find in Job no real solutions for the problem of theodicy, we at least know how to act: piously fearing God and maintaining righteousness. Christians today should not be ashamed to vent their anger toward God, as long as they do not allow it to cause them to become bitter and eventually lose their faith. God expects a give-and-take relationship with human beings, a personal relationship. God expects prayer and the venting of emotions. Though God may not answer back directly as in the days of Job, we can still see providential answers in our daily lives.

FOR FURTHER STUDY

Manlio Simonetti and Marco Conti, *Job* (Downers Grove, Ill.: InterVarsity, 2006).

Stephen J. Vicchio, *The Image of the Biblical Job*: A History (3 vols.; Eugene, Ore.: Wipf & Stock, 2006).

WORKS CITED

Robert Alter, *The Art of Biblical Poetry* (New York: Basic Books, 1985).

Anonymous, "Naamathite," *Interpreters' Dictionary of the Bible* 3 (1962): 491.

Harrell Beck, "Shuah," *Interpreters' Dictionary of the Bible* 4 (1962): 341.

Joseph Blenkinsopp, *Wisdom and Law in the Old Testament*: The Ordering of Life in Israel and Early Judaism (Oxford: Oxford University Press, 1983).

Roger Boraas, "Seba, Sabeans," *Harper-Collins Bible Dictionary* (1996): 991.

Lennart Boström, "Patriarchal Model of Piety," in *Shall Not the Judge of All the Earth Do What Is Right?* (ed. D. Penchansky and P. Redditt; Winona Lake, Ind.: Eisenbrauns, 2000): 57–72.

David Clines, *Interested Parties*: The Ideology of Writers and Readers of the Hebrew Bible (Sheffield: Sheffield Academic Press, 1995).

———, *Job 1–20* (Dallas: Word, 1989).

James Crenshaw, "Job," *Anchor Bible Dictionary* 3 (1992): 858–68.

Edwin Good, "Job," in *Harper Collins Bible Commentary* (ed. James L. Mays; San Francisco: HarperSanFrancisco, 1988): 407–32.

Ronald Green, "Theodicy," *Encyclopedia of Religion* 14 (1987): 430–41.

Norman Habel, *The Book of Job* (Philadelphia: Westminster John Knox, 1985).

Mark Hamilton, "In the Shadow of Leviathan: Kingship in the Book of Job," *Restoration Quarterly* 45 (2003): 29–40.

Richard Hays, *The Moral Vision of the New Testament* (San Francisco: HarperSanFrancisco, 1996).

Alexander Heidel, *The Babylonian Genesis* (Chicago and London: University of Chicago Press, 1951).

William Holladay, *A Concise Hebrew and Aramaic Lexicon of the Old Testament* (Leiden: Brill; reprint Grand Rapids: Eerdmans, 1982).

Gerhard Lenski, *Power and Privilege*: A Theory of Social Stratification (New York: McGraw-Hill, 1966).

Victor Matthews and Don Benjamin, *Social World of Ancient Israel*: 1250–587 BCE (Peabody, Mass.: Hendrickson, 1993).

Amihai Mazar, *Archaeology of the Land of the Bible*: 10,000–586 BCE. (New York: Doubleday, 1992).

Carol Newsom, "The Book of Job," in vol. 4 of *The New Interpreters Bible* (ed Leander Keck; Nashville: Abingdon, 1996): 319–637.

James Pritchard, ed., *Ancient Near Eastern Texts Related to the Old Testament* (3rd ed.; Princeton: Princeton University Press, 1969).

Cyril Rodd, *The Book of Job* (Philadelphia: Trinity, 1990).

Alexander Rofé, *Introduction to the Prophetic Literature* (trans. J. Seeligmann; Sheffield: Sheffield Academic Press, 1997).

Joel Rosenberg, "Firmament," *Harper-Collins Bible Dictionary* (1996): 309–10.

Brian Rosner, *Paul, Scripture & Ethics: A Study of 1 Corinthians 5–7* (Leiden: Brill, 1994).

H. H. Rowley, *The Book of Job* (Grand Rapids and London: Eerdmans and Marshall, Morgan & Scott, 1980).

Choon Leong Seow, "Job," in *The New Oxford Annotated Bible* (ed. Michael Coogan; Oxford: Oxford University Press, 2001): 726–74.

Terrence Tilley, *The Evils of Theodicy* (Georgetown, S.C.: Georgetown University Press; reprint Eugene, Ore.: Wipf and Stock, 2000).

James Weinstein, "Uz," *Harper-Collins Bible Dictionary* (1996): 1108.

Psalms

Rick R. Marrs

CHAPTER CONTENTS

Contexts 445

Commentary & Theological Reflections 448
- Book 1 · Psalms 1–41 448
- Book 2 · Psalms 42–72 465
- Book 3 · Psalms 73–89 476
- Book 4 · Psalms 90–106 483
- Book 5 · Psalms 107–150 490

For Further Study 504

Works Cited 504

MAPS, TABLES, & FEATURES

The Language of Poetry 445
"Gods" or "Rulers"? 471

The book of Psalms has challenged and nourished the faith of God's people throughout the centuries, both in public worship and private devotion. It provides profound glimpses into the character of God and offers language for worship. The Psalter, or biblical collection of Psalms, is unique in Scripture, containing not only God's word to humanity but also human words to God. As such, it provides a vocabulary for subsequent believers to utilize in public and private conversation with God.

CONTEXTS

The Psalter is ancient Israel's equivalent to a modern hymnbook. Although many modern readers of Scripture utilize the book of Psalms primarily as a rich resource for private devotion, the bulk of the psalms functioned originally in corporate worship. A quick perusal of most hymnbooks confirms that these ancient hymns have provided a treasure trove for later hymn writers. Just as modern hymnody speaks to a variety of occasions, so the psalms of ancient Israel give voice to the cry of despair that comes during suffering and tumultuous life experiences and the joyous exclamations of celebration that come during times of deliverance and well-being. The Psalter overflows with poignant imagery and gripping poetic language.

Like all lyrics, the language of the Psalter is poetry. Hebrew poetry is characterized by two features: meter and semantic parallelism (that is, saying the same thing twice in different words). Scholars continue to debate the details of Hebrew metrics. Virtually all Hebrew poetry occurs in two-line (bicolon) or three-line (tricolon) units. Earlier discussions of Hebrew parallelism relied heavily upon the taxonomy of Bishop Robert Lowth (*De sacra poesi Hebræorum*, 1753), who categorized parallel lines as synonymous, antithetic, or synthetic. Synonymous parallelism states the same thing twice (with semantic variation; see Pss 21:8; 22:16; 24:1–2; 27:3; 37:1; 59:1–2; 113:7). Antithetic parallelism states similar thoughts by stating the opposite (such as Pss 1:6; 20:8; 32:10; 34:10; 37:16, 21–22; 55:20–21; 68:6). In synthetic parallelism, the two lines are related, but the precise nature of the relationship varies (for example, intensification, furtherance, movement from abstract to concrete; see Pss 27:1; 29:1–2; 30:11; 36:11; 38:3, 13; 50:14; 51:7; 69:10–12).

The Language of Poetry

Poetry is characterized by the heightened use of language. We recognize that words can convey literal meaning as well as figurative meaning through elements such as simile, metaphor, personification, or irony. Such terms may baffle students in English classes, but in actual practice we all use figurative language from time to time. When we say, "he's a regular Einstein" to portray a bright student, or we describe a marine as a "lean, mean, fighting machine," we are using figurative language. While Einstein refers to a literal person named Albert Einstein, we also associate Einstein with genius. We relate the marine with the finely tuned operation of a machine even while knowing the marine is not literally a machine. Poetry relies on such figurative language to evoke an emotional response from the reader through associations. Thus, we should read poetry with an eye for the literal meaning and an ear for the figurative meanings.

Recent analyses of Hebrew poetry have revealed other forms of the relationship of parallel Hebrew lines. Hebrew poetry comes in parallel lines; the reader must determine the precise relationship between the two lines. Recognizing the repetitive nature of Hebrew poetry enables the interpreter to utilize clear lines to clarify obscure lines and to avoid unnecessarily finding unrelated meanings in parallel lines. Hebrew poetry manifests such poetic features as: *chiasmus* (stating matters in reverse order); *ellipsis* (creation of gaps); statements in the first line followed by a reason, question, or answer in the second line; "better than" statements; movement from the abstract to the concrete; *synecdoche* (interchange of a part and the whole); *merismus*; refrain; and *inclusio* (beginning and ending a section in the same way).

> **Imagery in Psalms**
> The poetry of the Psalms is rich with emotive language. Imagery abounds, often captured through simile or metaphor, hyperbole, personification, and apostrophe (address to a nonhuman object). The rhetoric flows with alliteration (repeated sounds) and onomatopoeia. The Psalter contains several acrostic poems.

Through an evaluation of the genre and rhetorical features of the psalm, the reader can often determine the social setting of the psalm and its original purpose. The interpreter can only very rarely determine a specific historical setting for a psalm (see the later discussion on the headings of the psalms). However, rather than this limitation resulting in a lessening of a psalm's use, it actually allows a greater use of the psalm for later listeners. The psalms speak to typical situations, such as illness and life-threatening disease, abuse by enemies, defeat by foreign powers, slander, guilt and the need for forgiveness, thanksgiving for blessings both individual and communal, and future hope. The most common types of psalms are laments, songs of thanksgiving, hymns, penitential psalms, royal psalms, and psalms of enthronement, Zion, and wisdom.

The lament (or complaint) psalm is the most prevalent type in the Psalter. It can derive from an individual or a community. The most common backdrop for the individual lament is the loss of health or the experience of abuse by adversaries. Communal laments typically follow natural disaster or military defeat. Laments contain the following elements: address to God; lament (over the suffering, enemies, or against God); profession of innocence; petition and a vow of praise. Contrary to popular opinion, laments are generated not by the faithless, but by those faithful who cannot align their faith with their present experience. Convinced that God is faithful, the lamenter cries out to God to address the present situation. Lament use stark language, for the one crying to God is desperately attempting to find God's healing and delivering presence in the midst of life-threatening circumstances. Because of this, some scholars prefer the designation "psalm of trust" (confidence) for these texts. In contrast to Mesopotamian laments, virtually all the laments in the Psalter end with expressions of confidence.

The song of thanksgiving is largely an answered lament. Appropriately, the vow to praise that concludes most laments moves to the beginning of this psalm. These psalms thank God for intervening. Like the lament, songs of thanksgiving can be individual or communal.

In contrast to the song of thanksgiving, the hymn praises God in more general terms; the praise is descriptive. Hymns typically begin with imperative calls to praise that are quickly followed by reasons for offering the praise. Hymns address God's majesty as creator and lord of history. They speak eloquently of God's awesome acts of deliverance in the lives of people.

Several psalm categories derive from the content of the psalm (rather than more formal characteristics). Thus a penitential psalm presumes the presence of sin and guilt; forgiveness is requested (in contrast to a lament that professes innocence). A royal psalm centers about the king and his welfare. The king in ancient Israel was central not only to political life, but also to religious life. An enthronement psalm also speaks of kingship, but the king is heavenly (Yahweh), not earthly. These psalms celebrate Yahweh's royal rule over the universe and its earthly inhabitants. As king, Yahweh judges his world. A Zion psalm focuses upon Jerusalem and praises it as Yahweh's city. In Jerusalem, Yahweh's royal rule shines brightest; the Lord's people dwell secure in that city, for there Yahweh has chosen to dwell. A didactic or wisdom psalm teaches a lesson or provides reflection. Worship not only provides opportunities for praise and petition, but also for reflection and instruction. Through these psalms, Israel reminded itself of God's will and way in the world.

STRUCTURE & MESSAGE

The reader of a particular psalm must determine the meaning of that psalm by the contents rather than the appended heading. The superscriptions were attached later to the psalms, providing helpful insights into how a particular psalm was understood and used by a later (but still ancient) worshiping community (but not necessarily providing an accurate reflection of its original intention or use). That the psalm headings were later additions is confirmed by the substantially different headings that appear in the Septuagint, Syriac translation, and Targums. Psalm headings are of three basic types: those that provide a historical context; those that connect a psalm to a particular person; and those that designate the type of psalm, its liturgical use, or musical features.

> **Targums**
> Ancient Aramaic translations and running commentary on the Bible, Targums were a sort of amplified Bible, and they served Jews who read little or no Hebrew and needed explanation of the biblical text.

Thirteen psalms carry headings that allude to events in David's life, ranging from his flight from Saul (for example, Pss 7; 43; 52; 56; 57; 59; 142) to his adultery with Bathsheba (Ps 51). Sometimes a psalm heading provides information not found in the corresponding narrative account (for example, Psalm 7 mentions an unknown Cush of Benjamin) or information in tension with a narrative account (for example, Ps 34 mentions Abimelech, where 1 Sam 21:10–15 has Achish).

The most common heading links a psalm with a biblical person: David · 74 psalms (the Septuagint adds nine more); the sons of Korah · 12 psalms (see 2 Chron 20:19); Asaph · 12 psalms (see 1 Chron 6:35; 25:1–2); Solomon · 2 psalms; Moses · 1 psalm; Heman · 1 psalm; Ethan · 1 psalm; and Jeduthun · 3 psalms. While the superscriptions intend often to identify the author of the psalm, such is not the case in every situation (particularly with famous persons such as David, Solomon, and Moses). The Hebraic construction, "a psalm *le-David*," may equally be translated "to David" or "for David." That is, although David may have written several psalms (see 1 Sam 16:16–18; 2 Sam 1:17–27), several of the Davidic psalms may have been penned in his honor or for a royal collection of psalms bearing his name. Support for this interpretation derives not only from the grammatical construction of the heading but from the fact that the various psalms often use language forms dating long after the Davidic era.

Several psalms provide information relating to the musical execution of a psalm. Some headings provide information about the nature of the psalm: *tehillah* [praise]; *shir* [song]; *mizmor* [perhaps a song with accompaniment]; *maskil* [didactic song]; *miktam* [perhaps a psalm inscribed on a stele or stone monument]; and *shiggayon* [lament]. Some psalms provide musical information, listing the musical instrument to be used in accompaniment (for example, the harp) or providing the title of a popular melody to use (for example, "Do Not Destroy"; "Hind of the Dawn"). Several psalms carry the notation, "for the choirmaster." The obscure term *selah* appears seventy-one times, possibly demarcating a pause or musical interlude.

Several smaller collections of psalms comprise the Psalter. Like Proverbs, the Psalter shows evidence of a long and complex editorial history. Smaller collections of psalms survive in the Psalter, as we see from the presence of doublets and duplicate psalms within and outside the Psalter (for example, Psalm 14 and Psalm 53; Psalm 22 and 2 Sam 22), notations such as Psalm 72:20, "the prayers of David, son of Jesse, are ended" (though psalms with a Davidic heading appear in later psalms), and collections such as the "Egyptian *Hallel*" (Pss 113–118), the Songs of Ascents (Pss 120–134), and the "Elohistic Psalter" (Pss 42–83, where *Elohim* dominates as the preferred designation for God).

The obvious arrangement of the Psalter appears in its subdivision into five books: Psalms 1–41; 42–72; 73–89; 90–106; 107–150. Each book concludes with a doxology; in Book Five, Psalm 150 functions as the doxological conclusion (arguably for the whole Psalter).

While the Psalter seems to reflect a purposeful editorial arrangement, much work remains to determine that purpose in specific sections. In general, laments dominate the beginning of the Psalter, giving way to hymns and songs of praise toward the end. The bulk of the psalms attributed to David appear in the first half of the book. Psalm 1 provides an introduction to the entire collection, inviting worshipers to meditate on God's instruction (torah) day and night. Psalm 119, another torah psalm, concludes this large section, immediately preceding the small collection of the Songs of Ascents (Pss 120–134). Royal psalms conclude books Two (Ps 72) and Three (Ps 89). Just as the torah psalms (Pss 1 and 119) may balance each other, so the royal psalms (Pss 2 and 110) show striking similarities. The bulk of the psalms celebrating Yahweh's kingship appear together (Pss 93; 95–99). Although each psalm must be read in its own light, it is also often productive and illuminating to read the surrounding psalms to hear linguistic and thematic links.

The psalms provide a rich repository for theological reflection and spiritual nourishment. Although language addressed to God predominates over language from God, the language provides wonderful insights into the nature of God's relationship with creation, particularly humankind. The Psalter reveals the character of God both through God's names and the events it attributes to God.

In the Old Testament, a person's name captures his or her essence and identity. For ancient Israel, the pivotal question is not "does God exist," but "who is this God we worship?" Through various names, God is revealed as the majestic creator of the universe [*El*], the Almighty [*El Shaddai*], the Most High [*El Elyon*], and the Lord of the heavenly armies [*Yahweh Sebaoth*]. God is the one who "makes things happen" [*Yahweh*], both in creation and in history. Through such various labels, the psalmists affirm Yahweh's power ("Rock") and protection ("Shelter"). In the Psalter, Yahweh's royal status dominates ("King, Judge, Shepherd").

God is also revealed through actions in creation and in the history of his people Israel. The expanse and intricacy of the universe reflects the majesty and grandeur of its creator. Appropriately, all creation joins the chorus of praise to the one who establishes and sustains everything. Creation vibrates with praise and celebration. Similarly, history reveals the character and purposes of God. In worship, numerous psalms recount the mighty acts of God in dealing with the people. However, the psalmists never recount history for history's sake. Rather, the rehearsing of history functions to provide encouragement, chastisement, or warning. God's actions in history reflect the essence of God's character as the faithful lover who keeps promises. This monarch who reigns supreme over the universe is also involved in the daily routines of Israel.

The Psalter provides contemporary worshipers an invaluable liturgical and devotional resource. The language of prayer and worship comes primarily in two forms – petition and praise. The Psalter teems with vocabulary for both. One genius of these psalms is their ability to give voice to sufferers in the midst of tragedy and turmoil and to provide vocabulary for those experiencing the salvation and blessings of an all-merciful God. Throughout history, these ancient psalms declared the anxieties and hopes of God's people and offered compassionate promises from the majestic Lord of all. Even the royal psalms experienced transformation after the fall of the kingdom. These songs celebrating Yahweh's original choice of David became resources for messianic hope, for God's faithful followers knew this faithful and loving God would not end their story with loss. Modern worshipers read these ancient royal hymns ultimately through the lens of God's mighty act in Jesus Christ. The Psalter powerfully reminds its readers that worship is nothing less than coming into the presence of the King of the universe to express gratitude, to offer praise, to celebrate the attributes of this Lord who chooses to shepherd subjects with grace and compassion, and to realign themselves to the will and way of this majestic Lord who stands with them and for them.

COMMENTARY & THEOLOGICAL REFLECTIONS
BOOK 1 · PSALMS 1–41
Psalm 1

This wisdom poem contrasts the lives of the righteous and wicked. The psalmist opens with a beatitude that speaks to the nature of two ways of living, following with metaphors that capture the essence of those

> **Numbering the Psalms**
> *Throughout this commentary, verse numbers are those in the English Bible. Hebrew verse numbers are often one digit higher.*

two manners of life in their positive and negative dimensions. The psalm divides into three sections: verses 1–3 (the way of the righteous); verses 4–5 (the way of the wicked); and verse 6 (a final contrast).

1 The *blessed* are those whose conduct and character receive God's commendation and benefits (compare Matt 5:3–10). The psalmist first states the activity of the righteous negatively (*walk, stand, sit*), then positively (*meditates*). **2** *The law of the Lord* refers to God's torah (instruction) that, like that of a parent to a child, manifests the care and concern of the parent and intends protection, security, and blessing (see Deut

4:5–8; 6:20–25). **3** The *tree* metaphor demonstrates that blessing is not a *reward* for a righteous life, but a result. The tree produces fruit because it stands near a source of inexhaustible nourishment (Jer 17:7–8). **4** In contrast to the stable and productive tree, the *chaff* is insubstantial and rootless. **5** The *judgment* reference is not to final judgment nor to the legal court system, but to the communal assembly of the Lord's followers. Cut off from the assembly, the wicked are denied the blessings of such communion.

Theological Reflection · This psalm introduces the Psalter, ably declaring that those who make these psalms the focus of their lives will experience blessings from Yahweh. True to the spirit of the Torah, the psalmist acknowledges the delight that comes from meditating upon God's ways and will and the proper conduct that results from such reflection upon God. Faithful living blesses not only the righteous but those who live in their presence. This psalm provides a model for faithful piety; humans either follow God's torah or create their own!

Psalm 2

This royal psalm (compare Pss 18; 20; 21; 45; 72; 89; 101; 110; 132) likely presents the liturgical elements of a coronation ceremony (see 2 Sam 7:14; Isa 9:6–7; Pss 89:27–28; 110:3). Royal transitions in power provide opportunities for exploitation. The surrounding nations are plotting to take advantage of God's people during this transition to a new ruler. However, the psalmist presents the scene through the eyes of God. The Lord laughs at the schemes of the nations, having already decreed promises. God will not fail Israel. The psalm divides into four sections: verses 1–3 (the nations plot); verses 4–6 (God reacts); verses 7–9 (the king recites the royal promises); and verses 10–12 (the nations are warned).

1 *Why* expresses surprise more than anxiety. Theologically, a revolt against God's people is a revolt against Yahweh. **2** The *anointed one* [Hebrew *mashiach*, "Messiah"] is the legitimately appointed king. Typically, a prophet consecrates the new king with a sacred horn of oil. **4–6** The scene shifts from the earthly arena to the heavenly courts. **6** *Installed my King on Zion, my holy hill* summarizes the Davidic promise, the selection of the Davidic dynasty and the city of Jerusalem as Yahweh's dwelling. **7** *You are my Son; today I have become your Father* captures the essence of the relationship between Yahweh and the earthly royal representative. Since Yahweh designated the Davidic king "son," his coronation would be the day of his "adoption" (compare Pss 72:1; 89:3–4, 26). **8** See Deuteronomy 32:8–9. **10–12** A plausible reading of these verses understands the king here applying the divine decree of verses 7–9 to rebellious subjects. Several of the lines of these verses are textually uncertain and unclear.

> **"Kiss the Son..."**
> While some translations read "kiss the son," others read "kiss his feet" (*a gesture of political obedience; see Ps 72:9; Isa 49:23; Mic 7:17; also see the Black Obelisk of Shalmaneser III that depicts the Judean king kissing the Assyrian king's feet*).

Theological Reflection · This psalm may link with Psalm 1 to provide a second introduction to the Psalter. The two psalms exhibit linguistic links. Psalm 1 addresses how the individual chooses the right path in life in the midst of wicked surroundings, while Psalm 2 addresses how the community lives faithfully in the midst of the surrounding nations. Although the immediate circumstances may seem threatening, the psalmist calls God's people to see historical circumstances through the eyes of the all-powerful and always faithful God. Like the other royal psalms, this psalm provided the early church powerful language to articulate God's ultimate act of fidelity and commitment to the promise to David: the entrance and enthronement of Jesus into the world.

Psalm 3

This individual lament alternates between desperate cries for deliverance and strong affirmations of confidence in Yahweh. This is the first psalm that begins with a superscription; only Psalms 1–2, 10, and 33 lack the heading *of David* in Book One. The psalm falls naturally into three sections: verses 1–2 (a desperate cry to the Lord acknowledging the taunt of the enemies); verses 3–6 (an assertion of confidence in the Lord's power to deliver); and verses 7–8 (a call to Yahweh to effect deliverance).

1 *How many...* the wicked are typically expressed in the plural in the Psalms and Wisdom literature; the righteous are usually expressed in the singular. **2** The wicked boast that *God will not deliver him*, perhaps because of divine inability or the presumed sin of the psalmist.

3 The psalmist stridently affirms his faith in God his protector three times: *shield; you bestow glory on* *me and lift up my head.* **5** *I lie down and sleep* affirms confidence in Yahweh's ability to protect against any nocturnal attacks.

7 *Arise*: the psalmist knows his deliverance is only awaiting divine attention. Since the enemies have spoken evil of the psalmist, the psalmist asks God to incapacitate their speech organs (*strike all my enemies on the jaw, break the teeth of the wicked*). Alternately, the imagery may envision the destruction of a wild animal (see Ps 58:6; Job 29:17). **8** The final blessing (*may your blessing be on your people*) may suggest a royal identity for the psalmist.

Theological Reflection · Though the enemies appear daunting, the psalmist's faith remains resolute, for he rests confident that the Lord's willingness and ability to deliver can overcome any predicament. Because of his faith in the Lord, the psalmist defines himself and his tenuous situation less by his immediate situation and more by his relationship with Yahweh.

Psalm 4

The motif of trust dominates this individual lament. Though in dire circumstances, the psalmist remains resolute in his conviction that God will once again intervene and deliver him. The psalm divides into three sections: verse 1 (appeal to God); verses 2–5 (outcry against the adversaries); and verses 6–8 (affirmation of trust in the Lord).

2 The interrogative *how long* is a typical lament marker. The expression *O men* (literally "sons of man") connotes either mortality or social influence. In the ancient Near East, honor (NIV: *glory*) and *shame* were driving forces in social behavior. The psalmist contrasts his commitment to the Lord with the delusional worship of *false gods* (literally, "seek falsehood"). **3** The psalmist identifies himself as *godly*, or faithful. The psalmist rests his plea on the faithfulness of his relationship with God. **4–5** The psalmist is either exhorting his adversaries to cease worshiping false gods and turn to the right worship of the true Lord, or he is exhorting his companions who are wavering in their devotion to the Lord because of the severe treatment of the psalmist by his enemies.

6 *Let the light of your face shine upon us, O Lord*: Compare the Aaronic blessing in Numbers 6:25–26. **7–8** The psalm ends with an affirmation of serene trust – the psalmist sleeps peacefully, knowing that his Lord allows him to *dwell in safety*.

> **Answer & Call**
> The word pair answer/call occurs frequently throughout the Psalter. The psalmist appeals to his righteous God (*that is, the God who does what is right and just*). The psalmist portrays his distress through spatial imagery: he is in *a narrow spot and seeks spaciousness* (compare Pss 18:7, 20; 118:5; so Kselman and Barré 527).

> **Enemies**
> In Psalms, problems of all sorts come from the "enemies," whether real or metaphorical. Older scholars (Mowinckel) thought of these enemies as sorcerers, but usually the description applies more broadly.

Theological Reflection · This psalm affirms the confidence that results when trust in the Lord's ability to deliver surpasses the immediate distress caused by those who mock God's faithful and engage in idol worship.

Psalm 5

This individual lament alternates between appeals to God to hear the prayer of the faithful (who can then joyously stand in God's presence in the temple), and the devastation wrought by the wicked and their devious ways. The psalmist calls upon God to hear his prayer and grant him a presence in the temple and to punish the evildoers who rebel against God. The psalm divides into five sections: verses 1–3 (appeal for a hearing); verses 4–6 (an affirmation of God's just ways); verses 7–8 (a pledge to worship God in the temple); verses 9–10 (a call to God to declare the deceitful wicked guilty); and verses 11–12 (a call to God to provide refuge and blessing to the righteous).

1–3 *In the morning* is a common motif in the Old Testament (Pss 46:5; 59:16; 90:14; 143:8; Lam 3:22–23). **4–6** In contrast to the psalmist, who longs for the presence of the Lord, the wicked can neither *dwell* nor *stand* in the Lord's *presence* (compare Pss 15; 24; 26:4–5). The wicked are characterized by deceit (*tell lies*) and violence (*bloodthirsty*). **7–8** The psalmist *in reverence…bow*(s) *down* and seeks God's guidance. **9–10** From the *mouth, heart, throat*, and *tongue* of the evildoers issue deception and destruction. Outwardly, they speak flattery, while inwardly they plot destruction (Clifford 58). **11–12** In contrast to the evildoers whose speech organs spew forth deceit, the speech of the righteous issues forth in praise (*joy, rejoice*). Though the evildoers may intend harm against the righteous, the latter are secure, since *you surround them with your favor as a shield*.

Theological Reflection · This psalm powerfully contrasts the ardent desires of the righteous to dwell securely in God's presence (in the temple) with the blatant disregard for God by the wicked (reflected in their disdain for truth-telling and integrity). The psalmist contrasts the *many sins* (verse 10) with God's *great mercy* (verse 7). The psalmist knows he will not receive a fair hearing from the wicked, and so he relies solely upon Yahweh for his security.

Psalm 6

This individual lament belongs to the seven penitential psalms (so labeled by the early church; also Pss 32; 38; 51; 102; 130; 143). The psalmist leaves his "sin" unspecified; he is more focused on its debilitating effects on his life. The psalm divides into four sections: verses 1–3 (lament and petition); verses 4–5 (appeal); verses 6–7 (lament); and verses 8–10 (thanksgiving and trust).

> **Divine Significance of the Body**
> *Physical distress and serious illness (verses 1–3) were regularly considered the result of divine disfavor. My bones ... my soul is a Hebraic way of saying "I." Ancient Hebrews did not compartmentalize themselves into body, soul, and spirit, but considered themselves a unity.*

4–5 The psalmist appeals to God not on the basis of merit but on the basis of God's character (*unfailing love*) and the human inability to offer praise when dead (*who praises you from the grave*?). The absence of God and the lack of human praise (see Pss 30:9; 88:10–12; 115:17; Isa 38:18) characterize Sheol, the realm of the dead. **6–7** Constant weeping produces physical exhaustion and deteriorating eyesight. As so often in Psalms, internal distress leads to physical illness and vice versa. Israel had a keen appreciation of the bodily dimension of spirituality. **8–10** *All you who do evil* "are not the cause of the psalmist's affliction; rather, they are its exploiters and exacerbators" (Mays 61). The sudden mood shift puzzles scholars; some suggest the sufferer receives a salvation oracle between verses 7 and 8 (akin to that Eli offered Hannah); others simply highlight the transforming power that worship generates.

> **Shubah & Surah**
> *Through wordplay, the psalmist invokes God to* turn *[Hebrew* shubah*] ... and deliver* him, *while simultaneously asking God to* turn away *[Hebrew* surah*] his enemies.*

Theological Reflection · Profound faith often is articulated through simple piety. Though apparently mortally ill, the psalmist focuses his energies upon God's *unfailing love* and faithful willingness to hear the prayers of his followers. This psalm presents the theological dynamics of illness.

Psalm 7

This individual lament focuses upon the innocence of the psalmist in the face of violence. The psalmist places his own situation in a global context (verses 7–8) and asks God to bring upon the evildoers the harm they intend to do to him. The psalm divides into five sections: verses 1–2 (an appeal for deliverance); verses 3–5 (an assertion of innocence); verses 6–9 (a strident call for divine justice); verses 10–13 (an expression of confidence in God's protection); and verses 14–17 (a thanksgiving for God's "poetic justice"). The psalmist envisions a finale in which the wicked suffer destruction from their own weapons.

1–2 The phrase *tear me like a lion* (means literally, "tear my throat" see Pss 50:22; 22:13). **3–5** *If I have done evil to him who is at peace with me* echoes ancient Near Eastern treaties, where vassals swear loyalty to the suzerain (Kselman and Barré 528). The psalmist does not claim moral perfection, but rather innocence in these particular matters. **6–9** *Arise ... rise up*: Just as a time element often characterizes the lament ("how long"), so the lamenter often calls upon God to act swiftly on the matter at hand (see Ps 44:23–24; for a contrast, Ps 121:4). The psalmist pleads for retribution rather than forgiveness. He places his personal struggle against his foes within a larger context of world justice, and boldly affirms his own *righteousness* and *integrity* to the *righteous God, who searches minds and hearts* (see Jer 11:20). **10–13** The subject of the verbs beginning in verse 12 is disputed. Several scholars consider God the subject (so NIV); others consider the enemies the subject (so NJPS; REB); some consider the wicked the initial subject (verse 12a) against whom God prepares himself for battle (verse 12b–13) (so NRSV). **14–17** The psalmist seeks poetic justice against his enemies (see Pss 9:15; 35:8; 57:6; Prov 26:27; 28:10; compare 1 Kgs 8:31–32).

Theological Reflection · Though pursued by vicious and voracious enemies, the psalmist relies exclusively upon his conviction that the just God of the universe knows everything and will rule decisively in his favor.

Psalm 8

This first hymn of praise in the Psalter extols the creative majesty of God, manifested both in the grandeur of the universe and in the intricate detail of the creation of humanity. The psalmist traffics in contrasts: the expansive sky with tiny infants; the divine majesty with human insignificance; the status of humanity with the rest of creation. The psalm divides into two sections: verses 1–2 (praise for Yahweh's glory); and verses 3–9 (the place of humanity in God's creation).

1 *O Lord, our Lord*: this refrain begins and ends the psalm and provides the appropriate context from which to read the intervening reflection on humanity. **2** While this verse is textually difficult, the main point seems clear. God's invincible power makes it possible to choose the weakest and most vulnerable (*children and infants*) for protection against the *enemies*. **5** *Heavenly beings*: literally, "gods" (see Ps 7:8; 1 Kgs 22:19; Job 1:6). Later interpreters understood here a reference to angels.

> **The "Son of Man"**
> *The expression* son of man *(Ps 8:4), in parallelism with* man, *is simply a Hebraic way of expressing humanity (rather than a reference to Jesus).*

Theological Reflection · This psalm provides the poetic counterpart to Genesis 1; it is a symphonic celebration of creation. In worship, the community of faith marvels at the incomprehensible choice that God has made to elevate humans to such lofty status – they truly are royal creatures (*crowned with glory and honor*). Such lofty status carries within it the dangerous temptation for human pride and arrogance; because of this, the psalmist provides also the antidote to potential egocentrism – all of life begins and ends with the exclamation *O Lord, our Lord, how majestic is your name in all the earth*! Thus we find that "human power is always bounded and surrounded by divine praise. *Doxology* gives *dominion* its context and legitimacy" (Brueggemann 37–38).

Psalms 9–10

These psalms probably originally comprised a single psalm (so the Septuagint and a few Hebrew manuscripts). Psalm 10 has no superscription (the only psalm lacking a heading in Pss 3–41). The two psalms form an acrostic (with a few letters missing due to textual corruption). Though the order of the psalms is somewhat rare (thanksgiving followed by lament), it is not unique to the Psalter (see Pss 44; 89). The psalms shift quickly back and forth between despair at the arrogance of the wicked and confident assertions of trust in divine justice. The psalmist seeks the defeat of his enemies (who are God's enemies). The two psalms divide into five sections: 9:1–12 (thanksgiving for past deliverance); 9:13–20 (lament); 10:1–11 (lament); 10:12–15 (a plea for vindication); and 10:16–18 (an affirmation of God). The psalmist struggles to reconcile his conviction in God's justice and defense of the powerless with the current conditions of rampant oppression by the powerful.

> **Acrostic Psalms**
> *Several psalms use an acrostic pattern as an organizing technique. Successive verses start with successive letters of the Hebrew alphabet. (These acrostics, unlike English examples, do not spell out words.) Simple examples are Psalms 111 and 112. Lamentations 1–4 are acrostic psalms. The most elaborate is Psalm 119, with each verse in each eight-verse cluster starting with the same letter of the alphabet.*

9:1–2 The psalm begins with a promise to extol God's mighty saving acts. **3–6** Part of the psalmist's anguish is that God's past acts of deliverance are not forthcoming in the present. **7–10** God, as king and judge, impacts directly the lives of the powerless who have no other recourse for aid. **11–12** The psalmist calls the oppressed to join him in song (a return to verses 1–2). **13–14** The psalmist quickly shifts from praise to ardent appeal to God for deliverance, so that praise may follow. He desperately desires a transfer from *the gates of death* to the *gates of the Daughter of Zion* (better, "Daughter Zion") so that he might offer his praise. *Gates* stand for the entire cities or realms of good and evil. **15–16** Like Psalm 7, Psalms 9–10 envision God's justice bringing on the oppressors the suffering they intend for the afflicted. **19–20** The stakes are high, for if the actions of the oppressors remain unaddressed, the nations may conclude that these mere mortals are invincible.

10:1 Since God is just, oppression can only occur when God is absent or aloof. **3–11** These verses offer a poignant depiction of the disastrous social effects of arrogance; the wicked act as a law unto themselves. Having affirmed that God does not forget or ignore the plight of the afflicted (9:12, 18), the psalmist now graphically portrays the misbehavior of those who live convinced that God neither cares nor remembers his commitments to the poor (10:11). **12–15** *Arise*: see Psalm 7:6. **16–18** Yahweh as king functions as defender and vindicator of the helpless.

Theological Reflection · Psalms 9–10 reflect the struggle of a community engulfed in social oppression. The faithful struggle to balance their faith in God's will to act on their behalf with the seeming delay of that action. The repeated use of temporal terms (*forever and ever, always, never*) reflects this tension. The psalmist lives with "the conviction that what he is now experiencing cannot be the last word" (Davidson 46). The psalmist ardently longs for the oppressors to experience the oppression they exact upon the poor and helpless.

Psalm 11

This psalm of trust contrasts the advice given the psalmist, who is in dire straits, with his resolute rejoinder to rely upon God. The psalmist rejects the advice to flee the situation; he stands firmly, trusting in God to rectify the current grievances. The psalm divides into two sections: verses 1–3 (advice to flee the present difficulties); and verses 4–7 (response to remain and wait for God's saving presence).

1–3 Scholars dispute the extent of the advice to the psalmist. Some consider the advice only verse 1b; others extend the advice through verses 2–3 (see Davidson 47; Clifford 76). Clearly, the psalmist rejects the despondent perspective offered by his advisor(s), namely, that one is helpless against the onslaught of the wicked. The wicked are depicted as snipers who *shoot from the shadows*. Though the enemies may have superior weaponry, the psalmist has the Lord. *When the foundations are being destroyed* may suggest concretely the temple foundations (see Pss 48:4; 76:3–6) or more generally social order (Mays 75). *What can the righteous do* more likely refers to a human than to God. **4–7** In the context, the psalmist likely envisions experiencing the presence of God in the temple, which represents heaven on earth. Whereas God *observes* and *his eyes examine* all humanity, only the *upright men will see his face* (a clear indicator of divine favor, Num 6:24–26). On *fiery coals … burning sulfur*, see Genesis 19:24.

> **"Flee like a bird …"**
> The imagery *flee like a bird* suggests less a reasoned retreat and more a panic-stricken (and thoughtless) flight (see Prov 27:8; Isa 16:2).

Theological Reflection · This psalm is a clear reminder that God gives the faithful courage. They need not react in panic to difficult circumstances; God enables them to choose whether they will flee in fear or stand fast in faith (Clifford 80). Psalm 11 simply yet eloquently demonstrates what *in the Lord I take refuge* looks like in daily life.

Psalm 12

This individual lament contrasts the speech of the wicked with Yahweh's speech. The speech of the wicked features deception and arrogance. They traffic in flattery and unapologetic self-reliance. In contrast, Yahweh's speech is pure and flawless. This psalm contains echoes of the Wisdom literature (see Prov 28:12, 28). The psalm divides neatly into three sections: verses 1–4 (an appeal to God to remove the destructive speech); verses 5–6 (Yahweh's promise of deliverance); and verses 7–8 (a petition for protection from the wicked).

1–4 Deception and boastful self-absorption characterize this society (compare Mic 7:1–7). *Their flattering lips speak with deception* literally says, "with smooth lips with heart and a heart they speak" (that is, they are "double-minded" as Jas 3:1–12 would say). *We own our lips – who is our master* literally says, "our lips are with us" (a perversion of "the Lord is with us" [Mays 76]). **5–6** This is a salvation oracle, possibly delivered by a prophet or priest at the sanctuary. *Silver refined*: in contrast to the worthless and polluted speech of the wicked, Yahweh's promises are as precious and pure as refined silver (see Prov 2:4; 3:14; 8:10, 19; 10:20). **7–8** *You will keep us safe … protect us*: though NIV reads these imperfect Hebrew verbs as future tense, they are better read as a plea or command ("may you …") since the danger remains present. The psalm concludes with a proverbial comment.

> **Yahweh's Protection of the Weak**
> Ironically, the oppressed suffer at the hands of their oppressors because they are weak; however, it is this quality of helplessness that triggers Yahweh's move to protect them.

Theological Reflection · This psalm captures the devastating consequences that deceptive speech has upon a society. Though depressing, the psalmist relies upon the powerful counterbalance that Yahweh's speech on behalf of the needy brings.

Psalm 13

This individual lament epitomizes the lament genre in the Psalter, with its emphasis on timing (*how long*), loss of meaningful life in the presence of God (*hide your face*), abuse from enemies, and profound faith in God's *unfailing love* [Hebrew *chesed*]. The psalm divides into two sections: verses 1–2 (lament); and verses 3–6 (petition and expression of trust).

1–2 The absence of God (*forget me ... hide your face*) results in mental anguish, intensified by scorn from the psalmist's adversaries. To forget is to cease providing protection (Kselman and Barré 528). **3–6** The psalmist pleads with God for deliverance (*answer*), presumably from a debilitating illness (*or I will sleep in death*). The specific nature of the psalmist's troubles is unclear; however, he clearly understands his demise as a victory for his foes.

Theological Reflection · This psalm powerfully reflects the struggle between faith in God's promises of salvation and current circumstances that seemingly belie those promises. The psalmist refuses to reject the divine promises; rather, he ardently calls upon his Lord to recognize the stakes: God's failure to intervene is nothing less than a victory for the psalmist's foes.

Psalm 14

The genre of this psalm is disputed; it has wisdom, prophetic, and liturgical characteristics. The psalmist pictures the Lord of heaven looking down upon earth (compare Gen 11; 19) to see if anyone engages in right behavior. Though the scene is dismal, the psalmist remains convinced that the righteous will prevail, since *the Lord is their refuge*. This psalm occurs again in Psalm 53 (one of the "Elohistic" Psalms) with minor variations. The psalm consists of three sections: verses 1–3 (description of the fool); verses 4–6 (rebuke of the fool); verse 7 (prayer for deliverance).

1 *The fool* [Hebrew *nabal*] *says in his heart* envisions the person who completely misreads a situation and thus makes wrong assumptions (as in 2 Sam 15), particularly about God's sovereignty. The *heart* houses the essence of a person's character. **3** *There is no one who does good, not even one* offers a prophetic critique of the social character of his society rather than providing a comprehensive view of humankind (Mays 82; compare Mic 3:1–3; Rom 3:10–12). **5–6** These verses are difficult. The term *there* may be better translated "then" (see Pss 53:5; 66:6; 132:17). **7** The clause *when the Lord restores the fortunes of his people* appears as an expression of hope in exilic and postexilic literature (see Jer 30:18; Ezek 29:14; compare Ps 126:1).

Theological Reflection · Psalm 14 exhibits no interest in the theoretical dimensions of atheism. It solely concerns itself with the behavioral consequences. The morality of a community sinks to a dismal level when humans do not consider themselves accountable to God (Mays 81).

Psalm 15

Worshipers entering the temple precincts may have intoned this psalm to remind themselves that worship is essentially the offering of one's life to God. The psalm manifests both prophetic (compare Isa 1:12–17; Ezek 18:5–9; Mic 6:6–8) and wisdom influences. The psalm divides into three sections: verse 1 (question); verses 2–5b (answer); and verse 5c (concluding promise).

1 This question may have been asked by a presiding priest at the temple gate as worshipers entered. See also Psalm 24:3 for a similar situation. **2** *Blameless*: compare Deuteronomy 18:13; Psalm 101:2, 6. **3–5** The psalmist cites specific examples of misconduct.

> **Usury**
> *Interest rates in the ancient Near East were often set at astronomical rates, resulting in the endless impoverishment of the lower classes.*

Theological Reflection · This psalm (compare Ps 24) reminds readers of the inseparable connection between worship and ethics. Since worship is the offering of one's life to God, the ethical quality of the life offered matters. This psalm manifests no legalistic mentality that worship results in merit before God; rather, it simply yet compellingly reminds listeners that God truly cares about the moral character of Israel. Ethical introspection plays a vital role in meaningful worship. To accept God's steadfast love involves acceptance of the discipline that love calls forth (Davidson 57). Genuine preparation for worship reminds the worshiper of the need for worship (Craigie 153).

Psalm 16

This psalm of trust extols the joyous security, both present (verses 5–6) and future (verses 10–11) that

> **"The fool says in his heart ..."**
> There is no God *expresses a "practical atheism" that denies the engagement of God in the daily affairs of humans (see verse 4).*

results from sole allegiance to Yahweh (verse 2). The psalmist disavows other gods and their worshipers. The psalm divides into two major sections: verses 1–6 (a confession of faith in Yahweh alone); and verses 7–11 (a promise of praise and expression of confidence in Yahweh).

2–4 The NIV interprets these difficult verses as a profession linking the psalmist with other saints in the land who refuse to *run after other gods*. The psalmist stridently distances himself from the worship of foreign gods. **5** Compare Psalm 142:5. **6** The language is reminiscent of the tribal allotments in Joshua 13–21 (see Josh 18:8, 10; Ps 78:55). **10** *Grave* literally means, "pit." Both Peter and Paul utilize this verse in their preaching about Christ's resurrection (Acts 2:25–31; 13:35). *Your Holy One* is better rendered "your faithful one" [Hebrew *hasid*]. **11** *You have made known* is better translated "you (will) make known." The psalmist experiences the *path of life* in the presence of God in the temple.

> **The "Path of Life"**
> In the Wisdom literature, path of life *typically refers to proper conduct; here it may specifically intend the proper behavior of sole allegiance to Yahweh.*

Theological Reflection · This psalm celebrates the joy and contentment that come both in the present and in the future to one who chooses exclusive devotion to Yahweh (compare Ps 23:6). God offers life, not death.

Psalm 17

This individual lament graphically rehearses the innocence of the psalmist, the callousness of his enemies, and his ardent confidence in God to right current wrongs. Some scholars (unnecessarily) envision a night vigil in the temple. The psalmist confidently asserts his willingness to have his own integrity examined (verses 3–5), characterizing his treatment at the hands of his enemies as nothing less than a lion attack (verses 11–12). The psalmist concludes (verse 15) where he began (verses 1–2) through reiteration of key terms (*righteousness*; *see*; *face*). The psalm divides into 3 sections: verses 1–5 (petition for help rooted in the psalmist's innocence); verses 6–12 (petition for help from present enemies); and verses 13–15 (reiteration of petition and assertion of hope).

1–2 The psalmist emphasizes sight (*eyes see*), sound (*hear*, *give ear*), speech (*lips*, *mouth*), activity (*ways*, *steps*, *feet*, *right hand*), and integrity (*heart*). **3–5** Compare Psalm 1. **8** This is the center of the psalm. Two images coalesce: *the apple of your eye … shadow of your wing* (see Deut 32:10–12). The pupil was regarded as the most precious portion of the eye; God as a protective mother bird spreading her wing over her vulnerable young occurs elsewhere (Pss 36:7; 57:1; 61:4; 91:4; Ruth 2:12; Matt 23:37). **10–12** The psalmist first describes concretely the wickedness of his adversaries (verses 10–11); he then visually describes them as a rapacious predator (verse 12; see Pss 7:2; 10:9; 22:21). **14** Though the ancient manuscripts read its text differently, this verse seems to contrast the evildoers who think only of self-concern with the righteous, for whose children God provides a meaningful future (compare Luke 22:21). **15** Though often read as an implicit reference to future resurrection (*when I awake*), the meaning more likely reflects a confident assertion from the psalmist that God will protect him through the night and bring vindication on the morrow.

Theological Reflection · This psalm portrays the theological implications of suffering at the hands of adversaries. Nothing less than the integrity of the psalmist is at stake. The first half of the psalm highlights his or her integrity; the second half depicts the viciousness of the evildoers. The psalmist remains undaunted; his security lies in the middle (verse 8): he rests secure that he is the *apple of God's eye* and dwells beneath the *shadow of his wings*.

Psalm 18

This royal psalm of thanksgiving, found in a slightly different form in 2 Samuel 22, praises God for deliverance past and present. The psalm alternates between lyrical exclamations of the majesty of God and detailed recounting of royal victories through divine power. The psalm

> **Royal Psalms**
> *Psalms 2, 18, 20, 21, 45, 72, 89, 101, 110, 132, 144, and possibly others focus on the king and his political, military, and religious roles. These psalms probably came originally from the royal court, which lay near the temple in Jerusalem.*

divides into two major sections (verses 1–30, 31–50) with several subsections: verses 1–3 (introductory praise of God); verses 4–6 (deathly distress); verses 7–19 (theophany and deliverance); verses 20–30 (divine deliverance of the just); verses 31–45 (God empowers the king's victories); and verses 46–50 (concluding praise of God).

1–3 Eight epithets for God begin the psalm (*strength, rock, fortress, deliverer, rock, shield, horn of my salvation, stronghold*). *Rock* is a favorite image for God (Deut 32:4, 30–31, 37). The images are primarily military. **4–6** The psalmist portrays his near death experience graphically as a binding and dragging to the Underworld [*grave*; Hebrew *Sheol*]. *Temple*: God's heavenly abode. **7–15** The psalmist depicts God's deliverance with language that pictures God's arrival as divine warrior through spectacular (and often cataclysmic) natural and geological phenomena (for example, thunder, lightning, earthquake, tempest, torrential rain; compare Exod 19:16–20; Pss 29; 50:2–3; 68:7–8; 97:2–5; 144:5–8). **16** Deliverance is depicted as rescue from drowning (rather than release from entanglement). **20–24** *Righteousness*: the language is not self-righteous, but covenantal. Since the psalmist has remained faithful to God's demands, God has fulfilled his promises. **23** *Blameless* [translates the Hebrew *tamim*, which means coherent, reliable, or wholehearted, not "perfect"]. **28** *Lamp burning*: God dispels the darkness. **31–45** The psalmist emphasizes that his victories are solely due to the divine equipping he has received. These verses portray the effects of God's appearance on behalf of his king in battle (see Eph 6:10–17). **46–50** The psalmist concludes where he began. *Anointed* [literally translates *mashiach*, as in Ps 2:2].

> **Cherubim**
>
> The cherubim *are winged lions (or bulls) (see Gen 3:24; Exod 25:17–22; compare Isa 6:1–8). The imagery echoes God's decisive victory at Jezreel (see Judg 5).*

Theological Reflection · This royal psalm utilizes cosmic language to depict God's divine intervention and deliverance of his earthly king. Conflicts between nations transcend national interests. Theologically, they raise questions about covenantal loyalty (divine and human). This psalm celebrates Yahweh's willingness and power to deliver the king and his subjects when they live in fidelity to his ways and will.

Psalm 19

This hymn celebrates God's majesty, manifested first in his creation and second in his law. Creation declares its praise of God; the law reflects the glory of God. Both creation and the law proclaim God's wisdom. The psalm divides into three sections: verses 1–6 (creation offers its praise of God); verses 7–10 (the law reflects the glory of God); and verses 11–14 (a final plea acknowledging the need for forgiveness and protection).

1 God is called *El* in verses 1–6; in verses 7–14 he is called *Yahweh*. **2–4** The NIV translation is somewhat confusing. These verses state the paradox that God's inanimate creation declares his glory without speech; creation reflects God's divine grandeur and majesty through being what God created it to be (compare Rom 10:18). A supreme example of that glorious reflection is the sun, whose warmth and brilliance reaches everything. The psalmist pictures the movement of the sun across the sky as that of a royal bridegroom marching forth to meet his bride. **7–9** The psalmist uses six synonyms for the law (Ps 119 uses eight). The psalmist talks of the law's qualities (*perfect, trustworthy, right, radiant, pure, sure, righteous*),

> **The Torah**
>
> *God's law* [Hebrew Torah] *is quintessentially "instruction," and it is not burdensome. Rather, it brings wholeness and health to those who embrace it (Deut 4:1–8).*

its effects (*reviving the soul, making wise the simple, giving joy to the heart, giving light to the eyes, enduring forever*), and its value (*pure gold, honey*). **12–14** The psalmist concludes first with an acknowledgment that righteousness comes not through perfect obedience but through forgiveness (praying that God would forgive him of both unintentional and deliberate sins). He then prays that *the words of* [*his*] *mouth and meditation of* [*his*] *heart* will match the qualities possessed by God's law (verses 7–9).

Theological Reflection · Although some scholars consider this psalm to be composed of two originally independent poems, the final line, *my Rock and my Redeemer*, brings unity to the work, which views creation and law as twin manifestations of God's majesty. Both declare God's glory, the former through nonverbal communication, the latter through verbal tones. Just as the sun dominates the daytime sky, so God's instruction dominates human life. The psalmist comes seeking protection (*Rock*) and forgiveness (*Redeemer*). This psalm reminds the reader that worship involves both celebration (offering praise like creation) and obedience (heeding divine instruction).

Psalm 20

This royal psalm articulates first a prayer for the king and then a pledge of allegiance to celebrate the kingship of both Yahweh and his anointed. The psalm divides into two sections: verses 1–5 (prayer for the king) and verses 6–9 (profession of confidence). The setting may reflect the eve of battle (compare 2 Chron 20).

1–5 The fortunes of the king are crucial, for as the king goes, so goes the country. *Answer* is equivalent to *save* (verse 9). The *name of God* captures his essence. The king was responsible for maintaining the *sanctuary* (where God's name dwelt). **6** *Now I know* shifts from prayer to pledge. **7** For similar sentiments, see Isaiah 30:15–18; 31:1–3. **8** Note the contrast: *they are brought to their knees and fall*, but *we rise up and stand firm*.

Theological Reflection · Psalm 20 captures the essence of ancient Israelite theology: "salvation belongs to the Lord" (Mays 101; compares Isa 12; Rom 8:31). Israel needed constant reminding that its royal deliverer (the king) first needed deliverance himself by the ultimate Deliverer, and that dependence upon Yahweh always trumps military weaponry.

Psalm 21

This royal psalm of thanksgiving may mirror Psalm 20, with the first (20) being a prayer for the king's deliverance, and the second (21) praise for that deliverance (note the verbal links – 20:4/21:2; 20:6/21:9, 13; compare similar links with Ps 18). The psalm divides into three sections, with verse 7 functioning as midpoint: verses 1–6 (Yahweh's blesses the king); verse 7 (transition); and verses 8–13 (Yahweh commissions the king for victory).

1 *The king rejoices in your strength*: note the inclusio with verse 13. **3** *Blessing*: God's positive, though often nondramatic, presence in the lives of his people (note *joy of your presence* [verse 6]). The blessings God bestows upon his royal agent are *joy in victories*, *the desire of his heart* (that is, answered prayer), *crown of pure gold/glory/splendor/majesty, life/length of days*. **7** This verse provides the hinge of the psalm, looking back to the king in verses 1–6 and forward to Yahweh in verses 8–13. **9** The *fiery furnace* was a portable oven used for cooking. (For Yahweh's devouring fire, see Exod 24:17; Deut 9:3). **10** *Descendents* and

> **Inclusio**
> The practice of beginning and ending a text or section of text with the same or nearly the same words is known as inclusio.

posterity are Hebraic expressions that declare the removal of any future for the king's opponents.

Theological Reflection · Psalm 21 celebrates kingship as a divine gift and blessing to the people. The Lord tasks his anointed with protecting Israel and ruling justly so that the divine grandeur would shine forth (Clifford 119). To make sure the Lord's centrality is not forgotten, the psalm is wrapped in *O Lord, in your strength*.

Psalm 22

This individual lament captures the extremes experienced in suffering. The psalmist depicts both the despair and the hope that come during those most agonizing times. This prayer for help moves between petition and praise. Perhaps most notably, this psalm concludes with a lengthy hymnic section where one expects a succinct vow of praise. The psalm divides into three sections: verses 1–11 (the present distress contrasted with past mercy); verses 12–21 (a depiction of the enemies); and verses 22–31 (an invitation for all to join in praise of God).

1–11 The opening section contains two laments (verse 1–2, 6–8) and two assertions of confidence (verses 3–5, 9–10). **1** *My God, my God, why have you forsaken me* captures the heartrending tension between experience and faith that comes during suffering. The most painful suffering is the experience of divine absence. **3** Although unique, "enthroned on the praises of Israel" is preferable to the NIV rendering *you are the praise of Israel*. **4–5** Compare Psalm 44:1–3. **6** *Worm*: compare Job 25:6; Isaiah 41:14. **12–21** Two laments (verses 12–15, 16–18) are followed by a petition (verses 19–21 [that balances the earlier petition, verse 11]). The psalmist alternates between describing his physical conditions (*bones out of joint, heart turned to wax, tongue sticks…*, etc.) and the ferocity of his enemies (depicted as ravenous predators or powerful beasts). **16** *Pierced my hands and feet* is the reading of the Septuagint; the Masoretic Text reads "like a lion my hands and feet." The preferable rendering is "my hands and feet have shriveled." **21** *Save me*: literally, "you have answered me" (verse 2). The NIV assumes the divine answer comes in the form of deliverance. **22–31** The praise for aid begins with a summons (verses 22–23) followed by the reason (verses 24–26). Verses 27–31 expand the praise to all humanity, reaching beyond the barriers of space (verses 27–28) and time (verses 29–31).

Theological Reflection · Most contemporary readers know this heartrending lament best from its use to portray the climax of Jesus' suffering and death. In its original context, the psalm powerfully reminds the listener that suffering and tribulation are not the final chapter in God's relationship with faithful followers. Because of that, the psalmist ends not with lament, but with praise and an invitation to all the earth to join in worship of the Lord of the universe. Similarly, as Jesus utters the memorable words of this lament, contemporary listeners remember that the final chapter in God's relationship with all peoples is not the crucifixion, but the resurrection.

Psalm 23

This psalm of trust celebrates the protection of Yahweh in the midst of the most difficult of circumstances. The psalmist utilizes the metaphors of God as shepherd and as host to trump the present dangers that surround him. Although the psalmist delineates no specific danger, the language echoes that of the Exodus and wandering (compare Ps 78:43–55). The psalm divides into two sections: verses 1–4 (the Lord is my shepherd); and verses 5–6 (the Lord is my host).

> **Psalm 23 in History**
> *In the nineteenth century, this psalm became part of American public lore. Although the image of God or Jesus as shepherd plays a major role in Christian art throughout the centuries, Psalm 23 was not a prominent part of Christian thinking about death and hope until the 1850s. Henry Ward Beecher contributed to its popularity more than anyone else, and by the end of the century it had gained the prominence it still enjoys.*

1 The term *shepherd* carries royal connotations as well as pastoral. In the ancient world, the king often described himself as shepherd of his people. For Yahweh as shepherd, see Psalms 80:1; 95:7; 100:3; Genesis 49:24; Isaiah 40:11; Ezekiel 34; and John 10:11–15. **3** *His name's sake*: compare Psalm 106:8. **4** *Shadow of death*: Better, "the darkest valley." **5** *You prepare a table*: The image of host highlights both the protection the host assumes for the guest and the provisions the host provides (see Gen 19:8; Exod 24; Judg 19:23). **6** Although enemies might pursue the psalmist, he focuses upon the *goodness and mercy* that *follow* (literally, "pursue") him.

Theological Reflection · This psalm presents a profound theological reality. The psalmist simply yet eloquently describes the numerous dangers that can harm believers. Dangers abound; however, the psalmist demonstrates how the believer can call upon the overriding reality of God as protecting shepherd and provisioning host to overshadow the reality of present dangers, especially the ultimate danger of death. The psalm captures this most profound theological truth with *you are with me*.

Psalm 24

This psalm (like Ps 15) probably reflects an entrance, a time when ritual processions that involved the ark of the covenant entered the temple. The overarching theme is God's kingship; the three sections of the psalm each speak to that theme: verses 1–2 (God as creator retains ownership of his world); verses 3–6 (the ethical standards expected of those who enter the heavenly king's sanctuary); and verses 7–10 (a call to the gates of the city to admit the glorious king).

1–2 These verses declare God's comprehensive and exclusive ownership of the earth; humans inhabit and have responsibility for God's world; they do not own it. **3–6** Four qualifications of the worshiper are purity of deeds (*clean hands* [although equally a designation for ritual purity]), purity of speech (*swear…false*), inward truthfulness (*pure heart*), and unadulterated faith (*not lift up his soul to an idol*) (Terrien 247–48). **7–10** Compare 1 Samuel 6:12–19.

Theological Reflection · This psalm provides a theology for the integration of ethics and worship. The ethical quality of the worshiper's life does not function as an entrance requirement. However, since worship is the offering of one's life to God, ethical quality matters. God is the holy king; of utmost importance is who may inhabit his kingdom (compare Isa 6 for the twin themes of God's kingship and holiness). This psalm challenges those who would be subjects in this kingdom. This psalm also captures the nature of worship by affirming first that Yahweh is sole owner of the universe who comes to his people and then that humans must order the character of their lives to be in right relationship to that king.

Psalm 25

In this acrostic psalm, the psalmist seeks divine guidance and forgiveness. The theme of instruction in Yahweh's *way* (verses 4–5, 8–10, 12) dominates. The psalm divides into three sections: verses 1–7 (prayer for God's instruction and mercy); verses

8–14 (affirmation of God's faithful guidance and forgiveness); and verses 15–21 (a final plea for divine intervention). The concluding refrain (verse 22) begins with the letter *p*, resulting in an overarching alphabetic structure of: *a* (beginning), *l* (middle), and *p* (end), signifying *aleph*, the first letter of the Hebrew alphabet and the verbal root for "to learn."

1 *I lift up my soul* provides the psalm's keynote (compare Pss 86:4; 143:8). The *soul* [Hebrew *nephesh*] denotes the life and conscious identity of the person, not an entity completely separate from the body. **2–3** In the ancient world, honor offered inclusion and acceptance into the community, while *shame* resulted in exclusion from and ridicule by the community. **4–7** The psalmist seeks both divine guidance and forgiveness. Forgiveness comes through God's willingness to *remember* God's *great mercy* and *not remember* the sins of his worshipers. **5** *Truth* might better be rendered "faithfulness, reliability." The term connotes less objective reality and more a trustworthy relationship. *In you is my hope all day long*: compare Isaiah 40:31. **8–14** The psalmist details the nature of the divine/human relationship. Clifford (139–40) finds here allusions to Israel's national salvation history (exodus, wilderness, conquest). **11** *Forgive*: the psalm uses three common terms for sin. They are *sin* [Hebrew *chata*, verses 7, 8, 18]; *rebellious ways* [or "transgression"; Hebrew *pasha*, verse 7]; *iniquity* [or "guilt"; Hebrew *awon*, verse 11]. **13** Compare Deuteronomy 1:35–36; 6:18. **16–21** The psalmist seeks relief from two troubles that create a paradox: he experiences loneliness (and loss of friendship with God) yet feels surrounded by enemies (who deal him distress and violence).

Theological Reflection · Psalm 1 presents the two ways one may travel; Psalm 25 offers a travel guide for the one choosing God's way (Davidson 89). Trusting God does not mean blind obedience. Rather, it involves instruction and guidance. Psalm 25 simply yet eloquently provides a primer on the relational dimension of religious education (Limburg 81) and its centrality to worship (Mays 125).

Psalm 26

This psalm defies categorization. It may be an individual lament, a national lament prior to a disaster, an entrance liturgy, or a protestation of innocence by one falsely accused. Given the concrete references in verses 6–8, many scholars envision a liturgical setting in the temple with a priest as the psalmist (Clifford 142). The psalm divides into a five-part chiastic arrangement (A B C B' A'): verses 1–3 (a plea for vindication based on the supplicant's integrity); verses 4–5 (a profession rejecting association with the wicked); verses 6–8 (praise for the Lord and his temple); verses 9–10 (a plea for protection from the wicked); and verses 11–12 (a plea for redemption based on the supplicant's integrity).

> **Entrance Liturgy**
> *A ritual for celebrating and consecrating the movement of worshipers into the temple.*

> **Chiasm**
> *A reversal of order of words or phrases in otherwise parallel parts of a text is known as chiasm or chiasmus. This pattern of arranging material appears often in the Bible. The book of Lamentations, for example, is arguably a very large chiasm.*

1 There is an inclusio (*led a blameless life*; *lead a blameless life* [verse 11]). *Blameless* here is better translated as "integrity" (see Ps 25:21; Jas 1:26–27). **2** Compare Psalms 7:9; 11:4; 17:3. **4** *Sit ... consort* means to be partners with (see 1 Sam 2:8; Pss 101:6; 113:8; Prov 31:23). **6–8** The focus shifts from persons (wicked) to place (the temple). **3–5** See Psalm 1. **5** *I abhor the assembly of evildoers* is balanced by *I love the house where you live, O Lord* (verse 8; compare Pss 23:6; 84:1, 3). The nuance may more closely intend "reject/choose" than any emotion-laden sense of "hate/love." **6** *Wash my hands* expresses either innocence (see Deut 21:6; compare Matt 27:24), purity (Ps 73:13), or preparation for sacrifice (Exod 30:21). The psalmist's pure hands contrast strikingly with the *hands* of the wicked that are filled with *wicked schemes* and *bribes* (verse 10). **8** *Glory dwells* refers to God's illuminating presence in the temple. **9–12** The psalmist's plea is stated first negatively (verses 9–10) and then positively (verses 11–12).

Theological Reflection · Psalm 26 dresses the sentiments of Psalms 1 and 101 in priestly attire. A life of integrity involves choices for and against – for God and against those who reject him.

Psalm 27

This psalm consists of a psalm of trust (verses 1–6) and an individual lament (verses 7–12) (see Ps 40). It concludes with a reiteration of trust (verses 13–14).

1 *Light* is a favorite metaphor for divine protection (see Pss 36:9; 43:3; 56:13 where it is also associated with the sanctuary; compare also Isa 2:5; 10:17). **3** The militaristic imagery need not suggest a royal psalmist; it may simply reflect metaphorical language highlighting the level of the psalmist's confidence. **4–6** The psalmist eloquently affirms the joy that comes from experiencing the presence of the Lord in worship (*gaze upon the beauty of the Lord*; *keep me safe in his dwelling*; compare verse 13). Three metaphors for desire in verse 4 (*dwell ... gaze ... seek*) are balanced in verse 5 with three metaphors for hope (*dwelling ... shelter of his tabernacle ... rock*). **11** The psalmist makes two requests: *teach me ... lead me*. **13** *Land of the living* (or "life") may refer to the temple (see Pss 52:7; 56:14; 116:9; Isa 38:11). **14** The final exhortation echoes the Lord's charge to Joshua – "be strong and of good courage" (Josh 1:6–9; Deut 31:7–8).

Theological Reflection · Psalm 27 ably reminds the readers of the realities of life: trust in the Lord makes most sense when dire circumstances (for example, unjust accusations and potential harm) are powerfully present. The key to balancing life in such circumstances comes through worship (verse 4). Though the imagery differs, the theology mirrors Psalm 23.

Psalm 28

This psalm has elements of an individual lament (verses 1–5), song of thanksgiving (verses 6–7), and appeal of one falsely accused (verses 8–9). The psalmist may be a king (note the reference to the *anointed* [verse 8] and prayer for the *people* [verse 9]; compare Hab 3:13). The psalm divides into four sections: verses 1–2 (appeal for a hearing); verses 3–5 (appeal for vindication); verses 6–7 (anticipated thanksgiving); and verses 8–9 (prayer for God's protection of his people).

1–2 Initially, the psalmist complains of God's nonresponsiveness (arguably a sign of indifference or powerlessness) rather than his opponents' attacks. *I lift up my hands* is a common prayer posture in ancient Israel (Pss 63:4; 134:2; 141:2; Neh 8:6; Lam 2:19; 1 Tim 2:8). Often, praise occurred with uplifted hands and petition with prostration. The *Most Holy Place* occurs only here in the Psalter; it is the usual term for the temple's holy of holies in Kings and Chronicles. **3–4** The psalmist designates his opponents in three ways (*wicked*; *do evil ... speak cordially ... harbor malice*) and offers three requests for retribution. **5** While the psalmist *lifts up* his *hands* for prayer (verse 2), the evildoers' *hands* engage in *evil work*; fittingly, he seeks retribution from God because his opponents *show no regard for the works of the Lord and what his hands have done*. **6–7** The silence of God has been broken; God has responded. **8–9** The psalmist asks God as the *shepherd* of the people, to *save* them, *bless* the land allotments to the ancestors, and *carry them forever* (for God as shepherd, see Pss 74:1; 80:1; Isa 40:11; Ezek 34).

Theological Reflection · The psalmist seeks justice; specifically, he desires the wicked to receive repayment in kind for their deeds. He trusts this will occur when God "hears" his case. The psalmist looks beyond his own circumstances and seeks God's vindication for all the people.

Psalm 29

Most scholars consider this psalm an Israelite adaptation of an original Canaanite hymn celebrating Baal's power. The poetic style is akin to early Canaanite poetry. The Israelite psalmist effectively transforms the language to remove any doubt that it is the Lord of Israel who exercises absolute control over the natural realm (the name Yahweh appears eighteen times in the psalm). The psalm describes in gorgeous detail the thunderous path of a storm from the Mediterranean Sea southeastward across the mountain ranges of Lebanon. The psalm divides into three sections: verses 1–2 (address to the heavenly court); verses 3–9 (awesome depiction of God's "glory"); and verses 10–11 (acclamation of the glorious Lord by the heavenly court).

1–2 The threefold *ascribe to the Lord* reflects early Israelite poetic style. *O mighty ones*: literally, "sons of El" (compare Pss 82:1, 6; 89:7; Job 1:6; 2:1; 1 Kgs 22). Whereas Canaanite thought envisioned numerous gods and goddesses who vied for supremacy, Israel believed in angelic beings that functioned solely to offer praise and obedience to the one creator of the universe. The call to worship addresses these divine beings, not the earthly realm (see Ps 96:7–8; 1 Chron 16:28–29). **3–4** *The voice of the Lord* is thunder (compare Exod 9:28; 19:16; 20:18; Pss 18:13; 77:18). **5** The ferocity of the storm buckles and breaks even the mighty *cedars of Lebanon* (symbols of power and prestige; see Ps 104:16; Isa 2:13). **6** *Sirion*: Mount Hermon (Deut 3:9). **8** *Kadesh*: given the usual tracking of a Mediterranean thunderstorm, this locale is more likely Kadesh on the Orontes in Syria than the better known Kadesh in the southern desert. **9** *Twists the oaks*: literally, "causes hinds to give birth." However, the parallelism with *strips the forests bare* favors this NIV correction. **10–11** *Enthroned over the flood*: the imagery clearly pictures Yahweh royally seated atop his universe and holding court (symbolically captured in the Jerusalem temple).

> **Mabbul**
> The term flood [Hebrew *mabbul*, used elsewhere only in Gen 6–9] portrays God fully in control above the roiling seas.

Theological Reflection · This psalm demonstrates the importance and hermeneutical power of articulating faith in the language and thought-world of the surrounding culture. People of ancient Mesopotamia and Canaan considered the world they inhabited the result of a primordial battle between the beneficent god of nature and the adversarial powers of the god of the cosmic oceans. Ancient Israel, recognizing the incomparable power and majesty of Yahweh, the creator of the universe, utilized these ancient Near Eastern images and forms to profess faith in Yahweh. In Genesis 1, the all-powerful God simply speaks the world into existence; combat is entirely absent. Elsewhere in the Old Testament (see Pss 24:1–2; 74:13–15; 89:10–11; 93:4–5), biblical writers transform the story of primordial combat to declare the uniqueness of Yahweh. Perhaps most importantly, the heavenly realm bursts forth in praise of Yahweh.

Psalm 30

This individual thanksgiving offers praise to God for deliverance from a life-threatening situation. The psalmist contrasts the dramatic reversal of his life through the imagery of *going down into the pit* (verse 3) where there is no praise (verse 9) with being *lifted out of the depths* and *grave* so that the psalmist and other *saints* might *praise his holy name* (verse 4) (Clifford 158). Though the precise circumstances of the psalmist are uncertain, the type of situation resembles that encountered in Psalm 6 and Isaiah 38. The psalm divides into four sections: verses 1–3 (praise for deliverance); verses 4–5 (a call to join in praise); verses 6–10 (rehearsing of the crisis); and verses 11–12 (reiteration of praise).

1 The psalmist praises the Lord who "drew him up" out of the *depths* as one draws water from a well (see Exod 2:16). **5** The directional ("up/down") contrast of the opening verses is matched by a temporal contrast — *anger lasts only a moment ... favor lasts a lifetime* (see Exod 20:4–5; 34:6–7). **6** The psalmist may have become complacent. **7** *Dismay* comes with the absence (*hid your face*), not presence, of the Lord **9** Sheol lacks praise: the psalmist rightly notes his death would have resulted in one fewer voice of praise upon earth. **11** *Dancing* is a customary reaction to deliverance and restoration (see Exod 15:20; Ps 150; Jer 31:12–13; Lam 5:14–15).

Theological Reflection · This psalm highlights the responsibility deliverance by God calls from the one rescued. Joy must be shared. Praise involves acknowledgement of the nature of God, specifically of the ability of divine grace to overwhelm anger (verse 5).

Psalm 31

This individual lament alternates between expressions of anguish and affirmations of trust. The psalmist seeks *refuge* (*rock*, *fortress*) and direction (*lead*, *guide*). The psalm unevenly divides into two major sections: verses 1–18 (lament); and verses 19–24 (thanksgiving). The first section is arranged in a chiasm: prayer (verses 1–4); expression of trust (verses 5–8); lament (verses 9–13); expression of trust (verses 14); and prayer (verses 15–18).

1 *I have taken refuge*: compare Psalms 7; 11; 16; 71. Honor and *shame* figure prominently throughout the Psalter (4; 25). **5** *Into your hands I commit my spirit* are uttered later by Jesus (Luke 23:46) and Stephen (Acts 7:59). **9–10** The societal shame of the psalmist impacts his entire body. **13** *Slander* and *conspire* designate the specific circumstances triggering the lament. *Terror on every side*: compare Jeremiah 6:25; 20:10; 46:5. **15** *My times are in your* (that is, Yahweh's) *hands* contrasts with "hands" of the enemies (verses 5, 8). The affirmation is less about confidence in death and more about confidence in life. **16** *Let your face shine*: see Numbers 6:24; Psalms 4:6; 80:3, 7, 19; 119:135. **21** The dramatic mood change may reflect a positive response in worship from the priest, or simply the joy that comes after honestly expressing one's deepest sufferings to God.

Theological Reflection · Psalm 31 reminds us that being in right relationship with God does not assure a life free from trouble and suffering. It demonstrates how to respond to challenging moments in faith. Trust bridges the gap between suffering and the goodness of the Lord (Eaton 147).

Psalm 32

This individual song of thanksgiving is the second of the seven psalms known as the penitential psalms (Pss

6; 38; 51; 102; 130; 143). The psalmist first celebrates the blessings that come from divine forgiveness and contrasts his life before and after forgiveness. He then utilizes his own experiences to instruct his listeners in the proper way to live. The psalm divides into two sections: verses 1–5 (blessing and thanksgiving); and verses 6–11 (thanksgiving and instruction).

1–2 *Blessed* [Hebrew *ashre*; see also Pss 1:1; 128:1; Matt 5:1–10] ... *transgressions are forgiven*: The Old Testament offers numerous examples of the forgiveness of sins. Three terms for sin appear in this psalm (*transgression...sin...iniquity* [NIV "sin" verse 2]), matched by three terms for forgiveness (*forgiven...covered...count against*). **3–4** The psalmist graphically depicts the physical impact that sin effects (Ps 51:8). **5** *Not cover*: For examples of "covering sin," See Genesis 3 (Adam and Eve), Genesis 4 (Cain), or 2 Samuel 12 (David and Bathsheba). **8–10** The conclusion echoes themes familiar to the Wisdom literature (Prov 1–4; 26:3). The psalmist exhorts his listeners to avoid the mistakes he has made.

Theological Reflection · This psalm reminds its readers of the frequent impact that sin has upon the emotional and physical health of the believer and the joyous release and health that comes only through forgiveness. It also rightly notes the responsibility that forgiven sinners have to not keep their experience of forgiveness private but to share those moments with other believers.

Psalm 33

This hymn invites the righteous to praise the Lord's steadfast love, manifested first in creation and then in history. The psalm divides into two major sections: verses 1–11 (imperative call to praise [verses 1–3] and basis for the praise [verses 4–11]); and verses 12–22 (God's critique of the peoples of the earth and possible human responses to that divine assessment).

2 The first reference to instrumental music in the Psalter occurs here. **3** The "newness" of the *new song* is not the content but the singer's ever-new daily experience of God's love (see Pss 40:3; 96:1; 98:1; 144:9; 149:1; Isa 42:10; Rev 5:9). **6** Through his *word*, the Lord speaks his creation into existence (Gen 1). **10–11** The psalmist transitions from God's acts in creation to God's will to preserve justice in the earth. **16–17** Compare Isaiah 31:1–3.

Theological Reflection · The first half of this psalm celebrates the creative power of God's mouth, with which he speaks the universe into being. The second half highlights the care and concern of this creator, whose eyes are on those who rely upon him. The Lord's *chesed* (*unfailing love*) is evident in both. The *righteous* are those who both praise God for his power and grace and who call others to join in that praise.

Psalm 34

This individual song of thanksgiving highlights first the deliverance experienced and then engages in extended instruction regarding the implications of divine deliverance for daily life. The poem is an acrostic and bears a similar uniqueness to Psalm 25 (neither has a verse for the Hebrew letter *waw*, and both conclude with a *pe* verse). Several terms occur multiple times: *hear*, *deliver*, *fear*, *good*, *evil*, and *righteous*. The psalm divides into two major sections: verses 1–10 (individual thanksgiving) and verses 11–22 (instruction).

2 Although the term *boast* normally has a negative connotation when used with humans, when directed toward God its nuance changes (see Jer 9:23–24). **5** *Radiant*: see Isaiah 60:5. **7** Compare Jeremiah 6:25; 20:3. Rather than focusing upon the "fear" of the surrounding enemies, the psalmist centers his focus upon the Lord's protection that surrounds the one who fears the Lord (compare Exod 14:19; Josh 5:13–15). **8** *Taste*: that is, experience or think about. **10** The contrast to the *young lions* (the self-reliant) are *those who seek the Lord* (those dependent upon God). **12** Compare Proverbs 3:13–18; 9:4–6. **18** Compare Isaiah 61:1–3; Luke 4:18–19. **19–22** The vision here is that of traditional wisdom; God protects the righteous from harm and punishes the wicked.

Theological Reflection · This psalm rightly reminds its readers of the responsibility for those whom God delivers to instruct others. Simple praise is insufficient; the lessons learned during difficulties and the implications for faithful living call for instruction to the coming generation. The theology of this traditional wisdom instruction is not simplistic, for the psalmist recognizes that the righteous do not escape trials.

Yahweh the Creator

The psalm first celebrates God's creative power in the universe, manifested in the heavens, sea, and earth. It then celebrates God's involvement in the lives of the earthly creation. Humans have two options: they can trust in themselves (verses 16–17) or can fear and hope in Yahweh's unfailing love (verse 18).

Rather, he acknowledges that God is present throughout those difficult moments and sides always with the faithful. First Peter 3:10–12 appropriately reapplies verses 12–16 as a Christian response to suffering.

Psalm 35

This individual lament depicts in detail the devastating manner in which the psalmist's enemies impact him. The three sections of the psalm alternate among appeal, imprecation, and complaint, with each section concluding with a vow of praise: verses 1–10 (initial pleadings), verses 11–18 (case for the defense), verses 19–28 (final appeal).

1 *Contend*: a technical Hebrew term [*riv*] for legal confrontation. **2–3** The psalmist piles up the offensive and defensive weaponry (*shield, buckler, spear, javelin*). **4–8** Seven petitions are leveled against the foe. The poet utilizes both hunting and military imagery. **11–16** The main complaint against the foes highlights their false and vicious slander that is completely unjustified (*without cause*; verse 11, *I know nothing about*). **19–26** Seven more petitions against the enemies. **19** *Wink the eye*: that is, conspiracy (see Prov 6:12–14).

Theological Reflection · The psalmist skillfully mixes images of God (warrior, judge), the enemies (warriors, hunters, perjurers, betrayers), and himself (a victim both in court and on the battlefield) (Clifford 180). Though mistreated, the psalmist resolutely continues to call upon God to right the present wrongs.

Psalm 36

This psalm contains elements of lament, hymn, and wisdom instruction. Though the psalmist provides an extensive description of the wicked, no danger seems imminent. The psalm divides into three sections: verses 1–4 (portrayal of the wicked); verses 5–9 (affirmation of trust in God); and verses 10–12 (appeal for help from God).

1 *An oracle is within my heart*: The NIV dramatically rereads the Hebrew (which literally reads, "an oracle of rebellion in his heart"). The line may parody the normal use of *oracle* (see Ps 110:1). Here it is not God who provides the revelation but solely the self-generated transgression of the wicked. **2** This is not the usual term for the *fear of God*; the term suggests becoming awestruck and rendered obedient (Clifford 183). **4** Compare Micah 2:1–5. **5–6** *Heavens…skies* evokes the expanse of God's *love*; *mighty mountains…great deep* highlights the immensity of God's *righteousness*; *man and beast* notes the inclusiveness of God's care (see Eph 3:18–19). **7** *Both high and low among men*: the NIV rereads the Hebrew (literally "gods and humans"). *In the shadow of your wings*: for God as a protective bird, see Psalms 17:8; 36:7; 57:1; 61:4; 63:7; 91:4; compare Matthew 23:37. **8** Perhaps a reference both to God's general provisions and specific care at the temple (*house*). *River of your delights* [Hebrew *adaneyka*]: perhaps an implicit echo of the garden of Eden (*eden*). *In your light we see light*: the phrase is puzzling; it perhaps refers to true life that comes only in the presence of God.

Theological Reflection · This psalm contains echoes of wisdom thought. Wisdom involves both correct cognition and proper moral behavior. The fool has no fear of God; he lives solely for and from himself (see Prov 6:12–15). The wise desire to share God's banquet table (Prov 9) and recognize God as the *fountain of life* and *light* (see John 1:4; 4:14).

Psalm 37

This wisdom psalm discusses the lot of the righteous and the wicked, encouraging its listeners to take a longer range view of God's actions and avoid hasty conclusions. This acrostic poem almost forms an anthology of traditional wisdom sayings. The psalm divides into four sections: verses 1–11 (exhortation to resist the lure of the wicked lifestyle); verses 12–20 (the wicked plot harm, but God protects the faithful); verses 21–26 (the righteous generously lend); and verses 27–40 (exhortation to resist evil and cling to righteousness).

> **Traditional Wisdom**
> *Through proverbial sayings and personal observation, the psalmist engages more in pastoral exhortation than in rigorous intellectual dissection of the ways of God in the world.*

1–2 Compare Proverbs 24:19; 23:17; 24:1. Throughout, the psalmist contrasts the fleeting nature of the seeming success of the wicked (compare Pss 90:5–6; 103:15–16; Isa 40:6–7). **5–6** See Proverbs 16:3. **11** See Matthew 5:5. **16–17** See Proverbs 15:16; 16:18. **21–22** See Proverbs 3:33. **23–24** Also, Proverbs 24:6. **3–31** See Proverbs 10:31–32. **32–33** Compare Proverbs 1:11, 15–19. **35–36** A reversal of Psalm 1:3. **37–38**. See also Proverbs 23:18.

Theological Reflection · The psalmist intends not to provide intellectual solutions to the social inequities between those faithful to God and those rejecting

God's ways. Rather, the psalmist's provides encouragement and hope for believers who may stumble in the midst of present difficulties. He exhorts his listeners not to allow the difficulties of the present to negate their commitment to God's ultimate purposes. Although the present may cause anxiety (*fret not*), the psalmist draws upon the larger corpus of his own experience to argue that, over a lifetime, God is faithful to his righteous followers and ultimately attends to the wickedness in his world.

Psalm 38

This psalm, the third of the so-called penitential psalms (see Pss 6; 32; 51; 102; 130; 143), possesses characteristics of the individual lament. The psalmist graphically details the physical and emotional toll his own sins and his unjust treatment at the hands of his adversaries have taken upon him. Appeals to God (verses 1–2, 9–10, 15–16, 21–22) punctuate the descriptions of the psalmist's physical ruin (verses 3–8, 17–20) and exposure to his enemies (verses 11–14, 17–20).

> **Responses to Suffering**
> Psalm 38 depicts the tragedy when onlookers exploit the suffering of another or regard themselves as better than the sufferer. Such responses only increase the anguish of the sufferer, leaving that one solely in the hands of a caring God.

1 *O Lord, do not rebuke me*: so Psalm 6:1. **2** *Arrows*: symbolize harmful, painful interactions, as in Job 6:4; Deuteronomy 32:23; Psalm 7:12–13; Lamentations 3:12. **4** The term for *guilt* implies something bent or twisted (see the verb in verse 6 – *bowed down*). **10** The psalmist is near death (see Ps 13:3). **11** Social isolation exacerbates the physical suffering of the psalmist. **13–14** The sufferer is either silent to the slander of his foes (see Ps 39:1–2) or unaware of their plotting (Jer 11:19–20) (so Kselman and Barré 532).

Theological Reflection · Psalm 38 struggles with the murky connection between sin and physical ailments. Whatever the connection, it has theological implications. The psalm rightly notes that any connection between the two comes from the sufferer.

Psalm 39

In this individual lament, the psalmist gives voice to the anguish he experiences initially through silent suffering and ultimately through his sense of being an outsider in the presence of God. The psalm echoes themes from the Wisdom literature (particularly Job and Ecclesiastes) and continues the themes and mood of Psalm 38. The psalm divides into four sections: verses 1–3 (silent suffering); verses 4–6 (the transient life); verses 7–11 (appeal to God for deliverance); and verses 12–13 (final plea for relief). Verses 1–3 and 7–11 highlight the silence and suffering of the psalmist, while verses 4–6 and 12–13 highlight the fragility of human life.

2 *Silent and still*: the psalmist gives no reason for his silence; perhaps he wants to give no additional language to his adversaries for use against him. When he does speak (verses 4–6), he speaks not to his opponents, but prays to God. **3** *Heart grew hot*: in Egyptian literature, the wise person is the "silent" person, and the fool is the "hot" person. **4–6** *Life's end and number of my days*: though most consider this a reference to the brevity of life, some envision more a plea for God to divulge the length of the period of suffering (so Clifford 199; Kselman and Barré 532). The language and worldview resembles that of Ecclesiastes (note especially *breath*). **11** *Rebuke and discipline*: compare Psalm 38:1. The psalmist attributes his plight directly to God. **12** *Alien, stranger*: see Exodus 22:21; 23:9, 12; Deuteronomy 24:17; Job 7:16–21.

> **"Look away from me ..."**
> Like Job, the suffering psalmist seeks God's withdrawal from him rather than the customary desire to rejoice in his beneficent presence.

Theological Reflection · This psalm demonstrates the place of theological reflection in worship. The psalmist struggles with his suffering, how he should respond verbally to it, and the anguish that comes from realizing that life, already transitory, may be consumed with pain. This psalm provides language for those who suffer silently.

Psalm 40

This psalm (like Pss 9–10, 27, and 89) begins with a song of thanksgiving (verses 1–10) and concludes with a lament (verses 11–17). The psalmist vocalizes the dual nature of life lived in relationship with God, praise and petition.

1–2 The language of rescue from a muddy bog resembles that of the river ordeal known in Mesopotamia, where survival signifies innocence (Kselman and Barré 532). Conversely, *pit* often occurs in parallel with Sheol (Ps 30:3; Isa 14:15; 38:18). **3** *New song*: see Psalm 33:3. This song celebrates Yahweh's incomparability and the psalmist's resolve to obedience (verse 5; Clifford 205). **6** *Sacrifice and offering you did not desire* resonates with the prophetic perspective (see 1 Sam 15:22–23; Hos 6:4–5; Amos 5:21–24; Mark 12:33; compare Pss 50:8–15; 51:16; 141:2); the psalmist substitutes public praise for public sacrifice. The Septuagint reads this line, "a body you have prepared," which the Hebrews writer ably utilizes to contrast the once-for-all death of Christ with the sacrificial system of the Old Testament (Heb 10:5–7). **7** *Here I am*: compare Isaiah 6:8; Numbers 22:38 (Balaam). What is *written about me in the scroll* is unclear. Though some suggest the Shema of Deuteronomy 6:4, the specific contents of this scroll may be the joyous recounting of *the wonders* God has done in the psalmist's life (verses 5, 9; see Ps 139:16; Isa 65:6). **9** *I proclaim righteousness*: the Hebrew term finds its counterpart in the Greek term *evangelizo*. To "evangelize" is simply to proclaim the mighty gracious acts of God in one's own life. **13–17** See Psalm 70, a virtual duplicate.

> **"My ears you have pierced..."**
> Literally "*my ears you have dug,*" the imagery here is likely less that of a slave linked to his master (as in Exod 21:6) and more that of an "open ear" that listens attentively to the will and ways of God (Isa 50:5).

Theological Reflection · This psalm evidences the inseparable connection between praise and petition. The psalmist celebrates the deliverance and marvelous graciousness of the Lord (verses 1–10), and only his reexperience of dire circumstances necessitates another appeal to this same gracious Lord for deliverance. The psalmist lives in a world of gracious deeds *too many to declare* (verse 5) and *troubles without number* (verse 12).

Psalm 41

Though disputed, this psalm is better read as a song of thanksgiving for past deliverance than a lament seeking future relief. The psalm opens with a beatitude that folds neatly into instruction from the sufferer. The psalm divides into three sections (plus the final doxology concluding Book One of the Psalter [verse 13]): verses 1–3 (beatitude); verses 4–9 (a lament from the past illness); and verses 10–12 (final statement of trust).

1 *Blessed ... regard for weak*: Active concern for the poor demonstrates faithfulness to God (Clifford 210; see Pss 15:3; 37:11; Prov 16:20). **5–8** The vile gossip the enemies whisper intensifies the psalmist's illness. **9** *Close friend*: literally, "friend of my *shalom*." *Lifted up his heel*: though elsewhere unattested, the phrase envisions crushing one's opponent underfoot (Davidson 138). **10** Usually a psalmist seeks redress (*that I may repay them*) from God (as in Pss 31:23; 62:12; 137:8). This verse forms an inclusio with verse 4 (*O Lord, have mercy on me*). **11–12** The psalmist states how he knew God had heard him.

Theological Reflection · This psalm graphically portrays the exquisite joy of experiencing God's healing touch and the oppressive agony of life-threatening illness that onlookers regard as the just deserts from a punishing God. Although his foes may consider his situation hopeless, the psalmist experiences God's faithfulness through his dramatic recovery.

BOOK 2 · PSALMS 42–72

Psalms 42–43

Though appearing as two psalms in most Hebrew manuscripts, there is little doubt these were originally one psalm (as with Pss 9–10) because they share common language and imagery, Psalm 43 has no heading (the only other psalm without a heading in Book Two is Ps 71), and these psalms are joined in some Hebrew manuscripts. This individual lament divides into three sections, with a common refrain concluding each section (42:5, 11; 43:5); 42:1–5 (an anguished longing for God and memories of past worship); 42:6–11 (further longing for God from afar); and 43:1–5 (an appeal to God for vindication and hope of renewed worship).

> **The Elohistic Psalms**
> *Psalm 42 is the first of the "Elohistic psalms," a group of psalms (42–83) in which the generic term for God [Hebrew* elohim] *is far more common than "Yahweh," which is prevalent elsewhere in the Psalter.*

42:1–2 *Deer pants ... soul thirsts*: The psalmist eloquently compares his longing for the presence of God to that of a thirsty deer seeking life-sustaining water (see Pss 63:1; 143:6). **3** *Tears*: water imagery runs throughout the psalm (verse 7). **3–4** The psalmist suffers a triple indignity: absence from God and the communion with his fellow worshipers, and the presence of mockers taunting him regarding God's absence (*Where is your God?*). **6** The geographical references are somewhat obscure (though the distance from the Jerusalem temple is clear). *Hermon* refers to the highest mountain range in the Anti-Lebanon. The location of *Mount Mizar* (literally, "Mount Tiny") is unknown. **7** *Deep calls to deep* may allude to the headwaters of the Jordan River. *All your waves and breakers have swept over me*: see Jonah 2:3–4. **9** The taunting questions in verses 3, 10 are matched by the psalmist's own query, *Why have you forgotten me?* **43:3** The psalmist longs for God's *light* to dispel the "dark night of his soul," for God's *truth* to *vindicate* his cause against the *ungodly…deceitful and wicked* (verse 1). **3–4** *Holy mountain…altar of God* refer to the Jerusalem temple.

> **The Waters of Mount Hermon**
> *Runoff from Mount Hermon supplies most of the water for the Jordan River, and thus its ecological and economic importance can hardly be overestimated. The mountain also symbolized for ancient Israelites majesty and isolation.*

Theological Reflection · These psalms poignantly capture the anguish this faithful worshiper experiences in his current distance from the presence of God's temple. He longs to stand in God's presence and offer heartfelt worship. For him, worship and communion with God are as necessary for life as food and water for an animal in the hostile, arid desert. In his anguish, his memories of past worship nourish his *soul* (used seven times in these psalms).

Psalm 44

This community lament (Pss 74; 80) remembers longingly God's former victories, made bittersweet by a recent devastating military loss. The defeat is inexplicable, since the people have remained loyal to the covenant. The psalmist knows theologically the issue ultimately concerns not Israel's military might but God's reputation as all-powerful Lord, and so it is to that that he appeals. The psalm divides into three sections: verses 1–8 (remembrance of past victories); verses 9–22 (present distress and complaint); and verses 23–26 (appeal for divine aid).

1–2 The victories remembered appeal to the period of the exodus and conquest. **3–7** For Israel, victories always come through God, not military expertise (compare Deut 8; Josh 24). **13–15** Joshua's appeal to God following the initial defeat at Ai (Josh 7:6–10). **17–18** The key to the complaint: Israel professes its faithful allegiance to the Lord. **19** *Jackals* live at the edge of the desert, that area immediately adjacent to death. **23–24** The language is graphic. The psalmist believes that the only reason for a defeat in these circumstances is that God has become inattentive (*awake…rouse yourself*; compare 1 Kgs 18:27; contrast Ps 121). The irony is poignant. Since the people have not *forgotten the name of God* (verse 20), why does God *forget* [their] *misery and distress*?

Theological Reflection · This psalm poignantly depicts the consternation that results in the community of faith when defeat occurs instead of an expected victory. The psalmist bluntly calls to mind God's past fidelity and apparent present inattentiveness, and he remains assured God will rectify these egregious wrongs and *redeem* Israel with *unfailing love*.

Psalm 45

This royal wedding song illustrates the importance of all facets of royal life in ancient Israel. The poet first announces the splendor of the king and then invites the royal bride to join in the festal celebration. The psalm divides into two major sections enwrapped by a prescript and postscript (verses 1, 17): verses 2–9 (praise and blessing on the king); and verses 10–16 (praise of the bride and her presentation to her royal groom).

1 The poet functions almost like a muse; his scribal praise is oral (Ezra 7:6). **2** Gracious speech reflects inner integrity (as in Prov 22:11). **2–5** The king enters in all his military *splendor and majesty*. **6** Scholars debate the referent of *your throne, O God*. Several scholars consider the addressee the king; that is, this line reflects ancient Near Eastern hyperbole that depicts the king with divine attributes (*splendor, majesty*) and divine titles (elsewhere the psalmists call the king "son of God" and regard his enthronement as his "adoption"; see 2 Sam 7:14; Pss 2:7; 89:28; Isa 9:6). Other scholars consider Yahweh the subject of the invocation (elsewhere in this psalm, Yahweh is clearly the subject of the references to "God"). **7–8** Most likely

> **Queen Mother**
> *In Israel and surrounding states, the king's (widowed) mother played some role in government. In a polygamous society, the dominant wife of a king could help her son gain the throne. Kings lists two queen mothers for Israel (1 Kgs 11:26; 16:31; 22:52; 2 Kgs 3:2; 9:22) and fifteen for Judah (1 Kgs 14:21; 15:2, 10; 22:42; 2 Kgs 8:26; 12:1; 14:2; 15:2, 33; 18:2; 21:1, 19; 22:1, 31; 23:35; 24:8, 18). Several mothers gave birth to more than one monarch.*

a description of the royal regalia the king wears at his wedding. **9** The *royal bride* may refer to either the bride or her new mother-in-law, the queen mother, since in verse 13 the bride is still in her chamber (Clifford 225; see 1 Kgs 2:19). The location of *Ophir* is unknown. **12** *Daughter of Tyre* is better read "Daughter Tyre" (a reference to the inhabitants of the city).

> **Ophir**
>
> The Bible thinks of Ophir primarily as the location of gold (1 Kgs 9:28; 22:49; 2 Chron 8:18; Job 22:24; 28:15; Isa 13:12). Locations from Arabia (the most likely site) to India or north Africa are possible.

Theological Reflection · The poet offers as his gift to the newlyweds an ode that both extols their beauty and character and seeks blessings from God, the blessings of future military victories and progeny. The king needs both for future security and prosperity (see Ps 127). The Song of Solomon offers perhaps the best parallel to this psalm, with its similar imagery.

Psalm 46

This first of the songs of Zion (also Pss 48; 76; 84; 87; 122) contains several of the key motifs associated with Zion (the river of paradise; Yahweh's victory over the waters of chaos; Yahweh's defeat of the foreign nations). Though the world may swirl in turmoil and danger surround the psalmist, he stands resolute, for Yahweh securely upholds his royal city, Jerusalem. The psalm divides into three sections (with refrains concluding two of them [verses 7, 11]): verses 1–3 (God rules over creation); verses 4–7 (God rules over history); and verses 8–11 (an invitation to acknowledge God's acts in creation and history).

1 The opening refrain captures the essence of the song: *God is our refuge and strength*. **2–3** The imagery reflects the terror that nature generates through sea storms and earthquakes. **4–5** The tumult the earth experiences misses the *city of God*, for God *is within her*. The *river* likely echoes themes from Genesis 2. **6** The *uproar* among the *nations* matches the chaos in the created order. **8–9** The psalmist calls his listeners to see God's powerful splendor displayed both in creation and military victories. **11** *Be still* calls the audience to quit fearing the military prowess of the adversary and acknowledge the supremacy of Yahweh's power (*know that I am God*).

Theological Reflection · This psalm captures the essence of faith for difficult times: *God is our refuge and strength, an ever-present help in trouble*. Though the natural disasters or military conflagrations may cause the world to appear futureless, the promises and presence of Yahweh remain secure.

Psalm 47

This hymn celebrates Yahweh's kingship over all the earth, manifested in the selection and protection of the people of Israel. The psalmist intermingles universal and national (or cosmic and covenantal) themes throughout the poem. The psalm divides into two summons to praise, with each summons describing an aspect of Yahweh's divine rule: verses 1–4 (call to praise plus an account of how Yahweh came to rule), and verses 5–9 (call to praise plus a description of the enthroned Lord).

1–2 The language echoes that of a royal coronation (compare 2 Kgs 11:12, 19–20). **6–9** On the interrelation of universalism and nationalism in the Old Testament, see Genesis 12:1–3 and Isaiah 2:2–4. Yahweh elected Israel to be a medium through which to benefit all of humankind.

Theological Reflection · This psalm calls upon all the earth to offer the praise due Yahweh as the ultimate Lord of all the nations, who cares for and guides Israel particularly. God is no divine being limited in power or influence. God's sovereignty extends throughout all the earth, whether all nations acknowledge that or not. In worship, we declare that the Lord has made a place for us among the nations so that we might call the nations to enter the place of his people (verse 9).

Psalm 48

This song of Zion builds upon Psalms 46 and 47. Like Psalm 46, the text lauds Zion as Yahweh's dwelling and the sign of God's victory over the forces of chaos. The mighty God whose enthronement is celebrated in Psalm 47 receives the accolades of worshiping pilgrims in Psalm 48. The psalm divides into four sections: verses 1–3 (the beauty of Mount Zion); verses 4–8 (Zion's grandeur scatters kings); verses 9–11 (Yahweh's victory generates praise); and verses 12–14 (laudatory beauty of Mount Zion).

2 Theological rather than geographical reality drives the psalm. Mount Zion is one of the smaller peaks in Jerusalem, but as the temple locale, it overshadows the surrounding hills, theologically speaking. The *heights of Zaphon* (literally, "north") is the phrase Canaanite texts apply to Baal's abode in the far north (Jebel el-Aqra'). The true *great king* (a title employed by the rulers of Mesopotamia and Egypt) of the universe is none other than Yahweh, God of Israel. **4** *Kings joined forces*: see Psalms 2:3–8; 46:6; 76:6–8. Although the reference may envision a decisive defeat of one of Israel's foes, it more likely echoes ancient Near Eastern language of the Lord of the universe conquering and controlling the forces of chaos (compare Pss 77:16–19; 89:9–10; 114). **9–10** This psalm may reflect a pilgrimage of worshipers to the temple at one of the great festivals. As they *meditate on his unfailing love*, they realize the all-encompassing power of the Lord (*like your name ... your praise reaches to the ends of the earth*). **12–13** If a pilgrimage, the worshipers conclude their celebration of praise with a "tour" of the city.

> **Canaan & Israel**
> *Although the Bible remembers the Canaanites as idolaters, several elements of Israelite religion are similar to those in Canaanite religion. These include the tie of holidays to the agricultural year, the use of some sacrificial terminology, and even common divine names such as El and Elohim. At the same time, Israel carefully sorted through aspects of Canaanite religion in the light of Yahweh's self-revelation.*

Theological Reflection · Although out of proportion to Jerusalem's geographical and political reality, this psalm ably captures Mount Zion's theological reality as the locale of the majestic creator of the universe – Yahweh. The expanse of Yahweh's control spatially is matched by his expanse temporally (*forever and ever*).

Psalm 49

This wisdom psalm treats death. The psalmist reflects upon the great *riddle* (verse 4) of life: no level of wealth can purchase release from death. It is inevitable for all. The psalmist first notes that apparent differences between rich and poor ironically fade against the common experience of death, and both share fate with animals! The language and thought match Ecclesiastes. The psalm divides into three sections: verses 1–4 (a call of instruction to all); verses 5–12 (the futility of trusting in wealth to avoid death); and verses 13–20 (death is the great equalizer).

4 The *proverb* and *riddle* address the enigma of death's inevitability. **8** The wealthiest person cannot afford his own ransom. **11–13** Compare Ecclesiastes 2:18–21; 3:19; Luke 12:13–21. **11** This text is difficult; the Masoretic Text reads, "in their thoughts their houses remain." **14** The irony is poignant: while the rich graze confidently from their wealth, death already is grazing on them! Note the striking contrast with Psalm 23. **15** The precise intent of this verse is unclear. The psalmist may intend a statement about future life; alternately, he may simply intend a statement about present protection in this life. The verse hauntingly echoes verse 7 (whereas the rich cannot purchase an exemption from death, Yahweh intervenes for the poor). **17–20** A return to the themes of verses 6–8, 11–12.

Theological Reflection · This psalm addresses a perennial dilemma, the relationship of death to the inequities of daily life. The psalm offers a compelling reminder that death comes to all with no respect. The psalm provides a powerful poetic counterpart to Luke 12:13–21 (the parable of the rich fool) and 16:19–31 (the parable of the rich man and Lazarus). The seemingly sure substance of the rich and powerful becomes inconsequential in the moment of greatest need (the presence of death). In contrast, the poor and powerless in that same moment experience the inexhaustible richness of God (verse 15).

Psalm 50

This psalm contains elements of a covenant lawsuit (Deut 32; Isa 1:2–20; Hos 4:1–6; Mic 6:1–8). It likely functioned in covenant renewal ceremonies. The psalm manifests several of the features of covenant proceedings: theophany (verses 1–6); the calling of witnesses (verses 1, 4, 6); and charges of disloyalty to the covenant and Torah violation (verses 7, 17–20). In true prophetic fashion, this psalm

> **Ancient Covenants**
> *Ancient nations made treaties setting forth mutual obligations and prescribing blessings and curses for those who keep or violate the covenant. For Israel to violate the covenant is to tear apart the links between the people and God. The prophets spoke often of Yahweh executing the curses of the covenant so as to bring it to an end.*

affirms the inseparable relationship between worship and ethical behavior. The psalm divides into three sections: verses 1–6 (the appearance of God and summoning of the earth); verses 7–15 (the charge, namely an improper understanding of sacrifice); and verses 16–23 (a final condemnation and call to change).

1–6 God comes as judge (verses 4, 6). He summons heaven and earth as witnesses on his behalf (verses 1, 4, 6). **2** Only God can *shine forth* from the heavenly realm and Jerusalem simultaneously. **5** The *consecrated ones* [Hebrew *chasidim*] are those loyal to the covenant. **7** *I am God, your God*: The charge is simple, yet profound – God is the sole God of the universe. **8–15** God's people have completely perverted the proper understanding of sacrifice. Sacrifice derives from gratitude to the one who has first given it. It in no way insinuates dependency on God's part, for God owns the universe. These verses do not reject sacrifice but the misunderstanding and misuse of sacrifice. In the ancient Near East, sacrifice was often understood as providing for the needs of the divine realm. **16–20** These verses succinctly state the ethical misbehavior that results when God's Torah is rejected; the Decalogue is violated on multiple fronts (theft; adultery; false and malicious speech; see Hos 4:1–3). **21** The wicked have taken divine silence as approval (that is, "God is one of us"). **23** *Thank offering* [Hebrew *todah*] the one sacrifice never required of the worshiper in the Old Testament).

Theological Reflection · This psalm captures the essence of prophetic religion for a worship setting and thus of a correct relationship with God. As verse 7 puts it, *I am God, your God*, this psalm's equivalent to "I am the Lord your God" (Exod 20:2; Deut 5:6). Put simply, false religion centers upon the human; true religion centers upon God. False religion results in offerings given from a premise that God needs them and they obligate God to the giver. True religion results in true sacrifice, offerings that come from thanksgiving and gratitude (verse 23), acknowledging human dependence upon the creator and sustainer of everything.

Psalm 51

This penitential psalm (also Pss 6; 32; 38; 102; 130; 143) revolves entirely around petitions for forgiveness and restoration. The psalmist roots his multiple appeals for forgiveness in the character of God as gracious and ever willing to restore frail followers. The psalm divides into four sections: verses 1–6 (petition for pardon and confession of sin); verses 7–12 (prayer for restoration); verses 13–17 (promise of humble praise); and verses 18–19 (prayer for the restoration of Jerusalem).

1–3 *Have mercy on me*: Compare Psalms 56; 57. The psalmist rightly roots his appeal in God's character (*unfailing love, great compassion*) rather than self-justification. The psalmist uses three terms for his sin: *transgression* (*pasha*, "rebellion"); *iniquity* (*awon*, "distortion"); *sin* (*chat'ah*, "missing the mark"). The counteractions he seeks are: *blot out* (see Num 5:23); *wash* (see Exod 19:10; Lev 11:25); *cleanse* (see Num 8; Lev 13). **5** This difficult verse does not imply original sin or that sexual intercourse or childbirth are sinful. Rather, the psalmist uses exaggerated language to express his inability to deliver himself from his sinful predicament. Sin is a constant reality for the psalmist. **6** *Desire truth*: that is, faithfulness. *Teach me wisdom*: see Proverbs 1:7. **7** Compare Isaiah 1:18. **8** *Bones you have crushed*: see Psalms 6:2; 22:14. **11** *Holy Spirit*: This is not the personal indwelling Spirit of the Trinity; it is the "spirit" of God, which is by definition holy (because it derives from a holy God). God's spirit in the Old Testament is often God's power to create and transform life (compare Gen 2:7; Jer 31:33–34; Ps 104:29–30; Ezek 36:26–27; 37:10). **13** Acceptance of God's healing forgiveness always assumes a responsibility to share that forgiveness with others. **17** Compare Psalm 34:18. **19–21** These verses match the preceding private prayer with a public prayer.

Theological Reflection · This psalm provides the fullest exposition of the true nature of penitence. The psalm focuses not solely upon human failure and inability to remove guilt but more on the consoling reality of God's willingness and pleasure to forgive and restore followers to a right relationship. This psalm affirms that the confession of sin implies the profession that God is gracious, compassionate, and able to transform human weakness into obedience. Only through confession of sinfulness comes renewal.

Psalm 52

This psalm of trust contrasts the arrogant evildoer with the righteous God-fearer. While the boastful wicked *plots destruction* and relies upon his own power, the *righteous…trust in God's unfailing love*. The psalm divides into three sections: verses 1–4 (a denunciation of the arrogant evildoer); verses 4–7 (divine judgment and the reaction of the righteous); and verses 8–9 (trust and praise from the psalmist).

1 The psalmist derisively contrasts the evildoer's self-assessment (*you mighty one*) and God's verdict (*you who are a disgrace in the eyes of God*). **2** *Tongue…sharpened razor*: Speech often provides the external proof of inner corruption (see Ps 36:1–4;

Prov 6:12–15). **5** The psalmist utilizes four verbs to emphasize the gravity of the Lord's response (*bring you down ... snatch you up ... tear you ... uproot you*). *Your tent*: "Your" is missing in the Hebrew. The tent more likely is the temple than the evildoer's own house. **7** See Proverbs 11:28. **8** *Olive tree*: see Psalms 1:3; 92:12–15; Jeremiah 17:5–8.

Theological Reflection · This psalm likely reflects the turmoil experienced by the righteous living within the same community as those who actively plotted harm against them. Rather than sink into despair, the psalmist contrasts his own future as one planted and nurtured by God with that of the wicked, who have no future.

Psalm 53

See the discussion of Psalm 14, which is the same psalm with minor variations.

Psalm 54

In the midst of life-threatening difficulties, in this simple individual lament the psalmist relies upon the essence of God's character – his name (verses 1, 6). The psalm divides into three sections: verses 1–2 (petition); verses 3–5 (lament); and verses 6–7 (vow of praise).

1 *Name*: the essence of a person's character. **3** *Seek my life*: Compare 1 Samuel 23:15. *Without regard*: literally, "who do not set God in front (of them)." **5** An example of when something intended for another boomerangs upon oneself.

Theological Reflection · Psalm 54 articulates the faithful cry of one unjustly harassed by ruthless enemies. The psalmist trusts the "name" of God to rectify the present unjust situation.

Psalm 55

This individual lament graphically recounts the anguish and betrayal the psalmist experiences when his most intense enemies are his comrades. Although he may briefly long for the solitude and safety of the desert (verse 7) and removal from the *destructive forces at work in the city* (verse 11), he knows that refuge and relief come solely from Yahweh. The psalm divides unevenly into two fairly parallel panels: verses 1–15, 16–23. Both sections express the complaint of the psalmist and highlight the tragedy of betrayal by close associates. The second section moves from the agony of betrayal to trusting hope in a faithful Lord.

6 *Wings of a dove*: The dove nests in the safety of the inaccessible face of the cliff (see Ps 11; Jer 48:28; Song 2:14). **9–11** The violent city is unidentified. **12–14, 20–21** For a similar depiction of a treacherous society, see Micah 7:1–6.

Theological Reflection · This psalm captures the terrifying nature of a community where deceit and deception characterize the behavior and speech of its inhabitants. The psalmist rightly notes that no greater sorrow comes than that from betrayal by one's closest friends and fellow worshipers. In such a situation, the psalmist knows that flight solves nothing; he can only place his hope in God's unfailing love and commitment to final justice.

Psalm 56

This individual lament calls for God to intervene against plotting enemies and promises praise following the deliverance. The refrain in verses 4, 10–11 captures the essence of the psalmist's plea. The customary elements of the lament (petition, complaint, trust, vow of praise) are present in the two sections of this psalm: verses 1–7, and 8–13.

1 *Be merciful to me*: the psalmist considers this simple plea sufficient to overcome the violent plots of his opponents. **2** *In their pride*: though difficult, this line is better read "many are attacking me, O Most High" (see NRSV etc.). **3** Two contrasts dominate this lament: *afraid/trust ... God/mortal* (literally, "flesh" [Hebrew *basar*]; compare verse 11 [Hebrew *adam*]). **4** The *word I praise* is God's promise of protection. **8** To counter the evildoers who are *plotting to harm* (verse 5), the psalmist begs God to *record my lament* (literally, "my tossings"); *list my tears on your scroll* (or alternately, "put my tears in your bottle"). Either reading produces graphic imagery: the psalmist either asks God to keep a ledger of his numerous tearful moments or fill a bag with his tears, as one might fill a leather skin with life-giving liquid. **13** *Death ... feet ... walk ... life*: note the chiasm (compare Ps 116:8–9; John 8:12).

> **God & Trials**
> *Trust in God does not remove the reality of dangerous threats and difficult moments, but it does transform them (see Luke 12:4–7; Rom 8:31–38).*

Theological Reflection · This psalm ably captures the determining factor for life lived in fear or trust.

Psalm 57

As in Psalm 56, trust in God's saving presence dominates the landscape of this individual lament. Where Psalm 56 talks of trust in God, this psalm accents God's *love and faithfulness* (verse 3). The enemies may have ravenous appetites for evil, but the psalmist knows that God's love is greater, reaching even to the heavens (verse 10). The psalm divides into two sections (verses 1–5, 6–11), with a refrain concluding each section (verses 5, 11).

1–3 *Refuge in the shadow of your wings*: the psalmist pictures God as a mother bird protecting her defenseless young (compare Deut 32:10–12). The psalmist fully relies on God, who *sends from heaven and saves...rebuking those who hotly pursue*. **3** *Love...faithfulness*: the psalmist depicts these twin attributes of God as divine messengers sent for protection. **4–6** The psalmist likens his foes first to ravenous predators (verse 4) and then to hunters (verse 6); however, the extent of their deadly power pales in comparison to the expanse of Yahweh's love and glory (verse 5). **7–11** These same lines occur in Psalm 108:1–5. **8** *I will awaken the dawn*: the psalmist "orchestrates" a musical to hasten the dawn (Clifford 270–72 notes that predators typically hunt prey at night).

Theological Reflection · As in Psalm 56, the author here lives fearlessly in the midst of danger, for he takes refuge under the expansive shadow of the divine wings and recognizes the all-encompassing reach of God's love, faithfulness, and glory (compare Lam 3:22–23).

Psalm 58

This psalm challenges the interpreter. Several verses defy translation; perhaps more importantly, the identity of the addressees in verse 1 remains uncertain. The psalm divides into three sections: verses 1–5 (judgment against the judges); verses 6–9 (a prayer for divine intervention); and verses 10–11 (hope for divine retribution).

1 *Rulers*: the confusing term *elem* ("silence") is usually revocalized *elim* ("gods"). The question then becomes whether this term intends divine beings or is a euphemism for pompous earthly rulers. **3–5** The psalmist employs graphic metaphors to describe the extent and uncontrollable nature of the wickedness – it is *from birth, from the womb...the venom of a snake...like that of a cobra...that will not heed the tune of the charmer*. **6–9** The psalmist utters seven "curses" upon the evildoers. **10** The vindictive tone of the righteous is troubling.

Theological Reflection · This psalm challenges modern readers, both because of the worldview it envisions (similar to the "principalities and heavenly powers" of Eph 6:12) and because of the intensity of the retribution the psalmist desires for his adversaries. While not justifying the spirit driving the desire, contemporary readers should also acknowledge the lack of experience many of us have with rampant social injustice. The psalmist, ardently awaiting God's justice and reign, longs for those who have been "from birth" evildoers and venomous adders to be "defanged" and experience stillbirth.

Psalm 59

Given the nature of the danger, this individual lament plausibly derives from the king or his spokesperson. The psalmist focuses upon the threats to the city (verses 6, 14) and seeks vindication against the nations (verses 5, 8). The psalm graphically portrays the foes as dogs prowling about the city (verses 6, 17). The psalm divides into two sections (verses 1–10, 11–17) that have the elements typical of a lament (petition, complaint, expression of trust, anticipated thanksgiving) and a key refrain (verses 9, 17). The psalmist leads his listeners twice through the situation to underscore the gravity of the dangers.

4–5 *Arise to help...rouse yourself*: The appeal pictures God as a sleeping warrior needing awakening for battle (see Pss 7:6; 44:24; contrast 121). **6** *Snarl like dogs*: this line occurs again in verse 14. These wild street dogs initially do not attack; in verse 7 they spew vitriol; in verse 15 they scavenge to fulfill their voracious appetites. **8** Compare Psalm 2:4. **11** *Do not*

"Gods" or "Rulers"?

Scholars debate whether the addressees in Psalm 58:1 are powerful earthly judges (so NIV, etc.) or minor deities of the heavenly court (so NRSV, etc.). Both readings marshal compelling supports. Given the desire for avenging the rampant injustice running throughout the earth, a strong case can be made for the first reading. However, since ancient Israelites understood earthly events to reflect the machinations of the divine realm, this may reflect a polemic against competing foreign deities (so Kselman and Barré 535). The first reading links with the hyperbolic language of Psalm 52; the second reading finds its analogy in Psalm 82.

kill them: this line is puzzling, especially in light of verse 13 (*consume them*). Two readings seem plausible: some scholars emend the Hebrew *al* ("not") to *el* ("God"); others suggest the psalmist desires a period of public humiliation before the final destruction.

Theological Reflection · Like Psalms 57–58, this psalm carries a troublingly vindictive tone. Interestingly, the author's perspective matches what he envisions for God (*But you, O Lord, laugh at them; you scoff at all those nations*). Rampant injustice in the earth raises questions for the righteous regarding the presence of God as the just and righteous one.

Psalm 60

This national lament mourns a devastating military defeat and begs God to reverse the plight of his people with a victory. The psalmist graphically depicts the impact upon the people first as that of an earthquake upon a land (verse 2) and then as a drunken stupor (verse 3; compare Ps 75:8). Structurally, the psalm enwraps a divine oracle (verses 6–8) with complaint and petition (verses 1–5, 9–12).

6–8 The divine oracle envisions God majestically enthroned over Israel (*Gilead, Manasseh*) with the surrounding nations (*Moab, Edom, Philistia*) subject. *Ephraim* and *Judah* take pride of place (*helmet, scepter*). **6–12** These verses appear also in Psalm 108:7–13.

Theological Reflection · The psalm bespeaks the theological crisis military defeats created for God's people. The divine oracle at the center of the psalm calls upon God to resume former saving activity, affirming that only *with God will we gain the victory* (verse 12).

Psalm 61

This individual lament may have a royal voice (verses 6–7) or may merely reflect the centrality of the king's future to that of his people. The psalmist currently resides far from the temple and longs to return. Although arguable, one may plausibly divide the psalm into two main sections: verses 1–4 (a cry to God for rescue and refuge); and verses 5–8 (a prayer for the king and promise of praise).

2 *Ends of the earth*: Although some consider this a reference to the realm of death (that is, the netherworld), in the context of the psalm it more likely indicates the distance separating the psalmist from the temple (see verse 4, *tent*). **6** Compare Psalm 72:5, 15. **5** The phrase *you have heard my vows* occurs only here in the Bible. The vow may refer to a promise to return to the sanctuary (Clifford 288). **7** *Love and faithfulness* function as "guardian angels" (see Eaton 231).

Theological Reflection · This psalm demonstrates that, though the foe may cause geographical distance from God, the desire for worship and praise for God always remains.

Psalm 62

This psalm of trust ably articulates the challenges to faith that duplicitous foes can exact; however, the psalmist remains resolute in his faith and employs his own difficulties as an opportunity for exhortation to others. The psalm divides into three sections: verses 1–4 (trust in God in the midst of an enemy assault); verses 5–10 (trust in God with an exhortation to the congregation to do the same); and verses 11–12 (reason for trust in God).

2 *He alone*: The Hebrew term *ak* ("truly, surely, indeed") introduces six of the lines of this poem (verses 1, 2, 4, 5, 6, 9). **3–4** The psalmist pictures himself as a teetering wall and his foes as a wrecking crew (Limburg 206). **9** *Lowborn men...highborn*: literally, "sons of man." Many commentators consider the contrast a reference to varying degrees of social status (see Ps 49:2). Others consider the lines synonymous. With either interpretation, the emphasis falls upon the fragility of life (*only a breath*; see Ecclesiastes for the same view). **11–12** *One...two things*: Although a common rhetorical device (see Prov 30:18; Amos 1:3), here the number seems significant. Two elements paradoxically capture God's essence, power, and steadfast love (that is, God can and will requite a human *according to what he has done*) (Mays 217).

Theological Reflection · Psalm 62 reminds the reader of the theological importance of not simply offering praise to God during difficult circumstances but of using those moments to encourage others.

> **"He is my fortress ..."**
> Psalm 62 echoes sentiments about the brevity and fragility of human life found elsewhere in Ecclesiastes and Isaiah 40:12–31. *The confessional refrain captures the psalm's essence*: He alone is my rock and my salvation; he is my fortress, I will never be shaken.

Psalm 63

This psalm of trust expresses the ardent longings of one far from God's sanctuary. Though most commentators interpret this psalm as the words of one having returned from a distance and entered the Lord's sanctuary (so NIV, etc.), other interpreters consider the psalmist yet apart from the sanctuary and desiring desperately a future restoration to God's presence (so NJPS). In other psalms where longing for the temple plays a prominent role, the hope is yet to be realized (see Pss 27:4–6; 42:3–5; 84:1–2; Clifford 294). A determination of this issue results in two different divisions. Those following the first interpretation divide the psalm into three sections (with each section marked by the Hebrew term *nephesh*, "soul" [verses 1, 5, 9]): verses 1–4 (praise for a safe return to the sanctuary); verses 5–8 (an affirmation of praise for God's protective presence); and verses 9–11 (a request for justice and final praise). Those following the latter interpretation divide the psalm into two sections: verses 1–5 (hope for coming into God's presence in the future); and verses 6–11 (a recognition that God is present now) (Clifford 295).

1 Compare Psalm 42. **2** *I have seen you*: NIV reads the Hebrew perfect as past tense; alternately, some read it as "that I might see you…." Either is possible. **3** *Your love is better than life*: a dramatic comment highlighting the meaninglessness of life without God's steadfast love (compare Rom 8:38–39). **5–8** These verses intensify the previous verses: "the minor chords [are] transformed into the major key" (Davidson 199). *My soul thirsts* becomes *my soul will be satisfied as with the richest of foods*; *my lips will glorify you* becomes *with singing lips my mouth will praise you*. **6** *On my bed*: a night vigil? **11** *But the king*: perhaps the speaker of the psalm.

Theological Reflection · This psalm manifests the dramatic transformation God's presence exacts upon the worshiper, whether past or eagerly anticipated. Whatever the geographical dynamics of the psalmist's life, the theological dynamics remain clear – *You are my God* (verse 1; compare verse 8).

Psalm 64

This individual lament gives voice to one suffering from the injustices of malicious plots. The psalmist eloquently likens the verbal assault upon him to an ambush by archers and hunters. Fittingly, the retribution he seeks against his foes entails God turning their verbal weapons back upon them (note *arrow(s)* [3b/7a], *tongue(s)* [3a/8a], *suddenly* [4b/7b], *shoot* [4/7a], *fear* [4b/9a]; see Clifford 299). The psalm divides into two sections: verses 1–6 (appeal for divine help); and verses 7–10 (hopeful affirmation that God will intervene).

2 *Conspiracy*: The threat envisioned throughout is verbal, perhaps slander. **3–6** For similar graphic imagery, see Psalm 10:6–11; James 3:5–6, 9–10. **4** *From ambush*: literally, "from hiding places," an echo of the psalmist's earlier cry, *hide me* (verse 2). **8** *Shake their heads*: a gesture of contempt.

Theological Reflection · This psalm portrays the personal anguish vicious plots and verbal assaults can create in the righteous. Without condoning the principle of *talion* (that is, retribution) articulated in this psalm, one can nonetheless understand the desire for justice, especially so that the rest of *mankind will fear* and *proclaim the works of God and ponder what he has done* (verse 9).

Psalm 65

This song of thanksgiving likely has as its backdrop the Festival of Tabernacles (Exod 23:16; 34:22; Deut 16:13–15), that autumn festival celebrating God's bounty in the harvesting of the vineyards and seeking God's renewing presence in the land through the winter rains (see Lev 23:33–43; Num 29:12–39). During that festival, the worshipers acknowledge sin and seek forgiveness (verse 3), celebrate God's mighty acts in creation (verses 6–7), and appeal to God to renew fertility to the arid soil. The psalm divides into three sections: verses 1–4 (praise for God who forgives sins and blesses his people); verses 5–8 (praise for God who manifests his mighty power in creation); and verses 9–13 (thanks for the life-giving rains).

3 *Forgave*: The language of atonement is common in the priestly materials (Exod 12:48; 40:32; Lev 16:1). For confession and forgiveness of sins preceding rain, see 1 Kings 8:35–36; Amos 4:7–8 (Kselman and Barré 536). **4–5** *We are filled … you answer us*: The Hebrew may also be read as a prayer: "May you fill … may you answer." God is the object of the praise, the temple the location. **5** The phrase *awesome deeds* usually references the exodus and God's mighty acts in history, but here, the

> **God of the Rains**
> *The language of Psalm 65:9–13 also likely echoes the Canaanite language for Baal sending rain as he drove his chariot across the mountain ridges. Israel, however, knew the great chariot rider was none other than Yahweh (see Deut 33:26; Pss 68:4, 33; Hab 3:8).*

worshipers celebrate God's mighty acts in nature. **9–13** The image is graphic, picturing God as a regal farmer preparing his soil, irrigating his fields, and harvesting a bumper crop. **12** The winter rains cause even the desert to bloom and produce grass.

Theological Reflection · This psalm provides a stunning reminder that the productivity of the earth ultimately resides in the hands of the Lord of the universe, not in some mechanistic and impersonal regulations of nature.

Psalm 66

This song of thanksgiving is a somewhat unusual blend of communal (verses 5–12) and individual (verses 13–19) voices. The community of faith gathers in worship and celebrates the impact of God's ancient saving acts upon present believers. An individual (possibly the king) then extols God's recent gracious deliverance. The psalm divides into five sections (each marked by *Selah*): verses 1–4 (an invitation to praise); verses 5–7 (an invitation to acknowledge God's lordship manifested in the exodus); verses 8–12 (an acknowledgement of recent difficulties); verses 13–15 (an offering of a fulfilled vow); and verses 16–20 (an offering of thanksgiving).

> **Selah**
>
> *A refrain that appears 71 times in Psalms, the meaning of the word* selah *is unknown. However, it is likely some sort of musical notation.*

1, 5, 8 Each opening section begins with an imperative summons to praise (*Shout…Come and see…Praise*). **6** The *sea…waters* (literally, "river") reference either the exodus, or the exodus and crossing of the Jordan. **9** *Feet from slipping*: see Psalm 121:3. **10** *Tested us…refined us like silver*: see Isaiah 1:25. **12** *Fire and water*: figure of speech for "every conceivable difficulty" (Isa 43:2).

Theological Reflection · This marvelous psalm demonstrates the influence of past events on the present. Where Psalm 65 celebrates God's mighty acts in creation, Psalm 66 celebrates God's mighty acts in history. The worshiping community lives in the present with the reality of those defining past moments of salvation history (especially the exodus). Against that glorious backdrop, the individual plays out his or her recent personal experience of God's deliverance (verse 16). The psalmist reminds the listening congregation that difficulties can be borne faithfully with the memory of God's faithfulness. The response of the individual and corporate worshipers provides powerful testimony to the nations of God's sovereign lordship in the earth.

Psalm 67

How one interprets the verb tenses in this psalm determines its understanding. All the verbs are imperfect (indicating incomplete action) except for the lone perfect (indicated completed action) verb in verse 6 (*yield*). If this verb is read as past tense, then this psalm is most likely a communal thanksgiving for a bountiful harvest, but if it indicates a prayer or wish, then this psalm is best read as a communal petition for the productivity of the land. Either interpretation is grammatically possible. Though numerous translations follow the first reading (NRSV, REB), the latter reading seems preferable (NIV, NJPS). The psalm has a chiastic arrangement, where the prayer for God's blessing (verses 1, 7) and call for the people's praise (verses 3, 5) encircle the central goal of the psalm (verse 4).

1 This verse creatively echoes the Aaronic blessing in Numbers 6:24–26, asking that God *bless* (that is, extend well-doing) and *make his face shine* (look approvingly) upon the people. **6** *Land will yield its harvest*: reading the Hebrew perfect as a wish.

Theological Reflection · This psalm goes beyond a simple request for a bountiful harvest and promise of thanksgiving in return. Its ultimate goal is global, for it seeks a successful yield so that the *nations* and *peoples* (the terms occur seven times) may see God's benevolence and offer praise in return. As the nations see God's care and sustenance of Israel, they will themselves enter into celebration and rejoicing (verse 4).

Psalm 68

Most scholars rightly consider this psalm the greatest interpretive challenge in the Psalter. The genre and structure are less than obvious, and the text bristles with unclear terms and lines defying translation. With all these obscurities, some basic contours seem clear. The psalm seems to reflect a liturgical march (the three references to procession in verses 1, 7, 17) that reenacts God's movement from Sinai to Zion. Along the way, the worshipers celebrate various moments in that historical march. The psalmist utilizes language familiar from Israel's ancient traditions and language about the universe familiar throughout the ancient Near East. The psalm begins with a call to Yahweh to march forth victoriously; it concludes with a call to the whole earth to praise Yahweh as Lord of the universe.

1 The language echoes Numbers 10:35–36 (language spoken at the beginning of a military processional with the ark). In the ancient Near East, war was not merely between armies; it was ultimately between the gods of those armies. **2** *Wax melts*: see Psalm 97:5; Micah 1:4. **4** The phrase *rides on the clouds* occurs repeatedly in Canaanite texts for Baal; here Yahweh is the true Lord of the mountaintops (compare Deut 33:26; Ps 18:10; Isa 19:1). **5–6** For similar presentations of God as protector of the vulnerable, see Deuteronomy 10:18; 27:19; Psalm 82:2–3; Isaiah 35:3–6; 61:1–2). **7–14** The scene is that of the march from Sinai to Zion (as in Deut 33:3–5; Judg 5:4–5; Hab 3:3–15). **12–14** Extremely obscure. **14** *Wings...dove...feathers...gold*: uncertain. Some scholars find here a reference to the coloring of the homing doves released to relay the news from the battlefield (Eaton 249); others find a reference to the capture of booty, which may have included figurines of the goddess Astarte. **15–16** The more majestic mountains in northern Israel envy Yahweh's choice of the geographically less impressive Mount Zion! **18** Through verse 18 the focus is on God's coming; from verse 19 on the focus is on God's presence (Davidson 211). **23** Compare 1 Kings 22:38. **24–25** The liturgical procession is comprised of *singers*, *musicians*, and *maidens playing tambourines* (see Exod 15:20–21; Isa 40:9). **27** The four tribes mentioned may represent the northern (*Zebulun*, *Naphtali*) and southern (*Judah*) borders. *Benjamin* is puzzling; some scholars cite the practice of the least powerful entity leading the procession. **29** *Kings bring gifts*: see Isaiah 60:6–7, 11–14. **33** *Who rides...thunders* is a reference to God as the Lord of nature (as in Ps 29); the language returns the listener to the beginning of the psalm (verse 4).

Theological Reflection · Although the language is dense and confusing at times, this psalm clearly portrays the prominent place in worship that celebrating the mighty acts of God should play. The psalmist powerfully intertwines past saving moments with present circumstances. In so doing, present worshipers affirm their place in Yahweh's salvific scheme.

Psalm 69

This lengthy individual lament captures the gravity of the distress through dramatic repetition. The psalmist rehearses more than once his anguish, the intensity of his foes' scorn, and the need for God to rectify the situation. Despair surrounds him as the ground beneath his feet gives way, he sinks in a river, the waters rise to his throat, and his enemies hurl insults at him. The psalm divides into five sections: verses 1–4 (a prayer for deliverance); verses 5–12 (a lament of alienation); verses 13–18 (a renewed appeal for deliverance); verses 19–28 (a curse upon the enemies); and verses 29–36 (a promise of thanksgiving).

3 The psalmist's *throat is parched* and his *eyes fail* from weeping and wailing (see Pss 31:9–10; Lam 2:18–19). **4** *Did not steal*: the language highlights the general injustice of the psalmist's circumstances rather than specifically citing his specific "crime." **7–8** *Shame...stranger*: In the ancient world, shame led to ostracism from the community. **9** *Zeal for your house*: likely a reference to the temple. **12** *Those who sit at the gate...drunkards*: the former are the influential of the city (see Deut 21:19; Amos 5:12, 15); the latter are the despised. All mock the psalmist (compare Job 30). **14–15** The appeal echoes the lament (verses 1–2). **17** Yahweh's *face* figures prominently in Psalms 67–69. **22–28** The psalmist desires the suffering he has experienced to come upon his adversaries. **33** *Captive people*: perhaps a reference to the exile. The previous references to *ox* and *bull* may similarly indicate an inability to sacrifice in a foreign land (see Ps 137).

Theological Reflection · The dramatic linguistic repetition captures the seriousness of the psalmist's circumstances. Verbal abuse matches physical suffering. The psalmist refuses to abandon faith in God; rather, he pleads for deliverance, seeking God to *answer*, *out of the goodness of [his] love* and *great mercy* (verse 16). The psalmist bases his plea not solely on the character of God, who *hears the needy and does not despise his captive people* (verse 33). The anguish of his social alienation pales in comparison to his fear of alienation from God (verse 17).

> **Psalms in Early Christianity**
> Psalm 69 is second only to Psalm 22 in verses utilized to capture the experience of Jesus and the early church.

Psalm 70

This individual lament duplicates Psalm 40:13–17, with minor variations. Since this psalm makes sense on its own, it was probably incorporated into Psalm 40, rather than extracted from it (Mays 233). The motif of shame provides a dominant focus of the psalm (four times in verses 2–3). The psalm divides into two sections: verses 1–3 (an appeal for God to shame the foes); and verses 4–5 (a plea for God's aid to come quickly).

Psalm 71

This psalm of trust reflects the spirit of one who has lived a long life in faithful relationship with God (verses 6, 9, 17–18) and now is experiencing threats and malicious plots (verses 10–13, 20). Refusing to abandon God, he promises to proclaim the gracious power of the Lord to the next generation (verse 18). The psalm moves easily among lament, petition, and praise. The psalm divides into three sections, each concluding with a note of praise: verses 1–8 (an affirmation of trust and appeal for deliverance); verses 9–16 (an appeal to thwart the plans of the foes); and verses 17–24 (a promise of continuing praise).

1–3 Compare Psalm 31:1–3. **5–6** The psalmist has belonged to God since birth. **7** A *portent* can be positive or negative. A positive nuance understands the sufferer seeing himself as a living example of God's protective presence (so NJPS; Clifford 328–29); a negative nuance understands the sufferer seeing himself as a current victim of God's wrath (so NIV, NRSV; Mays 235). **16** *Proclaim your righteousness* is God's right way of acting in the lives of his followers. **19** See Isaiah 40:12–31. **20** *Restore my life again* more likely refers to restoration of health than future life. **22** *Harp...lyre* may indicate that the psalmist was a temple musician.

Theological Reflection · This psalm reflects the trials and tribulations that may come at the end of one's life. Although old age carries its share of troubles (Eccl 12:1–8), this psalmist chooses to focus more upon the potential to praise God for repeated acts of kindness and righteousness. The psalmist is a realist, acknowledging that the threats of his foes hurt, and the dangers are severe. However, he has taken refuge in Yahweh, who is his rock and fortress.

Psalm 72

This royal psalm (like Pss 2; 18; 20; 21; 45; 89; 101; 110; 132) prays that the king will practice social justice and experience a long reign. The psalm articulates the essential purpose of the king as God's agent in the dispensing of justice. The psalmist structures his prayer in four sections: verses 1–4 (prayer that the king imitate Yahweh in executing justice and righteousness); verses 5–7 (prayer for a long and successful reign); verses 8–14 (prayer that the king have worldwide dominion); and verses 15–17 (prayer that the king have a long life and wealth). Verses 18–20 provide a blessing and conclusion to Book Two of the Psalter.

1 *Royal son*: The king, as Yahweh's earthly representative (see 1 Sam 10:1–2), was understood as his adopted son. The motif of *Justice* and *righteousness* runs throughout the Old Testament (Ps 82:2–4; Prov 29:14; Isa 9:7; 11:3–5; Amos 5:24; Mic 5:4–5). Justice is clearly central to this psalm, occurring 25 times in some form. **5–7** The king enhances; he does not give life. **5** As the *sun* shines upon the land and blesses it, so the king shines upon his people and blesses them. **6** *Rain...showers*: see Isaiah 45:8; 55:10–11; Hosea 6:3. **8** *Sea to sea...river* spans the Mediterranean to the Persian Gulf (Euphrates River). **9** *Lick dust*: A metaphor for subjection. **10** *Tarshish... Sheba...Seba* encompasses western Spain to Arabia (Isa 60:6–10). **15–17** See 1 Samuel 10:24; 2 Samuel 16:16; 1 Kings 1:31, 34, 39.

Theological Reflection · This psalm ably articulates the intricate and intimate relationship among God, the ruler, and the people. The ethical behavior of God's leaders has ramifications not only for the people of the land but for the well-being of the land itself.

> **God & King**
>
> *The king as God's earthly representative was responsible for insuring that justice and righteousness proliferated throughout the land. When that occurred, the people could pray that the king rule "forever."*

BOOK 3 · PSALMS 73–89

PSALM 73

This wisdom psalm grapples intensely with the inequities in life. Like Job, Jeremiah, and Habakkuk, it struggles to work through the dilemmas that the prosperity of the wicked and the poverty of the righteous create. The psalm reads like a series of internal dialogues the psalmist has with himself about justice and social inequity. Although internal, the psalmist "thinks out loud," for he knows the decisions he makes in his own life have profound consequences for the community of faith. The psalm divides into three sections: verses 1–12 (the lot of the wicked); verses 13–17 (the dilemma of the psalmist); and verses 18–28 (the final lot of the psalmist and the wicked).

1–2 *Surely*: see also verses 13, 18 (compare Jer 12:1). These opening verses have been called "the great nevertheless." The psalmist does not doubt God's goodness, only how to reconcile it with current events. **7** *From their callous hearts comes iniquity* follows the Septuagint. The Hebrew reads, "their eyes bulge with fat." **11** A classic description of the neglect of God and self-absorption. **13** The psalmist laments the futility of living righteously in the face of immoral prosperity. **15** The psalmist refuses to reject his faith; surrendering trust in God betrays the coming generation. **17** The "solution" to the psalmist's dilemma – the presence of God in worship. **23** The term *always* speaks less to the quantity and more to the quality of life. **24** The precise nuance of *glory* remains uncertain; this term is not used elsewhere in the Old Testament of heavenly glory. Most of the references involve earthly situations (Exod 14:4, 17–18; 16:7, 10; 24:16–18; 34:29–35; Isa 35:2; 40:5; 59:19). **28** *Near God* is typically a technical term for access to the temple.

Theological Reflection · This psalm eloquently grapples with the dilemma of speaking of the goodness of God in the midst of rampant wickedness. The psalmist, faithful throughout, cannot solve this vexing dilemma. However, rather than forsake his faith, he enters the sanctuary, and in worship discovers reality as God intends it for the faithful. As in other wisdom psalms (though with a different emphasis tenor [for example, Pss 37; 49]), he experiences the transforming power of God's presence in his life.

> **Worship**
>
> Psalm 73 is a powerful reminder of the necessity of worship. While worship is no substitute for serious intellectual effort, it functions effectively as a place where God meets struggling followers and reorients them. In worship, believers reaffirm that God's goodness is not about prosperity but about presence.

Psalm 74

This communal lament focuses solely upon the destruction of the temple and the impact of that event upon worshipers. The enemy's path of destruction across the land and within God's sanctuary has left the people reeling. The psalmist's despair is heightened by the absence of any sense of how long the destruction will continue. The psalm divides into three sections: verses 1–11 (an appeal to God to remember the people and stop the senseless violence); verses 12–17 (an affirmation of God's mighty acts in creation); and verses 18–23 (an appeal to God to remember his people and intervene).

1–3 The psalmist employs riveting phrases (*sheep of your pasture; people you purchased from of old; tribe of your inheritance* [see Ps 78:52–55]) to incite God to action. **3** *Everlasting ruins*: The motif of punishment with no time limit runs throughout the psalm (verses 10, 19; *how long* in verses 9–10). **4** The *standards* are military banners. **9** That no divine word is forthcoming regarding the length of the oppression heightens the tragedy. *Prophets* should have a word from the Lord in these situations (Pss 39:4; 90:11–12; Jer 25:11–12). While the enemy's military *signs* (verse 4) proliferate, *signs* (verse 9) from God are noticeably absent. **12–17** The psalmist articulates God's majestic power at creation in military language, where God defeated the awesome powers of chaos (*heads of Leviathan*). The psalmist employs cosmic language of a primordial battle familiar to the inhabitants of the ancient Near East (Pss 77:16–20; 89:9–10; Isa 51:9–11). Just as God destroyed the potentially destructive forces of chaos at creation, so God should now engage the destroyers of his temple. **13** *Split open*: similar language is used of the Red Sea crossing. **18–23** The call to *remember* intensifies with an additional *do not forget*. Just as the psalmist utilizes emotive language in the opening appeal, so now he concludes with equally compelling language to pull Yahweh into the fray: *enemy has mocked you … foolish people have reviled your name … covenant … poor and needy … defend your cause*.

Theological Reflection · Space and time matter in the lives of believers. For the faithful community, the destruction of the temple raises questions about God's control over the forces of evil in the world; the silence of God and absence of any indication of "how long" this reign of terror will last raise questions about God's control of history. The psalmist pleads with God to intervene in the melee in ways comparable to the defeat of chaos at the origins of the world.

Psalm 75

This psalm manifests several literary forms in its thanksgiving. Within the psalm several voices speak: the congregation offering praise, and God (or a spokesman for God, who expands on the divine oracle). The text comes from a ritual in the temple. The psalm divides into three sections: verse 1 (opening thanksgiving); verses 2–8 (divine oracle with elaboration); and verses 9–10 (closing praise).

2–5 God declares a plan to hold the inhabitants of creation accountable; all arrogant self-reliance should stop. **2** The *appointed time* refers either to a set time or place (for example, an assembly). **4** *Horns* are a symbol of power. The *arrogant* and *wicked* opponents of God may be earthly foes (as in Pss 5:5; 73:3), or possibly heavenly adversaries (as in Pss 58:1; 82:1; Clifford 30). **8** God's *cup* of *foaming wine* can contain either beneficial or harmful drink (see Job 21:20; Pss 60:3; 116:13; Isa 51:17; Hab 2:16; Rev 14:10). **9–10** Yahweh promises to "dehorn" the wicked and exalt the *horns* of the righteous.

Theological Reflection · Through this psalm, the gathered community remembers that the future and destiny of the world lay not in the hands of the earthly powers but in the hand of the one who first fashioned the earth and continues to hold it securely in place.

Psalm 76

Although most scholars categorize this psalm as a song of Zion (like Ps 46), the psalmist speaks more of the Lord who dwells there than of the city itself. Zion figures prominently as the locale where the majestic warrior Yahweh won victories and now receives deserved acclaim. Wordplay makes the psalm more memorable. The psalm divides into three sections: verses 1–3 (praise for the "renowned" God); verses 4–6 (praise for the "resplendent" God); and verses 7–12 (praise for the "awesome" God; so Kselman and Barré 538–39).

> **Alliteration**
> *The repetition of sounds in poetry, alliteration is not uncommon in Psalms. Here, the psalmist punctuates his praise with key words, beginning with the letter "nun": he calls the worshipers to make vows [nideru, verse 11] to their God who is known [noda`, verse 1], resplendent [na'or, verse 4], and feared [nora', verses 7, 12].*

2 *Salem*: Jerusalem. **3** God shatters the war weapons of his opponents. **10** *The survivors of your wrath are restrained*: literally, "a remnant of wrath(s) you will gird on."

Theological Reflection · The militaristic tone of this psalm may give modern readers discomfort. Israel sang this song as a tiny, beleaguered nation among superpowers. Nonetheless, as God's people, they affirmed each time they beheld the beauty and splendor of Zion and the temple perched atop it, that Yahweh, the fearsome and all-powerful ruler of the universe, held their future in his hands. In a world riddled with injustice and the oppressive abuse of power, faithful Israel knew no force could withstand the withering judgment of a God who *rose up … to save all the afflicted of the land* (verse 9).

Psalm 77

This psalm uses two distinct genres: individual lament (verses 1–10) and hymn (verses 11–20). Some scholars consider this an example of the merging of two originally distinct poems; other scholars suggest that the sufferer places his personal turmoil in the context of Israel's earlier deliverance by Yahweh. The lamenting sufferer in the opening lines speaks as a representative (king?) of the people, who personalizes the anguish of God's people and reminds God through hymnic praise of past acts of deliverance, especially the exodus (Clifford 37–38). Each of the sections (verses 1–10, 11–20) divides into three subsections: verses 1–2, 3–6, 7–10, 11–12, 13–15, 16–20.

2 *Stretched out untiring hands* provides a unifying theme to the psalm (verses 10, 15, 20; Kselman and Barré 539). **4–7** Remembrance of the past triggers sorrow, given the gap between past and present divine treatment. **7–9** Questions of the extent and duration of the suffering highlight the plight of the psalmist. **10** This verse, variously interpreted, transitions the reader to the next section. The psalmist's appeal is striking; he chooses to *remember* God's former saving acts (*the years of the right hand*). **13** See Isaiah 40:12–31. **16–19** See Exodus 15. **17–18** Just as the psalmist *cried out* twice (verse 1), so God "thunders" twice (Kselman and Barré 539). **20** Yahweh formerly led his people by the *hand of Moses and Aaron*; earlier the psalmist *stretched out* [his] *untiring hands* (verse 3). **19** The *footprints were not seen* line is noticeably absent from Exodus 15! Perhaps the psalmist longs for God to become visible again.

Theological Reflection · Worship leaders must articulate the concerns of the congregation in the language of faith. Here the psalmist, presumably an influential worship leader, personalizes the community's suffering. He speaks his appeal to the all-powerful God, who currently seems absent, in the hymnic language well known to his listening worshipers, the language of deliverance at the Red Sea. Utilizing the powerful language of that defining event in the people's history, he eloquently calls upon God to reactivate that same saving power in the present circumstances.

Psalm 78

This psalm (like Pss 105; 106; 136) utilizes history for instruction. The psalmist begins with the reason for reciting history; he intends to keep his audience from repeating the failures of previous generations of God's people. The psalm divides into three major sections, with the two historical panels having several subsections: verses 1–11 (didactic introduction –"do not be like us"); verses 12–39 (from the Red Sea through the wilderness); verses 40–72 (from Egypt to Canaan). The two recitals of history follow a common theological pattern: gracious divine acts (verses 12–16, 40–55); rebellion (verses 17–20, 56–58); divine anger and punishment (verses 21–32, 59–64); and divine merciful response (verses 33–39, 65–72).

> **God & History**
> The history of God's people is read theologically as one of God's fidelity to Israel, contrasted with the people's rebellion.

1–11 The introduction bears marks of wisdom terminology and influence (see Prov 3:1; 4:2). **2** The *parables* (or proverbs) emphasize the comparison; the *hidden things* (or riddles) highlight the present relevance of a past event (see Judg 14:12; Matt 13:35). **7** *Not forget* connotes not a slip of memory but deliberate disregard (note the contrast, *keep his commands*). **12** *Zoan*, in the eastern part of the Nile delta, was the ancient capital of the Hyksos (known as Avaris) and later of Ramesses II and his successors. **13** *Stand firm like a wall*: see Exodus 15:8; 14:9–20; Numbers 20:8–13. **21** *Lord ... very angry*: God's anger results from the failure of his people to entrust their lives to the God who could supply their every need. **38** See Exodus 34:6. **44–51** The psalmist arranges the plagues theologically rather than chronologically. **65** See Psalm 44:23. **60–72** God's rejection and destruction of Shiloh is contrasted with the selection of Zion and David.

Theological Reflection · This psalm expresses in poetic verse what Deuteronomy 6:20–25 affirms in narrative prose: the importance of teaching the following generation about faithful living. However, biblical instruction is ironic, for those who pass on the traditions of the faith simultaneously acknowledge their own failures to entrust themselves fully to God.

> **Materialism & Idolatry**
> Psalm 78 also highlights two constant failures that plague every generation of God's people: the desire to have more than is necessary (materialism) and the tendency to worship self rather than God (idolatry).

Psalm 79

This communal lament matches the language and setting of Psalm 74. The psalmist depicts the enemy's invasion and desecration of God's holy city and temple. He complements the violent image of bodies strewn about the city streets with the taunting scorn the faithful survivors currently experience at the hands of their captors. The stakes are high, for the rebuke God's people receive is nothing less than a mocking of the God they worship. The psalm divides into three sections: verses 1–4 (a description of devastation); verses 5–10 (a plea for God to intervene); and verses 11–13 (final petition).

1 *Inheritance* is the covenant term for God's land (or people). **2** The bodies lie unburied as *food to the birds* (an act of desecration in the ancient Near East). **5** *How long* is not merely rhetorical but genuinely seeks insight into the length of the punishment (Pss 39:4–5; 74:9). **6** The psalmist asks God to *pour out* [his] *wrath on the nations*, just as they *poured out blood like water* around Jerusalem (verse 3). **12** *Pay back ... seven times*: the desire for vengeance is graphic and should not be minimized. The survivors remain surrounded by the dead bodies of their compatriots and verbally assaulted with taunts about their God and their faith.

Theological Reflection · A community experiences deep anguish when a key symbol of God's protective and sustaining presence lies in ruins. The vindictive expressions are troubling, but worthy of hearing. They invite the reader to consider seriously a setting in which God's presence, power, and nature are ridiculed and scorned, especially a setting where evil (where those *that do not acknowledge* or *call upon your name* [verse 6]) seemingly triumphs over good, and no evidence of relief is in sight. Moments such as these are critical, for faith in God is at stake (see Isa 40–55).

Psalm 80

This communal lament pleads with God for restoration, rooting its plea in the ancient image of the people as God's handpicked vine brought from Egypt. The psalm divides into four sections, punctuated by a refrain seeking restoration and the blessing of God's presence (verses 3, 7, 19; also 14): verses 1–3 (an appeal to restore

Israel); verses 4–7 (a description of the tragedy); verses 8–13 (a description of Israel as a vine); and verses 14–19 (an appeal to restore Israel and her ruler).

1–2 A king in the ancient Near East often designated himself *shepherd* of his people. For Yahweh as shepherd, see Psalms 23:1; 28:9; Isaiah 40:11; Ezekiel 34:15. *Enthroned between the cherubim* reminds one of the picture of Yahweh sitting on the outstretched wings of the cherubs flanking the ark (2 Sam 7:6; Ps 99:1). *Cherubim* are winged lions or bulls (based on ancient Near Eastern iconography). **3** Compare Psalm 126; Numbers 6:24–26. **8–11** The imagery of Israel as Yahweh's transplanted vine occurs most prominently in the prophetic literature (see Isa 5:1–7; Jer 2:21; 6:9; Ezek 17:1–6; Hos 9:10; 10:1). **11** *Sea...river* likely refers to the Mediterranean Ocean and Euphrates River. **17** *Man...son of man*: for similar parallelism, see Psalm 8:4. In Ezekiel 19:10–14, the vine is transplanted in Canaan, and its strongest branch becomes a ruler's scepter (see Clifford 56). The language probably refers to the king (as in Ps 110:1).

> **Indicators of Northern Composition**
> *The references to Israel, Joseph, Ephraim, and Manasseh make a northern origin for Psalm 80 plausible.*

Theological Reflection · The beleaguered people cry out for God to return to them. They remind God of prior care in bringing the "vine" into the land and question whether it will all now be for naught. Like the previous psalm, this one appeals for help by employing the treasured traditions of the ancestors. Faith employs the past to weather the present.

Psalm 81

This psalm most likely functioned as a prophetic liturgy for the Feast of Tabernacles (see Lev 23:33–43; compare Ps 50). A temple official delivers an oracle on God's behalf (verses 6–16). The psalmist implores his hearers not to emulate their ancestors, who refused to listen to God, but to *listen* to the God who calls and claims them. The psalm divides into two sections: verses 1–5 (hymnic call to worship); and verses 6–16 (divine oracle).

3 *Ram's horn*: the *shofar* (used not as a worship instrument, but as a call to worship). *New moon... moon is full*: two weeks (the length of the Feast of Tabernacles). **5** *Where we heard a language we did not understand* (literally, "a language I did not know I hear") is incredibly difficult to interpret (Jer 5:15). **6–16** For other examples of divine oracles, see Psalms 2:7; 12:6; 32:8–9; 101:6–7. These verses present in compressed form the experience from exodus to the entrance into the land. **7** *I tested...Meribah*: in Exodus 17:1–7 and Numbers 20:2–13, the people test Yahweh. **9** The first commandment captures the purpose of the exodus (see Exod 20:2–3). **11–13** Yahweh wants his people to *listen* (that is, obey) (see Exod 19:3–6). **16** *Wheat...honey*: see Deuteronomy 32:13–14.

Theological Reflection · Worship must involve rehearsing the saving deeds of God. However, to remember is not simply a stroll down memory lane. To hear and remember what God has done can only result in grateful obedience.

Psalm 82

This psalm may challenge the modern reader unfamiliar with the ancient Near Eastern world. Ancient peoples believed the divine realm was populated with numerous gods; early on, the issue was less the existence of these gods and more who reigned over the divine realm (that is, these gods were real, but clearly subordinate to Yahweh; see Deut 4:19). This psalm pulls back the curtains of heaven and presents a divine council hearing (see Job 1–2; 1 Kgs 22; Ps 29). Yahweh presides over the divine council; however, its members have actively sided with the evildoers of the earth. Yahweh charges them with dereliction of duties and threatens the ultimate punishment – mortality (verse 7). The psalm divides into three sections: verses 1–5 (the trial of the assembly of gods); verses 6–7 (the verdict); and verses 8 (a concluding prayer for justice).

1 *Great assembly*: literally, "assembly of El." *Gods*: although some scholars consider this hyperbolic language for arrogant earthly judges and rulers, the language fits the worldview of the ancient Near East. The best text of Deuteronomy 32:8–9 suggests that each nation had its own god (responsible for maintaining justice), but Yahweh maintained justice in Israel and oversaw the affairs of all the nations. For a court hearing, see Isaiah 41:21–24. **2–3** The members of the divine assembly have failed miserably in their most crucial task, maintaining social justice. **6–7** *Die like mere men*: mortality comes to these presumed divine beings.

Theological Reflection · The psalmist first reminds his listeners that, in a world where numerous people make claims for their gods, Yahweh stands supreme as Lord of the universe and calls all other gods to account. Second, a key component to a god's power and viability is the ability to generate and maintain social justice for all, especially the powerless.

Psalm 83

This national lament asks God to intervene in current affairs in a manner similar to past saving actions with Israel. The psalm moves between labeling this crisis an assault upon God's people and as an attack upon God. The psalm divides into two sections: verses 1–8 (introduction and complaint against Israel's foes); and verses 9–18 (plea for destruction of the enemy).

1 *Silent ... quiet*: that is, inactive. **2–4** The psalmist designates the enemy's threat a conspiracy (Ps 2). **5–7** No known historical period evidences an alliance including all these participants. The list is simply a shorthand for "everybody." Significantly, ten nations are mentioned (a symbol of completeness). **9–11** See Judges 4–8. **13–15** The language portrays the devastating waste upon the landscape left behind by the scorching east wind (see Isa 29:5–6; Hos 13:15).

Theological Reflection · Modern readers rightly wince at the intensity of the vindication desired by the psalmist. For the psalmist, the stakes are high because God's reputation hangs in the balance. Accordingly, he cries out for justice that responds violently to the overwhelming injustice that surrounds God's people. Interestingly, the ultimate goal he desires in such desperate circumstances is *that men will seek your name, O Lord* (verse 16) and to *let them know that you ... alone are the Most High over all the earth* (verse 18).

Psalm 84

This song of Zion (Pss 46; 48; 76; 122) eloquently verbalizes the intense joy pilgrims felt as they journeyed to Jerusalem to worship at the temple (see Ps 42:1–2). The attraction of Zion is obvious; it is the dwelling place of Yahweh (the terms "God" and "Yahweh" occur seven times each). Blessing ("happiness") comes to those associated with Zion who trust in the God who dwells there (verses 4, 5, 12). The psalm divides into four sections: verses 1–4 (longing for the temple); verses 5–7 (the pilgrimage); verses 8–9 (prayer for the king); and verses 10–12 (blessing that comes from Yahweh and the temple).

1 *Lovely*: better "beloved" (the focus is less upon the aesthetic beauty of Zion and more its religious significance; see Mays 274.). **3** The psalmist longs to experience the same security defenseless birds find in dwelling in God's sanctuary. *My king and my God* presents two key facets of God, his power to protect (*Lord Almighty*, literally, "Lord of the armies") and a gracious willingness to care for each follower (*my king and my God*). **7** *Strength to strength* is unclear. It may refer to the increased confidence the worshipers feel as they get closer to the city (Davidson 278). **9** *Shield ... anointed*: a reference to the king. **10** The psalmist captures the joy of experiencing God's presence through contrast (*one day ... thousand*); *doorkeeper* may be better translated *at the threshold* (contrasting with *dwell*). **11** *Sun ... shield*: the only place in the Psalter where Yahweh is compared to the sun (but see Isa 60:19–20; Rev 21:23). The former image highlights God's life-giving presence, the latter his protective presence (Limburg 286).

> **The Valley of Baca**
> *In verse 6, the valley of Baca is not a specific locale, but a place of drought (Hebrew* baka *is a desert shrub).*

Theological Reflection · This psalm captures the sentiment of all faithful worshipers who joyfully anticipate coming into God's presence for praise and celebration. Appropriately, the believer's life is characterized as pilgrimage toward a complete experience of the presence of God.

Psalm 85

The setting of this national lament intrigues modern commentators. The psalmist longs for God to manifest the same forgiving deliverance in the present as he has in previous times (verses 1–3). The psalm divides into three sections: verses 1–3 (praise for past blessings); verses 4–7 (lament over the current situation); and verses 8–13 (salvation oracle).

1 *Restored the fortunes* most often refers to return from exile (see Deut 30:3; Ps 126; Jer 29:14; 31:23; Ezek 29:14; Amos 9:14). The phrase is virtually synonymous with

> **"Our land will yield its increase ..."**
> *Some scholars envision Psalm 85 as a plea for rejuvenating fall rains that must come following the autumn Feast of Tabernacles (note verses 11–12). Others see a postexilic setting:* Yahweh has restored the fortunes *of the people by returning them from exile (verses 1–3), but a complete realization of all the former glories of the land remains a future hope (verses 4–7).*

forgave. Although some read the verbs in verses 1–3 as prayer or as announcing a future event, they are best read as occurring in the past. **4–7** The language and questions are typical of laments (see Pss 13; 44). **8–13** This "word from the Lord" (oracle) the psalmist seeks is punctuated by key theological terms – *peace, salvation, love, faithfulness, righteousness*. **10** *Meet…kiss* utilizes the metaphor of two royal courtiers meeting and greeting after a long absence (see Clifford 77).

Theological Reflection · Communal laments remind the reader that current difficulties are often heightened by memories of past gracious actions by Yahweh. However, while the memories magnify the present distress, they simultaneously provide a basis for appeal to God. Perhaps most striking is the language employed to capture the essence of life when God restores the fortunes of the people; the language is relational (*peace, salvation, faithfulness, righteousness*). The lamenting community knows that the "present crisis cannot be God's final word to his people" (Davidson 281).

Psalm 86

This individual lament seeks rescue from unspecified problems. The psalm divides into three sections: verses 1–7 (request for divine aid); verses 8–13 (statement of confidence in the Lord); and verses 14–17 (lament and petition).

1–4 The psalmist first bases his appeal upon his circumstances (*poor and needy*) and then upon his relationship with God (*servant*). **5** The adjective *forgiving* occurs only here; the verb occurs only with God (Pss 25:11; 103:3; 130:4). **8** For God's incomparability, see Exodus 8:6; Psalms 35:10; 71:19; Isaiah 40:12–31. **11** The psalmist characterizes right conduct as a *walk* in a single direction; loyalty and single-minded devotion he calls an *undivided heart* (literally, "united in heart").

Theological Reflection · This model petition names God 22 times. The psalmist appeals to God's nature as a forgiving God and his relationship to this sovereign God as a needy and humble servant.

Psalm 87

This song of Zion (like Pss 46; 48; 76; 84; 122) highlights Yahweh's choice of Jerusalem and the possibility of all peoples becoming citizens of that sacred abode. The brevity of the psalm creates questions for the modern interpreter; the psalmist assumes information modern readers lack. The psalm divides into two sections: verses 1–3 (Yahweh's choice of Zion); and verses 4–7 (Zion, the potential abode of all peoples). The psalm manifests a concentric circle: *of you* (verse 3) > *in Zion* (literally, "there," verse 4) > *in her* (verse 5) > *in Zion* (literally, "there," verse 6) > *in you* (verse 7) (see Clifford 82).

1–2 *Foundation*: The notion that gods chose and built their own cities was common to the ancient Near East. *Loves*: that is, "chooses" (see Deut 4:37; 10:15; Ps 78:68; Isa 41:8). *Gates of Zion*: the essence of the city, the judicial and commercial center. **4** *Rahab* is best known as the chaos monster of the deeps (see Ps 89:10; Job 9:13; 26:12; Isa 51:9); here it refers to Egypt (Isa 30:7). (The name in Josh 6 is spelled differently in Hebrew.) *Cush* is Ethiopia. The nations listed are either perennial enemies of Israel or distant lands. The meaning of *this one was born in Zion* is difficult to determine. It either refers to Israelites born in foreign lands (that is, Diaspora Jews) but pledging allegiance to their faith and homeland (Zion) or perhaps on a more grandiose scale to non-Israelites who acknowledge the sovereignty of Yahweh (as in Ps 86:9). **6** *Write in the register*: see Psalm 69:28; Isaiah 4:3.

Theological Reflection · This psalm highlights the central importance Zion played in the lives of its inhabitants. Physical birth was not necessary for citizenship in God's city (see Gal 4:26; Phil 3:20; Heb 12:22–24; Rev 21:2).

Psalm 88

This individual lament is distinctive in the Psalter primarily for two reasons: it has no expression of confidence (nor any glimmer of hope), and it obsesses on one topic, death. No enemies threaten this psalmist; the only enemy present is death itself, and the only one who might fight off that enemy is God (who seems unwilling to do so). The psalm divides into three sections (with the first and third section echoing each other): verses 1–9a (appeal of one facing imminent death); verses 9b-12 (death removes any possibility for divine wonders or for praise); and verses 13–18 (repeated appeal with a more accusatory tone).

> **Death**
>
> *Death in the context of Psalm 88 is less physiological and more relocation to a thoroughly unpleasant place* (Mays 282).

3–6 The terms for death proliferate (*grave, pit, slain, darkest depths*). **8** The psalmist faces death in isolation. **10–13** In desperation, the psalmist challenges God with six rhetorical questions. The psalmist captures the utter bleakness of the realm of the dead by noting its two qualities: God works no wonders there; God receives no praise there. **11** *Destruction*: The Hebrew word here is *Abaddon*.

Theological Reflection · This psalm challenges the assumptions of death as a natural part of life. The psalmist cries out in despair as he faces his imminent demise. This psalm unfolds the complete distress that comes when facing death alone and finding no indicators that God wills to change the course of the mortal illness. Rightly, some label this the "dark night of the soul" (Davidson 289). However, in the midst of the overwhelming cruelty and finality of death, the psalmist continues to beg God for intervention; while he may feel abandoned by God, he will not abandon his Lord.

Psalm 89

This royal psalm details a recent military disaster. The psalmist questions not God's power but God's fidelity to the promises to David. The psalm rehearses those promises and the manifestations of God's majestic power in creation. Against that backdrop, he laments the current inexplicable situation in which the king and his army retreated disgracefully from the enemy. The psalmist knows this cannot be the final chapter; God's promises are sure and simply need reactivation. The psalm divides into three major sections: verses 1–18 (hymn celebrating God's incomparable power manifested in creation); verses 19–37 (rehearsal of God's promises in oracle form); verses 38–51 (lament for the king and his followers).

1–4 The psalm opens with general covenant language: *great love* [Hebrew *chesed*] *forever*; *faithfulness* [Hebrew *emunah*] that leads to covenant language specifically relating to David (*chosen one*; *servant*; *establish*; see 2 Sam 7; Ps 132). **5–18** The psalmist recounts God's powers manifested in creation; the language utilizes images of the cosmic battle. In creation, God overwhelms the forces of chaos and establishes orderly rule once and for all. **10** *Rahab*: see Job 9:13; Isaiah 51:9. **12** *North...south*: perhaps better read as "Zaphon" and "Amanus," resulting (with *Tabor and Hermon*) in four (symbolizing completeness) principal mountains (Clifford 93), all in the north of Israel or Lebanon. **14** *Righteousness and justice* secure Yahweh's throne; *love and faithfulness* serve as royal attendants. **19–37** The psalmist recounts in great detail the divine promise Yahweh made to David. **20** *Anointed* [Hebrew *mashiach*] designates any legitimate king Yahweh appoints. **25** *Seas...rivers* emphasizes the massive extent of the kingdom (Mesopotamia to the Mediterranean). **26** *My father*: Yahweh "adopted" David and his royal descendents as his "sons" (Ps 2:7). **27** *Firstborn*: Although Yahweh reigned over all peoples and had control of the kings of all nations, the Davidic king was his *most exalted* [Hebrew *elyon*, a term used mostly for Yahweh the "Most High"; see Gen 14:19–20; Pss 47:2; 82:6]. **30–37** A poetic equivalent to 2 Samuel 7:12–16. **38–51** The psalm concludes with the distress of military defeat. Shame covers the landscape. Appropriately, the psalmist desperately seeks to know the duration of the current disaster (*how long*).

Theological Reflection · This psalm provides an invaluable glimpse at the interplay between the Davidic promises and daily reality in ancient Israel. The fate of the king loomed large over the national horizon. The psalmist rests sure in God's majestic power; creation attests to Yahweh's ability to control the most threatening forces. The pressing question of the present is Yahweh's fidelity to his long-standing promises to David. The psalmist knows only too well that Israel's future rests solely upon Yahweh's constant commitment to those promises (see verse 49).

BOOK 4 · PSALMS 90–106

Psalm 90

This national lament (like Pss 44; 74) highlights the despair caused by lengthy suffering. The psalmist talks of the frailty of human life and of the misery resulting from living under God's wrath. The psalm divides into three sections: verses

---

> **The Holy Ones**
>
> As the phrases *Assembly of the holy ones ... heavenly beings ... council of the holy ones* display, in Israelite monotheism, the Canaanite gods and goddesses vying for supremacy are nothing more than beings serving Yahweh (see 1 Kgs 22; Job 1–2; Ps 82).

> *"He will command his angels ..."* Although modern readers often employ Psalm 90 as a reflection on the transience of human life, it more likely reflects the despair of a community living for an extended period under oppressive conditions (perhaps exile).

1–6 (eternal God and frail humanity); verses 7–12 (the endless wrath of God); and verses 13–17 (a plea for divine relief).

2 Birth language is used for creation (see Deut 32:18). **3** *Back to dust*: see Genesis 3:19. **5** The psalmist graphically depicts human frailty as grass scorched by the midday heat (Isa 40:6–7; 51:12–13). The issue of days and years continues throughout the psalm (verses 9–10, 12–15). **10** *Seventy years*: Although regarded as a traditional lifespan, few lived this long in ancient Israel. The length (*seventy ... eighty*) emphasizes the seemingly interminable length of the oppression. **11–12** The psalm echoes Wisdom language.

Theological Reflection · This psalm reflects the despair of a community that has experienced only the wrath of God. Fully aware of its finitude, the community laments its miserable lot of unrelenting suffering. The psalm views the reality of suffering theologically as the result of divine anger. The tragedy of the situation is that even the oldest members of the community can only remember God's anger; apparently no one has experienced his gracious presence, although they longingly await its arrival. The psalmist seeks not only relief but also wisdom to make sense of such a tragic plight (verse 12). Fully aware of their sin, the community pleads with God to allow compassion and grace to trump their sinfulness.

Psalm 91

This psalm of trust concludes with a divine oracle. The psalmist encourages his listeners in instructional tones to rely upon the Lord, who is their *shelter* and *shadow* (verse 1). Refuge language dominates the psalm, which divides into three sections: verses 1–8 (trust in God, who protects from the snares of the enemy); verses 9–13 (trust in God, who provides guardians); and verses 14–16 (God promises to protect his faithful).

4 For the image of God as a protecting eagle, see Exodus 19:4; Deuteronomy 32:10–12; Psalms 17:8; 36:7. **11** The notion of angelic guardians occurs infrequently in the Old Testament period (but see Exod 23:20; Ps 34:8; Matt 4:6). **12–13** The image of protected feet goes from passive protection (*not strike your foot*) to active aggression (*tread ... lion, cobra ... trample ... great lion, serpent*). **14–16** The divine oracle, although briefer than the preceding affirmations of security, provides the climactic assurance because of its speaker.

Theological Reflection · The psalmist exhorts his audience in a didactic manner to trust the Lord, who provided refuge in the exodus and continues to offer protection. The psalmist reminds his audience that God's protective care demonstrates itself not only defensively, but offensively.

Psalm 92

This song of thanksgiving utilizes hymnic elements recalling God's mighty deeds in creation and in history and applies them to the psalmist's own personal experience. Having experienced God's deliverance and protection in his own life, he acknowledges that only the *senseless* would not recognize Yahweh's way in the world (verse 6). The psalm divides into three sections: verses 1–5 (praise for Yahweh's works); verses 6–11 (Yahweh's contrasting treatment of the wicked and the righteous); and verses 12–15 (blessings that come to the righteous).

2 *Morning ... at night*: Since God protects his followers throughout the night (see Ps 91:5–6), the psalmist fittingly offers praise at each end of that period. **6** *Senseless*: literally, "boorish one, dullard." Fools fail to grasp the bigger picture of life. **7–11** The righteous psalmist and his foolish opponent are contrasted from several angles: the latter *does not know/understand*; the psalmist's *eyes have seen/ears have heard*; fools *spring up like grass/flourish ...* (but are) *forever destroyed*; the psalmist is refreshed *with fine oils*; fools *perish* and are *scattered*; the psalmist is *exalted*. **12–13** Compare Psalms 1; 52:8; Jeremiah 17:8. This tree appropriately flourishes within the temple precincts.

Theological Reflection · This psalm reminds its listeners of the importance of making connections between God's mighty deeds in creation and history and God's specific attention to the daily protection of human beings. The psalmist contrasts the ways of the fool and the wise in the world, noting the failure of the former to make and acknowledge these connections. Because of this, the wicked may flourish for a brief time, but ultimately their lives end in failure. In contrast, although the righteous may experience momentary setbacks, they know and acknowledge that the mighty Lord of creation and history nourishes and sustains them like trees in his sanctuary.

Psalm 93

This enthronement psalm celebrates Yahweh's control over all forces that seek to disrupt the order of the universe (Pss 24; 29; 47; 93–99). The psalmist graphically depicts the unseen God seated in splendor upon a throne. The seas may thunder and waves may crash upon the shore, but Yahweh sits enthroned forever. The psalm moves from Yahweh's "coronation" as monarch (verses 1–2) to triumph over the opposing forces of chaos (verses 3–4) to secure decrees that stand forever (verse 5).

> **Enthronement Psalms**
> *Psalms 24, 29, 47, 93, and 95 through 99 celebrate Yahweh's role as king of the universe. These psalms may have their original setting in an annual New Year Festival (that is, the autumn Festival of Tabernacles) celebrating the successful harvest of the past year and seeking the return of the needed fall rains for the beginning of a new season. The label "enthronement" derives from the opening line of several of these psalms – "Yahweh reigns (is enthroned)," that could also be read, "Yahweh has become king." The latter translation in no way suggests that Yahweh had been deposed and was now returning to rightful rule. Rather, it is a liturgical acclamation that reaffirms past reality in the present.*

1 *The Lord reigns* is variously rendered ("the Lord is king" or "the Lord has become king"). For relevant passages, see Psalms 47:8; 96:10; 97:1; 99:1; 1 Kings 15:33; 2 Kings 9:14. *The Lord reigns* captures both the present moment ("has become") and the eternal significance ("is"). **3–4** The images echo the cosmic language well-known to the ancient Near East, imagery acknowledging the triumph of the Lord of creation and nature over the chaotic forces of the destructive *seas*. **5** These *statutes* are either decrees Yahweh initiated at the completion of creation (to govern the natural world) or those laws instituted for the inhabitants of his world. Just as Yahweh is *robed in majesty* (verse 1), so *holiness adorns* [*his*] *house* (most likely a reference to his heavenly abode, of which the temple functions as an earthly representation).

Theological Reflection · This psalm reminds its audience of the eternal implications of living in a world Yahweh has created. Although elements within the universe may reveal deadly powers (for example, the devastating waters), the world remains firm and sure, for it has been established by one who sits enthroned above those chaotic waters.

Psalm 94

This cry for social justice has features of a communal lament; however, the speaker at the conclusion of the psalm is singular and seems throughout the psalm intent on instruction. The psalmist graphically depicts the ruinous effects of injustice upon the widow, alien, and orphan. He cries out for God to vindicate their cause, chastising the foolish evildoers for undoing God's will. As in Psalm 73, he ultimately assures himself that God cannot forever delay justice. The psalm divides into three major sections, each with contrasting subsections: verses 1–7 (appeal to God to judge the wicked and a lament over their arrogant evil); verses 8–15 (rebuke of the foolish and commendation of the wise); and verses 16–23 (affirmation of confidence in God as helper of the righteous and judge of the wicked).

1 *God who avenges* derives not from the world of emotion but from the legal realm. The psalmist asks God to address the severe injustices plaguing the community. **2** *Pay back* (literally "return") appears again in verses 15 and 23 and captures the essence of the psalmist's plight. **4–7** The psalmist details the social oppression created by God's failure to defend the *widow*, *alien*, and *fatherless*. Social injustice reflects the arrogant assumption that God *pays no heed* (compare Ps 73:11). The psalmist responds with a powerfully emotive term – *inheritance* (see verse 14). **8–11** The rhetorical questions are similar to those found in the Wisdom literature (for example Job 38–39).

Theological Reflection · This psalmist breathes the same air as the author of Psalm 73 and offers a chilling picture of a society overrun by fools (see Ps 1). He pleads with God to restore justice, instructing his listeners not to delude themselves into thinking this present lapse in social equity means that God lacks the care or the power to stop the wicked from doing whatever they please.

Psalm 95

This hymn (with divine oracle) praises God as the supreme ruler of the universe and calls upon the listening community to worship this Lord and not engage in rebellion (like their ancestors). This psalm divides into two sections: verses 1–7a (call to worship); and verses 7b–11 (warning exhortation).

> **Yahweh's Power**
> *This psalm celebrates Yahweh's incomparable power (manifested at creation) and his supremacy over any other presumed divine beings.*

3 *Great King* occurs often in the ancient Near East as a technical term for the sovereignty of the world. **4–5** Through creation, Yahweh reveals his superiority over any other claimants to divinity. **7** Having asserted Yahweh's supremacy (*great King*), the psalmist now asserts his personal involvement (*he is our God...people of his pasture, the flock under his care*). Often kings called themselves shepherds of their people (see Pss 23; 80; 100; Ezek 34). **8** *Massah...Meribah*: see Exodus 17:1–7; Psalm 78. Here the people test Yahweh; in Exodus 17, God tests the people (compare Ps 81:8). **10** *Forty years* is a stock designation for a generation. **11** *Rest*: that is, the promised land (see Deut 12:10; 25:19; Josh 22:4).

Theological Reflection · This psalm follows a pattern similar to Psalms 50 and 81 – praise with final admonition. While celebrating Yahweh's incomparable majesty and willingness to be involved intimately in the lives of Israel, the psalmist warns his listeners not to make the same tragic mistake their ancestors made, rejecting God for pseudogods.

Psalm 96

This enthronement psalm sings in lofty tones, inviting not only Israel but all the earth to join in praise and celebration to Yahweh (compare 1 Chron 26:23–33; Ps 98). Three calls to *sing* are followed by three challenges to *ascribe* to the Lord appropriate honor. Because the Lord sits firmly enthroned as king and judge of the universe, the world is secure. All nature joins the praise. The psalm divides into three sections: verses 1–6 (invitation to sing about Yahweh's greatness); verses 7–10 (invitation to ascribe sole honor to Yahweh); and verses 11–13 (invitation to the heavens and earth to join in the praise).

1 *New song*: see Psalm 33:3. **5** *All the gods of the nations are idols* takes the affirmation that Yahweh is supreme among the gods to its logical conclusion – all other gods are in reality nothing more than idols [Hebrew *elilim*, likely a pun on the word for God, *elohim*]. **6** Just as kings have royal courtiers about them, so Yahweh's divine attendants are *splendor, majesty, strength, and glory*. **7–9** These verses duplicate Psalm 29:1–2, with the notable exception that Psalm 29 calls upon the divine realm to *ascribe to the Lord glory*, while this psalm calls upon the *families of nations* to do so. **11–12** The psalmist captures every element of God's creation: *heavens, earth, sea...all that is in it, fields...everything in them, trees* (compare Isa 44:23; 49:13).

Theological Reflection · This hymn, though similar to Psalm 98, exhibits a uniquely missionary thrust. The psalmist is not content simply to call Israel to worship; he invites all nations to acknowledge Yahweh's supremacy. The psalmist powerfully articulates the ethical implications of God's reign over an ordered universe. The stability of God's natural realm ultimately will be reflected in social stability.

Psalm 97

This enthronement psalm (like Pss 47; 93; 95–99) rejoices in the social justice Yahweh's reign brings to the earth. The Lord sits enthroned in splendor; rejoicing fills the earth. The psalm divides into three sections, with the themes of joy, righteousness, and justice linking each section: verses 1–5 (a divine appearance celebrating Yahweh's reign); verses 6–9 (a joyful response to God's appearance); and verses 10–12 (a call to the righteous to rejoice).

1 *Distant shores* highlights the extent of Yahweh's reign. **2–5** Traditional language of a divine appearance (Deut 4:11; Pss 18:7–15; 50:3; 89:5–14; 77:16–18; Ezek 34:12; Mic 1:4). **10** *Love the Lord hate evil* intends less emotion and more language emphasizing choice (as in Deut 6:5; 30:16). Yahweh's followers are called to embrace him and reject other deities. **12** Even though *clouds and thick darkness surround* Yahweh (verse 2), *light is shed upon his faithful followers*.

> **Yahweh's Supremacy**
> *In a polytheistic world, the psalmist denies divine reality to the gods of the surrounding nations (see Ps 96:5; Isa 42:17). The psalmist emphasizes Yahweh's supremacy by repeating* all *five times.*

Theological Reflection · This psalm captures the splendor of Yahweh's reign, the impact it has upon the faithful, and the ethical implications of that reign. Yahweh's rule triggers multiple reactions from various quarters of the earth: the natural realm simultaneously rejoices and shudders; evildoers are shamed; and the faithful joyfully embrace the Lord in worship.

Psalm 98

This enthronement psalm, while echoing sentiments similar to other enthronement hymns (see Pss 47; 93; 95–99), also exhibits its own distinctive flavor. Most similar to Psalm 96, this text highlights Yahweh's saving activity. The psalmist calls upon the faithful to join with all nature in praise of the Lord, who repeatedly acts on behalf of creation. The psalm divides into three sections: verses 1–3 (call to praise Yahweh for saving deeds); verses 4–6 (call to all the inhabitants of the earth to join in the praise); and verses 7–9 (call to the earth itself to join the praise).

1 *New song*: see Psalm 33:3; Isaiah 42:10–12. God's *salvation* (better, "victory, deliverance") appears three times in verses 1–3. **7–9** Various elements of nature join in the celebration (see Ps 96:11–13). **9** *Equity*: compare 2 Samuel 8:15.

Theological Reflection · This psalm focuses almost solely upon Yahweh's victorious deeds on behalf of Israel. The nations and their presumed deities lie in the distant background. The psalmist invites all peoples to acknowledge Yahweh's rule and join in joyous celebration with the full symphony of the natural realm.

Psalm 99

This final enthronement psalm in the Psalter (like Pss 47; 93; 95–99) highlights the holiness of the Lord who reigns supreme. The psalm celebrates Yahweh's activity in righting social wrongs and responding appropriately to the cries of his people. The psalm divides into three sections, with the key term *holy* concluding each section: verses 1–3 (exaltation of the holy Lord as the one who reigns); verses 4–5 (exaltation of the holy Lord as the one who does justice); and verses 6–9 (exaltation of the holy Lord as the one who answers prayer).

1 *Enthroned between the cherubim*: Yahweh is pictured seated upon the outstretched wings of the cherubs (winged lions or bulls) with the ark as a *footstool* (verse 5; see 1 Kgs 8:6–7; Ps 18:10; Isa 6:1–8). **4** See Psalms 96:13; 98:9. **6** *Moses, Aaron ... Samuel*: Although scholars suggest numerous reasons for the selection of these three figures (for example, the greatest of the ancestors, [in]direct communicators, lawgiver, priest, prophet), the context highlights their intercession on behalf of the people and their fidelity to the divine *decrees and statutes* (compare Jer 15:1). *Pillar of cloud*: see Exo-dus 33:7–11.

> **"Forgiving God ... punished their misdeeds..."**
> Numerous scholars find here a contradiction which they attempt to resolve. However, as Davidson notes (325), forgiveness never implies casual dismissal of wrongs. Divine grace is costly, and this verse captures the tension between the consequences of action and response of grace.

Theological Reflection · This psalm fittingly concludes the enthronement psalms, highlighting Yahweh's distinctiveness. Yahweh's uniquely *holy* way of interacting with creation and its inhabitants manifests itself in willingness to dwell intimately with the people as their king. God responds to the cries of the people and works for justice throughout the earth. In return, the psalmist acknowledges the only fitting response to such a King – exaltation and adoration.

Psalm 100

This brief hymn of praise captures the essential elements of Israelite faith and worship. The psalmist uses seven imperative verbs to call God's people to worship, with reasons for such worship. The call to worship highlights that God is present as shepherd and is fundamentally good. This psalm likely functioned as an entrance song of praise. The psalm divides into two calls to praise with attendant reasons: verses 1–3 (call to worship because Yahweh alone is God); and verses 4–5 (call to worship because Yahweh is faithful).

2 *Worship* (literally, "serve") functions in the book of Exodus as a contrast to "serving Pharaoh" (see Exod 3:12; 4:23; 7:16; 8:1; 10:26). In Deuteronomy, the contrast is between serving Yahweh or the gods of Canaan. **3** *Know* is less cognition and more recognition. *Sheep of his pasture* likely echoes royal imagery (see Pss 23; 80:1; Isa 40:11; Ezek 34:11–15). **4** *Gates ... courts* likely refers to the Jerusalem temple. **5** *Lord is good*: Yahweh's goodness manifests itself in enduring *love* and constant *faithfulness*.

Theological Reflection · This psalm eloquently articulates both the focus of worship (the name Yahweh appears fifteen times) and the reasons for worship (Yahweh's presence and never-failing attributes). The psalm captures both the religious and political dynamics of worship. Religiously, worship is first and foremost coming into the presence of the one God who is Israel's originator and protector. Politically, worship involves acknowledging that only Yahweh merits sole allegiance and adoration.

Psalm 101

This royal psalm details the king's commitment to justice and integrity in his kingdom. While the identity of the speaker seems relatively clear (the king [although some consider verses 6–7 a divine response; so Kselman and Barré 543]), the setting for this psalm's use is obscure. Several scholars propose a setting during a possible annual ceremony of royal investiture; a few consider the backdrop a lament situation (for a fuller discussion, see Davidson 328). The king employs language familiar to the Wisdom literature; the structure and focus of the psalm is somewhat akin to Psalm 32. The psalm divides into two sections: verses 1–2a (a royal promise and question); and verses 2b-8 (a royal commitment to ethical excellence).

2 *I will be careful*: literally, "study." *Blameless life* [Hebrew *tamim*] denotes completeness or wholeness. The intent of *when will you come to me* is difficult to determine. **2B-8** The king makes twelve promises: three are stated positively, nine are stated negatively. **2** The *house* is the palace. **3** *Vile thing*: literally, "matter of *belial*." **4** A *perverse heart* is the opposite of the *blameless heart*.

> **Belial**
> A Hebrew word for "wickedness." "Men of Belial" or "sons of Belial" means "wicked persons," a highly insulting or even profane term. In 2 Cor 6:15, the term becomes a name for Satan.

Theological Reflection · This psalm presents not a portrait of a king but the actions of a king (Limburg 341). This psalm reflects the ideals of kingship found elsewhere in the Wisdom literature (for example, Prov 2:7; 10:9; 13:6; 19:1). Psalm 101 presents Psalm 1 in royal dress. The king pledges to *sing* (worship) praise to God, study (*be careful*, verse 2) God's way, and to *walk* (conduct himself) with integrity and blamelessness. The king commits himself and his officials to the highest ethical standards.

Psalm 102

This individual lament, given its significant emphasis upon communal concerns (especially the welfare of Zion), is best understood as the cry of an important representative of the community (most likely the king). The psalm moves fluidly between individual concerns and despair and concerns for Zion and its inhabitants (as in Ps 77; Lam 1–5). This psalm is designated one of the seven penitential psalms (also Pss 6; 32; 38; 51; 130; 143). The psalmist highlights physical suffering, loneliness, and despair as his life comes too quickly to an end. While lamenting his own miserable situation, he pleads on behalf of Zion, calling upon Yahweh to love the beloved city again and restore it to fullness. The psalm divides into three sections, with each contrasting human frailty and mortality with Yahweh's eternal nature and power: verses 1–11 (lament); verses 12–22 (confession of trust); and verses 23–28 (renewed lament and celebration).

2 *Hide your face*: compare Psalms 13:1; 27:9; 69:17; 88:14; 143:7. **3–11** The psalmist graphically depicts his current plight. Specifically, he laments the fleeting nature of life (*smoke, embers, withered grass, evening shadow*), physical dissolution (*heart is blighted, forget to eat my food, skin and bones, eat ashes, mingle my drink with tears*), and abject loneliness (*desert owl...among ruins, bird alone on a roof*). **12–22** The psalmist first appeals, not for divine intervention in his personal case, but for Yahweh to restore Zion. From the midst of his present despair, he calls upon God to act on behalf of the *future generation* (verse 18). **23–24** The psalmist contrasts the tragically short and frail nature of his own life with God's eternal and powerful nature.

Theological Reflection · This psalm, although addressing God as king and creator of the universe, lives in the midst of despair and present tragedy. The psalmist significantly appeals for God to act out of self-interest by delivering Jerusalem. God's reputation is at stake; the presence of future worshipers of God is in question. In the midst of this seeming self-interest on behalf of the psalmist, it is equally clear that his appeal is consistently rooted in a belief in God (the divine name appears seven times in confession of trust in verses 12–22).

Psalm 103

This individual thanksgiving song articulates the reverse of Psalm 102. Whereas the previous psalm struggles with human frailty and transience in the context of God's power, this psalm offers heartfelt gratitude for the Lord's willingness to express that power in compassionate ways to frail human beings. The psalmist begins and ends with a personal call to *praise the Lord, O my soul*. God's merciful activity in the life of this psalmist trumps all concerns with human frailty. The psalm divides into four sections that balance each other: verses 1–5 (thanksgiving for divine healing of the individual); verses 6–14 (thanksgiving for divine healing of the nation); verses 15–18 (Yahweh and earthly beings); and verses 19–22 (Yahweh and heavenly beings) (Clifford 144).

1 *Praise the Lord* (literally, "bless") entails declaring the wonderful acts God manifests upon his followers.

The psalmist specifically highlights praise for God, who *forgives all your sins and heals all your diseases*. Apparently, the psalmist has recently recovered from a life-threatening illness. *All* occurs five times in the opening six verses (four times in the closing verses). **5** *Renewed like the eagle*: compare Isa 40:31. **7–18** The psalmist ably incorporates Exodus 34:6–7 into worship. **19** The psalmist affirms that divine intimacy in no way negates the awesome power of this Creator and King of the universe.

> **"Bless the Lord, O my soul …"**
> *Although the psalmist is fully aware of his own frailty and transience, he celebrates the distance the Lord creates between sin and redemption (verse 12) and the divine willingness to act as a loving parent (verse 13) toward feeble humanity.*

Theological Reflection · This psalm beautifully captures the language of gratitude that should dominate the life of the believer. Because of his recent illness, the psalmist can never forget the fragility of his own life and his need for the Lord's gracious intervention. However, he fixates upon the overwhelming divine attributes that dominate Yahweh's character: forgiveness, compassion, redemption, renewal, and grace.

Psalm 104

This hymn of praise celebrates the majestic greatness of God reflected in the creation of the innumerable creatures made and sustained by the wisdom of this Lord. The psalm reflects on God's creative grandeur from several angles, dividing into six sections: verses 1–9 (God as royal creator); verses 10–18 (God as dispenser of nourishment); verses 19–23 (God as master of seasons); verses 24–26 (God as Lord of earth and sea); verses 27–30 (God as controller of life and death); and verses 31–35 (a final prayer).

> **Creator & Creation**
> *Scholars have noted similarities with the thoughts of this psalm and other ancient Near Eastern materials, especially the Egyptian hymn to the sun god Aten and Canaanite texts about the storm god. However, in this psalm, the sun is created by Yahweh, who controls creation with confidence.*

1–9 God's creation is an architectural marvel, and God moves majestically throughout it as its royal architect and builder. The heavens function as the roof (verses 2–3); the waters, initially spread across the expanse of the earth, are driven to their final locale in the seas (verses 7–9). Compare Psalm 18:7–15. **10–18** Yahweh nourishes creation through springs, brooks (verses 10–12), and refreshing rains (verses 13–18). The potentially harmful waters of verses 7–9 provide life for the animals of verses 14–18. **15** *Wine … oil … bread* reflect main crops of the land. **19–23** Yahweh creates the heavenly bodies (unlike ideas in Egypt and Mesopotamia, where they are independent divine entities); they function as servants in his entourage. **24–26** See Psalm 89:10–11; Isaiah 51:9–10. **27–30** All of creation lives only through Yahweh's life-giving Spirit (see Gen 2).

Theological Reflection · This psalm invites readers to reflect on the world theologically through the eyes of faith. Like Psalm 8, it expresses the theology of Genesis 1 through poetry and song. Creation marvelously displays God's constant care for all creatures. God possesses infinite wisdom and uses that wisdom to coordinate and insure that all of his creation flourishes and thrives. The images for God are powerful and numerous – God functions as architect, builder, field general, farm manager, and father.

Psalm 105

This hymn of praise celebrates the mighty acts of God on behalf of people, as Psalm 104 does for creation, rehearsing events from the choice of the patriarchs to the exodus. First Chronicles 16:7–36 utilizes sections of Psalms 96, 105, and 106 to celebrate David's installation of the ark in Jerusalem. The psalm divides into two major sections, with the second section subdividing according to the early history of Israel: verses 1–6 (call to praise); and verses 7–45 (the mighty acts of God). The subdivisions of the second part are verses 7–15 (God covenants with Abraham, Isaac, and Jacob); verses 16–25 (God protects Joseph); verses 26–41 (God delivers Moses and Aaron); verses 42–44 (God remembers); and verse 45 (a call to praise).

6 The *descendents of Abraham* are called to praise the God who entered into covenant with the ancestor. **7–11** The imperative verbs of verse 1–6 give way to predicate-nominative sentences (*he is the Lord our God*). The reference to the patriarchs is unique in the historical recitals in the Psalter. **12** *Strangers*: literally, "sojourners." **14** *Rebuked kings*: for example, Pharaoh (Gen 12:17); Abimelech (Gen 20:3). **15** *Anointed*

PSALMS

ones ... prophets: elsewhere, only Abraham is called a prophet; nowhere else are the patriarchs called anointed ones (literally "messiahs"). This may refer to their designation for a task (anointed) as spokesmen (prophets) for God. **26–36** The order of the plagues differs from that in Exodus. **37** For the despoiling of the Egyptians, see Exodus 12:35–36. The dramatic reversal is apparent, for the people impoverished in Egypt leave enriched. **41** *Opened the rock*: the same term is used in verse 20 of Joseph (*released*).

Theological Reflection · This psalm reminds readers of the centrality of history to faith. Historical reflection, specifically rehearsing the mighty interventions of God's saving hand, gives identity, meaning, and purpose to the lives of his followers. Ancient history enriches faith. Through the exercise of memory in worship, ancient stories of God's work in the world become truly present and empower a hopeful stance toward the future. The God who has repeatedly secured covenantal promises on Israel's behalf will continue to do so.

Psalm 106

Like Psalm 105, this communal lament recites the history of God's dealings with the people. However, where the previous psalm highlights God's marvelous works, this psalm focuses upon his people's rebellion. This psalm thus aligns more with Psalm 78, although the former uses historical recitation as a teaching moment, while history in this psalm creates a confessional moment in worship. The psalm divides into three major sections, with hymnic celebration on each side of the historical recitation: verses 1–5 (appeal for favor); verses 6–46 (recounting of the rebellious acts of God's people); verse 47 (prayer for salvation and promise of praise).

6 This verse links the current rebellious situation with previous rebellions. **7–12** See Exodus 14. The psalmist fittingly depicts the people's sin at the Red Sea as failure of memory (*did not remember*,

> **Rebellion & Grace**
> *Psalm 106 recounts seven instances of human rebellion and God's gracious forgiveness in the lives of people. Each of the seven incidents are linked with a place: rebellion at the Red Sea, testing God in the wilderness, the rebellion of Dathan and Abiram in the camp, the golden calf at Horeb, the disaster at Baal-Peor (Num 25), rebellion at the waters of Meribah, and the sacrifice of children in Canaan.*

see Deut 4:9, 23) and inattentiveness to Yahweh. Conversely, *name* offers the explanation for Yahweh's acts, which come from the divine nature. The emphasis on Yahweh's *name* derives ultimately from Deuteronomy. **13–15** See Numbers 11:18–24, 31–34. **16–18** See Numbers 16. **19–23** See Exodus 32–34. **20** *Bull, which eats grass* is likely a sarcastic aside contrasting Yahweh with a futile idol (Davidson 349). Various ancient deities were represented as bulls (especially *El*). **23** *Stood in the breach* is imagery of a soldier using his body to plug a hole in the defense (see Ezek 22:30). **24–31** See Numbers 13–14, where the Israelites refuse to enter the promised land and instead (Num 25) worship Baal at Peor. Where Moses intervenes in the previous event, Phinehas intervenes in this situation. **32–33** See Exodus 17:1–7; Numbers 20:2–13. The people receive the blame for Moses' sin. **34–46** See Exodus 23:23–24; 34:10–16; 2 Kings 16:13; Jeremiah 19:5. **47** The final appeal for one more act of forgiveness and restoration provides the setting for the appeal – exile.

Theological Reflection · Given the human propensity to forget God's saving actions on behalf of Israel, recounting biblical history functions not merely as an exercise in memory or data gathering. It functions powerfully in worship to provide a confessional moment and position from which to seek God's continued gracious intervention.

BOOK 5 · PSALMS 107–150

Psalm 107

This communal song of thanksgiving extols the steadfast love [Hebrew *chesed*] of the Lord from the perspective of those who have experienced it (the *redeemed*). Two refrains punctuate a major portion of the psalm: *they cried out to the Lord in their trouble, and he delivered them from their distress* (verses 6, 13, 19, 28) and *let them give thanks to the Lord for his unfailing love and his wonderful deeds for men* (verses 8, 15, 21, 31). The psalm is neatly structured: after an opening call for praise (verses 1–3) the psalmist recounts four examples of divine redemption – lost wanderers in a desert wasteland (verses 4–9), released prisoners (verses 10–16), fools with near fatal illnesses (verses 17–22), and storm-tossed sailors (verses 23–32). Each example follows a similar pattern: a life-threatening danger, a desperate cry to the Lord, response and rescue by the Lord, praise and thanksgiving from the redeemed. The final section (verses 33–43) departs from this pattern, moving the theme from deliverance to sustenance in the land (although vocabulary from verses 4–32 reappears).

2 *Redeemed* is the same term as that used in the book of Ruth (for Boaz), levirate marriage, and the next of kin blood avenger. **3** The four directions suggest the totality of the redemption. **10–16** Unlike the wanderers in verses 4–9, these *prisoners* deserve their punishment, having *rebelled against the words of God* and *despised the counsel of the Most High*. **17** Some emend *fools* to read "ill," (see NRSV, REB, NAB), but *fools* adequately captures the understanding that rejecting God's will may result in serious illness. **23–32** Like the wanderers, no connection is made between the plight of these *merchants* and their behavior. Unlike the Phoenicians who ruled the sea, ancient Israelites lived as farmers and typically feared the sea. **33–43** These verses use terminology from the first example (verses 4–9) and resonate with language and imagery from Isaiah 40–66.

Theological Reflection · This psalm provides an excellent illustration of how personal experiences of divine redemption can have long-range impact in the lives of later believers. Through the use of early examples of deliverance and rescue (whether deserved or not), the psalmist calls upon his community to thank Yahweh for sustaining them in current difficult circumstances. He concludes with the fitting reminder that true wisdom entails seeing the presence of God's unfailing love in daily life (verse 43).

Psalm 108

This lament psalm contains materials found elsewhere in the Psalter. Verses 1–5 appear in Psalm 57:7–11 (an individual lament); verses 6–13 appear in Psalm 60:5–12 (a communal lament).

Psalm 109

This individual lament arguably presents the most caustic accusatory language in the Psalter. The psalmist finds himself overwhelmed by the verbal assaults of his adversaries. He begs God to come to his rescue. At the center of this psalm (verses 6–19) lies a series of brutal curses. Historically, scholars have understood these imprecatory comments as utterances from the afflicted psalmist against his adversaries. More recently, some scholars have suggested that these lines are actually quotes from the adversaries against the psalmist (so NRSV). Although this interpretation initially tempers the shock of the psalm, ultimately it does little to lessen the emotional intensity of the psalmist, since the psalmist asks that the Lord execute all these curses against his foes (verse 20). The psalm divides into two major sections (verses 1–19, 20–31), each with two subsections: verses 1–5 (opening plea and description of distress); verses 6–19 (series of curses); verses 20–25 (prayer and second description of distress); and verses 26–31 (final prayer and promise of praise).

1–3 The silence of God contrasts strikingly with the verbal assault of the psalmist's enemies. For God's silence, see Psalms 35:22; 50:3; 83:1. **6** *Accuser*: [Hebrew *satan*] This term literally means "the accuser, adversary" (Job 1–2; 1 Kgs 22). Only much later does it become the designation for the ultimate adversary, Satan. **6–19** The psalmist has experienced betrayal by his friends (verse 4) and groundless attacks. He responds in kind. **21–25** The psalmist rests his plea in two places: Yahweh's *name* and the *goodness of [God's] love* versus his own neediness.

Theological Reflection · This psalm rightly troubles modern readers. The psalmist leaves no doubt regarding the severity of the distress in which he finds himself. Feeling abandoned by God and betrayed by his friends, he pleads with God to speak (rectify the wrongs engulfing him). Such language appears also in Job 29–31 and Jeremiah 17:14–18. This psalm reminds the reader of the extreme challenge to faith that overwhelming injustice creates.

Psalm 110

This royal psalm (like Pss 2; 18; 20; 21; 45; 72; 89), the most quoted in the New Testament, contains verses that virtually defy translation. Two divine oracles constitute the psalm; its setting is likely a coronation ceremony (or perhaps an anniversary of the same). The psalm celebrates the political, military, and religious significance of the Davidic monarch. It divides neatly into two sections; each begins with an oracular introduction: verses 1–3 (Yahweh installs his king in victory); and verses 4–7 (Yahweh repeats earlier promises of victory to his priest-king).

> **Imprecation**
>
> *An imprecation is a curse placed by one person on another. The Psalms sometimes use this form to express the anger at injustice that humans feel.*

1 *The Lord says to my Lord*: literally, "an utterance of Yahweh to my lord" (see Num 14:28; 1 Sam 2:30; Isa 1:24). In its original context, this verse depicts Yahweh inviting the Davidic monarch to take the throne next to him as he brings his enemies into subjection. **2** Yahweh sat enthroned in the Jerusalem temple with the ark as his *footstool*; in ancient Near Eastern art and literature, defeated foes were often depicted bowing at the footstool of the victorious monarch (Josh 10:24). **3** *Your troops will be willing*: literally, "your people are willing" (compare Judg 5:2). The remainder of verse 3 is obscure. **4** *Priest forever … Melchizedek*: In Canaanite ideology, the king also functioned as supreme priest. In Genesis 14:18–24, Melchizedek, the priest-king of Salem (Jerusalem) who worships El Elyon, greets Abraham following his successful military venture. David, upon his accession to the throne in Jerusalem, received from Yahweh both royal and priestly responsibilities (2 Sam 6:17; 8:18; 1 Kgs 3:4). **5–6** The imagery quickly returns to the military prowess of the king. Just as Yahweh earlier invited the king to sit on the right, so Yahweh now delivers crushing military victories at the right hand of the installed monarch. **7** This verse is obscure. It may simply refer to a tired warrior stopping for a refreshing drink, or it may reflect a moment in the enthronement ritual (as in 1 Kgs 1:9, 33, 39).

Theological Reflection · Information from other royal psalms aids in fleshing out the details of this psalm. The installation of a monarch in ancient Israel was an especially significant military, political, and religious moment. During the ceremony, an official rehearsed the divine promises made to David. However, with the passing of the monarchy, these royal psalms received new life with the rise of messianic thought in Israel. God's people looked forward to a day when Yahweh would once more raise a Davidic descendent and subject all nations to him.

> **"Messiah" in Israel**
> *Although the Old Testament never used the Hebrew word* mashiach *to designate a future, coming king, Jews in the Second Temple period (539–70 CE) did use the term that way. Expectations of the messiah's roles were diverse. For example, some of the Dead Sea Scrolls expect two messiahs, one from David and one from Aaron.*

Psalm 111

This acrostic hymn of thanksgiving is the first of three "hallelujah psalms." In typical hymnic fashion, it calls the congregation to praise and provides reasons for the praise. The language echoes Exodus 34:6 and Psalm 103:17–18, suggesting that the mighty acts envisioned in this psalm are the exodus, desert wanderings, and giving of the law at Sinai. The psalm revolves entirely around praise: verse 1 (call to praise); verses 2–6 (praise for God's actions in the exodus, wilderness, and giving of the land); verses 7–9 (praise for God's trustworthiness); and verse 10 (praise and the fear of the Lord).

2 *Pondered* (literally, "studied"): Those who delight in God's works investigate them to gain fuller understanding of the character of God. **3** *Glorious and majestic* is royal language (Ps 8). **7–9** God's mighty acts in deliverance and in offering his law are inextricably linked; both manifest God's gracious provision. **10** *Fear of the Lord* (see Prov 1:7; 3:4; 13:15) connotes awesomeness and reverence, not terror. To fear God is to live in obedience.

Theological Reflection · Grateful praise and humble obedience are the proper responses to a God fully available to people in covenant. God saves and teaches.

Psalm 112

This acrostic psalm takes its theme from the last verse of the preceding psalm (Ps 111:10). Through language at home among teachers of wisdom, the psalmist describes the life of one who *fears the Lord*. The thought alternates between descriptions of the blessings the God-fearer experiences and his or her behavior. Several of the themes common to the wisdom tradition are present: the fear of the Lord; the veneration of Torah; the contrast between the righteous and the wicked and their futures. The psalm begins with a call to praise (verse 1) followed by a description of one who fears the Lord (verses 1b-10).

1 *Blessed*: see Psalm 1:1. **5** Compare Psalm 37:21. **9** The behavior of the God-fearer is described in language often used for God (as in Matt 5:48).

Theological Reflection · Like Psalms 1 and 119, this psalm depicts the joy and satisfaction that comes to one who studiously attends to God's Torah. The psalm moves from *the fear of the Lord is the beginning of wisdom* to *blessed is the man who fears the Lord*. The previous psalm developed the praise that issues from those who fear the Lord; this psalm describes how reverence works itself out in the life of the upright.

Psalm 113

This hymn is the first of the so-called "Egyptian Hallel" psalms. In later Judaism, Psalms 113–118 were sung during the Passover meal (Pss 113–114 before the meal; Pss 115–118 after the meal). The psalm calls upon the worshiping community to praise Yahweh's incomparable greatness. The psalmist notes God's greatness in two areas: exaltation of the poor and powerless, and giving children to the barren woman. The psalm divides into three sections: verses 1–3 (call to praise); verses 4–6 (the Lord reigns from the heavens); and verses 7–9 (the Lord reigns on earth).

1 *Servants of the Lord*: The term connotes both honor and subservience for those who serve the incomparable Lord of the universe (Clifford 189). **5** *Who is like the Lord*: compare Isaiah 40:12–31. **9** *Barren woman*: see 1 Samuel 2; Luke 1:46–55.

Theological Reflection · The Lord of the universe majestically shows compassionate concern for the poor and needy and those unable to secure their future. This psalm reminds careful listeners of God's powerful intervention in the lives of such faithful women as Sarah, Rebekah, Hannah, and Mary.

Psalm 114

This second of the Hallel hymns celebrates the exodus from Egypt at the Red Sea and the entrance into the promised land at the Jordan River. Although several key elements of a hymn are absent, the language is hymnlike and speaks of these historic events in cosmic terms. The psalm divides into two sections: verses 1–4 (the exodus from Egypt and entrance into the land); and verses 5–8 (questions and warning to the Red Sea and Jordan River).

1 Although *foreign tongue* is a unique phrase in the Old Testament, the expression captures the reality that the Egyptian language is non-Semitic. **2** *God's sanctuary*: literally, "his holiness." **3** The Red Sea and Jordan crossings summarize the entire deliverance; no mention is made of the intervening wilderness period (in contrast to Pss 78; 105; 107). **4** The *mountains* and *hills* are likely the Canaanite landscape celebrating the entrance of God's people. The rhetorical return to this moment in verse 6 may envision the divine encounter at Sinai (Exod 19:18; Judg 5:5; Ps 68:9). **5** Compare Joshua 3:15–17; Psalm 77:16. **6** See Psalm 29:5–6. **8** See Exodus 17:1–7; Numbers 20:8–13.

Theological Reflection · This psalm captures the historic and cosmic significance of the exodus from Egypt and entrance into the land. Using cosmic imagery, the psalmist taunts the fearful and impotent waters of the Red Sea and Jordan to stop the victorious march of Yahweh and the people into the new land.

Psalm 115

This psalm contains elements from a variety of genres, gathered here to serve liturgy. The psalm opens like a communal lament, but moves quickly into a polemic against idolatry. It follows with a call to the worshipers and closes with assurances of divine blessing. The moves in the psalm likely reflect different voices in worship. The psalm divides into four sections: verses 1–2 (communal lament); verses 3–8 (polemic against idols); verses 9–11 (a call in response); and verses 12–18 (assurance of divine blessings and congregational response).

> **Psalm 115**
> *Numerous early translations merge Psalm 115 with the preceding psalm, even though their tone and style differ (Davidson 375).*

4–8 This tirade against idolatry has its setting within Israel, not in debate with Gentiles (since at a deeper level ancient peoples knew that idols merely represented the divine being). For similar language and rhetoric, see Isaiah 40:18–20; 41:6–7; 44:9–20; Jeremiah 10:1–16. These verses recur in Psalm 135:15–18. **9–11** Scholars debate whether the three groups mentioned here (*house of Israel, house of Aaron, those who fear the Lord*) are simply variations for all Israel (Clifford 196) or three distinct groups (Israel; the priests; proselytes). **12–15** For a similar priestly blessing, see Numbers 6:22–26. **15** In contrast to idols that humans make, Yahweh is the *Maker of heaven and earth*. **16** In concert with Genesis 1:26–31, Yahweh keeps the heavenly realm under dominion (no pseudogods share his dominion) but entrusts the earthly realm to humanity. **17** *Dead...go down to silence*: The realm of the dead offers no praise to God (also Pss 88:11–13; 94:17). In contrast, the worshiping community offers ceaseless praise.

Theological Reflection · This psalm plausibly fits a context where God's people dwelt surrounded by powerful nations extolling their "more powerful" gods (for example, in the exile). Against that backdrop, this psalm provides language and rhetoric to the worshiping community to address faithfully the present difficulties. In contrast to the lifeless idols of the foreign powers, Israel's God is the *Maker of heaven and earth*. This mighty God *does whatever pleases him*, and what pleases him most is to remember and bless Israel.

Psalm 116

This individual song of thanksgiving expresses praise and gratitude for deliverance from almost certain death. In response to God's rescue, the psalmist offers praise and thanks in the congregation of the faithful. Although the Septuagint divides this psalm into two (making verses 1–9 into Psalm 114 and verses 10–19 into Psalm 115), the unity of the psalm in the Masoretic Text reflects the psalmist's true intent. The psalm divides into two major sections (verses 1–9, 10–19), with each consisting of two subsections: verses 1–4 (cry of distress); verses 5–9 (Yahweh's answering deliverance); verses 10–14 (promise to praise Yahweh); and verses 15–19 (fulfillment of the vow to praise).

1 The phrase *I love the Lord* [Hebrew *ahav*] is unique to the Psalter, although the sentiment occurs elsewhere (Ps 18:1 [Hebrew *racham*]; compare Prov 12:1; 20:13; Isa 41:8; 1 John 4:19). *Love* is more akin to "choose" than an emotional feeling. **4** The plea is simple: *save me*. **5** Like Exodus 34:6–7, the psalm focuses more on the divine attributes than on the divine deeds. **6** *Simplehearted*, familiar from the Wisdom literature, more likely refers to vulnerability (note the parallel line, *in great need*) than to naiveté or gullibility. **12–14** The psalmist *repays* the Lord in two forms: he *lift*(s) *up the cup of salvation* (possibly a reference to a liturgical act during worship or a drink offering [see Exod 29:40–41; Num 15:5–7]) and he *fulfill*(s) [his] *vows to the Lord*. Whereas he earlier called on the name of Yahweh for deliverance (verse 2), he now calls on Yahweh in praise. **15** *Precious* means "costly" or "grievous" (Mays 370). The death of God's faithful can hardly cause delight; rather, loss of praise is costly. **16** The psalmist increases the linguistic intensity of his relationship to the Lord – *servant ... son of your maidservant ... freed me from my chains*.

Theological Reflection · The appropriate response to deliverance from deathly dangers is complete thankfulness. The psalmist fulfills the promises he made during his life-threatening circumstances. In the assembly of the worshiping congregation, he acknowledges the Lord as his savior and deliverer, he fulfills his vow, and he offers a freewill offering. As Clifford (200) rightly notes, verses 9–11 are about obedience, while verses 12–19 are about worship, two sides of the same coin.

Thank Offerings

The thank offering [Hebrew *todah*] *is the only sacrifice never required; it derives solely through the voluntary expression of overwhelming gratitude from the worshiper.*

Psalm 117

This briefest psalm captures the essence of Israelite faith in two verses. This thanksgiving song thinks on a grand scale, calling all the nations to offer praise to Yahweh. The psalm divides into two sections: verse 1 (call to praise) and verse 2 (reason for praise).

Theological Reflection · This psalm provides the poetic counterpart to Exodus 34:6. True praise ultimately derives from God's faithfulness, and until every nation engages in that praise, God's true sovereignty has not been fully acknowledged.

Psalm 118

This individual thanksgiving song is the final of the so-called Egyptian Hallel psalms (Pss 113–118) and is memorably sandwiched between the shortest and longest psalms in the Psalter. It incorporates themes found in each of the earlier psalms. Psalm 118 fluctuates between first person singular ("I") and plural ("they") language. Although much discussed, the psalm is best understood as a liturgical rendering (perhaps a victory processional) of events that impacted the king and his people. The psalm divides into four sections: verses 1–4 (call to praise); verses 5–9 (affirmation of trust in Yahweh); verses 10–18 (declaration of deliverance in battle); and verses 19–29 (appeal to open the gates so that praise may be offered).

1 See Psalms 106:1; 107:1; 136:1. **2–4** See Psalms 115:9–11; 135:19–20. **12** *Bees*: compare Deuteronomy 1:44. **14** See Exodus 15:2; Isaiah 12:2. **19** Best understood as a request of the processional party entering the Temple Mount following a decisive victory. **22** *The stone the builders rejected* refers either to the king's unexpected military victory or to his people Israel. The line may have become proverbial in ancient Israel. **24** *Day the Lord has made*: alternately, "the day Yahweh has acted." **25** *O Lord, save us*: [Hebrew *hoshianna*] This is the word Hosanna. **26** Perhaps spoken by the presiding priest (as in Pss 15; 24).

Theological Reflection · This psalm keeps the focus throughout on Yahweh, whose name occurs 28 times. The psalmist utilizes gripping imagery to praise Yahweh's intervention: Yahweh transposed him from narrow straits to a spacious place (verses 5–9) just as with Israel at the Red Sea; the stone considered useless and consigned to the scrap heap Yahweh selected for a place of prominence in a new building (verses 22–24). Such decisive divine action can only result in unabashed praise and public celebration.

Psalm 119

This massive acrostic poem contains 176 verses, divided into 22 sections of eight verses each. Each line of each section starts with the same Hebrew letter. The psalm is best understood as an individual petition built around the central theme of the place of God's Torah in the life of the believer. God's word, or law, is best understood as divine self-revelation and an expression of God's will for humanity. The language and vision of this psalm are most compatible with that found in Deuteronomy and Proverbs. Although much of the structure is created by the acrostic formatting and so is highly repetitive, the 22 sections of this psalm manifest some movement: verses 1–8, 9–16 (prologue); verses 89–96 (lamed stanza, the turning point [moving somewhat from lament to praise]); verses 169–176 (conclusion).

> **The Word of God**
> *The psalmist utilizes eight Hebrew synonyms for God's word: law [torah]; word [dabar]; promise(s) [imrah]; ordinances [mishpatim]; statutes [chuqqim]; commandments [mitzvot]; decrees [edot]; and precepts [piqqudim]. Together, these words appear 177 times in the psalm, 88 times in verses 1–88 and 89 times in verses 89–176.*

1–8 Happiness is found in obedience to the Torah. **9–16** Yahweh is the model wisdom teacher. **17–48** The psalmist complains and pleads with God for aid and promises obedience. **49–80** The psalmist talks of his past, admits guilt, and pleads for future help. **81–112** The psalmist moves forward with new energy to face impending dangers. **113–144** The psalmist declares his loyalty to Yahweh, who is righteous. **145–176** The psalmist concludes his extended petitions with further statements of loyalty and promises to praise (see Clifford 213–15 for further elaboration of each of these sections).

Theological Reflection · This extended meditation on the virtues of the Torah reminds the reader of the powerful and positive role of God's instruction in believers' lives. This is no simple legalism but an extended reflection on the struggle to live faithfully to God's word in difficult circumstances. This text exemplifies the transformative nature of faithful obedience to God's word.

Psalm 120

This psalm is most akin to an individual lament. The psalmist is far from home and the object of malicious slander. The psalm divides into three sections: verses 1–2 (prayer for deliverance); verses 3–4 (complaint about slanderous attacks); and verses 5–7 (lament about living among warmongers).

1 *Call...answer*: See Psalms 3:4; 4:1; 27:7. The psalmist anticipates God's deliverance even prior to the answer (compare Jonah 2 for a similar prayer). **3** *What...what*: see 2 Samuel 3:9; 1 Kings 2:23. The psalmist engages in a form of self-curse ("may God do to me if nothing is done to you!"). **4** For the interplay of weapons and speech, see Psalms 52:4; 57:5; 64:3; Proverbs 12:8. **5** *Meshech...Kedar*: that is, the far northern and southern extremities. The psalmist emphasizes his distance from his homeland.

> **Psalms of Ascent**
> *Psalms 120–134 are a collection of psalms labeled the "songs of ascents." The precise meaning of this designation is uncertain. Some scholars interpret these psalms as pilgrimage psalms, considering the "ascent" a reference to the climb to the Jerusalem Temple Mount for worship (a few of these psalms [122; 132] mention pilgrimage). Other scholars understand "ascents" as a reference to the stairlike parallelism in these psalms. That is, each line takes up one word from the previous line and builds upon it. Finally, some scholars understand "ascents" as a reference to the steps of the temple (so understood by the Septuagint, Vulgate, and Mishnah) and suggest these psalms were sung as worshipers ascended the temple steps to praise Yahweh.*

Theological Reflection · The psalmist agonizes over his plight – he lives far from the community of faith and experiences the violence that comes with evil speech. He longs for God to answer him, presumably by returning him to his homeland.

Psalm 121

This psalm of trust highlights the dual role of Yahweh as creator and protector. The psalmist notes several activities that might cause injury to the believer and then affirms the divine attributes that keep those events from occurring. This psalm may envision a pilgrimage setting or a dialogue between the entering worshiper and a temple officiant (as in Pss 15; 24). The psalm divides into two sections: verses 1–2 (Yahweh as creator); verses 3–8 (Yahweh as protector).

1–2 These lines may intend a contrast between the Canaanite idols that dot the hilltops and Yahweh who dwells supreme atop Mount Zion (Pss 48:2–3; 87:1–2). **3** *Slumber*: Yahweh's presence, absence, and attention to matters at hand are expressed through his "sleep" or lack thereof (Ps 44:23; 1 Kgs 18:27). **5** The primary reference here is likely the brutal heat of the desert sun; however, the psalmist may also intend a secondary reference to the Canaanite notion that the sun and moon had independent powers to harm humans. **7–8** With each verse, Yahweh's care as guardian expands (*all harm ... life ... forevermore*).

Theological Reflection · This psalm beautifully articulates God's gracious care as creator and protector over all facets of human life. In the midst of terrifying and potentially hostile surroundings, the psalmist's Lord remains ever vigilant to protect Israel's future.

Psalm 122

This song of Zion (like Pss 46; 48; 76; 84; 87; 122) celebrates the anticipated arrival of worshipers to the city. Where the preceding psalm describes the dangerous journey, this one extols the goal of the journey. The psalm divides into three sections: verses 1–2 (pilgrimage and arrival); verses 3–5 (praise of Zion); and verses 6–9 (prayer for the peace of Jerusalem).

3 Jerusalem sits atop a slender ridge and thus is densely populated. **4** Compare Exodus 23:17; 34:23; Deuteronomy 16:16. **5** Compare Deuteronomy 17:8–13.

Theological Reflection · The psalmist marvels at the wonders of God's faithfulness to the people, manifested in Jerusalem's architectural features, in its ability to unite the tribes in common worship, and in its legal statutes. The confluence of these features results in peace and security for all citizens.

Psalm 123

This simple prayer of confidence utilizes compelling similes to portray the nature of petition and the psalmist's stance before God. The *eyes* of the community are fixated upon Yahweh; the psalmist beseeches the Lord to *have mercy* upon an attentive people. The psalm divides into two sections: verses 1–2 (affirmation of trust); and verses 3–4 (petition).

1 *Eyes ... throne ... heaven*: the psalmist contrasts his abject need (verse 4) with Yahweh's exalted royal status (see Gen 13:10; 18:2; Isa 40:26). **2** *Slaves ... maid*: the gist of the comparison seems to be the powerlessness of the servant to protect himself and the overwhelming attentiveness of that same servant to the overseer who provides protection (*master/mistress*). **3** *Shows mercy* occurs three times; *eyes* occurs four times.

Theological Reflection · This psalm highlights the fact that "prayer begins and ends with dependence on God and openness to divine action" (Clifford 228).

Psalm 124

In this communal song of thanksgiving, the psalmist calls upon the worshiping community (*let Israel now say*) to join in grateful acknowledgment of the deliverance Yahweh effected on their behalf. The psalm divides into three sections: verses 1–5 (acknowledgment of past deliverance); verses 6–7 (praise for the deliverance); and verse 8 (confessional statement of trust).

1 *On our side*: see Psalm 94:17. **3** *Swallowed us alive*: so Proverbs 1:10–12. **6** *Torn ... teeth*: Although the psalmist may

> **Images of Vulnerability & Salvation**
> *Through gripping imagery, the psalmist expresses both the complete vulnerability of the people and the Lord's miraculous deliverance. The first image envisions the threat as a raging flood (itself embodied as a ferocious predator); the second image envisions the deliverance as that of a captured bird freed from the hunter's trap.*

intend a second image for the danger (a ravenous predator), more likely he is using this imagery to capture the devouring aspect of the torrent. Elsewhere in the ancient Near East, torrential floods and sea storms are likened to devouring beasts (Ps 89:9–10). **7** *Bird ... snare*: the imagery of a trapped bird released from the snare highlights the miraculous nature of Yahweh's deliverance (see Pss 91:3; 140:5). Escape from the snare is only possible when it *has been broken*.

Theological Reflection · This psalm notes the decisively different nature of life when the Lord intervenes. Dangers that should result in destruction end instead with deliverance and acknowledgment of Yahweh's intervention. Life is qualitatively and quantitatively different when *the Lord [is] on our side.*

Psalm 125

This psalm of confidence compares God's faithful followers with the holy city and contrasts them with their wicked foes. The psalmist emphasizes the key motif of the stability and inviolability of Zion (Pss 46; 48; 76). The psalm divides into two sections: verses 1–3 (affirmation of trust); and verses 4–5 (appeal for help).

1–2 Two similes are set in chiastic (A B B' A') arrangement (trusters in the Lord are immovable like Mount Zion ... mountains surround Jerusalem like Yahweh surrounds his people). **3** If *the scepter of the wicked* refers to a royal foreign oppressor, then *those who turn to crooked ways* (verse 5) may refer to Jews who abandon their faith to follow the foreign oppressors (Davidson 415). *Land allotted*: compare Numbers 26:55–56; Joshua 15:1; 17:1; 18:6; Psalms 25:12–14; 37:29. **5** Although the NIV reads this verse as a simple declaration, it is better read as a prayer ("may ... ").

Theological Reflection · This psalm likens the future of God's people to Jerusalem. The psalm refuses to offer a sophisticated delineation of the multiple stances humanity might take before the Lord; one is either a follower (variously identified as one who trusts in the Lord, is righteous, is good, and is upright in heart) or an opponent of God (variously identified as wicked, turning to crooked ways, or evildoers).

Psalm 126

This prayer expresses joy for God's deliverance of the people from exile and asks God to "complete" their return with abundance in their daily lives. The psalmist follows his two references to the restoration of fortunes (the first in past tense, the second an imperative) with similes. The psalm is set at a time when the exiles have returned home, eliciting joyous elation, but do not enjoy prosperity. The psalm divides into two sections: verses 1–3 (declaration of joy following deliverance); and verses 4–5 (prayer for complete renewal).

1 *When the Lord brought back the captives*: literally, "when the Lord returned the restoration of Zion" (see Pss 14:7; 53:7; 85:1; Jer 29:14; Amos 9:14; Joel 3:1; Zeph 2:7). Reading the text in past tense (so NIV, NRSV) is preferable to a future rendering (so NJPS). *Like men who dreamed* is preferable to the more pedestrian reading, "like those healed" (see Isa 29:7–8). The transformation from captivity to freedom surely had a surreal quality. **4** *Like streams in the Negev* refers to the dry ravines that flood during the winter rainy season. **5–6** The imagery (possibly proverbial) is poignant and likely reflects the reality desired – the psalmist seeks abundant crops to follow the expectant planting.

Theological Reflection · God's intervention in the lives of Israelites occurs in stages. Faith involves the offering of heartfelt thanksgiving for what the Lord has already done as well as the earnest pleas for God's complete restoration and continued involvement.

Psalm 127

This wisdom psalm contrasts human endeavor with divine blessing. Human effort apart from divine involvement often results in futile activity. The psalmist links two sayings, highlighting the importance of divine involvement in work and family. The psalm divides into two sections: verses 1–2 (the futility of human endeavor apart from God) and verses 3–5 (family as a gift from God).

1 A classic example of syntactic parallelism. *Builds the house* may secondarily refer to Solomon's palace (compare 2 Sam 7). For God as builder, see Psalms 78:69 (the sanctuary); 102:16; 147:2 (Zion); 28:5 (the people); 89:4 (the Davidic dynasty). **2** *Sleep to those he loves*: see Deuteronomy 33:12; Psalms 60:5; 108:6; 132:4; Proverbs 6:4; Jeremiah 11:15. Sleep conveys both the nuance of rest and the prosperity that comes from fruitful labor. For worrisome toil, see Proverbs 10:22; Matthew 6:23–24. **3** *Sons are a heritage* [Hebrew *nachalah*]: Children are second only to salvation in the highest level of blessing God bestows on his people. This verse succinctly captures the angst barrenness created in the lives of ancient Israelites (for example, Rachel; Hannah). **4–5** *Like arrows ... quiver*: The imagery is graphic – sons born to a young father become his protectors in his old age; his wife's womb functions as his quiver.

> **"Contend ... in the gate ..."**
> Contend ... in the gate *may intend either verbal disputes in legal and business matters or physical altercations (since the gate was the most vulnerable military point of a city).*

Theological Reflection · This psalm elaborates the old adage, "Man proposes, but God disposes." Like other wisdom materials, this psalm notes the anxiety and often unsuccessful enterprises that result when humans do not align their actions with God. Conversely, blessing in the workplace and the home is nothing less than a gracious gift from God.

Psalm 128

This wisdom psalm matches the previous psalm in themes (work, family) and vocabulary, though using different imagery. The psalm divides into two sections: verses 1–4 (the life of the person who fears the Lord); and verses 5–6 (divine blessings on the one who fears the Lord).

1 *Blessed*: compare Psalm 1:1. *Fear the Lord*: see Psalm 111:10. **2** Also Psalm 127:2. **3** Compare Psalm 80:8; Song of Songs 7:8. Here the imagery derives from the cultivation of vines; in Psalm 127:4–5, it derives from archery. **5** See Psalm 134:3. **6** As in Psalms 29:11; 127:5.

Theological Reflection · This psalm links the *way* one chooses to live with the outcome of one's life. One who lives in right relationship with God (that is, chooses the right *way*, a notion equivalent to *fears the Lord*) enjoys the blessings of fruitful labor and family. Here the psalmist links personal well-being with the larger well-being of Jerusalem.

Psalm 129

This communal lament differs from most laments in that it mourns an extended period (*from my youth*) rather than a single event. In contrast to the life of blessing noted in the previous two psalms, this song portrays a life filled with suffering and the absence of God's blessing (verse 8). The psalm divides into two sections: verses 1–4 (statement of suffering); and verses 5–8 (prayer for vindication against the enemies causing the suffering).

1 *From my youth* most likely refers back to Egyptian captivity (as in Hos 11:1). *Let Israel say*: see Psalm 124:1. **3** *Plowmen have plowed*: Compare Micah 3:12. The punishment is extensive (*made their furrows long*), since Israelite farmers typically made short rows to rest the oxen (Clifford 245). *Cut ... cords* may refer to cutting the lines to the plow. **5–7** This futility curse utilizes the graphic image of grass with poor roots that withers quickly in the sweltering desert heat (see Isa 37:27). **8** For a contrast of blessing spoken in harvest, note Ruth 2:4.

Theological Reflection · This psalm reminds its readers that faithfulness to the Lord often involves painful circumstances.

Psalm 130

This individual lament is one of the seven so-called "penitential psalms" (with Pss 6; 32; 38; 51; 102; 143). The psalmist pleads with God merely to listen to his appeal, depending on God's willingness to extend forgiveness rather than keep a record of wrongs. The psalmist waits with eager anticipation for God to exercise redemption on his behalf. The psalm divides into four short sections: verses 1–2 (petition for a hearing); verses 3–4 (statement about the forgiving Lord); verses 5–6 (confession of faith); and verses 7–8 (a call to the community to trust in the Lord).

1 *Out of the depths*: See the language of Psalm 69:3, 15; Isaiah 51:10; Ezekiel 27:34. **2** *Hear my voice*: the psalmist seeks first a hearing, knowing deliverance can only come after sins are forgiven. In the context, *hear* and *forgive* are virtually synonymous. **3** *Who could stand*: as in Amos 7:2. **4** *Forgiveness ... feared*: Divine forgiveness results in awe and reverence from the one forgiven (1 Kgs 8:39–40). **5** *Word*: most likely the divine promise to deliver.

Theological Reflection · The psalmist founds his relationship (and that of his community) in Yahweh's willingness to forgive rather than keep an account of sin. He acknowledges the depths of human alienation and therefore dependence on God.

Psalm 131

This song of trust beautifully portrays the relationship between the psalmist and Yahweh as that of a weaned child with her mother. The psalmist first expresses the relationship negatively (with a threefold denial, verse 1), then follows with a positive description of the relationship (with a double affirmation, verses 2–3).

1 *Heart ... proud ... eyes ... haughty*: The heart and eyes signify the inner and outer character of the person (Pss 18:28; 73:6–9; Prov 6:17; 18:12; 30:13; Ezek 28:2).

Theological Reflection · This is the second psalm of ascent that utilizes

> **"Like a weaned child ..."**
> A weaned child *is no longer totally dependent upon the mother for all sustenance, but certainly needs the mother for continued health, well-being, and protection (compare Matt 18:2–4).*

female imagery for God (the other being Ps 123:2), contrasting divine power and willingness to comfort with human weakness and need.

Psalm 132

This royal psalm rehearses the events of 2 Samuel 6–7 in poetic verse. The psalm features prominent themes from the David and Zion traditions, focusing upon David's commitment to securing a prominent dwelling place for Yahweh and Yahweh's covenantal commitment to David and his successors. The psalm divides into two major sections, each containing an oath and multiple balancing phrases: verses 1–10 (David's oath to Yahweh); verses 11–18 (Yahweh's oath to David).

1 *Hardships he endured* is better read "his piety." Securing a dwelling place for a god was the ultimate act of piety for an ancient king. **2** *Mighty One of Jacob*: see Genesis 49:24; Isaiah 49:26; 60:16. **6** *Ephratah* is a region near Bethlehem (according to Gen 35:16, 19; Mic 5:1). *Jaar* is likely Kiriath-Jearim (1 Sam 7:12). **8–10** See 2 Chronicles 6:41–42. **8** *Arise, O Lord* echoes Numbers 10:35, where this expression is used when the ark was transported to and from a battle. **10** *Anointed one*: see Psalm 2:2. **11–12** In contrast to Psalm 89:20–38, the promise here is conditional. **14** David refuses "rest" until he secures a *resting place* for Yahweh. **17** *Horn grow*: see Psalms 18:2; 75:4. **18** *Clothe his enemies with shame*: earlier, the priests are clothed with *righteousness* (verse 9) and *salvation* (verse 16). The image of virtues as clothing is common in the Old Testament.

Theological Reflection · This psalm reflects the importance of momentous events in the life of God's people. God's people recognized in worship that their fortunes and lives were enmeshed in the divine promises made to David and his descendents. They regularly reminded themselves of their ancestor's willingness to commit himself fully to Yahweh.

Psalm 133

This psalm defies classification; most scholars label it a wisdom or pilgrimage psalm. The psalm extols the virtues of harmonious communal life through the use of the similes of oil and dew (images symbolizing refreshment).

2 *Precious oil ... beard of Aaron*: See Exodus 30:22–32; Leviticus 8 (priestly ordination). The officiating priest wears a vestment bearing twelve precious stones. *Brothers ... unity*: compare Deuteronomy 25:5 (in a context of levirate marriage). **3** *Dew of Hermon*: Mt. Hermon, the highest mount in the Antilebanon range just north of Israel (approx. 9,100 feet), was proverbial for heavy dew. In an arid climate, nightly dew provides welcome relief.

Theological Reflection · Just as communal togetherness today creates tensions and challenges to unity, so this ancient text notes the joyous blessings that harmonious fellowship brings to community life.

Psalm 134

This final psalm of ascent appropriately travels in two liturgical directions as it intones the doxology. The psalm calls upon the worshipers to bless Yahweh and Yahweh to bless his people.

1 *Praise*: literally, "bless." Since God lacks nothing, "blessing" the Lord is simply offering deserved praise. *Servants ... minister by night* likely identifies sanctuary personnel (Deut 10:8; 1 Chron 9:33; 23:30). **2** *Lift up your hands*: that is, "pray" (see Pss 28:2; 63:4; 141:2). **3** Compare Numbers 6:24–26.

Theological Reflection · This psalm captures the cyclical nature of blessing in the life of believers. God, originator and owner of all the universe, blesses followers from creation with the necessities for meaningful life. In return, worshipers offer God praise and adoration.

Psalm 135

This hymn of praise calls upon the servants of the Lord (see Ps 134) to praise the Lord for power manifested in deliverance from Egypt and safe passage into the promised land. The psalm focuses on two primary themes: God's selection of Israel and his incomparable dominion over the idols of the nations. The psalm gathers together traditional themes found elsewhere in the Psalter and weaves them into a powerful liturgical moment. The psalm divides into five sections, with the outer sections encircling the central section: verses 1–4 (call to praise); verses 5–7 (Yahweh the incomparable creator); verses 8–12 (Yahweh the sovereign Lord of Israel); verses 13–18 (Yahweh the incomparable Lord against idols); and verses 19–21 (call to praise).

1–2 *Servants ... minister*: see Psalm 134:1–2. **4** *Treasured possession* denotes the most cherished possession of the owner (see Exod 19:5; Deut 7:6; 1 Pet 2:9). **8** The psalmist references the entire exodus experience by simply citing the final plague.

11 *Sihon...Og*: see Numbers 21:21–35. **15–18** See Psalm 115:4–8; compare Isaiah 44:9–20.

Theological Reflection · This psalm ably notes the greatness of Yahweh in two areas: the deliverance and choice of Israel and God's incomparable superiority over the idols of the nations. The first Yahweh establishes through the overthrow of pharaoh at the Sea; the second he establishes through Yahweh's creation. Lifeless images pale in comparison to the life-giving power of Yahweh.

Psalm 136

This hymn calls upon the entire community to affirm the steadfast love of the Lord (26 times). The psalm celebrates the goodness of the Lord manifested in creation and the redemption of the people. Grammatically, participles (-ing verbs) dominate the syntax until verse 21, where the psalmist switches to past tense and then brings the worshipers to the present request for God to manifest this same enduring love for contemporary Israel.

5–9 See Genesis 1. **10–22** See Exodus 12:29–15:21; Numbers 21:21–35; Deuteronomy 3:1–7; Joshua 12:1–6; Psalms 78; 105; 106.

> **Pictures of History**
> In Psalm 136, "history unfolds like a series of photographs arranged in a gallery of divine interventions" (Schaefer 319).

Theological Reflection · This psalm provides a fitting poetic commentary on Exodus 34:6–7. The most appropriate offer of thanks involves declaring publicly God's mighty acts in the cosmos and in Israel's history.

Psalm 137

This communal lament eloquently depicts the plight of the Babylonian exile. The captors taunt their beleaguered captives. The crisis generates a twofold response: the captives affirm their remembrance of Zion, and they call upon God to remember Zion and its inhabitants. The psalm divides into three sections: verses 1–3 (taunt about Zion); verses 4–6 (response); and verses 7–9 (call for deliverance and retribution).

1–3 See Psalm 42:3 (compare Pss 46; 48; 76; 84; 122). **5–6** The psalmist utters a futility curse against himself. He cannot forget Zion, on pain of self-annihilation. **7–9** The psalmist seeks retribution through a curse. Edom often operated as a "scavenger nation" (that is, profiting at the expense of others) in the ancient world (compare Lam 4:21; Ezek 25:12–14; 36:5; Obad 8–14).

Theological Reflection · This psalm exhibits the use of lament in a particular setting. It functioned powerfully as resistance literature in a most difficult setting. Memory plays a powerful role in faith and worship. The people declare their commitment to remember Zion always; they call upon God to remember a troubled people.

Psalm 138

This individual song of thanksgiving takes on communal significance with its focus on the temple and the kings of the earth. The psalmist offers his praise not only before the community, but more importantly, *before the gods*. The psalm divides into three sections: verses 1–3 (praise for answered prayer); verses 4–6 (call for kings of the earth to praise); and verses 7–9 (affirmation of trust and request for help).

1 *Before the gods*: literally, "in the face of the gods" (an almost polemical denial of their divinity); compare Isaiah 41:21–24. **4–6** NIV rightly reads this section as a petition rather than a declaration (NRSV). **6** Compare 1 Samuel 2:-1–10.

Theological Reflection · Believers live with a fundamental tension, for the experience of grace does not ultimately negate a daily sense of neediness and desire for God's renewing presence. This psalm holds in balance God's awesome transcendence and gracious immanence.

Psalm 139

Meditative reflections on divine attributes dominate this individual lament (the psalmist expands a protestation of innocence into a reflective meditation). The psalmist focuses on God's omniscience (verses 1–6), omnipresence (verses 7–12), and unlimited creative power (verses 13–16), highlighting especially the personal implications of each. The lament motifs appear primarily in verses 19–24. The psalm divides into four major sections: verses 1–6 (Yahweh is all-knowing); verses 7–12 (Yahweh is all-present); verses 13–18 (Yahweh's personal knowledge of the psalmist); and verses 19–24 (prayer against the enemies) (Kselman and Barré 550).

1 *Searched me* begins and ends the psalmist's reflection (verses 23–24; compare Prov 18:17; 25:2; Job 5:27; 13:9; 28:3, 27). **5** *Hem me in*: see Job 1:10;

3:23). **8** *Depths*: literally, *Sheol*. This thought is unusual, since Sheol is usually considered the one realm beyond God's presence. **11–12** *Darkness...light*: see Job 3; John 1:5. **13** *Knit*: the imagery of God as knitter functions similarly to the more common image of God as sculptor. **18** *When I awake*: literally, "I come to an end." The end refers either to the thoughts of God, or to death. **20–22** These enemies are first and foremost God's enemies.

Theological Reflection · This psalm takes the abstract theological concepts of God's omniscience, omnipotence, and omnipresence and personalizes them. Through such personalization, theological concepts that might bring anxiety result in comfort and joy. The psalmist speaks specifically of God's knowledge (and care) of him, of God's presence (and protection) with him. The psalmist declares that he will give as much attention to God as his creator has given to him; such is the life of faith.

Psalm 140

This individual lament may reflect the cry of one falsely accused. The psalmist utilizes three images to express his plight: war (verse 2), a venomous snake (verse 3), and the hunter (verses 4–5). The psalm highlights God's care for the powerless (as in Pss 145:14–21; 146:7–9; 147:3, 6). Chiasm characterizes the psalm's language – *evil/violence* (verses 1, 11); *lips* (verses 3, 9); *wicked* (verses 4, 8). The psalm divides into five brief sections: verses 1–3 (an initial cry for deliverance); verses 4–5 (a second appeal for help); verses 6–8 (confession); verses 9–11 (an appeal for divine justice); and verses 12–13 (a declaration of confidence).

1–5 The psalmist first cites the verbal abuse of his enemies (verses 1–3) and then speaks of their physical abuse (verses 4–5). **10** The language evokes imagery from Sodom and Gomorrah (Gen 19:24).

> **Justice**
> Verse 12 captures the theme of the psalm – I know that the Lord secures justice for the poor and upholds the cause of the needy.

Theological Reflection · In this world, injustice often reigns, creating numerous victims. The psalmist holds forth an eschatological vision: he declares the reign of God in the midst of circumstances that seemingly deny God's sovereign power.

Psalm 141

This individual lament seeks discipline in the midst of troubling circumstances. The psalmist prays both for relief from evildoers and for the strength not to succumb to the lure of their lifestyle. The psalm divides into four sections: verses 1–2 (a request for a hearing); verses 3–4 (a request for strength to withstand temptation); verses 5–7 (a declaration of willingness to submit to discipline); and verses 8–10 (a profession of trust and petition for deliverance).

2 *Incense*: compare Exodus 30:7–8. *Lifting up of my hands* is the posture of prayer (Pss 28:2; 63:4; 134:2). **3–5** See Psalm 140:1–3, 9. **6–7** NIV reads these verses as an affirmation of God's will; they may be better read as a complaint. **8–10** Compare Psalm 123:1–2.

Theological Reflection · Succumbing to the enticement of evil in the midst of suffering is a constant danger. Trying circumstances tempt the faithful to divert their allegiance for God to possessions and ease. The psalmist articulates a faithful response both to the struggles evildoers present and to the temptations a materialistic lifestyle offer.

Psalm 142

This individual lament captures the lonely despair that troubles create. The psalmist pleads for God to rescue him in his most desperate hour of need. The psalm divides into three sections: verses 1–2 (plea for a hearing); verses 3–4 (cry of abandonment); and verses 5–7 (renewed plea for deliverance).

1, 5 The psalmist first cries to the Lord in general terms, and then cries more personally (*my* – verse 5). **4** *Right*: see Psalms 16:8; 110:5. **5** *Portion* perhaps echoes the Levite tradition (Josh 18:5, 6, 9). **7** It is unclear whether *my prison* is literal or figurative (see Isa 42:7).

Theological Reflection · The psalmist intertwines lament and praise, knowing that suffering and injustice cannot be the final chapter of his story. Though in desperate straits, he refuses to abandon his conviction that God intends good for him (verse 5).

Psalm 143

This individual lament is the last of the seven penitential psalms (with Pss 6; 32; 38; 51; 102; 130). Only verse 2 manifests any indication of penitence; the remainder of the psalm contains lament. The psalmist roots his appeals to the Lord in divine faithfulness and righteousness. The psalm has been variously divided; the divisions of the NIV are plausible: verses 1–2 (appeal for relief); verses 3–4 (lament about the present dangers); verses 5–6 (profession of loyalty); verses 7–10 (appeal for deliverance and instruction); and verses 11–12 (a final appeal for deliverance from the enemies).

1 *Hear my prayer*: the psalmist seeks God's acceptance based on God's *faithfulness and righteousness*. **2** *No one living is righteous before you*: the psalmist seeks God's grace, not justice. **3** *Darkness* may refer to the exile (see Isa 42:16; Lam 3:6). **5–6** Compare Psalm 77. **8–10** The psalmist contrasts himself with his enemies, taking for himself the primary identification of a *good servant* (as in Neh 9:20).

Theological Reflection · Any appeal for God's faithful response to one's plight must be rooted first and last in God's essence and character, namely, gracious faithfulness. God's justification of frail humanity comes from grace.

Psalm 144

This royal prayer seeks the two fundamental hopes manifested in the Old Testament: God's salvation and God's blessing (Limburg 488). The psalm divides into five sections: verses 1–4 (praise and reflection); verses 5–8 (a petition for Yahweh to appear); verses 9–11 (a vow of thanksgiving); verses 12–14 (an affirmation of the blessing that will follow the deliverance); and verse 15 (concluding blessing).

> **"Make the lightning flash ..."**
> *The psalmist seeks God's intervention through God-revealing storms, using language reminiscent of Psalms 18 and 33.*

1–2 Compare Psalm 18:2, 34, 46–47. **3** See Psalm 8:3–4; Job 7:17–18. In Psalm 8, humans are spatially insignificant; here they are temporally insignificant. **5–8** See Psalm 18:7–19. The crisis behind this appeal may involve broken treaties with foreign nations. **9** *New song*: see Psalm 33:3; Isaiah 42:10–12. **12–15** The shift to agrarian imagery and blessing, though awkward at first glance, indicates that ancient Israel understood blessing as a natural outcome of salvation.

> **Plants & Pillars**
> *The psalmist mixes imagery: sons are likened to healthy plants (Ps 127); daughters are likened to pillars adorning a palace entrance. Often, the pillars had capitals in the shape of lilies, hence the connection to the prior image.*

Theological Reflection · This psalm reflects the proper vision of leadership in ancient Israel. The king put aside his own will, seeking first God's deliverance of his people from foreign oppression and then agricultural abundance for continued well-being and security.

Psalm 145

This hymn of praise serves as an overture to the final song of praise in Psalms 146–150. Celebration of the divine attributes dominates this acrostic poem, providing its structure and overarching theme: Yahweh's greatness as king. The praise is comprehensive; the term "all" occurs seventeen times in the Hebrew. The psalm divides into four sections (verses 1–3, 4–9, 10–13, 14–21); the first three begin with praise followed by attributes, while the last section reverses this order.

1–2 These verses extol Yahweh as king; verses 11–13 laud his kingdom. **3** *Great ... greatness*: see Psalms 48:1; 96:4. **4** *One generation ... another*: compare Deuteronomy 6:20; Psalm 78:4. **8** Compare Exodus 34:6. **14–21** These concrete illustrations of divine activity reveal God's grace.

Theological Reflection · Just as lament dominates the beginning of the Psalter, so doxology dominates its conclusion. This psalm invites worshipers to view God's world in a celebratory way (Clifford 303). God's greatness, goodness, and mercy are never merely abstract attributes. They repeatedly manifest themselves in concrete acts.

Psalm 146

This hymn begins the lengthy concluding doxology of the Psalter (Pss 146–150 all begin and end with *Praise the Lord* [Hebrew *halleluyah*]). This psalm instructs the faithful community to avoid the pretentiousness of earthly rulers and put its trust solely in the faithful graciousness of the creator and ruler of the universe. The psalm divides into four sections: verses 1–2 (call to praise); verses 3–4 (admonition to reject human power); verses 5–9 (blessing upon those who make Yahweh their help); and verse 10 (concluding affirmation).

1 Compare Psalms 103; 104. **2** *All my life ... as long as I live*: the psalmist pledges lifelong allegiance to the *Lord* [who] *reigns forever* (verse 10). **3–4** Compare Genesis 2:7. **5–9** These verses echo themes familiar to the prophetic literature, but with a didactic style at home in the Wisdom literature.

Theological Reflection · This psalm grounds praise in its true locale, God's eternal nature and will to act with justice and equity in lives. Human powers fail to deliver permanent deliverance; only Yahweh reigns forever. The psalmist recognizes the importance of instruction in worship, since the temptation to trust in human strength is perennial (Mays 441). Worship transforms reality, reminding the worshipers that true happiness is not the absence of suffering but the presence of a God who cares about it (Fretheim).

Psalm 147

This hymn invites Israel to praise God's activity in the life of the people and care of the universe. Each section calls for praise and states the reasons for that praise. The psalmist moves easily between God's particular care for Israel in daily acts and a more general care for them through the maintenance of the world. The psalm divides into three sections: verses 1–6 (a call to praise for God's restoration of Israel); verses 7–11 (a call to praise for God's care for the universe and provision of Israel); and verses 12–20 (a call to praise God for his provision of Israel through the gift of his word).

1 *How good it is* replaces the more usual "for" (see Psalm 133:1). **2** *Exiles*: compare Nehemiah 1:9. **9** A popular view among ancients was that *ravens* abandoned their young to fend for themselves (Davidson 472).

Theological Reflection · This psalm demonstrates the organic nature of the life of faith. The psalmist glides effortlessly between celebrating God's care for various creatures and God's care for Israel. He praises God for creating the majestic universe and Jerusalem, for caring for animals and the brokenhearted and powerless. All this God does simply through the power of the word!

Psalm 148

This hymn invites all God's creation to join in praise. Where praise predominates in the preceding psalm, summons to praise dominates this psalm. This psalm divides into two major sections: verses 1–6 (praise from the heavens); and verses 7–14 (praise from the earth).

1–6 *Heavens ... heights*: The outermost reaches of God's universe are invited to offer praise: the angels, all angelic beings, the sun, the moon, the shining stars, the supraterrestrial waters (see Gen 1). **7–14** The corresponding terrestrial choir consists of sea monsters and ocean deeps, lightning, hail, snow, clouds [literally "smoke"], storm winds, towering mountains, fruit trees, majestic cedars, wild animals, domestic cattle, crawling creatures, birds, rulers, nations, and all ages and sexes of humanity; in short, everything. **14** *Horn* is either a symbol for the king or perhaps a metaphor for the strength with which Yahweh endowed Israel.

> **"Praise the Lord ..."**
> *Clearly, the summons to heaven and earth to offer Yahweh praise implicitly affirms that the entire universe properly owes it existence and continued well-being to Yahweh, the sole creator and ruler of everything.*

Theological Reflection · Although somewhat oversimplified, a few scholars have read the poetic sections of this psalm against the backdrop of Genesis 1–2 (verses 1–6 connect with Gen 1:1–19; verses 7–14 connect with Gen 1:20–2:4).

Psalm 149

This hymn challenges the reader with its linkage of praise for God and call to arms (verse 6). The key to this psalm lies in its connection with Psalm 148:14 (this psalm uses all but two of the terms from that verse) and Psalm 2. Psalm 148 summons heaven and earth to praise Yahweh, while Psalm 149 summons Israel to proclaim the Lord's sovereignty. Both Psalms 149 and 2 address the refusal of the kings of the earth to acknowledge God's kingship. The psalm divides into two sections: verses 1–4 (an invitation to praise God as king in worship); and verses 5–9 (an invitation to praise God as king through military victories).

1 *New song*: compare Psalm 33:3; Isaiah 42:10. **3** See Exodus 15:20–21. **5** *On their beds*: the first call is for public praise (verses 1–3); the psalmist now calls for praise in private devotion. **6** *Double-edged sword* (literally, "sword of mouths") is likely a metaphor for proclaiming Yahweh's sovereignty. **7–9** Some scholars suggest that verses 1–4 reference the exodus, while verses 5–9 reference the entrance into the land.

Theological Reflection · Acknowledging God's sovereignty and offering praise cannot always remain an abstract activity with no practical implications. Here the psalmist addresses the ramifications of celebrating Yahweh's kingship. Those who attempt to squelch such a proclamation suffer the consequences.

Psalm 150

This hymn of praise fittingly provides the concluding doxology for the whole Psalter. The psalmist calls the congregation to *praise* thirteen times, and mentions the Lord an equal number of times. The psalmist invites a full orchestra (seven instruments are mentioned) to join the heavenly chorus in praise. The psalm divides into three sections: verses 1–2 (summons to praise); verses 3–5 (the instruments for praise); and verse 6 (conclusion).

1 *Sanctuary* most likely refers to God's heavenly dwelling, although a secondary reference to Zion is possible. **6** *Everything that has breath* encompasses all creatures in heaven and earth.

Theological Reflection · This psalm fittingly addresses the crucial questions regarding worship: who is to be praised, why God is to be praised, how God is to be praised, and who offers the praise (Mays 450).

FOR FURTHER STUDY

John Eaton, *The Psalms* (London: T&T Clark, 2003).

Erhard Gerstenberger, *Psalms: Part 1 with an Introduction to Cultic Poetry* (Grand Rapids: Eerdmans, 1988).

———, *Psalms, Part 2 and Lamentations* (Grand Rapids: Eerdmans, 2001).

William L. Holladay, *The Psalms through Three Thousand Years* (Minneapolis, Minn.: Fortress, 1993).

Sigmund Mowinckel, *The Psalms in Israel's Worship* (2 vols.; Nashville: Abingdon, 1962).

Samuel Terrien, *The Psalms: Strophic Structure and Theological Commentary* (Grand Rapids: Eerdmans, 2003).

WORKS CITED

Leslie C. Allen, *Psalms 101–150* (Waco, Tex.: Word, 1983).

Walter Brueggemann, *The Message of the Psalms* (Minneapolis: Augsburg, 1984).

Richard J. Clifford, *Psalms 1–72, 73–150* (Nashville: Abingdon, 2002, 2003).

Peter C. Craigie, *Psalms 1–50* (Waco, Tex.: Word, 1983).

Robert Davidson, *The Vitality of Worship: A Commentary on the Book of Psalms* (Grand Rapids: Eerdmans, 1998).

John Eaton, *The Psalms* (London: T&T Clark, 2003).

Terence Fretheim, *Psalms* (Nashville: Abingdon, 2002).

John S. Kselman and Michael L. Barré, "Psalms," in *The New Jerome Biblical Commentary* (ed. Raymond Brown, Joseph Fitzmyer, and Roland Murphy; Englewood Cliffs, N.J.: Prentice Hall, 1990).

James Limburg, *Psalms* (Louisville: Westminster John Knox, 2000).

James L. Mays, *Psalms* (Louisville: John Knox, 1994).

Sigmund Mowinckel, *The Psalms in Israel's Worship* (2 vols.; Nashville: Abingdon, 1962).

Konrad Schaefer, *Psalms* (Collegeville, Minn.: Liturgical Press, 2001).

Marvin E. Tate, *Psalms 51–100* (Waco, Tex.: Word, 1990).

Samuel Terrien, *The Psalms: Strophic Structure and Theological Commentary* (Grand Rapids: Eerdmans, 2003).

Proverbs

Jennifer S. Green

CHAPTER CONTENTS

Contexts 505

Commentary 508
- The Prologue · 1:1–7 508
- The Way of Wisdom & the Way of Folly · 1:8–9:18 509
- The Proverbs of Solomon · 10:1–22:16 513
- The Words of the Wise & Additional Sayings of the Wise · 22:17–24:34 517
- Solomon's Other Proverbs Copied by Hezekiah's Officials · 25:1–29:27 518
- The Words of Agur Son of Jakeh · 30:1–33 519
- The Words of Lemuel & His Mother · 31:1–9 520
- The Woman of Strength · 31:10–31 520

Theological Reflections 521

For Further Study 522

Works Cited 522

A desire for wisdom unites people from countless cultures and time periods, including ours today. The book of Proverbs presents ancient Israel's ideas of wisdom, what it is, and how to achieve it. Both a gift of God and something attained through deliberate human effort, wisdom comes through the fear of the Lord and by following traditional teachings passed on from other contexts. Its acquisition leads to great benefits. Through the development of moral character, wisdom leads to a life of ethical integrity as well as success in material and social dimensions. This occurs as wise ones live in accordance with principles of wisdom that permeate the entire cosmos and reflect the nature of God. The book of Proverbs sets forth how wisdom is taught, acquired, sought, and admired in numerous areas of life, from the home to the workplace to political settings.

CONTEXTS

Though Proverbs offers what many consider to be straightforward, "common sense" observations about the world, the presentation of the book creates particular challenges in interpretation due to its historical and literary complexities. Historical questions about the date, authorship, and social setting of Proverbs reflect the book's multiple layers of composition: the original sources of the various sayings, secondary usages of the sayings, and the sayings in the final form of Proverbs. For example, a particular proverb may have originated in a rural home setting in ancient Egypt and then come into use later in Israel in a royal context to make a political statement. At a still later time, the editors of Proverbs used it for their own purposes to construct a picture of wise living.

Many sayings in Proverbs point to daily life in agrarian contexts and so may reflect an original setting of village or farm life among farmers, laborers, craftspeople, and family members (Westermann 17). A school setting may have given rise to other proverbs, but conclusive evidence for Israelite schools before the Hellenistic period is lacking (Crenshaw 601–5; Jamieson-Drake; Weeks 132–56). A number of sayings relate to the king (such as 10:1; 25:1; 31:1) or his advisors, courtiers, clerks, and other officials (Fox, *Social Location*, 10). Of these, only the reference to Hezekiah offers a firm date, the late eighth century BCE (around 728–700). The other references indicate additional time periods and royal administrations.

As with Ecclesiastes, the Song of Songs, and the apocryphal book of *Wisdom*, the attribution of the book to Solomon points less to actual authorship and more to the legacy of the king famous for his wisdom. In addition to these sources within Israel, some sayings in Proverbs appear to have originated in other parts of the ancient Near East. In particular, Proverbs 22:17–23:11 seems to make use of proverbs from the ancient Egyptian *Instruction of Amenemope*, written in the second millennium BCE.

> **Sources of Proverbs**
> *Proverbial sayings come from several sources. Some originate as oral folk sayings and may circulate for many centuries without being written down. Their precise origins often remain obscure, but their content may provide general clues to earlier use.*

Drawing on these diverse sources, editors chose and arranged particular proverbial sayings to create a new piece of literature as it now exists in the final form of Proverbs. This occurred in the Persian or early Hellenistic period (early sixth century BCE through the late third century BCE). Some linguistic forms appearing in the text would not have been known in Israel until that time (Yoder 15–38). The writers probably were scribes or royal servants employed to compile and create literature for the royal temple and court (Fox, *Social Location*, 227–39). As such, their writings reflect aristocratic concerns, and furthermore, as they were probably all men, their male perspective on life often comes to light in the text. At the same time, readers can still glimpse perspectives from other social settings in which proverbial sayings were used. Ultimately, however, the perspective of the learned editors remains dominant as a result of their careful filtering and shaping of the myriad sayings and ideas available to them from other contexts.

Literary elements also shape Proverbs in vital ways. Here the form is inseparable from the meaning. At the outset, the prologue emphasizes that wisdom involves understanding a variety of literary forms: *proverbs and parables, the sayings and riddles of the wise* (1:6). In its most fundamental sense, a proverb is a saying that is current and familiar among people (Fox, *Proverbs 1–9*, 54). In the majority of the sayings in Proverbs, two short lines appear together as parallel couplets. With remarkable conciseness, the couplets juxtapose words or phrases so that they bring out comparisons and contrasts, wordplays, ambiguities, sound patterns, or other relationships between ideas. The couplets stand on their own without further comment or elaboration so that they offer a "maximum of meaning in a minimum of words" (Williams 39). Many of the sayings resemble the genre of "instructions" common in ancient Egypt and elsewhere in the ancient Near East that deal with a wide range of topics, from family life to advice about women to how to act in the presence of the king.

The proverbial sayings in this book take three general forms (see Alter 169–77). First, lines based on principles of antithesis set up contrasts between opposite ideas, with the second line essentially stating the converse of the first line. For example, *A wise son brings joy to his father, but a foolish son grief to his mother* (10:1). These lines present what appear to be three pairs of opposites: wisdom/folly, joy/grief, and father/mother. The proverb contrasts a wise son with a foolish son in the way that he influences his parents' emotions. In a clever twist, however, the final pair of terms sets up not a straightforward antithesis but an intensification of the idea of "father." Though "father" and "mother" might be opposites in another context, here they state the same idea of "parent." This brings an element of surprise and expansion to the proverb even as it maintains structure emphasizing contrast.

Second, lines based on principles of equivalence or elaboration comprise the second category of proverbial sayings, with the second line showing some development or nuance of the first line. Proverbs 18:6 features this structure: *A fool's lips bring strife, and his mouth invites a beating.* One may read these lines as essentially synonymous, as reflected in the NIV translation of the first line.

> **"Better Than" Sayings**
>
> Some proverbs appear as what is often called a "better than" saying. For example, Better a meal of vegetables where there is love than a fattened calf with hatred (15:17). These sayings deem one concept that is normally undesirable to be superior to something typically desirable in order to stress the value of a principle or character trait. In this case, love makes even a meatless meal superior to a fattened calf. Similarly, tranquility (as opposed to strife) makes a sparse meal more desirable than a feast in 17:1.

While that reading is possible, the Hebrew of the first line does not have the object "him" and so allows a more general reference, simply saying that the fool's speech brings strife. Thus it may refer to the trouble that the fool's speech brings to himself (10:8; 14:3; 17:20; 18:7, 21; 21:6) and/or to other people (10:14; 11:9; 12:6; 20:19; compare 14:7). The second line of the couplet, then, might be understood as making a more specific statement in reference to the first line. One may read it as an ironic observation: the fool's speech brings strife…and it is strife to himself! Or one may read it as inclusive: the fool's speech not only brings strife to others but also to himself. Read as synonymous, the second line intensifies the first line by providing an image of strife brought to a fool. Either way, the second line develops or elaborates on the first in some way.

Often, lines of this structure form a short vignette with a mini-plot enacting consequences of an action or character trait (Alter 169). For example, *The sluggard buries his hand in the dish; he will not even bring it back to his mouth!* (19:24; see 26:15). Here, the second line humorously thwarts what one would expect from the action of the first line. Instead of a person eating after putting his hand to a dish, laziness causes him simply to leave his hand there! Elaboration and intensification also occur in the "how much more" sayings (that is, 15:11; 19:10), which are comparable with the "better-than" sayings of antithetical proverbs.

Third, riddles make up a third basic form of proverbial sayings. As in the proverbs based on equivalence and elaboration, in riddles the second line develops the first line but to a greater degree. In these proverbs, a baffling or incomplete statement in the first line receives explanation in the second line (Alter 169). Often these occur as outlandish similes, a number of which cluster together in chapters 25–26. Proverbs 26:17 provides an example: *Like one who seizes a dog by the ears is a passer-by who meddles in a quarrel not his own.* The first line presents a vivid image of a dog being grabbed, but its point is unclear. The second line then becomes something of a "punchline" to that image, explaining its significance in a narrower context (Alter 176). In this case, the proverb warns that meddling can lead a person to get bitten.

The form of a proverb has important rhetorical implications in communicating its message. For one, the concise form makes a proverb easy to remember, as does its play on sounds or images. In English, for example, the saying "look before you leap," with its shortness and alliterative "L" sounds, stays in the mind much easier than "Consider your situation before you get involved in it." So also form makes a proverb persuasive on an intuitive level. Simply put, a proverb sounds correct due to its satisfying linguistic qualities. It gives a sense of familiarity and rightness, so that the truth of the proverb seems self-evident once it is expressed (Alter 171). On an even deeper level, proverbial form implies a worldview of predictability and order, corresponding to the structures of creation itself (see discussion on 8:23–29). Just as one parallel line "matches" another in some expected way, behaviors have matching consequences, and causes have predictable effects in the world. Even when this order is disrupted (just as when a proverb introduces an element of surprise), we still assume an underlying pattern that normally is present. Furthermore, the concise and unadorned form of a proverb aids in its application to various contexts. Lacking commentary or elaborative details, it preserves an openness that keeps it from being bound to only a few situations. As Murray Salisbury puts it, proverbs are "wisdom in a nutshell" that can stand on their own (438), and this makes diverse applications of them possible. Wisdom is required for discerning the situations in which a proverb is fitting and appropriate.

Proverbial sayings have meaning as self-contained poems, but literary contexts around them may influence their meaning, whether within the book of Proverbs or elsewhere in the Old Testament or other ancient Near Eastern wisdom materials. In Proverbs, literary influence occurs sometimes on a small scale. One proverb, for example, may refer directly to another proverb that immediately precedes or follows it (that is, 18:10–11; 26:4–5), or proverbs may "debate" with each other from afar (see 10:15; 18:11). Various literary devices emphasize connections between proverbs, including

> **The Functions of Proverbs**
> *In the end, each proverbial saying presents an interpretive challenge to the reader, who must figure out relationships between lines and words. A proverb does not spell out connections between images. It relies less on formal logic than on wordplays, sounds, rhythm, irony, and other imaginative elements of language. Therein lies part of a proverb's power, as it draws in the reader's participation. As such, each proverb gives the reader the opportunity to experience exactly what the prologue states: to gain skill in understanding proverbs, sayings, and riddles (1:5–6).*

> **Juxtaposition & Context in Proverbs**
> *Read together, proverbs may intensify, disagree with, or modify one another. The sayings of 26:4–5 famously provide two perspectives on dealing with fools:* Do not answer a fool according to his folly, or you will be like him yourself. Answer a fool according to his folly, or he will be wise in his own eyes. *Indeed, both sayings are true, and the intentional placement of the sayings side by side highlights the real tension that a person feels in trying to determine the proper response to a foolish person. Proverbs are not absolute rules but depend on context for their relevance.*

catchwords, puns, synonym sequences, and wordplays (see Hildebrandt 207–24).

The sayings of Proverbs appear within six collections in 10:1–31:9, each introduced by a superscription. Contrary to assertions that the proverbial collections in these chapters appear as haphazard lists, William Brown has argued persuasively that they show some deliberate literary development in their portrayals of wise living. While the earlier collections show more simplistic or binary understandings of wisdom, the later collections contain more nuances and emphasize the need for developing keen powers of discernment in order to live ethically and successfully in a complex world. The implied reader of Proverbs progresses from the figure of a receptive child ("son") in earlier chapters to the more mature figure of a king who becomes the object of critique and must engage in serious self-reflection (Brown, "Pedagogy," 180–81). Such development reflects a similar movement in the opening and closing chapters of Proverbs, where the reader moves from silent son in chapters 1–9 to the respected spouse of the valiant woman in 31:10–31 (Brown, "Pedagogy," 153).

On a broader scale, the overall structure of Proverbs also provides an important interpretive context for the sayings. The collections of 10:1–31:9 sit between two poetic sections in chapters 1–9 and 31:10–31. These sections use vivid metaphors to portray wisdom as a path to be traveled with care, a woman to be loved and pursued, a house to be built, and a feast to be savored. All of these flesh out what it is to live in fear of the Lord (1:7). Within this frame, diverse details of life mentioned in the proverbs of 10:1–31:9, whether farming issues or advice about building or parents' discipline of children, come to be seen as related to wisdom.

The Old and New Testaments, of course, offer an even larger literary context for interpreting Proverbs. Proverbs shares with the rest of the canon many thematic and theological points of contact, such as the fear of the Lord, righteousness and wickedness, and creation.

> **The "Woman of Strength"**
> *It is perhaps not surprising that in the Hebrew arrangement of books, the story of Ruth, a "woman of strength" [Hebrew 'eshet chayil; Ruth 3:11], follows the poem praising the "woman of strength" [eshet chayil] in Proverbs 31:10–31; that title occurs only one other time in the Old Testament (Prov 12:4).*

In addition, moral virtues taught in Proverbs such as self-control, honesty, fidelity, and concern for the poor are the subject of many biblical stories and the portrayals of various characters. So also wisdom texts of the ancient Near East, particularly those that contain the genre of "instruction," provide an important literary context for Proverbs. The parental guise prevalent in Proverbs, for example, occurs also in most ancient Egyptian instructional texts. Proverbs' portrayal of wise living, furthermore, shares much in common with the "silent one," a figure who models prudence and self-control in the Egyptian text *The Instruction of Ptahhotep*. It also shows points of contact with the sixth century Aramaic *Instructions of Ahiqar*. Along with sayings about careful speech, the discipline of children, self-control, and behavior before the king, *Ahiqar* contains a section praising heavenly wisdom, showing similarities with Proverbs 8.

COMMENTARY

THE PROLOGUE · 1:1–7

Proverbs opens with a sweeping statement of its ambitious goals in 1:1–7. The verses pile up wisdom terms in order to convey the comprehensiveness of the book's aims. In the Hebrew, the cumulative effect of the terms comes across noticeably, as each verse except one begins with the preposition "for." Presented in a chiastic structure, the literary presentation of the prologue shows the scope of the book's program, which covers intellectual, rhetorical, practical, and moral dimensions:

   A Comprehensive, intellectual values (2a)
   B Literary expression of wisdom (2b)
   C Instrumental virtue (3a)
   D Moral, communal virtues (3b)
   C' Instrumental virtues (4–5)
   B' Literary expressions of wisdom (6)
   A' Comprehensive, intellectual virtues (7)
                        (Brown, *Character*, 25)

Wisdom, the virtue that the prologue emphasizes along with instruction, refers both to the faculty of the human mind and to the knowledge one may possess. Similarly, instruction [Hebrew *musar*], also translated as "discipline," may point to something learned as well as the means by which a person learns. Due to the importance of language in teaching and learning wisdom, the prologue also emphasizes literary expressions of wisdom. So also the book aims to teach practical virtues that allow a person to achieve certain objectives. These include "wise dealing" (*prudent life*) that leads to prosperity (Prov 17:8; 1 Sam 18:15; Jer 10:21; 20:11) and reputation (Prov 3:4; 12:8; 13:15). Other practical virtues include prudence (often equated with caution; Prov 15:5; 14:15) and discretion (paired with resourcefulness and good sense; Prov 3:21) as well as skill at problem solving (Prov 11:14; 20:18; 24:6) (Brown, *Character*, 24–27).

> **Reader Participation in Proverbs**
> *Proverbs, figures, and riddles (verse 6) all require participation by the reader, stressing the active nature of acquiring wisdom.*

At the center of the prologue, the ethical principles of righteousness, justice, and fairness come into focus, emphasizing the fact that wisdom is a moral quality as well as an intellectual one, and it deals with community relations as well as individual success or character. The rest of Proverbs fleshes out the meaning and nuances of these terms in 1:2–7 by referring to them specifically or portraying them through images and metaphors. In addition to setting forth what Proverbs seeks to teach, the prologue also identifies whom it seeks to teach: the "simple" or inexperienced, the young, and even the wise, who never cease needing further instruction in wisdom.

The prologue culminates with the fear of the Lord, the primary motto of Proverbs. The importance of this theme comes across as it also concludes chapters 1–9 (9:10) and the entire book (31:30). As the *beginning of knowledge* (1:7), the fear of the Lord is the posture one must assume to become a wise and virtuous person (Brown, *Character*, 28). It may involve a real emotion of fear (14:27; 24:21) or awe at God's mysterious freedom that can supersede human plans (16:1, 9; 19:21; 21:30-31; 27:1). At the same time, it involves intellectual knowledge of the nature of God (2:5). Importantly, this attitude and knowledge brings a *relational* dimension to ethical behavior. Grounded in the fear of the Lord, proverbial sayings do more than simply lay out rules for correct behavior. They articulate a response that people have as they recognize their position in relation to God (Brown, *Character*, 28).

> **The "Fear of the Lord"**
> *The understanding of the fear of the Lord in 2:5 may equate with human conscience; it is an often unverbalized orientation deep within a person that recognizes a divine force in the cosmos and leads to an inner sense of right and wrong (Fox, Proverbs 1–9, 111).*

THE WAY OF WISDOM & THE WAY OF FOLLY · 1:8–9:18

Running throughout Proverbs 1–9 is a foundational metaphor of "the way." The text continually portrays life as a journey on two opposite paths: one traveled by the wise and righteous, the other by the foolish and wicked. Using this image, the text brings out many nuances of the pursuit of wisdom and the contrasting path of folly and evil. The journey through life involves movement, shown through images of walking (1:15; 2:13; 4:12, 14) and running (1:16; 4:12; 6:18). To stay on the right path requires intentional navigation, since obstacles can lead a person off course. Such obstacles include stumbling (4:19), getting caught in traps (3:26), getting lost in darkness (2:13; 4:19), or being led astray by bad influences (1:15-16). Various navigational aids, however, help a person to stay the course, such as parental instruction (4:11; 6:22), the example of wisdom (8:20), God's guidance (2:18; 3:6; 5:21), virtuous living (2:11-15), and deliberate effort to stay on the right path by walking past distractions (4:15, 25-27; 9:15). In Proverbs, navigation in the right way involves human effort, help from others, and divine guidance. Finally, the paths lead to certain destinations. The way of wisdom leads to brightness and light (4:18), increased wisdom and other virtues (righteousness, justice, equity, knowledge; 2:9-10), life in the land (2:21), and security (3:23). In stark contrast, darkness (4:19) and death (2:18; 5:5; 7:27) lie at the end of the road for the wicked and foolish.

A Father's Instruction, A Mother's Teaching · 1:8–19; 2:1–3:12; 3:21–7:27

The voice of a parent speaking to a child opens the instructions of Proverbs and resounds throughout chapters 1–9 in a series of ten lectures. Again and again, this persona addresses the reader as *my son* (1:8, 10; 2:1; 3:1, 11; 4:1, 10, 20; 5:1, 7; 6:1, 3, 20; 7:1). Instruction directed to the son (and not the daughter) reflects the male orientation shown in the sexual imagery used in these chapters.

The parental instructions [Hebrew *musar*] typically take the form of warnings and commands accompanied by promises about rewards and punishments. Repeatedly, the parent puts these instructions in terms of the heart (that is, 2:2, 10; 3:1, 3, 5, 4:4, 21, 23). In Hebrew, the word for heart (*leb*) is the same as for "mind," and its usage in Proverbs (and elsewhere in the Old Testament) shows it to be the center both of cognitive understanding (2:2; 3:1; 16:1; 18:15) and emotion (3:5; 7:25; 13:12; 14:13; 15:13; 16:5). The exhortation to *write* [*love and faithfulness*] *on the tablet of your heart* (3:3; see 6:21; 7:3; Jer 31:31–34; Ezek 11:19) aims to ingrain those virtues deep in the son's character. In urging the son to [*apply*] *your heart to understanding* (2:2), the parent seeks to instill in him a wholehearted desire for wisdom and righteousness. It is not simply a call to pay attention or to memorize certain principles but a call for enthusiastic receptivity to wisdom and parental teaching (Fox, *Proverbs 1–9*, 109). The parent's teaching reflects this by comparing wisdom to a relationship with a desirable woman. At the same time, it warns against seduction by the "strange woman" and "sinners" who vie for the son's heart.

> **The Parental Persona**
> *Along with Proverbs, most ancient Egyptian wisdom texts also use a parental guise in order to engender wisdom and foster moral character (see Ecclesiasticus 12:12). The parental persona brings authority to the instructions as well as a degree of intimacy, since parents have their children's best interests at heart and understand (Fox, Proverbs 1–9, 347–50).*

The Sinners · 1:8–19

In 1:8–19, the parent warns against "sinners" who move along the wrong path, trying to lure the son into destructive behavior with promises of valuable rewards (see Prov 16:29). Ironically, their being "swift to shed blood" (1:16), ostensibly the blood of their victims, turns out to lead to the shedding of their own blood (1:18). The adage about the bird in 1:17 underscores this point: the sinners even walk right into an obvious trap, but the son should avoid the trap set before him (compare 7:23). The parent, then, dismantles the credibility of the "birdbrained" thugs who entice the son and shows that their behavior leads not to the quick riches they promise but to self-destruction.

The Strange Woman · 2:16–22; 5:1–23; 6:20–35; 7:1–27; 9:13–18

Also traveling the path of wickedness and destruction is the figure of the "strange woman" (NIV *adulteress*), who epitomizes the folly of adultery. Forsaking her own marital commitment to her husband (2:17; 6:24; 7:19), she shamelessly tries to seduce young men in public places (7:10–12; compare 9:13–15). Not only does she ambush [Hebrew *te'erob*, used most often in military contexts] passersby with kisses (7:13), but like the sinners in 1:8–19, she tries to lure men to her evil path by offering pleasurable delights. Her bed, adorned with expensive Egyptian linens and perfumed with fragrant spices, appeals to the senses of sight and smell, leaving no question as to her intentions (7:16–17). But it is through the sense of hearing that she works her greatest charms with her "smooth" speech (2:16; 5:3; 6:24; 7:5, 21; compare 22:14). Though lovely to the ear, smooth speech entraps (29:5), ruins (26:28), and deceives (Ps 55:21; Prov 28:23; 29:5; Isa 30:10; Ezek 12:24). Proverbs 7:21 describes the woman's *persuasive words* [Hebrew *liqahah*] as *smooth talk* [Hebrew *heleq*]. The two words, heard one after the other in the Hebrew, create play on sounds to communicate how the woman's so-called instruction sounds smooth even though it leads to destruction (7:22–23). In the end, the pleasures offered by the strange woman turn out not to be so pleasant, after all. Much like the rewards promised by the sinners in 1:8–19, the strange woman "rewards" men by trapping them (5:22; 6:25; 7:22–23; see 1:17) and leading them to death and destruction (2:18; 5:5; 6:32; 7:23, 27; see 1:18–19).

The figure of the strange woman serves to warn how lust and adultery can turn a person away from the path of wisdom. To avoid that, the parent urges the son to stay faithful to his own wife instead of being seduced by other women (5:15–23). More broadly, seduction by the strange woman points ahead to 9:13–18, where the text presents folly, personified as a woman, in direct opposition to personified wisdom (9:1–6).

> **The "Strange Woman"**
> *The "strange woman" and other voices of wickedness and folly compete with the voice of the parent, as well as with Woman Wisdom, whose speeches appear in 1:20–33 and 8:1–36. Ironically, the words of the strange woman and Woman Folly often resemble the words of Woman Wisdom, as do the locations where they call out, showing the need for discernment when listening to the voices of the world.*

Woman Folly shares noticeable traits in common with

the strange woman: she speaks loudly (9:13; compare 7:11), tries to lure her victims in public places (9:14; compare 7:12), and leads to death and Sheol (9:18; compare 2:18; 5:5; 7:27). These characteristics link the adulterous exploits of the strange woman to folly in general, hinting that other foolish behavior in life can be just as seductive and destructive as adultery.

The Woman Wisdom · 1:20–33; 8:1–36; 9:1–6

Instruction in wisdom comes not only from the voice of the parent in Proverbs, but also from the voice of Wisdom herself. Wisdom speaks through the literary device of personification, a technique also used elsewhere in the Old Testament such as with the figure of Zion in Lamentations and elements of nature that sing and clap their hands in Psalm 98:8 and Isaiah 55:12. Far from being a mere "decoration" or fancy way of writing, presenting wisdom as a person brings out and develops aspects of wisdom that are not seen or felt when speaking of wisdom in other ways.

In Wisdom's first speech (1:20–33), she shouts out her message (emphasized by two verbs of calling) in the streets, public squares, crossroads, and city gates. These busy locations pick up on Proverbs' underlying metaphor of "the way" and emphasize the very public nature of Wisdom's message. City streets in antiquity bustled with animals, stores, beggars, children playing, and people going about their business. Public squares were the city plazas, and the *head of the noisy streets* was the place at the city gate where the roads fanned out into the city (Fox, *Proverbs 1–9*, 97).

> **Wisdom's Call**
> *The public location and loud volume of Wisdom's message stresses her accessibility to all people rather than a select few, such as the educated (see Deut 30:11–14). This leaves no excuse for ignoring her call.*

Like a prophet preaching in public places (Jer 11:6) to those who refuse to hear her words (Jer 6:19; Ezek 3:7), Wisdom tells her audience to "turn back" [Hebrew root *shub*, NIV *if you had responded*]; prophets frequently use that term in calls for repentance. In 1:31, she denounces *waywardness* [Hebrew *meshubah*], a word from the same Hebrew root. Other prophetic language includes calling and not being heard (1:24, 28; compare Isa 65:12; 66:4; Mic 3:4; Jer 7:13; 35:17; Zech 7:12) and seeking and not finding (1:28; compare Amos 8:12; Hos 5:6, 15). Wisdom promises that disaster and calamity will hit like a storm and whirlwind, along with distress and trouble. When calamity hits, she will mock the mockers (1:22). She promises that *they will eat the fruit of their ways*, highlighting the principle of act-consequence prevalent in Proverbs (see discussion below in 10:1–22:16) and summarizing the fate of the sinners from the parent's speech in 1:16–19. Also looking back to the parent's speech, disaster comes from failing to heed Wisdom's *rebuke*. On the heels of the parent's instruction [Hebrew *musar*] in 1:8–19, Wisdom's rebuke may address an unwillingness to heed the warnings of that earlier speech. In this way, the voice of Wisdom blends to some extent with that of the parent (see Prov 8:32, where Wisdom addresses readers as *my sons*).

Wisdom speaks again in the great poem of Proverbs 8. The form of this poem has parallels to speeches of self-presentation by gods and goddesses in ancient Egypt and Mesopotamia (Van Leeuwen, *Proverbs*, 90). As in her earlier speech, once more she calls out with a loud voice so that all may hear (1:1–3). Again she takes her stand in public places where all the details of life occur. At the city gate, in particular, people engaged in such activities as conducting business dealings, administering justice, getting married, and interacting with friends (Van Leeuwen, *Proverbs*. 89). The last line of Wisdom's speech (36) echoes her warnings in 1:20–33, but the overall tone of the poem is more positive as she stresses the rewards of wisdom instead of punishments for not pursuing it. Those who seek her *will* find her (8:17; compare verses 9, 35; 1:28). Listening to her words and choosing her instruction [Hebrew *musar*; 10, 33] results in happiness (32–35; compare 1:33). It also leads to great treasures (10–11, 18–19, 21; see 2:4; 3:14–16; Job 28:15–29) as opposed to the empty promises of the sinners (1:13–14). Wisdom's warnings in 1:20–33 now make way for Wisdom's promises of rewards as wise ones enjoy her fruit (8:19; compare 1:31).

Wisdom's virtues and benefits also stand in striking contrast to the portrayal of the strange woman who competes with her for attention in public places (7:11–12). In contrast to the smooth speech of the strange woman (7:21; compare 2:16; 5:3; 6:4), Wisdom speaks honest and righteous words with truth and justice (8:6–8). Following Wisdom leads to life (8:35), whereas the strange woman leads to death (7:23, 26–27; compare 2:18; 5:5). Wisdom actively brings wealth and treasure to those who follow her (8:21; compare 10–11, 18–19, 21), while association with the strange woman leads to poverty (5:10). The honor that Wisdom brings to public officials (8:15-16) further contrasts with the ruin in the public assembly that the strange woman brings (5:14). Wisdom calls on humans to love her (8:17, 21; compare 5:6, 8; 7:4), and remarkably, she too loves humans (8:17) and delights in them (8:31). This stands against the love and delight the strange woman claims to have for her lovers (7:15, 18).

> **The Love of Wisdom**
> Love of Wisdom guards against inappropriate love of the "strange woman" (7:4–5; compare 8:31 and 5:8). Even more, it characterizes a reciprocal relationship with Wisdom marked by desire, and it involves all the senses of the body, drawing on the emotions as well as the intellect.

Even more dramatically setting Wisdom apart from the strange woman – and anything else – are her extraordinary origins and her unique relationship to God and the world (8:22-31). These form the basis for her promises in verses 6-21. She was created [Hebrew *qanah*, a different word from Genesis 1's *bana*] by God, and the divine acquisition of wisdom serves as the prototype for humans who also acquire wisdom, though in different ways (Prov 4:7: *Get* [*qanah*] *understanding*; see also *qanah* in 1:5; 4:5; 15:32; 16:16; 17:16; 18:15; 19:8; 23:23) (Fox, *Proverbs 1–9*, 280). God created Wisdom before anything else (8:22-26), and then Wisdom was present in the creation of the world (8:27-31). The poem moves through the creation of all realms of the universe, going upward from the deeps (8:24a) to the springs leading to the earth's surface (8:24b) to the mountains and hills and land (8:25-26) to the heavens and horizons and clouds (8:28), and then going downward to the wellsprings (8:28b) and seas (8:29) and foundations of the earth (8:29). The systematic presentation highlights the coherence and orderliness of the natural world, all of which is imbued with wisdom. On a subtle level, the symmetrical and predictable patterns of proverbial sayings throughout Proverbs attest to this order. Such order extends also to the order of the social world, as indicated by the way that human *decrees* (8:15 NIV *make laws*; see also 31:5) reflect how God *marked out* (8:27, 29) the structures and limits of nature (both texts use the same Hebrew verb).

In verse 30, Wisdom declares that during creation, she was *the craftsman at* [*God's*] *side*. The translation *craftsman* comes from an Akkadian word that signifies skill, expertise, and artisanship. In Akkadian texts, it refers to scribes, officers, and scholars as well as a group of divine sages who brought arts and culture to the human race (Greenfield 17-20). Other translations for this term include "little child" or "nursling," indicating one who is in God's care; this reading reflects several verbs in 8:23-25 associated with giving birth.

Continuing Wisdom's invitation in 8:32–36, the poem of chapter 9 also shows Wisdom's contrast with the strange woman, who herself invites humans to eat and drink. The

> **Wisdom's Playfulness**
> Wisdom also declares herself to be a source of delight to God as she "frolics" before God (NIV attributes *delight* and *rejoicing* to Wisdom, but instead 8:30 actually indicates God's pleasure in Wisdom and her frolicking activity). This reflects a playful quality of Wisdom, often embodied in the witty sayings of Proverbs, as well as the satisfaction and pleasure brought by the joy of learning and creation itself (for example *it is good* in Gen 1; see Job 38:7; Ps 104:15, 31, 34). Thus, Wisdom says in 8:32, Happy are those who keep my ways (compare 8:34; 3:12–13).

seven pillars of Wisdom's house (9:1) show its completeness and perfection, and her preparation of wine and meat, typically reserved only for special occasions, demonstrates her value (9:2); Folly, by contrast, serves bread and water (9:17). Wisdom's nourishment leads to life (9:9), while Folly's provision, though seemingly sweet and delicious on some levels (9:17), brings death (9:18).

Between the portrayals of Wisdom and Folly in 9:1-6 and 9:13-17, an interlude offers counsel about advising others (9:7-12). Verse 10a, *The fear of the Lord is the beginning of wisdom*, almost exactly quotes 1:7 in the prologue to Proverbs, making a frame to chapters 1–9 and at the same time highlighting this motto in the sayings that follow this section. The instructional form of verses 7-12 also anticipates the sayings in chapters 10-30, as does the linking of wisdom and righteousness (9:9) in contrast to the wicked (9:7). The interlude also shows literary development in chapters 1–9 as the child moves from the recipient of advice to one who gives advice. Wisdom's portrayal in 9:1-6 serves a similar purpose. Having joined the parent in sternly rebuking the child in the opening chapter (1:20-33), Wisdom now offers joy and sustenance in the home she opens to her followers.

THE PROVERBS OF SOLOMON · 10:1–22:16

With this collection, the first of the six collections in 10:1–31:9, Proverbs shifts from the extended poetical form to sayings presented one after the other with less literary development than seen in chapters 1–9. The Solomonic collection stands out most immediately for the repetitive grammatical structures of its sayings. The first five chapters (10:1–15:33) feature a large number of sayings of antithesis that contrasts various moral behaviors and attitudes: wise/foolish, righteous/wicked, silence/speech, honesty/dishonesty, wealth/poverty, or diligence/laziness.

Among the many topics scattered throughout the chapters of this collection, several emerge as distinct themes. The first eight proverbs (10:1–8) highlight these themes which include the household (10:1, 5), righteousness as contrasted with wickedness (10:2, 6, 7), wealth and poverty (10:3–5), and speech (10:8). In addition, some proverbs discuss kingship and the nature of God (Brown, "Pedagogy," 158–64). They also show noticeable connections to themes in chapters 1–9, including the metaphor of the two paths (10:17; 10:29; 12:28; 14:2, 12; 15:9, 21, 24; 23:19).

A strong connection between acts and consequences comes through in many of the proverbs dealing with these themes, especially in chapters 10–15 (exceptions appear more frequently in 16–22). In general, bad deeds or character lead to bad consequences, and good deeds/character lead to some kind of reward, as in Proverbs 11:21: *Be sure of this: The wicked will not go unpunished, but those who are righteous will go free.* Often, evildoers seem to bring about their own punishment through the natural consequences of their actions. In 11:6, for example, *The righteousness of the upright delivers them, but the unfaithful are trapped by evil desires.* The second line plays on the word "desires" which in Hebrew also means "disaster" (this wordplay occurs also in 10:3). The desires of the wicked, then, are themselves disastrous (compare 13:6; 14:32; Ps 5:9–10; 7:15–16; 9:15–16). Outside of this collection, Proverbs 26:27 communicates a similar idea: *If a man digs a pit, he will fall into it; if a man rolls a stone, it will roll back on him.* Other sayings attribute the consequences of one's actions directly to God (10:3; 15:25; 22:14). Ultimately, these two ideas of retribution merge in a view of God as creator and ruler of a just and orderly world. Thus any "natural" consequence of an action may be understood as ordained or set in motion by God (see Ps 9:15–16).

The Household

Just after the poem in which Wisdom builds a house (Prov 9), the Solomonic collection opens with a proverb emphasizing the familial context of wisdom (10:1). This theme dominates much of 10:1–22:16, with over fifty references to the father, mother, son, wife, servant, and house; only chapter 16 lacks mention of them (Clifford 109). The household context sets the stage for learning wisdom as well as for enjoying wisdom's benefits, which include happy family relations (10:1; 15:20; 17:21, 25; 19:13, 26; see 23:22–26; 29:15; *Ecclesiasticus* 16:1–3), blessings from God (15:25), and general flourishing (12:7; 14:11; 15:6).

Among the many ways that a person can learn wisdom, parental discipline or instruction [Hebrew *musar*] stands out as one of the most important. While *musar* can be either verbal or physical in nature, most of the sayings on this topic clearly refer to verbal instruction or discipline. At times, the term *musar* appears as the object of verbs of listening (19:27), or it parallels words for verbal "reproof" (10:17; 12:1; 13:18; 15:5, 32) or "rebuke" (13:1) (compare 19:20; 23:12). The physical aspect of discipline comes across in only two sayings in the collection (13:24; 22:15 [also 23:12; 29:15]), both of which refer to the use of a rod in disciplining children.

> **Disciplining a Child**
>
> In 13:24, *the parent who loves the child applies physical discipline carefully* (NIV), or "early," another possible reading of the Hebrew word. Translated as "early," the word highlights the importance of disciplining soon after an offense is committed as well as when a child is young.

The proverbs say little about the actual content of instruction but instead stress its importance and provide motivation for it. Some sayings do this by appealing to the parents. For example, instruction shows a parent's love (13:24) and drives away folly (22:15). Picking up the metaphor of "the way," Proverbs 22:6 points out that discipline helps children not to stray when they grow up. Furthermore, discipline saves children from destruction, according to Proverbs 19:18. The grammar of that saying allows different readings. Whereas the NRSV stresses the timeliness of discipline: *Discipline your children while there is hope*, the NIV presents discipline as that which brings hope. The second line, *do not be a willing party to his death*, emphasizes its point by using two words with the same Hebrew characters:

to (*his death*) [Hebrew *'el*] and *do not* [Hebrew *'al*]. The saying likely points out how discipline saves children from the destruction they would otherwise bring on themselves. Some scholars, however, read this as counsel to parents not to chastise their children excessively when disciplining them (Whybray 283). Outside of this collection, other proverbs motivate discipline by promising rest and delight to parents who discipline their children (29:17) and warning that an undisciplined child disgraces a parent (29:15).

Most sayings speak directly to children by spelling out the benefits of listening to instruction. It leads to understanding (15:32), knowledge (12:1), honor (13:18), and wisdom for the future (19:20). Proverbs 19:16 shows a direct connection between keeping [Hebrew *shamar*] instruction and keeping [*shamar*] one's life. So also Proverbs 10:17 portrays instruction as preserving life. The Hebrew form of the verb used in that saying may indicate that following instruction *shows the way to life* to other people (NIV) or that it preserves the life of the person who takes instruction (NRSV).

A number of proverbs speak more generally about the importance of learning from others and not relying on one's own opinions (18:1-2; compare 12:15; 15:12, 22, 31). In this vein, the triad of Proverbs 15:31-33 stresses the humility required in a willingness to accept instruction from others. Such humility comes from the fear of the Lord and leads to honor (15:33; see 13:18).

Righteousness & Wickedness, Justice & Injustice

Contrasts between righteousness and wickedness make up one of the most distinctive features of the Solomonic collection. Appearing among the other contrasts set up in the sayings (for example: wisdom/folly, justice/injustice, or diligence/laziness), a general overlap develops between righteousness and the positive states of being and between wickedness and the negative ones. Like wisdom, righteousness has a cosmic dimension to it as a sense of right and wrong imbues all of creation (see Pss 50:6; 72:3, 16; 97:6). At the same time, righteousness has a narrower range of meaning than wisdom.

Since righteousness coincides with the order of the cosmos, a righteous life leads to blessing and rewards that are the natural consequences built into reality by God. These include a good reputation (10:7), deliverance from death and trouble (10:2; 11:4, 8), nourishment from God (10:3), life (10:16; 11:19; 12:28; 21:21), longevity (16:31), having desires granted (10:24), and being loved by God (15:9). A righteous person also blesses others, whether a friend who gets good advice (12:26) or an entire nation that is exalted (14:34). Wickedness, on the other hand, leads to a bad reputation (10:7), an inability to prosper (10:2), trouble (11:8; 12:21), death (11:18), a lack of security (12:3), and trouble for others (16:29; 17:4)

Righteous behavior entails doing what is right and correct. Often, sayings about righteousness and wickedness overlap to some degree with those about justice and injustice, such as in Proverbs 1:7 and 2:9. Other proverbs note that the righteous person hates falsehood (13:5), shows thoughtfulness in speech (15:28), gives without holding back (21:26), and has mercy even for animals (12:10). These indicate that righteousness involves both inner purity as well as ethical relations with others.

In addition to proverbs that use some form of the term "righteousness" [Hebrew *tsedeq*], other sayings describe righteous living even when they do not use that term. In some cases, the proverb implicitly refers to righteousness by setting up a direct contrast with wickedness, as in Proverbs 10:27, which contrasts wickedness and the fear of the Lord. In other cases, similarities between two separate proverbs bring out nuances of righteousness, such as in Proverbs 15:16 and 16:8, which also link righteousness and the fear of the Lord: 15:16: *Better a little with the fear of the Lord than great wealth with turmoil*; 16:8: *Better a little with righteousness than large income with injustice*.

The second of these sayings (16:8), furthermore, shows the close connection between righteousness and justice that comes through in the collection. The link first appears in the prologue's association of "righteousness, justice, and equity" (1:3; compare 2:9), and sayings throughout the book advocate these virtues in all areas of life. For one, they relate them to worship. In ranking righteousness and justice as more desirable to God than sacrifice (15:8; 21:3),

> **Wisdom & Righteousness**
> *A person can do a righteous deed such as an act of charity but do it unwisely. One cannot, however, be wise and be unrighteous. A person cannot steal or murder wisely, since such deeds are destructive and go against the moral order of the world. Wisdom, then, includes righteousness but extends beyond the realm of righteousness* (Van Leeuwen, Proverbs, 105).

Proverbs shares the vision of ethical life laid out in the prophets and Psalms (Isa 1:12–17; Amos 5:21–24; Mic 6:6–8; Ps 50:8, 16–23).

Second, some of the sayings deal with justice in legal settings (17:15, 23, 26; 18:5; compare 24:23; 28:21). Among these, Proverbs 19:28 uses a pun to characterize *a corrupt witness* [Hebrew *'ed beliyya'al*] as one who *gulps down* [Hebrew *bala'*] *evil*. Third, the sayings emphasize justice in business dealings and economic life. Several deal specifically with the practice of using balances and scales in commerce, such as Proverbs 11:1 (see Lev 19:35–37; Deut 25:13–16; Ezek 45:10; Hos 12:7–8; Amos 8:5; Mic 6:11). A translation of this proverb, more literal than the NIV, reads: "scales of falsehood, an abomination to the Lord /a weight of completeness, his delight" (compare 16:11; 20:10, 23). Showing almost symmetrical opposition between the kinds of business that God detests and appreciates, the literary balance of lines and concepts in the saying cleverly brings out the notion of weights and balances. Proverbs 20:10 makes the same point but through a riddle: *weight and weight, measure and measure, an abomination to the Lord are they both*. What on the surface looks like a balance of equals in the first line turns out to be the dishonest practice of double standards that the Lord hates. The two proverbial forms in 11:1 and 20:10 imply that unfair business dealings are blatantly wrong and at the same time subtly present in economic life.

Wealth & Poverty

Issues of wealth and poverty come to the fore repeatedly in the collection. Some proverbs, clustered mostly in the first half (chapters 10–15), refer to poverty in terms of acts (or character) and resulting consequences. Typically, poverty results from character deficiencies, whether laziness or stubbornness, and wealth comes from diligence and toil (10:4; 12:24, 27; 13:18; 14:23). Proverbs 14:23 contrasts hard work with *mere talk* (literally "a word of the lips"), showing a link to the sayings about speech.

The sayings present mixed views of wealth. Though some sayings recognize benefits of wealth (10:15; 18:11) and attribute its acquisition to good character or divine blessing (10:22), other sayings note that wealth may come from dishonest or unjust means (13:11; 21:6; 22:16), aggression (11:16), or greed (20:21). For those who gain wealth through such wickedness, their income is ultimately valueless (10:2; compare 11:4) or marked by trouble (15:6). This comes across in the second line of 10:3, where the Hebrew word for *craving* [Hebrew *hawwa*] also means disaster. The Lord "thrusts forward the *craving* [NIV *disaster*] of the wicked" (Van Leeuwen, *Proverbs*, 107). The wicked, then, get what they crave, but it has disastrous ramifications. As one proverb puts it, *Whoever trusts in his riches will fall, but the righteous will thrive like a green leaf* (11:28). Another points out, *wealth is worthless in the day of wrath* (11:4). Likely, the *day of wrath* refers to a person's death or disasters that occur in life (Van Leeuwen, *Proverbs*, 117). Certainly, wealth does have benefits, as Proverbs 10:15 makes clear in describing wealth as a *fortified city*. At the same time, Proverbs 18:11 provides another perspective: the rich only *imagine* their wealth to be a fortified city. Actually, *the name of the Lord is a strong tower* that provides security to those who are righteous (Prov 18:10).

> **Poverty & Wickedness**
> Some proverbs also associate poverty or hunger with wickedness and the avoidance of it with righteousness (10:3; 13:25; see Pss 34:10; 37:19, 25). The theological problems with such statements are obvious. Clearly, some righteous people do experience hunger and poverty, as do some people who are diligent. Proverbs 13:23 acknowledges that there may be more to such situations: *a poor person's good harvest may be eradicated through injustice* rather than any laziness or wickedness on his or her part. Experience allows the reader to evaluate the truth of proverbs like these and to determine in which contexts they may be appropriate.

Along with proverbs recognizing negative aspects of wealth, other proverbs point out that poverty actually has positive value relative to moral flaws in character. Often, these take form as "better than" sayings, such as in 15:16–17: *Better a little with the fear of the Lord than great wealth with turmoil. Better a meal of vegetables where there is love than a fattened calf with hatred*. Other sayings extol poverty as better than injustice (16:8), pride (16:19), perverse speech (19:1), and lying (19:22). The sayings certainly do not celebrate poverty but instead use it, a condition understood as undesirable, to point out that other conditions are even more undesirable. In doing so, however, they acknowledge that poverty is not necessarily linked to moral deficiency. This also comes through in the proverbs that encourage charity to the poor (14:21; 21:13; 22:9) and recognize that both the poor and the rich have in common

Speech

In Proverbs, speech is one of the most important ways of distinguishing between the righteous and the wicked, the wise and the foolish. A large percentage of the sayings on this topic appear in the Solomonic collection, with over sixty sayings discussing proper speech and many others dealing with improper speech. The sayings continually extol the great value of proper speech as a facet of wisdom. For example: *Gold there is, and rubies in abundance, but lips that speak knowledge are a rare jewel* (20:15; see 3:14; 8:10, 19; 10:20; 16:16). The proverb obviously plays on the availability of gold and "rubies." Though extremely rare, both are abundant compared to *lips that speak knowledge*. The Hebrew word for "rubies" may also be translated as "pearls" or "corals," and it is rare in the Old Testament, appearing only five times (Job 28:18; Prov 8:11; 20:15; 31:10; Lam 4:7). Three of these references (Job 28:18; Prov 8:11; 20:15) mention precious stones in relation to the value of wisdom, and the usage in Proverbs 31:10 also points to wisdom. The focus on wisdom continues in the second line with its reference to Hebrew "lips of knowledge." While this may include the speaking of knowledgeable or impressive things (reflected in the NIV), it also would include wisdom more subtly displayed in speaking gently (15:1, 4; 25:15), judiciously (16:23), graciously (15:26; 22:11), openly and directly (10:10; 16:13; 25:12), and honestly (12:17, 19; 14:5, 25; compare 12:22; 19:5, 9). Proper speech in Proverbs is never a superficial quality but reflects the inner character of a person.

As Proverbs 17:7 puts it, "Fine speech" (NIV *arrogant lips*) is *unsuited to a fool, how much worse lying lips to a ruler!* (see 14:7, 15:2, 7, 14)

Individuals demonstrate their wisdom and virtue not only in their speech but also in their silence. Silence shows deliberation in responding to a situation (15:28) and allows wise ones to avoid saying something they might later regret (20:25). In Proverbs 17:27, one who *uses words with restraint* parallels one who is *even-tempered* (Hebrew "cool in spirit"); the self-control one shows in speech reflects his or her knowledge and understanding. On the other hand, *He who answers before listening – that is his folly and shame* (18:13). The theme continues in a number of sayings (10:19; 12:23; 15:2, 28), with the very brevity of the proverbial form reflecting the brevity in speech that it often recommends.

The sayings enumerate benefits that result from wise and righteous speech. Many of these benefits come directly to the speaker. For one, they enjoy protection from disaster. The saying in 21:23 uses the word "guard" in both of its lines: ones who *guard* their mouths and tongues *guard* their lives from calamity (compare 14:3). Positively, the "fruit" of one's own speech fills one's mouth with good things (12:14; 13:2; 18:20, 21). So also the tongue may be a "tree of life," the fruits of which may nourish other people (15:4; compare 10:21), and it may bring healing (12:18; 16:24). In contrast, the speech of the wicked and foolish lead to destructive consequences for themselves (10:8; 14:3; 17:20; 18:6, 7, 21; 21:6) and for others (10:14; 11:9; 12:6; 20:19).

The Nature of God

Aspects of the nature of God come into focus in a number of proverbial sayings. For one, God comes across as keenly interested in and responsive to human activity and thought. As Proverbs 15:3 puts it, *The eyes of the Lord are everywhere, keeping watch on the wicked and the good* (see 22:12; 16:2; 17:3; 21:2). Proverbs 20:27 also emphasizes divine attention to human thoughts (though not reflected in the NIV, the Hebrew wording of this proverb also stresses a person's own self-reflective attention to his or her inner thoughts; see Van Leeuwen, *Proverbs*, 188). At times, God's interest in human action and thought leads to divine reward or punishment for deeds (10:22; 12:2; 14:9, 29; 15:29a; 16:4, 5, 7, 20; 18:10; 19:17; 21:12; 22:12, 14), but God's emotion itself remains central in many of the proverbs, with human activity often described as God's "delight" or an abomination to God (11:1, 20; 12:22; 14:31; 15:8, 9, 26a; 20:10, 23; 21:3). The motto of the fear of the Lord winds through the sayings as well; it prolongs life (10:27; 14:27), brings confidence (14:26), is more valuable than great treasure (15:16), allows a person to avoid evil (16:6), and brings security and life (19:23; compare 14:2; 15:33).

Restraint in Speech

Whether or not one has restraint in speech can have life or death consequences (13:3; 18:21). This idea comes across also in the ancient Sumerian proverb, "An open mouth draws flies" (Alster 100), and the World War II saying, "Loose lips sink ships" (Van Leeuwen, Proverbs, 31). At the same time, the consequences may be less drastic but still noticeable by others. Proverbs 17:28 points out that even fools may be thought wise if they keep silent.

The second half of the sayings opens with a noticeable theocentric orientation in 16:1-9. All but one of the first nine sayings focus directly on God. Attention turns especially to God's will in relation to human intentions. The concise Hebrew wording of 16:1 sets up a stark contrast: "from a person the plans of the heart, from the Lord the answer of the tongue." Verse 9 continues the theme, forming a kind of frame with verse 1 around the opening sayings. Again, Proverbs 16:9 distinguishes between divine plans and human ones: *In his heart a man plans his course, but the Lord determines his steps* (compare 19:21); this picks up the metaphor of "the way" pervading much of Proverbs. All human activity falls within the divine domain as *the Lord works out everything for his own ends* (16:4). Even actions that may be attributed to human preparation or technological advantages come about as a result of God's intentions: *The horse is made ready for the day of battle, but victory rests with the Lord* (21:31). Because of God's active role in the ways of the world, the sayings advise humans to *commit to the Lord whatever you do, and your plans will succeed* (16:3). Importantly, this aspect of God's nature orients all human wisdom, which must conform to God's will if it is to lead to a happy and successful life. In sum, if it goes against the Lord's will, it is not wisdom (21:30). Wisdom entails both listening to the counsel of other people (11:14; 15:22) and living in the fear of the Lord. The wise person always remains aware of both the potentials and limits of human understanding and power in navigating the world.

THE WORDS OF THE WISE & ADDITIONAL SAYINGS OF THE WISE · 22:17–24:34

This section of Proverbs features *thirty sayings...of counsel and knowledge* (22:20) in 22:17-24:22, along with an appendix in 24:23-34 introduced in 24:23 (*These also are sayings of the wise*). As the NIV marginal note indicates, the Hebrew term translated as *thirty sayings* is complicated. In light of the puzzling Masoretic Text, many translators emend this word to read "thirty" and understand it to refer to the "thirty chapters" of the *Instruction of Amenemope*, an ancient Egyptian wisdom text that appears to be a source of many of the sayings in this section, especially 22:17-23:1.

Themes common to the Solomonic collection continue in this group of proverbs (the family, righteousness and wickedness, wealth and poverty, the nature of God). Immediately, however, one can recognize a different tone and style from the Solomonic proverbs. For one, the "antithetical" and "equivalent" parallelism typical of the Solomonic collection almost completely falls out of usage (exceptions include 23:17; 23:23; 24:3-7). Along with this, sayings set within the metaphorical framework of "the way" also disappear. Replacing them are positive and negative admonitions with motive clauses giving reasons for obedience. Though typically briefer than the extended instructions of chapters 1-9, some instructions cover several lines, such as the comical poetic riddle about the dangers of wine in 23:29-35 (compare 24:30-34).

Second, language of direct address appeals to the reader in first person: *Incline your ear and hear my words, and apply your mind to my teaching* (22:17; see 22:20; 23:15-16, 26). Reminiscent of the parent figure in Proverbs 1-9, the speaker of the proverbs in 22:17-24:34 calls to the "son" (23:15, 19, 26; 24:13, 21; see especially 1:8; 6:20; 23:22). Also like the parent in the early part of Proverbs, this figure shares intimacy with the "son" in rejoicing in the child's wisdom (23:15, 16) and modeling good behavior (23:26). The family context of wisdom comes through further in admonitions dealing specifically with family life or the maintenance of family property.

> **Household Wisdom**
> Along with exhortations to heed parental instruction (23:22–25), one saying emphasizes the role of wisdom in establishing a successful and prosperous house (24:3–4; compare 9:1–3; 14:1). Another saying offers practical advice about preparing land before building a house (24:27), in contrast to the lazy person whose field becomes overgrown with thorns (24:30–31).

A political context of wisdom also marks some sayings in this collection. Though one should respect and obey the king (24:21), one should also be discriminating in viewing aspects of royal life. Skill may allow a privileged position in relation to the king; a wordplay in 22:29 between "his work" [Hebrew *mela'kto*] and "kings" [*melakim*] stresses the connection of a skilled worker to royalty. This highlights technical skill and craftsmanship as one domain of wisdom, also seen elsewhere in the Old Testament (Exod 35:31; 36:4; Isa 40:20). With such skill come privileges, such as dining in royal settings, which may stir up greed in a person. Putting a knife to the throat rather than in one's food guards against feeding one's desires (23:2). The point is not to kill oneself but to suppress the appetite, since such luxuries are deceptively fleeting (23:5; compare Eccl 4:7-8; 5:13-17) and the pursuit of them can be nauseating (23:7-8). One proverb advises, *Do not wear yourself out to get rich; have the wisdom to show restraint* (23:4).

Along with such warnings against preoccupation with wealth in political contexts, other sayings offer additional instruction related to wealth and poverty. Picking up the dinner table setting of 23:1-8, Proverbs 23:20-21 urges restraint in the presence of overindulgent *drunkards and gluttons* whose behavior will lead them to poverty. In much different contexts, two sayings denounce oppression of the poor based on God's special advocacy of the poor and the orphan (22:22-23; 23:11). Related to this are instructions against moving "boundary stones," markers of land understood to be given to families by God (22:28; 23:10; compare 15:25; Deut 19:14). Even poor families might lay claim to land through a divine inheritance such as this, so robbing families by moving their markers in order to reduce their portion could take away their primary possession in life.

> **Boundary Markers**
> *Israel and its neighbors took boundary markers very seriously, so that violating them was understood as going against divinely established order. One may read this in light of the order created by God as presented in Proverbs 8:27-29 (Van Leeuwen, Proverbs, 205; Keel 96-100).*

In this collection, the portrayal of God serves mainly to warn against specific behaviors, whether oppression of the poor (22:23; 23:11), gloating at the failings of one's enemies (24:17-18), the envy of sinners (23:17), or disobedience to God or the king (24:21). The wicked person receives greater emphasis in this section than the righteous person. As described in the Solomonic collection, the wicked come to disaster (24:16) and have no future (24:20a; compare 23:18; 24:14). Readers, then, should not envy the wicked (24:19) or even associate with them (24:1; 22:24-25). Still, instead of overlooking the guilt of the wicked, they should rebuke them (24:24-25), though Proverbs 24:29 does not encourage retribution (compare 20:22; 24:17-18).

SOLOMON'S OTHER PROVERBS COPIED BY HEZEKIAH'S OFFICIALS · 25:1-29:27

The sayings of this collection show great variety in topics and forms. Along with the antithetical sayings common to the collections preceding this one, these proverbs appear in the form of rhetorical questions (26:12a; 27:4; 29:20), "better than" sayings (25:7, 24; 27:5, 10c), "happy is" sayings (28:14a; 29:18b), and conditional sentences (25:16, 21; 29:9, 12, 14). Some proverbial units extend past the typical two-line sentence. The longest is eleven lines long. Stylistically, the sayings feature some of the most vivid metaphors and similes in the book, showing a higher level of sophistication than usually seen in the collections of chapters 10-24. With their striking variety and elegance of poetic forms and features, these sayings model the art of good speech as well as prescribe it (Brown, "Pedagogy," 169-71).

Proverbs' familiar themes appear in this collection, though often the sayings put a new spin on topics covered elsewhere. Sayings about righteousness and wickedness, for example, offer standard observations about their opposition to each other (29:27) and the expected consequences of such behavior (28:18). One saying even points out an ironic aspect of wickedness: *The wicked man flees as though no one pursues, but the righteous are as bold as a lion* (28:1). Running from imagined dangers, the wicked show on one level their failure to grasp reality – and on another level perhaps a deep recognition (through an uneasy conscience) of their self-induced destruction. Other sayings acknowledge that sometimes the wicked prevail instead of being defeated (28:12, 28; 29:2).

A number of the sayings situate righteousness and wickedness within the realm of politics. From the beginning of the collection, royal leadership receives much attention. Proverbs 25:2 sets a high standard for kings: *It is the glory of God to conceal a matter, to search out a matter is the glory of kings*. In seeking to understand God's mysteries and the divine order of the world, kings should model wisdom to the highest degree, showing their minds to be "unsearchable" (25:3). Even as these two sayings recognize the important place of kingship and respect that comes with that position, the collection also creates space for more critical reflection of the office, as in 29:12, 16 (Brown, "Pedagogy," 171). This differs from the other collections, which stress the benefits of royal favor (16:15; 19:12; 20:2) and the king's good judgment (16:10; 20:8, 26), even comparing him to God (16:10, 15; 19:12; 21:1; 24:21-22). In this section, however, the sayings offer criteria for evaluating the king, including his treatment of the poor (28:3, 15; 29:14) and administration of justice (29:4). Ultimately, God is the one who brings justice, and this is superior to any favor bestowed by a ruler (29:26). Clearly, the sayings do not presume that "might makes right." Instead of assuming inherent righteousness in rulers, they point out that sometimes wicked people make their way to positions of authority (28:12, 28; 29:2) and that a ruler may lack understanding (28:12). Recognizing that leaders often need guidance, Proverbs 25:15 advises, *Through patience a ruler can be persuaded, and a (soft) tongue can break a bone.*

Other familiar themes in this section include the household (27:8, 11; 28:7, 24; 29:3, 15, 17), but it receives considerably less emphasis than in other collections. Instead, attention focuses on social relations in political contexts and with other people such as masters (27:18), friends (27:9, 17), and neighbors (25:17; 26:18-19; 27:14), some of whom are even better than family in certain situations (27:10). Because of their value, relationships with neighbors and friends should be nurtured. Proverbs 25:17 thus warns against overstaying one's welcome: *Seldom set foot in your neighbor's house – too much of you, and he will hate you.* Various sayings also discuss wealth and poverty, though here they rarely link poverty to laziness or other flaws in character, as in other collections (but see 24:33-34). In fact, several sayings speak of a poor person with integrity (28:6) and discernment (28:11). Rich people, on the other hand, receive condemnation if they are greedy (28:20, "in a hurry to get rich"; compare 28:22). Instead, true riches come to those who give to the poor (28:27), remain faithful (28:20), and trust in the Lord. Proverbs 28:25 makes the final point by contrasting the greedy person (literally, "wide of appetite") with the person who becomes rich (literally, "grows fat") through trust in God.

Another example of misplaced trust comes from the fool, a figure who frequently enters the spotlight in the Hezekian sayings. Fools trust in themselves, or literally, in their own hearts, rather than walking in wisdom (28:26). Fools also may be *wise in their own eyes* (26:4); that phrase, appearing only in this collection (see Prov 3:7), describes sluggards (26:16) and rich people (28:11), as well.

According to Proverbs 26:7, 9, another characteristic of fools is their inability to use proverbs appropriately. A fool's incompetence with words thus makes him a poor choice as a messenger. Instead of being an extra pair of feet for the one sending him, the botched job has more of an effect of cutting off one's feet, as one has to go back and clear up misunderstandings (Van Leeuwen, *Proverbs*, 224). A fool's bungling of a proverb brings out the truth of Proverbs 25:11: *A word aptly spoken is like apples of gold in settings of silver.* To interpret and appropriate a proverb (or any part of the Bible, for that matter) correctly, one must sensitively "read" the proverb as well as life situations.

> **The Misuse of Proverbs**
> *Wisdom involves more than simply having access to information but knowing when and how to apply that information, especially with something as dependent on context as a proverb. Not having such discernment makes a proverb ineffective (26:7) or painfully annoying (26:9). Like a thornbush in a drunkard's hand, a misappropriated proverb can bring pain either to oneself or to others.*

So also fools fail to learn from their mistakes, as Proverbs 26:11 vividly points out: *As a dog returns to its vomit, so a fool repeats his folly.* Since they cannot correct themselves, fools require external means of improvement (26:3). Even the most stringent of efforts, however, may not suffice in correcting them (27:22). The need for discernment when dealing with fools comes out in the proverb pair of 26:4-5. Different situations call for different responses. At the same time, both statements may be true at once, showing the difficulty of dealing with a fool effectively.

THE WORDS OF AGUR SON OF JAKEH · 30:1-33

The first lines of this chapter make up one of the most difficult sections in Proverbs to interpret, due to textual complexities and unclear meanings of obscure words. The figure Agur himself is unknown. The Hebrew term that follows his name may identify him as a foreigner from the Arabian tribe of Massa (see Prov 31:1), or it may label the section as an "oracle" or "pronouncement" (also indicated by the Hebrew term *ne'um*, "oracle," in the first line).

The first four verses, at the least, seem attributable to Agur; some argue that the oracle extends to verse 6 or 14. The perplexing declaration in 30:1b in the NIV (*to Ithiel, to Ithiel and to Ucal*) is better read as a confession of Agur's weariness over failing to understand God. The NRSV and others translate the line this way by redividing the Hebrew consonants and repointing the vowels (see Clifford 260): *I am weary, O God, I am weary, O God. How can I prevail?* (NRSV). Agur calls himself a *beast* (NIV *most ignorant*) when it comes to grasping the divine (similarly Pss 73:22; 92:5-6). The four rhetorical questions in verse 4 anticipate a negative answer: no human or child of a human can have perfect knowledge of wondrous divine activity in the world (hence the divine questions in Isa 40:12-17 and Job 38-42). Ironically, this admission of not knowing reveals that Agur actually does grasp something of God's mysterious creative work and the limits of human knowledge. This, too, is wisdom. Following the questions are an affirmation of God's reliable and sufficient word (30:5-6; see also 2 Sam 22:31; Ps 18:30) and a prayer (30:7-9) to avoid false words and to avoid profaning God's name, since that may come with excessive greed or oppressive poverty. Both the affirmation and the prayer uphold divine sufficiency and the name of God, presupposed in the questions of 30:4.

A series of numerical sayings follows the prayer. The numerical form, often following an "x, x + 1" pattern, appears also in 6:16-19 as well as Amos 1-2, Greek poems of Homer, and Ugaritic (northern Canaanite) sayings. Less formally a numerical saying, 30:11-14 present various groups of wicked people who violate wisdom principles presented elsewhere in Proverbs through family disloyalty (30:11; compare 10:1; 20:20; 30:17), deceptive self-righteousness (30:12; compare 16:2; 20:9; 26:12; 30:20), pride (30:13; see also 6:17; *haughty eyes* in 2 Sam 22:28; Ps 18:27; Prov 30:32), and oppression of the poor (30:14; see 14:31). These correspond to other social disruptions that appear in 30:17, 20.

Interwoven with these observations of the (violated) social order are elements of the social and created order that are insatiable (30:15-16), awe-inspiring (30:18-19), terrifying (30:21-23), impressive (30:29-31), and indicative of wisdom permeating nature (30:24-28). In the end, these sayings testify to the intertwining of the social realm and the realm of nature, both of which are sustained by principles of wisdom. Both realms display a sense of order, modeled by the very "x, x + 1" pattern of the numerical sayings and leading to earth's trembling when something subverts that order (30:21-23). They also display awe-inspiring qualities that are too amazing to understand (30:18). Such mysteries of creation and humanity should provoke the kind of humility that Agur exhibits in 30:1-4 in light of God's wondrous and transcendent activity. Humility also comes with a proper perspective on God's sufficiency as opposed to human sufficiency (30:5-9) and honest reflection on human nature (30: 12, 13, 20). The chapter concludes by advocating such humility (30:32-33). The Hebrew word for anger is the same as for nose, presenting a clever pun in 30:33. In the end, humility becomes a cardinal virtue of wisdom. It arises from observations about human limits and divine transcendence.

THE WORDS OF LEMUEL & HIS MOTHER · 31:1-9

Again a parental voice offers instruction in Proverbs, though here alone the voice is explicitly that of a mother. Similar to royal instruction common in ancient Egyptian wisdom literature, the parent gives advice about proper conduct for a king. The wise mother begins with negative commands against sexual impropriety and strong drink and then turns them into positive commands, all of which focus on just treatment of the poor and powerless. Use strong drink not for self-indulgence, she says, but to alleviate the suffering of the downtrodden. Her warning, *Do not spend your strength* [Hebrew *chayil*] *on women* (31:3) looks ahead to the woman of strength (in 31:10 and 17), as does the mother's advice to attend to the poor and the needy (31:9). At the same time, the mother's counsel looks back to the household setting of proverbs that opened the Solomonic collection (10:1) and chapters 1-9. Concluding in the same household context, the proverbial collections come full circle but with significant development in themes and the presentation of the "child" who now is a king (Brown, "Pedagogy," 179-82)

THE WOMAN OF STRENGTH · 31:10-31

Proverbs culminates in an acrostic poem praising the *wife of noble character* [Hebrew *'eshet chayil*], also translated as "a woman of strength" (see 31:17), "capable wife," or "woman of worth." The theme of nobility [*chayil*] or

---

Pressing the Mouth
Putting one's hand on the mouth symbolizes humiliation and restraint (Job 21:5; 29:9; Judg 18:19) and reverence before God (Job 40:3-5). Pressing the mouth is better than pressing anger (which often arises from a lack of humility).

Acrostic Poems
Like other acrostic poems in the Old Testament (Ps 9-10; 24; 34; 37; 111; 119; Lam 1-4), each line of "The Woman of Strength" begins with a letter of the Hebrew alphabet, moving in order from the first to the last. This lends the poem a sense of order and comprehensiveness reflecting the order that the woman brings to her household.

strength frames the poem in 31:10 and 20, with another reference in 31:17, and links the poem to the earlier part of the chapter (31:3). Her resourcefulness encompasses both land (31:16) and sea (31:14), and private (31:11, 15, 21, 23, 27, 28) and public realms (31:14, 18, 20, 23, 24, 31). In the public domain, her hands do good work in business (31:13, 16, 19; see verse 17), and they also reach out to the poor (31:20), linking her activity to the mother's exhortation to Lemuel in 31:5-9. She works not only in the day but well into the night (31:15, 18). The various activities reflect the work of actual women in the Persian period (Yoder).

References to clothing and textile materials weave through the poem, bringing out aspects of the woman's remarkable character and abilities. First, the references highlight her adeptness at her work (see 31: 16). She selects quality materials for making cloth and delights in working with her hands (31:13). She skillfully uses the distaff (31:19), the staff for holding flax or wool which is then twisted or spun into yarn by the spindle (Clifford 275). Through her excellent work, she makes and sells linen garments, and she makes sashes for merchants (literally, "Canaanites" who were so famous for their work as merchants that their name became synonymous with it; see Job 41:6; Zech 14:21; Van Leeuwen, *Proverbs*, 262). Second, the references to clothing emphasize the woman's care for members of her household as they all wear fine garments, their superior quality indicated by their scarlet color and durability in harsh weather (31:21). Third, clothing reveals something about the woman herself. Not only does she wear clothing of fine linen and purple (22), showing her great worth, but she wears figurative clothing of strength and dignity (31: 25; compare 31:17). Not insignificantly, in Exodus and Jeremiah, the making of garments (and in particular, garments of fine purple) is associated with *a spirit of wisdom* (Exod 28:3-6; 31:1-10; Jer 10:9), and this woman also exhibits wisdom when she *opens her mouth* (31:26). Verse 27 subtly emphasizes the woman's wisdom through the first word of that verse [Hebrew *tsophiya*], which transliterates as *sophia*, the Greek word for wisdom (Wolters 577-87).

In a number of ways, the portrayal of this remarkable woman merges with that of Woman Wisdom in Proverbs 1–9. In addition to the wisdom attributed to the woman in 31:26-27, her care for her household and provision of food (31:14-15) resemble the way that Wisdom builds her house in 9:1-6 and offers bread and wine to those who enter. The description of the woman as "worth far more than rubies" also sounds like Wisdom, whose value and rarity are described in terms of precious jewels in 3:13-15 and 8:11 (compare Job 28:18). So also the question asking "who can find" a woman like this (31:10) calls to mind the exhortations to "find" Wisdom (3:3:13; 8:17; see Eccl 7:24), and her husband's admiration for her (31:11, 28-29) recalls the love language for Wisdom in 4:6, 8 and 8:17. The words describing Wisdom in 4:6 could just as easily be said of the woman of strength: *Do not forsake wisdom, and she will protect you; love her, and she will watch over you.* The woman's provision for her husband and household (31:11-12, 15, 21, 27) offers the same kind of security and freedom from fear of disaster promised by Woman Wisdom to those who listen to her (1:33; see also especially 31:21).

> **"Rubies"**
> The rare Hebrew word for "rubies" refers to wisdom in three of the four other times it is used in the Old Testament (Prov 8:11; 20:15; Job 28:18; compare Lam 4:7).

The woman in 31:10-31, then, provides a composite portrayal of actual women who model an ideal, virtuous life for women and present an ideal wife for men. Along these lines, the recitation of *midrash* on this poem by a husband to his wife makes up part of the weekly Sabbath ritual in Jewish tradition. At the same time, the woman is a remarkable depiction of Wisdom herself, also highly desirable to men. As such, she draws the everyday activities of private and public life into the sphere of wisdom. Wisdom belongs not only to the educated elite but also to the life of the farmer, artisan, and textile worker. This reflects the ancient Egyptian wisdom saying from *The Instruction of Ptahhotep*: "Wisdom…may be found among maids at the grindstones." The portrayal of the woman in this poem provides a remarkable artistic conclusion to the book of Proverbs. Having opened with a child being warned by his parent in a crisis situation, the book ends with the son in a marital relationship with of the woman of strength. The final scene shows a productive and generous household enjoying the fruits of wise living (Brown, "Pedagogy," 153).

THEOLOGICAL REFLECTIONS

Proverbs collects and arranges pithy statements on everyday life, often without an attempt at an overall viewpoint. It does so because the wisdom teachers of ancient Israel, as in many other cultures, recognized that much of life can be understood only in part. Wisdom has limits.

At the same time, Proverbs is not merely a self-help book aimed at making more successful secular people. Its final editors, by prefacing long series of proverbs by an overall call to wisdom in chapters 1–9, asked their audience to pay attention to their own character. As the prologue to the book (1:1–7) makes explicit, the wise person continued to learn and to aid others in learning. Such a lifestyle has profound religious implications because it orients the person living this way to the ultimate reality, and thus to God.

Compared to other books of the Bible such as Deuteronomy or Romans, Proverbs speaks little explicitly about God or theology. Yet the book does not espouse the view that one can be wise while ignoring religion. Quite to the contrary, it argues that a life of balance, insight, self-restraint, and care for others will inevitably lead to a kind of faith. For this reason, the book deserves an honored place in the biblical canon.

FOR FURTHER STUDY

Claudia Camp, *Wisdom and the Feminine in the Book of Proverbs* (Sheffield: Almond, 1985).

James L. Crenshaw, *Education in Ancient Israel* (New York: Doubleday, 1998).

Tremper Longman III, *How to Read Proverbs* (Downers Grove, IL.: InterVarsity, 2002).

Alyce M. McKenzie, *Preaching Proverbs*: *Wisdom for the Pulpit* (Louisville: Westminster John Knox, 1996).

WORKS CITED

Bendt Alster, *Proverbs of Ancient Sumer*: *The World's Earliest Proverb Collections*, vol. 1 (Bethesda, Md.: CDL Press, 1997), 100.

Robert Alter, *The Art of Biblical Poetry* (San Francisco: Harper Collins, 1985), 163–84.

William P. Brown, *Character in Crisis*: *A Fresh Approach to the Wisdom Literature of the Old Testament* (Grand Rapids: Eerdmans, 1996).

———, "The Pedagogy of Proverbs 10:1–31:9," in William P. Brown, ed., *Character and Scripture* (Grand Rapids: Eerdmans, 2002), 179–82.

Richard J. Clifford, *Proverbs* (Louisville: Westminster, 1999).

James L. Crenshaw, "Education in Ancient Israel," *Journal of Biblical Literature* 104 (1985): 601–15.

Michael V. Fox, *Proverbs 1–9*: *A New Translation with Introduction and Commentary* (New York: Doubleday, 2000).

———, "The Social Location of the Book of Proverbs," in M. V. Fox, et al., eds., *Texts, Temples, and Traditions*: *A Tribute to Menahem Haran* (Winona Lake, Ind.: Eisenbrauns, 1996), 227–39.

Jonas C. Greenfield, "The Seven Pillars of Wisdom (Prov 9:1): A Mistranslation." *Jewish Quarterly Review* 76 (1985): 13–20.

Ted Hildebrandt, "Proverbial Pairs: Compositional Units in Proverbs 10–29," *Journal of Biblical Literature* 107 (1988): 207–24.

David Jamieson-Drake, *Scribes and Schools in Monarchic Judah* (Sheffield: Almond, 1991).

Othmar Keel, *The Symbolism of the Biblical World*: *Ancient Near Eastern Iconography and the Book of Psalms* (New York: Seabury, 1978).

Murray Salisbury, "Hebrew Proverbs and How to Translate Them," in Robert D. Bergen, ed., *Biblical Hebrew and Discourse Linguistics* (Dallas: Summer Institute of Linguistics, Eisenbrauns, 1994), 434–61.

Raymond C. Van Leeuwen, *Context and Meaning in Proverbs 25–27* (Atlanta: Scholars Press, 1988).

———, "Liminality and Worldview in Proverbs 1–9," *Semeia* 50 (1990): 111–44.

———, *Proverbs* (Nashville: Abingdon, 1997), 19–264.

Harold C. Washington, *Wealth and Poverty in the Instruction of Amenemope and the Hebrew Proverbs* (Atlanta: Scholars Press, 1994).

Stuart Weeks, *Early Israelite Wisdom* (Oxford: Clarendon, 1994).

Claus Westermann, *The Roots of Wisdom*: *The Oldest Proverbs of Israel and Other Peoples* (Louisville: Westminster John Knox, 1995).

R. N. Whybray, *Proverbs* (Grand Rapids: Eerdmans, 1994).

James G. Williams, "The Power of Form: A Study of Biblical Proverbs," *Semeia* 17 (1980): 35–58.

Al Wolters, "Sopiyya (Proverbs 31:27) as Hymnic Participle and Play on *Sophia*," *Journal of Biblical Literature* 104 (1985): 577–87.

Christine Yoder, *Wisdom as a Woman of Substance*: *A Socioeconomic Reading of Proverbs 1–9 and 31:10–31* (Berlin and New York: de Gruyter, 2001).

Ecclesiastes

Thomas H. Olbricht

CHAPTER CONTENTS

Contexts 523

Commentary 524
- Superscription · 1:1 524
- Earth's Features are Cyclical · 1:2–11 524
- Reflections of the Teacher-King on his Own Experiences · 1:12–2:26 524
- For Everything a Season · 3:1–15 525
- Injustice & Oppression · 3:16–4:8 525
- Proverbs or Aphorisms · 4:9–6:12 525
- Miscellaneous Reflections · 7:1–8:17 526
- Life's Outcomes Cannot be Anticipated · 9:1–16 527
- The Benefits of Wisdom · 9:17–10:20 527
- Wise Enterprises · 11:1–8 527
- Instructions for the Young · 11:8–12:8 527
- Conclusion · 12:9–14 527

Theological Reflections 528

For Further Study 528

Works Cited 528

MAPS, TABLES, & FEATURES

Ecclesiastes' Radicalism 523

Scholars locate Ecclesiastes among the wisdom books of the Old Testament, and appropriately so, since the author is highly interested in the outcomes of wisdom and folly. Traditionally, readers assumed the author to be Solomon, who authored "three thousand proverbs, and his songs numbered a thousand and five" (1 Kgs 4:32). The contemporary consensus among critical scholars is that the book was written at a later date. Seow places it no earlier than the fifth century BCE because of the language. The superscription identifies the author as "the son of David" (1:1), and he himself professes to be a king in Israel (1:12) but following a long succession of kings (1:16), thereby making Solomonic authorship problematic.

CONTEXTS

Several proposals have been put forth regarding the structure of Ecclesiastes, but none enjoys majority support. Parallels to the book occur in other biblical and ancient documents, but no counterpart exists for the overall composition. The theme "all is vanity" pervades the whole work. The major topics are toil and laziness, wisdom and folly, pleasure, a fixed world, justice and injustice, God's gifts, and rules. Each topic comes up several times without an emerging logical sequence. The structure thus resembles the cycle of human life and nature depicted in chapter 1. Ideas about a fixed world, toil and indolence, and pleasure occur mostly in the early part of the book. Themes of justice and injustice commence in chapter 3. Rules first enter in chapter 5 and reoccur periodically. Wisdom and folly and God's gifts weave in and out through the whole book. Some of the sections are descriptive, especially the four major poetic sections (1:3–8; 7:1–13; 9:17–10:4; 10:8–11:4). Some sections set out rules after the fashion of legal materials (5:1–12; 7:1–13). Exhortation is minimal (but

---

Ecclesiastes' Radicalism

Why does the Bible include a work as contemptuous of the conventional as the book of Ecclesiastes?

In the commentary of the Puritan John Cotton (1654), Ecclesiastes is an exhortation against attachment to possessions, achievements, and relationships since death ends all. For T. B. Larimore (about 1890), the baffling work demonstrates the futility of labor, experience, and ownership if treasured in the place of service to God. Most modern commentators highlight the challenge to conventional wisdom (such as the theme that virtue is rewarded and vice punished.

For Christians, this work is a poignant depiction of the predictable hopelessness prior to the abundant life now and forever, accomplished in the works, words, and resurrection of Jesus Christ.

see 7:14; 9:7–10; 12:1–7, 13–14). Blocks of materials are in the form of aphorisms or proverbs (10:1–11). The book's reasoning is often dialectical. Major sections close with the teacher advising the enjoyment of food and drink that God has supplied (2:24–26; 3:12–13; 5:18–20; 8:15; 9:7–10; 11:9).

COMMENTARY

SUPERSCRIPTION · 1:1

The Hebrew *Qoheleth* means "one who summons an assembly"; therefore, the title is translated Ecclesiastes (a Latinized form of the Greek word for "assembly"). The author is a *teacher* (1:1, NRSV) of the assembly, a term more appropriate than "preacher" (used by Jerome and Luther). His central claim is that *all is vanity* [Hebrew *hevel*].

EARTH'S FEATURES ARE CYCLICAL · 1:2–11

Ecclesiastes begins with the theme "all is vanity." Various words have been employed to translate the Hebrew word *hevel*. Towner and others argue that the best translation into contemporary English is "absurdity." The lot of humankind is "absurdity of absurdities."

Human efforts fail to challenge or make a dent in the normal cycles of nature. People have little to show for their incessant labors. Humans come and go, but the earth remains the same. Nature repeats the same cycles over and over. Individuals scrutinize all that goes on around them but never perceive enough. Nothing disturbs the cycles. The tenacity of the status quo pervades Ecclesiastes and runs counter to the view that God creates anew (Isa 43:19; 65:17). This feature of Ecclesiastes exhibits the limits of applying the mind *to seek and to search out by wisdom all that is done under the sun* (1:13). The affirmation that God creates the new is revealed to the prophets. According to Ecclesiastes 1:11, even people experience this vicious cycle because, though memory might preserve the worth of the individual, even memory fails. Personal merit might survive awhile in the family's memory or on monuments, but the teacher thinks that over the long range, these too will disappear.

REFLECTIONS OF THE TEACHER-KING ON HIS OWN EXPERIENCE · 1:12–2:26

After the exile (587 BCE), no king ruled in Jerusalem for some centuries. The author assumes the persona of a king in Jerusalem and probably assumes that Solomon will come to mind. Perhaps "all those in Jerusalem before him" (1:16) includes pre-Davidic Jebusite kings. The teacher declares that he will investigate wisdom, pleasure, power, and toil. He finds them all to be meaningless, that is, absurd. Fulfillment only comes from gratefully accepting food and drink from God.

1:12–18 The teacher first turns his mind to ascertain whether wisdom can satisfy. He concludes that though wisdom is the business of humans, the whole search is unfulfilling. What is crooked cannot be straightened nor can what is absent be counted (Seow 123). Having wisdom does not provide the means for resolving the unresolvable. The wisdom of the teacher surpassed that of all his predecessors. Solomon's wisdom achieved such renown that the Queen of Sheba traveled to Jerusalem (1 Kgs 10:1–13). The teacher seeks to distinguish between wisdom and folly but finds that wisdom may increase sorrow.

2:1–11 The teacher seeks pleasure in all possible locations. The building projects sound like those any king or noble would celebrate. He becomes greater than everyone in Jerusalem before him. He pursues every possible pleasure and delights in his labors. But when he considers all his experiences and achievements, he finds that he has gained nothing.

2:12–26 Since pleasure is in the end unfulfilling, the teacher once again takes up wisdom and its opposites, madness and folly. He contemplates what a successor to the great king might do in addition, but concludes that his heir could only repeat what has been done. Thus wisdom exceeds folly as light does darkness. Nevertheless the fate, that is, the death, of both fools and wise persons is identical. So what is the benefit of being wise? He seems not to dispute the value of wisdom for life's ongoing activities, but since all die life is absurd (2:17).

Furthermore, the hard working wise person cannot control his or her achievements after death. Accomplishments may fall into the hands of fools or at least of those who have not worked for them and so may fail to appreciate them. Toil is accompanied by pain, vexation, and anxiety (2:23). Regardless, human labor makes no permanent impression upon the world or the persons who live in it. So what is there to life? What is left is to enjoy food and drink and toil (2:24). This is a gift of God. Gordis (123) affirms that the enjoyment of life's basics is actually the central claim of the teacher. Enjoyment is the remarkable solution to the enigma of life. The wise profit from the toil of sinners, for God transfers it to them. The exertions of sinners do not result in benefit to them.

> **Pleasure in Ecclesiastes & Epicureanism**
> Both Qoheleth and Epicurean philosophers share an emphasis on noble pleasures as the secret to human life. (Contrary to their popular image, the Epicureans did not advocate hedonism or debauchery.) Ecclesiastes, however, connects human pleasure to the will of God.

FOR EVERYTHING A SEASON · 3:1–15

3:1–8 This section is unparalleled both in construction and substance. To concretize the claim that for everything there is a season, the teacher sets forth seven contrasting parallels. Such antithetical parallels are common in Proverbs (for example, Prov 15:1–2), but almost always limited to one set. In the teacher's run of parallels, except for birth and death, the matter of timing involves human choice. One decides when to plant and when to pluck up. The key is choosing the right time. The teacher has no advice as to how to go about choosing the right time. His point is that such choices must be made even at one's own peril. Humans have the sense that God has determined what time is proper and what not, yet God has provided few clues upon which to base decisions (3:11).

3:9–11 Humans continually struggle over the appropriate times to do things. God puts in their minds a sense that there is such a time. What it is that God has put into the minds of humans (3:11) has puzzled scholars for centuries. The key word in Hebrew is *ha'olam*. The KJV translates it *world*, the NIV and RSV *eternity*, and the NRSV *a sense of past and future*. To translate the word as *world* is to employ a meaning from a later period. Better, in light of the context, is God plants in the mind the concept of time's infinity, that is, eternity, but does not enable humans to access insight other than from their own lifetime. The author does not envision the eternity of the soul or heaven.

3:13–15 The teacher brings this conundrum to a close by claiming that rather than bemoaning what they cannot know, humans should enjoy food, drink, and toil, and stand in awe of God who supplies these needs. Nothing can change what God has done. The meaning of the phrase *God seeks out what is gone by* (3:15) is difficult. The noun literally means "what is pursued," and Seow (165) suggests that it refers to that which humans pursue but cannot know. Again it is pointless to pursue comprehension beyond God's limits.

INJUSTICE & OPPRESSION · 3:16–4:8

Here for the first time the teacher introduces themes of justice and injustice. He notices that justice and wickedness do not always reside in their proper spheres but are sometimes reversed or mixed. He decides, however, that eventually the wicked will receive their just deserts from God. There is then a time for the mixture of uprightness and evil, and a time for their separation. In fact, according to the teacher, death is the end of both humans and animals, for all return to dust. Genesis 2:7 comes to mind. According Genesis 1:20, 30, animals have *nefesh* [KJV *soul*, NIV *living being*] as well as humans (Gen 2:7). According to the teacher, no one knows whether the human spirit goes up and that of the animals down. He insists that humans cannot be certain of survival in heavenly realms beyond the grave. Because the future is concealed, the enjoyment of work here and now must suffice (3:22).

As an additional injustice, the teacher recounts oppression from the hands of the powerful. The powerless have no one to comfort them (4:1). To be dead may be better than to be alive, but the state of the unborn is preferable because they have not witnessed oppression. Toil and skill are motivated by envy, which is absurd (4:4). The one who will not work, however, destroys himself. It is better to accept less than to risk the stress that arises through aspiring for more. Some individuals work ceaselessly even though they have neither sons nor brothers for whom to leave their estates. Some workaholics absurdly deprive themselves of pleasure.

PROVERBS OR APHORISMS · 4:9–6:12

The teacher now introduces sayings in the form of proverbs. Two working for the same end are better than one working alone. They can encourage and support each other against enemies (4:12). A poor wise youth is better than a king who will not accept advice, but still new generations will not praise him (4:16).

Additional aphorisms provide rules by which to relate to one's superiors. One should show proper decorum when going to the house of the Lord. To listen (apparently instruction was available) is better than to offer sacrifices as do fools (5:1). One should be careful and not hasty to speak in the house of God. A vow made in the temple must be kept (compare Deut 23:21). It is perilous, in view of God's punishment, to declare to the one who requests fulfillment that you did not mean it after all (5:6). The teacher clearly knows of and respects the guidelines provided by the Torah. That he ends therefore by declaring *Fear God, and keep his commandments* should not come as a surprise (12:13). Many dreams may produce an unwarranted multiplying of words (5:7).

> **The Importance of Dreams**
> *Ancient Israelites and their neighbors believed dreams to be a vehicle for communication from the divine realm. Ecclesiastes cautions against excessive reliance on such experiences.*

The next section of aphorisms reflects on wealth. The economic arrangements are such that the poor are oppressed because they are at the bottom of a hierarchy of officials, each of whom takes his cut from what the farmer produces. Verse 9 is best translated by the NIV (Towner 318–19): *The increase from the land is taken by all; the king himself profits from the fields.* The money-lover is never satisfied since his only gratification is to see his goods (5:11). Laborers sleep, but the overabundance of the wealthy engenders fitful nights. Sometimes persons of wealth enter ventures and lose all they have, ending up ill and bitter (5:16). All their abundance turns into emptiness. With the comments on power and wealth complete, the teacher again encourages those who keep their wealth to acknowledge that God has provided such abundance.

The final section on wealth makes clear that possessing things is of no consequence if one cannot enjoy them. Some spend a lifetime accumulating an estate only to die before enjoying it. A stranger enjoys it instead (6:2). No matter how many children a person conceives, they are pointless unless enjoyed. A stillborn child is better off than one who does not enjoy what he has. Eating offers another example along the same lines (6:8). Verses 10–12 provide a summary of some of the key points of the first half of Ecclesiastes.

MISCELLANEOUS REFLECTIONS · 7:1–8:17

7:1–13 This sections offers another set of aphorisms in poetic form. These set out positive guidance for a rewarding life through seeking after a good name all the way to the end, accentuating the serious side, listening to wisdom, treating others with justice, being patient, and locating meaning in the present. As the teacher has argued before, one cannot change the reality God has made (verse 13). Therefore, one should take each day as it is, whether it brings prosperity or adversity (verse 14).

7:14–21 This unit reflects on unfair events. The length of life does not seem to coincide with uprightness (7:15). Therefore moderation is the best policy. Through proper action, though not in excess, one will attain both righteousness and wisdom if one fears God (7:18–20). Persons must believe gossip only with caution since they too have spoken ill of others, as they will discover through inventorying their own thoughts and actions (7:22).

7:22–29 The teacher returns to the value of wisdom that he has declared worth more than the strength of ten rulers (7:19). Wisdom is, however, elusive even though wickedness is folly. He also discerns that a seductive woman is to be avoided at all costs (compare Prov 1–9), and that both men and women are schemers (7:26–29). So immediate wisdom is of great value for maneuvering the pathways of life (8:1), but long-term wisdom is inaccessible.

8:1–17 Ecclesiastes 8:2–14 recommends keeping the king's commands as well as the moral codes. The teacher is more concerned with lawful observance than those admit who contend that 12:13 comes as a surprise and therefore must have been added by a scribe (but see Seow 390). One keeps the commands as a master of integrity and because of the king's power to punish evildoers (8:4). Royal punishment is as inevitable as nature (8:8–9). Retribution may not occur quickly but is certain to come (8:11–13). Yet things will go well with those who fear God (8:12). On the other hand it seems absurd then that wicked people receive praise while the righteous suffer (8:14). Now that the teacher has arrived at what seems to him an impasse, he once again declares that such enigmas must not lead to bitterness and despair, but rather to enjoyment (8:15). It is not possible for humankind to discern what God is doing through these conflicting developments (8:16–17).

LIFE'S OUTCOMES CANNOT BE ANTICIPATED · 9:1–16

It is not known whether love or hate is in a human's heart, and therefore one cannot second guess the fate of others (9:1). The same fate – death – comes to everyone. Yet, it is better to be alive than dead (9:4). Ancient Near Easterners admired the majestic lion but disdained dogs. Even so, it is better to be a live dog than a dead lion. The dead know nothing, and they are not remembered (9:5). Once again, life is absurd but worthwhile if one enjoys what God has provided. To his earlier lists of food, drink, and toil the teacher now adds enjoying the wife one loves (9:9). Rewards seldom come as expected, nor can calamity be anticipated (9:12). Sometimes a person on the fringe of power in a city provides escape in a time of attack. Even so, no one remembers his wise strategy.

> **Life after Death**
> *The Old Testament does not offer a systematic theory of life after death but does assume a great gap between this life and any other.*

THE BENEFITS OF WISDOM · 9:17–10:20

The teacher proposes that wisdom is advantageous over loud shouting or weapons (9:17–18), but folly is more noticeable (10:1–3, 5–7). Calmness is important to offset anger (10:4). Wisdom helps overcome potential injury from dangerous occupations and actions (10:8–11). Fools suffer from their words and deeds (10:12–15). A land does well when the king and princes manifest nobility and wisdom (10:16–20).

WISE ENTERPRISES · 11:1–8

Undertake, commence, and expect return, but do not put all your eggs in one basket (11:1–2). Before planting and sowing, observe the weather conditions (11:3–6). Life will bring both days of light and darkness, all a cause for rejoicing.

INSTRUCTIONS FOR THE YOUNG · 11:8–12:8

The young should rejoice and follow their hearts. The teacher then seems to stress that God will judge misdeeds, but he may mean that God will judge those who do not follow their hearts (so Towner 353–54). The young should not be anxious, but should also realize that the youthful years are also absurd (11:10).

Early Jewish and Christian interpreters scrutinized 12:1–8 to uncover metaphorical depictions of the aging stages of life. Some modern translations have interpreted the section accordingly, including the Amplified Bible, the Today's English Version, and the New Living Word Translation. The metaphor in part depicts a storm or a house falling into ill repair. The teacher encourages his audience to remember their creator in the days of their youth before the ills at the end of life befall them (12:1; Fox 322; Seow 353). The best understanding of this striking extended metaphor is that these signs from earth and heaven (see parts of Isa 24–27) anticipate the fateful moment of death. Darkness pervades this vision, storm clouds gather, strong men and women tremble, activities of humans and birds cease, trees and grasshoppers behave as in a blight, and mourners go about in the streets. The silver cord or tendril likely portrays a lampstand depiction of the tree of life (Seow 364). The golden bowl is the lamp on the stand containing the oil in which the wick is submersed. The destruction of both vividly denotes the extinguishing of the lamp, or of life itself.

Today's English Version (12:3–5), in contrast, interprets the guards as the trembling of arms and the weakening of legs due to old age, the women who grind as the teeth decaying, those who look through the window as failing eyes, and the door and street noises as the deterioration of the ears. Aged persons fear high places since walking is dangerous. The almond tree, because of its white blossoms, depicts the graying of the hair; the dragging of the grasshopper is the elderly person being barely able to hobble along. The rest, beginning in verse 5b, is perceived in a conventional manner. Perhaps the extended metaphor may be taken in different ways, but the aging human body interpretation seems overly creative, if not misdirected.

CONCLUSION · 12:9–14

The teacher sets forth what he perceives as his achievements (12:9–10). Some think this summary is the addition by an editor since it is in the third person. The sayings of a wise person serve as goads. Verses 11–12 suggest that additional wise reflections are unnecessary. While a later editor may have wished to discourage the production of a stream of wisdom books, at the same time, the statement seems consistent with the view of the teacher that a later king can only repeat the investigations he has undertaken. Many scholars suggest that verses

13–14 are an addition by an editor who was bewildered by the teacher's cynical observations and his neglect of the esteemed Torah. But the keeping of the commandments is consistent with earlier claims that the attentive believer lives by the rules.

THEOLOGICAL REFLECTIONS

The author's observations on life's diverse experiences sometimes seem contradictory. At the same time, he is the pessimistic cynic (1:3–9; 2:11) who acknowledges God's gifts and the merits of human relationships (4:9; 5:18–20; 9:9). Sometimes he seems to affirm that nature runs its own course (3:2–8), but at others that all is dependent upon God (6:1–2). Certain commentators despair of reconciling the diverse declarations in the book, but a somewhat consistent picture may be set forth in six predominant themes:

- God determines the course of the universe (3:1–3; 3:10–11; 7:13–14);
- humans have freedom within limits (1:14–15; 2:18–21);
- human wisdom is advantageous above folly over the short term, but no one knows whether such is the case for the long haul because of the finitude of human insight (2:13–16; 3:11; 7:14);
- one should accept life as a gift from God (2:24–25; 5:18–20; 9:7–10);
- the hope is that virtue will be rewarded and vice punished, but conflicting outcomes persist (3:17; 7:16–18; 10:5–8); and
- a fruitful life results from keeping the rules of existence (8:2–6; 11:9; 12:1–3; 12:12–14).

FOR FURTHER STUDY

Dave Bland, *Proverbs, Ecclesiastes & Song of Songs* (Joplin, Mo.: College Press, 2002).

William P. Brown, *Ecclesiastes* (Louisville: John Knox, 2000).

Norbert Lohfink, *Qoheleth: A Continental Commentary* (trans. Sean McEvenue; Minneapolis, Minn.: Fortress, 2003).

WORKS CITED

Michael V. Fox, *A Time to Tear Down and a Time to Build up: A Rereading of Ecclesiastes* (Grand Rapids: Eerdmans, 1999).

Robert Gordis, *Koheleth, the Man and His World: A Study of Ecclesiastes* (New York: Schocken, 1968).

Roland E. Murphy, *Proverbs, Ecclesiastes, Song of Songs* (Peabody, Mass.: Hendrickson, 1999).

Choon-Leong Seow, *Ecclesiastes: A New Translation with Introduction and Commentary* (New York: Doubleday, 1997).

W. Sibley Towner, "The Book of Ecclesiastes" in vol 5 of *The New Interpreter's Bible* (ed. Leander E. Keck; Nashville: Abingdon, 1997).

Song of Songs

Mark W. Hamilton

CHAPTER CONTENTS

Contexts 529

Commentary 530
- Superscription · 1:1 530
- Desire · 1:2–4 530
- Conversing about Love · 1:5–2:7 530
- The Female Lover's First Long Speech · 2:8–3:11 530
- The Male Lover's First Long Speech · 4:1–5:1 531
- The Female Lover's Second Long Speech · 5:2–6:3 531
- The Male Lover's Second Long Speech · 6:4–7:9 531
- The Female Lover's Reply · 7:10–13 532
- Conversing about Love Again · 8:1–14 532

Theological Reflections 532

For Further Study 532

Works Cited 532

According to a famous story in the Talmud, the second century CE rabbi Aqiva, when asked whether the Song of Songs belonged in the Bible, replied "all the writings are holy, but the Song of Songs is the Holy of Holies" (m. Yadayim 3:5 in Neusner 1127). Later, Origen (185–254 CE) forbade any Christian under thirty from studying the book, since such a person would likely see it as mere love poetry. And Bernard of Clairvaux (1090–1153), in a series of 86 sermons on the book, sought to draw his audience to hear "the music of the heart" (Bernard 7). Ancient and medieval readers understood the book in four main ways: as an allegory of God's love for Israel; as an allegory of Christ's love for the church; as an allegory of the Holy Spirit's love for the soul; or as some combination of options two and three. Jews opted for the first interpretation, and Christians for one of the last three. In these cases, eroticism was seen as serving the higher end of spiritual maturity.

> **Is *Song of Songs* Scripture?**
> The collection of Jewish law called the Mishnah, which dates to about 225 CE, records a series of rabbinic discussion about whether certain books "soil the hands," that is require ritual purification because they are holy Scripture. The debate is settled by the great rabbi Aqiva, who says that Song of Songs has a prominent place in the Old Testament canon.

CONTEXTS

Modern scholars are less inclined to find spiritual meanings here, though all acknowledge the book's beauty as it speaks of human love. The poems here use some of the conventions of ancient Near Eastern love poetry (Exum 47–63; Loprieno), such as speaking of the lovers as brother and sister, or mentioning odors, sights, plants, and animals.

Although 1:1 says that the book *pertains to Solomon*, this is not necessarily a claim that he wrote the book, and indeed 3:7, 9, 11 and 8:11 refer to him in the third person, indicating that someone else wrote or edited the book. In fact, Song of Songs collects a number of poems written over a long time yet woven together into an intricate whole (Pope 21–33). The date of the book also remains uncertain. The use of a Greek loanword for "litter" in 3:9 may date the text as late as the third century BCE, and many other expressions seem to reflect Hebrew of the fifth through the third centuries BCE (Dobbs-Allsopp). On the other hand, some Hebrew word forms seem to point to an earlier date, and some parts of the poem may date as early as Solomon, or alternatively the book may deliberately use archaic spelling.

The book presents a story of unconsummated love and longing. It is difficult to trace out a precise sequence of events because the book repeats episodes, telling them from a range of perspectives. The main characters are not married, and the book does not take a stand on the need for premarital chastity, although some contemporary moralists read it that way. By leaving the reader to wonder whether the lovers will or will not meet in bed, the text heightens the sexual tension.

SONG OF SONGS

The characters of the Song include a male lover, a female lover, Solomon, and a chorus. This small cast of characters resembles that of a Greek play, and so it is not impossible that the text was to be acted out, although we do not have direct evidence of the staging of plays in ancient Israel. The Song is the only book in the Bible that consists entirely of dialogue.

Finally, commentators have outlined the text differently (see Exum 39 for options). Here I follow the recent work of Exum, which she admits is tentative. The difficulty of outlining the book stems from the fact that it weaves together different images, voices, and episodes seamlessly.

COMMENTARY

SUPERSCRIPTION · 1:1

Like headings of Psalms, this verse probably is later than the rest of the book. The phrase "song of songs" means "the best song" or "the song par excellence." The Hebrew word *lishlomo* can mean "by Solomon," "for Solomon," "in the manner of Solomon," or most likely, "concerning Solomon." It does not necessarily claim authorship for him. The verse may, however, seek to associate Solomon with wisdom in a broad sense, implying that love poetry speaks to the nature of reality in a profound way (see Dell 15–17).

DESIRE · 1:2–4

The poem opens with the woman's expression of desire for physical displays of love. Exum compares the disembodied speaking voice to that in Genesis 1: like God, the woman in this poem creates a world of beauty and delight with her words (Exum 92). The reference to *wine* (1:2) is a recurring image throughout the book (2:4 [where NIV spoils the translation – it should say "house of wine"]; 4:10; 5:1; 7:9; 8:2), as is *perfume* (literally "oil"; 1:3; 4:10; compare Prov 21:17). These liquids signify comfort and even luxury. Throughout the book, liquids serve as metaphors for the pleasures of love and sex. Verse 4 refers to the *king* and his *chambers*, again a metaphor for the male lover, not a literal reference to a monarch. Royal images for the lovers appear throughout the book. *How rightly they are to adore you* implies that the female lover must vie for the male's attention, apparently because he has a virtual harem, as in 6:8–9. Kings enjoyed such privileges, suggesting the image to the poet at this point.

> **Lover & Beloved**
> The NIV labels the male lover as Lover and the female as Beloved, implying that one is active and the other passive. This choice of wording is unfortunate because in the book both lovers receive equal attention and each actively pursues the other. The translators seem to project onto the text their own views of gender relationships.

CONVERSING ABOUT LOVE · 1:5–2:7

This section alternates the male and female voices, each describing the other. Verse 5 has received a great deal of attention – does darkness contribute to, or work against, beauty? Either translation could fit the Hebrew grammar, but NIV's translation *yet* is probably mistaken because the woman celebrates her own beauty. It comes from living naturally and avoiding the pampered life of the city, which would allow her skin to remain pale. Verse 7's *like a veiled woman* could refer to prostitutes (as in Genesis 38), but may be better translated as "like one who wanders" (Exum 108). The male lover as the shepherd par excellence deserves the woman's undivided attention; she should not follow other men. Verses 9–11 offer the male's view of his lover: she is like a *mare* among the chariot horses. Egypt was a well-known source of chariot horses (see Deut 17:16), most of which, as contemporary art indicates, were male. The presence of a female would arouse the stallions, just as the female lover arouses men who see her. Verses 12–14 return the compliment. *Myrrh* comes from the Arabian peninsula or Ethiopia and was a major ingredient in perfumes and incense. *Henna* blossoms provide a red dye for coloring hair. The woman speaks in 2:1, 3–7 with the man responding in 2:2. Verse 4 uses military imagery to describe love's triumph, and thus to subvert illusions of military glory (Exum 115; Longman 113).

THE FEMALE LOVER'S FIRST LONG SPEECH · 2:8–3:11

The speech expresses the woman's passion for her lover, whom she portrays as athletic and attractive. The speech contains three scenes, 2:8–17, 3:1–5, and 3:6–11. They do not connect chronologically, but thematically, as ways of expressing frustrated love. The first scene opens and closes with the image of the *stag*. The lovers' meeting takes place in the late spring after the winter rains (2:11–13) but before the full harvest. The two lovers cannot yet consummate their love, hence the male's location outside the house and the woman's sequestration inside it (verse 14). They cannot leave the city and wander the countryside away from parental supervision.

The second scene portrays her sleepless longing, so powerful that she roams the city streets at night. She expects to find him in bed, indicating that they often lie together and therefore that they have consummated their love. The *watchmen* in ancient walled cities must guard against outside banditry as well as internal strife.

The third scene describes a procession of Solomon in his luxurious litter, but it is not clear whether the female lover also rides the litter or what relationship Solomon has to her lover. Longman (133) suggests that the poet simply focuses on Solomon's wealth as a metaphor for the richness of love, though it is also possible that the woman thinks of her lover as regal and opulent, like Solomon (Exum 143). NIV's *carriage* (3:7) is incorrect; the Hebrew word *mittah* usually refers to a bed or couch, and thus here a litter. Verse 11 apparently refers to a wedding custom of which no other evidence exists.

THE MALE LOVER'S FIRST LONG SPEECH · 4:1–5:1

This unit contains three speeches from the male lover (4:1–7, 8–15; 5:1); 4:16 represents the woman's voice, and 5:1b that of the chorus. The male responds to his lover's speech in chapter 3 with a description of her body (4:1–7) and an invitation to leave her place of refuge and join him (4:8–15). Though the praise of her *teeth* and *neck* seem odd, her excellent dental hygiene and graceful body would have marked her as unusually beautiful. A *flock of goats* undulates down a hillside like the female's wavy, well-coiffured hair. The image of *fawns* (4:5) appears also in 7:3. Since the male's lips are lilies in 5:13, the poet is describing him kissing her breasts, a scene of tender lovemaking (Exum 166).

The invitation in 4:8–14 begins by placing the female in northern mountains (all lie in southern Lebanon), a symbol of her hiddenness and unobtainability, comparable to that in 2:14. The mountains of Lebanon, a favorite destination of ancient kings on campaign (beginning in the "Gilgamesh Epic"), were famed for their grandeur. So now is the female's body. The poem ends in verses 12–15 by describing a private garden like those that ancient kings created for their recreation (see Neh 2:8; Esth 7:7–8; Eccl 2:5; Nebuchadnezzar's so-called "Hanging Gardens" are the most famous example). The scents, colors, and textures of the female's body, like a magnificent garden's, overwhelm the male. Identifying the spices is difficult, hence the variety of English translations. Song of Songs 5:1 echoes 4:11; drinking occurs when the lovers kiss.

THE FEMALE LOVER'S SECOND LONG SPEECH · 5:2–6:3

This section returns thematically to chapter 3. The woman speaks twice, and the chorus asks her questions that advance the drama (5:9; 6:1). One might expect their questions to occur in the reverse order, since 6:1 responds directly to 5:2–8. Yet the poet builds suspense by delaying the question. Verses 2–8 substantially repeat 3:1–5 but enhance the sense of anticipation of sexual union (verse 3). (Most commentators believe that verses 2–6 describe sexual intercourse but disagree on the specific allusions of the metaphors.) This unfulfilled anticipation adds to the erotic charge of the entire book: sex must wait. Verse 7 also adds the beating by the *watchmen*, again a poetic exaggeration of legal practice, but one that allows the poet to state that love merits suffering. Verses 10–16 describe the male body as a statue. Its value and strength commend it to the female lover. Song of Songs 6:2–3 places the male in a *garden*, namely at the side of the female.

THE MALE LOVER'S SECOND LONG SPEECH · 6:4–7:9

The male makes two speeches (6:4–10; 7:1–9) that repeat much earlier material. The identity of the speakers in 6:11–13 is unclear, and verse 12 is notoriously difficult to translate (though it does describe a rendezvous between the lovers [Longman 184]).

The first poem introduces two new elements: the regal status of the female (6:8) and her similarity to heavenly bodies (6:10). The comparison to *queens* need not be taken literally, for the lovers think of each other in grandiose terms. The astronomical imagery reflects the poet's comprehensive interest in nature. The NIV translation *stars in procession* is probably incorrect: "noteworthy in splendor" would be better.

The break between the two poems speaks of "the *Shulammite*," which may designate someone from

> **Tirzah**
>
> *A city located at modern Tell el-Far'ah (North), near modern Nablus, and once capital of the northern kingdom of Israel (Joffe). The poet, fond of wordplay, uses this word because it sounds like the verb "you are pleasant."*

Shunem; a Solomon-like woman; or, most likely, an exemplary person (the Hebrew root *sh-l-m* means "whole" or "peaceful"). The dance of Mahanaim is otherwise unknown. Mahanaim in Transjordan was the capital for Ish-bosheth (2 Sam 2:8).

The male's second poem (7:1–9) continues the royal imagery but moves immediately to another description of the woman's body. Some scholars have seen here a parody of the woman's beauty, but this is highly unlikely (Exum 230–31; Longman 188–89). The woman may be dancing, but this is also uncertain. The locations in the poem lie at the boundaries of an idealized Israel and also indicate military preparedness. Again, the poet describes graphically the male's desire for his lover's body.

> **Heshbon**
> *A city in Jordan 19 kilometers southwest of Amman, Heshbon's inhabitants dug a large reservoir south of the city during the ninth or eighth century BCE, probably the pool of Song of Songs (Geraty 20).*

THE FEMALE LOVER'S REPLY · 7:10–13

The woman accepts the male's invitation to leave the city and make love in the countryside. Ancient people believed *mandrakes* to possess aphrodisiacal properties (Gen 30:14–16).

CONVERSING ABOUT LOVE AGAIN · 8:1–14

The concluding dialogue (female: 8:1–4, 5b–10, 14; male: 8:11–13; the chorus: 8:5b) presents the lovers side-by-side in a lifelong embrace. The sibling imagery in 8:1 comes from a literary tradition in ancient Near Eastern love poetry (seen also in Egypt) and did not seem incestuous to early readers. The lovers lie arm in arm (verse 3) at a place where his parents made love (verse 5b).

Verses 6–10 use a series of images of protection and ownership. Ancient Israelites used a *seal* of semiprecious stone to attest to legal documents and thus indicate possession. The building images, attributed to the woman's brothers (her protectors before marriage [but see Exum 255–56 for objections]), break down because she has already committed herself to her lover. Love overcomes all forces, even death itself.

The reference to Solomon and his sharecroppers works as a contrast on several levels: the woman's *garden* (body) is better than anything Solomon owns, her lover is better than any king, and her love excels any legal transaction. The book ends with the two lovers heading off to their life together.

THEOLOGICAL REFLECTIONS

Song of Songs says virtually nothing about God, worship, ethics, or any of the other key topics of biblical theology. It lives in the extraordinary world of everyday love. The poem celebrates mutual human fulfillment in a beautiful world. If love truly is "stronger than death," then humans have hope under God that a greater love than ours can translate human failing and evil into something exceeding our imagination. The Song offers a foretaste of just such a world.

FOR FURTHER STUDY

André LaCocque, *Romance, She Wrote: A Hermeneutical Essay on Song of Songs* (Harrisburg, Pa.: Trinity Press International, 1998).

John G. Snaith, *Song of Songs* (Grand Rapids: Eerdmans, 1993).

WORKS CITED

Bernard of Clairvaux, *On the Song of Songs I* (trans. Kilian Walsh; Spencer, Mass.: Cistercian, 1971).

Katherine Dell, "Does the Song of Songs Have Any Connections to Wisdom?" in *Perspectives on the Song of Songs, Perspektiven der Hoheliedauslegung* (ed. Anselm C. Hagedorn; Berlin: de Gruyter, 2005), 8–26.

F. W. Dobbs-Allsopp, "Late Linguistic Features in the Song of Songs," in *Perspectives on the Song of Songs, Perspektiven der Hoheliedauslegung* (ed. Anselm C. Hagedorn; Berlin: de Gruyter, 2005), 27–77.

J. Cheryl Exum, *Song of Songs* (Louisville: Westminster John Knox, 2005).

Lawrence T. Geraty, "Hesban," *Oxford Encyclopedia of the Archaeology of the Ancient Near East* 3 (1997): 19–22.

Alexander Joffe, "Far'ah, Tell el-," *Oxford Encyclopedia of the Archaeology of the Ancient Near East* 2 (1997): 303–4.

Tremper Longman III, *Song of Songs* (Grand Rapids: Eerdmans, 2001).

Antonio Loprieno, "Searching for a Common Background: Egyptian Love Poetry and the Biblical Song of Songs," in *Perspectives on the Song of Songs, Perspektiven der Hoheliedauslegung* (ed. Anselm C. Hagedorn; Berlin: de Gruyter, 2005), 105–35.

Jacob Neusner, trans., *The Mishnah* (New Haven: Yale University Press, 1988).

Marvin Pope, *Song of Songs* (New York: Doubleday, 1977).

Isaiah

John T. Willis

CHAPTER CONTENTS

Contexts   533

Commentary   533
- Superscription · 1:1   533
- Doom & Hope for Judah & Jerusalem · 1:2–12:6   534
- Yahweh's Work among the Nations · 13:1–23:18   542
- Yahweh's Punishment of the Wicked & Redemption of the Righteous · 24:1–27:13   549
- Yahweh Punishes & Restores the People through Invasion & Exile · 28:1–39:8   551
- Yahweh's Promise to Return Judah's Remnant to Jerusalem · 40:1–55:13   558
- Objectives & Controversies in Yahweh's Postexilic Community · 56:1–66:24   567

Theological Reflections   573

For Further Study   575

Works Cited   575

MAPS, TABLES, & FEATURES

- The Assyrian Empire, 9th to 8th Centuries BCE   538
- The Structure of Isaiah   551
- Critical Issues in Isaiah 36–39   556

The book of Isaiah contains materials originating over four centuries. Several specific, datable historical events are referenced in Isaiah and provide the framework for the book: the year King Uzziah of Judah died (742 BCE; 6:1); the Syro-Ephraimite War (734–732 BCE; 7:1–9:7; 17:1–11); the fall of Samaria (721 BCE; 10:9–11); the siege of Ashdod (711 BCE; 20:1–6); Sennacherib's invasion of Judah and siege of Jerusalem (701 BCE; 1:2–20; 28–33; 36–39); the Babylonian conquest of Judah and subsequent exile of the Judeans (587 BCE; 40:1–2; 47:6; 48:3–6); the rise of Cyrus, king of Persia and his capture of Babylon (540–539 BCE; 44:24–45:7; 46:11–13; 48:14–15); the Jewish return from Babylon and the rebuilding of the temple (536–516 BCE; 60:11–14; 62:9); and the rebuilding of the walls of Jerusalem (445 BCE; 58:12; 60:18; 62:6).

CONTEXTS

The book's composer uses a variety of specific events and God's message derived from them to present relevant truths to his contemporaries in Jerusalem at the end of the fifth century BCE. He assumes that what God has done in the past God can and will do again, and God's centuries-old messages still speak to contemporary audiences.

The composer did not construct the book to be read silently in isolated settings but to be performed orally by trained readers or dramatic actors before assembled audiences. Accordingly, he used many traditional "oral transmission" techniques, giving special attention to structure, rhetoric, repetition, plays on words and phrases, dialogue, quotations, sign acts, symbolic names, allegories, gestures, and other means of communication to assure that those responsible expressed God's message clearly and effectively.

Like all the prophetic books, Isaiah contains a great deal of Hebrew poetry, which relies on parallelism, or some form of repetition, for its overall effect.

COMMENTARY

SUPERSCRIPTION · 1:1

The contents of Isaiah extend far beyond the chronological limits of the four Judean kings mentioned in Isaiah 1:1. Since there are superscriptions at 2:1 and 13:1, perhaps 1:1 is not intended as a superscription for the whole book, but only for 1:2–31 or 1:2–12:6 (compare Jer 1:1–3, which clearly does not cover all the contents of Jeremiah). *Vision* here does not refer to a particular type of divine revelation, but is a very broad term for all kinds of divine messages. *Judah and Jerusalem* do not adequately describe the intended audience for the contents of Isaiah, which also contains oracles for north Israel (9:8–10:4) and several other nations (13–23; 46–48).

DOOM & HOPE FOR JUDAH & JERUSALEM · 1:2–12:6

The first major section of the book consists of four parts (1:2–5:30; 6:1–9:7; 9:8–10:4; 10:5–12:6) that together portray Israel under threat and promise. Isaiah 1:2–5:30 forms a chiasmus. The outer sections (1:2–31 and 5:1–30) emphasize justice and righteousness, while the center section (2:1–4:6) calls humans to be humble and praise God.

> **Chiasmus**
> A way of structuring texts so that the first and last parts are parallel, the second and next-to-last are parallel, and so on, chiasmus is very common in the Bible and seems to reflect how Israelites thought texts should be written in order to be most compelling. In citing a chiasmus, the first and last parts are referred to as A and A', respectively, the second and next-to-last, B and B', and so on.

1:2–31 This section uses three metaphors for Yahweh's relationship to Judah: parent-child (verses 2–4), doctor-patient (verses 5–6), and husband-wife (verse 21). The wealthy and powerful oppress orphan, widow, and the helpless for personal gain, but scrupulously observe rituals at the temple (verses 11–15). The prophet declares Yahweh's punishment for this injustice but redemption for the penitent (verses 5–9, 18–20, 24–31).

For the Lord has spoken (verse 2b) and *for the mouth of the Lord has spoken* (verse 20c) form an inclusio. In this covenant lawsuit, Yahweh is plaintiff; the prophet, Yahweh's lawyer; Israel, the defendant; and heavens and earth, witnesses to the validity of Yahweh's claims (Wildberger 12). Although Yahweh lovingly raised children as a parent, operated on the patient as a doctor, and besieged Jerusalem like an enemy army, Israel continues to rebel. Publicly they present large numbers of sacrifices, festivals, and prayers, but privately they oppress the defenseless. Hence they are sick, desolate, and threatened with the sword. Their only hope is that Yahweh has left them a few survivors and beckons them to be willing and obedient in order to wash their sins clean and make them like snow and wool.

Not know, not understand (verse 3cd) parallels *rebel* (verse 2d), *forsake, spurn, turn … backs on* (verse 4e-g), but contrasts with *the ox knows his master* (verse 3a), which refers not to intellectual information, but to a personal relationship. *The Holy One of Israel* (verse 4f) is a major title for Yahweh in Isaiah (28 times), along with affirmations that Yahweh is "holy" (for example, 6:3; 57:15), indicating one significant theme in this work. Yahweh inflicts the people with *wounds* (verse 6c) to motivate them to repent in order to heal them (see Jer 30:12–17), but they refuse to return.

Descriptions of the *desolate country*, *cities burned with fire*, hostile *foreigners* (*strangers*) in the land, Jerusalem *like a city under siege*, and *some survivors* point to Sennacherib's invasion of Jerusalem in 701 BCE (Isaiah 36–37), when he conquered 46 Judean towns and exiled 200,150 prisoners (Pritchard 288). *Remnant*, a term prominent in Isaiah, here means those remaining after invasion.

Yahweh punishes the people as he did *Sodom* and *Gomorrah* (verse 9) because they sin like those cities (verse 10). The verse assumes the *lex talionis* (Gen 18:16–19:29). Isaiah uses terms like *multitude* (verse 11a), *more than enough* (verse 11c), *trampling* (verse 12c), *burden* (verse 14c), and *many* (verse 15c), to show God's people assuming that if they bring large quantities of sacrifices in public worship, Yahweh will ignore their unjust treatment of others. Yahweh *hates* those who hide their sins under elaborate worship. Uplifted palms and eyes are common in prayer throughout Scripture (1 Kgs 8:22, 54; Ps 28:2; Lam 3:41; 1 Tim 2:8).

> **Lex Talionis**
> Biblical law states a principle of reciprocity in punishment: "an eye for an eye, and a tooth for a tooth." Such a law fits punishment to the crime but also insists on punishment.

Justice, especially toward the *oppressed*, *fatherless*, and *widow*, is central to godliness (Jas 1:27). Legal decisions favoring the powerful above the weak contradict justice (Isa 10:1–2).

The lament in verses 21–31 expresses Yahweh's frustration with the unfaithful wife, Jerusalem. She who formerly practiced *justice* and *righteousness* now teems with *murderers*, *rebels*, and *thieves* who oppress the *fatherless* and the *widow*. These oppressors are Yahweh's *enemies*, whom God will *remove* and replace with righteous *judges* and *counselors*. God's people fall into two groups: the *penitent*, whom Yahweh will *redeem*, and *rebels*, whom Yahweh will destroy. Foreign idols and worship practices provide little help for the unfaithful.

Verses 21–26 are chiastic. Yahweh will transform his wife, the *harlot*, who abandoned *justice* and *righteousness* (A – verse 21), into a *City of Righteousness*, a *Faithful City* (A' – verse 26), like one eliminates the *dross* that adulterates *silver* (B – verse 22; B' – verse 25). On Judah's *rulers*, who oppress the *fatherless* and *widows* for selfish gain (C – verse 23), he will *avenge* misdeeds (C' – verse 24). NIV's *the Lord Almighty* inadequately translates the Hebrew *Yahweh tseva'ot* (NRSV: *the Lord of hosts*); "hosts" may refer either to angels (Ps 103:20–21), Israel's armies (1 Sam 17:45), or foreign armies (Jer 25:8–9); the latter option seems most likely here (Wildberger 29–30).

Scripture frequently distinguishes between professed and true believers (verses 27–28; Rom 2:17–29). Yahweh will punish his people who practice foreign cults under *oaks* (57:5) and in *gardens* (65:3; 66:17).

2:1–4:6 This section is chiastic, with the following structure:

A Zion's Mission to the Nations (2:1–5)
B Humbling arrogant people (2:6–22)
B' Humbling arrogant leaders (3:1–15)
B" Humbling arrogant women (3:16–4:1)
A' Exaltation of Zion's penitent remnant (4:2–6).

In 2:1–5, the prophet quotes a "Song of Zion" (Ps 137:3): Yahweh will exalt abased Zion and the temple. A faithful people will go out from Zion proclaiming God's redeeming message to the nations, who will respond enthusiastically, make pilgrimages to Zion, and learn Yahweh's word more fully. Yahweh will mediate among them, bringing peace. This vision can become reality if God's people walk in Yahweh's light.

In the last days (verse 2a) means "sometime in the future" (Gen 49:1; Deut 31:29). *Law* (verse 3f) is Yahweh's "teaching," as the synonymous parallelism with *word* (verse 3g) shows.

In 2:6–22, alternating recurring refrains (verses 9, 11, 17 and verses 10, 19, 21) emphasize that Yahweh will humble the arrogant, including Judah, and they will flee in terror. Because God's people trust in foreign cult practices and the pursuit of wealth and military strength (verses 6–8, 12–18, 20), the *day of Yahweh* will come (verses 11, 12, 17, 20), when Yahweh will punish them for their infidelity.

In verses 6–9, the prophet addresses Yahweh concerning the people's misplaced trust, which fuels arrogance, and beseeches Yahweh not to forgive them. In verses 10–22, the prophet urges the people to hide from the *day of Yahweh*, when Yahweh will humble human arrogance in all of its manifestations.

As 3:1–15 points out, corruption abounds among the leaders of God's people. Soon, all strata of society will oppress people indiscriminately. Conditions will become so chaotic that the populace will allow anyone to rule. Sin is everywhere; Jerusalem is *like Sodom* (verse 9). Yahweh will punish *the wicked* but sustain *the righteous* (verses 10–11). God will bring a "covenant lawsuit" against the wicked *elders and leaders* of the people, because they oppress *the poor*. God does not call all Judah *my people*, but only the faithful ones (verses 14–15).

> **The Day of the Lord**
> *In the Old Testament, the theme of Day of the Lord appears frequently. It does not refer to the end of time, but to a period of God's dramatic intervention in human history in order to right wrongs. See, for example Amos 5:18–20.*

According to verses 1–7, all Judah's leaders, whether military, political, judicial, religious, moral, or practical, are corrupt (verses 2–4).

In verses 8–12, Jerusalem *staggers*; Judah *is falling* like a drunkard (verse 8). *They have brought disaster upon themselves* (verse 9). Yahweh will deliver the righteous remnant but punish his people as a whole (verses 10–11); their leaders have misled them (verse 12).

The "covenant lawsuit" in verses 13–15 is similar to 1:2–20: Yahweh accuses the rich and powerful of oppressing the poor and defenseless. God's true *vineyard* is not Israel or Judah as a whole, but only those faithful to him, who practice justice and righteousness (5:1–7).

According to 3:16–4:1, influential women in Judah and Jerusalem are *haughty*, parading their beauty, clothing, ornaments, perfumes, and accessories in public, extolling their importance and wealth. Yahweh has a *day* (3:18; 4:1) when he will make these women repulsive eyesores, with the accompanying hideous smells, garments, sounds, and social conditions.

In 4:2–6, Yahweh punishes the arrogant not to destroy, but to refine. Yahweh's *fire* will *wash away the filth of the women of Zion* and *cleanse* the *bloodstains* of the oppressed *from Jerusalem*. He will *create* for *the survivors in Israel, who remain in Jerusalem*, a *shelter* from *heat* and a *refuge* from *storm and rain*.

5:1–30 Isaiah 5 contains three parts: the parable of a disappointing vineyard (verses 1–7); six "woes" against injustice (verses 8–23); and an announcement that Yahweh will punish the unjust (verses 24–30).

In verses 1–7, probably playing a lyre or harp (Ps 33:2–3), Isaiah appears before an audience as a minstrel and sings about his best friend and his vineyard. His friend expended much time and energy preparing the ground for a vineyard and a vat for its fruit. His expectations of bountiful good grapes are very high. But the vineyard produces *wild grapes*. His friend's disappointment is immeasurable. He resolves to demolish his vineyard. The audience empathizes with the vinedresser. Then the prophet declares: "You are that vineyard!"... and Yahweh is the vinedresser. Using Hebrew wordplays, the prophet declares that the good grapes are *justice* [*mishpat*] and *righteousness* [*tsedaqah*]; but the wild grapes, *bloodshed* [*mispach*] and *a cry* [*tse'aqah*, NRSV].

Isaiah 5:8–23 pronounces six "woes" against injustice, examples of the sin condemned in the song of the vineyard. The first woe denounces the rich and powerful for endless property expansion (removing a neighbor's boundary marker; see Deut 19:14) and home improvement. As just punishment, Yahweh will despoil *the great houses* and deplete the crops of the rich. The second woe rebukes powerful, rich leaders of God's people who try to escape impending punishment for their sins by becoming absorbed in drunkenness and salving music; these individuals show *no respect* for Yahweh's *deeds* or *work* of humbling the people (see 2:11, 17) by sending powerful armies to overthrow them and carry them into *exile*, demonstrating that God is *holy* by *justice* and *righteousness*. The third woe reproaches Isaiah's opponents who mock his announcement that Yahweh has a *plan* to send enemies to punish his people for their sins, asking, "If Yahweh really plans to do this, why hasn't it happened yet?"

In verse 20, context suggests that the fourth woe censures those who proclaim all is well in Judah although God's people are approaching calamity (compare verse 30); yet it may also condemn people who reverse God's moral standards.

In verse 21, the fifth woe rebukes those who assume they can live by norms derived from their own wisdom apart from Yahweh's guidance. In verses 22–23, the sixth woe condemns indulgence in drunkenness (compare verse 11) and undermining justice in court by giving and receiving *bribes* (compare Exod 23:8; Deut 16:19), thereby refusing *justice to the innocent* (1:17, 23).

According to 5:24–30, Yahweh will punish his people as *fire* consumes *straw* or *dry grass* because they have ignored *instruction* (or his *word*). Prophets did not establish a new religion but evaluated people by God's existing law, as these six "woes" illustrate. Yahweh unleashes *anger* once and again, because the people persist in sin (verse 25ef recurs in 9:12, 17, 21; 10:4). As army commander, Yahweh *lifts up a banner* (11:12; 13:2; 18:3; 31:9; 49:22; 62:10) to and *whistles for* (7:18) a distant *nation* (NRSV), Assyria, summoning its soldiers to move against Judah. The army advances *swiftly*, refreshed, well-equipped, deafening, and swarming, making the land appear *darkened* (8:21–22).

6:1–9:7 This large subsection begins with a theophany and ends with visions of a deliverer. In between, stories and oracles of conflict and salvation appear.

> **Theophany**
> A divine being's appearance to a human is known as theophany. Israelites believed that seeing God would lead to death, but such did not occur for Isaiah in this text. Isaiah 6 marks the beginning of the prophet's career.

6:1–13 Isaiah 6:1–9:7 addresses the question: who is king? Within that section, chapter 6 relates Yahweh's commission to Isaiah (742 BCE), while 7:1–9:7 recounts four "son" oracles bearing on the Syro-Ephraimite War (734–732 BCE).

Isaiah worships at the Jerusalem *temple* (verses 1, 4), Yahweh appears as *King* (verses 1, 5), *the Lord of hosts* (NRSV, verses 3, 5), that is, the heavenly hosts of seraphim and attending angels (1 Kgs 21:19; Ps 103:20–21) under a universal sovereign (verse 3). Yahweh strongly contrasts with the earthly King Uzziah who has just died (742 BCE). Angelic beings, *seraphs*, attend him, proclaiming to all that he is *holy, holy, holy* (Ps 99:3, 5, 9; Rev 4:8), which manifests itself in *glory* disseminated throughout *the whole earth*.

Immediately, Isaiah realizes he is a spiritual leper among leprous people. For public protection, lepers covered their upper lip and warned anyone approaching: *Unclean, unclean* (Lev 13:45–46), in contrast to the seraphs' cries to God: *Holy, holy, holy* (verse 3). Yahweh sends a seraph with a *live coal* to touch the prophet's *lips*, inflicting pain as punishment but granting forgiveness in mercy.

Yahweh must send someone to expose his people's spiritual disease: *calloused heart*, *dull ears*, *closed eyes*. The choice falls on Isaiah, one formerly with the same disease but now recovered. Although the Judeans' infirmity is chronic, the great physician yearns for them to *turn* to him and *be healed* (1:5–6), as Isaiah has been (verses 6–7). The prophet asks *how long* he must preach to this hardened people; Yahweh replies: *Until* the land is completely devastated and only *the holy seed* remains (4:3), a small group of penitent believers surviving the fall of Samaria (721 BCE), Sennacherib's invasion (701 BCE), the overthrow of Jerusalem and Babylonian exile (587 BCE).

7:1–9 Isaiah 7:1 (which parallels 2 Kgs 16:5) sketches circumstances surrounding the Syro-Ephraimite war (734–732 BCE), preparing the hearer for 7:2–9:7. *Rezin, king of Aram* (Syria) and *Pekah, king of Israel* (or *Ephraim*), rebelled against Tiglath-pileser III of Assyria (2 Kgs 16:7), who controlled the small western states along the Mediterranean. They invited *Ahaz, king of Judah*, to join, but he refused. So they *marched ... against Jerusalem* to dethrone Ahaz and put *the son of Tabeel* (perhaps an offspring of Uzziah or Jotham by a Syrian woman from Tabeel in Syria) on the throne, because he would join them.

Ahaz and the Judeans greatly fear Pekah and Rezin. Yahweh sends Isaiah to Ahaz with this message: *Don't be afraid. Do not lose heart*. To encourage Ahaz, Isaiah presents a *son* as a *sign* (Isa 8:18) and an illustration.

The *son* is Isaiah's own *son Shear-Jashub*, "a remnant shall return," here apparently meaning: "[Only] a remnant [of the armies of Syria and Ephraim] shall return [from this attack on Jerusalem]," implying: "If you [Ahaz and the Judeans] trust Yahweh to overthrow Syria and Ephraim, you will not ask Tiglath-pileser III and the Assyrians for help, but will trust Yahweh to act." The "illustration" supports this interpretation: Rezin and Pekah are merely *two smoldering stubs of firewood*, able to harm no one. Briefly they burn brightly like two large pieces of wood used to start a new fire, but Yahweh will quench their power so that they cannot execute their plan against Judah. Syria and Ephraim will fail because each has the wrong *head*, or king: Rezin and Pekah, respectively. Ahaz and the Judeans (*you* in verse 9cd is plural) must decide whether they will accept the prophet's message with trust: *If you do not stand firm in your faith, you will not stand at all*. Ahaz and the Judeans must believe this *sign* will occur before it happens (Exod 3:12; 1 Sam 2:34).

7:10–25 Yahweh sends Isaiah to Ahaz again to tell the king to ask for a miraculous *sign*. Ahaz refuses, asserting he would never *put the Lord to the test* by demanding a sign. Isaiah replies that Ahaz is *trying God's patience* with his religious hypocrisy, since he was considering sending to Tiglath-pileser III for help rather than trusting in Yahweh (2 Kgs 16:7–9).

Upon Ahaz's refusal, Yahweh gives him a *sign*, again involving a *son*, then an illustration (verse 20). Gesturing toward or pointing at an unnamed young woman nearby (Tucker 112), perhaps one of Ahaz's wives (Watts 99; Wildberger 306–12) or Isaiah's wife (Clements 86, 88). The young woman does not refer to Mary (see Motyer 84–87). Isaiah declares: *Look, the young woman is with child* (NRSV, Masoretic text) *and will give birth to a son* (not twins or a daughter) *and will call him Immanuel* [with us (Judeans) is God, so we have nothing to fear]; baby Immanuel *will eat curds and honey* (when his mother weans him, the only food available; verses 21–22); but before little Immanuel *knows how to refuse the evil and choose the good* (NRSV) food, *the land of the two kings* (Rezin and Pekah) *you* (the singular pronoun refers to Ahaz) *dread will be laid waste*. If

> **Who is Immanuel?**
> *Throughout history, readers of Isaiah have identified Immanuel with several figures, including Hezekiah, Maher-Shalal-Hash-Baz, and others. In the context of the original events of Isaiah 7, the child must have been someone living in Isaiah's lifetime, since otherwise Ahaz could not see the sign. Early Christians understandably connected the verse to the boy who was most fully "God with us," Jesus.*

Ahaz and the Judeans believe this, Yahweh will deliver them. But if they make a treaty with Tiglath-pileser III, *the king of Assyria*, after he subdues Syria and Israel, he will oppress Ahaz and the Judeans, bringing devastation worse than had been experienced *since Ephraim broke away from Judah* after Solomon's death (1 Kgs 12–14).

Here four oracles, each beginning with *in that day*, announce devastating conditions threatening Judah because Ahaz and his advisors refuse Isaiah's pleas to trust in Yahweh. First, Yahweh, king of the nations (Jer 10:7), will *whistle for* (that is, summon, 5:26) *Assyria* (*Egypt* parallels Assyria in Hos 9:3; 11:5, 11) to decimate Judah (verses 18–19). Second, the prophet uses an illustration to convey the same message as the Immanuel sign. Yahweh, the barber, will use his *razor, the king of Assyria* (Tiglath-pileser III), to *shave the head* (Rezin), *the hair of the feet* (Pekah), and *the beard* (Ahaz; NRSV; verse 20), because Ahaz

ISAIAH

The Assyrian Empire, 9th to 8th Centuries BCE

and Judah reject trust in Yahweh (2 Kgs 16:5–18). Third, the Assyrians will reduce Judah's population so drastically that *a young cow and two goats* can supply sufficient food for them. All remaining in Judah will eat *curds and honey* (including little Immanuel, verse 15), since this will be the only food available (verses 21–22). Fourth, the small size of the population will make cultivation impossible, allowing *briers and thorns* to engulf the land. People will hunt game in the fields, and let their livestock run free, searching for pasture.

8:1–15 For the third time, to encourage Ahaz not to fear Rezin and Pekah but to trust Yahweh, Isaiah gives Ahaz a *son* as a *sign* (8:18) and an illustration.

Yahweh instructs Isaiah to *write* on a *large scroll* the words *This scroll stands for Maher-Shalal-Hash-Baz*, and to certify it legally using *reliable witnesses*. Isaiah is to put it in a public place for all to read.

Further, Isaiah goes to *the prophetess* (his wife), and she *conceived* and *gave birth to a son*. Yahweh instructs him to name him *Maher-Shalal-Hash-Baz*, which means, "The Spoil Speeds, The Prey Hastens." Yahweh tells Isaiah: *Before the boy knows how to say* "Dada" *or* "Mama," *the wealth of Damascus and the plunder of Samaria will be carried off by the king of Assyria*. The details and point of this "sign" are identical with the "sign" of Immanuel (7:14–17), occurring approximately a year later. By the time little *Maher-Shalal-Hash-Baz* says his first words (at about one year), Syria and Ephraim will no longer threaten Judah. Hence, it is unnecessary to send to Assyria for help.

The illustration accompanying this sign involves two rivers (verses 5–10). One is *the gently flowing waters of Shiloah*, a channel supplying water to Jerusalem during siege (7:3; 36:2), symbolizing trust in Yahweh (28:16; 30:15). Ahaz and his advisors (*this people*) rejected this river because they *melt in fear* (NRSV) before Rezin and Pekah. Therefore, Yahweh will bring against them *the mighty flood waters of the River … the king of Assyria*, which will *overflow all its channels* (into Syria), and *run over all its banks* (that is, destroy Israel, or Ephraim), and it will *sweep on into Judah*, as well. Judah's alliance with Assyria (2 Kgs 16:7–9) will backfire: after Tiglath-pileser III overthrows Syria and Ephraim, he will subjugate Judah (2 Kgs 16:10–18; 2 Chron 28:16–25). While making this declaration, Isaiah holds the year-old *Immanuel* in his arms, representing the small population that will survive (7:21–22), addressing him by name (verse 8c). In verses 9–10, Isaiah proclaims to Syria and Ephraim his message to Ahaz in 7:7–9: their *plan* to dethrone Ahaz and replace him with *the son of Tabeel will not stand* (7:6).

Next, the prophet tells an audience (imperatives in verses 12–13 are plural) what Yahweh said to him (verse 11). His audience is different from *this people* (NRSV; verses 11–12), which usually refers to Ahaz and his associates (7:2, 17; 8:6), but in this case probably indicates Isaiah's comrades. God's message is the same as that to Ahaz and his advisors in the *sign* of Shear-Jashub: *do not fear* Syria and Ephraim; *let the Lord of hosts* (NRSV) *be your fear*; trust God (7:4, 9). Yahweh *will be a sanctuary* from the Syro-Ephraimite alliance for those who trust in him, but *a stone that causes men to stumble for both houses of Israel*: Ephraim, because she has joined Syria against Assyria; and Judah, because she has not trusted in Yahweh but asked Tiglath-pileser III for help against the Syro-Ephraimite invaders (2 Kgs 16:7–9). This political maneuvering will cripple Ephraim and Judah.

8:16–20 Ahaz, his advisors, and most Judeans refuse to accept Isaiah's advice to trust in Yahweh. Isaiah decides to quit preaching until his announcements occur, but he leaves two witnesses. First, he instructs one of his associates (imperatives in verse 16 are singular) to *bind up the testimony* and *seal the teaching* (NRSV) among his *disciples*, to write his oracles now preserved in Isaiah 7:3–8:15 and keep them among Judeans who share his trust in Yahweh. When the events Isaiah has announced occur, the Judeans will *consult mediums and spiritists* (NRSV *ghosts* and *familiar spirits*), seeking in vain explanations for them from *their gods* (NRSV). Then they must resort to the *teaching* (NRSV) and to the *testimony*! (verse 20; verse 16); at that point, it will be time to read Isaiah's oracles written on the little scroll his disciples preserved. Second, Isaiah and *the children the Lord has given* him (*Shear-Jashub* [7:3], *Immanuel* [7:14; 8:8, 10], and *Maher-Shalal-Hash-Baz* [8:3]) will be *signs and symbols in Israel*. Whenever Judeans see Isaiah or these *children*, their symbolic names will recall Isaiah's message.

Necromancy & Divination
In the ancient world, it was common to consult the gods or the dead ancestors about the future. Techniques for doing so included reading entrails of sacrificed animals, studying stellar movements, looking for unusual behaviors of animals or persons, and digging holes into the ground so as to induce ghosts to rise from the netherworld. Israel's prophets forbade all these practices as incompatible with worshiping the God of life.

8:21–9:7 The placement and content of 8:21–9:7 date this oracle near the beginning of Hezekiah's reign (715 BCE; 2 Kgs 18:13). It contains four contrasts between Judah's devastation at the end of Ahaz's reign and the renewal Hezekiah brings: where Ahaz's reign brought distress (8:21, 22; 9:1), Hezekiah's brings joy (9:1, 3); where Ahaz's brought defeat (9:1, 4), Hezekiah's brings victory (9:4–5); where Ahaz was an evil king (8:21), Hezekiah is a good king (9:6–7); and where Ahaz brought darkness (8:22; 9:2), Hezekiah brings light (9:2).

Judeans remaining after Assyrian subjugations live in chaos and despair. They *curse their king* (Ahaz), in whom they had great confidence; and *their gods* (NRSV), whom they adopted from the nations (2 Kgs 16:3–4, 10–18; 2 Chron 28:2–4, 22–25) and whom they trusted instead of Yahweh. Tiglath-pileser III overran *the land of Zebulun and the land of Naphtali*, that is, *Galilee of the Gentiles*, in Ephraim west of the Jordan, and Gilead in Ephraim east of the Jordan (2 Kgs 15:29); so only Samaria in southern Ephraim west of the Jordan remained.

According to 9:2–5, as Yahweh miraculously defeated the large Midianite army with 300 poorly equipped, inexperienced soldiers under Gideon on *the day of Midian* (NRSV; Judg 6:2–6; 7:1–25), so Yahweh, through his angel, will defeat the large Assyrian army with a much smaller Judean army under Hezekiah (Isa 37:36). Isaiah likens God's people's ensuing *joy* with joy *at the harvest* (Ps 126:6) and the joy an army experiences *when dividing the plunder* [Hebrew *shalal*, recalling the name *Maher-Shalal-Hash-Baz*, 8:1, 3] of its defeated enemy (Judg 5:28–30; 1 Sam 30:16–20).

In verses 6–7, the statements *for a child has been born for us, a son given to us* (NRSV) refer not to physical birth of a royal prince (Wildberger 398–402; Blenkinsopp, *Isaiah 1–39*, 248–49), but to a king's accession, which has already occurred when the prophet utters this (Clements 107; Hayes and Irvine 180–81). This *son* is Hezekiah, Ahaz's successor. The king of Israel is Yahweh's *son* (2 Sam 7:14; Pss 2:7; 89:26–27). His accession is his *begettal* (Ps 2:7) or *birth* (Isa 9:6). As *son*, the king is *heir* of Yahweh's estate (Ps 2:8), the world, and its nations. Yahweh gives his *son* victory and rule over all nations through Yahweh's universal rule (Pss 47:1–3, 8–9; 99:1–2).

Hezekiah's *name* (verse 6b) is symbolic, consisting of four parts: *Wonderful Counselor* [Hebrew *pele' yo 'ets*], who acts wisely, as Solomon did (1 Kgs 3:3–14); *Godly Hero* (or "mighty warrior") [Hebrew *'el gibbor*], who derives his strength from Yahweh, enabling him to lead his people against their enemies (Wildberger 403–4); *Father of Eternity* [Hebrew *'abi 'ad*], one responsible for the king's public and private affairs and estate (see 22:21; Gen 45:8), whose durability Yahweh assures; and *Prince of Peace* [Hebrew *sar shalom*], promoting peace by submitting himself to Yahweh and promoting *justice and righteousness* among Yahweh's people (Isa 1:17; 5:7).

9:8–10:4 As in Leviticus 26:14–24 and Amos 4:6–11, Isaiah 9:8–10:4 declares that Yahweh has smitten the people repeatedly to bring them to repentance, but they persist in sin. This section contains four oracles, each ending with: *Yet for all this, his anger is not turned away, his hand is stretched out still* (NRSV; 9:12, 17, 21; 10:4).

Yahweh delivered Israel from Egypt *with an outstretched arm* (Exod 6:6) and now *stretches out his hand* against his own people, who refuse to repent. The prophet addresses Ephraim in the first three oracles, Judah in the fourth. The first three oracles describe what Yahweh has done recently.

Yahweh punished *Ephraim* and her capital *Samaria* because of *pride and arrogance*. A possible reconstruction of the setting of this oracle is that the anti-Assyrian Pekah, incited by Syrians and Philistines, murdered the pro-Assyrian Pekahiah, but the Ephraimites confidently resolve they will *rebuild* and *replace* their losses (2 Chron 28:5–6, 18). Yahweh's "hand is stretched out still" (NRSV) to punish Ephraim more severely by sending the Assyrians under Tiglath-pileser III against them and their allies.

According to 9:18–21, Yahweh consumed Ephraim like *fuel for the fire*, because her *wickedness burned like a fire* (NRSV). Northern Israelites opposed each other (*Manasseh devoured Ephraim, and Ephraim Manasseh*): one group after another murdering the reigning king and enthroning its own candidate (2 Kgs 15:8–26); and, *together*, they fought against Judah: they joined Syria and attacked Jerusalem to dethrone Ahaz and enthrone *the son of Tabeel* (2 Kgs 15:37; 16:5; Isa 7:1–6). *His* [Yahweh's] *hand is stretched out still* to punish the Ephraimites, because they did not repent when Yahweh punished them previously.

Isaiah's announcement (10:1–4) that Yahweh will punish the rich, powerful, influential leaders of Yahweh's people for oppressing the *poor, oppressed, widows,* and *fatherless* recalls Isaiah 1:10–17 and 5:8–23, oracles addressed to Judah, so it is likely that the prophet is addressing Judah here. Authorities made laws allowing them to oppress the helpless legally (29:20–21). *Their spoil* (verse 2c) is *shelalam*; *make their prey* (verse 2d) is, in Hebrew, *yabozzu*, recalling the name *Maher-Shalal-Hash-Baz* (8:1, 3). Yahweh has a *day of punishment* (NRSV) which they cannot avoid, when they will become *captives* or *slain. His hand is stretched out still* to punish the powerful for oppressing the defenseless.

10:5–12:6 Just as most of 7:1–10:4 concerns the Syro-Ephraimite War, 10:5–12:6 fits Sennacherib's invasion of Judah in 701 BCE, reapplied to the Jews' return from Babylonian exile in 536 BCE and afterward. This section falls into two parts: Yahweh will overthrow Assyria after using that nation to punish Judah (10:5–32); and Yahweh will then restore the remnant of the people under a *new David* (10:33–12:6).

Isaiah 10:5–32 is a woe oracle (compare 5:8–23) against Assyria (see 33:1). It reflects a conflict in purposes between Yahweh and Assyria regarding Assyria's invasion of Judah. Yahweh intends to use Assyria to punish Judah (verses 6, 12), then to restore a faithful remnant (verses 20–25); Assyria intends only to *destroy* Judah (verses 7, 11).

Yahweh sends Assyria against Judah because the latter is *a godless nation,* a *people who angers* him, intending for Assyria to *take spoil* [Hebrew *lishlol shalal*] and *seize plunder* [Hebrew *laboz baz*], once again recalling the name *Maher-Shalal-Hash-Baz* (8:1, 3). Yahweh is like a lumberjack wielding an *ax* (Assyria) to fell a tree (Judah), a carpenter handling a *saw* (Assyria) to cut a board (Judah, verse 15), and a parent using a *rod* (Assyria) to discipline a child (Judah, verses 5, 15). As the lumberjack controls the ax, not the ax the lumberjack, so Yahweh controls Assyria, not Assyria Yahweh.

The "Outstretched Hand" of the Lord

Yahweh cut off Ephraim's religious leaders, elders *and* prominent men (the head), *and* prophets (the tail), *because they "led this people ... astray," so that "everyone was godless and an evildoer"* (NRSV; Isa 19:15). *Perhaps this refers to murders of Ephraimite kings between 746 and 737 BCE (Hos 7:3–7). His "hand is stretched out still" to punish Ephraim's rulers and people for not returning to him.*

The king of Assyria brags in his *arrogant boasting* and *haughty pride* (NRSV, verse 12) that he will destroy *Jerusalem and her images* as Assyria has destroyed other cities and their idols, including *Samaria* (verses 8–11), which Assyria overthrew after a three-year siege under Shalmaneser V and Sargon II (724–721 BCE).

> **Assyrian Propaganda**
>
> *According to Isaiah, the king of Assyria exalts his own strength and wisdom (verses 13–14), boasting that he is so terrifying that he vanquishes enemies like one gathering eggs out of nests mother birds feared to protect: not one flapped a wing or opened its mouth to chirp. This simile resembles Sennacherib's boast that he made Hezekiah "a prisoner in Jerusalem, his royal residence, like a bird in a cage" (Pritchard 288). Indeed, the book of Isaiah knows a great deal about Assyrian propaganda and quotes it several times.*

Yahweh, the *Light* and *Holy One of Israel*, will overthrow Assyria like a deadly illness suffocates an invalid (verse 18c) or like a rapidly spreading *fire* destroys fields of *thorns* and *briers* (7:23–25) and *forests* (verses 16c–18b), leaving only a few trees (verse 19). The *wasting disease upon* Assyria's *sturdy warriors* (verse 16b) refers to Yahweh's angel killing 185,000 Assyrian soldiers (Isa 37:36).

Yahweh *decreed* the *destruction* of Judah by Assyria, so *only a remnant will return* (verses 20–22), a clause recalling the Hebrew name *Shear-Jashub* (7:3). But the remnant will not *rely on him who struck them down* (the Assyrians), as Ahaz relied on Tiglath-pileser III (2 Kgs 16:7–9), but on Yahweh (7:9; 31:1; 36:4–7). Hebrew *'el gibbor* in verse 21b refers to Yahweh and means *Mighty God*, recalling Hezekiah's throne name (9:6).

According to 24–27b, since Yahweh is punishing Judah, she must *not be afraid of* the Assyrians whom Yahweh is using to do this. When Yahweh finishes using the Assyrians, he will overthrow them as he did the Egyptians at the Red Sea (Exod 3:7–10; 14:26–31) and the Midianites when they oppressed Israel in the time of Gideon (Judg 7:24–25; Ps 83:9–12; Isa 9:4), thus breaking *the yoke* on Judah's neck.

The prophet's intensely dramatic rhetoric in verses 27c–32 enables his audience to envision and hear the Assyrians (*he* in verses 28, 32 [NRSV]; *they* in verse 29) tramping methodically and irrepressibly from *Rimmon* (NRSV) southward through *Aiath*, then *Migron*, then *Michmash* (NRSV), onward, until *he* reaches the village of *Nob* about a mile and a half north of Jerusalem on Mount Scopus overlooking the city, where *he* shakes his fist at Jerusalem, signifying his imminent attack on the city. Sennacherib's annals do not mention an approach from the north. Micah 1:10–16 describes a similar approach of this army from the west, which Sennacherib's annals corroborate. This sets the stage for the second part of Isaiah 10:5–12:6.

Isaiah 10:33–12:6 completes the picture begun in 10:5–32, reapplying the aftermath of Sennacherib's invasion in 701 BCE to the Jews in Babylonian exile after 587 BCE. This section falls into three parts: Yahweh will devastate Judah, then restore justice, righteousness, and peace to Judah through a *new David* (10:33–11:9); Yahweh will work through the *new David* to restore his faithful remnant to their land (11:10–16); and the remnant will praise Yahweh (12:1–6).

10:33–11:9 Using Assyria as an *ax* (10:15), Yahweh fells the *lofty trees* and *forest thickets* of *Lebanon*. The mention of *Lebanon* indicates that 10:33–34 announces Yahweh's devastation of Judah, not Assyria. The situation looks bleak for Judah. But Yahweh will cause a *shoot* to come forth from the *stump of Jesse*, a *new David* (1 Sam 16:1–13; 2 Sam 23:1–2), infused with ample *wisdom and understanding* to restore and maintain *righteousness* and *justice* in the land by slaying the *wicked* and vindicating the *needy* and *poor*. Yahweh will establish peace between former enemies. Some scholars understand verses 6–9 literally, reasoning that human sin produces enemies in the animal kingdom (Genesis 3), and these verses announce that Yahweh will end that hostility by enacting peace among human beings (Brueggemann, *Isaiah 1–39*, 102). However, "context suggests that the talk of harmony in the animal world is a metaphor for harmony in the human world. The strong and powerful live together with the weak and powerless because the latter can believe that the former are no longer seeking to devour them" (Goldingay 85; see Seitz, *Isaiah 1–39*, 96, 106–7).

> **The New David**
>
> *Isaiah 10 does not identify the "new David." He might be Hezekiah or Josiah, but the promise of return from exile as a "second exodus" (11:12, 15–16) indicates that most likely he is Zerubbabel, or perhaps an ideal future ruler.*

The setting of 11:10–16 comes near the end of the Babylonian exile (550–536 BCE). The prophet announces that Yahweh will do four things. First, God will duplicate the mighty act of delivering Israel from slavery to Pharaoh at *the Egyptian sea*. He will send *a scorching wind* to part the waters of *the Euphrates River* so the remnant may *cross over* on dry land and escape from foreign bondage, effecting a "second exodus" (verses 15–16; Exod 14:21–22). Second, God will *gather the remnant* from their various habitations in exile (verses 10–12) and lead them along a *highway* back to their land, thus repeating the entrance of Israel into the promised land (verses 11–12; Exod 15:13, 17). Third, Yahweh will remove the *jealousy* of Ephraim over Judah, and the *hostility* of Judah against Ephraim (verse 13). The hope that Yahweh will end the animosity between Ephraim and Judah, which dates at least to the time of David (2 Sam 2:12–3:39; 19:41–43), is prominent in late preexilic and exilic texts (Jer 30:1–3; 31:1–14, 31–34; Ezek 37:15–28), suggesting that Isaiah 11:10–16 (and probably all of 10:33–12:6) originated in that era. Fourth, Yahweh will use the reunited people to overthrow their enemies, *Philistia*, *Edom*, *Moab*, and *the Ammonites* (verse 14), essentially the same peoples who trembled upon learning that Yahweh delivered Israel from Egypt (Exod 15:14–15). The phrase *they will plunder* [Hebrew *yabozzu*] recalls the name *Maher-Shalal-Hash-Baz* (8:1, 3).

As 12:1–6 points out, after Yahweh delivered Israel from Egypt (Exod 14:21–31), Moses and the Israelites sang praises (Exod 15:1–18). Similarly, after Yahweh delivers the Jews from Babylonian exile in a "second exodus" (Isa 11:10–16), they will sing praises (Isa 12:1–6). *You* is singular (referring to Israel as a whole) in verses 1–2, 6 but plural in verses 3–5 (indicating individual Israelites). *In that day you will say* in verses 1 and 4 divides this song into two equal parts.

The prophet urges Israel to praise Yahweh for having *comforted* them (verse 1), a term normally referring to return from exile (Isa 40:1; 49:13). *I will trust, and will not be afraid* (verse 2b) is a major teaching in Isaiah (Isa 7:2, 4, 9; 8:12–13). Verse 2c-d is almost identical to Exodus 15:2a-b. *You will draw water from the wells of salvation* (verse 3) is a metaphor meaning that Yahweh will sustain the restored people by being constantly present and delivering them (Ps 36:8–9).

When Yahweh delivers Israel from powerful oppressors by a mighty act, they cannot but *give thanks* (verses 1, 4) and *make known among the nations what he has done* (verses 4–5; Pss 66:1–12; 105:1–6). Those recently returned from exile and now living in *Zion* must *sing for joy* because Yahweh is in their midst (verse 6).

YAHWEH'S WORK AMONG THE NATIONS · 13:1–23:18

Isaiah 13–23 contains fourteen oracles proclaiming Yahweh's work among nations and individuals (compare Jer 46–51; Ezek 25–32; Amos 1–2): Babylon (13:1–14:23) and Egypt (19:1–20:6); Assyria (14:24–27) and Babylon (21:1–10); Philistia (14:28–32) and Edom (21:11–12); Moab (15:1–16:13); Arabia (21:13–17); Aram and Ephraim (17:1–11) and Judah (22:1–14); Assyria (17:12–14) and Shebna and Eliakim (22:15–25); and Ethiopia (18:1–7) and Phoenicia (23:1–18).

These oracles date from the late eighth (14:24–32; 17:1–11; 20; 22) to late sixth centuries BCE (13:1–14:23; 23). In the fifth century BCE book of Isaiah, they convey important theological messages. First, Yahweh governs all nations and uses them to accomplish holy purposes (13:2–5, 17; 19:1–4; 23:8–12). Second, Yahweh punishes Israel (17:1–11) and Judah (22:1–14), along with other nations (see Amos 3:1–2). The fate of Yahweh's people is bound up with the fate of the nations. Third, humanity's universal pervasive sin is pride, arrogance, self-sufficiency, hubris, ingratitude (13:11, 19; 14:12–15; 16:6; 17:4; 19:11–12; 22:15–19; 23:7–12), already affirmed of Judah (2:6–22) and Assyria (10:5–19). Fourth, Yahweh's "plan" alone prevails (14:24–27; 19:3, 11–12, 17; 23:8–9). Fifth, Yahweh has a *day* to punish or redeem nations (13:6, 9, 13; 17:4, 7, 9, 11; 19:18, 19, 21, 23, 24; 22:5, 8, 12, 20, 25).

13:1–14:23 The two-step sequence noting that Yahweh will restore his people and then overthrow his people's conqueror is common in Isaiah (see 11:10–12:6; 13:1–14:23; 30:18–26; 30:27–33).

Some have claimed that 13:2–14:27 was originally a unit denouncing Assyria for its arrogance in attacking Judah in 701 BCE, including an announcement that Assyria will destroy Babylon in 689 BCE (13:19–22; 14:22–23; see Erlandsson 109–27, 160–66). Similarly, some scholars believe that 13:2–14:23 contains prophetic fragments originating from Merodach-baladan II's rebellions against Assyria in the eighth to the fourth centuries BCE (Clements 129–38). It is more likely, however, that, as in 21:1–10, 47 and 48:14–20, a prophet in Babylon at the end of the exile (540 BCE) announces that Yahweh will incite the *Medes* (Medo-Persians under Cyrus, 41:25) to overthrow Babylon (13:17), slay her king, and return the Jews to Israel.

> **Cyrus the Great**
> *Cyrus the Great (about 590–530 BCE) was founder of the Persian empire.*

This oracle contains four parts: Yahweh will use Medo-Persia to overthrow Babylon (13:1–22); Yahweh will restore Israel to Canaan (14:1–2); those restored will sing a taunt, mocking Babylon's defeated and dead king (14:3–21); and Yahweh reaffirms a promise to destroy Babylon (14:22–23).

The oracle announcing Babylon's defeat in 13:2–14:23 fits well with the message of *Isaiah son of Amoz* (verse 1). *The Lord of hosts* (verse 4; NRSV), *the Almighty* [Hebrew *shadday*], *raises a banner* (verse 2; 5:26; 11:10, 12; 49:22; 62:10) to summon *warriors* (verse 3), an *army* (verse 4), *the Medes* (verse 17) *from a distant land* (verse 5; NRSV), to overthrow *Babylon* (verse 19). The terms *the whole earth* (verse 5; NRSV), *the earth* (verse 9; NRSV), and *the world* (verse 11) reflect Babylon's far-flung dominion in its prime.

The day of the Lord (verses 6, 9), *the day of his fierce anger* (verse 13; verses 3, 5, 9), *is near* to punish Babylon for its sins (verses 9, 11) especially *pride* (verses 11, 19). *The day of Yahweh* refers to Yahweh's intervention in history to punish or redeem a nation. Yahweh's coming impacts all creation in several ways: *the heavens tremble* and *the earth shakes* (verse 13; Joel 2:10; 3:16; Hag 2:6–7, 21); the *light* of the sun, moon, and stars becomes *dark* (verse 10; Zeph 1:15; Joel 2:1–2, 10, 31); *pain and anguish* seize the hearts of the Babylonians and their sympathizers *like a woman in labor* (verses 7–8; Ps 48:6; Mic 4:9–10; Jer 4:31); and they flee in fear before their attackers (verse 14).

The prophet announces that the Median devastation of Babylon and its allies will be cruel and thorough. They will make their victims *more rare* than *pure gold* (verse 12), looting houses, ravishing women (verse 16), slaughtering young men and children (verses 16, 18), vacating cities and buildings so that wild animals may inhabit them (verses 20–22), like *God overthrew* (NRSV) *Sodom and Gomorrah* (verse 19; Gen 19:24–28; Isa 1:9–10; 3:9).

14:1–2 Babylon's overthrow means freedom from captivity and return of the Jewish exiles to *the Lord's land*, Canaan, which Yahweh gave Israel after the wilderness wanderings (Josh 1:2–4, 11; 21:43–45). Yahweh rejected Israel for rebelling and sent Babylon to defeat and deport the nation (42:24–25; Jer 25:1–29). But now, in *compassion*, Yahweh will *choose* Israel again (Deut 7:6–8), execute "a second exodus," and *settle them in their own land*. *Aliens* (that is, non-Jews) will *unite with* them, aid them in their return (Ezra 1:1–4; 6:1–5), and become their slaves (45:13–17; 49:7, 22–23; 60:4–16; 61:5–7; Jer 30:16).

According to 14:3–21, after the Jewish exiles return home, they will take up a *taunt*, a mocking and satirical funeral lament, *against the king of Babylon*, Nabonidus, symbolizing all oppressive Babylonian rule. This taunt declares that: Yahweh has overthrown the king of Babylon (verse 5); the Babylonian king was cruel (verses 6, 17, 20); nations subject to him rejoice in his death, because now they can be at peace (verses 7–8); and rulers of other nations who preceded him in death come to meet him as he approaches Sheol, joyfully declaring that the world will remember them more favorably than Nabonidus, because of his ruthlessness (verses 9–21).

A tyrant who oppresses people (verse 4) recklessly diminishes the ecological system. Forests suffer. When the tyrant dies, trees *exult* because they can rest from mistreatment (verse 8).

Death levels all humans, demonstrating that all are *weak* (verse 10) despite their *pomp* (verse 11). Verses 12–14 apply portions of a Canaanite myth about the god Baal to Babylon's deceased king. Like the *Day Star* (NRSV), the planet Venus (the Canaanite deity *Athtar*), which attempts to seize supremacy from Elyon (*the Most High*), Nabonidus (representing all Babylonian kings) tries to usurp Yahweh's place as presider over the gathering of the gods *on the mount of assembly* (*the heights of Zaphon*; NRSV), Syria's Mount Casius in the north where the gods assembled in Ugaritic mythology. Babylon's

> **Cyrus's Conquest of Babylon**
> *Babylon gladly surrendered to Cyrus without resistance in 539 BCE* (Pritchard 315–16), *apparently owing to the unpopularity of the city's last king, Nabonidus. The city prospered until Seleucus I, Alexander the Great's successor, built Seleucia (end of fourth century BCE); then Babylon's citizens moved to Seleucia.*

> **The Death of Nabonidus**
> *Nations usually give their rulers honorable funerals and burials. Babylon's king is an exception because he destroyed his land and killed his people (verse 20a-c). Maggots and worms swarm over his body (verse 11c-d) as it lies on the ground for all passers-by to humiliate (verses 18–20c). In Isaiah 14, the Jewish remnant prays that this king will have no descendants to arise and repeat his brutalities (verses 20d–21). Yahweh will redeem a "remnant"* (NRSV) *of Judah (verses 1–2), will but sweep Babylon clean with the broom of destruction.*

king's sin is pride, reflected in his self-assessment: *I will ascend* (twice), *I will raise, I will sit, I will make myself* (verses 13–14). He assumes he is equal to or above God.

14:24–27 As in Isaiah 10:5–27b, here *the Lord of hosts* (NRSV) promises to execute a *plan* for Assyria. Having sent them to punish sinful Israel/Judah, Yahweh will next *stretch out his hand* to overthrow Assyria and expel them from the promised land, as when delivering Israel from Egypt (Exod 15:12; Deut 4:34; 5:15; Isa 5:25), removing the *yoke* and *burden* confining his faithful remnant's mobility (Isa 9:4; 10:27).

14:28–32 This oracle dates from *the year King Ahaz died* (verse 28; probably 715 BCE). Isaiah addresses Philistine *envoys* who come to Jerusalem to encourage Ahaz's successor, Hezekiah, to join a rebellion against Assyria (verse 32). Shalmaneser V, the *rod* or *root of that snake* (verse 29), died in 722 BCE. A usurper, Sargon II (721–705 BCE), claimed the Assyrian throne, causing internal strife in Assyria. Philistia and other western states celebrated, hoping to throw off Assyrian domination. Isaiah tells the Philistine envoys that this rejoicing is premature. *A viper* (verse 29), Sargon II, will come with his army, pictured as *smoke...from the north* (verse 31), and subject the western states to Assyria again. Isaiah counsels Hezekiah to reject the proposal to join this rebellion and to trust in Yahweh to provide *refuge* for the *poor, needy*, and *afflicted* in *Zion* (verses 30, 32), advice similar to that which he gave Ahaz when Rezin of Syria and Pekah of Israel threatened in 734 BCE (Isa 7:1–9). Apparently Hezekiah rejected this advice, as Sargon II says he invaded the western states and besieged Ashdod in Philistia because of an alliance between Philistia and Judah (711 BCE; Pritchard 287).

15:1–16:14 Isaiah 16:13–14 indicates that the description of Moab's devastation preserved in 15:1–16:12 was *in the past* (NRSV). The one who preserved this description (perhaps Isaiah or a later compiler) declares that *within three years* Moab will fall. At this point, a later prophet or author interjects earlier oral or written material in his work. There are striking similarities between Isaiah 15–16 and Jeremiah 48 (Isa 15:2c-7a parallels Jer 48:37a, 38, 34a, 31, 34b, 5, 34d, 36c; Isa 16:6–11 parallels Jer 48:29, 30b, 36a, b, 32c, b, a, d, 33, 36a, b), indicating borrowing from earlier statements concerning Moab. Isaiah 15–16 announces that Yahweh will overthrow Moab because of its pride (16:6), a major theme in Isaiah 13–23. Isaiah 15–16 contains four parts: the Moabites lament over their desperate condition (15:1–9); the Moabites seek help from Judah (16:1–5); Yahweh reluctantly rejects the Moabites' plea (16:6–12); Isaiah says the description of Moab's devastation in 15:1–16:12 will occur within three years (16:13–14).

Isaiah 15:1–9 describes how recently an enemy army has ravaged Moab *in a night* (verse 1), shedding much *blood* (verse 9), so that *her fugitives flee* (verse 5), carrying paltry possessions (verse 7); also, grievous drought devastated the land (verse 6; 16:8–10). Every Moabite city and village laments (verses 5, 8; 16:7, 11), practicing customary mourning rites: weeping (verses 2, 3, 5; 16:9), wailing (verses 2, 3, 8; 16:7), crying out (verses 4, 5, 8), shaving heads (verse 2; compare Job 1:20; Jer 16:6; Amos 8:10; Mic 1:16) and beards (verse 2; Jer 41:5), and wearing sackcloth (verse 3; Job 16:15; Amos 8:10). Yahweh himself is deeply touched by Moab's plight and cries out over her (verse 5; *I* in verse 9 indicates that Yahweh is the speaker throughout verses 1–9 as in 16:9, 11; Goldingay 109, 111). People rush to *temple* and *high places to weep* (verse 2) and pray (16:12). But Yahweh refuses to listen; he *will bring still more punishment on the fugitives*, or *the remnant* (NRSV), *of Moab* (verse 9; 16:12).

> **Moab**
> The Transjordanian kingdom of Moab was organized by Mesha (see 2 Kgs 3) in the ninth century BCE. He revolted against his Israelite overlord to establish an independent entity that lasted until it became part of the Assyrian and subsequent empires.

Moabite refugees temporarily stay in *Sela*, Edom's capital (verses 1–5). Their leaders advise them to *send lambs as tribute* (2 Kgs 3:4) by envoys to Judah's ruler in *Zion* (verse 1). These envoys should describe Moab's desperate circumstances: their *women* are helpless and homeless *at the fords of the Arnon* river, the boundary between Moab and Judah (verse 2). They should beg Judah: *Grant justice* (NRSV); *let the Moabite fugitives stay with you*; give them protection and asylum from their assailants in your land (verses 3–4b). The envoys should also reassure Judah that, when this crisis ends, a descendant of David *who in judging seeks justice and speeds the cause of righteousness* will reign over Judah (verses 4c-5).

Judah's ruler and his advisors (*we*, verse 6) reject the pleas and assurances of Moab's envoys as self-centered and self-serving, and therefore *false*.

Accordingly, Yahweh (*I*, verse 9; *my heart*, verse 11) decrees that Moab go on lamenting because its deplorable condition will continue (verses 7, 9) in spite of its fervent prayers for relief (verse 12). Yahweh's heart goes out to these grieving people (verses 9, 11), but their *overweening pride and conceit* (verse 6) demand continued suffering.

17:1–11 The setting of this oracle, like the one of chapter 7, is early in the Syro-Ephraimite war (734–732 BCE). Rezin of Aram (Syria) and Pekah of Ephraim (North Israel) allied to rebel against Tiglath-pileser III of Assyria and invited Ahaz of Judah to join them, but he refused. They marched toward Jerusalem to replace Ahaz with the son of Tabeel (Isa 7:6). Ahaz and Judah thought the best political strategy was to ally with Assyria, but Isaiah urged them to trust in Yahweh alone (Isa 7:7–9). Apparently, Isaiah delivered the message of 17:1–11, as he had in 7:1–9, to Ahaz and Judah, assuring them Yahweh would overthrow Aram and Ephraim and urging them to trust in Yahweh alone for deliverance. *In that day* (verses 4, 7, 9) divides this oracle into four parts.

Isaiah assures Judah that Assyria will reduce *Damascus*, Aram's capital, to *a heap of ruins* (on this expression, see Mic 1:6; 3:12), so that only animals will live there. As predicted, Tiglath-pileser III later conquers Damascus and carries its inhabitants into captivity to Kir (732 BCE; 2 Kgs 16:9).

Further, Isaiah assures Judah that northern Israel (called *Ephraim* in verse 3 and *Jacob* in verse 4) will experience defeat, describing their destruction with several metaphors, such as physical deterioration of the sick (verse 4), *a reaper* collecting *grain* (verse 5), and harvesters *gleaning olives* (verse 6). Tiglath-pileser III overthrew Israel's territory east of the Jordan (Gilead) and in the north, west of the Jordan (Galilee), carrying the survivors into captivity (732 BCE; 2 Kgs 15:29; Isa 9:1) and leaving only Samaria.

The destruction of Damascus and devastation of Galilee and Gilead will convince some northern Israelites to abandon their self-initiated, human-manufactured *Asherah poles* (symbols of the goddess Asherah, whom some ancient Israelites considered the consort of Yahweh) and *incense altars*, and return to *their Maker, the Holy One of Israel*.

Ephraim will desert its *strong cities* in the same way that *the Hivites* (Josh 9:1–2) *and the Amorites* (Gen 15:16, 21) (NRSV, following the Septuagint) deserted their fortified cities when the Israelites attacked them during the conquest of Canaan (verse 9). In verses 10–11, *you* is second feminine singular, thus referring to the nation of Ephraim or its capital, Samaria. The prophet denounces the northern Israelites for forgetting (forsaking) their *Rock*, God their protector (30:29; 44:8; Deut 32:4, 15; 1 Sam 2:2; Pss 18:2, 31) and engaging in foreign worship practices. Yahweh will bring such idolatrous practices to an end (Isa 2:8–9, 18–21).

17:12–14 The prophet pronounces a woe [Hebrew *hoy*] oracle (compare 5:8–23) against unnamed *nations* and *peoples* who are looting and plundering God's people (*us*). He compares the invaders with *the raging sea* and *the roaring of great* or *surging waters*, the simile Isaiah 8:7–8 uses to describe an attack of the Assyrians. In 17:12–14, the prophet declares that Yahweh will drive Assyria away *like chaff before the wind* and like *whirling dust before the storm* (NRSV). Apparently the setting is Sennacherib's siege of Jerusalem (701 BCE), when Yahweh's angel killed 185,000 Assyrian soldiers *in the evening, before the morning*—that is, in one night (Isa 37:36). *Plunder* translates Hebrew *bazaz*, recalling the symbolic name of Isaiah's son *Maher-Shalal-Hash-Baz* (Isa 8:3; 10:2, 6).

> **Illicit Worship Practices**
> Isaiah's audience practiced many religious rites that connected them to deities other than Yahweh. For example, they induced small plants to grow rapidly in pots or baskets in ritual gardens (Isa 1:29–31; 65:3), symbolizing the rising of the deity from the netherworld. This was a form of sympathetic magic guaranteeing bountiful crops and other blessings, a practice borrowed from Babylonian Tammuz worship (Ezek 8:14) and later incorporated into the Hellenistic Adonis cult.

18:1–7 Ethiopia controlled Egypt during the Twenty-fifth (Nubian) Dynasty (715–663 BCE). Twice during this period, western states, including Egypt under the Ethiopian Shabaka and Judah under Hezekiah, plotted to rebel against Assyria. First, in 713–711 BCE, Philistia, Judah, Egypt, and other nations rebelled against Sargon II, but he suppressed their efforts by routing Ashdod (Isa 14:28–32; 20). Some scholars think this is the historical setting for Isaiah 18 (Clements 163–64). Second, in 705–701 BCE, Babylon, Judah, Egypt, and other nations rebelled against Sennacherib. Sennacherib brought his Assyrian army to the west, overthrew Judah's forty-six fortified cities, and besieged Jerusalem. This seems to be the setting for Isaiah 18 (Childs 138).

The prophet begins by declaring *woe* [Hebrew *hoy*] against Ethiopian authorities who sent *envoys* to Jerusalem *by sea in papyrus boats* (verses 1–2b), apparently to negotiate an alliance with Judah (and perhaps other nations) to rebel against Assyria. He counsels these *messengers* to return home and abandon their mission (verse 2c-g). Then he summons *all ... people of the world* to watch for Yahweh's *banner* and listen for his *trumpet* (verse 3) as signals to execute his plan to overthrow the Assyrians by his own power, which should convince all nations that Yahweh alone is God.

Until the time is right, Yahweh will calmly observe human activities from his heavenly abode, like one watches motionless wisps of *shimmering heat* and *a cloud of dew* hang over a valley or hill on a windless day (verse 4), suggesting that Hezekiah and Judah do likewise. At the right moment, Yahweh will *cut off, cut down and take away* the Assyrians as a tree surgeon severs *shoots* and *spreading branches* from overgrown, cumbersome foliage, leaving the bare plants exposed to *birds of prey* and *wild animals* (verses 5–6). This prophecy was fulfilled when Yahweh's angel killed the Assyrian soldiers as they besieged Jerusalem (Isa 37:36). Yahweh's victory over the Assyrians will convince the Ethiopians that Yahweh alone is God, and they will bring *gifts ... to Mount Zion*, showing homage, submission, and reverence to *the Lord of hosts* (NRSV) who rules over all the earth (verse 7; Isa 45:14, 23).

19:1–20:6 While it is impossible to determine the historical setting of the oracles in Isaiah 19, Isaiah 20:1 dates chapter 20 to the year the Assyrians under Sargon II conquered Ashdod (711 BCE). These chapters contain three oracles concerning Egypt: soon Yahweh will punish Egypt (19:1–15); afterwards, Yahweh will bless Egypt (19:16–25); and, finally, Isaiah urges Hezekiah and his advisors not to trust in Egypt and Ethiopia for help against Assyria (20:1–6).

In 19:1–15, the prophet portrays Yahweh as the one who *rides on a swift cloud* (Deut 33:26; 2 Sam 22:11; Ps 68:4, 33), a common description of and title for Baal in the Ugaritic texts. Yahweh strikes terror into the *idols of Egypt* and all *the Egyptians* (verse 1).

Yahweh's coming will have extensive consequences for Egypt. First, it will affect national stability. Yahweh will *stir up Egyptian against Egyptian*, causing civil war and political unrest (verse 2), *bring their plans to nothing* (verses 3, 12), causing them to *consult* frantically *the idols, the spirits of the dead, the mediums*, and *the spiritists* to no avail (verse 3; 8:19), and then *hand* them *over to ... a cruel master, a fierce king* (verse 4).

Second, Yahweh's coming will cause a drought (verses 5–6), decimating four major industries in Egypt: farming (verse 7), fishing (verse 8), linen manufacturing (verse 9), and weaving (verse 10; NRSV).

Third, Yahweh's presence will expose the counterfeit wisdom of Egypt's political officials, counselors, wise men, and *leaders*, who are like *head or tail, palm branch or reed* (verse 15), also terms for Ephraim's leaders in Isaiah 9:14–15. They are *fools* (verses 11, 13), *give senseless advice* (verse 11), *are deceived*, *have led Egypt astray* (verse 13), and exhibit a *spirit of dizziness. They make Egypt stagger ... as a drunkard staggers around in his vomit* (verse 14), also a simile for Judah's prophets and priests in Isaiah 28:7–8.

> **Fine Linens**
> *Egypt was a major grower of flax for the production of linen. Since the land of Israel also grew flax suitable for manufacturing everyday clothing, the book of Isaiah must have in mind the trade in luxury textiles, in which Egypt was a significant player.*

Verses 16–25 abruptly shift from announcing destruction of Egypt to announcing Yahweh's delivery of that nation. Isaiah 19:16–25 contains five promises, each beginning with the phrase *in that day* and each amplifying the previous promise.

The first promise (verses 16–17) is that Yahweh's *uplifted hand* and *plan* (NRSV) and Judah's *land* will strike *fear* and *terror* into the hearts of the Egyptians. This sounds like the announcements of devastation in verses 1–15, but verse 22 may put it in a different light. As a surgeon must hurt a sick patient by operating in order to make the patient well, so Yahweh *strikes* in order to *heal*, not in order to destroy (compare 1:5–6; Jer 30:12–17).

The second promise (verse 18) states that *five cities in Egypt* will *swear allegiance* to *the Lord of hosts* (NRSV), Israel's God; and they will *speak the language of Canaan* (namely, Hebrew). This reflects the exilic or postexilic period, when Jews lived in Egypt (Jer 42–44) and converted some of their Egyptian neighbors to the worship of Yahweh.

The third promise (verses 19–22) declares that the Jews (perhaps along with their Egyptian proselytes to Yahweh) will set up an *altar* to Yahweh somewhere deep in Egypt and a *pillar* at some place on its border as a *sign and witness* that some in Egypt worship Yahweh. When enemies oppress Egypt, and the Egyptians cry out to Yahweh, Yahweh will send a *savior and defender* to *rescue* them, as he had rescued Israel from the Egyptians in the days of Moses (Exod 6:2–8; 14:21–31). Consequently, Egyptians will come to *know* Yahweh (NRSV). "The verb 'know'... does not mean to have information about, ... [but] to acknowledge fully and embrace as sovereign" (Brueggemann, *Isaiah 1–39*, 163). This will lead these Egyptians to *worship* Yahweh *with sacrifices and grain offerings* and to *make vows* to Yahweh and *keep* them (Deut 23:21–23). Yahweh will *strike*, then *heal*, the Egyptians, as a surgeon operates on a patient in order to heal that patient. When the Egyptians repent, Yahweh will answer their prayers and heal them.

The fourth promise (verse 23) is that Yahweh will make a *highway from Egypt to Assyria* (Isa 11:16; 35:8; 40:3–4 also use the highway metaphor), and the Egyptians and Assyrians will *worship* Yahweh *together*.

The fifth promise (verses 24–25) announces ecumenical fellowship between Yahweh's chosen people and *Egypt and Assyria*, symbolic of all nations. Yahweh calls Egypt *my people*, Assyria *my handiwork*, and Israel *my inheritance*, making all humanity equal before God (Amos 9:7).

> **God's Blessing to the Nations**
> *Yahweh's purpose in choosing a people was not to exalt them above the rest of humankind (exclusivism), but to use them as his instrument to convert the rest of the world to himself (inclusivism; Isa 2:2–4). He told Abraham: through your offspring all nations on earth will be blessed (Gen 22:18; 12:1–3; 26:3–5; 28:13–14; Ps 72:17; Jer 4:1–2). Isaiah 19:24–25 repeats that promise, using the term "bless" three times.*

Chapter 20 relates a symbolic act of Isaiah. He appears in public, *stripped and barefoot for three years*, in obedience to Yahweh, before Sargon II sends his army to crush the western states, including Philistia (*the people who live on this coast*, verse 6), *Egypt*, and *Ethiopia* (NRSV), for rebelling against Assyria (verse 1; 711 BCE). This act indicates that the Assyrians will defeat the Egyptians and Ethiopians and lead them into exile *with buttocks bared* (verse 4), bringing *shame* on Egypt and those who *trusted* in *Ethiopia* (NRSV) and *boasted in* or *relied on Egypt* (verses 5–6), statements designed to dissuade Hezekiah and his advisors from allying with Egypt against Assyria.

21:1–10 This oracle's composer addresses God's people *crushed on the threshing floor* (verse 10), that is, oppressed in Babylonian exile, announcing that Babylon will soon fall (verse 9), ending the Israelites' captivity and actuating hope. Like 13:1–14:23, the setting is the end of the Babylonian exile (540 BCE). Yahweh or his spokesperson summons *Elam* and *Media* (equivalent to the Persian Empire under Cyrus the Great; Isa 13:17) to *attack* Babylon and *end all the groaning she caused* (verse 2; Isa 44:24–45:7). Arguments defending the setting of this oracle as Sennacherib's overthrow of Merodach-baladan II of Babylon in 700 BCE are unconvincing; some scholars suggest that the oracle originated in 700 BCE, and a later prophet reapplied it to the situation in 540 BCE (Childs 148–53).

Yahweh shows the prophet a *vision* (verse 2). *An invader*, *Elam* and *Media* (verse 2), approaches like *whirlwinds sweeping through the southland* (verse 1; Jer 4:11–13) to attack *Babylon* (verse 9). Thoughts of intense suffering by Babylon overwhelm the prophet, like Yahweh's anguished empathy for Moab's misery (Isa 15:5; 16:9, 11). *Pangs seize* him, *like those of a woman in labor* (verses 3–4; Ps 48:6; Isa 13:8; Jer 4:31; 6:24). He sees Babylon's army and *officers* sharing a banquet, oblivious to imminent danger (verse 5; see Dan 5); then he sees a *lookout* observing approaching *chariots*, *horses*, *riders* invading Babylon. The lookout shouts dolefully: *Babylon has fallen!* (verses 6–9). Isaiah concludes the oracle by assuring Jewish exiles in Babylon that he is repeating to them what he has *heard from the Lord of hosts, the God of Israel* (verse 10).

21:11–12 Edom (*Dumah* is a misspelling or wordplay), or *Seir* (Num 24:18; Judg 5:4; 2 Chron 25:14), allied with Babylon to plunder Jerusalem in 587 BCE (Obad 10–14; Ps 137). Now it suffers oppression by the Persians under Cyrus the Great, who recently captured Babylon (539 BCE). Edomites ask the prophet, *the watchman* (Ezek 3:16–21): *What is left of the night?* How long will Edom's suffering continue? The prophet replies that it will end soon, but return later.

21:13–17 The NIV and NRSV interpret this oracle differently. The NIV omits the word *for* [Hebrew *ky*] beginning verse 16, separating verses 13–15 from verses 16–17. In verses 13–15, according to the NIV, the prophet urges *Dedanites* and inhabitants of *Tema* to provide *water* and *food* for unnamed *fugitives*, which an unnamed army had recently defeated in battle. In verses 16–17, the prophet tells an unnamed audience that Yahweh informed him that *within one year*, *Kedar* will be decimated. However, the NRSV retains the word *for* at the beginning of verse 16. According to this translation, the prophet admonishes the *inhabitants ... of Tema* to supply *water and bread* to the *Dedanites* who recently fled to *the scrub of the desert plain* after *Kedar's warriors* defeated them in battle; Yahweh declares that *within a year, all the glory of Kedar will come to an end*. The NRSV more correctly reflects the Masoretic text.

> **Dedan, Tema & Kedar**
> *Dedan is a city in Arabia about 300 miles southeast of the Dead Sea; Tema, a region in Arabia about 250 miles southeast of the Dead Sea (Job 6:19; Jer 49:7–8; Ezek 25:13); and Kedar, a region in northern Arabia (Isa 60:7; Jer 2:10; Ezek 27:21). It is impossible to know the dates and occasions of the battle and of Kedar's defeat mentioned here.*

22:1–14 Like Amos 1–2, Isaiah 13–23 contains oracles concerning Ephraim (17:1–11) and Judah (22:1–14, 15–25) alongside oracles concerning other nations. God considers all nations sinful and yet objects of love and care (Pss 47; 67; Isa 2:1–5; 19:16–25; Amos 9:7).

Isaiah 22:1–14 relates an oracle Isaiah initially delivered when the Assyrian army lifted the siege around Jerusalem to join Sennacherib at Libnah to fight Tirhakah and the Egyptians approaching from the south (701 BCE; 2 Kgs 19:8–9; Isa 37:8–9); the author of the book of Isaiah preserved and repeated this oracle because its message spoke afresh to the people of Jerusalem when the Babylonian army under Nebuchadnezzar II lifted the siege around Jerusalem to fight Pharaoh Hophra and the Egyptians also approaching from the south (588 BCE; Jer 34:8–22; 37:5–10).

Yahweh sent the Assyrians to punish his people for their sins (verses 5–8a; Isa 10:5–6), expecting them to repent, using customary mourning rites (verse 12; Isa 15:2–3, 5, 8; 16:7, 9–11). Instead of trusting in *the One who planned* the Assyrian invasion (Yahweh; verse 11c-d), Judah's *leaders* and soldiers *fled* before the invaders in fear (verses 2c-3) or relied on their military strategies, including *weapons* stored in *the Palace of the Forest* (verse 8b-c; 1 Kgs 7:2–5; 10:17), diverting the water supply inside the city walls (verses 9c-d, 11a-b; Isa 7:3; 36:2), and tearing down houses inside the city to *strengthen the wall* where the Assyrians had made *many breaches* (verses 9a-b, 10; Jer 33:4). And when the Assyrians lifted the siege, instead of expressing deep remorse for their sins, the people of Jerusalem went up on the *housetops, full of shoutings* (NRSV), *tumult, revelry, joy,* festive *eating* and *drinking* (verses 1–2b, 13), inappropriate responses to Yahweh's plan and actions (Ps 51:17; Joel 2:12–17). Contrariwise, the prophet weeps bitterly over Judah's spiritual bankruptcy (verse 4) and declares the reaction Yahweh revealed to him: *Till your dying day this sin will not be atoned for* (verse 14), since the people's behavior demonstrated they had apostatized so far from Yahweh they would never return (see Luke 13:34; Rom 1:24, 26, 28).

22:15–25 A comparison of Isaiah 22:15–25 with 36:3, 22 and 37:2 suggests that Isaiah delivered the message in 22:15–25 to Shebna shortly before Sennacherib's invasion of Judah in 701 BCE. At that time, Shebna was *steward* of the royal estate (verse 15); by the time the Assyrians besieged Jerusalem, Hezekiah replaced him with Eliakim and demoted him to *secretary* (Isa 36:3, 22; 37:2). Isaiah 22:15–25 appropriately follows another oracle initially delivered during the Assyrian siege of Jerusalem (22:1–14).

Shebna held the office of steward under Hezekiah shortly before Sennacherib's invasion. Isaiah rebukes Shebna for arrogance, which led him to abuse his office by misdirecting government funds to have a *grave* hewn out for himself in a wealthy section of Jerusalem (verse 16) and using *splendid chariots* for travel (verse 18). Isaiah says that Yahweh will *throw* him into *a large country* (perhaps have him carried into Assyria as a prisoner), where he will die as a *disgrace* to his master's (Hezekiah's) house (verses 17–18), thus removing him from his *office* (verse 19).

> **The Royal Steward**
> *Solomon established the political office of* steward *as one who is in charge of the palace (literally "over the house"; verse 15), sometimes called* father *(verse 21; Gen 45:8; Isa 9:6) or he who wears on his shoulder the key to the house of David (verse 22), terms that describe one who governs the public and private possessions and functions of the king (Gen 41:41–45; 1 Kgs 4:6; 16:9; 2 Kgs 10:5; 2 Chron 19:11).*

Yahweh will *hand* Shebna's *authority over to Eliakim* (verses 20–23). However, slowly but surely, Eliakim will commit nepotism, putting members of *his* own *family* in high governmental positions, which will ultimately lead to his own downfall (verses 24–25).

23:1–18 The prophet announces that Yahweh (verses 8–9, 11–12) will punish Phoenicia (that is, *Sidon* [verses 2, 4, 12] and *Tyre* [verses 5, 8, 13, 15, 17]), the *inhabitants of the coast* [NRSV; verses 2, 6), for their arrogance (verses 7, 9, 12). Yahweh will *bring low* and *humble* a region that is influential, powerful, and wealthy (verses 8–9).

> **Phoenicia**
> *The cities on the coast of what is now Lebanon were major ports connecting the Near East with the central and western Mediterranean. Tyre, in particular, served as the major point of commerce for the entire world of ancient Israel.*

Scholars suggest several historical backgrounds for this oracle. Verse 13 indicates that the setting is the Babylonian siege of Tyre under Nebuchadnezzar II (585–573 BCE; see Jer 27:3–7; Ezek 26–28), who devastated the mainland portion of Tyre (Childs 165–67). Alexander the Great later destroyed its island portion (332 BCE).

Tyre's fall adversely affects Phoenicia's merchant trading with *Tarshish*, that is, Tartessos in southern Spain (verses 1, 6, 10, 14), as well as with *Egypt* (verses 3, 5, 10), *Cyprus* (verses 1, 12), and other Mediterranean ports. But after *seventy years* (a normal human lifetime [Ps 90:10] but also the period of Babylonian captivity [Jer 25:11–12]), Yahweh will restore Tyre so that she will *ply her trade with all the kingdoms on the face of the earth as a prostitute* now aged and *forgotten* (verses 15–17); however, now *her profit and her earnings* will help sustain Yahweh's people returned from exile (verse 18; Isa 18:7).

YAHWEH'S PUNISHMENT OF THE WICKED & REDEMPTION OF THE RIGHTEOUS · 24:1–27:13

The meaning of Isaiah 24–27 is difficult. Hebrew *'erets* can mean "earth," "land," or "ground." The identity of the *city* (sometimes wicked; sometimes righteous) varies from passage to passage. Different voices speak to different audiences with different messages and purposes. The overall thrust of these chapters suggests their author was a Jew living in the last half of the fifth century BCE in Judah, addressing a small community of fellow believers who felt overwhelmed by their Persian overlords, in order to inspire them to trust in Yahweh as creator, sustainer, and controller of heaven and earth. A God who can control the universe can also deliver a struggling faith community. Isaiah 24–27 falls into six sections: Yahweh will punish the wicked of both heaven and earth (24:1–23); Yahweh will save earth's penitent (25:1–12); the faithful remnant prays that Yahweh will deliver his people (26:1–27:1); Yahweh will revive his vineyard (27:2–6); Yahweh will restore North Israel (27:7–11); and Yahweh will gather faithful exiles (27:12–13).

24:1–23 The prophet declares that Yahweh *is about to lay waste the earth* and all its inhabitants (verses 1–3) because they have *broken the everlasting covenant* (verses 5, 20c) Yahweh made with Noah and thus with the whole earth (Gen 9:1–17); even *the heavens languish* (verse 4; NRSV). Yahweh will remove all joy and pleasure from the earth (verses 6–13), desolating *the ruined city* (verses 10, 12), that is, all worldly cities: "every concentration of human power that functions effectively but is rooted in disobedience and defiance of Yahweh" (Brueggemann, *Isaiah 1–39*, 192). Voices rise *from the west*, and the prophet summons peoples *in the east* to join them in praising Yahweh for punishing the wicked (verses 14–16b); but the prophet cannot join this chorus, because earth's sins and devastation disturb him too much (verse 16c-f). No one can escape Yahweh's punishment. God will gather the wicked of heaven and earth, *like prisoners bound in a dungeon* (Mic 4:11–13), and punish them *after many days* (verses 17–23b). Then *the Lord of hosts* (NRSV) *will reign on Mount Zion*, and *before his elders ... manifest his glory* (verse 23c-e; NRSV) as they strive to lead the small community of returned exiles *in Jerusalem* in faithful service to Yahweh.

> **The Wicked in Heaven**
> *The Bible often speaks of wicked forces "in heaven," that is, forces of larger than ordinary strength and scope. Examples of such forces can include the prince of Persia (Dan 10:13, 20), the prince of Greece (Dan 10:20), "the cosmic powers of this present darkness," "the spiritual forces of evil in the heavenly places" (compare Eph 6:12; NRSV), among others.*

25:1–12 Yahweh punishes to remove corruption – to refine, not to annihilate. After punishing heaven's and earth's wicked (24:1–23), God will save earth's penitent. The faithful community or its representative (*I*, verse 1), including *all peoples* (verses 3, 6–7), *praise* Yahweh for punishing *the fortified town* (verse 2; 24:10, 12) – that is, all self-centered cities. Yahweh *planned* (14:26–27; 19:12, 17; 22:11; 23:8–9) this *long ago* (verse 1). Such mighty deeds will lead people from all nations to *honor* and *revere* that God (verse 3) who has been *a refuge for the poor* and *needy* from *the ruthless* (verses 4–5).

Yahweh will prepare a sumptuous banquet *on this mountain* (that is, Zion; verses 6–7) for *all peoples* (2:2–4; 19:23–25), and then will *destroy* the *shroud* or *sheet* of death and mourning which covers all peoples, *swallow up death forever*, and *wipe away the tears from all faces*. The remnant of the nations will praise Yahweh for saving those who *trusted in him* (verses 6–10a).

Simultaneously, Yahweh will *trample down* Moab, "a figure for all detested powers that resist Yahweh and abuse Yahweh's people" (Brueggemann, *Isaiah 1–39*, 201), for its *pride* (16:6; 13:11, 19; 14:11–14; 23:9, 12), a fate from which it cannot escape, no matter how hard it tries (verses 10b-12).

26:1–27:1 Orally uttered, *in that day* in 26:1, 27:1, 2, 12, 13 indicates to hearers that Isaiah 24–27 envisions the same future period. When Yahweh punishes heaven's and earth's wicked and restores earth's penitent (chapters 24–25), the restored (*we*: 26:1; *trust* in 26:4 is plural) will sing songs of praise (26:1–6), exalt and commit themselves to prayer (26:7–19), and wait for the punishment of the wicked (26:20–27:1).

According to 26:1–6, in their song, *the righteous nation ... that keeps faith* (verse 2) or *trusts* (verses 3–4) in Yahweh will declare that it has *a strong city* in *Judah*, namely Jerusalem (verse 1; 24:23; 25:6–7), which shall enjoy *peace* (verse 3) because Yahweh protects it. Conversely, Yahweh will *humble the lofty city* (verses 5–6), *the city of chaos* (24:10, 12; NRSV), and *the fortified town* (25:2) – that is, all worldly cities.

In their prayer (26:7–19), the restored extol Yahweh for disciplining them because they had *not brought salvation to the earth* through example and teaching (verses 16–18), vindicating *the righteous* (verse 7), that is, the penitent, and thereby expanding *the nation* (verses 15, 19). They will applaud Yahweh for their accomplishments (verse 12) and for overthrowing their oppressors (verse 14), expressing *desire* to serve and honor Yahweh alone (verses 8–9b, 13), and beseeching Yahweh to *consume* those who persist in wickedness (verses 10–11).

Verses 9c-11 declare that *the people of the world learn righteousness* by observing Yahweh's *judgments* on the wicked (Ps 65:5–8; Amos 3:9–11). Yahweh's genuine servants never take credit for their accomplishments but recognize that their achievements are Yahweh's doing (verse 12). The metaphor of the pregnant woman experiencing labor (verses 17–18) to denote penitence and grief occurs often in the Old Testament (13:8; Jer 4:31; 6:24). Verse 19 does not announce physical resurrection of individuals after death, but the re-enlivening, reviving, and restoring of penitent Jewish exiles to their homeland to resume faithful service to Yahweh (Ezek 37:1–14). Yahweh will rejuvenate his dejected people *like the dew* rejuvenates parched grass (Mic 5:7).

Accordingly, the prophet admonishes Yahweh's faithful remnant to wait for Yahweh to finish destroying evil persons and the power of evil itself, the mythological monster *Leviathan* (compare Ps 74:12–14).

27:2–6 The prophet summons hearers (plural) to *sing about Yahweh's vineyard* (verse 2). Yahweh promises to reverse the punishment of the vineyard announced in 5:1–7. Previously Yahweh removed the hedge and broke down the wall around his vineyard, abandoning it to vagabonds (5:5), but now God will *watch over* and *guard it day and night* to prevent its harm (27:3). Reversing the previous command to the clouds not to rain upon it (5:6), God will now *water it continually* (27:3). Previously angry with the vineyard (5:5–6), God now will *not* be *angry* (27:4). Previously he caused it to be overgrown with briers and thorns (5:6); now if his vineyard produces *briers and thorns*, he will go to battle against it, hoping it will seek protection and make peace (27:4–5; NRSV). Ultimately, the penitent remnant of *Jacob will take root, bud and blossom and fill all the world with fruit* (27:6),

> **The Leviathan**
> *Leviathan*, or the sea monster, functions primarily as a symbol of chaos and terror in the Bible. Yet this fearsome creature also falls under the control of Yahweh. Thus the reader need not fear it at all, but can express gratitude and awe before God, who defends the human race from its worst nightmares.

suggesting efforts by true Israelites to convert other nations to Yahweh (2:2–4; 19:23–25; 45:22–23).

27:7–11 The meaning of Isaiah 27:7–11 is uncertain. *Jacob* may mean northern Israel. *The fortified city* (verse 10) apparently refers to Samaria, which must destroy its *altar stones*, *Asherah poles*, and *incense altars* (typical elements of northern Israelite worship; see 2 Kgs 17:5–18) to *atone for* its *guilt* so that Yahweh can *remove* its *sin* (verse 9). Otherwise, Yahweh will have *no compassion on* them (verse 11). Yahweh punished northern Israel, but less severely than he did the Assyrians (verses 7–8; compare 10:16–19; 14:24–27).

27:12–13 Yahweh will *thresh* the exiles (verse 8), separating wheat (true Israelites) from chaff (counterfeit Israelites), cause a *great trumpet* to *sound*, summoning the people to a great feast, and *gather* penitent, faithful exiles from *Assyria* and *Egypt to worship the Lord on the holy mountain in Jerusalem*.

YAHWEH PUNISHES & RESTORES THE PEOPLE THROUGH INVASION & EXILE · 28:1–39:8

In chapters 28–33, the prophet directs the first five *woes* (28; 29:1–14, 15–24; 30; 31–32) against Hezekiah and Judah for allying with Egypt against Assyria, and the last *woe* against Assyria (33). In each case, beyond the punishment, Yahweh promises redemption for the faithful remnant.

28:1–29 This chapter has three parts: Yahweh will punish *Ephraim*, or northern Israel, and save *the remnant* (verses 1–6); Yahweh will punish Judah for allying with Egypt but deliver those who *trust* in him (verses 7–22); and Yahweh punishes to restore, not to destroy (verses 23–29).

Probably speaking to Judean leaders in about 703 BCE, verses 1–6 repeat part of an oracle delivered originally to northern Israelite leaders about 724 BCE. Yahweh will punish *Ephraim* because of the *pride* of the *wreath* resting on its head, that is, its capital, Samaria (Isa 7:9). Punishment especially falls on Ephraim's self-indulgent leaders, who are *gluttons* (NRSV), *bloated with rich food*, and *drunkards* (verses 1–4). Yahweh will send *one who is powerful and strong* (verse 2), namely, Assyria (Isa 8:7) under Shalmaneser V (2 Kgs 17:1–6), *like a storm* (verse 2) and like one eating *a first-ripe fig* (verse 4; Isa 17:4–6). Judean leaders would have approved of this message. The next two verses add that Yahweh will be *a beautiful wreath for the remnant of his people* (verse 5) and *a spirit of justice* to its rulers (verse 6).

Suddenly, in verses 7–22, Isaiah turns on Judean *priests and prophets*, accusing *these also* of being drunkards like their northern counterparts (verses 7–8). A spokesman for these religious leaders angrily asks his associates: *Who is he* (that is, Isaiah) *trying to teach*? Does he think we are *children* recently *weaned* that he addresses us so? He acts like one trying to teach little children the alphabet.

> **Teaching Children the Alphabet**
> *Verse 10 plays on two letters of the Hebrew alphabet*, tsadhe and qoph, *apparently mimicking the chants of schoolchildren* (Clements 228; Brueggemann, Isaiah 1–39, 223; verses 9–10).

Isaiah immediately throws his opponents' words in their teeth. Yahweh will indeed *speak to this people* (Judah), not in Hebrew, but *with foreign lips and strange tongues*, that is the Assyrian dialect of Akkadian. Since the Judeans have rejected *rest* based on trust in Yahweh (30:15), Yahweh will teach them the ABCs of his response to sin – that is, punishment by invaders who speak a foreign language (verses 11–13).

Isaiah denounces those who *rule* Yahweh's people for making *a covenant with death* (alliance with Egypt; 30:1–7; 31:1–3) to protect themselves from Assyrian invaders, because Yahweh will send *an overwhelming*

> **The Structure of Isaiah**
> *Three concepts hold together Isaiah 28–39: Yahweh punishes the people to purify them, not to destroy them; Yahweh works in parallel ways through Sennacherib's invasion and the Babylonian exile; the people must trust Yahweh, not in foreign allies and everything associated with them. These chapters fall into three parts: six "woe" sections (chapters 28–33); Yahweh will punish the nations, especially Edom, and restore Israel's faithful remnant (chapters 34–35); a narrative concerning Sennacherib's invasion and siege of Jerusalem and Yahweh's deliverance of the city (chapters 36–37); and Hezekiah's illness and recovery (chapters 38–39). The author combines materials from various earlier times and circumstances and inserts some of his own, but "the crucial exegetical question remains ... whether one can in the end discern any element of coherence in the rendering of the chapters in their final form"* (Childs 200).

scourge, a storm with much *hail* and rain – that is, Assyria – to punish the rebellious people (verses 14–15, 17c-19; 8:7–8). Yahweh offers a safe haven from this storm, using the metaphor of a building. Its *foundation* is *a precious cornerstone*, bearing the inscription: *One who trusts will not panic* (NRSV; 7:9; 30:15; 31:1). The *measuring line* and *plumb line* for constructing its walls and roof are *justice* and *righteousness* (verses 16–17b; 1:21, 27; 5:7, 16; 32:1, 16; 33:5; 59:9, 11, 14). Egypt gives no protection; it is like a *bed* that is *too short* and a *blanket* that is *too narrow* (verse 20). Yahweh, who defeated the Philistines before the Israelites led by David at *Mount Perazim* (2 Sam 5:17–25), and who defeated the king of Jerusalem and his Canaanite allies before the Israelites led by Joshua in the *Valley of Gibeon*, where the sun stood still (Josh 10:1–15), will do a *strange work* (contrast *strange tongues*, verse 11) by defeating the Judeans before the Assyrians. Nothing, including alliance with Egypt, can change the *destruction* Yahweh has *decreed against the whole land* (verses 21–22).

In verses 23–29, the words *Listen, hear, pay attention* (plural) demonstrate that the composer of the book of Isaiah intended for professional performers or readers to present it orally to gathered worship audiences, and that verses 23–29 proclaim the core message of this composition. The speaker relates two similar parables in wisdom style. In the first, Yahweh is like a *farmer* who *plows soil* to prepare it for *planting* seed at strategic places to get maximum yield (verses 24–26). In the second, Yahweh is like a skilled processor who prepares each foodstuff for consumption using the procedure suitable to that grain: beating *caraway with a rod* and *cummin with a stick*, and grinding *grain to make bread* (verses 27–29). Yahweh's judgment is violent, like plowing and processing, but necessary to produce proper spiritual growth in people's hearts and lives, like a farmer produces good crops, or a processor, good consumer products. Accordingly, the fundamental message of the book of Isaiah is that Yahweh punishes sinners (including Israel), using means suitable to their nature and temperament, seeking not to destroy, but to refine for spiritual maturity, productivity, and divine blessing.

> **Agricultural Imagery**
>
> The Bible often uses agricultural imagery, which was familiar to ancient audiences of farmers. Since farming both destroys and creates, and involves both hard work and joyful productivity, it supplies numerous opportunities for spiritual and moral reflection.

29:1–14 The second woe contains two parts: Yahweh will send the Assyrians to besiege Jerusalem but will ultimately deliver the city (verses 1–8); and the prophet denounces Jerusalem's prophets for being blind to Yahweh's ways and Jerusalem's citizens for counterfeit worship (verses 9–14).

In verses 1–8, Yahweh announces a siege of *Ariel*, the altar hearth, which refers to the altar of burnt offering before the temple (Ezek 43:15–16) in Jerusalem. Jerusalem had previously been besieged by David when he captured it from the Jebusites (2 Sam 5:6–9). Now, a second seige will take place: Sennacherib's siege of Jerusalem (701 BCE). But just when the Assyrians think Jerusalem will fall, *as when a hungry man dreams that he is eating, but he awakens, and his hunger remains, suddenly, in an instant, the Lord of hosts* (NRSV) will deliver *Mount Zion* (37:36).

In the conclusion of this oracle (verses 9–14), the prophet condemns Jerusalem's *prophets*, or *seers*, for their inability to understand the *vision* Yahweh revealed concerning Jerusalem, because they are spiritually *blind, drunk*, and asleep. The text also criticizes Jerusalem's inhabitants for "follow[ing] the rules and regulations of prescribed piety ... lacking in ... serious commitment of the heart" (Brueggemann, *Isaiah 1–39*, 235). At this point in Isaiah 28–32, this woe oracle may denounce Jerusalem's leaders and people for sending to Egypt for help rather than trusting in Yahweh.

29:15–24 The third woe oracle contains a short section of condemnation (verses 15–16) and a long section of assurance (verses 17–24).

In verses 15–16, Isaiah reproves Hezekiah and his counselors for allying with Egypt to protect Judah from Assyria (30:1–7; 31:1–3). They try to *hide* their *plan* from Yahweh by keeping their intentions from Isaiah. How naïve of *what is formed* (the clay pot represents human beings) to think that he *who formed it* (*the potter*, that is, Yahweh: 45:9; 64:8; Jer 18:1–6) is unaware of its activities!

In verses 17–24, Yahweh proclaims hope for the remnant of penitent believers *in a very short time* (verse 5): the *deaf, blind, humble*, and *needy*, whom Judah's *ruthless, mockers*, and *all who have an eye for evil* oppress by giving *false testimony* against them in court. Yahweh sent the Assyrians against Judah to punish it for its rampant injustice against the poor and afflicted (10:1–6). Soon, Assyria's work will end: Judean oppressors will fall, and innocent victims will enjoy vindication, leading them to *rejoice in*, *acknowledge the holiness of*, and *stand in awe of the Holy One of Israel* (or *Jacob*). Then those trying to serve Yahweh who are *wayward in spirit* and *complain* against Yahweh because Assyria invaded the land will *gain understanding*, or *accept instruction*, by observing how Yahweh works (28:23–29).

30:1–33 In this fourth woe oracle, the prophet denounces Hezekiah and his advisors for allying with Egypt against invading Assyrians under Sennacherib in 701 BCE (verses 1–17). He then assures Yahweh's true followers that Judah will survive the Assyrians (verses 18–33). Those who trust in Yahweh have no need for Egypt.

> **Israel & Egypt in Isaiah's Day**
> During Isaiah's time, Egypt fell under the rule of the Cushites, from northern Sudan. Their Twenty-fifth Dynasty competed with Assyria for domination of Palestine, as well. Judah, as a minor state between two superpowers, tried to negotiate its own survival. Isaiah criticized this political gamesmanship as both unwise and unfaithful to Yahweh.

When Isaiah delivers this oracle, Hezekiah has already sent envoys to Egypt carrying tribute to persuade Pharaoh Shebitku to ally with Judah against Assyrian invaders (verses 1–2); the envoys have traveled through dangerous terrain to avoid detection (verse 6); some negotiate *in Zoan*, while others *have arrived in Hanes* for consultations (verse 4). Such efforts contradict Yahweh's *plans* (verse 1). Egypt's powerlessness (verses 5, 7) suggests the symbolic name: *Rahab the Do-Nothing* (verse 7). *Pharaoh's protection*, symbolized as *Egypt's shade*, will bring *only shame and disgrace* to Judah (verses 3, 5).

Hezekiah and his advisors ignore Yahweh's message. Yahweh instructs Isaiah to *write it on a tablet for them* so that when Egypt fails and Yahweh delivers Judah's remnant, Isaiah's hearers cannot deny that Yahweh warned them, but they refused *to listen* (verses 8–11). Because they *rejected this message* and *depended on* Egypt, they will *collapse like a high wall* and *break in pieces like pottery* (verses 12–14). Yahweh offered them *salvation* and *strength* through *repentance*, *rest*, *quietness*, and *trust* in him, "the heart of Isaiah's message of trust in God through a quiet, unshakeable faith" (Childs 226), but they preferred to trust in *horses*, representing military might (Pss 20:7; 33:17; 147:10–11).

By sending Assyria to devastate Judah for its sins (10:5–6), Yahweh gave them *the bread of adversity and the water of affliction* (verse 20) and *inflicted* them with *bruises* and *wounds* (verse 26; 1:5–6; Jer 30:12–15), as a *Teacher* (verse 20; Job 35:10–11; 36:21–22) attempting to remove their sin (Isa 6:5–7) and humble them to repentance (verse 22). Yahweh's severe blows were meant *to be gracious* and *to show mercy* so his faithful ones would *wait for* (or hope) in him (verses 18–19).

The future of God's people is bright. Yahweh will *send rain*, increase crops, multiply livestock, and heal the battered people (verses 23–26). Further, Yahweh will come as *a consuming fire* and *a rushing torrent*, *with cloudburst, thunderstorm and hail* (verses 28, 30) to *shatter Assyria* (verse 31) and overthrow her *king* (verse 33), Sennacherib, referring to the Lord's slaughter of 185,000 Assyrian soldiers in one night to end Jerusalem's siege (37:36), causing joyous celebration on *the mountain of the Lord* (verses 29, 32). Jews returning from Babylonian exile in the last half of the fifth century BCE would have readily understood the relevance of Isaiah 30's message to their own situation.

31:1–32:20 The fifth woe oracle contains two parts: it is futile for Hezekiah and his advisors to seek Egypt's protection, because Yahweh will deliver the people from Assyria and establish a king and rulers to govern them with justice and righteousness (31:1–32:8); and Yahweh will devastate Jerusalem, with its complacent women, until the divine spirit instills justice and righteousness in the people (32:9–20).

In 31:1–32:8, Isaiah denounces Hezekiah and his associates because they *go down to Egypt for help*, *rely on horses*, and *trust in … chariots* rather than relying on Yahweh (31:1–3; 30:1–7). Yahweh will protect Jerusalem from Assyria *as a lion* protects his slaughtered prey from shepherds, and *like birds hovering overhead* protect their young on the nest (Luke 13:34); accordingly, Isaiah urges Yahweh's people to return (31:4–7). Further, Yahweh will overthrow the Assyrians: *a sword*, *not of mortals*, *will devour them* (31:8–9; 30:31–33; 37:36).

Then Yahweh will establish a new government in Judah, a *king* (Hezekiah after he repented for relying on Egypt and sought Yahweh's help [37:8–20]) and *rulers* who will maintain *righteousness* and *justice* (5:7,

16; 9:7; 28:17; 59:9, 14), providing protection and relief to the oppressed (verses 1–2). The wise leader of Yahweh's people will *see*, *hear*, *know*, *understand*, *be fluent and clear*, and *make noble plans* with regard to Yahweh and his fellow human beings (verses 3–5, 8), shaming *the fool* whose *mind is busy with evil* to afflict the defenseless, depriving *the hungry* of food and *the thirsty* of *water*, and destroying *the poor* and *needy with lies* in court (verses 6–7; 1:16–17, 23; 10:1–4).

> **The "Good Leader"**
> The Bible speaks often of the goals and character traits of good leaders. All biblical traditions agree that a leader's primary responsibility is the protection of the vulnerable, particularly of widows, orphans, the poor, and resident aliens. Leaders who use their power for self-aggrandizement or the building of military might come under divine judgment (see Deut 17:14–20; Ps 101; and many texts in the prophets).

In 32:9–20, the prophet announces affliction on the rich, powerful, *complacent* Judean women *who feel secure*, who receive and maintain their enviable position in society at the expense of the oppressed and mistreated, along with the securities on which they depend: good *harvest* (verses 10, 12–13b), *houses of merriment* (verse 13c), *fortress, citadel and watchtower* (verse 14; 3:16–4:1; Amos 4:1–3).

This affliction will continue *until a spirit* (or power, Luke 1:17) *from on high is poured out* (NRSV) on Yahweh's (*my*) *people* (verse 18), transforming *the desert* into *a fertile field* (verse 15), producing abundant crops and bountiful grazing for *oxen and donkeys* (verse 20), nullifying *the forest* and *the city* as exponents of wealth and power and corruption (verse 19), and promoting *justice* and *righteousness* between people as harbingers of *peace*, *quietness*, and *trust* (NRSV; verses 16–18).

33:1–24 The sixth woe oracle is a liturgy designed for oral presentation by six trained speakers, or singers, before a worshiping community. The first orator (verse 1) notifies Assyria (*destroyer*) that when Yahweh finishes using it to punish his people, he will *destroy* it (10:5–19). The second spokesperson (verses 2–6), representing the faith community (*we, us, our*), prays that Yahweh will give the people strength and protection daily (verse 2), and be *the stability of your* (the community's) *times* (NRSV), *a rich store of salvation and wisdom and knowledge* (verse 6a-b), as formerly (verses 3–5 refer to Yahweh's mighty acts in the past [NRSV], not the future [contrary to NIV]), filling *Zion with justice and righteousness* (verse 5b; 5:16; 9:7; 32:1, 16). *The fear of the Lord* means genuine reverence for Yahweh (as opposed to false reverence [see 29:13]) and connects Yahweh's people with this *treasure* (verse 6c).

The third speaker (verses 7–9) describes an extensive drought in northern Israel – *Lebanon, Sharon, Bashan, Carmel* (or "the whole land") – as Yahweh's punishment of Judean aristocrats for rejecting *envoys of peace* and breaking a *treaty* (that is, not honoring business agreements) and for defrauding the poor (5:22–23; 10:1–4; 32:6–7).

The fourth voice (verses 10–12) is Yahweh's through the prophet (*says the Lord*), reacting to the previous speaker's description of Judah's dismal situation. Yahweh will *arise, be exalted, be lifted up* (2:11, 17, 19, 21; 31:2). Judah's leaders' corruption indicates they have no spiritual substance but *conceive chaff* and *give birth to straw*, so that their own *breath is a fire that consumes* them, as well as *the peoples* (5:24; 30:27–30).

The fifth orator (verses 13–16) is also Yahweh, now addressing worshipers seeking entrance into the Jerusalem temple. These verses contain an "entrance liturgy," or "Torah liturgy," similar to Psalms 15 and 24. First, Yahweh summons those who are *far away* and those who are *near* spiritually (29:13) to *hear* of Yahweh's deeds and acknowledge them, as worship leaders proclaim them before the assembly (Pss 66:5–20; 105:1–6). Then *sinners* and the *godless* who have come with penitent hearts ask how they can survive Yahweh's *devouring fire* (verses 11–12).

> **Yahweh's Requirements for the Righteous**
> Yahweh enumerates six qualities one must possess to survive. One must: walk righteously; speak what is right (Ps 15:2); reject gain from extortion (Exod 22:25; Lev 25:35–37); decline to accept bribes (1:23; 5:23; compare Deut 16:19; Ps 15:5; Prov 15:27); refuse to participate in plots of murder or in schemes to kill or oppress others (Prov 1:10–19); and avoid contemplating evil (Mic 2:1–2). Such people will enjoy Yahweh's security and provisions.

The sixth spokesperson (verses 17–24) announces that Yahweh will revive and restore the destitute people. God will enthrone a righteous *king* (verse 17; 32:1), perhaps the penitent Hezekiah (37:1–7, 14–32), Josiah (2 Kgs 22–23), or an ideal descendant of David (Jer 33:14–26). Yahweh will also remove the Assyrian invaders (verses 18–19; 28:11; 30:31–33; 31:8–9), make Jerusalem a *peaceful* and secure *abode* (verses 20–21), be the people's *judge* (or deliverer; Judg 3:9–10, 15; 11:27), *ruler* (NRSV) and *king* (verse 22; 6:1, 5). God will give the remnant the enemies' *spoils* [Hebrew *shalal*] and *plunder* [Hebrew *bazezu*] (Isaiah here again makes wordplay on the name *Maher-Shalal-Hash-Baz* [see also 8:1, 3; 10:2, 6]) in spite of the remnant's weakness (verse 23), and *forgive those who dwell* in *Zion* of their *sins* (verse 24). *Our* (verses 20, 21, 22) and *us* (verse 22) refer to the prophet and his comrades. *Your* (verses 17, 18, 20, 23), *you* (verses 19), and *look* (verse 20; masculine singular) are the whole assembly addressed as one individual.

34:1–35:10 The setting of Isaiah 34–35 is near the end of the Babylonian exile (540–536 BCE) or later; this is firstly evident because 34:5–17 announces the destruction of Edom, who helped Babylon overthrow Jerusalem in 587 BCE, using language like Obadiah 1–16; Jeremiah 49:7–22; Ezekiel 25:12–14; Psalm 137:7; and secondly, because 35:3–4 and 8–10 proclaim that Judean exiles in Babylon will return to Zion, which occurred under Zerubbabel and Joshua in 536 BCE (Ezra 1:1–2:2), Ezra in 458 BCE (Ezra 7:1–10), and Nehemiah in 445 and 433 BCE (Neh 2:1–16; 13:4–9). Such Scriptures use the highway metaphor, which is characteristic of passages comparing the return from Babylon (the "second exodus") with the exodus from Egypt (Isa 11:15–16; 40:3–5; 43:14–21). Blenkinsopp (*Isaiah 1–39*, 450, 456) details striking contrasts between Isaiah 34 and 35, demonstrating the coherence of these chapters. Isaiah 34–35 announce that Yahweh will punish the wicked of both heaven and earth (especially Edom [34:1–17]) and restore Zion's faithful remnant (35:1–10).

In 34:1–4, the prophet declares that Yahweh is *angry with all nations*, *peoples*, *earth*, *world*, and *all the host of heaven* (that is, rebellious angels) (verses 4–5; 24:21–23; Dan 10:13, 20–21; Matt 25:41; Eph 6:12; Rev 12:7–9) and *will give them over to slaughter*.

Specifically, Yahweh will destroy *Edom* (verses 5, 6, 9, 11; 63:1–6) as a priest slaughters a lamb for *sacrifice* (verses 6–7; Zeph 1:7–8; Jer 46:10). Yahweh has a *day of vengeance* and *retribution* (verse 8; 61:2; 63:4; Jer 46:10) against Edom, bringing complete *desolation* so that only *thorns*, *nettles*, *brambles* (verse 13a-b; 7:23–25; 9:18; 10:17), wild animals, and birds can live there (verses 9–15). Human beings can inhabit it no longer, but will give it the symbolic name *No Kingdom There* (NRSV, verse 12). For confirmation, hearers may consult *the book of the Lord* (NRSV), where Yahweh decreed that these creatures would inhabit Edom (verses 16–17).

In bold contrast to Isaiah 34's description of the desolation Yahweh will bring on Edom, chapter 35 announces Yahweh's redemption for Zion's faithful remnant. This redemption is presented in an alternating pattern which describes Yahweh as transforming the wilderness (A) and Yahweh as restoring the weak, exiled, faithful devotees of Zion into a fertile land (B):

A verses 1–2
B verses 3–6b
A' verses 6c-7
B' verses 8–10

According to 35:1–2, Yahweh will change the *desert*, *parched land*, or *wilderness* into the *glory* or *splendor* of Yahweh manifested in *Lebanon, Carmel and Sharon* (33:9), producing great joy. In verses 3–6b, the prophet encourages despondent Judean exiles in Babylon (plural imperatives): *strengthen* your *feeble hands*, *steady* your *knees that give way* (Heb 12:12–13), and *say to* the *fearful*, *Be strong, do not fear*; *your God will come ... to save you*; he further promises that Yahweh will give sight to *the blind*, hearing to *the deaf*, agility to *the lame*, and speech to *the dumb*.

According to verses 6c-7, Yahweh will cause abundant *water* to *gush forth* in the *wilderness*, or *desert*, just as the Israelites received water from the rock (Exod 17:1–7; Num 20:1–13), and magnificent plants will grow there (41:17–20).

Verses 8–10 depict Yahweh preparing a *highway* in the wilderness, *the Way of Holiness*, not for *the unclean* (6:5; 52:1, 11) or *wicked fools*, but *only the redeemed*, the *ransomed of the Lord*, Judean exiles who have genuinely repented and turned to Yahweh (1:27–28; 57:14–15). They will return to *Zion* with great *joy*, free from threatening dangers on the road (11:11–16; 40:3–5; 51:11; 65:17–25).

36:1–39:8 Isaiah 36–39 parallel 2 Kings 18–20 and 2 Chronicles 32, omitting some sections (notably 2 Kgs 18:14–16), adding others (significantly, Isa 38:9–20), and changing the order of others (Isa 38:21–22 appears after verse 20, but belongs after

ISAIAH

> **Critical Issues in Isaiah 36–39**
>
> Space allows only brief discussion of the critical issues posed by Isaiah 36–39. First, how are 2 Kings 18–20 and Isaiah 36–39 related? Since both accounts are theologically relevant in their present positions in these two books, the authors probably adapted a common tradition, either oral or written, to their own respective compositions (Childs 260–62).
>
> Second, how many sources lie behind the account of Sennacherib's invasion in 2 Kings 18–19 and Isaiah 36–37? John Bright thinks these chapters present one account of two invasions: one in 701 BCE and one in 688 BCE (Bright 298–309). Most scholars believe these chapters combine three accounts: A (2 Kgs 18:14–16), B1 (2 Kgs 18:17–19:9a = Isa 36:1–37:9a), and B2 (2 Kgs 19:9b-35 = Isa 37:9b-36).
>
> Another possibility is that Isaiah 36–37 reports one Assyrian siege of Jerusalem, which the Assyrians lifted briefly to fight against the Egyptians.
>
> Third, why are Isaiah chapters 36–39 in their present position in the book? Most scholars agree they function as the bridge from the Assyrian to the Babylonian periods (chapters 40–55) in the book of Isaiah.

verse 6, as 2 Kings 20 and common sense demonstrate). Isaiah 36–39 breaks down as follows: Assyria overthrows Judah's fortified cities and besieges Jerusalem (36:1–37:7); the Assyrians withdraw to Libnah to encounter the Egyptians (37:8–9a); the Assyrians resume the siege of Jerusalem; Yahweh's angel kills 185,000 Assyrian soldiers (37:9b-38); Yahweh heals Hezekiah (38); and Judah and Babylon ally against Assyria (39).

36:1–37:7 According to 36:1, in 701 BCE *Sennacherib king of Assyria* devastated the forty-six *fortified cities of Judah* (Pritchard 287–88). According to verses 2–21, Sennacherib sent his *field commander with a large army from Lachish* near the Mediterranean to Jerusalem to negotiate with Hezekiah's officials: *Eliakim the palace administrator, Shebna the secretary, and Joah the recorder*. The Assyrian field commander chides Hezekiah and Judah for having *confidence* in *strategy and military strength* (such as *chariots and horsemen, Egypt*, and *Yahweh*, who, according to the field commander, are no match for Assyria). In fact, he asserts, *The Lord himself told me to march against this country and destroy it*, which Isaiah 10:6 confirms (Pharaoh Neco of Egypt made a similar claim to Josiah, 2 Chron 35:21).

> **The Punishment of the Gods**
> Ancient Near Eastern nations believed the gods of a city or nation gave that city or nation to invading armies to punish their followers for disloyalty or sin. Thus Babylon's priests gave Babylon to Cyrus without a battle.

Hezekiah's officials request that the field commander speak in *Aramaic*, fearing he is tearing down the morale of Judean soldiers on Jerusalem's walls by speaking in Hebrew (verses 2–11).

The field commander, however, responds loudly in Hebrew, admonishing the Judean soldiers not to *trust in* Hezekiah or Yahweh, boasting that no *god of any nation* had successfully resisted *the king of Assyria*, including *Samaria* (which allegedly served Yahweh), concluding: *how then can the Lord deliver Jerusalem from my hand?* The soldiers remain silent in obedience to Hezekiah's instruction (verses 12–21).

Hezekiah's officials report the field commander's words. Hezekiah laments, tearing his clothes (Jer 36:24; Ezra 9:3) and wearing *sackcloth* (2 Sam 3:31; 1 Kgs 21:27), as do his officials. Hezekiah sends his officials to *Isaiah*, asking him to *pray for the remnant that still survives* so that Yahweh will deliver them from the Assyrians. Isaiah encourages Hezekiah with the words: *do not be afraid* (7:4; 8:12–13), because Sennacherib *will return to his own country* and die there by *the sword* (verse 38; 31:8).

Another report occurs in 37:8–38: while the Assyrian field commander and his army besiege Jerusalem, the Egyptians under *Tirhakah* move north to fight against the Assyrians. Sennacherib learns of this and withdraws from *Lachish* north to *Libnah*. The Assyrian field commander lifts the siege of Jerusalem so his soldiers may join Sennacherib at Libnah to fight against the Egyptians (22:1–14).

When Sennacherib learns that Tirhakah and the Egyptians are advancing from the south to fight against his forces, he sends a *letter* (verse 14) to Hezekiah, threatening to destroy the Judeans if they do not surrender. He alleges that Yahweh and his king Hezekiah have no more chance to resist *the king of Assyria* than *the gods of* other *nations* and their kings whom the Assyrians overthrew earlier.

Hezekiah takes the letter to the Jerusalem temple and asks Yahweh to deliver Jerusalem, *so that all kingdoms on earth may know* the truth of Israel's faith. The primary reason Yahweh works mightily for the people is to convince the nations that he alone is God. Hezekiah extols Yahweh as Lord of hosts, king, creator (verse 16), the only God (verses 16, 20), *the living God* (verse 17). He acknowledges that Assyria's kings overthrew other nations and their gods but affirms that the gods they overthrew are *not gods*, since they are *fashioned by human hands* (2:8, 20; 44:9–20).

According to verses 21–35, *Isaiah sends Yahweh's word against Sennacherib* to *Hezekiah*, responding to Sennacherib's letter. The response includes several elements: *Zion, or Jerusalem, despises and mocks* Sennacherib (verse 22); Sennacherib has boasted *in pride* and *insolence* (verses 23, 29) of his victories over *foreign lands*, but the real reason for his triumphs is that Yahweh, *the Holy One of Israel, brought to pass* events *planned long ago* (verses 23–27); and, finally, because of Sennacherib's arrogance, Yahweh will *make* him *return by the way* he *came* (verses 28–29), leading him home like captors lead prisoners into exile (Amos 4:2–3; Blenkinsopp, *Isaiah 1–39*, 477) or "the way a hunter treats a wild ox on the way to putting it in the royal zoo" (Goldingay 212; see Ezek 19:1–4).

Yahweh's *sign* to Hezekiah that this will occur (7:14–16; 8:4, 18) is that, three years hence, Judean agriculture will return to normal, and *out of Jerusalem will come a remnant* (7:3; 10:20–22), due to *the zeal of the Lord of hosts* (NRSV; verses 30–32). Yahweh assures Hezekiah and the Judeans that Sennacherib *will not enter this city* (Jerusalem), but *by the way that he came he will return*. Yahweh will *defend* and *save* Jerusalem (30:31–33; 31:5) for his sake and *for the sake of David* (verses 33–35; 29:1–8;

> **Sennacherib's Invasion**
> *The story of Sennacherib's invasion closes with three events that validate Isaiah's message: the angel of the Lord puts to death 185,000 Assyrian soldiers besieging Jerusalem (29:6; 31:8); the Assyrians return to Nineveh and do not invade Judah again; twenty years later (681 BCE), two of Sennacherib's sons murder him, and Esarhaddon his son becomes king of Assyria (Ezra 4:2).*

see 1 Kgs 11:13; 15:4; 2 Kgs 8:19; Ps 78:68–72).

Following 2 Kings 20:1–11, it seems best to rearrange Isaiah 38 as verses 1–6, 21–22, 7–20. This chapter reports Hezekiah's illness, Yahweh's cure, and Hezekiah's thanksgiving. These events occurred before Sennacherib's siege of Jerusalem in 701 BCE (chapters 36–37), which verse 6 anticipates, probably during 705–703 BCE.

In verse 1, Yahweh smites Hezekiah with a fatal boil (verse 21) as punishment for his pride (verse 17; 2 Chron 32:24–26); Isaiah declares that the king will die. When Isaiah leaves, Hezekiah prays that Yahweh will spare him, weeping bitterly. Yahweh sends Isaiah back to Hezekiah (2 Kgs 20:4 says that Yahweh apprehended the prophet *before Isaiah had left the middle court* of the palace) with Yahweh's message: *I have heard your prayer and seen your tears*; *I will add fifteen years to your life* (Hezekiah died in 687 BCE), and *I will deliver you and this city from ... the king of Assyria* (verses 2–6).

Isaiah tells those attending Hezekiah to apply *a poultice of figs* to the boil to promote recovery. Hezekiah asks what *sign* Yahweh will give that he will recover (7:14–16; 37:30–32). Isaiah says Yahweh *will make the shadow cast by the sun go back the ten steps it has gone down on the stairway of Ahaz*. By lengthening the day, Yahweh symbolically assures Hezekiah that he will lengthen his life (verses 21–22, 7–8). The text also emphasizes the contrast between Hezekiah's faithfulness in seeking a sign and his father Ahaz's stubborn refusal to do so (see 7:10–17).

Hezekiah's prayer song (verses 9–20), thanking Yahweh for healing, falls into two parts. First, Hezekiah describes his despondent feelings when he was near death. He lamented that he would die *in the prime of ... life* (verse 10). No more would he commune with *the Lord* or *mankind* (verse 11). His illness arrested his life so abruptly that he could hardly believe or bear it (verse 12). But Yahweh was the one afflicting him to humble him, causing great pain which he could hardly endure. In his distress, he cried out: *O Lord, come to my aid!* (verses 13–15). Second, Hezekiah thanks Yahweh for answering his prayer: *Oh, restore me to health and make me live!* (NRSV; verse 16). He acknowledges that he *suffered such anguish* for his own good. But Yahweh forgave him and spared his life (verse 17). Therefore, he will tell the next generation as well as his fellow-believers *in the temple of the Lord* what Yahweh did for him (verses 18–20).

In 39:1–8, Merodach-baladan II (Marduk-apla-Iddina II) learns of Hezekiah's *illness and recovery*, and sends *envoys with letters and a gift*, "ostensibly to inquire about his health, but probably to encourage his rebellion against Assyria" (Tucker 304).

Hezekiah haughtily shows them all *his treasures* (verses 1–2). Isaiah questions Hezekiah concerning the identity of his visitors and transactions between them; Hezekiah responds (verses 3–4).

Isaiah rebukes Hezekiah for allying with Babylon, declaring that all Judah's treasures *will be carried off to Babylon*, and some of Hezekiah's direct descendants *will be taken away, and…will become eunuchs in the palace of the king of Babylon*, portending the carrying off of Jehoiachin, 10,000 citizens of Jerusalem, and Judah's treasures to Babylon by Nebuchadnezzar II in 597 BCE (2 Kgs 24:8–17; Jer 29:1–2; Ezek 19:5–8). Hezekiah accepts Isaiah's message, selfishly comforting himself that its realization will not affect him, since he will die in peace.

> **Parallels in Isaiah**
> *The book of Isaiah teems with parallels. As Yahweh delivered Judah from Assyrian siege* (30:31–33; 31:4–5, 8; 37:36–38), *so will Judah escape Babylonian exile* (40:1–11; 48:20–21; 52:7–12). *Yahweh sent Assyria* (10:5–6) *and Babylon* (40:2) *to punish Judah for its sins. Assyria destroyed Judah's fortified cities* (36:1); *Babylon destroyed the cities of Judah, Jerusalem, and the temple* (44:26–28). *As Babylon rose up against Assyria* (39:1–8), *Cyrus and Medo-Persia will rise up against Babylon* (41:2–4, 25–27; 44:28–45:3; 45:13). *Isaiah's author(s) theologically connect chapters 1–39 and 40–55 (or 40–66).*

YAHWEH'S PROMISE TO RETURN JUDAH'S REMNANT TO JERUSALEM · 40:1–55:13

Approximately 160 years separate the setting of Isaiah 1–39 (742–701 BCE) from that of Isaiah 40–55 (about 540 BCE), during which time disciples of Isaiah and/or advocates of his messages preserved, deleted, modified, rearranged, and expanded them in chapters 1–39 orally for application in new situations; later, the composer/s of chapters 40–55 attached their oracles to chapters 1–39. Many earlier and some contemporary scholars see great incoherence between these two sections (Blenkinsopp, *Isaiah 40–55*, 41–55), while several contemporary scholars find coherence throughout the book (Seitz, "Isaiah 40–66," 309–21, 327–30). This commentary follows the latter approach.

40:1–11 Four voices are evident in verses 1–11, consistent with the notion that "in antiquity all writing was meant to be heard, to be read out loud, and therefore writers would be drawn to use phenomena characteristic of oral delivery" (Blenkinsopp, *Isaiah 40–55*, 64). The sixth century BCE exilic prophet (first voice) proclaims Yahweh's word (*says your God*) to his associates (*comfort, your, speak, proclaim* are masculine plural): *Comfort my people* addresses *Jerusalem*, assuring them they have stayed long enough in exile to pay for *all* their *sins*, which led Yahweh to send them into exile (Lam 1:2–5, 8, 12–14, 17–18, 22). *Jerusalem* may mean exiles from Jerusalem in Babylon, or it may refer to the the uninhabited city itself.

In verses 3–5, an angelic member of the heavenly council (second *voice*) encourages his fellow angels (in the masculine plural) to *prepare in the desert a highway for our God*, as forerunners prepare a road for a victorious king's journey home, for Yahweh will bring the redeemed, transformed people back to Jerusalem from Babylon (35:8–10) as he lead the people to the promised land from Egypt (Deut 4:37–38; Ps 78:51–55). This mighty defeat of Babylon and restoration of the exiles will make clear Yahweh's *glory* to *all mankind*, convincing them that Yahweh alone is God.

In verses 6–8, another angel (third *voice*) instructs the prophet (referred to as *I*): *Cry out* (singular) that *all men* (the arrogant Babylonians; Whybray 51) *are like grass* that thrives briefly, then *withers*. In bold contrast, *the word of our God* (Yahweh's assurance that he will restore his redeemed exiles to Jerusalem) *stands forever*.

In verses 9–11, the sixth century BCE spokesperson of Isaiah 40–55 (fourth voice) summons *Zion*, calling *Jerusalem* to be Yahweh's *herald of good tidings* (NRSV) to *the towns of Judah*, announcing that Yahweh is coming from Babylon to Jerusalem as a victorious king, bringing *his reward*, or *recompense* (spoils; redeemed exiles), with him; *like a shepherd* ("shepherd" symbolizes king; see, for example, 2 Sam 5:2; Ps 78:70–72), he *tends, carries, leads* his flock on safe paths to good pasture.

40:12–31 Hoping to convince Judean exiles in Babylon around 540 BCE to trust in Yahweh, the prophet emphasizes Yahweh's incomparability to all creation, using rhetorical questions (verses 12–14, 18–19, 21, 25–28) like *To whom…will you liken God?* (verses 18, 25), expecting the reply "no one."

In verses 12–14, Yahweh constructs *waters, heavens, earth, mountains, hills* (in other words, the universe) according to predetermined dimensions (compare Job 38:4–7); no one, including Babylonian gods, *directed* (NRSV), *instructed*, *enlightened*, *taught*, or *showed* him.

According to verses 15–20, *the nations*, including Babylon, *are like a drop from* (NRSV) *a bucket*, *dust on the scales*, *nothing*, *worthless*, *less than nothing* compared with Yahweh. One cannot *compare* Yahweh with persons or things, so one cannot symbolize Yahweh with an *image* or *idol* (Deut 4:15–20), which people must nail to a solid surface so it *will not topple*, and carry from place to place (Jer 10:3–5).

> **"There is No God but Yahweh"**
> *Isaiah 40 engages in interreligious polemic. Against Babylonian claims that Marduk created the world and thus sustains the power structure of their empire, Israel's prophet speaks of Yahweh as creator and the nations as insignificant and temporary. He then describes the foreign gods as mere fetishes, objects without power, feeling, or meaning. This chapter is thus the first in the Bible to deny the very existence of gods other than Yahweh, and it illustrates a major turning point in biblical religion.*

According to verses 20–26, one cannot *compare* Yahweh with persons or things, because Yahweh *created* everything and constantly sustains *the earth*, *its people*, *the heavens*, and *the starry host* by *his great power and mighty strength* (Neh 9:6; Ps 104:1–4, 10–30; Job 36:26–37:24; compare Heb 1:2–3). He *sits enthroned* as king above the earth, bringing its *princes to naught* and its *rulers to nothing*; before him, its *people are like grasshoppers*.

At last, in verses 27–31 the spokesperson or persons of verses 12–26 addresses his audience specifically: *Jacob* (that is, *Israel*) in Babylonian exile (verse 27), the *faint*, *weary* (verses 28–31), and despondent, and the heartless (Ezek 37:11). His message is that Yahweh has not *disregarded* the people; *the everlasting God*, *the Creator of the ends of the earth*, who never becomes *tired or weary*, *will renew* the *strength* of *those who hope* in him, empowering them to *walk*, *run*, and *soar*.

41:1–42:17 In this speech, Yahweh (*I*, *my*, *me* throughout) addresses the nations and their gods (41:1–7, 21–29; 42:10–17) and Judean exiles in Babylon (41:8–20; 42:1–9). On the one hand, Yahweh challenges the nations and their gods to themselves be able to identify events they predicted and caused to happen (41:4, 21–29; 42:14–17); on the other hand, the prophet assures Judean exiles of Yahweh's presence in their oppression and impending deliverance from their bondage (41:8–20; 42:1–9, 16).

In 41:1–7, summoning *the nations* to *come forward and speak*, Yahweh asks rhetorically: *Who has stirred up one from the east* (Cyrus) and subdued *nations* and *kings*? It is Yahweh. This strikes *fear* in the hearts of all who see it; they hire a *craftsman* to make an *idol* to protect them; they *nail* it to a solid surface *so it will not topple* (40:20).

Verses 8–20 portray Yahweh encouraging *Israel*, or *Jacob*, the *servant*, whom he *chose* by delivering it from Egyptian bondage: *Do not fear* (verses 10, 13, 14), *for I am with you* to *strengthen* and *help* you. Israel's opponents are *as nothing* (40:17). By Yahweh's power, Israel will *thresh* and *crush* them. Yahweh will supply abundant resources to *the poor and needy* to make their journey to Jerusalem enjoyable.

In verses 21–29, Yahweh challenges the nations' gods to announce *what is going to happen*, *what the future holds* and cause it to occur, as proof they are gods. They cannot do this, because they are *less than nothing* (37:18–20; 40:17). In contrast, Yahweh has *stirred up one from the north* (Cyrus; verse 2), who *treads on rulers* of many nations, performing what he announced earlier (verse 27). One should conclude that gods other than Yahweh *are all false*.

In 42:1–9, Yahweh turns back to present (verses 1–4) and addresses (verses 5–9) his *servant*, Israel (not Cyrus, contrary to the claims of Blenkinsopp, *Isaiah 40–55*, 210–212; 41:8–9). Yahweh has *chosen* Israel to *bring justice to the nations*, *on earth*, faithfully, gently, quietly, and unobtrusively (verses 1–4), "the reordering of social life and social power so that the weak (widows and orphans) may live a life of dignity, security, and well-being" (Brueggemann, *Isaiah 40–66*, 42).

He who created the heavens and *spread out the earth* and sustains people who live on it, who announces events before they occur and makes them happen, assures Israel he will protect it and *make* it *a light to the Gentiles* to *open blind eyes* and to *free* prisoners (verses 5–9; 2:2–4; 49:8–12).

Verses 10–17 summon *the ends of the earth* to *sing* to Yahweh *a new song* (Pss 96:1; 98:1), to *give glory to* him, to *proclaim his praise*, because he will *march out like a warrior* (Exod 15:3) and *triumph over his enemies* (such as Babylon) (verses 10–13). Yahweh has *kept silent for a long time*, but now he will come, devastate

Babylon as one drains *pools*, and *lead the blind* (the Judean exiles) (verses 18–19; 43:8) *by ways they have not known*, home to Jerusalem, turning *darkness into light before them*; at the same time, he will reject *those who trust in idols* (verses 14–17).

42:18–44:8 As Yahweh's messenger, the sixth century BCE prophet among Judean exiles in Babylon (43:14) rebukes his comrades for not understanding (42:25) the message Yahweh tried to communicate to his people by sending them into exile: Yahweh was punishing them for sin (42:24) to bring them to repentance. He compares their spiritual obtuseness with being *deaf* and *blind* (42:18–19). This message falls into six units: the prophet chides Judean exiles for not understanding Yahweh's message taught by the exile (42:18–25); Yahweh admonishes penitent exiles to *fear not*, because Yahweh will restore his people safely to Judah (43:1–7); Yahweh summons the nations and Judean exiles to testify that their respective gods are true (43:8–13); the prophet declares that Yahweh will overthrow Babylon and prepare a way for penitent Judeans to return to Jerusalem (43:14–21); Yahweh resolves to destroy Judean exiles for persistent sins (43:22–28); and, finally, Yahweh admonishes penitent exiles, *do not be afraid*, because God will multiply their offspring in order to unite all the nations in worship (44:1–8).

> **The Decree of Cyrus**
> Cyrus of Persia decreed that deported populations within the former Babylonian Empire could return to their homelands. The so-called "Cyrus Cylinder," a barrel-shaped clay text written in cuneiform, gives one version of his decree. Ezra 1:2–5 gives another.

In 42:18–25, Yahweh accuses his *servant/messenger* Israel (41:8–9) of being spiritually *deaf* and *blind* (verses 18–20), although Yahweh *handed Jacob* (*Israel*) *over* to Babylonian *plunderers* [Hebrew *bozezim*, recalling Isaiah's son's name, *Maher-Shalal-Hash-Baz*, 8:3] to bring them to their senses (verses 22, 24–25) because they *sinned* by failing to *obey his law* (verses 21, 22, 24). Although the Babylonians *consumed* them, *they did not understand* (verse 25).

In 43:1–7, the prophet announces Yahweh's message to the people Yahweh *created* and *formed* (verses 1, 7) at the exodus, penitent exiles who understood the message of the exile: *fear not, for I am with you* (verses 1–2, 5). They may *pass through waters, rivers, fire*, but Yahweh will protect them. The exiles' deliverance is costly, necessitating Yahweh giving a *ransom* of *Egypt, Ethiopia* (NRSV), and *Seba in exchange for them* (verse 3), since he considers them *precious and honored* and loves them (verse 4). Yahweh will reassemble Israelites throughout Babylon, and return them to Judah (verses 5–6).

In 43:8–13, while generally the Judean exiles are spiritually *blind* and *deaf*, Yahweh's exiling his people opened the eyes and ears of a few (the remnant). Yahweh summons them and *all the nations* to appear for a court trial or international debate concerning the identity of the true God. The summons says, *Bring forth the people* who are *blind, yet have eyes*, who are *deaf, yet have ears"* (NRSV). The nations are *witnesses* to their gods (verse 9), and penitent Judean exiles are *witnesses* (verse 10) to Yahweh (verses 10, 12). A god is true if he or she *declared* or *foretold* events and caused them to happen (verses 9, 12; 41:21–24). Only Yahweh can satisfy such a condition, and therefore only Yahweh is God (verses 10–13).

> **Yehud**
> Under the Persian Empire, some Israelites returned to Judah, now called Yehud. There they took on the name Yehudim, or "Jews." (And after this period, we speak of Jews, whereas before the Exile, the proper title was Israelites.) However, some remained in Babylonia and elsewhere. The Jewish community in Iraq lasted until the 1949, when it immigrated en masse to the new state of Israel.

In 43:14–21, the sixth century BCE exilic prophet announces that Yahweh, *the Holy One of Israel*, will *send* Cyrus and the Medo-Persians to overthrow *Babylon*, preparing a *way* (verse 19; 11:15–16; 35:8–10; 40:3–5; 42:16) for penitent Judean exiles to return to their homeland from Babylon to Jerusalem. Their migration will relive the key events of Israel's history, such as the deliverance from the Egyptians at the Sea of Reeds (verses 16–17) and the provision of *water in the desert* (verse 20). Yahweh will once again supply traveling Israelites with water from a rock, just as at Meribah and Massah (Exod 17:1–7; Num 20:1–13; Ps 78:15–16). Yahweh urges penitent Judean exiles *not* to *dwell on the past* (the exodus) but to observe the *new thing* Yahweh is doing by returning exiles to Jerusalem and to *praise* him for it (verses 18–21).

Although Yahweh had not *burdened* or *wearied* the people with *demands* for sacrifices, they *burdened* and *wearied* him with their *sins* (1:14; 7:13), like their *first father*, Jacob (43:22–28; 58:14; Deut 26:5). Yahweh repeatedly forgave their sins, but they persisted in rebelling against him, so he *delivered Jacob to utter destruction* (verse 28b, NRSV) through the Babylonian exile.

Isaiah 44:1–8 proclaims Yahweh *Israel's King, Redeemer, the Lord of hosts* (NRSV, verse 6), *the first and … the last* (verse 6), the only *Rock* (verse 8), who alone is *God* (verses 6, 8), as demonstrated by predicting events and making them happen (verses 7–8; 41:22–23, 26–27). The prophet again admonishes penitent Judean exiles: *do not be afraid* (verses 2, 8; 41:10, 14; 43:1). The fact that Yahweh created (verse 2) and *chose* (verses 1–2) *Jacob* (*Israel* or *Jeshurun*) (compare Deut 32:15; 33:5, 26) to be a *servant* (verses 1–2; 41:8–9; 42:19) and *witness* (verse 8; 43:10, 12) proves to the world that Yahweh alone is God. Thus the main example of executing a publicly declared plan is the creation and redemption of Israel, both originally and in a new time.

Yahweh next promises faithful Judean exiles to *pour out* his *spirit* (NRSV; principle of life), or *blessing*, on their *offspring*, causing them to grow and flourish (verses 3–4; Ezek 37:1–14), like *water* causes plants to spring up and thrive on *thirsty land*. The cycle of promise and fulfillment will continue in the future, and this reality will lead people from other nations to devote themselves to Yahweh (verse 5; 45:14, 20–23; Whybray 95; Baltzer 187).

> **Idol Making**
>
> *In the ancient Near East, the manufacture of statues of deities was a high art. After the artists finished their work, priests would wash out the statue's mouth, offer numerous prayers and incantations – often in a garden – and then move the statue to its proper place in a temple. The whole process could require an extended time, and was regarded as a highly spiritual occurrence. The book of Isaiah points out, however, that no created thing can possibly symbolize the sovereign Lord of the universe, and therefore to worship the creation instead of the creator makes little sense.*

44:9–20 The prophet contrasts the only God (verses 6, 8) with idols. Yahweh created and sustains all who make idols (verses 9, 10, 15, 17, 19), such as *craftsmen* (verse 11), *the blacksmith* (verse 12), and the *carpenter* (verse 13), who get hungry and thirsty (verses 12, 16, 19). They shape, cast, and *forge* iron (verses 10, 12, 13) and *wood* (verses 14–17, 19) into an idol *in the form of man* (verse 13) and cover it with gold and silver (40:18–20; 41:6–7). Artisans can do only so much with wood: burn it for warmth or cooking (verses 15–16, 19) and *fashion a god* out of it (verses 15, 17, 19), *which can profit* them *nothing* (verse 10). The maker is superior to what he/she makes. Thus one who makes an idol, then *bows down* and *worships* it (verses 15, 17, 19) and *prays* to it to *save* him/her (verse 17), is *blind* (verses 9, 18), *ignorant* (verse 9), *deluded* (verse 20), and *knows* and *understands nothing* (verses 18–19).

44:21–45:25 Resuming the declaration that Yahweh alone is God *and there is no other* (45:5, 6, 14, 18, 21, 22) from 44:6, 8, the prophet announces in 44:21–45:25 that Yahweh will send Cyrus, king of Medo-Persia, to overthrow Babylon (44:28; 45:1–3) and deliver the Judean exiles (45:13), convincing the nations that he alone is God and converting them (45:20–23).

Through the prophet, Yahweh, creator of everything (verse 24) and confounder of *false prophets*, *diviners*, and *the wise* (verse 25), addresses *Jacob*, or *Israel*, his servant (NRSV verses 21, 26), namely, the Judean exiles, whom he *formed* (NRSV verse 21; verse 24) and *redeemed* (verses 22, 23, 24). God assures those who *return* of forgiveness for their sins

> **Cyrus**
>
> *Isaiah 44–45 recognizes that Cyrus was a Zoroastrian and not technically a follower of Yahweh. Yet Cyrus himself, in his inscriptions, honors various local deities. The book of Isaiah makes a theological claim (that Yahweh is ruler of the political order), not a historical one (that Cyrus believes in Yahweh).*

(verse 22) and proclaims that he will *fulfill the predictions* of the prophets that *Jerusalem* and Judah's fortified *towns* will be *rebuilt*, the *foundations* of the *temple laid*, and *Cyrus*, Yahweh's *shepherd*/king (2 Sam 5:2; 7:7; Ps 78:70–72), *will accomplish all that* Yahweh wants (verses 26–28), including Babylon's overthrow, using the metaphor of evaporating the sea (verse 27; 42:15; 50:2; Koole, *Isaiah 40–48*, 424). The prophet thus summons the basic features of the universe to rejoice over Yahweh's mighty deeds (verse 23).

Generally, Judean exiles opposed the prophet's declaration that Yahweh chose a foreign king to deliver Israel. In 45:1–13, the prophet counters this reluctance to accept foreign domination. He declares that *Cyrus* is Yahweh's *anointed* [Hebrew *meshiach*, "messiah"], whom Yahweh selected *to subdue nations* (notably, Babylon). Yahweh will precede Cyrus to prepare the way for him to do Yahweh's bidding so Cyrus will not misunderstand Yahweh's uniqueness (verses 5, 7), even though Cyrus does *not acknowledge* Israel's God (verses 4, 5). This is *for the sake of* Yahweh's *servant, Jacob/Israel* (verse 4). One proof that Yahweh can do this is that he is creator: of *light* and *darkness, prosperity* and *disaster* (verse 7; literally: "good and evil," evil referring to "punishment," not "sin"; see, for example, Jer 1:14; 6:1). Yahweh summons the *heavens*, or *clouds*, to *rain down* Yahweh's *righteousness* and *salvation* (deliverance of Judean exiles) on *earth*, indicating that Yahweh is the source and support of Cyrus's work for a renewed Israel (Seitz, "Isaiah 40–66," 395).

Yahweh, creator of *earth* and *heavens* (verse 12), is *the potter*, Israel's *Maker*, and Judean exiles in Babylon are *the clay*; Yahweh is the Judean exiles' *father* and *mother*, and they his *children* (verses 9–10). Thus, it is inappropriate for them to *question* or instruct him (verse 11) about appointing *Cyrus* to *rebuild* Jerusalem and liberate the *exiles* (verse 13).

In 45:14–25, Yahweh promises through the prophet that Yahweh's faithful people will receive goods from prisoners coming from *Egypt* and *Ethiopia* (NRSV), and the *Sabeans* as subjects, who will acknowledge that Yahweh is God and *there is no other god* (verse 14). The prophet addresses Yahweh, *who hides himself* while working invisibly in history to carry the people into exile and release them without any visible idol to represent him (Deut 4:15–20). Yahweh will put *makers of idols to shame* but will *save* Israel, who *will never be put to shame* (verses 15–17).

Yahweh, creator of everything, has *not spoken in secret* (verses 18–19), but rather summons idol worshipers to testify that their *gods* announced future events and caused them to happen. Idols cannot respond, demonstrating that Yahweh alone is God. Thus Yahweh invites: *turn to me and be saved, all you ends of the earth*; declaring that *every knee will bow* and *every tongue swear* (compare Rom 14:11; Phil 2:9–10), and proclaiming *in the Lord alone are righteousness and strength*. Yahweh will *put to shame* all opponents, and bestow righteousness on *all Israel's descendants* (verses 20–25).

46:1–48:22 Yahweh's message in Isaiah 46–48 is that he will send Cyrus to defeat Babylon and its gods and deliver penitent, faithful Judean exiles from exile. These chapters fall into three parts: Yahweh promises to summon Cyrus to overthrow Babylon and restore a faithful remnant to Zion (46:1–13); Yahweh informs Babylon and its enchanters of their impending defeat (47:1–15); and Yahweh charges penitent Judean exiles to leave Babylon to return home (48:1–22).

Isaiah 46:1–13 addresses *all the remnant* (NRSV; 7:3; 10:20–22; 11:11, 16; 28:5; 37:31–32) of the *house of Jacob/Israel* (verse 3), whom he *carried since birth* and *will carry to old age* (verses 3–4), assuring them that the Babylonian gods *Bel* and *Nebo*, which are so helpless that *beasts must carry* them, will themselves *go into captivity* (verses 1–2). The sharp contrast between Yahweh carrying his people and the nations carrying their

> **The Parade of Deities**
> In the ancient Near East, deities periodically went on parade during major festivals. Worshipers would move their statues around a pre-appointed circuit and offer sacrifices at each stop. The book of Isaiah uses this practice as evidence that the "gods" were helpless, since humans had to move them.

gods on *their shoulders* (verse 7) or on animals' backs (verse 1) demonstrates Yahweh's incomparability (verse 5). How foolish to *worship* a *god* a *goldsmith* fashions. Humans must decide its location, from which it can do nothing for worshipers (verses 6–7; 40:18–20; 41:7; 44:9–20).

Yahweh addresses the remnant a second time, as *rebels* (verse 8) because they refuse to accept what he *planned* (14:24–27; 22:11; 30:1; 37:26): to *summon a bird of prey from the east*, namely, Cyrus, to overthrow Babylon and deliver his people (verse 11; 44:24–45:7; 45:13). He charges them to *remember the former things*, when he proved to be the only God by announcing events and making them happen (verses 9–10; 41:21–29; 45:20–21).

Yahweh addresses the remnant a third time, as *stubborn-hearted*, *far from righteousness*, resisting Yahweh's *righteousness*, or *salvation*, through Cyrus (verse 11), who is returning faithful Judean exiles to *Zion* to begin again Yahweh's work through his people (Goldingay 269).

In 47:1–15, Yahweh turns to address *Babylon*, or *Chaldea* (NRSV; verses 1, 5), announcing that he will *take vengeance* on her (verse 3) because: the city claims to be God, using the language of Yahweh's exclusiveness, *I am, and there is none besides me* (verses 8, 10; 45:5,

6, 14, 18, 21, 22; 46:9); it believes itself invincible, declaring, *I will continue forever – the eternal queen* (verse 7), *lounging in … security* (verse 8); it *showed no mercy* to Judeans whom Yahweh gave into its hands to punish for their sins (54:7–8), but *laid a very heavy yoke* upon them (verse 6); and it is confident that its sorcerers (verses 9, 12), conjurers (verse 11), magicians (verse 12), astrologers, and stargazers (verse 13) can stave off Yahweh's wrath (verses 13–15). Like Judah (2:6–22) and other nations (16:6; 23:9), Yahweh overthrows Babylon for its pride (13:11, 19; 14:4, 11–14). Yahweh will demote Babylon from *mistress* (NRSV, verses 5, 7) to slave (verses 1–2, 5), remove its *throne*, or exalted position, among the nations (verses 1, 5), expose the city's *nakedness* and *shame* (verses 2–3; compare Jer 13:26), and defeat *her* (verses 3, 11, 14) so *she* will suffer *loss of children and widowhood* (verses 8–9).

> **Cities & Nations as Female**
> *The prophets often use sexual imagery to describe cities and nations. Since place names in Hebrew are feminine, such a metaphorical use of gender must have seemed an easy shift to make for the ancient writers. The extremely graphic images of debasement in texts like this caught the attention of an audience.*

Again, verses 48:1–22 address the citizens of *Jacob* (Israel/Judah) in Babylonian exile (verses 1, 12; 46:3), some of whom pretend to *rely on the God of Israel but not in truth or righteousness* (verses 1–2), are *citizens of the holy city* (Jerusalem) in name only (verse 2), are *stubborn* (verse 4), *treacherous*, rebellious (verse 8), and ignore Yahweh's *commands* (verse 18). Some, however, are faithful to Yahweh and have genuinely repented after being *refined* or *tested in the furnace of affliction*, that is, the Babylonian exile (verse 10; 30:20, 26).

Yahweh, not the *idols* that Judah tended to serve (verses 5, 14; Judg 2:17, 19; 3:6), *foretold former things long ago* (possibly Judah's fall and exile, Jer 1:13–19; 6:26; 25:8–11); later, he *acted, and they came to pass* (verses 3, 18–19). Now, Yahweh announces *new things* (verses 6–7): a *delay* in executing *wrath* on an apostate people and a refusal to *cut* them *off* (verse 9). Rather, the creator and sustainer of *earth* and *heavens* (verse 13) will send Cyrus to *carry out his purpose against Babylon* (verses 14–15).

Against Judean exiles who reject Yahweh's decision to use Cyrus to overthrow Babylon and deliver a penitent people, the prophet (verse 16d; some say Yahweh's servant) declares Yahweh's promise to *teach* the people *what is best for* them and to *direct* them *in the way* they *should go* (verse 17), as they should have learned from their ancestors' disobedience (verses 18–19). The prophet proclaims, *the Lord has redeemed his servant Jacob* (verse 20; verse 17; 41:14; 43:1; 44:23; 50:2; 52:9) from Babylonian captivity. Thus, Yahweh summons the exiles to *leave*, or *flee from, Babylon* (verse 20; 52:11–12; compare Jer 50:8), just as the Israelites left Egypt (Exod 12:41; 13:3–4; Deut 9:7; 16:3). On the way home, Yahweh will supply *water from the rock*, as he did for Israel in *the deserts* (verse 21; Exod 17:1–7; Num 20:1–13; Neh 9:15; Pss 78:15–16, 20; 105:41; 114:8). Not all Judean exiles will heed Yahweh's call: they are *the wicked*, for whom *there is no peace* (verse 22; compare verse 18; 57:21).

49:1–53:12 Yahweh's purpose to use his servant, faithful Israel, to bring back the majority of Israel and the nations is the fundamental declaration of Isaiah 49–53. Speakers and addressees vary from passage to passage. These chapters fall into seven units: Yahweh's servant tells the nations his God-given mission (49:1–6); Yahweh encourages the servant to lead Judean exiles to Canaan (49:7–13); Yahweh promises to restore deserted Jerusalem (49:14–50:3); Yahweh's servant declares his steadfast trust in Yahweh and summons the faithful to do likewise (50:4–11); Yahweh promises faithful exiles to deliver them from captivity (51:1–8); Yahweh's servant beseeches Yahweh to deliver the faithful exiles from Babylon (51:9–11); and, finally, Yahweh calls faithful exiles to leave Babylon and return to Judah (51:12–52:12).

49:1–6 Yahweh's *servant* (verses 3, 5–6), *Israel* (verse 3; 41:8; 44:1–2, 21; 48:20), tells the *islands* and *nations* (verse 1) the mission Yahweh gave him: *to bring Jacob* (Israel) *back to him* (verse 5), *to restore the survivors of Israel/Jacob* (verse 6), and to be *a light to the nations* that Yahweh's

> **The "Servant" Israel**
> *The identity of the servant in these chapters is difficult to discern. As Childs (387) puts it, "The extension of the servant's role in chapter 49 is not an attempt to replace an earlier corporate understanding of the servant Israel with that of an individual prophetic figure. Rather, the servant always remains Israel, but Israel is now understood within the dynamic movement of the prophetic history as embodied in a suffering, individual figure who has been divinely commissioned to the selfsame task of the deliverance of the chosen people and the nations at large."*

salvation may reach to the end of the earth (verse 6; 42:1–4; 45:20–25). Despite the servant's feeling that he failed in executing this mission (verse 4), Yahweh offers him *strength* to persist (verses 5–6). Baltzer (295–317, 393–429) argues the *servant* is Moses, and Koole (*Isaiah 49–55*, 1–25) calls him "the great Saviour of the future." But verses 3, 5–6 state he is (the faithful remnant of) *Israel*, *formed* to bring unfaithful Israel and the nations to Yahweh.

In chapter 49, through the prophet (see the formula *This is what the Lord says*, verses 7, 8), Yahweh promises the faithful *servant* (verse 7) (that is, *his people* or *his afflicted ones* [verse 13]), whom *the nations* (verse 7; NRSV) *despised and abhorred* when Jerusalem fell and the Jews went into exile (60:14; Jer 33:24; Lam 1:7–8; 2:15–16), that God will *help* him and *make* him *a covenant for the people* (verse 8). Yahweh charges the servant to embolden Judean *captives* to *come out* of Babylonian exile and *be free* (verse 9a-b; 42:6–7), offering to provide food, water, protection, guidance, and roads conducive to travel (40:3–4; 42:16) for the journey home (verses 9c-12), just as when Israel in the wilderness followed God like a flock does its shepherd (40:11; Pss 78:52–53; 80:1). Then, through the servant, Yahweh will *restore the land* of Canaan and *reassign its inheritances* to a faithful people (verse 8; Josh 13–21). The prophet summons *heavens*, *earth* and *mountains* to *rejoice* because Yahweh *comforts* oppressed *people* in this way (verse 13).

49:14–51:11 In this section, personified, uninhabited *Zion* (Jerusalem) (40:9; 41:27; 52:1–2, 7–8) protests, *the Lord has forsaken me* (verse 14). Yahweh replies through the prophet (*This is what the Lord says*, 49:22, 25; 50:1): *a mother* may *forget* her *baby*, but *I will not forget you* (verse 15). Several biblical texts present God as mother (Num 11:12; Isa 42:14; 66:13; Matt 22:37; Luke 13:34). Yahweh *engraved*, inscribed, or tattooed a blueprint (outline) of Jerusalem bounded by *walls on the palms of* his *hands* as he eagerly contemplates her rebuilding (verse 16; 44:26, 28), paralleling "the outline of the Sumerian city of Lagash in the lap of the statue of its ruler, King Gudea" (around 2000 BCE; Blenkinsopp, *Isaiah 40–55*, 311; Whybray 144; Koole, *Isaiah 49–55*, 56–57). Jerusalem's *sons* (verses 17, 18, 22), her *people* (verse 19), and *children* (verses 20, 25), will *hasten back* (verse 17) to Zion in such numbers the city cannot accommodate them, to its amazement (verses 19–21). Jerusalem will *wear them as ornaments like a bride* (verse 18), giving the city new splendor.

As "the great King over all the earth" (Ps 47:2, 7) or "the nations" (compare Jer 10:7; Ps 47:8), Yahweh will do the impossible: overthrow Judah's captors and *oppressors* (Babylon) and subject them to his people (verses 23c-26b), raising a *banner* as a signal (5:26; 11:10, 12; 13:2; 18:3; 30:17; 62:10) to the nations to do Yahweh's bidding. As *foster fathers* and *nursing mothers*, the nations will *bring* (carry, 40:11; 46:3–4, or escort) God's *sons* and *daughters* (namely, the Judean exiles in Babylon) safely to Judah (verses 22–23b).

To Zion's children (49:17–18, 20, 25), Yahweh denies being arbitrary in allowing Judah to be deported, since he gave her a *certificate of divorce* (compare Deut 24:1–4; Hos 2:2; Jer 3:1–11) – that is, he *sold* her as a slave into Babylonian exile *because of* her *sins* (verse 1). Recently Yahweh *came* and *called* the exiles to leave Babylon and return to Judah in order to *ransom* and *rescue* them, but they did not respond (see 65:1–5; 66:4). Consequently, Yahweh will bring drought and *darkness* upon them (verses 2–3).

Abruptly, Yahweh's servant (Israel's faithful remnant in exile) speaks again (50:1–11; compare 49:1–6) to fellow exiles (*you* and *your* in verses 10–11 are plural), affirming three things: Yahweh *sustains the weary* (40:29–31) with the *word* the prophet had been *taught* (verses 4–5); the prophet tolerated persecution, mockery, and false accusations that opponents brought against him, confident that since Yahweh *helps* him (verses 7, 9), he will *not be disgraced* (verses 6–9); and he admonishes the larger group of exiles to *fear*, *obey*, *trust*, and *rely on* Yahweh through the servant's *word*, warning those who *walk in the light of* their own *fires* that they will *lie down in torment* (verses 10–11).

Suddenly in 51:1–8, Yahweh speaks again through the prophet (*Listen to me*: verses 1, 4, 7; 49:7–50:3) to Judean exiles *who pursue righteousness* by *seek[ing] the Lord*. He says that, just as Yahweh transformed Judah's ancestor, *Abraham*, *one* man, into *many*, so will he *comfort Zion* (verse 19; 40:1; 61:2–3; 66:13), transforming her *ruins* (*deserts* and *wastelands*) into *the garden of Eden* (35:1–2, 6–7; 41:17–20), producing *joy*, *gladness*, *thanksgiving*, and *singing*. Yahweh's *justice*, *righteousness*, and *salvation draws near speedily* and, unlike *the heavens* and *the earth* (verse 6) and those who *reproach* or *insult* Yahweh's true followers (verses 7c-8b), *will last forever* (verses 5, 6, 8). God will restore a faithful people, *who know what is right* and *have* Yahweh's *law in* their *hearts* (verse 7), from exile to Jerusalem (verse 3) and to be *a light to the nations* (verses 4, 5; 42:6; 49:6).

In 51:9, the speaker again changes abruptly, this time to Yahweh's servant (referring to the faithful exiles), who implores Yahweh's strong *arm* to *awake* (three times) *as in days of old* (Exod 6:6; 15:16; Deut 4:34; 5:15; 7:19), that is, at creation, when God defeated the mythological monster *Rahab*, or *the dragon, the sea* and *the waters of the great deep*, or chaos (Gen 1:2; Job 26:12–13; Pss 74:12–15; 89:9–10); and at the Sea of Reeds, when God parted the waters so that Israel could escape from Egypt on dry land (43:16; 50:2; Exod 14:21–22; Ps 77:16–20). Then *the ransomed of the Lord will return* to *Zion* with *singing, everlasting joy,* and *gladness* (verse 3; 35:10; 44:23–28; 55:12).

51:12–52:12 Yahweh responds to the servant's pleas. He urges faithful exiles not to *fear mortal men* (that is, their Babylonian oppressors), for they cannot stand before Yahweh, Israel's *Maker* (45:9, 11; 54:5), creator of *the heavens* and *the earth* (51:12–13, 15–16; 40:21–22, 26; 42:5; 45:18; 48:13). Yahweh *will soon set* Judah's *prisoners* in Babylon *free* (51:14; 52:2) and *put* his *words in* the *mouth* of the servant (here again equaling the faithful exiles) and *cover* him *with the shadow of* his *hand* (51:16a-b; 49:2). Yahweh assures *Zion* (51:16–17; 52:1–2), which is in *ruins* (51:19; 52:9) as a result of the Babylonian destruction of the city (2 Kgs 25:1–12; Jer 39:1–10; 52:3–16), having *drunk* deep of *the cup of* Yahweh's *wrath* (51:17, 20–22; Jer 25:15–29), that he is *her God* (51:20) and *she* is *his people* (51:16, 22; 52:5, 6, 9). Yahweh will *comfort* (51:12, 19; 52:9), *defend* (51:22), *redeem* (52:3, 9), and, in short, save Jerusalem (52:7, 10). The prophet cries out to Zion, *Awake, awake!* (51:17; 52:1). Yahweh will fill the city with Judeans returning from exile and *put* the *cup of* Yahweh's *wrath into the hands of* Zion's *tormentors* (51:22–23). Yahweh will deliver the people from Babylon in a way reminiscent of their earlier deliverance from *Egypt* and *Assyria* (52:4–6). A *messenger* (NRSV) *brings good tidings* to the uninhabited, devastated *ruins of Jerusalem* (compare Nah 1:15), announcing, *your God reigns* and *returns to Zion*, leading the exiles home. Jerusalem's *watchmen* will spot evidence of God's intervention when it first appears on the horizon and will *shout* the wonderful news for all to hear.

The prophet says that there will be two responses to Yahweh's salvation of the Jewish people. First, *all the nations* and *all the ends of the earth will see* Yahweh's *salvation* (52:7–10). Second, the prophet urges the exiles to *depart, depart* from Babylon with *the vessels of the Lord* (Ezra 1:7; 6:5). *Haste* and *flight* are unnecessary, unlike Israel's departure from Egypt (Exod 12:11; Deut 16:3), because *the Lord will go before you, the God of Israel will be your rear guard* (52:11–12), just as the angel and pillar of cloud protected Israel from the Egyptians (Exod 14:19–20; 13:21–22; 23:20; 33:2; Deut 1:30–33).

> **The Audience of Isaiah**
>
> As throughout the book of Isaiah, and indeed much of the rest of the Bible, here Yahweh's saving actions have two audiences, the nations of the earth and Israel itself, both of whom should respond with awe and thanksgiving.

52:13–53:12 The theme of this section is the humiliation and exaltation of Yahweh's servant. This poem contains three parts: in the first and last, Yahweh will exalt his servant (52:13–15 and 53:11–12); in the middle unit, Jewish exiles whom Yahweh's servant restored extol his vicarious suffering for them (53:1–10). Probably "a double chorus was used in the dramatic performance" of this passage (Baltzer 404). Secondary literature and diverse interpretations of this passage are vast and humbling. No one can claim definitive understanding of its meaning. Provisional suggestions follow.

The section opens in 52:13–15. Here Yahweh speaks concerning *my servant*, probably the remnant of Jewish exiles whom Yahweh restored through the exile (49:1–6; 50:4–11), declaring *he will be highly exalted*. Formerly, *many nations were appalled at him*, because he was *so disfigured*, but now he will awe *kings* because, through him, Yahweh will empower them to *see* and *understand what they were not told* and *have not heard* – that is, Yahweh's servant will be a light to the nations (42:6; 49:6).

The larger body of Judean exiles in Babylon (*we, us, our, my people*) proclaim that the remnant suffered vicariously because of its *transgressions* and *iniquities* and stubborn impenitence. Yahweh's servant *grew up before* Yahweh with *no beauty or majesty to attract* his fellows to him; they *despised and rejected* him (verses 1–3).

Initially, the larger exile group considered Yahweh's servant *stricken, smitten,* and *afflicted by God,* but now they realize that *he was pierced* and *crushed* because of their *transgressions*, and *by his wounds* they *are healed*. They *have gone astray*, and Yahweh *has laid on* his servant (namely, the faithful remnant) the *iniquity* of the larger group (verses 4–6; 50:6).

Yahweh's servant voluntarily went *like a lamb to the slaughter* to be *stricken* because of *the transgression of* Yahweh's *people*, the larger exiled body. Reflecting his sacrificial attitude, *he did not open his mouth*. Though he was innocent, he suffered the indignity of burial in *a grave with the wicked* and *rich for the sake of his comrades*. In this way, *the Lord's will will prosper in his hand* (verses 7–10).

In verses 11–12, Yahweh speaks again concerning his servant (*my righteous servant*). Not only will Yahweh's servant, the faithful Judean exiles, restore some of their fellows, but he will also *bear the sin of* and thereby *justify many* nations (52:15; 49:5–6), or in other words, make *intercession for the transgressors*. "The individual servant's suffering and death are Israel's, on behalf of the nations" (Seitz, "Isaiah 40–66," 462).

54:1–55:13 Yahweh admonishes personified, abandoned Jerusalem not to be afraid (54:4, 14), for he will take her back because of his unfailing love for her (54:10) and will populate her with numerous people (54:1–17), as a husband takes back a wife he divorced (54:5–6). Yahweh summons faithful, penitent Judean exiles in Babylon to forsake their evil ways, receive his forgiveness (55:6–7), enter an everlasting covenant with him (55:4), and leave Babylon for Jerusalem (55:12) to attract the nations to Yahweh (55:1–13, especially 5).

54:1–17 Yahweh, through the prophet, addresses Jerusalem, the *afflicted city* (54:11), using the metaphor of a *barren woman who never bore a child*, and declares she will have many children (verses 1–3).

> **Isaiah 53 in Early Christian Interpretation**
>
> *In the time of Jesus, Jews interpreted the Suffering Servant of Isaiah 53 to be Israel as a whole. This is notably true of the Targum of Isaiah, a work finished in about 200 CE but including older interpretations of the biblical book (see Hayes 550). Early Christians read the story of the Servant typologically. Since Jesus took on many aspects of Israel (see Matt 1–4 especially), it was fitting that his career as the Suffering Servant par excellence should be interpreted in light of the beautiful images of Isaiah 53. Whatever the original intent of the chapter, it became an ideal portrayal of the one who died so that all might live.*

He admonishes her *not* to *be afraid*, for Yahweh her *Maker* is her *husband* and will *call* or *bring* her *back* into a *covenant of peace* (verse 10; Mal 2:14), that is, their marriage relationship. Yahweh's actions come out of *deep compassion* (verses 7–8, 10), *everlasting kindness* (verse 8), and *unfailing love* for her (verse 10), although he formerly *rejected*, *abandoned*, *hid* his *face from*, and *divorced* her (verses 4–6; 50:1; Hos 2:2–15) out of anger (verses 8–9). God's punishment of the people in the Babylonian exile is like the destruction of humankind by the flood in *the days of Noah*. Yet, just as God *swore* never to destroy humanity again by flood (Gen 8:21–22), so now God vows never to punish Israel again by exile.

Yahweh promises to *build* abandoned Jerusalem, including its *foundations*, *battlements*, *gates*, and *walls*. Yahweh will teach its residents, establishing the city *in righteousness* (1:26), liberating it from *fear*, and defeating all enemies. Accordingly, *the heritage of* Yahweh's faithful *servants* (namely the core group who urged their fellow exiles to return to Yahweh), is a bright future because of Yahweh's *vindication* (verses 11–17).

In chapter 55, Yahweh offers the exiles free, *good*, *rich* drink and food that can *satisfy* their deepest longings, in contrast to Babylon's expensive, insipid, non-nutritious fare that *does not satisfy*. Yahweh desires to enter into *an everlasting covenant* with them, thus demonstrating the *unfailing kindnesses* (54:8, 10) promised to David (2 Sam 7:11–16; Ps 89:19–37). Like David, they will be *a witness to the peoples*, and *nations* that *do not know* them *will hasten to* them, or to be concrete, will depend upon them economically and will bring tribute to build up Jerusalem and provide her protection (Ps 18:43), *because* Yahweh *has endowed* them *with splendor* (verses 1–5).

> **The Land & the People Will Be Healed**
>
> *Isaiah 55 says that, just as war and deportation led to ecological degradation, so now the recovering land itself will symbolize the return of God's people to their promised state of wholeness under God, who created nature as well as them.*

Yahweh admonishes the exiles to *seek*, *call on*, and *turn to* him, promising that *his ways* and *thoughts* will prevail. As *rain and snow* nourish plants to produce grain for *bread*, Yahweh's *word* that he will deliver

Judean exiles and restore them to their land *will accomplish what* Yahweh *desires* (verses 6–11). *The wicked* (verse 7) are Judean exiles "who are so settled in Babylon and so accommodated to imperial ways that they have no intention of making a positive response to Yahweh's invitation to homecoming" (Brueggemann, *Isaiah 40–66*, 160).

The prophet concludes by promising faithful Judean exiles that they will exit Babylon *in joy* (52:11–12), as Israel *went out* from Egypt (Exod 12:41; 13:3; Deut 9:7; 11:10). In short, they will experience a new exodus. All creation, and in particular, the *mountains*, *hills*, and *trees*, will rejoice in Yahweh's magnificent salvation of his people.

OBJECTIVES & CONTROVERSIES IN YAHWEH'S POSTEXILIC COMMUNITY · 56:1–66:24

According to Isaiah 56–66, both penitent and non-receptive Judean exiles have now heard Yahweh's announcements in chapters 40–55 of deliverance from Babylon and return to Judah. Passages in chapters 56–66 date originally from the period of rebuilding the Jerusalem temple (536–516 BCE) to rebuilding its walls (about 445–432 BCE). But despite the fact that they post-date the events of Isaiah, they are nevertheless an integral part of the book as they continue, combine, reinterpret, reapply, and emphasize with greater clarity major teachings of chapters 1–55. Chapters 56–66 fall into seven sections (56:1–8; 56:9–57:21; 58:1–59:21; 60:1–62:12; 63:1–6; 63:7–64:12; 65:1–66:24).

56:1–8 Some Judean exiles now inhabiting Jerusalem wish to exclude *eunuchs* and *foreigners* from Yahweh's people. The fifth century BCE prophetic composer of Isaiah 56–66 denounces this practice. Yahweh declares through the prophet (*This is what the Lord says* [verses 1, 4]) that *salvation* and *righteousness* (46:13; 51:5–6, 8) are very near (verse 1). Therefore, the prophet charges his followers to *maintain justice and do what is right* (verse 1; 1:16–17; 5:7, 16; 10:1–2), which in this context means especially to *keep the Sabbath* (verses 2, 4, 6; Exod 20:8–11; Jer 17:19–27) and to *keep* one's *hand from doing any evil* (verse 2) by hold[ing] *fast to* Yahweh's *covenant* (verses 2, 4, 6).

Yahweh will *bless* anyone *who does this*: the chosen *people* (verse 3), *foreigners* (verses 3, 6), *eunuchs* (verses 3–4), and *all nations* (verse 7; 2:2–4; 25:6–8; 45:20–23; 51:4–5; 66:18–19; Zech 2:11; Ruth 2:10–12). He will *exclude* none *joined to the Lord* (verse 3), *who bind themselves to serve, love, and worship the name of the Lord* (verse 6). Although eunuchs cannot have *sons and daughters* to preserve their memory (Job 18:16–17), Yahweh will *give them* something better: incessant fellowship with him (verses 3–5). He will *give* foreigners *joy in* his *house* and *accept their sacrifices* (verse 7). Yahweh has already *gathered* some *exiles of Israel*, but he *will gather others* (verse 8). Judean exiles returned from Babylon in several waves.

56:9–57:21 Division arose among different exiled groups who returned to Judah. The prophet uses several introductory formulas (*This is what the high and lofty One says* [57:15]; *says the Lord* [57:19]; *says my God* [57:21]) to show that Yahweh speaks directly to denounce sinners and announce punishment upon wicked leaders (56:9–12; 57:3–13b, 20–21). At the same time, God commends and promises to bless *the righteous* (57:1–2, 13c-19).

In 56:9–12, Yahweh summons *all beasts* to *devour Israel's blind watchmen* (*shepherds*) (Jer 12:9–13; Ezek 34:1–10), namely the wicked leaders of the small Jerusalem community, here false prophets (Jer 6:17; Ezek 3:16–21; Koole, *Isaiah 56–66*, 34–35). They *lack knowledge* and *understanding*; they should warn the community of spiritual dangers, but they are *mute dogs*. They should be alert to protect the people, but they *lie around* and *love to sleep*. Their primary care should be the flock, but their only concern is to satisfy their own appetites and acquire their *own gain* (compare Jas 4:1–4).

Chapter 57 opens with the wicked killing *the righteous*; but this is a blessing, because in death Yahweh spares the righteous from further ill treatment by their oppressors; he gives them *peace* and *rest* from additional affliction *in death* (see Job 3:11–19).

According to 57:3–13b, the exile did not cure God's people of idolatry. Jeremiah condemned fellow Jews who went to Egypt after Jerusalem's fall for worshiping idols (Jer 44). In Isaiah 57:3–13b, Yahweh condemns certain groups of exiles returned to Judah for worshiping Baal and Molech, labeling them *sons of a sorceress*, *offspring of adulterers and prostitutes* (verse 3), *brood of rebels*, *offspring of liars* (verse 4). By turning to idols, God's people *mock*, *sneer at*, *stick out* their *tongue at* (verse 4), *forsake* (verse 8), are *false to*, do not *remember*, and *do not fear* Yahweh (verse 11). *Among the oaks*, *under every spreading tree* (verse 5), *on a high and lofty hill* (verse 7; Deut 12:2–3; 1 Kgs

14:22–24; 2 Kgs 17:9–11; Jer 2:20; Ezek 20:27–29; Hos 4:11–13), they practice cult prostitution as an act of worship to the fertility god Baal (verses 5, 7–8); and *in the ravines, under the overhanging crags* (verse 5), they *sacrifice* their *children to* the Ammonite deity *Molech*, or Milcom (Deut 12:31; 1 Kgs 11:7; 2 Kgs 16:3; 17:31; 21:6; 23:10; Jer 19:4–5; Ezek 16:20–22; Mic 6:6–7; Zeph 1:4–6). They offer *drink offerings* and *grain offerings* to foreign deities (verse 6). All these religious activities *weary* the participants, but they find *strength* to proceed (verse 10). Thus, Yahweh resolves to be *silent* no longer, but to *expose* the wicked exiles' *righteousness* and *works* (verses 11–12). When they petition for *help*, Yahweh will summon their gods to rescue them. Their gods can do nothing, so *the wind carries them off* (verse 13a-b).

> **False Gods in Israel after the Exile**
> *After reading the gorgeous promises of Isaiah 40–55, it is disturbing to find in chapters 56–66 that Judah returned to some of its old ways. However, the book of Isaiah offers hope even under such difficult circumstances, since Yahweh continues to work to redeem the people and to win them to worship of the one true God.*

In 57:13c-19, there are some returned exiles who *make* Yahweh *the high and lofty One, who lives forever, whose name is holy*, who *lives in a high and holy place* (verse 15), their *refuge* (verse 13c) and are *contrite and lowly* (verse 15); these Yahweh will maintain in Judah (verse 13c), *revive* (verse 15), *heal* (verses 18–19), *guide and restore comfort to* (verse 18), *creating praise* from mourners (verse 19) and *peace* for those who trust in Yahweh. At one time, Yahweh was *angry* and *enraged by* the people's *sinful greed* and *punished* them, but in vain (verses 16–17). Yet, to keep them from tiring or losing all hope, the prophet now summons his forerunners to *prepare the road* for additional exiles to return from Babylon (verse 14; 40:3–5). God has resolved to save the people, even though their *ways* are *willful* (verse 17). By contrast (verses 20–21), *the wicked* among the restored Judean exiles have *no peace* but are continually miserable and restless (48:22).

58:1–59:21 Isaiah 58–59 reflects the situation shortly before Nehemiah rebuilt the walls of Jerusalem (445 BCE, 58:12). Yahweh's people are oppressing one another, and Yahweh is punishing them; they hold a great fast and strictly observe the Sabbath to persuade God to stop the punishment. The prophet declares that Yahweh desires justice and righteousness, that is, right treatment of one's fellow human beings, not mere external fasting and observing the Sabbath (58:1–14). Yahweh yearns to save the people but cannot do so as long as they treat each other with violence, oppression, and injustice (59:1–21).

In 58:1–14, Yahweh charges the fifth century BCE prophet to *declare to* his *people their sins* (verse 1) of pride, arrogance, and self-centeredness. In a line reminiscent of charges in the book of Judges, the prophet notes that they *do as they please* (verses 3, 13). Outwardly, *they seem eager* to have a close relationship with Yahweh *as if they* kept Yahweh's *commands* (verse 2). They meticulously *fast* and keep the *Sabbath*, but Yahweh *has not noticed* (verses 3a-b, 4c-5), because in daily life they *exploit all* their *workers* (verse 3c), *quarrel, strive, strike* each other with *wicked fists* (verse 4a-b), and utter *malicious talk* against their fellows (verse 9). *The kind of fasting* Yahweh desires is to *loose the chains of injustice* from the mistreated, *set the oppressed free* (verses 6, 9, 10), *share food with the hungry* (verses 7, 10), *provide the poor wanderer with shelter*, *clothe the naked*, and care for needy relatives (verses 6–7; Matt 25:31–46).

If they do this, Yahweh will transform their *darkness* into *light* (verses 8, 10), *heal* them, protect them, *answer their cries for help* (verses 8–9b), *guide* them, *satisfy* their *needs*, *strengthen* them, be their spiritual fountain (verse 11; Jer 2:13), and empower them to rebuild Jerusalem, bearing the symbolic names *Repairer of Broken Walls, Restorer of Streets with Dwellings* (verse 12). They will now *find* their *joy in the Lord* and prosper in the promised *land* (verse 14).

> **Dialogue with the Prophet**
> *In chapter 59, the themes of Isaiah 58 continue. However, the speaker is no longer Yahweh. Chapter 59 is a dialogue between the fifth century BCE prophet (verses 1–8, 15c–21) and the sinful people (verses 9–15b).*

The prophet declares that Yahweh is ready and able to *save* the people (verse 1), but their *iniquities* drown out their cries for deliverance (verses 1–2). Their fundamental sin is *injustice, unrighteousness* in dealing with other human beings (verses 4, 8). Their hearts devise wicked plans to hurt others: they *conceive trouble* (verse 4), and *their thoughts are evil* (verse 7). These erupt in sinful speech: their *lips* and *tongues* make *empty arguments* and *speak lies* in court cases (verse 4) and daily speech (verse 3). They *mutter wicked things* (verse 3) and engage in sinful actions, especially violence against the vulnerable. Thus the prophet charges that their *hands are stained with blood* of *innocent*, unsuspecting victims they killed or mistreated in *evil deeds* and *acts of violence* (verses 3, 6, 7; Prov 1:10–19). In addition, *their feet rush into sin* (verse 7), destroying the *peace* that should prevail among God's people (verse 8).

Some of the prophet's hearers respond (*we, us, our*), confessing guilt for sins of which he accused them. The prophet uses a series of synonyms to illustrate how odious is the behavior of the people of God: *offenses, sins, iniquities, rebellion, treachery,* turning their *backs on God, oppression, revolt, uttering lies* their *hearts conceived,* absence of *truth* or *honesty* (verses 12–15). The people acknowledge that this is why Yahweh's *justice, righteousness, light, and deliverance do not reach* them, and they *feel* their *way like the blind, stumble at midday*, having become *like the dead* (verses 9c–11b).

The prophet responds to the penitent. He declares that Yahweh *was displeased* that *no one* in Judah's restored community arose to promote *justice* among God's people. So Yahweh donned a warrior's uniform: the *breastplate* of *righteousness, helmet of salvation, garments of vengeance,* and *cloak* of *zeal* (verses 15b–17; compare 1 Thess 5:8; Eph 6:10–17) and marched forth *like a pent-up flood* (see 8:7–8) to punish his *enemies*, namely, the Judeans in the community who oppressed and mistreated their fellow Jews (verses 18–19). Yahweh acted in order to motivate foreign peoples to *fear* the divine *name* and *revere his glory* (verse 19), and to redeem *those in Jacob who repent of their sins* (verse 20; 1:27–28). Yahweh assures those who faithfully keep his *covenant* that his *spirit* (NRSV), or power or energy, and *words* (or law) will be with their descendants *forever* (verse 21).

60:1–62:12 Zion is the central focus of Isaiah 60–62. Zerubbabel and his companions finished the temple in 516 BCE (60:7; Ezra 6:13–18), but Nehemiah's rebuilding of Jerusalem's walls (445 BCE; Neh 6:15–7:4) is yet to come (60:10, 18). The population of Jerusalem is small (Neh 7:4); religious division plagues the returned exiles. The fifth century BCE prophet persuaded some to repent (59:20). In Isaiah 60–62, he announces that Yahweh will restore other penitent exiles to Zion, who will convert foreigners to Yahweh.

In chapter 60, the fifth century BCE prophet informs Zion through second-person imperatives [*arise, shine, lift up*, etc.] and feminine singular pronouns [*you, your*] that Yahweh's *light* (glory and deliverance) (58:8, 10) *has come*, while *the peoples* are in *darkness* (verses 1–2, 19–20). The prophet announces that *nations will come to* this *light* (verse 3; 2:2–4; 42:6; 49:6). They will *serve* God's people (verses 10, 12, 14), escort Zion's *sons* and *daughters* home (verses 4, 8–9, 22; 49:22–23), provide their *riches* to help faithful Judeans recuperate (verses 5–6, 11, 16–17), *rebuild* the *walls* of Jerusalem with *gates* (verses 10–11, 18; 54:12), and join Yahweh's people in *praise* and *honor of the Lord* (verses 6, 10), including making *offerings* to Yahweh at the Jerusalem *temple* (verses 6–7).

Yahweh will replace Zion's *violence, ruin, destruction,* and *sorrow* (verses 18, 20; 58:3–4, 6, 9–10; 59:6–7) with *peace* and *righteousness* (verse 17). Zion will become *radiant* (verse 5) and full of *splendor* (verses 9, 21), and God will *adorn* and *glorify the place of* the *sanctuary* (verse 13) and multiply their numbers (verse 22). By sending the Babylonians to devastate Judah (587 BCE; Jer 25:8–10), *in anger* Yahweh *struck* that nation (verse 10; 54:7; 57:16–17) so that it was *forsaken and hated* (verse 15; 49:14; 54:6; 62:4). However, God will

> **The Message of Isaiah 60–62**
> The prophet's message has several elements. First, he declares that Yahweh will use the nations to increase Jerusalem's population by restoring more exiles to it, and Yahweh's people will bring foreigners into their religious community (60:1–22). Second, the penitent Judean remnant declares that Yahweh sent the prophet to encourage returning exiles to be faithful to Yahweh (61:1–11). Third, the prophet and his associates beseech Yahweh to restore Zion. Graciously, Yahweh consents (62:1–12).

> **Symbolic City Names**
> In the ancient Near East, parts of cities or their fortifications often bore symbolic names. The most famous case was in Babylon, which bore several dozen poetic names for the city itself and many more for various temples, shrines, and other locales within it. The book of Isaiah thus uses a common practice in naming parts of Jerusalem's walls, but does so for highly spiritual reasons.

now restore the nation (verse 10; 49:15; 54:7–10). Zion will receive symbolic names such as *The City of the Lord* and *Zion of the Holy One of Israel* (verse 14). This will be true even of the city walls (verse 18).

In chapter 61, it is impossible to identify the speaker in verses 1–7, 10–11: possibly the fifth century BCE prophet; more likely, the penitent, faithful remnant of restored exiles distinguished from the larger body of Jews (42:1–7; 57–59). Yahweh speaks in verses 8–9. The faithful remnant recognizes that Yahweh's *spirit* (NRSV) is upon it, because Yahweh *anointed* (designated) and *sent* it on a mission to announce to the people that they will soon exchange their great problems for great blessings. Like their capital city, these new converts will receive a symbolic name, *Oaks of Righteousness*, *a Planting of the Lord*, and thus will become Exhibit A *for the display of* Yahweh's *splendor* (verses 1–3; 60:9, 21).

The new converts will *rebuild, restore,* and *renew* neglected *ruins* in Judah and Jerusalem. *Aliens* and *foreigners* will join them to care for Judah's *flocks, fields, vineyards,* or, in other words, the primary elements of the nation's economic life (49:22–23; 60:10). The converts receive another symbolic name, *priests,* or *ministers of the Lord,* selected by Yahweh to bring to reality the original purpose for all Israel to bring the nations to God (Exod 19:4–6). Yahweh's faithful *people will rejoice* in receiving their *inheritance in their land*, which Yahweh intended for the people all along (verses 4–7; see Gen 13:14–18; 15:7–21).

Yahweh responds to the cries of the chosen people, promising to *reward* and *make an everlasting covenant with* the faithful remnant who practices *justice* (1:27–28; 58:1–12; 59:15c-19), declaring that *all the nations who see them* as they faithfully serve Yahweh *will acknowledge they are a people the Lord has blessed* (verses 8–9; 19:24–25; 44:3).

Judah's faithful remnant responds to Yahweh's assurances with joy, because Yahweh *clothed* them *with garments of salvation, a robe of righteousness,* and deliverance like an adorned *bridegroom* and *bride*. Moreover, Yahweh offers to bring all the nations into a state of well-being and justice like *soil causes seeds to grow* (45:8; 55:10–11). As Whybray (246) says, "The nations will be observers and witnesses of the salvation conferred upon God's people" (compare Isa 52:10).

In chapter 62, just as Amos interceded for Israel (Amos 7:2, 5), the prophet (verse 1) and his associates (*watchmen,* verse 6) resolve *not* to *keep silent* but to "nag" Yahweh incessantly, *till* Jerusalem's *righteousness* (*vindication* (NRSV) or *salvation*) occurs – that is, until Yahweh elevates Jerusalem to a position of international prominence so that it can bear witness to the glory of its God (verses 2, 6–7). Yahweh will change Jerusalem's symbolic name from *forsaken* [Hebrew *'azuvah*; 49:14; 54:6–8] and *Desolate* [Hebrew *shemamah*] to *My Delight Is In Her* [Hebrew *cheftsivah*] and *Married* [Hebrew *be'ulah* = Beulah; NRSV], indicating *the Lord will take delight in* the city (verses 4–5). Restored Jerusalem *will be a crown of splendor* and *a royal diadem* that Yahweh holds so that all may admire it (verse 3; compare verses 1–7). The possibly embarrassing idea of Jerusalem's *sons* marrying their own mother city (verse 5a-b) has provoked numerous textual emendations and interpretations, none of which is satisfactory (Koole, *Isaiah 56–66,* 310–11). One aspect of the solution must be that "the prophet proceeds from such a close relationship between Zion and her land that he identifies both here" (Koole, *Isaiah 56–66,* 311).

Yahweh swears *never again* to *give* the *grain* and *new wine for which* the faithful returned exiles *have toiled* to *enemies* and *foreigners* (65:21–22; Deut 28:30; Amos 5:11). Instead, the returned people will benefit from their own labor and enjoy its use (compare Amos 9:14), and so they will *praise the Lord* (verses 8–9).

The fifth century BCE prophet responds by summoning Judeans already returned to Jerusalem to *prepare the way* (40:3–5; 57:14) for others still in foreign lands to return. "Apparently the majority of this people is in the Diaspora, and the people present in Jerusalem are responsible for their return.... Given the salvation... they themselves have experienced, Zion's inhabitants can make the way of salvation attractive to those who are absent" (Koole, *Isaiah 56–66,* 321–22). Then, the prophet summons these Judeans to *raise a banner* (5:26; 11:12; 13:2; 18:3; 49:22) *for the nations* to abandon their gods in order to worship and serve Yahweh (verse 10; 2:2–4; 19:23–25; 42:1–7; 45:20–23; 49:1–7).

Yahweh instructs *the ends of the earth* to tell Zion that its *salvation* (NRSV) *comes*. By fighting for

---

Yahweh's Promise

Isaiah 62 relates a dialogue between the prophet (verses 1–7, 10, 12) and Yahweh as reported by the prophet (verses 8–9, 11). Notice the clauses, the Lord has sworn *(verse 8) and* the Lord has made proclamation *(verse 11).*

Jerusalem, Yahweh has earned the *reward*, or *recompense*, of *salvation* for Zion (verse 11; 40:10).

To emphasize Yahweh's restoration of Jerusalem, the prophet declares additional *new names* (verses 2, 4) that Yahweh gives its inhabitants: *the Holy People* (6:13; 63:18), *the Redeemed of the Lord* (1:27–28; 35:8–10), *Sought After* (Jer 30:14, 17), *the City No Longer Deserted* (verse 4; 54:7–8). As before, these symbolic names reinforce the hearers' sense of God's care for them.

63:1–6 Edom joined Babylon to overthrow Judah when it concluded that Babylon would prevail (Ps 137:7–8; Obad 10–14). Like chapter 34, this section announces Yahweh's *day of vengeance* against *Edom* (verse 4; 34:8; 61:2) for oppressing Judah. A watchman (21:11–12; 62:6–7) asks two questions (verses 1a-d, 2), each of which Yahweh answers (verses 1e-f, 3–6). The first is: *Who is this coming from Edom*? [Hebrew *'edom*]. The question is much like our "Who goes there?" Yahweh replies to the question, *It is I, announcing vindication* (NRSV), *mighty to save*; that is, God comes to punish Israel's oppressors and captors and to deliver them from them (verse 1).

> **Israel & Edom**
> *Edom's historical relationship with Israel was a complex one. The two nations thought of themselves as kin, as the stories of Jacob and Esau, their ancestors, show. During the Persian and Hellenistic eras, the Edomites moved west into the land of Israel proper and converted to Judaism.*

The second question is: *Why are your garments red*? [Hebrew *'adom*], a wordplay on *Edom* (Gen 25:30). Yahweh answers this question by saying, *In my anger* (see verses 3, 5, 6), *I have trodden the winepress* (that is, Edom) *alone* (verses 3, 6; 59:16; compare Lam 1:15; Joel 3:13; Rev 14:19–20; 19:15) without using other nations. The prophet quotes God as saying that the Edomites' *blood spattered my garments* on my *day of vengeance* (verses 3–4; Isa 61:2). Red wine suggests *blood* (verses 1–3, 6).

63:7–64:12 Here the sixth century BCE prophet speaks on behalf of Yahweh's faithful people (*we, us, our*: 63:7, 15, 16, 17, 18; 64:3, 5, 6, 7, 8, 9, 11, 12; compare the labels in 63:17, 18; 64:4, 5, 9). He rehearses Yahweh's past mighty deeds on behalf of the people (63:7–14), then beseeches Yahweh to redeem them yet again (63:15–64:12). The text uses the form of communal laments seen in Psalms 44, 85, 89, and so on. This oracle originally dates between 587 BCE and 536 BCE, since the *sacred cities* of Judah lie in ruins, *Zion*, or *Jerusalem*, is uninhabited, and the Jerusalem *temple has been burned with fire* (64:10–11). In the flow of the final form of Isaiah, concern for the restoration of Yahweh's faithful exiles (63:7–64:12) naturally follows a description of Yahweh's destruction of Edom and its allies, especially Babylon, who demolished Judah and Jerusalem (63:1–6).

In 63:7–14, as in Psalms 44:1–8, 85:1–3, and 89:1–37, the prophet, as spokesperson for Yahweh's faithful servants, rehearses Yahweh's former mighty *deeds for the house of Israel* (verse 7), especially in *the days of Moses* (verses 11–12). He enumerates the key events of the crossing of the Reed Sea (verses 11–13; Exod 14:21–15:18) and the wilderness wanderings (Ps 78:51–55). In order to emphasize Yahweh's immediate presence with the people, the prophet also mentions *the angel of his presence* (verse 9; Exod 23:20–23; 32:34; 33:2; Num 20:16; Judg 2:1–5; following the NIV contra the NRSV; Blenkinsopp, *Isaiah 56–66*, 260–61) and *God's holy spirit* (NRSV), or presence (Pss 51:11; 139:7), whom *he set among them* (verse 11), and by whom he gave them *rest* (verse 14; Westermann 389). These deeds reveal Yahweh's *mercy* and *steadfast love* (verses 7, 9; NRSV), which accrue *everlasting renown* and *a glorious name* in the eyes of Israel and the rest of the nations (verses 12, 14). The prophet notes that Yahweh assumed that the redeemed people would be faithful (verse 8), but they *grieved his holy spirit* (NRSV; verse 10; compare Gen 6:6; Ps 78:40) so that he *became their enemy* (verse 10; Isa 1:24; see Lam 2:5).

The appeals to God follow several lines. First, the prophet says that with the Judeans in exile, there is no evidence of Yahweh's *zeal*, *might*, *tenderness and compassion* toward the people. In other words, God's basic characteristics seem obscured (63:15). Second, God's people depend on Yahweh, not on *Abraham* or *Israel*

> **The Prophet Appeals to God**
> *In Isaiah 63:7–64:12, just as in Psalms 44:9–26, 85:4–13, and 89:38–51, as the faithful exiles' spokesman, the prophet uses several incentives to persuade Yahweh to help the oppressed people (63:15; compare 57:15; Pss 14:2; 33:13–15; 80:14). The prophet asks God to return (63:17) and to* rend the heavens and come down *as at Mount Sinai when the* mountains trembled, fire *burned hot as in a kiln, and people* quaked *(64:1–3; Exod 19:16–20). That is, the prophet appeals to divine honor and the precedents of the past in order to shape a present reality.*

(*Jacob*) as their *Father* to protect and nurture them. Therefore, his absence can seem a way of making the people *wander from* his *ways* and *harden their hearts* (Exod 4:21; 7:3; 9:12; 14:4, 8, 17; Josh 11:20) so they *do not revere* him (63:16–17). Third, Yahweh's temple has fallen to hostile pagans, making Yahweh's people *like those whom* Yahweh does *not rule, like those not called by Yahweh's name* (63:18–19; NRSV, contra NIV). The loss of the temple seems to nullify Yahweh's role as the people's *Redeemer* (63:16). Fourth, Yahweh's people are in an unsolvable dilemma: their incomparable God delivers obedient, faithful people, but their sins have made them like an *unclean* menstrual cloth. The prophet uses a series of disgusting images to illustrate their disgusting behavior (compare Rom 1:22–32). *How then can* they *be saved*? (64:4–7). They wonder whether Yahweh would consider delivering them in spite of their stubbornness. Fifth, Yahweh is Israel's *Father* (63:16) and *potter* (29:16; 45:9–10), while they are Yahweh's *people* (63:8, 18) and the *clay* Yahweh *formed* (43:1, 21; 44:2, 21). Therefore, they beseech Yahweh not to keep punishing them for their *sins forever*, but, considering this intimate relationship, to forgive and restore them (64:8–9; Ps 103:8–14). Sixth, the prophet notes that the *sacred cities* of Judah, *Zion* (that is, *Jerusalem*), and the *temple* have all experienced destruction at the hand of the Babylonians (2 Kgs 24:1–4; 25:1–12). He then asks whether God can remain aloof from the sufferings of the chosen people (64:10–12; compare 42:14; 57:11). These appeals to God cumulatively paint a picture of a penitent people who have lost everything and seek to regain the one thing that matters – their relationship with the redeeming God who repeatedly rescued them and who will, they hope, do so again.

65:1–66:24 Responding to Israel's complaint that Yahweh did not answer them when they called to him for help (63:15, 17; 64:1, 7, 9, 12), Yahweh declares that he repeatedly *called* to them, but most of them *did not answer*; he *spoke* to them, but they *did not listen* (65:1, 12, 24; 66:4); instead, they were *obstinate*, pursued *their own imaginations* (65:2), and *did evil in* Yahweh's *sight* (65:12; 66:4). But a small remnant returned to him; ultimately, he will restore them (65:8–10, 17–25; 66:2, 10–16), and they will bring peoples from *all the nations* to Yahweh (66:18–23). Yahweh distinguishes between his true *servants* and those who pretend to be his people (65:8–16; 66:5). Isaiah 65–66 falls into three sections: Yahweh will destroy his people who rebelled against him but restore a remnant (65:1–16); Yahweh will bless his true servants (65:17–25); Yahweh promises his true servants in Zion (Jerusalem) a bright future but decrees harsh punishment for his people who worship idols (66:1–24).

65:1–16 Yahweh denounces Judean exiles as a whole for rejecting the call, *Here am I, here am I.* They refused to *ask for* or *call on* his *name* (55:6–7; 58:2; 64:7), practicing illicit *sacrifices*, sitting *among graves*, keeping secret vigil at night, eating pork and other *unclean meat*, maintaining that they were holier than others (65:1–5b, 7b-c; 1:29–31; 57:4–10; 66:3). Consequently, they are *smoke in* his nostrils, *a fire that keeps burning all day* and provokes him to anger (Deut 32:22; Pss 18:8; 74:1; Jer 15:14; 17:4). Accordingly, Yahweh will punish them (65:5c-7b, 7e-f).

The text uses several agricultural images to indicate that, conversely, Yahweh will rescue those from *Jacob* (that is, northern Israel) and *Judah*. First, just as viticulturists save a *cluster of grapes* still containing *juice*, so will God preserve them. Second, they will graze their *flocks* and *herds* in choice *pasture* and *resting place*[s] in their land, *Sharon* (35:2) and *the Valley of Achor* (Hos 2:15). In other words, their territory will extend well beyond the tiny limits of the Persian province of Yehud into the original territory of the kingdom of Judah.

On the other hand, God will destroy with the *sword* the majority of Israel. The prophet defends this destruction by noting that the majority *forsake the Lord*, do *not answer* when he calls, and do *evil in* his *sight*, including practicing idolatry by spreading *a table for* the god *Fortune* [Hebrew *Gad*] and filling bowls of mixed wine for the deity *Destiny* [Hebrew *Meni*] as means of communing with them (65:8–12).

> **Gad & Meni:**
> *The identities of the deities Gad and Meni are obscure. The names may be epithets of otherwise known ancient gods (much as one calls George Herman Ruth "Babe" or "The Sultan of Swat"). Or they may have been minor deities that Israelites worshiped in order to forestall bad things happening to them. Whatever their identity, worshiping them illustrated a lack of confidence in Yahweh's management of the future. Hence the prophet's strong condemnation.*

Summarizing, Yahweh's true *servants will eat, drink, rejoice, sing,* receive *another name* (56:5; 62:2–4, 12), *invoke a blessing,* and *swear by the God of truth* (compare Deut 10:20) *in the land,* forgetting their *past troubles.* On the other hand, apostate worshipers will experience physical, mental, and spiritual deprivation, and ultimately they will die ignominiously (65:13–16).

For his small band of true servants in Judah, Yahweh will remove *the former things* – that is, their past troubles (65:16) and *the sound of weeping and crying,* and he will *create new heavens and a new earth* so that Jerusalem can be a delight *and its people a joy* (65:17–19). There are three dimensions to this new creation. First, Yahweh's true servants will not die in infancy but will live to a very old age (65:20, 23). Ancient peoples considered long life a great blessing, particularly since their childhood mortality rate was so high. Second, Yahweh's true servants *will long enjoy the works of their hands* and realize the benefits and blessings of their labors (65:21–22; 62:8–9; Deut 6:10–11; 8:12; but see Deut 28:30, 38–44). Another great blessing was meaningful work. Third, Yahweh will *answer* the prayers of his true servants *before they call*; he will be eager to provide for their needs, and he will promote peace between hostile groups and individuals in society (65:24–25; compare 11:6–9).

In chapter 66, the fifth century BCE prophet proclaims Yahweh's message, using standard formulas for introducing divine speech (*this is what the Lord says*; *hear the word of the Lord*; *declares the Lord*; *says the Lord* [see 66:1, 5, 12, 17, 21, 22, 23]). He speaks to the small Judean community in Jerusalem, consisting of both counterfeit and true servants of Yahweh.

On the one hand, Yahweh announces *harsh treatment* on the people who worship other gods and treat their fellow human beings unjustly; all others will despise them (66:3–4, 17, 24). Yahweh rejects the sacrifices and other forms of worship of this group because: *they have chosen their own ways* rather than Yahweh's (55:8–9); *their souls delight in their abominations* (idols) (verses 3, 17; compare 44:19; 65:2–4; Ezek 5:9, 11); they did not *answer* when Yahweh *called* (65:1–2, 12); and *they did evil in* Yahweh's *sight* (65:12) by oppressing the poor and defenseless (58:1–12; 59:3–8). All of these indictments repeat themes of 1:10–17.

On the other hand, Yahweh, who *made all things* and rules the universe from the *heavenly throne, esteems* people who are *humble and contrite in spirit and* [who] *tremble at* the divine *word* (verses 1–2; 57:15). Their wicked opponents in the faith community *hate* and want to *exclude* them, but Yahweh promises to make things right. God will come as a mighty warrior to bless the true followers and *execute judgment upon* counterfeit worshipers with *fury, fire, chariots, anger and sword* (verses 5–6, 14–16; 65:6–7). Yahweh will empower *Zion (Jerusalem)* to *give birth* to numerous *children* (that is, to grow rapidly in population), and *will extend prosperity* (NRSV) *to her like a river* and *the wealth of nations like a flooding stream* (60:5–14; 61:5), so that Yahweh's true servants who live there, those who now *love her* and *mourn over her, will drink deeply and delight in her overflowing abundance* (verses 7–12). *As a mother comforts her child,* Yahweh will *comfort* his new faith community in Jerusalem (verse 13; 49:14–15).

The book concludes with a vision of Yahweh assembling all *nations and tongues* to *see his glory.* The righteous remnant will also *proclaim* God's *glory among the nations* and will reassemble the chosen people from their various locations throughout the Near Eastern world. All Jews will return to *the temple of the Lord in Jerusalem as an offering to the Lord.* Yahweh will *select some of the foreigners from other nations to be* his *priests and Levites.* Jerusalem's *name and descendants will endure* throughout the generations, and *all mankind will come and bow down before* Yahweh there (verses 17–23; 45:20–25; 56:6–8). "This is ... a great inclusive, universal reach of Yahweh to claim sovereignty over all peoples and to include all nations in the protected, blessed, covenanted community" (Brueggemann, *Isaiah 40–66*, 258).

> **Universalism in Isaiah**
>
> The final vision of the book of Isaiah, like so much of the rest of the book, offers a picture of universal human well-being under the rule of God. Israel does not exist for its own sake alone, but for the sake of all humanity. The universalizing vision of the book draws deeply from the biblical tradition and leads to both Judaism's views of itself as a chosen people bearing witness to God and to Christianity's desire to heal all the nations (see Rev 22:2).

THEOLOGICAL REFLECTIONS

The authors of the book of Isaiah in its present form were addressing a small Jewish community in and near Jerusalem in the mid- to late-fifth century BCE, consisting of both faithful servants of Yahweh and counterfeit worshipers. The authors reapplied Yahweh's former activities to this new situation, emphasizing the characteristics of Yahweh that these activities demonstrated as denunciations of the wicked and encouragements to the righteous.

Yahweh *created, formed, made, stretched or spread out* the universe and all that is in it, including humankind (29:16; 37:16; 40:26, 28; 42:5; 45:12, 18; 48:13; 51:13, 16; 54:16; 66:1–2); God created different physical conditions on earth (41:17–20); he made Jacob (Israel) (43:1, 7, 15; 44:2, 21–24; 45:9, 11; 49:5 [the remnant]; 54:5); God is the author of righteousness, punishment, and blessing (45:7, 8), and of new and hidden things previously unknown (48:6–7); he will create a new heaven and a new earth, with Jerusalem as a joy (65:17–18). All creatures belong to God, demonstrating God's power, wisdom, love and care.

Yahweh acts in human history to accomplish eternal purposes, controlling kings, nations, and events. After destroying human life on earth with the flood, Yahweh promised never to do so again (54:9). He redeemed Abraham from Ur of the Chaldees (29:22) and promised to multiply his descendants greatly (51:1–2). He delivered the Israelites from Egyptian bondage (10:24–26; 11:11, 15–16; 43:12, 16–17; 63:7–9), supplied their needs during the wilderness wanderings (48:20–21), and gave them the promised land as a precursor to delivering their descendants from Assyria (11:15–16; 30:15; 37:20, 35) and Babylon (35:8–10; 40:3–4; 43:14–17; 52:3–6) to prosper in the promised land again (60:21; 61:7; 62:4). Yahweh established David and his dynasty, empowering David to capture Zion/Jerusalem and make it Yahweh's dwelling place (1:27–28; 2:2–4; 4:2–6; 8:18; 12:6; 14:32; 18:7; 24:23; 29:1–8; 31:4–5; 33:20; 35:10; 51:3, 11; 52:1–8; 55:3; 60:14; 62:11–12); God raised up penitent Hezekiah of the Davidic lineage to restore justice and righteousness in Judah (8:21–9:7; 32:1–8). Yahweh used Tiglath-pileser III of Assyria to overthrow Syria and North Israel and to punish Ahaz and Judah (7:17, 20; 8:7–8); Sennacherib, to destroy the cities of Judah and besiege Jerusalem as punishment for the sins of Hezekiah and Judah (1:2–9; 10:5–19; 36–37); Nebuchadnezzar, to devastate Jerusalem and carry many Judeans into exile (47:6–7; 54:6–8); and Cyrus, to *redeem* (1:27–28; 41:14; 43:1, 14; 44:6, 22–24; 47:4; 48:17, 20; 49:7, 26; 52:9; 54:5, 8; 59:20; 60:16; 63:16) or *save* (35:4; 43:3, 11; 45:15, 17, 21; 49:25–26; 60:16) Yahweh's faithful servants from captivity and return them to their land (13:17–19; 14:1–2; 41:2–3, 25; 44:24–45:7; 45:13; 46:8–11).

Yahweh is *the Lord, and there is no other; besides him there is no god* (44:6; 45:5, 14; 46:9). Other gods are false because they are the work of human hands and can do nothing (2:8, 18–21; 21:9; 40:19–20; 44:9–20; 46:1–2), whereas Yahweh is *the living God* (37:4, 17) who intervenes in nature and history to accomplish holy purposes. Yahweh is incomparable (40:18, 25; 46:5, 9). To emphasize God's transcendent majesty, Isaiah affirms that God is *holy* (5:16; 6:3; 52:10; 57:15), calls him *the Holy One [of Israel, or Jacob]* (29 times; for example, 1:4; 5:19, 24; 29:19, 23; 54:5; 55:5), and extols his *glory* (3:8; 6:3; 10:16; 35:2; 40:5; 42:8; 48:11; 58:8; 59:19; 60:1–2; 62:2; 66:18–19). Yahweh is *king* of the individual (6:1, 5), of Israel (33:22; 41:21; 43:15; 44:6; 52:7), of the nations (24:21), and of all creation, including the angelic hosts (24:21–23).

Yahweh has an intimate, daily, personal relationship with the chosen people Israel, which Isaiah compares with the relationship of king to people (6:1–5; 33:22; 40:1–11; 52:7–12), husband to wife (50:1; 54:1–8; 62:1–5), parent (father and mother) to child (1:2–4; 45:9–11; 49:14–15; 63:16; 64:8; 66:13), shepherd to sheep (40:11), vinedresser to vineyard (5:1–7; 27:2–6), doctor to patient (1:5–6), potter to clay (29:15–16; 45:9; 64:8), and teacher to student (28:5–13; 30:19–26; 48:17–19).

This relationship experienced certain vicissitudes, which essentially form the backbone of Isaiah's message. First, Yahweh chose Israel as a people in the exodus, wilderness wanderings, giving of the law at Sinai and settlement of the land (14:1; 41:8–10; 44:1–2; 51:10), like a husband marrying *the wife of his youth* (54:5–8). God chose Israel to be his *servant* (41:8–10; 43:10; 44:1–2, 21, 26; 45:4; 48:20; 49:3, 5–7; 50:10; 52:12; 53:11) and *witnesses* (43:10, 12; 44:8), *messenger(s)* (42:19; 44:26), and a *light* (42:6; 49:6) to the nations to open their blind eyes and deaf ears (42:7; 52:13) so they will serve Israel's God. As Yahweh's *servant*, Israel's "great task is to bear testimony that Yahweh alone is God, that there is no savior beside him" (Muilenburg 405), and by doing this attempt to bring the nations to Yahweh.

Second, Israel *forsook* Yahweh (1:4, 28; 65:11) like a wife forsakes her husband for other lovers (50:1). Pride, arrogance, self-centeredness, and ingratitude ruled Israel's heart (2:11–17; 5:15, 21), motivating them to abandon Yahweh for other gods (2:8, 18–21; 10:10–11; 31:6–7; 44:9–20; 57:5–10; 65:2–5), trust in military strength and foreign nations rather than Yahweh (7:1–17; 8:3–10; 30:1–7; 31:1–3), practice external religious rituals although the worshipers' hearts were far from Yahweh (29:13–14), and oppress the defenseless and poor (1:10–17, 21–26; 3:13–15; 5:1–17, 22–23; 10:1–4; 58:1–14). Israel, whom Yahweh appointed to help the nations *see* and *hear* was itself *blind* and *deaf* (6:9–10; 42:18–20; 43:8).

Third, Yahweh punished Israel like a husband *forsakes*, *abandons*, and *divorces* his wife as a last resort for her infidelity (50:1; 54:5–8). On *the day of Yahweh* (2:12–17; 7:18–25; 22:5–14), God *sent* Assyria (7:16–20; 8:7–8; 10:5–19; 28:1–4) and angrily gave *Israel into Babylon's hand* (39:1–6; 47:6).

Fourth, however, Yahweh still loves Israel (54:5–8; 62:4–5) and yearns for her to return to him (65:1, 12, 24; 66:4).

Fifth, Yahweh will woo and marry the penitent in Israel, the remnant (46:3), once more (54:5–8; 62:4–5). The authors of Isaiah have placed 28:23–29 strategically to summarize how Yahweh works with his rebellious, then penitent, people. Sweeney comments that the farmer "plows, harrows, and overturns the earth, but it is of limited duration. Because his purpose is to provide food, he plants seeds and orders his land so that cummin and the various grains will grow. Likewise, when he harvests his crops, his actions are essentially destructive, but again they are not thoroughly destructive in that they lead to a positive result. In this manner, the actions of the farmer are compared to those of the coming invader. There will be destruction and hardship, but the result will be the reestablishment of Yahweh's glory and justice once the incompetent leadership is removed" (Sweeney 366; compare Beuken, *Isaiah Chapters 28–39*, 59–68).

Yahweh's comprehensive plan is to use his faithful elect to *save* the nations. Though world powers, the nations *are like a drop from a bucket*, *as dust on the scales* (40:15), *as less than nothing* (40:17), *like grasshoppers* (40:22) before Yahweh. He uses the nations to punish his people (5:26–30; 10:5–19; 44:24–45:7) and to return them from captivity (49:22–23; 60:10–16). Like Israel (2:6–22), the nations are full of pride, arrogance, self-centeredness, and ingratitude (13:11, 19; 14:11–15; 16:6; 23:7–12; 47:8–11). Therefore, like Israel, on *the day of Yahweh*, Yahweh punishes them (13:6–13; 19:1–15; 23:1–18; 47:1–15). But Yahweh's ultimate purpose is to draw in the nations in order to *save* them (2:2–4; 19:23–25; 45:20–25; 49:1–6; 52:13–53:12).

Jesus, born and raised a Jew, took up this Isaianic vision and gathered around himself a *little flock* (Luke 12:32) of twelve Jewish disciples, first commissioning them to *go nowhere among the Gentiles, and enter no town of the Samaritans*, *but go rather to the lost sheep of the house of Israel* (Matt 10:5–6). But after his resurrection, he commissioned them to *go and make disciples of all nations* (Matt 28:19). Everywhere Paul, *a Hebrew born of Hebrews* (Phil 3:5), traveled proclaiming God's message of salvation, he went first to the Jews, then to the Gentiles (Rom 1:16; Acts 13:44–48). He designated those who came to God through Christ the *true Israel* of God (Rom 9:6–8; Gal 6:11–16). Like Isaiah, the New Testament distinguishes between faithful, penitent servants of God and those who pretend to serve him (Titus 1:16; 1 John 2:19; Heb 10:32–39).

The Remnant

"Remnant" in Isaiah refers to different groups in different contexts: *physical survivors of northern Israel after Tiglath-pileser III's invasion* (7:3–9; 17:6; 28:5); *Judah after Sennacherib's invasion* (1:9; 4:3; 37:4, 31–32); *Babylon* (14:22), *Philistia* (14:30), *Moab* (15:9; 16:14), *and Aram (Syria)* (17:3); *spiritual survivors of northern Israel after Tiglath-pileser III's invasion* (10:20–23; 11:11, 15–16); *and Judah after Babylon destroyed Jerusalem* (46:3). Isaiah's author addresses the book to the remnant of Judah in Jerusalem and its environs in the mid- to late-fifth century BCE. This remnant consists of faithful "servants" of Yahweh, as well as counterfeits (54:11–17; 63:15–19; 65:8–16; 66:14–16); Yahweh's future lies with the faithful.

FOR FURTHER STUDY

John Goldingay, *The Message of Isaiah 40–55: A Literary Theological Commentary* (London: T & T Clark, 2005).

D. N. Premnath, *Eighth Century Prophets: A Social Analysis* (St. Louis: Chalice, 2003).

WORKS CITED

Klaus Baltzer, *Deutero-Isaiah: A Commentary on Isaiah 40–55* (Minneapolis, Minn.: Fortress, 2001).

ISAIAH

Willem A. M. Beuken, *Isaiah Part II*, vol. 2: *Isaiah Chapters 28–39* (Leuven: Peeters, 2000).

Joseph Blenkinsopp, *Isaiah 1–39* (New York: Doubleday, 2000).

———, *Isaiah 40–55* (New York: Doubleday, 2002).

———, *Isaiah 56–66* (New York: Doubleday, 2003).

John Bright, *A History of Israel* (3rd ed.; Philadelphia: Westminster, 1981).

Walter Brueggemann, *Isaiah 1–39* (Louisville: Westminster John Knox, 1998).

———, *Isaiah 40–66* (Louisville: Westminster John Knox, 1998).

Brevard S. Childs, *Isaiah* (Louisville: Westminster John Knox, 2001).

Ronald E. Clements, *Isaiah 1–39* (Grand Rapids: Eerdmans, 1980).

Seth Erlandsson, *The Burden of Babylon: A Study of Isaiah 13:2–14:23* (Lund: Gleerup, 1970).

John Goldingay, *Isaiah* (Peabody, Mass.: Hendrickson, 2001).

John H. Hayes, "Isaiah, Book of," in vol. 1 of *Dictionary of Biblical Interpretation* (Nashville: Abingdon, 1999): 549–56.

John H. Hayes and Stuart A. Irvine, *Isaiah the Eighth-Century Prophet: His Times & His Preaching* (Nashville: Abingdon, 1987).

Jan L. Koole, *Isaiah III*, vol. 1: *Isaiah 40–48* (Kampen: Kok, 1997).

———, *Isaiah III*, vol. 2: *Isaiah 49–55* (Kampen: Kok, 1998).

———, *Isaiah III*, vol. 3: *Isaiah 56–66* (Kampen: Kok, 2001).

J. Alec Motyer, *The Prophecy of Isaiah: An Introduction and Commentary* (Downers Grove, Ill.: InterVarsity, 1993).

James Muilenburg, "The Book of Isaiah Chapters 40–66: Introduction and Exegesis," in vol. 5 of *The Interpreter's Bible* (ed. George Buttrick et al.; Nashville: Abingdon, 1956): 381–773.

John N. Oswalt, *The Book of Isaiah Chapters 1–39* (Grand Rapids: Eerdmans, 1986).

James Pritchard, ed., *Ancient Near Eastern Texts* (3rd ed.; Princeton: Princeton University Press, 1969).

Christopher R. Seitz, *Isaiah 1–39* (Louisville: John Knox, 1993).

———, "The Book of Isaiah 40–66: Introduction, Commentary, and Reflections" in vol. 6 of *The New Interpreter's Bible* (ed. Leander Keck; Nashville: Abingdon, 2001): 307–552.

Marvin A. Sweeney, *Isaiah 1–39, With an Introduction to Prophetic Literature* (FOTL XVI; Grand Rapids: Eerdmans, 1996).

Gene M. Tucker, "The Book of Isaiah 1–39: Introduction, Commentary, and Reflections," in vol. 6 of *The New Interpreter's Bible* (ed. Leander Keck; Nashville: Abingdon, 2001): 25–305.

John D. W. Watts, *Isaiah 1–33* (Waco, Tex.: Word, 1985).

Claus Westermann, *Isaiah 40–66: A Commentary* (Philadelphia: Westminster, 1969).

R. N. Whybray, *Isaiah 40–66* (London: Oliphants, 1975).

Hans Wildberger, *Isaiah 1–12* (Minneapolis, Minn.: Fortress, 1991).

Jeremiah

Keith N. Schoville

CHAPTER CONTENTS

Contexts 577
Commentary 579
   Historical Prologue · 1:1–3 579
   Prophecies of Deserved Disaster · 1:4–29:27 579
   Sin & Punishment · 8:4–9:26 584
   The People, the Covenant & Jeremiah's Prophecy · 10:15–29:32 585
   Prophecies of Restoration · 30:1–33:26 597
   The Last Days of Judah · 34:1–38:13 602
   Zedekiah Questions Jeremiah Again · 38:14–28 606
   Jeremiah's Witness after Jerusalem's Fall · 40:1–45:5 608
   Prophecies Against Foreign Peoples · 46:1–51:64 611
   Historical Appendix · 52:1–34 615
Theological Reflections 615
For Further Study 616
Works Cited 616

MAPS, TABLES, & FEATURES

The Ark of the Covenant 581
The Prophet as Mediator 583
Child Sacrifice 584
The Potter & the Clay 588
Distinguishing True from False Prophets 591

The Book of Jeremiah is a collection of oracles revealed to the inspired prophet. These are primarily poetic in form, as is true of other prophets. The main feature of Hebrew poetry is parallelism, that is, a line that repeats or supplements the thought in a previous line. For example, in Jeremiah 1:5–6 we read:

> Before I formed you in the womb I knew you,
> before you were born I set you apart;
> I appointed you as a prophet to the nations.

In addition to poetic oracles, however, prose elements may appear within or between oracles (as in 9:12–16), including biographical information. Most contemporary English translations identify these elements and set them off appropriately, so that it is relatively easy to identify poetry from prose. Being aware of poetic expression helps us to appreciate the cooperative creativity of the Lord and the prophet. Jeremiah's words combine the inspirational activity of God with the verbal activity of the prophet, making the combined effect memorable.

CONTEXTS

Jeremiah lived and fulfilled his ministry in a crucial period in the history of God's people. As the historical prologue (1:1–3) indicates, Josiah was in his thirteenth year as king of Judah when Jeremiah heard the Lord's call to prophesy (627 BCE). Josiah was eight years old when he became king (640 BCE), so he was 21 when Jeremiah answered the Lord's call. We do not know Jeremiah's age at the time; perhaps he was about the same age as the king. Five years later, workers found the scroll of the Law in the temple as they refurbished the building (2 Kgs 22). The young king was horrified at the sorry state of the religion of his people when compared to the covenant stipulations in the scroll (probably Deuteronomy or part of it). After the reign of Hezekiah in the days of the prophet Isaiah, Manasseh and his son Amon, grandfather and father of Josiah, led the nation astray. In the aftermath of the discovery of the scroll, Josiah instituted the reforms for which he is famous (2 Kgs 24:25). This involved cleansing the temple of all its unorthodox elements, eliminating worship at places other than Jerusalem, purifying the priesthood, and reestablishing the religious practices of the Law of Moses.

Thirteen years later (609 BCE), Josiah met his death when he and his kingdom became involved in the international politics of the day. Three major power centers—Egypt, Assyria, and Babylonia (Chaldea)—struggled for dominance over the region between the Euphrates River and the Sinai Peninsula. Assyria, which had dominated the region for over a century and carried the northern kingdom Israel into exile in 722 BCE, declined in power after the fall of Nineveh in 612 BCE. Egypt was allied to Assyria at the time, and Pharaoh Neco moved north through Palestine to thwart the growing power of Nabopolassar of Babylon. King Josiah attempted to stop the Egyptians in a battle at Megiddo but died in battle. Pharaoh Neco then replaced Josiah's immediate successor, Jehoahaz (Shallum; Jer 22:11), with his brother, Eliakim, and gave him the throne name Jehoiakim. Neco also required an excessive tribute from the Judeans.

In order to maintain their dominance in the region, the Egyptians had to confront the growing power of Babylon. The decisive battle was at Carchemish, a ford over the Euphrates River, in 605 BCE. The new king of the Babylonians was Nebuchadnezzar, who succeeded his father upon Nabopolassar's death. King Jehoiakim of Judah then became a vassal of Babylon for three years, but rebelled against Nebuchadnezzar when the latter fought Egypt in 601 BCE. Ultimately, Nebuchadnezzar put down the rebellion by besieging Jerusalem and capturing it in 597 BCE. No details survive about Jehoiakim's death in 598 BCE, but Jeremiah had predicted that he would not receive a king's burial (Jer 22:19; 36:30). Jehoiakim's son Jehoiachin, who assumed the throne as Jeconiah, or Coniah, surrendered to the Babylonians after a three-month reign. Nebuchadnezzar then placed Jehoiachin's uncle, Mattaniah, on the throne of Judah and gave him the throne name Zedekiah. Zedekiah was caught between pro-Egyptian and pro-Babylonian political groups in Judah. Despite the warning of Jeremiah that Nebuchadnezzar was the Lord's instrument to punish his rebellious people, Zedekiah entertained an anti-Babylonian conference of leaders of neighboring peoples in 594 BCE (Jer 27:3). Finally, in 589 BCE the Judeans revolted, expecting support from Egypt.

The Babylonians rampaged across the country, and by early 588 BCE the siege of Jerusalem had begun. Jeremiah remained in Jerusalem throughout the siege. Zedekiah sought and received the prophet's counsel – that the only way to save himself and the city was to surrender (21:1–14). Zedekiah, however, did not follow that advice in the face of the strong pro-Egyptian element in his advisory court. The Egyptian army did move into the region, causing the Babylonians to lift the siege briefly to shift their forces against the Egyptians (Jer 37:5), but soon the Egyptians withdrew, and the siege of Jerusalem resumed. The Babylonians breached the walls and stormed the city, probably in July, 587/6 BCE (the exact year remains uncertain). Nebuchadnezzar deported a large number of people, particularly leaders of the Judeans, and appointed a governor, Gedaliah, to administer the region. Insurgents murdered the governor within months and forced a considerable number, including Jeremiah and Baruch the scribe, to seek refuge in Egypt, apparently fearing Babylonian reprisals. This brought a third and final round of deportation to Babylon (Jer 52:28–30). The Babylonians continued to control the region until Cyrus the Great wrested control of the empire from them in 539 BCE, ushering in a new era allowing those in exile to return to their homelands.

Other commentators may and often do perceive the structure of the book somewhat differently.

Chapters 1–25:14 form the core of the book, which, except for the words of a compiler(s) or editor(s), Baruch wrote on a scroll at the prophet's dictation (Jer 36:4). This material was expanded after King Jehoiakim burned the original scroll (36:23; 32). Many scholars believe that Baruch was the major compiler or editor of the book, but we may assume that at least the final verses (52:31–34) were written some time after the death of both Jeremiah and Baruch in approximately 560 BCE. Other editorial additions appear in the text.

> **The Masoretic Text**
>
> All English translations of Jeremiah are based on the Masoretic Text. This Hebrew text had a history of development, and it reached its final form after about 250 BCE. At that time, the Greek translation of Hebrew Scriptures (the Septtuagint, or LXX) began, and the Greek version of Jeremiah came to be sometime after that date. The Septuagint is shorter than the Masoretic Text, and the arrangement of the materials of the book differ. This indicates some fluidity in the transmission of the text.

> **The Compilation of Jeremiah**
> According to Timothy Willis,
>
> The author/compiler (probably Baruch) is inspired by God to present particular prophecies in a particular arrangement for the purpose of giving a written message from God to readers living long after these events had transpired. Some prophecies that were spoken originally at separate times and under separate circumstances are now placed side by side. Such placement has an intended (and inspired) effect on later readers (Willis 21).

Initially intended for the Jerusalem audience of his contemporaries, Jeremiah gave his prophecies orally. Later they were written down, making them available to other audiences and in particular those in exile in Babylon.

There are similarities in vocabulary and ideas between Jeremiah and Deuteronomy. Critical scholarship has related the composition of Deuteronomy to the time of Josiah, based on the discovery of the "book of the law" (2 Kgs 22:8). The scholarly perception also identifies Deuteronomy as the beginning of a Deuteronomistic History that ends with 2 Kings. The German scholar Martin Noth, the primary formulator of the theory in a 1943 publication, attributed the authorship of the history to "a single exilic author/compiler." Whether or not a single individual or a group of Deuteronomists compiled the prophecies, many scholars suspect that individual or group largely formed the book of Jeremiah. Such scholars search for and highlight evidences within the book to support their views of its composition.

The details of the composition of the book elude us, and space does not allow an extended discussion of the matter. But the observations of at least one scholar who deals with the subject even-handedly are useful:

> Jeremiah *himself* may have been a Deuteronomist of sorts in that he grew up in a Levitical community north of Jerusalem in which this tradition was rooted....
>
> If then, when dictating his messages for reading at the temple, he did so in a Deuteronomic style, it would not be surprising. That was the style he grew up with....
>
> (Miller 154)

COMMENTARY

HISTORICAL PROLOGUE · 1:1–3

The opening words of the book of Jeremiah place the prophet in his historical time and place. These words were not written by the prophet himself, but by the final person(s) involved in the collecting, editing, and arranging of the materials in the book. However, readers learn more about Jeremiah than any other prophet. He was from a priestly family from Anathoth in Benjamin, about 3 miles northeast of Jerusalem.

The dates in this superscription range from 627/6 BCE, *the thirteenth year of the reign of Josiah*, through 609–598 BCE, *the reign of Jehoiakim*, to 586 BCE, *down to the fifth month of the eleventh year of Zedekiah*. The text mentions neither the three-month reign of Jehoahaz, nor that of Jehoiachin (598–597 BCE), who was also known as Jeconiah or Coniah. (See 2 Kgs 23–24 for Jehoahaz and Jehoiachin.)

PROPHECIES OF DESERVED DISASTER · 1:4–29:27

1:4–19 *The word of the Lord came to me* marks the beginning of a communication from Yahweh to Jeremiah, but we do not know by what means the prophet received that word. It may have come through a vision, a dream, audibly, or through some kind of mental awareness. Whatever the mode of transmission, the message was personal and specific. The call came in 627/6 BCE, but we do not know Jeremiah's age at the time of the call. He was but a *child* [Hebrew *naar*], or better, a *youth* (RSV).

The Lord rejected Jeremiah's sense of inadequacy and reluctance and countered with: *you must go ... and say whatever I command you*. The Lord's words, *Do not be afraid ... I ... will rescue you*, and action, *reached out his hand and touched my mouth*, reassure and empower, similarly to Isaiah's experience (Isa 6:8–10).

The Lord's agenda for Jeremiah lays out in general terms the career of the new spokesperson. He is to speak the Lord's words, which have extraordinary power to bring destruction and reconstruction, not just to Judah (Israel) but also to other nations and kingdoms. The collected materials from the prophet's work, that is, the rest of the book of Jeremiah, illustrate his faithfulness to the divine call.

Two visions follow. The first in Hebrew has a play on words: *almond branch* [Hebrew *shaqed*] and *for I am watching* [Hebrew *shoqed*]. This literary nicety cannot be translated into English, but it reveals the book's linguistic creativity. In the second vision Jeremiah sees a *boiling pot, tilting away from the north* toward the south. It symbolizes the disaster that will reach Jerusalem from the north in the person of unnamed invaders. Historically, Babylonian armies under Nebuchadnezzar invaded Judah. The plural *kings* refers to the great king of Babylon and his vassal kings. The boiling pot will spill over Judas as Yahweh's judgment on their paganized

> **"The People of the Land"**
> *The prophet learns again of God's presence and power to protect him as he faithfully confronts the entrenched political and priestly powers and* the people of the land. *The latter group are not the poor, common people but the "landed gentry" (Bright 6).*

religious practices, a refrain that echoes throughout Jeremiah (for example, 2:26–28; 7:9; 10:3–5). Similar expressions of God's righteous judgment on his people appear in 2 Kings (21:10–15; 22:14–17).

2:1–3:5 Immediately following the prophetic call are a series of pronouncements in which Jeremiah confronts the Judean powers with the charges the Lord brings against them.

The Septuagint in verses 1–2a say only *And he said, Thus saith the Lord*. The city is personified in the expression: *in the hearing of Jerusalem*.

In verses 2b–3, with imagery harking back to Hosea 1–3, the Lord reminds Judah of their mutual love and expresses care for, and protection of, them in the wilderness wanderings. What their forefathers had experienced, Jeremiah's generation shared in potential as descendants of that first generation. *Israel was holy to the Lord*, sanctified, set apart for special purposes. The generation to which Jeremiah spoke should also have been holy to the Lord. The imagery of the Lord's people as bride continues in the New Testament with the church as the bride of Christ (2 Cor 11:2; Eph 5:23–27).

The expression *declares the Lord* is a recurring divider between independent prophetic sayings. *House of Jacob* and *clans of the house of Israel* exhibit the characteristic parallelism of Hebrew poetry; they are equivalent. Though the northern kingdom, Israel, ended with the Assyrian conquest in 721 BCE, the Judean contingent of God's people is also a remnant of Israel – that is, Jacob's descendants.

Verse 5's rhetorical question begins this word of the Lord. The implicit answer to the question is that your ancestors did not find a fault in me, yet they strayed far from me! According to verses 6–9, memory of Yahweh's past care should have played a vital role in Israel's religious understanding, but the priests had failed as teachers and transmitters of the Torah (Lev 10:11; Deut 24:8). They had lost an intimate awareness of the Lord; they *did not know me*. *Kittim* (Crete) and to the east *Kedar* (Arabia) indicate the extremities of east and west. An individual may change deities, but never had an entire nation done so, except for Judah. *Their Glory* refers to God, who had blessed them with a land flowing with milk and honey. The *lions* are a metaphor for foreign rulers from both Egypt and Mesopotamia (the latter referring to Assyria and Babylonia). Israel fears foreign powers because they *have no awe* before God.

The charges God brings through the prophet speak both of *long ago* and of *this generation*. Theirs was a persistent practice. The prophet depicts their rebellion in terms of prostitution and of a choice vineyard whose stock has reverted to wild, bitter fruit. Their pursuit of other *Baals* (lords) is as persistent as eager males pursuing a she-ass in estrus. God's people have been caught red-handed, serving gods of their craftsmanship – until a crisis strikes. Then they cry out to the Lord. The entire nation is guilty, but the text mentions the leaders – kings and their advisors, priests, and prophets – specifically. They bear the greater responsibility. The Lord's punishment serves for the ultimate good of his people, but they *did not respond to correction*. Again and again, Scripture describes them as a stiff-necked people (Exod 32:9).

The Lord now focuses upon Jeremiah's generation. The rhetorical question pairs *desert* with *land of great darkness*. Desert and darkness bear negative connotations. Deserts largely lack the necessities of life; deep darkness restricts movement. The truth to be understood is exactly the opposite. The Lord brought them into a fertile land, a land where one is *free to roam* and live. But they used their freedom to forget and forsake Yahweh. The *lifeblood of the innocent poor* offers clear testimony against them. Protesting innocence will not save the guilty from the Lord's judgment. Rather than trusting in the Lord, they trusted in Egypt. But just as the Assyrians had carried away the Lord's people with their hands bound above their heads, so Judeans in Jeremiah's time will be captives.

Jeremiah 3:1–5 emphasizes the sacredness of the marriage bond. Once sundered by divorce and remarriage, it is an abomination to the Lord for the first husband to take his former wife back (Deut 24:1–4). God's people had played the harlot with pagan gods, though they had been like a bride to him (verse 2). God had sought to get their attention to correct them. He withheld the precious rains, resulting in drought. Yet they *refuse to blush with shame* while they blame God, asking, *Will your wrath continue forever*? Their

---

Yahweh as Water

In contrast to worthless idols, *Yahweh is* the fountain of living waters, *like a spring, an ever-flowing source of pure, life-sustaining liquid. In ancient Israel, the only other source of precious water was rain caught in plastered cisterns. In contrast, the* worthless idols *are* broken cisterns..

deeds speak louder than their talk, even though their words are couched in the endearing, *My Father*. They had forsaken the Lord while deluding themselves, saying, *I am innocent; he is not angry with me*. Self-delusion is the most pernicious kind.

3:6–4:4 *During the reign of King Josiah* is the book's first historical reference since the superscription. What is written is a reminder to the prophet of the history of *faithless* Israel, again using metaphors of marriage, adultery, and divorce. Israel's intimate relationship with the Lord was sullied and sundered. Because of northern Israel's idolatry and pernicious practices, God sent them into exile over a century before Jeremiah heard this word from the Lord. *On every high hill and under every spreading tree* denotes pagan worship at high places where there were sacred oaks. A related expression, *committed adultery with stone and wood*, refers to the materials for making images. Despite the example Israel set for Judah, the southern kingdom only pretends to return to the Lord. Their *pretense* of repentance is an abomination to the Lord.

In verses 11–13, God tells Jeremiah to focus his message *toward the north*, in the direction of the land Israel once occupied and even beyond, toward Assyria, the land of their captivity. The long-suffering of God exceeds human comprehension. Even in their deserved captivity, God asks only for the acknowledgment of guilt, an action associated with repentance, so that he could show them his mercy.

According to verses 14–18, God is faithful and will save a remnant (see Isa 10:22; 28:5), *one ... from every town and two from every clan* of those who will turn from faithlessness. He will bring the remnant back, not to Samaria, but to Zion. He will provide *shepherds*, leaders wise in the ways of the Lord and dedicated to the welfare of the people, unlike their former leaders (2 Kgs 17:21–23). In that time, *the ark of the covenant of the Lord* will fade from memory, replaced by the city of Jerusalem, *The throne of the Lord*, and so recognized by *all nations*. The remnant will represent a reunification of Israel and Judah. This section looks to the distant future and is a hopeful word injected into the preceding condemnation of the faithlessness of God's people, both in Israel's past and in Jeremiah's own time.

After the word of hope for restoration, 3:19–4:4 continues with themes we have heard before. The contrast between the Lord's kindly intention and the faithless people's rejection is clear. The *cry* of those who *have forgotten the Lord their God* draws a response urging them to return. Whether the dialogue between the Lord and the people is real or an expression of what the Lord desires is not clear. Verses 22b–25 indicate what God wants to hear: faithlessness turned to faith (*you are the Lord our God*), and a confession of guilt, the preliminary of repentance. Words alone are not sufficient; appropriate actions must follow (4:1–2).

The prophetic instruction and hope contained in 3:14–4:2 appear to have come from a later time than Josiah's reign. These words address those in exile, assisting them to understand God's intent for a future restoration. Jeremiah 4:2–4 returns to the Lord's effort to call *the men of Judah and people of Jerusalem* to repent.

4:5–31 History proves that Judah ignored the Lord's call for repentance. Jeremiah must now announce the coming disaster, the Lord's *wrath* that *will ... burn like fire ... with no one to quench it*. Jeremiah must announce the coming invasion and the necessity to prepare for it. The unnamed *lion* can be none other than Nebuchadnezzar, *a destroyer of nations*. All that happens will be an expression of *the fierce anger of the Lord*. All the leaders, to whom the people might have looked for hope, will themselves be hopeless *in that day*.

The Ark of the Covenant

Bezalel, chief craftsman, constructed the ark (Exod 37:1–9) as a container for the Ten Commandments (Deut 10:2–5), a pot of manna (Exod 16:33–34), and Aaron's rod (Num 17:8–10). The dimensions of the ark were "two and a half cubits long, a cubit and a half wide, and a cubit and a half high" (50 × 30 × 30 inches). Made of acacia wood, and covered with gold foil, the ark resided in the inner sanctum, the most holy place, of the tabernacle and later the Jerusalem temple. The ark signified God's presence in those holy places and in the midst of his people. While the Bible does not document the disappearance of the ark from the temple, it occurred either prior to or during the Babylonian conquest and destruction of Jerusalem. It is very doubtful that a substitute ark was ever in the Second Temple, for the Roman general Pompey found its inner sanctum empty in the first century BCE (See Josephus, Antiquities, *14:71–72; Jewish War, 1:152–53).*

JEREMIAH

In verse 10, the prophet's identification with his audience is evident in this aside remark to the *Sovereign Lord*, particularly as he notes that the sword of the invader is at *our* throats. In verse 11, the desert wind from the east (sirocco) is a metaphor for destruction. The prophet enlarges the image in the following poetic lines, then interrupts with the urgent plea of verse 14. The warning of the invader's approach comes from the north, *from Dan...from...Ephraim*.

The Lord's words are followed by the heart-rending verses 18–21, expressing the prophet's (or God's) deep anguish. He must not only speak the word of the Lord; he must also witness and experience as *disaster follows disaster*. The Lord's own assessment of the tragedy (verse 22) unfolding before the prophet's eyes provides a pause before Jeremiah continues to describe the ultimate outcome of the conflict.

> **God's Emotions**
> The Bible often portrays God with human emotions (anger, love, joy, dismay, though not fear or uncertainty). Yahweh relates to human beings at their most basic level of understanding.

In a prophetic vision, Jeremiah in verses 23–26 paints a picture of the chaotic results of the invasion on the environment and the people, the result of the Lord's *fierce anger*.

The word of the Lord continues in verses 27–31 with a description of inevitable results. This is what war was like for Judah in the face of overwhelmingly superior Babylonian forces. The image of the harlot expresses again the implacable nature of Judean idolatry. And so Jerusalem, *the Daughter of Zion*, is in her final travail, like a woman in the throes of birthing just before she dies. The Lord would not turn back from that decision (verse 28).

> **Rich & Poor in Jeremiah**
> In conversation with the Lord, Jeremiah responds in verses 3–6. The poor are set in their unrepentant ways because they do not know the way of the Lord. *But the leaders, who have leisure time to learn, have cast off all restraints. Like cattle on the loose, prey for predators, both the leaders and their followers will suffer for their rebellion and backslidings.*

5:1–31 The Lord urges the prophet to search for one honest, truth-seeking individual in Jerusalem. The people of Jerusalem were guilty of swearing falsely because they had rejected the living God for gods of "stone and wood" (3:9; 4:1b–2).

The word of the Lord (verses 7–11) against Judah again pours forth from the lips of the prophet. The God of all grace rejects forgiveness for his people who swear by *gods that are not gods* in place of truly believing and swearing, *As surely as the Lord lives* (verse 2). Jeremiah depicts their sins of sexual obsession and immorality with the metaphor of *lusty stallions*. The metaphor of a stripped vineyard depicts the land stripped of its inhabitants, but even here the grace of God is visible when God declares *do not destroy them completely*.

In verses 12–13, Jeremiah here injects his own observations on the self-delusion of the people. In self-denial they scoff at the idea that Yahweh would allow *harm to come to us*. The same twisted mentality appears in 7:4. The relationship of verse 12 to verse 13 is enigmatic. Those who *lied about the Lord* and denied that he would bring any harm may have been false prophets. In that case, verse 13 is "Jeremiah's indignant rejoinder" (Bright 40). Or these may be words of disdain aimed at Jeremiah and other true prophets, "...so they treated his prophets as false, and said that the punishment would fall on them" (Cawley and Millard 658). The Septuagint supports the latter view, with the people saying, *Our prophets became wind, and the word of the Lord was not in them*.

Jeremiah responds in verse 15 to what the people have said with a word from the *Lord God Almighty*. He emphasizes the awesome supremacy of Yahweh, whom he serves. The people may disdain his words, but the Lord has made them a consuming fire which the people will experience.

In verses 15–17, Jeremiah brings the word of the Lord to this people whose faces are harder than stone. In poetic form it is a graphic description of the coming invasion and destruction. In verses 18–19, God gives a passionate word of hope for the future for Jeremiah to deliver to the puzzled people.

Echoing Isaiah 6:9–10, verses 20–25 remind Jeremiah's hearers that Yahweh deserves respect, for almighty power is manifested in the barrier between land and sea. But they, spiritually deaf and blind, fail to recognize, respect and fear the God who sustains life through the cycles of the seasons.

In private conversation with Jeremiah, which he will make public, the Lord explains (verses 26–29) why he is justified in bringing calamity to his people. Many are guilty of exploiting the most vulnerable among their people, the widows and orphans, rather than assisting and defending them.

Before the division of Jeremiah into chapters and verses, verses 30–31 would have been a prelude to 6:1–3 (Willis 85). They highlight the moral morass that (false) prophets and priests create and in which the people wallow. Generally, the morality of the populace will rise no higher than that of their religious leaders.

6:1-30 In answer to the question, *But what will you do in the end?*, the Lord describes the *end* that is coming (verses 1–3), advising the people to *flee*. Benjamin, just north of Jerusalem, remained with Judah after the northern kingdom went into exile. *Tekoa*, (hometown of Amos) to the south of Jerusalem, and *Beth Hakkerem* to the west signify the coming encirclement of Jerusalem. The *shepherds* are the military leaders; *their flocks* are their warriors.

According to verses 4–5, God is privy to the battle plans of the invaders, and Jeremiah reveals those plans to his audience.

The Lord Almighty [literally "Lord of hosts," commander of the heavenly army] urges on the attackers in verses 6–9 because the city deserves punishment. He then uses his message as a last-ditch effort to urge them to change. But the coming devastation will be complete. Invaders will strip the land clean like a gleaned vineyard.

In verses 10–11a, Jeremiah bemoans his lack of an attentive audience. Those to whom he speaks will not listen; *the word of the Lord is offensive to them*. Yet he cannot refrain from speaking. He is the container of the burning wrath of the Lord and must empty himself of it.

The Lord responds in verses 11b–12 to Jeremiah, *Pour it out*. The prophet must proclaim the Lord's wrath to every segment of society, for all *who live in the land* will share the loss.

Following the instructions to Jeremiah, verses 13–15 describe the social and moral ills to which their lives testify. Rank materialism permeates their society. Though they speak peace, "there is no peace for the wicked" (Isa 48:22; 57:21). So calloused are they, they have no shame. They have even lost the ability to blush! God will punish them.

In verses 16–21, God offers the opportunity to return to *the ancient paths…the good way*, the way taught by Moses, but they refuse to go that way. The *watchmen* warn a city of approaching dangers. These were God's true prophets (Ezek 3:17), but the Lord's people would not listen to the prophetic warnings. Two witnesses, the nations and the earth, must thus witness the rightness of God's judgment. Though the Judeans act religiously, offering sacrifices, the odor is a stench to God, who desires that his people "act justly and…love mercy and…walk humbly" with their God (Mic 6:8). Therefore, the Lord will trip them up, and they *will perish*.

Verses 22–26 report a conversation. First the Lord, through Jeremiah, alerts the *Daughter of Zion* (Jerusalem) with a graphic description of the approaching army. Their fearful reply follows. Jeremiah appears to be speaking in verse 26; the use of *us* indicates his identification with his people. Jeremiah is not a disinterested bystander.

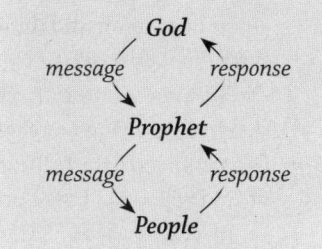

The Prophet as Mediator
In ancient Israel, the prophet spoke to God for the people and to the people for God.

In verses 27–30, the Lord speaks directly to Jeremiah. The metaphor of metallurgy indicates that the people are as hard as bronze and iron, and Jeremiah must test them. But testing and refining is fruitless; they cannot be purified *with fire*, so the Lord rejects them.

7:1-29 The "Temple Sermon" appears both here and in 26:1–6. Harrison calls this a "celebrated attack upon popular confidence in the Temple as an absolute guarantee of Jerusalem's inviolability" (Harrison 84). Jeremiah 26:1 places it *early in the reign of Jehoiakim*, thus in 609/608 BCE, likely at the time of one of the pilgrimage religious festivals (Deut 16:16–18; Lev 23:4–44; Exod 23:14–19). Recent translations, including NIV, indicate a change here from poetry to prose through 8:4.

In 7:1–15, Jeremiah must proclaim the word *at the gate of the Lord's house*, the entrance to a courtyard within the temple (26:2). Josiah's reforms focused the religion on the Jerusalem temple (2 Kgs 23:4–23). The Lord, through Jeremiah, rejects the inviolability of the temple and calls instead for moral and ethical change. The people's security is to be based on right actions rather than in impressive buildings. Shiloh [Arabic

Den of Robbers
Jesus, six hundred years later, would recall Jeremiah's words about the temple as a den of robbers *(Matt 21:13; Mark 11:17; Luke 19:46), though Jeremiah was not criticizing the temple establishment per se, as Jesus was.*

JEREMIAH

Seilun], eighteen miles north of Jerusalem, where the tabernacle and the ark were initially located, was apparently destroyed by the Philistines (1 Sam 4:10–11). *The people of Ephraim* are the people of Israel, the northern kingdom.

> **Kiriath-Jearim**
> Kiriath-Jearim is with modern Abu Ghosh, approximately eight miles northwest of Jerusalem. Here the ark rested for twenty years after its recovery from the Philistines before King David brought it into Jerusalem with great fanfare (2 Sam 6).

Yahweh addresses the remarks in verses 16–20 directly to Jeremiah. The prophet has a soft heart toward his people, so the Lord commands him to refrain from pleading for them. *The Queen of Heaven*, mentioned elsewhere in the Old Testament only in Jeremiah 44:17–25, is likely Ishtar (Assyrian-Babylonian religion), also identified with the Canaanite god Astarte (King 102–7). The righteous wrath of God will wreak havoc on both people and land.

In verses 21–26, Yahweh sarcastically instructs Jeremiah with an additional word for his audience. From the beginnings of Israel, the Lord has put obedience above the sacrificial system (1 Sam 15:22). The Lord's prophets repeatedly emphasize obedience.

The sober instruction in verses 27–29 concerns the prophet himself. Some commentators correctly connect verse 29 with the following section. The command, *Cut off your hair*, has a feminine pronoun in Hebrew; thus it refers not to the prophet but to the city or the nation.

7:30–8:3 Cutting off the hair and lamenting (verses 29–34) express profound sorrow. Such sorrow is appropriate; the Lord has *rejected and abandoned* Judah for practicing idolatry in the very temple of Yahweh. Further, they offered child sacrifices *in the Valley of Ben Hinnom* (on the western and southern bounds of Jerusalem). Such occurred in the reign of Manasseh (2 Kgs 21:5). In the place in which paganized Judeans sacrificed children, the bodies of those slain in the coming conflict would become carrion or be buried in mass graves. For a body to remain unburied was a terrible fate for an Israelite (Deut 28:26). A devastated and depopulated land would no longer witness the joys of weddings, the promise of a future for its people.

The litany of horror continues in 8:1–3. The attackers will ransack the rock-cut tombs of the elite, likely to contain valuable grave goods. In the process, they will cast out the bones, exposing them to the heavens, the astral deities they had honored. And the few survivors will wish they were dead.

SIN & PUNISHMENT · 8:4–9:26

Here the text returns to the poetic form that continues through chapter 10. The speaker(s) and audience vary. It is probable that the person(s) who assembled these prophetic statements, which may have come to and from the prophet over a long period of time, placed them here to supplement the Temple Sermon.

In verses 4–7, to return to the Lord is to repent. The Judeans do not follow normal human patterns, unlike migrating birds; they *do not know* what they should have known. Their teachers failed to instruct them in *the requirements of the Lord*.

According to verses 8–13, the scribes who copy the *law of the Lord* should know it better than anyone else; they were also teachers. But they *handled it falsely* and will pay the price for their folly. Verses 10–12 repeat 6:13–15. No doubt the prophet repeated himself over the years, particularly as he attempted to move his audiences to repentance and change. For a people who *all are greedy for gain*, the drought conditions promised will hit them where it hurts. In verses 14–16, the people respond with abject fear, but they put the blame on *the Lord our God*. Yet the invaders (in verse 17) cannot be dissuaded. They are like *vipers who cannot be charmed*.

A despairing cry comes from Jeremiah. The note with verse 18 identifies a textual problem, and *Comforter*

> **Child Sacrifice**
> Little material evidence for child sacrifice in ancient Israel exists, but biblical and other written sources testify to the practice among both Israelites and neighboring Moabites and Arameans. The descendants of the ancient Canaanites, the Phoenicians, practiced child sacrifice, and the predominant evidence for tophets have come to light at Phoenician (Punic) sites in North Africa, at Carthage and el Hofra (Albright 237). Topheth denotes a "hearth" or "roaster." A Punic tophet was the cultic installation where the sacrifices occurred and an adjacent burial ground for burned bones. The underlying motivation for all sacrifice is to obtain the favor of the unseen powers, for good or ill, that humans cannot control. Apparently to the pagan mind, the ultimate sacrifice of one's own offspring was sometimes necessary, but it was an abomination to Yahweh (see Mic 6:6–7).

indicates a title for God. The larger context, rather, suggests "Grief has overcome me" (Bright 62). A better reading for *from a land far away* is "from the length and breadth of the land," similar to Isaiah 33:17, where the same expression occurs (Hyatt 887). The question in verse 19b is a terse response to Jeremiah from the Lord, and in verse 20, the people cry out in dire circumstances.

Jeremiah's lament continues in 8:21–9:2. There is no healing salve nor anyone to apply it. The prophet's tear ducts cannot produce the flow of tears he longs to pour out for the fate of these people who have brought it upon themselves. Another alternative is his desire to withdraw far away from them and their sinfulness.

In verse 3, Yahweh supplements Jeremiah's complaint that the people are adulterers and unfaithful. They are also liars whose fundamental error is that they do not *acknowledge* (literally, "know") *me*.

> **Knowing God**
> Jeremiah often emphasizes the importance of knowing God, which he equates with living a highly ethical life and trusting and reverencing God.

The Lord warns the prophet (verses 4–6) not to trust anyone in his society. The masculine singular pronoun, *you*, confirms that Jeremiah is the audience.

In verses 7–9, the Lord again addresses Jeremiah with these poignant words, and God grieves (see 4:19–22) because there is no alternative to the punishment because of *the sin of my people*. Yet, he still calls them *my people*; God holds out hope for their redemption.

In verse 10, Jeremiah sorrows for the desolation of the countryside, and in verse 11, God responds that city and villages will also be desolate.

In the prose of verse 12, Jeremiah asks why *the land has been ruined and laid waste*. Some commentators consider this to be an insertion by an editor in the exilic period. But even Jeremiah in distress could ask it. The response of the Lord in verses 13–16 answers the question—his are a disobedient and stubborn people *who have followed the Baals*. Baal means "lord." They have chosen to submit to the false lords rather than to the Lord Almighty. The *bitter food* and *poisoned water* are metaphors for exile, slavery, and *the sword*.

With a word from the Lord (9:17–22), Jeremiah advises the people to summon the professional mourners. The funeral laments are for ruined Zion, all who dwell therein, and for all who die within it, "without respect to age or sex" (Harrison 91).

The word in verses 23–24 reveals the mind of the Lord and is timeless in its relevance. Neither wisdom, power, nor wealth is significant. To know God intimately is to reflect God's character of *kindness, justice, and righteousness*.

Verses 25–26 contrast the preferred circumcision of the heart with the less important circumcision of the foreskin. Circumcision for *the whole house of Israel* was supposed to signify a covenant relationship with Yahweh, but in reality they were no different from the neighboring nations.

THE PEOPLE, THE COVENANT & JEREMIAH'S PROPHECY · 10:15–29:32

10:1–5 In poetic speech, Jeremiah admonishes the *house of Israel* about the folly of the religious ideas and practices of other nations. He merely repeats *what the Lord says*. Verse 5 describes the well-attested Ancient Near Eastern practice of carrying statues of gods in parades during festivals.

Contemplating the Lord in contrast to pagan deities, Jeremiah praises Yahweh (verses 6–10). Even when made of silver imported from *Tarshish* (either in Spain or Sardinia) and gold from *Uphaz* (possibly identical with Ophir in the Arabian Peninsula [but see Baker 6:765]), the idols are nothing. Yahweh is *the true God*.

Only in verse 11 do we find a verse in Jeremiah written in Aramaic (see NIV note). It may be original with the prophet, used for rhetorical effect. Or it may have been a marginal scribal note that later merged into the text.

According to verses 12–16, in contrast to pagan gods, the creator controls his creation. Verse 13 echoes Psalm 29. *Portion of Jacob* (that is, Israel) is another biblical title for Yahweh, found elsewhere only in Jeremiah 51:19.

10:17–22 Direct from the Lord, Judah receives marching orders from Jeremiah (10:17–18). This warning sparks in Jeremiah, the bearer of the bad tidings, an outpouring of grief at the coming destruction described in the following verses.

Verses 19–22 offer the voice of Jerusalem personified as a woman in despair (note *my sons*) at the mortal wound she has suffered. Again, the destroyer comes from the north.

10:23–25 Jeremiah notes first the Lord's sovereignty over him;

> **Personified Places**
> The Old Testament often personifies places. Since most place names in Hebrew are feminine nouns, the places are often portrayed as women in various roles. Jerusalem as mother and wife also figures prominently in Lamentations.

the prophet had not chosen his path in life. It was the path of obedience to the divine director. He trusts the Lord to discipline him justly and to deal appropriately with *the peoples who do not call on your name*. Compare Psalm 79:6–7, which Jeremiah is apparently quoting.

11:1–17 Most commentators distinguish a change here from the preceding materials, with the initial focus on the broken covenant. The close of the new section may occur at 12:17, 15:21, 20:18, or 24:1. Such disparity of views illustrates the difficulty of identifying the relationships of the materials in the book of Jeremiah.

According to verses 1–8, the covenant to be heeded is that given at Sinai, given *when I brought them out of Egypt*. The Ten Commandments contain both religious and ethical requirements. Obedience brings blessings; disobedience brings curses (Deut 28). The text compares slavery in Egypt to an iron-smelting furnace (as in Deut 4:20; 1 Kgs 8:51). Verses 6–8 repeat and emphasize the message the prophet is to proclaim.

The reforms of Josiah seem to have been short-lived. The people have fallen back into their old ways (verses 9–11). They have broken the first commandment (Deut 5:6–7). Let them cry out to Baal and the other gods to whom they burn incense; these false gods *will not help them*. This passage is similar to 2:27–28.

As in 7:16, verses 14–17 command Jeremiah not to pray for *this people*; their moral and religious corruption is beyond the intercession of a righteous person. The Hebrew text of verses 15–16 "is exceedingly corrupt, and any reconstruction conjectural" (Bright 82). The translation of the NIV is a satisfactory guess. It emphasizes that sacrifices cannot replace covenantal obedience, and that which the Lord has deemed lovely may still be worthy of destruction by fire, the same element used in *burning incense to Baal*.

11:18–23 This incident may have occurred during the reign of Jehoiakim (reigned 609–598 BCE; Huey 136). The Lord had promised Jeremiah that he would be with him as he faced opposition (1:17–19). The plotters were his kindred, *the men of Anathoth*. Anathoth recalled the words of Jesus, *Only in his home town and in his own house is a prophet without honor* (Matt 13:57). Jeremiah asks Yahweh to bring divine *vengeance upon them*, a request that reflects the human character of the prophet. Yahweh promises to discipline Jeremiah's opponents.

12:1–4 Of all the prophets, only in Jeremiah do we find laments and confessions such as this. Similar material occurs in chapters 15, 17, 18, and 20. Here the prophet's concern is the timeless question, *Why does the way of the wicked prosper?* The question arises out of his reaction to being "like a gentle lamb led to the slaughter" (11:19).

12:5–17 The response in verses 5–6 evades the question. Instead, the Lord urges Jeremiah to stiffen his backbone for even more difficult situations. The text uses the metaphor of a runner racing against a swifter competitor in more difficult terrain.

The complaint of Jeremiah pales in comparison with the lament of the Lord (verses 7–13). While loving the people (*inheritance*), God will deliver both land and people into the destructive power of their foes. This saying of the Lord answers Jeremiah's question. Prosperity is not God's ultimate treatment of the wicked; in the end, they will encounter divine punishment.

In verses 14–17, the prophet emphasizes God's sovereignty over all nations. Although these neighbors – Edom, Moab, Ammon, etc. – are unwitting instruments of judgment against Judah, they also are subject to the Lord's judgment. Yet grace is also available to them under the conditions given here.

13:1–11 This is the first of several symbolic acts in the ministry of Jeremiah. Each is a stark, visual statement that underscores the related prophetic word.

> **Jeremiah's Linen Belt**
>
> The linen belt *described in 13:1–7 was more like a kilt worn under the outer garments. Commentators have struggled to identify the location where Jeremiah first buried, then later retrieved, the garment. The* NIV *identifies it as* Perath, *with a footnote giving the alternative location, the (River) Euphrates, as translated in many versions of the Bible. If the latter, Jeremiah had to make two round trips of approximately 700 miles each.* Perath (Khirbet el Fara), *however, is some six miles northeast of Jerusalem. Nothing in the text indicates that this symbolic act was public; it appears to have been instructive to Jeremiah alone.*

The Lord interprets the action for Jeremiah. God chose Israel to be as near to him as the linen garment was to the prophet. But they had become *ruined and completely useless*, as had the linen belt.

13:12–14 Wineskins do not smash; the Hebrew word *nevel* signifies a ceramic jar, holding about ten gallons of liquid. Every Judean, from king to commoner, like wine jars, will be stupefied by what they hold within them – confusion and panic in the face of the attackers. Jars shatter, and so will Judah.

13:15–17 The mode of expression in verses 15–27 returns to poetry. Jeremiah again urges his audience to honor *the Lord your God* to prevent the threatened catastrophe. Jeremiah takes no pleasure in the dark scene he describes for them. His sorrow will bring bitter tears to his eyes.

Verses 18–19 command Jeremiah to inform the king (Jehoiachin) and his mother (Nehusta) of their coming humiliation. Enemies will besiege cities in the southland (*Negev*), and no one can save them. *All Judah*, that is, the bulk of the people, even a few who remained after the exile, including Jeremiah, will be deported.

> **The Queen Mother**
> *The mention of the queen mother indicates the significant role of that position in the Judean monarchy (see 1 Kgs 2:19).*

The subject of verse 20 is Jerusalem (SEPTUAGINT and verse 27). The leaders (*shepherds*) will have no followers, and former allies will dominate the city. With euphemisms, verse 22 describes the rape of the city. The remainder of the section explains the national destruction as the result of idolatry.

14:1–15:21 In relaying a message about the drought, Jeremiah gives both the land and cities human characteristics, depicting them as mourning and crying out. In a land with few springs, people collected rainwater during the two rainy seasons (the "former" and "latter" rains, in the late fall and spring) in cisterns cut into the limestone bedrock and sealed with plaster. Wild animals acting in such uncharacteristic ways are evidence of the severity of the drought.

Verses 7–9 are likely the words of the people rather than a prayer of Jeremiah on their behalf (see 3:22b–25). Their plea for help includes a confession of sins which appears to be hypocritical, in light of their past practices. They also urge Yahweh to act on their behalf *for the sake of your name*, that is, to protect God's honor and reputation.

In verses 10–12, Jeremiah quotes the Lord directly in this response to their plea. Their treacherous past has caught up with them. Again the Lord tells Jeremiah not to petition on behalf of his people. Even when they do religious things, it will be to no avail. Their destruction is certain through war, starvation, and disease.

In verses 13–16, Jeremiah shows his compassion for his people because false prophets have led them into complacency. Yet following false prophets is no excuse. Both prophets and their followers will suffer exactly what the prophets say will never befall them – sword and famine. The prophet speaks a brief lament in verses 17–18 to the people on behalf of the Lord. The land and Jerusalem are in the midst of the Babylonian invasion. In verses 19–22, the people plead again for the Lord to save them, confessing their *wickedness and the guilt of our fathers*. In what appears to be sincere repentance, they confess that their only hope is in Yahweh their God. Yet according to 15:1–4, God has sealed their destiny. Even if the two great men of God from their past – Moses and Samuel – were to plead for this people, God would not relent. So awful is their end that the dead, from whatever cause, will lie unburied, carrion for vultures and dogs. Manasseh epitomized the guilty leader (compare 2 Kgs 21:3–16.)

The Lord had said that he would *make them abhorrent to all the kingdoms of the earth*. In verses 5–9, the prophet paints the sickening scene. Overwhelmed by the destruction to come, Jeremiah cries out in despair (verses 10–11). The Lord reassures him; those who curse him now will seek him in their disaster and distress (see 21:1–6; 37:3).

Yahweh speaks to the people through the prophet in 15:12–14. *Iron from the north* is the superior military technology the invader brings. Armed resistance will prove futile because of the anger of the Lord.

Again, Jeremiah laments to the Lord in verses 15–18. He pleads his loyalty and explains his devotion, even the joy he has known, in his prophetic duty. But now he experiences the resulting suffering. He asks, Can there be no end to it? Will Yahweh fail him? Thus he offers his own lament as counterpoint to Judah's.

> **The Lord Rebukes Jeremiah**
> *When Jeremiah is at his lowest ebb, the Lord responds (verses 19–21). Jeremiah must turn from self-pity and not speak worthless words if he is to continue to be God's spokesman. The Lord again reassures the prophet of divine power to strengthen him in every situation and to rescue him from all peril (compare 1:17–19).*

16:1–17:18 This section contains instructions to Jeremiah from Yahweh. They deal with his personal situation (16:1–13), with prophetic messages he is to deliver to the people (16:14–18), and with warnings and exhortations in poetic form (16:19–17:18). The latter begin with 16:19.

According to verses 1–4, Jeremiah's bachelorhood is a visual testimony to the truth of his warnings to the people. Thereby, the Lord also saves him from the personal loss and grief the coming disaster will bring upon others. Verses 5–10 forbid Jeremiah to participate in funerals or weddings. Such bizarre behavior sets the prophet apart from his society and adds to the burden of his service to the Lord. Jeremiah must tell his audience that he cannot participate in such normal human activities (verses 10–13) because of their disobedience to the Lord.

> **Prophetic Sign Acts**
> *Prophets often behaved strangely in order both to internalize in full their message and to symbolize its effect on their audience. They might walk around naked (Isaiah), play with model cities (Ezekiel), or bury a loincloth (Jeremiah).*

Verses 14–15 contain a word of hope similar to 23:7–8 (see also Isa 28:5–6; 29:5–8; Joel 3:18–21). The restoration *out of all the countries where [the Lord] banished them* will be more striking than was the exodus from Egypt. Restoration is in the future (verses 16–18); the present brings disaster. *Fishermen* and *hunters* – the invaders – will see to it that there will be no escapees from the *double* jeopardy the Lord intends, due to the people's wicked ways. In poetic form, Jeremiah praises Yahweh as his shelter (verses 19–21), and he anticipates the time when the Gentile nations will acknowledge Yahweh as the only true God. Jeremiah will teach them to recognize God's almighty nature.

The Septuagint omits 17:1–4. In the meantime in Judah, the people's corrupt natures are so immersed in sin that their sin is permanently inscribed on their hardened hearts and *on the horns of their altars* (stone altars with upward projecting corners). Expiation for sin came when the priest anointed the horns of the altar with the blood of the sacrifice (Lev 16:18), but Judah's sin, now engraved in stone, cannot be cleansed. The *Asherah poles* were symbols of the Canaanite goddess, Asherah. Archaeological evidence suggests the widespread mixture of Canaanite elements in Israelite folk religion, interrupted by the reforms first of Hezekiah and later of Josiah, but never completely eradicated until the Babylonian exile. The Temple Mount (*My mountain*) in the holy city contrasts with the high places (*bamot*) in the countryside; however, God will destroy both kinds of sanctuary.

Verses 5–8 are verses of wisdom, similar to Psalm 1, which distinguish the two ways open to individuals. Trusting God opens the way to a fruitful life. Wisdom continues in verses 9–13. The state of the unredeemed *heart* exceeds human comprehension, but God knows and deals justly with everyone. If a person's conduct resembles the proverbial partridge's, that person will ultimately be a loser. Those who forsake the *Lord, the hope of Israel,* forsake the sustenance of a life-giving water source. In the present context, the *glorious throne* that is *the place of our sanctuary* is not the temple itself but God who occupies the throne and makes it glorious. Inserted in verses 14–18 is Jeremiah's appeal for Yahweh's support in the face of those who doubt the prophet's word. He testifies that he has been faithful as the Lord's shepherd, and he prays for the continuing support of the Lord.

17:19–27 The Sabbath is an integral part of God's covenant with his people (Exod 20:8–11). Jeremiah instructs both king and people, on the authority of Yahweh, and he does this in the gates of Jerusalem through which many passed, assuring a wide distribution of this vital word. Keeping the Sabbath was crucial to the continuation of the Davidic dynasty and to the survival of the city. The Lord threatens to destroy Jerusalem's defenses unless the people uphold the sanctity of the Sabbath. The people's fate and that of their city ultimately lay in their own hands through obedience or disobedience.

> **The Potter & the Clay**
>
> In 1902, Adelaide Pollard wanted to serve as a missionary in Africa. Discouraged by her failure to raise funds, she overheard an old woman pray, "Lord, it doesn't matter what you bring into our lives – just have your way with us." That night she meditated on Jeremiah 18:1–6 and the old woman's prayer. Jeremiah's image of the potter and the clay inspired Pollard to pen the lines of one of America's best known hymns:
>
> Have Thine own way, Lord!
> Have Thine own way!
> Thou art the potter; I am the clay.
> Mold me and make me after Thy will,
> While I am waiting, yielded and still.
>
> Years later, Pollard went to Africa. During her lifetime, she wrote more than 80 other hymns. Pollard died in 1934 at the age of 72.

18:1–19:15 18:1–12 lays the foundation for the poetic word that follows. At the potter's house, Jeremiah observes the potter at work. That work becomes a paradigm for the sovereignty of Yahweh over the destiny of nations, including the *house of Israel*. The Lord warns all that remains of that house – *the people of Judah* – that *I am preparing a disaster for you*. Repentance and reformation can change the final form that will result, but the Lord anticipates that the people will reject Jeremiah's warning to them.

The oracle in verses 13–17 supplements the previous proverb of the potter's house by the editorial *Therefore*. *Virgin Israel* (see 14:17) experiences the original state of the people's relationship to Yahweh (2:2–3). The Lord asks two rhetorical questions; both questions expect "No!" as a response. *The snow of Lebanon* translates the Hebrew *siryon*.

> **Mount Hermon**
>
> "Sirion" is the Phoenician name for the heights of Mount Hermon (Deut 3:8). At 9,100 feet above sea level, the peak is often covered with snow. Melting snows feed perennial springs. The constancy of nature is starkly contrast to the fickle ways of the Lord's people. Disaster will result, viewed in astonishment by all who pass by.

Verse 18 sets the stage for the following poetic section. Jeremiah continually warns the people of coming disaster, but they retort that things will remain the way they have been, with priests, sages, and prophets going about their business. They attack Jeremiah by spreading the word to ignore him.

In utter disgust, Jeremiah calls upon the Lord in verses 19–23 to bring the disaster of which he had faithfully prophesied on his opponents. Some scholars cannot accept such demands as being worthy of a true prophet of God. But the prophet's humanity surfaces in this outburst of righteous indignation at the plots posed against him.

Instructed by the Lord, Jeremiah in 19:1–15 executes another symbolic action that illustrates what he will tell both leaders and people. *Some of the elders of the people and of the priests* come along as witnesses. Jeremiah carries the jar he had purchased to the valley on the southern boundary of Jerusalem. It is the valley for the refuse dump, where people sacrifice infants to Molech (see 7:29–34). There the prophet smashes the clay jar. In like manner, God will smash Judah and Jerusalem. So horrible will be the siege that the living will practice cannibalism in a desperate effort to stop their hunger (see Deut 28:53–57; Lam 4:10). After delivering his message to the witnessing elders of the people and priests, Jeremiah returns to the *court of the Lord's temple* and renews his warning to *all the people* on the authority of God.

20:1–6 We must distinguish between this Pashhur and Pashhur son of Malkijah (21:1). This *son of Immer* is the priest in charge of temple security. He considers Jeremiah a threat to temple order. Apparently the threat was short-lived, and he releases Jeremiah the following day. None of this escapes the all-seeing eye of the Lord. Jeremiah clearly describes the terror this man and his associates will experience and their ultimate end in Babylon. To prophesy is to speak out, and Pashhur has spouted lies. *Magor-missabib* means "terror all around," a favorite phrase of Jeremiah's (Jer 6:25; 20:10; 46:6; 49:29; compare Ps 31:14).

20:7–8 In poetic form, Jeremiah voices his inner struggles to Yahweh. He charges the Lord with deceiving him (verses 7–10). The NIV note, *persuaded*, is too weak. The Hebrew word translated here means to "seduce" (a virgin) in Exodus 22:16, and to "lure" in 1 Kings 22:20. Jeremiah must be a perpetual prophet of doom; none react positively to his messages. But he cannot withhold the Lord's announcement of punishment, even when he tries to do so.

His ultimate hope for validation is in the presence of the Lord (verses 11–13). Jeremiah is confident that he has been true to his calling and that the Lord will vindicate him by bringing vengeance on his persecutors. The thought sparks a psalm of praise: a "brief note of hope and joy pervades the gloom of the section as a whole" (Harrison 114).

Sentiments similar to Job 3 in verses 14–18 reflect Jeremiah's deep depression, "the result of his impossible task" (Overholt 628). *The towns the Lord overthrew without pity* apparently refer to Sodom and Gomorrah (Gen 19:24–28).

21:1–14 Unlike the difficulty of dating much of the previous material, the mention of King Zedekiah (597–586 BCE) clearly dates this section. Apparently, this incident occurred relatively late in his reign, just before the city fell to Nebuchadnezzar. In extreme duress, the king and his associates finally seek a word from the Lord from the very prophet they have rejected so often (see also 37:3–10).

Despite the devastating reply of Jeremiah to his visitors, he communicated an alternative which the

Lord offered to those who would surrender to the Babylonians – life rather than death by *plague, sword and famine*. The contrast between life and death is reminiscent of Deuteronomy 30:15–16. But to the royal house, who should have, but failed to administer, daily justice to the oppressed, the Lord threatens punishment.

22:1–30 Chapter 22 opens after the preceding poetic judgment above with a similar condemnation in narrative form. Here the identity of the *king of Judah* is not certain, but the righteous requirements for every ruler remain the same. The Lord demands social justice. If this demand goes unmet, destruction will follow.

Verses 6–8 promise to destroy the king's grand palace and the entire city. The ruins will become a conversation piece for foreigners passing by. And the explanation for the destruction will be covenant breaking and idolatry on the part of the former inhabitants.

Verse 10 instructs survivors for whom to mourn. Weep for the exiled, who shall never return; but to not grieve for dead kings. Jehoiakim was guilty of oppressing his people and exhibiting presumptuous pride (verses 13–14). This was in contrast to Josiah (verses 15b–16). Verses 18–19 poetically describe the nation's demise. The NIV uses *Babylonians* and footnotes *Chaldeans*, the actual word in the Masoretic Text. Nebuchadnezzar was from the Chaldean tribe. Jehoiakim spent three years under Babylonian control, then rebelled in concert with neighboring allies. *Bashan* is to the north; *Abarim* is a mountainous region in Moab. The *Lebanon* of verse 23 is "the house of the forest of Lebanon" (1 Kgs 7:2–5; Isa 22:8), the palace of the kings in Jerusalem.

The Last Kings of Judah	
Josiah	640–609 BCE
Jehoahaz/Shalum	609 BCE
Jehoiakim	609–598 BCE
Jehoiachin	598–597 BCE
Zedekiah	597–598 BCE

Jehoiachin the Captive
Jehoiachin *is also called Coniah* (37:1) *and Jeconiah* (24:1). *The condemnation of Jehoiachin in verses 24–30 proclaims the judgment of Yahweh delivered by Jeremiah to the king before he was taken as a hostage to Babylon, from which he never returned. Archaeologists discovered ration tablets allocating provisions to Ya'u-kin, dating to around 570 BCE in the excavations of Babylon (Pritchard 308). He will be known as Jehoichin the captive, and none of his heirs* (1 Chron 3:17) *will inherit his throne.*

23:1–8 This *Woe* in narrative form (verses 1–4) provides the backdrop for the future-oriented pronouncement (verses 5–6) in poetic form. The figure of irresponsible under-shepherds explains the scattering of the flock in exile. Yahweh, the Good Shepherd, will *gather the remnant*, restoring them from exile to *their pasture*. He will also appoint responsible leaders to care for them.

Verses 5–6 promise the restoration of *a righteous Branch* sometime in the future. This king from the line of David will do all that previous Davidic kings failed to do.

The Branch is a messianic designation (see 33:15; Isa 9:2–7; 11:1–9; Mic 5:1–5; Zech 3:8; 6:12). In the New Testament, the name *The Lord Our Righteousness* is applied to Jesus by Paul (1 Cor 1:30), though Zechariah 3 and 6 apparently connect the image to Zerrubbabel. Verses 7–8 repeat 16:14–15.

23:9–32 The preceding oracles dealt with political leaders; this section focuses upon religious leaders. In verses 9–10, Jeremiah speaks out of personal anguish when he contrasts *the Lord and his holy words* with the evil of the prophets. Yahweh agrees and adds that evil fills the holiest place in the land (2 Kgs 21:5; Ezek 8:6–18). The Lord will punish them with disaster. As disgusting as were the prophets of Samaria, *the prophets of Jerusalem* are far worse. Their lying, immoral lives encourage others toward wickedness, recalling the degraded inhabitants of Sodom and Gomorrah. Ungodliness is poisonous and bitter in its results. The prophets who exhibit and encourage ungodliness will suffer poetic justice – *bitter food … and … poisoned water* (figures of speech for bitter judgment).

According to verses 16–22, the false prophets con the people with exactly the opposite of Jeremiah's warnings. They have never *stood in the council of the Lord*. Other references to the heavenly council are in 1 Kings 22:19–22; Job 1–2; 15:8; and Psalms 82:1; 89:6–7. Jeremiah warns his audience of the coming *storm of the Lord*, the anger of the Lord pouring forth on people and prophets alike.

The two questions in verses 23–24 focus attention on the transcendence (*far away*) and immanence (*nearby*) of Yahweh, the God of the universe. God sees everything (see also Ps 139:7–16; Isa 66:1; Amos 9:2–4).

Verses 25–32 compare the practices of false prophets with those of a genuine prophet (Dreams are one means by which the Lord reveals his will. Two others are by *Urim* and by prophets [1 Sam 28:6].). But dreams can also be delusional. The true prophet will not *lead my people astray*. The word of the Lord will burn away dross; it is a hammer that "shatters all pretension and self-confidence" (see also Heb 4:12; Huey 218). Beware false prophets; they lead people astray in every age.

23:33–40 The Hebrew word *massa* connotes both "burden" and "oracle." Thus, an oracle is the burden of the word of God the prophet delivers to an audience (Nah 1:1; Hab 1:1). The Lord, through Jeremiah, informs the false prophets who seek a message from God that they are the *burden*. The following verses expand on this theme and end with the condemnation of the false prophets.

24:1:1–10 This vision is datable to mid-summer, when figs begin to ripen, in the year 597 BCE. The vision has immediate and distant connotations. In the near future, the bad figs (Zedekiah and others) would end disastrously. In the distant future, the good figs (descendants of the deportees listed in 24:1) would lead in the restoration of the Lord's people *in this land*. All this is the work of *the Lord, the God of Israel* who sends away and restores.

25:1–14 This word of the Lord to Jeremiah actually precedes that of the two baskets of figs, an illustration that the scribes did not arrange the book of Jeremiah chronologically. Because events recorded in 36:2–4 occurred at about the same time as those in 25:1, some scholars believe 25:1–7 is the introduction to the scroll dictated by Jeremiah to Baruch.

In verses 1–17, for the first time since the historical prologue (1:2), we can firmly date part of Jeremiah's prophecies. His ministry began in 627 BCE, when Josiah was twenty-one years old and had been on the throne thirteen years. Five years later (622 BCE), "the Book of the Law was found in the temple of the Lord" (2 Kgs 22:8). It is interesting to note that it was the prophetess, Huldah, whom the king's advisors consulted about the implications of this discovery. As one would expect from a true prophetess, her response was very similar to the content of Jeremiah's prophecies (2 Kgs 22:15–17). By the time of the events in chapter 25, Jeremiah had been faithfully fulfilling his calling for twenty-three years – with little evidence of success. The majority of the people, and particularly the religious and political leaders, had not responded positively to his call for repentance in order to escape the coming calamity. The very survival of his oracles, however, indicates that a remnant of his audience believed his prophecies and saved them. Yahweh showed graciousness toward Judah *again and again* with offers of clemency and encouragement toward reconciliation, but to no avail. They continued to provoke Yahweh *with what [their] hands have made*, namely, representations of deities in ceramics, wood, and metal, as well as cakes for the Queen of Heaven. They ignored the invisible Yahweh, God of hosts.

Nebuchadnezzar, upon the death of his father, Nabopolassar, in 605 BCE, became ruler of the Babylonian Empire. In securing his dominance over the region from the Euphrates to Egypt, he became the Lord's *servant*. (The Septuagint omits *my servant*.) The Babylonians did not realize that they were instruments of Yahweh to *completely destroy* Judah. The same Hebrew word describes the total destruction of the Canaanites by Israel during the conquest (see Deut 20:17; Josh 6:21, 10:28; 1 Sam 15:3). Theirs was to be *an everlasting ruin*. The Hebrew word rendered "everlasting" can mean "forever," but it can also be translated "a long, long time." In fact, the destruction layer left by the Babylonians in Jerusalem and in other Judean sites still remains, hidden beneath subsequent layers of occupation. With the physical destruction and slaughter or deportation of much of the population, the usual

---

Distinguishing True from False Prophets

The outward appearance of Jeremiah did not differ much from that of the false prophets, and both claimed to be speaking what God had revealed to them. The uncritical listener could not tell the difference, and uncritical individuals prefer that which they want to hear: there is no necessity to turn from *their* wickedness (23:14), they should trust in false hopes that they will have peace (23:17), and adultery is permissible because the false prophets do it and, therefore, so can the people (23:14). False prophets ignore the revealed will of God, the moral and ethical teachings of the Mosaic covenant.

The more discerning listener could recognize the moral and ethical integrity of the prophet from Anatoth. "Absolute loyalty and obedience to the revealed will and word of the Lord was the ultimate criterion for distinguishing between true and false prophets" (Harrison 123). *Jeremiah is the epitome of the faithful and true spokesman for Yahweh.*

cultural sounds will cease. This devastation would not only occur with Judah, but also with any other peoples who opposed the Babylonians.

The Babylonian empire lasted just over seventy years, from 612–539 BCE, counting from the fall of Nineveh, the Assyrian capital, to the capture of Babylon by Cyrus, king of the Medes and Persians. But from the destruction of Jerusalem in August, 586 BCE until the fall of Babylon in 539 is less than seventy years. Scholars have struggled to determine whether the seventy years in this prophecy is literal or symbolic. If the seventy-year period is literal, then the difficulty is in deciding when to begin the count. If the number is symbolic, it could signify whatever the appropriate time of punishment might be. The number seven and its multiples occur symbolically throughout the Bible (for example, Gen 4:24; Matt 18:22). Second Chronicles 36:21, in the postexilic period (about 400 BCE), notes that *the land enjoyed its Sabbath rests; all the time of its desolation it rested, until the seventy years were completed in fulfillment of the word of the Lord spoken by Jeremiah*. Since the Sabbath is the seventh day, and seventy is a multiple of seven, symbolism may underlie the seventy years. Another way to compute the time, however, is to count back seventy years from the fall of the Babylonian Empire in 539 BCE, that is, 609 BCE. The latter date was the seventeenth year of the reign of Nabopolassar, the father of Nebuchadnezzar, and the Babylonians were not yet in control of Judea and Jerusalem. So the puzzle remains unsolved.

The phrase *written in this book* probably refers not to the book of Jeremiah as we presently have it, since at that time it was not yet completed, but to the earlier book (or scroll) destroyed by King Jehoiakim (36:23). The book likely consisted of most if not all of the materials we have in chapters 1–25 (Bright 163).

Verse 13 in the Septuagint does not include the last part of the verse, *and prophesied by Jeremiah against all the nations*. In the Greek version of Jeremiah, immediately following *written in this book*, are the oracles against the nations (chapters 46–51), beginning with Elam. The order of the nations does not exactly follow the Hebrew text, which begins with Egypt (46:2). The Septuagint picks up 25:15 at the beginning of its chapter 32.

25:15–29 Here the NIV follows the order of the Hebrew Masoretic Text rather than that of the Septuagint. Scribes likely inserted the section on God's judgment against the nations here in order to expand on the coming destruction of Babylon prophesied in verses 12–14. Perhaps, too, 25:15–38 stands as a fit conclusion to the initial section of Jeremiah (Masoretic Text), acting as a closing envelope (called an *inclusio*) to the beginning: *I appointed you as a prophet to the nations* (1:4) and *See, today I appoint you over nations and kingdoms to uproot and tear down, to destroy and overthrow, to build and to plant* (1:10). This section consists of two parts – verses 15–29 are prose while verses 30–38 are poetic.

> **Inclusio**
> *The practice of beginning and ending a literary section with identical or very similar material.*

To understand verses 15–29 literally is to assume that Jeremiah visited all the places indicated in verses 17–26. This seems to be a physical impossibility, since he would have to have traveled to *all the kingdoms on the face of the earth* (verse 26). And it would have been virtually impossible for him to have access to the throne rooms of the Pharaoh of Egypt or that of Nebuchadnezzar or the other kings; powerful monarchs limited access to their persons as a precaution against possible assassination. An alternative is to interpret the passage symbolically. This alternative assumes that each of the nations named had representatives present in Jerusalem. Jeremiah would have offered these representatives the "cup." Chapter 27:3 mentions envoys in Jerusalem from several nations, which may support this approach. However, another more reasonable approach is to understand this passage as a visionary experience (see for example Gen 15:1; Rev 9:17). With this interpretation, Jeremiah told his audience in Jerusalem all that the Lord revealed. Jeremiah also remembered and wrote down these prophecies for the further instruction of those in exile in Babylon, as well as for succeeding generations, including our own.

The *cup filled with the wine of my wrath* is a graphic image of the reality of Almighty God's righteous disgust and anger with not only Jerusalem and Judah but also all the kingdoms of this earth. The rebellious nature of all humanity leads to a form of madness as nation rises against nation in cycles of seemingly endless wars and conflicts. This is *the sword I will send among them*. The cup of God's wrath is a symbol of his judgment found elsewhere in Scripture (for example, Ps 11:6; Isa 51:17; Jer 8:14). Above all else, this prophetic unit speaks clearly of the sovereignty of God over all nations and peoples. His righteous judgment begins with his chosen people but extends to all nations.

Harrison (126) notes that "All the peoples mentioned in chapters 46–51 are included here except for Damascus." Egypt, Philistia, Edom, Moab, Ammon, Tyre, Sidon, and Arabia are generally well-known and identifiable on maps of the biblical period. *Uz*, associated with Job (1:1), was a country in northwest Arabia. *Dedan* was "an important commercial settlement located at one of the major oases in northwest Arabia" (Gen 10:7; 25:3; Graf). *Tema* is identified with Tayma, a caravan city on an oasis in northern Arabia (Knauf), and *Buz* also was in northern Arabia – likely a tribal region rather than a particular place. Buz was Elihu's country (Job 32:2). The phrase, *all who are in distant places* (verse 23) is more accurate in the NIV footnote and appears again in 49:32 in connection with Kedar. These were Bedouin tribes of north Arabia and related to the Ishmaelites of Genesis 25:13. *Zimri* as a place name is otherwise unknown, although it is possibly associated with *Elam* (Bright 161), in the highlands of modern Iran known as Khuzistan (Vallat). *Media* was in northwestern Iran.

> **Athbash**
>
> *The last kingdom to drink of the cup of the Lord's wrath is the king of Sheshach, apparently a cryptogram (also found in 51:41) for Babylon formed by exchanging the order of the Hebrew alphabet from first to last. Thus* BBL, *consisting of the second* (beth) *and twelfth* (lamedh) *consonants, is written* SHSHKH, *consisting of the next to the last* (shin) *and the eleventh letter counting backward from the end of the* (Hebrew) *alphabet. This system of reverse writing is called* athbash.

There is no possibility of escaping or refusing to experience the wrath of the Lord Almighty. As Jesus stated, *for all who draw the sword will die by the sword* (Matt 26:52).

In verses 30–31's arresting imagery of the deafening roar of a lion and the loud noise of those trampling grapes in the wine press, this poetic prophetic saying emphasizes again the awful and inevitable judgment of the Lord *against the nations ... on all mankind*. While the preceding prophecy speaks of the coming judgment, verse 32 describes the immediacy and expansion of the rising storm of disaster.

Verses 33–38 depict the catastrophic scope of the spreading disaster in terms of *those slain by the Lord*. There will be either no survivors or an insufficient number to mourn and bury the dead, and the worst fears of those dying will be realized – they will remain unburied, scattered across the landscape. The leaders of the people, the shepherds, will die also. All this will be the result of *the fierce anger of the Lord*, realized by means of *the sword of the oppressor* – unknowing instruments in the hand of the Lord. The NIV footnote alerts us to the possibility that the original word here was *anger* rather than *sword*. The expression "sword of the oppressor" does occur in the indicated verses. It is possible here, however, that the "anger of the oppressor" balances and equates to *the Lord's fierce anger*. The imagery of Yahweh as a lion in verses 30 and 38 act as an envelope for the poetry within, another *inclusio*.

26:1–24 Chapters 26–29 focus on conflicts Jeremiah faced as he faithfully presented the word of the Lord to the Judeans, particularly in the time of the kings Jehoiakim and Zedekiah. Other prophets, priests, and certain political leaders opposed Jeremiah. The opposition was so intense that they threatened Jeremiah's very life. Nevertheless, he remained true to his calling and mission, which included not only warnings and exhortations to his contemporaries in Jerusalem but also encouragement and instructions to those already in exile in Babylon. All this material from Jeremiah has been called "Baruch's Book" because of the scribe's role revealed within the section. The first incident relates to the "Temple Sermon," the same incident as Jeremiah 7:1–15.

> **Baruch**
>
> *It is likely that the scribe Baruch was instrumental in preserving Jeremiah's prophecies, which devout people in Babylon during the exile then assembled and enhanced with explanatory comments.*

Early in the reign of Jehoiakim places this event in 609 BCE (but see 28:1). Again, the chronological order of events was a secondary concern to the compilers of Jeremiah, since 25:1 is set in *the fourth year of Jehoiakim*. The *courtyard of the Lord's house* lay within the gate(s) of the temple compound. Priests alone had access to the temple structure proper. The particular pilgrim feast when most of the men of Judah came to Jerusalem is not identified; it could have been Passover, Pentecost, or Tabernacles. The latter occurs in the fall, while the first two are spring festivals (Lev 23).

Jeremiah reveals in these verses the general instructions Yahweh is giving to him. The verses that follow give the exact message he is to communicate to his audience. The Lord's intent is to bring the people to repentance, that they might turn from their evil ways and escape the coming disaster. God offers grace, but it is conditional.

Verses 7–9 are not a first-person account; rather, they are a report. For the content of Jeremiah's message, see 7:1–15. The religious assembly (priests, prophets, and people), who trusted in religious ritual but ignored the moral requirements of the covenant relationship with God, found Jeremiah's ultimatum unbearable. They were all ready to silence him forever. The intensity of the situation is clear. They were prepared to commit murder *in the house of the Lord*. (The Septuagint identifies the prophets as *pseudoprophets* in verses 7, 8, 11, and 16. The expression "false prophet" does not occur in the Masoretic Text.)

The sound of the commotion in verses 10–16 drew the attention of *the officials of Judah*, who must have feared a riot. The royal palace was adjacent to but south of the Temple Mount. The location of the *New Gate* is uncertain, but it was likely in the southern wall of the temple facing the palace compound. (The current southern wall of the Temple Mount enclosure is farther south than that of the Solomonic complex, since Herod the Great enlarged the Temple Mount.) It may be a reference to the gate constructed by Jotham (2 Kgs 15:35; Harrison 127).

The officials *took their places*, that is, they sat in the places of authority within the city gate to hear and judge matters of dispute. This was a common practice (see Deut 21:19; 22:15; Josh 20:4). Jeremiah's defense in court repeats what the Lord had instructed him to say, and what he had said to the priests, prophets, and people. His life was in their hands to do with him as they wished, but if they put him to death, they would be guilty off shedding *innocent blood*. Jeremiah insists he is innocent because Yahweh truly sent him to deliver the message they had heard. Written words on a page cannot capture the tone of voice, posture of body, and intensity of Jeremiah's compelling response. Jeremiah won supporters, who demanded that *the priests and the prophets* release him. The phrase *all the people* is a general expression. Clearly, many of them were open to persuasion by those who held positions of authority. The judgment of the officials became their opinion as well.

Further strengthening that judgment, the elders recall the case of *Micah of Moresheth* in verses 17–19. The quotation of Micah 3:12 makes the point that the great king of former days, Hezekiah, took Micah's message seriously, rather than threatening him with death. And the result was that the Lord relented and did not bring the threatened disaster. If the Judeans reject Jeremiah's message, the disaster he predicted could happen to them. As it happened, Jehoiakim, though a descendant of Hezekiah, did not seek God's favor.

> **Micah**
> Micah's name is a shortened form of Micaiah, "Who is like Yah(weh)?" His hometown, Moresheth-Gath, was a small village near the larger Philistine city of Gath, now tentatively identified with the site Tell el-Judeideh in the foothills some twenty-five miles southwest of Jerusalem.

Note that verses 20–23 form a parenthetic remark. The final editors of the book, or more likely Baruch himself, could have inserted the incident. We know nothing more of the prophet Uriah. His name means, "Yah[weh] is my light." Scribes included the account of Uriah's activities and subsequent death at the hands of King Jehoiakim here to emphasize the danger Jeremiah confronted in his resolute stance as a true prophet of Yahweh. The fact that the king had Uriah buried with *the common people*, rather than returning him to his family burial place, underscores the king's disdain for him. The common people were buried in the Kidron Valley rather than in rock-cut family tombs which the upper classes possessed.

Apparently the support of *Ahikam son of Shaphan* (verse 25) was significant in saving Jeremiah from dying at the hands of his accusers. This man and his father were both important in Josiah's reign (2 Kgs 22:3–14), and he clearly was still a powerful and respected person in Jerusalem at this time.

27:1-22 Chapters 27–28 are a unit involving a symbolic act. A yoke, first worn by Jeremiah, Hananiah (a false prophet) removes. Hananiah then breaks the yoke as a symbolic act to illustrate the supremacy of his own prophecy, which contradicted that of Jeremiah.

As the NIV footnote to verse 19 states, most Septuagint manuscripts do not have this verse, which provides the historical setting for the yoke incident. Another note indicates that the name of the king, either Zedekiah or Jehoiakim, varies in

Hebrew manuscripts. The context that follows supports the identification as Zedekiah. The date for the incident is likely 594 BCE. It is worth noting that the Septuagint varies considerably from the Masoretic Text in this chapter. It is shorter, indicating that the Hebrew original behind the Septuagint translation was shorter. These textual differences, however, do not alter the basic message of this section.

The yoke which Jeremiah fashioned and wore symbolized the yoke worn by a work ox. A yoked animal obeys its master's commands. Jeremiah is to speak directly to the envoys of the surrounding nations who had come to Jerusalem, apparently to plan with Zedekiah rebellion against the Babylonians (2 Kgs 25:1). Even though Zedekiah's predecessor was in exile in Babylon because he had rebelled against Nebuchadnezzar, Zedekiah did not shrink from following the same course. The message to *Edom, Moab, Ammon, Tyre and Sidon* was by a superior authority than even the Babylonian king – *the Lord Almighty* [the word "Almighty" here translates *tsevaoth*, "hosts/armies (of heaven)"]. Yahweh controls all the powers of heaven and earth and can determine whatever shall occur. At the present, God wills that these minor kingdoms shall wear the yoke of the Babylonian monarch and serve him. To rebel against Nebuchadnezzar is to rebel against God, and the punishment for rebellion is *sword, famine, and plague*.

The counselors of kings included *prophets, diviners ... interpreters of dreams ... mediums ... [and] sorcerers*. It should come as no surprise that other kingdoms than Judah had prophets (Huffmon). The confrontation of Elijah with the religion of Baal involved prophets of Baal (1 Kgs 18:19). To wear the yoke of Nebuchadnezzar was to survive as his servant in one's own land.

In verses 12–15, Jeremiah gave the same message to Zedekiah and offered the same alternatives: the possibility of survival as a servant of Nebuchadnezzar or disaster and death for both Zedekiah and those who were *prophesying lies* to him in the name of Yahweh.

In verses 16–22, Jeremiah's message from the Lord to the political leaders of Judah and the surrounding kingdoms was to submit to the rule of Babylon and survive. To the priests and people of Judah, however, his message was in opposition to the false prophets.

True prophets, Jeremiah emphasizes, would be praying for the lesser treasures of the temple that yet remained, not those already plundered. These were larger items made of bronze. By the word of the Lord, Jeremiah prophesied that they, too, would be carried away to Babylon *until the day I come for them*. Even in a message of doom and destruction, the Lord provides a word of hope and a glimpse into a future restoration.

> **Ancient Divination**
> *Diviners sought to determine the future by looking for "signs," such as observing the pattern of drops of oil in a cup of water (lecanomancy) or examining the entrails of a sacrificed animal (extispicy). Mediums consult with ghosts or spirits; a necromancer is a medium who inquires of the dead (Kuemmerlin-McLean 469). Sorcerers are magicians and practitioners of witchcraft. Jeremiah, speaking verbatim for the Lord Almighty, warned the rulers of these nations not to listen to the advice of such counselors. To heed their advice would lead to exile.*

> **The Temple Vessels**
> *The Jerusalem prophets falsely anticipate the imminent end of the exile and the return of the holy vessels that Nebuchadnezzar had taken to Babylon in 597 BCE, when he first conquered Jerusalem and Judah (2 Kgs 24:13). Daniel 5:2 also mentions Nebuchadnezzar blasphemously drinking wine from the holy vessels and praising false gods; later Jews who returned from exile under Cyrus, the Persian king, after he conquered Babylon in 539 BCE, restored the holy vessels.*

28:1–17 The incidents in this chapter grow directly out of the previous account regarding false prophets. Here the false prophet *Hananiah son of Azzur* personifies the opposition to Jeremiah and to his message from Yahweh. We know nothing more about this prophet than is given here – his name, his father's name, and his hometown, Gibeon (modern Tell el-Jib, located five miles north of Jerusalem). Gibeon was a town assigned to priests (Josh 21:17), so he may have been a priest, as was Jeremiah. Different manuscript traditions have different kings in verse 1.

In a very public place before *the priests and all the people*, Hananiah flatly contradicted the message of Jeremiah, using the exact introductory words that Jeremiah had used (27:4). Rather than accepting the yoke of Babylonian domination, Hananiah insists that Yahweh will act the opposite of what Jeremiah had predicted. *Within two years* the Lord would remove Babylonian rule and restore all the holy vessels to Jerusalem. The restoration would include the captive King Jehoiachin and the other exiles.

Jeremiah had earlier prophesied that Jehoiachin would never return (22:26–27).

The *Amen!* of Jeremiah's response (verse 5) has been translated variously: *I hope so* (JB), *So be it* (NJB), *May it be so* (NEB), and *Amen* in the NIV, KJV, NRSV, NAB, and NJPS (Huey 248 note 17). We cannot recover the tone, but it may have been tinged with sarcasm.

The only way to prove the validity of Hananiah's prophecy was to see if it came true. As events unfold, Jeremiah did not believe that Hananiah's hope for the future was true and from the Lord.

Verses 10–11 offer a report of what followed, written in the third person, perhaps by Baruch, who could have been an eyewitness to these events. Hananiah took the yoke from Jeremiah's neck and broke it before the audience in his own symbolic act, giving the meaning of his actions by the repetition of his prophecy. God would break Nebuchadnezzar's rule over Judah and the surrounding nations within two years. Having faithfully carried out the Lord's mandate, Jeremiah departed. The people who heard the two prophets were left to decide which to believe. Human nature would tend to embrace the message of Hananiah, encouraging those who were conspiring to revolt against Nebuchadnezzar. Those in captivity in Babylon who heard Hananiah's words would oppose settling down in their place of exile (29:5–6).

Jeremiah accuses Hananiah of lying. The lies were twofold: Hananiah had lied about receiving a word from the Lord, and by persuading the nation that it would be free of Nebuchadnezzar's rule within two years. The nation would not have to wait two years to see whether or not Hananiah's words were true. Jeremiah warned Hananiah that he would die within the year; two months later, he died. His death authenticated the validity of Jeremiah's prophetic ministry, though many continued to oppose him.

> **Jeremiah versus Hananiah**
> *No word of the Lord had come to Jeremiah in the midst of his confrontation with Hananiah, and so he had departed, but in verses 12–17 the word of the Lord came to Jeremiah. Jeremiah does not give an exact indication of the time that had elapsed. He quotes Yahweh directly to Hananiah. The nations will serve Nebuchadnezzar as surely as it is impossible to break a yoke of iron. Even animals will submit to him, perhaps a reference to the hunting prowess of Mesopotamian monarchs illustrated in the reliefs of Assyrian palaces.*

29:1–23 Those responsible for assembling the materials in the book of Jeremiah placed this letter immediately following the account of Jeremiah's confrontation with Hananiah. This arrangement is appropriate, since the letter deals with unwarranted assumptions by some Judeans in exile that they would soon return home to Jerusalem and their native land.

Verses 1–3 enable readers to understand details about the letter not revealed in the text of the letter itself. Someone other than Jeremiah authored them. The letter includes the intended recipients. *Surviving elders* would include those not slain by the Babylonians who survived the long journey into exile. They and the others named were leaders of Judean society in Babylon, including political and religious officials as well as artisans, officers, and fighting men. According to 2 Kings 24:14, "a total of ten thousand" were carried away in the initial exile in 597 BCE.

Jeremiah gave the letter to *Elasah son of Shaphan and to Gemariah son of Hilkiah* to deliver to the exiles. Elasah may have been the brother of Ahikam son of Shaphan (26:24) and of Gemariah son of Shaphan (36:10).

> **Gemariah Son of Hilkiah**
> *Gemariah son of Hilkiah is unknown other than in this text. Although both he and Jeremiah are called* son of Hilkiah, *they were probably not brothers, since Hilkiah was a common name. Clearly Gemariah and Elasah were aides of Zedekiah, and Jeremiah trusted them to carry the letter to Babylon. Communications between Judah and Babylon were a normal feature of life under Nebuchadnezzar's rule.*

The letter consists of four prophetic sayings that Jeremiah passes along to the exiles. Verses 4–9 comprise the first message. It is noteworthy that the people in exile learn that the Lord was the cause of their transfer from Jerusalem to Babylon; Nebuchadnezzar was simply an instrument in God's hands. Immediately, the letter informs the recipients that they will live there a long time. They should, therefore, establish a normal pattern of life, seeking *the peace and prosperity* of their new home rather than dreaming of the old homeland. They must *pray to the Lord* for the welfare of their new home. That Judeans could worship the Lord in a foreign land was a new idea. They had thought that the temple of the Lord in Jerusalem was inviolable (7:4) and shared the widespread idea that national deities were territorial (1 Sam 26:17–20; 1 Kgs 20:28).

The prophets and diviners were clearly stirring up the people and urging them on with ideas about an imminent return to Jerusalem. This was exactly the activity of the false prophets in Jerusalem, with whom Jeremiah contended. In both instances, the Lord insists, *I have not sent them*.

The second word from the Lord (verses 10–14) offers hope. The seventy years are an approximate figure (see 25:12–14 above). "From the fall of Nineveh (612) to the fall of Babylon (539) was seventy-three years; from Nebuchadnezzar's accession (605) to the fall of Babylon was sixty-six years" (Bright 209). Yahweh promises to come to those in exile to fulfill his *gracious promise* to restore them, because of positive plans for them. For every generation these words are precious: *You will seek me and find me when you seek me with all your heart*.

The third word from the Lord (verses 15–19) concerns those remaining in Jerusalem, and it contrasts starkly with the word of hope for those in exile in Babylon. They shall experience *the sword, famine and plague*. Implicit in this word is that a quick return from exile would put returnees back into the terrible disaster that was coming upon Jerusalem. The coming disaster was due to their failure to listen to *my servants the prophets*. But Jeremiah asserts the same charge of failure to heed the word of the Lord against the recipients of this letter. They have escaped the coming disaster in Judah by grace.

Except for one manuscript, the Septuagint does not contain verses 16–20, suggesting that they are a secondary addition. There is a natural flow of the text from the end of verse 15 to the beginning of verse 21. Nevertheless, the contrast between the bad figs in Jerusalem and the good figs in Babylon (see 24:1–10) offers a motivation for those in exile to squelch further thoughts about an early return to Jerusalem.

The two doomed prophets, Ahab and Zedekiah, are under God's judgment for *prophesying lies*. Further, they are morally corrupt. It is likely that Nebuchadnezzar executed them for stirring anti-Babylonian aspirations among the community in exile.

> **Punishment by Fire**
> *The Babylonian practice of punishment by fire appears also in Daniel 3:20. The Persians who conquered the Babylonian Empire used other forms of punishment (Dan 6:16), for fire was sacred to them (Harrison 132).*

29:24–32 Although incorporated in chapter 29, these events occurred some time after Jeremiah's letter had reached Babylon. Apparently, that letter had so angered the false prophets in Babylon that Shemaiah had sent a letter of complaint back to the religious authorities in Jerusalem.

We do not know anything else about *Shemaiah*. *Nehelamite* is likely a reference to his place of origin, but *Nehel* is unknown. Shemaiah sent his letter to all the priests, but in particular to *Zephaniah son of Maaseiah*. His name appears also in 21:1 and 37:3. Zephaniah was second in rank to Seraiah, the high priest (52:24; 2 Kgs 25:18). He may have been a brother of the false prophet Zedekiah *son of Maaseiah* mentioned in verse 21.

Note that the Lord charged him with sending letters *in your own name*. That is in contrast to Jeremiah, who consistently attributed what he wrote to the Lord. Shemaiah testifies that Zedekiah's appointment came from the Lord, but then urges the priest to reprimand Jeremiah. Shemaiah was clearly aligned with the other Babylonian false prophets who were pushing the exiles to believe in an early return.

Rather than reprimand Jeremiah, Zephaniah reads the letter from Shemaiah to the prophet (verses 29–32). The Lord instructed Jeremiah to send his second letter to the community in exile rather than to Shemaiah alone. Yahweh was informing the entire community that Shemaiah spoke lies; he had never received his message from the Lord. The entire community would witness in due time the punishment of Shemaiah indicated in the letter. Neither he nor any of his descendants would live to see the development of a flourishing life in the exilic community nor to share in the promised return.

> **Jeremiah & Zephaniah**
> *As both a prophet and a priest, Jeremiah may have been on friendly terms with the priest Zephaniah. The word from the Lord apparently came to Jeremiah immediately as he stood before Zephaniah.*

PROPHECIES OF RESTORATION · 30:1–33:26

Following Jeremiah's correspondence with those in exile encouraging them to adjust patiently to life in their new location, the compilers of the book inserted a series of prophetic sayings expressing hope for the future. These are undated prophesies, for the most part consisting of poetic expressions. Each begins with the introductory refrain, *This is what the Lord says*, with the added occasional insertion *declares the Lord*. Some of the prophecies anticipate events long after the Babylonian and Persian periods. Because of the content, scholars call this section "The Book of Consolation" or "The Book of Comfort."

30:1–24 Verses 1–3 are a prose introduction to the collection. As a faithful prophet, Jeremiah is to *write in a book* (scroll), but behind the writing are the words of Yahweh. Jeremiah probably called upon the writing skills of Baruch the scribe and dictated the words to him. It is useful to remember that the Old Testament prophets often had a circle of supporters and assistants, often unnamed (see Isa 8:16).

Verse 4's *the Lord* (Yahweh), in verse 2 appears as "the God of Israel." Israel represents the ideal and totality of God's people, but here the two groups – Israel and Judah – are recognized. The prophet expresses interest in the entire nation, not just Judah.

Verses 5–7 depict the agony of days of disaster here with a striking word picture. *Every strong man looks like a pregnant woman at the time of delivery*, as he suffers fear and terror *in a time of trouble for Jacob*. Jacob is Israel, God's people. It is impossible to know whether the time of trouble refers to the fall of Jerusalem, the fall of Babylon, or some other unspecified calamity. The important truth is that *he will be saved out of it*.

In that day (verse 7) is equivalent to "the day of the Lord," usually destructive, as in Amos 5:18–20, Isaiah 2:12–21 and Zephaniah 1:14–18. Here, however, *that day* will mean freedom from serving foreigners and freedom to serve Yahweh *their God and David their king*. The promise is not to resurrect the dead David, but to raise up a worthy successor of David (see also in 23:5–6; Ezek 34:23–24; Hos 3:5).

Verse 10 picks up from verse 7 with references to "Jacob" and "save." This allows for the possibility that verses 8–9 intrude between verses 7 and 10. However, the reference to *that day* in both verses 7 and 8 weakens that interpretation. Scholars note a similarity in expression between verse 10 and Isaiah 41:8–10, 13–14; 43:1, 5; and 44:1–2 (Hyatt 1024).

These verses speak particularly of the trouble out of which God will save Israel. Rather than fear and terror, *Jacob will again have peace and security*. Even in a distant place of exile, the Lord is present and in the future will save. Yahweh will bring all nations and peoples to just judgment, as he has in the past. However, God may obliterate other nations but *not completely destroy you*.

The Septuagint omits verses 10–11, but they do appear in that version in 26:27–28. With minor variations, the Masoretic Text repeats them in 46:27–28.

The initial focus of verses 12–17 is upon the sorry state of Judah, described in terms of a person suffering deadly injuries for whom no healing or healer is available. *All your allies* may be the surrounding peoples mentioned in 27:3: Edom, Moab, Ammon, Tyre, and Sidon. Yahweh caused this incurable situation, which is fully deserved. Although this declaration from the Lord is distinct from the preceding prophecy, it contains a similar promise that God will punish the oppressors of Yahweh's people and heal the people. What no human being can do, the Lord is fully capable of accomplishing, and God will care for the place *for whom no one cares*, Zion.

The reference to Zion in verses 18–22 may have been the cause for placing this prophecy immediately following the preceding sayings. Here the promise is for the restoration of Jerusalem and her inhabitants, identified as *Jacob*. The expression *Jacob's tents* recalls the former days when Israel followed Yahweh through the desert (2:2) and dwelt in tents (Num 24:5–6). Jerusalem *will be rebuilt on her ruins*, literally, "on her tell." Verse 19 is a reversal of the disaster described by Jeremiah in 5:14–17. The *songs of thanksgiving* could refer to joy at the harvest and *the sound of rejoicing* to wedding festivities, although both may also refer to worship in a restored city and sanctuary. The Lord promises peace and security after punishing *all who oppress them*. One of their own will rule them rather than a foreigner, fulfilling the promise of Moses (Deut 17:15). Since the leader will *arise from among them*, which suggests a lowly beginning like that of David, this hints that it will be a fulfillment of verse 9. To draw near to God unbidden or unauthorized is to risk death

> **Archeological Tells**
> A "tell" is an archaeological term for a mound of debris built up by successive periods of occupation and destruction.

> **Messianic Prophecy**
> Though there are interpreters who deny the messianic tones of this passage, the messianic interpretation is the stronger one. Verse 22 foresees the reestablishment of a close relationship between the Lord and Israel, and its basis will be a new covenant (31:33–34; verse 22 is lacking in the Septuagint).

(Exod 28:34–35), so that even priests must follow the correct protocols. But this ruler in the future will have close fellowship with God, who will himself *bring him near*.

Verses 23–24 occur with slight variation in 23:19–20. The final compiler may have wanted to emphasize that the restoration would come only on the Lord's timetable. The promises lay in the future as he wrote, but in the future they would come to understand divine providence.

Recalling that chapter divisions were not in the original book, some scholars associate 31:1 with these verses (Hyatt 1027). *In days to come* (verse 24), in this interpretation, refers to *At that time* (verse 24). All these promises will come to pass in the future, after *the storm of the Lord* has passed. When the renewed relationship between God and the people becomes a reality, understanding will come.

31:1–40 God's interest is not in the exiles of Judah alone. As in the wilderness of Sinai and until the division of Israel and Judah, Yahweh was *God of all the clans of Israel*. God intends the reuniting of all the people, including a remnant of the exiled northerners who will be reestablished in Samaria. Watchmen, usually stationed atop city walls to warn of an approaching enemy, now in time of peace stand atop the fruitful hills, "watching for the first appearance of the new moon or for the arrival of other pilgrims" (Huey 270). They now summon their people to worship *the Lord our God* in Jerusalem. There is no longer any hint of pagan deities or places of worship. All of this is due to the activity of God, who exhibits *everlasting love* and *loving-kindness*.

Verses 7–9 call for exuberant, joyful singing. The words to the song pray to Yahweh to *save your people*; the Lord will gather the remnant that remains *in the north* and from every place on the earth. Even those who might have lost hope will return – *the blind … the lame … the pregnant* and even those in labor, probably referring to those who would give birth along the way. As they travel, they will be weeping (tears of joy) and praying (thanksgivings). As a father sees to the needs of his family, so God will meet the needs of the travelers. This return will be like a second exodus, with *streams of water* in a dry and thirsty land, recalling the rock which Moses smote to satisfy the thirst of the Israelites in the wilderness (Exod 17:1–7).

What Yahweh does for Israel is a story to tell to the nations (verses 10–14). First Jeremiah calls them to attention – *Hear the word of the Lord*. Then the story begins. Yahweh has scattered the people, but *like a good shepherd* has never lost sight of them. God will *ransom*, buy back, and *redeem* them. To redeem is to deliver from a hopeless situation, such as slavery (Mic 6:4). The redeemed will express unrestrained joy in the city of the Lord and in *the bounty of the Lord*. They will return to a land of milk and honey (Exod 3:8) where they will know *comfort and joy instead of sorrow*. The fields, flocks, and herds will be bountiful, providing abundant sacrifices in which the priests share, and feasting rather than famine for the Lord's people.

Verse 15 introduces a new prophecy (verses 15–22). Long before the time of Jeremiah, Rachel died giving birth to Benjamin at Ramah (Gen 35:16–21). She was buried nearby at Zelzah, according to 1 Samuel 10:2. Located five miles north of Jerusalem, Ramah is the modern er-Ram, the place from which the Judeans taken into exile departed for Babylon (40:1). In poetic imagery, the long-deceased Rachel weeps at the loss of her children being taken into exile. Due to a scribal explanatory note (gloss) in Genesis 35:19, Israelites came to associated Rachel's burial place with Bethlehem. This association may have come about by the confusion of Ephrath with Ephratah (see also Ruth 4:11 and Mic 5:2). The tradition that Rachel was buried near Bethlehem, however, was already well-established by about 250 BCE, for it appears in the Septuagint of Genesis 35:19. This reading provided Matthew (2:18) with grounds for a typological reading of Jeremiah 31:15.

But the word of the Lord consoles the weeping matriarch and those in exile. *Your work* (verse 16) apparently refers to Rachel's grief and tears. The consolation is that *They will return … there is hope for your future*.

> **Typology**
> *Early Christians and their Jewish contemporaries often read biblical texts as referring to persons or events in their own times by way of analogy. The pattern of ancient biblical realities repeated themselves in a new situation.*

Those in exile have responded to the harsh discipline that Yahweh rightly imposed on them. *An unruly calf* fights against rope and halter, refusing to follow its master, an apt figure of God's rebellious people. Now disciplined, they pray for restoration. They now submit to the lordship of God.

The heart of the Lord is touched by their confession. Verse 20 is a timeless portrait of the love, longing, and compassion of God for Israel. God encourages them with instructions for the way back *to your towns*. They are to mark the way into exile so that they can find their way back home again. His address to them, *O Virgin Israel*, signifies that Yahweh has cleansed them and restored them to a virginal condition. With God, nothing is impossible. All of this lies in the future for those in exile. Until that time, the question in verse 22 remains.

The final sentence of the verse is so puzzling that the original intent escapes us. The saying may have been proverbial, understandable to Jeremiah's audience but not to us. It is clear, however, that the *new thing on earth* is a creation of the Lord. A woman encompassing a man is a reversal of the normal order, so traditional readers have assumed a messianic message within the saying, that is, that the new thing was God in Christ reconciling the world to himself. This meaning would not have been apparent to those in exile.

The revelation in verses 23–30 came to Jeremiah while he was sleeping. The previous section refers to Ephraim. Here the Lord explicitly names Judah. The Lord will act to restore them, and they will acknowledge their redemption by blessing the (rebuilt) temple on the holy mountain in a rebuilt Jerusalem.

Farmers in ancient Israel lived in villages and went to and from their outlying fields, vineyards, and olive orchards. Herdsmen pastured their flocks on untillable areas and, after the harvest, benefited by letting their sheep and goats feed in the harvested fields. Refreshment and sustenance for the weary came from the produce of the land to which the Lord had restored Judah. Jeremiah's vision of harmony and prosperity was sweet, for he had observed the desolation of conflict and famine (verse 28).

The Lord assures him (and those who would hear or read his words) that he will protect those restored *in those days*. The sour grapes proverb, also found in Ezekiel 18:2, contrasts the present point of view among the exiles of collective, communal, and intergenerational guilt and responsibility (Lam 5:7) with the view that will hold *in those days*, in the future. Set as it is just before the prophecy of the new covenant, the new sour grapes saying points to the time when individual responsibility will be normal.

The promise of a new covenant with *the house of Israel* (and) *Judah* was an important word of hope for those in exile (verses 31–34). They, as well as *their forefathers*, had broken the covenant even though Yahweh *was a husband to them*. This expression, appearing also in 3:14 and in Hosea 2:16, reflects the close relationship Yahweh desired with Israel within the Sinai covenant. Their rebellious ways generation after generation resulted in the estrangement of the exile. The new covenant Yahweh will establish at an undetermined *after that time* will realize in full an intimate relationship with the people. Those who *know the Lord* will mean complete forgiveness of their sins. Sin will not be eliminated, but forgiven and forgotten by the Lord.

> **"Know the Lord ..."**
> *Jeremiah calls Israel to "know the Lord" (9:24; 22:16), that is to imitate God's treatment of the oppressed. Jeremiah understands the Torah to concern the people's relationship to each other, as well as to God.*

Two brief sayings from the Lord (verses 35–37) emphasize Yahweh's sovereign power over the universe. God's limitless power guarantees that he will never completely forsake his people Israel. (The Septuagint has reversed the order of these two prophecies.)

Verses 38–40, a final word of hope for the future, must have come to Jeremiah as Jerusalem lay in ruins after the Babylonian assault. Just as the Lord promised to bring people back from exile to the land, he promises that Jerusalem *will be rebuilt for me* (literally, "for Yahweh"). Although some of the places can no longer be identified with certainty, the description moves from the north wall (Neh 3:1; 12:39; Zech 14:10) along the western side of the city down the Valley of Gehenna (*where dead bodies and ashes are thrown*) to the south and east (*the Kidron Valley*). God would forever reverse the defilement caused by Judah's sins (2:7, 23; 7:30–34; 19:13; 32:34–35; Huey 288). Once again, Jerusalem would become the Holy City.

32:1–44 Verses 1–2 sketch the environment and time frame in which Jeremiah purchased the field. Written in the third person, they are clearly the work of an editor/compiler. Nebuchadnezzar had placed Zedekiah on the Davidic throne after he had captured the city. Zedekiah replaced his nephew, Jehoiachin, whom the Babylonians deported. But Zedekiah had revolted (2 Kgs 25; Jer 39:1), bringing the Babylonian siege of the city. *The courtyard of the guard* must have included related rooms in which Jeremiah was detained.

Possibly written by the same hand as verses 1–2, verses 3–5 explain why Jeremiah was incarcerated.

Restricting his freedom also restricted his morale-destroying prophecy from spreading through the besieged population. *Until I deal with (visit) him* does not appear in the Septuagint. Nebuchanezzar did deal with Zedekiah face to face (2 Kgs 25:4–7). Zedekiah was blinded and taken to prison in Babylon, where he died.

The purchase of the field was not Jeremiah's idea but was initiated by the Lord (verses 6–8). It was another symbolic act with implications for *this people* (verses 15, 42–44). Leviticus 25:25–28 contains rules for redeeming property. The war may have impoverished Hanamel. It was Jeremiah's right to purchase the field, but it was also his *duty*. By all means possible, it was to remain within the (extended) family. Family land was a sacred inheritance (see 1 Kgs 21:1–16). Because of Jeremiah's imprisonment, the transaction of necessity took place in *the courtyard of the guard*.

Hyatt notes that verses 9–12 represent "the only occurrence in the O.T. where such details [of a land purchase] are given" (1044). *Seventeen shekels of silver* refers to weight (see NIV footnote), not to coins; the use of coinage did not develop until the sixth century BCE. We have no information on the source of Jeremiah's income. Although not stated, *Baruch son of Neriah* must have been the scribe who drafted the documents. This is the first mention of Jeremiah's secretary and associate.

Archaeological evidence indicates that such deeds of sale (verses 13–15) were tri-folded, tied with a string with a small lump of clay spread over the knot, which a scribe then impressed with a signet ring. This guaranteed that the unopened document was the original and unaltered. The clay jar provided a virtually moisture-free environment for long-term storage of the documents. The discovery of the Dead Sea Scrolls in jars in 1947 proves the effectiveness of this method.

> **Baruch's Ring**
> *The impression of a signet ring bearing an inscription relating to Baruch surfaced on the antiquities market of Jerusalem and is now on display in the Israel Museum. Although not recovered in an excavation, few doubt its authenticity. Published by Israeli scholar Nahman Avigad, the inscription reads "Belonging to Berekyahu (Baruch) son of Neriyahu (Neriah) the scribe."*

Some scholars are skeptical that the entire prayer in verses 16–25 comes from Jeremiah, claiming only verses 16, 17a, and 24–25 are from the prophet (Bright 298). However, their skepticism is due to their presuppositions; there is nothing in the prayer foreign to Jeremiah's thought.

The first section of the prayer (verses 17–19) acknowledges the greatness of God. The second part of the prayer (verses 20–23) illustrates the power of God. Jeremiah recalls how Yahweh redeemed Israel from Egyptian bondage and gave them the promised land. But as he prayed, Jeremiah noted the present siege and the reason for it: disobedience to Yahweh's law. The third section of the prayer (verses 24–25) reminds the Lord of the siege and the end of it now revealed to the prophet. Expressing surprise at God's instructions to buy a field, "…Jeremiah could scarcely believe that a reliable and consistent deity would instruct him to acquire property when the end of organized life in Judah was at hand" (Harrison 42).

Following Jeremiah's prayer, the Lord responds to his confusion (verses 26–440). Jeremiah had prayed, *Nothing is too hard for you*, and Yahweh reaffirms that truth, with the self-description *the God of all mankind*, literally, *all flesh* (KJV, RSV). Yes, the city is destined for destruction at the hands of the Babylonians. Its inhabitants had turned from rather than to the Lord. They had refused the Lord's teaching and discipline. They had polluted the temple that bore Yahweh's *Name*, just as they had polluted their homes with idols. And they had served their master, Baal, by offering their children to Molech in the Valley of the Sons of Hinnom.

Jeremiah had prophesied *sword, famine and plague* for Jerusalem (14:12; 21:7; 24:10; 27:8; 29:18). These were words which he had heard from the Lord, and they were valid. However, *the Lord, the God of Israel* now had an additional word for both prophet and people. God would restore them to *this place*, Jerusalem and Judah, a safe place for them in the future. Verses 38–41 are an expansion of 31:33.

With limitless power, the Lord will ultimately turn calamity into prosperity for *this people*. Many would perish before their descendants would participate in the fulfillment of these promises, yet the promises will become reality. Family properties will be restored in the place Jeremiah calls *a desolate waste*. Thus a modest land transaction had exploded into a magnificent hope because nothing is too hard for the Lord.

33:1–26 This chapter continues the theme of restoration that began in chapter 30. Three aspects of restoration come into focus here: of the people to the land (verses 1–8), of the land to prosperity (verses 9–13), and of a Davidic king (verses 14–26).

The expression *a second time* ties verses 1–9 to 32:2. Yahweh as creator echoes 32:17. The Lord invites Jeremiah to pray for new and added insights or revelations.

The NIV translation of verses 4–5 veils a difficult and obscure Hebrew text. Some words appear to have dropped out of the original. As rendered, the translation points to a military strategy in which city leaders remove buildings adjacent to the besieged walls at strategic points along them to improve the defenses of the city.

Yahweh has ordained the destruction of Jerusalem, but aims at *health...healing...peace* and *security* for the future. Verse 8 echoes and expands upon 31:34b, "For I will forgive their wickedness and will remember their sins no more." Because people will recognize the future prosperity of Jerusalem as coming from Yahweh, they will offer praise and honor *before all nations*. Isaiah 62:2, 7 express similar thoughts.

Another brief saying from the Lord (verses 10–11) continues the theme of restoration. Jeremiah speaks of what he sees – total desolation – describing the aftermath of the siege of the Babylonians. What Yahweh sees for the future is the return of inhabitants to *towns of Judah* and *Jerusalem*, with the restoration of normal social and religious activities. These are marked by joyful events such as weddings. The people rightly recognize *the Lord* as the *Almighty*, who has brought this about and is worthy of praise and thanksgiving. The praise comes from Psalm 136:1, and the editor of Jeremiah probably intends it as a reminder of the entire psalm.

In verses 12–13, another promise for the future looks to the restoration of flocks grazing over an area from the north of Jerusalem (Benjamin) to the south (*Negev*). Similar territorial descriptions occur in 17:26 and 32:44. Shepherds will keep tabs on their flocks, counting them as they come into the fold to see that none is missing.

Verses 14–26 are lacking in the Septuagint, but textual variations do not negate the importance of the passage. The focus of restoration now turns to the promise of the continuation of the Davidic kingship and the Levitical priesthood. Verses 15–16 reflect the announcement in 23:5–6, which is in the Septuagint. In contrast to the string of wicked and unjust kings of Judah in the past, the coming monarch *will do what is just and right*. His character will be so dominant that the city will wear the name *The Lord, our Righteousness*, the name of the coming king in 23:6.

Historically, the Davidic monarchy ended in Babylon with the death of Jehoiachin (unrecorded in the Bible), the last mentioned king of Judah (2 Kgs 25:27). Although some argue that Zedekiah was the last king of Judah, he too died in exile in Babylon. Zerubbabel, a prince of the Davidic line, was a leader in the return to Jerusalem (Ezra 2:2), but neither he nor anyone else became king. He is called "governor" in Haggai 1:1, 14; 2:2, 21.

Verse 18 foresees the restoration of the Levitical priesthood in a functioning temple. The second temple was rebuilt and dedicated in 516 BCE (Ezra 6:14–15). The priestly leader in the first return of the Jews from Babylon was Jeshua (Joshua) son of Jehozadak, of the line of Aaron. The priesthood in the Second Temple period undergoes transitions and a loss of prestige due to political changes. The Hasmonean priest-kings replaced the Zadokite priestly line in the second century BCE. Controversy over the legitimacy of the high priest resulted in the establishment of the community responsible for the Dead Sea Scrolls. Beginning with the Roman period, the civil rulers appointed the high priests. With the destruction of the temple by the Romans in CE 70, the high priesthood ended, although priestly family connections (the Jewish family name Cohen and its variations) continue to the present.

> **The Coming King**
>
> *Like other prophetic texts, Jeremiah 33 expects a future monarch to restore Israel's fortunes. Jeremiah does not specify his identity. Here and in chapter 31, he expects this king to rule alongside a renewed priesthood in answer to charges that God has reneged on his promises (verse 24). Later Jewish and Christian interpreters connected these and similar passages to the coming messiah.*

THE LAST DAYS OF JUDAH · 34:1–38:13

Turning from the Book of Consolation (30:1–33:36), the compilers of the book of Jeremiah present next a series of events (34:1–38:28) in which Jeremiah interacts with the Judean rulers prior to the final fall of

Jerusalem to Nebuchadnezzar's army. These events are of varied dates and not necessarily sequential.

34:1–7 Verses 1–7 give the timing of this prophetic warning and promise to Zedekiah. The Babylonian ruler had engaged Jerusalem; however, his main focus lay on destroying all the fortified cities of Judah outside the capital. His forces included *all the kingdoms and peoples in the empire*. As vassals of the mighty king, they provided whatever support he required. Only Lachish (Tell ed-Duweir, about thirty-five miles southwest of Jerusalem) and Azekah (about 10 miles north of Lachish) remained unconquered before the entire Babylonian force turned against Jerusalem. Both sites are in the Shephelah, the foothills between the Philistine Plain and the Central Highlands.

The Lord told Jeremiah to warn Zedekiah that Yahweh is about to hand over Jerusalem to the Babylonians. Zedekiah will not escape. He will appear before King Nebuchadnezzar, who will deport him to Babylon. All this happened according to the word of the prophet. However, after having looked into the eyes of Nebuchanezzar, Zedekiah fell blind or became blind. He was captive in Babylon, but he never saw the place (39:7; 52:10–11). The prophet also transmits a promise of Yahweh to Zedekiah. He will not die in battle. The *funeral fire* is not a reference to cremation. It will be a fire to honor him, as was the custom (2 Chron 16:14; 21:19).

34:8–22 King Zedekiah apparently initiated the emancipation of slaves some time after the siege of the city began, early in 588 BCE. It seems to have been an effort to placate the Lord. The slaveholders entered into a solemn agreement before Yahweh (verse 15) to free all *Hebrew slaves*. The text does not mention slaves who were not Hebrews. Then they reneged on their promise and reenslaved those freed. This covenant-breaking *profaned* the Lord's name. The law forbade lifelong enslavement of Hebrews by Hebrews unless willingly entered into (Exod 21:5–6). Otherwise, the slave must be freed after six years of servitude (Exod 21:2; Lev 25:39–46; Deut 15:1, 12–18). The prophetic word reminded the slaveholders of the Lord's will, which they and their forefathers had disdained.

In an ironic statement, the Lord gave the slaveholders their *freedom* – to suffer the consequences of their rebellious ways. *The calf they cut in two* refers to the ancient practice of sacrificing an animal when making a solemn covenant (see Gen 15:9–17). The Hebrew expression for making a covenant is "to cut" a covenant.

The timing of this event is related to the lifting of the siege by the Babylonians (verse 21). Jeremiah 37:5–8 indicates that the withdrawal of the Babylonians was due to the approach of an Egyptian army coming to the aid of the Judeans; however, according to Ezekiel 17:15–17, the Egyptian effort failed, and when they returned to Egypt, the Babylonians took Jerusalem.

The Lord takes covenants very seriously (Num 30:2; Deut 21–23; Josh 9:15–18; Eccl 5:4–5; Matt 21:28–32).

35:1–9 Verses 1–5 occur *during the reign of Jehoiakim*, probably dating to 598 BCE. The incident is related to the raiding parties of *Babylonian and Aramean armies* (verse 11). Second Kings 24:2 provides the setting for the invaders's activities. Both chapters 35 and 36 relate to the reign of Jehoiakim and appear between the preceding and following chapters associated with King Zedekiah. There is no apparent explanation for why the compilers made this arrangement.

The invitation to the Recabites came *from the Lord* via Jeremiah. What Yahweh commands, the prophet faithfully does. The *side rooms* were built adjacent to the sanctuary proper and served as storerooms, meeting rooms, and as temporary living quarters for the priests on duty. *Jaazaniah son of Jeremiah* points to the popularity of the name Jeremiah, and was not the prophet's son. The people mentioned are otherwise unknown, except for *Maaseiah son of Shallum*, probably the father of the priest Zephaniah (21:1; 29:25; 37:3). Door-keeping at the temple was an important priestly function, preventing the entry of ritually unclean persons. The

> **The Recabites**
>
> The Recabites were a clan begun by Jonadab (Jehonadab), *a supporter of the revolt of Jehu against the house of Ahab* (2 Kgs 10:23). He apparently became disillusioned by the subsequent actions of Jehu, who "was not careful to keep the law of the Lord" and "did not turn away from the sins of Jeroboam" (2 Kgs 10:31). *So he withdrew from the urban and agrarian culture of Israel to a nomadic way of life*. The Recabites were related to the Kenites (1 Chron 2:55), who may have been metalworkers, also an itinerant trade. The event in Jeremiah 35 provides the bulk of biblical information about the group – they dwelt in tents, neither drank wine nor owned vineyards, and never built houses nor practiced agriculture. Noteworthy is the fact that they had been carrying on this lifestyle for two and a half centuries by Jeremiah's time.

doorkeepers were also in charge of funds set aside for the repair of the temple (2 Kgs 12:9–10). The name *Igdaliah* occurs only here. The Septuagint has Gedaliah, so the longer form is simply an alternative spelling of the name.

As with other symbolic acts of the book, Jeremiah publicly offered wine to the Recabites, knowing they would refuse to drink it, to make a point. Even in the temple of the Lord at the invitation of the prophet of the Lord, they refused to break the covenant of the clan. That they were dwelling in Jerusalem was a temporary interlude in their normal life away from settled places. For their safety and survival, they had entered the city to escape the rampaging *Babylonian and Aramean armies*.

Instruction to Jeremiah from Yahweh was immediate (verses 12–17). The people of Judah and Jerusalem saw an example of obedience to a family covenant by the Recabites. Would they be moved by that example to observe the covenant relation with Yahweh that he had established? Past performance gave little hope that they would. Disaster awaits those who *did not listen* and *did not answer*.

The Lord promised condemnation to Judah (verses 18–19) but gave commendation to the Recabites. Because of their faithfulness, the Recabites would survive to serve Yahweh "while the earth remains" (Septuagint).

36:1–32 This second event during Jehoiakim's reign occurred in 605 BCE, the year in which Nebuchadnezzar defeated Egypt at Carchemish, a ford across the Euphrates River. After this victory, the Babylonians began to extend their control over the rest of the ancient Near East. Jeremiah was then in his twenty-third year of ministry.

What Jeremiah had spoken over the years for the Lord was now to be written down (verses 1–3). Some who had heard the prophecies had died. What Jeremiah presented orally in the past now would take on a more permanent form, so that the current generation would know the warning. The reason for writing is that they might repent and escape from the disaster to come.

Although Jeremiah mentions Baruch in 32:12, verses 4–7 mark his earliest appearance in the events of Jeremiah's ministry. Why Jeremiah was *restricted* (prevented from entering the temple) is unclear. He may have been ceremonially unclean, or he may have been barred from entry by temple officials who considered him a troublemaker (see chapters 7, 26). He does not seem to have been under arrest, because he is free to move about in verses 19 and 26. Baruch is to read the scroll in public on a fast day when the people are likely to pray (*bring their petition*). The Old Testament does not establish any set fast days (but see Zech 7:5), but with the threat of foreign invaders, priests had announced a special fast day. This fast was apparently related to Nebuchadnezzar's sack of Ashkelon in the nearby Philistine plain.

According to verses 8–10, The scroll contained *the words of the Lord*, although dictated by Jeremiah. Baruch faithfully carried out Jeremiah's instructions, reading to those assembled from the *room of Gemariah*. This was likely a portico, opening on the *upper courtyard* in which those entering the New Gate could congregate. Shaphan, father of Gemariah, was high official under Josiah (2 Kgs 22:3, 8). Gemariah's brother, Ahikam, stood by Jeremiah when he was threatened (26:24), so Baruch was in a friendly environment as he read Jeremiah's words to the people. Gemariah, however, was not present (verse 12).

Micaiah reported the gist of what Baruch had read to his father and the others in conference (verses 11–19). The officials were meeting in the office of *Elishama*, another official. He is likely the same individual mentioned in 41:1 and 2 Kings 25:25, and was related to the royal family. All these men were high-ranking members of the king's court. The Bible does not mention *Jehudi son of Nethaniah* elsewhere, but noting his ancestors to the third generation suggests that he was an important individual; normally only the father is named. While commanding Baruch to bring the scroll to them, these officials treated him respectfully, inviting him to be seated. The words of Jeremiah struck fear in the hearts of the listeners, as the officials heard Baruch read them. As the king's advisors, they determined that the king should hear what the message

> **Gemaraiah**
> *Archaeologist Yigael Shiloh found evidence for "Gemaryahu son of Shaphan" in the city of David excavations in the form of a* bulla, *a piece of clay that authenticated a sealed papyrus document which had been impressed by Gemaryahu's seal. (Gemaryahu is a longer form of Gemariah.) Fire destroyed the papyrus document but hardened the clay so it survived until its recent discovery (King 94).*

in the scroll. After learning that Jeremiah dictated the message that Baruch read, and anticipating a negative reaction on the part of Jehoiakim that would endanger both Baruch and Jeremiah, they ordered both men to hide for their personal safety. (Much later unconfirmed tradition identifies their hiding place north of the Damascus Gate in what is now called the Grotto of Jeremiah.)

The reaction of Jehoiakim to the prophetic word testifies to his unbelief and disdain (verses 20–26). In mid-winter, he was keeping warm with heat from a *firepot* (brazier), probably burning charcoal. Despite the suggestion that the scroll was made of parchment (Harrison 150), it was more likely a papyrus scroll. Burning leather would have given off a terrible stench; furthermore, parchment was not invented until the second century BCE. Unlike the fear felt by the group of court officials who heard Baruch read the scroll, the king and his circle of closest advisors treated the prophetic words skeptically. They rejected the wise counsel of *Elnathan, Delaiah and Gemeriah*. As *Jehudi* read column after column of the scroll, the king cut off a few columns, adding it to the fuel in the brazier. His actions contrast sharply with those of his father, Josiah, when the scroll was discovered in the temple during his reign (2 Kgs 22:8–13). *Son of the king* was a title that indicated a close but not necessarily a blood relationship to the monarch. The king did not discover Baruch and Jeremiah.

> **Jeremiah's Second Scroll**
> *To the second copy, Jeremiah added many similar prophecies. This second scroll was likely the beginning of our Book of Jeremiah. Just as Yahweh provided the second set of tablets for Moses (Exod 32:19; 34:1), so he provided for the survival of the word Jehoiakim destroyed (Huey 326).*

The anger of Jehoiakim against Jeremiah and Baruch subsided in due time, and the Lord instructed Jeremiah to dictate again to Baruch the contents of the destroyed scroll (verses 27–32).

The Lord also gave a personal word to Jehoiakim through Jeremiah. He would fall to the very force he denied – *the king of Babylon*. He would die and have no proper burial, nor would a son succeed him. His son and successor, Jehoiachin, ruled but three months (2 Kgs 24:8).

37:1–21 The text now returns to events in the reign of Zedekiah (see 2 Kgs 24:17–25:7). From 37:1 through 44:30, the book of Jeremiah focuses upon events just prior to the fall of Jerusalem, the fall itself, and its aftermath. The section is almost entirely written as a narrative, probably by Baruch.

Verse 1 is a succinct version of 2 Kings 24:17–20, which states that Zedekiah *did evil in the eyes of the Lord*. He ignored the prophetic warnings of Jeremiah, and *the people of the land* followed the example of their leader. *Jehucal son of Shelemiah* was no friend of the prophet. In 38:1, 4, he, among others, urges Jeremiah's execution. *Zephaniah*, the next in rank after the high priest, treated Jeremiah with respect in 24:24–29. Zedekiah will not accept the word of the Lord from the prophet, but he recognizes Jeremiah's intimate relationship with Yahweh and asks him to pray to Yahweh *our God*. The Babylonians had temporarily halted their siege of Jerusalem, due to the threat from the Egyptian forces of Pharaoh Hophra, identified by name in 44:30 (589–570 BCE). Zedekiah perhaps hoped prayer would make the withdrawal permanent, as verse 7 indicates. This event occurred before the prophet was imprisoned (32:2).

The king had requested that Jeremiah pray (verses 6–10). There is no indication that Jeremiah did as requested. However, the revelation he received from the Lord is clear. The Lord denies the desire of Zechariah. Egypt will withdraw, and the Babylonians will return to destroy Jerusalem. The city's doom is inevitable, even in the unlikely but extreme circumstances depicted in verse 10.

The arrest of Jeremiah also occurred during the period in which the Babylonian forces had withdrawn from besieging the city (verses 11–16). The prophet had personal business to attend to outside Jerusalem in the territory of the tribe of Benjamin. The property involved is apparently not that which he purchased as a symbolic act (chapter 32). *Irijeh* is otherwise unknown in the Bible, but he was not related to the false prophet Hananiah (28:1, 10). The captain of the guard arrested Jeremiah and charged him with *deserting to the Babylonians*. He was likely under suspicion because he had urged people to surrender to the enemy (21:9; 38:2), and some had done so (38:19). The *officials* are here unnamed, but

> **The Benjamin Gate**
> *The* Benjamin Gate *was in the north of the city wall (compare 38:7; Zech 14:10); gates bore the name of the places toward which traffic was headed, as with the modern Jaffa Gate.*

they were probably those listed in 38:1. These were not the officials of 36:12, 19, who had been sympathetic to Jeremiah. A decade had passed and an earlier group had accompanied Jehoiachin into exile.

Although he was imprisoned in a *house*, his was not a benign house arrest. He endured beating and isolation in *a vaulted cell in a dungeon*. The dungeon was in the basement of the house; vaulting supported the the floor above.

King Zedekiah's secret desire for a (good) *word from Yahweh* finally brought Jeremiah out of his prison and into the palace (verses 17–21). Apparently, the king feared what his officials, who were pro-Egyptian, might do to him, if he asked Jeremiah the question publicly (Huey 331). A man of courage and integrity, despite the possible consequences, Jeremiah gave the word of doom from the Lord.

Taking advantage of the opportunity to speak directly with the king, Jeremiah pled his case. The reality of current events had proven the false prophets were false. Jeremiah's prophecies had proven true. To his credit, Zedekiah removed Jeremiah (still under arrest) to better surroundings and rations.

38:1–13 There are similarities between this and the previous incident: in both, officials charged the prophet with treason and threw him in prison; both have private interviews with the king; and in both Jeremiah ends up in *the courtyard of the guard*. But there are differences as well. The setting for the arrests differ. Jeremiah stays in two different prison environments, and the king deals with each incident differently. Either this chapter is an alternative version of chapter 37 or, more likely, a separate incident.

Gedaliah son of Pashhur may be the son of the Pashhur who had mistreated Jeremiah (20:1–6). *Jehucal*, mentioned in 37:3, has a shortened name, *Jucal*, here. *Pashhur son of Malkijah* appears in 21:1. Jeremiah had frequently spoken the same or similar prophetic words given in verse 2 (21:9; 34:2, 22; 37:8). The charge is not that of encouraging people to escape the doomed city, but the effect of Jeremiah's prophecies on the morale of the defenders.

The king's response to his officials reminds one of Pilate handing Jesus over to the mob. By referring to himself in the third person, (*The king can do nothing to oppose you*), Zedekiah distances himself from his actions. Surprisingly, the officials who had deemed Jeremiah worthy of death, rather than executing him immediately, put him in a cistern. Perhaps they intended that he die there slowly, by starvation. The cistern was much worse than the dungeon in Jonathan's house.

But Jeremiah had a friend in the royal court – *Ebed-Melech*, a Cushite. When he heard what officials done with Jeremiah, he went directly to the king. Zedekiah was at the same gate where Jeremiah had been arrested in the previous incident, probably seeing to the

> **Cisterns**
> *Cisterns were cut into bedrock and plastered to hold water in many ancient cities. That only mud remained in the cistern puts the event late in the summer dry season, likely in July or August, shortly before the Babylonians breached the wall in 587 BCE (52:5–7).*

> **Cush**
> *Modern northern Sudan. In Jeremiah's time, the Cushites were heavily Egyptianized. Earlier they ruled Egypt as the Twenty-Fifth Dynasty (eighth through the seventh centuries BCE).*

defenses. Invaders had always approached Jerusalem from that direction due to the strategic value of the heights of Mount Scopus. While the king had earlier put the fate of Jeremiah in the hands of his angry officials, he acted forthrightly here, even assigning a considerable contingent of men to assist Ebed-Melech, perhaps to prevent any interference from the officials mentioned in 38:1. (On the other hand, one Hebrew manuscript has three rather than thirty men; and RSV follows this translation.) We see the thoughtfulness of Ebed-Melech for the condition of Jeremiah in the cushioning he provided from the pressure of the ropes on his malnourished body. He would receive his reward from the Lord (39:16–18).

ZEDEKIAH QUESTIONS JEREMIAH AGAIN · 38:14–28

Rather than questioning Jeremiah "in the palace" as previously (37:17), the king is in *the third entrance to the temple of the Lord*. The location of this gate in the Solomonic temple is unkown; it may have been an entrance adjacent to the king's palace (Hyatt 1076). Verses 15–16 reflect Jeremiah's previous experience with the king; however, the king's oath convinced the prophet to respond to Zedekiah's request. Yahweh offers the king two dismal outcomes (verses 17–18).

Surrender offered a better result than capture, but fear of mistreatment at the hands of Judeans who had already surrendered to the Babylonians dominated the king's mind (verse 19). Jeremiah first urges Zedekiah to surrender for his own personal good. Then the prophet paints a stark picture of what will happen to the king's *women* (his harem of concubines and wives) and children. Four lines of poetry that will be uttered by his wives will utterly shame and humiliate the king if he refuses to surrender. These words possibly point to the pro-Egyptian officials of Zedekiah's court, his advisors (verse 1). These men had earlier desired to slay Jeremiah, as the king knows, so he commanded Jeremiah not to reveal the content of their discussion to the *officials*, should they inquire of him. Jeremiah obeyed the king. He did not reveal the heart of his conversation with the king, but he did tell them what the king wanted them to hear.

39:1–18 What Jeremiah had prophesied happened (verses 1–7). The Babylonians had sacked Jerusalem. For reasons we cannot discern, the compiler(s) of our book repeat the fall of the city in 52:4–16, which itself comes almost verbatim from 2 Kings 25:1–12. The shortened version of the Septuagint does not include verses 4–13. The siege "began in January 588 and lasted until July 587 (with a brief interlude, probably in the summer of 588)" (Bright 242). The approach of Egyptian forces noted earlier caused the interlude. The breach of the walls occurred on *the ninth day of the fourth month*, still observed by Jews as the Ninth of Av.

The leaders of the Babylonian forces held an immediate conference in the *Middle Gate*. That location is uncertain. The manuscript tradition has garbled some of the names of the officers. *Nergal-sharezer*, though mentioned twice (verse 3), may be the same individual as in verse 13. The Babylonians, upon entering the city, would have moved cautiously and methodically into unfamiliar streets with armed defenders still within the walls. Zedekiah and his soldiers fled the city under cover of darkness through *the gate between the two walls* (a narrow postern gate). They entered the Kidron Valley on the east side of the city and fled toward the Jordan Valley. Pursued and captured, they appeared before Nebuchadnezzar at his headquarters in central Syria, *Riblah in the land of Hamath*. There the mighty ruler took his vengeance on the petty king who had caused him so much grief. As excessive as the Babylonian treatment of prisoners seems, it was normal in the warfare of the ancient Near East.

Verses 8–10 offer an account of the destruction of the rebellious city. The account telescopes events. *Nebuzaradan* arrived in the city a month after its capitulation rather than the day the walls fell (52:12). The destruction of the city was complete, making it virtually uninhabitable. The phrase *and the rest of the people* at the end of verse 9 is a scribal error. The correct reading should follow 52:15, "the rest of the craftsmen." Those whom Nebuzaradan left behind and to whom he gave *vineyards and fields* could be an asset to the meager provincial government formed by the captors and to the "Babylonian soldiers" who served with Gedaliah (41:3).

Verses 11–14 give the first of two slightly differing accounts of the release of Jeremiah. The second follows in 40:1–6. Jeremiah's release from his imprisonment in the *courtyard of the guard* came at the hand of the Babylonians, not by action of Zedekiah's officers. This apparently occurred on the day the city fell to the Babylonians. Nebuzaradan, however, was not in the city that day and did not arrive for another thirty days. The key to understanding Jeremiah's initial release is the word *sent* (verse 14). Apparently, the leading officers were at their field headquarters in "Ramah" (40:1) and sent the orders for Jeremiah's release. The succinct text does not give many particulars. Jeremiah may have been brought to Ramah (modern er-Ram), some five miles north of Jerusalem. They also placed him in the custody of *Gedaliah*. As governor, he stayed in Mizpah (40:5), three miles north of Ramah.

> **Nebuchadnezzar & Jeremiah**
> *Skeptics might insist that Nebuchadnezzar would not have known about Jeremiah nor have given orders for his welfare. Yet Zedekiah had feared* the Jews who have gone over to the Babylonians (38:19). *Surely they informed their Babylonian interrogators about the prophet who had encouraged them to surrender and foretold the conquest of the city by Nebuchadnezzar's forces. Although the Babylonian king knew about Jeremiah, it is doubtful that they ever met face to face.*

Verses 15–18 logically connect with 38:28. Scribes placed this section here because it relates to Jeremiah's confinement in *the courtyard of the guard*. Acting out of a compassionate heart, *Ebed-Melech the Cushite* had rescued Jeremiah from a deadly situation in the cistern. Now the Lord had compassion upon him because of his faith in Yahweh. The Hebrew is more emphatic than *I will save you*. The grammatical construction (infinitive absolute + imperfect) means, "I will surely save you" (compare NRSV).

JEREMIAH'S WITNESS AFTER JERUSALEM'S FALL · 40:1–45:5

40:1-6 *The word came to Jeremiah from the Lord* should introduce a prophetic oracle, but none follows. The next mention of a word from the Lord to the prophet occurs in 42:7. The text has a history we do not know. Clearly it has suffered damage here. On the other hand, Willis (319) thinks that Nebuzaradan's words to Jeremiah comprise the oracle.

Lacking details, we cannot know how Jeremiah ended up in chains in Ramah, where he was again freed. Another possibility is that the account in 39:11–14 has compressed within it the events in this section. In other words, Jeremiah went from the courtyard of the guard in chains to Ramah to see Nebuzaradan, who released him there. Yet Nebuzaradan's advice to Jeremiah to *Go back to Gedaliah* indicates that Jeremiah had been with Gedaliah before ending up in Ramah. Whatever the actual sequence of circumstances, Jeremiah chose to remain in the land. *Gedaliah son of Ahikam* was the grandson of Shaphan (39:14). Shaphan, in the service of Josiah, had a role in the discovery of the scroll of the law (2 Kgs 22:3–20). Ahikam was a supporter of Jeremiah (26:24).

> **Gedaliah's Seal**
> A stamp seal found at Lachish in 1935 bearing the inscription, "[Belonging to] Gedalyahu, the one over the house," may be related to Gedaliah. If so, he was serving Zedekiah as the royal steward (manager of the palace staff) until the city fell (King 98). Nebuchadnezzar would thus have appointed an experienced administrator to be governor.

40:7–41:16 The text does not mention Jeremiah or Yahweh again until 42:2. We learn much about Jeremiah in this book, but it is not a biography of the prophet. According to verses 7–10, the *army officers and all their men* had apparently escaped the conquerors, finding temporary refuge *in the open country*. Harrison (160) suggests that they were guerrilla fighters. Variants of the names of the officers occur in the Septuagint and some Hebrew manuscripts. *Ishmael*, of the house of David, perhaps had an attitude of superiority over Gedaliah. A clay bulla reading "Belonging to Ishmael the son of the king" exists, and may refer to this person; however, it came from the antiquities market and may be a forgery (King 98–99).

Gedaliah was intent on pacifying the countryside. He attempted to reassure the officers and their men by oath (presumably taken before Yahweh) and by his political authority. Gedaliah was rightly concerned about the harvest of vintage grapes, summer fruits, and olives. The survival of the remnant that remained in the land depended upon an adequate food supply. Harvest times for these crops occured in August/September.

Besides the remnant of the Judean army, refugees in Transjordan and elsewhere returned (verses 11–12). Combined with *the people who were left behind in the land* (verse 6), the military group and the refugees were able to enjoy an abundant harvest.

Johanan son of Kareah led a deputation to warn Gedaliah of the plot against his life (verses 13–14). The Ammonite king, Baalis, orchestrated the plot in concert with Ishmael son of Nethaniah. Baalis probably hoped to control the Judahite territory with Gedaliah out of the way. Gedaliah could not believe such a thing could be true, and he rejected Johanan's offer to preemptively assassinate Ishmael.

> **The Bulla of Baalis**
> Archaeologists discovered a bulla of Baalis in excavations at Tell el-Umeiri south of Amman, Jordan in 1984.

In the seventh month was less than three months after Gedaliah became governor (41:1–3). The assassination of the governor may have occurred one or more years later than the year in which Jerusalem fell, however. The text does not specify the year, and three months seems insufficient time for the return of the refugees and the harvest.

Ishmael and his men were guests at the table of Gedaliah. They broke the key custom of hospitality in the ancient Near East by slaying their host. So awful was the deed that the Jews observed a fast day in October in the Second Temple period as a memorial (Zech 7:5; 8:19). The others killed – a small contingent of Babylonian soldiers and *all the Jews who were with Gedaliah* – probably refers to others at the meal, not to all the inhabitants of Mizpah (see verse 10).

The murder of all present at the dinner apparently left no one to escape and spread the alarm (verses 4–15). The men arriving from *Shechem, Shiloh and Samaria* were coming from the north, apparently on a religious pilgrimage to the ruined holy place in Jerusalem. While Leviticus 19:28, 21:5, and Deuteronomy 14:1 forbid the religious act of cutting oneself some people apparently practiced it. Ishmael went out to meet them, falsely showing evidence of a similar grief, and drew them into his deadly ambush. Only ten survived; the others were thrown into a mass burial in an empty cistern, *along with Gedaliah*, and we can assume the rest of those murdered at the meal. The text includes a historical note, associating the construction of the cistern with the defenses built by *King Asa* (1 Kgs 15:22).

Besides *the king's daughters*, Jeremiah was apparently among the captives (42:2 mentions him among those rescued). Ishmael, his men and his captives, headed eastward toward Ammonite territory across the Jordan.

Johanan and his associates rescued the captives *near the great pool in Gibeon*. Perhaps Ishmael was aware of pursuers and was attempting to circumvent them. In the melee, Ishmael and eight of his men escaped to the Ammonites.

> **Gibeon**
> *Gibeon (Tell el-Jib) is actually southwest of the site identified as Mizpah (Tell en-Nasbeh) rather than east.*

41:16–43:13 Johanan and his men realized that the assassination of Gedaliah represented rebellion against Nebuchadnezzar and Babylon (verses 16–18). Rather than return to Mizpah, they and those whom they had rescued headed south past ruined Jerusalem. Fearing Babylonian reprisals, they headed toward Egypt for refuge. They stopped to assess their situation at *Geruth Kimham near Bethlehem*. We cannot now identify the location. It may have been a piece of property given by King David to Kimham in recognition of his support (2 Sam 19:38), and the name of which continued through the centuries.

According to 42:1–6, the entire group was uncertain what they should do, but they all acted in one accord to approach Jeremiah to pray to Yahweh (*your God*) on their behalf. In a crisis, this irreligious group turned to the one person who had a relationship with Yahweh. They do not seek spiritual guidance, simply physical safety.

Jeremiah agrees to pray to "Yahweh *your God*," perhaps using the occasion as a teachable moment. They swear a modest form of oath to obey whatever the Lord *your* God requires; however, they finally acknowledge Yahweh as *our* God. It should be noted, however, that the Septuagint reads *our God* in verses 4–5.

The duration *ten days later* presents a test of their faith and patience (verses 7–12). Jeremiah presents the reply in the Lord's words. The ultimate decision is in their hands. Yahweh's word comes in "if/then" clauses, urging them to stay and benefit from what God promises to do for them. The Lord has compassion on them because of their suffering. And as sovereign of all nations, God will see to it that Nebuchadnezzar will treat them compassionately. The Lord promises his sustaining presence with them.

In verses 13–18, Jeremiah injects his own preliminary warning to the group about what will happen to them if they refuse to stay in the land, thus disobeying the Lord. From the practical point of view, Egypt looked like a haven from the horrors of their recent experiences, but asylum in Egypt was not God's will for them. *The word of the Lord* substantiates the word of his prophet. In Egypt, they would suffer the very things they seek to escape. All of this would come upon them, despite the compassion of the Lord, if they chose to rebel.

Jeremiah completes his presentation in verses 19–22 by emphasizing in his own words what the oracle from the Lord had stated. He sensed that they had *made a fatal mistake* by asking him to seek the Lord's direction for them because they had already determined that they were going to go on to Egypt. They had not made their petition in good faith. They sought only Yahweh's confirmation of their plans. Apparently, Jeremiah could tell by the body language of his audience that they *still have not obeyed the Lord* [their] *God in all he sent* [Jeremiah] *to tell* [them].

In 43:1–3, the *arrogant* men flatly rejected the prophet's reply, accusing him of lying. For the first time, we learn that *Baruch* is also among the group rescued at Gibeon. Likely he conferred with Jeremiah during the ten days' wait for the word of the Lord. The arrogance of the men comes through in their accusations against Jeremiah and Baruch. Baruch himself no doubt penned the narrative that connects the flow of the dialogue.

The arrogance of these men is also evident in their breaking of the solemn pledge that they would all obey whatever the Lord revealed to Jeremiah concerning their future (42:5–6). The text emphasizes their rebellion by the repeated words *disobeyed* (verse 4) and *disobedience* (verse 7). *Tahpanhes* (meaning "the Fortress of Penhase") is the modern Tell ed-Defenna/Dafna, a site in the eastern Delta bordering Sinai.

> **Jeremiah in Egypt**
> *Jeremiah and Baruch entered Egypt, too. Some commentators think they went of their own free will, in order to assist the* remnant of Judah. *Others think that the group forced them to go along, which seems the more likely alternative.* Huey (362–63) speculates, "The question remains unanswered why they would want Jeremiah to accompany them, since they repudiated him as God's spokesman."

The remnant who sought safety in Egypt receive a further word from the Lord (verses 8–13) by means of another symbolic act by Jeremiah in view of the assembled group. Basically, the action and the word of the Lord assure the group that has sought safety from Nebuchadnezzar in Egypt that they will not escape. Jeremiah lays the foundation stones on which the Babylonian monarch will place his throne. He will bring *death ... captivity ... the sword*. These are the very horrors the remnant from Judah sought to escape. And it will be the Lord's doing. The *temple of the sun* may refer to a temple in Heliopolis (also known as On), "the city of the sun," located about ten miles northeast of Cairo.

A fragmentary inscription, now in the British Museum, provides evidence that Nebuchadnezzar made a brief invasion of Egypt in his thirty-seventh year (568–567 BCE). He did not, however, conquer the country or depose the ruling pharaoh, Amasis (570–526 BCE). Some commentators, however, do not believe the subjugation of Egypt by Nebuchadnezzar, as depicted here, ever took place. Rather, Jeremiah uses the symbolic action and related oracle to assure the disobedient Jews that what had happened to Jerusalem would also reach them (Willis 377).

44:1-30 This chapter consists of a dialogue between Jeremiah and the people from Judah who had come to Egypt. It naturally divides into three parts: Jeremiah first presents the Lord's charges against them of idolatrous worship and the consequences (verses 1–14); the people responded (verses 15–19); and the Lord described their fate followed by the promise of an historic event that would be a sign assuring their punishment.

The message from Yahweh concerns *all the Jews living in Egypt*, not just the recent refugees at Tahpanhes (verses 1–14). Some of these people had migrated to Egypt at least since the fall of Samaria in 722 BCE. The location of *Migdol* is uncertain, but it was in Egypt's northeastern sector. *Memphis* (Noph), the capital of Lower Egypt, is at the head of the delta, just south of modern Cairo. *Upper Egypt* (Pathros) is southern Egypt, from Cairo to Aswan. A colony of Jews were living on the island of Elephantine (Yeb) near Aswan, perhaps before the destruction of Jerusalem.

Destroyed Jerusalem and the towns of Judah are examples of what Yahweh has done when *provoked ... to anger* by idolatrous worship.

> **The Elephantine Papyri**
> *The Jewish mercenary colony on Elephantine Island, near Egypt's southern border near the First Cataract, left behind numerous letters, contracts, and even one literary text, all dating from about 500 to 400 BCE. The letters in particular give important evidence for Jewish life in the Diaspora just after Jeremiah's time.*

The anger in part also stemmed from their treatment of his *servants the prophets*. The "why?" questions caused the audience to consider the tragic results of failing to *humble themselves*, *show reverence*, and obey the *law* of *the Lord God Almighty*. Thus the same end will befall those who sought refuge in Egypt as happened to Jerusalem and Judah – *sword, famine and plague*, except for a very few fugitives.

In verses 15–19, the people reply, rejecting the appeals voiced by Jeremiah. From their point of view, when they turned from idolatrous worship to serve Yahweh, likely referring to the religious reforms of Josiah, they lost everything, often including their lives. This is in contrast to the prosperous former times when they had burned incense to the *Queen of Heaven*. (As noted earlier, this deity is a version of the Mesopotamian goddess Ishtar or the Canaanite Astarte [King 102–7].) This is probably a reference to the time of Manasseh, prior to the Josianic reforms. The wives and husbands had acted in concert and would continue to do so in pagan worship; the women may have led the way (Willis 341).

Jeremiah responds in verses 20–28 with an oracle of the Lord. To paraphrase, "Do what you have vowed to do – and suffer the consequences." Yahweh swears by his *great name*. No more emphatic word could be offered. Since they had chosen the Queen of Heaven, never more would they be able to validate any statement by the name Yahweh. Verse 28 reiterates the end of verse 14. Time will validate the truth of the word of the Lord. In contrast to all other ancient religions, the prophet's understanding of Israel's faith demanded exclusive worship of only one god.

Verses 29–30 promise a validating sign for the near future, a historical event. Behind the circumstances that will bring *Pharaoh Hophra* down is the sovereign Lord, the same Yahweh who ended Zedekiah's reign. In 566 BCE, Hophra was put to death by his rival and successor, Amasis. Whether Jeremiah lived to see that day is unknown. These are the last recorded words of Jeremiah.

45:1–5 The date of this oracle to Baruch is 605 BCE, *the fourth year of Jehoiakim*. It is associated with the scroll incident in chapter 36. Bright moves the passage to place it in conjunction with that chapter (184–86). The compiler of the book of Jeremiah, however, who may have been Baruch himself, may have placed it here to contrast with the texts that immediately precede it (Willis 345). It may also have been placed here because the first readers, those in exile in Babylon, had, like Baruch, also escaped with their lives.

Baruch's woe, whether expressed verbally or only in his mind, reached the Lord. Scholars have likened his groanings to the confessions of Jeremiah, who also struggled with the horrendous weight of his prophetic ministry (15:10–21; 20:7–18). Jeremiah brought to his faithful scribe and associate the response of the Lord, similar to the Lord's words to Ananias concerning Saul, "I will show him how much he must suffer for my name" (Acts 9:16). In a world experiencing *disaster*, Baruch can expect nothing for himself, but he learns that he will *escape with [his] life*. (God gave the same promise to Ebed-Melech, 39:18.)

The biblical record leaves both Jeremiah and Baruch in Egypt. One can speculate, however, that Baruch either ended up in Babylon or saw to it that those in exile received the oracles of Jeremiah. The Lord chose those in exile in Babylon to initiate the restoration, and that community cherished and preserved the words of Jeremiah that Baruch faithfully recorded.

PROPHECIES AGAINST FOREIGN PEOPLES · 46:1–51:64

46:1–28 The Lord appointed Jeremiah "a prophet to the nations." His oracles to the nations comprise chapters 46–51. Originally they may have followed immediately after 25:13a, which is where they appear in the Septuagint. The order of the nations differs in the Septuagint, as well. We find similar oracles against foreign nations in a number of other prophets (Isa 13–23, Ezek 25–32, and Amos 1–2). Jeremiah 46:1 introduces prophecies concerning surrounding peoples. The verse is lacking in the Septuagint. The oracles are in poetic style with an occasional line or two of narrative prose interspersed between poems.

The initial oracle in verses 2–12 concerning Egypt dates to 605 BCE, *the fourth year of Jehoiakim*. Four years earlier, *Pharaoh Necho* had been responsible for the death of King Josiah, as the Judean king, allied with the Babylonians, moved to prevent the Egyptians from assisting the Assyrians, who were their allies (2 Kgs 23:29–30).

> **Carchemish**
>
> The Egyptian defeat in 605 BCE at Carchemish, a ford of the Euphrates River, was decisive in opening Syria and Palestine to the advancing Babylonian forces.

Those preparing for battle are infantrymen, charioteers, and calvarymen. The Egyptians are *terrified* and flee in disorder. The swelling Egyptian forces rise up like the Nile when the annual flood surges down the valley from the highlands of Ethiopia and Central Africa. Necho's Egyptian forces also included men from regions south of Egypt–Ethiopians, Somalis, and Luds (not Lydians; compare Gen 10:13).

Despite the urging of the leaders, the day belongs to Yahweh, *the Lord Almighty*. The day of *vengeance* will avenge the death of good king Josiah. The slain Egyptians will be a *sacrifice* that the Lord will offer by means of the Babylonian sword. The Lord urges wounded Egypt to obtain the legendary balm of Gilead (compare 8:22), but to no avail. Its defeat is certain and *the nations* will witness the debacle.

The second word concerning Egypt (verses 13–24) relates to the invasion of Egypt by Nebuchadnezzar. Although the Babylonians were on the Philistine plain in 604 BCE, threatening Egypt, Nebuchadnezzar's invasion of Egypt did not occur until 568 BCE. That event probably occurred after Jeremiah's death, "but the prophet seems years earlier to have regarded such an invasion as certain" (Bright 308). The Babylonians, however, were never able totally to conquer and devastate Egypt. It seems more likely that the Babylonians, when they withdrew early in the siege against Jerusalem, posed a serious threat to the Egyptians (37:6–8). This oracle, then, describes the psychological impact of the Babylonians upon Pharaoh Hophra's army. No matter the efforts of the Egyptian warriors, *the Lord will push them down*.

As a result, people everywhere will scorn *the king of Egypt*. The *one who will come* refers to Nebuchadnezzar. His prominence as a military leader is as visible as are the two mountains, Tabor, near Nazareth, and Carmel, rising from the sea at modern Haifa.

Using bovine, reptilian, forest, and insect imagery, the text depicts the demise of the Egyptian forces. Egypt had no actual forests, depending upon Lebanon for timber.

Almighty God will punish Amon, the chief deity of Egypt, who was worshiped in a temple in Thebes (verses 25–280). Despite the calamity to befall Egypt, there is a word of hope: the land will be *inhabited as in times past*.

Appended to this last oracle to Egypt is a word of hope for Yahweh's chosen people. The text here basically repeats 30:10–11. Whether or not Egyptians ever heard these oracles, they were instructive for the Lord's people in exile. Thus the word of hope for Egypt provides a setting to recall the word of hope for *Israel*.

47:1–7 Verse 1, an editor's remark, establishes the time when the oracle came to Jeremiah. The phrase *before Pharaoh attacked Gaza* is missing in the Septuagint. The exact date for the oracle is not clear – perhaps before Josiah's death at Megiddo (609 BCE); perhaps after the battle at Carchemish (604 BCE). Gaza was a major Philistine city. The figure of *waters ... rising in the north*, however, points to the Babylonian attack. After his victory at Carchemish, Nebuchadnezzar overran Philistia.

Whether Egyptian or Babylonian, the overwhelming horde of armed men struck terror in the hearts of the Philistine people. Even parents abandoned their children in a desperate effort to escape. *Tyre and Sidon* were Phoenician coastal cities to the north of Philistia; apparently they had some sort of mutual defense arrangement. In poetic parallelism, Jeremiah associates *Philistines* with *Caphtor* (that is, Crete, a stop in their migration eastward to Canaan). *Ashkelon* was the next Philistine city on the coast north of Gaza. The *remnant on the plain* likely refers to the two inland Philistine cities, Ekron and Gath. Ultimately, the oracle testifies to the sovereignty of Yahweh. Though foreign armies destroy Philistia, they are but the outward manifestation of *the sword of the Lord*.

48:1–47 Moab occupied a part of the Transjordanian plateau between the deep, east-west valleys of the Arnon to the north and the Zered to the south. The boundaries of the Moabites, however, fluctuated over time. According to Genesis 19:37, the Moabites were descended from Lot.

This long poem has two main segments divided by *This is what the Lord ... says* (48:1, 40). It is rich in place names, not all of which are identifiable. Some of them occur on the famous Moabite Stone (about 840 BCE),

> **The Mesha Inscription**
> *The best evidence for Moabite history comes from an inscription of the ninth century Moabite king, Mesha (also mentioned in 2 Kgs 3). The so-called Moabite Stone, or Mesha Stele, reports his defeat of Israel, his building projects, and his trust in his patron god, Chemosh.*

discovered at Dibon in 1868. Although we find no date, the oracle clearly relates to the time of Jeremiah and to the conquests of Nebuchadnezzar.

Nebo here refers to a Moabite city rather than the mountain. The plotters in *Heshbon* are likely that city's conquerors as they prepare to continue their conquests. *Madmen* is the transliteration of a Hebrew place name. *Chemosh* is the chief deity of Moab. His image and those who believe in him will go into exile. They are powerless against the God of Israel, who orchestrates the destruction of Moab.

Like well-aged wine, Moab has survived undisturbed, but that will change by the will and word of the Lord (verses 11–17). *Bethel* is in poetic parallelism with Chemosh and refers to the name of a deity rather than a place (Hyatt 1113). The fall of Moab is at the word of *the King ... the Lord Almighty*. The broken scepter and staff are symbols of "the end of its power and glory" (Huey 391).

The description of the calamity to befall Moab continues in verses 18–25. The long list of place names emphasizes the totality of the conquest. The *horn* is a symbol of power (see Ps 18:2).

Moab is to drink the cup of God's wrath (verses 26–28; compare 25:15–16, 27–29) to the point of drunkenness, that is, utter devastation. With poetic justice, the nation that had ridiculed Israel will now face ridicule.

Many similarities exist between verses 29–39 and other biblical texts: verse 29 to Isaiah 16:6; 31–35 to Isaiah 16:7–10; 34 to Isaiah 15:4–6; 36 to Isaiah 15:7 and 16:11; and 37–38 to Isaiah 15:2–3 (Hyatt 1115–16).

This lament over Moab points not only to God's sovereignty over all nations but also to divine sorrow at the price they must pay for their sins.

The *eagle* likely is a figure of speech referring to Nebuchadnezzar and his army (verses 40-47). The destruction of Moab *as a nation* began with the Babylonian conquest. Then came the incursion of the Nabateans, an Arab tribe, into which the remnant of the Moabites assimilated by the time of Christ. Verses 43-44 echoes ideas similar to Amos 5:18-19.

Verses 45-47 are missing in the Septuagint. Yet the restoration of Moab *in days to come* is a word of hope, perhaps to encourage Israel (Huey 397). In light of the subsequent history of the Moabites, it may ultimately be messianic in intent (Harrison 178).

> **"In later days ..."**
> The Hebrew phrase "in later days" (Jer 48:47) usually refers to an unspecified future, not the eschatological turning point of New Testament texts. For Jeremiah, God is ultimately a restorer of nations, not their destroyer.

49:1-6 The Ammonites also derived from Lot (Gen 19:38). They occupied a region to the north of the Moabites in Transjordan. *Molech* (also known as Milcom) was the chief deity of the Ammonites. Gad, an Israelite tribe living east of the Jordan River, went into exile with the Assyrian conquest (721 BCE). *Rabbah* was the Ammonite citadel atop one of the seven hills in what is today Amman, Jordan. As with Moab, the Ammonites succumbed to Babylon. As a result, Arabs encroached on their territory and ultimately absorbed them into their tribes. Similar to the oracles against Egypt and Moab, this one ends with a word of hope.

49:7-22 The Edomites descended from Esau (Gen 36:1). Edom occupied the territory south of Moab from the Dead Sea to the Gulf of Aqabah. The territory extended eastward into the Arabian desert.

There is no word of hope in the oracle about Edom (verses 7-11). The rhetorical question about the departure of *wisdom* expects a "yes" response. Traditionally, Edom was a seat of oriental wisdom (Obad 8), and one of Job's wise visitors was Eliphaz from Teman (in Edom). Dedan was an oasis in the Arabian desert southeast of Edom. Because they are neighbors, Jeremiah warned them of the coming disaster. The imagery indicates total devastation, but the compassion of the Lord for the most vulnerable among the Edomites is instructive. Widows and orphans cannot trust in humans, but they can trust in the Lord.

A prose insertion in verses 12-13 recalls the metaphor of the cup of wrath in 25:15-29. The solemn oath of the Lord certifies the destruction of Edomite Bozrah.

Verses 14-16 have close parallels to Obadiah 1-4. The early Edomite center was a mesa-like stronghold alluded to in verse 16. The Asiatic lion inhabited the jungle-like growth along the River Jordan; only a few survive today in reserves in India. Verse 18 also occurs in 50:40, and verses 19-21 appear in 50:44-46, referring to Babylon. The clause *Who is the chosen one I will appoint for this*? is an effort to translate a problem passage in Masoretic Text. The NRSV renders it, *and I will appoint over it whomever I choose*. The text does not name anyone; however, it is God who will appoint the destroyer of Edom, most likely Nebuchadnezzar.

The disdain against Edom expressed in the Bible is to a large degree surely due to their failure to aid Judah during the Babylonian conquest. Rather, Edom took advantage of the opportunity to migrate into the depopulated area of southern Judah. Eventually, they occupied the region as far north as Hebron, and their descendants were the Idumeans. At the same time, the Nabatean Arabs moved into the former Edomite territory.

> **Idumeans**
> The Edomites who moved into former Israelite territory converted to Judaism beginning in the second century BCE. Herod the Great was the most famous Idumean.

49:23-27 Damascus was the power center of Aram (a kingdom in Syria), located north of Israel. Hamath and Arpad were small Aramean city states to the north of Damascus. An occasional ally of Israel and often an enemy, Aram fell first to the Assyrians, then to the Babylonians (2 Kgs 16:9). They formed a part of the Babylonian forces attacking Judah (2 Kgs 24:2). Verse 26 is also found in 50:30, and verse 27 is a quotation from Amos 1:4. *Ben-Hadad* was both a personal and a dynastic name. All that befalls Damascus is due to the sovereign will of *the Lord Almighty*.

49:28-33 Kedar and Hazor denote tribes and tribal areas in the Syrian desert east of Palestine (Harrison 182). Rather than *kingdoms*, these were desert chiefdoms. Babylonian records confirm Nebuchadnezzar's attack on Kedar in 599 BCE (Huey 405). Why attack Bedouins? "Perhaps the purpose for including these relatively insignificant peoples was to show that no one, however unimportant by our standards, would escape God's judgment" (Huey 405).

49:34-39 Elam was a significant kingdom east of Babylon in what is now southwestern Iran. The oracle dates to 597 BCE, *early in the reign of Zedekiah*. The Elamites were famed archers (Isa 22:6). The text mentions Elam among the nations that must drink the cup of the Lord's wrath (25:25) but gives no theological reason. Yet Yahweh is sovereign over all nations and peoples, even those far distant from Judah and Jerusalem. After they have tasted *disaster*, the Lord promises restoration *in days to come* (better with NRSV *in the latter days*).

50:1–51:55 The oracles against Babylon form an appendix. We can assume scribes assembled them during the exile. There is practically no internal evidence for dating these writings, except that they do not mention Persia, Babylon's conqueror in 539 BCE, so they must predate that event. We can date only 51:59-64 to year four of Zedekiah's reign. It is difficult to distinguish one oracle from another, but one theme unites them all: the downfall of Babylon and the restoration of the Jews to their homeland. For convenience, we will follow the divisions of the material employed by Timothy Willis.

In the oracle consisting of 50:1-32, Jeremiah predicts a reversal of Israel's catastrophe. In the Septuagint, verse 1 is shorter, reading "The word of Yahweh, which he spoke concerning Babylon" (Bright 339).

Bel ["lord"] is the Akkadian equivalent of the Northwest Semitic "Baal," with an identical meaning. Bel signifies the chief deity of Babylon, Marduk [Hebrew *Merodach*].

Just as Babylon, the nation from the north, had threatened Judah, so *a nation from the north* will attack Babylon. In fact, it will be *an alliance of great nations*. At that time, the people of Yahweh will turn their faces toward their homeland. Despite the fact that the Lord employed first Assyria then Babylon as instruments to chasten Israel, Babylon *has sinned against the Lord* and faces punishment (verses 11-17). Like a shepherd leading his flock, Israel shall *graze on Carmel and Bashan*, referring to the highland extending westward from Megiddo to modern Haifa and to today's Golan Heights south of Mount Hermon. By his grace the Lord *will forgive the remnant*.

God's anger against Babylon will occur because *she has defied the Lord* (verse 29) and because she is *the arrogant one* (verses 31-32). *I will kindle a fire in her towns* recalls similar actions by the Lord in the oracles against the nations in Amos 1-2.

Despite the oppression of the exile, *the Lord Almighty* will redeem the people of Israel. They will know *rest*; Babylon will experience *unrest* (verses 33-46). Once a thriving city, Babylon will be uninhabited. The ruins of Babylon have lain vacant for centuries. In spite of excavations and reconstruction for tourism in the last century, the city remains uninhabited.

The army from the north included those who *ride on their horses*, probably Scythian horsemen allied with the Medes and Persians and renowned for their horsemanship. Verses 44-46 are practically identical to 49:19-21 where they refer to Edom.

Though a shepherd to Israel, Yahweh will be as a hungry lion decimating the flock Babylon.

Turning to 51:1-32, the people of *Leb Kamai* are the Chaldeans. This is another instance of *athbash* – that is, as the NIV notes, "a cryptogram for Chaldea." The Hebrew *Leb Kamai* actually means "the heart of those who rise against me."

The *gold cup in the Lord's hand* occurs as a figure elsewhere (13:12f; 49:12). The *vengeance* of the Lord (verse 6) means vindication for Israel (verse 10). God takes vengeance *for his temple*. Those who return are to tell the good news *in Zion*. Cyrus the Great of Persia will conquer the *Medes*, whom the Lord has stirred up (550 BCE).

Jeremiah praises the power of Yahweh and contrasts it with the impotent idols created by *every goldsmith*. Jeremiah 51:15-19 repeat 10:12-16, where we examined the *Portion of Jacob*. The text does not identify the *war club* that shatters, but it probably symbolizes a reversal of Babylon's role. "The description [is] applied to Babylon (see 50:23) as well as to her conqueror, both instruments in God's hands" (Cawley and Millard 657). *Ararat, Minni and Ashkenaz* were peoples north of the Medes. Ararat (ancient Urartu) was north of Lake Van in modern east Turkey. Minni (ancient Mannai) was south of Lake Urmia. Ashkenaz were the Scythians, horse nomads to the east of Lake Urmia. Those who attack Babylonia will burn the marshes, preventing escapees from hiding in them. Because of what Babylon had done to Jerusalem and its people, those in exile from Zion pronounce a curse on Babylon (51:33-35).

Yahweh will fulfill the curse against Babylon (verses 36–57) by preparing a drunken *feast for them*. As they slumber in a stupor, they will never awaken. The *Sheshach athbash* occurred in 25:26. As the Lord destroys *Bel in Babylon*, he calls for his people to be prepared to flee for their lives. The Lord's vengeance is certain. It is a case of poetic justice. Just as Babylon slew *the slain in all the earth*, so Babylon must fall. God's people in exile must be mindful of the Lord and not forget Jerusalem. As they well know, *the Lord is a God of retribution*. Just as God had repaid them in full for their sins and follies, so will Babylon receive full punishment. God is not a respecter of persons.

Nebuchadnezzar built *Babylon's thick wall* and it was wide enough to drive chariots on it (verse 58). The *peoples whose work is in vain* are probably those carried into exile whom the Babylonians put to work in constructing the revamped city under Nebuchadnezzar.

Seraiah Son of Neriah
Seraiah son of Neriah (*verses 59–64*) *was very likely the brother of Baruch. Archaeologists have discovered a bulla of Seraiah. The scroll he carried to Babylon when Zedekiah was king must have included the material in chapters 50–51. In this symbolic action, after having read the prophecy against Babylon, he was to cast the weighted scroll into the Euphrates, demonstrating that the great city would sink into oblivion.*

The note at the end of verse 64 marks the end of the oracles of Jeremiah. It closes the book that begins in verse 1 with "The words of Jeremiah." This provides a verbal envelope called an *inclusio* – a fitting end to the great prophet's work (Huey 430).

HISTORICAL APPENDIX · 52:1–34

52:1–30 There is little variance between this appendix and 2 Kings 24:18–25:30. Scribes probably added it to Jeremiah's oracles to show their fulfillment in the fall of Jerusalem and the exile of most of its people. There are two major differences between the accounts. The events relating to Gedaliah are missing here but are in the account in 2 Kings. However, Jeremiah 40–41 gives the details concerning Gedaliah. The second difference is the list of three deportations in verses 28–30, absent in 2 Kings 25. This listing does not occur in the Septuagint. The third group, taken *in his twenty-third year*, probably experienced deportation after the murder of Gedaliah. The total taken into exile does not agree with 2 Kings 24–25, where the text records 10,000 taken in the first exile. Discrepancies could occur if the criteria for counting varied – for example counting only the men.

52:31–34 It is not likely that Jeremiah was alive when Jehoiachin was released from prison; he would have been about ninety years old by then. Also, the text makes no mention of Zedekiah, who must have died in prison prior to this event.

No doubt the final compiler(s) of the book of Jeremiah ended with the release of Jehoiachin from prison because it was a hopeful note for those in exile. He was of the Davidic line. With God nothing is impossible.

THEOLOGICAL REFLECTIONS

What can we discern about the nature of God and humans and their interrelationships from this book? Every author dwells and writes within a particular environment, as did Jeremiah. Deuteronomy fueled the reforms of Josiah and undergirded Jeremiah's understanding of himself and the developing history of his people.

As Willis observes, "Deuteronomy sets the stage for Israel's entrance into the Promised Land. Jeremiah sets the stage for Israel's expulsion from the Promised Land" (Willis 13).

Jeremiah lived through the demise of his city and country at the hands of foreigners.

In the midst of crisis, Jeremiah provides both teaching and example to the person called of God to live to the praise of his glory. While he sometimes struggled to understand and survive the Lord's tests, he remained faithful to the end. We can say the same of Yahweh. God fulfilled promises to Jeremiah at his call, including his abiding presence and strength. Jeremiah's opponents could not overcome him because of the Lord was with him and enabled him (1:19).

While at times Jeremiah seemed to suffer alone at the hands of those in political and religious power, he drew supporters, especially Baruch. The Lord sustained him. This was because he understood that Yahweh, the Lord God Almighty, is both creator and sustainer.

Against paganized people, false prophets, compromised priests and unprincipled politicians,

Jeremiah stood in his determination to fulfill faithfully his mission as a spokesperson for God. The religious and political institutions of Judah, temple and palace, had undermined the covenantal relationship with God established through Moses at Sinai. This brought the destruction and exile about which Jeremiah warned. God is holy and righteous and will punish the unrepentant. But the Lord is willing and will save a remnant. So there is a word of hope at the very time that seems hopeless.

God is gracious. Not only is there a promise of restoration, there is the promise of a new level of relationship between the faithful and the Lord. For Jeremiah, "the ... future was not focused on temple or king but on a new covenant by which God would establish a new individualized relationship with his people (31:31–34)" (Huey 34). Jeremiah spoke and wrote to his people and their times, but by God's grace, he has spoken to generation after generation, including our own.

FOR FURTHER STUDY

Walter Brueggemann, *To Pluck Up, To Tear Down: A Commentary on the Book of Jeremiah* (Grand Rapids: Eerdmans, 1988).

William L. Holladay, *Jeremiah I: A Commentary on the Book of the Prophet Jeremiah* (2 vols.; Minneapolis, Minn.: Fortress, 1986–1989).

Philip J. King, *Jeremiah: An Archaeogical Companion* (Louisville: Westminster/John Knox, 1993).

Jack R. Lundbom, *Jeremiah 1–20: A New Translation with Introduction and Commentary* (New York: Doubleday, 1999).

William McKane, *A Critical and Exegetical Commentary on Jeremiah* (2 vols.; Edinburgh: T & T Clark, 1986–1996).

T. W. Overholt, *The Threat of Falsehood: A Study in the Theology of the Book of Jeremiah* (Napierville, Ill.: Allenson, 1970).

Jorge Pixley, *Jeremiah* (St. Louis: Chalice, 2004).

J. A. Thompson, *The Book of Jeremiah* (Grand Rapids: Eerdmans, 1980).

François Vallat, "Elam," *Anchor Bible Dictionary* 2 (1992): 424–29.

WORKS CITED

William F. Albright, *Yahweh and the Gods of Canaan* (Winona Lake, Ind.: Eisenbrauns, 1968).

David W. Baker, "Uphaz," *Anchor Bible Dictionary* 6 (1992): 765.

John Bright, *Jeremiah* (Garden City, N.Y.: Doubleday, 1965).

F. Cawley, and A. R. Millard, "Jeremiah," *The Eerdmans Bible Commentary* (ed. D. Guthrie, J. A. Motyer, A. M. Stibbs and D. J. Wiseman; Grand Rapids, 1970), 5:626–58.

David Graf, "Dedan," *Anchor Bible Dictionary* 2 (1992): 121–23.

R. K. Harrison, *Jeremiah & Lamentations* (Downers Grove, Ill.: InterVarsity, 1973).

F. B. Huey Jr. *Jeremiah/Lamentations* (Nashville: Broadman, 1993).

H. B. Huffmon, "Ancient Near Eastern Prophecy," *Anchor Bible Dictionary* 5 (1992): 477–82.

James P. Hyatt, "The Book of Jeremiah," in vol. 5 of *The Interpreter's Bible* (ed. George A. Buttrick; Nashville: Abingdon, 1956), 775–1142.

Richard Jones and Zbigniew Fiema, "Tahpanhes," *Anchor Bible Dictionary* 6 (1992): 308–9.

Josephus, *Works* (ed. H. St. John Thackeray; 10 vols.; Cambridge: Harvard University Press, 1926–1965).

Philip J. King, *Jeremiah: An Archaeogical Companion* (Louisville: Westminster/John Knox, 1993).

Ernst Axel Knauf, "Tema," *Anchor Bible Dictionary* 6 (1992): 346–47.

Joanne Kuemmerlin-McLean, "Magic (OT)," *Anchor Bible Dictionary* 4 (1992): 468–71.

John W. Miller, *Meet the Prophets* (New York: Paulist Press, 1987).

T. W. Overholt, *The Threat of Falsehood: A Study in the Theology of the Book of Jeremiah* (Napierville, Ill.: Allenson, 1970).

J. B. Pritchard, ed., *Ancient Near Eastern Texts Relating to the Old Testament* (3d ed.; Princeton: Princeton University Press, 1969).

D. W. Thomas, ed., *Documents from Old Testament Times* (London: Nelson, 1958).

Timothy M. Willis, *Jeremiah-Lamentations* (Joplin, Mo.: College Press, 2002).

Lamentations

Mark W. Hamilton, Nathaniel D. Lollar, & David I. Shaw

CHAPTER CONTENTS

Contexts 617

Commentary 617
- The Deserted City · 1:1–22 617
- The Anger of God · 2:1–22 618
- One Who Has Seen Affliction · 3:1–66 619
- The Gold Without Luster · 4:1–22 619
- Does God Remember? ·5:1–22 620

Theological Reflections 620

For Further Study 620

Works Cited 620

MAPS, TABLES, & FEATURES

The Suffering Female in Lamentations & the Prophets 618

Lamentations consists of five discrete poems mourning the Babylonian destruction of Jerusalem in 586 BCE. The first four poems are acrostics, with each verse or cluster of verses beginning with a successive letter of the Hebrew alphabet. Even the last poem, though not an acrostic, contains 22 lines, the number of letters in the Hebrew alphabet. The use of acrostics allows singers not only to memorize the songs but also to make interconnections among the poems (Renkema 50). The poems gorgeously express Israel's dismay at their fate, their questioning of God, and their timid hope for restoration.

> **City Laments**
>
> A few texts survive from the ancient Near East that mourn the fall of a city. From about 2000 BCE comes the Sumerian "Lamentation over the Destruction of Sumer and Ur," whose 436 lines mourn the fall of the Ur III empire. Its opening and closing lines are reminiscent of Lamentations: "He has abandoned his stable … the lord of all lands has abandoned it…. Enlil has abandoned the shrine of Nippur," and "O Nanna in your city again restored, may your praise be sung!" The Israelites may not have known that already ancient song, but they were familiar with the literary conventions for lamenting the tragic fall of a city.

CONTEXTS

Multiple voices appear in each chapter. Probably inhabitants of Jerusalem, especially surviving priests, sang them in their communal worship settings during the Babylonian exile. Perhaps women composed these songs, since they were primarily responsible for mourning in ancient Israel. Someone later wrote down these orally performed texts in order to preserve them for a postexilic community. Lament of the present reminded the future of the precariousness of life and everyone's dependence on God.

Jewish tradition attributed Lamentations to Jeremiah, but no evidence for this exists in the book itself or elsewhere in the Bible. The laments of Jeremiah mentioned in 2 Chronicles 36:25 cannot refer to this book, since they concern Josiah's death twenty years earlier. Like many biblical books, this one is anonymous.

COMMENTARY

THE DESERTED CITY · 1:1–22

Like most Hebrew dirges, the poetry of chapter 1 uses the *qinah* meter, in which the first half of the line is roughly 50 percent longer than the second half, though with frequent exceptions. *Qinah* poetry has a musical association and is sung as a lament over the dead (see 2 Sam 1:17–27; 2 Chron 35:25; Garr 60). The speaker's point of view changes from third person ("he"; 1:1–11) to first person ("I"; 1:12–16) to third again (1:17), and back to first (1:18–22)

1:1–11 In verse 2, the word for *comfort* here (and in verse 16) has the connotation of a gift that shows respect or pays homage to the receiver, or it can show an alliance between kings (2 Kgs 20:12; Isa 39:1). The clause *no one shows me/her mercy* creates a refrain here and in 1:9, 17, 21. In verse 5, *children*

LAMENTATIONS

> **The Suffering Female in Lamentations & the Prophets**
>
> The Old Testament often uses female imagery for Israel or the cities in it.
>
> Two controlling metaphors lead to the elaborate set of female images that appear in these texts. First, place names in Hebrew are feminine, and second the idea of a "male" God having a wife was common in the ancient world. Since Yahweh was not really male and did not have a goddess as a wife, Israel became that spouse.
>
> Starting from the metaphoric equation Yahweh is to Israel as a husband is to a wife, the texts can spin out images of marriage and fertility (as in Isa 62:4, an answer to Lamentations), but also of rape, adultery, and so on. However problematic we may find this imagery, and however shocking the prophets and lamenters themselves meant it to be, it powerfully captures a sense of the estrangement between God and God's people.

really means "infant" or "toddler," evoking the even more poignant image of babies as captives of war. In verses 8–10, the poet uses the intensive form of the verb ("she sinned, O how she sinned!") twice to convey the magnitude of Jerusalem's sin (House 354). *Unclean* in verse 8 refers to a woman's menstrual discharge (Lev 12:2, 5; 15:19; House 354), as does *filthiness* on her skirts. This kind of exposure and public nudity in the Israelite mind was a source of insufferable shame. Verse 10's *treasures* refers at one level to the temple treasures, but it is also a euphemism for the private parts of the personified woman Jerusalem. Thus the looting of the temple is metaphorically a rape of Yahweh's wife, Jerusalem.

1:12–22 In verse 13, the fire burns inside the city, and the net spreads around and prevents the inhabitants from escaping. As a result the poet is weak and overcome, unable to escape (House 358). The *winepress* imagery moves in two directions: the red color of wine suggests the gush of warriors' blood, and the fragility of the grape compares to Judah's inability to stop its enemy from crushing it.

THE ANGER OF GOD · 2:1–22

The second chapter begins like the first, with *How*. This new dirge, like chapter 1, follows an acrostic pattern and *qinah* (3:2) meter. Chapter 2 divides into two sections, each with a different speaker. The chapter also links verses with catchwords: for example, verses 1 and 22 both speak of *the day*, and 2 and 21 mention God's lack of *pity*.

> **The Hebrew Alphabet**
>
> The stanzas beginning with the Hebrew letters ayin and pe (NIV verses 2:16, 17; 3:46–48, 49–51; 4:16, 17) are reversed (thus pe, ayin) in chapters 2, 3, and 4, indicating that when the poems were written the Hebrew alphabet may not have been rigidly set.

2:1–10 Verses 1–10 speak of Yahweh in the third person ("he") and the divine destruction of the physical structures in Israel and particularly Jerusalem. Focusing on the physical destruction of the nation, the poet uses the acrostic pattern to take a tour through the city and especially the temple precincts. We should imagine the poet walking in a line of captives past the structures he or she describes. The Lord burned every house (verse 2) with fire (verses 3–4). The royal palaces lie in ruins (verse 5), along with the city's fortifications (verse 5). Then the Lord destroys the temple, where key festivals (NIV *meetings*) occur (verse 6), and the poet sees the sanctuary and the altar (verse 7).

Princes in verse 2 is the masculine form of the word translated *queen* in 1:1 (see 2:9). In 2:4 and 5, *like an enemy* is one Hebrew word and occurs in both of these verses as the third word of the first line, giving the verses assonance and rhythm. Verses 9 and 10 give a beautiful transition from the destruction of the landscape to the devastation of the people. The destruction of Jerusalem's gates (verse 9) symbolizes God's refusal to interact with the people through the traditional mediators – the priesthood, prophecy, and kingship. Verse 10 has a very potent connection that links the 1–9 with 11–22. Verses 10a and 10c deal with the people – the honored and respected elders and the lowly but cherished young women. These groups represent both ends of the social spectrum, but they both sit in the ground, recalling verse 1's declaration that the Lord has cast Israel from heaven to earth (*ground* in verse 10 is the same word for *earth* in verse 1). Verse 10b fully captures the connection between the physical destruction and the destroyed people, when the people cover themselves with dirt (a different word that connotes dust or filth rather than the word translated *ground* in 10a and c). The chosen people are social rubble.

2:11–22 Verses 11–22 change to the point of view of a single lamenter speaking in the first-person. The poet is now one exile among many on the road outside the city. Verses 15–17 recount the horror that has befallen the population. The poet does not mention the city anymore in this poem, save an outburst to the city wall in verse 18; the deportees see the wall last and speak to it as their failed protector. In verse 12, *wounded* is literally "pierced," so that the corresponding *wound* in verse 13 is deep as the sea. In verses 15–16, clapping of hands here is a mocking, derisive act. *Clap* may mean slapping one's thigh (Jer 31:19; Ezek 21:17); striking hands out of anger (Num 24:10); slapping a person (Job 34:26); striking or splashing (Jer 48:26); or mocking (Job 27:23). The image accompanies similar mocking acts and may have elements of physical hostility associated with it, as well (House 389). *Scoff* in verses 15 and 16 is literally "hiss," another hostile and insulting act (compare 1 Kgs 9:8; Job 27:23; Isa 5:26; 7:18; Jer 19:8; 49:17; 50:13; Ezek 27:36; Zeph 2:15; Zech 10:8). *Hissing* and *clapping* hands occur together also in Job 27:23. In Zechariah 10:8, the Lord hisses to signal Israel to gather together again.

In 2:20, the poet puns *treated* [Hebrew *olalta*] and *children* [Hebrew *olaley*], and the latter word ties verse 20 back to verse 19. In 2:22, the Hebrew literally says, "You summon as a day of feasting," implying that the Lord's proclamation goes out as though it were an invitation to a celebration, but with a disappointing result.

ONE WHO HAS SEEN AFFLICTION · 3:1–66

Chapter 3 abandons the third person perspective, and a man speaks out as the personified city. The text falls into three sections (verses 1–25; verses 42–51; verses 52–58) with several expansions between them (verses 26–41; verses 59–63), and with a small conclusion at the end (verses 64–66). Unlike the rest of the book, chapter 3 contains hopeful verses as well as direct address toward God.

3:1–25 The poem maintains the traditional Jewish lament pattern except for the address to God at the beginning. However, 2:22 sets up the divine addressee as the antagonist through the first portion of chapter 3. The vivid imagery of God's actions against the warrior persona of Zion takes on the language of military engagement. Yahweh has *surrounded* and *built up walls* and *targeted [Zion] with His bow*, creating an image of siege tactics employed to take a city. Yet the speaker suddenly counters images of broken teeth (verse 16), humiliation (verse 14), and debasement (verse 15) with a declaration of hope. While laments in the Psalms usually express some kind of hope or praise for God (for example, Ps 22; 129; 140), this hopeful refrain in Lamentations 3 does not perform the customary role of ending of the song. Perhaps the narrator falls back into lament because the magnitude of his suffering is too great, or perhaps the text wants to contemplate further possible transgressions against God (verses 31–42; Dobbs-Allsop 120). Either way, the sudden hope seems short-lived.

3:26–41 The poetic content of this section is different than the rest of Lamentations. The author makes a theological move, remembering Yahweh's justice and willingness to equalize suffering and blessing (verse 31–36), shifts to rhetorical questions magnifying God (verse 37–39), and ends by blaming his suffering on himself (verse 40). While hopeful, this section does not reach the apex of emotion that verses 22–25 do; nor does its logical treatment of affliction soothe the afflicted heart of chapters 1 and 2. But whatever reasons the author has for taking up this tune, it is insufficient to alleviate his pains, and, again, he relapses into brooding.

3:42–66 The NIV treats this section as a quote originating from the exhortation in verse 41. The Hebrew text gives no such indication, but rather the narrator returns to the poetic style of chapters 1 and 2. This time, however, the narrator portrays God not as an enemy of Israel but as the liberator who looks upon the plight of the oppressed and acts mightily on behalf of the scorned, and, in typical lament fashion, the narrator issues a call for retribution.

THE GOLD WITHOUT LUSTER · 4:1–22

After three chapters of lament, the poet has grown exhausted or perhaps uses a disjointed poetic style to create a feeling of despair (Dobbs-Allsop 130). In any case, the narrator turns back to the style of chapters 1 and 2.

4:1–16 The *how* of 1:1 is repeated. The couplets primarily function to show different ways in which Zion is depraved and thus to lead the reader to understand the depths of Israel's suffering. The infant images are abundant (verses 2, 3, 4, 10) and are paralleled with other images of delicacy or purity (milk, snow) to contrast sharply with the mention of cannibalism in verse 10. These forms of purity in the early verses of chapter 4 also contrast with the uncleanness of the nation in verses 14–16.

4:17–20 A final voice appears in the book in verse 20, indicating the community. The first plural ("we") perspective begins here and continues for the rest of the book, except in 4:21–22. The community in its own voice, rather than the narrator's, now recounts the story of their oppression by the enemy and relives the horror of chapters 1 and 2. The reference to Yahweh's *anointed* at one level mourns the demise of the monarchy as a symbol of the nation, and phrases like *our very life breath* remind the audience of the king's crucial role as a protector. The community's wistful regret at no longer living *under his shadow* expresses a loss of hope in both human and divine kingship (compare Ps 89:20–26).

4:21–22 The poem ends with mixed words of hope and revenge. Lament psalms often emphasize poetic justice (Westermann 207). Some have thought the initial words of rejoicing to be sarcastic (Dobbs-Allsop 137). As in 3:22–26, the narrator expresses hope that all will be equalized. The narrator's future is set and the section makes clear the expectation of divine justice. The *cup* is presumably that of God's vengeance.

DOES GOD REMEMBER? · 5:1–22

This communal lament begins with a list of calamities (verses 1–18) and ends with a sad cry to God for mercy (verses 19–22). The people have settled into everyday hardship (Lee 192), with the siege of Jerusalem as a memory. The poem ends the book on a note of uncertainty and faint hope.

5:1–18 The list of disasters includes emotional, economic, and social elements. Verse 6 comments on public policies of the last years of Judah's independence, when its kings courted Assyria and Egypt. Verse 7 follows the basic claims of the prophets and of 1–2 Kings, which argued that the fall of the nation was a divine punishment. However, the poet turns this theological claim around by noting that the present sufferers did not commit the sins that led to the downfall. The text thus questions an easy equation between present suffering and past sin. Verse 8's *slaves rules over us* refers to the Babylonians' use of minor officials, some of them royal eunuchs, to control subject populations. The *crown* (verse 16) may be that of a king (as in 2 Sam 12:30; 1 Chron 20:2; Ezek 21:31; Song 3:11) or of partygoers (Isa 28:1, 3; Ezek 23:42). The crown can also signify honor (Job 19:9; 31:36; Prov 17:6), which Israel has lost.

5:19–22 The closing lament of the book appeals to God's pity and majesty. God's eternal splendor should lead to the healing of Israel, but the song ends not knowing whether it will.

THEOLOGICAL REFLECTIONS

As texts by and about refugees, the elegant poems of Lamentations challenge easy assumptions about divine benevolence or the correlation between sin and suffering. This text protests God's treatment of the people while still reverencing God. Living in the narrow space between blind faith in God and defiance, the poet seeks to honor human suffering without giving it the last word. Like Job, he or she seeks to vindicate both God and suffering humanity without opting for moralism or implacable anger. For that reason, Lamentations is a text for all times when people suffer.

FOR FURTHER STUDY

F. W. Dobbs-Allsopp, *Lamentations* (Louisville: Westminster John Knox, 2002).

Tod Linafelt, *Surviving Lamentations: Catastrophe, Lament, and Protest in the Afterlife of a Biblical Book* (Chicago: University of Chicago Press, 2000).

WORKS CITED

F. W. Dobbs-Allsopp, *Lamentations* (Louisville: Westminster John Knox, 2002).

Randall Garr, "The Qinah: A Study of Poetic Meter, Syntax and Style." *Zeitschrift für die Alttestamentliche Wissenschaft* 95 (1983): 54–75.

Paul R. House, *Lamentations* (Nashville: Nelson, 2004).

Jacob Klein, "Lamentation over the Destruction of Sumer and Ur," in *The Context of Scripture*, vol. 1: *Canonical Compositions from the Biblical World* (Leiden: Brill, 1997), 535–39.

Nancy C. Lee, *The Singers of Lamentations: Cities under Siege, from Ur to Jerusalem to Sarajevo…* (Leiden: Brill, 2002).

Johan Renkema, *Lamentations* (Leuven: Peeters, 1998).

Ezekiel

Brandon L. Fredenburg

CHAPTER CONTENTS

Contexts 622

Commentary 623

- Superscriptions & Ezekiel's Conscription · 1:1–3:15 623
- Ezekiel's Message, Phase I: Covenant Curses · 3:16–11:25 625
- More Covenant Curses for Jerusalem & Judah · 12:1–24:27 629
- Interlude: Judgment on Judah's Neighbors · 25:1–32:32 639
- Ezekiel's Message, Phase II: Covenant Blessings · 33:1–48:35 644

Theological Reflections 650

For Further Study 651

Works Cited 651

MAPS, TABLES, & FEATURES

- Blessings & Curses of the Mosaic Covenant 625
- Distinguishing True from False Prophecy 629
- Ezekiel & Ancient Near Eastern Mythology 633
- Nations of the Ancient Near East 640
- The Fulfillment of Ezekiel's Promises of Blessing 645
- Ezekiel's Visionary Temple 649

The images, visions, and actions of Ezekiel have always challenged audiences. Some influential Jewish teachers in the early Common Era nearly succeeded in keeping Ezekiel from being widely read, fearing it would be misunderstood. Jerome (about 340–420 CE) noted that some rabbis prohibited men under thirty from reading large sections of the work (see *b. Hag.* 13a) because of the complex and sometimes disturbing visions at the beginning and end. Contemporary interpreters, regardless of age, also find their task daunting.

Ezekiel's words and actions are intentionally hard to understand. Because his Israelite audience is exceptionally unreceptive (2:3–8), Ezekiel speaks and acts in often grotesque ways to arouse an interest in Yahweh's activity. Through Ezekiel, Yahweh tries to elicit a response – any response! – from a hard-hearted people.

Yahweh's activity through Ezekiel and other prophets is intimately bound to the covenant with Israel. Yahweh repeatedly pleads with, threatens, and disciplines Judah to get them to repent. Yet divine actions meet increasing resistance. Yahweh sends Ezekiel not to entice with words of hope and redemption, but to announce the end of God's patience and the time for national repentance. God will soon fulfill the most painful threats of the covenant: Israel will be exiled from its land and the temple will be demolished. These calamities would surprise Ezekiel's audience.

> **Warning & Hope**
>
> Many prophets preceded Ezekiel with words of both warning and hope. This pattern of warning and comfort reflected the structure of the Mosaic covenant, particularly its rehearsal of blessings for loyal behavior and curses for infidelity (see Lev 26; Deut 28; see comments at 4:9).

Another surprise is that Yahweh enlists hardhearted Ezekiel, whose name in Hebrew means "God hardens" (see 3:8–9). Ezekiel is at best reluctant and at worst, a liability in need of strong control (3:26–27). Yahweh's command that he *not rebel like that rebellious house* (2:8) and Ezekiel's admission of going into his task *in bitterness* and *anger* (3:14) signal his unruly nature. Only after Jerusalem falls does Yahweh allow Ezekiel his own voice (33:21–22). Then Ezekiel extends comfort and hope.

We know Ezekiel only from the book that bears his name. He obviously knew the oracles of Jeremiah and others (Zimmerli, *Ezekiel 1*, 42–46). Born into a priestly family (1:1), Ezekiel may have heard Jeremiah both denounce his birthright occupation as a priest and denigrate Israelite prophets (Jer 2:8; 5:31; 6:13; 8:10). Yet it is unknown whether Ezekiel ever acted as a priest. His reluctance to be a prophet may originate from familiarity with Jeremiah's career. Summoned to be a prophet of doom, Ezekiel could hardly have welcomed the same treatment from his kinsmen that Jeremiah received. This would have

EZEKIEL

been especially true since, unlike Jeremiah, Ezekiel was married (24:15–27). Some scholars speculate on Ezekiel's mental health, but the text provides no certain support for their theories.

CONTEXTS

Nineteenth and twentieth century critics used methods of literary analysis to separate many supposed later additions to the book from Ezekiel's "original" material. Zimmerli's more balanced work substantially slowed this trend, and more recent commentators, influenced by newer literary approaches, usually regard the content of the book as substantially from Ezekiel.

The process by which Ezekiel's words (perhaps written at various times, see 24:1–2; 37:16; compare Jer 36; Wilson, "Ezekiel," 656–57) and actions became written text is unknown. Some Jewish rabbis suggested "the men of the Great Synagogue" (in Ezra's day, about 450 BCE) collectively edited the book (b.Baba Bathra 15a), but this assertion cannot be proved. The essential composition may be dated to about the mid fifth century BCE (see Fredenburg 24–25), but significant variations of order and content in the book's oracles appear in copies and versions through the sixth century CE.

Ezekiel was born during a tumultuous period of Israelite history. Manasseh (697–642 BCE), Amon (642–640), and Josiah (640–609) had successively been client-kings of Assyria's Ashurbanipal (668–627). Their client status obligated them to promote the worship of Assyria's gods and pay tribute. Assurbanipal's death in 627 BCE sparked a power struggle among his sons that allowed Judah and other subject nations to reassert independence. Josiah did this through religious reforms designed to eradicate Judean idolatry. His initial efforts around 628 BCE coincided with Yahweh's call of Jeremiah; Josiah intensified his program in 622 BCE (2 Kgs 22–23). Ezekiel was probably born near this time.

> **Tribute**
> In the ancient Near East, a nation under threat of attack paid tribute with silver and/or gold objects and/or treasure taken from royal or temple stocks to the nations threatening to attack it (see 1 Kgs 20:1–7; 2 Kgs 18:13–16; 2 Chron 28:16–21).

The Babylonians also took advantage of Assyria's civil strife. In 614 BCE, Babylon allies, the Medes, conquered the Assyrian capital, Asshur; in 612 BCE, the new capital of Nineveh fell. Concerned about Babylon's growing power, the Egyptian pharaoh Necho II allied with Assyria and tried to aid them against Babylon at Harran in 609 BCE. However, Josiah engaged and delayed Necho's forces at Megiddo; Josiah died in that battle and his son, Jehoahaz, took his father's throne.

> **Ezekiel's Life & Times**
> 612 Nineveh falls to the Babylonians and Medes
> 609 The battle of Carchemish and the final fall of Assyria
> 605 Nebuchadrezzar subjects Judah to his rule
> 586 Jerusalem falls to the Babylonians, and the exile begins

Returning through Judah from defeat at Harran, Necho took Jehoahaz to Egypt, replaced him with his pro-Egyptian brother Jehoiakim, and demanded heavy tribute. By 605 BCE, Babylonia's Nebuchadrezzar had defeated the Assyrians and taken Palestine from Necho. Nebuchadrezzar made Jehoiakim his client and deported many leading Judeans to Babylon (see Dan 1:1–6). In 601 BCE, Jehoiakim allied with Egypt again. Nebuchadrezzar returned to Palestine to deal with Jehoiakim's rebellion in 598 BCE. Around this time, Jehoiakim died and his son Jehoiachin replaced him (Jer 22:18–23). Nebuchadrezzar besieged Jerusalem in December 598 BCE, and Jehoiachin surrendered on 16 March 597 BCE. Nebuchadrezzar again took leaders of Judah, including Ezekiel, into exile in Babylon (2 Kgs 24:14–16; Ezek 1:1–3). Nebuchadrezzar appointed Josiah's son Zedekiah as client-king over Judah. Over the next decade, Zedekiah was eventually influenced to ally with Egypt again. He did so around 588 BCE; Nebuchadrezzar responded by destroying Jerusalem in 586 BCE.

> **Nebuchadrezzar**
> This spelling of the king's name, rather than the more common Nebuchadnezzar, better reflects the Babylonian original, Nabukudurri-usur ("may the god Nabu guard the boundaries").

The exile raised serious theological problems for the Judeans, including Ezekiel. Those who remained in Judah believed they were the remnant of the true Israel (11:3) and that the deportees deserved their fate. In their view, Yahweh had rejected and removed the wicked from his land. The deportees understood matters even more darkly.

Fully embedded in the ancient Near Eastern view that earthly events reflect realities of the unseen realm, many exiles regarded the defeat of their nation and king as a reflection of the defeat of Yahweh by Marduk and the Babylonian pantheon. To them, their situation demonstrated the inability of Yahweh to protect his territory and people. Ezekiel and his companions, now in Babylon, lived far from the comfort of any promises made by their defeated Judean territorial god, Yahweh. Intra-Judean debates about who are Yahweh's chosen people, and interest in Yahweh's covenant blessings and curses, seemed fruitless to those who viewed Yahweh as an impotent god recently conquered.

Yahweh's invocation of the blessings and curses of the Mosaic covenant pervades Ezekiel (see Lev 26; Deut 28; see comments at 4:9). Yahweh was not defeated; the dispirited exiles had simply failed to recall the curses, chief among which was deportation and the subjugation of Jerusalem and its environs. Rather, citing the curses demonstrated the same covenant fidelity as the providing of blessings. Moreover, in Deuteronomy 30, Yahweh promises that he will once again receive the people in covenant – after the blessings and curses are fulfilled. This covenanted order – curses followed by renewed covenant blessings – forms the fundamental outline of the book.

> **The "Recognition Formula"**
> *Not only had Yahweh's people forgotten the covenant, they had forgotten him. The phrase, "then they will know that I am Yahweh," called a "recognition formula" by scholars, occurs in the book over sixty times and reminds Ezekiel's audience that the enactment of both the covenant blessings and the curses inextricably points to Yahweh's activity. Yahweh brings the same fidelity to enact the covenanted curses as to enact the blessings. Hardly impotent, Yahweh is powerful enough to act.*

Yahweh's actions are not limited by territorial boundaries, either. Yahweh's sovereignty over all nations appears throughout, most notably in the "oracles against the nations" (25:1–32:32). Judah's oppressive neighbors will come under Yahweh's judgment. Moreover, Yahweh's manipulation of Nebuchadrezzar's interests and armies demonstrates who the true "king of kings" is (compare 26:7). Ezekiel also shows Yahweh's control over ancient Near Eastern myths (see comments after 17:24). Ezekiel transforms several well-known polytheistic mythical symbols and narratives into oracles praising God.

Finally, the three named visions (1:4–3:15; 8:1–11:25; 40:1–48:35) show Yahweh's essential holiness. Israel and the nations around them misunderstand the unique nature of God. Even as Moses learned, "I am who I am" refuses to be pigeonholed into familiar ancient Near Eastern categories. Among the severest mistakes of Ezekiel and his companions was their settled theological notions about how their covenanted God would and could act. Their views of a domesticated Yahweh had to be shattered. Ezekiel and his audience come to experience a much more dynamic God.

> **Structure of Ezekiel**
> *The book is organized in a two-part structure reflecting the coming curses and subsequent blessings. The "oracles against the nations" separate these sections. Also, several chronological notices indicate the progress of Ezekiel's ministry.*

COMMENTARY

SUPERSCRIPTIONS & EZEKIEL'S CONSCRIPTION · 1:1–3:15

1:1–3 The first-person autobiographical superscription is elaborated by a third-person editorial superscription that identifies the event that launches Ezekiel's career; it does not provide career dates. The *thirtieth year* may refer to Ezekiel's age, but this is uncertain. David lowered the age for priestly duty from thirty to twenty (Num 4:3; 2 Chron 23:24, 27). Thus, this reference to thirty may indicate that in the year Ezekiel would have become a priest, Yahweh called him to be a prophet instead. Boadt (310) suggests the number refers to the years since Josiah's reform. Ezekiel views himself as one of *the exiles by the Kebar River*.

> **The Kebar River**
> *The Kebar was a man-made irrigation channel near Nippur in southern Iraq.*

Geographical location here is less significant than the fact that Ezekiel is near the center of Babylonian empire but far away from a demolished homeland and his presumably defeated patron god. Against all expectation, here *the heavens were opened and he saw visions of God*.

A later editor correlates the date with *the fifth year of the exile of King Jehoiachin*. The date is 31

July 593 BCE (for dates adopted here, see Block, *Ezekiel 1–24, 28–29*). Ezekiel's visions are *the word of* Yahweh; this frequent Old Testament phrase indicates that the content is authoritative, not necessarily the medium by which the message was delivered. To underscore that Yahweh encountered Ezekiel away from Judah, the editor writes that the visions come in *the land of the Babylonians* and that *there the hand of* Yahweh *was upon him*. The contrast between Ezekiel and his fellow exiles' view of their plight and Yahweh's view is stark. Forced to march to Babylon and see the immense temples and tile relief images of Babylonian gods, the exiles assumed their God's defeat. Yet, *there*, in the land protected by powerful Babylonian deities, the *hand of* Yahweh – symbolic of overwhelming compulsion and control upon those it grasps (Deut 4:34; Ps 136:12) – presses upon Ezekiel.

1:4–3:15 Two stylistic elements stand out in this first vision (1:4–28a). First, the Hebrew has a highly energetic quality and is difficult to translate in places. The display of power and the images are unexpected and confusing. Ezekiel tries to relate the indescribable. Second, he is reduced to simile and analogy, using *looked like*, *like*, *appearance of*, and *form of* throughout.

1:4–28A The vision begins when a wall of cloud with intense *flashing lightning* comes from *the north* (Ps 18:9–14; Nah 1:3b–6). Ezekiel may have believed this cloud harbored Babylonian gods rather than Yahweh. Whether Ezekiel literally saw a storm cloud or the entire episode was a vision is unclear. In the cloud, he sees *four living creatures*, each with *four faces and four wings*. Some scholars suggest the creatures' faces generically represent humanity, wild and domesticated animals, and birds. More likely, the faces reflect composite representations of Babylonian gods similar to the tile reliefs in Babylon. Moreover, Ezekiel's focus on their wings recalls the throne-bearing cherubim of Israelite theology (Exod 25:17–22; Isa 6:2). Ancient Near Eastern deities are often depicted on thrones borne by winged creatures (Allen, *Ezekiel 1–19*, 26–33). Ironically, the Babylonian gods are portrayed as Yahweh's throne-bearers. Ezekiel also describes a war chariot/wagon with unusual *intersecting wheels* with studded rims (*full of eyes all around*). The Hebrew says the wheels were tall and fear-inspiring. When the creatures moved the wagon, which may resemble wheeled wash stands found in Cyprus as well as chariots, the noise was deafening and awe-inspiring.

On a platform above the creatures rode a *figure like that of a man* surrounded in *brilliant light* (compare Exod 40:34). Ezekiel does not claim to see Yahweh; rather, he uses *like* ten times to express separation from what he sees and its reality. He describes *the appearance of the likeness of the glory of* Yahweh, whose *radiance* reminded him of *a rainbow in the clouds on a rainy day*. This recalls Yahweh's covenant promise to Noah (Gen 9:13) after the flood to be merciful in future cataclysmic judgments.

> **The Glory of the Lord**
> God's "glory" pervades creation (Ps 19:1; Isa 6:3) and dwells in the tabernacle (Exod 40:34–37), temple (Ps 76:4), Zion (Isa 60:1–2), the ark of the covenant (1 Sam 4:19–22; 1 Kgs 8:1–13; Ps 24:7–10), and God's heavenly dwelling (Jude 24–25). It defies precise definition. Psalm 145:5 speaks of the glorious splendor of God's majesty.

This vision forms the backdrop for the rest of Ezekiel's ministry. It rejects the view that Yahweh now serves the Babylonian gods. It challenges the notion that Yahweh is constrained by territorial boundaries: both the storm cloud and war wagon easily move over the terrain. And it hints that the theophany is about Yahweh's ability to keep covenant promises even when Israel leaves the world they once knew.

1:28B–2:2 Ezekiel prostrates himself (compare Esth 4:11) and awaits his summons. The figure commands, *Son of man, stand up on your feet and I will speak to you*. *Son of man* (2:1) highlights Yahweh's right to command his human subjects rather than Ezekiel's mortality (against NRSV's *mortal one*). Each use of *son of man* reminds Ezekiel of his obligation to obey immediately and completely. *The Spirit* who will direct his ministry helps him to his feet (Block, *Ezekiel 1–24*, 115).

2:3–8 Like Isaiah (Isa 6:8–13), Ezekiel is sent to a *rebellious* people. So severe is Israel's faithlessness, Yahweh calls them a *goy*, an Old Testament term often used of non-Yahwistic, non-Israelite people. To this *obstinate and stubborn* people, Ezekiel is to declare *what the Sovereign Lord says*. He is to declare Yahweh's faithfulness in fulfilling his covenant obligations to bring curses upon Israel. Ezekiel, too, must now choose to rebel or to obey. Thus, Yahweh presses, *You must speak my words to them ... listen to what I say* to you. Do not rebel.... Open your mouth and eat what I give you.

3:4–15 Once again, Yahweh reminds Ezekiel that his *hardened and obstinate audience will refuse to listen*. To help, Yahweh will make him *as unyielding and hardened as they are*, impervious to ridicule. Yahweh commands Ezekiel to *take to heart all the words I speak to you*, that is, to be convicted by his own ministry. This will not occur until Jerusalem falls. Yahweh commands Ezekiel to *go now to your countrymen in exile and speak to them* and removes him from the visionary throne room while "the glory of Yahweh rose from its place" (verse 12, a textual emendation). In a rare self-reference, Ezekiel admits his deep *bitterness* and *anger* at Yahweh's heavy-handedness. He is so outraged he daringly refuses to speak to his companion exiles *where they were living* at *Tel Abib* for seven days. The site must have been one of the ancient citymounds in southern Mesopotamia (Zimmerli, *Ezekiel 1*, 139), and has nothing to do with the modern city Tel Aviv.

Prophetic "Call Narratives"

Biblical *"call narratives"*—reports about the prophet's entrance into that role—often highlight the prophet's mouth (Exod 4:10–12; Isa 6:5–8; Jer 1:6–9). In Ezekiel's call narrative (2:9–3:3), Ezekiel must eat a scroll *with writing on both sides full of lament and mourning and woe*. Yahweh has much to say; there is no room for Ezekiel's comments. Yahweh commands him four times to eat, an indication of Ezekiel's reluctance. That the woeful words tasted as sweet as honey (*see Ps 19:7–11*) is ironic and may even be sarcastic.

EZEKIEL'S MESSAGE, PHASE I: COVENANT CURSES · 3:16–11:25

3:16–21 After seven days, Yahweh gives an ultimatum. Yahweh has *made* Ezekiel *a watchman for the house of Israel*. The task is irrevocable, and Ezekiel's

Blessings & Curses of the Mosaic Covenant

The primary task of Yahweh's prophets was to call the people back to a full, sincere observance of the Mosaic covenant. The messages of Amos, Hosea, Isaiah, and the rest are impossible to understand fully without grasping the core of the covenant restrictions and the incentives Yahweh provides for keeping them.

The heart of the Mosaic covenant is the unique, uncompromising confession of monotheism, "Yahweh is our God; Yahweh alone. You shall love Yahweh your God with all your heart, and with all your being, and with all your might. Observe these words I am commanding you today in your heart" (Deut 6:4–6).

One statement of the basic principles of the Mosaic covenant appears in Exodus 20:2–17, and Deuteronomy 5:6–21, the Ten Commandments. The first four commandments summarize Israel's obligations to Yahweh: recognize God's uniqueness, give uncompromising loyalty amid rampant polytheism, respect Yahweh's character by one's actions, and confess Yahweh as sole provider by observing Sabbath. The remaining six summarize the obligations of Israelites to one another: respect authority, life, family structures, property rights, and personal rights, and beware of temptations to undermine the community by failing to meet one's obligations (Kaufman).

Many scholars think that the Mosaic covenant follows the structure of ancient Near Eastern treaties between conquering kings (suzerains) and defeated kings (vassals). These treaties ended with incentives for each party to keep its obligations to the other, known as "blessings" and "curses." Such agreements called upon the gods of the conquered and conquering nations to enforce the treaty. The Mosaic list of blessings and curses appear predominantly in Leviticus 26 and Deuteronomy 28 and are enforced by Yahweh alone.

A list of blessings includes seasonal rain, crops, orchards, vineyards, herds, wives, and children that are productive, abundant food, secure personhood and property, domestic calm, no wild animal attacks, no foreign invaders, victory in battle, international prosperity, respect, acclaim, and Yahweh's presence in their midst.

Covenant curses reversed the blessings: pestilence, all kinds of diseases and maladies on people, crops, and livestock; drought, famine, military defeat, improper burial, persecution, assault, rape, destruction of property, theft, slavery, idolatry, taunts and mockings by foreigners, deportation from their land, international disdain, oppressive debt and poverty, besieged villages and cities, cannibalism, paranoia, terror, shame, and Yahweh's abandonment of his people to every physical, social, environmental, political, financial, and agricultural enemy.

The governing principle behind the blessings and curses is simple: Yahweh blesses covenant fidelity and punishes infidelity. When Israel disobeys, it faces increasingly harsh curses until it proffers fidelity once again. Reception of the blessings depends on Israel's repentance and fidelity. These fundamental promises and expectations provide the foundation for Ezekiel's message (see Stuart, xxi–xliii).

life depends on his response. Echoing Jeremiah 6:17, the text presses Yahweh's demand in four scenarios: Ezekiel's warning or not warning the *wicked* and the *righteous*. The cases survey Ezekiel's choices, not responses to his message. Yahweh will *hold* Ezekiel *accountable for* the *blood* of those he does not warn and will deliver him if he does warn them.

3:22–27   After rehearsing Ezekiel's options, Yahweh gives him room to obey. Yahweh requests a rendezvous, this time without calling him "son of man." Now, without coercion, Ezekiel *got up and went to the plain* and *fell facedown* before the *glory of the Lord*. He relents to Yahweh's demand. Yahweh responds in verses 24–27 by constraining him physically and vocally – symbolic gestures that communicated to an ancient Near Eastern audience Yahweh's complete control over his prophet's actions and words (Wilson, "Dumbness").

4:1–7:27   Ezekiel begins with pantomimes (4:1–5:4) and oracles (5:5–7:27) against Jerusalem, its surrounding mountains, and the land of Judah. These undermine the concept that Jerusalem is inviolable (compare Jer 7). The pantomimes describe what will occur; the oracles explain why and by whom.

4:1–3   Yahweh constrains Ezekiel's actions and words through fourteen months of prophetic sign acts. These actions probably occurred within a regular daily routine. In the first, Ezekiel is to *draw the city of Jerusalem* on a *clay tablet* and to *lay siege* against *it*. The Hebrew is highly repetitive: the models of *siege works*, a *ramp*, *camps*, and *battering rams* are to be "against" the diorama. An *iron pan* separates the "city" from Ezekiel, who plays the role of Yahweh. Ezekiel is to *turn* his *face toward it* (literally, "set your face against it" in hostility). Yahweh's hostility reflects Leviticus 26:14–20. This pantomime is a *sign to the house of Israel* that Yahweh will soon invoke the covenant curses. After building the diorama, Ezekiel lies near it on his *left* side 390 days, then on his *right* side 40 days, representing the years of Israel's and Judah's history of sin and punishment. These numbers in the Masoretic text and the Septuagint do not agree; thus, their precise referents are uncertain (compare Num 14:33–34; Boadt 312). While lying down, Ezekiel is to "set his face against" the siege scene *and with bared arm prophesy against* it. This depicts Yahweh as a warrior ready to do battle against Jerusalem as he had done against Egypt (see Deut 5:17).

4:9–17   Daily, Ezekiel interrupts his pantomime to eat. Depicting the severity of the siege (see Lev 26:26), he is to mix flour from ground *wheat and barley*, *beans and lentils*, *millet and spelt*. *Twenty shekels* (8 oz.) of bread and *a sixth of a hin* (11 oz.) of water are meager daily rations. Ezekiel is to cook a *barley cake* on the embers of *human excrement*. Ordinarily, one used animal dung as a fuel for cooking. This depicts both the scarcity of combustibles and the harsh, ritually unclean conditions of a siege. Ezekiel objects (compare Deut 23:12–14), and Yahweh permits him to use *cow manure* instead.

5:1–4   In carnival-like manner, Ezekiel is to *shave* his *head* and *beard* with a *sword* when his previous pantomime ends (compare Lev 21:5; 26:33). Ezekiel represents both Yahweh and the city; the *hair* is the Jerusalemites. His mangy, nicked appearance depicts a destroyed, humiliated Jerusalem. He is to weigh the hair, *divide* it into thirds, *burn* a third, *strike* out at a third, *scatter* a third, and *tuck* a few strands into his *garment*. Babylonian priests used hair to divine omens; Ezekiel's audience may (wrongly) have thought he was doing the same. Three of these four actions depict curse fulfillments (Lev 26:17, 24–25). In an unexpected mercy, Yahweh will save a small remnant (see 11:16–21).

5:5–17   In verse 5, Yahweh says the shaved hair is *Jerusalem* and indicts the disobedient city. As the *center of the nations*, Jerusalem was to lead the world by example (see Exod 19:5–6); instead, it grew worse than *the nations and countries around her*. Echoing Leviticus 26:17, Yahweh promises by his life to punish Jerusalem *in the sight of the nations*. Twenty six times, Yahweh uses "I" and "my" to ensure Jerusalem knows whence its punishment comes. Cannibalism will occur before deportation (see Deut 28:53–57; Lam 2:20), but Yahweh will have no pity. Yahweh's patience is ended because (in a foreshadowing of chapters 8–11) the people *defiled my sanctuary* with *vile images and detestable practices*. Israel had forgotten Yahweh by engaging in illicit religious practices. Jerusalem will indeed be *the center* (of attention) *of the nations* as *a ruin*, *a reproach*, *a taunt*, *a warning and an object of horror to the nations* (5, 15).

Prophetic "Sign Acts"

The prophets performed "symbolic acts," or "sign acts," before live audiences to arouse the curiosity of their hearers (Ezek 37:18) and to make their messages unforgettable in the memory of those who saw them (1 Sam 15:24–28; 28:16–17).

6:1–14 Yahweh's judgment expands to the *mountains of Israel* surrounding Jerusalem. As announced in Leviticus 26:30, Yahweh *will destroy* Israel's idolatrous *high places*, or open-air worship places, by enforcing the covenant curses. The *altars* will be desecrated with pulverized Israelite bones (Amos 2:1–3; 2 Kgs 23:16) and corpses. In the first of thirty-eight times, Ezekiel crassly uses a mocking pun in Hebrew to call the idols Yahweh will eradicate "little dung pellet gods" (verse 4; compare Jer 8:12). These idols are as worthless as excrement, both as objects of worship and protectors of their subjects. In a note of mercy (verses 8–10), Yahweh promises to *spare some* Judeans by deporting them. These deportees, Yahweh hopes, will recall their sins and realize their punishment comes as part of Yahweh's faithfulness to the covenant. The final section (verses 10–14) reverts to gestures of judgment and repeats descriptions of covenant curses seen already. In verse 14, one should read "Riblah" instead of *Diblah*. Riblah is north of Israel in Syria (2 Kgs 25:20–21), while Diblah is unattested (see Blenkinsopp 43–44).

7:1–27 The three sections of chapter 7 repeatedly refer to *the day* [of Yahweh] (verses 7, 10, 12, 19) as an approaching day of judgment. Each section ends with a variation of the recognition formula (verses 4, 9, 27). As Wilson remarks, "Over and over the prophet repeats his devastating message until his words pound the reader like a hammer" ("Ezekiel," 666).

7:1–9 Until Amos, the phrase *the day of the Lord* evoked notions of Yahweh's protection and comfort for Israelites. Amos turned that tradition on its head (Amos 5:18, 20), and Ezekiel follows suit: Yahweh will *unleash* his *anger against* Judah, *judge* the nation *according to* its *conduct*, *repay* it *for all* its *detestable practices*, and *not look on* it *with pity or spare* it from Babylonian exile. This calamity will come while people's abominable idols (*detestable practices*) are present. Their dung gods cannot save Judeans from their God. The terse Hebrew of verse 5 makes Ezekiel's announcement more shrill: *Thus says the Lord God, A disaster, a singular disaster – behold*! *It comes*! The coming day will bring *panic, not joy, upon the mountains*. Also, the Hebrew of verses 10–12a is somewhat confusing and chaotic. Ezekiel skillfully conveys the chaos of the day he describes through his language.

7:10–22 After a reference to Korah's rebellion (Num 16–17), Ezekiel announces the suddenness of the impending calamity. *Buyers* and *sellers* will have time neither to savor their gain nor to grieve their loss. The trumpeted call to arms will come too late. In another coarse reference, Ezekiel describes the cowardly Judahite soldiers: *every hand will go limp* ("a limp hand" describes impotence or weakness) and *every knee will* flow with water (better, "men will wet themselves"; NIV needlessly adds *weak as*). Attempts to bribe soldiers with *their silver and gold* will be unsuccessful: one cannot be bribed with what one is taking anyway. Most shocking of all, Yahweh will permit the temple to be looted and desecrated.

After the Judeans are deported, the Babylonians will *take possession of their houses*, just like ancient Israelites received Canaanite homes. In exile, Yahweh will render all four kinds of leaders, *prophet*, *priest*, *elder*, and *king*, unable to function.

8:1–11:25 Chapters 8–11 comprise a single vision in five sections framed by the guiding Spirit's entrance into (8:1–4) and departure from the temple (11:22–25). The first section (8:5–18) displays Israel's idolatry in the temple; the last four (9:1–11; 10:1–22; 11:1–15; 16–21) portray Yahweh's responses. Chief among these is Yahweh's progressive exit from the temple (9:3; 10:3; 11:23).

8:1–4 On 18 September 592 BCE, while still on his side, Ezekiel hosts *the elders of Judah* in his house. Their mission is unclear; perhaps they inquire about Ezekiel's pantomimes or seek comment on news from Judah (compare Jer 27–29). Unexpectedly, the *hand of the Sovereign Lord* falls on him, and Ezekiel lapses into a vision as he did in his first vision. *The Spirit* brings Ezekiel to the temple in Jerusalem.

8:5–18 Ezekiel sees four distinct foreign worship practices, probably reflecting the successive obligations to worship foreign gods that began during Manasseh's servitude to Assyria. Manasseh had erected an *idol of jealousy* (2 Kgs 21:7), likely an Asherah pole; Josiah had removed it (2 Kgs 23:6–7), since it violated Deuteronomy 5:8 (also Deut 12:3; see Smith 111–18). Ezekiel next encounters the *seventy elders of the house of Israel* (Num 11:16–25) secretively worshiping images of creeping animals, perhaps representations of Egyptian gods. That

> **Shackling of Prisoners**
> In 7:23–27, the call to prepare chains refers to the manner of deportation. Both Assyria and Babylon shackled deportees together. Assyrians also ran chains through rings that pierced the nose, cheek, or lower lip (see 19:4; 38:4; Isa 37:29; 2 Kgs 19:28; Amos 4:2).

Jaazaniah son of Shaphan is among them indicates the quick return to idolatry after Josiah's death (2 Kgs 22:3–14; Jer 26:24). Finally, Ezekiel sees priests *bowing down to the sun in the east*, thus turning their backsides to Yahweh. The phrase, *putting the branch to their nose* is enigmatic. Fisch (46) notes the Masoretic scribes intentionally changed its wording because it offensively referred to breaking wind in God's nose (see Boadt 314). Yahweh decides to pursue judgment upon the guilty without mercy.

> **The God Tammuz**
> In some forms of Babylonian mythology, Tammuz would die (and rise) yearly in tandem with seasonal changes. In contrast to the elders' clandestine worship, Ezekiel sees the women openly lamenting a dead Babylonian god.

9:1–11 Yahweh summons *six* armed *men* to carry out the judgment; they are accompanied by a scribe *clothed in linen*. They approach from the location of the idol of jealousy (8:3). When they assemble for duty, *the glory of the God of Israel* moves to the *threshold of the temple* (or perhaps the podium on which it stood). Before executing judgment, Yahweh commands the scribe to mark the innocent with the Hebrew letter *taw*. The six are to spare these while slaughtering the guilty among the *old men, young men and maidens, women and children* – a foreshadowing of the slaughter to come. The first to be killed are *the elders in front of the temple* (see 1 Pet 4:17) who had insulted Yahweh. Ezekiel, deeply distressed, pleads for Yahweh to preserve a *remnant*. Yahweh does not directly answer, but instead, justifies the slaughter because of Judah's *bloodshed*. After Yahweh promises to *bring down on their own heads what they have done*, the scribe returns to report that his job is done.

10:1–22 Yahweh orders the scribe to go *among the wheels beneath the cherubim* to receive burning coals. Evidently, this is a superhuman figure able to be in the holy of holies. Unlike their purifying use in Isaiah 6, these *coals* are to be scattered over the city to foreshadow its destruction (2 Kgs 25:9). In this vision, Ezekiel notes that the cherubim have shifted to the *south side* of the holy of holies in anticipation of leaving. The scribe *stood beside a wheel* and receives the coals from the midst of the cherubim. He leaves to complete his task. The cherubim and chariot resemble those in 1:15–28 (see Block, *Ezekiel 1–24*, 314–17). In the first vision, Ezekiel describes *living creatures* and demonstrates Yahweh's power over Babylonian deities in their own territory. Here, the thronebearers conform to Israelite artistic traditions as *cherubim*. The *glory* of Yahweh turns from the entrance to the holy of holies and sits *above the cherubim* for transport out of the temple. For the first time since his presence filled the temple in Solomon's day (1 Kgs 8:10–11), Yahweh leaves. On the way out, *the glory of the God of Israel* stops at the *east gate* of the temple for one final look. When the glory is gone, the temple and the city lack their divine protector. Verses 20–22 identify the *living creatures* of the first vision with the *cherubim* of this vision. Ezekiel twice notes he had seen them before *by the Kebar River*. By paralleling the two visions, he demonstrates that Yahweh may have abandoned the city and temple but not the people themselves. The temple and city are vitally important, but they are not essential for Yahweh's presence among the people. Yahweh is not distant but is among the people in their plight.

> **Cherubim**
> In the Old Testament, the cherubim protect sacred space (Gen 3:24; Exod 25:17–22). They are fearsome creatures with both human and animal features. They stand ready to protect Yahweh's holiness by escorting God away.

11:1–15 Chapter 11 reinforces the point that Yahweh's people reside in Babylon, not Jerusalem. Before its destruction in 586 BCE, Jerusalem's leaders and people regarded the exiles as castaways and themselves as Yahweh's favored subjects (verses 1–6). Ezekiel's reactions to the vision (9:8; 11:13) show he believed the same. The *leaders* are Zedekiah's anti-Babylonian, pro-Egyptian advisors. Their call to *build houses* may be variously translated (see NIV alternate translation). It looks forward to prosperous days under Egyptian rule. *Meat* was not a staple of ancient Near Eastern diets; the city leaders' metaphor is an arrogant claim to Yahweh's special favor. Their arrogance devalues the lives of others to the point that they commit murder. The wicked leaders' judgment will come through what they most fear: they *will fall by the sword … at the borders of Israel*. This is later realized when the Babylonian general Nabuzaradan takes the officials to Riblah and executes them (2 Kgs 25:10–21; Jer 52:10). In verses 13–15, *Pelatiah's* death is ironic since his name means "Yahweh delivers (a remnant)." Ezekiel is aghast; he considers the Jerusalemites, not the exiles, as the remnant. Yahweh disabuses him of this view in verse 15. He calls Ezekiel's exilic companions *the whole house of Israel*: the faithless exiles are the remnant.

11:16–21 Verse 16 shows that the Jerusalemites have arrogantly rejected the exiles as their kin and people. Ezekiel's sympathies for those who have rejected him and his companions are misplaced. This oracle of hope is a rejoinder to the Jerusalemites. Yahweh shockingly claims to be a *sanctuary* for the exiles *in the countries where they have gone*. In contrast to the Jerusalemites' claims to the land, Yahweh promises it only to the remnant-in-exile. In terms explained more fully in chapters 34–48, the exiles will return to a renewed land with *undivided hearts* and *new spirits* ready for obedience. The promise concludes with the covenant formula, *They will be my people, and I will be their God*.

11:22–25 After the *glory of* Yahweh departs from the east gate to *the mountain east* of the city (that is, the Mount of Olives), the spirit returns Ezekiel to his fellow exiles. This time, Ezekiel tells *the exiles everything* Yahweh *had shown* him.

MORE COVENANT CURSES FOR JERUSALEM & JUDAH · 12:1–24:27

Chapters 12–24 comprise one third of the book and offer extended reasons for Yahweh's judgments just announced. These oracles show why the exiles should abandon their view that Yahweh's blessings must be tied to the land and the temple. Editors arranged the oracles into six sections: 12:1–20 and 24:1–27 are sign acts about the destruction of Jerusalem that form an inclusio; 12:21–14:11 are about prophets and prophecy; 14:12–16:63 explain why Jerusalem will fall; 17:1–22:31 relate causes for Jerusalem's fall; and chapter 23 contains oracles about *Oholah* and *Oholibah*.

12:1–16 The phrase *eyes...hear* is common in the Bible (see also Isa 6:9–10; Jer 5:21, 23; Mark 4:9, 23). Ironically, the following pantomimes provide much to see and hear: *while they watch* appears six times in verses 3–7. Ezekiel appears to prepare for an imminent end to the exile (see Jer 27–28). *During the day*, he is to set his bags out. At twilight, he is to go into exile (the exiles do not know where he is going) after he digs through his own house wall. As he goes off into the evening, he is to *cover* his face. This sign act is an object lesson for his companions.

In a double entendre, *oracle* [Hebrew *massa'*] may be translated "burden," or "load": "The prince is the *burden* in Jerusalem and the whole house of Israel who are there." Thus, as a *sign*, Ezekiel portrays Yahweh hauling Zedekiah and his associates out of Jerusalem and *into exile as captives*. Ezekiel also plays Zedekiah (2 Kgs 24:20c–25:7). The phrases *spread my net* and *caught in my snare* are common prophetic metaphors for destruction (Hos 7:12; Isa 8:14–15; 24:17–18; Jer 48:43–44), similar to formulas in ancient Near Eastern treaty curses (Block, *Ezekiel 1–24*, 376–77 notes 66–68). This oracle ends with the recognition formula tied to enforcing the covenant curses (see Lev 26:33a).

12:17–20 This eating enactment, also about *those in Jerusalem and in the land of Israel*, is more

---

Distinguishing True from False Prophecy

The phenomenon of prophecy was widespread in the ancient Near East, finding its place in Israel and in other nations (see Nissinen, Seow, and Ritner). Because prophetic activity was widespread, it was difficult for ancient Israelites to discern true from false prophecy.

Little wonder, then, that Ezekiel's audience despairs of genuine prophetic messages. The only certain course was to reject prophets who openly encouraged the pursuit of other gods (Deut 13:1–5), but false prophets usually had more sense than to mount a direct frontal assault. Even genuine prophets could not always discern a false prophet, as the sad episode of 1 Kings 13 relates: a false prophet speaking a true message hoodwinks a true, but disobedient, man of God.

Despite these formidable obstacles, most true prophets shared three characteristics. First, they show an overwhelming compulsion to speak or enact their messages under extreme difficulty or at great personal cost (compare 1 Kgs 18:40; 19:1–2; 22:8, 27; Isa 20:2–4; Jer 12:6; 16:1–2; 38:1–28; Ezek 24:15–27; Hos 1:2). Second, they address the sins of the people rather than downplay them (Jer 23:22; Zech 1:4), whereas false prophets wink at sin (Lam 2:14). Finally, true prophets apply the covenant blessings and curses in proper order. The covenant is arranged in a blessings-curses-blessings restored sequence. The false prophets grasped this superficially, too quickly announcing coming blessing. False prophets were often guilty, not because of the hope they offered, but because of the time when they offered it. A true message spoken too soon offers false hope.

animated than 4:9–17. It applies the covenant curse of extreme anxiety in Deuteronomy 28:65–67 to those in Judah. In Deuteronomy, the curse applies to worshipers of foreign gods on foreign land. Ezekiel's allusion implies that those in Jerusalem are foreigners. This view is supported when verse 19 calls the exiles *people of the land*, a phrase reserved for inhabitants of Judah. The preceding oracles thus dash the hopes of the exiles for a quick return and demolish their rosy view of those left in the land. Such views had been fueled by false prophets – a subject to which Ezekiel turns next.

12:21–28 Before addressing false prophecy, Ezekiel challenges his audience's cynicism and apathy about prophets and prophecy as seen in their terse, four-word proverb: *Days amass, visions vanish!* Which prophecies are being referenced is unknown – perhaps Ezekiel's, Jeremiah's, Hananiah's, Shemaiah's or others' (see Jer 27–28). Yahweh, weary of being charged with the inability to fulfill his words, will *put an end to this proverb* by bringing the calamities soon, *in your days*.

13:1–16 Yahweh charges false prophets of Ezekiel's day with seven offenses: they *follow their own spirit* and are not inspired by Yahweh; they have no recourse to Yahweh's heavenly council, and so they *have seen nothing* (see 1 Kgs 22:19–22; Isa 6:1–13; Jer 23:16–22); they are mercenary, *like jackals among ruins*, scavenging for believers among Israelites; they are careless – they do not *repair* the *breaks in the wall* (a metaphor for protecting against spiritual intrusions); their genuine *visions* give *false* comfort; their real *divinations* tell a *lie*; their worst offense is to claim Yahweh's approval of their deceit with "Yahweh *declares*" after their words. Therefore, Yahweh is *against them* (see Lev 26:17) and will completely exclude them from his people. They *will not belong to the council of my people*; they will be removed from the *records of the house of Israel*, losing all inheritance rights; and they will not *enter the land of Israel* upon return. The false prophets' messages are like an incompetent plaster job on an adobe house (verses 10–16).

> **The "Book of Life"**
> *Several biblical texts refer to the ancient Near Eastern practice of "recording" or "enrolling" names in a scroll or book to denote people who are included in or excluded from a certain group or activity (for example, Exod 32:3; Isa 4:3; Ps 69:28; Mal 3:16; Phil 4:3; Rev 21:27).*

Ezekiel puns on the word *plaster* (not NIV's *whitewash*). Instead of "plaster," Ezekiel uses "malicious folly" [Hebrew root *tpl*]. The bad plaster job – that is, the malicious folly – of the false prophets will become evident when the Babylonians storm Jerusalem.

13:17–23 There are female false prophets, too. They use *magic charms* and *veils* to *ensnare people like birds*. The exact practices are impossible to determine with current evidence. The point is clear enough: Yahweh is deeply angered by female diviners (*witches*) who beguile the people with their magic instead of calling them to *turn from their evil ways*. Yahweh will *save* the *people* from them.

14:1–11 *Some elders* consult Ezekiel as a prophet while harboring *idols in their hearts*. Their idolatry is mental and probably includes their misguided favor of Judah and Jerusalem. To whatever inquiry they make, Yahweh *will answer...in keeping with* the inquirer's *great idolatry*, that is, tell the fool what he wants to hear (Prov 26:5). Yahweh wants to *recapture the hearts* (literally, "seize by the hearts") of the people and so calls them to *repent* of their duplicity. Inquirers of Yahweh's prophets are not to be double-minded. Additionally, the prophets ought not be quick with answers; they must wait on Yahweh. The problem of divine *entice*ment is difficult, but Block (*Ezekiel 1–24*, 437) catches the sense of verses 9–10: "So-called prophets of the Lord who acquiesce before the flattery...of hypocritical inquirers become accomplices in their crimes and may expect the same punishment." Once duplicity and vanity are removed from Israel, *Israel will no longer stray* from Yahweh, and the covenant formula will be fulfilled.

14:12–23 Echoing the four punishments listed in the covenant curses of Leviticus 26:21–26 – *famine*, *wild beasts*, *sword*, and *plague* – and reinforcing the point with the oath *as surely as I live* (verses 16, 18, 20), Yahweh declares his policy of individual merit in bringing about deliverance. In a rejection of the earlier episode with Sodom (Gen 18:16–33), Yahweh insists that even the renowned righteousness of *Noah, Daniel, and Job* would only benefit themselves and not their children in the current situation. Noah and Job are well known, but scholars dispute the identity of *Daniel*. He is most likely not the biblical Daniel, but rather an ancient, non-Israelite (like Noah and Job) character, known also to Canaanites in the second millennium BCE, legendary for his righteousness, justice, and care of widows and orphans. Whoever *Daniel* is, the point remains: the righteousness of the fathers does not overcome the treachery of the children. Despite the totality of the hypothetical calamities, when Jerusalem is punished, some children of the exiles will unexpectedly survive, but not because of their righteousness. Instead, they will serve to vindicate Yahweh's decision: Jerusalem must be destroyed.

15:1–8 A similar viticulture metaphor appears in Psalm 80 (compare Hos 10:1; Jer 2:21). This *wood of the vine* alludes to Israel as Yahweh's vineyard (Deut 32:32; Isa 5:1–7). Grapevine wood, otherwise unusable, is useful for fuel. The metaphor turns to an analogy about *the people of Jerusalem*. Yahweh has set his face against them (Lev 26:17) and is pruning the vine and burning the branches. *Come out of the fire* refers to Nebuchadrezzar's siege of 598–597 BCE. *The fire will yet consume them* in the destruction of 586 BCE. Once again, an enforcement of a covenant curse supports the repeated recognition formula.

16:1–63 Ezekiel uses gutter language to reach his insensitive audience. So far, he has referred to idols as "little dung gods" (6:1–7), crassly described soldiers as impotent, incontinent old men (7:17), and mentioned priests "breaking wind in God's face" (8:17). Ezekiel uses no euphemism here (but English translators still do); instead, he bluntly describes Jerusalem as a whoring nymphomaniac [Hebrew *zonah*] and freely employs sexual, sometimes pornographic, images throughout. The shocking language seeks to rehabilitate Judah by alerting the people to their true state.

This oracle rounds out a series defending the justice of Yahweh's destruction of Jerusalem (14:12–16:63), and it serves as an opening frame for a series exploring its causes (17:1–22:31). The concluding frame oracle is the similarly sexually graphic chapter 23.

16:1–14 Born to *Canaanites* – an *Amorite father* and *Hittite mother*, Jerusalem begins with idolatry in her blood (Deut 7:1–5). Girls in the ancient world were often *thrown* naked *out into the open field* at birth to die. Yet Yahweh finds and adopts Israel, an unusual and negative take on Israel's election. Verse 7 parallels her infancy with puberty: she *grew up*, her *breasts were formed*; she *developed* pubic *hair*; she was completely nude (see Block, *Ezekiel 1–24*, 478), *naked and bare*. When she is *old enough* for sexual intercourse, Yahweh marries her with his *solemn oath* and *covenant* pledge (see Ruth 3:9). This practice would not have been unusual or shocking to Ezekiel's contemporaries, whatever our sensibilities. This symbolic marriage occurred when David took the city and Solomon built the temple there (2 Sam 5:6–12; 6:12–19; 7:1–17). The remaining description shows Yahweh's extravagant tenderness in providing sexual relations, clothing, and food. Jerusalem owed its life, *fame*, and *beauty* to Yahweh's affection.

16:15–22 As a betrayed husband, Yahweh indicts Jerusalem for using his gifts to buy sex with others. She used her *beauty* and *fame* to become promiscuous and *lavished* her *favors on anyone who passed by*. From her *garments*, she *made gaudy high places*; from her *gold and silver*, she made *male idols* (possibly cast metal phalluses; NJPS: *phallic images*; see Isa 57:8; Exod 32:2–4) that she adorned with clothes and provided with food. Worst of all, she sacrificed *my children to the idols* because she ungratefully forgot *the days of* her *youth* when she was rescued from death.

> **Ungrateful Nations**
> *The book of Ezekiel tells stories of three ungrateful cities or nations who abused the "beauty" Yahweh had given them for selfish goals, so that Yahweh destroyed each one: Jerusalem, the beautiful bride (Ezek 16); Tyre, the beautiful ship (Ezek 27); and Egypt, the beautiful cedar (Ezek 31).*

16:23–34 Verses 23–34 focus on Jerusalem's sexual partners, a metaphor for political alliances (Hos 8:9; Jer 22:20). *Woe! Woe to you* shows Yahweh's anger and condemnation. At *shrines* to foreign gods, Jerusalem *offered* her *body* (literally, "threw the legs open") to any passer-by. This lecherous behavior shows Israel's desire to achieve security through alliances with other countries rather than through fidelity to Yahweh. Alliances with *Egypt* began with Solomon's horse trading (1 Kgs 10:28–29); compare the crude, *your neighbors with the huge penises* (NIV translates it, more politely, *your lustful neighbors*; compare 23:20). Even the notoriously uncivilized *Philistines* find Jerusalem's deeds offensive. Unfulfilled by the Egyptians, she turns to the *Assyrians* (under Ahaz; 2 Kgs 16:7–18); still not sated, she engages the *Babylonians* (beginning with Hezekiah; 2 Kgs 18:5–8;

> **Child Sacrifice**
> *The Israelites borrowed the practice of child sacrifice from their pagan neighbors, especially in very stressful circumstances, as a desperate means of persuading Yahweh to help them (2 Kgs 16:3; 21:6; Jer 7:30–31; Mic 6:6–7).*

Isa 39:1–8). In verse 30, Yahweh declares his fury (literally, "How incensed I am at you." NIV's *How weak-willed you are* is inaccurate; see Allen, *Ezekiel 1–19*, 229 note 30a). Jerusalem both refuses her husband and *scorned payment* for sex. Worse than other whores, she *gives payment* (that is, tribute).

16:35–43 Before sentencing, Yahweh summarizes the indictment. She *poured out* her *lust* (NIV alternate translation). Ezekiel's pornographic phrase clinically means "your genitals became lubricated." Then she *exposed* her genitals and engaged in brazen sex. Yahweh also recalls the "dung pellets of your abominations" and the murder of children.

41–43 Metaphor merges with the reality of 586 BCE in this description of Jerusalem's destruction. Yahweh strikes an alliance of sorts with Jerusalem's *lovers* to punish her; here, it is Babylon. When Jerusalem's death sentence is completed, Yahweh's *jealous anger will turn away*.

16:44–52 Even in *death*, Jerusalem will suffer the shame of a bad reputation (see 2 Sam 18:18; Ps 83:4) and be the butt of an unflattering *proverb* – just like her bigger (not *older*) *sister Samaria* and smaller (not *younger*) *sister Sodom*. By comparison, Jerusalem *became more depraved* than Sodom. Yahweh rehearses Sodom's sins: Sodom was *arrogant*, *overfed and unconcerned* about *the poor and needy*, and *did detestable things*. Note that Sodom's sins here are not primarily (if at all) sexual. Whatever sins *Samaria* committed, she *did not commit half the sins* Jerusalem *did*. Indeed, both sisters *seem righteous* by comparison. Samaria and Sodom had been utterly destroyed for crimes less egregious than Jerusalem's; therefore, Jerusalem's punishment is just.

53–58 Yet destruction is not Jerusalem's end, because the covenant promises blessings after curses. Yahweh promises to *restore the fortunes of Sodom* and of *Samaria* when he restores Jerusalem. Justice requires that, if he restores Jerusalem to her former glory (verses 8–14), Yahweh must also restore those whose crimes were less.

16:59–63 In another unexpected oracle of hope, Yahweh promises to *establish an everlasting covenant* with Jerusalem (compare Jer 32:40). Yahweh's graciousness will arouse shame for *all they have done*, and they will be unable to *open* their *mouth* in complaint at their harsh punishment.

17:1–24 Told to *riddle a riddle and allegorize an allegory*, Ezekiel presents a historical fable about two eagles and two plants. *A great eagle* comes to *Lebanon* and snaps off *a cedar shoot*. It transplants the sprig to *a city of traders*. The eagle also plants an indigenous grapevine seedling, tends it, and it grows well, spreading *toward* the great eagle. When another *eagle* comes, the grapevine alters course and grows toward it. The fable refers to the shifting reliance of Judah upon Babylon and Egypt. In a series of questions (verses 9–10), Ezekiel asks his audience to judge the fate of the vine. Similar to Amos's rhetorical strategy (Amos 1:2–2:16), Ezekiel has his hearers deliver their verdict before they realize it is a self-judgment. They are obtuse (see 12:2–3).

The riddle allegorically rehearses Israel's recent changing allegiances and condemns Zedekiah for disloyalty to Nebuchadrezzar (verses 11–24). The great eagle is Nebuchadrezzar, *the king of Babylon*. *Lebanon* is Jerusalem. The cedar shoot *carried off* is Jehoiachin and his advisors. Zedekiah is the *member of the royal family* with whom Nebuchadrezzar *made a treaty*. Zedekiah *rebelled* in 588 BCE *by sending his envoys to Egypt*'s Pharaoh Hophra. In a surprising turn, Yahweh holds Zedekiah accountable to his vassal obligations to Nebuchadrezzar. No doubt their treaty contained typical blessings and curses, as well as the invocation of the two parties' gods (including Yahweh) as covenant enforcers. Thus, Yahweh can call Zedekiah's oath *my oath that he despised and my covenant that he broke*. The phrase *as surely as I live* reflects Yahweh's intention to fulfill his own obligation: Zedekiah *shall die in Babylon*. Yahweh's fidelity again calls forth the recognition formula.

With Jehoiachin in Babylon and Zedekiah's death imminent, it appears Yahweh's "forever" oath to David (2 Sam 7:1–17) is ended. Recycling images from the preceding fable, Yahweh promises that, even though the covenant is suspended, it will continue. Unlike the humble vine Nebuchadrezzar planted, Yahweh's plant will *become a splendid cedar*. Yahweh

---

A Husband's Wrath

As depicted in Ezekiel 16:37–40, ancient Near Eastern custom allowed a betrayed husband to publicly strip (a reversal of verses 10–13) and humiliate his wife. The community participated, sometimes throwing feces on the woman to demonstrate communal outrage (Isa 47:3; Nah 3:5–6). Ancient people believed such jealous anger *to be appropriate to the marriage relationship*.

underlines his fidelity to reestablish a Davidic king with *I Yahweh have spoken, and I will do it*.

18:1–32 In 14:12–20, Yahweh rejected a prior policy of delivering a sinner through the righteousness of another. In verses 1–4, he rejects the exiles' view of punishment for them because of the sins of their ancestors, voiced in their proverb, *The fathers eat sour grapes, and the children's teeth are set on edge* (but see Exod 20:5; 2 Kgs 24:3–4). Yahweh rejects such fatalism because it dismisses the value of each person (verse 4) The text then cites as its warrant Deuteronomy 24:16: *The* person *who sins is the one who will die*.

To persuade his audience, Ezekiel reviews the cases of three successive generations (verses 5–9). The first, *a righteous man*, evinces qualities generally described in Deuteronomy 24:6–22 and Exodus 22:21–27. He abstains from idolatrous practices, observes sexual purity, and engages others with concern, care, and integrity. "Life" here means being delivered from a premature death in exile and a general enjoyment of tangible, material blessings. No afterlife is in view.

Then appears *a violent*, murderous *son* (verses 10–13). Whatever his father did not do, he does. In addition, he does *detestable things* – a general charge for good measure. Ezekiel asks and immediately answers a rhetorical question about his fate: *Will such a man live? He will not!*

In the third generation (verses 14–18), the grandson is entirely unlike his father and like his grandfather, except that *he does not ... require a pledge* (compare verse 7). Ezekiel does not ask "Shall he die?" because this is the point at issue with his audience: *He will not die for his father's sin; he will surely live*.

Ezekiel & Ancient Near Eastern Mythology

Biblical scholars do not agree on a single definition of the term "myth" when applied to biblical literature. They do, however, agree that Ezekiel and his audience not only knew their neighbors' myths, but that many Israelites subscribed to them. This is the essence of Israelite idolatry. It is hardly surprising that Ezekiel would adapt familiar elements of polytheistic mythology to communicate his points effectively to his audience. Myths are not "false," but are stories about the deep structure of reality.

Ezekiel adapts at least five major mythological elements in his oracles. First, the throne-chariot vision in chapters 1 and 10 contains elements similar to Canaanite depictions of the storm gods Baal and El riding their chariots in pursuit of enemies. This image is widely used in the Old Testament, but biblical writers adapt it to describe Yahweh instead of Baal or El (for example, Deut 33:26; Pss 18:9; 68:4, 33; 104:3; Isa 18:1; Nah 1:3).

Second, Ezekiel also refers to the mythological symbol of the cosmic tree (17:22–24; 19:10–11; 31:1–19; compare Dan 4:10–12). Similar tree symbols appear in Akkadian, Sumerian, Babylonian, and Egyptian literature, sometimes in association with another mythological tree, the tree of life. Usually, the cosmic tree symbolized the grandeur of an empire.

Third, Ezekiel uses the cosmic, deep watery chaos prevalent in biblical references to creation (the deep in Gen 1:25; Pss 65:6–7; 89:9; 95:4–5; 124:4–5). This primeval, chaotic sea represented the initial state of all that existed; it stood against all order and harmony. From it, dry land emerged. In Ezekiel, this watery chaos swallows Tyre (26:19), the ship Tyre (27:26–27), and, in a reversed image, appears as the river of life flowing from the new temple (47:1–12).

Fourth, adaptations of the myth of the great sea monster Tiamat (or Rahab or Leviathan) appear throughout the Old Testament, especially in the Psalms (Job 3:8; 7:12; 26:12; 41:1; Pss 74:13–14; 77:16; 89:10; 104:26; Isa 27:1; 51:9; Amos 9:3). Ezekiel uses this image in oracles against Egypt's Pharaoh Hophra (29:3–5; 32:2–8). The biblical accounts of Yahweh's easy victory over this sea creature undermines some Israelites' view that everything is ultimately chaotic. Instead, when Yahweh is involved, matters move quickly from chaos to order.

Finally, ancient Near Eastern creation myths often describe a garden paradise of the gods. One popular Sumerian myth described this paradise, Dilmun, as a fertile, well-watered land free of all pollutants, sickness, death, and hostility among animals. Ezekiel's references to "the trees of Eden in the garden of God" (28:13; 31:8–9, 16, 18) are adaptations of the idyllic state. Ezekiel adapts various strands of ancient Near Eastern paradise myths for his own purposes and transforms them through the language of Genesis. Ezekiel's usage need not suggest that he viewed the Genesis account of the garden as fictional. Rather, he uses old images for monotheistic ends.

Ezekiel's adaptation of these and other mythical elements are part of his "by any means necessary" communication strategy to his hard-hearted and rebellious audience. His tactic also demonstrates that Yahweh is not bound to any particular means of communicating but is sovereign even over the polytheistic myths that would deny God's uniqueness.

Ezekiel next words his audience's question: *Why does the son not share the guilt of his father?* They assume that their exile is the consequence of others' sins. Ezekiel rejects a corporate fatalism and insists on individual responsibility. Fishbane (141) explains the transition:

> [W]hile the first [section] argued that there was no transfer of guilt from one generation (person) to another, nothing was said about the sinner in his own lifetime. Was a (repentant) person considered guilty in later years for sins committed earlier, and vice versa?

The answer is similar in both the generational and individual cases: Yahweh deals with people in their present state. Current Israel perpetuates former Israel's sins. In their hard-heartedness, *Israel* declares Yahweh's policy absurd (NIV's *not just* is misleading). Yahweh twice hurls the charge back: *Is it not your ways that are* ridiculous?

Ezekiel's attempt to persuade fails, so he pronounces God's judgment: *I will judge you, each according to his ways* (verses 30–32). Israel's refusal to agree with Yahweh's policy does not hinder its implementation. Yet Yahweh's judgment allows for repentance: Yahweh does not want the people to die. He commands them to *get a new heart and a new spirit*. Usually these are a divine grant (11:19; 36:26), but this oracle focuses on Israel's obligation to take responsibility for its state rather than claim to be a victim of its ancestors' sins.

19:1–14 Chapter 19 presents two allegorical, ironic laments for Judah's last four rulers. The first (verses 1–9) uses a zoological metaphor. A *lioness* raises a *cub*. When grown, he becomes violent, is captured, and is taken to *Egypt*. The lioness rears another cub. When grown, he becomes more violent than the previous cub. He is captured and taken to the *king of Babylon*. These cubs are *princes of Israel*. The first is undoubtedly Jehoahaz (2 Kgs 23:34). The second cub probably represents Jehoiakim.

The second lament uses another viticultural simile (see chapters 15, 17). The *mother is like a vine in your vineyard*. It had *many and strong branches*. However, the hot *east wind* dried up the branches, and fire burned *one of its main branches*. What remains is unfit *for a ruler's scepter*. The mother is the Davidic dynasty and the branches its succession of kings. Babylon is the hot *east wind*; the *fruit and strong branches* are Jehoiachin, his sons, and the other deportees taken into exile *in a dry and thirsty land*. Zedekiah, deemed unfit as king by Ezekiel, is the smoldering *main branch* that remains.

20:1–44 Most of this chapter surveys Israel's history from its origin to its end in five eras. The hallmark of this historical review is Yahweh's patience. From each God requires fidelity, Israel rebels, God intends to punish it utterly, but avoids punishment to defend God's honor, and so gives limited punishment and new regulations to assist Israel's fidelity. Yet the people rebel.

On 14 August 591 BCE, *some of the elders come to inquire of* Yahweh. Yahweh emphatically swears (*as surely as I live* is an oath formula) they will receive no response. He also asks Ezekiel whether he will *judge them*. Despite Ezekiel's oracles, Yahweh realizes that he is still sympathetic to the exiles' views. Nevertheless, Ezekiel is to *confront them with the detestable practices of their fathers*. The review is unlike anything they had heard before (see Pss 78; 106).

Israel never had a golden age; the nation's idolatry began in Egypt (but see Josh 24:14–15). When Joseph comes to Egypt, he assimilates by taking the Egyptian name Zaphenath-Paneah and marrying the daughter of the high priest of On (Gen 41:44–45). Moses, reared in Pharaoh's house, is also thoroughly Egyptianized (Exod 2:19). Even his name is Egyptian. Nevertheless, Yahweh *chose Israel* (Deut 7:6–11), reaffirmed the original oath *with uplifted hand* to be their *God*, was *revealed* through Moses (Exod 6:6–9), determined to *bring them out of Egypt*, and give them a land *searched out for them*. In return, Yahweh requests singleminded loyalty (Exod 20:2–6).

> **Historical Summaries**
>
> The Bible contains several "historical" summaries of Yahweh's dealings with his people, proclaiming various messages (Josh 24:2–15; Judg 11:14–28; 1 Sam 12:6–18; Neh 9:6–37; Pss 78; 105; 106).

Predictably, *they rebelled* and did not *forsake the idols of Egypt*. Ezekiel tells what Exodus does not. While still *in Egypt*, Yahweh determines to punish them. Yet, not wanting to become a laughingstock *in the eyes of the nations they lived among*, Yahweh refrains.

Instead, God brings them to Sinai and gives *decrees*, *laws*, and *Sabbaths*, that is, Saturday, Sabbath years, Jubilee (compare Lev 23:24, 39). Again, they *rebelled* and *desecrated* the *Sabbaths*. Yahweh determines to *destroy them in the desert* and then relents.

Moses' critical role in this goes unmentioned (but see Exod 32:7–14). Instead, Yahweh suspends the blessing of his promise (the promised land and abundant fertility) to the first generation because of their sins; he has greater hopes for their children.

Incredibly, during the wilderness wanderings, *the children rebelled*. Rather than destroy them, Yahweh disperses that generation *among the nations and scatters them through the countries* (Deut 28:64), thus anticipating the deportations of Ezekiel's own time. For them, the land will be but a temporary grant. Verses 25–26 are a difficult passage (Allen, *Ezekiel 1–19*, 11–12; Block, *Ezekiel 1–24*, 637–41; Fisch 126), but the solution is reasonably clear. A slight stylistic variation in the gender and presence of a possessive suffix ("my") for *statutes* [Hebrew *chuqqotay* in verses 11, 13, 16, 19, 21, 24 versus *chuqqim* in verse 25], usually inconsequential, signals a differentiation in this context. These statutes do not come from Yahweh (compare *the statutes of your fathers*, verse 18) because *they could not live by* them, whereas Yahweh's laws bring life (verses 11, 13, 21; compare Ps 119:93). Verse 26 seems to explain the generalized *statutes* and *laws* of verses 18 and 25: Yahweh allowed them to follow their own rules with the expectation that they would become horrified at their child *sacrifice*.

In verses 27–29, Ezekiel broadly describes all the generations between those Yahweh *brought into the land* and his own day. The entire sweep is characterized by idol worship: the forefathers *blaspheme* Yahweh by *forsaking* (literally "acting traitorously against") him to present idols with *sacrifices*, *offerings*, *incense*, and libations on the *high places*. Ezekiel thus dismisses all Israelite history with one rhetorical flourish. For greater nuance on this subject, see Joshua-Kings.

According to verses 30–38, The exiles are not punished for their forefathers' sins, but like them, they continue (*to this day*) to lust after and *sacrifice* their children to *all* their *idols* (also 16:36). This disqualifies them from inquiring of (that is, obtaining information from) Yahweh. Despite their desire *to be like the nations ... who serve wood and stone*, Yahweh *will never* let them be like all others. Using the metaphor of a shepherd (seen again in chapter 34), Yahweh will *gather* his sheep *from the countries* to examine each one and *purge* the flock of rebels. These *will not enter the land of Israel*.

Go serve your idols (verses 39–44) offers a temporary, ironic permission because judgment is set. The consequences of its future arrival will be true Yahwistic worship, a resumption of blessing of promised land to *the entire house of Israel*, a thorough repentance and a fulfillment of the recognition formula by Israel and the nations (16:59–63).

20:45–21:32 Four oracles comprise this section developed thematically around the word "sword"– a sign of Babylon's imminent invasion of the eastern Mediterranean basin and the destruction of Jerusalem. The English chapter and verse divisions diverge from the Hebrew divisions until the end of chapter 20.

> **The Four Oracles**
> *The oracles show a progression: from Yahweh's decision to bring the sword upon Judah, to preparing the sword and giving it to a slayer, to the slayer making ready, to the aftermath.*

20:45–21:7 The first oracle, like the one in chapter 17, is divided into metaphorical presentation and allegorical explanation. The words *south*, *south*, and *southland* represent different Hebrew words. The first, *teman* [literally "to the right"], refers to that side of a map when east is the orienting direction, as is common in ancient Near Eastern cartography. The second [*darom*] is the usual directional word for south. *Southland* in Hebrew is *negev* and refers to the Negev wilderness south of Jerusalem. That the Negev was never *forest*ed in historical times indicates that the oracle has other than literal meaning. In an unusual move, Ezekiel objects that his use of figures of speech brings the disdainful dismissal, *Isn't he just telling parables*? It is unclear whether Ezekiel laments his unpopularity or the use of an ineffective medium for his message.

The overall explanation is clear, however. *Jerusalem*, *the sanctuary*, and *the land of Israel* are the intended referents. The fire is the *sword* of Babylon; the trees are *both the righteous and the wicked*. *Cut off* may refer to deportation rather than death, although death for the wicked cannot be excluded. Ezekiel's sign act of *groan*ing focuses on the effect of the raid.

21:8–17 This sword song, spoken separately from the earlier oracle, is difficult in places. The meter is unclear, but it approaches the limping meter of a lament. Ezekiel likely brandished a sword

> **The Sword Song**
> *In this poetic form, the first line of a couplet has three stressed syllables, while the second line has two stressed syllables. Hebrew poetry rarely has regular meter or rhyme.*

wildly as he proclaimed this oracle. Verse 10b is hopelessly corrupt in Hebrew; it appears to rebuke the exiles for their view that Jerusalem is inviolable because of its Davidic connections. Similarly, verse 13 is incomprehensible: "Indeed, it looks like a group of words randomly thrown together, opening with an enigmatic reference to *testing*" (Block, *Ezekiel 1–24*, 679). NIV adds *Judah* to both verses without any textual support. Ezekiel is to accompany this song with actions: *wail*, *beat* his chest, *strike* his hands together three times. The threefold repetition signifies the completeness of the violence against its victims. When done, Yahweh's *wrath will subside*.

21:18–27 In another sign act, Ezekiel depicts Nebuchadrezzar's decision to go to Jerusalem and destroy it rather than Rabbah. He uses three divinatory actions to receive an *omen*. Correct procedures were outlined for ancient Near Eastern diviners in omen texts. To *cast lots with arrows* simply required pulling a premarked arrow from a quiver. Scholars are uncertain about how the idols were *consult*ed. To *examine the liver* required a sheep sacrifice. The size, shape, color, density, and amount of fat around the liver all required careful interpretation to ascertain the gods' decisions. The decision, Yahweh claims, is his, not theirs. Not only will the people be deported, but also Zedekiah (*O profane and wicked prince of Israel*) will be removed for disloyalty to his vassal oath (compare 17:16–21). The NIV's *A ruin!* is better translated "Upside down!" All social structures will be inverted. Verse 27 echoes Genesis 49:10, but ironically inverts it: the reference is not to a messianic deliverer, but to Nebuchadrezzar, as the similar phrase at 23:24b confirms.

21:28–32 Verses 28–29 repeat phrases from the earlier sword song to announce the Ammonites' impending destruction. Another oracle about Ammon appears in 25:1–7. At verse 30, Yahweh addresses Babylon, telling its king, *Return the sword to its scabbard*; the executioner's task is done. Yahweh then claims to have *created* Babylon and thus to be entitled to *pour out wrath* on it. The point is the same here as in the inaugural vision: Nebuchadrezzar does Yahweh's work.

22:1–31 Three oracles asserting Jerusalem's impurity have been loosely assembled here. The first oracle (1–16) opens with a focus on Ezekiel. Just as in chapter 20, Yahweh asks whether Ezekiel *will judge this city of bloodshed*, highlighting again where his sympathies lie. Nahum (3:1) had earlier called Nineveh a *city of bloodshed*. If the parallel is intentional, Nineveh's fate forecasts Jerusalem's. Jerusalem's sins break both segments of the Ten Commandments (to worship idols is to reject Yahweh, while bloodshed destroys community) and violate portions of the priestly legislation of Leviticus 17–26. Jerusalem has become the *infamous city*, an *object of scorn to all the nations*.

The first list (verses 6–8) enumerates a rejection of Yahweh's values by *the princes of Israel*: parents are maligned, perhaps cursed (Exod 20:12; 21:17); *alien*, *fatherless*, and *widow* are exploited (see Exod 22:21–22); and *Sabbath* is violated (Num 15:32–36; Ezek 20:12–13, 16, 21, 24).

Next comes a list of sexual boundary violations (verses 9–11). *To eat at mountain shrines* and *commit lewd acts* may refer to ritualized sexual intercourse with cult prostitutes (Num 25:1–3), but more likely simply means casual sex during community gatherings. The other matters listed are violations of purity laws found in Leviticus 18.

Finally (verse 12), the legal and economic foundations are flouted by judges who *accept bribes* (Exod 23:8; Isa 5:23; Amos 5:12) and those who charge *excessive interest* to a *neighbor*, that is, a fellow Israelite. All the sins listed are attributable to one cause: *You have forgotten me, declares the Sovereign Lord* (Deut 4:9, 23; 6:12; 8:11, 14; 26:13). Jerusalem's problems were no lapse in judgment but a wholesale defection.

Yahweh's sentence compactly rehearses the covenant curses (verses 13–16). When they are invoked, the recognition formula will be fulfilled.

22:17–22 The second oracle mentions no sins; instead, it presses a silver refining analogy, perhaps adapted from Isaiah 1:22, 25 and/or Jeremiah 6:27–30. In Ezekiel's analogy, the *dross* represents those left in the land after the deportations of 605 and 597 BCE; after Yahweh's fiery blast of 586 BCE, nothing salvageable remains. Bringing the *dross* into Jerusalem reflects the reality of ancient Near Eastern siege warfare. Rural Judeans would rush to fortified Jerusalem ahead of an advancing army. Jerusalem, however, became not the place of protection but a prison. This oracle also ends with the recognition formula.

> **Metal Refining**
> *Refining was a two-stage process in which lead ore was melted to extract trace amounts of silver. The process also yielded copper, tin, and iron.*

22:23–31 The final oracle echoes previous indictments of Judean leaders and is addressed to the land. That the *land...has had no rain* [literally "deluge"] *...in the day of wrath* implies that on the day of wrath, it will be deluged. This echo of Genesis 6:5–7 foreshadows the cleansing rain of judgment ahead. Fishbane (461–63) suggests that the indictments against Judah's leaders echo Zephaniah 3:3–4. The *princes*, *priests*, *officials*, and *prophets* fail in their respective duties as trustees of the land and examples to the people to the point that *the people of the land* exploit the *poor*, *needy*, and *alien* among them. Rather than move to immediate sentencing, Yahweh mercifully searches for an intermediary *among them* and finds none. Because of the leaders' dereliction, Yahweh will *bring down on their own heads all they have done*.

23:1–49 Chapter 23 shares, multiplies, and intensifies the coarse sexual images of chapter 16 in an extended allegory of judgment against Yahweh's two "wives," Oholah and Oholibah. The allegory focuses on the alliances Israel and Judah made with Assyria and Babylon – alliances of a type strongly forbidden in the Mosaic covenant (Deut 7:1–7). The influence of Hosea 1–3 and Jeremiah 3:6–13; 5:8; and 13:27 is evident throughout.

Sensitive readers will find this section particularly vulgar. Nevertheless, Ezekiel seeks to offend his audience. As Taylor (170–71) puts it:

> Despite the distasteful theme and the indelicate language, the reader of these verses must appreciate that this is the language of unspeakable disgust and must try to recognize Ezekiel's passion for God's honour and his fury at the adulterous conduct of his covenant people. The feeling of nausea which a chapter like this arouses must not be blamed on the writer of the chapter, nor even on its contents, but on the conduct which had to be described in such revolting terms.

In verses 1–4, Ezekiel returns to a pornographic portrayal of Jerusalem's sins; Samaria is added to highlight Jerusalem's depravity by comparison. If the names *Oholah* (for Samaria/Israel) *and Oholibah* (for Jerusalem/Judah) once had significance, scholars can no longer recover it. The dalliances of the Israelites with foreigners begins in Egypt *from their youth* (compare 20:5–9). Ezekiel describes their willing participation with Egypt as *prostitution* in which *their breasts were fondled and their virgin bosoms caressed*. Hosea-like, Yahweh takes both as his wives and they bear him *sons and daughters*. Yahweh knew their character before he married them. Again, as in chapter 16, the practice of marrying two sisters did not in itself offend an ancient audience.

In verses 5–10, Ezekiel portrays Yahweh's marriage to *Oholah* (Israel) first. Oholah lusts after Assyrian men in uniform, a cipher for Jehu and Menahem of Israel currying favor with the Assyrian rulers Shalmanezer III and Tiglath-Pileser III in the ninth and eighth centuries BCE. Ezekiel describes their cravings in autoerotic terms (*defiled herself with all the idols of everyone she lusted after*). Moreover, her actions simply continued her previous whorings *in Egypt*, where she serviced men in her youth who squeezed her pubescent breasts and ejaculated on her. In return for her infidelity, Yahweh allows her *Assyrian* lovers to shame her in public, take *away her sons and daughters* for the slave trade, and *kill her with the sword*. This metaphorical description matches Israel's fate in the Assyrian deportation of 721 BCE, as well as standard treatment of women caught in adultery in the ancient Near East.

The historical recital continues in several stages (verses 11–13). The historical referent is the alliance between Ahaz of Judah and Tiglath-pileser III against Rezin of Aram and Pekah of Israel during the Syro-Ephraimite skirmishes against Assyria in the mid-730s BCE (compare 2 Kgs 16:5–14; Isa 7:10–16). The Assyrians, however, were conquered by the Babylonians (that is, the *Chaldeans*; verses 14–18). Oholah (Israel) had only one lover; Oholibah (Judah) will have three. Oholibah sought, but was ultimately left unsatisfied with, the Babylonians, and she *turned away from them in disgust*. This briefly alludes to the history of Judean-Babylonian relations from Hezekiah's rebellious invitation to Merodach-baladan in the late 700s BCE to Zedekiah's rebellion against Nebuchadrezzar in 588 BCE. Ezekiel saves his most graphic description for Zedekiah's alliances

---

Oholibah

"Queen Oholibah" is a character in British poet Algernon Charles Swinburne's (1837–1909) "The Masque of Queen Bersabe": "I am the Queen Oholibah:/My lips kissed dumb the word of Ah / Sighed on strange lips grown sick thereby."

with Egypt in 588 (verses 19–21). In extremely crude and graphic language that alludes to Leviticus 18:22–23, Yahweh attacks Oholibah's desire to return to the same Egypt from which he delivered her. In Egypt, she "fixated upon (becoming one of) their concubines," not NIV's *lusted after her lovers*. "Concubines" refers to women used sexually by men. Oholibah's (Judah's) desire is explained by a vulgar equine simile, possibly instigated by Jeremiah's metaphor (Jer 2:24; 5:8; see Ezek 16:26): her lovers had donkey-sized penises and profuse ejaculations. In the ancient world, such bawdy references bespoke an insatiable and debauched sexual appetite. Thus, Ezekiel combines the Mosaic prohibition against bestiality (Lev 18:23) with a culturally negative description of Egyptian lewdness. Still, Judah wanted to return to the sexual escapades of her youth in Egypt.

In response (verses 22–31), Yahweh will bring her lovers from *Pekod*, *Shoa*, and *Koa* to wage merciless war on her. Ezekiel likely chooses these places, not for their geographic location, but because their names have symbolic meanings: "punish," "cry for help," and "scream," respectively. The description of punishment is graphic.

> **Punishment of Adulteresses**
> It was common ancient Near Eastern practice to disfigure adulteresses by cutting off their noses and ears. These responses metaphorically anticipate the horrors of Jerusalem's destruction.

Yahweh's sentence ends oddly with a drinking song (verses 32–35). The Hebrew is incomprehensible at places, giving the impression that it is a drinking song about drinking sung by a drunk (Blenkinsopp 101). Ezekiel brilliantly mimics the complete loss of decorum to which Judah has sunk. The *cup* metaphor here represents Yahweh's full wrath (compare Isa 51:17, 22; Jer 25:15–29; 49:12–13; Ps 75:9) brought against both Oholah (Samaria) in 721 BCE and Oholibah (Jerusalem) in 586 BCE because they had *forgotten* Yahweh (8:17; 22:16).

The chapter ends with yet more charges (verses 36–49). Again, Yahweh calls Ezekiel to indict the sisters for sins already mentioned. To these, Yahweh adds blatant religious hypocrisy: *On the very day they sacrificed their children to their idols, they entered my sanctuary and desecrated it*. He again describes Israel's and Judah's foreign alliances in sexual terms, describing the *noise of a carefree crowd* indulging in an orgy. The sisters invite *drunkards* (NIV alternate translation) and *men from the rabble* for an exhausting round of sex. Verse 45 is an aside from Yahweh to Ezekiel and his audience, guiding them to an appropriate response: *Righteous men will sentence them* as adulteresses, rather than sympathize with their kinspersons in Jerusalem. The oracle ends with references to both the covenant curses and the recognition formula.

24:1–27 Two sections comprise this chapter, a parable song (verses 1–14) and a parabolic drama (verses 15–27). This is the final chapter in which the covenant curses are the primary message. Ezekiel has been prophesying for five and a half years.

Yahweh tells Ezekiel to take up, perhaps even enact, the *cooking pot* metaphor used by the Jerusalem leaders in 11:3. A celebration seems in the offing; the preparation is quite routine: a pot is filled with water, meat, and choice bones and is then set on a fire to simmer. *Woe!* is the first clue that the parable is an enacted judgment for *the city of bloodshed* (compare 22:1–12). The pot is Jerusalem, the meat is the leading Jerusalemites, the cooking is the siege of 587–586 BCE. The pot, however, had not been cleaned beforehand. Its patina (or "rust") and charred food deposits ruined the meal; the choice pieces must be removed. According to verses

> **The Seige & Fall of Jerusalem**
> Despite the accuracy intended by having Ezekiel record this date, this very date of Jerusalem's siege, scholars disagree on the date it represents. The Old Testament unanimously describes an eighteen-month siege before Jerusalem fell. According to 2 Kings 25:1, 3, 8 (which parallels Jer 39:1–3), Jerusalem was overrun in Zedekiah's eleventh year, which was Nebuchadrezzar's nineteenth year. By modern reckoning, this year ran from March/April 586 BCE to March/April 585 BCE. Almost all scholars agree that Jerusalem was captured in mid-July and the temple razed in mid-August 586 BCE. The siege, therefore, probably began on 5 January 587 BCE, Jerusalem fell on 17 July 586, and the temple was destroyed on 14 August 586. (Some scholars follow the chronology of Parker and Dubberstein and place the siege on 15 January 588 BCE and the fall of Jerusalem in July 587 BCE.)

7–8, the contamination is *the blood she shed in her midst*. Disregarding the purity laws for kosher preparation, the blood was not properly discarded (Lev 17:10–14); this symbolizes the improper burial rites of those unjustly slain. Their blood cries out to be requited (Gen 4:10; Job 16:18). So Yahweh stokes the fire; instructs someone to *cook the meat well* (literally, "completely" – that is, burned to a crisp). Instead of NIV's *mixing in the spices*, we should read RSV's "empty out the broth" to reduce everything to carbonized residue. Then, the *copper* pot is to be superheated to remove the residue. Verse 12, although quite difficult in Hebrew, claims that even this does not work; the pot is contaminated beyond use. Verses 13–14 sum up the point: Yahweh has tried to cleanse Jerusalem to no avail. The extreme covenant curses are being invoked.

As in previous sign acts, Ezekiel is to incarnate the role of Yahweh: he is not to lament, weep, cry, or perform any mourning rituals over (presumably) Jerusalem's fall (verses 15–27). Throughout, Yahweh has said he will have no pity on Jerusalem (5:11; 8:18; 9:10). The message, however, is about more than Jerusalem; it refers to Ezekiel's wife, also. Unawares, he *spoke to the people in the morning, and in the evening* his *wife died. The next morning* he *did as* he *had been commanded*.

Ezekiel's audience expects the sign acts to have application for them, and they inquire what the death of Ezekiel's wife foreshadows. The significance is, Yahweh will *desecrate* his *sanctuary, the delight of* their *eyes, the object of* their *affection* (compare 7:21–22). Like Ezekiel, they are not to mourn the loss because whoring, blood-shedding Jerusalem's demise is deserved. Verses 25–27 directly address Ezekiel and form an inclusio with 3:24–27. When a Jerusalemite escapee (compare 14:22) appears with the news of Jerusalem's fall, the constraints imposed some seven years earlier will be lifted. Throughout, Ezekiel has been, and will remain, a *sign to them* of Yahweh's character as their covenant-keeping God. A further reflection on this event and its consequences appears in 33:21–22.

INTERLUDE: JUDGMENT ON JUDAH'S NEIGHBORS · 25:1–32:32

Chapters 25–32 separate the announcements of Jerusalem's siege (24:2) and fall (33:21). The oracles against Judah's neighbors serve both as a literary interlude – biding time while Jerusalem languishes in its siege – and as the beginning of hope for all who love the homeland. Those neighbors that welcomed Jerusalem's fall will fall themselves. All the undated oracles in this section assume Jerusalem has fallen and may be dated after July–August 586 BCE.

Isaiah, Jeremiah, Zephaniah, and Amos have similar collections of oracles against the nations. These oracles have been editorially arranged both geographically and literarily, beginning in the northeast with Ammon and then proceeding clockwise to Moab, Edom, Philistia, Tyre, and Sidon. Finally, the seventh nation, Egypt, is decried in seven doom oracles, as is Tyre. The arrangement by sevens may be a literary figure symbolizing the totality of enemy nations and their complete punishment (compare Deut 7:2).

25:1–28:24 Five of these six neighbors gloated over the fall of Jerusalem. Yahweh had warned his own people against such arrogance: *Do not gloat when your enemy falls; when he stumbles, do not let your heart rejoice, or the Lord will see and disapprove and turn his wrath away from him [and toward you]* (Prov 24:17–18). Faithful to the people, Yahweh will be an enemy to their enemies.

25:1–17 The first five oracles are short and formulaic. After Yahweh is identified as speaker comes an indictment ("Because X did Y") and sentence ("therefore I will ..."). The oracles criticize the nations for their war crimes. Each oracle ends with a variation of the recognition formula.

> **Israel & the Nations**
> Isaiah (15–16; 21:11–12; 14:28–32) and Jeremiah (49:1–6; 48; 49:7–22; 47) also contain oracles concerning Ammon (in Jeremiah only), Moab, Edom, and Philistia in collections of oracles concerning foreign nations (Isa 13:23; Jer 46–51).

Longstanding animosity between Israel and Ammon (compare Josh 13:25; Judg 11:1–32; 2 Sam 10–12) had recently flared when the Ammonites harassed Judah around 600 BCE (2 Kgs 24:2). Most recently, Ammon gloated (*said "Aha!"*, an interjection of glee; see Ps 35:21–25) when the temple was *desecrated*, when Israel was *laid waste*, and when Judeans *went into exile*. As punishment, *the people of the East* (the Babylonians) will deport them. Nebuchadrezzar destroyed Ammon in about 570 BCE (see 21:28–32).

The *Moabites* denied the special bond between Yahweh and Israel by claiming *the house of Judah has*

become like all the other nations. In one sense, this was sadly true. However, Moab took advantage of Yahweh's apparent inability to protect Judah after the exile by plundering Judean territory. Like the Ammonites, Moab, too, will belong to *the people of the East* as punishment for their treachery.

The kinship ties between Edom and Judah (Gen 25:21–34) make Edom's aid of Babylon's siege of Jerusalem in 587 BCE reprehensible, but the longstanding rivalry (Isa 34; Ps 137:7) makes it understandable. Yahweh's agent of *wrath* will, surprisingly, be *my people Israel* (see Obad 19–21) Significantly, the recognition formula has Edom coming to know *vengeance* rather than Yahweh.

The Philistines' vengeful attitude toward Judah is condemned. *Vengeance* is the key term here and the linkword to the previous oracle. They *acted in vengeance, with malice in their hearts,* and *with ancient* (better, "never ending") *hostility.* Yahweh will repay their vengeance with his own.

26:1–21 Seven well-arranged oracles against Tyre appear in 26:1–28:19. The first (26:1–7) follows the pattern of the four in chapter 25. The next three (26:7–14, 15–18, 19–21) follow a death-mourning-burial pattern. Chapter 27 is an extended metaphor. The series ends with an irony-filled indictment and judgment (28:1–10) and a mock lament (28:11–19) against Tyre's ruler.

The Hebrew text does not preserve the correct date, but the Septuagint corrects the year number to twelve, yielding the date 3 February 585 BCE (compare Allen, *Ezekiel 20–48*, 71 note 1a; Block, *Ezekiel 25–48*, 34–35). Tyre gloats (*Aha!*) that Jerusalem's lost commerce will now come to it. Ancient Tyre was the chief eastern Mediterranean port for trade from Egypt, Palestine, Anatolia, Arabia, and Babylonia, toward the west as far as Spain. It consisted of a mainland city and an offshore island port. In response to its glee, Yahweh will *bring many nations* against the mainland city and besiege it. The island port will also be destroyed. The oracle ends with the recognition formula.

Verses 7–14 are a detailed expansion of verses 1–6. Here, Yahweh names Nebuchadrezzar and his forces as the besieging conqueror of Tyre. The details of the siege are stereotypical. The *strong pillars* (verse 11) of Tyre's celebrated temple to Melqart (Hercules/Heracles) *will fall to the ground.* Yahweh promises that after Nebuchadrezzar's victory, Tyre *will never be rebuilt.* This promise cannot be taken literally, since the city was rebuilt.

This prophecy was not fulfilled literally. Nebuchadrezzar besieged Tyre in 585 BCE but withdrew in 572 BCE without breaching its walls. Yahweh acknowledges Nebuchadrezzar's failure in 29:17–19 and thus admits the essential failure of this prophecy. Sixty-five years later, Zechariah prophesies against Tyre (Zech 9:3–4), corroborating Nebuchadrezzar's failure. Tyre was ransacked by Alexander the Great in 332 BCE. Attempts to circumvent the clear admission of Scripture of this oracle's failure by transferring this prophecy from Nebuchadrezzar to Alexander fail the text's specific mention of Nebuchadrezzar as the conqueror, Tyre's history as a thriving commercial center into the Middle Ages, and the city's continual habitation into the present. Contemporary readers must not try to salvage this prophecy when even Yahweh admits its failure. Biblical prophecies were still under Yahweh's control and were not predictions that referred to irreversible, inevitable developments.

Verses 15–18 describe the anticipated international reaction to Tyre's destruction. The *coastlands* will *tremble* and their rulers (*princes of the coast*) will be *clothed with terror*. Tyre's fall jeopardizes these city-states' economic prosperity and signals their own vulnerability to attack. The *lament* both admits their own fear of Tyre as the *power on the seas* and their fright at having to negotiate the new situation its *collapse* brings.

Verses 19–21 are infused with ancient Near Eastern mythological views of death and the afterlife, and also assume Tyre's destruction by Nebuchadrezzar. Drawing on associations of *the ocean depths* with the primeval chaos, Yahweh will bring a cosmic tidal wave to *cover* the city to bring it *down to the pit*. Ezekiel's description of the realm of the dead (those who *dwell in the earth below*) assumes the three-tiered universe (subterranean world, earth, sky) of ancient Near Eastern thought. Tyre's consignment is permanent; it *will never again be found*.

27:1–36 Chapter 27 provides a single, extended metaphor of the trading ship *Tyre* loaded with cargo from around the known world that sinks in a storm on the open sea. The point is clear: Tyre's fall described in 26:1–14 will have a devastating impact on international trade in the ancient Mediterranean world. In verses 1–3a, Ezekiel presents this as a *lament*.

Israelites used *perfect in beauty* to describe Jerusalem (16:13–15; Lam 2:15); Ezekiel applies this description to Tyre to reflect the arrogance mentioned in 26:2. The city's fate will match Jerusalem's. Tyre (pictured here as a ship) was beautifully built and extravagantly outfitted. The craftsmen used the best local wood for its decking, mast, and oars. Its sails, banners, and awnings were of the finest *linen*. Its *veteran* crew were only the most experienced. Because of its expensive cargo, it also employed mercenary guards from *Persia*, *Lydia*, *Put*, *Arvad*, *Helech*, and *Gammad* – locations from around the known world.

The *merchandise* that flowed through Tyre's docks was extensive. Among the goods listed are metal commodities and ores; slaves; all kinds of animals for work, wool, food, and fur; precious gemstones, ivory, and ebony; manufactured and dyed fabric goods; and consumable commodities like wheat, honey, oil, and wine. In short, the raw and manufactured wealth of the whole ancient Near East came to market in Tyre.

At verse 16, the sequence shifts from south to north, beginning with Edom (NIV alternate translation; "Aram" and "Edom" differ only in the middle letter, *resh* or *daleth*, in Hebrew; see comment at 6:14). Next are *Judah and Israel*. *Minnith* is directly east of Israel in Ammon. North of Israel lay *Damascus*, with *Helbon* and *Zahar* to its north. Because of another letter confusion, NIV's *Danites and Greeks from Uzal* should be "and casks of wine from Uzal." *Dedan*, *Arabia*, *Kedar*, *Sheba*, and *Raamah* are Arabian locales; *Haran*, *Canneh*, *Eden Asshur*, and *Kilmad* are to the distant northeast. *Tyre's* loss would cripple the worldwide economy.

A gale, or *east wind*, clearly a cipher for Nebuchadrezzar and Babylonian armies, *will break Tyre to pieces*. All cargo and hands will be lost.

Ezekiel describes the response to Tyre's loss in stereotypical terms. Fellow sailors will mourn their lost comrades with loud wailing, *dust on their heads*, *rolling in ashes*, shaved heads, *sackcloth*, and lament.

> **The Nations Who Trade with Tyre**
>
> *The number of nations mentioned here rivals the list in Genesis 10:1–30 and partly corresponds to it. Ezekiel's listing by nation has a discernible geographical order of west to east, south to north, and far northeast.* Tarshish (*Tartessos in Spain*) *marks the farthest western place name.* Greece, Tubal, Meshech, Beth Togarmah, *and* Rhodes *are in Asia Minor and are listed among the Japhethites in Genesis 10:2–4.*

The lament proper in verses 32b–36 echoes 26:17–18. It rehearses Tyre's importance in international trade, bemoans Tyre's calamitous loss, and finally admits that those who formerly reveled in associations with Tyre now find their relationship potentially problematic. Tyre's loss portended the same fate for its trading partners.

> **Ancient Mourning Customs**
> *Putting dust on the head, rolling in ashes, shaving the head, tearing one's garment, wearing sackcloth, and loud wailing were all cultural means of expressing grief in Israel and the ancient Near East (see Amos 8:10; Isa 15:2–3; Mic 1:8, 16; Jer 25:34; 49:13).*

Although the oracle itself is remarkably free of references to Yahweh or to various sins, it is clear that the metaphorical *Tyre*, filled with arrogance, drowns in the watery chaos because Yahweh sends an east wind. Yahweh will ultimately destroy all forms of arrogance, Tyrian or otherwise.

28:1–10 This oracle denounces Tyre's *ruler*, Ethbaal III, for arrogance. He is portrayed as claiming to *sit on the throne of a god* in an ancient Near Eastern pantheon and thus be unassailable. Yahweh responds that he is *a man and not a god*, but with caustic, sarcastic irony, he "admits" that Tyre's king is wiser than *Daniel* (NIV's rhetorical questions in verse 3 are better read as ironic assertions; see RSV). The figure may refer to the Canaanite sage (compare 14:14) or to the biblical prophet *Daniel* who refuses to use his powers for gain (Dan 5:13–17). Verses 6–8 reflect the same punishment seen in earlier oracles against Tyre. In verse 9, with grotesque humor, Ezekiel portrays the defiant "god" Ethbaal informing his attackers (literally, "his desecrators") of his divine invulnerability. He will be as shocked at his fatal wound as his executioners will be delighted. Finally, in a sneering insult, Yahweh consigns Tyre's ruler to *the death of the uncircumcised* (Tyrians practiced circumcision). Once again, Ezekiel uses an offensive sexual term, much like some contemporary slurs question the marital status of one's parents.

28:11–19 Because this oracle lacks standard features of a *lament* and its description *concerning the king of Tyre* unmistakably reflects elements found in Genesis 1–3, it is best read as a satire of Ethbaal: if he is divine, he should be addressed and treated as such. Interpretations that perceive in this oracle the fall of Satan, as Calvin remarks on Isaiah 14:12, arise "from very gross ignorance, ... these inventions have no probability whatever, let us pass by them as useless fables." The phrases *model of perfection*, *full of wisdom*, and *perfect in beauty* begin the extravagant satire. The remaining description weaves together elements of ancient Near Eastern mythology, Genesis 1–3, and prophetic denouncement (see comments on 17:24). The imagery and meaning are complex, but the lesson is not. The arrogance of Tyre, especially its *dishonest trade*, must be punished in a manner befitting its own grandiose view of itself.

28:20–24 This oracle against Sidon contains no specific charges. It ends in verse 23 with the standard recognition formula. Yahweh's purpose in punishment is simply to *gain glory*. Verse 24 rounds out the oracles against Judah's six closest neighbors by describing them as *painful briers and sharp thorns* (compare Num 33:55) and again closes with the recognition formula.

28:25–26 This brief announcement of blessing comes midway among the oracles against the nations and reiterates Yahweh's intent to bless his people after the covenant curses have been expended (compare Deut 30:1–10). *My servant Jacob* implicitly recalls the condition of blessing: Jacob/Israel will serve God in the manner they were created to do. Their regathering is not simply for their own sake, but so that Yahweh may appear *holy among them in the sight of the nations* (Exod 19:6). The promise of restoration ends with the recognition formula mixed with a shortened covenant formula.

29:1–32:32 As with the previous ones against Tyre, the seven oracles against Egypt follow no obvious sequence.

29:1–6A Ezekiel received this first oracle on 7 January 587 BCE, a few days after Jerusalem fell under siege. It is against both *Pharaoh* and *all Egypt*; as goes Pharaoh,

> **Pharaoh as Monster**
> *Pharaoh is described as an arrogant mythical great monster lying among your streams, that is, the crocodile, an oft-used symbol of the pharaoh.*

so goes the nation. For Pharoah to claim *I made* the Nile *for myself* supplants Yahweh's role in creation. Yahweh, in the image of a crocodile hunter, will capture the beast and fling it into the desert to die.

Its carcass will be *food for the beasts of the earth and the birds of the air*, a common ancient Near Eastern description of a shameful death without burial (Deut 28:16; 1 Sam 17:44, 46; 1 Kgs 14:11).

29:6B–12 Shifting metaphors, Yahweh calls Pharaoh a *staff of reed* (compare Isa 36:6). In 587 BCE, Hophra proved to be an insufficient military ally to Zedekiah during Jerusalem's siege (Jer 37:1–10). Although Yahweh forbade Israel to make military alliances with Egypt, he still holds Hophra accountable for his failure (17:18). Yahweh's punishment will encompass all Egypt *from Migdol to Aswan as far as the border of Cush*, that is, from the northern frontier in the Sinai to the southern border in northern Sudan. *Forty years* is a stereotypical, not literal, number that occurs throughout the Old Testament in similar contexts (for example, Num 14:33–35; 32:13).

29:13–16 Unexpectedly, Yahweh promises a diminished restoration for Egypt after its punishment (compare Isa 19:16–25). Unlike the other nations that are erased entirely, perhaps Egypt is spared because it did not gloat over Jerusalem's demise and attempted aid. This oracle contains three recognition formulas.

29:17–21 Ezekiel learns on 26 April (New Year's Day) 571 BCE that Nebuchadrezzar's forces made an unsuccessful thirteen-year attempt to starve and overrun Tyre. *Every head was rubbed bare and every shoulder made raw* from carrying dirt and fill for siege ramps in baskets atop the head or next to the head on the shoulders. Since the Babylonians *got no reward* from Tyre, Yahweh transfers the fulfillment of 26:7–14 to Egypt as a consolation prize. Yahweh also promises that, when Nebuchadrezzar conquers Egypt (*on that day*), the news will give Israel confidence that its restoration is near (*a horn will grow for the house of Israel*), and they will happily acknowledge that Ezekiel was right after all (*open your mouth among them*). Nebuchadrezzar invaded Egypt in 568 or 567 BCE; no extrabiblical records indicate the extent of his success.

30:1–26 This unit contains two oracles. The first is undated, but its opening lines connect to *on that day* in 29:21. It describes Nebuchadrezzar's defeat of Egypt and its allies *Cush, Put, Lydia*, all the rabble, *Libya, and the people of the covenant land*. Cush and Put lie in modern Sudan, and Lydia is in southwestern Asia Minor. The several uses of *that day, the day, the day of* Yahweh, and *a day of clouds* recall similar terms in 7:7, 10–12 (also Joel 2:1–2; Zeph 1:15). Egypt's destruction will come from both Nebuchadrezzar and Yahweh (verses 9–19). Nebuchadrezzar and his army will *destroy the land* and *fill the land with the slain*. Yahweh will bring drought (verse 12) and fire (verse 16). The major urban centers *Memphis, Zoan, Thebes* (see Nah 3:8–10), *Pelusium, Heliopolis, Bubastis,* and *Tahpanhes* (most in northern Egypt) will be destroyed. All of these sites were major centers of Egyptian worship. As with the ten plagues, Yahweh's actions will demonstrate sovereignty over the gods of Egypt (Exod 12:12). *Memphis*, the principal city and capital during most of Egypt's history, was associated with the god Ptah. Both Ptah and Pharaoh (*prince of Egypt*) will be removed. *Thebes*, in the south, was the center of Amun worship. *Pelusium* was an important eastern fortress; it would have been an initial casualty of Nebuchadrezzar's invasion. *Heliopolis* (On; 20:5–9) was the center of sun worship; *Bubastis* served as the center of feline worship. *Tahpanhes*, like Pelusium, was a northeastern fortress city. The terms *dark* and *clouds* may refer to the smoke of its destruction; more likely, this is apocalyptic imagery (32:7–8; Isa 13).

> **God & the Gods**
> The Bible frequently affirms that battles which "seem" to be taking place on earth among human beings are actually taking place in heaven between Yahweh and other gods or heavenly beings (see Exod 18:8–12; Judg 16:23–30; 1 Sam 5:4–7; 17:43–47; 2 Kgs 19:14–19).

30:20–26 This oracle, received on 29 April 586 BCE, reflects Hophra's defeat by the Babylonians when he tried to aid Zedekiah (compare Jer 37:1–11). Ezekiel uses *arm* as a theme in a deliberate, ironic attack on Hophra's self-given pharaonic title, "Strong Arm." Babylon's victory against part of Hophra's army broke an arm of "Strong Arm." The broken arm symbolizes a severely crippled army division unable any longer to *hold a sword*. The oracle also suggests Babylonian troops will receive reinforcements against Egypt. The oracle applies two recognition formulas to Egypt.

31:1–18 Ezekiel speaks this three-part, single-chapter oracle on 21 June 586 BCE. The oracle begins and ends with a reference to *Pharaoh and his hordes*. "Hordes" (literally, "abundance") has a double meaning, referring to Pharaoh's armies and to his arrogance. Verse 2b asks Pharaoh to identify a peer in greatness; verses 3–8 present Ezekiel's hyberbolic portrayal of Pharaoh's "answer." Drawing from the ancient Near Eastern myths of the cosmic tree and the garden of the gods, "Pharaoh" allegorically compares his empire with Assyria. This tall "cedar" was well-watered by the heavy tribute from its vassal kingdoms. Assyria was a ruthless collector of *all the great nations*. Verse 7 summarizes; verse 8 makes an even more grandiose claim: *no tree in the garden of God could match its beauty* (compare 28:12–15). Yahweh interrupts to take credit for Assyria's might in verse 9.

The comparison is double-edged (verses 10–14). If Egypt is equal in Assyria's grandeur, it must also be equal in its downfall. Assyria is judged *because it was proud of its height*. Its demise, here allegorically described as the felling of the cosmic tree, came when Nebuchadrezzar defeated Assyria at Harran in 609 BCE and at Carchemish in 605 BCE.

The *grave* [Hebrew *sheol*] welcomes all equally. Assyria's subjects, allies, rivals, and conquerors all become equal in the *pit* (verses 15–18). For all its hubris, Pharaoh's Egypt will meet the same fate as the once great Assyria and also *the uncircumcised* (Egyptians practiced circumcision; Jer 9:25–26). Yahweh's last word against arrogance is the silence of a common grave of nations and people.

32:1–16 This sixth oracle occurs on 3 March 585 BCE. NIV misses the contrast of the opening lines; it is "You seemed like a lion …; instead, you are (merely) a monster in the seas" (compare NRSV). Instead of a *lion*, Egypt is more like a crocodile constrained by its habitat (29:3). The description of the captured crocodile left in the open to bloat, burst, rot, and be eaten by scavengers parallels gruesome Assyrian descriptions of discarding enemies' bodies (Greenberg 656). Egypt's destruction is described in apocalyptic terms similar to Isaiah's oracle of Babylon's fall (see Isa 13:1–14:27). The thorough darkness described is a lampoon of Egypt's chief deity, Ra the sun god (compare Exod 10:21–23).

32:17–32 The final oracle lacks a month in the date notice; it is probably 18 March 585 BCE. The force of this oracle is the same as chapter 31: both the great and the ignominious *go down to the pit*. NIV adds *say to them* in verse 19 without warrant. Egypt is addressed, not by Ezekiel, but by *the mighty leaders from within the grave*, a "Sheol welcoming committee." With a series of frequently repeated phrases, Ezekiel describes the rogue's gallery of dead nations where Egypt will take its place. Each nation, regardless of its earthly prestige, meets an identical fate: its demise occurs through shameful military defeat (compare Isa 14:3–21). These defeats are presumably handed out by Yahweh for each one's contribution to general chaos and terror. Boadt (324) may be correct that the quality of "sleeping arrangements" corresponds to one's honor in life. Significantly, after Egypt arrives, seven nations inhabit this netherworld. The nations are listed by decreasing geographical distance from Egypt: *Assyria*, *Elam*, *Meshech and Tubal*, *Edom*, *all the princes of the north and the Sidonians* (that is, Phoenicians), and *Pharaoh*. Verse 27 in NIV reverses the point by making the first sentence into a question; it should read "They do not lie.…" Also, *punishment for their sins* should read "shields" (so NRSV, JB, REB).

EZEKIEL'S MESSAGE, PHASE II: COVENANT BLESSINGS · 33:1–48:35

Chapters 33–48 recognize that Jerusalem has fallen (see 33:21); Ezekiel's doom oracles are fulfilled. While Jerusalem's fall vindicates Ezekiel's early ministry, it drives the exiles to greater despair (33:10; 37:11). If they had suspected Yahweh was impotent because of their exile, Jerusalem's demise cemented the notion. However, Yahweh's enforcement of the covenant curses was the necessary prelude to recreating a full relationship with Israel (Lev 26:40–45). Ezekiel's later ministry is even more difficult than before. It will be hard to convince his companions in exile that Yahweh can now fulfill the covenant blessings.

33:1–33 This chapter has two purposes. First, it serves to renew Ezekiel's call. With Jerusalem's fall,

---

The "Day of the Lord"

The language of darkened sun, moon, and stars appropriately describes a "day of the Lord" (Joel 2:2, 10, 31; 3:15; Amos 5:18–20; Zeph 1:15) and demonstrates that language which seems to describe the historical end of the world does not necessarily do so. As verses 9–10 demonstrate, the apocalyptic terms merely describe a calamitous international political, military, economic, and culture-shaping event. Its fulfillment is described in more common terms in verses 11–15: Babylon's destruction of Egypt.

Ezekiel's doom oracles are not only vindicated, but he is now permitted to tell of coming glory days. Yet the oracles of blessings do not assume unilateral action by Yahweh; the exiles must respond obediently. Preceding the oracles of blessing, this chapter lays the foundation for understanding them properly. Just as the covenant curses were not imposed apart from Israel's faithlessness, so the blessings will not be accomplished without Israel's future obedience. Israel's repentance is the necessary condition to enjoy these proferred blessings.

> **Oracles of Blessing**
> *The oracles of blessing generally reverse the doom oracles, though not in a simple way. These oracles of blessing contain transhistorical and apocalyptic elements, along with heightened symbolism. Scholars disagree on the manner of fulfillment of these oracles.*

Verses 1–20 rework themes from 3:16–21 and allegorize Ezekiel's own ministry among the exiles. He indeed has been a faithful *watchman*. But the point now is not about Ezekiel's faithfulness. It is about his hearers' response: will they *take warning* or not?

In verses 10–20, Ezekiel voices the exiles' despair and remorse. Their complaint echoes the final curse named in Leviticus 26:39. Ironically, Leviticus 26:40–41 announces the conditions of national restoration: the people must confess their sins and humble themselves. Yahweh's answer consistently repeats the call in 18:21–32: *Turn! Turn from your evil ways!* (see 18:30). Their national death will not please Yahweh, but, just as the watchman's warning could not make one respond (verses 4–5), so Yahweh cannot force *the house of Israel* to turn.

Out of proportion to its importance, the announcement that vindicates Ezekiel's doom oracles and lays the groundwork for the blessing oracles is composed merely of two Hebrew words that mean "the city is struck." The report arrives on 8 January 585 BCE, almost five months after the temple was razed on 14 August 586 BCE. The night before, Yahweh *opened* Ezekiel's *mouth and he was no longer silent* (see 24:25–27). Ezekiel's silence had kept him from announcing blessings before their time. This announcement does little to change Ezekiel's audience.

Old attitudes die hard. Both those left in Judah (verses 23–26) and those in exile (verses 30–36) maintain views that prevent them from experiencing blessing. Nebuchadrezzar's forces do not deport everyone in Judah. The poorest are left to tend the fields (Jer 39:10). Yet even these *people living in those ruins in the land of Israel* still maintain the same arrogant attitude as their now-dead leaders. Their expectation to possess the land as Abraham's descendants fails to recall that Abraham's claim was a divine grant related to his fidelity to Yahweh. Ezekiel lists at least six different ways these inhabitants fail in their covenant commitments. For them, Yahweh invokes the covenant curses again to cleanse the land. After they are removed, Israel's only hope will be among the exiles. As verses 30–33 emphasize, many in exile are also faithless, coming to Ezekiel only to hear his erotic *songs*. They feign sincerity, but they come under no conviction. As Ezekiel had already recognized (20:49), his medium hampered his message. The reference to *all this* in verse 33 is unclear; whatever *it* is will vindicate Ezekiel. The chapter, strategically placed to guide

> **The Fulfillment of Ezekiel's Promises of Blessing**
> *Although modern interpreters sometimes argue over possible future fulfillment of Ezekiel's prophecies, his exilic audience would have expected the blessings to be fulfilled in as tangible, material, and literal a way as the curses, for both curses and blessings are announced in the same covenant and do not await Ezekiel's distant future (12:25–28; 36:8).*
>
> *Biblical prophecy has within it the seeds of its own nonfulfillment. Jeremiah 18:7–10 articulates the principle of conditional prophecy: all prophecy regarding a people's well-being or woe has an inherent element of conditionality in it. For example, the Ninevites repented and were spared even though Jonah offered no conditions of repreive (Jonah 3:6–10), as Jeremiah 18:7–8 allows. Ezekiel's exilic audience's situation confirms Jeremiah 18:9–10: the blessings were not fulfilled, presumably because they did not obey.*
>
> *The category of unfulfilled prophecy recognizes that Yahweh's promises of blessing extend genuine offers to Israel that give tangible expressions to God's ultimate desires for them, but that such offers must be received in faithful obedience as the covenant relationship demands (Lev 26:40–45).*

the reading of the prophecies of blessing that follow, offers no real optimism that the exiles will return in heart to Yahweh.

34:1–39:29 In the following blessings, Yahweh frees Ezekiel to announce a period of unity, prosperity, security, and relationship with God. These oracles fall into three sections: oracles about Yahweh's sheep (34:1–31), about mountains (35:1–36:15), and about the land of Israel (36:16–39:29). The unexpressed purpose is to call the exiles to obedience by showing them what is in store if they obey. By once again extending the covenant blessings to exiled Israel, Yahweh demonstrates a readiness to act on "behalf of his holy name" by keeping covenant. Each section begins with Yahweh's determination to remove the defilements that make obedience difficult.

34:1–31 Ezekiel recycles and expands the oracle in Jeremiah 23:1–8. Both assume the Davidic covenant language of 2 Samuel 7. Verses 1–10 are indistinguishable from a doom oracle. *Shepherds* assumes the common ancient Near Eastern theme of a king as a shepherd over his people. The plural suggests that all leaders are in view. They are guilty of selfishness, seen in both passive neglect and active oppression, leaving the flock effectively with *no shepherd*. Fisch (229) suggests this neglect applies most pointedly to the most vulnerable in Israelite society, the widow, orphan, and alien. Yahweh, then, claims them as *my sheep*. The scattering here reflects the Assyrian and Babylonian deportations, and *wild animals* is a cipher for their deporters. It was customary to hold shepherds accountable for lost sheep. They either had to pay for those lost or bring a piece of a mangled sheep to the owner (Exod 22:13; Amos 3:12). Here, Yahweh *removes them*.

Yahweh, the primary actor in the remainder of the chapter, will regather his flock and protect it from external threats. *Scattered on a day of clouds and darkness* refers to the deportations that came with the falls of Samaria and Jerusalem (32:7–8). Yahweh's care is portrayed in idyllic fashion, and the justice lacking earlier will be abundant. In addition to scrutinizing the shepherds, Yahweh will also cull the sheep (verses 10–17). This section suggests that Israel's leaders were not the only problem. Some among the exiles made life difficult for others. As in 20:37–38, the *rams and goats* are the oppressing upper classes that victimize those weaker among them. By removing the *shepherds of Israel*, however, Yahweh appears to cancel the Davidic covenant, particularly for a Davidide to be Israel's king perpetually. Verses 23–24 reaffirm Yahweh's pledge to be *their God*. Also, his *servant David will be prince among them*. This promise is irrevocable, but it is not unconditional (see Waltke 130–32).

Yahweh's blessings include more than a new leader; they will inaugurate a new phase of relationship with his people, a *covenant of peace* (compare especially Isa 54:7–10). *Peace* [Hebrew *shalom*] conveys many meanings here: harmony between Yahweh and the people, between Yahweh and nature, between oppressive and oppressed people, and between people and nature. The *wild beasts* could either be literal or refer to Nebuchadrezzar's armies or to the bad leaders. Verses 27–30 offer curse reversals to prove to *the house of Israel* that the faithful Judeans have Yahweh among them, even without a temple. Verse 31 echoes the covenant formula ("They will be my people, and I will be their God").

35:1–15 Having removed Israel's bad leaders and people and promised its ideal ruler, Yahweh addresses the external obstacles to Israel's coming prosperity. The oracle begins with the need to remove Edom (35:1–15) before the restoration of the mountains of Israel (36:1–15). The oracle against *Mount Seir* (a metonymy for Edom) is punctuated with four recognition formulas, a clear indication of Yahweh's severe hostility. The opening segment announces the outcome twice, *you will be desolate*. Yahweh will destroy Edom because it willingly assisted the Babylonians against Israel during Jerusalem's siege and afterward (Obad 11–14; Ps 137:7). This betrayal was the culmination of *an ancient* (better, "enduring") *hostility* going back to Jacob and Esau. Verse 6 mentions blood [Hebrew *dam*] four times in a veiled wordplay on Edom [Hebrew *edom*]. The latter part is better rendered, "Surely, it was bloodshed borne of hatred, and the blood avenger will pursue you." Edom will also fall because it annexed parts of Judah after it helped

---

The Tasks of Shepherds

Ezekiel 34:4, 16 delineate seven tasks of shepherds: seek lost sheep; bring back the strayed; bind up the injured; strengthen the weak; heal the sick; remove or destroy belligerent sheep that harm the peaceful; and treat the sheep gently, not harshly. The New Testament describes the responsibilities of elders in similar language (Acts 20:17; 28:30; 1 Pet 5:1–4).

deport Judah's population. Like other nations, Edom *boasted against* Yahweh; like them, it will fall. The oracle ends with another twofold reference to *desola*ti*on*. Yahweh has not deserted the land; he still guards *the inheritance of the house of Israel*.

36:1–15 Verses 1–15 are spoken to the *mountains of Israel* and assume the oracles against *the rest of the nations, and against all Edom*. Zimmerli (*Ezekiel 2*, 231–32) suggests this oracle is an editorially manufactured composite, evident from the sevenfold repetition of *This is what the Sovereign Lord says*. On the other hand, the repetition supplies strong reinforcement to Yahweh's claim to be able to act. It also reverses the curses of chapter 6. The initial section (verses 1–7) responds to the enemies' gloating over the land's depopulation. In *typical fashion*, the nations uttered *gossip*, *slander*, *insults*, and *disgrace* against God's vanquished people (verses 3, 15). In an application of *lex talionis* ("an eye for an eye"), the *scorn of the nations* against *the land of Israel* will return to the nations who gave it. Yahweh had always intended the land of Israel to be the site of blessing for his people (verses 8–15). Landedness was an essential element of the promise to Abraham (Gen 12:6–7; 13:14–18; 35:11–13). Yahweh promises to make the land fertile (compare Lev 26:1–13) and to bring the exiles home (compare 11:7). Ezekiel's words clearly limit this promise to the exiles in Ezekiel's day. In retrospect, they did not return soon, and the land did not literally become all that was described for it here. The reason lay in the dispirited exiles' failure to repent.

Landedness was but one leg of a three-sided relationship (deity-people-land) assumed across many ancient Near Eastern theologies (see Block, *Gods*, 21–153). So interconnected were these concepts that, when a nation's land suffered natural calamities, or when a nation's people were massacred or deported, other nations assumed the defeat or impotence of that nation's gods. Thus, by invoking the covenant curses, Yahweh created a bad reputation for himself in the eyes of the nations. The remaining oracles through chapter 39 address these problems. Yahweh rehearses why the deportation was necessary (36:16–21), he reasserts the people's purpose to be a witness to the surrounding nations (36:22–38), and promises to reenliven the demoralized exiles so that they will reinhabit the land with joy, hope, and unity (37:1–28). Finally, events will confirm both Yahweh's power toward the nations and concern for the people and land when defeating Israel's enemies (38:1–39:29).

36:16–38 With a revolting simile, Yahweh explains Israel's deportation. Like blood in a menstruant's rag, the Israelites had saturated the land with defilement. Of necessity they were *scattered through the countries*. Significantly, in Leviticus, exile is among the last curses threatened. While Yahweh's people are off their land, it can *rest and enjoy its sabbaths* (Lev 26:34). Israel's exile, however, had the unwelcome effect of bringing Yahweh's ability and reputation into disrepute (*they profaned my holy name*). In response, Yahweh determines that divine honor is too important to allow the profanation to continue. In a replay of the exodus, Yahweh will reestablish the people-land relationship by bringing Israel *back into your own land* (see "my land," verse 5). In a reenactment of the covenant ceremony at Sinai (Exod 24:1–11), God will *sprinkle clean water on* them. The cleansing theme recalls the menstruant's responsibilities before reestablishing social contact (Block, *Ezekiel 25–48*, 347). In addition, God will supply them with a *new spirit*. This is not the indwelling Holy Spirit but the renewed national spirit described in 37:1–14. The reestablished deity-people-land relationship will be complete: *You will live in the land I gave your forefathers; you will be my people and I will be your God*. Wilson ("Ezekiel," 690) fails to see the conceptual parallels with Deuteronomy 30:1–10 and so wrongly asserts that Israel will return while still wicked. Verses 29–38 are typical expansions of previous language, with one surprise. Whereas before Yahweh refused to hear Israel's pleas (8:18; 14:3; 20:3, 31), he will *once again yield* to their cries (verse 37).

> **God & People**
>
> "I am [will be] your God and you are [will be] my people" occurs frequently throughout the Bible to denote the intimate mutual commitment of God and his people to each other (for example, Deut 29:13; Hos 2:23; Jer 7:23; 11:4; 24:7; 2 Cor 6:16; Rev 21:3).

37:1–28 The two oracles of chapter 37 continue to describe Israel's restoration. The elements of the vision of verses 1–14 arise from the exiles' despairing complaint in verse 11: *Our bones are dried up and our hope is gone; we are cut off*. This description is a metaphor for Yahweh's ability to inspire the dispirited exiles to renewed hope, obedience, and trust in his power to revivify them nationally. The envisioned bones are remains of bodies left unburied (29:5; 32:4–6). When asked, *Can these bones live?* Ezekiel defers answering, finally appearing to comprehend that Israel's fortunes lie with Yahweh's power. The *wind/breath/spirit* [Hebrew *ruach*] wordplay throughout echoes Yahweh's giving life to Adam in Genesis 2:7. The "resurrection" here is metaphorical, echoing a new exodus motif. NIV misleadingly capitalizes *Spirit*, wrongly implying fulfillment in the Christian era.

The exiles are at their lowest point, so low that the dead-in-the-grave metaphor is apt (verses 15–28). To motivate them, Yahweh offers like terms of Israel's zenith: the peaceful days of the undivided kingdom under David and Solomon. In this final sign act, Ezekiel is to *join* sticks representing Judah and Ephraim (Israel) in his hand. The ancient rivalries will be more than permanently undone, as the thematic words *one/single* [Hebrew *echad*] and *forever/everlasting* [Hebrew *olam*] demonstrate. The promises repeat earlier ones. Since Yahweh is one (Deut 6:4), so Israel must be one. This intention will be realized most fully in their future combined worship in Yahweh's abiding *sanctuary*.

> **Reuniting Israel & Judah**
> Hezekiah (2 Chron 30), Josiah (2 Chron 35:1–19), Jeremiah (Jer 30:1–11; 31:1–9, 15–20), *and* Ezekiel (Ezek 37:15–28) championed a reunification of all Israel, which had been divided since the split under Jeroboam I and Rehoboam (1 Kgs 12:1–19).

38:1–39:29 The oracles against Gog and his allies continue Yahweh's promises of a bright future for the dispirited exiles. Modern readers, eager to discover the identity of an end time antagonist to God's people, wholly miss the point. While the language echoes ancient Near Eastern myths, contains apocalyptic symbolism, and groups a variety of elements by sevens, the audience is *my people Israel* (that is, the exiles), portrayed as having returned to *the mountains of Israel*. Given the exiles' present location and despairing attitude, Yahweh's promise once again addresses their deepest psychological fears, namely, that after their hoped-for return, Yahweh will summon the worst enemy imaginable to invade Israel, only to have it meet catastrophic and final defeat by Yahweh himself. In short, after Israel's future return, there will never again arise an enemy like Babylon.

38:1–9 All attempts to identify *Gog of the land of Magog* are speculative. Although some claim Gog refers to Gyges of Lydia, or stands as a cipher for Babylon, Gog and his seven allies simply personify the exiles' deepest fears that their ruinous experiences with Assyria and Babylon will be repeated in the future when they least expect it. The image of unfortified villages assumes that the covenant of peace (34:25–31) is in force. Three new allies join, bringing the number to ten, symbolically representing all of Israel's enemies. Just as he had previously used a willing Nebuchadrezzar for his purposes, Yahweh will now *show* himself *holy through* Gog *before* everyone's *eyes*.

> **Apocalyptic Language**
> The answer to the question in 38:17 is, "No, not literally, but yes, typologically." Apocalyptic language pervades verses 19–22. A literal fulfillment would bring untold destruction on the very land Yahweh is protecting! Here, the earthquake symbolizes Yahweh's direct intervention to change spiritual realities (compare Exod 19:18; Ps 97:4–5; Isa 24:18–20; Zech 14:4–5; Matt 27:51–53). The symbolic seven weapons Yahweh uses against Gog recall Yahweh's actions against Canaan (Deut 7:17–24).

39:1–16 Ezekiel farcically describes Yahweh's dispatch of Gog and his allies. Like a puppeteer, Yahweh twirls, drags, brings, and flings Gog *against the mountains of Israel*. Upon arrival, the ominous, menacing Gog, leader of the world's best-equipped armies, face-to-face with Yahweh, has his weapons knocked from his hands and drops dead before firing an arrow. Yahweh abandons the enemy to the *carrion birds and to the wild animals* – an image expanded upon in verses 17–20. After watching Yahweh defeat Gog from the sidelines, Israel collects seven types of arms to burn for *seven years*: *weapons, small and large shields, bows and arrows, war clubs and spears*. Gog and his allies will eventually be buried; it will take *seven months* to do so. The repetition of *seven* represents the finality of Yahweh's action. Removing all traces of Gog will finally *cleanse the land*. Ezekiel serves up humorously grotesque fare in this out-of-sequence expansion of verse 4. It is not hard to imagine a banquet hall, scavengers seated in an orderly fashion, garnished platters of dismembered body parts on the tables, and goblets filled with blood raised in toast to Yahweh's victory. Surprisingly, Yahweh serves the sacrificial meal of human flesh. Verses 21–24 summarize the negative themes of the book. Verses 25–29 summarize the essence of chapters 34–39. The final verse reasserts Yahweh's intention to revitalize the nation, seen in 37:1–14.

40:1–48:35 For ancient Hebrew readers, the details of chapters 40–48 provided the climactic end of Ezekiel's book. For contemporary readers, these same details seem almost insurmountably ancient and beyond our ability to grasp. Perhaps more than any other section of the Old Testament, these details remind us that this vision was not written to us; it was preserved for us. Earlier readers struggled, too, as Fisch (265) notes:

> The Rabbis of the Talmud (Men. 45a) remarked that only the prophet Elijah, who will herald the ultimate redemption, will elucidate these chapters. They added the observation that had it not been for Rabbi Chanina ben Hezekiah, who explained several of these difficulties, the Book of Ezekiel would have been excluded from the Scriptural canon.

Many contemporary interpreters hold that these chapters are best understood eschatologically (see Wilson, "Ezekiel," 693). While this view has a long history, it is fundamentally flawed. This vision represents Yahweh reaching out to his people in Babylonian exile. Despite the exiles' idolatrous attachment to Solomon's temple, Yahweh here amazingly offers to build another at which they can worship and offer atoning sacrifices (compare 45:13–46:15). These chapters provide for the returning exiles what the Mosaic instructions provided for the first generation of Israelites. As a vision preserved for us (not written to us) that was not and will not be fulfilled, these words still offer a glimpse into Yahweh's heart for Israel.

After a brief introduction (40:1–4), the vision falls into four large sections: the description of a new temple (40:5–43:11), its regulations for operation (43:12–46:24), its geographical setting (47:1–48:29), and the new city of Yahweh's people (48:30–35). In some sections, a large number of unique words and technical architectural terms make understanding precise details difficult.

40:1–4 Ezekiel saw this vision on 28 April 573 BCE, the second latest date notice in the book. The typical elements of a transport vision are present: the *hand of* Yahweh, the relocation to Israel, and the guide. The preponderance of multiples of five and twenty-five (for example, 40:7, 13, 15, 19, 21, 30, 47; 41:9, 14; 42:2, 16–20; 45:1–6; 48:8–22, 30–35)

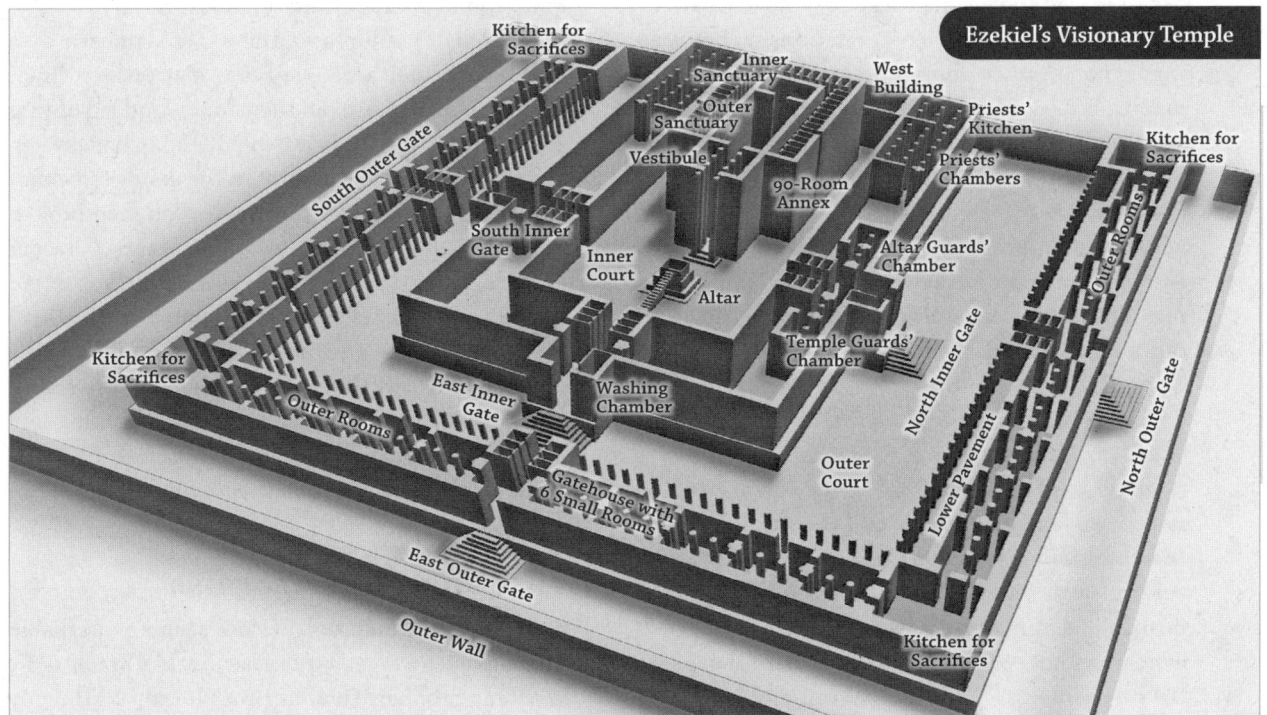
Ezekiel's Visionary Temple

leads scholars to discern allusions to the Jubilee Year (Lev 25:8–38).

40:5–43:11 The guide takes Ezekiel through the visionary temple complex, meticulously measuring every area outside and inside. In all these, only one vertical measurement is taken (40:5). The temple's *outer wall*, too thin and short to be a fortification wall, marks boundaries and controls access. The *burnt offerings*, *sin offerings*, and *guilt offerings* (40:39) mean the same things they did in Solomon's temple and in the tabernacle. Ezekiel also provides for the organization of temple space for priests and underscores the holiness of the entire building complex.

43:1–11 The meticulous measuring of the temple and its perimeter structures demonstrates to Ezekiel and his audience its perfect suitability for its divine inhabitant, who now returns. Ezekiel describes *the glory of the God of Israel* in terms similar to his earlier visions, but without mentioning the cherubim, previously protectors of Yahweh's holiness. Yahweh declares the temple to be *where I will live among the Israelites forever* (see 37:26–28). This indwelling, however, is conditioned upon Israel's renewed fidelity (verse 9). Ezekiel's audience would have been overwhelmed at the size and detail with which the new temple was constructed. The symmetrical perfection of the structures and Yahweh's meticulous attention to order demonstrates a deep desire to woo the people back.

43:12–46:24 With a new relationship between Yahweh and Israel, and a new temple in which to maintain it, comes the need for a new sacrificial system, administrators, and regulations. In this new environment, Ezekiel is cast as a new Moses, a new lawgiver. These new instructions [Hebrew *torah*] address many different issues. The new torah begins with the consecration of the new altar so that the relationship between Yahweh and the returned exiles can continue. In another clue that this vision offered a potential future to the exiles, Yahweh commands Ezekiel himself to be the inaugural priest at the altar (43:18–27; compare Lev 1–7). Ezekiel also receives *torah* for the Levites and Zadokites, the prince, the new tribal land allotments, and the ritual calendar. The exclusion of foreigners in 44:9 differs from the rule in Isaiah 56:1–8. Ezekiel 44:10–16 explains the postexilic distinction between priests and Levites, which does not seem to have been so hard and fast in the preexilic era. On the festival rules in 45:18–46:2, compare the somewhat different instructions in Leviticus 23 and Numbers 28–29. Again, Ezekiel's rules never went into effect, but they do show a powerful insight into the prophet's concern to express the beauties of Yahweh's renewed presence with Israel.

47:1–48:29 As noted earlier, a harmonious deity-people-land relationship was crucial for any ancient Near Easterner. So far in this vision, Yahweh has returned to his temple and has provided instruction to his people about how to maintain their renewed relationship through careful observance of sacrificial ritual. It remains for the final leg of the stool to be repaired. Yahweh's sanctification of the land comes by means of a *river* that inexplicably deepens without tributaries, flows over and through hills, makes fresh the most salty water on earth, and causes trees perpetually to produce fruit. But, in a vision, anything can happen. The near-mythical claims reinforce Yahweh's magnanimous offer. Life on their land, with Yahweh and the temple in its midst and as its life-giving source, would be indescribably and unimaginably wonderful... when they returned. Ezekiel 47:13–48:29 instructs Israel as to how to parcel their property properly. This passage calls to mind Joshua 13–19.

48:30–35 In a wordplay, the former capital, the "City of Peace" [Hebrew *yerushalayim*] is replaced with "Yahweh is There" [Hebrew *Yahweh-shammah*]. In keeping his promises to Jerusalem (16:53, 55), Yahweh reconstructs and renames the city.

This vision addresses the exiles' concern over the severed deity-people-land relationship. Their deportation had broken the people-land leg of that theological triad. The invasion of Judah had broken the deity-people leg, at least in the dispirited exiles' minds. The destruction of the temple had broken the third leg. But Ezekiel's visions assert Yahweh's faithfulness. God had reestablished the temple with exquisite care, then reinhabited it. God had destroyed Israel's enemies in the guise of Gog. One more leg was left to mend: the people must return from exile, both physically and spiritually. Yet, Yahweh cannot coerce this most important move. The exiles' return must be their own doing.

THEOLOGICAL REFLECTIONS

That Yahweh would use Ezekiel seems remarkable. Throughout, we get hints that Ezekiel was hardly a willing prophet. The few times he speaks directly to Yahweh, he shows ignorance, recalcitrance, or irritation. His sympathies lay with Jerusalem and its leadership rather than Yahweh. One wonders whether Ezekiel's vulgar language was given by Yahweh, or whether Yahweh used a priest already practiced in coarse speech. The latter view should not surprise; Yahweh seems to delight in choosing the problematic and unpolished to speak for him, as the choices of Moses, Balaam's ass, Micaiah ben Imlah, Amos, Jeremiah, and Jonah make clear. These choices show that Yahweh is prone to act through difficult and unlikely means. His primary covenant partner Abraham was a polytheist (Josh 24:14), prone to half-truths and stubborness. The nation descended from him was barely worth notice from the start, and had adopted Egypt's religious views as its own. Its second king, a "man after God's own heart," was arguably a rapist, certainly a murderer, and a negligent father. Israel's third king was the very model of inconstancy: he built Yahweh's temple but married the daughters of the nations.

Yet remarkably Yahweh persists in working through all these and others like them. That Yahweh chooses to use imperfect spokespersons to declare faithless, despairing Israelites in exile his "remnant" should give his imperfect, sometimes doubting servants of today hope.

Many view Ezekiel's repetitious use of the recognition formula "Then they will know that I am the Lord" as a claim that Yahweh is in omnipotent control. Perhaps more than any other Old Testament book except Psalms, Ezekiel proclaims Yahweh's sovereignty over history. Or so it seems. Most often the formula functions to assert that, when the covenant curses come to fruition, both the exiles and those remaining in Judah will perceive the calamities as intentional invocations of the curses by Yahweh (Ezek 6:7, 10). The realization that Yahweh faithfully executed the covenant curses will permit Israel to anticipate his faithful orchestration of the covenant blessings. The exiles had experienced the curses: they had survived Jerusalem's siege in 597 BCE, witnessed the deaths of friends in that event, and suffered deportation. Nevertheless, Ezekiel's companion exiles never turned their minds to the covenant. Instead, they despaired at Yahweh's inability to protect them and sneered at prophetic pronouncements. That the blessings were not materially fulfilled to them suggests that most never came to recognize Yahweh's invocation of the curses as the prelude to the certainty of his blessings. The blessings-curses-blessings restored sequence of the covenant was not realized as Yahweh hoped.

What, then, is one to make of Ezekiel's portrayal of Yahweh's sovereignty? Contemporary readers who assign all events to Yahweh's omnipotent, omniscient control are rightly caught short by Yahweh's unrealized plans and prophecies. Fundamentally, the conditions for Yahweh to enact blessings are limited by the same covenant condition that assigns the curses (see 18:30–32; 33:10–20). The essential nature of the relationship between Yahweh, intoned by the covenant formula, "I will be their God and they will be my people," requires reciprocal fidelity. Yahweh self-limits sovereignty to allow room for free, genuine response. Despite Yahweh's intense desire for Israel's happiness, and equally intense dislike for sin, Yahweh awaits Israel's genuine repentance (Lev 26:40–46; Deut 30). To act unilaterally after invoking the curses, apart from Israel's return, would undermine the very faithfulness the recognition formula communicates. Yahweh faithfully waits for Israel to turn. Until then, self-imposed covenant limitations only permit Yahweh to plead for Israel's return.

FOR FURTHER STUDY

Michael Fishbane, "Sin and Judgment in the Prophecies of Ezekiel," *Interpretation* 32 (1984): 131–50.

R. A. Parker and W. H. Dubberstein, *Babylonian Chronology 626 BCE–CE 75* (Providence, R.I.: Brown University Press, 1956).

Bruce K. Waltke, "The Phenomenon of Conditionality within Unconditional Covenants," in *Israel's Apostasy and Restoration: Essays in Honor of Roland K. Harrison* (ed. Avraham Gileadi; Grand Rapids: Baker, 1988), 123–39.

WORKS CITED

Leslie C. Allen, *Ezekiel 1–19* (Dallas: Word, 1994).

———, *Ezekiel 20–48* (Dallas: Word, 1990).

Joseph Blenkinsopp, *Ezekiel* (Louisville: John Knox, 1990).

Daniel I. Block, *Ezekiel 1–24* (Grand Rapids: Eerdmans, 1997).

———, *Ezekiel 25–48* (Grand Rapids: Eerdmans, 1998).

———, *The Gods of the Nations: Studies in Ancient Near Eastern National Theology* (2d ed.; Grand Rapids: Baker, 2000).

Lawrence Boadt, "Ezekiel," in *The New Jerome Biblical Commentary* (ed. Raymond Brown et al.; Englewood Cliffs, N.J.: Prentice-Hall, 1990), 305–28.

John Calvin, *Commentary on the Book of the Prophet Isaiah* (4 vols.; trans. W. Pringle; Grand Rapids: Christian Classics Ethereal Library, 1999).

Solomon Fisch, *Ezekiel* (London: Soncino, 1960).

Michael Fishbane, *Biblical Interpretation in Ancient Israel* (Oxford: Clarendon, 1985).

Brandon L. Fredenburg, *Ezekiel* (Joplin, Mo.: College Press, 2002).

John Goldingay, *Models for Interpretation of Scripture* (Grand Rapids: Eerdmans, 1995).

Moshe Greenberg, *Ezekiel 21–37* (Garden City, N.Y.: Doubleday, 1997).

Stephen A. Kaufman, "The Structure of the Deuteronomic Law," *Maarav* 1/2 (1978–1979): 105–58.

Johan Lust, "Ezekiel 36–40 in the Oldest Greek Manuscript," *Catholic Biblical Quarterly* 43 (1981): 517–33.

Marti Nissinen, C. L. Seow, and Robert K. Ritner, *Prophets and Prophecy in the Ancient Near East* (Atlanta: Society of Biblical Literature, 2003).

Mark S. Smith, *The Early History of God* (2d ed.; Grand Rapids: Eerdmans, 2002).

Douglas Stuart, *Hosea–Jonah* (Waco, Tex.: Word, 1987).

John B. Taylor, *Ezekiel* (Downers Grove, Ill.: InterVarsity, 1969).

Emanuel Tov, "Recensional Differences between the MT and LXX of Ezekiel," *Ephemerides theologicae Lovanienses* 62 (1986): 89–101.

Bruce K. Waltke, "The Phenomenon of Conditionality within Unconditional Covenants," in *Israel's Apostasy and Restoration: Essays in Honor of Roland K. Harrison* (ed. Avraham Gileadi; Grand Rapids: Baker, 1988), 123–39.

Robert R. Wilson, "Ezekiel," in *Harper's Bible Commentary* (ed. James L. Mays; San Francisco: HarperSanFrancisco/Society of Biblical Literature, 1988): 652–94.

―――, "Interpretation of Ezekiel's Dumbness," *Vetus Testamentum* 22 (1972): 91–104.

Walther Zimmerli, *Ezekiel 1* (trans. Ronald E. Clements; Philadelphia: Fortress, 1979).

―――, *Ezekiel 2* (trans. James D. Martin; Philadelphia: Fortress, 1983).

Daniel

Mark W. Hamilton

CHAPTER CONTENTS

- Contexts 653
- Commentary 654
    - Life at Court · 1:1–6:28 654
    - Visions of the Future · 7:1–12:13 660
    - A Final Vision · 10:1–12:13 662
- Theological Reflections 663
- For Further Study 664
- Works Cited 664

MAPS, TABLES, & FEATURES

- Events in the Book of Daniel 653
- Babylon & Susa 654
- Additions to Daniel 654

The book of Daniel has long inspired Jews and Christians with its lessons of faithfulness in adversity. In reading this story of people who remained faithful to God even when great powers threatened their existence, it is important to keep a few things in mind.

CONTEXTS

Daniel is really two books in one. Chapters 1–6 contain a series of stories about wise Jews at the royal court. Chapters 7–12 contain several visions about a future resolution of the conflict between good and evil. Also, the book is written in two different languages: 1:1–2:4a and 8:1–12:13 are in Hebrew, while 2:4b–7:28 are in Aramaic. Originally, the court stories in the book circulated orally apart from the apocalyptic section at the end. By combining these differing materials, the author of Daniel captures a flavor of foreignness and alienation.

The two parts of the book are nevertheless interlinked, not only because they are about the same person, but also because they consider the same problem – how to be God's people under foreign rule. Literarily, chapters 2–7 are arranged in a ring structure: 2 and 7 report visions of the coming divine kingdom; 3 and 6 discuss potential martyrdom of Jews who worship God alone; and 4 and 5 expose arrogant kings. This careful arrangement, with chapter 7 as a bridge between the book's two parts, creates an overarching unity.

The book covers events over a period of several centuries. The stories describe the Jews' exile under the Babylonians in the 500s BCE, while the visions concern mostly events from Alexander the Great down to the Jewish revolt of the 160s BCE. Whatever the time period, however, the major theological issues are the same.

The first half of the book concerns the era of the Neo-Babylonian and early Persian empires. Here we see life at court, as a courtier like Daniel tries to live faithfully to God and loyally to his king, despite the fact that some of his royal masters are less than sensible. Here the book echoes a theme that is widespread in Jewish literature of the Second Temple period, the foolishness of the Gentile king. Compare the drunken, out-of-control Ahasuerus in the book of Esther or

---

Events in the Book of Daniel
(all dates below are BCE)

- **605** Nebuchadnezzar of Babylon makes Judah a vassal state
- **586** Nebuchadnezzar destroys Jerusalem and ends the state of Judah
- **539** Babylon's last king, Nabonidus, and his son Belshazzar lose their kingdom to the Persian emperor Cyrus
- **322** Alexander the Great, king of Macedonia, destroys the Persian empire
- **301** Alexander's successor divide his empire; Palestine comes under the rule of Ptolemy, now king of Egypt
- **200** Palestine passes to the Seleucid dynasty, rulers of Syria and Mesopotamia
- **164** Antiochus Epiphanes, king of Syria, tries to impose the worship of Greek gods on the Jewish population, which in turn revolts
- **164** Antiochus dies; there are no later events referred to in the visions of Daniel

DANIEL

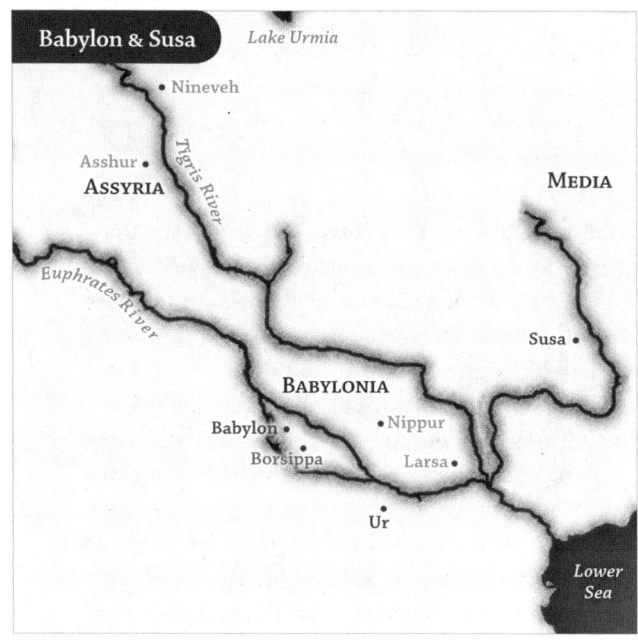

dismissive statements about kings in Ecclesiastes. Jews took a dim view of foreign royalty. In this they share the attitudes of other people subject to the great empires. Greek texts also portray Persian kings as drunken tyrants, much as Esther does, for example.

These chapters do, however, believe that faithful people can survive in the dominant system. By attending to prayer and food laws and by avoiding idolatry and acts of injustice, the good Jew can excel, even at court. Indeed, such a person's success can be a sign of God's protection of the chosen people.

The second half of the book takes a different view. Here events have darkened the picture. No longer can Jews survive under the present conditions of empire. And so God will intervene to rectify the situation and bring in the eternal kingdom. The shift is understandable in the light of the changing conditions of the second century BCE, as Jews came under increasing pressure to assimilate to Hellenistic (Greek) ways of life.

The hero of these stories is God, who speaks to the powerful through Daniel. God's words of judgment and hope inspire the book's readers with the knowledge that the powers that be do not survive forever and that present adversity will soon give way to a time of triumph.

The book's human heroes, Daniel and his three friends, must make tough decisions about how to live faithfully in a foreign land. These stories must have inspired Jews living under similar constraints.

The visions of the last half of the book do not describe a far distant future. Rather, they describe a time in real history, the early second century BCE, when Jews in Palestine had to fight for the very survival of their faith and their people. The visions do not merely recount history. They offer hope.

Finally, the book of Daniel provided visionary language for later prophets to use in interpreting their own times. The most obvious example of this process is the book of Revelation, which applies Daniel's language to the Roman Empire of the first century. Whenever religious people live under duress, such language helps express hope and trust in God. However, Daniel and Revelation do not refer to the same historical events, but only parallel ones.

COMMENTARY

LIFE AT COURT · 1:1–6:28

The stories in chapters 1–6 portray life at the royal courts in Babylon and Susa, not in a systematic way but from the point of view of a Jewish community struggling to maintain its existence under foreign

---

Additions to Daniel

The text of Daniel differs extensively between the Hebrew/Aramaic version and the Greek translation (the Septuagint). The latter includes three significant additions, all predating the time of Jesus. Between 3:23 and 3:24 the revisers of the book inserted the "Prayer of Azariah and the Song of the Three Young Men," a poem that is 68 verses long and that combines lament and praise. After chapter 12, they inserted two detective stories, "Bel and the Dragon" and "Susanna." In the first, Daniel proves that the Babylonian god Marduk does not eat the sacrifices that people give him; the priests of Marduk do. In the second, Daniel defends a wrongly accused Jewish woman from lecherous old men she has spurned. All the stories pick up themes seen elsewhere in the book, especially the dangers of living under pagan rule and the need to honor God in spite of adversity. Most editions of the Apocrypha print these additions separately from the biblical book, often under the label "Additions to Daniel," even though no ancient text transmits them separately from the rest of the book.

control. The stories identify major boundary markers of Jewish identity, especially diet, avoidance of idolatry, and prayer to Yahweh. Other possible markers, such as names or careers, appear less important, and indeed Daniel and his friends take Babylonian names and work in the royal bureaucracy. Thus the stories do not value separation from the pagan society but rather steady application to ways of life that will succeed within it while still remaining loyal to the faith of Israel. The stories also address the crucial theological question of how Yahweh rules over the nations when Israel no longer experiences political independence (Albertz 20).

1:1–21 The opening story connects Daniel's life with the end of the kingdom of Judah, though with a problematic dating of his deportation to the third year of Jehoiakim (606 BCE). Jeremiah 25:1 dates Nebuchadnezzar's invasion to the following year at the earliest, while Babylonian records indicate a date of about 598 BCE for the first siege of Jerusalem (see Collins 130–31). However one resolves the problem, the book aims to portray Daniel and his friends as typical of all Jews (though extraordinarily talented) living in the Diaspora.

> **The Diaspora**
> After the destruction of Jerusalem in 586 BCE, Jewish communities sprang up all over the Near Eastern and Mediterranean worlds. The resulting Diaspora, or "dispersion," remains a major factor in Jewish history until the present day. Until the twentieth century, Jerusalem remained only one center of Jewish life, and life outside the promised land became a standing issue for Jewish thinkers and leaders.

Verses 3–7 describe a process of recruiting and training potential leaders in the Babylonian government. Such a practice did occur in the ancient empires, and some evidence exists for Assyrian, Babylonian, and Persian bureaucrats who were members of subject peoples, even if such persons rarely rose to the top of the political structure. Verses 3–4 describe qualifications of ideal leaders, at least according to ancient thinking: descent from leaders, physical excellence, and intelligence. The NIV's *language and literature of the Babylonians* should be translated more literally "the book and language of the Chaldeans." That is, the boys learn to write Akkadian cuneiform (on clay tablets), especially texts related to telling the future (divination). Thousands of such texts exist from ancient Mesopotamia.

Changing the names of the captives (verse 7) integrates them to some extent into Babylonian society. Like many ancient names, some of theirs constitute sentences making explicitly theological statements. Thus Belteshazzar means "protect the king's life," and Abednego is a distortion of "servant of Nabu" (a major Babylonian deity). The other two names' meanings are less clear (Collins 141). Jews in the sixth through the third centuries BCE often used Babylonian or Persian names (for example Esther equals "Ishtar" and Mordecai equals "Marduka"). However, such names did not indicate unfaithfulness to Judaism, a point this book emphasizes in the following stories.

The test of Daniel's resolve (verses 8–16) involves food. No specific law in the Pentateuch forbids consuming Gentile food or wine, but Daniel opts for a vegetarian diet in order to avoid eating non-kosher meat. Later Jewish law forbade the eating of Gentile food for the same reason. The head eunuch (NIV *chief official*) allows a ten-day test, which results in Daniel's success. The eunuch's fear for his *head* (verse 10) is surely a figure of speech calculated to intimidate Daniel into eating. Daniel makes a counter-offer, however. The story reminds ancient readers of the importance of observing the food laws and of negotiating openly with Gentiles in order to live an observant Jewish life. It assumes that such a diet will prove its superiority so that no one need worry about further concessions.

Verse 17 summarizes the boys' early career in a way reminiscent of 1 Samuel 2:26 (compare Luke 2:52). Their accomplishments, all gifts from God, include a high level of literacy ("understanding in every book"). Scribes in antiquity specialized in certain kinds of documents, though the most highly skilled ones could produce everything from literary texts to royal inscriptions to letters to transcripts of rituals.

> **Divination & Magic**
> Ancient readers assumed that these practices had some validity. They worked. However, they involve danger, and so many parts of the Bible severely restrict them (for example Lev 19:26; Deut 18:9–13). Yet Joseph (Gen 44:5) as well as Daniel and his associates tell the future and excel others in doing so.

Daniel, apparently unlike the other boys, could interpret dreams and thus gain access to the ultimate source of knowledge, heaven.

2:1–49 Daniel 2 describes a dream of Nebuchadnezzar's. The text contrasts the Babylonian diviners, who have no access to divine insight, with Daniel, who does. Thus the contrast works on two levels: Daniel versus the pagan soothsayers, and Yahweh versus the idols. Even more importantly, the dream sets up a contrast between God's eternal kingdom and those transient human kingdoms that dominate Israel.

Verse 4 marks the transition from Hebrew to Aramaic as the language of the text. This shift heightens the exotic nature of the following stories of life at court.

While some Christian readers continue to identify the kingdoms mentioned in chapter two with whatever empire dominates their own time, scholars have fallen into two basic camps. Conservative scholars have identified them as Babylon, Persia, the Hellenistic kingdoms, and Rome. This typology rests on the assumption that the kingdoms of Daniel coincide exactly with those of the book of Revelation. Christian readers historically have understood the text in this way and have seen the triumphant kingdom of 2:34, 45 as the church. Most scholars, however, understand the kingdoms to be Babylon, Media, Persia, and the Hellenistic realms. The second interpretation rests on two facts: the visions of chapters 7–12 concern the Hellenistic kingdoms and nothing later (Rome is mentioned only as the Kittim in 11:30; they are not yet a dominant empire); and Greek ideas about four successive kingdoms, dating to the centuries just before and after the life of Jesus, identify Babylon, Media, Persia, and Greece as a series. On the other hand, the fact that Media never dominated Israel presents a problem for this interpretation.

Although the second interpretation is more probable, either view yields the same theological point: God will intervene in the affairs of the oppressive dominant powers in order to vindicate truth and right. The kingdoms of the world will give way to the kingdom of God.

Daniel 2 shares basic elements with Genesis 41: a king has a dream that no diviner can interpret; an Israelite in God's name offers the correct understanding; and the king rewards the Israelite. Daniel's story adds a level of challenge in that Nebuchadnezzar demands that his diviners guess the dream itself. Perhaps this element illustrates his basically tyrannical nature (verse 15), but it especially highlights Daniel's (and thus Yahweh's) superiority to the Babylonians. Daniel's foreign colleagues argue that Nebuchadnezzar's request is unprecedented, thus implying that, since kings should rule according to ancient custom (as the Babylonians certainly believed), his request lacks merit. They also argue that only the gods can do what he asks (verse 11). For the author of Daniel, this is the critical point. Only the hero Daniel has access to divine knowledge.

Verses 20–23 contain an eloquent prayer for help by Daniel. He seeks not to impress Nebuchadnezzar, but to survive the test. The opening in verse 20 offers phrases typical of psalms of praise (for example, Pss 113; 134; 135; compare Ps 122). Verse 21 in this context pointedly criticizes the Gentile kings, noting their subjection to the God of Israel. Verse 22 alludes to an idea of God as the knower and revealer of secrets (see Job 28; Prov 25:2). The specific secret now revealed concerns Nebuchadnezzar's dream (verse 23).

The audience with the king, like Joseph's (Gen 41:15–36), focuses attention on Yahweh. Daniel agrees with the Babylonian diviners that no human being can both tell and interpret the king's dream, but this impossibility becomes further proof of the might of the God of Israel (verse 28).

The description of the dream (verses 31–46) maps out the history of Jewish subjection prior to the Maccabean revolt (Collins 166–68). The metals become progressively stronger and less valuable, indicating the decreasing status of Jews under foreign rule. The division of the fourth kingdom symbolizes the breakup of Alexander's empire into several major powers. Two of them, Egypt under the Ptolemies and Syria-Mesopotamia under the Seleucids, fought over Palestine, which lay at the border of their realms.

The theological climax of the vision comes in verses 44–45, which expects God's decisive intervention in human history. The *rock cut out of a mountain* refers to the chosen people of Israel, as in Isaiah 51:1–2 (Seow 47). God will not abandon Israel even when Gentile kingdoms seem most powerful. The vision closes with a notice of the elevated status of Daniel and his colleagues (verses 48–49).

3:1–30 The text opens and closes with the actions of Nebuchadnezzar, indicating the degree to which faithfulness is a matter of response to the decisions of

---

The Kingdom of God

The term "the kingdom of God" is rare in the Old Testament, but it appears in 1 Chronicles 28:5 and 2 Chronicles 13:8. God is often called king. But the kingdom does not equal Israel, nor is it necessarily something lying far in the future. "Kingdom" is a metaphor for the perfect reign of God, which is breaking into the world. And so it is in Daniel.

others. The three Hebrew men, now provincial governors, fall victim to slander by opportunistic opponents, who charge them with not worshiping the king's gods and thus of being disloyal. According to the slanderers, true worship shows disloyalty to the dominant system. The chapter follows a seven-part narrative flow: an introduction (verses 1–7); an accusation (verses 8–12); the confrontation with the king (verses 13–18); the king's condemnation of the Jews (verses 19–23); the king's astonishment (verses 24–25); God's deliverance (verses 26–27); and the king's proclamation (verses 28–30). The proclamation of tolerance in verses 28–29 makes the story's main point. Since only Yahweh can save in such a dramatic fashion, ridiculing either Jews or their faith makes no sense. A sensible ruler, even if a pagan, should honor Israel and its God, and the state has an interest in insuring religious tolerance of the Jews. The story thus, ultimately, makes the same point as the book of Esther.

Although enforced idolatry was rare in antiquity, Jews undoubtedly experienced the pressure to conform as they engaged in business dealings and other kinds of relationships with their polytheistic neighbors. Also, martyrdom was uncommon, though it did happen. Stories about martyrdom – or as here, the divine rescue from impending martyrdom – encouraged Jews to be faithful even under the most extreme circumstances.

Gigantic statues (verse 1) did exist in antiquity (Collins 180). This one may have been overlaid in gold (compare Isa 40:19). Its odd dimensions (a height ten times its width) would have made it unstable. Possibly, the author is satirizing the Babylonians' lack of realism (compare Haman's 75-foot-high gallows [Esth 5:14]), a stupidity finding its fullest expression in their idolatry.

Verse 2 lists officials in the Babylonian empire (though the titles actually come from Persian administration). The list highlights the bravery of the three Jews, who resist such a large crowd. The story does not mention Daniel, probably because the author wishes to portray the bravery of a wider assortment of Jews, not just of one man.

Several verses focus on idolatry as a theme. Verse 12 contrasts the worship of the king's gods with the Jews' behavior. Failure to worship equaled disloyalty to the state, according to the magicians. Verse 15's *what God could deliver you from me?* changes the story to one of direct challenge to Yahweh (like Pharaoh's role in Exod 1–14).

The major transition of the story takes place at verse 24. Nebuchadnezzar's question about the number of men in the furnace draws attention to the miracle of God's deliverance of the three Jews. The *one like a son of the gods* must be an angel. Some early Christian interpreters thought that Nebuchadnezzar saw Jesus, but this is unlikely for many historical and theological reasons.

4:1–37 This text, framed as a first-person narrative by Nebuchadnezzar himself, begins with a dream in which the mighty tree is leveled. Then Daniel interprets the dream as a divine judgment on the king for his arrogance. Curiously (given the events of the previous chapter), Daniel mourns the message of the dream, Nebuchadnezzar's impending punishment.

There is a significant historical problem regarding this text. The Dead Sea Scrolls contain a similar story (see Flint 332–38), but with Nebuchadnezzar's successor Nabonidus as the absentee king. In fact, we know that Nabonidus abandoned Babylon for several years in order to live in Teima, in what is now Saudi Arabia. Some scholars suggest, therefore, that this move serves as the basis of the story, which then gets transferred to Nebuchadnezzar, the better-known king.

In the book of Daniel, however, the story functions as a morality tale about the arrogance of power (see Henze). Note verse 27, the king's analysis of his own actions (*I built ... my power, my glory*). Failure to give glory to God (in contrast with 3:29) provokes divine punishment.

The chapter's six parts (verses 1–3; 4–8; 9–18; 19–27; 28–33; and 34–37) move from a royal decree in the first person ("I") to a third-person ("he") narration. (The Old Greek translation of the chapter significantly reorganizes it, indicating that the story remained unfixed early on.) Hebrew verse numbers differ from those in English; this commentary follows the latter.

> **What Did the Men Pray?**
> At Daniel 3:24, the Septuagint adds the "Prayer of Azariah and the Song of the Three Jews," a beautiful hymn of praise (verses 1–22), description of the Babylonians' troubles in intensifying the fire (verses 23–27), and a second prayer of praise (verses 28–68). The first part of this addition, the "Prayer of Azariah," highlights the loss of the temple and true worship and the resulting emotional trauma that Jews experienced.

Like chapter 2, the story begins with a royal dream. The "tree in the middle of the earth" (better than NIV's *land*) symbolizes the universe itself; like Pharaoh in Ezekiel 31, Nebuchadnezzar claims universal rule (compare 4:1). The *watcher* (see NIV footnote) is a type of angel, also discussed in *1 Enoch* and *Jubilees*, Jewish books from the third and second centuries BCE. This being conveys God's decree of judgment (the cutting of the tree symbolizing Nebuchadnezzar).

> **1 Enoch**
> The First book of Enoch *is a collection of teachings and visions written between 350 BCE and 1 CE. Chapters 72–82 come from the Persian period and describe heavenly beings. Chapters 1–36 date to the second century BCE and resemble Daniel 7–12.*

Verses 19–27, like 2:36–45, interpret the dream in a robustly theological way. The dream emphasizes God's rule over human kingdoms. The *seven times* (verses 16, 23, and 32; compare 7:25) equals seven years. No Babylonian evidence exists for an interruption in Nebuchadnezzar's reign, and Nabonidus's trip to Teima lasted ten years. The number seven is thus symbolic, not historical. It symbolizes a complete cessation of royal rule and thus a complete testimony to the power of God.

Verses 34–35 offer the main theological claims of the chapter. The prayer of a pagan king, lately a dumb animal, attests to the sovereignty of Israel's God and the truth of Israel's faith. God is the *Most High*, who reigns over an eternal kingdom, ordering human kingdoms in whatever way ensures the greatest possible degree of justice. Verse 34 alludes to Psalm 145:13 and verse 35 to Isaiah 40:17, with its claim that the nations ultimately fail (compare Isa 24:21; 34:4). Given the ability of the powerful to act arrogantly to claim an ever greater share of power, status, and wealth, God's pursuit of justice leads inevitably to a disruption of the status quo.

5:1–31 Chapter 5 contains a story of royal extravagance, a popular theme in postexilic Jewish literature (compare Esther), as well as in contemporary Greek stories about the Persian court. The royal court serves as a moral universe counter to the one in which faithful Jews should live (see Mills). Belshazzar, the son and viceroy of Nabonidus, the last Babylonian king, throws a party using the vessels from the Jerusalem temple while the city lies under siege by the Persian armies. He thus combines sacrilege with obliviousness. The chapter consists of four sections: the introduction (verses 1–6); the failure of the diviners (verses 7–12); Daniel's audience with Belshazzar (verses 13–28); and the conclusion (verses 29–30). Earlier themes of the book appear here: the superior insight of Daniel and thus the superior wisdom of God, the lack of awareness of the king, revelation through dreams, contempt for luxury and privilege (verse 17), and the importance of submission to God on the part of the king, since the king should model moral behavior for his subjects.

Nebuchadnezzar had taken the temple's metal kitchenware as booty (2 Kgs 25:13–15). Since only the priests could use them, their use by Belshazzar's *concubines* (verses 2–3) only adds to the offense. Verse 3's reference to Babylonian deities as mere statues underscores the folly of the king's party. Jewish texts of the Diaspora highlight their dismay at idolatry.

The story portrays the king's weakness and folly in several ways. He loses control of his limbs (and possibly his bowels; see Seow 79) and *cried out* (NIV *called out* does not capture his fear). Unlike Nebuchadnezzar, he cannot command himself. His promise to make the interpreter of the words on the wall *third highest ruler* (verse 7) need not be taken literally (Collins 247). The title refers only to a very high rank.

In contrast to the king, the *queen* (probably the queen mother since she knows more than he) calmly plans a solution. She calls for Daniel. Unlike his polite response to Nebuchadnezzar's praise of him (2:27–45), Daniel brushes off Belshazzar's promises (verse 17). His answer reports past history for a present purpose, to remind the king of the price of arrogance. His condemnation of the king (verse 22) is reminiscent of the prophets.

> **Queen Mothers**
> *Stories of remarkable queen mothers survive from ancient Mesopotamia. For example, the mother of Nabonidus (and thus grandmother of Belshazzar), Adad-guppi, left an important inscription commemorating her worship of the moon-god Sin. In the late ninth century, the queen mother Shammuramat ruled Assyria. She may be the basis of the many later legends of an Assyrian queen Semiramis. Those legends circulated among the Greeks and Armenians for many centuries.*

The Aramaic words in verses 25–28 present several problems. First, it is hard to understand why no Babylonians can read the words, since some of them must have read Aramaic. Thus the problem was not one of reading but of interpretation. Second, the words at first appear to be nouns and possibly the names of weights (see Collins 251–52; Seow 82–83). If the words refer to weights, then the first two minas (*mene, mene*) might indicate the superiority of the early Babylonian rulers to the last ones, who were a mere shekel (*tekel* being the Aramaic equivalent of the Hebrew *sheqel*). Third, however, verses 26–28 interpret the first words as verbs, all referring to Belshazzar and his rule, and the last as a pun on "Persia" (*peres* is the singular form of *parsin*). The chapter, like the older biblical prophetic books, pronounces God's judgment on foreign powers that behave arrogantly (see for example Isa 13–23; Jer 46–51; Ezek 26–32; Amos 1–2; Obadiah; Nahum).

> **Ancient Weights**
> *The value of ancient weights fluctuated in antiquity. A talent varied from 45 to 90 pounds. A mina was usually 1/60 of a talent, and a shekel was 1/60 of a mina.*

The text also emphasizes the importance of memory. Belshazzar's courtiers remember the aged Daniel, who reminds the king of Nebuchadnezzar's rise and fall, which he interprets theologically in light of Israel's central ideas about the nature of God and God's actions in the world. The record of the past becomes a moral example for the present. Remembering the past is important because it helps us avoid mistakes through self-understanding and self-examination.

6:1–28 As in chapter 3, slanderers again blame a potential Jewish martyr for not praying to idols. Again, the story ends with divine rescue and the king's worship of God. The king's confession in verse 27 acknowledges (as before) God's eternal reign and, by implication, the temporariness of the king's own.

Chapter 6 adds a new ingredient, the emphasis on prayer. Daniel's faithfulness is marked by the thrice daily practice of prayer toward Jerusalem. Prayer thus moves in several directions: upward to God; outward to Jerusalem; and inward to the faithful person's soul. Daniel prays in the direction of Jerusalem to illustrate the Jews' reverence for that city as the location of God's saving actions.

The chapter consists of six parts: an introduction (verses 1–3); the plot (verses 4–9); Daniel's "crime" and sentence (verses 10–18); his deliverance (verses 19–24); the royal proclamation (verses 25–27); and the conclusion (verse 28). The story's structure closely resembles that of chapter 3.

Verse 1 offers several historical problems. First, the identity of *Darius* remains difficult. Babylonia fell to Cyrus the Great, and the three kings named Darius all lived after any historical figure named Daniel. Attempts to connect Darius to the governor of Babylonia named Gubaru are extremely speculative. Second, the Persian empire never had 120 *satraps*; the number usually ran around two dozen. Apparently Daniel uses the title loosely to include lower ranking officials (such as Nehemiah), as also some Greek writers did (see Collins 264). Third, the Persian government normally had seven cabinet officials, not three (see Ezra 7:14; Esth 1:14). The number must thus be symbolic, not literal.

The conspirators against Daniel appeal to the king's vanity (verse 7). Ancient monarchs did not think of themselves as gods (except in Egypt), but the elaborate royal protocol of the Persians did bother the Greeks, and it may lie behind the idea that a king would demand worship.

The text portrays the king as regretting his decree and fretting for Daniel's safety. Even the king must obey the law. His inability to save Daniel, however, only highlights the power of Yahweh. Again the story climaxes when a foreign king praises Israel's God (verses 16, 26–27; compare 2:47; 3:28–29; and 4:34–37).

> **The Law of the Medes & the Persians**
> *The idea that no one could repeal the laws of the Medes and Persians also appears in Esther 8:8. However, no evidence for this legal practice exists from Persia itself. In Esther such an approach to jurisprudence highlights the folly of the Persian regime, since the irrevocability of the law leads to street violence.*

Verse 17 describes a practice for sealing rooms. The king and nobles stamp their rings into clay or wax placed on the edge of the stone. Such *signet rings*, often of semiprecious stones, were common for ancient persons of means as ways of attesting to documents.

The decree in verses 26–27 does not call for an end to polytheism, but merely respect for Jewish religion. The theology of the decree draws heavily on Exodus,

Psalms and other biblical texts in portraying God as a rescuer and wonderworker (see Pss 78; 105).

VISIONS OF THE FUTURE · 7:1–9:27

While chapters 1–6 portray survivable dangers for Jews in the Diaspora, chapters 7–12 reflect an uglier reality. Jews in these visions do not flourish and so must await God's coming deliverance.

7:1–28 The chapter repeats much of the material of chapter 2, with a similar notion of a succession of kingdoms. The narrative contains five sections: an introduction in the third person (verses 1–2a); the vision proper (verses 2b–14); interpretation of the dream (verses 15–18); a clarification regarding the fourth beast (verses 19–27); and the conclusion (verse 28).

The story begins in a flashback. The *four beasts* come from the cardinal directions. The story vaguely resembles the Babylonian creation story in that creatures from the sea fight against the main deity, but Daniel differs significantly from the older story (Lacocque; Collins 286). Daniel may draw the species of beast from Hosea 13:7–8 (Collins 295), but sculptures of beasts of mixed species (especially winged lions) appeared throughout the ancient Near East. The monsters equal kingdoms who devour prey (hence the bear's *three ribs* from its prey). They may or may not equal the four kingdoms of chapter 2.

The fourth beast, because of its ferocity, receives extended comment in the text. Coins from Alexander the Great and his immediate successors portrayed a ruler wearing a horned crown, and such an image may have triggered the author's imagination here. On the other hand, horned gods and kings figured in Near Eastern art much earlier, as well. Speechmaking was an important role for monarchs, but to speak *boastfully* (verse 8) marked a king as an opponent of God (see Isa 37:23; more generally Ps 12:2–3).

The vision of God's throne (verses 9–10; compare *1 Enoch* 14), portrays the victor over the evil beasts/kingdoms. The *Ancient of Days*, namely God, sits amid a vast staff of angels. The throne consists of fiery wheels (see Ezek 1:15–21). The idea of the opened *books* echoes the ancient Near Eastern image of the "tablets of destiny," documents recording in advance all human and divine activities. Here, however, the books fall under the control of the victorious God. The figure of the *one like a son of man* (or "human being"; verse 13), like the image of God as an aged person, receives no explanation here. Traditional Christian readers read verse 13 as a reference to Jesus, but the text does not make this figure messianic or even human. It may be an angel, perhaps Michael (Collins 310; Seow 108). The vagueness of the reference did, however, warrant the later Christian interpretation. In any case, God's kingdom endures forever, in contrast to the human kingdoms that dominate Israel in Daniel's dream.

Verses 15–24 begin an extended analysis of the dream, focusing especially on the fourth kingdom. The "three and half times" of verse 24 equals three and a half years, half of seven years, and roughly the lapse between the desecration of the temple by Antiochus IV Epiphanes and its cleansing by the Maccabees (167–164 BCE). More importantly, the *time* of trouble contrasts with the *everlasting kingdom* soon to replace it (verse 27; Seow 112–13).

The climax of the crisis comes in verses 25–27, which envision the Syrian persecution of Jews. Daniel announces the divine decision to bring an end to the persecution. The text also tries to set this persecution in the context of the era's rapid political and social changes, over which Jews had no control. Such rapid change could suggest either that the world is so unstable that we can be confident in nothing; or that the world's instability is proof that momentary evils will pass away because underneath the instability is a calm stability anchored in the steadfastness of God. The writer wants us to elect the second conclusion.

> **The Ten Kings**
> Various theories exist for how to account for the ten kings of Daniel 7. They seem to include the first seven Seleucid rulers, possibly Alexander the Great, and probably Seleucid rulers down to Antiochus IV. However, the number ten may be a symbolic round number.

8:1–27 The text depicts the rise and fall of Alexander the Great. The description of him as a he-goat probably comes from the fact that his coins portray him with horns, because he sought to present himself as the offspring of the Egyptian chief god, Ammon, who was a ram. Alexander invaded the vast Persian empire in 334 BCE and gradually destroyed it. He died at age 33, master of the known world. Jews in Jerusalem welcomed Alexander and generally got on well with his successors for the next century. But the instability following his invasion and death, and then the struggle for domination among his generals, inevitably created uncertainty for everyone in the region, including Jews.

The chapter consists of four parts: an introduction (verses 1–2); a vision report (verses 3–14); the interpretation of the vision (verses 15–26); and the conclusion (verse 27). The vision takes place in Susa, a city in present-day Iran not part of the Neo-Babylonian Empire but one of the capitals of the Persian Empire (see Neh 1:1; Esth 1:2), apparently as a result of visionary transportation to the site (compare Ezek 8:3; 11:24; 40:2; see Collins 329). The *Ulai Canal*, a human-made irrigation work, has the same name in Greek sources.

The *ram* of verse 3 signifies the Persian Empire, which fell to the *goat* from the west (Alexander the Great from Macedonia; verse 7). The *four prominent horns* (verse 8) signify the breakup of Alexander's empire after his death, when his generals partitioned the region. The little horn of verses 9–12 is, again, Antiochus Epiphanes, who defiled the temple in the *Beautiful Land* (verse 9; that is, the land of Israel) and claimed semidivine status. The *Prince of the host* must be God. As in the previous chapter, the audience must recognize that even the gravest threats to their faith cannot separate them from God.

Verses 11–14 focus upon the defilement of the temple by Antiochus Epiphanes. The end of sacrifice could conceivably mean that Israel's sins were not atoned for and thus that God might not protect the people, but the text reminds its readers that such a conclusion is unwarranted. The angelic speaker (*a holy one*) presents this conclusion as beyond dispute, since only an arrogant Gentile king would argue with a heavenly being! Atonement does not depend on human actions alone, but on the sovereign choice of God, who hears a contrite people crying out for relief, and who will restore the sacrifices after 2,300 *evenings and mornings*. Since the priests in Jerusalem sacrificed each evening and morning (at the beginning and midpoint of each day), verse 14 envisions a break in the temple worship lasting 1,150 days, or about three and a half years (compare 7:25). Again, the text speaks of the crisis under Antiochus Epiphanes.

Verses 15–25 give the foregoing interpretation of the vision. The vision ends with a notice that Daniel must keep the vision a secret though it overwhelms him emotionally (the same themes appear in 7:28). Obviously, the vision did not remain secret since it appears in this book. Secrecy functions as a literary device – a fiction – emphasizing the importance of the vision as a way of encouraging a Jewish audience to persist against persecution by reminding them that God knew all along what would befall them.

9:1–27 This chapter reflects on the nature of divine revelation, particularly as it relates to human activity in the present. The chapter includes three parts: an introduction (verses 1–2); a prayer of repentance (verses 3–19); and an answer promising deliverance (verses 20–27).

Verses 1–2 introduce *Darius* as the son of *Ahasuerus* the Median, both otherwise unknown characters, and portray Daniel contemplating Jeremiah's prediction of exile (Jer 25:11, 12; 29:10). *Seventy years* is a round number, but Daniel's vision roughly corresponds with the time preceding the prophecies of Haggai and Zechariah, whose work led to the rebuilding of the Jerusalem temple. Verse 3 introduces the prayer itself by noting Daniel's discipline of his body in preparation for confronting God. Sackcloth and ashes symbolized mourning (see Isa 58:5; Lam 2:10; compare Seow 140).

The prayer of verses 4–19 resembles the penitential prayer of Nehemiah 9:5b–37 (compare Pss 78; 79; Lam 2). Daniel's prayer alternates praise to God and blame for himself and his people. Verses 11–14 recall the covenant curses of Deuteronomy 28, though with the expectation that God will eventually relent from punishing Israel when they repent (as in 1 Kgs 8:35–40, 46–51). Verses 15–18 center God's (and the reader's) attention on the distress in Jerusalem and Judah. Restoration of the temple equals restoration

---

The Prayer of Daniel

Three major theological moves occur in the prayer. First, verses 10–11 call God (and implicitly the prayer's Israelite audience) to reflect on the promises and laws of the ancient Scriptures (Law and Prophets) and thus on human sinfulness and redemption, the need for ethical behavior on the part of humans, and the reality of steadfast love and graciousness on the part of God. Second, the prayer of Daniel seeks to understand the disaster that has befallen the nation as earned punishment for sin, specifically for idolatry and social injustice (the paired sins prevalent throughout the prophetic books). Third, the return to the promised land, actually fulfilled in the late sixth century, is a prominent theme. God will restart the clock on the covenant people (see also Jer 31) and thus bless all humankind (see Isa 49; 56).

of the nation. Such a request thus functions at several literary levels: in the world of the story set in the sixth century BCE, Daniel prays for the restoration of the temple under Zerubbabel; while in the world of the ancient reader of Daniel, the prayer both anticipates the cleansing following Antiochus's desecration and reminds Jews that God has done such a thing before. Thus Daniel's prayer, though on the surface sounding desperate, invites the one praying to hope.

Verses 20–27 explicitly address the problem of the meaning of Jeremiah's prophecy. Since restoration should not give way to further devastation, any Jewish interpreter of history must try to connect experiences of the second century with the words of the already ancient book of Jeremiah. Daniel denies that the rebuilding of the temple under Zerubbabel completely fulfills Jeremiah's prophecy. His *seventy sevens* (verse 24) would equal 490 years, but the number is probably symbolic (since it does not correspond to any known sequence of events in the first millennium BCE). Daniel merely states that the final fulfillment of Jeremiah's prophecy will come when the Jews purge the temple after Antiochus's desecration. Verse 24 envisions a probationary period when God's people will put an end to sin and fulfill Daniel's prophecies and perhaps others (*seal up vision and prophecy*; see Collins 354; Seow 148). The consecration of the *most holy* [Hebrew *qodesh qodashim*, a name for the innermost part of the temple (1 Kgs 6:16; 7:50; 8:6; 2 Chron 3:8, 10; 4:22; 5:7; Ezek 41:4)] refers to the cleansing of the temple and thus the institution of regular sacrifice.

The *Anointed One* of verse 26 refers to Onias III, murdered in 171 BCE (2 *Maccabees* 4:23–28). This beginning to a turbulent period climaxes in the erection of the *abomination that causes desolation*, almost certainly the altar to Zeus that Antiochus erected in the Jerusalem temple. Chapter 9 ends without a resolution of the conflict, but that will come in the conclusion of the book.

A FINAL VISION · 10:1–12:13

Chapters 10 through 12 form a continuous vision, the longest in the book. The chapters consist of five sections: an introduction (10:1); report of an angelic vision (10:2–9); conversation with an angel (10:10–11:1); the angel's historical discourse (11:2–12:4); and a final conversation and revelation (12:5–13). Chapters 10–11 repeat much of the previous visions. Again we read a lesson on Hellenistic history, particularly as it affected Jews in Palestine. Alexander's empire broke into several parts. The Seleucids in Syria and the Ptolemies in Egypt fought over Palestine, with the Seleucids eventually prevailing. The Seleucid monarch Antiochus Epiphanes sought to destroy Jewish religion. The text responds to this by indicating God's ultimate ability to overcome even the most terrible evil.

The angelic vision in 10:2–9 begins with Daniel fasting to prepare himself for his encounter with the divine realm. Since the vision occurred in the first month, he must have fasted through Passover, indicating the seriousness of the events that the vision recounts (see Seow 155–56; but Collins 373). Daniel refrains from the celebration of the happiest time of the Jewish year in order to highlight the terrible times awaiting the book's readers.

The figure appearing in 10:4–6 resembles that in Ezekiel 9–10; the angel may be Gabriel as in chapters 8–9. *Chrysolite* (a semiprecious mineral, often greenish, of magnesium iron silicate) and other aspects of his appearance resemble the elements of the throne of God in Ezekiel 1. Since the vision terrifies Daniel, the angel assures the prophet that he is *highly esteemed* and therefore that no harm will befall him (verse 10; for the comforting of an anxious prophet, see Isa 6:7; Jer 1:9).

The conversation with the angel in 10:10–11:1 portrays Daniel's humility and relentless search for truth (verse 12) so as to benefit his people. The prince of Persia (apparently the angel in charge of Persia) resisted the angel of the vision for *twenty-one days* (verse 13), the duration of Daniel's fast (Collins 375). After explaining his delay in appearing, the angel again comforts Daniel (10:18–19), states the

---

Daniel & Jesus' Apocalyptic Visions

Mark 13 (which parallels Matt 24 and Luke 21:5–28) employs much of the language of Daniel. It is a mistake, however, to assume that they refer to the same historical events. Indeed, they cannot possibly do so without serious rearrangements of early Christian history and even understandings of Jesus. Rather, Mark recycles the images of Daniel to describe a parallel event, the destruction of Jerusalem by the Romans in 70 CE and to offer hope of God's ultimate restoration of all things in Christ. The powerful images of Daniel thus serve a new purpose in a new situation.

key point of his vision (10:20), and explains that the angel Michael will also help him.

The vision proper (11:2–12:4) describes the conflict between the Seleucid rulers of Syria and the Ptolemaic rulers of Egypt, who fought over Palestine throughout the late third and early second centuries BCE. It also mentions the marriage alliance between Berenike of Egypt and Antiochus II of Syria (11:6), the rise of Ptolemy III, Berenike's brother (11:7), the changes of military fortunes under Seleucus III and Antiochus III of Syria (11:8–13), the conflicts in Judea between supporters of Syria and Egypt (11:14–19), and the rise of Antiochus IV, the great foe of the Jewish people (11:20–12:4).

Antiochus comes in for severe criticism, not only for his arrogance, but for his mad attitude toward the God of Israel, and even his own gods (11:36–39; compare *1 Maccabees* 1:41–50). Antiochus emphasizes the worship of Olympian Zeus, even, says Daniel, to the detriment of other gods. The *one desired by women* (verse 37) was the god Tammuz/Adonis, who died and rose from the dead and whose worship especially drew women. Despite initial successes, however, Antiochus's actions lead to his downfall and thus to the deliverance of the faithful among the Jews.

Daniel ends with a reflection on the differences between the faithful and the unfaithful. The former have their names *written in the book* (12:2), that is, the book of life (related to other books in Dan 7:10; 10:21; compare the so-called *Book of the Heavenly Luminaries* from the Dead Sea Scrolls). The righteous dead experience resurrection. Again, Daniel 12 is the only text in the Old Testament that unequivocally expects a resurrection of the dead, though it does not explicitly describe their subsequent state, nor does it mention the fate of the wicked dead.

According to 12:7, the crisis under Antiochus Epiphanes would last three and a half *times* (or years). By emphasizing its relative brevity, the vision encourages readers to persevere until the resurrection. As a time of trial, it can only lead to the refinement of the saints. Daniel 12:11 describes the gap in sacrifice between the desecration of the temple by Antiochus and its cleansing by the Maccabees, an event now commemorated in the Feast of Hanukkah.

Like the New Testament, Daniel does not try to explain the precise timing of the resurrection, the nature of the resurrected human body, the specifics of the life of the blessed with God, or other questions that we as readers (and believers!) naturally ask. The focus is exclusively upon the divine promise that we will someday be saved, and evil will no longer threaten in any way. In the meantime, we persevere.

THEOLOGICAL REFLECTIONS

The theology of Daniel takes the shape of stories and visions, not systematic treatises. Still, several major themes emerge. First, Yahweh, the God of Israel, is in fact the only God. God reveals the future to whomever he wishes. God judges kingdoms and rulers on the basis of their behavior, particularly as regards their treatment of the poor and vulnerable. Second, God insures the continuity of the story of Israel. Even in exile, under the most terrible conditions, God redeems the chosen people and provides for them. Since many Jews never returned to the land of Israel but continued to live in the Diaspora, such a vision of the universality of God was extremely important. Third, Israel thus does not exist as a group of people by virtue of their location in a given locale, even a land "flowing with milk and honey" promised to the ancestors (as Deuteronomy emphasizes), but because of their commitment to the basic norms of the law. Daniel especially emphasizes observance of the food laws (chapter 1), avoidance of idolatry, and prayer toward Jerusalem. These boundary issues make a person a Jew, and thus a faithful person. Fourth, prayer in this view is an act of radical orientation to the ultimate reality. Prayer brings the faithful person into contact with both God and other people at prayer, and thus with the Jewish people throughout the ages. Fifth, Israel lives in a hostile world (especially in chapters 7–12) in which the powerful both worship false gods and live by false mores. The visions of the crisis of the

> **Daniel & Resurrection**
> *Daniel 12 is the only text in the Old Testament that clearly talks about a resurrection from the dead, which will result from God's decisive saving action. Like Jesus in Matthew 24, Daniel merges the saving events of a particular time (here the second century BCE) into the final time of salvation, in which the dead are really raised. Timing is not the text's particular concern. The ultimate destiny of God's people is.*

second century in particular wish to portray the fragility of the seemingly invincible evil empires. They fall under God's judgment because of their unethical behavior.

FOR FURTHER STUDY

Donald E. Gowan, *Daniel* (Nashville: Abingdon, 2001).

Theodoret of Cyrus, *Commentary on Daniel* (trans. by Robert C. Hill; Atlanta: Society of Biblical Literature, 2006).

WORKS CITED

Rainer Albertz, *Israel in Exile: The History and Literature of the Sixth Century BCE*. (Atlanta: Scholars Press, 2003).

John Collins, *Daniel* (Minneapolis, Minn.: Fortress, 1993).

Peter W. Flint, "The Daniel Tradition at Qumran," in *The Book of Daniel: Composition and Reception* (ed. John J. Collins and Peter W. Flint; 2 vols.; Leiden: Brill, 2001), 2:328–67.

Matthias Henze, *The Madness of King Nebuchadnezzar* (Leiden: Brill, 1999).

André Lacocque, "Allusions to Creation in Daniel 7," in *The Book of Daniel: Composition and Reception* (ed. John J. Collins and Peter W. Flint; 2 vols.; Leiden: Brill, 2001), 1:114–31.

Tim Meadowcroft, "Exploring the Dismal Swamp: The Identity of the Anointed One in Daniel 9:24–27," *Journal of Biblical Literature* 120 (2001): 429–49.

Mary Mills, "Household and Table: Diasporic Boundaries in Daniel and Esther," *Catholic Biblical Quarterly* 68 (2006): 408–20.

Uriel Rappaport, "Maccabean Revolt," *Anchor Bible Dictionary* (1992) 4:433–39.

C. L. Seow, *Daniel* (Louisville: Westminster John Knox, 2003).

Hosea

Philip G. Camp

CHAPTER CONTENTS

Contexts 665
Commentary 666
   Superscription · 1:1 666
   Hosea's Wife & Children · 1:2–2:1 666
   The Marriage Analogy Applied to God & Israel · 2:2–23 666
   Reconciliation Illustrated · 3:1–5 667
   Israel on Trial · 4:1–19 667
   Judgment on the Brazen Prostitute · 5:1–7 667
   An Ineffective Cure · 5:8–15 668
   An Exhortation to Return to God · 6:1–3 668
   God Longs for His Children · 6:4–11a 668
   A Self-Destructive Nation · 6:11b–7:16 669
   Illegitimate Kings & Gods · 8:1–6 669
   Reaping the Whirlwind · 8:7–10 669
   Displeasing Sacrifices & Misplaced trust · 8:11–14 669
   The Return to Captivity · 9:1–6 669
   The Prophet: Watchman or Madman? · 9:7–9 670
   Bereaved of Children · 9:10–17 670
   The Beginning & End of Israel's Idolatry · 10:1–8 670
   Breaking New Ground · 10:9–15 670
   God's Parental Love for Israel · 11:1–11 670
   Past Examples, Present Evil · 11:12–12:14 671
   A Matter of Life & Death · 13:1–16 671
   An Invitation to Return · 14:1–9 672
Theological Reflections 672
For Further Study 673
Works Cited 673

MAPS, TABLES, & FEATURES

   The Assyrian Empire in the 8th-Century BCE 668

The Book of Hosea presents God as one who longs for Israel and desires their wholehearted devotion, but Israel refuses such a relationship with God by trusting in idols and foreign alliances. Therefore, Hosea announces both the judgment of God upon his people but also God's desire to restore them. The primary audience is the northern kingdom, Israel, though some oracles also address Judah (1:7, 11; 4:15; 5:5, 10–15; 6:4, 11; 8:14; 10:11; 11:12; 12:2).

CONTEXTS

Little is known about the prophet Hosea. He is the *son of Beeri* (1:1), who is otherwise unknown, the husband of *Gomer* (1:2–3), and the father of at least three children (1:3–9). According to the superscription (1:1), Hosea's activity extends from sometime in the reign of King Jeroboam II of Israel (786–746 BCE) to sometime in the reign of King Hezekiah of Judah (715–687 BCE), a minimum of about thirty years.

Hosea witnessed one of the most turbulent times in the histories of Israel and Judah. His career began as an era of peace and prosperity for Israel and Judah, during the reign of Jeroboam II, was coming to a close. Following Jeroboam's death, Israel experienced a period of turmoil that lasted until the kingdom's end in 721 BCE. The final twenty-five years saw six kings take the throne of Israel, usually through violence (see 2 Kgs 15:8–31). Beginning around 734 BCE, the Assyrians asserted control over Syria-Palestine, and eventually both Israel and Judah became Assyrian vassals. In 734 BCE, kings Pekah of Israel and Rezin of Aram allied to oppose Assyria. When Jotham of Judah and his son, Ahaz, refused to join them, the allied kings attacked Judah with the intent of replacing the king, the so-called Syro-Ephraimite War. Ahaz appealed to the Assyrian king Tiglath-Piliser III for help, and he responded by wiping out Aram and subduing Israel, which was spared only because Hoshea seized the throne and surrendered (2 Kgs 15:37–16:9; Isa 7:1–9). When Hoshea later rebelled against Assyrian rule, the Assyrians brought the northern Israelite kingdom to an end (2 Kgs 17:3–6).

The book of Hosea presents at least three noteworthy critical issues. First, the bulk of the book is essentially from Hosea, but the superscription and the biographical account in chapter 1 indicate that the book was edited, probably after Hosea's death and probably in Judah. Second, the references to Judah and the predominance of Judean kings in the superscription (1:1) have led some scholars to conclude that the book was not only edited but also updated after the fall of Israel in order to address Judah. While possible, such a conclusion is not necessary. A prophet in Israel could have addressed Judah at times, as well. Third, the text of Hosea has been poorly preserved in ancient manuscripts, leading to notorious translation problems in places. However, the general message of the prophet remains clear.

The contents of the book of Hosea fall into two major divisions. Chapters 1–3 draw parallels between the prophet's relationship to his wife and children and Yahweh's relationship with Israel. Chapters 4–14 contain a collection of oracles, most announcing judgment on Israel for various transgressions but others extending hope of restoration after the judgment.

COMMENTARY

SUPERSCRIPTION · 1:1

The content of the book of Hosea is *the word of the Lord*, and the prophet *Hosea* is merely the messenger. The references to the *kings of Judah* draw Judah into a message primarily aimed at Israel and serve as a warning to Judah. The only king of Israel mentioned is *Jeroboam son of Jehoash*, though six kings would follow him during Hosea's career. Perhaps the omission of their names implies that the "glory days" of Israel ended with Jeroboam.

HOSEA'S WIFE & CHILDREN · 1:2–2:1

1:2 God commands Hosea to take *an adulterous wife and children of unfaithfulness*, which serves as a symbol of the relationship between God and his people. *Adulterous* and "unfaithfulness" are the same word in Hebrew. The root (*zanah*) often refers to prostitution in the Old Testament and is better understood that way here. While the root can refer to literal prostitution (for example, Gen 38:24; Lev 19:29; 1 Kgs 3:16), it often indicates spiritual prostitution, selling oneself to other gods or foreign nations, in exchange for what they seem to offer (compare 2:12a; 4:10–15; 9:1; Exod 34:15–16; Deut 31:16). Scholars debate whether *Gomer* is a prostitute prior to the marriage (see McComiskey 11–17), but the parallels drawn in the next chapter suggest her prostitution begins after their marriage (see Anderson and Freedman 116).

1:3–9 She gives birth to three *children of unfaithfulness* (or "prostitution"), which means that the children are born to a prostitute. The text specifies that she *bore him* (Hosea) a child only with respect to the firstborn (1:3; compare verses 6, 8), leaving the paternity of the other two a question (2:4–5). Each child's name anticipates judgment. *Jezreel* refers to the judgment coming upon the *house of Jehu for the massacre at Jezreel* (compare 2 Kgs 9–10). This word is fulfilled with the overthrow of Jeroboam II's son, Zechariah (2 Kgs 15:10). *Lo-Ruhamah*

> **Jehu's Punishment**
> *Curiously, God punishes the dynasty of Jehu for a coup d'état commanded by one of God's own prophets (2 Kgs 9:6–10). This is not a case of inherited guilt, but rather of poetic justice. Since Jehu's family practiced the same sins as Ahab's, they will meet the same fate (see Anderson and Freedman 180).*

means "no mercy," and *Lo-Ammi* means "not my people," both signaling God's rejection of Israel. God will *no longer show love* (better translated "mercy") to Israel, though he will be merciful to Judah and *save them*. The fulfillment comes when Assyria destroys northern Israel (2 Kgs 17:3–23).

1:10–2:1 Then God announces an amazing reversal. Recalling the promise to Abraham (Gen 22:17), the Israelites *will be like the sand on the seashore*. The judgments signified by the children's names will be reversed, and a reunited Israel and Judah will *come up out of the land*, which is language of sprouting and a play on the meaning of *Jezreel* ("God sows"; 2:21–23).

THE MARRIAGE ANALOGY APPLIED TO GOD & ISRAEL · 2:2–23

2:2–4 The *mother* symbolizes God's estranged "wife" Israel (collectively), who has destroyed the covenantal bond. The word translated *rebuke* sometimes functions in prophetic texts to indicate that God is putting his people on trial (4:1; 12:2; Isa 3:13–14; Jer 2:9; Mic 6:1–2). God warns Israel to stop playing the whore with other gods, or she will be humiliated and her *children* (individual Israelites) shown no mercy.

2:5–13 Israel has pursued idols, including *Baal*, thinking they provide her with the necessities of life.

Because Israel has not *acknowledged* the true origin of these gifts, God withholds them, proving that her *lovers* cannot *pay* what they promise.

2:14–23 God intends to return to the "honeymoon" era with Israel in the *desert* following the exodus *out of Egypt*. Given the volatile nature of Israel's relationship with God in the wilderness, such an idealization of the past seems strange. However, in the wilderness Yahweh provided food and drink for Israel (Exod 16:1–17:7; Num 11), things Israel now attributes to *Baals*, that is, local versions of the Canaanite storm and fertility god. In this way, God will *remove the names of the Baals from her lips* because she will no longer see a need for them. Israel will no longer even utter a common designation for a husband: *my master* (ba`al). *In that day*, an unspecified future time, God will reestablish the covenantal bond, rooted in the very qualities of God, *righteousness, justice, love, compassion,* and *faithfulness*. When Israel *will acknowledge* God's overtures, they will receive the things they need. The reversal of Hosea's children's names in verse 23 symbolizes the healing of the relationship with God.

RECONCILIATION ILLUSTRATED · 3:1–5

> **Prophets & Symbolic Actions**
> *God often commanded his prophets to perform symbolic actions, some of which involved personal pain and humiliation (Isa 20:1–5; Jer 16:2; Ezek 4:4–6). The command for Hosea to marry a woman of prostitution falls into this category. Such prophetic acts created vivid, memorable illustrations of the prophets' messages and underscored the depth of both God's love and the people's estrangement. While difficult for the individual prophets, these acts served God's larger loving intention of calling the people to account in order to redeem them. So the dignity of the individual is sacrificed for the greater good of the whole community (compare Luke 23:11; 35–39; 1 Cor 4:9–13).*

To illustrate his ultimate intention to restore Israel, God commands Hosea to *show love again to his wife*, despite her unfaithfulness. Some scholars argue that the woman here is not Gomer but a second wife, but the parallels with chapter 2 indicate that Hosea reclaims Gomer with the condition that she remain faithful from now on. Like Gomer, Israel must experience separation prior to reconciliation. Verse 4 describes the key institutions of a well-functioning ancient society. Their absence highlights the impending desperate plight of Israel.

ISRAEL ON TRIAL · 4:1–19

4:1–10A God again brings *a charge* (2:4) against the *Israelites*, who show *no faithfulness, no love*, and *no acknowledgement of God*. The absence of these qualities leads to breakdown within the community: *cursing, lying, murder, stealing, adultery* (see also Exod 20:13–17; Deut 5:17–21). The people's sinfulness derives in part from the malfeasance of the *priests* and *prophets*, who have failed in their duty to teach the people covenant faithfulness. Therefore, God will *punish* them through deprivation of food and offspring (Deut 28:17–18).

4:10B–19 The *prostitution* discussed in these verses may not be simply figurative. The Israelite women may have become cult prostitutes at the shrines of their gods and are patronized by the men of Israel. *Judah* is warned not to patronize such cults at *Gilgal* and *Beth Aven*, the latter being a pun of the name *Bethel* ("house of God" versus *Beth Aven*, "house of iniquity"). Because Israel is *stubborn* in their idolatry, God's judgment will *sweep them away*. Beginning here in the book (except for 13:1), *Ephraim*, the main northern tribe and after the Syro-Ephraimitic War the only remaining dependent territory, indicates the whole northern kingdom of Israel.

> **"Prostitution" in Canaanite Religion**
> *Earlier scholars believed Canaanite religion to include cult or sacral prostitution, in which a female worshiper of the god would offer sexual services to men. According to this view, males could also serve as cult prostitutes, likewise offering their services to men (Deut 23:18). The term translated* shrine prostitute *in 4:14 has been particularly associated with cult prostitution (Gen 38:21–22; Deut 23:17–18; 2 Kgs 23:7). More recent research, however, has cast considerable doubt on this interpretation. More likely, Hosea uses the sexual language here as a graphic metaphor, perhaps reflecting the excesses of some festival-goers, but more generally playing off the key metaphor of God's "marriage" to Israel (see Ackerman).*

JUDGMENT ON THE BRAZEN PROSTITUTE · 5:1–7

This oracle continues the theme of Israel's prostitution. The *judgment* against Israel is inclusive. The *priests* and the *royal house* may have led Israel into apostasy, but the *Israelites* are guilty for following. Theoretically, they could repent, but their *spirit of*

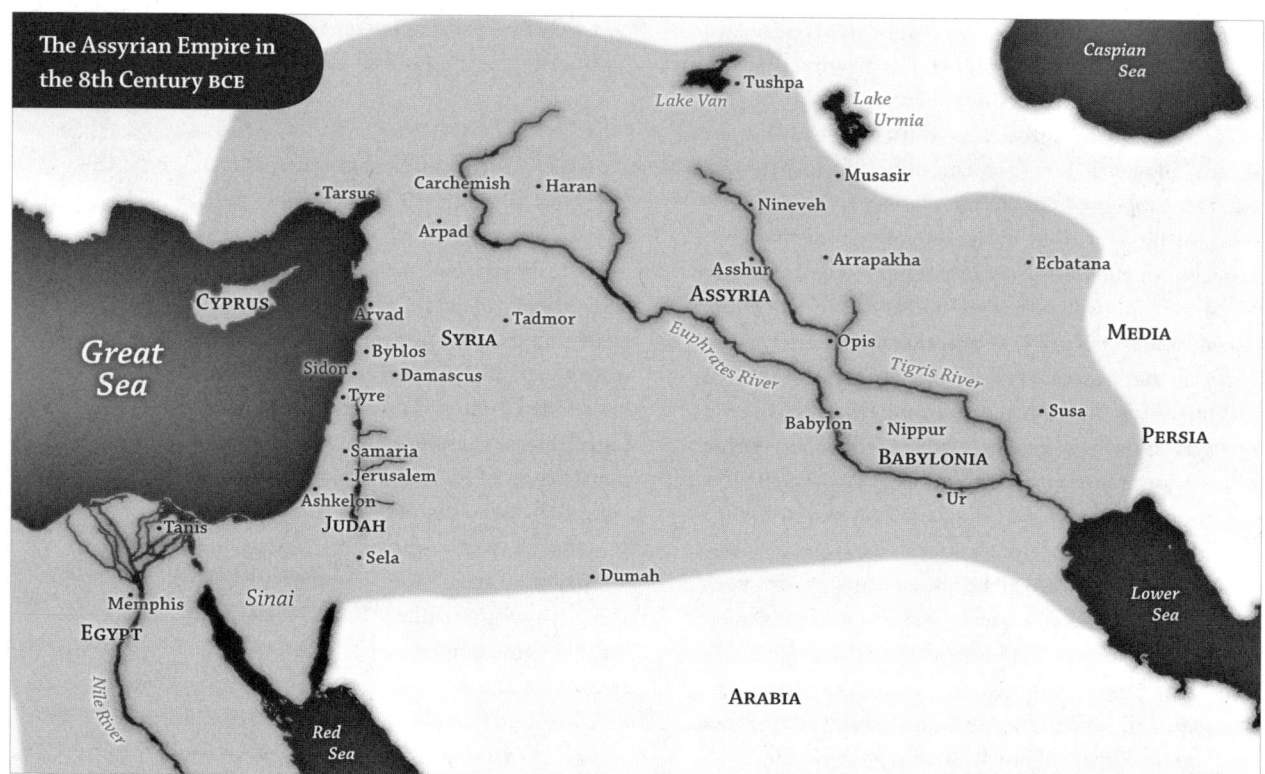

prostitution is so ingrained on their *heart* that they cannot *return to their God*. When they do *seek the Lord, they will not find him* because they continue to be *unfaithful*. *Mizpah* and *Tabor* may have been worship sites, but this is unclear.

AN INEFFECTIVE CURE · 5:8–15

5:8–12 The context for this oracle is the Syro-Ephraimite War (Achtemeier 47). The comparison of *Judah's leaders* to *those who move boundary stones* (see Deut 19:14; 27:17; Prov 23:10) points to Judah's takeover of territory to the north of Jerusalem (*Gibeah, Ramah*, and *Bethel*) outside Judah's territorial boundaries, probably after Israel withdrew from attacking Judah in order to meet the approaching Assyrians. God had set the tribal boundaries, and Judah had no right to violate them (Stuart 104). Even in warfare, nations must observe humanitarian limits.

5:13–15 Both Israel (2 Kgs 15:19–20) and *Judah* (2 Kgs 16:7–9) had turned to *Assyria* for security. Their vulnerability to the nations was their *sickness*, and this superpower seemed the obvious *cure*. They do not see that they are vulnerable precisely because they have failed to trust God for their security, and he will show them the futility of relying upon Assyria. He will attack Israel, ironically through Assyria, who will wipe out Israel and nearly destroy Judah (see 2 Kgs 18:13). Only then will the people *admit their* guilt and seek God.

AN EXHORTATION TO RETURN TO GOD · 6:1–3

Hosea calls on his people to *return to the Lord*. Drawing on the language of the previous oracle, Hosea says that, though *Yahweh* inflicted injury on Israel, he will *heal* them. However, the people must first *acknowledge the Lord* (2:8; 4:1; 5:4). The result will be God's assured presence, which will be an ongoing blessing like *winter rains* and *spring rains*. Most rain falls in Palestine between November and January, with annual totals ranging from about four inches in the Negev (southern desert region) to 25–30 inches in northern Galilee. The NIV distinction between winter and spring rains is misleading; verse 3 refers to the rains of October and March beginning and ending the season. Rainfall was essential to Israel's agricultural productivity, and the symbolism reminds Israel that God alone is the source of rain.

GOD LONGS FOR HIS CHILDREN · 6:4–11A

Like a parent pleading with a child, God asks both *Israel* and *Judah*, "What can I do with you?" Their *love* for God is fleeting, like the *morning mist* and *dew*. Therefore, through the *prophets*, he announces and executes *judgments* against his people. Their attempts to appease God through *sacrifices* and *burnt offerings* are meaningless because they think they can divorce worship from *mercy* toward others and *acknowledgement of God* (Matt 9:13; 12:7). They sacrifice in an attempt to pacify or manipulate God, yet they remain violent and *defiled*.

A SELF-DESTRUCTIVE NATION · 6:11B–7:16

6:11B–7:2 This passage again displays God's desire to *restore* and *heal* his people, but they make it impossible. They think they have hidden their *sins*, but their transgressions *are always before* God. The prophet's extreme language, again, aims at healing Israel, not merely indicting it.

7:3–16 Three additional problems, all political, illustrate the degeneration of Israel. First, Israel's *king* is pleased with their *wickedness* and *lies* and even *joins hands* with drunken revelers (contrast Ps 101). Second, the Israelites *devour their rulers* through repeated violent *coups d'état*. Third, the Israelites flit back and forth between *Egypt* and *Assyria*, the two superpowers of the time, in search of security, but these nations *sap Israel's strength* (for example, resources and manpower). Israel slides closer to death but *does not notice*. In *arrogance*, Israel thinks it can manage its own security, but God sees this as a rejection of him as Israel's true protector. Thus, God will not protect Israel, and, ironically, Israel *will be ridiculed* by those they thought would protect them. The prophet thus comments on the politics of small states like Israel as they seek to play the great power games. Without justice and piety, they will be pawns in a game whose rules they cannot control.

ILLEGITIMATE KINGS & GODS · 8:1–6

The prophet warns that *an eagle* (Assyria) will carry out God's judgment on Israel for breaking God's *covenant* (Deut 28:49). God sees through Israel's *cries* of desperation, knowing that they have *rejected what is good*, namely God himself. The oracle specifies two offenses. First, they *set up kings* without God's consent. Choosing kings was God's prerogative (Deut 17:15; compare 1 Sam 8–12), and in the past God designated Israel's kings through prophets (1 Sam 9:15–10:7; 16:1–13; 1 Kgs 11:29–39; 2 Kgs 9:1–10; 10:30). The second offense is idolatry. The *calf-idol of Samaria* refers to the image set up in Bethel by Jeroboam I (1 Kgs 12:26–33), and the reference to *Samaria* is a case of synecdoche, a literary device in which a part (in this case the capital city) represents the whole (Israel).

REAPING THE WHIRLWIND · 8:7–10

For Israel to *sow the wind and reap the whirlwind* means they invest themselves in what is useless, and the return is disastrous. Israel thinks their security rests in *Assyria* or other *nations*. They fail to see God as the source of their security. Instead of providing safety, the Assyrians will *swallow* the productivity of Israel, and Israel *will* suffer *oppression* under Assyrian rule.

DISPLEASING SACRIFICES & MISPLACED TRUST · 8:11–14

Israel's worship rituals are useless. From God's perspective, the very *altars* that are intended for atonement from sin have become *altars for sinning*. Israel disregards God's *law*, so to appeal to him for forgiveness through sacrifice is useless and even blasphemous. The same is true of fellowship offerings, after which Israel would *eat* a portion of *the meat* symbolizing a fellowship meal with God (Lev 7:11–18; Deut 16:2–4; 27:7). Since they have broken that fellowship, God is *not pleased* with such offerings. God's judgment will reverse the exodus: *They will return to Egypt*, that is, to captivity (compare Amos 9:7–10).

> **The "Sin Offering"**
> The "sin offering" (Lev 4:1–5:12; Num 15:22–31) served not to remove an individual's sin but to purify the sanctuary from human impurity. Thus, Hosea is saying that Israel's worship does not work anymore.

Israel *has forgotten* the one who made them, as illustrated by their trust in their kings (signified by *royal palaces*), and so has Judah, who trusts in their *fortified ... towns*. God's *fire* of judgment will demonstrate that their trust is misplaced.

THE RETURN TO CAPTIVITY · 9:1–6

In Israel, harvest time was supposed to be characterized by joy and thanksgiving to God (Deut 16:9–15), but Hosea instructs the people not to *rejoice*, because they are *unfaithful to God*. The *threshing floor* may have served as a location for worshiping non-Israelite gods – or treating Yahweh like one of those gods, through cult prostitution (Achetmeier 72–73; Stuart 142). Thus, the reference to Israel's prostitution here may be both symbolic and literal. In any case, the produce of these *threshing floors* and of the *winepresses* will *fail* to meet the people's needs (Deut 28:38–39). Israel will also be exiled and will eat *unclean food*, which will make them unclean and no longer holy to God (see Lev 11:1–47; Deut 14:3–21). Furthermore, *their sacrifices* in exile will not *please* God because he will consider them like food used in mourning rituals, which was unacceptable as an offering to God (Deut 26:14). Finally, Israel should not view Egypt as a place to *escape from destruction*, because those who go there will die there (see Jer 41:16–44:30).

THE PROPHET: WATCHMAN OR MADMAN? · 9:7–9

> **Hosea & Tradition**
> *Hosea cites many older stories of the Exodus, wandering, and the period of the so-called judges. Presumably, Israel knew and treasured these stories, and Hosea can appeal to a common stock of ideas and beliefs in order to rehabilitate Israel's relationship to God. Conspicuously absent is any reference to southern traditions about David.*

God graciously sends his *prophet* to act as a *watchman* to warn *Israel* that their *punishment* is *at hand*. But the people consider *the prophet* a *maniac* (2 Kgs 9:11; Jer 29:26) and do not heed his warning. The depth of Israel's corruption is here compared to *the days of Gibeah*, when that town's violence and corruption led to civil war in Israel (Judg 19–21).

BEREAVED OF CHILDREN · 9:10–17

9:10–13 This passage compares Israel's *fathers* in the wilderness generation to the Israelites in Hosea's day. The ancestors were initially pleasing and promising in God's eyes, but they continually broke faith with him, as evidenced in their participation in idolatry at *Baal Peor* (Num 25:1–10). The implication is that not much has changed. The hyperbolic language of verses 11–13 points to the end of Israel because its offspring are cut off in one way or another.

9:14–17 Hosea and God engage in dialogue. Hosea beseeches God to exact vengeance on the wicked, invoking God's judgment on Israel in the form of *wombs that miscarry* (Deut 28:18). To say God *hated them* refers to the intensity of God's rejection and his plan to *drive them out* into exile. *Gilgal* was once a site for sacrifices to God (1 Sam 10:8; 15:21), but it also served as a place for problematic worship (Judg 3:19; Hos 4:15; 12:11; Amos 4:4; 5:5).

THE BEGINNING & END OF ISRAEL'S IDOLATRY · 10:1–8

Like a fruitful *vine* (compare Isa 5:1–7; Jer 2:21), Israel *prospered*, but their apostasy grew in proportion to their prosperity (Deut 8:10–20), as evidenced in their multiplication of *altars* and *sacred stones* (Deut 16:22). Despite the announcement that God will *demolish* these sacred objects and will take away their *king*, Israel's concern is for the *calf-idol* of Bethel (see 8:5–6). Verse 4 describes abuses in the court system (compare Deut 17:8–13). The idol, like their king, who may be God's patron, is powerless to save even itself. *Assyria* will take both away along with the people of *Samaria*. The cry for the *mountains* to *cover* them indicates great despair (see Lk 23:30; Rev 6:16).

BREAKING NEW GROUND · 10:9–15

The sinfulness at *Gibeah* in the days of the judges (Judg 19–21) has characterized God's people from that time to Hosea's day. Therefore, God will place the *yoke* of Assyrian domination on both Israelite nations (Deut 28:48; Isa 14:25). God intends this judgment to be ultimately redemptive, but Israel and Judah must begin anew. They must *break* new *ground* by suffering through judgment until they *seek the Lord*. This judgment will clear away those things in which Israel misplaces trust: its *own strength* and *fortresses*, idols like the one at *Bethel*, and its *king*. The identity of *Shalman* (for suggestions, see Stuart 171–72) and the location of *Beth Arbel* are uncertain, but the Israelites well remember his brutality there. The prophets, like Deuteronomy, have strong ethical scruples against war crimes, even those involving the victimization of non-Israelites (Deut 20; Amos 2:1–3).

GOD'S PARENTAL LOVE FOR ISRAEL · 11:1–11

This passage depicts God as the devoted parent of a rebellious child. God brought the *son*, Israel (Exod 4:22), up *out of Egypt* (Matt 2:15) in the exodus and lovingly taught Israel *to walk* and *healed them* (On childbearing as symbols

> **Matthew's Use of Hosea**
> *Matthew reuses this verse, not to claim that Hosea somehow predicted Jesus' flight to Egypt, but to help construct an artistic picture of Jesus as living out, this time in perfect obedience to God, Israel's early life. Thus Matthew 1–4 portrays Jesus as hunted like Israel by an evil king, as moving to Egypt, as living in the wilderness, and so on.*

of God's care and provision for Israel, see also Deut 1:31). But Israel did not return God's love, worshiping instead *Baals* and other *images*.

In light of Israel's rebellion, God exercises "tough love," giving them over to foreign nations. But because of his deep affection for his people, God cannot *give* them *up* to the fate of *Admah* and *Zeboiim*, cities that fell along with Sodom and Gomorrah (Deut 29:23; see also Gen 19). God's *compassion* leads him to new plans for Israel. However, that redemption comes through judgment because Israel must first return to God.

PAST EXAMPLES, PRESENT EVIL · 11:12–12:14

This passage indicts Israel and *Judah* for a variety of transgressions, centering primarily on *deceit* (Wolff 207–8).

11:12–12:6 Israel is duplicitous in its foreign policy. While allied to *Assyria* through *treaty*, Israel attempts to woo *Egypt* with bribes. Such machinations lead the Assyrians to destroy Israel (2 Kgs 17:3–6). Thus, as Israel's *lies* multiply, so does *violence*. Israel's ancestor *Jacob* was notorious for his deceitfulness (Gen 27:5–36), and his descendants follow in his footsteps. Again, the ancient stories give the prophet a way of talking about current realities. The differences are that Jacob *begged for* the *favor* of God's *angel* (Gen 32:22–32) and that he *found* God at *Bethel* (28:10–19; 35:1–15). Likewise, Israel *must return* to the God of Jacob.

12:7–8 The Old Testament repeatedly condemns *dishonest scales* (for example, Deut 25:13–16; Amos 8:5; Mic 6:11; Prov 11:1; 20:23). Those who are *very rich*, presumably because of such unscrupulous business practices, believe that no one will find them guilty of *iniquity or sin*. Such *boasts* are likely rooted in the corruption of the judicial system through bribery and favoritism toward the wealthy, which the Old Testament also repeatedly condemns (for example, Exod 23:8; Deut 16:19; Prov 17:23; Isa 1:23; 5:22–23; Amos 5:12).

12:9–10 These verses point to the wilderness period (see also 2:14–15; Amos 5:25), a time when all Israelites were equally dependent on God. The reference to the prophets reminds the reader of God's mercy in sending prophets to warn Israel, which also leaves Israel without excuse.

12:11–14 Hosea contrasts Israel with Jacob and Moses. On *Gilead*, see 6:8, and on *Gilgal* see the discussion on 9:14–16 above. Jacob's duplicity led him to be "exiled" from his home and to suffer equivalent justice of a sort when he *served to get a wife* from a duplicitous Laban (Gen 29:1–30). Yet, he eventually turned to God and was restored (see above on verse 4). Also, God used the faithful *prophet* Moses (Deut 18:15, 18; 34:9–10) to deliver *Israel* from *Egypt* and to *care* for Israel in the wilderness. But Israel shows neither the faith of Moses nor the proper response to God's commands in Moses' law or to subsequent prophets. Therefore, God will *repay* Israel for such *contempt*.

A MATTER OF LIFE & DEATH · 13:1–16

13:1–3 Life and blessing for Israel naturally flow from being faithful to the covenant relationship with God (Deut 5:32–33; 30:15–20), but Israel is unfaithful and so invites death. The phrase *Ephraim … was exalted in Israel* suggests that here *Ephraim* means the tribe rather than the whole northern kingdom. This tribe was prominent and powerful within Israel, and it was also the tribe of the northern kingdom's first king, Jeroboam I (1 Kgs 11:26). Following his rise to the throne, Israel rapidly fell into idolatry, particularly *Baal worship* and worship of Jeroboam's *calf-idols*. A translation problem makes it uncertain whether Israel really was practicing *human sacrifice* (see the NIV note on verse 2), but such a meaning here is certainly possible (see 2 Kgs 17:17). Israel's idolatry means that they will soon vanish.

> **Human Sacrifice in Pagan Worship**
>
> *Human sacrifice occurred in the ancient world, especially at times of crisis (see Judg 11; 2 Kings 3:27; Mic 6:7). The Greeks told the story of Agamemnon's sacrifice of his daughter Iphigeneia during the Trojan War, and the Carthaginians, who were descendants of Phoenician colonists, sacrificed huge numbers of children and buried them in a special cemetery, the Tophet. The Bible condemns this practice.*

13:4–8 Verse 4 echoes of the first commandment (Exod 20:3; Deut 5:7), reminding that God demands exclusive loyalty from Israel. He has the right to do so because he delivered them from *Egypt*, *cared for* them *in the desert*, and also *fed them* in the land. But they have forgotten that he is the one who provides (Deut 8:10–20). Therefore, in a vivid image of judgment, God will attack and destroy them like a predator attacks its prey.

13:9–11 These verses allude to the stories of Samuel and Saul. God was Israel's *helper* (*ezer*), the one who delivered them in their battle with the Philistines at Ebenezer ("stone of help"; 1 Sam 7:12). Yet Israel demanded *a king* to lead them in battle (1 Sam 8:20), indicating a lack of trust in God. He granted their request, anointing Saul then later rejecting him for disobedience (1 Sam 9–15). Until Hosea's day, Israel has continued this pattern of rejecting God's help and installing kings who disobey. But these kings are powerless to *save*, and, thus, Israel is *destroyed*.

13:12–16 God knows well the sins of Israel, and, thus, Israel will "die," like a stillborn child, when Assyria destroys the nation. The meaning of verse 14a–d is debated (see 1 Cor 15:55). If one follows the NIV's translation, the first two lines are assertions – God will *ransom* and *redeem* Israel *from death* – and the next two lines taunt *death*. On this reading, there is hope that restoration will follow judgment. Such an abrupt shift from judgment is not unprecedented in Hosea (for example, 2:14–23; 11:8–9; McComiskey 223–24). However, many commentators and several translations (NASB 95, NRSV, NLT), understand the first two lines as questions: *Shall I ransom them from the power of Sheol*? *Shall I redeem them from Death*? (NRSV). On this reading, the answers to the first two questions are "no," and the third and fourth questions are God's invitation to "death and Sheol ... to loose all their pestilent powers from the underworld upon this faithless people" (Achtemeier 107). The latter view fits better contextually. Verses 14e–16 continue the images of death. The scorching *east wind* from the *desert* represents the Assyrians, who will sweep into Israel and kill violently and indiscriminately.

AN INVITATION TO RETURN · 14:1–9

14:1–3 The prophet summons the people to *return* to their *God*, even providing *words* of confession to *take* with them. They are to ask God to *forgive all* their *sins*, and they must acknowledge they have misplaced their trust. Neither *Assyria*, nor their own military might (symbolized by *war horses*), nor their *gods* can *save* them.

14:4–8 God offers to *heal* and *love* Israel in response to such a confession. He must *heal* them because they cannot do it for themselves (Hos 7:1; Jer 30:17; 33:6). Israel will again grow and prosper (2:21–23). When they sincerely call upon God rather than *idols*, he will then *answer* and *care* for them.

14:9 This wisdom statement addresses the reader of the book. The *wise* person is the one who takes to heart *these things*, that is, what this book has said. The reader is left with a choice: to walk in God's *ways* as *the righteous do* or to be like *rebellious* Israel and *stumble* (Ps 1; Prov 4:18–19).

THEOLOGICAL REFLECTIONS

With images of God as a husband and father, Hosea gives us glimpses into the heart of God, who loves the covenant people. Like the husband of an unfaithful wife, God's heart is broken by idolatry or unwise political alliances. Like the loving parent of a rebellious child, God longs for Israel to realize the error of their ways and come home. God takes the covenant seriously, even when Israel does not.

Because of this love, God is willing to send judgment upon them in order ultimately to restore them (see also Lev 26; Deut 27–28). In this light, the frequent caricature of the Old Testament's God as one of anger and wrath falls flat. Certainly, God's anger and wrath appear in Hosea, but God's judgment comes because of Israel's sin and rebellion, and it serves a loving and merciful intention to eradicate injustice and idolatry within Israel so as to bring life (compare Deut 30:11–20). Such judgment is a last resort. God graciously sent prophets to warn the people, but they refused to listen.

Israel's God is also not impotent like the gods and nations to whom Israel turned. God has repeatedly demonstrated his ability to protect the people (Exod 14–15; 17:8–16; Judg 4–5; 7) and provide for them (Exod 16:1–17:7). In Hosea, God intends to demonstrate his power and the powerlessness of those whom Israel pursues by withholding the security and provision that Israel seeks from them. When they realize the futility of their pursuit and turn again to God, they will receive restoration and blessing again (Deut 30:1–10).

Following Hosea, the New Testament characterizes the church as the bride of Christ (2 Cor 11:2; Rev 19:7) and its members as God's children (Gal 3:26; 1 John 3:1). Hosea's words warn us against entrusting and devoting ourselves to anything other than God for provision and security. Yet when we do prostitute ourselves to such impotent "gods," Hosea reminds us that God will pursue us, discipline us, and, if we turn back to him wholeheartedly, graciously restore us.

FOR FURTHER STUDY

Bruce Birch, *Let Justice Roll Down: The Old Testament, Ethics, and Christian Life* (Louisville: Westminster John Knox, 1991).

Enrique Nardoni, *Rise Up, O Judge: A Study in Justice in the Biblical World* (Peabody, Mass.: Hendrickson, 2004).

WORKS CITED

Elizabeth Achtemeier, *Minor Prophets I* (Peabody, Mass.: Henrickson, 1996).

Susan Ackerman, "Cultic Prostitution," *Eerdman's Dictionary of the Bible* (2000): 300.

Francis I. Anderson and David N. Freedman, *Hosea* (Garden City, N.Y.: Doubleday, 1980).

Thomas E. McComiskey, "Hosea" in *The Minor Prophets: An Exegetical and Expository Commentary* (ed. Thomas E. McComiskey; Grand Rapids: Baker, 1992), 1:1–237.

Douglas Stuart, *Hosea-Jonah* (Waco, Tex.: Word, 1987).

Hans Walter Wolff, *Hosea* (trans. Gary Stansell; Philadelphia: Fortress, 1974).

Joel

John T. Willis

CHAPTER CONTENTS

Contexts 675
Commentary 675
    Superscription · 1:1 675
    Locust Plague & Drought; Call to Repentance · 1:2–2:17 675
    Restoration of the Penitent & Their Enemies' Defeat · 2:18–3:21 676
Theological Reflections 677
For Further Study 677
Works Cited 677

Scholars debate Joel's structure. Prinsloo describes eight units, each one intensifying the preceding unit. Wolff claims that Joel contains two parts, arranged in reversed chiasm, but this view requires rearranging and omitting several verses. A productive way to view Joel's structure is to divide it into two sections, the first describing doom and demanding repentance; the second announcing hope and enemies' destruction. Joel and his audience would have been familiar with several such organizational Old Testament traditions (Gray 208–225; Crenshaw 27–28).

> **Chiasm or *Chiasmus***
> *A way of arranging parts of a text in a repetitive pattern in which the first part parallels the last, the second part the next to last, and so on (A B C C'B'A'). Chiasmus appears frequently in the Bible.*

CONTEXTS

The book of Joel originated about 400–350 BCE. We know this because the Babylonian exile is spoken of in the past (3:1–3, 17), and the community leaders are elders (1:2, 14) and priests (1:9, 13; 2:17), not kings. Since the temple (1:13–14, 16; 2:17) and the city wall of Jerusalem (2:7, 9) exist in this book, a date of composition sometime after 445 BCE is necessary. Chapter 3:4–6 mentions that the Phoenicians and Philistines have confiscated Judah's riches and sold Judean slaves to Greeks, *far from their homeland*, therefore indicating that the text precedes Alexander the Great's defeat of Tyre in 332 BCE. If these events had occurred after the conquest of Tyre, slaves sold to the Greeks would not necessarily have been sent far from Israel.

All but verses 1:1 and 2:30–3:8 are in poetry. From the 1870s to the 1960s, most scholars believed Joel to consist of two originally independent works (1:1–2:17 and 2:18–3:21), or an expansion of an earlier work. Most current scholars, however, think it is essentially a unity.

COMMENTARY

SUPERSCRIPTION · 1:1

Joel son of Pethuel appears only here in the Old Testament. In prophetic books, it is often difficult to distinguish between Yahweh's and the prophets' words. Joel 1:1 designates Yahweh as the source of Joel's message but does not specify how Yahweh communicated it.

LOCUST PLAGUE & DROUGHT; CALL TO REPENTANCE · 1:2–2:17

1:2–20 Joel names five groups that locusts and drought have harmed: elders and people (verses 2, 14); drunkards (verse 5); priests (verses 9, 13); farmers and vinedressers (verse 11); and animals (verses 18, 20). In verses 2–3, *Hear* and *Give ear* elicit audience attention (Hos 5:1).

> **Locust Swarms**
> *Locust swarms may cover many square miles and include trillions of insects. Their devastating passage leads to human famine and disease.*

Elders are civil leaders (see Ruth 4:4) or older people (see Psalm 37:25) who can testify that no locust plague or drought like this has occurred in decades (Exod 10:6, 14). Each generation of Israelite parents would *tell* their children about the community's problems and needs, and how Yahweh had overcome them (Deut 6:6–7; Ps 78:1–8). In verse 4, the four locust groups (compare 2:25) are not symbols for nations, as some have claimed, but possibly reflect stages of locust development: larva, pupa, young locust, and mature locust; or, more probably, they refer to different types of locusts.

Locusts devour grapevines and fig trees so that *drunkards* lack wine. Locusts are innumerable and irrepressible, like an attacking *nation* (2:4–9). According to verses 8–10, cultic officiants cannot function, because sacrifices require *grain*, *wine*, and *oil* (Hos 2:8–9). Ancient Near Easterners wore *sackcloth* (verse 8) for mourning (Lam 2:8–11) or repentance (Isa 32:9–15). The trauma gripping priests is like that of a young widow bemoaning her husband's death.

Owing to the locust plague, farmers have no grains to harvest; vinedressers, no fruits to glean (11–12). These verses list all the main agricultural products of the land of Israel. Joel thus envisions the total devastation of the land. In verses 13–14, Joel charges priests to assemble elders and people to *the temple* (mentioned in verse 16). *A fast* demonstrated sadness (Neh 1:4) or repentance (Isa 58:1–12). In verses 15–17, locusts and drought signal *the day of the Lord*, which in the Old Testament refers to Yahweh's intervening to punish or bless his people or their enemies. Joel 1:15; 2:1–2, 11 denote God's judgment on Judah (Isa 2:10–17; Zeph 1:7); and 2:31; 3:14, the overthrow of nations and the deliverance of Judah. Verse 1:15 recalls Isaiah 13:6. *Almighty* translates the Hebrew name *Shaddai* (Exod 6:3). Verses 16–17 reiterate verses 4–13. In 18–20, locusts and drought harm fodder crops, causing animals to starve. In verses 19–20, Joel begs Yahweh to remove the devastation (compare Amos 7:1–6). *Fire* and *flames* accompany drought (Amos 7:4), which verses 10, 12, and 17 imply.

2:1–11 Verses 1–11 do not envision an "apocalyptic army" (Wolff 39–43) or Yahweh's earthly army (Crenshaw 116–32), but actual locusts, as the words *appearance* (verse 4) and *like* (verses 5, 7) show. Joel 1:2–20 describes locusts in the country, and 2:1–11 announces the advance of locusts into Jerusalem. Joel's comrades must proclaim calamity: *the day of Yahweh* is near, and Yahweh's locust *army* (verses 2, 5, 11, 25) threatens Zion (verses 4–5, 7). In the first two verses, a trumpet blast means an enemy army approaches (verse 1; Hos 5:8). Ironically, the warning achieves nothing. *Darkness* signifies God's punishment (Amos 5:18–20; Zeph 1:15). The plague has no precedent. In verses 3–11, Joel proclaims the locusts' advance into and through Jerusalem. These verses graphically describe the sound and movements of the enormous locust swarms, which may include billions of insects. Their whirring wings are like *rumbling of chariots and crackling of … fire* (verse 5). The hyperbolical comparison *like the garden of Eden* (Gen 2:8–14) contrasts with *a desolate wilderness* (verse 3). Devouring fire precedes Yahweh (Psalms 50:3; 97:3). Fear overwhelms the people (verses 6, 11).

2:12–17 Yahweh does not wish to annihilate Judah but to deliver it. God addresses first the people (verses 12–14), then the priests (verses 15–17). The people should *return* [Hebrew *shuv*; verses 12, 13] so that Yahweh might *turn* [Hebrew *shuv*] away punishment and bless them (verse 14; Mal 3:7). Genuine *return* begins in the heart and produces appropriate external actions (verse 12; Jer 24:7).

> **To "Rend Garments"**
> *Rending clothing (verse 13) signifies displeasure (2 Kgs 5:7–8), mourning (2 Sam 3:31), shame (2 Sam 13:19), or repentance (1 Kgs 21:27). It did not prove genuine repentance.*

External actions include *fasting, weeping, mourning* (verse 12; see Esth 4:3). The text states two motivations for repentance: Yahweh is *gracious and merciful*, a stereotyped portrayal (Exod 34:6); and Yahweh may yet *relent and leave a blessing* (verse 14). God is free even to avert promised destruction (Ps 115:3). Often Yahweh *relents*, changing plans (Jer 18:7–10; Jonah 3:4, 6–10). The *blessing* is grain, wine, and oil for sacrifices (1:9–10, 13; compare 1:13–14). Yahweh charges the priests to assemble Judah for repentance. Verse 15a repeats verse 1a; verse 15b repeats 1:14a. Since locusts and drought devastated all, all must come to the temple. The priests must *lament* over sins – that is, they must lead the people in praying in the manner of the psalms of lament. As Yahweh's *heritage* (or private possession; see Exod 19:5–6), Israel must escape destruction so nations cannot mock them. When God's people suffer economic setbacks or military defeats, nations ask scornfully, *Where is their God?* (verse 17; Ps 79:10).

RESTORATION OF THE PENITENT & THEIR ENEMIES' DEFEAT · 2:18–3:21

2:18–32 Joel addresses a changed audience. Between 2:17 and 2:18, the hearers repented, following the pattern of the psalms of lament. Like a husband (Prov 6:34), Yahweh *became jealous* for the devastated land; like a father (Ps 103:13), he *had pity on his people*. The paternal imagery here parallels other instances of its use in the Old Testament (for example, Deut 11:31). *The eastern sea* equals the Dead Sea, and the *western sea* is the Mediterranean. Pastures will flourish (verse 22; 1:10, 18–20), fig trees and grapevines bear fruit (verse 22; 1:5, 7, 12), rain pour (verse 23; 1:10, 12, 18–20), grain, wine, oil (verse 24; 1:10), and food abound (verse 26; 1:16), and Yahweh will remove the people's shame (verses 26–27; 2:17). Again, the text lists the major agricultural crops and thinks of national distress as a matter of honor and shame. Joel discourages fear (verses 21–22; 2:6) and encourages joy (verses 21, 23; 1:5, 8, 11–13, 16) and praise (verse 26).

3:1–15 Yahweh will punish the nations who afflicted Israel. Verse 1b recalls Jeremiah 29:14. Yahweh will gather all nations to *the valley of Jehoshaphat* (a symbolic name; verses 2, 12) for punishment. This may be a literal valley lying near Jerusalem, or it may refer to the fact that Jehoshaphat of Judah defeated the Moabites, Ammonites, and Meunites in the valley of Beracah (2 Chron 20:20–26). Joel announces that Yahweh will act similarly now in punishing Israel's foes. Verses 2e–3 enumerate crimes the nations committed that warrant Yahweh's punishment. Invaders *cast lots* to determine ownership of captives (Obad 11). In verses 4–8, Yahweh specifies Phoenicia and Philistia, asking what prompted them to oppress the Israelites. They stored Judah's wealth in their temples (a common practice in antiquity) and sold Judeans to Greeks. Were these retaliations for Judah's crimes? Yahweh summons *the nations* for judgment (verse 12), mockingly charging them to make weapons, deliberately reversing the language of Isaiah 2:4 (verse 10); Yahweh's *warriors* will fight them (verses 11–12). Yahweh will destroy the nations like harvesting grain (Isa 17:5) or treading grapes (Isa 63:1–6). Verse 15 reiterates 2:10.

Joel 3:16–21 highlights Yahweh's presence in Judah, which is like a roaring lion (verse 16; Amos 1:2), striking fear in the nation's enemies (Amos 3:4, 8) but protecting God's people (Hos 11:10–11). *The Lord dwells in Zion* (verses 17, 21) evokes a centuries-old understanding of the temple and Jerusalem as being under God's protection (Pss 2, 84; but see Jer 7). Verse 18d recalls Ezekiel 47:1–12.

THEOLOGICAL REFLECTIONS

Joel is an encouragement to penitent believers. It affirms Yahweh's presence and sovereignty over nature and nations. Locusts and drought punish God's people for sins by removing essentials for physical life and worship. Sin is serious to the holy God. Like a mighty warrior, Yahweh leads a locust "army" across the countryside and into the city. The ultimate intention is not to destroy but to save the penitent. When they recognize their destitute circumstances, God calls them to genuine repentance, not to mere external actions. Gracious and merciful, God may relent, and knowledge of this possibility leads the people to repent. God will then punish their enemies and restore their losses, making Jerusalem a "refuge" and "stronghold."

FOR FURTHER STUDY

Bruce Birch, *Hosea, Joel, and Amos* (Louisville: Westminster John Knox, 1997).

Richard James Coggins, *Joel and Amos* (Sheffield: Sheffield Academic Press, 2000).

WORKS CITED

James L. Crenshaw, *Joel* (New York: Doubleday, 1995).

George Buchanan Gray, "The Parallel Passages in 'Joel' and Their Bearing on the Question of Date," *Expository Times* 8 (1893): 208–25.

W. S. Prinsloo, *The Theology of the Book of Joel* (Berlin: de Gruyter, 1985).

Hans Walter Wolff, *Joel and Amos* (Philadelphia: Fortress, 1977).

The Divine Spirit

Yahweh will heal Judah's spiritual despondency (1:12; 2:6), pouring out the divine spirit *(a life-giving force, according to Zech 4:6) on* all flesh, *that is, the survivors of locusts and drought (verse 32). Peter quotes 2:28–32 in Acts 2:17–21, applying it to his context and message.*

Amos

Philip G. Camp

CHAPTER CONTENTS

Contexts 679

Commentary 679
- Superscription · 1:1–2 679
- Oracles Against the Nations · 1:3–2:16 679
- Oracles of Judgment Against Israel · 3:1–6:14 680
- Amos's Vision Reports with Interludes · 7:1–9:15 682

Theological Reflections 684

For Further Study 684

Works Cited 684

MAPS, TABLES, & FEATURES

Justice & Righteousness 682

The book of Amos announces God's judgment on the northern kingdom of Israel, especially for the injustices perpetrated by the wealthy and powerful upon the poor and weak.

CONTEXTS

Amos's oracles address Israel in a period of national expansion and prosperity sometime during the first half of the eighth century BCE. The long, stable reigns of Israel's King Jeroboam II (786–746 BCE) and Judah's King Uzziah (1:1), the peace between their nations, and their secure borders allowed for such conditions. However, the influx of wealth did not benefit the entire nation. The rich got richer through the manipulation and exploitation of the poor.

Amos was a *shepherd* from *Tekoa* who also *took care of sycamore-fig trees* (1:1; 7:14). God called him to prophesy to the northern kingdom, Israel. The reference to Amos in the third person in the superscription (1:1) and the narrative in 7:10–15 suggest that someone other than Amos edited the book. However, there is no scholarly consensus on the nature and extent of the editing process (see Paul 16–27; Stuart 294–95).

COMMENTARY

SUPERSCRIPTION · 1:1–2

In addition to the information covered in the "Introduction," the superscription also says that Amos *saw* (compare Isa 1:1; 2:1; Mic 1:1) these things *two years before the earthquake* (see Zech 14:5). The date of this event is uncertain (Paul 35), but it would have been fresh in the mind of Amos's audience.

Verse 2 sets the stage for the rest of the book. God's judgment booms with devastating effect from *Zion/Jerusalem* (see Jer 25:30; Joel 3:16), the site of his holy temple. Note that a lion *roars* after it has caught its prey (see 3:4), indicating that, while judgment is still to come, Israel is as good as dead.

ORACLES AGAINST THE NATIONS · 1:3–2:16

Oracles against nations usually announce God's sovereignty over and judgment upon foreign nations (Isa 13–23; Jer 46–51; Ezek 25–32), but Amos also uses the genre to lump *Israel* (and *Judah*) in with all the other neighboring nations, implying there is no real distinction. The oracles in 1:3–2:16 share several common features. First, the N, N+1 pattern *for three sins ... even for four* (1:3, 6, 9, 11, 13; 2:1, 4, 6) is a literary device that sometimes specifies an exact number (as in Prov 30:15–31), but here it indicates the totality of these nations' sins (Paul 27–30). Thus, with the exceptions of *Judah* and *Israel*, each oracle specifies only one sin that characterizes the general wickedness of that nation. Second, with the exception of *Israel*, God says he will send *fire* that will *consume* the *fortresses* of these nations (1:4, 7, 10, 12, 14; 2:2, 5). That is, the nations' defenses will not withstand the judgment of God. Third, the agent of God's judgment is not specified, but historically conquests by Assyria and later Babylon accomplish these judgments.

1:1–5 *Damascus* is the capital of *Aram* (Syria). The *house of Hazael* refers to the line of a usurper who murdered his predecessor (2 Kgs 8:7–15), and *Ben-Hadad* is Hazael's son (2 Kgs 13:3, 24). Both violently oppressed Israel, including attacks on *Gilead*, in the late ninth and early eight centuries BCE (2 Kgs 8:28–29; 9:14–15; 10:32–33; 13:22–25). God will "reverse Aram's history" (Achtemeier 180) by sending them back to *Kir*, the place of their origin (9:7).

1:6–8 *Gaza, Ashdod, Ashkelon,* and *Ekron* are four of the five city-states of the Philistine Pentapolis (Gath is the fifth; see 6:2). Selling captives as slaves was not an unusual practice in ancient warfare, but this reference suggests the *Philistines* raided *communities* expressly for the purpose of capturing people to sell into slavery (compare Exod 21:16; Joel 3:4–6).

> **The Philistines**
>
> *Derived from the Hebrew* plish-tim, *the Philistines were a people who inhabited the southern coast of Canaan during Old Testament times, but who had probably migrated there in the 12th century BCE from Crete.*

1:9–10 *Tyre* is also charged with selling *captives to Edom*, which is seen as a violation of *a treaty of brotherhood*. If Israel is the treaty partner, then this refers to David's and later Solomon's cordial relationship with King Hiram of Tyre (1 Kgs 5:1, 12).

1:11–12 *Edom* is Israel's *brother* nation because the Edomites descend from Esau, the brother of Jacob (Gen 25:30; 36:1). Since Edom has taken up the *sword* against Israel, God's judgment is coming (as in Obad 1–21). *Teman* and *Borzah* are principle cities of Edom.

1:13–15 *Ammon*, whose capital is *Rabbah*, is charged with massacring *pregnant women of Gilead* (2 Kgs 8:12; 15:16; Hos 13:16). This practice was rare in ancient warfare and was considered especially brutal. This reference probably represents a wide range of similarly heinous acts by the Ammonites (Cogan 755–57).

> **Gilead**
>
> *The area northwest of the Dead Sea. Israel, Ammon, and Moab each ruled the area at different times. A recently discovered Moabite text records the capture of Ammonite settlers in this area and their deportation to Moabite work projects. An earlier Moabite text, the Mesha Stele from the ninth century BCE, records the massacre of Israelites in the same general area.*

2:1–3 *Moab* is charged with burning *the bones of Edom's king*, namely the desecration of his tomb. In the ancient Near East, not receiving a burial was a great disgrace. *Kerioth* is the site of a sanctuary for Moab's chief god, Chemosh.

2:4–5 Pointing out the impending judgment of *Judah*, Israel's sister nation, for violating God's *law*, including following *false gods*, should open Israel's eyes to their own precarious situation (Jer 3:6–11).

2:6–16 The oracle against *Israel* expands on the pattern of the previous seven oracles. Amos names several *sins*, all examples of oppression and injustice. Human life is devalued as people are sold into slavery for insignificant amounts, probably to pay off their loans. The powerful abuse those unable to defend themselves and *deny* them *justice* (Exod 23:2–3, 6; Lev 19:15; Deut 16:19–20). *Father and son* disgracefully use the same *girl*, probably a slave, for sexual gratification (see Gen 35:22; 49:3–4; Lev 18:8, 15). Furthermore, the worship of *their god* takes place alongside the use of clothing as collateral, in violation of Israelite law (see Exod 22:26–27; Deut 24:12–13, 17) and levying undeserved *fines*.

By reciting God's gracious deeds on Israel's behalf, Amos places responsibility for the coming judgment squarely on Israel. God also raised up *prophets* (Deut 18:15–22; 2 Kgs 17:13, 23) and *Nazirites* (Num 6:1–21) for the benefit of Israel, but Israel turned against both. Therefore, severe judgment is coming upon them.

ORACLES OF JUDGMENT AGAINST ISRAEL · 3:1–6:14

3:1–2 Chapter 3 contains three judgment oracles. The first oracle couches the judgment of Israel in the context of its special relationship with God, based on the election of the Israelites from among *all the families of the earth* and their deliverance from *Egypt*. God's intention was to bless the Israelites and, through them, the nations (compare Gen 12:3; 18:18–19; Deut 4:5–8). Their refusal to live up to their calling, as evidenced in their idolatry and treatment of the poor, jeopardizes God's intentions for them and the world. Thus, their election will not insulate them from God's judgment (Paul 101).

3:3–8 This oracle begins with seven rhetorical questions. The obvious answers of the first six lead the audience to the obvious answer of the seventh question: Of course, *disaster* does not *come* to a *city* unless *the Lord has caused it*. The larger context of Amos indicates that cities deserving of God's judgment are in view here (as in 1:3, 5, 6–10, 12, 14; 2:5; 3:14; 5:5–6) and not every city that experiences a tragedy. However, God mercifully does not send judgment without first warning the people through *prophets* (see Gen 18:16–33; 2 Kgs 17:13, 23), and Israel should take Amos's message as just such a warning.

3:9–12 God calls both Philistines and Egyptians to *assemble* in order to witness the *unrest* and *oppression* in Israel and to witness the resulting judgment, implying that Israel is worse than these nations that the Israelites would consider the epitome of oppressors (Exod 1:11–12; 3:9; Judg 10:7–8; 31:1). The image of the rescued bits of a sheep indicates the totality of the judgment.

3:13–4:13 This long oracle announces God's judgment on the wealthy and idolatrous oppressors of Israel. The opening verses connect idolatry and injustice by announcing judgment on symbols of each one: *altars* and *houses* of the wealthy, respectively. The two offenses are linked because forsaking God for idols means forsaking divine standards in all matters, including justice. The *altars of Bethel* include Jeroboam I's altar at the shrine of his calf image (1 Kgs 12:26–13:5) and may include unauthorized altars for God, as well.

In 4:1–3, the prophet then addresses the rich *women*, who stand for all those who *oppress the poor*. Amos derogatorily compares them to *cows* fattened for the slaughter. They will be dragged through breaches in the city wall, tethered by *hooks*, an image of defeat and humiliation (see 2 Kgs 19:28; 2 Chron 33:11; Ezek 38:4; Hab 1:15). The meaning and location of *Harmon* is uncertain (Stuart 333; Paul 135–36).

The call to *sin* at *Bethel* and *Gilgal* (4:4–5; compare Hos 4:15; 9:15) is ironic. If the wealthy Israelites continue to live as they do now, no amount of *sacrifices* or *offerings* can save them. True worship and ethical living are inextricably intertwined.

> **Alternative Sanctuaries**
>
> *In ancient Israel, temples or open-air sacred spaces existed at several locales. Bethel and Dan, the border cities of the northern kingdom of Israel, were the largest and best known. Gilgal had been in use since the earliest days of Israelite life in Palestine. Amos does not condemn the sanctuaries per se, but rather the actions that occurred within them and the worshipers' neglect of ethical living.*

In keeping with the curses in the law (Lev 26:14–26; Deut 28:15–48), God sent judgments of increasing severity upon the people, even completely destroying *some* in the manner of *Sodom and Gomorrah* (4:6–12; compare Gen 19:1–29). However, to this point, God has been unwilling to destroy everyone (2 Kgs 13:23). The goal of such judgments is corrective and redemptive, intending to lead the people back to God, as indicated by the refrain *yet you have not returned to me* (verses 6, 8, 9, 10, 11; see Lev 26:18, 21, 23, 27, 40).

Because the wealthy refuse to respond to such correction, Amos warns them to *prepare to meet* their awesome *God*. The word *this* in verse 12 probably refers back to destruction and exile predicted in 3:13–4:3. Exile is the final and most severe of the curses of the law (Lev 26:27–35; Deut 28:49–68).

5:1–17 God, who takes no pleasure in bringing judgment, laments the impending "death" of *Israel* (verses 1–3). In verses 4–6, God's intention is to bring the people to repentance. Therefore, Amos calls on them to *seek* him and *live* (Deut 30:15–20) instead of turning to the idolatrous shrines of *Bethel*, *Gilgal*, or *Beersheba* (8:14), which will all perish in the coming judgment.

Verses 7–13 draw a fearful picture of a God who will not allow injustice to continue unpunished in the land. *Justice* and *righteousness* should characterize the people of God, as they characterize God himself, but Israel has undermined both. They *hate* those who testify truthfully in *court* (literally "gate," where legal matters were handled; also in verses 12, 15) and use bribery to corrupt the system in their favor (Exod 20:16; 23:1, 8; Deut 16:19). They grow wealthy on the backs of the *poor* by coercing them *to give* over their livelihood, perhaps by manipulating the courts against them (Stuart 348), or through excessive taxation (Paul 172–73), or through making debt repayment impossible. But God assures the rich that they will not long enjoy the fruits of their corruption (see Deut 28:30). The *prudent man* here could refer to those who simply remain quiet in order to avoid being crushed by the corrupt system, or it could refer to the unjust, who should resist any attempt to justify themselves before God.

Verses 14–15 again call Israel to repent, particularly by ensuring *justice in the courts*. The use of *perhaps* (verse 15) indicates that the extension of God's *mercy* to Israel is not guaranteed. Israel has violated the covenant, so restoration can occur only because of God's mercy. However, if things continue as they are, God's judgment will result in great *wailing* as God *passes through* their midst, a scene reminiscent of the plague on the firstborn of Egypt (verses 16–17; Exod 11:4–6; 12:29–30).

Justice & Righteousness

Justice and righteousness are central to the character and action of God (Pss 33:5; 36:6; 37:6; 89:14; Jer 9:24; Hos 2:19), whom Israel should imitate. These concepts are related, and, thus, they are often paired in the Old Testament. Justice [Hebrew mishpat*] derives from the root* shaphat, *"to judge," which indicates the restoration of harmony and wholeness [Hebrew* shalom*] between individuals or within a community. A disruption of that wholeness can occur when two parties have a dispute or when one party wrongs another. A third party (for example, a judge, the king, or God) intervenes to restore* shalom, *and justice* [mishpat] *is the act and result of this intervention (hence* mishpat *is also often translated "judgment"). Thus, justice is active. The term frequently applies to a legal setting, as is often the case in Amos, but it is not limited to this setting (Liedke 1392–99; Birch 155–56, 259). Righteousness [Hebrew* tsedaqah *or* tsedeq*] is a relational term that entails both the act and results of faithfully maintaining the integrity of the relationship so that both parties enjoy the benefits of the relationship. Thus God delivers and preserves Israel, and Israel keeps God's commands, most of which focus on how humans treat each other (see Birch 153–55, 259–60; Koch 1046–62; von Rad 370–83).*

Injustice, violence, and oppression are antithetical to justice and righteousness because they disrupt the harmony and wholeness of the community and violate the relationships between God and Israel and between fellow Israelites (see Isa 1:21; 5:7; Jer 22:3; Ezek 45:9). Once Israel becomes unfaithful to its covenant relationship with God, love of neighbor also disappears, and violence and oppression erupt. God sends prophets like Amos to warn the people to restore justice and righteousness, but, when they refuse, God intervenes to save the oppressed and to judge and punish the oppressors (Ps 103:6, 17–18).

5:18–27 The *day of the Lord* refers to a time when God will decisively intervene in history to judge and to save. Israel mistakenly expects that such a day will benefit them because they think that their religious exercises appease or manipulate God. But God hates their worship and refuses to *accept* their *offerings* because they have subverted *justice* and *righteousness* (compare Isa 1:10–15), both of which should flourish in Israel. Furthermore, their worship to God is only half-hearted because they also worship *idols*.

The question in verse 25 is curious. In light of verses 21–23, the expected answer is "no," but several passages indicate that *Israel*, in fact, made *sacrifices and offerings* during the wilderness period (for example, Exod 24:5; Lev 9:8–22; Num 7:87–88). The complete sacrificial system, however, came into force only after Israel settled in the land (Deut 12). Faithfulness, rather than performing rituals, is the central element of a proper relationship with God (Stuart 355; Achtemeier 212; Paul 193–94).

6:1–14 The rich are *complacent* and *feel secure* because their wealth continues to increase and their borders are safe. In their own eyes, they are indeed *notable men of the foremost nation* and are better than *Calneh*, *Hamath*, or *Gath*, states neighboring Israel or Judah. These cities fell under Assyrian control around Amos's time. Israel's wealth does not indicate God's favor. They sin not simply by enjoying luxuries but by ignoring the *ruin* of their fellow Israelites, whom they oppress in order to obtain those luxuries.

God reveals deep disgust for Israel's misplaced *pride*. Past military victories at *Lo Debar* and *Karnaim* should not make them confident in their own strength or in God's favor upon them. Because they pervert *justice* and *righteousness*, God will *deliver up* Israel to foreigners who will leave nothing but *bodies* behind. Any survivor will not want *the name of the Lord* mentioned, lest he draws God's attention and die, too. The geographical range from *Lebo Hamath* (in the gap between the Lebanon and Antilebanon mountain ranges) to *the valley of the Arabah* (the rift valley south of the Dead Sea) represents the northernmost and southernmost conquests of Jeroboam II (2 Kgs 14:25).

AMOS'S VISION REPORTS WITH INTERLUDES · 7:1–9:15

7:1–9 Three visions of God's judgment arouse Amos's compassion for his people so that he intercedes on their behalf (like Moses in Exod 32:11–14). Twice God *relented* because of his compassion for Israel (2 Kgs 13:23), but Israel cannot presume upon God's mercy, since God is also just and righteous (Jer 7:16; 11:14). The first vision is of a devastating plague of *locusts* (verses 1–3; compare Joel 1:2–12; 2:1–11). The second vision (verses 4–6), *judgment by* *fire*, may symbolize severe judgment in general or may hyperbolically picture a terrible drought (see. 4:7–8). The third vision (verses 7–9) is of a *plumb line*, a tool that provides a standard for making sure that walls are straight or *true*. God finds that his people are not *true* to his calling for them (compare 2 Kgs 21:13; Isa 28:17; 34:11). Another possible translation for the word translated *plumb line* [Hebrew *'anak*] is "tin." If this translation is correct, it may be an auditory wordplay on similar sounding Hebrew words (see 8:1–2) for groaning or moaning (*'anach* or *'anaq*), or it may be an image of a tin wall, which would be weak and offer little protection for Israel (see Holladay 492–94; Stuart 373; Paul 233–35). Whatever the correct translation, the point of the oracle is clear: God will no longer withhold judgment against Israel's *sanctuaries* and the royal family (see 2 Kgs 15:8–12).

> **Prophetic Intercession**
> In the Old Testament, three great prophets succeed in changing God's mind regarding the destruction of a people: Abraham for the number of citizens of Sodom required to save the city, Moses after the golden calf episode, and Amos here. The Bible does not portray God as an inflexible manipulator of human actions.

7:10–17 The encounter between Amaziah the priest and Amos interrupts the series of vision reports, but it explains Amos's words against the house of Jeroboam (7:9). Amaziah accuses Amos of treason. Since Amos never specifically predicts the death of Jeroboam, this accusation probably reflects Amaziah's own interpretation of Amos's prophecy in verse 9. Amaziah sees Amos as a prophet-for-hire (as in 1 Kgs 22:6; Mic 3:5) and orders him to return to Judah and earn his living there. Amos denies that he is the kind of prophet Amaziah has in mind. He is neither a professional prophet nor a disciple of a prophet (*a prophet's son*). Rather, God *took* him and sent him to prophesy (see Deut 18:15, 18). Amos then announces degradation and death for Amaziah's family and exile for Amaziah.

8:1–3 This vision report involves a wordplay between two similar sounding Hebrew words, "ripe fruit" (*qayits*) and "end" (*qets*), which the NIV translates the "time is ripe," preserving the sense of the wordplay. The picture of that day of God's judgment is mayhem followed by desolation.

8:4–14 This extended oracle reviews the sins of Israel before giving several pictures of the day of God's judgment upon them. According to verses 4–6, the oracle addresses those who gain wealth by cheating *the poor* through deceptive business practices (Lev 19:36; Deut 25:13–16; Prov 11:1; 20:23) and by treating their lives as cheap commodities (see above on 2:6). The rich formally observe the *Sabbath* but forget its significance as a reminder that God is the creator and sustainer of all (Exod 20:8–11) and that God delivered all Israel from slavery (Deut 5:12–15). Thus, Sabbath observance was to serve as the great equalizer in the Israelite community, reminding Israel that they all benefited from God's care and thus should show each other similar care and compassion. However, God is well aware of their practices and will soon respond by convulsing Israel like the rising and falling of the *Nile* in its annual flood cycle (verses 7–8).

> **Amos & Foreign Cultures**
> Amos and other biblical writers knew a great deal about the geography, patterns of life, and even religious traditions of neighboring cultures. The active trading culture of the time would have made such broad knowledge possible.

Three descriptions of *that day* of God's judgment then follow. First, the images of the cosmos darkening (Amos 5:18, 20; Isa 13:10; Jer 4:28; Ezek 32:7–8; Joel 2:10; 2:31; 3:15; compare Matt 24:29) and of celebration turned to *mourning* (Isa 24:6–13; Jer 16:8–9; Hos 2:11; Rev 18:21–22) are common images of severe judgment. Second, there will be a *famine* of God's *words* (11–12). Israel had already rejected God's word in the Law, which was to truly sustain them (Deut 6:1–2; 8:3), and now God will withhold the prophetic word. When God no longer sends prophets, Israel will face judgment (1 Sam 3:1; 28:6; Lam 2:9; Ezek 7:26). Third, the judgment will be so severe that even the most vigorous will *faint* and not be revived.

9:1–6 Amos sees the image of God striking a temple, probably the Bethel sanctuary, so that it collapses on the worshipers within. Any survivors are *killed with the* sword, which illustrates the point of this oracle: *none* of those under God's judgment *will escape*. No place is low enough, high enough, or far enough to *hide* from God (Rom 8:38–39) who intends *evil*, that is harm, for them rather than *good*.

9:7–10 With this final oracle of judgment, the book of Amos comes full circle, again proclaiming

God's sovereignty over all nations and again lumping Israel among the nations (Amos 1:3–2:16). God brought both *Israel* into its land, and other nations into theirs (Deut 2:2–23; 32:8). However, God promises not to *totally destroy* Israel but rather to scatter *Israel among the nations*, but *the sinners*, those who arrogantly believe that they will not *meet* judgment, *will die*.

9:11–15 Following the judgment, God announces another *day* for the pitching again of *David's fallen tent*, which anticipates the restoration of all Israel. Territorial expansion, rebuilding, replanting, and abundance will mark this restoration. God will *plant* Israel so that it will never be *uprooted* (Jer 31:27–28; 32:41; Hos 2:21–23). Thus, God's ultimate goal is to restore and bless the people.

THEOLOGICAL REFLECTIONS

Does the book of Amos present good news or bad news? For those who gain and maintain wealth through the oppression of the poor and corruption, it is bad news. It is bad news for those who divide their loyalties between God and idols. Whatever they think, abundance does not prove that they have pleased, appeased, or manipulated God.

However, for those among the poor and oppressed, Amos's words are good news. God is indeed aware of their plight and will act on their behalf. Within the Law, God has repeatedly expressed a concern for the weakest of society and an intention to intervene on their behalf (see Exod 22:21–24; Lev 19:33–34; Deut 10:17–19; 15:1–11). Through the prophets, like Amos, God announces that such intervention is at hand because Israel refuses to maintain justice and righteousness, especially for the poor and weak (compare Isa 1:10–20; Jer 22:1–9; Mic 3:1–4, 9–12; Hab 1:1–11).

Even to those under God's judgment, however, Amos reveals that God's mercy and compassion are at work. First, God sends prophets like Amos to warn the people to repent, and judgment comes only after they reject the prophet's message (2:11–12; 3:17). Second, God delays judgment repeatedly and refrains from executing it totally (4:11; 7:3, 6). Third, God announces a plan to restore and bless the people (9:11–15).

Amos's words are a timely warning for the American church today, especially in light of our great wealth compared to the world at large and to fellow Christians abroad. Amos warns us against acquiring our wealth, directly or indirectly, through the oppression of the poor and weak. He further warns us against manipulating the system against the weak by favoring the rich over the poor or by denying the poor access to the same level of justice we enjoy. Amos reminds us that we, as the people of God, are responsible to care for fellow Christians in need, wherever they are, to ensure that there is no favoritism toward the wealthy or powerful in our churches, and to fulfill our calling by living as people of justice and righteousness in this world. Jesus came to proclaim release for the oppressed (Luke 4:18), and we must join him on the side of the oppressed.

FOR FURTHER STUDY

Philip J. King, *Amos, Hosea, Micah: An Archaeological Commentary* (Philadelphia: Westminster, 1988).

Enrique Nardoni, *Rise Up, O Judge: A Study in Justice in the Biblical World* (Peabody, Mass.: Hendrickson, 2004).

WORKS CITED

Elizabeth Achtemeier, *Minor Prophets I* (Peabody, Mass.: Hendrickson, 1996).

Bruce C. Birch, *Let Justice Roll Down: The Old Testament, Ethics and the Christian Life* (Louisville: Westminster John Knox, 1991).

Mordecai Cogan, "'Ripping Open Pregnant Women' in Light of an Assyrian Analog," *Journal of the American Oriental Society* 103 (1983): 755–57.

William L. Holladay, "Once More, 'anak = 'tin.' Amos 7:7–8," *Vetus Testamentum* 20 (1970): 492–94.

Klaus Koch, "ṣdq," *Theological Lexicon of the Old Testament* 2 (1997): 1046–62.

Gerhard Liedke, "špt," *Theological Lexicon of the Old Testament* 3 (1997): 1392–99.

Shalom M. Paul, *Amos* (Minneapolis, Minn.: Fortress, 1991).

Gerhard von Rad, *Old Testament Theology* (trans. D. M. G. Stalker; 2 vols.; San Francisco: Harper San Francisco, 1962).

Douglas Stuart, *Hosea-Jonah* (Waco, Tex.: Word, 1987).

Obadiah

Mark W. Hamilton

CHAPTER CONTENTS

Contexts 685
Commentary 686
    Superscription · 1a 686
    Yahweh's Indictment of Edom · 1–14, 15b 686
    Yahweh's Deliverance of Zion · 15a, 16–21a 687
    Conclusion · 21b 687
Theological Reflections 688
For Further Study 688
Works Cited 688

The book of Obadiah has the twin distinctions of being both the shortest book in the Old Testament and the only one that substantially duplicates part of another book. At twenty-one verses, it is only 1.7 percent as long as Jeremiah, the longest prophetic work, and it extensively parallels Jeremiah 49.

Importantly, Obadiah offers a powerful reflection on the morality of world politics, as God perceives it. In addressing the question of God's interest in Israel's enemies, it also complements Jonah's gracious universality with a realistic perception of the complexities of international affairs and the true effects of war upon conquered peoples.

CONTEXTS

The date, career, and background of the prophet Obadiah remain obscure. Scholars have dated his work anywhere between 900 and 450 BCE, although his reference to Edomite betrayal of Judah makes best sense in the context of events surrounding Nebuchadnezzar's destruction of Jerusalem in 586 BCE (see Ps 137; Lam 21:22; Ezek 25:12–14). Raabe and Wolff have proposed, plausibly, that Obadiah's prophecy may come from a service of lamentation at the location of the destroyed temple in Jerusalem during the years immediately preceding its rebuilding at the end of the sixth century BCE (Wolff 20–21; Raabe 55–56). See also Psalm 74.

While scholars have offered various scenarios by which originally separate, brief oracles could have coalesced in this single book, the more recent trend has been to try to understand the book as a coherent unit originating probably in one situation. (However, the opening words *the vision of Obadiah* (1a) probably come from the editor of the Book of the Twelve.) Since verses 1b–18 are poetry, and 19–21 are prose, the end of the book may stem from a separate occasion in the prophet's life, but even this hypothesis remains unproven. As they stand, verses 19–21 explicate the previous lines, explaining concretely what the generalized talk of Israel's restoration in verses 17–18 will mean. Admittedly, the book does seem to jump from metaphor to metaphor in a slightly bewildering way, but this can be explained by its origins in oral performance (as was true of most prophetic oracles), and in its rich use of wordplays and a kaleidoscope of images to carry its message.

> **"Book of the Twelve"**
> *"Book of the Twelve" is a Hebrew term for the twelve minor prophets in the Old Testament canon.*

One of the simplest, yet powerful, examples of wordplay revolves around a series of puns in Hebrew. For example, verse 12 mentions the *day of their destruction* [Hebrew *yom avedam*], which sounds like verse 13's *day of their disaster* [*yom eydom*], which in turns sounds like "day of Edom." Whenever the hearer of Obadiah's oracle thinks of Edom, he or she also thinks of disaster. A second series of wordplays centers around the name of the Edomite capital Bozrah [*Botsrah*]. For example, verse 12 refers to Edom's behavior in Judah's *day of trouble* [*beyom tsarah*], and verse 5 uses the word for *grape pickers* [*botserim*]. The fondness for wordplay is common in Hebrew poetry, and skill at such punning must have marked the successful poet. Since this poetry was probably originally oral, the punning also allows easy memorization of the words.

As one expects from Hebrew poetry, the lines of Obadiah consist of strings of couplets linked by numerous wordplays and chains of imagery. For example, verses 3–4 open with a reference to the mountainous home of the Edomites (*you who live in the clefts of the rocks*), then refer to something that also nests among the mountains (*the eagle*), then imagines such birds nesting higher still, among the stars, and finally concludes by reversing the boast of verse 3 (*Who can bring me down to the ground?*) with God's taunt in verse 4 (*I will bring you down*).

> **Yahweh's Servant**
> *Obadiah places his great poetic gifts in the service of the theological proclamation of the absolute sovereignty of Israel's God.*

COMMENTARY

The book consists of two large intertwined blocks of material, plus a superscription and concluding tag line.

THE SUPERSCRIPTION · 1A

Befitting the brevity of the book, *The vision of Obadiah* is the shortest superscription in the prophetic works. Typically, the superscription locates a prophet in time and space by naming his father or birthplace and dating the prophetic words to a king's reign. For example, Micah 1:1 introduces: *The word of the Lord that came to Micah of Moresheth during the reigns of Jotham, Ahaz, and Hezekiah, kings of Judah*…. The terseness of the heading of the book of Obadiah allows the editor who combined it with other parts of the Book of the Twelve to connect its reference to the day of Yahweh with prior discussions of that theme in Joel and Amos. We hardly notice that one book has ended and another has begun.

YAHWEH'S INDICTMENT OF EDOM · 1B–14, 15B

1B Opening with the typical prophetic style of introduction, the messenger formula *This is what the Sovereign Lord says*, the oracle immediately shifts to a different point of view, *We have heard*. The *We* may include other prophets, or the divine council, or simply Obadiah's hearers, as well as the prophet himself. The rest of the verse calls someone, probably foreign nations though possibly Israel, to battle.

2–4 After the call to battle, God taunts Edom, referring to its mountainous terrain. While the Edomites think of this territory as impregnable, Yahweh knows better. The metaphor of rising to the *stars* typically symbolizes the arrogance of political leaders, notably the king of Babylon in Isaiah 14:12–14 (see also Gen 11:1–9). Numbers 24:21 describes the nomadic tribe of the Kenites nesting in the strongholds of the mountain. *Declares the Lord* marks the end of the first paragraph of the oracle.

5–7 The second paragraph emphasizes the Edomites' vulnerability. *Grape pickers* alludes to the extensive grape production around the capital, Bozrah (see LaBianca and Younker 403). Even those who should enhance Edom's economic prosperity become potential enemies. Verse 7 makes the threat concrete: *All your allies* will abandon you. Obadiah faults Edom's choice of *allies*, which led to its betrayal of its natural partner, Judah. How ironic, then, that these very allies should now abandon Edom! *Allies* translates the Hebrew "men of your covenant." A "covenant" here means a political agreement – that is, a treaty. Often in the Bible, the term designates God's agreement with Israel.

> **Edom**
> *The land of Edom lies south and east of the Dead Sea in what is today Jordan and northern Saudi Arabia. An arid region that receives 4–8 inches of rain per year, Edom relied on herding and limited agriculture to make a living. After the Babylonian conquest of Judah, Edomites gradually moved west into southern Judah. The region became known as Idumaea (the Greek form of "Edom").*
>
> *Egyptian sources mention the region as early as the reign of Ramesses II (1304–1237 BCE). However, extensive settlement of the area dates only to the centuries after 1000 BCE (see MacDonald; LaBianca and Younker).*

8–10 These verses describe the *day* of the Lord, a recurring theme in the prophets. The day may not appear on any calendar. Rather, it marks any moment of decisive divine intervention. While Edom may not have enjoyed more *wise men* than other nations (though Job hailed from the region), their demise meant the loss of practical skills and of social memory. *Teman* is a town in northwest Saudi Arabia (for its link to Edom, see Amos 1:12). Curiously, the last Neo-Babylonian king, Nabonidus, spent most of his reign in *Teman* pursuing religious enlightenment. So his contemporary

Obadiah may envision here the destruction both of Edom and of the geopolitical system into which it has placed itself.

11–14 Obadiah uses the Hebrew imperfect verb in verses 12–14 to make the terrible events surrounding the sack of Jerusalem seem more real, more current. For an even more graphic description of the city's fall, see the book of Lamentations. *Gates* symbolizes the entire fortification system of a city (13). The breach of a city's gates by enemy armies spells doom for its inhabitants.

15B The conclusion of Yahweh's indictment refers to the *lex talionis*: *As you have done, it will be done to you*. Leviticus 24:17–21 establishes a basic principle of Israelite justice: punishment fits the crime. Punishment should not be excessive, arbitrary, or prejudiced. Since Edom has betrayed its friends and participated in ethnic cleansing, it must suffer the consequences. The final line, *your deeds will return upon your head*, reflects a slightly different idea, namely, that actions have consequences irrespective of the intervention of others (including God).

> **Lex Talionis**
> The legal principle of exact reciprocity, or "mirror punishment," sometimes called "eye for an eye" justice, which was common in ancient legal systems.

YAHWEH'S DELIVERANCE OF ZION · 15A, 16–21A

15A This verse links the two major sections of the book, the indictment of Edom and the deliverance of Zion. The prophet describes both events, which are ultimately one event, as *the day of the Lord* (see Joel 3:14; Zeph 3:14–16). As in Psalm 2, Yahweh saves Jerusalem from foreign powers threatening it.

16–18 Scholars debate the identity of the subject of *you drank*. Since drinking can sometimes in the Bible symbolize suffering and calamity (for example, Ps 75:8; Isa 51:17–23; Hab 2:16), some argue that *you drank* must refer to Israel, the group that has suffered *on my holy hill*, which is to say, Jerusalem (Raabe 203). On the other hand, since Edom has been the addressee so far in the book, others argue that it must be so here, as well (Wolff 64). This would mean that *drink* in 16a means "to drink in celebration," while in 16b it means "to drink in suffering." This more poetically elegant double entendre, probably the better interpretation of the verse, would emphasize the reversal of fortune awaiting Edom. NIV's rendering *they will drink and drink* obscures the change of verb in the Hebrew text: "they will drink and guzzle" would capture the original text's intensification better.

The promise of deliverance, paralleled in roughly contemporaneous texts such as Isa 40–55 and Jer 31, extends to all Israelites. *House of Jacob* and *house of Joseph* must include even those deportees from the northern kingdom of Israel. All will return to *Mount Zion*, meaning that all the people will once again worship Yahweh in one place as one people. In some unspecified way, their relocation around Jerusalem will involve the destruction of Edom, like *stubble* burned in *fire* (an image readily understandable to dwellers in arid regions like Edom).

19–21A The author describes the various parts of the land of Israel. The Negev in the south, the *foothills* (*Shephelah*) separating Judah from the Coastal Plain, the plain itself (*land of the Philistines*), the *fields* (fertile hills) *of Ephraim and Samaria*, *Gilead* (in modern Jordan), and southern Lebanon (*Zarephath*) – all of these regions will once again fall under Israelite control. In other words, the nation will recover all the territory it has ever occupied. Moreover, deportees from as far away as Sardis in Asia Minor (*Sepharad*) will resettle in the land. *Deliverers*, presumably Israelites who work to free their people from foreign domination, will also *govern* Mount Esau. NIV's *govern* translates the Hebrew word *shaphat*, "to rule as judge," the word normally associated with the premonarchic chieftains in the book of Judges. Obadiah thus does not envision the restoration of an earthly king, but of a looser kind of organization, directed by God. NIV's *mountains of Esau* would be better translated "Mount Esau." Obadiah coined this term to parallel *Mount Zion*: God will rule over both Israelites and Edomites.

> **The Negev**
> The Negev is a rocky desert region of southern Israel. The word "negev" derives from a Hebrew word that denotes both "dry" as well as "south."

CONCLUSION · 21B

And this is, of course, the point. Yahweh, not the Babylonian superpower, not the pesky Edomites, will rule: *the kingdom*, or better, "kingship," belongs to God. See Psalm 22:27–28.

THEOLOGICAL REFLECTIONS

Obadiah's fierce denunciation of Edom challenges the comfortable notions of divine love to which Christians in the prosperous West often subscribe. We ask, can God truly seek the destruction of a whole people, as this book envisions? Nor is Obadiah alone, for extended oracles against Edom appear also in Isaiah 34 and 63; Jeremiah 9, 27, and 49; Ezekiel 25 and 35; and Amos 1. (Shorter oracles appear elsewhere.) Indeed, the prophets frequently denounce foreign nations, not only for their mistreatment of Israel, but for their abuse of each other (see Amos 2:1).

The criticism of foreign powers reflects Israel's understanding of God as a God of justice who becomes involved in the messiness of history. Since politics and warfare inevitably involve injustice, a God who is concerned with the realities of human existence must work within their parameters. Edom, Obadiah charges, has betrayed its "brother" Jacob (note the stories in Gen 27 and 32–33 that serve as a background of this book) by allying itself with foreign, oppressive powers. Babylonia cut a swathe of destruction across the whole of southwest Asia, destroying cities of every nation and slaughtering or enslaving numerous populations. Most of Palestine lay underpopulated throughout their rule. To conspire with such a power, as Edom did, is to commit a range of injustice (see verses 11–13 for the catalogue) that a just God cannot overlook. This belief inspires Obadiah's seemingly hate-filled speech.

In reading this book, we become keenly aware of the injustices that humans can inflict on each other. Like the author of Jonah, the next book in the canon, we question to what degree violence can ever compensate for previous violence. Since the last verse of Obadiah envisions Yahweh's rule over both Israel and Edom, the prophet himself, ever the political realist, may have understood the punishment of the latter to be merely a prelude to a glorious time of international harmony and piety. Still, we ask what oracles like those of Obadiah tell us about the nature of God. If the book leaves us with more questions than answers, we nevertheless find in it a keen sense of hope. If the desperate refugees from Jerusalem can find their way home and can live anew as God intended them to do, perhaps we may also hope for something better.

FOR FURTHER STUDY

William P. Brown, *Obadiah through Malachi* (Louisville: Westminster John Knox, 1996).

Harold Shank, *Minor Prophets* (Joplin, Mo.: College Press, 2001).

WORKS CITED

John Bartlett, *Edom and the Edomites* (JSOT Supplement 77; Sheffield: Sheffield Academic Press, 1989).

Øystein LaBianca and Randall Younker, "The Kingdoms of Ammon, Moab and Edom: The Archaeology of Society in Late Bronze/Iron Age Transjordan (ca. 1400–500 BCE)," in Thomas Levy, ed., *The Archaeology of Society in the Holy Land* (New York: Facts on File, 1995) 399–413.

Burton MacDonald, "Early Edom: The Relation between the Literary and Archaeological Evidence," in Michael Coogan, J. Cheryl Exum, and Lawrence Stager, eds., *Scripture and Other Artifacts* (Louisville, Ky.: Westminster John Knox, 1994) 230–46.

Paul Raabe, *Obadiah* (AB 24D; New York: Doubleday, 1996).

Hans Walter Wolff, *Obadiah and Jonah* (trans. Margaret Kohl; Minneapolis, Minn.: Augsburg, 1986).

Jonah

John T. Willis

CHAPTER CONTENTS

Contexts **689**
Commentary **689**
    Jonah's Actions · 1:1–3:10 **689**
    Jonah's Attitude · 4:1–11 **691**
Theological Reflections **691**
For Further Study **691**
Works Cited **692**

MAPS, TABLES, & FEATURES

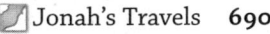 Jonah's Travels **690**

Various scholars have thought of Jonah as a historical account, legend, fable, novella, allegory, parable, satire, narrative, midrash, or didactic story. It is probably a religious drama, meant to be memorized and performed or recited before God's people.

> **Midrash**
> An ancient approach to biblical texts, the midrash sought not to explain the texts so much as to use them to illuminate current issues.

One of the purposes of this book is to challenge the audience's assumption that God loves only them. The book of Jonah was most likely written to Jews in Judah who had returned from Babylonian exile in the sixth through the fourth centuries BCE, as Persian customs, Aramaisms, themes of God's justice and the possibility of repentance are evident in the book.

> **Aramaisms**
> Although written in Hebrew, Jonah uses words and expressions borrowed from the closely related language Aramaic. This familiarity with Aramaic suggests a postexilic date for the book.

CONTEXTS

To facilitate memorization and performance, Jonah uses striking rhetorical and literary strategies, such as:

Contrast · Jonah contrasts actions and attitudes of God and Jonah, Jonah and the sailors, and Jonah and the Ninevites.

Intensification · Jonah progressively "moves downward" (1:3–5; 2:6), metaphorically indicating spiritual decline. For example, the storm worsens (1:4, 11, 13); the sailors' fear increases (1:5, 10, 16).

Repetition · The word *great* occurs 15 times (1:2, 4, 10, 12, 16, 17; 3:2, 3, 5, 7; 4:1, 6, 10, 11). *Evil*, with various nuances, occurs nine times (1:2, 7, 8; 3:8, 10 [where it occurs twice]; 4:1, 2, 6); and Yahweh *provides* four times (1:17; 4:6, 7, 8).

Questions · Jonah contains thirteen questions (1:6, 8 [where we find five questions], 10, 11; 3:9; 4:2, 4, 9, 11), each playing an important role in the message.

STRUCTURE & MESSAGE

James Limburg (*Hosea–Micah* 137) identifies five sections of the book: "Israel," which explores the relationship between Yahweh and Jonah (1:1–3); "Sea," which examines Jonah and the sailors (1:4–16); "Fish" which shows Yahweh and Jonah (1:17–2:10); "Nineveh" which shows the interplay between Yahweh, Jonah, and the Ninevites (3); and "Outside Nineveh," which again portrays the relationship between Yahweh and Jonah (4). Another possible structure has been developed by Leslie C. Allen (181, 200), who proposes two basic sections of Jonah: "Hebrew Sinner Saved" (1–2); and "Heathen Sinners Saved" (3–4). Either of these organizational templates makes sense, but this commentary proposes a third way to view the structure of the book of Jonah (1–3, 4).

COMMENTARY

JONAH'S ACTIONS · 1:1–3:10

1:1–3 That Yahweh charges *Jonah* to preach to the great city of *Nineveh* shows confidence in Jonah, but more importantly, it emphasizes that Yahweh is a universal ruler, dedicated to saving all people. Nineveh's *wickedness* is *violence* (3:8) and oppression

JONAH

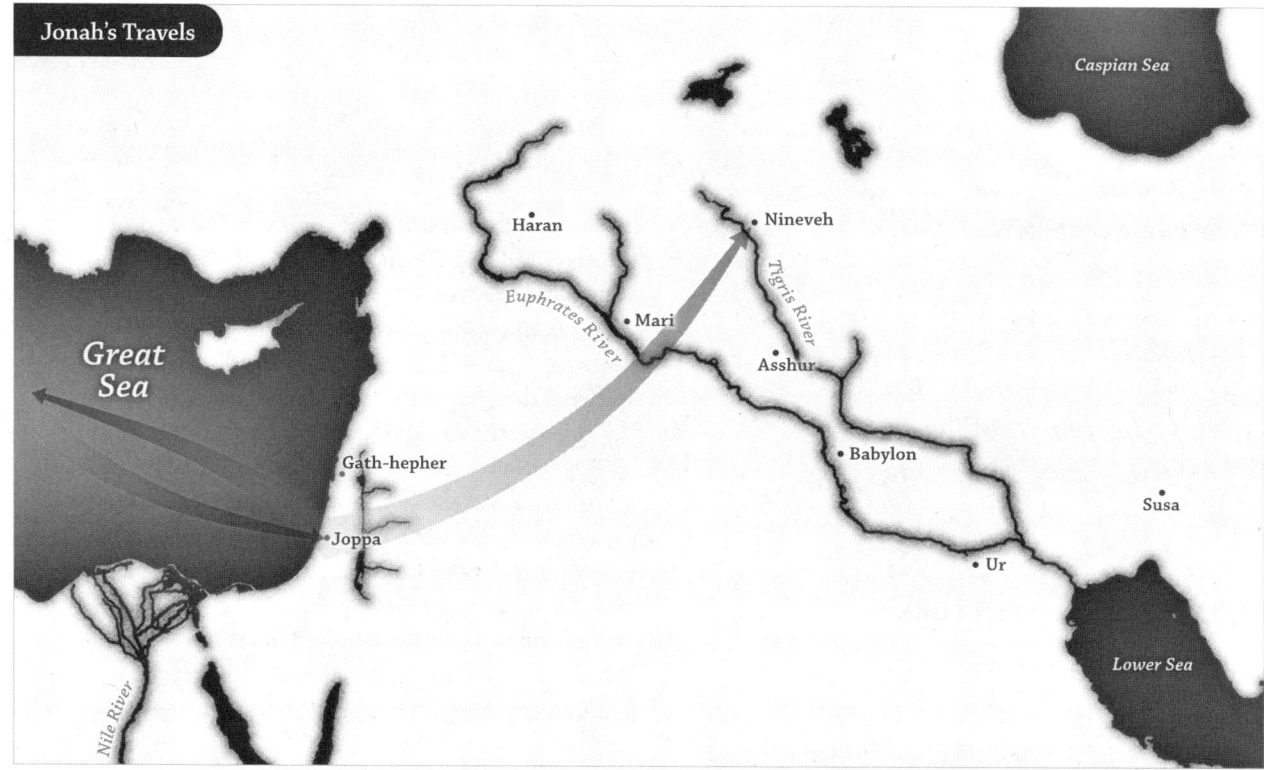

(Nah 2:11–12; 3:19). Jonah betrays Yahweh by fleeing (verse 10). Yahweh tells Jonah to go east to Nineveh, but instead, Jonah flees west to *Tarshish*, probably Tartessos in southern Spain. Gradually he *went down*, away from the will of God.

1:4–16 This section emphasizes Jonah's flight from Yahweh. Yahweh *sent* a *violent storm* to intercept Jonah. The harder the sailors work, the rougher the storm becomes (1:11, 13), threatening to wreck the ship and provoking the sailors to pray, in startling contrast to Jonah's indifference. To save their lives, the sailors risk economic ruin by jettisoning their cargo. The *captain* urges Jonah to pray, recognizing Yahweh's sovereign freedom to respond as he wills (verse 14). Again, the pagan sailor's piety contrasts with Jonah's impiety. Lot casting was a legitimate means of determining a guilty party in ancient times (Josh 7:14–18). The sailors' questions expose Jonah. *Who is responsible*? Jonah is, for striving to avoid doing Yahweh's commission. *What do you do*? Jonah is Yahweh's messenger. *From what people are you*? Jonah is an Israelite charged to "bless" the nations (Gen 22:18) by Yahweh's message (Isa 49:1–6). Jonah's reply *terrified* the sailors (verse 5). The question *What have you done?* is intended to force Johah to admit the seriousness of his actions (Gen 3:13; Jer 8:6). Jonah tells the sailors to throw him overboard to calm the storm, since Yahweh has sent it to punish him. Jonah had rather die than preach to Nineveh. Jonah tries everything to avoid preaching to Nineveh, while the sailors try everything to save the ship and passengers. The sailors' prayer, rooted in their desire to preserve life, evinces great hesitation to throw Jonah overboard and contrasts sharply with Jonah's preference for death. However, in desperation, they eventually acquiesce. Immediately the sea grows calm. The sailors, again unlike Jonah, worship Yahweh with gratitude.

1:17–2:10 Yahweh provides a fish to save Jonah from drowning, and Jonah, evincing a change of heart, thanks Yahweh for deliverance. As is often the case for those praying during times of great distress, Jonah's prayer (2:2–9) is composed largely of quotations, particularly from psalms (Sasson 159–215; Limburg, *Jonah*, 63–71). The fish carries Jonah for *three days and three nights* before bringing him back to dry land, giving

> **Merchant Ships & Their Cargo**
> *The cargo of ships in the ancient Mediterranean often consisted of large copper ingots or vast storage jars full of wine or oil.*

him much time to pray. In the book of Jonah, the three-day duration of Jonah's ordeal has no obvious significance, although, of course, in the New Testament Jesus uses it to describe the time he will spend in the tomb (Matt 12:39).

> **Jonah's Prayer**
> In his prayer inside the fish, Jonah uses the traditional language and structural formula of "thanksgiving psalms": a summary of experience (verse 2; Pss 31:22; 120:1); a description of peril (verses 3–6b; Pss 31:22; 42:7; 69:1; 102:10); deliverance (verse 6cd; Ps 103:4); a summary of experience (verse 7; Pss 102:1; 142:3; 143:5); and a message to congregation (verses 8–9; Pss 3:8; 31:6; 116:17–18).

Following his liberation from the fish, Jonah thanks Yahweh for saving him from drowning (verses 3–7). Jonah deserved to die, but Yahweh has been gracious. The storyteller here takes center stage (2:8–9) to contrast the *pagans*' trust in *worthless idols* and Jonah's (the believer's) thanksgiving for deliverance. Verses 5–6 portray an ancient view of the structure of the world, with mountains resting upon deep waters (see Pss 24:2; 148:4, 7, 9).

3:1–10 Jonah is now safe at home, but Yahweh repeats his earlier instructions to go to Nineveh, and this time, having experienced Yahweh's wrath, Jonah obeys. His message is: *Forty more days and Nineveh will be destroyed* (verse 4), indicating Yahweh's seriousness yet leaving open the possibility of forgiveness. A condition is understood (Jer 18:7–10): the fulfillment of Old Testament predictions and prophecies depends on the hearers' response. In this case, the Ninevites repent, using the traditional symbols of fasting (Joel 2:12), wearing sackcloth, and sitting in dust or ashes (Dan 9:3). Their hope is that *God may yet relent*. As Jonah has feared (4:2), Yahweh *changed his mind* (see also Exod 32:11–14); Yahweh's *compassion* extends to the penitent nation.

> **Jonah & Assyria**
> Given Assyria's historical role in the destruction of the Israelite monarchy and annexation of the land, the story of Jonah must have seemed daring to ancient Israelites. The repentance even of the Assyrian animals (3:7–8) both signals the comedic side of the book of Jonah and paints a serious picture of the possibilities of human repentance and God's forgiveness.

JONAH'S ATTITUDE · 4:1–11

4:1–8 Jonah 1–3 seem complete, yet the drama continues as the author, reflecting God's point of view, seeks to change the attitude both of Jonah and of the Jewish audience, who presumably agrees with Jonah about the repentance of the Ninevites. Yahweh turns from his *fierce anger* (3:9), but Jonah, in turn, now becomes *angry*. Here he reveals his motivation for running from God's command in chapter 1: he did not go to Nineveh at first (1:3) because he knew that Yahweh would be merciful even to pagans of the cruelest type. Jonah is upset when Yahweh forgives the penitent sinners of Nineveh, presumably because they are "pagan." When God confronts Jonah about his attitude, Jonah stalks off, unwilling even to answer. The death of the plant reveals Jonah's selfishness and failure to understand Yahweh's graciousness. Jonah complains that he is miserable and wants to die (verse 3). Jonah chooses death in protest if Yahweh saves people or destroys plants.

4:9–11 The storyteller takes center stage again (2:8–9) with Yahweh's question: Should one be like Jonah, who loves a plant that has no eternal destiny? Or should one be like Yahweh, *concerned* with *people* whose lives have their own integrity?

THEOLOGICAL REFLECTIONS

Jonah is written for people convinced that they alone are saved and all others are doomed. Against such arrogance, it proclaims that Yahweh is creator of everything (1:9), not merely of the chosen people, who have the task of proclaiming God's message to all nations in order to save them (Isa 49:1–6). Jonah represents the chosen people. The audience shares his attitude and must decide how to respond. The Ninevites are lost but will listen to Yahweh's messengers. Yahweh loves all peoples and desires their salvation.

FOR FURTHER STUDY

Uriel Simon, *Jonah* (Philadelphia: Jewish Publication Society, 1999).

Ehud Ben Zvi, *Signs of Jonah* (Sheffield: Sheffield Academic Press, 2003).

JONAH

WORKS CITED

Leslie C. Allen, *The Books of Joel, Obadiah, Jonah and Micah* (Grand Rapids: Eerdmans, 1976).

James Limburg, *Hosea–Micah* (Atlanta: John Knox, 1988).

———, *Jonah* (Louisville: Westminster John Knox, 1993).

Jack M. Sasson, *Jonah* (New York: Doubleday, 1990).

Micah

John T. Willis

CHAPTER CONTENTS

- Contexts **693**
- Commentary **693**
    - Superscription · 1:1 **693**
    - Punishment & Restoration: Israel & Judah · 1:2–2:13 **693**
    - Denunciation of Injustice & Restoration: Judah · 3:1–5:15 **695**
    - Punishment & Restoration: Samaria & Jerusalem · 6:1–7:20 **696**
- Theological Reflections **697**
- For Further Study **698**
- Works Cited **698**

MAPS, TABLES, & FEATURES

- Israel & Judah **694**

Material in the book of Micah dates from before the fall of Samaria in 724–721 BCE (1:5–7) to near the return from Babylon in 536 BCE (2:12–13; 4:6–10). Micah addressed Israel (1:5–7) and Judah (3:9–12) in about 725–700 BCE. Those passing on Micah's words (see Jer 26:17–19) assembled the book in about 536 BCE.

CONTEXTS

Recurring themes in Micah include the notion that punishment must fit the crime, calls for justice, and the importance of a restored remnant. Similarly, a number of images recur in the book: a shepherd and sheep, Zion, and the Davidic dynasty. Micah's reproof of Israel's and Judah's leaders is contrasted with the image of Yahweh's just and righteous leadership. The book thus demonstrates an overall coherence. Wordplays abound, and it appears that Micah's composers arranged the book for oral reading or dramatic performance before religious assemblies.

English versification from 5:1–15 (adopted here) equals the Hebrew versification of 4:14–5:14.

COMMENTARY

SUPERSCRIPTION · 1:1

Micah 1:1 affirms that the source of Micah's message is Yahweh. Micah's hometown was *Moresheth-gath* (1:14), twenty-five miles southwest of Jerusalem. Micah preached to *Samaria* and *Jerusalem* during the reigns of *Jotham* (742–735 BCE), *Ahaz* (735–715 BCE), and *Hezekiah* (715–687 BCE).

PUNISHMENT & RESTORATION: ISRAEL & JUDAH · 1:2–2:13

1:2–7 This passage portrays a "covenant lawsuit." Yahweh is the plaintiff; the prophet, the plaintiff's lawyer; Israel and Judah, the defendants; and the peoples and earth, witnesses that Yahweh's charges are valid. Micah summons the *peoples* and *earth* to learn from Yahweh's response to the people (Amos 3:9). Yahweh *comes down* from *his holy temple*, heaven (Gen 11:5–8), dissolving mountains and valleys. This language is common in poetic descriptions of God's appearances.

Yahweh will punish *Israel*'s and *Judah*'s sins, which are radiating from *Samaria* and *Jerusalem*. Israel's sins infect Judah; Yahweh's punishments follow (1:9, 13). Yahweh will make Samaria and Jerusalem a *heap of rubble* (1:6; 3:12). Invaders will destroy Samaria's walls and idols (1:6–7). The translation of verse 7d–e is debatable. Samaria prospered by allying with foreign nations (see Hos 8:8–10), so the nation will lose its prosperity to foreign nations. The oracle anticipates the Assyrians' destruction of the northern kingdom.

> **Prophets & Lament**
> *Prophets lamented disasters and sins (compare Amos 5:1–3), expressing grief traditionally by loud weeping (Jer 9:17–20), going barefoot and naked (Isa 20:2–4), howling like jackals, moaning like owls or ostriches (Job 30:29–31), and shaving their heads bald (Amos 8:10). Simundson observes:* "The message was contained both in the words and in the acting out of the lament" *(Simundson 546).*

1:8–16 This section reflects Sennacherib's invasion in 701 BCE (2 Kgs 18–19; Pritchard 287–88). The towns in 1:10–15 lie between Lachish – Sennacherib's

MICAH

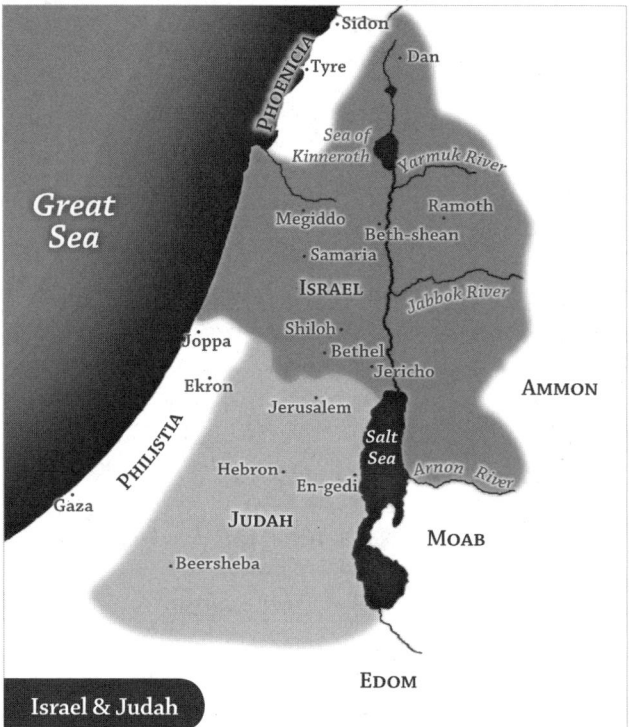

Israel & Judah

headquarters near the Mediterranean (2 Kgs 19:8) – and Jerusalem. The Assyrians destroyed them while approaching Jerusalem. Because Micah 1:10–15 does not proceed in geographical order west to east (compare Isa 10:27c–32), it presents translational difficulties. Experts have proposed various explanations for these problems, including the possibility that the beginning of each line was damaged, so that parallelism, wordplays, ancient versions, and "educated guesses" must be used to restore the text (Andersen and Freedman 253).

Her *wound* in verses 6–7 refers to Samaria's devastation in 721 BCE, which *has come to Judah* by Sennacherib's invasion. The *gate of my people* is Jerusalem (Obad 13). The verse begins with a pun: Hebrew *taggidu* (*tell*) sounds like the word for *Gath*. *Tell it not in Gath* (2 Sam 1:20) implies that Philistines will plunder or gloat over Israel if they discover Israel's defeat.

> **Places & Wordplay in Micah**
> Several place names here form word plays: Beth Ophrah *sounds like the word for* dust; Zaanan, *like* come out; Lachish, *like the Hebrew for* team; Achzib, *like the word for* deceptive; Mareshah, *like* conqueror.

Verbs in verse 16 are feminine singular, thus referring to Jerusalem; *the children* in whom Jerusalem delights are Judah's fortified cities. *They who go into exile* are the 200,150 Judeans Sennacherib carried into exile, according to his Annals.

2:1–11 Micah 2:1–11 explains why the Assyrians devastate Judah. Because powerful Judeans seize inheritances of the poor, Yahweh sends the Assyrians to seize and divide their land. This woe oracle might have ended at verse 5, but prophetic opponents challenged Micah (verses 6–7). Micah insists his charges are true and his opponents are liars and deceivers (verses 8–11).

I am planning disaster (verse 3) counters *those who plan ... evil* (verse 1) with just retribution (see Gal 6:7–8). Sin begins within, then erupts externally (verse 1). Oppressors *covet* others' possessions, then *seize* them (verse 2; see Amos 5:11–12), violating the tenth commandment (Exod 20:17). Yahweh's punishment is threefold: he crushes the oppressors' pride (verse 3b); enemies remove them from the land (verse 4); and invaders seize the possessions that the oppressors had previously claimed, ridiculing their impotence (verses 4–5).

Verses 6–11 are difficult. In verses 6–7, Micah relates prophetic opposition to his message in verses 1–5: these so-called prophets claim that they will not experience *disgrace* (verse 4); they say that Yahweh does not unleash anger against the people (verse 3), for he is *slow to anger* (Exod 34:6–7); and they point out that, because Yahweh blesses the *upright*, and God's people are prospering, therefore the people are upright.

Verses 8–11 contain Micah's response to these false prophets' rebuttal in verses 6–7. Verse 8a in the NRSV indicates certain prophets who rose up against defenseless Judeans as an enemy, while the NIV points to wealthy, powerful Judeans (verses 1–2) rather than to prophets. Whether prophets or the wealthy, these miscreants stole travelers' outer garments (Job 22:6), or kept garments taken in pledge (Deut 24:10–13), and drove women from their homes, leaving their children without an inheritance. Micah encourages the oppressed to flee, calling his opponents liars and deceivers. He satirizes his opponents for selling out for alcohol.

2:12–13 Here, the mood, setting, and message change, and a different performer speaks. His hearers are in Babylonian exile (compare 4:9–10). He summarizes major themes of other Mican hope oracles: that Yahweh, as Judah's *king*, will *gather* the exiles; and that he will *bring* together the remnant of Israel (in Jerusalem) as a shepherd assembles his *flock*.

DENUNCIATION OF INJUSTICE & RESTORATION: JUDAH · 3:1–5:15

The first part of this section balances a denunciation of injustice in Judah with a vision of the restoration of the righteous remnant.

3:1–8 Micah reproves Judah's *leaders*, responsible for maintaining *justice*, for oppressing the defenseless in the same way that cannibals flay and consume victims, demonstrating that they *hate good and love evil*. This gory image works rhetorically to gain the audience's attention. According to verse 4, Yahweh's punishment fits the crime (2:1–3). Oppressors will suffer oppression and *cry out to the Lord*; yet God will not play the role of deliverer (Ps 27:7–9).

The second person plural "you" (verse 6a) indicates that Micah addresses his prophetic opponents' criticism (verse 8). Micah censures the other prophets for preaching to please powerful rulers, who reward them liberally.

God's punishment of *prophets*, *seers*, *diviners* (three synonyms for technicians who seek to understand the divine will for the future) fits the crime. They proclaim peace; Yahweh sends the Assyrians to punish Judah (night and darkness represent such punishment; Amos 5:18–20), publicly disgracing them. *Cover the lips* (NRSV) signifies disgrace (Ezek 24:17, 22). Micah affirms that he is *filled with power*, the *spirit* (or presence) of Yahweh (compare Ps 51:11), *justice* and *might*, proclaiming Yahweh's displeasure with Judah's *sin*.

> **The Will of the Gods**
>
> *Ancient peoples went to great lengths to discern the will of the gods. They studied the entrails of sacrificed animals, the movement of the stars (astrology), and unusual events. They collected and systematized omens so as to create a body of precedents for predicting the future. The Bible forbids many, but not all, such practices (Lev 19:31; Deut 18:9–13).*

3:9–12 Micah denounces Judah's *leaders*, *priests*, and *prophets* for oppressing the helpless (2:2, 8–9), accumulating wealth, and assuming exemption from *disaster* (see 2:3) no matter how they live. Again, as in verses 6–7, Micah refers to a triad of leaders.

Yahweh says that he will devastate Jerusalem, as he did Samaria (1:6–7), and destroy the temple. This does not happen immediately, because Hezekiah and Judah repent (Jer 26:17–19). Although doom oracles sound superficially as if they allow no alteration of God's will, in fact they function as calls to repentance. They are revocable.

The prophet borrows from a Song of Zion (see Isa 2:2–4), affirming Zion's elevation of status and the pilgrimage of all nations to it. He adds a description of peace, using traditional metaphors (verse 4), then states that this peace will occur when Israel follows Yahweh's ethical standards (verse 5). Verses 1–5 contain five contrasts to 3:9–12: a description of an elevated (4:1) versus ruined Temple Mount (3:12); Yahweh's empowering (4:2) versus the priests' debasing teaching (3:11); Yahweh's equitable (4:3) versus the leaders' unjust judging (3:9, 11); *Zion*, or Jerusalem, characterized by Yahweh's instruction (4:2) versus the leaders' wickedness (3:10); and divine peace (4:3–4) versus human chaos (3:9–10).

4:1–5 The word *for* in verse 2f (NRSV) is crucial to understanding the sequence. First, Yahweh will exalt the Temple Mount (verse 1a–c). Second, Yahweh's messengers (prophets or priests) will carry teachings from Zion to the nations (verse 2f–g). Third, receptive nations will stream to Zion to receive Yahweh's further instruction (verses 1d–2e). The NRSV's *in days to come* and *instruction* are preferable to the NIV's *In the last days* and *law*.

Yahweh decides disputes between nations; they assent and live at peace (1 Kgs 4:25). Far from being merely the god of a small kingdom, Yahweh is actually the sovereign of the universe.

The prophet and his associates resolve to *walk in the name of the Lord* as they carry Yahweh's message to the nations (verse 2f–g), so the hopes of verses 1–4 may become reality.

4:6–7 Verses 6–7 (compare 2:12–13) assume that God's people are in Babylonian exile. Yahweh *afflicted* (NRSV) them (verse 6d) through the Babylonians (Jer 25:8–11). Yet Yahweh will next reassemble the deportees, transform them into a *remnant* (compare Isa 10:20–23) and *a strong nation*, and reconstitute them as a political entity on *Mount Zion*.

4:8–11 The verses from 4:8 to 5:2 contain the chiastic, or sandwiching, wordplay: *we attah* ("and you") (4:8); *attah* ("now") (4:9); *we attah* ("and now") (4:11); *attah* ("now") (5:1); and *we attah* ("and you") (5:2). The punning focuses on the hearers' deep involvement in the crisis of national destruction. Micah 4:9–10 assumes Jews are in Babylonian exile but will soon return to Jerusalem (550–538 BCE), depicting the fate of *daughter Zion* (NRSV) in four stages: distress due to *enemies*; the rigors of deportation (*camp in the open field*); travel to *Babylon*, and a final hopeful word concerning Yahweh's rescue.

The *king and counselor* may be Zedekiah, the last king of Judah, who failed in his plot to throw off Babylonian rule (2 Kgs 25:1–21). *A woman in labor* is a metaphor for terror during military attack (see Jer 4:31). To *redeem* [Hebrew *gaal*; Isa 44:22–24] is the task of the avenger of blood [Hebrew *goel*; Deut 19:6, 12], a term which is sometimes used to describe Yahweh delivering Israel from Egypt (Exod 6:6).

Many nations gather to destroy Jerusalem (see Psalm 2), yet Yahweh gathers them *like sheaves to the threshing floor* (Isa 21:10) to pulverize them. The use of farming imagery to describe military action occurs elsewhere in the Bible (for example, see Amos 1:3). The word *devote* is a technical term for giving spoils of holy war to God (see Josh 6:17–19).

5:1–6 *Now* (NRSV) in verse 5:1 begins a new oracle. This oracle comprises verses 1–6, and its setting was Sennacherib's invasion in 701 BCE. *Israel's ruler* is Hezekiah. The blow *on the cheek with a rod* symbolizes the destruction of most of his kingdom because he used human strategies, such as tribute to Sennacherib (2 Kgs 18:13–16) and alliance with Egypt (Isa 31:1–3). The ruler from Bethlehem (verse 2) refers to Hezekiah when he trusts in Yahweh after Sennacherib sends a letter demanding Judah's surrender. Victory over the Assyrians (verses 5b–6) refers to the angel of Yahweh smiting 185,000 Assyrians and the rest of the army returning to Nineveh (2 Kgs 19:35–36). Verse 1 is best translated by the NRSV: *Now you are walled around with a wall*. In verse 2, as David's descendant, the king is from *Bethlehem* (1 Sam 16:1–13). *From of old* parallels *former dominion* in 4:8 and thus David's dynasty.

> **Sennacherib & Hezekiah**
> *Sennacherib (who reigned 705–689 BCE) wrote about his siege of Lachish and Jerusalem:*
>
> As for Hezekiah, the Judean, I besieged 46 of his walled cities.... Using packed down ramps and applying battering rams, infantry attacks by mines, breeches, and siege machines, I conquered them.... [As for Hezekiah] I locked him up within Jerusalem, his royal city, like a bird in a cage.
>
> (translation by Mordechai Cogan, in Hallo and Younger, Contexts of Scripture, 2: 303).

Israel [Judah] is *abandoned* by Yahweh until *she who is in labor* (Jerusalem, 4:9–10) *gives birth* (that is, produces a righteous king). The *rest of his brothers* are those in Assyrian exile, who will return to help the besieged in Jerusalem.

> **Feminine Imagery for Jerusalem**
> *In Hebrew, all place names are feminine nouns. The prophets very often, therefore, use female metaphors such as birthing, nursing, and childbearing to describe the actions of the nations of Israel and Judah and their capitals.*

A transformed Hezekiah will *shepherd his flock* (Judah) in the *strength of the Lord*. "Shepherd" is one biblical term for "king" (for example, 2 Sam 5:2). Yahweh's people "living securely" parallels 4:4. *He* (Hezekiah transformed) *shall be the one of peace* (NRSV); through him, Yahweh will expel the Assyrian invaders. Verses 5b–c and 6d–e form an *inclusio*. When the Assyrians invade, the Judeans will raise against them *seven shepherds, even eight leaders of men*. This number pattern (similar to the one in Amos 1–2) simply implies that there will be adequate leadership (*the ruler* of 5:2d), not literally fifteen leaders (compare Prov 30:15–31).

5:7–15 According to verses 7–8, depending on the nations' actions, the *remnant* will bless them *like dew* and *showers* nourish grass (4:1–3), or crush them *like a lion* mauls sheep (4:11–13). As Yahweh's spokesman (verse 9), the prophet assures the remnant that it will triumph.

Yahweh's threat, *I will cut off* (NRSV), makes verses 10–14 cohere, denouncing Judah's objects of trust (Isa 2:6–8), such as military armaments (verses 10–11) and idolatrous paraphernalia (verses 12–14). Such punishments should refine Yahweh's people (Isa 1:21–28). Verses 12–14 list several idolatrous practices aimed at providing national security without loyalty to Israel's God.

PUNISHMENT & RESTORATION: SAMARIA & JERUSALEM · 6:1–7:20

This section contains three parts: Yahweh reproves Judah for infidelity due to ingratitude for Yahweh's blessings (verses 1–5); a hearer asks what Yahweh wants, according to the prophet (verses 6–7); and the prophet declares that Yahweh wants fidelity and care for others (verse 8). In verse 1, the prophet summons his audience to heed (imperative plural) Yahweh's instructions to announce the case against Israel. The *mountains* and *hills* serve as witnesses to the case because they have been around long enough to judge Israel's conduct. Mountains and hills witness to Yahweh's covenant with Israel at Sinai, as do the heavens and earth (Deut 32:1), and thus can vouch for Yahweh's integrity in his lawsuit.

6:1-5 Micah reports Yahweh's accusations against Israel. Yahweh speaks as defendant, asking for the people's grounds for their infidelity. The proof of Yahweh's fidelity comes from the ancient story of the exodus and deliverance in the desert (see Num 22-24; Josh 3-4).

6:6-7 An imagined hearer sarcastically asks what Yahweh desires. The list of possible religious acts, up to and including human sacrifice, serves rhetorically to contrast Israel's actions with God's desires.

6:8 The prophet responds with three teachings of Yahweh's law: *do justice* (NRSV) rather than enact oppression (2:1-11; 3:1-4, 9-12); love steadfast love, not fickle or hypocritical love; and *walk humbly with your God*, not arrogantly.

6:9-16 These verses may resume Yahweh's lawsuit (verses 1-5) following the interruption (verses 6-7), or verses 9-16 may be a separate announcement of Yahweh's judgment. *The city* mentioned here may be Samaria (1:5-7), Jerusalem (3:9-12), or both, since Micah closely connects Samaria's and Jerusalem's sins and punishment (1:5-7, 9, 13). Yahweh reproves merchants for using a substandard *ephah* (a vessel for measuring grain), *dishonest scales*, and *bag[s] of false* (irregular-sized stone) *weights* to weigh commodities, thus gaining wealth unethically (Deut 25:13-16; Amos 8:5).

> **Dishonest Scales**
> *In the absence of governmentally standardized weights and measures, customers were often at the mercy of unscrupulous merchants. Basic ethics dictated the use of fair measures and weights on scales. Buyers often paid in silver chunks (before the invention of coinage).*

In verses 13-15, Yahweh will send unspecified armies to divest oppressors of their objectives (Lev 26:26; Deut 28:38-41).

Verse 16a-c summarizes verses 10-12; and verse 16d-f, verses 13-15. Since oppressors mimic the injustices of *Omri* and *Ahab* (for example 1 Kgs 21), kings of the century before Micah, Yahweh will destroy them.

7:1-6 The prophet laments that Judah's corruption (verses 1-4b, 5-6) requires Yahweh's punishment (verse 4c-e). First, the prophet bemoans the oppression and dishonesty of Judah's leaders (3:9-12). The search for honest leaders proves disappointing, like a hungry person seeking grapes or figs on already gleaned plants (verse 1). Leaders hunt the defenseless, giving and accepting *bribes* to favor the rich in lawsuits, and *they all conspire together*.

Second, the prophet deplores untrustworthiness of *neighbor*, *friend*, spouse, and other family members (compare Matt 10:21; Luke 12:51-53).

7:7-20 These verses form a four-part liturgy (verses 7-10, 11-13, 14-17, 18-20), composed for oral reading (Neh 8:1-9; 1 Tim 4:13) or dramatic performance.

Personified Jerusalem (*I*) addresses her mockers (see Ps 115:2; 137:7-8), who say: *Where is the Lord your God?* (verse 10), implying that Yahweh is weak or indifferent. This liturgy dates from the late exilic or early postexilic period. The former inhabitants of Jerusalem (verse 8) acknowledge their sins as the cause of their downfall (Lam 1:1-14), but they are confident that Yahweh will deliver them.

A priest, prophet, or messenger promises Jerusalem (*your ... you* is feminine singular in Hebrew) that her exiles will return from captivity and rebuild the city's fortification (Neh 6:15-16).

Jewish exiles in Babylon (the NRSV's *us* in verse 15; NIV's *our* in verse 17) beseech Yahweh to carry out a new exodus and *shepherd* them like a *flock*. Nations will *be ashamed* for mocking Yahweh and the people and will acknowledge Yahweh alone as God (4:1-3; compare Isa 56).

Jewish exiles in Babylon (*remnant*, verse 18; *us*, *our*, verses 19-20) declare Yahweh to be incomparable (Exod 15:11) for forgiving their sins out of *steadfast love* (verses 19-20) and *compassion*, anticipating return to Jerusalem. In *anger* (NRSV), Yahweh sent the Babylonians to devastate Judah, but that anger is temporary (verse 9; Ps 30:5); Yahweh's steadfast love prevails. The phrases *Tread ... iniquities under foot* and *hurl ... sins into the depths of the sea* (NRSV; echoing Exod 15:4-5) denote complete forgiveness.

THEOLOGICAL REFLECTIONS

Micah's message is not new but is based on the law and earlier prophets. Deliberate, prolonged sin in

Israel and Judah brings Yahweh's wrath through the Assyrians and Babylonians. Sin is self-centeredness, manifested in arrogant rebellion against Yahweh and oppression of others in government, economic life, and religion. However, Yahweh's punishment is redemptive. There is hope for the penitent remnant, Yahweh's flock, to return to Jerusalem, enjoy protection, rebuild ruins, reestablish the Davidic dynasty, and be Yahweh's witness to the nations.

FOR FURTHER STUDY

Joseph Jensen, *Ethical Dimensions of the Prophets* (Collegeville, Minn.: Liturgical Press, 2006).

Harold Shank, *Minor Prophets* (Joplin, Mo.: College Press, 2001).

WORKS CITED

Francis I. Andersen and David Noel Freedman, *Micah* (New York: Doubleday, 2000).

James B. Pritchard, ed., *Ancient Near Eastern Texts Relating to the Old Testament* (3rd ed. with supplement; Princeton: Princeton University Press, 1969).

Daniel J. Simundson, "The Book of Micah: Introduction, Commentary, and Reflections," *The New Interpreter's Bible* (Nashville: Abingdon, 1996), 7:533–89.

Nahum

John T. Willis

CHAPTER CONTENTS

Contexts 699
Commentary 699
  Superscription · 1:1 699
  Poem Praising Yahweh · 1:2–8 699
  Addresses to Nineveh & Judah · 1:9–15 700
  Description of Nineveh's Imminent Destruction · 2:1–3:19 700
Theological Reflections 701
For Further Study 701
Works Cited 701

The book of Nahum dates from between the Assyrian king Assurbanipal's sack of Egypt's capital, Thebes (also called No-Amon), in 663 BCE (3:8–10), and Babylon's overthrow of Nineveh in 612 BCE (2:1–13).

CONTEXTS

Chapters 2–3 expect imminent attack, dating the book to about 612 BCE. Recurring expressions, similes and metaphors, water imagery, and the focus on Nineveh's fall create the book's cohesion. The book is designed for oral reading or dramatic performance before worshiping communities.

COMMENTARY

SUPERSCRIPTION · 1:1

Nahum 1:1 calls the book *an oracle* [Hebrew *massa*, which also means "burden" (as in Isa 13:1; Hab 1:1)], a genre generally employed in responding to community questions about Yahweh's intentions regarding some situation. This *oracle* concerns *Nineveh*, Assyria's capital (2:8; 3:7; NIV unjustifiably adds Nineveh in 1:8, 11, 14; and 2:1). Verse 1 calls Nahum the *book of the vision* (compare Isa 1:1; Hab 2:2), affirming that Yahweh answers community questions. No information exists about either the man *Nahum* or the location of *Elkosh*.

POEM PRAISING YAHWEH · 1:2–8

This text constitutes a broken acrostic, with each verse beginning with a different letter of the Hebrew alphabet halfway through (see also Pss 34, 119). It praises Yahweh, the mighty warrior, for overthrowing enemies and protecting followers. Yahweh is *slow to anger* (verse 3) *but* (not *and* as the NIV translates it in verse 3) *great in power*. He is *good*, a *stronghold* (NRSV; verse 7); but *jealous, avenging, wrathful* (verses 2, 3, 6), punishing enemies (verses 2, 3, 6). *Jealous* on Israel's behalf (Ezek 38:18–23), God takes vengeance on Nineveh for cruelty. Yahweh's fearsome appearance brings whirlwind, storm, dark clouds, the evaporation of the sea and rivers, withering foliage on mountains and hills, quaking mountains, melting hills, and trembling of the earth and all its inhabitants (compare Mic 1:3–4; Hab 3:3–15; Ps 18:7–15). Such language speaks to the overwhelming nature of any appearance or action by God. Yahweh's opponents cannot endure his *indignation, anger*, and *wrath*. The phrase *even in a rushing flood* (verse 8a in NRSV, which completes verse 7 rather than contrasting with it, as indicated in the NIV) echoes a favorite Assyrian image for destruction. In verse 8b, Hebrew reads *her place*, the NIV reads *Nineveh*, and the NRSV reads *his*

> **A Hymn to Yahweh**
> *Nahum opens with a hymn to Yahweh. Its literary strategy of setting up a series of contrasting attributes was not unusual in the ancient world. For example, the Babylonian wisdom text called "I Will Praise the Lord of Wisdom" (Ludlul bel nemeqi) opens with a hymn to the god Marduk, "whose anger is like a raging tempest, but whose breeze is sweet as the morning's breath." For Nahum, the sovereign God is not that of the Mesopotamian oppressors but of the now liberated Israelites (Hallo and Younger).*

> **Nahum & the Assyrian Empire**
> *Nahum celebrates the collapse of the Assyrian Empire in the 610s BCE, hoping for the end to oppression in the Near East. The Assyrians practiced widespread deportations of populations in an effort to reorganize their world in a way fitting the alleged decrees of the gods.*

adversaries. All these interpretations are possible, but a preferable reading is "he will put an end to opposition [Hebrew *mequmah*]."

ADDRESSES TO NINEVEH & JUDAH · 1:9–15

The prophet next addresses Assyrians (verses 9–11, 14) and Judeans (verses 12–13, 15). Baselessly, NIV inserts *Nineveh* twice (verses 11, 14), and *Judah* once (verse 12). *Judah* is in verse 15. Context suggests *you* (plural, (verse 9, as in the NRSV; not *they* as in the NIV) are Assyrians who oppress Yahweh's people. Yahweh's onslaught demolishes all foes, leaving them *entangled thorns*, *drunkards* (NRSV), and *dry stubble* (verse 10; Isa 28:7–8; 33:11–12). *You* (verse 11) is feminine singular, referring to Nineveh/Assyria. The *one* who *has come forth* from her and *plots evil against the Lord* is probably Sennacherib, who besieged Jerusalem in 701 BCE (Isa 36–37). *Wickedness* [Hebrew *beliyaal*; also verse 15], comes from the verb meaning "to swallow," suggesting the image of the god of death swallowing his victims (Isa 5:14; Hab 2:5).

The messenger formula *thus says Yahweh* (verse 12a) introduces encouraging words from God (*I*) to Judeans (*you* [verses 12–13] is feminine singular, referring to Jerusalem/Judah) *afflicted* by Assyria. Although enemies have maximum strength, Yahweh will defeat them, and although Yahweh has used Assyria to *afflict* sinful Judah (compare Isa 10:5–6), Yahweh will *break his* [that is, *Assyria's king's* as in NRSV not *their* as in the NIV] *yoke* (slave collar) and *shackles* from Judah's *neck* (see Isa 58:6, 9; Jer 28:10, 12). Assyria has served its purpose and now must pay for oppressing others excessively.

Assyria's destruction is *Judah's good news*. The messenger formula (verse 14a) introduces Yahweh's intention to vanquish Assyria's king (*you*, *your*; the pronouns are masculine singular and cannot refer to *Nineveh*, as the NIV suggests): the punishments meted out to Assyria are harsh: the king *will have no descendants*; Yahweh *will destroy* Assyria's *carved images* and *cast idols* (of Ashur, Bel, Marduk, Ishtar, etc.), whom the king sponsored to legitimate his rule; and Yahweh will assign him (the king) a despicable *grave* (verse 14). Suddenly, the *feet* (symbolizing the entire person) of a *good news* messenger (perhaps God) appear *on the mountains* (see also Isa 52:7; Rom 10:15) to announce the end of foreign domination. *Wicked* again translates the Hebrew word *beliyaal*, as in verse 11. Israel can begin its religious life anew in its own land.

DESCRIPTION OF NINEVEH'S IMMINENT DESTRUCTION · 2:1–3:19

2:1–13 The prophet graphically depicts a battle between invading Babylonians, Medes, and Scythians and the invaded Assyrians, portraying the attackers as charging Nineveh ("*you*," feminine singular) to prepare for battle (verse 1). He assures both north Israel and Judah (*Jacob* and *Israel*) that, by overthrowing Assyria, Yahweh will restore the *splendor* that Assyria removed from them when it defeated Samaria (722 BCE; 2 Kgs 17:1–6) and besieged Jerusalem (701 BCE; Isa 36–37) like thieves strip grapes from *vines* (verse 2). The prophet also describes terrifying attacking *warriors* bearing blood-stained (*red*) armor, driving technologically advanced *chariots* and sacking a city (the graphic depiction of a battle sounds like an eyewitness account) (verses 3–6). He depicts capture and *exile* of some and flight of others, amid commands (*Stop! Stop!*) as useless as a leaky *pool* (verses 7–8). He portrays invaders inciting each other to *plunder* Nineveh's vast *treasures* (verse 9). And he summarizes widespread fear in Nineveh: *Devastation, desolation, and destruction!* (NRSV; verse 10).

The prophet taunts demolished Nineveh, formerly a *lions' den* where Assyrian soldiers felt confident bringing captives and spoils of war to benefit the city (Isa 5:29). He reports a message from *the Lord of* [*the heavenly*] *hosts* [not the *Lord Almighty*, as the NIV translates it]: *I am against you* (feminine singular, referring to Nineveh; 3:5); Nineveh will fall (verses 11–13).

The *city* is interpreted in verse 7 (in the Masoretic Text) as *she*. Some propose that the "she" refers to Nineveh's *mistress* (see the RSV translation) – that is, the city's queen, or goddess, Ishtar. It was common in ancient Assyrian and Babylonian warfare to remove images from a defeated enemy's temple. Wall reliefs from Assurbanipal's palace at Nineveh depict the king ritually hunting lions. He imported lions from Syria for hunts and was proud of his

> **The Fall of Ninevah**
> British Museum text 21901 gives Babylon's account of Nineveh's fall in the fourteenth year of Nabopolassar, king of Babylon (Pritchard 304–5).

accomplishments as a lion hunter. Verses 11–13 report the end of such imperial boasting.

3:1–19 The prophet utters *woe* against Nineveh, *city of bloodshed* (verse 1; NRSV), whose sophisticated army exploited helpless victims, murdering ruthlessly with *swords* and *spears*, leaving *piles of dead bodies* (verses 2–3), practicing deceitful diplomacy (Isa 36:16–17) like a *harlot* using *sorcery* (verse 4; NRSV). Yahweh reacts: *I am against you, says the Lord of hosts* (verse 5; NRSV, 2:13). Since place names in Hebrew are feminine, Nahum (like other prophets) can use female imagery for Nineveh. He chooses images of gradation. God will punish her: exposing her shame to the nations (verse 5), *treating* her *with contempt, making* her *a spectacle* so onlookers will *flee* from her, leaving none to *mourn* for or *comfort* her (verses 6–7).

Ironically, Nineveh will suffer like its former victim *Thebes* (Jer 46:25; Ezek 30:14–16). *Ethiopia* (NRSV), *Put, and Libya* were African areas whose peoples suffered Assyrian brutality under Assurbanipal in the 660s, fifty years earlier than Nahum. The succeeding images graphically describe such destruction. Some images also appear elsewhere: *first ripe figs* that *fall* from the tree into the *eater's mouth* (compare Isa 28:1–4), female soldiers (Isa 19:16; 50:37; 51:30), *wide open gates*, and burned *bars* for the gates (verses 8–13).

> **Thebes**
> *Located in upper Egypt about 440 miles south of Memphis, Thebes was the capital of Egypt under Ethiopian kings during Egypt's Twenty-fifth Dynasty (716–663 BCE).*

Satirically, the prophet summons Assyria/Nineveh (feminine singular imperatives and pronouns) to prepare for attack. *Fire* and *sword* will *devour* Nineveh like *locusts* (NRSV) devour vegetation (verses 14–15c). Three *locust* metaphors describe Nineveh's desperate situation: rapid numerical growth cannot thwart overthrow; Assyrian and foreign *merchants* will abandon the city, leaving unattended shops like *locusts shed* their *skins* (NRSV; not *strip the land* as in the NIV), and *fly away*; *guards* and omen interpreters appointed to advise the king freeze before invaders *on fences* (NRSV; not *in the walls* as in the NIV) who *fly away* at sunrise (NRSV) (verses 15d–17).

The prophet reprimands the *king of Assyria* because his *shepherds* (leaders) or *nobles* provide no guidance for their *people* (1 Kgs 22:17). The king's *wound is fatal*. *All who hear* will *clap their hands* (approvingly; see Lam 2:15), because Assyria inflicted *endless cruelty* on defenseless peoples (verses 18–19).

THEOLOGICAL REFLECTIONS

Learning, power, and wealth stoked Assyria's pride. It had no qualms of conscience about practicing cruelty. Extended domination reinforced her atrocities. But eventually Yahweh intervened, declaring: *I am against you!* Though *slow to anger*, God releases his wrath against persistent sin through Babylon to destroy Assyria. Such prophetic messages are not nationalistic. Amos and others proclaim similar messages against God's chosen people, as well. Sin is serious; God deals with it accordingly. God comforts the oppressed and punishes oppressors (Exod 22:21–24; Luke 16:19–31).

FOR FURTHER STUDY

Francisco O. García-Treto, "The Book of Nahum," in *The New Interpreters' Bible* (ed. Leander Keck; Nashville: Abingdon, 1996): 7:593–619.

Julia Myers O'Brien, *Nahum* (London: Continuum, 2002).

WORKS CITED

William Hallo and K. Lawson Yonger, eds., *The Context of Scripture*, vol. 1: *Canonical Composition from the Biblical World* (Leiden: Brill, 1997).

James B. Pritchard, ed., *Ancient Near Eastern Texts Relating to the Old Testament* (3d ed.; Princeton: Princeton University Press, 1969).

Habakkuk

John T. Willis

CHAPTER CONTENTS

Contexts 703

Commentary 703
- Superscription · 1:1 703
- Dialogue between Habakkuk & Yahweh · 1:2–2:4 703
- Woe Oracles against Babylon · 2:5–20 704
- Prayer extolling Yahweh as Victorious Warrior · 3:1–19 705

Theological Reflections 705

For Further Study 706

Works Cited 706

MAPS, TABLES, & FEATURES

The Babylonian Empire 704

Habakkuk's flow of thought and structure demonstrates coherence. The book is designed for dramatic performance or oral presentation before worshiping assemblies.

CONTEXTS

References to Babylon's rise (1:6) and overthrow of small nations (2:5–17) suggest 612–587 BCE as Habakkuk's historical setting. The psalm in Habakkuk 3, with its superscription *on* (according to) *Shigionoth* (verse 1 is similar to the superscription of Psalm 7), *selah* (verses 3, 9, 13), and subscription *to the leader, with stringed instruments* (verse 19; see Ps 4:6 superscription), indicates that Habakkuk borrows structure, terminology, and theology from the worship at the temple.

COMMENTARY

SUPERSCRIPTION · 1:1

Habakkuk declares he *saw* (NRSV) the *oracle* (which is the same as the Hebrew word for "burden") . The use of the word "burden" in this context suggests a response to doubt about Yahweh's intentions.

DIALOGUE BETWEEN HABAKKUK & YAHWEH · 1:2–2:4

1:2–4 Habakkuk complains because Jehoiakim and his associates abuse their power against defenseless victims (see Jer 22:13–19), but when Habakkuk *cries out* to Yahweh to redress this, Yahweh does not *listen* and *save*. Cries of *how long*? (Ps 13:1–2) and *Why*? (Ps 22:1–2) seek to persuade Yahweh to act, just as in the Psalms. Again, Habakkuk draws on the language of the temple's worship.

> **Jehoiakim**
> Jehoiakim, king of Judah from 609–598 BCE, was the son of Josiah by Zebidah, daughter of Pedaiah of Rumah. He married Nehushta and fathered King Jehoiachin. His name means, "he whom Yahweh has set up."

1:5–11 Yahweh addresses all Judah (using masculine plural imperatives and pronouns *you*, *your* [verse 5]), promising to use the *Babylonians* to punish Judah for injustices (verses 5–6). This is probably immediately after Babylon defeated Assyria and Egypt at Carchemish (605 BCE; Jer 46:2–12). Babylonians are *ruthless*, *violent*, arrogant warriors, *sweep*ing swiftly *across the whole earth like a desert wind* to *seize* others' *dwelling places*. The images of speed emphasize their skill as warriors and thus the depth of the danger to Judah. They *gather prisoners like sand* and besiege *fortified cities*, *building* massive earthen ramps to scale walls and *capture* inhabitants. Siege technology had advanced a great deal by this period. They boast *they are a law to themselves* and claim their *own strength* as *their god* (Amos 6:13).

1:12–2:1 Yahweh's announcement that he is *raising up the Babylonians* (1:6) to punish Judah perturbs Habakkuk: How can the *everlasting* (translated literally *You [Yahweh] shall not die* [NRSV], verse 12c), *holy*, invincible (literally *Rock*, verse 12e; compare Deut 32:30–31; Ps 18:2), *pure* God use a foreign nation to destroy *those more righteous than themselves* (verse 13d–e)? Babylon purposes to *destroy*, not merely punish, *nations*, using massive military machinery, like fishers use *hooks* and *nets* to *catch fish*, unconcerned about human dignity and

HABAKKUK

value (verses 14–15). Babylonians worship instruments that increase their wealth and power (verse 16). Will Yahweh tolerate such cruel oppression forever (verse 17)? Habakkuk *stations* himself on Jerusalem's *ramparts*, eagerly awaiting Yahweh's *answer* to his *complaint* (2:1).

2:2–4 Unlike 1:5–11, here Habakkuk's composer introduces Yahweh as speaker (verse 2a). Yahweh charges Habakkuk to *write plainly on tablets* the *vision* (NRSV) Yahweh is giving him so *that a herald* (that is, Habakkuk himself) proclaims it to Judean audiences (verse 2b-d; compare Jer 23:21); to *wait* patiently for Yahweh to restore justice, guaranteed by the written record of the *vision* (verse 3; Isa 30:8); and to be faithful to Yahweh and endure steadfastly (verse 4).

> **The Babylonian Empire**
>
> *After the collapse of Assyria in 612 BCE, most of its empire fell to Babylon. Its great ruler Nebuchadnezzar (sometimes spelled Nebuchadrezzar) ruled 605–562 BCE and was a brilliant general. Judah was a Babylonian vassal state from 605–586 BCE, after which the Babylonians utterly destroyed the little kingdom, deporting most of its population.*

Scholars interpret verse 4 variously. In verse 4a, one should probably emend the Hebrew for "swollen" (NIV, *puffed up*; NRSV, *proud*) to more directly contrast with *the righteous* in 4c. Thus, unlike the righteous, this "swollen" person will not walk in the vision's message. Further, the Hebrew word *emunah* in verse 4c does not mean "faith" as acceptance of doctrine or as an inner attitude toward God, but rather as steadfast endurance, or "faithfulness." Interpreters have often understood Paul (Rom 1:16–17; Gal 3:10–11) and the author of Hebrews (10:32–39) as reading the Septuagint's rendition of "faith" in the former sense rather than the latter in 4c, although there is some reason to question this reading of the New Testament texts.

WOE ORACLES AGAINST BABYLON · 2:5–20

Verses 5–6a introduce five *woes* against Babylon (verses 6b–20), returning to the theme of 1:5–17. The addressee is in the third person masculine singular (*he, him*), referring to Babylon collectively. The proclaimers of the *woes* are all *nations* whom Babylon had *taken captive*. They cry *woe*, a funeral lament (similar to the one in Jer 22:18–19), to mock Babylon for excessive atrocities. The prophet indicates that all nations, not just Israel, have a stake in Babylon's downfall and thus the end of oppression.

The first *woe* (2:6b–8) denounces Babylon for accumulating wealth from plunder, exacting *goods taken in pledge* (NRSV; compare verse 17). Babylon's

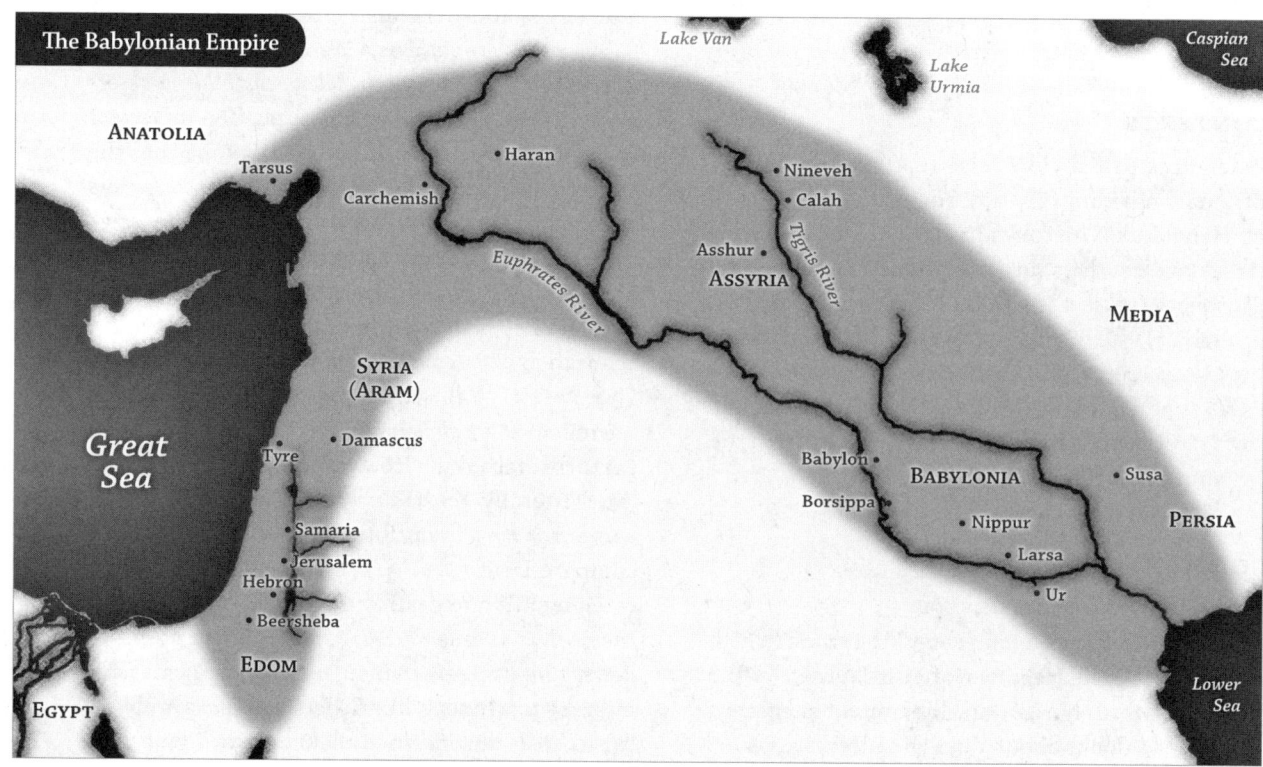

debtors will *suddenly arise*, make it *their victim*, and *plunder* it. Babylon reaps what it sowed (Gal 6:7).

The second *woe* (verses 9–11) reprimands Babylon for striving to make itself impregnable by amassing *unjust gain* to build the royal palace, like an eagle *setting* his *nest on high* (Obad 4). The very materials Babylon collected to build the royal palace *will cry out* in protest against Babylon's cruelty and ask for punishment. The prophet uses images of invulnerability to emphasize the futility of Babylon's relentless pursuit of power.

The third woe reproves Babylon for killing and subjugating nonsupporters and opponents (compare Mic 3:9–10). Yahweh thwarts the unjust use of *labor*, particularly by Babylon. Babylon's policy of forced resettlement, well-known from the Babylonian sources themselves, comes under scrutiny here (Floyd 143). Verse 14 echoes Isaiah 11:9, where the image of flooding waters comes ultimately from the royal propaganda of the Mesopotamian empires.

The fourth woe reproaches Babylon for making his *neighbors drunk* to *gaze on their naked bodies* (compare Gen 9:20–25), using sexual imagery to trigger disgust at their behavior. *Violence done to Lebanon* refers to indiscriminate tree felling for building, etc. (Isa 14:8) and random *destruction of animals* for sport or to hector enemies, both of which were activities for displaying royal power. Retributively, Yahweh will *fill* Babylon with *shame* and force it to *drink the cup* of Yahweh's wrath (compare Jer 25:15–29) to *expose* its own nakedness.

The fifth woe ridicules Babylon for idolatry, labeling their gods as human *creations* (Ps 135:15–18). Idol makers control images they make and so determine their own theology and lifestyle. By contrast, Yahweh creates and sustains humanity. In verse 20, God's *temple* equals heaven (see Ps 11:4); *silence* does not mean absence of sound, but humility and trust (as in Zech 2:13).

PRAYER EXTOLLING YAHWEH AS VICTORIOUS WARRIOR · 3:1–19

Habakkuk 3 relates a prayer of Habakkuk (3:2, 16–19) responding to an ancient vision (perhaps referred to in 2:2) of Yahweh's appearance, or "theophany," to overthrow enemies (verses 3–15), thus restoring order to creation. The song itself may be much more ancient than Habakkuk himself (Hiebert; but see Floyd 147–48), and it has elements of both a psalm of praise and one of complaint. The prophet functions here as a temple singer (Floyd 157–58). After the superscription (3:1), the chapter contains three parts, arranged chiastically:

    A Prayer (3:2)
    B Description of Yahweh's coming & victory (3:3–15)
    A′ Prayer (3:16–19)

The superscription calls this poem a *prayer of Habakkuk*. *On shigionoth* indicates it was composed for singing. Habakkuk first acknowledges God's deeds, drawing on the ancient language of theophany (verses 3–15), afterwards resuming his prayer with: *I hear* (verse 16). He petitions Yahweh to *renew* deeds of *mercy* for Israel. Yahweh approaches from *Teman* (northwest Edom) and *Mount Paran* (hills west of the Gulf of Aqaba) (as in Deut 33:2; Judg 5:4–5), producing *glory* and *splendor*. God walks with an entourage – *plague* and *pestilence* – as would a mighty warrior approaching his enemies. God traverses the sky in *chariots* (see Pss 18:9–10; 68:32–33), shoots *arrows*, and brandishes a *spear*. The poem thus draws on one of Israel's oldest metaphors for God, the divine warrior.

Yahweh stupefied his enemies in nature and history, combating nature by inflicting cataclysmic upheavals on *earth*, *mountains*, *waterways*, *sun*, and *moon*. When battling human foes, Yahweh *made the nations tremble, crushed the leader of the land of wickedness, and pierced his head* when his warriors *came like a whirlwind* (NRSV) to scatter Yahweh's people. *Anointed one* refers to the Davidic king in Jerusalem. This vision does not refer to specific historical events, though in the context of the book, the fall of Babylon must be in view.

Rehearsal of Yahweh's appearance terrified Habakkuk. Like lamenters in the Psalms, he experiences bodily dislocation. He imagines massive failures of crops and herds. Yet he resolves to *wait patiently* for Yahweh to overthrow Babylon and to rejoice in Yahweh as his strength, indicating acceptance of Yahweh's assurance in 2:4.

THEOLOGICAL REFLECTIONS

Habakkuk struggles with how a just and loving God could permit personal, political or social,

HABAKKUK

and international injustice to rule in his world. Yahweh does not resolve this by restoring justice in Habakkuk's day but by challenging him to trust in Yahweh's eventual intervention to punish the wicked and vindicate the righteous.

FOR FURTHER STUDY

Elizabeth Achtemeier, *Nahum–Malachi* (Louisville: Westminster John Knox, 1986).

Maria Eszenyei Szeles, *Wrath and Mercy: A Commentary on Habakkuk and Zephaniah* (Grand Rapids: Eerdmans, 1987).

WORKS CITED

Michael Floyd, *Minor Prophets Part 2* (Grand Rapids: Eerdmans, 2000).

Theodore Hiebert, *God of My Victory* (Atlanta: Scholars Press, 1986).

Zephaniah

John T. Willis

CHAPTER CONTENTS

Contexts 707

Commentary 707
- Superscription · 1:1 707
- The Day of Yahweh's Wrath Against Judah · 1:2–2:4 707
- The Day of Yahweh's Wrath Against the Nations · 2:5–3:8 708
- The Day of Yahweh's Salvation of the Nations & Judah · 3:9–20 709

Theological Reflections 709

For Further Study 710

Works Cited 710

Apparently, Zephaniah was a great-great-grandson of King Hezekiah of Judah, who reigned 715–687 BCE (1:1). Zephaniah prophesied in the reign of Josiah (640–609 BCE), during whose reign Hilkiah discovered the book of the law in the temple during its repairs (621 BCE), on which Josiah based his reforms (2 Kgs 22:3–23:25).

CONTEXTS

The setting explains Zephaniah's condemnation of idolatry and child sacrifice (Zeph 1:4–9, 11–12; 3:1–4; 2 Kgs 23:4–15), which Manasseh brought into Judah (2 Kgs 21:2–9, 16) and which Josiah removed. Philistines, Moabites, and Ammonites taunted Judah (2:4–11); Cushites (that is, inhabitants of Sudan who then ruled Egypt) seemed weak but threatening (2:12); Babylon had not yet destroyed Nineveh (2:13–15). These facts indicate that the book dates from between 621 and 612 BCE. Zephaniah and Jeremiah, the first prophetic voices since Isaiah and Micah roughly 75 years previously, likely helped initiate and encourage Josiah's reform. Zephaniah's familiarity with Jerusalem (1:10–13), its officials (1:8–9; 3:3–4), and sacrifices at the temple (1:7–8), as well as his insights into the attitudes and circumstances of Jerusalem's residents (1:12–13; 3:7) and joy over anticipating Yahweh's deliverance of a faithful remnant (3:14, 17) suggest he was a Jerusalemite who frequented the temple and knew people in the city personally, including officials. The book's structure and content indicate it was composed for oral reading or dramatic performance at a major pilgrim festival at the Jerusalem temple, probably the Feast of Booths, also called Tabernacles or Ingathering (see Exod 23:16–17; Lev 23:33–44; Num 29:12–40; Deut 16:13–17).

COMMENTARY

SUPERSCRIPTION · 1:1

Zephaniah 1:1 declares that Zephaniah's message *came* from Yahweh, that Zephaniah was the descendant of king *Hezekiah*, and that he prophesied *during the reign of Josiah*.

THE DAY OF YAHWEH'S WRATH AGAINST JUDAH · 1:2–2:4

Declares the Lord (1:2, 3, 10) is a version of the "messenger formula" that ancient heralds used to proclaim the sender of their message. As a royal messenger, the prophet relates Yahweh's announcement to all nations (1:2–3, 18; 2:4), especially Judah (1:4, 10–12; 2:1), using the first personal singular pronoun "I" and the third person singular "Yahweh" to emphasize the speaker's significance. Yahweh announces the nearness of the *great day of the Lord* (1:7, 14). As in Amos 5:18–20, the intended day of national deliverance will bring instead national judgment. It will be a *day* of *sweep*ing *away* (1:2, 3, 4; 2:2; as in Noah's flood, Gen 6:7), of a *sacrifice* of apostate Judean officials (1:7–9), of Yahweh's *punishment* (1:8, 9, 12) and *wrath* (1:15, 18; 2:2, 3), as well as a series of graphic signs of destruction (1:15–17). Zephaniah portrays his audience as people practicing idolatry (1:4) and foreign religious rites (1:5, 8, 9), abandoning Yahweh (1:6), and full of *violence* (1:9), smugness (1:12), and dependence on their riches. Their silver and gold (1:11, 13, 18) provoke this punishment. The effect will be extensive destruction of humans and all the surrounding ecosystem (1:2, 3, 17, 18), of physical property (1:13), and of *fortified cities* (1:16; 2:4), with *cry*ing and *wailing* (1:10, 11, 14). Whereas many citizens of Judah saw the collapse of the Assyrian Empire as a chance for independence, Zephaniah correctly foresaw only anarchy.

1:2–6 Under Manasseh and Amon, many Judeans worshiped at the same time *Baal*, the Canaanite deity of fertility and battle (compare Hos 2:2–20); the *starry host* (sun, moon, and stars) (Deut 4:19); *Molech* (NIV), or *Milcom* (NRSV), perhaps an Ammonite deity or one to whom they sacrificed babies (Lev 18:21; 1 Kgs 11:5, 7; Jer 32:35); as well as Yahweh (1:4–6). For ancient persons, this mixture of religious elements (or syncretism) would have seemed perfectly normal.

> **Molech**
> *Phoenician texts, especially from Carthage in North Africa, a Phoenician colony, speak of a* mulk *sacrifice – a lamb offered along with a child sacrifice or perhaps sometimes in substitution for it. "Molech" is not ordinarily a god. The better reading of verse 5, in any case is "their king," with no god's name present at all (Sweeney 71).*

1:7–9 *Leaping over the threshold* (verse 9, NRSV) of a temple was a superstitious act of Philistine religionists of the deity Dagon (1 Sam 5:5), perhaps indicating fear of demons or of terrifying consequences.

> **Dagon**
> *Dagon was a god of grain and agriculture worshiped by the early Amorites and popular in the ancient cities of Ugarit and Ebla. Dagon is mentioned in extrabiblical sources as early as 2300 BCE.*

1:10–13 Invaders will attack Jerusalem from the north, the direction of the road from Mesopotamia. The places in verses 10–11 mostly lie in the western part of the city. Yahweh, using assailants, will search every inch of *Jerusalem with lamps* (verse 12a; see Ps 139:12); none will escape (Amos 9:1–4). Many Judeans are complacent, *like wine left on its dregs* (as in Jer 48:11). Numerous Jerusalemites settled into a spiritually and morally deteriorating, indolent lifestyle, assuming that *the Lord will do nothing, either good* (blessing) *or bad* (punishing) (verse 12b–e; Jer 5:12; 23:17; Amos 9:10; Mic 3:11). When the Israelites settled Canaan, they lived in houses they did not build and drank wine from vineyards they did not plant (see Deut 6:10; Josh 24:13), but Yahweh will reverse this: Babylonian invaders will dwell in houses Israelites built and drink wine of vineyards Israelites planted (verse 13), as the law threatened if Israel forsook Yahweh (Deut 28:30).

> **New Wine & Dregs**
> *To give wine strength and flavor, vintners let new wine stand with grapes' sediment ("dregs") temporarily, straining it through a cloth before drinking.*

1:14–18 As a mighty *warrior*, Yahweh will lead Babylon's army (1:14d; Jer 25:8–11). Judah's citizens' blood and *flesh* (NRSV) will cover the ground *like dust* and *dung* (1:17d–e; compare NRSV; Jer 8:2; 9:22). Assailants will refuse exorbitant bribes from victims to cease attacking (verse 18a–c).

2:1–4 Even while announcing Judah's severe mass destruction, Yahweh contemplates deliverance. There is time for repentance as the phrases in verse 3 indicate. *The humble* accept Yahweh's instruction, leadership, and teaching (see Mic 6:8; Ps 25:8–9). *For* (verse 4a, NRSV) joins verse 4 to verses 1–3; verse 4 describes impenitent Judah's fate through previous Philistine devastation. This verse names four of five Philistine cities (omitting Gath, as does Amos 1:6–8; compare 1 Sam 6:17), using metaphors of a woman jilted before marriage, abandoned by her husband, divorced, or rendered barren to depict pain of enemy atrocities.

THE DAY OF YAHWEH'S WRATH AGAINST THE NATIONS · 2:5–3:8

Woe (2:5; repeated for emphasis in 3:1) begins a new section, which again heralds Yahweh's punishment of *the nations* (3:6, 8) or the *whole world* (3:8), including Judah (3:1–5, 7), but now especially other nations. The prophet names the nations by their position relative to Judah: *Kerethites* or *Philistines* westward by the sea (2:5–7; Ezek 25:15–16); *Ammon* and *Moab* eastward (verses 8–11; Jer 48:1–49:6); *Ethiopians* (NRSV) southward (12; Isa 18:1); *Assyria* northward (13–15; Nah 1:12–3:7); and finally Judah (3:1–5, 7). Yahweh will punish the nations for oppressing Judah (2:8, 10) and for *pride* (2:10). The warrant for this divine punishment comes in 2:15: *I am, and there is none besides me* (2:15; Isa 47:8, 10; Ezek 28:2). The following verses lay out the abuses

> **"There is none besides me …"**
> *The nations ignore their dependence on God, boasting superiority to Yahweh, who alone claims dominance successfully (as in Isa 45:5–6, 18). Judah falls under the same judgment.*

of power by leaders (compare Ezek 22:23–19), the priests' defilement of the temple, and the idolatrous attitudes of the people.

Yahweh's intention in *dispens*ing *justice* (3:5c) through severe retribution is to refine and redeem. The soaring language of the text glorifies Yahweh, who works to transform human hearts and bring justice among individuals and nations. Ultimately, Yahweh blesses the people in several ways: Philistine territory *will belong to Judah* for pasturage, indicating economic recovery for Judah (verses 6–7d); Yahweh *will care* for Israel (verse 7e–f; 3:20; Jer 30:18; 33:26); Yahweh's *people* will occupy Moab and Ammon (verse 9g–h). In short, a restored Israel will occupy the entire region. Yahweh also blesses the nations and destroys their gods. The restoration of Israel has implications for everyone else. The idea that other gods will fall under Yahweh's overarching rule also appears elsewhere (Exod 12:12; 18:11; Ps 82:6–7).

2:5–7 Yahweh, hence Yahweh's *word*, opposes evildoers (verse 5c; 2 Sam 12:9–10).

2:8–11 Moab's and Ammon's destruction resemble that of *Sodom* and *Gomorrah* (verse 9c–d; Gen 19:24–29; Isa 13:19; Jer 49:18).

2:12 Yahweh's sword in the hands of human soldiers (compare Ezek 21:1–23) will kill Judah's former allies against Assyria, the *Cushites* under Tirhakah (Isa 37:9).

> **Cush & Tirhakah**
> *Cush* (or *Kush*), *an ancient civilization in Nubia (now northern Sudan), was one of the earliest Nile civilizations. Tirhakah (or Taharqa), an Ethiopian king during the time of Hezekiah, fought against Sennacharib in 701 BCE, preventing the latter from conquering Jerusalem and deporting its citizens.*

13–15 The prophet describes *Nineveh's* total desolation (612 BCE): this previously large, powerful, bustling city is now a ruin and the habitation of frightening animals (Isa 13:19–22; 34:8–15; compare Rev 18:2). The political revolution of the late seventh century came, says the prophet, because of Yahweh's search for human justice.

3:1–5 Jerusalem's wicked officials prowl against defenseless victims at night, leaving *nothing for the morning* (verse 3). By contrast, Yahweh appears *morning by morning*, as regular and dependable as the sunrise, to punish oppressors and deliver the oppressed (verse 5).

3:6–8 Since all the *nations*, including Judah, refuse to *fear* (that is, stand in awe of, reverence, honor) Yahweh, they will experience divine punishment (Mic 4:11–13).

THE DAY OF YAHWEH'S SALVATION OF THE NATIONS & JUDAH · 3:9–20

Yahweh's will is to heal wounds as well as inflict them (Isa 30:26). Deliverance follows punishment. Zephaniah's theme continues to be *at that time* (3:9, NRSV; 3:11, 14), the Day of Yahweh, now *a day of festival* (3:18a, NRSV), probably equaling the Feast of Tabernacles. Yahweh will *change the speech of the peoples to a pure speech* (verse 9a, NRSV) so that they may join in prayer to God (verse 9b; Joel 2:32) and *serve* God *with one accord* (verse 9c; NRSV), reversing the confusion of tongues at Babel (Gen 11:1–9). Yahweh's *worshipers*, those *scattered* from all nations who will be converted to him, will *bring his offering* (NRSV) in adoration and praise (verse 10; 2:11).

Further, Yahweh will remove from Judah the proud oppressors of the defenseless, leaving behind only the pious (verses 11–13, 19). In a series of images reminiscent of Isaiah 54–55 and 60–62, Zephaniah describes the glorious renewal of the nation. Hearers of the prophets *should be glad and rejoice* (verse 14), avoid *fear* (verses 13, 15, 16), and quit being terrified by enemies or circumstances (verse 16c; Isa 13:7; Jer 6:24; Heb 12:12), because Yahweh, the *King of Israel*, is *mighty to save* (verses 15, 17). God will not *shame* them (verses 11, 19) but will *give them praise and honor* (verses 19–20); they will be secure in their land (verse 13); Yahweh himself will *take great delight in* them, *renew* them *in his love* (NRSV), rejoice over them *with singing* (verse 17), and *restore* their *fortunes* (verse 20; 2:7). These climactic verses turn the book's message into one of hope. The word of condemnation in chapter 1 gives way to a love song in the finale.

THEOLOGICAL REFLECTIONS

Yahweh, creator of all humanity, is deeply concerned about and cares for all peoples, including the people chosen to bring blessing to all nations and all nations to God. Yahweh has a "Day of Wrath" for all peoples, since all persist in sinning. Since sin is very serious and debilitating, God deals with it severely, yet not in order to annihilate, but to cleanse and redeem. Thus, beyond punishment, Yahweh has a "Day of Deliverance" (or salvation) for all peoples, on which all false gods perish, and meek, humble, and faithful people throughout the world convert to worshiping and serving God in *pure speech* and *with one accord*.

FOR FURTHER STUDY

Elizabeth Achtemeier, *Nahum–Malachi* (Louisville: Westminster John Knox, 1986).

Maria Eszenyei Szeles, *Wrath and Mercy: A Commentary on Habakkuk and Zephaniah* (Grand Rapids: Eerdmans, 1987).

WORKS CITED

Michael H. Floyd, *Minor Prophets Part 2* (Grand Rapids, Eerdmans, 2000).

Marvin Sweeney, *Zephaniah* (Minneapolis, Minn.: Fortress, 2003).

Haggai

Paul L. Watson

CHAPTER CONTENTS

Contexts 711

Commentary 711

　Is It a Time for Yourselves? · 1:1–11 711

　I Am with You · 1:12–15 712

　How Does It Look to You Now? · 2:1–9 712

　From This Day On, I Will Bless You · 2:10–19 712

　I Have Chosen You · 2:20–23 712

Theological Reflections 712

For Further Study 712

Works Cited 712

Haggai is unique in the prophetic canon of the Old Testament. Whereas other prophets critique the worship of the people of Israel (Amos 5:21–24; Isa 1:10–17) and their uncritical loyalty to the temple (Jer 7:1–4), Haggai urges the reconstruction of the temple and a renewal of temple worship. Because of this, many readers have depreciated his message, feeling that it has little current relevance. However, an understanding of Haggai's historical context and a close reading of his oracles affirm the validity of his prophecy.

CONTEXTS

All five of Haggai's oracles date to 520 BCE, the third year of the reign of the Persian king Darius the Great (522–486 BCE). While it was a time "of [the] beginnings of regional autonomy" (Peterson 27), Judah was still a subprovince of the new Persian Empire. Moreover, it was a time of land redistribution and of economic decline (March 709–10).

> **"Beyond the River"**
>
> *The Persian Empire was organized into several satrapies, or regions. The satrapy "Beyond the River" included most of today's Syria, Lebanon, Israel, Palestine, and Jordan. Judah, or Yehud, was a small division of this larger satrapy, as was Samaria.*

Such was the situation Haggai faced as he joined a contingent of exiles returning from Babylon to Jerusalem and Judah (Ezra 3:1–13; 5:1–2; 6:13–15). Haggai saw that such an impoverished, unfocused community could not survive without having a center – God – and a common commitment to worship and service. In this context, the message of Haggai makes sense.

Of Haggai the messenger we know very little. His name comes from the Hebrew word meaning "observe a pilgrimage feast." The book is written in a third-person, narrative style, suggesting that a disciple of Haggai composed it shortly after Haggai's ministry.

COMMENTARY

IS IT A TIME FOR YOURSELVES? · 1:1–11

Haggai's first oracle, dated 29 August 520 BCE, explicitly addresses *Zerubbabel, son of Shealtiel, governor of Judah, and to Joshua, son of Jehozadak the high priest* (1:1), and implicitly all the residents of Jerusalem and Judah (1:5–6). The people are experiencing crop failure, scarcity of goods, and inflation (1:6). But the heart of their problem lies in their priorities: *These people say, The time has not yet come for the Lord's house to be built* (1:2). The people intend to rebuild God's temple – some day. But, for now, their primary attention is on themselves. So God puts this penetrating question to them: *Is it a time for you yourselves to be living in your paneled* [or, "finished"] *houses, while this house* [God's temple] *remains a ruin?* (1:4).

All of this amounts to a violation of their covenant with God. By enacting the covenant-curses of Leviticus 26 and Deuteronomy 27–28, God reminds his people "that not foreigner nor fate nor workings of nature control the Judeans' lives, but God" (Achtemeier 99). Even the date of this first oracle is significant. Apparently, it is a feast day, connected with the Sabbath (2 Chron 31:3; Amos 8:5) – one they cannot observe "because of the lack of both altar and sanctuary" (Peterson 44).

Therefore, God says, *Give careful thought* [literally "set your heart"] *to your ways* (1:7). By shifting their focus from themselves to their relationship with God, they will in fact secure the prosperity they currently seek in vain.

I AM WITH YOU · 1:12–15

About three weeks later, on 21 September 520 BCE, Haggai delivers this message of divine approval. Leaders and people alike have *obeyed the voice of the Lord their God* (1:12). In response, God says, *I am with you* (1:13) – well before the temple was rebuilt – and God *stirred up the spirit* of all to carry out his will (1:14).

HOW DOES IT LOOK TO YOU NOW? · 2:1–9

Almost a month later – at the end of the Feast of Tabernacles (or *Sukkoth*, 17 October 520 BCE) – Haggai speaks again. Based on the recollections of the oldest members of the community (2:3a), it is clear that this will be "a half-baked building compared with the old temple that Solomon built" (Craigie 145).

God's response to the people's disappointment is twofold. First, *Be strong ... for I am with you* (2:4–5). The size and beauty of the temple are not important; God's presence is. Second, God gives them a greater vision of the future that includes *all nations*, when God will *fill this house with glory* and will *grant peace* (2:6–9).

FROM THIS DAY ON, I WILL BLESS YOU · 2:10–19

"The ultimate danger of temple building, and indeed of all works of religion, is the temptation to become self-righteous" (Achtemeier 102). That temptation apparently lies behind this oracle, dated 18 December 520 BCE. God warns the community that holiness is not contagious (2:11–12), but corruption is (2:13–14). God then urges the community to *give careful thought* to how it has been – empty silos and wine vats, unproductive labor (2:16–17) – compared with how it can be: *From this day on I will bless you* (2:18–19). Here holiness refers to the ritual purity of objects, but Haggai expands a technical argument among priests into a discussion with wider implications.

> **"Give careful thought ..."**
> *Although their forefathers had believed that technically correct worship was all that God required (Mic 6:1–8), Haggai warns that this generation needs to beware of that trap.*

I HAVE CHOSEN YOU · 2:20–23

Haggai's final oracle, also delivered on 18 December 520 BCE, is God's personal promise to Zerubbabel to honor his commitment to the house of David (2 Sam 7:11b–16). In a reversal of Jeremiah 22:24, God will empower Zerubbabel – *make you like my signet ring* – for *I have chosen you* (2:23).

> **Signet Rings**
> *A signet ring served ancient tradespeople and rulers as a tool for certifying documents.*

THEOLOGICAL REFLECTIONS

The message of Haggai, which at first glance seems to contradict that of the rest of the prophets, turns out to be one with theirs. God yearns to be present with Israel and to give them peace. But God will not do so unless they become persons of faith (Exod 20:1–3; Deut 6:4–6). The size and splendor of their accomplishments are not important to God; their wholehearted dedication to him is.

FOR FURTHER STUDY

William P. Brown, *Obadiah through Malachi* (Louisville: Westminster John Knox, 1996).

Carroll Stuhlmueller, *Rebuilding with Hope: A Commentary on the Books of Haggai and Zechariah* (Grand Rapids: Eerdmans, 1988).

WORKS CITED

Elizabeth Achtemeier, *Nahum–Malachi* (Atlanta: John Knox, 1986).

Peter Craigie, *Twelve Prophets*, vol. 2: *Micah, Nahum, Habakkuk, Zephaniah, Haggai, Zechariah, and Malachi* (Louisville: Westminster John Knox, 1985).

W. Eugene March, *Haggai* (Nashville: Abingdon, 1996).

David L. Peterson, *Haggai and Zechariah 1–8* (Philadelphia: Westminster, 1984).

Zechariah

Tim Sensing

CHAPTER CONTENTS

Contexts 713

Commentary 714

    Introduction · 1:1–6 714

    Eight Night Visions with Corresponding Oracles · 1:7–6:15 714

    Sermonic Response to the Present Situation · 7:1–8:23 715

    The Restoration of Judah & Israel · 9:1–11:17 716

    God's War to Purify Israel ·12:1–14:21 717

Theological Reflections 718

For Further Study 718

Works Cited 718

Zechariah, which means "Yahweh remembers," is the name of 29 biblical characters. The Zechariah of this book is a prophet (Zech 1:1, 7), and he responds as a prophet to the delegation's question in Zechariah 7–8. He may be the priest referred to in Nehemiah 12:16. This Zechariah was a contemporary of Haggai, and both prophesied in Jerusalem after the return from Babylonian exile sometime after 539 BCE. The edict of Cyrus (Ezra 6:3–5) allowed them to rebuild the temple. Ezra 5:1, 6:14, and Nehemiah 12:16 mention the career of both prophets, as well. Zechariah's first prophecy follows Haggai's by two months (Zech 1:1), and his work continued until 518 BCE, *the fourth year of King Darius* (Zech 7:1). Both Haggai and Zechariah advocated the completion of the temple.

> **Eschatology in Zechariah**
> *Many of Zechariah's themes are eschatological in nature, describing Yahweh as the lord of the whole earth (4:14) who rules from Zion over all the nations (compare Psalm 2). Peace and justice will characterize God's reign, which completely depends on God's action and will be a reversal of the devastation of Judah in former times. Although Zechariah's vision of God's recreated future seems utopian, it still expects conflict and death.*

CONTEXTS

Differences in literary style between Zechariah 1–8 and 9–14 have led many scholars to attribute the two sections to different authors. For example, chapters 9–14 contain no visions and no historic references to the restoration of Jerusalem, the temple, or the reign of Darius, while chapters 1–8 strongly emphasize those elements. Similarly, chapters 9–14 make no mention of Zechariah, Joshua, and Zerubbabel, who are so prominent in chapters 1–8. Chapters 9–14 also demonstrate considerable differences in vocabulary and other literary features (Coggins 61–62).

> **Yehud in the Persian Empire**
> *The district around Jerusalem, called Yehud (a short form of Yehudah, or Judah), was part of the larger Persian satrapy "Beyond the River," which covered modern Syria, Lebanon, Jordan, Israel, and the Palestinian Authority. The high priest of Jerusalem functioned as a local leader subject to the imperial Persian government. Coins from Yehud often bear the names of these high priests.*

Yet certain themes appear in both sections: the prominence of the Zion tradition, the stress on the cleansing of the community, universalistic tendencies, the appeal to earlier prophecy, and the role of proper leadership as a sign of the new age. Such similarities suggest some historical relationship between the two parts of the book.

Dating of chapters 9–14 becomes problematic since there are no concrete references to people or events. The reference to *Greece* in 9:13 may represent a later time period for these oracles. Scholars tend to date 9–14 later than 1–8 due to the differences in literary style. Yet it is more helpful to try to understand the entire book as a single work, with the historical setting of chapters 1–8 leading into a more generalized vision of the world later in the book. The emphasis on divine judgment throughout the book can certainly refer to many historical periods. On the other hand, chapters 1–8 more often envision the restoration as a present reality, whereas chapters 9–14 depict the restoration as an eschatological hope still in the future (see Conrad).

ZECHARIAH

COMMENTARY
INTRODUCTION · 1:1–6

Zechariah has long stymied interpreters. It stands between the utopian picture of the future represented in Isaiah 40–55 and the hard realities of postexilic Palestine. Much of the apocalyptic language defies concrete historical connections. However, in association with Haggai, Zechariah gives readers a rare glimpse into the state of affairs in postexilic Jerusalem.

Zechariah, *son of Berekiah*, *the son of Iddo*, joined with Yahweh in forming a new community fit for the new age promised by the earlier prophets. Zechariah reiterates the message of the *former prophets*, calling the community to *return* to God. Even his name reminds the community to remember God's past action and promise. The people during Zechariah's day, unlike their ancestors, repented of their sins (6b). Zechariah believed that the return from exile and the rebuilding of the temple would inaugurate God's eschatological future. Zechariah looks back at an earlier era, the time of the *former prophets* (Zech 1:2–6; 7:4–14; 8:9), namely those like Amos or Jeremiah, and understands the exile to have been the fulfillment of their words. He declares that he and his fellow Jews now stand at the threshold of the new era.

EIGHT NIGHT VISIONS WITH CORRESPONDING ORACLES · 1:7–6:15

Much of the imagery in the night visions describes common sights in Jerusalem during the rebuilding of the temple. The visions are arranged in a chiastic (A B B′ A′) fashion and consistently depict Yahweh's return to Zion. The first and last visions encompass the whole world. The second and seventh visions narrow the focus to Judah. The third and sixth visions focus on Jerusalem. The fourth and fifth visions examine the roles of Joshua and Zerubbabel. Fishbane (448) notes a pattern of each vision except the fourth: Zechariah reports a vision: "I saw…"; he describes a sign: "and there before me was/were…"; he asks: "What is this/are these?"; the angel identifies the sign: "This is/these are…"; the angel interprets the sign.

A major feature of each oracle is the prophetic introduction: the messenger formula *thus says Yahweh*, the oracle formula *says Yahweh*, and the revelation formula *the word of Yahweh came to…*.

Hanson observes that the structural arrangement of the visions focuses on the temple as the center of a symbolic universe (see also Halpern). Yet the visions themselves do not directly mention the temple reconstruction. No matter how the visions are numbered, the two visions of chapters 3 and 4, which focus on the political power of Joshua and Zerubbabel in the temple, are the centerpiece of the entire section.

1:7-7 Soon after the initial prophecy, while the temple is being reconstructed, Zechariah receives night visions full of hope concerning what God has already begun to do in the new age (Zech 1:11b, 16; 2:4–5, 10). The first night vision raises the question of the delay of the promise that underlies Haggai's work, by referring to *seventy years* (verse 12) of punishment, perhaps an echo of the equal time span predicated by Jeremiah (Jer 25:11; 29:10). The world Zechariah envisions does not correspond to the reality the people experienced.

1:18–21 The *four craftsmen*, divine agents of God, will destroy the *four horns*, representing the oppressive nations that *scattered Israel, Judah, and Jerusalem*. The horns symbolize military powers, and the number four represents the four corners of the world and thus its totality. God will accomplish

---

Zechariah's Visions

Meyers and Meyers (Zechariah 1–8, 179, 213–15) *exclude 3:1–10 from the list of visions and renumber 5–8 as 4–7. Chapter 3 does break from the pattern of the other visions by lacking the interpreting angel and Zechariah's subsequent answer, the naming of a historical person, and the mention of the satan. Someone else shows Zechariah the vision. I have followed here the more usual arrangement of the visions, however.*

Apocalypse in Zechariah

These chapters contain an early form of apocalyptic literature. John Collins says that it is

> a genre of revelatory literature with a narrative framework, in which a revelation is mediated by an otherworldly being to a human recipient, disclosing a transcendent reality which is both temporal, insofar as it involves another, supernatural world, intended for a group in crisis with the purpose of exhortation and/or consolation by means of divine authority (Collins 9).

These visions work by piling up images that collectively evoke certain responses.

the promised restoration by crushing the oppressive powers.

2:1–13 Jerusalem is being measured as a symbol of its restoration. It will be *without walls*, not because foreign armies have destroyed them, but because the population of returnees grows too large. People will again dwell there in prosperity and God's *glory* will fortify the city. The oracle that follows, 2:6–13, interprets the first three night visions by affirming the restoration of Judah and Jerusalem as God's holy dwelling, ensuring the destruction of the oppressive nations, and envisioning prosperity in the future. The phrase *Holy Land* (2:12) occurs only here in the Old Testament.

3:1–10 Joshua served as the first high priest after the exile (Ezra 2:2; 3:2; see also 2 Kings 25:18; 1 Chron 6:15; Jer 52:24; Zech 4; 6:9–15). He helped build the altar and the temple, and he offered sacrifices (Ezra 3:1–13; 5:1–2). By omitting the name of the governor, Zerubbabel, this vision emphasizes the central role of the high priest in postexilic Judaism.

Verses 1–5 describe the heavenly courtroom where *the satan* accuses Joshua. The Lord rebukes the satan for undercutting Joshua. The angel orders the cleaning of Joshua's priestly garments (see Exod 28:31–38), signifying the cleansing of sin and the restoration of relationship between Yahweh and his people.

> **"The Satan"**
> The satan, *with the definite article*, occurs in the Bible elsewhere only in Job 1–2 and 1 Chronicles 21:1, where it names a member of the divine council, not a demonic figure.

Verse 6 introduces an oracle from the Lord describing the duties or privileges of Joshua. Subsequently, the future ruler from David's line, the *Branch* (see Jer 23:5–6; 33:14–15), will remove the sin from all the people in the land. Zerubbabel may be the Branch (see Hag 2:23), since 6:12–13 designates the figure as the one to build the temple, while 4:7–10 presents Zerubbabel as the one to do so. However, the prophet also presents the Branch as a future messiah who will demonstrate the inclusive nature of God's protection among the nations.

4:1–14 The central feature of this vision is the *lamp stand* symbolizing God's presence in the temple and in Jerusalem. If chapter 3 is a later addition, then the lamp stand representing God's presence sits at the center of all the visions and coincides theologically with the first and last. Verses 8–14 describe Zerubbabel's reconstruction of the temple. The *plumb line* of verse 10 links the prophecy to Amos 7:7–9: the new prophecy reverses the doom oracle of Amos. The *two who are anointed* are Joshua and Zerubbabel.

> **Apocalyptic Vision**
> In Revelation 5:6, the eyes of the Lamb take over the function of Yahweh's eyes in Zechariah 4:10b.

5:1–4 The *flying scroll* symbolizes the word of God going forth among the people, cursing violators of the Mosaic law, especially the eighth and ninth commandments. The *curse* consumes those who are an internal threat to the community and thus preserves the people as a whole. Like all the night visions, this one lodges no judgment against the community as a whole. The scope of God's restoration begins to expand here to include the whole earth, a move climaxing in the final vision.

5:5–11 The theme of protecting the community from internal threat continues in the seventh and most complex of the visions. The *basket* of *iniquity* goes to *Babylonia*. The sin of the people has been removed.

6:1–8 The eighth vision structurally parallels the first in setting and theme, emphasizing God's presence. The horses represent God spreading his reign throughout the world with an emphasis on the *north country*, the land of exile, where God's *Spirit* is at *rest* and the cosmos is now ordered. The inclusive nature of God's future reign encompasses the east and west in 8:7–8 and the south in 9:14.

6:9–15 Mason (197) observes that the last oracle has little literary connection with the final vision but may serve as an "appendix" to the whole series. The central feature of the section is the crowning of Joshua and the building of the temple. Though Joshua is the true representative of God, he also functions as a sign of the unnamed "Branch" and an unspecified future to come.

SERMONIC RESPONSE TO THE PRESENT SITUATION · 7:1–8:23

7:1–3 A two-year gap occurs between the dating of the night visions and the arrival of a delegation from Bethel. According the 2 Kings 25:8–9, Jerusalem fell in the fifth month. For decades, the lamentations and fasting have beseeched the throne of God on behalf of the land, Jerusalem, and the people. And during their exile, the prophets proclaimed a coming age of grace, a time when a remnant of the people would return to the land. Now with the return of the prophets Haggai and Zechariah, the temple itself was being reconstructed. In the second year of that reconstruction process, about halfway through, a delegation came asking whether the mourning remained appropriate in light of new circumstances.

7:4–8:23 The remainder of this section consists of a series of oracles responding to the question of 7:3 (7:4–7; 7:8–14; 8:1–8; 8:9–13; 8:14–17; 8:18–19; and 8:20–23). The oracles begin in the same way and weave together images of restoration (often drawn from earlier prophets) and call for ethical living. Nineteen times throughout the sermon in chapters 7 and 8, either the messenger formula (*thus says Yahweh of hosts*), the revelation formula (*the word of Yahweh came to*), or the oracle formula (*Says Yahweh*) constitutes Zechariah's understanding of the continuation and authority of the prophetic tradition to interpret the present in light of the past, in order to reorient the future. Mason (224) notes, "Such a homiletical practice serves at least three purposes. It explains why the promises of the prophets have not yet been fully experienced; it puts the stress on moral regeneration which is where the preacher believed it must be; and it serves to keep hope and faith alive in face of any temptation to despair and disillusion."

These oracles of Zechariah refer repeatedly to the "former" or "earlier" prophets. Mason (203) states, "It is interesting that the prophetic word is now becoming regarded as authoritative teaching on a par with Torah, for that is what the paralleling of the legal terms *statutes* with *my words* must imply." He also identifies (218) in chapter 7 allusions and images from the former prophets (for example Deut 29:25; 32:17; 2 Chron 29:8; 30:7; Isa 29:6; Jer 3:19; 19:4; 23:19; 25:32; 44:3; Ezek 32:9; Amos 1:14; Hos 13:3).

> **Tradition**
> *For Zechariah, the tradition acted as testimony to faith and practice that allowed the emergence of a new understanding in his own context. He proclaims the former words as his word in order to reshape his community. Even though Zechariah's and the former prophets' message was the same, the contexts, intents, and responses were different. The former prophets' words brought devastation, Zechariah's hope.*

The delegation's question in 7:3 afforded Zechariah the opportunity to interpret the past, present, and future of God's intent for his people. Verses 9–10 state the core ethical practices of Israel. However, the people did not listen in those former days. The God of the past, who had brought prosperity, also brought judgment. Consequently, the land of prosperity became desolate (Zech 7:11–14).

Ollenburger sees the structure of the unit 7:7–14 as comprising an introduction (7:7), a summary of the words of the former prophets (7:9–10), a report of the people's response (7:11–12a), and the consequences of their response (12b–14). Zechariah refers to the adversity in the past as the reversal of an earlier prosperity due to the people's rejection of the former prophets. The scope of restoration will be broad, extending from Babylonia to the Mediterranean (8:7). It will even encompass foreigners (compare Isa 2:55).

Finally comes the answer to the question asked by the delegation (Zech 8:14). Zechariah calls his people *to be strong and not afraid* and not to interrupt the rebuilding of the temple but to continue to strive to join with God's salvation (Zech 8:10, 13c). Fast days of mourning will become seasons of celebration (8:4–5, 18–19). In the past, God's word involved a reversal from prosperity to adversity, but now the future involves a reversal from fasts to feasts. God's return to Jerusalem inaugurates the beginning of the future now (Zech 8:20–23).

THE RESTORATION OF JUDAH & ISRAEL · 9:1–11:17

The eschatological oracles of Zechariah 9–14 do not forecast international history but create a vision of the future by reenvisioning the past. The need to see the future in more distant terms was a response to the failure of the return to the land under Persian rule to produce the utopia envisioned by earlier eschatological expectations (see Isa 40–55). The oracles in Zechariah 9–14 address the disparity between present realities and unfulfilled hopes (for example, Zech 4:10). The shepherds have failed to tend the flock of God, and the flock of God has detested the shepherds. The mastery of the Lord over the whole earth is therefore called into question (chapters 9–11). Chapters 12–14 look to the future, *on that day*, when God's reign over the whole earth commences.

The promises of restoration awaited fulfillment. Four passages (9:1–17; 10:3b–12; 12:1–13:6; 14:1–21) present a bright and glorious future hope that includes a Davidic king and a reunited kingdom. This future will involve conflict, war, and death, but God will purge Jerusalem and protect Judah. Uniting these four passages are three sections (10:1–3a; 11:1–17; 13:7–9) describing the failures of the shepherds that ultimately led to the unrealized hope for king and kingdom and the intermingled texts of war against Jerusalem.

9:1–8 The divine warrior, Yahweh, sweeps across Syria-Palestine north to south toward Jerusalem on his march to restore the land. After his victory, all the people *rejoice* because their king is arriving at the temple, victorious and in peace (9:9–10). The list of nations includes Jerusalem's nearest foreign neighbors. The connection between conquest and temple building goes back before the Israelites and underlies many biblical texts (for example Exod 15).

9:9–17 This section begins with a call to praise (verses 9–10) and continues with a word of deliverance and encouragement (verses 11–17). As such, these verses resemble a psalm of praise. The restored people of Israel return to the land once the future king has come in victory and sealed their relationship by *the blood of my covenant*. Although there is peace, not all is well. There is an announcement of war, for some people remain prisoners in far away lands. The Lord desires a full return and restoration of Israel. The reference to *Greece* (verse 13) may echo the conflict between Persia and Greece in the fifth century BCE (Meyers and Meyers, *Zechariah 9–14*, 148) or date the oracle to the Maccabean struggle in the 160s, depending on one's view of the entire book.

10:1–12 The promising vision of God's restoration continues in chapter 10 with only a hint of trouble in 10:2 that anticipates the internal collapse in chapter 11 (Ollenburger 802). Other than Isaiah 57, Zechariah 10:2 and 13:2 are the only mentions of *idols* in postexilic writings. Chapter 10 parallels and extends the vision of restoration found in chapter 9. God, as the creator and sustainer of life, directs his anger toward the shepherds in order to bring about the future restoration of all the scattered people and a son of David of the house of Judah who will again sit on a throne of a united kingdom.

11:1–17 Chapter 11 calls into question the vision of chapters 9–10 by using a parable, or allegory, describing the symbolic act of the prophet becoming a shepherd in a tenuous relationship with the people (11:4–17). The oracle uses a first person report, or prophetic autobiography, to communicate the failure of the shepherd. The shepherd breaks a staff, symbolic of a covenant, draws his wages, and hurls the money into the temple. He breaks a second shaft, symbolic of the union between Israel and Judah. The breaking of this staff is a reversal of the symbolic act of Ezekiel 37:15–23. The prophet then becomes the foolish shepherd who abuses the people of God.

> **Corrupt Leadership**
> The postexilic community must see the corruption of its leadership depicted by the prophet, for this precludes the coming of God's mercy. Numerous attempts to identify the shepherds with historical figures pervade the literature, but to no satisfying consensus.

The reference to the *thirty shekels* of 11:13 possibly alludes to the same amount paid to a slave owner as compensation when an ox gores a slave (Exod 21:32). The passage concludes with a woe oracle directed against the worthless shepherd who neglects the flock. The shepherd usually refers to a king but in this context may include other religious leaders. The solution envisions a restored Davidic throne. The woe of 11:17 anticipates the description of the purging of Jerusalem in 12:10–13:6.

> **Matthew's Use of Zechariah**
> Matthew 26:16–16 and 27:3–10 recycle Zechariah 11:13 to describe Jesus' betrayal and Judas's fate.

GOD'S WAR TO PURIFY ISRAEL · 12:1–14:21

12:1–14 This section depicts a war by the nations against Judah, with God bringing Judah to victory. The cryptic text defies identifying the circumstances described with any particular international setting. The future orientation of these oracles of promise (12:1–14:21) and thematic unity of God's victory as divine warrior is heightened by the repeated use of eschatological scenarios of what will transpire *on that day* (12:3, 4, 6, 8, 9, 11; 13:1, 2, 4; 14:4, 6, 8, 9, 13, 20, 21 – 17 times total).

The God of creation (12:1) declares that, as the nations gather to attack Jerusalem, they will be frustrated (12:2–9). The encouraged people recognize that *the Lord Almighty is their God* (12:5). Verse 10 suggests various echoes used in the New Testament (Matt 3:17; Luke 2:7, 9:35; John 1:18, 19:37; Rom 8:29; Col 1:15).

Mourning and supplication will follow God's victory as the people realize that their salvation has come through God's intervention (12:10–14).

13:1–9 This unit describes the cleansing that follows God's victory and the elimination of idols, prophets, and prophecy (13:2–6). Prophets come under such disdain that even their parents will slay them. Even the language of Amos 7:14, *I am not a prophet*, plays against the prophets. Finally, even a good shepherd of the people is slain, scattering two-thirds of the people; however, a third of the people will be purified and remain in the land. Thus this chapter picks up the ancient ideas of the remnant.

14:1–21 The war imagery of chapter 12 is repeated in chapter 14, with the latter making no mention of prophets, shepherds, or a Davidic house. Both chapters affirm the theology of Zion prevalent in Isaiah. In 14:1–2, the nations are gathered to fight against Jerusalem (compare Psalm 2). In 14:3, God will fight for the people and the nations will be defeated. God alone will be king (14:9, 16, 17). And after Jerusalem is purged, it will be the center of God's universal reign and re-creative order. Survivors from all nations will come to celebrate the Feast of Tabernacles (see Exod 23:16; Neh 8:18). Zechariah concludes with his final word about the temple (14:20–21). *On that day*, the day of God's consummate victory in the age to come, the temple will finally be fit for worship for the whole world. The inclusive vision of the nations gathering in Jerusalem characterizes the endings of both parts of the book (8:20–23; 14:20–21).

THEOLOGICAL REFLECTIONS

Zechariah must find a way to make the words of the older prophets relevant to a new day. The book bearing his name deals with specific problems such as the rebuilding of the temple, the relationship of Jews to their Gentile rulers, and especially the meaning of Israel's preexilic history. It addresses these problems by reclaiming the hopeful language and high ethical standards of the past as it seeks to rebuild Israel as a fit location for the residence of the God of all the earth.

FOR FURTHER STUDY

Paul Hanson, *The Dawn of Apocalyptic* (Philadelphia: Fortress, 1975).

Rex Mason, "The Relation of Zech.9–14 to Proto-Zechariah," *Zeitschrift für die alttestamentliche Wissenschaft* 88 (1976): 227–39.

WORKS CITED

R. J. Coggins, *Haggai, Zechariah, Malachi* (Sheffield: JSOT Press, 1987).

John Collins, "Introduction: Toward the Morphology of a Genre," *Semeia* 14 (1979): 1–20.

E. W. Conrad, *Zechariah* (Sheffield: Sheffield Academic Press, 1999).

Michael Fishbane, *Biblical Interpretation in Ancient Israel* (Oxford: Clarendon, 1985).

Baruch Halpern, "The Ritual Background of Zechariah's Temple Song," *Catholic Biblical Quarterly* 40 (1978): 167–90.

Paul Hanson, "In Defiance of Death: Zechariah's Symbolic Universe," in *Love and Death in the Ancient Near East* (ed. J. H. Marks and R. M. Good; Guilford: Four Quarters, 1987): 176–77.

Rex Mason, *Preaching the Tradition: Homily and Hermeneutics after the Exile* (Cambridge: Cambridge University Press, 1990).

C. L. Meyers and Eric M. Meyers, *Haggai and Zechariah 1–8* (New York: Doubleday, 1987).

———, *Zechariah 9–14* (New York: Doubleday, 1993).

B. C. Ollenburger, *New Interpreters Bible*, vol. 7: *The Book of Zechariah* (Nashville: Abingdon, 1996).

David Petersen, *Haggai and Zechariah 1–8* (Louisville: Westminster John Knox, 1984).

———, *Zechariah 9–14 and Malachi* (Louisville: Westminster John Knox, 1995).

Malachi

Paul L. Watson

CHAPTER CONTENTS

Contexts 719

Commentary 719
- Introduction · 1:1 719
- I Have Loved You, Says the Lord · 1:2–5 719
- If I Am a Father, Where Is the Honor Due Me? · 1:6–2:9 720
- Have We Not All One Father? · 2:10–16 720
- Where Is the God of Justice? · 2:17–3:5 720
- I the Lord Do Not Change · 3:6–12 720
- It Is Futile to Serve God · 3:13–4:3 720
- Epilogue · 4:4–6 721

Theological Reflections 721

For Further Study 721

Works Cited 721

The book of Malachi provides a fitting conclusion to the "Book of the Twelve" (that is, the Minor Prophets). Malachi sets forth many great themes of the biblical witness: the universal rule of God; the steadfast love of God for Israel, in spite of their sins; the absolute necessity of covenant-keeping from the heart; and the certainty of divine judgment, tempered with mercy.

CONTEXTS

We know virtually nothing about Malachi. In fact, "Malachi" may be his actual name or simply his title – "my [God's] messenger" (see 3:1). His messages address the restored Jewish community in Palestine during the postexilic (Persian) period. It was "a small and relatively poor community, without solid economic resources or great hopes" (Schuller 848), with the population of Judah numbering at most a few thousand. Most scholars date that community to a few decades after the rebuilding of the Jerusalem temple in 520 BCE (see Haggai and Zech 1–8), but before the time of Nehemiah and Ezra.

> **The Persian Empire**
> The Persian Empire extended from present-day Afghanistan to Greece and existed from 539–334 BCE before falling to Alexander the Great. Darius the Great came to the throne of Persia in 522 BCE after a brief civil war. He was a junior member of the royal family.

Between a brief introduction (1:1) and an epilogue (4:4–6), the book of Malachi has six distinct units. Each unit typically includes an accusatory statement and/or question by God (for example, 2:17a); a response from Israel that deflects the accusation, often by asking a counterquestion (2:17b); and God's rebuttal, often cast as a summary statement or question (2:17c), which is then expounded upon (3:1–5). This format has been labeled a disputation, a dialogue (Schuller 850), a priestly trial (Achtemeier 172), and a diatribe (Petersen 31). Whatever the book's form, the function is clear: to urge the people to recognize and repent of their sins before it is too late.

COMMENTARY

INTRODUCTION · 1:1

Oracle is a technical term used to designate prophetic speech (see Isa 13:1; Nah 1:1; Hab 1:1). In the introduction, *Israel* expresses God's inclusive view of his people (see 4:4 and Deut 1:1).

I HAVE LOVED YOU, SAYS THE LORD · 1:2–5

This is the topic sentence of Malachi. It conveys both God's feelings for Israel and a covenant commitment to them (see Deut 7:7–9; Hos 11:1). The community's response, *How have you loved us?* (1:2b), challenges that commitment.

God responds, somewhat surprisingly, by reminding Israel of its "half-brother," Esau/Edom. Even though Esau was the firstborn twin, God chose to love Jacob/Israel (Gen 25:23; 28:13–15). Edom subsequently became Israel's implacable enemy (Obad 1–21; Jer 49:7–22). *Great is the Lord – even beyond the borders of Israel* (1:5) is Malachi's first reminder of God's worldwide sovereignty and honor (see 1:11, 14; 3:12).

MALACHI

IF I AM A FATHER, WHERE IS THE HONOR DUE ME? · 1:6–2:9

This unit illustrates the people's contempt for God. God has loved them (1:2); but in return they have dishonored him with their *defiled* offerings – *blind, crippled, diseased* (1:8), and *injured* (1:13) animals – contrary to the explicit instructions of Leviticus 1:3; 22:17–25, and Deuteronomy 15:21. Even offering the culls from their herds is a *burden; and* [*they*] *sniff at it* (NIV; NRSV, *me*) in contempt (1:13). To God, absence of worship is preferable to disrespectful worship (1:10; see Amos 5:21–24; Isa 1:12–14), particularly since *my name will be great among the nations*, that is, honored by others worldwide (1:11).

The last half of the unit (2:1–9) is directed to Israel's priests. It may be that *two* groups of priests are involved – the Aaronic priests, who are condemned (2:2–3), and the Levitical priests, whose covenant with God is salvageable (2:4–5; see Deut 33:8–11 and Jer 33:19–22; see Petersen 189–190). The priestly blessings of unfaithful priests will become a curse (2:2; see Num 6:22–27). Priests who offer *defiled* sacrifices (1:7, 12) will themselves be defiled by having the excrement of the sacrificial animals spread over their own faces (2:3), thus disqualifying them from serving at God's altar.

HAVE WE NOT ALL ONE FATHER? · 2:10–16

At stake in this unit is the integrity of the community. By *breaking faith with one another*, the people are also breaking faith with their forefathers and with God (2:10). Some are marrying outside the covenant community (2:11–12; see Solomon in 1 Kgs 11:1–6). Others are abandoning their longtime mates – *your partner, the wife of your marriage covenant* (2:13–14). God himself has made them one (2:15a; see Gen 2:24 and Mark 10:6–9), and he expects *godly offspring* from such unions (2:15b; see Gen 1:27–28). The faithless behavior of Israelite husbands *in flesh and spirit* (2:15) has made that impossible. No wonder God says, *I hate divorce* (2:16): "The ruined lives, the collapse of hopes, and the loss of faithfulness make it a hateful practice" (Craigie 238).

WHERE IS THE GOD OF JUSTICE? · 2:17–3:5

The dialogue now turns to Israel's accusation that Yahweh is not just and fair because God accepts evildoers as good and because there is no justice in God's world (2:17).

The *wearied* Lord replies that his justice will surely become evident, first through *my messenger, who will prepare the way before me*, then by his own arrival at his temple (3:1). Verse 5 cites six specific examples of covenant-breaking and spells out the nature of God's coming – *for judgment*, on all who have rejected the messenger.

> **The Role of God's Messenger**
> The messenger's role is elaborated upon in 3:2–4. His will be a ministry of refining and purifying God's people, in preparation for the Lord's arrival (see Matt 3:1–12 and 11:7–15, where Jesus quotes Mal 3:1).

I THE LORD DO NOT CHANGE · 3:6–12

The next issue in the dispute is unfaithful stewardship. God begins the dialogue by reminding Israel of his consistency (3:6a). Far from being unjust (2:17), God rightly could have *destroyed* the *descendants of Jacob* (3:6b). Instead, God urges the audience to *Return to me, and I will return to you* (3:7b). Their return, however, must be in deed as well as in word. They must produce "fruit in keeping with repentance" (see Matt 3:8), specifically the *tithes and offerings* (3:8c) that they owe to God.

Such *tithes* (given to support the Levites; Num 18:21–24) and *offerings* (one-tenth of the tithe, given by the Levites to God; Num 18:25–32) are not gifts but are God's due (Lev 27:30–33). To withhold them is truly to *rob God* (3:8). Conversely, to *bring the whole tithe* (3:10) will lead to God abundantly blessing them (3:10–11). While it is more common for God to test people, here God audaciously invites his people to *test me in this* (3:10b). The results will be *a delightful land* for them, and worldwide commendation for them and their God (3:12).

IT IS FUTILE TO SERVE GOD · 3:13–4:3

In this summary debate, the recalcitrant members of the community expand their complaint against God. Having previously asked, *Where is the God of justice?* (2:17), they now assert, *It is futile to serve God. What did we gain by carrying out his requirements?* … [*E*]*vildoers prosper, and even those who challenge God escape* (3:14–15).

Interestingly enough, God does not respond immediately to their charges. Instead, *those who feared the Lord* (3:16) talk things over among themselves and conclude that God *is* right. God *listened and heard* them, records their faithfulness and promises to *spare them* and make them his *treasured possession* (3:16b–18; see Exod 19:3–6).

Then God reveals the future: *Surely the day is coming …* (4:1a; see Amos 5:18–20, 8:11; Isa 2:12). It will be a day of disaster for *all the arrogant and every evildoer* (4:1), but a day of deliverance for *you who revere my name* (4:2a). Like *calves released from the stall*, the faithful will *leap* in the warm sunlight (4:2b) and *trample* the *ashes* of the wicked (4:3a) who have already met their fate (4:1).

EPILOGUE · 4:4–6

These last three verses of Malachi are a divine admonition (4:4) and a divine promise (4:5–6). The admonition is to *remember the law* (*teaching*, NRSV; Hebrew *torah*) *of my servant Moses* (see Deut 8:1–2, 10–18). The promise is *I will send you the prophet Elijah* (4:5), whose mission will be one of reconciliation and preparation for the Lord's own coming (4:6).

THEOLOGICAL REFLECTIONS

For such a short and relatively unfamiliar biblical book, Malachi is theologically full and rich. Themes that merit further reflection include the primacy of God's love (1:2; John 3:16), worship (1:6–14; Mark 11:15–17), ministry (2:1–9; 2 Cor 4:1–2), marriage and divorce (2:10–16; Mark 10:1–12), and stewardship (3:6–12; 2 Cor 8:1–7). The theme of God's justice – present and future – rounds out the book (2:17–3:5; 3:13–4:3), leaving its readers with both an admonition and a promise (4:4–6; 2 Pet 3:10–13).

FOR FURTHER STUDY

William P. Brown, *Obadiah through Malachi* (Louisville: Westminster John Knox, 1996).

Eileen M. Schuller, "The Book of Malachi," in *The New Interpreters' Bible* (ed. Leander Keck; Nashville: Abingdon, 1996): 7:841–77.

WORKS CITED

Elizabeth Achtemeier, *Nahum–Malachi* (Atlanta: John Knox, 1986).

Peter Craigie, *Twelve Prophets*, vol. 2: *Micah, Nahum, Habakkuk, Zephaniah, Haggai, Zechariah and Malachi* (Louisville: Westminster John Knox, 1985).

David L. Petersen, *Zechariah 9–14 and Malachi* (Louisville: Westminster John Knox, 1995).

Eileen M. Schuller, "The Book of Malachi," in *The New Interpreters' Bible* (ed. Leander Keck; Nashville: Abingdon, 1996): 7:841–77.

Matthew

Gregory M. Stevenson

CHAPTER CONTENTS

- Contexts **724**
- Commentary **730**
  - Genealogy of the Christ · 1:1–17 **730**
  - Birth Narrative of the Christ · 1:18–2:23 **732**
  - Jesus as the Faithful Son of God · 3:1–4:25 **734**
  - Discourse 1: The Sermon on the Mount · 5:1–7:29 **736**
  - Ministry of Miracles · 8:1–9:38 **740**
  - Discourse 2: Missionary Instructions to the Twelve · 10:1–42 **741**
  - Growing Conflict with Israel · 11:1–12:50 **742**
  - Discourse 3: Parables of the Kingdom · 13:1–52 **744**
  - Opposition from Without & Growing Enlightenment From Within · 13:53–16:12 **745**
  - The Demands of Discipleship · 16:13–17:27 **747**
  - Discourse 4: The Life of the Community · 18:1–35 **748**
  - From Galilee to Judea · 19:1–20:16 **749**
  - To Jerusalem · 20:17–21:11 **749**
  - Teaching & Conflict in the Temple · 21:12–23:39 **750**
  - Discourse 5: Instructions on the End of the Age · 24:1–25:46 **751**
  - The Passion · 26:1–27:56 **753**
  - Burial & Resurrection · 27:57–28:15 **756**
  - The Great Commission · 28:16–20 **756**
- Theological Reflections **756**
- For Further Study **759**
- Works Cited **759**

MAPS, TABLES, & FEATURES

- Syrian Antioch **725**
- Jesus' Discourses **727**
- Women in Christ's Genealogy **731**
- Herod the Great **733**
- Nazareth & Sepphoris **734**
- Capernaum **736**
- The Pharisees **738**
- The Jerusalem Temple **753**

The gospel of Matthew enjoys both priority in the New Testament canon and popularity in the church. The church widely embraced Matthew early on, a development that assured its easy acceptance into the New Testament canon of Scripture. Although several early Christian writers (Clement of Alexandria, Origen, Eusebius) viewed Matthew as the first of the canonical gospels written (in contrast to most present-day scholars who opt for Mark), its placement as the first book in the New Testament probably owes more to the belief that it offers the most suitable introduction to the story of Jesus. Matthew opens with an extensive presentation of Jesus that includes his genealogy, birth narrative, baptism, and temptation in the wilderness (Matt 1–4). These stories introduce a Jesus deeply rooted in Israelite history and tradition, who comes not to break with Israel's past but to bring God's promises to Israel to fulfillment. Consequently, Matthew contains abundant quotations, allusions, and echoes of Old Testament Scripture. With approximately fifty direct quotations of the Old Testament, most of which come from the Pentateuch (the first five books of the Bible) and prophetic literature, Matthew crafts a narrative that defines Jesus in light of the Law and the Prophets. With this emphasis on continuity, Matthew serves as an appropriate choice to open the New Testament because it links the new to the old by connecting the church to Israel through Jesus Christ.

Another likely factor in the placement of Matthew was its popularity in the church. Matthew was the most prominent and frequently quoted gospel of the early church, and that popularity has continued throughout most of the church's history. Matthew betrays its interest in the church by being the only gospel to use the term *church* [Greek *ekklesia*], which it does twice (16:18; 18:17). Matthew also emphasizes the teachings of Jesus, which are prominently displayed in five major discourses spread throughout the gospel, the most notable being the Sermon on the Mount (Matt 5–7). These teachings instructed the apostles and the church in how to live lives of righteousness

MATTHEW

after the pattern of Christ. Consequently, the common use of this gospel for the instruction of disciples and for the edification of the community led to its designation as "the Church's Gospel."

CONTEXTS

Determining the circumstances behind any gospel is difficult because the gospels were written several decades after the events they describe. The gospels tell the story of Jesus for their contemporary audience, yet how their individual narrations reflect that contemporary situation is often obscure. Nevertheless, most scholars agree that Matthew provides sufficient clues to reconstruct several important aspects of the occasion. These clues arise out of the tension between Matthew's competing themes of particularism and universalism.

Matthew's Jewish Christology (indicated by his use of the titles "son of David," and "son of Abraham"), limitation of Jesus' ministry to Israel, lack of explanation for several Jewish customs, and emphasis on the abiding validity of the law (5:17–19) make it the most Jewish of the gospels. Matthew's particularism finds distinct expression in texts that appear to represent a preference for Jews over Gentiles. Several texts offer sharp criticism of Gentiles (5:47; 6:7, 32; 18:17), while others limit Jesus' saving activity to Israel.

> **Jesus' Jewish Ministry**
> At Jesus' birth, the Magi proclaim him *the shepherd of my people Israel* (2:6). *This metaphor of shepherd and sheep structures Jesus' self-understanding of his ministry. Upon sending out the twelve apostles, Jesus instructs them to stay away from the Gentiles and Samaritans, instead commanding them,* Go rather to the lost sheep of Israel (10:5–6). *When confronted by a Gentile woman seeking help, Jesus replies,* I was sent only to the lost sheep of Israel (15:24).

The prominence of Israel in Matthew, combined with the dominant Jewish tone of the book, points to a predominantly Jewish Christian audience. Although most scholars accept this conclusion, they qualify it either by asserting a minority presence of Gentiles as well or by emphasizing that these are Hellenistic Jews (Jews heavily influenced by Greek culture). These clarifications result from an awareness that Matthew's particularism stands in tension with his universalism.

Alongside the limitation of Jesus' ministry to Israel are the themes of Israel's rejection for its treatment of God's Messiah and the turn towards a Gentile mission. Contrasting with the pro-Israel, anti-Gentile texts are Matthew's anti-Israel, pro-Gentile texts.

Because Israel's leaders rejected God's Messiah, God has rejected them. This idea finds fullest expression in the theme of the transference of the kingdom. In Matthew 8:11–12, Jesus promises that many Gentiles will come to sit at *the feast with Abraham, Isaac, and Jacob in the kingdom of heaven*, while *the subjects of the kingdom will be thrown outside*. In the parable of the Tenants, Jesus tells about a landowner who entrusts his vineyard to tenants who represent Israel's leaders. This becomes clear when they kill the landowner's son (verses 38–39; see also verse 45). Jesus summarizes the message of the parable to the chief priests and Pharisees by stating that *the kingdom of God will be taken away from you and given to a people who will produce its fruit* (verse 43).

> **Jesus & the Pharisees**
> *Jesus regularly condemns Israel's leaders for their opposition to him and to God's plan. The primary recipients of his attack are the Pharisees, who represent Jesus' main opponents in Matthew. Jesus rebukes the Pharisees for their misguided priorities (12:38–39) and warns his disciples against their dangerous teachings (16:12). In his lengthiest attack on them (Matt 23), Jesus condemns them for their love of public honor (verses 5–7), their hypocrisy, and their neglect of the more important matters of the law (verse 23).*

Matthew stands in tension between these two poles of particularism and universalism. In assessing the historical occasion that gave rise to the gospel, it is vital to maintain that tension (Hagner, *Sitz im Leben*, 36). The question is what kind of occasion accounts for both poles?

Most recent scholars propose a strained relationship between Matthew's Christian community and Judaism as the key to identifying the occasion of the gospel. These proposals fall broadly into three categories. First, the most traditional interpretation asserts that Matthew's community is in complete separation from Judaism and in full embrace of the Gentile mission. The theme of the transference of the kingdom asserts that God has rejected Israel and now turns to the Gentiles. The church, for Matthew, has broken continuity with Israel and is now a "new people" (Stanton 11). A second view holds that Matthew's community still operates within Judaism. They do not desire a break with Judaism, but may see such a development as inevitable owing to increasing opposition from their fellow Jews and increasing pressure to address the Gentile issue (see Saldarini; Overman). The third view proposes a relatively recent break with Judaism and a church trying to deal with the resulting situation. As evidence, scholars point to Matthew's tendency to refer to "their" synagogues (4:23; 9:35; 10:17), indicating an institution from which his audience is now separated. In support of a recent break, scholars cite the harshness of Matthew's anti-Israel language as an indication that the wounds are still fresh. This mediating view posits a church in transition. They have broken with Judaism but do not wish to lose their claim on Jewish history and tradition, especially in the context of a church that is becoming increasingly more Gentile. Although the third option most closely resembles the view represented in this commentary, all three of these proposals are essentially variations of a single occasion. That occasion is that Matthew writes to a community in need of defining itself with respect to both Judaism and the larger Gentile world.

Scholarly discussions on the occasion of Matthew also impact decisions on Matthew's place of writing and date. Scholars typically place Matthew's gospel in an urban setting with a large Hellenistic Jewish population and a strong Gentile Christian community (Hagner, *Sitz im Leben*, 63). This accounts for both Matthew's interest in the Gentile mission and his concern for continuity with Judaism. The most common suggestion is Syrian Antioch because it meets these criteria and played an initial role in the early church's movement out into the larger Gentile world (Acts 11:19–26). Furthermore, the earliest known reference to the gospel of Matthew comes from the early second-century writings of Ignatius, bishop of Antioch. Nevertheless, several other cities (Alexandria, Cæsarea Maritima) are also possible locations of origin.

The majority of scholars date Matthew after the destruction of Jerusalem in 70 CE because they believe the uncertainty that characterized those years eroded Judaism's tolerance for diversity, thus facilitating the break between church and synagogue. Also, the expanded authority that the Pharisees enjoyed in post-70 Judaism accounts for the hostility toward them in Matthew. Some tie the dating of Matthew specifically to the year 85 CE because of a curse upon Christians that was supposedly introduced into the synagogue liturgy around that time. The assumption is that 85 CE marked a change in relations between Jews and Christians that led to the cessation of the Christian mission to Israel and to the need for a gospel like Matthew that defends Christianity against Pharisaic Judaism while paving the way for the Gentile mission. Such

> **"Go out into all the world …"**
> *Matthew sows the seeds for the turn to the Gentiles throughout the gospel. He quotes Old Testament prophetic texts that highlight the significance of Jesus for all nations (4:15–16; 12:18–21). Certain Gentiles receive praise for their faith in Jesus (8:10; 15:28) or exhibit faith in contexts where most Israelites fail to do so (27:54). That the gospel is to be proclaimed throughout the world is a repeated refrain (13:38; 24:14; 26:13). Matthew closes with the Great Commission, mandating a mission to all nations (28:19).*

> **Syrian Antioch**
> *Located on the bank of the Orontes River, Antioch was the capital of the Roman province of Syria. Antioch was a large and important city, with population estimates ranging from 200,000 to 600,000. A cosmopolitan city, its population enjoyed a wide mixture of nationalities and races, leading to a religiously diverse city. Antioch's Jewish population numbered at least 25,000. The integration of Jews and Gentiles in Antioch created an ideal setting for the Gentile mission. The church at Antioch was the first to inaugurate an official Gentile mission, and it became an important base for Paul's missionary activities. One of the leaders of the Hellenistic wing of the Jerusalem church was Nicolas, a Gentile convert to Judaism from Antioch (Acts 6:5). Although no specific tradition supports the theory, many scholars suggest Antioch of Syria as the probable origin for Matthew's gospel. Located in a diverse city and displaying a vested interest in the Gentile mission, the church at Antioch possesses many of the qualities that scholars envision for Matthew's audience.*

a specific dating for the gospel, however, seems increasingly unlikely to other scholars who argue that we have no knowledge of the extent or influence of this curse, and the gospel itself betrays no knowledge of it. Furthermore, the Matthean community's break with Judaism could have occurred at any time, including during the decades prior to 70 CE, just as the curse upon Christians probably did not represent a new development in relations between Christians and Jews but a continuation and culmination of longstanding hostilities (Hagner, *Matthew*, 287). Although the Gospel of Matthew reads well against a post-70 setting, the evidence from the gospel itself does not demand it. Consequently, a cautious estimate would allow for a date anytime during the period of 60–90 CE.

STRUCTURE & MESSAGE

Matthew does not write with one overarching purpose that accounts for every feature of his gospel. He has many concerns of a broad, pastoral nature (Stanton 380). Nevertheless, scholars identify one major concern of Matthew's that arises out of the gospel's proposed occasion. Matthew's Christian community stands in the tension between a past lived within the confines of Judaism and a future increasingly characterized by Gentile involvement. As Matthew envisions a church that will become more Gentile in orientation, he writes to define Christian community in a manner that affirms this Gentile mission while preserving the church's connection to its Jewish roots and heritage (Senior, "Between Two Worlds," 6, 21; Meier 625).

Although Israel's leaders rejected God's Messiah and the Christian community, Matthew does not see a break with the synagogue as a definitive exclusion of the church from Israel. Unfaithful Israelites, he believes, have forfeited their claim on God's promises to Israel, for those promises find fulfillment in the Messiah they rejected. It is thus in the community of the Messiah, the church, that the heritage of Israel persists; and so, as the church embraces the Gentile mission, it must not forget that it stands in continuity with Israel. Yet, the church is not merely an extension of Israel, for with Jesus comes something new. Many scholars point to Matthew 9:16–17 as a key passage for unlocking Matthew's purpose. Jesus contrasts the *old* with the *new*. Just as *new wine* poured into *old wineskins* causes the skins to burst and both to be destroyed, "the new spirit of the Kingdom cannot be contained within the old forms of Judaism" (Hill 177). For the religion of Israel to survive, it must find renewal in the Messiah and in the kingdom of heaven.

> **New Wineskins**
> Jesus does not here envision the complete rejection of Israel, for he argues that when new wine *inhabits* new wineskins, both are preserved. *The statement that both are preserved occurs only in Matthew's version of the account*, indicating that the phrase may hold special import for Matthew. By accepting the messiahship of Jesus and conforming itself to the righteousness of the kingdom of heaven, Israel can become a new wineskin *and find preservation in the community of the Messiah*.

Forming the heart of Matthew's message is its distinctive presentation of Christ. Traditionally scholars would analyze the titles given to Jesus in a gospel as a way to understand that gospel's doctrine of Christ. More recently, scholars recognize that titles alone are an insufficient source of meaning unless also connected to the function of Christ within the narrative. At his birth, Christ receives two names that establish important functions that he will fulfill. Both names and the concepts they represent form an *inclusio* in the gospel. He receives the name *Jesus* ("the Lord saves") *because he will save his people from their sins* (1:21). The saving activity of Jesus unfolds throughout the gospel in his healing and teaching ministries, but culminates in the death, burial, and resurrection scenes. At his birth, Jesus also receives the name *Immanuel*, meaning *God with us* (1:23). The Great Commission that concludes the gospel returns to this theme when Jesus announces to his disciples that *I am with you always* (28:20). This Jesus thus represents God come near to save.

> **Inclusio**
> *The repetition of a term or idea at the beginning and end of a literary section is known as inclusio.*

A notable feature of Matthew is its "Son Christology." Jesus is the son of David, Abraham, God, and Man. These titles highlight specific functions of Jesus in God's dealings with humanity. As son of Abraham and son of David, Jesus embodies the fulfillment of

God's promises to Israel. This theme of fulfillment permeates Matthew, especially the fulfillment quotations. Matthew introduces approximately ten of his Old Testament citations with some variation on the formula: *All this took place to fulfill what the Lord had said through the prophet* (1:22; 2:15, 17, 23; 4:14; 12:17; 13:14; 13:35; 21:4; 27:9). Although the heavy use of Old Testament quotations in Matthew underscores Jesus' faithfulness to Israel, this fulfillment formula also introduces two quotations that hint at Jesus' saving activity expanding beyond the border of Israel (4:14; 12:17). God promised Abraham that he would make him into a *great nation* and *all peoples on earth will be blessed through him* (Gen 12:3). Whereas Matthew's particularism signals God's fidelity to Israel, his universalism signals that God's selection of Israel was for a greater purpose – the blessing of all peoples. As son of Abraham, Jesus stands in continuity with a nation that from the beginning was created to be *a light for the Gentiles* (Isa 42:6; 49:6), thus justifying the future mission to Gentiles as a part of God's promises to Israel.

Not only does Jesus fulfill God's promises as spoken through the prophets, but he also comes to fulfill the Law (5:17). The Hebrew term *torah* often translates as "law" or "instruction," but more broadly represents "the source of wisdom" and "the reflection of the mind of God" (Johnson 183). As God come near to dwell among humanity, "Immanuel" embodies Torah. As such, he has not come *to abolish the Law*, but to reveal the true meaning of the Law in all its fullness.

Jesus therefore functions in Matthew as the preeminent teacher and interpreter of the law. Although the term "teacher" as an address to Jesus occurs in Matthew only on the lips of outsiders to the kingdom (in contrast to insiders who consistently address him as "Lord"), he fills the role of Israel's authoritative teacher of the law.

For Matthew to call Jesus the son of David points to Jesus' legitimacy as the "Messiah" [Hebrew *meshiach*] or "Christ" [Greek *christos*]. As son of David, Jesus rules faithfully over a kingdom, but Matthew makes it clear that this kingdom is of no earthly origin or design. Matthew's preference for the phrase *kingdom of heaven* (32 times) highlights the spiritual nature of this kingdom. The kingdom of heaven becomes in Matthew the lens through which Jesus' followers must view the law. When Jesus says that *every teacher of the law who has been instructed about the kingdom of heaven is like the owner of a house who brings out of his storeroom new treasures as well as old* (13:52), he suggests that instruction on the law (*old*) finds *new* meaning in the kingdom of heaven. In Matthew the law thus becomes the foundation for kingdom ethics.

Also permeating the teachings of Jesus in Matthew is the language of judgment and reward.

> ### The "New Moses"
> Based upon Jesus' association with the Law and certain events in his story that parallel those of the exodus, some scholars have termed the Matthean Jesus a "new Moses" come to bring a "new Torah." The similarities between Jesus and Moses in Matthew are unmistakable, yet to call Jesus a "new Moses" is too limiting, for he is one greater than Moses. Like Moses, Jesus offers deliverance and instructs in the law. But Jesus is also the Son of God, and it is in this capacity that he offers a greater deliverance than Moses, for he *will save his people from their sins* (1:21). As one who wields the authority of the Son of God, he offers an interpretation of the law that faithfully renders the spirit of the Mosaic law while bringing it into conformity with the newness of the kingdom of heaven.

> ### Jesus' Discourses
> The discourses of Jesus in Matthew involve ethical instructions on the requirements for kingdom living.
>
> Jesus asserts that entrance into the kingdom of heaven requires that one's righteousness should surpass that of the Pharisees and the teachers of the law (5:20). This righteousness surpasses not because it is fundamentally different from the law, but because it dwells upon and embraces that which comprises the very heart of the law: justice, mercy, and faithfulness (23:23).
>
> Twice, the Pharisees receive condemnation from Jesus for their failure to recognize that God desires mercy, not sacrifice (9:13; 12:7). The ethical demands of the Sermon on the Mount are transformational, calling for a surpassing righteousness by taking the requirements of the law and holding them up to the light of God's mercy.

In fact, warnings of judgment occur at or near the end of each of Jesus' five major discourses (Meier 632). Threats of punishment and promises of reward confront all those who encounter Jesus in Matthew's gospel. John the Baptist announces that this Christ comes with a *winnowing fork* in his hand to clear the threshing floor, *gathering his wheat into the barn and burning up the chaff with unquenchable fire* (3:12). Matthew's contrast of punishment and reward finds further expression in the metaphor of fruit bearing. John the Baptist proclaims that *every tree that does not produce good fruit will be cut down and thrown into the fire* (3:10). Jesus makes virtually the same statement, only changing John's future tense to present. Whereas John says unproductive trees *will be* thrown into the fire, Jesus asserts that every unproductive tree *is* thrown into the fire (7:19). With Jesus the kingdom of heaven is near, and so is the judgment for those who fail to serve faithfully. Jesus twice announces, *By their fruit you will recognize them* (7:20; see also 12:33). This is the line that demarcates righteous and unrighteous, wheat and chaff. In Jesus' conflict with the religious leaders of Israel, he condemns them because they fail to bear fruit appropriate to the kingdom of heaven, particularly as represented by their killing of God's son (21:33–44; see also 21:19). It is this rejection of Christ that leads to their expulsion from the kingdom and the transference of their inheritance to *a people* (Gentiles) *who will produce its fruit* (21:43).

It is in this context of judgment that Jesus most prominently functions as Son of Man. As a title, "Son of Man" is unique in that it is the one Jesus typically uses of himself. Scholars debate the meaning of this title because, outside of the Gospels, it connotes two very different ideas. In the book of Ezekiel, "son of man" refers to any human being. By contrast, in Daniel, the author describes a divine "son of man" who comes with the clouds of heaven and wields authority and power over the world (Dan 7:13–14).

Perhaps, however, the two options are not mutually exclusive. Jesus primarily uses "Son of Man" when engaged in public discourse. It is his preferred title for self-identification to outsiders to the kingdom. The inherent duality of the title – that it can represent both humanity and divinity – may be the key to unlocking Jesus' attraction to it. Since Jesus represents "God with us" in human form, the title "Son of Man" best captures two sides of his existence. He is both the divine Son of God and the human born of Mary. Thus, rather than choose one option over the other, it seems best to preserve the ambiguity of the title. For when Jesus employs this title in public discourse, his identity remains shrouded in mystery. Is he the human "son of man" or the divine "Son of Man"? The title leaves both options open. Like the parables that challenge the hearer to accept the identity of God's Christ while couching that challenge in language that can be hard to interpret, this title deliberately leaves his identity open to interpretation. So just as outsiders to the kingdom in Matthew's gospel address Jesus only as "teacher," thus acknowledging only the human Jesus, insiders to the kingdom address him as "Lord," recognizing that Jesus embodies the presence of God in human form.

On one level, the theological message of Matthew is deceptively simple. The Messiah (or Christ), the son of David, the Son of God has come into this world to announce the fulfillment of God's promises to Israel. In true prophetic fashion, he calls upon Israelites to live lives of righteousness based upon the true meaning of the law, a meaning revealed in the teachings of Jesus. Israel, influenced by its religious leaders, spurns this invitation to share in the kingdom of heaven and thus brings itself under God's judgment. Consequently, the invitation is now fully open to the Gentiles who will receive the pride of place rejected by Israel. Yet all subjects of the kingdom must conduct themselves faithfully as they await their Lord's return. In light of the coming judgment inaugurated by the divine Son of Man, Jesus instructs his disciples to embody the kingdom

> **The Son of Man**
>
> *With respect to Matthew, some scholars interpret Jesus' self-referential use of the term "Son of Man" as a generic description of himself that bears no christological weight. As such, the term means little more than "this man" (Kingsbury 95–100). Yet others believe that Jesus' choice of this title reveals a deliberate attempt to identify himself as the divine judge who brings his authority to bear in God's kingdom (Luz 113). That a large number of the "Son of Man" passages in Matthew occur in texts that highlight Jesus' authority or his role as judge supports this latter view (see 9:6; 10:23; 12:8, 40–41; 13:37, 41; 16:27–28; 19:28; 24:27–30, 37–39, 44; 25:31–33).*

ethics modeled on his own example and to continue his proclamation that the kingdom of heaven is near to all. Matthew's message is simple, but only to the extent that the major movements in his story are relatively straightforward. The depth of his story unfolds through the telling of it.

The Gospel of Matthew employs a variety of stylistic features in the formation of its message to create a sense of order and purpose. Summary statements orient the audience to the beginning or end of vital material. Matthew introduces his fulfillment quotations with some form of the statement, *All this took place to fulfill what the Lord had said through the prophet*. Similarly, each of the five major discourses conclude with some variation on the formula, *When Jesus had finished saying these things* (7:28; 11:1; 13:53; 19:1; 26:1). Matthew also uses numerical schemes by organizing elements with reference to the numbers 3 and 7. There are three summary sections (4:23–25; 9:35–38; 11:1), the first two of which highlight Jesus' threefold function as teacher, preacher, and healer (4:23; 9:35). In the wilderness, Jesus encounters three temptations (4:3–10). Within the Sermon on the Mount, he offers 9 (3×3) beatitudes and 6 (3×2) contrasts. Likewise, there are 7 petitions in the Lord's Prayer (6:9–13), 7 parables in chapter 13, and 7 woes directed against the teachers of the law and Pharisees in chapter 23. In a combination of these two, Matthew divides Jesus' genealogy into 3 parts based on a multiple of 7 (1:17). These stylistic features both organize features of the gospel and emphasize the orderliness of God's plan.

Matthew's gospel alternates between story and speeches, with the formula that concludes each major discourse serving as a transition between the two. The determination of Matthew's structure hinges on whether one gives priority to the narrative sections or to the discourse sections. Outlines for the book of Matthew typically center on two models. The first model derives from B. W. Bacon who argued that the five discourses in Matthew allow for a division of Matthew into five books. These five books form an intentional parallel to the Pentateuch. For Bacon, this meant that Matthew deliberately presents Jesus as a new Moses bringing a new Torah (Bacon). Scholars today generally reject the idea that the five discourses point to Jesus as the bringer of a new Torah because the five-book structure occurs elsewhere in Jewish writings (the Psalms, for example) and because Jesus in Matthew fulfills the law and does not replace it with a new one. Nevertheless, many scholars retain the five-book outline for Matthew more as a structural device than a theological one. Others argue that an outline based on the five discourses does not adequately account for chapter 23 and effectively reduces the genealogy/birth narrative (Matt 1–2) and the passion narrative (Matt 26–28) to a prologue and an epilogue.

The second major influence on the determination of Matthew's structure is a theory popularized by Jack Dean Kingsbury. Kingsbury divides Matthew into three sections based upon two markers of time in the text. At 4:16 Matthew says, *From that time on Jesus began to preach*. At 16:21 Matthew states, *From that time on Jesus began to explain to his disciples that he must go to Jerusalem and suffer many things*.

Both methods of outlining, along with their countless variations, have supporters and both offer helpful insight into Matthew's structure. However, neither one fully accounts for every significant feature of Matthew's gospel. In fact, scholars' inability to agree on a coherent structure for Matthew may be an indication that Matthew was less systematic in the organization of his work than we demand of him (Senior, *What Are They Saying*, 25–26). Rather,

> **Jesus' Discourse on the Pharisees**
> *One of the difficulties attached to the identification of Matthew's five discourses is determining what to do about Jesus' criticism of the Pharisees in chapter 23. At 39 verses, it certainly qualifies as a major discourse, yet many scholars exclude it from the five because it does not conclude with the normal formula. Others include it with the fifth major discourse in Matthew 24–25. However, the change in scene and shift in audience that occurs between chapter 23 and chapter 24 requires one to be cautious in linking them.*

> **Time in Matthew**
> *The recurring temporal markers (From that time on…) highlight significant transitions in the flow of the story and allow for a division of Jesus' life into three stages (Kingsbury 40). Matthew 1:1–4:16 forms the presentation of Jesus to Israel, Matthew 4:17–16:20 relates his ministry to Israel, and Matthew 16:21–28:20 recounts his journey to Jerusalem and subsequent suffering.*

MATTHEW

Matthew offers a variety of important textual markers (5 discourses, the formulaic conclusions to the discourses, the temporal markers of 4:16 and 16:21, fulfillment quotations, and summary passages) that highlight certain sections and point to shifts in the narrative. All are important pieces of Matthew's structure. Although outlines are helpful and often necessary guides for the interpretation of a text, they are scholarly creations and not necessarily intrinsic to the text itself.

COMMENTARY

GENEALOGY OF THE CHRIST · 1:1–17

The first two chapters of Matthew establish the identity of Jesus as son of David and Messiah by means of a genealogy (1:1–17) and an extended birth narrative (1:18–2:23). These two chapters also form a fitting introduction to the gospel as a whole in that many of Matthew's distinctive themes appear here (Stanton 360). Matthew constructs his genealogy in three parts: an introductory heading (1:1), the list of names (1:2–16), and a summary conclusion (1:17).

1:1 A genealogy is fundamentally about identity, and this one asserts its identity claims from the outset. The three identity claims (*Christ, son of David, son of Abraham*) are the primary focus of the genealogical listing that follows. This *Jesus* is a descendant of Israel's royal family. Yet, he is more than just someone with royal ancestry, for he is also the *Christ*. The Greek term *Christ* and its Hebrew counterpart *messiah* simply mean "anointed one," a phrase that took on royal connotations in ancient Israel. Just as *Christ* and *son of David* connect Jesus to Israelite expectations of a coming king, *son of Abraham* connects him to an Israel that was founded upon a promise made by God. *David* and *Abraham* thus represent kingship and the fulfillment of promise, two themes that resonate throughout the Gospel of Matthew.

1:2–16 Matthew divides the genealogical list into three distinct parts: from Abraham to David (1:2–6), from David to the Babylonian exile (1:7–11), and from the exile to Jesus (1:12–16). This structure highlights the three most important figures in the genealogy: Abraham, David, and Jesus. The Babylonian exile is the only event of Israelite history that Matthew mentions in the genealogy. The choice to highlight the exile and these three people is intentional, and the connection between them may provide the key to this genealogy.

Both Abraham and David received promises from God that became foundational for Israelite faith and identity. To Abraham God promised, *I will make you into a great nation ... and all peoples on earth will be blessed through you* (Gen 12:2–3). To David, God promised, *Your house and your kingdom will endure forever before me; your throne will be established forever* (2 Sam 7:16). God promised Abraham and David to create a nation and a dynasty that would rule forever. The fulfillment of these promises in the nation of Israel became a focal point for Israelite self-identity. They were the people of God because God had kept his promises to them and was working faithfully through their nation and king. The year 586 BCE changed everything. The Babylonians destroyed Jerusalem and took many Jews away into exile. Suddenly, the nation ceased to exist, and there was no longer a king. The very identity of Israel and its relationship to God became an issue. More importantly, the faithfulness of God came into question. Had God failed to keep his promises?

The prophets of Israel who prophesied at the time of the exile defended the fidelity of God by pointing Israel toward the future fulfillment of God's promises. Over time, the expectation of such fulfillment became intertwined with the expectation of a Messiah or Christ. This Messiah would restore the nation of Israel and rule over it faithfully as a son of David.

The central theme of Matthew's genealogy is the faithfulness of God in fulfilling the promises to Abraham and David. The first two parts of the genealogy demonstrate that, up to the time of the exile, God was faithful to Israel through its nation and king. The third part demonstrates that, after the exile, God continued to work powerfully in Israel, culminating in the birth of Christ. Therefore, Jesus appears as more than one who merely stands in continuity with great figures of Israel's past. He is, in fact, the fruition of God's promises to Abraham and David.

Israelite interpretation of the promises also sheds light on Israel's eventual rejection of God's Christ. Following the exile, the Jews developed very distinct expectations concerning the Christ: that he would fulfill God's promises to Abraham and David by ruling as king over a restored nation. One reason why Israel rejected Jesus is that he did not act like the Christ many were expecting. For Matthew, Jesus does fulfill those promises, but in a way that demonstrates how God's plan transcends human expectation.

> **Messianism in the First Century**
> *Jews in the time of Jesus held many different views of the coming Messiah. The Dead Sea sectarians (traditionally called the Essenes) expected two messiahs, one from David (a royal warrior) and one from Aaron (a priest).*

The most distinctive feature of Matthew's genealogy is the unexpected mention of five women: Tamar (verse 3), Rahab (verse 5), Ruth (verse 5), Bathsheba (verse 6), and Mary (verse 16). Mary's mention derives in part from her obvious connection to Jesus. But why are these other four women singled out? Their mention is unnecessary for the development of the genealogy since Matthew is tracing Jesus' lineage through the male descendants. This question is "the most debated issue in the interpretation of the genealogy" (Bauer 147).

Most scholars recognize that these four women serve a dual function. First, all four are likely foreigners to Israel (Bauer 148; Luz 26; Stanton 379). Mary, of course, is not a foreigner. However, the inclusion of these four women in the genealogy of the Christ shows that the child Mary bears will be the source of salvation for Gentiles as well as for Jews. As such, the presence of these women points both backward and forward. These women support the point that Jesus is indeed *the son of Abraham* (1:1), and not strictly in the genealogical sense. He is the heir of God's promise to Abraham to bless all nations through his descendants. Therefore, these women foreshadow the future Gentile mission of the church. God's promise to Abraham, combined with the presence of four Gentile women in the lineage of the *son of David*, reveals that the Gentile mission is neither an afterthought nor a "Plan B," but an integral part of God's plan from the beginning.

The second function of these four women derives from another characteristic that they share. Each has some form of irregular or suspect sexual activity. Tamar acts as a prostitute in order to secure a child from her father-in-law (Gen 38). Rahab is a prostitute (Josh 2:1; 6:17). Ruth attempts to seduce Boaz at the threshing floor (Ruth 3:7–9). Bathsheba engages in an adulterous affair with David (2 Sam 11). In fact, Matthew does not list Bathsheba by name but only describes her as one who *had been Uriah's wife* (Matt 1:6). This highlights both the adulterous nature of her relationship with David and his complicity in the death of Uriah.

This last point raises the question of how these four women connect to Mary. Matthew clearly does not assign any sexually suspect activity to Mary. He explicitly states that Mary is a virgin whose child is of miraculous conception (1:18, 20, 23). However, the birth of Jesus looks different to those who are outsiders to the kingdom than it does to insiders. Those who do not recognize Jesus as the Christ do not accept the idea of the virgin birth. To those outside, Jesus appears to be an illegitimate child. In fact, Joseph himself initially jumps to this conclusion (1:19). Matthew's genealogy, therefore, also defends against attacks on the legitimacy of Jesus' birth. We know, for instance, that in the second century, both pagans and Jews attacked the virgin birth of Jesus as a deception and viewed Mary as an adulteress (see Origen, *Against Celsus*, 1.28).

> **Women in Christ's Genealogy**
> *Matthew takes an apologetic approach at several key moments in the narrative, such as when he constructs his resurrection narrative to defend against Jewish charges that the disciples stole Jesus' body (28:11–15).*
>
> *In terms of Christ's birth, he builds a careful argument by focusing on the women in Christ's genealogy. Against those who would argue that God would not allow Christ to be conceived to a poor girl out of wedlock, Matthew counters that such is exactly how God works.*
>
> *According to human expectation, the four women of the genealogy are all unlikely choices for divine favor. Yet Tamar becomes an ancestor of David; Rahab receives praise for her faith (Heb 11:31; Jas 2:25); Ruth becomes the great-grandmother of David; and Bathsheba becomes the mother of Solomon. By grouping Mary with these women, Matthew argues that the birth of Jesus to an unknown girl from Galilee and in circumstances that easily lend themselves to false perceptions of infidelity is a testimony to a God who constantly confounds human expectations. Christ's birth to this girl thus sets the stage for the advent of the Christ who will likewise confound the expectations of Israel.*

1:17 The genealogy concludes with a brief summary that divides it into three parts, emphasizing the key figures and events: *Thus there were fourteen generations in all from Abraham to David, fourteen from David to the exile to Babylon, and fourteen from the exile to the Christ.* The numbers three and seven represent concepts of completeness and fullness in Jewish thought. The division of the genealogy into three parts of fourteen (twice seven) generations shows the divine plan at work. The history of Israel, begun with Abraham, thus culminates in the birth of the Christ. Scholars also suggest that the number fourteen may have another significance for Matthew. Each letter of the Hebrew alphabet, as with Greek, has a numerical value. In Hebrew, the numerical value of the letters in the name "David" adds up to fourteen. It is therefore possible that Matthew emphasizes this number as another way of identifying the Christ as *the son of David* (1:1).

BIRTH NARRATIVE OF THE CHRIST · 1:18–2:23

Matthew's extended narrative of the birth of Christ emphasizes the theme of fulfillment. The narrative divides into five parts, each centered on a fulfillment quotation from the Old Testament. This alternating pattern of narrative and fulfillment quotation makes the point that the child Jesus represents the climax of prophecy.

1:18–25 The first section of Matthew's account records the events of Jesus' birth. The angel who corrects Joseph's misperception of Mary's pregnancy addresses him as *Joseph son of David* nine times in order to connect the birth narrative to the genealogy and further stress the messianic identity of this child. Matthew uses the title *son of David* nine times in contrast to only three in Mark, thus pointing to the significance of this title for Matthew's identification of Jesus.

The repeated emphasis on the role of the Holy Spirit in Jesus' conception (1:18, 20) establishes his divine origin. The announcement of this child's miraculous conception then leads into the first fulfillment quotation. Matthew abruptly stops the narrative to proclaim in verse 22, *All this took place to fulfill what the Lord had said through the prophet.* He then quotes Isaiah 7:14: *The virgin will be with child and will give birth to a son, and they will call him Immanuel* (Hebrew for "God with us"). In this way Matthew identifies Jesus both as the fulfillment of prophecy and as the presence of God at work among the people.

2:1–6 The second narrative section recounts the arrival of magi from the east following Jesus' birth in Bethlehem. They come searching for *the king of the Jews* (verse 2). This news disturbs Herod, the king of Judea, who learns that the Christ is to be born in Bethlehem. This information comes from the chief priests and teachers of the law, who inform Herod that *this is what the prophet has written* (verse 5). The fulfillment quotation that follows, which comes from Micah 5:2, establishes that out of Bethlehem *will come a ruler who will be the shepherd of my people Israel.* As the second fulfillment quotation establishes Bethlehem as the birthplace of the Christ, the third will connect him to Egypt.

> **The Magi**
> *The magi were Zoroastrian astrologers from Iran.*

2:7–15 The third narrative section of Matthew's birth story relates Herod's attempt to discover the location of the newborn Christ. He instructs the magi to find the child and report back to him so that he can go to worship the child. Being warned about Herod in a dream, however, the magi return to their own country after finding and worshiping the infant. That these Gentiles from the East are the first to worship the Christ foreshadows the inclusion of Gentiles that will characterize the mission of the church and, to a lesser extent, the ministry of Jesus.

After the return of the magi to their own land, Joseph receives a warning in a dream that Herod seeks to kill Jesus. Herod's antagonism toward the child results from a misperceived threat to his kingdom. He, the king of Judea, must protect his interests against this child heralded as *king of the Jews* (2:2). Herod assumes that the nature of the Christ's kingdom is the same as his, political sovereignty. But Christ's kingdom is one of spiritual sovereignty, and it is the failure on the part of Israel and its leaders to recognize this that creates antagonism and opposition, culminating in the crucifixion of *the king of the Jews* (27:37).

To escape the clutches of Herod, Joseph takes the child to Egypt. Matthew's primary interest in this section is to explain the reason for their move to Egypt so that he can tie these events to prophecy. Again he stops the narrative to announce: *And so was fulfilled what the Lord had said through the prophet.* He then quotes Hosea 11:1: *Out of Egypt I called my son* (2:15).

2:16–18 The fourth narrative section records Herod's anger at learning that the magi are not returning, and that he will therefore not know the identity of the Christ. Consequently, he decrees the death of all boys in the area of Bethlehem who are two years of age or younger. This leads into the fourth fulfillment quotation as Matthew announces, *Then what was said through the prophet Jeremiah was fulfilled* (verse 18). His subsequent citation of Jeremiah 31:15 addresses the *weeping and great mourning* that accompanies the loss of Israel's children.

Matthew constructs his birth narrative in a manner that emphasizes connections between Jesus and the exodus. Herod, who slaughters the young boys of Bethlehem, mirrors the Egyptian Pharaoh who decrees the slaughter of all male Jewish infants (Exod 1:22). The quotation in Matthew 2:15 from Hosea 11:1, *Out of Egypt I called my son*, refers in Hosea to God bringing Israel (the *son*) out of slavery in Egypt. Here, applied to Jesus (God's Son), it establishes solidarity between Jesus and the Israelites of the exodus.

2:19–23 The fifth and final section of the birth narrative continues the exodus motif. As God brought the Jews out of Egypt and into the land of promise, he now commands Joseph to *take the child and his mother and go to the land of Israel* (2:20). Warned in a dream against settling in Judea, they journey north to the town of Nazareth in Galilee. Matthew's interest in geography (Bethlehem, Egypt, Nazareth) derives from his interest in prophecy. He thus concludes his birth narrative with a fifth fulfillment quotation introduced with, *So was fulfilled what was said through the prophets: 'He will be called a Nazarene'* (2:23). The source of this final quotation is puzzling, as no Old Testament text contains these words. Many scholars assume that *through the prophets* in 2:23 means that Matthew sees this as a combination of prophetic utterances rather than as a direct quotation. Perhaps he envisions a connection to the messianic branch [Hebrew *netser*] of Isaiah 11:1 or to one who is under a Nazirite vow, as in Judges 13:5–7 (Hill 87–88; Mounce 19). Regardless of its origin, the reference serves the same function as the other four fulfillment quotations in the birth narrative: to demonstrate that this child Jesus represents the fulfillment of God's promises to Israel.

Herod the Great

King Herod the Great became governor of Galilee in 47 BCE. The Parthian invasion in 40 BCE forced him to flee to Rome where he received an appointment by the emperor Augustus to be king of Judea. By 37 BCE, Herod regained control of Galilee and included it under his authority. Herod ruled as king until his death in 4 BCE.

Herod was an Idumean, meaning he was half-Jewish. His compromised heritage, coupled with his overt friendship to the Romans, created suspicion in the minds of many Jews. Nevertheless, much of Herod's reign was a time of peace and prosperity. Some of his most lasting and significant contributions came in the form of immense building programs. Herod constructed many theaters, hippodromes, amphitheaters, palaces, and fortresses throughout the land. Many of his construction projects were Hellenistic by design and function as an attempt to curry favor with Rome. For instance, Herod built temples in honor of Roman and Greek deities and constructed an entire city (Cæsarea Maritima) in honor of the emperor Augustus Cæsar. However, in an act of concession to the Jews, Herod also enacted a massive rebuilding and renovation program for the Jerusalem temple, although even here several of the renovations contained distinct Hellenistic flourishes.

Toward the latter part of Herod's reign, domestic troubles took their toll. Herod had ten wives and each desired that one of their sons succeed him (Hochner 488). This, combined with Herod's naturally jealous disposition, was a recipe for disaster. Plots and rumors of plots led Herod to execute his wife Mariamne, his mother-in-law Alexandra, his brother-in-law Costobarus, and his sons Alexander, Aristobulus, and Antipater. At Herod's death, two of his remaining sons, Archelaus and Antipas, inherited his kingdom. This portrait of Herod's latter years as a time of suspicion, jealousy, and violence accords well with Matthew's portrayal of Herod's attempt to kill the Christ. That Herod would order the deaths of young boys in the vicinity of Bethlehem in response to the rumored birth of a rival king is fully conceivable in one who refused to spare his own family (Matt 2:1–5, 16).

Nazareth & Sepphoris

The village of Nazareth sits in the hills of lower Galilee. Small and relatively unimportant, Nazareth was capable of accommodating no more than about 480 people (Strange, "Nazareth," 1050). It was primarily devoted to agriculture, as remains of winepresses, olive presses, and grain storage facilities testify. The rural and agricultural nature of Nazareth created the longstanding impression that Jesus grew up in a backwards and uncultured environment. During the late twentieth century, however, focused attention on the nearby city of Sepphoris has revolutionized perceptions about the early environment of Jesus.

Located just three miles to the northwest of Nazareth, Sepphoris was the capital of Galilee and the primary residence of Herod Antipas, tetrarch of Galilee. When Herod the Great died, the citizens of Sepphoris revolted, with the tragic result that the Roman governor Varus destroyed the city. Antipas rebuilt Sepphoris as a Roman city, with the palaces, colonnaded streets, and theater characteristic of prominent Greco-Roman cities. Josephus characterizes first century Sepphoris as the "ornament of all Galilee" (Antiquities 18.2.1). Despite the Romanization of Sepphoris, the population remained largely Jewish, and, by the second century, Sepphoris became a "great Jewish intellectual center" (Strange, "Galilee," 397).

The importance of Sepphoris for the New Testament lies in its impact upon our understanding of the early years of Jesus prior to the start of his public ministry. The environment in which Jesus grew up was not simply rural and agricultural but also urban and hellenized. It is difficult to imagine Jesus growing up three miles from a major urban city and not spending significant time in it. During the early years of the first century, much of Sepphoris was under construction, and local laborers would have made up a significant portion of the work force. Although the precise date for the completion of the theater at Sepphoris remains debated, some scholars see the influence of the theater on Jesus' language in the Gospels (Batey). The term "hypocrites," which literally means "actors," derives from the theater and serves as Jesus' primary label for the Pharisees. Likewise, the description of Pharisees as actors ("hypocrites") who disfigure their faces when they fast recalls the stage actors who painted their faces or wore masks to convey certain moods (Matt 6:16).

JESUS AS THE FAITHFUL SON OF GOD · 3:1–4:25

Matthew 3:1–4:25 records Jesus' preparation for and beginning of his ministry. The theme running through this section is Jesus as the faithful Son of God whose ministry serves as an invitation for all to subject themselves to the kingdom of heaven.

3:1–12 Before Jesus arrives on the scene, John the Baptist heralds his coming. The essence of John's message is: *Repent, for the kingdom of heaven is near* (3:2). This plea for repentance is a plea for renewal. The baptism that John performs on all who confess *their sins* (3:6) enacts a new state of being, the state of repentance and moral reformation. Although possibly modeled after it, John's baptism is not proselyte baptism (an act in which Gentiles convert to Judaism) because he baptizes fellow Jews. Rather, it is a sign that entrance into the kingdom of heaven demands moral purity. Some scholars see a stronger parallel between John's baptism and the baptism practiced at the desert community of Qumran. This baptism involved repentance and confession of sins and served as a sign of one's entrance into a new covenant (Hill 91).

John combines his plea for repentance with a harsh warning of judgment that highlights the division between the righteous and unrighteous in Israel. Whereas the crowds confess their sins and receive baptism from John, the Pharisees and Sadducees receive words of condemnation. In line with warning them *to flee from the coming*

Baptism among the Dead Sea Community

The community that produced the Dead Sea Scrolls, conventionally called the Essenes, immersed themselves regularly to signify moral and ritual purity. Many other Jews did so as well. For example, large pools were constructed in Jerusalem just south of the Temple Mount for just such washings. Christian baptism thus built on an old and widespread Jewish practice, while giving it new significance.

"With the Holy Spirit & with fire …"

The precise meaning of a baptism with Spirit and fire is unclear. Baptism with the Holy Spirit probably refers to the refining, purifying, and redemptive power of the Spirit for all those who repent and subject themselves in obedience to the teachings of Christ. A connection to the reception of the Spirit in Christian baptism is not out of the question but does not seem to be the primary focus in this text. Baptism with fire, however, is the fire of judgment that John just warned about.

wrath, John assures these leaders of Israel that their historical connection to *Abraham* is not sufficient for entry into the kingdom of heaven. After all, *out of these stones God can raise up children for Abraham* (3:7, 9). Entry into the kingdom requires that one *produce fruit in keeping with repentance* (3:8). This establishes a theme that runs throughout the gospel. The metaphor of bearing fruit marks the distinction between insiders and outsiders to the kingdom. In fact, because the kingdom is near, John warns the Pharisees and Sadducees that they now stand at the moment of decision: *The ax is already at the root of the trees, and every tree that does not produce good fruit will be cut down and thrown into the fire* (Matt 3:10).

As the herald of Jesus, John preached to lay the foundation for Christ's ministry. A focus of Jesus' preaching in Matthew is the same as that of John: repentance and judgment. As John announces the Christ to the gathered crowd (including the Pharisees and Sadducees), John says, *He will baptize you with the Holy Spirit and with fire* (3:11). Matthew 3:1–12 bears the influence of Malachi 4. The book of Malachi concludes with a warning from God: *Surely the day is coming; it will burn like a furnace. All the arrogant and every evildoer will be stubble, and that day that is coming will set them on fire ... See, I will send you the prophet Elijah before that great and dreadful day of the Lord comes* (Mal 4:1, 5). Matthew identifies John the Baptist as this Elijah who is to herald the day of fire (Matt 17:10–13). Throughout Matthew, fire frequently serves as a metaphor for judgment (5:22; 7:19; 13:40–42; 18:8–9; 25:41). So, when John precedes his reference to a baptism *with fire* by warning that every unproductive tree *will be cut down and thrown into the fire* (3:10) and then follows it with a statement that the one who will baptize *with fire* comes with a *winnowing fork* and will *clear his threshing floor, gathering his wheat into the barn and burning up the chaff with unquenchable fire*, it becomes clear that the baptism *with fire* functions as a symbol of judgment.

3:13–17 In his first appearance in the gospel as an adult, Jesus travels from Galilee to the Jordan River to receive baptism from John. He does this not as a confession of sin but *to fulfill all righteousness*, an ambiguous phrase that in the broad sense probably refers to his self-subjection to the will of God (Luz 35) and his conformity to the standards of righteousness that characterize the kingdom of heaven. As a result of Jesus' obedience in baptism, the Spirit of God descends upon him and *a voice from heaven* declares, *This is my Son* (3:17). Thus Jesus prepares to embark on his ministry as the faithful and obedient Son of God.

4:1–11 Matthew reveals the identity of Jesus as the faithful Son of God at his baptism. That identity is then immediately put to the test. The temptation narrative in Matthew is less about Jesus overcoming the same kinds of temptations we all face than it is about him overcoming challenges to his identity and to the focus of his ministry. The connection between Jesus and the story of the exodus continues in this passage in a climactic way. Just as the Israelites, following their exodus from Egypt, were tempted and tested in the wilderness for forty years, so also Jesus, who has been called out of Egypt, enters the wilderness for forty days to be tempted and tested. The Hosea 11:1 passage that Matthew quotes in 2:15 (*Out of Egypt I called my son*) describes Israel as God's son who, though called out of Egypt by God, fails to live faithfully. Hosea 11:2a adds, *But the more I called Israel, the further they went from me*. Israel faltered in the wilderness and repeatedly failed in their time of testing. In his own time of testing in the wilderness, however, Jesus reverses that faithlessness. He demonstrates himself to be the obedient and faithful Son of God and as such can now call Israel to relinquish the historical baggage of their ancestors' failure in the wilderness and to follow his model of faithfulness.

The temptation that Jesus experiences in the wilderness is the temptation to subvert the very identity affirmed at his baptism. Each of Satan's first two challenges begins with the statement, *If you are the Son of God* (4:3, 6). The use of *if* with the indicative mood in Greek establishes a perceived reality. Consequently, this phrase may carry the sense of "*Since* you are the Son of God." Thus, the issue is not Jesus needing to prove his sonship, but needing to decide what it means to be the Son of God. Satan exhorts Jesus to turn stones to bread and to cast himself off the temple. He is tempting Jesus to use his relationship with God in self-centered and misguided ways. The third temptation offers world dominion in return for worshiping Satan (the kingdoms of the world versus the kingdom of heaven). These temptations are Satan's attempt to persuade Jesus to choose a different path than the one God has planned for him. It is a path on which Jesus would exercise his own will. That Jesus responds to each temptation by quoting Scripture demonstrates his fidelity to the plan of God and the subjection of his own will to God's.

4:12–17 Following the wilderness temptations, Jesus embarks on his public ministry. He returns to Galilee and settles down in the city of Capernaum, a move that Matthew highlights as fulfillment of prophecy due to its proximity to Zebulun and Naphtali. Matthew quotes Isaiah 9:1–2, which says that *Zebulun* and *Naphtali* in the *Galilee of the Gentiles* are a *people living in darkness* who *have seen a great light*. From the very beginning of Jesus' ministry, therefore, Matthew informs his readers that the Christ of Israel will also be a light to the Gentiles.

This section concludes with the first of two important temporal markers that begin with, *From that time on* (4:17). Here, Matthew announces that Jesus now begins *to preach, 'Repent, for the kingdom of heaven is near.'* This summary statement reveals the heart of Jesus' message, one that echoes the plea of John the Baptist (3:2) for repentance and proclamation of the kingdom.

4:18–25 As Matthew leads into the first of Jesus' major discourses, he provides an account of Jesus calling three of his apostles, Andrew, James, and John (4:18–22), and a summary statement of his early ministry activities (4:23–25). The summary highlights the threefold function of his ministry (teaching, preaching, and healing). Resulting from this activity, large crowds follow him and create the setting for the first major discourse.

DISCOURSE 1: THE SERMON ON THE MOUNT · 5:1–7:29

Jesus directs his first major discourse in Matthew to his disciples (5:1). The primary function of this discourse is therefore not evangelism to outsiders but instruction to insiders. The Sermon on the Mount conveniently summarizes kingdom ethics to instruct readers in how to live righteously in the kingdom of heaven.

5:1–12 The Sermon on the Mount begins with nine beatitudes that attribute blessing to various categories of people. The first eight beatitudes form a unit, with the ninth one deviating from the pattern. Each of the first eight beatitudes consists of two parts: a pronouncement of blessing on a category of people and the reason for the pronouncement. The first and eighth beatitudes each contain as their reason a statement, thus binding all eight with an inclusio: *for theirs is the kingdom of heaven* (5:3, 10). The beatitudes announce that *the poor in spirit*, *those who mourn*, *the meek*, those who *thirst for righteousness*, *the merciful*, *the pure in heart*, *the peacemakers*, and *the persecuted* are the very kinds of people who make up the kingdom of heaven (Albright and Mann 46). In line with the already established theme in Matthew that the kingdom of heaven confounds human expectations, the beatitudes call for a reversal. The categories of people they exalt are the exact opposite of what human society typically identifies as successful, powerful, and blessed.

The first and eighth beatitudes also differ from those they bracket in that their reason statements are in the present tense (*theirs is the kingdom*), while the reason statements in beatitudes two through seven

Capernaum

Capernaum was located on the northwest shore of the Sea of Galilee. Jesus lived in Capernaum during the time of his ministry, possibly in the home of Simon Peter (4:13; 8:14). Two archaeological discoveries from Capernaum may shed light on the gospel story. Archaeologists uncovered a synagogue at Capernaum that dates somewhere between the second and fourth century CE. Beneath this later synagogue, however, are the remains of an earlier synagogue building, possibly from the first century. This find is intriguing because the discovery of first-century synagogue buildings is rare and because some scholars identify it with the synagogue built in Capernaum by the Roman centurion who later encounters Jesus (Luke 7:1–5; Corbo 868).

Archaeologists also discovered a first-century house at Capernaum that later Christians identified as a holy site and upon which they built a church building. The house is similar to other such houses in Capernaum, with narrow walls indicating that the roof had been made of wood and earth as opposed to stone (McRay 164–65). Although the identification remains conjecture, church tradition identified this house as the home of Simon Peter and the site where Jesus may have stayed while in Capernaum.

are in the future. The present tense asserts that the kingdom of heaven belongs to such as these, while the future tense asserts that those who live such lives in the kingdom of heaven will receive a future reward. They *will be comforted, inherit the earth, be filled, be shown mercy, see God,* and *be called sons of God*.

This theme of reward leads into the ninth beatitude (5:11–12), which is more extensive than the others. Its shift from the third person address of the first eight beatitudes to second person address (*Blessed are you*) indicates that this is a more all-encompassing category that incorporates all of the others. All in the kingdom of heaven are blessed *when people insult you, persecute you and falsely say all kinds of evil against you because of me*. This is a cause for rejoicing *because great is your reward in heaven*. This statement foreshadows the further development of the idea of reward in 6:1–18 where it highlights divine favor as a response to kingdom righteousness.

5:13–16 Following the beatitudes come two statements of identity that mark the purpose for the kingdom ethics outlined in the Sermon on the Mount. Jesus informs his disciples that they are *the salt of the earth* and *the light of the world*. Foundational to the promises God made to Israel is the idea that God chose Israel not so that it could be a blessing unto itself but so that it would become the vessel through which blessing would flow to all nations (Gen 12:2–3; Isa 42:6; 49:6). The Sermon on the Mount is a plea to Israel to live up to that calling. By fulfilling their mission as a "light for the Gentiles," Israel glorifies God. The disciples function as salt and light in the world by conforming their conduct to the kingdom ethics outlined in the sermon. By doing so, the world will *see your good deeds and praise your Father in heaven* (5:16).

5:17–20 Matthew 5:17–20 provides the key for unlocking the meaning of the Sermon on the Mount. The ethical admonitions that follow this section derive from the law of Moses. In fact the entire Sermon on the Mount represents the law of Moses as interpreted by Jesus the Messiah. Therefore prior to offering specific ethical admonitions, Jesus summarizes his attitude towards the law by stating, *Do not think that I have come to abolish the Law or the Prophets; I have not come to abolish them but to fulfill them* (5:17). For Jesus, the law has an abiding validity in the kingdom of heaven. Hyperbole is at work in 5:18–19, where Jesus says that *until heaven and earth disappear, not the smallest letter, not the least stroke of a pen, will by any means disappear from the Law* and that those who break *one of the least of these commandments* (of the law) *and teach others to do the same will be called least in the kingdom of heaven*. Yet, the point of these statements is that the law remains valid in the kingdom of heaven and that inclusion in the kingdom does not allow for a relaxing of the law (Snodgrass 125; Martin 64).

Jesus claims that his concern is not to do away with the law nor to present a new law, but to bring the old law to fullness. By fulfilling the law, Jesus means that he reveals its true meaning and intent. Verse 20 provides a context for interpreting verse 17. In it, Jesus lays out the central theme of the Sermon on the Mount when he says that *unless your righteousness surpasses that of the Pharisees and the teachers of the law, you will certainly not enter the kingdom of heaven*. Jesus thus offers an interpretation of the law that contrasts with that taught by the Pharisees and teachers of the law. From Jesus' perspective, the Pharisees corrupted the true meaning of the law either by "limiting it to the outward act or by evading its radical prescriptions" (Martin 70).

In Matthew 23:23, Jesus attacks the Pharisees for focusing on lesser matters of the law while ignoring *justice, mercy, and faithfulness*. So when Jesus calls for a *righteousness* surpassing *that of the Pharisees*, he is advocating an interpretation of the Law and the Prophets that focuses upon *the more important matters*. In the context of Matthew, this means that one must read the entirety of the Law and the Prophets in light of the principles of love and mercy. In Matthew 22:37–40, Jesus claims, *All the Law and the Prophets hang on these two commandments*: *Love the Lord your God* and *Love your neighbor as yourself*. Elsewhere, Jesus twice quotes Hosea 6:6 (*I desire mercy, not sacrifice*) in contexts of disputes with the Pharisees over the interpretation of the law. The application of love and mercy to the requirements of the law are what distinguishes Jesus' interpretation from that of the Pharisees and teachers of the law and what characterizes the ethics of the Sermon on the Mount (Luz 52; Snodgrass 106, 108).

5:21–48 Scholars call these verses "the antitheses" because this section contains Jesus' instruction on six topics, each of which begins with an initial statement (*You have heard that it was said*) that quotes a teaching from or on the law, and then

> **The Pharisees**
>
> The information we have about the Pharisees derives from three sources: Josephus, the New Testament, and possibly the later rabbinic writings known as the Mishnah (finished about 225 CE), which may contain some earlier teachings of prominent Pharisees. The origin of the Pharisees probably dates to the time of the Maccabean Revolt or shortly thereafter (mid-second century BCE).
>
> Scholars recognize that the destruction of Jerusalem in 70 CE brought about a paradigm shift in the religious organization of Judaism. After 70, the Pharisees became the dominant religious influence in Judaism, while the Sadducees virtually disappeared. Prior to 70, the Pharisees were a minority group within Judaism, although one that wielded great influence and popularity with the masses. Scholars debate whether the Pharisees were primarily a political or religious reform movement, yet such debates represent more of a modern distinction than an ancient one. Politics and religion were thoroughly intermingled, and the Pharisees represent both. All sources agree that the Pharisees' main concern was the interpretation of the law and its application to all areas of life. In contrast to the Sadducees, who restricted religious observance solely to the written law of Moses, the Pharisees supported a twofold law, written and oral. The oral law was a collection of oral traditions external to the law of Moses that were designed to enhance religious observance and relate the law to everyday life. Despite this pious focus, the Pharisees were also politically influential and jealously protective of their power base.
>
> The evaluation of the Pharisees in the New Testament is far from uniform. The Pharisees come off much more positively in Luke-Acts than in Matthew, Mark, or John. The most thoroughly negative portrayal of them belongs to Matthew, which presents them as religious hypocrites and violent enemies of Jesus.

follows with a second statement (*But I tell you*) that appears antithetical to the first. Yet the term "antitheses" is a misnomer because the statements that Jesus introduces with *But I tell you* are not antithetical to the law of Moses at all (Stanton 301). Rather, these six topics offer specific examples of the kind of righteousness that surpasses that of the Pharisees (5:20). The contrast in the two statements, then, is not between Jesus' teaching and the teaching of the law, but between two opposing interpretations of the law, that of Jesus and that of the Pharisees. Jesus points his disciples to a radical view of the law that corresponds to the law of Moses, while simultaneously extending the prescriptions of the law in line with the principles of love and mercy. Jesus' teaching here is not a new law, but a novel perspective on the law governed by the realities of the kingdom of heaven (Martin 56, 58).

Jesus extends or heightens the prescriptions of the law in three ways (Johnson 187–88). In the first two antitheses (5:21–30), he exalts interior motivation over exterior action by arguing that prohibition of anger and lust is the true intent of the commandments against murder and adultery. With respect to divorce and the breaking of oaths (5:31–37), he advocates a more absolute ethic that demands keeping marital relationships intact and living by a code of honesty that negates the need for oaths. In the final two sayings, Jesus instructs his disciples to go beyond the letter of the law by showing more love and mercy than the law strictly requires. Instead of seeking *eye for eye*, the disciple must respond to oppressors with unlimited mercy (5:38–42). Instead of merely loving his *neighbor*, the disciple receives the call to love his *enemies* (5:43–48). For Jesus, the righteousness of the kingdom of heaven surpasses the strict adherence to commands by advocating love for God and for others that sees the law as a starting point that transcends boundaries and allows one to become *perfect, therefore, as your heavenly Father is perfect* (5:48).

6:1–18 Matthew 6:1 establishes the theme that governs this section. It concerns the exercise of practical piety or *acts of righteousness*. Jesus contrasts those acts done *before men* with those performed before *your Father in heaven*. At issue is the nature of the *reward* received, based upon the motivation driving the action. Jesus warns against performing *acts of righteousness* for public approval, for in doing so one forfeits one's heavenly *reward*.

Matthew 6:2–18 singles out three particular *acts of righteousness*: giving to the needy (verses 2–4), prayer (verses 5–15), and fasting (verses 16–18). In all three, Jesus contrasts genuine righteousness with that practiced by those he terms *hypocrites* (verses 2, 5, 16). The term *hypocrites* [Greek *hypokritai*], which means "actors," identifies those who play a role for public applause. That Jesus later applies the term specifically to the Pharisees and teachers of the law (Matt 23) indicates that he likely has the same group in view here. This section is therefore a further clarification of the kind of righteousness that surpasses that of the Pharisees and teachers of the law. Whereas the hypocrites perform their *acts of righteousness* as if on a stage seeking public approbation, inhabitants of the kingdom of heaven seek commendation from God alone.

Two standardized statements structure Jesus' teaching on the three acts of piety. Following each description of the *hypocrites* who desire *to be seen* and *honored* in public, Jesus states, *I tell you the truth, they have received their reward in full* (verses 2, 5, 16). In contrast, Jesus admonishes his disciples to act *in secret* before the one who is *unseen*. Each of these admonitions then contains the promise that *your Father, who sees what is done in secret, will reward you* (verses 4, 6, 18). This contrast between lust for public recognition and anonymous piety highlights a distinguishing characteristic of the surpassing righteousness of the kingdom of heaven.

6:19–7:12 The main section of the Sermon on the Mount, which runs from 5:17 to 7:12, concludes here with a call to seek after the kingdom of heaven as opposed to the kingdom of earth. The programmatic statement, *For where your treasure is, there your heart will be also* (6:21), provides the motivation for these admonitions. The dichotomy between seeking *treasures on earth* (6:19) versus *treasures in heaven* (6:20) determines one's attitude toward wealth (*money* versus *God*: 6:24) and toward physical necessities like food, clothing, and shelter (*worry* versus *faith*: 6:25–32). The proper attitude for the disciple is to *seek first his kingdom and his righteousness* (6:33) and to *ask* of God, to *seek* the kingdom, and to *knock* on the door (7:7), trusting that God will provide for earthly needs (6:30–32; 7:8–11).

Matthew 7:12, which concludes this section, appears out of place in its context as it does not logically follow from the preceding discussion of the Father who gives good gifts to children (verses 9–11). The verse actually serves more as a conclusion to the entire main section of the Sermon on the Mount (5:17 –7:11). In fact, the references to the *Law* and *the Prophets* that occur at the beginning (5:17) and the end (7:12) of this section form an *inclusio* that brackets the material. Matthew 7:12, commonly known as the Golden Rule, states: *So in everything, do to others what you would have them do to you*. The additional statement that *this sums up the Law and the Prophets* parallels Matthew 22:34–40, with its assertion that love of God and love of neighbor forms the essence of *the Law and the Prophets*. So as the concluding statement of 5:17–7:12, the Golden Rule asserts that what ultimately characterizes a righteousness surpassing that of the Pharisees and what ultimately provides the basis for interpreting the law and the prophets is love and mercy.

7:13–29 The Sermon on the Mount ends with three summary admonitions. First comes the call to *enter through the narrow gate* as opposed to the *wide gate* that *leads to destruction* (7:13–14). In this context, the *narrow gate* would be the path of surpassing righteousness that leads to the kingdom of heaven. This is in contrast to the *wide* path of the Pharisees and teachers of the law. Second is the invitation to *bear good fruit*, interpreted as doing *the will of my Father who is in heaven* (7:15–23). Again, the sermon defines the *will* of God and the *good fruit* that is to characterize the disciple as the application of love and mercy to the demands of the law and the prophets. Finally, the sermon closes with a parable that contrasts the *foolish* person and the *wise* person (7:24–27). What identifies one as *foolish* or *wise* is whether that person *hears these words of mine and puts them into practice*. These final three admonitions thus set up two opposing options for how one may respond to this sermon. The *foolish* person enters through the *wide gate* and bears *bad fruit* by failing to subject his or her religious practice to the guidance of love and mercy. The *wise* person enters through the *narrow gate* and bears *good fruit* because he or she seeks first the kingdom of heaven and the righteousness of God.

"Teach us how to pray …"

In the midst of his teaching on prayer, Jesus instructs his disciples on the proper content of prayer in contrast to the pagans who keep on babbling with many words *(6:7). Two themes structure this prayer (6:9–13). First is the plea for the establishment of God's sovereignty over all of creation (verse 10). Second is the plea for God's mercy as expressed in provisions for material needs (verse 11), forgiveness of sins (verse 12), and deliverance from spiritual danger (verse 13).*

MINISTRY OF MIRACLES · 8:1–9:38

The summary statement in Matthew 4:23 describes Jesus' ministry in terms of teaching, preaching, and healing. Whereas the Sermon on the Mount (Matt 5–7) exemplifies Jesus' teaching and preaching, chapters 8–9 present his healing ministry. Jesus' ministry creates a two-sided response within Israel as it provokes amazement and acceptance by the crowds, while sowing seeds of conflict with the religious leaders. The structure of the chapters unfolds in three sets of three miracle stories, each set divided by nonmiracle stories.

> **Miracles**
>
> *Although the New Testament does not explain in detail what a miracle is, early Christians and their pagan contemporaries all believed that some events were extraordinary. Christians attributed such events to God, not the miracle-worker. Christian miracles thus became ways for the Spirit-led church to live out the gospel of redemption in their own time.*

8:1–17 The first triplet of miracle stories begins with Jesus healing an Israelite leper (8:1–4). Jesus is the Christ bringing the healing mercy of God to Israel. Yet, in the second story, Jesus encounters a Roman centurion in Capernaum who begs Jesus to heal his paralyzed servant (8:5–13). The centurion's request that Jesus simply command the healing from afar prompts Jesus to announce, *I have not found anyone in Israel with such great faith* (8:10). Jesus then uses this event to foreshadow the extension of God's mercy to faithful Gentiles at the expense of faithless Israelites. He says that the *feast with Abraham, Isaac and Jacob* will incorporate Gentiles who come *from the east and the west*, while *the subjects of the kingdom* will find themselves cast out *into the darkness* (8:11–12). The third story in this first triplet records Jesus' healing of Peter's mother-in-law and then concludes with a fulfillment quotation from Isaiah 53:4: *He took up our infirmities and carried our diseases* (8:14–17). This quotation provides the prophetic context within which Jesus' healing activity occurs. It is a display of divine mercy to Israel, although the previous approval of the centurion's faith indicates that Matthew understands the *our* of Isaiah 53:4 to include Gentiles.

> **The Messianic Banquet**
>
> *Many Jewish texts just before and after the first century speak of an eschatological banquet in which the Messiah and the nations will join Israel in praise to God. Early Christians saw this as a symbol of their successful Gentile mission. Sometimes the banquet is thought of as a wedding feast.*

8:18–22 Following the first triplet of miracle stories comes an interlude that exposes the cost of discipleship. Those who choose to follow Jesus as a result of these miracles must do so understanding the demands of the kingdom.

8:23–9:8 The first story of the second triplet of miracle stories records a nonhealing miracle: the calming of a storm (8:23–27). This story contrasts the faith of the disciples with the faith of the centurion in the previous triplet. Both the disciples and the centurion address Jesus as *Lord* (8:8, 25), yet the nature of their requests reveals differing levels of trust. The disciples' desperate and uncertain plea for rescue, followed by amazement after the fact, contrasts with the centurion's certainty and trust that Jesus is capable of more than people expect. As a result, Jesus distinguishes between the *great faith* [Greek *tosauten pistin*; 8:10] of the centurion and the *little faith* [Greek *oligopistoi*; 8:26] of the disciples.

The second miracle story in this triplet corresponds with the second story in the first triplet in that both involve Gentiles. Jesus travels across the Sea of Galilee to *the region of the Gadarenes*, a Gentile area. His healing of two demon-possessed men, however, does not provoke the acclaim and acceptance it does with the Israelite crowds, as the Gentiles of the region ask him to leave (8:34).

In the third miracle story, Jesus returns *to his own town* of Capernaum and encounters a paralytic (9:1–8). Jesus forgives the paralytic's sins, and the subsequent healing done to buttress that act exposes the tension that Jesus' ministry creates in Israel. For the first time in the gospel, Jesus comes into direct conflict with leaders of Israel, *the teachers of the law*. They describe his act of forgiveness as *blasphemy* (9:3), yet the crowd praises God for the healing (9:8).

9:9–17 Set between the second and third triplets of miracle stories are two stories that deal with the dissonance between the activities of Jesus and his disciples and the activities of the Pharisees. A question concerning the lack of fasting on the part of Jesus' disciples leads Jesus to compare his presence among them to a wedding celebration during which fasting is inappropriate (9:14–17).

The dispute regarding Jesus' social practice of eating with *tax collectors and sinners* offers a pointed insight into the nature of his ministry. The healing miracles in Matthew 8–9 are a display of divine mercy by the one who takes up *infirmities* and carries *diseases*. The connection of healing and forgiveness of sins in the story of the paralytic (9:1–8) sets up this conflict with the Pharisees by linking physical needs to spiritual needs. By eating with *tax collectors and sinners*, Jesus violates the Pharisaic interpretation of purity regulations that demand separation from the unclean. However, according to Jesus, the Pharisaic interpretation of purity regulations violates the principle of divine mercy that demands interaction with the unclean.

> **The Great Physician**
> When Jesus says that the sick are the ones in need of a doctor and that his call is for sinners (9:12–13), he stresses that his outpouring of mercy flows equally to the spiritually infirm and the physically infirm. Jesus thus places the Pharisees in the position of physicians who avoid sick people. So his admonition to them to go and learn what this means: 'I desire mercy, not sacrifice' *is an admonition to prioritize love and mercy over ritual and tradition.*

9:18–34 Matthew 9:18–34 offers the final triplet of miracle stories. The first story actually contains two miracles: the healing of a woman with a hemorrhage and the raising of a dead girl (9:18–26). The next two record the healing of two blind men (9:27–31) and a demoniac (9:32–34).

Matthew's organization of miracle stories in chapters 8–9 shows an increasing tension between Jesus and Israel's leaders that culminates in dual responses to his ministry (Luz 64). When the two blind men first encounter Jesus, they plead, *Have mercy on us, Son of David!* (9:27). By including this address, Matthew marks Jesus' healing ministry as a sign of his messianic identity (Stanton 180). Similarly, the crowds of Israelites respond to Jesus' displays of mercy to the sick and to sinners with amazement. The first two stories conclude by noting how news about Jesus spreads throughout the region (9:26, 31). The third story makes the crowds' response to Jesus even more emphatic when they proclaim, *Nothing like this has ever been seen in Israel* (9:33).

> **Jesus as Messiah**
> *Although Matthew stops short of suggesting that the crowds accept Jesus' messianic identity, they clearly respond favorably. By contrast, the Pharisees reject any association of Jesus with the Christ, assigning his miraculous activity to demonic origin (9:34). Thus, Jesus' application of mercy over sacrifice sets the stage for division in Israel.*

9:35–38 This transitional summary section completes the presentation of Jesus' healing ministry by noting his *compassion* for *the crowds* who appear as *sheep without a shepherd* (see Matt 2:6). It also sets up the major discourse of chapter 10 (Jesus' instructions to the twelve apostles as he sends them out to preach) by including Jesus' request that the disciples pray that God would *send out workers into his harvest field* (9:38).

DISCOURSE 2: MISSIONARY INSTRUCTIONS TO THE TWELVE · 10:1–42

Following Jesus' request of them to pray that God send workers out into the field (9:38), the twelve disciples learn that they themselves are the workers. After imparting to them *authority to drive out evil spirits* and the power *to heal every disease and sickness* (10:1), Jesus sends them out into the field with specific instructions (10:5). The first admonition concerns the beneficiaries of their ministry. Jesus instructs them *not to go among the Gentiles* or to *the Samaritans* (10:5). Instead, they are to focus solely upon *the lost sheep of Israel* (10:6; see also verse 23b). Given favorable references to Gentiles earlier in the gospel, this restriction of the disciples' ministry to Israel is all the more striking. However, the promise to Abraham that the divine plan includes blessing for all nations assumes the priority of Israel: it is through Israel that nations will be blessed. Consequently, Jesus' invitation to partake of the kingdom of heaven comes first to Israel.

One of the functions of the major discourses in Matthew is to shape the lives and ministries of the disciples after the pattern of Jesus' own life and ministry. As the disciples go out, therefore, they do as Jesus does. The message they are to preach is the same: *the kingdom of heaven is near* (10:7; see 4:17). Like Jesus, they *freely give* of God's divine mercy by healing the sick, raising the dead, and driving out demons (10:8). If they preach the message of the kingdom faithfully, it will create division in Israel. Jesus tells his disciples, *I did not come to bring peace, but a sword* that divides (10:34). Consequently, faithful proclamation of the kingdom of heaven will lead to unrest on earth and to families torn asunder and turned against each other (10:21, 35–36).

Jesus assures his disciples that they will receive harsh persecution for their efforts. They are *sheep among wolves* who will become prey to powerful and committed adversaries (10:16–18). He announces to the disciples that *all men will hate you because of me* (10:22). In their persecution, they stand in solidarity with their Lord, for Jesus tells them that *a student is not above his teacher, nor a servant above his master* (10:24). If the *teacher* and *master* suffer, then the *student* and *servant* shall suffer *much more* (10:25). Yet in the face of this persecution, they are neither to worry nor to fear. Three times in 10:26–31 Jesus tells them, *Do not be afraid* (verse 26, 28, 31). The source of their courage is the knowledge that their *Father* protects them and speaks through them (10:19–20, 29–31). The book's theme of judgment and reward plays out here as well, made dependent upon how one welcomes these disciples.

> **Welcoming the Disciples**
> *Those who reject the disciples will find it unbearable on* the day of judgment (10:14–15), *while everyone who welcomes them* will certainly not lose his reward (10:40–42).

GROWING CONFLICT WITH ISRAEL · 11:1–12:50

11:1–24 While Jesus preaches *in the towns of Galilee*, John the Baptist sends his followers to question Jesus about his messianic identity (11:1–2). Matthew introduces John's question by stating, *When John heard in prison what Christ was doing* (11:2). The single word *Christ* as the identifier for Jesus stands out because it is not Matthew's typical means of referring to Jesus. By using this term, Matthew points to the crux of John's question, which is the messianic identity of Jesus. Through his messengers, John asks, *Are you the one who was to come, or should we expect someone else?* (11:3). John is beginning to doubt whether Jesus is in fact the Christ. When John announced the advent of the Christ in Matthew 3, he did so with the expectation that Jesus would be a proclaimer of repentance and judgment. Yet, now, John apparently does not recognize in Jesus' activities the kind of prophetic edge that he expects of the Christ. The beginning of Matthew 11 thus sounds a note of uncertainty with respect to Jesus' identity. The question *Are you the one who was to come?* provides an organizing theme for the section that extends from 11:1 to 16:12 (Matera 248). It is the very question with which Israel wrestles. The heightening tension between Jesus and Israel derives from Israel's increasingly negative response to that question.

Jesus replies by sending John's messengers back to report on what they *hear and see*, and then he lists his miraculous and preaching activities (11:5). For Jesus, the proof of his identity as Christ is the very kind of preaching and healing activities recorded in chapters 5–9. He expects John to recognize his messianic identity through these activities. He then closes his reply with a warning that refers as much to the leaders and people of Israel as to John: *Blessed is the man who does not fall away on account of me* (11:6).

The narrative then turns to address the crowd's response to the preaching of John and Jesus. Once again, Israel repudiates the prophetic witness. Their failure to recognize Jesus as *the one who was to come* leads to a pronouncement of judgment. In 11:20–24, Jesus condemns the very towns in which he performed *most of his miracles* (11:20), indicating that the miraculous and merciful activity of chapters 8–9 functioned as a plea to repentance. Yet, *because they did not repent*, the Galilean cities of *Korazin*, *Bethsaida*, and *Capernaum* will find *the day of judgment* less bearable than will the notoriously sinful Gentile cities of *Tyre*, *Sidon*, and *Sodom* (11:20–24). In this context, Jesus looks very much like the figure expected by John: the prophet who commands people to *repent*, for the

> **John the Baptist**
> *Acknowledging John as both the messenger of Malachi 3:1 and Elijah of Malachi 4:5, Jesus challenges the crowd to make a decision concerning John (11:10, 14). He who has ears, let him hear (11:15) suggests that only those who are able to hear the truth about John will be able to hear the truth about Jesus (see 17:12). Jesus makes this point by comparing the crowd to children who refuse to dance at the sound of a flute and to mourn at the singing of a dirge (11:16–17). The stubborn crowd fails to recognize the presence of God in its midst regardless of the form it takes. They reject both John's strict asceticism and Jesus' free approach (11:18–19).*

kingdom of heaven is near (4:17; see also 3:2) and then brings *his winnowing fork* to bear on those who reject that command (3:12).

11:25–30 Following this harsh pronouncement of judgment, Jesus offers words of comfort to those who heed his call for repentance. He distinguishes between *the wise and learned* from whom God has *hidden these things* and the *little children* to whom God has *revealed them* (11:25). The *little children* in this context represent the disciples who, like children, are able to recognize Jesus in a simple display of trust (see 10:42), while the *wise and learned* represent the spiritually blind leaders of Israel. As caretakers of Israel's wisdom, they should have been attuned to the presence of God but instead are blind and deaf to it, lacking the *eyes to see* (13:13–15) or the *ears to hear* (11:15; 13:14–15).

Jesus then beckons all these "little children" who are *weary* and *burdened* to take his *yoke* upon them (11:28–29). The *yoke* in this text refers to the observance of the law, not in the sense that observance of the law itself is a burden, but that the Pharisees, with their innumerable regulations and conditions, had turned law observance into a burden (see 23:4, 13). By contrast, Jesus offers a *yoke* that is *easy* and a *burden* that is *light*, meaning that the true intent of the law is to help, not burden, God's people. The following story (12:1–14) serves as an illustration of this. Jesus' dual offer of *rest* (11:28, 29) sets up his conflict with the Pharisees over their differing interpretations of the Sabbath rest.

12:1–14 In Matthew 12:1–8, the Pharisees accuse Jesus' disciples of violating the Sabbath law by picking and eating heads of grain. As a command to rest, the Sabbath law (Exod 20:8–11) was a blessing to Israel, a chance for physical refreshment and spiritual renewal. Keeping the Sabbath law, therefore, should be a *yoke* that is *easy* and a *burden* that is *light* (11:30). Nevertheless, the Pharisees focused less on the "rest" part of the command and more on the "you shall not do any work" part. They developed restrictions on behavior and regulations for governing activity with the intent of facilitating Israel's ability to avoid work on that day. Rather than promoting rest, however, these additional regulations became burdensome for some people or even an obstacle to love and mercy.

Jesus replies to the Pharisees' accusation by directing their attention toward Scripture. He refers to 1 Samuel 21:1–6 in which David and his companions *entered the house of God* and, out of hunger, *ate the consecrated bread – which was not lawful for them to do* (Matt 12:3–4). For Jesus, the David story represents the principle that human need takes precedence over ritual and law. By exalting ritual and law over human need, some Pharisees miss the heart of the law and so miss God. The Pharisees' strict adherence to the letter of the law, without the application of love and mercy, led to a corruption of the Sabbath law. In an earlier dispute with the Pharisees, Jesus challenged them to *go and learn what this means*: *'I desire mercy, not sacrifice'* (9:13). Now he returns to this theme by saying, *If you had known what these words mean, 'I desire mercy, not sacrifice,' you would not have condemned the innocent* (12:7). The words *if you had known* shows that the Pharisees failed to heed Jesus' earlier admonition to *go and learn*. Their failure to learn the priority of mercy blinds them to the presence of the kingdom of heaven. As if to prove his point, Jesus then enters a synagogue and heals a man with a shriveled hand while announcing that *it is lawful to do good on the Sabbath* (12:9–12). The Pharisees, rather than praising the mercy of God, go out and plot *how they might kill Jesus* (12:14), thus marking an intensification of the conflict between the Christ and Israel.

12:15–21 As a result of the increasing animosity of the Pharisees, Jesus leaves the area, healing the sick among his followers. This leads to a fulfillment quotation from Isaiah 42:1–4, which announces that *he will proclaim justice to the nations* and *in his name the nations will put their hope* (Matt 12:18, 21). This foreshadows once again that Israel's rejection of the Christ will lead to the proclaiming of the message to *the nations*.

12:22–37 Jesus' healing of a demoniac prompts the crowd to ask, *Could this be the Son of David?* (12:23). This variation of John's question (*Are you the one who was to come?*; 11:3), highlights that Jesus' messianic identity is the central focus of these chapters. While the people continue to struggle with the possible messianic identity of Jesus, the

> **Beelzebub**
> 2 Kings 1 mentions this figure as the god of the Philistine city of Ekron. His real name was not Baalzebub ("lord of the flies"), an obvious insult, but Baalzebul ("lord of princely estate"). The name in later Judaism became a name for the demonic opposition to God.

Pharisees reject it outright and attribute his miraculous activity to *Beelzebub, the prince of demons* (12:23–24). This blasphemous accusation compels Jesus to lecture the Pharisees on the distinction between bearing good fruit and bad fruit, which Jesus compares to the words that come out of a person (12:33–37). Because *a tree is recognized by its fruit* (12:33), the Pharisees' blasphemy marks them as a bad tree producing bad fruit and leads Jesus to declare to them that they will *give account on the day of judgment for every careless word they have spoken* (12:36).

12:38–45 The Pharisees' request *to see a miraculous sign* from Jesus leads to another harsh rebuke (12:38). Jesus condemns them by employing an argument from the lesser to the greater, which reveals that Jesus himself is the sign to which they must respond. First, he tells them that the only sign they will receive is *the sign of the prophet Jonah*, but then he compares Jonah's *three days and three nights in the belly of a huge fish* to the Son of Man's *three days and three nights in the heart of the earth* (12:40). This indicates that *the sign of the prophet Jonah* is in fact the resurrection of the Son of Man. The primary reason for Jonah's mention here, however, is the theme of repentance. Jonah preached to *the men of Nineveh*, and they repented. But *now one greater than Jonah is here*, and so Israel's failure to repent at the preaching of one who is *greater* will lead to a greater *judgment* (12:41). Likewise, *the Queen of the south* (see 1 Kgs 10) traveled *from the ends of the earth to listen to Solomon's wisdom*, yet Israel refuses to hearken to the wisdom of *one greater than Solomon* (12:42). He who is *greater than Jonah* and *greater than Solomon* is the sign that stands before the Pharisees, and their refusal to heed that sign condemns them (12:1–42).

12:46–50 Chapter 12 concludes with a short vignette in which Jesus redefines the nature of his family. Prompted by the attempt of his mother and brothers to speak with him, Jesus identifies his family as *whoever does the will of my Father in heaven* (12:50). This declaration forms an implicit attack on Israel. It is not those who can trace their ancestry to Abraham who can claim to be children of God, but only those who bear good fruit. (Jesus here says much the same thing as the Old Testament prophets.) This opens the door to the kingdom to faithful Gentiles as well.

DISCOURSE 3: PARABLES OF THE KINGDOM · 13:1–52
Matthew's third major discourse is a compilation of seven parables. All seven are parables about the nature of the kingdom, yet the last six more properly receive the title of "kingdom parables" because each one begins with the phrase, *The kingdom of heaven is like ...* (13:24, 31, 33, 44, 45, 47). Significantly, Jesus suddenly begins teaching the crowds in parables, whereas his previous teaching in this gospel occurred in open discourse. Jesus explains only two of the parables, and these only to his disciples. The increasing hostility from the people and leaders of Israel provokes Jesus to teach in parables that obscure the message of the kingdom from all but those with *ears* to *hear* (13:9, 43).

13:1–23 Surrounded by crowds of people, Jesus begins to teach them *many things in parables* (13:2–3), beginning with the parable of the Sower. This parable serves a programmatic function in this discourse in that the three themes that characterize the subsequent parables (growth, decision, and judgment) are all present here (Johnson 183). Jesus publicly recites the parable to the crowds (verses 3–9), then privately responds to a question from his disciples (verses 10–17), and finally explains the parable to them (verses 18–23). Following the recitation of the parable, with its four kinds of soil producing four different results, the disciples ask the relevant question for this chapter, *Why do you speak to the people in parables*? (13:10).

> **Jesus' Parables**
> *Jesus' parables in Matthew are a means of distinguishing between insiders and outsiders of the kingdom (Johnson 182). Whereas unfaithful Israelites are blind and deaf, the disciples are blessed because their eyes* see *and their ears* hear *(13:16). Jesus then explains to his disciples that the parable is about how people* respond *to the message about the kingdom (13:19).*

Jesus replies that *the knowledge of the secrets of the kingdom of heaven* is for the disciples and not for rebellious Israel. In fact, what rebellious Israel has will be taken away from it (13:11–12). Jesus says that the reason *why I speak to them in parables* is that they failed to understand the message of the kingdom when he proclaimed it openly (13:13). He then quotes from Isaiah 6:9–10, revealing that the people of Israel fail to understand plain teaching (13:14–15).

The four different kinds of soil on which the sower plants seed represent the different responses by Israel to Jesus' teaching (Luz 87). The first three types of soil illustrate three reasons for Israel's rejection of Jesus' message: failure to understand (verse 19), inability to weather hardship (verse 21), and worldliness (verse 22). The person whose heart represents *good soil*, however, *hears* and *understands* the message, thus producing the good fruit of the kingdom (13:23).

13:24–43 The parable of the Weeds also involves the sowing of seed. This time, however, an *enemy* sows *weeds among the wheat*. The owner of the field refuses to pull up the weeds for fear of damaging the wheat, opting instead to wait until the harvest (13:24–30). Next, Jesus recites the parable of the Mustard Seed and the parable of the Yeast, both of which illustrate the rapid and pervasive growth of the kingdom (13:31–33). These two parables about the growth of the kingdom sit between the parable of the Weeds (13:24–30) and the explanation of that parable (13:36–43). The parable of the Weeds reveals that the kingdom initially contains both the righteous and the wicked due to the influence of the *enemy*, or the *devil* (13:39). Unlike in the parable of the Sower where the seed represents the message of the kingdom, here the *seed* are the righteous *sons of the kingdom* (the wheat), in contrast to *the sons of the evil one* (the weeds). The *harvest* is the judgment at which the angels will separate the weeds from the wheat and burn them in *the fiery furnace* (13:41–42).

13:44–52 The parable of the Hidden Treasure and the parable of the Pearl both highlight the value of the kingdom and its demand for a committed decision (13:44–46). The parable of the Net concludes Jesus' discourse in parables on the note of judgment. The parable of the Net and the parable of the Weeds are companion pieces. Just as the field contains both wheat and weeds, the fisherman's net contains both *good* and *bad* fish (13:48). Just as the angels will separate the weeds from the wheat and cast them into the fiery furnace, so also the angels will separate the righteous (good fish) from the wicked (bad fish), who will likewise be cast into *the fiery furnace* (13:49–50).

At the conclusion of his teaching, Jesus asks the disciples if they have *understood all these things* (13:51). He explains the necessity of their understanding in verse 52 by noting that those who receive *the secrets of the kingdom of heaven* (13:11), the disciples, are to serve as the teachers of the law for the new community of believers (Johnson 182). They will bear the responsibility for teaching the church about the kingdom of heaven and the *new treasures* that it offers alongside (not in opposition to) the *old* treasures of Judaism.

OPPOSITION FROM WITHOUT & GROWING ENLIGHTENMENT FROM WITHIN · 13:53–16:12

Because the disciples are to be the teachers of the community of believers (13:52), they must understand their responsibilities in the kingdom and learn to trust in God. Consequently, from Matthew 13:53 to 16:12, Jesus continues to instruct his disciples in the way of the kingdom while fending off opposition from without.

13:53–14:12 The first two stories in the section of 13:53 to 16:12 testify to the continuing difficulty that Israelites face in coming to terms with the identity of Jesus. First, Jesus returns to Nazareth only to be rejected by his hometown people. Unable to reconcile his *wisdom* and *miraculous powers* with his identity as the *carpenter's son* whose mother, brothers, and sisters they know (13:54–57), the people of Nazareth fall away on account of him (13:57–58; see also 11:6). Their familiarity with the human Jesus blinds them to the divine Christ.

Balancing the rejection of Jesus at Nazareth is Herod Antipas's confusion over Jesus' identity. Herod, who is *tetrarch* of Galilee, mistakenly concludes from reports about Jesus that he is John the Baptist resurrected. This reference to the death of John the Baptist leads Matthew to review the events surrounding John's beheading by Herod (14:3–11).

> **Tetrarch**
>
> *A tetrarch is the ruler of a fourth of a kingdom. Herod the Great divided his kingdom amongst his sons, with Herod Antipas ruling Galilee and Perea for more than 40 years.*

14:13–36 Following the two stories about confusion over the identity of Jesus come two stories about the disciples' inability to understand and trust in the power of Jesus. First, Jesus challenges them to feed a crowd of 5,000 men plus women and children (14:13–21). When he tells the disciples to *give them something to eat*, the disciples demonstrate a lack of understanding by protesting that *five loaves of bread and two fish* are insufficient to accomplish the task (14:17). Jesus responds by multiplying the food and feeding the crowd. Then, Jesus sends the disciples away on a boat (14:22). *During the fourth watch of the night* (from 3:00 to 6:00 a.m.), Jesus comes to them walking on the water (14:25). His admonition to them of *Don't be afraid* represents the point of this story (14:27). They are to trust in the presence and power of Jesus. Peter initially displays this trust by stepping out of the boat and walking on the water toward Jesus; yet, contrary to Jesus' admonition, he becomes *afraid* and begins to sink (14:30). Whereas Peter demonstrates *little faith* due to his inability to trust, the other disciples in the boat confess Jesus as *the Son of God* (14:31, 33). Their failure to comprehend fully the significance of Jesus' presence among them thus stands alongside their growing enlightenment.

15:1–20 Matthew 15:1–20 begins as a story about the Pharisees but ends as one about the disciples. The Pharisees and teachers of the law question Jesus over why his disciples *break the tradition of the elders* by not washing their hands before eating (15:1–2). The *tradition of the elders* refers to a body of oral instructions developed in addition to the written law. The Pharisees viewed these oral traditions as equally binding as the law, while the Sadducees rejected them (Hill 250–51; Mounce 148). The washing of hands before eating was not a hygienic exercise but a ceremonial one designed to ward off ritual uncleanness. The issue here is not violation of the written law, which does not require the washing of hands before eating, but violation of *the tradition of the elders*.

> **An Oral Torah**
>
> Christians often misrepresent Jewish oral law as a legalistic, mindless, or even oppressive system. However, the Pharisees and the later rabbis simply sought to make the written Torah as applicable to life as possible. As the early (before 200 CE) collection Pirqe Avot ("Sayings of the Ancestors") puts it: "The World is sustained by three things, the Torah, worship, and deeds of steadfast love." Or consider the saying attributed to Jesus' older contemporary Hillel, "Be among Aaron's disciples, loving peace and pursing it, loving your fellow creatures, and drawing them near to Torah."

Jesus responds not by immediately addressing the issue of ritual purity, but by accusing the Pharisees of violating the written law *for the sake of your tradition* (15:3). The example he gives is of the Pharisaic teaching that a man who has dedicated a *gift* [Greek *doron*] to God is then unable to use that gift to aid his parents (15:5–6). In Mark's account of this story, he terms the gift *Corban* [Greek *korban*, a loanword from Hebrew: Mark 7:11]. "Corban" refers to a votive offering to God, which is therefore removed from secular use. In some cases, a person might dedicate property to God in order to make it unavailable to others who might have a legitimate claim upon it (Hill 251). In the situation Jesus describes, the Pharisees teach that the dedication of a gift to God takes priority over responsibility to one's parents. Jesus, however, counters that any refusal to take care of one's parents violates the law to *Honor your father and mother* (15:4). The Pharisees *nullify the word of God* by exalting their tradition over love and mercy (15:6). Their failure to comprehend the heart of the law leads Jesus to apply to them the divine accusation of Isaiah 29:13 that *their hearts are far from me* (15:8).

Jesus now addresses the purity issue initially raised by the Pharisees but connects it to purity of heart. He tells the crowd a brief parable the point of which is that only what comes out of a person makes him or her *unclean* (15:10–11). The meaning of the parable is that things from without, like foods and the dirt of unwashed hands, do not make a person unclean, but only those things that come from within *the heart*, such as *evil thoughts*, *murder*, *adultery*, *sexual immorality*, *theft*, *false testimony*, and *slander* (15:19).

When Peter asks Jesus to explain this parable, it prompts the rebuke, *Are you still so dull?* (15:15–16). That Jesus uses second person plural address indicates that the rebuke encompasses all of the disciples, not Peter alone. The word *still* reveals that Jesus expects the disciples to be more astute in their comprehension of the kingdom than they have so far shown themselves to be.

15:21–28 Traveling through Tyre and Sidon, Jesus encounters a Gentile woman who recognizes his messianic significance and addresses him as *Son of David* (15:22). Her constant pleas on behalf of her ailing daughter, however, fall on deaf ears. Jesus ignores her, justifying it by referring to the priority of Israel in his ministry (15:24). When she persists, he responds with the proverb, *It is not right to take the children's bread and toss it to their dogs* (15:26). "Dog" is a Jewish way of referring to Gentiles (Hill 254), although Jesus' use of the diminutive form

[Greek *kynarion*] indicates a little dog or puppy. The context of the proverb clearly implies a domesticated animal. Jesus is pointing out the inappropriateness of taking what belongs to Israel (the children) and giving it to the Gentiles. Her clever reply that even *dogs eat the crumbs that fall from their masters' table* is an acknowledgement that she seeks not to usurp the place of Israel but only to share in the mercy of God. Thus, Jesus grants her request, praising her *great faith* in the process. Just as in the story of the centurion (8:5–13), Jesus commends a Gentile for *great faith* in the context of stories that chastise the disciples for exhibiting *little faith* (14:31; 16:8).

15:29–16:4 These verses contain two stories that create a sense of déjà vu. First comes a story in which Jesus again feeds a large crowd. Just as with the feeding of the 5,000 in 14:13–21, the feeding of the 4,000 opens with Jesus healing large crowds of people and feeling *compassion* for them (14:14; 15:30–32). The story focuses on the reaction of the disciples to the need of the crowd. They question how anyone could *get enough bread in this remote place to feed such a crowd* (15:33), an echo of their request in the feeding of the 5,000 that Jesus send the crowd home because they are in *a remote place* (14:15). The second feeding story illustrates the inability of the disciples to grasp the power of Jesus. Not only had they recently witnessed him multiplying food for a crowd of 5,000, but this time there are fewer people to feed (4,000) and marginally more food with which to begin (seven loaves and a few fish). Jesus once again feeds the crowd, with an abundance left over (15:35–37).

The second story involves the Pharisees and Sadducees asking Jesus for a sign. This passage is almost a mirror image of Matthew 12:38–39. Jesus replies with language virtually identical to chapter 12 when he calls the Pharisees and the Sadducees *a wicked and adulterous generation* and promises that no sign *will be given it except the sign of Jonah* (16:4; compare 12:39). As the second feeding story highlights the disciples' continuing failure to understand, the second conversation over signs highlights the Pharisees' continuing obstinacy. These two stories, therefore, set up the confrontation between Jesus and his disciples that occurs in 16:5–12.

16:5–12 Following the multiplication of bread for a crowd of 4,000 and the dispute with the Pharisees and Sadducees over signs, Jesus draws from both events by warning his disciples to *be on your guard against the yeast of the Pharisees and Sadducees* (16:6). The disciples misinterpret Jesus and think he is talking about their lack of bread (16:7). This misunderstanding leads to the climax of this section, where Jesus declares the disciples to be those of *little faith* and asks them, *Do you still not understand?* (16:8–9). When Jesus reminds them of how much food was left over after feeding the crowds of 5,000 and 4,000 (16:9–10), he deliberately links those feeding events to his warning about the teaching of the Pharisees and Sadducees. In fact, Jesus asks the disciples, *How is it you don't understand that I was not talking to you about bread?* (16:11). Something was going on in those feeding stories that the disciples should have grasped, but they missed it. Only when it becomes clear that the real issue is *the teaching of the Pharisees and Sadducees* can Matthew say of the disciples, *Then they understood* (16:12).

In 13:52, Jesus compares the disciples to *teachers of the law* who will instruct the people of God *about the kingdom of heaven*. The two feeding stories and Jesus' confrontation with the disciples over the teaching of the Pharisees and Sadducees can be read against that backdrop. The satisfying of hunger that occurs in each feeding story teaches the disciples about the nature of their ministry. As instructors in the kingdom of heaven, they are to feed the people with knowledge of the higher righteousness of God. Doing so, however, means guarding their teaching against the Pharisees and Sadducees.

THE DEMANDS OF DISCIPLESHIP · 16:13–17:27

Chapters 16–20 focus upon the nature of discipleship. In 16:13–17:27 Peter's confession of Jesus as the Christ becomes the catalyst for examining the implications of that identity for discipleship.

16:13–28 Jesus himself raises the question of his identity at Cæsarea Philippi. After the disciples describe the confusion among the crowds (16:14), Jesus asks them, *But what about you?* (16:15). When Peter declares Jesus to be *the Christ*, Jesus

> **Peter the Rock**
> *Early Christians like Origen (died 254) interpreted this text to refer to any spiritually insightful Christian teacher. Not Peter as a person, much less as the holder of an office, but Peter as the one who knows the truth about Jesus receives the blessing here. Peter's successor is thus the entire church as it confesses Jesus as Lord.*

commands them to tell no one (16:16, 20). At this stage, the knowledge is only for the disciples. In fact, Jesus' blessing of Peter for his confession further places this discussion in the context of discipleship as Jesus refers to *my church* for the first time and to the authority that Peter will exercise in that community (16:18–19).

Peter's declaration of Jesus as the Christ leads to Jesus' first prediction of his suffering and death (16:21). It is because he is the Christ that he *must go to Jerusalem and suffer*. The temporal marker (*From that time on*) signifies this important shift in the narrative. This also introduces the literary device of the journey to Jerusalem (Kingsbury 77), although actual movement toward Jerusalem does not begin until 19:1.

Peter's refusal to accept that the Christ is to suffer and die (16:22) reveals his expectations of what the Christ is to do. Peter and the other disciples still misperceive the nature of the kingdom, viewing it according to worldly models of success and authority (18:1; 20:21). Jesus tells Peter *Get behind me Satan!* because Jesus recognizes that Peter's objection to the idea that the Christ should suffer and die functions as a temptation, like that in the wilderness, to choose an easier path that leads to worldly glory (16:23). Peter's misconception stems from his misplaced concern for *the things of men* as opposed to *the things of God* (16:23).

Jesus, however, clarifies the truth about messiahship and discipleship. He says that everyone who wishes to be his disciple *must deny himself and take up his cross and follow me* (16:24). To follow Christ means to accept where that journey leads: to a cross. The life of the disciple demands a lifestyle of self-denial and self-sacrifice that rejects earthly glory and comfort in favor of solidarity with the sufferings of Christ. This self-denial and rejection of the world (16:25–26) constitutes *the things of God*.

> **The Suffering Servant**
> *Jesus' passion prediction explains what it means for him to be the Christ: suffering and death. This is the nature of Jesus' own discipleship and obedience to God. For those who understand the kingdom to be about the things of men, this makes no sense. If the Son of David is to restore the kingdom to Israel and rule it faithfully, he cannot be dead.*

17:1–13 The transfiguration addresses whether the disciples understand the implications of discipleship outlined in the previous section. Taking Peter, James, and John to *a high mountain*, Jesus becomes transfigured before them while Moses, the lawgiver, and Elijah, a prophet, appear to talk with him (17:1–2). It is likely that Moses and Elijah here serve as representatives of the law and the prophets. After a voice from the cloud states, *This is my Son ... Listen to him!* (17:5), the disciples look up and see Jesus standing alone. The sudden disappearance of Moses and Elijah, with God singling out Jesus as his *Son*, defines discipleship for Peter, James, and John as obedience to the *Son*, who is greater than the Law and the Prophets. The transfiguration scene essentially makes visual what Jesus elsewhere states: that he is *greater than the temple* (12:6) and *greater than Jonah* (12:41).

17:14–27 This section concludes with two more stories that focus on the disciples. In the first, their failure to heal a possessed boy prompts Jesus to chastise them for their *little faith* for the fourth time in the gospel (8:26; 14:31; 16:8; 17:20). Then comes a discussion about the temple tax (an annual tax upon adult Jewish males for support of the temple sacrifices). Although Jesus teaches that the disciples are exempt from the temple tax, he urges them to pay in order to avoid causing offense. The message is that even though the disciples are distinct from the world, discipleship demands involvement in the world.

DISCOURSE 4: THE LIFE OF THE COMMUNITY OF DISCIPLES · 18:1–35

Jesus' fourth discourse builds on the theme of discipleship by addressing responsibilities in the community of faith. The discourse begins with a question from the disciples, *Who is the greatest in the kingdom of heaven?* (18:1). This question shows their resistance to the idea of self-denial and servanthood as the essence of discipleship (Kingsbury 130). Jesus replies by using a *little child* to illustrate self-abasement as the path to greatness in the kingdom (18:2–4). Jesus then shifts the discussion from little children to *little ones* (18:6–14), these being those disciples who exhibit such childlike humility. He warns those who would cause the *little ones* to sin or who would look down on them because God values each one of the *little ones* (18:6, 10, 12–14).

The second part of the discourse focuses on reconciliation and church discipline. If one disciple sins against another, the wronged party is to seek reconciliation privately (18:15). If the disciple who sinned refuses to repent, the community then intervenes. Continued resistance can lead to exclusion from the community (18:16–17). The famous statement, *For where two or three come together in my name, there am I with them* (18:20), is often taken as a blanket comment on worship; yet, it pertains more directly to church discipline. In the church's response to the stubborn disciple, the purpose of bringing the community in on the process is to subject the matter to *the testimony of two or three witnesses* (18:16). Jesus' statement to Peter that *whatever you bind on earth will be bound in heaven* is here applied to the church in the sense that God will ratify the church's decision concerning the stubborn disciple (18:18). Consequently, the promise of Christ's presence whenever two or three come together in prayer is a promise that he is active in matters of church discipline (Hill 276; Mounce 176–77).

Following the topic of discipline for the unrepentant disciple, the discourse concludes with a parable about how believers are to respond to the repentant disciple (18:21–35). They are to forgive without limits because the divine mercy that disciples receive will be based upon the mercy they show.

FROM GALILEE TO JUDEA · 19:1–20:16

19:1–12 With Matthew 19:1, Jesus begins his journey from Galilee to Judea and toward the fate awaiting him there. Along the way, he continues to explain to his disciples what it means to be a follower of Christ. The ensuing discussions contrast the kingdom values of Jesus with the more worldly values of the disciples (Kingsbury 15). When the Pharisees test Jesus with a question about divorce, he emphasizes that God intends the permanency of marriage (19:4–9). The disciples, however, conclude that it would then be *better not to marry* (19:10). Jesus replies that the dual choices of commitment in marriage or celibacy are both marks of discipleship and that his teaching on marriage is for *the one who can accept this* (19:11–12).

19:13–15 Jesus' attempt to pray for *little children* conflicts with the values of the disciples who try to hinder them, leading Jesus to reiterate that *the kingdom of heaven belongs to such as these*.

19:16–20:16 The third conflict of values between Jesus and his disciples occurs over wealth. Jesus tells a wealthy man, *If you want to enter life, obey the commandments* (19:17). Jesus then lists several commandments from the Decalogue and the command to *love your neighbor as yourself* (19:18–19). When the man claims to have kept all these, Jesus amends his earlier charge of *If you want to enter life* to *If you want to be perfect* (19:21). The man has kept the commandments, but has he demonstrated the higher righteousness of the kingdom of heaven? *To be perfect*, to go beyond the minimum requirements of the law in an act of mercy, the man is to renounce his wealth and *give to the poor* (19:21).

The focus then shifts to the disciples as Jesus informs them that a *camel* would have an easier time squeezing through the eye of a sewing *needle* than would a rich man getting into *the kingdom of God* (19:24). The impossibility of the wealthy entering the kingdom is due to money binding people to the world and blinding them to the spiritual. Renunciation of wealth is a persistent theme in Matthew (Luz 109–110; see 6:19–34; 10:9–10; 13:22; 16:26). Yet Jesus' statement is clearly hyperbole, for he qualifies it in verse 26 by adding that it is indeed *impossible* for the wealthy to enter heaven, but by God's power it can become *possible*.

> **The Needle's Eye**
> *Contrary to popular belief, there is no evidence that a city gate was ever called the "eye of a needle."*

When Peter then notes that the disciples have *left everything to follow* Jesus and inquires about their reward (19:27), Jesus says that all who renounce the world for his sake will *inherit eternal life*, yet he counsels them that *many who are first will be last, and many who are last will be first* (19:29–30). Jesus then tells the disciples a parable to illustrate this point (20:1–16). A landowner hires workers for his vineyard at different times during the day, but then pays them all equally. Those hired last receive the same reward as those present from the beginning, so that the *last* are *first* and the *first* are *last* (20:16). This parable reminds the disciples that their place as the first followers of Jesus does not necessarily garner them a greater reward than those who come later to the kingdom.

TO JERUSALEM · 20:17–21:11

20:17–28 While Jesus is *going up to Jerusalem*, he predicts his imminent suffering and death for the third time (20:17–19). This expectation of suffering stands against the expectation of a messianic kingdom. The request by two of his disciples to sit at his *right* and *left* in the kingdom reveals that they still interpret the kingdom in terms of glory rather than service. With the cross just around the corner, time grows short for Jesus to impress upon them that the essence of discipleship is not glory and power, but humility and service. In the kingdoms of the world, glory and power are the norm; but, Jesus says, *Not so with you* (20:26). The one who is *great* in the kingdom of heaven is the one who becomes a *servant* (20:26–27). It is vital for Jesus that the disciples understand the value of servanthood, for without it they will never comprehend the cross (20:28).

20:29–34 The journey from Jericho to Jerusalem and the entry into Jerusalem (21:1–11) are both marked by proclamations of Jesus as the expected king, the son of David. On the way from Jericho, Jesus encounters two blind men who twice implore him as *Lord, Son of David* (20:30–31). These physically blind men are the ones who can see the spiritual truth, in contrast to the physically sighted Pharisees who are spiritually *blind* (23:16).

21:1–11 Jesus' entry into Jerusalem sparks praise for the *Son of David* (21:9). Nearly half of Matthew's uses of this title occur at Jesus' entry into the city and temple (20:30, 31; 21:9, 15). The crowds who follow Jesus to Jerusalem announce him as the Christ whom they expect to bring freedom from Roman oppression and to restore the kingdom of Israel. The citizens of Jerusalem, however, ask, *Who is this*? (21:10). The issue of identity is thus central to this text, and the irony is that the crowds who hail him as the Christ fail to comprehend the true significance of that designation, as their ultimate rejection of him shows (27:22–25).

TEACHING & CONFLICT IN THE TEMPLE · 21:12–23:39

21:12–27 Jesus' first act in the *temple area* is to drive out the money changers whose economic pursuits have turned the *house of prayer* into *a den of robbers* (21:12–13). Next come three stories that interpret each other. First, the chief priests and the teachers of the law protest when children in the temple area proclaim Jesus as *the Son of David* (21:14–17). Then the next day as Jesus is returning to the temple area, he curses a fig tree for not bearing fruit (21:18–22). Finally, Jesus returns to the temple courts where the chief priests and elders question the source of his authority (21:23–27). Matthew places the cursing of the fig tree between two stories in which religious leaders in Jerusalem challenge Jesus' identity and authority as the Son of David. The tree that bears no fruit thereby serves as a symbol for the religious leaders who bring the curse of God upon themselves through their opposition to the Christ.

21:28–22:14 Jesus addresses three parables to the chief priests and Pharisees, all of which teach that because Israel's leaders reject Jesus, their place in the kingdom will transfer to others (Meier 634). In the parable of the Two Sons (21:28–32), the religious leaders are the second son who professes obedience but then fails to do the father's will, while *the tax collectors and the prostitutes* are the first son whose prior disobedience gives way to repentance. Consequently, Jesus tells the chief priests and Pharisees that these sinners *are entering the kingdom of God ahead of you* (21:31).

In the parable of the Tenants (21:33–46), a vineyard owner sends his servants (the prophets) to collect the fruit from the vineyard's tenants (the Jewish leaders). The tenants kill the servants and then the landowner's son. Jesus gives the Pharisees and chief priests an opportunity to pronounce their own sentence when he asks them what the owner of the vineyard should do to those tenants (verse 40). They reply that *he will rent the vineyard to other tenants* (verse 41). By this, they unknowingly foreshadow the transference of their place in the kingdom to the Gentiles, for Jesus states, *Therefore I tell you that the kingdom of God will be taken away from you and given to a people who will produce its fruit* (verse 43).

In the parable of the Wedding Banquet (22:1–14), invitees to a wedding banquet for the son of a king serve as representatives of the Jewish leaders. Their refusal to attend the banquet prompts the king to reject them and instead fill the wedding hall with others who accept the invitation (22:8–10).

22:15–46 As a result of Jesus' parables, the Jewish leaders desire to arrest him, but they fear the crowds (21:46). Instead they attempt *to trap him in his words* (22:15). The Pharisees and Herodians challenge him on the issue of Roman taxation (22:16–22);

Cursing the Fig Tree

This story is troubling because figs do not bloom until long after Passover and because Jesus in Matthew heals and blesses, not curses. Like the Old Testament prophets, Jesus performs a symbolic act. But what does it symbolize? The story shows both judgment on the leaders' failure to produce fruit and the power of the prayer of faith.

the Sadducees on the question of marriage at the resurrection (22:23–33), an obviously disingenuous question since the Sadducees do not believe in the resurrection (22:23); and a Pharisee tests Jesus' knowledge of *the greatest commandment in the Law* (22:34–40). In each instance, Jesus avoids the trap and responds in a manner that silences his opponents and instills amazement in the crowds.

> **The Herodians**
> Supporters of the Herod family and thus pro-Roman sympathizers, Herodians would have typically been at odds with staunchly Jewish authorities. Agreement between the Herodians and the Pharisees must therefore have been extremely unusual.

In Matthew 22:41–46, Jesus turns the tables and traps the Pharisees by quoting Psalm 110:1 (*The Lord said to my Lord*) and asking the Pharisees how the Christ could be the son of David if David calls him *Lord*. Unable to answer, the Jewish leaders no longer *ask him any more questions* (22:46). Jesus here undercuts the identity assigned to him at his entrance into Jerusalem by asserting that the Christ is more than a son of David, for he is greater than David.

23:1–39 Concluding Jesus' time in the temple is a lengthy denunciation of the Pharisees and teachers of the law. The specified audiences for this speech are *the crowds* and the *disciples*, not the Pharisees, indicating that its primary function is to contrast the way of Jesus with that of the Pharisees for the benefit of the listeners. Jesus begins by noting that the Pharisees *sit in Moses' seat*, likely a reference to an actual stone seat in the synagogue where the authoritative teacher sat (Hill 310; Mounce 214).

> **"Do everything they tell you ..."**
> In advocating obedience to what the Pharisees teach, but not conformity to their actions, Jesus employs hyperbole as a means of emphasizing Pharisaic hypocrisy. After all, Jesus has not only attacked teachings of the Pharisees elsewhere in Matthew, but even does so in this discourse (23:16–19). At the same time, Jesus agrees with the Pharisees on the importance of obedience to God.

Jesus' invective against the Pharisees and teachers of the law unfolds in three parts. In the first part, Jesus contrasts the Pharisees' lust for public honor (*Everything they do is done for men to see*; 23:5) with the disciples, who are to exchange public approbation for humble service (23:5–12).

The second part (23:13–33) contains seven pronouncements of *Woe* against the Pharisees and teachers of the law for their hypocrisy. Jesus condemns them for opposition to the kingdom of heaven and for their corrupting influence on believers (23:13–15); for disingenuous manipulation of oaths (23:16–22); for neglecting *the more important matters of the law – justice, mercy, and faithfulness* in favor of obsessive attention to lesser legal matters (23:23–24); for proudly presenting an external appearance of righteousness while internally decaying from wickedness and greed (23:25–28); and for sharing in the sins of their ancestors by rejecting and murdering God's prophets (23:29–33), a foreshadowing of their involvement in the death of Jesus.

> **"Woe to you ..."**
> The pronouncement of woes against the Pharisees contains some of the most vitriolic language anywhere in the teachings of Jesus. The Pharisees are *blind guides* and *blind fools* (23:16, 17). *They go to great lengths to make a convert only to succeed at making the convert twice as much a son of hell as you are* (23:15). *Inside they are full of dead men's bones and everything unclean* (23:27). Jesus concludes the seven woes with a final denunciation, *You snakes! You brood of vipers! How will you escape being condemned to hell?* (23:33). The harshness of this language is a reminder that the Jesus who counsels love and mercy also pronounces judgment and condemnation.

The third part of the address builds on the final woe in which Jesus condemns the Pharisees for their role in the killing of the prophets. He announces that the Pharisees will kill or persecute the *prophets and wise men and teachers* that Jesus will send to Israel (23:34–36). This denunciation of the Pharisees leads then into a similar condemnation of *Jerusalem* for its rejection of Jesus and the prophets (23:37–39).

DISCOURSE 5: INSTRUCTIONS ON THE END OF THE AGE · 24:1–25:46

Matthew 24–25 is an apocalyptic discourse on the signs preceding the destruction of Jerusalem in 70 CE and the coming of Jesus. The symbolic language of this discourse, characteristic of apocalyptic, makes any specific interpretation treacherous. Jesus seems to vacillate between those signs preceding his coming [Greek *parousia*] at the destruction of Jerusalem and his coming prior to the final judgment, and it is not always clear when he shifts from one to the other (Mounce 221).

24:1-3 The setting for this discourse occurs as Jesus leaves the temple complex and declares its eventual destruction to his disciples (verses 1–2). In response, the disciples ask two questions: when will this predicted destruction of the temple occur and *what will be the sign of your coming and of the end of the age*? (verse 3). The discourse that follows must be read as an answer to both questions, even if it is not always certain when Jesus addresses one as opposed to the other.

24:4-28 From verses 4 through 28, Jesus clearly responds to the disciples' first question by addressing the signs that will precede the destruction of the temple in 70 CE at the end of the Jewish war with Rome. From verse 29 on, Jesus' language becomes much more difficult to correlate with specific events. Preceding the destruction of the temple are *the beginning of birth pains* (verse 8), which include the appearance of false Christs (see Acts 5:36; 21:38), wars, famines, and earthquakes (verses 5–7). Persecution of the disciples will increase and the gospel will be preached among the Gentiles (verses 9–14).

These precursors lead up to the appearance of *the abomination that causes desolation*, which they will *see standing in the holy place* (24:15). In 167 BCE, the Seleucid king Antiochus IV Epiphanes profaned the Jerusalem temple by erecting a pagan altar on top of the Jewish altar (1 Maccabees 1:54). This polluting object is Daniel's *abomination that causes desolation* (Dan 9:27; 11:31; 12:11). Jesus picks up this tradition and applies it to a similar act of sacrilege in the temple that will precede its destruction, although the exact referent for his language is a matter of much scholarly debate. That it is to occur shortly before the destruction of the city is clear from the verses that follow: *those who are in Judea* must *flee to the mountains* (verse 16); people are to leave valuables behind (verses 17–18); it will be especially hard on *pregnant women and nursing mothers* (verse 19); and they are to pray that these events *not take place in winter or on the Sabbath* (verse 20), for both are times when travel becomes either difficult or restricted. Jesus describes the events of Matthew 24 as *the coming of the Son of Man* (verse 28), a phrase that need not mean his final end-time appearance, but can refer to his coming in judgment upon Jerusalem for its rejection of God's Christ.

24:29-35 When Jesus says, *Immediately after the distress of those days* (24:29), he appears to link verses 29–35 with the preceding discussion. However, the language at this point becomes much more generic and symbolic, leading some to conclude that 24:29 is the point at which Jesus begins to address the disciples' second question concerning *the end of the age* (24:3; Luz 125). The ambiguity of the language makes either possible.

> **"The sun will be darkened …"**
> *The cosmic disruption language in 24:29 of the sun and moon becoming dark, the stars falling from the sky, and the shaking of the heavenly bodies does not necessarily point to end-time activities as it is common prophetic language for God acting in history, often in the sense of bringing judgment upon a nation. See Isaiah 13:10 (Babylon), 34:4 (Edom), Ezekiel 32:7–8 (Egypt), and Amos 8:9 (Israel).*

Concluding this section is Jesus' promise that *this generation will certainly not pass away until all these things have happened* (24:34). Scholars interpret this statement in a variety of ways (see Mounce 227), but the most natural reading of it in its context is that the current generation will live to see the fulfillment of these signs. This verse makes sense if 24:4–35 deals with the events surrounding 70 CE in response to the disciples' first question, but it becomes problematic if the preceding verses refer to the final return of Jesus.

24:36-51 In Matthew 24:36–51, the language of the discourse becomes less specific and more strongly eschatological (dealing with the end time). The illustrations of Noah (verses 37–39), of the workers in the field and at the mill (verses 40–41), and of the owner of the house (verse 43) all make the point that *the coming of the Son of Man* will occur at a time that no one, not even the Son himself, can predict (verses 36, 42, 44).

Matthew 24:45 presents a question that governs the remainder of the discourse and places it in the context of discipleship: *Who then is the faithful and wise servant*? The answer is the servant who remains watchful and fulfills his or her charge while the master is away (24:46–47). Yet those servants who become disobedient because the master takes too long in returning will be dismembered and placed *where there will be weeping and gnashing of teeth* (24:48–51). This juxtaposition of faithfulness and judgment leads into three parables that expand upon these themes.

25:1–46 The parable of the Ten Virgins (25:1–13) compares *the kingdom of heaven* to five foolish and five wise virgins whose inclusion or exclusion from the wedding banquet depends upon their preparation for the arrival of the bridegroom. The parable of the Talents (25:14–30) describes the reward for servants who make money for the master during his absence. The servant who fails to produce such results ends up *where there will be weeping and gnashing of teeth*. Jesus' teaching on the sheep and the goats (25:31–46) is less a parable than an account of the criteria for final judgment (Meier 635). The coming of Jesus will inaugurate the separation of people, just as sheep are separated from goats. What distinguishes the righteous (sheep) from the unrighteous (goats) are deeds of mercy performed for the *hungry*, the *thirsty*, the *stranger*, the *naked*, the *sick,* and those *in prison* (25:35–36). Jesus thus ties his coming promises of punishment and reward to one's recognition that God desires mercy, not sacrifice. Those who grasp this earn *eternal life*, while those who fail to learn *go away to eternal punishment* (25:46).

THE PASSION · 26:1–27:56

Two motifs run throughout the Matthean passion account: the identity of Jesus and the meaning of his death.

26:1–13 The opening scenes of the passion account establish the impending death of Jesus. Two days before *the Passover*, Jesus predicts his death for the fourth time (26:2), while the chief priests and elders plot to arrest and kill him (26:3–5). Then, a woman anoints Jesus with expensive perfume for burial (26:6–13).

26:14–29 At the Passover meal, Jesus announces that one of his disciples will betray him, a disciple already revealed to the reader as Judas (26:14–16, 21). During his description of the Passover meal, however, Matthew employs a subtler means of identifying the traitor. Throughout the gospel, Matthew consistently distinguishes between insiders and outsiders to the kingdom by means of the title they use to address Jesus. Outsiders, such as the Pharisees and other religious leaders, address him as "Teacher" or "Rabbi" (the Aramaic term for "teacher"; see 12:38; 17:24; 19:16; 22:16, 24, 36). Insiders address him as "Lord" (8:2, 6, 25; 9:28; 14:28; 15:22; 16:22; 17:4, 15; 18:21; 20:30). After Jesus predicts that a disciple will betray him, all those eating with him protest, *Surely not I, Lord?* (26:22). Judas alone replies, *Surely not I, Rabbi?* (26:25). This subtle shift in title identifies Judas as the outsider and betrayer (Johnson 181).

Matthew begins the passion account by noting the proximity to *the Passover* (26:2). Then, at the outset of the passage in which Jesus institutes the Lord's Supper, Matthew includes three more references to *the Passover* (26:17–19). For Matthew, it is vital that his readers understand that the meal Jesus shares with his disciples is the Passover meal. The Passover is a celebration of God's deliverance

---

The Jerusalem Temple

Solomon built a temple in Jerusalem that became the successor to the tabernacle. Eventually this temple became a national shrine, uniting the people and providing a center for worship. The temple consisted of a porch or vestibule, the holy place that contained the lampstand, table, and golden altar of incense, and the most holy place, which originally contained the ark of the covenant. The Babylonians destroyed Solomon's temple in 586 BCE, but under the leadership of Joshua and Zerubbabel, a new temple was begun in 520 BCE and finished in 515 BCE. Throughout its history, this second temple underwent numerous alterations, culminating in the extensive rebuilding program of Herod the Great, which began in 20/19 BCE and did not conclude until about 63 CE. Only a short time later in 70 CE, the Romans destroyed the temple during the course of the Jewish War with Rome (66–70 CE).

The significance of the Jerusalem temple for the Jewish people should not be underestimated. This temple was the location of the presence of God, the sign of the covenant between God and the people, and the evidence of Jewish election. It provided both social and economic stability and became a dominant symbol of Jewish nationalism. Many Jews even ascribed cosmic significance to the temple, viewing it as the point of unification for the universe. This explains why Jesus' prediction of the destruction of the temple created such opposition and confusion (Matt 24:1–2; 26:61–62).

of the Jews from slavery in Egypt. The shedding of lamb's blood and the placing of it above the doorpost caused the angel of death to pass over the houses of the faithful during the final plague (Exod 12:12–13). For the Jews, the exodus event was God's greatest act of deliverance on behalf of the people, and that deliverance was celebrated each year with the Passover meal. Matthew's deliberate identification of the Lord's Supper with the Passover meal is thus highly significant. *While they were eating* the Passover meal, Jesus took the *bread* and the *cup* and gave it to his disciples as a reminder and celebration of his *body* and of his *blood of the covenant, which is poured out for many for the forgiveness of sins* (26:26–28). Jesus here invests the Passover meal with new meaning for a new occasion. He forces the disciples to view the cross in the context of the exodus. Just as God delivered the people from slavery in Egypt, God is now about to deliver the people from slavery to sin.

26:30–56 Jesus' prediction of Peter's denial (26:30–35), the Gethsemane event (26:36–46), and the arrest of Jesus (26:47–56) are bound together by the theme of discipleship. Retreating to the Mount of Olives, just east of the temple mount, Jesus predicts that all of the disciples will *fall away on account of me* in fulfillment of Zechariah 13:7 (Matt 26:30–31). Peter's vehement protest prompts Jesus to announce that Peter in particular will disown him three times (26:34).

Then Jesus and the disciples go to Gethsemane, a small cave with a garden nearby located at the base of the Mount of Olives. Here Jesus prays that he not have to endure *this cup*, meaning the suffering he is about to experience (26:39). Despite Jesus' own desire to avoid crucifixion, he bends his will to God's and declares, *May your will be done* (26:42). By this act, Jesus defines discipleship as sacrificing one's own will to the will of God. His decision in Gethsemane forms a model of discipleship for others to imitate.

While Jesus is at Gethsemane, Judas, who again addresses him as *Rabbi* (26:49), arrives with the authorities who arrest Jesus (26:47–56). He offers no resistance in order that *the Scriptures be fulfilled that say it must happen in this way* (26:54), a reference that all these events conform to the divine will. After Jesus again asserts that all these events occur so that *the writings of the prophets might be fulfilled*, Matthew tells us that *all the disciples deserted him and fled* (26:56).

Gethsemane is the hinge event in this section. It asserts a specific model of discipleship with Jesus subjecting his will to that of the Father. During his arrest, Jesus once more demonstrates this model as he refuses to defend himself, because to do so would violate the will of God (26:53–54). Flanking this positive show of discipleship are two events that highlight the failure of the disciples. Just prior to Jesus' arrest, a disciple betrays him (26:47–49). Then, immediately after, they all flee (26:56). This accompanying failure of the disciples further highlights Jesus' faithfulness as a disciple of God.

26:57–68 Jesus makes his first custody appearance before the Jewish high priest, Caiaphas. Matthew emphasizes the innocence of Jesus by noting the *false evidence* and *false witnesses* marshaled against him (26:59–60). Despite the false charges, the primary issue of contention is not lawless or criminal behavior but the question of Jesus' identity. Caiaphas demands an answer to this question when he says, *Tell us if you are the Christ, the Son of God* (26:63). Jesus' affirmative reply leads to a charge of blasphemy and a pronouncement of death (26:65–66).

> **Caiaphas**
>
> *Josef bar Kayafa, or Joseph son of Caiaphas (called simply Caiaphas in the gospels) was appointed by the Romans as high priest and served in that role from 18–37 CE. Caiaphas is also mentioned extra-biblically in the writings of first century Jewish historian Josephus.*

26:69–75 While the trial before Caiaphas unfolds, the crowds outside confront Peter over his association with Jesus. In fulfillment of Jesus' earlier prediction, Peter disavows knowledge of Jesus three times (26:70, 72, 74). Peter's denials, coming after Jesus' own confession of his messianic identity (26:63–64), are noteworthy for what they actually deny. Peter disowns any association with the human Jesus. The two girls who place Peter with Jesus refer to Jesus by the mundane titles of *Jesus of Galilee* and *Jesus of Nazareth* (26:69, 71). Furthermore, Peter repudiates Jesus by denying any familiarity with *the man* (26:72, 74). In this way, Peter's rejection of Jesus is more than a denial of Jesus' divine sonship or of his messianic identity, for it disowns any connection to the person of Jesus at all.

27:1–31 In Matthew 27, the death of Judas (verses 1–10), Jesus' appearance before the Roman governor Pilate (verses 11–26), and the mocking of Jesus by Pilate's soldiers (verses 27–31) form the prelude to the crucifixion. Before committing suicide out of remorse, Judas returns to the chief priests the thirty silver coins earned for his act of betrayal (27:5). The chief priests use the money to purchase a potter's field *as a burial place for foreigners* (27:7). This sets up a fulfillment quotation that Matthew attributes to *Jeremiah the prophet*, even though the subsequent quotation derives primarily from Zechariah 11:12–13, with various words and phrases contributed by Jeremiah (Hill 349). This may be an example of the practice of "assigning a composite quotation to the more prominent individual" (Mounce 253).

As with Caiaphas, Pilate also asks Jesus a direct identity question: *Are you the king of the Jews?* Jesus again offers an affirmative response (27:11). Although the charge that Jesus claims to be *the king of the Jews* appears calculated to sway Pilate (Hill 349–50), Pilate instead affirms the innocence of Jesus (27:18, 23), a position buttressed by his wife's dream (27:19). Pilate's offer to the crowd to release either Jesus or Barabbas is an attempt to wiggle out of a tense political situation, a move that fails to produce the desired result.

The scene in which Pilate's soldiers mock Jesus abounds with irony (27:27–31). They adorn him with *a scarlet robe*, *a crown of thorns*, and *a staff*. Feigning obeisance, they bow before him and hail him as *king of the Jews*. The irony is that the very identity they mock is in fact true.

27:32–56 At the outset of the Gospel of Matthew, Matthew emphasizes the identity of Jesus as the Christ, the king of the Jews, (1:1; 17, 18; 2:2, 4) and as the Son of God (2:15; 3:17; 4:3, 6). Both of these identity claims dominate Matthew's telling of the crucifixion account. To those outside the kingdom of heaven, the cross is proof that Jesus is neither *king of the Jews* nor *Son of God*, but to insiders the cross demonstrates both claims.

Written above Jesus' head on the cross is the charge laid against him: *The King of the Jews* (27:37). Those who mock him use language that echoes the early chapters of the gospel. In Matthew 1:21, the child receives the name *Jesus* because his purpose will be to *save his people*. It is also difficult not to see the return of Satan in the taunts of the crowd, for the language recalls those of the temptation narrative. Satan tempted Jesus to take matters into his own hands by turning stones into bread and by casting himself off the top of the temple. Each time Satan prefaced his temptation with the challenge, *If you are the Son of God* (4:3, 6). Likewise, the crowd beckons Jesus to take himself off the cross by adding the challenge, *if you are the Son of God* (27:40). Then, they say that Jesus should prove his identity by letting God *rescue him ... for he said, 'I am the Son of God'* (27:43). In Matthew 4, Satan tempted Jesus to assert his identity through self-centered means. In Matthew 27, Jesus now demonstrates that identity through the selfless act of the cross. Furthermore, Matthew contrasts the doubt of the Jewish crowd with the response of the Gentile centurion and the other guards who respond to Jesus' death and the subsequent earthquake by exclaiming, *Surely he was the Son of God!* (27:54).

Shortly before his death, Jesus shouts out the first verse of Psalm 22: *My God, my God, why have you forsaken me?* The recitation of the first verse of a psalm was often a means of evoking the entire context of the psalm (Hill 355). By reciting the opening of a lament, Jesus may be identifying himself with the suffering righteous man of the psalm (Meier 636). That Matthew sees the larger context of Psalm 22 as fulfilled in the crucifixion event is clear. Several aspects of Psalm 22, such as the mocking of the crowds (22:7), the taunt that God rescue the psalmist (22:8), the piercing of hands and feet (22:16), and the dividing of clothes by casting lots (22:18), all appear in Matthew's account of the crucifixion (Matt 27:35, 39–44).

One event that accompanies Jesus' death is the tearing of the temple curtain (27:51). Within the Jerusalem temple, a curtain separated the holy place from the most holy place where the presence of God resided. Matthew does not comment on the meaning of this event, but the tearing of the curtain could represent either the removal of the

> **"He saved others ..."**
> At the crucifixion, the crowds derisively call upon Jesus to *save yourself* (27:40). They point out the irony of one who saved others but appears unable to save himself (27:42). In this way, Matthew subtly highlights the continuing blindness of the crowds who fail to see that the cross is the means by which Jesus is saving his people.

MATTHEW

barrier between God and the people or an act of judgment upon Jerusalem for its rejection of God's Son, and thus a foreshadowing of the destruction of the temple in 70 CE.

BURIAL & RESURRECTION · 27:57–28:15

27:57–66 A recitation of details surrounding the burial of Jesus in a rock-cut tomb with a stone rolled in front (27:57–61) leads into a story with an apologetic edge (27:62–66). Showing the chief priests and Pharisees to be aware of Jesus' resurrection prophecy (27:63), Matthew recounts their efforts to seal the tomb and place a guard there (27:64–66). Matthew's goal is to defend the legitimacy of the resurrection by demonstrating the inability of the disciples to steal the body.

28:1–15 Matthew offers a straightforward description of the resurrection: an angel rolls back the stone of the tomb, Jesus appears to two of the women, and he announces that he will go ahead of the disciples into *Galilee* (28:1–10). Then, Matthew follows this with another apologetic story. Responding to the persistent rumor that the disciples stole the body of Jesus during the night (28:15b), Matthew assigns the origin of this rumor to an attempted cover-up by the chief priests who pay the guards to circulate it (28:12–15a).

THE GREAT COMMISSION · 28:16–20

In Galilee, Jesus meets with his eleven disciples and commands them to *make disciples of all nations* by *baptizing them* and *teaching them* (28:19–20). Matthew 1:1 announced Jesus as *the son of Abraham*, thus linking him to the covenant with Abraham through whom God promised to bless all nations. Although Jesus in Matthew orients his ministry to Israel, he also sows seeds for the Gentile mission. Here at the close of the gospel, Jesus now fully exhorts his disciples to spread the message of the kingdom of heaven to *all nations* in fulfillment of the promise to Abraham.

This final event of the gospel teaches that the appropriate response to the resurrected Jesus is worship and confidence in his continuing presence (Matera 242). The use of *inclusio* here is strong, connecting back to the opening of the gospel. Just as the magi worshiped the infant Jesus (2:11), the disciples worship the resurrected Lord (28:17). Just as the infant Jesus received the appellation of *Immanuel*, meaning *God with us* (1:23), the resurrected Lord promises that *I am with you always* (28:20).

THEOLOGICAL REFLECTIONS
ANTI-SEMITISM & SUPERSESSIONISM

More than any other biblical book, the Gospel of Matthew stands at the center of current debates over anti-Semitism. The gospel's harsh attack on Israel for its historical treatment of the prophets and the gospel's condemnation of Israel's leaders prompts accusations of anti-Semitism. Furthermore, when the Jewish crowd convinces Pilate to crucify Jesus, they do so by vowing that *his blood be on us and on our children* (27:25). This statement appears at first glance to place the blame for Jesus' death on all Jews throughout history. Indeed, it has been used to justify persecution of and animosity toward subsequent generations of Jewish people.

Matthew was a Jewish author writing to a predominantly Jewish community about issues relevant to Jewish tradition and faith. At issue is the acceptance or rejection of Jesus of Nazareth as the Jewish messiah, a choice that has profound implications for the future of Judaism. Matthew's Jesus is a prophet who, much like the Israelite prophets before him, rebukes Israel for its stubbornness, immorality, and refusal to submit to the divine plan. The plea that *his blood be on us and on our children* is not a placement of blame upon all generations of Jews, but simply an idiomatic means by which the current crowd accepts responsibility for the choice they are making. The language and theology of Matthew is thus in no way anti-Semitic in the modern sense. It is rather a dispute involving differing visions for the future of Israel. The irony is that many read Matthew as a condemnation of Judaism, when in fact it seeks

> **Matthew & Anti-Semitism**
> *Christians do themselves and others a disservice when they deny or ignore the historical influence of Matthew on atrocities against the Jewish people. However, Christians also must draw a sharp distinction between misguided interpretations and Matthew's actual teaching. Because the seemingly anti-Jewish language of Matthew operates within the context of an intra-Jewish debate (Jews arguing with Jews), charges of anti-Semitism are difficult to maintain.*

to preserve the Jewish heritage of the church (Senior, "Between Two Worlds," 6).

Closely tied to charges of anti-Semitism are charges of supersessionism. According to this charge, Matthew teaches that the church supersedes Israel. Israel stands in complete rejection by God who turns to the church as its replacement and superior. This charge is more difficult to defend against because there is an element of truth to it. Matthew does hold that God will bring judgment upon Israel for its rejection of the Christ and that such judgment involves the loss of Israel's place in the kingdom (21:43), a place that will go to the Gentiles.

However, this stress on discontinuity between church and Israel operates under the umbrella of continuity. For Matthew, the church is not a completely new entity nor an afterthought designed to cover for the unexpected faithlessness of Israel. The church is both *new* and *old* (9:16–17; 13:52). Matthew's concern is not the continuity of the nation of Israel as a political entity, but the continuity of God's promises to Israel. These promises find fulfillment in the community of the Christ so that the church does not supersede Israel, as though the issue were the faithlessness of Israel versus the faithfulness of Christians; rather, the church embodies God's faithfulness to his promises.

THE CHURCH IN TRANSITION

Matthew addresses a community in need of defining its relationship to both the past and the future. The growing chasm between Judaism and Christianity, coupled with the increasing influx of Gentiles into the church, is forcing the church to break with its past. Matthew's concern is that the church not lose its heritage and forget its Jewish roots as it moves into the future.

The church took seriously the mandate of the Great Commission to *make disciples of all nations* (28:19). In the twenty-first century, Christianity is almost exclusively Gentile. The real issue for today's church is whether we have successfully fulfilled Matthew's desire that the Gentile church not divorce itself from its Israelite heritage. A church that embraces its Israelite heritage is a church that recognizes that Abraham, Isaac, and Jacob are our ancestors and that the history, tradition, and heritage of Israel is ours. It is a church well aware that the promises God made to Israel are also promises to us.

Jesus says that the teacher who is trained about the kingdom of heaven discovers *new treasures as well as old* (13:52). The church that ignores its Jewish roots, however, abandons the old treasures in favor of the new. The Lord's Supper offers an illustration of this phenomenon. The church that has lost connection to its roots sees in the Lord's Supper only a new meal that memorializes the death of Christ and establishes a new commemorative practice for the church. The church that maintains its Jewish roots, however, recognizes the Lord's Supper as the Passover meal reinterpreted for a new context. When these Christians eat this supper, therefore, they do so in solidarity with the Israelites who have gone before them. They see the exodus in the reflection of the cross and recognize this supper as a celebration of the God of deliverance.

PARTICULARISM & UNIVERSALISM

The nation of Israel owes its origin to God's promise to Abraham to make him *into a great nation* through which *all peoples on earth will be blessed* (Gen 12:2–3). Israel is thus a nation that exists for the benefit of all nations, to become a light for the Gentiles (Isa 42:6; 49:6). The elect nation of Israel (particularism) was not chosen for its own benefit or due to its own merit, but to serve as the instrument through which God blesses all peoples (universalism). Unfortunately, Israel consistently forgot the reason for its election. When Israel turned its focus inward by exalting itself over other nations and by prioritizing the protection and maintenance of its traditions over acts of mercy, then Israel failed to fulfill its universal mission. Yet if Israel often faltered by embracing particularism to the detriment of universalism, at other times it faltered by not being particular enough.

> **Christ's Mission**
> *Matthew renews the call to Israel to fulfill its purpose in the context of the church. His interest in Jewish history and tradition and his concern that the church not lose touch with its roots betrays his particularist bent. By representing the restriction of Jesus' ministry to the lost sheep of Israel, Matthew asserts the uniqueness and election of Israel; yet Jesus' acts of mercy toward Gentiles and the Great Commission support a universal mission. The Roman centurion, the Canaanite woman, and many other Gentiles will take their places at the feast with Abraham, Isaac, and Jacob in the kingdom of heaven (8:11).*

Whenever Israel became too much like the nations around it through immorality, idolatry, and cultural compromise, it ceased to be a light.

For Matthew, the church is the community of Israel's Messiah. As such, the purpose of this community is the same as that of Israel: to be a blessing to the nations. As with Israel, the church does not exist for its own sake. Yet also like Israel, the church faces the constant temptation to lose sight of its purpose. Matthew envisions a community of believers whose light shines among the nations as they model the surpassing righteousness of the kingdom of heaven.

MERCY, NOT SACRIFICE

Many Christians view the Bible's teaching on the law of Moses as irrelevant to a church founded upon the cross of Christ. Some turn to Paul in Romans and learn that the law cannot justify one before God and then mistakenly conclude that the law is therefore no longer worthy of reflection. Yet this simplistic view stands at odds with Paul's own complex position on the law in Romans. The same Paul who argues that no one achieves justification by *observing the law* (Rom 3:28) adds that this concept in no way nullifies the law (Rom 3:31). For Paul *the law is spiritual* and *holy*, and *the commandment is holy, righteous and good* (Rom 7:12, 14). Consequently, Paul can say, *I delight in God's law* (Rom 7:22).

Such a multifaceted perspective on the law characterizes Matthew as well. Although Jesus in Matthew frequently counters common interpretations of the law and rebukes Israel's leaders for exalting legalistic observance of the law over acts of mercy, Jesus also views a correct understanding of the law as essential to his followers' understanding of the kingdom of heaven. Jesus assures us that he did not come *to abolish the Law*, but *to fulfill* it (Matt 5:17). Fulfillment of the law does not mean that he brings it to completion so that it can be abolished; otherwise Jesus would contradict himself. Fulfillment of the law means that in Jesus the law becomes that which it was intended to be from the beginning. For Jesus, mercy and love constitute the intent of the law and govern its application. Unless one reads the law through the lenses of mercy and of love for God and neighbor, one does not read the law correctly. In this Jesus and Paul agree (see Rom 13:8, 10).

The conflict between Jesus and the Pharisees in the gospel of Matthew holds profound implications for the church. Jesus identifies the key distinction between his view of the law and that of the Pharisees as their inability to grasp the meaning of Hosea 6:6: *I desire mercy, not sacrifice*. Jesus encourages them to *go and learn what this means* (Matt 9:13) but then later rebukes them for failing to do so. His statement, *If you had known what these words mean* (12:7), indicts the Pharisees for their lack of understanding. Their hypocrisy stems from a blindness to *the more important matters* (23:23).

> **Religious Complacency**
> *The unfortunate temptation is to discount Jesus' attack on the Pharisees as a first century dispute with a religious party that no longer exists. However, Jesus' condemnation of the Pharisees stands as a constant warning to all disciples. Not all Pharisees were of the sort that Jesus condemns. His words are less an attack on a religious party than they are an attack on a corrupted understanding of the kingdom of heaven. All disciples are in danger of falling into the same deception. The question that the church should constantly ask itself is whether Jesus would confront it with the same accusation,* If you had known what these words mean, 'I desire mercy, not sacrifice,' you would not have ... (12:7).

REPENTANCE & JUDGMENT

Much of contemporary Christianity currently shies away from the topics of repentance and judgment. Love and grace are far more palatable messages in our culture, and they grant us a view of God and of Jesus that allows us to feel more comfortable when we lie down to sleep. Yet this perception of God is not a more accurate one. Scripture tells us that *God is love* (John 4:8), but Scripture also affirms that *God is a consuming fire* (Heb 12:29). Throughout the Bible, God's grace and God's wrath stand in constant tension. The God who loves and forgives and rains down mercy is the same God who destroys and punishes and rains down fire. Until the church learns to become comfortable living within that tension, it does not accurately reflect the God of Scripture.

Matthew's Jesus embodies this tension. He is a proclaimer of love and mercy, yet he is also a fire and brimstone preacher. Warnings about the fire of judgment permeate his teaching (Matt 5:22; 7:19; 13:40–42; 18:8–9; 25:41). He follows the model of John the Baptist in calling upon people to repent of their sins. Jesus in Matthew is both prophet and divine judge, calling people to repent and warning of God's judgment. This message does not, however, contradict Jesus' proclamations of love and mercy. Grace does not nullify judgment but stands alongside it. The key to repentance, the proof of righteousness, and the basis for judgment or reward in Matthew is whether one bears fruit in acts of love and mercy (see 24:34–46).

Matthew models for the church a balanced theological message that embraces the tension between grace and mercy rather than recoiling from it. It suggests that Christians are to proclaim and live lives of love and mercy yet also be a prophetic voice in the world calling for repentance and warning of the reality of divine judgment. The message of grace is more comfortable for us, and it allows us to coexist more peacefully with our culture, but unless the message of grace walks hand in hand with that of divine wrath, it is not a faithful representation of the preaching of Jesus.

THE AUTHORITY OF CHRIST

Matthew's presentation of Jesus is rich and multi-layered. I have discussed much of Matthew's Christology elsewhere in this commentary and it does not bear repeating here. But central to Matthew's presentation is the authority of the Christ. The most significant theological titles for Jesus in Matthew are Son of God and Son of Man, especially if Son of Man derives from Daniel 7, because they are titles that communicate divine authority. Throughout Matthew, Jesus, in both word and action, presents himself as greater than Moses, Solomon, Jonah, the Sabbath, and even the temple. Possibly Jesus' self-proclamations of superiority may represent an assertion of authority surpassing that of the Jewish Scriptures represented by the threefold division of the Law, the Prophets, and the Writings (Johnson 189).

As Son of Man, Jesus has *authority* [Greek *exousia*] to forgive sins (9:6). He grants *authority* to his disciples to heal and cast out evil spirits (10:1). His authority creates division in Israel. The crowds marvel at the *authority* displayed in his teachings and actions (7:28–29; 9:8), while debate over the source of his authority forms a crucial part of the conflict with Israel's leaders (12:24; 21:23–27). Finally, the gospel concludes with Jesus' assurance that *all authority in heaven and on earth has been given to me* (28:18).

The authority of the Christ is the lifeblood of the church. Without that authority, the church withers and dies. It is only because Jesus possesses *all authority in heaven and on earth* (28:18) that the church can make disciples and teach (28:19). The church, however, must continually acknowledge the authority of Christ over it or risk losing connection to Jesus through assertions of self-will. The church is the obedient disciple, bending its will to the authority of its Lord and acknowledging that the same authority that allows it to teach and make disciples will also stand in judgment of the church as faithful servant. But if the authority of Christ carries with it a note of warning, it primarily serves the church as a source of great comfort. That Jesus possesses *all authority* is the basis for the church's confidence. All disciples can move boldly forward, carrying their crosses after the pattern of Christ and witnessing fearlessly to the world because they know that the one they worship possesses *all authority in heaven and on earth*, and that that authoritative presence will be with them *always, to the very end of the age* (28:20).

FOR FURTHER STUDY

David E. Aune, ed. *The Gospel of Matthew in Current Study* (Grand Rapids: Eerdmans, 2001).

Craig L. Blomberg, *Jesus and the Gospels: An Introduction and Survey* (Nashville: Broadman and Holman, 1997).

W. D. Davies, *The Sermon on the Mount* (Cambridge: Cambridge University Press, 1966).

Robert A. Guelich, *Sermon on the Mount: Foundation for Understanding* (Waco: Word, 1982).

Craig S. Keener, *A Commentary on the Gospel of Matthew* (Grand Rapids: Eerdmans, 1999).

John P. Meier, *The Vision of Matthew: Christ, Church and Morality in the First Gospel* (New York: Paulist, 1979).

Mark A. Powell, *God With Us: A Pastoral Theology of Matthew's Gospel* (Minneapolis: Fortress, 1995).

Calvin J. Roetzel, *The World That Shaped the New Testament* (Louisville: Westminster John Knox Press, 2002).

WORKS CITED

W. F. Albright and C. S. Mann, *Matthew* (New York: Doubleday, 1971).

B. W. Bacon, "The 'Five Books' of Matthew against the Jews," *The Expositor* 15 (1918): 56–66.

Richard A. Batey, "Jesus and the Theatre," *New Testament Studies* 30 (1984): 563–74.

David R. Bauer, "The Literary and Theological Function of the Genealogy in Matthew's Gospel," in *Treasures New and Old: Recent Contributions to Matthean Studies* (eds. David R. Bauer and Mark Allan Powell; Atlanta: Scholars Press, 1996), 129–59.

Virgilio C. Corbo, "Capernaum," in *Anchor Bible Dictionary* 1 (1992): 866–69.

Donald A. Hagner, "Matthew, Gospel According to," *International Standard Bible Encyclopedia* (1986) 3:280–288.

———, "The *Sitz im Leben* of the Gospel of Matthew," in *Treasures New and Old: Recent Contributions to Matthean Studies* (eds. David R. Bauer and Mark Allan Powell; Atlanta: Scholars Press, 1996), 27–68.

David Hill, *The Gospel of Matthew* (Grand Rapids: Eerdmans, 1972).

H. W. Hochner, "Herodian Dynasty," in *Dictionary of New Testament Background* (2000): 485–94.

Luke Timothy Johnson, *The Writings of the New Testament: An Interpretation* (Philadelphia: Fortress, 1986).

Josephus, *Complete Works* (ed. H. St. John Thackeray; Loeb Classical Library; 10 vols.; Cambridge: Harvard University Press, 1926–1965).

Jack Dean Kingsbury, *Matthew As Story* (2d ed.; Philadelphia: Fortress, 1988).

Ulrich Luz, *The Theology of the Gospel of Matthew* (trans. J. Bradford Robinson; Cambridge: Cambridge University Press, 1993).

Brice L. Martin, "Matthew on Christ and the Law," *Theological Studies* 44 (2001): 53–70.

Frank J. Matera, "The Plot of Matthew's Gospel," *Catholic Biblical Quarterly* 49 (2001): 233–53.

John McRay, *Archaeology and the New Testament* (Grand Rapids: Baker, 1991).

John P. Meier, "Matthew, Gospel of," in *Anchor Bible Dictionary* 4 (1992): 622–41.

Robert H. Mounce, *Matthew* (Peabody, Mass.: Hendrickson, 1991).

Origen, *Contra Celsum* (trans. and ed. Henry Chadwick; Cambridge: Cambridge University Press, 1953.

J. A. Overman, *Matthew's Gospel and Formative Judaism: The Social World of the Matthean Community* (Minneapolis, Minn.: Fortress, 1990).

A. J. Saldarini, *Matthew's Christian-Jewish Community* (Chicago: University of Chicago Press, 1994).

Donald Senior, "Between Two Worlds: Gentiles and Jewish Christians in Matthew's Gospel," *Catholic Biblical Quarterly* 61 (2001): 1–23.

———, *What Are They Saying about Matthew?* (New York: Paulist Press, 1983).

Klyne Snodgrass, "Matthew and the Law," in *Treasures New and Old: Recent Contributions to Matthean Studies* (eds. David R. Bauer and Mark Allan Powell; Atlanta: Scholars Press, 1996), 99–127.

Graham N. Stanton, *A Gospel for a New People: Studies in Matthew* (Edinburgh: T. & T. Clark, 1992).

James F. Strange, "Galilee," in *Dictionary of New Testament Background* (2000): 391–98.

———, "Nazareth," in *Anchor Bible Dictionary* 4 (1992): 1050–51.

Mark

Allen Black

CHAPTER CONTENTS

Contexts 761
Commentary 762
    Prologue · 1:1–13 762
    The Galilean Ministry · 1:14–8:30 763
    The Journey to Jerusalem · 8:31–10:52 773
    The Last Week: Jerusalem, the Cross & the Resurrection · 11:1–16:8 777
Theological Reflections 787
For Further Study 788
Works Cited 788

MAPS, TABLES & FEATURES

The Messianic Secret 764
The Twelve 766
"Sandwiches" in Mark 767
Jesus & Divorce 776
Interpreting Mark 13 780
Jesus & the Safe People 782
Jesus' Trial Before the Sanhedrin 784
Other Endings for Mark's Gospel 787

Mark's story of Jesus focuses on two major themes – Christology and discipleship – and develops them in two sections. The two halves of the book turn on Peter's confession (8:27–30).

With respect to Christology, the first half of Mark centers on Jesus' authority. Mark informs the reader that Jesus is the Christ, the Son of God, in the first verse. The characters in the story (the crowds, the religious authorities, and the disciples) do not know his identity but repeatedly encounter his authority from 1:2–8:29. John the Baptist teaches it, Jesus' teachings reveal it, the demons reveal it (although he then silences them), and his miracles reveal it. Yet until Peter's confession, no human being identifies Jesus as the Messiah. Multiple texts in the first eight chapters either use the word "authority" (for example, 1:22, 27) or imply the concept (for example, 4:41).

The first half of the gospel emphasizes the need for faith and submission to Jesus' authority. Disciples are called to "follow" (1:17–18, 20; 2:17–18). The importance of faith is consistently emphasized (explicitly in 1:15; 2:5; 4:40; 5:34, 36; 6:6). Throughout the first half of the gospel, the disciples struggle to discern what they are to believe about Jesus (4:41).

The second half of the gospel begins when Peter confesses Jesus to be the Christ in 8:29. Throughout the second half, the focus of both the Christology and discipleship themes revolves around servanthood. In the stories that begin with Peter's confession, it becomes apparent that the disciples misunderstand Jesus' messiahship as an earthly kingship and their own discipleship as routes to chief places in that kingdom. Jesus repeatedly seeks to teach them that *whoever wants to become great among you must be your servant, and whoever wants to be first must be slave of all. For even the Son of Man did not come to be served, but to serve …* (10:44–45). He had come to show them how to give themselves up in service to others. This is the heart of Mark's teaching for the church.

CONTEXTS

We can be much more confident of the themes and structure of Mark than of its authorship, date, place of composition, and so on. The majority of scholars consider Mark to be the first of the four canonical Gospels and date it at least as early as the early 70s. Beyond that there are many opinions.

It is reasonable to believe that the title is correct in assigning the book to Mark and that Papias was correct when he described Mark as the companion of Peter and claimed that Mark's gospel contained Peter's

> **Papias**
> *Papias was a bishop of Hierapolis who wrote about 120–130 CE. Martin Hengel has written the best defense of the title and of the Papias tradition, even arguing the surprising conclusion that a biographical writing would have needed a title from the beginning and that Mark himself was responsible for it (Hengel 48–56, 96–106).*

stories of Jesus (Eusebius 3.39.15). Acts 12:12 and 1 Peter 5:13 connect Mark to Peter.

The often untrustworthy late second-century writer Clement of Alexandria places the composition of Mark in Rome (Eusebius 6.14.5–7). On this he may be correct. The reference to Babylon in 1 Peter 5:13 is apparently a cipher for Rome and would place Mark there. And there are many Latinisms in the book, although mostly for military, judicial, or economic items that would be found outside of Rome as well as in it (see Guelich xxix–xxxi).

Wherever Mark worked, he wrote to an audience that included a large number of Gentiles. This becomes clear especially in 7:3–4 where he explains ritual cleansing practices that he says are common to all Jews. His readers are also probably Christians. He often assumes they know about certain Christian concepts that he mentions but does not explain, such as Jesus baptizing in the Spirit (1:8). He is writing for Gentiles who do not know Jewish customs, yet he often assumes familiarity with the Old Testament. Modern scholars have often assumed Mark wrote for a particular church or regional group of churches to address issues arising there. But recently Hengel and others have challenged this model (Hengel 77, 101; Bauckham 9–48). It may be preferable to think of Mark as writing for Gentile Christians in various geographical locations across the Roman Empire.

Many assume Mark's readers are undergoing persecution (Lane), but few texts in Mark specifically address persecution, and there are many texts on subjects that do not seem particularly relevant in a tract to support persecuted Christians. Perhaps we should conceive more broadly of Christians needing a call to servant discipleship, sometimes in persecution and sometimes in other circumstances (see Best 52–53).

The late-second century church fathers Irenæus and Clement of Alexandria differ over whether Mark wrote before or after Peter died (Clement's *Hypotyposes* according to Eusebius 6.14.5–7; Irenæus 3.1.1). Modern discussion usually revolves around the predictions in Mark 13 or the probable use of Mark by Matthew and Luke (Donahue and Harrington 41–46). Mark is rarely dated past the early seventies. A date as early as the late fifties would be possible.

COMMENTARY
PROLOGUE · 1:1–13

The opening verses of Mark provide an important orientation for the reader. Here one learns (among other things) that Mark is a theological narrative that presents Jesus as Christ and Son of God, interprets his story as the fulfillment of Old Testament prophecy, and issues a summons to confess sins and repent.

1:1 In Mark's opening line, *the beginning of the gospel about Jesus Christ, the Son of God*, the reference to *the beginning* probably refers to the preparatory work of John the Baptist rather than to the entire Gospel of Mark (Guelich 6–7). But the entire book of Mark could, of course, be fairly labeled *the gospel about Jesus Christ*. The word *gospel* [Greek *euangelion*] had a wide range of use in the first century similar to our modern phrase "good news." Its use in early Christianity is particularly reminiscent of its use in the Septuagint, the Greek translation of the Old Testament, to refer to God's coming salvation (for example, Isa 61:1).

In this opening verse, Mark tells his audience that Jesus is *Christ* and *Son of God*. The English words "Christ" and "Messiah" are respectively based on the Greek *christos* and Hebrew *mashiah*, words that both mean "anointed one." Because of the convention of anointing kings, it was common to use the terms "christ" or "messiah" for the expected eschatological king of Israel.

1:2–3 In the best manuscripts, Mark mentions only Isaiah in his introduction to the quotation. However, verses 2–3 are a blended

> **The Son of God**
> *God refers to Jesus as* Son *at Jesus' baptism (1:11) and transfiguration (9:7); and at the foot of the cross, a centurion describes Jesus as God's son (15:39). This idea also appears in 3:11; 5:7; 12:6; 13:32; and 14:36, 61. In the Old Testament, the "son of God" concept does not indicate deity. It is used for angels, the nation of Israel, and Israel's kings (for example, Exod 4:22–23; 2 Sam 7:14; Job 1:6). God's statement in 2 Samuel 7:14 concerning David's descendant that "I will be his father and he will be my son" apparently led some Jews to describe the hoped-for messiah as son of God, but without any idea that he would be deity (Collins 154–72). However, in the early Christian context in which Mark wrote, it is appropriate to consider deity as a potential connotation of the concept.*

citation of Malachi 3:1, elements of Exodus 23:20, and Isaiah 40:3. By inserting elements of Exodus 23:20 into Malachi 3:1, altering "my way" to *your way*, and altering "paths for our God" to *paths for him*, Mark has made the citation more fitting for the activity of John the Baptist as a forerunner for Jesus (Donahue and Harrington 61).

This citation is important not only for setting the activity of John the Baptist in the framework of prophecy, but also for indicating that the entire story of Jesus is a fulfillment of Old Testament prophecy. It resonates with the statement in 1:15 that *The time has come … The kingdom of God is near*. Mark does not use the fulfillment theme as frequently as the other Gospel writers, but he does use it in several key instances.

1:4–8 Verses 2–3 say that God will send a messenger to prepare the way. Verses 4–8 show who that messenger was, where he delivered his message, what it was, and for whom he was preparing. In accord with the citation, John began his ministry before Jesus, conducted it in a desert region, and called upon the people to confess their sins and repent in view of one who was coming after him.

For the large crowds who came to John (verse 8), he administered a *baptism of repentance for the forgiveness of sins*. Apparently those who repented and were baptized in the Jordan by John received forgiveness of sins as would those who responded to Peter a few years later on the day of Pentecost (Acts 2:38). However, unlike that later Christian baptism, those who accepted John's baptism did not receive the Holy Spirit. John specifically differentiates between himself and Jesus with *I baptize you with water, but he will baptize you with the Holy Spirit*. This baptism in the Spirit is not explained in Mark's gospel, suggesting Mark presumed that his audience would already know about it. It is equivalent to the *gift of the Holy Spirit* received in Christian baptism according to Acts 2:38 (see the interconnections of Acts 1:4–5; 2:16–21, 33, and 38–39).

1:9 *At that time Jesus came from Nazareth* is the only naming of Jesus' hometown in Mark, although he is repeatedly called a Nazarene (1:24; 10:47; 14:67; 16:6), and one event takes place in "his hometown" (6:1–6).

1:10–11 Jesus' baptism highlights his identity through the rending of the heavens, the descent of the Spirit, and God's declaration from heaven (verses 10–11). *Heaven being torn open* suggests a revelation from God as in Ezekiel 1:1, Acts 7:56, and Revelation 19:11. Mark does not say why the Spirit descends upon Jesus at his baptism. Perhaps it identifies Jesus as the one who will baptize in the Spirit (see 1:8) or commissions him for his mission (see 1:14–15; Isa 61:1–3). The declaration from heaven confirms Jesus' divine sonship. It echoes the end of 1:1 and is in turn echoed by the heavenly voice at the transfiguration in 9:7. *You are my Son* probably alludes to Psalm 2:7 and *whom I love; with you I am well pleased* to Isaiah 42:1.

1:12–13 Mark's account of Jesus' temptation in the desert is brief, although it is possible that he presumes his audience knows more about the story than he reports. At the least, his Christian readers knew that Jesus did not succumb to temptation. His primary point here is continued emphasis on Jesus' unique identity: he is led by the Spirit, unharmed by wild animals, and served by angels.

THE GALILEAN MINISTRY · 1:14–8:30

1:14–15 The work of John the Baptist, Jesus' baptism, and the forty days in the desert are all preparatory. They set the stage for Jesus' public ministry, which takes place in and around *Galilee*, and *after John was put in prison*. Mark's one-word characterization of Jesus' message is that it is the "gospel," the same word found in 1:1, but in 1:14 and 15 translated *good news* in the NIV. Unlike 1:1, where "gospel" seems to refer to the good news about Jesus, here it refers to the good news Jesus preached. This word "gospel" is modified by *of God*, meaning either the good news about God or the good news from God, or both.

In more than one word, Jesus' message is the gospel that *The time has come … The kingdom of God is near*. The first clause is better translated by the NRSV's *the time is fulfilled*, which rightly reflects the idea of the fulfillment of prophecy. The second clause has been the subject of much discussion for over a century. Some have argued that for Jesus the kingdom is wholly in the future, others that it is already realized (and so the sentence means "the kingdom is here"). Most now agree that Jesus believed the kingdom was both dawning in his own ministry and yet still to come in its fullness, giving birth to the common proposal that for Jesus the kingdom was "already, but not yet" (France 91–93).

According to Mark, the essence of Jesus' message is that the kingdom is dawning and that this good news calls for a response of repentance and belief.

Repentance is perhaps first because only those who repent and seek God will be able to see and believe in the dawning of the kingdom of God.

Some consider the introduction to Mark to be 1:1–15. I have chosen to treat 1:14–15 as the opening verses of the Galilean ministry. They clearly serve an introductory function in either case. At the end of the first fifteen verses, Mark introduces his two major themes of Christology and discipleship. Most of the introduction is about Jesus' identity as Christ and Son of God. But Mark also indicates that the gospel involves a summons to belief and repentance.

1:16–20 To some extent, these two short episodes highlight the authority of one whose *Come, follow me* brings about an immediate and radical following. More prominently, they are stories of discipleship, introducing the first disciples and describing discipleship as imitating Jesus in fishing for people, a metaphor for preaching the gospel of the kingdom. Peter, Andrew, James, and John form the nucleus of followers who will be both positive and negative examples of discipleship for Mark's audience.

1:21–28 Capernaum was a small village on the western shore of the Sea of Galilee. The central theme of this story is Jesus' authority. It is demonstrated by both his teaching and his exorcism. Verses 23–26 report the first of four exorcisms Mark describes. The exorcisms demonstrate Jesus' identity in two ways – by his ability to cast out the unclean spirit (Mark calls them *unclean spirits*, or *demons*, not *evil spirits* as in the NIV) and by the spirits' identification of Jesus as God's Son (see 1:34; 3:11; 5:7). When this spirit identifies Jesus as *the Holy One of God*, Jesus *sternly* commands him to *Be quiet*! This is the first occurrence of a phenomenon in Mark commonly designated the "messianic secret."

Verse 28 marks the first of many times that Mark comments on the spreading fame of Jesus. Some of the phenomena usually included under the messianic secret theme are not directed at keeping Jesus' messiahship secret but at reducing the spread of his fame as a miracle worker.

1:29–34 Capernaum is identified as the location of the home of Peter and Andrew. When the sun had set, the Sabbath was over and so the people *brought to Jesus all the sick and demon-possessed*. Concerning his refusal to allow the demons to identify him, see the comments above on 1:24–25.

1:35–39 Mark tells us little about Jesus' personal prayer life. On three occasions (1:35; 6:46; 14:32–42) he seeks a place of solitude to be alone with the Father. *Everyone is looking for you!* suggests that there are other sick and demon possessed persons waiting for Jesus in Capernaum. However, Jesus' fundamental mission is not to heal but to preach the good news of the kingdom. He therefore sets out on a preaching tour *throughout Galilee*, often preaching in synagogues. His message is accompanied by healing.

1:40–45 Healing a leper is a remarkable miracle. It is also remarkable that *Jesus stretched out his hand and touched him*, since leprosy causes uncleanness. But in Jesus' case the influence of touch reverses directions.

In verse 41 instead of *filled with compassion* the TNIV begins with *Jesus was indignant*. This reflects a textual variant accepted as the preferred reading by many commentators who commonly suggest that Jesus is angry at the suffering caused by the disease (for example, France 117–18).

Mark describes Jesus' commands to the former leper in strong language, perhaps suggesting that Jesus anticipates the leper's noncompliance. Although some include Jesus' command to silence in the messianic secret theme, what is to be kept

---

The Messianic Secret

The clearest instances of Mark's messianic secret are when Jesus tells the disciples not to tell anyone he is the Christ (8:30) and when he tells Peter, James, and John not to tell about the transfiguration until after he has risen from the dead (9:9). The instances in which he silences demons seem to be along the same line. This is not as clear in 1:25 when he tells the demon to be quiet *as it is in 1:34 when he would not let the demons speak because they knew who he was* and *in 3:11–12 when the demons identify Jesus as the Son of God and he gave them strict orders not to tell who he was.*

Mark does not explain the rationale behind Jesus' request for secrecy. Two suggestions have the most merit. Jesus may be concerned about stirring up messianic fervor and through it, stirring up political powers such as Herod Antipas who might be interested in bringing his ministry to an end before its time. Or he may urge secrecy because no one, as is later illustrated even by his disciples, could understand his messiahship properly until after his death (see France 31–32, 330–31).

secret here is not Jesus' messiahship, but the healing miracle itself (compare 5:43; 7:36; 8:26). The motivation for this command to silence is provided in verse 45: *Jesus could no longer enter a town openly but stayed outside in lonely places.* The second part of the command, *go, show yourself to the priest and offer the sacrifices that Moses commanded for your cleansing*, may have caught Mark's attention because it shows Jesus' adherence to the Mosaic law, an issue that arises in the controversy stories of 2:1–3:6.

The five stories in 2:1–3:6 report conflict between Jesus and the religious authorities. They are loosely related to each other in time and place and are gathered together by common themes. In each story Jesus or his disciples violate the recognized norms among many pious Jews, especially the religious authorities. This results in a challenge, which usually comes from those authorities. Jesus then defends his or his disciples' behavior, usually by asserting his special authority.

2:1-12 Jesus returns to Capernaum, presumably to Peter's house (the NIV's *he had come home* is an unlikely paraphrase of *he was in a [the] house*). There are so many people that they overflow into the street. This creates a situation in which four men who are bringing a paralytic to be healed decide to go up on the roof, work their way through it, and lower him down to Jesus.

All five men (assuming the paralytic himself was part of the plan) thus give a powerful demonstration of great faith. Mark 1:15 has already mentioned the importance of faith, and Mark will highlight faith repeatedly throughout the book. But everyone present must have been shocked when Jesus forgave the paralytic's sins. (In this case, there may be a connection between the man's sins and his paralysis; compare John 5:14). The teachers of the law are appalled, thinking within themselves, *Who can forgive sins but God alone?* In defining what Jesus does here as blasphemy, the scribes are using a broad definition which could include any "word or act detracting from the power and glory of God" (Twelftree 75).

Jesus defends his authority to forgive sins by healing the paralytic and enabling him to carry his mat before the crowd. His remark in verse 10 contains the first use of the title *Son of Man*. This is the title Jesus uses most frequently for himself in Mark (14 times), but it is also the most difficult title to define. The allusion to Daniel 7:13 in connection with this title in Mark 14:62 indicates that Jesus would relate it to Daniel's vision of one "like a son of man" who receives a kingdom from God. It may be that Jesus uses it partly because it is ambiguous at the time of his ministry and yet if understood correctly it points to the exalted figure of Daniel 7 (Marshall 775–81).

2:13-17 Although the parallel in Matthew 9:9–13 may indicate that *Levi* is another name for the apostle Matthew, Mark does not make the connection. In Mark, the point of the call of Levi is that he is a tax collector, a member of a despised group from which one would not expect Jesus to call a disciple. From the standpoint of the religious authorities, it was shameful for Jesus to have table fellowship at a tax collector's house, especially with other *tax collectors and "sinners."* (The NIV's quotation marks around *"sinners"* suggests the term refers primarily to breaking ritual rules rather than to immorality. I am inclined to see the term as including both.) Jesus responds that it is precisely sinners that he has come to find. Jesus does not mean to imply that the religious authorities are healthy and *righteous*.

2:18–22 This time it is not the religious authorities (the teachers of the law or the Pharisees) who interact with Jesus. However, the issue at hand involves the behavior of the Pharisees, although John's disciples fasted as well. In the Old Testament fasting was only required on the Day of Atonement, but it was commended as pious behavior (for example, Esth 4:1–3).

> **Fasting**
> *The seventh chapter of the early Christian text* Didache *(dated to about 100 CE) instructs Christians,* "Do not fast like the hypocrites on the second and fifth days of the week, but fast on the fourth and the sixth days...."

In the time of Jesus, as verse 18 indicates, many pious Jews fasted regularly.

Jesus responds with three brief metaphors (Mark would call them parables). In the first, he compares himself (or his teachings about the kingdom) to a *bridegroom*. As long as the bridegroom is present at the wedding feast, no one fasts. It is a time of joy and feasting. *When the bridegroom is taken from them*, then it is appropriate to fast. From our standpoint, we can see here an allusion to Jesus' death that would not have been recognizable to his contemporaries.

The metaphors of the *patch* and the *wineskins* are parallel to each other. The point is that the new circumstances (the *unshrunk cloth*, the *new wine*) created by the inbreaking kingdom of God bring about a situation in which, at least for a time, fasting (part of the old garment, the old wineskins) is not appropriate (see verse 20).

2:23–28 From most modern Christians' point of view, the disciples' picking and eating grain as they pass through a field is not an instance of *doing what is unlawful on the Sabbath*. We might want to suggest that Jesus' reply should have been that the disciples were innocent of the charge leveled against them (see 3:2–4). However, Jesus accepts the accusation and argues that their violation of the law is justified. By way of defense, Jesus uses a case in which David and his men violated the law of God and did so legitimately. It was another case involving food and hunger, although David and his men did not break the Sabbath law but rather the law concerning who can eat the consecrated bread. He was justified because he and his men were hungry and because he was God's anointed king.

According to 1 Samuel 21:1–6, Ahimelech was the high priest who gave David and his men the consecrated bread. Abiathar was Ahimelech's son who became high priest at a later time. The translation of the Greek preposition governing Abiathar in Mark 2:26 is subject to debate. The NIV translation *in the days of Abiathar the high priest* opens the possibility that the bread incident happened during Abiathar's life but before he became high priest.

Either verse 27 or verse 28 could serve as the climactic saying of this story. The first would put the emphasis on human need in interpreting the law. In the case of Jesus' disciples and in the case of David and his men, hunger justified the violation involved: *the Sabbath was made for man*. The second would place the emphasis on the special status of the two leaders involved. David could make the decision to eat the consecrated bread because he was God's anointed, and Jesus could grant his disciples their violation because *the Son of Man is Lord even of the Sabbath*. Both points are important conclusions, but the context of the five controversy stories of 2:1–3:6 tends to highlight verse 28 and the issue of Jesus' authority. Sabbath violation cannot occur at will or for light reasons.

3:1–6 Each gospel has one or more stories about controversy over Jesus healing on the Sabbath (Mark 3:1–6 = Matt 12:9–14 = Luke 6:6–11; Luke 13:10–17; 14:1–6; John 5:1–18; 7:21–24; 9:13–16). Note that in the present case, Jesus' comments (*Which is lawful on the Sabbath*: *to do good or to do evil, to save life or to kill?*) contrast what he is doing with what the religious authorities are doing. Jesus is doing good and saving life. They are doing evil and killing (see verse 6).

Ironically, the Pharisees who are so concerned about Jesus working on the Sabbath go out *immediately* (a better translation than the NIV's *then*) while it is still the Sabbath and plot to kill Jesus. This plot is the climax of the five controversies in 2:1–3:5. The Pharisees plot with the *Herodians*, concerning whom we know very little. They are only mentioned here, in Mark 12:13, and once in Josephus (*War* 6.16.6). The name suggests they were supporters of the Herods.

3:7–12 In chapter 1, Mark calls attention to Jesus' growing fame and popularity in Capernaum (1:33, 37) and then throughout Galilee (1:39, 45). Now he extends the scope of that fame southward to *Jerusalem* and all *Judea* and even down to *Idumea*, eastward to regions *beyond the Jordan*, and northwest to *Tyre and Sidon*. Jesus was not only famous in those regions, but people were coming from them to see and hear him and to be healed by him. The reference to the need for the boat is another of Mark's several comments about the intensity of the crowds (1:45; 2:4). On the demons' identification of Jesus and his silencing of them, see the comments on 1:24–25.

3:13–19 Mark describes the calling of the four fishermen in 1:16–20 and of Levi in 2:13–14 (although he does not identify him as Matthew). He has spoken of Jesus having disciples in 2:18, 23 and 3:9. Now

---

The Twelve

In the list of the Twelve, the order of the names has some significance. Peter is listed first and is the most prominent apostle in Mark. James and John are next – even though it would seem natural to list Andrew after Peter. But the three listed first are singled out as a special group on more than one occasion. It is also interesting that they are the only ones who receive special nicknames from Jesus. Judas Iscariot is listed last, and the reason is stated.

Matthew 9:9 identifies Matthew as the tax collector known in Mark 2:14 as Levi. Luke 6:16 uses the name Judas son of James for Thaddaeus. The NIV's description of Simon as the Zealot *comes from Luke 6:15. Mark 3:18 and Matt 10:4 call him Simon "the Cananaean," from an Aramaic word meaning "enthusiast" or "zealot."*

> **"Sandwiches" in Mark**
>
> This is the first of Mark's "sandwich sections" in which one story is framed by another. The story of the family coming to seize Jesus resumes in verse 31 after the story of the accusation that Jesus casts out demons by the power of the prince of demons.
>
> The complete list of sandwich stories in Mark includes Jairus's daughter and the woman with the hemorrhage (5:21–43), the mission of the Twelve and the death of John the Baptist (6:6b–44), the cursing of the fig tree and the cleansing of the temple (11:12–25), Judas betrays Jesus and a woman anoints Jesus with oil (14:1–11), and Peter's denials and Jesus' trial before the Sanhedrin (14:53–72). In these special "sandwich sections," the two stories relate thematically to each other.
>
> In the case of the family coming to seize Jesus and the accusation that he casts out demons by demons, they present two incorrect views of Jesus: that he is a lunatic or that he gets his power from Satan.

Jesus selects twelve of those disciples whom he can send out as his apostles (the phrase *designating them apostles* is omitted from most ancient textual witnesses but is present in two of the most reliable manuscripts). The word "apostle" is the noun form of the verb "send." These twelve men will be sent to extend Jesus' preaching mission and will even receive from him *authority to drive out demons*.

3:20–30 Mark has little to say about Jesus' family (see also 6:3). Here, in chapter 3, they seem concerned about Jesus' mental health because someone is saying, *He is out of his mind*. At least some in the family seem to take this seriously and go with the intention to *take charge of him*.

As the NIV footnote indicates, the Greek text does not say *Beelzebub*, but Beelzeboul. The NIV is relating the accusation to the god of Ekron referred to in 2 Kings 1. Whether or not that is correct, it is clear that Jesus' accusers intend this word to point to Satan, *the prince of demons*.

Note that verses 23–27 call Jesus' proverbial replies "parables." We usually use the term "parable" in a more narrow sense. The Gospels use it broadly, including any proverbial or metaphorical statement. Jesus' point is a simple one. Why would Satan fight against himself? In fact, Jesus' ability to cast out demons shows that he has been able to bind Satan.

By identifying the Spirit that empowered Jesus as Beelzebul, Jesus' opponents have blasphemed, or come dangerously close to blaspheming, the Holy Spirit. He says that other sins and blasphemies *will be forgiven…. But whoever blasphemes against the Holy Spirit will never be forgiven; he is guilty of an eternal sin*. France makes the useful observation that "the vast majority of pastoral cases involving those who fear that they have committed or might commit 'the unforgivable sin' have little or nothing to do with what this saying is talking about. It is a warning to those who adopt a position of deliberate rejection and antagonism, not an attempt to frighten those of tender conscience" (France 177). Blasphemy of the Holy Spirit is contextually defined in verse 30.

3:31–35 These verses resume the story begun in verses 20–21. Jesus' family now arrives with the intention of taking charge of him because of his presumed mental impairment. In a society that was much more oriented toward family honor than ours, Jesus' remarks must have seemed even more startling than they do to modern readers. He often uses startling, even shocking, rhetoric to teach important spiritual principles. Jesus' true family are those who do God's will.

4:1–9 The setting for Jesus' teaching in parables resonates with 3:9, where the great crowds by the sea caused him to use a boat. Jesus describes the results of a farmer sowing seed on four different types of ground: a path, a rocky area, an area full of thorns, and good soil. The results are predictable. The one yield that needs the most explanation for modern readers is the good soil. A yield of 30-, 60-, or 100-fold means a yield of thirty, sixty, or one hundred times the amount of seed sown. With ancient farming methods a yield of 4- or 5-fold would be typical and a yield of 30- to 100-fold would be wildly successful (McIver 606–08).

Immediately before the parable of the Sower, Jesus urges his audience to *Listen*. And here at the end of it he says, *He who has ears to hear, let him hear*. He is not calling for physical hearing, but for understanding. The problem of understanding Jesus' parables continues throughout this section (compare verses 10–13, 23, 24–25, 33–34).

4:10–12 It is evident from verse 13 that when his followers ask Jesus *about the parables*, at least part of what they do not understand is the meaning of the parable of the Sower. In response Jesus says that *the secret of the kingdom of God has been given to* the disciples, *but to those on the outside everything is said in parables*. The secret may be the fact that the kingdom of God was dawning in Jesus, which would provide an important hermeneutical clue for understanding the parables (Lane 158). The parables obscure as much as they explain.

Jesus spoke in parables to those on the outside *so that* they would not understand, repent, and be forgiven. The words are from Isaiah 6:9–10. In both cases God has already passed judgment on the guilty. *Those on the outside* would presumably be Jesus' opponents, as in 3:6 and 3:22–30. Jesus' use of parables was not meant to obscure the message from everyone, or he would not have repeatedly urged his listeners to hear and understand (for example, 4:9).

4:13–20 This is the first of many occasions when the disciples do not understand Jesus. The relationship between Jesus' two questions is not clear. The point may be simply that the Sower is a typical parable; so if the disciples do not understand it, they will also fail to understand others. But Jesus may be treating the Sower as key to understanding the other parables (France 204).

Jesus interprets the parable in an allegorical fashion. It describes four different ways in which people receive the word, the gospel of the kingdom. Some, under Satan's influence, refuse to receive it. A second group receives it joyfully, but in a shallow manner: *when trouble or persecution comes ... they quickly fall away*. A third group receives it but allows *the worries of this life, the deceitfulness of wealth and the desires for other things* to choke it out. The fourth group receives it, and in them the word produces an incredible harvest. The main thrust of the parable is to summon the listeners to respond like the fourth group. Because of the superabundant harvest, the parable also serves to encourage those who sow the word.

> **Allegory**
> Normally, parables have just one key point, with the details of the story contributing to it. Jesus interprets some parables' details in specific symbolic ways, however.

4:21–25 As noted in the comments on 3:23, the evangelists use the term "parable" broadly. Mark would call these sayings parables. Unfortunately, they are more difficult to understand than most of Jesus' parables.

Beginning with verse 21, it appears that Jesus addresses the crowds again. He has been speaking with the disciples alone in verses 10–20. But verses 33–34 indicate that at some point after verse 20 he turns again to the crowds, to whom he speaks in parables. The parabolic form of verses 21–25 indicates that they are addressed to the crowds. So does the appeal for understanding in verse 23 (see verse 9).

The statement about the lamp is easy to understand on a literal level. But what spiritual concept does Jesus have in mind? Verse 22 indicates that it is something that is hidden or concealed that is meant to be disclosed or brought out into the open. Many suggest that it is the presence of the kingdom of God in the ministry of Jesus (for example, Guelich 231–32).

4:26–29 The last two parables of chapter 4 are similitudes, extended similes, introduced with explicit comparisons: *the kingdom of God is like*. The first is a declaration that the kingdom of God will reach fruition. The seed being sown will reach a harvest. The ending of verse 26 and beginning of verse 27 also have special significance: the sower *does not know how* the seed sprouts and grows because it grows *all by itself*. So also the sower of the word of the kingdom does not know how the results are brought about: God is in charge of the harvest.

> **The "Good Soil"**
> The key to being like good soil in one's reception of the word, or to grasping the sometimes hidden gospel of the kingdom's presence in Jesus, lies in the heart of the listener. Those with spiritual hearts will be drawn even closer to God. Those with hard hearts will find their hearts growing harder.

4:30–32 In this similitude, the point is made by contrasting the smallness of the mustard seed with the large size of the plant. The beginnings of the kingdom of God in the ministry of Jesus may appear unimpressive, but the outcome will be great.

4:33 This verse indicates that Jesus did not intend for his parables to conceal the message from all who came to hear him who were not his disciples. He used parables to the extent that they could be understood. On the other hand, verses 10–12 and 24–25 suggest they also deliberately hide the message from the hardhearted. Mark says that parables dominated Jesus' public teaching and that he made a regular practice of explaining them to his disciples.

4:35–41 This is the first of four miracles (4:35–5:43) that together demonstrate Jesus' power over nature, demons, disease, and death. They are powerful demonstrations of Jesus' authority in a variety of areas. But they also teach important lessons about discipleship, emphasizing faith in Jesus and how it can conquer fear.

The *furious squall* on the Sea of Galilee must have been serious to scare even the fishermen into thinking they might drown. Yet Jesus easily stills the storm and then rebukes the disciples for their lack of faith and their consequent fear. Presumably, they should have had faith in Jesus and known that God would protect him and his mission. The unanswered question *Who is this*? will be answered by the disciples in chapter 8. But at this point in Mark, the disciples do not know his identity.

5:1–20 The location of this story is plagued by text critical problems stemming from the geographical problems associated with each possible locale: Gerasa is 30 miles from the southeast shore of the lake, Gedara is 5 miles, Gergesa is an unknown location, but possibly associated with a site known as Kursi on the northeast shore (Gundry 255–56). The southeast shore has no steep banks.

The description of the demoniac in verses 2–5, the name of the demon (Legion, a Roman military division of several thousand men), and the demons' control of two thousand pigs combine to underscore the radical nature of this case of demon possession. This appears to be the worst case Jesus encounters.

As in other cases (1:24, 34; 3:11–12) the demon recognizes and identifies Jesus, although we do not know whether Jesus ordered him to be silent. If not, it could be because the only ones present besides Jesus and the demoniac were the disciples. It is unusual that Jesus permits the demons to enter the pigs, but the outcome is that their hosts are drowned.

The reaction to Jesus in the Decapolis, a predominantly Gentile region, is different than the reaction in Galilee. Instead of flocking to him, this crowd is afraid and asks him to leave. The difference helps explain the difference in Jesus' instructions to the former demoniac. In Galilee, he had told many not to tell others that he had healed them. In the Decapolis, he urges the former demoniac to *go home ... and tell them how much the Lord has done for you*. In modern terms, he has too much publicity in Galilee, not enough in the Decapolis.

5:21–43 This is another example of two sandwiched episodes. The story of the woman with the hemorrhage occurs within the story of Jairus's daughter. The two stories are thematically interrelated as both demonstrate Jesus' awesome power and call for faith to triumph over fear.

As Jesus walks with *Jairus* to heal his *daughter*, a noteworthy miracle occurs that illustrates Jesus' power and emphasizes the need for faith. Mark sets the scene by noting that the woman had suffered *for twelve years* and *spent all she had* on many doctors but only *grew worse*. She believes that if she could but touch Jesus' clothes, she will be healed. And so it is. It is also striking that Jesus, pressed by the crowd on every side, knows of the touch and the healing. He uses this moment to commend the woman for her faith. She is perhaps fearful partially because the cleanliness laws forbid her to touch Jesus. Yet Mark's readers know she need not be (see 1:41–45).

The climactic miracle of this sampler of sorts is the raising of Jairus's daughter, the story begun before the healing of the woman with the hemorrhage and completed after it. Jairus has already demonstrated great faith in asking Jesus to come and heal his dying daughter. However, the real test comes when he hears that his daughter has died. In the clearest summons yet, Jesus urges both Jairus and the reader, *Don't be afraid; just believe.*

At Jairus's house, Jesus first singles out Peter, James, and John as witnesses of a special incident. In the little girl's room he takes her by the hand, speaks to her one brief phrase in Aramaic, the common language of Palestine in Jesus' day, and she stands up and walks. In the light of his other use of Aramaic, it is unlikely that Mark intends the Aramaic to take on the connotations of a magical phrase. More likely, he is using it for vivid portrayal of the scene (France 240). The command *not to let anyone know about this* is problematic, since many already knew that the girl had died. What Jesus may have intended was that no one know for a period of time until he could leave (so Lane 198–99).

6:1–6A Jesus' hometown was, of course, Nazareth (see 1:9 and comments). This incident in Nazareth is a story about faith, or rather, the lack of it. Despite their knowledge of his miracles and their amazement at the wisdom of his teaching, the people of Nazareth are offended at the local boy whose family they know and whom they know as just a carpenter. Mark says the extent of their disbelief amazed Jesus and kept him from working many miracles there. Christology and discipleship continue to wind their way through each unit of Mark's collection and often in the form of Jesus' authority and the need to accept it in faith. In this case, Jesus' healing ministry is hindered by the Nazarenes' lack of faith. See Matthew 13:53–58 and Luke 4:18–30 for other versions of this episode.

6:6b–13 When Jesus called the fishermen in 1:16–20 he told them they would fish for people. In 3:13–19 he chose twelve apostles to send out to preach. He now sends the Twelve to extend his own mission both in preaching the message of repentance and in miraculous healing. There are ongoing questions concerning the rationales behind Jesus' specific instructions (Gundry 308–9). He may send the apostles in pairs for moral support, because of the danger of traveling alone, or due to the need for two witnesses according to the Old Testament (Deut 17:6; 19:15; see Guelich 321). The instructions about provisions and not changing (to better?) quarters perhaps enhance their dependence on the Lord to provide through others (Moloney 122).

Jesus gives the apostles authority to heal and exorcize. Anointing the sick with oil is also mentioned in James 5:14. Oil was used medicinally in antiquity (see Luke 10:34), but it was also used symbolically (as in the anointing of kings and priests). Here it surely has some symbolic value, for the apostles have received the authority to work miracles (and not just to heal by normal means).

6:14–29 Although other instances stand out more clearly, this account is part of a sandwich section recounting the death of John before the story of the mission of the Twelve (6:7–13) is completed in 6:30–31. In most of the sandwich sections, there is a clear thematic relationship between the two stories. In this case the relationship is more distant, but apparently John's death foreshadows the eventual fate not only of Jesus but also of the Twelve as they carry out their ultimate mission.

In keeping with Mark's messianic secret theme, both here and in 8:27–28 the popular speculations about Jesus do not include that he might be the Messiah. Rather, the people think he might be a great prophet like those of the Old Testament, or Elijah (see Mal 4:5–6), or John the Baptist raised from the dead.

Herod Antipas, one of the sons of Herod the Great, ruled Galilee and Perea from 4 BCE to 39 CE. The Jewish historian Josephus (about 37–120 CE) includes information about Antipas's illegitimate marriage to his half-brother's wife and about his putting John the Baptist to death, although he differs from Mark at some points (Black 117–20). Apparently, Antipas had two half brothers both named Philip, sharing the same name because they had different mothers. Philip the tetrarch later married Salome, Herodias's daughter who danced for Antipas. Herodias herself was married to another Philip. John's criticism focused on incest: *It is not lawful for you to have your brother's wife*. The Old Testament commands levirate marriage, but only after a woman is widowed.

The primary points for Mark are John's courage in standing for God's will and how his story foreshadows the treatment of Jesus, the Twelve, and others. It is a story that encourages others to imitate John in the face of evil.

6:30–44 The feeding of the 5,000 is the only one of Jesus' miracles that all four gospels record (Matt 14:13–21; Luke 9:10–17; John 6:1–15). The importance of this miracle for Mark is apparent in his reference to it in 6:52 as a key incident for the disciples' understanding, in the way he develops the feeding of the 4,000 (8:1–10), and in Jesus' use of both feeding incidents in his rebuke of the disciples in 8:17–21. Multiplying five loaves of bread and two fish to feed 5,000 men is spectacular both in the nature of what Jesus does and in the scope of the witnesses.

As on many previous occasions, Mark highlights the massive crowds that come to see Jesus (1:45; 2:2; 3:7–10, 20; 4:1; 5:24). He and his disciples go to a remote place to rest, but his compassion compels him to teach the crowd.

At the end of the story, we learn why it would take two hundred *denarii*, each one worth approximately one day's wage for a common laborer, to feed the crowd. It is composed of thousands. When Mark reports the number fed at the end of the story, he says there were 5,000 *men*. The term he uses is not the generic term for men and women, but a more specific reference to males. Matthew 14:21 says, *there were about five thousand men, besides women and children*. Jesus feeds them with a few loaves and fish and recovers leftover food.

6:45–52 This is the second of three boat scenes (4:35–41; 8:13–21) in which there are significant encounters between Jesus and his disciples. Sending the disciples ahead in a boat, Jesus again seeks a place of solitude to pray (see 1:35). Although Mark's references to Jesus' prayer life are brief, they indicate Jesus' seriousness about prayer. In chapter 1, he goes out early while it was still dark. In chapter 6, he prays into the fourth watch of the night, which begins about 3:00 a.m.

This incident is found in every gospel except Luke (Matt 14:22–33; John 6:16–21). There are two miracles involved: walking on water (against a strong wind) and calming the wind (upon entering the boat).

Many interpreters see added christological import in two phrases of this story. First, based on Exodus 33:19–23; 34:6; 1 Kings 19:11; and Job 9:8–11, they believe that the statement *he intended to pass them by* (NRSV; the NIV translation obscures the idea) is an allusion to appearances of God (Donahue and Harrington 213). However, the context of Mark suggests the phrase be taken literally (according to France 272). He is not concerned that the disciples will not outlast the wind. Second, many see the statement "It is I" as an allusion to Exodus 3:14 where Moses learns God names as "I Am" (Donahue and Harrington 213). However, in Mark's context it is more natural to understand it as a simple response to the disciples' fear that Jesus is a ghost. *It is not a ghost*, he implies; *no, it is I* (see France 272–73).

The disciples' amazement resonates in their reaction to Jesus calming the storm in 4:41. Mark says they were amazed because *they had not understood about the loaves*. As noted in the comments on 6:30–44, he puts a heavy emphasis on the feeding miracles. He also says that the disciples do not understand because *their hearts were hardened*. In 3:5 Jesus' opponents' hearts are also hardened. This is Mark's strongest indication yet that the disciples are not developing as well as they should be.

6:53–56 The disciples had started sailing for Bethsaida (6:45), but land at Gennesaret, perhaps due to the wind. Mark tells us that there, and wherever else Jesus goes, people bring the sick to him for healing. They are healed, even if they only touch the edge of his cloak.

7:1–23 In comparison with most sections of Mark, this one is long (23 verses). It has significance for Mark's interest in Jesus' authority, in discipleship, and in the controversy between Jesus and the religious authorities. Mark may also be interested in the cleanliness issue as it bears upon the church of his own day and the relationship of Jews and Gentiles within it.

Exodus 30:17–21 requires priests to wash their hands and feet before entering the tabernacle, but there are no Old Testament laws requiring everyone to engage in regular ritual cleansing of their hands or of various utensils except at certain festivals. However, the Pharisees extended these purity rules to all Jews in an effort to enhance the piety of the nation. By the phrase *and all the Jews*, Mark indicates both that this perspective was widespread among the Jews and that the readers of his gospel included many non-Jews.

The essence of Jesus' reply is in verse 8: they *are holding on to the traditions of men* and *have let go of the commands of God*. He supports this charge with a citation from Isaiah 29:13, an example from the *Corban* tradition, and a statement about what truly makes a person unclean. In Jesus' context, the words from Isaiah refer to those who ostensibly honor God but are upholding human traditions. Jesus here does not contradict Jewish tradition, only abuses of it.

As a specific example of adhering to a human tradition in a way that overrules God's commands, Jesus brings up the *Corban* tradition. It was a vow by which one gave his or her possessions to God but still could retain use of them. Jesus criticizes the way some abused this vow so that even if a person's parents were in need, he or she could not help them (and so fulfill the divine command to honor them) because of the vow (see Marcus 445–46).

Jesus also sees the case at hand as another instance where the religious authorities were committed to human rules but did not care much about God's commands. He states his point in a proverbial and parabolic (see verse 17) manner. What goes into a person is not what defiles him or her. Rather, it is what comes out: evil thoughts, sexual immorality, theft, murder, etc.

Mark 7:19 notes that in the words of 7:14–23 Jesus declared all foods clean. It is doubtful that any of Jesus' hearers on that day thought he was permitting them to violate the Old Testament dietary laws.

> **Caring for the Sick**
>
> *Jesus and early Christians addressed the health care of some populations partially excluded from normal society by the Levitical system of purity. Some healings are miraculous, while others use known medical techniques (see James 5).*

The discussion was, from the beginning, not about the law, but about traditions. However, decades after Jesus spoke these things, Christians like Mark could look back in the light of later revelation and see that the implications of Jesus' words extended beyond what could be understood at that time (Lane 255–56). In the church of Mark's day, it might have been important to bring out this inference due to the issues that divided Jews and Gentiles.

7:24–30 Jesus attempts to escape the crowds of Galilee by going into the Roman province of Syria to the *vicinity of Tyre*. Mark clearly portrays the mother of the demon-possessed child as a *Greek*, not a Jew. He is attracted to this story for several reasons: it illustrates Jesus' authority in a spectacular way (he casts out the demon without going to where the girl is), it illustrates the importance of faith, and it touches on the Jew/Gentile issue (as had 7:1–23). The second and third topics are both portrayed in a way that unnerves modern readers. Jesus' parabolic statement about *children* and *dogs* strikes contemporary readers as racist. However, in their ancient setting the important feature that would stand out is that Jesus crosses racial barriers by talking to the woman and healing her daughter. It is also significant that the word he uses for "dog" is the diminutive form (that is, for pets, not wild dogs) and that his saying has a proverbial ring to it. Both observations diminish the idea that he is simply calling Gentiles "dogs."

> **Jewish Missionaries**
>
> *In the first century, some Jews sought to convert Gentiles to the worship of the one true God. Evidence for their work comes mostly from Christian sources, however, so it is difficult to know how extensive such Jewish missions were or what vision of the Law they espoused.*

7:31–37 The route Mark describes for Jesus is certainly not a direct journey to Galilee. However, a deliberately circuitous route fits well with verses like 7:24 (which tells us Jesus went to Tyre to keep his presence unknown) and 9:30 (in which Jesus and his disciples are traveling through Galilee, but he does not want anyone to know because he is teaching his disciples). This route brings Jesus through the Decapolis, which causes many to conclude that the man involved in 7:31–37 is a Gentile (see Guelich 394). However, many Jews also lived in the Decapolis, and Mark could easily have indicated that this man was a Gentile if he had wished (as he did for the Syrophoenician woman).

Several features of this healing are unusual. Jesus does not normally use physical gestures such as putting his fingers in the man's ears or putting saliva on his tongue. (See the comments on 8:23 concerning the use of saliva.) On the other hand, Jesus does occasionally use such conventional miracle-working gestures. The sigh and the Aramaic *Ephphatha* ("be opened") are also unusual. In a few instances, such as this one and 5:41, it is hard to discern why Mark provides the Aramaic except as local color.

Again Mark says Jesus tries to keep those whom he heals from spreading the word everywhere, but to no avail. The public reaction is by now expected. The last part of verse 37 alludes to Isaiah 35:5–6.

8:1–10 As noted in the comments on the feeding of the 5,000, Mark puts significant emphasis on the feeding miracles, particularly their importance as signs for the disciples. Verse 4 indicates that the disciples still do not understand the theological significance of the feeding of the 5,000 (compare 6:52). But Jesus performs a roughly equivalent miracle, feeding 4,000 (Matt 15:38 says *besides women and children*) using only seven loaves of bread and a few fish, with seven basketfuls of food left over. Some argue that the feeding of the 4,000 was primarily for Gentiles because Jesus is still in the Decapolis where he had been since 7:31 (France 305). This is questionable, however, since many Jews lived in the Decapolis and Mark makes no reference to Gentiles in this story (see Gundry 396).

8:10 Once again Jesus and his disciples cross the Sea of Galilee, this time to Dalmanutha, a location unknown outside of Mark's gospel.

8:11–13 Although the Gospel of John uses the term "sign" repeatedly to designate Jesus' miracles, Mark does not. Here the word designates something Jesus refuses to grant his opponents, probably either a cosmic apocalyptic event or a direct message from God (Guelich 413–14).

8:14–21 Jesus' metaphorical statement about the evil influence of the Pharisees and Herod Antipas becomes the catalyst for his rebuke of the disciples' lack of understanding. This is the third occasion in which a boat trip across the Sea of Galilee is the setting for an important interaction between Jesus and his disciples (see 4:35–41; 6:45–52).

Mark 3:5 describes Jesus' opponents as hard-hearted. The word in Mark does not mean lacking in compassion, but lacking in perception and thus unable to act appropriately. But in chapter 8 it is the disciples whose hearts are hard. After the feeding of the 5,000, *they had not understood about the loaves; their hearts were hardened* (6:52). Now, after the feeding of the 4,000, Jesus rebukes them for not understanding the implications of the miraculous feedings, reminding them of the spectacular numbers in each case. What is it that Jesus expects them to understand (verses 17–18, 21)? Certainly, they should grasp the metaphorical nature of Jesus' reference to yeast (see Matt 16:8–12). But they should grasp the implications of the feeding miracles for the messianic identity of Jesus.

8:22–26 The healing of the blind man contains several intriguing features. One is that Jesus takes the man out of the village to perform the miracle and then sends him home, instructing him not to return to the village. This maneuver is often considered part of the messianic secret theme. But it might be simply a means of avoiding the massive crowds that such miracles incite (see, for example, 1:23–45; 7:24).

The most intriguing feature of this story is that at first the blind man does not see clearly. He only sees clearly after Jesus put his hands on his eyes a second time. Although this detail may seem inexplicable, it makes excellent sense when understood in the light of Mark's narrative as a whole and its portrait of Jesus and the disciples. In Mark, the disciples have exhibited blindness with respect to Jesus' identity throughout the first half of the narrative. Just before the blind man's healing, Jesus makes the point using the metaphor of sight: *Do you still not see …? Do you have eyes but fail to see …?* (8:17–18). In the story immediately after the healing of the blind man, they do come to see that Jesus is the Christ, but their vision is impaired. Throughout the remainder of the book they do not understand what it means for Jesus to be the Christ. Jesus performs the healing of the blind man in two stages to symbolize the stages in the disciples' developing understanding. Read in the light of Mark's narrative as a whole, it is an appropriate miracle to appear immediately before Peter's confession in 8:27–30.

8:27–30 *Cæsarea Philippi* was east of Galilee and roughly as far north as Tyre. In both cases, Jesus leads his disciples to the surrounding villages, presumably to spend time alone with them. Cæsarea Philippi was Herod Philip's capital, named Cæsarea to honor Augustus and Philippi for himself.

When Jesus asks who people say he is, the disciples' response mirrors the opinions Mark reports in 6:14–15. In both cases, speculation that Jesus is the Messiah is absent.

Peter's response on behalf of the disciples marks the climax of the first half of Mark's gospel. The disciples now understand that Jesus is the Messiah. In 4:41 they ask, *Who is this that even the wind and the sea obey him*? Now they know the answer. Unlike the crowds, the disciples know that Jesus is the Christ. (On the terms "Christ" and "messiah," see the comments on 1:1.) Although there were divergent ideas among first century Jews about what the Messiah would be like, there is reason to believe that many, including Jesus' disciples (see Mark 10:35–37), were looking for "the Davidic messiah as the warrior king who would destroy the enemies of Israel and institute an era of unending peace" (Collins 68).

Jesus implicitly affirms Peter's identification, but he *warned them not to tell anyone about him*. This is the fundamental text in Mark for the messianic secret theme. Related texts include 1:24–25, 34 and 3:11–12 in which Jesus prohibits demons from identifying him, and 9:9 where he orders three disciples not to tell about the transfiguration until after his resurrection. Unfortunately, Mark never explains Jesus' motive. See the comments on 1:23–25 for two possibilities.

THE JOURNEY TO JERUSALEM · 8:31–10:52

8:31–9:1 Peter's confession marks a turning point in Mark's gospel in terms of geography, Christology, and discipleship. Geographically, Jesus begins to journey toward Jerusalem, a point that becomes clearer with each passion prediction (9:30; 10:32). Christologically, he begins to tell them about his coming rejection,

---

Healing with Saliva

Modern readers find it odd that Jesus uses saliva in healing the blind man, but Mark's audience would not. The first century author Pliny the Elder wrote of the medicinal value of saliva as an eye salve (Natural History 28.7.37). *And saliva was sometimes used for miraculous healing. In his* Histories (4.81), *the Roman historian Tacitus describes an incident in which a blind man is healed by the saliva of the emperor Vespasian (reigned 69–79 CE). Apparently Jesus chose to use a culturally recognized method of miraculous healing.*

death, and resurrection. And with respect to discipleship, he begins to tell them what following a suffering, dying messiah means for his followers.

The first prediction begins with the enigmatic phrase *Son of Man*. As stated in the comments on the first use of this title in 2:10, Jesus may have used it partly because it was ambiguous, but it could be tied into his own interpretation of the son of man figure of Daniel 7:13. The substitution of *Son of Man* for *Christ* would not provide any clues to help the disciples to grasp the idea that Jesus was going to be rejected and killed. His prediction was virtually incomprehensible to Jews of his day, including his disciples. It compounded the problem to think that those who would oppose him would be the Jewish leaders who make up the Sanhedrin: *the elders, chief priests and teachers of the law*.

In referring to the resurrection, Mark is the only gospel to say that Jesus will rise *after three days* (8:31; 9:31: 10:34); Matthew and Luke say *on the third day* (Matt 16:21; 17:23; 10:19; Luke 9:22; 19:33; see 24:7, 46). Mark is perhaps using an idiom in which "after three days" means "the day after tomorrow" (as in Josephus, *Jewish Antiquities*, 7:280–281; 8:214, 218; see France 336–37).

Peter finds Jesus' prediction unacceptable and *began to rebuke him*. But Jesus turns the tables quickly and strongly, calling Peter *Satan* and accusing him with *you do not have in mind the things of God, but the things of men*. After rebuking Peter, Jesus calls the other disciples and the crowd together and teaches the implications of a suffering, dying savior for those who would follow him. Jesus has just mentioned his death but has not designated the way in which he will die. Verse 34 indicates crucifixion: those who would follow Jesus must take up their own crosses. Of course, for most disciples the crosses are metaphorical. The same is true of the concept of losing one's life. For most it is metaphorical, but for some it is literal. In cases where losing one's life is metaphorical, saving one's life could be understood as a spiritual reality that begins before physical death. However, the context of verse 38 suggests Jesus might primarily have in mind life after death as the reward. Those unwilling to deny themselves and who try to save themselves in this life will lose out in the life to come when the Son of Man comes in glory. The concepts in verses 34–38 lie at the heart of Mark's purpose in writing and will appear again in chapters 9 and 10.

Mark 9:1 fits closely with 8:38 and should have been identified as 8:39. It underscores the warning of 8:38 with assurance of the coming of the kingdom. It is a highly debated text with several possible interpretations. Some believe it refers to an event soon after Jesus' death, like the resurrection or the day of Pentecost (Moloney 177). However, the contextual connection to 8:38 seems to require a close relationship to the second coming. Taking *the kingdom of God having come with power* to refer to what will happen at the second coming does not necessarily mean Jesus was wrong about the timing, for his prophecy could be considered conditional, like some predictions in the Old Testament (Gundry 466–69, 790). However, a number of interpreters believe he is speaking of the transfiguration, when a few of those present at the prophecy of 9:1 will see Jesus in a prefiguring of the glory of his second coming (Lane 312–14; compare 2 Pet 1:16–18).

9:2–13 Whether or not the transfiguration is the fulfillment of the prophecy in 9:1, it is clearly confirmation of Peter's confession in 8:29. Jesus takes the three that he had chosen to witness the raising of Jairus's daughter and allows them a dazzling mountaintop glimpse of his coming glory.

Further wonders accompany the awesome glory of the transfiguration of Jesus. One is that Elijah and Moses appear to talk to Jesus. Mark does not explain why these two might be chosen, but perhaps it is because they were both associated with eschatological expectations (Deut 18:5; Mal 4:5–6). In any event, it is not surprising that the disciples are frightened. Peter's suggestion of building something (perhaps shelters of branches and leaves; see France 354) for each man becomes the catalyst for yet other startling events: the cloud and the voice. The first part of the message uttered by the voice echoes the beginning of the message from heaven at Jesus' baptism. The NIV obscures the parallel. The NRSV shows it clearly: *You are my Son, the Beloved* in 1:11 mirrors *This is my Son, the Beloved* in 9:7. Here, in the center of his text, Mark has placed a clear affirmation of Jesus' identity as the Christ (8:29) the Son of God (9:7; 1:1).

This is the classic text providing a time frame for the messianic secret. The disciples are not to proclaim what they have seen *until the Son of Man had risen from the dead*. It seems odd that the disciples would wonder *what "rising from the dead" meant*. They may wonder this because they did not accept

Jesus' prediction of his death or because they associated rising from the dead only with the corporate resurrection of all humans at the end time.

Mark has already made reference to people speculating that Jesus is Elijah in 6:15 and 8:28. The disciples' question refers to the belief that Elijah will come before the Day of the Lord or perhaps before the Messiah. Since we have no pre-Christian sources for a belief that Elijah would precede the Messiah, the former is more likely (see Mal 3:1; 4:5; *Ecclesiasticus* 48:10; see Collins 116). When Jesus says Elijah has come, he presumably has John the Baptist in mind (compare Matt 11:13–14; 17:13). The remark about doing to him (Elijah) as it is written about him probably is a typological use of the sufferings of the Old Testament Elijah. As Elijah was, so Jesus will be. Jesus wants to change their focus to the sufferings of the Son of Man, which he says are also a matter written about in the Scriptures. In other parts of Mark he alludes to or quotes at least three passages that predict his passion: Psalm 118:22–23 (Mark 12:10–11), Isaiah 53 (Mark 10:45), and Zechariah 13:7 (Mark 14:27). The focus on Jesus as the messianic Son of Man and on his coming suffering are the primary thrusts of the transfiguration account and the accompanying discussion.

9:14–29 Mark tells this story, in which Jesus casts out a demon the disciples have been unable to exorcize, as a call to prayer and faith. The first clear call for faith comes in verse 19, when Jesus decries the *unbelieving generation* he must *put up with*. In this he includes his own disciples, who do not have the faith needed to cast out this demon (Moloney 184–85).

Some of the boy's symptoms are similar to epilepsy, but clearly Mark presents this case as more than epilepsy. It involves loss of speech and hearing (verses 17, 25), and the convulsions are guided by a malevolent force (verses 20, 22). The call to faith continues in Jesus' conversation with the boy's father. Jesus tells the father and the reader of Mark: *Everything is possible for him who believes*, to which the father responds for us all. The focus rests on the one in whom we believe, not on the act of belief itself.

Jesus indicates that some demons are more difficult to cast out than others. The statement that *this kind can come out only by prayer* suggests that the disciples are not showing adequate faith in and dependence on God but have perhaps become confident in their own powers. The importance of faith appears a third time in this story.

9:30–32 Jesus' attempt to find time alone with his disciples begins at the point of Peter's confession in chapter 8, if not earlier (compare 7:24). This is the second of three similar reports of teaching about his coming death and resurrection. The only addition here over 8:31 is that he will *be betrayed into the hands of men*. Mark's response that *they did not understand what he meant* seems to be a regression from their initial reaction in 8:32 (Donahue and Harrington 284; compare Luke 9:45). After the interchange with Peter in 8:32–33, it is understandable that they *were afraid to ask him about it*.

9:33–37 There is a pattern in the context of each of the three passion predictions: the prediction, the disciples' failure to understand Jesus and themselves, and Jesus teaching what his suffering servanthood means for them. Verse 32 declares that the disciples do not understand Jesus' prediction concerning himself. Verses 33–34 demonstrate they do not understand their own role as being one of servanthood. They are arguing about who is the greatest. In verses 35–37, Jesus addresses their selfish attitudes and urges them to be willing to *be the very last, and the servant of all*.

9:38–41 This story continues the theme of humility and servanthood. The issue here is not that the man was a charlatan or only appeared to be casting out demons in Jesus' name. The issue for the disciples is *he was not following us* (NRSV; the NIV mistranslates this clause). Once again Jesus needs to correct the disciples' attitude. The disciples should not oppose those who support them. They should be thankful for anyone who even *gives ... a cup of water* because they *belong to Christ*.

9:42–50 The context of verses 36–41 provides a fluid basis for the antecedents of *these little ones who believe in me*. There is the little child in verses 36–37, the unknown exorcist in 38–40, and the one who gives a cup of water in verse 41. Jesus probably means any fragile believer. It would be better to drown in the sea than to cause one of these to sin.

The parallel comments about dismembering the hand, foot, and eye stress the dire importance of not being a cause of sin to others. In each case, the consequence of causing others to sin is being *thrown into hell* [Greek *gehenna*]. Verse 48 quotes Isaiah 66:24, that in hell *their worm does not die, and the fire is not quenched*. Certainly, any sacrifice is worth it if one can avoid such a place.

Verses 49–50 are difficult to understand and to connect to the context. To some extent they are connected by catchword association (verses 48–49 "fire"; verses 49, 50a, and 50b "salt"). Perhaps the reference to being *salted with fire* in verse 49 is based on the practice of salting grain offerings before offering the sacrifice (Lev 2:13). These verses probably speak about those who do not enter hell but pass through another kind of fire, a sacrifice. Verse 50b connects these two verses to the main point of verses 33–48. The disciples must make the necessary sacrifices to maintain peace with each other. They must consider themselves last and servants of others. This attitude seems to be the metaphorical meaning of salt in this text (Moloney 192).

> **"If the salt loses its saltiness ..."**
> *Concerning verse 50a, ancient salt could lose its saltiness because it was contaminated. The salt itself could be leached out leaving other minerals (France 385).*

10:1–12 This story is another example of controversy between Jesus and the religious authorities (see 2:1–3:6; 3:22–30; 7:1–15; 8:11–13). The Pharisees' question about divorce sits against two well-known backdrops: the marriage of Herod Antipas and Herodias (who divorced their spouses to marry one another), and the debate between the rabbinic schools of Hillel and Shammai. According to later tradition, Shammai held that divorce was only acceptable to God if one's spouse had violated the marriage sexually, but Hillel accepted a wide range of reasons, even if one's wife "spoiled a dish for him" (*m. Gittin* 9.10). The response to Jesus' question indicates that this group of Pharisees were probably Hillelites: divorce is permissible as long as one provides *a certificate of divorce* (see Deut 24:1–4).

Jesus is no Hillelite. In his response, he cites Genesis 1:27 and 2:24, interpreting 2:24 to mean that in marriage God takes two persons and makes them one. The divorces Moses permitted are a concession to the hardheartedness of human beings and do not reflect God's true will. Later, in the house, Jesus explains to his disciples that either a husband or a wife who divorces a spouse and marries another commits adultery against the first spouse.

10:13–16 This is another incident in which the disciples demonstrate that they do not have a heart of servanthood. Jesus rebukes the disciples for their arrogant attitude toward the children and then uses the children as examples of the attitude the disciples need to develop.

10:17–31 Mark does not describe this rich man as young (Matt 19:20) or as a ruler (Luke 18:18). All three gospels make the central point that the man is rich. Jesus' *Why do you call me good*? *No one is good but God alone* may suggest that he knows the man thinks of himself as good because he has kept the commandments. In the original context the rich man would not have known to think about the doctrine of Jesus' sinless nature, which has raised some question, with which perhaps even Matthew 19:16–17 must deal.

Jesus knows the one thing this man will not give up for God. The rich man becomes a paradigm for

---

Jesus & Divorce

Three questions need to be considered concerning verses 11–12: First, how does this text, which gives no exceptions for divorce and remarriage, relate to Matthew 5:32; 19:9; and 1 Corinthians 7:15 that provide permission to divorce and remarry under certain limited conditions? The text in Mark is probably intended as a general principle that admits of exceptions, rather than as a specific law.

Second, were women in Jesus' audience allowed to initiate divorce as verse 12 implies? Jesus might have in mind the famous case of Herodias. Some have argued there is evidence for Jewish women initiating divorce (see Gundry 543 for references). On the other hand, Mark may be balancing verse 11 for those in his readership, since Gentiles did permit women to initiate divorce.

Third, does "Anyone who divorces his wife and marries another woman commits adultery against her" mean that such a man is still married to the first wife? That is the most common view. However, another possibility should be considered. Jesus does not explicitly say, "Whoever appears to divorce his wife and marry another but does not really do so in the eyes of God commits adultery against her because he is still married to her." He speaks as if the divorce and remarriage were real. In verse 9 he does not say "humans should not try to separate what God has joined," but he speaks as if humans do actually separate it. Jesus' statement in verses 11–12 could mean, "Whoever [actually] divorces his wife and [in the eyes of God and humanity] marries another commits adultery [in the sense that what he does is tantamount to adultery in God's eyes]."

Jesus' statement that it is hard for a rich person to enter God's kingdom. There is no evidence to support the old idea that the eye of the needle referred to a small, low gate in the walls of Jerusalem that a camel could enter only with great difficulty. Jesus is referring to a literal eye of a needle. He chooses an illustration that is impossible. Only God can make it possible for a rich man to be saved.

Peter uses the rich man's refusal to give up his riches as an opportunity to commend himself and other disciples for what they have given up to follow Jesus. Jesus' reply contains both encouragement and warning. Those who leave *homes, brothers, sisters, mothers, children and fields* to follow Jesus *will receive a hundred times as much in this present age* [metaphorically speaking; see Mark 3:34] ... *and in the age to come, eternal life.* On the other hand, what they receive in the present age will be accompanied by *persecutions* (13:12–13). Jesus' last statement is paradoxical and may be taken to apply to more than one aspect of the context: *Many who are first will be last, and the last first* may mean those like the rich man would end up last and those like the disciples would end up first. Or perhaps Peter must think about his own "I am superior" attitude expressed in his "we have left everything" statement (compare Matt 19:27–20:16).

10:32-34 It is now clear to all that Jesus' destination is Jerusalem. He continues to instruct his disciples about what will happen there. This is the most specific of the three prediction sections (see also 8:31–32; 9:30–31).

10:35-45 There is a three-part narrative pattern that occurs in connection with each of the three passion predictions: the prediction itself, the disciples' rejection or misunderstanding of it, and Jesus' clarification of what his suffering messiahship means for discipleship. In this third instance James and John demonstrate an obvious (to the reader) misunderstanding of the nature of Jesus' messiahship and its implications for themselves as his disciples. By saying that they want to sit at his right and his left when he comes into his glory, they imply an earthly kingdom in which Jesus will reign as the Davidic messiah (Moloney 205).

Jesus replies that they do not know what they are asking. *The cup* and *the baptism* he refers to are metaphors for his coming passion (compare Mark 14:36; Luke 12:50). James and John only further demonstrate their ignorance by their easy affirmation of their ability to share in these experiences. Even so, Jesus says, he does not have the authority to grant their request.

The angry reaction of the ten in verse 41 reflects the fact that all twelve of the disciples have the same self-serving attitudes as James and John. But Jesus demands a new social order among his followers. The two paradoxes of verses 43–44 create a new counterintuitive social economy that turns the normal way of thinking on its head (see 9:35; 10:31).

In verse 45 Jesus provides the pattern for his new social order: his own sacrificial death. His followers can be servants and slaves because *the Son of Man did not come to be served but to serve.* And that service would be the ultimate: *to give his life.* Verses 43–45 make explicit what each of the two preceding passion predictions and their following discussions of discipleship (8:31–37; 9:30–35) imply: that Jesus' coming sacrifice creates the pattern for discipleship.

The last phrase of verse 45, *as a ransom for many*, is one of two statements in Mark (see also 14:24) that alludes to the atoning nature of Jesus' death as a sacrifice for sin. *As a ransom for many* probably alludes to Isaiah 53:10. A ransom was a price paid for the freedom of a slave or prisoner and is used metaphorically for the vicarious suffering of Jesus who paid the price for the sins of others.

10:46-52 This blind man sees what those with sight could not. In calling Jesus the *Son of David* he recognizes Jesus' identity as the Messiah. He exhibits a strong and persistent faith that Jesus can heal him and bring him sight. He refuses to be quieted by the crowds, and he boldly asks Jesus for healing. As a result, he receives it and models the right reaction to Jesus' life-changing power by becoming a follower.

Many connect this healing with that of the blind man in 8:22–26 as bookends around Mark's key section on discipleship (for example, Donahue and Harrington 319–20). According to this view, both miracles have metaphorical overtones as they introduce and conclude a section focusing heavily on the disciples' need to come to see the true identity of Jesus as a suffering servant and the implications of that identity for discipleship.

THE LAST WEEK: JERUSALEM, THE CROSS & THE RESURRECTION · 11:1–16:8

11:1-11 This event begins the last week of Jesus' life. *Bethphage* and *Bethany* are small towns on *the Mount of Olives*, just east of the city of Jerusalem and overlooking the temple. Mark does not say whether Jesus had made prior arrangements with the owner of the colt. In any case, the disciples find the situation to be just as he said it would be (see 14:12–16).

The people honor Jesus as a king as he rides down the Mount of Olives and into Jerusalem on the colt. They spread out their cloaks and fresh-cut branches as a carpet for him to ride on (see 1 Kgs 9:13), and they form a procession shouting words of acclamation reminiscent of Psalm 118:25–26. The words *Blessed is the coming kingdom of our father David!* show that these people see Jesus as the coming messiah. He seems to encourage such messianic fervor by his method of entry into the city. At the beginning of the final week, he is ready to reveal the messianic secret.

> **The Triumphal Entry**
> *Matthew 21:4–5 and John 2:4–16 specify that this event fulfills Zechariah 9:9. Mark does not explicitly refer to that text, but he has it in mind.*

During his final week, Jesus spends the nights in Bethany (11:11–12, 19; 14:3).

11:12–25 Why would Jesus curse a tree, especially since *it was not the season for figs*? The answer comes in the next story, which is sandwiched in before the conclusion of the fig tree incident. The cursing of the fig tree symbolizes God's punishment on the Jewish leadership because they have not borne the fruit he wants from the temple.

There are several possibilities for what Jesus intends by his actions in the temple. He would not have disagreed in principle with exchanging money for the temple tax (see Matt 17:24–27) or with selling sacrificial animals to those who have come long distances. Stopping such practices would have shut down the temple altogether. He was probably protesting doing those things in the Court of the Gentiles (the large region of the temple court in which Gentiles could worship). His citation of Isaiah 56:7 focuses in this direction because it says the temple should be *a house of prayer*. That *he would not allow anyone to carry merchandise through the temple courts* might also be something that he perceives as detracting from the temple's use as a house of prayer. This sounds similar to the Mishnah's instruction that one must not "enter into the Temple Mount with his staff or his sandal or his wallet … nor may he make of it a short by-path" (*m. Berakoth* 9:5). Jesus may also be protesting the prices as exorbitant, as suggested by his allusion to Jeremiah 7:11 concerning making the temple *a den of robbers*. Some argue that his action symbolizes not just a cleansing or purification of temple practices but the coming destruction of the temple itself (Moloney 225–26). But nothing in his words of explanation points specifically in this direction.

Jesus' actions, according to verses 18–19, target most of all the Jewish leadership. *The whole crowd* is not offended at his teaching, but is amazed. The evening marks the end of Monday of the passion week.

As Tuesday begins, we hear the rest of the story of the cursed fig tree. Peter observes that it has withered. This completes the sandwich effect with the cleansing of the temple episode. But Mark is not finished with the significance of the fig tree. It becomes an object lesson for the prayer of faith. Jesus' teachings about faith in prayer are the strongest in the New Testament. His disciple can even cast a mountain into the sea if he *does not doubt in his heart but believes that what he says will happen,* if in fact, when he asks for something he *believe[s] that [he] has received it*. This is a difficult passage. On the one hand, it does mean that faith figures in the efficacy of prayer (compare 9:17–19, 28–29). But on the other hand, it would be incorrect to claim that if we truly believed, we would always get what we want (see 14:35–36; 2 Cor 12:7–9). There are some literary markers of hyperbole here: casting mountains into the sea does not seem the sort of thing Jesus would intend his disciples to take literally, and it is logically problematic to believe that in a literal sense one already has what one is asking for. Prayer involves the radical trust in God by the one praying.

The somewhat unnerving idea that God's forgiveness of us depends upon our forgiveness of others is also found in Matthew 6:14–15 and 18:35. Verse 26 is omitted in modern translations because it is not found in the best manuscripts. It is a negative version of verse 25, very similar to Matt 6:15.

11:27–33 This question begins a series of controversy segments similar to 2:1–3:6 in which Jesus opposes the Jewish authorities. There are five units in this series that include not only the Jewish authorities attacking Jesus but also his counterattacks against them.

The first group to question him consists of the segments of the Sanhedrin (see 8:31). The questions arise from Jesus' controversial behavior in the temple on the day before. Jesus' counterquestion in verse 30 sets up a dilemma for the authorities. They certainly do not accept John's baptism as authorized by God, but they want to stay in the favor of those who do. In a public forum, they have no acceptable answer.

> **The Sanhedrin**
> Taken from the Greek synedrion, meaning "sitting together," the Sanhedrin was a Jewish governing council of men that existed in every ancient Jewish city.

12:1–12 Jesus responds to the religious authorities' questioning with an allegorical parable that even they realize is *spoken ... against them* (verse 12). He constructs the parable using elements from a similar parable in Isaiah 5:1–7 where the vineyard is Judah and its owner is Yahweh. In Jesus' version, the owner is also God. The tenants are the religious authorities. The servants are the prophets. And the beloved son is Jesus himself, who thereby sets himself above all the prophets. The leaders of the Jews not only had failed to give God what they owe, but they had beaten or killed God's prophets and would soon kill the son.

Verse 10 cites Psalm 118:22–23 to say that, although the beloved son Jesus is *the stone the builders* (the authorities) *rejected*, he will *become the capstone* of God's building. The word translated *capstone* might also be translated "cornerstone" (Gundry 691).

The leaders of the Jewish Sanhedrin determine to arrest Jesus, but not in front of the crowds, many of whom favor him. They decide to wait, hoping to find a more discreet opportunity (Mark 14).

> **"Render to Cæsar ..."**
> Early Christians struggled with their involvement in the Roman government. They paid taxes and obeyed the laws, but their non-participation in worship of the emperor or deified city of Rome left them out of many civic pursuits. Jews escaped state disapproval because their religion was established, but Christians had no such advantage. The second century apology for Christianity, the Epistle to Diognetus, took pains to emphasize that "Christians do not differ from the rest of humanity in location, speech, or lifestyle."

12:13–17 The Pharisees and Herodians appear together earlier in 3:6, plotting Jesus' destruction. By their question about taxes they hope to trap Jesus between the government and the people. There is a wonderful irony in Mark's record of their praise of Jesus' integrity and willingness to speak the truth before all (11:31–32). Jesus' response avoids the horns of the dilemma. The face on the silver denarius belonged to the emperor Tiberius and the inscription read "Tiberius Cæsar Augustus, Son of the Divine Augustus." The coin belongs to Tiberius, and he can demand its return. On the other hand, one should only give God what belongs to God. Jesus does not clarify what belongs to God, but his comment raises questions about the last part of the motto on the coin.

12:18–27 This is Mark's only specific reference to the Sadducees, although they would be included in his references to the chief priests, elders, and teachers of the law. They did not accept oral tradition and denied the resurrection (Sanders 317–40). Their question, of course, seeks to negate the idea of a resurrection of the dead. The woman marries each of the seven brothers because of the levirate marriage law in Deuteronomy 25:5–10 that requires a man to marry his brother's widow if his brother has not fathered children. Jesus' reply to the conundrum is that there is no marriage in the world to come. Rather, resurrected people will be like angels. We have no record of married angels from the Bible or from extrabiblical literature before or during the New Testament period.

In the absence of chapter and verse references, Jesus identifies his text as coming from *the account of the bush* (see Rom 11:2). How Jesus uses Exodus 3:6 to make his point is a matter of debate. Some argue his point rests on the present tense of "I am," but the verb does not actually appear in Mark's Greek or the underlying Hebrew. More likely the point is based on what is implied in God's covenant commitment to Abraham, Isaac, and Jacob. As France puts it, "If ... God chooses to be identified by the names of his long-dead servants Abraham, Isaac, and Jacob, with whom his covenant was made, and whom he committed himself to protect, they cannot be simply dead and forgotten ..." (471).

12:28–34 Mark does not clarify whether this teacher of the law's question was a genuine inquiry or another test. Matthew considers it a test (Matt 22:35; compare Luke 10:25). Jesus' response uses Deuteronomy 6:4–5, the famous *Shema* that has been repeated every day by Jews from before the time of Jesus (*Letter of Aristeas* 160; *Jubilees* 6:14 [both in Charlesworth]). He adds the second greatest commandment from Leviticus 19:18. Jesus does not invent this connection, since the lawyer of Luke 10:25–27 draws the same conclusions. The teacher of the law who asks Jesus the question immediately recognizes the validity of his response and rightly observes that Jesus' words agree with the prophets' emphasis that love of God and neighbor are *more important than all burnt offerings and sacrifices*. Jesus' remark that the man was close to the kingdom shows that love of God and neighbor lies at the heart of the kingdom. This dialogue silences Jesus' opponents.

12:35–37 The last three pericopes – or sections – of chapter 12 portray Jesus on the offense. In this case, he has his own question to ask. As in the triumphal entry and the parable of the Tenants, Jesus is once again publicly provocative about his identity. In his question, Jesus uses "Christ" to refer to "the Messiah." Since other texts in Mark imply that Jesus as the Christ is in fact David's son (10:47–48; 11:10), the text focuses on the meaning of the claim. Jesus makes a messianic interpretation of Psalm 110:1 (compare Heb 7) in which the second *lord* is interpreted to refer to the messiah so that David, as the author of the Psalm, is said to call the messiah *my lord*. The implication is that, in some way, the messiah will be greater than David. Many in the crowd are pleased to hear it. They probably understood the last part of Psalm 110:1 to refer to the defeat of Rome.

12:38–44 In these verses, Jesus makes a strong and direct attack on the behavior and motives of the teachers of the law. Wherever they are, the marketplace, the synagogue, or a banquet, they look for attention and praise. Furthermore, that they *devour widows' houses* presumably means they defraud them for financial support (France 491–92). The observation that they *will be punished most severely* is one of very few New Testament references to the idea of degrees of eternal punishment.

In contrast to the teachers of the law who use widows for financial gain is a poor widow who gives the temple treasury all she has. Her gift also stands in contrast to wealthy people who give large amounts. Her two *leptons* were worth one *quadrans*, a tiny fraction of a denarius (Gundry 729). Jesus' point is that her gift is more valuable because it represents a deeper sacrifice on her part than that of the rich people who give from the overflow of their abundance (compare 2 Sam 24:24).

13:1–27 The temple complex was truly magnificent. Roughly 35 acres were enclosed by walls built of stones, most of which were two to five tons each. The largest stone weighed about 400 tons. The inner wall around the temple itself had ten gates with double doors, each 45 feet high and 22 feet wide (Sanders 54–69, 306–14).

The *Mount of Olives* east of the city provides a beautiful vantage point for viewing the temple. The question the four former fishermen ask indicates that they have in mind a series of events (*these things … all*).

The central theme of the chapter is expressed in the verb the NIV translates *watch out* or *be on guard* (verses 5, 9, 23, 33). The disciples must *be on guard* so that they do not go astray and can face persecution and Jesus' return. One way they might be misled is that during the last days many false messiahs and prophets would appear (verses 6, 21–22). Furthermore, there would be wars, earthquakes, and famines (verses 7–8) that would lead many to believe that the end must be upon them. Jesus says these are

> **Psalm 110 in Second-Temple Judaism**
> *Psalm 110, a royal psalm originally about the king of Judah, gained popularity among early Christians (see Heb 5 and 7). Its chief character, Melchizedek, served as a model for the messiah, and alternatively, as a mighty angel for the Dead Sea Scrolls community (11Q 13).*

> **Interpreting Mark 13**
> Jesus' cleansing of the temple and his subsequent conflicts with the Jewish authorities lead naturally to his comments about the destruction of the temple complex. When the disciples ask about that destruction, Jesus provides an extended discourse on various events of the "last days," focusing particularly on the destruction of the temple, the destruction of Jerusalem, and on his second coming.
>
> The discourse is notoriously difficult to interpret. The first major issue is to determine in each segment whether Jesus is speaking about: general characteristics of the last days, the destruction of Jerusalem in 70 CE, or his return at the end of human history.
>
> The second major issue is to determine how he relates these elements chronologically. In my book on Mark, I discuss seven views of these issues, clearly dismissing three and allowing for the possibility of four (Black 223–27). Owing to space limitations in this chapter, however, I here only discuss the view I consider most likely.

the beginning of birth pains. Jesus' use of the imagery of a woman in labor resembles the Old Testament texts that use the same imagery to describe the horrors of people under siege (Isa 13:8; 26:17; Jer 4:31; 6:24). Some non-Christian Jewish writings also portray the last days of human history as times of great turmoil (for example, *2 Baruch* 27:1–7).

The turmoil of the last days will be a time of persecution for the disciples, but Jesus gives them two assurances. First, the Holy Spirit will guide them when they are brought up on trial. And second *he who stands firm to the end will be saved*. *The end* here may be the same as in verse 7, where it appears to refer to the end of the age (Donahue and Harrington 371). France argues that the absence of the article with the noun in this case suggests otherwise. He takes the phrase as idiomatic for something like "right through" or "forever," and understands *will be saved* not in the literal sense of staying alive, but in a spiritual sense (519).

In verse 14, Jesus moves from general characteristics of the last days to the events of 66–70 CE. He takes the phrase *abomination that causes desolation* from Daniel 8:13; 9:27; 11:31; and 12:11, which *1 Maccabees* 1:54 had correctly interpreted as a reference to Antiochus IV, when he offered sacrifices to Zeus on the altar of the temple in Jerusalem. There is no agreement concerning what Mark has in mind. Perhaps Luke's reference to the Roman armies surrounding Jerusalem explains Mark's phrase (Luke 21:20), but Luke may also be providing a separate sign. In Mark, Jesus may have reference to the desecration of the temple by the Zealots who committed murder there and who appointed a usurper as high priest (Lane 468–69; France 525).

When the time comes, Jesus emphasizes the need to leave Jerusalem immediately. His remarks about not entering the house from the rooftop or going back for one's coat from the field place a dramatic emphasis on the necessity of immediate flight.

The comment in verses 17–19 about pregnant women and nursing mothers may reflect the difficulties of flight or the situations in the caves they would be hiding in. The language describing the distress as the worst that ever has been or will be should not be taken literally (compare similar rhetoric in Exod 10:14; 11:6; Joel 2:2).

The *days* of verse 20 (*those* does not precede *days* in the Greek text of verse 20) appear to most interpreters to refer to *those days* of verse 19: that is, the days of the siege and destruction of Jerusalem. Alternatively, verse 20 may continue Jesus' description of the general characteristics of the last days from verses 5–13 (Carson 488–511). *The elect* in verse 20 most naturally applies to Christian believers who should have escaped the tribulation in the city. *All flesh* in verse 20 (which the NIV combines with the negative conjunction and translates *no one*) most naturally applies to people in general rather than only to those within the walls of Jerusalem. And the *false Christs* of verses 21–22 have already been mentioned as characteristic of the last days (verse 6). These features suggest that verses 20–23 continue the general characteristics of the last days, the treatment of which the description of the destruction of Jerusalem has interrupted.

The celestial imagery of verses 24–25 occurs in several Old Testament texts to refer to events within human history (Ezek 32:7–8; Amos 8:9; Joel 2:10; 3:15; and especially Isa 13:10; 34:4). France argues that verses 24–27 speak of the destruction of Jerusalem (530–37).

This view deserves serious consideration, and verses 24–25 could easily be explained in the light of their Old Testament precursors. However, it is not appropriate to interpret the idea that the Son of Man will be seen *coming in clouds with great power and glory* and that he will *send his angels and gather his elect* without reference to the New Testament texts concerning the second coming of Jesus (see especially Matt 13:37–43; 25:31; 2 Thess 1:7; Rev 1:7). These texts show that it is likely that verses 24–27 refer to the second coming, not to the destruction of Jerusalem.

13:28–31 The lesson of the fig tree is that one can look at the signs given by a fig tree and know that summer is near. Similarly, Jesus says, *when you see these things happening you know that it* (or *he* as in the NRSV) *is near*. Furthermore, *all these things* will happen before *this generation* passes away. In verse 29, *these things* refer to signs of the second coming. That would be the things in verses 5–23, including the destruction of Jerusalem and some of the other events (wars, famines, false messiahs, etc.) characterizing the last days. *These things* in verse 29 do not include the things in verses 24–27 because those verses describe the second coming. *All these things* in verse 30 should be understood in the light of *these things* in verse 29. The second coming is not included. Jesus is stating that the destruction of Jerusalem and the other events predicted in verses 5–23 as precursors to the second coming will occur within one generation. The destruction of Jerusalem took place in 70 CE.

13:32–37 Having stated in verse 30 that the destruction of Jerusalem and the other signals of the second coming would happen within one generation, Jesus turns to the specific date of the second coming, which *not even the angels … nor the Son* knows. The chapter ends with an emphasis on constant vigilance, because no one knows when Jesus will return. Note the repeated urging: *Be on guard! Be alert! … keep watch …. Watch!* These words are thematic for the chapter.

14:1–11 All of chapters 14–15 relates to Jesus' death. The first two sections are sandwiched stories. In this case, there is an obvious contrast in how the characters of each story treat Jesus.

With the time reference at the beginning of this chapter, Mark moves to Wednesday of the final week of Jesus' life. The Feast of Unleavened Bread was a weeklong celebration of the exodus beginning with the Passover meal (Exod 12:15–20; 23:15; 34:18; Deut 16:1–8). The story of the authorities' attempt to arrange for a secret arrest of Jesus is completed in verses 10–11, creating a sandwich with verses 3–9.

The NIV addition of *known as* before *Simon the Leper* reflects the opinion of the translators that Simon was not a leper at the time, or he could not have invited guests to his house. The unidentified woman brings *nard*, an oil from a plant native to India and praised by the first century author Pliny as "the foremost possible rank among perfumes" (*Natural History* 12.25.42). She brings it in *an alabaster jar*, for as Pliny said, "the best ointment is preserved in alabaster" (13.3.19). So costly is all of this that she is criticized because the perfume *could have been sold* for more than 300 denarii (*more than a year's wages*) and *given to the poor*.

Jesus, however, defends the woman's action, interpreting it as preparing his body for burial. Jewish burial customs included putting perfume-like substances on the corpse, which was laid in a cave until it decomposed enough to put the bones in an ossuary (bone box) so the space in the cave could be used for another body. Jesus' comment about the poor alludes to Deuteronomy 15:11. Jesus commands care for the poor, and such care included the proper burial of the dead.

The story begun in verses 1–2 is now completed. The religious authorities find their accomplice in *Judas Iscariot, one of the Twelve*. An unnamed woman has poured out a year's wages to anoint Jesus for his burial; Judas has taken money to betray his master to those who will send him to his death.

14:12–16 The Passover meal and the weeklong Feast of Unleavened Bread commemorated the exodus, the most important event in Israel's history. Verse 12 moves forward one day to Thursday, the 14th of the month of *Nisan*, the day of the sacrifice of the Passover lambs. The Passover meal would be eaten that evening as the 15th of *Nisan* began. Like his earlier instructions about getting the colt for the triumphal entry, Jesus does not say whether he had made any prior arrangements concerning the upper room.

14:17–21 Psalm 41:9 says, *Even my close friend, whom I trusted, he who shared my bread, has lifted up his heel against me*. Jesus alludes to this verse as he predicts his betrayal and says that

---

Jesus & the Safe People

As author of the Lord Peter Wimsey mysteries, Dorothy L. Sayers felt a keen irony about social respectability. Her comments about Jesus' crucifixion are startling but true: "The people who hanged Christ never, to do them justice, accused Him of being a bore – on the contrary; they thought Him too dynamic to be safe. It has been left for later generations to muffle up that shattering personality and surround Him with an atmosphere of tedium."

Sayers showed her brilliance as one of the first women graduates of Oxford University (1915) and author of theological books, religious dramas, boisterous articles, and speeches, and a translation of Dante's Divine Comedy. Along with C. S. Lewis, Charles Williams, and other Inklings, she called on Christians to take Jesus seriously in a century awash in secularism, psychological fads, and greed. "We have very efficiently pared the claws of the Lion of Judah, certified Him 'meek and mild,' and recommended Him as a fitting household pet for pale curates and pious old ladies. To those who knew Him, however, He in no way suggested a milk-and-water person; they objected to Him as a dangerous firebrand."

– Chris Willerton

it will be carried out by *one of the Twelve ..., one who dips bread into the bowl with me*. Mark says the Twelve are *saddened*. They must also have been shocked. The comment that *the Son of Man will go just as it is written about him* may include Psalm 41:9, but see also the texts mentioned in the comments on 9:11–13.

14:22–25 Jesus takes two items from the Passover meal and gives them a new significance in relationship to his impending death. The bread represents his body. It is unlikely that the disciples would understand *this is my body* in a literal sense with Jesus sitting directly before them. The Passover meal itself was full of symbolism and formed a background for how to understand Jesus' words.

The wine symbolizes his *blood of the covenant*. A useful backdrop to this concept is Exodus 24:8, where "blood of the covenant" describes part of the process of Israel's confirmation of the covenant at the foot of Mount Sinai. Jesus' statement that this blood was *poured out for many* echoes Isaiah 53:12 and, like Mark 10:45, portrays Jesus' death as a vicarious sacrifice for the sins of the many.

Jesus declares that his days of drinking wine with the disciples are over until a time when he will *drink it anew in the kingdom of God*. He probably intends the time of the messianic banquet, which Jews believed would come in the new age of the kingdom (Matt 8:11; Rev 19:9; compare Isa 25:6; *1 Enoch* 62:13–16; *2 Baruch* 29:5–8). He is predicting his imminent death and giving assurance of his and his disciples' triumph.

14:26–31 Jesus bases his prediction of the disciples' failure on Zechariah 13:7. (Zech 9:9 lay behind the triumphal entry and John 19:37 cites Zech 12:10 concerning the soldiers piercing Jesus.) Jesus goes on to predict his resurrection and the reunion with his fallen disciples. The prediction in verse 28 serves as the basis for the words of the angelic messenger in 16:7 that Jesus would meet the disciples in Galilee as he had told them.

Peter and the rest protest that they will not fall away. The second cock crow, associated with Peter's denial, normally came at dawn (Brown 137, with ancient references). Variant readings in ancient Greek manuscripts to the text in verses 30, 68, and 72 seek to reduce the cock crowing in Mark to one time, but the original readings are probably the ones indicating two cock crows (Metzger 96–98).

14:32–42 The name "Gethsemane" means "olive presses" and probably refers to an olive grove. It becomes the scene of a startling portrait of both Jesus' frailty and his submission. In contrast to Jesus, the disciples fail even to recognize what is happening. Mark paints a dark picture of Jesus' sorrow. He begs three times to escape the cross and yet ends each time with *not what I will but what you will*. Here is an important insight into Christ's nature and a model for prayer.

The word *abba* appears three times in the New Testament (Mark 14:36; Rom 8:15; and Gal 4:6). It is an Aramaic word transliterated into Greek. Since we have no relevant examples of others using this word to address God, Jesus' use of the term probably expresses his special relationship with God. However, the claim that it was a term used by little children to address their fathers is no longer accepted (Brown 172–73).

The remainder of the pericope focuses on the failure of the disciples. In verses 37–38, Jesus singles Peter out because he boasted that he would not fall away like the rest. The phrase *fall into temptation* could be translated *come into the time of trial* as in the NRSV. All of them do come into a time of trial almost immediately and fail. In verse 41 the question *Are you still sleeping and resting*? is a rebuke. But now the time has come. Verse 35 says that Jesus *prayed that if possible the hour might pass from him*, but in verse 41 Jesus observes that *the hour has come*.

14:43–50 The swords indicate that the crowd with Judas is not an unruly mob but a military delegation dispatched by the Sanhedrin (compare Matt 26:47; John 18:3). The kiss that Judas uses to identify Jesus was probably a common method of greeting (Brown 254–55).

14:51–52 John 18:10 identifies the one who cut off the ear of the high priest's servant as none other than Peter. But his courage fades. The NIV's translation *Am I leading a rebellion*? is questionable, for it treats a general Greek word for criminal as meaning "rebel" (Brown 283–84). The NRSV's *as though I were a bandit* is better. Jesus also complains that they have not arrested him during his many open visits to the temple courts. Nevertheless, he sees the arrest as the fulfillment of Scripture.

These verses provide the fulfillment of Jesus' prediction in verse 27. The notion that the young man was Mark himself is speculative. The flight of the young man is described as a particularly striking illustration of the flight of all of Jesus' followers.

14:53–65 Verses 53–54 begin two sandwiched stories. The story of Jesus' trial contrasts with the informal trial of Peter in the courtyard outside. Jesus' courage contrasts with Peter's cowardice. The high priest that year from 18 to 37 CE was Caiaphas.

Mark suggests the purpose of the hearing was not to determine the truth, but to secure a conviction for a death sentence. The specific accusation of verse 58 sounds similar to what Jesus is quoted as saying in John 2:19: *destroy this temple and I will raise it again in three days*. However, in John he does not say that the temple he has in mind is *man-made*, and John says that he was speaking of his own body, not the *temple* proper. It is not surprising that the witnesses' *statements did not agree*. In a capital offense, the nonagreement of the witnesses should have resulted in the dismissal of the case.

When the witnesses fail, the high priest begins questioning Jesus directly. Initially, he questions him about the witnesses' accusations, but Jesus remains silent. Then he poses a direct question about his identity as the Messiah: *Are you the Christ, the Son of the blessed One?* The high priest probably intends "Son of the Blessed One" as appositional to "Christ," and as having similar meaning – not a connotation of deity, but a royal son of God as expected according to 2 Samuel 7:14 (see the comments on Mark 1:1). This time Jesus responds to the high priest's question forthrightly. *I am*, he declares, and then adds to the offense of his response. He claims that the high priest and the others (*you* is plural) *will see the Son of Man sitting at the right hand of the Mighty One and coming on the clouds of heaven*. His statement blends elements of Daniel 7:13 and Psalm 110:1. These statements exceed all bounds for anyone who found Jesus' prior hints and allusions to messiahship disturbing.

Tearing one's clothes expressed great grief (Gen 37:34; 2 Sam 1:11–12; Cassius Dio 54.14.1–2; 56.23.1). As noted in the comments on Mark 2:5, the notion of *blasphemy* was a loose one. Spitting in someone's face signifies public shaming in many cultures (Num 12:14; Deut 25:9). The spitting and beating fulfill Isaiah 50:6–7: *I gave … my cheeks to slaps; I did not turn my face from the shame of spitting*.

14:66–72 These verses pick up the story of Peter in the courtyard begun in verse 54. Peter has his own trial by interrogation. As predicted, Peter denies Jesus three times. On the third instance, the NIV says *he began to call down curses on himself*. This may be correct, but the Greek text does not provide an object for *curse*, and other interpreters believe he is actually cursing Jesus (Brown 604–605). In any event, he is sorrowful when the second cock crow reminds him of Jesus' words.

15:1–15 Pilate governed Judea from 26–36 CE. He lived in Cæsarea Maritima, on the Mediterranean coast, but resided in Jerusalem for the feast days. According to John 18:31, the Sanhedrin turned to Pilate because they could not administer the death penalty. They might have be able to execute certain types of criminals, but not a case like Jesus' (see Brown 363–72). The charge before Pilate was not blasphemy, but insurrection. The title is therefore shifted from "Christ" to "king."

The NIV's interpretation of Jesus' response to Pilate as an unqualified affirmation, *Yes, it is as you say*, is a questionable interpretation of the two Greek words which the NRSV more literally translates *You say so*. Probably Jesus wants to

---

Jesus' Trial Before the Sanhedrin

The historicity of Mark's account of the trial before the Sanhedrin has been challenged by observing that the "trial" breaks rules set forth in the Mishna. However, two responses are appropriate. One is that the Mishna was written about 200 CE and may not reflect the practices of Jesus' time. Second, the hearing before the Sanhedrin was probably not a formal trial and would not follow the usual legal rules for such a trial (Carson 549–52; France 601–03). In the first century, the high priest played a prominent role in the Sanhedrin but was not its executive (see Vanderkam, 428–29).

The Gospels' portrayals of the trials of Jesus are often accused of being anti-Semitic. It is true that many have shamefully used them for anti-Semitic purposes. However, to ascribe condemnation of Jesus to the majority of the Sanhedrin is not in itself anti-Semitic, since Jesus and his disciples were also Jews. The differences between Jesus and his opponents reflect a debate among Jews (Carson 551–52).

agree and disagree: I am the king, but not in the way you suppose.

It is difficult to determine whether Pilate had any genuine interest in releasing Jesus or was taunting the crowd with his comments about Jesus. Even if he had some serious interest in releasing Jesus, it was not strong enough for him to choose to save Jesus. It is ironic that Pilate does release a violent threat to the Roman authorities. The gospel writers do not describe Jesus' flogging or crucifixion. Their readers were all too familiar with both forms of punishment. Floggings were commonly done with leather thongs studded with pieces of bone or metal (Brown 851). The facts that Jesus had difficulty carrying his cross (15:21) and died more quickly than usual (15:44) suggest that his flogging was severe.

15:16–20 At the end of his hearing before the Sanhedrin, Jesus is mocked as the messiah. At the end of his trial before Pilate, he is mocked as the king of the Jews. The term *prætorium* is the common name for a governor's palace. The trial takes place outside the prætorium. Mark now shifts to an inner courtyard. The term he uses for a *company* of soldiers is "cohort," typically about 600 soldiers. A large number of soldiers may have participated in this scene. The purple robe, crown, and falling to the knee are all mockeries of royalty. The thorns on the crown may have symbolized the image of a diadem with the sun's rays radiating from the ruler's head.

> **Crucifixion As Shame**
> *All who lived in the Roman empire knew about crucifixion and associated it with two things: pain and shame. Mark emphasizes shame: Jesus is mocked as a king, he is paraded through the city, his clothes are divided by his executioners, he has a plaque with the charge against him affixed to his cross, he is crucified between robbers, passersby insult him, the religious authorities mock him, and even those who are crucified with him heap insults on him.*

15:21–41 Typically the criminal carried his own crossbeam out to where the vertical beams were left planted (Brown 914). Jesus may have been weakened by a severe flogging. Mark assumes his audience knows something about *Alexander and Rufus*. Perhaps they had become Christians after their father *Simon* carried the cross (Gundry 953–54). The word *Golgotha* is Aramaic, so Mark translates it for his Greek audience as *the Place of the Skull*. Many readers suppose that the *wine mixed with myrrh* refers to a drugged drink that some Jewish women offer Jesus. However, there is no reference to Jewish women in the text; the idea comes from the Babylonian Talmud, which was written several centuries after Jesus lived, and which speaks of women who gave condemned criminals wine mixed with frankincense (*b. Sanhedrin* 43a; Brown 941). In Mark, the soldiers offer Jesus the wine. The actual event of the crucifixion itself is described with extreme brevity: *and they crucified him*. Mark feels no need to explain the brutality of the act itself. The account of the soldiers casting lots emphasizes Jesus' humiliation and fulfills Psalm 22:18: *They divide my garments among them and cast lots for my clothing*.

Chapter 15 includes a series of time references in connection with the day of Jesus' crucifixion: *very early in the morning* (verse 1), *the third hour* (verse 25), *at the sixth hour … until the ninth hour* (verse 33), *at the ninth hour* (verse 34), and *as evening approached* (verse 42). *The third hour* would be about 9:00 a.m. After this time reference, Mark highlights features of the story that involve shame: Jesus has a placard describing his crime, as was common for criminals (Brown 963), and robbers flank him on each side. Three groups mock and insult him: passersby blaspheme [Greek *blasphemeo*] him in a way that alludes to Psalm 22:18 (*All who see me mock me; they hurl insults, shaking their heads*), the leaders of the Sanhedrin call on him to come down from the cross, and even those crucified with him berate him.

From roughly noon until 3:00 p.m., *darkness came over the whole land*. The darkness is a sign of divine displeasure (see Jer 15:9; Amos 8:9–10). Perhaps we should think of the plague of darkness God brought to the Egyptians (so Lane 572; Brown 1035). At about 3:00 p.m., Jesus cries out the only statement he makes from the cross in Mark. It is a quotation of Psalm 22:1 in Hebrew or Aramaic (concerning which see Brown 1051–53), which Mark translates into Greek for his audience: *"My God, my God, why have you forsaken me?"* The reason Mark first gives the quotation in Hebrew or Aramaic is to clarify why some thought Jesus is calling Elijah [*Eloi, Eloi*]. Although Psalm 22 ends on a note of confidence in God, like most Old Testament laments, Jesus cites only the first verse to express a feeling of abandonment in the midst of his suffering. Misunderstanding his words as a call for Elijah, one of those nearby makes one last mocking gesture.

Although the *vinegar wine* [Greek *oxos*] he offers Jesus was a common drink (Brown 1063), Mark probably intends to allude to Psalm 69:21 (Septuagint, Psalm 68:11) where it has negative connotations: *They put gall in my food and gave me vinegar (oxos) for my thirst.* The context of the other mockings would suggest that the man was not serious about thinking *Let's see if Elijah comes to take him down.* Following this final insult, Jesus cries out and dies.

There are two different *curtains of the temple* that Mark might have in mind in verse 38: the outer veil that marks the entrance to the holy place and the inner veil that marks the entrance to the holy of holies. We cannot determine which he intends. In either case, the tearing of the curtain is a miraculous sign that connects the coming destruction of the temple to the crucifixion of Jesus (Brown 1113–16).

A *centurion* (verse 39) was a commander of 100 men. Something about Jesus' death led the one in charge of the crucifixion to make a confession that Jesus was *the Son of God*.

Verses 40–41 make Mark's first reference to Jesus' women followers. They appear at the crucifixion, burial, and resurrection. The three he names here are the three who go to the tomb after Jesus' resurrection. The term *Magdalene* means that the first *Mary* comes from a small village called Magdala. *James the younger* and *Joses* may be known to Mark's audience so that Mark can use them to identify their mother, *Mary*. Matthew 27:56 might suggest that *Salome* was the mother of the apostles James and John. These and other women had ministered to Jesus in Galilee and had followed him to Jerusalem.

15:42–47 The NIV translation *as evening approached* is incorrect. Mark says, as in the NRSV, *when evening had come*. Joseph's plan was to complete the burial before the new day began at sundown. Although archaeologists have only found the remains of one crucified body in Palestine, Josephus claims, "The Jews are so careful about funeral rites that even those who are crucified because they were found guilty are taken down and buried before sunset" (*War* 4.317). This practice followed Deuteronomy 21:22–23: *If a man guilty of a capital offense is put to death and his body is hung on a tree, you must not leave his body on the tree overnight. Be sure to bury him that same day, because anyone who is hung on a tree is under God's curse.*

Joseph was from *Arimathea*, the location of which is no longer known. He was a prominent member of the Sanhedrin. He needed *boldness* because neither the Sanhedrin nor Pilate would accept his support of Jesus. Jesus had died more quickly than most victims of crucifixion (Brown 1222), and so Pilate investigates and confirms his death. His burial was a typical Jewish burial in which mourners placed a linen-wrapped body in a niche in a natural or (as in this case) carved-out cave. The stone would have been a large boulder or perhaps a disc-shaped stone that rolled in a track across the cave's entrance (Brown 1248). Mark points out that the women saw the place so that they could return on Sunday.

16:1–8 Mark introduces these three women at the crucifixion and identifies two of them as seeing where Jesus was buried. It was customary to put oil and/or spices on the corpse. Since Jesus was buried just before the beginning of the Sabbath, early Sunday morning offered the first opportunity for the women to carry out this ritual. Their remark about the stone serves to underscore their surprise at the resurrection.

The young man's *white robe* suggests that he is an angel. That *they were alarmed* is typical for those who see an angel, as is his reassurance that they should not be alarmed. Every word of the angel's message is significant, especially *He is risen!* and *He is going ahead of you into Galilee. There you will see him, just as he told you.* The angel declares the resurrection and the coming appearances. The promise to appear to them in Galilee *just as he told you* refers back to 14:28, the same context in which Jesus had predicted Peter's denials. Perhaps that is why the angel's comments single out Peter.

Mark's gospel probably originally ended at verse 8. The primary focus of Mark's ending with 16:1–8 is that Jesus has risen! Verse 8 especially emphasizes the fact that the women who first see the empty tomb and hear

---

The Centurion's Confession

Scholars debate whether to translate the centurion's confession "a son of God" or "the Son of God." The former emphasizes the centurion's probable (but not necessary—see Acts 10) background as a pagan. The absence of the Greek article before "Son" is sometimes wrongly seen as strongly favoring this understanding (but see Matt 4:3, 6; 27:40, 43; Luke 1:32, 35). However, the Son of God more appropriately emphasizes the context of Mark's use of the theme (1:1; 1:11; 9:7) and sees this verse as an important climax of the Son of God theme.

> ### Other Endings for Mark's Gospel
>
> Unfortunately we do not know for certain how the Gospel of Mark originally ended. I have treated it as intentionally ending at 16:8.
>
> Some would argue that the original ending is lost (Gundry 1009–21). The manuscript tradition offers two very short endings, one represented in only one manuscript. There is also the long ending, verses 9–20, that is well known to English readers from the King James Version tradition.
>
> On the one hand, we do know from an allusion by Irenæus that the content of verses 9–20 existed in the late second century (Irenæus 3.10.6). On the other hand, the evidence against Mark having originally ended with these verses is strong. The two oldest and best manuscripts end at verse 8, as do several ancient versions and church fathers (Metzger 102–3). Furthermore, in the early fourth century and the late fourth/early fifth respectively, Eusebius (Quaestiones ad Marinum 1) and Jerome (Epistle 120.3) say that "almost all" of the Greek manuscripts they know end at verse 8.
>
> Two other arguments are often used against these verses. One is that their vocabulary and grammar differ significantly from Markan style (Metzger 104). Another, which I find more significant, is that if Matthew and Luke were using Mark as sources, they both essentially quit using him at 16:8.
>
> The long ending of Mark stresses two themes: faith and mission. The emphasis on faith can be seen in the following phrases: they did not believe it (verse 11), they did not believe them either (verse 13), he rebuked them for their lack of faith and their stubborn refusal to believe (verse 14), whoever believes and is baptized will be saved, but whoever does not believe will be condemned (verse 16), and these signs will accompany those who believe (verse 17). The theme of faith is also supported by the appearances of Jesus, the testimony of those who see him, and the emphasis (in verses 17–18 and 20) on confirmatory signs.
>
> The emphasis on mission comes through in the following phrases: she went and told those who had been with him (verse 10), they returned and reported it to the rest (verse 13), go into all the world and preach the good news to all creation (verse 15), and then the disciples went out and preached everywhere (verse 20).
>
> These verses would form a fitting ending to the gospel. They call the reader to believe the message and to proclaim it to others.

the angel's words are filled with overwhelming awe. The NRSV's more literal translation makes the point better than the NIV: *So they went out and fled from the tomb, for terror and amazement had seized them; And they said nothing to anyone, for they were afraid.*

Three words describe their state after seeing the tomb and the angel: terror, amazement, and fear. As a result, their initial reactions are flight and silence. This last verse of Mark emphasizes the awe elicited by the resurrection of Jesus.

THEOLOGICAL REFLECTIONS

In the first eighteen hundred years of church history, Mark suffered from relative neglect compared to the other gospels. After all, most of its stories are also found in Matthew and Luke. And those gospels add birth and resurrection narratives plus many important teachings of Jesus. Then in the late 1800s, Mark began to be heavily studied as scholars became convinced that it was the first gospel. But, until the latter 1900s, much of the interest in Mark remained academic, using Mark to reconstruct the so-called "historical Jesus."

The rise of more theological and literary perspectives (like redaction and narrative criticism) have helped Mark's gospel to find its deserved place in the church's theological reflection. It is important to see that although Matthew and Luke gain by their additions to Mark, they also lose something. The church would be impoverished without Mark's perspective on Jesus and his story.

Mark's gospel clearly summons us to deny ourselves, take up our crosses, and follow Jesus (8:34); to lose our lives rather than save them (8:35); to be last of all and servant of all (9:35); and that *whoever wants to become great…must be your servant, and whoever wants to be first must be slave of all* (10:43–44). Mark in his brevity keeps our attention on the key elements: Christology (who Jesus is) and discipleship (what it means to follow him). In terms of Christology, the first half of the book emphasizes Christ's authority, and the second half, his sacrificial service. In terms of discipleship, the first half calls for faithful submission, and the second for imitating him in sacrificial service. The sharpness of the emphasis, especially in connection with the passion predictions in chapters 8–10, is lost in Matthew and Luke. Mark's gospel is a powerful challenge to follow the path of the Son of God as he gives his life up in service to God and others.

FOR FURTHER STUDY

Morna D. Hooker, *The Gospel according to St. Mark* (Peabody, Mass.: Hendrickson, 1991).

David Rhoads, Joanna Dewey, and Donald Michie, *Mark As Story, An Introduction to the Narrative of a Gospel* (2nd ed.; Minneapolis, Minn.: Fortress, 1999).

WORKS CITED

Richard Bauckham, "For Whom Were the Gospels Written?" in *The Gospels for All Christians: Rethinking the Gospel Audiences* (ed. Richard Bauckham; Grand Rapids: Eerdmans, 1998), 9–48.

Ernest Best, *Mark: The Gospel As Story* (Edinburgh: T & T Clark, 1983).

Allen Black, *Mark* (Joplin, Mo.: College Press, 1995).

Raymond E. Brown, *The Death of the Messiah* (2 vols.; New York: Doubleday, 1994).

Donald A. Carson, "Matthew," in *The Expositor's Bible Commentary*, vol. 8 (ed. Frank E. Gaebelein; Grand Rapids: Zondervan, 1984).

James H. Charlesworth, ed., *The Old Testament Pseudepigrapha* (2 vols.; Garden City, N.Y.: Doubleday, 1983–1985).

John J. Collins, *The Scepter and the Star: The Messiahs of the Dead Sea Scrolls and Other Ancient Literature* (New York: Doubleday, 1996).

Cassius Dio, *Dio's Roman History* (ed. Earnest Cary; 9 vols.; Cambridge: Harvard University Press, 1955–1961).

John R. Donahue and Daniel J. Harrington, *The Gospel of Mark*, (Collegeville, Minn.: Liturgical Press, 2002).

Eusebius, *The Ecclesiastical History* (ed. Kirsopp Lake; 2 vols.; Cambridge: Harvard University Press, 1926–1932).

Joseph A. Fitzmyer, "The Aramaic Qorban Inscription from Jebel Hallet et-Turi and Mark 7:11/Matt 15:5," *Journal of Biblical Literature* 78 (1959): 60–65.

Richard T. France, *The Gospel of Mark: A Commentary on the Greek Text* (Grand Rapids: Eerdmans, 2002).

Joel B. Green, Scot McKnight, and I. Howard Marshall, eds., *Dictionary of Jesus and the Gospels* (Downers Grove, Ill.: InterVarsity Press, 1992).

Robert A. Guelich, *Mark 1:1–8:26* (Dallas: Word, 1989).

Robert H. Gundry, *Mark: A Commentary on His Apology for the Cross* (Grand Rapids: Eerdmans, 1993).

Martin Hengel, *The Four Gospels and the One Gospel of Jesus Christ: An Investigation of the Collection and Origin of the Canonical Gospels* (trans. John Bowden; Harrisburg, Pa.: Trinity Press International, 2000).

Michael W. Holmes, ed. and trans., *The Apostolic Fathers* (Grand Rapids: Baker Academic, 2007)

Larry W. Hurtado, *Mark* (NIBC; Peabody, Mass.: Hendrickson, 1989).

Irenæus, *Against Heresies*, in vol. 1 of *The Ante-Nicene Fathers* (reprinted; Grand Rapids: Eerdmans, 1956).

Josephus, *Works* (ed. H. St. John Thackeray; 10 vols.; Cambridge: Harvard University Press, 1926–65).

William L. Lane, *The Gospel according to Mark* (Grand Rapids: Eerdmans, 1974).

Joel Marcus, *Mark 1–8: A New Translation with Introduction and Commentary* (New York: Doubleday, 2000).

I. Howard Marshall, "Son of Man," in *Dictionary of Jesus and the Gospels* (eds. Joel B. Green, Scot McKnight, and I. Howard Marshall; Downers Grove, Ill.: InterVarsity Press, 1992): 775–81.

Robert K. McIver, "One Hundred-Fold Yield – Miraculous or Mundane? Matthew 13.8, 23; Mark 4.8, 20; Luke 8.8," *New Testament Studies* 40 (1994): 606–8.

Bruce M. Metzger, *A Textual Commentary on the Greek New Testament* (2nd ed.; New York: United Bible Societies, 1994).

Francis J. Moloney, *The Gospel of Mark* (Peabody, Mass.: Hendrickson: 2002).

Pliny the Elder, *Natural History* (ed. H. Rackham; 10 vols.; Cambridge: Harvard University Press, 1997–2001).

E. P. Sanders, *Judaism: Practice and Belief, 63 BCE–66 CE* (Philadelphia: Trinity Press International, 1992).

Tacitus, *Histories* (4 vols.; trans. and ed. Clifford Moore; Cambridge: Harvard University Press, 1970–1981)

G. H. Twelftree, "Blasphemy," in *Dictionary of Jesus and the Gospels* (eds. Joel B. Green, Scot McKnight, and I. Howard Marshall; Downers Grove, Ill.: InterVarsity Press, 1992) 75–77.

James Vanderkam, *From Joshua to Caiaphas: High Priests after the Exile* (Minneapolis, Minn.: Fortress, 2004).

Luke

Kenneth L. Cukrowski

CHAPTER CONTENTS

Contexts **789**

Commentary **790**
- The Prologue · 1:1–4 **790**
- The Birth & Youth of Jesus · 1:5–2:52 **790**
- The Beginnings of Jesus' Ministry · 3:1–4:13 **793**
- Jesus' Ministry in Galilee · 4:14–9:50 **795**
- The Road to Jerusalem · 9:51–19:27 **802**
- Jesus' Ministry in & around Jerusalem · 19:28–21:38 **813**
- The Passion, Resurrection & Ascension Narratives · 22:1–24:53 **816**

Theological Reflections **821**

For Further Study **823**

Works Cited **823**

MAPS, TABLES & FEATURES

Women Unique to Luke's Gospel **822**

Paired Men & Women in Luke **823**

Reading the Gospel of Luke is like examining an enormous tapestry. This gospel is vast and intricate, incorporating more material about Jesus than any of the others and interweaving a number of themes throughout the book. It should not surprise readers to know that Luke wrote more of the New Testament than any other single writer – including Paul.

Luke, however, is no mere encyclopedist; he writes with his mind and heart fully engaged. Only Luke reports the shepherds' awe at Jesus' birth, Jesus' stay in Jerusalem at age twelve, Martha's call for Mary to help, and Zacchaeus's climb up a tree to see Jesus. Luke's gospel contains some of the most famous and demanding parables – the Good Samaritan, the rich fool, the prodigal son, the dishonest steward, the rich man and Lazarus, and the Pharisee and the tax collector. With the epic scope of Homer and the mind of a disciple, Luke stretches out a compelling vision of the kingdom of God.

CONTEXTS

Along with Matthew and Mark, Luke is one of the Synoptic Gospels. These three gospels are so called because they can be "seen" [-optic] "together" [syn-], meaning that the three accounts have some relationship. The wording is often similar, and for some verses, the wording is almost exactly the same in the original Greek (see Matt 3:10; Luke 3:9). This evidence points to a literary relationship among the Synoptic Gospels. Among the many proposals to explain this relationship, the one that commands widest acceptance proposes that Mark wrote his gospel first, and both Matthew and Luke used it as a source. In addition, Luke used another work named "Q," for the German word *Quelle*, meaning "source," as well as still another work named "L," which contains material distinctive to Luke's work.

More than the other gospel writers, Luke reveals details about the nature and composition of his gospel. Luke 1:1–4 calls the gospel a *narrative*. As such, it continues the record of God's activity. God's work did not stop with the Old Testament, and Luke's style and content make that continuity clear. He imitates Old Testament narrative style, especially in the initial chapters of the book. His content echoes the Old Testament constantly and shows God at work within the world.

Because a gospel differs from a letter, it is much more difficult to determine the audience to whom Luke wrote. Clear, however, is the first recipient, named Theophilus (1:3). From the description

> **Writing Luke**
> Luke put a considerable amount of work into the composition of his gospel; the length alone shows the extent of his industry. Luke also reveals, to some extent, how he prepared for the writing of his gospel. "He carefully investigated everything from the beginning," using accounts of "eyewitnesses and servants of the word" (1:2–3). In other words, Luke did research for his composition. Furthermore, he indicates that his gospel was not the first written when he says "many have undertaken to draw up an account of the things that have been fulfilled among us" (1:1). This detail fits with the proposal that Luke used other gospels in the composition of his own.

of Theophilus as *most excellent*, some have thought he held a political office (see Acts 23:26; 24:3; 26:25). Although possible, the theory about Theophilus's political stature is not as probable as his high social and economic standing. Because he is mentioned in the preface, Theophilus likely functioned as the patron for Luke, paying for the writing of Luke-Acts.

Because Luke is such a long book, encompassing a number of topics, many different emphases have been stressed as "Luke's purpose." Luke wanted to tell some yet untold parts of the story of Jesus. Had he been entirely content with the *many* who had written accounts before him, there would be no reason to pen another gospel. Luke wrote in order that Theophilus might have *certainty* about the things that he had been *taught* (1:4).

In translating the gospel for Gentile ears, Luke undertook challenges that many Christians have – to tell the story of Jesus in terms a non-Christian can understand. Luke also wants to tell what it means to be a disciple in God's kingdom. As Luke works through a number of themes, such as the use of possessions, the treatment of outcasts, roles for women, and prayer, readers of Luke will see how contemporary antiquity can be.

COMMENTARY

THE PROLOGUE · 1:1–4

From his very first words, Luke signals that he is writing in the tradition of the historians of his time. His chosen form, content, and style resemble those same features in other prologues in the ancient world. For example, a comparison of Luke's prologue with those in Josephus's *Jewish War* and *Antiquities of the Jews* illustrates this point well. Luke's style is polished and literary, the form brief. The content, densely packed, reveals a number of things about the author, the recipient, and the gospel itself.

Concerning the author, one finds three direct references – the only ones in the gospel – in the first three verses (*among us*; *to us*; *I myself*). Luke describes his work on the book with two verbs (*investigated*; *write*). In addition, Luke indicates the purpose of his work in 1:4 (*so that you may know the certainty of the things you have been taught*). His references to *many* (1:1) who have undertaken accounts and *eyewitnesses* (1:2) show that Luke is not the first to write such an account and that he is not a first-generation Christian. Instead, Luke writes to supplement what has been recorded, adding features and emphases that others have not included.

What can be known about the recipient, "Theophilus"? Although some interpreters understand Theophilus as a generic designation (that is, "friend of God") rather than a real name, it is acceptable to take Theophilus as the actual name of the recipient, given that the name "Theophilus" occurs in both pagan and Jewish literature. Given the practice in other ancient prologues, it is also likely that Theophilus was the patron of Luke's work. Furthermore, Theophilus likely enjoyed high social status, given the designation *most excellent*. One should not, however, necessarily infer that he was a Roman official (compare Acts 23:26; 24:3; 26:25).

> **Who Was Theophilus?**
> *Two factors make it likely that Theophilus was a Christian. First, Luke apparently includes Theophilus in the us of 1:1–2. Second, Luke speaks about Theophilus* coming to *know the certainty of the things you have been taught (1:4), most likely a reference to Christian teaching to Theophilus.*

Luke gives several clues about the nature of the work itself. His own designation of the work is a *narrative* (NIV's *account*; 1:1). Furthermore, Luke's gospel is an accurately researched (*carefully investigated*), comprehensive (*everything*), thorough (*from the beginning*), and *orderly account* (1:3).

THE BIRTH & YOUTH OF JESUS · 1:5–2:52

1:5–56 Luke intentionally parallels the accounts of the births of John and Jesus. Among the parallels, the following are clear: an angel makes an announcement (1:11–13, 26–28) about a child to be born (1:13, 31) who will be great (1:15, 32) and born under extraordinary circumstances. Within this larger parallel, Luke also compares and contrasts Zechariah and Mary, revealing the first of a number of male/female pairings in Luke. From the perspective of social status, Zechariah and Mary stand at opposite ends of the spectrum. Luke places Zechariah *in the temple* in *Jerusalem*, and Mary in the small town of *Nazareth* in the north. Zechariah is married, Mary single (although both are childless). Zechariah is male, Mary female. Zechariah serves as a *priest*; Mary has no official position. Virtually every single social marker places Zechariah at the top and Mary at the bottom (Johnson 39). Understandably, Mary wonders about Gabriel's greeting, *Greetings, you who are highly favored! The Lord is with you* (1:28).

Nevertheless, when Gabriel tells Zechariah that his *prayer has been heard*, Zechariah responds with disbelief. Because he *did not believe* (1:20) Gabriel's words, Zechariah must remain silent until Gabriel's words *come true* (1:20). Mary, on the other hand, even though she is *greatly troubled* and *wondered what kind of greeting this might be* (1:29), responds with belief (1:45), modeling Luke's view of discipleship. In the face of God's surprising and powerful acts, Mary answers, *I am the Lord's servant* (1:38, 48; 2:29).

Luke concludes the foretelling of the births with Mary's visit to Elizabeth and a song of Mary. Mary's visit to Elizabeth confirms Gabriel's words. In the first place, Mary finds Elizabeth with child, confirming Gabriel's announcement (1:36, 41). Second, in language that echoes Zechariah's prophetic speech (1:15, 41, 67), Elizabeth, *filled with the Holy Spirit*, pronounces a threefold blessing over Mary and the child Mary carries (1:42), because of her belief (1:45).

> **Vulgate**
> *The Latin translation of the Bible by Jerome around 400 CE. The Vulgate was the dominant translation in the West for the next thousand years.*

Mary's song, often called the Magnificat (after the first word in the Latin Vulgate), expresses several prominent themes in Luke (compare 1 Samuel 2:1–10). First, Mary *praises the Lord* because *God has done great things* (1:46–49). Second, God shows *mercy* (1:50, 54) on the lowly in society – the *humble* (1:48, 52) and the *hungry* (1:53). Third, God shows judgment on the *proud*, the *rulers*, and the *rich* (1:51–53), foreshadowing Luke's interest in the use of possessions and the theme of reversal. Fourth, Luke portrays God as faithful *to Abraham and his descendents forever* (1:55).

1:57–80 John's birth brings joy, astonishment, and praise – *joy* for Elizabeth, her neighbors, and her relatives (1:58); *astonishment* for everyone at the naming of the infant John (1:63); and *praise* by Zechariah for the loosening of his tongue (1:64). God continues to act in surprising and powerful ways, creating *awe* and causing *everyone* to wonder (1:65–66). Those who hear about these events ask, *What then is this child going to be?* Luke answers this question with the song of Zechariah in 1:67–79.

Like Mary's song, Zechariah's song foreshadows several Lukan emphases. The first half of the song focuses on God, the second on John the Baptist. As always, *praise* is due to God for acting on behalf on his people (1:68). *Salvation*, which will play a significant role in Luke and later in Acts, dots Zechariah's song at several points (1:69, 71, 77). Both of these themes are combined as Zechariah extols God for his *mercy* and faithfulness to his people (1:68–75, 78), *as he said through his holy prophets of long ago* (1:70).

Luke expands on John's role in the final verses of Zechariah's song (1:76–80). Like the voice of Isaiah 40, John will *prepare the way for God* (1:76). Thus, John becomes an agent of God's *mercy*, which is compared to the *sun* shining *on those living in darkness* (1:78–79). Finally, John grows physically and spiritually (*in spirit*) until he appears *publicly to Israel* (1:80).

2:1–20 Luke recounts the birth of Jesus in three parts: the setting, the birth, and the witnesses to his birth. Luke describes the setting in two ways; the first connects the birth to contemporary Roman history, the second to Israel's history. Luke's linking of God's action and human history (1:5; 3:1–2) results in the naming of two Roman leaders. First, the emperor *Cæsar Augustus* (emperor 29 BCE–14 CE) issues *a decree that a census should be taken*. Given Luke's earlier connection of the birth of Jesus and the rule of Herod the Great (1:5), the timing of this *census* is difficult to reconcile (Fitzmyer 1:399–405) with the three known censuses during Augustus' reign (28 BCE, 8 BCE, and 14 CE according to the *Res gestae divi Augusti* 8.2–4) and the one known governorship of Quirinius over the province of Syria (6–7 CE; compare Acts 5:37).

> **Quirinius**
> *Quirinius (died 21 CE) served as a consul of Rome in 12 BCE, as mentor to Augustus's grandson Gaius in 2 CE, and as legate of Syria.*

Luke places Jesus in Israel's heritage through *Bethlehem, the town of David*, and through Joseph, who *belonged to the house and line of David* (2:4). This repeated emphasis on David is consistent with Luke's stress on David elsewhere in the gospel (1:27, 32, 69; 2:11; 3:31; 6:3; 18:38, 39; 20:41, 42, 44). Two significant passages are 1:32–33, which link Jesus to David's *throne* and a *kingdom that will never end*, and 20:41, which expresses the conviction that *the Christ is the Son of David*.

Luke narrates the birth of Jesus in a surprisingly brief manner with few details (2:6–7). Jesus is the *firstborn*, a detail that anticipates the presentation of Jesus in the temple (2:23). Mary wraps him in *cloths* and places him *in a manger*. This second detail doubles as a *sign* to the shepherds in the subsequent passage (2:12, 16). Third, Jesus is placed in a manger *because there is no room for them in the inn* [Greek *katalyma*], a word that could also be translated "guest room" (as in 22:11).

Luke describes the visit of the shepherds in densely packed language. Luke stresses the identity of the child. The threefold description in 2:11 lies at the center. As *Savior*, Jesus will bring *salvation* to the *Gentiles and…glory to Israel* (2:30–32). As *Christ*, Jesus fulfills the promises of God (2:26, 29). As *Lord* – the most frequently used title for Jesus in Luke-Acts (Fitzmyer 1:200–01) – Jesus wears the same title God has in the Old Testament (1:68).

Luke uses four different witnesses to continue his portrait of God as powerful and worthy of praise. Structurally, the language of *praise* (2:13, 20) and *glory* (2:14, 20) frames the passage. An *angel of the Lord* announces the birth of the child. *A great company of the heavenly host* (2:13) responds to God's mighty work with a song (2:14), just as Mary and Zechariah did (1:46–55; 67–79). The shepherds leave quickly, find the *baby* (2:16), *spread the word…about this child* (2:17), and glorify and praise God (2:20). The description of Mary's response builds on the previous description in 1:29–38, this time with an echo of Jacob's reflection on his son (Gen 37:11). In the face of God's surprising work, she *ponders*, rather than doubts (see also 2:51; compare 1:66). Each of these responses appropriately acknowledges God's mighty deeds.

2:21–40 Luke next turns his attention toward two more male/female pairs, first to Joseph and Mary, and then to Simeon and Anna. For all four individuals, the setting is the temple in Jerusalem. The major theme for this section is faithfulness to the law. Both the introductory and concluding verses focus on Joseph and Mary's obedience (2:21–24, 39–40). First, Jesus is circumcised *on the eighth day* (2:21; compare 1:59). Second, the child is *named Jesus* (1:31; 2:21). Third, rites of *purification* (Lev 12:2–4) are completed *according to the Law of Moses* (2:22). Fourth, Joseph and Mary *present him to the Lord as it is written in the Law of the Lord* (2:22–23). Fifth, they *offer a sacrifice in keeping with what is said in the Law of the Lord* (2:24). Through the description of these five actions and with two citations from Scripture (Exod 13:2; Lev 5:11), Luke depicts Joseph and Mary as devout and obedient. Luke concludes by saying that they return to Galilee after completing *everything required by the Law of the Lord*. With these faithful parents, the child grows *strong* and is *filled with wisdom*; moreover, the *grace of God was upon him* (2:40; compare 1:80).

Luke portrays further aspects of discipleship with Simeon and Anna. Simeon is *righteous* and *devout*. He waits for (2:25, 38; 23:5) the *consolation of Israel*. The *Holy Spirit* is upon him (2:25), having promised him life until he saw *the Lord's Christ* (2:11). With Simeon, Luke reveals his interest in the Holy Spirit, a theme seen throughout Luke-Acts. Previously, Luke connects the activity of the Holy Spirit to John (1:15), Mary (1:35), Elizabeth (1:41), and Zechariah (1:67). To be a disciple is to be filled with and led by the Holy Spirit.

Taking the child *in his arms*, Simeon *praises God* for acting as he had *promised* and for the *salvation* that will be for all people (2:28–32). Like Mary, Simeon is God's *servant* (1:38; 2:29). With this brief speech, Simeon introduces some Lukan themes. More important, however, at this juncture in the gospel are the concluding words of Simeon. These verses are programmatic for the response to Jesus throughout the rest of the gospel. True, with Jesus comes salvation for all. Yet, not all will embrace God's gracious offer. In fact, the order of the phrase *falling and rising* foreshadows the strong negative response to Jesus; the language of the *sword* foretells his ultimate fate.

Luke's vignette of Anna portrays another faithful disciple. She is a *prophetess* and *very old* (2:36). Luke's description of her as a *prophetess* foreshadows other female prophets active in the early church (Acts 2:17–18; 21:8–9). She never leaves the *temple*, *worshiping night and day*, *fasting and praying* (2:37; compare Psalm 23:6). Her devotion is all-consuming; her life is filled with acts of piety, notably prayer (also a major theme in Luke). As other disciples do, she gives *thanks to God* and *speaks about the child to all who were looking forward to the redemption of Jerusalem* (2:38). Anna's and Simeon's recognition, praise, and witness mirror the responses of the shepherds.

2:41–52 At this point, the narrative about the twelve-year-old Jesus shows some continuities and discontinuities within the larger narrative structure (Cukrowski, "Pagan Polemic," 64-68). Regarding the discontinuities, several features are clear. First, the narrative has moved beyond the birth of Jesus. Second, the parallelism between Jesus and John the Baptist breaks apart. Third, the narrative could end with 2:40, as a comparison with the wording of 2:52 reveals.

Nevertheless, Luke connects this section to the birth narrative. First, the emphasis on temple continues (1:5–23; 2:22–40) with the infancy narrative beginning and concluding in the temple – as does the entire gospel. Second, the statement about Mary in 2:50 echoes the refrain in 2:19. Third, the statement about her pain (2:48) continues the theme of 2:35. And finally, as already mentioned, the refrain in 2:52 repeats the ideas in 2:40.

What, then, does Luke stress in this temple narrative? The central feature seems to be Jesus' first words in the gospel, *Why were you searching for me? Didn't you know I had to be in my Father's house?* (2:49). These words stress the sonship of Jesus, especially with the reference to Joseph in the previous verse (*your father*; 2:38). In addition to the other titles for Jesus, Jesus is also the Son of God, a theme appearing earlier in the gospel (1:32, 35). Their response also foreshadows the lack of understanding that other disciples will show (9:45; 18:34; 19:42; 24:16).

> **Luke's Portrayal of Jesus**
> Luke's emphasis on the wondrous understanding of Jesus connects Jesus to typical descriptions of the youth of great men (Philo, Moses, 1.20–21; Lucian, Demonax, 3; Josephus, Antiquities, 2:230–231). In other words, Luke describes Jesus in a way that Hellenistic readers would expect a great person to be depicted.

Luke brings this section of narrative to a close with several assurances. As Jesus grew up in *Nazareth*, he was *obedient* to his parents (2:51). Mary continues to model reflective discipleship – she *treasured all these things in her heart* (2:51), even though she does not fully understand (see 8:10; 9:45; 18:34). In turn, Jesus continues to grow *in wisdom* [intellectually] *and stature* [physically], *and favor with God* [spiritually] *and men* [socially; compare 1 Samuel 2:26].

THE BEGINNINGS OF JESUS' MINISTRY · 3:1–4:13

3:1–20 Luke 3 begins with an extended section on John the Baptist, a highly influential person in early Christianity. A measure of John's influence appears in both extrabiblical and biblical sources. In one passage, Josephus mentions John's preaching and baptism, as well as his death under Herod Antipas (*Antiquities*, 18.116–119). In Luke 11:1, Luke reveals that John the Baptist had disciples: "*Teach us to pray just as John taught his disciples.*" Apparently, John's disciples were known for their fasting and prayer (5:33).

In the book of Acts, Luke tells of two interactions between Christianity and John's disciples. Acts 18:24–28 describes Apollos as one who *taught about Jesus accurately, though he knew only the baptism of John*. Priscilla and Aquila explain to Apollos *the way of God more adequately* (18:26). In the very next passage in Acts, Luke recounts how more than twelve disciples of John were baptized *into the name of Jesus*, even though they had already received *John's baptism* (19:1–7). It seems that followers of John the Baptist were widespread from Judea to Egypt (Apollos) to Asia Minor (twelve disciples), even more than a generation after John's death.

Not only is John significant historically and religiously, but he is also significant theologically for Luke. John goes *in the spirit and power of Elijah...to make ready a people prepared for the Lord* (1:17). Zechariah sings of his son's prophetic role as a messenger of God's redemption (1:67–77). John comes at a turning point in God's plan; as Luke 16:16 states, *The law and the Prophets were proclaimed until John. Since that time, the good news of the kingdom of God is being preached.*

Luke's discussion of John begins with another synchronism (1:5; 2:1–2). Luke correlates John's ministry with seven individuals. The successor to Augustus, *Tiberius Cæsar*, ruled from 14–37 CE. Thus, the *fifteenth year* of his reign was 29 CE. *Pontius Pilate* governed Judea as prefect 26–36 CE. One of the many children of Herod the Great, *Herod* Antipas ruled as the *tetrarch of Galilee* (4 BCE–40 CE) until the emperor Caligula sent him into exile. Another son of Herod the Great, *Philip the tetrarch*, governed *Iturea and Traconitis* (regions northeast of the Sea of Galilee) from 4 BCE–34 CE. Philip married Salome, the unnamed girl who danced before Herod Antipas (Mark 6:21–29). In addition, Philip rebuilt the city of Panion and named it Cæsarea Philippi in honor of Augustus. *Lysanius* ruled as *tetrarch of Abilene*, an area about twenty miles northwest of Damascus with its capital at Abila.

The final two individuals correlate with the Jewish high priesthood and function as a transition to John's ministry among the Jews. *Annas* was high priest 6–15 CE; *Caiaphas*, who was the son-in-law of Annas, served as high priest 18–36 CE. Since these men did not share in a joint high priesthood, it is not clear what Luke means by connecting them as he does.

Echoing the language of a prophetic call (see Jeremiah 1:1–2), Luke describes John as a prophet. His message is *a baptism of repentance for the forgiveness of sins* (3:3). With the phrase *in the wilderness* (3:2, 4), Luke connects John the prophet to a quotation from *Isaiah the prophet* (Isa 40:3–5). Luke's quotation from Isaiah is longer than Mark's, probably because Luke wants to include the last phrase – *All mankind will see God's salvation* – a phrase that emphasizes Luke's theme of universal salvation (3:6).

In the following verses, Luke moves from general admonitions to repentance (3:7–9) to specific examples (3:10–14; Craddock 48). Luke connects the specific examples together with the thrice-repeated question, *What should we do?* The examples involve violence and the use of possessions in several forms.

Luke then contrasts John and Jesus. In each case, John's words tell how Jesus is superior. Jesus is *more powerful*; John is *not worthy to untie* Jesus' sandals; Jesus baptizes *with the Holy Spirit and fire* (3:16). Given the immediate context, the "fire" probably refers to judgment (3:9, 17). In fact, the next verse describes Jesus' role as judge. The last verses about John describe his preaching *good news* and his imprisonment by Herod the tetrarch (3:18–20).

3:21–38 Interestingly, Luke does not mention John in the context of Jesus' baptism. Luke, however, is the only gospel writer to mention that Jesus *was praying* at his baptism (3:21). Luke also stresses the presence of the *Holy Spirit* and concludes with God's words, *You are my son, whom I love; with you I am well pleased*. With the word "son," Luke links this section with the genealogy in 3:23–38.

Luke's genealogy differs from Matthew's in four key respects. First, Luke's genealogy is much longer. Second, Luke moves backward in time to *Adam*, allowing Luke to stress the antiquity of Christianity, since the newness of Christianity was a point of criticism by opponents. Going back to Adam (versus Matthew's beginning with Abraham) also connects Jesus to all of humanity. Third, it is difficult to resolve all of the questions about specific individuals in Luke's genealogy, given the extant information. Fourth, Luke ends with the phrase *Son of God*, a phrase that both affirms Jesus' identity and connects the genealogy to the temptation narrative (4:3, 9).

4:1–13 With a different order than Matthew, the temptation of Jesus in Luke both begins and ends with the phrase *If you are the Son of God*, echoing both 3:22 and 38 (compare 4:41). Two other distinctive features in Luke's account include his emphasis on the Holy Spirit (4:1) and the additional information about the devil in 4:6 and 13. Juxtaposed beside Jesus' ministry at Nazareth, Luke first uses the temptation narrative to describe what Jesus' ministry is not and then tells what Jesus' ministry is with the episode in Nazareth.

Luke describes the setting for the temptation in 4:1–2. Jesus, *full of the Holy Spirit*, has returned from the *Jordan*, a probable reference to his baptism (3:3). Jesus *was led by the Spirit in the desert, where for forty days he was tempted by the devil*. Jesus *ate nothing during those days* and was *hungry*. In this context comes the first temptation, the command, *Tell this stone to become bread*. A physical temptation, this first demand shows that Jesus does not exercise his ministry in a self-directed way; his efforts go toward the feeding and healing of others. As with the next two temptations, Jesus responds with Scripture: *It is written: 'Man does not live on bread alone'* (Deut 8:3).

The second temptation appeals to a desire for power. The devil offers the *authority and splendor* of *all the kingdoms of the world* if Jesus will *worship* him. Jesus rejects this offer of power and quotes Deuteronomy 6:13: *Worship the Lord your God and serve him only*. The third temptation finds the devil quoting Scripture, this time Psalm 91:12. Undaunted, Jesus responds with a third quotation from Deuteronomy: *Do not put the Lord your God to the test* (Deut 6:16). This temptation shows Jesus' rejection of a ministry of style over service. Jesus refuses to amaze crowds by throwing himself from *the highest point of the temple*. Instead, he focuses on a ministry to others that leads to the cross. Luke, however, knows that the story has just begun. Further temptations await *an opportune time* (22:3, 31). Disciples learn about the role of Scripture

> **Discipleship**
>
> Luke not only focuses on the nature of Jesus' ministry; he also gives information about discipleship. Disciples learn about the context of temptation. Jesus has just returned from his baptism and the heavenly affirmation. Yet he is also hungry and alone, conditions for temptation to take hold.

in responding to temptation. Scripture informs Jesus each time; yet a shallow understanding of Scripture makes a disciple susceptible to its misuse. Finally, disciples learn about different types of temptation and a way of doing ministry.

JESUS' MINISTRY IN GALILEE · 4:14–9:50

4:14–30 The Nazareth account is not the first time Jesus has ministered. Already, he has been in *Galilee*. Already, *news about him spread through the whole countryside* (4:14, 37). Already, Jesus *taught in their synagogues, and everyone praised him* (4:14–15, 31). Luke focuses on and expands this account in Nazareth because it is paradigmatic for Luke's understanding of Jesus' ministry.

Jesus entered the synagogue *as was his custom*, showing his faithfulness to his religious heritage (see 2:42). After receiving the scroll, Jesus *found* (a word showing intent) the passage in Isaiah, which he reads. The Isaiah quotation from chapters 61 and 58 shows the typical Lukan interest in the Spirit: *The Spirit of the Lord is upon me*. In addition, Luke's interest in the dispossessed is evident in the four groups that are served: the *poor* (6:20; 7:22; 14:13, 21; 16:20, 22; 18:22; 21:3), *prisoners*, *blind* (7:21–22; 14:13, 21; 18:35), and *oppressed*.

The first response to Jesus is positive. *The eyes of everyone ... were fastened on him.... All spoke well of him and were amazed at the gracious words*. The reaction changes dramatically with the second part of Jesus' sermon. Jesus utters two proverbs; the first, unique to Luke, shows the desire for miracles in Nazareth (4:23): *Physician, heal yourself! Do here in your home town what we have heard that you did in Capernaum*. The second proverb, *No prophet is accepted in his own town* (see 4:16), foreshadows the rejection of Jesus in Nazareth.

In a passage unique to Luke, Jesus tells of two Gentiles, the *widow in Zarephath* (1 Kgs 17:7–24) and *Naaman the Syrian* (2 Kgs 5:1–19). With this part of Jesus' sermon, Luke stresses the universal extent of Jesus' ministry and the difficulty of the inclusion of the Gentiles (compare the responses to Cornelius and the mention of Gentiles in Acts 10–11 and 22:21–22). The second responses from the synagogue are anger and attempted violence. Given the prediction by Simeon that Jesus would *cause the falling and rising of many in Israel* (2:34), the opposing reactions to the different parts of the sermon are not surprising. Most likely, Jesus *walked right through the crowd* because his hour had not yet come (see Luke 22:53).

4:31–37 In the first of three extended exorcism accounts (8:26–39; 9:37–43a), the contrast to Nazareth's response to Jesus could hardly be stronger. As Jesus teaches at a *synagogue* in *Capernaum* [4:23, 31], *a town in Galilee*, three emphases become clear. Luke first stresses Jesus' *teaching* (4:31, 32 [literally *word* in verses 32 and 36]), a basic component of Jesus' ministry (4:15, 31; 5:3). In the second place, Luke stresses Jesus' *authority* (4:32, 36; 5:24) with the exorcism of an *evil* [literally "unclean"] *spirit* (4:33, 36). Third, with two synonyms, Luke reports that the people are *amazed* (4:32, 36). Luke concludes by noting that *news about him spread* (4:14, 37).

4:38–44 In summary fashion, Luke reports more healings and exorcisms. The healing of *Simon's mother-in-law* reflects the language of exorcism: Jesus *rebuked the fever* (4:35, 39, 41). After successful healings of various kinds of sickness and casting out of demons, Jesus *went out to a solitary place* (4:32; 5:16). Although the people attempt to keep Jesus from *leaving*, Jesus does leave because he *must preach the good news of the kingdom of God to the other towns also* (8:1). With these concluding accounts in chapter 4, Luke gives a summary of Jesus' ministry, with its teaching, preaching, healing, and exorcisms (Craddock 64).

5:1–11 The calling of Simon illustrates a new aspect of Jesus' ministry, the enlisting of disciples, as well as the *power and authority* (4:36) of Jesus' word. In this account, Luke records an individual's response to the *word of God* (5:1; see 4:32, 36). The first three verses give the context of Simon's call. Jesus preaches beside the *Lake of Gennesaret*, another name for the Sea of Galilee. Because of the crowd, Jesus enters a boat *belonging to Simon*, sits down, and teaches the people from it.

After this introduction, Luke focuses on the interaction between Jesus and Simon in the encounter

> **Jesus' Authority**
>
> In 5:4, Jesus tells Simon to go out *into deep water and* let down the nets for a catch. Simon responds in the following ways: he answers Jesus and obeys, despite not understanding completely (see 1:34, 38; Johnson 90); *he lowers the nets; he catches* a large number of fish; *and he signals to his* partners in the other boat. Simon obeys because Jesus says so (literally "at *your word*"). *Each of Simon's actions emphasizes Jesus' authority.*

that begins the calling of Simon. Luke shows the power of Jesus' word in the large number of *fish* caught, the *nets* brought to the point of breaking, and the near sinking of the *boat*.

Luke records the protest of Simon in 5:8–10a. Peter falls at Jesus' knees, tells Jesus to leave, and confesses his sinfulness. Luke will show Jesus regularly in the company of sinners (5:8, 30; 7:34, 37, 39; 15:1–2; 19:7) and stresses forgiveness of sins in subsequent accounts (see 5:20, 21, 23, 24, 32; 7:34). Simon's response is a mixture of astonishment (4:36; 5:9) and fear (5:10). In addition, there is an important change of address from *master* (5:5) to *Lord* (5:8), indicating Simon's transition to a disciple. Next, Jesus reassures Simon and gives him a commission in 5:10b-11. From now on, Simon *will catch men*. Luke ends with a refrain characterizing discipleship – *left everything and followed him* (5:11, 28). The one who told Jesus to *go away* (5:8) now follows. The call is now complete. From encounter to response to protest to reassurance and commission, Luke uses these features of a call to show Simon's progress to discipleship.

5:12–16 With this account, Luke shows the authority and power of Jesus' word through the healing of a leper (7:22; 17:11–19). At Jesus' word, *immediately the leprosy left* (5:13). Luke also depicts Jesus' faithfulness to the law; here, Jesus commands the man to show himself *to the priest and offer sacrifices that Moses commanded* (5:14). Finally, Luke again shows Jesus at prayer (3:21; 5:16).

5:17–26 Luke extends his stress on the power and authority of Jesus in this passage. The focus of the *power* (5:17; 6:19; 8:46) begins with healing (5:17, 25) and extends to the *authority* [4:32, 36] *on earth to forgive sins* (5:24; 7:48). In fact, Jesus' role in the *forgiveness of sins* becomes the primary emphasis in this passage (5:20, 21, 23, 24). Conflict with *the Pharisees and the teachers of the law* begins to grow; Jesus is aware of their thinking (2:35; 5:21–22). The account concludes in a typically Lukan fashion; that is, when a miracle is performed, God is praised. Here, after the healing of the paralytic, *everyone ... gave praise to God*.

5:27–31 Luke records another calling (see 5:1–11) of a disciple, this time a tax collector. Luke connects this passage to the calling of Simon by stressing discipleship and possessions. Luke records that Levi *left everything and followed him* (5:11, 28).

Two other factors merit attention. Luke introduces the first of a number of scenes in the gospel where a banquet is the setting (7:36–50; 11:37–54; 14:1–24). This setting, similar to a symposium, or pagan drinking party, illustrates a common Hellenistic feature of first century culture. Second, the conflict between Jesus *and the Pharisees and the teachers of the law* continues (5:21, 30), this time over Jesus' contact with social and religious outcasts. Additionally, the issue of contact with tax collectors and sinners dominates this passage, from the initial contact with Levi the *tax collector* (5:27) to the *large crowd of tax collectors* at Levi's house (5:29), to the accusation in 5:30, to Jesus' explanation in 5:31–32: *I have not come to call the righteous, but sinners to repentance*. In his ministry, Jesus continues to attend to those marginalized by society (4:18–19).

5:33–39 In the context of the banquet at Levi's house, Luke introduces a conflict connected to eating. The charge is that the disciples of Jesus *go on eating and drinking*, while *John's disciples* (7:18–24; 11:1) and the Pharisees *fast*. Jesus responds in two ways. The first response is an analogy. Jesus is like a *bridegroom* and his disciples like wedding *guests*. Jesus asks if it is reasonable for guests to fast while the bridegroom is with them (5:34). A time will come, however, when the bridegroom *will be taken away* and the guests *will fast* (5:35). Jesus' second response is a double *parable*. Both parts connect through the language of *old* and *new*. The first image is that of a *new garment*, from which a patch is torn to mend an old garment. The ruin associated with the tearing of the new garment and the patching of the old is evidence of the radical difference that the kingdom inaugurates. The second image is that of *new wine*, which, if put in old wineskins, *will burst the skins* (5:37). The final verse explains why some hearers, accustomed to the old, reject the new (5:39).

6:1–12 Moving from one act of piety to another, Luke turns from fasting to observance of the Sabbath. The two episodes in 6:1–11 show Luke's interest in Jesus' faithfulness to Jewish piety. It is not surprising that Luke here explains Jesus' actions on the Sabbath, as he does later in the gospel (13:10–17; 14:1–6). In the first account, the disciples *pick some heads of grain, rub them in their hands and eat the kernels*. Perhaps alluding to the fourth commandment (Exod 20:8–11; see Deut 25:23), but even more likely to the oral traditions that had arisen regarding the Sabbath, some Pharisees ask, *Why are you doing what is not lawful on the Sabbath?* Jesus' first response uses a precedent from the life of David (1 Sam 21:1–6). Because of hunger, *David* and his companions ate *consecrated bread* reserved *only for priests to eat*. The law is superseded by human need, a principle that foreshadows the second Sabbath account.

> **Jesus' Lordship**
> Luke concludes this first account with a claim about the identity of Jesus: *The Son of Man is Lord of the Sabbath*. Compared with his comparison of Jesus to David, this is obviously the more remarkable of the two warrants, since this statement affirms Jesus' lordship and places him above both David and the Sabbath.

The second account concerns the healing of a man *whose right hand was shriveled*. The Pharisees and the teachers of the law become more aggressive in their opposition; they were *looking for a reason to accuse Jesus, so they watched him closely* (14:1; 20:20) *to see if he would heal on the Sabbath*. The crucial point of the passage comes in Jesus' question in 6:9, *Which is lawful on the Sabbath: to do good or to do evil, to save life or to destroy it?* Here the principle builds on the idea of human need in the previous passage and then goes beyond that idea to the intent of the law: what is lawful is what is good and what preserves human life. In a striking show of opposition to the views of those leaders, Jesus tells the man to stretch out his hand, which becomes *completely restored*. The response of those leaders, anger and discussion *with one another what they might do to Jesus* (6:11), foreshadows future conflicts in the gospel.

6:12–16 One of four passages with lists of the twelve apostles (Matt 10:1–4; Mark 3:13–19; Acts 1:13–14), this text provides little comment. Four items are noteworthy, however. First, as is characteristic of Luke, he mentions that Jesus prays at important points in his life (3:21; 22:41). Here Jesus spends *the night praying to God*. Second, as apostles, the Twelve will be sent out, consistent with the meaning of the Greek word *apostolos* (9:1–2). Third, the lists diverge on one of the names; where Matthew and Mark have Thaddaeus, Luke and Acts have *Judas son of James*. Perhaps Matthew and Mark call *Judas son of James* Thaddaeus to avoid confusion with Judas Iscariot. In any case, outside of these four passages the only other possible direct reference to Judas son of James is John 14:22. Fourth, Luke, as do all the gospel writers, lists *Judas Iscariot* last because Judas *became a traitor* (22:3–6, 47–48).

6:17–26 After describing Jesus' teaching (4:15, 31, 32; 5:3, 17; 6:6), Luke now offers a sample of it, here called the Sermon on the Plain. The first few verses give the setting. Jesus stands *on a level place*. Two groups are present: *a large crowd of his disciples* and *a great number of people from all over Judea, from Jerusalem, and from the seacoast of Tyre and Sidon*. The people come *to hear him and to be healed*. They also try to *touch* Jesus because *power was coming from him and healing them all*. Luke's reference to power is likely another reference to *the power of the Lord…to heal the sick* first mentioned in 5:17 (see also 8:46), although a reference to the *power of the Spirit* is not impossible (4:14).

> **Tyre & Sidon**
> Two ancient Phoenician cities often appearing in the Bible. Their presence here bespeaks Luke's interest in the Gentile mission.

Jesus directs his words to his disciples (7:1); notice the phrase *looking at his disciples*. The blessings and woes are equally balanced among four groups. With the blessings on the poor, hungry, weeping, and hated, Jesus emphasizes the upside-down nature of the kingdom. The values that the kingdom promotes differ from those of the world. Thus, disciples will need to transform their understandings because of the nature of God's kingdom. In contrast to Matthew's beatitudes, Luke emphasizes physical difficulties; for example, note the following: *poor* versus the poor in spirit (Matthew); *hunger* versus hunger and thirst for righteousness (Matthew). Both the blessings and the woes end with a similar refrain, *For that is how their fathers treated the [false] prophets*, that functions as an encouragement and a warning respectively.

6:27–36 Luke continues to describe the upside-down nature of God's kingdom in this next section. With the first four categories (that is, *your enemies, those who hate you, those who curse you*, and *those who mistreat you*), Jesus calls his disciples *to love, do good, bless*, and *to pray*. With the next four categories (*strikes you on one*

> **"Do to others…"**
> Although the proverbial nature of some of Jesus' sayings may make the literal performance of them problematic (for example, give to everyone who asks), *the final saying helps interpret questions that may arise*: Do to others as you would have them do to you.

cheek, *takes your cloak*, *asks you*, and *takes what belongs to you*), the response of the disciples is equally counter-cultural.

The second part of this section (verses 32–36) shows how Jesus calls disciples to a higher standard than that of the world; they must embody grace. With a threefold refrain, *what credit* [literally "grace"] *is that to you* (verses 32, 33, 34), Jesus asks disciples to consider whether their actions imitate God's graciousness. In fact, Luke is the only Synoptic writer to use the word *grace*. Jesus discourages disciples from doing the minimum with a thrice-repeated refrain that begins *even 'sinners.'* The *reward* for the disciples is *great*; they *will be sons of the Most High* because they behave like God, who is *kind to the ungrateful and wicked*. Thus, the call for disciples is to be like God.

6:37–49 Each of the four sayings (6:37–38) and five parables (6:39–49) in this next section shape the identity of a disciple of the kingdom. Disciples should *not judge* or *condemn*; the disciples *forgive* and *give*. Each of these activities not only blesses the world but also the disciple, as all four sayings describe. The first *parable* in 6:39 consists of two questions: *Can a blind man lead a blind man? Will they not both fall into a pit?* Only in Luke is this *parable* connected with the saying in 6:40: *A student* [literally "disciple"] *is not above his teacher, but everyone who is fully trained will be like his teacher*. This saying ties these behaviors to discipleship, which is described as becoming more like Jesus, *his teacher*. The second parable, as in Matthew, shares the context of judging and reproves the person who criticizes others for a *speck* but who does not see the *plank* in his or her own eye. Such a person is a *hypocrite*.

With agricultural images (*tree*, *figs*, *thornbushes*, *grapes*, *briers*), the third and fourth parables stress how the heart leads to behavior. The repetition of the word *heart* (twice in verse 45) and the climactic placement of the final saying link heart and action in an integral way. Jesus concludes this instruction with a fifth parable stressing the obedience of the disciple, who is someone who *hears my words and puts them into practice* (8:15, 21; 11:28). The true disciple builds his *foundation on rock*, and a *flood* cannot *shake* it; the false disciple builds *without a foundation*, and his *destruction is complete*. The disciple's words should lead to deeds (8:15, 21; 11:28).

7:1–10 After speaking about words and deeds in 6:46–49, Luke moves from the words of Jesus to the ministry of Jesus in chapter 7. Luke connects the first two accounts with the exclamation in 7:16, *A great prophet has appeared among us ... God has come to help his people*. For in both 7:1–10 and 7:11–17, Jesus acts in ways reminiscent of the prophets Elijah and Elisha, although the allusions are more explicit in the second account. In the first account, Jesus heals a Gentile soldier, echoing Elisha's healing of the Syrian Naaman (2 Kgs 5:1–14). In the second account, Jesus raises the dead son of a widow, an allusion to Elijah's raising of a widow's son (1 Kgs 17:20–24). Jesus mentions these same two examples in his sermon at Nazareth (4:25–27). Through these allusions, Luke indicates that the power of God working in the prophets also works in the ministry of Jesus.

> **Jesus & the Gentiles**
> With Jesus' encounter with the centurion, Luke stresses the inclusive nature of the kingdom. Religious and ethnic differences do not block the healing. In addition, this account foreshadows and provides a precedent for the inclusion of the Gentile Cornelius in Acts 10–11.

Luke further continues his comment on the *power* (5:17; 6:19) and *authority* of Jesus' word (4:32, 36; 5:5). The centurion explains in 7:7–8, *But say the word, and my servant will be healed. For I myself am a man under authority*. In this account, the power of Jesus is such that he heals despite being absent (7:10).

The main point in this passage, however, is Jesus' exclamation in 7:9, *I tell you, I have not found such great faith even in Israel*. In extolling the *faith* of the centurion, Jesus highlights another characteristic of disciples (18:8). In addition, Luke depicts the centurion's humility in the wordplay between the elders' assessment (*deserving*; literally "worthy") and his self-assessment (*I did not even consider myself worthy*). It is likely that his humility contributed to his *great faith*.

7:11–17 The power to heal (5:17; 6:19) finds its ultimate expression in the raising of a widow's son from the dead. This miracle foreshadows Jesus' statement in 7:22, as well as other resurrections (8:40–42, 49–56; Acts 9:36–43; 20:7–12). The allusions to Elijah are strong: Jesus goes (7:11; 1 Kgs 17:10), to the gate of a city (7:12; 1 Kgs 17:10), where he meets a widow (7:12; 1 Kgs 17:9), her son is raised from the dead, and he gives him to his mother (7:15; 1 Kgs 17:23). The last allusion repeats the same six words (in Greek). In the gospel, other people recognize similarities between Jesus and the prophets Elijah and Elisha (9:8, 19), perhaps in part because of Jesus' own words (4:24–27). Nevertheless, the term prophet cannot entirely describe Jesus, as Peter's confession (9:18–20) and other allusions to Elijah reveal (see 9:54–55). Furthermore, healing comes through the power of Jesus' word, in contrast to the threefold actions of Elijah (Fitzmyer 1:655–658).

In *Nain*, a town only a few miles southwest of Nazareth, Jesus sees a widow whose *only son* (see also *only* in 8:42; 9:38, a Lukan characteristic) has died. Luke highlights the compassion of Jesus (10:33; 15:20), whose *heart went out to her*. That compassion is seen as God's coming to *help his people* (1:68). As is characteristic after a miracle, the people *praise God*.

7:18–35 The first part of this story (verses 18–23) describes an exchange between two disciples of John the Baptist (5:33; 11:1) and Jesus. The disciples ask, *Are you the one who is to come, or should we expect someone else?* Their question, repeated twice, echoes John's statement back in 3:15–16, connecting the *Christ* to one who *will come*. Jesus performs many miracles and replies, *Go back and report.... The blind receive sight, the lame walk* [14:13, 21], *those who have leprosy are cured* [5:12–13; 17:11–19], *the deaf hear* [see 1:22; 11:14], *the dead are raised* [7:15], *and the good news is preached to the poor* [7:23], an obvious reference to Jesus' previous self-description of his ministry in 4:18–19 (see also 14:13, 21).

In 7:24–35, the messengers leave, and Jesus addresses the crowd about John. After a series of questions, Jesus reveals that John is a *prophet – and more than a prophet* (1:76; 20:6; compare 7:16, 39) because John fulfills the prophecy of Malachi 3:1. John's earthly role is to *prepare* the way for Jesus. Yet, because kingdom status is greater than earthly status, *the one who is least in the kingdom of God is greater than he*. As Simeon had predicted of Jesus (2:34), the response to Jesus is divided in 7:29–30. Jesus compares those who rejected John and who now reject him to children who are unhappy when others do not conform to their desires. They criticize John for indulging too little (1:15; 5:33) and Jesus for indulging too much. To his critics, Jesus is *a glutton and a drunkard, a friend of tax collectors and sinners*. The references to "sinners" and eating and drinking provide the transition to the next passage, where Luke tells about a *sinful* woman at a banquet (7:37, 39; also 5:27–32; 15:1–2).

7:36–50 This passage is a narrative explaining the previous passage in this chapter. While eating *dinner* (7:34, 36–37) at a *Pharisee's house* (11:37–54; 14:1–24), Jesus encounters a *sinner* (7:34, 37, 39) who responds with love, while the Pharisee Simon does not recognize that Jesus is a *prophet* (7:16, 39; Johnson 129). One of several banquet scenes (5:27–31; 11:37–53; 14:1–24), this passage shows Jesus teaching using a parable (verses 41–43) and then pointing out three contrasts between the sinful woman and Simon: tears versus no water for my feet; kisses for my feet versus no kiss; and perfume versus no oil on my head. To her Jesus says, *Your sins are forgiven. Your faith has saved you; go in peace* (1:79; 2:14; 8:48; 19:38; compare 12:51). His action raises questions about his identity (5:21; 7:49; 8:25), a question that Luke will address directly in chapter 9. Here Luke is content to emphasize faith, forgiveness, and salvation (7:47–50), all key interests in this gospel (7:9; 8:12).

8:1–21 The first three verses provide a brief but valuable transition to the parable of the Sower. In Jesus' ministry, Luke shows the *Twelve* along with *some women*, namely *Mary (called Magdalene), Joanna the wife of Cuza, Susanna,* and *many others*.

Although Matthew and Mark also contain the parable of the Sower, Luke's version presents a different emphasis. Luke concludes with *consider carefully how* [compare "*what*" in Mark 4:24] *you listen* (8:18). Thus, Luke stresses the individual's reception of the word, the responsibility of the hearer. Notice the emphasis on the heart (8:12, 15), faith (8:12, 13), and patience (8:15), all of which are only in Luke's version. Previously, Luke has stressed the heart (6:45) and faith (7:9, 50); and later he will highlight patience (21:19). Luke's account also has the only reference to salvation (8:12),

> **Women Who Followed Jesus**
> Luke indicates that women supported Jesus and his disciples financially (compare 23:49, 55; 24:1–11, 22–25). This concise report highlights Luke's interest both in the contributions of women to Christianity and in the proper use of possessions.

> **Jesus' Family**
> Only in Luke does the account of Jesus' mother and brothers coming to see Jesus follow the parable of the Sower. With this placement, Luke comments on the parable. Thus Jesus' final words are not surprising: My mother and my brothers are those who hear God's word and put it into practice. Here Luke stresses the need for disciples to study God's word and do God's will (6:47; 8:15; 11:28).

which accords with his previous emphasis on salvation (1:69, 77, 79; 2:11; 7:50).

8:22–25 In Luke 8:22–25, Luke begins a series of accounts focused on miracles. In recounting the stilling of the storm, Luke shows a dual emphasis. First, the gospel focuses on Jesus' identity. Although the disciples call Jesus *master*, Jesus is more than master, a fact the disciples do not yet recognize. In the midst of a *squall* and *great danger*, Jesus calmly sleeps in the boat. Upon awaking, Jesus *rebukes* the wind and waters, and the storm *subsides*. The climax of the scene is the disciples' question, *Who is this? He commands even the winds and water, and they obey him?* In part, this question echoes other previous questions that begin with the phrase, *Who is this …?* (5:21; 7:49). Luke's answer to this question, though not direct, is that Jesus controls creation. With a powerful word (4:36; 5:5; 7:7; 8:11) of rebuke, Jesus commands, and nature obeys. Jesus has authority (7:8–10) over disease, demons, death, and nature. With that power and authority, Jesus protects the disciples from *great danger*. Luke's second focus is on the faith of the disciples. Again, a question highlights Luke's emphasis: *Where is your faith?* Addressed to the disciples, this question contrasts the disciples' lack of faith with the faith of others in the narrative (7:9, 50). With this account, Luke continues to make faith, here in the midst of *fear* (7:16; 8:25, 35, 37, 50), a key part of discipleship.

8:26–39 In showing the full range of Jesus' power and authority, Luke recounts another exorcism (4:31–37, 41; 6:18; 7:21; 9:37–43a). Ironically, the demons know the answer to the question posed to the disciples in the previous account (8:25). Who is this Jesus? He is *the Holy One of God* (4:34), *the Christ* (4:41), and *Son of the Most High God* (8:28). Because Jesus is who he is, he can *command* evil spirits to come out, even if they are *legion*. Only by begging *repeatedly* and with Jesus' *permission* can demons secure a different fate. Rather than go *into the Abyss*, the demons enter *pigs* and drown in the *lake*. The *Abyss* most likely refers to the final destination of demons (Rev 9:1, 11; 11:7; 17:8; 20:3; Fitzmyer 1:739). Jesus' power is further seen in the contrast between the *demon-possessed man* before and after the exorcism. After the exorcism, the man is *sitting at Jesus' feet* (see 10:39), *dressed and in his right mind*. Free from his violent, unsettled life under the power of the demon (8:29), the man begs to go with Jesus. Instead, Jesus calls this disciple to *tell how much God has done for you*. The man goes and tells *how much Jesus had done for him*; with the change of *Jesus* for *God* in these last phrases, Luke again emphasizes the identity of Jesus. As Luke has consistently done, he again depicts the divided response to Jesus (2:34), here clearly seen in the responses of the cured man and *the people of the region*, who are *overcome with fear* (8:25, 35, 37, 50) and ask *Jesus to leave them*.

8:40–56 Luke retains the structure of Mark's telling of the raising of Jairus's *only daughter* (7:12; 9:38) and the healing of the woman with a flow of blood. Luke begins with the daughter, cuts to the account of the woman, and then returns to the daughter. The two accounts link up not only structurally but also verbally (note the use of the words *daughter* [8:42, 48] and *twelve* [8:42, 43]), and thematically. Both are females in hopeless situations. Several matters are worthy of note. First, Luke continues to stress the *power* of Jesus (5:17; 6:19; 8:46), here over disease and death (7:11–17). Second, with the phrase *your faith has healed* [literally "saved"] *you*, Luke adds further stress on faith (7:9, 50; 8:25) and salvation. Unclean from her continued bleeding (Lev 15:25–30), this woman and her faith form a contrast to the disciples, who lack sufficient faith earlier in this chapter (8:25). In fact, the faith shown by the woman is precisely the type Jairus needs, when he learns, *Your daughter is dead*. Jesus tells him, *Don't be afraid; just believe, and she will be healed*. Third, with these two females, Luke continues his stress on women and the lowly of society (here an "unclean" woman).

9:1–9 Jesus extends his ministry through the sending of the twelve disciples. *The Twelve* will come to represent the restoration of Israel (22:29–30) and function as witnesses to Jesus (Acts 1:8). At this point, however, Jesus gives the Twelve *power and authority to drive out demons and to cure diseases and … to preach the kingdom of God and to heal the sick*. With that description, Luke reiterates the power and authority of Jesus (4:36); furthermore, Luke's description summarizes the ministry of Jesus (4:18–19; 7:21–23; 9:2, 6, 11). Jesus' instructions include a call to depend on God: *Take nothing for the journey – no staff, no bag, no bread, no money, nor extra tunic*. Later, Luke reveals that the Twelve lacked nothing on this mission (22:35).

A Roman Legion
In the Roman army, a legion typically consisted of 6,000 men.

In a summary fashion, Luke records that the Twelve go, preach, heal, return, and report to Jesus (9:6, 10). This sending, however, also sets up the reaction of *Herod the tetrarch*. Grandson of Herod the Great, Herod Antipas hears reports linking Jesus' activity with *John* the Baptist, *Elijah*, and *the prophets of long ago*. Puzzled, Herod wonders, *I beheaded John. Who, then, is this I hear such things about?* This question of Jesus' identity, asked so many times already (5:21; 7:49; 8:25), comes to the forefront in chapter 9. The options mentioned in this passage help connect the various parts of Luke 9 together.

9:10–17 After the apostles return from their mission (9:1–6), they report to Jesus *what they had done*. Jesus then takes them to *Bethsaida*. Near the northeast shore of the Sea of Galilee, Bethsaida is named (only by Luke) as the place for the feeding of the 5,000. Interestingly, Luke's account of the feeding uncharacteristically ends without any report of the crowd's reaction, probably anticipating Jesus' criticism of Bethsaida's lack of response to the miracles he performed there (10:13).

Jesus continues the work of the kingdom, preaching and healing (9:11). But in this passage, three allusions give shape and meaning to this passage. First, Luke probably alludes to God's provision of manna in the wilderness. The *bread* is *eaten* in a *remote* place, here in Bethsaida (literally "in a deserted place"; 9:12). The second allusion is to the feeding of a hundred men by Elisha. Both 2 Kings and Luke contain a command to give the bread for others to eat (2 Kgs 4:43; Luke 9:13) and a report that all eat with some left over (2 Kgs 4:44; Luke 9:17). With these two allusions, Luke anticipates the focus on Jesus' identity in 9:18–27: Jesus is like Moses and a great prophet (Elijah/Elisha). Finally, Luke also echoes the language of the Lord's Supper; in the feeding of the 5,000, Jesus takes the loaves and fishes, looks up to heaven, gives thanks, breaks the loaves, and gives them to the disciples (22:19; compare 24:30).

> **The Bread of Life**
> As the disciples come to know Jesus through both the Lord's Supper and the meal in Emmaus (22:14–23; 24:30–32), so too the crowds and disciples in chapter 9 should recognize who Jesus is.

9:18–27 As is typical, Luke describes Jesus *praying* when the other gospel writers do not. In this scene, Luke answers the question, *Who is this?* (5:21; 7:49; 8:25; 9:9). The crowds say that Jesus is *John the Baptist, Elijah*, and *one of the prophets of long ago...come back to life*. Jesus continues, *But what about you? Who do you say I am?* Peter responds, *The Christ of God* (9:20; 23:35). Jesus warns *them not to tell this to anyone*, which is, at first thought, a curious command. However, from the following description of the suffering of the Christ, it appears that the disciples may hold other, perhaps earthly and political, views of what the Christ will be. Such a misunderstanding is probably also shared by the crowds to whom Jesus ministers.

Luke concludes with the first of several passion predictions (9:22, 44; 18:32–33; compare 17:25) and the first of a number of extended discussions on discipleship (9:23–27, 47–48, 57–62; 14:25–35). Probably the most puzzling aspect of this section is Jesus' statement that *some who are standing here will not taste death before they see the kingdom of God*, a prediction fulfilled in the transfiguration account that follows.

9:28–36 The context of the transfiguration shows consistently Lukan features. From the twelve apostles, Jesus takes *Peter, John, and James* (8:51; see 5:1–11), an order foreshadowing the pairing of Peter and John in Acts. As before (3:21; 6:12), Luke shows Jesus *praying* at a time of great importance.

With this scene, Luke focuses on the identity of Jesus, using Moses, Elijah, and perhaps the Son of Man from Daniel 7. The language bears striking similarities among these individuals. In Exodus 24:13–18, Moses has an encounter with God on a *mountain*, God appears *in a cloud*, and *the glory of the Lord* is present (see also Exodus 34:2, 5, 29–35). Two other uniquely Lukan touches emphasize this allusion to Moses: the mention of Jesus' departure [Greek *exodus* in 9:31] and the command *Listen to him* (Deut 18:15; Luke 9:35). In 1 Kings, Elijah also has an encounter with God on a *mountain* (19:8, 11), God acts through a *cloud* (18:44), and Elijah experiences the presence of God (19:11–13). The Son of Man (see 9:26) may also play a role; Johnson (155) remarks, "The elements of white clothes, clouds, glory, and kingdom all recall Daniel 7:9–13." Luke's account emphasizes Jesus' identity. Jesus is not

> **The Transfiguration**
> In Luke's narrative, Jesus himself is *not* transfigured [Greek metamorphein], *as he is in Mark* (9:2), perhaps to avoid the connotations of transformation in Hellenistic mythology.

merely human like Moses and Elijah, as God's voice makes clear (9:35; compare 3:22). Luke concludes with the phrase *The disciples kept this to themselves*, possibly in obedience to Jesus' command in 9:21.

9:37–45 With his focus on the identity of Jesus, Luke shortens Mark's account and stresses the power of Jesus to heal in this text, the last of three extended exorcism stories (4:31–37; 8:26–39). After the transfiguration, Jesus encounters a father whose *only child* (7:12; 8:42) has an evil spirit that the disciples cannot drive out. Apparently, the disciples should have been able to drive out this demon (see 9:1–2), because their failure prompts Jesus' rebuke. The healing of the child leads to Luke's conclusion – *And they were all amazed* [2:48; 4:32; 9:43] *at the greatness of God*.

Luke places Jesus' second prediction of his death (9:22; 18:31–33) in the context of this exorcism (9:43b). Luke concludes with a description of the incomprehension of the disciples. This incomprehension anticipates the next three accounts, in which the disciples fail to grasp the meaning of discipleship. Luke's theme of the incomprehension of the disciples continues (18:34; 19:42) even after the resurrection (24:16, 25–27, 44–47).

9:46–50 Perhaps prompted by Jesus' selection of Peter, John, and James to accompany him (9:28), the disciples argue about *which of them would be the greatest* (see 22:24–27). Jesus, *knowing their thoughts* (2:35; 5:22; 6:8), stands a *child* [9:37–43; 18:15–17] *beside him*. With this child, Jesus teaches how his ministry concerns receiving those esteemed *least*, so that *whoever welcomes this little child in my name welcomes me*. As to who is the greatest, Jesus concludes that the least among the disciples is the *greatest*, because greatness comes from the sender, not the sent.

In the next two verses, when the disciples try to stop a man from casting out demons, Jesus replies, *Do not stop him, for whoever is not against us is for us* (see 11:23). Here, recalling the language of Numbers 11:28, where Joshua tries to stop some Israelites from prophesying, Luke illustrates the attitude that disciples should have for outsiders who are acting in ways consistent with the ministry of Jesus.

THE ROAD TO JERUSALEM · 9:51–19:27

9:51–56 With this passage, Luke begins a long section, extending through Luke 19:27, where he depicts Jesus on the way to *Jerusalem* (9:51, 53; 13:22; 17:11; 18:31; 19:11, 28). Luke also uses two echoes of Elijah to define the identity of Jesus and his disciples. Luke's phrase, *As the time approached for him to be taken up to heaven*, alludes to Elijah's being *taken up to heaven* (2 Kgs 2:9–11). Next, after being rejected by people in a *Samaritan* village (10:25–37; 17:11–19), James and John ask Jesus whether they should *call fire down from heaven to destroy them*, an echo of Elijah's calling down of fire from heaven (2 Kgs 1:10–12). So, like Elijah, Jesus will be taken up to heaven; unlike Elijah, however, Jesus' ministry does not involve destroying those who oppose him.

9:57–62 With three examples, Luke illustrates the cost of discipleship. Disciples of Jesus forego comfort and security (9:58), and they have commitments that surpass family duty (9:60) and affection (9:62). The last saying, *No one who puts his hand to the plow and looks back is fit for service in the kingdom of God*, alludes to Elijah's selection of Elisha (1 Kgs 19:19–21) and shows how Jesus' call to follow surpasses that of even Elijah and Elisha.

10:1–24 Unique to Luke, this long section divides into two parts: the sending and the return of the seventy-two (10:1–16, 17–24). It is difficult to decide whether 10:1, 17 should read seventy or *seventy-two* (NIV), because the textual evidence is virtually evenly split between the two options. An allusion to Numbers 11:16 is the most probable reason for the mention of the number seventy (or seventy-two, with the addition of the two elders in 11:26; see Garrett 47). These seventy-two disciples help Jesus in the same way that the seventy-two elders helped Moses in his work. The sending of the seventy-two may also anticipate the sending of Christians other than the twelve apostles in Acts.

Jesus sends them out *two by two...where he was going to go*. Thus, their ministry both prepares the way for Jesus and anticipates the pairs found in Luke and Acts (see Luke 19:29; 22:8; in Acts, note Peter and John; Paul and Silas). Jesus warns them about opposition, those he calls *wolves*. Jesus' instructions parallel his instructions to the twelve apostles in chapter 9. Here Jesus adds *sandals* to the list of things to leave behind and offers the admonition *do not greet anyone on the road*, presumably because of the urgency of the mission (see 2 Kgs 4:29). Jesus then gives instructions about suitable behavior in the face of acceptance and opposition. If a house accepts them, they should eat and drink whatever they are given, avoiding moving *around from house to house* searching for better food.

If a town receives them, they should *heal the sick who are there and tell them*, *The kingdom of God is near you* (10:9, 11; 11:20; 17:21).

If a house rejects them, Jesus tells them that *peace will return to you* (that is, not be lost or wasted; Fitzmyer 2:848). If a town rejects them, they are to proclaim, *Even the dust of your town that sticks to our feet we wipe off against you* (Acts 13:51; 18:6). *Yet be sure of this*: *The kingdom of God is near*. Jesus promises that *it will be more bearable on that day for Sodom than for that town*, echoing the account in Genesis 19, which portrays Sodom as an example of inhospitality.

Jesus continues with pronouncements against three towns that rejected him: *Korazin*, which is thought to be located in Galilee, about two miles north of Capernaum (Smith 912); *Bethsaida*, the location of the feeding of the 5,000 (9:10–17); and *Capernaum*, a city on the northwest shore of the Sea of Galilee and where Jesus ministered (4:23, 31; 7:1). The judgment against these three cities will be worse than that for *Tyre and Sidon*, Phoenician cities remembered for their sinfulness (Ezek 28). From those cities where Jesus served and ministered, much is expected.

The return of the seventy-two has three components: the report to Jesus, Jesus' words to them, and Jesus' words to the other disciples. The report to Jesus is brief but enthusiastic: *Lord, even the demons submit to us in your name*. Their ability to exorcise demons is somewhat surprising because, in contrast to the disciples (9:1), the seventy-two do not explicitly receive the ability to cast out demons at their commission (10:9).

Jesus responds to the seventy-two with a mysterious statement, *I saw Satan fall like lightning from heaven*. The saying likely alludes to Isaiah 14:12. Garrett thinks (50–54) that Jesus anticipates his own resurrection with these words. Nevertheless, more important than their *authority to trample on snakes* [see Acts 28:1–6; Psalm 91:13] *and scorpions, and to overcome all the power of the enemy* is that their *names are written in heaven*. Jesus, *full of joy through the Holy Spirit*, concludes with a prayer praising God for hiding these things *from the wise and learned* and revealing them *to little children*.

To the disciples, Jesus says *privately*, *Blessed are the eyes that see what you see*. This blessing likely refers back to God's revelation of hidden things (10:21) and Jesus' revelation of the Father (10:22).

10:25–37 The last two accounts in chapter 10 form a contrasting yet complementary pair. The parable of the Good Samaritan shows the need to do acts of righteousness and mercy, while the story of Mary and Martha highlights the necessity to hear the word. Luke introduces the parable with a lawyer – one of the *wise and learned* (10:22) – asking, *What must I do to inherit eternal life?* This question illustrates Luke's theme of salvation and parallels other similarly phrased questions in Luke and Acts (3:10, 12, 14; 10:25; 18:18; Acts 2:37; 16:30; 22:10). When questioned, the lawyer responds by quoting the *Shema* (Deut 6:5), an answer that wins Jesus' approval. Unfortunately, the lawyer *wanted to justify himself* (16:15), so he next asks, *And who is my neighbor?*

Jesus then relates a parable wherein a traveler falls *into the hands of robbers* who leave him *half dead*. In order, a *priest* and *Levite* pass by *on the other side* of the road. In contrast, a *Samaritan* takes *pity* (7:13; 15:20), bandages his *wounds*, *pouring on oil and wine*, puts the man on his own donkey, takes him to an *inn*, takes *care of him*, leaves money for his care, promises to pay for *extra expense*, and plans to *return* – nine actions that emphasize the kindness of the Samaritan.

When asked, *Which of these three do you think was a neighbor*, the expert in the law replies, *The one who had mercy shown to him*. Jesus concludes, *Go and do likewise*. This climactic emphasis on doing recalls the lawyer's initial question and stresses the need to perform acts of mercy. The use of the Samaritan highlights Luke's interest in ministering to the outcasts in society, an emphasis that Luke picks up again in the following story of the women Mary and Martha.

The Heavenly Book

The idea that a book existed that recorded human deeds and destinies began in the ancient Near East. In the Bible, God owns this book, and its mention offers hope to faithful persons facing adversity. For the idea of a book in heaven with the names of the saved, see Exodus 32:32; Isaiah 4:3; Philippians 4:3; Hebrews 12:23; Revelation 3:5; 13:8; 17:8; 20:12, 15; 21:27.

Samaritans

The use of the Samaritan as the hero taps into popular prejudice about Samaritans, who offered (9:51–53) and received hostility from Jews (9:54–56; John 4:9). Even the name "Samaritan" was an insult among some Jews (John 8:48), who viewed a Samaritan as a "foreigner" (Luke 17:11–19). Despite this hostility, the Christian mission will reach Samaria and bear fruit (Acts 1:8; 8:4–25; 9:31; 15:3).

10:38–42 As Luke does so often, he does here as well, pairing an account about a man (the Samaritan) with one about a woman (see below). The two accounts also go together as a contrast between doing (10:25, 37) and hearing (10:39). Yet, both doing and hearing are necessary, as 8:21 indicates; but some people need to hear one message more than the other—hence the separate stress given to hearing in this passage.

Luke tells of Jesus' visit to the village of Mary and Martha. Martha opens *her home* to Jesus and begins preparations for his stay. Mary, on the other hand, *sits at the Lord's feet listening* to Jesus. The posture of Mary is the posture of a disciple; note the description of Paul's training *under* [literally "at the feet of"] *Gamaliel* (Acts 22:3). When Martha protests, *Lord, don't you care that my sister has left me to do the work by myself? Tell her to help me!* Jesus chides Martha and praises Mary because *Mary has chosen what is better, and it will not be taken away from her.* His praise of Mary's choice of learning over domestic preparations counters prevailing expectations for women in first century culture.

11:1–13 Luke continues his emphasis on prayer with this passage. After Jesus *finished* praying, the disciples ask him, *Lord, teach us to pray, just as John taught his disciples* (5:33; 7:18–24). From this request, Luke indicates that the disciples recognized Jesus as a person of prayer and that prayer is a learned practice; Jesus also teaches about prayer in Luke 18:1–8.

> **"Teach us to pray …"**
> Commonly known as the Lord's Prayer, the five-part prayer in Luke is shorter than its parallel in Matthew. The first part asks that God's name be recognized as holy. In the second part, Jesus prays that God's rule be established. The next two parts contain requests for physical and spiritual health. The final line exhorts disciples to pray that they do not fall into temptation, *an idea also found later in Luke* (22:40, 46; compare 22:31–32).

With the word *bread* connecting 11:5–8 with the preceding teaching, Luke continues his teaching on prayer with a brief parable about a persistent friend. This *friend* arrives at *midnight* and asks for *three loaves of bread.* The householder does not want to be bothered because his *door is already locked*, and his *children* are with him *in bed.* The final lines of the parable demonstrate Jesus' stress on persistence in prayer. Later in the gospel, Jesus will again emphasize persistence in prayer (18:1–8). In 11:9–10, Jesus further stresses the importance of making requests to God with three different words for asking (*ask, seek,* and *knock*), each followed by a promise of giving, finding, and opening respectively.

The final section is a parable composed of three questions (compare 17:7–10), comparing disciples to children and God to a *father*. The word *father* (11:2, 11, 13) connects this last instruction to Jesus' initial teaching. Jesus presumes that no earthly father will give a *snake* or a *scorpion* (compare 10:19) to his child, but rather *good gifts*. How much more will God *give the Holy Spirit* [compare *good gifts* in Matt 7:11] *to those who ask him?* This brief parable illustrates God's willingness to bless human beings and presumes that disciples will ask for and receive the Holy Spirit.

11:14–28 Using the context of Jesus *driving out a demon* (11:14, 15, 18, 19, 20), Luke treats two faithless responses (11:14–20), explains Jesus' relationship with Satan (11:21–23), and concludes with two positive admonitions (11:24–28). After Jesus drives out *a demon that was mute*, some in the crowd say, *By Beelzebub, the prince of demons, he is driving out demons.* Others test Jesus *by asking for a sign from heaven.* Jesus offers two rebuttals. First, it does not make sense for Jesus to cast out demons by Beelzebub because *a house divided against itself will fall.* Second, Jesus asks, *Now if I drive out demons by Beelzebub, by whom do your followers drive them out?* Next, Jesus offers his interpretation of the situation: *the kingdom of God has come to you* (compare 10:9, 11; 17:21). With the phrase

> **Beelzebub**
> "Beelzebub" is another name for Satan, probably coming from the Beelzebub of 2 Kings 1:2–3, 6, 16 and meaning the "Lord of the Flies" (Fitzmyer 2:920).

> **Jesus & Satan**
> Luke illustrates Jesus' relationship with Satan with the story of a strong man (Satan) who is safe, *unless* someone stronger (Jesus) attacks and overpowers him. The stronger can claim victory with the taking of the strong man's armor and the dividing up of the spoils. With this parable, Jesus argues that Satan is defeated. Jesus characterizes the one who claims otherwise with the following saying: *He who is not with me is against me* [see 9:50], *and he who does not gather with me, scatters.*

finger of God, Jesus alludes to Exodus 8:19, where Pharaoh's magicians acknowledge the power of God. With this phrase, Jesus also associates magic, a significant theme in Acts, with the demonic and explains that each exorcism is a demonstration of God's victory over Satan and an advancement of the kingdom of God.

Illustrated by an account about an *evil spirit*, the complete story about evil includes both expulsion of the bad and inclusion of the good. After leaving someone and wandering about, the evil spirit returns to him or her, *finds the house* [that is, the person] *swept clean and put in order*, and *takes seven other spirits more wicked than itself, and they go in and live there*. Because his life was not filled with kingdom activities, the man's final condition is *worse than the first*.

Luke balances the brief account about the man taken over by evil spirits in 11:24–26 with an exclamation by a woman in 11:28–29. She blesses Jesus. Jesus responds by indicating that true blessedness in the kingdom is not tied to social expectations or biological functions, but rather to faithfulness in the kingdom of God. Thus those who *hear the word of God and obey it* (6:47; 8:15; 21) are *blessed*.

11:29–32 To those seeking signs (11:16), Jesus replies that judgment awaits that generation. In fact, one *greater than* both *Solomon* and *Jonah is here*. The sign given to this generation is *the sign of Jonah*, which in Luke is Jesus' preaching (11:32), not the resurrection, as in Matthew's account (Matt 12:39–40).

11:33–36 Luke sums up a series of sayings about light (see 8:16–18) with the admonition in 11:35, *See to it, then, that the light within you is not darkness*. Thus, with respect to signs (11:29–32), disciples are responsible for recognizing them and their significance.

11:37–54 Again in the context of a meal (5:27–31; 7:36–50; 14:1–24), Jesus describes people who do not live by the *light* mentioned in the preceding verses. Initially, Jesus criticizes *greed* (11:39); then, with the first three woes, he condemns the neglect of *justice and the love of God* (11:42), the desire for prominence (11:43; 14:7–8; 20:46), and the hidden contamination (11:44) in the lives of Pharisees. With the last three woes, Jesus condemns the *experts in the law*, who struggle with hypocrisy (11:46), with opposition to God's prophets (11:48), and with hindering others from knowing God (11:52). Because of Jesus' strong critique, *the Pharisees and the teachers of the law began to oppose him fiercely and to besiege him with questions, waiting to catch him in something he might say*, thus ignoring Jesus' warning and confirming his critique in 11:47–51.

12:1–12 Luke follows the six woes of 11:37–54 with a series of six admonitions *to his disciples*. First, Jesus warns about *hypocrisy* (12:1). Second, as disciples live *in the daylight*, they may be tempted to retreat to *the dark* and to whisper in *inner rooms*, rather than to proclaim the kingdom from the *housetops*. Third, Jesus admonishes disciples to *fear* those who have *power to throw you into hell*, not those who can merely *kill the body* (12:4–5; compare 21:16). Fourth, after this mention of death, Jesus comforts the disciples by telling how much God values them, using analogies of *sparrows* (12:6–7, 24) and the *hairs* on people's heads. Fifth, Jesus encourages disciples to *acknowledge the Son of Man*, and warns those who *disown* (compare 9:26) Jesus and blaspheme *against the Holy Spirit*. Sixth, Jesus assures the disciples that the *Holy Spirit will teach you … what you should say when you are brought before synagogues, rulers and authorities*. Thus, disciples should not *worry* (8:14; 10:41; 12:11, 22, 25, 26; 21:34).

12:13–21 Apparently worried about losing some possessions, *someone in the crowd* says to Jesus, *Teacher, tell my brother to divide the inheritance with me*. Jesus first addresses his *greed*, then his attachment to his possessions. After affirming that life does not consist in the abundance of possessions, Jesus tells the parable about *a certain rich man*. In the abundance of *a good crop*, the man thinks only of himself, as the many uses of "I" and "my" within this story demonstrate. Such a person is not only a *fool* because of his shortsighted focus on this life, but also not *rich toward God* because of his singular focus on himself. Jesus calls for those with plenty to bless others with their possessions.

12:22–34 Turning to *his disciples* and picking up again the themes of worry (12:11) and fear (12:4, 5, 7), Jesus calls disciples to a life free from worry (12:22, 25, 26) and fear (12:32). In the first place, disciples should not worry, because *life is more than food, and the body more than clothes*. Then, using God's feeding of *ravens* as an example, Jesus tells disciples not to worry about *food* and *clothes*. Thus, God's providence in the physical world provides confidence for disciples. Furthermore, worry is not productive – *Who of you by worrying can add a single hour to his life?* After using *lilies* as another example of God's care, Jesus depicts worry as evidence of *little faith* and as a characteristic of *the pagan world*. In contrast, disciples *seek his kingdom*, confident in receiving basic necessities, as well.

Disciples should not be *afraid*, because they have received a *kingdom* (22:29). Instead, disciples should *sell* their possessions and *give to the poor* (11:41; 18:22), so providing for themselves *a treasure in heaven that will not be exhausted*. How disciples use their possessions is a vital indicator of spiritual health; Jesus concludes, *For where your treasure is, there your heart will be also*.

12:35–48 After calling the disciples to consider their possessions in light of the kingdom, Jesus encourages them to consider their actions in that same light, specifically admonishing them to be watchful and ready. To this end, Jesus tells three parables. The first (12:35–38), describing servants who are *watching* for their master's arrival, praises disciples who are active and shows them receiving the master's favor in a shocking way. The master *will dress himself to serve, will have them recline at the table and will come and wait on them*. In the second parable (12:39–40), Jesus admonishes disciples to be *ready* (12:38), just like the *owner* of a house should be to thwart a *thief*. The third and fourth parables (12:41–46, 47–48) also encourage disciples to be ready, but here Jesus stresses the punishment for those who are not *ready* (12:47). Punishment consists of cutting one servant *to pieces* (12:46) and beating another. Note other strong depictions of punishment (13:28; 16:23–24; 19:27; 20:16). Jesus concludes with the recognition that not all disciples have the same opportunities or gifts, but *from the one who has been entrusted with much, much more will be asked*.

12:49–53 Jesus' discussion of punishment (12:46–48) leads to statements about judgment and the divisive nature of the kingdom. Jesus comes to *bring fire on the earth*, likely a reference to judgment (see 3:16–17). In this context, Jesus' *baptism* probably refers to his impending suffering at Jerusalem (see 11:47–51; 18:31–33). As predicted earlier in Luke 2:34, Jesus' preaching of the kingdom provokes a divided response, which Jesus articulates in terms of family divisions (see 9:59–62; 14:26; 17:34; 18:29; 21:16).

12:54–59 Now turning to *the crowd*, Jesus encourages those who interpret the signs for *rain* and for *hot* weather to apply those interpretive skills to the important matter of assessing *what is right*. Since judgment is inevitable, the crowd needs to *try hard to be reconciled*, lest they be thrown *into prison*; here reconciliation and prison imply repentance and judgment, respectively.

13:1–9 Jesus' teaching about judgment in the two previous passages (12:49–53, 54–59) leads to two passages about repentance. The first passage, marked by the repeated phrase *But unless you repent, you too will all perish* (13:3, 5), describes two historical events not recorded in historical sources outside the New Testament. Some people in the crowd tell how *Pilate*, the prefect of Judea, killed some *Galileans* who were offering *sacrifices*. The second event, told this time by Jesus, is the falling of a *tower in Siloam*, which killed *eighteen* people; the tower was likely located near the pool of Siloam in Jerusalem (John 9:7, 11). Here Jesus' call for repentance demands that each person be ready, not knowing what injustice or accident life may bring.

The second part of Jesus' teaching on repentance consists of a parable about a *fig tree*. In this parable, a man who planted a fig tree in his vineyard expresses his frustration to the caretaker of the vineyard. The caretaker asks for one more year to tend the tree. Then, if the tree does not bear fruit, the man can *cut it down*. This parable shows how, in the context of judgment, the call to repentance is an offer of mercy.

13:10–17 Verbally connected to the previous section by the catchword *eighteen* (13:4, 11), this passage, unique to Luke, describes another controversy on the *Sabbath* (6:1–5, 6–11; 14:1–6). *Teaching in one of the synagogues* (4:15, 31; 13:10, 22, 26), Jesus sees a woman *who had been crippled by a spirit for eighteen years*. After calling her *forward*, Jesus heals her. Luke again shows two contrasting responses to Jesus (2:34). The woman praises God, and the people are *delighted* (13:17), but the *synagogue ruler* is *indignant*. Jesus responds with a comparison; if it is permitted to *untie* [Greek *luo*] an *ox* [see 14:5] *or donkey on the Sabbath* and give it water, how much more should this *daughter of Abraham* [see 3:8; 13:28; 16:22; 19:9] *be set free* [Greek *luo*] *on the Sabbath*? With this teaching, Jesus shows the merciful nature of God's kingdom.

13:18–21 As is typical of Luke, he puts two passages side by side, one with a man as the main figure, the other with a female. In the first parable, a *man* plants a *mustard seed*, which grows into a *tree*. The second parable tells of a *woman* who mixes *yeast* into a *large amount of flour* (about a bushel, or 35 liters;

Danker) until it works *through all the dough*. Both parables show how seemingly small things can have a significant impact, illustrating generally the nature of the kingdom and specifically the previous account, in which Jesus' healing of the crippled woman banishes disease, overturns calcified opinions, and loosens Satan's hold. These parables invite disciples to participate in the transforming activity of the kingdom.

13:22–30 Jesus continues his *teaching* about the kingdom of God (13:18, 20, 28, 29) with a characteristic prompt, a question from another person (11:1; 12:13, 41; 13:1; Craddock 172). Someone asks, *Lord, are only a few people going to be saved?* Jesus' answer begins with an exhortation to *make every effort to enter through the narrow door*. Then, Jesus tells a parable about the *owner* of a house, who, after closing the door, will tell those knocking outside, *I don't know you or where you come from*. Despite their further plea, the owner will deny them entry. Finally, Jesus describes the judgment, where there will be *weeping and gnashing of teeth* (see 12:46–47; 16:23–24; 19:27; 20:16) for some, and a *feast* with *Abraham, Isaac, and Jacob and all the prophets in the kingdom of God* for others.

> **The Great Feast**
> *The image of gathering God's people from all directions draws from the Old Testament (Isa 43:5–6), as does the image of an end-time banquet (Isa 25:6; see Luke 14:15; 22:16, 18, 30; Rev 3:20; 19:9; Fitzmyer 2:1026).*

13:31–35 Luke follows Jesus' warning about judgment (13:25, 27, 28) with *some Pharisees* warning Jesus about Herod's desire to harm him. Apparently, *Herod* Antipas, the tetrarch of Galilee (3:1; 9:7, 9; 23:7), had plans to *kill* Jesus (see 3:19–20). Here Luke shows the Pharisees in a positive light (Acts 5:33–40; 15:5; 23:6). Jesus shows his resolute determination to fulfill his destiny in Jerusalem – *I will reach my goal…. I must keep going…for surely no prophet can die outside Jerusalem*.

The catchwords "kill" (13:31, 34) and "Jerusalem" (13:33, 34) link Jesus' reply in 13:31–33 to his lament in 13:34–35. In this lament, despite Jerusalem's history of killing the *prophets*, Jesus longs to *gather* the children of Jerusalem together, *as a hen gathers her chicks under her wings*; but Jerusalem is *not willing*. Thus, Jerusalem is left *desolate*. As Jesus predicts in 13:35, *You will not see me again until you say, 'Blessed is he who comes in the name of the Lord,'* so the fulfillment comes later in the gospel (19:38). Luke shows Jesus as a faithful prophet, fulfilling his mission despite the threat of death.

14:1–14 Jesus again dines at the house of a *Pharisee* (7:36–50; 11:37–54). This half of the meal narrative has three parts. The meal itself occurs under an ominous shadow, with the threat of traps (11:53–54) in the background, with Luke's comment that Jesus *was being carefully watched* (6:7; 14:1; 20:20), and with the event taking place on the *Sabbath* (6:1–5, 6–11; 13:10–17). Seeing a man with *dropsy*, the swelling of the body caused by the accumulation of fluid, Jesus asks the *Pharisees and experts in the law* whether it is *lawful to heal on the Sabbath or not*. After they remain *silent*, Jesus heals the man and sends him away. He justifies this with a question that implies a lesser to greater argument. This passage continues the theme of the escalation of the Pharisees' conflict with Jesus.

The second part of the meal narrative treats the issue of humility (16:15; 18:14), a virtue for Christians, but not in Greco-Roman culture. Prompted by guests who *picked the places of honor* [11:43; 14:7, 8; 20:46] *at the table*, Jesus tells a *parable*. In this parable, Jesus warns guests not to take the place of honor because a person *more distinguished* may be invited. Then, the host will tell the guest, *Give this man your seat*, and the guest will be humiliated. Rather, if a guest takes the *lowest place*, the host will say, *Friend, move up to a better place*. Jesus here teaches against self-exaltation; he is not advocating a crafty way to gain honor.

Third, Jesus turns his attention to his *host*, instructing those who have wealth to invite others to dine with them. With a balanced group of four on each side, Jesus discourages invitations to those who *may invite you back*. Rather, *invite the poor, the crippled, the lame, the blind, and you will be blessed* because *they cannot repay you*. Luke shows a continuation of Jesus' concern for the outcasts (4:16–19; 7:21–23; 14:21). In addition, Jesus' teaching overturns the cultural expectations of the patron/client relationship, in which a "you scratch my back, I scratch yours" type of relationship defined first century personal interactions.

14:15–24 Connected by the catchword *blessing* (14:14, 15) and the four groups of outcasts (14:13, 21), the last half of the meal narrative consists of an exclamation by *one of those at the table* and a parable told by Jesus. A guest exclaims, *Blessed is the man who will eat at the feast in the kingdom of God* (13:29), and Jesus tells a parable about a *great banquet*. Calls to the banquet go out in three waves. First, a servant tells those who had been invited, *Come for everything is now ready*. But the invitation is met with three sets of excuses. After reporting back, the servant is commanded a second time to go and *bring in the poor, the crippled, the blind and the lame*. Since there is *still room* after the second invitation, the master sends the servant a third time, this time outside the city. Yet the master concludes by determining not to invite his originally intended guests. With this parable, Jesus again emphasizes the call to reach out toward those who are less fortunate (14:21). In addition, Jesus teaches about the mercy of God, with the three sendings (14:17, 21, 23), and the judgment of God for those who reject the invitation of the master (14:24). As for the three excuses, they strongly parallel the legitimate exemptions for going to war described in Deuteronomy 20:5-7, suggesting that the call to be a disciple surpasses even valid excuses (Craddock 179). Luke next turns to describe more explicitly the nature of the call of a disciple in the following passage.

14:25-35 Again emphasizing the cost of discipleship (9:57-62), Jesus treats three aspects of discipleship in his teaching to the *large crowds*. Each time his teaching ends with the refrain *cannot be my disciple* (14:26, 27, 33). To those who do not agree with these descriptions of discipleship, Jesus essentially says "I don't want you." Disciples who hear this passage need to listen seriously, as the final verse cautions, *He who has ears to hear, let him hear*.

The first call is expressed in hyperbolic language. Although the call to *hate* cannot be taken literally, it must be taken seriously, because disciples will have to face divisions within families (9:59-62; 12:51-53; 14:26; 18:29; 21:16) and family challenges to their commitments. In summary, the call to discipleship surpasses even the demands of family.

The second call flows naturally from the first description; note the earlier aside, *yes, even his own life* (14:26). The call to *carry* one's own *cross* (9:23) *and follow* implies suffering and even death for disciples. Earlier, Jesus had issued that same demand to his disciples (12:4-7).

Two parables, both illustrating the need to count the cost before committing, precede the third call. The first parable admonishes one who *wants to build a tower* to *estimate the cost to see if he has enough money to complete it*. The second parable counsels a *king* with *ten thousand men* to consider whether he is able to defeat another with *twenty thousand*. With both these parables, when the risks of shame or danger are high, careful consideration should precede action. *In the same way*, those who aspire to be disciples need to know that the cost is high. Jesus asks for them to *give up everything* (better, "all they own"). Earlier in the narrative, disciples have shown this level of commitment (5:17, 28), and Jesus has addressed the allure of possessions (12:13-34). Disciples who do not live up to these demands are useless, like *salt* that *loses its saltiness*. The concluding saying about salt suggests that uncommitted disciples are not only useless but also under judgment.

15:1-7 Although all three parables in chapter 15 begin with something that is lost (a lost sheep, coin, and son), the point of each parable is *joy* (15:5-7, 9-10, 32; see *celebrate* in 15:23-24, 29, 32), when each thing or person is *found* (4, 5, 6, 8, 9, 24, 32). The first two verses provide the context for the three parables. Jesus again is found in the company of *tax collectors and 'sinners'* (5:27-32; 7:34, 37, 39; 19:1-10), which prompts the *Pharisees and teachers of the law* to mutter (better "complain, grumble"; 19:7; compare 5:30), *This man welcomes sinners and eats with them*. The Pharisees' absence of joy contrasts strongly with the joy depicted in each parable.

The first two parables pair a man and a woman, respectively, as the main character, a trait characteristic of Luke. Found also in Matthew, the first parable nevertheless has a different emphasis than the parable in Matthew. Matthew's version stresses the need to go after a sheep that *wanders away* (Matt 18:12). In Luke, the sheep is *lost* (15:4, 6). In Matthew, the finding is uncertain (*if he finds it*), whereas in Luke the sheep is actually found – *when he finds it*. Luke also emphasizes the tenderness of the shepherd, who puts the sheep *on his shoulders* [see Isa 66:12 in LXX] *and goes home*. With the phrase *over one sinner who repents* (15:7, 10), Jesus verbally connects this parable with the conflict in 15:1-2 over *sinners* and anticipates the use of humans in the third parable.

15:8-10 Only found in Luke, this parable tells of a woman who *has ten silver coins and loses one*; the coin is a drachma, equivalent to one day's wages. Like the shepherd in the previous parable, the woman searches *carefully until she finds it* (15:4, 8), *calls her friends and neighbors*, and says, *Rejoice with me* (15:6, 9). As in the previous parable, Jesus concludes by noting that *rejoicing* is the attitude of those *in the presence of the angels of God* ("in heaven" in 15:7) when there is *one sinner who repents*. With these two parables, Jesus establishes that even in everyday life, joy is the natural response to finding what was lost.

15:11–32   With this third parable, Jesus raises the stakes in two ways: first, the story takes place on the human level, precisely where the conflict lies (15:1–2), and second, Jesus directly addresses the bad attitude of the *Pharisees and teachers of the law* with the introduction of the *older brother*. Each of the three people in the introductory sentence plays significant roles: the younger son illustrates the *sinner who repents* (verses 7, 10); the *father* provides the divine perspective, showing the lavish and disturbing nature of grace; and the *older brother* embodies and expresses the attitude of the Pharisees and teachers of the law (verses 1–2).

After the opening line, which introduces the three characters, the younger son asks for *my share of the estate*. According to inheritance practices, the older son would receive a *double share* (Deut 21:17; Fitzmyer 2:1087). Not much later, the younger son gathers his belongings, leaves for a *distant country*, and squanders his *wealth in wild living*. With the coming of a *famine*, the younger son is reduced to feeding *pigs*, animals unclean for Jews (Lev 11:7). Still hungry, he longs to *fill his stomach with the pods that the pigs were eating*. At this point, the younger son comes *to his senses*, decides to return to his father, and prepares his confession.

The parable now stresses the actions of the father toward the younger son; upon seeing his son, the father is filled with *compassion* (compare 7:13; 10:33), runs to his son, throws his arms around him, and kisses him. The father's gracious actions are matched by his many gifts. The final comment to the younger son is echoed in the final words to the older son (verses 24, 32).

Nearing the house, the older son hears *music and dancing*. Upon hearing that his brother had returned and that his father had killed a fattened calf to celebrate, the older brother becomes *angry* and refuses to go in. So, the father goes out and pleads with his older son. The older son reminds his father about his hard work and obedience; yet he was never given even a *young goat* to celebrate. The characters of the father and the two sons teach the lessons of a grace that is lavish but sometimes offensive, a repentance that is necessary but always available, and a joy that is godly and natural but sometimes difficult.

16:1–18   With three parts, this passage presents one of the more difficult texts in Luke. Luke continues his treatment of possessions (see 12:13–34; 16:19–31; 18:18–30; 19:1–10; 21:1–4), although the connection to the last part (16:14–18) is none too clear. In the first part, Jesus tells a parable to his disciples. Accused of *wasting* (15:13) his master's possessions, a *manager* (12:42) is called to *give an account* of his management. The manager reflects, *What shall I do now* [see 12:17; 20:13]? *My master is taking away my job. I'm not strong enough to dig, and I'm ashamed to beg* (18:35). With a plan in mind, he calls in *each one of his master's debtors* (7:41). To the first, who owed *eight hundred gallons of olive oil* [literally "100 *baths*"], the manager says, *Take your bill, sit down quickly, and make it four hundred* [literally "50 *baths*"]. To the second, who owed *a thousand bushels of wheat* [literally "100 *kors*"], the manager says, *Take your bill and make it eight hundred*. Surprisingly, the master commends the *dishonest manager* because he acted *shrewdly*. The parable ends with two comments. First, in 16:8b, Jesus answers the question, "On what basis can such a manager be commended?" It is because *the people of this world* [20:34] *are more shrewd in dealing with their own kind than are the people of the light*. Thus, Jesus commends shrewdness, not the dishonesty, in that the manager used possessions in a way that insured his future. Second, disciples should use their possessions in a way that secures their futures in God's kingdom (16:9). In sum, Jesus calls disciples to use their possessions with an eternal, not merely a worldly, perspective.

In the second part (16:10–13), Jesus teaches on the use of wealth. He contends that how disciples handle their wealth reveals their character. Thus one can conclude, *Whoever can be trusted with very little* [19:17] *can also be trusted with much, and whoever is dishonest with very little will also be dishonest with much*. With "how much more" reasoning, Jesus then adds, *So if you have not been trustworthy in handling worldly wealth, who will trust you with true riches?* Addressing the lure of wealth, Jesus concludes, *No servant can serve two masters.... You cannot serve both God and Money*.

The third section (16:14–18) presents a mystery. When he turns to some greedy *Pharisees* (see 20:47) who *were sneering* (see 23:35), Jesus appears to continue his teaching about money, as his first comment shows. Jesus then, however, speaks about the *Law and the Prophets*, the endurance of the *Law*, and marriage and divorce. Despite efforts to connect these two sets of teachings together, an entirely satisfactory solution still awaits discovery.

> **The Law & the Prophets**
> *The stock expression "the law and the prophets" designated two of the three major sections of the Jewish Bible (equivalent to the Christian Old Testament). The third section was the "Writings."*

16:19–31 Connected to the parable of the shrewd manager by the catch phrase *there was a rich man* (16:1, 19; 18:23; 19:2; 21:1), the parable in 16:19–31 continues Jesus' teaching on wealth. The narrative is characterized by a number of contrasts and reversals. As the parable begins, the rich man is *dressed in purple and fine linen* and lives *in luxury every day* (compare 12:19; 15:23–32). In contrast, *a beggar* [literally "poor man"] *named Lazarus* is covered with *sores* and longs to *eat what fell from the rich man's table*. *Dogs* lick his sores. Both Lazarus and the rich man die. *Angels*, however, carry Lazarus to *Abraham's side* (see 3:8; 13:16, 28; 19:9), while the rich man finds himself *in hell* [Greek *Hades*] and *in torment* (see 12:46–47; 13:28; 19:27; 20:16). After the rich man makes the first of two requests to Abraham, the patriarch (speaking for God) explicitly describes the reversal of fortune between the rich man and Lazarus (compare 6:24). Abraham then explains that this request is impossible to grant because one cannot *go from here to you*. This first request functions as an encouragement to share possessions with those in need and as a warning to those who *loved wealth* (verse 14).

The rich man counters with a second request, this for his relatives. Abraham says that they should listen to *Moses and the Prophets*; that is, they should consider scripture. The rich man says that his brothers *will repent*, if *someone from the dead goes to them*. Abraham responds, *If they do not listen to Moses and the prophets, they will not be convinced even if someone rises from the dead*. The second request of the rich man functions as a statement about the nature of repentance. Those with hearts closed to God's revelation will not open their hearts, even in the presence of a miracle.

17:1–10 Jesus next turns to his disciples and teaches them about sin, faith, and duty with three brief sayings. Although Luke is moving on to new topics in chapter 17, he links this discussion to the previous passage with the word *repent* (16:30; 17:3, 4). With respect to sin, Jesus warns his disciples to avoid causing others to sin, concluding with the admonition *So watch yourselves*. Concerning *a brother* who sins, Jesus instructs his disciples to *rebuke* and then *forgive* him if he *repents*, even up to seven times, indicating the seriousness of the demand to forgive. Here Jesus teaches his disciples how to live in community when sin enters that community.

> **"Small as a mustard seed…"**
> *Because of those strong words about sin, the apostles ask,* Increase our faith. *Jesus indicates that even a small amount of faith – as small as a mustard seed – has incredible power, enough to uproot a* mulberry tree *and plant it in the sea. Here Jesus calls on disciples to exercise their faith, trusting in God to work powerfully in his kingdom.*

In Jesus' teaching about duty, he introduces a parable about *a servant plowing or looking after the sheep*. He tells the parable itself through a series of three questions with obvious answers (compare 11:11–13): first, a master would not invite a servant to eat. Second, he would demand that the servant *Prepare my supper*. And third, he would not *thank the servant*. Jesus then concludes that disciples have an obligation to obey their master; their obedience – namely every good work – does not count as extra credit but as their *duty*. There is no way to earn or merit God's grace.

17:11–19 After reminding the reader that Jesus is progressing *on his way to Jerusalem* (9:51, 53; 13:22; 18:31; 19:28), Luke tells an account about *ten lepers* (5:12–16; 7:22) that shows the appropriate response to God's grace. Leviticus 13:45–46 states that lepers must live separate from others and cry out, *Unclean*. These ten lepers cry out, *Jesus, Master, have pity on us!* (compare 18:38, 39). In accordance with Old Testament law (Lev 14:1–2), Jesus tells them, *Go, show yourselves to the priests*. Interestingly, they are *cleansed, as they* go. One leper, however, returns, praises *God in a loud voice*, throws himself *at Jesus' feet* (5:12), and thanks Jesus. At this point, Luke adds that this leper *was a Samaritan*, continuing his mention of Samaritans (9:51–56; 10:30–37) and anticipating the coming of the gospel to Samaria in Acts (Acts 1:8; Acts 8:4–25; 9:31; 15:3). Jesus praises *this foreigner*, saying, *Rise and go*; *your faith has made you well* [literally "saved you" 7:50; 8:48; 18:42]. Thus, with the Samaritan, Luke demonstrates both physical and spiritual healing. The Samaritan also embodies the proper response to God's gracious action – praise and thankfulness. Luke records a number of times when humans give *praise* or *glory* to God after a manifestation of power (2:20; 4:15; 5:25–26; 7:16; 13:13; 18:43; 19:37–38; 23:47). In fact, the last words of Luke's gospel describe the Eleven *praising God* [24:53; literally "blessing"].

17:20–37 The last part of Luke 17 includes a brief exchange between some Pharisees and Jesus and a longer exchange between Jesus and his disciples, both regarding the kingdom of God. After the *Pharisees* ask *when the kingdom of God would come*, Jesus responds, *The kingdom of God does not come visibly, nor will people say, 'Here it is,' or 'There it is,' because the kingdom of God is within you* (10:9, 11; 11:20). The NIV translation obscures two points. First, the noun translated *visibly* is better translated "with close observation," because the Greek word echoes the accounts where the Pharisees were *watching* Jesus *closely* (6:7; 14:1; Johnson 263). In other words, Jesus is saying, "The kingdom does not come with the kind of close observation that you are doing of me." Second, a better translation of the last phrase in 17:21 is "the kingdom of God is among you," because it is unlikely that the Pharisees embody a kingdom attitude at this point in the narrative, and Luke has already described how the kingdom can be perceived by the type of kingdom activity that is occurring (11:20; compare 7:21–23). In other words, the kingdom of God is among the Pharisees in the person of Jesus and the deeds that he and his disciples perform.

In comments to *his disciples*, Jesus addresses the consummation of the kingdom. With both present and future aspects, the kingdom has been inaugurated in the ministry of Jesus, but God's rule is not fully realized until the coming of the *Son of Man*. Jesus' audience *will not see it* come. Nevertheless, Jesus tells about its arrival. First, the coming will be evident *like the lightning, which flashes and lights up the sky from one end to the other*. Second, the coming will follow Jesus' suffering and rejection *by this generation*. Third, it will come while people are going about their earthly business, whether *eating, drinking, and marrying* as it was in the days of *Noah*, or *eating and drinking, buying and selling, planting and building* as in the days of Lot. In both those circumstances, those who were unprepared were *destroyed*. Fourth, the arrival will be a time of sorting between those who strive to *keep* or *lose* their lives. *Lot's wife*, who looked back at her home in Sodom and became a *pillar of salt* (Gen 19:26), serves as a negative example for attraction to the world. Fifth, the sorting will divide even those who sleep side-by-side *in one bed* or those who work side-by-side *grinding grain together*. Still not understanding, the disciples ask Jesus, *Where?* Jesus replies with a proverb: *Where there is a dead body, there the vultures will gather*, meaning that the arrival will be obvious because of the signs. Jesus' teaching calls disciples to live – not in calculation, but in expectation – prepared for the final realization of the kingdom by living according to the standards of the kingdom.

18:1–8 Luke's commentary on this parable is explicit: *Jesus told his disciples a parable to show them that they should always pray and not give up* (see 21:36). In this parable, a *widow* keeps coming to a judge with her plea. The *judge, who neither feared God nor cared about men* (18:2, 4), refuses her request *for some time*. Finally, the judge relents (see 12:17; 15:17; 16:3), so that she will quit bothering him. With a "how much more" kind of argument, Jesus asks, *And will not God bring about justice for his chosen ones, who cry out to him day and night?* Jesus assures his disciples that they will get *justice* (18:3, 5, 7). The twist comes at the end with Jesus' final question, *However, when the Son of Man comes, will he find faith on earth?* This question assumes that persistence in prayer is both a sign of a disciple's faith and proper preparation for the judgment that all will face.

18:9–14 Connected to the parable in the previous verses by the topic of prayer (18:1, 10, 11), this parable addresses *some who were confident of their own righteousness and looked down on everybody else*. In the parable, two men go *up to the temple to pray*. The first, a Pharisee, prays *about himself*, thanking God that he is *not like all other men* (that is, a sinner) and recounting his good works, namely fasting and tithing (Deut 14:22).

> **The Son of Man**
> *The phrase "Son of Man" connects the second coming of Jesus to the imagery from Daniel, in which this figure comes to bring a kingdom that* will never be destroyed *(Dan 7:14).*

Although despised by society (5:30; 7:29, 34; 15:1), the tax collector shows humility in his prayer, as Johnson (272) notes: the tax collector stands *at a distance*; he does *not even look up to heaven*; he beats *his breast* (see 23:48); and he asks God for *mercy*, confessing that he is a *sinner* (5:8). Because of his humility and repentance, the tax collector goes home *justified before God*. Here Jesus commends humility in prayer as a mark of a disciple (compare 14:11).

18:15–17 The disciples rebuke people who *were bringing babies* [9:47] *to Jesus to have him touch them*. Jesus tells the disciples to invite *the little children*. Jesus blesses the children by receiving them without any claim of merit on their part (see 17:7–10; 18:11–12), since they are among the weakest of society.

18:18–30 Certainly a part of Luke's emphasis on possessions, the account of the rich ruler also likely contrasts with the previous verses. The *little child* receives the kingdom as a gift, while *a certain ruler* (compare the *young man* in Matt 19:22) strives to obtain the kingdom on his own terms. The ruler's question, *Good teacher, what must I do to inherit eternal life?* arises numerous times in Luke and Acts (Luke 3:10, 12, 14; 10:25; Acts 2:37; 16:30; 22:10), showing Luke's interest in conversion and salvation. Jesus' first response is somewhat puzzling: *Why do you call me good? No one is good – except God alone*. Here Jesus does not deny his goodness; rather, he calls the ruler to attribute the goodness "to its rightful source" (Fitzmyer 2:1199), much in the same way that, in the miracle stories, Luke focuses attention on praise, glory, and thanks to God (see 17:11–19 above). Then Jesus, quoting five of the Ten Commandments, calls the ruler to obey *the commandments*, which he has kept since he was *a boy*. Jesus next calls the ruler to *sell everything* [see 5:11, 28; 14:33], *give to the poor* (see 11:41; 12:33), and then *come* and *follow* him. Upon hearing these words, the ruler, however, is *very sad because he was a man of great wealth* (compare 16:1, 9; 18:23; 19:2; 21:1). Jesus observes that it is *hard for the rich to enter the kingdom of God*, warning disciples about the spiritual threat of possessions (6:24; 8:14; 12:16; 16:14–15, 19; 21:1).

Some then ask, *Who then can be saved?* Jesus replies, *What is impossible with men is possible with God*. Within Luke-Acts, Jesus' words ring true, as Luke describes some rich people who use their possessions appropriately (12:33, 48; 14:13; 19:1–10; Acts 4:34–37; 16:14, 40). Wondering, perhaps anxiously, where he stands, Peter says, *We have left all we had to follow you!* Jesus assures Peter that those who have left possessions and family *for the sake of the kingdom of God* (9:57–62; 14:25–35) will receive *eternal life*, precisely what the ruler was asking for in his initial question to Jesus (18:18).

18:31–34 Taking the *twelve aside*, Jesus predicts his suffering for the third time (9:22, 44). He is on his way to Jerusalem (9:51; 13:33) where *everything that is written by the prophets about the Son of Man will be fulfilled*. Luke has a strong interest in showing how Jesus fulfills Scripture (22:37; 24:25–27, 44). After the longest of the three descriptions of Jesus' suffering, the disciples still do *not understand* the necessity of the Messiah to suffer (9:45; 24:16; Johnson 279).

18:35–43 In the first of three scenes set in Jericho, a town about twelve miles from Jerusalem, Jesus encounters a *blind man*. From the beginning, the "blind" have played a key role, illustrating Jesus' ministry to the outcasts (4:18; 7:21–22; 14:13, 21). The blind man calls out, *Jesus, Son of David, have mercy on me!* Despite being rebuked (18:15), the man cries out *all the more*. As *Son of David*, Jesus is heir to a *kingdom* (2 Sam 7:12–14; Luke 1:27; 2:4; 20:41). Jesus heals the man and says, *Your faith has healed you* (7:50; 8:48; 17:19). The man follows Jesus, *praising God* (2:20; 18:43; 19:37), as do all the people in attendance when they see what has happened. Both of the man's actions – following Jesus and praising God – identify him as a disciple (9:57–62; 17:11–19), in contrast to the rich ruler, who does not heed Jesus' call to *follow* (18:22).

19:1–10 While in Jericho (10:30; 18:35), Jesus encounters Zacchaeus, who models the response of repentance. Luke gives a number of details about Zacchaeus. A *chief tax collector* (see 5:27–32) and *wealthy* (see 16:1, 9; 18:23, 25; 21:1), Zacchaeus *wanted* [literally "seeks"] *to see who Jesus was*; interestingly, Jesus *seeks* Zacchaeus, as well (19:10). Because of his *short* stature and the *crowd* around Jesus, Zacchaeus

---

"Through the eye of a needle ..."
Jesus says that "it is easier for a camel to go through the eye of a needle than for a rich man to enter the kingdom of God." *Jesus' exaggeration, using one of the largest animals in Judea and an object with the smallest opening, is meant to catch the attention of his hearers and make them take his words seriously; there is not an opening in city walls called the "eye of the needle" through which camels could crawl, as commentators sometimes report* (Fitzmyer 2:1204).

runs ahead and *climbs a sycamore-fig tree*. With these details, Luke depicts Zacchaeus as someone despised by society, yet striving to overcome the obstacles between him and Jesus. When Jesus says, *Zacchaeus, come down immediately. I must stay at your house today*, Zacchaeus's response is immediate; he comes down and welcomes Jesus *gladly*. In response, *all the people mutter* (15:2; see also 5:30), *He has gone to be the guest of a 'sinner'*, a response that echoes that of the Pharisees in Luke 15:2. Zacchaeus's promise to *give half of my possessions to the poor* exceeds the general requirements for restitution found in the Law (Num 5:6–7; compare Exod 22:1, 4). Zacchaeus's repentance results in praise from Jesus: *Today salvation* (see 18:42) *has come to this house, because this man is a son of Abraham* (compare 3:8; 13:16, 28–30; 16:19–31). Jesus defends Zacchaeus's salvation and his contact with Zacchaeus with a statement of his purpose: *For the Son of Man came to seek and to save what was lost*, a claim similar to the one that concludes the account about Levi, another tax collector and *sinner* (5:31–32).

19:11–27 As Luke has done in previous passages (18:1, 9), he introduces a parable and describes its function. According to Luke, Jesus tells the parable *because he was near Jerusalem and the people thought that the kingdom of God was going to appear at once* (17:20; Acts 1:6). The parable has two foci, perhaps echoing the divided response to Jesus (2:34): for those who accept Jesus' kingdom, there is a message of responsibility and activity; for those who reject Jesus' kingdom, there is a message of warning and judgment.

In the parable, *a man of noble birth* goes to a *distant country to have himself appointed king*. Before leaving, the man calls *ten of his servants* and gives them ten *minas*, charging them, *Put this money to work until I come back*. Some *subjects* send a delegation to report: *We don't want this man to be our king* (19:14, 27). Nevertheless, the man becomes king and returns home to see how his servants have done. Both of the first two servants have earned ten and five more minas, respectively. *Trustworthy in a very small matter* (19:17; 16:10), they are rewarded with *ten* and *five cities*. The third servant, however, *hid* his mina, earning nothing, not even *interest*, which was the minimum

> "Put this money to work …"
> A "mina" is a Greek monetary unit equivalent to 100 drachmas, which is about 100 days' wages (Danker 654).

that the king expected. For the punishment, compare 12:46; 13:28; 16:23–24; 20:16. For those who have differing expectations about the responsibilities and the validity of Jesus' kingship, Jesus offers this parable warning against inactivity and rebellion.

JESUS' MINISTRY IN & AROUND JERUSALEM · 19:28–21:38

19:28–44 As Jesus approaches Jerusalem, he passes through Bethphage and Bethany. Although Bethphage has not been located, the context indicates that it is near Bethany and the Mount of Olives, probably a small suburb of Jerusalem (Carroll 1.715.). Bethany, however, is about *two miles from Jerusalem* (John 11:18) near the place of Jesus' ascension (24:50). Jesus tells *two* (10:1) of his disciples to go and bring a *colt, which no one has ever ridden* (23:53), perhaps indicating that the animal is for holy use (Num 19:2; Deut 21:3; 1 Sam 6:7; Fitzmyer 2:1249). Obeying his instructions, the two disciples find it *just as he had told them* (22:13; compare 24:24). As Jesus proceeds, *people spread their cloaks on the road*; for this practice, compare the placing of cloaks before king Jehu (2 Kgs 9:13). Luke is clear that joy (15:5–7, 9–10, 32; compare *celebrate* in 15:23–24, 29, 32) and praise are characteristics of disciples (2:20; 18:43; Acts 2:47; 3:8–9). The first exclamation comes from Psalm 118:26, with the insertion of "king" for "he" (see 13:35b), while the second exclamation echoes the angelic chorus in Luke 2:14. *Some of the Pharisees* tell Jesus to *rebuke* his disciples, to which Jesus replies, *I tell you if they keep quiet, the stones will cry out*. This detail, found only in Luke, probably supports Luke's portrayal of Jesus as king (1:32–33; 12:32; 19:12–27; 22:28–30; 23:2, 40–43) and echoes language associated with Roman triumphs (Cicero, *In Pisonem*, 52; Cukrowski, "Blessed Is the King"). Yet, in contrast to a Roman emperor who slaughters his enemies before entering the temple of Jupiter to sacrifice, Jesus weeps (13:34–35; 23:28) over Jerusalem before he enters the temple. Jesus *wept* because those in Jerusalem *did not recognize the time of God's coming* to them. God's revelation is *hidden* (9:45; 18:34; 24:16) because the kingdom does not come in the ways they expect or desire. Nevertheless, the consequences of rejection mean destruction for the city and death to its inhabitants.

19:45–48 Luke's account of the cleansing of the temple is the shortest in the Synoptic Gospels.

Luke omits Jesus' driving out buyers, overturning the tables of the moneychangers, knocking over the seats of the pigeon-sellers, and forbidding anyone to carry anything through the temple (Matt 21:12–13; Mark 11:15–19) – all probably because Luke does not want his audience to misunderstand Jesus as socially disruptive (Luke emphasizes the same theme about Christians throughout the book of Acts). Instead, with allusions to Isaiah 56:7 and Jeremiah 7:11, Jesus condemns the activity of *selling* in the temple. Luke illustrates the divided response to Jesus (2:34) with his description of *the chief priests, the teachers of the law, and the leaders,* who were trying to *kill* Jesus (20:19), and the *people,* who *hung on his words* while he was *teaching at the temple* (21:37; 22:53).

20:1–8 The description of Jesus as *teaching the people in the temple* (19:47–48; 20:1) connects Luke 19 with Luke 20. Luke 20 contains a series of controversy stories, the first one treating Jesus' authority. Luke describes Jesus' opponents as *the chief priests and the teachers of the law, together with the elders.* The chief priests include not only the high priest but also other priests over temple worship and the treasury and probably those priests in the Sanhedrin, the council ruling on religious matters (Fitzmyer 1:780). Sometimes also called *scribes* or *lawyers* (7:30; 10:25; 11:45, 46, 52; 14:3), the *teachers of the law* (5:17) are experts in Torah. The *elders* are Jewish leaders, in this case also likely part of the Sanhedrin. When asked, *Tell us by what authority you are doing these things. Who gave you this authority?* Jesus replies, *I will also ask you a question, Tell me, John's baptism – was it from heaven or from men?* Craddock (232) correctly describes Jesus' counter-question as "designed to see whether his inquirers are open to an answer. If they are not open to an answer, then no answer will satisfy." Realizing that their answer will expose their hypocrisy or disbelief (see 7:33), the leaders answer, *We don't know where it was from.* Thus, Jesus, recognizing their lack of openness (see 22:67–68), refuses to answer their question.

20:9–19 Again, Jesus uses a parable to warn those who reject the kingdom (19:11–27). In this parable, *a man* plants a *vineyard* (see Isa 5:1–7), rents it out to some *farmers,* and goes away *for a long time.* Three times the man sends *a servant* to collect some *fruit of the vineyard;* each time, the tenants treat the servant *shamefully.* Next, the owner of the vineyard decides, *I will send my son, whom I love* (3:22; 20:13). The tenants, however, decide to *kill* the son and throw him out of the vineyard, thinking that the inheritance will then be theirs. The owner of the vineyard will *kill those tenants and give the vineyard to others* (see 12:46–47; 13:28; 16:23–24; 19:27). Upon hearing the conclusion, the people cry out, *May this never be!* Quoting Psalm 118:22, Jesus asks what the rejection of the capstone means (see 9:22; 17:25). His opponents look for a way to *arrest* Jesus *because they knew he had spoken this parable against them;* their *fear* of the people (22:2; compare 20:6), however, stops them. From the responses of the people and the leaders, it seems clear that both groups understand that, in the parable, the *owner* is God, the *servants* are God's leaders, such as prophets (6:26; 11:49–51), the *son* is Jesus, and the *tenants* are the leaders who reject Jesus.

20:20–26 *Keeping close watch* (6:7; 14:1; 20:20) on Jesus, some Jewish leaders send *spies* who pretend to be *honest.* They *hope to catch* (20:20, 26) Jesus in something he says, *so that they might hand him over to … the governor.* After some words of flattery, the spies ask, *Is it right for us to pay taxes to Cæsar or not?* Seeing through their *duplicity,* Jesus asks for a denarius, a small silver coin, and asks whose face is on the obverse. The spies reply, *Cæsar's,* to which Jesus responds, *Then give to Cæsar what is Cæsar's, and to God what is God's.* Unable to *trap* Jesus and *astonished by his answer,* the spies become *silent.* Jesus' reply not only recognizes that people owe Cæsar taxes but also relativizes the claim of Cæsar by pointing out that God is also owed his due, which includes and surpasses any claim of Cæsar's.

20:27–40 The Sadducees face Jesus in this next controversy story. Tracing their roots to Zadok, a priest in King David's time (2 Sam 8:17; 1 Kgs 1:39), the Sadducees hold priestly and political power

> **Sadducees**
> *The Sadducees did not believe in resurrection or angels (Acts 23:8) and viewed only the Law of Moses as authoritative.*

among the Jews (Acts 4:1; 5:17), although they were fewer in number than the Pharisees. Paraphrasing the teaching on levirate marriage, which required a man to marry the childless widow of his brother (Deut 25:5), the Sadducees describe a situation where a woman ends up marrying *seven brothers.* They ask Jesus, *Now then, at the resurrection whose wife will she* be, since the seven were married to her? First, Jesus points out that the Sadducees do not understand the nature of the resurrected life, in which people *neither marry nor [are] given in marriage*. Second, he offers a defense for the resurrection with a reference to Exodus 3:6, which states that the Lord is *the God of Abraham, and the God of Isaac, and the God of Jacob*. Since God is *not the God of the dead, but of the living*, then Abraham, Isaac, and Jacob must be *alive. Some of the teachers of the law,* who are probably Pharisees and agree with Jesus about the resurrection, congratulate him: *Well said, teacher.* After Jesus bests the Sadducees in that discussion, *no one dared ask him any more questions.* Nevertheless, the conflict does not end. In fact, in the next account, Jesus asks them a question and criticizes the *teachers of the law.*

20:41-47 Luke records that Jesus asks *them* (probably the Sadducees of 20:27–28) a question: *How is it that they say the Christ is the Son of David?* Quoting from Psalm 110:1, Jesus continues, If *David calls the Christ Lord,* then how can the Christ be *his son* (that is, "only an earthly descendent of David"; Johnson 314)? For Luke, Jesus is both *Son of David,* because he is an earthly descendent of David, and *Lord,* because of what Scripture says.

Turning to the disciples, Jesus warns them about six actions of the *teachers of the law* (11:45–54): they *like to walk around in flowing robes;* they *love to be greeted in the marketplaces*; they love to *have the most important seats in the synagogues* (11:43); they love *the places of honor at banquets* (14:7–8); they *devour widows' houses*; and *for a show they make lengthy prayers.* For such actions, they will be *punished more severely.* Five of the actions deal with the desire to seem important or pious. The criticism of *devouring widows' houses* addresses greed (compare 16:14) and links this account to Luke's next account about a widow. All six descriptions warn disciples about behavior inappropriate for God's people.

21:1-4 In a brief but touching account, Luke records an incident in which Jesus sees gifts being placed *into the temple treasury.* Jesus notices both rich people and a poor widow offering their gifts, the widow offering only *two very small copper coins* [Greek *lepta*]. Yet, Jesus claims that *this poor widow has put in more than all the others.* How is this claim possible? Jesus explains, *All these people gave their gifts out of their wealth; but she out of her poverty put in all she had to live on.* Thus, in relationship to possessions, disciples are to ask, "How much does one have remaining after the offering is made?" (Craddock 242).

21:5-38 One of the more difficult passages, this long discourse demands that the reader keep in mind the different topics being addressed. The first part (21:5–11) describes the time preceding the destruction of Jerusalem. Prompted by a comment about the beauty of the *temple,* Jesus predicts its destruction (see also 19:44; 21:6). The disciples ask, *When will these things happen? And what will be the sign that they are about to take place?* In his response, Jesus mentions several items: *watch out* for false prophets and false claims about timing; it will be a time of national upheaval, with *wars and revolutions;* it will be a time of judgment (21:22), illustrated with prominent Old Testament images for judgment, namely "earthquakes, famines, and pestilences" (Johnson 321).

The second part of the discourse (21:12–19) describes the trials that Jesus' disciples will face before the fall of Jerusalem. Others will *persecute* them, deliver them to *synagogues and prisons,* and bring them *before kings and governors.* In this context, disciples should be *witnesses to them.* Disciples should not *worry* how to *defend* (12:11) themselves. Disciples will face betrayal by family members (see 9:61–62; 14:26; 18:29); for some disciples, this betrayal will mean *death* (12:4–5; 21:16). Disciples will face hate because of Jesus (6:22; 21:17). In light of the *death* mentioned in 21:16, Jesus' statement *not a hair of your head will perish* (21:18) offers assurance about a disciple's spiritual standing before God, especially since the next verse speaks in spiritual, not physical, terms (8:15; 21:19).

In the third part (21:20–24), Jesus describes the fall of Jerusalem and offers advice. The fall is terrible and tragic. This destruction will continue *until the times of the Gentiles are fulfilled,* which in this context refers to the sack of Jerusalem by the Romans in the year 70 CE.

Jesus' description of the judgment of Jerusalem leads to a description of judgment for all *nations* in the fourth part of this discourse (21:25–28). Because the judgment is universal, the language reflects this cosmic event. *There will be signs in the sun, moon and*

> **The Widow's Mite**
> *Small and bronze, a lepton is the lowest denomination of coinage, not even enough money to buy half a sparrow (Luke 12:6).*

stars (Joel 3:15); the *sea* will roar and toss (Ps 46:3); *heavenly bodies will be shaken* (Isa 34:4); and the *Son of Man* will come in a *cloud* (Dan 7:13). Jesus uses images from the apocalyptic tradition in the Old Testament to describe this time of judgment, which will also be a time of *redemption* for God's people.

Returning to the destruction of Jerusalem in the fifth part (21:29–33), Jesus tells a parable about a *fig tree* (see 13:6–9). Just as fig trees *sprout leaves*, indicating that *summer is near*, so *these things happening* show that *the kingdom of God is near*. In fact, the fall of Jerusalem will happen within the *generation* to whom Jesus is speaking.

The sixth and last part of the discourse (21:34–36) tells disciples how to live, regardless of whether the judgment is *about to happen* or in the future *before the Son of Man*. Disciples should avoid *dissipation, drunkenness, and anxieties of life* (8:14; 10:41; 12:11, 22, 25, 26); they should be *on the watch*; and they should *pray* (compare 18:1). Luke concludes (21:37–38) with a description of Jesus' activity in Jerusalem. Jesus taught *in the temple* daily (19:47; 22:53), attended by *all the people*, who *came early in the morning*; he spent each *night* on the *Mount of Olives* (22:39), a hill less than half a mile east of Jerusalem.

THE PASSION, RESURRECTION & ASCENSION NARRATIVES · 22:1–24:53

22:1-6 As *Passover* approaches, the *chief priests and teachers of the law* look for *some way to get rid of Jesus* (see 19:47; 20:20). Passover, followed by the one-week *Feast of Unleavened Bread*, celebrates God's redemption of his people from Egypt (Exod 12:1–51). At this time, *Satan enters Judas, one of the Twelve*, who in turn goes to the Jewish leaders and discusses *how he might betray Jesus*. Without any attempt to resolve the two, Luke describes both the spiritual, with this reference to Satan (22:3), and the human dimensions (22:1–2, 5–6, 22) of Judas' betrayal. *Delighted*, the leaders agree to give Judas *money*. Meanwhile, Judas looks for an opportunity to betray Jesus *when no crowd was present*.

> **Pilgrimage Festivals**
> *Passover is one of the three pilgrimage festivals in first century Judaism, the others being the Feast of Tabernacles and the Feast of Weeks, or Pentecost. For these festivals, Jews traveled to Jerusalem, if possible (2:41), and the city of Jerusalem swelled to many times its normal size.*

22:7-38 Luke explicitly puts the Last Supper in the context of the Passover meal; Jesus sends *Peter and John* (10:1; 19:29) saying, *Go and make preparations for us to eat the Passover*. Jesus tells them that, as they enter the city, they will see *a man carrying a water jar*, that they are to follow him to the *house* he enters, that they are to ask the *owner of the house* for a *guest room* (compare 2:7), and that they should *make preparations* there. Following Jesus' instructions, Peter and John find things *just as Jesus had told them* (19:32; 24:24).

After taking the bread and giving thanks, Jesus breaks the bread, gives it to the disciples, and says, *This is my body given for you; do this in remembrance of me*. Two things are noteworthy. First, Jesus' body is given for their sake; it is a vicarious sacrifice. Second, the practice of the Lord's Supper is a remembrance. But it is more than a mere remembrance of the facts; it is a commemoration, much like the Passover in which the Last Supper is set. As for the cup, it is also a vicarious sacrifice; the cup is *poured out for you*. In addition, the cup is a *new covenant* (see Jer 31:31–34). Finally, the cup is connected to Jesus' *blood*, an image that first century Jews would associate with sacrifice and atonement (Lev 17:11).

> **The Lord's Supper in Luke**
> *One difficulty with Luke's account of the Last Supper is the cup-bread-cup sequence. Why is there an extra cup? There is precedent for accounts describing the cup before the bread* (1 Cor 10:14–17; Didache 9). *In this case, however, the first cup (22:17–18) is probably one of the four cups associated with the Passover meal (Johnson 337), especially since the first cup is preceded by Jesus' statement*, I have eagerly desired to eat this Passover with you (22:15). *In addition, the second cup is linked with the bread by the transitional phrase in the same way* (22:20).

In Jesus' discourse to the disciples (22:21–38), three topics emerge: the betrayal of Jesus, greatness and service, and the role of the disciples in Jesus' suffering. Regarding his betrayer, Jesus says that the hand of the betrayer is with his *on the table*. Maintaining the tension between providence and free will (see 22:1–6), Jesus says, *The Son of Man will go as it has been decreed, but woe to that man who betrays him*. In response to a dispute among the disciples about who was the *greatest* (9:46), Jesus talks about the nature of God's kingdom, which demands leaders who *serve*.

Disciples are not like the *kings of the Gentiles* who *lord over* others; disciples are not *benefactors*, distributing benefits and expecting benefits in return (14:13–14). In the kingdom, those who *rule* are *like the one who serves*. Jesus himself models that ideal: *I am among you as one who serves*.

Jesus describes the disciples' role in this final act of his life and in the future. In the first place, Jesus confers on them a *kingdom* (12:32; 22:29) that they may *eat and drink at my table...and sit on thrones, judging the twelve tribes of Israel*. Jesus' description echoes previous language about an end-time banquet (13:29; 14:15; 22:16, 18; compare Isa 25:6). The twelve apostles represent a reconstituted Israel. Second, Jesus warns, *Satan has asked to sift you* [plural, referring to all the disciples] *as wheat*. Focusing on Simon Peter, Jesus tells him that he has *prayed* that his *faith may not fail* and that he repent and then strengthen his brothers. Peter insists that he is *ready* to go with Jesus *to prison and to death*. Jesus responds, *Before the rooster crows today, you will deny three times that you know me*. Third, Jesus warns the disciples about the new context they will soon face. They can expect hostility, not the hospitality that they received earlier (22:35). Jesus tells them, *If you don't have a sword, sell your cloak and buy one*, which they mistakenly understand literally; they tell Jesus, *See, Lord, here are two swords*. Jesus' reply, *That is enough*, should be understood as a rebuke, given Jesus' actions at his arrest (22:49–51). Moreover, a sword will not help Judas, Peter, or the rest of the Twelve in the types of battles they will face (Craddock 260). Instead, Jesus' words about a sword point to a future context of hostility, which is in *fulfillment* (18:31; 24:25–27, 44) of Isaiah 53:12: *He was numbered with the transgressors*. Later in the narrative, this prediction proves true as Jesus is arrested like a common criminal, traded for the murderer Barabbas, and crucified between two criminals (22:52; 23:18–19, 25, 32–33).

22:39–46 Jesus goes *as usual to the Mount of Olives* (21:37; compare *Gethsemane* in Matt 26:36; Mark 14:32), and his disciples follow. Jesus himself prays, and Jesus asks his disciples to pray. This emphasis on prayer is not surprising, since Luke has regularly portrayed Jesus teaching about prayer (11:1–13; 18:1–8). In this passage, Jesus twice tells the disciples to pray that they not *fall into temptation* (22:40, 46; compare 11:5; 22:31–32). Jesus withdraws *about a stone's throw*, kneels, and prays; he prays that God take this *cup*, which is going to require his blood (22:20), from him and that God's *will*, not his, *be done*. There is textual uncertainty regarding 22:43–44, since the manuscript evidence is about evenly divided. In these verses, an *angel* appears to Jesus and strengthens him (1:11; 4:10–11). In *anguish*, Jesus sweats profusely, as though bleeding. In his final words to the disciples before his arrest, Jesus tells them, *Pray that you will not fall into temptation*.

22:47–53 With Jesus' arrest, Luke shows three responses to Jesus. *Judas* approaches Jesus *to kiss him*, leads a *crowd* to Jesus, and so betrays him. Judas does not reappear in the narrative until Acts 1:15–20, where his actions are described as *wickedness*. On the other hand, when the disciples see that Jesus is about to be betrayed, they ask Jesus, *Lord, should we strike with our swords?* (22:36–38). One of them does cut off the *right ear* of the *servant of the high priest*; only John reports that the wielder of the sword is Peter and the servant is Malchus (John 18:10). In response, Jesus calls for a stop to the violence, touches the man's ear, and heals him. Thus Luke depicts the eleven as bold but misguided. Jesus then addresses the crowd, which is the third group. The crowd is composed of the *chief priests, the officers of the temple guard, and the elders*. Apparently, the *officers* (22:4) guard the temple and serve as a sort of police force for the temple (Acts 4:1; 5:24, 26). Jesus asks the leaders why they are coming for him *with swords and clubs*, as though he were a criminal (22:37), since he was with them *every day* in the *temple courts* (19:47; 21:37). Their weapons and secrecy point to evil plans on their part, which Jesus describes when he says, *But this is your hour* [see 12:12] – *when darkness reigns* (23:44).

22:54–62 Peter's denial of Jesus takes place *at the house of the high priest*, elsewhere identified as Caiaphas (Matt 26:57). In contrast to the other disciples, Peter initially follows Jesus. However, Peter later falters in the face of temptation as well, denying Jesus to *a servant girl* (22:56), to *someone else* (22:58); finally, to someone who calls him a *Galilean* (compare Matt 26:73). As Peter denies Jesus for the third time, a rooster crows in fulfillment of Jesus' prediction

> **Peter's Confession**
>
> In Acts 1–12, Peter fulfills the last part of Jesus' prediction and *strengthens his brothers* (22:31). Luke shows the predictions of Jesus fulfilled and Peter as a model of repentance.

(22:34). Only Luke records that after the third denial, the *Lord turned and looked straight at Peter*. Peter remembers Jesus' words, goes *outside,* and weeps *bitterly,* an act that also fulfills Jesus' prediction that Peter would repent (22:31).

22:63–65 This brief account shows how Jesus' predictions of his suffering are fulfilled (9:22, 44; 18:31–33). The *men who were guarding Jesus* are likely the officers of the temple guard (22:52), although they could include some of the Jewish leaders, as well (22:52). The officers *begin mocking* [18:32] *and beating* (20:10–11) Jesus. Luke then gives details about this mocking and beating: *They blindfolded him and demanded, Prophesy! Who hit you?* Luke closes with a general statement: *And they did many other insulting things to him*; although similar, the term in 22:65 [Greek *blasphemein*] is stronger than the language in 18:32 [Greek *hubrizein*; insult]. As the prophets were mistreated, so too is Jesus (4:24; 6:22–23; 11:47–51; 13:33–34; compare 20:9–12).

22:66–23:25 In contrast to the NIV heading, Jesus stands before three separate groups: the Sanhedrin (22:66–71), Pilate (23:1–5, 13–25), and Herod (23:6–12). *At daybreak,* Jesus is led before the Sanhedrin, which Luke calls *the council of the elders of the people, both the chief priests and teachers of the law*. After two rounds of interrogation, they render a decision. First, they ask Jesus for a confession: *If you are the Christ, tell us*. Jesus' response recognizes their attempts to trap and kill him (19:47–48; 20:19, 20–26; 22:1–6): Jesus recalls their refusal to answer (20:1–7). When Jesus mentions the *Son of Man* seated at the right hand of God (20:42–44; Ps 110:1; Dan 7:13), the council turns to Jesus a second time and says, *Are you then the Son of God?* Jesus' ambiguous response leaves the interpretation up to them (literally *you say that I am*; see 23:3), unlike the NIV translation. The condition of their hearts is seen in their response (compare the dissent of Joseph in 23:50–51).

Jesus is then led to *Pilate,* the prefect of the province of Judea. As the governor of the province, Pilate has *imperium,* the right to inflict the penalty of death. Three times Pilate will declare Jesus innocent (23:4, 14–15, 22). The Jewish leaders begin to accuse Jesus, saying, *We have found this man subverting our nation. He opposes payment of taxes to Cæsar and claims to be Christ, a king*. Pilate does not care about their first point; he does care about the payment of taxes, but their charge is false (20:20–26). Pilate follows up on their third charge, asking Jesus: *Are you the king of the Jews?* Despite the NIV's translation, Jesus replies with virtually the same ambiguous answer he gave the Sanhedrin, *Yes, it is as you say* (literally *you say*; see 22:70). After declaring that he finds *no basis for a charge* against Jesus, Pilate hears another accusation: *He stirs up the people all over Judea by his teaching*. Pilate takes a charge of social unrest seriously, especially with Jerusalem swelled with enthusiastic pilgrims celebrating Passover. He is, however, even more interested in passing the problem of Jesus to *Herod's jurisdiction*. As tetrarch of Galilee (3:1), Herod has jurisdiction over that area.

Pilate sends Jesus to Herod, who is *greatly pleased* because he hopes that Jesus will *perform some miracle*. Herod asks Jesus *many questions,* but Jesus gives him *no answer,* like the suffering servant of Isaiah 53:7. The Jewish leaders continue their accusations (23:10). Herod and his soldiers ridicule and mock (18:32; 22:63; 23:36; compare 23:35, 39) Jesus, involving, at least, dressing him *in an elegant robe*.

After Jesus has returned from Herod, Pilate summarizes the investigation thus far: he has investigated the accusation of *rebellion* and found *no basis for the charges*, and *neither has Herod*. After this second statement of Jesus' innocence, Pilate proposes, *I will punish him* [23:16, 22] *and then release him*. The leaders, and perhaps the people (23:13), cry out for the release of *Barabbas*.

Wanting to release Jesus, Pilate appeals a *third time,* but the crowd continues to ask for Jesus, now with cries of *Crucify him!* Despite his affirmation of Jesus' innocence and a second proposal to *punish* Jesus (23:16, 22; compare *flog* in 18:32), Pilate is persuaded by the loud shouts of the crowd. On Pilate's decision to crucify Jesus, compare the descriptions elsewhere in which Pilate is anxious about a riot developing (Matt 27:24) or desires to *satisfy the crowd* (Mark 15:15). This scene before Pilate fulfills Jesus' prediction that he would be *handed over to the Gentiles* (18:32).

23:26–43 As Jesus is crucified, Luke mentions six individuals or groups of people. First, Luke mentions *Simon from Cyrene,* which is a town in North Africa located in the Roman province of Cyrenaica (modern Libya). In the book of Acts, Luke mentions Jews (2:10; 6:9) and Christians (11:20; 13:1) from Cyrene. Little is known about Simon, other than that he carries Jesus' cross. Mark records that Simon was the *father of Alexander and Rufus* (15:21). Perhaps he and his sons had become Christians.

The second group mentioned by Luke is *a large number of people* who follow, but Luke focuses on the *women* in that group, who mourn and wail for Jesus. A bit later, Luke briefly notes that the *people* stand and watch the crucifixion (23:35). Turning to the women, Jesus tells them not to weep for him, but for themselves and their children (19:41). The reason is stated as a reversal of the earlier blessing in 11:27. *Barren women* will be *blessed* because it will be better not to have children, so great will be the trials that Jerusalem will face (21:23; 23:29). Referring to Hosea 10:8, Jesus again emphasizes the severity of the coming suffering for Jerusalem. People will prefer a speedy death, calling to the *mountains, 'Fall on us!' and to the hills, 'Cover us!'* Jesus concludes with a proverbial saying, *If men do these things when the tree is green, what will happen when it is dry?* meaning, "If people do these sorts of things when Jesus is present, imagine what will happen in his absence."

The third and the fourth groups of people continue to mock Jesus (18:32; 22:63; 23:36; see 23:35, 39) and call on Jesus to *save [him]self* (23:35, 37, 39). The *rulers* sneer (22:35; compare 16:14), *He saved others; let him save himself if he is the Christ of God* [9:20; 22:67], *the Chosen One* (9:35). The Roman *soldiers* mock him, offer him *wine vinegar* (Ps 69:21), and say, *If you are the king of the Jews, save yourself*. The reference to the *king of the Jews* echoes the charge before Pilate (23:3) and restates the wording on the *written notice* above Jesus: *This is the king of the Jews*. The soldiers also divide up Jesus' *clothes by casting lots*, an allusion to Psalm 22:19. From the cross, Jesus says, *Father, forgive them, for they do not know what they are doing*. This verse is omitted in some manuscripts (22:34; compare Acts 7:60).

Jesus' crucifixion takes place at a location called *The Skull*; Matthew and Mark call the place *Golgotha*, a word reflecting the Aramaic word for skull [*gulguta*; Matt 27:22; Mark 15:22; Fitzmyer 2:1503]. The word *Calvary*, found in the KJV, comes from the Latin word for skull [*calvaria*]. Notice that Luke also omits the Aramaic *Gethsemane*, preferring *Mount of Olives* (22:39; compare Matt 26:36; Mark 14:32). At *The Skull*, perhaps so named because the place of crucifixion resembled a skull, Jesus is crucified with *two other men, both criminals, one on his right, the other on his left*, fulfilling Isaiah 53:12 (Luke 22:37). Matthew and Mark call the criminals *robbers* (Matt 27:38; Mark 15:27). This fifth group reflects the divided response to Jesus (2:34). One criminal, like the rulers and the soldiers, hurls *insults* at Jesus. Also like the rulers and soldiers, this criminal calls on Jesus to *save [him]self* (23:35, 37, 39). Unlike the rulers and soldiers, he asks Jesus to save him. Apparently, this request is an insult, because the other criminal rebukes the first one: *Don't you fear God, since you are under the same sentence?* The second criminal continues with a statement regarding Jesus' innocence: *But this man has done nothing wrong* (23:4, 14–15, 22, 41, 47). The second criminal also has a request: *Jesus, remember me when you come into your kingdom*. Jesus grants the request, saying, *Today you will be with me in paradise*. Thus, despite undergoing taunts three times to save himself, Jesus saves not himself, but a criminal.

23:44–49 Luke shows different reactions to Jesus' death. Creation itself responds with *darkness from the sixth hour* [noon] *until the ninth hour* [3:00 p.m.]. The darkening of the sun plays a role in Old Testament descriptions of God's judgment (Joel 2:10, 31; Amos 8:9). The darkness can also be seen as a sign of evil's power at this moment; earlier Jesus said, *But this is your hour – when darkness reigns* (22:53). In addition, the *curtain of the temple* is *torn in two*.

Before dying, Jesus cries out, *Father, into your hands I commit my spirit*, an allusion to Psalm 31:5. As before, Luke shows how Jesus fulfills Scripture (18:31; 19:38; 22:37; 23:34, 36; 24:25–27, 44). The *centurion* glorifies God (2:20) and says, *Surely this was a righteous* [Greek *dikaios*] *man*. Thus, the centurion declares Jesus innocent [Greek *dikaios*], as Pilate, Herod, and the second criminal do earlier (23:4, 14, 15, 22, 41). *All the people who had gathered to witness* the crucifixion *beat their breasts* in sorrow (18:13) and go away. *All those who knew him, including the women who had followed him from Galilee*, stand at a distance and watch these events. Luke mentions

> **The Torn Curtain**
> Most commentators think that the curtain *is the curtain at the entrance to the holy of holies* (Exod 26:31–33, 36); *the meaning of the sign, however, is variously understood with no agreement: God's punishment for the rejection of Jesus, God's departure from the temple, the end of the old covenant, the end of divisions between Jews and Gentiles, and/or the new possibility of direct access to God* (Johnson 379; Craddock 275).

the women here because of the role they will play in the burial (23:55–56) and resurrection (24:1–10).

23:50–56 In this passage, Luke introduces Joseph and continues to comment on the role of Jesus' female disciples: Luke describes Joseph as *a member of the Council, a good and upright man, who had not consented to their decision and action.* Among the Jewish leaders, there is not complete agreement about Jesus (see 8:41–56; 13:31–33; 22:1–6; 22:66–23:1). Joseph comes from the Judean town of *Arimathea*; Luke also reveals that Joseph is *waiting for the kingdom of God* (2:25, 38; 23:51). Joseph asks *Pilate* for Jesus' body, takes it down from the cross, wraps it *in linen cloth,* and places it *in a tomb cut in the rock, one in which no one had yet been laid* (see 19:30). Joseph does all these things on *Preparation Day,* meaning the time before the *Sabbath was about to begin.* The women, meanwhile, follow Joseph, see the tomb and the placement of Jesus' body, go home, prepare *spices and perfumes,* and rest *on the Sabbath in obedience to the commandment.* Luke shows both Joseph and the women honoring Jesus after his death with flurries of activity.

24:1–12 Present at the death, burial (23:49, 55), and now the resurrection, the women will become eyewitnesses of these events to others (24:9; see 1:2). *On the first day of the week,* the women bring *the spices they had prepared* (23:56; 24:1) to the tomb, find *the stone rolled away,* and enter, but do *not find the body* of Jesus. As they are *wondering, two men in clothes that gleam like lightning* stand beside them. Later, the narrative identifies these two men as *angels* (24:23; compare Acts 1:10). The two men rebuke the women: *Why do you look for the living among the dead? He is not here; he has risen!* Next, they ask the women to *remember* Jesus' predictions about his suffering (9:22, 44; 18:31–34), which the women then do (24:6, 8). The women return from the tomb and tell *all these things to the Eleven and to all the others.* This mention of *the others* anticipates the two disciples on the road to Emmaus (24:13) and those with the eleven (24:33). Luke names three of the women, including *Mary Magdalene* and *Joanna* (8:1–3). Although Luke omits Susanna here (but 8:3), he does include *Mary the mother of James,* who is not mentioned in Luke 8 (compare Mark 15:40, 47; 16:1). The eleven and the others do *not believe the women because their words seemed to them like nonsense.* In fact, the men continue to struggle with their belief (24:11–12, 25, 37–39, 41; compare 24:16). Prompted by the women's account, Peter rises, runs to the tomb, sees *strips of linen lying by themselves,* and leaves, *wondering* to himself what happened. Peter's experience verifies the account of the women (24:24); yet the reader awaits an appearance of the risen Christ.

24:13–35 The first and second post-resurrection appearances of Jesus occur in a lengthy account of two disciples' journey to *Emmaus,* a city *about seven miles from Jerusalem.* One disciple is *Cleopas,* the other unnamed (24:9, 13, 18). The account moves in three stages: the journey to Emmaus, the meal in Emmaus, and the report to the eleven. On the *same day* as the resurrection, the two disciples discuss *everything that had happened* in Jerusalem as they journey to Emmaus. Although *Jesus* joins the pair, they are *kept from recognizing him* (9:45; 18:34; 19:42; see 24:31, 45). In the ensuing conversation between Jesus and the two disciples, Jesus asks about the events in Jerusalem, which the disciples summarize: Jesus was a *prophet*; the Jewish leaders handed him over to be *crucified*; they thought Jesus would *redeem Israel*; some *women* found the *tomb* empty, but a *vision of angels* said Jesus was *alive*; some *companions* went to the tomb, finding it *just as the women said* (see 19:32; 22:13; Johnson 395), but *they did not see* him. Jesus rebukes the pair for being slow of heart to believe (24:11, 25, 41) and explains to them *what was said in all the Scriptures concerning himself* (24:27, 32, 44–45). As they approach the village, the disciples urge Jesus: *Stay with us, for it is nearly evening; the day is almost over.*

At the meal in Emmaus, Jesus takes bread, gives thanks, breaks it, and gives it to them, actions that echo both the feeding of the 5,000 and the Last Supper (9:16; 22:19). The *eyes* of the disciples are *opened* (24:31–32, 45), and they recognize Jesus, who then disappears *from their sight.* They return to Jerusalem *at once.* Before they can speak, the eleven describe the second post-resurrection appearance of Jesus in Luke's account: *It is true! The Lord has risen and has appeared to Simon.* The two disciples then report *what happened on the way, and how Jesus was recognized by them when he broke the bread.* For Luke, this account functions to describe how disciples come to recognize and believe in Jesus (24:11, 25, 41; see Craddock 285–87). First, reflection plays a role, as the disciples discuss among themselves and with Jesus the events in Jerusalem. As Mary did (2:19, 51), they ponder the significance of their experiences. Second, that reflection also includes the witness of others (24:22–24, 48; Acts 1:8). Third, Scripture plays a key role (24:27, 32, 44–47). Fourth, their eyes are opened in the eating of the meal with Jesus (24:30–31), which echoes the Lord's Supper, anticipates the messianic banquet, and probably points to the role of worship in developing and growing faith.

24:36–49 The third post-resurrection appearance of Jesus addresses a question about Jesus' physical presence, reiterates previous themes, and anticipates themes in Acts. Some might wonder whether the appearance of Jesus was the appearance of a ghost. In fact, Luke records that the disciples think that they see a *ghost*. Jesus responds in two ways. He first asks them, *Look at my hands and my feet. It is I myself! Touch me and see; a ghost does not have flesh and bones as you see I have*. Then, when they still do *not believe*, Jesus asks them, *Do you have anything to eat?* Receiving *a piece of broiled fish*, Jesus eats it *in their presence*.

Jesus teaches his disciples, again stressing the fulfillment of Scripture (24:27, 32, 44–45) and the necessity of the Christ to *suffer* (24:26, 46). Jesus' final words give the disciples a task and a promise, as well as prepare the reader for prominent emphases in Acts: *Repentance and forgiveness of sins will be preached in his name to all nations, beginning in Jerusalem. You are witnesses of these things. I am going to send you what my Father has promised; but stay in the city until you have received power from on high*. From this instruction, one notes the following key themes: conversion (*repentance and forgiveness*; Acts 2:38), universalism (*all the nations*; Acts 1:8), the spread of the gospel (*beginning in Jerusalem*; Acts 1:8), witness (Acts 1:8), and the Holy Spirit (*what my Father has promised*; Acts 1:4–5, 8).

24:50–53 Luke recounts the fourth and last post-resurrection appearance with brevity. Jesus leads the disciples out *to the vicinity of Bethany* (19:29), lifts up his hands, and blesses them. While *blessing* them, Jesus departs from them and is *taken up into heaven*; for a discussion of the chronological difficulties with the ascension in Acts, see the treatment of Acts 1. The disciples worship and return to Jerusalem *with great joy*. Staying in the *temple*, they praise God. In Jesus' absence, their worship, obedience, joy, and praise model to later disciples how one behaves while waiting for Jesus' promises to be fulfilled.

THEOLOGICAL REFLECTIONS

Scholars have proposed various themes as the key to Luke. However, Luke displays more complexity than such a search assumes. In other words, Luke weaves a number of themes throughout his narrative, many of which come up again in Acts. This section highlights five prominent themes.

First, Luke emphasizes prayer more than any of the other gospels. Even in parallel passages, Luke mentions prayer when the other writers do not, such as at Jesus' baptism and at the transfiguration (3:31; 9:28). Above all, Luke shows Jesus as a person of prayer. Prayer is a persistent feature of Jesus' life; during his ministry, Jesus withdraws for solitude and prayer (5:16) and teaches about prayer (11:1–13). Jesus carves out time for prayer by seeking solitude (6:12; 9:18; 9:28; 22:39–42). In fact, Jesus' last words should probably be understood as a prayer (23:46).

Luke also shows Jesus praying at critical times in his life. He prays at his baptism before the beginning of his ministry (3:21–22). Remarkably, he spends all night in prayer before the selection of the twelve disciples (6:12) as well as before his death (22:39–42). Earlier, he encourages disciples to pray for strength in times of trial (21:36). These examples show Jesus seeking God's wisdom and strength at difficult times, modeling one role of prayer for disciples.

Not only Jesus' actions, but also his words, testify about the importance of prayer. At two points, Luke records Jesus' teaching about prayer. Through these teachings, Luke provides a model prayer (11:1–4), stresses the importance of persistence in prayer (11:5–8; 18:1–8), describes God's desire to bless those who pray (11:9–13), and cautions about the right attitude one brings to prayer (18:9–14; 20:47).

Jesus offers various kinds of prayer. He prays for himself and for Peter and the other disciples (22:31–34). Luke also shows Jesus offering prayers of thanks to God for food (9:16; 22:19; 24:28–30) and for the progress of the kingdom (10:21–22). In all of these accounts, Luke stresses the importance of prayer for the life of one who follows Jesus.

Second, more than any of the other Gospels, Luke stresses the contributions of women in the ministry of Jesus. Even with women mentioned in the other gospels, Luke often expands their significance in his narrative (for example, Mary).

Among the women in Luke, one finds Mary, a model of discipleship and faith (1:38, 45), Anna, a prophetess who speaks to everyone about Jesus in the temple (2:36–38), women who fund Jesus' ministry (8:1–3), Mary, who sits at Jesus' feet in the posture of a disciple (10:38–42), a woman who cries out with praise to God in the middle of a synagogue (13:13), one widow who models persistence (18:1–8), another widow who exemplifies generosity (21:1–4), and finally the women who first see the resurrected Jesus and tell about him to others (24:1–11). In Luke, Jesus appears to be ahead of his culture in his inclusion of women in the group that travels with him (8:1–3; 23:49, 55; 24:1–11, 22–25) and in his emphasis on theological definitions of identity versus social expectations (10:38–42; 11:27–28).

Third, Luke demonstrates a strong interest in how one uses possessions. In his account of the call of the disciples and then Levi, Luke alone records that they left *everything* (5:11, 28), a theme echoed later in the Lukan discussion of discipleship (14:33) and shown negatively in the story of the rich ruler (18:22). The *sinful woman* (7:36–50) provides an example of generosity, as do the women who support Jesus' ministry with their use of possessions (8:1–3). Jesus treats covetousness and the folly of trusting in a stockpile of riches in the Lukan parable of the rich fool (12:13–21). The responsible use of possessions looks beyond satisfying one's own desires to benefiting others (12:21, 33–34). In the treatment that follows this parable, Jesus also addresses the worry that accompanies possessions (12:22–34). The use of possessions reveals the heart of a disciple (12:34). Disciples who have been blessed must bless others (12:48).

In the narrative that follows, Luke shows that disciples invite the kind of guests who cannot repay them with an invitation (14:13). Luke uses unique material in chapter 16 to show that disciples should use their wealth wisely (16:1–9) rather than love money (16:14–15) and be selfish in their use of wealth (16:19–31). Luke uses scribes and widows to condemn dishonesty (20:47) and commend generosity (21:1–4). In the kingdom, the dishonest should repent (19:1–10).

> **Wealth & Stewardship**
> Luke's teaching on wealth challenges Christians today to give generously and to recognize the eternal consequences of the use of possessions (16:19–31; 18:24–25).

Fourth, from the very beginning of the gospel, Luke portrays God's interest in the weak of society. Mary exclaims that God regards *the humble state of his servant,* lifts up *the humble,* and fills *the hungry* (1:48, 52, 53). Also, Luke's programmatic description of Jesus' ministry at Nazareth focuses on the poor, the captives, the blind, and the oppressed (4:18), a focus that continues throughout the gospel (see poor in 6:20; 7:22; 14:13, 21; 16:20, 22; 18:22; 21:3; blind in 7:21–22; 14:13, 21; 18:35). In Jesus' Sermon on the Plain (6:20–22), blessings fall on the poor, hungry (1:53), those who weep (7:13, 38; 8:52), and those who are hated (see 1:71; 6:27; 21:17). Corresponding woes go out to the rich, the full, those who laugh, and those who are praised (6:24–26). When disciples come from John the Baptist, the validation of Jesus' ministry is that *the blind receive sight, the lame walk* [14:13, 21], *those who have leprosy are cured* [5:12–13;

Women Unique to Luke's Gospel

Among the Synoptic Gospels, Luke alone mentions the following women and female characters:

- Elizabeth (1:5–25, 36, 39–60)
- The daughters of Aaron (1:5)
- All women (1:42)
- Anna (2:36–38)
- Many widows in Israel (4:25)
- The widow of Zarephath (4:25–26)
- The widow of Nain (7:11–17)
- Wisdom (7:35)
- The forgiven woman (7:36–50)
- The women with Jesus – Joanna, Susanna, and many others (8:1–3)
- Mary & Martha (10:38–42)
- The woman who praises Jesus' mother (11:27–28)
- Maidservants (12:45)
- The crippled woman (13:10–17)
- A newlywed wife (14:20)
- Wife & sisters (14:26)
- The woman who lost a coin (15:8–10)
- Prostitutes (15:30)
- Lot's wife (17:32)
- The importunate widow (18:1–8)
- The wife who has been left for the sake of the kingdom (18:29)
- Parents (21:16a)
- The women wailing at the crucifixion (23:27–31)
- Barren women (23:29–30)

> **Paired Men & Women in Luke**
>
> In addition to including several women not found in the other Synoptic Gospels, Luke also emphasizes the inclusive nature of the gospel by pairing a story about a man with a corresponding story about a woman. This feature pervades Luke, as the following list shows:
>
> Zechariah & Mary (1:5–25, 26–38)
> Simeon & Anna (2:25–35, 36–38)
> The widow of Zarephath & Naaman (4:25–26, 27)
> The demoniac & Simon's mother-in-law (4:33–37, 38–39)
> The centurion's slave & the widow of Nain (7:1–10, 11–17)
> Simon the Pharisee & the forgiven woman (7:36–50)
> The good Samaritan & Mary and Martha (10:29–37, 38–42)
> The man with an unclean spirit & a woman in the crowd (11:24–26, 27–28)
> The Queen of the South & the men of Nineveh (11:31, 32)
> Father/son and mother/daughter pairs (12:53a, 53b)
> The Sabbath healing of a woman & of a man (13:10–17; 14:1–6)
> The man with the mustard seed & the woman with leaven (13:18–19, 20–21)
> The man who lost a sheep & the woman who lost a coin (15:3–7, 8–10)
> The man in a field & Lot's wife (17:31, 32)
> The two men in bed & the two women at the mill (17:34, 35)
> The importunate widow & the Pharisee/tax collector (18:1–8, 9–18)
> Scribes & a widow (20:45–47; 21:1–4)
> Simon of Cyrene & the women who lament (23:26, 27–31)
> Jesus' acquaintances & the women who followed him (23:49a, 49b)
> The women witnesses & the two men on road to Emmaus (24:1–11, 12–24)
>
> It is significant that fourteen of these pairs occur only in Luke: in seven, both parts are unique to Luke; in the other seven, Luke adds a figure – most often a woman – to create the pairing. Though many of the pairs involve parables and stories, the emphasis on inclusivity and balance is clearly important to Luke.

17:11–19], *the deaf hear* [compare 1:22; 11:14], *the dead are raised* [7:15], *and the good news is preached to the poor* (7:23). In his ministry, Jesus associates with sinners in general (5:8, 30; 7:34, 37, 39; 15:1–2; 19:7) and tax collectors specifically (5:27–32; 7:34; 15:1; 19:2). It may possibly be more accurate to say that Jesus seeks out those people (5:32; 19:10). Outcasts even star in some of Jesus' most famous parables, which feature Samaritans (10:29–37), sinners (15:18, 21; 18:13), and tax collectors (18:9–14). Those who have the least power, position, health, and wealth provide opportunities for disciples to serve.

And fifth, in Luke, God's kingdom is a topsy-turvy place. In this kingdom, surprises repeatedly punctuate the narrative. Prodigals, Samaritans, and tax collectors play the heroes, while Pharisees and hard-working older brothers function as negative examples (10:29–37; 15:11–32; 18:9–14). Elsewhere, Jesus praises friends who wake up other friends at midnight, while rich farmers turn out to be fools (11:5–8; 12:13–21). The *poor, the crippled, the blind, and the lame,* and street people feast at a banquet (14:15–24). A shepherd leaves ninety-nine sheep to search for the one lost sheep (15:3–7). Both the blessed and the oppressed experience reversals of fortune. Probably no parable illustrates this feature better than the account of the rich man and Lazarus (16:19–30). Expectations are turned upside down. In Jesus' Sermon on the Plain (6:20–22), blessings fall on the poor, hungry, those who weep, and those who are hated. Corresponding woes go out to the rich, the full, those who laugh, and those who are praised (6:24–26). The Messiah is the friend of tax collectors and sinners (5:8, 27–32; 7:34, 37, 39; 15:1–2; 19:2, 7). The kingdom of God is different from the world, which values power, position, and wealth. In God's kingdom, significance is found in service (22:24–27), and identity is defined by likeness to one's teacher (6:40) and by hearing and doing God's word (8:19–20; 11:27–28). Luke calls disciples to become citizens of God's kingdom, blessing others and shunning the false attractions of the world.

FOR FURTHER STUDY

Amy-Jill Levine, Dale C. Allison, and John Dominic Crossan, eds., *The Historical Jesus in Context* (Princeton: Princeton University Press, 2006).

V. George Shillington, *An Introduction to the Study of Luke-Acts* (London: T & T Clark, 2007).

WORKS CITED

Scott Carroll, "Bethphage," *Anchor Bible Dictionary* 1 (1992): 715.

Cicero, *Pro Milone, In Pisonem, Pro Scauro, Pro Fonteio, Pro Rabirio Postumo, Pro Marcello, Pro Ligario, Pro Rege Deiotaro* (Cambridge: Harvard University Press, 1953).

Fred B. Craddock, *Luke* (Louisville, Ky.: John Knox, 1990).

Kenneth L. Cukrowski, "Pagan Polemic and Lukan Apologetic," Ph.D. diss., Yale University, 1994.

———, "'Blessed Is the King': The Roman Triumph and Jesus' Triumphal Entry in Luke 19:37–40." *Bulletin of the General Theological Library of Bangor Theological Seminary* 87/3 (1996): 3–14.

F. W. Danker, ed. *Greek-English Lexicon of the New Testament and other Early Christian Literature* (3rd ed.; Chicago: University of Chicago Press, 2000).

Joseph Fitzmyer, *The Gospel according to Luke* (2 vols.; Garden City, N.Y.: Doubleday, 1981–1985).

Susan Garrett, *The Demise of the Devil: Magic and the Demonic in Luke's Writings* (Minneapolis, Minn.: Fortress, 1989).

Michael W. Holmes, ed. and trans., *The Apostolic Fathers* (Grand Rapids: Baker Academic, 2007)

Luke Timothy Johnson, *The Gospel of Luke* (Collegeville, Minn.: Liturgical, 1991).

Josephus, *Works* (ed. H. St. John Thackeray; 10 vols.; Cambridge: Harvard University Press, 1926-65).

Robert Smith, "Chorazin," *Anchor Bible Dictionary* 1 (1992): 911–12.

John

Mark A. Matson

CHAPTER CONTENTS

- Contexts 825
- Structure & Message 827
- Commentary 828
  - The Prologue to the Gospel · 1:1–18 828
  - The Early Ministry of Jesus · 1:19–4:54 830
  - The Controversies Over Jesus' Mission · 5:1–11:47 835
  - The Passion of Jesus · 12:1–19:42 843
  - The Resurrection Appearances of Jesus · 20:1–21:25 851
- Theological Reflections 853
- For Further Study 854
- Works Cited 854

MAPS, TABLES & FEATURES

- The Background of John's "Word" Metaphor 830
- The Adulterous Woman 838

The fourth gospel stands out in the collection of gospels because of its structure, its tone, and the picture it gives of Jesus' own self-revelation. It has been called the "spiritual gospel" in part because it deals so clearly with issues of the origination and destination of Jesus from heaven, and in part because Jesus speaks in longer units of dialogue that address spiritual issues. But this gospel is still a narrative presentation of Jesus as a man who interacts with people in his time. John presents a compelling account of Jesus' life and the conflicts which arise in response to his claims about his relationship with God. Alongside the spiritual interpretation of Jesus is a story of growing conflict, of differing choices about how to understand Jesus, and finally of his self-sacrifice in the name of love for all of humanity.

A quick look at the structure of John gives us some idea of the main emphasis of the gospel. First, before the plot begins, the author frames the story of Jesus with a theological prologue, set outside of time, in which the reader learns that this man Jesus is the preexistent Word of God. Second, the initial account of the life of Jesus is punctuated by a series of miracles, called "signs." This term suggests that miracles point to a deeper reality than simply powerful activity. Third, interspersed among the signs, Jesus engages in long discourses with various individuals. In these discourses, Jesus makes a number of dramatic revelations of who he is and how people should react to him. Fourth, as the story progresses, there is a growing opposition to Jesus on the part of a group called "the Jews." This growing opposition is a central feature of John's plot.

Fifth, following the raising of Lazarus in chapter 11, the focus shifts to Jesus' anticipated death. This death, in John's gospel, is framed as a "glorification." Sixth, by means of a series of recurring trips to Jerusalem, John emphasizes that Jesus' life centered on the temple and the Jewish religious calendar and its festivals.

All of these structural features suggest an approach to the life and work of Jesus that focuses on the nature of Jesus and the meaning of his ministry. John rhetorically underlines Jesus' special relationship to God and the misunderstanding of that relationship by many who claim to follow God.

CONTEXTS

The rather striking structure outlined above sets John apart from the other three gospels, the Synoptic Gospels (called synoptic because they are "seen together"). How should we understand the relationship between John and the Synoptics? On the one hand, all four gospels tell the story of Jesus, with a major focus being his crucifixion and resurrection. And in all the gospels Jesus performs miracles and faces opposition from the religious establishment

> **The Synoptic Gospels & the Synoptic Problem**
> *Matthew, Mark, and Luke relate closely to each other literarily. Many scholars believe that Matthew and Luke used Mark as one of their major sources. John agrees with them on the basic details of the final week of Jesus' life and on the key features of his life and ministry but overlaps very little with them in reporting the specific sayings and miracles of Jesus.*

of his time. But the gospels are told in such strikingly different ways that some explanation must be made for their similarities and differences.

The fourth gospel is not literarily dependent on any of the other gospels, but is rather based on eyewitness testimony and oral traditions. While there are similarities between the Synoptic Gospels and John at various points, the dissimilarities seem to be more telling. It would be harder to explain the differences between John and the Synoptics if there were indeed a textual relationship between them than if John is truly independent. More often than not, comparison with the other gospels will only be made in order to cast in sharp relief the distinctive nature of John's story of Jesus.

Traditionally, scholars have sought the background of John's thought in Hellenistic (or Greek) philosophy and religions, so much so that John was even deemed the "gospel of the Hellenists." But that view has shifted, and with good reason. In many ways it can be said that John is indeed the most Jewish of all the gospels. We can summarize this Jewish focus by means of three key features.

The first major feature is the strongly dualistic perspective of the author. He frequently interprets the mission of Jesus in terms of sharply contrasted opposites. The most striking one, of course, is the light/dark motif: Jesus is the light; he comes to a world of darkness. With the discovery of the Dead Sea Scrolls, this dualism can comfortably be located within Judaism of the first century.

The second major feature, already mentioned, is the strong opposition to Jesus by "the Jews." This viewpoint informs the entire gospel, being the basis for much of the plot of the story. In many ways the central focus of the dialogues with Jesus is an attempt to define him against misinterpretation by "the Jews." The arguments make best sense as apologetic arguments within Judaism about Jesus' relationship to God. To what extent might a prophetic messiah who has been charged to bring God's authoritative message be seen as uniquely related to God? Thus the christological arguments are framed from the perspective of a dialogue within Judaism, not a dialogue with Greco-Roman religions or ideology.

A third feature is the unique emphasis that John places on the temple and on Jerusalem as its location. John alone has Jesus frequently in Jerusalem, and the geographical center of his work when in Jerusalem is the temple. Moreover, Jesus' trips to Jerusalem are constructed around the major festivals of the Jewish calendar. Thus John pictures Jesus as an observant Jew.

AUTHORSHIP

Much ink has been spilled on the question of the authorship of the fourth gospel. The gospel text does make an explicit self-reference to the author in 21:24–25: the author of the gospel is *this disciple*, that is, *the disciple whom Jesus loved* (more commonly termed the "Beloved Disciple"). Yet it is very hard to determine precisely who the disciple is. Certainly the relationship of the Beloved Disciple to Peter suggests that the Beloved Disciple belongs to the inner circle of Jesus' disciples. If one extrapolates from the other gospels, one might well conclude that this was John, son of Zebedee. Early church tradition identifies the author of the fourth gospel with this John. The problem, of course, is that the Gospel of John itself is not specific about the authorship.

However, the gospel does link itself directly to a disciple of Jesus who was an eyewitness of the events that are recorded. In this respect, John is unique among the four gospels in asserting an eyewitness relationship. It is the same kind of assertion that 1 John also makes. While this may well be a literary construction, nonetheless the assertion is clearly made and must be acknowledged.

Generally in current scholarship the author of the fourth gospel is located within the "community" of the Beloved Disciple (Brown). In this view, the gospel comes from the Beloved Disciple in the sense that it represents the "traditions" of that disciple. This naturally is related to theories about the date of writing (see below), as well as the purpose of the gospel. If we presume a late writing as well as a gospel that is literarily derivative of the Synoptic Gospels, it is very hard to assert apostolic authorship directly. If the gospel is early and independent, then the question is more open.

While I am not entirely convinced that John, the son of Zebedee, wrote the fourth gospel, I am increasingly convinced of its early date and direct relationship to a disciple who was an eyewitness to at least some of Jesus' ministry. Attribution to a "community" of the beloved disciple is thus not necessary.

DATE

New Testament introductions routinely date John late, certainly at the end of the first century and often well into the second century. There has been an increasing attention, though, to a reevaluation of the date of John and its relationship to the other gospels. Beginning with John A. T. Robinson's posthumous work, *The Priority of John*, in 1985, questions about whether John might be early have increased.

The late date of John stems primarily from conclusions about its theology and its relationship to the Synoptics. John's distinctive Christology of the Word made flesh has been seen as more developed (and hence later) than the other gospels. Taken together with assumptions about its more Hellenistic nature and its dependence on the Synoptic Gospels, many have concluded that John was the latest of all the gospels. However, John is probably literarily independent of the Synoptics. Moreover, we now see John as fundamentally Jewish in tone and outlook, not Hellenistic. And John's Christology is no more developed than Paul's in Philippians 2 or Colossians 2, and Paul is undoubtedly the earliest New Testament author. The major arguments for a late John, therefore, have seemed less impressive in recent years. If we give any credence to the gospel's own claim to be based on some relationship to an eyewitness, then we might also move its date earlier.

STRUCTURE & MESSAGE

The fourth gospel has a number of distinctive features that set its narrative apart from the other gospels and suggest that we should give care to reading and interpreting the way the gospel has been constructed.

Jesus uses symbolic language in a distinctive way in John. Especially noteworthy is his use of the "I am" saying, often linked to striking metaphors. In particular, Jesus uses this construction to create the following striking symbolic pictures: *I am the bread of life* (6:48, 59); *I am the light of the world* (8:12); *I am the door of the sheepfold* (10:7, 9); *I am the good shepherd* (10:11,14); *I am the resurrection and the life* (11:25); *I am the way, the truth, and the life* (14:6); and *I am the true vine* (15:1, 5). In addition to these metaphorical "I am" sayings, Jesus used such symbolic language as his reference to rebuilding the temple (which is then understood later as his body, 2:22), and his statements that he will provide living water, that one must eat his flesh and drink his blood to have eternal life, and his allusive references to rebirth. Each metaphorical or symbolic statement is rich in meaning, and in each case points to some aspect of Jesus' identity as the unique agent of God.

While all the gospels have important statements from Jesus that are authoritative in tone, John is unique in presenting so much of Jesus' speaking. And rather than short enigmatic parables or didactic commands, Jesus in John often engages in extended arguments with opponents, or instructs others about his mission and the future. I would suggest that John has a very rhetorical purpose in mind. The discourses are major tools, together with the signs and symbolic language, that the evangelist uses to achieve the rhetorical thrust of the gospel.

CONFLICT WITH "THE JEWS"

One major motif in the Gospel of John is the theme of conflict with "the Jews." This conflict is really an essential component of the narrative fabric of John's gospel. The plot is structured around increasing tension and misunderstanding between Jesus and "the Jews," a tension that becomes outright opposition and persecution in the later stages.

However, we must ask, who are these "Jews"? I have deliberately enclosed the word in quotes to signal that the term is not identical with Judaism itself. Indeed John makes it clear that Jesus is a Jew, and that *salvation comes from the Jews*. Moreover, I hesitate to use the term without qualification because this gospel's use of the term "the Jews" has led to significant persecution of Jews throughout history. Instead of simply referring to Judaism in general, the term itself seems to be a "sign" or symbol of an abstraction.

One explanation is that John is referring by this term to the inhabitants of Judea (as the term "the Jews" is often translated), perhaps in contrast to the inhabitants of Galilee. While this certainly avoids any misuse of the term "Jews," it is hardly supported by the text. Not all of the Judeans oppose Jesus, and "the Jews" appear even in Galilee. An alternative explanation is that "the Jews" are the religious leaders of the Jewish nation, as opposed

> **"Signs" in John's Gospel**
> Perhaps one of the most striking features of the fourth gospel is the obvious use of symbolism in the actions and words of Jesus (Koester). Many of Jesus' actions have significance beyond their surface representation. This is apparent in John's use of the word *signs* to describe many of these actions.

to the average Jew. It is perhaps preferable, though, to see John's term "the Jews" as a designation for those Israelites who oppose Jesus and who actively seek to still his voice and his testimony. The term does not relate to any single geographical or political group, although John understands the religious leaders to be a major component of the opposition to Jesus. In short, "Jews" is a cipher for the spiritual forces of opposition and darkness.

JESUS' MINISTRY & RELATIONSHIP WITH GOD

Another significant feature of John's narrative is the length of Jesus' ministry that it displays. Much longer than that portrayed in the other gospels, John puts Jesus' ministry at around three years, as the references to at least three Passover celebrations make clear (chapters 2, 6, and 12). The longer ministry is not by itself significant, but in John, the narrative structure is built around Jesus' repeated visits to Jerusalem, always on the occasion of a Jewish festival. This structure highlights both Jerusalem as the site of many of Jesus' significant discourses, and the importance of the Jewish festival calendar as the background and source of imagery for many of his discourses (especially chapters 7–10).

Finally, the fourth gospel is unique in its focus on Jesus' relationship with God. Jesus, in John's view, is the preexistent Word, and as such has a very special relationship with God: as creative Word, as Son in a special Father-Son relationship, and even as participating in God's own (divine) nature. Jesus consistently maintains that he is God's unique agent to bring reconciliation to the world: *the Father has sent me* (5:36). And yet at the same time he consistently shows himself to be dependent on God: *I do nothing by my own accord* (8:27). Thus John portrays Jesus as being subordinate to God, and yet in a fundamental way the full manifestation of God: *Whoever has seen me has seen the Father* (14:9). Indeed, Jesus' relationship with God is sufficiently close that he can say that *I and Father are one* (10:30). Jesus' relationship with God is thus the focus of all the dialogues and is the basis for the plot of increasing opposition and rejection, and ultimately death.

COMMENTARY

THE PROLOGUE TO THE GOSPEL · 1:1–18

The fourth gospel is a story about Jesus. But it is also constructed as an argument for belief. We should, perhaps, always read the beginning of the gospel with the author's purpose in mind:

> *Jesus did many other signs in the presence of his disciples which are not written in this book; but these are written that you may believe that Jesus is the Christ, the Son of God, and that believing you may have life in his name* (20:30–31).

The opening of the book presents an interpretation of who Jesus is, his relationship with the God of Israel, and the purpose of his mission on earth.

The fourth evangelist has used a nonnarrative philosophic reflection to preface the gospel in order to signal his purpose: this gospel is to be a reflection on the importance of Jesus, not just a narration of his life. By using poetic language, the fourth evangelist sets the initial frame of Jesus outside of time and outside of human experience – Jesus truly has a cosmic and eternal significance. But despite the poem's opening perspective outside of time, and despite its point of view from beyond the merely human experience, it nonetheless has narrative structure to it as well. The poem of 1:1–18 sketches Jesus' descent, ministry, and return to God. The Jesus of history is part of the transhistorical Word. Time and eternity meet and interpret one another in the prologue to John.

The basic meaning of the prologue is clear. Jesus Christ was not just a prophet or a savior but was indeed the incarnation of the very Word of God. Thus Jesus was fully human, but also, in some unique way was God manifest, God come near, God come to bring humanity back to God.

Three central themes appear in this poem. The first identifies the Word with God's creative and life-giving activity. The second speaks of the incarnation of the Word in Jesus, an incarnation which both revealed

> **Docetism**
> *Docetism, one of the major heretical threats to early Christianity, was a denial of the incarnation of Jesus. Many of those who advocated that Jesus only seemed to have a human body also declined to partake of the Lord's Supper. Yet this gospel clearly testifies to the flesh-and-blood body of Jesus. These multiple explicit comments about Jesus' appearance in the flesh may be the fourth evangelist's attempt to put this misconception to rest.*

God's glory and the rejection of that glory by much of humanity. The third emphasizes the role of belief in the Word, based on testimony by and about Jesus. These themes are developed in consecutive units, but there are interruptions in the flow and a certain degree of overlapping of themes.

The first major unit, verses 1–5, deals with the Word, its relationship with God, and its role in the very act of creation. In the second major unit, verses 9–13, the theme is the Word's entry into and role in the world. And the third major unit, verses 14–18, focuses on the testimony of the community of faith to the Word's life as a human being. The text flows, then, from a cosmic role to an earthly mission, and then finally to the specific relationship with believers.

1:1–5 The first unit of the prologue begins outside of history and beyond the realm of human experience. The fourth gospel intended for the reader to "hear" the openings words of Genesis echoed in the opening verse of this poem: *In the beginning*.... Once one makes the connection with the creation story in Genesis, other images in the prologue begin to make sense. In Genesis, God "speaks" the world into being, and John refers to the Word as being the agent of all creation. In Genesis, light is the first thing created, and God then separated light and dark; John also speaks of the Word as light shining in the darkness. The opening verses of John thus invite the reader to enter into a dialogue between this text and the well-known opening verses of Genesis. This dialogue is itself creative, allowing a variety of comparisons and allusions to details in the Genesis story to enrich the understanding of the Word's creative work.

This first unit of the poem also anticipates the drama of the life and death of Jesus, connecting the past story of creation to the coming narrative of the Word incarnate. Light and darkness, which in Genesis are simply physical qualities, are transformed into spiritual qualities: light and darkness engage in a battle with one another. Light is clearly the positive force of God, and darkness thus takes on a malevolent quality in direct opposition to light. While this can be taken simply as an eternal battle, it also drops the first hint of the passion story.

1:6–8 Instead of moving directly to the incarnation itself, the poem is seemingly interrupted by the introduction of John the Baptist. This John is defined as a *witness* to the light, and not the light itself. This distinction clearly indicates that the author was already thinking about the human Jesus in the last sentence of the previous unit; John the Baptist's reference brings us suddenly to the historical situation of Jesus. More importantly, it indicates the role of persuasion in the mind of the author. Witnesses are crucial to making a convincing proof of a historical event.

1:9–13 The second major unit of thought begins with the previous theme of the Word as the light of the world and expands this idea into a truly incarnated phenomenon. The Word is now the light *come into* the world. The author has introduced a new concept, *the world*. Is this simply a reference to human events, to history, or is there a deeper meaning to the term? For John, *the world* carries a multiplicity of meanings. It is the object of God's love, not judgment (3:16–19), yet the world has judged itself by rejecting the light. The world is also the object of Jesus' mission, and yet it rejects him and hates his followers (17:14). For the fourth evangelist, then, the term *the world* is both the locus of fallen humanity and the object of a mission from God.

John goes on to say that Jesus came to *his own*. This term might be referring to humanity in general as being in some special way God's "own." But more likely this implies that Jesus was rejected by the Jewish people, God's chosen people.

1:14–18 With the third unit, the implication of the incarnation becomes completely clear. With the clear statement of the incarnation of the Word, we learn that Jesus is the physical manifestation of God, the only begotten (or unique) Son of God, who shows God's glory as has never before been seen.

As one examines the structure of the poem and how it develops its ideas, it is clear that recurrent themes are developed in successive "waves." That the Word came into the world to bring light and life to humanity is introduced vaguely in the first unit (*the light shines in the darkness, and the darkness has not overcome it*), then a bit stronger in the second unit (*He was in the world, and the world was made through him, yet the world knew him not*), and finally is made clear in the third unit (*and the Word became flesh and dwelt among us*). Similarly the interest in persuasion is introduced with John the Baptist (*He came for testimony, to bear witness to the light, that all might believe through him*), is raised a second time in the second unit (*to all who believed in his name, he gave power to become children of God*), and is reiterated in the third unit (*John bore witness to him*). And the

Passion Narrative is anticipated throughout. In the first unit, it is mostly an allusion (*and the darkness has not overcome it*). In the second unit, the anticipation of the passion is stronger still (*his people did not receive him*). The author, then, does present ideas in a linear fashion, but repeats important themes and concepts in varying ways throughout the poem.

THE EARLY MINISTRY OF JESUS · 1:19–4:54

Testimonies of John the Baptist · 1:19–34

After the prologue, the fourth gospel, like all the others, begins its narrative proper with John the Baptist. But the reader does not first hear of John's preaching in the wilderness, nor of his baptizing. Indeed, the reader must read a bit further to find that this John is indeed the baptizer (1:25, 28, 31). Instead, the Baptist is introduced first by his words of *testimony*, a testimony that declares that he is not the Christ, nor Elijah, nor *the prophet*. John's witness is complex and points to some important threads that continue in the narrative to follow.

> **John the Baptist**
> *Josephus* (Antiquities 18.5.2) *describes John as a "good man" who encouraged his hearers to "practice justice toward their fellows and piety toward God." The gospels also know him as a prophet who called Jews to repent before the coming of God's kingdom. Acts 19:1–7 implies that followers of John survived his death by decades and apparently had close contact with the early Christians.*

First, John identifies himself to the Jewish leadership at the outset in terms of what he is not. This emphatic negation serves primarily to anticipate who Jesus is.

Second, John's witness shows that there was a broad expectation for a coming prophet and/or Christ.

Third, upon seeing Jesus, John immediately confesses a feature about Jesus' identity that could only come by revelation: *Look the Lamb of God who takes away the sin of the world*. This comment may be suggestive of Isaiah 53, which likens the Suffering Servant of Israel to a lamb led to slaughter. This servant is said to be *an offering for sin* (Isa 53:10).

Fourth, the fourth gospel does not explicitly relate Jesus' baptism. Instead, it leaves it up to the reader to infer that John has baptized Jesus. But John does relate the coming of the Holy Spirit, descending as a dove on Jesus. John goes on to say that this person on whom the Spirit descends will himself baptize with the Holy Spirit. The baptism received from Jesus, then, would be better than that received from John the Baptist.

Fifth and finally, John makes a solemn testimony that Jesus is the Son of God. This echoes the statement in the prologue that Jesus was the only son of the Father (1:14, 18). The language identifies Jesus as more than a prophet or messiah. He is the only Son of God.

There are hints here and elsewhere that the author of the fourth gospel knew of a misapprehension of John the Baptist's role. The fourth evangelist goes to

---

> **The Background of John's "Word" Metaphor**
>
> *It is apparent that the fourth evangelist makes adept use of images that draw on preexisting ideas in his prologue. The opening verses draw on Genesis and in so doing invite the reader to remember that creation account and make comparisons between the two. John's term* the Word *also draws on previous literature or concepts with which the reader should compare it in order to draw out its full meaning.*
>
> *A likely conceptual background of John's use of the Word is the wisdom tradition of Israel. This tradition is especially found in the book of Proverbs in the Old Testament and in the books of Ecclesiasticus and Wisdom of Solomon in the Apocrypha. The Jewish wisdom literature often portrays God's wisdom as having an independent, even personal quality that is involved in the very creation and sustenance of the world:*
>
> The Lord created me [wisdom] at the beginning of his work, the first of his acts of long ago. Ages ago I was set up, at the first, before the beginning of the earth *(Prov 8:22–23; compare also Prov 8:27–30; Ecclesiasticus 24:9; and Wisdom of Solomon 9:9). This same wisdom was seen as a life-giving quality for those who draw on it, and a source of light and revelation.*
>
> *The author of John, then, appears to be drawing on traditions about wisdom already well known to those familiar with the Scriptures and has used this concept to interpret Jesus from an eternal and cosmological perspective. Thus the evangelist has provided two generative dialogue partners for the reader of the prologue, both found in the Scriptures of Judaism: the creation story in Genesis and the wisdom literature. The reader knowledgeable of these Scriptures will read the prologue with rich and varied interpretations, all pointing to God's creative activity with humanity.*

great lengths to differentiate between John the Baptist and Jesus. John the Baptist is a witness to the light but not the light itself (1:8, 15). In 1:20, John the Baptist explicitly proclaims, *I am not the Christ*. He reiterates this denial in 3:25 and acknowledges that as Jesus' ministry grows, his own importance will decrease.

The First Disciples · 1:35–51

Following John the Baptist's witness to Jesus, the gospel turns to a short series of scenes in which Jesus begins to collect disciples into his entourage. This short narrative serves to link John the Baptist with Jesus' disciples. But more importantly, we see the importance of testimony about who Jesus is. He is immediately understood to be the Messiah by Andrew and to be the Son of God by Nathanael. These, like John the Baptist, then become witnesses to Jesus. And they fulfill the mission for which Jesus came, that people should believe.

The stage is set, then, for the ministry of Jesus. Jesus has come to his own, and some of his own have understood who he is and believed. They testify to his nature. But the reader is also aware that rejection and disbelief are possible.

Wedding at Cana · 2:1–11

With the wedding at Cana, the ministry of Jesus enters a new phase, the phase of signs. Jesus' actions are dramatic and prophetic, and in some way signify his nature and his mission. Signs, like testimony, constitute evidence that can persuade a reader to believe in Jesus as the incarnate Word of God.

John introduces the wedding scene with the chronological marker, *on the third day*. But surely this cannot be referring to the time passed since the encounter with John the Baptist. There have already been more than three days specifically noted in chapter 1. The reference to the *third day* probably refers to the time after Jesus' promise to Nathanael that he would see greater signs. The time marker, then, links the disciples to the wedding story that follows. It is important for the point of the story that the disciples are said to be invited to the wedding with Jesus, for the focus of the story is ultimately on their reaction to the miracle.

The setting for the first *sign* is a wedding, and this story is unique to John. The story proper is fairly straightforward and is clearly miraculous. The wedding feast has run out of wine, and Jesus' mother informs Jesus of this fact. While Mary's comment to Jesus is not phrased as a request to do something, it seems to be implied; Jesus does respond by directing that certain stone jars be filled with water. When the water is subsequently tasted, it has become good wine. Based on this miracle, the disciples believe in Jesus.

While Jesus' mother is introduced as a central character, what follows is not a glowing or sentimental presentation. John's gospel never identifies Jesus' mother as "Mary," but as *woman*. She appears early in the gospel and again at the end when Jesus is on the cross (19:25–26), and in both cases she is presented in close connection with the disciples. This story set in Cana concludes with Jesus and his mother and brothers and disciples departing together to Capernaum. Only the disciples are positively portrayed as believing, while Mary's feelings about Jesus remain unclear.

This ambiguous presentation of Mary is especially seen in the exchange between her and Jesus. Jesus responds to her, *what concern is that to you and me?* (3:4). This phrase is difficult to translate; it literally says "what to me and to you?" It could mean "what have I done to you that you should bring this to me?" in which case it would indicate a strong sense of discord between Jesus and his mother. However, the context does not seem to point to this meaning. Instead, it is more likely meant to portray a mild form of distance: "why are you bothering me with this?" Or it may be a general remark on Jesus' relationship with his mother, as the RSV reads: *O woman, what have you to do with me*?

Another provocative feature in the exchange is Jesus' response to his mother: *it is not yet my hour* (3:4). The term "my hour" or "the hour" is usually used in the fourth gospel to refer to the passion: that time when Jesus' glory would be most evident (7:30; 8:30; 12:23, 27; 13:1; 17:1). Used in the context of the Cana wedding, however, the term "the hour" is a bit confusing. Is he saying, "don't bother me now, since my time of glorification is not yet come?" If the time of glory is when Jesus will show his power, then

---

Stone Water Pots

The water pots at Cana were of stone because stone could not transmit ritual impurity. Jesus' hosts may not have been overly religious, because traditionally, water for ceremonial washing was kept in a stone pool, a mikveh *(Keener 510).*

why does he proceed here and elsewhere to perform miracles (and thus show his glory)?

The focus of the passage, however, is primarily on Jesus' willingness to perform a "sign." This term for the miracle at Cana is not accidental but reveals the way John thinks of these powerful actions. Jesus' miracle at Cana points to his identity. The author emphasizes that with this sign Jesus *manifested his glory* (2:11), which is a key theme in the fourth gospel. By showing his glory, Jesus is actually displaying that he is the Son of God. The word *glory* (or *splendor*) is used extensively in John, and it implies the intensity of God's own presence. Thus, at Sinai God's presence among Israel is called *the glory of the Lord*, a glory that leaves an image on Moses' face even after departing from God's presence (Exod 24:15–17; 34:29–35). Glory indicates the presence of the divine. Jesus shows his glory in those cases where he demonstrates his divinity, and he is ultimately "glorified" (clothed in splendor, made to be seen as divine) when he is raised from the dead.

> **Signs & Jesus' Identity**
>
> *Signs in John's gospel point beyond themselves to something that gives them meaning. They serve as evidence of Jesus' very identity, and certain individuals may, based on their evidence, come to believe in Jesus. Throughout the fourth gospel, signs point to Jesus' divinity and identity, but are apprehended as such only by those who choose to be convinced.*

The Temple Incident · 2:13–25

The fourth gospel again shows its unique approach with the placement of the temple incident early in the ministry of Jesus. In all the other gospels, this disruptive action in the temple occurs in the last week of Jesus' life. Like the other gospels, the setting here is the Passover week. But John's gospel seems to refer to many times that Jesus goes to Jerusalem for Passover, and thus portrays at least a three-year ministry, rather than what appears to be a one-year ministry in the other gospels. Most importantly, in John's gospel the temple altercation marks the beginning of conflict with the Jewish leadership and thus introduces a thematic struggle early in the gospel that will serve to define the course of the narrative.

It is unfortunate that this incident has often been called a temple *cleansing*. There is nothing in the incident itself, or the practices Jesus disrupts, that would suggest that he sees anything "unclean" taking place. The temple practices required that a significant number of sacrificial animals be available for slaughter. So the sale of animals was necessary for the temple sacrificial system to be maintained. The temple tax was also required, and since it had to be paid not in Roman but in Tyrean coinage, the changing of money was necessary. It has been suggested that these animals and coins were sold by the temple priesthood at a high rate of profit, thus implicating them in corrupt practices. But there is nothing in the text that indicates any condemnation of profiteering.

Instead, Jesus' action in the temple is a prophetic act. By tipping over the tables of the money changers and driving out the sellers and their animals, Jesus symbolically both disrupts the activity that supports the temple worship and anticipates the violent destruction of the temple and the city that would occur in 70 CE. Indeed, the fourth evangelist has Jesus himself explicitly link his action to the destruction of the temple. When asked for a sign that would explain his actions in the temple (2:18), Jesus says *Destroy this temple and in three days I will raise it up*. The disciples later, following the resurrection, come to understand this as a reference to Jesus' body that was killed and resurrected. Moreover, in Christian theology Jesus' body, the church, does become the new temple built without hands (compare Mark 14:58) following his death and resurrection.

It is crucial for the development of John's story that "the Jews" are introduced here and are indeed seen in conflict with Jesus. Jesus begins to attract opponents, who become more strident and emphatic in their opposition to Jesus – which is an essential part of John's story of Jesus: *He came to his own, and his own did not receive him* (1:10).

The Dialogue with Nicodemus · 3:1–21

Nicodemus appears three times in John: here, again when the temple police attempt to arrest Jesus (7:45), and finally at the tomb of Jesus (19:39). He is, on the one hand, a leading member of the Jewish council and therefore participates in the council that has Jesus arrested and killed. On the other hand, he appears to be open to Jesus, as the dialogue with Jesus and the dispute with the Pharisees seem to indicate. He remains throughout the gospel a cryptic figure, about whom we are left to ponder and question.

3:1–4 The story of Nicodemus begins with a nighttime visitation. Perhaps this is because he is afraid of the reaction of the other "Jews." But perhaps the night is meant to signify the spiritual darkness that envelops Jewish leadership: the prologue has used light and darkness as spiritual motifs, and that must influence our reading of this passage. Jesus' own statements to Nicodemus draw on this dark/light motif: *And this is the judgment, that the light has come into the world, and people loved the darkness rather than light because their deeds were evil* (3:19).

3:5–21 Nicodemus' opening question implies an openness toward Jesus. But the resulting dialogue presents a miscommunication and failed understanding. The basis for the miscommunication lies in the double meaning of the phrase used for *born again*. The Greek adverb *anothen*, which modifies the verb "to be born," has two possible meanings. It can mean "again," as Nicodemus interprets it, or it can mean "from above." The latter meaning is what Jesus suggests, and this serves as the basis for his subsequent discussion about being a man from heaven who tells of heavenly things (3:12–13). He is "from above" and he brings the Spirit which allows others to be born "from above."

3:5–21 In the course of responding to Nicodemus' misunderstanding, Jesus introduces in his own words some of the key theological concepts of the book.

> **The Serpent in the Wilderness**
> *The story of the bronze serpent of Numbers 21 both intrigued and bothered many ancient Jewish (and later, Christian) interpreters. As* Wisdom of Solomon *16:5–8 puts it, the serpent was a "sign of salvation to remind them of the requirements of your law." Jesus simply takes contemporary interpretation one step further, by applying the sign to God's ultimate salvation, himself (see the discussion in Kugel 479–82).*

Jesus says that he has come to bring eternal life to all those who believe in him. This theme is a refrain repeated frequently in John. And Jesus' speech emphasizes the crucial importance of belief: those who believe have eternal life and escape judgment; those who do not believe do not receive eternal life and are condemned already by their actions. The essential and unique nature of Jesus is now made clear; only through belief in this *only Son* is eternal life bestowed to humanity.

Jesus' Baptizing Ministry · 3:22–4:3

According to the fourth gospel (thought not the Synoptics), Jesus practiced a ministry of baptism in Judea at the same time as John. There is good reason to believe that John is reflecting a historical feature from the early period of Jesus' ministry. That Jesus both drew some of his disciples from John's, and then followed with some similar ministry is very likely. The fourth gospel uses the report of parallel baptizing ministry to emphasize John the Baptist's role as a witness and to underline Jesus' unique role. Here and later, the gospel describes John the Baptist as a true witness, even though Jesus' own signs and testimony are greater and more valuable.

The Woman of Samaria · 4:4–42

4:4–9 Upon departing from Judea, Jesus has a dialogue with a Samaritan woman, a story which is unique to John's gospel. The narrative begins with Jesus meeting a Samaritan woman at Jacob's well. When Jesus asks her to draw some water from the well, she expresses surprise that he would ask for water from a Samaritan. Much to the woman's surprise (and the reader's also), Jesus turns the whole request around and suggests that if she only recognized who he was, she would be asking him for living water.

4:10–15 Jesus' initial response makes use of a double meaning of the term *living water*. It is the usual term for running water, water that flows from streams or springs, and is valued more than water from cisterns or wells because it is fresher and less full of sediments. Jesus' response to the woman suggests that he knows of a spring with living water, which would be superior to the water from Jacob's well. The Samaritan woman's *give me this water* is the expected response, but it shows a failure to appreciate the real issue at stake. While

> **Jews & Samaritans**
> *"Jews" and "Samaritans" were originally labels for groups of Israelites living in adjoining districts in the Persian Empire. But by the time of Jesus – and even today – these labels apply to distinct ethnic and religious groups. Both groups worship one God, respect Moses as the lawgiver, attempt to follow the five books of Moses, and live similar ethical lives. The Samaritans expect the coming of a messiah called the Taheb. Until just before 100 BCE, Samaritans worshiped in a temple on Mount Gerizim (the* this mountain *of John 4:21). John Hyrcanus, king in Jerusalem, destroyed the Gerizim temple. However, today the 1,000 or so surviving Samaritans still pray on the mountain and offer sacrifices there at Passover (see Anderson and Giles,* The Keepers*).*

the Samaritan woman understands the term in this normal sense, Jesus seems not to be referring metaphorically to water at all, but rather to some life-giving quality that flows from belief in Jesus himself. Again, a dialogue with Jesus turns on the misunderstanding of a term which has acquired a metaphorical meaning.

4:16–26 Jesus then shifts the focus to the woman's situation. He demonstrates a miraculous knowledge, or at least a prophetic ability, when he states that she has had five husbands and that the man she lives with now is not her husband. Upon hearing this, the Samaritan woman, though acknowledging the prophetic nature of Jesus' speech, proceeds to test him within the context of the Jewish-Samaritan distinction. The deep antipathy between Judaism and the Samaritans prevents the woman from accepting Jesus simply on the basis of the "sign" given by his special knowledge of her situation. Instead, the woman asks a provocative question about the worship practices of the Samaritans. While Jesus does assert that the Samaritan worship practices are in error, he contextualizes this statement first by saying that both Jewish and Samaritan worship practices are transitory and will be superceded by worship *in spirit and in truth*. This understanding of an endtime worship levels the ground between Samaritan and Jew, and opens the door for the complete reconciliation of the two groups. Jesus embraces the Samaritans as equally worthy of God's attention and able to approach God in worship.

Jesus concludes the exchange, then, with a bold revelation of his own nature. *I am he, the one who is speaking to you.* He could simply say "I am the one speaking to you," but in this statement, Jesus first uses a term "I am" [Greek *ego eimi*] which occurs throughout the gospel, almost always with some emphatic christological context: *I am the light of the world*; *I am the bread which comes down from heaven*; *before Abraham was, I am*. It appears to be a form of self-revelation, although it is still cloaked in ambiguity and allows for possible misinterpretation. Keener (621) connects "I am" to the Septuagint's rendition of Isaiah 52:6.

4:27–42 But the woman correctly interprets Jesus' assertion about his own nature. She immediately returns to her village to tell of her encounter and to suggest that possibly this man is the Messiah. She phrases the question to leave open the possibility that such a conclusion is wrong; the NRSV has accurately captured the hesitancy in the question, *He cannot be the Messiah, can he*? The woman is only tentatively a believer in Jesus. But because of her statement, the Samaritans invite Jesus to stay with them, and many come to believe independently of her witness. The exchange between Jesus and the Samaritan woman bears fruit in many Samaritans' belief in Jesus' identity as the Savior of the world (compare Acts 8).

Healing of the Official's Son · 4:43–54

The account of the healing is fairly straightforward. A royal official's son is dying in Capernaum. The royal official begs Jesus for healing. After a response by Jesus that could be taken as a rebuff or as an encouragement, the official asks again, and Jesus declares that the son will live. The official returns home to find the son well and subsequently responds in faith.

A central question in understanding John's account is whether Jesus' statement in verse 48 offers a negative or positive assessment of signs. Scholars often

---

Christ & the Samaritan Woman

The Samaritan woman, drawing on Jesus' statement that the hour is coming, interprets his words messianically. Her response acknowledges that the Samaritans also expect a messiah who will prophetically reveal the will of God. In this statement, the woman is echoing the expectation of the Samaritans for the Taheb, whom Moses predicted in Deuteronomy 18:18: I will raise up for them a prophet like you from among their own people; I will put my words in the mouth of the prophet, who shall speak to them everything that I command. *But she sees this only as a future possibility. She has missed Jesus' strong statement of present fulfillment in verse 23.*

Signs & Wonders in John's Gospel

The fourth gospel's story of the healing of an official's son is similar to ones found in Luke and Matthew, and it provides another "sign" of Jesus' nature and gives rise to a positive response of faith. Furthermore, it structurally relates this healing to the wedding at Cana, Jesus' first sign, thus providing a sense of unity to Jesus' actions. Two significant markers point to the healing story's close relationship to the Cana miracle. First, the healing story begins with a reference to the miracle at Cana. Second, the incident closes with a comment that this was the second *sign that Jesus did after coming to Galilee.*

view Jesus' phrase *unless you people see miraculous signs and wonders you will not believe* as a negative statement, because faith engendered in this fashion is somehow secondary to faith that springs unaided by signs. But such a view, in my opinion, reads too much into the text at this point. Jesus simply states that signs and wonders can, in fact, be useful for bringing about faith.

The early ministry of Jesus thus opens and ends with positive notes on the linkage between signs and faith. The disciples believed based on his sign at Cana, the Samaritans believed based on his prophetic words, and here a royal official believes based on a healing. Signs are part of the way that Jesus reveals his glory. Granted, the signs might be misinterpreted or ignored, as the controversies in the next section of the gospel clearly show. Jesus finds it necessary to interpret himself to his audience. But signs and testimony are both validated by the fourth evangelist as ways to perceive Jesus for who he is – the creative Word of God.

THE CONTROVERSIES OVER JESUS' MISSION · 5:1–11:47

Following a more or less positive view of the reception of Jesus, in which signs engender belief, the fourth gospel moves to growing controversies about Jesus' words and actions. The first harbinger of these controversies appeared at the temple incident (2:13–25). In the next major unit of the gospel, the focus will be on increasing objection to, and discussion of, Jesus' ministry.

Healing on the Sabbath · 5:1–18

In what is beginning to take shape as a pattern for John's gospel, Jesus again journeys from Galilee to Jerusalem, this time on the occasion of an unnamed *festival of the Jews*. Thus a Jewish holiday is again the occasion for a trip to Jerusalem. It is possible, though not certain, that this unnamed festival is that of Pentecost or Weeks, celebrated in the late spring.

Once again, the fourth evangelist relates a miraculous sign. This time it is the healing of a paralytic who seeks a cure at the Sheep Pool (located just north of the Temple Mount). Jesus, upon inquiring whether the man wants to be healed, commands him to pick up his mat and walk. Jesus' words on this occasion are almost identical to the healing of the paralytic in the Synoptic tradition (Mark 2:11; compare Matt 9:7; Luke 5:24), although the setting and circumstances are completely different.

The focus of the story rests not on the healing itself, but on the controversy that follows. "The Jews" accuse Jesus of doing work on the Sabbath. In response, Jesus offers his defense: *My Father is still working, and I also am still working* (5:17). This response only serves to solidify "the Jews" in their opposition to Jesus, such that they seek to kill him. The basis for their opposition is summarized by John in a threefold argument: Jesus was breaking the Sabbath; Jesus was calling God his own Father; and thus, Jesus was making himself equal to God.

It is easy, of course, to dismiss the Jewish opposition to Jesus as blind and narrow. But protection of the Sabbath is a duty under the law, given by God, and is crucial for protecting the holiness of God among the people. Sabbath breaking would be a serious offense, but more serious would be any attempt by a Jew to deny its requirement. By claiming to be able to work on the Sabbath because God is also working, Jesus in fact claims a special exemption by virtue of his relationship with God. "The Jews," then, are quite correct in deducing that Jesus claims equality with God, or at least a special filial relationship.

The fourth evangelist portrays "the Jews" as making true statements about Jesus, and ironically the truth places them in complete opposition to him. The problem is not that they are wrong, but that they oppose Jesus because they do not, or will not, recognize Jesus' true identity. This reaction by "the Jews" anticipates the course of the developing narrative: Jewish opposition to Jesus develops not from a lack of knowledge, but from a lack of light and a lack of desire to accept the Son of God. Interestingly, mainstream Jewish legal interpretation would agree with Jesus in permitting preservation and enhancement of life on the Sabbath.

The Authority of the Witnesses to Jesus · 5:19–47

In response to the opposition of "the Jews," Jesus defends himself in a monologue. There is no response to Jesus' monologue, but no one in the story appears to have been convinced, because the opposition to Jesus only grows. But at the same time, the absence of a response to Jesus' monologue suggests a satisfactory rebuttal to the charges. The opposition is left speechless, in fact, if not in thought.

Jesus' response to the opposition rests on a bold claim that develops (and accepts) one of the charges placed against him by the Jews: that he contends God is his Father. If Jesus is, indeed, God's Son, then three conclusions must follow: the Son is sent from the Father, and thus his work is directly related to the Father's and receives its authority and power from him; the Son has received the authority to execute judgment; and finally, given the ample testimony to Jesus' identity, the failure to acknowledge him is not a failure of information, but a spiritual failure.

The first of these propositions serves, in part, to defend Jesus against the misapprehension that he is working in some way independently of God. Jesus, however, affirms that he is subordinate to the Father and he functions as God's designated agent. The second proposition is perhaps bolder still: the Son has received the power of judgment. Judgment is the prerogative of God, an idea that Jesus affirms by saying that God has given the activity of judging to the Son (5:22). And yet Jesus' judgment is never disconnected from God, but only expresses the divine will (5:30). The third proposition exonerates Jesus of charges of blasphemy, citing the testimony of John the Baptist, who was widely acknowledged as upright and prophetic, and the testimony of Jesus' own works. Signs were often used as evidence in antiquity, and in this case Jesus says that the signs are God's own testimony on behalf of Jesus (5:37). Finally, Jesus calls on the testimony of ancient witnesses, the Scriptures. In so doing, Jesus actually calls Moses as a witness against the prosecution. Their attempt to invoke Moses against Jesus is thus actually an indication of their failure accurately to discern God's will and is thus a sign of their spiritual darkness.

Feeding of the 5,000 & Walking on the Water · 6:1–24

6:1–15 John's report of the miraculous feeding of 5,000 is remarkably similar to that found in all the other gospels. Indeed, this miracle is the only one that appears in all the gospels. The essential elements are all here: Jesus goes with his disciples to a remote location, and a large crowd numbering 5,000 follows them. With concern over their lack of food, Jesus takes five loaves of bread and two fish and, after blessing them, distributes them to the crowd. The food is sufficient to satisfy the people, and the disciples are able to collect twelve baskets of fragments left over from the food.

John places this miracle close to the second Passover mentioned in the gospel. The specific notation of the Passover time reminds us again that John is very aware of the Jewish festival seasons. Moreover, since the Passover is also related to the exodus from Egypt, during which time they subsisted on manna, the subsequent comparison of bread and manna is also particularly appropriate to this festival season.

But for John, the miracle of the feeding of the 5,000 is not just a miracle: it is a sign. Here the crowd understands that something deeper has taken place and interprets this as a sign that Jesus is *the prophet who is coming*. As a result, they want to make him king. In this, they are drawing on messianic ideas, primarily the notion that one would come like David who would be king of Israel. Jesus' contemporaries had a variety of conceptions that were jumbled together. That these categories were not neatly divided has already been clear in the priests' questions to John the Baptist (1:19–21). There, too, the priests ask John if he is the Messiah, Elijah, or the Prophet.

> **Prophet & Messiah**
> *The crowd evidently thinks of the promise of Deuteronomy 18:15–18, which predicted the coming of a future prophet who would be like Moses himself. Or perhaps the reference is to Elijah; the language* the one who is coming into the world *is suggestive of Elijah (compare Mal 4:5).*

6:16–24 Just as John's feeding miracle is very similar to the account in the other gospels, so also is the fourth gospel's report of Jesus walking on the water, found also in Mark 6:45–46 and Matthew 14:22–36. The similarities are striking: there is a boat trip, strong winds, Jesus walks on the water, and his self-identification brings a close to the incident. What is striking in John's account is the lack of concluding reaction on the part of the disciples. The walking on the water, then, is not recognized as a sign, and little is made of it. It is the feeding which serves as the primary sign of who Jesus is. Apparently, the oral tradition behind both John and the Synoptics placed these stories alongside each other.

Bread from Heaven · 6:25–71

6:25–29 With the disciples' departure, and Jesus' subsequent walking on the water, the scene shifts to the western side of the lake, near Capernaum. The crowd has followed Jesus to that location, but he questions their motives for following. His criticism is potentially very illuminating for an understanding of the signs in the fourth gospel. Jesus makes a distinction between the miraculous aspect of a sign (sufficient food to eat), and the spiritual aspect of a sign (the feeding pointing to the real nature of Jesus). It is the latter issue that interests him.

When they hear Jesus' exhortation to work for food that leads to eternal life, the crowd misunderstands the point and asks instead how they might perform the works of God. In response to their failure properly to understand the nature of "doing work," Jesus simply states that the one work necessary is to *believe* in him who is sent by God, that is, Jesus. Belief once again comes to the forefront of John's understanding of the proper response to Jesus. But rather than believe, the crowd asks for another sign.

6:30-31 The sign the crowd has in mind is manna, because their view of Jesus as prophet is based on an expectation of a *prophet like Moses*. In other words, they confirm their "earthly" motives: they want more food, even that which perishes (as the manna did each day). In requesting this sign, or something like it, the crowd shows it misunderstands Jesus' exhortation for them to do works resulting in imperishable food. The phrase *bread from heaven* quotes the recital of the exodus story in Psalm 78:24 and 105:40. As the following discourse explains, Jesus' ministry both continues the story of salvation begun in Exodus and brings it to a new height.

> **Moses & Manna**
> *In Exodus 16, Moses provided the people with daily food as a sign that God was with them.*

6:32-59 This misunderstanding of the nature of Jesus' feeding miracle and his mission is the basis for the discourse to follow. Jesus clarifies exactly what this bread from heaven is: *I am the bread of life* (6:35). Jesus himself has come from heaven to give life to those who believe. In this he satisfies spiritual hunger and spiritual thirst. The theme that began in 6:29 – that the work that results in eternal food is belief in the sent one – is now made clear. Those who believe in Jesus as the bread of life will have eternal life, and Jesus will raise them up on the last day (6:40). The theme of Jesus as lifegiving food actually is developed in the discourse with two distinct, though linked, metaphors: first as *bread*, and secondly as *flesh and blood*. The first metaphor draws on the image of manna to equate Jesus with the *bread from heaven*. That metaphor is dominant in 6:35-51. But the metaphor shifts in 6:53-58 to language that appears to anticipate the Lord's Supper. At the close of the first section of his discourse (6:51), Jesus finally does connect the bread of heaven with his *flesh*, but the focus of the first section is a metaphorical *bread*. In the latter section, Jesus shifts the metaphor more explicitly to his *flesh and blood*, which is clearly eucharistic in nature. Not only is the metaphor more explicit, but the command is more urgent and essential: *unless you eat the flesh of the Son of Man and drink his blood, you have no life in you* (6:53). It is, of course, intriguing that the fourth gospel does not contain any eucharistic language in its depiction of the Last Supper (13:1-30). Such language is not absent from the book, and the response to the feeding miracle is fundamentally sacramental in nature.

It is not surprising that Jesus' audiences react to this very strong metaphorical language. Jesus has claimed to be one who has descended from heaven, who must be the object of the people's belief, and who must be feasted upon in order for the people to receive life. As one might expect, "the Jews" react immediately. They see Jesus as the son of Joseph; if so, he cannot be the one who came from heaven. When Jesus expands the metaphor to refer to his own flesh, "the Jews" react again. It is only surprising that there is no mention at this point of an attempt to kill him, as has occurred already in 5:18.

6:60-71 In response to these hard words, some of Jesus' own disciples draw back from following him. First they question the saying (6:60), then they withdraw (6:66). The reason for their turning back is stated clearly: they do not believe (6:64). As a counterpoint to the withdrawal by some, the Twelve assert their belief in him. In response to a question posed by Jesus, Peter speaks for all of them by making an explicit confession of faith – the fourth gospel's equivalent to the "good confession": *You have words of eternal life; and we have believed, and have come to know that you are the Holy One of God* (6:68-69).

Tabernacles Controversies · 7:1-52, 8:12-30

The Feast of Tabernacles is the context of the next large section of John's gospel (chapters 7-8; compare

Lev 23:33–43; Num 29:12–39). Jesus has traveled again to Jerusalem for a crucial Jewish feast, and we find again that his presence in Jerusalem and near the temple provides the setting for discourse that helps further define Jesus' role. The controversies that take place at tabernacles are notable because Jesus' proclamations are, in many ways, based on imagery drawn from the tabernacles practices, there is a clear distinction drawn between "the Jews" and the rest of the Jewish participants of the feast, and the controversies serve to force a reaction, a crisis of a decision on the hearers.

> **The Feast of Tabernacles**
> *This major Jewish festival occurs on the fourteenth through the twenty-first days of the seventh month, Tishri, and commemorates Israel's 40 years in the desert. Jews build an outdoor temporary shelter (tabernacle, or in Hebrew, sukkah) and have a week-long celebration.*

7:37–52 On the last day of the feast, Jesus taught publicly, this time saying that the believer would receive living water that would quench thirst. In many ways this is reminiscent of Jesus' teaching to the Samarian woman (4:10–15), although here the narrator interprets it as the gift of the Holy Spirit that would be given following Jesus' death and resurrection (his *glorification*, to use John's term). The introduction of the theme of *living water* at this point is better understood as a reaction to or interpretation of some of the activities at the Feast of Tabernacles. Each day of the feast, water was drawn from the pool of Siloam and carried in golden flasks to the altar, where it was poured out. Jesus employs this imagery of the drawn water to compare the gift of the Spirit, which would not be drawn or still water, but rather flowing water. It is quite likely that Jesus is also evoking the prophecy of Zechariah 14:8, which refers to the coming of the messianic end times with its description of living waters flowing out from the altar itself and watering all of the region of Israel.

As usual in the fourth gospel, Jesus' pronouncement prompts a response. Some of those listening think him to be the prophet, some think him to be the Christ, and others refuse to believe him to be anything special because he came from Galilee. Some of those disbelieving in Jesus want to arrest him. But no arrest or action against Jesus occurs. The officers sent to arrest Jesus (in 7:32 following a previous exchange) return to the leaders without him, because they are amazed at his teaching.

8:12–30 Jesus continues his self-disclosure by claiming to be the light of the world. From the prologue, the reader already knows that Jesus is the true light that comes into a darkened world. But at the close of the tabernacles celebrations, Jesus explicitly uses this metaphor with reference to himself. As with the living waters metaphor, the light metaphor also is based upon and interprets certain tabernacles festival activities. Each night during tabernacles large oil lights were set up, using the priest's linen garments for the wicks. According to the Mishnah, these lights were so bright that "there was not a courtyard in Jerusalem that did not reflect the light of the *Beth ha-She'ubah*" (*m Sukkah* 5:3). The most likely context for Jesus' self-revelation as the light of the world is this evening

> **The Mishnah**
> *About 225 CE, the rabbi Judah the Prince compiled a huge number of Jewish laws and traditions into an orderly work called the Mishnah. Many parts of the collection actually date to the first century. The Mishnah later became the basis of the Jerusalem Talmud and the Babylonian Talmud.*

> **The Adulterous Woman**
> *There are notorious textual problems with the account of Jesus and the adulterous woman in John 7:53–8:11. The earliest and best textual manuscripts of the New Testament do not contain the section. It is clear that the tradition was not fixed in the Gospel of John at its early stage; indeed, it might well have been an independent tradition initially added at various points in the already written gospels. But while the story is clearly not part of the "original" fourth gospel, it has nonetheless become an important part of the gospel tradition.*
>
> *The woman in the story is caught in the act of adultery and thus is liable to the punishment of stoning. The reader is immediately struck by the injustice of the whole arrangement, for it is apparent that if the woman was caught in the act of adultery, then so must also the man – but only the woman is charged. Moreover, the scribes and Pharisees are using this person to entrap Jesus, hence Jesus' challenge to the innocent to begin the trial. The story is reminiscent of the tale of Susanna in the* Additions to Daniel *in the Apocrypha.*

of the tabernacles feast when the lights are lit brightly and provide a spectacle for celebrants.

As with the previous discourses in the tabernacles feast, such a bold saying elicits a disagreement and a varying response. The Pharisees criticize Jesus for using the term *light* to refer to himself. In response, Jesus validates his witness by claiming that he alone knows from where he comes and where he is going, and that the true testimony is from God the Father, who bears witness to him. The reference to *where [he is] going* produces a misunderstanding in some (8:27), yet many believe in him (8:30).

Jesus & Abraham · 8:31–59

The initial series of exchanges and discourses at tabernacles results in many of the Jews believing in Jesus. But to what degree do they really believe? Was this a passing agreement with Jesus' words, or was it truly a full understanding that Jesus is the one sent from God? It would appear that in the further dialogues at the close of chapter 8, Jesus is asking just this question. Jesus, in addressing those who have come to believe in him, makes the claim that discipleship is based on continuing in Jesus' teaching. And this act of abiding in Jesus will result in knowledge of truth and thus freedom from the captivity of sin; *the truth will set you free* (8:32). This theme of "abiding" in Jesus' words and thoughts is an important theme in John (compare John 15:4–16) and reappears in the epistle 1 John as well.

But his reference to freedom causes a misunderstanding and hostility on the part of many in his audience. They invoke the memory and promise of Abraham to claim that they have always been free – a statement that blithely overlooks the Jewish history in Egypt, Babylon, and even the present occupation of Palestine by the Romans. By denying their enslavement to oppressive forces, whether political or spiritual, the audience is really disavowing its need to find freedom in Jesus, thus negating any affirmation of faith they may have made.

The conflict over freedom involves something more than simply a failure by the audience to perceive their past enslavement. For Jesus, enslavement is a fundamental spiritual quality, a turning away from God and an obedience to the created order rather than to the heavenly order. It is, in a word, sin, and sin itself is slavery. *Everyone who sins is a slave to sin* (8:34). Thus the hearers' claim to be free is itself a denial of the power of sin and evil. But in denying its power, people not only fail to acknowledge God but actually serve the darkness, the forces that oppose God (8:44).

The audience's insistence on their freedom, and the invocation of Abraham, leads Jesus to question their motives toward him. Certainly he now addresses not only these "believing" Jews but the entire Jewish leadership by criticizing their attempts to kill him. And in their protest against abiding in Jesus' word, the audience who had claimed to believe has actually aligned itself with Jesus' opponents, not his disciples. The "believing" Jews are really just a part of the broader opposition to Jesus – "the Jews." In their attempt on his life, they actually demonstrate that they are spiritually children of the devil rather than of Abraham (8:44; compare 8:41).

In a final appeal to them to remain in his teaching, Jesus openly says that by keeping his word, the believer will escape death. And Jesus goes on to insist that Abraham rejoiced to see the day when Jesus appeared. In other words, Abraham is alive, and he thus experiences the present situation. Jesus then adds one final comment which only makes sense if he was the preexistent Word of God: *Before Abraham was born, I am*. In doing so, Jesus makes a statement about his preexistence and perhaps even his divinity. By saying *I am* about a time long before his birth, he appears to be claiming the title Yahweh – for the Hebrew name for God is based on the verb "to be," perhaps meaning "he who is" (compare Exodus 2:13–15).

The Man Born Blind · 9:1–41

In the aftermath of the tabernacles controversies, and following his argument of who can best claim a relationship with Abraham, Jesus performs another Sabbath healing that produces a controversy between him and "the Jews." The story of the healing of the blind man contains a number of themes central to John's portrayal of Jesus, which also point to the growing hostility between Jesus and the Jewish leadership.

9:1–12 Jesus heals a man born blind as he is walking through Jerusalem. He instructs the man to wash his eyes in the pool of Siloam (on the south side of Jerusalem). It is interesting that Siloam is the pool from which the water libations were taken during tabernacles. And Jesus makes use of the light metaphor in this healing (*I am the light of the world*), which is reminiscent of his declaration in the tabernacles feast (compare 7:12). It is likely, then, that healing of the blind man is closely tied with traditions about Jesus' interaction during the tabernacles feast.

While all the gospels report healing of blind men, John's report is unique in that the man is born blind. This in itself is deemed a remarkable sign of power. Yet, the initial reaction to the miracle is low key, because the focus of the story is elsewhere; the controversy that ensues receives the main emphasis.

The theological discussion which initiates the healing centers on the relationship of sin to physical disability and suffering. The question, *who sinned, this man or his parents?* presumes that physical disability is the result of sin. This connection, of course, has old antecedents in the Old Testament wisdom tradition, where prosperity and health are indications of righteousness, and illness and poverty are indications of sin. The perceived relationship between sin and suffering can be seen in Job's three friends' accusations that his own difficulties must come from some hidden sin (Job 8; 15; 18). Jesus, however, does not accept the premise upon which the question is based. It is not an issue of sin but rather of whether illness can be used as an occasion to do God's works.

9:13–34 But the healing of the blind man is only the first act in this complex story. Initially, the neighbors of the blind man are perplexed when they see him sighted. All the blind man knows is that Jesus healed him when he did what Jesus said.

When the neighbors bring the blind man to the Pharisees, they ask the same basic question, and he again tells the story. But two crucial complexities are added in the second telling that determine the direction of the narrative. First, John tells us for the first time that the healing occurred on the Sabbath. Secondly, the blind man tells in more detail how he was healed: Jesus put mud in his eyes, then when he washed it he could see. The making of mud was a violation of the Sabbath – understood as a specific violation of the prohibition of work. The Pharisees, therefore, seize on this violation as an indication that Jesus could not be from God.

The opponents of Jesus, "the Jews," seek to resolve the issue by denying that the man was really blind from birth. While the parents confirm that he was born blind, they refuse to answer any other questions about the healing because "the Jews" threaten to expel Jesus' disciples from the synagogue (9:22). This particular statement has raised interesting historical questions relative to the date and occasion of the writing of the gospel; but from the point of view of the narrative, this statement focuses attention on the persecution of Jesus by "the Jews." They have been trying to arrest or kill him in the preceding narratives (5:18; 7:1; 7:32; 8:59), and now we learn that they have also been persecuting those who confessed Jesus as Messiah.

9:35–41 John continues the story, however, beyond the failed examination by the Pharisees and "the Jews." Once all the attackers have left, the focus returns to Jesus and the blind man with a group of Pharisees gathered around the periphery. Jesus' question is the central question of the gospel, that of faith (9:35). Once Jesus identifies himself as the Son of Man, the man who was once blind responds immediately with a confession, "*Lord, I believe,*" and with worship. The blind man, as a result of faith, is freed of sin. By the same word of judgment, the Pharisees are characterized as being blind and full of sin (9:41). Here the important role of faith is displayed in its full and complete form. On the one hand, the decision which arises out of the miraculous healing finds the blind man openly confessing Jesus and worshiping him. On the other hand, "the Jews" and the Pharisees fail to respond to the situation with faith. They are now seen as spiritually blind and full of sin.

The Good Shepherd Discourse · 10:1–42

The parable of the Good Shepherd, introduced with Jesus' *amen, amen* statement in 10:1, follows immediately on the disagreement with the Pharisees in 9:39–41. Without any indication of a passage of time or a change of location, 10:1–21 (known as the "Shepherd Discourse") continues the disputes that followed upon the blind man's healing. This is confirmed by the conclusion of the Shepherd Discourse: there we find a division among "the Jews," in which the text raises various themes from chapters 8 and 9. John's use of the shepherd metaphor serves both to interpret and further develop the conflict between Jesus and "the Jews," as well as to suggest the close relationship Jesus seeks with those who would believe.

10:1–6 The parable of the Shepherd begins with a description of sheep in a sheepfold. Two main characters are contrasted: thieves and the true shepherd. Thieves who would harm the sheep try to gain entrance by means other than the gate. In contrast, the true shepherd of the sheep enters by the gate. The gatekeeper recognizes him as the proper shepherd and gives him entrance. Furthermore, the sheep recognize him and follow him. It is clear that the contrasting images of shepherd and thief seen in reference to a flock are being used to contrast true leaders with false leaders of the people of Israel.

Jesus' imagery of the shepherd is not original to him; he is drawing upon images from the Old Testament. In numerous places, God is described as a shepherd and the people of Israel as a flock (Ps 23; 80; Isa 40:11; Jer 39:10; and especially Ezek 34:11–16). But the sheep/shepherd imagery also describes false shepherds who lead the flock astray (Jer 10:21; 12:10; 23:1–2; Ezek 34:2–4; Zeph 3:3; and Zech 10:3; 11:15). The Old Testament also uses the shepherd image to describe a future "good" leader who will serve as a good shepherd (Ps 78:70–2; Jer 3:15; 23:4–6; Ezek 34:23–24; 37:24; Mic 5:4; and Zech 13:7–9).

It is likely that these various images drawn from the Old Testament, especially the striking variety of images found in Ezekiel 34, provide the interpretive framework upon which Jesus builds this parable. Jesus draws creatively on this imagery and expects his audience to hear the references to Ezekiel as a backdrop to his own statements.

Given the scriptural antecedents, the central focus throughout is the contrast between good leaders and false leaders, a focus which should have been understandable to the Jewish audience. It would seem that at the very least the references to thieves and strangers is an indictment of the Pharisees and "Jews" who oppose Jesus and an assertion that Jesus is the true shepherd. That they do not understand speaks to spiritual blindness, not the rich metaphor that is invoked.

10:7–10 In a second movement of the parable, Jesus shifts the metaphor even while still using sheep as the central image. This time Jesus surprisingly identifies himself as the *gate* of the sheepfold. By identifying himself as the gate, he proclaims himself to be the sole legitimate means of access to the sheep.

When he turns, then, to consider the *thieves and robbers*, they are contrasted with him in two ways: first, he represents the legitimate leadership, while thieves and bandits are clearly illegitimate and contrary to what is proper, and second, he comes to save and protect, but thieves and bandits come only to kill and destroy. On this latter theme, Jesus returns to one of his previous topics, that he is a life-giver. Jesus gives life, and this result of Jesus' work must be contrasted with the result of false leadership.

10:11–21 In this section, Jesus brings the implications of the previous parable to its logical conclusion, which must have been unsettling to the leaders of the Jewish people. This conclusion emphasizes four elements: Jesus' own future role as one who will give up his life on behalf of humanity; the current leaders' interests, which are primarily focused on personal gain rather than concern for the people; Jesus' claim of intimate knowledge of *his own*, in the same way that he and God share intimate knowledge of one another; and a recognition that others outside of Israel are to be brought into the flock.

The prediction that Jesus would die has only been broached once previously in the fourth gospel (2:22), when the narrator tells us that the disciples remembered his words after he was raised from the dead (it is, then, a comment by the narrator told from the point of view of the end of the story). Now, in this section, Jesus himself introduces the theme of his dying on behalf of his people. This statement serves a similar purpose in John's gospel to Jesus' predictions of his passion in the Synoptic Gospels (for example, Mark 8:31; 9:31; 10:32): to begin to orient the reader to the central role the death and resurrection play in his ministry. But Jesus predicts not only his death but also his resurrection (10:17).

One facet of Jesus' shepherd role is his close identification with the sheep, the people of Israel. This is illustrated through the aspect of "knowing." Jesus *knows* his sheep, and they in turn *know* him. This implies, of course, that those who do not *know* him, that is, do not believe in him, are not his own. Like the word "abide," the word "know" implies a deep sense of belonging and identification with the object. This play on the word "to know" is further heightened by the way Jesus compares his relationship with those who identify with him with his own relationship with God. In just the same way that Jesus "knows" his people and they "know" him, so also God "knows" Jesus and Jesus "knows" God. Once again, the order of "knowing" is important. First God knows Jesus, and Jesus thus knows God. There is a reciprocity, but the reciprocity has an order. The priority is placed on God, and Jesus demonstrates the response; in the same way, Jesus first knows his people, and his people respond to him.

Finally, this concluding segment of the Shepherd Discourse adds an additional note that could have been deeply troubling to a Jewish audience. Jesus says that there are other sheep in other folds that will become part of his flock. This must surely imply the inclusion of non-Jews into the people of God.

10:22–42 The subsequent scene opens with another Jewish festival, the Feast of Dedication, or Hanukkah. While the introductory verse has signaled a change in time, the dialogue in the subsequent narrative still shows strong links to the preceding events. The exchange between "the Jews" and Jesus in the opening paragraph seems to be a continuation of the previous discourse of the Good Shepherd. "The Jews" ask Jesus directly if he is the Christ, and in his response he returns to the imagery of sheep and "belonging" that marked the Good Shepherd discourse.

> **Hanukkah**
>
> *This festival commemorates the defeat of the Hellenistic king Antiochus IV, in 165 BCE. The events of the revolt appear in 1–2 Maccabees.*

Using the metaphor of a flock, Jesus declares that he has already told them that he is the Christ; the fact that they still ask this only makes it clear that they are not part of his flock. And Jesus, echoing 10:15, amplifies the theme of his intimacy with God by stating flatly, *I and the Father are one* (verse 30). As in chapter 5, Jesus is once again charged with blasphemy for asserting his close connection with God.

In defending against the charge of blasphemy, Jesus again does not deny his basic equality with God. Instead he points to the validity of his work, a proof of his identity and his relationship with God. In John 5, Jesus defended himself by pointing to God's witness in the Scriptures; here he defends himself by pointing to God's nature manifested in his good works. These works are, in effect, God's witness to his status as Son of God. The narrative shows a consistency of what is at stake between Jesus and "the Jews": the nature of his relationship with God. And it demonstrates a growing momentum to the opposition, a momentum that will reach its apex in the raising of Lazarus and the reaction of "the Jews" to that sign.

Jesus and Lazarus · 11:1–44

The story of Lazarus's raising is well known. Jesus hears about his illness and, after a short delay, arrives in Bethany after Lazarus has already died. Jesus then raises Lazarus from the dead, even though he has been dead four days. The raising dramatically demonstrates Jesus' power over life and death. It is an extraordinary sign of his connection with God, for in reviving someone who has been dead this long, Jesus manifests a creative power over the world. The ultimate sign, of course, will be Jesus' own resurrection.

That the fourth evangelist wants to emphasize this raising of Lazarus as a dramatic "sign" is made clear by Jesus' deliberate two-day delay before going to heal Lazarus. The delay gives an occasion for a demonstration, or sign, of God's glory in and through the action of Jesus. Jesus says this illness *does not lead to death* (11:4). As the story progresses, of course, we do find that Lazarus actually does die, contrary to this statement of Jesus. But since Lazarus is ultimately raised back to life, Jesus' statement that this sickness *does not lead to death* is still true.

The narrative of Lazarus centers around two ironic word plays that give it much of its explanatory power. The first word play deals with Jesus' use of *sleeping* and *death*. Jesus said that the illness was not leading to death (verse 4), and so when he says that Lazarus is sleeping (verse 11) and he will go to wake him, his disciples naturally assume that he refers to normal sleep. But sleep can also be euphemism for death, and so Jesus must clarify that misunderstanding. The word play serves to make the raising from the dead all the more dramatic.

The second word play deals with the term *rise again*, or "resurrection." The same word is used to denote different meanings in the dialogue which ensues. When Jesus says, *Your brother will rise again* in verse 23, he uses the same verb "to raise" that Martha uses in her response in verse 24. But again there is a difference in emphasis. Jesus is speaking of the imminent resurrection of Lazarus, not the coming eschatological resurrection. The confusion over these two different kinds of resurrection, however, does imply that Lazarus's resurrection foreshadows the coming general resurrection. The confusion also allows Jesus to assert his authority over both kinds of resurrection in verse 25. Life and death are under the control of Jesus, and the believer participates in the victory over death.

The purpose of the raising of Lazarus, as with the previous signs, is to engender belief in Jesus as one working on behalf of God. Jesus asks Martha in a point blank fashion, *Do you believe this?* (verse 27). She responds with a confession of his role as Messiah and Son of God. Similarly, at the raising of Lazarus, many of the Jews who were present also believed in him (verse 45). In each case, the death and resurrection of Lazarus has presented an opportunity for a response to Jesus.

The Final Judgment of "the Jews" · 11:45–57

As indicated above, the raising of Lazarus does produce belief among some of "the Jews." But such a response of faith is not universal, even in the face of such a dramatic sign. As often before, "the Jews" are divided in their response (see 10:19; 2:23; 7:30–31, 43–44). Some who had seen the raising of Lazarus went instead to the Pharisees and chief priests, who assembled a formal council to consider what action might be necessary. Up until now, various groups of "Jews" had expressed opposition, often in potentially violent ways. They tried to stone (8:59; 10:31), kill (5:18; 7:1), and arrest Jesus (7:30, 7:44; 10:39). But all of these actions were unofficial. At the raising of Lazarus, however, the actions take on a more official tone when the Jews assemble a council (the Sanhedrin) to consider formal action.

> **The Sanhedrin**
> *The Sanhedrin was the major religious court in Jerusalem in the first century. Its exact role is known mostly from later sources and thus remains uncertain.*

Again, John's report of the council's action has an ironic undertone to it. The speech of the high priest, Caiaphas, is a masterful combination of insight and blindness. He argues that Jesus should die in order to protect the Jewish nation from retribution by the Romans. But the fourth evangelist presents his argument in the form of an ironically truthful statement: *it is expedient that one man should die for the people, and that the whole nation should not perish* (verse 50). As the fourth evangelist

> **Caiaphas**
> *High priest 18–37 CE, son-in-law of Annas and one of the most successful Jewish leaders the first half of the first century. His house and possibly his burial site have come to light in recent years.*

notes, this statement is true – not politically, but spiritually in that through Jesus all the children of God might find true life in him. Even opposition furthers God's plan in and through Jesus. The conclusion of the trial by the Sanhedrin is the judgment that Jesus should be put to death. This must be seen as a formal action, the official Jewish trial. The fourth evangelist knows of no trial by the Sanhedrin on the night Jesus was arrested – this trial had already taken place before the final passion week. In this early trial, as portrayed by John, Jesus is never examined but convicted in absentia, with no witnesses or charges of criminal behavior. Indeed the single charge raised, that he performs many signs, is completely true.

THE PASSION OF JESUS · 12:1–19:42

With Jesus formally charged, the story of Jesus' life moves to a new stage. His early ministry showed his power, leading to a series of controversies in which Jesus showed who he was. The final movements in this drama are his death and resurrection.

The Final Entry into Jerusalem · 12:1–36

At the close of chapter 11, the fourth gospel signals a chronological shift. The Passover of the Jews has arrived, and the stage is set for a final conflict. We have already seen Jesus' pattern of going to Jerusalem for each of the major feasts, and so the announcement of the Passover sets the stage for another trip to Jerusalem, his final one. The final journey begins at Bethany, just outside Jerusalem.

12:1–8 The arrival at Bethany once again links Jesus to the family of Lazarus, and especially Mary and Martha. The dinner setting establishes a close link between Jesus and this family: Lazarus is at the table, Martha serves, and Mary ministers to Jesus. The dinner in John's gospel is the setting for an anointing of Jesus, as well as the first sign of Judas's betrayal.

The fourth gospel's account of the anointing is significantly different than that in Matthew and Mark. Here Mary anoints not Jesus' head, but rather his feet with ointment, and then wipes it up with her hair. In this description, John is very close to another dinner setting (not about Mary) in Luke 7:36–50, in which a sinful woman wipes Jesus' feet with tears and her hair and then anoints his feet with ointment. The similarity of the anointing of the feet, and the wiping of them with the hair, set these two accounts apart from the other Synoptic accounts.

John's account of the anointing has another interesting variant from the Synoptic accounts. In Mark 14:8, Jesus answers criticism of the woman's act and responds that she has anointed him for burial in advance of his death. John's gospel, in contrast, has Jesus suggesting that Mary should keep the ointment for the day of burial. Perhaps this reflects another part of the gospel tradition, that women did indeed go to the tomb with spices with which to anoint Jesus after his death (compare Mark 16:1; Luke 24:1). In either case, Jesus is indicating the nearness of his upcoming death; the anointing is thus the initial act that introduces the series of passion events.

12:9–19 As in all the gospels, Jesus enters Jerusalem for a final time during a period of great festivity. As he enters Jerusalem on a donkey, the crowds welcome him with cries of *Hosanna* and wave branches. But John's version is more explicit in its image of Jesus being received as a king based on a messianic expectation. The following items seem to support the view that this was a royal reception: in John 12:13, the crowd adds the interpretation "even the King of Israel" at the end of the citation from the Psalm 118:26; Jesus' riding on the donkey is explicitly interpreted in light of Zechariah 9:9, which indicates that this is how the messianic king would enter Jerusalem; and the crowd waves palm branches, used as a sign of Jewish nationalism, as Jesus arrives (compare *1 Maccabees* 13:51).

Those who were present at Lazarus's raising play an important part in Jesus' entry into Jerusalem. The fourth evangelist says that this crowd from Bethany now bears witness to Jesus, thus linking them with another major theme in the gospel, that of testimony and witness. But they are met by another group that comes out because they have *heard* the witness about the *sign* of Lazarus. We have then in this short scene a full assortment of responses: those who testify (the crowds from Bethany), the object of their testimony (Jesus), a group that responds to the testimony (the crowd from Jerusalem), and the Pharisees, who stand apart from these crowds and complain, prophetically, that the *world has gone after him*.

12:20–36 In response to some Greek-speaking Jews' request to see him, Jesus instead announces that the Passion is upon them: *The hour has come for the Son of Man to be glorified*. John frequently uses the word *hour* to speak of the focus event of the gospel, the crucifixion of Jesus. This central moment was anticipated as early as 2:4, when Jesus responded to his mother that his hour had not yet come. At various points in the gospel the future event is obliquely referred to as the *hour*: in 5:25, 27 Jesus speaks of the hour when the dead will hear the voice of the Son of God; in 7:30 and 8:20, it is because his *hour* had not yet come that his captors are unsuccessful in their arrest. And following Jesus' announcement in 12:23, 27 that the *hour* had indeed arrived, he continues to use this term to refer to his coming death (13:1; 17:1). For John, the events of the passion are part of a preconceived plan to which only Jesus and his Father are privy.

The Final Supper · 13:1–20

In all the gospels, Jesus celebrates a final supper with his disciples on Thursday night before his crucifixion. John's depiction of this supper is significantly different in a number ways: the meal is not a Passover feast, there is no "Lord's Supper" language, and John highlights the washing of the disciples' feet.

In John's account, there is no mention of any preparation for the meal. More specifically, though, we learn when Jesus is tried before Pilate the subsequent day that the Jewish accusers will not enter into Pilate's palace so that they might avoid any possible impurity. This is important, John notes, because they had not yet eaten the Passover (18:28).

> **The Passover Meal**
> *In the Synoptic Gospels, the final meal on Thursday evening is the Passover meal. On this day, the Passover lamb was sacrificed in the temple and then cooked and eaten before sunup the next day. The Passover meal required some substantial preparation, as seen in the Synoptic Gospels' attention to the procuring of a room in which to meet. At the meal, by means of telling the story of the exodus, reciting prayers and blessings, and eating ritual foods and drinking cups of wine, Israel remembered the deliverance from Egypt.*

There is no obvious solution to the problem of the difference in dating between John's final supper and the Lord's Supper of the Synoptic Gospels. While it is possible that John has deliberately structured the account so that Jesus dies at the same time as, and symbolically stands for, the Passover Lamb, it is curious that John does not make a specific point about this potentially significant interpretation of his death.

Most probably John and the Synoptics derive from independent oral traditions. But John's dating is coherent and plausible and explains, in part, the absence of the language of the Lord's Supper at the meal, language which is instead found echoed at least in Jesus' discourse at the feeding of the 5,000 (6:48–59).

Equally striking, however, is the fourth gospel's portrayal of the footwashing. The central focus of this final meal is found in Jesus' action toward his disciples: he assumes the posture of a servant, taking a towel and a basin, and washes his disciples' feet. It is not clear how prevalent footwashing was in antiquity. There is some evidence that hosts would provide a basin for guests to wash their own feet (see Luke 7:44). But John's portrayal is unusual, since it has Jesus actively washing his disciples' feet during the dinner, not before it. It is the servant role that is clearly at issue, and Jesus' actions serve as an example for his disciples. Peter's resistance to the footwashing, and Jesus' adamant insistence on it, suggests the importance this action plays in John's portrayal of the final moments of Jesus' life.

A key question that the church must face is whether this example is to be interpreted literally, as a sacrament of footwashing, or figuratively, as simply an instruction on an appropriate servant posture. Few churches have taken the command literally, although some have; the resistance to a literal reading is interesting given that Jesus actually commands that his disciples should follow his example. Regardless of whether the footwashing command is construed literally, certainly the key teaching of servanthood must be seen as a central part of Jesus' teaching (compare Mark 10:43–44; Luke 22:25–27). Given the importance placed on the footwashing, it would at least suggest that serving, especially of those of lower stature, is an essential part of the command to love one another, a commandment that will soon be emphasized by Jesus.

Predictions of Betrayal & Denial · 13:21–38

The figure of Judas Iscariot is important in John's narration of the story of Jesus. John says two times in the story of the final supper that Satan *entered into* Judas. But such a connection of Judas to the devil is not a surprise. John has already prepared the reader for the betrayal, and Satan's involvement, early on in the gospel. In 6:71, following Peter's confession Jesus says, *Did I not choose you, the twelve, and one of you is a devil?* The narrator then informs us that he was speaking of Judas Iscariot.

Thus it is no surprise when, during the supper, Jesus announces openly to all the disciples that *one of you is going to betray me*. Jesus knows Judas as the betrayer, and yet they share this final meal together. Indeed, Jesus appears to be complicit in the act of betrayal, for after giving the bread to Judas, he bids him to *do quickly what you are going to do* (13:28). Judas's betrayal is both a violation of close friendship and a sign of a deeper spiritual battle.

John emphasizes the spiritual nature of the betrayal in the closing verse of the dinner scene. Upon receiving the morsel, Judas immediately leaves the dinner, and John tells us, *and it was night*. This final verse, so simple and stark, reinforces the darkness/light motif with which John has begun his gospel. Jesus is the light of the world, come into a dark world. Judas, in rejecting Jesus, has turned his back on the light and reentered the darkness. The fact that he goes into the night serves to punctuate the spiritual choice Judas has made.

After Judas departs, Jesus gives a final teaching that draws on the logic of his footwashing and summarizes the ethic of the new kingdom: love one another. He calls this a new commandment, and using his own life as an example of what this love should look like, he urges the disciples to pattern themselves after him. Moreover, love for one another is to be the distinguishing characteristic of true disciples of Jesus. This particular commandment will be repeated and reinforced in the final discourses that follow the meal.

Given both Jesus' commandment of love, and Judas's betrayal under the impetus of Satan, the subsequent portrayal of Peter only underlines his character as rash and impetuous and further serves as a warning about the tenuous nature of discipleship. When Jesus says that where he is going they cannot come (meaning death by crucifixion, and then heaven), Peter rashly asserts that he is willing to lay his life down for Jesus. But, as in all the gospels, Jesus predicts that Peter would instead deny him three times. Peter's intentions exceed his ability or his knowledge, a consistent part of all the gospels' portrayals of him.

The Farewell Sayings · 14:1–17:26

As noted in the introduction, the Gospel of John has a distinctive structure made up of a narrative about

Jesus and his signs that is periodically interspersed with dialogues or discourses. These dialogues usually follow and interact with the narrative story. Many of these discourses have involved some degree of self-revelation of Jesus' nature and his relationship to God, often using some form of the "I am" formula. Following the final supper, the evangelist presents a long discourse unit, chapters 14–17, which is self-revelatory in nature, this time functioning as a farewell speech to the disciples.

There is no apparent structure to the discourses of these chapters. Many times the same themes recur in variations (for example, the predictions about the Paraclete, teaching about "abiding" in him), creating a sense of overlapping ideas, and often echoing themes that have already appeared in the preceding narrative leading up to the Passion. It is worthwhile, then, to consider this long block of discourses thematically, not in the order it is presented.

Jesus' Departure & His Promise · Jesus begins his long series of discourses in the form of a farewell speech. While he has previously announced to both the Jews (7:33) and the disciples (13:33) that he is *going away*, and indeed to a place to which they cannot follow immediately, the beginning of his farewell speech develops this idea more fully. The departure theme is picked up in a number of places and serves as the thread that binds the entire discourse together. Jesus says he is going away, but that this departure is actually good news, for he will prepare a place for them and await them there (14:1–4). Jesus' departure will allow the Paraclete to come (14:18). His departure is good news, since he goes to the Father (14:29), the one who sent him (16:5). And the departure motif is an integral feature in Jesus' final prayer, chapter 17, where the use of the past tense assumes his life is over, and he is reflecting on the effect he will have on his followers.

In John's opening prologue, a clear spatial metaphor describes the relationship between the realm of God and the realm of humanity. These two realms are seen as "places" between which travel is possible. Thus, Jesus was *coming into the world* from the realm of God (1:9). In the dialogue with Nicodemus, Jesus had spoken of this entry as a descent from heaven. This spatial metaphor of heaven as a place "up there" to which Jesus will return is the backdrop of his departure sayings.

While such a spatial concept is implicit in many of the departure references, especially the opening verses of chapter 14, at a deeper level Jesus hardly holds to such a spatial sense. When Philip asks for him to show the Father, seemingly requesting that he show the way to the place where God is, Jesus' response turns the spatial metaphor on its head. Jesus has already shown the Father to them in his very person. God's place is already with them, for God dwells in Jesus, and Jesus is dwelling with them. Yet in response to Thomas's question, *how can we know the way?* Jesus says *I am the way, and the truth, and the life. No one comes to the Father except through me* (14:6). Here Jesus interprets the spatial concept in a different way. Not only is there a place to which Jesus will go, and to which he will also bring all believers, but the pathway between "the world" and "heaven" is Jesus himself. Thus, Jesus himself also becomes a part of this spiritual geography (just as his resurrected body is to become the new temple, the place at which humanity normally comes closest to God).

The Paraclete · A key promise that Jesus makes in discussing his departure is the coming of the Paraclete who will assist the believers in his absence. The distinctive word "Paraclete," has been translated in various ways: *counselor* (RSV, NIV), *advocate* (NRSV, JB), *comforter* (KJV, ASV), and *helper* (NKJV). Literally, it means "one who is called to the aid of another" [from Greek *para* = beside, and *klesis* = a calling]. Outside of the New Testament, the word meant a legal assistant or advocate, a slave who was called to assist, and an intercessor in matters of legal or administrative difficulties.

In John, the Paraclete will come to teach the disciples (14:26; 16:13); especially it will remind them of what Jesus had said while alive (14:26). Furthermore, it will provide testimony on behalf of Jesus, perhaps aiding the disciples in their own testimony on behalf of Jesus (15:26–27). The Paraclete is plainly identified as the Holy Spirit (14:26) and also as the Spirit of Truth (15:26; 16:13). It is, then, a spiritual presence for believers and closely connected with Jesus himself. Just as the disciples are to abide in Jesus, and Jesus in them, also the Holy Spirit is said to abide with the disciples (14:16). In this sense, then, Jesus can say that he will not leave the disciples orphaned, for in the Paraclete Jesus will simultaneously abide among the believers, even as he abides in the Father.

Abide in Me · A strong theme in the farewell discourses is the need for the followers of Jesus to abide, or remain, in Jesus even after his departure. In many ways, this "abiding" is one of the key ways that belief and love are manifested among believers. Indeed, these terms – abide, believe, and love – seem at times to be different ways of saying the same thing.

Jesus in this gospel has earlier sounded the theme of "abiding" in terms of the believers' continuing relationship with him. In 8:31, Jesus defined discipleship in terms of abiding in his words: *If you continue [abide] in my word, you are truly my disciples, and you will know the truth, and the truth will make you free*. Jesus was indicating that the close relationship between belief and "abiding" in Jesus' words represents a total approach to life.

Such an understanding of "abiding" that links belief and action takes shape in the first part of the farewell dialogue. In 14:10, when asked to show the Father to the disciples, Jesus says that the Father has been abiding in Jesus throughout his ministry, and that this close relationship is what has allowed him to speak with authority and act with power. Thus, Jesus' own relationship with God, and his own activity, is defined in terms of "abiding."

In chapter 15, Jesus further develops the theme using the metaphor of the grapevine. The disciples should have a close relationship with him, just as branches of the grapevine have with the main stem. The branches are unable to survive without being connected to the vine. The disciples are to "abide" in him in just such a close, intimate way. Drawing on the Paraclete's power, those "abiding" in Jesus obey *my commandments*. Abiding in Jesus' love is not matter of more belief or emotion; it is ultimately proven by action.

The Love Commandment · As already noted, Jesus' command to love one another is a bold and striking element in his final instructions to his disciples. This explicit commandment appears in 15:12 as well as 13:34. But this commandment that the disciples love one another is linked to a broader set of themes that runs through the entire gospel and especially the discourses in chapters 14–17. Consistently, Jesus' mission demonstrates God's love for humanity and calls for disciples to respond in a similar way.

In 15:12–17, Jesus uses his own ministry to interpret the commandment that he had already enunciated in 13:34. The disciples are to love one another in the same way that Jesus has already loved them. Jesus, then, is the preeminent example of love. In the statement *as I have loved you*, Jesus also points forward to the next statement about the willingness to lay down one's life for friends. Jesus is in the very process of laying down his life on behalf of the entire world, and this self-sacrificing attitude is to be the hallmark of love.

Jesus has introduced the word *friend* into the equation at this point. The true friend to others is willing to lay down his life for them. Jesus, then, defines his relationship with the disciples as friendship as opposed to a "master-servant" relationship. As friends, Jesus has included them in his plans and has revealed his nature and his future. But friendship is reciprocal, and the disciples will demonstrate that they, too, are friends, by following Jesus' commandment to love one another. As friends, therefore, they are to pattern their life for one another on his example as the friend who demonstrates the greatest love.

Unity Among Believers · Another key concept in the farewell discourses, and certainly linked to abiding in Jesus and to loving one another, is the idea of Christian unity. This comes to beautiful expression in the final chapter of the farewell discourse, commonly called Jesus' "high priestly prayer." In chapter 17, Jesus does not speak directly to the disciples, but rather allows them to overhear his prayer to God.

At the conclusion of Jesus' prayer, he especially asks that all followers of Jesus should be unified. The example of that unity is the relationship that Jesus himself has with God. Just as the disciples have understood that Jesus is in full harmony and communication with God, so also believers should be unified in action and belief (17:22). This unity among believers demonstrates God's love in Jesus for the world. Moreover, a true unity among believers is a visible manifestation of Jesus abiding in and with his community. In this prayer for unity, then, the key themes of abiding in Jesus and love are shown to be integrally related concepts.

The Importance of Belief in Jesus · The theme of belief, which has been a constant thread running throughout the gospel, appears often in the final discourses, as one might expect. The very opening verse of the discourse, 14:1, puts it as an entreaty or command: *Believe in God, believe also in me*. Here is the core message of the gospel: to know and believe in God is to believe in Jesus. And to know and believe in Jesus is truly to know God. If one wants to know God, one need only know Jesus as the true image of God (see 14:9–10).

For those who believe, the relationship with God offers a secure future. God loves those who have come to believe in Jesus as the one sent from God (16:27). These followers who believed in Jesus thus truly understand God's nature. Jesus prays for them (17:8, 20) and for the purpose of bringing about belief in the world when he entreats unity (17:21). By the same token, however, those who disbelieve are counted as outsiders to the promises. Jesus' prayer in chapter 17 very explicitly excludes those who do not believe, and the implication throughout is that they will face a judgment based on their own actions and attitudes.

Opposition · Throughout the gospel, there has been an escalating opposition to Jesus. This was anticipated in the prologue, where the evangelist portrays Jesus as one who comes into the world that he created, but his own people reject him (1:10–11). This opposition is often termed *the world*, and is portrayed as being in darkness.

This theme is developed in three sections in the final discourses: 15:18–25, 16:29–33, and 17:12–16. In the first of these units, Jesus says that *the world* will oppose his followers in the same way that it is currently opposed to him. This prediction suggests a fundamental opposition between the thinking of the world and that of God – it is the opposition of darkness to light. Those who hate the believers really hate God.

According to the fourth gospel, while this opposition to Jesus will extend to all who believe in him, this should not be seen as a failure on God's or Jesus' part. It is, instead, a part of the very nature of Jesus' mission – to shine light on the darkness and so bring about the crisis of judgment, either to belief or to death. Such activity by its very nature produces opposition. But Jesus makes clear that his mission is ultimately victorious. Neither the cross, nor subsequent opposition to his followers, should suggest any failure, for Jesus has conquered the world in his mission (16:33).

The Arrest of Jesus · 18:1–14

Following the final discourses of Jesus, the scene shifts from the room where the dinner has taken place to the Mount of Olives. In the fourth evangelist's description, this is a garden across the valley of Kidron, just east of the Temple Mount. Judas arrives at the scene with a contingent of soldiers and officers from the high priests and the Pharisees. When the arresting party arrives, there is no kiss of identification nor any need for it, as in the Synoptics. Jesus, instead, takes the initiative by asking whom they seek, and in response to their request for *Jesus of Nazareth*, he openly identifies himself to the arresting party. This particular scene has a very curious element to it. Upon hearing him identify himself – *I am he* – the arresting party steps back and falls to the ground. Why? It is possible that the Jewish guards, upon hearing him use the term *I am he* – literally, the "I am" [*ego eimi*] that he has used in his self-revelatory metaphors – prostrated themselves (in reverence or fear). More likely, however, this *falling down* is meant to symbolically illustrate that they "stumbled" at this point over the very one who has come as their savior.

The arresting officials then take Jesus to the house of the high priest. Curiously, the fourth evangelist reports that Jesus was taken first to Annas, the father-in-law of the current high priest and probably the high priest during Jesus' youth. Only secondarily is Jesus taken to the current high priest, Caiaphas (18:24), but nothing of this exchange is recorded.

> **High Priests**
> In Jesus' time, the high priests did not serve for life. Thus Annas held the office from 6–15 CE and was succeeded by several sons and by his son-in-law Caiaphas (18–36 CE).

The hearing before Annas underscores that Jesus is entirely open and self-confident in the face of persecution. The scene uses courtroom rhetorical language that has been used throughout the gospel: testimony, signs, truth, judgment, and proof (or belief). Jesus indicates that he has taught openly in the temple and synagogues. In other words, Jesus had functioned publicly as a faithful witness. In contrast, it would seem, this hearing before the high priest, being held at night and not open to all, is not just. In response to Jesus' simple statement affirming his openness, he is struck by the high priest's officer – a senseless act of brutality. What is at stake here are basic concepts of justice: true testimony and a fair trial. Jesus is both the true witness and the innocent victim of unjust persecution.

Pilate's Trial · 18:28–19:16

John's version of the trial before Pilate is striking in its construction and its more positive portrayal of Pilate. For John, the real opposition is "the Jews," not the Romans.

The trial begins with the Jewish leaders taking Jesus to Pilate's headquarters, the prætorium. Since later on John simply reports that "the Jews" respond to Pilate's questions, we might conclude that here the term "the Jews" equals the leadership of the Jewish council. Later on in the trial, Pilate refers to the group who have accused him as being *your own nation and the chief priests* (18:35). John is thus using the leadership of the Jews, the chief priests and Pharisees, to symbolize a deeper and more fundamental opposition.

> **The Prætorium**
>
> "Prætorium" is the standard name for Roman military headquarters. In Jerusalem, the prætorium is often identified with the Antonia Fortress, a large fortification built just north of the temple. The Roman authorities used this massive fortress to police the city.

The description of the trial setting reminds the reader of John's unique chronology of the Passover week: it is not yet Passover, and so the delegates from the chief priest are unwilling to enter the governor's headquarters lest they become ritually unclean and thus unable to enter the temple for the sacrifice of the Passover lambs. As a result of the fourth gospel's distinctive chronology, a very curious situation unfolds. On the one hand, Pilate's interrogation of Jesus takes place inside the prætorium. On the other hand, Pilate's interaction with the Jewish leaders and the crowds takes place outside. Thus, Pilate is portrayed as shuttling back and forth between Jesus and the crowd! This portrayal of two different scenes allows Pilate to have private conversations with Jesus, which is a distinctive feature of the fourth gospel's trial setting.

> **Pontius Pilate**
>
> Governor of Judea and Samaria from 26–36 CE, Pilate was well-known for his firm, not to say oppressive, rule (see Luke 13:1–5).

The trial begins with the formal accusation, which Pilate demands at the outset: *what is he accused of?* The response by "the Jews" is certainly weak and nonspecific: *If this man were not a criminal, we would not have handed him over to you* (18:30). Apparently, one of the charges is that he claims to be *King of the Jews*, since the first question Pilate asks him is whether he is King of the Jews. But Pilate never actually says the Jews have accused him of this, and the net effect is a vague accusation, heightening the image of injustice.

In the trial, Pilate interrogates Jesus gently. In response to numerous requests about this alleged kingship (18:36), Jesus responds with a riddle (18:37). Such indirect answers do not seem to perturb Pilate, and in response to Jesus' claim that he came into the world to testify to the truth, Pilate responds only with curiosity: *What is truth?* (18:38). Even later on, in 19:11, when Jesus says that Pilate only could have power over him if he (Jesus) willed it, Pilate does not get angry, but instead seeks to release Jesus. Still, Pilate is not painted with completely rosy colors. He has Jesus flogged and humiliated, apparently as a normal course of treatment for an accused criminal (19:1–5).

Pilate's judgment throughout this trial is that Jesus should be released. He repeats this three times (perhaps mirroring Peter's threefold denial). In the first instance, after his initial interrogation, he attempts to use the practice of releasing a convicted criminal on Passover as a means of releasing Jesus. But "the Jews" demand Barabbas, a rebel, instead. After having Jesus flogged and dressing him up as a king for public humiliation, Pilate again seeks to have him released. Finally, after a third interrogation, Pilate resolves again to release him. Only when he is accused by "the Jews" of opposing the emperor should he release Jesus does Pilate agree to the crucifixion.

"The Jews," on the other hand, demonstrate an increasing animosity toward Jesus that ultimately leads them ironically to convict themselves, at least before God. They not only bring Jesus to Pilate for conviction but demand the death penalty for vague and unsubstantiated charges. When Pilate seeks to release Jesus, they request a convicted criminal be released instead. When Pilate brings out Jesus dressed in purple, they cry out emphatically, with a doubled cry, *Crucify him! Crucify him!* (19:6). And when Pilate again seeks to release Jesus, they use political blackmail against Pilate, suggesting that such a release would indeed be treason against the Cæsar. The emotion of "the Jews'" reaction reaches a fever pitch in the last scene.

The ultimate irony of "the Jews'" opposition is found in their response to Pilate's request, *Shall I crucify your King?* (19:15). They respond by saying *We have no king but the emperor*. It is clear that they cannot accept Jesus as king, but their emphatic rejection of Jesus is also a betrayal of God: To affirm no king but the emperor is to deny God as king. This is a fulfillment, indeed, of what Jesus himself had accused them of earlier in the gospel: in rejecting him they were declaring that God was not their father, thus showing they were children of the devil who was a murderer and a liar (8:42–44).

In the end, Pilate agrees to the crucifixion, but the text is not clear whether it would be the Romans or "the Jews" who would crucify Jesus. While "the Jews" have earlier stated that they were not permitted by law to put anyone to death (18:31), still Pilate's handing over Jesus *to them* seems to suggest that "the Jews" actually carried out the crucifixion. As Pilate finally relents to the pressure of the crowd, it appears that he simply turns over Jesus to them for crucifixion, rather than actively subject him to Roman punishment.

The Crucifixion · 19:17–37

John interprets the crucifixion through a reading of the Old Testament. In particular, the way Jesus' clothes are claimed by the soldiers, especially the fact that his tunic is not torn into pieces but is distributed to the soldiers by lots, fulfills Psalm 22:29. All the gospels report that soldiers cast lots for Jesus' clothing, but only John's gospel explicitly sees this in light of the Old Testament. Similarly, the failure to break Jesus' leg is seen as a "fulfillment" of, or rather an analogy to, Exodus 12:46, which commands that the bones of the Passover lamb not be broken. And finally, when the soldiers pierce his side and it issues forth blood and water, John sees this as the fulfillment of Zechariah 12:10, which describes how they will *look upon the one whom they have pierced*. These last two events are unique to John, and Jesus' pierced side will become important in the post-resurrection appearances (20:20, 25, 27).

John also reports a poignant scene while Jesus hangs on the cross. Jesus' mother and the beloved disciple are present at the crucifixion, along with some other women. Jesus addresses his mother, as at Cana, as *woman* and, referring to the beloved disciple, says, *Here is your son*. Similarly he addresses the beloved disciple and says, *here is your mother*. The appearance of Jesus' mother again in this closing scene functions as a bookend to the gospel story. Previously, she had been present at his first sign, when he first revealed his glory, and the disciples believed. Here she appears again at the time of his glorification (crucifixion). In handing over his mother to the beloved disciple's care, to become his mother, Jesus concludes his life as the son of Mary. At Cana, Jesus says his hour is not yet come. But clearly this final moment of life is *his hour*. In making arrangements for his mother's (and the beloved disciple's) care, Jesus has completed his task. It is, then, certainly significant that Jesus' next words are, *it is finished*. At the same time, the handing over of Mary to the beloved disciple's care suggests that the community of believers is somehow a substitute for Jesus, a new family. Jesus' statement thus anticipates the church, even as the Paraclete's anticipated coming imagines a church to receive its instruction.

Jesus' death in the fourth gospel lacks any cry lamenting God's absence, as Mark and Matthew report. Instead, he resolutely cries *it is finished* and gives up his spirit. Here, as in his reply to Pilate, Jesus controls events. With him remains the power over his crucifixion and his death. Dying is his intentional act. For the fourth gospel, Jesus is the knowing and intentional Son, the preexistent Word, who now returns to the Father.

Jesus' Burial · 19:38–42

Even in the burial, the opposition of "the Jews" occurs. Joseph of Arimathea asks for and receives the body of Jesus. Joseph, the gospel tells us, is a disciple of Jesus, but a secret one because of fear of "the Jews." Here again we are reminded of the parents of the blind man (chapter 9), who fear being removed from the synagogue by "the Jews," as well as authorities in 12:42 who fear to declare their faith openly lest they also be removed from the synagogue.

Joseph is joined by Nicodemus, who has been a somewhat ambivalent character in the gospel. Is Nicodemus a disciple, too? In the previous scenes where Nicodemus appeared (3:1–15; 7:50), it was not clear whether he truly believed in Jesus or was only open to the possibility. While Joseph is called a secret disciple, Nicodemus is not. Here, at the burial scene, Nicodemus remains an ambivalent figure.

Thus the trial and crucifixion end on a note of sadness tinged as always with the continued opposition to Jesus – and this despite John's language of glorification. The burial happens in an atmosphere of *fear of the Jews*, even for Jesus' absent disciples.

THE RESURRECTION APPEARANCES OF JESUS · 20:1–21:25

The fourth gospel relates the crucifixion and death of Jesus as victory, one in which Jesus willingly dies in order to fulfill his mission and thus to glorify God. But the story is not finished. As Jesus had indicated in his farewell discourses, there is a future to the story that involves his followers. They are to receive the Spirit and to testify, so that future followers may come to believe.

The Empty Tomb · 20:1–10

As in all the gospels, the first to arrive at the empty tomb on Sunday morning is Mary Magdalene. In John's gospel she comes alone, not with other women. Mary's initial reaction seems to be based on the preceding opposition to Jesus. She concludes that, since the stone has been rolled away and Jesus' body is missing, his opponents have removed it.

Upon hearing Mary's report of the empty tomb, two key disciples rush to the tomb to confirm her claim. When Lazarus was raised, John was very explicit in detailing how he came forth from the tomb with the grave-clothes still wound around him (11:44). In contrast to Lazarus's experience, Jesus' grave-clothes are lying on the floor with the face cloth off to one side. The folded grave clothes suggest that something significant has happened; they also are a sign that the body was not simply taken.

> **Jesus' Tomb**
> *The traditional site of Jesus' burial is underneath the Church of the Holy Sepulchre. The tradition predates Constantine, and the site has strong claims to being at least approximately correct. The site known as Gordon's Calvary, though charming, was not a tomb in Jesus' time (it is older) and was proposed as the site only in the nineteenth century.*

In the report of the two disciples' race to the empty tomb, while Peter enters first, the beloved disciple nonetheless takes priority. Upon seeing the empty tomb and the graveclothes lying in piles, he is said to believe. But in what does he believe? The disciples have already come to believe that Jesus is the Messiah, the one sent from God. Given the editorial note that they did not yet know the Scripture that Jesus must rise from the dead, one must conclude that the disciple believed that Jesus was raised from the dead. The empty tomb, together with the folded grave-clothes, then, functions much as other signs in the gospel have: they point to a deeper significance that produces belief on the part of at least some present.

Mary in the Garden · 20:11–18

In contrast to the beloved disciple, however, stands Mary. She is portrayed as having returned to the garden where the tomb is, and her weeping indicates a lack of understanding or belief in the resurrection. Upon recognizing Jesus, however, she responds with a sincere emotional response, and touches him. But Mary's embrace only emphasizes the extreme disjuncture between the earthly Jesus and the risen Jesus. This Jesus has not come back to live among them, but is "on the way" to the Father. This "physical" appearance anticipates the later appearances to the disciples in the closed room.

The Closed Room Appearances · 20:19–29

Later that day the scene shifts to a gathering of the disciples in a locked room. The theme of the opposition of "the Jews" is continued, since they are meeting behind a locked door for fear of the "the Jews." Jesus miraculously appears in their midst. His initial words, *Peace to you*, are reminiscent of the promise given to them in his final discourse that he would give them peace (14:27). This distinctive greeting occurs a number of times in these final appearances.

Jesus then shows the marks of his crucifixion, his hands and his side. The presentation of his hands and side is a very important feature in John's gospel and pointedly affirms that the risen Jesus is truly a physical being, even when he is risen, just as he was truly a human being who suffered and died. In this emphasis on the hands and the side, reiterated in the appearance before Thomas, we find a continuity with the epistles of John. There, the author goes to great pains to emphasize the physical presence of Jesus, certifying that he truly saw Jesus and touched him with hands (1 John 1:1). Later on, John declares that only those with the Spirit of God confess that Jesus *came in the flesh* (1 John 4:2). The evangelist takes great pains to refute the misconception that Jesus did not come in the flesh but only in the spirit.

Jesus then proceeds to fulfill another of his promises from the final discourses, the giving of the Holy

Spirit. He breathes upon them and commands that they should receive the Holy Spirit. The very action of Jesus breathing on the disciples is suggestive, especially given the framework of the prologue. We should recall that the prologue insisted that Jesus was a coparticipant in creation, echoing Genesis. Here again Jesus' act mirrors God's gift of life to humans in Genesis 2, *then the Lord God ... breathed into his nostrils the breath of life; and the man became a living being* (Gen 2:7). In the same way, Jesus breathes on the disciples and imparts the Holy Spirit, thus creating a new humanity and a new life.

With the gift of the Holy Spirit, the disciples receive a charge as his apostles (literally "sent ones"); they are sent to participate in the very mission Jesus had as a human. Notice that Jesus uses commissioning language: *As the Father has sent* [Greek *apostellein*] *me, so I send* [Greek *apostellein*] *you* (20:21). The giving of the Holy Spirit, then, confirms this commission and empowers them. Finally, they are charged to engage in the very acts of forgiveness that has marked Jesus' ministry.

The sign to Thomas, however, illustrates the variety of ways in which faith may arise. While Thomas receives the "sign" of Jesus' resurrection by means of his actual touch, faith may also arise through the agency of the testimony, the true witness, that the disciples themselves will now offer. From this point on, belief will not come about by direct seeing, but instead by the testimony of those who have seen. Thomas's touch, then, is not meant primarily for him, but rather to enable others, through his witness and the witness of the fourth gospel itself, to come to know Jesus and believe in him. This action of letting Thomas touch him functions as a testimony for those who will follow in subsequent generations, that is the church (20:29).

The First Ending · 20: 30–31

This final sign to Thomas has thus set forth the purpose of the entire book, which the evangelist now makes clear in a concluding word. The signs recorded in this book should create life-giving belief in Jesus as the Christ, the Son of God. Each of the signs serves the purpose of evidence, or proof, that will convince people about the reality of this person, Jesus. Belief, for John, is the change of mind that comes about as a result of evidence and convincing arguments. Throughout the gospel, we have seen signs, testimony, and explanations by Jesus himself which have formed a complex argument: that God so loved the world that he sent his Word, his Son, as a human to lead people to life-giving community through his Son.

The Epilogue · 21:1–25

The fourth gospel does not end, however, with this conclusion in 20:30–31. Instead, an entire chapter follows with numerous appearances and more teaching. This story-after-the-story has certainly led to a vast amount of commentary. Many scholars believe that chapter 21 was added by a subsequent author, or perhaps by the community to which the fourth gospel was originally written. Others believe that the fourth evangelist himself added the final chapter as an afterthought. Its placement after a seeming conclusion certainly raises questions about the stages of the composition of the gospel. Yet the final chapter does retain much of the feel of the rest of the gospel, and even its literary style is not remarkably different from the rest of the gospel.

21:1–14 The final chapter of John begins with another appearance of Jesus, this time in Galilee. The miraculous catch of fish creates belief for both the disciple whom Jesus loved and Peter. These two men are thus once again at center stage, and once again it is Peter who races to Jesus, just like he raced to the empty tomb.

There are striking points of continuity and discontinuity between this story and the previous resurrection accounts. The narrator tells us that this is the third time Jesus has appeared to the disciples since his resurrection, and indeed this fits perfectly with the preceding chapter. As at those appearances, he is definitely a physical being; in chapter 20 he showed his hands and side, and here he eats with the disciples. Moreover, as with the appearance to Mary in the garden, Jesus is not immediately recognizable: it seems to be a knowledge of faith, borne out of the miracle, that leads the beloved disciple to understand that this must be Jesus. But why do they not recognize him after two previous appearances?

While the miracle does affirm the disciples' faith, more importantly it provides the setting for a dialogue between Simon Peter and Jesus that is oriented toward the future of the disciples. This subsequent appearance shifts the focus away from Jesus' own life and resurrection to the lives of the believers and their community. In doing so, however, this epilogue highlights several major themes of the final discourses (chapters 14–17), which also directed the attention to the subsequent life of the followers of Jesus: the function of the Paraclete, the importance of love for one another, and the need for unity.

21:15-19 The resulting dialogue between Jesus and Simon Peter both restores him to a central place following his denial and emphasizes his role in the developing community of believers. Jesus draws heavily on the imagery painted in chapter 10 of the good shepherd, applying it now, by extension, to Peter.

Previously, Jesus had personalized discipleship in terms of love – true disciples will love Jesus and will show it by keeping his commandments (14:15, 21) or keeping his word (14:23). Jesus' question to Peter, *do you love me?* (21:15) is thus consonant with this definition of discipleship. When Peter responds affirmatively, Jesus transfers his own role of the shepherd to Peter.

But Jesus does not simply ask this question and let it go. Instead, he asks Peter the question three times (21:15, 16, 17). This triple repetition of the question, with Peter responding affirmatively each time, reminds one of Peter's triple denial of Jesus. While Peter had failed there, he does not fail now. Despite having been denied, Jesus shows his love for Peter by giving him leadership, although that leadership will come at the price of suffering. But this, too, is the fulfillment of a previous word of Jesus. Peter, when faced with the prediction that he would deny Jesus, said he would follow Jesus even to the point of death. Jesus' response to Peter was that he could not follow him right then, *but you will follow later* (13:36). Peter would, like Jesus, be a shepherd but would also suffer and die in a similar way to Jesus (21:18–19).

21:20-23 The theme of Peter's role in the new community of believers is developed by comparison with the other key figure in the fourth gospel, the disciple whom Jesus loved. As we have frequently seen, where Peter is a major character, there also the beloved disciple appears as a companion figure. Here, in the final scene of the gospel, Peter asks about that disciple's role and his fate. It is not clear precisely what Peter's question is with regard to the beloved disciple. Is he asking what the beloved disciple's role in the community would be? Or is he asking about his fate? Jesus takes it as the latter, and the response simply defers an answer (21:22). It is clearly meant to reject comparisons, inviting instead total devotion on serving Christ. Apparently, a legend about the beloved disciple's immortality had grown up among his followers, and the gospel attempts to dispel that misconception.

21:24-25 With this final discourse between Jesus and the disciples, the gospel closes with a final ending. This ending is meant to certify the truth of the gospel itself. It returns to the theme of witness which has been a feature throughout the gospel. The validity of the author's witness and the truth of the message are based on eyewitness and thus are reliable. The author of the gospel is identified with the beloved disciple – this is the natural way to understand the *this* that introduces 21:24. Being based on the eyewitness of an actual disciple – the very disciple whom Jesus loved – the testimony of the gospel is thus true and reliable. While not necessarily complete, it is yet accurate.

THEOLOGICAL REFLECTIONS

As noted before, John's gospel is a narrative, but a narrative that is explicitly constructed to bring a reader to faith. John never uses the noun form of "faith," but rather uses the verb form, "to believe." The issue of faith is very common in John: there are almost a hundred occurrences of the Greek verb *pisteuein* in the fourth gospel, and the largest majority are explicit references to believing in Jesus, or believing that he is the one sent by God. The word "believe" in John, then, has the sense of a decision and commitment that arises from learning the truth about Jesus. This is seen clearly in the first conclusion to the gospel, John 20:30, which states the gospel's purpose to bring the reader to believe that Jesus is the Christ and thus to have life in his name. The frequent use of the word "believe" alone gives a clue to the nature and structure of the gospel: it is rhetorical and argumentative, a fact that is underlined by the debate-like features of many of the dialogues and discourses.

In addition to the word "believe," the word "witness" and its cognates "testify" and "testimony" also support the rhetorical point. Similarly, the word "signs," which can be seen as physical evidence in favor of an argument, also occurs repeatedly in the gospel.

John's gospel is constructed structurally and linguistically around the task of proving the proposition that Jesus is the Messiah, the unique Son of God.

FOR FURTHER STUDY

Raymond Brown, *The Gospel according to John* (2 vols.; Garden City, N.Y.: Doubleday, 1966–1970).

Craig S. Keener, *The Gospel of John: A Commentary* (2 vols.; Peabody, Mass.: Hendrickson, 2003).

WORKS CITED

Robert Anderson and Terry Giles, *The Keepers: An Introduction to the History and Culture of the Samaritans* (Peabody, Mass.: Hendrickson, 2002).

———, *The Literature of the Samaritans* (Peabody, Mass.: Hendrickson, 2005).

Raymond Brown, *The Community of the Beloved Disciple* (New York: Paulist, 1979).

Josephus, *Works* (ed. H. St. John Thackeray; 10 vols.; Cambridge: Harvard University Press, 1926–1965).

Craig S. Keener, *The Gospel of John: A Commentary* (2 vols.; Peabody, Mass.: Hendrickson, 2003).

Craig Koester, *Symbolism in the Fourth Gospel: Meaning, Mystery, Community* (Minneapolis, Minn.: Fortress, 1995).

James Kugel, *The Bible as It Was* (Cambridge: Harvard University Press, 1997).

John A. T. Robinson, *The Priority of John* (London: SCM, 1985).

Acts of the Apostles

Kenneth L. Cukrowski

CHAPTER CONTENTS

Contexts   855
Commentary   856
　Witnesses in Jerusalem · 1:1–8:3   856
　Witnesses in Judea & Samaria · 8:4–9:43   863
　Witnesses to the Ends of the Earth · 10:1–28:31   866
Theological Reflections   888
For Further Study   892
Works Cited   892

MAPS, TABLES & FEATURES

Luke's "Special" Conversions   889

Acts describes the spread of the gospel from the tiny province of Judea to the very heart of Rome. Guided by God, apostles, evangelists, and ordinary Christians carry the message of the cross across not only political, but also social and ethnic boundaries, beginning in the Jewish capital of Jerusalem, spreading through Samaria and even including outsiders such as eunuchs, and culminating in the conversion of Gentiles from virtually every corner of the Roman Empire. Despite imprisonments, beatings, stonings, plots, executions, internal disputes, riots, and shipwreck, Christians bear witness to God's power in their lives.

CONTEXTS

Although the book of Acts itself is anonymous, there is strong consensus that the author of Acts is the same person as the author of the Gospel of Luke. The argument for the common authorship of Luke-Acts is based mainly on literary, theological, and historical grounds (Parsons and Pervo). The literary features include similarity in genre and style, as well as parallels among the actions of the main characters. Common theological emphases include themes such as prayer, the activity of women, and possessions. The historical argument focuses on the common addressee Theophilus in the prefaces of both works.

Nevertheless, although almost everyone agrees that Luke-Acts has a common author, there is not agreement over the name of that author. Some scholars have focused attention on the four so-called "we passages" in Acts (16:10–17; 20:5–15; 21:1–18; 27:1–28:16), in which the "we" seems to be evidence of the author's direct involvement in the events in the narrative. Probably the best evidence that the author of Acts is also the author of the "we passages" is the consistent language and style between the "we passages" and the narrative surrounding them. However, other options remain possible. For instance, the "we" may be evidence for the author's use of a source, such as a diary, written by someone else. Or, the use of "we" may be a stylistic convention or variation.

Traditionally, the early church attributed the authorship of the Gospel of Luke and Acts to Luke. Although some have claimed that the use of medical language "proves" that Luke the physician was the author, this claim is not supportable because the language in these two books has no more medical vocabulary than similar ancient works (Cadbury 39–64). It is, however, noteworthy that the early church would attribute the authorship of Acts to someone so rarely mentioned in the rest of the New Testament (Col 4:14; Phlm 24; 2 Tim 4:11). This second argument, more than any other, is the strongest argument for calling Luke the author of Luke-Acts.

Although one can read the book of Acts like a simple adventure story, upon further examination the narrative betrays an underlying complexity. Several features reveal Luke's craftsmanship; he uses intertextual echoes, structural and stylistic features, and a number of literary forms to shape his narrative and emphasize his message. One finds not only echoes of Luke's story of Jesus in Acts, especially in the stories of

> **Intertextuality**
> *The citation or allusion by one text of another is known as intertextuality. This practice is very common in the New Testament and, more rarely, in the Old Testament.*

Peter and Paul, but also parallels between Peter and Paul themselves: the healing of a lame man (3:1–10; 14:8–10), extraordinary miracles (5:14–16; 19:11–12), bestowing the Holy Spirit (8:14–17; 19:1–7), battles against magic (8:18–25; 13:4–12; 16:6–18), raising the dead (9:36–43; 20:7–12), and misplaced honor (10:26; 14:15). These parallels show that God is working in similar ways through different individuals.

Structurally, Luke often places side-by-side stories that contrast with each other. Placing these opposites together makes the good appear better, and the bad worse, as these examples illustrate: good and bad giving (4:32–36; 5:1–11), the zeal of Simon and that of the eunuch (8:1–24, 25–40), the zeal of the eunuch and Saul (8:25–40; 9:1–9), responses at Thessalonica and Berea (17:4–6, 10–11), God's power versus magic (19:11–12, 13–17), and Christian and pagan attitudes toward money (19:18–20, 21–41). These contrasting panels signal the focus of the passage to the reader.

Luke also uses foreshadowing, often introducing characters briefly before they play a larger role in the narrative. For example, Barnabas sells his land (4:32–36), stands up for Paul in Jerusalem (9:27), and travels on behalf of the churches in Jerusalem and Antioch (11:22–30; 12:25) – all brief mentions – before the long account of his journey with Paul (13:1–14:28). The attentive reader will notice other instances of foreshadowing as well. Note the following eleven examples and their first appearance in Acts: Stephen (6:5), Philip (6:5), Saul/Paul (7:58), Simon the tanner (9:43), John Mark (12:12), James (brother of Jesus; 1:14; 12:17), Silas (15:22), Aquila (18:2), Priscilla (18:2), Trophimus (20:4), and Claudius Lysias (the tribune/commander; 21:31). All of these characters play more significant roles as the narrative progresses.

Within the narrative of Acts itself, Luke uses various literary forms: prologues, summaries, letters, and speeches. Acts begins with a prologue (1:1–2), just as the Gospel of Luke did (1:1–4). For the significance of the prologue, see the discussion below. Multiple summaries dot the narrative of Acts, providing transitions and connecting Luke's narrative (Acts 1:14; 2:41, 42–47; 4:4, 32–35; 5:12–16, 42; 6:1, 7; 8:25; 9:31, 42; 11:21, 24; 12:24; 13:48; 14:1; 16:5; 19:20; 28:30–31; compare Fitzmyer 97–98). Two letters, the first from the church in Jerusalem and the second from the tribune Claudius Lysias, lie embedded in Luke's narrative (15:23–29; 23:26–30).

Finally, speeches dominate Luke's narrative with at least twenty-six examples. In fact, about 25 percent of Acts consists of speeches. Peter gives eight (1:16–22; 2:14–40; 3:12–26; 4:8–12; 5:29–32; 10:34–43; 11:5–17; 15:7–11); James two (15:13–21; compare 21:20–25); Stephen one (7:2–53); and Paul ten (13:16–41; 14:15–17; 17:22–31; 20:18–35; 22:1–21; 23:1–6; 24:10–21; 26:2–29; 27:21–26; 28:17–20, 25–28). Non-Christians give another five: Gamaliel (5:35–39), Demetrius (19:25–27), an anonymous city clerk (19:35–40), Tertullus (24:2–8), and Festus (25:14–21, 24–27). Depending on how one defines a speech, even more instances may be found elsewhere (see 1:4–8; 6:2–4, 18:14–15, 27:33–34).

As most commentators note, the structure of the book of Acts mirrors that found in Acts 1:8. Jesus says: *You will be my witnesses in Jerusalem, and in all Judea and Samaria, and to the ends of the earth.* The spread of the gospel follows this same pattern in Acts.

COMMENTARY

WITNESSES IN JERUSALEM · 1:1–8:3

Within this first section, one finds a prologue to the book as a whole (1:1–2), as well as a description of the community as it waits in Jerusalem for the coming of the Spirit (1:3–26). The gospel then begins its spread in Acts 2 on the day of Pentecost. Statements about the growth of Christianity dot the narrative (2:41, 47; 4:4; 6:7). With the death of Stephen, the church scatters beyond the city of Jerusalem into Judea and Samaria (8:1–2).

1:1–11 Acts starts with a prologue (1:1–2), just like the beginning of Luke, followed by an ascension narrative (1:3–11), just like the ending of Luke. Luke mentions his *former book*, a reference to his gospel. The addressee in both documents, *Theophilus* connects the author of the gospel to the author of Acts. Meaning "lover of God," the name *Theophilus* can refer to anyone who loves God. It seems likely, however, that he is a real person and the patron of both Luke and Acts because *Theophilus* is a name

> **Theophilus's Status**
> *Since the description* most excellent *refers to both Theophilus (Luke 1:3) and the provincial governors Felix and Festus (Acts 23:26; 24:3; 26:25), it is likely that Theophilus was a socially prominent person.*

actually used for real people in the first century (see Josephus, *Antiquities*, 18.123; Haenchen 136) and because prologues often contain the name of an author's patron (for example, Josephus, *Against Apion*, 1.1). The rest of the prologue reviews the content of Luke (that is, *all that Jesus began to do and teach until the day he was taken up to heaven*) and introduces the beginning of Acts (*after giving instructions through the Holy Spirit to the apostles he had chosen*). Those *instructions* locate Jesus and the apostles in Jerusalem, which is where Acts begins.

Luke expands his brief report of Jesus' ascension in his gospel (24:50–51). In Acts, Jesus interacts with his disciples for *forty days*. Jesus shows himself to the apostles, offers *many convincing proofs*, and speaks about *the kingdom of God*. Jesus instructs the apostles *not* to *leave Jerusalem, but wait for the gift* God promised, which Jesus explains: *in a few days you will be baptized with the Holy Spirit*. Picking up the topic of the *kingdom* (1:3, 6), Luke records a question from the disciples and Jesus' response. The disciples want to know when the *kingdom* will be restored *to Israel* (see Luke 19:10; 21:7; 24:21). Jesus responds with a rebuke (*it is not for you to know the times or dates*), a promise (*you will receive power when the Holy Spirit comes*), and a commission (*you will be my witnesses*). The promise of the coming of the Holy Spirit is fulfilled in Acts 2:1–4. Their commission as *witnesses* consumes the rest of the narrative of Acts, not only for the apostles (1:22; 2:32; 3:15; 5:32; 10:39, 41; 13:31), but also for Paul (22:15; 26:16). The geographical place names in 1:8 function as an outline for the book of Acts.

After Jesus' response, he ascends and *two men dressed in white* appear. Jesus' ascension takes place on the *Mount of Olives* (Acts 1:12), which Luke equates with *Bethany* (Luke 24:50; see 19:29). Luke's description of the ascension of Jesus contains echoes of Elijah's ascension (2 Kgs 2:11; Acts 1:2, 11, 22). Like Jesus in 1:7, the *two men* (compare the angels in Luke 24:4, 23; Acts 10:3, 30) offer the disciples a rebuke (*why do you stand here looking into the sky*) and a promise (*Jesus ... will come back in the same way you have seen him go into heaven*). The ascension connects Luke to Acts and places the eleven in Jerusalem.

1:12–26 The account of the replacement of Judas consists of an introduction (1:12–14), Peter's speech (1:15–22), and Matthias's selection (1:23–26). The introduction places the eleven back in Jerusalem. The list of the eleven disciples corresponds to Luke's previous listing (Luke 6:13–16), except for the understandable absence of Judas and the order of the eleven; most notably, Luke pairs *Peter and John* together, anticipating the role that the pair will play in the upcoming narrative (3:1, 3, 4, 11; 4:13, 19; 8:14). After the list of the eleven, Luke mentions three noteworthy features about this group waiting in Jerusalem: their unity, prayer, and fellowship as believers. Unity characterizes the early Christian community here as elsewhere [Greek *homothumadon*; see Acts 1:14; 2:46; 4:24; 5:12], as does prayer. In addition to the eleven, *women* (compare Luke 8:1–3; 23:49, 55; 24:1–11, 22–25) *and Mary the mother of Jesus, and his brothers* meet with the eleven in an *upstairs room* (see 12:12). *Mary* will not play a role in the rest of Acts, but other women will. In his gospel, Luke mentions Jesus' brothers in passing (Luke 8:19–21; named in Mark 6:3), but in Acts, James will play a small but significant role, as a leader of the church in Jerusalem (12:17; 15:13; 21:18).

As Peter stands up to speak, those with him number *about a hundred and twenty*. Peter depicts Judas' death as a fulfillment of Scripture, citing Psalms 69:26 and 109:8. Within this argument, Peter relates four details of Judas's death: with the blood money, he *bought a field*; he *fell headlong*; *his body burst open and his intestines spilled out*; and the field is called *Akeldama, that is, Field of Blood*. The accounts of Judas's death in Acts and Matthew 27:3–10 differ slightly, but it is not clear how to resolve the issues (Johnson 39–40).

Peter says that it is necessary to choose another apostle who had been with the eleven *the whole time the Lord Jesus went in and out among* them. The selection of another apostle to replace Judas fits with Luke's view of the Twelve, who judge reconstituted Israel (Luke 22:29–30). Two candidates are put forth: *Joseph called Barsabbas* (see 15:22) (*also known as Justus*) *and Matthias*. Although Matthias is chosen, neither man appears again in Acts. With the full contingent of twelve, the apostles await the coming of the Holy Spirit and their role as witnesses.

2:1–13 This section falls into two parts: the coming of the Holy Spirit (2:1–4) and the reaction of the crowd (2:5–13). The Holy Spirit comes on the day of *Pentecost*, the fiftieth day after Passover, to those in the *house*, which may include the Twelve or the 120 (1:15). The phenomena are threefold: first, there is *a sound like the blowing of a violent wind*; second, those present see *what seemed to be tongues of fire that separated and came to rest on each of them*; and third, *all of them were filled with the Holy Spirit* and begin to *speak in tongues*. The first two phenomena probably signal God's arrival, since these signs are connected with other appearances of the divine in the Old Testament (see, for example, 1 Kgs 19:11–12; Johnson 42). Speaking in *tongues* here refers to speaking in other languages (2:4, 6, 8, 11). This phenomenon also occurs when the Gentiles and the disciples of John the Baptist receive the gospel (10:46; 19:6).

> **Pentecost**
> In ancient Israel, Pentecost was a festival connected to the beginnings of the barley harvest (Exod 23:16; Lev 23:15–22; Num 28:26–31). It also eventually came to be a celebration of the giving of the Torah at Sinai (see Exod 19:1).

Luke describes the divided response of the crowd (see Luke 2:34). On the one hand, four different verbs depict the *confusion* (2:6), *amazement* (2:7, 12), *wonder* (2:7), and *perplexity* (2:12; 10:17) of the crowd who hears the Twelve each *in his own native language*. On the other hand, others *make fun of* (2:13) the Twelve, claiming that they were intoxicated. The crowd consists of *God-fearing Jews from every nation under heaven*. With a listing of over a dozen different places, Luke emphasizes the universality of the gospel message and may also anticipate the spread of the gospel in the later narrative. Some commentators see this scene as a reversal of the tower of Babel story.

2:14–41 This sermon is the second of Peter's eight speeches in Acts. With this sermon, Peter explains the meaning of the phenomena (2:14–21) and preaches the story of Jesus (2:22–36). As Luke describes the response to the sermon, one reads the crowd's question (2:37), Peter's answer (2:38–40), and the results (2:41). Peter explains that the phenomena do *not* mean that *these men are drunk*. Rather, *this is what was spoken by the prophet Joel*. Thus, Peter introduces the long quotation from Joel 2:28–32 to explain the coming of the Holy Spirit (*I will pour out my Spirit on all people/in those days* in Acts 2:17–18) and the cosmic nature of this event (*the sun will be turned to darkness and the moon to blood*). In addition, the quotation from Joel anticipates the activity of men and women in the spread of the gospel (*your sons and daughters will prophesy; even on my servants, both men and women*) and the emphasis on conversions in the book of Acts (*everyone who calls on the name of the Lord will be saved*). Using the language of *wonders* and *signs* from the Joel quotation (2:19, 22), Peter launches into the story of Jesus, *who was a man accredited by God ... by miracles, wonders and signs*. With God's *foreknowledge*, Jesus was *handed over* and killed. God, however, *raised* (2:24, 32) Jesus *from the dead*. Using quotations from Psalms 16:8–11 and 110:1, Peter argues that David *spoke of the resurrection of the Christ* (2:31) and that David calls Jesus *Lord*. Peter concludes that *God made this Jesus*, whom the crowd *crucified, both Lord and Christ*.

Cut to the heart, the crowd asks: *Brothers, what shall we do*? (Luke 3:10, 12, 14; 10:25; 18:18; Acts 2:37; 16:30; 22:10). Peter answers with the first and fullest description among the eight conversion narratives in Acts (see below): *Repent and be baptized every one of you in the name of Jesus Christ so your sins may be forgiven*. In addition, those who respond *receive the gift of Holy Spirit*, who will guide and strengthen them. Luke summarizes the rest of Peter's sermon as a call to *Save yourselves from this corrupt generation*. Luke records the response of the crowd as the conversion of 3,000 persons. This remark is the first of many times that Luke comments on the growth of the church (2:41, 47; 4:4; 5:14; 6:7; 9:31; 11:21, 24; 12:14; 14:1; 16:5; 19:20).

2:42–47 In the longest summary in the book of Acts, Luke characterizes the Spirit-filled community of believers. The church devotes itself *to the apostles' teaching and to the fellowship, to the breaking of bread and to prayer*. The *breaking of bread* can refer to a normal meal (2:46) or to the Lord's Supper (20:7) or both, since the Lord's Supper was taken in the context of a meal. All the believers are *together*. They have *all things in common* (2:44; 4:32), showing Luke's emphasis on the proper use of possessions (see the discussion in the commentary on Luke). They meet *together in the Temple courts*; they eat together *in their homes with glad and sincere hearts*. They *praise God* and enjoy *the favor of all the people*. Even though Luke does not hesitate to show the flaws of the church (5:1–11; 6:1–6), here his portrait commends the standards toward which Christians should strive.

3:1–10 Although connected to the previous passage by the language of prayer (2:42; 3:1) and the setting of the temple (2:46; 3:1), this text begins a narrative that runs through 4:31. The passage breaks down into three parts: the setting (3:1–3), the healing of the beggar (3:4–7a), and the response (3:7b-10). The miracle takes place in *the temple at the time of prayer – at three in the afternoon*. Luke gives some details about the beggar: he was *crippled from birth, over forty years old* (4:22), and carried every day to *beg at the temple gate called Beautiful*, perhaps the ornate bronze door mentioned by Josephus (*Jewish War* 5.201). The beggar sees *Peter and John*, who are about to enter the *temple courts*, and asks them *for money*.

Luke's account of the healing begins with Peter's command: *Look at us!* (14:9). After the beggar directs his attention to them, Peter says that he does not have money to give him; then Peter adds: *but what I have I give you. In the name of Jesus Christ of Nazareth, walk*. A prominent theme in this extended account, *the name of Jesus* (3:6, 16; 4:7, 10, 12, 17–18, 30) refers to the person and power that come through Jesus, deflecting attention from the doer to the source of the power.

> **The Structure of Acts 3:1–8:3**
> This section begins a series of passages alternating between external conflict narratives (3:1–4:31; 5:12–42; 6:8–8:3) and internal conflict narratives (4:32–5:11; 6:1–7). The outside danger increases from threats to death within this cycle. Each of the external conflict narratives has a similar structure: a miraculous sign (3:1–10; 5:12–16; 6:8), an arrest (4:1–4; 5:17–26; 6:9–15), the response to authorities (4:5–22; 5:27–32; 7:1–53), and the result (4:23–31; 5:33–42; 7:54–8:3). The only exception to this pattern is Peter's sermon (3:11–26), which is not too surprising, given Luke's interest in speeches in the book of Acts.

The man responds with a burst of activity and thanks. *Walking* and *leaping* are mentioned three and two times respectively, *praising* twice (3:7–8). The *people* who recognize the beggar respond *with wonder and amazement*. These responses contrast strongly with the later reaction of the Jewish leaders (4:1–22).

3:11–26 Luke connects Peter's speech to the healing narrative with the theme of *amazement/ astonishment* (3:10, 11). The setting moves to *Solomon's Colonnade*, which is a place where some Jews confronted Jesus (John 10:23) and *believers used to meet together* (Acts 5:12). The speech falls into two parts (3:11–16, 17–26). The first part asks about and then identifies the source of the power for the miracle (3:12, 16). Peter begins: *Why do you stare at us as if by our own power or godliness we had made this man walk?* Peter then answers: *It is Jesus' name and the faith that comes through him that has given this complete healing to him, as you can all see*. Between this question and answer, Peter details the actions of God, the crowd, and the apostles. In contrast to God's action of exalting Jesus through resurrection (3:13, 15), the crowd *handed him over to death, disowned him, asked that a murderer be released*, and *killed the author of life*. The apostles function as *witnesses of this*.

> **Solomon's Colonnade**
> Herod the Great remodeled the temple precinct significantly. South of the temple proper sat a large, two-storied portico that could house thousands of visitors. Outside its southern wall were a massive staircase and a series of ritual bathing pools, or mikvehs, in which anyone entering the temple had to wash. These pools would have easily handled 3,000 baptisms.

The second half of the speech has two foci: the witness of the prophets to these events (3:18, 21, 22, 23, 24, 25) and the proper response to God's activity. In Peter's telling of the story of the witness of the prophets, he begins with *Moses* and concludes with *Abraham*; in between, Peter affirms that *all the prophets from Samuel on, as many as have spoken, have foretold these days*.

Even though the people and *leaders acted in ignorance*, Peter calls them to repentance. This call comes at both the opening and closing of this section (3:19, 26): *Repent then and turn to God*. If the people respond in this way, then their *sins* will *be wiped out*. Ultimately, *times of refreshing* will come, God will *send the Christ…even Jesus*, and God will *restore everything as he promised long ago through his holy prophets*. Although the phrases *times of refreshing* and *restore everything* (1:6) are cryptic, their import is clear: God is faithfully fulfilling his promises through Jesus to those who respond with repentance. The passage ends with a warning that those who do not listen *will be completely cut off from among his people*.

4:1–22 This passage divides into the arrest of Peter and John (4:1–4) and Peter's response to the authorities (4:5–22). The opposition to Peter and John consists of three groups: *the priests*, *the captain of the temple guard* (5:24, 26; see Luke 22:4, 52) *and the Sadducees*. The cause of their opposition to Peter and John is twofold: *the apostles were teaching the people and proclaiming in Jesus the resurrection of the dead*. The Sadducees, who do not believe in the resurrection of the dead, naturally oppose Peter and John on the latter point. *Teaching* will continue to be a source of conflict in the upcoming narrative (4:2, 18; 5:21, 25). Because of these two issues, Peter and John are put *in jail until the next day*, the first of a number of imprisonments in Acts (5:18; 8:3; 12:1; 16:23; 21:33). Luke concludes with a summary statement; the number of male converts grows to *about five thousand* (see 2:41).

Next, the leaders question Peter and John: *By what power or what name did you do this*? Peter's response is brief (4:8–12). He names the source of the healing: *by the name of Jesus Christ of Nazareth*. He then adds details about Jesus – some *crucified* him, but God raised him *from the dead*; Jesus is *the stone you builders rejected*, an allusion to Psalm 118:22. Finally, Peter tells them about the implications of Christ's death and resurrection: *salvation is found in no one else*.

The presence of the healed man silenced the rulers. So, after withdrawing to confer, the Sanhedrin reconvenes and commands Peter and John *not to speak or teach at all in the name of Jesus*. Peter responds: *Judge for yourselves whether it is right in God's sight to obey you rather than God*. After another round of *threats* (4:17, 21), they release Peter and John.

4:23–31 Peter and John return *to their own people*, report what happened, and pray together. The prayer has three parts. First, they begin by praising God as *Sovereign Lord*. The second and longest part of the prayer describes the futility of leaders who try to oppose God. After a lengthy quotation from Psalm 2:1–2, the prayer uses key words from Psalm 2 to describe how *Herod and Pontius Pilate with the Gentiles and the people of Israel in this city* conspired against Jesus. These two individuals and two groups, however, end up doing what God *had decided beforehand should happen*. Here as elsewhere, Luke uses the theme of God's *will* to explain the events of the cross (2:23; Luke 22:22); Luke affirms that God retains control in spite of human sin. In the prayer they ask for two items: for *boldness* to speak and for *signs and wonders* to be done *through the name of your holy servant Jesus*. The immediate response is the shaking of *the place where they were meeting* (4:31; compare 16:26), a filling with the *Holy Spirit*, and speaking of *the word of God boldly*. Soon, the apostles perform *signs and wonders* (5:12). Luke thus shows God equipping the believers for the challenges to their faith.

4:32–37 Luke places the next two passages (4:32–27; 5:1–11) side by side to emphasize the generosity of Barnabas and the sin of Ananias and Sapphira; unfortunately, the English chapter divisions obscure this connection. Luke shows how the church handles the challenges of possessions by giving a positive example followed by a negative example. The first passage moves from a general description of the community's use of possessions to a specific example. With an allusion to Deuteronomy 15:4, Luke highlights the faithful response of the Christian community: *There were no needy persons among them* (4:34). The church is able to achieve its result because of its unity (*all the believers were one in heart and mind*) and because of its generosity (*they shared everything they had*). The sharing is not based on a one-time selling of all they had, but on selling *lands or houses* as anyone *had need* (2:45; 4:35); the tense of the verb in Greek makes this point clearly.

Luke introduces *Joseph, a Levite from Cyprus*, as an example of this practice of the church. Joseph, more commonly known as *Barnabas*, sells a *field*, brings the *money*, and places it *at the apostles' feet* (4:35, 37; 5:2; compare 5:5, 10). The introduction of Barnabas foreshadows his role in the later narrative of Acts (9:27; 11:22–30; 12:25; 13:1–15:41) and functions as a contrast to *Ananias and Sapphira*.

5:1–11 The passage falls into four parts: the setting (5:1–2), Peter's confrontation of Ananias (5:3–6),

---

The Sanhedrin

Before Peter delivers his defense, Luke describes the composition of the Sanhedrin (4:15). As the ruling body over the internal affairs of the Jewish people, the Sanhedrin consists of rulers, *among whom are* elders and teachers of the law, *as well as* Annas the high priest *(see Luke 3:2) and other members of the* high priest's family, *of whom Luke names three individuals*: Caiaphas *(see Luke 3:2)*, John, *and* Alexander. *Later texts number the members of the Sanhedrin at 70, but too little is known of its first century composition and role to speak definitively about the body.*

Peter's confrontation of Sapphira (5:7–10), and the conclusion (5:11). Luke describes the setting as follows: *Ananias together with his wife Sapphira* sells a *piece of property; with his wife's full knowledge*, he *keeps back part of the money for himself*; he puts the *rest of the proceeds from the sale at the apostles' feet*. At this point, their actions seem to conform to the practice of the church described in the previous passage. The next section, however, makes clear that Ananias and Sapphira report the sale in a deceptive way.

Peter describes the nature of the sin and ownership of the property. Peter charges that Ananias has *lied* (5:3, 4), and not merely *to men but to God*. Apparently, Ananias indicated that he gave all the money from the land sale. Peter explains that the money belonged to Ananias *before it was sold*; and after the land was sold, the money remained at Ananias' *disposal*. After Ananias falls down and dies, *young men* bury his body. *About three hours later*, Sapphira enters, *not knowing what had happened*. Peter questions her about the *price of the land*, giving her an opportunity to act justly, which she does not do. Peter asks her how she could *agree to test the Spirit of the Lord*. She then falls down dead *at his feet*, ironically the very place where the money was first placed (5:2, 10). *Young men* bury her body as well (5:6, 10). Luke concludes with a summary statement: *great fear* (5:5, 11) *seized the whole church and all who heard about these events*.

> **Achan**
> Acts 5 alludes to the Old Testament story of Achan (note the use of the same verb held back/have kept in Acts 5:2, 3 and Josh 7:1). Luke makes the point that the church must hold onto the same high standard of purity that God had for Israel.

5:12–16 This passage is the beginning of the second of three cycles of external opposition (the other two being 3:1–4:31; 6:8–8:3). As with the other two cycles, this one begins with signs. The *apostles* perform *signs and wonders*, apparently as an answer to their prayer (4:30). Although the action begins back in *Solomon's Colonnade* (3:11; 5:12), it extends to the *streets* and ultimately to *crowds gathered also from the towns around Jerusalem*. In contrast to the 5,000 *men* (4:4), *women* are now explicitly mentioned along with *men* as part of the growth of the church in the first of several such statements (5:14; 8:3, 12; 9:2; 17:4, 12, 34; 22:4). Peter still functions as the lens through which Luke tells his account. The expectation about the healing power of Peter's *shadow* parallels the healings through *handkerchiefs and aprons* touched by Paul (5:15; 19:12).

5:17–42 This section of Acts divides into three parts: the arrest (5:17–26), the response to authorities (5:27–32), and the results of this opposition (5:33–42). Prompted by jealousy (5:17; 13:45; 17:5; see 7:9), the *high priest* and some *Sadducees* arrest the apostles and imprison them. In this second imprisonment (4:3; 5:18), those arrested increase from Peter and John to all the *apostles*. *During the night*, however, an *angel* releases the apostles (see 12:7) and tells them to *go to the temple courts* and *tell the people the full message of this new life*; *at daybreak*, the apostles go to the temple courts and begin to *teach* (5:21, 25, 28, 42).

When the authorities send for the apostles, the *officers* do not find them in jail. Instead, they find the *jail securely locked, with the guards standing at the doors*. When informed that the apostles are *teaching in the temple*, the *captain* and *his officers* bring the apostles back to the Sanhedrin. The *high priest* charges that the apostles make the authorities *guilty* of Jesus' *blood*.

Peter's response begins with a thematic statement: *We must obey God rather than men!* God has acted, and the apostles must obey. God worked through Jesus to *give repentance and forgiveness of sins to Israel*. Not only are the apostles *witnesses of these things* (1:8, 22), but so is the *Holy Spirit, whom God has given to those who obey him* (2:38).

After hearing Peter's reply, the Sanhedrin is *furious* (5:33; 7:54) wanting to put the apostles to *death*. Instead, *a Pharisee named Gamaliel, a teacher of the law, who was honored by all the people*, orders the apostles to be *put outside* (4:15; 5:34) and addresses the assembly. In his speech, Gamaliel uses two examples to warn the assembly not to act too rashly or harshly. Both *Theudas* (see Josephus, *Antiquities*, 20.97–99) and *Judas the Galilean* (Josephus,

> **Gamaliel**
> Later rabbinic texts contain several stories about Gamaliel, the founder of a succession of rabbis who were prominent Jewish leaders for several centuries. Sayings attributed to him concern ritual purity, protection of women in divorce proceedings, and the care for biblical paraphrases (targums) as though they were Scripture. All these views, though from later texts, make sense from a first century Pharisee (Chilton 904).

Antiquities, 18.3–9, 23–25; *Jewish War* 2.118) rallied followers; but each was *killed* and *all his followers were dispersed/scattered* (5:36, 37). Gamaliel's concluding advice is simple: *Leave these men alone! Let them go!* His rationale consists of two truisms: divinely motivated actions will inevitably succeed, and humanly motivated actions will inevitably fail. Instead of being killed, the apostles are *flogged*, which is still an increase in violence from the Sanhedrin's previous *threats* (4:21; 5:40). After hearing additional orders *not to speak* (5:28, 40), the apostles leave *rejoicing* that they have been *counted worthy of suffering disgrace for the Name*. Furthermore, the apostles continue *teaching and proclaiming the good news* not only *in the temple courts*, but also *house to house*. The increased hostility from the authorities does not stop the apostles. On the other hand, the apostles' continued teaching does not stop another increase in hostility; the death that was stayed by Gamaliel's advice looms on the horizon.

6:1–7 As he did previously, Luke places a narrative describing internal conflict after an external conflict narrative (3:1–4:31; 4:32–5:11). In this brief passage, Luke tells how some Jews who speak mainly Greek (see 6:2; 9:29) complain of mistreatment of their *widows*. The *Twelve* gather all the disciples together and ask them to *choose seven men from among yourselves who are known to be full of the Spirit and wisdom*. Given their primary role as witnesses (1:8, 22; 5:22), the apostles are unwilling *to neglect the ministry of the word of God in order to serve tables*. The proposal pleases the whole group, who choose *Stephen, a man full of faith and the Holy Spirit*; also *Philip, Procorus, Nicanor, Timon, Parmenas, and Nicolas from Antioch, a convert* (2:11; 6:5; 13:43) *to Judaism*. The first two names feature prominently in the immediate narrative: Stephen (6:8–8:3) and Philip (8:4–40). Although Luke does not mention the other five individuals again, it is worth noting that all seven have Greek names, indicating that Grecian Jews were chosen to oversee the daily distribution of food.

Should the seven be understood as the first deacons? On the one hand, the Greek noun *diakonia* (*distribution* in NIV; 6:1) and the verb *diakonein* (*wait on*; 6:2) describe the work that the seven do. On the other hand, the word *diakonos* ["servant, deacon"] is not used of the seven in Acts 6; the noun *diakonia* also describes work of the apostles (6:4); and later in Acts, two of the seven (Stephen and Philip) do work beyond table service. So, the presence of the words *diakonein* and *diakonia* does not necessarily make the seven "deacons." Actually, most translations rarely use the word "deacon" (Rom 16:1; Phil 1:1; 1 Tim 3:8, 12). Nevertheless, the possibility remains that the seven are deacons. Luke closes this section by noting that *a large number of priests* are among those who *became obedient to the faith*, indicating the extent to which Christianity is spreading (2:41, 47; 4:4; 5:14; 6:7; 9:31; 11:21, 24; 12:14; 14:1; 16:5; 19:20).

6:8–15 This passage begins the last of three consecutive cycles describing external opposition to Christianity (3:1–4:31; 5:12–42; 6:8–8:3). There are several new and distinctive features: the absence of an imprisonment (see 4:3; 5:18), opposition from the synagogue (6:9), and the production of false witnesses (6:11, 13). The most distinctive feature is the speech of Stephen, which is the longest speech in the book of Acts. As in the two previous cycles, miracles begin the narrative (6:8). Luke then describes opposition from the *Synagogue of the Freedmen*, which is composed of *Jews of Cyrene*

> **Synagogues in the First Century**
> In the first century, synagogues are known to have existed in Galilee and Jerusalem, at least. The building in Gamla in Galilee is particularly impressive. The "Theodotos Inscription," from a first century synagogue in Jerusalem, describes the organization as a place for prayer, hospitality to travelers, and community-building. The earliest literary texts mentioning synagogues come from the New Testament.

(2:10; 11:20; 13:1) *and Alexandria* as well as the provinces *of Cilicia* (21:39; 22:3; 23:34) *and Asia* (21:27; 24:19). Despite the NIV translation, it is also possible that Luke specifies five synagogues (see 24:12). Because these *men* cannot best Stephen in debate, they bring him before the Sanhedrin and produce *false witnesses*, who claim that Stephen speaks *against the holy place and against the law* (6:13; see 6:11; 21:28; 25:8).

7:1–53 Prompted by a question from the high priest (7:1), Stephen's speech divides into five sections: Abraham (7:2–8), Joseph (7:9–16), Moses (7:17–43), tabernacle/temple (7:44–50), and the conclusion (7:51–53). Peppering his speech with at least three quotations from Genesis (Gen 12:1 in Acts 7:3; Gen 48:4 in Acts 7:5; Gen 15:13–14 in Acts 7:6–7), Stephen begins his defense by demonstrating that he knows both Scripture and the "founding father" of Israel. Starting with the call of Abraham, Stephen then turns to the promise of a *land* (five times in 7:3–6) where Israel will *worship* God, only after centuries of slavery. The stress on the covenant of *circumcision* (7:8 twice) contrasts with the *uncircumcised hearts and ears* of the Sanhedrin later in the speech (7:51). The listing of Abraham's descendents down to the *patriarchs* (7:8–9) connects the Abraham section with the next section about Joseph.

Stephen retells the Joseph narrative (7:9–16) so that the hearers connect themselves to the story of Jesus. Like the Sadducees in the Sanhedrin (5:17) before and perhaps now, the *patriarchs were jealous* (7:9; see 13:45; 17:5) *of Joseph*. Like Jesus, Joseph is "rejected by his people … is empowered through God's intervention, and is now in a position to save the ones who rejected him" (Johnson 121).

In recounting the Moses narrative (7:17–43), Stephen emphasizes many details that parallel the life of Jesus so that those who rejected Moses act like those who now reject Jesus. Notice the following seven parallels: Moses' *birth* coincides with the fulfillment of God's *promise* (7:17, 20); a ruler tries to kill *newborn babies* (7:19), but Moses escapes; Moses grows in *wisdom* (7:22; compare Luke 2:40, 52); Moses is *powerful in speech and action* (7:22; Luke 24:19); Moses *visits* his people to *rescue* them (7:23, 25); Moses leaves his own people (7:29); and Moses is sent back to be *their ruler and deliverer*, but the *fathers refuse to obey him* (7:35, 39). Therefore, God exiles them (Amos 5:25–27 in Acts 7:42–43).

Stephen then turns to a discussion of the *tabernacle* (7:44–50). Stephen argues that from the time in the *desert* to the time of *David our forefathers* had the tabernacle. In time, *Solomon* builds the *house* for God, but *the Most High does not live in houses made by men*. Stephen quotes the prophet Isaiah to prove his point: *Or where will my resting place be? Has not my hand made all these things?* (Isa 66:1–2). In other words, God has already made a house for himself.

Stephen concludes with the string of five charges against his hearers: they are a *stiff-necked people*, with *uncircumcised* (see 7:8) *hearts and ears*; they *act just like* their *fathers* (7:9, 39; see Luke 11:47); they *resist the Holy Spirit*; they *betrayed and murdered* Jesus; and they have *not obeyed* the law. Luke shows Stephen speaking with great boldness, as did the apostles before him (compare 4:29).

7:54–8:1A Luke closes the story of Stephen with a description of the hearers' reaction, with three statements by Stephen, and with two asides about Saul. The hearers are *furious* (5:33; 7:54) and gnash their teeth. Stephen's first statement (*I see heaven open and the Son of Man standing at the right hand of God*) prompts a flurry of activity from his hearers; they cover their *ears*, yell *at the top of their voices*, rush at Stephen (19:29), drag *him out of the city* (Luke 4:29), and *begin to stone* him. Luke reveals that clothes are *laid at the feet of a young man named Saul* and that Saul gives *approval* (22:20; compare Luke 11:48) of Stephen's *death*. With this first mention of Saul, Luke foreshadows the role Saul, later named Paul, will play in the spread of the gospel.

> **Stephen's Last Words**
> *Stephen's last two statements are prayers*: Lord Jesus, receive my spirit *and* Lord, do not hold this sin against them (*compare Luke 23:43*).

While contemporary readers might find Stephen's speech an attack on the law or the temple, this could hardly be Luke's intention. Rather, as a careful read of texts from the Dead Sea Scrolls or the early rabbis would show, polemics between members of the same religion often take on the strong flavor that Acts 7 shows. In fact, Stephen's attitude toward the Old Testament and the temple is high: he opposes corruption of them.

8:1B-3 Luke briefly summarizes the beginning of persecution in Jerusalem, the end of Stephen's story, and Saul's role in the persecution. A *great persecution* breaks out *against the church at Jerusalem* on the day of Stephen's death. *Except for the apostles*, Christians are scattered *throughout all Judea and Samaria*, thus beginning the spread of the gospel beyond Jerusalem outlined in Acts 1:8. *Godly men bury* and *mourn* deeply for Stephen. Saul drags off *men and women* (5:14; 8:3, 12; 9:2; 17:4, 12, 34; 22:4) and puts them in *prison* (4:3; 5:18; 8:3; 12:1; 16:37).

WITNESSES IN JUDEA & SAMARIA · 8:4–9:43

The second phase of the spread of the gospel is the shortest as the gospel moves outside the city of Jerusalem into the province of Judea and the region of Samaria. Philip first brings the gospel to Samaria; Peter and John later preach in Samaritan villages (8:25). The gospel then comes to an Ethiopian through the witness of Philip (8:26–40). Saul comes to faith in

Acts 9. Peter travels through Lydda and Joppa, where the gospel has already arrived (9:32–43).

8:4–8 Luke begins a long section connected by the person of *Philip* (8:4–40; compare 6:5; 21:8). This first part (8:4–8) summarizes Philip's activity. *Scattered* by the persecution in Jerusalem, Philip goes to *a city in Samaria* and preaches the message of *Christ*. Philip also performs *miraculous signs* (4:30; 5:12; 6:8), three of which Luke names: the casting out of *evil spirits* (5:16; 8:7) and the healing of *paralytics* (8:7; 9:33) and *cripples* (3:2; 8:7; 14:8).

8:9–25 Though still present in this section (8:12–13), Philip fades into the background, and the story of *Simon* dominates the narrative. Luke tells about the conversion of Simon (8:9–13) and the interaction between Simon, and Peter and John (8:14–25). Luke gives some details about Simon in the opening verses: Simon *practiced sorcery, amazed all the people of Samaria*, and *boasted that he was someone great*. The *people* of the city, however, *believe* Philip's preaching and are *baptized*; Simon too converts and then follows *Philip*, amazed at his *miracles*.

After hearing about the conversion of Samaria, the *apostles* send *Peter and John*, who *pray* that the believers might *receive the Holy Spirit* (8:15, 17, 19), which is somewhat odd since the gift of the Holy Spirit comes at baptism in Acts 2:38. One notices, however, that as the gospel spreads to new peoples – Samaritans in Acts 8, Gentiles in Acts 10, and disciples of John the Baptist in Acts – the Holy Spirit is a consistent feature confirming the new direction that the gospel spreads. The Samaritans receive the Holy Spirit when *Peter and John* lay *their hands* (8:17, 18, 19) on them. When Simon sees that the Spirit comes by *the laying on of the apostles' hands*, he offers Peter and John *money*, resulting in a rebuke by Peter. Peter then calls on Simon to *repent* and *pray* because Simon's *heart* is *full of bitterness and captive to sin*. Simon asks that they *pray to the Lord* for him so that *nothing* may happen to him. Peter and John return to Jerusalem, *preaching the gospel in many Samaritan villages*. Along with the account of Ananias and Sapphira, this account shows a negative example of the early church's use of possessions.

> **Christianity & Magic**
> Acts 8 depicts the spread of the gospel to a new group of people and Christianity's conflict with magic (8:11). *This account is the first of Christianity's many encounters with magic in Acts; in each account, Luke distinguishes Christianity from magic and shows that Christianity is more powerful.*

8:26–40 Philip again moves into the foreground with this passage, which shows God's promises being fulfilled in the conversion of the *Ethiopian eunuch*. Eunuchs were excluded from worshiping with God's people (Deut 23:1). Isaiah, however, envisions a time when God will *bring* both *eunuchs* and *foreigners* to his *holy mountain* and *give them joy* in his *house of prayer* (Isa 56:3–8); *Ethiopia* (*Cush*) is specifically mentioned in a listing of those foreigners in another oracle (Isa 11:11–12). Luke's account unfolds in three parts: the angel's command and Philip's meeting (8:26–28), the encounter between Philip and the eunuch (8:29–35), and the conclusion (8:36–40).

The angel of the Lord (5:19; 8:26; 12:7, 8, 11, 23; compare 10:3, 7, 22; 11:13; 27:23) tells Philip to go south to *Gaza*, a city located about three miles from the Mediterranean coast and about 50 miles southwest of Jerusalem. Philip obeys and meets an *Ethiopian eunuch* who is *an important official in charge of all the treasury of Candace, queen of the Ethiopians*. After going to *Jerusalem to worship*, the eunuch is returning to Ethiopia and *sitting in his chariot reading the book of Isaiah the prophet*. Luke's characterization of the eunuch is important because it shows Luke's interest in high status converts to Christianity. Notice these five high status features of Luke's description: the eunuch has leisure time to travel from Ethiopia to Jerusalem and back; he has the position of treasurer in Ethiopia; he can read; he can afford a personal copy of Isaiah; and his chariot is large enough to seat at least three people (8:31, 38).

Like Philip's first appearance on the road (8:26) and last appearance with the eunuch (8:39), his encounter with the eunuch is divinely prompted. Although Philip's initial command comes from an *angel* (8:26), and his encounter and departure are connected with the *Spirit* (8:29, 39), all three events show God's initiative in spreading the gospel, which is also connected with Philip's actions showing the joint work of redemption typical in Acts. Philip runs up to the chariot, hears the man *reading Isaiah the prophet*, and asks him a question: *Do you understand what you are reading*? The eunuch invites Philip to *sit with him*, and the two discuss Isaiah 53:7–8. From that *passage*, Philip tells the eunuch the *good news about Jesus*. When they come *to some water*, the eunuch asks to receive baptism (8:37; 10:47; 11:17). After ordering the *chariot to stop*, Philip and the eunuch go *down into the water*, and Philip *baptizes* him. Luke spends considerable time describing this conversion, the second of at least eight in Acts, because of his interest in the theme of salvation. The *Spirit* takes Philip away to *Azotus* (a town about 20 miles north of Gaza); this description parallels the descriptions of the prophet Elijah (1 Kgs 18:9–12; 2 Kgs 1:15–16) and shows that the divine power at work with Elijah is at work in the church through Philip. From Azotus, Philip travels north about 55 miles, preaching the *gospel in all the towns*; he settles in the coastal town of *Cæsarea* where he later appears in Acts with his *four daughters* (21:8).

9:1–19A Starting in Jerusalem, the gospel spreads throughout the city reaching both outsiders, such as a crippled beggar (3:2–6), and insiders, such as priests (6:7). Outside Jerusalem, the gospel spreads to Samaritans and a eunuch from Ethiopia (8:4–40). Now, the gospel reaches the ultimate outsider, the one who has been persecuting the church (8:1–3), Saul himself. The importance of this story is clear since Luke tells it three times (Acts 9, 22, 26) and since Saul/Paul becomes the main character in the latter half of the book. The story of Saul's conversion falls into four parts: introduction (9:1–2), Saul's encounter with Jesus (9:3–9), Ananias's encounter with the Lord (9:10–16), and the responses of Ananias and Saul (9:17–19a). Luke introduces Saul's conversion by describing Saul's preparation to arrest Christians in Damascus. *Still breathing out murderous threats* (compare 4:17, 21, 29; 22:4; 26:10), Saul goes to the *high priest* asking *for letters to the synagogues in Damascus, so that if he found any of the Way…he might take them as prisoners to Jerusalem.*

Saul's encounter with Jesus has two components: a light and a voice. After *a light from heaven* flashes around Saul, he *falls to the ground*. A voice asks Saul: *Why do you persecute me?* Then, the voice identifies himself as *Jesus whom you are persecuting.* Finally, the voice instructs Saul to enter Damascus and await instructions.

Luke describes the results of this encounter. *The men traveling with Saul* hear the voice, but do not see anyone (see 22:9). *Blind*, Saul is *led by the hand* (9:8; compare 13:11) *into Damascus*, where *for three days he did not eat or drink anything.*

The disciple *Ananias* (9:10, 12, 13, 17; 22:12) also has an encounter with the divine in a *vision* (10:3, 17, 19; 11:5; 12:9; 16:9; 18:9) that results in three exchanges between him and the *Lord*. First, the Lord calls to Ananias, and Ananias answers. Second, the Lord instructs Ananias to visit Saul, who is waiting for him to *restore his sight*. Understandably, Ananias is reluctant because he knows about the *harm* that Saul has *done in Jerusalem* and that Saul has come to Damascus to *arrest* those who *call on your name/the name of the Lord*, an expression that means believe in the Lord (see Joel 3:5; Acts 2:21; 9:14, 21; 22:16; Rom 10:11–13). Third, the Lord advises Ananias that Saul will be *my chosen instrument to carry my name before the Gentiles and their kings* (25:13–26:32; compare 25:11–12, 21, 25; 26:32; 27:24; 28:19) *and before the people of Israel. I will show him how much he must suffer for my name.* This third statement encapsulates Paul's story in Acts by describing his call and the consequences of that call; Paul will take the gospel to Gentiles and Jews, and he will experience many trials.

9:19B–31 This passage tells about Saul's immediate response to his calling in two parallel accounts, one set in Damascus and the other in Jerusalem: Saul preaches, some opponents try to kill Saul, and the church aids Saul's escape. A brief summary (9:31) provides a transition to the material about Peter. *At once*, Saul begins to *preach in the synagogues* (9:20; 13:14; 14:1; 17:1–2, 10, 17; 18:4, 19; 19:8; compare 16:13; 18:26) of *Damascus* that *Jesus is the Son of God*. The hearers are *astonished* because Saul came to Damascus to take Christians *as prisoners to the chief priests*. Because Saul grows *more and more powerful* in his

> **Early Christian Worship & Identity**
> *It is worth nothing that at this point in the history of Christianity, Christians were still worshiping in synagogues and that they called themselves* the Way *(9:2; 19:9, 23; 22:4; 24:14, 22); it is not until later that disciples were first called* Christians *(11:26).*

> **The Conversion of Saul**
> *The stories of Saul and Ananias converge in 9:17–19. Ananias goes to the* house *of Judas, lays his* hands *on Saul, and tells Saul that Jesus sent him so that Saul could* see again *and* be filled with the Holy Spirit. *Saul regains his sight,* arises, *is* baptized, *eats some* food, *and regains his* strength. *With this flurry of activity the conversion of Saul is complete; now he is ready to undertake his new calling.*

presentation of the gospel, some Jews devise a *plan* (9:24; compare 9:29; 20:3, 19; 23:16, 30) to *kill* (9:23, 24, 29) him. Even though the conspirators *watch the city gates*, the church helps Saul escape by lowering him *in a basket through an opening in the wall* (2 Cor 11:32–33) of the city *at night* (9:25; 17:10; 23:31).

In *Jerusalem*, the same pattern occurs with minor variations. Saul attempts to *join the disciples* there. Understandably, they are *afraid* and do *not believe* that he really is a disciple. *Barnabas*, however, brings Saul *to the apostles* and tells about Saul's experience of the *Lord on his journey* and how in Damascus Saul preached *fearlessly* (9:27, 28) *in the name of Jesus*. As an advocate for Saul, Barnabas here lives up to the earlier description of him as a *Son of Encouragement* (4:36; 9:27; 11:23; 15:36–39). Saul lives up to Barnabas' expectations, by teaching Greek-speaking Jews, the same ones who had contributed to Stephen's death (6:9–14) and now try to *kill* Saul. The church learns about the plot, takes Saul to the coastal city and provincial capital of *Cæsarea*, and sends him to *Tarsus* (9:11, 30; 11:25; 21:39; 22:3), Saul's hometown located in modern Turkey. After Saul's departure, the *church throughout Judea, Galilee, and Samaria* (see the formula in 1:8) enjoys a time of *peace* and growth.

9:32–43 The final two accounts in Acts 9 depict Peter's healing of Aeneas and the raising of Dorcas, showing the *signs and wonders* typical of the apostles (4:30; 5:12) and setting up the story of Cornelius by placing Peter in *Joppa* (9:36, 38, 42, 43; 10:5, 8, 23, 32; 11:5, 13). Luke also connects both stories with the command to arise (9:34, 40). Traveling about, Peter visits the *saints* (9:32, 41) in *Lydda*, a town about 24 miles northwest of Jerusalem. He heals a man named *Aeneas, a paralytic* (8:7; 9:33; compare Luke 5:18, 24) *who had been bedridden for eight years*. The healing results in the conversions of those living in the town of *Lydda* and the coastal region of *Sharon*, which encompasses about 30 miles of a plain from just north of Cæsarea south almost to Joppa.

As he does in his gospel, Luke pairs the story of a man with that of a woman (see the conclusion of the commentary on Luke), showing his interest in depicting women impacting the history of the church. Luke translates the Aramaic name *Tabitha* into the Greek equivalent *Dorcas*, both names meaning "antelope" or "gazelle." After Dorcas's death, disciples send *two men* (see 10:7) to Peter asking him to come to *Joppa*, a town about 10 miles away. Peter comes, prays (9:40; 28:9), tells Tabitha to arise, and presents her alive to the *believers and widows*. As with Aeneas, many *believe*. Peter remains in Joppa with *a tanner named Simon*, setting up the story of Cornelius in Acts 10. These stories contain echoes of the activity of the prophets Elijah and Elisha and the ministry of Jesus, showing that the same power at work in them is also at work in Peter and later in Paul (20:7–12) (Johnson 180).

WITNESSES TO THE ENDS OF THE EARTH · 10:1–28:31

The third part of Luke's account is the longest, telling the story of the gospel's coming to the Gentiles and spreading across the Roman Empire. The gospel first comes to the Gentiles through Peter's preaching to Cornelius in Cæsarea (10:1–11:18). Those scattered by the persecution after Stephen's death preach the gospel in Phoenicia, Cyprus, and Antioch (11:19), anticipating the role that the church at Antioch will play in the spread of the gospel. Others preach to Greeks in Antioch (11:20). Acts 12 returns the action back to Jerusalem. In Acts 13, Luke begins his use of Paul as the lens through which to view the spread of

> **"The ends of the earth …"**
> The phrase ends of the earth in Acts 1:8 alludes to Isaiah 49:6, where those words are parallel to Gentiles (see also Isa 49:6 in Acts 13:47).

the gospel. Luke, however, includes a number of stops before the gospel finally reaches Rome. Barnabas and Paul preach in Cyprus and Asia Minor and return to Antioch (13:1–14:28). In Jerusalem, the church decides about requirements for Gentile Christians (Acts 15:1–35). Paul and Silas spread the gospel in Asia Minor, Macedonia, Athens, and Corinth (15:41–18:22). After a brief stop back at the home church in Antioch, Paul again leaves to preach in Ephesus, Macedonia, and Achaia (18:23–20:38). Paul does not make it back to Antioch because he is arrested in Jerusalem (21:27–40). He remains in prison, first in Jerusalem then in Cæsarea (22:1–26:32), until his trip to Rome (27:1–28:10). With Paul's arrival in Rome (28:11–31), the gospel has reached the Gentiles in the political and cultural heart of the Roman Empire.

10:1–8 This section contains a description of Cornelius (10:1–2), his vision (10:3–6), and his response to the vision (10:7–8). Luke locates *Cornelius* at *Cæsarea*, the capital of the province of Judea. Cornelius is a *centurion*, a soldier in charge of 100 men; he serves *in the Italian Regiment* (10:1; see 27:1). Luke depicts the piety of Cornelius in generous terms: *He and all his family were devout and God-fearing; he gave generously to those in need and prayed to God regularly*. It is not surprising that Luke mentions Cornelius's use of possessions and his habit of praying, since both topics are important throughout his two-volume work. In Cornelius's *vision*, an *angel* addresses him, and Cornelius answers: *What is it, Lord?* After commending Cornelius's *prayers* and *gifts to the poor* (10:2, 4), the angel instructs him to *send men to Joppa* (9:36, 38, 42, 43; 10:5, 8 23, 32; 11:5, 13) to bring back *Peter*. Cornelius responds by calling *two of his servants and one of his soldiers*, telling them *everything*, and sending them *to Joppa*. Luke shows the joint nature of God's initiative and Cornelius's obedient response.

10:9–23A Luke divides this passage into two parts: Peter's vision (10:9–16) and Peter's meeting with the messengers (10:17–23a). Peter's vision takes place *about noon the following day* when he goes *on the roof to pray*. In a *trance* (compare 10:10, 17; 11:5), Peter sees *heaven opened and something like a large sheet being let down to earth by its four corners*. It contains *all kinds of four-footed animals, as well as reptiles of the earth and birds of the air*. A *voice* tells Peter: *Get up, Peter. Kill and eat*. Peter declines, citing his faithfulness to biblical dietary law, but the voice replies, *Do not call anything impure that God has made clean*. Peter's refusal to eat reflects Jewish dietary restrictions about eating certain kinds of animals deemed *unclean* (Lev 11:1–47; Deut 14:1–21).

While Peter was *wondering about the meaning of the vision*, the men sent by Cornelius arrive. Luke shows the active role of the Holy Spirit in this encounter (8:29; 10:19; 11:12; 13:2; 21:11). The Spirit instructs Peter to *go with them, for I have sent them*. As this section ends, Peter tells the men who he is; the men tell Peter why they have come; and Peter invites *the men into the house to be his guests*.

10:23B-48 Luke divides this part of his narrative into three scenes: Peter's meeting with Cornelius (10:23b-33), Peter's sermon (10:34–43), and the coming of the Holy Spirit (10:44–48). *The next day*, Peter leaves with the messengers from Cornelius and *some of the brothers from Joppa* (10:23; 11:12). *On the following day*, Peter meets Cornelius who has *called together his relatives and close friends*. Cornelius falls at Peter's feet, but Peter makes him get up (10:25–26; compare 12:22–23; 14:11–15). Peter explains that God has shown him *not to call any man impure or unclean*. Peter asks why he was sent for, and Cornelius retells his encounter with and instructions from *a man in shining clothes* (see 10:3, 30). Cornelius invites Peter to speak, which introduces Peter's sermon.

The *Holy Spirit* (10:44, 45, 47) soon interrupts Peter's sermon by coming *on all who heard the message*. As in Acts 2 with the Jews, in Acts 8 with the Samaritans, here in Acts 10 with the Gentiles, and in Acts 19 with the disciples of John the Baptist, the coming of the Holy Spirit confirms the inclusion of a new people. Peter draws this conclusion and reiterates it several times in the later narrative: *they have received the Holy Spirit just as we have* (10:47; 11:15, 17; 15:8). Furthermore, one notices that the *speaking in tongues and praising God* roughly parallel the Spirit's activity in the other accounts (compare 2:4, 6, 8, 11, 47; 10:46; 19:6). Peter thus concludes that there is not anything *to keep these people from being baptized*. After being baptized, these new believers in Cæsarea (18:22; 21:16), who perhaps later join Philip (8:40; 21:8), invite Peter *to stay with them for a few days*. In this way, Cornelius ushers in a wave of Gentile converts into the church.

> **Peter's Sermon to Cornelius**
> Peter's sermon to Cornelius has several noteworthy features. With his first words, Peter connects the Gentiles to the gospel (verses 2, 22, 35) as potentially moral people (verses 22, 35). Peter continues with a concise summary of the message of the gospel, for which the apostles serve as witnesses (10:39, 41, 42) along with the prophets who testify (10:43) that everyone who believes in him receives forgiveness of sins.

11:1–18 In the Gospel of Luke, Jesus' comment on the faith of another centurion (Luke 7:1–10) sets the stage for readers of Acts's story of the conversion of Cornelius the centurion. The retelling of Cornelius's story in Acts 11 indicates that readers needed assistance working through both the issue of the inclusion of Gentiles and the implications of that inclusion. Luke presents the first criticism of Cornelius's conversion through the words of *the circumcised believers* (11:2; compare 15:5) *in Jerusalem* who confront Peter: *You went into the house of uncircumcised men and ate with them*. Table fellowship is a cause of tension in the first century because it assumes fellowship and agreement among those eating together (Luke 5:27–30; Gal 2:11–13). Luke's treatment proceeds as follows: criticism of Peter (11:1–3), Peter's retelling of God's activity and his experience (11:4–17), and the resolution (11:18).

By specifying the various ways that divine activity permeates Peter's retelling, Luke confirms that the inclusion of the Gentiles came by God's initiative with Peter as God's instrument. In his response, Peter makes three appeals. First, the Holy Spirit came on the Gentiles just as on the Jews *at the beginning* (11:16), showing a common experience between Jews and Gentiles. Second, Peter quotes the words of Jesus (11:16), not found previously in the first account in Acts 10 but in Acts 1:5, showing that the inclusion of the Gentiles fulfills Jesus' words. Third, Peter asks: *So if God gave them the same gift as he gave us, who believed in the Lord Jesus Christ, who was I to think that I could oppose God?* This rhetorical question, based on God's activity and a shared human experience, leaves little room to draw another conclusion. Peter's speech results in a threefold resolution. The opponents have *no further objections*; they *praise God*; and they conclude: *So then, God has even granted the Gentiles repentance unto life*. For now, the issue is at rest; Luke, however, will deal with further complications regarding the Gentiles in Acts 15.

> **God's Activity among the Gentiles**
>
> Acts 10 and 11 mention six kinds of divine activity: *a vision* (10:3, 17, 19; 11:5), *a trance* (10:10; 11:5), *a voice* (10:13, 15; 11:7), *an angel* (10:3, 7, 22; 11:13), *the Holy Spirit* (10:19, 44, 45, 47; 11:12, 15), and the direct mention of *God* (10:3, 15, 28, 33, 34; 11:9, 17). These signs of God's activity confirm the legitimacy of including the Gentiles.

11:19–30 Luke introduces the church in Antioch (see 6:5), which is going to play a pivotal role in the spread of the gospel (13:1–3; 14:26; 15:40; 18:22–23). The passage divides into four vignettes: more Gentiles convert in Antioch (11:19–21); Jerusalem sends Barnabas to Antioch (11:22–24); Paul ministers in Antioch (11:25–26); and the church in Antioch ministers to Judea (11:27–30). Some of those *scattered by the persecution in connection with Stephen* (8:1, 4) travel *as far as Phoenicia* (11:19; 15:3; 21:2; 27:3), *Cyprus* (4:36; 11:19; 13:4–12; 15:36; 21:16), *and Antioch* (13:1–3), *telling the message only to Jews*. Others, however, *men from Cyprus and Cyrene* (2:10; 6:9; 11:20) go to Antioch and speak to *Greeks too*. So, the conversion of Gentiles begun by Peter in Cæsarea continues in the city of Antioch. God's blessing of this work is seen in Luke's summary: *The Lord's hand was with them, and a great number of people believed and turned to the Lord*.

When these conversion stories reached Jerusalem, the church there sends *Barnabas* (4:36; 9:27; 11:22–30; 12:25; 13:1–15:41), who, upon seeing *evidence of the grace of God*, *encourages* the church in Antioch. Luke concludes with a description of Barnabas's character (*He was a good man, full of the Holy Spirit and faith*) and with a report on the church in Antioch (*a great number of people were brought to the Lord*).

At this point, Luke reintroduces Saul into the narrative. For his own protection, he had gone to Tarsus at the advice of the church in Jerusalem (9:30). Barnabas goes to Tarsus, finds Saul, and brings him back to Antioch. *For a whole year Barnabas and Saul* meet with the church in Antioch and teach *great numbers of people*, foreshadowing the success of their upcoming journey together (13:1–3). Luke ends by noting that *the disciples were first called Christians at Antioch*. The self-designation of the earliest Christians seems to have been the Way (9:2; 19:9, 23; 22:4; 24:14).

In the last vignette, Luke tells about one of the *prophets* (2:17; 11:27; 13:1; 15:32; 21:9) who comes *down from Jerusalem to Antioch*. Through the Spirit, *Agabus* (11:28; 21:10) predicts that *a severe famine would spread over the entire Roman world*. Luke dates the famine to *the reign of Claudius* (11:28; 18:2), who ruled from 41–54 CE. As an example of a good use of possessions, the disciples at Antioch aid the Judean disciples. They send *their gift to the elders by Barnabas and Saul* (11:30; 12:25).

12:1–19A Chapter 12 is a mixture of the familiar and the new. The church continues to experience opposition, women continue to figure in the life of the church, and Christians continue to pray. However, deadly opposition now reaches the Twelve for the first time, and that opposition comes not from Jewish religious leaders, but from a leader serving the Roman government. Throughout Acts 12, Luke's theme of reversal holds these various threads together; at the onset, James is dead, Peter is in prison, the angel *strikes* Peter (12:7), and King Herod is powerful. At the end of the chapter, Herod is dead, Peter is free, the angel strikes Herod (12:23), and the word of God is powerful (12:24; Stott 213).

Acts 12:1–5 describes the plight of the church. As the narrative begins, Herod arrests *James, the brother* of John, and executes him at Passover. The timing echoes Jesus' death and casts an ominous shadow across the passage. The mention of *four squads of four soldiers* stresses the apparently hopeless context in which Luke describes the church as *earnestly praying to God* for Peter.

> **Herod Agrippa**
> King Herod is also known as Herod Agrippa I. Although he only appears here in this passage, he has connections with a number of other people in the New Testament. He is the grandson of Herod the Great (Matt 2:1–22; Luke 1:5), the son of Aristobulus, and the brother of Herodias (Luke 3:19–20), as well as the father of Herod Agrippa II (Acts 25:13–26:32), Bernice (Acts 25:13, 23; 26:30), and Drusilla (Acts 24:24).

Luke recounts Peter's release in 12:6–11. On the night before his *trial*, Peter sleeps *between two soldiers, bound with two chains* (21:33); two other *sentries* stand guard. Peter's apparent calm may reflect the apostles' prayer for boldness in the face of opposition (4:29) or his memory of a previous release from prison (5:17–20); the latter seems less likely since Peter later thinks his release is not real but a *vision* (12:9). Luke stresses the divine aspects of Peter's release: an *angel of the Lord* appears, the *chains* fall off, they pass *the first and second guards*, and the *iron gate* opens *by itself*. Only after this series of events does Peter recognize God's role in the rescue (verse 11).

Luke records the response of the church in 12:12–19a. Peter goes to the *house of Mary the mother of John, also called Mark*, because he apparently expects to find the church gathered there. It follows, then, that Mary functions as the host of a house church in Jerusalem, as does Lydia in Philippi (Acts 16:40), Nympha (Col 4:15), and Prisca and Aquila in Rome (Rom 16:3–5) and Ephesus (1 Cor 16:19). Luke's mention of Mary reveals a role that women played in the life of the church. Mary also appears to serve Luke's apologetic purpose, showing a Christian of high status. Mary not only has a *servant girl named Rhoda*, but also a house large enough for *many people* and for Rhoda to run from the outer entrance to the gathering inside. Luke's passing reference to *John* (12:12) foreshadows the role that John will play later in Acts (12:25; 13:5, 13; 15:37, 39). Although it is noteworthy that Luke describes the church *praying* (12:5, 12), the joyful response of *Rhoda* contrasts with the church's doubt-filled response to Rhoda's news (verse 15: *You're out of your mind*) and its astonishment at seeing Peter (verse 16). Luke stresses that prayer must be accompanied by belief. Peter credits his escape to the *Lord* (verse 17), which fits with Luke's emphasis on divine activity in 12:6–11. Peter's instructions to tell *James and the brothers* anticipate the role of James, the brother of Jesus; James has two speeches later in Acts (15:13–21; compare 21:20–25).

Luke concludes the events in Jerusalem with the response of the soldiers and Herod. Peter's release causes *a great commotion among the soldiers* because they know that a soldier who loses his prisoner is subject to death (16:27; 27:42), a sentence that Herod commands after a cross-examination of the guard.

12:19B-25 The final scene takes place in Cæsarea, where Luke describes the response of God to Herod. Luke links this scene and the previous scene (12:1–19a) with *an angel of the Lord* who, this time, *strikes* Herod (12:7, 23). The context in Cæsarea involves a conflict between Herod and *the people of Tyre and Sidon*, who seek an audience with Herod through his personal servant *Blastus*. Luke, however, focuses on the conflict between God and Herod, who has killed James, arrested Peter, and now neglects to *give praise to God* when the people in Cæsarea shout, *This is the voice of a god, not of a man*. In the end, Herod is destroyed by *worms*, but the *word of God* continues to *increase and spread*. Acts 12 concludes with a report about the activity of Barnabas, Saul, and John Mark (compare 11:27–30). Unfortunately, there are two readings in the Greek texts (namely, *to Jerusalem* and *from Jerusalem*), between which it is extremely difficult to decide; it is clear, however, that the report in 12:25 provides a transition to Acts 13 where all three individuals play key roles.

13:1–3 These verses describe the composition and discernment of the church at Antioch. Given the outreach to Greeks in Antioch (11:19–26), it is perhaps not surprising to note the diversity in the church at Antioch. Luke names five *prophets and teachers* at Antioch (see 11:29; 15:32). *Barnabas*, a *Levite* from *Cyprus* and

> **Antioch**
> Founded around 300 BCE by Seleucus I, Antioch in the first century was the capital of the province of Syria and the third largest city in the Roman Empire, with a population of about 500,000. Its ethnic and cultural diversity made it an obvious location for the growth of an international religion like Christianity.

familiar from previous passages in Acts (4:36; 9:27; 11:22–30; 12:25), will go on to play a major role in the initial spread of the gospel into Asia Minor. *Simeon*, who is only mentioned here in the New Testament, also has the Latin name *Niger* (compare 1:23; 12:15); because *Simeon* reflects a Hebrew name (see Simon), he is likely Jewish; *Niger* refers to someone who is "dark-complexioned" (Danker 672; Josephus, *Jewish War*, 2.520). *Lucius* comes from *Cyrene* (Luke 23:26; Acts 2:10; 6:9), the capital city of the Roman province Cyrenaica, located in North Africa. Lucius may be one of those from Cyrene who went to Antioch and spoke to Greeks (11:20). Luke describes *Manaen* as one *brought up with Herod the tetrarch*, meaning Herod Antipas. Unfortunately, nothing more is known about *Manaen* or his relationship to Herod Antipas. The fifth person mentioned is *Saul*, who has come most recently from a mission in Jerusalem after a yearlong stay in Antioch (11:25–30; 12:25).

The *Holy Spirit* tells the church, perhaps through one of the prophets (see 8:29; 11:12; 13:1; 21:11): *Set apart for me Barnabas and Saul*. This call is preceded by the church *worshiping* and *fasting*, as they seek discernment. The commission of Barnabas and Saul occurs in the midst of *fasting* and *prayer* (14:23), and then concludes with the laying of *hands* (6:6; 13:3) on Barnabas and Saul.

13:4–12 Barnabas and Saul travel from Antioch to the port city of *Seleucia*, located about five miles inland on the Orontes River. From Seleucia, they sail to the island of *Cyprus*, both the homeland of Barnabas (4:36) and of those Christians who first spoke to Greeks in Antioch (11:20). The first stop on Cyprus is the city of *Salamis*, where Barnabas and Saul, along with *John as their helper* preach in *the Jewish synagogues*.

They next travel across the island to *Paphos*, the capital city, where Luke recounts Christianity's second major encounter with magic in the person of *a Jewish sorcerer named Bar-Jesus*. Luke relates several details about this sorcerer: he is *an attendant of the proconsul*, he has another name (*Elymas*), although the explanation of his name seems lost to modern interpreters, and he tries to *turn the proconsul from the faith*. At stake is the proconsul *Sergius Paulus*, who functions as the governor of the province of Cyprus. The sorcerer's opposition brings a rebuke and a curse of blindness from Saul (see 9:8). Two factors are noteworthy. First, before the rebuke and curse, Luke says that Saul is *filled with the Holy Spirit*. In other words, the curse is not a personal vendetta by Saul, but divine punishment. Second, the punishment is limited (*for a time*). The confrontation results in the blindness of Elymas and the conversion of Sergius Paulus. This second encounter with magic both shows the power of Christianity over magic and distinguishes Christianity from magic.

13:13–52 Barnabas and Paul next enter Asia Minor, where they remain until they return to their home church in Antioch of Syria (14:26–28). The first few verses (13:13–14) briefly relate their itinerary: Cyprus to Perga in Pamphylia to Pisidian Antioch. In *Perga*, which lies about 12 miles from the Mediterranean coast, *John* leaves Barnabas and Paul and returns to his home in *Jerusalem* (12:12). Although John's reason for leaving is unstated, his departure will be a source of contention later in the narrative (15:36–41). After this brief itinerary, Paul's sermon to the synagogue in Antioch dominates the rest of the chapter (13:16–41).

Paul opens the sermon with a recounting of God's activity among the people of Israel, from the exodus to the possession of the *land* to life under the *judges*, *Samuel*, *Saul*, and *David* (13:16–22). With the mention of David, Paul then describes Jesus as one of David's *descendents* and as the fulfillment of God's *promise*. The *message of salvation* begins with *John* the Baptist, encounters opposition by *the people of Jerusalem and their rulers*, includes Jesus' death under *Pilate*, culminates in *God* raising Jesus *from the dead*, and is now proclaimed by the *witnesses* who traveled with Jesus *from Galilee to Jerusalem* (13:23–31). Paul concludes in 13:31–41 with a series of three scriptures that also function as witnesses to this fulfillment of God's promises (Ps 2:7; Isa 55:3; Ps 16:10) and one passage that functions as a warning (Hab 1:5) *that what the prophets have said does not happen to* them.

Luke records the various responses to Paul's sermon in the remaining verses (13:42–52). Initially, the response is positive: Paul and Barnabas receive invitations to speak again, and *many of the Jews and devout converts to Judaism followed Paul and Barnabas*. On the next Sabbath, however, when the *whole city* gathers to listen, the *Jews* are filled with *jealousy* (5:17; 7:9; 17:5) and

> **Roman Proconsuls**
> *Since proconsuls were selected from a pool of former senators, Sergius Paulus, upon his conversion, became the Christian with the highest social status mentioned in the New Testament.*

talk *abusively against what Paul was saying*. This response prompts Paul and Barnabas to *turn to the Gentiles* (compare 18:6; 28:28), citing Isaiah 49:6 as support (see 1:8), which makes the Gentiles *glad and honored*, and causes the Jews to stir up (14:2) *persecution against Paul and Barnabas*, who shake the *dust from their feet in protest* (compare 18:6; Luke 9:5) and pass to *Iconium*.

14:1–7 Traveling southeast about 80 miles from Antioch, Paul and Barnabas enter *Iconium*. Although Luke's account is brief and functions primarily as a transition to the much longer account of the events at Lystra, this report connects a number of previous themes and anticipates others. As is typical with Paul's preaching in Acts, his proclamation begins in a *synagogue* (13:14; 14:1; 17:1–2, 10, 17; 18:4, 19; 19:8; compare 16:13; 18:26). At the same time, Luke emphasizes the universal scope of the gospel by noting that *a great number of Jews and Gentiles* [literally "Greeks"; 18:4; 19:10; 20:21] believe. Again, the Jews *stir up* (13:50) problems for Paul and Barnabas. Nevertheless, Paul and Barnabas spend *a considerable time* in Iconium. Luke often notes the length of Paul's stays, emphasizing his commitment to his converts, in contrast to some traveling philosophers and hucksters in the first century (9:23; 11:26; 14:3, 28; 16:39–40; 18:11, 18, 23; 19:8, 10, 22; 20:3, 31). The result is that the city is *divided*, a response that occurs again (23:7) and fits with Luke's view of what the message of Jesus does (Luke 2:34). The desire of some to *stone* Paul and Barnabas anticipates the actual stoning in the next account at *Lystra* (14:19).

14:8–20 The events at Lystra echo earlier accounts: parts of the healing at Lystra (14:8–10) parallel the healing of a lame man in Acts 3, and the response of the city (14:11–20) alludes to the story of Philemon and Baucis (see sidebar). In Acts 14, Luke repeats four phrases from his account of the healing of the lame man in Acts 3: *a certain man* (3:2; 14:8), *lame from birth* (3:2; 14:8), *look directly* (3:4; 14:9), and *jump and walk* (3:8; 14:10). This parallelism between the healing by Peter and now by Paul confirms that the same God who was at work with the apostle Peter is now at work with Paul. So, it is perhaps not by accident that in verses 4 and 14, Luke uses the word *apostles* to describe Paul and Barnabas. The word is meant to connect the actions of the Twelve with Paul and Barnabas.

The inhabitants of Lystra, which is within the bounds of the region of Phrygia, treat Paul and Barnabas as *Zeus* and *Hermes*, assuming that the gods have come down again to test the people of Phrygia. *The priest of Zeus* and the *crowd* attempt to offer sacrifices to Paul and Barnabas; this action prompts the *apostles* to tear their *clothes*, apparently as an indication that blasphemy has occurred (see Matt 26:65; Mark 14:63). The apostles then affirm that they are *only men*, *human like you* (10:26; compare 12:22; 28:6) and proceed to preach to the city. The sermon has two main points: a call to repentance and an appeal to creation as a witness to God's work as creator and to God's kindness. Paul's words barely stop the crowd *from sacrificing to them*. The delicate balance is broken with the arrival of Jews *from Antioch and Iconium*. It is surprising not only that those Jews travel about 100 and 20 miles respectively to hunt down Christians (see 9:1–2; 17:13), but also that those Jews are able to persuade these pagan inhabitants of Lystra to *stone* Paul; what those persuasive words are remain a mystery. Although Paul is left for *dead*, when *disciples* gather around him, Paul arises and reenters Lystra, and finally proceeds to *Derbe*, the last stop before Paul begins to retrace his steps.

> **The Story of Philemon & Baucis**
> *The latter part of the Lystra account probably reflects an understanding of a story in Ovid's* Metamorphoses *(8.611–725). In the story of Philemon and Baucis, the Roman equivalents of Zeus and Hermes (that is, Jupiter and Mercury) come in disguise to the region of Phrygia seeking hospitality, but time and again, they are turned away. Then enters the aged couple Philemon and his wife Baucis, who offer a meal and hospitality to the gods. The gods reward the kind couple and punish the other inhabitants severely.*

14:21–28 The return to Syria winds back through almost all of the same cities in Asia Minor: *Lystra, Iconium, Antioch, Perga*, and *Attalia*. Although Luke does not mention Attalia when Paul first arrived (13:13), it is possible, even likely, that Paul landed in this port city before passing to Perga. Luke describes Paul's activity on this return trip as *strengthening* and *encouraging*. Paul continues his work by *warning* the Christians about upcoming *hardships* and *appointing elders* in the churches. In an extremely condensed way, all four actions illustrate the range of Paul's pastoral activity, a focus that tends to be overlooked.

Upon returning to Antioch of Syria, Paul and Barnabas *gather* the church and *report all that God had done through them*. Again, Luke sees the spread of the gospel as the result of God and humans working together (8:26–27). As is typical, Luke reports that Paul stays *a long time* with the disciples (9:23; 11:26; 14:3, 28; 16:39–40; 18:11, 18, 23; 19:8, 10, 22; 20:3, 31).

15:1–21 This section lays out the setting that precedes the council (15:1–5) and records the speeches of Peter (15:6–11) and James (15:12–21). The conflict over circumcision begins with an anonymous group, of which little is known, except that they are *from Judea* and probably belong *to the party of the Pharisees*, if the people in 15:1 and 5 overlap. They advocate circumcision for Gentiles, which the Old Testament does not command; the practice of circumcision for Jews goes back to Genesis 17:9–14. This teaching brings *Paul and Barnabas into sharp dispute and debate with them*. Unresolved, the debate prompts the church to appoint Paul, Barnabas, and *some other believers* to go to *Jerusalem* to consult with the *apostles and elders* (15:2, 4, 6) there.

In his speech, Peter highlights God's activity. Peter notes that *God made a choice among you that the Gentiles might hear ... and believe*. God's choice is clear because *God showed that he accepted them by giving the Holy Spirit to them, just as he did to us* (10:45, 47; 11:15, 17). Peter concludes by appealing to the common Jewish Christian experience of failure to do the law (15:10) and to the common basis of salvation between Jews and Gentiles, namely *the grace of our Lord Jesus* (15:11).

Even though Luke reports that *Barnabas and Paul* give a speech, he only summarizes its content as *the miraculous signs and wonders God had done among the Gentiles through them*. Luke does not need to retell the events of Acts 13–14 for the reader, but he does want to provide an interpretation that again focuses on God's action.

James, the brother of Jesus, has the longest and apparently the most crucial speech in Acts 15. James makes two arguments. First, God chooses Israel itself *from the Gentiles* (or "nations"). For his second point, James, combining an allusion to the Septuagint text of Amos 9:11–12 and probably Isaiah 45:21, provides a warrant from Scripture that points to the inclusion of the Gentiles. Based on these two points, James makes this *judgment*: *we should not make it difficult for the Gentiles who are turning to God*. He asks that the Gentiles abstain from *food polluted by idols ... sexual immorality ... from the meat of strangled animals* and *blood*. These actions roughly parallel the kinds of requirements already in place for sojourners in Israel (Johnson 273; see Lev 17:8–9; 18:26–30; 17:13–14; 17:10–12 respectively).

> **Meat Offered to Idols**
> Acts 15:29 requires Gentile Christians to avoid meat offered to idols. Paul qualifies the command (1 Cor 10:25-30; compare Rom 14:1-21), allowing for exemptions under certain circumstances.

15:22–35 After choosing *Judas (called Barsabbas) and Silas*, the leaders and the church at Jerusalem send them with *Paul and Barnabas* back to *Antioch* with a *letter* describing the decision. Luke's brief mention of *Silas* foreshadows Silas's larger role in the upcoming narrative (Acts 15:40–18:5). *Judas (called Barsabbas)* disappears from the narrative after his role regarding the letter (15:30–32; compare the Joseph Barsabbas in 1:23). This letter is the first of two embedded letters in Acts 15:23–29 (see 23:26–30). The content of the letter makes clear four points: those who *disturbed* the church in Antioch did so without *authorization* from Jerusalem; Judas and Silas will *confirm* what is written in the letter; the decision is supported by the *Holy Spirit* (15:28); and the letter repeats the four *requirements* for the Gentiles.

Luke then describes the reception of the news by the church at Antioch. The church is *glad for its encouraging message*. *Spending some time there*, Judas and Silas *encourage and strengthen* the church before returning to Jerusalem. Absent from the best manuscripts, Acts 15:34 most likely keeps Silas in Antioch to explain his presence in Antioch in the immediately following narrative (15:40).

15:36–41 This passage records a proposal by Paul, another proposal by Barnabas, the split with Barnabas, and the beginning of a new journey with Silas. Paul suggests to Barnabas: *Let's go back and visit the brothers in all the towns where we preached the word of the Lord and see how they are doing*. Barnabas proposes that they take along *John, also called Mark*. Paul rejects Barnabas' idea because Mark *had deserted them in Pamphylia* (13:13). The ensuing disagreement is so *sharp* that Barnabas takes Mark to *Cyprus*, where Barnabas was raised (4:36), while Paul takes Silas through Syria and *Cilicia*, where Paul was raised and spent time after his conversion (22:3; 9:30; 11:25). Despite the split with Barnabas, Paul is *commended by the brothers* in Antioch. This passage functions as a transition to Paul's next journey and explains the absence of Barnabas and the presence of Silas.

16:1–5 In many ways, this section is compressed and transitional: it introduces *Timothy* as a coworker of Paul and Silas (16:1–3), relates their activity to the decisions reached in Jerusalem in Acts 15 (16:4), and summarizes the results of Paul's ministry (16:5).

Timothy will play a role in the later narrative of Acts, primarily as an emissary (18:5; 19:22) and a coworker (17:14, 15; 20:4) of Paul. In this section, Luke provides various personal details about Timothy: he is from the area of Derbe and Lystra (see 20:4); his mother was *a Jewess and a believer*; his father was a *Greek*; believers *spoke well of him* at Lystra and Iconium; and Paul *circumcised him because of the Jews that lived in that area*. The last item is the most controversial because of Paul's refusal to circumcise Titus (Gal 2:1–5). Some scholars doubt Luke's account; others see pastoral sensitivity, even pragmatism, in Paul's circumcision of Timothy. The latter option does not violate Paul's self-description, especially when one considers passages like 1 Corinthians 9:19–20 on ministry and Galatians 5:6 and 6:15 on circumcision.

According to Luke, Paul delivers the decisions reached by the leaders in Jerusalem to the churches (16:4). This account raises difficult questions. Why does the conference in Jerusalem seem to play such a small role in Paul's letters? Why does Paul not cite this decision, especially when the issue of eating food offered to idols arises (Acts 15:20; 1 Cor 8)? Was the decision at Jerusalem in force for a particular period of time or for a particular geographical area (see 21:25)? Unfortunately, Luke's abbreviated account does not provide answers to these questions.

Luke reports the results of Paul's activity with a summary, as is typical for both of his works: the churches were *strengthened* (14:22; 15:32, 41; 18:23) *in the faith and grew daily* (2:47; 6:7; 12:24; 19:20).

> **Timothy**
> *Paul's letters reveal further information about Timothy's service as a coworker (Rom 16:21; 2 Cor 1:1, 19; Phil 1:1; Col 1:1; 1 Thess 1:1; 2 Thess 1:1; Phlm 1:1) and emissary of Paul's (1 Cor 4:17; 16:10; Phil 2:19; 1 Thess 3:2, 6).*

16:6–10 Luke provides a clue, albeit a cryptic one, about God's leading in the spread of the gospel. Twice God prevents Paul and his companions from entering certain regions; once a vision directs the group to a particular area. In the first encounter, the *Holy Spirit* prevents Paul from preaching in the Roman province of *Asia* (see 19:10), located in the northwestern part of Asia Minor. So instead, Paul travels through *Phrygia and Galatia*, areas in the central part of Asia Minor to which Paul later returns (16:6; 18:23). When the group tries to enter *Bithynia*, a province in the north central part of Asia Minor, the *Spirit of Jesus* does not *allow them*. It is unclear whether Luke means the same thing by the *Holy Spirit* and the *Spirit of Jesus*. Given the role of God in the Macedonian *vision*, the third report of divine direction, it seems that Luke feels comfortable describing divine guidance in a variety of ways.

As a result of the direction from the Spirit of Jesus, the group travels to *Troas* (16:8, 11; 20:5–12), a port on the northwestern coast of Asia Minor. At Troas, Paul has a vision of a man begging, *Come to Macedonia and help us*. Paul concludes that God has called this group to preach in Macedonia. This passage is significant because 16:10 introduces the first of the four "we passages" in Acts (16:10–17; 20:5–15; 21:1–18; 27:1–28:16), passages that may give readers a clue about the authorship of Acts.

16:11–15 After spending one night on the island of *Samothrace*, the original home of the famous Winged Victory statue found in the Louvre today, Paul arrives in *Neapolis*, the port city for Philippi. Paul's landing signals the arrival of Christianity on European soil, thus continuing the march of the gospel to the heart of the Roman Empire. Located ten miles from Neapolis, *Philippi* was not only a *leading city* on the Egnatian Way, the main thoroughfare across modern Greece, but also one of the six cities in the Roman province of *Macedonia* that Paul visits on this journey (namely, Neapolis, Amphipolis, Apollonia, Thessalonica, and Berea).

> **Roman Roads**
> *The Romans built an elaborate network of roads, primarily for military use, throughout their empire. This road network provided ample opportunity for Christian travelers to spread the new faith to the major cities of the Mediterranean world.*

With Paul's arrival in Philippi also comes the conversion of Lydia and her household. *On the Sabbath*, Paul searches *outside the city gate* for a *place of prayer*, likely meaning a synagogue. He finds some *women* gathered there, among whom is *Lydia*. Luke discloses that Lydia sells *purple cloth* (a costly item) and hails from *Thyatira* (a city in the Roman province of Asia). Luke also identifies her as a *worshiper of God*, perhaps, but not necessarily, identifying her as a Gentile God-fearer (see 10:2, 22, 35; 13:16, 26, 43, 50; 16:14; 17:4, 17; 18:6–7). Paul speaks and the *Lord* opens *her heart to respond to Paul's message*, another example of divine-human joint work in Luke's account. The baptism of Lydia and *her household* is the second occurrence of household baptisms in Acts, as well as the only one in which Luke gives no further information beyond baptism regarding the response of the household to the gospel. Lydia persuades Paul and his companions to stay with her at her *house* (compare 18:20), which likely becomes the meeting place for the house church in Philippi (16:40). Earlier Luke identified Mary's house in Jerusalem as a place where Christians met (12:12–17).

16:16–40 If one considers only the narrative portions of Acts, then Luke's description of Paul's remaining time in Philippi is perhaps the longest account of a single day in the ministry of Paul. Paul battles pagan magic, confronts Roman opposition, and converts a jailer and his family. Previously, Paul had confronted a Jewish magician (13:4–12); here Luke recounts the first of two encounters with pagan magic (16:16–19; 19:11–20). The *spirit* by which the slave girl *predicted the future* is literally a "Pythian spirit." This phrase links her with the most famous of all the oracles in the first century world, the oracle of Apollo at Delphi, where the prophetess is called the Pythia. In this confrontation between the "king" of oracles and Christianity, Paul bests the spirit by casting it out of the *slave girl*, which causes her financially threatened *owners* to drag Paul before the *authorities* (16:16, 19). Luke connected greed and magic previously in the narrative as well (8:4–25).

The owners charge Paul with disruption of the social order, and perhaps the religious order as well: *These men are Jews, and are throwing our city into an uproar by advocating customs unlawful for us Romans to accept or practice.* As a result of this charge and the cries of the *crowd*, Paul and Silas are *stripped*, *beaten*, and *thrown into prison* (4:3; 5:17–21; 12:3–11). After hearing that Paul and Silas are *Roman citizens* (16:37–39; 22:25–29; 23:27; 25:10–12), the officials are *alarmed*.

Luke sandwiches another conversion story between the account of the slave girl and Paul's release from prison. In this conversion story, an *earthquake* (as in 4:31) opens the *prison doors* and loosens the *chains* of the prisoners. With the jailer about to *kill himself* because he thinks that the prisoners have escaped (12:19; 16:27; 27:42), Paul shouts, *We are all here!* The jailer asks, *Sirs, what must I do to be saved?* (2:37; 16:30; 22:10). Paul tells the jailer and his household to *believe*. After speaking *the word of the Lord to him and to all the others in his house*, Paul baptizes the jailer and *all his family*. With this third story of a household conversion, Luke stresses the speaking of *the word of the Lord*, the belief in this word, and the baptism of the hearers (16:31–33).

17:1–15 After encouraging the Christians at *Lydia's house* (16:40), Paul and Silas continue down the Egnatian Way about 95 miles, passing through *Amphipolis* and *Apollonia* to *Thessalonica*, the capital of the province of Macedonia. From Thessalonica, Paul flees to Berea, leaving the Egnatian Way. In Luke's portrayal of these events, the reception of the gospel in Thessalonica contrasts with the reception of the gospel in Berea. In addition, Luke shows the hostility that Christianity faces from some Jews and pagans, illustrating various aspects of Luke's apologetic interest.

This section begins in typical fashion. *As his custom was*, Paul begins preaching in the synagogue (13:14; 14:1; 16:13; 17:1–2, 10, 17; 18:4, 19; 19:8), reasoning *from the Scriptures*. Although some dispute Luke's depiction of Paul on this point, Paul's own letters show evidence of his ministry among Jews (Rom 1:16; 2:9–10; 1 Cor 9:20; 2 Cor 11:24, 26). Although Luke mentions only *three Sabbath days*, it is possible that Paul's ministry in the synagogue lasted three weeks, but that his ministry in Thessalonica lasted longer. The results of Paul's preaching are divided, with some Jews and Gentiles accepting his message, but with some Jews being *jealous* (5:17; 13:45; 17:4; compare 7:9).

Upon arriving in Berea, Paul does exactly the same thing; he enters the synagogue. Luke highlights,

---

The Innocence of Paul & Silas
Even though the Roman government imprisons Paul and Silas, Luke emphasizes their innocence by showing pagan greed as the source of the unrest and by recounting how the city magistrates personally come to the prison to appease Paul and Silas, to escort them from the prison, and to ask them to leave the city.

however, a different response in Berea. Luke explicitly states that *the Bereans were of more noble character than the Thessalonians*. Then Luke details how the Bereans were more noble. First, they *received the message with great eagerness*. Second, they *examined the Scriptures every day to see if what Paul said was true*. Third, *many* (as opposed to *some*) *of the Jews believed, as did also a number of prominent Greek women and many Greek men*. In his contrast of Thessalonica and Berea, Luke stresses the responsibility of the hearer.

Luke cannot deny that social disorder seems to follow the gospel wherever it goes (16:20–21; 17:5–6, 13; 19:23–41; 21:27–34; 23:7–10; 24:12, 18). He can, however, show the sources of the disorder. In this account, the problem begins with the *jealousy* of some Jews who gather a mob from the marketplace and start a *riot* in Thessalonica. They rush to Jason's house, which may function as a house church for the Christians at Thessalonica (12:12–17; 16:40). Not finding Paul and Silas, the crowd brings Jason and some other Christians before the city officials. The crowd charges the Christians with causing *trouble all over the world* and *defying Caesar's decrees, saying that there is another king, one called Jesus*. The first charge amounts to social disorder, the second to political disorder or treason. *Turmoil* results; *Jason and the others* are released after posting bond; later *at night* (5:19; 9:23–25; 12:6; compare 16:33), Paul and Silas depart for Berea. After hearing that Paul is preaching there, *the Jews in Thessalonica* travel about 60 miles south to Berea (see 14:19) to provoke further riots. With this dramatic account, Luke continues to defend Christianity and to show a divided response to the gospel (Luke 2:34).

Although it is somewhat difficult to track the movements of Paul, Silas, and Timothy after this point, the following movements are clear: Silas and Timothy remain in Berea (17:14); Paul goes to Athens (17:15); Paul tries to return more than once to Thessalonica (1 Thess 2:17–18); Timothy, and perhaps others, meets Paul in Athens (1 Thess 3:1–5); Paul sends Timothy back to Thessalonica (1 Thess 3:1–3); Paul goes to Corinth (18:1); and Silas and Timothy eventually rejoin Paul at Corinth (18:5).

17:16–34 The account of Paul's stay in Athens divides into three sections: an introduction to the speech (17:16–21), the speech proper (17:22–31), and the response to it (17:32–34). As Paul waits for Silas and Timothy to join him in Athens, he is *greatly distressed* (see 15:39) by the many *idols* in the city, a description that foreshadows elements in Paul's speech (17:22–23, 29). Paul debates in the *synagogue*, but Luke covers this preaching in one verse (17:17), while his preaching to pagans comprises the rest of the chapter.

> **Athens**
> Along with Alexandria and Tarsus, Athens was one of the three great centers of higher education in the Roman Empire during the first century.

In the *marketplace*, Paul engages members of the two most prominent philosophies of his day. Like the Christians, the *Epicureans* live in communities and communicate by letters. The Epicureans, however, seek pleasure as the highest good, though they mean by pleasure those actions that cause the least pain in the long run (that is, they are not hedonists in the common sense of that word). The gods, they argue, are not interested in the daily affairs of humans. Stoicism is the most popular Hellenistic philosophy; the *Stoics* argue for the suppression of emotions and seek to use reason to achieve happiness. Paul's preaching evokes a twofold response: *some* call Paul a *babbler* [Greek *spermologos*; literally a "seed picker"], which is a negative term meaning someone who sounds educated because he has picked up a few good "sound bites," but really has no depth. *Others* express interest because of the *foreign gods* Paul preaches, indicating that they misunderstood *Jesus and the resurrection* as gods. The result is that Paul stands in the *Areopagus*, which is both a place and Athens's highest court, which meets in that place. Luke lightly lampoons the Athenians for their interest in *listening to the latest ideas*.

Paul launches his speech with a reference to an *altar* he has seen. Paul then preaches about this god they worship as *something unknown*. Paul describes God as creator: *the Lord of heaven and earth ... who gives all men life and breath and everything else*. Because creation shows God's fingerprint, humans *seek* God. Paul quotes the pagan poet Aratus to support the connection between the divine and humanity: *We are his offspring*. In his conclusion, Paul makes four points: since humans are God's offspring, then God is not of human making, *gold or silver or stone*; God now calls all people to *repentance*; judgment *with justice* will come by the man God *has appointed*; and God gave *proof of this* by raising Jesus from the dead.

Not surprisingly, the response to Paul's message is divided (Luke 2:34). Some *sneer* when they hear about the *resurrection from the dead* (17:32; compare 25:19–20; 26:8; see 4:2; 23:8). Others want to hear more from Paul. Among those who believe are some prominent converts. With *Dionysius*, Luke continues to emphasize prominent converts to Christianity. The conversion of *Damaris* shows Luke's interest in detailing women who comprised the early church.

18:1–17 Paul leaves Athens and arrives at *Corinth*, where he stays *for a year and a half* (verse 11).

> **Corinth**
>
> A cosmopolitan city on the isthmus connecting mainland Greece and the Peloponnesian peninsula, Corinth functioned as the capital of the Roman province Achaia.

Luke's account divides Paul's time in Corinth into four scenes. In the first scene (verses 1–4), Luke introduces *Aquila* and his *wife Priscilla*, foreshadowing their role later in Acts. Luke reveals that Aquila is a *Jew* and a native of *Pontus*, a province in the northern part of Asia Minor. He has recently come from *Italy* because the emperor *Claudius* (compare 11:28) *had ordered all the Jews to leave Rome*. The Roman historian Suetonius records evidence of this expulsion dated to the year 49 (*Claudius* 25.4). Because Paul, Aquila, and Priscilla are tentmakers, Paul stays and works with them, probably using his time both to support himself and spread the gospel (Hock). Paul also goes to the *synagogue every Sabbath* to persuade *Jews and Greeks* (14:1; compare 19:10; 20:21).

Silas and Timothy arrive from Macedonia (see 17:1–15 above), introducing the second scene, which describes Paul's conflict with and success in the synagogue (verses 5–8). Paul preaches Jesus as the *Christ*, causing Jews to oppose and abuse Paul. In response, Paul shakes out his *clothes in protest* (13:5), proclaims his innocence of their blood with an allusion to Ezekiel 33:1–4, and turns to the Gentiles (13:46; 18:6; 28:28). With two named converts, Luke shows the extent of Paul's preaching. Paul enters the house of *Titius Justus*, a *worshiper of God* who lives *next door* to the synagogue, because Titius has converted and perhaps because Paul now uses his home as a house church (compare 12:12–17; 16:40; 17:5). Surprisingly, *Crispus, the synagogue ruler, and his entire household* convert to Christianity. In fact, many Corinthians believe and are *baptized*. Luke shows Paul's faithfulness to his people and the success of the gospel despite opposition.

In the third scene (verses 9–11), Luke briefly describes a *vision* of the Lord (compare 22:17–18; 23:11) to Paul one *night* (compare 16:9–10; 27:23–24) and summarizes Paul's stay of eighteen months in Corinth. In this vision, the Lord encourages Paul to continue preaching because the Lord is with Paul, providing protection, and the Lord has *many people in this city*. Paul in fact escapes harm, as the next scene details.

Luke uses the fourth scene to describe a typical "trial" of a Christian. Locals, in this case Jews, bring Paul *into court* [Greek *bema* in verses 12, 16, 17] before the *proconsul*, who functions as the governor of the province of *Achaia*. Achaia covers most of the southern part of modern Greece. The proconsul *Gallio* is the brother of the Stoic philosopher Seneca and the Roman poet Lucan. As proconsul, only *Gallio* can exercise *imperium*, the right to issue the death penalty in his province. The charge against Paul is as follows: *This man is persuading people to worship God in ways contrary to the law* (18:13; 21:28; 25:8; compare 6:13), an accusation that Gallio chooses to ignore because proconsuls decide which cases are heard and which are dismissed. Since the charge does not consist of *some misdemeanor or serious crime*, Gallio refuses to hear the case, prompting a beating of *Sosthenes the synagogue ruler* before Gallio, who, as is his prerogative as proconsul, shows *no concern whatever*. It is not clear why Sosthenes is beaten, perhaps because of the failure of the accusation, perhaps to prompt Gallio to act, perhaps because Sosthenes is suspected of Christian sympathies (see 1 Cor 1:1).

> **Prosecution of Legal Cases against Christians**
>
> Acts 18's portrayal of a trial fits with a pagan description of a trial of Christians (*Pliny*, Letters 10.96–97): prosecution, when present, is local and dependent on the decision of a governor to hear the case (see Acts 13:7; 19:38); prosecution begins with an accusation from an inhabitant of the province, not the Roman government; and prosecution, when present, is sporadic, since it depends on the accusations of locals and the willingness of a governor to hear such cases (Ste. Croix).

18:18–28 Priscilla and Aquila connect the account of Paul's return to Antioch (18:18–23) with the first of two stories that treat disciples of John the Baptist (18:24–28). As is Paul's custom, he spends extended time with a congregation, unless he is forced to flee. The same is true in Corinth, where Paul remains *for some time* before leaving (9:23; 11:26; 14:3, 28; 16:39–40; 18:11, 18, 23; 19:8, 10, 22; 20:3, 31). Luke then states Paul's itinerary: *Cenchrea*, *Ephesus*, *Cæsarea*, his home church at *Antioch*, and back out on another trip beginning with *the region of Galatia and Phrygia*. Brief events accompany each stop. At *Cenchrea*, about seven miles east of Corinth on the Aegean Sea, Paul has *his hair cut off* because of a *vow* (compare 21:23–24), which is likely part of a Nazarite vow (Num 6:1–21). With this vow, Luke shows Paul's respect for the Law (see 18:13; 21:28; 25:8). After crossing the Aegean Sea, Paul preaches in the synagogue at *Ephesus*, promises the church to return *if it is God's will*, and leaves Priscilla and Aquila at *Ephesus*. After arriving in *Cæsarea*, Paul greets the Christians who had once helped him escape to Tarsus (9:30). After spending *some time in Antioch*, Paul begins another journey by visiting *the region of Galatia and Phrygia* (verse 23; compare 16:6), *strengthening all the disciples* (14:22; 15:32, 41; 18:23).

Priscilla and Aquila's instruction of Apollos reveals the significance of followers of John the Baptist and of women in early Christianity. John the Baptist is a prominent first century personage, even mentioned by the Jewish historian Josephus (*Antiquities* 18.116–119). He apparently has disciples throughout much of the eastern Roman Empire, at least in Judea (Luke 5:33; 7:18–24; 11:1), Alexandria, Egypt (Acts 18:24–25), and Ephesus (19:1–7). What should Christians do when they encounter these "John the Baptist" Christians? Luke has two responses: John's disciples need more instruction (18:24–28), and they need to be baptized in the name of Jesus and receive the Holy Spirit (19:1–7).

Luke gives quite a bit of information about *Apollos*. He is a *Jew* and *a native of Alexandria* now living in *Ephesus*. He is *a learned man, with a thorough knowledge of the Scriptures*. He had been *instructed in the way of the Lord, and he spoke with great fervor and taught about Jesus accurately, though he knew only the baptism of John* (19:3). He spoke *boldly in the synagogue*. From this information, it is safe to say that when Priscilla and Aquila teach Apollos *the way of the Lord more accurately* (compare 18:25), their teaching goes beyond the basics. Furthermore, their teaching of Apollos apparently goes well because, when he wants to go to *Achaia*, the church supports his decision by writing *to the disciples there to welcome him*.

Luke's interest in showing the involvement of women in the life of the church continues in this passage. Elsewhere in his telling of the story of the church, he often mentions both men and women (5:14; 8:3, 12; 9:2; 17:4, 12, 34; 22:4). It is noteworthy that Priscilla's name precedes her husband's name, indicating her prominence in the instruction of Apollos. In fact, four of the six times that both appear in the New Testament, Priscilla's name comes before Aquila's (Acts 18:18, 26; Rom 16:3; 2 Tim 4:19; compare Acts 18:2; 1 Cor 16:19).

19:1–22 Paul's entrance into *Ephesus* connects this second narrative about the disciples of John the Baptist (verses 1–7) with all the rest of the material about Ephesus (verses 8–41). Despite the mention of Ephesus, the first section (verses 1–7) picks up the problem of disciples of John the Baptist that concluded Acts 18. In this passage, the question is whether or not disciples of John the Baptist need to be rebaptized. Luke presents Paul's encounter with these disciples through a dialogue between them. Paul's first two questions reveal that they do not know about the Holy Spirit and that they did receive John's baptism. With this knowledge, Paul places their baptism in the context of the greater revelation of Jesus. Luke then records the response and the results of their response. The disciples are *baptized into the name of the Lord Jesus*. Paul places his hands on them, and the *Holy Spirit* comes on them, with the result that they *spoke in tongues and prophesied*.

> **The Coming of the Holy Spirit**
> As with Pentecost and Cornelius in Acts 2 and 10, the coming of the Holy Spirit verifies the actions in chapter 19. That is, those disciples of John need a baptism that includes the reception of the Holy Spirit (see Acts 2:38).

Luke provides a capsule version of the events in Ephesus in 19:8–10. In a span of *two years*, Paul speaks in the *synagogue*, encounters opposition there, and turns to teach Gentiles daily in the *hall of Tyrannus*. The result is that *Jews and Gentiles* hear the *word of the Lord*. Luke then describes specific events that happened during Paul's stay.

In a brief account, Luke tells how *God* works *extraordinary miracles through Paul*. Luke's account of the powerful healing of the sick and demon-possessed stresses God's activity, parallels Peter's activity with Paul's (19:12; compare 5:15), and forms a contrast with the impotence of the Jewish "exorcists" in 19:13–17. These "exorcists" think that the power of God is akin to magic that can be manipulated with the correct "magic words." Thus they *invoke the name of the Lord Jesus over those who were demon-possessed*. These exorcists are *seven sons of Sceva, a Jewish chief priest*. Since Sceva is unknown as a chief priest, this designation may identify them as charlatans. The consequences of their attempted exorcism certainly supports this possibility, since the evil spirit, unimpressed by their incantation, jumps on, overpowers, and beats them so badly that they run out of the house *naked and bleeding*.

Luke recalls the response to this botched exorcism (19:18–20). The event became known to both *Jews and Greeks*, who fearfully praise Jesus. Then, *many of those who believed* confessed to *sorcery*, brought their *scrolls*, and *burned them publicly*. Luke differentiates Christianity from magic in a striking way; the value of the scrolls came to *fifty thousand drachmas*, the equivalent of almost 137 years of work for the average day laborer.

Before recounting the longest episode in Ephesus, Luke pauses to note Paul's travel plans: first a trip to *Jerusalem, passing through Macedonia and Achaia*, then a trip to *Rome*. In preparation, Paul sends *Timothy* and *Erastus* to Macedonia, while he remains *in the province of Asia a little longer*. Because this passage is the only place where *Erastus* occurs in Acts, there is not much information about him. Thus, it is difficult to determine whether this Erastus is the same person as the Erastus mentioned in Romans 16:23 and 1 Timothy 4:20, although it is certainly possible that two or more of these passages refer to the same Erastus.

19:23–41 Luke devotes a long narrative to his description of the riot in Ephesus. Through his narrative, one sees a number of ways that Christianity impacts the surrounding culture. First, there is an economic impact; specifically in this case, fewer people buy *silver shrines* of the Greek goddess *Artemis* from the silversmiths. Second, there is a religious impact. In Ephesus, Paul convinced many of the falsehood of idolatry. Third, there is the social impact of Christianity, namely a near-riot that breaks out and encompasses the whole city (19:29, 32, 40). In fact, social disturbances seem to occur fairly frequently when Paul is present (17:5; 21:30–36; 22:22–24; 23:7–10; 24:5). To each of these threats, Luke offers a response. The economic sacrifice of those Christians who burn 50,000 drachmas' worth of magic books (19:19) contrasts with the pagan silversmiths' greed. Regarding the threat to pagan religion, the city clerk points out that the Christians have done nothing wrong (verse 37). As for the social disturbances, Luke cannot deny that they occurred, but he can explain that the Christians were not at fault. In this passage, the riot begins with the demagoguery of *Demetrius* the silversmith (verses 25–28); it continues with the city pouring into the theater, even though *most of the people did not even know why they were there* (verse 32). Both the city clerk and some of the *officials of the province* [Greek *asiarchoi*] side with Paul and try to protect him (verse 31).

> **The Injustice of Demetrius' Attack**
>
> *The city clerk points out several ways in which the pagans are at fault: the Christians have been detained, even though they have done no wrong (verse 37); Demetrius and his fellow craftsmen have not followed the correct legal procedure (verse 38); any other charges should go to a proper court (verse 39); and, these pagans in the theater risk charges of rioting themselves because of the day's events (verse 40). In summary, the pagans cannot justify their baseless misbehavior (verse 41).*

20:1–6 In this section, Luke summarizes Paul's travels from *Ephesus* to *Macedonia* and *Greece*, back through *Macedonia* (20:3), including *Philippi*, and on to *Troas*. Paul begins this itinerary from *Ephesus*, which he leaves after *the uproar had ended* and *after encouraging* and saying *good-by* to the *disciples* there. Next, Paul travels through *Macedonia*, speaking many words of encouragement. Although Luke does not mention any specific cities, six have been named previously: Neapolis, Philippi, Amphipolis, Apollonia, Thessalonica, and Berea. Since it is likely that Paul visits churches that he established (see 15:36), some of these six cities are probable stops. His stay in *Greece*, which probably includes Corinth, lasts for *three months*. Because of a *plot* against him, Paul changes his plans to sail to *Syria*, and instead he goes back through *Macedonia*. After sailing from *Philippi*, Paul meets his traveling party *five days later* in *Troas*.

In addition to the list of places, Luke includes a list of seven named traveling companions. *Sopater son of Pyrrhus*, from *Berea* (17:10–15) in Macedonia, is mentioned only here in the New Testament. *Aristarchus*, a Thessalonian, appears first in Ephesus

(19:29) and later will accompany Paul on his trip to Rome (27:2). Elsewhere, Paul identifies him as a *fellow prisoner* and a *Jew* (Col 4:10–11), as well as a *fellow worker* (Phlm 24). Luke relates that *Secundus*, like Aristarchus, is *from Thessalonica*. *Gaius* hails from *Derbe*, a town of Galatia; he may or may not be identical with other mentions of Gaius (Acts 19:29; Rom 16:23; 1 Cor 1:14; 3 John 1). *Timothy*, discussed above (16:1) and last mentioned at 19:22, continues his work with the Pauline mission. Both *Tychicus* and *Trophimus* come from the *province of Asia*. Tychicus appears in a number of the Pauline letters (Eph 6:21; Col 4:7; 2 Tim 4:12; Tit 3:12). Trophimus, identified as an *Ephesian*, plays a significant role in the riot in Jerusalem (21:29) and falls ill at *Miletus*, the port city about 30 miles from Ephesus (2 Tim 4:20). Some also add Luke as a traveling companion of Paul because this "we passage" (20:5–15) begins again at Philippi, where the last "we passage" ended (16:10–17).

20:7–12 In *Troas* (16:8, 10; 20:5, 6), Luke's story about Eutychus contains echoes of other accounts when someone is raised from the dead. Note the accounts about Jesus (Luke 7:11–17; 8:49–56) and Peter (Acts 9:36–43), both of which allude to the raising of the widow's son by Elijah (1 Kgs 17:7–24, especially verses 15–24; similarly, Elisha in 2 Kgs 4:34–35). With these allusions, Luke shows that the power of God that was active in the prophet Elijah is also active in the ministries of Jesus, Peter, and Paul. Luke notes that the church gathers together to break bread, which probably refers to the Lord's Supper (see 2:42, 46; 20:11). Because Paul intends *to leave the next day*, he extends his speech past *midnight*. The *many lamps* that Luke mentions may offer assurance to pagans that there is nothing suspicious about this meeting at night (compare 12:6–17; Livy 39.8.3, 4, 8; Minucius Felix, *Octavius*, 9). While Paul is speaking, *Eutychus*, whose name ironically means "lucky," falls asleep in a *window* and then falls down *from the third story* window to the *ground* where he is *picked up dead*. Paul revives the boy in a way that echoes the actions of Elijah and Elisha (1 Kgs 17:21; 2 Kgs 4:34–35). After speaking *until daylight*, Paul departs for Assos. *Greatly comforted*, the people take the *young man* home *alive*.

> **"On the first day of the week ..."**
> *The early church gathered* on the first day of the week (*as in Rev 1:10*); *this practice marked a change from Jewish worship, which takes place on the Sabbath (Saturday). Christians began to meet on Sundays, most likely because it was the day of Jesus' resurrection (see the second century text*, Barnabas 15:9).

20:13–38 This unit consists of three sections: Paul's travels to Miletus (verses 13–16), Paul's speech at Miletus (verses 17–35), and his departure from there (verses 36–38). The first section functions as Paul's itinerary from Troas to Miletus. With no explanation by Luke, Paul separates from the rest of his traveling party and travels about 20 miles *on foot* from Troas to *Assos*, where he rejoins his party and boards a ship for *Mitylene*, which is the main city on the island of Lesbos. The next day, they sail and land on the mainland of Asia Minor opposite the island of *Kios*. The next two days, they stop on the island of *Samos* and arrive at the port city of *Miletus*. Paul avoids going to *Ephesus* (compare 18:21) because he wants to reach *Jerusalem* by *the day of Pentecost* (compare 16:3; 18:18; 20:6, 16; 21:20–26).

Paul's sermon to the Ephesian *elders* (11:30; 14:23; 21:18; compare 15:2, 4, 6; 16:4) is the only speech to Christians in the book of Acts. In this speech, whose form is a farewell discourse, Paul describes his ministry and warns the elders about future dangers to the church. As a minister, Paul was committed to the Ephesians, eventually spending a total of *three years* with them (verse 31; compare 18:19–21; 19:10). He *served with great humility and with tears* (verses 19, 31; see Luke 19:41), showing his character and personal investment in his ministry. Paul ministered, despite *being tested by the plots of the Jews* (9:24, 29; 20:3, 19; 23:16, 30; see 14:5), demonstrating his willingness to endure hardships. Thus far in Acts, Paul has already endured hostile audiences (13:45, 50; 14:2; 16:22; 17:5, 13, 18, 32; 19:9, 30), a stoning (14:19), an imprisonment (16:23), and a beating (16:23).

The phrase *I have not hesitated* (verses 20, 27) shows Paul's boldness to declare what his hearers need to hear. In fact, *boldness* is a key word in Luke's portrayal of those who preach; note Peter and John (4:13), the church (4:29, 31), Barnabas (13:46; 14:3), Apollos (18:26), and most of all Paul (9:27, 28; 13:46; 14:3; 19:8; 26:26; 28:31) who speak boldly. Paul's boldness does not tear down his hearers; rather, it provides what is *helpful* and what *teaches* them. His ministry is also inclusive, serving *both Jews and Greeks* (14:1; 18:4; 19:10, 17; 20:21).

As Paul reflects on his journey to *Jerusalem*, he knows through the *Holy Spirit* that *prison* (verse 23; 23:18, 35; 24:27; 25:14; 28:16–17) and *hardships* (14:22; 20:23) await him. The forthcoming narrative vividly depicts these trials.

Paul interrupts his speech to *warn* the elders about internal and external dangers to the church (verses 28–31). Those who will come from the outside to attack the *church of God* are harsh and fierce; Paul calls them *savage wolves*. From within the church will come men who *distort* (13:8, 10; 20:30) *the truth in order to draw away disciples*. Paul has warned *each* of the elders about these dangers during the whole *three years* that he has been with them, demonstrating his individual attention and consistent care for them and the church.

> **The Persecution of Paul**
> In the remainder of Acts, Paul faces more attempts on his life (21:31–32; 23:12–30; 25:3; 27:42–44), still more hostile hearers (22:22; 23:1–2), another beating (23:32; see 23:2), an arrest (21:33), imprisonments at Cæsarea (23:35–26:32) and Rome (28:30–31), storm (27:13–20), hunger (27:21, 33), shipwreck (27:41), and snakebite (28:3). Paul nevertheless disregards these hardships as long as he can fulfill his call. Luke insists that Paul ministers, despite hardships, because he has a divine commission to testify to the gospel (20:21, 23, 24; see 1:8; 20:26; 26:22).

Luke shows that Paul's ministry is free from the taint of personal gain. He notes that with his own *hands* and *hard work* (18:3; 19:11–12; 28:30), he strives to *help the weak*. Paul bases these convictions on the words of *Jesus*: *It is more blessed to give than to receive*. As Paul prepares to depart, he *prays* with them. *Grieved* because they will not *see his face again*, they all weep, embrace, and kiss Paul before accompanying him *to the ship*.

21:1–16 The section details Paul's journey as he travels from Miletus to Jerusalem. Luke names the people and places Paul visits, as well as the reception that he receives. With the peace brought by Augustus, travel is safer in the first century. A common language (Koine Greek) and coinage further enables mobility, as do over 50,000 miles of roads. With more people able to travel, hospitality becomes a prized virtue, especially among Christians (Rom 12:13; 1 Tim 3:2; 5:10; Tit 1:8; Heb 13:2; 1 Pet 4:9), since inns sometimes double as brothels.

In rapid succession, Luke details the first few stops on the journey: Miletus, the islands of *Cos* and *Rhodes*, and *Patara* on the mainland of Asia Minor. Cos was known as the birthplace of Hippocrates, the father of medicine, and for its medical school. Finding a ship for *Phoenicia*, they sail past the island of *Cyprus* and land at *Tyre*. Because the people of Phoenicia first heard the gospel from those scattered after the death of Stephen (11:20; compare 15:3; 21:2; 27:2), it is not surprising that Paul finds *disciples there*. After staying *seven days* and being warned about the danger ahead in Jerusalem, Paul prays with them and then departs, sailing from Tyre to *Ptolemais*. At the Phoenician city of Ptolemais, Paul again receives hospitality with the *brothers for a day*.

> **Rhodes**
> Rhodes boasted one of the "seven wonders of the ancient world," the Colossus of Rhodes. Measuring about 100 feet tall (Pliny, Natural History, 34.8), this huge statue collapsed long before Paul's time (in about 226 BCE) during an earthquake. Even on the ground, its size inspired the awe of travelers.

Leaving Phoenicia, Paul reaches *Cæsarea*, which he had visited before (18:22). His stay there dominates the rest of his itinerary (verses 8–16). Luke continues to highlight hospitality; the group first stays a number of days with *Philip*; then some *disciples from Cæsarea* accompany Paul to the home of *Mnason* in Jerusalem, giving a total of four acts of hospitality (verses 4, 7, 8–10, 16). Luke also highlights several Christians who live in Cæsarea: *Philip the evangelist, one of the Seven* (6:1–6; 8:40), his *four unmarried daughters who prophesied* (21:9), *Agabus*, and *Mnason*. It is not surprising to find women who prophesy, given Luke's quotation of Joel 2:28–32 in Acts 2:17. Also a prophet, Agabus again prophesies (11:28; 21:10–11). Mnason was originally *from Cyprus and one of the early disciples*, which could make him a follower of Jesus (1:15), a friend of Barnabas (4:36), one of those scattered after the persecution of Stephen (11:19), one of those who preached to the Greeks in Antioch (11:20), or some combination of the aforementioned. Luke's third stress is showing the way that *in every city the Holy Spirit warns* Paul that *prisons and hardships await him* (20:23). This stress is seen not only in Tyre (verse 4), but also in an expanded way in Cæsarea through the prophecy of Agabus (verses 10–14). Despite the hardships that await Paul, he will still continue toward Jerusalem; the church learns to conclude *the Lord's will be done*.

21:17–26 This unit has three parts: a brief description of Paul's arrival (verses 17–19), a "speech" (verses 20–25), and a brief report of Paul's actions (verse 26). When Paul and his traveling companions arrive at Jerusalem, the *brothers*, perhaps those at the house of Mnason, perhaps the church in Jerusalem, receive them *warmly*, showing their acceptance of Paul. Paul then goes to see the leaders in Jerusalem, who are *James* (12:17; 15:13–21) *and all the elders*. Paul reports *what God had done* (14:27; 15:4, 12; 21:19) *among the Gentiles*, stressing God's initiative among the Gentiles. One significant question remains: how is Paul's ministry perceived in Jerusalem?

Speaking to Paul, the leaders articulate their concerns, offer a proposal, and reiterate their policy on the Gentiles (verse 25). The leaders describe the reports heard about Paul among the *many thousands* (2:41; 4:4; 21:20) *of Jews* who believed that he has abandoned the teachings of the Old Testament (18:13; 25:8; 28:17). In response, Luke has already detailed the ways that Paul respects Jewish customs (18:18; 20:6, 16; 21:26), even circumcision (16:1–3). The leaders propose that Paul take *four men* who have *made a vow* (see Num 6:1–21 for the probable background of this vow), *join in their purification*, and *pay their expenses*. The leaders close with a summary of what was decided in Acts 15 (21:25). Paul honors their request by taking the men and purifying himself along with them on the *next day*, continuing Luke's portrayal of Paul's respect for Jewish customs.

21:27–36 In his record of Paul's arrest, Luke explains the cause (verses 27–29) and describes the response by both the crowd and the Roman officials (verses 30–36). To explain the reason for Paul's arrest, Luke introduces *some Jews from the province of Asia* (21:27; 24:19; compare 19:10). These Jews had previously *seen Trophimus the Ephesian* (20:4) *in the city with Paul* and assumed that Paul had brought him into *the temple area*. The entry of a Gentile into the temple was strictly forbidden. Multiple signs were posted in Greek and Latin "at equal intervals" (Josephus, *Jewish War*, 193–94; *Antiquities*, 417) around the temple; these signs stated: "No one of another nation may enter within the fence and enclosure round the temple. Whoever is caught shall have himself to blame that his death ensues" (Fitzmyer 698). When the Jews from Asia see *Paul at the temple*, they stir up the crowd and seize him, making four charges. Luke disposes of the fourth charge with an aside (verse 29). A more extensive rebuttal of the first three charges comes in Paul's next speech (22:1–21). A more extensive rebuttal of all three charges comes in Paul's next speech (22:1–21).

The crowd *drags* Paul from the temple and attempts to *kill him* (verses 31; 26:21). The commander of the Roman troops is a tribune named Claudius Lysias (23:26; 24:22); a tribune commands a cohort of 500–1,000 men. Hearing about the *uproar*, the commander takes *officers* [literally "centurions"] *and soldiers* to the crowd, who stop *beating Paul*. After arresting Paul and *binding* him *with two chains* (12:6; 21:33), the commander asks who he is and what he has done. This *binding* of Paul fulfills what the Holy Spirit and Agabus predicted (20:23; 21:11, 13, 33). As for the crowd, Luke records: *some in the crowd shouted one thing and some another*, the same language used to describe the pagans rioting in Ephesus (19:32; 21:34). So *great is the violence of the mob* that Paul has to be *carried by the soldiers* to the *barracks*, which refers to the Fortress Antonia.

> **The Antonia Fortress**
> The Antonia Fortress lay just northwest of the temple precinct, and its height allowed its garrison to overlook all activities in the temple. Herod the Great built the structure and named it in honor of Mark Antony before the latter's defeat by Augustus in 31 BCE.

21:37–22:21 Paul's speech to the crowd in the temple court falls into two parts: Paul's conversation with the commander (verses 37–39) and Paul's speech (verses 40–22:21). As the crowd was *shouting*, *Away with him!* (compare the trial of Jesus in Luke 23:18), Paul asks the commander a question in Greek, which surprises the commander who thought that Paul was *the Egyptian* (see Josephus, *Jewish War*, 2.261–63; *Antiquities*, 20.169–72) *who started a revolt and led four thousand terrorists out into the desert some time ago*. The commander confuses Paul with an Egyptian who led individuals from one of the Jewish sectarian groups called the *sicarii* (*terrorists*), who were so-named because they used daggers (*sica* means "dagger" in Latin) to kill those, even Jews, sympathetic to Rome. The *sicarii* were the most extreme faction of the Zealots, who opposed Roman rule in a variety of ways.

Paul answers that he is *a Jew, from Tarsus in Cilicia*. Located about ten miles inland from the Mediterranean Sea on the Cydnus River, Tarsus was the capital of the Roman province of Cilicia, which is in the southeast corner of Asia Minor. Along with Alexandria and Athens, Tarsus was known as a center of education (Strabo, *Geography*, 14.5.12–15). After requesting to speak to the people, Paul receives the *commander's permission* to do so.

As the story of Cornelius' conversion (Acts 10) is retold from the perspective of Peter (Acts 11), so now Paul tells the story of his own call (chapter 9) from his perspective (chapter 22). In his retelling, Paul answers the three charges against him (21:28); that is, Paul explains his ties with his people, the Jews, describes his zeal for the law, and reveals that the temple was the very place he received a revelation of Jesus. At the end of the speech, Paul reveals his ministry to the Gentiles.

Many details in the speech show Paul's ties to the Jews. Significantly, Paul's very first words are *I am a Jew*. Although born in Tarsus, Paul tells the crowd that he was *brought up* in *Jerusalem*. Twice Paul describes Israel as *our fathers* (22:3, 14). Ananias is described as *highly respected by all the Jews living* in Damascus.

Paul's zeal for the law is evident in various ways. *Under Gamaliel* (5:34; 22:3), Paul was *thoroughly trained in the law*; Gamaliel is a member of the Sanhedrin, a *teacher of the law*, and *honored by all the people* (5:34; 22:3). Paul then claims that he was *as zealous for God* as any of those listening. He details two examples of this zeal: his persecution of Christians in Judea and in Damascus (verses 4–5). At the close of this speech, Paul concludes with two more examples of his zeal, his persecution of Christians and his support of the martyrdom of Stephen (verses 19–20). It is noteworthy that only this account describes Ananias as *a devout observer of the law*.

Furthermore, only in this telling of the three accounts of Paul's call does one find the detail that Jesus' revelation to Paul occurs *at the temple*. While *praying*, Paul falls in a *trance*; the *Lord* tells Paul *to leave Jerusalem immediately* because his *testimony* will not be *accepted*. The mention of prayer highlights Paul's piety. When Paul reveals that his *witness to all men* (22:15) includes *testimony* (22:18) *to the Gentiles*, it both explains his contact with Trophimus and sends the crowd into another frenzy (see 21:30–31; 22:22–23). The near riot at Paul's mention of Gentiles parallels the response to Jesus' mention of Gentiles in his sermon at Nazareth (Luke 4:16–30; Acts 22:21–23; compare 28:25, 28), showing just how volatile this issue was. Even though Paul attempts to defend himself from the charges against him, his speech only angers the crowd further.

22:22–29 In these few verses, Luke briefly depicts the response of the crowd (22:22–23) and focuses on Paul's use of his Roman citizenship. The response of the crowd includes three actions: *shouting* (21:36; 22:22), *throwing off their coats*, and *flinging dust into the air*. Roman citizenship plays a dual role in the latter part of Acts. First, Paul's Roman citizenship exempts him from flogging, although he does not mention that right until after the flogging when he was in Philippi (16:22–39; 22:25–29). In this passage, the *commander* orders Paul to be *flogged and questioned* to find out why the crowd was so agitated (21:34; 22:24, 30; 23:28). About to be flogged, Paul challenges the punishment (verse 25). Upon learning from the centurion that Paul is a Roman citizen, the commander replies that he had to *pay a big price* for his *citizenship*. The second aspect of Roman citizenship plays a role later in Acts when Paul appeals directly to the emperor (25:11, 12, 21, 25; 26:32; 28:19).

> **Roman Citizenship**
> The commander's reply to Paul in 22:27–28 is consistent with reports that under the emperor Claudius, citizenship was extended much more widely and could even be bought (Cassius Dio, Roman History, 60.17.4). *The tribune's name, Claudius Lysias, also reflects the first century practice of taking the name of the emperor under whom one's citizenship was gained (see 23:26; Ferguson 62–63).*

22:30–23:11 Luke's description of Paul before the Sanhedrin has three parts: the introduction (22:30), Paul's speech (23:1–8), and the threefold response (23:9–11). In the introduction, the commander, still wanting to find out *why Paul was being accused by the Jews* (21:34; 22:24, 30; 23:28), summons *the chief priests and all the Sanhedrin*. One wonders whether Gamaliel, both Paul's teacher and a member of the Sanhedrin (5:21, 34), is present at this assembly. Previous to Paul, Peter, and John (4:5–6, 15), the apostles (5:21–41) and Stephen (6:12–15) have appeared before the Sanhedrin.

After having heard only the first sentence of Paul's speech, the high priest *Ananias* orders those standing near to *strike* Paul *on the mouth*. Paul responds with vehemence: *God will strike you, you whitewashed wall!* Paul's comment (*you sit there to judge me*) seems to indicate that he knows that Ananias sits as high priest. Yet, when Paul is rebuked, he claims not to know Ananias's rank and cites Exodus 22:27 as a warning. How does one explain this exchange? Some have posited that the high priest was out of Paul's view, that Paul's poor vision made him unable to recognize the high priest, or that Paul spoke without thinking. It is perhaps more likely that that Paul responded sarcastically, thus criticizing Ananias; this view fits with the term *whitewashed*, which probably connotes hypocrisy (23:3; see Matt 23:27) and which Paul uses of Ananias. So, Paul is saying that he did not realize that Ananias was the high priest because his behavior did not befit a high priest (see Lev 19:15). Nevertheless, none of these solutions is entirely satisfying.

Knowing the disputed issues between Pharisees and Sadducees, Paul divides the assembly with the next two sentences of his speech. He states that he is a *Pharisee* and that he stands *on trial because of his hope in the resurrection of the dead* (23:6; 24:21). In an aside (verse 8), Luke explains the source of the conflict between the Sadducees and Pharisees.

> **Pharisees & Sadducees**
> *Both the Pharisees and the Sadducees grew out of religious reform movements of the second century BCE. Because the Sadducees' power centered around the temple and the priesthood, they did not survive the war with Rome in 66–70 CE. The Pharisees supplied the early postwar leadership that eventually, with numerous changes, formed rabbinic Judaism.*

The response to Paul's speech is threefold. In the Sanhedrin, there is *a great uproar*, causing the Romans to fear for Paul. So, the commander orders the troops to remove Paul from the assembly *by force and bring him into the barracks*. This is the third time that this commander has rescued Paul from an angry crowd (21:31–32; 22:22–24; 23:10); his fourth and final rescue of Paul comes in the next passage (23:12–35). On the *following night*, Paul hears the third response, one of assurance from Jesus promising a trip to Rome (verse 11). Luke continues to stress God's involvement both in the lives of believers and in the spread of the gospel to Rome.

23:12–22 Although Paul has already faced plots on his life in Damascus (9:24), in Jerusalem (9:29), in Iconium (14:5), and in Greece (20:2–3; compare 20:19), with this plot the threat is elevated in at least four ways. The conspirators have *bound themselves with an oath not to eat or drink until they* have *killed Paul* (verses 12, 14, 21). *More than forty men* (verses 13, 21) are involved in this plot. In addition, they have asked the *Sanhedrin* (verses 15, 20) to *petition* the commander to bring Paul before the council for further interrogation. As planned, the *ambush* (verses 16, 21; 25:3) is imminent; it will happen *tomorrow* (verse 20).

The resolution is both intriguing and impressive, intriguing because of the involvement of Paul's family, impressive because of the show of military force. Somehow, the *son of Paul's sister* hears about the plot and tells *Paul*, who tells a *centurion* to take the boy to the *commander*. After hearing the boy, the commander dismisses the young man and swears him to silence. One wonders about Paul's parents, his sister, and this nephew. Do any of them, besides the nephew, still live in Jerusalem? Are any of them Christians? How does the nephew learn about the plot? Could family members have been involved in the plot? Albeit intriguing, these questions are not answerable. It is clear, however, that Paul's rescue confirms the divine assurance given in the preceding passage (23:11; see also 27:24–25). Next, Luke describes Rome's impressive show of military force as Paul is evacuated from Jerusalem.

23:23–35 Luke's account of Paul's transfer to Cæsarea consists of three parts: Lysias's instructions (verses 23–24), his letter to Felix (verses 25–30), and the journey from Jerusalem to Cæsarea (verses 31–35). Lysias summons two centurions and orders them to prepare a *detachment* of 200 legionnaires and 270 auxiliaries. From this point, Paul remains in Cæsarea until his departure for Rome (27:1). During his stay in Cæsarea, he will appear before a series of Roman officials; thus, at this point, it is helpful to explore Luke's description of the Roman government.

Luke's depiction of Rome is realistic; both positive and negative portrayals exist side by side. Despite Lysias's show of force to protect Paul, Lysias is not entirely honest in his letter to Felix (see below). *Felix* allows Paul *some freedom* and permits *his friends to take care of his needs* (24:23) Even though Felix keeps Paul safe for *two years*, he does so *hoping that Paul would offer him a bribe* (24:26). Moreover, when he is succeeded by Festus, Felix leaves *Paul in prison* because he *wanted to grant a favor to the Jews*; this very phrase occurs again with *Festus* (24:27; 25:9; compare 12:3; 25:3). Although Festus follows Roman law in both Paul's trial (25:4–5) and his *appeal to*

Cæsar, he also speeds up that appeal by asking Paul whether he wants to *stand trial* in *Jerusalem*. The centurion *Julius* refuses to listen to Paul, but does protect him (27:11, 43). Previous to these passages, the same depiction of Roman officials as inconsistent in their attitudes toward Paul emerges. In Philippi, Paul is wrongly beaten, but the officials apologize and release Paul after hearing that he is a Roman citizen (16:19–40). In Corinth, Gallio both dismisses Paul's case and ignores beatings in the middle of his court (18:12–17).

Lysias's letter to Felix is the second letter embedded in the narrative of Acts (15:23–29; 23:25–30). Luke explains that Lysias wrote a letter *having this type* (NIV *as follows*; see Danker 1020), which likely means that the letter is representative of the types of letter that a commander writes, not that Luke has access to the governor's mail. Lysias's letter both reveals his care for Paul and omits his mishandling of Paul's case. Lysias did *rescue* Paul at the temple and *send* Paul to Cæsarea when he was *informed of a plot* (23:27, 30). Lysias, however, neglects to mention that he found out about Paul's Roman citizenship after he rescued Paul and that he almost had Paul flogged (22:23–29).

Luke reports the journey from Jerusalem to Cæsarea as another travel itinerary. Paul travels about 40 miles *during the night as far as Antipatris*, making this journey the third night escape for Paul (9:25; 17:10; 23:31). On the *next day*, only the *cavalry* advances with Paul the 25 miles from Antipatris to Cæsarea. After reading Lysias's letter, Felix informs Paul that he will hear his case when his *accusers* arrive, setting the stage for Paul's defense in chapter 24.

Roman Perceptions of Christianity

Throughout his descriptions of the apostles' dealings with the government, Luke stresses the innocence of Christianity and explains the conflicts between Christians and Jews as intramural differences, not worthy of legal proceedings, thus showing that Rome can coexist peacefully with Christians. As the book of Acts comes to a close, Lysias, Festus, and Agrippa all affirm Paul's innocence (23:29; 25:25; 26:31–32). Paul too affirms his innocence and explains his imprisonment to the Jews in Rome (25:8; 28:17–19). Several times, Luke emphasizes that the accusations against Christians are not matters meriting the attention of Roman officials (18:14–16; 23:29; 24:20–21; 25:18–20; compare 24:10; 26:2–3). Because of his portrayal, Luke hopes that Rome can dismiss anxieties about Christians as a threat.

24:1–27 This passage breaks into three parts: Paul's accusers (verses 1–9), his speech (verses 10–21), and Felix's responses (verses 22–27). As the *governor* or procurator of Judea (52–60 CE), Felix lived in Cæsarea, the administrative center of the province. Surprisingly, Felix was a former slave who had gained his freedom. Appointed governor by the emperor Claudius, Felix ruled poorly according to both Jewish and Roman sources (Josephus, *Antiquities*, 20.182; Tacitus 5.9). He was married to Drusilla (24:24), who was Jewish; she was the daughter of Herod Agrippa I (Acts 12:1–23) and the sister of both Herod Agrippa II (25:13–26:32) and Bernice (25:13, 23; 26:30). Drusilla left her husband Azizus to marry Felix (Josephus, *Antiquities*, 20.139–144), a fact that may account for Paul's decision to speak about *righteousness* and *self-control* to Felix and Drusilla (24:25).

To begin his description of the trial, Luke lists the accusers who arrive *five days later*: the high priest *Ananias* (23:2–5; 24:1; compare 24:9), *some of the elders* (verses 1, 9), and a *lawyer* [Greek *rhetor*] named *Tertullus*. With the greatest level of education in the ancient world, a rhetor is a highly trained, professional speaker. Luke depicts his polished, if long-winded, style, especially in the introductory words of Tertullus's speech (verses 2–4). The actual accusations against Paul come in the following verses: Paul is a *troublemaker* in Jewish communities everywhere; he is a *ringleader of the Nazarene sect*; and he tried to *desecrate the temple*. The *Jews* who *join in the accusation* probably include Ananias and the elders (verses 1, 9).

Paul responds to the accusations, affirming his innocence in several ways. First, he just arrived in *Jerusalem twelve days ago*. Second, his accusers did not find him disputing in the temple, synagogues, or *anywhere else in the city* (verses 12, 18). Third, they *cannot prove* the *charges* they make (verse 13). The only so-called *crime* to which they can attest is what Paul said in the Sanhedrin: *It is concerning the resurrection of the dead that I am on trial before you today*, which does not qualify as a crime in a Roman court (18:14–16; 23:29; 24:20–21; 25:18–20).

Furthermore, Paul is not the ringleader of some sect, but one who *worships* the *God of our* (that is, the Jews') *fathers*, as a follower of the *Way* (verse 14). He came to *Jerusalem to worship* (verse 11); he also came to bring *gifts for the poor* and *to present offerings* (verse 17; see 21:26).

He believes in *the Law and…the Prophets*. He strives to keep his *conscience clear* (verse 16; compare 23:1).

As for desecrating the temple, Paul affirms that he was *ceremonially clean when they found* him *in the temple courts*. Then, he plays his trump card. Those who can attest to this charge, *the Jews from Asia* (21:27; 24:19; compare 19:10), are not in fact present to *bring charges against him*; thus, this charge, if not the whole case, should be dropped.

> **Roman Courts**
>
> Luke portrays Roman courts with considerable awareness of both their internal procedures and their significance to the larger culture. Thus he portrays Paul in Acts 24 as one who can make appeals on both the merits of his case and the failure of his opponents to follow proper procedure.

Luke shows both the long-term and immediate responses of Felix. To the speeches, Felix responds by *adjourning the proceedings*, deferring his decision *until Lysias the commander comes*, and keeping *Paul under guard* but with *some freedom* and care *from his friends*. *Several days later*, Felix and his wife *Drusilla* come to hear Paul speak; Paul's discourse *on righteousness, self-control, and the judgment to come* leaves Felix *afraid*. As the next *two years* pass, Felix sends for Paul *frequently* but only because he hopes that Paul will offer him a *bribe*. Upon leaving his position, Felix keeps Paul in *prison* as *a favor to the Jews* (24:27; 25:9; see 12:3; 25:3).

25:1–12 Luke's description of Paul's trial before Festus is extremely abbreviated; both the accusation and Paul's defense consist of only one verse each (verses 7–8). Rather than record Paul's trial speech, this passage explains why Paul appeals to Cæsar, why Festus consults with Agrippa, and why Paul speaks before Agrippa. The passage falls into two parts: the background to the trial (verses 1–5) and the trial itself (verses 6–12). Festus succeeds Felix as governor; immediately upon arrival he goes to *Jerusalem*, perhaps to build good relations with the Jewish leaders. *As a favor* (24:27; 25:3, 9; see 12:3), the leaders ask that Paul be *transferred to Jerusalem* because they were *preparing an ambush* (23:16, 21; 25:3) to *kill* him. Instead, Festus calls for the accusers to appear with Paul in Cæsarea. *After spending eight or ten days* with the leaders, Festus returns to Cæsarea, convenes the court, and orders Paul to be brought before him.

At the trial, the accusers stand around Paul, *bringing many serious charges against him, which they could not prove*. Although a single sentence, Paul's *defense* is threefold. He has done *nothing wrong against the law of the Jews or against the temple or against Cæsar*. Luke has already depicted Paul's zeal for the law in Paul's speech to the crowd (21:40–22:21; compare 18:13; 21:28; 25:8; 28:17) and in Paul's actions (16:3; 18:18; 20:6, 16; 21:20–26). Paul has already defended his actions in the temple as well (24:12, 18–19; see 21:28; 22:17–22). The new accusation is that Paul has acted *against Cæsar* (25:8; compare 17:8), which will catch the attention of the Roman officials.

Wishing to do the Jews a favor (24:27; 25:9; compare 12:3; 25:3), Festus asks Paul whether he is *willing* to *stand trial in Jerusalem*. At this point, Paul appeals to Cæsar, and after conferring with his council, Festus orders him sent to Rome. As a Roman citizen, Paul has the right to appeal to the emperor (25:11, 12, 21, 25; 26:32; 28:19).

> **An Appeal to the Emperor**
>
> Under Roman law of Paul's time, a citizen had the right to appeal to the emperor when a lower court had not yet reached a verdict in the case. Thus Paul did not appeal his case in the modern sense, but moved for a change of venue. This was a shrewd move in light of the unlikelihood of a fair trial in Cæsarea, much less in Jerusalem.

25:13–22 For the most part, this passage recounts the events of the previous section. In this retelling, however, Luke also begins to reveal the dilemma that Festus faces. On the one hand, Festus has for the most part (verses 9, 11) conducted the legal proceedings properly (verses 4–5, 12). Furthermore, he has attempted to begin his term of office by fostering good relations with the Jewish leaders (verses 1, 6). On the other hand, Festus has not been in office very long (verses 1, 6, 13), and he already has to send an appeal to the emperor, which does not make him appear competent. To make matters worse, he does not have a reasonable charge to record against Paul. Into this situation come *King Agrippa and Bernice*, who arrive *at Cæsarea to pay their respects to* the new governor of Judea. Since Agrippa is both a Roman official and a Jew, Festus may gain some insight as to how to handle this case.

The climax of this retelling explains Festus's problem more fully. Of the accusers, Festus states that *they had some points of dispute with him about their own religion and about a dead man named Jesus who Paul claimed was alive*. Luke first shows the case as an internal dispute between Jews and Christians (verses 18–20; 18:14–16; 23:29; 24:20–21; compare 24:10; 26:2–3). Then, with the mention of the resurrection, one sees how strange that concept is to pagan ears (17:32; 25:19–20; 26:8; compare 4:2; 23:8). Festus explains his quandary over the accusations: *I was at a loss how to investigate such matters*. Omitting his desire to do the Jews a favor (verses 9, 20), he tells about his proposal to send Paul to Jerusalem to stand trial. After mentioning Paul's appeal to Cæsar, Festus concludes his retelling, and Agrippa and Festus agree to hear Paul *tomorrow*.

25:23–26:32   Paul's speech has three main parts: Festus's introduction (25:23–27), Paul's speech (26:1–23), and the responses by Festus and Agrippa (26:24–32). Herod Agrippa II is the son of Herod Agrippa I (12:1–23); his sisters are Bernice (25:13, 23; 26:30) and Drusilla (24:24). Luke first sets the stage by listing all of the prominent people present for Paul's speech. Then, Festus names Paul's accusers. Before concluding, Festus reiterates his verdict; Paul has *done nothing deserving of death* (23:29; 25:25; 26:31–32; 28:18), but, since he has appealed to the *Emperor*, he will go to Rome. With a bit of understatement, Festus thinks *it unreasonable to send on a prisoner without specifying the charges against him*. And at this point, Festus cannot make specific charges against Paul, however. Festus declares that he has brought Paul before Agrippa and the rest so that he *may have something to write*.

In his speech, Paul both defends (26:1, 2, 24) himself and preaches, thus combining the two primary functions of previous speeches in Acts. After receiving permission to speak from Agrippa, Paul motions with his hand in the same way that orators began speeches in the first century (Apuleius, 2.21; compare Acts 12:17; 13:16; 19:33; 21:40). Five times (26:2, 7, 13, 19, 27) Paul directly addresses *Agrippa* as *King*; this speech thus fulfills Paul's call to speak *before Gentiles and their kings* (9:15). Following a polite introduction (26:2–3), Paul describes himself as a faithful Jew and *a Pharisee*. He is on trial for his *hope* (26:6–7) in the fulfillment of God's *promises*.

As Paul retells his call on the road to Damascus (verses 12–18), still more new details emerge; one is especially noteworthy, another surprising. In this account, Paul discloses that Jesus had already described Paul's call (26:16–18). So, while waiting for Ananias, Paul has three days to reflect on Jesus' call to send him *as a servant and as a witness* (verse 16; compare 1:8). With language reflecting the call of Ezekiel (Acts 26:16; Ezek 2:1) and God's servant in Isaiah (verse 18; Isa 42:7, 16), Jesus sends Paul *to open their* (that is, both Jews' and Gentiles') *eyes and turn them from darkness to light*. Surprising are Jesus' words to Paul – *It is hard for you to kick against the goads* – which echo a proverb found in Euripides (794–95).

Paul's response to the vision was obedience (26:19–23). He preached repentance to Jews and Gentiles; his contact with Gentiles prompted the *Jews* to *seize* him *in the temple courts* and to try to *kill* him. Paul affirms that what he preached is consistent with the Old Testament. In this way, Paul ends his defense with a summary of the gospel.

At this point, *Paul's defense* (verses 1, 2, 24) is *interrupted* (as in 17:32; 22:22; 23:2, 6; 26:23), and the scene closes with the responses of Festus and Agrippa. Festus declares that Paul's *great learning* is driving him *insane* (verse 24; compare verse 11). In response, Paul affirms that his message is *true and reasonable* and that the king must know the basic facts of the Christian story. Paul asks *Agrippa* whether he believes the prophets, a question that he deftly sidesteps with a question to Paul. After leaving the assembly, Agrippa and Festus agree that Paul has not done anything that merits serious punishment (23:9, 29; 25:18–19, 25; 26:31–32; 28:18) and that Paul *could have been set free if he had not appealed to Cæsar*. Thus, despite yet another affirmation of his innocence, Paul must go to Rome.

27:1–12   This passage begins a long travel narrative detailing the stops and trials in Paul's journey from Cæsarea to Rome (27:1–28:15). This first stage takes Paul from Cæsarea to Crete. As the journey begins, *Paul and some other prisoners* are handed over to *a centurion named Julius*. Accompanying Paul is *Aristarchus* (verse

---

Paul's History as Persecutor

In Paul's summary of his persecution of Christians (26:9–11), new details emerge. Paul says that *when the* saints were put to death, *he* cast *his* vote against them, *which should probably be understood as Paul's assent, not as Paul literally voting*. In either case, one also learns that more Christians than Stephen died (since 26:10 speaks of plural saints). *Furthermore, Paul reveals that he tried to* force *Christians to* blaspheme *and that he traveled to* foreign cities, *implying more trips to arrest Christians than his recorded trip to Damascus*.

2; see 19:29; 20:4); Luke may also be present, since Acts 27:1 begins the fourth "we passage."

The first stop is *Sidon*. The last time that Paul visited Phoenicia, he was hospitably received at both Tyre and Ptolemais (21:3–7). Now the same happens in Sidon. After sailing by the island of *Cyprus*, the travelers make their way west along the southern coast of Asia Minor, passing the provinces of *Cilicia* and *Pamphylia*, until they finally put ashore at *Myra* in the province of *Lycia*. Changing ships at Myra, Julius finds an *Alexandrian ship* (verse 6; 28:11) headed for *Italy*. After stopping at *Cnidus*, a city at the southwest tip of Asia Minor, they are driven south by the wind past Cape *Salmone*, on the northeast tip of *Crete*. *With difficulty*, they sail to a harbor called *Fair Havens*, near the Cretan town of *Lasea*.

By indicating that it was *after the Fast*, meaning the Day of Atonement, Luke sets the voyage in late September or early October. Because of *dangerous* conditions, almost all travel on the open sea stops from mid-October through March (Fitzmyer 775). At this point, Paul speaks for the first time during the shipwreck narrative (verses 10, 21–26, 31, 33–34) predicting loss of ship, cargo, and life. Instead of listening to Paul, Julius follows the advice of *the pilot and owner of the ship*; the *majority* decides to sail for the Cretan town of *Phoenix* and *winter* there. The fulfillment of Paul's words plays out in the following narrative.

27:13–26 Before the travelers reach Malta, they will endure storm and shipwreck (verses 13–44). In this portion of that narrative, Luke records a long description of the storm and the longest of Paul's "speeches" in the shipwreck narrative (verses 10, 21–26, 31, 33–34). After setting sail, *a wind of hurricane force* sweeps the ship away from Crete, past the small island *Cauda*, and out to sea. After taking a number of measures to save the ship (Stott 389) and being driven by the storm for *many days*, they finally give up *all hope of being saved*. Paul urges them to take *courage* (verses 22, 25) because their *lives* will not be lost, even though the *ship* (verses 22, 41–44) will still be destroyed (verse 22; compare verse 10). Paul bases this change in his prediction (verse 10) on the words of the *angel of the Lord* who assured Paul that he *must stand trial before Cæsar* and that his shipmates will survive. Despite the storm, God will bring Paul safely to Rome (see 23:11; 27:24–25). Paul adds another prediction that comes true in the following narrative: the ship will *run aground on some island* (verses 26, 41; 28:1).

27:27–44 This last section of the shipwreck narrative divides into two parts: an attempt to escape (verses 27–32) and the shipwreck itself (verses 33–44). On the *fourteenth night* (27:27, 33), the sailors sense that they are *approaching land*. *Fearing* that the ship will be *dashed against the rocks*, they drop *four anchors* and *pray for daylight* (verses 29, 39). Some sailors, however, try to escape in the *lifeboat*. Paul warns them to *stay with the ship* (verses 31, 44; 28:1). This time, the crew listens to Paul (verses 31–32; compare verse 10) and cuts the *lifeboat* away from the ship.

Before the ship runs aground, Paul speaks for the fourth and last time (verses 33–34). He encourages them to eat since no one will die. All 276 passengers and crew do so. When *daylight* comes, they decide to run the ship *aground* on the shore. Instead, they hit a *sandbar*, and the surf begins to break the ship *to pieces*. The *centurion* Julius prevents some *soldiers* from killing the prisoners whom they feared might *escape* (verse 42; compare 12:19; 16:27). Whether swimming or holding on planks, *everyone* reaches *the land in safety*. Luke shows that Paul's predictions, which are based on God's assurances (verses 22, 25, 31, 44), are true.

28:1–10 On Malta, Luke's narrative centers on two events: a snakebite (verses 1–6) and a healing (verses 7–10). The *islanders* on Malta show the travelers *unusual kindness* (verse 2; compare verse 7; 27:3), *welcoming* them and building a *fire*. As Paul adds wood to the fire, a *viper* bites him. The islanders think that Paul is someone whom the goddess *Justice* has found a way to punish. After shaking off the snake, Paul does not die, which astounds the islanders who now think that he is a *god* (compare 10:25–26; 12:22–23; 14:11–15; 28:6). This event may echo the *authority* that Jesus gave to the seventy-two *to trample on snakes* (Luke 10:19). It certainly fulfills God's promises of protection on Paul's way to Rome (23:11; 27:24–25).

The healing narrative associates Paul with a high status person, echoes previous healings, and emphasizes prayer. In an attempt to defend Christianity against criticisms, Luke has recorded high status individuals who are among the converts to Christianity. Though not a convert, Publius is still a high-ranking person who associates with Paul, much like the *officials of the province* who are *friends of Paul* (19:31). When Publius's *father* was suffering from *fever and dysentery*, Paul heals him, which is similar to Jesus' healing of a fever (verse 8; see Luke 4:38); Luke thus shows that the same power at work in the ministry of Jesus now works through Paul. Luke mentions that Paul prays before the healing, just as Peter prays before his healing of Dorcas (verse 9; see 9:40).

28:11–16 In a condensed way, Luke's final travel itinerary brings Paul from Malta to Rome. The travelers sail in *an Alexandrian ship* (verse 11; see 27:6) *that had wintered on the island*. On the figurehead, the ship has the *twin gods Castor and Pollux*, who are also known as the Dioscuri and "associated with protection at sea" (Johnson 463). On the island of Sicily, the traveling party lands at *Syracuse* and stays for three days. A brief sea voyage brings them to the mainland of Italy at *Rhegium*, located at the tip of Italy's boot. The final leg by ship lands them at *Puteoli*, a key commercial port on the Bay of Naples. At Puteoli, they *spend a week* with some *brothers* before passing through the *Forum of Appius*, a city named after the consul who initiated the building of the Appian Way. After stopping at the *Three Taverns*, they reach *Rome*, where Paul lives *for two years in his own rented house* (verse 30) *with a soldier to guard him* (verse 16).

28:17–31 The final section in the book of Acts contains an apologetic speech by Paul (verses 17–21), an evangelistic speech by him (verses 23–29), and the conclusion of the entire book (verses 30–31). *Three days after his arrival in Rome, Paul calls together the leaders of the Jews*. He offers the following points in his defense: he has *done nothing against* the Jewish *people* (22:3) or *against* the *customs* of the Jews (16:3; 18:18; 20:6, 16; 21:20–26); the *Romans examined* him *and wanted to release* him (25:25; 26:31–32; compare 23:29); and *when the Jews objected*, he was *compelled to appeal to Cæsar* (25:11, 12, 21, 25; 26:32; 28:19). Rather than offer something new, this speech summarizes Paul's defense in a concise way. The Jews say that they have heard *nothing bad* about him, but they want to hear his views about *this sect* that everyone is *talking against*.

Paul's second speech to the Jews in Rome is more of a sermon. Speaking all day, Paul argues for the Christian faith from the Old Testament. As predicted by Simeon (Luke 2:34), there is a divided response. After a long quotation from Isaiah 6:9–10, Paul's mention of Gentiles prompts dissent, as it does elsewhere (22:21; 28:25, 28; see Luke 4:16–30). As he has done in the past, so in Rome Paul speaks to the Jews first and then turns to the Gentiles (13:46; 18:6; 19:8–9). Paul continues for the next two years to *preach* the *kingdom of God* and teach *about the Lord Jesus Christ* unhindered.

THEOLOGICAL REFLECTIONS

The theology of Acts is very rich, for Luke has tried to show how the early Christian movement reflects the work of God. As such, the church both continues the story of Israel and transposes it into a new key. Let us examine several elements of the book's theology.

CONVERSION

Luke tells how the gospel spreads from Jerusalem throughout the Roman Empire to Rome itself. As the gospel spreads geographically, many respond to the message, and Luke describes a number of these conversions in some detail (2:1–42; 8:4–13; 9:1–20; 10:1–48; 16:13–15, 23–24; 18:8; 26:12–23). Luke's descriptions combine a retelling of God's initiative and human response (5:12–14; 6:7; 8:26–40; 9:1–18; 35, 42; 10:1–48; 11:21; 14:27), although in any single account Luke may emphasize one dimension over the other. For example, in Acts 2 Luke tells how God sends Jesus, provides miracles, raises Jesus, and works through the prophets (2:22, 25, 32); the crowd also responds with faith, repentance, and baptism (2:37–41).

When Luke describes conversion in terms of faith, repentance, and baptism, he works in a similar way; some accounts detail all three components (2:27–41; 19:1–7). Other accounts emphasize belief alone (4:4; 5:14; 6:7; 9:42; 13:12, 48; 14:1; 17:12, 34; 19:18), baptism alone (8:36–38; 9:18; 10:47–48; 16:15; 22:16), or repentance alone (9:35; 11:18). Luke appears confident that the reader knows that all these three aspects work together in a human's response to the gospel. Likely intentional, the first conversion account (Acts 2) is the fullest, functioning as the default mode for future descriptions, even though later descriptions may emphasize one aspect over the others.

DEFENSE OF CHRISTIANITY

Christians raised suspicions among pagans for various reasons. Luke seems not only to be aware

---

Luke's Focus

It may be natural to wonder what happened at Paul's trial or afterwards. Luke, however, has never been primarily interested in the story of any one individual, be it Peter, John, or Paul. It has always been about the spread of the gospel from Jerusalem *to the* ends of the earth *(1:8). With the arrival of Paul at the very heart of the Roman Empire, Luke's part of the story is complete.*

of these suspicions and subsequent criticisms, but also to respond in subtle ways through his narrative, thus defending Christianity (compare *defend* in 19:33; 24:10; 25:8; 26:1, 2, 24; *defense* in 22:1; 25:16; Cukrowski, "Pagan Polemic," 35–84). What are some of the aspects of Christianity that non-Christians find suspect? The crucifixion of Jesus, the resurrection, and the imprisonment of Paul rank high on any pagan's list. Not surprisingly, Luke spends a long time in his discussion of the crucifixion, highlighting Jesus' innocence (Luke 23:4, 14–15, 22, 41, and 47). Paul also tells how preaching *Christ crucified is foolishness to Gentiles* (1 Cor 1:23). Luke shows pagans sneering about (17:32) or doubting (25:19–20; 26:8; compare 4:2; 23:8) the resurrection. In his recounting of Paul's appearances before Roman magistrates, from the local *politarchs* (city magistrates) in Thessalonica to the provincial governors in Judea to King Agrippa, Luke repeatedly emphasizes Paul's innocence (17:5; 23:9, 29; 25:18–19, 25; 26:31–32; 28:18).

Apart from these three major features of Christianity, Luke treats other items that pagans find suspicious about any group. Pagans do not trust anything new, especially religions. Luke, however, connects Christianity to the God of creation and links pagans with interests in all things new (17:16–34). Pagans also mistrust a group that meets in secrecy; in response, Luke points out the worldwide (2:5–11) and the public nature of Christianity (4:16; 5:42; 9:32; 13:49; 16:37; 17:6; 18:28; 19:17, 26; 20:20; 21:28; 24:5; 28:22), with Paul's words to Agrippa typifying Luke's response: *These things were not done in a corner* (26:26). Upsetting the religious order also makes a group suspicious in pagan eyes (16:21; 19:25–27).

Because the Roman government also prizes social and political order, any group disturbing the peace will catch its attention (Acts 16:20–24; 17:5–9; 19:29–20:1; 21:27–36; 22:22–24; 23:7–10; 24:12, 18). Luke cannot deny that riots occurred, but he can show that the disturbances were due to pagan greed (16:19; 19:27), the jealousy of some Jews (17:5), the false assumptions of some Jews from Asia (21:27–29; 24:18–19), and disagreements between Pharisees and Sadducees (23:8). Luke also records political charges against Christianity (17:7; 25:8), but readers of Acts know that Christians are not interested in the political overthrow of the Roman government. Actual crimes also catch the attention of authorities, but Luke makes it clear that the Roman leaders do not find evidence for those charges (18:14–15; 25:18).

Finally, groups that attract only the rabble of society will raise suspicions. As a response, Luke points out that a number of socially prominent individuals convert to Christianity; the most surprising is Sergius Paulus, who, as the proconsul of Cyprus, ranks as a senator. Luke's list of Christians includes at least the following eight well-placed persons or groups: the treasurer of Ethiopia (8:27); Cornelius, a centurion (10:1); Manæn, brought up with Herod (13:1); Sergius Paulus, the proconsul of Cyprus (13:6–12); Lydia, a seller of purple (16:14–15); prominent women in Thessalonica (17:4); prominent women in Berea (17:4); and Dionysius, a member of the Areopagus in Athens (17:34).

To this list, one can probably add Mary (12:12) and Jason (17:5–9), who host house churches. From a Jewish perspective, the priests who convert (6:8) and Crispus, the ruler of the synagogue (18:8),

Luke's "Special" Conversions

Luke records three "special" conversions, special in that at key junctures in the spread of the gospel, God provides confirmation that the gospel is spreading according to God's will.

After the conversion of the Samaritans (8:1–25), Peter and John journey to Samaria. The Samaritans receive the Holy Spirit through the laying on of hands by the apostles, which differs from the reception of the Holy Spirit at baptism (2:38). The presence of the apostles and the coming of the Holy Spirit confirm the reception of the gospel by the Samaritans.

The conversion of Cornelius is Luke's second special case because with the conversion of Cornelius, the Gentiles have a Pentecost of sorts; the Holy Spirit comes on Cornelius, his relatives, and his friends before their conversion (10:44–48), just like the Spirit came on the Jewish converts in Acts 2. Luke makes this comparison between Acts 2 and 10 explicit: The Holy Spirit came on them as he had come on us at the beginning *(11:15).*

The third case is that of disciples of John the Baptist (19:1–7). These disciples receive the Holy Spirit when they are baptized in the name of Jesus; they also prophesy and speak in tongues; both of these actions function as confirmation of the inclusion of disciples of John within the community of Christian believers.

also qualify. In addition, Luke shows that Paul has high-ranking friends, from the provincial officials in Ephesus (19:31) to Publius, the chief official on the island of Malta (28:1–10). Of course, not all Christians are well educated (4:13), and not all high status people convert (13:50; 26:28); yet, throughout his narrative, Luke shows an awareness of criticisms against Christianity and equips his readers to respond to those criticisms.

DIVINE ACTIVITY

As Luke describes the spread of the gospel, God's role stands out. Two emphases especially pervade the narrative. In the first place, Luke stresses the will and plan of God (Squires 1–3); that is, events occur because God is directing and aiding the spread of the gospel. Although this theme appears in various ways, three deserve special attention.

First, Acts uses the word *plan* with reference to God five times (2:23; 4:28; 5:39; 13:36; 20:27). Second, the Greek word *dei* ("*it is necessary*") recurs frequently throughout Acts (1:6, 21; 3:21; 4:12; 5:29; 9:6, 16; 14:22; 16:30; 17:3; 19:21; 20:35; 23:11; 24:19; 25:10; 26:9; 27:24; compare Luke 2:49; 4:43; 9:22; 13:33; 17:25; 21:9; 22:37; 24:7, 26, 44). Third, Luke often shows God acting directly or through some other means, such as an angel or vision (1:3, 9–11; 2:3; 5:19–20; 9:3–6; 10:3–7, 10–16, 30–32; 11:5–10, 13–14; 12:7–11, 23; 16:9–10; 18:9; 22:6–8, 17–21; 23:11; 26:13–18; 27:23–24). Luke also records Jesus' words throughout the narrative of Acts (1:4–5, 7–8; 9:4–5, 10, 11–12, 15; 11:16; 20:35; 22:7–8, 10, 18, 21; 23:11; 26:14–18).

As a second emphasis, Luke affirms that God works in tandem with Christians with the result that divine activity and human activity occur side by side in the spread of the gospel. This joint work appears in various ways. Sometimes the human activity receives a greater stress (2:40–46), even though the divine activity undergirds the narrative (2:47). At other times, the divine and human stand side by side, with both receiving similar stress (8:26–40; 9:1–19a). At still other times, the divine activity stands out over the human, but the human role is not totally muted (Acts 10:1–47; 13:1–3). So, it is probably best to describe the divine/human relationship as synergistic. Although God works *through* (14:27; 15:12; 19:11) and with Christians, sometimes it is not clear exactly how to define that interaction (15:28; 23:11; 27:23–24). For instance, Paul preaches, Lydia responds, and God opens her heart (16:13–14); for Luke, that event shows the integration of divine and human activity. Thus Luke is not interested in unraveling how the divine and human work together. Rather, Luke wants to depict the partnership that Christians have with God in the spread of the gospel.

MAGIC

Although other New Testament writers address the issue of magic (Gal 5:20; Rev 21:8; 22:15), Luke's treatment is by far the most extensive (see Garrett; Cukrowski, *Demons*, 80–92). Luke probably treats magic because it was an issue between Christians and pagans; that is, pagans would see the miracles as evidence of magic, especially ones attributing power to Peter's shadow and Paul's handkerchiefs and aprons (5:14–15; 19:11–12). In the Gospel of Luke, opponents attribute Jesus' power to cast out demons to a demonic source (Luke 11:14–26).

In the four accounts treating magic (8:4–25; 13:4–12; 16:16–19; 19:11–29), Luke distinguishes Christianity from magic, showing God as the source of the miracles in Acts. In the first account, Simon the sorcerer attempts to buy the ability to pass on the Holy Spirit,

> **Luke & Magic**
> Luke's treatment of magic may function as a warning to Christians who have a hard time giving up their attachments to their earlier practices and forms of belief.

which results in a strong rebuke by Peter (8:24). The second occurs on the island of Cyprus when Paul encounters a Jewish magician named Bar-Jesus/Elymas. Because of Elymas's attempt to turn the proconsul from Christianity, Paul issues a strong rebuke, and Elymas becomes blind for a time (13:9–11). In Philippi, Paul faces a former priestess of the oracle of Apollo at Delphi. After casting out her spirit of divination, Paul has to deal with her angry owners, who present a bigger challenge than the slave girl's spirit (16:16–21). Known as the best city to purchase spells, Ephesus is the place where Luke treats magic most extensively. Luke contrasts God's power through Paul with seven Jews who try to use Jesus and Paul's names as "magic words" and who end up *naked and bleeding* after an attempted exorcism (19:11–16). Believers who still own scrolls associated with sorcery decide to burn these items, even though the scrolls have great monetary value (19:17–20). Luke neither denies nor omits the miracles of Christians in Acts, but he does make clear that they are not connected with magic, but rather with the power of God.

PRAYER

As in his gospel, Luke emphasizes prayer in Acts. For him, prayer permeates the life of Christians. Not surprisingly then, prayer is found in a number of different contexts in Acts. For instance, people of faith pray at times of decision. Thus Acts 1 records the apostles' prayer when faced with the choice between Joseph and Matthias as the replacement for Judas (1:24), and Saul prays in Damascus as he waits for further instruction from the Lord (9:11). In several places, Luke also reports that prayer occurs during the commission of a person for a task. The apostles pray when commissioning the seven (6:6), the church prays before sending out Barnabas and Saul (13:3), and Paul and Barnabas pray at the installation of elders (14:23). The third specific context is at a farewell. Before leaving the elders at Miletus (20:36) and before leaving the church at Tyre (21:5), Paul kneels and prays with each group. Fourth, Luke details that Peter and John pray that the Samaritan believers will receive the Holy Spirit (8:15), a type of prayer recorded nowhere else in Acts. As a fifth context, Luke regularly shows Christians praying at a time of crisis. The crises vary from the threat of physical harm (4:31), spiritual danger (8:22, 24), death (7:59–60; 12:5, 12; 27:29), and disease (28:8) to actual imprisonment (16:25) and death (9:40). Last, Luke depicts prayer as a constituent part of a godly life. Thus Luke often shows believers at prayer (1:14; 2:42; 6:4; 10:2, 9; 11:5; 16:16; 22:17). Sometimes prayer occurs at a regular time or place (3:1; 10:4, 30–31; 16:13). Among these prayers, one finds requests for guidance, blessing, safety, boldness, forgiveness, healing, deliverance, and the reception of the gospel. For Luke, the church is a body of people who are constantly in prayer.

WOMEN

As in Luke's gospel, women play a significant part in the book of Acts. In the opening chapter, Luke mentions that *women and Mary* meet with the eleven and other believers, and pray with them (1:12–14). These women probably include some of the women who accompany Jesus during his ministry (compare Luke 8:1–3; 23:49, 55; 24:1–11, 22–25). This initial group of men and women foreshadows Luke's interest in the lives of both the men and women who shaped the early life of the church. Throughout Acts, Luke mentions both men and women as converts (5:14; 8:12; 17:4, 12, 34), as objects of persecution (8:3; 9:2; 22:4), and, less positively, even as persecutors (13:50). As he did in his gospel, Luke pairs accounts of men and women. There are six such pairings in the narrative of Acts: Ananias and Sapphira (5:1–11); Aeneas and Dorcas (9:32–43), Timothy's mother and father (16:1); the conversions of Lydia and the jailer at Philippi (16:11–40); the conversions of Dionysius and Damaris at Athens (17:34); and Aquila and Priscilla (18:1–26).

Very early in his narrative (Acts 2:17–18), Luke signals his interest in the activities of men and women by quoting from Joel 2: *I will pour out my spirit on all people. Your sons and daughters will prophesy.... Even on my servants, both men and women, I will pour out my Spirit in those days. And they will prophesy.* Within a few more chapters, Luke devotes Acts 6:1–6 to the special needs of widows (compare 9:39, 41), and in 9:36, he records the only New Testament use of the female form of the Greek word for "disciple." Among the Christian women mentioned in Acts, one finds women serving in the following five functions: a husband and wife ministry team (Aquila and Priscilla in 18:1–26), hosts of house churches (Mary in 12:12; Lydia in 16:15, 40), prophetesses (the four daughters of Philip in 21:9; see 2:17–18), teachers (Priscilla and Aquila in 18:26), and patrons (the *prominent women* in 17:4 and 12 probably exercise influence on behalf of their fellow Christians).

Women appear within the narrative of Acts not only because they are Christians, but also because they are part of the daily life in the first century, as the following list demonstrates: Candace, queen of Ethiopia (8:27), a slave named Rhoda (12:13–15), women who meet to pray (16:13), the girl with a Pythian spirit (16:16–20), wives with their husbands and children (21:5), Paul's sister (23:16), Drusilla, the wife of the procurator Felix (24:24), and Bernice, the sister of Herod Agrippa II (25:13, 23; 26:30). In these ways, Luke continues in the book of Acts to highlight the activity of women so that the story of their contributions now stretches from the birth of Jesus to the arrival of Paul in Rome.

FOR FURTHER STUDY

David Tuesday Adamo, *Africa and Africans in the New Testament* (Lanham, Md.: University Press of America, 2006).

V. George Shillington, *An Introduction to the Study of Luke-Acts* (London: T. & T. Clark, 2007).

WORKS CITED

Apuleius, *The Golden Ass, Being the Metamorphoses* (trans. and ed. William Adlington and Stephen Gaselee; Cambridge: Harvard University Press, 1915).

Henry J. Cadbury, *The Style and Literary Method of Luke* (Cambridge: Harvard University Press, 1920).

Bruce Chilton, "Gamaliel," *Anchor Bible Dictionary* 2 (1992): 903–6.

Kenneth L. Cukrowski, "Pagan Polemic and Lukan Apologetic." Ph.D. diss., Yale University, 1994.

———, "Demons, Magic, and the Occult." Pages 80–92 in *Fanning the Flame: Probing the Issues in Acts* (ed. Mark E. Moore; Joplin, Mo.: College Press, 2003).

F. W. Danker, ed. *Greek-English Lexicon of the New Testament and Other Early Christian Literature* (3rd ed.; Chicago: University of Chicago Press, 2000).

Cassius Dio, *Dio's Roman History* (ed. Earnest Cary; 9 vols.; Cambridge: Harvard University Press, 1955–1961).

Euripides, *Bacchae* (trans. and ed. David Kovacs; Cambridge: Harvard University Press, 2002).

Everett Ferguson, *Backgrounds of Early Christianity* (3rd ed. Grand Rapids: Eerdmans, 2003).

Joseph Fitzmyer, *The Acts of the Apostles* (Garden City, N.Y.: Doubleday, 1998).

Susan Garrett, *The Demise of the Devil: Magic and the Demonic in Luke's Writings.* (Minneapolis, Minn.: Fortress, 1989).

Ernst Haenchen, *The Acts of the Apostles: A Commentary* (trans. B. Noble, G. Smith, H. Anderson; rev. R. McL. Wilson; Philadelphia: Westminster, 1971).

Ronald F. Hock, *The Social Context of Paul's Ministry: Tentmaking and Apostleship.* (Philadelphia: Fortress, 1980).

Luke Timothy Johnson, *Acts of the Apostles* (Collegeville, Minn.: Liturgical, 1992).

Josephus, *Works* (trans. H. St. John Thackeray and Ralph Marcus; 9 vols.; Cambridge: Harvard University Press, 1926–1963).

Livy, *History of Rome* (14 vols.; ed. and trans. B. O. Foster; Cambridge: Harvard University Press, 1922–1967).

Mikeal C. Parsons and Richard I. Pervo, *Rethinking the Unity of Luke and Acts* (Minneapolis, Minn.: Fortress, 1993).

Minucius Felix, *Octavius* (trans. G. W. Clarke; New York: Newman, 1974).

Pliny the Elder, *Natural History* (10 vols.; ed. and trans. H. Rackham, W. H. Jones, and D. E. Eichholz; Cambridge: Harvard University Press, 1938–1969).

Pliny the Younger, *Letters, and Panegyricus* (2 vols.; ed. and trans. Betty Radice; Cambridge: Harvard University Press, 1962).

G. E. M. de Ste. Croix, "Why Were the Early Christians Persecuted?" *Past and Present* 26 (1963): 6–38.

John T. Squires, *The Plan of God in Luke-Acts* (Cambridge: Cambridge University Press, 1993).

John R. W. Stott, *The Message of Acts* (Downers Grove, Ill.: InterVarsity, 1990).

Strabo, *Geography* (8 vols.; trans. and ed. Horace Jones; Cambridge: Harvard University Press, 1917–1932).

Suetonius, *Divus Claudius* (ed. Donna Hurley; Cambridge: Cambridge University Press, 2001).

Tacitus, *Histories* (4 vols.; trans. and ed. Clifford Moore; Cambridge: Harvard University Press, 1970–1981).

Romans

James Walters

CHAPTER CONTENTS

Contexts 893

Commentary 895
- Introduction · 1:1–17 895
- The Gospel as the Revelation of God's Impartial Righteousness · 1:18–4:25 897
- How the Revelation of God's Righteousness in Christ Is Effective · 5:1–8:39 902
- The Revelation of God's Righteousness & Israel's Unbelief · 9:1–11:36 907
- God's Righteousness & the Community's Ethics · 12:1–15:13 910
- Closing & Final Greetings, · 15:14–16:27 914

Theological Reflections 915

For Further Study 915

Works Cited 915

MAPS, TABLES, & FEATURES

Textual Sources in Romans 895
Paul & the Law 898
Paul's "Already but Not Yet" Eschatology 903

Paul's letter to the Romans has arguably affected the history of Christianity more than any other book of the Bible. Romans is the longest letter in the New Testament – for this reason it appears first in early collections of Paul's letters – but its influence far outstrips any analogy based upon length. Influential Christian thinkers traced their pivotal insights to Romans, and it has had unparalleled influence over the interpretation of Pauline theology. In recent scholarship, however, this understanding of the letter is disputed. With the aid of historical, literary, and theological studies, Romans is now read, not as a theological treatise, but as a genuine letter addressed to a specific situation.

CONTEXTS

Romans reflects ancient Greco-Roman letter writing. The letter begins with a structurally typical greeting followed by the letter body and a closing salutation (see White). Scholars have attempted to identify the Greco-Roman rhetorical forms in the letter in order to trace its argumentation (see Bryan 11–29). Although earlier scholars analyzed Romans as an *epideictic* speech (praise or censure), more recent analyses that call it a *logos protreptikos* (a speech of exhortation designed to win converts) are more promising (Aune in Donfried 278–96). This rhetorical form allows Paul to argue for his version of the gospel and also explains why Paul favors the diatribe style.

Perhaps the greatest debate concerns the purpose of Romans. It is important to distinguish the occasion of Romans from its purpose (for a variety of positions regarding the letter's purpose, see Donfried). Clearly, Paul's plan to extend his mission westward to Spain with the support of Christ-believers in Rome occasioned the letter (15:14–33). However, this does not mean that letter focused primarily on Spain (see Sampley, *Romans in a Different Light*, 109–29). Other factors in Paul's situation influenced his purpose as well.

When Paul wrote Romans, he was traveling east to deliver the money he had collected from Gentile churches for poor Christians in Jerusalem. He believed that acceptance of the collection by the Jerusalem leaders would validate his controversial law-free mission to Gentiles and preserve the unity of Jewish and Gentile Christians. Paul's understanding was based on his meeting with leaders of the Jerusalem church recounted in Galatians 2:1–10. According to Paul, they accepted that he was entrusted with the gospel to the Gentiles as Peter was entrusted with the gospel to the Jews, and they agreed not to require circumcision of Gentiles. All they required, according to Paul, was that *he remember the poor* (Gal 2:10). Paul began the collection project soon after this meeting (1 Cor 16:1–4). For Paul the collection symbolized the unity of Jews and Gentiles as Romans 15:25–29 makes clear.

> **Diatribe**
> *A rhetorical strategy that presents objections of an imaginary conversation partner in order to answer them.*

Yet for Paul the collection symbolized more than unity. It also expressed the spiritual debt Gentile Christians owe to Jews, an indebtedness acknowledged through material gifts. His hopes for the collection project now depend on Jewish Christ-believers accepting the Gentile gift. Therefore what awaits Paul upon his arrival in Jerusalem is a referendum on his entire mission. Because he is uncertain of the outcome, he asks for the prayers of Christ-believers in Rome (Rom 15:30–33). Although reading Romans as a letter to Jerusalem goes too far (as Jervell does in Donfried 53–64), Paul writes this letter with Jerusalem on his mind.

Rome figures into Paul's context because he hopes not only to visit Rome, but also *to be sent on* to Spain by Christians in the capital after he enjoys their *company for a little while* (15:24). No doubt this involves an expectation of financial support, but probably also a desire to tap social networks Roman believers may have in Spain. Paul probably considers Rome a strategic base for his westward mission, a base that is threatened by critiques of Paul and his gospel that he knows will reach the capital before he does (Rom 3:8).

However, Romans is much more than a letter of self-introduction seeking to gain support for the Spanish mission. As the apostle to the Gentiles, Paul believes that he has work to do in Rome as well (Rom 1:15). This letter is at least in part a first installment of his preaching.

The letter is addressed to those *called to be saints* in Rome. Although there is evidence that Christ-believers in Rome included Jews, Romans concentrates on Gentile readers. Some have argued that only Gentiles are addressed (Stowers, *A Rereading of Romans*, 21–33). In this view, arguments in the text between Paul and an imaginary Jewish interlocutor are written to be overheard by Gentiles. In my view, however, Paul also desired at least some Jews to overhear the same argument.

> **Paul's Rhetorical Care**
> *By noting that they are competent to instruct one another, and that his message is really only a "reminder" of what they already know, Paul protects himself against the charge of presumptuousness. Paul believes that the churches in Rome fall within the mandate of his ministry to the Gentiles even though he did not plant these churches. Recognizing the delicacy of Paul's intervention into Roman Christianity is critical for reading this letter.*

Reconstructing the historical situation in Rome is difficult. Not only are we ignorant of the beginnings of Christianity in Rome, we lack sources for sketching its early development. However, two texts offer important internal evidence for the historical context: Romans 11:11–32 and 14:1–15:13. The former rebukes arrogant Gentile Christ-believers for assuming that God has rejected the Jews and that Gentile Christ-believers have taken their place in salvation history. The latter admonishes the strong, who have no scruples regarding foods or special days, to accommodate those who do. If, as I argue below, the strong are primarily Gentile Christians and the weak are primarily Jewish Christ-believers, the connections between 14:1–15:13 and 11:11–32 become evident. The anti-Jewish outlook and arrogance of Gentile Christians reflected in 11:11–32 stands behind the "unwelcoming" posture of Gentile Christians toward Jewish Christ-believers with scruples over foods and special days (14:1–15:13). Christ-believers who rejected Paul's law-free mission to Gentiles probably exacerbated division among Roman Christians along Jew-Gentile lines as well. These opponents of Paul (see Rom 3:8 and 16:17–19) appear similar to those in Galatians.

If we step outside the literary evidence, we learn a few other things. Peter Lampe argues that earliest Christianity in Rome developed within a Jewish synagogue context (Lampe 7–79). Christianity made its way to Rome spontaneously as Jews, proselytes, and sympathizers brought faith in Jesus as messiah with them from the east (see Acts 2:10). They came to Rome as immigrants in business or as slaves. It is not surprising therefore that early Christians lived alongside non-Christian Jews primarily in areas where foreign peoples were concentrated. Christ-believing Jews – and Gentile sympathizers and proselytes – not only shared a religious outlook with non-Christian Jews, but also a common socialization. They were part of the Jewish *ethnos* and of the foreign population of ancient Rome (Lampe 42–47). Therefore, they assembled in synagogues with other Jews in the earliest period.

Over time, however, Christ-believers gathered in their own house churches as Romans 16 indicates. Although this transition was not uncommon in earliest Christianity, the process may have been accelerated in Rome by Roman administrative action (Walters, *Ethnic Issues*, 56–66). According to the ancient Roman historian Suetonius, the emperor Claudius evicted the Jews from Rome because of disturbances in the synagogues instigated by "Chrestus" (*Claudius* 25.4). If by "Chrestus," a common Roman slave name, Suetonius meant "Christus," not a common name, he would be referring to conflicts over issues related to the observance of the law and the inclusion of Gentiles. An eviction of Jews would have included Christ-believing Jews, such as Aquila and Priscilla (Acts 18:1–2), as well as Gentile Christians who "lived like Jews." The edict of Claudius (49 CE) would have been in force until Nero rescinded his decrees in 54 CE.

Claudius's edict would have contributed to a shift in the ethnic composition of these the Christian assemblies because Christ-believing Jews and Gentiles who lived like Jews were expelled. The Christians who played the chief roles in defining the character of the Christian gatherings after the edict, therefore, would have been those Roman Christians who were least shaped by the Jewish context of earliest Christianity in Rome.

It is possible to interpret Romans without relating it to the edict of Claudius. Yet, relating the two provides context for the anti-Jewish sentiments Paul addresses in 11:11–32 and 14:1–15:13. Within this context, Paul strongly argues that the extension of salvation to the Gentiles is rooted in God's promises to Israel, but God will not be *praised with one voice* (15:6) unless Gentiles recognize their spiritual debt to Jews.

As noted above, Paul wrote Romans from Corinth (see 16:21–24) sometime in the mid- to late-50s. The only major question regarding the textual integrity of the larger document concerns chapter 16, which many scholars believe was added later. Doubts about the chapter have arisen because of the number of persons greeted, and their connections to other regions, as well as irregularities in the manuscript tradition regarding the ending of the letter. However, Gamble has shown that the chapter belongs to the original letter, with the exception of the doxology in 16:25–27.

In turning to the structure of the book, note that the letter consists of an introductory section and a concluding section bracketing four large blocks of material. Although there is much scholarly debate over the descriptive headings that should identify these sections, there is widespread agreement regarding the divisions – though some would include 5:1–21 with the preceding block.

COMMENTARY

INTRODUCTION · 1:1–17

1:1–7 Paul begins his letters with a greeting that is structurally typical of Greco-Roman letter writing: sender to addressee, greetings. However, the way Paul describes himself as sender, as well as the way he describes the addressees, varies from letter to letter and often provides a window into the letter's context and purpose. What stands out in Romans is the way he describes his "calling" *to be an apostle* as one *set apart for the gospel of God*. This opens the door for Paul to introduce his Gentile mission in a manner that emphasizes his mission's continuity with Israel. The NIV's *Obedience that comes from faith* reflects the translators' nervousness. "*Obedience of faith*" is a better translation. In no other description of his gospel is its continuity with Israel so prominently on display: It was *promised beforehand through his prophets in the Holy Scriptures regarding his Son, who as to his human nature was a descendant of David*. Paul's mission to Gentiles is no bold move to start

---

Textual Sources in Romans

Numerous intratextual references in Romans indicate resources for Paul's argumentation. The Old Testament is his chief literary source – 53 Old Testament quotations occur in chapters 1–4 and 9–11 alone, but this is not Paul's only textual resource.

Another important resource for Paul is the Jewish apocalyptic tradition (see Collins 264–68). Paul reflects Jewish apocalyptic traditions when he interprets the death of Christ as an assault on the power of sin (Rom 5–6; compare 1 Enoch 1–36). An apocalyptic outlook also permits Paul to argue for human accountability before God, the righteous judge (Rom 1–3; compare especially 4 Ezra and 2 Baruch).

Greco-Roman philosophy also provided an important resource for Paul, as well as for other Jews who engaged in moral exhortation during this period (see Malherbe). Paul's argument in Romans 7, for example, shares much in common with ancient moralists' debates regarding the body and the problem of self-mastery (see Stowers, Rereading 258–84).

a new religion but is merely the continuation of God's work in and through Israel.

Because the idea that Jesus was *declared with power to be the Son of God by his resurrection from the dead* (based on Ps 2:7 and Ps 110:1) occurs nowhere else in Paul's letters (but see 2 Tim 2:8), both this phrase and the previous reference to Davidic descent (based on 2 Sam 7:11b-16) are often interpreted as a preexisting Jewish Christian formulation that Paul incorporated. The formulation reflects a two-stage Christology: before resurrection and after resurrection.

> **According to the Flesh**
> The NIV's *human nature is an unfortunate translation* – here and elsewhere in Romans – of Paul's complex phrase kata sarka, "according to the flesh" (see commentary on chapter 7; see also Wright 417–19).

Grace to you and peace is the standard way Paul greets his addressees. It replaces the common Greek greeting *chairein* with the related Christian word "grace" [*charis*], and adds the Hebrew greeting "peace" [*shalom*] in Greek [*eirene*]. What stands out in verse 7 is not this formulation but rather the phrase *To all in Rome who are loved by God and called to be saints*. Paul typically addresses his letters to a church in a city. Therefore, this greeting should catch our attention. Rome, by far the largest city in the world of Paul's day, had around a million inhabitants scattered over a large area. Instead of a single congregation or a cluster of interconnected house-church cells (as in Corinth), Rome probably had at least five house churches that were less connected (see chapter 16; Lampe in Donfried 216–30).

1:8–15 The thanksgiving and prayer, typical of Paul's letters and other Greco-Roman letters, provides opportunity for the apostle to praise Roman Christians *because [their] faith is being reported all over the world*, and to announce his prayer that *by God's will the way may be opened for me to come to you*. Later in 15:20–24, Paul explains what hinders him from visiting sooner. Such an overture to the readers helps connect Paul with his readers. Accomplishing this is especially critical in this letter because he is writing to congregations he did not plant in a city he has not visited. The delicacy of the rhetorical situation is evident when Paul balances his desire – and authority – to *impart to you some spiritual gift* with the more careful *that you and I may be mutually encouraged by each other's faith*. Compare the tone here with 1 Corinthians 4:14–21.

Verses 13–15 continue to build Paul's relationship to readers by underscoring his regret at not having been able to visit sooner as part of his larger mission. As one who has sought a *harvest* among *other Gentiles*, it is only natural for Paul to seek a harvest among Gentiles in Rome. This is strengthened by his obligation *to Greeks and non-Greeks, both to the wise and the foolish*. The NIV's *non-Greeks* [Greek *barbaros*] is better translated "barbarian" because it is a cultural rather than an ethnic identifier. The phrase means all Gentiles both educated – therefore Greek speaking – and uneducated. The second phrase *the wise and the foolish* restates the point.

1:16–17 Paul follows the statement that he is eager to preach the gospel in Rome with a stark affirmation of his confidence in it: *I am not ashamed of the gospel*. What reason does Paul have for such confidence? *It is the power of God for salvation of everyone who believes*: *for the Jew, then for the Gentile*. The last phrase is better translated "to the Jew first, and also to the Gentile" as in the NRSV because in Romans the distinction drawn here is not only temporal as becomes clear in chapters 9–11.

Explaining how the gospel is the power of God for salvation for *everyone* who believes while still affirming the priority of Israel is Paul's central task in the letter. The next verse gives an extremely condensed explanation: The gospel's power is effective because in it *the righteousness of God is revealed* (NRSV). The NIV's *righteousness from God* reflects one position in a long-standing debate. Is righteousness to be understood primarily as a gift God gives on the basis of faith, or is it God's own saving activity (as Rom 3:5, 25–26; and 10:3 seem to suggest)? The former became the dominant interpretation following the Reformation and reads Paul's argument in Romans primarily as a defense of God's grace against Judaizers (works righteousness). It assumes that the primary question in Romans has to do with how sinners are saved. The latter has been increasingly important in the interpretation of Romans since the 1960s (Käsemann, *New Testament Questions*, 168–82) and sees Paul defending God's saving activity in Christ. This reading assumes that Romans primarily focuses on God's covenant faithfulness (see 3:24–26).

Käsemann stressed the apocalyptic context of 1:17 by claiming that the revelation of God's righteousness involves God reclaiming "the fallen world into the sphere of his legitimate claim" (Käsemann, *Romans*, 29). The causal relation between verses 16 and 17 illustrates how God's "righteousness" in Romans is often shorthand for God's saving activity because it demonstrates God's covenant faithfulness.

The NRSV's *through faith for faith* follows the Greek text more closely than the NIV's *by faith from first to last*. The quotation of Habakkuk 2:4 does not correspond exactly to the Masoretic Text nor to that of the Septuagint. Paul adapts the quotation to connect "by faith," "the righteous person," and "shall live." However, it is a mistake to read them as a structural key to chapters 1–8. The terms and their interconnections are quite complicated in Romans and are better interpreted through reading the letter than parsing the grammar of this very condensed passage. Following this approach, I translate verse 17 as follows: "For in it the righteousness of God is revealed by faithfulness [God's] for faithfulness [of humans], just as it has been written, the righteous one will live by faith/faithfulness."

> **God's Salvation**
>
> *Romans is about the revelation of God's saving activity as an apocalyptic event through Jesus Christ for the Jew first, and also for the Gentile, as a demonstration of God's covenant faithfulness. The letter aims to persuade readers that although this saving activity is universal in scope, it does not undermine God's promises to Israel.*

THE GOSPEL AS THE REVELATION OF GOD'S IMPARTIAL RIGHTEOUSNESS · 1:18–4:25

In the first major block of material in Romans, Paul demonstrates that in the ways God both saves and judges, divine impartiality is apparent. God's activities of "saving" and "judging"– or "showing mercy" and "showing wrath"– are closely related in Romans because righteousness involves God's saving activity in the context of God's covenant faithfulness. The revelation of God's wrath (with its implications for divine impartiality) dominates 1:18–3:20, while the revelation of God's mercy (with its implications for divine impartiality) dominates 3:21–4:25.

It is difficult for modern readers to give divine impartiality its due weight in these chapters (see Walters, *Ethnic Issues*, 68–77). The Protestant Reformation and its theological legacy made justification by faith the center of Paul's thought and the basis of Christianity's "truth" in relation to Judaism. However, as Krister Stendahl puts it, "Paul was not chiefly concerned about on what terms we are to be saved (justification by faith), but rather about the relation of Jew to Gentile and justification by faith was one of his arguments" (Stendahl 3). Moreover, as Jouette Bassler has argued persuasively, the "pivot" of Paul's argument in chapters 1–4 is 2:11, *God does not show favoritism* (Bassler 121). For Paul, justification by faith and judgment by works both demonstrate this thesis.

1:18–32 Paul argues his case by first demonstrating that God's wrath justifiably falls on Gentiles. In verses 18–23 Paul seems to be answering a presumed objection to the "all" of verse 18 (see also 2:17–29). Should Gentiles be held accountable since the law was not given to them? Paul claims that God's *eternal power and divine nature* were plain in creation itself, leaving Gentiles without excuse for their idolatry. Paul connects idolatry with their *thinking becoming futile* and their *hearts being darkened*. This damage (see also 1:28) to one's thinking lies behind Paul's claim that "transformation" from conformity to "this world" requires *the renewing of the mind* (12:2).

Because *they exchanged the truth of God for a lie*, idolatry, *God gave them over* to enslaving passions. According to Paul, God's wrath is displayed against Gentiles in the present by *handing them over* to their passions resulting in unnatural sexual practices (1:24–27) as well as antisocial vices (Stowers, *Rereading*, 92). The causal relationship Paul draws between idolatry and sexual sins is strikingly similar to that found in *Wisdom of Solomon* 14:12–31. Paul's vice list (verses 29–32) confirms the moral decline that results from idolatry by reciting behaviors that were commonly condemned in the Greco-Roman world. Note that according to Paul these perverse actions are not the cause of God's wrath but rather the result. The cause is failure to glorify God.

2:1–16 The abrupt shift to the second person singular (*you*) in 2:1 coupled with the charge of hypocritical judging leads many to assume that the attention shifts from Gentiles to Jews at this point. Stowers argues, however, that such shifts are characteristic of the diatribe style in which one conducts an argument with an imaginary interlocutor. The literary function would be to sharpen the preceding argument into a more personal indictment for Paul's audience (Stowers, *Diatribe*, 93). No one – not even a moralist – may stand with God in judging evildoers. However, by focusing on those who claim special prerogatives, 2:1–13 also functions as a transition to the indictment of Jews beginning in 2:17 (Byrne 80).

The interlocutor is portrayed as one who passes judgment on others while doing the same things they do. Such persons will not escape God's eschatological wrath to be meted out on *the day of God's wrath*. There will be no escape because that judgment will be based strictly on deeds: God *will give to each person according to what he has done*. *Eternal life* will be given to those who do good, while those who are *self-seeking and who reject the truth* (see the indictment in 1:18–28) can expect *wrath and anger*.

The relation of this indictment to Paul's larger purpose in the letter becomes clear in the next paragraph: Judgment on the basis of actual deeds demonstrates God's impartiality. The repetition of the phrase *first for the Jew, then for the Gentile*, echoes the other occurrence of the phrase in the letter's thematic statement (1:16–17). Eschatological rewards, for the evil as well as for the good, are reserved *first for the Jew, then for the Gentile*. The phrase *for God does not show favoritism* looks both backwards and forwards in Paul's argument (Bassler 121, 160; compare the summation in 3:27–31).

However, divine impartiality appears open to dispute because God gave Israel the Law. In verses 12–16 Paul guards this vulnerability by affirming that God will judge those *under the law* and those *who do not have the law* by using standards appropriate to each. Because Gentiles will be judged by *the requirements of the law* and not the law itself, they are ostensibly in the same situation as Jews. Performance is what counts. Readers of Romans are sometimes surprised by this standard. Is salvation based on works after all? Although Paul says that salvation comes through God's grace, not by human deeds, he also says that the renewal God works in human beings must produce deeds that will be judged (see 14:4, 10–12; 2 Cor 5:10; Phil 2:12–13).

The phrases *do by nature things required by the law, they are a law for themselves*, and *the requirements of the law are written on their hearts* sound as if Paul holds a developed theory of natural law. If so, it is surprising that he so rarely bases his ethical arguments on it. Determining what was "according to nature" was a crucial but disputed topic among Greco-Roman moralists (Stowers, *Rereading*, 109–18), as is the meaning of this text for scholars. Are these non-Christian Gentiles, Gentile Christians, or hypothetical Gentiles? The first option seems more likely, though certainty is impossible (see Dunn, *Romans*, 98–107). Nonetheless, what Paul is arguing in this context should be kept firmly in view: because the requirements of the law are a reasonable standard, Gentiles, like Jews, are accountable for their deeds; therefore, God's impartiality in judgment stands.

2:17–3:8 In 2:17 Paul returns to the diatribe but this time his interlocutor is clearly a Jew. Stowers (*Rereading*, 144–50) is correct in identifying the interlocutor as a Jewish teacher of Gentiles, but the critique addresses more than just "Jewish teachers who behave like the one in 2:17–29," as the summation of 3:9 indicates. Verses 25–29 appear to be a generalizing development that prepares for the summation in 3:9. Paul reinforces God's impartiality by demonstrating that no one escapes accountability before God. Both Gentiles and Jews fall far short

Paul & the Law

Paul's understanding of "law" [Greek *nomos*] is complicated and not always clear (see Dunn, Paul and the Mosaic Law). Sometimes he seems to mean law as something like an abstract principle (see 3:27; 7:21, 23). However, in the vast majority of cases he means the law of Moses delivered at Sinai or some portion of it (see 5:13, 20). Sometimes, though, Paul uses *nomos* to refer to the Pentateuch (3:21) or to Scripture more generally (see 3:19 referring to 3:10–18; 7:1–3).

For Paul the law is especially what *distinguishes Jews from Gentiles*. Nonetheless, Gentiles are expected to obey the things required by the law (2:14). For Paul the law is holy, righteous, and good – even spiritual (7:12, 14). The problem with the law is that although it is effective in making one aware of sin, it is powerless to do anything about sin's dominion. Therefore, it cannot be the basis of one's standing before God.

As Paul argues, Christ's death accomplishes what the law could not do with the result that Christ-believers fully *meet* the righteous requirements of the law (8:3–4; see also 13:9–10).

and face God's eschatological wrath as other Jewish apocalyptic materials also claim (see especially *4 Ezra* and *2 Baruch*).

The questions posed in verses 17–23 highlight the prerogatives of Judaism (compare the list in 9:4–5) to undermine the notion that such prerogatives exempt Jews from God's wrath. In fact, as the quotation of Isaiah 52:5 in verse 24 indicates, the opposite is true: Jews are not only accountable for failing to keep the law, they are responsible for the slandering of God by Gentiles!

Verses 25–29 go further. Here Paul challenges the ethnic categories themselves by questioning their perceived boundaries. Recently scholars have emphasized that ethnic identities are not as "objective" as they seem (Cohen). Because Gentiles for centuries had been able to become "Jewish" by converting, Paul is able to exploit the definition of "Jewishness": a Jew is one who lives the life of a Jew. The ambiguity of the address in 2:17 (*if you call yourself a Jew*) prepared the reader for this move: keeping the law makes a person Jewish, not circumcision, and thus those who *keep the Law's requirements* will be *regarded as though they were circumcised* in spite of lacking the physical marks. This move sets up the distinction of verses 28–29, which claims that the real marks of Jewishness are not physical but spiritual. The Greek word *gar* ("for") at the beginning of verse 28 (omitted by the NIV) indicates that verses 28–29 explain verses 25–27. The law without these inward marks is reduced to *written code* [Greek *gramma*], Paul's shorthand for the law absent the Spirit (Rom 7:6; 2 Cor 3:6). Paul believes the *requirements of the law* are valid (see 8:4) but cannot be realized apart from God's revelation of righteousness in Christ Jesus and the Spirit. The Old Testament prophets and their critique of religion are crucial here. This argument, as well as the larger thesis of God's impartiality, creates common ground between Jews and Gentiles by undermining apparent differences. The situation of the Christians in Rome and/or Paul's own context must have accentuated these differences.

> **A Matter of the Heart**
> Like Paul, the Old Testament prophets frequently criticized those who used religion as a cover for sin. See for example the writings of Amos or Micah or Isaiah 1–39. Also like Paul, they believed that the covenant people should live in the context of God's saving activity – God's grace – and thus should lead obedient lives.

Returning to the diatribe style in 3:1–8, Paul deals with two objections. The first arises from the logic of the previous paragraph; the second arises from the first answer. However, he does not answer either objection. Rather, in order to protect his relationship with his readers, his *ethos* in Greek rhetoric, Paul denies radical inferences that could be drawn from his argument. The first objection involves God's faithfulness to promises made to Israel (see chapters 9–11), while the second concerns human accountability (see chapter 6). If those who are not circumcised will be regarded as though they were circumcised if they keep the law's requirements (2:26), it is reasonable to ask, *What advantage, then, is there in being a Jew, or what is the value in circumcision*? Paul claims that being Jewish remains an advantage because Jews were *entrusted with the very words of God*. The *words of God* probably mean "the promises of God" since the issue of God's faithfulness figures so prominently in the argument. Paul claims that being entrusted with God's promises remains an advantage because *lack of faith* on the part of Jews does not *nullify God's faithfulness* as 11:28–29 states even more starkly.

Paul's answer gives rise to the second objection: if God's faithfulness does not depend on human fidelity, and if, in fact, human *unrighteousness brings out God's righteousness more clearly*, does God's judgment of the world make sense? Paul apparently expected this critique of his gospel to have arrived in Rome prior to his letter, as 3:8 (*slanderously reported as saying*) indicates. Here Paul dismisses his critics harshly: *Their condemnation is deserved*.

3:9–20 This section is a summary as indicated by the language of 3:9 (*We have already made the charge*) and the temporal marker (*but now*) in 3:21. This section aims to gather together key elements of the preceding argument to set the stage for 3:21–31.

When Paul uses the phrase *under sin*, he anticipates the next section of the letter, using an idea that lacks development until chapters 5–8. The Greek word for sin, *harmartia*, occurs only two times in this opening argument (3:9 and 3:20), but occurs 41 times in chapters 5–8, typically denoting an enslaving power.

The litany of quotations in verses 10–18 emphasizes the universality of sin (verses 10–12, 18) and its character. Paul reads these Old Testament texts as proof that God holds everyone, both Gentiles and Jews, accountable under the law. That Gentiles are included with Jews in verse 19 as *under the law* catches many readers by surprise even though their obligation to keep the requirements of the law has been stressed throughout the argument (see 2:6–16; 25–29).

When verses 19 and 20 juxtapose the whole world's accountability to God with the law's ability only to make persons *conscious of sin*, as opposed to making them righteousness (compare chapter 7), the stage is set for the revelation of God's righteousness in verses 21–26.

3:21–26 This paragraph restates the thesis of 1:16–17 in light of the development of the argument to this point. Now we know that the phrase *to the Jew first and also to the Greek* (1:16, NRSV) holds in tension ideas about the faithfulness of God to promises made to Israel and God's impartiality, even though the complexities of Paul's solution must wait until chapters 9–11. As 1:17 anticipated, the emphasis falls on Jesus' death as the eschatological revelation of God's righteousness. It is the first time "Jesus Christ" appears in the argument of 1:18–4:25. Even though the efficacy of Jesus' death as *a sacrifice of atonement* is clear in 3:25, the implications of this sacrifice for the salvation of believers is not Paul's chief concern here. Paul primarily wants to show that the way God saves believers through Jesus' death demonstrates God's righteousness. The Greek word that the NIV translates as *righteousness* in verses 21 and 22 [*dikaiosyne*] is the same word it translates as *justice* in verses 25 and 26. The NRSV translates it as *righteousness* all four times. For Paul this word carries considerable freight including God's saving activity, God's covenant faithfulness, and God's justice. All three are interrelated and belong to the meaning of *dikaiosyne* in Romans. Scholars increasingly see God's saving covenant faithfulness as the most common meaning of *dikaiosyne* in Romans (Wright 464–68).

Verse 21 reveals why Paul's gospel is so controversial from Jerusalem to Rome. He claims that God's saving covenant faithfulness has been revealed *apart from law* – though not inconsistent with the testimony of *the Law and the Prophets* (see 1:1–2). Verses 22–24 depend on the thesis of God's impartiality argued previously and supported by God's wrath against both Gentiles and Jews (see especially 3:9).

The interpretation of verse 22 is tied to that of verse 26. There is considerable debate over the phrase the NIV translates *faith in Jesus Christ* in verses 22 and 26 (see Hays, "*Pistis*," and Dunn, "Once More"). Hays argues persuasively that the Greek phrases *dia pisteos Iesou Christou* (verse 22) and *ek pisteos Iesou* (verse 26) should be translated "through the faith [that is, faithfulness] of Jesus Christ," just as the latter phrase is understood when Abraham is the object of the preposition instead of Jesus (see Rom 4:16). According to this reading, the covenant faithfulness of God is revealed through the faithfulness of Jesus for all who believe. Christ's faithfulness is demonstrated in his obedience in the face of death on the cross (see Rom 5:18–21; Phil 2:5–8).

This understanding shifts the emphasis from human faith as the means of appropriating God's gift of righteousness to Christ's faithfulness as the means of enacting God's righteousness. The NIV's translation of *dikaiosyne tou theou* as *righteousness from God* in verse 22 reads righteousness here as a gift that is received by faith. Though Paul certainly believes this to be true (see Rom 4:3, 22–25; Phil 3:9), this is not the main point he is making in Romans 3:21–26. Yet, we

> **God's Faithfulness**
> Dikaiosyne *means the revelation of God's covenant faithfulness in God's saving activity – the eschatological death of Jesus – which demonstrates God's justice. God keeps his promises while not overlooking sin.*

> **Paul's View of Salvation**
> *In Paul's understanding of God's righteousness, salvation is still by* grace *and brings redemption (verse 24). The Greek word for* redemption, apolutrosis, *means to ransom a slave or a captive and anticipates the notion of slavery to sin that will be important in chapters 5–8. Christ's death as a sacrifice of atonement (verse 25) demonstrates God's justice [Greek* dikaiosyne] *because, though patient, God did not finally leave sins unpunished. Although Paul clearly thinks of Christ's death as an atoning sacrifice, modern readers often think this is the primary way he understands the cross. Although true of Hebrews, it is not true of Paul. Paul more commonly thinks of the cross as an apocalyptic event by which the powers of this present age are put on notice (as will become clear in chapters 5–8).*

should avoid making too sharp a distinction. Recently, Christopher Bryan (108) has argued that translators should preserve the ambiguity of the phrase *dia pisteos Iesou Christou* as the KJV did when it translated it as *through the faith of Jesus Christ*. Because scholars who read it as "faith in Christ" and scholars who read it as "Christ's faith" are both able to make their readings square with Paul's theology, he argues that Paul may have had both in mind.

The emphasis on the faithfulness of God and Christ strengthens the connection between faith and obedience for believers. Having the faithfulness of Jesus involves a greater expectation for the obedience of faith than many Protestants have understood faith in Jesus to imply. But this is why Paul described his apostolic mission in 1:5 as calling *people from among all the Gentiles to the obedience that comes from faith* (see also 15:18; 16:26).

3:27-31 This paragraph is a bridge. The opening question connects this paragraph to the previous one. How does the revelation of God's righteousness contribute to the larger argument of 1:18–4:25? By demonstrating that God's saving covenant faithfulness creates one worldwide family of God. The assumed conclusions that *boasting is excluded* and that *God is not the God of the Jews only*, depend on the reader connecting these questions with earlier arguments: there is no difference, for all have sinned (3:22–23); Are we any better? Not at all! We have already made the charge that Jews and Gentiles alike are all under sin (3:9); God does not show favoritism (2:11); the gospel is the power of God for the salvation of everyone who believes (1:16). By strongly excluding boasting, Paul adds the implications of 3:21–26 to the argument of chapter 2 against those who presumed themselves above criticism.

Again, using a dialogical argument, Paul claims that the two pillars of Judaism, monotheism and the law, are upheld in the way God's righteousness has been revealed. *Since God is one* (NRSV) is better than the NIV's *since there is only one God*, because it makes Paul's reference to the Shema (Deut 6:4) more transparent. Because God is one, there must be one people of God. Moreover, if we are justified by Christ's faithfulness and not by *observing the law* (literally "works of the law"), the law should no longer function as an ethnic marker between Jews and Gentiles. *Erga nomou* means those "works of the law" that differentiate Jews from Gentiles as opposed to *the just requirements of the law* (8:4; see Dunn, *Romans*, 1.lxii-lxxii). By making this distinction Paul avoids the charge that his understanding of faith and one worldwide people of God nullifies the law.

4:1-25 Abraham is the key to Paul's claim that one worldwide family of God is in fact testified to *by the Law and the prophets* (3:21). Central to the argument is the opposition between grace and works. However, the main point of the chapter is not to show how God justifies human beings (the bias of post-Reformation exegesis), but to show that the way God justified Abraham demonstrates God's parentage of one worldwide family.

Of course it is true that Abraham was justified by faith, not by works, as verses 2–8 argue. Abraham is exhibit A; David is exhibit B. The next part of the argument (verses 9–15) focuses on circumcision for two reasons: First, because circumcision is the sign of the covenant for Jews and the means by which male Gentiles become Jewish, and separating circumcision from justification opens the door for one worldwide people of God related to Abraham by faith, not circumcision (see also Gal 3). This is exactly the point Paul drives home in verses 16–17.

The phrase *not only to those who are of the law but also to those who are of the faith of Abraham* raises a much debated question: Does Paul mean that this worldwide family is made up of two parts, Jews who are justified by keeping the law and Gentiles who are admitted to the family through Christ? Although more scholars have signed on to this view recently (see Stowers, *Rereading*), it is difficult to reconcile such an idea with Romans 2:17–3:9 and chapters 9–11 (see Räisänen 178–206). *Those who are of the law* refers to Jews (including proselytes) who come to faith in Christ under the law's guidance (see Gal 3:24–29).

Verses 18–25 describe the nature of Abraham's faith (verses 18–22) in a way that parallels Christian faith (verses 23–25). *The fact that his body was as good as dead* when the promise of Genesis 15:5 was made clarifies that Abraham trusts in a God who can create life from the dead. This is the sort of faith that God *credited to him as righteousness* and will likewise be credited to those who *believe in [God] who raised Jesus our Lord from the dead*.

With the shift from the third person (he/she, him/her) and the second person (you, used to address the imaginary interlocutor) to the first person (I, we/us) in verses 24–25, Paul addresses the reader directly for the first time since the letter's introduction (1:5–15). This probably indicates that the phrase, *he was delivered over to death for our sins and was raised to life for our justification*, marks the end of the first major section of the letter by returning to the revelation of God's saving covenant faithfulness, probably in the words of a preexisting Christian confession.

HOW THE REVELATION OF GOD'S RIGHTEOUSNESS IN CHRIST IS EFFECTIVE · 5:1–8:39

The *therefore* of 5:1 indicates that this section depends on the previous argument. Nonetheless, a major transition has occurred. Key terms and phrases like "God's righteousness" and "faith" disappear as "death" and "life" (or "to live" and "to die") come to the forefront. References to "Jews" and "Gentiles" disappear completely and Paul quotes only twice from the Old Testament (there were 21 in chapters 1–4). In chapters 5–8 Paul places the death of Christ in the context of a cosmic struggle between the power of sin and death and the power of righteousness and life. The key players in this apocalyptic drama are Adam and Christ. The central claim of these chapters is that through Christ's death God has defeated the power of sin and accomplished a salvation that has already begun to be revealed.

The key to recognizing the relationship between this and the previous section is noticing the shift in Paul's apocalyptic reasoning in chapters 5–8 compared to chapters 1–4. Recently, De Boer (357–61) pointed out that there are two distinct "tracks" in the Jewish apocalyptic tradition, a cosmic track and a forensic track. A forensic apocalyptic outlook, most evident in *4 Ezra* and *2 Baruch*, emphasizes human responsibility and strict eschatological judgment based on the law. Paul uses the forensic track to drive home human accountability before God, the impartial judge, in Romans 1–4.

However, in chapter 5 Paul shifts to the cosmic track (compare *1 Enoch* 1–36) to develop more precisely how the revelation of God's righteousness has effected change in the larger predicament in which human beings and the whole creation find themselves. In this view, evil forces have entered the world and humans fall victim in a cosmic struggle that they did not initiate. The cosmic scope of the problem emphasizes the common predicament all human beings, both Jews and Gentiles, face. This is the context in which Paul chooses to explore why God's righteousness had to be revealed apart from the law (see chapter 7).

5:1–11 Unlike in the previous section, with the exception of 4:23–25, Paul here includes the reader with first person pronouns. By pointing out that *being justified* also means being at *peace with God*, he shifts the salvation metaphor. By *peace with God* he means the reconciliation of former enemies, as verses 9–10 make clear (see 2 Cor 5:18–19). Anticipating the cosmic conflict between God and sin that dominates the entirety of chapters 5–8, Paul asserts that through faith/faithfulness Christians have changed sides in the conflict. These verses introduce a number of terms that will be important in chapter 8 (hope, perseverance, God's love, and the Holy Spirit), where Paul distinguishes between *present sufferings* and *the glory that will be revealed* (8:18). One can already tell that the terms represent resources for those who have already been reconciled but not yet saved. Verses 3–5 assert that we are able to rejoice in our sufferings because of these resources, but the nature of the help they provide is developed in chapter 8 after Paul explains the cosmic problem and the nature of God's answer. Verses 6–10 elaborate the reason why believers should be hopeful as they await salvation: if God came to our aid while we were enemies, we can be confident that God will stand by us until our salvation is complete.

5:12–21 In this section Paul sets up a framework for explaining how the gospel is the power of God for salvation. He introduces two rival dominions: Adam and Christ. The negative side of the correlation is sketched in verses 12–14. Because of Adam, sin reigns over all human beings because

---

> **4 Ezra & 2 Baruch**
> *These two books were written by Jews around 100 CE. Some Christians have accepted* 4 Ezra *as canonical, and* 2 Baruch *appears in the Syriac Peshitta. Both texts display a heightened sense of apocalyptic expectation, a focus shared with early Christians and some Jews (for example, those at Qumran).*

> **"We will be saved ..."**
> *Salvation in Paul's vocabulary usually refers to final salvation, not to conversion, hence the future tenses in Romans 5:9–10. For Paul, believers have already been justified and reconciled but not yet saved (see 13:11).*

Adam's trespass was not just a simple human misstep, but a cosmic disaster that unleashed sin's dominating power into the world (see 1 Cor 15:21–26; *4 Ezra* 3:21, 26; *2 Baruch* 54:15, 19). Because the Vulgate Latin translation of verse 12c could be understood to assert that Adam was the one *in whom all sinned*, this verse became the key proof text for hereditary depravity (genetically transmitted sin). However, modern translations understand the Greek phrase as causal: *because all sinned*. Paul does not explain how sin spread; rather, he wants to show that because of Adam sin entered the world as a malevolent power. Adam's sin changed the nature of the cosmos in which humans live, including humans themselves. This is why verses 13–14 distinguish the period between Adam and Moses from the period after Moses. For Adam and those after Moses (that is, after the law was given), there was a command to be broken. However, sin was in the world as a power prior to the law of Moses, as indicated by death's reign, even though there was no command to break. It is this understanding of sin as a power that is critical to Paul in Romans 5–8.

Because Adam represents the dominion of sin, he is a *pattern of the one to come*, who represents the dominion of grace (namely, Christ). Although Adam and Christ are similar in that they are representative figures, verses 15–17 highlight their differences: gift versus trespass; condemnation versus justification; death versus life. Note that *death* and *life* are reigning powers according to verse 17. In verses 18–21 Paul associates *one trespass, condemnation, disobedience, sin,* and *death* with Adam while their counterparts are associated with Christ: *one act of righteousness, justification, obedience, grace,* and *life* (compare 1 Cor 15:54–55). In verse 19 Paul uses *obedience* to describe Christ's death supporting the idea that the Greek *pistis Christou* in 3:26 means not "faith in Christ" but "Christ's faith/faithfulness." Verses 20–21 make it clear that sin and grace are both powers in a cosmic struggle: *where sin increased, grace increased all the more.* Therefore, as 1:16 claimed, the gospel is the *power of God for salvation*.

The contrast Paul draws between these two rival dominions, his description of their character, and the way he portrays God as destroying the old age and establishing a new age share much with Jewish apocalyptic eschatology. Jewish apocalyptic scenarios typically depict two successive ages: an

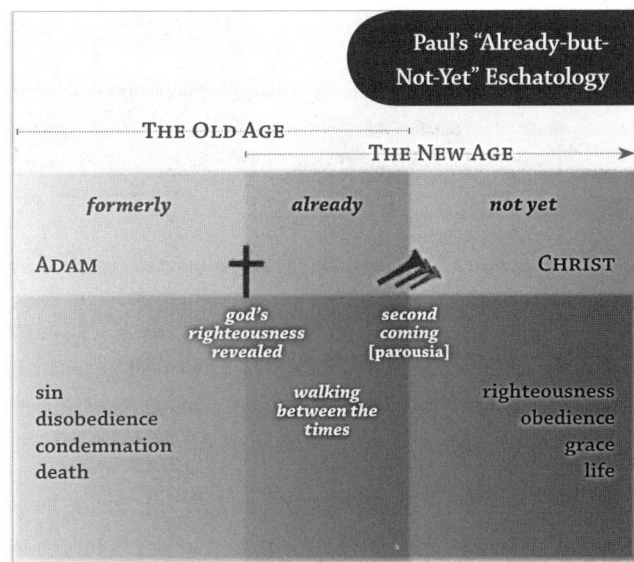

evil age in which the righteous inhabit a corrupted earth and suffer great hardship, followed by a new age in which God reigns over a new heaven and a new earth where the righteous are vindicated. The transition to the new age awaits God's dramatic action. Paul, however, was not waiting for God's dramatic action because he believed it had already occurred in the death and resurrection of Jesus. In the Jewish apocalyptic tradition, the earlier prophets' expectation that justice will occur within human history gives way to the expectation of justice through a general resurrection of the dead and final judgment. With Paul's Damascus Road vision of the risen Christ came not only the conviction that Jesus was God's Messiah, but also that God's eschatological intervention to set things right had begun. Yet God's redemptive work is not complete because the old age (Adam) has not met its end (see 1 Cor 15:20–28). The reign of Adam/sin predated the reign of Christ/grace, but now they coexist. In fact, their overlapping status explains the tensions believers experience in the present: joy and suffering, freedom from sin and assault by sin. Paul Sampley (*Walking*) aptly describes the present experience of believers as "walking between the times."

6:1–7:6 The question of whether Christ-believers should go on sinning is asked twice in this section (6:1, 15). Paul offers three answers. Romans 6:1–14 answers "no" because we have moved from death to life. Romans 6:15–23 answers "no" because those freed from sin are now slaves to righteousness. Romans 7:1–6 answers "no" because those freed from the law of their first marriage now belong to another, Christ (Meyer 1053–54).

According to 6:1–14, the resurrection of Christ demonstrates that the dominion of life is more powerful than the dominion of death. Paul's related claim that *where sin increased, grace increased all the more* raises an objection that Paul raised in 3:8 but now faces squarely: *Shall we go on sinning so that grace may increase*? Or to put it another way, does Christ's victory over sin and death render human obedience irrelevant? Paul answers, *By no means*! Since Christians are no longer *in Adam* but are *in Christ*, their new identities must be reflected in how they live. Jewish apocalyptic writers often divide the cosmos into spheres of influence as Paul does when he contrasts Adam and Christ. Hence, baptism is *into Christ* (see 1 Cor 12:13; Gal 3:27). Since Christians have shared in Christ's death by their baptism and have been raised to *live a new life*, while still waiting to be *united with him in his resurrection*, any continuation of a life dominated by Adam/sin is unthinkable. However, sin continues to look for an opportunity to reestablish Adam's dominion, indicating that Christ-believers are not yet out of Adam's reach (see 8:23; 1 Cor 15:35–57). The *old self* that *was crucified with him* (*Christ*), is the Adamic self. Wright (533–36) is probably correct that the association of baptism with changing dominions reflects the story of the exodus in which Israel passed through the sea to escape slavery (see 1 Cor 10:2).

An important feature of Paul's moral reasoning is reflected in verses 1–4 and then 5–14, often referred to as the "indicative" and the "imperative" in Pauline ethics. The "indicative" refers to Paul's declarative statements regarding God's redemptive work in Christ. The "imperative" refers to commands for believers that reflect the in-breaking of God's new creation. Once this structure is recognized, it becomes evident that the relationship between the indicative and the imperative is not haphazard. For Paul, the indicative always precedes the imperative. God has done X; therefore, believers must do Y. Verses 1–4 declare *you have died*, the indicative of God's redemptive work in Christ. The next paragraph (verses 5–14, especially verses 11–13) features commands based on God's redemptive work: *Therefore do not let sin reign in your mortal body* (the first explicit exhortation in Romans). The progression between the two paragraphs is essentially "you have died with Christ" (verses 1–4); "therefore, consider yourselves dead" (verses 5–14). What God has done through Christ is the necessary precondition for what those "in Christ" are able to do, illuminating again what Paul means by *obedience of faith*. Note that the reason given for not offering *the parts of your body to sin* (verse 13) is that we have been *brought from death to life*. Christ's death and resurrection have broken the dominion of sin and our baptism into Christ has freed us from its dominion. The rejection of sin as master (verse 14) because we are *under grace* reflects the apocalyptic notion of power that is so central to the argument. *Because we are not under law* raises the question of how the law figures into this apocalyptic drama: does the law belong to the dominion of Adam or to that of Christ? Chapter 7 faces this question more squarely.

As 6:15–23 continues the argument, freedom from law does not mean freedom to sin, because those freed from the dominion of sin (Adam) are now under to the dominion of righteousness (Christ). No one is without a master. In this section Paul moves from the death/life imagery of verses 1–14 to the image of slavery in order to clarify that his gospel does not allow a life of sin as opponents claimed (see 3:8; 6:1). For Paul baptism marks a transfer of allegiance resulting in *slavery to righteousness leading to holiness*, not *slavery to impurity and to ever-increasing wickedness*. The question is which master? The slavery to be preferred is obvious.

In 7:1–6, Paul is still answering the question *Shall we go on sinning*? (6:1). This paragraph restates the basic point made in 6:15–23, but by switching to a marriage metaphor adds that freedom to belong to another requires death. As in the previous paragraph, being "unbound" is not an option: one is freed to *belong to another*. This metaphor also marks a transition to the next section by asking how Christ's death affects obligation to the law. The marriage analogy works because death negates the prior obligation to the law without rejecting the validity of the law's instructions: Without the death she would be *called an adulteress*. The analogy is awkward because the one who dies is also the second husband. However, the basic point is clear enough: the woman represents the Christian who is freed from the law's condemnation by the death of Christ. The phrase, those *who know the Law*, does not indicate that Paul necessarily addresses only Jewish readers since many Gentile converts were already synagogue adherents (God-fearers or proselytes) prior to their conversions, and because the Jewish Scriptures were the Scriptures of the early church for both Jews and Gentiles. The *new way of the Spirit* versus the *old way of the written code* is shorthand for an important distinction: through the Spirit, Christians can fulfill the just requirements of the law while not being under the law. *Written code* equals the law without the Spirit, therefore bondage (see Rom 8:1–4; 2 Cor 3:6).

7:7–25 Paul again resorts to the diatribe to counter objections. The question *Is the Law sin?* arises for the same reason as the question, *Shall we go on sinning?* in 6:1. Paul's own argument raises it. Because Paul defends the law by dramatizing the enslaving power of sin, he must distinguish between the law's impotence in the face of sin's dominion and the identification of the law itself with sin.

> **"Had it not been for the law ..."**
> The switch to the first person singular, I," has led many readers to conclude that Paul is describing the frustration he faced trying to keep the law prior to his encounter with Christ. Most modern scholars, however, disagree with this reading because elsewhere (Phil 3:6) Paul describes his life under the law with great confidence, as "faultless." Therefore, in Romans 7, Paul is looking back as a redeemed person who now understands the unredeemed state.

Regarding chapter 7, Stowers has argued that using the rhetorical device of speech in character, Paul addresses Gentiles who are attracted to the law as a means of self-mastery. Paul identifies with his Gentile audience as one who uses the law to gain self-mastery but who finds that the law is not the answer to the problem of enslavement to appetites and passions (Stowers, *Rereading*, 258–84). Stowers's summary, "the law is not the problem but also not the answer" (280), captures Paul's argument nicely. Dramatizing the problem of self-mastery in light of the reign of sin in verses 13–25 helps remove responsibility from the law by placing it squarely on sin as verses 7–12 claim. Stowers is probably correct that Gentiles are in view but mistaken that they are the only ones in view.

In verses 7–12 Paul faces the issue of the law's association with sin by asking, *Is the Law sin?* His answer to the question is the same one he gave to the question of whether one should go on sinning: *certainly not* [Greek *me genoito*, 6:2, 15; see also 3:4, 6, 31]. Paradoxically, the law produced knowledge of sin but extended sin's power. The commandment against coveting (Exod 20:17; Deut 5:21) makes one aware of one's own *covetous desire*. What Paul means by *when the commandment came, sin sprang to life* finds its best commentary by comparing 5:13–14 and 5:20. In fact, verses 7–12 are closely related to 5:12–21. According to 5:20, sin increased when the law arrived (compare 5:13). Perhaps the existence of a prohibition generates desire, but Paul also thinks that with the arrival of the law there was an increase in trespasses because they were now being counted against people resulting in an increase in sin's power. The relation between sin and death in this paragraph is complex and depends on connections developed in 5:12–21 and 6:1–23. Paul understands the payment for sin to be death (6:23). However, death is not simply the end of one's life, it is also a power that entered the world as a result of sin and spread, a reading of Genesis with an apocalyptic worldview. To be under the mastery of sin is to die; to be under the mastery of righteousness is to live (see 5:17).

In verses 13–25, verb tenses shift from past to present dramatizing the impotency of the law as a tool for achieving self-mastery. All human beings, Jews and Gentiles alike, lack the power to escape sin's grip. The question, *Did that which is good, then, become death to me?* with the repeated answer, *By no means!* reminds the reader that Paul aims to defend the law in this argument. As noted above, the "I" of verses 13–25 is not autobiographical but rhetorical: It dramatizes the powerlessness of human effort in the face of sin's apocalyptic dominion. When the overwhelming power of sin is recognized, the law's failure to curb it deflects criticism from the law itself while underscoring the human predicament: *What a wretched man I am! Who will rescue me from this body of death?* Verse 25 anticipates the answer of 8:1–11. The NIV's *sinful nature* is an unfortunate translation of the Greek *sarx* (*flesh* in NRSV and other translations) because it encourages modern readers to equate sinful nature with the body itself. The problem with the body is not that it is sinful by its very nature (see 1 Cor 6:19–20), but that the body becomes subject to the dominion of sin.

8:1–17 If the law is not the problem but also not the answer according to 7:7–25, Paul is poised to give the answer in 8:1–11: *there is now no condemnation for* *those who are in Christ Jesus*. Being set free from *the law of sin and death* does not equate the law with sin and death – an equation Paul explicitly denies in chapter 7. Rather it recognizes that with the law came the recording of transgressions (see 5:12–21) and therefore death, because *the wages of sin is death* (6:23). Verses 3–8 give an explanation for the assertion of verses 1–2. Although Paul claimed already in 1:16 that the gospel is *the power of God* for salvation, only after 7:7–25 is it apparent why power is so critical: *For what the law was powerless to do in that it was weakened by the flesh* [Greek *sarx*], *God did by sending his own Son*. Chapter 7 explains how the law was *weakened by the flesh* [Greek *sarx*]. The problem of the flesh is how to do good while under the dominion of sin. Even those *in Christ* continue to live in a body that has kinship with Adam and, therefore, the dominion of sin. How does one navigate this eschatological predicament? By means of the Spirit, the eschatological gift of God for believers who are walking between the times. Because those *in Christ* have their *minds set on what the Spirit desires*, they *live according to the Spirit*. Consequently, they fulfill the *righteous requirements of the Law*.

The Spirit is not just a mindset; it is eschatological life-giving power. It is the power that raised Jesus from the dead and that already gives life to Christians while they await their final resurrection. Verses 9–11 use striking words for this eschatological power: *Spirit*; *Spirit of God*; *Spirit of Christ*; *Christ*; and *Spirit of him who raised Jesus*. In verses 12–17 Paul exhorts readers to live according to their new identity as God's children. As God's adopted children they are no longer under obligation to the flesh. The NRSV's translation of *huiothesia* as *adoption* is preferable to the NIV's *Spirit of sonship*. Continuing to live according to the flesh would be a denial of new adoptive status. That the Spirit is eschatological power is clear in verse 13: *if by the Spirit you put to death the misdeeds of the body, you will live*. The filial relationship created through adoption is attested by the Spirit through the child's cry: *Abba, Father* (*abba* is the Aramaic word for father; see Gal 4:6–7). The adoptees are now God's heirs and co-heirs with Christ. However, although the future inheritance promises a *share in his glory*, currently it involves a *share in his sufferings*.

8:18–39 The contrast in verse 18 between present sufferings and future glory open the clearest window into the eschatological outlook that is central to the entire letter. Christians, even the whole creation, live in hope of final redemption. In Paul's narrative of God's creation and redemption of the world, *present sufferings* are the result of God's cursing of the ground (creation *subjected to frustration* and in *bondage to decay* allude to Gen 3:17–19). Adam's sin affected not only human beings but all of creation. This cosmological aspect of the problem is crucial for understanding Paul. Forgiveness of individuals is not enough. Because sin is an issue of cosmic scope, God must redeem the entire cosmos, including human beings. Both creation and *we ourselves groan* in the pains of childbirth awaiting final redemption. Although not stated explicitly in this text, both the liberation from bondage anticipated by the creation and the *redemption of our bodies* will take place at the second coming of Christ (see 1 Cor 15:23). For Paul, God's future reign has already broken into the present with the death and resurrection of Christ. Those who are in Christ already participate in that reign even while still having bodies like Adam. Those who are *in Christ* were formerly slaves to sin but are now slaves of righteousness. Although they have not yet experienced the redemption of their bodies, they have already received the Spirit that attests their adoption and enables them to put to death the deeds of the body.

> **Adoption**
> In Greek law, adoption freed the adoptee from any debts that might otherwise be inherited from the natural parents and established new inheritance rights (see Walters, "Adoption").

> **Birth Pangs**
> The pains of childbirth provide an excellent analogy for Paul's apocalyptic outlook. Unlike other types of pain, labor pains are good news because they indicate that the sufferer is getting closer to joy. Yet this sufferer must understand clearly what is going on, because otherwise the expectant mother would anticipate death instead of life. The sufferings of believers, therefore, do not indicate that God's life-giving effort has failed. On the contrary, because these pains are birth pains, they offer assurance that everything is proceeding properly. Therefore, patient hope is the appropriate posture for Christ-believers who understand the drama of God's cosmic redemption and who already have the firstfruits of the Spirit.

In verses 26–30 Paul assures readers that during this period of birth pains the Spirit intercedes and that God acts on their behalf. In the beginning of chapter 5 Paul assured Christ-believers that the God who came to their aid while they were enemies can be counted on to work out their salvation (see 5:1–11; Phil 1:6; 2:12–13). It is no surprise, therefore, that the vocabulary of 8:18–30 is so similar to that of 5:1–11 (suffering; perseverance; hope, love, Spirit). Predestination language is common in apocalyptic literature as it emphasizes God's firm control in circumstances that may appear to be spinning out of control.

In a rhetorical flourish of courtroom language, verses 31–39 drive the point home by alluding to God's purpose in verse 28 and reflecting on the implications of God's loving commitment to those he has called. *The love of Christ* (verse 35) corresponds to the love of God (5:8). Two lists dramatize Christ's loving commitment: the first (verse 35) recounts physical human hardships; the second (verses 38–39) focuses on suprahuman, cosmic threats. Paul states eloquently that God is unfailingly on the side of those called.

THE REVELATION OF GOD'S RIGHTEOUSNESS & ISRAEL'S UNBELIEF · 9:1–11:36

In recent years, scholars have come to see these chapters as central to Romans, perhaps even the climax of the letter. Because "righteousness" in Romans means covenant faithfulness, these chapters are unmistakably bound to the previous argument. Paul noted two objections to his explanation of God's righteousness in 3:1–8. The first involves its implications regarding the faithfulness of God, while the second concerned its implications regarding morality. Chapters 5–8 explained how the revelation of God's righteousness in the death and resurrection of Christ was effective in a way that answered the second question. Now Paul focuses squarely on the question of God's faithfulness to the promises he made to Israel.

9:1–5 Paul's affirmation of God's unfailing commitment to those he has called in the previous paragraph launches Paul into a defense of God's apparent failed commitment to Israel. In verses 1–4a, Paul uses a personal oath to express his anguish over the people of Israel, wishing he could be cut off from Christ for their sake (see Exod 32:31–32). *Cursed* is very strong language (see 1 Cor 16:22; Gal 1:8–9). Instead of exploring the reason for his concern, Paul enumerates Israel's advantages in a list reminiscent of 3:1–2. The list of advantages in verses 4–5 climaxes in the affirmation of Christ's Jewish ancestry (see 1:3). In verse 5 it is unclear whether there should be a period after *Christ*, or a comma as in the NIV.

9:6–29 Elizabeth Johnson is correct that the central question of chapter 9 "concerns not who is in the family and who is out but who is in charge and to what purposes" (Johnson 225). As she (223) demonstrates, the progression of Paul's argument is straightforward. First, ancestry is determined by God's promise rather than by human descent (verses 6–9), and election is based on God's call rather than on human works (verses 10–13). Second, God's call is not arbitrary but serves the purposes of divine wrath and mercy, hence the examples of Pharaoh (verses 14–18) and the potter's vessels (verses 19–23). Third, both Jews and Gentiles have been called in the same way (verse 24): God mercifully calls Gentiles (verses 25–26); and God mercifully calls Israel (verses 27–29).

> **God's Election**
> *Paul assumes that if readers understand how God's election works, they will not conclude that God's word has failed. The issue is God and God's actions, not Jews or Judaism. This is easy for modern readers to miss.*

Verses 6–9 explore the difference between Isaac and Ishmael for insight into divine election. Both were descendants of Abraham, but only descendants of Isaac were *regarded as Abraham's offspring* (see Gen 25:12–18). If Israel does not equal the descendants of Abraham, what is the determinative factor? The answer is God's promise! Verses 10–13 demonstrate that works have nothing to do with justification. God's decision was made prior to birth. *Loved* and *hated* correspond to *chosen* and *not chosen* as in Malachi 1:2–3.

Verse 14 asks in diatribe style, *Is God unjust?* In other words, does the analysis above indicate that God's election is unfair or arbitrary? Paul answers "no" because there is a divine purpose: *God's mercy*. The hardening of Pharaoh (see Exod 7:3, 13–14; 8:19; 9:12; 10:1, 20, 27; 11:10), for Paul, demonstrates that the nature of God's elective purpose is to show mercy, in this case to Israel. The hardening of Pharaoh's heart, a Gentile, contributed to the salvation of Israel from Egypt.

Paul repeats the challenge to God's justice in verse 19 in view of the forceful claim of verse 18: *Therefore God has mercy on whom he wants to have mercy, and he hardens whom he wants to harden.* Now Paul shifts to the potter and the potter's wheel analogy (see Isa 45:9–13) to accentuate God's sovereignty as verses 20–21 make clear. The analogy focuses on God's freedom, not human bondage. The added feature is that God's election is governed by the desire to show both mercy and wrath. Paul is not concerned with the election of individuals, as the use of *Israel* indicates. Pharaoh represents Gentiles as the counterpoint to Israel; he is not "exhibit A" for individual predestination in this argument.

Paul's claim in verse 24 that God calls both Jews and Gentiles is supported in verses 25–29 with Old Testament quotations but in reverse order: Gentiles first, then Jews. Paul quotes Hosea 1:10 and 2:23 in verses 25–26 to portray God's love for the unloved as focused upon the Gentiles. In verse 27 Paul shifts to God's mercy toward Israel. Citing Isaiah 10:22 and 1:9, Paul emphasizes how pivotal were God's elective actions on Israel's behalf: without God's mercy, Israel, like Sodom and Gomorrah, would have been annihilated. This reinforces the central claim in 9:6 that God's word had not failed. Although there is a note of judgment here (*only the remnant will be saved*), it is important to remember that the subject is still God's elective purpose of showing mercy, as verses 23–24 indicate.

9:30–10:21 In the previous argument Paul maintained that God's election was not arbitrary but rather aimed at showing mercy both to Jews and to Gentiles. Using a rhetorical question (*What then shall we say?*), Paul finally states the historical fact that stands behind the entire argument of chapters 9–11: the proclamation of the gospel has proven more effective among Gentiles than Jews. Paul's reference to the grief he felt for Israel in 9:1–2 already assumed this fact, but it remained unstated until now: Gentiles *have obtained [righteousness] ... Israel has not.* In order to explain what happened to Israel, Paul employs the metaphor of a footrace. Although Israel ran with zeal, the Gentiles obtained the prize because Israel *stumbled over the "stumbling stone."* Ironically, Israel loses the race because she tries too hard – pursuing righteousness *as if it were by works. Gentiles, who did not pursue [strive for* in the NRSV] *righteousness, obtained it* because righteousness depends on faith/faithfulness, not on works of the law. For the meaning of *law of righteousness* in verse 31 compare the similar contrast between law and faith in 3:27 and recall that keeping the law is what distinguished Jews from Gentiles. This permitted Jews to "boast" of their ethnic identity as the people of God. They mistakenly thought that righteousness was something they could possess by observing the law instead of understanding it to be a divine possession, God's covenant faithfulness. This caused them to confuse God's faithfulness with partiality (see 10:11–13). The *stumbling stone* over which Israel tripped may refer to Christ. However, given Paul's elaboration in 10:14–16, the proclamation of the gospel may be more accurate.

In 10:1–17 Paul focuses on Israel's responsibility for the current state of affairs – in marked contrast to the emphasis on God's determinative role in chapter 9. Romans 10:1–4 covers much of the same ground as 9:30–33 but without relying on the footrace imagery. In language reminiscent of Philippians 3:9, Paul distinguishes between establishing one's own righteousness by observing the law and submitting to God's righteousness. Verse 4 describes what submitting to God's righteousness entails: Christ reveals God's saving covenant faithfulness *for everyone who believes* (see 3:21–26). By sending Christ, God demonstrated his faithfulness, and Christ's faithfulness (that is, his death) makes believers righteous. Therefore, *Christ is the end of the law*. The Greek word translated *end [telos]* can mean "termination" or "goal." In light of 8:3–4 and 13:8–10, "goal" is the better translation. The goal of the law is righteousness and through Christ it is realized.

Verses 5–13 elaborate on the claim of verse 4, particularly the universality of righteousness by faith. Quoting Leviticus 18:5 in verse 5 and Deuteronomy 30:12–14 in verses 6–8 Paul sets up a contrast between *righteousness that is by the law* and *righteousness that is by faith*. As verse 4 anticipated, what distinguishes the latter is its nearness: *The word is near you; it is in your mouth and in your heart*.

"I have run the race ..."
Paul and other early Christian writers regularly employed athletic imagery. In all major cities of the Roman Empire, gymnasia, stadiums for chariot races and track and field, and arenas for gladiatorial contests were common, drawing large crowds and often employing well-paid professional athletes. Paul's culture was as fond of sports as ours is.

The *mouth* and the *heart* in verse 8 correspond to *confessing* and *believing* in verses 9–10, providing Paul the bridge between early Christian worship practice and the language of Deuteronomy 30:14. That Paul understands the nearness of the word to indicate its accessibility and universality is evident in verses 11–13. The context places the emphasis in the quotation from Isaiah 28:16 on *anyone* in verse 11. *For there is no difference* reminds the reader of 3:22, while *the same Lord is Lord of all* closely parallels 3:29–30. As often in Paul, especially with Old Testament quotations, Lord here refers to God. To *call* on God in verse 12 means to trust or look to God, and anticipates the quotation of Joel 2:32 in verse 13 with the emphasis on *everyone*.

In verses 14–21 Paul assigns responsibility for the apparent breakdown of Israel's election. Although bringing righteousness near through Christ should have served God's elective purpose of showing mercy to Jews and to Gentiles, Israel rejected it. The rhetorical questions of verse 14 set up a causal relationship among calling, believing, hearing, preaching, and preachers being sent out. By interpreting the *message* as the *word of Christ* (Christ as the content of the preaching, not Christ's teaching), Paul presents Isaiah 53:1 as a prediction of Israel's rejection of the gospel in verse 16. The rhetorical questions and quotations in verses 18–19 make it clear that God satisfied every condition in the causal chain in verse 14. God has been faithful; Israel has not. Paul reads *their voice* in Psalm 19:4 to be Christian missionaries, leaving no doubt that Israel heard (verse 18). In verse 19 Paul again finds Moses predicting what has recently taken place: God has made Israel *envious* and *angry* by provoking them with Gentiles (Deut 32:21). He then reads Isaiah 65:1 as predicting the surprising response of the Gentiles to the gospel, and Isaiah 65:2 as its surprising rejection by Israel.

> **The People of God**
> Drawing together the threads of the preceding argument, Paul claims that because God has not rejected Israel, neither should Gentile Christ-believers. He asserts that the salvation of Jews and Gentiles are interdependent and that Israel's apparent replacement as God's elect people by Gentiles is an illusion. Israel's salvation has been delayed, not cancelled.

Verses 19–21 repeat the paradox of 9:30–33 while preparing the reader for the next chapter: Even though God was faithful to Israel while Israel was not faithful to God, God is not finished with Israel. When Paul claimed in 9:6 that *God's word had not failed*, he meant it. Even in Israel's defiance God's elective mercy is still at work making Israel envious through the Gentiles – a point he will develop further (see 11:11, 14).

11:1–10 The diatribe returns with the rhetorical question of 11:1, *Did God reject his people*? The question follows naturally from 10:18–21. For Paul, God has not rejected Israel since in the very act of showing mercy to the Gentiles God is pursuing Israel. He supports his answer to the question by once again appropriating remnant language (compare 9:27). Using himself as an example, he argues that Jewish Christ-believers are themselves evidence of God's continuing loyalty to Israel. As the story of Elijah demonstrates, God does not annul Israel's election because the majority disobeys (1 Kgs 19:10, 18). Underscoring that the present remnant is *a remnant chosen by grace* highlights the continuity of divine election by alluding to the claims of 9:11–12. Moreover, the claim that the *others were hardened*, supported by the quotations in verses 8–10, causes the reader to think of Pharaoh (9:16–18) and brings to the surface the paradox that underlies the whole argument of chapters 9–11: Israel cannot see because God blinded them; Israel stumbled because God tripped them. The passive voice, *were hardened*, indicates that God was the one who caused it.

11:11–16 This paragraph draws together two threads: The purpose of God's election is to show mercy (9:16–18), and God uses Gentiles to make Israel envious (10:19–21). God tripped Israel to show mercy to the Gentiles. By showing mercy to the Gentiles God will make Israel envious. *Their fullness* in verse 12 means "their full inclusion" (the remnant plus the others), anticipating 11:26. *I am talking to you Gentiles* is not a shift in audience since Gentiles are the primary audience throughout. The phrase underscores Paul's relationship to the readers as *apostle to the Gentiles* permitting him to associate his own ministry with God's larger purpose of making Israel envious. In the first fruits metaphor (see Num 15:17–21), the *part* and the *whole* in verse 16 are analogous to the *remnant* and the *others* in verses 5–7. This indicates again that Paul expects an influx of Jews as a result of the Gentile mission. The root and branches of verse 16b provide a bridge to the olive tree metaphor in the next section.

11:17–24 In this paragraph Paul puts aside the question of whether Israel's stumbling is permanent to deliver a warning. Gentile Christians are *a wild olive shoot* grafted into a tree whose *natural branches* are Jewish and whose nourishing roots are also Jewish. Arrogance on the part of Gentiles is out of place because *You do not support the root, but the root supports you* (see 15:27). The potential objection in verse 19 comes from a Gentile this time, as in 2:1–5. As Paul's exposition of divine election has shown, Jewish branches were indeed broken off so that Gentile branches could be grafted in (verse 19), but the reason is unbelief, not partiality. Therefore, fear, not arrogance, is the appropriate Gentile response. Verses 23–24 turn back to the question of whether Israel's stumbling is permanent by asserting that God has the power (see 1:16) to graft the broken branches back into the olive tree, all the more easily since they are *natural branches*. Paul extends the analogy for his own purposes beyond the actual practice of horticulture as *contrary to nature* signals.

11:25–36 The final section has two parts. In verses 25–32 Paul concisely repeats his defense of God's faithfulness to Israel, and in verses 33–36 he concludes with praise and a doxology. Paul, in good apocalyptic style, reveals a mystery in order to check Gentile conceit: although Israel is currently hardened, when *the full number of Gentiles has come in* God will turn his attention back to Israel *and so all Israel will be saved* (verses 25–26a). Paul continues to speak of ethnic Jews not the church as a "new Israel," or "true Israel." Paul expects an influx of ethnic Jews into the church when God's hardening of Israel has served its purpose. In remnant theology *all Israel* does not mean every single descendant of Abraham but, rather, the inclusion of many others; hence, no longer just a remnant. The brevity of the summary Paul offers in verses 28–32 depends on the argument in chapters 9–10. Verse 28 expresses the historical paradox dramatically: Israel's failure to respond to the gospel versus Israel's election. How can both be true? The phrase, *on your account*, is critical. The Jews are currently *enemies* (of God, or of the gospel?) because God hardened them in order to show mercy to Gentiles. This, however, does not negate Israel's election because *God's gifts and his call are irrevocable*. It does delay Israel's inclusion because an effective Gentile mission must occur first to make Israel envious. If this sounds unlikely, Paul offers a history lesson that reminds readers how God's elective mercy works: if Jews are now disobedient, they are in the same position Gentiles were once in prior to God's mercy being shown to them. As verse 32 makes clear, assigning both Gentiles and Jews to disobedience is a prerequisite for God's elective mercy. Therefore, God's faithfulness and impartiality remains intact.

The three exclamatory lines in verse 33 may come from an early Christian hymn. The content of the lines and the questions that follow in verses 34–35 draw loosely on Jewish wisdom and poetic traditions to acclaim a God who transcends human judgment and understanding, and thus a God whose actions require the revelation of a mystery (verse 25).

GOD'S RIGHTEOUSNESS & THE COMMUNITY'S ETHICS · 12:1–15:13

Beginning with 12:1 there is an unmistakable transition to moral exhortation for the community of Christ-believers. Gathering such material at the end of a letter is typical of Paul (see Gal 5–6; Phil 4; 1 Thess 4–5). In 12:1–13:14 we find more general exhortations while 14:1–15:13 focuses more narrowly on a single issue. The central message is clear: the revelation of God's saving covenant faithfulness involves an eschatological renewal that equips Christ-believing communities to function properly both in relations between insiders and with outsiders.

12:1–2 Two features of this introductory transition especially connect the exhortations that follow to earlier themes: offering your bodies as living sacrifices *in view of God's mercy*; and transformation from *the pattern of this world*. In chapters 9–11 Paul emphasized that God's hardening of Pharaoh and his subsequent hardening of Israel came from God's desire to show mercy. In 11:30–32 he summarized the sweep of the entire argument by stating:

Apocalyptic Imagery

In ancient Jewish apocalyptic literature, God sets numbers and times (see Dan 11:36 and 4 Ezra 4:36–37) and reveals mysteries (in apocalyptic literature, it is because the truth is hidden that it must be revealed [see 1 Cor 2:6–13]). Paul uses such literary devices because he believes that, in Christ, God has begun the eschatological age of cosmic transformation.

For God has bound all men over to disobedience so that he may have mercy on them all. Although Paul uses a different Greek word for mercy in 12:1 [*oiktirmos* instead of *eleos/eleeo*], the allusion is unmistakable: because God has been so faithful in mercifully pursuing Jews and Gentiles, recipients of God's mercy should respond with a *spiritual act of worship* (literally "*reasonable act ...*"), a sacrifice pleasing to God, namely, themselves.

Do not conform any longer to the pattern of this world reminds readers of the dominion of Adam and the dominion of Christ, so important in chapters 5–8. Using this apocalyptic image Paul exhorted readers no longer to submit to Adam/sin's mastery but to *live a new life* (6:4). Paul's assertion that radical transformation depends on *the renewing of the mind* recalls that Gentile impiety led God to *give them over to a depraved mind* (1:28) with the result that their *thinking became futile and their foolish hearts were darkened* (1:21). He embarks on this series of moral exhortations because he believes that with Christ's death and resurrection come new possibilities (see chapters 7–8). Because these new possibilities result from the revelation of God's righteousness, the exhortations of chapters 12–15 are inseparable from the argument of chapters 1–11. These exhortations, especially in chapters 12–13, focus especially on social relations.

> **Transformation**
> Because sin, in Romans, darkens the mind, it is no surprise that transformation *is required for* Christ-believers to be able to test or discern God's will (see 2 Cor 3:17–18; Phil 1:9–11). For Paul, forgiveness is not enough.

12:3–8 Using a social metaphor common in the ancient world, Paul appeals for humility so that a body of diverse members can realize the benefits of diversity – a variety of gifts available to the body – without sacrificing the unity of the community (see 1 Cor 12:12–30). A more sober self-assessment occurs when one recognizes *the measure of faith God has given you*. Because the capacities Paul mentions (prophesying, teaching, encouraging, contributing, leading, and showing mercy) are gifts from God, as well as the faith to exercise them, there is no room for self-aggrandizement. Not only do members have different gifts, they may also have a different *measure of faith* affecting how gifts are exercised (compare verse 3b with verse 6). This may be why Paul describes believers who eat only vegetables in 14:1–3 as weak in faith (see also 14:22–23), and why he counsels the strong to welcome them.

12:9–21 This series of concise exhortations flows from the opening admonition: *love must be sincere*. However, this passage lacks the careful exposition of love reflected in 1 Corinthians 13, which also follows a body metaphor. Although the structure is loose, verses 9–13 focus on relationships between insiders while verses 14–21 concern (primarily) relationships with outsiders. Paul emphasizes humility. Nonretaliation is the dominant admonition governing relations with outsiders. Because the Romans were suspicious of private religious associations, it was important for Christian house churches not to draw unnecessary attention to themselves or provoke hostility from neighbors (compare 1 Thess 5:15; 1 Pet 2:11–17; 3:8–12). Retaliation by members of despised minority groups against oppressors confirms the prejudices of suspicious outsiders.

13:1–7 Paul's general warnings against retaliation in 12:19–21 give way in this paragraph to more specific instructions that also suggest prudent steps to avoid conflict with outsiders – this time with political administrators. The recent Claudian edict that expelled Jews from Rome, including the Jewish Christians Prisca and Aquila (Acts 18:2; Rom 16:3–4), vividly illustrates the importance of staying off the radar of Roman administrators. Submitting to *the governing authorities*, as 13:1 directs, was the surest way to avoid attracting such unwanted attention (see also 1 Pet 2:13–14; 1 Tim 2:1–2; Titus 3:1). Most of this paragraph provides a theological rationale for such submission: because governing authorities exist under God's sovereignty, resisting them resists God. The

> **Government & Authority**
> Readers of Romans 13 must remember that Paul was a missionary, not a theologian composing systematic doctrine. He does not discuss governmental abuse of authority. Paul can be more negative about governmental authorities (see 1 Cor 6:1–6). For Paul, God may use governments to advance holy purposes, but in Paul's apocalyptic outlook they belong unquestionably to the sphere of Adam. By establishing and nurturing eschatological communities, Paul was in fact subverting Roman authority because Roman administrators viewed private associations as political threats (Horsley).

conviction that all authority ultimately rests on God's authority is reflected in the Old Testament prophets (Isa 41:1–4; 45:1–3), in the wisdom tradition (Prov 8:15–16; *Wisdom of Solomon* 6:1–3), and in apocalyptic writings (Dan 2:37–38; 4:17, 25, 32).

Here, Paul's goal is narrowly focused: to encourage Christians to keep their heads down by living peaceably with their pagan neighbors and by not engaging in rebellious activities. Tragically, Paul's attempt to provide a survival strategy for a tiny, vulnerable Christian minority has been used throughout history to encourage passive acquiescence on the part of powerful Christians and "Christian" governments who could have played a far greater role in standing up against oppressive policies and regimes (see Elliott). Paul operated in a very different context from that of modern democracies.

The specific reference to paying taxes, using Greek terms for direct and indirect taxes, in verses 6–7 may indicate special dangers associated with resisting payment of taxes in the context of tax riots during Nero's administration (Walters, *Ethnic Issues*, 65–66). Or, it may reflect common awareness of where political dissent often gets measured.

13:8–14 The transition in verse 8 places the "debts" enumerated in 13:7 in perspective: These debts should be settled so that *the continuing debt to love one another* might be the sole focus of attention. Love for one another was also central in the exhortations of 12:9–21. For love as the fulfillment of the law, see also Galatians 5:14. Paul's use of Leviticus 19:18 as a summary of the law, probably derived from Jesus' teaching (Matt 22:34–40; Mark 12:28–34; Luke 10:25–28; see also Matt 7:12). This text also provides important commentary for Paul's claim that those who walk according the Spirit fulfill the *righteous requirements of the law* (8:4).

The dualistic images of darkness and light, coupled with assurances that time is running out, remind readers of the apocalyptic character of Paul's gospel (see 1 Thess 5:4–10). *Salvation is nearer* refers to the second coming of Christ. *Clothe yourselves with the Lord Jesus Christ* is probably an allusion to baptism (see Gal 3:27) and the new life that is to follow (Rom 6:4; see also Eph 4:22–24; Col 3:9–14; 1 Thess 5:8).

14:1–15:13 The admonition in 15:7 provides an accurate summary of this entire section. Paul clearly calls upon the *weak* and the *strong* to accept one another. Yet, the persons or groups to which the labels refer are disputed. The one *whose faith is weak*, *eats only vegetables* (14:2), and *considers one day more sacred than another* (14:5) while the one whose faith is strong *eats everything* and *considers every day alike*. Is this a dispute about Jewish dietary laws and Sabbath observance? Jews were not generally vegetarians and *special days* sounds broader than Sabbath-keeping. However, verse 14 refers to food that is *unclean* [Greek *koinos*] and this Greek word was only used of Jewish dietary practices. Moreover, the summary call for mutual acceptance in 15:7 is buttressed by Old Testament quotations in the following verses that have Gentiles praising God together with Jews. Thus Paul uses the more general terms *vegetables* and *special days* because the labels *weak* and *strong* do not exactly fit as ethnic categories. Some Jews, like Paul, had fewer scruples about diet and Sabbath while some Gentiles had more. By using the more general terms Paul avoids treating the problem as a Jew versus Gentile issue. By formulating his argument in a more oblique fashion Paul is able to address a delicate Jew-Gentile problem without reflecting negatively on Jews and Judaism, the very thing he takes pains to avoid because of Gentile Christian arrogance (see 11:17–24). It is important to recognize that this passage is fundamentally about how persons with power, the strong, live with people who lack power, the weak, in a community of Christ that belongs to the new age.

From the opening admonition of 14:1–12, *accept him whose faith is weak*, the weight of Paul's exhortation falls on the *strong* though this label does not appear until 15:1. *Weak* must have been an epithet assigned to more scrupulous believers by their opponents, the *strong*. Designating the weakness to be a weakness of *faith* may be Paul's way of anticipating the argument he

> **Dietary Regulations**
>
> *Dietary restrictions and Sabbath observance were behaviors that clarified boundaries for Jews (see Gal 2:11–14). As Romans 14:5–6 makes clear, Paul has no problem with the behaviors themselves: God can be honored either way and the motives of both groups are commendable. However, he does have a problem with foods and days functioning as community boundaries; hence, his censure of judgment over such matters in verses 3–4.*

will make in 14:13–23, especially verses 22–23. *Without passing judgment* announces the central issue to be argued in this section. *Disputable matters* over which believers should not judge one another contrast with other matters (sexual immorality, greed, idolatry, slander, drunkenness, and swindling) that Paul argues elsewhere should be grounds for judgment within the community (see 1 Cor 5:9–13).

Verses 5–6 picture both groups carrying out their respective practices in honor of God while verses 7–9 claim that every activity is to be God directed, even death. In verse 9 Paul links the case for this universal lordship – over the living and the dead – to Christ's death and resurrection (see Phil 2:5–11). Everything in verses 5–9 flows from the question in verse 4a: *Who are you to judge someone else's servant*? Therefore, in verses 10–12, Paul brings the reader back to the issue of judgment with rhetorical questions in verse 10 unmistakably linked to the initial question of verse 4a, but now with more force. For Paul *God's judgment seat* and Christ's judgment seat are interchangeable phrases (see 2 Cor 5:10).

The next section (14:13–23) opens with a wordplay. Because the Greek verb translated *passing judgment* in the NIV in verse 13a is the same verb translated *make up your mind* in verse 13b, modern readers miss the wordplay. Making a decision is central to the meaning of *krinein* ["to judge"]. Therefore, Paul's wordplay means "Those determined to make a judgment should make this judgment: do not create an obstacle for a fellow believer." The remainder of the chapter underscores and defends this mandate. Food may be neutral to some, but not to everyone. The terms *clean* and *unclean* [Greek *koinon*] reflect Jewish dietary distinctions (see Mark 7:19), indicating that the *strong* are primarily Gentile believers. How one believer could *destroy* another by *eating* (verse 15) becomes clear in verses 20–23: because what does not proceed from *faith* (conviction) is sin, those who experience the food as *unclean* are guilty of sin when they eat it. Hence, if the *strong* pressure the weak to eat what their faith does not permit, they are clearly *no longer acting in love*. It should be noted that Paul introduced the whole section in 14:1–12 with this understanding of *faith* (compare his use of *knowledge* in 1 Cor 8). Verses 16–19 encourage readers to focus on the things that matter most: *righteousness, peace and joy in the Holy Spirit. Kingdom of God*, a rare phrase in Paul, indicates that *righteousness, peace and joy* should be understood as eschatological gifts (see chapters 1–8) which believers already experience in the present – though only partially (see 8:18). The association of *peace* with *mutual edification* in verse 19 suggests that for Paul peace with God (see 5:1) is the basis for peace between Christ-believers. *Whatever you believe* (verse 22) assumes that Christians could *believe* different things while leaving individual believers accountable to God for what each one *approved*.

In 15:1–6, Paul includes himself among the strong even though the strong were mostly Gentile believers. In the first paragraph (verses 1–6) Paul exhorts the strong to follow Christ's example of looking out for the interests of others. In verse 4 Paul defends reading the Old Testament eschatologically through the lens of the death and resurrection of Christ as a means of generating *hope* among Christ-believers. That Paul emphasizes *endurance* should come as no surprise for those who can imagine the complications involved in having Christ-believing Jews and Gentiles praising God *with one heart and mouth*.

> **The Pattern of Christ**
> *Although Paul's letters rarely appeal directly to Christ's example for moral exhortation, Christ's death on the cross reflected a pattern for Paul. It was a death for others. Christ's faithfulness was revealed most fundamentally when he did not please himself (see Phil 2:1–11). Thus Paul quotes Psalm 69:9 here in Romans 15 to drive the point home by reading insults to refer to the derision Christ endured (compare Mark 15:23, 36). Christians live as Christ lived.*

The argument about weak and strong, and in fact the main body of the letter, concludes in 15:7–13. The connections to chapters 9–11 are especially strong. Verse 7 repeats the exhortation that began the discussion in 14:1 but now – because of 14:1–15:6 – the reader knows what *Accept one another* will require. In this paragraph the specific problems of Jews and Gentiles dining together give way to an expansive vision of God's covenant faithfulness demonstrated by Christ becoming a *servant of the Jews* confirming *the promises to the patriarchs* so that Gentiles might glorify God together with Jews. The litany of Old Testament quotations emphasizes the inclusion of the Gentiles. The prayer in verse 13 closes the body of the letter by connecting the readers' experience of joy, peace, and hope to their continuing trust in God's covenant faithfulness.

CLOSINGS & FINAL GREETINGS · 15:14–16:27

15:14–33 This section, together with 1:1–17, forms the frame of the letter by which Paul builds his relationship to his readers. In verses 14–24 Paul gently defends his interference with churches he did not plant by balancing their competency *to instruct one another* with his *priestly duty* as *minister of Christ Jesus to the Gentiles*. In this metaphor the Gentiles are a sacrifice Paul offers to God. Referring to the letter's content was intended *to remind* them; also it guards against negative responses some might have to his encroachment.

Because his eastern Gentile mission is complete (Jerusalem to Illyricum), he is ready to embark on a westward mission to Spain and hoping to win the partnership of Roman Christians in that mission. However, even though Paul has *been longing for many years to see* the Romans, he is currently traveling east to Jerusalem rather than west toward Rome because he must deliver the collection to Jerusalem first. Delivering this collection will make good on a promise that Paul made at the Jerusalem conference (Gal 2:7–8). For Paul this collection recognizes the debt Gentile Christ-believers owe to Jews while obligating the Jerusalem church to accept Paul's Gentile churches and mission – thus tying up loose ends in the east before he heads west. The debt Gentile Christians owe to Jews, acknowledged in the collection, is consistent with the olive tree metaphor in chapter 11 and with the obligation the strong owe the weak in 14:1–15:13. Paul's request for prayer that he might be *rescued from the unbelievers in Judea* and that his *service in Jerusalem* might *be acceptable to the saints there*, reflects how important Paul understood the delivery of this gift to be as well as the anxiety he felt.

16:1–27 The conclusion of the letter contains five distinct parts: A recommendation of Phoebe who apparently carried the letter from Corinth to Rome (verses 1–2); personal greetings (verses 3–16); a warning against false teachers (verses 17–20a); greetings to Roman Christ-believers from persons with Paul in Corinth (verses 21–23); and, a formal doxology (verses 25–27).

Phoebe, a *servant* [Greek *diakonos*, deacon] *of the church in Cenchrea* (one of Corinth's ports), was likely a woman of some financial means. Her influence was related to her role as a patron [Greek *prostatis*; see Walters, "Phoebe"]. Paul's brief letter of recommendation suggests that she was the letter carrier, probably because she had other business in Rome.

Of special note in the greetings are Prisca and Aquila, Andronicus and Junia(s), and the various groupings of persons that are reflected (see especially verses 14–15). Prisca and Aquila (see also Acts 18:2, 26; 1 Cor 16:19; 2 Tim 4:19) had returned to Rome after being expelled when Claudius evicted the Jews (Acts 18:1–2). Paul's note that *all the churches of the Gentiles are grateful to them* not only indicates their Jewish ethnicity, but also underscores a key theme in the letter: Gentile Christ-believers have received spiritual blessings from Jews. The identification of *Andronicus and Junia(s)* as *outstanding among the apostles* and as apostles before Paul clearly highlights their status as Jewish missionaries whose work even predated that of Paul. Moreover, because the second name is more likely the feminine name *Junia* rather than the masculine *Junias*, we likely have here a missionary couple and a female apostle (see Walters, "Phoebe"). Paul's groupings of greeted individuals around households (see 16:10, 11, 14, 15) reflects the domestic setting of early churches and indicates as many as five to eight house churches in Rome. Whether some of the house churches included more Jewish Christians and were more law observant than others is uncertain but probable (see Lampe in Donfried).

The sharp warning against false teachers in verses 17–20a is reminiscent of Philippians 3:18–19. The harsh tone reflects Paul's concern that agitators, perhaps like those in Galatia, would pervert the gospel.

Why So Many Greetings?

Manuscript evidence indicates that the formal doxology at the end of Romans did not belong to the original letter. Many ancient manuscripts do not include it while others have it after 14:23 or 15:33. None of Paul's other letters concludes with a doxology. The letter originally ended with a benediction (verse 20b) that followed verse 23. Because of manuscript evidence that Romans circulated in shorter versions early on, many scholars have argued that chapter 16 was a separate letter addressed to another location (perhaps Ephesus). In recent years, however, most scholars accept chapter 16 as original with the exception of verses 25–27 (see Gamble). Paul greets more people (twenty-six) by name in this letter than any other because he had not visited Rome and needs to make the most of all connections he has there.

The God of peace will soon crush Satan refers to the final eschatological defeat of Satan (see 1 Cor 15:20–28).

Timothy is included among those offering greetings, but not as coauthor in the salutation of Romans (compare 2 Cor 1:1; Phil 1:1; 1 Thess 1:1; 2 Thess 1:1; Col 1:1). The church in Corinth meets in the house of *Gaius* (see 1 Cor 1:14), indicating that he is a person of financial means. Paul appears to be staying in his house while composing this letter. *Erastus* is the only Christian ever mentioned by Paul as holding an office outside the church. *Tertius* is a secretary to whom Paul dictated the letter – as was his usual practice (see 1 Cor 16:21; Gal 6:11; Col 4:18; 2 Thess 3:17; Phlm 19). It is unlikely that the closing doxology is original to the letter.

THEOLOGICAL REFLECTIONS

Romans addresses key Christian theological themes. Some of the most important are these:

The Righteousness of God · This is the central theological claim of Romans (1:16–17). When Christ's death is understood as *God's saving covenant faithfulness* (3:21–26), the continuity of Paul's gospel with the Law and the Prophets becomes clear. When Paul explores God's faithfulness in spite of Israel's faithlessness in chapters 9–11, God's mercy shines through and becomes a powerful and abiding basis for hope (see 11:28–36).

Justification · The insight of Luther and others that sinners are justified by grace through faith remains an important theological reflection for readers of Romans even though it is not the primary message of the letter. The recent scholarly trend of reading *pistis Christou* as the "faith of Christ" rather than "faith in Christ" encourages more reflection on the relation of faith and obedience in Paul (*obedience of faith*; 1:5) than has been characteristic of Protestant interpretation.

Eschatology and Ethics · Paul believed that with the death and resurrection of Christ God had already begun to overthrow the dominion of sin and death. Christ-believers, through baptism, have been transferred from the sphere of Adam into the sphere of Christ as they await their final adoption, the redemption of their bodies (6:1–11; 8:23). In the meantime, however, Christians must live out the new identity God has given them struggling to "walk between the times" with the aid of the Spirit (8:1–30). Because their "darkened minds" are being "renewed" they are increasingly able to determine God's will (12:1–2) and to live in community with others and in proper relation to outsiders (12:1–15:13).

FOR FURTHER STUDY

A. Andrew Das, *Solving the Romans Debate* (Minneapolis, Minn.: Fortress, 2007).

Jeffrey Greenman and Timothy Larsen, eds., *Reading Romans through the Centuries from the Early Church to Karl Barth* (Grand Rapids: Brazos, 2005).

WORKS CITED

Jouette M. Bassler, *Divine Impartiality*: *Paul and a Theological Axiom* (Chico, Calif.: Scholars Press, 1982).

Christopher Bryan, *A Preface to Romans* (New York: Oxford University Press, 2000).

Brendan Byrne, *Romans* (Collegeville, Minn.: Liturgical Press, 1996).

Shaye J. D. Cohen, *The Beginnings of Jewishness*: *Boundaries, Varieties, Uncertainties* (Berkeley: University of California Press, 1999).

John Collins, *The Apocalyptic Imagination*: An Introduction to Jewish Apocalyptic Literature (Grand Rapids: Eerdmans, 1998).

M. C. De Boer, "Paul and Apocalyptic Eschatology." Pages 357–61 in *The Encyclopedia of Apocalypticism*, vol.1: *The Origins of Apocalypticism in Judaism and Christianity* (ed. John Collins; New York: Continuum, 2000).

Karl P. Donfried, *The Romans Debate*: *Essays on the Origin and Purpose of the Epistle* (2d ed.; Peabody, Mass.: Hendrickson, 1991).

James D. G. Dunn, "Once More, *Pistis Christou*," *SBL Seminar Papers* (1991): 731–44.

———, *Romans* (Dallas, Tex.: Word, 1988).

———, *Paul and the Mosaic Law* (Tübingen: Mohr-Siebeck, 1996).

Neil Elliott, *Liberating Paul*: *The Justice of God and the Politics of the Apostle* (Maryknoll, N.Y.: Orbis, 1994).

Harry Gamble, *The Textual History of the Letter to the Romans* (Grand Rapids: Eerdmans, 1977).

Richard B. Hays, "*Pistis* and Pauline Christology: What Is at Stake?" *SBL Seminar Papers* (1991): 714–29.

———, *The Faith of Jesus Christ* (Chico, Calif.: Scholars Press, 1983).

Richard Horsley, ed., *Paul and Empire* (Valley Forge, Pa.: Trinity Press International, 1997).

E. Elizabeth Johnson, "Romans 9–11: The Faithfulness and Impartiality of God." Pages 211–39 in *Pauline Theology*, vol. 3: *Romans* (ed. David M. Hay and E. Elizabeth Johnson; Minneapolis, Minn.: Fortress, 1995).

Ernst Käsemann, *Commentary on Romans* (Grand Rapids: Eerdmans, 1980).

———, *New Testament Questions of Today* (Philadelphia: Fortress, 1969).

Peter Lampe, *From Paul to Valentinus*: *Christians at Rome in the First Two Centuries* (Minneapolis, Minn.: Augsburg Fortress, 1999).

Abraham J. Malherbe, *Paul and the Popular Philosophers* (Philadelphia: Fortress, 1989).

Paul W. Meyer, "Romans." Pages 1038–73 in *HarperCollins Bible Commentary* (ed. James L. Mays; San Francisco: Harper, 2000).

Heikki Räisänen, "Paul, God, and Israel: Romans 9–11 in Recent Research." Pages 178–206 in *The Social World of Formative Christianity and Judaism*: *Essays in Tribute to Howard Clark Kee* (eds. Jacob Neusner, Ernest Frerichs, Peter Borgen, and Richard Horsley; Philadelphia: Fortress, 1988).

J. Paul Sampley, "Romans in a Different Light: A Response to Robert Jewett." Pages 109–29 in *Pauline Theology*, vol. 3: *Romans* (ed. David M. Hay and E. Elizabeth Johnson; Minneapolis, Minn.: Fortress, 1995).

———, *Walking Between the Times*: *Paul's Moral Reasoning* (Minneapolis, Minn.: Fortress, 1991).

Krister Stendahl, *Paul among Jews and Gentiles* (Philadelphia: Fortress, 1976).

Stanley K. Stowers, *A Rereading of Romans*: *Justice, Jews, and Gentiles* (New Haven: Yale University Press, 1994).

———, *The Diatribe and Paul's Letter to the Romans* (Chico, Calif.: Scholars Press, 1981).

Suetonius, *Claudius* (trans. J. C. Rolfe; Cambridge: Harvard University Press, 1914).

James C. Walters, "Adoption and Inheritance." Pages 42–76 in *Paul in the Greco-Roman World*: *A Handbook* (ed. Paul Sampley; Harrisburg, Pa.: Trinity Press International, 2003).

———, *Ethnic Issues in Paul's Letter to the Romans*: *Changing Self-Definitions in Earliest Roman Christianity* (Harrisburg, Pa.: Trinity Press International, 1993).

———, "Phoebe and Junia(s)." Pages 167–90 in vol. 1 of *Essays on Women in Earliest Christianity* (ed. Carroll Osburn; Joplin, Mo.: College Press, 1995).

John L. White, *Light from Ancient Letters* (Philadelphia: Fortress, 1986).

N. T. Wright, *The Letter to the Romans*. Pages 395–770 in vol. 10 of *The New Interpreter's Bible* (ed. Leander Keck; Nashville: Abingdon, 2002).

1 Corinthians

Christopher R. Hutson

CHAPTER CONTENTS

Contexts   917
Commentary   918
   Epistolary Opening · 1:1–9   918
   Divisions in the Church · 1:10–4:21   918
   Keeping Christ's Body Holy · 5:1–6:20   921
   Marriage & Celibacy · 7:1–40   923
   Meat Offered to Idols · 8:1–11:1   924
   Hairstyles & Clothing · 11:2–16   926
   Not the Lord's Supper · 11:17–22   928
   Spiritual Gifts · 12:1–14:40   929
   The Resurrection of the Body · 15:1–58   932
   The Epistolary Closing · 16:1–24   934
Theological Reflections   934
For Further Study   935
Works Cited   935

MAPS, TABLES, & FEATURES

"But the greatest of these is love…"   930
"Death, Be Not Proud"   933

In Paul's day, Corinth was the capital of the Roman province of Achaia. The Romans had destroyed the classical city in 146 BCE, but in 44 BCE Julius Cæsar refounded Corinth as a Roman colony for freedpersons. Some of the colonists may have been ethnically Greek, but they had lived in Rome, so they spoke Latin and had absorbed Roman culture. Also, they were Roman citizens, since the Romans normally granted citizenship to freed slaves. Thus the aristocracy of first century Corinth was Roman, but the city also included local Greeks, as well as Jews and people from around the Mediterranean.

CONTEXTS

Corinth was wealthy due to its bronze (Murphy-O'Connor 199–218) and pottery manufacture, tourism, and especially commerce (Strabo, *Geography*, 8.6.20–23; Williams). Located on the isthmus, Corinth controlled the major trade route between Rome and Asia, and people and goods from around the Mediterranean passed through the harbors at Cenchreai and Lechaion. The Isthmian Games, sponsored by Corinth every other spring in honor of Poseidon, were second only to the Olympics in importance and drew a large tourist trade. Corinth also sponsored Cæsarean Games every four years in honor of the emperor. The traditional site of the games was in nearby Isthmia, but when Paul arrived, the facilities at Isthmia had not yet been rebuilt since the Roman destruction in 146 BCE, and the games were staged in Corinth (Gebhard 82–89).

The city supported a rich religious life. There were temples of the traditional Greek gods, including Aphrodite (love), Apollo (sun), Asklepios (healing), Demeter (fertile earth), Poseidon (sea), Tyche (fortune), and others. The Romans built a temple to the imperial family. There were also non-Greek religions, including the Egyptian cult of Isis, and a Jewish community.

Paul worked in Corinth for 18 months during his second journey, overlapping with Gallio's term as proconsul (governor) of Achaia (Acts 18:12–17). Gallio was proconsul most likely in 51–52 CE, so Paul first visited in about 50–51 (Murphy-O'Connor 161–169).

Paul is writing from Ephesus (16:8). According to Acts, when Paul left Corinth he went briefly to Ephesus, then to Jerusalem and Antioch (Acts 18:18–22). Then he launched his third journey through Galatia and Phrygia (Acts 18:23), eventually spending over two years in Ephesus (19:8–10). While away, Paul had received at least one letter from Corinth (7:1) and had written one (5:9). He had a report from *Chloe's people* (1:11) and a visit from three Corinthians (16:17–18). These exchanges must have occurred while he was in Ephesus, perhaps in the years 54–56. From Ephesus, Paul says he is coming (16:1–7) and threatens to bring a rod of discipline (4:18–23). Indeed, he will later make a brief "painful visit" and follow that with a "tearful letter" (2 Cor 2:1–4), but he is not yet ready to wind up his work in Ephesus (16:8). The Corinthians will become exasperated at his changes of plan (2 Cor 1:15–24). All of this suggests that Paul wrote 1 Corinthians sometime in the middle of his stay in Ephesus, about 54 or 55 CE (Murphy-O'Connor 170–74).

COMMENTARY

EPISTOLARY OPENING · 1:1–9

1:1–3 Paul identifies himself as *apostle of Christ Jesus by the will of God* (1:1). His need to establish his credentials implies that some of his target readers question his authority.

Although he is aware of factions in the community, Paul addresses his letter to *all who call upon the name of our Lord Jesus Christ in every place*, *theirs and ours* (1:2; NIV's *their Lord and ours* misses the point of the Greek). *Every place* reminds us that the Corinthian Christians met in several house churches (Cenchreai: Rom 16:1; house of Gaius: Rom 16:23; house of Titius Justus: Acts 18:7). Since Paul sometimes converted entire households (Crispus: Acts 18:8; Stephanas: 1 Cor 1:16; 16:15), it would have been natural for house churches to form around groups of family and friends that reflected different ethnic origins. Furthermore, house churches might have resulted from the work of different evangelists, Paul, Cephas, or Apollos. When Paul says *every place*, *theirs and ours* (1:2), he addresses all the Corinthian Christians, regardless of the evangelist who started each group. This anticipates the problem of factions in chapters 1–4. God had called all the Corinthian Christians into fellowship with Jesus Christ (1:9).

1:4–9 Paul often gives thanks at the beginning of a letter for things that he discusses later. Here the Corinthians are rich in *knowledge* (verse 5; compare 8:1, 7, 10; 12:8; 13:2, 8; 14:6); lack no *gift* (verse 7; compare 7:7; 12:4, 9, 28–31); expect the Lord ... to be *revealed* (verse 7; compare 2:10; 3:13); anticipate *the Day of the Lord* (verse 8; compare 3:13; 5:15); and are called into *fellowship* (verse 9; compare 10:16). So this prayer introduces some theological themes of the letter.

> **Martyrion Christou**
> Our testimony about Christ (1:6) would be the story Paul told (15:1–8), but the Greek phrase martyrion Christou could be translated "Christ's testimony," which would refer to Christ's willingness to die as a "witness" (*martyr*) to his faith.

DIVISIONS IN THE CHURCH · 1:10–4:21

1:10–17 The Christian community in Corinth was split into factions. In the first major section of the letter (1:10–4:21), Paul discusses the general problem of divisions before addressing specific issues in dispute. He needs to create community among converts from various ethnic groups and social classes. Some, like Aquila and Prisca, were transplants from Italy (Acts 18:2). Some followed other teachers (1:12). Paul could form this diverse group into a community because the cross points people away from the competition and distrust of this age and toward the end times in which Christians are all connected with one another through their common connection with Christ.

The report about divisions came from those *of Chloe* (1:11). Perhaps, as the NIV suggests, Chloe was head of her household, like Lydia (Acts 16:14–15). Or perhaps she hosted a house church like Aquila and Prisca (1 Cor 16:19). Possibly, she was the leader of yet another faction like those in 1:12, and it is possible that those *of Chloe* had appealed to Paul to settle a factional dispute. If so, Paul avoids taking sides.

The Corinthians were apparently behaving like students of rhetoric, with rivalries based on loyalty to different teachers (Dio Chrysostom, *Oratio*, 8.6; Winter, *Philo*, 123–29; Winter, *After*, 38–40). They claimed, literally, *I am of Paul, I am of Apollos, I am of Cephas, I am of Christ* (1:12). Apollos was a well-educated Jewish convert from Alexandria (Acts 18:24–28). Cephas was Peter's Aramaic name (Gal 2:6–14). Paul mentions three of the factions again in 3:22, and he focuses on the Paul and Apollos factions in 3:3–4 and 4:6. This suggests that the biggest problem lay between those two factions. But Paul never criticizes Apollos, whom he views as a coworker (3:6; 16:12).

Paul does not support any of the factions, even the group that claims to be *of Paul*. His rhetorical questions (1:13) all expect a "no" answer. Since the community had its basis in Christ, it should not wear any other name. Among the few Paul baptized in Corinth (1:14–16), *Crispus* had been a synagogue ruler (Acts 18:8), *Gaius* hosted a house church (Rom 16:23), and *Stephanas* was Paul's first local convert and a trusted leader (16:15–18). *Christ did not send me to baptize* (1:17) does not mean baptism is optional for Paul. He assumes all Christians are baptized (1:13; 12:13; Rom 6:3–4), but his point is that baptism identifies believers with Christ, not with the one who performs the baptism. *Words of human wisdom* (1:17) suggests sophisticated oratory (Winter, *Philo*). Some Corinthians thought Paul was not a polished speaker (2 Cor 10:10), whereas Apollos was a gifted orator (Acts 18:24). So perhaps some of the educated Corinthians favored Apollos's polished style. Paul does not criticize Apollos, but he does suggest that a focus on style over substance can *empty the cross of its power* (1:17).

1:18–2:5 Paul argues that the cross expresses the wisdom and power of God. He quotes Isaiah 29:14 (1:19) to show that God does not operate on the terms of *this age*. Those who are *perishing* (1:18) and *of this age* and *of the world* (1:20) do not understand how the cross of Christ reveals God. The *wise man* [Greek *sophos*, 1:20] refers to one who aspires to the best education, but here Paul has especially in mind the Sophists, orators who valued rhetorical display over truth (Clement, *Stromata*, 1.3; Winter, *Philo*, 123–202; Stowers, "Abuse," 255–62). The *scholar* [literally "scribe"] refers to a Jewish Torah scholar. Both Jews and Gentiles missed God's message. *The foolishness of what was preached* (1:21) is the story of the cross (15:1–8; compare 1 Thess 1:9–10). Paul preaches *Christ crucified* (1:23). The cross symbolizes that Jesus gave up wealth, power, reputation, and even his life. The scribes *demand signs* (1:22), but a crucified messiah did not seem miraculous. Sophists *seek wisdom* (1:22), but their worldly wisdom (1:21) is no search for truth. They seek only to expand their egos and their wallets. The cross and resurrection of Jesus reveal *God's foolishness* and *weakness* (1:25).

In 1:26–31, Paul appeals to the Corinthians' experience. The Corinthian Christians apparently included various social strata (Theissen 69–119), though most were not educated, influential, or aristocratic (1:26). God chose slaves and laborers, the *foolish things of the world*, the *weak*, *lowly*, and *despised*, the nothings of the world in order to put to shame the *wise* and *strong*, the somethings (1:27–28). Verse 31 paraphrases Jeremiah 9:24, and all of 1:26–31 echoes Jeremiah 9:23–24.

In 2:1–5, Paul recalls the example he set in Corinth. Depending on which ancient manuscript one reads, Paul proclaimed either the *testimony of God* (2:1; compare 1:6) or *the mystery of God* (2:1 NIV note; compare 2:7; 4:1; 13:2; 14:2; 15:51). Either way, the point is that Paul preached the cross of Christ (15:1–5). He did not come like a sophist delivering a showy oration to attract paying students (Winter, *Philo*, 144–47). Rather, like a true philosopher, he told people what they needed to hear to improve themselves, not what they wanted for entertainment (Plato, *Apology*, 17C; Epictetus, *Discourses*, 3.23; Dio Chrysostom, *Oration*, 8; Winter, *Philo*). He did not display *eloquence or superior wisdom* (2:1) but *weakness and much fear and trembling* (2:3; 4:10–13). He did not want people to marvel at his oratorical prowess but to trust in God's power (2:5).

2:6–3:4 Having argued that he did not preach wisdom (2:1–5), Paul now says, *we do speak a message of wisdom*, but *not the wisdom of this age* (2:6). Neither *mature* (2:6, NIV) nor *perfect* (KJV) quite expresses the apocalyptic nuance in Paul's word *teleios*, which might better be translated "end-time oriented." Paul is saying that people who orient themselves to the end time understand God's wisdom revealed in the cross. The *rulers of this age* do not understand God's wisdom (2:7–8), because they trust in wealth and military power rather than in God. Paul quotes Isaiah 64:4 and *Ecclesiasticus* 1:10 to affirm that God's ways are unheard of in *this age*.

> **Secret Wisdom**
> Literally "wisdom hidden in a mystery," secret wisdom (2:7) is only understandable to those initiated into the faith.

In 2:6–16, Paul's language reflects a quest for divine knowledge (Hunt 15–70). The word for *search* (2:10) often refers to inquiry into divine knowledge (1 Pet 1:11), including investigation of the Scriptures (John 5:39; 7:52). The *deep things of God* (2:10) cannot be known by secular means, because the message is taught not *by human wisdom* but only *by the Spirit* (2:13). Understanding is a gift *freely given* (2:12) by God through the Spirit (compare the gifts of the Spirit in 12:8, 28). God's wisdom is made known to *us* (2:10), the community collectively (Hunt 71–92).

Without the spirit (2:14) translates the Greek word *psychikos* (rendered *natural* in 15:43). The *psyche* or "mind" is still *earthly*, while the spirit is heavenly (15:42–50). According to Isaiah 64:4, God acts in surprising ways, but believers are not surprised, because *we*, the community, have the *mind of Christ* (2:16) reflected in how we live out the gospel (compare Phil 2:1–11). For people of *this age*, the cross is foolishness, because it is about giving up self-interest and trusting God. The rulers of "this age" know how to protect their image and enhance their financial and physical security. But from an end-times perspective, the only image that matters is what God sees in one's heart, and earthly treasures never last (Matt 6:19–21).

In 3:1–4, Paul shames his readers for childish behavior. Far from maturity (2:6), they are *infants* (3:1), too young for solid food (3:2). The NIV *worldly* (3:1, 3) is literally "fleshly" (KJV, RSV). They are motivated by physical appetites and not by the Spirit, as evidenced by their actions (3:3), especially their rivalries (3:4).

3:5–23 In chapters 2–3, Paul develops images that illustrate the interconnectedness of Christians: farm, temple, and family. First, the church resembles God's farm (3:6–9). Although Paul and Apollos perform different chores, each is a hired hand. The farm belongs to God (3:9).

Second, the church is God's temple (3:9–17). Paul was the *expert builder* (3:10) who laid the foundation in Corinth, but he is not the only one working on the building. Yet he admonishes anyone who would join the building crew to *be careful how he builds* (3:10). It is not appropriate to build shoddy construction upon the foundation of Jesus Christ. An end-times community is building for eternity. Paul says *the Day* (of Judgment, compare 1:8; 5:5; 2 Cor 1:14) will reveal poor building materials. If part of the building is poorly constructed, it will not survive the final judgment (3:13). Only a church built on end-times principles will survive the test.

The community of believers is where God's Spirit dwells. *You* in 3:16–17 and 3:21–23 is plural, so the temple is the body of all believers. Those who promote divisions are destroying the body, the temple of God. The divisive claim comes from a singular, self-interested voice, "I" (1:12). Paul does not endorse any individual who claims to be "of Christ" over against other Christians, because the whole body ("you" plural) is God's temple (3:16) and is *of Christ* (3:23). There is no room for divisions, since everything is *of God* (3:23).

> **Good & Poor Builders**
>
> Paul does not compound the problem of the poor building methods by attacking the builders. Even a poor builder "will be saved" (3:15). A poorly built structure can be remodeled, and builders can learn new tricks. But if we destroyed all the builders with whose methods we disagreed, nothing would get built. Paul appreciates even ill-equipped builders, but he predicts destruction for anyone who tears down God's building.

4:1–21 Paul does not merely want the Corinthians to be end-times oriented individuals. He is trying to create an end-times oriented community. He does not endorse the faction that favors him over Apollos, because rivalry and jealousy are "fleshly" and pertain to "this age." The teachers should be considered *servants of Christ* whom God *entrusted with the secret things* ("mysteries"; 4:1). They must answer to God, who will judge them on the Day of the Lord (4:4–6). Until then, there is no *human court* (4:3) for judgment. It is inappropriate for factions within the community to usurp the Lord's authority by judging God's servants prematurely.

Paul says, *I have applied these things to myself and Apollos for your benefit* (4:6). Some said, *I am of Apollos*, or *I am of Paul* (1:12), but Paul stands side-by-side with Apollos. As far as he is concerned, the rivalry is only in the minds of those *proud* [literally "puffed up," 4:6] who *boast* in "this-world" status, as if all they have were not a gift (4:7). In ironic tones, Paul portrays them as aristocrats *having all you want ... rich ... kings* (4:8), while he portrays the apostles as ideal philosophers with no worldly assets, wandering beggars in search of wisdom and often ridiculed (compare Epictetus, *Discourses*, 3.24.113–14; Philo, *Worse*, 34; Dio Chrysostom, *Oration*, 77/78.26–28, 33; Fitzgerald 47–116, 132–48). They appear inferior in every way (see 2:3), like condemned criminals destined to be the final act in a bloody gladiatorial show (4:9). The Corinthians are *wise*, *strong*, and *honored* (4:10). By contrast, we are fools, weak, dishonored, hungry, thirsty, in rags [literally "naked"], brutally treated, homeless [literally "unstable"], manual laborers (a mark of poverty; compare 1 Thess 2:9), *scum*, *refuse* (4:10–13). What could such a destitute wanderer offer the self-satisfied Corinthians? Only the Christlike behavior of blessing those who curse him and enduring persecution (4:12–13; compare Luke 6:27–36; Rom 12:14–21). Paul is a fool by the standards of this age. But he is *a fool for Christ* (4:10), living by the wisdom of God as displayed in the crucified Messiah.

But Paul's irony packs a rhetorical punch (Fitzgerald 119–22). A diplomat never criticizes a king directly but offers covert allusions and analogies and allows the king to make the application. Paul breaks all the rules by making a pointed analogy to the Corinthian factions (4:6). They are full of pride and boast of what they did not earn (4:7). *Do not go beyond what is written* (4:6) refers to the letters a child traces when learning to write (Plato, *Protagoras*, 326D; Fitzgerald 122–28). Paul puts a pin in their puffy pretensions. They are not kings but *infants* (3:1), Paul's *children*, whom he admonishes (4:14–15). He will come and give them a thrashing if they do not stop mistreating one another (4:21). Instead, they should trace the example set by Paul and Apollos (4:6, 16–17).

> **Paul's Family Imagery**
> *The father/child imagery (4:14–17) suggests a family. Paul sends Timothy, his* son, *who will remind you of my way of life in Christ (4:17). Timothy is like an older brother who shows the younger children what it means to follow their father's example. As a father, Paul can be gentle or harsh, depending on the Corinthians' behavior.*

KEEPING CHRIST'S BODY HOLY · 5:1–6:20

5:1–13 In chapters 5–6, Paul addresses three problems *reported* to him (5:1), perhaps by Chloe's people (1:11) or the Stephanas delegation (16:17), or by some other source. He deals with incest (5:1–13); then lawsuits (6:1–8); then prostitution (6:9–20). It is not clear what lawsuits have to do with sexual immorality. Perhaps Paul had in mind a specific lawsuit about the case of incest described in chapter 5. Or perhaps he used all three issues to discuss the larger topic of covetousness.

Paul is dismayed that the Corinthians tolerate gross sexual immorality within the community (5:1). He argues that the immoral brother should be expelled (5:2, 12, 13). Few would approve the behavior, as Paul points out (5:1), but many wrestle with how and why to discipline a member by withdrawing fellowship. When Paul refers to nonbelievers as "Gentiles" (5:1; NIV *pagans*), he implies that Christians constitute "Israel," even though many Christians in Corinth were not ethnically Jewish. From a Christian perspective, "Israel" and "Gentiles" are no longer defined in terms of ethnicity. Instead, "outsiders" are *immoral* people (5:9–13), with whom God's people should not mix. Paul offers two ways to think about excommunication theologically.

First, Paul wants the Corinthians to orient their behavior toward the eschatological kingdom of God. He says the community should *deliver this man to Satan* (5:5). In the Old Testament, Satan is God's prosecutor in heavenly court (Job 1–2; Zech 3:1–2), and Paul is thinking of the last judgment, the *day of the Lord* (5:5). Paul says literally, *for the destruction of the flesh* (5:5), that is, the destruction of self-seeking desires that are tied to "flesh" (NIV *sinful nature*). Paul wants him to face the final judgment as a spiritual person, not a fleshly person. In this context, Paul's own judgment (5:3) is only preliminary, and final judgment belongs to the Lord. Excommunication is done by the whole community assembled *in the name of the Lord Jesus*. Even though Paul has made up his mind, he urges the congregation to take action as a group.

Second, Paul considers each issue in terms of how it affects the whole body of Christ. He draws an analogy from the Passover. Just as Jews remove every speck of *yeast* from the house at Passover (Exod 12:15, 19–20), so Christians should remove every speck of sin from their midst (5:7–8). Paul lists the types of sins that cannot be tolerated within the group (5:11). The blood of the *Passover lamb* (5:8) marked the Israelites as God's people, so the so-called death angel *passed over* them and attacked only the Egyptians (Exod 12:13).

> **Excommunication**
> *Paul clarifies a point from a previous letter (now lost) that, although judgment of outsiders belongs to God, the Christian community should drive out the evil from among their members (5:13; compare Deut 13:5; 17:7; 19:19; 21:21; 22:22; 24:7). Excommunication is like an amputation that removes an infected body part to save the body. This drastic measure is a treatment of last resort.*

6:1–11 Paul's exhortation not to judge outsiders (5:12–13) now becomes a hook to which he connects his next point, that Christians should not allow outsiders to judge them (6:1–8). Christians should not ask secular courts to settle disputes between them (6:1). A lawsuit between Christians defeats the whole group (6:7). It violates the principle that Christ is not divided (1:13) and damages the community, which is the temple of God, thus incurring God's wrath (3:16–17). On the other hand, suffering injustice is consistent with the crucified Messiah, because the endurance of injustice manifests the wisdom of God (1:23; 2:8). Although some Corinthians boasted in wisdom (4:10), Paul is amazed at their lack of godly wisdom, and his question in 6:5 is deeply ironic.

Paul develops the insider/outsider idea using theological words. The technical term for setting apart something as holy to God is "sanctification." The words "saint," "holy," and "sanctify" all translate the same Greek root (the adjective *hagios*, the verb *hagiazo*). Paul uses the theological ideas of being *washed* (in baptism), *sanctified* (set apart as holy), and *justified* (put in a right relationship with God) to describe how the Spirit works (6:11). In this passage, believers are *saints* (6:1–2), *sanctified* (6:11), and *brothers* (6:6, 8). By contrast, outsiders are *unjust* [Greek *adikos*, 6:1, 9; NIV *ungodly*, *wicked*]. Indeed, Roman court systems heavily favored wealthy citizens over the poor and noncitizens (Winter, *After Paul*, 58–75). This is a symptom of the theological situation that nonbelievers are not in a "just" relationship with the living God. Some Corinthian Christians *cheat* [literally "act unjustly," 6:8]. Christians who use the secular courts to advance their claims play by the rules of this world, so that even if they do not break any secular laws, they are still theologically "unjust," because they are not oriented toward God. As Paul puts it, the unjust (NIV *wicked*) *will not inherit the Kingdom of God* (6:9). Those who have been *sanctified* and *justified* (6:11) should no longer play by the rules of the secular world. They should prefer to *be wronged* ("treated unjustly," 6:7), having confidence that being *justified* by God (6:11) is of more lasting importance than winning a case in this age.

6:12–20 In 6:9–12, Paul picks up where he left off in 5:11, with a list of sins that Christians should not tolerate. This vice list is not exhaustive but represents the types of sins that bar one from *the Kingdom of God* (6:9, 11). With this, Paul returns to the general topic of sexual immorality, once again discussing the ethics of this age in terms of Christian orientation toward the end times.

In 6:12–20, Paul refutes some slogans the Corinthians had adopted. The NIV places quotation marks around what seem to be the Corinthians' words that Paul is quoting back to them (6:12–13). The argument is interpreted in different ways, depending on which words one thinks represent the Corinthians' views and which are Paul's responses. I suggest that there are three pairs of Corinthian slogans and three pairs of responses.

The first pair is obvious (6:12), and there is wide agreement about it. Some Corinthians say, *Everything is permissible for me*, which may reflect their Greek philosophical background, since a Stoic slogan was that "everything is permissible to the wise" (Dio Chrysostom, *Oration*, 3.10; 62.3; Stowers "Debate," 63–67). Paul meets them where they are, responding also in Stoic terms, *Not everything is beneficial* (Epictetus *Discourses*, 1.28.5). Some Corinthians say, *Everything is permissible for me*, but Paul responds, *I will not be mastered by anything*. Paul makes a pun that is difficult to translate but something like this: "All things are appropriate for me, but I will not be appropriated by anything" (compare Dio Chrysostom, *Oration*, 14.13–17).

The second pair of Corinthian slogans appears in 6:13. The slogan *Food for the stomach, and the stomach for food* (6:13a) is clearly a this-age ethic, like saying, "Appetites are only natural." Paul offers an end-time alternative slogan: *The body for the Lord, and the Lord for the body* (verse 13). The body is not *for sexual immorality* (6:13). Like sex, both food and stomach are "fleshly." The slogan, *God will destroy the* [*food*] *and the* [*stomach*] (6:13) sounds as if some Corinthians had heard about the end times and thought what they did with their bodies in this age would not matter in eternity, since earthly things will be destroyed. But Paul appeals to the doctrine of bodily resurrection (6:14; see 15:32–34), arguing that our bodies and spirits are connected eternally. Notice that Paul refers to *body* here, not "flesh." The "flesh" will pass away, but the body will be transformed in the resurrection (15:51–53). Meanwhile, our bodies are already *members* of the body of Christ (6:15). Since deeds of the body affect the spirit, sex with a prostitute affects one's spiritual union with Christ (6:16–17).

The most difficult part of the argument occurs in verses 18–20. But this becomes clearer if we read 6:18 as a third pair of Corinthian slogans. Some

> **Body & Soul**
>
> The conflict between Paul and the Corinthians may lie in the Greek understanding of the relation between spirit and body. In Greek thought, the body is a tomb of the soul and is not essential to the real person (Seneca, Epistles, 65.16–17). In Jewish apocalyptic thought, by contrast, soul and body are inseparable, both essential to the whole person (1 Enoch 71). Even angels have bodies (Ezek 1:11, 23; Dan 10:6). In Jewish apocalyptic, what happens to the body affects the spirit, and vice versa.

Corinthians say, "Every sin a person commits is outside the Body," and "the sexually immoral person is sinning against his own body" (6:18; NIV's *every other sin ... makes nonsense of the verse. The word *other* is not in the Greek text; see KJV, NRSV). Both of these slogans imply that sex is a private matter that does not affect the community. But Paul counters, *your Body is a temple of the Holy Spirit* (verse 19). Even though *Body* here is singular, the word *your* is plural, which suggests that *Body* here refers to the community as the Body of Christ (as in 3:16–17; 6:15b). Thus, sexual immorality is not simply a private concern but affects the body of Christ. Paul concludes with an exhortation to *honor God with your body/Body* (6:20).

MARKIAGE & CELIBACY · 7:1–40

Beginning in 7:1, Paul responds to questions asked by the Corinthians, since the phrase *now for* introduces several topics (7:1, 25; 8:1; 12:1; 16:1, 12). Paul's responses build on principles laid down in chapters 1–6. The concern about celibacy (7:2) connects to the discussions of sex in chapters 5–6. This chapter shows Paul working out his opinions about an ethical question (7:12, 25, 40).

Some scholars think *It is good for a man not to marry* (7:1, literally, "not to touch a woman") is the view of some Corinthians, which Paul quotes from their letter. If so, they may have gotten the idea from philosophers who encouraged self-control over physical desires as essential to a higher, spiritual life (Yarbrough 32–34). Or possibly, they heard Paul's preaching against sexual immorality, as in chapters 5–6, and thought he meant that all sex is bad. If some members did argue for celibacy while others tolerated fornication, that would show again the diversity of the Corinthian community. On the other hand, a simpler reading of this chapter assumes that Paul is expressing his own preference for celibacy in 7:1, a view he clearly reiterates as his own (7:8, 25–26, 32–35, 38, 40).

Should married Christian couples stop having sex (7:1–9)? Paul prefers celibacy (7:1), but he regards it as a gift (7:7). Not everyone has the self-control to renounce sex altogether (7:5, 9), so Paul follows typical Jewish teaching that the proper outlet for sexual desire is marriage (Yarbrough 7–29), because *it is better to marry than to burn* (7:9; compare 1 Tim 5:11–15). Paul's view of marriage is that each spouse has a *duty* to satisfy the sexual needs of the other (7:3–4). Each spouse's body *belongs to* the other (7:4; literally, each "has authority over" the other's body; see 7:32–35). Such a reciprocal view of marriage was consistent with a philosophical emphasis on self-control (Winter, *Roman Wives*, 71). Paul's view reflects his orientation to the new creation "in the Lord," which does not favor the rights of one sex over the other (11:11–12; compare Gal 3:27–28). Just as Christians should consider how their behavior affects each other, so also Christian couples should depend upon and support one another as *one body* (6:16).

From this, it follows that Christian spouses should not divorce (7:10–11). This saying of *the Lord* resembles sayings in the gospels (Matt 19:9; Mark 10:10–12; see Matt 5:31–32; Luke 16:18). The canonical gospels were not yet published when Paul wrote this letter, but apparently he knew some of Jesus' teachings. Though Paul advocates celibacy, he takes into account Jesus' teaching on marriage as a commitment that should not be broken easily.

Should Christians separate from non-Christian spouses (7:12–16, 39–40)? Paul sometimes refers to unbelievers as *the rest* (1 Thess 4:13; 5:6; Phil 1:13), so in 7:12–16 he is discussing marriage between a Christian and a non-Christian. He thinks that if the unbelieving spouse seeks a divorce, there is no stigma for the Christian. But a Christian should not divorce a non-Christian spouse, since the Christian has an effect on the family for good.

In 7:17–24, Paul inserts an analogy from ethnicity and social class. His general rule, which he states three times, is that each one should remain in the situation *to which God has called him* (7:17, 20, 24). A Jew should not have surgery to mask his *circumcision* and thereby gain social access in Greco-Roman culture (7:18; Hall). On 7:19, compare Galatians 2:1–10; 6:15. Of course, Paul encourages *slaves* to take an opportunity for freedom (7:21; Bartchy 155–59). One's situation may change, and one may serve the kingdom in a different capacity. But it makes no difference whether one is Jew or Gentile, slave or free. God calls people from all walks of life. By analogy, it makes no difference whether one is married or single. Paul sees the single, celibate life as a gift and calling from God.

In 7:25, Paul returns to the discussion of celibacy, now focusing on whether unmarried persons should marry. Some have supposed that the *present crisis* (7:26) was a local famine that seems to have occurred in the year 51 (Winter, *After Paul*, 216–225). But even if such a crisis precipitated the questions, Paul's answer is based on his orientation to the end times, because *the time is short* (7:29). Paul seems to expect the return of Jesus in his own lifetime (1 Thess 4:13–18; compare Matt 24:34). But regardless of when the Lord comes, verses 29–31 describe what it means to be oriented to the end times. Family, friends, and possessions are all of this age. But *this world in its present form is passing away* (7:31), so Paul wants the Corinthians to think about the end times. Even a spouse can distract from eternal things (7:32–35). However, Paul recognizes the realities of married life and the obligation of married partners. You should be concerned about your spouse's needs, which is precisely why an unmarried, celibate Christian has a great opportunity for *undivided devotion to the Lord* (7:35). Marriage is good, but Paul urges his readers to consider whether they have the gift of celibacy (7:36–39).

Paul makes the same point for widows (7:39–40) that he made for virgins (7:25–38). He repeats his injunction against divorce (7:39; compare 7:10–16; Rom 7:2–3). Again, he says it is fine for a widow to remarry, but he stipulates that the new spouse *must belong to the Lord* (7:39). Still, Paul's opinion is that celibacy is a better option (7:40). This final comment contrasts sharply with 1 Timothy 5:11–15, which reminds us that the Bible often includes more than one view on important questions.

MEAT OFFERED TO IDOLS · 8:1–11:1

8:1–7 Idol meat posed various ethical dilemmas for early Christians. In some cases, banquets were part of religious rituals (Willis, *Idol Meat*, 7–47). More often, social gatherings of family groups or voluntary associations would include some offering or prayer to a god (Plutarch, *Moralia*, 696E; Willis, *Idol Meat*, 47–64), and such meals might be eaten in a temple compound (Plutarch, *Moralia*, 164D; Murphy-O'Connor 186–90). If a Christian attended a private dinner in a pagan temple, even if it were not primarily a religious event, some might well ask whether that constituted idol worship (8:10). Finally, there were civic banquets. In 51 CE, for example, the president of the Isthmian and Caesarean Games hosted a public banquet for all the citizens of the city. Such a banquet would have included offerings to various gods and to the divine emperor. Such a banquet for citizens might explain why Paul refers to dining as a "right" (NIV *freedom*, 8:9). Some Christian citizens might have felt pressure to attend in order to display civic pride and loyalty to the emperor (Winter, *After Paul*, 93–96). So idol meat challenged the faith of early Christians.

> **Epistolary Dialogue**
> The logic of chapter 8 becomes clearer if we read it as a running dialogue between Paul and the Corinthians, in which he quotes from their letter (8:1b; 4–6) and then responds (Willis, Idol Meat, 67–70, 83–87, 96–98).

We know that we all possess knowledge (8:1) seems to be a quotation from the Corinthians (NIV note), because Paul modifies it (8:1), doubts it (8:2), and finally denies it altogether (8:7). Paul counters, *knowledge puffs up, but love builds up* (8:1). Knowledge is desirable but inadequate apart from love (13:2). Being *puffed up* [Greek *phusioo*, translated elsewhere as "pride" or "arrogance"] leads to factionalism (4:6, 18, 19) and casualness toward sexual immorality (5:2). It is not characteristic of love (13:4). Paul is concerned about things that "build up" the body of Christ (10:23; 14:4, 17). One who *thinks he knows something* is puffed up by partial knowledge (8:2). Such a person *does not yet know* (8:2), whereas complete knowledge comes only at the end time (13:9–12; Phil 3:12–15). Complete knowledge comes with learning how to *love God* (8:3), which is expressed in how one loves people (13:4–8). Those who *love God* (8:3) are believers. Knowing correct doctrine about God is not as important as being *known by God* (8:3; 13:12).

In 8:4–6, Paul apparently quotes the Corinthians again: *We know that an idol is nothing ...* (8:4). This time, the Corinthians support their doctrine with an early Christian creedal statement (8:6). *There is no God but one* (8:4) and *there is but one God* (8:6) sound like the basic Jewish affirmation of monotheism (Deut 6:4). This creator God was a standard theme in Jewish preaching to Gentiles (Exod 20:11; Ps 146:6), but identifying Jesus Christ with the creator God is a distinctive Christian interpretation of the doctrine (compare Col 1:16). So we can surmise that the Corinthians had learned well about the one true God (Rom 11:36; compare Acts 14:15; 17:24), but this new knowledge of theirs seems to have been filtered through their prior philosophical views on the freedoms of the wise (Malherbe, "Determinism"). Paul offers an ethical consideration that eating idol meat could damage some Christians who do not have this knowledge (8:7).

8:8–9:23 In 8:8–13, Paul develops the point from 8:7 that love trumps knowledge. Reading 8:8 as containing another quotation from the Corinthians, they are right to say, "Food does not commend us to God" (compare Rom 14:17). But Paul says it is *not* true, as they claim, that "we are worse off if we do not eat," and *not* true that we are "better off if we do" (8:8). Whoever knows that an idol is a non-god, and that another Christian believes the superstition, should voluntarily refrain from eating idol meat rather than risking the faith of the less mature Christian (8:11). The weak Christian who sees another Christian eating in a pagan temple (8:10) might be influenced to participate in a meal that he or she would believe to be an endorsement of the idol. *Causes to fall* (8:13) means to lose faith in Christ. The Greek verb *skandalizo* (8:13) means "trip, cause to stumble, ensnare," and the Septuagint uses the word *skandalon* to describe idols as a "snare" to faith (Josh 23:13; Judg 2:3; 8:27).

In 9:1–23, Paul develops the point from 8:9 that, although we have certain rights, we also have the right to give up our rights (Malherbe, "Determinism," 238–41). His *defense* (9:3) is against those philosophical Corinthians who might possibly *sit in judgment* on his argument (Willis, "Apostolic," 37; Malherbe, "Determinism," 240). The *right to take a believing wife* [literally "a sister-wife"] *along* (9:5) may reflect an early Christian practice of husband-wife missionary teams (Rom 16:3, 7).

The *right* for evangelists to receive *food and drink* (9:4) is developed in 9:6–12. In Deuteronomy 25:4 (9:9), Paul finds an example *for us* (9:10). Elsewhere, he applies the correlation between "spiritual seed" (see Mark 4:14) and "material harvest" to his collection for famine relief (2 Cor 8:14; 9:10). But Paul gives up his right to support (compare 1 Thess 2:7–9), and the Corinthians will take offense at him for not accepting their money (2 Cor 11:7–8), even though he accepts aid from Philippi (2 Cor 11:9; Phil 2:25–30; 4:10–20). Paul does not preach for money. He is *compelled* (9:16) to preach the *trust committed to me* (9:17), all of which sounds like he has a prophetic call (see Gal 1:15–17; compare Exod 3; Isa 6; Jer 1:4–10; Ezek 2–3). At the same time, Paul engages the views of the Corinthians in terms of Greek philosophy (Malherbe, "Determinism," 242–51). Stoic philosophers asserted that only the sage is truly free, since he does not act under compulsion but yields voluntarily to the vicissitudes of fortune. Only the sage is a true king, since he alone knows good and evil, which are necessary to rulers (Diogenes Laertius 7.121–122; Epictetus, *Discourses*, 3.24.64–77). Paul could preach *voluntarily* for a *reward* or *not voluntarily* on assignment (9:17). He volunteers to preach for a *reward* (9:18), and his *reward* is that he gives up his right to payment (9:18).

Paul adapts the rule of giving up rights to reach specific groups (9:19–23). He is *free* but *became a slave to everyone* (9:19; compare Gal 5:13) by bending to their needs. Like a Cynic philosopher who freely endures hardships in order to *win* a greater good (Dio Chrysostom, *Oration*, 33.15; Epictetus, *Discourses*, 3.22.47–49; 3.24.64; Malherbe, "Determinism," 252–53), he became like *a Jew*, like *one under the Law* (9:20), like *one not having the Law* (9:21), but he became *weak* (9:22), not merely like the weak (2:3; 4:10). The *weak* cling to superstitions about so-called gods (8:11). Paul is willing to meet such people where they are and adjust to their scruples in order to help them grasp the gospel. Love trumps knowledge.

9:24–10:13 Paul offers an athletic illustration. No athlete wins a *prize* who loses sight of the goal. Winners at the Isthmian Games won a crown of withered celery (later of pine) that *will not last* (9:25). In the spiritual race, every runner can win a crown, but only those who keep their eyes on the goal will do so. A boxer does not win a prize for sparring (*beating the air*; 9:26) but for winning in the ring. Nevertheless, disciplined training is essential (9:27). The lesson applies to Christians, *on whom the fulfillment of the ages has come* (10:11). The con-

> **Spiritual Food & Drink**
> Spiritual food (10:3) *recalls the quails and manna that appeared miraculously (Exod 16; Num 11:4–34). Spiritual drink (10:4) recalls the stories of Moses striking a rock in Exodus 17:1–7 and Numbers 20:2–13. Some ancient rabbis thought these two stories were about the same rock, although they are set in different locations. So a tradition developed that a rock followed the Israelites through the wilderness (Pseudo-Philo, Biblical Antiquities, 11.15; Willis, Idol Meat, 133–42). Paul suggests that Christ is like that rock, who supplies support for believers along the way.*

cerns of this age must not distract us from the end-times goal.

Another illustration comes from Scripture. Many Israelites left Egypt, but most failed to reach the promised land because of worldly distractions. In their dramatic departure from Egypt, the Israelites were *under the cloud* and *passed through the sea* (10:1; Exod 14:19–22). *Baptized into Moses* (10:2) implies that the Red Sea crossing was like the initiation rite of baptism. It was where Israel began a new walk as the people of God.

Almost the entire generation that crossed the Red Sea died in the wilderness (10:5; Num 14), and their stories are examples for us (10:6). Paul simply alludes to these familiar stories in quick succession. He recalls the feasting and orgy that accompanied the golden calf at Sinai (10:7; Exod 32:6). The death of *twenty-three thousand* (10:8) recalls those who died after indulging in sexual promiscuity and worshiping the Baal of Peor (Num 25:1–9, though the Old Testament text reads 24,000. Paul seems to be working from memory, mentioning stories as they come to mind). Those *killed by snakes* (10:9) had complained about their food (Num 21:4–9). It is not clear what story Paul has in mind about a *destroying angel* (10:10), although several stories recount grumbling (Exod 15:24; 16:2; 17:3; Num 14:2; 16:41). Paul takes these stories as *warnings for us* (10:11). The resurrection of Jesus is the *firstfruits* (15:20) of a general resurrection. That is why Christians are those *on whom the fulfillment of the ages has come* (10:11). Christians are reoriented away from the present age toward the end time (compare 2 Cor 5:17; Gal 6:14–15). The warning is that, if God punished Israel after delivering them from Egypt, God will also punish Christians who compromise their faith through idolatry or selfish desires, regardless of their baptism or the spiritual food they eat each Sunday. Verse 13 is a comforting reminder that God will *provide a way out* of temptation. At the same time, it suggests that every circumstance in life is a test of whether we trust God.

10:14–22 Paul refers to the *cup we bless* and the *bread we break* (10:16), as if he assumes the Corinthians celebrate the Lord's Supper regularly. His language "the cup of blessing" (10:16) reflects the customs of Jewish Passover (NIV mistranslates this as *cup of thanksgiving…give thanks*). Paul's point is that both cup and bread are *participation* [Greek *koinonia*, "fellowship, communion"] in the blood and body of Christ. This is more than a memorial. Those who eat are in communion with Christ (similarly to baptism as participation in the death and resurrection of Jesus; Rom 6:1–11). So also, those who eat sacrificial meat commune with the deity to whom it is sacrificed (10:18–20), even if that god does not exist (10:19). Communion with the Lord contradicts communion with other gods (10:21). Idolatry arouses the Lord's jealousy (compare Deut 32:16, 21).

Additionally, the practice of using a single loaf for the whole group symbolizes the unity of the body (10:17). Members of a unified Body should be sensitive to avoid compromising one another's faith.

10:23–11:1 In 10:23–11:1, Paul sums up his discussion by returning to his opening points from chapter 8. He quotes a philosophical slogan used by some Corinthians to justify eating idol meat: *everything is permissible* (10:23; see the comments on 6:12). Paul's counter-slogan *not everything is constructive* [literally "does not build up," 10:23] echoes 8:1, while *seek…the good of others* (10:24) recalls 8:9–13 (compare 10:33; Phil 2:4).

Paul grants the Corinthians' freedom to *eat anything sold in the market* without worrying whether it was ritually slaughtered (10:25) and quotes Psalm 24:1 (10:26) to assert that the one true God created all. All food is available, if we *thank God* for it (10:30–31; compare 1 Tim 4:3–5). Paul also grants the right to accept a private dinner invitation (10:27–28). Note that these scenarios would pertain only to prosperous believers, since the poor would not likely have money for meat nor be invited to dinners. Paul insists that one should never do anything to create an obstacle to the gospel (10:28–29, 32–33; compare 9:19–23). Concern for others trumps one's rights. Paul extends this principle even to unbelievers – we should not do anything to hinder our Christian witness to unbelievers (10:28–29). After all, we are running for an eternal prize. Paul sets an example (see also 4:16–17), but the ultimate example is Christ (11:1; Phil 2:5–11).

HAIRSTYLES & CLOTHING · 11:2–16

In chapters 11–14 Paul discusses problems pertaining to the assembly, when the Corinthians *come together* (11:18, 20; 14:23, 26). These include disputes about attire in worship (11:2–16), abuses of the

Lord's Supper (11:17–34), and abuses of spiritual gifts (chapters 12–14).

The Christians in Corinth included Jews, Greeks, and Romans, slaves, artisans, and aristocrats. Different groups had different customs about how to dress for worship (Oster; Winter, *After Paul*, 121–23). A Jewish man would cover his head with a prayer shawl when he prayed. Roman men and women pulled their togas up over their heads when offering sacrifices, though other worshipers were usually bareheaded. Greeks usually worshiped bareheaded. Greek, Roman, and Jewish priests wore various headdresses.

Apart from worship, Jewish women in Palestine normally wore veils, but we do not know their practice in Greece. Greek and Roman women normally wore their hair tied up in public but were not necessarily veiled, although a woman might let her hair down when mourning. Wealthy women displayed their status with elaborate hairdos (Thompson). But the early Empire saw the emergence of the so-called "new woman," who was more liberated financially and sexually than her grandmothers (Winter, *After Paul*, 123–30; *Roman Wives*, 17–38). Augustus introduced new laws to uphold old-fashioned family values, including strong tax incentives for marriage and legitimate children (Suetonius, *Augustus*, 34; Winter, *Roman Wives*, 39–58). Amidst conflicting traditions about attire for worship, Paul does not lay down an absolute rule.

> **Worshipers of Isis**
>
> *In rites of the Isis cult, women wore veils, while men shaved their heads* (Apuleius, Golden Ass, 11.10).

11:2–7 This passage is full of ambiguities. One difficulty is that the Greek word *aner* can mean either *man* or "husband," and the word *gyne* either *woman* or "wife." Is every man the head of every woman? More likely, Paul is talking about husbands and wives here, as in chapter 7.

A second difficulty is the figurative meaning of *head*. The Greek word *kephale* could symbolize anything at the top or front and so could function as a metaphor for either authority or source (Fitzmyer). Some understand *head* here as a metaphor for authority, since Paul speaks of *authority* in 11:10. But in what sense is Christ the "head" of a man and not of a woman? Does a woman relate to Christ only through a man? And how does Paul's advice here square with his statement that a husband and wife each *has authority over* the other's body (7:4)? And what does it mean, *the head of Christ is God*? How does this fit with the doctrine of the Trinity, which holds that Father and Son are equal? This passage does not support a chain of command running from God to Christ to man to woman. Paul does not present the pairs in that order.

Others conclude that Paul here uses *head* as a figure for source, like the "head" of a river. Thus Christ was the source of the first man in that he participated in the creation (Col 1:16; John 1:3). And Adam was the source of the first woman, who was made from his rib. And God is the source of Christ in the birth of Jesus. This interpretation would fit with the reference to creation in verses 8–9.

Whichever way Paul intends the *head* metaphor in 11:3, what he emphasizes is shame (NIV *dishonor*). He asserts that for a man to pray or prophesy veiled *shames his head* (11:4). Likewise, for a woman to do so unveiled *shames her head* (11:5). This is another example of the communal nature of Christian worship.

For a woman to have cut or shaven hair in public was shameful (11:6; *Testament of Job*, 24.9–10). First century women might cut their hair as a sign of mourning or as a rite of passage, but in some places cutting a woman's hair was a penalty for adultery. Furthermore, the imperial family values agenda emphasized the veil as a symbol of a married woman's modesty when she was in public, and local magistrates enforced the dress codes (Winter, *Roman Wives*, 42–44, 78–91). A woman convicted of adultery or a prostitute had to wear a dark toga and could not wear a veil (Winter, *Roman Wives*, 42). Paul seems to have in mind this sort of shame associated with sexual immorality. Christians should wear clothing that conforms to societal norms for modesty. Above all, their attire should deemphasize themselves and emphasize their intent to honor God.

11:8–12 For his recommendation that women prophets cover their heads and men uncover theirs, Paul offers two supporting arguments, the first of which is from Scripture (11:7–12). *Image* (11:7) alludes to Genesis 1:27, while the order of creation (11:8–9) alludes to Genesis 2:18–24. The obscure phrase *because of the angels* (11:10) may allude to Genesis 6:2, where the *sons of God looked on the daughters of men that they were fair*. A popular, ancient interpretation of that passage was that angels lusted after human women (*1 Enoch* 6–11; *Jubilees* 5). Alternatively, we could understand the Greek word *angelos* here in the secular sense of "messenger" to refer to those who might inform against Christians to local magistrates (Winter, *After Paul*, 136–38; *Roman Wives*, 89–91).

Paul suggests that a wife is her husband's *glory* (11:7), but a man's glory should not be the focus in worship. Those who flaunt their appearance bring glory only to themselves, not to God. So man's glory should be covered (11:7), and God's glory should be exposed. Paul is not arguing that women's bodies should be covered because they are inherently shameful. What is shameful is a woman calling attention to herself, especially trying to gain the attention of men. In Roman culture, a veil announced that a woman was married and unavailable. But Paul does not want the veil to imply that she is secondary to her husband, because *in the Lord* neither gender takes priority (11:11–12). In the new creation in Christ, there is no room for arguing about who is first.

11:13–16 Paul's second supporting argument appeals to *nature* (11:14), but it is not about animal behavior. *Nature* is a technical, philosophical term parallel to what is *proper* (11:13). Stoics taught that one should always behave "according to nature" (Diogenes Laertius 7.85–89). But human nature differs from animal nature in that humans can reason (Epictetus, *Discourses*, 4.11). Therefore, to live "according to nature" for Stoics meant to live a rational life and develop one's moral character (Epictetus, *Discourses*, 3.1; fragment 18). Long hair on a man was associated with virility and thus carried overtones of sexual attraction. But Stoics claim that men have a higher nature than attracting sexual partners. Human nature is to develop one's reason, justice, and self-control. Hence, long hair on a man is "unnatural" (Epictetus, *Discourses*,

> **"Because of the angels ..."**
> An idea related to that found in 1 Corinthians 11 may be reflected among the Dead Sea Scrolls, which stressed the need for holiness because of the presence of angels with the community of the faithful. Among other things, at the end time, "No man shall go down with them on the day of battle who is impure because of his 'fount,' for the holy angels will be with their hosts" (1Q WarScroll 7.6; Stuckenbruck 223–32; on sexual purity, see 1 Sam 21:4–5).

3.1.24–26). Similarly, to say that a woman's long hair is her *covering* (11:15) is to suggest that her nature is modesty (compare 1 Tim 2:9–10). Paul agrees with Stoic philosophy on these points.

Paul recognizes that his suggestions may not be agreeable to everyone, so he says the issue is not worth fighting over. There is no one rule for all Christians, since "we have no such custom, neither the churches of God" (11:16). The NIV gives the opposite sense, *we have no other practice* (11:16, also RSV, NAS), which is a blatant mistranslation. The correct translation is found in KJV, NRSV, and ESV. Each local community should develop its own customs about worship attire, and members should respect one another's cultural differences.

NOT THE LORD'S SUPPER · 11:17–22

Ancient Greeks and Romans commonly held banquets as parts of religious rites. For many early Christians, then, it seemed natural to have a meal connected with the weekly assembly. Christians called these meals "love feasts" (Jude 12; Ignatius, *Smyrnaeans*, 8; Clement of Alexandria, *Instructor*, 2.1.4; Tertullian, *Apology*, 39.16–18).

To the Corinthians, it also seemed natural to arrange the meals like any other banquet. Dinner was typically at the ninth hour (3:00 p.m.), often a bring-your-own-meat affair, with a second table primarily for drinking later in the evening (Lampe 37–41). An afternoon schedule would accommodate wealthy men with leisure time but would be impossible for workers and slaves. This could explain why Paul criticizes the wealthy Corinthian Christians, that each one *goes ahead without waiting* (11:21, literally, "takes his own dinner beforehand"). Greek and Roman banqueters strictly enforced seating according to social status (Willis, *Idol Meat*, 47–64). Honored guests at the head table received better food and service than lower-ranking guests. In a home, a typical dining room might seat no more than twelve (Murphy-O'Connor 178–82; White 2:123–31; 152–59; 219–28); so poorer guests who came later would be seated in the courtyard, perhaps on the floor (Pliny, *Letters*, 2.6; Martial, *Epigrams*, 3.60). Such practices may have seemed normal to the Corinthians, but Paul says it is not the *Lord's Supper* (11:20), since Jesus would not host a dinner arranged in such a way. Paul wants the Corinthians to model a more egalitarian society and not simply accept local customs.

In response to their discrimination, Paul reminds the Corinthians of the meaning of the Lord's Supper (11:23–25). *I received* and *passed on to you* (11:23) shows that Paul was continuing an established Christian tradition. That he received it *from the Lord* (1:23) indicates that he understood Jesus as the originator of the tradition. The tradition emphasizes the function of the meal in *remembrance* (11:24–25). To this, Paul adds that the meal also *proclaims the Lord's death* (11:26) as a continual reenactment of the Last Supper.

> **The Lord's Supper**
>
> Paul's account of the origins of the Lord's Supper is very similar to those found in Matthew, Mark, and Luke: Jesus shared a meal with his disciples before he died, during which he blessed bread and wine, giving them new symbolic meanings, and he exhorted his followers to observe this ritual as a reminder of his death.

The behavior of Christians toward one another contributes to this proclamation. *In an unworthy manner* (11:27) is parallel to *without discerning the Body* (11:29). Paul is discussing discrimination in the assembly, so self-examination (11:28) applies to the behavior of the group as the Body of Christ. Recall his appeal when discussing idol meat: *Because there is one loaf, we, who are many are one body, for we all partake of the one loaf* (10:17). The unity of the body is Paul's concern (8:12; 12:12–27). The "unworthiness" he has in mind is discriminatory behavior that obstructs communion by reflecting the values of this age and so fails to *proclaim the Lord's death* (11:26). Apparently, some Corinthian Christians had become *weak and sick* (11:30) and even *fallen asleep* (euphemism for death, 7:39; 15:6, 20, 51; 1 Thess 4:13–15). Paul interprets these as divine judgments to *discipline* the community (11:32; compare Heb 12:6; Prov 3:11–12). He calls his readers to exercise greater judgment in disciplining themselves (11:31), lest they be *condemned with the world* at the final judgment (11:32; compare 5:4–5; 1 Pet 4:17).

SPIRITUAL GIFTS · 12:1–14:40

12:1–11 The new topic of *spiritual gifts* takes up chapters 12–14. Chapter 12 unfolds in three sections: varieties of gifts (verses 1–11), the unity of the body (verses 12–26), and varieties of gifts (verses 27–31). The overall theme is discerning the Spirit's operation in the community, especially in the worship assembly.

In contrast with *dumb idols*, the Spirit has something to say (12:2). One can discern the Spirit moving by being aware of what the Spirit says. In verse 3, the word *is* does not appear in the Greek, so the curse could be understood as, "Jesus [grants] a curse." This may reflect a Corinthian practice of writing a curse on a lead tablet and invoking a god against one's enemy (Winter, *After Paul*, 174–81). In any case, when you hear *Jesus is Lord*, you know the Spirit is operating (12:3). Since all who confess *Jesus is Lord* are animated by the Spirit (12:3), it is worth contemplating just how large the body of Christ is. We should be careful not to draw our circle of fellowship too tightly along doctrinal lines, lest we hack off vital body parts.

Paul describes the types of gifts given by the Spirit (12:4–11; compare 12:27–31; Rom 12:3–8): *wisdom*, *knowledge*, and *faith*. The Spirit gives these *to each [one] as he determines* (12:11). We may be surprised who is gifted in what ways, but we should discern at least one gift in each Christian.

12:12–26 The body metaphor is not unique to Paul (see Livy, *From the Founding of the City*, 2.32.9–11), but it serves his purposes in dealing with the conflicts that could spring from ethnic and class differences (Martin 92–96). The unity of the Christian body is not based on ethnicity or culture but on the idea that *we all [were] baptized by one Spirit into one Body … and we were given to drink from one Spirit* (12:13). The Spirit animates the body of Christ. Furthermore, Paul values the weaker and less honorable parts (12:22–24; compare 4:8–10). Paul wants those who are (self-) important to see their obligation to the weak in the community.

12:27–31 Once again, Paul uses the plural *you* when he says, *you are the Body of Christ*, namely, the community of believers. Even though the Spirit equips individuals for particular tasks within the body, it is the community collectively that the Spirit animates (2:10; 3:16; 6:19). Individual gifts are subordinated to the operation of the Spirit in the group as a whole.

The list of gifts in 12:28 is similar to that in 12:8–10 but not identical with it, and neither list is exhaustive. *Different kinds of tongues* (12:10, 28) anticipates *tongues of men and of angels* (13:1) and suggests that human speech is also a gift. Prophecy rises from sixth position in verse 10 to second in verse 28, which suggests that we should be careful about ranking the gifts in order of importance. In fact, to do so would violate Paul's main point that all are essential, and no member takes priority. The verb *eagerly desire* [Greek *zeloo*] in 12:31 is the same root translated "jealousy" [Greek *zelos*] in 3:3, where it is associated with strife and factional rivalry. The connection is clearer if we translate verse 31a as a question: "Are you jealously desiring the greater gifts? I will show you a more excellent way" (Hunt 118–19).

Spiritual Gifts
In both lists in chapter 12, intellectual gifts—wisdom, knowledge, and teaching—are portrayed as relatively higher, while miracles, healing, and tongues are shown to be relatively lower. Knowledge and teaching are also spiritual gifts. However, recognizing that this ranking was likely a product of Paul's rhetorical task, we should not rank the gifts.

13:1–3 In 13:1–3, Paul shifts into the first person, offering himself as an example (Holladay 83–94), since he himself *speaks in tongues* (14:6, 18), is a *prophet* (2:7–10; 7:40; Gal 1:15–16), can fathom *mysteries* (2:10; 15:51) and *knowledge* (2:12), has *faith* to perform miracles (2 Cor 12:12), and lives self-sacrificially (4:9–13; 9:12, 15; 2 Cor 6:4–10; 11:23–29). Instead of *to the flames* (13:3), the better ancient manuscripts read, "that I may boast" (NIV note), which in this context would be consistent with Paul's boasting in weakness (2 Cor 11:30). Although he values his spiritual gifts, including tongues and prophecy, Paul argues that no gift is meaningful apart from love.

13:4–7 Paul describes love in terms that correspond directly to the problems he discusses throughout the letter (Holladay 94–97). Love *does not envy* [Greek *zeloo*, 13:4], in contrast with the jealousy of 3:3; 12:31. Love *does not boast* (13:4), but the Corinthians do (4:7; 5:6). Love *is not proud* [literally "puffed up," 13:4], but the Corinthians are (4:6, 18–19; 5:2; 8:1). Love *is not rude* [literally "improper," 13:5], as in 7:36. Love *is not self-seeking* (13:5), as Paul models it (10:33). Love does not delight in *evil* [literally "injustice," 13:6], but some Corinthians delight in their unjust "cheating" (6:7–8). Thus, love is an antidote to many of the problems that plague the community.

13:8–13 Love *never fails* (13:8). Love is the greatest of those things that endure (13:13), even when such spiritual gifts as prophecy, tongues, and knowledge *pass away* (13:8). That will be when the *teleion* (*perfection*) comes (13:10). The Greek adjective *teleion* is usually translated "complete" (RSV) or "perfect" (KJV, NAS), because it stands in direct contrast to things that are "incomplete" or "partial" (13:9). But the word also carries an overtone of the end time. As long as we remain in this age with our human limitations, then even with the aid of the Spirit, we know and prophesy only *in part* (13:9). Our understanding is no clearer than a *reflection* in a mirror (13:12). But *then* (when the *teleion* comes, 13:10), *we shall know fully* (13:12). Paul is alluding to the end time, when God's kingdom will be "finally" and fully realized. After all the things of this age have passed away, love will remain (Holladay 97–98).

"In a mirror darkly …"
Ancient mirrors were made of polished bronze, so looking in one was like looking at yourself in a doorknob.

Love is the essence of that great apocalyptic event, the cross, when God intervened decisively

"But the greatest of these is love …"
Paul inserts chapter 13's description of love into his discussion about the abuse of spiritual gifts in the worship assembly. Several details cement this chapter into its context.

First, chapter 12 ends with I show you a more excellent way *(12:31), and chapter 14 opens with an exhortation to pursue love (14:1). Love, then, is the most excellent way (see Rom 12:9–21), and understanding love is essential to the discussion of tongues and prophecy in chapter 14. Second, Paul's exhortation to* seek the spiritual gifts, and especially that you may prophesy *(14:1) links chapter 14 back to desiring the greater gifts (12:31). Third, in 13:1–3, love gives meaning to tongues, prophecy, knowledge, faith, charity, and self-sacrifice (13:1–3).*

The gifts mentioned in 13:1–3 echo the lists in 12:8–10 and 12:28–30. But in chapter 13, tongues and prophecy move to the top of the list. These two gifts are the primary focus of chapter 14, which suggests that they were the main sources of trouble in the Corinthian assembly. Paul emphasizes love as the fundamental presupposition of how Christians relate to one another in the assembly.

in history and shook the earth to its foundations. And when the end time is fully realized at Christ's return, then everything that pertains to this age will vanish. Love is oriented toward the end time because it reflects the love of Christ. Paul wants the Corinthians to be end-times oriented in their relations to one another, to love one another now in ways that reflect the love of Christ and not the sort of things that pass for "love" in this age. Love is the *more excellent way* (12:31).

14:1–25 Of all the spiritual gifts listed in chapter 12, Paul now focuses on *tongues* and *prophecy*. Some Corinthian Christians were enthralled with these two gifts, and their self-centered use of them hindered corporate worship.

The nature of "speaking in tongues" at Corinth differs from the phenomenon described on Pentecost (Acts 2). There, tongues enabled the apostles to bear witness of the resurrection to pilgrims from all over the world. Here Paul talks about the *tongues of angels* (13:1) and says that one *speaks to God* and *utters mysteries in the Spirit* (14:2). This sounds like what happened at the Greek shrine of Delphi, where a priestess uttered oracles in an ecstatic trance (Plutarch, *Moralia*, 404E-405D; Plato, *Phaedrus*, 244; *Timaeus*, 71E; Martin 96–101).

The Corinthian tongue speakers found the experience edifying (14:4), and that was fine with Paul, who wanted every believer to speak in tongues (14:5, 18, 39) and prophesy (14:31, 39). But he did not want the Corinthians to concentrate on self-edification. Whatever one does in the assembly should edify the whole body (14:12).

Chapter 14 grows directly out of the discussion of love in chapter 13 and applies the ethic of community that we have seen throughout the letter. As Paul said before, love builds up (8:1); love is not self-seeking (13:5). Now he exhorts the Corinthians to aim for love (14:1). Tongue speakers and prophets should use their gifts to edify not themselves but the church (14:1–5).

In 14:6–19, Paul applies this community ethic to the worship assembly. The main idea is that love builds up the body. Those who exercise spiritual gifts only to edify themselves are like untrained musicians (14:7–9) or people speaking in a foreign language (14:10–13). They do not edify the group. The worship assembly is not about getting a spiritual high but about contributing to the spiritual growth of one's brothers and sisters. Paul encourages the Corinthians to sing and pray with the Spirit, but also with the mind to communicate with others (14:14–19).

In 14:16, Paul contemplated an outsider visiting the assembly, and so in 14:20–25 he discusses how spiritual gifts can address the spiritual needs of outsiders. He says Christians should be "mature" [Greek *teleios*] in their assemblies (14:20). He is calling for an end-times orientation to worship that takes into account the needs of others. Close-knit family groups may be able to edify one another, but they can present unseen barriers to outsiders. Corporate worship is part of a Christian witness to outsiders (14:20–25). Isaiah 28:11 suggests that foreigners will bear witness to Israel, but Paul turns this idea around to comment on Christian witness to non-Christians (14:21).

14:26–40 First century house churches consisted of small groups of mostly relatives and friends. Such a setting would surely have been more relaxed than our typical, large assemblies, and we can imagine that individuals would offer their various gifts to the Body. One might bring a *hymn*, another an *instruction*, another a *revelation* or an *interpretation* (14:26). But in 14:26–40, Paul clamps down on three specific groups who are hindering the edification of this sharing community by their self-centered behavior.

First, tongue speakers should take turns and address their gifts to the community. If there is no interpreter, Paul says the tongue speakers should *be silent in the church* (14:28). The NIV *keep quiet* obscures the fact that Paul uses the same verb "be silent" [Greek *sigao*] three times (14:28, 30, 34). Paul's emphasis on the communal quality of this gift serves as a caution against modern day individuals who claim private revelation.

Second, prophets should take turns, and other members of the community should evaluate their words. Paul would not agree with those who talk about being carried away in the Spirit. The spirits of the prophets are subject to the control of the prophets (14:32), so prophets can wait their turns. If a second prophet receives a revelation, *let the first be silent* (14:30). The NIV *the first speaker should stop* obscures Paul's second use of the verb "be silent" [Greek *sigao*, as in 14:28, 34]. The underlying principle is that *God is not of disorder but of peace, as in all the churches of the saints* (14:33). Self-serving exercise of spiritual gifts can lead to chaos. The NIV mispunctuates 14:33 by starting a new paragraph with *as in all the churches of the saints* (14:33). This phrase makes no sense as an introduction to verse 34, since Paul does not assume women are silent in *all the churches of the saints*, not even at Corinth (11:5). But it does make sense as the conclusion to verse 33 (as in KJV).

Third, Paul urges the women in Corinth to *remain silent in the churches* (14:34). It is not clear what *law* Paul had in mind to support this injunction (14:34). No Old Testament text says this, so perhaps he is thinking of a traditional Jewish interpretation (see Josephus, *Apion*, 2.201). But Paul did talk about shame before (11:4–6).

Three times in this section, Paul exhorts some Corinthian Christians to *be silent* (14:28, 30, 34). He is not making universal rules. In fact, he expressly hopes the Corinthians will continue to speak in tongues and prophesy (14:5, 39). This includes presumably also the women (11:5). But he exhorts that *everything should be done in a fitting and orderly way* (14:40). In this section, he is warning against self-serving, unedifying, or disruptive behaviors in Roman Corinth.

> **Women in Corinth**
>
> *In 11:5, Paul assumes women pray and prophesy in the assemblies, and he sees nothing wrong with that. His only concern is that women dress so as not to call attention to themselves when they do so. Likewise, it appears in 14:25 that the behavior of some women in Corinth was disruptive and self-seeking.*

THE RESURRECTION OF THE BODY · 15:1–58

15:1–11 In chapter 15, Paul reminds the Corinthians of *the gospel* he *preached* in the beginning. It seems they did not understand the resurrection, and that ignorance contributed to many of their problems (Martin 104–36). So by returning to the basic story, Paul tries to put their problems in a new perspective. He preached a gospel in three parts: that *Christ died ... was buried ... and was raised ...* (15:3–4). Paul elaborates on the last part. He stresses that Jesus was raised bodily and cites eyewitnesses (15:5–8). Then he argues that Christians will also be raised bodily in the end time. Finally, he argues that the resurrection of Jesus was a victory over death itself, which freed us from enslavement to the concerns of this age.

15:12–34 Most ancient Greeks and Romans thought of the body as a "tomb of the soul," something to be abandoned at death, while the soul lives forever (Seneca, *Epistles*, 65.16–17). Plato was not the first to promote this idea, but he made it popular, and it remains the dominant Western view today. But Paul follows the Jewish apocalyptic belief that, in the end time, God will resurrect the bodies of all the dead for a final judgment (see comments on 6:14; see Rev 20:11–15; *1 Enoch* 51). In 15:12–34, he argues his case along several lines.

First, *if there is no bodily resurrection, then not even Christ has been raised* (15:12–19). It is strange for a Christian to affirm that God raised Jesus' body from the grave and deny that he will raise ours. If we agree that God can raise the dead and that he has done so, how can we deny that God will do so again? Our hope is that what God did for Christ will also occur to those who are in Christ (Rom 6:3–10).

Second, the resurrection of Christ foreshadows a general resurrection of the dead at the end time (15:20–23). Christ was the *first fruits* (15:20, 23), which implies that a general harvest is coming (Col 1:18; Rev 1:5). Jewish apocalyptic theology typically expected that all the dead would be raised for the final judgment. But Jews did not believe the messiah would die, so the idea of a crucified messiah was a *stumbling block* for many (1:23). The distinctively Christian claim is that Jesus' messiahship was manifest when God raised him as the *first fruits* of a general resurrection. In Christ, the end time has already begun.

Third, Paul interprets Psalm 8:6 and Psalm 110:1 messianically (15:24–28) to argue that the end time will come when God's son has *destroyed all dominion, authority and power* and subdued *all his enemies*, including *death*. When Christ conquers death, then death will no longer be able to hold our bodies.

Fourth, Paul argues that baptism *for the dead* only makes sense if one believes in resurrection (15:29; compare sin offerings for the dead in 2 Maccabees 12:39–45). The practice may reflect a cultural preoccupation with providing for the dead (DeMaris). But it is not something Paul endorses, as he refers to the ones who practiced it as *they*, not *we*. His point is simply that the practice would be nonsensical unless one believed in the resurrection, since baptism symbolizes both death and resurrection.

Fifth, Paul argues that it makes no sense to risk your life for your faith, if you do not believe you would get your life back in the end time (15:30–31). On Paul's hardships, see 4:9–13.

Sixth, Paul argues that Christian ethics make better sense in terms of the resurrection (15:32). *Fighting with beasts* (15:32) was a Cynic metaphor for struggle against passions and desires (Dio Chrysostom, *Oration*, 1.84; Malherbe, "Beasts," 82–84), which Paul views from the perspective of the resurrection. If this life is all there is, then *Let us eat and drink, for tomorrow we die* (15:32; compare Isa 22:13). This slogan was a common caricature of Epicurean philosophy, which emphasized pleasure [Greek *hedone*] and denied any afterlife (Malherbe, "Beasts," 85). Of course, Epicureans were not really hedonists, because they taught that real pleasure derives from prudence and justice, not from satisfying physical appetites. Paul quotes the Greek poet Menander, a student of Epicurus, to make just this point: *Bad company corrupts good character* (15:33). *As you ought* (15:34) is literally, "justly." Hedonism is not true wisdom but results from being *ignorant of God* (15:34; compare Rom 1:18–32), including God's resurrection of the dead.

15:35–50 Paul's discussion of body types approximates some scientific theories of his day. It is not a simple question of physical/spiritual but a matter of degrees from plants to animals to humans to heavenly bodies (15:36–42; Martin 104–36). For Paul, the resurrection will be a sort of evolution from a relatively lower to a higher order. In theological terms, resurrection changes us from *dishonor* and *weakness* to *glory* and *power* (15:43). In the present age, Paul himself is *dishonorable* and *weak* (4:10), while some Corinthians are arrogant about their *glory* and *power* (4:10). They have their reward in this age. But in some ways, a Christian is already transformed from *perishable* and *natural* to *imperishable* and *spiritual* (15:42–43; compare 2:13–16). Baptism symbolizes the transforming resurrection and implies that Christians should live now in the new creation (6:9–11; compare Rom 6:1–14).

The *natural body* (15:44) breathes and thinks (15:45, quoting Gen 2:7); whereas the *spiritual body* is animated by the Spirit of God, bearing the *likeness of the man from heaven* (15:49; compare 11:7; Rom 8:29; 2 Cor 3:18). Paul develops the analogy between Adam and Christ more fully in Romans 5:12–21. If God could create a human (Adam) out of earth in the first place, God can recreate us in the image of Christ (15:47–49) with transformed bodies.

That *flesh and blood cannot inherit the Kingdom of God* (15:50) has ethical implications for this age (see 5:5; 6:10). Physical appetites are of the *flesh*. Citizens of the kingdom exercise self-control over fleshly desires and live for the end time. Instead of worrying about what our bodies will be like in the next life, we should consider how the promise of resurrection affects what we do with our bodies in this life.

15:51–58 Paul envisions the coming of Jesus as a triumphal procession (15:52; compare 1 Thess 4:15–17). Believers will be *changed* (15:51) by putting on new *clothes* in place of their perishable bodies (15:53–54), though at baptism believers have already donned one type of new clothes (Gal 3:27).

Death has been swallowed up (15:54) paraphrases Isaiah 25:8, from an oracle that describes God's new reign after the defeat of the fortified cities of oppressive powers. The problem with this age is that death has taken over and is trying to run it (Rom 5:12–14; 6:19–21; 7:7–25). In 15:55 Paul lifts language

---

"Death, Be Not Proud"

John Donne (1572–1631) was an Anglican priest and an acclaimed poet of the English metaphysical school. Though his early poetry often focused on worldly themes, his later poetry became increasingly religious in focus, often serving in his own private devotions. The following poem, "Holy Sonnet X," echoes the reminder in 1 Corinthians that Death has been swallowed up in victory ... *(15:54–55).*

Death, be not proud, though some have called thee
Mighty and dreadful, for thou art not so;
For those whom thou think'st thou dost overthrow,
Die not, poor Death, nor yet canst thou kill me.
From rest and sleep, which but thy pictures be,
Much pleasure; then from thee much more must flow,
And soonest our best men with thee do go,
Rest of their bones, and soul's delivery.
Thou art slave to fate, chance, kings, and desperate men,
And dost with poison, war, and sickness dwell;
And poppy or charms can make us sleep as well
And better than thy stroke; why swell'st thou then?
One short sleep past, we wake eternally,
And death shall be no more; Death, thou shalt die.

from Hosea 13:14 but rewords it into a taunt against death. Death rules us through fear that we will lose whatever we have built up to protect our physical bodies (see Rom 8:2). *The power of sin is the law* (15:56) suggests that sin influences even our attempts to follow Scripture, so that we tend to interpret and apply it in self-serving ways (Rom 7:7–13; 8:3). But in the end, death defeats all promises of security in this age. The gospel is that Jesus defeated death (15:57). Jesus' followers live in this world, subject to its fears and selfish desires. But we do not live for this world. We place our hope in the one who conquered death, and, even though our physical bodies are not yet transformed, we live for the end time, when Jesus will deal the final blow to death itself (15:24–28).

THE EPISTOLARY CLOSING · 16:1–24

A typical ancient letter closing had standard elements: travel plans, so correspondents would know where to send a reply; personal greetings to and from friends and family; and a closing salutation. First Corinthians has all three elements.

16:1–13 The last topic in the letter is the *collection* for famine relief (16:1–4), a project Paul undertook at the request of the Jerusalem elders (Acts 11:27–30; Rom 15:25–29; 2 Cor 8–9; Gal 2:10). Paul wants the Corinthians to prepare for his next visit by having their contribution to the fund ready and by selecting delegates to accompany him to Jerusalem. This collection is a reminder that the Christians in Corinth are part of a worldwide fellowship that crosses ethnic and political boundaries.

Although Paul plans to visit, he cannot come right away (16:5–9), so he is sending *Timothy* (16:10–11). *If Timothy comes* (16:10) may reflect the uncertainties of travel conditions. The NIV *see to it that he has nothing to fear while he is with you* (16:10) implies that Timothy is a timid greenhorn, but that contradicts what Paul says about Timothy elsewhere (4:17; Phil 2:19–24; 1 Thess 3:1–5). This could better be translated, "recognize that he comes to you fearlessly" (Hutson 61–65). Timothy is Paul's representative until he himself arrives, and Paul has already threatened to come with a rod (4:17–21).

Paul has also urged *Apollos* to come (16:5–13). Since some Corinthians regarded Apollos as a rival to Paul (1:12; 3:5–6; 4:6), this show of solidarity helps blunt the factionalism in the community.

16:14–20 This section provides information about Paul's contacts with Corinth. The delegation led by *Stephanas* was at least the second group to visit Paul in Ephesus (1:11). Paul's earliest convert in *Achaia* (16:15) and one of the few Corinthians baptized by Paul (1:16), *Stephanas* must have been one of Paul's sources of information. He is a community leader, but his authority derives not from any office. Paul urges the Corinthians to submit to *such as these*, who *have devoted themselves to the service* (16:15) and to recognize *such men*, who *refresh my spirit* (16:18). Christian leadership does not inhere in any title but in service to the church. Paul further urges submission to *everyone who joins in the work and labors at it* (16:16). Again, he refuses to side with any teacher against the others.

Paul sends greetings from *Aquila and Priscilla*, who were like old family, charter members of the Christian community in Corinth (Acts 18:2–3). But he also sends greetings from *all* the Christians in Asia (16:19–20). For Paul, the Christian family includes all who are related *in the Lord*.

16:21–24 Paul writes a benediction with his *own hand* (16:21–24). Of course, that original manuscript is lost to us, but the words indicate that Paul dictated the body of the letter to a scribe (as in Gal 6:11–18).

THEOLOGICAL REFLECTIONS

The letter is theologically significant because it illustrates the ethical implications of the gospel in concrete situations. Also, it shows Paul working across cultural boundaries. He comes with a Jewish apocalyptic theology that emphasizes monotheism, God's sovereignty, and an expectation that, at the end of the present age, God's reign will become undeni-

> **Paul on Division & Unity**
>
> 1 Corinthians speaks to the fractured nature of Christianity. Although Paul is addressing one local congregation, his principles apply to the denominational and sectarian impulses that divide all Christians. Indeed, Thomas Campbell referred to this letter no fewer than fifty times in his Declaration and Address (1809), the document that launched the Restoration Movement in America and helped inspire the ecumenical movement (Olbricht & Rollmann, 139–142).

able when God raises the dead for a final judgment. The Christian twist on this scenario is that, with the resurrection of Jesus, the end time has already begun, and believers should now orient their lives toward it. But Paul must argue in terms that make sense to converts steeped in Greek philosophy and religion. Readers often assume that the problems in Corinth arose from misunderstandings of Christian doctrine. That is partly true, but most misunderstandings derived from Corinthians' pre-Christian lives. The baggage converts brought to Christianity from their philosophies, religions, and social customs influenced how they (mis)understood Paul's teaching.

FOR FURTHER STUDY

Margaret M. Mitchell, *Paul and the Rhetoric of Reconciliation: An Exegetical Investigation of the Language and Composition of 1 Corinthians* (Louisville: Westminster/John Knox, 1992).

Rollin A. Ramsaran, *Liberating Words: Paul's Use of Rhetorical Maxims in 1 Corinthians 1–10* (Harrisburg, Pa.: Trinity Press International, 1996).

WORKS CITED

S. Scott Bartchy, Μαλλον Χρησαι: *First-Century Slavery & 1 Corinthians 7:21* (Missoula, Mont.: Scholars Press, 1973).

Richard E. DeMaris, "Corinthian Religion and Baptism for the Dead (1 Corinthians 15:29): Insights from Archaeology and Anthropology." *Journal of Biblical Literature* 114.4 (1995): 661–82.

Dio Chrysostom, *Discourses* (5 vols.; ed. H. Lamar Crosby; Cambridge: Harvard University Press, 1951).

Epictetus, *Discourses* (2 vols.; Cambridge: Harvard University Press, 1925–28).

John T. Fitzgerald, *Cracks in an Earthen Vessel: An Examination of the Catalogues of Hardships in the Corinthian Correspondence* (Atlanta: Scholars Press, 1988).

Joseph A. Fitzmyer, "*Kephale* in 1 Corinthians 11:3," *Interpretation* 47 (1993): 52–59.

Elizabeth R. Gebhard, "The Isthmian Games and the Sanctuary of Poseidon in the Early Empire," in *The Corinthia in the Roman Period* (edited by T. E. Gregory (Ann Arbor: University of Michigan Press, 1994), 78–94.

Robert G. Hall, "Epispasm: Circumcision in Reverse," *Bible Review* 8 (August 1992): 52–57.

Carl R. Holladay, "1 Corinthians 13: Paul as Apostolic Paradigm," in *Greeks, Romans, and Christians: Essays in Honor of Abraham J. Malherbe* (ed. D. L. Balch, E. Ferguson, and W. A. Meeks; Minneapolis, Minn.: Fortress, 1990), 80–98.

Allen R. Hunt, *The Inspired Body: Paul, the Corinthians, and Divine Inspiration* (Macon, Ga.: Mercer University Press, 1996).

Christopher R. Hutson, "Was Timothy Timid? On the Rhetoric of Fearlessness (1 Corinthians 16:10–11) and Cowardice (2 Timothy 1:7)," *Biblical Research* 42 (1997): 58–73.

Peter Lampe, "The Eucharist: Identifying with Christ on the Cross," *Interpretation* 48 (1994): 36–49.

Abraham J. Malherbe, "The Beasts at Ephesus," in *Paul and the Popular Philosophers* (ed. Abraham Malherbe; Minneapolis, Minn.: Fortress, 1989), 79–89.

———, "Determinism and Free Will in Paul: The Argument of 1 Corinthians 8 and 9," in *Paul and His Hellenistic Context* (ed. Troels Engberg-Pedersen; Minneapolis, Minn.: Fortress, 1995), 231–55.

Dale B. Martin, *The Corinthian Body* (New Haven: Yale University Press, 1995).

Jerome Murphy-O'Connor, *St. Paul's Corinth: Texts and Archaeology* (Collegeville, Minn.: Liturgical Press, 2002).

Thomas Olbricht and Hans Rollmann, *The Quest for Christian Unity, Peace, and Purity in Thomas Campbell's Declaration and Address: Texts and Studies* (Lanham, Md.: Scarecrow, 2000).

Richard Oster, "When Men Wore Veils to Worship: The Historical Context of 1 Corinthians 11.4," *New Testament Studies* 34 (1988): 481–505.

Plato, *Laches, Protagoras, Meno, Euthydemus* (ed. and trans. W. R. M. Lamb; Cambridge: Harvard University Press, 1924).

Seneca, *Epistles* (ed. R. M. Gummere; 3 vols.; Cambridge: Harvard University Press, 1917–25).

Stanley K. Stowers, "A 'Debate' over Freedom: 1 Corinthians 6:12–20," in *Christian Teaching: Studies in Honor of LeMoine G. Lewis* (ed. E. Ferguson; Abilene: ACU Bookstore, 1981), 59–71.

———, "Paul on the Use and Abuse of Reason," in *Greeks, Romans, and Christians: Essays in Honor of Abraham J. Malherbe* (ed. D. L. Balch, E. Ferguson, and W. A. Meeks; Minneapolis, Minn.: Fortress, 1990), 253–86.

Loren T. Stuckenbruck, "Why Should Women Cover Their Heads because of the Angels (1 Corinthians 11:10)?" *Stone-Campbell Journal* 4 (2001): 205–34.

Gerd Theissen, *The Social Setting of Pauline Christianity* (Philadelphia: Fortress, 1982).

Cynthia L. Thompson, "Hairstyles, Head-Coverings, and St. Paul: Portraits from Roman Corinth," *Biblical Archaeologist* 51 (1988): 99–115.

L. Michael White, *The Social Origins of Christian Architecture* (Valley Forge: Trinity, 1997).

Charles K. Williams, "Roman Corinth as a Commercial Center," in *The Corinthia in the Roman Period* (ed. T. E. Gregory; Ann Arbor: University of Michigan Press, 1994), 31–46.

Wendell Willis, "An Apostolic Apologia? The Form and Function of 1 Cor 9," *Journal for the Study of the New Testament* 24 (1985): 33–48.

———, *Idol Meat at Corinth: The Pauline Argument in 1 Corinthians 8 and 10* (Chico, Calif.: Scholars Press, 1985).

Bruce W. Winter, *After Paul Left Corinth: The Influence of Secular Ethics and Social Change* (Grand Rapids: Eerdmans, 2001).

———, *Philo and Paul among the Sophists: Alexandrian and Corinthian Responses to a Julio-Claudian Movement* (Grand Rapids: Eerdmans, 2002).

———, *Roman Wives, Roman Widows: The Appearance of New Women and the Pauline Communities* (Grand Rapids: Eerdmans, 2003).

O. Larry Yarbrough, *Not Like the Gentiles: Marriage Rules in the Letters of Paul* (Atlanta: Scholars Press, 1985).

References to ancient sources come chiefly from the Loeb Classical Library, published by Harvard University Press.

2 Corinthians

James W. Thompson

CHAPTER CONTENTS

Contexts 937

Commentary 937
- Salutation · 1:1–2 937
- Introduction of Themes · 1:3–11 938
- Paul's Reciprocal Boasting · 1:12–14 939
- Paul's Defense & Appeal · 1:15–7:16 939
- Paul's Appeal for the Collection · 8–9 943
- Final Defense and Appeal · 10:1–13:13 944

Theological Reflections 947

For Further Study 947

Works Cited 947

MAPS, TABLES, & FEATURES

Paul's Missionary Journeys 938

While most of Paul's letters provide a snapshot of his relationship with a church that he established, the Corinthian letters reflect the experience of a church over a period of time. Paul established the church at Corinth around 49 CE (Acts 18:1–18) and then remained with the new converts for eighteen months (Acts 18:11).

CONTEXTS

Some time after Paul left Corinth, he wrote a letter instructing Christians *not to associate with sexually immoral people* (1 Cor 5:9). During his stay in Ephesus (1 Cor 16:8), he wrote 1 Corinthians around 54 CE in response to reports from visitors (1 Cor 1:11; 16:15) and a letter from the Corinthians (1 Cor 7:1). After delivering the letter (1 Cor 4:17), Timothy returned to Paul with a report of a new crisis.

In response to Timothy's report, Paul first made a *painful visit* (2:1) in which someone led many members in a revolt against him (2:5; 7:12). After returning to Ephesus, he wrote a letter *with many tears* (2:4), which Titus delivered. After failing to find Titus, Paul finally met him in Macedonia, (7:5–6), where Titus brought a favorable report of improved conditions at Corinth (2:6; 7:8–12).

Despite these hopeful signs, Paul's defensive posture throughout 2 Corinthians indicates that all of the problems at Corinth had not been resolved. Indeed, some of the issues apparent in 1 Corinthians, including Paul's lack of oratorical ability (1 Cor 2:1–4; 2 Cor 10:10–11) and his refusal to accept payment (1 Cor 9:1–18; 2 Cor 11:7–11) continued without resolution. New issues had also emerged with the arrival of some who claimed to be *apostles of Christ* (11:13) and *servants of Christ* (11:23; see 11:5; 12:11). The dominant issue of the letter is the opponents' insistence on comparing their ministries to Paul (see 10:12; 3:1–5) and their boast that they are the true ministers. As a result, 2 Corinthians is the most autobiographical of Paul's letters. With the church caught between the two competing claims to authentic ministry, this letter is primarily a defense speech in which he responds to the charges against him by redefining the nature of Christian ministry.

The remarkable change of tone at certain points within the letter (for example, from 2:13 to 2:14; 6:13 to 6:14; 9:15 to 10:1) suggests to many scholars that 2 Corinthians is a composite of more than one letter that Paul sent to the Corinthians (that is, fragments of the letters that are mentioned (1 Cor 5:9; 2 Cor 2:4). However, the unified theme throughout 2 Corinthians, even though chapters 10–13 are more customarily intense than the rest of the letter, suggests that the entirety of the book is a single letter of defense in which Paul attempts to regain the allegiance of his converts.

COMMENTARY

SALUTATION · 1:1–2

Paul begins the letter with the customary epistolary form, identifying himself, his co-sender Timothy (Phil 1:1; Col 1:1; 1 Thess 1:1), and his readers. His claim to be *an apostle of Christ Jesus by the will of God* establishes his authority and anticipates the later

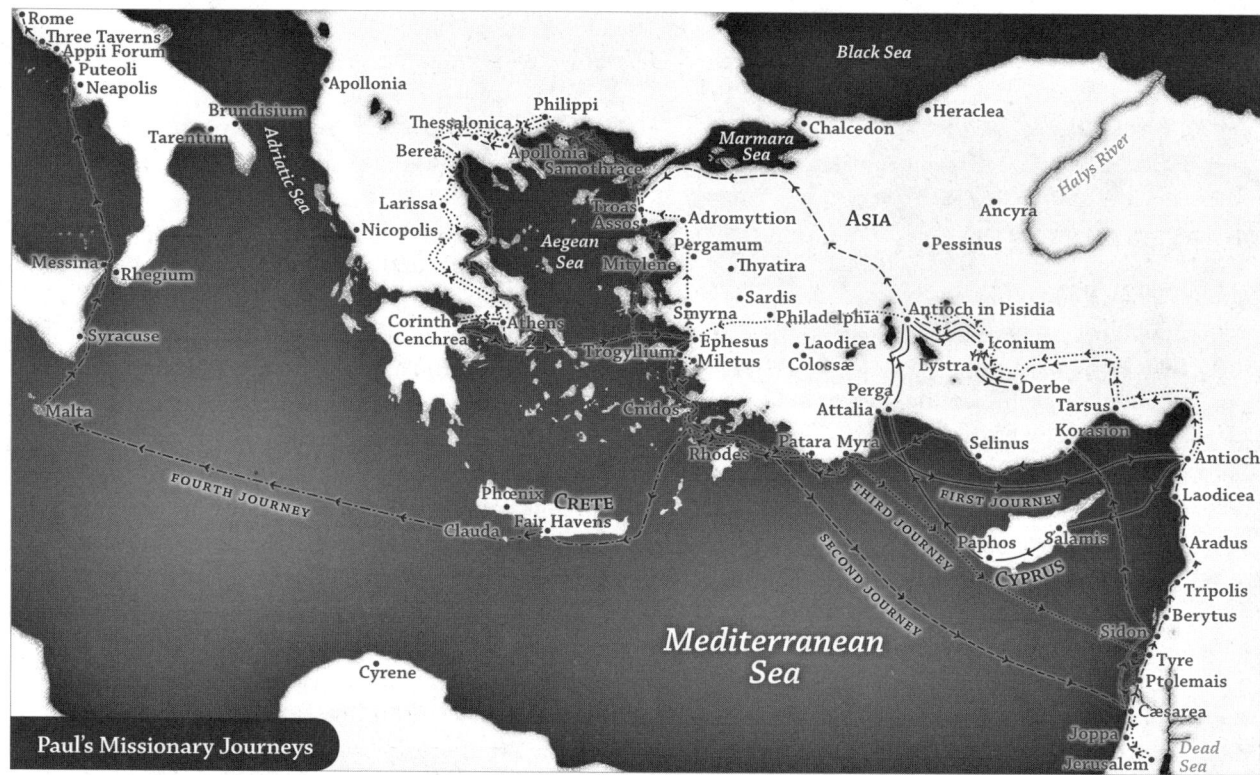

Paul's Missionary Journeys

argument against those who claim to be apostles (see 11:13). Paul addresses not only *the church of God in Corinth*, but also *the saints throughout Achaia*, indicating his expectation that people from the house churches throughout this Roman province will read his letter. A favorite term for Christians is *saints* [literally "*holy ones*"; see Rom 1:7; 1 Cor 1:2], a term that reflects God's call to ancient Israel to be *holy as God is holy* (Lev 19:2). As in all of his letters, Paul adapts the familiar greeting (*chairein*) from Hellenistic letters to words from Jewish worship, *grace to you and peace*.

INTRODUCTION OF THEMES · 1:3–11

Paul introduces the letter, not with the customary thanksgiving, but with *praise be to God* (see Eph 1:3; 1 Pet 1:3), followed by the description of God as *Father of compassion and God of all comfort, who comforts us in all of our afflictions*. The language echoes Israel's songs of praise (see Ps 116:1–11; 118:5; 119:50), introducing two related themes of the letter – affliction (*trouble*) and *comfort* – in a way that reorients the Corinthians' critique of Paul as a weak and suffering leader. Without raising the issue of their criticism of him, he affirms that *the sufferings of Christ overflow to us*, anticipating the later claim that his ministry is distinguished by his carrying of the death of Jesus (4:10). Later in the letter, Paul describes a specific instance when *God comforted* [him] *by the coming of Titus* (7:5–6) in the midst of his sufferings. That Paul is describing his own sufferings with the words *we* and *us* is evident in the movement from *us* in 1:3 to *you* (plural) in 1:6–7, when he declares that his sufferings are *for your comfort and salvation*. Paul's sufferings are not a sign of weakness, as his opponents suggest, but the occasion for God's comfort, which consists not only of encouraging words, but of God's empowering presence (see Isa 40:1). Thus Paul sets forth the argument of the book: that human weakness is the occasion for the power of God (see 4:7–15; 12:10).

1:8–11 Using the familiar disclosure formula, *We do not want you to be uninformed* (see Rom 1:13; Phil 1:12), Paul continues the theme introduced in 1:3–7, recalling an event that is otherwise unknown to his readers. In recalling the *hardships* that he *suffered in the province of Asia*, he describes his own experience in the language of the psalmist, who also had been desperate in the face of death (Ps 88:15). This instance is only one example of Paul's continuing theme of the *hardships* involved in his ministry (see 2 Cor 4:8–9; 6:4–6; 11:23–30) and God's power, the source of life in the midst of death (see 4:10–11).

PAUL'S RECIPROCAL BOASTING · 1:12–14

Paul's opponents, who *take pride* [literally "boast"] *in what is seen rather than in what is in the heart* (5:12) and *boast* of their achievements *in the way the world does* (11:18), have forced him to offer his own *boast* in 1:12–14, the thesis statement of the letter. Against those who have suggested that he makes plans "in a worldly manner" (see 1:17), Paul first speaks in the past tense (1:12), declaring that he has always acted with *holiness and sincerity*, and not according to *worldly wisdom* (see 2:17). In 1:13–14, he turns to the present tense, indicating that he writes in the hope that the Corinthians will understand his special relationship with them: *that you can boast of us just as we will boast of you on the day of the Lord Jesus*. At several points in the letter, Paul indicates that the Corinthians are his *boast*; that is, that he is proud of them (7:4; 8:24) or hopes that their conduct will make him proud of them (see 9:1–5). His defense throughout the letter is the basis for his appeal to reciprocate his pride in them.

PAUL'S DEFENSE & APPEAL · 1:15–7:16

1:15–22 Paul's insistence on his integrity (1:12) is the result of his recent change of plans. At the close of 1 Corinthians, Paul had promised to come to Corinth for an extended stay (1 Cor 16:5), but intervening events caused him to change his plans (see 2:1–4). Before Paul explains this change in itinerary (1:23–24), he places the immediate issue in the larger theological context. Paul would not say *"yes, yes"* and *"no, no"* like the flatterer because such behavior would be inconsistent with the nature of God, whose word is always reliable. The ultimate demonstration that *God is faithful* to his *promises* is Jesus Christ, God's *yes*. The Greek-speaking church has now made the Hebrew word *amen* a part of its own vocabulary, responding in the worship assembly to God's faithfulness with its own affirmation (1:21) of the faithfulness of God. The further indication of God's faithfulness is that God makes both Paul and the community *stand firm* in Christ. He has also indicated his faithfulness in the past: the memory that God anointed *us*, *set his seal of ownership on us*, and gave his Spirit as a *guarantee* recalls the moment of baptism. Paul's quasi-legal language (*seal*, *guarantee*) testifies that the community's existence rests on God's faithfulness.

> **Paul as Flatterer**
> Paul's inability to go to Corinth as he had promised suggested to the Corinthians that he was unreliable, saying, "Yes, yes" and "no, no." Such charges fit the profile of a stock character in the Greco-Roman world: the flatterer who tells others what they want to hear.

1:23–2:13 Since Paul has declared that he is no opportunist, changing his plans to fit his own ambitions, he now explains why he did not make the promised visit. He wrote a letter (2:3, 9; 7:8) rather than make the promised visit in order to *spare* the Corinthians (1:23). In keeping with Paul's goal for the Corinthians (1:14), his *work* aims at their *joy*. Since the planned visit would have been a source of grief rather than mutual *joy*, Paul chose to write a letter *out of much distress and anguish of heart* (2:4) rather than make another *painful visit* (2:1). His *love* for the Corinthians superseded the planned visit.

In 2:5–11, Paul moves beyond the pain of his past relationship with the readers to offer instruction for future conduct. Someone in particular had caused grief to Paul (2:5; see 7:11) on his previous visit. In response to Paul's letter (2:3–4), the *majority* of Corinthians had punished the offender. Now Paul indicates that the punishment is sufficient, and he encourages the readers to *forgive and comfort* the offender (2:7) and to affirm their *love* (2:8), noting that he also forgives him. Therefore, Paul's ultimate aim is the restoration of the offender (see 2:7) in order that he can fulfill his ambition of boasting of the entire community at the day of Christ (1:14).

Paul's commitment to the Corinthian church is evident in the anguish that he describes in 2:12–13. Despite his evangelistic success in Troas, he had no *peace of mind* because did not find Titus, who had delivered the letter to the Corinthians. His passion for the Corinthians led him to press on to Macedonia because he was desperate to know the outcome of the tearful letter.

2:14–17 Paul resumes the story of his search for news from Titus in 7:5–16. In the intervening section (2:14–7:4), he speaks in the present tense, defending his ministry, while 1:15–2:13 and 7:5–16 provide a continuous story in the past tense of his travel plans. The sudden shift from his expression of anguish (2:13) to *thanks be to God* (2:14) is so startling that many interpreters have suggested that 2:14–7:4 includes a separate letter that interrupts Paul's account of his relation to the Corinthians. However, the transition in 2:14 is not as sharp as many have supposed, inasmuch as *thanks be to God who leads us in a triumphal procession in Christ* (2:14) actually continues the theme of Paul's anguished ministry. Paul's imagery, taken from the Roman victory processionals, portrays him, not as a conquering general, but as a captive on his way to death. He is thankful to be involved in a victory parade (see Rom 8:37; 1 Cor 15:57), even as a captive on his way to death. In his preaching ministry, he *spreads everywhere the fragrance of the knowledge of* Jesus, and his work has life and death consequences for *those who are being saved and those who are perishing* (see 1 Cor 1:18). Elsewhere Paul describes himself as the priest offering a sacrifice (Rom 15:16) and as the sacrifice to God (Phil 2:17).

> **"The aroma of Christ ..."**
> The imagery of *fragrance and aroma may draw from the aroma of incense at Roman victory processionals, but these images also draw from Old Testament descriptions of sacrifices as a* pleasing odor *(Exod 29:18, 25, 41).*

The extraordinary claim of 2:14–16a leads to the rhetorical question, *who is equal to such a task*? In response to the opponents' challenge to Paul's competence, he identifies with Moses, who responded to God's call with the words, *I am not equal to the task*, according to the Septuagint's rendition of Exodus 4:10. Paul knows that his competence comes from God (3:5). Such a ministry is not for opportunists, as Paul indicates when he distinguishes himself from opponents, who *peddle the word of God for profit* (2:17). In refusing financial support from the Corinthians (see 11:7–11), Paul has raised suspicions about his conduct among the Corinthians, who compare him negatively with the opponents who demand financial support. Paul's response, like that of Plato centuries earlier, is that his opponents are simply merchants seeking financial gain rather than truth.

> **The Septuagint (LXX)**
> Also known by the abbreviation "LXX," this third century BCE Greek translation of the Old Testament was so named because 70 scholars were said to have been involved in its production. Paul and other early Christians often quoted from this version rather than from a Hebrew original.

3:1–6 Paul continues to defend himself against *some* (see 2:17; 3:2), introducing the theme of self-commendation, which he will develop throughout the letter (see 4:2; 6:4; 5:12; 10:12) in response to the opponents, who brought *letters of recommendation*. Just as this community is Paul's *boast* (1:14), they are also his *letter*, his continuing witness to the world (*known and read by everybody*). *Written by the Spirit of God on human hearts*, this letter is different from those brought by the opponents and the Ten Commandments *written on tablets of stone*. Thus his *ministry* is the realization of the promise of the New Covenant promised by Ezekiel (11:19; 36:26) and Jeremiah (31:31), a covenant *written with the Spirit of God ... on human hearts*.

3:7–18 Paul's claim to be the *minister of a new covenant* (3:6) implies a comparison to Moses, the minister of the first covenant. In 3:7–18, he continues the comparison, recalling the story of Moses' descent from Sinai with a shining face (Exod 34:29–35) and acknowledging that the Sinai covenant *came with glory* (3:7). However, he describes this covenant as *the ministry that brought death*

> **"A glory now set aside ..."**
> Although the Old Testament never mentions the *fading of Moses' shining face, Paul infers that its glory was transitory, contrasting Moses' glory with the* glory that lasts *in Paul's own ministry.*

(3:7) and *the ministry that condemns* (3:9), contrasting it with his own *ministry of the Spirit* (3:8) and of *righteousness* (3:9). Paul's purpose is not to deny the glory of the first covenant, but to claim *how much more glorious is the ministry* in which he is involved. Thus while opponents criticized the ineffectiveness of Paul's ministry, Paul insists that it is more glorious than that of Moses.

In 3:12–18, Paul reflects on his own ministry, answering his critics' charges against his courage (see 10:1) by comparing his own boldness with that of Moses, who placed the *veil* over his face to conceal the fading of the glory (Exod 34:33). Paul's primary concern, however, is to draw the parallel between the Israelites' hardness of heart (3:14) and the hardness of heart that Paul encounters (3:15). Whereas the *veil* still remains over many of Paul's listeners, Paul insists that it is removed when one *turns to the Lord* (3:16), just as Moses removed it whenever he turned to the Lord in the tent. In 3:18, Paul speaks not only of himself but of all Christians (*we all*) who have an *unveiled face*. All who have turned to the Lord are being transformed *into his likeness*. Thus, despite his apparent ineffectiveness, his ministry gains credibility in light of the transformation into the divine image that is already taking place in his churches.

4:1–6 Paul concludes this section on the glory of his ministry, summarizing what he said in the section that began in 2:14. His insistence that he does not *lose heart* (4:1, 16) indicates that the central issue is his ineffectiveness. According to 4:2–3, as in 2:17, he will not alter his message to fit the audience. In 4:3–4, as in 3:14–15, he suggests that most people do not accept his message, but he insists that their lack of response is the result, not of his own failure, but the work of *the god of this age*. Despite this lack of response, he is sure of his message: that *Jesus Christ is Lord* (4:5) because this message is the dazzling light that transformed his life (4:6) at his conversion.

4:7–15 In the striking metaphor, *We have this treasure in clay jars*, Paul makes the transition from the glory of his ministry (2:14–4:6) to his own weakness. The *treasure* is the gospel that transformed his life (4:6). The image suggests the paradoxical nature of his ministry, for breakable clay jars were a common metaphor for human fragility (Isa 29:16; 30:14; Lam 4:2). The trifling value of the jar cannot compare with the priceless treasure. Contrary to the claims of his opponents, Paul insists that his weakness is not a sign of failure, but an occasion *for the all-surpassing power* of God. Paul elaborates on the theme of divine power in human weakness in verses 8–12, describing the constant experience of his ministry. The repetition of *but not* (4:8–9) indicates that God never abandoned Paul to his own resources. The list of sufferings in 4:8–9 is the first of four instances in 2 Corinthians where Paul lists the hardships that characterize his ministry (see 6:4–10; 11:23–33; 12:10).

According to 4:10–12, Paul's sufferings share in the death and resurrection of Christ, the ultimate expression of power in weakness. He elaborates on the earlier claim that the *sufferings of Christ flow over into our lives* (1:5) with the statement that he *always carries around the death of Jesus*. However, in sharing the death of Jesus, he also shares the resurrection power of his *life* (4:10–11).

4:16–5:10 Paul now offers a second reason why he does not *lose heart*, turning from his present experience (4:7–15) to the future hope. In the statement that *we are wasting away*, he is not talking about mortality in general, but the conditions of his own ministry as he carries the death of Jesus (4:10). Just as his weakness opens doors for God's power, he is inwardly *being renewed day by day*. To his critics who see only the present moment, Paul indicates that his present troubles are only *momentary* and that he anticipates *an eternal glory*.

Paul's contrast between the momentary affliction and the eternal glory extends to 5:1–10, where he elaborates on the hope that undergirds his confidence. Instead of seeing his body as a fragile *clay jar* (see 4:7), he now describes his earthly existence as that of an *earthly tent* (5:1) that will be destroyed and replaced by the *building from God, an eternal house in heaven, not built by human hands*. In the meantime, Paul says, *we groan* (5:2, 4), *longing for* the heavenly dwelling. To live in the fragile body is to be *away from the Lord*. Unlike his opponents, who measure everything according to visible results, Paul says, *we walk by faith and not by sight* because God has given the Spirit, *guaranteeing what is to come* (5:5; see 1:22).

5:11–6:2 A transition in Paul's argument for the legitimacy of his ministry begins in 5:11, where his defense moves toward a series of appeals to the readers (5:20–6:2, 11–13; 7:2–4). Because Paul's desire to be the Corinthians' *boast* (1:14) remains unfulfilled, he continues to explain why he *persuades men* (5:11), hoping that the readers will *take pride* in him. Whereas he claims in 4:2 that he *commends himself*, here he insists that he does not commend himself, but offers a defense so that the Corinthians *may answer those who take pride in what is seen*. That is, the boasts of the opponents have forced Paul to explain his ministry, and he defends himself in order that the Corinthians can defend him. In the

---

Power in Weakness

Knowledge of God's power in weakness provides the basis for Paul's confidence in his ministry (4:13–15). In quoting the words, I believed; therefore I have spoken (Psalm 116:10), he identifies with the psalmist, who spoke in the context of affliction. The knowledge of the resurrection (4:14) gives Paul the courage to continue his work.

statement, *if we are out of our mind, it is for the sake of God; if we are in our right mind, it is for you*, which is reminiscent of his distinction between tongues and prophecy (1 Cor 14:4–5), Paul's primary aim is to declare that his ministry is *for you*. As in the thesis statement of the book (1:14), the outcome of his converts defines his ministry (see 1:23; 2:4; 4:15). In 5:14–16, Paul offers the theological explanation that determines why his ministry is *for you*. It is that *Christ's love compels us*; that is, it "has taken us captive" (see 2:14). The demonstration of *Christ's love* is the fact that *one died for all*. The phrase is a slight variant of the content of his original preaching (see 1 Cor 15:3). In the claim that *therefore all died*, Paul indicates that the cross is not only a singular event of the past but that believers share in the selfless love of the cross (see 4:10; Rom 6:6; Gal 2:20). Consequently, *those who live no longer live for themselves* (5:15; see Rom 14:7–9). Thus, in response to the opponents, Paul argues that his selfless ministry is determined by the ultimate manifestation of selflessness, the story of the cross.

Unlike those who boast *according to human standards* (11:18), Paul's approach to ministry is not based on a *worldly point of view* (5:16) but on the standard of a *new creation* (5:17). The Old Testament hope for a *new heaven and new earth* (Isa 65:17; 66:22) has become a reality for those who share the cross of Christ. Whereas the NIV translates Paul's words, *if anyone is in Christ, he is a new creation*, a more accurate reading is, "If anyone is in Christ, there is a new creation." Paul explains this new creation in a summary of the Christian message (5:18–19), which is parallel to the earlier summary in 5:14. Recalling that the prophets had anticipated a time of peace that would follow the exile (see Isa 41:3; 52:7; 54:10; 60:17), Paul announces that *God was reconciling the world to himself in Christ* (2 Cor 5:19). In the *new creation* and reconciliation in Christ, God has fulfilled Israel's hope for a new world of peace through the cross. In the parallel statements of 5:18–19, Paul insists that the God who acted in Christ also committed to him the *message of reconciliation*.

In 5:21, Paul refers to God's unfinished work, recalling the prophet's words, *the righteous one ... will make many righteous* (Isa 53:11). Only when the readers respond to God's invitation will they *become the righteousness of God* (5:21). The invitation in 6:1–2 echoes the voice of the prophet (Isa 49:8), who summoned Israel to respond to God's redeeming work. Paul's defense of his ministry is the basis for the appeal not *to receive God's grace in vain* (6:1).

6:3–13 Paul now offers a new defense of his ministry (6:3–10) followed by an appeal for a response (6:11–13), in the hopes that the Corinthians will reciprocate his affection for them. In 6:3, as in 5:12, Paul explains why he perseveres in the defense of his ministry. Here he defends himself *so that our ministry will not be discredited* in response to suspicions surrounding his ministry (see 7:2; 12:17), echoing ancient philosophical discussions about the necessity of the philosopher's concern not to do anything that would invalidate his message. In 8:20 Paul gives a specific instance of his care to avoid any appearance of impropriety in the handling of the collection.

Verses 4–10 demonstrate Paul's integrity. He "commends himself" as a minister (see 4:2; 5:12) in response to those who *commend themselves* (10:12). The pervasiveness of these lists of hardships reflects Paul's debates with opponents who offered their own list of hardships. Paul lists nine hardships in three groups of three. The first triad (*troubles, hardships, and distresses*) describes afflictions of a general nature (6:4), recalling a consistent theme of the letter (see 1:4, 8; 2:4; 4:17; 7:4; 12:10). The second triad lists afflictions associated with his ministry (*beatings, imprisonments, and riots*), while the third triad lists problems associated with Paul's work and his involvement with the churches (*hard work, sleepless nights, and hunger*).

In the list of virtues in 6:6–7, Paul indicates that he not only endured hardship but also served from the purest of motives. The qualities that he lists are common features in Paul's descriptions of Christian behavior (see Gal 5:22–23; Col 3:12; Rom 12:9). In verses 8–10, he describes the paradoxes of his ministry: his entire life is the expression of strength out of weakness (see 4:7–12) and the inversion of the world's values. These hardships and virtues are the basis for the appeal in 6:11–13, in which he asks for the Corinthians to reciprocate his affection, in keeping with the hope

> **Ambassadors of Christ**
>
> In his claim that *we are ambassadors* (5:20), *Paul recalls the ancient role of ambassadors, who spoke only the words their ruler authorized. Thus Paul's appeal in 5:20–6:2 to be reconciled to God comes not only from his own voice but also from the voice of God. Paul assumes that the Corinthians' alienation from him is nothing less than alienation from God.*

expressed at the beginning of the letter (1:14) that he will be their *boast* at the day of Christ.

6:14–7:4   Because 6:13 (*open your hearts also*) appears to fit naturally with 7:2 (*make room for us in your hearts*), many scholars assume that 6:14–7:1 is an interruption in the flow of Paul's defense of his ministry. The fact that the concern of the letter is not *unbelievers*, as in 1 Corinthians, supports this view. However, if one notes that the issue throughout the letter is Paul's concern over the Corinthians' alliances, this passage fits the context. Paul calls for the readers to disassociate themselves from the opposition, whom he describes as *unbelievers*. The rhetorical questions of 6:14–16a indicate the clear demarcation that separates the Christian community from sources of impurity. In the Scriptures cited in 6:16b–18, he reaffirms the community's identity, indicating that the church is the temple where God's Spirit dwells. Using promises once addressed to Israel (see Lev 26:11–12; Isa 52:11; Ezek 37:27), he draws the consequences of God's place in their midst: *Come out from among them and be separate … and touch nothing unclean*. Just as the prophet challenged ancient Israelites to leave the corrupt city of Babylon, Paul challenges readers to abandon their alliances with his opponents. God's promise to be a Father (6:18) is the basis for the renewed appeal in 7:1. The result of the community's return to God is reconciliation with Paul, as he indicates in the words *make room for us in your hearts* (7:2). In 7:2–4, Paul speaks of his unrequited love for the Corinthians, reiterating the goal he expresses in 1:14. He has *great pride* and *confidence* in the Corinthians (7:4).

7:5–16   Paul now completes the narrative of his anxious desire to learn about the Corinthians from Titus, which he interrupted in 2:13, turning from his constant use of the first person plural ("we") to the first person singular ("I"). He has delayed the outcome of the story until now because the good news that he reports in 7:5–16 illustrates his expression of confidence and pride in 7:4. His anguish (2:13) turned to joy when he met Titus in Macedonia (7:5). Paul's experience illustrates the claim that he made at the beginning of the letter (1:3–11): *God who comforts the downcast* (see 1:3–4), comforted both Titus and Paul in the midst of their anguish.

In 7:8–13, Paul offers the details of how his anguish turned to consolation at the coming of Titus. He recalls that the *sorrow* that his letter caused (see 2:4) led to *repentance* (7:9). The Corinthians had punished the offender described in 2:5–11, responding to Paul's letter with *longing* and *concern*, and indicating how devoted to Paul they were (7:12). As a result of these events, Paul is *encouraged* [literally "comforted"], and Titus is *happy* over the outcome of Paul's painful letter. Paul's *boasting* about the Corinthians (see 1:14) had been justified, giving Paul complete *confidence* in this community (7:16). He has seen a glimpse of the reciprocal pride that he desires in his relationship with the Corinthians.

PAUL'S APPEAL FOR THE COLLECTION · 8–9

At the end of 1 Corinthians (16:1–2), Paul had instructed the Corinthians to participate in the *collection for God's people*. Now a year has passed (2 Cor 8:10) since he first mentioned the collection, which is evidently the work of his life (see Rom 15:26–30). The questions about Paul's integrity (7:2; 12:17) have undoubtedly raised obstacles to his plans. The good news from Titus (7:5–16) now provides the setting for Paul's renewed appeal in chapters 8 and 9.

8:1–6   Paul lays the basis for his appeal by reporting about the *grace that God has given the Macedonians*, which has resulted in their *generosity*. Consistent with the letter's emphasis on God's power in the context of weakness, he insists that the Macedonians gave out of their *extreme poverty*, giving *beyond their ability*. Paul's terminology indicates the theological significance of the collection. It is God's *grace* (8:1, 6), fellowship (NIV *sharing*), and ministry (NIV *serving*). Just as the Macedonians *gave themselves to the Lord*, he desires that Titus, who has recently returned with the good report (7:5), *bring to completion this act of grace* (8:6).

8:7–15   As a skilled orator, Paul introduces the topic for discussion by offering the example of others and complimenting the listeners (8:7). As much as they may excel *in faith, in speech, and in knowledge* (verse 7), only by participating in the collection will they demonstrate the *sincerity of their love*. Paul offers the most powerful argument for the collection in 8:9. The ultimate act of *grace* was the gift of Jesus Christ for his people. Here, as

> **God's Comfort**
>
> *Just as God comforted despairing people in ancient Babylon (Isa 40:1; 49:13), God now comforts Paul with the knowledge of the Corinthians' affection for him (7:7).*

elsewhere, Paul appeals to the story of Jesus' sacrifice to shape the values of his listeners (Phil 2:6–11; see Rom 15:1–3). The fact that Jesus Christ *was rich* and *became poor for your sakes* gives Christians a new outlook on the giving of their funds. In verses 10 through 12, Paul offers a second argument, asking the Corinthians to *finish the work* that they began a year earlier, assuring them that the gift *is acceptable according to what one has*, *not according to what one does not have*. In verses 13 through 15, Paul offers a third argument, calling for *equality* among the churches, recalling Israel's experience of manna in the wilderness when he quotes Exodus 16:18, *he who gathered much did not have too much, and he who gathered little did not have too little*. For Paul, partnership is not only a spiritual matter, for he expects his affluent congregations to be financial partners with those who were financially deprived.

8:16–24 Before proceeding to a new argument in chapter 9, Paul pauses to reassure the Corinthians of his integrity. Paul does not collect the funds at all, but enlists three men who have impeccable credentials for the task. Titus (8:16–17) enjoys the full trust of the Corinthians. Paul sends with him the anonymous brother who is praised in all the churches (8:18) and another unnamed brother (8:22) who has often *proved*… that he is *zealous*. His purpose in sending them is *to avoid any criticism in his administration of the gift*. He is concerned not only to be honest in his dealings, but to avoid any appearance of impropriety. Their participation will demonstrate their *love* and reaffirm Paul's *pride* (or boasting) in them, which he mentioned in the thesis statement of the letter (1:14).

9:1–15 Paul's argument for the collection in chapter 9 begins as if it is a totally new appeal for the collection (9:1). Having boasted of the Macedonians in 8:1–6, he now tells the Corinthians that he is *boasting* about them to the Macedonians (9:2). He sends the *brothers* (see 8:18, 22) in order that his *boasting not prove hollow* (9:3). Paul's terminology once more indicates the distinctively theological nature of the collection (see 8:4). It is a *service* (*diakonia*) and a *blessing* (9:5) rather than something *grudgingly given*. Because Paul knows that all blessings come from God in abundance (see Rom 15:29; Gal 3:14; Heb 6:7), he notes that participation in the collection is involvement with what God is doing.

Paul now makes his case in 9:6–15, beginning with the thesis statement in 9:6: *Whoever sows sparingly will also reap sparingly* (see Ps 126:5–6; Gal 6:7–8), an image from farming that Paul now applies to giving. The remainder of the argument indicates the blessings that accompany giving. In the first place, he describes the blessings to the giver. As in 8:15, Paul's instructions echo ancient words to Israel. That *God loves a cheerful giver* (verse 7) was the ancient lesson to Israel (Deut 15:10). In keeping with the constant emphasis on God's power through human weakness (1:8; 4:7; 6:7; 8:3; 13:4), Paul insists that God can take meager funds and multiply them, again applying to the church the words once spoken to Israel (Ps 112:9). Paul does not promise wealth to those who give, but he assures them that the readers will have *all that* [they] *need* to abound *in every good work* (verse 9) and that they will be able to be *generous on every occasion* (verse 11). In the second place, Paul applies the ancient language of sacrifice, again insisting that *this service* [literally "ministry of service"] results *in many expressions of thanksgiving to God* (verse 12). In the third place, he indicates that giving will create solidarity between the givers and the recipients (verses 13–14), who will reciprocate with *prayers for your hearts* because of our *sharing with them* [Greek *koinonia*] in material things, a sign of the *surpassing grace God has given you*.

FINAL DEFENSE & APPEAL · 10:1–13:13

10:1–11 Paul follows his customary practice of describing his future plans (see Rom 15:22–29; 1 Cor 4:14–21; Phil 2:19–30; Phlm 22), turning from his expression of thanksgiving (9:15) to the combative and threatening tones (10:1–2; 13:1) of chapters 10–13. Since this passionate defense of Paul's ministry continues the same theme as chapters 1 through 7, one need not conclude, as many scholars do, that chapters 10 to 13 belong to a separate letter. The introductory words *I Paul*, are rare in the letters (see Gal 5:2), and anticipate the intensity and personal investment of Paul's argument. Paul's appeal by the *meekness and gentleness of Christ* (10:1) is a response to the opponents' charge that Paul is *timid* in their presence but *bold* when he is away. Paul's hope that he will *not have to be bold* refers to his forthcoming visit (see 13:2), when he will punish those who reject his leadership. In response to the charge that he lives by *the standards of this world*, he describes his ministry in military terms, indicating that he does not fight with the *weapons* of the world, but that he has the *power to demolish strongholds*. In this extended military metaphor, Paul follows the philosophers who regularly spoke of the battle for the mind in which they were engaged. Like the philosophers, Paul battles bad ideas. Like the prophets before him (Jer 24:6), he has the power for *building up* and not for *pulling down* (10:8). The opponents, who say, *His letters are weighty and strong, but his bodily presence is weak* (10:10), hold to the values of Hellenistic society. Paul's response in 10:11 indicates that his forthcoming visit will be the occasion for him to demonstrate the courage that the opponents find lacking when, in contrast to the previous visit (1:23), he will *not spare* them (13:2).

> **Early Schools of Philosophy**
>
> *In the first century, philosophers focused chiefly on training individuals for ethical, wise lives. The main schools were the Stoics, the Epicureans, the Neo-Pythagoreans, the Cynics, and the Middle Platonists. See also Acts 17:17–21. Paul shared many viewpoints with these philosophers while at the same time reconceiving their ideas about the pursuit of wisdom. For further information, see the chapter on Greco-Roman New Testament Backgrounds in this volume.*

10:12–18 Paul now indicates why the pervasive theme throughout the letter has been the subject of self-commendation (see 3:1–2; 4:2; 5:12; 6:4). Continuing the focus on the triangular relationship among the Corinthians, Paul refers in 10:12 to *some who commend themselves, measure themselves,* and *compare themselves*, indicating that the opponents engage in self-praise, a common practice among philosophers of antiquity. In response to their boasts, Paul indicates in 10:13–16, that *we do not boast beyond proper limits*. Unlike the opponents, who boast of extraordinary achievements, he desires only to *boast* of the work that he has done among the Corinthians. He confirms his outlook with the quotation of Jeremiah 9:22: *Let him who boasts boast in the Lord* (10:17; see 1 Cor 1:31).

11:1–21 After distinguishing himself from the boasting opponents in 10:12–18, Paul begins the "fool's speech" in 11:1–12:10, in which he talks *as a fool* (11:17; see 11:16, 21; 12:11), boasting as the opponents do. In the prologue to the speech in 11:1–21, he distinguishes himself from the opponents and asks the readers to *put up with* his *foolishness* (11:1), just as they "put up with" opponents who abuse them (11:20). The whole section is filled with references to the dangers threatening the church. As the founder of the church, Paul is the anxious father of the bride who *promised* [literally "betrothed"] the church to Christ (see Eph 5:26) and hopes to *present* it as a *pure virgin* to him at his return. Their conversion, therefore, only began a story that ends at the return of Christ (see 1:14). In the meantime, Paul shares God's *jealousy*, fearing that their minds may be led astray from pure devotion to Christ (see 10:3–6). In verse 4, Paul mentions hypothetical problems that the church may face, suggesting that they would *put up with* preaching a Jesus other than the one preached by Paul, and they would receive a *different spirit* or a *different gospel*. Paul's comments are probably not directed to specific false teachings in Corinth but against the Corinthians' vulnerability to a teaching other than what Paul delivered. Paul offers an example of these dangers in 11:5–6, recalling the criticism mentioned in 10:10–11. Their relationship to the so called *super apostles* endangers the outcome of the story. Despite the charges that he is not a *trained speaker* (see 10:10–11), Paul insists that he does not lack in *knowledge*.

Paul's insistence on working with his hands posed a problem for the Corinthians from the beginning, for wealthy people in antiquity wished to add to their esteem by becoming patrons of a philosopher. By working with his hands, Paul *lower*[ed] [literally "humiliated"] *himself*, placing himself in the lowest social class and alienating the wealthy members. His demeanor is the opposite of that of the opponents, who make demands on the Corinthians (11:20). Paul's conduct apparently led the Corinthians to ask if Paul actually cared for them. Although he does not say why he received funds from the Macedonians while refusing the support of the Corinthians (11:9), he insists his refusal was actually an act of *love* (11:11), reflecting a desire not to be a *burden* to them. As he indicates in 1 Corinthians (4:11–12), his refusal to accept payment was a way of being shaped by the cross. He chooses to exhaust himself for others (see 12:14–15) rather than allow them to exhaust themselves for him.

In 11:13–21, Paul leads to the body of the fool's speech with a clear description of the dangers to his work. Their distinguishing feature is the boasting through which they claim to be apostles (11:13).

Because they boast by human standards, they have forced Paul into matching their boasts (11:18, 21, 22). Paul speaks sarcastically, referring to the criticism of his weakness (10:11) when he contrasts his own humility with the overbearing false apostles *who take advantage of* [them] *and slap* [them] *in the face* (11:20), saying *we were too weak for that* (11:21).

11:21B–33 Paul now begins the actual boasting that the opponents and the church have forced upon him. Inasmuch as the entire letter is a defense of Paul's ministry, this *speaking as a fool* is the climax in which he incorporates earlier claims (see 4:7–15; 6:4–10). Scholars debate whether Paul is actually matching his opponents' claims or parodying their catalog of adversities, such lists being common among philosophers. This section reveals numerous instances that are unknown from Acts. In the first triad in 11:22, Paul indicates the extent of his Jewish heritage. In the claim to be a *Hebrew*, he indicates that he, unlike many others, speaks the ancestral language. The question, *Are they servants of Christ*? introduces the extensive list of Paul's ministerial credentials. In verses 23–26, his speech is characterized by comparatives and specific numbers, indicating how he is better. Whatever the opponents have done, he has done more. Whereas he has mentioned his imprisonments and floggings earlier (6:4–10), here he adds *more frequently* and *more severely*. In 11:24–25, he mentions events otherwise unknown to the Corinthians, supplying the number of occasions in each instance. Verse 26 indicates the difficulty of travel, as Paul mentions *danger* eight times. Verse 27 describes the deprivations associated with his work (see 6:4). Because constant travel has deprived him of a regular income, he has often *gone without food* and has been *cold and naked*. The constant *pressure of* [his] *concern for all the churches* is evident in his past relationship with the listeners (see 2:12–13; 7:5). In 11:29–30, Paul's summation interprets the list. Whereas his opponents probably employed similar lists to indicate their triumph over adversity, Paul's adversities are a sign of his *weaknesses*. The story in 11:31–33 (see Acts 9:24–25) offers a specific example of his weakness, for to escape the city in a basket would have made him the subject of ridicule.

12:1–13 In a new turn in the fool's speech in 12:1, Paul now *boasts of visions and revelations from the Lord*, apparently responding to the opponents' boasts. Although Paul speaks of a *man in Christ*, he is describing his own experience, as verses 6 through 10 indicate. Using the language common to apocalyptic literature (see 2 *Enoch* 8:1), Paul speaks of being *caught up* to *the third heaven* and *paradise*. Although the event happened *fourteen years ago*, long before the founding of the Corinthian church, Paul has never told the Corinthians because he chooses only to *boast* in his *weaknesses*. Although Paul obviously values such experiences, they do not constitute his credentials for ministry.

In verses 7 to 10, Paul juxtaposes the memory of this ecstatic moment with an account of the *torment* caused by the *thorn in* [the] *flesh*, which was apparently a chronic source of pain. To speculate on the nature of the *thorn in the flesh* is futile, for Paul only describes its continuing effect on him as he prayed *three times* (see Matt 26:44) that God *take it away*. God's answer, *My grace is sufficient for you, my power is perfected in weakness* (12:9), epitomizes Paul's message throughout 2 Corinthians. In contrast to opponents who measure themselves according to the Greek standards of physical stature and power, Paul boasts only in matters that show his weakness. He concludes the fool's speech with a final list of hardships in 12:10 and the slogan that summarizes the argument of the letter: *when I am weak, then I am strong* (12:10; see 4:7–10; 13:4).

Paul offers the epilogue to the fool's speech in 12:11–13, indicating that his boasts demonstrate that he is not inferior to the *super apostles*, who apparently boast of their *signs, wonders, and miracles*. He refers once more to Corinthian charges that his refusal of patronage was a sign of his low esteem for them (see 11:11), answering with sarcasm (*Forgive me this wrong!*) similar to his words at the beginning of the fool's speech (11:21).

12:14–13:13 Having obliquely mentioned his travel plans in 10:2 before making his final defense of his ministry, Paul returns to the topic in 12:14 and 13:1. He now reiterates his defense and expresses his fears for the outcome of his work. Against the charge that he has *exploited* them (12:16–18), he declares that he is like a parent who is ready to *spend…everything* for the sake of his children (12:14–15, 19). In the threefold *I am afraid…I fear…I am afraid* (12:20–21), he expresses his fear that he will find that the Corinthians hold to the same vices as before their conversion (*quarreling*, *jealousy*, *outbursts of anger*, *factions*, *slander*, *arrogance and disorder*; see 1 Cor 3:1–3; 6:9–11) and his concern that on the next visit *God will humble* him, causing him to *grieve* as he did on the second visit (2:1–4). Since everything Paul does is for their strengthening [Greek *oikodome*, literally "building up"], the church's failure to progress will mean failure for Paul's ultimate goal, which he stated at the beginning of the letter (1:14).

In 13:1–10, Paul reiterates the themes of 10:1–11, where he responded to the charge that he was *timid* (10:1) with the desire that he will not need to be *bold* (10:2) toward his opponents and the claim to authority (10:8), which he hopes not to use. In 13:1–10, his warning becomes explicit. The statement that *every matter must be established by two or three witnesses*, drawn from the Old Testament procedure for trials (see Deut 19:15), refers to Paul's *third visit* when he *will not spare those who sinned* (verse 2) as he did on the second visit (see 1:23). In keeping with the focus of the entire letter on the legitimacy of Paul's ministry, the center of the discussion in 13:1–10 is the *proof* of the legitimacy of Paul's ministry that the Corinthians require (13:3). Paul first answers in 13:4, reiterating the theme of the book: that his *power* is present in *weakness*, just as Jesus was *crucified in weakness*, *but lives by the power of God*. Finally, he indicates that the Corinthians who demand proof are themselves facing a test (13:5–10). What matters is not whether Paul has passed the test, but whether they *will do what is right* (13:7). Hence he prays for their perfection [literally "to be restored, to put in proper condition"] in order that he will not need to exercise the *authority the Lord gave* [him] *for building* [them] *up, not for tearing* [them] *down* (13:10; see 10:8). Paul's language echoes that of Jeremiah (Jer 1:10; 24:6), as he claims prophetic authority over the church. He has not given up on this troublesome church, despite their disloyalty to him.

13:11–13 Paul commonly includes ethical exhortations that delineate the consequences of his theological teachings near the end of his letters. In 2 Corinthians, however, he has said little about the concrete ethical demands of the Christian life until he comes to 13:11–12, which stands in contrast to the antisocial vices he lists in 12:20, 21 (see 1 Cor 1:10). These instructions are commonplace in Paul's letters (see Rom 15:5; 16:16; Phil 2:2; 1 Thess 5:13). Paul expands on his customary benediction (see Rom 16:20; 1 Cor 16:23; Gal 6:18) with the Trinitarian formula in 13:13, indicating that the future well-being of the church rests not on its own abilities, but on the resources that come from God.

THEOLOGICAL REFLECTIONS

As the last recorded stage in Paul's lengthy conversation with the Corinthians, this epistle addresses issues that continue to confront the church: the challenge of determining the nature of the church's mission and ministry in the context of competing voices. Churches today, as in Paul's time, are caught between competing visions of ministry – between a secular understanding and one that is shaped by the cross, between the desires for market-driven success and the challenge of faithfulness to the cross. Paul's defense of his ministry contributes to the contemporary conversation about ministerial identity and church leadership. The congregation that looks to secular models of leadership will find uncomfortable words in 2 Corinthians, where we discover that authentic ministers are the breakable jars who carry around in their bodies the dying of Jesus (see 4:10) and find power only in his weakness. The mark of the authentic church is its recognition of leadership that is distinguished by its understanding of the cross of Christ.

FOR FURTHER STUDY

Ralph P. Martin, *2 Corinthians*. Word Bible Commentaries (Waco, Tex: Word, 1986).

Sze-kar Wan, *Power in Weakness: The New Testament in Context* (Harrisburg, Pa: Trinity, 2000).

WORKS CITED

Frank J. Matera, *II Corinthians* (Louisville: Westminster John Knox, 2003).

Ben Witherington III, *Conflict and Community in Corinth* (Grand Rapids: Eerdmans, 1995).

Galatians

Richard E. Oster, Jr.

CHAPTER CONTENTS

Contexts · 949
Commentary · 949
   Address & Greeting · 1:1–5 · 949
   Occasion for the Letter · 1:6–10 · 949
   The Defense of Paul's Gospel · 1:11–4:31 · 950
   New Life Under the Law of Christ · 5:1–6:10 · 954
   Letter Summary & Final Appeal · 6:11–18 · 955
Theological Reflections · 956
For Further Study · 956
Works Cited · 956

MAPS, TABLES, & FEATURES

Paul's Journey Through Anatolia · 951

Paul addresses the letter of Galatians to a cluster of congregations (*the churches*), rather than to just one city. Because of the changes made in regional boundaries by the Romans, the identity of the Galatians is a matter of debate. The traditional home of ethnic Galatians lay in the highlands of Asia Minor. With the change in the boundaries, the province of Galatia included the cities of Derbe, Lystra, and Iconium, where Paul had established churches on his first missionary journey.

CONTEXTS

The alignment of the Pauline letters and the historical events in Acts is often uncertain. If Paul is writing to the Greek inhabitants of the Roman province, Galatians could be Paul's earliest letter, written shortly after the travels narrated in Acts 13–14. If Paul is writing to the ethnic Galatians, the letter would belong to a later period in Paul's ministry. Paul's location during the writing of this letter is unknown.

Shortly after the founding of the Galatian churches, Jewish-Christian missionaries had undermined Paul's work by insisting that these Gentile converts accept the authority of the Mosaic covenant. Since Jews had traditionally welcomed Gentiles who kept the covenant into the community, these Jewish missionaries compelled the new converts to be circumcised and keep the Torah (6:12). Paul calls the message of these teachers a perversion of the gospel.

COMMENTARY

ADDRESS & GREETING · 1:1–5

Paul expands the traditional salutation (see 1 Thess 1:1; Phil 1:1), indirectly confronting the issues that he will address in the letter. Since agitators in Galatia challenged Paul, he argues that as an *apostle* his authority and message come from *God the Father* and not through *men*, anticipating the claim that he makes in 1:10–2:10.

By describing Christ as the one *who gave himself for our sins to rescue us from the present evil age*, Paul summarizes the gospel that the Galatians originally accepted and that he will defend in the letter. The phrase *for our sins* focuses on a believer's righteousness before God because of Jesus' substitutionary (2 Cor 5:21) death. Paul's claim that Christ *delivered us from the present evil age* prepares the way for his later complaint that the Galatians have relapsed into their old ways (see 4:8–9). Paul's piety and doctrines revolve around God, and he emphasizes in several letters that *glory* belongs to *God the Father* (Rom 11:36; 16:27; Eph 3:21; Phil 4:20; 1 Tim 1:17; 2 Tim 4:18).

> **"Gospel" in Galatians**
>
> In Galatians, "gospel" should not be identified with the generic definition of the gospel as the death, burial, and resurrection of Jesus (1 Cor 15:3–5). Paul explicitly connects the gospel with the promise of God to bless Gentiles as Abraham's offspring (Gal 3:8–9) on the basis of faith rather than Mosaic law. The "different gospel" refers to the Jewish-Christian opposition to Paul, which taught that Gentiles must follow Moses in order to be offspring of Abraham.

OCCASION FOR THE LETTER · 1:6–10

Paul points to the Galatians' rapid *departure* from the true gospel. With so many polemical terms such as *different gospel*, *pervert*, *confusion*, and *eternally condemned*, it is crucial to understand what Paul means by "gospel" and "different gospel."

Paul identifies these *people* working to *pervert the gospel* as *false brothers* (compare Gal 2:4) rather than unbelieving Jews. These opponents believed in most Christian doctrines. They trusted in the saving significance of Jesus' death, burial, and resurrection and knew that the church had received the Holy Spirit.

These opponents did not teach that believers were saved on the basis of human merit and ritualistic self-righteousness (McKnight 19–46). Rather, their departure from the *truth of the gospel* (Gal 2:5, 14; 4:16) involved their resistance to Paul's making Abraham's faith (rather than Moses' laws) the foundation of Gentile Christianity (Barclay 378–82). They argued that to experience the blessing of Abraham required that one receive circumcision (2:3–9; 5:2–6; 6:12–5), observe sacred holy days (4:8–11), and live a life of holiness described by the purity and ritual cleanness portrayed in the Mosaic law (2:11–14).

> **Gentiles & Jewish Ritual**
>
> *Paul's opponents in Galatia, Jewish Christians closely connected to the Jerusalem church, sought to make Gentiles accept circumcisions as evidence of their faith in Christ. It is inappropriate to call them "Judaizers," however, because unlike these Christians, Jews did not seek to circumcise Gentiles, and most modern scholars avoid that term because of its obvious anti-Semitic undertones (see Martyn).*

The term *angel from heaven* may reflect the frequency of angelic revelations or the familiar association of angelic beings with the giving of the law (Acts 7:53; Gal 3:19; Heb 2:2).

THE DEFENSE OF PAUL'S GOSPEL · 1:11–4:31

1:11–17 Paul mentions his *previous way of life* in order to upstage his opponents. *In Judaism* he formerly advocated the *traditions of the fathers*. Galatians 1:13–24 reports Paul's conversion to *Jesus Christ* and also his commission as an apostle. Paul's words *set apart from birth* allude to similar statements about Jewish prophets (Isa 49:1; Jer 1:4–5). Galatians and Acts recognize the impact of Isaiah 49 on Paul's understanding of his apostleship (Gal 1:15; Acts 13:46–47; compare 2 Cor 6:1–2).

Pharisees (Phil 3:5; see Mark 7) were *extremely zealous* for enforcing purity rules. A dramatic reversal was required when Paul was called to leave *Judaism* and to *preach among the* impurest of the impure, namely the *Gentiles*. The *grace* that *called* Paul to this ministry was not the saving grace of God (Rom 3:24; Eph 2:8–10) but the *equipping grace* of God for ministry (as in Rom 12:3–8; 15:15–16; 1 Cor 15:10; 2 Cor 9:8; Eph 3:2, 7, 8; 4:7). Paul's ambivalence toward *Jerusalem* in 1:17–18 and 2:1 probably comes from his association of the city with his opponents, although his collection of money for the Jerusalem church shows his clear concern for them, as well.

1:18–24 The roles of *Peter* and *James, the Lord's brother*, agree with the picture of Acts (Peter: Acts 1–15; James: Acts 12:17; 15:13; 21:18; compare 1 Cor 15:7). Paul perhaps goes to *Syria and Cilicia* because of the region's importance in the Gentile mission (Acts 11:19–26; 15:23). This section asks: how could the opponents be correct in their assault against Paul and his Gentile converts since, in fact, even the *churches of Judea that are in Christ* have *praised God because of* Paul and his Gentile gospel?

2:1–10 Having established his independence from Jerusalem, Paul now emphasizes Jerusalem's support for his mission to *Gentiles*. Paul *fear[s]* in 2:2 that his entire mission could be *in vain* because he realizes that no legitimate Gentile mission can exist without Jewish roots (compare Acts 13:46–47; Rom 11:13–18). For that reason, Paul *set before them the gospel* that he preached *among the Gentiles*.

In an effort to refute the arguments from *some false brothers*, Paul reports that the Jerusalem church itself did not mandate the circumcision of the *Greek* Christian *Titus*. In Galatians, *freedom* and *slavery* have to do with issues (ceremonies and rituals of Moses) extraneous to the Gentile mission rather than with liberating Christians from the importance of good deeds and obedience.

Paul stresses that the gospel has two distinct facets, Paul's *message* for the *Gentiles* and Peter's for the *Jews*. The agreement of Peter and Paul *to remember the poor* points to the poor Christians in Judea. First Corinthians 16:1–2 attests to Paul's faithfulness to this commitment.

2:11–21 Just as the story of Titus demonstrated the *truth of the gospel* about circumcision, the Antioch incident demonstrates that holiness rules and dietary statutes concerning purity marked a departure from the *truth of the gospel*.

In earlier days, Peter had been comfortable in *eating with Gentiles*, having no concerns about

Paul's Journeys through Anatolia

Jewish holiness laws or pollution from foods sacrificed to idols. Since *Peter, Barnabas, and the other Jews were afraid* of those from *the circumcision group*, they *drew back and separated* from the Gentiles. The sin of these Christians at Antioch was their *hypocrisy*. By *separating himself* from eating with the Gentiles, Peter was *forcing Gentiles to follow Jewish customs* in order to be acceptable.

Paul's summary of the arguments against Peter and others at Antioch follows. Paul reminded Peter and Barnabas that being *justified* does not come *by observing the law* (compare Ps 143:2). A work of the law like circumcision *is nothing* (1 Cor 7:19) and does not have *any value* (Gal 5:6), or *mean anything* (Gal 6:15).

Paul's phrase "works of the law" (incorrectly translated in the NIV as *observing the law*) occurs only in Romans and Galatians (Rom 3:20, 28; Gal 2:16; 3:2, 5, 10), strongly indicating its limited significance except to specific discussions of the Gentile mission. Rather than depicting self-righteousness, legalism, or merit-based salvation, "works of the law" refers to visible acts of Judaism (circumcision, sacred days, and purity rules) that certain Jewish Christians required of Gentile converts.

Some advocate that *faith in Jesus Christ* refers to the faith (or faithfulness) of Jesus Christ. While Scripture does affirm that Jesus is faithful, that is not Paul's intent here.

Since the gospel provides justification only *in Christ* rather than in observing the law, Paul reminded those at Antioch *that we ourselves are sinners* also. If the removal of the works of the law for Gentiles came from Christ's death, does that mean that *Christ promotes sin*? Paul's gospel *absolutely does not* teach that! Paul would be a *lawbreaker* if he accepted the theology of the false teachers.

Before Christ, Israel was instructed to keep God's law to live (Deut 4:40; 5:33; 8:1). What, now, replaces the law for those who wish to *live for God*? Paul's answer: now Christ can *live in me*. Paul concludes that righteousness in the new covenant must be in *Christ* and not *through the law*, lest the Messiah *died for nothing*.

3:1–6 While Paul uses autobiography in the first two chapters, chapters 3 and 4 employ arguments from Scripture. Scripture is necessary not only to substantiate the truth of his gospel but also to refute the arguments from Scripture used by his opponents, for example, their use of Genesis 17:1–14.

Paul chooses Genesis 15:6 for its connection to terms such as *Abraham, believed,* and *righteousness*. Paul's dichotomy between *observing the law* (works of the law) and *believing what you heard* (Gal 3:2, 5) is worded with the theology of Galatians 3:6 (equals Gen 16:5) in mind. The threefold reference to the *Spirit* (Gal 3:2, 3, 5) does not primarily argue from the subjective spiritual experiences of the Galatians. Rather, it appeals to the Jewish understanding of the possession of the Spirit as proof of being Abraham's heir – an understanding accepted by both Paul and his opponents (as with Cornelius in Acts 10:1–11:18). During Paul's time in Galatia, none kept circumcision, holiness rules, or Sabbaths, but nevertheless each had the Spirit. Indeed, the *blessing* of Abraham comes to fruition in the *promise of the Spirit* (Gal 3:14).

3:7–9 Paul personifies the *Scripture* of Genesis 12:2–3 and states that it *announced the gospel to Abraham*. The point of connection between Paul's message and the proto-gospel revealed to Abraham is the *blessing* that God gives to the *Gentile nations* through Abraham. This straightforward connection between the call of Abraham as a blessing for the nations and Paul's gospel makes it clear that the "Gentile mission on the basis of faith" is the central issue of this epistle. Both Paul and the false brothers agree that the *blessing* that God pronounced on Abraham in Genesis 12 is essential for righteousness. Paul's gospel argues, however, that *faith* in Christ (not Sinai) offers access to this blessing.

3:10–14 The notion of the threat of *the curse of the law* probably originated with Paul's opponents. They disputed Paul's gospel at two points, both how Gentiles receive the inheritance and blessing of Abraham and how they stay in that covenant faithfully. The issue of the one-time act of circumcision relates to "getting in," while the threat of the curse of the law relates to "staying in." Yet Paul says that his opponents should fear the curse of the law and its statutes since they claim that they *will live by them*, and of course they cannot. In the new covenant (Gal 4:24) *no one is justified before God* by keeping *everything written in the Book of the Law*, but rather *by faith* (Rom 1:17; Heb 10:38).

> **The Cross of Christ**
> *The death of Christ* on a tree has more to do with facilitating the Gentile mission than with depicting a shift from works to faith in the Scriptures. Paul never implies that personal faith did not exist in the Old Testament (see Gal 3:6–9; Hab 2:4). Rather, he says redemption from the curse of the law came in order that the Gentiles might receive the promise of the Spirit.

Since *law is not based upon faith*, what did God do so that establishing "life through faith" took the place of establishing "life through law"? *Christ redeemed us* is Paul's emphatic answer.

3:15–18 To fight for the autonomy and authority of the Abrahamic covenant over the Mosaic, Paul employs *an example from everyday life* to argue that an earlier covenant cannot be *set aside* or overruled by a later one. Specifically the *law* of Moses, *introduced 430 years later* than God's covenant with Abraham, cannot annul *the covenant previously established by God*. Paul sees *Christ* as the ultimate and exclusive heir of the inheritance promised to Abraham's seed. To bring God's blessing to the nations as Genesis 12:3 *promises*, the term *seed* in Genesis 12:7 must point to *Christ* and not the *many people* who comprise historic and ethnic Israel. Paul's point about the collective singular word *seed* combines both "rhetorical play on the ambiguity" of the word and "an exegetical device" approved by his peers (Dunn, *Epistle*, 184). Paul asserts here that the pre-Sinai promise of the *inheritance* was based upon *grace* and that Sinai could not *do away with the promise*.

3:19–25 If Abraham's covenant and its blessing do not need Moses, *What, then, was the purpose of the law*? The law was not an addition to Abraham, but *was added as a later covenant because of transgressions*, not to create transgressions but to constrain them. Paul's opponents taught the law as the remedy for Gentile sins, a way to produce holy living. Paul believes that the law could only expose sin and only *until the Seed had come*, and that Jews themselves needed it because of their own sins.

> **The Purpose of the Law**
> *Deuteronomy 30 explains the law as the source of life for a people delivered from Egyptian tyranny. The law provided a system of communal and individual norms, attitudes, and commitments orienting Israel to God.*

Should one conclude, then, that the events of Sinai, requiring angels and a mediator, were *opposed to the promises of God*? No, for Paul knows that the law originated from God. Nevertheless, the spiritual *life* of the Gentile Christian is *imparted* on the basis of faith (Gal 3:11; Hab 2:4) and cannot *have come by the law. The whole world* that God promised Abraham he would bless (Gen 12:1–3) stands as *a prisoner of sin*, waiting for *righteousness* that comes *through faith in Jesus Christ*.

This radical antithesis between law and faith (compare 3:12) makes most sense in the particular Jew-Gentile situation in Galatia, where Paul is emphasizing the connection of law to a particular covenant even while insisting that faith is more fundamental than the law. Paul's uses of the temporal terms *430 years later*, *Before faith came*, *until faith was revealed*, *now that faith*, and *no longer* highlight this. The period of being *locked up* ends both when *faith should be revealed* and when the law has finished its task of *leading us to Christ*.

> **Gentiles & the Torah**
> Most Jews in Paul's time and later would have agreed with him that the Torah did not apply to Gentiles, even if they would disagree with his arguments for the position.

3:26-29 Paul introduces the central term *sons*, a term occurring over a dozen times in the section 3:26-4:31. *Faith in Christ Jesus* rather than observing the law is the means through which this adoption occurs. Their being *clothed with Christ* at baptism identifies them as *belong*[ing] *to Christ*. The depth of the union of believers with Christ at baptism means that believers take their place alongside Christ as *Abraham's seed*. As baptized believers, they also become *heirs according to the promise* given by God.

The immediate context of Galatians 3:28 is the discussion of who can be an heir of Abraham's. The wording *neither Jew nor Greek, slave nor free, male nor female* fits in that contextual argument. Once one is *clothed with Christ* these three traditional categories of exclusion from inheritance are no longer relevant.

4:1-7 Historic Israel was like a *child* under the tutelage of a guide (Gal 3:23-25). Israel *owned the whole estate* as God's elect, but only potentially. Until the time set by his Father, when God sent his Son, historic Israel was in *slavery* until it would be redeemed and receive the *full rights* of sonship that it potentially had for centuries under the law. The phrase *Abba, Father* goes back to the pattern of Jesus' relationship with God (Mark 14:36), thus explaining why Paul refers to the *Spirit of his Son*. Odd as this claim would have seemed to contemporary Jews reading the Old Testament, it follows from Paul's assumptions about the meaning of the death, burial, and resurrection of Jesus.

> **"Abba"**
> *Abba* is the ordinary Aramaic word for "father." Contrary to popular homiletics, the word does not narrowly mean "daddy" nor does it imply merely a term of affection.

4:8-11 Paul's monotheistic evaluation of paganism is typical of his Jewish contemporaries: polytheists do *not know God*. The myriad polytheists of antiquity were only *slaves* to idols, which were *not gods* (compare Isa 44:9-20). Some Gentile believers, however, had returned to a style of religion – ritual-based Jewish Christianity – that looked suspiciously like the paganism they left. The *basic principles of the world* that engendered the Jews' *slavery* under the law (Gal 4:3) now lured these former pagans *to be enslaved again* by observing Jewish *special days*.

4:12-20 Paul uses language of both endearment and chastisement. He wants to stabilize his relationship prior to the ensuing harsh theology and imperatives of 4:21-31. Paul's admonition to *become like me* certainly includes a freedom from works of the law. Paul's first meeting with the Galatians stemmed from an *illness* of Paul's (a fact not mentioned in Acts), and Paul reminds them that they had harbored no *contempt or scorn* for him, but only *joy*. The affection they had for Paul was so strong that they *would have torn out* their *eyes* and *given them* to Paul.

> **Paul's Eyesight**
> The description of the Galatians' affection for Paul need not be taken as proof of Paul's poor eyesight. It may have involved a proverbial notion (as in Matthew 5:29 and 18:9) that was not meant literally. Paul introduces an important term, *children* [Greek *teknon*], that guides his thoughts to the end of the chapter (4:19, 25, 27, 28, 31). He and the Galatians care for each other as family members do.

4:21-27 Paul attacks the spiritual status of those *who want to be under the law*. To undermine their spiritual claims, Paul reminds them that *Abraham had two sons*, one from the *slave woman* Hagar and the other from *the free woman* Sarah. Only the latter was *born as the result of a promise*.

These two women *figuratively* (see Dunn, *Epistle*, 247-48 for general use of allegory in antiquity) represent the distinct *covenants* advocated by Paul's gospel and the pseudo-gospel of his opponents. On the side of the false teachers are *Hagar*, the earthly *city of Jerusalem*, and the *children in slavery* who follow the false doctrine of Paul's opponents. On Paul's side are the heavenly *Jerusalem who is our mother*, *Isaac* (the child *of promise*), and Sarah, the *desolate woman* of the quotation from Isaiah 54:1.

4:28–31 Paul continues his figurative interpretation with a reference to Genesis 21:9–10, where Ishmael mocks Isaac (the Hebrew text merely says they were playing, but Paul and his contemporaries understood play in a negative sense). The behavior of the false teachers *is the same now* in Paul's day as was Ishmael's at the time of Abraham. Those of the flesh *persecute* those *born by the power of the Spirit*. Paul directs the Galatians to expel those who disagree with him, for they are the *children of the slave woman* and are destined to *be eternally condemned* (Gal 1:8–9).

> **Circumcision of the Heart**
> *In making his argument, Paul downplays the role of circumcisions in the Genesis account of Abraham and his sons.*

NEW LIFE UNDER THE LAW OF CHRIST · 5:1–6:10

While some of the themes of chapters 1–4 reappear in chapters 5–6, these final two chapters focus more upon ethical behavior. Paul's dual commitment to justification and sanctification best explains the shift in emphasis in chapters 5–6 (Porter 397–402). Given the occasion of the epistle, the issues of justification and sanctification most likely relate directly to the opponents' threats. Thus, Galatians 1–4 treat "getting in" on the basis of faith, while chapters 5–6 treat "staying in" on the basis of Spirit-controlled living.

5:1–6 The concepts of *freedom* and *slavery* in 5:1 come directly from the preceding treatment of Genesis 21 (Gal 4:21–31). Here this negative connotation of *yoke* is associated with ritual mandates of the law.

Circumcision commits one to *obey the whole law*, an idea already stated in Galatians 3:10 (compare also Gal 6:13). While *whole law* here points to the ritual aspects of Sinai, the later phrase *entire law* (Gal 5:14) points to its ethical demands. With the fulfillment of the Abrahamic covenant, justification is now revealed apart from *the law* (see Rom 3:21; 10:2–4; Phil 3:9). In wording similar to Galatians 2:21, Paul states that God's *grace* is only *of value* if one rejects observing the law and embraces only the cross of Christ. The Christians who have turned to the false gospel have become *alienated from Christ* and have *fallen away from grace*.

The wording *we eagerly await* [Greek *apekdechomai*] is eschatological language for Paul (Rom 8:19, 23, 25; 1 Cor 1:7; Gal 5:5; Phil 3:20). Paul so thoroughly anticipates the return of Christ that he emphasizes that no benefit of Christ's work can be fully experienced before his return, not even justification. While waiting, believers live *by faith* (Gal 2:20) and know that the *righteousness for which* they *hope* depends upon both a "saving faith" (Gal 2:15; Eph 2:8) and a "working faith" (1 Thess 1:3; Eph 2:10). The NIV's translation of the Greek *energeo* as *faith expressing itself* rather than "faith working" is misleading and reflects inconsistency in translation (see Rom 7:5; 2 Cor 4:12; Eph 3:20; Col 1:29; 1 Thess 2:13).

5:7–12 Paul portrays the spiritual life with athletic imagery, *running a good race*, in several letters (1 Cor 9:24–27; Phil 2:16; 2 Tim 4:7). The statement about *yeast* is a proverb cited verbatim in 1 Corinthians 5:6. It dismisses the corrupting influence of the *other view* held by the false brothers that is *throwing* the believers *into confusion*.

Paul's enigmatic statement about *still preaching circumcision* may reflect situations like Paul's circumcision of Timothy (Acts 16:3) or his becoming *to those under the law…like one under the law* (1 Cor 9:20). Since the *agitators* are zealous for circumcision, they should *go the whole way and emasculate themselves*.

5:13–18 Since Paul's Gentile converts *were called to be free* from the holiness laws, he must provide a different solution for the problem of the believer's struggle with *the sinful nature* [Greek *sarx*, "flesh"]. Paul disarms his opponents' insistence that Sinai provides the guidelines for the sanctification of Gentiles by affirming the obedience of Gentile Christians to Mosaic law as expressed in Leviticus 19:18. Believers are devoted to the *entire law summed up in love* and to service to *one another*.

Paul now turns to the role of *the Spirit*. Scripture had already anticipated the centrality of God's Spirit in law keeping: *I will give you a new heart and put a new spirit in you*; *I will remove from you your heart of stone and give you a heart of flesh. And I will put my Spirit in you and move you to follow my decrees and be careful to keep my laws* (Ezek 36:26–27; see also Rom 8:4–6). The *sinful nature* and God's Spirit *are in conflict with each other*. Whereas the false teachers hoped to control the *sinful nature* by the decrees of Sinai, Paul states that a believer who is *led by the Spirit* has no need to be *under law* to win over sin.

5:19–21 The deeds of a life contrary to God are easy to detect. Rebellious acts involve *sexual immorality*, dishonoring God through *idolatry and witchcraft*, and the mistreatment of the *neighbor* mentioned in Galatians 5:14 (echoing Lev 19:18) through, for example, *hatred*, *ambition*, and *envy*. These actions exclude people from the *Kingdom of God*, so Paul *warns* the Christians more than once about them so that they will not forfeit their inheritance.

> **Covenantal Nomism**
> A concept promoted by E. P. Sanders and others who argue for a post-Reformation understanding of Paul and Judaism, Covenantal Nomism focuses on the positive and necessary role of law (nomism, from the Greek work for law, nomos) in one's covenant relationship with God. Lawkeeping, in this view, does not earn or merit the covenant, but merits an obligation demanded by one's relationship to God in the covenant. God's mercy places demands upon the believer, and one's response to God serves as an indication of whether the mercy was received in vain. Thus, one is saved on the basis of grace and evaluated on the basis of behavior (compare Jesus' idea of identifying a tree by its fruit).

5:22–26 The Spirit of God leads those not under law and who *have crucified the sinful nature*. Like the flesh, the Spirit's *fruit* is visible. These virtues are possible only because of the Spirit's work and are to be expected in people that *belong to Christ Jesus*. Paul's opponents can quote *law* from Moses to forbid this fruit demanded by Paul's gospel.

6:1–6 Gentleness and humility should characterize the more *spiritual* Christian desiring to *restore* the Christian *caught in sin*. Introspection keeps the *spiritual* Christian from yielding to sin. The reciprocal idea of *each other* fits the paradigm of Leviticus 19:18. The concept that Christians must *fulfill the law* is known elsewhere in Paul (Rom 13:8, 10; see Matt 5:17). The idiom *law of Christ* focuses on what Jesus called in Mark 12:31 the second greatest commandment (Lev 19:18).

> **The Law & Christian Ethics**
> One curious aspect of Paul's thinking is his belief that Christians, led by the Spirit, keep the ethical demands of the Law. See also Romans 13:8–10.

Most interpreters are puzzled about the purpose of 6:6 in Galatians. It is perhaps the earliest reference to paid ministers (see also 1 Cor 9; 1 Tim 5:18). *Instruction in the word* was particularly necessary for churches under attack by heretical missionaries.

6:7–10 These verses present a summary of the two paths that lie before the Christian, one of *eternal life* and the other of *destruction*. Paul's covenantal nomism affirms that having *eternal life* depends on Christians' endurance. Christians can *be deceived*, but God's faithfulness is certain and he *cannot be mocked*. God's faithfulness, however, does not excuse Christians who abandon their faith (1 Cor 10:8–12; 2 Cor 13:5–6; and especially 2 Tim 2:11). Doing *good to all people* continues Paul's elaboration of Christian law. *The family of believers* should receive special consideration as believers go about *doing good*.

LETTER SUMMARY & FINAL APPEAL · 6:11–18

On occasion, Paul used a scribe to write his letters (Rom 16:22), and that is implied here. By using the phrases *large letters* and *with my own hand*, Paul underscores his message and attests that the letter was not a forgery (see 2 Thess 2:2). There is no surprise that the opposing teachers would make circumcision the boundary marker of their community, given the importance of the rite in Judaism. *Persecuted for the cross of Christ* can refer to harassment coming from either false brothers (Gal 4:29) or from non-Christian Jews (Gal 1:13, 23).

Reiterating the charge of hypocrisy, similar to one made against Peter and Barnabas at Antioch, Paul states that among his opponents *not even those who are circumcised obey the law*. Similar to Mark 8:31–7 and Luke 9:22–6, Paul sees *the cross of our Lord Jesus Christ* not only as the foundation of God's redemptive work but also as the paradigm for the believer's life (see Gal 2:20). God's *new creation* presupposes one's death (2 Cor 5:14–7) to the values and influence of the *world*. A crucial *rule* for the Galatians is to keep the cross at the center of their relationship both with God and with their neighbor. The *Israel of God* surely refers to Christians, since they are the only heirs of Abraham and the only ones who devote themselves to this cruciform theology. A final autobiographical reference to carrying *on my body the marks of Jesus* shows Paul's superiority to his opponents. The latter can only show the surgical marks of circumcision, while Paul can reveal the scars and wounds of one *persecuted for the cross of Christ*.

The benedictory words *grace of our Lord Jesus Christ* occur frequently in Paul's letters (2 Cor 13:14; Phil 4:23; 1 Thess 5:28; 2 Thess 3:18; Phm 1:25). Paul transliterates (rather than translating) the Hebrew term *Amen*, a practice evident in other New Testament texts (Mark 14:36; Rom 1:25; 1 Cor 14:16; 2 Cor 1:20; Gal 1:5; Eph 3:21; Phil 4:20; 1 Tim 6:16; 2 Tim 4:18; Rev 19:4).

THEOLOGICAL REFLECTIONS

Paul's gospel precludes Christian groups who require the keeping of Jewish ceremonial and holiness statutes for Gentiles. The truth of Paul's message also means that modern believers must be very careful not to place cultural and ethnic requirements upon others. The "traditions of my fathers" that Paul abandoned were not innately evil. They just could not be identified with the gospel of Christ. Even so today, when there are great insights from centuries of traditions of our Christian fathers, these cannot become necessary components of the truth of the gospel (McKnight).

FOR FURTHER STUDY

Mark J. Edwards, *Galatians, Ephesians, Philippians* (Downers Grove, Ill.: InterVarsity Press, 1999).

Pheme Perkins, *Abraham's Divided Children*: *Galatians and the Politics of Faith* (Harrisburg, Pa.: Trinity Press International, 2001).

Sam K. Williams, *Galatians* (Nashville: Abingdon, 1997).

Ben Witherington III, *Grace in Galatia*: *A Commentary on St Paul's Letter to the Galatians* (Grand Rapids: Eerdmans, 1998).

WORKS CITED

John M. G. Barclay, "Mirror-Reading a Polemical Letter: Galatians as a Test Case," Pages 367–382 in *The Galatians Debate*: *Contemporary Issues in Rhetorical and Historical Interpretation* (ed. by Mark D. Nanos; Peabody, Mass.: Hendrickson, 2002).

James D. G. Dunn, *The Epistle to the Galatians* (London: A & C Black, 1993; reprint ed., Peabody, Mass.: Hendrickson, 2002).

———, *The Theology of Paul's Letter to the Galatians* (Cambridge: Cambridge University Press, 1993).

J. Lewis Martyn, "A Law-Observant Mission to the Gentiles," pages 348–61 in *The Galatians Debate*: *Contemporary Issues in Rhetorical and Historical Interpretation* (ed. Mark D. Nanos; Peabody, Mass.: Hendrickson, 2002).

Scot McKnight, "Introduction: Legalism Then and Now," Pages 19–46 in *Galatians*: *The NIV Application Commentary* (Grand Rapids: Zondervan, 1995).

Stanley E. Porter, "Holiness, Sanctification," Pages 397–402 in *Dictionary of Paul and His Letters*: *A Compendium of Contemporary Biblical Scholarship* (ed. G. F. Hawthorne, R. P. Martin, and D. G. Reid; Downers Grove, Ill.: InterVarsity Press, 1993).

E. P. Sanders, *Paul*: *A Very Short Introduction* (Oxford: Oxford University Press, 1991).

Ben Witherington III, *Grace in Galatia*: *A Commentary on St Paul's Letter to the Galatians* (Grand Rapids: Eerdmans, 1998).

Ephesians

Ira J. Jolivet, Jr.

CHAPTER CONTENTS

Contexts   957

Commentary   958
- The Ephesians' Calling as Heirs · 1:1–3:21   958
- How God's People Must Live · 4:1–6:24   960

Theological Reflections   962

For Further Study   963

Works Cited   963

MAPS, TABLES, & FEATURES

Ephesians & Christian Moral Instruction   960

Those Christians who grew up listening to sermons and Bible class lectures would agree to the spiritual power of Ephesians. Most devout Protestants, for example, would recognize the emphasis on grace in 2:8–9, while, those who grew up in Restoration traditions, however, would no doubt immediately recognize the call to unity in 4:4–6. And people from all faith traditions have found inspiration in the stirring charge in 6:10–12.

People who read and recite passages such as these in isolation from the context in which they appear in Ephesians for devotional purposes rarely encounter difficulties on matters of interpretation. When New Testament scholars read Ephesians as a unified document, however, most of them detect enough stylistic, grammatical, and thematic differences between this letter and those which they with certainty attribute to Paul that they conclude that a later admirer of his actually wrote it.

How one answers the question of the authorship of Ephesians is significant, because if Paul wrote the letter, he probably did so from a prison in Rome shortly before his execution in the early 60s CE in order to encourage and instruct a church that he had fairly recently established. If someone else wrote the letter, however, he would have done so later from somewhere other than Rome to address a completely different set of circumstances from those Paul faced. Attributing authorship of Ephesians to someone other than Paul also raises a more fundamental question: would not an audience in whom a writer must engender trust consider one who admonishes them to cease lying to one another (4:25) and who at the same time claims to be the well-known and by then perhaps long-deceased apostle to the Gentiles (3:1–13) to be both a hypocrite and a liar?

CONTEXTS

A fundamental presupposition of this commentary is that Paul wrote Ephesians. This presupposition rests on careful examination of the text, which suggests that the coherence of Ephesians emerges only when it is read intertextually. In other words, understanding Ephesians requires attention to the fact that Paul believed that Gentiles such as those in the church at Ephesus, who had believed in the atoning death and resurrection of Jesus, had now become part of the continuing story of Israel's exile from their ancestral homeland and God's promise to give them a new restored land as an inheritance. More specifically, Paul saw the members of the church at Ephesus as beneficiaries of the promises that God made through the prophet Ezekiel to the Jewish exiles from the sixth century BCE Babylonian invasion. Familiarity with the book of Ezekiel is essential to understanding the literary references occurring in Ephesians.

Ephesians & Colossians

Ephesians closely parallels Colossians in both structure and basic ideas, raising the question of how the two relate to each other. For example, see:

Ephesians	Colossians
4:15–16	2:19
5:18–20	3:16–17
6:21–22	4:7–8

While older scholars saw Ephesians as a post-Pauline copy of an authentic letter, more recent approaches to the problem emphasize how both letters use older traditions, whether from Paul, from the church's worship, or from the Old Testament.

God had initially made these promises to the exiles after having "poured out his wrath" for their failure to "walk in" the way of God's statutes and ordinances. While the book of Ezekiel contains many oracles making related but different promises, for the purpose of this present commentary, we will consider only those four major promises that Paul deemed relevant enough to allude to in his letter to the church at Ephesus.

First, in Ezekiel 36:22–23, God promises one day to redeem Israel in such a way that the Gentiles will acquire knowledge about God. Paul and his Jewish contemporaries understand the promise to mean that "'Israel' refers to those who know God, and 'not-Israel' ('Gentiles') refers to idolaters, pure and simple. In Rabbinic Judaism there are no other categories of the social order formed by all humanity" (Neusner 91–92). In other words, the defining characteristic of God's people, Israel, was not ethnicity but knowledge. The important question then becomes, what is the exact source of this knowledge? No doubt most of the forms of Judaism that emerged in the periods after the return from the Babylonian exile would have answered that question by responding that "the Torah – the written mediated through the oral – contains that knowledge that God wishes to impart to humanity. For those who practice Judaism, the encounter with God takes place in the Torah, hence, in the study of the Torah" (Neusner 30).

Paul understands the promise in Ezekiel 36:22–23 concerning the Gentiles differently, however. For him, knowledge of God comes through an experience rather than through a strictly cognitive process (Zimmerli 37). An understanding of this knowledge is extremely important because it will be the basis of Paul's claims in Ephesians that the saving knowledge of God comes through faith in God's acts in Christ rather than through adherence to the letter of the written law and that this knowledge is accessible to Gentiles as well as Jews.

Second, Ezekiel 36:24–27 promises to give Israel a "new heart" free from idolatrous inclinations. God will return the exiles scattered among the nations to the restored land. This time, however, God will enable them to remain there by empowering them to keep Torah. Ephesians insists that God has given them the power of the promised new heart and new Spirit and also access to the knowledge of his new statutes and ordinances by which the inhabitants of the restored land may live in God's presence.

As we see in the third promise at the conclusion of the oracle of the valley of the dry bones in Ezekiel 37:12–14, the gift of the Spirit brings another benefit as well, the resurrection of the people of Israel and the gift of the Spirit. This promise was especially relevant to the exiles because their estrangement from God meant that they were dead, and God himself had brought about their deaths at the hands of his executioner, the king of Babylon. The promise of resurrection from the dead, then, gave hope to the exiles in a hopeless situation. And, as we will soon see in our commentary, Paul alludes to this promise to emphasize to the Ephesians that God had already raised them up from death to life when they by faith had become a part of God's reconciled people.

> **Ephesus**
> *Founded in 290 BCE by Lysimachus, by the first century CE, Ephesus had grown to a large city full of monumental buildings centering around the Tetragonos Agora. The population of the city in the second century probably reached about 200,000, with only slightly fewer living there in the mid-first century. Thus, Ephesus was easily one of the three or four largest cities in the early Roman Empire.*

The fourth and final promise appears in Ezekiel 43:1–7, according to which God's glory will fill a divinely constructed temple and thus reverse the departure of God's glory from Solomon's temple (Ezek 11:22–23) as a prelude to its destruction by the Babylonians. Further descriptions of this temple and its environs in chapters 40–48 in Ezekiel indicate that it will be the geographical and ritual center of the heavenly city in the restored land, which God will give to his new people as an inheritance. Ephesians uses a number of related terms to allude to the promise of the new temple to convince its readers that, through faith, they also have become heirs of the land where God promises to dwell forever.

COMMENTARY

THE EPHESIANS' CALLING AS HEIRS · 1:1–3:21

1:1–14 After a brief salutation (1:1–2), Paul begins the main body of his letter with a traditional Jewish blessing (1:3–14). In reciting the spiritual blessings bestowed by God upon the Ephesians through Christ, he makes several strong verbal and thematic allusions to the promises from Ezekiel. The first allusion is his proclamation in verse 7 that, as God's adopted children, they now *have redemption through his blood, the forgiveness of our trespasses, according to the riches of his grace which he lavished upon us*, a reference to God's promise to cleanse recipients of divine wrath on account of their sins. The term *grace* here echoes God's stated motivation for acting on the basis of the divine nature rather than for anything that Israel had done. In other words, God will pardon rather than acquit them.

The second allusion is Paul's assertion that God has now made known the *mystery of his will* (verses 8–10). This phrase indicates that God has finally fulfilled the promise to act to sanctify the divine name that Israel profaned so that the nations would submit to God's sovereign rule. That act is now understood to be the atoning death of Jesus and his subsequent resurrection from the dead by the power of God's Spirit. This supernatural act reveals God as the sovereign lord over nature as well as human history.

The third allusion consists of the references in verses 11 and 14 to the inheritance awaiting God's new people in the heavenly realm. Here, Paul is cryptically referring to the promise that God's people will one day inhabit the restored land, where God will reside with them forever in the new temple. Paul makes further references to this same promise by repeated uses of the phrase *to the praise of his glory* (verses 6, 12, 14), which are subtle allusions to God's glory returning to and filling the divinely constructed temple in Ezekiel 40–48. All these allusions anticipate Paul's more explicit mention of the spiritual temple in 2:21–22.

The fourth allusion is implicit in Paul's assertion that the Ephesian saints were sealed with *the promised Spirit* when they initially believed in the *word of truth*, that is, the gospel (verse 13). In other words, they responded correctly to the fulfillment of God's promise to act to bring about reconciliation by submitting to God. They are among the Gentiles who know that God is sovereign Lord over all through belief in the atoning death of Jesus and his resurrection from the dead. Paul is also telling them that, as a result of their obedience, they have received the benefit of the new heart and new Spirit so that they now can walk in God's statutes and follow God's ordinances.

1:15–23 From the opening blessing, Paul moves directly into another liturgical form, a prayer in which he asks God to give the Ephesians a *Spirit of wisdom and revelation*, which he goes on to describe as the power to comprehend the magnitude of various blessings that God has graciously bestowed upon those who have now accepted pardon and reconciliation through faith. More specifically, he prays that God would give them a more intimate knowledge of the divine nature and a more profound appreciation of the vastness of God's resources and power. He concludes his prayer with a benediction in which he equates the promised new temple with Christ's cosmic body, the church.

2:1–22 After the benediction, Paul goes on to describe the Ephesians' calling in a narrative form contrasting their former existence with their new life as the reconciled people of God (verses 1–10). The primary imagery conveying this contrast appears in verses 1–7: resurrection. The Ephesians have experienced a resurrection from among *the walking dead*, who were alienated from God because of their sins, to life in heavenly places with and in Christ. This image directly alludes to the vision in Ezekiel 37:1–11 of the revivification of the dead bones that represented the whole house of Israel; it also implies the promise that God would one day open their graves and put his Spirit within them so that they would live (37:12–14). Once again, Paul's allusion is intended to inform the Ephesians of their new status as the reconciled people of God.

Paul continues to contrast the benefits of this status with the dire situation of their former way of life in the second part of his narrative in verses 11–22. In verses 19–22, however, he now describes this contrast in different terms, replacing the imagery of resurrection with language that first evokes images of political and familial relationships and then shifts to architectural

> **The Fullness of Christ**
>
> *Ephesians 1:23 uses the Greek noun* pleroma *and the related verb* pleroumenos. *These words later became technical terms in Gnostic texts, but in the first century, Stoics used them to refer to the infinity of the deity, and Ephesians has the same basic idea. Since the verb can be either middle or passive, the verse could mean either that Christ is filling everything (Muddiman 96) or that Christ is being filled with God or some attribute such as wisdom (Best 156, 185). Either way, the church becomes a manifestation of the all-encompassing nature of God in Christ.*

images for an ancient religious building. All of these images call to mind the promise that God made in Ezekiel 43:1–7 to construct a temple in the center of the restored land. Here, however, Paul takes Ezekiel's description of the temple a step further by implying that God is now in the process of constructing this divine edifice out of the cosmic, spiritual material of Christ, the apostles and prophets, and the reconciled people of God rather than from stone or any other physical building materials.

3:1–13 In the next section of the letter, Paul relates the story of his divine commission to proclaim the "mystery of Christ" to the Gentiles. He begins that story with verses 1–6, which bring to mind God's commission of Ezekiel as a prophet to the house of Israel in Ezekiel 2:3: *I am sending you to the people of Israel*. The Greek word translated here as "I am sending" [*exapostello*] is the verbal form of the noun [*apostolos*] that Paul uses to describe himself as God's spokesperson to the Gentiles.

Paul's use of this specific term to describe his divine commission suggests the possibility that he envisioned himself as a priest/prophet like Ezekiel whom God had sent to proclaim the fulfillment of the promise to teach the Gentiles the truth about the Lord's sovereignty, so that they might act in faith and so be saved. That possibility becomes somewhat more probable when we consider other aspects of Ephesians, such as Paul's repeated use of highly liturgical forms and language and his many allusions to the promises in Ezekiel.

3:14–21 Paul brings the first major section of his letter to a fitting conclusion with a second prayer on behalf of the Ephesians, the focus of which is similar to that of his earlier one: that God might grant them the power of the Spirit so that they will have a more intimate knowledge of God and a greater appreciation of what it means to be among a reconciled people. Paul ends his prayer by succinctly summarizing all the promises to which he has previously been alluding in the benediction of verses 20–21.

HOW GOD'S PEOPLE MUST LIVE · 4:1–6:24

Having told the Ephesians that, as part of God's reconciled people, they had received, among other benefits, the new heart and new Spirit that enables them to live ethical lives, Paul now moves to enlighten them as to exactly what God's statutes and ordinances actually are. From his statement in 2:15 that Christ has *abolished the law with its commandments and ordinances* [Greek *dogma*], we may assume with some degree of certainty that these regulations will not take the same form as the prescriptions in the written Torah. A clue as to what form they will take is perhaps to be found in this passage on moral teachings from Seneca:

> What is the difference between the doctrines of philosophy and precepts other than the fact that the former are general precepts, the latter specific? Each of them prescribes things – the former quite generally, the latter in particular…. Weaker characters need someone to lead the way: "This you will avoid, this you will do." If, moreover, someone waits for the time when he will know through himself what it is best to do, he will go astray in the interim and thus be prevented from reaching the point when he can be content with himself; therefore, he needs to be ruled while he is beginning to be able to rule himself (*Letters* 94.2, 31, 50–1; translation in Long and Sedley 426)

Seneca's statements here reflect the widely held Stoic view that weaker characters need specific precepts to tell them exactly what to do in every situation, whereas stronger characters need only general doctrines to guide them until they reach the level of maturity which allows them to rule themselves through the virtue of wisdom.

4:1–6 Paul's ethical teachings in Ephesians 4–6 conform more to general doctrines than to specific precepts such as those found in the written law of Moses. The beginning of these teachings in verses 1–6, for example, forms an exhortation to strive for the peace and unity that mirrors both the harmony

---

Belief & Behavior in Ephesians
Since Ephesians uses liturgical language extensively and even addresses Christian worship explicitly in 5:18–20, some have argued that it was a sermon connected to baptism or the Lord's Supper. While possible, these theories do not explain why the letter barely mentions either practice (but see 4:5).

A better approach would be to see it as a sermon (Best 59–63) that evokes the most profound language of worship and itself often moves into prayer and praise (especially 1:15–23; 3:14–21). The combination of worship and ethical instruction creates a theological effect by which the reader learns to connect his or her own behavior with a deeper understanding of the "mystery" (a favorite word in Ephesians; see 1:9; 3:3; 5:32; 6:19).

between God the Father and the Lord Jesus Christ; it also calls Christians to seek the reconciliation that has come about through the Spirit between God and humanity and between Israel and the Gentiles, who had previously been separated by the *dividing wall of the written law* (2:14).

4:7–16 This section makes it even clearer that Paul gives God's new people statutes and ordinances in the form of general doctrines. In verses 11–13, for example, he lists church leaders as gifts to the body of Christ. These persons carry out the task of bringing other Christians to a state of maturity characterized as *attaining to the whole measure of the fullness of Christ* (verse 13). The language here is obviously descriptive rather than prescriptive as Paul describes a developmental process that involves education in *the knowledge of the Son of God* with the ultimate goal of maturity in Christ. In other words, God has given certain members of the body the gifts to guide his people into proper ethical conduct through doctrines until they attain the wisdom necessary to discern on their own the difference between right and wrong.

4:17–5:2 God has given Christians other sources of the knowledge of these new ethical guidelines to help them to attain the goal of maturity, as well. Paul implicitly identifies one of these sources in 4:20–24, exhorting them to recall his oral instruction that invited them to a higher ethical standard. Paul implies here that the Ephesians had at some point received teachings about Christ through which

---

Ephesians & Christian Moral Instruction

Like all the letters of the New Testament, Ephesians conducts a dialogue on moral issues between the Greco-Roman and biblical (Israelite) traditions. The book grounds its moral instruction, which draws on modified forms of the best insights of the day, in the story of God's redemptive work through Christ (3:1–20; notice the word "therefore" in 4:1 and 5:1). Morality does not arise from a vacuum but from the church's central convictions. Moreover, the Old Testament often provides a warrant for particular behaviors, and Ephesians calls for little that does not have numerous parallels in Israel's law and wisdom.

However, since the letter's readers are Gentiles who must not act like Gentiles (4:17), Ephesians uses the conventions of Greco-Roman moral philosophy. Like many contemporary authors, this text builds its case for a particular way of life through personal example (3:1), lists of virtues and vices (4:25–31), and explorations of conventional subjects like peace in a family or group, relations of family members or masters and slaves, and sexual conduct, among others. Much of the advice here fits well with the best insights of the first century (see Malherbe), even if it challenged individuals to live better than the pagans normally did.

Especially interesting is the ethical material in Ephesians 5. Verses 3–20 rehabilitate language, counseling readers to avoid destructive talk and to speak words of praise to God and encouragement to each other, instead. To cement this shift in the use of words, the author quotes (verses 2, 14) what seems to be fragments of ancient Christian hymns or confessions, using them to say, in effect, "since we seek to be like Christ in our lives and worship, let us speak in ways befitting that goal."

Verses 21–33 draw on a common theme in Greco-Roman moral philosophy, the relationships of married persons (see Malherbe 152–54), to speak more broadly about the life of the church. As verse 32 makes clear, the meditation on husbands and wives does not attempt to lay out a comprehensive view of marriage but rather uses marriage as a metaphor for the Christian life in general. Such a life should be characterized by loyalty between Christ and the church, with a sacrificial attitude on the part of each. On the other hand, the view of marriage that serves as the model for the church elevates women more than was common in the Greco-Roman world, in which many of even the most sophisticated philosophers thought of them as mentally or even morally inferior. Rather, Ephesians seems to join more progressive forces in ancient society that made marriage more of a consensual partnership of a man and a wife. For example, the late first century thinker Musonius Rufus wrote a series of short essays on marriage, in which he called for monogamy and for encouraging women to study philosophy. He also says, "With respect to character or soul one should expect that it be habituated to self-control and justice.... These qualities should be present in both man and wife" (Musonius Rufus 91).

While Ephesians assumes a more traditional understanding of marriage, it does so as an analogy for the relationship between Christ and the church. Analogies are always incomplete, and this one eventually breaks open new possibilities for the relationship on which the analogy is based. The mutual love of Christ and his people offers a new model for all human relationships, especially that deepest one between a husband and a wife.

– Mark W. Hamilton

they had learned to emulate the holy and righteous attributes of God rather than live in lust. What Paul implies here he makes explicit in 5:1–2. The general doctrine here is clear: God teaches saved people how to emulate God's own character by walking in love, the highest form of ethical behavior, through the example of Christ's ultimate self-sacrificial act.

5:3–20 While Paul goes on to give further ethical instructions in the form of general doctrines, he gives subtle clues along the way indicating that, through the gift of the Holy Spirit, God's people have already received great powers of discernment. One of these clues is his statement in 5:10, which exhorts the Ephesians to *try to find out what is pleasing to the Lord*. Another clue appears in the call in 5:15–17 to *live not as unwise [people] but as wise, making the most of the time, because the days are evil*. By using the language of wisdom and foolishness, Paul connects his teaching to the highest moral standards of Greco-Roman culture as well as to the biblical tradition. In both of these exhortations, Paul is strongly implying that the Ephesians have access to knowledge of God's ethical standards from an internal source completely distinct from the written Torah or from any other external source, even though it coincides at several points with the best ethical reflections of both Gentiles and Jews.

5:21–6:9 Paul concludes his moral instructions with a series of exhortations and admonitions to specific familial groups. He starts with wives and then addresses husbands, children, slaves, and masters in turn. A perfect example of the general nature of these doctrines occurs in Paul's exhortation to husbands in verses 25–28b. While Ephesians assumes the basic hierarchies of the ancient world, it also corrects their worst abuses and points beyond them to an ethical life in which traditional patterns of subordination and superiority break down in a context of responsibility and love.

6:10–17 Having now explained that the Ephesians are God's new people who are the beneficiaries of the promise of reconciliation with him and having given them God's statutes and ordinances in general form, Paul fittingly summarizes all that he has said with verbal allusions to the powerful image of the resurrection of the dry bones in the oracle of Ezekiel 37:1–14. The most obvious of these allusions appears in the exhortations of verses 10–13, in which the repetition of various forms of the word "*stand*" are strong indications that Paul is alluding to Ezekiel 37:10. The earlier story of God's command to prophesy to the lifeless bones serves Paul's purpose of encouraging the Ephesians. Just as Ezekiel saw bones into which *the breath came ... and they lived, and stood on their feet, a vast multitude*, so now Paul has seen Gentiles and Jews reconciled to God through faith in Christ.

With this allusion, Paul is implicitly restating the assertion that he made in chapter 2 that the Ephesians are beneficiaries of God's promise to raise Israel from the dead by infusing them with the Spirit (Ezek 37:14). The implicit reference to the power of the Spirit, then, is also a further reminder that God has also given them the power to live ethical lives and even to overcome mighty cosmic powers and spiritual forces that are arrayed against them and that seek their destruction.

> **The Spirit & the Word**
> *The Greek term translated here as* "breath" *is* pneuma, *the same word which is rendered elsewhere in the Greek version of the Hebrew Bible and also in the New Testament primarily as* "spirit." *On the thematic connection between the spoken word of God, the infusion of his Spirit, and the ability to stand, compare Ezekiel 2:1–2:* He said to me: O mortal, stand up on your feet, and I will speak with you. And when he spoke to me, a spirit entered into me and set me on my feet; and I heard him speaking to me. *Here the spirit enters into the prophet as God speaks to him, enabling him to stand on his feet in God's presence.*

6:23–24 Paul concludes his letter to the Ephesians with a postscript in which he asks the Ephesians to pray that he continue to fulfill his mission of proclaiming the gospel (verses 18–20), with an appeal to them to receive Tychicus as a brother and a faithful minister of the Lord (verses 21–22), and with this final liturgical benediction in 23–24.

THEOLOGICAL REFLECTIONS

Paul writes to the saints at Ephesus to give them the motivation to lead lives worthy of their calling as the new covenant people of God. He does this primarily by alluding to Ezekiel's story of Israel's exile from their land as a result of their alienation from God and of God's promise to return the exiles to the restored land through a gracious act of reconciliation. In alluding to this story, Paul intends to make the Ephesians aware of their new identity as those people from the nations who, along with a remnant from the exiles of the house of Israel, have come to know God by faith and thus will one day inherit the restored land.

In the church today, we often either forget why we should live differently from other people in the world, or we mistakenly turn the general doctrines of Paul's ethical teachings into new dogmatic commandments. If this is indeed the case, then we need to hear Paul's letter to the Ephesians as he intended his original audience to hear it. That means that we need to be reminded that we live to do God's will because God has also delivered us from a hopeless situation by raising us from death in our sins to a new life with Christ in heavenly places. And it also means that we must learn how to rely more on the power of God's promised Spirit. Finally, it means that we should live as those who have joined the exiles of Israel in a foreign land and who await the time when, in fulfillment of promises, we will forever behold God's glory in an eternal, holy temple.

FOR FURTHER STUDY

Tom Wright, *Paul for Everybody*: *The Prison Letters* (Louisville: Westminster John Knox, 2002).

Thomas R. Yoder Neufeld, *Ephesians* (Waterloo, Ont.: Herald, 2002).

WORKS CITED

Leslie C. Allen, *Ezekiel 20–48* (Dallas: Word, 1990).

Ernest Best, *Ephesians* (Edinburgh: T&T Clark, 1998).

Gordon Fee, *God's Empowering Presence: The Holy Spirit in the Letters of Paul* (Peabody, Mass.: Hendrickson, 1994).

Donald E. Gowan, *Theology of the Prophetic Books: The Death and Resurrection of Israel* (Louisville: Westminster John Knox Press, 1998).

Richard B. Hays, *The Faith of Jesus Christ*: *The Narrative Substructure of Galatians 3:1–4:11* (Grand Rapids: Eerdmans, 2002).

Andrew Lincoln, *Ephesians* (Dallas: Word, 1990).

A. A. Long and D. N. Sedley, *The Hellenistic Philosophers*, vol. 1: *Translations of the Principal Sources with Philosophical Commentary* (Cambridge: Cambridge University Press, 1987).

Margaret Y. MacDonald, *Colossians and Ephesians* (Collegeville, Minn.: Liturgical Press, 2000).

Abraham J. Malherbe, *Moral-Exhortation: A Greco-Roman Sourcebook* (Philadelphia: Westminster, 1986).

John Muddiman, *The Epistle to the Ephesians* (London/New York: Continuum, 2001).

Musonius Rufus, *The Roman Socrates* (trans. Cora E. Lutz; New Haven: Yale University Press, 1947).

Jacob Neusner, *Judaism When Christianity Began: A Survey of Beliefs and Practices* (Louisville: Westminster John Knox, 2002).

Walther Zimmerli, *I Am Yahweh* (trans. Douglas W. Scott; Atlanta: John Knox Press, 1982).

Philippians

Jeffrey Peterson

CHAPTER CONTENTS

- Contexts 965
- Commentary 966
    - Address · 1:1–2 966
    - Paul's Prayers for the Church · 1:3–11 966
    - Report on Paul's Circumstances · 1:12–26 967
    - Exhortation to Heavenly Citizenship · 1:27–4:1 967
    - Appeal to Euodia & Syntyche for Unity · 4:2–3 970
    - Summary Exhortation to the Church · 4:4–9 970
    - Concluding Expression of Joy · 4:10–20 971
    - Greetings & Benediction · 4:21–23 971
- Theological Reflections 971
- For Further Study 971
- Works Cited 971

MAPS, TABLES, & FEATURES

- Leadership Roles in the Pauline Churches 966

When Paul wrote this letter late in his career, the church in Philippi had existed for over a decade (see Acts 16:11–40; Phil 1:5–6). Philippians thus addresses Paul's most mature converts. Paul writes from captivity (1:7, 13–14, 17), probably in Rome (see the comment on 1:13; 4:22), to encourage the Philippians to persevere in the hard work of living out the salvation God has extended to them (2:12–13) by seeking unity in the mind of Christ (1:27; 2:1–5; 4:2). The nearly fatal illness Epaphroditus had suffered while staying with Paul (2:25–27) had prevented his return to Philippi, but now that his health is restored, Paul is eager to send this fellow worker back to the Philippians with news, with expressions of Paul's gratitude, and with a call to living a life focused on Christ.

CONTEXTS

Paul's letter to the Philippians addresses a church in a Roman colony, a settlement centered around retired soldiers and their descendants. Though Greek-speaking and surrounded by Greek traditions, the city followed Roman law. As a stop on the major highway, the *Via Egnatia*, it was a crossroads of many cultures and religions, being the home of temples for Egyptian gods such as Serapis, the Phrygian mother goddess Cybele, and others. Religious pluralism was a given in this, as in so many other, Roman cities.

The letter to Philippi followed the ministry that Paul had conducted there between 49 and 52 CE. As a typical Pauline letter, Philippians continues the apostle's oral teaching, emphasizing the centrality of Jesus' death and resurrection to a new way of life. By connecting the Christian story to the ethical behavior within the Christian community, Paul seeks to encourage his readers to follow key exemplars, notably Jesus, Timothy, Epaphroditus, and Paul himself.

Though brief and structurally simple, Philippians seems to jump from topic to topic in a way that has led some scholars to suggest that two or more letters of Paul have been spliced together. However, this seems unlikely, and the alleged roughness of the transition from chapter 2 to chapter 3, in particular, can be explained as owing to the fact that Paul intended the letter to be read aloud to a small group of people who would track his argument that they should model their life on Jesus and on the Christians they knew, including Paul.

Paul had helped found the church at Philippi (see Acts 16:11–40) and the relationship between the Philippians and Paul had been reciprocal, with the Philippians *sharing in the gospel from the first day* (1:5). They had also provided him with regular financial support. Writing to this established and active church, one of Paul's major themes is the call to lead a life of joy. The inescapable result of living a life focused on emulating Christ, he notes that joy (1:4), selflessness (1:20–26), humility (2:3), and a passion for the true gospel (3:1–3) are the key attributes of those in genuine relationship with God. Paul calls his readers to unity, asking them *not to [look to] your own interests, but to the interests of others* (2:4 NRSV). Doing so, they will *become*

PHILIPPIANS

blameless and pure, children of God without fault in a crooked and depraved generation, in which [they] *shine like stars in the universe* (2:15) through their good works and through their willingness to share joyfully in the sufferings and sacrifice of others for the sake of the gospel (2:17–18).

COMMENTARY

ADDRESS · 1:1–2

The address follows Paul's practice of adapting the conventional Greco-Roman letter opening ("A to B, greetings") by offering a theological characterization of the letter's senders (*servants of Christ Jesus*) and recipients (*all the saints* [literally, "ones sanctified," by God] *in Christ Jesus*). Paul substitutes for the standard Greek letter greeting *chairein* (as in Acts 15:23; 23:26; Jas 1:1) the similar blessing *grace and peace* [Greek *charis kai eirene*]. Such changes fit Paul's letters for reading aloud in ancient Christian worship assemblies (1 Thess 5:27; Col 4:16). Timothy is a co-sender of the letter, but the authorial references in the singular ("I"), which begin at 1:3–26, as well as the third person reference to Timothy in 2:19–23, imply that Paul is the principal author (Bockmuehl 49). This is the only letter in which Paul directly addresses the church's *overseers and servants* (NIV *deacons*), suggesting that he either intends to strengthen them (as in 1 Corinthians 16:15–16), or to draw attention to their responsibility to work toward the goals he articulates in the letter (as in Philemon), or both (Campbell 124, who suggests that the "overseers and servants" included: Epaphroditus, Euodia, Syntyche, and Clement).

PAUL'S PRAYERS FOR THE CHURCH · 1:3–11

As often in his letters, Paul opens the body of Philippians with a report of how the church has figured in his daily prayers to God. As usual, the things for which Paul gives thanks introduce themes that he will develop through exhortation. The phrase *with joy* (verse 4) initiates a theme that recurs with significant variations throughout the letter (1:18, 25; 2:2, 17–18, 28–29; 3:1; 4:1, 4, 10). Paul has given thanks for the Philippians' cooperation in his missionary endeavors (verse 5). This participation has taken concrete expression in periodic financial gifts (4:15–18), but it also includes the moral transformation begun at their conversion by God, which God will complete *until the day of Christ Jesus* (1:6). Paul has served as God's agent in the Philippians' transformation, and they thus share a special bond (1:7a, 8; compare 1 Thess 2:7–8; Paul's word employs the same root as *partnership* in 1:5). Paul's present circumstances, which involve *both ... imprisonment and ... the defense and confirmation of the gospel* (1:7b NRSV; there is no basis in the Greek text for the NIV's *whether*), take place in the context of this relationship.

Paul prays that the church that shares in his mission (verses 9–10) will find that their *love may abound more and more in knowledge and depth of insight* so that they may grow in their moral sensitivities. Transformation of behavior is the principal standard that Paul offers for evaluating the life of the church (see Rom 12:1–2; 8:3–4). As in 1:6, this transformation continues until Christ returns (compare 2:11).

Leadership Roles in the Pauline Churches

The term "overseer" for a leader in the Pauline churches [Greek *episkopos*, *traditionally translated "bishop"*] *occurs only here and in the Pastoral Epistles (1 Tim 3:2; Titus 1:7; see Acts 20:28 and* episkope *["overseership"] in Acts 1:20 and 1 Timothy 3:1). The functions of spiritual oversight and communal guidance that the word suggests, however, occur elsewhere in Paul's references to the structure of his churches.*

In his earliest letter, Paul encourages the church to respect those who labor among you and stand before you in the Lord and admonish you *(1 Thess 5:12–13). Even more clearly, in 1 Corinthians Paul appeals to the membership of the church to* submit *[literally, "order yourselves under"] such people as the household of Stephanas (1 Cor 16:15).*

"Deacons" is perhaps too specific a rendering of the other term for leaders that Paul uses in Philippians 1:1, as diakonos *is Paul's general term for ministers, used of Christ in his earthly ministry (Rom 15:8), Paul himself (1 Cor 3:5; 2 Cor 6:4; Col 1:23, 25) and his itinerant coworkers Apollos (1 Cor 3:5), Tychicus (Eph 6:21; Col 4:7), and Epaphras (Col 1:7); Phoebe is identified specifically as* a servant of the church in Cenchrea" *(Rom 16:1).*

REPORT ON PAUL'S CIRCUMSTANCES · 1:12–26

In this section, Paul shows how his imprisonment (see 1:7b), which his converts might find disheartening, instead provides further grounds for joy in thanksgiving. Most importantly, his personal adversity *has really served to advance the gospel* (verse 12), as evidenced by two results detailed in verses 13–14. First, the awareness that Paul was imprisoned for the sake of Christ spread *throughout the whole palace guard*, who rotated on four-hour shifts, as well as *everyone else* in the imperial service involved with the trial of Paul's case (Fee 113–14). And second, Christians had increased confidence in preaching the gospel presumably in Rome and perhaps beyond (for Paul's awareness of circumstances in Christian communities generally, see Rom 1:8; 15:31; 16:19; 1 Cor 15:11; Gal 1:23–24; 1 Thess 1:8; 2:14).

Paul expands on the second result of his imprisonment in verses 15–17 with a recognition of mixed motives among preachers of the gospel, some doing so *for the sake of* [God's] *good pleasure* (not NIV's *out of goodwill*, verse 15; compare 2:15, *according to his good purpose*) and *in love* (verse 16), but others for bad motives or even to *increase* [Paul's] *suffering in imprisonment* (verse 17 NRSV). Remarkably, Paul regards this situation with contentment, rejoicing that *whether from false motives or true, Christ is preached* (verse 18). This suggests that there is no fundamental disagreement in doctrine between Paul and the evangelists to whom he here attributes bad motives, as clearly is the case with those he opposes in Philippians 3:2, 18–19 (see 2 Cor 2:17; 6:14–16; 10:9–18; 11:4–6, 12–23)

Paul takes the preaching of Christ resulting from his imprisonment as an occasion to rejoice (verse 18), thus offering model behavior for the Philippians (2:17–18). In verses 18–26, Paul prepares them for the outcome of his court case. He will regard either conviction or acquittal as a divine *salvation* (verse 19; NIV *deliverance*) and no cause for shame so long as he joins other fearless preachers (verse 14) in preaching Christ with *courage* (verse 20). The fate of Paul's *body* serves to exalt Christ (compare 2 Cor 4:10–12; Gal 2:19–20). Paul declares himself prepared to glorify Christ either *by life or by death* (verse 20) and expresses uncertainty about which is more advantageous for him (verse 22), inasmuch as *to live is Christ* (see Gal 2:20) and death means that he will *depart and be with Christ* (see 2 Cor 5:8). The question of his personal preference aside, Paul recognizes that the preservation of his earthly life will benefit his converts (verse 24) and expresses his confidence that the Philippians' prayers on his behalf will lead to his release (1:25–26; compare 2:24). His attitude thus illustrates the sacrificial concern for one's fellow Christians that he commends to the church in the following exhortation.

> **Paul's Contemplation of Mortality**
> *Paul's meditation on whether life or death is preferable (verses 20–26) differs from typical pagan variations on this theme (for example, Plato's* Apology, *40c–42) in expressing confident trust in God rather than resignation to fate.*

> **"Those who have fallen asleep ..."**
> *Paul states that between death and resurrection the Christian (or at least the Christian martyr; see Rev 6:9–11) experiences an intermediate conscious state (2 Cor 5:4, 6–8; Luke 16:22–31), which suggests that only the body "falls asleep" in death (1 Cor 7:39; 11:30; 15:6, 18, 51; 1 Thess 4:13–15).*

EXHORTATION TO HEAVENLY CITIZENSHIP · 1:27–4:1

1:27–2:5 Paul turns next from his circumstances to the church's responsibilities. The Philippians need not be discouraged by Paul's trials but should focus their energies on living as a colony of God's heavenly kingdom. The first imperative verb in the letter (weakly rendered *conduct yourselves* in NIV) might more fully be translated "exercise your citizenship" [Greek *politeuesthe*, verse 27]; a noun form of the same root appears toward the close of the exhortation [Greek *politeuma*, "citizenship," 3:20]. Paul's evangelistic preaching evidently presented membership in the Christian community as preparation for life in the coming kingdom of God (1 Cor 6:9–11; Gal 5:21) in royal imagery drawn from the preaching of Jesus (Mark 1:15; 4:11, 26–32; 9:1, 43–47) and Jewish Scripture (Exod 15:18; Pss 93:1; 96:10; 97:1; 99:1; Isa 40:10–11). The language in which Paul develops this imagery in Philippians doubtless made sense in Philippi, a Macedonian city under Roman rule since 168 BCE, and a Roman colony since 30 BCE (Bockmuehl 2–6; Fee 25–26). The appeal to unity (verse 27b) also echoes ancient political rhetoric, in which faction was one of the greatest evils a city-state or federation faced (see Mitchell, especially 60–68, 180–83).

Paul understands the opposition the Philippians have experienced (verse 28) to be one of the woes attending the advent of the messianic age (see Mark 13:7–27; Rom 6:3–4; 8:17–18; 1 Pet 4:12–19). The Philippians' perseverance through this hostility proves God's favor for the persecuted and judgment on the persecutors (see 2 Thess 1:4–8). The Philippians' suffering for Christ (verses 29–30) also makes them Paul's partners in the gospel.

The appeal for unity, humility, and mutual concern in 2:1–5 introduces the letter's central example of Christ, the "first citizen" of the heavenly kingdom (2:6–11). In 2:1, Paul recalls the divine gifts (see 1:7) sustaining the Philippian community as a basis for the appeal that follows. The *if* is rhetorical and does not imply uncertainty about the presence of the *encouragement, comfort, fellowship with the Spirit,* or *tenderness and compassion* that accompany life *in Christ* (2:1 NRSV). The faithfulness of the Philippian community and other churches undergirds Paul's expectation of *joy* in God's impending judgment (verse 2; see 4:1; 2 Cor 1:14; 1 Thess 2:19). Christian unity *in spirit and purpose* (verse 2b) comes through the renunciation of *selfish ambition* and *vain conceit* and the cultivation of *humility.* The NIV softens the charge of verse 4 by the addition of *not only* and *also.* Paul in fact exhorts Christians, *Let each of you look not to your own interests, but to the interests of others* (2:4 NRSV). The example of Christ is the indispensable model for the Christian *mind* (verse 5).

2:6–11 The description of Christ falls into two sections roughly equal in length, the first (verses 6–8) describing Christ's lowering of himself and the second (verses 9–11) describing God's exaltation of him.

The narrative begins before Christ's earthly mission with his existence *in the form of God* (NIV margin), that is, "the visual characteristics of [God's] heavenly being" (Bockmuehl 129; compare 1 Kgs 22:19; Isa 6:1–5; Ezek 1:1–4, 26–28). This imagery is used both of Adam (Gen 1:26–28) and, more pertinently in this context, of the eternal Wisdom by which God created (*Wisdom of Solomon* 7:26). Elsewhere Paul designates Christ as *wisdom from God* (1 Cor 1:30), draws on Jewish wisdom tradition to describe Christ's role as God's agent in creation (1 Cor 8:6; see Prov 8:30; *Wisdom of Solomon* 9:1–2), and describes Christ's incarnation as abandoning heavenly riches for earthly poverty (2 Cor 8:9). The preexistent Christ's story becomes the photographic negative of Adam's (see Gen 3:1–7) and a positive example for Christians in that he *emptied himself* (NRSV) of heavenly glory and divine privilege, to assume *the form of a servant* (2:7; NIV margin), or *slave* (NRSV), echoing Isaiah 52:13–15. Jewish teachers understood divine Wisdom to be embodied in the Mosaic Law (*Sirach* 24:23), but only Christians thought of the image of God's eternal Wisdom (or Word, as in John 1:1, 14; compare *Wisdom of Solomon* 9:1–2) *being made in human likeness* (2:7). Christ further exemplified the life that Paul commends to Christians in that once he had descended from heaven, *he humbled himself.* Specifically, he *became obedient to death – even death on a cross* (2:8), the most shameful death known to Roman antiquity, reserved for slaves and enemies of the imperial order.

Paul's *therefore* (2:9) encourages Christians facing discouragement; because Christ's humility during the extremes of suffering and *death* led God to reward him with an incomparable position and *name* (2:9), so also the Philippians may look forward to sharing Christ's reward if they follow in his steps. Verse 9 reflects early Christian interpretation of Psalm 110:1 (in combination with Isa 52:13), according to which

---

A Hymn to Christ

The description of Christ in 2:6–11, the letter's centerpiece, has attracted much commentary (Martin and Dodd). Since ancient times, readers have scrutinized it for its understanding of the person and incarnation of Christ. Its lyrical style suggested to many scholars an origin in the worship of the early church, so that commentators often designate it the "Philippian hymn" or "Christ hymn." However, there is no proof that the passage existed in its present form before the composition of Philippians (see Bockmuehl 116–117; Fee 193 note 4). The passage offers a lyrical summary of the story of Christ as the fulfillment of Israel's hopes (for the idea, see Rom 1:2–3; 1 Cor 15:3–4). In its literary context, the passage offers the Philippians the supreme example of one who looked not to [his] own interests, but to the interests of others *(verse 4 NRSV).*

Apocryphal Books in the First Century

First century Jewish interpreters, including Paul, read the Wisdom of Solomon, Sirach, *and other such texts as commentary on the book of Proverbs, here on Proverbs 8:22–31.*

> **The Nature of God**
>
> Philippians 2 witnesses to the earliest Christians' "redefining the unique identity of God in a way that includes Jesus" (Bauckham 36). To account for such complex passages (see also John 1:1–18; 1 Cor 8:6; Col 1:13–20; Heb 1:1–4), teachers in the first Christian centuries elaborated the doctrines of the Trinity and the incarnation, in order to do justice both to the divine salvation Jesus has brought and to the model for believers his life supplies.

the risen Son now reigns at God's right hand (compare Rom 8:34). A further interpretation of this psalm verse appears in the statement that the Father bestowed on Christ *the name that is above every name*, which is to say the divine name. Since the Greek Old Testament renders the name Yahweh as "Lord," reference to the Lord Jesus connects him to God. The climactic scriptural allusion of the passage applies to Christ God's declaration in Isaiah 45:23 (*Before me every knee will bow; by me every tongue will swear*, or in the Greek translation, *every tongue will acknowledge me*).

2:12–18 In 2:12–13, Paul draws a lesson from the story of Christ. The plural pronoun in the phrase *work out your own salvation* (verse 12b NRSV) implies effort to secure *each other's* hold on salvation rather than exclusive concern for one's own fate (Thompson 48, note 30; compare 1 Cor 6:7; Heb 10:25). Psalm 2:11 encourages *fear and trembling* among Gentiles in the presence of the Lord and the anointed ones, where Paul has brought the Philippians. Paul does not endorse "works righteousness," for *it is God who works in* the faithful to transform both desires and actions (see Rom 12:1–2). This same interplay of divine and human agency also appears in 1:5–6, and Paul's frequent ethical appeals emphasize such actions for believers (Rom 12:1–15:1; Gal 5:1–6:10). The corollary of unity (2:1–4) is to leave aside *complaining or arguing* (verse 14), unlike the Israelites in the wilderness (Exod 16:7–12; 17:3; Num 11:1; 14, 27, 29). The phrase *crooked and depraved generation* (verse 15; see Deut 32:5) further refers to those opposing the church (1:28), in comparison with whom the Philippians *shine like stars in the universe* (see Dan 12:3) by *maintaining* [their] *hold on the word of life* (2:16, see NIV margin). As verse 16 makes clear, Paul views the church's present work of faithful endurance in terms of Christ's return (compare 1:6, 10; 4:5). Paul would have run the apostolic race and labored *for nothing* if his converts proved faithless *on the day of Christ* (also Gal 2:2), but in the present situation, Paul's life stands as *a libation* of wine *poured out over the sacrifice and the offering* of the Philippians' faith (2:18 NRSV; see 4:18b).

2:19–3:14 In 2:19–30, Paul surveys the travels of two of his missionary associates, because he expects them to return to Philippi soon (2:19, 23, 25), and because they provide the church with models of sacrificial faithfulness (see 3:17). Thus Paul's roving assistant Timothy *takes a genuine interest in* the Philippians' *welfare* (verse 20), as Paul has urged the Philippians to do for one another (2:4). As in 1 Corinthians 4:16–21, Paul now commends Timothy as a trustworthy authority whose visit will prepare the church for Paul's own return to them (Phil 2:24). Epaphroditus, who conveyed the church's offering to Paul (2:25; 4:18) and fell ill on the journey (2:26–27), *approached the point of death*, the same phrase that applies to Christ in 2:8. Epaphroditus's willingness to sacrifice all for the gospel embodies for the Philippians the virtue of Christ in their midst.

The appeal to the Philippians to receive Epaphroditus *with great joy* (2:29) prepares for a renewed exhortation to *rejoice in the Lord* (3:1). Commentators often find the transition in these verses abrupt, but comparing the church's conduct with that of outsiders occurs elsewhere in the letter (1:27–30; 3:17–20; and comment on 4:4–9). By asking them to *watch out for* (3:2), or perhaps simply *consider*, those requiring the circumcision of Gentiles, Paul contrasts such teachers with the Christian community, the true *circumcision* (3:3; see Rom 2:28–29; 8:3–4), *who put no confidence in the flesh* by trusting in the law.

In 3:1–14, Paul expands on his reasons for renouncing *confidence in the flesh* (3:4) and so puts himself forth as a further example of sacrificial obedience. Though he was *circumcised on the eighth day* (verse 5), as required by Leviticus 12:3 (see Luke 2:21), and *a Pharisee*, a member of a popular Jewish sect known for its faithfulness to ancestral tradition, Paul gave up his advantage among his peers. Paul's career in *persecuting the church* stemmed from his *zeal* for the Pharisees' understanding of the law (Gal 1:13–14). *Legalistic righteousness* (verse 6) is more neutrally translated *righteousness under the law* (NRSV). To embrace his call to apostleship, Paul left such achievements behind, regarding them as *loss* (verse 7) and even as *rubbish* (verse 8), to the extent of renouncing his own ancestral *righteousness ... that comes from the law* and accepting instead *the righteousness that comes from God and is by faith* (verse 9) as declared in the gospel (see Rom 3:20–31). Sharing in this righteousness involves imitating Christ's obedience even to the point of death (3:10–11; Rom 6:3–11). The word *somehow* (verse 11) emphasizes that this participation depends on the course run by Paul (and the Christians who follow his example) in the interim between our present and God's future (Bockmuehl 217).

> **"To win the prize ..."**
> Paul states his attitude in 3:12–14 as that of an athlete in competition, *straining ... toward the goal to win the prize* (1 Cor 9:24–27). His exaltation will be reminiscent of Jesus' (2:9). He then commends this attitude to all the *mature*, employing language that ties this exhortation back to the appeal to share the *mindset of Christ* (2:5). Finally, he expresses his confidence that God will continue to reveal his will to Christians who do not yet share Paul's understanding (3:15).

3:15–4:1 Paul concludes his central exhortation to Christian citizenship by drawing the church's attention to three related matters. First is the positive *example* the Philippians have in Paul and others who imitate his self-denying service in imitation of Christ (3:17), including Timothy and Epaphroditus (2:19–30). Second is the negative example of those whom Paul sorrowfully names *enemies of the cross of Christ*, perhaps the same teachers of circumcision opposed in 3:2, if their devotion to *their stomach* refers to their acceptance of material rewards for their teaching (compare 2 Cor 11:7–9, 19–21) and if *their mind* being set *on earthly things* indicates their concern to conform to the practices of the earthly Jerusalem (see Gal 4:25). Third, Paul contrasts their earthly orientation with the perspective of those whose *citizenship is in heaven* (3:20). Christians expect the *Savior* to return from there to transform *the body of our humiliation* (3:21 NRSV), a condition to which Christ was previously subject (2:8), into the *likeness* (a word recalling Christ's "form," 2:6–7) of his *glorious body* (see 2:9–11). Humiliation and suffering in the present prepare Christians for the glory to be revealed in God's accomplishment of his saving purpose (see Rom 8:17–18), and this hope constitutes the basis of Christian perseverance (4:1; compare 1 Cor 15:58).

APPEAL TO EUODIA & SYNTYCHE FOR UNITY · 4:2–3

The appeal to Euodia and Syntyche to *be of the same mind in the Lord* (verse 2 NRSV) and Paul's call to a fellow Christian at Philippi to mediate their dispute (verse 3) suggests a delicate situation involving significant members of the community

> **Euodia & Syntyche**
> Paul's direct intervention in this matter is understandable in the first century context, in which the existence and fortunes of the church in a given community depended on the informal network of personal relations surrounding a given household (Rom 16:5; 1 Cor 16:15, 19; Col 4:15; Phlm 2).

(compare Philemon or the role of Stephanas's household in 1 Cor 16:15–16). In this case, the women named *struggled beside* [Paul] *in the work of the gospel* (verse 3 NRSV), evidently as his close associates in missionary work.

SUMMARY EXHORTATIONS TO THE CHURCH · 4:4–9

A final appeal to *rejoice in the Lord always* (verse 4) introduces a concluding exhortation to the church at large, which emphasizes the Christian posture toward an often hostile society. Everyone should see the church's *gentleness* (verse 5), a refusal to retaliate in kind when attacked (2 Cor 10:1; 1 Tim 3:3; Titus 3:2; Jas 3:17; 1 Pet 2:18). The Christian community can sustain this posture even against hostility because of its confidence that *the Lord is near* (Rom 13:11) and will soon redress the wrongs suffered by his people (Rom 12:17–21). It can petition God boldly for its needs (verse 6) as the *peace that God's heavenly kingdom brings reshapes hearts and ... minds in Christ Jesus* (verse 7).

Paul next identifies specific qualities that the church should cultivate, which have in common their unchallengeable goodness (verse 8), which will also be *evident to all* (verse 5). Most striking is the prominence in this list of that which *is excellent*, evoking the Greek philosophical ideal of "human excellence" as the basis of ethics and politics. Paul's letter suggests that this ideal is fulfilled in the Christian life of self-denying service and humility (2:3, 8; 3:21; 4:12). Paul appeals to his ministry and his imprisonment as exemplifying such virtue and supplying a model for the Philippians' continued practice, which will ensure God's presence with the church even in suffering (verse 9).

CONCLUDING EXPRESSION OF JOY · 4:10–20

The letter's conclusion returns to Paul's circumstances and expresses his joy at having received the Philippians' tangible expression for concern for his well-being (verse 10). In context (verses 11–12), the climactic declaration *I can do everything through him who gives me strength* (verse 13) refers to the ability God grants Paul to endure external conditions rather than to perform impressive spiritual feats (but see Rom 15:17–19; 2 Cor 12:12). Paul acknowledges the Philippians' recent kindness (verse 14) and recalls their history of financial support of his ministry (verses 15–16; contrast 1 Cor 9:11–12, 15; 2 Cor 12:13), a corollary of their participation in its spiritual blessings (verses 17–18; see Rom 15:25–27). As before (1:18–26), Paul expresses his confidence in God's provision for the church's welfare (verses 19–20; see 1:25–26).

GREETINGS & BENEDICTION · 4:21–23

Paul invites the Philippians to *greet every saint* (verse 21a NRSV), by implication through the congregational exchange of the holy kiss (Rom 16:16; 1 Cor 16:20; 2 Cor 13:12; 1 Thess 5:26), and extends greetings from the Christians in his presence (verse 21b), singling out *the saints ... who belong to Cæsar's household* for special mention (verse 22). These perhaps included the households of Artistobulus and Narcissus (Rom 16:10–11), and in any case their mention increases the likelihood that Philippians was written from Rome (Bockmuehl 269–70; Fee 459). As is Paul's usual custom (Rom 16:20; 1 Cor 16:23; 2 Cor 13:13; Gal 6:18; Eph 6:24; Col 4:18; 1 Thess 5:28; 2 Thess 3:18), the letter concludes with a benediction pronounced on the congregation gathered for worship at the Lord's table (verse 23).

THEOLOGICAL REFLECTIONS

Three principal themes unite this encouraging book. First, the Philippians share a partnership in Paul's gospel (1:5, 7), which involves their suffering for Christ (1:29–30), imitating Paul's sacrificial service (3:3–4:1; 4:8–9), and financially supporting his mission (2:25; 4:10–20). Second, they adopt as the basis of their life together the sacrificial mindset of Christ in his earthly life (2:5–7), as well as of Paul (3:4–17; 4:9) and his coworkers (2:19–30; 3:17), more precisely characterized as "humility" (see 2:3, 8; 3:21; 4:12). And, third, they should embrace the joy that characterizes life in Christ (2:18, 28–29; 3:1; 4:4; compare 2:2), which Paul exhibits despite his captivity (1:4, 18; 2:17; 4:1, 10). This friendly letter thus encourages a vigorous Christian community life that can serve as a model for the church in any circumstance.

FOR FURTHER STUDY

Richard Bauckham, *God Crucified: Monotheism and Christology in the New Testament* (Grand Rapids: Eerdmans, 1999).

Markus Bockmuehl, *The Epistle to the Philippians* (Peabody, Mass.: Hendrickson, 1998)

Ralph P. Martin and Brian J. Dodd, eds., *Where Christology Began: Essays on Philippians 2* (Louisville: Westminster John Knox, 1998).

WORKS CITED

Richard Bauckham, *God Crucified: Monotheism and Christology in the New Testament* (Grand Rapids: Eerdmans, 1999).

Markus Bockmuehl, *The Epistle to the Philippians* (Peabody, Mass.: Hendrickson, 1998).

R. Alistair Campbell, *The Elders: Seniority within Earliest Christianity* (Edinburgh: T & T Clark, 1994).

Gordon D. Fee, *Paul's Letter to the Philippians* (Grand Rapids: Eerdmans, 1995).

Ralph P. Martin and Brian J. Dodd, eds., *Where Christology Began: Essays on Philippians 2* (Louisville: Westminster John Knox, 1998).

Margaret M. Mitchell, *Paul and the Rhetoric of Reconciliation: An Exegetical Investigation of the Language and Composition of 1 Corinthians* (Louisville: Westminster John Knox, 1991).

Plato, *Laches, Protagoras, Meno, Euthydemus* (ed. and trans. W. R. M. Lamb; Cambridge: Harvard University Press, 1924).

James W. Thompson, *Pastoral Ministry according to Paul: A Biblical Vision* (Grand Rapids: Baker, 2006).

Colossians

J. Paul Pollard

CHAPTER CONTENTS

Contexts **973**

Commentary **974**

    Greeting · 1:1–2 **974**

    The Body of the Letter · 1:3–4:6 **974**

    Final greetings · 4:7–18 **976**

Theological Reflections **977**

For Further Study **977**

Works Cited **977**

Colosse was located in western Asia Minor about 120 miles east of Ephesus in the Lycus Valley. In the time of Paul, it was smaller and less important than the nearby cities Laodicea and Hierapolis. Although discovered in 1835, the city has never been excavated (Reicke 429–30).

The Colossian church faced many spiritual problems. Most of the people were animists, believing in the existence of gods and goddesses along with the world of good and evil spirits. In this religiously pluralistic environment, the Colossians daily came into contact with a multitude of pagan deities. At the time, it was not the norm for pagans to worship only one deity. Instead, they worshiped several, frequently blending religious ideas and worship forms. Overshadowing their lives was an intense fear of the pagan divinities, whether good or bad. Spirits and powers filled their world, controlling fate and influencing daily life. Especially worrisome were the spirits of deceased ancestors. The Colossians turned to chants, amulets, and magic to ward off malevolent spirits, and numerous inscriptions indicate that people called on angels for help (Arnold, Syncretism, 21–29).

Paul did not establish the church in Colosse. In the mid-50s CE, he spent a long period of his ministry in Ephesus, where evidently Epaphras came into contact with the gospel and then carried it to Colosse (1:7). From there it probably spread to Laodicea. Philemon and Colossians are closely related, being addressed to some of the same people, and Tychicus carried both letters to Colosse (4:8–9).

CONTEXTS

It is difficult to identify precisely the problem Paul opposes in Colosse. Scholarly debate over the nature of this "heresy" continues and is one of the most difficult issues faced by interpreters of the letter. Two major options are Gnosticism and Jewish mysticism, or perhaps a combination of the two (Bornkamm 130; Lyonnet 137; see also Dunn 34–35). The Colossian "heresy" seems to have been a blending of pagan religion, traditional superstitions, Judaism, and Christianity. Apparently, Paul is dealing with a crisis in the church brought on by pressures to conform to the beliefs and practices of their pagan and Jewish neighbors (Hooker 329). In addition, certain leaders were pushing these ideas (2:8, 16).

The Colossian church faced a crisis caused by dangerous cultural and societal influences and attempted to find security by obeying Jewish regulations or rites promising relief from the evil forces. In 2:8, Paul characterized the church as embracing a destructive "philosophy" involving human tradition and the elemental spirits, perhaps rejecting Jesus as their mediator and depending instead on angelic beings (2:18) for protection from a vengeful spirit world. Because of the dangers threatening them, Paul urged the church to focus on the exalted Christ and resist all attempts to downplay his headship. In Paul's view, since salvation and redemption are complete in Christ, the Colossians should not look to other sources.

> **Authorship of Colossians**
>
> Although a significant number of scholars consider Paul the author of Colossians, a growing majority deem it inauthentic, largely on the basis of its style and eschatology ("last things"; see 2:12–13; 3:1). However, the style of Colossians resembles that of Philippians and Philemon, and the charge that eschatology in Colossians is different misconstrues the text. In short, the traditional attribution to Paul makes sense (Johnson 357–59).

COLOSSIANS

COMMENTARY

GREETING · 1:1–2

Paul mentions his status as an *apostle*, perhaps to enhance his authority in a congregation he did not establish. He warmly describes them as *holy and faithful*, assuming their devotion in the face of serious problems in the church.

THE BODY OF THE LETTER · 1:3–4:6

1:3–14 The thanksgiving and prayer section (1:3–8) provides important clues about the main concerns of the epistle. Noticeably, Paul does not attack the Colossian problem directly. Instead, he commends their *faith and love* (1:5) and their eternal *hope* (compare 1:23, 27). Paul asks the Colossians not to give up what they already have for some new philosophy or teaching. In contrast to the localized heretical influences, the gospel brought to them by Epaphras (a short form of Epaphroditus) is universal, *bearing fruit all over the world*. By commending faithful *Epaphras*, Paul validates their reception of the true apostolic gospel (O'Brien 16).

Paul prays that the Colossians will be filled with *knowledge* of God's will, especially needful in dealing with false approaches to spirituality (1:9–14). This "knowledge" involves two key ingredients: *spiritual wisdom and understanding*. Without being able to discern the situation around them, they cannot cope with the dangers they face. Paul also prays that their lifestyle would reflect their Christian commitment instead of the *false humility* and the *harsh treatment of the body* advocated by others (2:23). He prays as well for an increase in their *knowledge of God* (instead of the false knowledge others display). He says more about *knowledge* and *wisdom* later in the letter (*knowledge*, 2:2; 3:10; *wisdom*, 1:28; 2:3, 23; 3:16; 4:5; compare "understanding," 2:2).

He also prays for strengthening with the *power* that comes from the Lord's *glorious might* so that they can have the essential qualities necessary for survival, namely *endurance and patience*. Paul further reminds them that they have been given an inheritance of the *saints* in the light (NIV has *in the kingdom of light*), probably referring to God's presence. Before becoming Christians, they lived in the *dominion of darkness*, but God brought them into the *kingdom* of his son.

1:15–20 It is absolutely crucial for Paul's argument that he demonstrate the superiority of Christ over all other spiritual forces. He does this by showing Christ first as creator of all things (1:15–17) and also as head of the church. Although we cannot be sure whether Paul composed this hymn or adopted it in whole or in part, the general scholarly consensus today is that 1:15–20 is a pre-Pauline text (see Cannon 19–37; Sanders 75–97). In the first part, using language that connects with the Colossian problem, Paul asserts that Christ is superior to *thrones*, *powers*, *rulers*, and *authorities*. All of God's *fullness* dwells in him, and by his death and resurrection he reconciles all things to the Father. The reconciling work of Christ spills over into the next section (1:21–23), and the ideas found in 1:15–20 buttress the rest of the letter.

> **Early Christian Hymns**
> *The New Testament contains a few texts that apparently were early Christian hymns. The most famous is Philippians 2:5–11. These texts tend to confess the story of Jesus' surrender of heavenly glory for the sake of a sinful humanity and then his resumption of glory, which leads to our own ultimate resurrection.*

1:21–23 Though once *alienated from God* and *enemies*, the Colossians have been reconciled by Christ's death. The exact phrase is *reconciled by his physical body*. This may be Paul's way of emphasizing the realness of Christ's body over against views that deemphasize his corporeal nature (as later the Gnostics will do) or perhaps in preparation for discussion of the body in verse 24. *Reconciliation* [Greek *apakatallasso*] describes the removal of barriers between God and us. Having been *reconciled*, Paul advocates their firm stand in the *hope of the gospel*. Once they were *enemies*, and they must be careful not to return to that condition.

1:24–2:7 Paul rejoices at what was *suffered* on their behalf, saying that *I fill up in my flesh what is still lacking in regard to Christ's afflictions*. This suffering on Paul's part is for the *sake of his body, which is the church*. What the apostle means here is highly debated. Paul can hardly be saying that what Christ did on the cross was somehow lacking and that Paul is going to complete what shortage was needed. Rather, a better solution is to take *Christ's afflictions* in a broader sense, perhaps referring to the messianic afflictions of the end time, the woes of the Messiah (see Matt 24:8; Mark 13:8). Paul himself, like all Christians, shares in the messianic afflictions just as Christ did (though Christ surely suffered in a much fuller way by going to the cross), and through Paul's own service in Christ's corporate body (the church), he somehow lessens the sufferings of the righteous (Best 136).

The bottom line is that Paul's ministry involves *the mystery* hidden through the ages but now made known to the *Gentiles*. The content of that long kept secret is *Christ in you*, *the hope of glory*. Paul's goal is to make known this *mystery* so that everyone may be *perfect* (this may also be the claim of the opponents in Colosse); as a result, they can fathom the full *mystery of God* (2:2) – that in Christ are *hidden all the treasures of wisdom and knowledge*. Since they know where true *wisdom and knowledge* are found, they should stand *firm* against deceptive and *fine sounding arguments* (2:4). This means continuing to *live in him* (Christ) and producing Christian fruits (2:6–7).

2:8–23 For the first time in the letter, Paul discusses what the Colossians face, warning against empty and *deceptive philosophy* based on *human tradition* and *the best principles* [Greek *stoicheia*] *of this world*.

> **"Stoicheia"**
> Although variously interpreted, stoicheia most likely has to do with spirit beings and is another way of referring to the powers of darkness. Stoicheia takes its place alongside other terms in Colossians, such as "principalities," "powers," "authorities," and "thrones," indicating the demonic nature of the challenge the church faces (Arnold, Colossians, 384–85).

Because of deceptive teachings and demonic spirits, Paul emphasizes here, as he does repeatedly in Colossians, the superiority of Christ as the *head over every power and authority* (2:9–10). He invokes Old Testament terminology by arguing that those *in him* have experienced a type of *circumcision* by being baptized (2:12). Paul says that in baptism we put off the *sinful nature* (2:11). The NIV translation might imply (incorrectly) that we are born with a sinful nature (compare Matt 18:2–5; 19:13–14; Ridderbos 65–68, 93–95, 102–103), and so a better translation would be *fleshly body*, indicating our natural gravitation to the ways of the flesh rather than to the Spirit. In essence, we acknowledge by being baptized that sin and the flesh no longer dominate us.

The reality is that we were *dead* in our sins before Christ made us *alive* in him (2:13). Being made alive involves *canceling the written code* with all of its *regulations* [Greek *dogma*]. Since this *written code* was taken away by being *nailed to the cross*, it is frequently argued that this refers to the Old Testament, which was removed at the cross to make room for the new covenant. However, while it is true that the same word for *regulations* occurs in Ephesians 2:15, where it refers to the individual commands of the Mosaic law, here in verse 14 it is not linked to the usual word for law [Greek *nomos*] but to *cheirographon*, which means, "a handwritten document," specifically "a certificate of indebtedness" or "record of debts" (Bauer 1083). What is nailed to the cross is the agreement, or *contract*, with its binding demands of our indebtedness to God. God completely removes the papers proving our indebtedness (Yates, "Metaphor," 13). By doing this, he routs the *powers and authorities*, decisively defeating the evil supernatural forces, making a public show of them, just as defeated enemies were displayed in parade by victorious generals.

> **Baptism**
> Just as circumcision *set apart Israel from the nations as a covenant people, baptism sets apart Christians. Baptism is a burial and much like Paul's description in Romans 6, signifies our dying and rising with Christ by faith (Tannehill 70–71). Clearly, baptism's power lies in its connection to the cross and Christ's overcoming death.*

Evidently, those who practice asceticism criticize what Christians *eat or drink* and try to coerce them into observing certain Jewish *festivals*, *New Moon* celebrations, or *Sabbath* days which are bound up with serving the principalities and powers (2:16–23). These, however, are only a *shadow* of the reality God opens up for Christians and must not be added to the worship of Christ (compare Heb 10:1). Paul warns against those who parade about a *false humility* and *worship angels* (who might help them ward off evil forces). Following the lead of such persons can only disqualify the Colossian Christians from their heavenly prize. Paul further discredits the opponents by saying they are braggarts (2:18). By using the Greek word embateuo (NIV *goes into great detail*) which was used as a technical term for initiation into the mystery cults, Paul exposes the tactics of those who entice believers by claiming spiritual authority based on special knowledge and visionary experiences (Francis 197–207; Yates, "Worship," 13). Following such teachers, however, takes their focus off the *Head*, who is Christ.

Just as Christ died on the cross defeating evil forces, they also *died with Christ* (2:20; see also 2:12). They died to the *basic principles* [Greek *stoicheia*] *of this world* (see 2:8), and, that being true, they must not submit to rules and regulations that uphold the authority of evil spirit forces, such as *Do not handle! Do not taste! Do not touch!* Paul does not explain these terms, but they probably have to do with certain ascetic practices of those involved in *false humility* (perhaps fasting) and *harsh treatment of the body* (2:23). Outwardly, they look like people of *wisdom*, but their actions do not successfully discipline the flesh.

3:1–17 Ascetic practices do not promote ethical living, but being *raised with Christ* and setting the mind on things above does. Their lives are *hidden with Christ* (3:3), and when he returns, they will share in his *glory* (3:4) and judgment (contrast *the wrath of God* mentioned in 3:6). Vice and virtue lists (3:5–8) are very common in the New Testament (for example, Rom 1:29–30; 1 Cor 5:9–11; 6:9–10; Gal 5:19–23; Phil 4:8; 1 Tim 3:1–13; Titus 1:5–9; 1 Pet 4:3). Living ethically, as Paul argues in 3:9–10, involves taking off the *old self* (life in the old Adam) and putting on the *new self* (life in Christ as the new Adam). Racial, religious, cultural, and social barriers cannot exist in this new way of life (3:11).

> **"Barbarians" & "Scythians"**
> *From the Greek perspective, "barbarians" are non-Hellenic, non-Greek speaking people (Bauer 166), and the "Scythians," who lived in what is today Ukraine, were considered a "crude, ferocious, and inhuman people" (Martin 249).*

The virtue list in 3:12 stresses the importance of forgiving each other. Other qualities include *compassion, kindness, humility, gentleness and patience*. Above all else, they needed *love*, leading to *perfect unity* in their new community together. The currents of change sweeping through the church made *peace* especially important. In addition, they must meditate on the *word of Christ* as they teach and admonish each other by singing *psalms, hymns and spiritual songs* (see Eph 5:19). It is not possible to distinguish between the three terms (Schlier 164). Although the adjective *spiritual* is grammatically linked to the last term, it refers to all three nouns, indicating the Spirit's influence over the entire process. *In your hearts* does not mean silent worship by each Christian, else no admonishing or edification could take place (compare Ferguson 268–73).

3:18–4:1 Paul's advice to households (the so called "household codes") is most fully represented here and in Ephesians 5:22–33. Similar teaching appears in 1 Timothy 2:1–5; 5:1–2; 6:1–2, 17–19; Titus 2:1–3:8; and 1 Peter 2:13–3:7. The special form of the teaching involves advice to various members of the household concerning appropriate behavior. Many issues revolve around household codes, such as their source (Aristotle, Stoicism, or Hellenistic Judaism, especially Philo) and function in the New Testament (Crouch). Paul's practice differs from other such codes in antiquity in that he tries to shape believers' conduct based on Christ's lordship. He promotes social behavior that is respectable to outsiders in order to move the Colossians from infatuation with heresy to more practical matters (O'Brien 219).

> **Slaves & Masters**
> *Paul's advice to "slaves" and "masters" indicates that some early Christians owned slaves. Many slaves were Christians, and when the master was also a Christian, a new dynamic existed (see the letter to Philemon).*

4:2–6 Paul asks Christians to pray that he could continue preaching, though in prison. Ever concerned about influencing outsiders, Paul admonishes them to use every opportunity for making a good impression on nonbelievers. Their speech, therefore, was to be *full of grace, seasoned with salt*.

FINAL GREETINGS · 4:7–18

Paul concludes his letter as he usually does, with personal greetings and final comments. *Tychicus* and *Onesimus* will bring news from him and others in prison (in addition to bringing the letter). Various prisoners send their greetings, and he warmly notes the presence of several fellow Jews with him, especially commending *Epaphras* for his ministry. *Luke* is noted, along with *Demas* (but see 2 Tim 4:10). This is the first reference to Luke as *the beloved physician* (NIV reads *the doctor*). Efforts to prove conclusively by Luke's vocabulary that he was a medical doctor have not succeeded. Paul instructs the Colossians to share letters with the church at *Laodicea*, indicating the oral nature even of written material (see Havelock, Ong, Harvey). He closes with instructions to *Archippus* and adds his own signature to authenticate the letter.

THEOLOGICAL REFLECTIONS

The Christ-hymn of Colossians 1:15–20 sets the tone for the entire letter in its teachings about the person of Christ. Paul's central focus is on the supremacy of Jesus in contrast to all competing spiritual forces. He reinforces his argument by stating that Christ is the image of God (compare Genesis 1:26–27) and the firstborn over all creation. In stating that the preexistent Christ (1:17) created all things, Paul uses terminology that closely resembles pre-Christian Jewish references to personified Wisdom (compare Prov 8:22–25). Christ is also the head of the body, the church. As the head, he has an organic connection to the body, unlike the cosmic powers. Since he is the image of God and in him dwells the fullness of all that God is, this "Cosmic Christ" is preeminent in all things (1:18–19).

Those who have been delivered must lead a life that reflects the freedom Christ makes possible. This means staying free from human regulations and anything that tries to supplant Christ (2:8). Since we have died and been raised with Christ in baptism, we now live on a new plane (2:12), rejecting worldly living and old external distinctions (3:11). Instead, Christian virtues should dominate (3:12–14), and particularly love should prevail. Christian ethics and proper conduct must be displayed not only before outsiders (4:4–5) but also especially in the Christian household (3:18–25).

Christians today, like those at Colosse, find themselves involved in spiritual warfare. Although the Western world tends to discount the reality of spiritual forces, purely naturalistic explanations are not able to explain many forms of evil (Arnold, *Powers*, 176–82).

Finally, Colossians has an important message for the modern church, which also has many voices attempting to lure it away from the centrality of Christ. When Christ is supreme in our lives and in the church, we will not be led away by fine-sounding arguments and deceptive philosophy (2:4, 8). Instead, our hearts will be set on things above, where Christ sits at the right hand of God (3:1).

FOR FURTHER STUDY

Peter Gorday, *Colossians, 1–2 Thessalonians, 1–2 Timothy, Titus, Philemon* (Downers Grove, Ill.: InterVarsity Press, 2000).

Marianne Meye Thompson, *Colossians & Philemon* (Grand Rapids: Eerdmans, 2005).

WORKS CITED

Clinton E. Arnold, *Colossian Syncretism: The Interface between Christianity and Folk Belief at Colossae* (Grand Rapids: Baker, 1996).

———, *Colossians* (Grand Rapids: Zondervan, 2002).

———, *Powers of Darkness: Principalities & Powers in Paul's Letters* (Downers Grove, Ill.: InterVarsity Press, 1992).

Walter Bauer, *A Greek-English Lexicon of the New Testament and Other Early Christian Literature* (3rd ed.; ed. Frederick W. Danker; Chicago: University of Chicago Press, 2000).

Ernest Best, *One Body in Christ* (London: SPCK, 1955).

Gunther Bornkamm, "The Heresy of Colossians," in *Conflict at Colossae* (eds. Fred O. Francis and Wayne Meeks; Missoula: Scholars Press, 1973), 123–45.

George E. Cannon, *The Use of Traditional Materials in Colossians* (Macon, Ga.: Mercer University Press, 1983).

J. E. Crouch, *The Origin and Intention of the Colossian Haustafel* (Göttingen: Vandenhoeck & Ruprecht, 1972).

J. D. G. Dunn, *The Epistles to the Colossians and to Philemon* (Grand Rapids: Eerdmans, 1996).

Everett Ferguson, *The Church of Christ: A Biblical Ecclesiology for Today* (Grand Rapids: Eerdmans, 1996).

Fred O. Francis, "The Background of EMBATEYEIN (Col. 2:18) in Legal Papyri and Oracle Inscriptions," in *Conflict at Colossae* (eds. Fred O. Francis and Wayne Meeks; Missoula: Scholars Press, 1973), 197–207.

John D. Harvey, *Listening to the Text: Oral Patterning in Paul's Letters* (Grand Rapids: Baker, 1998).

Eric A. Havelock, *The Muse Learns to Write: Reflections on Orality and Literacy from Antiquity to the Present* (New Haven: Yale University Press, 1986).

M. D. Hooker, "Were there False Teachers in Colossae?" in *Christ and the Spirit in the New Testament* (eds. Barnabas Lindars and S. S. Smalley; Cambridge: Cambridge University Press, 1973), 315–31.

Luke T. Johnson, *The Writings of the New Testament: An Interpretation* (Philadelphia: Fortress, 1990).

Stanislas Lyonnet, "Paul's Adversaries in Colossae," in *Conflict at Colossae* (eds. Fred O. Francis and Wayne Meeks; Missoula: Scholars Press, 1973), 147–61.

Troy Martin, "The Scythian Perspective," *Novum Testamentum* 37 (1995): 249–61.

Peter T. O'Brien, *Colossians, Philemon* (Waco, Tex.: Word, 1982).

Walter Ong, *Orality and Literacy: The Technologizing of the Word* (London: Methune, 1982).

Bo Reicke, "The Historical Setting of Colossians," *Review and Expositor* 70 (Fall 1973): 429–38.

Herman Ridderbos, *Paul: An Outline of His Theology* (Grand Rapids: Eerdmans, 1975).

Jack T. Sanders, *The New Testament Christological Hymns: Their Historical Religious Background* (Cambridge: Cambridge University Press, 1971).

H. Schlier, "Ado," *Theological Dictionary of the New Testament* 1 (1964): 163–65.

Robert C. Tannehill, *Dying and Rising with Christ: A Study in Pauline Theology* (Berlin: Töpelmann, 1966).

Roy Yates, "Colossians 2,14: Metaphor of Forgiveness," *Biblica* 71 (1990): 248–59.

———, "'The Worship of Angels' (Col 2:18)," *Expository Times* (October 1985): 12–15.

1 Thessalonians

Christopher R. Hutson

CHAPTER CONTENTS

- Contexts 979
- Commentary 980
  - Epistolary Opening · 1:1–3:13 980
  - The Body of the Letter · 4:1–5:24 981
  - Epistolary Closing · 5:25–28 983
- Theological Reflections 983
- For Further Study 983
- Works Cited 983

The earliest writing in the New Testament (dating to about 50 CE), 1 Thessalonians offers the earliest written witness to the memory of Jesus. In it, Paul shapes new converts into a community and discusses resurrection and the coming of the Lord, so the letter is a resource for pastoral method and for eschatology.

CONTEXTS

Thessalonian Christians have been experiencing affliction (1:6; 2:14; 3:3–4; compare Acts 17:5–9; 2 Cor 8:2), so Paul has sent Timothy to *strengthen and encourage* them (3:2). This letter follows up on Timothy's work.

Several possible sources of pressure exist for the new converts (Still, 126–267). First, local synagogue officials are zealous defenders of Jewish identity (Acts 17:5, where NIV's *jealous* misses the point; see Acts 18:12) who may see Paul as a threat to their hard-won rights to practice their religion (Smallwood 121–43). Second, mob action (Acts 17:5) suggests that pagans could see Christians as undermining their cultural values by neglecting traditional gods (2:14; Donfried, "Cults," 337–42). Third, Thessalonica is a Roman provincial capital and has temples of Roma and the emperor (Hendrix 524–25; Donfried, "Cults," 342–46), so talk about the "coming of Lord Jesus" (2:19; 3:13) or a "king other than Cæsar" (Acts 17:7) could bring charges of sedition (Acts 16:20–21; 17:7). Fourth, any or all of these opposition groups might discredit Paul as a fly-by-night scam artist and so create doubt in the minds of his new converts (2:3–6; Malherbe, *Popular Philosophers*, 38–39). Paul's letter equips the Christians to respond to such opposition.

It is possible to analyze the letter according to ancient rhetorical or letter writing conventions. Both rhetorical and epistolary analyses are useful, and recent trends have been toward synthesizing approaches (Donfried and Beutler). This commentary favors epistolary analysis, but in any case, one must see how all parts of the letter function together to achieve the intended effect.

An ancient letter writer typically expressed thanks to the gods before beginning the letter body. This letter contains three thanksgivings (1:2–10; 2:13–16; 3:9–10), interspersed with two narratives (2:1–12; 2:17–3:10). Chapters 1–3 form an extended introduction as long as the body of the letter. Here, Paul describes the church as family, using kinship metaphors: *father* (1:1, 3; 2:11; 3:11), *brother* (1:4; 2:1, 9, 14, 17; 3:2, 7), *mother* (2:7), and *children* (2:7, 11). In addition, he praises the Thessalonians for what they already are (1:3, 6–8; 2:13–16, 19–20; 3:6–9). Further, he offers himself as a model to imitate (1:6; 2:1–12; 17–18). Finally, he recalls his previous teaching (1:9–10; 3:3–4). In these ways, Paul lays a foundation for exhortations and teaching in the body of the letter.

The letter body contains exhortations about how to live in God's eschatological family. Chapters 4–5 build on the kinship metaphors *brothers* (4:1, 6, 10, 13; 5:1, 4, 12, 14, 25, 27) and *brotherly love* (4:9). Paul exhorts Christians to care for one another (4:1–12, 18; 5:11, 12–22) in light of the *eschaton* (4:13–5:11). Each half of the letter ends with a prayer for sanctification (3:11–13; 5:23–24).

> **The *Eschaton***
>
> *The Greek word* eschaton *("end, last thing") has become a popular name for the end of time. Paul called his readers to live in expectation of the approaching return of Christ.*

1 THESSALONIANS

COMMENTARY

EPISTOLARY OPENING · 1:1–3:13

1:1 Greco-Roman letter openings typically included the names of the author(s), the addressee(s), and a greeting, in that order. *Paul* identifies himself by name only, reflecting his friendly relationship with the addressees. Although he identifies two coauthors and writes throughout in the first person plural (*we*), Paul expresses his own viewpoint, since he lapses into the singular (2:18) and writes about Timothy in the third person (3:1–2, 6). *Silas and Timothy* helped evangelize Thessalonica (Acts 17:1, 5, 10; 1 Thess 3:2, 6), and all three teachers maintain concern for the addressees.

As a family *in God the Father*, the church offers a home for new converts estranged from their biological families (Malherbe, *Popular Philosophers*, 117–20). *In the Lord Jesus Christ* describes the church's submission to the Messiah and thus the converts' tensions with their society, since they now worship a lord higher than Cæsar.

Grace [Greek *charis*] is a pun on the standard Greek letter opening, "greetings" [Greek *chairein*], while *peace* reflects the Jewish greeting, *shalom*.

1:2–10 In this first prayer, Paul introduces themes and portrays the Thessalonians as a model church, which serves to strengthen and encourage the readers amid suffering and doubt.

We remember you is thematic. Paul wants his readers to remember the story the way he does, so he constantly says, "you remember" (2:9), "as you know" (1:5; 2:1, 2, 5, 11; 3:4; 4:2), "you are witnesses" (2:10), and "we told you before" (3:4).

Work, *labor*, and *steadfastness* are concrete expressions of Christian *faith*, *love*, and *hope*. *Work* is how one earns a living (2:9; 4:11), so supporting oneself expresses faithfulness. Paul often uses *labor* [Greek *kopos*] to refer to evangelism (2:9; 3:5; 5:12; Gal 4:11; Phil 2:16), so here he implies that the Thessalonians are evangelistic. *Endurance* [Greek *hypomone*, "perseverance"] is a hallmark of faithfulness under duress (Rom 5:3; 2 Cor 1:6; compare Jas 1:3). As new converts, the readers may feel shaky, but *faith*, *love*, and *hope* protect them (5:8).

Paul preached *with power* and *the Holy Spirit*, which suggests that he worked miracles in Thessalonica, as at Philippi (Acts 16:16–18; see Rom 15:19). On Paul's *deep conviction*, see 2:1–12.

Imitators of Jesus expect to suffer (2:14; Acts 17:4; 1 Cor 4:16; 11:1). The Thessalonians' *suffering* [Greek *thlipsis*, "affliction," 3:3, 4, 7] must have included the anxiety of estrangement from family and friends (Malherbe, *Paul and the Thessalonians*, 34–52); however anxiety could also be triggered by real opposition. Yet affliction is an occasion for *joy* (2 Cor 7:4; 8:2), *given by the Holy Spirit* (Rom 14:17; Gal 5:22).

The Thessalonians in turn have served as a *model* for others (2 Cor 8:1), so that *the message rang out*. Their faithful actions (4:10) make them evangelists by example.

Paul recalls the main points he preached in Thessalonica, focusing on the cross (1 Cor 15:3–4) and judgment (Rom 2:16). *From idols* indicates that Paul's target readers were Gentiles, though Acts 17:4 mentions some Jewish converts. *The living and true God* (Jer 10:10) was a standard motif in Jewish preaching against idols (Acts 14:15; 15:19–20; compare Jer 51:17–19; Sirach 18:1; *Bel and the Dragon* 5). Paul preached that God *raised* Jesus *from the dead* (4:14); Jesus is coming *from heaven* (3:13); and he *rescues us* from slavery to death (Rom 7:24; 8:21; Col 1:13). *Wrath* refers to God's final judgment (2:16; 3:13; 5:9; Rom 1:18; 2:5; 12:19). Death/Sin has enslaved the world, because fear of Death leads to selfish sin. But the cross moves people to seek the interests of others even at personal risk, trusting God for resurrection. In sum, Paul preached an apocalyptic gospel according to which the resurrection mortally wounded death, and those who die to themselves and submit to the lordship of Christ escape slavery to death. When Jesus comes, he will destroy death (1 Cor 15:26) and vindicate those who submit to the lordship of Christ.

2:1–12 Paul's behavior in Thessalonica presents a model for readers to imitate (Malherbe, *Paul and the Thessalonians*, 52–60). *Opposition* (literally, "struggle") *in Philippi* (Acts 16:16–24) included resistance from the owners of a slave girl, anti-Jewish rhetoric, charges of treason, mob attack, and imprisonment. Yet Paul *dared to tell*, like one who frankly says what is true rather than what is popular (Malherbe, *Popular Philosophers*, 58–60). Family and friends might dismiss Paul as a charlatan (of the type popular in literature of his time; see Apuleius, *Golden Ass*, 2.12–14; 9.8; Lucian, *Professor of Rhetoric*; *Alexander the False Prophet*; *Peregrinus* 11–16; *The Runaways* 9–21; Plutarch, *Oracles at Delphi*, *Moralia* 407C).

But Paul was not a huckster who would preach with *impure motives* or *flattery* or *burden* converts with harsh demands. Rather, he was extremely gentle with them. *Like a mother* is literally, "like a nurse suckling her own children."

To share…our lives means they gave all they had, even risked death. Paul *worked night and day* to support himself (see comments on 1:3). *While we preached* suggests that his work and evangelism were not separate, and he may have taught in his workshop (Hock 31–42). *Toil and hardship* is better translated "labor and toil" (2 Thess 3:8). *Toil* [Greek *kopos*] is Paul's metaphor for evangelism (see 1:3). *Hardship* [Greek *mochthos*] is physical exertion or "toil." The NIV renders these as synonyms, but verse 9 forms a chiastic pattern (A B B' A'):

> A labor and
> B toil
> B' worked night and day …
> A' preached the gospel.

> **Chiasmus**
> A common rhetorical devise involving a reversal of words in two otherwise parallel phrases, such as "the loving acts of Yahweh never cease, indeed, never ending are his mercies" (Lam 3:22). There are many examples in the Bible of such a technique.

Like a *father*, Paul is sensitive to individual needs: *encouraging* people to do what they know; *comforting* (or "consoling") those who suffer loss; and *urging* [Greek *martyromai*], that is, affirming a proposition by calling others to bear witness (compare *you are witnesses* in 2:10; 4:6).

2:13–16 This prayer recalls the Thessalonians' conversion (1:2–10). *Word of God* echoes 1:8. The *word* is *at work in you* as the Holy Spirit animates the proclamation (1:5).

On *imitators*, see 1:6. What the *churches in Judea … suffered from the Jews* is unclear, but this may reflect a possible Judean backlash against Christianity in a time of Roman aggression against Jews (Bockmuehl 18–24). *Persecuted* (literally "chased out") and *prevented from speaking* may also describe Paul's experience with the synagogue in Thessalonica (Acts 17:5–9). Paul sympathizes with Gentiles who receive opposition from *their countrymen*. He does not expect all Jews to be destroyed (delete the comma after verse 14; and see Rom 9–11), but he exaggerates for rhetorical effect (Schlueter). God's *wrath* (1:10) falls on those who obstruct the gospel. *At last* refers to the end time (3:13; 5:23; Rom 2:5), which *has come upon them* in that they are in imminent danger of eternal destruction. Writer and readers have both experienced opposition, but in the following section, Paul puts hardships in apocalyptic perspective.

2:17–3:8 This section emphasizes the friendship between Paul and his addressees. *Torn away* (verse 17) literally means "orphaned from you." In 2:1–12, Paul described himself as brother, nursing mother and father; but now, separated from the Thessalonians, he feels like a motherless child. He depends on their love.

Paul views his mission as part of a cosmic struggle (2 Cor 10:3–5) between *Satan* and God (2 Cor 2:11; 11:14; 12:7). Verse 19 concentrates not on Paul's immediate problems but on the ultimate outcome *when Jesus comes*.

Paul trusted *Timothy* with difficult situations (1 Cor 4:17; Hutson). As *brother* and *fellow worker*, Timothy was a family member who could *strengthen and encourage*, which is also the purpose of this letter.

The Thessalonians' *trials* [Greek *thlipsis*, as in 1:6] have continued since their conversion, but Paul warned that they should expect to be *persecuted*. As in 2:18, Paul attributes afflictions to the *Tempter* (see 1 Cor 7:5), focusing on the cosmic battle between God and Satan rather than on human opposition. *Efforts* [Greek *kopos*] refers to evangelism (see comments on 1:3).

Despite hardships, the readers maintain *faith and love* (compare 1:3). Nor have they heeded any slander of Paul but have *pleasant memories*. The affection is mutual. Paul also experiences *persecution* [Greek *thlipsis*, 1:6], but he is *encouraged* by the Thessalonians' faith, again reflecting their friendship (2:17).

3:9–10 Paul's joy gives way to a third thanksgiving to God and a prayer that *we may see you again*. The exhortations in chapters 4–5 will address *what is lacking in* the practical expression of *your faith*.

3:11–13 This prayer summarizes the first half of the letter and forms a transition to the second. First, Paul's desire *to come* grows out of 3:9–10. Second, chapters 4–5 emphasize *love … for each other*, which is analogous to *ours … for you* in chapters 1–3. Third, Paul prays for the Thessalonians to be *blameless and holy* (5:23), in emulation of his own behavior (2:10). Fourth, the Christian life is wholly oriented toward *when our Lord Jesus comes* (1:9–10; 5:23–24).

1 THESSALONIANS

THE BODY OF THE LETTER · 4:1–5:24

4:1–12 *Finally*, Paul comes to the body of the letter. In chapters 4–5, he acts out his fatherly role (2:10–12), as he writes to *ask* (4:1; 5:12), *urge* [Greek *parakaleo* as in 3:2; 4:10; 5:14], and *warn* [Greek *diamartyromai*; see 4:6].

How to live (literally "walk," a Jewish metaphor for conduct) frames this section (4:1, 12). Paul encourages them to *do more and more* (4:10) what they already know from his *instructions* (4:6, 9, 11). In order to *please God*, they must first practice *holiness* (4:3, 4, 7, 8), described here as avoiding *sexual immorality*. The important distinction is not ethnic, but ethical, with a contrast between the *impure* and the *holy* (see 2:3, 10).

Lust is associated with the *heathen* (literally, "Gentiles"), but God *called* these Gentiles to a *holy life* enlivened by the *Spirit*. The Lord *will punish* at the judgment (Rom 12:19). *Lust* burns in this age, but holy lives are oriented to the end time (3:13; 5:23).

Pleasing God also entails *brotherly love, taught by God* through Paul (2:13) and definitively through the cross. A *quiet life* is not disruptive to society and so does not attract criticism (see 1 Tim 2:2, 12). *Work with your hands* implies that the addressees are not wealthy (2 Cor 8:2), but Paul dignifies manual labor as an expression of faith (1:3).

4:13–18 The formula *we do not want you to be ignorant* introduces information the readers do not know (contrast 4:1, 9). *Fall asleep* is a euphemism for death. If some converts died because of persecution, the readers might feel doubt as well as grief. Paul writes to console and to clarify the idea of bodily resurrection.

Others are nonbelievers, *who have no hope* to give them endurance (1:3). But since Jesus *died and rose again*, those who are *in him* share in his death and resurrection (compare Rom 6:1–10). *Coming* [Greek *parousia*] was a term for the arrival of any high official. It was customary to go out to *meet* a dignitary and escort him into town (Josephus, *Antiquities* 11.326–329; compare Matt 25:6; Acts 18:5). Paul describes Jesus' return like the arrival of an emperor, with a *shout*, a *voice*, and a *trumpet*.

As they continue to *encourage each other*, the Thessalonians follow Paul's example of encouragement (4:1, 10, 4:12; compare 3:2) and demonstrate mutual ministry to one another.

5:1–11 Those who try to match biblical phrases with newspaper headlines make nonsense of Scripture, because apocalyptic symbols do not predict events centuries in the future. Even though the images do not forecast our time, we see analogies between our time and Paul's, so we can learn from his exhortations to faithfulness. No one can predict when God will move (Matt 24:36–51).

The phrase *peace and safety* comes from Roman imperial propaganda (Koester 161–63), which lauded military might to secure world "peace." It also echoes Jeremiah 6:14, which criticizes religious leaders for their false sense of security in the face of God's impending judgment.

The word for *sleep* [Greek *katheudo*] is not the same as in 4:13–18. Here *wake/sleep*, *sober/drunk* and *day/night* are metaphors for moral and immoral behavior. Christians do not wage warfare against sinners (who face God's *wrath* at judgment) but against sin (2 Cor 10:3–6).

In verse 6, *others* are nonbelievers (see 4:13). Even believers who waver – *whether we are awake or asleep* – may live with Jesus, but Christians *encourage one another* (as in 4:18) to stay "awake" (Heil). *Build each other up* is literally, "build up, one on one." A private word may be more encouraging than a speech.

5:12–18 The Thessalonians should respond to one another according to varied individual needs and circumstances, as Paul modeled for them in 2:10–12.

Brotherly Love
Brotherly love *is practical*: Christians should not depend on outsiders. By taking care of their own, *they win the* respect of outsiders (3:14; compare Acts 2:42–47; Malherbe, Paul and the Thessalonians, 95–107). *They may even commend the faith to seekers*.

"They shall be caught up ..."
Paul uses *caught up* to describe his own mystical vision (2 Cor 12:2, 4). The Latin Vulgate used the verb *rapio*, from which we get the English "rapture." But modern notions of the Rapture miss Paul's point: believers will not be snatched out of the earth but will meet the Lord on his way down to reclaim the earth (see Rom 8:18–25).

Roman Patronage
In Roman society, patrons did not have official authority over their clients but social responsibility to advise, protect, and care for them, while clients owed social deference to their patrons. Patrons might provide money, a home where Christians could assemble, or other types of support.

Paul exhorts the Thessalonians to *respect* those who *work hard* [Greek *kopiao*, "labor"; see 1:3], that is, the teachers and evangelists. Those who *are over you* is literally, "who are your patrons." To *admonish* [Greek *noutheteo*] is to correct improper behavior. Paul does not identify these functions with any "office" but exhorts the Thessalonians to respect those who do them, whoever they may be.

To *warn* [Greek *noutheteo*, "admonish"] is not the exclusive domain of ordained leaders but, like encouragement, is a responsibility of all members toward one another (4:18; 5:11). *Idle* literally means "disorderly." The disorder is not specified here and could entail violations of any instructions in 4:1–12. In 2 Thessalonians 3:7–13, "disorderly" describes those who do not work, so a similar connotation here would build on 2:11; 4:11. *Encourage* (better: "console"; see 2:12) connects Paul's behavior with the way he wants the Thessalonians to behave toward one another.

Three exhortations on joy, prayer, and thanksgiving describe a Christian approach to life, which is possible amid afflictions, because Christians live oriented to the coming of the Lord (3:13; 5:34–34; compare Rom 12:12–13; Phil 4:4–6).

5:19–22 These four exhortations are about discerning the work of the Holy Spirit. While prophetic voices may come from unexpected corners, some claims of spiritual insight may be delusional, such as those justifying retaliation against persecutors. The Thessalonians should not blindly follow every so-called prophet, nor should they dismiss new ideas without exercising discernment (see 1 Cor 12:10; 14:29). The Thessalonians tested Paul's message in their persecutions and found by experience that it was from God (2:13–16).

5:23–24 This prayer, parallel to 3:11–13, closes the second half of the letter. There is no point in belaboring a distinction between *spirit* and *soul* here. Paul's emphasis is on the preparedness of the whole person as *blameless* at the *coming of the Lord*.

EPISTOLARY CLOSING · 5:25–28

A *kiss* was a typical greeting in ancient Mediterranean cultures. Whatever form is appropriate in modern societies, Christian greetings should reflect their *holy* relationship to one another. Paul's charge to *have this letter read to all the brothers* suggests that there was more than one house church in Thessalonica. Paul seeks to unify the community. The final benediction (verse 28) is typical of Pauline letters (1 Cor 16:23; 2 Cor 13:14; Gal 6:18; Phil 4:23; 1 Thess 4:28; Phlm 25).

THEOLOGICAL REFLECTIONS

This book illustrates pastoral care of new converts who are estranged from family, friends, and society. Congregations seeking to recover the spirit of first century Christianity should take to heart its emphasis on mutual support within God's family. Further, they should take seriously their submission to the lordship of Jesus, which supersedes all earthly pledges of allegiance.

FOR FURTHER STUDY

Peter Gorday, *Colossians, 1–2 Thessalonians, 1–2 Timothy, Titus, Philemon* (Downers Grove, Ill.: InterVarsity, 2000).

Abraham J. Malherbe, *The Letters to the Thessalonians: A New Translation with Introduction and Commentary* (New York: Doubleday, 1999).

WORKS CITED

Markus Bockmuehl, "1 Thessalonians 2:14–16 and the Church in Jerusalem," *Tyndale Bulletin* 52 (2001): 1–31.

Karl P. Donfried, "The Cults of Thessalonica and the Thessalonian Correspondence," *New Testament Studies* 31 (1985): 336–356.

Karl P. Donfried and Johannes Beutler, eds. *The Thessalonians Debate: Methodological Discord or Methodological Synthesis?* (Grand Rapids: Eerdmans, 2000).

J. P. Heil, "Those Now Asleep (Not Dead) Must be Awakened for the Day of the Lord in 1 Thess 5.9–10," *New Testament Studies* 46 (2000): 464–71.

Holland L. Hendrix, "Thessalonica," *Anchor Bible Dictionary* 5 (1992): 523–27.

Ronald S. Hock, *The Social Context of Paul's Ministry: Tentmaking and Apostleship* (Philadelphia: Fortress, 1980).

Christopher R. Hutson, "Was Timothy Timid? On the Rhetoric of Fearlessness (1 Corinthians 16:10–11) and Cowardice (2 Timothy 1:7)," *Biblical Research* 42 (1997): 58–73.

Helmut Koester, "Imperial Ideology and Paul's Eschatology in 1 Thessalonians," in *Paul and Empire: Religion and Power in Roman Imperial Society* (ed. R. A. Horsley; Harrisburg, Pa.: Trinity Press International, 1997), 158–66.

Abraham J. Malherbe, *Paul and the Popular Philosophers* (Minneapolis, Minn.: Fortress, 1989).

———, *Paul and the Thessalonians: The Philosophic Tradition of Pastoral Care* (Philadelphia: Fortress, 1987).

Carol Schlueter, *Filling Up the Measure: Polemical Hyperbole in 1 Thessalonians 2.14–16.* (Sheffield: Sheffield Academic Press, 1994).

E. Mary Smallwood, *The Jews under Roman Rule from Pompey to Diocletian: A Study in Political Relations* (Leiden: Brill, 1976).

Todd Still, *Conflict at Thessalonica: A Pauline Church and Its Neighbors* (Sheffield: Sheffield Academic Press, 1999).

References to ancient sources come chiefly from the Loeb Classical Library, published by Harvard University Press.

2 Thessalonians

Christopher R. Hutson

CHAPTER CONTENTS

- Contexts   985
- Commentary   985
    - Address · 1:1–2   985
    - Thanksgiving · 1:3–12   985
    - The Coming of the Lord · 2:1–15   986
    - Prayers · 2:16–3:5   987
    - Idleness · 3:6–16   987
    - Postscript · 3:17–18   987
- Theological Reflections   988
- For Further Study   988
- Works Cited   988

Modern day believers have neglected 2 Thessalonians, except for those who plunder its sensational second chapter for their own ideological ends. But one who studies the whole letter carefully will find encouragement for living with a view to the coming of the Lord.

CONTEXTS

Scholars debate whether 2 Thessalonians was really written by Paul: Possible references to a forged letter (2:2; 3:17) arouse suspicions that the author "doth protest too much," and similarities between 1 and 2 Thessalonians in phrasing, contents, and structure raise questions as to why Paul wrote two such similar letters. Did someone take 1 Thessalonians as a model and rewrite it, spinning it in a new direction? Some argue that the new spin moved away from an imminent coming of the Lord (1 Thess 4:17) to a delayed coming (2 Thess 2:3).

The issues are difficult, but pseudonymous authorship is not the only explanation. Malherbe, for example, argues that Paul realized his first letter had been misinterpreted and wrote this one as a follow-up to clarify himself (350–6). This commentary assumes that Paul wrote the letter but not that all the problems have been solved.

The authorship debate is really about historical context. If the letter is pseudonymous, it probably addresses a time of persecution late in the first century. If Paul wrote it, he probably did so close to the time of 1 Thessalonians. Both Thessalonian letters address contexts of persecution. The difference is that in 1 Thessalonians the crisis is past (1 Thess 2:14), whereas in 2 Thessalonians it is ongoing (1:5–6). But, assuming Paul wrote both, which letter was earlier? One could argue that soon after he left Thessalonica Paul sent a quick note (2 Thessalonians) via Timothy (Acts 17:13–15; 1 Thess 3:1–3). In that case, 1 Thessalonians was a follow-up after Timothy reported that the converts had weathered the crisis (Acts 18:5; 1 Thess 3:6). The more common assumption is that 2 Thessalonians addresses a new crisis of persecution that arose after Paul wrote 1 Thessalonians.

COMMENTARY

ADDRESS · 1:1–2

Although he identifies two coauthors (see 1 Thess 1:1) and writes throughout in the first person plural ("we"), *Paul* lapses into the singular at 2:5 and claims individual authorship at 3:17. *Silas and Timothy* helped evangelize Thessalonica (Acts 17:1, 5, 10; 1 Thess 3:2, 6), and all three teachers maintain concern for the readers.

THANKSGIVING · 1:3–12

Paul offers a two part prayer: thanks for the Thessalonians' perseverance to the present time (3–4) and a request that God will sustain them to the end (11–12). Between these, he puts their persecution in apocalyptic perspective (5–10), which sets a tone for chapter 2.

1:3–4 The language *we ... always thank God for you ... faith ... love ... perseverance* echoes 1 Thessalonians 1:2–3. For an example of Paul's *boast*, see 2 Corinthians 8:1–5. On the *persecutions and trials*, see the discussion above.

2 THESSALONIANS

1:5–10 The Thessalonians' perseverance and faith are *evidence* that God is *right* [Greek *dikaios*, verse 5] and *just* [Greek *dikaios*, verse 6], because, in ancient Jewish tradition, God is strict with the righteous in order to grant them eternal reward (2 Maccabees 6:12–16; Bassler 500–6). In the end, God will *pay back* (6) and *punish* (8–9) the persecutors and *give relief* to the afflicted (7). To *obey the gospel of our Lord* is to heed the crucifixion of Jesus as divine revelation. Those who do not will be punished *when the Lord Jesus is revealed* (7; see 1 Cor 1:7; 1 Pet 1:7, 13) *on the day when he comes* (10; see 2:2; 1 Thess 5:2, 4). Jesus' appearance will be startling, with *blazing fire* (see Rev 1:14; 2:18; 19:12) and *powerful angels* (see Matt 24:31; 1 Thess 3:13; 4:16). Believers do not avenge themselves but wait for God to punish evildoers (see Rom 12:14–21; Rev 19).

1:11–12 Paul prays that God's *power* will continue to invigorate the believers' *good purpose* and *faith* until the Lord comes.

THE COMING OF THE LORD · 2:1–15

This passage follows the basic model of apocalyptic theology: rebellion against God will grow stronger before the end of this age, when God will cut it off and reward the righteous in the age to come. The book of Daniel offers such an understanding to comfort righteous Jews persecuted under the Seleucid Empire (Dan 7:19–27; 8:23–35; 11:29–12:4), and Christians adapted Daniel's message to persecution by Roman authorities (Matt 24:5–31; Mark 13:9–27; Luke 21:10–28; Revelation).

> **Paul's Political Prophecy**
> Paul is not predicting specific events, and certainly not events twenty centuries in the future. He is commenting on his own time, but his apocalyptic symbols can be adapted to any context in which political powers claim divine authority.

2:1–2 The source of misunderstanding is uncertain, whether *prophecy* (literally, "spirit"), *report* (literally, "word"), or *letter*. Perhaps Paul suspected a forged letter was circulating in his name. Or perhaps some readers had misinterpreted Paul's first letter (Malherbe) and claimed the Spirit's guidance as they pressed their ideas. The point of misunderstanding was the timing of the *coming of the Lord*. It is unlikely that the Thessalonians thought the Day of the Lord had *already come* (the Greek does not say "already"), but they may have read 1 Thessalonians 4:15–17 to imply that the Day of the Lord was "at hand" (KJV). This chapter belies those who try to predict when the Lord will come by twisting phrases from Scripture to apply to current world events.

2:3 *Rebellion* (literally, "apostasy" or "departure," as in 1 Tim 4:1; Heb 3:12) suggests that the "lawless one" will come out of Christianity. Paul uses *lawlessness* [Greek *anomia*] as a synonym for uncleanness (Rom 6:19) and sin (Rom 4:7, quoting Ps 32:1; compare Heb 10:17, quoting Jer 31:24; 1 John 3:4). In 2 Corinthians 6:14–16, he associates *anomia* (NIV *wickedness*) with unbelief, darkness, Belial, and idols. The *man of lawlessness* is a human power who opposes God. He is also called, literally, "son of destruction" (the NIV's *doomed to destruction* misses the point). *Lawlessness* and *destruction* characterize his behavior.

2:4 Entering God's temple is a metaphor for claiming divine status. Political powers often claim divine authority, just as the Beast from the Sea (Rev 13) represents a political power supported by a false prophet, the Beast from the Earth. The irony is that, while he *opposes and exalts himself over everything that is called God*, the lawless one is *proclaiming himself to be God*. Any ruler can play this role.

> **Desecration of the Temple**
> There was historical precedent for pagan rulers or their agents literally entering God's temple: *Antiochus IV* in 167 BCE (1 Maccabees 1:54; 2 Maccabees 5:15–21); *the Roman general Pompey* in 63 BCE (Josephus, Antiquities 14.71–72); *and an attempt by Caligula to erect a statue of himself in 41 CE* (Josephus, Antiquities 18.261–309). However, Paul does not predict another such incident. Rather, he provides a symbolic framework for understanding earthly powers.

2:5–8 Since we do not know what Paul *used to tell* them when he was in Thessalonica, it is not clear *what is holding back* the lawless one nor *who now holds* [him] *back*. What is clear is that the restraint *will be taken out of the way*, so the lawless one will grow more powerful before the Lord *will overthrow* and *destroy* him. The *proper time* is not a date on a calendar but the opportune moment when God intervenes (Rom 9:9; Gal 6:9; 1 Pet 1:5; 5:6). *Secret*

> **"Mysteries" in Greco-Roman Religion**
>
> In Greco-Roman religion a "mystery" was a doctrine about a god, often portrayed in ritual. Paul refers to his proclamation about the cross as a "mystery" (often translated "secret" in NIV; see 1 Cor 2:1; 2:7; 4:1; 13:2; 14:1; 15:51).

power is literally, "mystery." Here the "mystery of lawlessness" is a counterfeit doctrine (9–10). *Breath of his mouth* is a metaphor for God's just and true judgment (Isa 11:4) that will expose the lies of the lawless one.

2:9 The lawless one will enjoy a *coming* (8–9) that parodies the coming of the Lord, with *counterfeit miracles, signs, and wonders*. The revelation and defeat of the lawless one will be when all earthly powers that claim religious authorization are exposed as *the work of Satan*, who promotes allegiance to human institutions and power structures as religious devotion.

2:10–12 But to those who *refuse to love the truth* (compare 1:8), God sends a *delusion*, that is, he allows them to persist in their self-delusion (Rom 1:18–32).

2:13–15 Paul's *thanks* is a rhetorical device for encouraging his readers to *stand firm* by reminding them that *God chose you to be saved* and *called you to share in the glory*. God is at work in them through the *Spirit* (compare 1:11–12). By ascribing *belief in the truth* to his readers, Paul implies that they are not deluded by Satan (10–12). The exhortation to *stand firm* and *hold to the teachings we passed on...by word of mouth or by letter* corresponds to the exhortation not to be unsettled by a word or letter in verse 2.

PRAYERS · 2:16–3:5

This section closes with two prayers (2:16–17; 3:5) that correspond to the prayer in 1:11–12.

3:1–2 By asking the Thessalonians to *pray for us*, Paul identifies with their affliction and shows that he needs their encouragement as much as they need his (see on 1 Thess 2:17; 3:6–8). Further, he models the behavior he expects from them (see 3:9).

3:3–4 Paul encourages his readers, even as he prays for God to encourage them (2:16–17). *The things we command* include *the teachings we passed on* (2:15), as opposed to any misrepresentations of Paul (2:2). It also includes the commands in the following paragraphs (3:6, 10, 12). Paul reminds the church of the teachings they have already received.

IDLENESS · 3:6–16

3:6–10 *We command you* opens a new topic (compare *we ask you*, 2:1). The word *idle* (3:6, 7, 11) is literally "disorderly," that is, out of line with the *name of the Lord* (verse 6; see 1 Thess 4:1–2) and with what *you received from us* (verse 7) and with *our instruction* (verse 14). Paul might also have in mind behavior out of line with the norms of society. The *teaching you received* refers to Paul's mission in Thessalonica, when he set an example of self-support (7–9; see comments on *labor and toil* in 1 Thess 2:7–9) and gave *this rule*: "If a man will not work ..." (verse 10; compare 1 Thess 4:11–12). Possibly, some able-bodied Christians were taking advantage of "brotherly love" (1 Thess 4:9–10), and their idleness was liable to attract criticism (Russell).

3:11–13 The wordplay *not busy* [Greek *ergazomai*] but *busybodies* [Greek *periergazomai*] continues in verse 12, where we might translate *earn* [Greek *ergazomai*] as "get busy." To *settle down* is literally to work "in quietness" (see 1 Tim 2:2), that is, not to disrupt society so as to provoke criticism from outsiders (see the discussion of 1 Thess 4:11–12; compare 1 Tim 5:11–14).

3:14–15 The community should *not associate* with a disobedient member. This is not retaliation against an *enemy*, but discipline to restore an erring brother (see 1 Cor 5:4–5; 2 Cor 2:5–11). Church discipline will only work if the member is loved by the group and wants their respect, so he will *feel ashamed* when they disapprove.

> **"The Lord be with all of you ..."**
>
> Paul's letters often end with benedictions, blessings, or prayers celebrating God's protection of the world (see Rom 16:25–27; 1 Cor 16:23; 2 Cor 13:14; Gal 6:18; Eph 6:23–24; Phil 4:23; 1 Thess 5:28; 1 Tim 6:21; 2 Tim 4:15; Phlm 25).

3:16 Closing the third section of the letter, this prayer corresponds to 1:11–12 and 2:16–3:5. At the same time, it is the benediction that closes the entire letter (see comments on 1 Thess 5:28).

POSTSCRIPT · 3:17–18

3:17–18 The *distinguishing mark* is Paul's signature, which indicates that the letter body was dictated to a secretary (Rom 16:22; Gal 6:11). *How I write* refers to handwriting style. The fact that Paul does not do this *in all his letters* arouses suspicions among some scholars that a pseudonymous author is trying to cover his tracks. Yet this signature would make sense

2 THESSALONIANS

if Paul suspected a document was circulating in his name that misrepresented his views.

THEOLOGICAL REFLECTIONS

Second Thessalonians discusses what it means to live as if the coming of the Lord is just around the corner. Persecutions and troubles diminish in perspective of the cosmic struggle between God and Satan. Because earthly powers are so easily used by Satan, submission to the Lord Jesus supersedes allegiance to any earthly realm. We must live ready for the Lord to come without pretending to predict when that will be.

FOR FURTHER STUDY

Beverly R. Gaventa, *First and Second Thessalonians* (Louisville: Westminster/John Knox Press, 1998).

Bonnie Bowman Thurston, *Reading Colossians, Ephesians, 2 Thessalonians: A Literary and Theological Commentary* (New York: Crossroad, 1995).

WORKS CITED

Jouette M. Bassler, "The Enigmatic Sign: 2 Thessalonians 1:5," *Catholic Biblical Quarterly* 46 (1984): 496–510.

Josephus, *Works* (ed. H. St. John Thackeray; 10 vols.; Cambridge: Harvard University Press, 1926–1965).

Abraham J. Malherbe, *The Letters to the Thessalonians: A New Translation with Introduction and Commentary* (New York: Doubleday, 1999).

R. Russell, "The Idle in 2 Thess 3.6–12: An Eschatological or a Social Problem?" *New Testament Studies* 34 (1988): 105–19.

1 Timothy

James W. Thompson

CHAPTER CONTENTS

Contexts   989

Commentary   990
- Salutation · 1:1–2   990
- Dangerous Teachings · 1:3–11   990
- Paul's Credentials · 1:12–17   990
- Thesis: A Charge to Keep · 1:18–20   991
- Maintaining Order & Confronting Danger · 2:1–6:2   991
- Summary of Major Themes · 6:3–21   995

Theological Reflections   995

For Further Study   996

Works Cited   996

Since the eighteenth century, the letters to Timothy and Titus have been known as the Pastoral Epistles because of their concern with the pastoral ministry of the church and because these letters share much in common with each other that they do not share with Paul's other letters. Stylistic features, including lists for officeholders and a distinctive vocabulary, distinguish these letters from Paul's earlier correspondence. Unlike those earlier letters, these all address Paul's envoys, who act in his absence. Timothy is the son of a Jewish mother and Gentile father (Acts 16:1–2). As the apparent deliverer of 1 Corinthians, Timothy will *explain* [Paul's] *ways* (4:17) to the church. He joins Paul as the cosender of several letters (2 Cor 1:1; Phil 1:1; Col 1:1; 1 Thess 1:1; 2 Thess 1:1). Titus, a Gentile convert, is Paul's emissary to the Corinthian church (2 Cor 2:12–13; 7:5–16; 8:16) and companion at the Jerusalem conference (Gal 2:1–3). In the Pastoral Epistles, as in the earlier correspondence, Timothy and Titus are Paul's messengers to the churches.

CONTEXTS

Those who gathered the letters of Paul into one collection apparently noted the distinctiveness of the Pastoral Epistles by placing them after the letters to the churches. Although the letters are written to individuals, they contain Paul's instructions for the churches and strengthen the hand of Timothy and Titus, indicating that Paul's authority lies behind them. First Timothy and Titus resemble ancient letters from a governor to a subordinate who is commissioned to implement the instructions of his superior. Second Timothy resembles the familiar "last will and testament" in which a dying patriarch passes on instructions to the next generation (see Genesis 49; Acts 20:17–35).

> **Paul's Letter Collection**
>
> *By the end of the first century, Christians collected Paul's letters, arranging them from longest to shortest (Romans to Philemon), and then adding the Pastoral Epistles as a sort of second collection. The earliest manuscripts of these letters date to the end of the second century. Other letter collections also circulated, both among Christians (for example, the letters of Ignatius) and non-Christians (for example, those of Cicero).*

In these three letters, Paul's envoys must confront false teaching (1 Tim 1:3–7; 4:1–6; 6:3–6; 2 Tim 2:14–18; Titus 1:10–15) and equip teachers who will guide the church. According to 1 and 2 Timothy, Paul's young coworker is in Ephesus (1 Tim 1:3; 2 Tim 4:6–8), and Paul is apparently in Macedonia (1 Tim 1:3). Titus receives his letter in Crete (Titus 1:5) as Paul is spending the winter in Nicopolis (Titus 3:12).

For more than a century, scholars have raised questions about the direct authorship of the Pastoral Epistles by Paul and have presupposed a date for the letters in the generation after Paul. The reasons for questioning Paul's authorship include the distinctive style of the letters; church organization that is more established than in earlier letters; the similarities between the heretics described and later Gnostic groups; and the fact that the setting described within the letters does not fit within the narrative of Acts. Not all of the questions raised (especially the second and third) are equally compelling. Scholars who maintain the Pauline authorship of the Pastoral Epistles have argued that changes in style can be the result of the role of a secretary (perhaps Luke) and that Acts does not offer a complete account of all of Paul's travels. In this commentary, we shall assume that Paul stands behind the instructions to his coworkers.

COMMENTARY

SALUTATION · 1:1–2

Like other letters of Paul, 1 Timothy begins with the name and credentials of the author, the name of the recipient, and the implied prayer for *grace*. The salutation adds other features that do not appear in the earlier letters of Paul but are present in the other Pastoral Epistles. Paul is *apostle of Christ Jesus by the command of God our Savior* (compare Titus 1:2–3; 2:10). Timothy, like Titus, is his *true son* in the faith (Titus 1:4). *Grace, mercy, and peace* expands on the familiar Pauline greeting (1 Tim 1:1) and prayer.

DANGEROUS TEACHINGS · 1:3–11

The warning in 1:3–11 provides the context for all of the instructions that follow, indicating that the central purpose of 1 Timothy is to combat false teaching. Timothy's central role is to *command* (better rendered as "instruct"– see NRSV) what Paul has handed on to him (see 1:18; 4:2, 11; 6:17). He faces *false doctrines* in Ephesus that involve *myths, endless genealogies, and controversies* (1:3–4). Some have *already wandered away from the faith and turned to meaningless talk* (1:6). Despite the numerous attempts to identify the false teachers, scholars have not been able to identify them with a specific group (see 4:1–6; 6:3–10, 20; compare also references in 2 Tim 2:14–17; Titus 1:10–16; 3:9–11), for the brief descriptions provide a warning rather than offer full details. The statement that the *goal of this command* is *love, which comes from a pure heart and a good conscience and a sincere faith* indicates the central focus of these letters. Whereas false teaching leads to immorality (6:3–9; 2 Tim 3:1–9), ethical behavior accompanies good teaching.

The opponents' desire to be *teachers of the law* (1:7) indicates a Jewish dimension to the false teaching and leads to an excursus (1:8–11) on the *law*, which *is made* to expose the vices listed in verses 9–10. This list corresponds to the consistent use of lists describing positive and negative qualities of character in the letter (3:1–13). It begins with three pairs (*lawbreakers and rebels, the ungodly and sinful, the unholy and irreligious*), followed by additional vices, some of which appear nowhere else in New Testament references to specific sins (for example, *those who kill fathers or mothers, slave traders, perjurers*). In describing these vices as *contrary to the sound doctrine* (1:10) that *conforms* to the *gospel*, Paul continues the theme, first indicated in 1:5, that the test of proper instruction appears in the qualities of character that it produces. This *sound teaching* corresponds to the gospel with which Paul was *entrusted*. The notion of the sacred trust is

> **"Sound Doctrine"**
> A frequent image throughout the Pastoral Epistles (1 Tim 6:3; 2 Tim 1:13; 4:3; Titus 1:9, 13; 2:1, 2), "sound doctrine" is a medical metaphor that literally means "healthy teaching."

another dominant image in the Pastoral Epistles (1 Tim 6:20; Titus 1:3). Paul's delegate should preserve the sacred trust that is threatened by false teaching.

PAUL'S CREDENTIALS · 1:12–17

The reference to the gospel *entrusted* to Paul (1:11) marks the transition to the autobiographical unit in 1:12–17, which establishes the credibility of the writer and provides the foundation for the instructions in the remainder of the book. As in other Pauline letters, autobiographical reflections precede the argument (see 1 Cor 15:1–11; 2 Cor 1:15–2:13; Gal 1:10–2:24; 1 Thess 2:1–12). Unlike the thanksgiving section in the earlier letters, expression of gratitude here focuses on the change from what Paul *once* was (1:13) to what he has become. He had been what the opponents are: a *blasphemer* (2 Tim 3:2; Titus 2:5; 3:2) as well as a *persecutor* and a *violent man*. This change is the act of God, who *gave him strength* (1:12), showed him *mercy* (1:13, 16), and *poured out grace* upon him. Like the Old Testament prophets, Paul serves as God's messenger only after God has called him and empowered him (see Isa 42:6; Mic 3:8).

A consistent feature of the Pastoral Epistles is the *trustworthy saying* (3:1; 4:9; 2 Tim 2:11; Titus 3:8). Here Paul summarizes the Christian faith in the statement that *Christ Jesus came into the world to save sinners* (1:15; see 2:5; 3:16 for other credal statements) in order to declare that his life is the demonstration of the saving power of the gospel. Consequently, he now serves as an *example for those who would believe* (verse 16). Paul establishes his own credibility before he instructs Timothy on Christian leadership (chapter 3) and encourages him to be an example also (4:12). He models the power of the gospel to change lives and lives as the opposite of the false teachers (see 6:3–6). This experience of God's grace leads to the doxology in 1:17.

THESIS: A CHARGE TO KEEP · 1:18–20

Paul's demonstration of his credibility (1:12–17) is the basis for the restatement of his charge to Timothy (1:3) and the thesis statement of the letter. Consistent with the claim that the gospel is a trust (1:11), Paul now proceeds to *give* Timothy *the instruction* that follows. The term for *give* means literally to "entrust something to the care or protection of someone for safekeeping." It often referred to bank deposits. The image appears again in the concluding words of the book in 6:20 (*guard what has been entrusted to you*), providing the framework for the entire letter. Timothy's task is to hold *to faith and a good conscience* and *fight the good fight* (see 1 Cor 9:7; 2 Cor 10:3; 2 Tim 2:4; 4:7) in the context of the dangers posed by the false teachings represented by *Hymenaeus and Alexander*, whom Paul has already *handed over to Satan* – apparently an act of expulsion from the church. The remainder of the letter consists of the instruction that Paul has "deposited" with Timothy.

MAINTAINING ORDER & CONFRONTING DANGER · 2:1–6:2

The instructions in 2:1–6:2 reflect the household setting of the early church and the nature of the church as an extended family. This section appears to be an expanded form of the household rules that appear in other letters (Eph 5:21–6:9; Col 3:18–4:1; 1 Pet 2:18–3:7). Here the rules extend beyond the immediate family to include instructions for men and women (chapter 2), household managers (that is, bishops and deacons, chapter 3), Timothy (4:6–16), old men and women (5:1–2), widows (5:3–16), elders (5:17–20), and slaves (6:1–2). Proper conduct in the house of God is necessary in order to preserve the trust that Paul has committed to Timothy.

2:1–15 *I urge, then* indicates that the charge to Timothy in 1:18–20 is the basis for the instructions for the house church that follow. Verses 1–7 offer instructions for prayer; verses 1 and 2 suggest the relationship of the church to the world. Paul's request that *prayers, intercession and thanksgiving* be made *for everyone*, including *kings and all those in authority*, may be a response to common rumors that Christians were disloyal to the governing authorities. The motivation *that we may live peaceful and quiet lives in all godliness and holiness* suggests Paul's concern for the reputation of the church (see 5:14) among outsiders. In verses 3–7, he indicates that prayer for everyone advances the mission of the church. As in 1:15, Paul cites the basic Christian story to make his claim. The focus on *everyone* (verse 1), *all men* (verse 4), and Jesus' ransom *for all* indicates that Christian prayer for everyone is consistent with God's plan to save the world. As in 1:12–17, Paul indicates in verse 7 that his own mission as a teacher *to the Gentiles* is based on the universality of God's plan.

The specific instructions for men and women in the meetings of the house church *everywhere* (verse 8) continue the thought of the impression made on outsiders. Just as the household rules in earlier letters give instructions for men and women, Paul here offers rules for men and women in the extended family. To *lift up holy hands in prayer* was common practice (Exod 9:29; 1 Kgs 8:54; Neh 8:6; Pss 28:2; 63:5; 77:3; Isa 1:15) in the Old Testament. The emphasis here is the request that men pray *without anger or disputing*, for this behavior would undermine the goal of living *peaceful and quiet lives* (2:2) in the presence of their neighbors.

As in the household rules, instructions for women parallel the instructions for men. The length of the instructions for women in 2:9–15 may suggest that Paul is addressing a particular problem (compare 5:14; 2 Tim 3:6). The concern about the wearing of *gold or pearls or expensive clothes* reflects the fact that such attire was associated in antiquity with rebellion against domestic order (1 Pet 3:4–5) and sexual immorality. The instruction for women to dress as *women who profess to worship God* suggests that Paul appeals to a common standard of appropriate dress in that society.

Parallel to the advice for women's attire is the instruction that women *learn in quietness and full submission*. The appeal for *quietness* [Greek *hesychia*] continues the earlier hope that the entire church will be able to live *quiet lives* [Greek *hesychion bion*; 2:2]. Because of the danger of false doctrine (1:3; 6:3), appropriate teaching is the central concern of 1 Timothy. Consequently, Paul's statement that he *does not permit a woman to teach or have authority over men* should be read in the context of the need to limit the teaching office, for some are appointed specifically for *preaching and teaching* (5:17). The NIV's *must be silent* is misleading since the same word is used here that is rendered as "quiet" in 2:2 and applied to all Christians.

> **Authoritative Teaching**
> The phrase *teach* or *have authority* indicates the kind of teaching that Paul has in view, indicating that the second verb (have authority) qualifies the first (teach). In ancient times, authoritative teaching would be most evident in the household rules that the father would lay down for those under his charge.

In verses 13–15, Paul offers the basis for his instructions about women, giving two arguments from Scripture. The first argument, that *Adam was formed first, then Eve*, is based on the common Jewish view that temporal priority corresponds to priority in importance (see Gen 2:7; 1 Cor 11:8). In the second argument, that *Adam was not the one deceived*, refers to the fall (Gen 3:13; see 2 Cor 11:1–3) and appears to suggest, along with many ancient writers, that the woman was especially vulnerable to false teachings. This statement may reflect the experiences in Ephesus, where the false teachers were taking advantage of the women (1 Tim 5:15; 2 Tim 3:6). Thus the statement suggests that Eve typified the women of Ephesus, who were being misled. The comment that *she will be saved through childbearing* reflects the domestic ideal of the Pastoral Epistles. In contrast to those who forbid marriage (4:3), Paul upholds the ideal of family life and the nurturing of children (1 Tim 3:4–5, 12; 5:4, 11–12) as appropriate roles for all members of the house church.

3:1–15 Having limited the teaching responsibilities in chapter 2, Paul now turns to those who exercise the leading roles in the house church. Since, in contrast to Titus 1:5, 1 Timothy 3 says nothing about the appointment of overseers and deacons, one may assume that these offices already existed at Ephesus. These instructions are introduced with the second *trustworthy saying* (see 1:15), *if anyone sets his heart on being an overseer, he desires a good work*, which is introduced in a way that suggests that it is a common expression. The NIV's *overseer* is an appropriate rendering of the Greek *episkopos* (often rendered "bishop"). The term occurred widely in both religious and secular contexts for people in charge of various functions. Here, as in Philippians 1:1, it functions alongside the term "deacon" for leadership roles in the church. The New Testament uses it as a synonym of "elder" (Acts 17:17, 28; Titus 1:5–7).

The list of qualities for overseer corresponds closely, but not precisely, with the list of attributes of the elder in Titus 1:5–9. The list enumerates qualities that ancient people highly respected in both religious and secular contexts. Indeed, several attributes listed also appear in an ancient list of qualities of the good general. The point of the list is that the overseer should be one of exemplary moral character, in contrast to the heretics who demonstrate the bankruptcy of their teaching in their behavior (6:3–10). The requirement that the overseer be *above reproach* is the heading of the list. Both this requirement and the concluding call for the overseer to *have a good reputation with outsiders* continue the emphasis on the reputation of the house church in the local community that appears in chapter 2.

The phrase *husband of but one wife* should be seen in the context of heretics who forbid marriage (4:3) and the letter's emphasis on the domestic life (2:15; 5:14–15). The emphasis falls on the exemplary nature of the leader's family life. Inasmuch as ancient people placed high regard on those who were *temperate*, *self-controlled*, and *respectable*, these qualities would have enhanced the leader's reputation in the community. The call to be *hospitable* reflects an especially important value in Greco-Roman and early Christian teaching (Rom 12:13; Titus 1:8; Heb 13:2; 1 Pet 4:9). The reference to hospitality probably indicates the leader's higher status and role as host of the house church. In the context of the false teaching that threatens the church, the overseer is expected to be *able to teach* (5:17; 2 Tim 2:24). The negative statements *not given to drunkenness*, *not violent but gentle*, *not quarrelsome* belong together as examples of the absence of self-control. *Not a lover of money* is a reminder that the list is intended to contrast the exemplary behavior of church leaders with the conduct of the false teachers (6:3–5).

Just as ancient writers considered the household the basic unit of the state and the proving ground for leaders, the instructions in 3:4–5 indicate the parallel functions between the management of the household and of the church. The task of the father is to *manage his own family*; the role of the overseer is to *take care of God's church*. The language suggests the overseer exercises the kind of caring authority that the father played in the ancient household.

The requirement that the overseer *not be a recent convert* indicates the importance of experience for this authoritative teacher. The concern that he might become *conceited* again indicates that the overseer is expected to be the opposite of the false teachers (6:4; 2 Tim 3:4).

Paul assumes that *deacons* are also present in the Ephesian church. His instructions indicate neither their task nor their relationship to bishops. The term [Greek *diakonos*] suggests that they were involved in acts of service. As with the bishops, the primary concern is their exemplary behavior. Some of the qualities are also those of the bishop (*not indulging in much wine, not pursuing dishonest gain, husband of one wife*). The requirement that they *be worthy of respect* is parallel to the call for the bishop to be *above reproach* (3:2). The requirement that deacons be tested and that they *serve only if nothing against them* is said parallels the prohibition of ordaining a new convert as a bishop (3:7).

> **Women as Deacons**
>
> *In the unusual sequence, Paul lists deacons (3:8), their wives (3:11 NIV), and then returns to the qualification for the deacon (3:12). This sequence can best be explained if we note that the Greek in 3:11 can be rendered either as "wives" or "women." The NIV's reading "their wives" interprets the phrase as a reference to the wives of deacons. The more likely reading in this context is "women" (that is, female deacons). Inasmuch as no requirements are given for the wives of bishops, the reference is probably to women who are appointed to do acts of service alongside the men who do similar deeds.*

In 3:14–16, Paul concludes this section with the familiar expression of desire to visit the reader (1 Cor 4:14–21; Phlm 22), indicating that the letter is a substitute for his presence. Having compared the church to a household (3:4–5), he summarizes the letter, expressing the intention that they will *know how people ought to conduct themselves in God's household*, the church. *Truth* is a central concern of the Pastoral Epistles (see 2:4, 7; 4:3; 6:4; 2 Tim 2:15, 18, 25; 3:7, 8; 4:4; Titus 1:1, 14). The ethical behavior that he describes throughout the letter is the appropriate way of life in *the church of the living God, the pillar and foundation of the truth* (2 Tim 2:19), in contrast with the conduct of the false teachers (1 Tim 6:3–10; see 2 Tim 3:8; 4:4), who have turned away from *the truth* (6:5; 2 Tim 3:8; 4:4). *Pillar and foundation* suggest the stability of the church as the foundation of truth (for the architectural language, see also 1 Cor 3:10–17; Eph 2:20).

In 3:16, Paul elaborates on the truth, introducing the conviction that is *beyond all question* among the readers. The New Testament commonly uses the term *mystery* for knowledge that is available only through divine disclosure (Rom 11:26; 16:25; 1 Cor 2:1, 7; 4:1; Eph 1:9; 3:3, 9; Col 1:26, 27; 1 Tim 3:9). *Godliness*, an important word in 1 Timothy (2; 4:7, 8; 6:3, 5, 6, 11), "sums up the entirety of the Christian life" (Collins 107). The recitation of the Christian story that follows is most likely an early Christian hymn, as the metrical form suggests. With its theme of the descent and ascent of Christ, it closely resembles the hymn in Philippians 2:6–11.

4:1–16 After the summation of the *mystery* that church leaders know, Paul begins a new unit that includes 4:1–6:2. The description of the false teachers in 4:1–5 provides the context for the instructions to Timothy, who has the task of confronting the impending dangers. In contrast to other descriptions of the heretics in the letter (1:3–11, 18–20; 6:3–10), which refer to a current crisis, here the Spirit warns that the heresies will arise in *later times* (compare 2 Tim 3:1). In contrast to the pure and clean conscience that results from healthy teaching (1:5, 19; 3:9), the *consciences of the false teachers have been seared as with a hot iron*. The destruction of living tissue has desensitized the false teachers to the truth (Collins 114). The

> **Gnosticism**
>
> *A cluster of ancient religions and practices that flourished during the first through the fourth centuries CE but survived into the Middle Ages. Although many forms of Gnosticism existed, most shared a dualistic view of the world and a belief that some persons could rise above the rest in enlightenment through various practices. Early Christian writers often opposed Gnostic teachings.*

reference to those who *forbid people to marry and order them to abstain from certain foods* may suggest that the false teachers hold to an early form of Gnosticism, a major force in the second century. Against their rejection of nature's gifts, Paul insists that *everything God created is good* (Gen 1:31), including sex and food.

In the new section that begins in 4:6–16, Timothy's task (compare 1:3–7, 18–20) as a *good minister* is to *point out* (4:6), *command and teach* (4:11). *These things* (4:6, 11) refers to the threat of false teachings. In 4:6–10, the focus is on Timothy's preparation for ministry, while 4:11–16 describes his teaching responsibility. The preparation of the *good minister* [Greek *diakonos*, the same word rendered "deacon" in 3:8, 13] involves both positive and negative aspects: to be *brought up in the truths of the faith and good teaching* that he received from Paul, his mentor, and from his home (2 Tim 1:3–5) and to *have nothing to do with godless myths and old wives' tales*. The reference to *old wives' tales* reflects a common ancient view that women were easily led astray (2:13–15; 5:11–13; 2 Tim 3:6). The alternative to *old wives' tales* is *to train* to *be godly*. "Godliness," a word that is rarely used outside the Pastoral Epistles (but see Acts 3:12; 2 Pet 1:3, 6; 3:11), is a comprehensive term for the duties performed by the person of faith (1 Tim 2:2; 3:16; 6:3, 5–6; 2 Tim 3:5). The image of *training* derives from athletics, suggesting the hard discipline required of the athlete. The contrast between *physical training* and the training to be godly recalls the common contrast by philosophers between the exercise of the body and the exercise of the mind. In the third *trustworthy saying* of the letter (see 1:15; 3:1), Paul continues the athletic image, *for this we labor and strive* [Greek *agonizometha*—"we strive," a term for athletes in the arena], quoting a saying that was apparently familiar to the readers. This struggle is with the false teachers.

Having described Timothy's preparation in 4:6–10, Paul now describes Timothy's task. He has been entrusted to *command and teach these things* (that is, the dangers from the false teachers). The first dimension of Timothy's teaching ministry is the example he sets before others. As a young man who will give instruction to older people (5:1–2), he needs to ensure that he does not conform to the common stereotype of young men (2 Tim 2:22; Titus 2:6). Rather than be *despised* (Titus 2:15) for youthful passions or arrogance, he should *set an example in speech, in life, in love, in faith and in purity*. That is, like his mentor Paul (1:16) and the church leaders mentioned in chapter 3, Timothy should be the opposite of the false teachers (6:3–10). As an example of good character, Timothy then conducts his duties in Paul's absence: *the public reading of Scripture, preaching, and teaching*. Timothy is empowered for this task by the *gift*, which was accompanied by the *prophetic message when the body of elders laid their hands on* him. Timothy looks back to his ordination by the elders, who commissioned him for his task (see also 2 Tim 1:6, where Paul indicates that he laid hands on Timothy to commission him for service). In the challenge to be concerned about his *life and doctrine*, Paul emphasizes two crucial aspects of Timothy's teaching ministry. The focus on his *life* recalls the comments about Timothy's role as an example of the faith trained in godliness. His *doctrine* refers to Timothy's role in communicating Paul's instructions (4:6, 11; 1:3, 18–20) to an embattled church.

5:1–6:2 After an interlude describing Timothy's character and teaching in chapter 4, this section comes under the general heading of "how to behave in the household of God," for it expands on the household rules of Paul's earlier letters to include the various members of the house church. The advice, *do not let anyone look down on you because you are young* (4:12), appropriately prefaces Timothy's role as the one who will *exhort the older man, younger men, and younger women*. To *exhort* (the same root word is rendered "preaching" in 4:13) is not to command, but to urge members of the family to conduct themselves appropriately in love (1 Thess 2:11–12, *as a father deals with his children, encouraging …*; Phlm 9).

5:3–16 Timothy's responsibilities within the house church extend to the wider circle, including widows (5:3–16), elders (5:17–22), and slaves (6:1–12). In 5:3, 17, Paul offers criteria for giving *honor* to widows and elders, suggesting that the church practices discernment in assuming financial responsibility (5:16). The church assumes responsibility for widows, but it should *honor* only *real widows* and not absolve their own families from responsibility (5:3–8). Those who should be *put on the list* should meet criteria indicated in 5:9–10, which closely parallel the qualities of character of bishops in 3:1–7. The extended limits on support of younger widows (5:11–15) reflect the problems that already exist in the church (5:15). Like others within the church (2:11–15; 3:4–5, 12), they should be models of the domestic ideal, for the good household is the basic unit of the church.

5:17–25 As Paul's delegate, Timothy has broad responsibility for the conduct of *elders* (5:17). He should ensure that they receive appropriate *honor*

(5:17), *entertain an accusation* against them (5:19), *rebuke those who sin* (5:20), and appoint them by the *laying on of hands* (5:22). Inasmuch as they *direct the affairs of the church* and are active in *preaching and teaching*, elders are most likely interchangeable with the overseers in 3:1 (see Titus 1:5–9). The explanation in 5:18 (1 Cor 9:9) indicates that the *double honor* involves financial support. As one who acts as judge (5:19–21), Timothy must hear *two or three witnesses* (Deut 19:15) and act without haste, *partiality*, or *favoritism*. His responsibility demands that he *keep* [himself] *pure* (5:22) and attend to his health by using *a little wine because of* [his] *stomach* (verse 23). The connection of verses 24–25, indicating the eternal consequences of one's deeds, emphasizes the consequences of Timothy's work.

6:1–2 As with other ancient communities, slaves belong to the household (Col 4:1) and the house church. As in 1 Peter (2:18–25), the advice to slaves reflects the church's concern to defend itself against the rumors that it undermined social institutions. The desire that *God's name and our teaching may not be slandered* reflects the letter's consistent concern about the church's reputation (see 2:2; 3:7; 5:14–15). Some slaves who have *believing masters* should not take advantage of their relationship as *brothers*. The phrase rendered in the NIV *those who benefit from their services* (that is, from the services of slaves) is unclear. It may also be read "those who devote themselves to service" (that is, the masters). In either case, the passage indicates the affection between masters and slaves within the house church. *These things* (see 4:6, 11), which Timothy is expected to *teach and urge*, are the instructions in 4:1–6:2.

SUMMARY OF MAJOR THEMES · 6:3–21

The major themes of the letter are summarized in this section, which is parallel in many respects to chapter 1. The dangers posed by the heretics is the focus of 6:3–10 (1:3–11), while Timothy's response is the topic of 6:11–20 (see 1:18–20; 4:6–16). With the medical imagery common in the Pastoral Epistles, 6:3–10 contrasts *sound* (literally "healthy") *instruction* with the *unhealthy* false teachers, whose *corrupt mind* indicates the spiritual illness that results from their separation from the *truth* and appears in the antisocial vices of 6:4–5. The final accusation is that they think *that godliness is a means to financial gain*.

This charge against the false teachers explains why attitudes toward wealth play an important role in 1 Timothy. Already bishops have been warned against love of money (3:3, 8). In 6:6–10, Paul lays out the appropriate view of money, contrasting *godliness with contentment* as the *great gain* in contrast to the desire for financial gain. Stoic philosophers commonly called for *contentment* and the desire for the simple life with only *food and clothing* (Phil 4:11). The primary concern is not with the possession of wealth, but with *the desire to be rich* and the *love of money*, which has led some to wander from the faith. These warnings may reflect the undue influence of wealthy converts within the house church who expect their wealth to give them power in the community.

In striking ways, 6:11–21 stand as the reverse image of 6:3–10. The false teachers' pursuit of wealth contrasts with Timothy's pursuit of godliness and his battle on behalf of the faith. Instead of pursuing wealth, he is to *pursue righteousness, godliness, faith, love, endurance and gentleness* and remember the *good confession* that he made at his baptism. Only by keeping *the command without spot or blame* can he *command those who are rich* (6:17) *not to be arrogant*, but to use their wealth for *good deeds* and to *be generous* with their possessions. Thus, although Paul condemns the pursuit of wealth, he acknowledges that wealthy people can make vital contributions to the house church if they place their hope in God and not on their riches.

The final charge to Timothy, like the opening one (6:18–20), returns to the banking metaphor to describe what has *been entrusted* (literally the "deposit") to Paul's representative. The preservation of the deposit is necessary to protect the church from the false teachers who have caused others to wander from the faith. The reference to *falsely called knowledge* is probably to early forms of Gnosticism. Like most New Testament letters, 1 Timothy concludes with a benediction requesting God's *grace* for the letter's recipient.

THEOLOGICAL REFLECTIONS

As the final letters in the Pauline collection, the Pastoral Epistles address a church in transition. The founding leaders are now passing from the scene, and the church faces a time of change. The major challenge of the church at the end of the apostolic era is scarcely different from the challenge facing the church in every age, for change is inevitable. Therefore, the task of the church is to maintain its continuity with the past while facing the future. According to the Pastoral Epistles, the church has inherited a deposit of healthy instruction – sound teaching – that will ensure that it maintains the legacy of the apostle. If the church is to maintain its identity, healthy teaching will be necessary to shape the minds of the people and provide an alternative to unhealthy ideas that confront God's people. Healthy teaching will result in transformed lives, as the Pastoral Epistles indicate. The church requires leaders who both teach and serve as examples of the power of the deposit of faith to create healthy lives.

FOR FURTHER STUDY

Jouette M. Bassler, *1 Timothy, 2 Timothy, Titus* (Nashville: Abingdon, 1996).

Deborah Krause, *1 Timothy* (London: T & T Clark, 2004).

WORKS CITED

Raymond F. Collins, *I and II Timothy and Titus* (Louisville: Westminster John Knox, 2002).

Gordon D. Fee, *1 and 2 Timothy, Titus* (rev. ed.; Peabody, Mass.: Hendrickson, 1988).

Luke Timothy Johnson, *The First and Second Letters to Timothy* (New York: Doubleday, 2001).

―――, *Letters to Paul's Delegates: 1 Timothy, 2 Timothy, Titus* (Valley Forge, Pa.: Trinity Press International, 1996).

Philip H. Towner, *1–2 Timothy and Titus* (Downers Grove, Ill.: InterVarsity Press, 1994).

2 Timothy

James W. Thompson

CHAPTER CONTENTS

Contexts   997

Commentary   997

   Salutation · 1:1–2   997

   Timothy's Legacy of Faith · 1:3–18   997

   Timothy's Ministry as Paul's Successor · 2:1–3:17   998

   Timothy's Charge to Keep · 4:1–22   999

Theological Reflections   1000

For Further Study   1001

Works Cited   1001

One of the so-called Pastoral Epistles, the second letter to Timothy resembles the familiar "last will and testament" in which a dying patriarch passes on instructions to the next generation (see Gen 49; Acts 20:17–35). At the time of the letter's composition, Timothy is in Ephesus (4:6–8 ; 1 Tim 1:3), and Paul is apparently in Macedonia (1 Tim 1:3).

CONTEXTS

Son of a Jewish mother and Gentile father (Acts 16:1–2), Timothy is one of Paul's young coworkers in the gospel and a frequent envoy, joining Paul as the cosender of several letters (2 Cor 1:1; Phil 1:1; Col 1:1; 1 Thess 1:1; 2 Thess 1:1). Although the letters are written to individuals, they contain Paul's instructions for the churches and strengthen the hand of Timothy, indicating that Paul's authority lies with him. As Paul's envoy, Timothy must confront false teaching (2:14–18) and equip teachers who will guide the church.

For a more detailed discussion of the historical and literary contexts of 2 Timothy, see the discussion of 1 Timothy's Contexts on page 989.

COMMENTARY

SALUTATION · 1:1–2

The salutation resembles that of Paul's other letters. A distinctive feature here is the phrase, *according to the promise of life in Christ Jesus*. Timothy is Paul's *child* in the faith (compare Acts 16:1; 1 Tim 1:2; 1 Cor 4:17). As in 1 Timothy, this letter to Paul's pupil also addresses the church.

TIMOTHY'S LEGACY OF FAITH · 1:3–18

The remainder of chapter 1 lays the foundation for the instructions to Timothy in chapters 2–4 by describing Timothy's legacy of faith. In the thanksgiving (1:3–5), a traditional introductory feature in Paul's letters, Paul *remember*[s] Timothy and *recall*[s] his *tears* and his legacy of *faith*. Hence, Paul now *remind*[s] Timothy of this legacy in order to *fan into flame* Timothy's *gift*, which empowers him for service. The image suggests that Timothy's gift has either grown cold or is like smoldering coals. The legacy includes Paul's ancestors, Timothy's *mother Eunice* and *grandmother Lois* (see Acts 16:1), and Paul's own work as the mentor who commissioned him by *the laying on of hands* at Timothy's ordination (1 Tim 4:14). This act of empowerment is reminiscent of the commissioning of Joshua by Moses through the laying on of hands (see Num 27:18–23; Deut 34:9).

8–14   The memory of Timothy's gift is the basis for the commands that provide the frame for verses 8–14 and serve as the thesis statement of the letter. In the first two commands, Timothy's task as Paul's successor is not to be *ashamed*, but to *join with* Paul in *suffering for the gospel*. As the first imperatives of the letter, these commands anticipate both the theme of the letter and Paul's destiny in 4:6–22. Chapter 1 offers both Paul and the household of Onesiphorus as examples of those who were not *ashamed* of the gospel (1:12, 16). In the third imperative (verse 14), Timothy should *guard the good deposit that was entrusted* to him. This banking metaphor (compare comments on 1 Tim 1:18; 6:20) refers to the good teaching that is a trust to be protected from the false teachers. The Holy Spirit who *lives in us* (see Rom 8:9) empowers Timothy for his task.

> **Discipleship & Suffering**
> *A major theme in 2 Timothy is that discipleship involves suffering with Christ (2:3, 9, 11; 3:11).*

2 TIMOTHY

The summary of the *gospel* in 1:9–10 offers insight into the nature of this *deposit*. In his claim that he was *appointed a herald and an apostle and a teacher* of this message, Paul suggests that he has been a trustee of this deposit already. The text literally says, "He is able to guard my deposit," that is, the deposit that God has given to Paul. In Paul's absence, Timothy will follow the example of his teacher, who is *not ashamed* to suffer.

In contrast to Paul's earlier letters, the Pastoral Epistles include numerous names of good and bad examples. As in 1 Timothy 1:18–20, Paul mentions those who have turned away from the faith. Here he contrasts *Phygelus and Hermogenes*, who deserted Paul (4:16), with the *household of Onesiphorus* (4:19), who were exemplary in not being *ashamed* of Paul's chains (1:8).

TIMOTHY'S MINISTRY AS PAUL'S SUCCESSOR · 2:1–3:17

Commission to Timothy to Continue with Paul in Suffering · 2:1–26

2:1–7 After laying the foundation for his message with the thesis statement in 1:8, 14 and the accompanying examples of faithful conduct, Paul now develops the message with the focus on Timothy as Paul's successor. *Be strong in the grace that is in Christ Jesus* develops the theme of empowerment from 1:7, 14 and continues the allusion to Moses and Joshua (Deut 31:7; Josh 1:6, 7; 1 Kgs 2:2; 1 Chron 22:13; 28:10, 20). This strength is the basis for the commission to Timothy, which Paul gives with two parallel commands. In the first place, he commands Timothy to *entrust to reliable men who will also be qualified to teach others*, where he again employs the language of the deposit (see 1 Tim 1:18). Although 2 Timothy, unlike the other Pastoral Epistles, does not mention specific offices within the church, the letter assumes that the preservation of the deposit of faithful instruction depends on Timothy and other teachers who transmit the teachings of Paul. In the second place, Timothy's must *endure hardship* (see 1:8), as the images of the *soldier* (compare 1 Cor 9:7; 2 Cor 10:3; 1 Pet 2:11), the *athlete* (1 Cor 9:25; Phil 3:12–18), and the *farmer* (1 Cor 9:7, 10) all indicate. These familiar images suggest commitment, hard work, and suffering that result in a desired outcome (victory, a crown, a crop).

2:8–13 Verses 8–13 provide the basis for the appeal, referring again to Timothy's memory (see 1:5, 8) of the basic Christian story. *Raised from the dead, descended from David* recalls early Christian summaries of the faith (1 Tim 1:15; 2:5–6; 3:16; 2 Tim 1:9–10). The *trustworthy saying* (1 Tim 1:15; 3:1; 4:9) in 2:11–13 contains parallel phrases and a rhythmic style that suggests that it is also a creedal statement known to Timothy. The parallel *if … we will also* focuses on the reward that comes to those who share in the suffering of Christ. As in 1:11–14, Paul is the example of *suffering*. He *endures all things* for the gospel, knowing that, although he is bound in chains, *God's word is not chained*.

2:14–21 Timothy's task is to *keep reminding them of* the Christian message stated in 2:8, 12–13. This unit contrasts what Timothy should shun with what he should become. According to verses 14–15, he should *warn* the church against *quarreling about words*, a practice of the heretics (2:23; 1 Tim 6:4; Titus 3:9), but *to do* [his] *best* to *present* [himself] *to God as a workman* who *correctly handles the word of truth* that is contained in the deposit of faith. According to verses 16–21, Timothy should avoid the *godless chatter* of the heretics (1 Tim 6:20), but should *stand firm* as God's *soldier*. The word of the false teachers *will spread like gangrene* (on the medical imagery of these letters, see comments on 1 Tim 1:11). Once more, Paul refers to specific names of those who *have wandered away from the truth* (see 1 Tim 1:18; 2 Tim 1:15). Their teaching *that the resurrection has already taken place* is probably a reference to an early form of Gnosticism.

As God's workman (2:15), Timothy should be equipped for this challenge (verses 19–21), knowing that God's *solid foundation stands*. This metaphor of the church as a building is well known (1 Cor 3:10–17; 1 Tim 3:15). The two citations from Scripture in 2:19 offer the implications of having a solid foundation. In the first place, one has the assurance that *the Lord knows those who are his* (Num 16:5). In the second place, one has the warning *to turn away from wickedness* (Lev 24:16; Isa 26:13). In the reference to the variety of building materials, the focus is on Timothy's task; if he *cleanses himself* from the vessels of dishonor, he will be prepared *to do any good work* (2:15). That is, he can only maintain the purity of the church against the onslaughts of the heretics if he has cleansed himself.

2:22–26 Continuing the contrast between Timothy and the false teachers, Paul contrasts what Timothy should *flee* with what he should *pursue* (compare 1 Tim 6:11). Verse 23 tells Timothy what to reject, while verses 24–26 portray the behavior that will have lasting results. Timothy should avoid the vices of the heretics (verse 23; 1 Tim 1:4; 6:3–10; Titus 3:9) and develop the qualities of character that are appropriate for Christian leaders (verses 24–25).

> **The "Evil Desires of Youth"**
> *The* evil desires of youth *is a theme of ancient writers, suggesting a common stereotype of young men (see 1 Tim 4:11; Titus 2:6). In contrast, healthy teaching should lead Timothy to righteousness, faith, love and peace (1 Tim 1:5; 4:12; 6:11).*

Timothy's Task in the Last Days · 3:1–17

An important transition occurs in chapter 3, as Paul turns from current dangers to the *terrible times* that will come in the *last days* with the emergence of the false teachers. Thus the chapter contrasts the false teachers (verses 1–9) with Timothy (verses 10–17), as *you, however* (verse 10) and *but as for you* (verse 14) indicate. In keeping with the consistent emphasis on ethical qualities that accompany healthy teaching (2:24–25), the extensive list of vices in 3:1–5 indicates the negative results of unhealthy teaching. The close resemblance to the list of vices in Romans 1:18–32 suggests that this list is drawn from a common description of the moral decay of those who do not know God. In verses 6–9, the emphasis shifts to the heretics' dangerous teaching activities. *They worm their way into homes* and take advantage of *weak-willed women*, who are easily swayed and filled with *evil desires*. This description again appeals to the common stereotype that women are controlled by emotion rather than reason. According to Jewish tradition, *Jannes and Jambres* were Pharoah's magicians, who opposed *the truth*. The false teachers, with their *depraved minds* (see 1 Tim 6:4), are unsuitable.

> **Jannes & Jambres**
> *Ancient Jewish tradition gave these names to the anonymous Egyptian magicians in Exodus. Sometime during or before the second century CE, a book bearing their name was written in Greek. The book contains their confession of sin, and it must have functioned as a warning to believers not to revolt against God.*

3:10–17 As *you, however* indicates in 3:10, Timothy must provide an education that is the opposite of that of the false teachers. His education draws on two sources. In the first place, he has learned from following Paul. The NIV's *know all about my teaching* should be, "having followed my teaching …," and the text uses the same Greek root word as when the disciples "followed" Jesus (Matt 8:23). This education involved adopting the *way of life, purpose, faith, patience, love, and endurance*, of which Paul was the example (1 Tim 1:16). This list of qualities contrasts with the list of vices in 3:1–6. The education also involved following Paul in *persecutions* and *sufferings* (1:8; 2:9) in Antioch, Iconium, and Lystra – the cities of the first missionary journey (Acts 13:13, 50). Unlike the false teachers, who go *from bad to worse*, the true disciple *will be persecuted*.

The *holy Scriptures* were a second source of Timothy's education. Unlike the teachings of the heretics, these writings (the Old Testament or the scrolls known to Timothy) *make* [one] *wise for salvation through faith in Christ Jesus*. Timothy has known *from infancy* from his mother and grandmother (1:3–5). In verse 16, Paul elaborates on the place of Scripture as the source of education with a general statement about Scripture. Since the Greek has no verb in the opening phrase in 3:16, one may translate either "every God-breathed Scripture is …" or "every Scripture is God-breathed …" Most translations render the NIV *God-breathed* as "inspired," a term [Greek *theopneustos*] that occurs in ancient writers but nowhere else in the Bible. The term makes the common affirmation that the Scriptures originate in God and thus are different from other books. The emphasis of the general statement about Scripture is that it is *useful for teaching, rebuking, correcting and training in righteousness*. Thus, insofar as Scripture is both *God-breathed* and *useful*, it is the basis for Timothy's ministry of educating the church. Those who are *equipped for every good work* will be the opposite of the heretics, whose vices are enumerated in 3:1–5.

TIMOTHY'S CHARGE TO KEEP · 4:1–22

The final chapter summarizes the letter with a poignant conclusion to Paul's "last will and testament," namely an emotional description of Paul's outlook at the end of his life and a plea for Timothy to carry on his work. The solemnity of the situation is evident in the words, *In the presence of God and of Christ Jesus ..., I give you this charge* (see 2:14; 1 Tim 5:21). Before Paul describes his own situation (verses 6–18), he highlights Timothy's role as his successor, restating the basic argument of the letter. Timothy (verses 2, 5) responds to the dangers facing the church (verses 3–4). Verse 3 focuses on Timothy's role in various forms of public proclamation. His task is to *preach the Word* (4:17). The *Word* is the message of Christ's saving work (1 Tim 4:6, 12; 5:17). Unlike the ancient philosophers who taught that one should learn to speak *in season* (that is, at the appropriate time), Timothy must speak *in season and out of season* – both when it is convenient and when it is not convenient. To *correct and rebuke* is to show people their faults (Titus 1:9, 13; 2:15); to *encourage* is to speak positively, especially within the circle of the family (1 Tim 5:1, 2), urging others to live ethically.

The urgency of Timothy's task comes through in 4:3–4. Here Paul summarizes previous warnings about the dangers that lie ahead (compare 3:1) when people *will not put up with sound doctrine* (1 Tim 6:3) but will follow other teachers (3:6–9) and turn from the *truth* to *myths* (1 Tim 1:4; 4:7). *But you* (verse 5) indicates that Paul's successor should meet these challenges by *keep*[ing] his head – that is, by demonstrating the self-control expected of other church leaders (compare 1 Tim 3:2; Titus 2:2) – enduring *hardship* (2:3), and doing the *work of an evangelist*. As Paul's successor, he will recognize that the *work of an evangelist* cannot be separated from hardship (1:8; 2:8–9).

4:6–8 *For* in verse 6 indicates the relationship between the charge to Timothy and Paul's own situation, which culminates his life of suffering for the gospel. As in the ancient last will and testament (compare Acts 20:17–35), Paul summarizes his life's work, using a variety of images to describe his impending death. Using the imagery of the sacrifice (compare Phil 2:17; Num 15:5, 7, 10), he indicates that he is now *poured out*. *Departure* (literally "untying") was an image for death (Phil 1:23). The athletic images in his claim that he has *fought the good fight* and *finished the race* (see Phil 3:12–16; 1 Tim 4:7–9) were commonly used for the hard struggle of martyrs who gave their lives for a cause. The *crown of righteousness*, the prize for winning the contest, makes the struggle worthwhile and serves as a motivation for Timothy's continued work.

4:9–22 At the beginning of this section, Paul appeals to Timothy to *come quickly* (verse 9), and at the end he says *come before winter* (verse 21). These requests reflect Paul's loneliness, which he describes in 4:9–21. *Demas*, *Luke*, and *Mark* are Paul's companions in Philemon (Phlm 24; compare Col 4:14). *Tychicus* is Paul's emissary in Ephesians (6:21), Colossians (4:7), and Titus (3:12). *Crescens* is unknown in the other letters. *Demas* has deserted Paul. Paul does not state why *Crescens* and *Titus* have left him. The emphasis is on the geographical reach of Paul's ministry and on the dwindling number of companions, leaving him with *only Luke*. The *books and parchments* are copies of the Scriptures written on scrolls.

> **Parchment**
> A writing material made from the tanned skins of sheep or goats.

Verses 14–18 continue the emphasis on Paul's isolation. *Alexander the coppersmith* may refer to the false teacher by that name in 1 Timothy 1:18. Everyone else *deserted* Paul. Nevertheless, Paul has already experienced God's strengthening presence (verse 17) as he *delivered* Paul from the *lion's mouth*. Furthermore, Paul is confident of future vindication from God, who *will repay* his opponent for what he has done (verse 14) and *bring* [Paul] *safely to* [God's] *heavenly kingdom*. Thus Paul is the model for Timothy, who will now act in Paul's absence.

The final greetings and benediction resemble the closing of other Pauline letters. Earlier letters mention *Priscilla and Aquila* (Rom 16:3–5; 1 Cor 16:19), as does Acts 18:2, 26. Trophimus is Paul's companion in Acts (20:4; 21:29). *Eubulus*, *Pudens*, *Linus*, and *Claudia* are otherwise unknown to us.

THEOLOGICAL REFLECTIONS

As the final letters in the Pauline collection, the Pastoral Epistles address a church in transition. The founding leaders are now passing from the scene, and the church faces a time of change. The major challenge of the church at the end of the apostolic era is scarcely different from the challenge facing the church in every age, for change is inevitable. Therefore, the task of the church is to maintain its continuity with the past while facing the future. According to the Pastoral Epistles, the church has inherited a deposit of healthy instruction – sound teaching—that will ensure that it maintains the legacy of the apostle. If the church is to maintain its identity, healthy teaching will be necessary to shape the minds of the people and provide an alternative to unhealthy ideas that confront God's people. Healthy teaching will result in transformed lives, as the Pastoral Epistles indicate. The church requires leaders who both teach and serve as examples of the power of the deposit of faith to create healthy lives.

FOR FURTHER STUDY

Jouette Bassler, *1 Timothy, 2 Timothy, Titus* (Nashville: Abingdon, 1996).

Raymond F. Collins, *I and II Timothy and Titus* (Louisville: Westminster John Knox, 2002).

C. Michael Moss, *1–2 Timothy & Titus* (Joplin, Mo.: College Press, 1994).

Thomas C. Oden, *First and Second Timothy and Titus* (Louisville: Westminster John Knox, 1989).

WORKS CITED

Raymond F. Collins, *I and II Timothy and Titus* (Louisville: Westminster John Knox, 2002).

Gordon D. Fee, *1 and 2 Timothy, Titus* (rev. ed.; Peabody, Mass.: Hendrickson, 1988).

Luke Timothy Johnson, *The First and Second Letters to Timothy* (New York: Doubleday, 2001).

———, *Letters to Paul's Delegates: 1 Timothy, 2 Timothy, Titus* (Valley Forge, Pa.: Trinity Press International, 1996).

Philip H. Towner, *1–2 Timothy and Titus* (Downers Grove, Ill.: InterVarsity Press, 1994).

Titus

James W. Thompson

CHAPTER CONTENTS

Contexts **1003**

Commentary **1003**
- Salutation · 1:1–4 **1003**
- The Dangers Facing the Church & the Qualifications for Elders · 1:5–16 **1003**
- Instructions to Various Groups to Adorn the Gospel · 2:1–3:7 **1004**
- Final Warnings to Titus · 3:8–11 **1005**
- Future Plans & Final Greetings · 3:12–15 **1005**

Theological Reflections **1005**

For Further Study **1006**

Works Cited **1006**

Like the two letters to Timothy, Titus is one of the so-called Pastoral Epistles. The common features found in these three letters – including lists for officeholders and a distinctive vocabulary not found in Paul's other letters – suggest a different purpose for a church that appears more established than those found elsewhere in his writing, leading some scholars to question Paul's authorship.

CONTEXTS

Titus, a Gentile convert, is Paul's emissary to the Corinthian church (2 Cor 2:12–13; 7:5–16; 8:16) and companion at the Jerusalem conference (Gal 2:1–3). In the Pastoral Epistles, as in Paul's earlier correspondence, Titus (along with Timothy) is represented as one of his messengers to the churches. Again, Paul's envoy must confront false teaching (1:10–15) and equip teachers who will guide the church. Titus receives his letter in Crete (1:5) as Paul is spending the winter in Nicopolis (3:12).

Written to Titus, this letter of Paul's instructions for the church indicates that the full force of Paul's authority lies with his emissary. Like First Timothy, Titus resembles ancient letters from a governor to a subordinate who is commissioned to implement the instructions of his superior.

For a more detailed discussion of the historical and literary contexts of Titus, see the discussion of 1 Timothy's Contexts on page 989.

COMMENTARY

SALUTATION · 1:1–4

In addition to the customary identification of the author and readers, the letter begins with Paul's credentials as an *apostle* and the description of his apostleship *for the faith of God's elect and the knowledge of the truth that leads to godliness*, anticipating the major themes of the letter. *The faith* refers to a body of doctrine (1:13; 2:2; compare 1 Tim 3:9; 4:1, 6; 5:8, 12; 6:10, 21) from which the false teachers have departed, just as they have abandoned the *knowledge of the truth* (2 Tim 3:8; 4:4). The Pastoral Epistles affirm consistently that this truth leads to *godliness*, which encompasses the entire Christian life (2:1; see also comments on 3:16). This faith has been *entrusted* to Paul for safekeeping (see 1 Tim 6:20; 2 Tim 1:12, 14) against the threats that undermine it.

THE DANGERS FACING THE CHURCH & THE QUALIFICATIONS FOR ELDERS · 1:5–16

In 1:5–16, Paul describes the dangers that threaten this trust (1:10–16) and the means he has already employed for ensuring its preservation. The indication that he left Titus *in Crete to straighten out what was left unfinished* suggests that Paul has been involved in a ministry on that island that is otherwise unknown to us. In Acts 27:7, Paul lands in Crete on his way to Rome but conducts no ministry there. As Paul's delegate, Titus's task is to *appoint elders in every town*. These *elders* are equivalent to the *overseers* mentioned in 1:7. The qualities of the elders stand in strong contrast to the conduct of the false teachers in 1:10–16. The emphasis on ethical characteristics suggests that the elders demonstrate the godliness that grows out of sound teaching. Several of the qualities (*blameless, husband of one wife, not pursuing dishonest gain, hospitable*) correspond to those listed for the overseer in 1 Timothy 3. Titus focuses on the elders as teachers who *hold firmly to the trustworthy message as it has been taught*. As Paul's delegate, Titus must ensure the presence of leaders in each community who know the faith, for they will be appointed to *encourage others in sound doctrine and refute those who oppose it*.

The description of the threats to the church in verses 10–16 indicate the urgency of the elders' task. As in 1 and 2 Timothy, the crisis comes from false teachers who are *ruining whole households* (1 Tim 5:14–15; 2 Tim 3:6). The false teachers resemble those in 1 and 2 Timothy. Their Jewish origins become clear in the identification of those *from the circumcision group* (verse 11) and Paul's charge to Timothy to ensure that the people *pay no attention to Jewish myths* (verse 14; 1 Tim 1:4; 4:7; 2 Tim 4:4). As *rebellious people*, *mere talkers* (1 Tim 1:6), and *deceivers*, they reflect the conduct of their culture, as the comment, a quotation from Epimenides, that *Cretans are always liars, evil brutes, lazy gluttons* suggests. Titus's task is to *rebuke them sharply* and to ensure *that they are sound in the faith*. The description of the false teachers in verses 15–16 indicates that the absence of *sound* teaching results in immoral conduct.

INSTRUCTIONS TO VARIOUS GROUPS TO ADORN THE GOSPEL · 2:1–3:7

2:1-15 After commissioning Titus to appoint elders, Paul emphasizes in the remainder of the letter Titus's commission. To teach what is *in accord with sound doctrine* is to show the ethical implications of the gospel, as chapter 2 indicates. Like 1 Timothy, this letter offers guidelines for everyone in the house church, extending the household rules of Colossians (3:18–4:1) and Ephesians (5:21–6:9). The behavior that is expected for older men (verse 2), older women (verse 3), younger women (verses 4–5), young men (verses 6–8), and slaves (verses 9–10) will demonstrate the countercultural ethics of a church that adorns the gospel (compare verse 10). The purpose clauses (*so that ...*) in verses 5, 8, and 10 indicate Paul's consciousness of the impact of the gospel on the surrounding culture. He assumes that this behavior will have an evangelistic impact on others.

Although not all *older men* are elders (see 1:5–9), the conduct expected of them is scarcely different from that of the elders. Like the elders, they should be *temperate* (1 Tim 3:2, 11), *worthy of respect* (1 Tim 3:8, 11), *self-controlled* (Titus 1:5, 8), and should exhibit the qualities of *love* and *endurance* that characterize all Christians (compare 1 Tim 1:5, 14; 4:12; 6:11; 2 Tim 3:10). The instruction that *older women* should not be *slanderers* or *addicted to much wine* reflects common stereotypes of the vices associated with them.

Although Titus is the teacher for the house church in general (2:1, 15), the older women should teach the *younger women*. The emphasis on the domestic duties of the younger women distinguishes them from those who go from house to house (1 Tim 5:13). Inasmuch as ancient writers valued those who *loved their husbands and children*, were *busy at home* and *subject to their husbands*, young Christian wives who conducted themselves according to these values would ensure *that no one will malign the word of God*.

2:6-8 Like others within the house church, *young men* should be *self-controlled* (1 Tim 3:2; Titus 2:2). As a member of this group, Titus should provide an *example* (1 Tim 4:12). Unlike the false teachers who are "unfit for doing anything good" (1:16), he should do *what is good*. Just as the appropriate behavior of young women will prevent others from maligning the word of God (2:5), Titus will ensure that opponents will *be ashamed because they have nothing bad to say about us* (2:8). He will make a good impression on outsiders through his character and actions.

2:9-10 Unlike the other instructions of chapter 2 that address the categories of age and sex (verses 2, 3, 4, 6), Titus's final instruction addresses the slaves in the house church. Like the household rules elsewhere (Col 4:2–5; Eph 6:5–6; 1 Tim 6:1–2; 1 Pet 2:18–25), this list encourages slaves to *be subject to their masters in everything*. This advice probably reflects the concern in ancient communities that Christians were undermining social order by encouraging the slaves to seek emancipation.

> **The Evangelistic Role of Slaves**
> *The instruction for slaves not to talk back and not to steal reflects common stereotypes about slaves. Once more (verses 5, 8), such behavior will make a good impression on outsiders and make the teaching about God our Savior attractive (literally, "adorn" or "dress up" the teaching). Proper behavior will have a missionary impact on unbelievers.*

2:11-14 As *for* indicates (verse 11), the memory of the Christian story is the motivation for the ethical behavior of each person in the house church.

Christians' behavior is counterculture in response to the *grace of God that brings salvation* and that *has appeared to all men*. Grace is not only a gift; it *teaches* the renunciation of *ungodliness and worldly passion* and the acceptance of *self-controlled, upright and godly lives in this present age*. These qualities correspond to the cardinal virtues known to the Greeks (of the four Greek cardinal virtues, Paul omits only courage). According to verse 13–14, Christians derive motivation to live ethical lives from the hope for the future and the knowledge of Christ's saving work in the past. They *wait for the blessed hope* of the *Savior, who gave himself to redeem us from all wickedness*. This description of the atoning significance of Christ is apparently a confession of faith summarizing the Christian story (1 Tim 1:15; 2:5–6; 3:16). To *redeem* in ancient times was to pay the price to ransom slaves or prisoners. The result of redemption is that God might *purify for himself a people ... eager to do what is good* (Exod 19:5; Deut 14:2; Ezek 37:23; 1 Pet 2:9). The chapter ends, as it began, with the charge to Titus *to teach* the new way of life to the Christians of Crete.

> **The Witness of the House Church**
> *In its ethical life, the house church demonstrates by its conduct that it has been purified by God and is motivated by the saving work of Christ.*

3:1–7 Paul next offers the final ethical instruction for Titus to deliver before recalling the Christian story as the motivation (3:3–8). The advice to *be subject to rulers and authorities* appears in several New Testament writings (Rom 13:1–7; 1 Pet 2:13–17; compare 1 Tim 2:1–2) and was important for ensuring the authorities that Christians were not subversive. The call t*o slander no one, to be peaceable and considerate, and to show true humility toward all men* continues the emphasis on the church's relationship to the outside world. This countercultural practice was motivated by the Christian story (3:3–7) and the radical change that took place in the lives of people. The "once-now" contrast is common in Paul to describe the ethical change that occurred at conversion (Rom 6:1–11; 1 Cor 6:9–11; Eph 2:2; 5:8; Col 1:21; 3:7; compare 1 Pet 4:3). This change involves God's *mercy* (3:5) and *grace* (3:7). The *washing of rebirth* and the *renewal by the Holy Spirit* suggests the close connection between baptism and the reception of the Spirit.

FINAL WARNINGS TO TITUS · 3:8–11

In the final charge, Paul summarizes the argument of the book, contrasting his goal of forming a community that does *what is good*, *excellent*, and *profitable*, which he has described in chapter 2, with the *controversies* (1 Tim 6:4; 2 Tim 2:23) and *genealogies* (1 Tim 1:4) that are *unprofitable and useless*. As Paul's emissary, Titus has the authority to conduct church discipline (see 1 Cor 5:1–11; 1 Tim 1:18–20).

FUTURE PLANS & FINAL GREETINGS · 3:12–15

The conclusion, with the request for Titus to come to Paul and the reference to future travel plans of others, parallels that of 2 Timothy. *Nicopolis*, a port city in Greece, was a natural place to *winter* (see 2 Tim 4:21). *Tychicus* and *Apollos* are Paul's coworkers in earlier correspondence (1 Cor 1:12; 3:4–6; 4:6; 16:12; Eph 6:21; Col 4:7; 2 Tim 4:12; compare Acts 18:24–19:1). *Artemas* and *Zenas* are otherwise unknown. The request that *our people* devote themselves to *what is good* and not live *unproductive lives* is an appropriate summary of a letter, with its emphasis on the need for members of the community to do *what is good* (compare 2:7, 14; 3:1). The final greeting and benediction are common in Paul's letters.

THEOLOGICAL REFLECTIONS

As the final letters in the Pauline collection, the Pastoral Epistles address a church in transition. The founding leaders are now passing from the scene, and the church faces a time of change. The major challenge of the church at the end of the apostolic era is scarcely different from the challenge facing the church in every age, for change is inevitable. Therefore, the task of the church is to maintain its continuity with the past while facing the future. According to the Pastoral Epistles, the church has inherited a deposit of healthy instruction – sound teaching – that will ensure that it maintains the legacy of the apostle. If the church is to maintain its identity, healthy teaching will be necessary to shape the minds of the people and provide an alternative to unhealthy ideas that confront God's people. Healthy teaching will result in transformed lives, as the Pastoral Epistles indicate. The church requires leaders who both teach and serve as examples of the power of the deposit of faith to create healthy lives.

FOR FURTHER STUDY

Peter Gorday, *Colossians, 1–2 Thessalonians, 1–2 Timothy, Titus, Philemon* (Downers Grove, Ill.: InterVarsity, 2000).

C. Michael Moss, *1–2 Timothy & Titus* (Joplin, Mo.: College Press, 1994).

WORKS CITED

Raymond F. Collins, *I and II Timothy and Titus* (Louisville: Westminster John Knox, 2002).

Gordon D. Fee, *1 and 2 Timothy, Titus* (rev. ed.; Peabody, Mass.: Hendrickson, 1988).

Luke Timothy Johnson, *The First and Second Letters to Timothy* (New York: Doubleday, 2001).

———, *Letters to Paul's Delegates: 1 Timothy, 2 Timothy, Titus* (Valley Forge, Pa.: Trinity Press International, 1996).

Philip H. Towner, *1–2 Timothy and Titus* (Downers Grove, Ill.: InterVarsity Press, 1994).

Philemon

Mark Black

CHAPTER CONTENTS

Contexts 1007
Commentary 1008
  Address & Greeting · 1–3 1008
  Prayer & Thanksgiving · 4–7 1008
  Plea for Onesimus · 8–21 1009
  Final Greeting & Farewell · 22–25 1010
Theological Reflections 1010
For Further Study 1011
Works Cited 1011

MAPS, TABLES, & FEATURES

Philemon & Slavery 1009

Whereas other New Testament letters deal with congregational matters, Philemon is the only truly personal letter in the New Testament. Philemon is therefore important not so much for its theological teaching but for the insight it gives into Paul's pastoral approach to a friend. Unlike the case with other letters, Pauline authorship of Philemon has never been seriously questioned.

CONTEXTS

Most interpreters agree about the most basic facts of the letter: a slave named Onesimus has left his master, Paul's friend Philemon. Onesimus has come into contact with Paul, who has converted him and must now send him back to his master Philemon. Paul writes the letter in order to encourage Philemon to forgive and accept Onesimus without harsh punishment. Philemon may be reluctant to do so because his pride and sense of justice would demand harsh punishment for a runaway slave, any other slaves in the home would need to know that such behavior would not be tolerated, and Philemon's peers might have ridiculed him.

Two approaches to this letter have gained prominence. The traditional interpretation understands Onesimus to be a runaway slave who had somehow wronged Philemon, had fled Philemon's home in Colosse, and ended up in prison with Paul in Rome or Ephesus (O'Brien 266; Garland 300). This reconstruction of events well accounts for most of the details in the letter. However, it fails to explain how the fugitive could find himself in the company of Paul, especially if Paul's "imprisonment" is actually the house arrest outlined in Acts 28:16–31, or how Paul would have authority to send him back to his owner.

In recent years a preferable solution has been offered, one based on literary evidence from the first century. Onesimus should not be seen as a fugitive slave so much as a slave seeking a mediator to intervene on his behalf after he has wronged his master (Rapske 195–96; Dunn 304–05, Fitzmyer 20). In other words, Onesimus went intentionally to his master's respected friend, Paul, knowing that Paul's favor would go far toward averting Philemon's anger. His intention was to return to his master, not to run away. He became a Christian while with Paul, and Paul became so fond of him that he found it difficult to send him back to Philemon.

> **The Rhetorical Structure of Philemon**
> *Like all Paul's letters, Philemon makes an argument through its careful organization. For example, verses 7 and 20 form an inclusio – that is, they use the same phrases to frame the lines in the middle. Philemon will continue to* refresh hearts *by treating Onesimus correctly. Also, Paul's refusal to make an explicit demand of Philemon is a deliberate strategy of persuasion. Subtle argument and gentle reminders of debt, rather than apostolic commands, should convince Philemon to treat his slave well.*

The literary evidence behind this reconstruction of events includes *The Digest of Justinian* 21.1.43.1:

> A slave who takes off to a friend of his master to seek intercession is not a fugitive; indeed, even if his thinking be that in the event of his not receiving assistance, he will not return home, he is not yet a fugitive, for flight requires not only the intention but also the act of flight.

There are also letters from Pliny to his friend Sabinianus with regard to a freedman who had wronged Sabinianus. In the following excerpts from one of the letters, Pliny pleads for Sabinianus to forgive his former slave:

> Your freedman, whom you had mentioned as having displeased you, has come to me; he threw himself at my feet and clung to them as he could have to yours.... You are angry now, I know, and rightly so, as I also recognize; but clemency wins the highest praise when the reason for anger is most righteous. You once had affection for this human being, and, I hope, you will have it again. Meanwhile it suffices that you let me prevail upon you.... (Pliny, *Epistles* 9:21)

Whether Paul was being held in Rome or in Ephesus is an interesting question that cannot finally be answered. Factors that suggest a Roman location include the fact that Luke narrates a Roman imprisonment (Acts 28:16, 23, 30). However, Rome is 1,300 miles from Philemon's home in Colosse. Other readers have therefore suggested that Paul was imprisoned at Ephesus, only 130 miles away from Colosse. Second Corinthians 1:8 may imply an imprisonment there (see also 1 Cor 15:32; 2 Cor 11:23). However, determining the precise location of Paul's imprisonment makes little difference for understanding the letter.

COMMENTARY

ADDRESS & GREETING · 1–3

Only in Philemon does Paul begin by identifying himself as a *prisoner*. Even though he was a prisoner when writing other letters, only here does he base the central rhetorical appeal on his status as a prisoner. It may seem strange that Paul names a co-writer (Timothy), since the letter is written in the first person singular from start to finish. This is also common in Paul's letters and is Paul's way of ensuring his readers that the co-sender is in full agreement with all that Paul has written. It may also be that Paul's co-writers were involved in the content, wording, and even transcription of the letters. In this case, Timothy was probably well known and loved by Philemon and the church in Colosse.

Philemon is clearly the primary recipient of this letter, since he is addressed in the second person singular throughout. However, Paul also greets *Apphia*, *Archippus*, and *the church* that gathers in Philemon's *home* ("your" in the phrase *to the church in your house* is singular). Paul may intend for Philemon to pass on his greetings, but more likely he expects the entire church to read the letter.

> **Apphia & Archippus**
>
> Most scholars believe that Apphia is Philemon's wife, and many think that Archippus is Philemon's son. Archippus appears to be a minister in the church at Colosse. Not only does Paul refer to him as a *fellow soldier*, but he also addresses him via the Colossians in Colossians 4:17.

If so, even such a personal matter as this one between master and slave is a topic for the whole church to consider. They would all need to welcome Onesimus upon his return, a difficult thing to do for these friends of Philemon. Paul may intend to add further pressure by having the church read over Philemon's shoulder. Paul's mention of the *church that meets in your home* reminds the reader that the earliest church met in private residences. As many as 35 or 40 Christians could have met regularly in the home of a wealthy Christian such as Philemon.

The greeting in verse 3 is like that in most of Paul's letters. Paul has replaced the Greek term, "greeting" [Greek *chairein*], typical in a letter of the time, with a similar sounding word, *grace* [Greek *charis*]. Additionally, Paul includes the standard Jewish greeting wishing the recipients *peace*.

PRAYER & THANKSGIVING · 4–7

This prayer section, as typical of Paul's letters, looks ahead to the primary themes of the body of the letter. As Paul mentions how Philemon has in the past shown his *love* for Christians, *refreshed their hearts*, and evidenced his *faith* in Jesus, Paul now wants Philemon to show that love to Onesimus, now a brother in Christ (verse 16), and to share that faith by sending Onesimus back to Paul (see notes below on verses 13 and 21) and thereby refresh his heart (verse 20). The NIV rendering of verse 6 is a poor one. This verse is not a prayer for the effectiveness of Philemon's evangelistic efforts but more likely a prayer for Philemon to make the right decision in regard to Onesimus. He wants Philemon to understand the importance of accepting Onesimus (Garland 319–22).

PLEA FOR ONESIMUS · 8–21

8–10 In verse 8, Paul begins his appeal to Philemon to do what he *ought to do*, but he never explains what he has in mind. At least he wants Philemon to accept Onesimus back without harsh consequences (verses 17–18). However, he wants more than that, as verse 21 makes clear. Some commentators think that Paul wants Onesimus released from slavery, while others believe that Paul wants Philemon to return Onesimus to help Paul while he is under house arrest. There will never be certainty on this matter, but the majority of scholars argue for the latter position.

Paul refuses to use his position as an apostle to force Philemon to accept Onesimus (verse 8). Paul knows that the action would not be truly Christian if it were undertaken for any reason other than *love* (see 1 Cor 13:1–3). At the same time, Paul does not mind telling Philemon how love behaves, reminding him of the fact that he is an *old man* and that he is a *prisoner* for precisely the activity (preaching) that led Philemon to Christ. He will remind him of this fact again in verse 19: *You owe me your very self*.

That *Onesimus* became Paul's *son* while Paul was *in chains* certainly means that Paul converted him to Christ. It is clear, however, that the father-son language refers to more than the fact of Onesimus' conversion, as Paul speaks twice of his great love for the slave (verses 12, 16).

11 The mention of Onesimus's usefulness in verse 11 seems unusual to English readers until they become aware that the name Onesimus meant *useful* or "profitable." As Paul makes a play on words, the reader should notice that he appears to place the blame on Onesimus (*he was useless to you*). Nowhere does Paul hint that Philemon is in the wrong.

12 Onesimus was not a prisoner, for Paul the prisoner would have had no authority to release him. Colossians 4:7–9 relates that Paul sent Onesimus with a brother named Tychicus, who is delivering the letters to Philemon and to the Colossian church. The phrase *my own heart* indicates just how much Paul had come to love Onesimus. Paul's continuing call on Philemon to accept Onesimus back may indicate doubt in Paul's mind about Philemon's reaction. He continues to apply pressure as the letter unfolds.

13 Paul not only loves Onesimus; he also needs his help. Reminding Philemon once again of his indebtedness, Paul wants Philemon to send Onesimus back to him to continue to serve him and the kingdom of God. This is also probably what Paul has in mind in verse 21, where he writes that he is confident that Philemon will do *even more* than he asks.

14 Paul reiterates that he does not want Philemon to feel forced but to act out of love, because only that which is motivated by love has real virtue. Paul does not mind putting pressure on Philemon to do what love demands – he simply refuses to command it. Paul does not hesitate to use strong words in order to encourage others to do what is right.

15–16 As unfortunate as Onesimus' wrongdoing and the ensuing separation were, God has used the situation for the advancement of the kingdom. Onesimus has become a Christian, so that he and his master can never again have simply a master-slave relationship. They will be brothers forever.

Paul's comment that Philemon would now have Onesimus *no longer as a slave* has led many to assume that Paul was requesting that Onesimus

Philemon & Slavery

Paul never calls for Christian slave-owners to release their slaves. His aim is rather to transform the master-slave relationship, not to overturn this societal structure. He instructs slaves to obey their masters as if serving the Lord, and he tells masters to be fair to their slaves since they also serve a master in heaven (see Eph 6:5–9; Col 3:22–41; and 1 Tim 6:1–2; but see also 1 Cor 7: 21–23, where he discourages Christians from becoming slaves).

Many scholars think that Paul simply accepts slavery, as did virtually everyone in the ancient world. While not a humane institution, slavery was often preferable to poverty in the ancient world; it was not based on racial identity; slaves were generally released by age 30; and slaves were often educated and had important positions. Others think that Paul did not approve of slavery but chose not to fight the institution because he had other priorities, especially the mission effort of the fledgling church. Still others think that Paul did not attack slavery because he expected the Lord to return soon. For more about slavery in the ancient world and especially about Paul's attitude toward it, see Bartchy 65–73 and Garland 342–75.

be released from slavery (Garland 335). It seems more likely that Paul's rhetorical language intends to remind Philemon that the more important relationship now between the two is that of brothers. As noted above, if Paul does hint at a release from slavery, this is a different teaching from that in Colossians 3:22–4:1, the letter sent to the whole Colossian church. The fact that Philemon and Onesimus would have an ongoing relationship *in the flesh* may further indicate that Paul was not requesting Onesimus's release from slavery.

17–19 Paul finally makes clear his most basic request, that Philemon would *welcome* back his slave just as he would welcome Paul, that is to receive the slave with love rather than anger. Verse 18 (*if he has done you any wrong*) may refer to Onesimus's having taken property or money from Philemon, or it may refer more simply to the loss of his work during his absence. In either case, it is clear that Paul knows that the loss of property and/or money would be a problem in Philemon's acceptance of his slave. After all, repentance and forgiveness demand the righting of wrong, to whatever extent possible. Paul therefore personally pens the words promising to repay whatever loss Philemon has experienced, all the while reminding Philemon that he owes Paul his *very self*, undoubtedly a reference to his salvation in Christ. Oddly enough, Paul says that he will not mention what he clearly mentions, apparently intending to remind Philemon that he is not calling in that debt.

20–21 Even though he refuses to force Philemon to do what he should do, Paul does not hesitate to ask for some *benefit* and refreshment from Philemon. The term translated *benefit* is from the same Greek stem from which the name Onesimus is derived ("useful, beneficial"), and the term *refreshed* is the term from verse 7 by which Paul praised Philemon for taking care of his fellow Christians.

> **Philemon & Grace**
> *This little letter focuses on forgiveness and reconciliation among God's people. Many readers have remarked how much this story parallels the parable of the Prodigal Son (although Onesimus comes from a lower social status and the cost of forgiveness is greater). Paul offers Philemon more than enough subtle reminders of how much grace he has received – how can he fail to offer the same grace to Onesimus?*

One wonders if Philemon truly felt that he had a choice by the time that he (and the whole church along with him) had read verse 21. Paul believes that Philemon will comply, and he expects Philemon to *do even more*. As suggested above, Paul most likely is requesting that Philemon send Onesimus back to him to attend to his needs and those of his churches (compare verse 13). Once again, however, Paul leaves the choice to Philemon.

FINAL GREETING & FAREWELL · 22–25

Paul hopes to be released soon, after which he will travel to Colosse to visit his friends, who he knows are praying for him. His desire to stay in his wealthy friend's *guest room* underscores their close relationship. As he does at the conclusion of most of his letters, Paul relays *greetings* to the church from those who are with him. Only Epaphras appears to be under arrest, whereas the others are there taking care of Paul and kingdom business. Epaphras would be well-known to Philemon and the church in his house, since he is a minister of the church there, according to Colossians 4:12–13. How he came to be arrested and why he was allowed to be confined with Paul are not stated. *Mark, Aristarchus, Demas, and Luke* are mentioned elsewhere as those who regularly worked with Paul. Paul's final words in this letter are his customary closing, in which he prays that Philemon will continue to receive the blessings [the *grace*] of the Lord Jesus Christ.

THEOLOGICAL REFLECTIONS

It is surprising that Philemon is in the New Testament canon, since it concerns a personal matter between friends. At the same time, we would be poorer without it, precisely because it shows how Paul deals with important interpersonal issues. The topic in this letter that receives the most discussion today is slavery. For good reason, Christians want to discuss ancient slavery over against slavery in America's past. They want to know why Paul does not speak out against slavery and what that means for contemporary Christians who stand opposed to oppressive societal structures. However, the letter to Philemon yields few answers to these questions. It is therefore difficult to speak of the theological implications of Paul's handling of the slavery question in this letter.

This story speaks to all ministers of reconciliation. Paul was apparently not certain that Philemon would forgive Onesimus, even though he had become a brother in Christ. Paul understands the difficulty of this situation, yet he does not demand Philemon's obedience. Philemon cannot be forced to forgive, because a decision that is not based on love is not a Christian decision (verses 8–9; compare 1 Cor 13:1–3). But Paul gives him many reasons to do what love demands. Paul reminds Philemon that forgiving Onesimus is God's will, even though Paul will not demand it, that Paul has sacrificed his whole life and now his freedom for the sake of people like Philemon, that Paul has come to love Onesimus like a son and would like to keep Onesimus, that he will pay any cost that Onesimus may owe, and that Philemon owes Paul his very life in Christ. The reconciled are called to be reconcilers. The comments of Martin Luther are most appropriate:

> Just as Christ did for us with God the father, so St. Paul does for Onesimus with Philemon. For Christ emptied himself of his right and overcame the Father with love and humility, so that the Father had to put away his anger and rights and bring us into favor for the sake of Christ, who so earnestly pleads our case and so heartily takes our part (from Luther's "Prologue to the Letter of Saint Paul to Philemon" (cited in Fitzmyer 36).

FOR FURTHER STUDY

John Knox, *Philemon among the Letters of Paul* (Nashville: Abingdon, 1959).

Eduard Lohse, *Colossians and Philemon* (trans. William R. Poehlmann and Robert J. Karris; Philadelphia: Fortress, 1971).

Marianne Meye Thompson, *Colossians and Philemon* (Grand Rapids: Eerdmans, 2005).

Bonnie B. Thurston and Judith M. Ryan, *Philippians and Philemon* (Collegeville, Minn.: Liturgical Press, 2005).

WORKS CITED

S. Scott Bartchy, "Slavery (Greco-Roman)," *Anchor Bible Dictionary*, 6 (1992): 65–73.

James D.G. Dunn, *The Epistles to the Colossians and to Philemon: A Commentary on the Greek Text* (Grand Rapids: Eerdmans, 1996).

Joseph A. Fitzmyer, *The Letter to Philemon* (New York: Doubleday, 2000).

David E. Garland, *Colossians and Philemon* (Grand Rapids: Zondervan, 1998).

Justinian, *The Digest of Roman Law: Theft, Rapine, Damage, and Insult* (trans. C. F. Kolbert; New York: Penguin, 1979).

Peter T. O'Brien, *Colossians, Philemon* (Waco, Tex.: Word, 1992).

Pliny the Younger, *Letters* (trans. William Melmoth and W.M.L. Hutchinson; 2 vols.; Cambridge: Harvard University Press, 1963).

B. M. Rapske, "The Prisoner Paul in the Eyes of Onesimus," *New Testament Studies* 37 (1991): 187–203.

Robert McL. Wilson, *Colossians and Philemon: A Critical and Exegetical Commentary* (London and New York: T & T Clark, 2005).

Hebrews

James W. Thompson

CHAPTER CONTENTS

Contexts **1013**

Commentary **1013**
- God's Ultimate Revelation · 1:1–4 **1013**
- God's Revelation in the Son · 1:5–4:13 **1014**
- The Ultimate Sacrifice · 4:14–10:31 **1017**
- A Call to Faithfulness · 10:32–13:25 **1023**

Theological Reflections **1025**

For Further Study **1026**

Works Cited **1026**

Although the Epistle to the Hebrews has exercised profound influence on the faith of Christians throughout the ages, it is surrounded by mystery. It says little about the identity or location of the author or readers. The statement "those from Italy send you their greetings" (13:24) suggests that either the author or the readers are in Italy. Nor is it actually an "epistle," as its unique introduction and style indicate.

CONTEXTS

The unknown author belongs to the second generation of Christians (see 2:3) and writes in an elegant Greek style. He describes the book as a "word of exhortation" (13:22), a term that commonly referred to the synagogue sermon (see Acts 13:15). Despite the title, "To the Hebrews," which a second century scribe added, this sermon provides no information about the identity of the readers.

Although we know little about the location of the author and readers, this sermon gives abundant evidence of the situation to which it is addressed. Like the author, the readers belong to the second generation, and they now suffer from "drooping hands and weak knees" (12:12). Having suffered persecution in the past (10:32–34), they now struggle primarily against the temptation to abandon the community (see 10:25) because of the general weariness now that tests them (see 10:36–39). The most basic question that the author attempts to answer is, "Is it worth it to be a Christian?" With its series of comparisons to people and institutions of the Old Testament, the author hopes to remind his readers of the greatness of the Christian faith and thus to renew their commitment.

COMMENTARY

GOD'S ULTIMATE REVELATION · 1:1–4

In a grand style, which is without parallel in the opening words to New Testament books, the "overture" to this sermon begins with the introduction of the themes that will follow. The contrast between God's speaking in the past but now in Jesus Christ introduces a theme that the author develops throughout the book (see 2:2; 12:25; see 4:12–13; 6:17). The motif of comparison between God's revelation in the past and present will dominate this sermon. The comparison between the Son and the prophets and angels anticipates the later argument for the superiority of Christ and his sacrifice to the high priests and sacrifices of the Levitical system.

> **Comparison as a Literary Tool in Hebrews**
>
> *Inasmuch as comparison was a common literary device for offering praise to a great person, one need not conclude that the readers are actually tempted to worship angels or return to the Levitical system. The author employs alliteration (five words in 1:1 begin with the letter "p" in Greek) and antithetical parallelism ("to the fathers … to us," "in many and various ways … in these last days," "in the prophets … in the son") to affirm the glory of the Christian faith for his weary readers.*

God's speaking occurred in the entire Christ event, as the poetry of 1:1–4 indicates. Indeed, the author describes the story of the Son in three acts, beginning with his place in creation (1:2b, 3a), his earthly existence and sacrificial death (1:3b), and his exaltation to the right hand of God (1:3c–4). This summary of the Christ event is remarkably similar to other passages that are commonly recognized to be early Christian hymns (Phil 2:6–11; Col 1:15–20) and contains themes that ancient interpreters commonly associated with God's wisdom or word (Prov 8:22; *Wisdom of Solomon* 7:22–26; see John 1:1–4). Unlike Jewish writers who commonly described wisdom's likeness to God and its presence and participation in the creation, the author of Hebrews describes the second act in which the Son *made purification for sins* in his death on the cross. This interpretation anticipates the central section of the book (4:14–10:31), which consistently interprets Jesus' death as the new counterpart to the Levitical purification rituals (9:14, 22–23; 10:2). In the third act of the story, the Son *sat down at the right hand of the Majesty in heaven*, returning to his exalted status. In this echo of Psalm 110:1, the author introduces another major theme of the sermon. The constant references to Psalm 110 in the sermon (1:13; 7:1–28; 8:1; 10:12) suggest that this psalm is the major text for the author's reflection on Christ. Christ is *superior to angels* and to all other potential competitors because he sits at God's *right hand*. The *name he has inherited* at his exaltation is that of Son. Although the author recognizes that Jesus was God's Son and heir (see 1:2) from the beginning, here he announces that the exaltation is also God's appointment as *Son*.

GOD'S REVELATION IN THE SON · 1:5–4:13

1:5–14 The quotations in 1:5–14 support the remarkable claim that Christ is *superior to the angels* (1:4), as the transitional *for* indicates in 1:5. Hebrews 1:5–2:18 develops this theme at length. Citations from Psalm 110:1 in 1:3 and 1:13 provide the frame for the quotations, indicating that the author is describing the status of the exalted Christ. Although the author quotes Old Testament passages without much comment in 1:5–13, his introductory statements and his arrangement of the passages set forth the major themes. The author interprets Old Testament passages through the lens of his faith in Christ, indicating that those words in another context tell the story of Christ. He introduces each of the passages as the voice of God (1:5, 6, 7, 8, 10, 13). Indeed, the citations in 1:5–13 restate the claim of the overture in 1:1–4, comparing Christ to the angels. The first three quotations in 1:5–6 reaffirm the claim of 1:4: as Son, Christ is greater than angels. Jewish and Christian interpreters commonly interpreted Psalm 2:7 (*you are my son ...*) and 2 Samuel 7:14 (*I will be to him a father...*) as messianic passages (see Matt 3:17; Acts 13:33). The third citation (*let all God's angels worship him*, 1:6) apparently combines Old Testament passages (Ps 96:7 and Deut 32:43) from the Septuagint.

> **The Septuagint (LXX)**
> Also known by the abbreviation LXX, this third century BCE Greek translation of the Old Testament was so named because 70 scholars were said to have been involved in its production. Early Christians often quoted from this version.

In 1:7–12, the author employs the citations from the Psalms to describe how Christ is superior to the angels. The contrast between angels, *whom he makes into winds* (1:7; see Ps 104:4), and the Son, whose throne is *forever and ever* (1:8; see Ps 45:6), assumes that the superiority of the Son rests on his eternal being. The lengthy quotation in 1:10–12 (see Ps 102:26–28) also indicates that only the Son *remains*, even if the creation grows old; the Son will *remain the same* although everything else will *wear out*. Thus the readers' faith does not depend on something transient, but on the one who is eternal. Placing Christ above the entire creation (1:10–12) restates the claims made in 1:2–4. The claim of the abiding nature of the Son becomes a major theme throughout the letter (see 7:1–3, 16, 24; 10:34; 12:27–28; 13:8, 14), serving as a constant reminder that Christians own a possession more permanent, and thus more valuable, than any alternative to which they might turn in their time of distress. The concluding contrast between the one who sits at God's *right hand* and those *angels* who merely *serve* (1:13–14) reinforces the claim for the superiority of the Christian faith by contrasting the royal person with the household servant.

> **Angels in First Century Thought**
> During the first century, Jews and Christians developed elaborate ideas about angels. A hierarchy of angels carried messages to human beings, teaching them the ways of God. The Essenes at Qumran believed in a war between good and evil angels in which humans were also involved. Hebrews, by contrast, downplays the importance of angels.

2:1–4 The purpose of the declaration of the superiority of Christ to the angels becomes clear in 2:1–4, as *therefore* in 2:1 indicates. Those who *inherit* the *salvation* described in chapter 1 (see 1:14) must *pay more careful attention*. That is, "God has spoken to *us*" (1:2), and now we *must pay attention to what we have heard*. Using the rabbinic argument "from the lesser to the greater," the author describes God's earlier revelation (1:1) as the *message spoken by angels* (see Deut 33:2; Acts 7:53; Gal 3:19), comparing it to *what we have heard*, concluding that disobedience of *a great salvation* has extreme consequences. Alluding to the variety of punishments for those who disobeyed God's commandments in the Old Testament (see Deut 17:6; Num 35:30; Heb 10:26–31), the author encourages the listeners to recognize the extraordinary consequences of abandoning this great gift. The description of this word first *announced by the Lord*, *confirmed to us by those who heard him*, and *confirmed by signs and wonders* indicates that the author and his readers belong to the second generation. Because they are separated in time from the revelation and now drifting from their original commitment, the author reminds them of their great possession.

2:5–18 The author continues the comparison of Christ to the angels in order to strengthen the resolve of the community. The claim, *It is not to angels that God has subjected the world to come* in 2:5 reiterates the content of 1:5–14. Using a customary way of introducing Scripture, the author continues the citation of Psalms with the phrase, *there is a place where someone has testified*, citing from the Septuagint of Psalm 8:4–5. After the lengthy quotation in Hebrews 2:6–8, the remainder of the chapter is composed of reflections about Christ based on the psalm.

Early Christians interpreted both Psalm 110:1 and Psalm 8:4–8 as references to Christ. Because the passages refer to the one who has subjected all things "under his feet" (Ps 8:6) or made the enemies "a footstool" (Ps 110:1), New Testament writers combined the two passages in order to describe the cosmic significance of Christ (1 Cor 15:27; Eph 1:22). Similarly, the author of Hebrews proceeds from the quotation of Psalm 110:1 (1:13) to the citation of Psalm 8. For the author, the *son of man* of the psalm is Jesus Christ, who is *crowned with glory and honor* and has *put everything under his feet*. In the explanatory comment (verse 8b), the author reiterates the conviction that *everything* is *subject to him*.

In verse 8b, the author concedes that *we do not see everything subject to him*, indicating that Christians do not actually *see* the triumph described in chapter 1.

What they *see* are the frustrations and temptations that accompany the fate of a minority group living in a hostile atmosphere (see 10:32–34). The author addresses this crisis, turning from the exalted Christ to the affirmation, *we see Jesus, who was made a little lower than the angels, now crowned with glory and honor because he suffered death*.

Jesus' suffering and death were not misfortunes, but deeds that were *fitting for God* (2:10) in *bringing many sons to glory*. Jesus was made *perfect through suffering* by completing his task through the cross. His people are *sons* (2:10), *of the same family* (2:11), *brothers* (2:11–12), and the *children* of God (2:13). The quotations in 2:12–13 (from Psalm 22:22 and Isa 8:17–18) indicate a kinship so strong that Jesus joins humans in placing his *trust* in God.

The extent of Jesus' solidarity with his people is evident in 2:14–17. Because he *shared flesh and blood* (2:14), he participated in death and liberated those who live *in fear of death*. In 2:17, the author describes Jesus as *high priest* for the first time, anticipating the argument of chapters 5–10. Jesus' humanity was total. The fact that he was *like his brothers in every way* qualifies him to be a *merciful and faithful high priest*. As one who was fully human, *he was tempted*, and thus able to help those *who are being tempted*. In describing Jesus' temptations, the author is reflecting on the specific temptations that face the church, encouraging the people with

> **"A little lower than the angels ..."**
> *In the Greek translation of the Old Testament, the words "little lower" can also be translated "little while lower." That translation offers the possibility of finding in the psalm the sequence in the life of Jesus that includes both his earthly life – "the little while" – and the time when Jesus was crowned with glory and honor. That is, his death for everyone preceded his glory. Thus, while the author affirms the cosmic superiority of Christ above the angels in chapter 1, chapter 2 describes the significance of his being lower than the angels – subject to suffering and death.*

> **The Author of Salvation**
> *The description of Jesus as the author of salvation (also in 12:2) evokes the image in Greek literature of a hero who founds a city and gives it his name. In the Septuagint, the term rendered "author" (archegos) often referred to a prince or judge (Num 13:2-3; 16:2; Judg 5:2, 15; 11:6ff) who leads the people. Only one who experiences solidarity with the people can assume the role of author, as 2:10–18 indicate.*

the fact that Jesus once faced the very temptations they are facing.

3:1–6 *Therefore* in 3:1 indicates that the consequence of having a *faithful high priest* (2:17) is that believers who *share in the heavenly calling* should consider Jesus, the high priest, who was *faithful to the one who appointed him*. Continuing the comparisons from the previous chapters, the author compares Jesus to Moses, who was *faithful in all God's house* (Num 12:7). The reference to the *builder of the house* evokes other passages from the Old Testament, including God's promise to Eli that his sons would not inherit the priesthood, but that God would raise up a "faithful priest" and "establish his house" (1 Sam 2:35) as well as the promise that God would *build* a dynasty (1 Kgs 11:38). In contrast to the Jewish tradition that described Moses as the greatest of revealers because he spoke to God "face to face" (Num 12:8), the author of Hebrews contrasts Moses the *servant* with Jesus the *Son* (3:6), just as he had compared angels as ministering spirits (1:14) to Jesus the Son. This extraordinary salvation is conditional, as 3:6b indicates. The author reminds readers who are tempted to "drift away" (2:1) of the obligation to *hold on* to the *courage* and the *hope* of which they *boast* because of the saving work of Christ.

3:7–4:11 Just as the comparison of Christ to angels in chapter 1 is followed by a warning (2:1–4), the author's comparison of Christ to Moses is followed by the lengthy warning in 3:7–4:11, as the word *so* in 3:7 indicates. The author quotes Psalm 95:7–11 in 3:7–11, introducing the citation with the *Holy Spirit says*. Scripture is the voice of God (1:5, 6, 7; 2:12), and the present tense (*says*) indicates that Scripture addresses the community directly. Psalm 95:7–11 is an ancient call to worship that invites the people to come before God in worship and calls for a decision *today* (Ps 95:7), recalling the ancient story of those who rebelled *in the time of testing in the desert* (Heb 3:8). The psalmist refers to the Israelites' complaints in the desert (Exod 17:7; Num 13–14) and warns the readers of his own time, recalling God's declaration that *they shall never enter my rest* (see Num 14:33).

In 3:12–19, the author applies this story to his own community, indicating the similarities between the temptations of his own community and those of ancient Israel in the desert. Inasmuch as the ancient Israelites failed to enter the promised land because of their lack of faith (3:19; 4:2), the author encourages his *brothers* to see to it that no one has a *sinful, unbelieving heart* (3:12). The *today* of the psalm (3:7) is also the *today* of the community (3:13), giving special urgency to the responsibility of members for each other. To ensure that *none of you* (4:1) abandons the faith is to take responsibility for each individual. The memory of Israel's failure to attain the promise moves the author again to indicate the conditional nature of salvation. In 3:14, as in 3:6, the author indicates that Christians hold the blessing only *if they hold firmly to the end* the *confidence* they had at the beginning.

> **House Churches in Early Christianity**
>
> *The fact that the author expects the members to encourage one another daily (3:13) suggests the rich community life of the house church with its daily meetings. Those who were alienated from their own families discovered in the new family a resource that would offer encouragement in times of temptation to abandon the faith.*

In the rhetorical questions in 3:16–19, the author returns to the story of the wilderness, indicating the totality of Israel's failure. He does not mention Joshua and Caleb, the exceptions to his claim that *all those Moses led out of Egypt* ultimately *fell in the wilderness*. According to the author, God's judgment was on all of Israel. The fact that they did not enter the promised land because of *unbelief* (3:19) is a lesson for the church (4:1–2) and a reminder of its responsibility to ensure that *none of you* (see 3:12) fails to enter God's *rest*. The journey toward the promised land is not solitary, but a communal activity in which members ensure the well-being of others. Anticipating the description of the great examples of faith in chapter 11, the author presents the negative example of those who did not *combine* the message with *faith* (4:2).

Having warned the readers with the negative example of Israel's *unbelief* (3:19; 4:2), the author turns to the promise that *we who have believed enter that rest* (4:3). Despite the fact that *rest* in the Old Testament refers to the promised land of Canaan (Josh 1:13, 15; 21:44; 22:4; 23:1), the *rest* that believers enter in Hebrews is not Canaan, but God's ultimate promise. The author repeats that promise in the assurance that there *remains a Sabbath rest for the people of God* (4:9), equating the *Sabbath rest* with the promised land and anticipating countless hymn writers with the association of the promised land with heaven. In 4:4–8 the author indicates how the rest promised centuries ago is still available for believers. Using the rabbinic rule of interpretation known as *gezera shewa*, the author associates the *rest* of Psalm 95:11 with the fact that God *rested* on the seventh day (Heb 4:4–5; see Gen 2:2). Since the psalmist spoke of *rest* long after the time of Joshua, the author concludes that Joshua did not give *rest* to the Israelites. The psalmist's words, *today if you hear his voice*, point to a new day which, for the author, is the urgent moment when the community hears his message. One may compare Paul's urgent plea to the Corinthians to recognize that the "day of salvation" of Isaiah 49:8 is "now" when the church hears his message. Thus God's rest is available for those who are faithful, and believers share in God's rest (4:10). The availability of the *rest* is the basis for the author's urgent plea in 4:11. Using his familiar "let us" style (which appears also in 4:14, 16; 6:1; 10:19; 12:1), he invites his readers to make *every effort to enter that rest* (4:11). Just as the heroes of faith in chapter 11 serve as examples of endurance for the church, Israel is an *example* of disobedience for the church to avoid.

> **Gezera Shewa**
> *The use of different passages containing the same word in which one passage "interprets" the other.*

4:12–13 The meditation on the *word of God* concludes the first major section of Hebrews, which began with the author's early description of the God *who has spoken* (1:1). The specific context for these reflections on the *word of God* is Psalm 95:7–11, the textual basis for 3:7–4:11. God's oath that *they shall never enter my rest* indicates the power of God's word and the consequences of disregarding it. The author warns elsewhere of the consequences of disobeying God's powerful *word* (see 2:1–4; 12:25). God does not speak "idle words" (see Deut 32:47); the divine word "does not return ... empty" (Isa 55:11), for it achieves the purpose for which God sent it. This *living and active word* can either promise hope or threaten God's judgment (compare 1 Kgs 17:1; Isa 40:8; Jer 1:9f; 5:14; 23:9; Amos 1:2). Here the author indicates that those who encounter God's word come under judgment. The believer is *uncovered and laid bare* before God's word. All of these images indicate the power of God's word to judge and expose the believer's innermost being. The author's reference to the one to whom *we must give an account* introduces a familiar theme: God's word is not to be taken lightly. God promises the heavenly rest and warns of the consequences of disobedience (see 10:26; 12:19, 25). God's oath to Israel (3:11) also speaks to the church.

> **The Sword**
> *The sword is a familiar image for God's word (Isa 49:9; Eph 6:17). The heavenly judge in Revelation has a two-edged sword in his mouth (1:16; 2:12; see Judg 3:16; Prov 5:4). The sharpness of God's word is evident as it penetrates between soul and spirit and judges the thoughts and intentions of the heart.*

THE ULTIMATE SACRIFICE · 4:14–10:31

4:14–5:10 The first section of Hebrews (1:1–4:13) focuses on Jesus as the Son of God, mentioning the high priesthood of Christ without elaboration (2:17; 3:1). In the reference to Jesus as *Son of God* and *high priest* 4:14, the author now makes the transition to the central section of this sermon (4:14–10:31), developing the theme of Christ as the high priest who offered the perfect sacrifice in the perfect sanctuary. The parallelism between 4:14–16 and 10:19–25 suggests that the exhortations at the beginning and end of the section are the frame for author's explanation of the work of Christ. The author's purpose in this lengthy section is to provide the foundation for his exhortation to a discouraged church.

In 4:14–16, the author alternates between affirmations of what *we have* and the exhortation, *let us....* In 4:14, the fact that *we have a great high priest who has passed through the heavens*, a heavenly exalted figure (as in 1:5–14), is the basis for the exhortation, *let us hold firmly to the faith we possess*. In 4:15, the fact that *we have* a high priest *who can sympathize with our weaknesses* and *has been tempted in every way* means that we can *draw near*. As in chapters 1 and 2, the author affirms both the heavenly exaltation and the full humanity of Christ. Expanding on the claim that he was "like his brothers in every respect" (2:17), he says that *he was tempted in every way* (4:15). The author is not making a theoretical statement, but is encouraging people who are being tempted not to abandon their faith, indicating that Jesus had experienced the same temptation that now confronts the readers. Because the high priest was both human and exalted, believers who now face temptation can approach *the throne of grace with confidence*. The author's claim that Jesus is *sympathetic* and *higher than the heavens* introduces the lengthy argument. Hebrews 5:1–10 develops the theme of Jesus' *sympathy*, while 7:1–10:18 elaborates on his status *higher than the heavens* – the two dimensions of his priesthood.

The author continues to demonstrate the greatness of Jesus by offering a comparison to others who are held in esteem (see 1:4; 3:1–6), indicating in 5:1–10 that Jesus fulfills the role (to *offer gifts and sacrifices for sins*; compare Lev 4:3–12; 9:7–8; 16:8; Num 15:22–31) and holds the qualifications expected of *every priest* (5:1). Instead of deriving the qualifications from the Old Testament (see Exod 28-29; Lev 8-10; Deut 33:8-11), the author defines the work of the priesthood in 5:1–4 in view of his claims about Christ in 5:5–10. According to 5:1–4, the high priest is *appointed* and is able to *deal gently* with sinners because he is subject to *weakness*. In 5:5–10, he demonstrates that God *appointed* (5:5) and *designated* (5:10) Christ for the task. His *weakness* was evident in the *loud cries and tears to the one who could save him from death* (compare Ps 116:8) during his life and the fact that *he learned obedience from what he suffered*. Whereas ancient priests could *deal gently* [5:2; Greek *metriopathein*, "moderate one's feelings"], Jesus is able to *sympathize* [4:15; Greek *sympathein*] with the people, transcending the work of the high priest. He *became perfect* in his path from weakness to divine exaltation, when God appointed him *Son* (see Heb 1:5) and *high priest in the order of Melchizedek* (5:5–6, 10). Only by completing this course is he the *source of eternal salvation* and thus an encouragement to discouraged Christians.

> **Jesus' Sufferings**
> Inasmuch as Jesus went to his death, despite the prayer, the statement that he *was heard* has puzzled commentators. The author is probably referring to Jesus' ultimate triumph over death. That is, in the days of Jesus' life on earth, he experienced the same sufferings that now test the readers (also 12:4–11), and he even shared the fear of death (compare 2:15).

5:11–6:12 The author will develop the theme of the *order of Melchizedek* (5:5, 10; see Ps 110:4) at length in 7:1–10:18, but interrupts this difficult section with the exhortation in 5:11–6:12 and the commentary on Abraham in 6:13–20. The NIV's *slow to learn* (5:11) and *lazy* (6:12) render the same Greek word [*nothros*], providing the frame for the discussion and indicating the author's concern for his readers' behavior. The message that is *hard to explain* is the discussion of Melchizedek, whom the author introduced in 5:5, 10 and discusses at length in chapter 7. In the only direct criticism of the readers in this sermon, the author indicates that the problem is not the subject matter, but the fact that the readers are *slow to learn*; that is, they are like poor students who make no progress in their studies. Despite the *time* that the readers have been Christians (see 10:32–34), they have not become *teachers* but remain in infancy. Like the philosophers, the author describes advanced teaching as *solid food* and compares the student to the athletes who *train themselves* through *constant use* (literally "through practice"). Thus the author associates the community's general lethargy (12:12) with an intellectual laziness that fails to advance in the knowledge of the faith. He challenges the whole church to progress in knowledge in order to have the strength to endure.

> **Childhood Imagery in Hebrews**
> The author employs language commonly used by philosophers to describe the educational progress of a child, who progresses from elementary truths *to higher learning* – from milk *to* solid food (see 1 Cor 3:1–3).

The author lists the *elementary teachings* in 6:1–2, urging the readers to *leave* them behind and *go on to* the *maturity* he describes in 5:14 rather than *again lay the foundation*. The items which the author lists (*repentance ... faith in God ... baptisms, laying on of hands, resurrection of the dead*, and *eternal judgment*) probably reflect items covered in the elementary instruction of new converts.

The author states the serious consequences of the community's failure to advance in 6:4–8, suggesting that the alternative is to *fall away* (6:6; see 3:12). In a reference to the readers' conversion, he recalls an event that happened only *once* in the life of the believers. In that moment, they were *enlightened, tasted the heavenly gift, became partakers of the Holy Spirit, and shared in the powers of the coming age*. In a stern warning, the author declares that it is *impossible* to renew to *repentance* believers who have turned away from this once-for-all event. He does not say why it is *impossible* (note the theme of the "impossible" in 6:18; 10:4; 11:6); nor is he addressing the problem of people who want to return after falling away. The stern warning declares only that the once-for-all event of conversion cannot be repeated. To do so would be to *crucify the Son of God all over again* (6:6). A similar warning appears in 10:26–31 and 12:17 (see Num 15:30, 36; Ezek 18:21ff; Mark 3:28ff; 1 John 5:16). The readers must recognize the need to consider the consequences of falling away; no one can hope to *fall away* and then return.

> **"Bear good fruit ..."**
> *The illustration from plant life in 6:7–8 compares Christians to plants that either produce a crop or thorns and thistles; those that are cursed and burned serve as a warning to Christians.*

6:9–12 Positive encouragement follows the stern indictment. Because God will remember the readers' acts of *love* and *help* for others from the time of their conversion to the present moment (see 10:32–34), the readers may choose the better of the two alternatives mentioned in 6:7–8. The community's previous deeds become the motivation for maintaining their commitment *to the very end*. Although the author has previously indicted the readers for being *slow to learn* [5:11; *nothros*], he expresses the hope that they will not be *lazy* [*nothros*]. Instead of imitating negative models (see 4:11), the community should *imitate those who through faith and patience inherit what has been promised*, overcoming their most persistent temptation. This appeal anticipates the argument in 6:13–20 (and chapter 11).

6:13–20 Abraham furnishes the example to imitate. According to Genesis 22:17, God made a promise to Abraham, who *received what was promised* after *waiting patiently*. Like the readers, Abraham did not receive the promise immediately. After telling the story in 6:13–15, the author offers the implications for the readers in 6:16–20, focusing on the certainty that the *oath* corroborates the *unchanging nature of his purpose* (6:17) as an assurance for believers who have also received God's promise. Like Abraham, believers have also received God's oath in the story of Christ and may now *take hold of the hope offered to us* and *be encouraged* (6:18). Christians are like refugees (*we who have fled*) who need something to *take hold of* to prevent them from perishing or becoming like people adrift at sea who need an *anchor* (6:19), and they have found this security in the hope that enters the sanctuary *behind the inner sanctuary* in the exaltation of Christ (see 9:1–14). Christ *went before us*, providing access to God so that we can also follow him (see 2:10; 12:1–2). His exaltation was the occasion when God *appointed him high priest forever, in the order of Melchizedek*. His triumph over death is his *oath* to believers, the assurance that gives them the endurance to remain faithful despite discouragement.

7:1–28 The author returns to the word that is "hard to explain" (5:11) in a commentary on the only two passages in the Old Testament that mention the mysterious figure of Melchizedek (Gen 14:17–20; Ps 110:4). In 7:1–3, he recalls the account in Genesis and offers the translation of his name [*Melchi*, king, *zedek*, righteousness] and his city [*salem*, peace] before declaring his attributes in four parallel phrases (7:3). The first two phrases (*without father or mother or genealogy*, having neither *beginning of days or end of life*) are inferences from the silence of Scripture, a common mode of interpretation among the rabbis. The latter two phrases (*like the son of God*, he *remains a priest forever*) echo Psalm 110:4, which describes a royal figure who *remains a priest forever*, thus becoming a priest-king. Taken together, these attributes describe the ideal priest, a heavenly exalted figure. The first two phrases in 7:3 were commonly used for the deity. The latter two phrases describe the one who sits at God's right hand (Ps 110:1). This "order of Melchizedek," to which Christ belongs, is now the basis for a comparison to the priesthood of Aaron.

> **Melchizedek**
> *Numerous Jewish writers had already demonstrated their fascination with this obscure priest. Some rabbis concluded that Melchizedek was another name for Shem, though this seems unlikely. Ancient interpreters understood the Genesis account of his encounter with Abraham as evidence of Abraham's superiority to him. One document in the Dead Sea Scrolls (11Q Melchizedek) describes Melchizedek as a heavenly judge. The author of Hebrews is probably aware of this fascination with Melchizedek and uses his mysterious priesthood as a means to explain the greatness of the priesthood of Christ.*

The claim that he *remains a priest forever* is the thesis for chapter 7 as the author compares not only two men but two kinds of priesthood. In 7:4–10, he contrasts *the men who die* with the one *declared to be living* (7:8). In 7:11–17, he argues that the Psalm's declaration about the priesthood forever assumes a change in the priesthood from one based on *ancestry* to one based on an *indestructible life* (7:16–17). In 7:18–19, the author anticipates chapter 9, arguing that the *former regulation* was set aside because of its *weakness* in favor of a better hope by which *we draw near to God*. That is, Jesus' exaltation to God's right hand is the entry into the transcendent world that opens the way for others to follow. In 7:20–22, the author recalls that Psalm 110:4 is God's *oath* ("he swore"), reaffirming the significance of God's oaths (compare 3:11; 6:13–20). In 7:23–28, he concludes with the affirmation of the Christians' access to the ideal priesthood in which Jesus, unlike the earthly priests who are *prevented by death from continuing, lives forever*. Because of his exaltation to God's right hand, he has been *made perfect forever* (7:28). The ideal high priest offers the certainty that is "firm and secure" (6:19), giving wavering Christians the reason to remain faithful.

8:1–13 Having proclaimed Christ as the ideal priest in chapter 7, the author now describes the work of the priest in the ideal sanctuary in 8:1–10:18, developing the themes announced in chapter 7. Earlier in the book, he presents the theme of the full humanity more thoroughly than any writer of the New Testament (see 2:17; 4:14–16; 5:7–8). In this section, however, he focuses on the exaltation of Christ to God's right hand (see 1:3, 13), indicating that the *point* of the argument is that *we have such a high priest, who sat down at the right hand of the Majesty in heaven*. This allusion to Psalm 110:1 appears at the beginning (8:1) and end (10:12–14) of this lengthy argument, forming the basis for the comparisons in 8:1–10:18. Because the Levitical sanctuary and sacrifices belong to this world, they are incomplete and ineffective in contrast to the work of Christ in the heavenly sanctuary.

In 8:1–5, the author introduces the contrast between the sanctuaries and the ministries performed in them. The exalted Christ serves in *the true tent, which God made* (8:2), while Levitical priests offer sacrifices at a sanctuary that is only a *copy and shadow* (8:5) of the *true* one. The author appeals to Exodus 25:40 to support the distinction between the earthly and heavenly tent, recalling that God instructed Moses to build the tabernacle *according to the pattern shown* him *on the mountain*.

In 8:6, the author contrasts the ministry of Jesus in the heavenly sanctuary to the one in the earthly tabernacle, declaring that Jesus' ministry is superior, just as the heavenly priesthood was also superior to the earthly one (chapter 7). In additional superlatives, he declares that this *superior* ministry is associated with Jesus' role as *mediator* of a *superior covenant* (compare 7:22; 9:15; 13:20) and the believers' reception of *better promises*. God's *promise*, a constant theme of the book (4:1; 6:12; 11:9, 13, 17, 33), intertwines with the *covenant* and oath (compare 7:20–22) as the basis for the believer's commitment. In keeping with the author's consistent attempt to reinforce the believers' commitment by pointing to the superiority of the Christian possession, he affirms here that the death and exaltation of Jesus is God's ultimate covenant.

With the extended Scripture citation in 8:8–12, the author equates the *superior covenant* with the new covenant promised by Jeremiah (31:31–34) and then develops this theme in 9:1–10:18, concluding the section by citing this passage from Jeremiah again in 10:15–18. He introduces the citation in 8:7–8a with the suggestion that the announcement of the *new covenant* suggests that the old covenant was not *blameless*. Just as the announcement of the priesthood of Melchizedek demonstrates the imperfection of the Levitical law (7:11–12), the promise of a *new covenant* is an implied critique of the old one (8:7). According to 8:8, however, the actual critique is directed at the people, inasmuch as God *found fault* with them when he announced the coming of the new covenant. In the lengthy quotation, the accent is on the final verse, "I will remember their sins no more" (8:12), a theme that the author will explore in 9:1–10:18 when he demonstrates that Christ is the perfect sacrifice for sin. The *new* covenant inaugurated at the death of Jesus makes the earlier covenant obsolete (8:13).

9:1–10:18 Although other New Testament writers speak of the new covenant (see Matt 26:28; 2 Cor 3:6), only Hebrews identifies the new covenant specifically with the sacrificial system. In 9:1–10 the

> **The World Below & the World Above**
> *Although the idea of the heavenly pattern for the sanctuary was common in the Old Testament (Exod 26:30; Ezek 42:15), the author's language suggests his acquaintance with Plato's view that everything in this world is a mere copy of the "true" things that exist in the unseen world. The Jewish philosopher Philo, a near contemporary of the author, employed this Platonic theory to indicate that the worship in the temple is patterned after heavenly models.*

author focuses his attention on the furnishings of the tabernacle and the sacrifices offered by the high priest in the *earthly sanctuary* before demonstrating that Christ offered a superior sacrifice in the heavenly sanctuary in 9:11–10:18. The annual sacrifice on the Day of Atonement (Lev 16) provides the basis for the comparison. The author enumerates the furnishings of the tabernacle in 9:1–5 (see Exod 25:23–30; 37:17–24) and then describes the activity of the priest in 9:6–10. The author describes the annual sacrifice of atonement as an *illustration* of the inadequacy of the Levitical sacrifices. His statement that the way into *the Most Holy Place had not yet been disclosed* anticipates the later claim that Christ has opened up the new and living way (10:19). In keeping with his consistent distinction between the heavenly and earthly levels of reality, he insists that the sacrifices in a material sanctuary were only *external regulations* (literally "regulations of the flesh"; compare 9:13) that could not cleanse the *conscience*. Although the Levitical passages state without reservation that the high priest offered sacrifices to take away sins, the author looks back on the Levitical sacrifices from the perspective of the work of Christ, the ultimate sacrifice for sin. Consistent with the argument throughout Hebrews, he insists that everything in the past – including the sacrificial system – pales in comparison with the work of Christ.

The description of the inadequacies of the sacrificial system in 9:1–10 is the background for the description of the work of Christ in 9:11–14, where the author, continuing the thought of 8:1–5, describes a sacrificial ministry in heaven, the more perfect tabernacle that is not human-made. Having previously described the exaltation of Christ as his entry "behind the curtain" into the sanctuary (6:19), the author now demonstrates the superiority of the sacrifice, bringing together in one thought the crucifixion and exaltation. Using the familiar argument from the lesser to the greater (also in 2:1–4; 12:9), he distinguishes between the sacrifices that cleanse *outwardly* and the one that *cleanses our consciences* (compare 9:9–10). These two levels of human existence correspond to the distinction between the earthly and heavenly tabernacles. The high priest offered *the blood of bulls and goats* (Lev 16:3, 14) on the Day of Atonement, and the *ashes of a red heifer* in a separate ritual of purification (Num 19:9, 17). In contrast, Christ is both high priest and sacrifice, cleansing the whole being of the people.

Having described Christ as the *mediator of a new covenant* already (8:6; 7:22; see 12:24), the author develops this theme in 9:15–22. Since the Greek word for *covenant* (*diatheke*) also means *will*, the author uses this legal metaphor in 9:15b–18 to explain that Jesus' death is the means by which the covenant *will* is *in force*. Like other New Testament writers (Rom 3:24; Eph 1:7), he describes the death of Jesus as a *ransom*, a term normally used for buying the freedom of a slave, and he returns to a major theme of this sermon in the reassurance to a discouraged community of the *inheritance promised by God* (compare 4:1; 6:12, 15, 17; 8:6) provided by the death of Jesus. In verses 18–22, the author moves from the legal image to sacrificial language, indicating that *the first covenant was not put into effect without blood* and demonstrating the importance of blood in the Levitical system. Although he finds the phrase *blood of the covenant* in Exodus 24:8, the scene he depicts in verses 19–22 draws on other Old Testament passages (Exod 40:9; Lev 8:12; 14:4; 17:11; Num 19:6) in order to show the importance of blood in the mediation of a covenant.

The description of the Levitical sacrifices in 9:15–22 is the basis for the comparison in verses 23–28, where Christ is the heavenly counterpart to the Levitical high priest, offering *better sacrifices* than the ones described above, insofar as he entered *heaven itself* and offered his own blood. The focal point of the comparison is that the sacrifice of Christ is *once for all at the end of the ages* (compare 1:1–2), unlike the sacrifices that the priests offered every year. Because the Lord will *appear a second time* to *bring salvation to those who are waiting for him*, the readers may take comfort in the assurance that the saving event of the past ensures their future.

> **The High Priest's Ministry & the Most Holy Place**
>
> *In placing the golden altar of incense within the most holy place rather than in the holy place, where it appears in the Old Testament accounts, the author is probably following established Jewish traditions. His primary interest in describing the furnishings is to delineate the demarcation between the most holy place and the holy place. The description of the high priest's ministry in the most holy place in 9:6–10 prepares the way for the comparison to the ministry of Christ in 9:11–14.*

The author summarizes the argument of this lengthy comparison of the sacrifice of Christ with the Levitical sacrifices. In 10:1–4, he repeats the claim of the ineffectiveness of the ancient sacrifices (see 9:9–10), concluding that the annual repetition of the sacrifices demonstrated their lack of finality in terms reminiscent of the argument in 7:23–25. Thus, although Old Testament passages indicate that the priests made atonement for sin, the author concludes that the overwhelming superiority of the sacrifice of Christ places all other sacrifices in a new perspective.

> **"The blood of bulls & goats ..."**
> *In adding that the ancient sacrifices were a reminder of sins, the writer of Hebrews may be referring to the Greek translation of Numbers 5:15, according to which the trial of the suspected adulteress was a reminder of sin. Other ancient writers, including the author's near contemporary Philo (Moses 2.107; Planting 108), also argued that physical sacrifices provided only a reminder of sins. Indeed, the author's conclusion that it is impossible for the blood of bulls and goats to take away sins was widely held by philosophers who concluded that the deity does not need sacrifices from humans.*

In 10:5–10, the author compares the sacrifice of Christ with those described in 10:1–4, quoting Psalm 40:7–9 as the words of Jesus when *he came into the world* at the incarnation. The parallelism of the psalm indicates two contrasts: *sacrifice and offering* with a *body*; and *burnt offerings and sin offerings* with doing God's *will*. The psalmist, like other Old Testament writers, indicates that sacrifices have no value without obedience to God (Amos 5:21ff; Isa 1:11-17; Hos 6:6; 1 Sam 15:22). In Hebrews, the psalm tells the story of Christ who, in doing God's *will*, replaced the sacrificial system; that is, he set aside the *first* (Levitical sacrifices) in order to establish the *second* (the sacrifice of Christ). In the comment that *he sets aside the first to establish the second*, the author employs a principle that he has used frequently – that a later passage renders an earlier one obsolete (4:8; 7:11; 8:7). The result of the argument is to provide assurance to the readers: because of the once-for-all sacrifice, *we have been made holy through the sacrifice of Jesus once-for-all*. The author concludes this lengthy argument by reinforcing the contrast between the finality of the sacrifice of Christ and the annual sacrifices that were repeated each year, returning to the two major Old Testament passages that he cited at the beginning of this section. In 10:11–14, the contrast between the priest who *stands* to perform his ministry and our high priest who *sat down at God's right hand* alludes to Psalm 110:1, also mentioned in 1:3, 13 and 8:1. The author then returns to the quotation of Jeremiah 31:33–34, cited in 8:7–13. For the author, both passages point to the finality of the sacrifice of Christ as a source of encouragement to the readers.

10:19–25 In keeping with his desire to write a "word of exhortation" (13:22), the author returns to the practical consequences of his discussion of the high priesthood of Christ (10:19–25) that he first mentioned at the beginning of this section (4:14–16), addressing the community in three "let us" passages that are consequences of the heavenly sacrifice of Christ. Christ has entered the heavenly world behind the curtain (6:19; 9:11–14), opening up *the new and living way* into the sanctuary for believers *through the curtain*, reversing the situation in which "the way into the most holy place" was not yet open (9:8). The *curtain* is his *body* insofar as his death on the cross was his entry into the true sanctuary. This *confidence* (see 3:6; 10:36) is the right to appear before someone of high rank. Because the way is open, the author first urges, *let us draw near to God*, using the language that the Old Testament employs for corporate worship (see Exod 16:9; 34:32; Lev 9:5; Num 10:3a). Unlike the ancient people, believers have a *conscience* (9:9, 14) through the work of Christ and *bodies washed with pure water* in baptism. The author urges secondly, *let us hold unswervingly to the hope we profess* (compare 3:3, 14), indicating that the sacrifice of Christ provides stability for a community tempted to abandon the faith (see 3:12). The third exhortation, *let us consider how we may stir one another toward love and good works*, suggests that discouragement has caused the community to diminish the *good works* that distinguished them in the earlier days (see 6:10–11; 10:32–34), but that now the reminder of the work of Christ is the basis for a new commitment. The author emphasizes corporate responsibility for the renewal of the church's commitment, insisting that they *stir one another up* and *encourage one another* when they *meet together* in the assembly (see 3:12). The frequent references to the community's temptation (2:1–4; 6:4–6; 12:12) suggests that the *habit* of some who *give up* on the congregation's meetings is the result of their general discouragement. The knowledge of the work of Christ and of the *Day* of his return (see 9:28) should motivate the members to recommit themselves to service. Expectation of the second coming leads to appropriate behavior in and for the community of believers.

10:26–31 Having shown the greatness of what Christians acquire through the work of Christ, the author now shows the consequences of rejecting this salvation, once more indicating that the superior salvation implies grave consequences for those who reject it (2:1–4; 6:4–6). Using the argument from the lesser to the greater (see 2:1–4), he points to the *fearful judgment* that awaits those who show contempt for the *blood of the covenant* and insult the Spirit of grace. The God who holds out a great promise for those who endure also *avenges* those who treat his gift with contempt (4:13; 12:25).

> **Willful Sin**
>
> The author of Hebrews assumes the Old Testament's distinction between unintentional sins and those committed "defiantly" (see Lev 4:1–2, 13, 22, 27; Num 15:27–31), warning those who deliberately keep on sinning that there is no more sacrifice for sin. The finality of Jesus' sacrifice (10:1–18) offers not only an assurance to believers, but also a warning to those who abandon the faith.

A CALL TO FAITHFULNESS · 10:32–13:25

10:32–39 The author concludes the central section of Hebrews (4:14–10:31) with a warning before introducing the final section of the book with the appeal to endure. He now motivates the readers by recalling the *earlier days* when they had both endured abuse and *sympathized* with others in their mistreatment, knowing that they owned *better and lasting possessions* than the material possessions *confiscated* from them. The memory of the community's past commitment undergirds both the appeal not *to throw away the confidence* (10:35) that they have gained as a result of the work of Christ (10:19) and the call to *persevere* in the midst of discouragement. While those who sin deliberately receive punishment (10:26–31), those who *persevere* receive what *he has promised* (10:36). The author concludes with the quotation of Habakkuk 2:4, which contrasts those who *live by faith* with those who *shrink back*, affirming that the community will make the appropriate choice between those two options.

11:1–39 The distinction between *faith* and *shrink*[ing] *back* introduces the discussion of faith in chapter 11, a theme that the author has anticipated earlier in this sermon (see 3:12, 19; 4:2; 6:1, 12). Noting that *we understand* the world's origin from what is *invisible*, the author summarizes the stories of the antediluvian heroes Abel, Enoch, and Noah before he gives the lengthy treatments of Abraham and his immediate descendants, and then Moses (verses 23–29). Hebrews 11:30–31 recall Joshua and the conquest before concluding with a comprehensive account of Israelite history from the judges to the prophets. In the list of heroes, the author pursues the themes that address the temptations that the readers now face. Repeatedly, the author emphasizes that faith is directed toward what one hopes for: thus the ancient heroes sought a *reward* (11:6, 26), a *promise* (11:9, 13, 17, 33), a *better country* (11:15–16), and a *city* (11:16). Because the heroes saw the invisible (see 11:27) and things *not yet seen* (11:7), they were alienated from the world around them. Noah "condemned the world" (11:7), and Abraham was a *stranger in a foreign country* (11:9). He, Isaac, and Jacob *lived in tents* (11:9); others "wandered in deserts and mountains, and in caves and holes in the ground" (11:38) as a sign of their homelessness. Moses chose to be mistreated and regarded *disgrace for the sake of Christ as of greater value than the treasures of Egypt* (11:26). The summaries in 11:32–38 highlight the abuse that accompanies those who see the invisible. The author concludes that *the world was not worthy of them* (11:38). Undoubtedly, his description develops the themes that will address his own community as it experiences the stress of alienation from its own culture and faces the temptation to abandon the faith under difficult circumstances. The refrain *they did not receive what was promised* (11:13, 39) reminds the readers that the great heroes lived their entire lives without seeing the fulfillment of the ultimate promise but held onto their faith in all circumstances.

> **"A great cloud of witnesses …"**
>
> *The distinctive literary form of Hebrews 11, with its list of heroes arranged around a theme, was common in Jewish literature (Ecclesiasticus 44:1–44:19; 1 Maccabees 2:51–61). Hebrews 11:1 is not a comprehensive definition of faith, but an introduction to the characteristics that distinguished the ancients, all of whom were sure and certain of what they hoped for but did not see.*

12:1–11 Just as the author consistently turns from a theological lesson to an appeal to his listeners, he turns from the list of heroes to encourage believers. After an implicit appeal in 11:40 (*only together with us would they be made perfect*), he speaks directly to them in 12:1–3, the actual climax of the list of heroes. Like many Jewish writers before him, he pictures the hardships of faithfulness as an athletic contest (also 10:32) in a stadium with a cloud of witnesses, and speaks with the familiar *let us* (4:14, 16; 10:22–24) to challenge them to *run with perseverance the race set before* [them]. The emphasis on *perseverance*, which the author equates with faith in 10:36–37, suggests that Christian existence is an exhausting long-distance run. While the readers do not see the ultimate reward in the present (11:39), they can *fix* [their] *eyes on Jesus*, who first persevered (NIV *endured*) to the cross and is now *seated at the right hand of God*. Jesus' status at God's right hand, a consistent theme (1:3, 13; 8:1; 10:12) comes only after he completed the journey the readers now travel (2:10–18; 5:5–10), and makes him both the *author and perfecter of faith* and the ultimate example of faithfulness. Since he *endured opposition* from *sinful men*, the listeners can take courage and not *lose heart*.

12:4–11 The author speaks directly to the anguish of the listeners and continues the theme of endurance, citing Proverbs 3:11–12 as a direct *word of encouragement* to the listeners. He resumes the familial language to describe the community (see 2:10–13; 3:1), applying the advice from father to son from Proverbs to a community of *sons*. He follows a familiar biblical theme of the Bible and the ancient world that hardship produces *discipline* (see Deut 8:5; 11:2; 2 Sam 7:14; Ps 118:18; Job 5:17-19), concluding that their hardships are not a sign of God's abandonment but of the *discipline* that benefits the children. This discipline will ultimately produce a *harvest of righteousness* for those who suffer.

12:12–17 This assurance is the basis for the exhortation in 12:12–13 to the readers *to strengthen their feeble arms and weak knees* (compare Prov 4:26; Isa 35:3). The imagery suggests that an entire community is near exhaustion on its long march. The call to *make level paths for your feet so that the lame may not be disabled* again indicates the importance of communal responsibility for its weakest members (3:12–19). The author's emphasis on communal responsibility continues in 12:14–17. To care for the weak is *to make every effort to live in peace with all men and to be holy* and to ensure that the entire community is holy, as the author indicates by the three clauses that follow the words *see to it*: *that no one misses the grace of God … that no bitter root grows up … that no one is sexually immoral like Esau*…. Here Esau exemplifies the opposite of the heroes of faith in chapter 11, insofar as he renounced the inheritance for something visible. The author appears to combine the stories of the birthright (Gen 25:29–30) and the blessing (Gen 27:1–40). The reference to Esau's futile attempt to repent, an apparent reference to the story of the blessing, is the third of the warnings about the irrevocability of the decision to abandon the faith (compare 6:4–6; 10:26–39).

> **Esau's Immorality**
> *Although the Old Testament never describes Esau as sexually immoral, Jewish tradition described him as one who chose the desires of the flesh over eternal matters.*

12:18–29 In keeping with the author's practice throughout this sermon of alternating exhortation with theological reflection, he reminds the readers of the greatness of their salvation and the consequences of rejecting it, again employing a comparison with the Old Testament. In the words *you have not come* (12:18) and *you have come* (12:22), he compares Israel at Mount Sinai with the listeners who have come to *Mount Zion, the city of the living God, the heavenly Jerusalem*. Whereas the Jewish tradition recalled the events of Mount Sinai with awe, the author contrasts *the mountain that can be touched* with Mount Zion. That is, the listeners, in coming to a heavenly *city*, have now come to something more awesome than Mount Sinai, with its thunder and lightning. Thus, in comparing two different assemblies, the author argues that, despite all appearances, the listeners *have come* to an awesome event in their corporate worship services that includes not only the little house church but also the heavenly host, as well. Such an event has severe consequences for those who do not pay attention. In contrast to the Israelites who heard a voice speaking words that terrified the people (12:19), the church hears a word from heaven announcing an earthquake far greater than the one at Mount Sinai (12:26). Consequently, the author calls on the church to worship God *with reverence and awe*, knowing that he is *a consuming fire* (see 4:13; 10:31). The great salvation poses great responsibility for the listeners.

13:1–25 Although Hebrews is a "word of exhortation" (13:22) rather than a letter, the conclusion in chapter 13 is similar to the ending of Paul's letters, which often contain specific ethical instructions (as in 1 Thess 4:1–5:22), requests for prayer (Rom 15:30; 1 Thess 5:26), his wish to see the readers (Phlm 22), a benediction (2 Cor 13:14), and final greetings (1 Thess 5:26). The ethical instructions in 13:1–6 describe the communal solidarity of those who live as family, *loving each other as brothers*, *entertain*[ing] *strangers*, and caring for prisoners in their midst as they have already (6:9–12; 10:32–34). The advice about *marriage* and the *love of money* further defines communal values that are present throughout the community. Those who are alienated from society because of their faith now express shared communal values that parallel the expectations that Paul had for his communities (1 Thess 4:3–12; Rom 12:9–12).

In 13:7–17, the author returns to the major themes of the sermon for a final exhortation, calling on them to *imitate the faith* of the leaders of the first generation, just as he has challenged them to imitate the faith of the heroes of Scripture (13:7). In the only reference to false teachings in the entire sermon (13:9), the author affirms that Jesus Christ is *the same yesterday, today, and forever* (see 1:10); hence the listeners do not need to be *carried away by all kinds of strange teachings*. In contrasting the *ceremonial foods* with the *altar* that *we have*, the author again compares the Christian possession with the alternatives described in chapter 9. The *altar* equals the heavenly sanctuary. Continuing the comparison with the Day of Atonement ritual of Leviticus 16, the author compares the ritual of taking the bodies of sacrificial animals *outside the camp* with Jesus' suffering *outside the gate* of Jerusalem (see John 19:17, 20) in a place of shame. He continues the theme of Christ as the forerunner (6:19; 10:19), with the summons to the listeners to follow him *outside the camp, bearing his shame*. For the readers to *go outside the camp* is to continue to suffer abuse within their own culture. Only the fact that they, like Abraham (see 11:10), *have a city* that is not here, but in heaven, gives them the resources to go *outside the camp*. In a sermon that has focused on the insufficiency of ancient sacrifices, he calls his listeners to offer the only sacrifices *that are pleasing to God*: the *sacrifice of praise*, good deeds, and the sharing of their possessions.

13:18–25 The author's request for the community's prayers for his return to them (13:19) indicates that, although he is unnamed, he is well known to the community. The reference to Timothy (13:23), a frequent companion of Paul, may suggest that the author and readers belong to circles familiar with the apostle. He describes his work as a *word of exhortation*, a term that refers to a synagogue sermon (Acts 13:15), asking his readers to *bear with* his message, which is intended to encourage them to hold fast in the midst of diversity. With the benedictions in 13:20–21, 25, he places the future of the community in the hands of God.

> **Obeying Leaders**
> Although the author has consistently called for communal responsibility for each other (3:12–14; 10:22–25; 12:14–17), *he now instructs them to obey their leaders, indicating that their responsibility for others does not preclude the role of* leaders *who keep watch over* [their] *souls. An earlier group of leaders had taught them the word of God* (13:7); *the community now submits to leaders who must* give an account *of their work.*

THEOLOGICAL REFLECTIONS

Although the themes of priesthood and sacrifice may appear obscure to contemporary readers, an understanding of the author's essential purpose will reveal the lasting significance of this work. Hebrews speaks to churches that face rejection from the larger society, declining numbers, and the distance between the faith they proclaim and the reality of actual experience.

Those who face the problems of church renewal in a changing world may find in Hebrews a model for addressing these challenges. Hebrews invites readers to see beyond the immediate context of suffering and discouragement and to recognize their place within the reality that is not limited by time and space. The author challenges his readers to envision a world that is unchanging, which will be an anchor for those who live in insecurity. He also invites readers to inhabit the world of Scripture and to recognize their place in a larger narrative that begins with creation and ends with the fulfillment of God's promises. By locating the readers within an alternative world, the author seeks to motivate readers to remain faithful.

FOR FURTHER STUDY

Alan C. Mitchell, *Hebrews* (Collegeville, Minn.: Liturgical Press, 2007).

James W. Thompson, *Hebrews*. Paideia: Commentaries on the New Testament (Grand Rapids: Baker Academic, 2008).

Tom Wright, *Hebrews for Everyone* (Louisville: Westminster John Knox, 2003).

WORKS CITED

David DeSilva, *Perseverance in Gratitude; A Socio-Rhetorical Commentary on the Epistle "To the Hebrews"* (Grand Rapids: Eerdmans, 2000).

Craig R. Koester, "Hebrews" *Anchor Bible Dictionary* 3 (New York: Doubleday, 2001).

James Kugel, *The Bible as It Was* (Cambridge: Harvard University Press, 1997).

Philo, *On the Life of Moses* (ed. F. H. Colson; Cambridge: Harvard University Press, 1935).

———, *On Planting* (ed. F. H. Colson; Cambridge: Harvard University Press, 1930).

James W. Thompson, *The Beginnings of Christian Philosophy* (Washington, D.C.: Catholic University of America Press, 1982).

James

Curt Niccum

CHAPTER CONTENTS

Contexts **1027**

Commentary **1027**
- Salutation & Introduction · 1:1–27 **1027**
- The Body of the Letter · 2:1–5:6 **1029**
- Conclusion · 5:7–20 **1031**

Theological Reflections **1032**

For Further Study **1032**

Works Cited **1032**

The popularity of the name *James* (literally "Jacob") in the first century CE prohibits ready identification of the author. Traditionally, commentators opt for the brother of Jesus. The simple description, *a servant of God and of the Lord Jesus Christ*, may support this, for no other James received such widespread recognition. (Note that James needs no introduction in Acts; see also Jude 1.) If Jesus' brother composed the letter, it predates 62 CE, the probable date of his death.

CONTEXTS

As with identifying the author, identifying the recipients of this letter also proves difficult. Although *the twelve tribes scattered among the nations* suggests a Jewish audience, it does not require it, since a similar salutation in 1 Peter 1:1 applies to Gentiles. Likewise James's emphasis on the law has a counterpart in Paul's letter to the predominantly Gentile churches in Rome (Rom 13:8–10).

Even the occasion for the letter remains obscure. James incorporates genres such as wisdom, *paranesis*, diatribe, among others that can address potential rather than actual situations. Although the recurring theme of trials probably reflects some type of opposition, the broad audience and the lack of any empire-wide persecution in the first century suggest that James merely offers advice on living under the general social and economic trials of the day. In other words, James probably presumes a situation of real, but sporadic, opposition similar to that documented in Acts.

> **Genres in James**
> *James combines different wisdom literary forms. Parenesis is moral instruction or advice like that at the ends of Paul's letters. Diatribe was a style of dialogue common in ancient schools and used by philosophers.*

COMMENTARY

SALUTATION & INTRODUCTION · 1:1

The salutation, following ancient custom, identifies the author, *James*, and the readers, the *twelve tribes*. The latter would be *scattered* from western Europe to eastern Persia (the result of deportations since the eighth century BCE, if James addresses Jewish Christians).

The introduction has five parts. The beginning (verses 2–4), middle (verses 12–15), and end (verses 26–27) state and expand on the thesis of "perfection," or spiritual maturity. The intervening sections prepare the reader for what this requires: appropriate speech (verses 5–11) and action (verses 16–25).

1:2–4 James paradoxically encourages his readers to consider *trials pure joy*, for these perfect the saints. James draws special attention to this goal of perfection with synonyms clustered at the end of the sentence (*perfect* [NIV *mature*], *complete*, and *not lacking in anything*; note also *pure and faultless* in 1:27) and with a series of wordplays in the Greek.

1:5–8 The word *lacks* (also in verse 4) links this discussion of appropriate requests to God with the preceding verses. Although *wisdom* is the specific object

> **Male & Female in James**
> *The gender-specific word for "man" occurs six times in James (1:8, 12, 20, 23; 2:2; 3:2), perhaps indicating a male-only audience. The context of wisdom and generalized advice, though, could still make this generic. The feminine "adulteresses" in 4:4 referring to a group that includes males suggests James employed traditional materials without regard to the gender(s) of his readers. His contrast between male and female resembles that in Proverbs 1–9.*

here, one may ask for other divine gifts (see 5:13–18). God gives generously and does so *without finding fault*. Hence, any imperfect saint can approach God expecting positive results rather than fearing reprisals for deficiencies. One *must*, therefore, *believe* in God's grace and mercy *and not doubt*. One who doubts God's willingness to answer prayers is *double-minded* and *unstable* (descriptors of sinful behavior in 3:8 and 4:8) and will receive no reward. Thus the faith of the petitioner determines the appropriateness of each request.

1:9–11 The subject moves to appropriate boasting before God. Those *in humble circumstances* (referring to Christians) can "boast" (NIV *take pride*, but see 4:16). God's generosity makes this acceptable, for God alone grants *high position*. On the other hand, James does not expect *the rich* (referring to non-Christians) to boast appropriately. Instead, their boasting *is evil* (4:16). A realistic evaluation, however, would cause them to recognize their *low position* and inevitable destruction alongside their possessions (verse 11). James here (and elsewhere) encourages the church by reminding them of the paradoxical nature of reality: God blesses the lowly and punishes those who appear blessed (see 1 Sam 2:8; Luke 1:52–53).

> **Rich & Poor**
> In James, "the rich" labels non-believers. This makes better sense of the context of judgment and the use of the phrase later in 2:1–7 and 5:1–6. James, however, recognizes the presence of some wealthy Christians, for they have the capacity to warm and feed the poor (2:16), actions which required means. Therefore one must conclude that James categorized wealthy Christians among those in humble circumstances and not among the rich. This approximates Jesus' own teachings (see Luke 6:20, 24; 18:18–25 and 19:1–10) and the lifestyles of the earliest Christians (see Acts 2:44–45 and 4:32–5:10).

The ending of the previous paragraph, *in all his paths* (NIV *in all he does*; verse 8), parallels the ending of this section, *in his ways* (NIV *while he goes about his business*; verse 11). Thus the speech of both groups, the doubters and the rich, leads down a destructive "path." Note, though, that one can be rescued from this *erroneous path* (NIV *error*; 5:20).

1:12–15 James repeats the elements of the thesis (*blessed, perseveres, test* [1:12], and *full grown* [1:15] parallel *joy, trials* [1:2], *perseverance* [1:3], and *mature* [1:4]). He also expands them. The result is the *victor's crown*, *the life* (literally "the crown of life") which *God promised*. At first glance, the claim that God cannot *tempt* anyone (verse 13) appears problematic, for God "tempted" Abraham. James, however, knows this, for he uses that very story later (2:21–23). Here he only concerns himself with trials coming from real *evil* (verse 13), and particularly those caused by the *rich* or *sin*. If the believer surrenders to such temptation, the *full-grown* (literally "perfect") end is *death*.

> **"When you face trials …"**
> Trials, test, and tempt/-ed/-ing in James all translate the same Greek root. No single English word adequately translates the spectrum of meaning covered by the Greek.

1:16–25 Three times James punctuates a call for action by preceding a reference to *the word* with a command. God's speech demands human action.

The first command, *don't be deceived*, sounds a note of warning. The believer recognizes that God provides *every good and perfect gift* rather than *evil* trials (verse 17). The consistency of God's nature guarantees the consistency of God's goodness. James offers convincing proof: whereas sin gives *birth to death* (verse 15), God gives *birth* (verse 18) to believers through *the word*.

> **The Greatest Commandments**
> James addresses the Christians as *dear* [literally "beloved"] for the first time in 1:16. James probably expresses God's love for the saints more than his own personal feelings. This adjective occurs only where James discusses loving God and loving neighbor (thus connecting "beloved" with the two greatest commandments) as a reflection of God's love for Christians.

The second command, *take note of this* (verse 19), reminds the readers that God's people must reflect his nature (that is, be consistently good and generous). Rash speech and anger *work* (NIV *bring about*) results contrary to God's will. In giving birth, God implants *the word*, which replaces *moral filth* and *evil*. The verb *take note* could be an indicative, "you know," referring to what precedes rather than what follows, but more likely the verb follows a pattern of beginning with a command and closing with a reference to "the word," and so looks forward.

Do not merely listen to the word … do what it says (verse 22) constitutes the third command. James reinforces this command by referring to the Law as a mirror. This analogy, at first, appears awkward. Johnson, though, has shown that the ancients frequently used the mirror in a context of moral reflection. Thus, one's ethics truly reflect oneself ("Mirror," 632–45). Because revelation is the source of Judeo-Christian ethics, *the word* becomes the mirror. God gives birth through the word and implants it. Therefore what one sees in the "mirror" should approximate what one finds in that word, *the perfect law* (verse 24). This correspondence between listening (verse 22)/seeing (verse 25) and doing makes one *blessed* (verse 25; creating an *inclusio* with verse 12).

> **Inclusio**
> *A literary device by which a nearly identical beginning and ending are used to frame a body of materials.*

1:26–27 In summary, perfect *religion* consists of keeping *a tight rein on* one's *tongue*, looking after *orphans and widows in their distress*, and keeping *oneself from being polluted by the world*. The following chapters examine these three topics.

THE BODY OF THE LETTER · 2:1–5:6

James associates caring for *orphans and widows* (a phrase from Deuteronomy referring to the poor) with "having faith." Faith shows no preference for the rich (2:1–13). Rather it expresses itself in action toward the poor (2:14–26).

2:1–4 James opens the letter body with the command to *have faith* (NIV *as believers*). Faith cannot brook partiality. On the contrary, *favoritism* derives from *evil thoughts* (verse 4). James illuminates this with a hypothetical situation: the entrance of a rich person and a poor person into the assembly [Greek "synagogue"], each welcomed in keeping with his or her social, rather than spiritual, status. He thus forbids copying the culture's social structures inside the church.

2:5–13 The imperative *listen*, occurring so close to 1:19, emphasizes the gravity of this error. Indeed, showing favoritism reverses God's mercy (see also 4:6), for God purposefully exalts *the poor* to be *rich in faith*. *In the eyes of the world* is not in the Greek; thus, the NIV waters down James' sharp distinction between the saints and the *rich*. The use of similarly sounding words further heightens this contrast. One must love the *neighbor* [Greek *plesios*] instead of coddling the *rich* [Greek *plousios*]. Furthermore, fawning over *the rich* makes little sense because they exploit believers, drag them before courts, and *slander* the Lord's name.

Keeping the *royal law* includes more than just loving one's *neighbor*. Johnson has convincingly shown that James relies upon the broader context of Leviticus 19 throughout the letter ("Use," 393–401). Of course, the connection between loving neighbor and loving God (verse 5) points to an even larger context, the entire Law (2:10; see also Matt 22:40 and Rom 13:9–10).

Showing partiality thus "works" *sin* (verse 9), and this results in the transgression of the entire law (verses 10–11). Speech and action (verse 12), therefore, must be consistent with this *law of freedom*, the measure of which is mercy (verse 13). James thus shares a view of law similar to that in Deuteronomy 30, which emphasizes the law's life-giving abilities.

2:14–26 To illustrate this, James creates a plausible scenario between a believer and a less fortunate sibling in the faith (verses 15–17). Saying *keep warm and well fed* accomplishes nothing without any attempt to warm and feed.

What good is speech without corresponding action (verses 14 and 16)? It only results in death (verses 17 and, by implication, 26). Indeed, *demons* acknowledge the two greatest commands yet remain excluded from salvation. (With the allusion to *one God* and the parallel statements *you are doing right* in 2:8 and 2:19 [NIV *Good*!], James again connects Deuteronomy 6:4–5 and Leviticus 19:18, just as Jesus did). One should rather desire the faith of *Abraham* and *Rahab* (verses 21–26). Actions consistent with speech *made* their faith *complete* (literally "perfect"). Faith goes beyond "right thinking." Faith is "right thinking producing right action."

3:1–12 Chapter three addresses *keeping a tight rein on* the *tongue* (see 1:26). Just as action must be consistent with speech, speech must be consistent with action. James advises many "not to become" *teachers* because of stricter judgment. If the transgression of one command makes one guilty of the entire law (2:10), how much more guilty, then, the one who stumbles while teaching others about that law? Yet who teaches without stumbling?

> **James's Rhetoric**
> *James uses the common Jewish strategy of arguing from the lesser to the greater (called in Hebrew qal wachomer, "light and heavy").*

Only the *perfect* can, because the one who controls the tongue can *keep his whole body in check* (verse 2).

James illustrates the power of the tongue with two classical analogies, that of the horse's bridle (verse 3) and the ship's rudder (verse 4). He also likens the tongue to a spark that ignites forest fires (verse 5). In dire terms he concludes that *the tongue is a fire, a world of evil. It corrupts the whole person* (literally "whole body," see verses 2–3), *sets the whole course of his life on fire, and is itself set on fire by hell.* If faith without works is dead, how much more so, then, the person with uncontrolled speech?

The ability to train animals serves as a counterexample (verse 7). Humans tame the deadliest of beasts, yet not the tongue. As before, a dreadful conclusion follows: The tongue *is a restless evil, full of deadly poison* (verse 8). The tongue proclaims praise to God yet curses those *made in* his *likeness* (verse 9). In verses 11–12, three comparisons from nature reveal how unnatural these contradictory uses of the tongue are.

3:13–18 In teaching, what one does (a *good life* shown *by deeds done in humility*) is as important as what one says. The necessary *wisdom* for the teacher descends *from heaven* (verse 15; also 1:5, 17) and reveals itself in all that is *pure, peace-loving, considerate, submissive, full of mercy and good fruit, impartial and sincere* (verse 17; in Greek, all the words in the list begin with the letters *alpha* or *epsilon*, a way of making the list memorable). *Bitter envy and selfish ambition*, on the other hand, derive from below. Such wisdom is *earthly, of the devil* (verses 14–15).

The incompatibility of these two wisdoms segues into the next topic: keeping *oneself from being polluted by the world*. Here the tone becomes sharper, and second person plural pronouns ("you") and verbs predominate. Although James does not necessarily address a specific situation in his readers' lives, the greater intensity draws a sharper distinction between the saints and the world. This distinction reaches its zenith with the prophetic denunciations of the *rich* in 4:13–5:6.

4:1–10 One worldly pollutant is strife. Strife originates from *desires*, in particular desires for pleasure. These *battle in your parts* (NIV *within you*). The NIV preserves the Greek's ambiguity. Does "parts" (NIV *you*) refer to the human body or members of the church? Although applicable to strife within the church, the previous use of this phrase (*in our parts*, 3:6; NIV *parts of the body*) favors the physical sense. Many problems in the church thus originate from sin's enticement of individuals (as in 1:14–15).

James notes two things about this strife. First, *fights and quarrels* result from desires that spawn lust (NIV *you want something*), murder, and covetousness (verse 2). Second, *you quarrel and fight* because "Christians" either do not approach God or they approach *with wrong motives* (verse 3). James gives a startling portrayal of God: "The gift-giving God is here manipulated as a kind of vending machine precisely for purposes of self-gratification" (Johnson, *Letter of James*, 278).

"One cannot serve both God and Mammon." Those wishing to maintain a relationship with both commit spiritual adultery. They are *adulterous people* (verse 4; literally "adulteresses"). Again James, like Proverbs, casts the life of faith in terms of the metaphor of marital fidelity. God demands single-minded devotion just as he gives to his own people. *Friendship with the world is hatred toward God!*

Verse 5 presents numerous problems for interpretation. Does James quote *Scripture*? How should one punctuate the verse? What is the subject of *tends* (literally "longs for")? *Scripture says* usually introduces biblical quotations, but the following words do not correspond to any known text, and the citation of Proverbs 3:34 (in 4:6) seems too remote. Perhaps James quotes an unknown Greek translation of an Old Testament passage or cites a noncanonical text. The syntax of the verse provides further confusion. *The* (human or Holy) *spirit* could be the subject or the object of *tends* (literally "longs for"). God must be the subject of *caused to live* (which is the original reading), but may also be of *tends*. (See NIV footnote.) If the phrase *toward envy* modifies *tends*, then only the human spirit can be the subject, because the Greek word translated *envy*, which is always negative, is incompatible with God. But that option basically strips the passage of any significant meaning. In the absence of any satisfactory solutions, I suggest that James relies here upon the larger context of Proverbs 3:27–35, which contains a number of parallels with James 4:4–6 (and elsewhere in the letter). In particular, Proverbs 3:31–32 sets those who envy at odds with God while the righteous have an intimate relationship with him.

To reflect this context, one could punctuate the verse differently, a reasonable option since ancient

---

The Fruits of Desire

The inclusion of murder as a result of worldly desire appears extreme to the modern reader, but Johnson has shown this to be common to ancient discussions about "envy" ("Topos"). Due to the traditional nature of the language, one should not conclude that James writes about a situation where a Christian had actually murdered another.

Greek texts lacked punctuation marks. The verse would then read, "Or do you think that Scripture speaks in vain about [literally "with respect *toward*"] *envy*? He (God) longs for *the spirit he caused to live in us*." If this reconstruction is correct, James uses Proverbs to support the mutual exclusion of friendship with the world (marked by *envy*) and friendship with God (marked by *the spirit*, already noted in verse 4). James then specifically quotes a passage from this same context which promises an even greater gift than *the spirit*.

Verse 6 thus emphasizes God's generosity rather than contrasting it with human jealousy (requiring the Greek conjunction to be translated "and" rather than *but*). *Greater* (NIV *more*) than the already tremendous gift of the Spirit is the reward given to *the humble* (that is, believers, 1:9). While exalting the faithful, God opposes *the proud*, the friends of this world.

Since eternal judgment hinges upon one's relationship with God, the subsequent call to repentance (verses 7–10) seeks immediate response. The primary invitations to conversion are *submit yourselves to God* (verse 7) and *humble yourselves before the Lord* (verse 10). These frame additional exhortations to those disloyal to God (called *sinners* and *double-minded*, see also 1:8). The clear allusion to 1:9–11 and the topic of 4:13–5:6 indicate that James specifically berates *the rich* here.

4:11–12 James now revisits the ideas of 2:1–4:10: speech and action (NIV *keeping*) must be consistent with the Law. One cannot sit in judgment on the Law or against one's neighbor, for God alone is lawgiver and judge. To *slander one another* disregards people and the will of their creator.

4:13–5:6 James closes the letter body by criticizing in prophetic fashion the speech (4:13–17) and actions (5:1–6) of *the rich*. They make plans based on their own business skill rather than God's will (4:13–17). James does not condemn setting long-term goals. Instead, he finds fault in the boasting. *All such boasting is evil* (verse 16; compare 1:9 and 4:6, 10). Because of the brevity of life and the sustaining power of God, the rich one *knows* that to recognize the sovereignty of the Lord is *good* (verse 17). For this reason, to omit offering one's life to God in prayer is sinful.

Practicing justice and mercy constitute the other good that the rich know to do (5:1–6), but they gain wealth at the expense of others instead. The *innocent* they *condemn* (by dragging them before the courts, 2:6) and *murder* (by withholding *wages*, 5:4). Although the weak offer them no opposition (verse 6), God opposes the oppressors (4:6). James, therefore, confidently speaks of their possessions as already tarnished (verses 2–3).

CONCLUSION · 5:7–20

5:7–8 To be perfect in imperfect times, saints must above all *be patient* (mentioned twice). Their reward is as sure as the corrosion of wealth. As a result, they should *strengthen their hearts* (NIV *stand firm*), whereas the rich must *purify* theirs (4:8). The motivation for action is *the Lord's coming* (also mentioned twice).

5:9–12 These verses attempt to rehabilitate human speech. First, Christians should not *grumble against one another* (verse 9). Like the prophets, they should use language to speak for God, whose deliverance is imminent.

Second, saints must *not swear*. In a statement clearly dependent on the teaching of Jesus (Matt 5:34–37), James discourages the making of oaths in order to convince another of one's fidelity or sincerity. Trickery or verbal sleight of hand does not characterize Christian speech.

> **Job**
> Like most first century Jewish writers, James would have included Job and other biblical figures among the prophets (see, for example, Acts 2:30). Job was famed for his endurance, though not necessarily patience (as in KJV), since his words hardly seem patient at times.

5:13–18 Two types of speech are consistent with patient suffering. First, those *in trouble* (same root as *suffering* in 5:10) *should pray*. Second, the *happy should sing songs of praise* (verse 13). Since James focuses on times of trial, he expands on the former. What follows emphasizes the need for prayer within community life. The inclusion of spiritual leaders is understandable (verse 14), but James extends the circle of accountability to the entire community (verse 16). Although nothing in this section proves difficult to interpret within its ancient setting, modern reluctance to associate physical illness with spiritual disease has resulted in attempts to qualify "sickness" here as something other than an ailment. Nonetheless, first century Jews and Christians connected the physical with the spiritual. For example, Jesus can say *Your sins are forgiven* or *Get up and walk* (Mark 2:1–12). Both mean the same thing. The man's paralysis stemmed from a sin problem. Likewise, Paul can speak of Christians being sick or dead because of their abuse of the Lord's Supper (1 Cor 11:30). Still, the healing of the blind man (John 9) reveals that not every disease had spiritual origins. James knows this. He makes the situation conditional: *if he* or she *has sinned* (verse 15).

Prayers are to be offered on behalf of the sick. In particular, the elders should come *pray and anoint* [the sick] *with oil* (viewed as medicinal in value). In the ancient world, holy people (such as prophets) could function as healers, especially if other medical means failed. This form of speech must also be *in the name of the Lord* (verse 14; see verse 10). (This does not refer to the tag "in Jesus' name" appended to prayers today, a modern invention derived from a misinterpretation of John 14:14.) Such prayers, if asked in faith (see 1:6), will *save* (NIV *make well*) and *heal* (verses 15–16). What better reason, therefore, for the saints to *confess sins to each other* and *pray for each other*?

As an example of the power of faithful prayer in times of suffering, James offers Elijah. He *was a man just like us* (literally "with the same nature" related to the Greek words for *suffering* and *trouble* in 5:10 and 13). Whereas Job provides an example for future hope, Elijah does for present action (see 1 Kgs 18:42–45). Here again God generously answers the prayer of faith (see 1:5–6 and 17–18).

5:19–20 As a final statement of churchwide accountability, James states that the correction of an errant one *will save him* or her *from death and cover many sins*. This translation probably comes closest to the actual meaning of the text, although the Greek is more ambiguous. This interpretation seems all the more probable if James alludes to Proverbs 10:12. This would then summarize the ultimate love for neighbor and perfection of the "royal law" (1:25; 2:8).

THEOLOGICAL REFLECTIONS

In a society where even the poor are rich by the world's standards, few Americans will appreciate the economic lines James draws between the faithful and sinners. According to James, unhealthy attitudes toward possessions creates partiality (despising the poor), causing neglect. They also beget materialism (envying the rich), causing strife. James firmly believes in God's generosity, but not so much in terms of wealth. The "good and perfect" gifts include wisdom, healing, and forgiveness, not mansions.

James does encourage the rich to aspire to God's kingdom, but he does not express much optimism. God does not exclude them, but their chances of survival seem remote. James does not specify how "the rich" become "poor," but that is because he writes only to "the poor," the community of faith. Since he presumes that some readers have wealth, we can extrapolate from the letter that "the rich" become humble only through faith in Jesus, and this is an active faith that displays itself in assisting the needy.

James's call for perfection poses an even greater challenge. Strongly influenced by Reformation theology, Western Christianity has often regarded perfection as unattainable this side of heaven. For James, though, Christ's near return makes perfection imperative now! He recognizes human shortcomings but suggests that with God's help these can be overcome. (Similar teachings also appear in the writings of John and Paul.) For James, perfection comes with speech and action that consistently benefit the community. In this interim period marked by suffering, one lives out one's faith by serving others, saving the sinner perhaps being the greatest service of all (5:20).

FOR FURTHER STUDY

Richard Bauckham, *James: Wisdom of James, Disciple of Jesus the Sage* (New York: Routledge, 1999).

Timothy B. Cargal, *Restoring the Diaspora: Discursive Structure and Purpose in the Epistle of James* (Atlanta: Scholars Press, 1993).

Peter H. Davids, *The Epistle of James* (Grand Rapids: Eerdmans, 1982).

Ralph P. Martin, *James* (Waco, Tex.: Word, 1988).

Todd C. Penner, *The Epistle of James and Eschatology* (Sheffield: Sheffield Academic, 1996).

———, "The Epistle of James in Current Research," *Currents in Research* 7 (1999): 257–308.

WORKS CITED

Luke Timothy Johnson, "James 3:13–4:10 and the Topos Περι Φθονου," *Novum Testamentum* 25 (1983): 327–347.

———, "The Mirror of Remembrance (James 1:22–25)." *Catholic Biblical Quarterly* 50 (1988): 632–45.

———, *The Letter of James* (New York: Doubleday, 1995).

———, "The Use of Leviticus 19 in the Letter of James," *Journal of Biblical Literature* 101 (1982): 391–401.

1 Peter

Mark Black

CHAPTER CONTENTS

Contexts   1033

Commentary   1033
- Greeting · 1:1–2   1033
- The Body of the Letter · 1:3–5:11   1034
- Final Words · 5:12–14   1039

Theological Reflections   1039

For Further Study   1040

Works Cited   1040

From the time of Irenæus (about 180 CE), early Christians explicitly named Peter as the author of this text. However, some modern interpreters claim that the letter was written by an unknown writer who used Peter's name to give it authority. They argue that the former Aramaic speaking Galilean could not have penned the excellent Greek found in the letter (see Achtemeier 1–7). However, Greek was widely spoken even in Galilee in the first century, and Peter spent many decades traveling and speaking. It is also possible that Silvanus was involved in the writing of this letter (see 5:12). Those skeptical of Petrine authorship also maintain that Peter would not have cited the Septuagint (the Greek version of the Old Testament used in 1 Peter) and that he would have referred more often to the teachings of Jesus (Senior and Harrington 4–7). These objections are not to be taken lightly; however, they are based on conjecture and are not weighty enough to overturn the testimony of the early Christians. In the present commentary, we will assume that Peter wrote the letter.

CONTEXTS

The circumstances behind the writing of 1 Peter are generally clear. Peter wrote from Rome (symbolically called Babylon in 5:13) to Christians undergoing persecution in Asia Minor. While there is no evidence of an organized empire-wide persecution during the time of Peter (Achtemeier 28–36), there is clear evidence within the New Testament and in Roman sources that Christians often faced persecution for their refusal to participate in the many local festivals and other public events that promoted idolatry. Peter writes to comfort and encourage faithfulness among Christians who no longer feel at home in their world. Peter wants his readers to remember that their blessings in Christ, both present and future, outweigh suffering.

> **Scapegoating Christians**
> *Nero's persecution of Christians in Rome after the great fire in 64 CE reminds the interpreter of the ease with which officials could make Christians scapegoats for society's ills.*

It is probable that Peter was imprisoned and martyred in Rome under the emperor Nero (1 Clement 5–6). Peter probably wrote this letter in the months or years just before his death, sometime between 64 and 66.

COMMENTARY

GREETING · 1:1–2

The beginning of the letter is typical of Greco-Roman letters, naming the author and recipients, including a greeting, and offering a prayer of thanksgiving to God (or the gods). Peter identifies himself simply as an *apostle*, perhaps emphasizing his authority since he is writing to Christians that he may not have visited. The five regions mentioned cover the larger part of Asia Minor (in modern Turkey), and their order may reflect the route that would be taken by the carrier of the letter (but see Achtemeier 85–86).

The reference to these Christians as *God's elect* and *chosen* by God recalls the foundational biblical idea that God chose Israel from among all the nations of the earth and that Christians were the heirs to that election. Early Christians, Gentiles included, saw themselves as the new or true Israel. Indeed, the Gentiles among the early Christians believed they were privileged to be allowed to join the essentially Jewish people of God. Peter will return to the theme of election again, using it as

1 PETER

his basis for calling these Christians to holiness (compare 2:9; 5:10).

Peter's appeal to the *foreknowledge of God* brings to mind the controversy over predestination, a topic that cannot be examined in depth here. Probably Peter means that God determined before the creation of the world (1:20) to redeem humanity by sending Jesus and creating a community who believe in him (the church). That is, *through the sanctifying work of the Spirit* God cleanses and empowers those who respond in faith to the message about Christ.

Just as the chosen people of Israel were *scattered* throughout the world and were therefore *strangers* in the lands in which they lived, Peter uses these terms to describe his primarily Gentile readers (Michaels xlix–lv). But in what sense were these Christians *strangers*, or as 2:11 refers to them, *aliens and strangers*? Some have argued that Peter's readers are literally exiles from their original lands, people who have lost social status and are now living without rights and under constant suspicion (Elliott 94, 101–03; McKnight 25–26). This understanding appears to stretch the evidence. Most scholars therefore understand the terms *aliens and strangers* to be used metaphorically. Christians are not at home wherever they live in this world, since their lives and beliefs are fundamentally different from those among whom they are living. They thus live under suspicion (Michaels 6). Their citizenship is in heaven (to use Paul's language in Phil 3:20).

Continuing the connection with Old Testament themes, Peter declares that God's act of calling Christians was ratified by the sprinkling of blood, just as was God's earlier redemption of the Israelites (Exod 24:7–8). Of course, the *sprinkling by his blood* in this instance refers to the blood of Jesus shed on the cross. Peter's prayer for *grace and peace* was a standard Christian greeting.

THE BODY OF THE LETTER · 1:3–5:11

1:3–12 Like Paul, Peter begins his letter with an extended thanksgiving to God for blessing the recipients of the letter. The emphasis is on the future life that God has prepared for them. Peter uses numerous metaphors as he describes their current situation. The *new birth* refers to their new lives since putting their faith in the word of God (see 1:23). Though they are children of the Father, they have yet to receive the full *inheritance* that is nonetheless sure, because Jesus has already been resurrected, and God is *shielding* them from any enemy. The *coming of the salvation* refers to the second coming of Jesus (see 1:13).

Verse 6 introduces a second dominant theme of the letter. Peter reminds his readers to *rejoice* even in the midst of persecution. Indeed, they are to rejoice *because of* their various *trials*, since these struggles will prove that their faith is real.

> **Persecution in 1 Peter**
> There is not enough information in the letter to specify precisely what sort of persecution its readers were undergoing (see Achtemeier 28–36). However, Peter hints at the nature of some of these trials, including verbal abuse, mistreatment of slaves by masters, harassment of wives by non-Christian husbands, and perhaps even false accusations before the authorities.

Peter follows by commending his readers for their willingness to suffer even for one whom they *have not seen*. The reason for their *joy* is the salvation that they *are receiving* (note the present tense). Even though the full experience of that salvation is in the future (see 1:5; 4:13; 5:4), they receive it in the present by faith.

Verses 10–12 inform Peter's readers that *the prophets* and *even angels* desired to know more about God's future plans. Despite their suffering, these Christians are blessed to live during the days of fulfillment rather than the days of promise. They understand better than the prophets the grace resulting from the *sufferings of Christ*, and they can feel assured about *glories that would follow*. This is Peter's first mention of Jesus as one who suffered, a theme that will become central later in the letter. The repeated references to the Old Testament prophecies offered an important means by which early Christian leaders reminded the church that God would therefore deliver the promised salvation.

1:13–16 Having encapsulated the whole of Christian belief in 1:1–12, Peter uses the next several sections in the letter to remind Christians of God's call to holiness and what that entails in relationships.

In 1:13, Peter writes of the gift of salvation and the call to holiness. God's people are saved by faith, and righteousness and good works are the response to God's grace. For these reasons, Peter begins this call to godly living with *therefore*. God has saved Christians, who should act like saved people.

The temptation to revert to paganism always lies close at hand for Peter's readers. Furthermore, their suffering only increases that temptation. Peter therefore tells them to *prepare* their *minds for action*, or literally, "gird the loins of your minds," a metaphor recalling the need to tuck their long garments into their belts in preparation for a journey or battle (Davids 66). Similarly, he tells them to be *self-controlled* or "sober," that is, not to allow their passions and habits to control them. Peter then reminds his readers that the key to living as they should is their constant reflection on their reward when Jesus returns.

Peter continues in verses 14–16 the father-child metaphor (compare 1:3–4) as he instructs these Christians to resemble their Father. They formerly did not know their true identity, but they must now be holy like their Father (compare Lev 19:2).

1:17–21 Peter continues his call for a holy lifestyle in 1:17, offering several motivating factors in these verses. First, God will not ignore disobedience simply because they are the children of God. The Father is impartial and will judge each person's actions fairly. Imperfection in obedient children is always forgiven, but willful rebellion is not. There is a place for *reverent fear* even among the children of God. The fact that Christians are *strangers here* provides a further reminder not to live too comfortably in this world.

Another motivation for holy living is the high cost of salvation (verses 18–19). The phrase *you were redeemed* envisions the payment of a price for the release of a captive from an enemy or a slave from a master (Michaels 64). Unlike slaves bought for money, they obtained release from their *empty way of life* with the blood of Christ.

To encourage their faithfulness, Peter informs his readers in verses 20–21 that God determined to save them by the blood of Christ *before the creation of the world*. They are fortunate to be living *in these last times*, after the coming of Jesus. They have the advantage of having entered into faith and hope in God because of Jesus' resurrection.

> **The Sacrificial Lamb**
> *Peter describes the death of Jesus in terms of sacrifice, the* lamb without blemish or defect. *Perhaps he has in mind the Passover lamb (Exodus 12) slain in Egypt to spare the life of the firstborn, or perhaps the lambs for sacrifices at the temple.*

1:22–2:3 Peter's readers have been purified and therefore are called to love each other. However, he wants them to make that love authentic. Verses 23–25 identify the source of this amazing love: they have experienced a new life after accepting the "living and enduring word of God" (see 1:3). They now experience eternal life instead of normal human life, and their new life calls them to a new way of relating to one another (McKnight 91). In support of this understanding of the Christian life, Peter quotes from Isaiah 40:6–8.

Peter continues his emphases on love and the "born again" imagery in 2:1–3. To love more deeply is to cast off the sins that destroy personal relationships. Instead, they are to behave as *newborn babies* of God the Father. Peter's desire that they *crave pure spiritual milk* probably means that they are to be eager for the Word of God rather than the prideful and selfish ways of the so-called mature people of the world. Peter once again bolsters his point by quoting the Old Testament (Ps 33:8).

2:4–10 Several images and metaphors relating to the theme of the new temple dominate this section. Jesus is the cornerstone of God's temple, and the church is the spiritual temple built upon him. The church, not the temple in Jerusalem, is the primary dwelling place of God. That Jesus is a *living* stone probably recalls his resurrection but also links him to Christians, who are also *living stones* that together make up the temple. In a shift of metaphors, Peter also calls them a *holy priesthood*. This image emphasizes Christians' holiness and leads to another metaphor, the *spiritual sacrifices* that Christians offer. Peter does not specify what sacrifices he has in mind, but we may assume that he would include all of the actions and attitudes encouraged in the letter.

Stringing together four descriptions of the church (*chosen people, royal priesthood, holy nation, people*

> **Christ, the Cornerstone**
> *Peter appears to follow a popular early Christian tradition when he writes of the church as the new temple built on Christ (see Eph 2:20–22), and he supports this image by appealing to well-known Old Testament texts. Romans 9:33 also cites the chosen and precious cornerstone (verse 6) passage from Isaiah 28:16. Mark 12:10–11 quotes (and parallels) Psalm 118:22 concerning the stone the builders rejected (verse 7). Finally, the idea that unbelievers stumble because they disobey the message (Isaiah 8:14) also occurs in Romans 9:33.*

belonging to God), verses 9–10 emphasize the surprising status of Gentile Christians. Whereas Israel had stumbled and refused to believe, God has now chosen Peter's readers to be objects of his favor. All four of the descriptive phrases appear to come from Exodus 19:6 and Isaiah 43:20–21, and they underscore God's election and his covenant with the new people of God. The most difficult of these phrases, *a royal priesthood*, probably implies that these priests (see verse 5) serve God the king (Black and Black 65). Continuing the connection to Isaiah 43, Peter writes that the reason for God's election of his people is for them to *declare the praises of him who called you out of darkness*. Finally, he alludes to God's earlier forgiveness of a sinful people in Hosea 2:4–10 when he tells his readers that God has declared them *the people of God* by showing them *mercy*.

> **The Importance of Symbols**
> 1 Peter 2:4–10 provides symbols that Christians can substitute for those of their dominant culture. This symbolic world gives them hope in a hostile Roman Empire.

2:11–12 Despite the NIV subheading after these verses, they properly belong with what follows. These verses point out that Christians, as a minority group, must live in ways recognizably good for all of society. Peter calls his readers *aliens and strangers*, recalling the words in his greeting. Christians are by definition strangers in the world, homeless and often mistreated and excluded by those among whom they live. Nevertheless, they are to *live such good lives* that *the pagans* will *glorify God* on the day of judgment, presumably because they will have turned to the Lord. This statement is the basis of the paragraphs that follow; how Christians relate to their culture, the state, their masters, and their spouses will lead others to accept and glorify God.

2:13–17 Oppressed people often rebel against their oppressors. However, Peter tells his readers that they are to *submit ... to the king* (the emperor) *or to governors*, because they *are sent by* God *to punish those who do wrong*. Peter, of course, knows that governments do not always carry out God's will; but he has a generally positive view of government, as does Paul in Romans 13:1–7 (Michaels 132). (Revelation 13, on the other hand, holds a negative view of the state.) The belief that submission serves to *silence the ignorant talk of foolish men* may mean that their accusers will be shown to have brought false charges against them. Peter affirms that Christians are truly free, since they are not really citizens of this world, but he also knows that Christians who do not see themselves as *servants of God* can misuse freedom (see 1 Cor 8:9). Faithful servants will draw the admiration of others, as they *show proper respect to everyone*.

2:18–25 Since many early Christians were slaves, the apostles instructed them concerning how to relate to their masters (see also Eph 6:5–9 and Col 3:22–4:1). It was common in the Greco-Roman world for philosophers to instruct slaves to obey their masters. Peter also demands obedience, but his goal is that God be glorified (see 2:12). Perhaps Peter implies that these slaves face punishment *because* they are Christians.

According to verses 21–25, Christ provides the model for abused slaves (and presumably wives and Christians in relation to the government). Just as *he committed no sin* (note the quotation of Isa 53:9) and *did not retaliate*, 1 Peter instructs his readers to trust in God and bear the suffering. Peter implies that God's gift of grace grants both forgiveness and transformation (see Rom 6:11; Senior and Harrington 79–80). Peter continues with clear allusions to Isaiah 53 as he reminds his readers of God's grace yet again.

> **Slaves, Masters & Oppression**
> Peter's demand that slaves obey even harsh masters is a very difficult teaching for modern readers, since he seems to be condoning oppression. However, we must remember that slavery as an institution was not questioned in the ancient world and that rebellion against a master was simply not tolerated. Slaves and other oppressed groups (citizens, abused wives, and others) had to obey or be harshly punished, perhaps even killed. This difference in social context means that the words of 1 Peter cannot apply directly today. All Christians, ancient and modern, must bear witness to the kingdom of God, not simply pursue personal rights.

3:1–7 Just as all Christians submit to governments and slaves to masters, Peter wants wives to submit to pagan husbands. Some interpreters argue that the authority of husbands over wives was culture-bound, just as were slavery and the reference to braided hair in verse 3. However, others point out that Paul in his letters links the hierarchical husband-wife relationship to creation, not to culture (1 Cor 11:7–9;

1 Tim 2:13–14). An enormous body of literature awaits the serious student interested in this topic.

Peter calls on wives to submit so that their *husbands* may be *won over by* their *behavior* (recall 2:12). They are not to wear symbols of wealth. Instead, they are to have a beautiful *inner self* or *spirit* like the *holy women of the past*, the great example being *Sarah who obeyed Abraham*. Wives should not succumb to pressure when their non-Christian husbands attempt to intimidate them. They are to be quiet and submissive, but unafraid and faithful.

Husbands are somehow to act *in the same way*, but how? Peter does not overturn the traditional relationship, but he does transform it in light of the example of Jesus (see Eph 5:25–33; Col 3:19). *Husbands* must realize that their wives are also recipients of God's *gracious gift of life*. The idea that failure to care for their wives would hinder the *prayers* of husbands is simply to acknowledge that one cannot expect God's blessings while mistreating others (Matt 5:23–24).

> **The "Weaker" Partner**
> The statement that wives are the "weaker" partner *probably means simply that females were weaker physically and thus were more susceptible to abuse* (Davids 122–23).

3:8–12 Peter writes about relationships between Christians, telling them to *love* each other *as brothers* and sisters. Slaves, wives, and all Christians should refrain from responding in kind when mistreated by masters, husbands, or the state. Once again he turns to the Scriptures for support of his teachings, Psalm 34:12–16 in this case. This passage explains why those who treat fellow Christians well will *inherit a blessing*.

3:13–17 Peter next offers several reasons for repaying evil with good. First, no one is likely to *harm* them if they *do good* instead of evil. Second, but *even if* they do *suffer for what is right*, they *are blessed*. The imperative, *Do not fear what they fear*, may mean that they must not share the fear of those who have no hope of eternal life with God (compare Matt 10:28). More likely, though, he means simply, "Do not fear their threats," (NIV footnote). Verse 14b

> **The Christian Difference**
> First Peter 3:15–16 explains what it means to set apart Christ as Lord. As Christians defend their hope to outsiders, they do so kindly.

adapts Isaiah 8:12, and Peter alludes to the next verse in Isaiah when he instructs his readers to *set apart Christ as Lord* (instead of fearing their oppressors). In this way their suffering, if it must occur (and is to that extent *God's will*), will be *for doing good* rather *than for doing evil*. This is the model of suffering Christ established (verses 18–22).

3:18–22 The primary intent of verses 18–22 is clear: Christians are to imitate Jesus, who suffered unjustly, even to the point of death, and then overcame death and was exalted to the right hand of God (compare Phil 2:5–11). Their suffering will lead to the same blessing. However, the details in this passage have baffled interpreters throughout the centuries (see Senior and Harrington 100–9).

Verse 18 expresses the central christological teaching of the New Testament: *Christ died for ... the unrighteous*. Difficulties arise when Peter writes that Christ *was made alive by the Spirit*. A better translation is that in the NIV footnote, that Christ was *made alive in the spirit*, a parallel phrase to *put to death in the body*. The phrase *made alive in the spirit* refers to Jesus' resurrection. The distinction, in other words, is not between body and soul, but between mortal existence and immortal existence (like Paul's distinction between the fleshly body and the spiritual body in 1 Cor 15:42–49).

Verse 20 has received three major interpretations (Elliott 647–50). The first is that Jesus' spirit left his body in the tomb and went to Hades (or hell) and preached to the spirits of people who were disobedient in the days of Noah, who may or may not have had the opportunity to repent. However, Peter writes that Christ preached to the spirits ... *who disobeyed*, not the spirits *of the people* who disobeyed. That is, his hearers were spiritual beings, not human beings.

A second interpretation is that Jesus preached through Noah to Noah's contemporaries, doing so through the (Holy) Spirit. These people did not heed Noah's warnings (they *disobeyed*) and therefore were punished *in prison*. This view has satisfied few, because it distorts the natural sense of the words.

The third and most likely interpretation can only be understood in light of specific Jewish traditions current in the first century. First century readers understood Genesis 6:1–4 to refer to spiritual beings who sinned by having children with human females and were then punished by God. The apocryphal book *1 Enoch* 6–16, 18 describes these beings as "spirits" and discusses in some detail their imprisonment in the heavenly realm (1 Enoch 6–16, 18). Early Christians knew these traditions (2 Pet 2:4; Jude 6). Peter's point thus seems to be that, after his resurrection, Jesus proclaimed victory over the spirit world as he ascended to heaven (Senior and Harrington 108–9; McKnight 216–17).

The mention of the increased sinfulness of humanity preceding the flood leads Peter to reflect on the fact that Noah's family was *saved through water*. Perhaps the analogy with baptism works for Peter because the Christians of his day passed *through* the waters of baptism, just as those in the ark passed through the waters of the flood. The statement that *baptism now saves you* reflects a high view of baptism but not a magical one, as the next statement makes clear. Baptism does not cleanse the exterior but expresses an interior transformation, *the pledge of a good conscience*. It is unclear whether Peter says that in baptism the believer is pledging to maintain a good conscience (by holiness and service), or, more likely, that the believer is appealing for a good conscience (based on the transformative power of this new birth [1:3–5]; Senior and Harrington 110–11).

It is Christ's *resurrection* that gives baptism its power to save. Because of Christ's resurrection, Peter's readers, who suffer as Christ suffered, will also through their baptism be saved and exalted just as Christ was exalted to *God's right hand*. These Christians need not fear evil spirits because they now obey Christ, who proclaimed victory over them in prison after his resurrection.

4:1–6 Again Peter encourages his readers to remain faithful in persecution. Since it is easy in such circumstances to revert to old patterns of living, he reminds them of Jesus' example.

Christians share with Christ a willingness to suffer *because* this attitude implies that one has conquered *sin*. Peter probably means that those who have *suffered in* the *body* thereby show that they have chosen holiness instead of sin (Achtemeier 280). Verses 2–3 instruct Christians to avoid pagan sins related to idolatry and abuses of sex and alcohol. Because Christians are unwilling to join them in their wild living, their pagan neighbors ridicule them (or God—the Greek term "blaspheme" does not specify an object). The mention of pagan sinfulness leads Peter to write of the coming judgment of both *the living and the dead*. The NIV translation, while possible, is confusing. Much better is the NRSV: *so that, though they had been judged in the flesh as everyone is judged, they might live in the spirit as God does.*

> **Christians & Death**
> Verse 6 does not refer to Jesus preaching to the dead during the time between his death and resurrection (compare 3:19). Rather, Christians who have died will be resurrected in order to live *in the spirit*.

Christians die like everyone else, but they will not miss out on the kingdom of God (1 Thess 4:13–18).

4:7–11 Peter and his readers apparently anticipated the return of Jesus and *the end of all things* in the near future. They, of course, were not alone in this belief, as is clear from other New Testament passages (for example, 1 Cor 7:29–31; Jas 5:13; Rev 1:1; compare 2 Pet 3:3–10).

Christian behavior is directly tied to the future coming of Christ, judgment, and eternal reward or punishment. Peter first calls for the discipline of mind and will needed for Christians to focus on prayer and *love* for *each other*. Hospitality was an important virtue in the mobile first century world. Christians, especially those who were missionaries, served and protected each other by being hospitable.

> **Love & Forgiveness**
> *The statement* love covers a multitude of sins *may mean either that ones who love have their sins forgiven or, more likely, that ones who are loved are forgiven. "There must be mutual love and forgiveness within the community itself"* (Achtemeier 295–96).

Another manifestation of love concerned Christians' use of their gifts (verses 10–11). Instead of acting selfishly, Peter's readers are *to serve others*. Whether their gifts involve teaching and prophesying or encouraging and showing mercy, they are to be conscious that it is *God's grace* they are *administering*. The goal is that *God may be praised*. Peter ends this section appropriately with just such praise in his doxology.

4:12–19 Peter expands his previous teachings related to suffering. Since Christ suffered, they should *not be surprised* at suffering. In fact, they should *rejoice*, because participation with Christ will lead to joy when he returns in judgment. Being verbally *insulted* was probably the most common type of persecution these Christians faced. Alluding to the teaching of Jesus (Matt 5:11–12), Peter reminds them that they are *blessed* when cursed, *Since the Spirit…of God rests on* them. Suffering for crime or meddling brings shame, but suffering *as a Christian* should lead one to *praise God*.

The statement that *it is time for judgment to begin with the family of God* would not have been surprising for the first readers of 1 Peter, since the prophets had said that Israel would be judged before the nations. Verse 17 refers to a purifying *judgment* that will lead to salvation (McKnight 251–52). Verse 18 quotes Proverbs 11:31 in support of this teaching regarding the future judgment of the disobedient. Peter ends the section with an exhortation for his persecuted readers to trust in God and to avoid retaliation.

> **Peter & the End Times**
> Many interpreters believe that Peter is proclaiming that the time of terrible troubles and sufferings preceding the end of time have begun (Michaels 270). Others think that the suffering of Christians is part of the final judgment itself (Achtemeier 315–16). Whatever the case, Peter contrasts the suffering of the faithful with the greater suffering that will befall those who do not obey the gospel of God.

5:1–11 The final section of 1 Peter begins by addressing the local leaders among the churches, the *elders* (compare Acts 14:23; 20:17–18; 1 Tim 5:17–19, Titus 1:5, Jas 5:14). Peter wants to identify with these men and therefore calls himself a *fellow elder*. His claim to be a *witness of Christ's sufferings* may recall that he was an eyewitness of Jesus, but it also connects him to church leaders who attest to the truth of the gospel (Senior and Harrington 138). Furthermore, he and they share the same hope in the future reign of God.

Peter uses traditional imagery as he calls on his fellow elders to lead well. They are to *be shepherds of God's flock* ("pastors"), and they are to serve as *overseers* ("bishops"). They carry on the work of Jesus, the "Shepherd and Overseer" of 2:25. Most importantly, they must have the proper spirit as they lead – not because of duty but out of love, not in order to profit but *to serve*, and not on the basis of power but by example. Such selfless leaders *will receive the crown of glory* at the coming of Christ, the *Chief Shepherd* (compare John 10:11–18; Heb 13:20). This crown of glory, unlike first century vegetable wreaths given as prizes in contests, *will never fade away*.

Peter next calls younger Christians to *submission to those who are older* and all Christians to mutual deference and respect. The warrant for this comes from Proverbs 3:34. Since God gives grace, Christians should *humble* themselves, so that God will *lift them up in due time*.

Just as one can only hope to escape a *roaring lion* by being aware of its presence and ready to react, these Christians must be *self-controlled and alert* (compare 1:13 and 4:7) if they wanted to escape *the devil*. Peter also tells them to take courage from their knowledge that all Christians suffer. There is strength in community. Peter's final encouragement comes in the form of a promise, summarizing earlier elements in the letter.

FINAL WORDS · 5:12–14

The conclusion of this letter is much like that of other New Testament letters, especially those of Paul. That Peter writes *with the help of* [Greek "through"] *Silas* [Greek "Silvanus"] may imply that Silas acted as his secretary. More likely, Silas was the bearer of his letter (as in Acts 15:23; see Michaels 306–7).

She who is in Babylon (verse 13) almost certainly refers to the church in Rome (where Peter is living). The Roman church, *chosen* by God just like the churches in Asia Minor, sends her greetings. So does *Mark*, undoubtedly John Mark who was with Paul in Rome (Phlm 23; Col 4:10) and is associated in Christian tradition as the one who put Peter's teachings about Jesus in the Gospel of Mark. Peter's final words (verse 14) encourage Christians to show their love for each other by giving the holy *kiss* and express his desire for them to experience *peace*, an appropriate prayer given their difficult circumstances.

> **"Babylon"**
> Rome is also called Babylon in Revelation and in a few Jewish writings, signifying the similarity between this powerful pagan capital of the empire with the enemy of God's people 600 years earlier (Senior and Harrington 155).

THEOLOGICAL REFLECTIONS

The distinctive message of 1 Peter concerns suffering as a Christian. For this reason, this short letter is not among the most popular with contemporary Christians. Peter's message addressed Christians living in a hostile pagan empire, a different social and political situation from ours. Today committed Christians can live exemplary lives of sacrificial service without the added burden of persecution and suffering.

On the other hand, authentic discipleship leads to suffering. Arguably, our comfort level with our world blunts the message of 1 Peter. If we regard ourselves as aliens and strangers and live a truly countercultural existence, we not only expose the sinfulness of our world – we also pay a price. Furthermore, there is much that we cannot learn about Christ until we have walked where he walked. In the words of Peter, *those who have suffered in their bodies are done with sin* (4:1); and Christians should *rejoice inasmuch as you participate in the sufferings of Christ, so that you may be overjoyed when his glory is revealed* (4:13).

FOR FURTHER STUDY

Wayne Grudem, *The First Epistle of Peter* (Grand Rapids: Eerdmans, 1988).

J. N. D. Kelly, *A Commentary on the Epistles of Peter and Jude* (New York: Harper & Row, 1969).

I. Howard Marshall, *1 Peter* (Downers Grove, Ill.: InterVarsity Press, 1991).

WORKS CITED

Paul J. Achtemeier, *1 Peter* (Minneapolis, Minn.: Fortress, 1996).

Allen Black and Mark Black, *1 & 2 Peter* (Joplin, Mo.: College Press, 1998).

Peter H. Davids, *The First Epistle of Peter* (Grand Rapids: Eerdmans, 1990).

John H. Elliott, *1 Peter* (New York: Doubleday, 2000).

Scot McKnight, *1 Peter* (Grand Rapids: Zondervan, 1996).

J. Ramsey Michaels, *1 Peter* (Waco, Tex.: Word, 1988).

Donald P. Senior and Daniel J. Harrington, S.J., *1 Peter, Jude and 2 Peter* (Collegeville, Minn.: Liturgical Press, 2003).

2 Peter

Charles B. Stephenson

CHAPTER CONTENTS

Contexts 1041

Commentary 1041
    Salutation · 1:1–2 1041
    True Knowledge · 1:3–21 1042
    False Knowledge · 2:1–22 1043
    The Lord Returns · 3:1–16 1044
    Conclusion · 3:17–18 1045

Theological Reflections 1045

For Further Study 1045

Works Cited 1045

The first direct reference to 2 Peter in early Christian writings comes from Origen (185–254 CE), though early Christians sometimes doubted the epistle's authenticity. Differences in writing style and vocabulary in 1 Peter and 2 Peter raised questions about authorship in some parts of the early church, as did 2 Peter's apparent dependence on Jude.

> **2 Peter & Jude**
> 2 Peter 2 overlaps with Jude to a huge extent. Medieval authors assumed that Jude borrowed from 2 Peter, but most modern scholars believe the relationship to have gone the other way.

CONTEXTS

The mention of what Paul does *in all his letters* leads to the assumption that this letter was written after the gathering of Paul's letters into one collection in the second century. Identifying Paul's writings as Scripture (3:15–16) also seems to require a second century date. However, these obstacles to Peter's authorship may not be as formidable as they seem. Peter may have used different scribes for each letter and given them wide latitude in composition. Moreover, the reference to Paul *in all his letters* may only mean all of Paul's letters known by the author.

The place of writing is not known, but this does not hinder the dating of the letter. Petrine authorship would require a date before Peter's death in the 60s. The mention of Paul's letters demands a date late enough to allow for the composition of several of Paul's letters.

Second Peter was written to *Christians* (3:1), the same audience as in 1 Peter. So 2 Peter may be to Christians who are *scattered throughout Pontus, Galatia, Cappadocia, Asia and Bithynia* (1 Pet 1:1). The *ours* in 1:1 with the very Jewish name *Simon Peter* may indicate a distinction between an audience of Jewish and Gentile Christians.

The letter faces the problem of capable and persuasive false teachers (2:1–3). The author's concern is heightened by the sense of his imminent death (1:13–14). He seeks to encourage his readers to continue what they have learned as Christians.

Second Peter's form has much in common with other New Testament letters. Following a salutation that introduces the author and the recipients comes the body of the letter and a short conclusion. There is a unified style throughout the letter (Green 41; Guthrie 846). The statement about the author's imminent death indicates this is a final testament from an honored leader speaking to the life of his people.

COMMENTARY

SALUTATION · 1:1–2

The author introduces himself as *Simon Peter, a servant and apostle of Jesus Christ*. This name, these titles, and the witnessing of the transfiguration (1:16–18) leave no doubt that this author claims to be Peter, although most modern scholars question this attribution (Senior and Harrington 235–37). *Apostle* and *servant* are titles of honor and authority for one commissioned to speak for Jesus Christ and owned by him. Also, *servant* has a rich Old Testament heritage in relation to God (for example, Exod 32:13).

To those who through the righteousness of our God and Savior Jesus Christ have received a faith as precious as ours can describe any Christian, and the materials in this letter still address Christians today. The description of Jesus Christ as our God and Savior in 2 Peter indicates a high christological understanding of Jesus (Blum 267).

The usual letter greeting of grace and peace expands into a request for an abundance of both. Interestingly, this abundance is through the knowledge of God and of Jesus our Lord. The beginning of the letter introduces the subject of knowledge, a central concern.

TRUE KNOWLEDGE · 1:3–21

This first major section describes the knowledge that is based in God's promises and reliable words from the Spirit. This knowledge stands in absolute contrast to the "knowledge" taught by the false teachers.

1:3–11 This section functions like the thanksgivings that appear in most New Testament letters. It serves to introduce some of the subjects discussed in the rest of the letter (Watson 335–36).

The knowledge of God and Jesus that brings abundant grace and peace also brings everything we need for life and godliness by Jesus' divine power. "Knowledge" [Greek *epignosis*] is a compound form of *gnosis* that gives the sense of "full knowledge." It is the knowledge that God and Christ reveal to bring us to life and godliness. This is the knowledge that moves us from the death of sin to life (1:2, 4, 8; 2:20–21). It forms the basis for godliness, an attitude of obedience to God's will in a life of moral excellence.

Not only has Jesus *called us by his own glory and goodness*, indicating that we can do nothing by ourselves, *his very great and precious promises* are confirmed by his glory and goodness. It is through Jesus' promises that Christians may participate in the divine nature and *escape the corruption in the world caused by evil desires*. Second Peter's claim resembles Paul's contrast of the Christian's life in Christ with the life (corruption, death) before knowing Christ (Rom 6:3–14). Evil desires are the tools of the false teachers (2:18–19) and the lifestyle of the scoffers (3:3). Material desires do not drive the Christian life. While participating in the divine nature, Christians are to make every effort to grow in the Christian life.

Faith is the foundation on which all of the virtues are built. Love is the last virtue in the list and ultimately involves all the others (Watson 336). Love in the Christian life is an expression of divine nature. The virtues listed before love seem to build on each other, but the list does not indicate that a Christian can have some of these virtues and not the others. The Christian must possess these qualities in increasing measure. It is only when Christians are growing in all of these that they are maturing properly.

Godliness is the same quality Jesus has made possible in Christians' lives by his power (1:3). *Goodness* also describes Jesus' goodness by which Christians are called to him (1:3). *Knowledge* (*gnosis*) comes from the experience of living life with God. This knowledge is always open to growth. This is possible because of the *saving knowledge* (*epignosis*) of God and Jesus (1:2, 3, 8). These characteristics, along with the other virtues, set high standards for the Christian's life. Living these will insure the promise of a rich welcome into the eternal kingdom of our Lord and Savior Jesus Christ.

1:12–21 Peter writes to remind the recipients of the truth they know. The encouraging words in the previous section are written to well-grounded and committed Christians. The author's sense of his imminent death drives his desire to help them always be able to remember these things. The mention of Peter's death recalls Jesus' prediction of his death

> **2 Peter & the Synoptic Gospels**
> Unlike most letters in the New Testament, 2 Peter extensively cites stories in the gospels. The letter seems to reflect a time when either those texts or the oral traditions immediately behind them were in circulation among Christians.

(John 21:18–19), though it is also possible that a more recent word from Jesus had made clear to the author the imminence of his death.

Peter addresses the accusation brought against him and the other apostles (*we* in 1:16). They were charged with teaching cleverly invented stories about the power, coming [Greek *parousia*], and majesty of Jesus. The Greek *mythos* means "stories," and most myths were stories about the gods. Peter was one of three privileged to witness the

> **Eyewitnesses**
> In contrast to tellers of myths, the apostles were eyewitnesses to the display of Jesus' power and glory.

transfiguration and hear God's voice saying, *This is my Son, whom I love; with him I am well pleased* (Matt 17:1–8). The transfiguration forecasts the glory and power of Jesus' coming.

The phrase *more certain* is open to two interpretations in relation to the word of the prophets. The apostles constantly confirm their teaching by reference to the Old Testament. The word of the prophets confirms the apostolic eyewitness testimony as the only light shining in a dark world until Christ's coming (3:4, 10, 12). The "morning star" in Greek texts usually identifies Venus or a royal or divine person (Green 88). The true light thus shines at the coming of Jesus Christ. Until then, Christians rely on the apostles' eyewitness word validated by the Old Testament.

False teachers had apparently made an accusation that the Old Testament prophets had spoken their own minds. Verses 20–21 counter that the true word from God came through human beings by the power of the Holy Spirit. The Spirit validates the Old Testament. Interpreters of Scripture read it in light of the life and work of Jesus Christ and vice versa.

FALSE KNOWLEDGE · 2:1–22

Second Peter now accuses the false teachers and describes their judgment and doom. Examples from tradition and Scripture support the book's arguments.

2:1–10A Peter moves from the certainty of true prophets to the reality of false prophets among God's ancient people. These teachers will secretly introduce their false teaching. Out of pure greed, they make up stories. They are doing what they falsely accused the apostles of doing (1:16). Swift destruction comes to them because they deny the sovereign Lord who bought them. The Greek word for "bought" [*agorazo*] is used in 1 Corinthians 6:20, 7:23 to speak of Christ's purchasing the Christian for himself. Because of theological presuppositions about Christians not losing their salvation, some interpreters try to explain away this meaning (Blum 276). Part of the horror of their destruction is what they have lost – their salvation in Christ.

> **Paying Teachers**
> *The practice of teaching for money was controversial in the Greek-speaking world. According to Plato, Socrates criticized those who sold wisdom for money. Paul discussed the problem in 2 Corinthians. Second Peter also raises the issue and criticizes his opponents for their greed.*

It is a great comfort to know that the Lord knows how to rescue. Peter states this on the basis of two examples. First, the sinful world of Noah's day was destroyed by water (3:5–6). Second, amid the destruction of Sodom and Gomorrah by fire, God saved Lot. Like contemporary Jewish and Christian texts, 2 Peter regards the Old Testament characters in the most positive possible light.

The previous examples also show that God knows how to punish the ungodly. The text finds warrant for this point in Jewish traditions related to Genesis 6:1–4. God did not exempt angels from punishment (see also Jude 6). These examples show that God holds the unrighteous for the day of judgment. The phrase *while continuing their punishment* (verse 9) speaks of the outcome of their unrighteous deeds in this life.

> **"If God did not spare the angels …"**
> *The celestial beings spoken of in 2 Peter are difficult to identify. If they are angels, the writer seems to be making a distinction between these and those who "will not speak against" the justified in God's presence. It has been suggested that the writer may be referring to fallen angels. Whatever they are, the point is that false teachers presume to speak when angels who are superior to them will not.*

2:10B–22 The pompous and arrogant false teachers are laughing in the face of their own destruction. Their moment in time is not the end of the story. They easily speak ill of "celestial beings," to their own doom. Compared to angels, these teachers are *brute beasts* to be caught and destroyed.

Their *wages* are what they have done against others. They continue in their shameful ways (see 2:2). Carousing constantly, desiring every woman, and sinning nonstop describe lives that are insults in the feasts they attend. False teachers look for the unstable to seduce. (2:2–3; 3:16; compare 1:12; 3:17). "Experts in greed" is a good translation of a phrase that actually says their hearts are *exercised* [Greek *gymnazo*] in greed. As an athlete trains, so they train for greed. Balaam is their role model for turning from God to greed and immorality (Num 22:5–24:25; 33:16).

> **Balaam**
> *In Jewish texts just before and after the first century, the Bible's troublesome but slightly comic figure of Balaam grows into the parade example of evil. Revelation 2:14 thinks of him as a model false teacher – one advocating sexual sin and idolatry. To associate one's opponents with Balaam is to dismiss their arguments and their character out of hand.*

False teachers are as useless as waterless springs and as directionless as mists. The life they offer is empty and leads to absolute darkness (Jude 13). Recent converts from polytheism (*unstable*, 2:14; 3:16) are the targets of their seductive mouthing that is as empty as they are. Ironically, Peter uses the same word to describe their empty mouths as he used to describe Balaam's donkey's speech [Greek *phthengomai*]. Empty talk promises life but brings slavery to depravity.

In 2:1, the false teachers were ones bought by Jesus. In 2:20, it seems that they have escaped from sin by *knowing* [Greek *epignosis*] *our Lord and Savior Jesus Christ* (contrast 1:2, 3, 8). Again, these false teachers turn away from Jesus to the world. Peter declares that the return to the world makes their end worse then if they had never known Jesus and salvation. Interestingly, Peter says the sacred command *was passed on* [Greek *paradidomi*] to them. This is a technical term for passing on traditions, especially gospel teaching (1 Cor 11:23). They turned away from gospel truth. Second Peter describes their sad end by two proverbs: one biblical and one traditional. *Dogs* (Prov 26:11) and *pigs* were both despised animals that well serve these proverbs.

THE LORD RETURNS · 3:1–16

The denial of the Lord (2:1) included a denial of his second coming, which the early church anticipated (1 Cor 16:22; Rev 22:20). As time progressed, the church had to deal with the delay of his return [Greek *parousia*].

3:1–10 Peter reminds his *dear friends* (3:1, 8, 14, 17) of his first letter, apparently 1 Peter. Both letters were to serve as reminders to keep focused on the holy prophets (Old Testament) and the command (the gospel) given through the apostles (1:16–21). This focus results in *wholesome thinking* or a purified mind, the opposite condition of the false teachers'.

The "scoffers" are false teachers who will be future problems for the church. Their own evil desires drive them (2:1, 10, 18; 3:3). These scoffers live in the last days: the days between Jesus' ascension and his return, the reality of which they deny. Nothing, according to them, has changed since creation. Here, 2 Peter uses the Old Testament to construct a view of God's word and promise as a creative force and therefore a certain guarantee of the final resolution of all things at the second coming.

The letter urges Christians not to forget God's different time perspective (Ps 90:4), since God's promise is not slow in coming. God does not want anyone to perish, but everyone to come to repentance, even the false teachers (3:15). Peter gives a stern warning to any who would not respect God's patience. The day of the Lord will come like a thief. Then, the heavens and the earth will be destroyed by fire.

3:11–16 The reality of the events at the Lord's return calls for Christians to live *holy and godly lives* looking forward to the Lord's return. Holiness is the pure life dedicated to God. Godliness is the life of moral purity and service (1:3, 6, 7). Christians must live in preparation for righteous living in a new heaven and a new earth. In waiting for this, how do Christians speed its coming? One early Christian understanding of this idea appears in Acts 13:19–20: *Repent, then, and turn to God, so that your sins may be wiped out, that times of refreshing may come from the Lord, and that he may send the Christ....* The last clause may imply that repentance and righteous living can affect the Lord's return.

The letter closes by exhorting the readers to prepare for the Lord's return. The same verb encourages these Christians to secure their salvation (1:10) and to remember Peter's teaching (1:15). Such an effort results in a spotless and blameless life, the opposite of that of the false teachers (2:13).

Verse 15 indicates that Peter's teaching on the Lord's patience (3:8–9) is corroborated by Paul. The letter's recipients knew Paul and associated him with Peter and the rest of the apostles. Not only did Paul write on the same subjects, he wrote with the wisdom that God gave him. This credits Paul's writings as from the same source as the writings of the Old Testament prophets (1:21). At the same time, 2 Peter recognizes that Paul's followers interpreted him in different ways.

In their lives and the lives of their followers, eternal destruction is the outcome of the false teachers' interpretations (2:14). Yet a brighter future awaits the recipients of 2 Peter. They know the Lord (1:3), are grounded in truth (1:12; 3:17), and know what Peter has written (3:17). They are at peace waiting for the Lord's return.

Cosmic Fire

The idea that the world would end in fire was widespread in the first century, notably among philosophers. Second Peter connects that common idea to the return of Jesus, thus placing it in the context of the Christian story.

CONCLUSION · 3:17–18

At the end, 2 Peter encourages Christians by calling them *dear friends* for the fourth time (see 3:1, 8, 14, 17). They know the apostolic teachings and their secure position in the Lord. Christians must be constantly aware of their teachers. Finally, the letter draws attention to what God and Christ have given them: grace and knowledge (1:2–3; 3:18). Christians must and can grow in the life God gives them through grace and knowledge (1:5–11).

The closing doxology is unusual because it is to Jesus alone. The author's high Christology is again evident.

THEOLOGICAL REFLECTIONS

This short epistle addresses small house churches struggling to maintain their faith against the overwhelming force of a pagan culture and the natural human tendency to lose sight of what matters. By appealing to the core of the Christian story – God through Christ is redeeming the world and will redeem it at the end of time – 2 Peter invites its readers to live ethical lives rooted in the promises of God.

The letter makes its appeal also in the context of the story of Israel. Citing numerous Old Testament stories, the author places his readers in the context of a tradition in which men and women must choose whether they will be faithful or not. Precisely because they face false teachers who deny the power of Scripture, the second coming, and the need for an ethical life under the lordship of Christ, these readers must remain vigilant. Remembering who they are and how they became that will help them do so.

Finally, 2 Peter sits tucked away in the back of the Bible. Yet its message of hope and sanity sounds a call to contemporary Christians who face similar challenges. The Jesus whom the letter extols as Lord of all remains such today for those who will submit to his gracious rule.

FOR FURTHER STUDY

Stephen Kraftchick, *Jude, 2 Peter* (Nashville: Abingdon, 2002).

Duane F. Watson, "The Second Letter of Peter" in *The New Interpreter's Bible*, vol. 12 (Nashville: Abingdon, 1998), 323–61.

WORKS CITED

Richard J Bauckham, *Jude, 2 Peter* (Waco, Tex.: Word, 1983).

Edwin A. Blum, "2 Peter" in *The Expositor's Bible Commentary*, vol. 12 (Grand Rapids: Zondervan, 1981).

Paul Feine, Johannes Behm, and Werner Georg Kümmel, *Introduction to the New Testament* (Nashville: Abingdon, 1966).

Michael Green, *The Second Epistle of Peter and the Epistle of Jude* (Grand Rapids: Eerdmans, 1968).

Donald Guthrie, *New Testament Introduction* (Downers Grove, Ill.: InterVarsity Press, 1990).

Donald Senior and Daniel J. Harrington, *1 Peter, Jude, and 2 Peter* (Collegeville, Minn.: Liturgical Press, 2003).

Duane F. Watson, "The Second Letter of Peter" in *The New Interpreter's Bible*, vol. 12 (Nashville: Abingdon, 1998), 323–61.

1 John

Wendell Willis

CHAPTER CONTENTS

Contexts **1047**

Commentary **1047**

    Prologue: The Surety of the Apostolic Message · 1:1–4 **1047**

    The True Faith & the False Faith · 1:5–3:10 **1047**

    Living in Love with Others · 3:11–4:7 **1049**

    Understanding the Love of God · 4:7–5:12 **1051**

    Conclusion: Christian Certainty · 5:13–21 **1053**

Theological Reflections **1054**

For Further Study **1054**

Traditionally, 1–3 John are dated near the end of the first century, but no events in the letters offer a real basis for dating. The three letters do not give an author. Because their language and style resemble that of the fourth gospel, tradition has assumed the same author. At least the author(s) represent the concerns and theology found in that gospel.

CONTEXTS

First John does not have the form of a genuine letter, but 2 and 3 John follow ancient letter style. Probably 2 John was a genuine letter accompanying the sermon we know as 1 John. Third John, while by the same writer, has a different concern.

These letters show two overarching concerns: love and a criticism of a flawed Christology. Some believers denied the genuine humanity of Christ, and because they considered themselves more spiritual, they left their previous Christian fellowship. Their faulty ecclesiology (or church practice) comes from their faulty Christology. Having broken away, they tried to recruit other Christians. These letters expose them in order to protect those abandoned Christians who felt insecure in their faith.

> **Docetism**
> *Docetism was the ancient heresy which taught that Jesus only seemed [Greek dokeo] to be human. These letters criticize such an idea.*

Second John continues the concern for those who deny Christ's humanity. Third John stresses hospitality because some Christians had rejected traveling missionaries.

COMMENTARY

PROLOGUE: THE SURETY OF THE APOSTOLIC MESSAGE · 1:1–4

First John 1:1–4 is a prologue for the entire letter, similar in style and function to John 1:18. It presents key themes ("life," "love," "fellowship," "testifying/testimony," "joy") and states the letter's purposes as building *fellowship* and *joy*.

First John 1:1–4 is one Greek sentence, asserting that Christianity begins with *the word of life*, which is either the message about Christ or the message of Jesus himself (John 1:4; 11:25, 26; 14:6). This *word of life* was made manifest by Jesus' coming in the flesh (John 1:14; 1 Tim 3:16; Heb 9:26).

Verse 2 points to the foundational work of the apostles as witnesses. *Testify* comes from the law court. The witnesses have *heard*, *seen*, *touched*, each verb bringing readers closer to Jesus. This testimony is about *eternal life*, an important concept in both John and 1 John. It is not simply "unending life" but also a quality of life.

In verse 3, *fellowship* [Greek *koinonia*] is a special term in John. Those who left the church may have stressed their close fellowship with God. Yet John insists that the true fellowship involves Jesus and other Christians. By breaking from the church, John's opponents show that they lack *koinonia* with God, too.

The prologue ends on the note of joy, a second goal of the letter (verse 4). The two goals are related, since, if they keep what they have known from the beginning (verse 1) and remain in fellowship with one another and with God, the readers have a secure basis for joy.

THE TRUE FAITH & THE FALSE FAITH · 1:5–3:10

1:5–2:2 Beginning in 1:5, John turns to disputes raised by those who left the congregation. The doctrinal issue is the incarnation, but those who left made other claims, as well (compare 2:9–11; 3:11).

In 1:6–10, several claims begin *If we claim*, each probably a claim of the heretics. In the next phrase, John rejects this claim. John evaluates these claims in verses 6–10 by reference to what one does. A verbal profession, even if genuine, is an inadequate test of true faith.

Verse 7 gives two results of *walking in the light*: *fellowship with one another* and the ongoing cleansing of our sin. The phrase *blood of Jesus* critiques the heretics, who deny the significance of Jesus' fleshly life. The true remedy is not to deny sin but to confess it openly and receive God's forgiveness. Forgiving sins manifests God's righteousness (Rom 1:16; 3:21–26), and righteousness provides the basis for forgiveness.

The third claim of the heretics is the most outlandish of all: "We have never committed a sin!" As with the previous quote, John (1:10) points to two faulty consequences: we make God a liar, and God's word has no place in us (parallel to verse 8: *the truth is not in us*).

In 2:1, John again states his purpose (see 1:4): *that you will not sin*. But he recognizes that Christians do commit sinful acts. John assumes that the Christian will sin, but Jesus is our advocate and our expiation.

> **Expiation & Propitiation**
>
> The terms "expiation" or "propitiation" are seldom discussed today. Both deal with the issue of how sin affects our relationship with God. Unlike John, we are prone to be either too lenient on sin (as John's opponents were), or too severe (thus eliminating hope for the believer who does sin). The "expiation" or "propitiation" (2:2, only here in 1 John, but see 4:10) *of our sins is* for the whole world, either in intent or prospect.

2:3–27 In 2:3, John describes what Christians do know and indicates that keeping God's commandments demonstrates our proper knowledge of God. The claim to know God also entails a horizontal dimension.

The second test is to live as Jesus lived (verse 5). If so, we "remain in him" (compare 3:2, 16). The new/old commandment epitomizes Jesus' life. *Old* probably goes back to the beginnings of Christianity (versus the opponents' interest in the "new" wisdom). Yet the commandment is also *new* because it is rightly defined by Jesus (John 13:34), it (God's power) is in you, and it is a new time – the old age is passing away.

If those who left claimed spiritual superiority, those left behind probably felt inadequate. So John reassures them based on what they know. In 2:12–14, he gives six reasons he has written, addressing three groups, each twice. The two claims that are repeated are that the fathers know *him who is from the beginning* (Jesus Christ), and the *youths* have mastered the evil one.

The first evidence for authentic faith (2:15–17) is how believers relate to the unbelieving world. John uses the word *world* slightly differently here than in John 3:16–17. John describes the world as a danger in three ways (2:16): the "desire" for the world's things, the desire of the eyes, and "empty pride" (see NEB's "all the glamour of its life"). Christians reject the world's desires because these desires are not from God and they are passing away.

In 2:18–27, John offers the first clear description of the false theology he refutes, the teaching of *antichrist*. The appearance of the antichrist is a clear sign that the last hour has come and that some have fallen away.

> **Antichrist**
>
> The word *antichrist* appears only in 1 and 2 John, although Jesus had warned about "false Christs" (Mark 13), and Revelation describes a fraudulent copy of Christ.

Verse 19 does not distinguish the "invisible church" from the "true church." But John's point is not about an invisible church. Rather, John points to the essential need to remain connected to the church if one claims to know God.

John stops to reassure his audience in verses 20–21 that he does not doubt the faith of those to whom he writes, but he writes to sustain them. Verses 22–23 explicitly name the heresy as those who deny that Jesus is the Christ. The *liar* denies that the human Jesus is essentially related to the divine Christ. John's response focuses on what Christians have always believed and taught (recalling 1:1–3). He insists that if this foundational truth remains in his readers, then they have eternal life. To continue in the apostolic teaching is to have an anointing of God.

2:28–3:10 This new section has three parts: 2:28–3:3 describes those who "do righteousness"; 3:4–6 those who "commit sin"; and 3:7–10 combines these two themes in a summary of the fundamental life choices: sin versus righteousness. Having corrected the false teaching that Christ was not really the human Jesus, John focuses upon the Christian demand for moral behavior based on Christian hope. Verses 28–29 mark a transition from the focus of chapters 1–2 (fellowship with God) to that of chapters 3–5 (love and sonship).

John frequently speaks of "abiding" in Christ (see also John 5). The word "confidence" [Greek *parresia*, elsewhere often translated "boldness"; see 4:17] is very common in the New Testament and important in John's writings. Verse 29 profoundly links behavior with Christian identity. The word *he* may refer either to Christ or to God, but since John closely links them with each other, the exact identification does not matter much.

Born of him (verse 29) signals a new theme, Christians as children of God. The hallmark of being God's child is "doing right" (see 3:10). The next verses (3: 1–3) develop this theme. Notice how the argument progresses: verse 1 tells what we are, verse 2 what we will be, and verse 3 (therefore) what we should be.

What sort of love (3:1) means "from what origin" (see Mark 8:27). It stresses the foreign character of God's love. The purpose of God's love is to make clear that we are God's children.

First John 3:1–3 explains positively, and 3:4–6 does so negatively. Verse 4's *everyone who sins* is a contrasting parallel to 2:29, *everyone who does what is right*. Occasionally Christians have the idea that, being free in Christ, they are not bound by laws (see Rom 6:1, 15; 1 Cor 9:21). Apparently, John's opponents thought this. But John insists that all *lawlessness* really is *sin*. Since Christ came to take away sin, no one who remains in sin really knows him. John now warns, "Let no one deceive you" (verse 7). This warning acknowledges that some were trying to deceive the readers (see 2:26). How will they be recognized for what they are? John gives a litmus test: "He who does righteousness is righteous."

Just as God is the father of children, those who live in sin (verse 8) also have a parent, the devil (compare verse 10). This idea reflects John 8:44. Verse 9 repeats the idea of verse 6. John's seeming predestination stems from the dramatic contrast he paints between the faithful and the heretics. But here he gives a reason, *God's seed remains in him*, which refers to the work of the Holy Spirit (4:13; Rom 8:9) or the "word of salvation" (John 5:38; Jas 1:18; 1 Pet 1:23, 25). Or perhaps he refers to the opponents' claims to have a "holy seed" that put them beyond sin. The author does not derive conduct from origins, but demonstrate origins from conduct (John 8:39–47). Verse 10 gives another test (parallel to 3:4) to identify the children of God and the children of the devil by their behavior. This idea summarizes 2:29–3:9. Then John introduces a new element as a test, love of fellow Christians (3:11–20).

LIVING IN LOVE WITH OTHERS · 3:11–4:6

3:11–24 The major section 3:11–4:6 focuses upon relationships within the church. Those who left clearly do not love these readers; but those who remain still need mutual love. The theme of love of the brother as the true sign of discipleship already appeared in 2:7–11. This is vital to John's viewpoint because: love is the opposite of hate, love is basic to the faith (*from the beginning*), and love defines precisely who are children of God and who are of the devil (3:10). First John 3:11–24 is very difficult to translate. Verse 11 seems clearly the beginning, but where to end the passage is not clear.

In his letter, John fights innovation in the faith, either in a so-called advanced view of Christ (2:22–24; 4:1–4) or neglected love for others (2:7–11; 3:11). Verse 11 thus sets forth the heart of the ancient gospel: we should love one another. Verses 12–18 explain the content of verse 11 in both negative (verses 12–15) and positive (verses 16–19) ways, contrasting the children of God and those of the devil. Humanity falls into two camps based on their love. To love one another (verse 11) is the opposite of being like Cain, the first murderer. This example clearly represents two life choices. Genesis 4 does not speculate on Cain's motives, but Jewish interpreters of the first century assumed a strong connection between the two brothers. For example, Hebrews 11:4 says that Abel offered a more acceptable sacrifice by faith.

Verse 13 reasserts 3:1 (compare John 15:18). The *world* will not acknowledge the righteous – and therefore hates them. This shows the world's alignment with the devil (see 5:19). Verse 14 emphatically contrasts *we* with the world in regards to knowledge. Christians have already passed (past tense) into the sphere of light (see John 5:24; 1 John 2:9–11). This is because *life* for John is qualitative and already

> **What is sin?**
> The basic idea of the Greek word for sin is "to miss the mark." But in the Old Testament, the master image is that God is King of Israel. Sin in that context is not only less than the best (missing the mark) but a rebellion against the King. This idea continues in the New Testament, so that sin equals rebellion or lawlessness.

present in the church. But this eternal, Christ-like life is not now fully visible but is manifested in our activities (John 3:8). Our actions indicate where our life is based. Verse 15 openly says that hate equals murder, which equals being without God's life.

> **Christian Charity**
> *Verse 17 gives a more common definition of love. To give our "goods" [Greek "things of life"—a pun on "lay down our life"] is the same as giving our life. This verse assumes that we do have the world's goods (a livelihood) and that we see others in need. If these criteria are met, then we are obligated by love to give (see 4:20).*

What does the word *love* mean? John defines it by example (verse 16). Christ laid down his life for us (John 3:16; 10:11; Rom 5:6). Christ's death is unique yet exemplary for Christians (compare John 15:12).

Verse 18 warns of the deceitful nature of claiming that we love but not acting in love (compare Jas 2:15). This verse continues the idea of *love*, but *dear children* points us to another section. The results of love are seen in verses 19–20. *This* refers to verse 18, that is by loving in deeds, not just words.

Verse 20's *whenever* recognizes that even the believer who lives as verse 19 demands may on occasions have doubts. Such doubts should not lead to despair, because God accepts us. John cites God's knowledge as a reassurance: those who love God, even if rejected by others, can be confident that God is aware of them (1:9). There is always some danger of complacency among Christians, which leads to slackness in love. But there is also a danger in being too self-critical, resulting in despair.

In concluding his argument, John discusses three ideas that exemplify three major themes: the believers' confidence before God, love for fellow Christians, and abiding in God's commandment(s) and in the Holy Spirit. With the high standards John has set forth (3:16, 17), his audience faces a real danger of losing heart.

Verses 19–20 try to prevent this. Verse 21 restates this case even more boldly: when we do examine our lives and find no basis in them for self-criticism, we can have boldness in prayer before God (verse 22; see also 2:28). John assumes that his hearers will keep God's commandments by doing what pleases God, especially loving other Christians (John 15:5–7).

Verses 23–24 summarize some points John has already made. Christians should believe in Jesus Christ and *love one another* (compare 2:5–8; 3:11). The phrase "Jesus is the Christ" was probably an early Christian confession at baptism (see John 6:29). This is the first mention of belief in this letter. John insists that the command to love one another is as necessary as the command to confess Jesus (compare Matt 22:34–40). Jesus says that to neglect one of these commands is also to break the other.

John seldom makes reference to the Holy Spirit's work in the Christian life. Verse 24 begins a discussion of the Spirit in the letter (but see 2:20, 27). The Spirit was part of Jesus' own power (John 14:16, 17; 16:7–15), a sign of his presence with his own (1 John 4:13).

> **Spirit & Commandment**
> *John refuses to set "spirit" and "commandment" in opposition. Instead, they are rather complementary. We show our abiding in God by keeping his commandment, and God continues abiding in us by the Spirit given to us. "Abide in God" is a standard concept in John. It has already been related to keeping the commandment of God (2:5, 6, 14, 24). Compare the vine/branch metaphor in John 15.*

First John 4:1–6 gives a more precise explanation of the antichrists and a fuller basis for Christian love (it is God's own nature). Verses 1–3 concentrate on the Spirit of God and the spirit of the antichrist and verses 4–6 focus on the contrast between the people of the world (*antichrist*), and the people of God.

Having pointed to the Spirit's work in the believer (3:24), John now turns to treat the other spirits—those not of God (see also 2:18–23). Since the church had Christian prophets, the problem of verification became significant (Acts 11:27; 13:1; 21:9, 10; 1 Cor 12; 14:1–5). Through these prophets, God revealed directions for the life of the early church. However, the situation John faces is that varied persons claimed the spirit of prophecy—the ability to speak for God under inspiration. Christians needed criteria to evaluate prophets under the Spirit. Behind this move lies the Old Testament tradition of testing prophets (Deut 13:1–5; 18:20–22). John presents ways of identifying "false" prophets.

That these false prophets have *gone out into the world* could simply mean that they have appeared, or that they have left the church for the world (compare 2:19). However, John says they are the *antichrist*, or *world*. Since 5:19 says that the *world* falls under the sway of "the evil one," then ultimately the devil is responsible for heresy. To discern these false prophets,

John gives a guideline (4:2): belief that *Jesus Christ has come in the flesh*. John says those claiming to speak by God's spirit are open to examination. The confession required is "Jesus Christ has come in the flesh." This is fuller than some earlier Christian confessions (see Acts 8:27; Phil 2:11).

The *you* in verse 4 is emphatic: "You, little children, are of God." Such a reminder encourages readers who feel defeated after the recent departure of some members who claimed a superior teaching about Christ. This victory over the false spirit is not due to their superiority as people but to the divine strength on which they have relied.

Verse 5 suggests that the false teachers, even if unsuccessful in getting a hearing in the church, did find some who liked their message – the *world* – namely "the world as the field of forces allied against God" (see John 15:19). Verse 6 represents the antithesis between those who have the Spirit of God ("us") and those who do not. This antithesis has a practical proof in who is receptive to the teachings of certain leaders. The ultimate test comes from the apostolic teaching.

UNDERSTANDING THE LOVE OF GOD · 4:7–5:12

4:7-16 First John 4:7–12 contains possibly the most profound biblical passage dealing with love. It combines the implications of love for Christian conduct with a discussion of God's nature. John says in verses 7–8 that God is love and love is of God, and to love God is to know God. First John uses *love* 43 times, 32 times in 4:7–5:4. First John 3:23 presented love as a commandment, but now John describes it as God's very nature. John stresses both that God's love is manifest in Christ and that we must love one another.

Both 4:7–10 and 11–18 begin with the phrase "beloved" (*dear friends*, NIV). The second unit contains two parts, verses 12–16 and 13–18. This is one of only four places in the New Testament discussing God's nature (see John 4:24; Heb 12:29; and 1 John 1:5). As in 1:5, John here does not speculate on the substance of the divine being but makes a claim about God's actions. All Christians believe that "God is love," but only 1 John says so explicitly (4:8, 16). This statement must not be taken out of context but rather focused upon the particularity of Jesus. Those whom John opposes defined the "real Christians" on the basis of their superior knowledge [Greek *gnosis*]

of God. John, however, defines the real Christians on the basis of love (similarly, 1 Cor 8:1–3).

Note the parallel structure of verses 7 and 8:
Beloved, let us love one another
love is of God
whoever loves is born of God and knows God
whoever does not love, does not know God
God is love

Failure to love (verse 8) invalidates any claim to *know God*. This is the fellowship test of truth. Since God expresses love toward us, not to love is to misunderstand God's nature. But what is this love that is of God? Verses 9–10 answer this question in a historical way (see John 3:16). God's love is self-sacrificial. Love is self-sacrifice, seeking another person's good at our expense. God's love preceded our love. We are able to love only because we have been loved (see Rom 5:8). Only when we understand how God has loved us can we love others. Unless we love others, we have not understood how God has loved us.

Verse 11 begins a new section, which says our love for one another must be modeled upon God's selfless sacrifice. Imitation of God demands love. The cross is the basis for, and limit of, Christian love.

Verse 12 may be the most radical statement in the letter: God's love is open only to those who love. Verse 12 offers three points about God and love (compare John 14:8–20): no one has ever seen God (John 1:18), God dwells in those who love each other, and the love of God reaches completion in us. John's letters rarely teach about the church (the word only occurs three times, all in 3 John). But John, without using the word, has as high a view of the church as does Paul, who speaks of it frequently. For John, the church functions as the completion of God's self-revelation in Christ.

In 4:13–16, John gives as proof of faith a debated point, the presence of the Spirit. John lists three proofs that God loves us and abides in us: God has given us the Spirit (verse 13; see 3:24; Rom 8:15), we abide in God as the apostles testify (verse 14), and we confess Christ (verse 15).

Notably, verse 14 describes *the world* as the object of Jesus' saving work. He is *Savior of the world* (see John 4:42). God has not rejected the *world*. God loved (John 3:16) the same world that rejected his son. Verse 16 combines the great themes of 1 John: knowing, believing, love of God, and abiding.

In 4:17–5:4, John continues the main theme: the love of God manifested in Jesus and its importance for believers' lives. Ideas tumble over themselves without any clear order. In 4:12, John declared that if we love each other, God dwells in us perfectly. First John 4:13–16 stresses indwelling divine love, and 4:17–21 elaborates upon the second idea. Just as we have confidence before God in the coming judgment, so also we can live now without fear. For fear is the present foretaste of an impending punishment. Believers in Christ who live out of this divine love have no cause for this fear. Indeed, if we fear judgment, we have not yet developed a right understanding of God's love.

> **Perfect Love**
> *What is the perfect love (4:18) that casts out fear? John may mean that when our love becomes flawless, we will no longer fear judgment, or that mature (see 2:15, 4:12) love comes from God. As we believe in God and love each other (4:16), God's love reaches its goal in us.*

Verse 19 sets out the basic thesis: *we love because he* [God] *first loved us*. The word *love* here has no object, but from 4:7, 11 "one another" seems the likely referent. The verb can mean either "we love" or "we should love." Although most translations go with the former option, in this section of exhortation, the second seems more likely.

Verse 20 applies this thesis to the problems in this congregation: *love* has an essential communal meaning. Here John again uses the "If anyone says …" form occurring in chapters 1 and 2. Since there these slogans represent the views of the opposition, they probably do here, as well. The heretics' indifference toward fellow Christians indicates their shallow understanding of the Christian faith.

This is not merely a logical deduction, it is a command from God or Jesus (verse 21). The gospels do not contain a command exactly like this, but it reflects Jesus' teaching, since the love for God and for fellow Christians are really a single commandment (3:23; compare Matt 22:34–39). John does not quote Jesus on the great commandment, but he seems to draw upon his thoughts.

Now the argument returns to logic (5:1; as in verse 20): 1 · everyone who believes Jesus is the Christ is a child of God; 2 · everyone who loves a parent, loves his child (a common proverb of the day); 3 · therefore to love God is to love all those who are "God-born" (4:7, 3:9, 10; compare John 1:12, 13).

First John 5:2 may refer back to verse 1, or to what follows, but John's key point is that, if we love the children of God, then we know that we are obedient to God (2:5; 2 John 6). Verse 2's *commands* probably refers to John 20:31 (and 1:12) as well as 1 John 3:23.

To obey God's command in 1 John has a specific content: love your fellow Christian (4:21). This command (verse 3) is not burdensome (a point already made in Deut 30:11–14 and restated by Jesus in Matt 11:28–39). John argues that God's power aids us (see Eph 3:16; Phil 4:13), God's demands recognize human limitations, and when we perceive God's love for us, we have strength to love others (see Rom 8:1–14).

Verse 4, our *faith* (better, "confidence") rests in God's power. This is the only time in either the gospel or letters of John that the noun *faith* occurs (the verb form, "believing," occurs often). Here *faith* probably means "the faith," that is, the Christian message about Jesus.

4:7–5:12 First John 5:5 gives a thesis and verses 6–12 offer three proofs of its truth: the birth and death of Jesus, the Spirit, and our faith. The word *believe* in verse 5 picks up the idea of *faith* in verse 4 (the same root word). This "believing," or "faith," is the basis of our victory over the world's hostile powers. This recalls 1 John 1:1–4, which also stresses belief's basis in Jesus.

The belief that gives victory is that "Jesus is the Son of God" (verse 5). Verse 6 elaborates the meaning of verse 5 by criticizing professed Christians who deny that Jesus came with *blood* and say it was only with *water*. John could be referring to the "water and blood" that flowed from Jesus' pierced side (John 19:34–35), baptism and the Lord's Supper (according to Luther and Calvin), or Jesus' baptism ("water") and death ("blood").

A textual problem exists in verses 7b and 8. Modern translations omit the verses because they do not appear in early manuscripts. Verse 7 says that the Spirit witnesses to Jesus' sonship. Since Jesus is the *Spirit of Truth* (John 15:26), his testimony is valid. The Spirit witnesses to Jesus at baptism, in apostolic preaching, and in Scripture, as well as in our hearts to our faith.

> **"Three Witnesses"**
> *Are the three witnesses of verse 8 the same as in verse 6? Apparently so, and more importantly, these three witnesses agree, looking back to the law (Deut 19:15), which required two or three witnesses to establish a case.*

Another testimony (verse 10) comes from confession of believers (see 4:13–14). (Note the NEB translation "in his own heart.") This inner testimony (verse 11) means that "God has already given us eternal life." In addition to the testimony about Jesus (verses 6–8) given by the Spirit (and God, verse 9), the believers also give testimony. Thus, a Christian is one who has accepted the testimony of God and has affirmed it personally (verse 10).

Verses 11–12 summarize the testimony that Christians have from God and the result of it. God has given us eternal life. To have the Son (not just the Spirit) is to have eternal life (verse 12). The opposite is also true: not to accept Jesus in the flesh means not to have life.

CONCLUSION: CHRISTIAN CERTAINTY · 5:13–21

The idea of the Son and eternal life also appears in 5:20 and marks off these verses as a unit. First John 5:13 closely resembles John 20:31 and serves as a conclusion to this letter, just as that passage originally did to the gospel. Verses 14–21 are an epilogue summarizing themes from throughout the letter: prayer, the world and the evil one, sin, God, the Son, and eternal life. The final verses (18–21) give a positive restatement of what *we know*. In the context of division and doctrinal dissent, it is vital to remind the readers of what they know. The sense of assurance about eternal life leads to confident prayer (verses 14–15). The basis of this is the reader's faith (2:28; 3:21–23). This confidence assumes a willingness to submit to the divine will.

Like John 14:13 and 15:17, 1 John emphasizes the privilege of "boldness" in prayer more than the assurance of results we wish for. The answered prayer has a particular focus (verses 16–17), the forgiveness of sin. As in 1:5–2:2, the author assumes that Christians do sin but that Christ effectively intervenes in lives. Here, however, other Christians intervene (not Jesus), and this leads to the restoration of life, a relationship with God.

The possibility of restoration leads to the consideration that sometimes this is not possible. Nothing here suggests a ranking of sins (but see Mark 3:28–29), although the Bible does describe some sins as beyond atonement (Num 15:27–31; Isa 22:12–14; Jer 7:16–20; 14:7–12). In John 8:21–24 and 9:39–41, the inescapable sin is the rejection of Jesus as the one sent by God, so the deadly sin in 1 John 5:11–13 may be the opponents' rejection of Jesus. The other mention of *death* in 1 John 3:14–15 concerns failure to love one's fellow Christians. To summarize then, John combines two "deadly" sins here to describe the *antichrists* as those whose lack of christological faith and brotherly love cuts them off from eternal life. It is essential that we not emphasize the wrong half of this verse. John's main point is the efficacy of prayer for the fallen Christian, not the existence of inescapable sin. Verse 17 says that while all wrongdoing is sin, and sin leads to death, we ought neither to obscure the seriousness of sin nor deny the possibility of repentance.

The final verses of 1 John state three things that *we know*, important affirmations to strengthen the readers' resistance to the opponents. All contrast the children of God with the evil one.

Verse 18 summarizes 2:3 and 3:9, emphasizing assurance of a good relationship with God. The verse has two difficulties: first, does the *anyone* and the *he* refer to the same person, or is the *he* Jesus (and therefore Jesus protects the person born of God)? Second, is there any significance of the verb tense shift from perfect ("born") to the aorist (the second "born")? From John 17:11–15 (and 1 John 2:13), it seems that it is God and Jesus who protect Christians from the evil one. That seems most likely to be the point here: the children of God are protected by the Son of God.

In verse 19, the second *we know* statement summarizes earlier statements (1:6; 2:15, 18; 3:10, 13) and acknowledges the great danger that surrounds the child of God. The phrase *whole world* here stresses the universality of sin's rule except over those who abide in the truth.

The third *we know* (verse 20) summarizes 4:9–11 and 5:1–12, and gives the full christological affirmation to "God's Son, Jesus Christ" (recalling 5:1–5 and John 20:31). These three titles, "God's Son," "Jesus" and "Christ," are essential to John's Christology, because the coming of God's true Son reveals God (John 17:3). It is probable that the one who is *true* here refers to God, not Jesus. But this is a meaningless distinction, since "I and the Father are one" (John 10:30, 20:28).

Verse 21 seems like a meteor fallen into this discussion. Nowhere previously in the letter has the topic of *idols* arisen. It relates to the preceding discussion either as a reference to the "false teachings" of those who left, as a comprehensive term for "sin" of all sorts, or as a traditional Jewish way of referring to any other god other than the God of Israel. Whatever he means precisely, perhaps John puts it this way to contrast strongly the beliefs he affirms with the beliefs of those who left claiming a more advanced understanding of God.

THEOLOGICAL REFLECTIONS

Although the structure of 1 John is not always easy to discern, or its argument to follow, it clearly seeks to connect the life of the church to the core of the Christian message. The love of God leads to a community faithful to the word of truth it has received, supportive of all its members, resolute in the face of adversity, and expectant of God's final victory over evil. Love for 1 John is not merely an emotion. It is a set of commitments that should always be the foundation of the church's life.

FOR FURTHER STUDY

Gerald Bray, *James, 1–2 Peter, 1–3 John, Jude* (Downers Grove, Ill.: InterVarsity, 2000).

David Rensberger, *The Epistles of John* (Louisville: Westminster John Knox, 2001).

David Rensberger, *1 John, 2 John, 3 John* (Nashville: Abingdon, 1997).

Stephen S. Smalley, *1, 2, 3 John* (Nashville: Word, 1984).

D. Moody Smith, *First, Second and Third John* (Louisville: John Knox, 1991).

2 John

Wendell Willis

CHAPTER CONTENTS

Contexts 1055

Commentary 1055

    Introduction · 1–3 1055

    The Command to Love · 4–6 1055

    Warning About the Deceivers · 7–11 1055

    Farewell · 12–13 1055

Theological Reflections 1055

For Further Study 1056

Second John shares two key topics with 1 John: some Christians have accepted a new view of Jesus, and this group has left those who do not share their "advanced" views. Behind this problem lies the early believers' custom of offering room and board to traveling evangelists, who depended upon such hospitality for their mission work (see Acts 16:15; 17:7; 21:8, 16). Christians, in fact, are commanded to greet such travelers and provide for them (Rom 12:13; Heb 13:2; 1 Tim 3:2; Titus 1:8).

CONTEXTS

The organization of the letter shows key sections between the greeting and the farewell: verses 4–6 praise those Christians who share mutual love, and verses 7–11 rebuke those who follow the "deceivers and antichrists." Second John thus illustrates that doctrine and conduct do connect, and that false doctrine lessens love.

COMMENTARY

INTRODUCTION · 1–3

The letter's opening resembles those of contemporary letters. The author addresses an individual congregation with the threefold Christian blessing.

THE COMMAND TO LOVE · 4–6

In three verses, *command* occurs four times. The "new/not new commandment" (verses 4, 5) is to love (compare 1 John 5:3). As the Lord taught, the command to love defines Christians.

WARNING ABOUT THE DECEIVERS · 7–11

Verse 7 connects verses 7–11 to what precedes. Christians must face a grave danger: "many deceivers have gone out into the world" (compare 1 John 2:18, 26; 4:1). Verse 8 poses a problem for many commentators, who are bothered by its suggestion that eternal life is a reward *worked for*. John need not speak like Paul, but both Paul and John (and Hebrews) know the need to persevere. Second John does not offer a theory of salvation but a call to endure.

Verse 9 speaks of those who abide in the "doctrine *of* Christ," which can be either the doctrine taught *about* Christ or the doctrine taught *by* Christ. The second suggestion implies all the Christian beliefs. The first specifically concerns teaching about Christ, and in view of the context and the focus on the humanity of Christ both in 1 John and here, the first interpretation seems more likely.

In verses 10–11, John says not to show hospitality to "deceivers." "Receive him *into your house*" may mean "welcome him to the church meeting held in your home." If this was the case, then John is really worried about the heretics participating or even teaching in house-church gatherings. In this confusion, Christians should measure teachings by the litmus test of faith in the incarnation. The deceivers are unwilling to affirm that Jesus "has come in the flesh" (verse 9; see 1 John 2:18–23; 4:1–3; 5:5). John instructs his readers to apply the simple test to traveling evangelists, whom simple Christians might welcome and then be led astray.

FAREWELL · 12–13

There is nothing special about this farewell. John explains his self-imposed limit (the size of the page on which he writes) and his preference for face to face conversations (literally, "mouth to mouth"). Ancient writing was very expensive.

THEOLOGICAL REFLECTIONS

This tiny letter calls an individual congregation to remain faithful to its commitment to love God and neighbor. Although it must originally have addressed a cluster of congregations known to the author, the letter quickly became more widely circulated as part of the Johannine collection. It thus addresses all churches everywhere seeking to navigate a troubled world in which love is too rare, and division too common.

FOR FURTHER STUDY

Gerald Bray, *James, 1–2 Peter, 1–3 John, Jude* (Downers Grove, Ill.: InterVarsity, 2000).

David Rensberger, *The Epistles of John* (Louisville: Westminster John Knox, 2001).

David Rensberger, *1 John, 2 John, 3 John* (Nashville: Abingdon, 1997).

Stephen S. Smalley, *1, 2, 3 John* (Nashville: Word, 1984).

D. Moody Smith, *First, Second and Third John* (Louisville: John Knox, 1991).

3 John

Wendell Willis

CHAPTER CONTENTS

Contexts   1057

Commentary   1057
> Introduction · 1–2   1057
> Gaius: A Model of Hospitality · 3–8   1057
> Diotrephes: A Bad Model · 9–10   1057
> An Exhortation · 11–12   1057
> Final Greetings · 13–14   1058

Theological Reflections   1058

For Further Study   1058

Unlike 2 John's defense of doctrine, the third letter of John – the shortest epistle in the New Testament – emphasizes the importance of extending hospitality, especially to those who are traveling and working for the gospel. This lesson is illustrated by the example of two Christians: Gaius, who regularly practices hospitality and whom John commends, and Diotrephes, *who loves to be first* (verse 9). Demetrius is also held up as someone *well spoken of by everyone*.

CONTEXTS

Generally parallel to 2 John in style, content, and length, 3 John is the only New Testament book that does not contain the name of Christ (although see "the Name" verse 7). After the introduction (verses 1–2), 3 John has messages to or concerning: Gaius (verses 3–8), Diotrephes (verses 9–10) and Demetrius (verses 11, 12), as well as a conclusion (verses 13–14).

COMMENTARY
INTRODUCTION · 1–2
The introduction closely resembles common letter-writing style in the first century. See further the introduction to 1 John.

GAIUS: A MODEL OF HOSPITALITY · 3–8
Gaius, a very common Roman name, is described as a man of *truth* (verse 3) and *love* (verse 6), especially hospitable to other Christians. Gaius walks *in the truth* (verse 3); that is, not only does he know the truth, but he leads his life in accordance with it. Christians should finance enterprises that the world will not support.

DIOTREPHES: A BAD MODEL · 9–10
As with Gaius, we know very little about *Diotrephes* except for his name [Greek "borne of God"]. John wrote the church and gave instructions, but Diotrephes opposed him. He may have kept the letter from being read or rejected the instructions that John wrote in the letter.

Here a local church leader feels that he can disagree with the author, despite the latter's authority. Interestingly, John does not invoke his apostolic status in this argument. Indeed, he does not seem to deny that Diotrephes remains a member of the church.

The letter does not give the reason for Diotrephes's inhospitality (beyond his inflated ego). It does not seem to have been regarding a doctrinal issue. Diotrephes himself may not have expressed any specific reasons for his opposition to John. As far as the letter reveals, this struggle is a personality conflict caused by Diotrephes's desire for power; thus it is about sin. Diotrephes not only opposed John's authority, he refused to receive traveling evangelists (from John?) and withdrew fellowship from local Christians who did support them. John promises (verse 10) to deal personally with the opposition of Diotrephes. The fact that this letter survives indicates that John did so successfully.

> **John's Other Letters**
> *What John had previously written to the church is unknown, though this probably does not refer either to 1 or 2 John, neither of which promotes the theme of hospitality. In some ways, John is receiving back here the treatment that he urges in 2 John 10–11 for those carrying on false teaching.*

AN EXHORTATION · 11–12
In Gaius and Diotrephes, John sets forth two examples of Christian hospitality: one good and one

lamentable. By these examples, he commends to Gaius a course of behavior ("do good and avoid evil"; verse 11). The concluding exhortation states a general principle about the Christian life and thus a test for Christian leaders (verse 11). It also holds up Demetrius as a model who bears witness to Christ. John commends Demetrius, perhaps the bearer of this letter, to Gaius in three respects: his reputation among Christians, his Christian life, and his relationship to John himself (verse 12). If Gaius wants to see a positive example of Christian living, Demetrius offers one.

FINAL GREETINGS · 13–14

As in 2 John, the author concludes by noting that a good deal more needs to be considered, but he prefers to communicate face to face rather than with *pen and ink*, probably because the issues are delicate.

Gaius cared for traveling preachers in his home. (On Christian hospitality as a virtue, see Rom 12:13; 1 Tim 3:2; 5:10; Titus 1; 8; Heb 13:2; 1 Pet 4:9). In the ancient world, travelers needed hospitality, and this was especially the case for those traveling missionaries who set out with minimal provisions (following Jesus' instructions in Mark 6:8 and Luke 10:4).

Christian preachers were reluctant to accept any payment from nonbelievers (literally "the Gentiles") for their preaching. They wished to avoid unfavorable comparison with the well-known street preachers of their day (see 1 Cor 9:6 and 2 Cor 11:7–11; 1 Thess 2:9).

THEOLOGICAL REFLECTIONS

The leaders of an individual Christian congregation sometimes face problems and temptations. Love can give way to power, and power can corrupt. This brief letter, however, orients readers to an alternative use of power and influence, not as a way to aggrandize the leader, but as a tool for service. By calling leaders to exercise the hospitality and graciousness of a Christian, 3 John gives a message still worth hearing.

FOR FURTHER STUDY

Gerald Bray, *James, 1–2 Peter, 1–3 John, Jude* (Downers Grove, Ill.: InterVarsity, 2000).

David Rensberger, *The Epistles of John* (Louisville: Westminster John Knox, 2001).

David Rensberger, *1 John, 2 John, 3 John* (Nashville: Abingdon, 1997).

Stephen S. Smalley, *1, 2, 3 John* (Nashville: Word, 1984).

D. Moody Smith, *First, Second and Third John* (Louisville: John Knox, 1991).

Jude

Charles B. Stephenson

CHAPTER CONTENTS

Contexts **1059**

Commentary **1060**
- Salutation · 1–2 **1060**
- The Reason for Writing · 3–4 **1060**
- Condemnation of False Teachers · 5–16 **1060**
- Appeal for Faithfulness · 17–23 **1061**
- Doxology · 24–25 **1062**

Theological Reflections **1062**

For Further Study **1062**

Works Cited **1062**

Jude was one of the last letters that all the church accepted, even though it was popular as early as the late second century (Kelly 223). Clement of Alexandria, Tertullian, and Origen accepted Jude during this period. However, in the fourth century Eusebius listed Jude among the disputed books. In 367, Athanasius listed the letter as one of the twenty-seven books of the New Testament, where it remains today.

CONTEXTS

The author identifies himself as *Jude, a servant of Jesus Christ and a brother of James* (1:1). This gives two clues for identifying the author: his name and his brother's name. *Jude* [Greek *Ioudas*, often rendered Judas] and James [Greek *Iakobos*] were common first century names. There are three Judases, other than Iscariot, named in the New Testament and associated with the apostles: Judas son of James (Luke 6:16; Acts 1:13), Judas called Barsabbas (Acts 15:22), and Judas brother of Jesus (Mark 6:3; Acts 1:13–14). As far as we know, Judas the brother of Jesus is the only one of these Judases who had a brother named *James* (Matt 13:55). Conceivably, then, the author of this book may have been Jesus' brother. *James* the brother of Jesus was a respected leader in the early Palestinian Jewish church (Acts 15:13; 21:17–19; Gal 1:19), and Jude may be associating himself with James's strong reputation. Thus this Jude is traditionally the brother of Jesus (Watson 473–74; Bauckham 14–16).

The date of the letter has to be rather early to fall within the lifetime of Jude, the brother of Jesus, probably sometimes between the 50s and the 70s of the first century. If Jude was a source used in 2 Peter, the letter would fall in the first half of this period.

Jude does not specifically identify the recipients of his letter. *To those who have been called, who are loved by God the Father and kept by Jesus Christ* (verse 1) is a general description that can fit any group of Christians. He calls the recipients his *dear friends* (verses 3, 17, 20), possibly a description of Christians anywhere with a relationship to Jude. But with a family home in Palestine and his brother James as the well-known leader of the church in Jerusalem, it seems reasonable that Jude ministered in Palestine and wrote to Christians in or near Palestine.

The addressees are churches plagued by false teachers. These false teachers have rejected all authority but their own (verses 4, 8, 11). Their rejection of authority comes from their misunderstanding of the freedom Christians have in Christ. Such a misunderstanding has resulted in immoral sexual activity (verse 7). These teachers are destroying the spiritual health of the churches (verses 12–13), and Jude writes to counter this effect.

Jude uses the form of an ancient Jewish letter: salutation (1–2), theme and occasion (3–4), body (5–19), appeal to action (20–23), and the concluding doxology (24–25). Because of the closing doxology, Jude might be described as an "epistolary sermon."

Anyone who reads Jude and 2 Peter 2 notices overlap between them. Most scholars argue that 2 Peter revised Jude, following the basic outline of the older letter but retaining little of the original wording. Both writers used similar materials to confront false teachers who were bothering churches. Material from Jude appears in 2 Peter, but in a new garb to suit the needs of a new audience.

COMMENTARY

SALUTATION · 1–2

The letter opening identifies the author as *Jude, a servant of Jesus Christ and a brother of James*. Jude's self-identification as *a servant of Jesus Christ* calls for his readers to give attention to his letter. He writes as one who has authority, using the Old Testament usage of *servant* as one of God's leaders (Deut 34:5; Neh 9:14; Ps 89:3). In the New Testament, *servant* can be used to identify apostles and evangelists (Rom 1:1; Col 4:12; 2 Tim 2:24; 2 Pet 1:1; see Richard 245–46).

When Jude writes that *James* is his brother, he is noting his relation to one of the most respected men in the Jewish church (Acts 15:13; Gal 1:19; 2:9). This association brings Jude's relation to Jesus to the attention of his readers. The opening is a humble statement of Jude's authority for writing.

The recipients are identified as *called, loved,* and *kept*. *Called* points to God's initiative in the salvation shared by these Christians. *Loved* identifies God's motivation for calling them to salvation. And *kept* demonstrates Christ's commitment to their salvation (Moo 222–23).

Jude desires that *mercy, peace and love* be in their lives *in abundance*, an unusual greeting for New Testament letters, and the only one not to mention grace. Also, it is the only one to contain *love*. *Love* and *mercy* are among the book's favorite terms.

THE REASON FOR WRITING · 3–4

The body begins with a declaration about why Jude was written. In verses 3, 17, and 20, where the NIV translates *dear friends*, Jude has *beloved* [Greek *agapetoi*], a common early Christian form of address. Jude identifies with his audience by calling them *beloved* and by focusing on *the salvation we share*.

> **The Confession of Faith**
> In the New Testament, "faith" has an objective content and it prompts a subjective experience. Summaries of the content appear in 1 Corinthians 15:3–5; 1 Timothy 1:15; 3:16; 2 Timothy 2:11–13; and Titus 3:4–7. Christians probably recited such confessions in worship, and they became ways of testing the faithfulness of teaching.

In instructing his readers *to contend for the faith that was once for all entrusted to the saints*, Jude uses an athletic metaphor, *contend*, to describe the struggle for faithfulness in the presence of *godless men*. Then, the need for continued commitment to *the faith* because of some who have *slipped in* to draw others away draws his attention. These *godless men* pervert *grace* into immoral *license* and deny *Jesus Christ*. Their sin and condemnation has been predicted *long ago*.

CONDEMNATION OF FALSE TEACHERS · 5–16

Jude moves from declaring the presence of *godless men* to a discussion of their condemnation and certain judgment. This section opens with Jude's desire *to remind you* (verse 5) and continues until the next section is opened by *dear friends, remember* (verse 17). Both emphasize the significance of what follows.

5–7 The certainty of judgment is illustrated by three examples of judgment against sin: the Israelite rebels in the wilderness (Num 14), the wicked angels (Gen 6:1–4), and Sodom and Gomorrah (Gen 19:1–29). These examples seem to increase in the severity of punishment (Watson 488).

In Numbers 14, when all but Joshua and Caleb refuse to listen to God's intention to give them the promised land, God condemns all others above age 20 to die in the wilderness. Genesis 6:1–4 records the story of *the sons of God* who married *the daughters of men*. Finally, Sodom and Gomorrah (Gen 19:1–29) experienced the fires of judgment.

> **"Sons of God"**
> 1 Enoch 6–19 identifies the sons of God as evil angels bound in chains by the archangel Michael. These evil angels were kept in darkness for the coming judgment. Jude uses this story as a dramatic comparison to the disturbers of the church's peace against whom he writes.

8–11 Having established precedents for God's judgment against sinners, Jude now offers reasons for judgment against those his audience is confronting (verses 4, 8, 11, 15, 16). These men are *dreamers* who *pollute their own bodies, reject authority and slander celestial beings*. They are *dreamers* like the false prophets in Israel (Deut 13:1–5). The three sins condemning these teachers are all found in the Sodom and Gomorrah story: illicit sex, disobedience to God, and sinning against angels.

Such sinful arrogance is magnified in comparison to the humility of *the archangel Michael* who would not rebuke *the devil* in a dispute over Moses' body. This story is apparently from the lost pseudepigraphical writing, *Testament of Moses* (Bauckham 47–48). Jude quotes an accepted Jewish tradition to illustrate a truth. In this text, *Michael* quotes Zechariah 3:2 where the Lord says, *The Lord rebuke you, Satan!* Even in his august position, *Michael* will not speak against his great adversary. In comparison, Jude's opponents *speak abusively against whatever they do not understand.* Their sinful arrogance denies all but what *they do understand by instinct, like unreasoning animals. And these are the very things that destroy them.* They reach for power and authority yet only gain destruction.

Their great sin causes Jude to pronounce a *Woe* oracle against them. These men have followed *Cain, Balaam,* and *Korah* (Gen 4:1–16; Num 22:1–24:25, 31:8; Num 16:1–35). Later Jewish tradition viewed each of these characters as the epitome of the sinful life (Richard 276–77). The reality of judgment is expressed when God curses *Cain, Balaam* dies, and the earth swallows *Korah*. Similar ends are already at work in the corrupt lives of these false teachers.

12–13 *These men are blemishes at your love feasts* raises the image of fellow Christians who take lightly their relationship to Christ and the church. The word for *blemishes* [Greek *spilades*] may also be translated "reefs." These men hidden in the love feast are a threat to others as rocks and reefs are to ships (2 Pet 2:13 changes the Greek slightly to "stain"; see Kelly 270; Bauckham 85–86).

These *godless men are shepherds who feed only themselves* (compare Ezek 34:1–3). Beyond being a hidden threat, they have no concern for others and their needs. Their role as *shepherds* is seen as a means to get for self and not for serving others (compare Acts 20:29).

> **Jude's Imagery**
>
> Jude uses nature imagery to illustrate the emptiness of his opponents. They are *wind-driven clouds without rain; twice dead trees without fruit or root.* The semiarid region of Palestine knew well the disappointment of rainless clouds and their end result: dead, fruitless fields. Also such men are like *wild waves of the sea, foaming up their shame* (see Isa 57:20). Finally, *they are wandering stars, for whom blackest darkness has been reserved forever:* a description of the planets as erratic stars that seem to move without direction into darkness (see Richard, 280–81).

14–16 Jude next introduces Enoch of the seventh generation from Adam (Gen 5:24; Heb 11:5). The story of his dramatic ascent to heaven gave rise to speculation among the Jews about a man with no real history. During the Second Temple period, pseudonymous writings appeared under Enoch's name. These writings were respected and popular. Although today *1 Enoch* is not considered a canonical writing (except among Ethiopian Christians), it appears to have been highly regarded by numerous Jews and some early Christians. Therefore, it is not surprising that Jude quotes *1 Enoch* 1:9 to give weight to his judgments against *godless men* (Moo 268–74; Richard 282–84).

Jude uses Enoch to picture the Lord coming with a great host of *his holy ones to judge everyone.* This beginning puts even Christians on warning about judgment (1:22–23). As the scene shifts to the judgment of *godless men,* Jude pictures God coming *to convict the ungodly.*

Verse 16 further describes the *ungodly acts,* the *ungodly way* these acts are accomplished, and the *harsh words* spoken by these *godless men*. They are *grumblers and faultfinders.* This identification relates them to the condemned Israelites who grumbled against God and his chosen leaders (Exod 16:1–8; Num 14:1–38; 1 Cor 10:10; Phil 2:14). These *faultfinders* are never happy with their lot. Their *evil desires* drive them always to want something more. Every act and word is an expression of their greed in all things.

APPEAL FOR FAITHFULNESS · 17–23

As noted earlier, *dear friends, remember* introduces a significant section. After studying verses 5–16, one may forget that Jude was written to faithful Christians. But here Jude again addresses *beloved* Christians whom he encourages to remain faithful and to overcome the work of the false teachers (verse 3).

17–19 Like verses 3–4, so also verses 17–19 call the recipients *dear friends,* describe ungodly men, and then appeal to past teaching. Jude clearly returns to his call for Christians *to contend for the faith* (Moo 279–80).

The appeal to *remember* the apostles' past teaching parallels Jude's desire *to remind* them of the Lord's past actions (verse 5). These Christians were to call on what they already knew when faced with false teaching. The apostles had warned them against *scoffers who will follow their own ungodly desires.* This knowledge should have armed their faith to face what came against them. *Scoffers* who question God and *follow their own ungodly desires* naturally cause divisions. These teachers act as natural men because they *do not have the Spirit*. In spite of their claims, there is no sign of spiritual life in them.

20–21 Jude again calls attention to his relationship with his *dear friends* as he urges them to persevere. *Keep* is the only actual imperative in these two verses. *Build*, *pray*, and *wait* are participles that the NIV translates as imperatives. With *keep* as a command, the other actions indicate how one should remain *in God's love* (see verse 1).

22–23 Those who anticipate *mercy* at our Lord's coming must show mercy to those who have been damaged by the false teachers – *those who doubt*. Also this *mercy* should extend to those who have been *stained by corrupted flesh*. Apparently, the false teachers had caused doubt in some and had caused others to share in their corrupted lifestyle. There is no sin in the life of another, even a false teacher, which is beyond a Christian's call to show *mercy*. Christians are to reach out to turn others *from the fire and save them* (verse 7).

Those who show *mercy* must do so with caution. They must hate the sin that pollutes. But the gravity of approaching those who are actively affected by sin should always humble those who move to correct others (see Matt 7:3–5). The whole church is waiting for *the mercy of our Lord Jesus Christ*.

DOXOLOGY · 24–25

Jude concludes with encouragement to *dear friends*. He had introduced them to Jesus' power to keep them when he began this letter (verse 1). He warned them of the seriousness of their lives for the keeping (verse 21). Now he declares the fullness of God's power to preserve the faithful for eternal life. The false teachers had denied *Jesus Christ our only Sovereign and Lord* (verse 4), and so Jude now reiterates the church's most basic convictions about the relationship of God and Christ to each other and to believers.

THEOLOGICAL REFLECTIONS

Jude's highly polemical letter seeks to defend the church from heretics whose theology denied essential Christian teaching about the nature of Jesus and whose loose morality undermined Christian practices. Because of the book's abundant use of metaphor and frequent allusions to biblical stories (or interpretations of them), working out the precise theology of Jude is difficult. Certainly, he believes in the Old Testament as sacred Scripture, in the core ethical standards of early Jewish Christianity, in the importance of angels (like those Jews who read *1 Enoch*), and in the imminent return of the Lord in glory. That is, he falls into the broad mainstream of the New Testament, first impressions about his book notwithstanding.

FOR FURTHER STUDY

D. A. Carson, Douglas J. Moo, and Leon Morris, *An Introduction to the New Testament* (Grand Rapids: Zondervan, 1992).

Peter H. Davids, *The Letters of 2 Peter and Jude* (Grand Rapids: Eerdmans, 2006).

Daniel J. Harrington, *Jude and 2 Peter* (Collegeville, Minn.: Liturgical Press, 2003).

WORKS CITED

Richard J. Bauckham, *Jude, 2 Peter* (Waco, Tex.: Word, 1983).

J. N. D. Kelly, *A Commentary on the Epistles of Peter and Jude* (New York: Harper & Row, 1969).

Douglas J. Moo, *2 Peter and Jude* (Grand Rapids: Zondervan, 1996).

Earl J. Richard, *Reading 1 Peter, Jude, and 2 Peter* (Macon, Ga.: Smyth & Helwys, 2000).

Duane F. Watson, "The Second Letter of Peter," *The New Interpreter's Bible*, vol. 12 (Nashville: Abingdon, 1998).

Revelation

Allan J. McNicol

CHAPTER CONTENTS

- Contexts 1064
- Commentary 1066
  - Prologues · 1:1–3 1066
  - John's Vision on Earth · 1:4–3:22 1066
  - John's Visions in Heaven · 4:1–22:5 1071
  - Epilogues · 22:6–21 1084
- Theological Reflections 1085
- For Further Study 1086
- Works Cited 1086

MAPS, TABLES, & FEATURES

- Apocalyptic Literature in Ancient Times 1063
- The Structure of the Letters to the 7 Churches 1067
- The 7 Churches of Asia Minor 1068
- The Roman Provinces of Asia Minor 1068
- Revelation & the Legend of Nero's Return 1076
- Armageddon 1079
- Dispensational Premillenialism 1083

Of the four major types of literature in the New Testament (gospel, history, epistle, and apocalypse), Revelation is the prime example of the fourth. The first words of the book state that it is *the revelation* [Greek *apokalypsis*] *of Jesus Christ*. While the book is primarily apocalyptic in form, parts of an epistolary form (beginning and ending) are attached. The apocalypse falls into two major parts. In 1:4–3:22 John, on earth, has a vision of Jesus and receives a message to the seven churches. In 4:1–22:5, John is taken into heaven where he receives information about the future. Both prologue (1:1–3) and epilogue (22:6–21) create the impression that the collected visions of 1:4–22:5 constitute a completed literary work.

A better translation of the word *apokalypsis* in Revelation 1:1, usually translated "revelation," is "unveiling." As in ceremonies where a dignitary unveils the covering over a statue, Revelation claims to unveil the secrets and purposes of God for his people in the first century. But this should not be misunderstood. Unlike Nostrodamus, the medieval mystic who wrote coded prophecies, Revelation does not contain coded symbols giving us specific information about the future course of history; rather, it reminds us of who is in charge of history. It teaches that life is not the sum of what we experience with our senses. Such perspectives on reality are often incomplete and distorted. It presumes that, despite appearances to the contrary, the Lamb of Calvary (and not the Roman Cæsar) is the sovereign Lord of history.

Apocalyptic Literature in Ancient Times

In common speech, the word apocalypse *[Greek* apokalypsis*] refers to extreme crisis situations ending in a train-wreck type of event. This is a complete misrepresentation of the nature and function of an ancient apocalypse. Although Revelation may be the first instance in ancient literature where a literary work actually calls itself an apocalypse (1:1), by no means is this the first time that we find in ancient literature writings that claim to unveil divine secrets and the course of history. The prophets were taken by inspiration into the heavenly places and the councils of God's advisors, focusing on problems in Israel (see 1 Kgs 22:19–28). This information was always limited in scope. God chose not to reveal to humans all divine counsel and wisdom (Job 38:–39; 42:1–4; Ecclesiasticus 3:21–24). Later, certain scribes claimed to have access to the wisdom of great sages of the past such as Enoch, Baruch, and Ezra. They believed the sages had made trips into the heavenly world accompanied by angels and learned about the universe, the state of the dead, and the end times. Written accounts of this legacy were very common not only among the Jews but throughout the Greco-Roman world. To the ancients, such writings as 1 Enoch provided insight into unknown matters and built hope that there existed a transcendent realm guaranteeing ultimate justice and order in the universe.*

REVELATION

CONTEXTS

John couches the divine message in a bewildering variety of literary devices and images besides the major forms of the letter and prophetic-apocalyptic structure. Without being exhaustive, we take note of the occurrence of hymnic fragments (4:8, 11; 5:9; 7:15–17; 11:17–18; 15:3–4; 19:6b); taunts (18:2–24); bizarre symbolism and numerology (9:1–6; 12:1–17; 13:17–18; 17:1–14); and a creative use of personification (such as Rome pictured as a temple prostitute [17:1–6]). It adds up to an enthralling literary work that captivates a careful reader.

Above all, what is characteristic of Revelation is its partiality for what scholars today call intertextuality. Although the writer of Revelation does not quote directly from other Scriptures, he echoes, interweaves, and evokes an amazing number of motifs and images from most of the Old Testament in an effort to bring a working closure to the biblical story. Intertextuality in Revelation does not just involve giving references to an isolated image (for example, teaching of Balaam in 2:14) but brings to the surface major biblical ideas such as judgment and exodus, reworked from their Old Testament context, in the interest of finishing the Christian story (7:9–17; 15:2–4). Sometimes even the outline of several chapters has a close correlation with the structure of a biblical book (namely Rev 20–21 with the closing chapters of Ezekiel). Thus Revelation cannot be fully appreciated without considerable acquaintance with the rest of the biblical story.

> **Intertextuality**
> Intertextuality is the use by one text of the words, ideas, or images of one or more other texts. Revelation recycles images and even quotations from Daniel, Isaiah, Ezekiel, and elsewhere, all the while creating something entirely new.

The writer calls himself John (Rev 1:1, 4, 9; 22:8). His visions occur on Patmos, an island off the west coast of present-day Turkey (1:9). There is no claim of apostleship; John clearly considers himself a Christian prophet (1:3; 19:10; 22:7–10; 22:18–19). Important second century authors such as Justin Martyr and Irenæus presume that the apostle John was the author. This seems to be the mainstream position of the second century church. The idea that the author was someone other than the author of the fourth gospel gained currency in the church in later centuries. Certainly the style and theology of Revelation are different from those of the gospel and epistles of John. But whoever the author of Revelation was, he was a major leader in the church in Asia Minor.

Revelation appears to be a response to a crisis facing the church. Identification of this crisis is often thought to be the key for dating the writing. But what is the nature of the crisis? There are two possibilities. Some claim that the crisis was the persecution of Christians by Nero that followed in the wake of the great fire in Rome in July 64 CE. However, Nero's persecution did not go beyond Rome, and Revelation emerges in the eastern provinces, a long way from Rome. A second position argues that Revelation offers religious criticism of the influence of Roman imperial power, especially through its sponsorship of cults where the emperors and their families were worshiped (Friesen, *Imperial Cults*, 150–51). These cults were widespread in Asia Minor, especially during the reign of Domitian, and could be the crisis that precipitated the production of the book. The editing of the book likely took place in the latter years of the reign of Domitian. This dating is confirmed by Irenæus, *Against Heresies* 5:30.3.

> **Domitian**
> Son of Vespasian, Domitian ruled as Roman emperor 81–96 CE. After his death, the senate condemned his memory because of his tyrannical acts.

STRUCTURE & MESSAGE

Revelation is a message from the divine realm addressed through the prophet John to the seven churches of Asia. Spiritual slackness is abroad in the churches, and believers are compromising with the dominant idolatrous culture. John argues that the churches must not surrender – especially in the area of emperor worship. To do so would make the churches both an accessory to Rome's excesses and a shared victim of its final doom. Among those advocating accommodation with Rome are some prophets in the church. In response, John calls the church to live as a contrast-society to the dominant idolatrous culture based on absolute faith in the lordship of Jesus.

The plot structure of Revelation supplies key literary indicators for readers to note. In the first part of the book, action centers around the appearance of a sealed scroll with a mysterious message

(5:1–5). The message is that sovereignty over the world is in the hands of Christ (the Lamb), and not Rome or the evil power of Satan, which stands behind it. This is the heavenly viewpoint that most humans do not see.

In order to read God's message, the seals of the scroll must be opened. One by one this takes place in 6:1–8:1. A short vision accompanies the opening of each seal. These visions summarize God's action in the world until the end of the age. As the seals are opened, we discover that God is sending a series of woes to a rebellious world to stimulate it to repent (6:1–8). The faithful suffer persecutions from the world and wonder how long this will last (6:9–11). They are told *a little longer, until the number of their fellow servants and brothers who were to be killed as they had been was completed* (6:11). This period of *a little longer* encompasses most of the action of the book. In 6:12–17, the reader receives a preliminary description of the horrors of God's wrath coming on the Lamb's opponents at the end. Revelation 7 focuses on the final victory of the righteous. What follows in two successive cycles of visions of the seven trumpets and bowls of wrath (8:2–16:16) are detailed vignettes of the unfolding conflict. Like viewing a kaleidoscope, it is simply recapitulation and elaboration of the events already given in 6:1–8:1 (Lambrecht, "Structuration," 85–92). Progression takes place only to the extent of describing the future conflict of the *little longer* in more detail. Although the intensification of the conflict in chapters 8–16 gives the appearance of chronological progression, this is only the effect of the literary format (Resseguie 165).

Finally, at 16:17, the crisis, that is the *little longer* has elapsed (*It is done!*). Revelation 16:17–22:5 explains the fate of two cities personified as women. The first is Babylon (a transparent reference to Rome). The second is Jerusalem (the people of God). Both cities are introduced in amazingly similar language in the text (17:1 parallels 21:9). Rome, the prostitute, collapses under its own excesses and is devoured and destroyed. Jerusalem, the new triumphant people of God, celebrates the transfer of power to the Lamb. The nature of the crisis with Babylon and its resolution is the key revelatory message of the scroll.

Responsible interpreters of Revelation understand the book in one of four ways.

PERPETUAL STRUGGLE BETWEEN GOOD & EVIL

The thrust of this view is that history is marked by a perennial clash between good and evil, with good finally winning out. The problem is that this lofty philosophical perspective never directly engages the text of Revelation. It minimizes the urgency of the eschatological setting of the already emerging crisis of emperor worship.

> **Eschatology**
> Eschatology involves a reflection on the end of the world or at least a major turning point in the basic structure of reality.

OUTLINE OF CHURCH HISTORY

This view takes the position that the visions of Revelation predict events of world history affecting the church. The approach suffers from lack of controls, so that virtually every historical crisis has been found in its pages, from the emergence of Islam and the rise of the papacy to Hitler or the Soviet Union. Ultimately, it fails on the grounds that only those at the end of history can understand the full symbolic code. And yet Revelation was written to encourage Christians in the first century.

MILLENNIAL INTERPRETATIONS

The claim is that chapters 2–3 concern events in the first century. But then there is an interlude. From 4:1–22:5, John sketches a series of events that will take place immediately before the return of Christ or immediately thereafter (depending on the interpreter). Then a literal millennium will follow. But there is no hint in the text of any gap between chapters 3 and 4. And it is questionable whether the 1,000 years of Revelation should be taken literally.

HISTORICAL INTERPRETATION

This view presumes that a reader will interpret the letters and visions of the book primarily in its historical context: the crisis of the growth of cults and emperor worship in the Roman province of Asia in the first century. This view seems to offer the most defensible procedure for interpreting the book. When one is forced to ask, "Would my interpretation be plausible to a first century reader?" one has a built-in means of control over idiosyncratic readings of the text.

On the other hand, one must guard against thinking that this writing only had meaning for people of the first century. Such views frequently emerge because of statements such as these *things must soon take place* (1:1). True, all literary works emerge in some historical context, but good literature dealing with universal issues always transcends local contexts. Revelation was produced in a community that did not worry about a particular "time line" of history. Rather, John sought to illumine events from the perspective that all earthly powers had been subjugated by the exaltation of the Lamb (Christ) to his heavenly throne (1:12–18; 5:5–14). The Roman Empire appeared self-sufficient and ultimate; and to a later reader this is true of other idolatrous powers. Visible political reality is not the last word. The divine perspective reveals something different. In the form of Rome John sees an ultimate end to this state of affairs. Babylon will be destroyed. As it is now in heaven, so will it be on earth (22:3–5). This is an abiding message that is as relevant for the church today as it was in the first century. Believers, under God's seal, wait for the time when they will see their cause vindicated. In the language of the apocalypse, they long for the coming of their sparkling new city of God's people, replacing the polluted earthly realm.

COMMENTARY

THE PROLOGUE · 1:1–3

1:1–2 The opening words *the revelation of Jesus Christ* function as a title for the book. Our present title, "Revelation," was probably placed on the original manuscripts at a later time. The phrase *of Jesus Christ* could mean "about Jesus Christ," but most likely it means "from Jesus Christ." The content of this revelation is the major focus of the book.

The revelation has its origin with God (1:1b). Like links in a chain, it is given to the Son (see John 5:19–24; 8:27–28), then to an angel, and finally to John. The purpose is *to show* (God's) *servants what must soon take place*. Specifically, this refers to the outcome of events that will take place during the period described as *a little longer* in 6:11 (that is, the coming conflict between believers and the idolatrous forces of the world). The terminology *what must soon take place* directly echoes the text of the earlier apocalyptic work of Daniel. John views his book as the ultimate explanation of the mysteries of the older book (Dan 2:28–29; 12:4, 9–10; see Bauckham, *Climax*, 251–57).

1:3 The discerning readers of the book are promised a blessing. Couched in the terminology of Jesus' beatitudes given on the mountain (Matt 5:1–12), the heavenly Lord offers the first of seven special blessings to the readers of the book (14:13; 16:15; 19:9; 20:6; 22:7, 14). These blessings will accrue to those remaining faithful to the Lord during the coming period of testing, of which *the time is near*.

JOHN'S VISION ON EARTH · 1:4–3:22

1:4–8 Before John enters heaven (4:1), he brings a message from Jesus Christ to the churches. This message follows the basic form of the early Christian letter. First there is the sender: John. Then follows the recipients: *the seven churches in the province of Asia*. Then follows a direct echo of the Pauline letter greeting, *Grace and peace to you*. The grace comes from God, who is described as the one *who is and who was, and who is to come*, as well as *the seven spirits before his throne*, and *from Jesus Christ*. The threefold expression appears to be a version of an early Trinitarian formula for the Godhead. God and Jesus Christ are clearly identifiable. The reference to *the seven spirits before his throne* (see 3:1; 4:5; 5:6), with seven representing perfection, suggests the total complement of the Holy Spirit's force (Isa 11:2; Zech 4:1–14).

The description of God as *who is, and who was, and who is to come* appears also in 1:8 and 4:8. To complete the emphasis on the number three, it is noteworthy that the eulogy in 5b–7 has a threefold analogy of saving accomplishments to the description of Christ:

faithful witness loves us
firstborn from the dead freed us from our sins by his blood
ruler of the kings of the earth made us to be a kingdom and priests.

It would be good news for the Christians in Asia to learn that they are kings and priests. Standing in tension with 5:10, the reader gets an object lesson in the eschatology of Revelation. Through the first coming of Jesus Christ, believers have direct access to God as a king and a priest. Yet they wait until the second coming before this rule and priesthood is fully realized (5:10).

The eulogy concludes in 1:7. Jesus is praised as the one who *is coming with the clouds* when *every eye will see him* and *will mourn because of him*. The verse is very close to Matthew 24:30, which has some similar changes in wording to Old Testament texts. Matthew 24:30 refers to the return [Greek *parousia*] of Jesus. Likewise, 1:7 functions as a promise of Jesus' return. There is an issue whether the mourning of *the peoples of the earth* will be an expression of their embracing Jesus in repentance or their showing sorrow because it is too late. The latter view is more plausible.

Revelation 1:8 repeats verse 4's description of God as the one *who is, and who was, and is to come*, as John concludes the opening salutation. *Alpha and Omega* are the first and last letters of the Greek alphabet. John is saying that God is all in all, from beginning to end. The same expression is given to Jesus at the end of the book (22:13).

> **God Almighty**
> The predicate of God as "Almighty" appears seven times in the book. The composition of Revelation was not haphazard. John composed the Apocalypse with attention to every detail, and readers should study it accordingly.

1:9–20 John is on Patmos. The language of 1:9b, *because of the word of God and testimony of Jesus* suggests a banishment of some kind by the Roman authorities, but additional speculation is fruitless.

The first message occurs *on the Lord's Day*. This is our Sunday. Just as the meal in the Christian assembly in honor of Jesus belongs to the Lord (Jesus), so the Greek phrase here literally means the "day belonging to the Lord" (see 1 Cor 11:20). Based on the resurrection of Jesus on the first day after the Jewish Sabbath, Sunday quickly became the day of Christian assembly (1 Cor 16:2; Acts 20:7; *Didache* 14:1; *Epistle of Barnabas* 15:9). John is told to write the message *on a scroll*. This pertains to 1:12–3:22. Another scroll (see 5:1) will play a major role in the heavenly visionary section of 4:1–22:5.

John's vision opens with the odd observation in verse 12 of "seeing a voice" ("seeing a voice" is a Hebrew idiom that John has carried over into Greek). This probably means that John heard something from behind and turned to see who was speaking. What he sees is *someone like a son of man* in the middle of seven lampstands. We learn from 1:20 that the seven lampstands stand for the seven churches, among whom Christ is walking.

> **The Structure of the Letters to the 7 Churches**
>
> The seven letters from Jesus to the churches of Asia function as an evaluation. As with all evaluations, there are both positive and negative elements to report. Several structural features can serve to draw attention to the central thrust of the evaluation.
>
> First, it is noticeable that the church that comes in the middle of the sequence (three before and three after), Thyatira, receives the longest evaluation (Rev 2:19–29). This invites attention. The church is criticized because it tolerates Jezebel, who calls herself a prophetess, *who is leading believers* into immorality and the eating of food sacrificed to idols *and into Satan's so-called deep secrets* (2:20, 24). The eating of food sacrificed to idols and the reference to immorality (an ancient Jewish metaphor for idolatry) were common practices of the various civic gatherings and temple practices of the major cities of Asia. The prophetess Jezebel (probably a pseudonym for an actual prominent woman in the church), no doubt for both economic and social reasons, saw no problem with a culture where these things were commonplace. Opposing the practices of the Nicolaitans (2:6:15) *and* the teaching of Balaam (2:14), John urges readers not to adapt to the popular culture of the time. By placing this strong admonition to the church of Thyatira at the center of the message, John foreshadows the coming central crisis of an impending conflict with the Roman social orders addressed by the later visions.
>
> Second, it is noticeable that each letter seems to be based on a five-fold structural model. This can be illustrated by an analysis of the message to the church at Ephesus:
>
> 1. *Addressee*: to the angel of the church (2:1);
> 2. *Estimate*: I know your deeds ... You have persevered ... You have forsaken your first love (2:2–4);
> 3. *Call to repentance*: Repent and do the things you did at first (2:5)
> 4. *Exhortation*: hate ... the Nicolaitans (2:6–7a);
> 5. *Promise*: To him who overcomes ... (2:7b).
>
> Finally, the promises all have some analogue in a fulfillment in the closing chapters of the book when the new creation comes. This is further evidence of the book's carefully organized composition incorporating the message to the seven churches with the later visions.

Christ is no longer the humble, winsome figure of his earthly ministry, but a powerful ruler who pulsates with otherworldly power. He wears the garments of both priest and king. *In his right hand* he holds *seven stars*. To ancient people, the stars were personifications of the powers that shaped human history.

> **The 7 Stars**
> Ancient coins depict Roman emperors among seven stars (*the Sun, Moon, Mars, Mercury, Jupiter, Venus, and Saturn*). John is saying that it is not the Roman emperor who rules the cosmos but Christ.

In verses 17–18, as with the Old Testament manifestation of God (see Isa 6; Ezek 1), in the presence of overwhelming power, the terrified John receives a hand of blessing and a word of grace, *Do not be afraid*. A triadic formula follows. Jesus is *the First and the Last* (see 1:8). As conqueror of death he is also *the Living One*; and he takes *the keys of death and Hades* from whoever guarded the unseen world, and thus exercises power over the life beyond.

In verse 19, some read *what you have seen* as 1:12–20, *what is now*, as the message to the seven churches, and *what will take place later* as the heavenly visions of 4:1–22:5. But this reads too much into the text. Past, present, and future intermingle in 1:12–3:22. Christ reveals a complete word to the seven churches. Nothing is withheld.

Yet in 1:20, the *mystery* of this message is about to unfold. The *seven lampstands* giving light to the world by faithful obedience (compare Matt 5:15) are the *seven churches*. The *seven stars* are the seven angels of the churches. In a world where angels and unseen powers are thought to be dominant in the affairs of everyday life, John probably means the angels of heaven. In nearby Colosse, Paul had already alluded to a group in the church who were engaged in worship either of or with angels (Col 2:18), and in Daniel angels serve as guardians of the nations (Dan 10:13; 20–21; 12:1). Probably many Christians in Asia believed that their churches had representative angels. Because Jesus holds the seven stars (angels) in his right hand (1:16), John is saying that angels in the heavenly court cannot change the words of evaluation to come (19:10; 22:8). Jesus is the cosmic Lord and is sovereign over all powers.

Message to the Seven Churches · 2:1–3:22

2:1–7 After the initial statement of address (2:1), Jesus gives his basic assessment of the church at Ephesus (2:2–4). The statement *I know your deeds* (2:2) appears with four other churches (2:19; 3:1, 8, 15). Often, but not always, it introduces a positive evaluation; in this case, the Ephesians had tested and rejected false apostles.

The years of service have taken a toll, however. Jesus tells them, *you have forsaken your first love* (2:4). This does not refer to a decline in enthusiasm but a tendency to forsake the obligations of the love commandment (1 John 4:7, 11).

Their resistance to *the Nicolaitans* is striking. Probably there is no connection with the Nicolaus of Acts 6:5; rather, it is more promising to see a connection in the later reference to *the Nicolaitans* with the teachings of Balaam (see 2:14–15). Balaam is a model for one who enticed the people of God into idolatry and fornication (see Num 22–25). The analogue exists in Ephesus, a center of imperial cults, emperor worship, and the locus of the main temple to Artemis, local goddess of the hunt and fertility. For John, participation in a lifestyle dominated by these forces was the practical equivalent of acknowledging another Lord than Jesus.

The promise in 2:7 to eat from *the tree of life*, which will return in paradise, God's new world (22:2), functions as a counterpoint to the devotion given to a sacred tree in the Artemis cult in Ephesus (Hemer 41–52).

2:8–11 Along with the church at Philadelphia (3:7–13), Smyrna receives the most positive evalu-

Seven Churches of Asia Minor

ation of the seven churches. Neither are called to repent. At the heart of Smyrna's evaluation (2:9) is a polemic against certain Jews who are labeled *a synagogue of Satan*. Some Jews were later complicit in the martyrdom of Polycarp, a second century overseer of the church in Smyrna (*Martyrdom of Polycarp* 17–18). John regularly claims the promises of Israel for the church. He attributes Jewish resistance to Satan.

In verses 10–11, anticipating the coming eschatological crisis, John does not distinguish between hostility from the synagogue and the imperial cults. Ironically, however, the reference to the *persecution for ten days* echoes Daniel 1:12, 14, where the Jew Daniel and his friends did not submit to the enticements of the pagan Nebuchadnezzar. The promise to the faithful is a victory crown (*crown of life*) that in the ancient world is accorded to winners of contests (1 Cor 9:24; Phil 3:14; Jas 1:12). The victor will not undergo *the second death*, a final separation from the benefits of the new age (2:11; 20:14; 21:8).

2:12–17 Pergamum was the Roman administrative center of the province of Asia, the province covering the western third of modern Turkey. For John, it was the place of all things evil. At its summit was a huge altar to Zeus; elsewhere were temples dedicated to the Roman emperors, deities, and local gods who received imperial patronage. John refers to it as the place *where Satan has his throne* and *where Satan lives* (2:13). Yet, despite Antipas's martyrdom, Christ comes to this church with a double-edged sword of judgment (see 1:16).

The heart of the problem, according to verses 14–15, is found in the reproof for those who harbor *the teaching of Balaam* and *the Nicolaitans* (compare 2:6). In the Old Testament, Balak of Moab hired Balaam to curse Israel. After a bizarre series of events, this all ended in a blessing for Israel (Num 22:1–24:25). Later, under the counsel of Balaam (or so John's contemporaries interpreted the story), the Israelites intermingled with the culture of Moab and engaged in many of their idolatrous practices (Num 25:1–18; 31:16). Balaam becomes a symbol to describe a false prophet who advocates worshiping other gods. Despite what the

> **Balaam**
>
> *Although Numbers 22–24 portrays Balaam as a somewhat ambiguous character, later traditions about him made him progressively worse (Deut 23:2–5; Josh 24:9–10). Philo depicted him as a sophist and false prophet, and* Pirque Avot *contrasts him with Abraham (faith versus lack of faith). Revelation continues in the mainstream of ancient Jewish interpretation of this figure.*

prophets say, John believes that attending the meals and festivals of the various local pagan temples is a denial of the lordship of Christ (1 Cor 10:14–33).

2:16–17 There is a call to repentance (2:16). After the exhortation (2:17a), there is a two-fold promise: to receive *the hidden manna*, and to have *a white stone with a new name* (2:17). First, there was a belief among the apocalypticists that the manna of the wilderness would reappear as the food of the messianic age (*2 Baruch* 29:8; *Sibylline Oracles* 7:148–149). John claims this promise.

> **The White Stone**
> *The stone here is clearly connected with the victory of the age to come. A white stone was often given as a token of admission, acquittal, or recognition.*

2:18–29 Thyatira was famous as a trading center, especially in cloth. It was the home of Lydia, Paul's famous convert in Philippi (Acts 16:14). As with Ephesus, *I know your deeds*, indicates that the church is commended for its faithfulness and good works (2:19). These words come from *the Son of God*, a rare title for Jesus in Revelation (12:5). His description as a figure *whose eyes are like blazing fire and whose feet are like burnished bronze* (1:15) indicates his message is serious.

The message of verses 20–25 is straightforward: banish *Jezebel*, a prophetess in the church in Thyatira. As with Balaam (2:14), the symbolism of Jezebel is well chosen. The Old Testament Jezebel sponsored the worship of gods with fertility religions such as Baal (1 Kgs 21:1–19; 2 Kgs 9:30–37). Her endorsement of *sexual immorality* and *the eating of food sacrificed to idols* validates the conclusion that the church is accommodating the pagan local civic culture. Five verses are devoted to the call to repentance (20–24). This call to refute the teaching of Jezebel stands at the center of the message to the seven churches, indicating its supreme importance. Indeed, in the heavenly visions that will follow in the later chapters, the center of conflict is between Christ (the Lamb) and the Dragon (Satan), the spiritual supporter of the imperial cults and emperor worship. Thus the forces of accommodation with the pagan cults, *Satan's so-called deep secrets*, must be purged.

Verses 26–29 make promises to the faithful. The word of promise echoes Psalm 2, which promises the Davidic King *authority over the nations* (Ps 2:8–9).

The *morning star*, a symbol of Venus, was claimed by the Cæsars. Based on messianic interpretation of Numbers 24:17 (note again the Balaam connection), Christ is the *morning star* (22:16). What benefits accrue to him in his reign in God's new world also will come to the believer (see also 2 Pet 1:19).

3:1–6 In the message to Sardis, Jesus *holds the seven spirits and seven stars* (see 1:4, 16, 20; 2:1). The *seven stars* refer to the entire body of angelic representatives of the churches in God's heavenly sanctuary (1:20). This message comes with the full authoritative force of heaven. Despite their good reputation for their *deeds* (works), they are (spiritually) *dead*.

Built around a wordplay on death/life and similes, the church is called to come back from death to life (verses 2–3). The Greek word for "wake up" is used in Mark 13:35, 37 to exhort the disciples to watch for the Lord's coming at the end of the age. The image of the Lord's coming unexpectedly, as a thief, is also drawn from the words of Jesus (Matt 24:43–44; Luke 12:39–40; 1 Thess 5:2; see McNicol 19–23).

Sardis was a center of the woolen industry. The church is told that there are still those who have not soiled their garments (that is maintained good conduct). The opposite to a soiled garment is a pure white one (3:4, 5). Ancient Christians came before the assembly after their baptism in a white garment. The church must return to their original state of holiness in order to participate in salvation with the redeemed on the last day (7:9, 13; 19:8). Then their names will not be erased from *the book of life* (20:12).

3:7–13 While the ruins of a major second century CE synagogue at Sardis have been discovered, attesting to longstanding Jewish social influence there, Philadelphia (as Smyrna, 2:9) is the site of the greatest opposition from the Jewish community (3:9). The low social standing of the church in opposition to the synagogue is the theme around which the positive word occurs in this message. The opening address is significant. The salutation comes from Christ, who is *holy* and *true*. In 6:10, the same terminology is used of God – another place in Revelation where descriptions of Christ and God are interchangeable. In Isaiah 22:15–25, the key to the royal household rested with the steward of an earthly king David dynasty. Revelation claims Jesus has *the key*. Despite the synagogue's social influence, it is Christ *alone* who has the keys to the kingdom.

The motif of doors and entrances continues in verses 8–9. Despite their relative insignificance, the Philadelphians have *an open door*. Christ, not the powerful forces of the local synagogue, decides the conditions of entrance to the kingdom (see 2:9). And, astonishingly, John claims that there will come a time when the tables are turned and the synagogue will acknowledge the Lord of the church.

In this letter, there is no call for repentance. Exhortation and promise are interwoven. Strikingly, the promise is that the faithful will be kept from the coming *hour of trial* that is about *to test those who live on the earth*. The Greek construction for *those who live on the earth*, occurs ten times in Revelation and always refers to those who are hostile to the people of God (3:10; 6:10; 8:13; 11:10 twice; 13:8, 14 twice; 17:8, compare 17:2). The wrath of God, in the three plague visions (6:1–16:21), comes upon these people. This will take place in *the hour of trial that is going to come upon the whole world*, when the righteous are sealed (7:2–3; 9:4). As Peter, James, and John were the pillars of the earliest Christian community in Jerusalem (Gal 2:9), believers who remain faithful will also play a pivotal role (as *pillars*) in the life of the renewed people of God: the new Jerusalem (21:1–22:5).

3:14–22 In a triangular geographical relationship with Hierapolis and Colosse, Laodicea was a thriving commercial and trading center. The church in Laodicea mirrored this prosperity. The description of Christ as *ruler of God's creation* may echo the Colossian hymn (1:15–20).

After the formulaic *I know your deeds* comes a negative evaluation: *because you are lukewarm – neither hot nor cold – I am about to spit you out of my mouth*. The water of Laodicea was neither.

> **"Because you are lukewarm ..."**
> *Generations of interpreters have connected this evaluation with the city water, routed through a lengthy aqueduct system that delivered a supply of lukewarm water – an apt analogy to the spiritual level of the church. Specifically, the contrasts are to the medicinal value of the hot water in the pools near Hierapolis and to the refreshment of the cold springs of Colosse (Mounce 109).*

Accommodating to the culture, they claim to be wealthy but are miserable and poor. They need *gold* (works based on faith passed through a refiner's fire) or eye *salve*, a spiritual equivalent of the famous local medical product (Hemer 196–201).

In verses 19–22, on the basis of love, God calls the church to shape up. Probably echoing Jesus' parable of servants waiting for the return of the Lord (Luke 12:35–38; Mark 13:34–36), John, ironically, describes Jesus as standing outside of his church waiting for entrance. The servants are to be awake and waiting at the master's return. Jesus calls the church at Laodicea to be alert (through spiritual service done in deeds of love) to welcome him at his return.

> **"Come in and eat ..."**
> *The reference to eating is a call to spiritual reformation. Since the words of Revelation were meant to be read aloud in the assembly (1:3), some commentators have even concluded that this may be the first of several literary pauses in the book where it was appropriate to stop reading and enter into the observance of the Lord's Supper (for example, Garrow sees these pauses at 3:20; 7:16; 11:17; 14:14–20; and 19:7, 9).*

JOHN'S VISIONS IN HEAVEN · 4:1–22:5

Vision of God and the Lamb · 4:1–5:14

The opening theological question of this section (indeed of the whole book) asks "who is Lord of the world?" Does the world belong to Cæsar or his modern counterpart? Or does it belong to God and the Lamb (Jesus Christ)? This vision says that 3:21 is correct: God exercises lordship over the world. The image of the throne is central to the whole unit. Revelation 4 is a vision of the Holy One enthroned and worthy of praise. Revelation 5 introduces the Lamb as equally worthy of praise.

4:1–11 This unit has two overlapping scenes. First, there is a description of God in the sanctuary (4:1–6a). Second, there is the description of the praise at God's throne (4:6b–11).

To begin, John is taken in a vision into heaven. The throne scene echoes Isaiah 6, Ezekiel 1, and perhaps Daniel 7:9–10. God is in a heavenly throne room analogous to the sanctuary of the second temple in Jerusalem. In keeping with biblical revelation, there is no description of God. To describe God would be to control him. (However, note the reference to his right hand in 5:1; such an Old Testament image need not have been taken literally in the first century.) The similes of the glory of precious stones is as close as we get to a picture of God. The rainbow may allude to God's covenantal faithfulness. Around the throne are the twenty-four elders, the heavenly counterparts of the twenty-four priestly orders of the temple (1 Chron 24:4; 25:9–31). As representatives of the people of God who are also kings (1:6, 5:10), they sit on thrones and cast their crowns before God (4:4, 10).

Around the throne are also the *four living creatures*. These are cherubim-type figures symbolic of the all pervasive seeing and knowing that comes from God's throne. Domitian may have been venerated in the emperor cult, but his would only be a pale imitation of God's heavenly court.

5:1–14 Like the previous chapter, this unit has two scenes. First there is the cosmic search to find one who is worthy to open a scroll found in God's hand (5:1–7). Second, after the Lamb is found worthy, there is a description of his praise (5:8–14).

John sees in God's right hand a scroll *with writing on both sides and sealed with seven seals*. Possibly the scroll's outer covering had a summary of its contents. Scrolls written on both sides were comparatively rare in the ancient world, though they did exist. Seals were placed on wills and other official documents in the Greco-Roman world. In Ezekiel 2:9–10 the prophet receives a scroll with the divine purpose for the future. Likewise, the content of this scroll represents God's will for the future, which will unfold throughout the book.

The immediate question raised by *a mighty angel* (10:1; 18:21) of God's heavenly court is *who is worthy to break the seals and open the scroll?* Such a task demands no ordinary person. The whole cosmos is searched without success (5:3–4). Then, in imagery reminiscent of Abraham's discovery of the "ram caught by its horns in the thicket" (Gen 22:13), almost overlooked, standing by God's throne, is a *Lamb looking as if it had been slain*. The Lamb is worthy. He conquers. From the tribe of Judah (Gen 49:9–10) and the family of David (Isa 11:1, 10; Rev 22:16), he triumphed by way of the cross. The "search" for the worthy one, though the choice is a foregone conclusion, nevertheless underscores the majesty of Jesus as Savior.

Evoking the traditional temple practices of musical instruments accompanying the offering of sacrifices, the twenty-four elders, to the accompaniment of a *harp* (better, lyre), exalt the sacrificed Christ with a hymn of praise (5:9–10). With his blood the Lamb has purchased a new empire (the church). Far superior to anything imaginable in the emperor cult, John sees a huge crowd of angels giving sevenfold praise to the Lamb (5:12). In 4:11 it is God who is *worthy ... to receive glory and honor and power*. In 5:13, coming full circle, both God (the one who sits on the throne) and the Lamb receive *praise and honor and glory and power*.

The Seven Seals · 6:1–8:1

The visible world, according to Roman propaganda, was experiencing the *pax Romana*, the Roman peace. The *Aeneid* and other Roman literary works, as well as the emperor cult, celebrated it. But John sees something different. He envisions a time of crisis about to come on the whole world (3:10). Despite what Rome says, this is not the Golden Age. In three sets of seven visions (seals, trumpets, and bowls of wrath: 6:1–16:21), John chronicles the collapse of the present order. Only then he will focus on the final outcome of history.

6:1–8 The time has come for the Lamb to open the seals, initiating insight into God's secret purposes for the future. Zechariah saw horsemen patrol the earth (Zech 1:8–10; 6:1–8); in sequence John sees a white, red, black, and pale horse, each having a different rider. Because the rider of Revelation 19:11–16 is on a white horse, some have viewed the *rider* on the *white horse* in 6:2, *bent on conquest* with his *bow*, as Christ. But the rider in 6:2 introduces a time of devastation and death for the world, hardly typical of the rule of Christ. The rider on the white horse represents armies gathering for future conflict. This is the first hint of the disintegration of Rome. The rider on the red horse carries a sword *to take peace from the earth*. The rider on the black horse with *scales* symbolizes social inequities with widespread famine for many; and the sequence ends with the fourth rider whose *name was death*. This is an expression of God's retribution about to

---

Cherubim

Ancient Israelites believed the cherubim, fierce creatures that were part human and part beast, lived in the heavenly realm. John reuses Old Testament imagery for his own purposes. Later exegesis of the church fathers associated them with the four canonical gospels; but this was not John's intention. The total scene is one of awesome power.

The Lamb

The description of Jesus as "the Lamb" occurs twenty-eight times in Revelation. It is the preferred word for Jesus in the book. On the chronology of the Gospel of John, Jesus is lifted on the cross at the time the Passover lambs are slain. Jesus as the antitype of the Passover lamb is central in Revelation. Revelation uses the Greek diminutive for Lamb (arnion) and not the usual word (hamnos) chosen by other New Testament writers, including the author of the fourth gospel (John 1:29, 36; Acts 8:32; 1 Pet 1:19). The simplest explanation is that John prefers to say "little lamb." As the perfect antitype, Jesus' sacrifice removes human need to utilize innocent animal life for religious purposes.

fall upon a rebellious creation. In the beginning, it is limited to a *fourth of the earth* (6:8). But in the literary sequence of the book, it develops to a third (9:18), and finally, there are no restrictions (16:1–4). God's purpose is not merely to punish but to draw humankind away from its idolatry and to bring about repentance (9:20–21). Alas, to the end many will shake their fists at this call (16:9–11).

6:9–11 The scene shifts entirely. John sees souls in heaven – below the heavenly altar. In the earthly temple, sacrificial blood was poured on the altar of burnt offering. The souls are in heaven because of martyrdom (6:9). John is vague about their identity. They may include those of the past among the people of God (Matt 23:33–36); but, in an anticipatory sense, they include those who will die for the faith in the coming clash with the sponsors of emperor worship.

The martyrs cry out for justice and ask how long it will be before God's wrath will be poured out on these *inhabitants of the earth* (see 3:10–13). This is not a plea to get even but comes out of concern for the reputation of God (Mounce 148). How long will God's sovereignty be repudiated until it is embraced in the human community (Matt 6:9–10)? Then comes the shock. Each martyr *receives a white robe* as a token of the Lamb's victory (compare 3:5; 7:9, 13, 14; 19:14). But they are also told that they must wait *a little longer* until the total complement of martyrs is complete.

> **The Crisis of Emperor Worship**
> *John alludes to the emerging crisis of emperor worship. Although the martyrs are addressed, the real audience is the church on earth. It must live patiently through tremendous testing before God's new world comes.*

6:12–17 After the time of testing comes the visit of God's final judgment on the unrighteous, akin to the Old Testament "Day of the Lord." Beginning with a terrible earthquake (8:5; 11:13, 19; 16:18), even in this preliminary introduction, we sense its horror. John emphasizes that all strata of society will be held accountable. Even those at the pinnacle of power will not escape (6:15). All will be forced to recognize the sovereignty of Christ (6:16–17; Phil 2:10).

7:1–17 In the narrative world of John, after the time of crisis and judgment day comes God's new world. But what happens to the people of God before this time? The interlude answers this question.

Verses 1–8 focus on the situation of the faithful who will live through the time of coming crisis. They are to receive God's protective *seal* against God's final judgment of evildoers (7:3). This means that their cause will triumph. Some will die. The guarantee is not against martyrdom but against being abandoned by God.

Before war there is a census of warriors (Num 1:3; 2 Sam 24). This holy war imagery describes the church of the time of crisis (Bauckham, *Climax*, 215–229). Various sectarian groups often appropriate the nomenclature of *144,000* for themselves. Other interpreters see the *144,000* in opposition to the "great multitude" of 7:9, as Jewish Christians. However, the number *144,000* is not actual but symbolic. It is the square of the twelve tribes of Israel multiplied by one thousand (compare Num 13:4–16). John understands the *144,000* to be the church under God's seal forcefully engaging idolatry, such as the emperor worship of his time.

Verses 1–8 focus on the beginning of the crisis. In an all-encompassing vision of the future, under the image of *a great multitude*, John describes its end: the faithful of all ages celebrating the victory of the Lamb (7:9–17). For example, *palm branches* are a symbol of triumph (1 Maccabees 13:51; John 12:13).

The seven-fold description of praise in verses 11–12 before God's throne ties the scene back into the initial manifestation of God's awesome power in 4:11 and 5:13. The world has finally come under the sovereignty of God. The *great tribulation* refers to the great crisis of testing that John believes the church was about to face.

The scene around God's throne in verses 15–17 is drawn from the Feast of Tabernacles. Normally at this feast, tents are stretched out to house the joyous people. But in God's final victory celebration, God will shelter Christians.

From 6:1 to 7:17, John highlights the major features of future events anticipated in breaking the seals of the scroll. The rest of the action from 8:2–16:21 expands these details.

8:1 In his famous movie *The Seventh Seal*, director Ingmar Bergman took the *silence in heaven* as a metaphor for the absence of God in the modern world. But for John it is the opposite. The brief quiet interlude, *about half an hour*, functions only as a short pause before the events of 6:1–7:17, which are about to be reenvisioned in the seven trumpets (8:2–11:18).

The seventh seal as a literary device catapults the reader into new perspectives on the coming crisis.

8:13 The action begins in heaven. John sees *seven angels*. These are archangels or "the angels of the presence" (Isa 63:9). They stand in the immediate presence of God (1 Enoch 20:2–8). As heralds of the coming crisis, each receives a trumpet. Still in God's throne room, John sees *another angel* at the altar of incense (8:3). Incense symbolizes the prayers of the saints (6:9–11). The prayers come from those who are faithful in the time of crisis. The faithful ask how long it will be before God's will in heaven is accomplished on earth.

> **Angelology**
> Although angels are rare in the Old Testament, Jews in the Second Temple period (538 BCE–70 CE) developed an elaborate set of ideas about angels, assigning them names and functions in heaven and on earth. Compared to some of the Dead Sea Scrolls, the New Testament's interest in angels is subdued.

Then, suddenly, comes an answer. God acts. God's angel puts the burning coals from the altar into a *censer* (a vessel used to throw incense) and hurls them down upon the earth in the form of intense plagues. The scene is reminiscent of Isaiah 6, but here the angel does not purify but destroy.

Each trumpet blast signals a plague. The imagery echoes expressions of God's retributive power, where Moses' God shows his superiority over the god of Pharaoh (Exod 7:8–11:10). The marking off of the first six trumpets with an interlude echoes Joshua 6:3–20, when the Israelites marched around Jericho for six days prior to its destruction on the seventh day (Garrow 23).

The combination of hail, fire, and blood in verse 7 is reminiscent of the seventh Egyptian plague (Exod 9:13–25). Some see the contemporary era as the *pax Romana*. John views it as similar to the times of plagues falling on Egypt.

The eruption of Vesuvius in CE 79 had a tremendous impact on the ancients. John alludes to this event in verse 8, perhaps as a metaphor to describe the horrors of the time of crisis.

The bitter-tasting plant wormwood signifies pollution of the fresh waters, a vivid metaphor for a marginalized person's view of Rome's justice (verses 10–11). In verse 13, John introduces another structural motif into his composition with this threefold statement of, *Woe*! Perhaps this is a counterpoint to the threefold statement of God's holiness in 4:8. Three woes corresponding to the last three trumpets mark the climax of God's wrath on a rebellious creation (9:12; 11:14). *An eagle* voices the woe. The same Greek word can mean vulture, perhaps a better translation here (see Matt 24:28; Luke 17:37).

9:1–21 Convergent with the movement from the fourth to the fifth trumpet, the emphasis shifts from the impact of God's wrath on creation to the suffering of humanity. A mysterious being (an angel?) is given a key to the underworld. Even as Pandora released evil by opening her box, so *he opened the Abyss* and all things evil pour out upon the earth.

Locust-like creatures (as in Joel 1–2) are let loose on the earth. These are demonic and demented figures, part human and part creature.

The first woe of the *eagle* (vulture) is ended. Two more are yet to come. Reverting to the heavenly altar (8:2–5), a sixth angel (verses 13–21) now allows the demonic forces east of the Euphrates (the traditional eastern boundary of the Roman Empire) to enter the Roman Empire and wreak untold destruction. Genteel Roman society looked on the Parthians (a major Iranian culture east of the Euphrates) as fierce warriors capable of inflicting tremendous havoc on them at any time. The exaggerated numbers of horsemen and mythical descriptions of their powers highlight the destructiveness of evil (Koester 100). Such disorder ought to result in a turning away from idolatry to the one true God. Yet, *the rest of mankind ... still did not repent* (9:20).

> **Abaddon & Apollo**
> Like cartoon figures, demonic figures represent the power of evil men. They have a ruler from whose name John makes a crude pun. In Hebrew his name is Abaddon, which means "destruction." The Greek equivalent is Apollyon, which is too similar to Apollo to escape the notice of John's audience. In the Greek pantheon, Apollo epitomizes beauty and vigor. Many Roman rulers claimed a relationship to Apollo. But, ironically, their rule promoted neither beauty nor vigor, but destruction. The faithful remain under God's protection (9:4).

10:1–11:14 As with the vision of the seven seals, there is an interlude between the sixth and seventh trumpets. Likewise, the interlude falls into two parts (10:1–11 and 11:1–14). Another point of similarity is that the focus is on the people of God moving to ultimate victory.

Since the Lamb took the scroll from God's right hand (10:1–2; compare 5:1–8), we have only heard that its seals were opened (6:1–8:1). The opening of the seals provides a summary of the events that *must soon take place*. The focus returns to the scroll and its message. The angel of 5:2 reappears, holding the now-open scroll. Some have questioned whether this is the same scroll as the one in 5:1–8. Although John used a different Greek word here, he probably intends the same scroll. The angel strides the whole created order. The contents of the scroll will have significance for the whole world.

In verses 3–7, the angel is about to set forth more words of judgment (seven thunders). But everything halts dramatically. *There will be no more delay* (10:6). Instead of more words of judgment, focus shifts to the unfolding of the scroll's message: *the mystery of God ... just as he announced to his servants the prophets* (10:7). This is a momentous point for the progression of the book. The revelation [Greek *apocalypsis*] starting with God (1:1), is now about to come to John, and through his word to God's servants (compare 1:1, 10:7). The *mystery* echoes Daniel 12:1–10. There Daniel hears a conversation between angelic figures about events that must take place in a 3 1/2 year period before the end. Daniel does not understand them. The words are sealed until the end (Dan 12:4, 9). Now the angel is about to unfold their meaning to John. He will make them known to his readers (God's servants), because the time is at hand (10:7; 11:15–18).

In verses 8–11, John eats the open scroll, internalizing its message. The message is *as sweet as honey* in his mouth, but it will turn *sour* upon reaching his *stomach* (10:9). The message is sweet because the elect will be protected and eventually saved (11:15–17), yet sour because God's people must go through a terrible crisis (Mounce 210).

In 11:1–2, John begins to expound the mystery of the scroll. He is *given a reed like a measuring rod* to measure the temple (similar to Ezek 40:3–5). Usually, such a rod is a builder's tool. John uses it for drawing lines. Those in the temple sanctuary are God's sealed (7:2–8; 9:4). Those in the *outer court* will be overrun by hostile forces (that is, the idolatrous nations). The focus is on the destiny of the church during the coming crisis. Earlier, the church was viewed as Israel (7:2–8); now it is the Jerusalem temple. The people of God will be preserved through the coming assault (10:1). But those in the church (outer courts) who assimilate to pagan culture will suffer a similar fate as those in Jerusalem in 70 CE. But this time of crisis is limited: by Daniel's reckoning, 1,260 days, or about 3 1/2 years (Dan 7:25; 12:7). Later exegesis connects the number with Elijah's sojourn in the wilderness, and it emerges as a fixed biblical symbol for a limited time of testing (Matt 24:15; Luke 4:25; Jas 5:17).

Attention in verses 3–4 moves to God's protection of the church's prophetic witness in the coming crisis. More explicitly, the two witnesses of verses 5–6 echo Elijah (fire from his mouth, 2 Kgs 1:9–12, and drought by his prayer, 1 Kgs 17:1) and Moses (the plagues of Exod 7:14–18). Out of the Abyss, opened in 9:2, steps a terrible beast who engages the witnesses (13:7) and kills them. A faithful church becomes a martyr church.

> **The Two Witnesses**
> *Symbolizing mission to an idolatrous world, the two witnesses become the center of attention in this part of Revelation. John interprets Zechariah's postexilic vision of the two olive trees (Zerubbabel the king and Joshua the high priest) as the prophetic witness of the kings and priests of the people of God (11:4; compare Zech 4:1–14).*

In verses 8–10, the reference to the great city as Jerusalem, *where also their Lord was crucified*, is puzzling. Presumably this is Jerusalem. Elsewhere the great city (16:19 et al.) refers to Babylon (Rome). Earlier prophets referred to Jerusalem as Sodom and Gomorrah (Isa 1:9–10). By correlating 3 1/2 days with 3 1/2 years, and picking up Old Testament imagery of Jerusalem as a defiled city, John is saying that the forces that were behind Jesus' death in Jerusalem are now attacking his faithful followers. Jesus was killed in public view outside the city wall. The nations under the spell of the beast openly exchange gifts over the demise of the witnesses and do not even allow them the dignity of a basic burial.

As the interlude of the vision of the seven seals ends with the vindication of the faithful (7:9–15), so resurrection vindicates the two witnesses in verses 11–12. After Elijah preached, the prophets of Baal were slaughtered (1 Kgs 18:40), yet seven thousand Israelites were found to be faithful (1 Kgs 19:18). In contrast, in verses 13–14 comes another act of judgment: an earthquake. But in Revelation, instead of seven thousand being found faithful, seven thousand are killed. But in anticipation of God's ultimate victory, under the pressure of the calamity, the rest of the people acknowledge the glory of God (compare Dan 2:46–49; 1 Kgs 18:39). The second woe is passed. Another woe (the destruction of wicked Babylon) will come soon.

11:15-18 This word is similar to the song of those who came out of the great tribulation in 7:11–17. The crisis has ended. The twenty-four elders praise God (4:10–11; 5:8–14; 7:11–17). God is described as *the one who is and who was*. The usual description of *is to come* is absent. The chronological progression of the visions brings us to the time of God's coming in judgment. The future is here.

Based on Psalm 2 the judgment of the nations alluded to 2:26–27. Now John will focus on this judgment. This will be the third and final woe (11:18–18:24).

The Seven Bowls of Wrath · 11:19–16:21

Two successive sequences have sketched details of a coming crisis (6:1–8:1; 8:2–11:18). A third sequence both repeating and expanding upon these events begins in 11:19. Once again it involves a series of seven visions: the seven bowls of wrath featuring the full wrath of God falling upon a rebellious creation (15:5–16:20). These visions also have an intervening sequence. It (11:19–15:4) precedes the seven bowls of wrath instead of following the sixth episode as in the visions of the seals and trumpets. Probably John changed his order for purposes of context and emphasis. In chapter 11 the time of crisis is 1,260 days. Chapters 12–13 have a similar emphasis (compare 11:3 with 12:6, 14). The logic of chapters 11–13 creates an orderly flow contributing to the overall message of the scroll: God protects his people in the coming crisis.

11:19-12:17 As in the earlier visions, action begins in heaven. The sanctuary of *heaven is opened* and John is even allowed to look into the holy of holies to view the *ark of the covenant*. As at Sinai (Exod 19:16–19), the language of theophany indicates something mighty about to take place.

Still in heaven in 12:1–2, John sees *a great and wondrous sign*: a woman whose description parallels an astral constellation. Medieval interpretation venerated Mary as the queen of heaven. But for John the woman with her crown of twelve stars (the totality of twelve tribes 7:4–8) is simply the people of God who are destined to rule the nations (2:26–27). The woman is in labor (Isa 26:16–17, Mic 4:10). She is about to bring forth a child (Jesus) who will be the Messiah, the one who will subdue the nations.

The appearance of the woman in labor in verses 3–6 attracts the attention of a frightening figure: *an enormous red dragon* writhing like a serpent. John identifies him as Satan (12:9). The description of the dragon uses biblical terminology for ancient monsters (Job 40:17; Ps 74:13–15). Satan, like Herod (Matt 2:1–12), is interested in stopping the male child from ruling the nations. Satan does not succeed. Jesus is exalted to God's right hand (Phil 2:6–10). But like Elijah going into the wilderness to escape Jezebel's wrath (1 Kgs 19), so Jesus' followers must suffer Satan's wrath for a short time (1,260 days, compare 11:3): a period of intense pressure to assimilate with pagan culture. The wilderness is not hostile to the woman (compare Elijah) but becomes her place of protection (see 11:1). It is *a place prepared for her by God*.

Revelation & the Legend of Nero's Return

A bizarre feature of modern life is the number of accounts of alleged sightings of Elvis Presley after his death. Indeed caricature of this belief is an industry in itself.

A similar belief that Nero was not dead but alive and living in Parthia, existed in this era. Political movements in the Empire tapped into this belief. John works a version of it into his description (13:3) of the sea beast emerging from a mortal wound. Here he describes the revival of the Roman Empire after its unraveling with the demise of Nero and the subsequent civil war.

A similar motif seems to inform the vision of the seven kings and the Beast of 17:9–18. Five emperors have come and fallen. A sixth (the revived Flavian dynasty?) emerges and a seventh follows in a short while. Then an eighth king, apparently "the revived Nero," emerges. With Rome at its zenith, ten of its client imperial kings yield power to this horrific figure who is a parody (was, is not, and is to come") of the godhead (1:4, 8, 17; 4:8; 21:6, 13). John uses "the returned Nero" as a metaphor for final resistance of early power to God. The returned Nero conquers all (even Rome itself), only to be routed by the Lamb (17:13–14; 19:17–21).

Even though Revelation 13 and 17 have more than their fair share of obscure features, such a reading is consistent with the social conditions of the Flavian dynasty, especially in the reign of Domitian (Bauckham, Climax, 423–452).

In 12:7–12, John gives additional information about the dragon. He sees a *war in heaven*. Michael, an archangel of God's court associated with events of the last days (Dan 12:1), hurls Satan down to earth. A loud voice in heaven announces that Satan has lost his place as the accuser of the righteous (see Job 1:9–11; 2:1–6). On earth he will make a last stand because *he knows the time is short*. Meanwhile those destined to suffer martyrdom during the crisis can be assured that they too will share in the Lamb's divine victory (12:11).

> **Satan**
> In the Old Testament, the Hebrew word satan *meant an adversary, an angel tasked with challenging human claims to righteousness (Job 1–2; Zech 1–2). In later tradition, this figured merged with the snake of Genesis 3 to become the very embodiment of evil, as here. However, Christian theology is never truly dualistic, since forces of evil ultimately give way to God.*

Despite the promises of victory in 12:7–12, John's readers are urged to prepare for a ferocious onslaught from Satan. Perhaps as a parody of the Apollo myth, the woman (people of God) *was given the two wings of a great eagle* to protect her during the time of crisis (see Exod 19:4, Isa 40:31). Notice that *the rest of her offspring – those who obey God's commandments and hold to the testimony of Jesus*, are marked especially for Satan's attention. What the NIV calls *her offspring* is in Greek "her seed," which echoes Genesis 3:15. By the unusual use of "seed" (usually associated with the male), John hints that the ancient conflict starting in the garden between Satan and the people of God will come to a head in the time of crisis. It will be the darkest just before the dawn of God's new world.

> **The Apollo Legend & the Roman Emperors**
> *Roman emperors frequently associated themselves with the legends of Apollo, a god of masculine beauty and manly prowess, viewing themselves as part of his family. In one myth widespread in Asia, Apollo's mothers, Leto, pregnant by Zeus, was pursued by a dragon trying to kill her. The north wind carried her to a safe place on an island. Protected by the gods, she gives birth to twins: Artemis (worshiped in Ephesus) and Apollo, who shortly after birth kills the dragon and, among other things becomes the legendary initiator of an age of prosperity. Stories like these undergirded the civic cults and emperor worship in the cities of Asia. In chapter 12, John may be alluding to elements of these stories. But for John, the real clash between the woman and a dragon was between the people of God and Satan.*

13:1–18 The dragon proceeds to make war against the people of God (12:17). He stands *on the shore of the sea*, traditional home of monsters, as if in expectation that one will come to his aid.

A beast emerges out of the sea, the place of chaos in the mindset of the biblical world (that is, *the deep* of Gen 1:2); he becomes Satan's first ally. The beast has seven heads and ten horns. This symbolism is not interpreted fully until 17:7–17. The beast embodies the characteristics of the world empires described in Daniel 7:3–7.

One of the heads of the sea beast appeared *to have a fatal wound*. Astonishingly, the same Greek word for *fatal wound* is also used in 5:6 to describe the Lamb; thus the Lamb was sacrificed at Calvary, but now vindicated, has all authority and power. The Roman emperors claim authority illegitimately. The *fatal wound* refers to the terrible power lost at the supposed demise of Nero (54–68 CE). But after the ensuing civil war of slightly more than a year, it had come back to life in John's day with even greater ferocity (*had been healed*) with the revival of the current dynasty.

The reference to *forty-two months* clearly identifies the beast's rule with the time of crisis that John sees on the horizon (11:2; 12:6, 14). Four times, 13:5–7 uses the verb "was given" in 13:5–7 (NIV *was given* and *to exercise*). Even though the people of God suffer under the beast (13:7), there are limitations. The reader learns that God both permits and limits even the work of evil people. In other words, good and evil are not on even terms; rather, evil can only go so far. The reference to *names … written in the book of life* and *the Lamb … slain from the creation of the world* may evoke the idea of predestination. But note that in 3:5 the implication is that it is only by unfaithfulness that believers can forfeit their place in the book of life. Verse 10 has many variants in the textual tradition, and so the exact text is uncertain. The general idea is that those who live by the sword will die by the sword (see Matt 26:52). John asserts that it will not be through taking up the sword that the faithful will defeat the idolatry of the emperor cult.

In verse 11, a land beast joins the sea beast. This indicates the universal scope (land and sea) of the

REVELATION

shadowy Satanic triad. Deceit is a major feature of the description of the earth beast. Already this is hinted in the description of his *two horns like a lamb*, which is a parody of the true Lamb of God. Later this beast which *spoke like a dragon* is called "the false prophet" (16:13; 19:20).

The work of the earth beast culminates in the erection of a statue of the sea beast: the Roman emperor. Temples with huge statues of the Roman emperors have been unearthed in this area. As with slaves, various cults marked or tattooed their followers as a sign of adherence. The Greek word *charagma*, "mark" (13:16–17), often denoted the official seal of Cæsar. Without the approval of the elite indicated by the mark, Christians were regularly excluded from ordinary economic activity. Christians were, however, sealed or marked by the Holy Spirit.

> **The Earth Beast**
> *The role of the earth beast is to facilitate emperor worship (13:12). Scholars are unclear as to its specific identity. One interpreter has argued that it was the wealthy elite of Roman society in Asia who furnished the various ruling offices including the priesthood (Friesen, "Beast," 62). In any case, the imperial cults elicit genuine devotion from their adherents. They even have their counterpart to the miracles of the Elijah-like prophetic witness (11:5; compare 2 Kgs 1:10). Already John sees their influences at work. In coming days, it will be inescapable.*

The sea beast is awarded a special number. In ancient Hebrew, since Arabic numbers were not used, each letter in the alphabet had a numerical value. The numerical equivalent for Cæsar Nero(n) (the "n" being a regular variant of Nero) was 666. Sometimes the "n" was dropped, decreasing the value by 50. In some manuscripts of Revelation, the number is 616. John is simply saying that in the coming crisis, the idolatrous forces will attack with the ferocity of Nero's attack of the Christians in Rome.

14:1–5 John concludes the intervening section with brief vignettes on the status of the faithful (14:1–5; 15:1–4) and the fate of their enemies (14:6–20).

At the earlier muster, the Lamb's followers numbered *144,000* (7:2–7). Now in the midst of battle they stand on *Mount Zion* (see Ps 2:6). *Mount Zion*, or the Holy City, is a place of protection and salvation. As if to indicate its symbolic nature and to show that it refers to no locale in particular, John mixes elements of both earth and heaven in his description to emphasize that believers remain safe and secure. In contrast to the followers of the beast who wear his mark (13:15–16), Christ's followers have the names of the Lamb and the Father symbolically *on their foreheads*.

The sounds of heaven accompany John's vision of the protected people. They hear the new song of vindication (5:8–10). In 7:2–7, *the 144,000* prepare for holy war. Israelite troops abstained from sexual activities in preparation for military duty (Deut 23:9–14). Celibacy becomes a metaphor for faithfulness and readiness. *Those who did not defile themselves with women* are, symbolically, all the faithful. The *pure* are the *first fruits* of God's ultimate harvest of the nations.

14:6–13 The scene shifts to the fate of the enemies. As if to emphasize the magnitude of their judgment, in a brief retort, John gives the reader an anticipatory picture of the horrors to come.

Three angels in 14:6, 8, 9 deliver a series of announcements. In 14:6–7, echoing the essence of the message of the two witnesses (11:3–14), the first angel issues a general call for the earth dwellers to forfeit their idolatry and turn to the God of heaven (see 9:20–21). *The eternal gospel* is not the message of salvation in Jesus but echoes Isaiah 52:7 (LXX) where the good news is that God comes to vindicate the righteous and judge the evil. Those under the spell of emperor worship should take note. The second angel identifies Babylon (Rome) as the source of abominations. And the third angel (14:9–11) gives a poignant warning to all those who succumb to the enticements of this evil system. Those in the seven churches should especially take note and *remain faithful*. They are called to practice *patient endurance* and to *obey God's commandments* (14:12). The seven beatitudes of Revelation are all addressed to the faithful. The second beatitude (14:13, compare 1:3) promises rest in the Lord.

> **The Septuagint (LXX)**
> *The ancient Greek translation of the Old Testament. Early Christians often quoted from this version.*

14:14–20 As Son of Man, Jesus gathers the faithful as the first fruits of the final harvest (14:4). Now in two graphic images of the grain harvest (14:14–16) and vintage (14:17–20), John predicts the fate of the unrepentant. The imagery of putting the *sickle* into the harvest echoes Joel 3:13 (compare the parable of the weeds in Matthew 13:24–30; 36–43). Also echoing Daniel 7:13–14, this passage pictures one *'like a son of man,' seated on the cloud* who swings *his sickle* over the whole earth.

Judgment is also the theme of the vintage scene of verses 17–20. The common linking word of the two units is *sickle*. Reusing the language of Isaiah 63:1–6, the gathering and crushing of *grapes* and a *winepress*, serves as a vivid metaphor of God's final wrath against the unrepentant. With imaginative literary exaggeration, John likens the carnage to a river of *blood* that will rise *as high as horses' bridles* (see 1 Enoch 100:3).

> **1,600 Stadia**
> 1,600 stadia (180 miles) is symbolic. Being a multiple of ten and four (ten rebellious kings, 17:12–14 and the four corners from the earth), the reference is probably to the envisioning of the universal defeat of God's enemies (Bauckham, Climax, 47).

15:1–4 As in 12:1, 3, John sees yet another *marvelous sign in heaven*. Revelation connects the earlier sign with the emerging crisis of emperor worship. This sign, *seven angels with the seven last plagues*, focuses on the resolution of the crisis: the unreserved visitation of God's wrath.

John sees again the heavenly ocean around God's throne, *a sea of glass* (see 4:6). But there is one crucial difference to the earlier description. The sea of glass is *mixed with fire*. The celebration of victory in God's throne room comes after a conflagration. The clash with *the beast* and his followers resulted in martyrdom. Therefore, the sea is mingled with fire. Pharaoh's defeat was followed by a song of Moses' triumph (Exod 15:1–18). With the new exodus, God's victory over the idolatrous nations will be complete. The victors sing *the song of Moses* and *the Lamb*. Significantly, in Exodus 15:11, 16, the nations were in terror and disarray after their defeat at the sea. But anticipating the defeat of the dragon and his allies, John points to the time when *all nations will come* in praise of God (compare 21:24; 22:2).

15:5–16:21 In 5:8, the four living creatures before God's throne hold *golden bowls full of incense, which are the prayers of the saints*. Now the four living creatures, as if in answer to these prayers, give *seven golden bowls filled with the wrath of God* to the angels who come out of God's sanctuary (see 6:9–11; 19:1–2). The full fury of God's wrath falls upon the rebellious creation (as in 11:19).

As in the two earlier sets of visions (seals, trumpets), the first four plagues are correlated. The plagues first fall upon people in the land *who had the mark of the beast*. It comes in the form of terrible sores (just as in Exod 9:10–11). Next, the *sea* turns to blood (compare Exod 7:20–21). Likewise, the *fresh waters* become blood. Like a chorus from a Greek drama, an angel pronounces the judgments are just. Finally, from the cosmos the *sun* scorches rebellious humankind. These plagues no longer fall on a fourth of the earth (6:8), or a third (8:7). The full fury of God's wrath comes upon the idolaters; yet, hardened in their rebellious ways, they refuse to repent.

As with the fifth trumpet (9:1–11), the wrath of God centers on the evil powers, here defined as the throne of the beast (that is, civic cults and places of emperor worship). Tormented, they still refuse to disavow their ways.

> **Civic Cults**
> Major cities in the Roman Empire competed for the right to build temples to Roma (the deified city of Rome) and various emperors. Leading citizens served as priests, and these temples joined those of traditional gods as centers of community life.

Expanding the sixth vision of the seven trumpets (9:13–19), John returns to the Euphrates. There he sees *the kings from the East*. Almost certainly these are the ten kings of 17:12–16. Embodying the triad of demonic powers (*three*

> **Armageddon**
> Armageddon is etched in popular imagination as an image for a terrible catastrophe, such as nuclear war. In Scripture, it appears only once, in Revelation 16:16, where the writer refers to the place of a final showdown between the forces of a world leader and the people belonging to the Lamb.
>
> Like most things in Revelation, this reference is symbolic. Armageddon in Hebrew literally means "mountain" of Megiddo, yet the mountain reference has puzzled commentators. Megiddo is a region of plains in the north of Israel and the site of numerous battles owing to its strategic location.
>
> For John, the mountain image functions as the place of judgment, probably counterbalancing Mount Zion, which symbolizes God's protection of his people (14:1–5). Thus, Armageddon symbolizes the final defeat of God's enemies. One today can stand on the ruins of the mound of Megiddo and survey the plains where numerous battles (often between the people of God and their enemies) took place. As such, Megiddo serves as the perfect symbol to describe God's final judgment on the forces of evil.

evil spirits ... like frogs), they are an incarnation of evil. Later interpreters refer to their leader as the antichrist, although Scripture reserves this term for others who deny Christ's deity (1 John 2:18, 22; 4:3, 2 John 7). John gives a fuller discussion of the final battle in chapter 17 where he focuses on a final gathering of the forces against the Lamb and his followers reminiscent of the Old Testament Day of the Lord (16:14//17:14). The place of gathering is *Armageddon*. The outcome of this battle is detailed in 17:14 and 19:17–21. But, in the middle of this terrifying scene, a third beatitude (16:15) gives relief. Believers are assured that if they persist keeping their *clothes* (good work) they will not fall (*go naked*) under judgment.

Before Armageddon, Babylon (Rome) must be destroyed (verses 17–21; compare 17:15–16). The reader has been prepared for its destruction in the vision of the seven trumpets (8:2–9:21) where Joshua 6 is clearly echoed. John describes Rome's fate with language drawn from God's dramatic appearance at Sinai (Ex 19:16–19). For the people of Israel, the exodus constituted the movement out of Egypt, coming to Sinai and ending with possession of the land. For John, the new exodus involves the defeat of resistance to the Lamb. Huge hailstones (echoing Josh 10:11) pound Babylon. With *flashes of lightning* and *a severe earthquake*, God defeats Bablyon (Rome). Then, because of its significance, John gives a lengthy description of Babylon's rise and fall (17:1–18:24).

The Fate of the Apostate Woman · 17:1–21:8

17:1–6 Because of its destruction of Jerusalem in 586 BCE, Scripture portrays Babylon as the traditional enemy of the people of God. After Rome destroyed Jerusalem in 70 CE, in Jewish apocalyptic literature, Rome, now encoded as Babylon, takes over this mantle (4 *Ezra* 11–12; *Sibylline Oracles* 5:12–51). John adopts a similar use of the symbols.

The Greek text of 17:1 opens with twelve words almost identical to 21:9, which introduces the description of the other city: the New Jerusalem. The Apocalypse's major closing structural feature is the contrast of two woman-cities. Readers must decide to which they belong. An angel shows John the first woman: a prostitute. *Many waters* (Jer 51:13) makes the Babylon connection. Ancient Babylon rested on the Euphrates and a number of canals. Later in 17:15 John allegorizes the reference to the waters to describe the ubiquitous wealth and power of Rome.

In verse 2, by attacking regional states, Rome had built an empire. As one who focuses on the spiritual battles, John is not impressed. He calls these physical conquests adultery.

John is carried to a *desert*, which for the Old Testament prophets is what Babylon will become (Jer 51:26, 29, 43). Those prophecies find fulfillment in the fate of (the new) Babylon, Rome. Chapter 17 pictures Rome under several images. It is both the prostitute and the *scarlet beast* identified in chapter 13. The focus at first is on the prostitute. As the sponsor of emperor worship and allied abominations, Rome carries a cup of enticements: *the blood of the saints*, a clear reference to those who have died for Jesus in the great crisis. Encoded on her forehead is a name. Counterbalancing her is the Lamb whose name, known by the insight of his followers, is not on open display for all to see (19:12–13).

17:7–18 The introduction to the woman's name in 17:5 begins with the word "mystery." The identity of the woman as Rome is clear. The angel promises to give a full explanation of the mystery. As it unfolds, the beast who *once was, now is not* is a grim parody of Christ, "who is, and who was, and who is to come" (1:8). The general reference is to chapter 13 with its chronicle of the rise, fall, and rebirth of the Roman Empire under the Flavians. Its splendor tricks *the inhabitants of the earth* into idolatrous allegiance (13:8, 12, 14; 17:2).

> **The Flavians**
> *Three emperors near the end of the first century CE made up the Flavian dynasty: Vespasian (ruled 69–79), Titus (79–81), and Domitian (81–96). Again, Domitian was likely the emperor opposed by the book of Revelation.*

John unfolds the meaning of the seven heads of the beast in verses 9–11 (13:1). First he compares the seven heads with seven hills, an obvious reference to the seven hills of Rome. But there is another meaning. The seven heads also stand for seven kings (Roman emperors). In John's symbolic world, the specific identity of the emperors is not the point. Seven is the number for totality. Six have come. The next king will rule *for a little while*. He will be followed by an eighth, a returning Nero-like figure (*who once was, and now is not*). He embodies the worst of the earlier rulers. Paradoxically, he will bring Rome's destruction through civil war (17:11, 16). John is not giving a history lesson but making a theological point. Idolaters have a limited time on stage. Rome will *remain for a little while* and then collapse.

After explaining the meaning of the seven heads of the beast (17:3, 7), John now interprets the ten horns in verses 12–18. These are the potentates and rulers of the eastern part of the empire (17:12) who, along with their leader, the beast incarnated, return with one ultimate purpose – to defeat the Lamb, *Lord of lords and King of kings* (17:14, compare 16:12, 16). Drunk with their own power, first they demolish the prostitute – Rome itself (17:16–17). John is saying that, in the end, the city personified as a woman collapses from its own excesses. Then for a short period, *one hour*, the forces that destroyed Rome set their sights on the Lamb. But before the denouément (19:11–19), more must be said about Rome's fall.

18:1–24 Isolated as he was on Patmos, John would watch ships going to and fro across the empire. From an earthly perspective, Rome seemed invincible. But from the heavenly dimension, drunk with her power and self-adulation, Rome is already *fallen* (18:2; see 16:17–21). In a mocking funeral dirge John draws up a bill of particulars against it.

In verses 1–3, an angelic messenger repeats the earlier announcement of 14:8 that Babylon is fallen (see 16:19). Rome is stripped of her power (compare Jer 50–51; Ezek 26–27).

In verses 4–8, John hears another voice warning the people of God not to assimilate themselves with Rome. *Come out of her, my people, so that you will not share in her sins* describes well a constant theme that resonates throughout the book. Christians should avoid merger with the dominant culture.

Three groups connected with the power structure within the empire appear successively in verses 9–10, expressing deep grief over their loss. The provincial rulers (*kings of the earth*) who were sharers of Rome's wealth (*committed adultery with her*) are the first to mourn. Most likely, these are not those kings of the east who rebelled (17:12, 16) but many administrative leaders who grieve over their enormous loss of power. Note that the woe (18:10) is repeated for each group (18:16, 19). Of the three groups, *the merchants* receive the greatest attention (verses 11–17a). The catalog of items traded (18:12–14) is an accurate assessment of ancient commerce. The last reference to *souls of men* (see Ezek 27:13) is a euphemism for slave trading. Rome's glorious splendor was built on human degradation.

> **Roman Trade**
>
> *As verses 17b–19 point out, Rome's wealth was not in the city itself but in trade; thus, seafarers are important for this system. They lament over the fall of the empire.*

Meanwhile, 18:20 and 24 serve as bookends around the final statement of doom over Babylon (18:21–23). These critical verses answer the martyrs' cry in 6:9–11. Heaven, including the founding apostles and prophets of the church (compare 21:14), is invited to share in God's praise over this victory.

19:1–10 Babylon is destroyed. A brief celebration ensues before the account of the final defeat of the dragon and his allies. Reminiscent of 7:9–10 and 15:2–5, John hears *the roar of a great multitude in heaven. The smoke* of the evil city ascends to God, counterbalancing the earlier prayers of the saints that also ascended (17:3–4). With alternating chants, *twenty-four elders and the four living creatures* make their last appearance in Revelation. It is praise time, with *a voice from the throne*. Prominent are the four uses of *Hallelujah* (Hebrew for "praise Yahweh"), the only occurrences in the New Testament (19:1, 3, 4, 6). The wedding of the Lamb is announced. The bride in fine linen (symbolizing good deeds of the church) stands in stark contrast to the tawdriness of the prostitute of chapter 17.

An interpreting angel reminds the readers with the fourth beatitude that faithfulness to the Lamb is a precondition to a participation in this wedding party. Overwhelmed, John falls before the representative of the heavenly court in a posture of adoration. But he is chastened. Only God is worthy of worship (1:20; 22:9). The angels, on the same level as John himself, are not to be worshiped.

19:11–16 After the interlude of 19:1–10, John depicts the fate of the opponents of the Lamb. In reverse order to their appearances in Revelation 12–13, the beast and the false prophet (earth beast) are thrown *into the fiery lake of burning sulfur* (19:20) to be followed by the dragon (Satan) in 20:10. The refrain *I saw* (19:11, 17, 19, 20:1, 4, 11; 21:1–2) structures the movement to the new heaven and new earth.

The rider on the white horse in verses 11–12 refers to the coming of Christ. In 3:14, he is called the *faithful and true witness*. He is no longer the tender earthly Jesus but a warrior judging a rebellious creation. His *eyes are like blazing fire* (see 1:14, 16). In stark contrast to Babylon, who openly flaunted her name (17:5), *He has a name ... that no one knows but he himself*. Here John seems to hint at the mystery of the interrelationship of Father and Son in the Godhead.

Astonishingly, before the final battle *he is dressed in a robe dipped in blood*. His victory already was won at Calvary (5:12; 12:5, 11). As the *Word of God* came from heaven to destroy the Egyptians (*Wisdom of Solomon* 18:15–16) so Jesus, the Word of God, comes with his armies to vanquish his enemies. The armies that accompany the Lamb are *dressed in fine linen, white and clean*. The angels may well be present. But the description also parallels that of the faithful witnesses who have survived the great crisis (6:11; 7:13–14; 19:8). They too will share in the victory.

As promised in 2:26–27 (echoing Psalm 2), verses 15–16 say that the rebellious nations will be crushed (see 12:5). It is time for the Lord's anointed as *King of kings and Lord of lords* to suppress his enemies and bring them into *the winepress of God's wrath* (14:19).

19:17–18 An angel (as in 14:6) summons the soaring birds to the great supper of God (compare 17:7–8). Instead of the human adversaries of Christ feasting on animals and other expressions of bounty, the birds feed on them. The scene echoes Ezekiel 39:17–20, where the prophet envisions the birds and animals feasting on the bodies of Prince Gog's warriors (compare Rev 20:7–10). Gog and Magog, traditional northern enemies of Israel, become a metaphor for the Lamb's enemies (16:13–14, 16; 17:12–14). John spares the reader battle details. It is no contest (19:15, 21).

19:19–21 Significantly, while the warriors are killed (19:21), the two allies of the dragon (13:1–18) are taken captive. These two allies symbolize all opposition against the Lamb. They are *thrown alive into the fiery lake of burning sulfur*. Apocalyptic literature regularly speaks of fire as the final punishment for evildoers (*1 Enoch* 54:1; Matt 13:42). Whether this represents annihilation or is unending punishment is unclear from the text. What is evident is that the verdict against evil is final. The Lamb, through the power of his word, has conquered absolutely.

20:1–10 Following the structure centering on the connecting words "I saw" (19:11, 17, 19), the next unit focuses on the defeat of Satan. Earlier in 12:7–9, 13–17, Satan (the Dragon) was deposed from a place in the heavenly court. On earth he pursued the people of God furiously (12:17–13:18). Now Satan is about to go one step lower. A nameless angel appears holding *a great chain*. Satan is confined in *the Abyss* (11:7). For *a thousand years* he will be unable to deceive *the nations*. John describes the defeat of Satan in two stages (20:1–3; 7–10). This emphasizes that Satan's defeat is not partial but absolute. Satan's total rout functions as bookends to a beautiful description of the faithful who enjoy their reward under God's protection (20:4–6). God protects the martyrs, who will enjoy life in the New Jerusalem under the continual reign of the Lamb.

Concurrent with the confinement of Satan, Christ reigns with the martyrs for 1,000 years. Highly symbolic, this is the only reference to the millennial reign of Christ in Scripture. It is controversial because many refuse to see it merely as symbolic and anticipate a literal thousand-year reign of Christ on earth.

The repeated phraseology (*And*) *I saw* opens the unit in verse 4. John sees *thrones* – a clear echo of Daniel 7:9 where thrones were set up for the Ancient of Days to judge the nations. However, here the martyrs have dominion. The NIV presumes that only the martyrs assumed the thrones and exercise dominion. The Greek text is less clear. John sees *souls ... beheaded ... because of the word of God*. But the following Greek relative pronoun then changes to the nominative case to speak of those who *had not worshiped the beast*.... Whether this is another group or refers back specifically to the martyrs is grammatically unclear. Probably John is indicating that all who were faithful through the crisis, whether they lived or died, would have their place in this time of dominion. They enjoy the blessings of victory (1:5–6; 7:14; 12:11). The millennium reveals God's triumph. It states symbolically that those who contested the beast's right to rule and suffered for it will in the end be the victors (Bauckham, *Theology*, 107). The origin of the number *one thousand* is unclear. Some take it as a version of an ancient idea of world history being divided into seven thousand years (a day = 1000 years) ending in a seventh (or eighth) day of timeless rest (*Epistle of Barnabas* 15:3–9; *2 Enoch* 33:1–2). The general idea is that the end of creation repeats the beginning.

According to verse 5, the reign with Christ is the *first resurrection*. Looking ahead to 20:7–10, the implication is that it is on earth. But place is not significant (14:1–5) because the old order is about to transition into a new heaven and new earth (21:1).

If one understands that all the faithful share in the millennial reign (7:11–14; 12:11–12; 14:1–5), then one should interpret this as the promised resurrection to life of the faithful. The implied "second resurrection" is the final judgment of the wicked (see below 20:12–15).

The fifth beatitude in verse 6 again exhorts believers in the seven churches. They should strive to reign with Christ and not suffer *the second death*, the fate of those who do not belong to the Lamb (20:14).

Satan's armies had made their stand against the Lamb in 19:19–21. They were defeated, and his two allies were consigned to the *fiery lake of burning sulfur* (19:21). It is time in 20:7–10 to describe *the devil* (the Dragon) receiving the same fate. Satan is only a shadow of his former self – totally impotent, he is consigned to the lake of fire.

20:11–15 Although this unit skips steps in its reasoning, its overall logic is relatively clear. Echoing Daniel 7:9–10, John describes a throne. In contrast to 20:4, *God comes to the great white throne*. John sees the dead standing there. Books are opened; anyone *not found written in the book of life* is *thrown into the lake of fire*. This passage is frequently cited as a description of universal judgment. But this is not John's point. John already assumes the vindication of the people of faith (20:4–6). Revelation 20:11–15 describes a punitive judgment (Lambrecht, "Final Judgments," 402). The dead of the "second resurrection" are the unrighteous "whose names have not been written in the book of life" (17:8). Their fate, along with the underworld (*death and Hades*) is sealed.

21:1–8 John starts to shift attention to another city personified as a woman, introduced in 21:9. As with 19:1–10, this unit anticipates this great event. It is both visionary (21:1–2) and auditory (21:3–5). The loud voice of 21:3–4 corresponds to seeing the *new heaven and new earth* of 21:1. And God's voice of 21:5–8 corresponds to John's glimpse of the *New Jerusalem* in 21:2.

> **The New Jerusalem**
>
> At the center of the new earth is the New Jerusalem. Hymn writers focus on the Holy City as a place, but for John, its center will be the people enjoying direct access to the glory of God. After Jerusalem's apostasy, the prophets looked for a new, ideal Jerusalem (Isa 65:18–19). Apocalyptists envisioned a heavenly prototype (4 Ezra 7:26; 8:52; 13:36; 2 Baruch 4:2–6). Now God's promise is about to be realized (3:12).

> **Dispensational Premillennialism**
>
> Throughout Christian history, a number have believed that God has a "prophetic timetable" ending in the defeat of evil and the coming of the golden age. The reference to the binding of Satan and reign of Christ for 1,000 years in 20:1–6 figures strongly in these speculations.
>
> From the second century, many in the church (Papias, Justin Martyr, and Tertullian) took the thousand years of Revelation 20:1–6 literally. They deduced from this that a thousand-year reign of Christ on earth would take place. The term for this view is chiliasm (Latin for "a thousand years"). Some call this "historic premillennialism" because it asserts that the world will go through a time of horrors shortly before ("pre") the return of Christ to reign 1,000 years ("millennium").
>
> When Christ did not return, many began to interpret the millennium as the heavenly reign of Christ in the church (Tyconius and Augustine). In the Middle Ages, Joachim of Fiore (1135–1202) was influential. He took the 1,260 days to be 1,260 years of testing for the church. Later commentators linked this with the papacy. Romanism would be cast aside through the preaching of the pure gospel, and after a new era of peace ("the millennium"), Christ would return (postmillennialism).
>
> A significant development took place in nineteenth century Britain. John Nelson Darby (1800–1882), founder of the Plymouth Brethren, linked the 1,260 days with Daniel 9:24–27 (the prophecy of 70 weeks) and concluded that 69 weeks of years (483 years) had elapsed before Pentecost. But then – as it were – God's prophetic time-clock was put on hold until the time of the restoration of Israel to its historic land. Shortly thereafter, the church would be "raptured" to heaven by Christ. Those "left behind" would suffer seven years (two 1,260 day periods). After this, a renewed Israel would rule with Christ on earth for one thousand years followed by the final judgment. This theory is known as "dispensational premillennialism." After the rebirth of Israel, it became very popular among American evangelicals. Recently, Hal Lindsey (author of The Late Great Planet Earth) and the Left Behind series of novels and films have popularized it.
>
> This view is exegetically dubious but remains popular because it caters to a constant human weakness: the conviction that the present generation is more significant than others because it will witness the climactic end of history.

The *new heaven* and *new earth* should be understood in biblical terms. God is creator of both (Gen 1:1). John, echoing Isaiah 65:17, sees a totally renovated creation (Rom 8:19–21; Rev 21:5). The old *sea* of chaos is no more. Creation is about to work properly.

Strongly reminiscent of 7:15–17, John hears an announcement of God coming to dwell with people (verses 3–4). The central image is the Feast of Tabernacles. Already in Christ, God has come and "tented" among us (John 1:14). Now in the new creation, God's tent lives with peoples of all races. Death, tears, and pain, so typical of the old creation, are gone.

21:5–8 As in 1:8, God announces he is *the Alpha and the Omega*. But more significantly, he announces, *It is done*. In 16:17, a similar expression announced judgment on Babylon. Here the renovation of the creation is complete. The new creation is for the faithful. With special focus on those enticed by cults and emperor worship (*who practice magic arts*, *the idolaters*), John reminds us that their fate is *the second death*.

The Appearance of the Pure City · 21:9–22:5

To create his picture of God's city, John pieces together various images of paradise and the ideal world as visualized by Old Testament prophets. Yet this set of elaborate descriptions is metaphorical. It is "people as place, not place for people" (Gundry 254).

21:9–14 John introduces the unit in almost the same language as 17:1. The unusual word for *come* [Greek *deuro*] marks a major transition of the book, from description to invitation. The reference to the *bride* is clearly to the faithful church now enjoying its moment of vindication (19:8–9).

Babylon was set on seven hills (verse 10; compare 17:9). John is carried to a *mountain great and high*. Ezekiel's vision (Ezek 40:2) is about to be fulfilled and transcended. The city is filled with the *glory of God* according to verses 11–14. God's glory rested in the temple (Ezek 43:2) and then in Jesus Christ (John 1:14). Here his resting place is likened to the presence of a rare jewel (4:3). Similar to those on ancient cities, over the twelve gates are inscriptions of benefactors' names. The names of *the twelve tribes of Israel* over the *gates* and of *the twelve apostles* on the "rock" foundation (Matt 16:16–20) symbolize the city as the totality of the people of God.

21:15–21 The city is a perfect cube, about 1,400 miles in diameter. As a literal description, this is impossible; instead the cube symbolizes the holy of holies of the temple and serves as a symbol of God's presence with his people. Compared to the height of the city, the height of the wall (216 feet) is trifling. The wall and its foundations are built out of precious stones from paradise (Ezek 28:13–14; Isa 54:11–12). Lost after the human banishment from paradise, the stones now return as adornments for the bride-city.

21:22–22:5 At the center of any ancient city was a *temple*. Ezekiel envisioned an ideal temple to be the crucial structure of the New Jerusalem (Ezek 40–48). The Temple Scroll of the Dead Sea sectarians portrayed an even more elaborate imaginary temple. But the New Jerusalem is a people! *The glory of God gives it light, and the Lamb is its lamp*.

21:24–27 The city is a blessing to *the nations*. Those enthralled by the beast have suffered their just fate (19:15, 17–21). But people from every tribe who have given allegiance to the Lamb now have their day (7:9; 21:7). Isaiah looks for "the glory of the Lord" to appear in Zion (Isa 60:1) and describes "the nations" making a pilgrimage in recognition of Zion's status (Isa 60:2–6). Here all the redeemed access the city, since its *gates* are never *shut* (21:25).

Closing off this section, John portrays the end time as the return of the beginning of paradise (Gen 2:10–14; Ezek 47:1–2). Ezekiel's life-giving river (47:1–2) flows *from the throne of God*. The *tree of life* (Eden), promised to return in 2:7, becomes a great orchard covering both banks of the river and providing full healing for the nations. God and his people exist in full communion (22:3–5). In the stunning presence of God's light, *there will be no night there*! (21:25, 22:5).

> **Waiting for the New Jerusalem**
> *Faithful readers living on the other side of the collapse of Rome sometimes wonder, if this is the case, why God's new world is delayed. One should remember that the crisis John saw coming recurs through the centuries, and versions of Rome in the culture are always enticing believers to accommodate to idolatrous claims. At an appropriate time, God will bring the end of history.*

EPILOGUE · 22:6–21

The concluding verses return us to a form and style similar to the prologue and the opening salutations of the letters to the seven churches (1:1–8).

22:6–7 The angel who showed John the restored paradise (22:1) attests to the trustworthiness of the prophecy (see 1:1–2). There follows a reminder, reinforced by the sixth beatitude, that these things *must soon take place*.

22:8–9 As with 19:10 (see 2:1), John is told that it is only the Holy One who is worthy of absolute homage. Even the heavenly council of angels is subordinate to God.

22:10–11 Unlike Daniel, who was told to seal up his message (12:9), John is warned not to follow this earlier precedent. The heavenly secrets of the earlier apocalyptic writings would be revealed in the last days. For John, the last days are here.

22:12–13 In 1:8 and 21:6, God is *the Alpha and the Omega*. In 1:17 and 2:8 Jesus is *the First and the Last*. Throughout the Apocalypse, the view that God and the Lamb are equally worthy of worship prevails.

22:14–15 The seventh beatitude honors those *who wash their robes*. The words echo 7:14 and an interpretation of Christ's redemption based on an exodus motif. Israel was saved from Egypt through the protection of the Lamb's blood. Christian believers and martyrs claim similar protection through Christ, their sacrificial Lamb. Revelation 7:14 speaks about the "washed" in the past tense; however, John uses the present tense in these verses (*those who wash*). John repeatedly exhorts his readers, people who face the prospect of martyrdom, to reclaim the power of their faith; otherwise, they may be numbered with the profligate.

22:16 John features Jesus' messianic credentials. He is *the Root* (Isa 11:10), *Offspring of David* (5:5; Rom 1:3), and the *Morning Star* (2:26–28; compare Isa 60:3; Num 24:17).

22:17 Not only is the wording an expectation of Christ's coming, but it also reflects a call to participate in the Lord's Supper, which may well have followed the reading of these words in the churches.

22:18–19 The warning not to add or take away from the prophetic message echoes the earlier words of Moses with respect to God's word (Deut 4:2; 12:32). John's message is the word of the risen Lord and should not be distorted. Although this warning specifically refers to the message of the Apocalypse, Christian readers appropriately apply it to all the canonical books, which is God's word to the church.

22:20 Moving to closure, the writing takes on a doxological note. The constant refrain of *Come, Lord Jesus* echoes the ancient Aramaic cry *Maranatha* ("O Lord, come"; 1 Cor 16:22).

22:21 The doxological theme continues with the book ending in a benediction. As the salutation of the message to the seven churches opens with "grace and peace" (1:4), so John uses a similar formula to close the book.

THEOLOGICAL REFLECTIONS

When John edited his visions at Patmos, he could hardly have conceived that this prophetic letter addressed directly to several churches would conclude the New Testament canon, which did not exist yet. Yet, perhaps providentially, certainly appropriately, this book brings the biblical story to a resounding climax. Revelation is not a book of doom and gloom, but a promise to a marginalized church that, after hard times, victory is at hand. In John's day, the church faced a bitter choice: either assimilate with the culture or face severe persecution. Throughout history, as Christians long for God's new world, they continue to face a similar choice. In name they are kings and priests. One day, in reality they will reign with Christ. The Christian life revolves around a tension between these two claims. Although the church is a struggling counter-cultural community, it is not bereft of resources. Behind and above all is an awe-inspiring God whom John describes as "Ruler of all" (1:8; 4:8; 11:17; 15:3; 16:7, 14; 19:6, 15; and 21:22). Before God, even mighty Rome, or any other human empire, is no match. In the first century, to one looking around, Rome seems invincible; but it is the Lamb, the Son of God (2:18), who has conquered. He holds the keys of death and Hades (1:18) and will eventually inaugurate a new world as King of kings and Lord of lords (17:14). Yet both God and the Lamb, possessors of cosmic power, acknowledge human freedom. Rebellious creation is patiently urged to repent (9:20–21). And, ironically, even though the Lamb (Jesus), the heavenly Lord, will be the center of the redeemed New Jerusalem, in a key scene he stands outside the door of one of his recalcitrant churches, quietly asking for entrance. God gives us the freedom, on the basis of love, to choose to reject or accept him.

But this winsome word of grace is not to be disdained. Above all, to the skeptic who cries out that, in the end,

"God must forgive – after all it is his trade," Revelation is a wake-up call. Evil will be punished. Through the seven beatitudes, John warns that even the churches must take note of that. And so Revelation ends with an invitation. All are invited to join the Lamb in God's new world: "Let whoever is thirsty come" (22:17).

FOR FURTHER STUDY

M. Eugene Boring, *Revelation* (Louisville: Westminster John Knox, 1989).

Richard Bauckham, *Climax of Prophecy* (Edinburgh: T & T Clark, 1993).

William C. Weinrich, *Revelation* (Downers Grove, Ill.: InterVarsity Press, 2005).

WORKS CITED

Richard Bauckham, *Climax of Prophecy* (Edinburgh: T & T Clark, 1993).

———, *The Theology of the Book of Revelation* (Cambridge: Cambridge University Press, 1993).

Steven J. Friesen, "The Beast from the Land: Revelation 13:11–18 and Social Setting," in *Reading the Book of Revelation* (ed. David L. Barr; Atlanta: SBL, 2003): 49–64.

———, *Imperial Cults and the Apocalypse of John: Reading Revelation in the Ruins* (New York: Oxford University Press, 2001).

A. J. P. Garrow, *Revelation* (London/New York: Routledge, 1997).

R. Gundry, "The New Jerusalem: People as Place, Not Place for People," *Novum Testamentum* 29 (1987): 254–64.

Colin J. Hemer, *The Letters to the Seven Churches of Asia in Their Local Setting* (Sheffield, England: Sheffield Academic Press, 1989).

Irenæus, *Against Heresies*, in vol. 1 of *The Ante-Nicene Fathers* (reprinted; Grand Rapids: Eerdmans, 1956).

Craig R. Koester, *Revelation and the End of All Things* (Grand Rapids: Eerdmans, 2001).

Jan Lambrecht, "A Structuration of Revelation 4:1–22:5," *L'Apocalypse johannique et l'apocalyptique dans le Nouveau Testament* (ed. Jan Lambrecht; Leuven: Leuven University Press, 1980): 77–104.

———, "Final Judgments and Ultimate Blessings: The Climactic Visions of Revelation 20, 11–21, 8," *Biblica* 81 (2000): 362–85.

Allan J. McNicol, *Jesus' Directions for the Future* (Macon, Ga.: Mercer University Press, 1996).

Robert H. Mounce, *The Book of Revelation: Revised Edition* (Grand Rapids: Eerdmans, 1998).

James L. Resseguie, *Revelation Unsealed: A Narrative Critical Approach to John's Apocalypse* (Leiden: Brill, 1998).

SIDEBARS, MAPS & GRAPHICS
Topical Index

A

Aaron
- The Ark of the Covenant 581
- Interspersed Thematic Summaries 190
- "Messiah" in Israel 492
- Messianism in the First Century 731
- An Oral Torah 746
- Priesthood 174
- The Prophetic Call 148

Abel
- Cain's Offering 112

Abraham
- The Arameans 228
- Children & the Israelite Family 273
- Eliezer 118
- God's Name 70
- Israel's Ancestors 209
- Map of Abram's Migration to Canaan 117
- Prophetic Intercession 683
- Sacrificing Isaac 124
- Sarai & Hagar 119
- The "Ten Righteous" 121

Absolom
- The Death of Absalom 302
- A King's Harem 293
- Wise Women 304

Achan 861

Adoption · See Family

Afterlife · See Resurrection & Afterlife

Agriculture & Farming
- Agricultural Imagery 552
- Cain's Offering 112
- Dagon 708
- Edom 686
- Fine Linens 546
- Food Laws 175
- The Kenites 253
- Law Codes in the Pentateuch 161
- Mysteries 52
- Sedentarization 59
- The Sling 282
- The Tasks of Shepherds 646
- Threshing Sledges 442
- Wells in Ancient Times 147

Ahab
- God & Deception 379
- Jehu's Punishment 666
- The Mesha Stele 331
- The Recabites 603
- Shalmaneser & Ahab 326

Alexander the Great
- Chariots 245
- The Persian Empire 719

Ammon
- Gilead 680
- Map of Israel & Judah 694
- Map of Philistia 286

Amorites 136
- Dagon 708

Andrew
- The Twelve 766

Angels
- 1 Enoch 658
- "A little lower than the angels..." 1015
- Angelology 1074
- Angels in First-Century Thought 1014
- Angels & Mediators 439
- "Because of the angels..." 928
- Cherubim 456, 628, 1072
- The Heavenly Council 425
- The Holy Ones 483
- "If God did not spare the angels..." 1043
- Jacob's Wrestling Partner 131
- Sadducees 814
- "Sons of God" 1060

Annas
- Caiaphas 843
- High Priests 848

Anthropomorphism & Personification
- Fables 258
- Imagery in Psalms 446
- Jacob's Wrestling Partner 131
- Jeremiah versus Hananiah 596
- Jonah & Assyria 691
- The Language of Poetry 445
- Medieval Chant 102
- Personified Places 585

Antichrist 1048

Anti-Semitism
- Hebrews & *Hapiru* 145
- Matthew & Anti-Semitism 756

Apocalypse & Eschatology
- 4 Ezra & 2 Baruch 902
- Apocalypse in Zechariah 714
- Apocalyptic Imagery 910
- Apocalyptic Language 648
- Apocalyptic Literature in Ancient Times 1063
- Apocalyptic Vision 715
- Armageddon 1079
- Cosmic Fire 1044
- Daniel & Jesus' Apocalyptic Visions 662
- Daniel & Resurrection 663
- The "Day of the Lord" 644
- Dispensational Premillennialism 1083
- Eschatology 1065
- Eschatology in Zechariah 713
- The Eschaton 979
- God's Salvation 897
- The Great Feast 807
- Interpreting Mark 13 780
- The Messianic Banquet 740
- The New Jerusalem 1083
- Paul's "Already but Not Yet" Eschatology 903
- Paul's Political Prophecy 986
- Peter & the End Times 1039
- Revelation & the Legend of Nero's Return 1076
- The Son of Man 811
- Textual Sources in Romans 895
- "They shall be caught up..." 982
- Waiting for the New Jerusalem 1084

Apollo
- Abaddon & Apollo 1074
- The Apollo Legend & the Roman Emperors 1077

1087

TOPICAL INDEX

Apostles · See also Andrew; James (apostle); John (apostle); Judas Iscariot; Matthew; Peter; Simon the Zealot (apostle); Thaddaeus
    Jesus' Authority 795
    The Messianic Secret 19, 764
    "Sandwiches" in Mark 767
    The Twelve 766
    Welcoming the Disciples 742

Apphia & Archippus 1008

Aram · See Syria

Archaeology & Artifacts
    Ai 241
    Amarna Letters 60
    Ancient Documents 35
    Ancient Musical Notation 38
    Ancient Near-Eastern Flood Stories 114
    Ancient Piety 38
    Archaeology & Biblical Events 57
    Archeological Tells 598
    Baal & Ashtoreth 276
    Balaam Son of Beor 196
    Baruch's Ring 601
    Basic Chronology of Ancient Israel & Its Neighbors 58
    Ben-Hadad III 338
    The Bronze Snake 195
    The Bulla of Baalis 608
    Caiaphas 843
    The Campaign into Judah 320
    Capernaum 736
    Ceramic Assemblage 60
    Children & the Israelite Family 273
    Cuneiform 400
    Dating the Exodus 315
    The Dead Sea Scrolls 31
    The Decree of Cyrus 560
    The Destruction of Israel 341
    Divorce Decrees 226
    Elaborate Worship 364
    The Elephantine Papyri 402, 610
    The Fall of Ninevah 700
    Faunal Assemblage 63
    Gedaliah's Seal 348, 608
    Gemaraiah 604
    Gibeon 609
    Gilead 680
    Hebrews & *Hapiru* 145
    Heshbon 206
    Hezekiah's Reforms 342
    The Iran Stele 341
    Ivory 318
    Jehoiachin the Captive 590
    Jericho 240
    Jerusalem's Walls 408
    Jesus' Tomb 851
    John's Historical Value 21
    Judah & Taxation 313
    Kingship & Divinity 313
    "Kiss the Son…" 449
    Lachish Letters 347
    Law & Justice 227
    Life in Babylonia 396
    The Megiddo Seal 340
    The Mesha Inscription 612
    The Mesha Stele 331
    Monotheism in Egypt 186
    The Mount Ebal Worship Complex 229
    Negative Evidence in Archaeology 57
    Non-Israelite Ancient Near-Eastern Prophets 66
    Omri 322
    Papyrus 28
    The Pentateuch & Ancient Near Eastern Law Codes 3
    The Philistines 275
    Poetry as Prophecy 369
    Royal Inscriptions 307
    Seraiah Son of Neriah 615
    Shalmaneser & Ahab 326
    The Siloam Tunnel 344
    The Sling 282
    Synagogues in the First Century 862
    Tel Dan 263
    Tel Dan Inscription 324
    The Tel Dan Inscription 336
    Tell 55
    Tent Shrines 187
    The War Scroll 187
    The Water Tunnel 295

Ark of the Covenant
    The Ark of the Covenant 238, 581
    Diagram of the Tabernacle 163
    Kiriath-Jearim 584
    Praise for David 362

Armageddon 1079

Armies · See War & Military Matters

Art, Sculpture & Literature
    The Ark of the Covenant 238, 581
    The Bible & Literature 85
    The Code of the Warrior 257
    "Death, Be Not Proud" 933
    Fantasy & the Young Adult 88
    The Followers of Bacchus 52
    Greco-Roman Public Buildings 42
    "His face was radiant…" 165
    Iconoclasm 389
    Idol Making 561
    Ivory 318
    Jeremiah versus Hananiah 596
    Jesus & the Safe People 782
    Literature & Its Influence 91
    Personal Reactions to Literature 89
    Poetry as Prophecy 369
    The Potter & the Clay 588
    Psalm 23 in History 458
    Rhodes 880
    Sin Depicted in Literature 86
    The Sling 282
    The Temple's Furnishings 374
    Trade in Cedars 314
    The Wings of God 268

Asceticism
    Fasting 214
    John the Baptist 742
    Nazirites 273

Assyria · See also Pagan Deities; Sennacherib
    Alliances 334
    Assyrian Empire in the 8th-Century BCE 668
    Assyrian Propaganda 541
    The Babylonian Empire 704
    Ben-Hadad III 338
    Critical Issues in Isaiah 36–39 556
    The Destruction of Israel 341
    Ezekiel's Life & Times 622
    The Fall of Ninevah 700
    God & His Sanctuary 208
    The Iran Stele 341
    Israel & Egypt in Isaiah's Day 553
    Jonah & Assyria 691
    Kings of Aram & Damascus 339
    "Kiss the Son…" 449
    Map of Babylon & Susa 654
    Map of the Assyrian Empire, 9th–8th Centuries BCE 538
    Map of the Babylonian Empire 704
    Map of the Nations of the Ancient Near East 640
    Map of the Persian Empire 396
    Nahum & the Assyrian Empire 699
    Non-Israelite Ancient Near-Eastern Prophets 66
    Omri 322
    Parallels in Isaiah 558

TOPICAL INDEX

Prophets & Foreigners 67
Pul or Tiglath-pileser 358
Queen Mothers 658
Sennacherib & Hezekiah 696
Sennacherib's Invasion 557
Shackling of Prisoners 627
Shalmaneser & Ahab 326
The Sling 282

Athanasius of Alexandria 25

Atheism & Unbelief
Christ, the Cornerstone 1035
Epicurus' Four-Fold Way 47
The Evangelistic Role of Slaves 1004
"The fool says in his heart..." 454

Atonement & Reconciliation
Ambassadors of Christ 942
Atonement Sacrifice & Grace 171
The Census 306
Daniel & Jesus' Apocalyptic Visions 662
The Day of Atonement 178
Fasting 214
Justice & Righteousness 682
Paul's View of Salvation 900
Philemon & Grace 1010
The Purpose & Object of Atonement 170
"We will be saved..." 902

Audience · See Textual Sources & Issues

Augustine of Hippo
Augustine's Canon 32

Authorship · See Textual Sources & Issues

B

Baal
Baal & Asherah 219
Baal & Ashtoreth 276
Baal-Zebub 329
Beelzebub 743
Cherem Warfare 162
Clouds in Biblical Symbolism 189
Cultic Sites 337
Early Ecstatic Prophets 284
God of the Rains 473
Hadad 321
Non-Israelite Ancient Near-Eastern Prophets 66
Watery Chaos 316

Babylon & Babylonia · *See also Nebuchadnezzar; Pagan Deities; Tammuz*

Additions to Daniel 654
Ancient Piety 38
Athbash 593
The Babylonian Empire 704
Carchemish 611
Critical Issues in Isaiah 36–39 556
Cyrus's Conquest of Babylon 543
The Death of Nabonidus 543
The Death Penalty 225
Divorce Decrees 226
Events in the Book of Daniel 653
Ezekiel's Life & Times 622
The Fall of Ninevah 700
Gemariah Son of Hilkiah 596
The God Tammuz 628
A Hymn to Yahweh 699
Jehoiachin the Captive 590
Lachish Letters 347
Law in the Ancient Near East 159
Life in Babylonia 396
Map of Abram's Migration to Canaan 117
Map of Babylon & Susa 654
Map of Jonah's Travels 690
Map of the Assyrian Empire, 9th–8th Centuries BCE 538
Map of the Babylonian Empire 704
Map of the Nations of the Ancient Near East 640
Map of the Persian Empire 396
Merodach-Baladan 387
Nebuchadnezzar & Jeremiah 607
Parallels in Isaiah 558
The Pentateuch & Ancient Near Eastern Law Codes 3
Poetic Descriptions of Creation 427
Prophets & Foreigners 67
Pul or Tiglath-pileser 358
Punishment by Fire 597
The Punishment of the Gods 556
The Seige & Fall of Jerusalem 638
Seraiah Son of Neriah 615
Shackling of Prisoners 627
The Temple Vessels 595
What Did the Men Pray? 657

Balaam 1043, 1069
Balaam Son of Beor 196
Non-Israelite Ancient Near-Eastern Prophets 66

Baptism · *See also Christian Practices & Customs*
Baptism 975
Baptism Among the Dead Sea Community 734

The Model of Jesus 78
Solomon's Colonnade 859
"With the Holy Spirit & with fire..." 734

Bathsheba
Women in Christ's Genealogy 731

Battles · *See War & Military Matters*

Biblical & Religious Texts
4 Ezra & 2 Baruch 902
Additions to Daniel 654
The Ahiqar Tradition 9
Apocryphal Books in the First Century 968
Athanasius of Alexandria 25
Augustine's Canon 32
Biographies of Jesus 18
The Book of Jashar 292
Books in the Hebrew Bible 185
Clement of Alexandria 27
The Dead Sea Scrolls 31
Early Christian Texts 28
Famous Last Words 247
Intermarriage in Israel 403
Is Song of Songs Scripture? 529
Jerome 29
Jesus' Trial before the Sanhedrin 784
"Know the Lord..." 600
The Law & the Prophets 810
The Masoretic Text 578
"Meditate on God's law..." 238
Mesopotamian Wisdom Literature 9
Mezuzot 216
Midrash 689
The Mishnah 838
The New Testament's Authority 29
An Oral Torah 746
Other Endings for Mark's Gospel 787
Papias on Matthew 17
The Pentateuch & Contemporary Literature 3
The Pharisees 738
The Prayer of Manasseh 388
A Prophet Like Moses 221
Reading the Torah 411
The Samaritan Pentateuch 1
Samson Reinterpreted 261
The Septuagint (LXX) 132, 940, 1014, 1078
Sirach 31
Synoptic Gospels 18
The Talmud 199

1089

TOPICAL INDEX

Tanakh 29
Targum 13
Targums 447
The Torah 456
Torah or Law? 4
Traditional Jewish Commentary 5
The Two Ways 231
Vulgate 125, 791
The War Scroll 187

Blasphemy & False Worship
Baal & Ashtoreth 276
Balaam 1043
Bethel 319
Cherem Warfare 162
Cultic Sites 337
False Gods in Israel after the Exile 568
God's Punishment of Idolatry 384
Hezekiah's Reforms 342
High Places 310
Human Sacrifice 331
"If God did not spare the angels…" 1043
Illicit Worship Practices 545
Sacrifice 247
The Temple Vessels 595

Blessing & Cursing
Babel 81
"Bear good fruit…" 1019
Blessings & Curses of the Mosaic Covenant 625
Cain's Offering 112
The Cross of Christ 952
Cursing the Fig Tree 750
Distinguishing True from False Prophecy 629
Esau's "Service" 127
The Fulfillment of Ezekiel's Promises of Blessing 645
"Gospel" in Galatians 949
Imprecation 491
"The Lord be with all of you…" 987
Oracles of Blessing 645
Peter the Rock 747
The Prayer of Daniel 661
The Twelve Curses 229

Body & Soul 922
"Death, Be Not Proud" 933
Divine Significance of the Body 451
Docetism 828
The Love of Wisdom 512
Philosophy 45
The Sword 1017

"Those who have fallen asleep…" 967

Buildings & Architecture
The Antonia Fortress 881
The Benjamin Gate 605
Building the Temple 368
Building the Wall 409
Capernaum 736
"Contend… in the gate…" 497
Ezekiel's Visionary Temple 649
Greco-Roman Public Buildings 42
Hosting Meals 48
Jeremiah versus Hananiah 596
Jerusalem's Walls 408
Jesus' Tomb 851
Mezuzot 216
Plants & Pillars 502
The Prætorium 849
Praise for David 362
Roofs in Ancient Architecture 332
Solomon's Colonnade 859
Synagogues in the First Century 862
Trade in Cedars 314
Urban Organization & Trade 42

Business · See Commerce & Trade

C

Cæsarea Maritima
Herod the Great 733

Caiaphas 754, 843
High Priests 848

Cain
Cain's Offering 112

Canaan
Amarna Letters 60
The Anakites 214
Baal & Asherah 219
Baal & Ashtoreth 276
Dagon 262, 288
Elaborate Worship 364
Forced Labor 317
Map of Abram's Migration to Canaan 117
The Philistines 275
Poetic Descriptions of Creation 427
The Rivers of Eden 111

Canon
1 Esdras 354
Additions to Daniel 654
Additions to Esther 417
The Ahiqar Tradition 9

Augustine's Canon 32
Books in the Hebrew Bible 185
The Canon 25
Is Song of Songs Scripture? 529
Luke-Acts or Luke & Acts? 20
The New Testament's Authority 29
Papias on Matthew 17
Paul's Letter Collection 989
The Placement of Chronicles 353
The Prayer of Manasseh 388
Sirach 31
The "Woman of Strength" 508

Celebrations · See Festivals & Holidays

Charity
Christian Charity 1050
"Do to others…" 797
Rich & Poor 1028
Wealth & Stewardship 822

Children · See Family

Christ · See Jesus; See also Messiah

Christian Art · See Art, Sculpture & Literature

Christian Doctrine
Athanasius of Alexandria 25
Clement of Alexandria 27
Ephesians & Christian Moral Instruction 961
"Gospel" in Galatians 949
The New Testament's Authority 29
Patristics 17
The Son of God 762

Christianity & Culture
Christianity & Magic 864
Christians & Cultural Influence 90
Fantasy & the Young Adult 88
Government & Authority 911
Jesus & the Safe People 782
Luke & Magic 890
Meat Offered to Idols 872
Motets 103
Philemon & Slavery 1009
"Render to Cæsar…" 779
Roman Perceptions of Christianity 884
Roman Proconsuls 870
Slaves & Masters 976
Slaves, Masters, & Oppression 1036
The Structure of the Letters to the 7 Churches 1067

Christian Living · See also Charity; Discipleship; Faith; Grace &

TOPICAL INDEX

Forgiveness; Mission & Ministry; Prayer; Teaching
The Bread of Life 801
Caring for the Sick 771
The Christian Difference 1037
Christianity & Magic 864
Covenantal Nomism 955
Dietary Regulations 912
Discipleship 794
Discipleship & Suffering 997
"Do everything they tell you…" 751
"Do to others…" 797
Ephesians & Christian Moral Instruction 961
The Evangelistic Role of Slaves 1004
Fasting 765
The "Good Soil" 768
The Greatest Commandments 1028
Jesus' Discourses 727
Jesus & Divorce 776
The Law & Christian Ethics 955
Love & Forgiveness 1038
A Matter of the Heart 899
Obeying Leaders 1025
Paul on Division & Unity 934
Perfect Love 1052
Philemon & Grace 1010
Religious Complacency 758
Rich & Poor 1028
"Small as a mustard seed…" 810
Spirit & Commandment 1050
"Teach us how to pray…" 739
"Teach us to pray…" 804
Transformation 911
Wealth & Stewardship 822
Welcoming the Disciples 742
"Woe to you…" 751

Christian Practices & Customs · See also Baptism; Church; Deacons; Elders; Lord's Supper; Spiritual Gifts; Worship (Christian)
Augustine's Canon 32
Baptism 975
Baptism Among the Dead Sea Community 734
Brotherly Love 982
Charlemagne & Music 102
Christian Charity 1050
Codex 26
"Come in and eat…" 1071
The Confession of Faith 1060
Early Christian Music 101
Early Christian Worship & Identity 865

Excommunication 921
Fasting 214, 765
Gentiles & Jewish Ritual 950
Isaac Watts & the Wesleys 104
The Lord's Supper 929
Martin Luther & Music 103
"On the first day of the week…" 879
The Passover 155
Sabbath for Christians 414
"Take up your cross…" 80
"With the Holy Spirit & with fire…" 734
Women in Corinth 932

Christian Sects & Denominations
Augustine's Canon 32
Paul on Division & Unity 934

Christian Thought · See also Apocalypse & Eschatology; Resurrection; Theology; Trinity
The Ahiqar Tradition 9
Challenges & Opportunities 96
Christians & Cultural Influence 90
Christology 22
Clement of Alexandria 27
Cosmic Fire 1044
The Dangers of Integration 96
Dispensational Premillennialism 1083
Early Christian Texts 28
Ecclesiastes' Radicalism 523
Faith Versus Science 94
Fantasy & the Young Adult 88
Forms of Marriage 160
Galileo on Science & Faith 93
Genesis 1 & Modern Science 110
Gnosticism 21
Holy War 223
Hugh of St. Victor 31
Interpreting Mark 13 780
Irenæus 27
Isaiah 53 in Early Christian Interpretation 566
Jerome 29
Jesus & Divorce 776
Jesus & the Safe People 782
John's Historical Value 21
Literature & Its Influence 91
Matthew & Anti-Semitism 756
Medieval Chant 102
The Messianic Banquet 740
Miracles 740
The New Jerusalem 1083
The New Testament's Authority 29

New Testament Theological Models 83
An Oral Torah 746
Other Endings for Mark's Gospel 787
Papias 761
Patristics 17
Paul on Division & Unity 934
Peter & the End Times 1039
Peter the Rock 747
Priesthood 174
A Prophet Like Moses 221
Psalms in Early Christianity 475
Sacrifice 172
Satan in Chronicles 367
Sin Depicted in Literature 86
The Son of God 762
"Take up your cross…" 80
Tertullian 27
"Those who have fallen asleep…" 967
The Two Ways 231
Waiting for the New Jerusalem 1084

Church
Athanasius of Alexandria 25
Christ, the Cornerstone 1035
Cities in Early Christianity 41
Euodia & Syntyche 970
The Fullness of Christ 959
House Churches in Early Christianity 1016
Irenæus 27
The Kingdom 81
Leadership Roles in the Pauline Churches 966
"On the first day of the week…" 879
Origen 26
Peter the Rock 747
Tertullian 27
The Witness of the House Church 1005
Women in Corinth 932

Church Fathers · See Athanasius; Augustine; Clement; Ignatius; Irenæus; Jerome; Origen; Papias; Philo; Tertullian

Cities & Peoples · See also Jerusalem; Rome
Ai 241
The Amalekites 281
Amorites 136
The Amorites 205
The Anakites 214

TOPICAL INDEX

Antioch 869
Aram 251
The Arameans 228
Athens 875
The Ban 281
Beersheba 123
Bethel 319, 330
Capernaum 736
Carites 337
Cherethites & Pelethites 311
Cities in Early Christianity 41
Cities of Refuge 246
Corinth 876
Dedan, Tema & Kedar 548
Edom & Israel 226
Ephesus 958
Extents of the Lands 244
Ezion Geber 380
The Fall of Ninevah 700
Gibeon 609
Gilead 680
Gilgal 239
Hazor 243
Heshbon 206, 532
Hospitality 264
Hyksos 146
Jericho 240
Jerusalem 346
Jerusalem & Its Names 294
Jews or Israelites? 399
Joseph & Egyptian History 135
The Kenites 253
Kerethites & Pelethites 300
Kiriath-Jearim 584
Map of Abram's Migration to Canaan 117
Map of a Possible Route of Wilderness Wandering 156
Map of Babylon & Susa 654
Map of Geshur 300
Map of Gezer 312
Map of Israel & Judah 694
Map of Jacob's Travels to Esau 130
Map of Jacob's Travels to Paddan-Aram 128
Map of Jonah's Travels 690
Map of Paul's Journeys Through Anatolia 951
Map of Philistia 286
Map of the 7 Churches of Asia Minor 1068
Map of the Anatolian Provinces of Rome 1069
Map of the Assyrian Empire, 9th–8th Centuries BCE 538
Map of the Assyrian Empire in the 8th-Century BCE 668
Map of the Babylonian Empire 704
Map of the Land of Midian 145
Map of the Nations of Genesis 10 116
Map of the Persian Empire 396
Map of the Twelve Tribes 61, 137, 250
Micah 594
Midian 255
Nazareth & Sepphoris 734
The Philistines 260, 275
Places & Wordplay in Micah 694
Rhodes 880
Symbolic City Names 569
Syrian Antioch 725
Tel Dan 263
Thebes 701
Tirzah 531
Travel in the First Century 44
Tyre & Sidon 797
Ungrateful Nations 631

Clement of Alexandria 27
The Ahiqar Tradition 9
Early Christian Texts 28

Clothing
Ancient Mourning Customs 642
Crucifixion As Shame 785
Fine Linens 546
The Iran Stele 341
Jeremiah's Linen Belt 586
Law & Justice 227
Prophetic Sign Acts 588
Removing Sandals 269
To "Rend Garments" 676

Commerce & Trade
Amos & Foreign Cultures 683
Ancient Coinage 397
Corvée 319
Divorce Decrees 226
The Incense Trade 317
Just Scales 227
Loans in Ancient Times 183
Merchant Ships & Their Cargo 690
Pledging Human Beings 188
Trade in Cedars 314
Urban Organization & Trade 42

Community & Relationship
Amos & Foreign Cultures 683
Ancient Covenants 468
Angels & Mediators 439
"Bless the Lord, O my soul..." 489
"Circumcise your hearts..." 215
Community Rededication 412
The Day of Atonement 178
The Fulfillment of Ezekiel's Promises of Blessing 645
God & People 647
God's Standards of Holiness 179
"He will command his angels..." 483
Individual & Communal 213
Intermarriage in Israel 403
A "Jealous" God 212
Justice & Righteousness 682
"Know the Lord..." 600
Law & Relationship 144
Loans in Ancient Times 183
"Look away from me..." 464
The Message of Isaiah 60–62 569
The Name of Yahweh 217
The People of God 359
The Prophet Appeals to God 571
Prophets & Symbolic Actions 667
Reading the Torah 411
The Remnant 575
Responsibility 435
Ritual Purification 176
Sabbath for Christians 414
Symmetrical Relationships 44
Worship 477

Cornelius
Jesus & the Gentiles 798
Luke's "Special" Conversions 889

Cosmology
The 7 Stars 1068
Cosmology 435
Diagram of Ancient Near-Eastern Models of the Cosmos 109
Ezekiel & Ancient Near Eastern Mythology 633
Faith Versus Science 94
Jude's Imagery 1061
"The sun will be darkened..." 752

Covenant
Ancient Covenants 468
Blessings & Curses of the Mosaic Covenant 625
"Circumcise your hearts..." 215
Covenant 204
Covenantal Nomism 955
Covenants 72
The Deuteronomist 272

TOPICAL INDEX

Dismembering the Concubine 264
The Falls of Israel & Judah 350
The Fulfillment of Ezekiel's Promises of Blessing 645
God's Faithfulness 900
God's Salvation 897
"Gospel" in Galatians 949
Israel's Ancestors 209
Israel's Faithlessness & God's Faithfulness 199
A "Jealous" God 212
A Matter of the Heart 899
Messianic Prophecy 598
The Mosaic Covenant 72
The Name of Yahweh 217
Nazirites 273
The "Recognition Formula" 623
Sacrificing Isaac 124
Theodicy 423
The Torn Curtain 819
Yahweh's Promise 570

Creation & the Material World
Ancient Creation Stories 437
Body & Soul 922
Cosmology 435
Creator & Creation 489
Diagram of Ancient Near-Eastern Models of the Cosmos 109
Docetism 828
Ezekiel & Ancient Near Eastern Mythology 633
Genesis 1 & Modern Science 110
Gnosticism 21
"Gods" or "Rulers"? 471
Humans as Caretakers 69
"O sun, stand still..." 242
Poetic Descriptions of Creation 427
Watery Chaos 316
The World Below & the World Above 1020
Yahweh the Creator 462

Crucifixion
The Centurion's Confession 786
The Cross of Christ 952
Crucifixion As Shame 785
"He saved others..." 755
The Torn Curtain 819

Cush 343, 606
Israel & Egypt in Isaiah's Day 553
Map of the Nations of Genesis 10 116
The Rivers of Eden 111

Cyrus 561
Cyrus's Conquest of Babylon 543
Cyrus the Great 542
The Decree of Cyrus 560
God's Control of History 405, 414
The Punishment of the Gods 556

D

Dagon 262, 288, 708
Daniel
1 Enoch 658
Additions to Daniel 654
Daniel & Jesus' Apocalyptic Visions 662
Daniel & Resurrection 663
Divination & Magic 655
Events in the Book of Daniel 653
The Prayer of Daniel 661

Darius
God's Control of History 405, 414
The Persian Empire 719

Dating & Periodicity
1 Enoch 658
Ai 241
Amorites 136
The Amorites 205
Ancient Coinage 397
Angelology 1074
Antediluvian & Postdiluvian 112
Archaeology & Biblical Events 57
Basic Chronology of Ancient Israel & Its Neighbors 58
Cave Burials 312
Cuneiform 400
The Deuteronomist 272
Early Christian Texts 28
Edom & Israel 226
God's Control of History 405, 414
The Hasmonean Kingdom 31
Hazor 243
Heshbon 206
History & Prophecy 30
Hosea & Tradition 670
Hyksos 146
Ivory 318
Jews or Israelites? 34, 399
Joseph & Egyptian History 135
Judah/Yehud 396
Life in Babylonia 396
"Messiah" in Israel 492
Messianism 392

Monotheism in Egypt 186
Negative Evidence in Archaeology 57
The People of the Land 398
The Placement of Chronicles 353
Poetry as Prophecy 369
The Samaritan Pentateuch 1
Second Temple Period 10
The Second Temple Period 185
The Septuagint (LXX) 132
Sheol 193
Targum 13
Tel Dan 263
Tell 55
Urim & Thummim 234
Yehud 560

David
The Bride Price 283
Building the Temple 368
Cherethites & Pelethites 311
The Code of the Warrior 257
David's Mighty Men 361
The Death of Absalom 302
The Death Penalty 225
Hosea & Tradition 670
Hospitality 264
Jerusalem & Its Names 294
Kerethites & Pelethites 300
Kiriath-Jearim 584
Lord of Hosts 74
Map of Ancient Jerusalem 294
Messianism 392
Messianism in the First Century 731
Perspectives on the Kings 377
The Philistines 275
Poetry as Prophecy 369
Praise for David 362
Primogeniture 357
Psalm 110 in Second-Temple Judaism 780
Royal Inscriptions 307
Satan in Chronicles 367
The Sling 282
The Teraphim 284
The "Wise Woman" 146
Women in Christ's Genealogy 731

Deacons · *See also Church*
Leadership Roles in the Pauline Churches 966
Women as Deacons 993

Death & Burial Practices
Abode of the Dead 287
Burial 385

TOPICAL INDEX

Cave Burials 312
Christians & Death 1038
Death 482
"Death, Be Not Proud" 933
The Death of Absalom 302
The Death Penalty 225
Famous Last Words 247
Honoring the Dead 51
Life after Death 527
Paul's Contemplation of Mortality 967
Sheol 193, 428
"Those who have fallen asleep…" 967
Water Symbolism 146

Demons & Evil Spirits
Abaddon & Apollo 1074
Beelzebub 743, 804
Jacob's Wrestling Partner 131
"Sons of God" 1060
"Stoicheia" 975
The Wicked in Heaven 549

Devil · See Satan; Demons & Evil Spirits

Diagrams & Graphics
Diagram of Ancient Near-Eastern Models of the Cosmos 109
Ezekiel's Visionary Temple 649
Paul's "Already but Not Yet" Eschatology 903
The Prophet as Mediator 583
Table of the Greek Alphabet viii
Table of the Hebrew Alphabet vii
The Tabernacle 163

Diaspora · See Exile

Disciples · See Apostles

Discipleship 794 · See also Christian Living
Discipleship & Suffering 997
Jesus' Family 799
Religious Complacency 758
The Suffering Servant 748

Disease · See Health & Healing

Distance · See Location & Distance

Divided Kingdom · See Israel & Judah

Divination 65
Ancient Divination 39, 595
Divine Approval 326
Lot-Casting 279
Necromancy & Divination 539
The Spirit of the Lord 256
Teraphim 129
The Teraphim 284

Urim & Thummim 234
The Will of the Gods 695

Dreams · See Visions & Dreams

E

Economics · See Money & Economics

Edom 686
Edom & Israel 226
Idumeans 613
Israel & Edom 571
Map of a Possible Route of Wilderness Wandering 156
Map of Israel & Judah 694
Map of the Babylonian Empire 704
Seir 206
Tent Shrines 187

Education · See Teaching & Education

Egypt · See also Pagan Deities
Amarna Letters 60
The Campaign into Judah 320
Carchemish 611
Cush 343, 606
The Elephantine Papyri 402, 610
Events in the Book of Daniel 653
Fine Linens 546
God's Leaders Oppose Injustice 150
Hardening Pharaoh's Heart 150
Hebrews & *Hapiru* 145
Hyksos 146
Israel & Egypt in Isaiah's Day 553
Jeremiah in Egypt 610
Joseph & Egyptian History 135
Map of Abram's Migration to Canaan 117
Map of a Possible Route of Wilderness Wandering 156
Map of Jacob's Travels to Paddan-Aram 128
Map of the Assyrian Empire, 9th-8th Centuries BCE 538
Map of the Land of Midian 145
Map of the Nations of the Ancient Near East 640
Map of the Persian Empire 396
Map of the Twelve Tribes 61, 137
Matthew's Use of Hosea 670
Monotheism in Egypt 186
Moses' Name 147
Origin Stories 138
Pharaoh as Monster 642
A Pharaoh's Heart 152

The Philistines 275
Prophets & Foreigners 67
References to the Exodus 70
The Rivers of Eden 111
Thebes 701
Ungrateful Nations 631

Elders · See also Church
Leadership Roles in the Pauline Churches 966
The Tasks of Shepherds 646

Elijah
Early Ecstatic Prophets 284
Elijah & Enoch 330
John the Baptist 742
Prophet & Messiah 836
Theophany 323

Elisha
Lord of Hosts 74
Roofs in Ancient Architecture 332

Elohim · See God

Emmaus
The Bread of Life 801

Esau
The Amalekites 281
"Esau despised his birthright…" 126
Esau's Immorality 1024
Esau's "Service" 127
Jacob's Wrestling Partner 131
Map of Jacob's Travels to Esau 130

Essenes · See Jewish Sects

Esther
The Law of the Medes & the Persians 659

Eucharist · See Lord's Supper

Euodia & Syntyche 970

Evangelism · See Christian Living

Evil · See Sin; Demons & Evil Spirits

Exile
The Babylonian Empire 704
"Beyond the River" 711
Building the Wall 409
Corrupt Leadership 717
The Destruction of Israel 341
The Deuteronomist 272
The Diaspora 655
The Elephantine Papyri 402, 610
Ezekiel's Life & Times 622
The Falls of Israel & Judah 350
The Fulfillment of Ezekiel's Promises of Blessing 645
God's Control of History 414

TOPICAL INDEX

Intermarriage in Israel 403
Jehoiachin the Captive 590
Jeremiah in Egypt 610
Jews or Israelites? 399
Life in Babylonia 396
The Message of Isaiah 60–62 569
Nahum & the Assyrian Empire 699
The New David 541
"Our land will yield its increase…" 481
The People of the Land 398
The Prayer of Daniel 661
The Remnant 575
Shackling of Prisoners 627
Theodicy 423
Yehud 560

The Exodus
Ai 241
The Amalekites 281
Cherem Warfare 162
The Feast of Tabernacles 838
God's Name 70
Hardening Pharaoh's Heart 150
Holy War 223
Hosea & Tradition 670
Israel's Faithlessness & God's Faithfulness 199
Law in the Ancient Near East 159
Map of a Possible Route of Wilderness Wandering 156
Monotheism in Egypt 186
Moses & Manna 837
The Order of the Plagues 152
The Passover 155
The Passover Meal 844
A Pharaoh's Heart 152
Red Sea or Reed Sea? 155
References to the Exodus 70
The Serpent in the Wilderness 833
Spiritual Food & Drink 925
Taking the Land 242
The Theology of the Exodus 279
Water from the Rock 157
Water Symbolism 146

Ezekiel
Ezekiel & Ancient Near Eastern Mythology 633
Ezekiel's Life & Times 622
Ezekiel's Visionary Temple 649
The Fulfillment of Ezekiel's Promises of Blessing 645
Structure of Ezekiel 623

F

Faith & Faithfulness
"A great cloud of witnesses…" 1023
Individual & Communal 213
Israel's Faithlessness & God's Faithfulness 199
Job's Fortitude 433
"Meditate on God's law…" 238
Other Endings for Mark's Gospel 787
"Small as a mustard seed…" 810

False Teaching
Balaam 1043, 1069
"If God did not spare the angels…" 1043
Jesus & the Pharisees 724

Family
Authoritative Teaching 992
The Bride Price 283
Children & the Israelite Family 273
Disciplining a Child 513
Eliezer 118
Fantasy & the Young Adult 88
God's Standards of Holiness 179
The Hearth 50
Jesus & Divorce 776
Jesus' Family 799
The "Kinsmen Redeemer" & Levirate Marriage 268
Levirate Marriage 133
"Like a weaned child…" 498
Options for Women 322
The Parental Persona 510
Patrilineal & Matrilineal 188
Paul's Family Imagery 921
Phratries 51
The Teraphim 284
Violated Women 299
Women in the Greco-Roman World 45

Featured Discussions
Additions to Daniel 654
Ai 241
Apocalyptic Literature in Ancient Times 1063
The Ark of the Covenant 581
Armageddon 1079
Baal & Ashtoreth 276
The Background of John's "Word" Metaphor 830
Blessings & Curses of the Mosaic Covenant 625
Building the Temple 368
"But the greatest of these is love…" 930
Capernaum 736
Cherem Warfare 162
Children & the Israelite Family 273
Child Sacrifice 584
Cosmology 435
Critical Issues in Isaiah 36–39 556
The Day of Atonement 178
"Death, Be Not Proud" 933
The Deuteronomist 272
Dispensational Premillennialism 1083
Distinguishing True from False Prophecy 629
Distinguishing True from False Prophets 591
The Doctrine of Retribution 428
Early Ecstatic Prophets 284
Ecclesiastes' Radicalism 523
Ephesians & Christian Moral Instruction 961
Events in the Book of Daniel 653
Ezekiel & Ancient Near Eastern Mythology 633
Fantasy & the Young Adult 88
Food Laws 175
Forms of Marriage 160
The Fulfillment of Ezekiel's Promises of Blessing 645
Genesis 1 & Modern Science 110
"Gods" or "Rulers"? 471
Hardening Pharaoh's Heart 150
The Heavenly Council 425
Herod the Great 733
The High Place 278
Interpreting Mark 13 780
Interspersed Thematic Summaries 190
Jericho 240
The Jerusalem Temple 753
Jesus & Divorce 776
Jesus & the Safe People 782
Jesus' Trial before the Sanhedrin 784
Joseph & Egyptian History 135
Justice & Righteousness 682
A King's Harem 293
Known Postexilic High Priests 413
The Language of Poetry 445
Law Codes in the Pentateuch 161
Law in the Ancient Near East 159

TOPICAL INDEX

Laying on of Hands 168
Leadership Roles in the Pauline Churches 966
Lord of Hosts 74
Luke's "Special" Conversions 889
The Messianic Secret 764
Monarchy & Hardships 277
Monotheism in Egypt 186
The Mosaic Covenant 72
Mysteries 52
Nazareth & Sepphoris 734
"O sun, stand still…" 242
Paired Men & Women in Luke 823
Paul & the Law 898
The Pharisees 738
Philemon & Slavery 1009
The Philistines 275
Pledging Human Beings 188
Poetry as Prophecy 369
The Potter & the Clay 588
Priesthood 174
The Prophetic Call 148
The Purpose & Object of Atonement 170
Revelation & the Legend of Nero's Return 1076
Royal Inscriptions 307
Sacrifice 172
Sacrificing Isaac 124
"Sandwiches" in Mark 767
Shalmaneser & Ahab 326
Sheol 428
Sin Depicted in Literature 86
The Structure of Isaiah 551
The Structure of the Letters to the 7 Churches 1067
Syrian Antioch 725
The Teraphim 284
Textual Sources in Romans 895
Theodicy 423
The Theology of the Exodus 279
The Twelve 766
The Twelve Curses 229
Violated Women 299
The Water Tunnel 295
Wise Women 304
Women in Christ's Genealogy 731
Women Unique to Luke's Gospel 822

Festivals & Holidays
Celebrating Purim 421
The Day of Atonement 178
Elijah & Enoch 330
Enthronement Psalms 485
Fasting 214
The Feast of Tabernacles 232, 838
Haman & Mordecai 418
Hanukkah 842
Holidays of the Jewish Year 181
Keeping Passover 386
Law Codes in the Pentateuch 161
Origins of Purim 421
"Our land will yield its increase…" 481
The Passover 155
The Passover Meal 844
Pilgrimage Festivals 816
The Purpose & Object of Atonement 170
The Purpose of Festivals 181
The Theology of the Exodus 279

Food & Drink
Dietary Regulations 912
Fasting 765
Food Laws 175
Hospitality 264
Hosting Meals 48
Kneading Trough 229
The Lord's Supper in Luke 816
Meals 44
Meat Offered to Idols 872
Moses & Manna 837
New Wine & Dregs 708
The Passover 155
Prophetic "Call Narratives" 625
Reflection on the Purity Laws 177
Spiritual Food & Drink 925
The Theology of the Exodus 279
"A young goat in its mother's milk…" 218

Fortune-Telling · See Divination

G

Gamaliel 861
Genealogy
Biblical Genealogies 355
Edom & Israel 226
Israel's Ancestors 209
Lineal & Branched Genealogies 356
Patrilineal & Matrilineal 188
The People of God 359
Phratries 51
Primogeniture 310, 357
The Psalms of Korah 193
Toledoth 107

Genre & Structure
2 Peter & Jude 1041
2 Peter & the Synoptic Gospels 1042
Acrostic Poems 520
Acrostic Psalms 452
Apocalypse in Zechariah 714
Authorship of Colossians 973
Chiasm 459
City Laments 617
The Compilation of Jeremiah 578
Critical Issues in Isaiah 36–39 556
The Doctrine of Retribution 428
Early Christian Music 101
The Elohistic Psalms 465
Ephesians & Colossians 957
Epistolary Dialogue 924
Etiologies 244
Ezekiel & Ancient Near Eastern Mythology 633
Fables 258
Famous Last Words 247
Fantasy & the Young Adult 88
Genres in James 1027
The Hebrew Alphabet 618
Historical Summaries 634
Imprecation 491
Interspersed Thematic Summaries 190
Law Codes in the Pentateuch 161
Law in the Ancient Near East 159
Lineal & Branched Genealogies 356
"The Lord be with all of you…" 987
The Mosaic Covenant 72
The New Testament's Authority 29
Parallels in Isaiah 558
The Pentateuch & Contemporary Literature 3
Performance & the Prophets 67
The Prophetic Call 148
Prophetic "Call Narratives" 625
Psalms of Ascent 495
The "Recognition Formula" 623
Royal Psalms 455
Sign Stories in John 79
The Song of the Sea 156
The Structure of Acts 3:1–8:3 859
Structure of Ezekiel 623
The Structure of Isaiah 551
The Structure of Psalms 13
The Sword Song 635
Synchronisms 331
Synoptic Gospels 18
Teaching Children the Alphabet 551
Theodicy 423

TOPICAL INDEX

Toledoth 107
Typology 599
Warning & Hope 621
War Poems 254

Gentiles & Christianity
The Centurion's Confession 786
Christ's Mission 757
The Cross of Christ 952
God's Activity Among the Gentiles 868
God's Salvation 897
"Go out into all the world…" 725
"Gospel" in Galatians 949
Jesus' Jewish Ministry 724
Jesus & the Gentiles 798
The Messianic Banquet 740
Paul's Rhetorical Care 894
Paul & the Law 898
Theophilus 21
Tyre & Sidon 797

Gentiles & Judaism
Ancient Creation Stories 437
Food Laws 175
Gentiles & Jewish Ritual 950
Gentiles & the Torah 953
Jewish Missionaries 772
Paul & the Law 898
Samson Reinterpreted 261
Syrian Antioch 725

Geography & Environment
Armageddon 1079
"Because you are lukewarm…" 1071
Boundary Markers 518
Gods & Mountains 324
Heshbon 206
The Incense Trade 317
Jeremiah's Linen Belt 586
Judah/Yehud 396
The Kebar River 623
The Levant 313
Locust Swarms 675
Map of Abram's Migration to Canaan 117
Map of Ancient Jerusalem 294
Map of a Possible Route of Wilderness Wandering 156
Map of Babylon & Susa 654
Map of Geshur 300
Map of Gezer 312
Map of Israel & Judah 694
Map of Jacob's Travels to Esau 130
Map of Jacob's Travels to Paddan-Aram 128
Map of Jonah's Travels 690
Map of Paul's Journeys Through Anatolia 951
Map of Paul's Missionary Journeys 938
Map of Philistia 286
Map of the 7 Churches of Asia Minor 1068
Map of the Anatolian Provinces of Rome 1069
Map of the Assyrian Empire, 9th–8th Centuries BCE 538
Map of the Assyrian Empire in the 8th-Century BCE 668
Map of the Babylonian Empire 704
Map of the Land of Midian 145
Map of the Nations of Genesis 10 116
Map of the Nations of the Ancient Near East 640
Map of the Persian Empire 396
Map of the Twelve Tribes 61, 137, 250
Mount Hermon 589
The Nations Who Trade with Tyre 641
"Near East" & "Middle East" 33
The Negev 687
Ophir 467
Personified Places 585
Red Sea or Reed Sea? 155
The Rivers of Eden 111
Seir 206
Symbolic City Names 569
Trade in Cedars 314
The Waters of Mount Hermon 466
The Water Tunnel 295

God
Ancient Near-Eastern Flood Stories 114
Apocalyptic Vision 715
The Army of the Lord 240
Atonement Sacrifice & Grace 171
The Audience of Isaiah 565
Blessings & Curses of the Mosaic Covenant 625
Building the Wall 409
Cherem Warfare 162
Clouds in Biblical Symbolism 189
Covenant 204
Creator & Creation 489
The Day of the Lord 535
Divine Council 113
The Divine Spirit 677
The Divine Warrior 207
Enthronement Psalms 485
Eschatology in Zechariah 713
False Gods in Israel after the Exile 568
The Glory of the Lord 624
God Almighty 1067
God Changes His Mind 71
God & Deception 379
God & His Sanctuary 208
God & History 479
God & King 476
God & People 647
God's Control of History 405, 414
God's Election 907
God's Emotions 582
God's Leaders Oppose Injustice 150
Gods & Mountains 324
God's Name 70
God's Standards of Holiness 179
God & the Gods 643
God & Trials 470
Hardening Pharaoh's Heart 150
How Deuteronomy Makes Arguments 204
A Hymn to Yahweh 699
"In later days…" 613
Jacob's Wrestling Partner 131
A "Jealous" God 212
Job & Psalm 8 430
Justice & Righteousness 682
The Kingdom 81
The Kingdom of God 656
Knowing God 585
The Leviathan 550
Lord of Hosts 74
Monotheism or Monolatry 210
The Name of Yahweh 217
Origin Stories 138
Paul's View of Salvation 900
Poetic Descriptions of Creation 427
"Praise the Lord…" 503
The Prophet Appeals to God 571
The Prophetic Call 148
Prophetic Intercession 683
Prophets & Symbolic Actions 667
The Purpose of Festivals 181
The "Recognition Formula" 623
Sacrificing Isaac 124
The "Shadow" of the Canaanites 192
The Spirit of God 108
The Spirit of the Lord 256

TOPICAL INDEX

Tetragrammaton 149
Theodicy 423
Theophany 323, 536
There is No God but Yahweh 559
"There is none beside me..." 708
The Wings of God 268
Yahweh as Water 580
"Yahweh is not with you..." 382
Yahweh's Power 485
Yahweh's Promise 570
Yahweh's Protection of the Weak 453
Yahweh's Servant 686
Yahweh's Supremacy 486
Yahweh the Creator 462

Gods & Goddesses · *See Pagan Deities*

Gospels · *See Biblical & Religious Texts; See also Canon*

Government & Politics
The Census 306
Cyrus 561
Dishonest Scales 697
Emperor Worship 53
Gedaliah's Seal 608
God & Deception 379
The "Good Leader" 554
Government & Authority 911
Greco-Roman Aristocracy 43
The Innocence of Paul & Silas 874
Israel & Egypt in Isaiah's Day 553
A King's Harem 293
The Mosaic Covenant 72
Paul's Political Prophecy 986
The Pharisees 738
Queen Mother 466
"Render to Cæsar..." 779
The Royal Cupbearer 408
The Royal Steward 548
Slaves 42
Taxation in Rome 43
Tetrarch 745
Who Were the Judges? 249

Grace & Forgiveness
The Adulterous Woman 838
Atonement Sacrifice & Grace 171
"Forgiving God... punished their misdeeds..." 487
The Fulfillment of Ezekiel's Promises of Blessing 645
Jonah & Assyria 691
Justice & Righteousness 682
Love & Forgiveness 1038
Perfect Love 1052

The Prayer of Daniel 661
The Prayer of Manasseh 345
Priesthood 174
The Purpose & Object of Atonement 170
Rebellion & Grace 490

Greco-Roman Culture
The 7 Stars 1068
Adoption 906
"The aroma of Christ..." 940
The Author of Salvation 1015
"Barbarians" & "Scythians" 976
Body & Soul 922
Codex 26
Cynics 46
Early Schools of Philosophy 945
Education 45
Emperor Worship 53
Ephesians & Christian Moral Instruction 961
Epicurus' Four-Fold Way 47
Epicurus & Pleasure 47
"Equestrian" 43
The Followers of Bacchus 52
Gods in Pantheism 47
Government & Authority 911
Greco-Roman Aristocracy 43
Greco-Roman Polytheism 48
Greco-Roman Priesthood 48
Greco-Roman Public Buildings 42
Healing with Saliva 773
The Hearth 50
The Herodians 751
Herod the Great 733
Hosting Meals 48
Human Sacrifice in Pagan Worship 671
"I have run the race..." 908
Luke's Portrayal of Jesus 793
Meals 44
Mithras 53
Mysteries 52
"Mysteries" in Greco-Roman Religion 986
Nazareth & Sepphoris 734
Paul as Flatterer 939
Paul's Contemplation of Mortality 967
Paying Teachers 1043
Philo of Alexandria 30
Philosophy 45
Phratries 51
Pleasure in Ecclesiastes & Epicureanism 525

"Put this money to work..." 813
Roman Citizenship 882
Roman Courts 885
A Roman Legion 800
Roman Patronage 982
Roman Perceptions of Christianity 884
Roman Proconsuls 870
Sacrifice & Society 50
Slaves 42
Stoics 46
The Story of Philemon & Baucis 871
Symmetrical Relationships 44
Syrian Antioch 725
Textual Sources in Romans 895
The Transfiguration 801
Travel in the First Century 44
Urban Organization & Trade 42
The White Stone 1070
The Widow's Mite 815
Women in the Greco-Roman World 45
The World Below & the World Above 1020

Greece
Ancient Coinage 397
Chariots 245
Events in the Book of Daniel 653
Greco-Roman Polytheism 48
Map of the Persian Empire 396
Phratries 51
"Put this money to work..." 813
Sacrifice & Society 50
Table of the Greek Alphabet viii
The Ten Kings 660

Greek Culture · *See Greco-Roman Culture*

H

Hagar
Sarai & Hagar 119

Health & Healing
Food Laws 175
The Great Physician 741
Healing with Saliva 773
Leprosy 333
Medicine & God 378
Ritual Purification 176

Heaven & Hell
Abode of the Dead 287
Angelology 1074
Angels & Mediators 439

TOPICAL INDEX

Apocalyptic Literature in Ancient Times 1063
Cherubim 1072
Divine Council 113
God & the Gods 643
The Heavenly Book 803
The New Jerusalem 1083
The Pentateuch & Contemporary Literature 3
Sheol 428
The Sword 1017
The Wicked in Heaven 549
"Woe to you…" 751
The World Below & the World Above 1020

Hebrews · *See Israel & Judah*

Hell · *See Heaven & Hell*

Hellenism · *See Greco-Roman Culture*

Heresy
Athanasius of Alexandria 25
Docetism 828, 1047
Gnosticism 21, 993
Irenæus 27
The Structure of the Letters to the 7 Churches 1067

Herod Agrippa 869

Herod Antipas
The Herodians 751
The Messianic Secret 764
Nazareth & Sepphoris 734
Tetrarch 745

Herod the Great
The Antonia Fortress 881
Edom & Israel 226
The Herodians 751
Herod the Great 733
Idumeans 613
Jerusalem's Walls 408
The Jerusalem Temple 753
Nazareth & Sepphoris 734
Solomon's Colonnade 859

Hezekiah
Assyrian Propaganda 541
Cush & Tirhakah 709
Hezekiah's Reforms 342
Jerusalem 346
Keeping Passover 386
The New David 541
Perspectives on the Kings 377
Reuniting Israel & Judah 648
Seeking Yahweh 392
The Siloam Tunnel 344
The Structure of Isaiah 551
The Water Tunnel 295
Who is Immanuel? 537

Hillel
Life in Babylonia 396
An Oral Torah 746

Holiness & Righteousness
"Because of the angels…" 928
Biblical Holiness 158
Cherem Warfare 162
Cherubim 628
The Doctrine of Retribution 428
The "Fear of the Lord" 509
Food Laws 175
God & King 476
God's Standards of Holiness 179
Job's Integrity 429
Law & Relationship 144
Medicine & God 378
The Purpose & Object of Atonement 170
The Reformation of Israel 414
Sacrifice 172
Syncretism 398
Wisdom & Righteousness 514
Yahweh's Requirements for the Righteous 554

Holy Spirit · *See Spirit*

Hosea
Hosea & Tradition 670
Matthew's Use of Hosea 670
Prophets & Symbolic Actions 667
"Prostitution" in Canaanite Religion 667
References to the Exodus 70
The "Sin Offering" 669

Hospitality
Hospitality 264
Hosting Meals 48
John's Other Letters 1057
Meals 44
The Story of Philemon & Baucis 871
Symmetrical Relationships 44
Synagogues in the First Century 862

Huldah
Finding the Book of the Law 389
Jerusalem 346

Humanity & Personhood
According to the Flesh 896
The Bible & Literature 85
Biblical Holiness 158
Body & Soul 922
The Doctrine of Retribution 428
Faith Versus Science 94
The "Fear of the Lord" 509
Hardening Pharaoh's Heart 150
"He is my fortress…" 472
"He will command his angels…" 483
Humans as Caretakers 69
Individual & Communal 213
New Testament Theological Models 83
Personal Reactions to Literature 89
Reflection on the Purity Laws 177
Responsibility 435
The "Sin Offering" 669
The "Son of Man" 452
Stoics 46
Universalism in Isaiah 573

I

Idols & Idolatry · *See Worship (Pagan)*

Ignatius
Early Christian Texts 28
Paul's Letter Collection 989

Immorality · *See Morals & Morality*

Incarnation
The Nature of God 968

Integrity · *See Holiness & Righteousness*

Interpretation & Hermeneutics
Abode of the Dead 287
According to the Flesh 896
"A little lower than the angels…" 1015
Angels & Mediators 439
Athbash 593
The Bible & Literature 85
Cain's Offering 112
Cherem Warfare 162
Clouds in Biblical Symbolism 189
"Contend…in the gate…" 497
Corrupt Leadership 717
Critical Issues in Isaiah 36–39 556
The Dangers of Integration 96
Divine Significance of the Body 451
Enemies 450
"Esau despised his birthright…" 126
Faith Versus Science 94
Fantasy & the Young Adult 88
The "Fear of the Lord" 509
"Forgiving God…punished their misdeeds…" 487
The Fullness of Christ 959

TOPICAL INDEX

The Functions of Proverbs 507
Genesis 1 & Modern Science 110
God & Deception 379
"Gods" or "Rulers"? 471
Haman & Mordecai 418
Hardening Pharaoh's Heart 150
The Heavenly Council 425
"He will command his angels…" 483
"His face was radiant…" 165
"I know that my redeemer lives…" 434
Inclusio 197
Interpreting Mark 13 780
Ishmael and Isaac 123
Ishmael the "Wild Donkey" 119
Jacob's Wrestling Partner 131
Jesus' Discourse on the Pharisees 729
Jesus & Divorce 776
Jesus & the Safe People 782
Juxtaposition & Context in Proverbs 507
The Language of Poetry 445
Literature & Its Influence 91
Lot's Daughters 122
Love & Forgiveness 1038
Lover & Beloved 530
Mabbul 461
Messianic Prophecy 598
The Messianic Secret 764
Midrash 689
The Misuse of Proverbs 519
The Order of the Plagues 152
"O sun, stand still…" 242
Other Endings for Mark's Gospel 787
The "Path of Life" 455
The People of the Land 398
Personal Reactions to Literature 89
Poverty & Wickedness 515
Pressing the Mouth 520
Rabbinic Interpretation 198
"Record of his reign…" 419
Retribution 376
"Rubies" 521
The "Safe Way" 403
Samson Reinterpreted 261
Sarai & Hagar 119
Selah 474
The "Servant" Israel 563
The "Shadow" of the Canaanites 192
"She laughs at horse and rider…" 441
Sheol 428
The "Son of Man" 452
The Spirit of God 108
The Talmud 199
Targums 447
The Ten Commandments 159
The "Ten Righteous" 121
The Theology of History 375
"They shall be caught up…" 982
Traditional Jewish Commentary 5
The Two Ways 231
Water from the Rock 157
Who is Immanuel? 537
"A young goat in its mother's milk…" 218

Irenæus 27

Isaac
Beersheba 123
Christ's Mission 757
Esau's "Service" 127
God's Name 70
Human Sacrifice 260
Ishmael and Isaac 123
Israel's Ancestors 209
Primogeniture 357
Sacrificing Isaac 124
Wells in Ancient Times 147

Isaiah
Dialogue with the Prophet 568
The Message of Isaiah 60–62 569
The Prophet Appeals to God 571
Theophany 536
There is No God but Yahweh 559
Yahweh's Promise 570

Ishmael
Ishmael and Isaac 123
Ishmael the "Wild Donkey" 119

Israel & Judah
Alternative Sanctuaries 681
The Amalekites 281
The Babylonian Empire 704
The Ban 281
Basic Chronology of Ancient Israel & Its Neighbors 58
"Beyond the River" 711
The Campaign into Judah 320
Canaan & Israel 468
Carites 337
The Census 306
Cherem Warfare 162
Covenant 204
David's Mighty Men 361
The Destruction of Israel 341
The Deuteronomist 272
The Divine Spirit 677
Edom & Israel 226
Eschatology in Zechariah 713
Extents of the Lands 244
The Falls of Israel & Judah 350
Forced Labor 317
The Four Oracles 635
Gilead 680
Gilgal 239
"Give careful thought…" 712
God's Salvation 897
Hanukkah 842
The Hasmonean Kingdom 31
Hebrews & *Hapiru* 145
History & Prophecy 30
Hosea & Tradition 670
Humor in the Story of Ehud 253
Israel & Edom 571
Israel & Egypt in Isaiah's Day 553
Israel's Ancestors 209
Israel's Faithlessness & God's Faithfulness 199
Israel & the Nations 639
Jehoiachin the Captive 590
Jehoiakim 703
Jeremiah in Egypt 610
Jews or Israelites? 34, 399
Judah & Taxation 313
Judah/Yehud 396
Justice & Righteousness 682
The Kenites 253
Lachish Letters 347
The Land 211
The Last Kings of Judah 590
Map of Gezer 312
Map of Israel & Judah 694
Map of Philistia 286
Map of the Assyrian Empire, 9th–8th Centuries BCE 538
Map of the Nations of the Ancient Near East 640
Map of the Persian Empire 396
Map of the Twelve Tribes 61, 137, 250
Merodach-Baladan 387
The Mesha Stele 331
The Names of Leah's Sons 129
Omri 322
The People of God 909
The People of the Land 398
Perspectives on the Kings 377
The Philistines 260, 275
Queen Athaliah 381

1100

TOPICAL INDEX

The Recabites 603
The Reformation of Israel 414
The Remnant 575
Reuniting Israel & Judah 648
The Samaritan Pentateuch 1
Second Temple Period 10
Shalmaneser & Ahab 326
The "Sin Offering" 669
The Sins of Manasseh 347
Table of the Hebrew Alphabet vii
Taking the Land 242
Tel Dan 263
Tel Dan Inscription 324
The Tel Dan Inscription 336
"There is none beside me…" 708
"Yahweh is not with you…" 382
Yehud 560
Yehud in the Persian Empire 713

J

Jacob
Bethel 319
Esau's "Service" 127
God's Name 70
Israel's Ancestors 209
Jacob's Wrestling Partner 131
Map of Jacob's Travels to Esau 130
Map of Jacob's Travels to Paddan-Aram 128
The Names of Leah's Sons 129
Primogeniture 357
The Purpose & Object of Atonement 170
Wells in Ancient Times 147

Jairus
"Sandwiches" in Mark 767

James (apostle)
The Twelve 766

James (brother of Jesus)
James' Rhetoric 1029
The Greatest Commandments 1028

Jannes & Jambres 999

Jehoiakim 703

Jeremiah
Distinguishing True from False Prophets 591
Gemariah Son of Hilkiah 596
"In later days…" 613
Jeremiah in Egypt 610
Jeremiah's Second Scroll 605
Jeremiah versus Hananiah 596
Know the Lord…" 600
The Lord Rebukes Jeremiah 587
Nebuchadnezzar & Jeremiah 607
References to the Exodus 70

Jerome 29
Vulgate 125, 791

Jerusalem 346
Baptism Among the Dead Sea Community 734
The Benjamin Gate 605
Cultic Sites 337
Daniel & Jesus' Apocalyptic Visions 662
The Diaspora 655
Edom & Israel 226
Events in the Book of Daniel 653
Ezekiel's Life & Times 622
Feminine Imagery for Jerusalem 696
God & His Sanctuary 208
Jerusalem & Its Names 294
Jerusalem's Walls 408
Judah/Yehud 396
Map of Ancient Jerusalem 294
The Needle's Eye 749
Pilgrimage Festivals 816
The Prætorium 849
The Remnant 575
Sacrifice 247
The Seige & Fall of Jerusalem 638
Sennacherib & Hezekiah 696
The Siloam Tunnel 344
The Water Tunnel 295
Yehud in the Persian Empire 713

Jesus
The Adulterous Woman 838
"A little lower than the angels…" 1015
Apocalyptic Vision 715
The Author of Salvation 1015
Biographies of Jesus 18
The Bread of Life 801
The Centurion's Confession 786
Christology 22
Christ's Mission 757
Christ, the Cornerstone 1035
Christ & the Samaritan Woman 834
Cities in Early Christianity 41
Crucifixion As Shame 785
Cursing the Fig Tree 750
Daniel & Jesus' Apocalyptic Visions 662
The Day of Atonement 178
Den of Robbers 583
"Do everything they tell you…" 751
"Do to others…" 797
The Great Physician 741
Healing with Saliva 773
Herod the Great 733
"He saved others…" 755
A Hymn to Christ 968
Interpreting Mark 13 780
Isaiah 53 in Early Christian Interpretation 566
Jesus as Messiah 741
Jesus' Authority 795
Jesus' Discourse on the Pharisees 729
Jesus' Discourses 727
Jesus' Family 799
Jesus' Jewish Ministry 724
Jesus' Lordship 797
Jesus' Origins 80
Jesus' Parables 744
Jesus & Satan 804
Jesus' Sufferings 1018
Jesus & the Gentiles 798
Jesus & the Pharisees 724
Jesus & the Safe People 782
Jesus' Tomb 851
Jesus' Trial before the Sanhedrin 784
John's Historical Value 21
John the Baptist 742
The Lamb 1072
Lex Talionis 182
The Lord's Supper in Luke 816
Luke's Portrayal of Jesus 793
"*Martyrion Christou*" 918
Matthew's Use of Hosea 670
Matthew's Use of Zechariah 717
The Messianic Secret 19, 764
Messianism in the First Century 731
Nazareth & Sepphoris 734
The Needle's Eye 749
The "New Moses" 727
New Wineskins 726
The Pattern of Christ 913
Priesthood 174
Prophet & Messiah 836
Psalm 110 in Second Temple Judaism 780
Psalms in Early Christianity 475
Religious Complacency 758
The Sacrificial Lamb 1035
"Sandwiches" in Mark 767

1101

TOPICAL INDEX

The Serpent in the Wilderness 833
Signs & Jesus' Identity 832
Sign Stories in John 79
Signs & Wonders in John's Gospel 834
The Son of God 762
The Son of Man 728, 811
Spiritual Food & Drink 925
The Suffering Servant 748
Syrian Antioch 725
"Teach us how to pray…" 739
"Teach us to pray…" 804
The Transfiguration 801
The Triumphal Entry 778
Water from the Rock 157
Who is Immanuel? 537
"Woe to you…" 751
Women in Christ's Genealogy 731
Women Who Followed Jesus 799

Jewish Practices & Customs · See also Passover; Priests & Priesthood; Sabbath; Sacrifice; Worship (Jewish)
Baptism Among the Dead Sea Community 734
Burial 385
Caring for the Sick 771
Cave Burials 312
Celebrating Purim 421
The Census 306
Children & the Israelite Family 273
Chronicles & Psalms 364
"Circumcise your hearts…" 215
Cities of Refuge 246
Community Rededication 412
The Day of Atonement 178
Diagram of the Tabernacle 163
Dietary Regulations 912
Elaborate Worship 364
Elijah & Enoch 330
Enthronement Psalms 485
Entrance Liturgy 459
Fasting 214
The Feast of Tabernacles 232, 838
Finding the Book of the Law 389
Food Laws 175
Forms of Marriage 160
Gender in Leviticus 170
Haman & Mordecai 418
Hanukkah 842
High Priests 848
Holidays of the Jewish Year 181
Hospitality 264
Instrumental Music in Jewish Tradition 100
Intermarriage in Israel 403
Interspersed Thematic Summaries 190
The Jerusalem Temple 753
Jesus' Trial before the Sanhedrin 784
Jewish Missionaries 772
Keeping Passover 386
The "Kinsmen Redeemer" & Levirate Marriage 268
Law Codes in the Pentateuch 161
The Law & the Prophets 810
Laying on of Hands 168
Levirate Marriage 133
Lot-Casting 279
Mezuzot 216
Nazirites 273
Origins of Purim 421
The Passover 155
The Passover Meal 844
Pilgrimage Festivals 816
Primogeniture 357
The Purpose & Object of Atonement 170
The Purpose of Festivals 181
Reading the Torah 411
Reflection on the Purity Laws 177
Removing Sandals 269
Ritual Purification 176
Rules of Warfare 73
Sabbath for Christians 414
Sacrifice 172, 247
The "Safe Way" 403
The Samaritan Pentateuch 1
The Sanhedrin 779, 843, 860
Sheol 428
Solomon's Colonnade 859
Stone Water Pots 831
Synagogues in the First Century 862
Taking the Land 242
Teraphim 129
Thank Offerings 494
The Theology of the Exodus 279
Urim & Thummim 234

Jewish Sects
4 Ezra & 2 Baruch 902
Angels in First-Century Thought 1014
Baptism Among the Dead Sea Community 734
"Do everything they tell you…" 751
The Great Physician 741
The Herodians 751
Jesus as Messiah 741
Jesus' Discourse on the Pharisees 729
Jesus' Discourses 727
Jesus & the Pharisees 724
Jews & Samaritans 833
Messianism in the First Century 731
The Pharisees 738
Pharisees & Sadducees 883
Psalm 110 in Second Temple Judaism 780
Religious Complacency 758
Sadducees 814
"Woe to you…" 751

Jewish Thought · See also Apocalypse & Eschatology; Messiah; Resurrection & Afterlife; Theology
An Oral Torah 746
The Author of Chronicles 386
Biblical Holiness 158
The Dead 432
The Deuteronomist 272
The Diaspora 655
Divine Significance of the Body 451
God & His Sanctuary 208
Holy War 187, 223
Humans as Caretakers 69
Iconoclasm 389
Interspersed Thematic Summaries 190
Is Song of Songs Scripture? 529
The Jerusalem Temple 753
John's Historical Value 21
Keeping Passover 386
The Land 211
Lex Talionis 223
"Messiah" in Israel 492
Messianism 392
The Mishnah 838
Monotheism or Monolatry 210
The Pharisees 738
Pleasure in Ecclesiastes & Epicureanism 525
Poetry as Prophecy 369
Pressing the Mouth 520
A Prophet Like Moses 221
Psalm 110 in Second-Temple Judaism 780
Reflection on the Purity Laws 177
Sadducees 814

TOPICAL INDEX

The Son of God 762
Sources of Proverbs 505
The Structure of Psalms 13
The Theology of History 375
Torah or Law? 4
Traditional Jewish Commentary 5
The Two Ways 231
Universalism in Isaiah 573

Jews · *See Israel & Judah*

Job 1031
Dishonest Scales 438
Job & Darkness 440
Job & Psalm 8 430
Job's Fortitude 433
Job's Integrity 429
Job & Worship 426

John (apostle)
John's Historical Value 21
John's Other Letters 1057
"Signs" in John's Gospel 827
The Twelve 766

John the Baptist 742, 830
Luke's "Special" Conversions 889
Preparing the Way 78
"Sandwiches" in Mark 767
"With the Holy Spirit & with fire…" 734

Jonah
Jonah & Assyria 691
Jonah's Prayer 691
Jonah's Travels 690

Joseph
Finishing the Story 248
Joseph & Egyptian History 135

Josephus
The Ark of the Covenant 581
Caiaphas 754
Desecration of the Temple 986
History & Prophecy 30
John the Baptist 830
Josephus 29
Luke's Portrayal of Jesus 793
The Pharisees 738

Joshua
Extents of the Lands 244
Jericho 240
The Jerusalem Temple 753
"Meditate on God's law…" 238
Sacrifice 247

Josiah
1 Esdras 354

Finding the Book of the Law 389
Iconoclasm 389
The New David 541
Reuniting Israel & Judah 648
Seeking Yahweh 392

Judah · *See Israel & Judah*

Judas Iscariot
Matthew's Use of Zechariah 717
"Sandwiches" in Mark 767
The Twelve 766

Judas (son of James) · *See Thaddaeus*

Justice · *See Law & Justice*

K

Kings & Kingship 220 · *See also Ahab; David; Hezekiah; Josiah; Solomon*
Ben-Hadad III 338
Building the Temple 368
Burial 385
Charlemagne & Music 102
The Coming King 602
Cush & Tirhakah 709
David's Mighty Men 361
The Death of Absalom 302
The Death of Nabonidus 543
Divine Approval 326
Enthronement Psalms 485
Events in the Book of Daniel 653
The Falls of Israel & Judah 350
Finding the Book of the Law 389
God & Deception 379
God & King 476
God's Control of History 405, 414
Hadad 321
Iconoclasm 389
Jehoiachin the Captive 590
Jehoiakim 703
Jehu's Punishment 666
Joseph & Egyptian History 135
The Kingdom 81
The Kingdom of God 656
The Kingly Ideal 365
A King's Harem 293
Kingship & Divinity 313
Kings of Aram & Damascus 339
The Last Kings of Judah 590
Medicine & God 378
The Megiddo Seal 340
Monarchy & Hardships 277
The New David 541
Omri 322

Perspectives on the Kings 377
Praise for David 362
Preparing the Way 78
A Prophet Like Moses 221
Psalm 110 in Second-Temple Judaism 780
Queen Athaliah 381
The Recabites 603
Righteous Kings & Sinful Kings 383
Royal Inscriptions 307
Royal Property 370
Royal Psalms 455
Seeking Yahweh 392
Sennacherib & Hezekiah 696
The Sins of Manasseh 347
The Tel Dan Inscription 336
The Ten Kings 660
The "Wise Woman" 146
Wise Women 304
Women in Christ's Geneaology 731

L

Languages & Translation
"Abba" 953
Abode of the Dead 287
According to the Flesh 896
Additions to Daniel 654
The Ahiqar Tradition 9
Aliens 179
"A little lower than the angels…" 1015
Antediluvian & Postdiluvian 112
Aramaisms 689
Athbash 593
Babel 81
Belial 488
Books in the Hebrew Bible 185
The Centurion's Confession 786
Cuneiform 400
Disciplining a Child 513
"A double portion…" 273
The Elohistic Psalms 465
"Esau despised his birthright…" 126
The Fullness of Christ 959
Gilgal 239
God's Faithfulness 900
Hardening Pharaoh's Heart 150
The Hebrew Alphabet 618
Hebrew & Aramaic 401
Hebrews & *Hapiru* 145
The High Place 278
"His face was radiant…" 165

TOPICAL INDEX

Indicators of Northern Composition 480
Individual & Communal 213
"In later days..." 613
Ishmael and Isaac 123
A "Jealous" God 212
Jerome 29
Jews or Israelites? 399
"Kiss the Son..." 449
The Lamb 1072
The Land 211
Lot's Daughters 122
Love & Forgiveness 1038
Mabbul 461
Martin Luther & Music 103
"Martyrion Christou" 918
Mezuzot 216
Molech 708
Moses' Name 147
The Names of Leah's Sons 129
The Names of Moses' Sons 158
Papias on Matthew 17
Paul's View of Salvation 900
The People of the Land 398
The Philistines 275
Places & Wordplay in Micah 694
"Plastering with lies..." 432
Psalm 115 493
Red Sea or Reed Sea? 155
The "Safe Way" 403
Sarai & Hagar 119
Secret Wisdom 919
The Septuagint (LXX) 132
Shubah & Surah 451
Sirach 31
The Song of the Sea 156
The "Son of Man" 452
The Spirit of God 108
The Spirit & the Word 962
Syriac 25
Table of the Greek Alphabet viii
Table of the Hebrew Alphabet vii
Targum 13
Targums 447
Teaching Children the Alphabet 551
Temple or Tabernacle? 274
Tent of Meeting 173
Tetragrammaton 149
"They shall be caught up..." 982
Vulgate 125
"When you face trials..." 1028
Who Were the Judges? 249
Wisdom 164

Law & Justice
The Adulterous Woman 838
An Appeal to the Emperor 885
Cities of Refuge 246
Covenant 204
Covenantal Nomism 955
Covenants 72
Crucifixion As Shame 785
The Death Penalty 225
Dishonest Scales 438, 697
Divorce Decrees 226
Forms of Marriage 160
God's Leaders Oppose Injustice 150
"Had it not been for the law..." 905
The Injustice of Demetrius' Attack 878
Jesus' Trial before the Sanhedrin 784
Justice 501
Justice & Righteousness 682
Just Scales 227
A King's Harem 293
The Law & Christian Ethics 955
Law Codes in the Pentateuch 161
The Law in Deuteronomy 225
Law in the Ancient Near East 159
Law & Justice 227
The Law of the Medes & the Persians 659
Law & Relationship 144
Legal Imagery in Job 431
Lex Talionis 182, 223, 534, 687
The "New Moses" 727
Paul's View of Salvation 900
Paul & the Law 898
The Pentateuch & Ancient Near Eastern Law Codes 3
The Pharisees 738
Pledging Human Beings 188
The Prayer of Daniel 661
Primogeniture 310, 357
Prosecution of Legal Cases Against Christians 876
Punishments in Leviticus 180
The Purpose of the Law 952
"Render to Cæsar..." 779
Roman Courts 885
Roman Perceptions of Christianity 884
Royal Property 370
Signet Rings 712
The Son of Man 728
The Ten Commandments 159

"Three Witnesses" 1052
Torah or Law? 4
The Twelve Curses 229
Usury 454
Violated Women 299
Why Ten Commandments? 210
"A young goat in its mother's milk..." 218

Leah
The Names of Leah's Sons 129

Levi (apostle) · See Matthew

Levites
The Author of Chronicles 386
Building the Temple 368
Interspersed Thematic Summaries 190
Keeping Passover 386
Pledging Human Beings 188
The Poverty of the Levites 215
Second Temple Worship 363

Literary Techniques · See Rhetorical & Literary Techniques

Liturgy · See Worship (Christian); Worship (Jewish)

Location & Distance
Bethel 330
Dedan, Tema & Kedar 548
Ezion Geber 380
Gibeon 609
Hazor 243
Heshbon 206, 532
Jeremiah's Linen Belt 586
Kiriath-Jearim 584
Midian 255
The Nations Who Trade with Tyre 641
Nazareth & Sepphoris 734
"Near East" & "Middle East" 33
Ophir 467
The Rivers of Eden 111
Syrian Antioch 725
Thebes 701
Tirzah 531
The Valley of Baca 481
Water from the Rock 157

Lord's Supper · See also Christian Practices & Customs
The Bread of Life 801
"Come in and eat..." 1071
The Lord's Supper 929
The Lord's Supper in Luke 816
The Passover 155

TOPICAL INDEX

Lot
    Lot's Daughters 122
    The "Ten Righteous" 121

Luke
    The Lord's Supper in Luke 816
    Luke-Acts or Luke & Acts? 20
    Luke & Magic 890
    Luke's Focus 888
    Luke's Portrayal of Jesus 793
    Luke's "Special" Conversions 889
    Paired Men & Women in Luke 823
    Who Was Theophilus? 790
    Women Unique to Luke's Gospel 822
    Writing Luke 789

M

Maccabees
    Desecration of the Temple 986
    Hanukkah 842
    The Pharisees 738

Magic & Sorcery
    Ancient Divination 39, 595
    Christianity & Magic 864
    Divination & Magic 655
    Enemies 450
    Fantasy & the Young Adult 88
    Jannes & Jambres 999
    Luke & Magic 890
    Necromancy & Divination 539

Maps
    The 7 Churches of Asia Minor 1068
    Abram's Migration to Canaan 117
    The Anatolian Provinces of Rome 1069
    Ancient Jerusalem 294
    The Assyrian Empire, 9th–8th Centuries BCE 538
    Assyrian Empire in the 8th-Century BCE 668
    The Babylonian Empire 704
    Babylon & Susa 654
    Geshur 300
    Gezer 312
    Israel & Judah 694
    Jacob's Travels to Esau 130
    Jacob's Travels to Paddan-Aram 128
    Jonah's Travels 690
    The Land of Midian 145
    Nations of the Ancient Near East 640
    Paul's Journeys Through Anatolia 951
    Paul's Missionary Journeys 938
    Philistia 286
    A Possible Route of Wilderness Wandering 156
    The Nations of Genesis 10 116
    The Persian Empire 396
    The Twelve Tribes 61, 137, 250

Mark
    Daniel & Jesus' Apocalyptic Visions 662
    Interpreting Mark 13 780
    The Messianic Secret 764
    Other Endings for Mark's Gospel 787
    Papias 761
    "Sandwiches" in Mark 767

Marriage & Divorce
    The Bride Price 283
    Children & the Israelite Family 273
    Divorce Decrees 226
    Endogamous Marriage 197
    Ephesians & Christian Moral Instruction 961
    Forms of Marriage 160
    Gender in Leviticus 170
    God's Standards of Holiness 179
    A Husband's Wrath 632
    Jesus & Divorce 776
    A King's Harem 293
    The "Kinsmen Redeemer" & Levirate Marriage 268
    Levirate Marriage 133
    Removing Sandals 269
    The Suffering Female in Lamentations & the Prophets 618
    Violated Women 299
    Women in the Greco-Roman World 45

Mary (Mother of Jesus)
    Medieval Chant 102
    Sign Stories in John 79

Matthew
    "Go out into all the world..." 725
    Jesus' Discourses 727
    Matthew & Anti-Semitism 756
    Matthew's Use of Hosea 670
    Matthew's Use of Zechariah 717
    The Son of Man 728
    Time in Matthew 729
    The Twelve 766
    Women in Christ's Geneaology 731

Melchizedek 1019
    Jerusalem & Its Names 294
    Psalm 110 in Second-Temple Judaism 780

Messiah
    Christ & the Samaritan Woman 834
    The Coming King 602
    Elijah & Enoch 330
    Isaiah 53 in Early Christian Interpretation 566
    Jesus as Messiah 741
    Jesus' Lordship 797
    John the Baptist 742
    "Messiah" in Israel 492
    The Messianic Banquet 740
    Messianic Prophecy 598
    The Messianic Secret 19, 764
    Messianism 392
    Messianism in the First Century 731
    The "New Moses" 727
    New Wineskins 726
    A Prophet Like Moses 221
    Prophet & Messiah 836
    Psalm 110 in Second-Temple Judaism 780
    Signs & Jesus' Identity 832
    The Son of God 762
    The Suffering Servant 748
    The Son of Man 728
    Women in Christ's Genealogy 731

Micah 594

Midian
    Map of a Possible Route of Wilderness Wandering 156
    Map of the Land of Midian 145
    Midian 255

Midrash · *See Interpretation & Hermeneutics*

Miracles
    Caring for the Sick 771
    Healing with Saliva 773
    Jesus as Messiah 741
    Miracles 740
    "Signs" in John's Gospel 827
    Signs & Jesus' Identity 832
    Sign Stories in John 79
    Signs & Wonders in John's Gospel 834

Mishna · *See Biblical & Religious Texts*

Mission & Ministry
    The Christian Difference 1037

TOPICAL INDEX

Christ's Mission 757
The Evangelistic Role of Slaves 1004
"Go out into all the world..." 725
Jesus' Jewish Ministry 724
Map of Paul's Journeys Through Anatolia 951
Map of Paul's Missionary Journeys 938
The Model of Jesus 78
The Potter & the Clay 588
Time in Matthew 729
Universalism in Isaiah 573

Moab
The Ban 281
Gilead 680
Humor in the Story of Ehud 253
Map of a Possible Route of Wilderness Wandering 156
Map of Israel & Judah 694
Map of Philistia 286
The Mesha Inscription 612
Moab 544

Molech · See Pagan Deities

Money & Economics
The 7 Stars 1068
Aliens 179
Ancient Coinage 397
The Bride Price 283
Corvée 319
Denarius 42
Dishonest Scales 697
Gender in Leviticus 170
The Importance of Provinces 43
Ivory 318
Judah & Taxation 313
Just Scales 227
Loans in Ancient Times 183
Paying Teachers 1043
Rich & Poor in Jeremiah 582
Roman Patronage 982
Royal Inscriptions 307
Talent 366
Taxation in Rome 43
Tribute 622
The Widow's Mite 815
Yehud in the Persian Empire 713

Monsters & Mythical Beasts
The Anakites 214
The Earth Beast 1078
The Leviathan 550
Pharaoh as Monster 642
Poetic Descriptions of Creation 427

Morals & Morality
Agricultural Imagery 552
Baptism among the Dead Sea Community 734
Biblical Holiness 158
Distinguishing True from False Prophets 591
Ephesians & Christian Moral Instruction 961
Esau's Immorality 1024
Fables 258
Food Laws 175
Forms of Marriage 160
Genres in James 1027
God's Standards of Holiness 179
The Parental Persona 510
The Pattern of Christ 913
Philosophy 45
Reflection on the Purity Laws 177
Samson Reinterpreted 261
The Talmud 199
The Two Ways 231
Wisdom & Righteousness 514

Moses
"A glory now set aside..." 940
Blessings & Curses of the Mosaic Covenant 625
God Changes His Mind 71
"His face was radiant..." 165
Interspersed Thematic Summaries 190
Monotheism in Egypt 186
Moses & Manna 837
Moses' Name 147
Moses, the Greatest Prophet 191
The Names of Moses' Sons 158
The "New Moses" 727
The Prophetic Call 148
Prophetic Intercession 683
A Prophet Like Moses 221
Prophet & Messiah 836
Theophany 323

Mountains · See Geography & Environment

Mourning & Lament
Ancient Mourning Customs 642
City Laments 617
The God Tammuz 628
Job & Worship 426
John the Baptist 742
To "Rend Garments" 676

Music & Praise
Ancient Musical Notation 38
Charlemagne & Music 102
Chronicles & Psalms 364
Clouds in Biblical Symbolism 189
Early Christian Hymns 974
Early Christian Music 101
Elaborate Worship 364
A Hymn to Christ 968
A Hymn to Yahweh 699
"I know that my redeemer lives..." 434
Instrumental Music in Jewish Tradition 100
Isaac Watts & the Wesleys 104
Liturgical Revival 105
Martin Luther & Music 103
Medieval Chant 102
Motets 103
The Names of Leah's Sons 129
The Potter & the Clay 588
"Praise the Lord..." 503
Psalms of Ascent 495
The Psalms of Korah 193
Second Temple Worship 363
Selah 474
The Song of the Sea 156
The Sword Song 635
What Did the Men Pray? 657

N

Nations · See also Amorites; Babylon & Babylonia; Egypt; Persia; Philistia; Phoenicia; Rome
Alliances 334
The Amorites 205
Ancient Coinage 397
Aram 251
Athbash 593
Cherem Warfare 162
Cush 606
Cush & Tirhakah 709
Edom 686
Edom & Israel 226
God's Blessing to the Nations 547
Humor in the Story of Ehud 253
Israel & the Nations 639
Map of Abram's Migration to Canaan 117
Map of a Possible Route of Wilderness Wandering 156
Map of Gezer 312
Map of Israel & Judah 694
Map of Philistia 286

TOPICAL INDEX

Map of the Assyrian Empire, 9th–8th Centuries BCE 538
Map of the Land of Midian 145
Map of the Nations of Genesis 10 116
Map of the Nations of the Ancient Near East 640
Map of the Persian Empire 396
Map of the Twelve Tribes 61, 137
The Mesha Stele 331
Nations of the Ancient Near East 640
The Nations Who Trade with Tyre 641
Omri 322
The Philistines 275
Prophets & Foreigners 67
The Remnant 575
Tribute 622
Ungrateful Nations 631
War Poems 254

Nature
"Bear good fruit…" 1019
Clouds in Biblical Symbolism 189
Cosmology 435
Cursing the Fig Tree 750
"If the salt loses its saltiness…" 776
Ishmael the "Wild Donkey" 119
Jude's Imagery 1061
The Land & the People Will Be Healed 566
Locust Plagues 154
The Magi 732
"Make the lightning flash…" 502
Medieval Chant 102
Mount Hermon 589
"O sun, stand still…" 242
"Our land will yield its increase…" 481
Stoics 46
"The sun will be darkened…" 752
The Waters of Mount Hermon 466
Water Symbolism 146

Nebuchadnezzar
The Babylonian Empire 704
Gedaliah's Seal 608
Jeremiah versus Hananiah 596
Nebuchadnezzar & Jeremiah 607
Nebuchadrezzar 622
The Seige & Fall of Jerusalem 638
The Temple Vessels 595

Nehemiah
Building the Wall 409
The Nehemiah Memoir 409
The Royal Cupbearer 408

Noah
Ancient Near-Eastern Flood Stories 114
The Ark 147

Nomadism
The Kenites 253
The Recabites 603
Sedentarization 59

O

Onesimus · *See Philemon*
Origen 26, 395, 407
Peter the Rock 747
Outcasts, Aliens & the Oppressed · *See also Samaritans; Women & Gender*
Aliens 179
The Alien, the Widow & the Orphan 228
Caring for the Sick 771
God's Leaders Oppose Injustice 150
The "Good Leader" 554
The Great Physician 741
Hebrews & *Hapiru* 145
The Law in Deuteronomy 225
Options for Women 322
The Poverty of the Levites 215
"She laughs at horse and rider…" 441
The Twelve Curses 229
Usury 454
Women in Christ's Genealogy 731
Yahweh's Protection of the Weak 453

P

Pagan Deities · *See also Apollo; Baal; Dagon; Tammuz*
Abaddon & Apollo 1074
Additions to Daniel 654
Ancient Near-Eastern Flood Stories 114
Ancient Piety 38
The Apollo Legend & the Roman Emperors 1077
Baal & Asherah 219
Baal & Ashtoreth 276
Baal-Zebub 329
Beelzebub 743
Cherem Warfare 162
Civic Cults 1079
Dagon 262, 288, 360, 708
The Followers of Bacchus 52
Gad & Meni 572
Gods in Pantheism 47
Gods & Mountains 324
The God Tammuz 628
God & the Gods 643
Greco-Roman Polytheism 48
Hadad 321
Hardening Pharaoh's Heart 150
The Holy Ones 483
Honoring the Dead 51
A Hymn to Yahweh 699
Illicit Worship Practices 545
Mesopotamian Wisdom Literature 9
Mithras 53
Molech 708
Monotheism in Egypt 186
Monotheism or Monolatry 210
Mysteries 52
Non-Israelite Ancient Near-Eastern Prophets 66
Origin Stories 138
The Parade of Deities 562
The Philistines 275
Poetic Descriptions of Creation 427
The Punishment of the Gods 556
The Story of Philemon & Baucis 871
There is No God but Yahweh 559
The Will of the Gods 695
The Wings of God 268
Worshipers of Isis 927

Papias 761
Papias on Matthew 17

Parables
Allegory 768
Fables 258
Fantasy & the Young Adult 88
The "Good Soil" 768
The Great Feast 807
Jesus' Parables 744
Jesus & Satan 804
Paired Men & Women in Luke 823
"Put this money to work…" 813
Samaritans 803
Women Unique to Luke's Gospel 822

TOPICAL INDEX

Parenting · See Family

Passover
- Jews & Samaritans 833
- The Lamb 1072
- The Lord's Supper in Luke 816
- The Passover Meal 844
- Pilgrimage Festivals 816
- The Sacrificial Lamb 1035

Patriarchs · See Abraham; Isaac; Jacob

Patristics · See Athanasius; Augustine; Clement; Ignatius; Irenæus; Jerome; Origen; Papias; Philo; Tertullian

Paul
- An Appeal to the Emperor 885
- Authorship of Colossians 973
- The Conversion of Saul 865
- "Had it not been for the law..." 905
- The Innocence of Paul & Silas 874
- Leadership Roles in the Pauline Churches 966
- "The Lord be with all of you..." 987
- Map of Paul's Journeys Through Anatolia 951
- Map of Paul's Missionary Journeys 938
- Paul as Flatterer 939
- Paul on Division & Unity 934
- Paul's "Already but Not Yet" Eschatology 903
- Paul's Contemplation of Mortality 967
- Paul's Eyesight 953
- Paul's Letter Collection 989
- Paul's Political Prophecy 986
- Paul's Rhetorical Care 894
- Paul's View of Salvation 900
- Paul & the Law 898
- The Persecution of Paul 880
- Roman Perceptions of Christianity 884
- Theophilus 21
- "They shall be caught up..." 982
- "To win the prize..." 970
- Water from the Rock 157
- "We will be saved..." 902

Peace · See Shalom

Penitence · See Repentance

Pentecost
- The Coming of the Holy Spirit 877
- Pentecost 858
- Pilgrimage Festivals 816

People of God
- The Ark 147
- Christ's Mission 757
- Corrupt Leadership 717
- Covenant 204
- Dialogue with the Prophet 568
- God & History 479
- God's Blessing to the Nations 547
- God's Control of History 405
- God's Salvation 897
- Haman & Mordecai 418
- "He saved others..." 755
- The Jerusalem Temple 753
- Jesus' Jewish Ministry 724
- Jesus' Parables 744
- The Land & the People Will Be Healed 566
- Law & Relationship 144
- Materialism & Idolatry 479
- The Message of Isaiah 60–62 569
- The "New Moses" 727
- New Wineskins 726
- Obeying Leaders 1025
- Parallels in Isaiah 558
- The People of God 359, 909
- The Prophetic Call 148
- The Reformation of Israel 414
- The Role of God's Messenger 720
- The "Servant" Israel 563
- The Structure of Isaiah 551
- The Suffering Servant 748
- Tradition 716
- Universalism in Isaiah 573
- Yahweh's Requirements for the Righteous 554

Persecution · See also Suffering & Trials
- The Injustice of Demetrius' Attack 878
- Persecution in 1 Peter 1034
- The Persecution of Paul 880
- Roman Perceptions of Christianity 884
- Scapegoating Christians 1033
- "When you face trials..." 1028

Persia · See also Cyrus; Darius
- 1 Enoch 658
- "Beyond the River" 711
- Cuneiform 400
- Cyrus 561
- Cyrus's Conquest of Babylon 543
- Cyrus the Great 542
- The Decree of Cyrus 560
- Edom & Israel 226
- Events in the Book of Daniel 653
- God's Control of History 405, 414
- Jews or Israelites? 34
- Judah/Yehud 396
- The Law of the Medes & the Persians 659
- Map of the Assyrian Empire, 9th–8th Centuries BCE 538
- Map of the Babylonian Empire 704
- Map of the Nations of the Ancient Near East 640
- Map of the Persian Empire 396
- Mithras 53
- Parallels in Isaiah 558
- The Persian Empire 719
- Punishment by Fire 597
- Second Temple Period 10
- The Temple Vessels 595
- Yehud 560
- Yehud in the Persian Empire 713

Peter
- Capernaum 736
- The Divine Spirit 677
- Food Laws 175
- Jesus' Authority 795
- Persecution in 1 Peter 1034
- Peter's Sermon to Cornelius 867
- Peter & the End Times 1039
- Peter the Rock 747
- "Sandwiches" in Mark 767
- The Twelve 766

Pharisees · See Jewish Sects

Philemon
- Apphia & Archippus 1008
- Philemon & Grace 1010
- The Rhetorical Structure of Philemon 1007

Philistia
- Baal & Ashtoreth 276
- Beelzebub 743
- Dagon 288, 360
- Kerethites & Pelethites 300
- Map of Gezer 312
- Map of Israel & Judah 694
- Map of Philistia 286
- Map of the Twelve Tribes 61, 137, 250
- The Philistines 260, 275, 680

Philo of Alexandria 30
- Balaam 1069
- "The blood of bulls & goats..." 1022
- Luke's Portrayal of Jesus 793

TOPICAL INDEX

The World Below & the World Above 1020

Philosophy
"The blood of bulls & goats..." 1022
Challenges & Opportunities 96
Childhood Imagery in Hebrews 1018
Christians & Cultural Influence 90
Clement of Alexandria 27
Cosmic Fire 1044
Cynics 46
Early Schools of Philosophy 945
Epicurus' Four-Fold Way 47
Epicurus & Pleasure 47
Genres in James 1027
Gods in Pantheism 47
Hugh of St. Victor 31
Literature & Its Influence 91
Paul's Contemplation of Mortality 967
Philo of Alexandria 30
Philosophy 45
Pleasure in Ecclesiastes & Epicureanism 525
Stoics 46
The World Below & the World Above 1020

Phoenicia
Ivory 318
Map of the Twelve Tribes 61, 137, 250
Molech 708
Phoenicia 549
Prophets & Foreigners 67

Pontius Pilate 849

Prayer
Jonah's Prayer 691
The Prayer of Daniel 661
The Prayer of Manasseh 345
Prophetic Intercession 683
Stephen's Last Words 863
"Teach us how to pray..." 739
"Teach us to pray..." 804
The Theology of History 375
What Did the Men Pray? 657

Priests & Priesthood
Caiaphas 754, 843
Community Rededication 412
The Day of Atonement 178
Elaborate Worship 364
Greco-Roman Priesthood 48
High Priests 848

The High Priest's Ministry & the Most Holy Place 1021
Interspersed Thematic Summaries 190
Jeremiah & Zephaniah 597
Keeping Passover 386
Known Postexilic High Priests 413
Lot-Casting 279
Melchizedek 1019
Messianism in the First Century 731
Priesthood 174
Reading the Torah 411
Rules of Warfare 73
The Sanhedrin 779, 843, 860
Yehud in the Persian Empire 713

Prophets & Prophecy · See also Elijah; Elisha; Huldah; Isaiah; Jeremiah; Jonah; Melchizedek; Micah; Nehemiah; Samuel; Zechariah
1 Enoch 658
Amos & Foreign Cultures 683
Ancient Divination 39, 595
Apocalypse in Zechariah 714
Balaam Son of Beor 196
"Book of the Twelve" 685
The Coming King 602
Corrupt Leadership 717
Cursing the Fig Tree 750
Daniel & Jesus' Apocalyptic Visions 662
Daniel & Resurrection 663
Dialogue with the Prophet 568
Distinguishing True from False Prophecy 629
Distinguishing True from False Prophets 591
Divine Approval 326
Early Ecstatic Prophets 284
Ezekiel & Ancient Near Eastern Mythology 633
Ezekiel's Visionary Temple 649
The Four Oracles 635
The Fulfillment of Ezekiel's Promises of Blessing 645
Gemariah Son of Hilkiah 596
The High Place 278
History & Prophecy 30
Israel & the Nations 639
Jehu's Punishment 666
Jeremiah in Egypt 610
Jeremiah's Second Scroll 605
Jeremiah versus Hananiah 596

Jeremiah & Zephaniah 597
John the Baptist 830
Jonah & Assyria 691
Justice & Righteousness 682
The Lord Rebukes Jeremiah 587
A Matter of the Heart 899
Matthew's Use of Hosea 670
Micah 594
Monarchy & Hardships 277
Moses, the Greatest Prophet 191
Nebuchadnezzar & Jeremiah 607
Non-Israelite Ancient Near-Eastern Prophets 66
Oracles of Blessing 645
Paul's Political Prophecy 986
"The People of the Land" 579
Performance & the Prophets 67
Poetry as Prophecy 369
The Prayer of Daniel 661
The Prophet Appeals to God 571
The Prophet as Intermediary 158
The Prophet as Mediator 583
The Prophetic Call 148
Prophetic "Call Narratives" 625
Prophetic Intercession 683
Prophetic "Sign Acts" 626
Prophetic Sign Acts 588
A Prophet Like Moses 221
Prophet & Messiah 836
Prophets & Foreigners 67
Prophets & Lament 693
Prophets & Symbolic Actions 667
Righteous Kings & Sinful Kings 383
The Role of God's Messenger 720
The "Safe Way" 403
Seraiah Son of Neriah 615
The Spirit of the Lord 256
The Spirit & the Word 962
The Suffering Female in Lamentations & the Prophets 618
"The sun will be darkened..." 752
Theophany 323
Tradition 716
The Triumphal Entry 778
Warning & Hope 621
Wise Women 304
Zechariah's Visions 714

Psalms · See Music & Praise

Punishment
Cherem Warfare 162
God's Punishment of Idolatry 384
Jehu's Punishment 666
Law Codes in the Pentateuch 161

TOPICAL INDEX

Lex Talionis 182, 223, 534, 687
The "Outstretched Hand" of the Lord 540
Paul's View of Salvation 900
The Prayer of Daniel 661
Priesthood 174
Punishment by Fire 597
Punishment of Adulteresses 638
Punishments in Leviticus 180
References to the Exodus 70
Responsibility 435
Retribution 376
Slaves, Masters & Oppression 1036
"So you will plunder the Egyptians…" 149
The Story of Philemon & Baucis 871
Theodicy 423
"There is none beside me…" 708

Purity · See Holiness & Righteousness

Q

Queens
Oholibah 637
Queen Athaliah 381
Queen Mother 466
The Queen Mother 587
Queen Mothers 658

Quirinius 791

R

Rachel
The Teraphim 284
Wells in Ancient Times 147

Rahab
Women in Christ's Genealogy 731

Reconciliation · See Atonement & Reconciliation

Redemption · See Salvation

Repentance
Blessings & Curses of the Mosaic Covenant 625
Fasting 214
Job & Darkness 440
Jonah & Assyria 691
The Prayer of Manasseh 345
The Reformation of Israel 414
Righteous Kings & Sinful Kings 383
To "Rend Garments" 676

Transformation 911

Resurrection & Afterlife
Abode of the Dead 287
Christians & Death 1038
Daniel & Resurrection 663
The Dead 432
"Death, Be Not Proud" 933
The God Tammuz 628
Life after Death 527
A Pharaoh's Heart 152
Sadducees 814
Sheol 193, 428
"Those who have fallen asleep…" 967

Retribution · See Punishment

Rhetorical & Literary Techniques
Acrostic Poems 520
Acrostic Psalms 452
Allegory 768
Alliteration 478
Answer & Call 450
Apocalyptic Language 648
"Better Than" Sayings 506
Building the Temple 368
Chiasm 459
Chiasm or *Chiasmus* 675
Chiasmus 534, 981
Circumcision of the Heart 954
Comparison as a Literary Tool in Hebrews 1013
The "Day of the Lord" 644
Diatribe 893
"Do everything they tell you…" 751
Epistolary Dialogue 924
Ezekiel & Ancient Near Eastern Mythology 633
The Fruits of Desire 1030
Genres in James 1027
Gezera Shewa 1017
"A great cloud of witnesses…" 1023
The High Priest's Ministry & the Most Holy Place 1021
Hosea & Tradition 670
How Deuteronomy Makes Arguments 204
Imagery in Psalms 446
Inclusio 197, 457, 592, 726, 1029
Interspersed Thematic Summaries 190
Intertextuality 855, 1064
James' Rhetoric 1029
Jesus' Discourses 727
Juxtaposition & Context in Proverbs 507

The Language of Poetry 445
The Messianic Secret 19
Paired Men & Women in Luke 823
Paul's Rhetorical Care 894
Personified Places 585
Poetic Descriptions of Creation 427
The "Recognition Formula" 623
The Rhetorical Structure of Philemon 1007
"Sandwiches" in Mark 767
"Signs" in John's Gospel 827
The Son of Man 728
The Structure of Psalms 13
The Structure of the Letters to the 7 Churches 1067
"Through the eye of a needle…" 812
Time in Matthew 729
The "Wise Woman" 146
Wise Women 304
The Word of God 495
"Yahweh is not with you…" 382

Righteousness · See Holiness & Righteousness

Ritual · See Worship (Christian); Worship (Jewish); Worship (Pagan)

Rivers · See Geography & Environment

Roman Culture · See Greco-Roman Culture

Roman Emperors & Authorities
The 7 Stars 1068
Abaddon & Apollo 1074
The Antonia Fortress 881
The Apollo Legend & the Roman Emperors 1077
An Appeal to the Emperor 885
The Crisis of Emperor Worship 1073
Domitian 1064
The Earth Beast 1078
Emperor Worship 53
The Flavians 1080
Healing with Saliva 773
Herod the Great 733
Pontius Pilate 849
The Prætorium 849
Quirinius 791
Revelation & the Legend of Nero's Return 1076
Roman Citizenship 882
Tetrarch 745

Rome
"Babylon" 1039

TOPICAL INDEX

Denarius 42
The Earth Beast 1078
Education 45
Emperor Worship 53
The Importance of Provinces 43
Map of the Anatolian Provinces of Rome 1069
"Render to Cæsar…" 779
Roman Roads 873
Roman Trade 1081
Second Temple Period 10
Taxation in Rome 43
Wealth in the First Century 41

Ruth
Women in Christ's Genealogy 731

S

Sabbath
Aliens 179
Dietary Regulations 912
Jesus' Lordship 797
"On the first day of the week…" 879
The Purpose of Festivals 181

Sacrifices & Offerings
"The aroma of Christ…" 940
Atonement Sacrifice & Grace 171
"The blood of bulls & goats…" 1022
Cain's Offering 112
Child Sacrifice 584, 631
Dismembering the Concubine 264
Greco-Roman Priesthood 48
The Hearth 50
Honoring the Dead 51
Human Sacrifice 260, 331
Human Sacrifice in Pagan Worship 671
The Lamb 1072
Laying on of Hands 168
Molech 708
Offerings of the Poor 176
Phratries 51
"Prostitution" in Canaanite Religion 667
Religious Complacency 758
Sacrifice 172, 247
Sacrifice & Society 50
The Sacrificial Lamb 1035
Sacrificing Isaac 124
The "Sin Offering" 669
Thank Offerings 494
Willful Sin 1023

Sadducees · *See Jewish Sects*

Salvation
"Bless the Lord, O my soul…" 489
The Cross of Christ 952
Expiation & Propitiation 1048
God's Election 907
God's Salvation 897
The Heavenly Book 803
Images of Vulnerability & Salvation 496
Paul's View of Salvation 900
The People of God 909
The Serpent in the Wilderness 833
"We will be saved…" 902

Samaritans
Christ & the Samaritan Woman 834
Jews & Samaritans 833
Luke's "Special" Conversions 889
Samaritans 803

Samson
Nazirites 273
Samson Reinterpreted 261

Samuel
The High Place 278
Hospitality 264
Wise Women 304

Sarah
Ishmael and Isaac 123
Sarai & Hagar 119

Satan 1077
Beelzebub 804
Belial 488
The Heavenly Council 425
Jesus & Satan 804
"The Satan" 715
Satan in Chronicles 367
Zechariah's Visions 714

Saul
Baal & Ashtoreth 276

Saul (King)
The Amalekites 281
Dismembering the Concubine 264
A King's Harem 293
Seeking Yahweh 392
Weaponry & Warfare 280

Saul (of Tarsus) · *See Paul*

Science & Religion
Challenges & Opportunities 96
The Dangers of Integration 96
Faith Versus Science 94
Galileo on Science & Faith 93

Genesis 1 & Modern Science 110
Reason & Creativity 95

Scripture · *See Biblical & Religious Texts; See also Canon*

Second Coming
Cosmic Fire 1044
The Son of Man 811
"They shall be caught up…" 982

Sennacherib 557
Assyrian Propaganda 541
Critical Issues in Isaiah 36–39 556
Cush 343
Sennacherib's Invasion 557
The Structure of Isaiah 551

Sex & Sexuality
Ancient Creation Stories 437
Baal & Asherah 219
Balaam 1043
"Because of the angels…" 928
Borrowed Images for God 36
Cities & Nations as Female 563
Distinguishing True from False Prophets 591
Esau's Immorality 1024
God's Standards of Holiness 179
"Prostitution" in Canaanite Religion 667
Reflection on the Purity Laws 177
The "Safe Way" 403

Shalom
Eschatology in Zechariah 713
The "Evil Desires of Youth" 999
Justice & Righteousness 682
The Land & the People Will Be Healed 566
An Oral Torah 746
The Torah 456

Sheol 193, 428
Abode of the Dead 287

Silas
The Innocence of Paul & Silas 874

Simon Peter · *See Peter*

Simon the Zealot (apostle)
The Twelve 766

Sin
The Adulterous Woman 838
"The blood of bulls & goats…" 1022
The Day of Atonement 178
Esau's Immorality 1024
The "Evil Desires of Youth" 999
The Falls of Israel & Judah 350

TOPICAL INDEX

The Fruits of Desire 1030
God's Punishment of Idolatry 384
Laying on of Hands 168
Materialism & Idolatry 479
Medicine & God 378
The Prayer of Daniel 661
Punishment of Adulteresses 638
Punishments in Leviticus 180
Rebellion & Grace 490
Sin Depicted in Literature 86
What is sin? 1049
Willful Sin 1023
"Woe to you..." 751

Slavery
The Evangelistic Role of Slaves 1004
Forced Labor 317
Philemon & Slavery 1009
Slaves 42
Slaves & Masters 976
Slaves, Masters, & Oppression 1036
"So you will plunder the Egyptians..." 149

Solomon
Building the Temple 368
Dating the Exodus 315
Forced Labor 317
Map of Ancient Jerusalem 294
Perspectives on the Kings 377
The Royal Purge 311
The Royal Steward 548
Solomon 373
Solomon's Colonnade 859
The Theology of History 375
Women in Christ's Genealogy 731

Spirit
The Coming of the Holy Spirit 877
Luke's "Special" Conversions 889
Spirit & Commandment 1050
The Spirit of God 108
The Spirit of the Lord 256
The Spirit & The Word 962
"With the Holy Spirit & with fire..." 734

Spiritual Gifts
"But the greatest of these is love..." 930
God's Activity Among the Gentiles 868
Spiritual Gifts 930

Stephen
Stephen's Last Words 863

Stewardship · See Wealth & Poverty

Suffering & Trials · See also Persecution
Birth Pangs 906
Discipleship & Suffering 997
Divine Significance of the Body 451
Enemies 450
Epicurus & Pleasure 47
The Falls of Israel & Judah 350
God & Trials 470
Isaiah 53 in Early Christian Interpretation 566
Jesus' Sufferings 1018
Job's Fortitude 433
"A little lower than the angels..." 1015
"Look away from me..." 464
The Model of Jesus 78
Persecution in 1 Peter 1034
Peter & the End Times 1039
Responses to Suffering 464
Rich & Poor in Jeremiah 582
The "Servant" Israel 563
The Suffering Servant 748
"Take up your cross..." 80
Theodicy 423
"When you face trials..." 1028

Sumer
City Laments 617
Cuneiform 400

Symbols & Imagery
1,600 Stadia 1079
The 7 Stars 1068
Agricultural Imagery 552
Ambassadors of Christ 942
Ancient Creation Stories 437
Answer & Call 450
Apocalyptic Imagery 910
Apocalyptic Language 648
The Ark 147
Armageddon 1079
The Army of the Lord 240
"The aroma of Christ..." 940
Assyrian Propaganda 541
Atonement Sacrifice & Grace 171
The Author of Salvation 1015
Babel 81
"Babylon" 1039
The Background of John's "Word" Metaphor 830
"Bear good fruit..." 1019
"Because you are lukewarm..." 1071
Biblical Genealogies 355
Birth Pangs 906
The "Book of Life" 630
The Bread of Life 801
The Centurion's Confession 786
Cherubim 1072
Childhood Imagery in Hebrews 1018
Christ, the Cornerstone 1035
"Circumcise your hearts..." 215
Cities & Nations as Female 563
Clouds in Biblical Symbolism 189
The Coming King 602
"Contend... in the gate..." 497
Corrupt Leadership 717
Cursing the Fig Tree 750
The Day of Atonement 178
The "Day of the Lord" 644
Dishonest Scales 438
The Divine Spirit 677
The Divine Warrior 207
"The ends of the earth..." 866
Ezekiel & Ancient Near Eastern Mythology 633
Fables 258
Feminine Imagery for Jerusalem 696
Finding Wisdom 437
"Flee like a bird..." 453
Food Laws 175
The Four Oracles 635
Genesis 1 & Modern Science 110
"A glory now set aside..." 940
Good & Poor Builders 920
The "Good Soil" 768
The Great Feast 807
The Great Physician 741
The Heavenly Book 803
"He is my fortress..." 472
"If the salt loses its saltiness..." 776
"I have run the race..." 908
Imagery in Psalms 446
Images of Vulnerability & Salvation 496
The Importance of Symbols 1036
"In a mirror darkly..." 930
Interpreting Mark 13 780
Isaiah 53 in Early Christian Interpretation 566
Ishmael the "Wild Donkey" 119
Jeremiah's Linen Belt 586
Jesus' Authority 795
Jesus' Jewish Ministry 724
Jesus & Satan 804
Jude's Imagery 1061
The Kingdom of God 656

TOPICAL INDEX

Kingship & Divinity 313
"Kiss the Son…" 449
Kneading Trough 229
The Lamb 1072
The Land 211
Legal Imagery in Job 431
The Leviathan 550
"Like a weaned child…" 498
The Lord's Supper in Luke 816
"Make the lightning flash…" 502
Matthew's Use of Hosea 670
Medieval Chant 102
The Messianic Banquet 740
Mount Hermon 589
"My ears you have pierced…" 465
The Needle's Eye 749
The "New Moses" 727
New Wine & Dregs 708
New Wineskins 726
Oracles of Blessing 645
The Order of the Plagues 152
The Parental Persona 510
The Passover 155
Paul's Eyesight 953
Paul's Family Imagery 921
Personified Places 585
Pharaoh as Monster 642
Pictures of History 500
Places & Wordplay in Micah 694
Plants & Pillars 502
"Plastering with lies…" 432
The Potter & the Clay 588
Prophetic "Call Narratives" 625
Prophetic "Sign Acts" 626
Prophetic Sign Acts 588
"Prostitution" in Canaanite Religion 667
Psalm 23 in History 458
Psalm 110 in Second Temple Judaism 780
Punishment of Adulteresses 638
Rebellion & Grace 490
Rich & Poor in Jeremiah 582
"Rubies" 521
The Sacrificial Lamb 1035
The "Safe Way" 403
Samaritans 803
Seraiah Son of Neriah 615
The Serpent in the Wilderness 833
The "Shadow" of the Canaanites 192
"She laughs at horse and rider…" 441
"Signs" in John's Gospel 827

Signs & Jesus' Identity 832
"Small as a mustard seed…" 810
The Son of God 762
The Son of Man 811
"Sound Doctrine" 990
Spiritual Food & Drink 925
The "Strange Woman" 510
The Suffering Female in Lamentations & the Prophets 618
"The sun will be darkened…" 752
The Sword 1017
Symbolic City Names 569
"Take up your cross…" 80
The Tasks of Shepherds 646
The Temple's Furnishings 374
The Ten Kings 660
"Three Witnesses" 1052
"Through the eye of a needle…" 812
Tirzah 531
To "Rend Garments" 676
The Torn Curtain 819
"To win the prize…" 970
The Two Witnesses 1075
Ungrateful Nations 631
Water from the Rock 157
The Waters of Mount Hermon 466
Water Symbolism 146
The White Stone 1070
Why Ten Commandments? 210
The Wings of God 268
Yahweh as Water 580

Syncretism & Comparative Religion

Ancient Creation Stories 437
Ancient Near-Eastern Flood Stories 114
The Apollo Legend & the Roman Emperors 1077
Baal & Ashtoreth 276
Borrowed Images for God 36
The Bronze Snake 195
Canaan & Israel 468
Clouds in Biblical Symbolism 189
Creator & Creation 489
Dagon 262
The Divine Warrior 207
The Doctrine of Retribution 428
Early Ecstatic Prophets 284
Elaborate Worship 364
God of the Rains 473
Gods & Mountains 324
The High Place 278
The Holy Ones 483
Human Sacrifice 260

Illicit Worship Practices 545
Mezuzot 216
Monotheism in Egypt 186
The Mosaic Covenant 72
Mysteries 52
Non-Israelite Ancient Near-Eastern Prophets 66
Origin Stories 138
The Parental Persona 510
The Pentateuch & Ancient Near Eastern Law Codes 3
The Pentateuch & Contemporary Literature 3
Poetic Descriptions of Creation 427
Punishment by Fire 597
Queen Mothers 658
Revelation & the Legend of Nero's Return 1076
Sabbath for Christians 414
The "Shadow" of the Canaanites 192
Syncretism 398
"There is No God but Yahweh" 559
Watery Chaos 316
Yahweh's Supremacy 486

Syria

The Amorites 205
Aram 251
The Arameans 228
Events in the Book of Daniel 653
Hadad 321
Ivory 318
Kings of Aram & Damascus 339
Map of the Anatolian Provinces of Rome 1069
Map of the Assyrian Empire, 9th–8th Centuries BCE 538
Map of the Babylonian Empire 704
Map of the Nations of the Ancient Near East 640
Map of the Persian Empire 396
Pledging Human Beings 188
Shalmaneser & Ahab 326
Tel Dan Inscription 324
The Tel Dan Inscription 336
Tent Shrines 187
Watery Chaos 316

T

The Tabernacle

The Ark of the Covenant 581
Diagram of the Tabernacle 163
The Glory of the Lord 624

TOPICAL INDEX

    The Jerusalem Temple 753
    Sacrifice 172
    Temple or Tabernacle? 274
    Tent of Meeting 173

Tamar
    Women in Christ's Genealogy 731

Tammuz
    The God Tammuz 628
    Illicit Worship Practices 545

Teaching & Education
    Authoritative Teaching 992
    Disciplining a Child 513
    Education 45
    Ephesians & Christian Moral Instruction 961
    Fantasy & the Young Adult 88
    Greco-Roman Public Buildings 42
    Paying Teachers 1043
    Performance & the Prophets 67
    Peter the Rock 747
    Rabbinic Interpretation 198
    Scribes 401
    The Ten Commandments 159
    The Torah 456
    Why Ten Commandments? 210

Technology
    Ancient Documents 35
    Cisterns 606
    Codex 26
    Cuneiform 400
    "In a mirror darkly..." 930
    Metal Refining 636
    Papyrus 28
    Parchment 1000
    The Philistines 275
    Roman Roads 873
    Scribes 401
    Signet Rings 712
    The Water Tunnel 295
    Wells in Ancient Times 147

The Temple
    Baptism Among the Dead Sea Community 734
    Building the Temple 368
    The Census 306
    Community Rededication 412
    Den of Robbers 583
    Desecration of the Temple 986
    Entrance Liturgy 459
    Ezekiel's Visionary Temple 649
    The High Priest's Ministry & the Most Holy Place 1021
    Instrumental Music in Jewish Tradition 100
    Interpreting Mark 13 780
    The Jerusalem Temple 753
    Map of Ancient Jerusalem 294
    Psalms of Ascent 495
    The Psalms of Korah 193
    Second Temple Worship 363
    Solomon 373
    Temple or Tabernacle? 274
    The Temple's Furnishings 374
    The Temple Vessels 595
    The Torn Curtain 819
    What Did the Men Pray? 657

Temptation · See Suffering & Trials

Tertullian 27

Textual Sources & Issues
    1 Esdras 354
    2 Peter & Jude 1041
    2 Peter & the Synoptic Gospels 1042
    Additions to Daniel 654
    Additions to Esther 417
    The Adulterous Woman 838
    Ancient Authorship 7
    The Audience of Isaiah 565
    The Author of Chronicles 386
    The Background of John's "Word" Metaphor 830
    Baruch 593
    The Bible & Literature 85
    The Book of Jashar 292
    The Canon 25
    Chronicles & Psalms 364
    The Compilation of Jeremiah 578
    Dagon 360
    Dating the Exodus 315
    David's Mighty Men 361
    The Deuteronomist 272
    Ephesians & Colossians 957
    The Ezra Memoir 411
    Finishing the Story 248
    The Functions of Proverbs 507
    The Heavenly Council 425
    Hebrew & Aramaic 401
    The High Place 278
    History & Prophecy 30
    Indicators of Northern Composition 480
    Jeremiah's Second Scroll 605
    Joseph & Egyptian History 135
    Lover & Beloved 530
    Luke-Acts or Luke & Acts? 20
    The Masoretic Text 578
    Minor Judges 259
    The Nehemiah Memoir 409
    Numbering the Psalms 448
    Other Endings for Mark's Gospel 787
    Papias on Matthew 17
    The Placement of Chronicles 353
    Psalm 115 493
    Reader Participation in Proverbs 509
    "Record of his reign..." 419
    Removing Sandals 269
    The Royal Purge 311
    The Samaritan Pentateuch 1
    Samson Reinterpreted 261
    The Song of the Sea 156
    Sources of Proverbs 505
    Synchronisms 331
    Synoptic Gospels 18
    The Synoptic Gospels & the Synoptic Problem 825
    Temple or Tabernacle? 274
    Textual Sources in Romans 895
    Torah or Law? 4
    Writing Luke 789

Thaddaeus
    The Twelve 766

Theodicy · See Suffering & Trials

Theology
    Blessings & Curses of the Mosaic Covenant 625
    Challenges & Opportunities 96
    Cherem Warfare 162
    Christology 22
    Clement of Alexandria 27
    The Deuteronomist 272
    The Doctrine of Retribution 428
    Ezekiel & Ancient Near Eastern Mythology 633
    Faith Versus Science 94
    The Fullness of Christ 959
    Genesis 1 & Modern Science 110
    God Changes His Mind 71
    God & History 479
    God's Emotions 582
    Hardening Pharaoh's Heart 150
    The Heavenly Council 425
    Humans as Caretakers 69
    A "Jealous" God 212
    Jesus & Divorce 776
    John's Historical Value 21
    The Kingdom 81

TOPICAL INDEX

The Kingdom of God 656
Law in the Ancient Near East 159
Lord of Hosts 74
Miracles 740
Monotheism in Egypt 186
The Name of Yahweh 217
The Nature of God 968
New Testament Theological Models 83
Origen 26
Power in Weakness 941
The Prayer of Daniel 661
Satan 1077
"The Satan" 715
The Spirit of God 108
"Teach us how to pray…" 739
Theodicy 423
The Theology of History 375
The Theology of the Exodus 279
There is No God but Yahweh 559
Universalism in Isaiah 573

Theophilus 21
Theophilus's Status 856
Who Was Theophilus? 790

Time & Seasons
Canaan & Israel 468
Cisterns 606
Dating the Exodus 315
Enthronement Psalms 485
The Feast of Tabernacles 838
The God Tammuz 628
Holidays of the Jewish Year 181
Law Codes in the Pentateuch 161
"Our land will yield its increase…" 481
The Seige & Fall of Jerusalem 638

Timothy 873

Torah · See Biblical & Religious Texts

Tradition
The Ahiqar Tradition 9
Hosea & Tradition 670
Tradition 716
Traditional Jewish Commentary 5

Trinity
Jesus' Origins 80
The Nature of God 968
The Spirit of the Lord 256

Tyre
The Nations Who Trade with Tyre 641
Ungrateful Nations 631

U

Unbelievers · See Atheism & Unbelief

United Kingdom · See Israel & Judah

Units of Distance · See Distance & Location

Units of Measure · See Weights & Measures

V

Visions & Dreams
Balaam Son of Beor 196
Ezekiel's Visionary Temple 649
Food Laws 175
God's Activity among the Gentiles 868
The Importance of Dreams 526
"They shall be caught up…" 982
The Two Witnesses 1075

Vows
Alliteration 478
Nazirites 273
Vows 189

W

War & Military Matters
Armageddon 1079
The Army of the Lord 240
The Babylonian Empire 704
The Ban 281
The Campaign into Judah 320
Chariots 245
Cherem Warfare 162
Cherethites & Pelethites 311
The Code of the Warrior 257
Cush 343
Dedan, Tema & Kedar 548
The Destruction of Israel 341
Divine Approval 326
The Divine Warrior 207
The Four Oracles 635
God & the Gods 643
Hazor 243
Holy War 187, 223
Kerethites & Pelethites 300
Lord of Hosts 74
Nebuchadnezzar & Jeremiah 607
Psychological Warfare 257
The Punishment of the Gods 556
A Roman Legion 800
Royal Inscriptions 307
Rules of Warfare 73
The Seige & Fall of Jerusalem 638
Sennacherib & Hezekiah 696
The "Shadow" of the Canaanites 192
Shalmaneser & Ahab 326
The Sling 282
Tel Dan Inscription 324
Tribute 622
War Poems 254
The War Scroll 187
Weaponry & Warfare 280
Who Were the Judges? 249

Wealth & Poverty
Ecclesiastes' Radicalism 523
"Equestrian" 43
Greco-Roman Aristocracy 43
Justice 501
Offerings of the Poor 176
"The People of the Land" 579
The Poverty of the Levites 215
Poverty & Wickedness 515
"Put this money to work…" 813
"Render to Cæsar…" 779
Rich & Poor 1028
Royal Generosity 220
Slaves 42
"Through the eye of a needle…" 812
Usury 454
Wealth in the First Century 41
Wealth & Stewardship 822
The Widow's Mite 815
Women Who Followed Jesus 799

Weapons & Weaponry · See War & Military Matters

Weights & Measures
Ancient Weights 659
Dishonest Scales 697
Dry & Liquid Measures 193
Talent 366

Wholeness · See Shalom

Widows & Widowhood · See Women & Gender

Wisdom
The Background of John's "Word" Metaphor 830
The Doctrine of Retribution 428
Ecclesiastes' Radicalism 523
The "Fear of the Lord" 509
Finding Wisdom 437
The Functions of Proverbs 507
Household Wisdom 517

TOPICAL INDEX

    Juxtaposition & Context in Proverbs 507
    The Love of Wisdom 512
    Mesopotamian Wisdom Literature 9
    The Misuse of Proverbs 519
    The Parental Persona 510
    The "Path of Life" 455
    Poverty & Wickedness 515
    Reader Participation in Proverbs 509
    Restraint in Speech 516
    "Rubies" 521
    Secret Wisdom 919
    Solomon 373
    The "Strange Woman" 510
    Traditional Wisdom 463
    Wisdom 164
    Wisdom & Righteousness 514
    Wisdom's Call 511
    Wisdom's Playfulness 512
    The "Wise Woman" 146
    Wise Women 304
    The "Woman of Strength" 508

Witness
    Eyewitnesses 1042
    Martyrion Christou 918
    The Two Witnesses 1075

Wit, Wordplay & Humor
    Abaddon & Apollo 1074
    Baal-Zebub 329
    Beelzebub 743
    Beersheba 123
    Christian Charity 1050
    The Functions of Proverbs 507
    Humor in the Story of Ehud 253
    Ishmael and Isaac 123
    Job & Psalm 8 430
    Places & Wordplay in Micah 694
    Reader Participation in Proverbs 509
    The Royal Purge 311
    Shubah & Surah 451
    Teaching Children the Alphabet 551
    Tirzah 531
    Wisdom's Playfulness 512

Women & Gender
    The Alien, the Widow & the Orphan 228
    Cities & Nations as Female 563
    Dismembering the Concubine 264
    Ephesians & Christian Moral Instruction 961
    Feminine Imagery for Jerusalem 696
    Finding the Book of the Law 389
    Forms of Marriage 160
    Gender in Leviticus 170
    God's Standards of Holiness 179
    A Husband's Wrath 632
    Inclusio 197
    Jesus & Divorce 776
    A King's Harem 293
    Male & Female in James 1027
    Options for Women 322
    Paired Men & Women in Luke 823
    Personal Reactions to Literature 89
    Personified Places 585
    Punishment of Adulteresses 638
    Queen Mother 466
    The Queen Mother 587
    Queen Mothers 658
    Sarai & Hagar 119
    The "Strange Woman" 510
    The Suffering Female in Lamentations & the Prophets 618
    Violated Women 299
    The "Weaker" Partner 1037
    The Widow's Mite 815
    The "Wise Woman" 146
    Wise Women 304
    The "Woman of Strength" 508
    Women as Deacons 993
    Women in Christ's Genealogy 731
    Women in Corinth 932
    Women in the Greco-Roman World 45
    Women Unique to Luke's Gospel 822
    Women Who Followed Jesus 799

Worldview · See Christian Thought; Jewish Thought; Philosophy

Worship (Christian)
    Belief & Behavior in Ephesians 960
    Charlemagne & Music 102
    Early Christian Music 101
    Early Christian Worship & Identity 865
    Isaac Watts & the Wesleys 104
    Liturgical Revival 105
    Martin Luther & Music 103
    Medieval Chant 102
    Motets 103

Worship (Jewish)
    Alternative Sanctuaries 681
    Bethel 319
    Capernaum 736
    Community Rededication 412
    Cultic Sites 337
    Elaborate Worship 364
    Gilgal 239
    "Give careful thought…" 712
    Hezekiah's Reforms 342
    Instrumental Music in Jewish Tradition 100
    Job & Worship 426
    Monotheism or Monolatry 210
    The Mount Ebal Worship Complex 229
    Pentecost 858
    Sacrifice 247
    Second Temple Worship 363
    The "Sin Offering" 669
    The Teraphim 284
    Thank Offerings 494
    What Did the Men Pray? 657
    Worship 477

Worship (Pagan) · See also Apollo; Baal; Dagon; Tammuz
    Additions to Daniel 654
    Ancient Piety 38
    A Pharaoh's Heart 152
    Baal & Ashtoreth 276
    Canaan & Israel 468
    Child Sacrifice 584, 631
    Civic Cults 1079
    Creator & Creation 489
    Cultic Sites 337
    Dagon 708
    Early Ecstatic Prophets 284
    The Earth Beast 1078
    Emperor Worship 53
    Events in the Book of Daniel 653
    Ezekiel & Ancient Near Eastern Mythology 633
    Gad & Meni 572
    The God Tammuz 628
    Greco-Roman Priesthood 48
    The Hearth 50
    Herod the Great 733
    The High Place 278
    High Places 310
    Honoring the Dead 51
    Hosting Meals 48
    Human Sacrifice in Pagan Worship 671
    Idol Making 561
    Illicit Worship Practices 545

TOPICAL INDEX

The Magi 732
Mithras 53
Molech 708
Mysteries 52
"Mysteries" in Greco-Roman Religion 986
Non-Israelite Ancient Near-Eastern Prophets 66
The Parade of Deities 562
Phratries 51
The Prayer of Daniel 661
"Prostitution" in Canaanite Religion 667
"Render to Cæsar…" 779
Sacrifice & Society 50
"Teach us how to pray…" 739
Tent Shrines 187
Teraphim 129
The Teraphim 284
Worshipers of Isis 927
"A young goat in its mother's milk…" 218

Y

Yahweh · *See God*
Yehud · *See Judah*

Z

Zechariah
Apocalypse in Zechariah 714
Eschatology in Zechariah 713
Tradition 716
Zechariah's Visions 714

Zion
Eschatology in Zechariah 713
The Glory of the Lord 624
Jerusalem & Its Names 294
The Message of Isaiah 60–62 569